REFERENCE

Black's Law Dictionary®

Abridged Ninth Edition

Black's Law Dictionary®

Abridged Ninth Edition

Bryan A. Garner
Editor in Chief

A Thomson Reuters business

Mat #41040632

COPYRIGHT © 1891, 1910, 1933, 1951, 1957, 1968, 1979, 1990 WEST PUBLISHING CO.
© West, a Thomson business, 1999, 2004, 2005
© 2010 Thomson Reuters
      610 Opperman Drive
      St. Paul, MN 55123
      1–800–313–9378

Printed in the United States of America
ISBN: 978–0–314–26578–4

Black's Law Dictionary

Abridged Ninth Edition

EDITOR IN CHIEF

Bryan A. Garner

President, LawProse, Inc.
Distinguished Research Professor of Law
Southern Methodist University
Dallas, Texas

ASSOCIATE EDITOR

Tiger Jackson

LawProse, Inc.
Dallas, Texas

ASSOCIATE EDITOR

Jeff Newman

LawProse, Inc.
Dallas, Texas

CONTRIBUTING EDITORS

Karolyne H. Cheng
Dallas, Texas

Herbert J. Hammond
Dallas, Texas

Brian Melendez
Minneapolis, Minnesota

Ann Taylor Schwing
Sacramento, California

Fred Shapiro
New Haven, Connecticut

Joseph F. Spaniol Jr.
Bethesda, Maryland

PRONUNCIATION EDITOR

Charles Harrington Elster
San Diego, California

PANEL OF ACADEMIC CONTRIBUTORS
Page vii

PANEL OF PRACTITIONER CONTRIBUTORS
Page viii

Black's Law Dictionary — Abridged Ninth Edition
PANEL OF ACADEMIC CONTRIBUTORS

Hans W. Baade
The University of Texas

Lynn A. Baker
The University of Texas

Thomas E. Baker
Florida International University

Barbara Aronstein Black
Columbia University

Hon. Thomas Buergenthal
*International Court of Justice
(George Washington University)*

Edward H. Cooper
University of Michigan

Daniel Robert Coquillette
Boston College

David Crump
University of Houston

A. Darby Dickerson
Stetson University

James Joseph Duane
Regent University School of Law

David G. Epstein
Southern Methodist University

(the late) E. Allan Farnsworth
Columbia University

Martha A. Field
Harvard University

Monroe H. Freedman
Hofstra University

Richard D. Freer
Emory University

S. Elizabeth Gibson
University of North Carolina

Alex Glashausser
Washburn University

Richard J. Graving
South Texas College

Alan Gunn
University of Notre Dame

Egon Guttman
American University

Geoffrey C. Hazard Jr.
*University of California–
Hastings College of Law*

R.H. Helmholz
University of Chicago

Tony Honoré
Oxford University

Heidi M. Hurd
University of Illinois

Julian Conrad Juergensmeyer
Georgia State University

Sanford H. Kadish
*University of California
at Berkeley*

Gideon Kanner
Loyola Law School

Joseph Kimble
Thomas M. Cooley Law School

Edward J. Kionka
Southern Illinois University

Douglas Laycock
The University of Michigan

Saúl Litvinoff
Louisiana State University

John S. Lowe
Southern Methodist University

(the late) Julius J. Marke
St. John's University

Thomas William Mayo
Southern Methodist University

Lucy S. McGough
Louisiana State University

Joseph W. McKnight
Southern Methodist University

John K. McNulty
*University of California
at Berkeley*

Ernest Metzger
University of Aberdeen

James E. Moliterno
College of William & Mary

James A.R. Nafziger
Willamette University

John B. Oakley
University of California

John V. Orth
University of North Carolina

Alan N. Resnick
Hofstra University

O.F. Robinson
University of Glasgow

Jean Rosenbluth
*University of
Southern California*

Paul Frederick Rothstein
Georgetown University

Ronald Daniel Rotunda
George Mason University

Stephen A. Saltzburg
*The George Washington
University*

Frederic S. Schwartz
*Oklahoma City University
School of Law*

Charles Silver
The University of Texas

Lawrence M. Solan
Brooklyn Law School

Marc I. Steinberg
Southern Methodist University

Michael F. Sturley
The University of Texas

Symeon Symeonides
Willamette University

Peter Meijes Tiersma
Loyola Law School

Mark V. Tushnet
Georgetown University

William D. Underwood
Baylor University

David Walker
University of Glasgow

Robert Weisberg
Stanford Law School

Mary Whisner
University of Washington

Peter Winship
Southern Methodist University

Charles W. Wolfram
Cornell Law School

Richard C. Wydick
*University of California
at Davis*

A.N. Yiannopoulos
Tulane University

Judith T. Younger
University of Minnesota

Black's Law Dictionary — Abridged Ninth Edition
PANEL OF PRACTITIONER CONTRIBUTORS

Sherri K. Adelkoff
Pittsburgh, Pennsylvania

Daniel Alexander
Los Angeles, California

Suzanne Antley
San Diego, California

Leslie Karyn Arfine
Ridgefield, Connecticut

John R. Armstrong II
Irvine, California

Brad D. Bailey
Evergreen, Colorado

William P. Baker
Baltimore, Maryland

Judith M. Bambace
San Diego, California

Daniel P. Barer
Los Angeles, California

Ben A. Baring Jr.
Houston, Texas

Chad Baruch
Dallas, Texas

Isabel Barzun
New York, New York

Eric S. Basse
Bremerton, Washington

Laurie T. Baulig
Lancaster, Pennsylvania

Hugh C. Beck
Littleton, Ohio

Adron W. Beene
San Jose, California

Bill C. Berger
Denver, Colorado

Xanthe M. Berry
Oakland, California

Nathan V. Bishop
East Hills, New York

Michael R. Blum
San Francisco, California

Deborah L. Borman
Chicago, Illinois

Sara E. Bouley
Salt Lake City, Utah

Kevin J. Breer
Westwood, Kansas

Mark A. Bregman
Scottsdale, Arizona

Beth A. Brennan
Missoula, Montana

Joyce Murphy Brooks
Charlotte, North Carolina

Diana Brown
Houston, Texas

Lynne Thaxter Brown
Fresno, California

James Andrew Browne
San Francisco, California

Julie A. Buffington
Dallas, Texas

B. Chad Bungard
Fredericksburg, Virginia

Beverly Ray Burlingame
Dallas, Texas

Fritz Byers
Toledo, Ohio

H. Thomas Byron III
Washington, D.C.

Christopher A. Camardello
Minneapolis, Minnesota

David D. Cardone
San Diego, California

David L. Cargille
New York, New York

Robert J. Carty Jr.
Houston, Texas

Thomas L. Casey
Lansing, Michigan

Bradley Charles
Grand Rapids, Michigan

Li Chen
Dallas, Texas

Jordan B. Cherrick
St. Louis, Missouri

Peter Clapp
Richmond, California

Kristina A. Clark
Washington, D.C.

Randall B. Clark
Boston, Massachusetts

A. Craig Cleland
Atlanta, Georgia

Michael Scott Coffman
Salt Lake City, Utah

Elizabeth J. Cohen
Chicago, Illinois

Charles Dewey Cole Jr.
New York, New York

Samuel Scott Cornish
New York, New York

Emily Côté
San Jose, California

Jefferson Coulter
Seattle, Washington

Jim Covington
Springfield, Illinois

Bernadette S. Curry
Fairfield, California

Jonathan A. Darcy
Philadelphia, Pennsylvania

Elaine Maier Deering
Boca Raton, Florida

A. Charles Dell'Ario
Oakland, California

C. David Dietz
St. Paul, Minnesota

Michael J. Dimino
Washington, D.C.

Richard S. Dodd II
Reston, Virginia

Leah Domstead
Dallas, Texas

Preston Saul Draper
Norman, Oklahoma

John C. Duncan
Norman, Oklahoma

Gerald F. Dusing
Covington, Kentucky

Steve C. Eggimann
Minneapolis, Minnesota

Daniel P. Elms
Dallas, Texas

Ann Erickson Gault
Pontiac, Michigan

Michael T. Fackler
Jacksonville, Florida

Michael E. Faden
Rockville, Maryland

John D. Faucher
Thousand Oaks, California

Bruce Ellis Fein
Washington, D.C.

Janet Rosenblum Fipphen
Fairfield, Connecticut

Angela Fisher
Knoxville, Tennessee

Neil Fried
Arlington, Virginia

Elizabeth Klein Frumkin
Cambridge, Massachusetts

Mark W. Gaffney
Pelham Manor, New York

Duane H. Gall
Denver, Colorado

Nicole S. Gambrell
Dallas, Texas

Baldemar Garcia Jr.
Laredo, Texas

Kathryn Gardner
Topeka, Kansas

Anne W. Gill
Castle Rock, Colorado

Black's Law Dictionary — Abridged Ninth Edition
PANEL OF PRACTITIONER CONTRIBUTORS

Alexander C.D. Giza
Culver City, California

Kevin W. Grierson
Norfolk, Virginia

Ellen B. Gwynn
Tallahassee, Florida

Matthew C. Hans
St. Louis, Missouri

Yaakov Har-Oz
Beit Shemesh, Israel

William H. Hart
Minneapolis, Minnesota

Molly Hatchell
Austin, Texas

Scott M. Heenan
Cincinnati, Ohio

Marie Hejl
Austin, Texas

Susan Hoffman
San Luis Obispo, California

Jeffrey A. Hogge
Elk Grove, California

Brian John Hooper
Arlington, Virginia

Henry W. Huffnagle
Washington, D.C.

Hon. Lynn N. Hughes
Houston, Texas

Roger N. Hughes
Virginia Beach, Virginia

Maryanne Burnes Hutchinson
Braintree, Massachusetts

Amy B. Ikerd
Coldwater, Ohio

Peter O. Israel
Los Angeles, California

Dianne L. Izzo
Austin, Texas

Matthew A. Jacober
St. Louis, Missouri

Robert A. James
San Francisco, California

Eric K. Johnson
Murray, Utah

David R. Johnstone
Washington, D.C.

Richard B. Katskee
Washington, D.C.

Stuart B. Katz
Chappaqua, New York

Paul D. Keeper
Austin, Texas

Darlene Azevedo Kelly
Oakhurst, California

H. Dennis Kelly
Fort Worth, Texas

Clark D. Kimball
Rochester, New York

James A. King
Columbus, Ohio

Andrew D. Klein
Cherry Hill, New Jersey

Melissa Lin Klemens
Washington, D.C.

William M. Klimon
Washington, D.C.

Heléna Klumpp
Deerfield, Illinois

Jonathan H. Koenig
Wauwatosa, Wisconsin

Thomas J. Koffer
New York, New York

Christina M. Kotowski
San Francisco, California

Mike Kueber
San Antonio, Texas

Nanda P.B.A. Kumar
Philadelphia, Pennsylvania

Robert J. Lally
Cleveland, Ohio

Hon. Harriet Lansing
St. Paul, Minnesota

Geoffrey Larson
Minneapolis, Minnesota

James Hays Lawson
Louisville, Kentucky

Hon. Steve Leben
Topeka, Kansas

Michelle Thomas Leifeste
Boulder, Colorado

Andrew D. Levy
Baltimore, Maryland

Janet Li
Foster City, California

Dryden J. Liddle
Alameda, California

Raymond J. Liddy
San Diego, California

Jacob R. Lines
Tucson, Arizona

Morris D. Linton
Salt Lake City, Utah

David W. Long
Washington, D.C.

Thomas G. Lovett IV
Minneapolis, Minnesota

Margaret I. Lyle
Dallas, Texas

David P. Lyons
Chicago, Illinois

Robert N. Markle
Fairfax, Virginia

Anthony J. Marks
Los Angeles, California

Catherine M. Masters
Chicago, Illinois

Jeffrey Matloff
Bellevue, Washington

Michael J. Mauro
Stamford, Connecticut

Olga I. May
San Diego, California

Jeffrey T. McPherson
St. Louis, Missouri

John W. McReynolds
Dallas, Texas

Edward R. Mevec
Buchanan, New York

Andrew E. Miller
Los Angeles, California

Matthew C. Miller
Kansas City, Missouri

Daphna H. Mitchell
New York, New York

Michael S. Mitchell
New Orleans, Louisiana

Andrew W. Moeller
Amherst, New York

Thomas J. Moses
San Francisco, California

R. Eric Nielsen
Bethesda, Maryland

Siobhán Nurre
San Jose, California

Consuelo Marie Ohanesian
Phoenix, Arizona

Erin J. O'Leary
Orlando, Florida

Kymberly K. Oltrogge
Drippings Springs, Texas

William S. Osborn
Dallas, Texas

James C. Owens
Washington, D.C.

Christine C. Pagano
Oakland, California

Paul I. Perlman
Buffalo, New York

Arthur R. Petrie II
Newport Beach, California

Rebecca B. Phalen
Atlanta, Georgia

Black's Law Dictionary — Abridged Ninth Edition
PANEL OF PRACTITIONER CONTRIBUTORS

David Pickle
Washington, D.C.

Mark D. Plaisance
Baker, Louisiana

Matthew Eliot Pollack
Topsham, Maine

Jeffrey D. Polsky
San Francisco, California

Christina E. Ponig
Houston, Texas

Steve Putman
Houston, Texas

Robert M. Redis
White Plains, New York

James M. Reiland
Chicago, Illinois

Tracy L. Reilly
Dallas, Texas

David E. Robbins
Broomall, Pennsylvania

Armando Rodriguez-Feo
Washington, D.C.

Susan L. Ronn
Kohimarama Auckland, New Zealand

Joseph E. Root
Montara, California

Hon. Janice M. Rosa
Erie County, New York

Glenn F. Rosenblum
Philadelphia, Pennsylvania

Joseph M. Russell
Chicago, Illinois

James B. Ryan
San Diego, California

Patrick M. Ryan
San Francisco, California

James F. Schaller II
Toledo, Ohio

Edward Schiffer
San Francisco, California

Daniel J. Schultz
Tempe, Arizona

David W. Schultz
Houston, Texas

Herbert R. Schulze
Truckee, California

Benjamin G. Shatz
Los Angeles, California

Denise Wimbiscus Shepherd
Solon, Ohio

Richard A. Sherburne Jr.
Baton Rouge, Louisiana

Anne M. Sherry
Riverswood, Illinois

Jordan M. Sickman
Southfield, Michigan

Marshall Simmons
Dallas, Texas

Fred A. Simpson
Houston, Texas

Adam Snyder
Wadsworth, Illinois

Randall J. Snyder
Bismarck, North Dakota

William C. Spence
Chicago, Illinois

Scott A. Stengel
Washington, D.C.

Heather E. Stern
Los Angeles, California

Scott Patrick Stolley
Dallas, Texas

Victor R. Stull
Redlands, California

Michelle Dimond Szambelan
Spokane, Washington

Tony Tanke
Davis, California

Craig D. Tindall
Phoenix, Arizona

Nick Tishler
Niskayuna, New York

Peter J. Toren
New York, New York

Renée Maria Tremblay
Ottawa, Ontario, Canada

Craig J. Trocino
Fort Lauderdale, Florida

R. Collins Vallée
Mandeville, Louisiana

Arthur A. Vingiello
Baton Rouge, Louisiana

Kristin P. Walinski
Richmond, Virginia

Richard S. Walinski
Toledo, Ohio

Alison Wallis
Harvey, Louisiana

Mark R. Wasem
Dallas, Texas

Christine E. Watchorn
Columbus, Ohio

M. John Way
Tumwater, Washington

Philip Weltner II
Atlanta, Georgia

Garner K. Weng
San Francisco, California

Eric R. Werner
Fort Worth, Texas

Donald C. Wheaton Jr.
St. Clair Shores, Michigan

Carla L. Wheeler
Chevy Chase, Maryland

Daniel R. White
Los Angeles, California

Malcolm E. Whittaker
Houston, Texas

Jamison Wilcox
Hamden, Connecticut

Hon. Bruce Donald Willis
Plymouth, Minnesota

Conrad R. Wolan
Elmira, New York

Craig M. Wolff
Yarmouth, Maine

Sara T.S. Wolff
Yarmouth, Maine

Albert J. Wollerman
Tallahassee, Florida

William C. Wright
West Palm Beach, Florida

GARNER LAW SCHOLARS — SMU SCHOOL OF LAW

JoAnn Dodson
Plano, Texas

Arrissa K. Meyer
Dallas, Texas

Shayna Edwards
Dallas, Texas

Jonathan Michael Thomas
Dallas, Texas

Timothy D. Martin
The Colony, Texas

Laurie M. Velasco
Plano, Texas

Contents

Guide to the Dictionary.............................. xiii
List of Abbreviations in Definitions................... xvii

Dictionary... 1

Appendix
   The Constitution of the United States 1391

Guide to the Dictionary

1. Alphabetization

All headwords, including abbreviations, are alphabetized letter by letter, not word by word. Spaces, apostrophes, hyphens, virgules, and the like are ignored. An ampersand (&) is treated as if it were the word *and*. For example:

Pan-American Convention
P & L
Panduit **test**
per annum
P/E ratio
per capita
percentage lease
per diem
peremptory

Numerals included in a headword precede the letter "a" and are arranged in ascending numerical order:

Rule 10b–5
Rule 11
rule absolute
rulemaking
rule of 72
rule of 78

A numeral at the beginning of a headword is alphabetized as if the numeral were spelled out:

Eighth Amendment
eight-hour law
8–K
ejection

Commas break the letter-by-letter alphabetization if they are backward-looking (e.g., *attorney, power of*), but not if they are forward-looking (e.g., *right, title, and interest*).

2. Pronunciations

Boldface syllables receive primary stress:

oligopoly (ol-ə-**gop**-ə-lee), *n.*

If a word has more than one acceptable pronunciation, the preferred pronunciation appears first and the variant form after *or*:

talesman (**taylz**-mən *or* **tay**-leez-mən).

A pronunciation of dubious standing is preceded by *also*:

condition precedent (prə-**seed**-ənt *also* **pres**-ə-dənt).

For variably pronounced syllables, often only the changed syllables are included.

> *ejusdem generis* (ee-**jəs**-dəm **jen**-ə-ris *also* ee-**joos**- or ee-**yoos**-).

Brackets in pronunciations indicate an optional sound:

> **fiduciary** (fi-**d[y]oo**-shee-er-ee), *adj.*

For handy reference, the pronunciation guide is located inside the front cover.

3. Etymologies

The origins of most foreign words and phrases are given in brackets. By far the most frequent etymologies are "Latin" (i.e., classical Latin used during the Roman Empire) and "Law Latin" (i.e., the Anglicized Latin formerly used in legal documents and proceedings). Essentially, the *Law Latin* tag corresponds to what some dictionaries call *Late Latin* and others call *Medieval Latin*. Other languages of origin are listed as well, including French, Law French (i.e., medieval common-law French), Old English, Greek, German, and Dutch.

4. Dates

The parenthetical dates preceding many of the definitions show the earliest known use of the word or phrase in English. For some words, the date is merely a century (e.g., *14c*), but for most of the recently emerging vocabulary a precise year is given. The editors hope to extend this feature to most or even all the entries in future editions. Interested researchers should know that we welcome certifiable antedatings.

5. Tags

Two types of tags appear. First, there are usage tags:

> *Hist.* = historical; no longer current in law
> *Archaic* = old-fashioned and declining in use
> *Rare* = very infrequent in modern usage
> *Slang* = very informal

Second, there are many subject-matter tags that identify the field of law that a particular term or sense belongs to (e.g., *Antitrust*, *Commercial law*, *Insurance*, and *Wills & estates*). Two of these tags deserve special mention. *Roman law* indicates a term that can be traced back to the legal system of the ancient Romans. *Civil law* indicates a term that is used in modern civil-law systems, including much of the law in Louisiana.

6. Angle Brackets

Contextual illustrations of a headword are given in angle brackets:

> **avail**, *n.* **1.** Use or advantage <of little or no avail>. **2.** (*pl.*) Profits or proceeds, esp. from a sale of property <the avails of the trust fund>.

7. Bullets

Bullets are used to separate definitional information (before the bullet) from information that is not purely definitional (after the bullet), such as encyclopedic information or usage notes.

8. Cognate Forms

This dictionary lists corresponding parts of speech. For example, under the definition of *consultation*, the corresponding verb (*consult*) and adjectives (*consulting, consultative*) are listed.

If a cognate form applies to only one sense of a headword, that form is denoted as follows:

> **enjoin,** *vb.* **1.** To legally prohibit or restrain by injunction <the company was enjoined from selling its stock>. **2.** To prescribe, mandate, or strongly encourage <the graduating class was enjoined to uphold the highest professional standards>. — **enjoinment** (for sense 1), *n.* — **enjoinder** (for sense 2), *n.*

9. Cross-references

a. See

The signal *See* is used in three ways.

(1) To indicate that the definition is at another location in the dictionary:

> **call loan.** See LOAN.

> **perpetuities, rule against.** See RULE AGAINST PERPETUITIES.

(2) To refer to closely related terms:

> **nationalization,** *n.* **1.** The act of bringing an industry under governmental control or ownership. **2.** The act of giving a person the status of a citizen. See NATURALIZATION.

> **cognovit** (kog-**noh**-vit). [Latin "the person has conceded (a debt or an action)"] An acknowledgment of debt or liability in the form of a confessed judgment. See *confession of judgment* under JUDGMENT.

(3) To refer to a synonymous subentry:

> **binding instruction.** See *mandatory instruction* under JURY INSTRUCTION.

b. Cf.

Cf. is used to refer to related but contrastable terms:

> ***Gallagher* agreement.** A contract that gives one codefendant the right to settle with the plaintiff for a fixed sum at any time during trial and that guarantees payment of the sum regardless of the trial's outcome. *City of Tucson v. Gallagher*, 493 P.2d 1197 (Ariz. 1972). Cf. MARY CARTER AGREEMENT.

> **false imprisonment.** A restraint of a person in a bounded area without justification or consent. ● False imprisonment is a common-law misdemeanor and a tort. It applies to private as well as governmental detention. Cf. *false arrest* under ARREST.

c. Also termed

The phrase also termed at the end of an entry signals a synonymous word or phrase. Variations include also spelled, also written, and often shortened to.

d. Terms with multiple senses

If the cross-referenced term has multiple senses, the particular sense referred to is indicated in parentheses:

> **light work.** See WORK (1).

> **rule day.** See return day (3) under DAY.

10. Subentries

Many terms in this dictionary are collected by topic. For example, the different types of contracts, such as *bilateral contract* and *gratuitous contract*, are defined under the main term *contract*. (Cross-references in B and G will redirect the reader who looks up *bilateral contract* or *gratuitous contract* to *contract*.) If a term has more than one sense, then the corresponding subentries are placed under the appropriate sense of that term.

11. Typefaces

The typefaces used in this dictionary are mostly self-explanatory. For instance, all headwords and cognate forms are in boldface type, and all subentries are italicized. As for headwords of foreign origin, those that are fully naturalized are in boldface Roman type, while those that are not fully naturalized are in boldface italics. Generally, small caps are used with "See" and "Cf." cross-references to main entries. There are, however, three other uses of small caps deserving special mention.

a. Small caps refer to a synonymous headword. In the following example, the small caps suggest that you review the definition at *contiguous* for more information:

> **adjoining.** Touching; sharing a common boundary; contiguous. — **adjoin,** *vb.*

b. Small caps also refer to the predominant form when it may be phrased or spelled in more than one way. For example, the following uses of small caps direct you to the entries at *perjury* and *payor*:

> **false swearing.** See PERJURY.

> **payer.** See PAYOR.

c. Small caps also refer to the spelled-out form of abbreviations (the term is defined at the spelled-out headword, not the abbreviated form). For example:

> **FDIC.** *abbr.* FEDERAL DEPOSIT INSURANCE CORPORATION.

> **Federal Deposit Insurance Corporation.** A federal corporation that protects bank and thrift deposits by insuring accounts up to $100,000, examining banks that are not members of the Federal Reserve System, and liquidating failed institutions. — Abbr. FDIC.

11. Abbreviations

For a list of abbreviations used within entries see p. xvii.

List of Abbreviations

abbr.	=	abbreviated as; abbreviation for
adj.	=	adjective
adv.	=	adverb
BrE	=	British English
ca.	=	circa
cap.	=	capitalized
cf.	=	(*confer*) compare with
ch.	=	chapter
conj.	=	conjunction
ed.	=	edition; editor
e.g.	=	(*exempli gratia*) for example
esp.	=	especially
et seq.	=	(*et sequentes*) and those (pages or sections) that follow
fr.	=	from; derived from
id.	=	(*idem*) in the same work
i.e.	=	(*id est*) that is
l.c.	=	lowercase
n.	=	noun; note
no.	=	number
¶	=	paragraph
pl.	=	plural
pp.	=	pages
p.pl.	=	past participle
prep.	=	preposition
pt.	=	part
repr.	=	reprinted
rev.	=	revised by; revision
§	=	section
sing.	=	singular
specif.	=	specifically
usu.	=	usually
vb.	=	verb

A

a. 1. (*usu. cap. & often ital.*) A hypothetical person <*A* deeds Blackacre to *B*>. **2.** [Latin] From; by; in; on; of; at. **3.** [Law Latin] With. **4.** [Law French] Of; at; to; for; in; with. **5.** *Securities.* A letter used in a newspaper stock-transaction table to indicate that cash was paid during the year in addition to regular dividends. **6.** *Securities.* A letter used in a newspaper mutual-fund transaction table to indicate a yield that may include capital gains and losses as well as current interest. **7.** (*cap.*) *Securities.* A letter used in a newspaper corporate earnings report to identify the American Stock Exchange as the primary market of a firm's common stock. **8.** (*cap.*) *Securities.* An above-average grade given to a debt obligation by a rating agency. ● The grades, as ranked by Standard & Poor's, range from AAA (highest) down to CCC. The equivalent standards from Moody's are Aaa, Aa, A, Baa, and so on down to C. **9.** *Marine insurance.* A rating assigned in *Lloyd's Register of Shipping* to ships considered to be in first-class condition. **10.** *abbr.* ADVERSUS. **11.** (*cap.*) *Hist.* A scarlet letter worn as punishment by a person convicted of adultery. **12.** *Roman law.* An abbreviation for *absolvo* written on wooden tablets by criminal-court judges to indicate a vote for acquittal. **13.** *Roman law.* An abbreviation for *antiquo* ("for the old law") written on wooden tablets by the participants in a popular assembly to indicate a vote against a proposed bill. **14.** (*cap.*) *abbr.* ATLANTIC REPORTER.

A.2d. *abbr. Atlantic Reporter Second Series.* See ATLANTIC REPORTER.

AAA. *abbr.* **1.** AMERICAN ARBITRATION ASSOCIATION. **2.** AMERICAN ACCOUNTING ASSOCIATION. **3.** AMERICAN ACADEMY OF ACTUARIES. **4.** AGRICULTURAL ADJUSTMENT ACT. **5.** See *accumulated-adjustments account* under ACCOUNT.

AALL. *abbr.* American Association of Law Libraries, founded in 1906 to promote law libraries and scholarship in the field of law-library science.

AALS. *abbr.* ASSOCIATION OF AMERICAN LAW SCHOOLS.

AAU. *abbr.* Amendment to allege use. See TRADEMARK APPLICATION AMENDMENT.

AB. *abbr.* See *able-bodied seaman* under SEAMAN.

ab, *prep.* [Latin] From; by; of.

ABA. *abbr.* **1.** AMERICAN BAR ASSOCIATION. **2.** AMERICAN BANKERS ASSOCIATION.

abacinate (ə-**bas**-ə-nayt), *vb.* To blind (a person) by placing a red-hot iron or metal plate in front of the eyes.

abalienation (ab-**ayl**-yə-nay-shən), *n.* [fr. Latin *abalienare* "to alienate"] *Civil law.* The transfer of an interest in or title to property; ALIENATION (2). ● In Roman law, the term was *abalienatio* ("a perfect conveyance from one Roman citizen to another"), which was anglicized to *abalienation*. — **abalienate**, *vb.*

abandoned application. *Patents & Trademarks.* An application removed from the U.S. Patent and Trademark Office docket of pending applications because the applicant (or the applicant's attorney or agent of record) filed an express notice of abandonment, failed to take appropriate or timely action at some stage in the prosecution of a nonprovisional application, or failed to pay the issue fee. ● Abandonment of a patent or trademark application does not automatically result in abandonment of the invention or the mark because an abandoned application may be revived by petition. Cf. *abandoned invention* under INVENTION; *abandoned mark* under TRADEMARK.

abandoned experiment. *Patents.* An unsuccessful attempt to reduce an invention to practice. ● Unless it is publicly known, an abandoned experiment does not qualify as prior art under § 102 of the Patent Act, so it does not bar future patents.

abandoned invention. See INVENTION.

abandoned mark. See *abandoned trademark* under TRADEMARK.

abandoned property. See PROPERTY.

abandoned, suppressed, or concealed, *adj. Patents.* Intentionally or accidentally hidden from public notice, not reduced to practice, or not patented. ● Another person's earlier invention will not be considered prior art if the first inventor abandoned the field to others or is held to have lost the right to patent by suppressing or concealing the invention. But if the suppression or concealment occurred after the art was known to the public, then it still qualifies as prior art. *See* MPEP § 2138.03.

abandoned trademark. See TRADEMARK.

abandonee (ə-ban-də-**nee**). (1848) One to whom property rights are relinquished; one to whom something is formally or legally abandoned.

abandonment, *n.* (1809) **1.** The relinquishing of a right or interest with the intention of never reclaiming it. ● In the context of contracts for the sale of land, courts sometimes use the term *abandonment* as if it were synonymous with *rescission*, but the two should be distinguished. An abandonment is merely one party's acceptance of the situation that a nonperforming party has caused. But a rescission due to a material breach is a termination or discharge of the contract for all purposes. **2.** *Property.* The relinquishing of or departing from a homestead, etc., with the present, definite, and permanent intention of never returning or regaining possession. **3.** *Family law.* The act of leaving a spouse or child willfully and without an intent to return. ● Child abandonment is grounds for termination of parental rights. Spousal abandonment is grounds for divorce. Cf. DESERTION.

malicious abandonment. 1. The desertion of a spouse without just cause. See *criminal desertion* under DESERTION. **2.** See *voluntary abandonment.*

voluntary abandonment. 1. As a ground for divorce, a final departure without the consent of the other spouse, without sufficient reason, and without the intention to return. **2.** In the law of adoption, a natural parent's willful act or course of conduct that implies a conscious disregard of or indifference to a child, as if no parental obligation existed. — Also termed *malicious abandonment.*

4. *Criminal law.* RENUNCIATION (3). **5.** *Bankruptcy.* A trustee's court-approved release of property that is burdensome or of inconsequential value to the estate, or the trustee's release of nonadministered property to the debtor when the case is closed. **6.** *Contracts.* RESCISSION (2). **7.** *Insurance.* An insured's relinquishing of damaged or lost property to the insurer as a constructive total loss. Cf. SALVAGE (2). **8.** *Trademarks.* A mark owner's failure to maintain the mark's proper use in commerce or failure to maintain its distinctive character. ● Abandonment is an affirmative defense to an action for trademark infringement. — Also termed *nonuse.* **9.** *Hist. Copyright.* An affirmative defense to a copyright-infringement claim governed by pre-1989 law, based on the author's general publication of the work without a copyright notice. ● Before March 1989, authors who did not affix a copyright notice to their published works risked losing legal protection for those works. Congress eliminated the copyright-notice requirement when it ratified the Berne Convention. **10.** *Intellectual property.* The loss of an intellectual-property right, as by disuse, neglect of formalities, failure to pay a required fee, or (for a trade secret) failure to ensure concealment. — **abandon,** *vb.*

abandonment by operation of law. See *constructive abandonment.*

actual abandonment. 1. *Patents.* Intentional relinquishment of the right to patent protection, evidenced, for example, by more than mere inactivity or delay in filing the application. ● Actual abandonment may be express or implied, but every reasonable doubt about intent will be resolved in the inventor's favor. **2.** *Trademarks.* Intentional loss of trademark protection by discontinuing commercial use of the mark with the intention of not using it again.

constructive abandonment. 1. *Patents.* The closing of a patent-application prosecution by the U.S. Patent and Trademark Office when an applicant fails to respond to an office action within the time allowed, usu. six months, or fails to pay an issue fee. ● If the delay was unintentional or unavoidable, the application may be revived. **2.** *Patents.* Abandonment of an invention by operation of law regardless of the inventor's intention, such as when the inventor forfeits the right to patent by selling or offering to sell the invention or by describing it in a publication more than a year before seeking patent protection. 35 USCA § 102. **3.** *Trademarks.* An owner's loss of trademark protection, regardless of whether the mark is registered, by allowing the mark to lose its distinctiveness, such as by letting the name become a generic term for that type of goods, or by otherwise failing to maintain the mark's distinctive character. ● For example, licensing the use of the mark without retaining control over how it is used may result in constructive abandonment. — Also termed *abandonment by operation of law.*

express abandonment. *Patents.* An applicant's intentional and clear termination of a patent prosecution. ● An express abandonment must be made in a signed writing and received by the U.S. Patent and Trademark Office in time for the Office to act before the patent issues. Once an application is expressly abandoned, it cannot be revived, and the applicant cannot preclude the public from freely availing itself of the invention's benefits. Unless there is an express abandonment filed, abandonment of a patent application does not result in abandonment of the invention. — Also termed *formal abandonment.*

formal abandonment. See *express abandonment.*

implied abandonment. *Patents.* An inventor's failure to take steps to protect an invention, such as by failing to claim the invention when disclosed in a patent application or by permitting an application to be abandoned, esp. by failing to file an answer to an office action within the time allowed.

abandonment of contest. *Patents.* A party's withdrawal from an interference contest. ● The abandonment of contest must be in writing. The contest is dissolved as to the abandoning party.

abatable nuisance. See NUISANCE.

abatement (ə-**bayt**-mənt), *n.* (14c) **1.** The act of eliminating or nullifying <abatement of a nuisance> <abatement of a writ>. **2.** The suspension or defeat of a pending action for a reason unrelated to the merits of the claim <the defendant sought abatement of the suit because of misnomer>. See *plea in abatement* under PLEA (2) **3.** The act of lessening or moderating; diminution in amount or degree <abatement of the debt>. **4.** *Wills & estates.* The reduction of a legacy, general or specific, as a result of the estate's being insufficient to pay all debts and legacies <the abatement of legacies resulted from the estate's insolvency>. Cf. ADEMPTION. **5.** *Archaic.* The act of tortiously entering real estate after the owner dies and before the legal heir enters <abatement of freehold>. — Also termed (in sense 5) *abatamentum.* — **abate,** *vb.* — **abatable,** *adj.*

abatement clause. (1890) A lease provision that releases the tenant from the rent obligation when an act of God or other specified reason precludes occupancy.

abater (ə-**bay**-tər *or* -tor). **1.** One who abates something. **2.** A plea in abatement. See *plea in abatement* under PLEA (2).

abator (ə-**bay**-tər *or* -tor). (16c) **1.** A person who eliminates a nuisance. See ABATEMENT (1). **2.** *Hist.* A person who tortiously intrudes on an heir's freehold before the heir takes possession. See ABATEMENT (5).

abbacy (**ab**-ə-see). *Eccles. law.* An abbot's jurisdiction or term of tenure.

abbess (**ab**-is). *Eccles. law.* A female superior or governess of a convent. Cf. ABBOT.

abbey (**ab**-ee). *Eccles. law.* A monastery governed by an abbot, or a convent governed by an abbess.

abbot (**ab**-ət). *Eccles. law.* A superior or governor of an abbey. Cf. ABBESS.

abbreviated term sheet. See TERM SHEET.

Abbreviatio Placitorum (ə-bree-vee-**ay**-shee-oh plas-i-**tor**-əm), *n.* [Law Latin "summary of the pleas"] *Hist.* An abstract of pleadings culled from the rolls of the *Curia Regis,* Parliament, and common-law courts from the 12th to 14th centuries, compiled in the 17th century, printed in 1811, and attributed variously to Arthur Agarde, Deputy Chamberlain of the Exchequer, and to other keepers of the records. Cf. YEAR BOOKS.

abbreviator. 1. One who abbreviates, abridges, or shortens. **2.** *Eccles. law.* An officer in the court of Rome appointed as assistant to the vice-chancellor for drawing up the Pope's briefs and reducing petitions, when granted, into proper form to be converted into papal bulls.

ABC test. The rule that an employee is not entitled to unemployment insurance benefits if the employee (A) is free from the control of the employer, (B) works away from the employer's place of business, and (C) is engaged in an established trade. ● The name derives from the A, B, and C commonly used in designating the three parts of the test.

ABC transaction. *Oil & gas.* A sale of a working interest from an owner (A) to an operator (B) in return for a cash payment and the right to another (usu. larger) payment when the well produces, followed by A's sale of the right to the production payment to a corporation (C), which pays A in cash borrowed from a lender on C's pledge of the production payment. ● Thus A receives cash taxed at capital-gains rates, and B pays part of the purchase price with nontaxable production income. The tax advantages of this transaction were eliminated by the Tax Reform Act of 1969.

abdication (ab-di-**kay**-shən), *n.* The act of renouncing or abandoning privileges or duties, esp. those connected with high office <Edward VIII's abdication of the Crown in 1936> <the court's abdication of its judicial responsibility>. — **abdicate** (**ab**-di-kayt), *vb.* — **abdicable** (**ab**-di-kə-bəl), *adj.* — **abdicator** (**ab**-di-kay-tər), *n.*

abditory (**ab**-di-tor-ee), *n.* [Law Latin *abditorium* "box, receptacle"] A repository used to hide and preserve goods or money. — Also termed *abditorium* (ab-di-**tor**-ee-əm).

abduction (ab-**dək**-shən), *n.* (17c) *Criminal law.* **1.** The act of leading someone away by force or fraudulent persuasion. ● Some jurisdictions have added various elements to this basic definition, such as that the abductor must have the intent to marry or defile the person, that the abductee must be a child, or that the abductor must intend to subject the abductee to concubinage or prostitution. **2.** *Archaic.* The crime of taking away a female person, esp. one who is below a certain age (such as 16 or 18), without her effective consent by use of persuasion, fraud, or violence, for the purpose of marriage, prostitution, or illicit sex. **3.** Loosely, KIDNAPPING. See ENTICEMENT OF A CHILD. — **abduct,** *vb.* — **abductor,** *n.* — **abductee,** *n.*

abearance (ə-**bair**-ənts), *n. Archaic.* Behavior; conduct.

***Abercrombie* classification.** *Trademarks.* A characterization of a trade designation — whether by mark, name, or dress — as generic, descriptive, suggestive, and arbitrary or fanciful, in increasing order of distinctiveness. *Abercrombie & Fitch Co. v. Hunting World, Inc.,* 537 F.2d 4, 9 (2d Cir. 1976).

aberrant behavior (a-**ber**-ənt). (1924) A single act of unplanned or thoughtless criminal behavior. ● Many courts have held that aberrant behavior justifies a downward departure — that is, a more lenient sentence — under the federal sentencing guidelines, based on a comment in the introduction to the *Guidelines Manual* to the effect that the guidelines do not deal with single acts of aberrant behavior. *U.S. Sentencing Guidelines Manual*, ch. 1, pt. A, ¶ 4.

abet (ə-**bet**), *vb.* (14c) **1.** To aid, encourage, or assist (someone), esp. in the commission of a crime <abet a known felon>. **2.** To support (a crime) by active assistance <abet a burglary>. See AID AND ABET. Cf. INCITE. — **abetment,** *n.*

abettor. A person who instigates the commission of a crime or advises and encourages others to commit it. — Also spelled *abetter.* See *principal in the second degree* under PRINCIPAL (2).

ab extra (ab **ek**-strə), *adv.* [Latin] From outside; extra; beyond.

abeyance (ə-**bay**-ənts), *n.* (17c) **1.** Temporary inactivity; suspension. **2.** *Property.* A lapse in succession during which no person is vested with title. — **abeyant,** *adj.*

abide, *vb.* (bef. 12c) **1.** To tolerate or withstand <the widow found it difficult to abide the pain of losing her husband>. **2.** To obey; (with *by*) to act in accordance with or in conformity to <try to abide the doctor's order to quit smoking> <abide by the rules>. **3.** To await <the death-row prisoners abide execution>. **4.** To perform or execute (an order or judgment) <the trial court abided the appellate court's order>. **5.** To stay or dwell <the right to abide in any of the 50 states>.

abiding conviction. See CONVICTION.

ability. (14c) The capacity to perform an act or service; esp., the power to carry out a legal act <ability to enter into a contract>.

   present ability. The actual, immediate power to do something (esp. to commit a crime).

ab initio (ab i-**nish**-ee-oh), *adv.* [Latin] (16c) From the beginning <the injunction was valid *ab initio*>.

abjudge (ab-**jəj**), *vb. Archaic.* To take away or remove (something) by judicial decision. Cf. ADJUDGE.

abjuration (ab-juu-**ray**-shən), *n.* A renouncing by oath.

   abjuration of the realm. An oath taken to leave the realm forever.

abjure (ab-**joor**), *vb.* **1.** To renounce formally or on oath <abjure one's citizenship>. **2.** To avoid or abstain from <abjure one's civic duties>. — **abjuratory** (ab-**joor**-ə-tor-ee), *adj.*

ablative fact. See *divestitive fact* under FACT.

able, *adj.* Legally competent and qualified <able to transfer title>.

able-bodied seaman. See SEAMAN.

ablegate (ab-lə-gayt), *n.* A papal envoy on a special mission, such as carrying a newly appointed cardinal's insignia of office.

ableism. Prejudice against or disregard of disabled people's needs and rights; discrimination that unreasonably favors able-bodied persons. See DISCRIMINATION (1), (2). — **ableist,** *adj.*

able seaman. See *able-bodied seaman* under SEAMAN.

able to work. *Labor law.* (Of a worker) released from medical care and capable of employment; esp., not qualified to receive unemployment benefits on grounds of illness or injury.

ablocation (ab-loh-**kay**-shən). *Archaic.* The leasing of property for money. Cf. LOCATIO.

abnormal law. The law as it applies to persons who are under legal disabilities such as infancy, alienage, insanity, criminality, and (formerly) coverture.

abnormally dangerous activity. (1957) An undertaking that necessarily carries with it a significant risk of serious harm even if reasonable care is used, and for which the actor may face strict liability for any harm caused; esp., an activity (such as dynamiting) for which the actor is held strictly liable because the activity (1) involves the risk of serious harm to persons or property, (2) cannot be performed without this risk, regardless of the precautions taken, and (3) does not ordinarily occur in the community. ● Under the *Restatement (Second) of Torts*, determining whether an activity is abnormally dangerous includes analyzing whether there is a high degree of risk of harm, whether any harm caused will be substantial, whether the exercise of reasonable care will eliminate the risk, whether the activity is a matter of common usage, whether the activity is appropriate to the place in which it occurs, and whether the activity's value to society outweighs its dangerousness. Restatement (Second) of Torts § 520 (1977). — Also, esp. formerly, termed *abnormally hazardous activity*; *extrahazardous activity*; *ultrahazardous activity*. See *strict liability* under LIABILITY.

abode. (13c) A home; a fixed place of residence. See DOMICILE; PLACE OF ABODE.

abolish, *vb.* To annul, eliminate, or destroy, esp. an ongoing practice or thing.

abolition. (16c) **1.** The act of abolishing. **2.** The state of being annulled or abrogated. **3.** (*usu. cap.*) The legal termination of slavery in the United States. **4.** *Civil law.* Withdrawal of a criminal accusation; a sovereign's remission of punishment for a crime. **5.** *Hist.* Permission granted to the accuser in a criminal action to withdraw from its prosecution. See NOLLE PROSEQUI.

abominable and detestable crime against nature. See SODOMY.

aboriginal cost. See COST (1).

aboriginal title. See TITLE (2).

abortee (ə-bor-**tee**). A woman who undergoes an abortion.

aborticide. See ABORTIFACIENT.

abortifacient (ə-bor-tə-**fay**-shənt), *n.* A drug, article, or other thing designed or intended to produce an abortion. — Also (rarely) termed *aborticide.* — **abortifacient,** *adj.*

abortion, *n.* (16c) **1.** An artificially induced termination of a pregnancy for the purpose of destroying an embryo or fetus. ● In *Roe v. Wade,* the Supreme Court first recognized a woman's right to choose to end her pregnancy as a privacy right stemming from the Due Process Clause of the 14th Amendment. 410 U.S. 113, 93 S.Ct. 705 (1973). Sixteen years later, in *Webster v. Reproductive Health Services,* the Court permitted states to limit this right by allowing them to enact legislation that (1) prohibits public facilities or employees from performing abortions, (2) prohibits the use of public funds for family planning that includes information on abortion, or (3) severely limits the right to an abortion after a fetus becomes viable — that is, could live independently of its mother. 492 U.S. 490, 109 S.Ct. 3040 (1989). In 1992, the Court held that (1) before viability, a woman has a fundamental right to choose to terminate her pregnancy, (2) a law that imposes an undue burden on the woman's right to choose before viability is unconstitutional, and (3) after viability, the state, in promoting its interest in potential human life, may regulate or prohibit abortion unless it is necessary to preserve the life or health of the mother. *Planned Parenthood of Southeastern Pa. v. Casey,* 505 U.S. 833, 112 S.Ct. 2791 (1992). In 2000, the Court again considered abortion rights and reaffirmed *Casey* in holding the Nebraska law at issue unconstitutional because (1) it failed to provide an exception to preserve the health of the mother, and (2) it unduly burdened a woman's right to choose a late-term abortion, thereby unduly burdening her right to choose abortion itself. *Stenberg v. Carhart,* 530 U.S. 914, 120 S.Ct. 2597 (2000). — Formerly also termed *procuring an abortion; criminal operation; criminal miscarriage; procuring miscarriage.* **2.** The spontaneous expulsion of an embryo or fetus before viability; MISCARRIAGE. — **abort,** *vb.* — **abortionist,** *n.*

forced abortion. An abortion performed without the mother's consent.

induced abortion. An abortion purposely and artificially caused either by the mother herself or by a third party. See ABORTIFACIENT.

late-term abortion. An abortion performed during the latter stages of pregnancy, usu. after the middle of the second trimester.

partial-birth abortion. An abortion in which a fetus is partly extruded from the womb and then destroyed.

spontaneous abortion. See MISCARRIAGE.

therapeutic abortion. An abortion carried out to preserve the life or health of the mother.

above, *adj. & adv.* (Of an appellate court) having the power to review the case at issue; having dealt with an appeal in the case at issue;<the court above> <when the case was heard above, the issue was not raised>. Cf. BELOW (2).

above-mentioned, *adj.* See AFORESAID.

above-stated, *adj.* See AFORESAID.

above-the-line, *adj.* (1973) (Of a deduction) taken after calculating gross income and before calculating adjusted gross income. ● Examples of above-the-line deductions are IRA contributions and moving expenses. Formerly, individual tax returns had a dark line above which these deductions were written. Cf. BELOW-THE-LINE.

A-B-Q trust. See *bypass trust* under TRUST.

abridge, *vb.* (14c) **1.** To reduce or diminish <abridge one's civil liberties>. **2.** To condense (as a book or other writing) <the author abridged the treatise before final publication>.

abridgment. 1. The reduction or diminution of something concrete (as a treatise) or abstract (as a legal right). **2.** A condensed version of a longer work **3.** *Hist.* A legal digest or encyclopedia.

abridgment of damages. The right of a court to reduce the damages in certain cases. See REMITTITUR.

abroad, *adv.* Outside a country; esp., other than in a forum country.

abrogate (**ab**-rə-gayt), *vb.* (16c) To abolish (a law or custom) by formal or authoritative action; to annul or repeal. Cf. OBROGATE. — **abrogation,** *n.*

abrogation of adoption. *Family law.* An action brought by an adoptive parent to terminate the parent–child relationship by annulment of the decree of adoption. ● An adoption may be nullified if it resulted from fraud, misrepresentation, or undue influence, or if nullification is in the child's best interests. — Also termed *annulment of adoption.* Cf. WRONGFUL ADOPTION.

ABS. *abbr.* **1.** AMERICAN BUREAU OF SHIPPING. **2.** AUTOMATED BOND SYSTEM. **3.** See *able-bodied seaman* under SEAMAN.

abscond (ab-**skond**), *vb.* (16c) **1.** To depart secretly or suddenly, esp. to avoid arrest, prosecution, or service of process. **2.** To leave a place, usu. hurriedly, with another's money or property. — **abscondence** (ab-**skon**-dənts), *n.* — **absconder,** *n.*

absconding debtor. See DEBTOR.

absence, *n.* (14c) **1.** The state of being away from one's usual place of residence. **2.** A failure to appear, or to be available and reachable, when expected. **3.** *Louisiana law.* The state of being an absent person. — Also termed (in sense 3) *absentia.*

absentee, *adj.* Not present <absentee voter>.

absentee, *adv.* In the manner of one who is not present <Debby voted absentee>.

absentee, *n.* (17c) **1.** A person who is away from his or her usual residence; one who is absent. **2.** A person who is not present where expected. **3.** A person who either resides out of state or has departed from the state without having a representative there.

absentee ballot. 1. See BALLOT (2). **2.** See *absentee voting* under VOTING.

absentee landlord. See LANDLORD.

absentee management. See *absentee landlord* under LANDLORD.

absentee vote. See *absentee voting* under VOTING.

absentee voting. See VOTING.

absentia. 1. See ABSENCE (3). **2.** IN ABSENTIA.

absent parent. See *noncustodial parent* under PARENT.

absent person. See PERSON (1).

absoile (ab-**soyl**), *vb.* See ASSOIL.

absolute, *adj.* (14c) **1.** Free from restriction, qualification, or condition <absolute ownership>. **2.** Conclusive and not liable to revision <absolute delivery>. **3.** Unrestrained in the exercise of governmental power <absolute monarchy>. — **absolute**, *n.*

absolute assignee. See ASSIGNEE.

absolute assignment. See ASSIGNMENT (2).

absolute auction. See *auction without reserve* under AUCTION.

absolute-bar rule. The principle that, when a creditor sells collateral without giving reasonable notice to the debtor, the creditor may not obtain a deficiency judgment for any amount of the debt that is not satisfied by the sale. • The rule governs commercially unreasonable sales made in violation of the UCC.

absolute contraband. See CONTRABAND.

absolute conveyance. See CONVEYANCE (1).

absolute covenant. See COVENANT (1).

absolute deed. See DEED.

absolute defense. See *real defense* under DEFENSE (4).

absolute delivery. See DELIVERY.

absolute disparity. (1976) *Constitutional law.* The difference between the percentage of a group in the general population and the percentage of that group in the pool of prospective jurors on a venire. • For example, if African-Americans make up 12% of a county's population and 8% of the potential jurors on a venire, the absolute disparity of African-American veniremembers is 4%. The reason for calculating the disparity is to analyze a claim that the jury was not impartial because the venire from which it was chosen did not represent a fair cross-section of the jurisdiction's population. Some courts criticize the absolute-disparity analysis, favoring instead the comparative-disparity analysis, in the belief that the absolute-disparity analysis understates the deviation. See FAIR-CROSS-SECTION REQUIREMENT; DUREN TEST; STATISTICAL-DECISION THEORY. Cf. COMPARATIVE DISPARITY.

absolute divorce. See *divorce a vinculo matrimonii* under DIVORCE.

absolute duty. See DUTY (1).

absolute estate. See ESTATE (1).

absolute gift. See *inter vivos gift* under GIFT.

absolute guaranty. See GUARANTY.

absolute immunity. See IMMUNITY (1).

absolute interest. See INTEREST (2).

absolute law. (16c) A supposed law of nature thought to be unchanging in principle, although circumstances may vary the way in which it is applied. See NATURAL LAW.

absolute legacy. See LEGACY.

absolute liability. See *strict liability* under LIABILITY.

absolute majority. See MAJORITY.

absolute martial law. See MARTIAL LAW.

absolute novelty. See NOVELTY.

absolute nuisance. See NUISANCE.

absolute nullity. See NULLITY.

absolute obligation. See OBLIGATION.

absolute pardon. See PARDON.

absolute pollution exclusion. See *pollution exclusion* under EXCLUSION (3).

absolute presumption. See *conclusive presumption* under PRESUMPTION.

absolute-priority rule. *Bankruptcy.* The rule that a confirmable reorganization plan must provide for full payment to a class of dissenting unsecured creditors before a junior class of claimants will be allowed to receive or retain anything under the plan. • Some jurisdictions recognize an exception to this rule when a junior class member, usu. a partner or shareholder of the debtor, contributes new capital in exchange for an interest in the debtor. 11 USCA § 1129(b)(2)(B)(ii).

absolute privilege. See PRIVILEGE (1).

absolute property. See PROPERTY.

absolute right. See RIGHT.

absolute sale. See SALE.

absolute simulated contract. See CONTRACT.

absolute title. See TITLE (2).

absolute veto. See VETO.

absolution (ab-sə-**loo**-shən). **1.** Release from a penalty; the act of absolving. **2.** *Civil law.* An acquittal of a criminal charge. — Also termed *absolutio*. **3.** *Eccles. law.* Official forgiveness of a sin or sins.

absolutism (**ab**-sə-loo-tiz-əm), *n.* In politics, the rule of a dictator whose power has no restrictions, checks, or balances; the belief in such a dictatorship. — **absolutist** (**ab**-sə-loo-tist), *adj.* & *n.*

absolve (ab- *or* əb-**zolv**), *vb.* (15c) **1.** To release from an obligation, debt, or responsibility. **2.** To free from the penalties for misconduct. — **absolver,** *n.*

absorbable risk. See RISK.

absorption, *n.* (18c) **1.** The act or process of including or incorporating a thing into something else; esp., the application of rights guaranteed by the U.S. Constitution to actions by the states. **2.** *Int'l law.* The merger of one nation into another, whether voluntarily or by subjugation. **3.** *Labor law.* In a postmerger collective-bargaining agreement, a provision allowing seniority for union members in the resulting entity. **4.** *Real estate.* The rate at which property will be leased or sold on the market at a given time. **5.** *Commercial law.* A sales method by which a manufacturer pays the reseller's freight costs, which the manufacturer accounts for before quoting the reseller a price. — Also termed (in sense 5) *freight absorption.* — **absorb,** *vb.*

absque (**abs**-kwee), *adv.* [Latin] Without.

absque hoc (**abs**-kwee **hok**), *adv.* [Latin] *Archaic.* Without this. ● The phrase was formerly used in common-law pleading to introduce the denial of allegations. — Also termed *sans ce que.* See TRAVERSE.

ABS Rules. *Maritime law.* Industry standards for the construction, maintenance, and operation of seagoing vessels and stationary offshore facilities, as set and enforced by the American Bureau of Shipping. See AMERICAN BUREAU OF SHIPPING.

abstain, *vb.* **1.** To voluntarily refrain from doing something, such as voting in a deliberative assembly. **2.** (Of a federal court) to refrain from exercising jurisdiction over a matter.

abstention. (16c) **1.** The act of withholding or keeping back (something or oneself); esp., the act of abstaining from voting. **2.** A federal court's relinquishment of jurisdiction when necessary to avoid needless conflict with a state's administration of its own affairs. **3.** The legal principle underlying such a relinquishment of jurisdiction. Cf. COMITY; OUR FEDERALISM.

Burford abstention. (1967) A federal court's refusal to review a state court's decision in cases involving a complex regulatory scheme and sensitive areas of state concern. *Burford v. Sun Oil Co.,* 319 U.S. 315, 63 S.Ct. 1098 (1943).

Colorado River abstention. (1976) A federal court's decision to abstain while relevant and parallel state-court proceedings are under way. *Colorado River Water Conservation Dist. v. United States,* 424 U.S. 800, 96 S.Ct. 1236 (1976).

equitable abstention. A federal court's refraining from interfering with a state administrative agency's decision on a local matter when the aggrieved party has adequate relief in the state courts.

permissive abstention. Bankruptcy. Abstention that a bankruptcy court can, but need not, exercise in a dispute that relates to the bankruptcy estate but that can be litigated, or is being litigated, in another forum. ● In deciding whether to abstain, the bankruptcy court must consider (1) the degree to which state law governs the case, (2) the appropriateness of the procedure to be followed in the other forum, (3) the remoteness of the dispute to the issues in the bankruptcy case, and (4) the presence of nondebtor parties in the dispute. 28 USCA § 1334(c)(1).

Pullman abstention. (1963) A federal court's decision to abstain so that state courts will have an opportunity to settle an underlying state-law question whose resolution may avert the need to decide a federal constitutional question. *Railroad Comm'n v. Pullman Co.,* 312 U.S. 496, 61 S.Ct. 643 (1941).

Thibodaux abstention (**tib**-ə-doh). (1974) A federal court's decision to abstain so that state courts can decide difficult issues of public importance that, if decided by the federal court, could result in unnecessary friction between state and federal authorities. *Louisiana Power & Light Co. v. City of Thibodaux,* 360 U.S. 25, 79 S.Ct. 1070 (1959).

Younger abstention. (1972) **1.** A federal court's decision not to interfere with an ongoing state criminal proceeding by issuing an injunction or granting declaratory relief, unless the prosecution has been brought in bad faith or merely as harassment. *Younger v. Harris,* 401 U.S. 37, 91 S.Ct. 746 (1971). — Also termed *equitable-restraint doctrine.* **2.** By extension, a federal court's decision not to interfere with a state-court civil proceeding used to enforce the criminal law, as to abate an obscene nuisance. See OUR FEDERALISM.

abstinence (**ab**-stə-nənts). The practice of refraining completely from indulgence in some act; esp., the practice of not having sex or of not consuming alcoholic beverages.

abstract, *n.* (15c) **1.** A concise statement of a text, esp. of a legal document; a summary. See AB-STRACT OF JUDGMENT; ABSTRACT OF TITLE. **2.** *Patents.* A one-paragraph summary of an invention's design and function, including its nature, structure, purpose, and novelty. • The abstract is a required part of a patent application, and also appears on the front page of the patent itself. It may not exceed 150 words. For the purpose of determining adequacy of disclosure, the abstract is considered to be part of the specification. See 35 USCA § 112. — Also termed *abstract of the disclosure*; *abstract of the specification*.

abstract compromis. See *general compromis* under COMPROMIS.

abstracter. See ABSTRACTOR.

abstract idea. *Intellectual Property.* A concept or thought, removed from any tangible embodiment. • An abstract idea is one of the categories of unpatentable subject matter, along with natural phenomena and laws of nature. But a process that uses abstract ideas to produce a useful result can be patented. Copyright law likewise will not protect an abstract idea, but only its expression. The law of unfair competition, on the other hand, does protect abstract ideas that meet the other criteria of a trade secret. See *business-method patent* under PATENT.

abstraction (ab- *or* əb-**strak**-shən), *n.* (16c) **1.** The mental process of considering something without reference to a concrete instance <jurisprudence is largely the abstraction of many legal particulars>. **2.** A theoretical idea not applied to any particular instance <utopia in any form is an abstraction>. **3.** The summarizing and recording of a legal instrument in public records <abstraction of the judgment in Tarrant County>. **4.** The act of taking with the intent to injure or defraud <the abstraction of funds was made possible by the forged signature on the check>. — **abstract** (ab-**strakt**), *vb.*

abstraction-filtration-comparison test. *Copyright.* A judicially created test for determining whether substantial similarity exists between two works in an action for infringement. • First, the court dissects the copyrighted work's structure and isolates each level of abstraction or generality (abstraction test). Second, the court examines each level of abstraction and separates out the unprotectable elements such as ideas, processes, facts, public-domain information, and merger material (filtration test). Finally, the court compares the resulting core of protectable expression with the accused work to determine whether substantial elements of the copyrighted work have been misappropriated (comparison test). This test was first applied by the Second Circuit in *Computer Associates Int'l, Inc. v. Altai, Inc.*, 982 F.2d 693 (2d Cir. 1992). Although that case involved computer software and the test is usu. applied in software-infringement cases, the test has also been applied to nonsoftware works. — Also termed *abstraction-filtration test*. See SIMILARITY. Cf. ABSTRACTIONS TEST.

abstractions test. *Copyright.* A means of comparing copyrighted material with material that allegedly infringes the copyright by examining whether the actual substance has been copied or whether the two works merely share the same abstract ideas. • The primary authority for the abstractions test is Judge Learned Hand's opinion in *Nichols v. Universal Pictures Corp.*, 45 F.2d 119 (2d Cir. 1930). Although referred to as a "test," it is not a bright-line test, but an approach to discerning the boundaries of protectable expression by isolating and comparing each level of abstraction in the two works, from the lowest (most detailed) to the highest (most conceptual). Cf. ABSTRACTION-FILTRATION-COMPARISON TEST; LOOK-AND-FEEL TEST.

abstract of conviction. A summary of the court's finding on an offense, esp. a traffic violation.

abstract of judgment. (1812) A copy or summary of a judgment that, when filed with the appropriate public office, creates a lien on the judgment debtor's nonexempt property. See *judgment lien* under LIEN.

abstract of record. An abbreviated case history that is complete enough to show an appellate court that the questions presented for review have been preserved.

abstract of the disclosure. See ABSTRACT (2).

abstract of the specification. See ABSTRACT (2).

abstract of title. (1858) A concise statement, usu. prepared for a mortgagee or purchaser of real property, summarizing the history of a piece of land, including all conveyances, interests, liens, and encumbrances that affect title to the property. — Also termed *brief*; *brief of title*.

> **good and merchantable abstract of title.** An abstract of title showing clear, good, and marketable title, rather than showing only the history of the property. See *clear title*, *good title*, and *marketable title* under TITLE (2).

abstractor (ab- *or* əb-**strak**-tər). A person who prepares abstracts of title. — Also spelled *abstracter*.

abstract question. See HYPOTHETICAL QUESTION.

absurdity, *n.* The state or quality of being grossly unreasonable; esp., an interpretation that would lead to an unconscionable result, esp. one that the parties or (esp. for a statute) the drafters could not have intended and probably never considered. Cf. GOLDEN RULE.

A-B trust. See *bypass trust* under TRUST.

abuse (ə-**byoos**), *n.* (15c) **1.** A departure from legal or reasonable use; misuse. **2.** Physical or mental maltreatment, often resulting in mental, emotional, sexual, or physical injury. — Also termed *cruel and abusive treatment.* Cf. NEGLECT; CRUELTY.

    abuse of the elderly. (1971) Abuse of a senior citizen, esp. by a caregiver or relative. ● Examples include deprivation of food or medication, beatings, oral assaults, and isolation. — Also termed *elder abuse.*

    carnal abuse. See *sexual abuse* (1).

    child abuse. (1891) **1.** Intentional or neglectful physical or emotional harm inflicted on a child, including sexual molestation; esp., a parent's or caregiver's act or failure to act that results in a child's exploitation, serious physical or emotional injury, sexual abuse, or death. **2.** An act or failure to act that presents an imminent risk of serious harm to a child. ● Child abuse can be either intentional or negligent. The first case of child abuse actually prosecuted occurred in New York City in 1874. An eight-year-old girl named Mary Ellen was found to have been severely abused. Her abusers were prosecuted under the law for prevention of cruelty to animals, since no law protecting children then existed. Child abuse was first recognized as a medical concern in 1962, when Dr. C. Henry Kempe introduced the medical concept of battered-child syndrome. — Also termed *cruelty to a child*; *cruelty to children*; *child maltreatment.* See *abused child* under CHILD; *battered child* under CHILD; BATTERED-CHILD SYNDROME. Cf. *secondary abuse.*

    domestic abuse. See *domestic violence* under VIOLENCE.

    elder abuse. See *abuse of the elderly.*

    emotional abuse. Physical or verbal abuse that causes or could cause serious emotional injury. — Also termed *mental abuse*; *psychological abuse.*

    mental abuse. See *emotional abuse.*

    psychological abuse. See *emotional abuse.*

    secondary abuse. Emotional harm suffered by children who, although they are not physically abused, witness domestic violence within their families.

    sexual abuse. (1874) **1.** An illegal or wrongful sex act, esp. one performed against a minor by an adult. — Also termed *carnal abuse.* **2.** RAPE (2).

    spousal abuse. (1978) Physical, sexual, or psychological abuse inflicted by one spouse on the other spouse; esp., wife-beating. See BATTERED-WOMAN SYNDROME.

    verbal abuse. Emotional abuse inflicted by one person on another by means of words, esp. spoken words, in a way that causes distress, fear, or similar emotions. ● Verbal abuse may include name-calling, insults, threatening gestures, excessive and unfounded criticism, humiliation, and denigration. — Also sometimes termed *vulgar abuse.*

    vulgar abuse. See *verbal abuse.*

abuse (ə-**byooz**), *vb.* (15c) **1.** To damage (a thing). **2.** To depart from legal or reasonable use in dealing with (a person or thing); to misuse. **3.** To injure (a person) physically or mentally. **4.** In the context of child welfare, to hurt or injure (a child) by maltreatment. ● In most states, a finding of abuse is generally limited to maltreatment that causes or threatens to cause lasting harm to the child.

abused child. See CHILD.

abusee (ə-byoo-**zee**), *n.* One who is or has been abused.

abuse excuse. (1994) *Criminal law.* The defense that a defendant cannot tell right from wrong or control impulses because of physical or mental abuse suffered as a child. ● Like the traditional excuse of insanity, the abuse excuse is asserted by a defendant in an effort to mitigate or avoid culpability for the crime charged. Cf. BATTERED-CHILD SYNDROME; BATTERED-WOMAN SYNDROME.

abuse of discovery. See DISCOVERY ABUSE.

abuse of discretion. (18c) **1.** An adjudicator's failure to exercise sound, reasonable, and legal decision-making. **2.** An appellate court's standard for reviewing a decision that is asserted to be grossly unsound, unreasonable, illegal, or unsupported by the evidence. See DISCRETION (4).

abuse of distress. *Hist.* The wrongful seizure and use of another's property as a means of collecting damages or coercing the property's owner to perform a duty.

abuse of process. (1809) The improper and tortious use of a legitimately issued court process to obtain a result that is either unlawful or beyond the process's scope. — Also termed *abuse of legal process*; *malicious abuse of process*; *malicious abuse of legal process*; *wrongful process*; *wrongful process of law.* Cf. MALICIOUS PROSECUTION.

abuse of rights. 1. *Int'l law.* A country's exercise of a right either in a way that impedes the enjoyment by other countries of their own rights or for a purpose different from that for which the right was created (e.g., to harm another country). **2.** *Louisiana law.* A person's exercise of a right in an unneighborly spirit that provides no benefit to the person but causes damage to the neighbor.

abuse-of-rights doctrine. *Civil law.* The principle that a person may be liable for harm caused by doing something the person has a right to do, if the right is exercised (1) for the purpose or primary motive of causing harm, (2) without a serious and legitimate interest that is deserving of judicial protection, (3) against moral rules, good faith, or elementary fairness, or (4) for a purpose other than its intended legal purpose.

abuse of the elderly. See ABUSE.

abuse-of-the-writ doctrine. (1973) *Criminal procedure.* The principle that a petition for a writ of habeas corpus may not raise claims that should have been, but were not, asserted in a previous petition. Cf. SUCCESSIVE-WRIT DOCTRINE.

abuser (ə-**byoo**-zər), *n.* **1.** One who abuses someone or something. **2.** ABUSE (1).

abusive (ə-**byoo**-siv), *adj.* **1.** Characterized by wrongful or improper use <abusive discovery tactics>. **2.** (Of a person) habitually cruel, malicious, or violent <abusive parent>. — **abusively,** *adv.*

abut (ə-**bət**), *vb.* (15c) To join at a border or boundary; to share a common boundary with <the company's land in Arizona abuts the Navajo Indian reservation>. — **abutment** (ə-**bət**-mənt), *n.*

abuttals (ə-**bət**-əlz). (17c) Land boundaries; the boundary lines of a piece of land in relation to other contiguous lands. — Also termed (archaically) *buttals.*

abutter (ə-**bət**-ər). **1.** The owner of adjoining land; one whose property abuts another's. **2.** Land that adjoins the land in question.

abutting foot. See FRONT FOOT.

a/c. *abbr.* ACCOUNT (4).

academic, *adj.* **1.** Of or relating to a school or a field of study; esp., of or relating to a field of study that is not vocational or commercial, such as the liberal arts <academic courses>. **2.** Theoretical; specif., not practical or immediately useful <academic question>.

academic freedom. (1863) The right (esp. of a university teacher) to speak freely about political or ideological issues without fear of loss of position or other reprisal.

academic lawyer. A law professor, usu. one who maintains a law practice on the side.

Académie de Droit International de La Haye. See HAGUE ACADEMY OF INTERNATIONAL LAW.

academy. 1. An institution of higher learning. **2.** An association dedicated to the advancement of knowledge in a particular field, such as the American Academy of Matrimonial Lawyers. **3.** A private high school. **4.** (*cap.*) A garden near Athens where Plato taught; hence, the school of philosophy that he led.

accede (ak-**seed**), *vb.* **1.** To consent or agree. **2.** To be added (to something else) through accession. **3.** To adopt. See ADOPTION (5). **4.** (Of a body politic) to accept unification with or annexation into another body politic. — **accession,** *n.* — **accedence** (ak-**see**-dənts), *n.*

Accelerated Cost Recovery System. An accounting method that is used to calculate asset depreciation and that allows for the faster recovery of costs by assigning the asset a shorter useful life than was previously permitted under the Internal Revenue Code. ● This system applies to property put into service from 1981 to 1986. It was replaced in 1986 by the Modified Accelerated Cost Recovery System. — Abbr. ACRS.

accelerated depreciation. See DEPRECIATION.

accelerated depreciation method. See DEPRECIATION METHOD.

accelerated disclosure. See *accelerated discovery* under DISCOVERY.

accelerated discovery. See DISCOVERY.

accelerated-reentry theory. See POST-EXPIRATION-SALES THEORY.

accelerated remainder. See REMAINDER.

acceleration, *n.* **1.** The advancing of a loan agreement's maturity date so that payment of the entire debt is due immediately. **2.** The shortening of the time for vesting in possession of an expectant interest. — Also termed *acceleration of remainder.* **3.** *Property.* The hastening of an owner's time for enjoyment of an estate because of the failure of a preceding estate. **4.** *Securities.* The SEC's expediting of a registration statement's effective date so that the registrant bypasses the required 20-day waiting period. — **accelerate,** *vb.*

acceleration clause. (1905) A loan-agreement provision that requires the debtor to pay off the balance sooner than the due date if some specified event occurs, such as failure to pay an installment or to maintain insurance. Cf. DEMAND CLAUSE; INSECURITY CLAUSE.

acceleration of remainder. See ACCELERATION (2).

Acceptable Identification of Goods and Services Manual. *Trademarks.* A U.S. Government publication that sets forth, for goods and services, known acceptable international class categorizations and descriptions that may be used in trademark applications submitted to the U.S. Patent and Trademark Office. ● This manual is available from the U.S. Government Printing Office, Washington, D.C. 20402 and through the PTO's website at http://www.uspto.gov.

acceptance, *n.* (16c) **1.** An offeree's assent, either by express act or by implication from conduct, to the terms of an offer in a manner authorized or requested by the offeror, so that a binding contract is formed. • If an acceptance modifies the terms or adds new ones, it generally operates as a counteroffer. Cf. OFFER.

acceptance by silence. Acceptance of an offer not by explicit words but through the lack of an offeree's response in circumstances in which the relationship between the offeror and the offeree justifies both the offeror's expectation of a reply and the offeror's reasonable conclusion that the lack of one signals acceptance. • Ordinarily, silence does not give rise to an acceptance of an offer.

qualified acceptance. A conditional or partial acceptance that varies the original terms of an offer and operates as a counteroffer; esp., in negotiable instruments (bills of exchange), an acceptor's variation of the terms of the instrument.

2. A buyer's assent that the goods are to be taken in performance of a contract for sale. • Under UCC § 2-606, a buyer's acceptance consists in (1) signifying to the seller that the goods are conforming ones or that the buyer will take them despite nonconformities, (2) not making an effective rejection, or (3) taking any action inconsistent with the seller's ownership. If the contract is for the sale of goods that are not identified when the contract is entered into, there is no acceptance until the buyer has had a reasonable time to examine the goods. But if the buyer deals with them as owner, as by reselling them, a court may find constructive acceptance. 3. The formal receipt of and agreement to pay a negotiable instrument. 4. A negotiable instrument, esp. a bill of exchange, that has been accepted for payment.

acceptance au besoin (oh bə-**zwan**). [French "in case of need"] An acceptance by one who has agreed to pay the draft in case the drawee fails to do so.

acceptance for honor. An acceptance or undertaking not by a party to the instrument, but by a third party, for the purpose of protecting the honor or credit of one of the parties, by which the third party agrees to pay the debt when it becomes due if the original drawee does not. • This type of acceptance inures to the benefit of all successors to the party for whose benefit it is made. — Also termed *acceptance supra protest*; *acceptance for honor supra protest*.

accommodation acceptance. (1807) The acceptance of an offer to buy goods for current or prompt shipment by shipping nonconforming goods after notifying the buyer that the shipment is intended as an accommodation. • This type of "acceptance" is not truly an acceptance under contract law, but operates instead as a counteroffer if the buyer is duly notified.

banker's acceptance. A bill of exchange drawn on and accepted by a commercial bank. • Banker's acceptances are often issued to finance the sale of goods in international trade. — Abbr. BA. — Also termed *bank acceptance*.

blank acceptance. Acceptance by a bill-of-exchange drawee before the bill is made, as indicated by the drawee's signature on the instrument.

conditional acceptance. An agreement to pay a draft on the occurrence or nonoccurrence of a particular event.

express acceptance. A written or oral expression indicating that the drawee has seen the instrument and does not dispute its sufficiency. • While a written acceptance is typically signified by the stamped or written word "accepted" or "presented," usu. on the instrument itself, an oral acceptance must be made directly to a drawer or holder who has waived the right to a written acceptance.

implied acceptance. An acceptance implied by a drawee whose actions indicate an intention to comply with the request of the drawer; conduct by the drawee from which the holder is justified in concluding that the drawee intends to accept the instrument.

special acceptance. An acceptance that departs from either the terms of a bill or the terms added to but not otherwise expressed in a bill. • An example is an acceptance of a draft as payable in a particular place even though the draft contains no such limitation.

trade acceptance. A bill of exchange for the amount of a specific purchase, drawn on and accepted by the buyer for payment at a specified time.

5. An insurer's agreement to issue a policy of insurance. 6. An heir's agreement to take an inheritance. See TACIT ACCEPTANCE. 7. See ADOPTION (5). — **accept**, *vb.*

acceptance au besoin. See ACCEPTANCE (4).

acceptance by silence. See ACCEPTANCE (1).

acceptance company. See *sales finance company* under FINANCE COMPANY.

acceptance credit. See *time letter of credit* under LETTER OF CREDIT.

acceptance criteria. *Intellectual Property.* Agreed-on performance standards that custom-made products such as computer software or hardware or a commercial website must meet before the customer is legally obligated to accept the product and pay for it.

acceptance doctrine. *Construction law.* The principle that, once a property owner accepts the work of a contractor, the contractor is not liable to third parties for an injury arising from the contractor's negligence in performing under the contract, unless the injury results from a hidden, imminently dangerous defect that the contractor knows about and the owner does not know about. — Also termed *accepted-work doctrine*.

acceptance for honor. See ACCEPTANCE (4).

acceptance-of-the-benefits rule. (1972) The doctrine that a party may not appeal a judgment after having voluntarily and intentionally received all or some part of the relief provided by it.

acceptance sampling. The practice of examining only a few items from a shipment to determine the acceptability of the whole shipment.

acceptance supra protest. See *acceptance for honor* under ACCEPTANCE (4).

acceptance testing. *Intellectual Property.* Formal experiments conducted by or on behalf of the customer to determine whether computer software or hardware or a commercial website satisfies the customer's acceptance criteria. ● Usu., an acceptance-testing provision in a sales contract or license agreement is accompanied by a termination provision allowing the customer to back out of the contract if the product is not acceptable. — Also termed *requirements testing*. See ACCEPTANCE CRITERIA.

accepted-work doctrine. See ACCEPTANCE DOCTRINE.

acceptilation (ak-sep-tə-**lay**-shən), *n.* [fr. Latin *acceptilatio* "release"] *Roman & civil law.* An oral release from an obligation even though payment has not been made in full; a complete discharge, esp. through a fictitious payment. — Also termed (in Roman law) *acceptilatio*. Cf. APOCHA.

acceptor. A person or entity that accepts a negotiable instrument and agrees to be primarily responsible for its payment or performance.

acceptor supra protest. One who accepts a bill that has been protested, for the honor of the drawer or an indorser. See *acceptance for honor* under ACCEPTANCE (4).

accept service. To agree that process has been properly served even when it has not been. — Also termed *accept service of process*.

access, *n.* **1.** An opportunity or ability to enter, approach, pass to and from, or communicate with <access to the courts>. **2.** *Family law.* VISITATION (2). **3.** *Family law.* The opportunity to have sexual intercourse. Cf. NONACCESS.

multiple access. *Hist.* In a paternity suit, the defense that the mother had one or more sexual partners other than the defendant around the time of conception. ● The basis for the defense is that because the mother bears the burden of proof, she must be able to prove that only the defendant could be the child's father. In some jurisdictions, this is still known by its common-law name, the *exceptio plurium concubentium* defense, or simply the *plurium* defense. Juries or judges who wished to dismiss the case because of the mother's promiscuity, rather than because of the improbability of the defendant's paternity, often accepted this defense. Most states have now abrogated the defense. In recent years the issue of multiple access has declined in importance with the rise of highly accurate paternity testing.

4. *Patents & Trademarks.* The right to obtain information about and to inspect and copy U.S. Patent and Trademark Office files of patents, patent applications, trademark applications, and *inter partes* proceedings pertaining to them. **5.** *Copyright.* An opportunity by one accused of infringement to see, hear, or copy a copyrighted work before the alleged infringement took place <the duplication of the error proved that the defendant had access to the work>. ● Proof of access is required to prove copyright infringement unless the two works are strikingly similar. **6.** *Copyright.* The right to obtain information about and to inspect and copy U.S. Copyright Office files and deposited materials. See (for senses 3 & 4) POWER TO INSPECT. — **access,** *vb.*

access easement. See EASEMENT.

accession (ak-**sesh**-ən). (16c) **1.** The act of acceding or agreeing <the family's accession to the kidnapper's demands>. **2.** A coming into possession of a right or office <as promised, the state's budget was balanced within two years after the governor's accession>. **3.** *Int'l law.* A method by which a nation that is not among a treaty's original signatories becomes a party to it. <Italy became a party to the nuclear-arms treaty by accession>. *See* Vienna Convention on the Law of Treaties, art. 15 (1155 U.N.T.S. 331, 8 I.L.M. 679 (1969)). — Also termed *adherence; adhesion*. See INSTRUMENT OF ACCESSION. **4.** The acquisition of title to personal property by bestowing labor on a raw material to convert it to another thing <the owner's accession to the lumber produced from his land>. — Also termed (in Roman law) *accessio*. See ADJUNCTION (2). **5.** A property owner's right to all that is added to the property (esp. land) naturally or by labor, including land left by floods and improvements made by others <the newly poured concrete driveway became the homeowner's property by accession>. ● In Louisiana law, accession is the owner's right to whatever is produced by or united with something, either naturally or artificially. La. Civ. Code arts. 483, 490, 507. Cf. ANNEXATION. **6.** An improvement to existing personal property, such as new shafts on golf clubs. **7.** The physical uniting of goods with other goods in such a manner that the identity of the original goods is not lost. UCC § 9-102(a)(1). **8.** ACCESSORYSHIP.

access order. See VISITATION ORDER.

accessorial (ak-sə-**sor**-ee-əl), *adj.* **1.** (Of a promise) made for the purpose of strengthening another's credit <an accessorial pledge by way of guaranty>. — Also termed *accessory*. **2.** *Criminal law.* Of or relating to the accessory in a crime <accessorial guilt>.

accessorial obligation. See COLLATERAL OBLIGATION.

accessory (ak-**ses**-ə-ree), *n.* (15c) **1.** Something of secondary or subordinate importance. **2.** *Criminal law.* A person who aids or contributes in the commission or concealment of a crime. ● An accessory is usu. liable only if the crime is a felony. Cf. PRINCIPAL (2). — **accessory,** *adj.* — **accessoryship,** *n.*

accessory after the fact. (17c) An accessory who was not at the scene of the crime but knows that a crime has been committed and who helps the offender try to escape arrest or punishment. 18 USCA § 3. ● Most penal statutes establish the following four requirements: (1) someone else must have committed a felony, and it must have been completed before the accessory's act; (2) the accessory must not be guilty as a principal; (3) the accessory must personally help the principal try to avoid the consequences of the felony; and (4) the accessory's assistance must be rendered with guilty knowledge. An accessory after the fact may be prosecuted for obstructing justice. — Sometimes shortened to *accessory after.*

accessory at the fact. See *principal in the second degree* under PRINCIPAL (2).

accessory before the fact. (17c) An accessory who assists or encourages another to commit a crime but who is not present when the offense is actually committed. ● Most jurisdictions have abolished this category of accessory and instead treat such an offender as an accomplice. — Sometimes shortened to *accessory before.* See ACCOMPLICE.

accessory building. See BUILDING.

accessory contract. See CONTRACT.

accessory obligation. See OBLIGATION.

accessory right. See RIGHT.

accessoryship. The status or fact of being an accessory. — Also termed (loosely) *accession.*

accessory thing. See THING.

accessory use. See USE (1).

access to counsel. See RIGHT TO COUNSEL.

access to justice. The ability within a society to use courts and other legal institutions effectively to protect one's rights and pursue claims.

access-to-justice commission. An agency of a state's judicial system designed to encourage the judicial, executive, and legislative branches of government, the bar, law schools, legal-aid providers, and others to work together to provide civil legal services to low-income citizens.

accident, *n.* (14c) **1.** An unintended and unforeseen injurious occurrence; something that does not occur in the usual course of events or that could not be reasonably anticipated. **2.** *Equity practice.* An unforeseen and injurious occurrence not attributable to the victim's mistake, negligence, neglect, or misconduct; an unanticipated and untoward event that causes harm.

culpable accident. An accident due to negligence. ● A culpable accident, unlike an unavoidable accident, is no defense except in those few cases in which wrongful intent is the exclusive and necessary basis for liability.

unavoidable accident. An accident that cannot be avoided because it is produced by an irresistible physical cause that cannot be prevented by human skill or reasonable foresight. ● Examples include accidents resulting from lightning or storms, perils of the sea, inundations or earthquakes, or sudden illness or death. Unavoidable accident has been considered a means of avoiding both civil and criminal liability. — Also termed *inevitable accident*; *pure accident*; *unavoidable casualty.* Cf. ACT OF GOD.

accidental, *adj.* **1.** Not having occurred as a result of anyone's purposeful act; esp., resulting from an event that could not have been prevented by human skill or reasonable foresight. **2.** Not having been caused by a tortious act.

accidental death. See DEATH.

accidental-death benefit. An insurance-policy provision that allows for an additional payment (often double the face amount of the policy) if the insured dies as a result of an accident, as defined in the policy, and not from natural causes. — Abbr. ADB.

accidental harm. See HARM.

accidental injury. See INJURY.

accidental killing. (17c) Homicide resulting from a lawful act performed in a lawful manner under a reasonable belief that no harm could occur. — Also termed *death by misadventure; homicide by misadventure; killing by misadventure; homicide per infortunium.* See *justifiable homicide* under HOMICIDE; *involuntary manslaughter* under MANSLAUGHTER. Cf. MALICIOUS KILLING.

accidental stranding. See STRANDING.

accident and health insurance. See *health insurance* under INSURANCE.

accident-based insurance. See *occurrence-based liability insurance* under INSURANCE.

accident insurance. See INSURANCE.

accident policy. See INSURANCE POLICY.

acclamation. *Parliamentary law.* **1.** Approval or election by general consent, usu. demonstrated by applause or cheering. ● Election by acclamation is common in large conventions where only one candidate has been nominated. **2.** Voting by applause or shouting.

accomenda (ak-ə-**men**-də). *Hist. Maritime law.* A contract between a cargo owner and a shipmaster whereby the parties agree to sell the cargo and divide the profits (after deducting the owner's costs). ● This contract actually consists of two agreements: a *mandatum*, by which the owner gives the shipmaster the power to dispose of the cargo, and a partnership contract, by which the parties divide any profits arising from the sale. See MANDATE (5).

accommodated party. A party for whose benefit an accommodation party signs and incurs liability. Cf. ACCOMMODATION PARTY.

accommodation, *n.* (17c) **1.** A loan or other financial favor. **2.** The act of signing an accommodation paper as surety for another. See ACCOMMODATION PAPER. **3.** The act or an instance of making a change or provision for someone or something; an adaptation or adjustment. **4.** A convenience supplied by someone; esp., lodging and food.

public accommodation. (1859) A business that provides lodging, food, entertainment, or other services to the public; esp. (as defined by the Civil Rights Act of 1964), one that affects interstate commerce or is supported by state action.

reasonable accommodation. An adaptation, adjustment, or allowance made for a disabled person's needs or an employee's religious beliefs or practices without imposing an undue hardship on the party taking the action. ● Under the Americans with Disabilities Act, an employer must make reasonable accommodations for an employee's disability. Examples of reasonable accommodations that have been approved by the courts include providing additional unpaid leave, modifying the employee's work schedule, and reassigning the employee to a more appropriate, vacant position. See *undue hardship* under HARDSHIP.

accommodation acceptance. See ACCEPTANCE (4).

accommodation bill. See ACCOMMODATION PAPER.

accommodation director. See *dummy director* under DIRECTOR.

accommodation indorsement. See INDORSEMENT.

accommodation indorser. See INDORSER.

accommodation land. See LAND.

accommodation line. *Insurance.* One or more policies that an insurer issues to retain the business of a valued agent, broker, or customer, even though the risk would not be accepted under the insurer's usual standards.

accommodation loan. See LOAN.

accommodation maker. See MAKER.

accommodation note. See NOTE (1).

accommodation paper. (18c) A negotiable instrument that one party cosigns, without receiving any consideration, as surety for another party who remains primarily liable. ● An accommodation paper is typically used when the cosigner is more creditworthy than the principal debtor. — Also termed *accommodation bill*; *accommodation note*.

accommodation party. (1812) A person who, without recompense or other benefit, signs a negotiable instrument for the purpose of being a surety for another party (called the *accommodated party*) to the instrument. ● The accommodation party can sign in any capacity (i.e., as maker, drawer, acceptor, or indorser). An accommodation party is liable to all parties except the accommodated party, who impliedly agrees to pay the note or draft and to indemnify the accommodation party for all losses incurred in having to pay it. See SURETY. Cf. ACCOMMODATED PARTY.

accommodation subpoena. See *friendly subpoena* under SUBPOENA.

accommodation surety. See *voluntary surety* under SURETY.

accommodatum (ə-kom-ə-**day**-təm), *n.* See COMMODATUM.

accompany, *vb.* To go along with (another); to attend. ● In automobile-accident cases, an unlicensed driver is not considered accompanied by a licensed driver unless the latter is close enough to supervise and help the former.

accomplice (ə-**kom**-plis). (1854) **1.** A person who is in any way involved with another in the commission of a crime, whether as a principal in the first or second degree or as an accessory. ● Although the definition includes an accessory before the fact, not all authorities treat this term as including an accessory after the fact. **2.** A person who knowingly, voluntarily, and intentionally unites with the principal offender in committing a crime and thereby becomes punishable for it. See ACCESSORY. Cf. PRINCIPAL (2).

accomplice liability. See LIABILITY.

accomplice witness. See WITNESS.

accord, *n.* (14c) **1.** An amicable arrangement between parties, esp. between peoples or nations; COMPACT; TREATY. **2.** An offer to give or to accept a stipulated performance in the future to satisfy an obligor's existing duty, together with an acceptance of that offer. • The performance becomes what is known as a *satisfaction.* — Also termed *executory accord*; *accord executory.* See ACCORD AND SATISFACTION; SATISFACTION. Cf. COMPROMISE; NOVATION. **3.** A signal used in a legal citation to introduce a case clearly supporting a proposition for which another case is being quoted directly.

accord, *vb.* **1.** To furnish or grant, esp. what is suitable or proper <accord the litigants a stay of costs pending appeal>. **2.** To agree <they accord in their opinions>.

accord and satisfaction. (18c) An agreement to substitute for an existing debt some alternative form of discharging that debt, coupled with the actual discharge of the debt by the substituted performance. • The new agreement is called the *accord*, and the discharge is called the *satisfaction.* Cf. COMPROMISE; NOVATION; SETTLEMENT (2), (3).

accordant (ə-**kor**-dənt), *adj.* In agreement <accordant with these principles>.

accord executory. See ACCORD (2).

accouchement (ə-**koosh**-mənt *or* ak-oosh-**maw***n*). [French] Childbirth.

account, *n.* (14c) **1.** ACCOUNTING (3) <the principal filed an action for account against his agent>. — Also spelled (archaically) *accompt.* **2.** ACCOUNTING (4) <the contractor filed an action for account against the nonpaying customer>. **3.** A statement by which someone seeks to describe or explain an event <Fred's account of the holdup differed significantly from Martha's>. **4.** A detailed statement of the debits and credits between parties to a contract or to a fiduciary relationship; a reckoning of monetary dealings <the trustee balanced the account at the end of each month>. • In wills and estates, an account is a brief financial statement of the manner in which an executor or administrator has performed the official duties of collecting the estate's assets and paying those who are entitled. An account charges the executor or administrator with the value of the estate as shown by the inventory, plus any increase, and credits the executor with expenses and costs, duly authorized disbursements, and the executor's commission. — Abbr. acct.; a/c. — Also termed *accounting.* See STATEMENT OF ACCOUNT. **5.** A course of business dealings or other relations for which records must be kept <open a brokerage account>.

account in trust. An account established by an individual to hold the account's assets in trust for someone else.

account payable. (*usu. pl.*) (1936) An account reflecting a balance owed to a creditor; a debt owed by an enterprise in the normal course of business dealing. — Often shortened to *payable*;

payables. — Also termed *note payable.* Pl. *accounts payable.*

account receivable. (*usu. pl.*) (1936) An account reflecting a balance owed by a debtor; a debt owed by a customer to an enterprise for goods or services. — Often shortened to *receivable*; *receivables.* — Also termed *note receivable.* Pl. *accounts receivable.*

account rendered. An account produced by the creditor and presented for the debtor's examination and acceptance.

account settled. An account with a paid balance.

account stated. (17c) **1.** A balance that parties to a transaction or settlement agree on, either expressly or by implication. • The phrase also refers to the agreement itself or to the assent giving rise to the agreement. **2.** A plaintiff's claim in a suit for such a balance. **3.** *Equity practice.* A defendant's plea in response to an action for an accounting. • The defendant states that the balance due on the statement of the account has been discharged and that the defendant holds the plaintiff's release. — Also termed *stated account.*

accumulated-adjustments account. *Tax.* An item on the books of an S corporation (usu. an equity item on the corporation's balance sheet) to account for taxable-income items passed through to shareholders, such as accumulated earnings — earned before the corporation converted from a C corporation to an S corporation — that would have been distributed as a dividend to the shareholders if the corporation had remained a C corporation. • One of the theories underlying the accumulated-adjustments account is that the shareholders should not be permitted to avoid dividend-tax treatment on a corporation's accumulated earnings just because the corporation converts from C status to S status. IRC (26 USCA) § 1368(e)(1). — Abbr. AAA.

adjunct account. An account that accumulates additions to another account.

annual account. See *intermediate account.*

assigned account. An account receivable that is pledged to a bank or factor as security for a loan.

bank account. A deposit or credit account with a bank, such as a demand, time, savings, or passbook account. UCC § 4-104(a).

blocked account. An account at a bank or other financial institution, access to which has been restricted either by the government or by an authorized person. • An account may be blocked for a variety of reasons, as when hostilities erupt between two countries and each blocks access to the other's accounts. — Also termed *frozen account.*

book account. A detailed statement of debits and credits giving a history of an enterprise's business transactions.

capital account. An account on a partnership's balance sheet representing a partner's share of the partnership capital.

charge account. See CHARGE ACCOUNT.

client trust account. See CLIENT TRUST ACCOUNT.

closed account. An account that no further credits or debits may be added to but that remains open for adjustment or setoff.

community account. An account consisting of community funds or commingled funds. See COMMUNITY PROPERTY.

contra account (**kon**-trə). An account that serves to reduce the gross valuation of an asset.

convenience account. An apparent joint account, but without right of survivorship, established by a creator to enable another person to withdraw funds at the creator's direction or for the creator's benefit. • Unlike a true joint account, only one person, the creator, has an ownership interest in the deposited funds. Convenience accounts are often established by those who need a financial manager's help and want to make it easy for the manager to pay bills. Although the manager's name is on the account, he or she does not contribute any personal funds to the account and can write checks or make withdrawals only at the direction of or on behalf of the creator.

current account. 1. A running or open account that is settled periodically, usu. monthly. **2.** A partner's account that reflects salary, withdrawals, contributions, and other transactions in a given period. **3.** *Banking.* A depositor's checking account. **4.** The portion of a nation's balance of payments that represents its exports, imports, and transfer payments.

custodial account. An account opened on behalf of someone else, such as one opened by a parent for a minor child, and usu. administered by a responsible third party. • Custodial accounts most often arise under the Uniform Transfers to Minors Act (1983). All states have enacted either that act or its earlier version, the Uniform Gifts to Minors Act. Property can be set aside by a donor or transferred to a third party as custodian for the benefit of a minor, usu. as an irrevocable gift. This is a much simpler mechanism than a trust. The custodian has powers and fiduciary duties similar to those of a trustee, except that the custodian is not under a court's supervision. The custodian must account for the property

and turn it over to the beneficiary when he or she reaches majority. See UNIFORM TRANSFERS TO MINORS ACT.

deposit account. A demand, time, savings, passbook, or similar account maintained with a bank, savings-and-loan association, credit union, or like organization, other than investment property or an account evidenced by an instrument. UCC § 9-102(a)(20). — Abbr. D.A.

drawing account. A temporary owner's equity account used by a sole proprietorship or a partnership to record an owner's or partner's withdrawals of cash or other assets from the business for personal use.

escrow account. 1. A bank account, generally held in the name of the depositor and an escrow agent, that is returnable to the depositor or paid to a third person on the fulfillment of specified conditions. — Also termed *escrow deposit.* See ESCROW (2). **2.** See *impound account.*

frozen account. See *blocked account.*

impound account. An account of accumulated funds held by a lender for payment of taxes, insurance, or other periodic debts against real property. — Also termed *escrow; escrow account; reserve account.* See ESCROW (2).

intermediate account. An account filed by an executor, administrator, or guardian after the initial account and before the final account. • This account is usu. filed annually. — Also termed *annual account.*

joint account. (17c) A bank or brokerage account opened by two or more people, by which each party has a present right to withdraw all funds in the account and, upon the death of one party, the survivors become the owners of the account, with no right of the deceased party's heirs or devisees to share in it. • Typically, the account-holders are designated as "joint tenants with right of survivorship" or "joint-and-survivor account-holders." In some jurisdictions, they must be so designated to establish a right of survivorship. — Abbr. JA. — Also termed *joint-and-survivorship account.*

lien account. A statement of claims that fairly informs the owner and public of the amount and nature of a lien.

liquidated account. An account whose assets are clearly ascertained, either by agreement of the parties or by law.

long account. An account involving numerous items or complex transactions in an equitable action, usu. referred to a master or commissioner.

margin account. A brokerage account that allows an investor to buy or sell securities on credit, with the securities usu. serving as collateral for the broker's loan.

multiple-party account. An account that has more than one owner with a current or future interest in the account. • Multiple-party accounts include joint accounts, payable-on-death (P.O.D.) accounts, and trust accounts. Unif. Probate Code § 6-201(5).

mutual account. An account showing mutual transactions between parties, as by showing debits and credits on both sides of the account.

mutual-fund wrap account. An investment account that allocates an investor's assets only among mutual funds rather than stocks or other investments. See *wrap account.*

negotiable-order-of-withdrawal account. See *NOW account.*

nominal account (**nahm**-ə-nəl). An income-statement account that is closed into surplus at the end of the year when the books are balanced.

nominee account. *Securities.* A brokerage account in which the securities are owned by an investor but registered in the name of the brokerage firm. • The certificate and the records of the issuing company show the brokerage as the holder of record. But the brokerage records show the investor as the beneficial owner of the securities in the nominee account. — Also termed *street-name security.*

NOW account (now). An interest-bearing savings account on which the holder may write checks. — Also termed *negotiable-order-of-withdrawal account.*

offset account. One of two accounts that balance against each other and cancel each other out when the books are closed.

open account. (18c) **1.** An unpaid or unsettled account. **2.** An account that is left open for ongoing debit and credit entries by two parties and that has a fluctuating balance until either party finds it convenient to settle and close, at which time there is a single liability.

partial account. (18c) A preliminary accounting of an executor's or administrator's dealings with an estate.

pay-on-death account. A bank account whose owner instructs the bank to distribute the account's balance to a beneficiary upon the owner's death. • Unlike a joint-and-survivorship account, a pay-on-death account does not give the beneficiary access to the funds while the owner is alive. — Abbr. POD account. — Also termed *pay-on-death bank account.*

pledged account. A mortgagor's account pledged to a lender in return for a loan bearing interest at a below-market rate.

profit-and-loss account. A transfer account of all income and expense accounts, closed into the retained earnings of a corporation or the capital account of a partnership.

real account. An account that records assets and liabilities rather than receipts and payments.

reserve account. See *impound account.*

revolving charge account. See *revolving credit* under CREDIT (4).

running account. (18c) An open, unsettled account that exhibits the reciprocal demands between the parties.

sequestered account. An account (such as a joint bank account) that a court has ordered to be separated, frozen, and impounded.

share-draft account. An account that a member maintains at a credit union and that can be drawn on through the use of share drafts payable to third parties. • A share-draft account operates much like a checking account operates at a bank. — Also termed *share account.*

suspense account. A temporary record used in bookkeeping to track receipts and disbursements of an uncertain nature until they are identified and posted in the appropriate ledgers and journals. • A suspense account does not appear in a final financial statement. It is a useful tool when, for example, a lump-sum receipt or expenditure must be broken down to match several transactions before posting.

tax-deferred account. An interest-bearing account whose earnings are not taxable as income to the account holder before the earnings are withdrawn. • Tax-deferred accounts include most types of IRAs, variable annuities, 401(k) plans, cash-value life insurance, and most other types of tax-deferred savings instruments.

trust account. See CLIENT TRUST ACCOUNT.

wrap account. An investment account for which the investor, helped by a stockbroker, selects an account manager and pays a fee based on a percentage of the total assets to be managed. • Most wrap accounts contain a portfolio of investments, including stocks, bonds, and cash. Investors generally provide a risk profile but do not select the investments or give instructions to buy or sell. — Also termed *wrap-fee account.* See *mutual-fund wrap account.*

accountable, *adj.* (14c) Responsible; answerable <the company was held accountable for the employee's negligence>. — **accountability,** *n.*

accountable receipt. See RECEIPT.

accountant. 1. A person authorized under applicable law to practice public accounting; a person whose business is to keep books or accounts, to perform financial audits, to design and control accounting systems, and to give tax advice. • For some purposes, the term includes a professional accounting association, a corporation, and a partnership, if they are so authorized.

> **certified public accountant.** An accountant who has satisfied the statutory and administrative requirements to be registered or licensed as a public accountant. — Abbr. CPA.

2. A defendant in an action of account.

accountant–client privilege. See PRIVILEGE (3).

accountant's lien. See LIEN.

account book. A journal in which a business's transactions are recorded. See SHOP BOOKS.

account debtor. See DEBTOR.

account duty. See DUTY (4).

account executive. See STOCKBROKER.

account for. (17c) **1.** To furnish a good reason or convincing explanation for; to explain the cause of. **2.** To render a reckoning of (funds held, esp. in trust). **3.** To answer for (conduct).

accounting. (18c) **1.** The act or a system of establishing or settling financial accounts; esp., the process of recording transactions in the financial records of a business and periodically extracting, sorting, and summarizing the recorded transactions to produce a set of financial records. — Also termed *financial accounting.* Cf. BOOKKEEPING. **2.** A rendition of an account, either voluntarily or by court order. • The term frequently refers to the report of all items of property, income, and expenses prepared by a personal representative, trustee, or guardian and given to heirs, beneficiaries, or the probate court. See ACCOUNT (4). **3.** A legal action to compel a defendant to account for and pay over money owed to the plaintiff but held by the defendant (often the plaintiff's agent); AC-COUNTING FOR PROFITS. — Also termed *account render*; *account*; *action of account.* **4.** More broadly, an action for the recovery of money for services performed, property sold and delivered, money loaned, or damages for the nonperformance of simple contracts. • Such an action is available when the rights of parties will be adequately protected by the payment of money. — Also termed *action on account*; *account*; *action of book debt.* **5.** *Commercial law.* An equitable proceeding for a complete settlement of all partnership affairs, usu. in connection with partner misconduct or with a winding up. See WINDING UP. **6.** *Secured transactions.* A record that (1) is authenticated by a secured party, (2) indicates the aggregate unpaid secured obligation as of a date no more than 35 days before or after the date of the record, and (3) identifies the components of the obligations in reasonable detail. UCC § 9-102(a)(2).

accounting for profits. (1871) An action for equitable relief against a person in a fiduciary relationship to recover profits taken in a breach of the relationship. — Often shortened to *accounting.*

accounting method. (1908) A system for determining income and expenses, profit and loss, asset value, appreciation and depreciation, and the like, esp. for tax purposes.

> **accrual accounting method** (ə-**kroo**-əl). (1942) An accounting method that records entries of debits and credits when the revenue or liability arises, rather than when the income is received or an expense is paid. — Also termed *accrual basis.* Cf. *cash-basis accounting method.*

> **capitalization accounting method.** A method of determining an asset's present value by discounting its stream of expected future benefits at an appropriate rate.

> **cash-basis accounting method.** (1954) An accounting method that considers only cash actually received as income and cash actually paid out as an expense. Cf. *accrual accounting method.*

> **completed-contract accounting method.** A method of reporting profit or loss on certain long-term contracts by recognizing gross income and expenses in the tax year that the contract is completed.

> **cost accounting method.** The practice of recording the value of assets in terms of their historical cost. — Also termed *cost accounting.*

> **direct charge-off accounting method.** A system of accounting by which a deduction for bad debts is allowed when an account has become partially or completely worthless.

> **equity accounting method.** A method of accounting for long-term investment in common stock based on acquisition cost, investor income, net losses, and dividends.

> **fair-value accounting method.** The valuation of assets at present actual or market value. • When this method is used to determine the value of a security or other financial instrument, it is also termed *mark-to-market accounting method.*

> **installment accounting method.** (1954) A method by which a taxpayer can spread the recognition of gains from a sale of property over the payment period by computing the gross-profit percentage from the sale and applying it to each payment.

> **mark-to-market accounting method.** See *fair-value accounting method.*

> **percentage-of-completion method.** An accounting method in which revenue is recognized gradually during the completion of the subject matter of the contract.

physical-inventory accounting method. A method of counting a company's goods at the close of an accounting period.

purchase accounting method. A method of accounting for mergers whereby the total value paid or exchanged for the acquired firm's assets is recorded on the acquiring firm's books, and any difference between the fair market value of the assets acquired and the purchase price is recorded as goodwill.

accounting period. (1903)A regular span of time used for accounting purposes; esp., a period used by a taxpayer in determining income and related tax liability.

Accounting Research Bulletin. A publication containing accounting practices recommended by the American Institute of Certified Public Accountants. — Abbr. ARB.

Accounting Series Release. A bulletin providing the Securities and Exchange Commission's requirements for accounting and auditing procedures to be followed in reports filed with that agency. — Abbr. ASR.

account in trust. See ACCOUNT.

account party. The customer in a letter-of-credit transaction. — Also termed *applicant*.

account payable. See ACCOUNT.

account receivable. See ACCOUNT.

account render. See ACCOUNTING (3).

account rendered. See ACCOUNT.

account representative. See STOCKBROKER.

account settled. See ACCOUNT.

accounts-receivable insurance. See *accounts-receivable insurance* and *credit insurance* under INSURANCE.

account stated. See ACCOUNT.

account statement. See STATEMENT OF ACCOUNT.

accouple, *vb. Archaic.* To unite; to marry.

accredit (ə-**kred**-it), *vb.* **1.** To give official authorization or status to. **2.** To recognize (a school) as having sufficient academic standards to qualify graduates for higher education or for professional practice. **3.** *Int'l law.* To send (a person) with credentials as an envoy. — **accreditation** (ə-kred-i-**tay**-shən), *n.* — **accredited,** *adj.*

accredited investor. See INVESTOR.

accredited law school. See LAW SCHOOL.

accredited representative. See REPRESENTATIVE.

accretion (ə-**kree**-shən). (1830) **1.** The gradual accumulation of land by natural forces, esp. as alluvium is added to land situated on the bank of a river or on the seashore. Cf. ALLUVION; AVULSION (2); DELICTION; EROSION. **2.** Any increase in trust property other than increases ordinarily considered as income. **3.** *Civil law.* The right of heirs or legatees to unite their shares of the estate with the portion of any coheirs or legatees who do not accept their portion, fail to comply with a condition, or die before the testator. **4.** A beneficiary's gain through the failure of a coheir or colegatee to take his or her share. **5.** *Scots law.* The perfection of an imperfect or defective title by some act by the person who conveyed title to the current holder. — **accretive, accretionary,** *adj.*

accroach (ə-**krohch**), *vb.* (16c) To exercise power without authority; to usurp. — **accroachment** (ə-**krohch**-mənt), *n.*

accrual, clause of. See CLAUSE OF ACCRUAL.

accrual accounting method. See ACCOUNTING METHOD.

accrual basis. See *accrual accounting method* under ACCOUNTING METHOD.

accrual bond. See BOND (3).

accrue (ə-**kroo**), *vb.* (15c) **1.** To come into existence as an enforceable claim or right; to arise <the plaintiff's cause of action for silicosis did not accrue until the plaintiff knew or had reason to know of the disease>. **2.** To accumulate periodically <the savings-account interest accrues monthly>. — **accrual,** *n.*

accrued asset. See ASSET.

accrued compensation. See COMPENSATION.

accrued depreciation. See *accumulated depreciation* under DEPRECIATION.

accrued dividend. See *accumulated dividend* under DIVIDEND.

accrued expense. See EXPENSE.

accrued income. See INCOME.

accrued interest. See INTEREST (3).

accrued liability. See LIABILITY.

accrued right. See RIGHT.

accrued salary. See SALARY.

accrued tax. See TAX.

accruer. See CLAUSE OF ACCRUAL.

accruing costs. See COST (3).

acct. *abbr.* ACCOUNT (4).

accumulated-adjustments account. See ACCOUNT.

accumulated deficit. A business's net losses that are carried over on the balance sheet from earlier periods. ● The deficit is shown under owners' or stockholders' equity.

accumulated depreciation. See DEPRECIATION.

accumulated dividend. See DIVIDEND.

accumulated-earnings credit. See CREDIT (7).

accumulated-earnings tax. See TAX.

accumulated income. See INCOME.

accumulated legacy. See LEGACY.

accumulated profit. See PROFIT (1).

accumulated surplus. See SURPLUS.

accumulated taxable income. See INCOME.

accumulation, *n.* **1.** The increase of a thing by repeated additions to it; esp., the increase of a fund by the repeated addition of the income that it creates. **2.** The concurrence of several titles to the same thing. **3.** The concurrence of several circumstances to the same proof. **4.** The retention of dividends for future distribution. **5.** *Insurance.* An increase in the principal sum insured for, effective upon renewal of a policy, without a change of premiums. — **accumulate,** *vb.*

accumulations, rule against. (1924) The rule that a direction to accumulate income from property — the income to be distributed later to certain beneficiaries — is valid only if confined to the perpetuity period. Cf. RULE AGAINST PERPETUITIES.

accumulation trust. See TRUST.

accumulative (ə-**kyoo**-myə-lay-tiv *or* -lə-tiv), *adj.* Increasing by successive addition; cumulative.

accumulative damages. See DAMAGES.

accumulative dividend. See *cumulative dividend* under DIVIDEND.

accumulative judgment. See JUDGMENT.

accumulative legacy. See LEGACY.

accumulative sentences. See *consecutive sentences* under SENTENCE.

accusation, *n.* (14c) **1.** A formal charge of criminal wrongdoing. ● The accusation is usu. presented to a court or magistrate having jurisdiction to inquire into the alleged crime. **2.** A statement that a person has engaged in an illegal or immoral act.

malicious accusation. An accusation against another for an improper purpose and without probable cause. See MALICIOUS PROSECUTION.

accusatorial system. See ADVERSARY SYSTEM.

accusatory (ə-**kyoo**-zə-tor-ee), *adj.* Of, relating to, or constituting an accusation.

accusatory body. (1877) A body (such as a grand jury) that hears evidence and determines whether a person should be charged with a crime.

accusatory instrument. See CHARGING INSTRUMENT.

accusatory part. The section of an indictment in which the offense is named.

accusatory pleading. See PLEADING (1).

accusatory procedure. See ADVERSARY SYSTEM.

accusatory stage. (1954) *Criminal procedure.* The point in a criminal proceeding when the suspect's right to counsel attaches. ● This occurs usu. after arrest and once interrogation begins. Cf. CRITICAL STAGE.

accuse, *vb.* (14c) To charge (a person) judicially or publicly with an offense; to make an accusation against <she accused him of the crime> <he was accused as an accomplice>.

accused, *adj.* Of or relating to someone or something implicated in wrongdoing <accused infringer>; esp., of or relating to a product that allegedly infringes someone's intellectual-property rights <accused device> <accused work>.

accused, *n.* (16c) **1.** A person who has been blamed for wrongdoing; esp., a person who has been arrested and brought before a magistrate or who has been formally charged with a crime (as by indictment or information). **2.** A person against whom legal proceedings have been initiated.

accuser. *Eccles. law.* A person who accuses another of a crime. ● In ecclesiastical courts, an accuser cannot be a person who has been convicted of a crime, has been excommunicated, or is otherwise disqualified.

accusing jury. See GRAND JURY.

ACF. *abbr.* ADMINISTRATION FOR CHILDREN AND FAMILIES.

acid-test ratio. See QUICK-ASSET RATIO.

acknowledge, *vb.* (15c) **1.** To recognize (something) as being factual or valid <acknowledge the federal court's jurisdiction>. **2.** To show that one accepts responsibility for <acknowledge paternity of the child>. **3.** To make known the receipt of <acknowledged the plaintiff's letter>. **4.** To confirm as genuine before an authorized officer <acknowledged before a notary public>. **5.** (Of a notary public or other officer) to certify as genuine <the notary acknowledged the genuineness of the signature>.

acknowledged father. See FATHER.

acknowledgment. (16c) **1.** A recognition of something as being factual. **2.** An acceptance of responsibility. **3.** The act of making it known that one has received something. **4.** A formal declaration made in the presence of an authorized officer, such as a notary public, by someone who signs a document and confirms that the signature is authentic. ● In most states, the officer certifies that (1) he or she personally knows the document signer or has established the signer's identity through satisfactory evidence, (2) the signer appeared before the officer on the date and in the place (usu. the county) indicated, and (3) the signer acknowledged signing the document freely. Cf. VERIFICATION (1). **5.** The officer's certificate that is affixed to the document. — Also termed (in sense 5) *certificate of acknowledgment*; (loosely) *verification*. See PROOF OF ACKNOWLEDGMENT. **6.** A father's public recognition of a child as his own. — Also termed *acknowledgment of paternity*.

formal acknowledgment. 1. A father's recognition of a child as his own by a formal, written declaration that meets a state's requirements for execution, typically by signing in the presence of two witnesses. • In Louisiana law, this recognition may also be made by a mother. La. Civ. Code art. 203. **2.** A father's recognition of a child as his own in the child's registry of birth or at the child's baptism. • In this sense, a formal acknowledgment typically occurs when a man signs the birth certificate or baptismal certificate as the father or announces at the baptismal service that he is the father. The fact that a man is named as the father on a certificate of birth or baptism is not a formal acknowledgment unless the father signs the document.

informal acknowledgment. A father's recognition of a child as his own not by a written declaration but by receiving the child into his family or supporting the child and otherwise treating the child as his own offspring.

acknowledgment of debt. *Louisiana law.* Recognition by a debtor of the existence of a debt. • An acknowledgment of debt interrupts the running of prescription.

acknowledgment of paternity. See ACKNOWLEDGMENT (6).

ACLU. *abbr.* (1936) AMERICAN CIVIL LIBERTIES UNION.

ACP. *abbr.* ADMINISTRATIVE DOMAIN-NAME CHALLENGE PANEL.

ACPA. *abbr.* **1.** ANTICYBERSQUATTING CONSUMER PROTECTION ACT. **2.** ANTICOUNTERFEITING CONSUMER PROTECTION ACT.

ACP challenge. *Trademarks.* An administrative procedure to settle disputes over Internet domain names, conducted by an Administrative Domain-Name Challenge Panel (ACP) under the auspices of the World Intellectual Property Organization and in accordance with the WIPO (Revised) Substantive Guidelines. • The guidelines are viewable at http://www.gtld-mou.org/docs/racps.htm.

acquaintance rape. See RAPE.

acquest (ə-**kwest**). See ACQUET.

acquet (a-**kay** or ə-**kwet**), *n.* [French *acquêt* "acquisition"] (*usu. pl.*) *Civil law.* **1.** Property acquired by purchase, gift, or any means other than inheritance. • The term is most commonly used to denote a marital acquisition that is presumed to be community property. — Also termed *acquets and conquets.* **2.** Property acquired by either spouse during the marriage. — Also termed *acquest.* See COMMUNITY PROPERTY.

acquiesce (ak-wee-**es**), *vb.* To accept tacitly or passively; to give implied consent to (an act) <in the

end, all the partners acquiesced in the settlement>. — **acquiescent,** *adj.*

acquiescence (ak-wee-**es**-ənts). (17c) **1.** A person's tacit or passive acceptance; implied consent to an act.

commercial acquiescence. *Patents.* Action or inaction by a patentee's competitor that reflects the competitor's belief that the patent is valid. • A patent owner may use another person's actions or inactions, such as taking a license or attempting to design around a patent, as circumstantial evidence of the nonobviousness of a patented invention or of a patent's validity or enforceability.

2. *Int'l law.* Passivity and inaction on foreign claims that, according to customary international law, usu. call for protest to assert, preserve, or safeguard rights. • The result is that binding legal effect is given to silence and inaction. Acquiescence, as a principle of substantive law, is grounded in the concepts of good faith and equity.

acquire, *vb.* To gain possession or control of; to get or obtain.

acquired allegiance. See ALLEGIANCE.

acquired corporation. See CORPORATION.

acquired distinctiveness. See DISTINCTIVENESS.

acquired federal land. See LAND.

acquired land. See LAND.

acquired right. See RIGHT.

acquired-rights doctrine. The principle that once a right has vested, it may not be reduced by later legislation. • The Universal Copyright Convention applies the doctrine to copyright protections, esp. terms, that controlled before the Convention took effect. — Also termed *doctrine of acquired rights.*

acquired servitude. See SERVITUDE (2).

acquired surplus. See SURPLUS.

acquisition, *n.* (14c) **1.** The gaining of possession or control over something <acquisition of the target company's assets>. **2.** Something acquired <a valuable acquisition>.

creeping acquisition. The gradual purchase of a corporation's stock at varying prices on the open market. • As a takeover method, a creeping acquisition does not involve a formal tender offer, although the SEC may classify it as such for regulatory purposes. — Also termed *creeping tender offer.*

derivative acquisition. An acquisition obtained from another, as by sale or gift.

new acquisition. An estate not originating from descent, devise, or gift from the paternal or maternal line of the owner. • For example, an estate acquired from a nonrelative is a new acquisition. See *nonancestral estate* under ESTATE (1).

original acquisition. An acquisition that has never been the property of anyone else, such as a copyright owned by an author.

acquisition cost. See COST (1).

acquisitive offense. See OFFENSE (1).

acquisitive prescription. See PRESCRIPTION (5).

acquit, *vb.* (13c) **1.** To clear (a person) of a criminal charge. **2.** To pay or discharge (a debt or claim).

acquittal, *n.* (15c) **1.** The legal certification, usu. by jury verdict, that an accused person is not guilty of the charged offense.

acquittal in fact. (17c) An acquittal by a jury verdict of not guilty.

acquittal in law. (17c) An acquittal by operation of law, as of someone who has been charged merely as an accessory after the principal has been acquitted.

implied acquittal. (1858) An acquittal in which a jury convicts the defendant of a lesser included offense without commenting on the greater offense. • Double jeopardy bars the retrial of a defendant on the higher offense after an implied acquittal.

2. *Contracts.* A release or discharge from debt or other liability; ACQUITTANCE. **3.** *Hist.* The obligation of a middle lord to protect a tenant from a claim, entry, or molestation by a paramount lord arising out of service that the middle lord owes the paramount lord.

acquittance, *n.* (14c) A document by which one is discharged from a debt or other obligation; a receipt or release indicating payment in full. — **acquit,** *vb.*

acquitted, *adj.* **1.** Judicially discharged from an accusation; absolved. **2.** Released from a debt.

acre. An area of land measuring 43,560 square feet. Cf. COMMERCIAL ACRE.

foot acre. A one-foot-deep layer of coal, water, or other material spread over one acre. • This measurement method is used to value coal land for tax purposes. It is also used to measure the volume and capacity of reservoirs.

acreage-contribution agreement. *Oil & gas.* A support agreement under which one party promises to grant leases or interest in leases in the area of a test well to the party who drills the test well in exchange for drilling or geological information if the test well is drilled to a certain depth. See SUPPORT AGREEMENT.

acre-foot. A volume measurement in irrigation, equal to the amount of water that will cover one acre of land in one foot of water (325,850 gallons).

acre right. *Hist.* In New England, a citizen's share in the common lands. • The value of the acre right varied among towns but was fixed in each town. A 10-acre lot in a certain town was equivalent to 113 acres of upland and 12 acres of meadow, and an exact proportion was maintained between the acre right and salable land.

across-the-board, *adj.* Applying to all classes, categories, or groups <an across-the-board tax cut>.

ACRS. *abbr.* ACCELERATED COST-RECOVERY SYSTEM.

act, *n.* (14c) **1.** Something done or performed, esp. voluntarily; a deed. — Also termed *action.* **2.** The process of doing or performing; an occurrence that results from a person's will being exerted on the external world; ACTION (2). — Also termed *positive act; act of commission.*

abstract juridical act. *Civil law.* A juridical act whose validity may be independent of the existence or lawfulness of the underlying cause. • In some systems, examples include negotiable instruments, debt remission, debt acknowledgment, and the novation of an obligation. See *juridical act.*

act in pais (in **pay**). [Law French] An act performed out of court, such as a deed made between two parties on the land being transferred. See IN PAIS.

act in the law. (1829) An act that is intended to create, transfer, or extinguish a right and that is effective in law for that purpose; the exercise of a legal power. — Also termed *juristic act; act of the party; legal act.*

act of court. See JUDICIAL ACT.

act of God. See ACT OF GOD.

act of hostility. See ACT OF HOSTILITY.

act of law. See *act of the law.*

act of omission. See *negative act.*

act of the law. (17c) The creation, extinction, or transfer of a right by the operation of the law itself, without any consent on the part of the persons concerned. — Also termed *legal act; act of law.* Cf. LEGAL ACT.

act of the party. See *act in the law.*

administrative act. (1818) An act made in a management capacity; esp., an act made outside the actor's usual field (as when a judge supervises court personnel). • An administrative act is often subject to a greater risk of liability than an act within the actor's usual field. See IMMUNITY (1).

bilateral act. (1895) An act that involves the consenting wills of two or more distinct parties, as with a contract, a conveyance, a mortgage, or a lease; AGREEMENT (1).

conversionary act. An act that, unless privileged, makes the actor liable for conversion.

external act. (16c) An act involving bodily activity, such as speaking.

intentional act. (17c) An act resulting from the actor's will directed to that end. • An act is intentional when it is foreseen and desired by the doer, and this foresight and desire resulted in the act through the operation of the will.

internal act. (16c) An act of the mind, such as thinking.

judicial act. (16c) An act involving the exercise of judicial power. — Also termed *act of court.*

jural act (**joor**-əl). (1860) An act taken in the context of or in furtherance of a society's legal system. — Also termed *jural activity.*

juridical act. *Civil law.* A lawful volitional act intended to have legal consequences. See *abstract juridical act.*

juristic act. See *act in the law.*

legal act. See LEGAL ACT.

ministerial act. An act performed without the independent exercise of discretion or judgment.• If the act is mandatory, it is also termed a *ministerial duty.* See *ministerial duty* under DUTY (2).

negative act. (17c) The failure to do something that is legally required; a nonoccurrence that involves the breach of a legal duty to take positive action. • This takes the form of either a forbearance or an omission. — Also termed *act of omission.*

negligent act. An act that creates an unreasonable risk of harm to another.

predicate act. An act that must be completed before legal consequences can attach to it or to another act or before further action can be taken. • In statutes, words such as "if" often precede a description of a predicate act.

quasi-judicial act. See QUASI-JUDICIAL ACT.

tortious act. An act that subjects the actor to liability under the principles of tort law.

unilateral act. (1861) An act in which there is only one party whose will operates, as in a testamentary disposition, the exercise of a power of appointment, or the voidance of a voidable contract.

unintentional act. (1820) An act not resulting from the actor's will toward what actually takes place.

verbal act. (18c) **1.** An act performed through the medium of words, either spoken or written. **2.** *Evidence.* A statement offered to prove the words themselves because of their legal effect (e.g., the terms of a will). • For this purpose, the statement is not considered hearsay.

3. The formal product of a legislature or other deliberative body; esp., STATUTE. • For the various types of acts, see the subentries under STATUTE.

act and deed. A formally delivered written instrument that memorializes a bargain or transaction.

acting, *adj.* (18c) Holding an interim position; serving temporarily <an acting director>.

acting chargé d'affaires. See CHARGÉ D'AFFAIRES.

acting executor. See EXECUTOR.

acting officer. See OFFICER (1).

act in pais. See ACT.

act in the law. See ACT.

actio (**ak**-shee-oh *also* **ak**-tee-oh), *n.* [Latin] **1.** *Roman & civil law.* An action; a right or claim. **2.** A right of action. **3.** *Hist.* At common law, a lawsuit. Pl. ***actiones*** (ak-shee-**oh**-neez).

actio ad exhibendum (ak-shee-oh ad ek-si-**ben**-dəm). *Roman law.* An action to compel a defendant to produce property so as to establish that it is in the defendant's possession. Pl. ***actiones ad exhibendum.***

actio arbitraria (ak-shee-oh ahr-bi-**trair**-ee-ə). *Roman law.* An action in which a judex issued an interlocutory decree ordering the defendant to do something (such as restoring property to the plaintiff) on pain of a monetary judgment payable to the plaintiff. • This action was so called because the judex could assess the damage at a high figure if the defendant failed to comply with the interlocutory order. Pl. ***actiones arbitrariae*** (ak-shee-**oh**-neez ahr-bi-**trair**-ee-ɪ).

actio bonae fidei (ak-shee-oh **boh**-nee fɪ-dee-ɪ). *Roman law.* One of a class of actions in which a judge could take equitable considerations into account in rendering a decision. Pl. ***actiones bonae fidei.***

actio calumniae (ak-shee-oh kə-**ləm**-nee-ee). *Roman law.* An action to restrain, or collect damages for, a malicious civil suit. • The victim could also pursue criminal charges. Pl. ***actiones calumniae.***

actio civilis (ak-shee-oh sə-**vɪ**-lis). [Latin "a civil action"] *Roman law.* An action founded on the traditional Roman law, rather than the innovations of magistrates. Cf. *actio honoraria.* Pl. ***actiones civiles.***

actio commodati (ak-shee-oh kom-ə-**day**-tɪ). [Latin "action on loan"] *Roman law.* An action for the recovery of a thing gratuitously lent but not returned to the lender. — Also termed *commodati actio.* Pl. ***actiones commodati.***

actio commodati contraria (ak-shee-oh kom-ə-**day**-tɪ kən-**trair**-ee-ə). *Roman law.* An action by a gratuitous borrower against a lender for extraordinary expenses or damage caused by the lender's default. Pl. **actiones commodati contrariae.**

actio commodati directa (ak-shee-oh kom-ə-**day**-tɪ di-**rek**-tə). *Roman law.* An action by a lender against a borrower for restitution for an item gratuitously lent. Pl. **actiones commodati directae.**

actio condictio indebiti (ak-shee-oh kən-**dik**-shee-oh in-**deb**-ə-tɪ). See *condictio indebiti* under CONDICTIO. ● Strictly speaking, the headword is a solecism, since a *condictio* is a type of *actio*, but this phrase is occasionally found in legal literature. Pl. **actiones condictio indebiti.**

actio conducti (ak-shee-oh kən-**dək**-tɪ). [Latin "action for the thing hired"] An action by the lessee of a thing or the hirer of another's services to enforce the contract or claim damages for breach. — Also termed *actio ex conducto.* Cf. *actio locati.*

actio confessoria (ak-shee-oh kon-fə-**sor**-ee-ə). [Latin "action based on an admission"] **1.** See *vindicatio servitutis* under VINDICATIO. **2.** An action in which the defendant admits liability but does not express it in a fixed sum. ● A judge therefore assesses the damages.

actio contraria (ak-shee-oh kən-**trair**-ee-ə). *Roman law.* A counterclaim. Cf. *actio directa.* Pl. **actio contraria.**

actio criminalis (ak-shee-oh kri-mə-**nay**-lis). *Roman law.* A criminal action. Pl. **actiones criminales.**

actio damni injuria (ak-shee-oh **dam**-nɪ in-**joor**-ee-ə). *Roman law.* An action for damages for tortiously causing pecuniary loss. See *actio legis Aquiliae.* Pl. **actiones damni injuriae.**

actio de communi dividundo (ak-shee-oh dee kə-**myoo**-nɪ di-vi-**dən**-doh). [Latin "for dividing a thing held in common"] *Roman & civil law.* An action to partition common property. — Sometimes shortened to *de communi dividundo.* Pl. **actiones de communi dividundo.**

actio de dolo malo (ak-shee-oh dee **doh**-loh **mal**-oh). *Roman law.* An action of fraud. ● This type of action was widely applied in cases involving deceitful conduct. — Also termed *actio doli.* Pl. **actiones de dolo malo.**

actio de peculio (ak-shee-oh dee pə-**kyoo**-lee-oh). *Roman law.* An action against a paterfamilias or slave owner concerning the value of the child's or slave's separate funds (*peculium*). Pl. **actiones de peculio.**

actio de pecunia constituta (ak-shee-oh dee pə-**kyoo**-nee-ə kon-sti-**t[y]oo**-tə). *Roman law.* An action on a promise to pay a preexisting debt. Pl. **actiones de pecunia constituta.**

actio depositi contraria (ak-shee-oh di-**poz**-ə-tɪ kən-**trair**-ee-ə). *Roman law.* An action that a depositary has against the depositor for unpaid expenses. Pl. **actiones depositi contrariae.**

actio depositi directa (ak-shee-oh di-**poz**-ə-tɪ di-**rek**-tə). *Roman law.* An action that a depositor has against a depositary for the return of the deposited item. Pl. **actiones depositi directae.**

actio de tigno juncto (ak-shee-oh dee **tig**-noh jəngk-toh). [Latin "action for joining timber"] *Roman law.* An action by the owner of material incorporated without payment into the defendant's building. ● It was akin to a theft action. The plaintiff could recover up to twice the value of the material. Pl. **actiones de tigno juncto.**

actio directa (ak-shee-oh di-**rek**-tə). *Roman law.* **1.** An action founded on strict law and conducted according to fixed forms; an action based on clearly defined obligations actionable at law based on a statute or a praetor's edict. **2.** A direct action, as opposed to a counterclaim (*actio contraria*). Cf. *actio in factum; actio utilis.* Pl. **actiones directae.**

actio empti (ak-shee-oh **emp**-tɪ). *Roman law.* An action by a buyer to compel a seller to deliver the item sold or for damages for breach of contract. — Also termed *actio ex empto.* Pl. **actiones empti.**

actio ex conducto (ak-shee-oh eks kən-**dək**-toh). See *actio conducti.* Pl. **actiones ex conducto.**

actio ex contractu (ak-shee-oh eks kən-**trak**-t[y]oo). *Roman law.* An action arising out of a contract. ● This term had a similar meaning at common law. Pl. **actiones ex contractu.**

actio ex delicto (ak-shee-oh eks də-**lik**-toh). *Roman law.* An action founded on a tort. Pl. **actiones ex delicto.**

actio exercitoria (ak-shee-oh eg-zər-si-**tor**-ee-ə). *Roman law.* An action against the owner or lessee (*exercitor*) of a vessel, esp. for contracts made by the master. Pl. **actiones exercitoriae.**

actio ex locato (ak-shee-oh eks loh-**kay**-toh). See *actio locati.*

actio ex stipulatu (ak-shee-oh eks stip-yə-**lay**-t[y]oo). *Roman law.* An action brought to enforce a *stipulatio.* See STIPULATION (3).

actio familiae erciscundae (ak-shee-oh fə-**mil**-ee-ee ər-sis-**kən**-dee). [Latin "action to divide an estate"] An action for the partition of the inheritance among heirs. — Sometimes shortened to *familiae erciscundae.*

actio furti (ak-shee-oh **fər**-tɪ). *Roman law.* An action by which the owner of stolen goods can, according to the circumstances, recover a multiple of their value from the thief by way of penalty, without prejudice to a further action to recover the goods themselves or their value.

actio honoraria (**ak**-shee-oh [h]on-ə-**rair**-ee-ə). Pl. ***actiones honorariae.***

actio in factum (**ak**-shee-oh in **fak**-təm). *Roman law.* An action granted by the praetor when no standard action was available. • The closest Anglo-American equivalent is *action on the case* or *trespass on the case.* See *trespass on the case* under TRESPASS. Cf. *actio directa; actio utilis.*

actio in personam (**ak**-shee-oh in pər-**soh**-nəm). Pl. ***actiones in personam.*** See *action in personam* under ACTION (4).

actio in rem (**ak**-shee-oh in **rem**). Pl. ***actiones in rem.*** **1.** See *action in rem* UNDER ACTION (4). **2.** See *real action* under ACTION (4).

actio institoria (**ak**-shee-oh in-sti-**tor**-ee-ə). [Latin] *Roman law.* An action against a principal by one who contracted with the principal's business agent, limited to matters arising out of the business.

actio judicati (**ak**-shee-oh joo-di-**kay**-tɪ). *Roman law.* An action to enforce a judgment by execution on the defendant's property. Pl. ***actiones judicati.***

actio legis Aquiliae (**ak**-shee-oh lee-jis ə-**kwil**-ee-ee). *Roman law.* An action under the Aquilian law; specif., an action to recover for loss caused by intentional or negligent damage to another's property. — Also termed *actio damni injuria; actio damni injuria dati.* See LEX AQUILIA.

actio locati (**ak**-shee-oh loh-**kay**-tɪ). [Latin "action for what has been hired out"] *Roman law.* An action that a lessor (the *locator*) of a thing might have against the hirer, or an employer against a contractor. — Also termed *actio ex locato* (**ak**-shee-oh eks loh-**kay**-toh). Cf. *actio conducti.*

actio mandati (**ak**-shee-oh man-**day**-tɪ). **1.** *Civil law.* An action to enforce a contract for gratuitous services or remuneration. **2.** *Hist.* An action to enforce a contract for gratuitous services. See MANDATUM. Pl. ***actiones mandati.***

actio mixta (**ak**-shee-oh **mik**-stə). *Roman law.* A mixed action; an action in which two or more features are combined, as an action for damages and for a penalty, or an action *in rem* and *in personam.* Pl. ***actiones mixta*** (**ak**-shee-**oh**-neez **mik**-stə).

actio negatoria (**ak**-shee-oh neg-ə-**tor**-ee-ə). *Roman law.* An action brought by a landowner against anyone claiming to exercise a servitude over the landowner's property. — Also termed *actio negativa.* Pl. ***actiones negatoriae.***

actio negotiorum gestorum (**ak**-shee-oh nə-goh-shee-**or**-əm jes-**tor**-əm). *Roman law.* An action

against a *gestor* for the mismanagement of the principal's property, or for any acquisitions made in the course of management. • The *gestor* could bring a counter action to recover management-related expenses *(actio contraria negotiorum gestorum).* See NEGOTIORUM GESTOR. Pl. ***actiones negotiorum gestorum.***

actio non accrevit infra sex annos (**ak**-shee-oh non ə-**kree**-vit seks **an**-ohs). [Latin "the action did not accrue within six years"] *Hist.* A plea to the statute of limitations by which the defendant asserts that the plaintiff's cause of action has not accrued within the last six years. Pl. ***actiones non accreverant infra sex annos.***

actio non ulterius (**ak**-shee-oh non əl-**teer**-ee-əs). [Latin "an action no further"] *Hist.* The distinctive clause in a plea to abate further maintenance of the action. • This plea replaced the *puis darrein continuance.* Cf. *plea to further maintenance to the action, plea puis darrein continuance* under PLEA. Pl. ***actiones non ulterii.***

actio perpetua (**ak**-shee-oh pər-**pech**-oo-ə). *Roman law.* An action that is not required to be brought within a specified time. Pl. ***actiones perpetuae.*** Cf. *actio temporalis.*

actio personalis (**ak**-shee-oh pər-sə-**nay**-lis). *Roman law.* A personal action. Pl. ***actiones personales.***

actio pigneratitia (**ak**-shee-oh pig-nə-rə-**tish**-ee-ə). *Roman law.* An action of pledge; an action founded on a contract of pledge. — Also spelled *actio pigneraticia; actio pignoratitia.* — Also termed *pigneratitia actio.* See PIGNUS. Pl. ***actiones pignoratitiae.***

actio poenalis (**ak**-shee-oh pi-**nay**-lis). *Roman law.* An action in which the plaintiff sued for a penalty rather than compensation. Pl. ***actiones poenales*** (**ak**-shee-**oh**-neez pi-**nay**-leez).

actio praejudicialis (**ak**-shee-oh pree-joo-dish-ee-**ay**-lis). *Roman law.* A preliminary action; an action begun to determine a preliminary matter on which other litigated matters depend. Pl. ***actiones praejudiciales.***

actio praetoria (**ak**-shee-oh pri-**tor**-ee-ə). *Roman law.* A praetorian action; one introduced by a praetor rather than founded on a statute. Pl. ***actiones praetoriae*** (**ak**-shee-**oh**-neez pri-**tor**-ee-ɪ).

actio pro socio (**ak**-shee-oh proh **soh**-shee-oh). *Roman law.* An action brought by one partner against another. Pl. ***actiones pro socio.***

actio Publiciana (**ak**-shee-oh pə-blish-ee-**ay**-nə). *Roman law.* An action allowing a person who had acquired bonitary ownership of land to recover it from a third party, so that the person would in due course acquire full title by prescription. • This action is named for Publicius, who might have been the first praetor to grant the action. — Also termed *actio Publiciana in rem*. See *bonitary ownership* under OWNERSHIP.

actio quod jussu (ak-shee-oh kwod jəs-[y]oo). *Roman law*. An action against a paterfamilias or a slave owner for enforcement of a debt contracted on behalf of the paterfamilias or slaveowner by a son or a slave.

actio quod metus causa (ak-shee-oh kwod mee-təs kaw-zə). *Roman law*. An action to penalize someone who wrongfully compelled the plaintiff to transfer property or to assume an obligation. • The plaintiff could obtain damages of four times the value of the loss suffered. Pl. **actiones quod metus causa**.

actio realis (ak-shee-oh ree-ay-lis). [Law Latin] *Hist*. A real action. See *real action* under ACTION (4). Pl. **actiones reales**.

actio redhibitoria (ak-shee-oh red-i-bi-tor-ee-ə). *Roman & civil law*. An action for restoration to cancel a sale because of defects in the thing sold. Pl. **actiones redhibitoriae**.

actio rerum amotarum (ak-shee-oh reer-əm am-ə-tair-əm). *Roman law*. An action to recover items stolen by a spouse shortly before a divorce. Pl. **actiones rerum amotarum**.

actio rescissoria (ak-shee-oh re-si-sor-ee-ə). *Roman law*. An action to restore to the plaintiff property lost by prescription. • This action was available to minors and other persons exempt from prescriptive claims against their property. Pl. **actiones rescissoriae**.

actio serviana (ak-shee-oh sər-vee-ay-nə). *Roman law*. An action by which a lessor could seize, in satisfaction of unpaid rent, the lessee's personal property brought onto the leased premises. Pl. **actiones servianae**.

actio stricti juris (ak-shee-oh strik-tı joor-is). *Roman law*. A class of personal actions enforceable exactly as stated in the *formula* without taking equitable considerations into account; an action of strict right. • This type of action was often used to recover a definite sum of money or a particular object that was the subject of a formal promise (*stipulatio*). See FORMULA (1). Pl. **actiones stricti juris**.

actio temporalis (ak-shee-oh tem-pə-ray-lis). *Roman & civil law*. An action that must be brought within a specified time. Cf. *actio perpetua*. Pl. **actiones temporales**.

actio tutelae (ak-shee-oh t[y]oo-tee-lee). *Roman law*. An action arising from a breach of the duty owed by a guardian (*tutor*) to the ward, such as mismanagement of the ward's property. Pl. **actiones tutelae**.

actio utilis (ak-shee-oh yoo-tə-lis). *Roman law*. An extension of a direct action, founded on utility rather than strict right, available esp. to persons having an interest in property less than ownership. • This type of action was modeled after the *actio directa*. Cf. *actio directa*; *actio in factum*. Pl. **actiones utiles**.

actio venditi (ak-shee-oh ven-də-tı). *Roman law*. An action by which a seller could obtain his price or enforce a contract of sale. — Also termed *actio ex vendito*. Pl. **actiones venditi**.

actio vi bonorum raptorum (ak-shee-oh vı bə-nor-əm rap-tor-əm). *Roman law*. A penal action to recover goods taken by force. • A successful plaintiff would also receive three times the value of the taken property.

actio vulgaris (ak-shee-oh vəl-gair-is). *Hist*. An ordinary action, as opposed to one granted in special circumstances. Pl. **actiones vulgares**.

action. (14c) **1.** The process of doing something; conduct or behavior. **2.** A thing done; ACT (2). **3.** *Patents*. OFFICE ACTION.

advisory action. *Patents*. See *advisory office action* under OFFICE ACTION.

4. A civil or criminal judicial proceeding. — Also termed *action at law*.

action at law. A civil suit stating a legal cause of action and seeking only a legal remedy. See *suit at law* and *suit in equity* under SUIT.

action de die in diem (dee dı-ee in dı-em). [Law Latin "from day to day"] *Hist*. **1.** An action occurring from day to day; a continuing right of action. **2.** An action for trespass for each day that an injury continues.

action de in rem verso (dee in rem vər-soh). [Latin "action for money applied to (the defendant's) advantage"] **1.** *Roman & civil law*. An action for unjust enrichment, in which the plaintiff must show that an enrichment was bestowed, that the enrichment caused an impoverishment, that there is no justification for the enrichment and impoverishment, and that the plaintiff has no other adequate remedy at law, including no remedy under an express or implied contract. **2.** *Roman law*. An action brought against a paterfamilias or a slaveowner who benefited from the transaction of a child or slave. — Also termed (in both senses) *actio de in rem verso*.

action en declaration de simulation. *Louisiana law*. An action to void a contract. See *simulated contract* under CONTRACT.

action ex contractu (eks kən-trak-t[y]oo). A personal action arising out of a contract.

action ex delicto (eks də-lik-toh). A personal action arising out of a tort.

action for money had and received. At common law, an action by which the plaintiff could recover money paid to the defendant, the money usu. being recoverable because (1) the money had been paid by mistake or under compulsion, or (2) the consideration was insufficient.

action for money paid. At common law, an action by which the plaintiff could recover money paid to a third party — not to the defendant — in circumstances in which the defendant had benefited.

action for poinding. *Hist.* A creditor's action to obtain sequestration of the land rents and goods of the debtor to satisfy the debt or enforce a distress.

action for the loss of services. *Hist.* A husband's lawsuit against one who has taken away, imprisoned, or physically harmed his wife in circumstances in which (1) the act is wrongful to the wife, and (2) the husband is deprived of her society or services.

action for the recovery of land. See EJECTMENT.

action in equity. (18c) An action that seeks equitable relief, such as an injunction or specific performance, as opposed to damages. See *suit in equity* under SUIT.

action in personam (in pər-**soh**-nəm). (1800) **1.** An action brought against a person rather than property. • An *in personam* judgment is binding on the judgment–debtor and can be enforced against all the property of the judgment–debtor. **2.** An action in which the named defendant is a natural or legal person. — Also termed *personal action*; (in Roman and civil law) *actio in personam*; *actio personalis*. See IN PERSONAM. Pl. **actiones in personam; actiones personales.**

action in rem (in **rem**). (18c) **1.** An action determining the title to property and the rights of the parties, not merely among themselves, but also against all persons at any time claiming an interest in that property; a real action. **2.** *Louisiana law.* An action brought for the protection of possession, ownership, or other real rights in immovable property. La. Civ. Code arts. 3651 *et seq.* **3.** *Louisiana law.* An action for the recovery of possession of immovable property. La. Civ. Code art. 526. — Also termed (in Roman law) *actio in rem*; *actio realis*; *real action*. See IN REM. Pl. **actiones in rem. 4.** An action in which the named defendant is real or personal property.

action of account. See ACCOUNTING (3).

action of assize. *Hist.* A real action by which the plaintiff proves title to land merely by showing an ancestor's possession. See ASSIZE.

action of book debt. See ACCOUNTING (4).

action of debt. See CONDICTIO.

action of declarator. *Scots law.* An action brought in the Court of Session for the purpose of establishing a legal status or right. — Also termed *declarator*; *action for declaratory*.

action of ejectment. See EJECTMENT (3).

action on account. See ACCOUNTING (4).

action on expenditure. An action for payment of the principal debt by a personal surety.

action on the case. See *trespass on the case* under TRESPASS.

action per quod servitium amisit (pər kwod sər-**vish**-ee-əm ə-**mi**-sit). [Latin] *Hist.* An action for the loss of a servant's services.

action quasi in rem (**kway**-si in **rem** *or* **kway**-zi). (1883) An action brought against the defendant personally, with jurisdiction based on an interest in property, the objective being to deal with the particular property or to subject the property to the discharge of the claims asserted. See *quasi in rem* under IN REM.

action to quiet title. (1837) A proceeding to establish a plaintiff's title to land by compelling the adverse claimant to establish a claim or be forever estopped from asserting it. — Also termed *quiet-title action*.

action to review judgment. *Rare.* **1.** MOTION FOR NEW TRIAL. **2.** A request for judicial review of a nonjudicial body's decision, such as an administrative ruling on a workers'-compensation claim. • The grounds for review are usu. similar to those for a new trial, esp. patent errors of law and new evidence.

amicable action. See *test case* (1) under CASE.

civil action. (16c) An action brought to enforce, redress, or protect a private or civil right; a noncriminal litigation. — Also termed (if brought by a private person) *private action*; (if brought by a government) *public action*.

class action. See CLASS ACTION.

collusive action. (18c) An action between two parties who have no actual controversy, being merely for the purpose of determining a legal question or receiving a precedent that might prove favorable in related litigation. — Also termed *fictional action*.

common-law action. An action governed by common law, rather than statutory, equitable, or civil law.

criminal action. (16c) An action instituted by the government to punish offenses against the public.

cross-action. An action brought by the defendant against the plaintiff based on the same subject matter as the plaintiff's action. See CROSS-CLAIM.

derivative action. See DERIVATIVE ACTION.

direct action. See DIRECT ACTION.

fictional action. See *collusive action.*

fictitious action. An action, usu. unethical, brought solely to obtain a judicial opinion on an issue of fact or law, rather than for the disposition of a controversy.

Good Samaritan action. See GOOD SAMARITAN ACTION.

hypothecary action (hɪ-**poth**-ə-ker-ee). *Roman & civil law.* An action for the enforcement of a mortgage (*hypotheca*); a lawsuit to enforce a creditor's claims under a hypothec or hypothecation. — Also termed *actio hypothecaria.*

innominate action (i-**nom**-i-nət). An action that has no special name by which it is known. Cf. *nominate action.*

joint action. 1. An action brought by two or more plaintiffs. 2. An action brought against two or more defendants.

local action. An action that can be brought only in the jurisdiction where the cause of action arose, as when the action's subject matter is a piece of real property.

matrimonial action. An action relating to the state of marriage, such as an action for separation, annulment, or divorce.

mixed action. An action that has some characteristics of both a real action and a personal action.

nominate action (**nom**-i-nət). An action that is known by a name, such as a confessory action, a petitory action, or a possessory action. Cf. *innominate action.*

nonpersonal action. An action that proceeds within some category of territorial jurisdiction other than in personam — that is, jurisdiction in rem, quasi in rem, or over status.

penal action. (16c) 1. A criminal prosecution. 2. A civil proceeding in which either the state or a common informer sues to recover a penalty from a defendant who has violated a statute. ● Although civil in nature, a penal action resembles a criminal proceeding because the result of a successful action is a monetary penalty intended, like a fine, to punish the defendant. See COMMON INFORMER. 3. A civil lawsuit by an aggrieved party seeking recovery of a statutory fine or a penalty, such as punitive damages.

personal action. (17c) 1. An action brought for the recovery of debts, personal property, or damages arising from any cause. — Also termed *remedial action.* 2. See *action in personam.*

petitory action (pet-ə-tor-ee). (17c) 1. *Roman & civil law.* An action to establish and enforce title to property independently of the right to possession. 2. *Civil law.* An action for the recognition of ownership or other real right in immovable (or sometimes movable) property. ● In civil-law systems, the petitory action (revendication) is a much broader and more effective remedy than the *rei-vindicatio*, the Roman prototype. This action is based on, and tends to protect, real rights, that is, ownership and its dismemberments. It is therefore a real action, distinguishable from personal actions based on (and tending to protect) personal rights. Generally, the petitory action is available for the protection of the ownership of both movables and immovables. In Louisiana, however, the petitory action is for the recognition of ownership or other real right in immovable property, brought by a person who is not in possession of it. La. Code Civ. Proc. art. 3651. An action for the recognition of such a right in movable property is an innominate real action, known as a *revendicatory action.* — Also termed *petitory suit; petitorium; revendication.*

plenary action (**plee**-nə-ree *or* **plen**-). (1837) A full hearing or trial on the merits, as opposed to a summary proceeding. Cf. *summary proceeding* under PROCEEDING.

possessory action (pə-**zes**-ə-ree). (17c) 1. An action to obtain, recover, or maintain possession of property but not title to it, such as an action to evict a nonpaying tenant. — Also termed *possessorium.* 2. *Maritime law.* An action brought to recover possession of a ship under a claim of title.

private action. See *civil action.*

public action. See *civil action.*

real action. (16c) 1. An action brought for the recovery of land or other real property; specif., an action to recover the possession of a freehold estate in real property, or seisin. 2. *Civil law.* An action based on, and tending to protect, a real right, namely, the right of ownership and its dismemberments. ● It is distinguishable from a personal action, which is based on (and tends to protect) a personal right. 3. *Louisiana law.* An action brought for the protection of possession, ownership, or other real rights in immovable property. La. Code Civ. Proc. arts. 3651 *et seq.* — Also termed *action in rem; actio in rem; actio realis.* See SEISIN.

redhibitory action. *Civil law.* An action brought to void a sale of a thing having a defect that renders it either useless or so flawed that the buyer would not have bought it in the first place. See REDHIBITION.

remedial action. 1. See REMEDIAL ACTION. 2. See *personal action* (1).

representative action. 1. See CLASS ACTION. 2. See DERIVATIVE ACTION (1).

rescissory action. *Scots law.* An action to set aside a deed.

revendicatory action (ree-**ven**-di-kə-tor-ee). See *petitory action.*

separate action. (18c) **1.** An action brought alone by each of several complainants who are all involved in the same transaction but either cannot legally join the suit or, not being required to join, choose not to join it. **2.** One of several distinct actions brought by a single plaintiff against each of two or more parties who are all liable to a plaintiff with respect to the same subject matter. — Also termed *several action.*

several action. See *separate action.*

sham action. An objectively baseless lawsuit the primary purpose of which is to hinder or interfere with a competitor's business relationships. *See Professional Real Estate Investors, Inc. v. Columbia Pictures Indus., Inc.,* 508 U.S. 49, 113 S.Ct. 1920 (1993). — Also termed *sham lawsuit; sham suit.* See SHAM EXCEPTION.

statutory action. An action governed by statutory law rather than equitable, civil, or common law.

test action. See *test case* (2) under CASE.

third-party action. (1872) An action brought as part of a lawsuit already pending but distinct from the main claim, whereby a defendant sues an entity not sued by the plaintiff when that entity may be liable to the defendant for all or part of the plaintiff's claim. • A common example is an action for indemnity or contribution.

transitory action. An action that can be brought in any venue where the defendant can be personally served with process.

Action. A former independent federal agency that administered various volunteer-services programs including Foster Grandparents, Retired Senior Volunteers, Senior Companions, Volunteers in Service to America, and Student Community Service Projects. • Its functions were transferred to the Corporation for National and Community Service in 1995. See CORPORATION FOR NATIONAL AND COMMUNITY SERVICE.

action, cause of. See CAUSE OF ACTION.

action, form of. See FORM OF ACTION.

action, right of. See RIGHT OF ACTION.

actionable, *adj.* (16c) Furnishing the legal ground for a lawsuit or other legal action <intentional interference with contractual relations is an actionable tort>.

actionable per quod (pər **kwod**). (Of potentially defamatory words) not inherently defamatory and therefore requiring allegation and proof of special damages. • For example, if the defendant says, "The plaintiff is crazy," the utterance

is actionable per quod. That is, the plaintiff must prove, in addition to the utterance, that the defendant intended the words to mean that the plaintiff was mentally impaired or deficient in business or professional capacity, and that these words caused the plaintiff to suffer special damages. See PER QUOD.

actionable per se (pər **say**). (Of defamatory words) legally and conclusively presumed defamatory. • In the law of defamation, words actionable per se are inherently libelous or slanderous. For example, if a person says of a fiduciary, "That person embezzles client funds," the utterance is actionable per se. The plaintiff does not have to allege or prove special damages. See PER SE.

actionable negligence. See NEGLIGENCE (1).

actionable nuisance. See NUISANCE (3).

actionable per quod. See ACTIONABLE.

actionable per se. See ACTIONABLE.

actionable word. A term that is defamatory in itself. See *libel per se* under LIBEL.

action agenda. See *action calendar* under CALENDAR (4).

action at law. See ACTION (4).

action calendar. See CALENDAR (4).

action de die in diem. See ACTION (4).

action de in rem verso. See ACTION (4).

actio negativa. See *actio negatoria* under ACTIO.

actio negatoria. See ACTIO.

actio negotiorum gestorum. See ACTIO.

actiones legis. See LEGIS ACTIO.

action ex contractu. See ACTION (4).

action ex delicto. See ACTION (4).

action for money had and received. See ACTION (4).

action for money paid. See ACTION (4).

action for poinding. See ACTION (4).

action for the loss of services. See ACTION (4).

action for the recovery of land. See EJECTMENT.

action in equity. 1. See ACTION (4). **2.** See *suit in equity* under SUIT.

action in personam. See ACTION (4).

action in rem. See ACTION (4).

action of account. See ACCOUNTING (3).

action of assize. See ACTION (4).

action of book debt. See ACCOUNTING (4).

action of debt. See CONDICTIO.

action on account. See ACCOUNTING (4).

actio non accrevit infra sex annos. See ACTIO.

action on decision. A legal memorandum from attorneys in the Internal Revenue Service's litigation division to the Service's Chief Counsel, containing advice on whether the Service should acquiesce, appeal, or take some other action regarding a court's decision that is unfavorable to the Service. — Abbr. AOD.

action on expenditure. See ACTION (4).

action on the case. See *trespass on the case* under TRESPASS.

actio non ulterius. See ACTIO.

actio noxalis (**ak**-shee-oh nok-**say**-lis), *n.* See NOXAL ACTION.

action *per quod servitium amisit.* See ACTION (4).

action quasi in rem. See ACTION (4).

action to quiet title. See ACTION (4).

action to review judgment. See ACTION (4).

actio perpetua. See ACTIO.

actio personalis. See ACTIO.

actio pigneratitia. See ACTIO.

actio poenalis. See ACTIO.

actio praejudicialis. See ACTIO.

actio praetoria. See ACTIO.

actio pro socio. See ACTIO.

actio Publiciana. See ACTIO.

actio Publiciana in rem. See *actio Publiciana* under ACTIO.

actio quod jussu. See ACTIO.

actio quod metus causa. See ACTIO.

actio realis. See ACTIO.

actio redhibitoria. See ACTIO.

actio rerum amotarum. See ACTIO.

actio rescissoria. See ACTIO.

actio serviana. See ACTIO.

actio servi corrupti. See ACTIO.

actio stricti juris. See ACTIO.

actio temporalis. See ACTIO.

actio tutelae. See ACTIO.

actio utilis. See ACTIO.

actio venditi. See ACTIO.

actio vi bonorum raptorum. See ACTIO.

actio vulgaris. See ACTIO.

active adoption-registry statute. See ADOPTION-REGISTRY STATUTE.

active breach of contract. See BREACH OF CONTRACT.

active case. See CASE.

active concealment. See CONCEALMENT.

active conduct. See CONDUCT.

active-control-of-vessel duty. See ACTIVE-OPERATIONS DUTY.

active debt. See DEBT.

active duty. 1. *Military law.* The full-time status of being in any of the U.S. armed forces. **2.** See *positive duty* under DUTY (1).

active euthanasia. See EUTHANASIA.

active income. See INCOME.

active inducement. See INDUCEMENT.

active negligence. See NEGLIGENCE.

active-operations duty. *Maritime law.* A shipowner's obligation to provide safe working conditions, in the work areas that it controls, for the longshoremen who are loading or unloading the ship. — Also termed *active-control-of-vessel duty.* Cf. TURNOVER DUTY; INTERVENTION DUTY.

active supervision. *Antitrust.* Under the test for determining whether a private entity may claim a state-action exemption from the antitrust laws, the right of the state to review the entity's anticompetitive acts and to disapprove those acts that do not promote state policy. See STATE-ACTION DOCTRINE; MIDCAL TEST.

active trust. See TRUST.

active waste. See *commissive waste* under WASTE (1).

activist lawyering. See CAUSE LAWYERING.

activity. 1. The collective acts of one person or of two or more people engaged in a common enterprise.

commercial activity. An activity, such as operating a business, conducted to make a profit.

2. See MARKET VOLUME.

activity incident to service. An act undertaken by a member of the armed forces as a part of a military operation or as a result of the actor's status as a member of the military. • For example, if a member of the military takes advantage of that status by flying home on a military aircraft, the flight is activity incident to service, and a claim against the government for any injuries received may be barred under the *Feres* doctrine. See FERES DOCTRINE.

act of attainder. See BILL OF ATTAINDER.

act of bankruptcy. An event, such as a debtor's fraudulent conveyance of property, that triggers an involuntary bankruptcy proceeding against a debtor. • The 1978 Bankruptcy Reform Act abolished this requirement as a condition to an involuntary bankruptcy proceeding.

act of commission. See ACT (2).

act of Congress. (18c) A law that is formally enacted in accordance with the legislative power granted to Congress by the U.S. Constitution. • To become a law, or an act of Congress, a bill or resolution must be passed by a majority of the members of both the House of Representatives and the Senate. Bills or resolutions may generally be introduced in either chamber, except that bills for generating revenue must be introduced in the House of Representatives. When a bill or resolution is introduced in a chamber, it is usu. assigned to a committee. If it is passed by the committee, it is reported to the full chamber. If it passes in the full chamber, it is reported to the other chamber, which then usu. assigns it to a committee in that chamber. If it passes by majority votes of the committee and full body in that chamber, it is reported back to the originating chamber. If its terms have changed in the second chamber, it is submitted to a conference committee, consisting of members from both chambers, to work out a compromise. When the bill or resolution is passed, with the same terms, by both chambers, it is signed by the Speaker of the House and the President of the Senate (usu. the President Pro Tempore), and is presented to the President of the United States for signature. If the President signs it or fails to return it to Congress within ten days, the bill or resolution becomes law. But if the President vetoes the bill or resolution, it must be passed by a two-thirds majority of the House of Representatives and the Senate to become law. U.S. Const. art. I, § 7; 3 *The Guide to American Law* 165–66 (West 1983).

act of court. 1. See *judicial act* under ACT. **2.** *Scots law.* A memorandum setting forth the proceedings in a lawsuit. **3.** *Scots law.* A rule made by a sheriff regulating proceedings within the sheriffalty.

act of God. (18c) An overwhelming, unpreventable event caused exclusively by forces of nature, such as an earthquake, flood, or tornado. • The definition has been statutorily broadened to include all natural phenomena that are exceptional, inevitable, and irresistible, the effects of which could not be prevented or avoided by the exercise of due care or foresight. 42 USCA § 9601(1). — Also termed *act of nature*; *act of providence*; *superior force*; *vis major*; *irresistible superhuman force*; *vis divina.* Cf. FORCE MAJEURE; *unavoidable accident* under ACCIDENT.

act of grace. An act of clemency; esp., such an act performed at the beginning of a monarch's reign or at some other significant occasion.

act of honor. *Commercial law.* A transaction, memorialized in an instrument prepared by a notary public, evidencing a third person's agreement to accept, for the credit of one or more of the parties, a bill that has been protested. • The UCC eliminated this type of transaction.

act of hostility. An event that may be considered an adequate cause for war; CASUS BELLI. — Also termed *hostile act.*

act of indemnity. 1. A statute that relieves specified persons, esp. government officials, from some penalty to which they might be subject as a result of having exceeded their powers or having otherwise acted illegally. **2.** A statute that compensates persons for damage incurred as a result of either some public measure or government service.

act of law. 1. See *act of the law* under ACT. **2.** See LEGAL ACT.

act of legislation. 1. A formal change in the law that existed previously. **2.** A statute.

act of nature. 1. See ACT OF GOD. **2.** See VIS MAJOR.

act of omission. See *negative act* under ACT.

act of Parliament. A law made by the British sovereign, with the advice and consent of the Lords and the Commons; a British statute.

act of Parliament of Scotland. 1. A statute passed by the Parliament of Scotland between its creation in the 14th century and 1707. **2.** See ACT OF THE SCOTTISH PARLIAMENT.

act of petition. *Hist.* A summary proceeding in which litigants provide brief statements supported by affidavit. • This procedure was used in the English High Court of Admiralty.

act of possession. (16c) **1.** The exercise of physical control over a corporeal thing, movable or immovable, with the intent to own it. **2.** Conduct indicating an intent to claim property as one's own; esp., conduct that supports a claim of adverse possession.

act of providence. 1. See ACT OF GOD. **2.** See VIS MAJOR.

act of sale. An official record of a sale of property; esp., a document drawn up by a notary, signed by the parties, and attested by witnesses.

Act of Settlement. *Hist.* An act of Parliament (12 & 13 Will. 3, ch. 2, 1701) that resolved the question of royal succession unsettled after the Glorious Revolution of 1688. • The question was resolved by limiting the Crown to Protestant members of the House of Hanover. The Act also provided that the sovereign must be a member of the Church of England, and it established that judges would hold office during good behavior rather than at the will of the sovereign.

act-of-state doctrine. *Int'l law.* The principle that no nation can judge the legality of a foreign country's sovereign acts within its own territory. • As originally formulated by the U.S. Supreme Court in 1897, the doctrine provides that "the courts of one country will not sit in judgment on the acts of the government of another done within its own territory." *Underhill v. Hernandez*, 168 U.S. 250, 252, 18 S.Ct. 83, 84 (1897). The Supreme Court later declared that though the act-of-state doctrine is compelled by neither international law nor the Constitution, it has "institutional underpinnings." *Banco Nacional de Cuba v. Sabbatino*, 376 U.S. 398, 423, 84 S.Ct. 923, 937 (1964).

Act of Supremacy. *Hist.* A statute that named the English sovereign as supreme head of the Church of England (26 Hen. 8, ch. 1). ● The Act was passed in 1534 during Henry VIII's reign and confirmed in 1559 (1 Eliz., ch. 1) to counteract pro-Catholic legislation enacted during the reign of Mary Tudor. In addition to making the monarch both head of state and head of the church, the Act defined some of the monarch's powers as head of the church, such as the power to issue injunctions relating to ecclesiastical affairs.

act of the law. See ACT.

act of the party. See *act in the law* under ACT.

Act of Uniformity. *Hist.* Any of several 16th- and 17th-century acts mandating uniform religious practices in England and Ireland; specif., an act requiring the use of the *Book of Common Prayer*.

Act of Union. Any of several acts of Parliament uniting various parts of Great Britain. ● The term applies to (1) the Laws in Wales Act (1535), which united Wales with England and made that principality subject to English law, and (2) the Union with Ireland Act (1800), which abolished the Irish Parliament and incorporated Ireland into the United Kingdom of Great Britain and Ireland. It is used loosely in reference to the Union with Scotland in 1707, which was made not by statute but by treaty, approved by separate acts of the parliaments of Scotland and England. The treaty dissolved each parliament and created the new state of Great Britain with one parliament, the Parliament of Great Britain.

actor. **1.** One who acts; a person whose conduct is in question.

    bad actor. An actor who is shown or perceived to have engaged in illegal, impermissible, or unconscionable conduct. ● A presumption that a person is a bad actor may be created by an adverse-inference instruction.

2. *Archaic.* A male plaintiff. **3.** *Hist.* An advocate or pleader; one who acted for another in legal matters. Cf. REUS (1). **4.** *Roman law.* (*ital.*) A person who sues; a claimant. — Also termed (in sense 4) *petitor.* Pl. (in sense 4) *actores.*

acts of assembly. See SESSION LAWS.

actual, *adj.* (14c) Existing in fact; real <actual malice>. Cf. CONSTRUCTIVE.

actual abandonment. See ABANDONMENT (10).

actual agency. See AGENCY (1).

actual allegiance. See ALLEGIANCE.

actual assent. See ASSENT.

actual authority. See AUTHORITY (1).

actual bailment. See BAILMENT.

actual bias. See BIAS.

actual capital. See CAPITAL.

actual cash value. See VALUE (2).

actual cause. See *but-for cause* under CAUSE (1).

actual change of possession. A real, rather than constructive, transfer of ownership. ● A creditor of the transferor cannot reach property that has actually changed possession.

actual consumer confusion. See CONSUMER CONFUSION.

actual controversy. **1.** See CONTROVERSY (2). **2.** See CONTROVERSY (3).

actual damages. See DAMAGES.

actual delivery. See DELIVERY.

actual escape. See ESCAPE (2).

actual eviction. See EVICTION.

actual force. See FORCE.

actual fraud. See FRAUD.

actual-injury trigger. *Insurance.* The point at which an insured suffers damage or injury (such as the time of an automobile accident), so that there is an occurrence invoking coverage under an insurance policy. — Also termed *injury-in-fact trigger.* Cf. EXPOSURE THEORY; MANIFESTATION THEORY; TRIPLE TRIGGER.

actual innocence. See INNOCENCE.

actual knowledge. See KNOWLEDGE.

actual loss. See LOSS.

actually litigated. (1969) (Of a claim that might be barred by collateral estoppel) properly raised in an earlier lawsuit, submitted to the court for a determination, and determined. ● A party is barred by the doctrine of collateral estoppel from relitigating an issue that was actually litigated — usu. including by summary judgment but not necessarily by default judgment — in an earlier suit involving the same parties, even if that suit involved different claims. Restatement (Second) of Judgments § 27 cmt. d (1980).

actual malice. See MALICE.

actual market value. See *fair market value* under VALUE (2).

actual notice. See NOTICE.

actual physical control. (1880) Direct bodily power over something, esp. a vehicle. ● Many jurisdictions require a showing of "actual physical control" of a vehicle by a person charged with driving while intoxicated.

actual possession. See POSSESSION.

actual reduction to practice. See REDUCTION TO PRACTICE.

actual-risk test. The doctrine that, for an injured employee to be entitled to workers'-compensation benefits, the employee must prove that the injury arose from, and occurred in the course and scope of, employment.

actual seisin. See *seisin in deed* under SEISIN.

actual service. See *personal service* (1) under SERVICE (2).

actual taking. See *physical taking* under TAKING (2).

actual total loss. See LOSS.

actual user confusion. See CONSUMER CONFUSION.

actual value. See *fair market value* under VALUE (2).

actuarial equivalent. The amount of accrued pension benefits to be paid monthly or at some other interval so that the total amount of benefits will be paid over the expected remaining lifetime of the recipient.

actuarially sound retirement system. A retirement plan that contains sufficient funds to pay future obligations, as by receiving contributions from employees and the employer to be invested in accounts to pay future benefits. Cf. NONACTUARIALLY SOUND RETIREMENT SYSTEM.

actuarial method. A means of determining the amount of interest on a loan by using the loan's annual percentage rate to separately calculate the finance charge for each payment period, after crediting each payment, which is credited first to interest and then to principal.

actuarial present value. The amount of money necessary to purchase an annuity that would generate a particular monthly payment, or whatever periodic payment the plan provides, for the expected remaining life span of the recipient.

actuarial surplus. An estimate of the amount by which a pension plan's assets exceed its expected current and future liabilities, including the amount expected to be needed to fund future benefit payments.

actuarial table. An organized chart of statistical data indicating life expectancies for people in various categories (such as age, family history, and chemical exposure). • Actuarial tables are usu. admissible in evidence. — Also termed *expectancy table*; *mortality table*; *mortuary table*. Cf. LIFE TABLE.

actuary (**ak**-choo-air-ee), *n.* A statistician who determines the present effects of future contingent events; esp., one who calculates insurance and pension rates on the basis of empirically based tables. — **actuarial** (ak-choo-**air**-ee-əl), *adj.*

actus (**ak**-təs), *n.* [Latin] **1.** An act or action; a thing done. **2.** *Hist.* An act of Parliament; esp., one passed by both houses but not yet approved by the

monarch. **3.** *Roman law.* A servitude for driving cattle or a carriage across another's land. — Also termed (in sense 3) *jus actus*.

actus reus (**ak**-təs **ree**-əs *also* **ray**-əs). [Law Latin "guilty act"] (1902) The wrongful deed that comprises the physical components of a crime and that generally must be coupled with *mens rea* to establish criminal liability; a forbidden act <the *actus reus* for theft is the taking of or unlawful control over property without the owner's consent>. — Also termed *deed of crime*; *overt act*. See CORPUS DELICTI. Cf. MENS REA.

ACUS. *abbr.* ADMINISTRATIVE CONFERENCE OF THE UNITED STATES.

A.D. *abbr.* ANNO DOMINI.

ad (ad), *prep.* [Latin] At; by; for; near; on account of; to; until; upon; with relation to; concerning.

ADA. *abbr.* AMERICANS WITH DISABILITIES ACT.

adaptation right. *Copyright.* A copyright holder's exclusive right to prepare derivative works based on the protected work. 17 USCA § 106(2). • For example, before a movie studio can make a film version of a book, it must secure the author's adaptation right. See *derivative work* under WORK (2).

ADB. *abbr.* ACCIDENTAL-DEATH BENEFIT.

ad damnum **clause** (ad **dam**-nəm). [Latin "to the damage"] (1840) A clause in a prayer for relief stating the amount of damages claimed. See PRAYER FOR RELIEF.

added damages. See *punitive damages* under DAMAGES.

addendum (ə-**den**-dəm). (17c) Something to be added, esp. to a document; a supplement.

addict (**a**-dikt), *n.* A person who habitually uses a substance, esp. a narcotic drug. — **addict** (ə-**dikt**), *vb.* — **addictive,** *adj.* — **addiction,** *n.*

  drug addict. A person who is psychologically or physiologically dependent on a narcotic drug.

addict, *vb. Roman law.* **1.** To adjudge (to); to deliver under court order. **2.** More broadly, to surrender a thing (to someone else).

addiction. 1. The habitual and intemperate use of a substance, esp. a potentially harmful one such as a narcotic drug. • The usual requisites are (1) an emotional dependence that leads to compulsiveness; (2) an enhanced tolerance of the substance, leading to more potent doses; and (3) physical dependence such that withdrawal symptoms result from deprivation. **2.** ADDICTIO.

addictive drug. See DRUG.

ad diem (ad **dɪ**-əm). [Latin] At a day; at the appointed day.

addition. (17c) **1.** A structure that is attached to or connected with another building that predates the structure; an extension or annex. • Although some courts have held that an addition is merely an appurtenant structure that might not actually be in physical contact with the other building, most courts hold that there must be physical contact. **2.** A title or appellation appended to a person's name to show rank, occupation, or place of residence. • In English law, there are traditionally four kinds of additions: (1) those of estate, such as yeoman, gentleman, or esquire; (2) those of degree (or dignity), such as knight, baron, earl, marquis, or duke; (3) those of trade or occupation, such as scrivener, painter, mason, or carpenter; and (4) those of place of residence, such as London, Bath, or Chester. It was formerly required by the statute of additions (1 Hen. 5, ch. 5) that original writs and indictments state a person's addition, but the practice has long since been abolished.

additional claims after allowance. *Patents.* Claims submitted for the first time by amendment after the U.S. Patent and Trademark Office has informed the applicant of the patent application's allowance. • Once a notice of allowance has been issued, the applicant may not by right submit additional claims. But in some circumstances, such as when the applicant seeks to add only dependent claims, the supervisory examiner has authority to enter an amendment containing additional claims after allowance but on or before the date when the issue fee is paid. See *amendment after allowance* under PATENT- APPLICATION AMENDMENT.

additional-consideration rule. *Employment law.* An exception to the employment-at-will principle, whereby an employee who does not have a written contract but who undertakes substantial hardship in addition to the normal job duties — as by relocating to a different city based on oral assurances of job security — can maintain a breach-of-contract claim if the employer does not fulfill its agreement.

additional damages. See DAMAGES.

additional extended coverage. *Insurance.* A policy endorsement providing supplemental residential coverage for a variety of perils, including vandalism, damage from falling trees, and water damage from the plumbing system.

additional grand jury. See *special grand jury* under GRAND JURY.

additional instruction. See JURY INSTRUCTION.

additional insurance. See INSURANCE.

additional insured. See INSURED.

additional legacy. See LEGACY.

additional-perils clause. See INCHMAREE CLAUSE.

additional servitude. See SERVITUDE (2).

additional standard deduction. See DEDUCTION.

additional tax. See *stopgap tax* under TAX.

additional term. See TERM (5).

additional work. See WORK (1).

additur (**ad**-ə-tuur). [Latin "it is added to"] (1894) A trial court's order, issued usu. with the defendant's consent, that increases the jury's award of damages to avoid a new trial on grounds of inadequate damages. • The term may also refer to the increase itself, the procedure, or the court's power to make the order. — Also termed *increscitur.* Cf. REMITTITUR.

add-on clause. (1965) An installment-contract provision that converts earlier purchases into security for new purchases.

add-on interest. See INTEREST (3).

add-on loan. See LOAN.

address, *n.* **1.** The place where mail or other communication is sent. **2.** In some states, a legislature's formal request to the executive to do a particular thing, such as to remove a judge from office. **3.** *Equity practice.* The part of a bill in which the court is identified. See DIRECTION (5).

address to the Crown. Upon a reading of a royal speech in Parliament, the ceremonial resolution by Parliament expressing thanks to the sovereign for the gracious speech. • Formerly, two members were selected in each house for moving and seconding the address. With the commencement of the 1890–1891 session, a single resolution was adopted.

adduce (ə-d[y]oos), *vb.* (15c) To offer or put forward for consideration (something) as evidence or authority <adduce the engineer's expert testimony>. — **adduction** (ə-dək-shən), *n.* — **adducible** (ə-d[y]oo-sə-bəl), *adj.*

ADEA. *abbr.* AGE DISCRIMINATION IN EMPLOYMENT ACT.

adeem, *vb.* To revoke or satisfy (a willed gift) by some other gift.

ademption (ə-demp-shən), *n.* (16c) *Wills & estates.* The destruction or extinction of a testamentary gift by reason of a bequeathed asset's ceasing to be part of the estate at the time of the testator's death; a beneficiary's forfeiture of a legacy or bequest that is no longer operative. • There are two theories of ademption. Under the *identity theory of ademption*, a devise of a specific piece of property will fail if that property is not a part of the testator's estate upon his or her death. Under the *intent theory of ademption*, by contrast, when a specific devise is no longer in the testator's estate at the time of his or her death, the devisee will receive a gift of equal value if it can be proved that the testator did not intend the gift to be adeemed. The intent theory has been codified in § 2-606 of the 1990 Uniform Probate Code. — Also termed *extinguishment of legacy.* Cf. ABATEMENT (4);

ADVANCEMENT; LAPSE (2). — **adeem** (ə-**deem**), *vb.* — **adeemed, adempted,** *adj.*

ademption by extinction. (1847) An ademption that occurs because the unique property that is the subject of a specific bequest has been sold, given away, or destroyed, or is not otherwise in existence at the time of the testator's death.

ademption by satisfaction. (1916) An ademption that occurs because the testator, while alive, has already given property to the beneficiary in lieu of the testamentary gift.

adequacy of disclosure. *Patents.* Satisfaction of the statutory requirements that the specification in a patent application (1) gives enough detailed information to enable one skilled in the art to make and use the claimed invention (the enablement requirement); (2) discloses the best way the inventor knows to make and use the invention (the best-mode requirement); and (3) shows that the inventor was in full possession of the claimed invention on the application's filing date (the written-description requirement). • A patent that fails to meet any one of these requirements may be rejected under 35 USCA § 112. Any issued patent with an inadequate disclosure is invalid, although the challenger has to overcome the presumption of validity. — Also termed *sufficiency of disclosure.* See ENABLEMENT REQUIREMENT; BEST-MODE REQUIREMENT.

adequacy test. See IRREPARABLE-INJURY RULE.

adequate, *adj.* Legally sufficient <adequate notice>.

adequate assurance. See ASSURANCE.

adequate care. See *reasonable care* under CARE.

adequate cause. See *adequate provocation* under PROVOCATION.

adequate compensation. See *just compensation* under COMPENSATION.

adequate consideration. See CONSIDERATION (1).

adequate notice. See *due notice* under NOTICE.

adequate protection. *Bankruptcy.* Consideration that a debtor provides to secured creditors to protect them from the deteriorating condition or diminishing value of their collateral during the pendency of the bankruptcy. • The consideration, which can be in any form, is most commonly an additional payment, additional lien, or replacement lien.

adequate provocation. See PROVOCATION.

adequate remedy at law. See REMEDY.

adequate representation. See REPRESENTATION (3).

adequate-state-grounds doctrine. (1962) A judge-made principle that prevents the U.S. Supreme Court from reviewing a state-court decision based partially on state law if a decision on a federal issue would not change the result.

adequate warning. See WARNING.

adesse (ad-**es**-ee), *vb. Civil law.* To be present.

ADF. *abbr.* AFRICAN DEVELOPMENT FOUNDATION.

ad finem (ad **fɪ**-nəm), *adv.* [Latin] To the end. • This citation signal, abbreviated in text *ad fin.*, formerly provided only the first page of the section referred to, but now usu. directs the reader to a stated span of pages.

adherence. 1. ACCESSION (3). **2.** *Scots law.* The duty of spouses to live together.

adhesion. See ACCESSION (3).

adhesionary contract. See *adhesion contract* under CONTRACT.

adhesion contract. See CONTRACT.

adhesory contract. See *adhesion contract* under CONTRACT.

ad hoc (ad **hok**), *adj.* [Latin "for this"] Formed for a particular purpose <the board created an ad hoc committee to discuss funding for the new arena>. — **ad hoc,** *adv.*

ad hoc arbitration. See ARBITRATION.

ad hoc committee. See COMMITTEE.

ad hoc compromis. See COMPROMIS.

ad hominem (ad **hom**-ə-nəm), *adj.* [Latin "to the person"] (16c) Appealing to personal prejudices rather than to reason; attacking an opponent's character rather than the opponent's assertions <the brief was replete with ad hominem attacks against opposing counsel>. — **ad hominem,** *adv.*

ad infinitum (ad in-fə-**nɪ**-təm). [Latin "without limit"] To an indefinite extent <a corporation has a duration *ad infinitum* unless the articles of incorporation specify a shorter period>.

ad interim (ad **in**-tər-im), *adv.* [Latin] *Hist.* In the meantime; temporarily.

ad interim copyright. See COPYRIGHT.

adjacent, *adj.* Lying near or close to, but not necessarily touching. Cf. ADJOINING.

adject (a-**jekt**), *vb.* To annex or adjoin. — **adject,** *adj.*

adjective law (**aj**-ik-tiv). (1808) The body of rules governing procedure and practice; PROCEDURAL LAW. — Also termed *adjectival law.*

adjoining (ə-**joyn**-ing), *adj.* (15c) Touching; sharing a common boundary; CONTIGUOUS. Cf. ADJACENT. — **adjoin** (ə-**joyn**), *vb.*

adjoining owner. See OWNER.

adjourn (ə-**jərn**), *vb.* (15c) *Parliamentary law.* To end or postpone (a proceeding). Cf. RECESS (2).

adjourn sine die (**sɪ**-nee [or **sin**-ay] **dɪ**-ee). [Latin "without date"] To end a deliberative assembly's or court's session without setting a time to reconvene. — Also termed *adjourn without day.* See SINE DIE. Cf. RISE (4).

adjourn to a day certain. To end a deliberative assembly's or court's session while fixing a time for the next meeting. — Also termed *adjourn to a day and time certain; fix a day to which to adjourn.*

adjourn without day. See *adjourn sine die.*

adjourned. See STAND ADJOURNED.

adjourned meeting. See MEETING.

adjourned term. See TERM (5).

adjournment (ə-**jərn**-mənt), *n.* **1.** The act of adjourning; specif., a putting off of a court session or other meeting or assembly until a later time. See ADJOURN.

adjournment sine die (ə-**jərn**-mənt sɪ-nee [or sin-ay] dɪ-ee). The ending of a deliberative assembly's or court's session without setting a time to reconvene. — Also termed *adjournment without day.*

conditional adjournment. An adjournment that does not schedule another meeting, but provides for reconvening the assembly at an officer's or board's call or under other defined circumstances.

2. The period or interval between adjourning and reconvening.

adjournment day. See DAY.

adjournment day in error. See DAY.

adjourn sine die. See ADJOURN.

adjudge (ə-**jəj**), *vb.* (14c) **1.** ADJUDICATE (1). **2.** To deem or pronounce to be. **3.** To award judicially. Cf. ABJUDGE. **4.** *Scots law.* (Of a creditor) to take a debtor's estate through adjudication. See ADJUDICATION (3). **5.** To award (some or all of a debtor's estate) to a creditor.

adjudicate (ə-**joo**-di-kayt), *vb.* **1.** To rule upon judicially. **2.** ADJUDGE (2). **3.** ADJUDGE (3). — Also termed *judicate.*

adjudicatee (ə-joo-di-kə-**tee**). *Civil law.* A purchaser at a judicial sale.

adjudication (ə-joo-di-**kay**-shən), *n.* (17c) **1.** The legal process of resolving a dispute; the process of judicially deciding a case. **2.** JUDGMENT.

former adjudication. See FORMER ADJUDICATION.

3. *Scots law.* The Court of Session's transfer of heritable property to a creditor as security for or in satisfaction of a debt, or its vesting title in an entitled claimant.

adjudication hearing. See HEARING.

adjudication withheld. See *deferred judgment* under JUDGMENT.

adjudicative (ə-**joo**-di-kə-tiv), *adj.* **1.** Of or relating to adjudication. **2.** Having the ability to judge. — Also termed *adjudicatory; judicative.*

adjudicative-claims arbitration. See ARBITRATION.

adjudicative fact. See FACT.

adjudicative law. See CASELAW.

adjudicator (ə-**joo**-di-kay-tər). A person whose job is to render binding decisions; one who makes judicial pronouncements.

adjudicatory hearing. See *adjudication hearing* under HEARING.

adjudicatory proceeding. See *adjudication hearing* under HEARING.

adjunct (**aj**-əngkt), *adj.* (16c) Added as an accompanying object or circumstance; attached in a subordinate or temporary capacity <an adjunct professor>. — **adjunct,** *n.*

adjunct account. See ACCOUNT.

adjunction (ə-**jəngk**-shən). **1.** The act of adding to. **2.** *Civil law.* The union of an item of personal property owned by one person with that owned by another. See ACCESSION (4).

adjuration (aj-ə-**ray**-shən), *n.* **1.** The act of solemnly charging or entreating. **2.** A swearing; a solemn oath.

adjure (ə-**juur**), *vb.* (14c) To charge or entreat solemnly <the President adjured the foreign government to join the alliance>. — **adjuration** (aj-ə-**ray**-shən), *n.* — **adjuratory** (ə-**juur**-ə-tor-ee), *adj.* — **adjurer, adjuror** (ə-**juur**-ər), *n.*

adjust, *vb.* **1.** To determine the amount that an insurer will pay an insured to cover a loss. **2.** To arrive at a new agreement with a creditor for the payment of a debt.

adjustable-rate mortgage. See MORTGAGE.

adjustable-rate preferred stock. See STOCK.

adjusted basis. See BASIS.

adjusted book value. See BOOK VALUE.

adjusted cost basis. See BASIS.

adjusted gross estate. See ESTATE (3).

adjusted gross income. See INCOME.

adjusted ordinary gross income. See INCOME.

adjusted present value. See PRESENT VALUE.

adjuster. One appointed to ascertain, arrange, or settle a matter; esp., an independent agent or employee of an insurance company who investigates claimed losses, and negotiates and settles claims against the insurer. — Also termed *claims adjuster.*

average adjuster. *Maritime law.* An adjuster who determines the proportionate value of sacrificed cargo as a percentage of the total value of the ship, cargo, and freight, and who allocates contribution among the owners of the surviving properties. See CONTRIBUTION (4).

independent adjuster. An adjuster who solicits business from more than one insurance company; one who is not employed by, and does not work exclusively for, one insurance company.

adjusting entry. An accounting entry made at the end of an accounting period to record previously unrecognized revenue and expenses, as well as changes in assets and liabilities.

adjustment board. An administrative agency charged with hearing and deciding zoning appeals. — Also termed *board of adjustment*; *board of zoning appeals*.

adjustment bond. See BOND (3).

adjustment of status. *Immigration law.* The changing of an alien's classification from nonimmigrant or parolee (temporary) resident to immigrant (permanent) resident. ● This is a technical term used only in United States immigration filings. Cf. 245(I) WAIVER.

adjustment security. See SECURITY.

adjutant general (**aj**-ə-tənt), *n.* (*usu. cap.*) **1.** The administrative head of a military unit having a general staff. **2.** An officer in charge of the National Guard of a state.

ad litem (ad **lı**-tem *or* -təm). [Latin "for the suit"] (18c) For the purposes of the suit; pending the suit. See *guardian ad litem* under GUARDIAN.

admeasurement (ad-**mezh**-ər-mənt), *n.* (16c) **1.** Ascertainment, assignment, or apportionment by a fixed quantity or value, or by certain limits <the ship's admeasurement is based on its crew, engine, and capacity>. **2.** A writ obtained for purposes of ascertaining, assigning, or apportioning a fixed quantity or value or to establish limits; esp., a writ available against persons who usurp more than their rightful share of property. — **admeasure** (ad-**mezh**-ər), *vb.*

admeasurement of dower. *Hist.* A writ available to an heir (or the heir's guardian if the heir is an infant) to reduce the dower of the ancestor's widow who, while the heir was an infant, was assigned more dower than she was entitled to. — Also termed *admensuratione dotis*.

admeasurement of pasture. *Hist.* A writ against a person whose cattle have overgrazed a common pasture.

adminicle (ad-**min**-i-kəl), *n.* **1.** Corroborative or explanatory proof. **2.** *Scots law.* A writing that tends to establish the existence or terms of an otherwise unavailable document, such as a lost will or deed. — Also termed *adminiculum*.

adminicular (ad-mə-**nik**-yə-lər), *adj.* Corroborative or auxiliary <adminicular evidence>.

administration, *n.* (14c) **1.** The management or performance of the executive duties of a government, institution, or business. **2.** In public law, the practical management and direction of the executive department and its agencies. **3.** A judicial action in which a court undertakes the management and distribution of property. ● Examples include the administration of a trust, the liquidation of a company, and the realization and distribution of a bankrupt estate. See JOINT ADMINISTRATION. **4.** The management and settlement of the estate of an intestate decedent, or of a testator who has no executor, by a person legally appointed and supervised by the court. ● Administration of an estate involves realizing the movable assets and paying out of them any debts and other claims against the estate. It also involves the division and distribution of what remains. — **administer,** *vb.* — **administrative,** *adj.*

administration cum testamento annexo (kəm tes-tə-**men**-toh ə-**nek**-soh). [Latin "with the will annexed"] An administration granted when (1) a testator's will does not name any executor or when the executor named is incompetent to act, is deceased, or refuses to act, and (2) no successor executor has been named or is qualified to serve. — Abbr. c.t.a. — Also termed *administration with the will annexed.*

administration de bonis non (dee **boh**-nis **non**). [Latin "of the goods not administered"] An administration granted for the purpose of settling the remainder of an intestate estate that was not administered by the former administrator. — Abbr. d.b.n.

administration de bonis non cum testamento annexo (de **boh**-nis non kəm tes-tə-**men**-toh ə-**nek**-soh). An administration granted to settle the remainder of a testate estate not settled by a previous administrator or executor. ● This type of administration arises when there is a valid will, as opposed to an *administration de bonis non*, which is granted when there is no will. — Abbr. d.b.n.c.t.a.

administration durante absentia (d[y]uu-**ran**-tee ab-**sen**-shee-ə). An administration granted during the absence of either the executor or the person who has precedence as administrator.

administration durante minore aetate (d[y]uu-**ran**-tee mi-**nor**-ee ee-**tay**-tee). An administration granted during the minority of either a child executor or the person who has precedence as administrator.

administration pendente lite (pen-**den**-tee **lı**-tee). An administration granted during the pendency of a suit concerning a will's validity. — Also termed *pendente lite administration*; *special administration*. See PENDENTE LITE.

administration with the will annexed. See *administration cum testamento annexo.*

ancillary administration (an-sə-ler-ee). (1814) An administration that is auxiliary to the administration at the place of the decedent's domicile, such as one in another state. ● The purpose of this process is to collect assets, to transfer and record changed title to real property located there, and to pay any debts in that locality. — Also termed *foreign administration.*

caeterorum administration (set-ə-**ror**-əm). [Latin "of the rest"] An administration granted when limited powers previously granted to an administrator are inadequate to settle the estate's residue.

domiciliary administration (dom-ə-**sil**-ee-er-ee). (1850) The handling of an estate in the state where the decedent was domiciled at death.

foreign administration. See *ancillary administration.*

general administration. (18c) An administration with authority to deal with an entire estate. Cf. *special administration.*

limited administration. (18c) An administration for a temporary period or for a special purpose.

original administration. An administration that is not ancillary to a domiciliary administration.

pendente lite administration. See *administration pendente lite.*

public administration. (1893) In some jurisdictions, an administration by an officer appointed to administer for an intestate who has left no person entitled to apply for letters (or whose possible representatives refuse to serve).

special administration. (18c) **1.** An administration with authority to deal with only some of a decedent's property, as opposed to administering the whole estate. **2.** See *administration pendente lite.* Cf. *general administration.*

temporary administration. (18c) An administration in which the court appoints a fiduciary to administer the affairs of a decedent's estate for a short time before an administrator or executor can be appointed and qualified.

administration bill. See BILL (3).

administration expense. *Tax.* A necessary expenditure made by an administrator in managing and distributing an estate. ● These expenses are tax-deductible even if not actually incurred by the time the return is filed.

Administration for Children and Families. A unit in the U.S. Department of Health and Human Services responsible for health, economic, and social well-being issues involving children and families, refugees, legalized aliens, and people with developmental disabilities. — Abbr. ACF.

administration letters. See LETTERS OF ADMINISTRATION.

administration of justice. The maintenance of right within a political community by means of the physical force of the state; the state's application of the sanction of force to the rule of right.

Administration on Aging. A unit in the U.S. Department of Health and Human Services responsible for promoting the welfare of the elderly, often in collaboration with governmental agencies that provide services to the elderly and to caregivers of the elderly.

administration pendente lite. See ADMINISTRATION.

administration with the will annexed. See *administration cum testamento annexo* under ADMINISTRATION.

administrative act. See ACT.

administrative adjudication. The process used by an administrative agency to issue regulations through an adversary proceeding. Cf. RULEMAKING.

administrative agency. See AGENCY (3).

administrative collateral estoppel. See COLLATERAL ESTOPPEL.

Administrative Conference of the United States. A former independent federal agency that provided a forum where agency heads, private attorneys, university professors, and others studied ways to improve the procedures that agencies use in administering federal programs. ● It was abolished in 1995. — Abbr. ACUS.

administrative-control rule. *Tax.* The rule making the grantor of a trust liable for tax if the grantor retains control that may be exercised primarily for the grantor's own benefit. IRC (26 USCA) § 675.

administrative-convenience exception. *Bankruptcy.* A provision permitting a bankruptcy plan to have a separate classification for small, unsecured claims, to the extent that the separate classification will assist in a more efficient disposition of the estate, as by paying or eliminating the small claims earlier than other claims. 11 USCA § 1122(b).

administrative crime. See CRIME.

administrative deviation. A trustee's unauthorized departure from the terms of the trust.

administrative discharge. See DISCHARGE (8).

administrative discretion. See DISCRETION (4).

Administrative Domain-Name Challenge Panel. *Trademarks.* A board of experts convened under the auspices of the World Intellectual Property

Organization to decide Internet domain-name disputes. — Abbr. ACP.

administrative expense. 1. See OVERHEAD. **2.** *Bankruptcy.* A cost incurred by the debtor, after filing a bankruptcy petition, that is necessary for the debtor to continue operating its business. ● Administrative expenses are entitled to payment on a priority basis when the estate is distributed. 11 USCA § 503(b). See *general administrative expense* under EXPENSE.

administrative freeze. *Bankruptcy.* The refusal by a debtor's bank to permit withdrawals from the debtor's bank account after the bank learns that the debtor has filed bankruptcy, usu. because the debtor owes money to the bank in addition to maintaining funds on deposit.

administrative hearing. An administrative-agency proceeding in which evidence is offered for argument or trial.

administrative interpretation. See INTERPRETATION.

administrative law. (1896) The law governing the organization and operation of administrative agencies (including executive and independent agencies) and the relations of administrative agencies with the legislature, the executive, the judiciary, and the public. ● Administrative law is divided into three parts: (1) the statutes endowing agencies with powers and establishing rules of substantive law relating to those powers; (2) the body of agency-made law, consisting of administrative rules, regulations, reports, or opinions containing findings of fact, and orders; and (3) the legal principles governing the acts of public agents when those acts conflict with private rights.

international administrative law. **1.** The internal law and rules of international organizations. **2.** The substantive rules of international law that directly refer to the administrative matters of individual states. **3.** Domestic administrative law specifically concerned with international problems or situations. — Also termed *administrative international law.*

administrative-law judge. (1972) An official who presides at an administrative hearing and who has the power to administer oaths, take testimony, rule on questions of evidence, and make factual and legal determinations. 5 USCA § 556(c). — Abbr. ALJ. — Also termed *hearing examiner*; *hearing officer*; *trial examiner.*

Administrative Office of the United States Courts. An office in the judicial branch of the federal government responsible for administering the nonjudicial business of the federal courts (except the Supreme Court), disbursing funds, collecting statistics, fixing certain salaries, and purchasing supplies and equipment. ● Created in 1939 the Office is supervised by the Judicial

Conference of the United States. 28 USCA §§ 601 et seq. — Abbr. AOUSC; AO. See JUDICIAL CONFERENCE OF THE UNITED STATES.

administrative officer. See OFFICER (1).

administrative order. See ORDER (2).

administrative patent judge. See JUDGE.

Administrative Procedure Act. 1. A federal statute establishing practices and procedures to be followed in rulemaking and adjudication. ● The Act was designed to give citizens basic due-process protections such as the right to present evidence and to be heard by an independent hearing officer. **2.** A similar state statute. — Abbr. APA.

administrative proceeding. (1841) A hearing, inquiry, investigation, or trial before an administrative agency, usu. adjudicatory in nature but sometimes quasi-legislative. — Also termed *evidentiary hearing*; *full hearing*; *trial-type hearing*; *agency adjudication.*

administrative process. 1. The procedure used before administrative agencies. **2.** The means of summoning witnesses to an agency hearing.

administrative remedy. See REMEDY.

administrative review. See REVIEW.

administrative rule. (1856) An officially promulgated agency regulation that has the force of law. ● Administrative rules typically elaborate the requirements of a law or policy.

administrative rulemaking. See RULEMAKING.

administrative search. See SEARCH.

administrative search warrant. See *administrative warrant* under WARRANT (1).

administrative subpoena. See SUBPOENA.

administrative tribunal. An administrative agency before which a matter may be heard or tried, as distinguished from a purely executive agency; an administrative agency exercising a judicial function.

administrative warrant. See WARRANT (1).

administrator (ad-**min**-ə-stray-tər). (15c) **1.** A person who manages or heads a business, public office, or agency.

court administrator. An official who supervises the nonjudicial functions of a court, esp. the court's calendar, judicial assignments, budget, and nonjudicial personnel.

local administrator. Conflict of laws. An administrator appointed in the state where property is located or where an act is done.

2. A person appointed by the court to manage the assets and liabilities of an intestate decedent. ● This term once referred to males only (as opposed to *administratrix*), but legal writers now generally use *administrator* to refer to someone of either sex. In the Restatement of Property, the term *administrator* includes the term *executor* unless specifically stated otherwise. Cf. EXECUTOR (2).

administrator ad colligendum (ad kol-i-**jen**-dəm). An administrator appointed solely to collect and preserve the decedent's estate. — Also termed *administrator ad colligendum bona*.

administrator ad litem (ad **lı**-tem *or* -təm). A special administrator appointed by the court to represent the estate's interest in an action usu. either because there is no administrator of the estate or because the current administrator has an interest in the action adverse to that of the estate.

administrator ad prosequendum (ad prahs-ə-**kwen**-dəm). An administrator appointed to prosecute or defend a certain action or actions involving the estate.

administrator c.t.a. See *administrator cum testamento annexo*.

administrator cum testamento annexo (kəm tes-tə-**men**-toh ə-**nek**-soh). An administrator appointed by the court to carry out the provisions of a will when the testator has named no executor, or the executors named refuse, are incompetent to act, or have died before performing their duties. — Also termed *administrator c.t.a.*; *administrator with the will annexed*.

administrator d.b.n. See *administrator de bonis non*.

administrator de bonis non (dee **boh**-nis **non**). An administrator appointed by the court to administer the decedent's goods that were not administered by an earlier administrator or executor. • If there is no will, the administrator bears the name *administrator de bonis non* (abbr. *administrator d.b.n.*), but if there is a will, the full name is *administrator de bonis non cum testamento annexo* (abbr. *administrator d.b.n.c.t.a.*).

administrator durante absentia (d[y]uu-**ran**-tee ab-**sen**-shee-ə). An administrator appointed to act while an estate's executor or an administrator with precedence is temporarily absent.

administrator durante minore aetate (d[y]uu-**ran**-tee mi-**nor**-ee ee-**tay**-tee). An administrator who acts during the minority of a person who either is named by the testator as the estate's executor or would be appointed as the estate's administrator but for the person's youth.

administrator pendente lite. See *special administrator*.

administrator with the will annexed. See *administrator cum testamento annexo*.

ancillary administrator (**an**-sə-ler-ee). (1825) A court-appointed administrator who oversees the distribution of the part of a decedent's estate located in a jurisdiction other than where the decedent was domiciled (the place of the main administration).

domiciliary administrator. A person appointed to administer an estate in the state where the decedent was domiciled at death.

foreign administrator. An administrator appointed in another jurisdiction.

general administrator. (18c) A person appointed to administer an intestate decedent's entire estate.

public administrator. (1809) A state-appointed officer who administers intestate estates that are not administered by the decedent's relatives. • This officer's right to administer is usu. subordinate to the rights of creditors, but in a few jurisdictions the creditors' rights are subordinate.

special administrator. (18c) **1.** A person appointed to administer only a specific part of an intestate decedent's estate. **2.** A person appointed to serve as administrator of an estate solely because of an emergency or an unusual situation, such as a will contest. — Also termed (in sense 2) *administrator pendente lite*.

administrator ad colligendum. See ADMINISTRATOR (2).

administrator ad colligendum bona. See ADMINISTRATOR (2).

administrator's bond. See *fiduciary bond* under BOND (2).

administrator's deed. See DEED.

administratrix (ad-min-ə-**stray**-triks *or* ad-**min**-ə-strə-triks). *Archaic.* A female administrator. Pl. **administratrixes, administratrices.** See ADMINISTRATOR (2).

admiral's mast. See MAST (1).

admiralty (**ad**-mə-rəl-tee), *n.* **1.** A court that exercises jurisdiction over all maritime contracts, torts, injuries, or offenses. • The federal courts are so called when exercising their admiralty jurisdiction, which is conferred by the U.S. Constitution (art. III, § 2, cl. 1). — Also termed *admiralty court; maritime court.* **2.** The system of jurisprudence that has grown out of the practice of admiralty courts; MARITIME LAW. **3.** Narrowly, the rules governing contract, tort, and workers'-compensation claims arising out of commerce on or over navigable water. — Also termed (in senses 2 & 3) *admiralty law.* — **admiralty,** *adj.*

Admiralty, First Lord. See FIRST LORD OF THE ADMIRALTY.

admiralty and maritime jurisdiction. The exercise of authority over maritime cases by the U.S. district courts sitting in admiralty. See 28 USCA § 1333. — Often shortened to *admiralty jurisdiction; maritime jurisdiction.* See ADMIRALTY (1);

SUPPLEMENTAL RULES FOR CERTAIN ADMIRALTY AND MARITIME CLAIMS.

Admiralty Clause. The clause of the U.S. Constitution giving the federal courts jurisdiction over admiralty and maritime cases. U.S. Const. art. III, § 2, cl. 1.

admiralty court. See ADMIRALTY (1).

Admiralty Extension Act. A 1948 statute extending admiralty-tort jurisdiction to include all cases in which damage or injury is caused by a vessel on navigable water, regardless of where the injury or damage occurred. 46 USCA app. § 740. ● Specifically, the Act extended jurisdiction over damages and injuries that a vessel causes on land, such as to bridges and piers or to people on them. — Abbr. AEA.

admiralty jurisdiction. See ADMIRALTY AND MARITIME JURISDICTION.

admiralty law. 1. See ADMIRALTY (2). **2.** See ADMIRALTY (3). **3.** See MARITIME LAW.

admissibility (ad-mis-ə-**bil**-ə-tee), *n.* (18c) The quality or state of being allowed to be entered into evidence in a hearing, trial, or other official proceeding.

 conditional admissibility. (1904) The evidentiary rule that when a piece of evidence is not itself admissible, but is admissible if certain other facts make it relevant, the evidence becomes admissible on condition that counsel later introduce the connecting facts. ● If counsel does not satisfy this condition, the opponent is entitled to have the conditionally admitted piece of evidence struck from the record, and to have the judge instruct the jury to disregard it.

 curative admissibility. (1904) The rule that an inadmissible piece of evidence may be admitted if offered to cure or counteract the effect of some similar piece of the opponent's evidence that itself should not have been admitted.

 limited admissibility. (1910) The principle that testimony or exhibits may be admitted into evidence for a restricted purpose. ● Common examples are admitting prior contradictory testimony to impeach a witness but not to establish the truth, and admitting evidence against one party but not another. The trial court must, upon request, instruct the jury properly about the applicable limits when admitting the evidence. Fed. R. Evid. 105.

 multiple admissibility. (1904) The evidentiary rule that, although a piece of evidence is inadmissible under one rule for the purpose given in offering it, it is nevertheless admissible if relevant and offered for some other purpose not forbidden by the rules of evidence.

admissible (ad-**mis**-ə-bəl), *adj.* (17c) **1.** Capable of being legally admitted; allowable; permissible <admissible evidence>. **2.** Worthy of gaining entry or being admitted <a person is admissible to the bar upon obtaining a law degree and passing the bar exam>.

admissible evidence. See EVIDENCE.

admission (ad-**mish**-ən), *n.* (15c) **1.** Any statement or assertion made by a party to a case and offered against that party; an acknowledgment that facts are true. Cf. CONFESSION.

 admission against interest. (1828) A person's statement acknowledging a fact that is harmful to the person's position, esp. as a litigant. ● An admission against interest must be made either by a litigant or by one in privity with or occupying the same legal position as the litigant; as an exception to the hearsay rule, it is admissible whether or not the person is available as a witness. Fed. R. Evid. 801(d)(2). A declaration against interest, by contrast, is made by a nonlitigant who is not in privity with a litigant; a declaration against interest is also admissible as an exception to the hearsay rule, but only when the declarant is unavailable as a witness. Fed. R. Evid. 804(b)(3). See *declaration against interest* under DECLARATION (6).

 admission by employee or agent. An admission made by a party-opponent's agent during employment and concerning a matter either within the scope of the agency or authorized by the party-opponent.

 admission by party-opponent. (1959) An opposing party's admission, which is not considered hearsay if it is offered against that party and is (1) the party's own statement, in either an individual or a representative capacity; (2) a statement of which the party has manifested an adoption or belief in its truth; (3) a statement by one authorized by the party to make such a statement; (4) a statement by the party's agent concerning a matter within the scope of the agency or employment and made during the existence of the relationship; or (5) a statement by a coconspirator of the party during the course of and in furtherance of the conspiracy. Fed. R. Evid. 801(d)(2).

 admission by silence. (1867) The failure of a party to speak after another party's assertion of fact that, if untrue, would naturally compel a person to deny the statement.

 admission in judicio. See *judicial admission.*

 adoptive admission. (1940) An action by a party that indicates approval of a statement made by another, and thereby acceptance that the statement is true.

 extrajudicial admission. (1824) An admission made outside court proceedings.

implied admission. (18c) An admission reasonably inferable from a party's action or statement, or a party's failure to act or speak. — Also termed *tacit admission.*

incidental admission. An admission made in some other connection or involved in the admission of some other fact.

incriminating admission. An admission of facts tending to establish guilt.

judicial admission. (18c) A formal waiver of proof that relieves an opposing party from having to prove the admitted fact and bars the party who made the admission from disputing it. — Also termed *solemn admission*; *admission in judicio*; *true admission.*

quasi-admission. (1813) An act or utterance, usu. extrajudicial, that creates an inconsistency with and discredits, to a greater or lesser degree, a present claim or other evidence of the person creating the inconsistency.

solemn admission. See *judicial admission.*

tacit admission. See *implied admission.*

true admission. See *judicial admission.*

2. Acceptance of a lawyer by the established licensing authority, such as a state bar association, as a member of the practicing bar, usu. after the lawyer passes a bar examination and supplies adequate character references <admission to the bar>. ● The entry of a lawyer on the rolls of an integrated bar, usu. after the fulfillment of two prerequisites: graduating from law school and passing a state bar examination. — Also termed *admission to practice law.*

admission on motion. Permanent admission of a lawyer who is in good standing in the bar of a different state without the need for a full bar examination.

admission pro hac vice (proh hak **vi**-see *or* proh hak **vee**-chay). Temporary admission of an out-of-jurisdiction lawyer to practice before a court in a specified case or set of cases. See PRO HAC VICE.

3. *Patents.* A concession or representation by a patent applicant that an activity, knowledge, or a publication is prior art. ● An admission requires the U.S. Patent and Trademark Office examiner to consider the relevant item as prior art, even if it does not technically qualify as prior art. — Also termed *admission of prior art.*

admission tax. See TAX.

admission to bail. An order to release an accused person from custody after payment of bail or receipt of an adequate surety for the person's appearance for trial. See BAIL (1).

admission to practice law. See ADMISSION (2).

admission to sufficient facts. See SUBMISSION TO A FINDING.

admittance. 1. The act of entering a building, locality, or the like. **2.** Permission to enter. **3.** *Hist.* The act of giving seisin of a copyhold estate. ● Admittance corresponded with livery of seisin of a freehold. Copyhold estates were abolished by the Law of Property Act of 1922. See COPYHOLD.

admitted asset. See ASSET.

admitted corporation. See CORPORATION.

admixture (ad-**miks**-chər). **1.** The mixing of things. **2.** A substance formed by mixing.

admonition (ad-mə-**nish**-ən), *n.* (14c) **1.** Any authoritative advice or caution from the court to the jury regarding their duty as jurors or the admissibility of evidence for consideration <the judge's admonition that the jurors not discuss the case until they are charged>. **2.** A reprimand or cautionary statement addressed to counsel by a judge <the judge's admonition that the lawyer stop speaking out of turn>. **3.** *Eccles. law.* An authoritatively issued warning or censure. — **admonish** (ad-**mon**-ish), *vb.* — **admonitory.**

adoptability, *n. Family law.* **1.** A child's availability to be adopted, esp. by reason of all legal impediments having been removed. **2.** The likelihood of a child's being adopted; a prospective adoptee's desirability from the prospective parents' point of view. — **adoptable,** *adj.*

adopted child. See CHILD.

adoptee. A person who has become the legal child of one or two nonbiological parents. — Also termed *adopted child.*

adoption, *n.* (14c) **1.** *Family law.* The creation of a parent–child relationship by judicial order between two parties who usu. are unrelated; the relation of parent and child created by law between persons who are not in fact parent and child. ● This relationship is brought about only after a determination that the child is an orphan or has been abandoned, or that the parents' parental rights have been terminated by court order. Adoption creates a parent–child relationship between the adopted child and the adoptive parents with all the rights, privileges, and responsibilities that attach to that relationship, though there may be agreed exceptions. Adoption is distinguishable from legitimation and from fosterage. Adoption usu. refers to an act between persons unrelated by blood; legitimation refers to an act between persons related by blood. Universally, a decree of adoption confers legitimate status on the adopted child. Adoption is permanent; fosterage is a temporary arrangement for a child's care. See *adopted child, foster child* under CHILD. Cf. LEGITIMATION (2); FOSTER CARE (1).

adoption by estoppel. (1933) **1.** An equitable adoption of a child by one who promises or acts in a way that precludes the person and his or her estate from denying adopted status to the child. **2.** An equitable decree of adoption treating as done that which ought to have been done. • Such a decree is entered when no final decree of adoption has already been obtained, even though the principal has acted as if an adoption has been achieved. A petitioner must show an agreement of adoption, relinquishment of parental authority by the child's biological parents, assumption of parental responsibility by the foster parents, and a de facto relationship of parent and child over a substantial period. Such a claim typically occurs when an adoptive parent has died intestate, and the child tries to be named an heir. In a minority of states, adoption by estoppel may be a basis for allowing a child to participate in a wrongful-death action. — Also termed *equitable adoption; virtual adoption*. See ESTOPPEL (1). **3.** See *de facto adoption*.

adoption by will. *Roman law.* A posthumous adoption effected by a testator's written statement declaring the intention to adopt and naming the person adopted. • The only legal effect of such an adoption was to entitle the adopted person to assume the testator's family name and be regarded as the testator's child. Because the adopted person was never subject to the testator's legal control (*patria potestas*), the person could not acquire agnatic rights or make a claim on the estate beyond any specific testamentary grants.

adult adoption. The adoption of one adult by another. • Many jurisdictions do not allow adult adoptions. Those that do often impose restrictions, as by requiring consent of the person to be adopted, but may not look too closely at the purpose for which adoption is sought.

agency adoption. An adoption in which parental rights are terminated and legal custody is relinquished to an agency that finds and approves the adoptive parents. • An agency adoption can be either public or private. In all states, adoption agencies must be licensed, and in most they are nonprofit entities. Parents who voluntarily place a child for adoption most commonly use a private agency. Cf. *private adoption*.

black-market adoption. **1.** An illegal adoption in which an intermediary (a broker) receives payment for his or her services. **2.** Baby-selling.

closed adoption. An adoption in which the biological parent relinquishes his or her parental rights and surrenders the child to an unknown person or persons; an adoption in which there is no disclosure of the identity of the birth parents, adopting parent or parents, or child. • Adoptions by stepparents, blood relatives, and foster parents are exceptions to the no-disclosure requirement. — Also termed *confidential adoption*. Cf. *open adoption; cooperative adoption*.

cooperative adoption. A process in which the birth parents and adoptive parents negotiate to reach a voluntary agreement about the degree and type of continuing contact after adoption, including direct visitation or more limited arrangements such as communication by telephone or mail, the exchange of either identifying or nonidentifying information, and other forms of contact. Cf. *open adoption; closed adoption*.

de facto adoption. An adoption that falls short of the statutory requirements in a particular state. • The adoption agreement may ripen to a de jure adoption when the statutory formalities have been met or if a court finds that the requirements for adoption by estoppel have been met. — Also termed *adoption by estoppel*.

de facto stepparent adoption. See *second-parent adoption*.

direct-placement adoption. See *private adoption*.

embryo adoption. *Slang.* The receipt of a frozen embryo that is implanted into a recipient's womb. • Donors must waive all parental rights before the recipients of the embryo assume legal ownership or custody. The process is not considered to be a legal adoption because American law does not treat embryos as children.

equitable adoption. See *adoption by estoppel*.

gray-market adoption. See *private adoption*.

identified adoption. See *private adoption*.

independent adoption. See *private adoption*.

intercountry adoption. See *international adoption*.

international adoption. An adoption in which parents domiciled in one nation travel to a foreign country to adopt a child there, usu. in accordance with the laws of the child's nation. • International adoptions first became popular after World War II and escalated after the Korean Conflict because of the efforts of humanitarian programs working to find homes for children left orphaned by the wars. More recently prospective parents have turned to international adoption as the number of healthy babies domestically available for adoption has steadily declined. — Also termed *transnational adoption; intercountry adoption*. See MULTIETHNIC PLACEMENT ACT OF 1994.

interracial adoption. See *transracial adoption*.

interstate adoption. An adoption in which the prospective parents live in one state and the child lives in another state. See INTERSTATE COMPACT ON THE PLACEMENT OF CHILDREN.

joint adoption. An adoption in which the prospective parents apply as a couple and are approved or rejected as a couple, as opposed to filing separate and individual applications to adopt a child. • Although the term most often applies to adoption by a married couple, it also applies to an adoption petition by two unmarried partners who are adopting a child.

open adoption. An adoption in which the biological mother (sometimes with the biological father) chooses the adoptive parents and in which the child often continues to have a post-adoption relationship with his or her biological family. • Typically the birth parents meet the adoptive parents and participate in the separation and placement process. The birth parents relinquish all legal, moral, and nurturing rights over the child, but usu. retain the right to continuing contact and to knowledge of the child's welfare and location. Cf. *closed adoption*; *cooperative adoption*.

posthumous adoption. An adoption that becomes legally final after the death of either an adoptive parent or the adopted child. • Few states recognize posthumous adoptions; most require all parties to an adoption to be alive at the time the final judgment is rendered.

private adoption. (1865) An adoption that occurs independently between the biological mother (and sometimes the biological father) and the adoptive parents without the involvement of an agency. • A private adoption is usu. arranged by an intermediary such as a lawyer, doctor, or counselor. Legal custody — though sometimes not physical custody — remains with the biological parent or parents until the termination and adoption are complete. — Also termed *private-placement adoption*; *direct-placement adoption*; *direct adoption*; *gray-market adoption*; *identified adoption*; *independent adoption*. Cf. *agency adoption*.

private-placement adoption. See *private adoption*.

pseudo-stepparent adoption. See *second-parent adoption*.

second-parent adoption. An adoption by an unmarried cohabiting partner of a child's legal parent, not involving the termination of a legal parent's rights; esp., an adoption in which a lesbian, gay man, or unmarried heterosexual person adopts his or her partner's biological or adoptive child. See Restatement (Third) of Property: Wills and Other Donative Transfers § 2.5 cmt. i. • Although not all jurisdictions recognize second-parent adoption, the practice is becoming more widely accepted. *See In re Adoption of B.L.V.B.*, 628 A.2d 1271 (Vt. 1993); *In re Adoption of Tammy*, 619 N.E.2d 315 (Mass.

1993); *In re Adoption of Evan*, 583 N.Y.S.2d 997 (Sur. Ct. 1992). — Also termed *de facto stepparent adoption*; *pseudo-stepparent adoption*. Cf. *stepparent adoption*.

stepparent adoption. The adoption of a child by a stepfather or stepmother. • Stepparent adoptions are the most common adoptions in the United States. Cf. *second-parent adoption*.

transnational adoption. See *international adoption*.

transracial adoption. An adoption in which at least one adoptive parent is of a race different from that of the adopted child. • Under federal law, child-placement agencies may not use race as a factor in approving adoptions. 42 USCA § 5115a. — Also termed *interracial adoption*. See MULTIETHNIC PLACEMENT ACT OF 1994.

virtual adoption. See *adoption by estoppel*.

wrongful adoption. See WRONGFUL ADOPTION.

2. *Roman law.* The legal process of creating a parent-child relationship with a young person who is still under the power of another father. • The adopted person became part of the new *paterfamilias*'s agnatic family with exactly the same standing as children (or grandchildren) by blood. This was later modified by Justinian. **3.** *Contracts.* The process by which a person agrees to assume a contract previously made for that person's benefit, such as a newly formed corporation's acceptance of a preincorporation contract. Cf. ADROGATION. **4.** *Trademarks.* The mental act necessary to acquire legal rights in a trademark, consisting of knowledge and intention to use a trademark on or in connection with a product or service in commerce. **5.** *Parliamentary law.* A deliberative assembly's approval or endorsement by vote of a motion or report. — Also termed *acceptance*; *consent*; *passage*; *ratification*. — **adopt,** *vb.* — **adoptive,** *adj.*

adoption agency. A licensed establishment where a biological parent can voluntarily surrender a child for adoption. See *agency adoption* under ADOPTION.

Adoption and Safe Families Act. A 1997 federal law that requires states to provide safe and permanent homes for abused and neglected children within shorter periods than those required by earlier state and federal laws. • The primary focus is on the safety and well-being of the child, in contrast to the previously paramount rights of the parents. The ASFA signaled a dramatic shift in the philosophy of child-protection proceedings that had controlled since 1980 under the Adoption Assistance and Child Welfare Act. — Abbr. ASFA. See ADOPTION ASSISTANCE AND CHILD WELFARE ACT; FOSTER-CARE DRIFT.

Adoption Assistance and Child Welfare Act. A 1980 federal statute whose purpose was to force states to use reasonable efforts (1) to avoid removing children from their homes, (2) to reunite families when children had been removed because of abuse or neglect, and (3) when reunification failed, to terminate parental rights and place the children in permanent homes. 42 USCA §§ 620 et seq.; §§ 670 et seq. • The Act provided funds for foster-care placement, Child Protective Services, family preservation and reunification, and foster-care reform to states complying with the Act. Its aim was to prevent the unnecessary removal of children from homes and to hasten the return of children in foster care to their families. It has now been essentially overruled in philosophy by the 1997 enactment of the Adoption and Safe Families Act. See ADOPTION AND SAFE FAMILIES ACT.

adoption-assistance plan. An employer-sponsored program that provides financial assistance to employees for adoption-related expenses.

adoption by estoppel. See ADOPTION (1).

adoption by reference. See INCORPORATION BY REFERENCE (1).

adoption by will. See ADOPTION.

adoption-registry statute. A law that provides for the release of adoption information if the biological parent, the adoptive parent, and the adoptee (after he or she reaches a certain statutorily prescribed age) all officially record their desire for its release. — Also termed *voluntary-registry law.*

active adoption-registry statute. A registry statute that authorizes a state authority to seek out parties' desires to obtain or release adoption information when one party expresses a desire for that information.

passive adoption-registry statute. A registry statute allowing parties to register their desires for release of adoption information after an adopted child reaches a specified age.

adoptive admission. See ADMISSION (1).

adoptive-admissions rule. (1949) *Evidence.* The principle that a statement offered against an accused is not inadmissible hearsay if the accused is aware of the statement and has, by words or conduct, indicated acceptance that the statement is true. See *adoptive admission* under ADMISSION (1).

adoptive father. See *adoptive parent* under PARENT.

adoptive mother. See *adoptive parent* under PARENT.

adoptive parent. See PARENT.

adpromission (ad-prə-**mish**-ən). [fr. Latin *adpromissio*] *Roman law.* **1.** A suretyship contract in which the surety promises to be liable for no more than the debtor owes. • Roman law had three types of adpromission: (1) sponsion; (2) fidepromission; and (3) fidejussion. In addition, *mandatum* and *pactum de constitutio* could indirectly be used by way of guarantee. **2.** A suretyship relation. — Also termed *adpromissio.*

ad quem (ad **kwem**), *adv.* [Latin] To which. • This term is used as a correlative to *a quo* in computation of time or distance. For example, the *terminus a quo* is the point of beginning or departure; the *terminus ad quem* is the end of the period or point of arrival.

ad quod damnum (ad kwod **dam**-nəm). [Latin "to what damage"] *Hist.* A writ directing the sheriff to inquire of jurors under oath to what damage a grant (as of a fair, market, liberty, or other franchise) would be to various people if the king were to make the grant. • The writ was issuable from the court of chancery. — Also termed *writ of ad quod damnum.*

ADR. *abbr.* **1.** See ALTERNATIVE DISPUTE RESOLUTION. **2.** See ASSET-DEPRECIATION RANGE. **3.** See AMERICAN DEPOSITORY RECEIPT.

ad respondendum (ad ree-spon-**den**-dəm). [Latin] To answer. See *capias ad respondendum* under CAPIAS; *habeas corpus ad respondendum* under HABEAS CORPUS.

adrogate (**ad**-roh-gayt), *vb. Roman law.* (Of a man) to adopt a son or daughter who is not already under another father's power (*patria potestas*). • Daughters became eligible for adoption in the later Empire.

adrogation (ad-roh-**gay**-shən), *n.* [fr. Latin *arrogatio* (a-roh-**gay**-shee-oh)] *Roman law.* An adoption of a person of full capacity (*sui juris*) into another family. — Also termed *adrogatio* (ad-roh-**gay**-shee-oh). Cf. ADOPTION (3). — **adrogate,** *vb.*

ad satisfaciendum (ad sat-is-fay-shee-**en**-dəm). [Latin] To satisfy. See *capias ad satisfaciendum* under CAPIAS.

ad testificandum (ad tes-ti-fi-**kan**-dəm). [Latin] To testify. See *habeas corpus ad testificandum* under HABEAS CORPUS; *subpoena ad testificandum* under SUBPOENA.

adult (ə-**dəlt** *or* **ad**-əlt), *n.* (17c) A person who has attained the legal age of majority, generally 17 in criminal cases and 18 for other purposes. — Also termed *major.* Cf. MINOR (1). — **adult** (ə-**dəlt**), *adj.*

vulnerable adult. An adult who is physically or mentally disabled; esp., one dependent on institutional services.

adult adoption. See ADOPTION.

adult correctional institution. See PRISON.

adult disabled person. See PERSON (1).

adulter (ə-**dəl**-tər), *n.* [Latin] *Roman law.* An adulterer; a man guilty of adultery.

adulterate (ə-dəl-tə-rayt), *vb.* To debase or make impure by adding a foreign or inferior substance. — **adulteration**, *n.*

adulterated drug. See DRUG.

adulterator (ə-dəl-tə-ray-tər), *n.* [Latin fr. *adulterare* "to adulterate"] *Civil law.* A corrupter; a forger; a counterfeiter, as in *adulteratores monetae* ("counterfeiters of money").

adulterine (ə-dəl-tə-rin), *adj.* **1.** Characterized by adulteration. **2.** Illegal; unlicensed. **3.** Born of adultery. **4.** Of or involving adultery; adulterous.

adulterine, *n. Archaic.* An illegitimate child.

adultery (ə-dəl-tə-ree), *n.* (15c) Voluntary sexual intercourse between a married person and someone other than the person's spouse. ● In many jurisdictions, adultery is a crime, but it is rarely prosecuted. In states that still permit fault divorce, proof of adultery is a ground on which a divorce may be granted. A court may also use proof of adultery as a reason to reduce the offending spouse's marital-property award in a property division. Judges traditionally viewed adultery as a reason for denying the offending spouse primary custody of a child in a child-custody dispute. But today, only the deleterious effect of immoral behavior on the child is typically considered relevant. — Formerly also termed *spouse-breach*; *avowtry.* Cf. FORNICATION; INFIDELITY. — **adulterous**, *adj.* — **adulterer, adulteress**, *n.*

   double adultery. Adultery between persons who are both married to other persons.

   incestuous adultery. Adultery between relatives; adultery committed by persons who are closely related.

   open and notorious adultery. Archaic. Adultery in which the parties reside together publicly, as if married, and the community is generally aware of the living arrangement and the fact that the couple is not married.

   single adultery. Adultery in which only one of the persons is married.

adult offender. See OFFENDER.

Adult Protective Services. A governmental agency with responsibility for investigating allegations of elder abuse and neglect and for responding appropriately. ● Every state has such an agency. — Abbr. APS.

ad valorem (ad və-**lor**-əm), *adj.* [Latin "according to the value"] (Of a tax) proportional to the value of the thing taxed. — **ad valorem**, *adv.*

ad valorem duty. See DUTY (4).

ad valorem tariff. See TARIFF (2).

ad valorem tax. See TAX.

advance, *n.* (17c) **1.** The furnishing of money or goods before any consideration is received in return. **2.** The money or goods furnished.

advance bill. See BILL (6).

advance-decline index. See INDEX (2).

advance directive. (1984) **1.** A document that takes effect upon one's incompetency and designates a surrogate decision-maker for healthcare matters. ● The Uniform Health-Care Decision Act (1993) states that the power of attorney for healthcare must be in writing and signed by the principal. Unless otherwise stated, the authority is effective only upon a determination that the principal lacks capacity, and it ceases to be effective once the principal regains his capacity. The agent must make decisions in accordance with the principal's relevant instructions, if there are any, or in the principal's best interests. — Also termed *power of attorney for healthcare; healthcare proxy.* See POWER OF ATTORNEY; UNIFORM HEALTH-CARE DECISION ACT. **2.** A legal document explaining one's wishes about medical treatment if one becomes incompetent or unable to communicate. — Often shortened to *directive.* — Also termed *medical directive; physician's directive; written directive.* See NATURAL-DEATH ACT; PROXY DIRECTIVE. Cf. LIVING WILL. **3.** See DO-NOT-RESUSCITATE ORDER.

Advanced Television Enhancement Forum. A standard-setting organization that defines the protocols for HTML-based enhanced television. ● The organization is an alliance of representatives from broadcast and cable networks, the consumer electronics and personal-computer industries, and television-transport companies. — Abbr. ATVEF.

advance-fee fraud. See FRAUD.

advancement, *n.* (15c) A payment or gift to an heir (esp. a child) during one's lifetime as an advance share of one's estate, with the intention of reducing, extinguishing, or diminishing the heir's claim to the estate under intestacy laws. ● In some jurisdictions, the donor's intent is irrelevant if all the statutory elements of an advancement are present. A few jurisdictions define the relationship between the donor and donee to include inter vivos transfers between ancestors and descendants. See SATISFACTION (4). Cf. ADEMPTION. — **advance**, *vb.*

advance payment. See PAYMENT.

advance premium. See PREMIUM (1).

advance pricing agreement. *Tax.* A usu. binding arrangement made between a multinational company and one or more national tax authorities about what method the company will use to calculate transfer prices. ● The agreement's purpose is to reduce or eliminate double taxation. — Abbr. APA.

bilateral advance pricing agreement. An advance pricing agreement made between a company and two tax authorities.

multilateral advance pricing agreement. An advance pricing agreement made between a company and more than two tax authorities.

unilateral advance pricing agreement. An advance pricing agreement made between a company and one tax authority. • This does not necessarily allow a company to avoid double taxation. A tax authority that is not a party to the agreement is not bound by the transfer-pricing method specified in the agreement.

advance sheets. (1868) A softcover pamphlet containing recently reported opinions by a court or set of courts. • Advance sheets are published during the interim between an opinion's announcement and its inclusion in a bound volume of law reports. Cf. *slip opinion* (1) under OPINION (1); REPORT (3).

advancing market. See *bull market* under MARKET.

adventure. (17c) **1.** A commercial undertaking that has an element of risk; a venture. Cf. JOINT VENTURE. **2.** *Marine insurance.* A voyage involving financial and insurable risk, as to a shipment of goods. — Often shortened to *venture.*

common adventure. A maritime enterprise, characterized as an undertaking in which all participants, including the carrier, everyone with an interest in the cargo, and the insurers of all share the risks of the perils of the sea. • The principle of shared risk is fundamental to maritime law. — Also termed *joint adventure*; *common venture.*

gross adventure. A loan on bottomry, so called because the lender will be liable for the gross (or general) average. See BOTTOMRY.

joint adventure. 1. See *common adventure.* **2.** See JOINT VENTURE.

adventurer. A person who undertakes a hazardous action or enterprise; one with a stake in a commercial adventure.

adversary (**ad**-vər-ser-ee), *n.* (14c) An opponent; esp., opposing counsel. — **adversary, adversarial,** *adj.*

adversary procedure. See ADVERSARY SYSTEM.

adversary proceeding. (1744) **1.** A hearing involving a dispute between opposing parties <Judge Adams presided over the adversary proceeding between the landlord and tenant>. **2.** *Bankruptcy.* A lawsuit that is brought within a bankruptcy proceeding, governed by special procedural rules, and based on conflicting claims usu. between the debtor (or the trustee) and a creditor or other interested party <the Chapter 7 trustee filed an adversary proceeding against the party who received $100,000 from the debtor one week before the bankruptcy filing>.

adversary system. (1936) A procedural system, such as the Anglo-American legal system, involving active and unhindered parties contesting with each other to put forth a case before an independent decision-maker. — Also termed *adversary procedure*; (in criminal cases) *accusatorial system*; *accusatory procedure.* Cf. INQUISITORIAL SYSTEM.

adverse. 1. Against; opposed (to). **2.** Having an opposing or contrary interest, concern, or position. **3.** Contrary (to) or in opposition (to). **4.** HOSTILE.

adverse action. A decision or event that unfavorably affects a person, entity, or association. • Common examples of adverse actions include a decrease in one's pay by an employer or a denial of credit by a lender.

adverse-agent doctrine. The rule that an agent's knowledge will not be imputed to the principal if the agent is engaged in fraudulent activities that are concealed as part of the fraud.

adverse authority. See AUTHORITY (4).

adverse-domination doctrine. The equitable principle that the statute of limitations on a breach-of-fiduciary-duty claim against officers and directors (esp. a corporation's action against its own officers and directors) is tolled as long as a corporate plaintiff is controlled by the alleged wrongdoers. • The statute is tolled until a majority of the disinterested directors discover or are put on notice of the claim against the wrongdoers. The purpose of this doctrine is to prevent a director or officer from successfully hiding wrongful or fraudulent conduct during the limitations period. *FDIC v. Shrader & York*, 991 F.2d 216, 227 (5th Cir. 1993). This doctrine is available only to benefit the corporation. — Also termed *adverse dominion*; *doctrine of adverse domination.*

adverse dominion. 1. See ADVERSE-DOMINATION DOCTRINE. **2.** *Torts. Rare.* The unlawful exercise of authority or control over goods so that the true owner is dispossessed. See CONVERSION (2). **3.** *Rare.* See ADVERSE POSSESSION.

adverse easement. See *prescriptive easement* under EASEMENT.

adverse employment action. An employer's decision that substantially and negatively affects an employee's job, such as a termination, demotion, or pay cut. — Also termed *adverse job action.*

adverse enjoyment. See ENJOYMENT.

adverse impact. See DISPARATE IMPACT.

adverse inference. See INFERENCE.

adverse-inference rule. See ADVERSE-INTEREST RULE.

adverse interest. (17c) An interest that is opposed or contrary to that of someone else.

adverse-interest rule. (1904) The principle that if a party fails to produce a witness who is within its power to produce and who should have been produced, the judge may instruct the jury to infer that the witness's evidence is unfavorable to the party's case. — Also termed *empty-chair doctrine*; *adverse-inference rule*.

adverse job action. See ADVERSE EMPLOYMENT ACTION.

adverse opinion. See OPINION (2).

adverse party. See PARTY (2).

adverse possession. (18c) **1.** The enjoyment of real property with a claim of right when that enjoyment is opposed to another person's claim and is continuous, exclusive, hostile, open, and notorious. • In Louisiana, it is the detention or enjoyment of a corporeal thing with the intent to hold it as one's own. La. Civ. Code art. 3421. — Also termed *adverse dominion*. Cf. PRESCRIPTION (5).

   constructive adverse possession. (1823) **1.** Adverse possession in which the claim arises from the claimant's payment of taxes under color of right rather than by actual possession of the land. **2.** *Louisiana law.* Adverse possession by operation of law. • When a possessor holds title to the property and corporeally possesses part of it, the possessor is deemed to have constructive possession of the rest of the property described in the title. La. Civ. Code art. 3426.

2. The doctrine by which title to real property is acquired as a result of such use or enjoyment over a specified period of time. See POSSESSION.

adverse presumption. See *adverse inference* under INFERENCE.

adverse title. See TITLE (2).

adverse use. See USE (1).

adverse witness. See *hostile witness* under WITNESS.

advertent negligence. See NEGLIGENCE.

advertising. **1.** The action of drawing the public's attention to something to promote its sale. **2.** The business of producing and circulating advertisements.

   comparative advertising. Advertising that specifically compares the advertised brand with another brand of the same product.

   competitive advertising. Advertising that contains little information about the advertised product, and that is used only to help a producer maintain a share of the market for that product.

   informative advertising. Advertising that gives information about the suitability and quality of a product.

advertising injury. See INJURY.

advertising substantiation. A doctrine of the Federal Trade Commission making it an unfair and deceptive act to put out an advertisement unless the advertiser first has a reasonable basis for believing that each claim in the advertisement is true.

advice (ad-VIS). **1.** Guidance offered by one person, esp. a lawyer, to another. See ADVICE OF COUNSEL. **2.** Notice of the drawing of a draft for goods or services. See LETTER OF ADVICE; ADVICE OF CREDIT. — **advise** (ad-VIZ), *vb.*

   remittance advice. Notice that a sum of money has been sent (esp. by mail) for goods or services. See REMITTANCE.

advice and consent. The right of the U.S. Senate to participate in making and ratifying treaties and appointing federal officers, provided by U.S. Const. art II, § 2. • As to treaties, the Senate's advice and consent generally includes Senate involvement in the negotiation process, and the need for a two-thirds majority of the Senate for ratification. As to public officers, the Senate's advice and consent generally includes the right to vote on approval of an appointment.

advice of counsel. (17c) **1.** The guidance given by lawyers to their clients. **2.** A defense in which a party seeks to avoid liability or punishment by claiming that he or she acted reasonably and in good faith on the attorney's advice. • Such a defense usu. requires waiver of the attorney–client privilege, and the attorney cannot have knowingly participated in implementing an illegal plan. **3.** In a malicious-prosecution lawsuit, a defense requiring both a complete presentation of facts by the defendant to his or her attorney and honest compliance with the attorney's advice. See MALICIOUS PROSECUTION.

advice-of-counsel defense. *Patents.* In an action for infringement, an assertion that after learning of the owner's rights, the defendant sought, obtained, and relied on an attorney's well-reasoned opinion before continuing the challenged act. • Courts treat the assertion as a factor in determining whether an act was willful (to support enhanced damages). It is not a true defense. Cf. *willful infringement* under INFRINGEMENT.

advice of credit. Notice by an advising bank of the issuance of a letter of credit. Cf. ADVICE.

advisement (ad-VIZ-mənt). (14c) Careful consideration; deliberation <the judge took the matter under advisement and promised a ruling by the next day>.

advisory action. *Patents.* See *advisory office action* under OFFICE ACTION.

advisory committee. A committee formed to make suggestions to an executive or legislative body or to an official; esp., any one of five committees that propose to the Standing Committee on Rules of Practice and Procedure amendments to federal court rules, the five committees being responsible for appellate, bankruptcy, civil, criminal, and evidence rules.

advisory counsel. See COUNSEL.

advisory jury. See JURY.

advisory office action. See OFFICE ACTION.

advisory opinion. See OPINION (1).

advocate (**ad**-və-kit), *n.* (14c) **1.** A person who assists, defends, pleads, or prosecutes for another.

> **public advocate.** An advocate who purports to represent the public at large in matters of public concern, such as utility rates or environmental quality.

2. *Civil & Scots law.* A barrister; specif., a member of the Faculty of Advocates (the Scottish counterpart of a barrister) or of the Society of Advocates in Aberdeen (a society of solicitors). • A member of the Aberdeen society is designated "advocate in Aberdeen." Cf. BARRISTER. **3.** *Hist. Eccles. law.* A person who is trained in both canon and secular law and can (1) appear in an ecclesiastical or admiralty court on another's behalf, and (2) give legal advice. • Members of the College of Advocates (also known as Doctors' Commons) bore the title of *advocate.* After the dissolution of the College in 1857, the term became indistinguishably associated with *barrister.* — **advocate** (**ad**-və-kayt), *vb.* — **advocacy** (**ad**-və-kə-see), *n.*

advocate's bias. See BIAS.

advocate-witness rule. See LAWYER-WITNESS RULE.

advocatus diaboli (ad-voh-**kay**-təs dI-**ab**-ə-lI), *n.* [Latin "devil's advocate"] *Eccles. law.* An official who argues against a person's beatification or canonization.

advowee (ad-vow-**ee**). A patron who holds an advowson; ADVOCATUS (2). — Also spelled *avowee.*

> **advowee paramount.** The sovereign, or highest patron.

advowson (ad-**vow**-zən). *Eccles. law.* The right of presenting or nominating a person to a vacant benefice in the church. • The person enjoying this right is called the "patron" (*patronus*) of the church, and was formerly termed "advocatus," the advocate or defender, or in English, the "advowee." The patron presents the nominee to the bishop (or, occasionally, another church dignitary). If there is no patron, or if the patron neglects to exercise the right within six months, the right lapses and a title is given to the ordinary (usu. the bishop) to appoint a cleric to the church. Cf. PRESENTATION (2); INSTITUTION (5).

> **advowson appendant** (ə-**pen**-dənt). An advowson annexed to a manor, and passing as incident to it, whenever the manor is conveyed to another. • The advowson passes with the manor even if it is not mentioned in the grant.

> **advowson collative** (kə-**lay**-tiv). An advowson for which there is no separate presentation to the bishop because the bishop happens to be the patron as well. • In this case, the one act by which the benefice is conferred is called "collation."

> **advowson donative** (**don**-ə-tiv *or* **doh**-nə-tiv). An advowson in which the patron has the right to put a cleric in possession by a mere gift, or deed of donation, without any presentation to the bishop. • This type of advowson was converted into the *advowson presentative* by the Benefices Act of 1898. — Also termed *donative advowson.*

> **advowson in gross.** An advowson that is separated from the manor and annexed to a person. • All advowsons that have been separated from their original manors are advowsons in gross.

> **advowson presentative** (pri-**zen**-tə-tiv). The usual kind of advowson, in which the patron has the right to make the presentation to the bishop and to demand that the nominee be instituted, if the bishop finds the nominee canonically qualified.

> **donative advowson.** See *advowson donative.*

AEA. *abbr.* See ADMIRALTY EXTENSION ACT.

aedile (**ee**-dIl). *Roman law.* A magistrate charged with policing the city, managing public buildings and services, supervising markets, and arranging public games. — Also spelled *edile.*

aesnecia (ees-**neesh**-ee-ə). [Law Latin] See ESNECY.

aesthetic functionality. See FUNCTIONALITY.

aesthetic zoning. See ZONING.

AFDC. *abbr.* AID TO FAMILIES WITH DEPENDENT CHILDREN.

aff'd. *abbr.* Affirmed.

affect, *vb.* **1.** Most generally, to produce an effect on; to influence in some way. **2.** *Civil law.* To pledge (property or revenues) as security for a loan; HYPOTHECATE. **3.** *Scots law.* To seize (debtor's property, etc.).

affection doctrine. See AFFECTS DOCTRINE.

affecting commerce. (Of an industry, activity, etc.) touching or concerning business, industry, or trade; esp., under the Labor–Management Relations Act, burdening or obstructing commerce, or having led or tending to lead to a labor dispute that burdens or obstructs the free flow of commerce. 29 USCA § 152(7).

affection. 1. Fond attachment, devotion, or love <alienation of affections>. **2.** *Hist.* The pawning or mortgaging of a thing to ensure the payment of money or performance of some other obligation.

affects doctrine. (1996) *Constitutional law.* The principle allowing Congress to regulate intrastate activities that have a substantial effect on interstate commerce. ● The doctrine is so called because the test is whether a given activity "affects" interstate commerce. — Also termed *effects doctrine* or (erroneously) *affectation doctrine.*

aff'g. *abbr.* Affirming.

affiance (ə-**fı**-ənts). **1.** *Archaic.* The act of confiding. **2.** The pledging of faith; specif., the act of promising to wed.

affiant (ə-**fı**-ənt). (1807) **1.** One who makes an affidavit. — Also termed *deponent.* **2.** COMPLAINANT (2).

affidavit (af-ə-**day**-vit). (16c) A voluntary declaration of facts written down and sworn to by the declarant before an officer authorized to administer oaths. ● A great deal of evidence is submitted by affidavit, esp. in pretrial matters such as summary-judgment motions. Cf. DECLARATION (1), (8).

affidavit after appeal. Patents. A sworn statement submitted to the U.S. Patent and Trademark Office after the filing of a notice of appeal from an adverse determination by an examiner. ● An affidavit or declaration submitted after a case has been appealed will not be admitted without a showing of good and sufficient reasons why it was not presented earlier.

affidavit after final rejection. Patents. A sworn statement submitted to the U.S. Patent and Trademark Office after an application's final rejection. — Also termed *declaration after final rejection.*

affidavit for the record. An affidavit made by a surveyor or engineer to supplement, correct, update, or otherwise alter existing information in official real-estate records.

affidavit of claim. An affidavit in which a plaintiff asserts that he or she has a meritorious cause of action.

affidavit of continued use. See DECLARATION OF USE.

affidavit of defense. See *affidavit of merits.*

affidavit of incontestability. See DECLARATION OF INCONTESTABILITY.

affidavit of increase. Hist. An affidavit that lists — and seeks reimbursement from the opposing party for — the additional costs (above the filing fee and other basic fees charged by the court clerk) incurred by a party in taking a matter through trial. ● Attorney fees, witness payments, and the like were included in this affidavit. See COSTS OF INCREASE.

affidavit of inquiry. (1925) An affidavit, required in certain states before substituted service of process on an absent defendant, in which the plaintiff's attorney or a person with knowledge of the facts indicates that the defendant cannot be served within the state.

affidavit of merit. See *certificate of merit.*

affidavit of merits. An affidavit in which a defendant asserts that he or she has a meritorious defense. — Also termed *affidavit of defense.*

affidavit of nonprosecution. An affidavit in which a crime victim requests that the perpetrator not be prosecuted. ● In many cases, if the victim files an affidavit of nonprosecution, the prosecutor will withdraw or not file criminal charges against the perpetrator on grounds that there is no victim. Sometimes, though, the prosecutor will go forward with the prosecution even if the victim files an affidavit of nonprosecution.

affidavit of notice. An affidavit stating that the declarant has given proper notice of hearing to other parties to the action.

affidavit of service. (18c) An affidavit certifying the service of a notice, summons, writ, or process.

affidavit of use. See DECLARATION OF USE.

affidavit of verification. See VERIFICATION (1).

affidavit under § 8. See DECLARATION OF USE.

affidavit under § 15. See DECLARATION OF INCONTESTABILITY.

counteraffidavit. An affidavit made to contradict and oppose another affidavit.

IFP affidavit. See *poverty affidavit.*

in forma pauperis affidavit. See *poverty affidavit.*

pauper's affidavit. See *poverty affidavit.*

poverty affidavit. (1887) An affidavit made by an indigent person seeking public assistance, appointment of counsel, waiver of court fees, or other free public services. 28 USCA § 1915. — Also termed *pauper's affidavit; in forma pauperis affidavit; IFP affidavit.*

search-warrant affidavit. An affidavit, usu. by a police officer or other law-enforcement agent, that sets forth facts and circumstances supporting the existence of probable cause and asks the judge to issue a search warrant.

self-proving affidavit. (1964) An affidavit attached to a will and signed by the testator and witnesses certifying that the statutory requirements of due execution of the will have been complied with. • The affidavit, which recites the facts of the will's proper execution, permits the will to be probated without the necessity of having the witnesses appear and prove due execution by their testimony.

sham affidavit. An affidavit that contradicts clear testimony given by the same witness, usu. used in an attempt to create an issue of fact in response to a motion for summary judgment.

supplemental affidavit. An affidavit made in addition to a previous one, usu. to supply additional facts.

affidavit for the record. See AFFIDAVIT.

affile (ə-fɪl), *vb. Archaic.* To file.

affiliate (ə-fil-ee-it), *n.* (1930) **1.** A corporation that is related to another corporation by shareholdings or other means of control; a subsidiary, parent, or sibling corporation. **2.** *Securities.* One who controls, is controlled by, or is under common control with an issuer of a security. SEC Rule 10b-18(a)(1) (17 CFR § 240.10b-18(a)(1)). See CONTROL PERSON. Cf. ASSOCIATED PERSON. — **affiliate** (ə-fil-ee-ayt), *vb.* — **affiliation** (ə-fil-ee-ay-shən), *n.*

affiliate click fraud. See FRAUD.

affiliated director. See *outside director* under DIRECTOR.

affiliated group. A chain of corporations that can elect to file a consolidated tax return because at least 80% of each corporation is owned by others in the group.

affiliated purchaser. See PURCHASER (1).

affiliation order. See *filiation order* under ORDER (2).

affine (ə-fɪn). A relative by marriage.

affinity (ə-fin-ə-tee). (14c) **1.** A close agreement. **2.** The relation that one spouse has to the blood relatives of the other spouse; relationship by marriage. **3.** Any familial relation resulting from a marriage. Cf. CONSANGUINITY. See *relative by affinity* under RELATIVE. Cf. CONSANGUINITY.

collateral affinity. The relationship of a spouse's relatives to the other spouse's relatives. • An example is a wife's brother and her husband's sister.

direct affinity. The relationship of a spouse to the other spouse's blood relatives. • An example is a wife and her husband's brother.

quasi-affinity. Civil law. The affinity existing between two persons, one of whom has been engaged to a relative of the other.

secondary affinity. The relationship of a spouse to the other spouse's marital relatives. • An example is a wife and her husband's sister-in-law.

affinity fraud. See FRAUD.

affirm, *vb.* (14c) **1.** To confirm (a judgment) on appeal. • Sometimes, the verb is used without a direct object <We affirm>. The equivalent expression in British English is *to deny the appeal.* **2.** To solemnly declare rather than swear under oath. **3.** To testify or declare by affirmation.

affirmance, *n.* (16c) **1.** A ratification, reacceptance, or confirmation. **2.** The formal confirmation by an appellate court of a lower court's judgment, order, or decree. **3.** The manifestation of a choice by someone with the power of avoidance to treat a voidable or unauthorized transaction as valid or authorized. **4.** The manifestation of a choice, by one on whose behalf an unauthorized act has been performed, to treat the act as authorized. Restatement (Second) of Agency § 83 (1958). — **affirm,** *vb.*

affirmance day general. See DAY.

affirmant. A person who testifies under affirmation and not under oath.

affirmation, *n.* (15c) A solemn pledge equivalent to an oath but without reference to a supreme being or to swearing; a solemn declaration made under penalty of perjury, but without an oath. Fed. R. Evid. 603; Fed. R. Civ. P. 43(b). • While an oath is "sworn to," an affirmation is merely "affirmed," but either type of pledge may subject the person making it to the penalties for perjury. Cf. OATH. — **affirm,** *vb.* — **affirmatory,** *adj.*

affirmative, *adj.* (15c) **1.** Supporting the existence of certain facts <affirmative evidence>. **2.** Involving or requiring effort <an affirmative duty>.

affirmative action. (1961) A set of actions designed to eliminate existing and continuing discrimination, to remedy lingering effects of past discrimination, and to create systems and procedures to prevent future discrimination. See *reverse discrimination* under DISCRIMINATION.

affirmative charge. See *affirmative instruction* under JURY INSTRUCTION.

affirmative condition. See *positive condition* under CONDITION (2).

affirmative converse instruction. See JURY INSTRUCTION.

affirmative covenant. 1. See COVENANT (1). **2.** See COVENANT (4).

affirmative defense. See DEFENSE (1).

affirmative duty. See DUTY (1).

affirmative easement. See EASEMENT.

affirmative injunction. See *mandatory injunction* under INJUNCTION.

affirmative instruction. See JURY INSTRUCTION.

affirmative misconduct. See MISCONDUCT.

affirmative plea. See *pure plea* under PLEA (3).

affirmative pregnant. (1807) A positive statement that ambiguously implies a negative; a statement that does not explicitly deny a charge, but instead answers an unasked question and thereby implies culpability, as when a person says "I returned your car yesterday" to the charge "You stole my car!" Cf. NEGATIVE PREGNANT.

affirmative proof. See PROOF.

affirmative relief. See RELIEF.

affirmative representation. See REPRESENTATION (1).

affirmative servitude. See *positive servitude* under SERVITUDE (2).

affirmative statute. See STATUTE.

affirmative testimony. See TESTIMONY.

affirmative warranty. See WARRANTY (3).

affirmative waste. See *commissive waste* under WASTE (1).

affix (ə-**fiks**), *vb.* (16c) **1.** To attach, add to, or fasten on permanently. See FIXTURE. **2.** *Trademarks.* To attach, physically or functionally, a trademark or servicemark to the goods or services it represents. • A mark must be affixed to show that it is used in trade. Where physical attachment is impossible or impracticable, the mark may be used on a container or tag, or (esp. with service marks) displayed prominently in advertising. — **affixation,** *n.* (af-ik-**say**-shən).

afforce (ə-**fors**), *vb.* To strengthen (a jury) by adding new members.

afforcement (ə-**fors**-mənt), *n.* [Law Latin] *Hist.* **1.** A reinforcement or fortification; esp., the reinforcing of a court on a solemn or extraordinary occasion. **2.** A fortress. — Also termed *afforciament* (ə-**for**-shə-mənt); *afforciamentum* (ə-for-shee-ə-**men**-təm).

afforcing the assize. *Hist.* A method of securing a jury verdict from a hung jury either by denying food and drink to the members until they reached a verdict or by bringing in new jurors until 12 would agree.

afforest, *vb.* To convert (land) into a forest, esp. by subjecting it to forest law. — **afforestation,** *n.*

affray (ə-**fray**). (14c) The fighting, by mutual consent, of two or more persons in some public place, to the terror of onlookers. • The fighting must be mutual. If one person unlawfully attacks another who resorts to self-defense, the first is guilty of assault and battery, but there is no affray. — Also termed *fray.* Cf. RIOT; *unlawful assembly* under ASSEMBLY; ROUT.

casual affray. See CHANCE-MEDLEY.

mutual affray. See MUTUAL COMBAT.

affrectamentum (ə-frek-tə-**men**-təm). See AFFREIGHTMENT.

affreightment (ə-**frayt**-mənt). The contracting of a ship to carry cargo. — Also termed *charter of affreightment*; (in French law) *affretement*; (in Law Latin) *affrectamentum*. See CONTRACT OF AFFREIGHTMENT.

affretement. See AFFREIGHTMENT.

a fine force (ay fin **fors**). [Law French] Of pure necessity.

AFIS. *abbr.* AMERICAN FORCES INFORMATION SERVICE.

AFL-CIO. *abbr.* AMERICAN FEDERATION OF LABOR AND CONGRESS OF INDUSTRIAL ORGANIZATIONS.

AF of M. *abbr.* AMERICAN FEDERATION OF MUSICIANS.

aforesaid (ə-**for**-sed), *adj.* (14c) Mentioned above; referred to previously. — Also termed *aforementioned; above-mentioned; above-stated; said.*

aforethought (ə-**for**-thawt), *adj.* (16c) Thought of in advance; deliberate; premeditated <malice aforethought>. See MALICE AFORETHOUGHT.

a fortiori (ay for-shee-**or**-ı *or* ah for-shee-**or**-ee), *adv.* [Latin] (16c) By even greater force of logic; even more so <if a 14-year-old child cannot sign a binding contract, then, *a fortiori*, a 13-year-old cannot>. Cf. A MULTO FORTIORI.

African Development Foundation. A nonprofit federal foundation that supports the self-help efforts of poor people in African countries by making grants and by making and guaranteeing loans to any African entity engaged in peaceful activities that enable African people to develop more fully. • ADF was created by the African Development Foundation Act and began operating in 1984. 22 USCA § 290h. — Abbr. ADF.

after-acquired domicile. See DOMICILE.

after-acquired-evidence doctrine. *Employment law.* The rule that, if an employer discharges an employee for an unlawful reason and later discovers misconduct sufficient to justify a lawful discharge, the employee cannot win reinstatement. • The doctrine either shields the employer from liability or limits the available relief when, after an employee has been terminated, the employer learns for the first time that the employee engaged in wrongdoing that would have resulted in a discharge anyway. *McKennon v. Nashville Banner Publ'g Co.*, 513 U.S. 352, 115 S.Ct. 879 (1995).

after-acquired property. 1. *Secured transactions.* A debtor's property that is acquired after a security transaction and becomes additional security for payment of the debt. UCC § 9-204. — Also termed *future-acquired property.* **2.** *Bankruptcy.* Property that the bankruptcy estate acquires after commencement of the bankruptcy proceeding. 11 USCA § 541(a)(7). **3.** *Wills & estates.* Property acquired by a person after making a will. • The old rule was that a testamentary gift of personal property spoke at the time of the testator's death, whereas a gift of lands spoke from the date of the will's execution (so that after-acquired property was not disposed of), but this has been changed by legislation in most states.

after-acquired-property clause. A mortgage provision that makes any later-acquired real estate subject to the mortgage.

after-acquired title. See TITLE (2).

after-acquired-title clause. *Oil & gas.* A provision in an oil-and-gas lease extending the lease's coverage to include any interest in the property that the lessor may obtain after the lease is signed. ● A common formulation is "This lease covers all the interest now owned by or hereafter vested in the lessor . . . ."

after-acquired-title doctrine. (1940) The principle that title to property automatically vests in a person who bought the property from a seller who acquired title only after purporting to sell the property to the buyer.

afterborn child. See CHILD.

afterborn heir. See HEIR.

aftercare. See *juvenile parole* under PAROLE.

after cost. See COST (1).

aftermarket. See *secondary market* under MARKET.

after the fact. (16c) Subsequent to an event of legal significance <accessory after the fact>.

AFTRA. *abbr.* AMERICAN FEDERATION OF TELEVISION AND RADIO ARTISTS.

AG. *abbr.* (1889) ATTORNEY GENERAL.

against the form of the statute. (16c) Contrary to the statutory requirements. ● This formal phrase, which traditionally concludes an indictment, indicates that the conduct alleged contravenes the cited statute and therefore constitutes a criminal offense. In modern contexts, the full conclusion often reads: "against the form of the statute in such case made and provided." The phrase is a translation of the Law Latin *contra formam statuti.*

against the peace and dignity of the state. (18c) A concluding phrase in an indictment, used to condemn the offending conduct generally (as opposed to the specific charge of wrongdoing contained in the body of the instrument). ● This phrase derives from the Law Latin *contra pacem domini regis* ("against the peace of the lord the king"), a charging phrase formerly used in indictments and in civil actions of trespass. Cf. KING'S PEACE.

against the weight of the evidence. (18c) (Of a verdict or judgment) contrary to the credible evidence; not sufficiently supported by the evidence in the record. See WEIGHT OF THE EVIDENCE.

against the will. (15c) Contrary to a person's wishes. ● Indictments use this phrase to indicate that the defendant's conduct was without the victim's consent.

agalma (ə-**gal**-mə). [Greek] A figure or design on a seal.

age, *n.* (13c) A period of time; esp., a period of individual existence or the duration of a person's life. ● In American usage, age is stated in full years completed (so that someone *15 years of age* might actually be 15 years and several months old). State statutes define various types of ages, as shown in the subentries.

    age of capacity. (1847) The age, usu. defined by statute as 18 years, at which a person is legally capable of agreeing to a contract, maintaining a lawsuit, or the like. ● A person may be authorized to make certain critical personal decisions at an earlier age than the general age of capacity, such as the decision whether to bear a child, to donate blood, to obtain treatment for sexually transmitted diseases, to marry, or to write a will. The age of capacity to write a will is typically not 18, but 14. — Also termed *age of majority*; *legal age; lawful age.* See CAPACITY (2).

    age of consent. (16c) The age, usu. defined by statute as 16 years, at which a person is legally capable of agreeing to marriage (without parental consent) or to sexual intercourse. ● If a person over the age of consent has sexual intercourse with a person under the age of consent, the older person may be prosecuted for statutory rape regardless of whether the younger person consented to the act. See *statutory rape* under RAPE.

    age of criminal responsibility. The age at which a child may be held responsible for a criminal act. ● In American criminal law, some state statutes allow a child as young as 7 to be held responsible (as a juvenile) for some acts. See, e.g., N.D. Cent. Code § 12.1-04-01. The minimum age for imposing adult liability is as low as 10. See, e.g., Ind. Code Ann. § 31-30-3-4(3). But in some circumstances, at least one state allows an offender to be tried as an adult at any age. See, e.g., Mich. Comp. Laws Ann. § 712A.2d.

    age of discretion. **1.** The age at which a person is considered responsible for certain acts and competent to exercise certain powers. ● For example, a person must be a legal adult to be eligible to serve a summons. **2.** PUBERTY.

    age of majority. (16c) **1.** The age, usu. defined by statute as 18 years, at which a person attains full legal rights, esp. civil and political rights such as the right to vote. ● The age of majority must be the same for men and women. In almost all states today, the age of majority is 18, but the age at which a person may legally purchase and consume alcohol is 21. — Also termed *lawful age*;

legal age. **2.** See *age of capacity.* — Also termed (in both senses) *full age.*

age of reason. (1884) The age at which a person becomes able to distinguish right from wrong and is thus legally capable of committing a crime or tort. ● The age of reason varies from jurisdiction to jurisdiction, but 7 years is traditionally the age below which a child is conclusively presumed not to have committed a crime or tort, while 14 years is usu. the age below which a rebuttable presumption applies. A child of 14 or older has traditionally been considered legally competent to commit a crime and therefore held accountable. With the creation of juvenile courts and their investiture of delinquency jurisdiction over children from birth to age 18, these traditional distinctions have nearly vanished. They surface from time to time in murder cases when a juvenile court considers whether to certify or transfer a very young child for trial in criminal court or when a prosecutor seeks to bypass the juvenile court by filing criminal charges against a young child.

drinking age. The age at which it is legal to purchase and consume alcoholic beverages in a given jurisdiction.

fighting age. The age at which a person becomes eligible to serve in (or liable to conscription into) a military unit.

full age. See *age of majority.*

lawful age. **1.** See *age of capacity.* **2.** See *age of majority* (1).

legal age. **1.** See *age of capacity.* **2.** See *age of majority* (1).

age discrimination. See DISCRIMINATION.

Age Discrimination in Employment Act. A federal law prohibiting job discrimination based on a person's age, esp. unfair and discriminatory employment decisions that negatively affect someone who is 40 years old or older. 29 USCA §§ 621–634. ● Passed in 1967, the Act applies to businesses with more than 20 employees and to all governmental entities. — Abbr. ADEA.

agency. (17c) **1.** A fiduciary relationship created by express or implied contract or by law, in which one party (the *agent*) may act on behalf of another party (the *principal*) and bind that other party by words or actions. See AUTHORITY (1).

actual agency. (1835) An agency in which the agent is in fact employed by a principal.

agency by estoppel. (1882) An agency created by operation of law and established by a principal's actions that would reasonably lead a third person to conclude that an agency exists. — Also termed *apparent agency; ostensible agency; agency by operation of law.*

agency by necessity. See *agency of necessity.*

agency by operation of law. See *agency by estoppel.*

agency coupled with an interest. (1844) An agency in which the agent is granted not only the power to act on behalf of a principal but also a legal interest in the estate or property involved. ● This type of agency is irrevocable before the interest expires, unless the parties agree otherwise when creating the interest. The agency survives even if the principal becomes insane or dies. See *power coupled with an interest* under POWER (3).

agency from necessity. See *agency of necessity.*

agency in fact. An agency created voluntarily, as by a contract. ● Agency in fact is distinguishable from an agency relationship created by law, such as agency by estoppel.

agency of necessity. An agency arising during an emergency that necessitates the agent's acting without authorization from the principal; the relation between a person who in exigent circumstances acts in the interest of another without being authorized to do so. ● It is a quasi-contractual relation formed by the operation of legal rules and not by the agreement of the parties. — Also termed *agency from necessity; agency by necessity.* See NEGOTIORUM GESTIO.

apparent agency. See *agency by estoppel.*

exclusive agency. (1805) The right to represent a principal — esp. either to sell the principal's products or to act as the seller's real-estate agent — within a particular market free from competition. ● Strictly speaking, an exclusive agency merely excludes all other brokers, but not the owner, from selling the products or property. — Also termed *exclusive agency to sell; exclusive franchise; sole selling agency.* Cf. EXCLUSIVE RIGHT OF SALE.

express agency. (18c) An actual agency arising from the principal's written or oral authorization of a person to act as the principal's agent. Cf. *implied agency.*

financing agency. A bank, finance company, or other entity that in the ordinary course of business (1) makes advances against goods or documents of title, or (2) by arrangement with either the seller or the buyer intervenes to make or collect payment due or claimed under a contract for sale, as by purchasing or paying the seller's draft, making advances against it, or taking it for collection, regardless of whether documents of title accompany the draft. UCC § 2-102(a)(20).

general agency. (18c) A principal's delegation to an agent, without restriction, to take any action connected with a particular trade, business, or employment. — Also termed *universal agency.*

implied agency. (18c) An actual agency arising from the conduct by the principal that implies an intention to create an agency relationship. Cf. *express agency.*

ostensible agency. See *agency by estoppel.*

special agency. (1808) An agency in which the agent is authorized only to conduct a single transaction or a series of transactions not involving continuous service.

undisclosed agency. (1871) An agency relationship in which an agent deals with a third party who has no knowledge that the agent is acting on a principal's behalf. ● The fact that the agency is undisclosed does not prohibit the third party from seeking redress from the principal or the agent.

universal agency. See *general agency.*

2. An agent's place of business. **3.** A governmental body with the authority to implement and administer particular legislation. — Also termed (in sense 3) *government agency; administrative agency; public agency; regulatory agency.*

federal agency. (1859) A department or other instrumentality of the executive branch of the federal government, including a government corporation and the Government Printing Office. ● The Administrative Procedure Act defines the term *agency* negatively as being any U.S. governmental authority that does not include Congress, the courts, the government of the District of Columbia, the government of any territory or possession, courts-martial, or military authority. 5 USCA § 551. The caselaw on this definition focuses on authority: generally, an entity is an agency if it has authority to take binding action. Other federal statutes define agency to include any executive department, government corporation, government-controlled corporation, or other establishment in the executive branch, or federal regulatory board.

independent agency. (1902) A federal agency, commission, or board that is not under the direction of the executive, such as the Federal Trade Commission or the National Labor Relations Board. — Also termed *independent regulatory agency; independent regulatory commission.*

local agency. A political subdivision of a state. ● Local agencies include counties, cities, school districts, etc.

quasi-governmental agency. (1904) A government-sponsored enterprise or corporation (sometimes called a *government-controlled corporation*), such as the Federal National Mortgage Corporation.

state agency. An executive or regulatory body of a state. ● State agencies include state offices, departments, divisions, bureaus, boards, and commissions. — Also termed *state body.*

agency adjudication. See ADMINISTRATIVE PROCEEDING.

agency adoption. See ADOPTION.

Agency for Healthcare Research and Quality. An agency in the U.S. Department of Health and Human Services responsible for conducting research into improving the quality of healthcare, reducing its cost, and broadening access to essential healthcare services.

Agency for International Development. See UNITED STATES AGENCY FOR INTERNATIONAL DEVELOPMENT.

Agency for Toxic Substances and Disease Registry. An agency in the U.S. Department of Health and Human Services responsible for evaluating the impact on public health of the release of hazardous substances into the environment, for maintaining a registry of contaminated waste sites, and for conducting research on the effects of hazardous substances on human health. — Abbr. ATSDR.

agency jurisdiction. See JURISDICTION.

agency records. Under the Freedom of Information Act, documents that are created or obtained by a government agency, and that are in the agency's control at the time the information request is made. 5 USCA § 552; *United States Dep't of Justice v. Tax Analysts*, 492 U.S. 136, 109 S.Ct. 2841 (1989).

agency regulation. See REGULATION (3).

agency security. See *government security* under SECURITY.

agency shop. See SHOP.

agency-shop membership. See FINANCIAL-CORE MEMBERSHIP.

agenda. A list of things to be done, as items to be considered at a meeting, usu. arranged in order of consideration. — Also termed *calendar; calendar of business; order of business.* Cf. PROGRAM (1).

action agenda. See *action calendar* under CALENDAR (4).

consent agenda. See *consent calendar* under CALENDAR (4).

debate agenda. See *debate calendar* under CALENDAR (4).

final agenda. An agenda that a deliberative assembly has adopted, or that has been adopted for a deliberative assembly by an officer or board charged with setting such an agenda.

proposed agenda. An agenda offered, usu. with the notice calling the meeting that the agenda covers, for a deliberative assembly's consideration. — Also termed *tentative agenda*.

report agenda. See *report calendar* under CALENDAR (4).

special-order agenda. See *special-order calendar* under CALENDAR (4).

tentative agenda. See *proposed agenda*.

unanimous-consent agenda. See *consent calendar* under CALENDAR (4).

agent. (15c) **1.** Something that produces an effect <an intervening agent>. See CAUSE (1); ELECTRONIC AGENT. **2.** One who is authorized to act for or in place of another; a representative <a professional athlete's agent>. — Also termed *commissionaire*. Cf. PRINCIPAL (1); EMPLOYEE.

apparent agent. (1823) A person who reasonably appears to have authority to act for another, regardless of whether actual authority has been conferred. — Also termed *ostensible agent*.

bail-enforcement agent. See BOUNTY HUNTER.

bargaining agent. A labor union in its capacity of representing employees in collective bargaining.

broker-agent. See BROKER.

business agent. See BUSINESS AGENT.

clearing agent. *Securities.* A person or company acting as an intermediary in a securities transaction or providing facilities for comparing data regarding securities transactions. • The term includes a custodian of securities in connection with the central handling of securities. Securities Exchange Act § 3(a)(23)(A) (15 USCA § 78c(a)(23)(A)). — Also termed *clearing agency*.

closing agent. See *settlement agent*.

co-agent. A person who shares with another agent the authority to act for the principal. — Also termed *dual agent*. Cf. *common agent*.

commercial agent. **1.** BROKER. **2.** A consular officer responsible for the commercial interests of his or her country at a foreign port. **3.** See *mercantile agent*.

common agent. An agent who acts on behalf of more than one principal in a transaction. Cf. *co-agent*.

corporate agent. (1819) An agent authorized to act on behalf of a corporation; broadly, all employees and officers who have the power to bind the corporation.

county agent. See *juvenile officer* under OFFICER (1).

del credere agent (del **kred**-ə-ray *or* **kray**-də-ray). (1822) An agent who guarantees the solvency of the third party with whom the agent makes a contract for the principal. • A del credere agent receives possession of the principal's goods for purposes of sale and guarantees that anyone to whom the agent sells the goods on credit will pay promptly for them. For this guaranty, the agent receives a higher commission for sales. The promise of such an agent is almost universally held not to be within the statute of frauds. — Also termed *del credere factor*.

diplomatic agent. A national representative in one of four categories: (1) ambassadors, (2) envoys and ministers plenipotentiary, (3) ministers resident accredited to the sovereign, or (4) chargés d'affaires accredited to the minister of foreign affairs.

double agent. See *dual agent* (2).

dual agent. **1.** See *co-agent*. **2.** An agent who represents both parties in a single transaction, esp. a buyer and a seller. — Also termed (in sense 2) *double agent*.

emigrant agent. One engaged in the business of hiring laborers for work outside the country or state.

enrolled agent. See ENROLLED AGENT.

escrow agent. The third-party depositary of an escrow; ESCROW (3). — Also termed *escrow holder*; *escrowee*; *escrow officer*.

fiscal agent. A bank or other financial institution that collects and disburses money and services as a depository of private and public funds on another's behalf.

foreign agent. A person who registers with the federal government as a lobbyist representing the interests of a foreign nation or corporation.

forwarding agent. **1.** See FREIGHT FORWARDER. **2.** A freight-forwarder who assembles less-than-carload shipments (small shipments) into carload shipments, thus taking advantage of lower freight rates.

general agent. (17c) An agent authorized to transact all the principal's business of a particular kind or in a particular place. • Among the common types of general agents are factors, brokers, and partners.

government agent. (1805) **1.** An employee or representative of a governmental body. **2.** A law-enforcement official, such as a police officer or an FBI agent. **3.** An informant, esp. an inmate, used by law enforcement to obtain incriminating statements from another inmate. • An accused's Sixth Amendment right to counsel is triggered when the accused is questioned by a government agent.

high-managerial agent. An agent of a corporation or other business, having authority to formulate corporate policy or supervise employees. — Also termed *superior agent*.

independent agent. (17c) An agent who exercises personal judgment and is subject to the principal only for the results of the work performed. Cf. *nonservant agent.*

innocent agent. (1805) *Criminal law.* A person whose action on behalf of a principal is unlawful but does not merit prosecution because the agent had no knowledge of the principal's illegal purpose; a person who lacks the mens rea for an offense but who is tricked or coerced by the principal into committing a crime. ● Although the agent's conduct was unlawful, the agent might not be prosecuted if the agent had no knowledge of the principal's illegal purpose. The principal is legally accountable for the innocent agent's actions. See Model Penal Code § 2.06(2)(a).

insurance agent. See INSURANCE AGENT.

jural agent. See JURAL AGENT.

land agent. See LAND MANAGER.

listing agent. (1927) The real-estate broker's representative who obtains a listing agreement with the owner. Cf. *selling agent.*

local agent. An agent appointed to act as another's (esp. a company's) representative and to transact business within a specified district.

managing agent. (1812) A person with general power involving the exercise of judgment and discretion, as opposed to an ordinary agent who acts under the direction and control of the principal. — Also termed *business agent.*

mercantile agent. An agent employed to sell goods or merchandise on behalf of the principal. — Also termed *commercial agent.*

nonservant agent. An agent who agrees to act on the principal's behalf but is not subject to the principal's control over how the task is performed. ● A principal is not liable for the physical torts of a nonservant agent. See INDEPENDENT CONTRACTOR. Cf. *independent agent*; SERVANT.

ostensible agent. See *apparent agent.*

patent agent. A specialized legal professional — not necessarily a licensed lawyer — who prepares and prosecutes patent applications before the Patent and Trademark Office ● Patent agents must be licensed by the Patent and Trademark Office. — Also termed *patent solicitor*; *registered patent agent.*

primary agent. An agent who is directly authorized by a principal. ● A primary agent generally may hire a subagent to perform all or part of the agency. Cf. *subagent.*

private agent. An agent acting for an individual in that person's private affairs.

process agent. (1886) A person authorized to accept service of process on behalf of another.

procuring agent. A person who obtains drugs on behalf of another person and delivers the drugs to that person. ● In criminal-defense theory, the procuring agent does not sell, barter, exchange, or make a gift of the drugs to the other person because the drugs already belong to that person, who merely employs the agent to pick up and deliver them.

public agent. A person appointed to act for the public in matters pertaining to governmental administration or public business.

real-estate agent. An agent who represents a buyer or seller (or both, with proper disclosures) in the sale or lease of real property. ● A real-estate agent can be either a broker (whose principal is a buyer or seller) or a salesperson (whose principal is a broker). Cf. REALTOR.

record agent. See INSURANCE AGENT.

registered agent. (1809) A person authorized to accept service of process for another person, esp. a corporation, in a particular jurisdiction. — Also termed *resident agent.*

selling agent. (1839) The real-estate broker's representative who sells the property, as opposed to the agent who lists the property for sale. Cf. LISTING AGENT.

settlement agent. An agent who represents the purchaser or buyer in the negotiation and closing of a real-property transaction by handling financial calculations and transfers of documents. — Also termed *closing agent.* See also *settlement attorney* under ATTORNEY.

soliciting agent. 1. *Insurance.* An agent with limited authority relating to the solicitation or submission of applications to an insurance company but usu. without authority to bind the insurer, as by accepting the applications on behalf of the company. 2. An agent who solicits orders for goods or services for a principal. 3. A managing agent of a corporation for purposes of service of process.

special agent. 1. An agent employed to conduct a particular transaction or to perform a specified act. 2. See INSURANCE AGENT.

specially accredited agent. An agent with whom a third person has been specially invited to deal by the principal under circumstances leading the third person to believe that he or she will be notified if the authority is altered or revoked.

statutory agent. (1844) An agent designated by law to receive litigation documents and other legal notices for a nonresident corporation. ● In most states, the secretary of state is the statutory agent for such corporations.

stock-transfer agent. An organization that oversees and maintains records of transfers of shares for a corporation.

subagent. A person to whom an agent has delegated the performance of an act for the principal; a person designated by an agent to perform some duty relating to the agency. ● If the principal consents to a primary agent's employment of a subagent, the subagent owes fiduciary duties to the principal, and the principal is liable for the subagent's acts. Cf. *primary agent.* — Also termed *subservant.*

successor agent. An agent who is appointed by a principal to act in a primary agent's stead if the primary agent is unable or unwilling to perform.

superior agent. See *high-managerial agent.*

transfer agent. An organization (such as a bank or trust company) that handles transfers of shares for a publicly held corporation by issuing new certificates and overseeing the cancellation of old ones and that usu. also maintains the record of shareholders for the corporation and mails dividend checks. ● Generally, a transfer agent ensures that certificates submitted for transfer are properly indorsed and that the right to transfer is appropriately documented.

undercover agent. (1930) **1.** An agent who does not disclose his or her role as an agent. **2.** A police officer who gathers evidence of criminal activity without disclosing his or her identity to the suspect.

universal agent. (18c) An agent authorized to perform all acts that the principal could personally perform.

vice-commercial agent. *Hist.* In the consular service of the United States, a consular officer who was substituted temporarily to fill the place of a commercial agent who was absent or had been relieved from duty.

3. *Patents.* A person who is not an attorney but who has fulfilled the U.S. Patent and Trademark Office requirements as a lay representative and is registered to prepare and prosecute patent applications before the PTO. ● To be registered to practice before the PTO, a candidate must establish mastery of the relevant technology (by holding a specified technical degree or equivalent training) in order to advise and assist patent applicants. The candidate must also pass a written examination (the "Patent Bar") that tests knowledge of patent law and PTO procedure. — Also termed *patent agent.* Cf. PATENT ATTORNEY.

agent not recognized. *Patents.* A patent applicant's appointed agent who is not registered to practice before the U.S. Patent and Trademark Office. ● A power of attorney appointing an unregistered agent is void.

associate agent. An agent who is registered to practice before the U.S. Patent and Trademark Office, has been appointed by a principal agent, and is authorized to prosecute a patent application through the filing of a power of attorney. ● An associate agent is often used by outside counsel to assist in-house counsel.

agent provocateur (ay-jənt prə-vok-ə-**tər** *or* a-zhaw*n* praw-vaw-kə-**tuur**), *n.* (1877) **1.** An undercover agent who instigates or participates in a crime, often by infiltrating a group suspected of illegal conduct, to expose and punish criminal activity. **2.** A person who entraps another, or entices another to break the law, and then informs against the other as a lawbreaker.

agent's lien. See LIEN.

agent's power. See POWER (3).

age of capacity. See AGE.

age of consent. See AGE.

age of criminal responsibility. See AGE.

age of discretion. See AGE.

age of majority. See AGE.

age of reason. See AGE.

aggravated, *adj.* (17c) **1.** (Of a crime) made worse or more serious by circumstances such as violence, the presence of a deadly weapon, or the intent to commit another crime <aggravated robbery>. Cf. SIMPLE (1). **2.** (Of a tort) made worse or more serious by circumstances such as intention to cause harm or reckless disregard for another's safety <the defendant's negligence was aggravated by malice>. **3.** (Of an injury) harmful to a part of the body previously injured or debilitated <an aggravated bone fracture>. See AGGRAVATION RULE.

aggravated arson. See ARSON.

aggravated assault. See ASSAULT.

aggravated battery. See BATTERY.

aggravated damages. See *punitive damages* under DAMAGES.

aggravated kidnapping. See KIDNAPPING.

aggravated larceny. See LARCENY.

aggravated misdemeanor. See *serious misdemeanor* under MISDEMEANOR.

aggravated robbery. See ROBBERY.

aggravated sodomy. See SODOMY.

aggravating circumstance. See CIRCUMSTANCE.

aggravating element. See *aggravating circumstance* under CIRCUMSTANCE.

aggravating factor. See *aggravating circumstance* under CIRCUMSTANCE.

aggravation. 1. The fact of being increased in gravity or seriousness. **2.** *Eccles. law.* A censure threatening the recipient with an increase in the penalties associated with excommunication, usu. because the recipient disregarded an earlier sentence. ● For example, a person who spurned a sentence of excommunication might be subjected to an anathema (a formal ban or curse). — **aggravate,** *vb.*

aggravation rule. *Workers' compensation.* The principle that when an on-the-job injury combines with a preexisting injury, resulting in a greater disability than that which would have resulted from the on-the-job injury alone, the entire disability is compensable as if it had occurred at work.

aggravator. 1. One who commits a crime with an aggravating circumstance. **2.** See *aggravating circumstance* under CIRCUMSTANCE. Cf. MITIGATOR.

aggregate (**ag**-rə-git), *adj.* (15c) Formed by combining into a single whole or total <aggregate income>. — **aggregately,** *adv.*

aggregate (**ag**-rə-git), *n.* An assemblage of particulars; an agglomeration <aggregate of interests>.

aggregate (**ag**-rə-gayt), *vb.* To collect into a whole <aggregate the claims>.

aggregate concept. *Tax.* An approach to taxing business organizations whereby an organization is viewed as a collection of its individual owners, not as a separate taxable entity.

aggregate corporation. See CORPORATION.

aggregate demand. See DEMAND (4).

aggregate income. See INCOME.

aggregate sentence. See SENTENCE.

aggregate supply. See SUPPLY.

aggregate theory of partnership. (1913) The theory that a partnership does not have a separate legal existence (as does a corporation), but rather is only the totality of the partners who compose it. Cf. ENTITY THEORY OF PARTNERSHIP.

aggregation. *Patents.* **1.** A set of parts that do not cooperate in structure or function, and are therefore unpatentable as an invention; the opposite of a combination. **2.** *Hist.* A patent examiner's label for a claimed invention that may or may not be a patentable combination but whose claims do not clearly explain how the parts cooperate to produce a new or unexpected result. ● As a term of art, *aggregation* lost its usefulness when it was replaced by a statutory test in § 103 of the Patent Act of 1952. — Also termed *juxtaposition.* Cf. COMBINATION (4).

aggregation doctrine. (1942) **1.** The rule that precludes a party from totaling all claims for purposes of meeting the minimum amount necessary to give rise to federal diversity jurisdiction under the amount-in-controversy requirement. See *diversity jurisdiction* under JURISDICTION; AMOUNT IN CONTROVERSY. **2.** *Constitutional law.* A rule that allows Congress, under its Commerce Clause powers, to regulate purely private acts, such as growing wheat for one's own consumption, if the consequences of many such acts, taken together, would have an effect on interstate commerce. See *Wickard v. Filburn,* 317 U.S. 111, 63 S.Ct. 82 (1942).

aggregation of claims. *Patents.* In a patent application, an excessive number of claims that do not differ significantly in scope and are essentially duplicative. ● Although a patent applicant may claim an invention and its various features in a reasonable number of ways, each claim must differ materially from the others. — Also termed *multiplicity of claims; undue multiplicity of claims.*

aggregation rejection. See REJECTION.

aggression. *Int'l law.* A grave breach of international law by a nation. ● The prohibition of aggression is a peremptory rule (*jus cogens*). Aggressors are guilty of an international crime. But there is no generally accepted definition of what constitutes aggression despite many attempts over the years to devise one. In 1974, the United Nations General Assembly adopted a Resolution on the Definition of Aggression (Resolution 3314 (XXIX) of December 14, 1974). It defines aggression, in part, as "the use of armed force by a State against the sovereignty, territorial integrity, or political independence of another country, or in a manner inconsistent with the Charter of the United Nations. . . ." The definition does not extend to measures that, in certain circumstances, might constitute aggression, nor does it recognize exceptional circumstances that would make the enumerated acts defensive rather than offensive. The U.N. Security Council has never expressly relied on the resolution when determining whether a nation's acts constitute a "threat to the peace, breach of the peace, or act of aggression." See U.N. Charter art. 39, 59 Stat. 1031. The difficulty of finding a generally accepted definition of *aggression* is reflected in Article 5 of the Statute of the International Criminal Court (37 I.L.M. 999). It confers jurisdiction on the Court over "the crime of aggression" but also requires the parties to the Statute to define the crime before the Court can exercise jurisdiction.

    direct aggression. Aggression in which a state's regular armed forces participate.

    indirect aggression. Aggression carried out by some means other than through a state's regular armed forces.

aggressor corporation. See CORPORATION.

aggressor doctrine. (1947) The principle precluding tort recovery for a plaintiff who acts in a way that would provoke a reasonable person to use physical force for protection, unless the defendant in turn uses excessive force to repel the plaintiff.

aggrieved, *adj.* (Of a person or entity) having legal rights that are adversely affected; having been harmed by an infringement of legal rights.

aggrieved party. See PARTY (2).

AGI. *abbr.* See *adjusted gross income* under INCOME.

aging of accounts. A process of classifying accounts receivable by the time elapsed since the claim came into existence for the purpose of estimating the balance of uncollectible accounts as of a given date.

aging-out, *n.* A foster child's or minor ward's reaching the age at which any legal right to care expires. ● Aging-out usu. occurs when the child reaches the age of majority and becomes ineligible for foster care. Some states allow an extension of eligibility up to age 21 if the child is still in school or cannot live independently, or if it is otherwise in the child's best interests to remain in foster care and the child consents. See INDEPENDENT-LIVING PROGRAM.

agio (aj-ee-oh *or* ay-jee-oh). The premium paid for the exchange of one kind of money for another, such as paper currency for coin or one country's currency for another's.

agiotage (aj-ee-ə-tij). **1.** The business of dealing in foreign exchange. **2.** The speculative buying and selling of securities.

agist (ə-jist), *vb.* To allow animals to graze on one's pasture for a fee.

agister (ə-jis-tər). One who takes and pastures grazing animals for a fee; a person engaged in the business of agistment. ● An agister is a type of bailee for hire. — Also spelled *agistor.* — Also termed *gisetaker.*

agister's lien. See LIEN.

agistment (ə-jist-mənt). **1.** A type of bailment in which a person, for a fee, allows animals to graze on his or her pasture; the taking in of cattle or other livestock to feed at a per-animal rate. **2.** A charge levied upon the owner or occupier of land. — Also termed *gisement.*

agnate (ag-nayt), *adj.* Related or akin through male descent or on the father's side.

agnate, *n.* (16c) **1.** A blood relative whose connection is through the male line. **2.** A relative on the father's side, whether or not traced exclusively through the male line. Cf. COGNATE.

agnatic (ag-nat-ik), *adj.* (Of a relationship) restricted to affiliations through the male line. — Also termed *agnatical* (ag-nat-i-kəl).

agrarian (ə-grair-ee-ən), *adj.* Of or relating to land, land tenure, or a division of landed property. — **agrarian,** *n.*

agrarian law. *Roman & civil law.* The body of law governing the ownership, use, and distribution of rural land.

a gratia (ay gray-shee-ə). [Law Latin] EX GRATIA.

agree, *vb.* **1.** To unite in thought; to concur in opinion or purpose. **2.** To exchange promises; to unite in an engagement to do or not do something. **3.** *Parliamentary law.* To adopt (usu. in the phrase *agree to*). See ADOPTION (5).

agreed-amount clause. An insurance-policy provision that the insured will carry a stated amount of coverage.

agreed boundary. See BOUNDARY.

agreed-boundary doctrine. (1941) The principle by which adjacent landowners resolve uncertainties over land boundaries by permanently fixing the boundaries by agreement; specif., the rule that owners of contiguous land may agree on the boundary between the parcels, as long as the actual boundary is uncertain, there is agreement between the two owners about the boundary line, there is acquiescence in the agreed line for a time exceeding the statute of limitations, and the agreed boundary is identifiable on the ground. — Also termed *doctrine of practical location.* See *agreed boundary* under BOUNDARY.

agreed case. See *agreed statement of facts* under STATEMENT OF FACTS.

agreed decree. See DECREE.

agreed dismissal. See *dismissal agreed* under DISMISSAL (1).

agreed judgment. See JUDGMENT.

agreed price. See PRICE.

agreed statement of facts. See STATEMENT OF FACTS.

agreed statement on appeal. See *agreed statement of facts* under STATEMENT OF FACTS.

agreed value. See VALUE (2).

agreement. (15c) **1.** A mutual understanding between two or more persons about their relative rights and duties regarding past or future performances; a manifestation of mutual assent by two or more persons. **2.** The parties' actual bargain as found in their language or by implication from other circumstances, including course of dealing, usage of trade, and course of performance. UCC § 1–201(3).

agreement incident to divorce. See DIVORCE AGREEMENT.

agreement of sale. An agreement that obligates someone to sell and that may include a corresponding obligation for someone else to buy.

agreement to agree. **1.** An unenforceable agreement that purports to bind two parties to negotiate and enter into a contract; esp., a proposed agreement negotiated with the intent that the final agreement will be embodied in a formal written document and that neither party will be bound until the final agreement is executed. **2.** A fully enforceable agreement containing terms that are sufficiently definite as well as adequate consideration, but leaving some details to be worked out by the parties.

agreement to sell. An agreement that obligates someone to sell.

antenuptial agreement. See PRENUPTIAL AGREEMENT.

binding agreement. (18c) An enforceable contract. See CONTRACT.

business-continuation agreement. An agreement for the disposition of a business interest in the event of the owner's death, disability, retirement, or withdrawal from the business. • The agreement may be between the business and its individual owners, among the individual owners themselves, or between the individual owners and a key person, family member, or outsider. — Abbr. BCA. Cf. *cross-purchase agreement*; *third-party business-buyout agreement*.

closing agreement. *Tax.* A written contract between a taxpayer and the Internal Revenue Service to resolve a tax dispute.

cohabitation agreement. See COHABITATION AGREEMENT.

criss-cross agreement. See *cross-purchase agreement*.

cross-purchase agreement. An agreement between a business's individual owners to purchase the interest of a withdrawing or deceased owner in order to continue operating the business. — Also termed *criss-cross agreement*. Cf. *business-continuation agreement*; *third-party business-buyout agreement*.

divorce agreement. See DIVORCE AGREEMENT.

exchange agreement. An agreement to exchange real properties, usu. like-kind properties. See 1031 EXCHANGE; TAX-FREE EXCHANGE.

formal agreement. (17c) An agreement for which the law requires not only the consent of the parties but also a manifestation of the agreement in some particular form (e.g., a signed writing), in default of which the agreement is unenforceable. Cf. *formal contract* under CONTRACT.

integrated agreement. See INTEGRATED CONTRACT.

invalid agreement. See *invalid contract* under CONTRACT.

living-together agreement. See COHABITATION AGREEMENT.

marital agreement. See MARITAL AGREEMENT.

marital settlement agreement. See DIVORCE AGREEMENT.

negotiated agreement. See NEGOTIATED AGREEMENT.

noncircumvention agreement. See NONCIRCUMVENTION AGREEMENT.

outsourcing agreement. See OUTSOURCING AGREEMENT.

point-and-click agreement. See POINT-AND-CLICK AGREEMENT.

postnuptial agreement. See POSTNUPTIAL AGREEMENT.

prenuptial agreement. See PRENUPTIAL AGREEMENT.

property settlement agreement. See PROPERTY SETTLEMENT (2).

reconciliation agreement. See RECONCILIATION AGREEMENT.

redemption agreement. See STOCK-REDEMPTION AGREEMENT.

separation agreement. See SEPARATION AGREEMENT.

side agreement. **1.** An agreement that is ancillary to another agreement. **2.** *Int'l law.* An international accord that is specifically negotiated to supplement a broader trade treaty. • For example, NAFTA contains no provisions about labor standards or environmental protection. But two side agreements about those areas were negotiated separately and designed to supplement NAFTA, making the treaty more attractive to the ratifying bodies. — Also termed *supplemental agreement*.

simple agreement. (18c) An agreement for which the law requires nothing for its effective operation beyond some manifestation that the parties have consented.

stock-retirement agreement. See STOCK-REDEMPTION AGREEMENT.

subordination agreement. An agreement by which one who holds an otherwise senior interest agrees to subordinate that interest to a normally lesser interest, usu. when a seller agrees to subordinate a purchase-money mortgage so that the buyer can obtain a first-mortgage loan to improve the property.

supplemental agreement. See *side agreement*.

surrogate-parenting agreement. See SURROGATE-PARENTING AGREEMENT.

takeover agreement. An agreement under which a defaulting party's surety agrees to perform the original contract in the defaulting party's stead.

third-party business-buyout agreement. An agreement by a business's owners to sell all or part of the business to an outside person who will continue to operate it. Cf. *business-continuation agreement*; *cross-purchase agreement*.

trust agreement. See *declaration of trust* (2) under DECLARATION (1).

unconscionable agreement (ən-**kon**-shə-nə-bəl). (1817) An agreement that no promisor with any sense, and not under a delusion, would make, and that no honest and fair promisee would accept. • For commercial contexts, see UCC § 2-302. — Also termed *unconscionable contract*; *unconscionable bargain*.

underwriting agreement. An agreement between a corporation and an underwriter covering the terms and conditions of a new securities issue.

valid agreement. See *valid contract* under CONTRACT.

voidable agreement. See *voidable contract* under CONTRACT.

void agreement. See *void contract* under CONTRACT.

agreement of imperfect obligation. See *unenforceable contract* under CONTRACT.

agreement of rescission. See RESCISSION (2).

agreement of sale. See AGREEMENT.

Agreement on Trade-Related Aspects of Intellectual Property Rights. See TRIPS.

Agreement Relating to Liability Limitation of the Warsaw Convention and The Hague Protocol. See MONTREAL AGREEMENT.

agreement to agree. See AGREEMENT.

agreement to marry. See *marriage promise* under PROMISE.

agreement to sell. See AGREEMENT.

agribusiness. The pursuit of agriculture as an occupation or profit-making enterprise, including labor, land-use planning, and financing the cost of land, equipment, and other necessary expenses. • This term generally excludes smaller family-owned and -operated farms.

Agricultural Adjustment Act. A 1933 federal statute that paid farmers not to produce crops in an effort to raise crop prices. • The U.S. Supreme Court declared the Act unconstitutional in 1936 on grounds that Congress had overstepped its power to regulate commerce. A second, more limited Agricultural Adjustment Act was enacted in 1938. — Abbr. AAA.

Agricultural Cooperative Service. The federal agency within the U.S. Department of Agriculture responsible for helping farmers to organize farm cooperatives. • The Service also collects statistical information on co-ops and publishes *Farmer Cooperatives*, a monthly magazine.

agricultural-disparagement law. A statute designed to protect food producers from and provide remedies for pecuniary harm resulting from false and malicious reports of food contamination. • A typical statute applies to false and disparaging public statements implying or claiming that a perishable food product is unsafe for human consumption. It typically applies when the speaker or writer knows that the statements are false because the claim or implication has no basis in reliable scientific inquiry, facts, or data. — Also termed *veggie-libel law*; *perishable-food-disparagement act*; *agricultural-product-disparagement law*; *food-disparagement law*.

agricultural fixture. See FIXTURE.

agricultural labor. Work that is performed on a farm or ranch, or that pertains to the production of commodities, such as harvesting crops, raising livestock, or obtaining milk, honey, or other animal products. • Agricultural labor is often excluded from certain labor laws, such as unemployment insurance and workers' compensation.

agricultural lien. See LIEN.

Agricultural Marketing Service. An agency in the U.S. Department of Agriculture responsible for compiling and publishing marketing information, establishing and enforcing quality standards for agricultural products, testing those products, and making grants to states and farmers. • It was established by the Secretary of Agriculture in 1972. — Abbr. AMS.

agricultural-product-disparagement law. See AGRICULTURAL-DISPARAGEMENT LAW.

Agricultural Research Service. An agency in the U.S. Department of Agriculture responsible for conducting agricultural research to ensure the production of high-quality food and food products. — Abbr. ARS.

agriculture. The science or art of cultivating soil, harvesting crops, and raising livestock.

Aguilar–Spinelli test (ah-gee-**lahr** spi-**nel**-ee *or* **ag**-wə-lahr). *Criminal procedure.* A standard for determining whether hearsay (such as an informant's tip) is sufficiently reliable to establish probable cause for an arrest or search warrant. • Under this two-pronged test — which has been replaced by a broader, totality-of-the-circumstances approach — the reliability of both the information and the informant must be assessed independently. *Aguilar v. Texas*, 378 U.S. 108, 84 S.Ct. 1509 (1964); *Spinelli v. United States*, 393 U.S. 410, 89 S.Ct. 584 (1969). Cf. TOTALITY-OF-THE-CIRCUMSTANCES TEST.

ahupuaa (ah-hoo-poo-**ah**-ah). [Hawaiian] A variable measure of Hawaiian land, traditionally understood to stretch from the sea to the mountains, to allow the people to obtain the various materials needed for subsistence offered at different elevations. — Also spelled *ahupua'a.*

AICPA. *abbr.* American Institute of Certified Public Accountants.

AID. *abbr.* **1.** See *artificial insemination by donor* under ARTIFICIAL INSEMINATION. **2.** UNITED STATES AGENCY FOR INTERNATIONAL DEVELOPMENT.

aid, *n.* **1.** A contribution toward defense costs from a third party who has a joint interest in the defense but has not been sued. **2.** *Hist.* A subsidy or tax granted to the king for an extraordinary purpose. **3.** *Hist.* A benevolence or tribute (i.e., a sum of money) granted by the tenant to his lord in times of difficulty and distress. ● Over time, these grants evolved from being discretionary to mandatory. The three principal aids were: (1) to ransom the lord's person if he was taken prisoner; (2) to contribute toward the ceremony of knighting the lord's eldest son; and (3) to provide a suitable dowry for the lord's eldest daughter.

aid and abet, *vb.* (17c) To assist or facilitate the commission of a crime, or to promote its accomplishment. ● Aiding and abetting is a crime in most jurisdictions. — Also termed *aid or abet*; *counsel and procure.* — **aider and abettor,** *n.*

aid and comfort. (16c) Help given by someone to a national enemy in such a way that the help amounts to treason. ● The phrase is a loan translation of the French *aide et confort*, which appears in the early 15th century in a French translation of the Bible. The first English-language use appears to have been in Grafton's *Chronicles* of 1568.

aided-awareness survey. *Trademarks.* A trademark survey in which interviewees are asked to choose from a spectrum of choices that prominently feature the desired response. ● Aided-awareness surveys are often discounted or entirely disregarded by courts in trademark-infringement actions. — Also termed *aided-recall survey.*

aide-mémoire (ayd-mem-**wahr**). [French] *Int'l law.* A diplomatic document that a diplomatic agent leaves with the receiving state's department of foreign affairs on the occasion of a *démarche.* ● The *aide-mémoire* presents the receiving state with a precise record of the substance of the diplomatic agent's mission. It is typically written in an impersonal style, without mentioning either the addressee or the author. It appears on printed letterhead and is dated, but it is not signed, initialed, or embossed with a seal. See DÉMARCHE.

aider, *n.* **1.** An act of aiding; the curing of a defect. **2.** One who aids another.

aider by pleading over. (1860) The cure of a pleading defect by an adversary's answering the pleading without an objection, so that the objection is waived.

aider by subsequent pleading. The cure of a pleading defect by an adversary's answer that refers to or admits a material fact or allegation that was not mentioned in the pleading, or an answer that shows the correct basis for the plaintiff's pleading. — Also termed *express aider.*

aider by verdict. (1824) The cure of a pleading defect by a trial verdict, based on the presumption that the record contains adequate proof of the necessary facts even if those facts were not specifically alleged. — Also termed *cure by verdict.*

aiding an escape. The crime of helping a prisoner escape custody.

aid or abet. See AID AND ABET.

aid or abet infringement. *Patents.* Through some affirmative act or conduct, to actively induce or assist with another person's infringement. ● Aiding or abetting patent infringement is actionable under § 271(b) of the Patent Act. Cf. *infringement in the inducement* under INFRINGEMENT.

aid prayer. *Hist.* A plea by a life tenant or other holder of less than a fee simple to bring into the action another who holds an interest in the estate (such as a reversioner or remainderman) to help defend the title. — Also termed *prayer in aid.*

aids. See AID (2).

aiel (**ay**-əl), *n.* [Law French] *Hist.* **1.** A grandfather. **2.** A writ by an heir of a grandfather for recovery of the grandfather's estate, which had been wrongfully possessed by a stranger. — Also spelled *aile; ayel; ayle.* — Also termed (in sense 2) *writ of aiel.* Cf. COSINAGE.

AIH. *abbr.* See *artificial insemination by husband* under ARTIFICIAL INSEMINATION.

Aiken exemption. *Copyright.* An exception in the law of infringement that permits retail establishments with less than 2,000 square feet of space to play radio and television broadcasts for employees and patrons without obtaining a license. *Twentieth Century Music Corp. v. Aiken*, 422 U.S. 151, 95 S. Ct. 2040 (1975). — Also termed *store-receiver exemption.*

aimable compositeur (ay-**mah**-blə kon-poh-zee-**tuur**). [French] See AMIABLE COMPOSITOR.

AIP. *abbr.* See AMERICAN INSTITUTE OF PARLIAMENTARIANS.

AIPA. *abbr.* AMERICAN INVENTORS PROTECTION ACT.

AIPLA. *abbr.* AMERICAN INTELLECTUAL PROPERTY LAW ASSOCIATION.

airbill. A document serving as a bill of lading for goods transported by air. ● The term includes air consignment notes and air waybills.

aircraft piracy. See *air piracy* under PIRACY (2).

air law. The part of law, esp. international law, relating to civil aviation.

airman's certificate. A license that every aircraft pilot must have to operate an aircraft in U.S. airspace. 49 USCA §§ 44701–44711; 14 CFR § 61.3.

Airman's Information Manual. A publication of the Federal Aviation Administration, providing the fundamental requirements of any pilot who flies in national airspace.

air piracy. See PIRACY (2).

air pollution. *Environmental law.* Any harmful substance or energy emitted directly or indirectly into the air, esp. if the harm is to the environment or to the public health or welfare.

air-quality-control region. *Environmental law.* A federally designated area in which communities share an air-pollution problem, often involving several states; an interstate area or major intrastate area that the Environmental Protection Agency designates for monitoring and ameliorating ambient air-quality standards. 42 USCA § 7407(c).

air-quality criteria. *Environmental law.* The legal limits that the Environmental Protection Agency sets for atmospheric or airborne pollutants in a defined area and at a specified time.

air right. (1922) The right to use all or a portion of the airspace above real property.

air-services agreement. See AIR-TRANSPORT AGREEMENT.

airspace. The space that extends upward from the surface of land, esp. so far as is necessary for the owner or possessor to have reasonable use and enjoyment of the incidents of its ownership or possession. Cf. OUTER SPACE.

   national airspace. *Int'l law.* The pillar of air above a nation's territory — including internal waters and the territorial sea — over which it has complete and exclusive sovereignty and through which foreign aircraft have no right of innocent passage. ● There is no agreement on the boundary between national airspace and outer space.

   navigable airspace. The area above the legally established minimum flight altitudes, including the area needed to ensure safe takeoffs and landings of aircraft. 49 USCA § 40102(a)(30).

air-transport agreement. A contract governing the operation of air services; esp., an intergovernmental agreement governing the operation of international air services between their territories. — Also termed *air-services agreement.*

air waybill. See WAYBILL.

AJS. *abbr.* AMERICAN JUDICATURE SOCIETY.

a.k.a. *abbr.* (1955) Also known as.

a large (ah **lahrzh**). [Law French] Free; at large.

Alaska trust. See *asset-protection trust* (1) under TRUST (3).

alcalde (ahl-**kahl**-day *or* al-**kal**-dee). [fr. Arabic *al-qadi* "the Cadi" or "the judge"] *Spanish law.* **1.** *Hist.* A judicial officer. ● The alcalde's functions typically resembled those of a justice of the peace. **2.** The mayor of a Spanish or Spanish-American town, usu. with a judicial element. ● This is the modern sense.

Alcohol and Tobacco Tax and Trade Bureau. A bureau in the U.S. Department of the Treasury that administers the laws governing the production, use, and distribution of alcohol and tobacco products, and collects excise taxes on firearms and ammunition. ● The Bureau has the tax-enforcement functions of the former Bureau of Alcohol, Tobacco, and Firearms. — Abbr. TTB.

alcoholometer. See BREATHALYZER.

alderman. A member of a city council or other local governing body. — Also termed *alderperson.*

alderperson. See ALDERMAN.

alderwoman. A female member of a city council or other local governing body.

aleatory (ay-lee-ə-tor-ee), *adj.* (17c) Dependent on uncertain contingencies. ● The word *aleatory* derives from the Latin word *aleator,* meaning "a gambler," which itself comes from *alea* (a die used in gaming). — Also termed *aleatoric.*

aleatory contract. See CONTRACT.

aleatory promise. See PROMISE.

alegal, *adj.* (1991) Outside the sphere of law; not classifiable as being legal or illegal <the law often treats the promises of unmarried cohabitants as contractual words rather than alegal words of commitment>. — **alegality,** *n.*

Alford plea. (1971) A guilty plea that a defendant enters as part of a plea bargain, without actually admitting guilt. ● This plea is not considered compelled within the language of the Fifth Amendment if the plea represents a voluntary, knowing, and intelligent choice between the available options <the defendant — realizing the strength of the prosecution's evidence and not wanting to risk receiving the death penalty — entered into an *Alford* plea>. *North Carolina v. Alford,* 400 U.S. 25, 91 S.Ct. 160 (1970). Cf. NO CONTEST.

algorithm. *Patents.* A mathematical or logical process consisting of a series of steps, designed to solve a specific type of problem. ● Algorithms were long considered abstract ideas and therefore unpatentable subject matter. But in 1998, the U.S. Court of Appeals for the Federal Circuit found valid a patent on financial software as "a practical application of a mathematical algorithm [that] produces a useful, concrete and tangible result." *State St. Bank & Trust Co. v. Signature Fin. Group*, 149 F.3d 1368 (Fed. Cir. 1998). That precedent makes it easier to patent computer software, which consists almost entirely of algorithms.

algorithm exception. *Patents.* The general rule that an abstract mathematical function, such as an algorithm, cannot be patented. • The exception was first articulated by the U.S. Supreme Court in *Gottschalk v. Benson*, 409 U.S. 63, 93 S.Ct. 253 (1972). The rule was undermined by *State St. Bank & Trust Co. v. Signature Fin. Group*, 149 F.3d 1368 (Fed. Cir. 1998). In that case, the court decided that a machine's transformation of numerical data into a calculated share price was a sufficient and practical application of a mathematical algorithm, formula, or calculation, because the final share price was "a useful, concrete and tangible result." — Also termed *mathematical-algorithm exception.*

ALI. *abbr.* AMERICAN LAW INSTITUTE.

alias (**ay**-lee-əs), *adj.* Issued after the first instrument has not been effective or resulted in action.

alias, *adv.* **1.** Otherwise called or named; also known as <William Grimsby, alias the Grim Reaper>. **2.** At another time.

alias, *n.* (17c) **1.** An assumed or additional name that a person has used or is known by. — Also termed *assumed name; fictitious name.* Cf. PSEUD-ONYM. **2.** *Hist.* A second writ issued after the first has failed. See *alias writ* under WRIT. Pl. **aliases.**

alias execution. See EXECUTION.

alias process. See PROCESS.

alias subpoena. See SUBPOENA.

alias summons. See SUMMONS.

alias writ. See WRIT.

alibi (**al**-ə-bi), *n.* [Latin "elsewhere"] (18c) **1.** A defense based on the physical impossibility of a defendant's guilt by placing the defendant in a location other than the scene of the crime at the relevant time. Fed. R. Crim. P. 12.1. **2.** The fact or state of having been elsewhere when an offense was committed.

alibi, *vb.* To offer or provide an alibi for <the conspirators alibied for each other>.

alibi witness. See WITNESS.

alien (**ay**-lee-ən *or* **ayl**-yən), *n.* (14c) A person who resides within the borders of a country but is not a citizen or subject of that country; a person not owing allegiance to a particular nation. • In the United States, an alien is a person who was born

outside the jurisdiction of the United States, who is subject to some foreign government, and who has not been naturalized under U.S. law.

   alien ami. See *alien friend.*

   alien amy. See *alien friend.*

   alien enemy. A citizen or subject of a country at war with the country in which the citizen or subject is living or traveling. — Also termed *enemy alien.*

   alien friend. An alien who is a citizen or subject of a friendly power. — Also termed (in Law French) *alien amy*; *alien ami.*

   alien immigrant. See IMMIGRANT.

   deportable alien. A alien who has entered the United States but is subject to removal.

   enemy alien. See *alien enemy.*

   excludable alien. A alien ineligible for admission or entry into the United States.

   illegal alien. (1901) An alien who enters a country at the wrong time or place, eludes an examination by officials, obtains entry by fraud, or enters into a sham marriage to evade immigration laws. — Also termed *undocumented alien.*

   inadmissible alien. A deportable or excludable alien. See 8 USCA § 1182(a).

   nonresident alien. (1801) A person who is neither a resident nor a citizen of the United States.

   resident alien. (18c) An alien who has a legally established domicile in the United States. See NATURALIZATION.

   undocumented alien. See *illegal alien.*

alien, *vb.* See ALIENATE.

alienable (**ay**-lee-ə-nə-bəl *or* **ayl**-yə-), *adj.* Capable of being transferred to the ownership of another; transferable <an alienable property interest>. — **alienability,** *n.*

alienage (**ay**-lee-ə-nij *or* **ayl**-yə-nij), *n.* The condition or status of being an alien.

   declaration of alienage. See DECLARATION (1).

alien ami. See *alien friend* under ALIEN.

alien amy. See *alien friend* under ALIEN.

Alien and Sedition Acts. *Hist.* Four statutes passed in 1798 designed to silence critics of the Federalist party by tightening residency requirements for citizenship, granting to the President the power to jail aliens considered dangerous to the country, and restricting freedoms of the press and speech by criminalizing speech hostile to the government. • All the acts had expired or been repealed by 1802.

alienate (**ay**-lee-ə-nayt *or* **ayl**-yə-), *vb.* (16c) To transfer or convey (property or a property right) to another. — Also termed *alien.* — **alienator,** *n.*

alienation (ay-lee-ə-**nay**-shən *or* ayl-yə-**nay**-shən), *n.* (14c) **1.** Withdrawal from former attachment; estrangement <alienation of affections>. **2.** Conveyance or transfer of property to another <alienation of one's estate>. — **alienative** (ay-lee-ə-nay-tiv *or* **ayl**-yə-), *adj.*

> **involuntary alienation.** Alienation against the wishes of the transferor, as by attachment. — Also termed *involuntary conveyance.*

alienation clause. (1877) **1.** A deed provision that either permits or prohibits the further conveyance of the property. **2.** *Insurance.* A clause in an insurance policy voiding coverage if the policyholder alienates the insured property.

alienation of affections. (1867) A tort claim for willful or malicious interference with a marriage by a third party without justification or excuse. ● Where the cause of action still exists, the elements are (1) some wrongful conduct by the defendant with the plaintiff's spouse, (2) the loss of affection or loss of consortium of the plaintiff's spouse, and (3) a causal relationship between the defendant's conduct and the loss of consortium. Only a few states allow this cause of action. But the doctrine thrives elsewhere. For example, a North Carolina court has upheld a $1 million award to an ex-wife who filed an alienation-of-affections action against her ex-husband's new wife. *Hutelmyer v. Cox*, 514 S.E.2d 554 (N.C. Ct. App. 1999). See CONSORTIUM; HEARTBALM STATUTE.

alienation office. See OFFICE.

alienative fact. See FACT.

alien corporation. See *foreign corporation* under CORPORATION.

alienee (ay-lee-ə-**nee** *or* ayl-yə-**nee**), *n.* (16c) One to whom property is transferred or conveyed. — Also termed *disponee.*

> **fraudulent alienee.** One who knowingly receives an asset by means of fraudulent alienation.

alien enemy. See ALIEN.

alien friend. See ALIEN.

alien immigrant. See IMMIGRANT.

alienism. The state, condition, or character of an alien.

alienist. (1864) *Archaic.* A psychiatrist, esp. one who assesses a criminal defendant's sanity or capacity to stand trial.

alienor (**ay**-lee-ə-nər *or* -nor), *n.* (16c) One who transfers or conveys property to another. — Also termed *disponor.*

Alien Tort Claims Act. A section in the Judiciary Act of 1789 giving federal courts jurisdiction to hear tort claims brought by foreigners who allege a violation of international law or a treaty to which the United States is a party. 28 USCA § 1350. ● The statute was largely dormant until the 1980s,

when it was invoked in several cases involving torture, disappearances, or killings committed by non-Americans in foreign countries. *See, e.g., Filartiga v. Pena-Irala*, 630 F.2d 876 (2d Cir. 1980). Later, alien plaintiffs began using the law to sue large corporations and the United States government or those acting at the government's direction. *See, e.g., Sosa v. Alvarez-Machain*, 542 U.S. 692, 124 S.Ct. 2739 (2004); *Bano v. Union Carbide Corp.*, 273 F.3d 120 (2d Cir. 2001). — Also termed *Alien Tort Statute.*

alimenta (al-ə-**men**-tə). [Latin] *Roman law.* Things necessary to sustain life, such as food and clothing.

alimentary-canal smuggling. See SMUGGLING.

alimony (**al**-ə-moh-nee). (17c) A court-ordered allowance that one spouse pays to the other spouse for maintenance and support while they are separated, while they are involved in a matrimonial lawsuit, or after they are divorced. ● Alimony is distinct from a property settlement. Alimony payments are taxable income to the receiving spouse and are deductible by the payor spouse; payments in settlement of property rights are not. The Supreme Court has held unconstitutional a statute that imposed alimony obligations on the husband only. *Orr v. Orr*, 440 U.S. 268, 99 S.Ct. 1102 (1979). — Also termed *spousal support; maintenance.* Cf. CHILD SUPPORT; DIVORCE AGREEMENT.

> ***alimony in gross.*** Alimony in the form of a single and definite sum not subject to modification. — Also termed *lump-sum alimony.*

> ***alimony pendente lite*** (pen-**den**-tee **lɪ**-tee). [Latin *pendente lite* "pending litigation"] See *temporary alimony.*

> ***final alimony.*** See *permanent alimony.*

> ***lump-sum alimony.*** See *alimony in gross.*

> ***periodic alimony.*** See *permanent alimony.*

> ***permanent alimony.*** Alimony payable in usu. weekly or monthly installments either indefinitely or until a time specified by court order. ● This kind of alimony may usu. be modified for changed circumstances of either party. It terminates upon the death of either spouse and usu. upon the remarriage of the obligee. — Also termed *final alimony; periodic alimony.*

> ***provisional alimony.*** See *temporary alimony.*

> ***rehabilitative alimony.*** Alimony found necessary to assist a divorced person in acquiring the education or training required to find employment outside the home or to reenter the labor force. ● It usu. has time limitations, such as a maximum of one or two years. — Also termed *short-term alimony; transitional alimony.*

> ***reimbursement alimony.*** Alimony designed to repay a spouse who during the marriage made

financial contributions that directly enhanced the future earning capacity of the other spouse. • An example is alimony for a wife who worked full-time supporting herself and her husband with separate-property earnings while he earned a medical degree.

temporary alimony. Interim alimony ordered by the court pending an action for divorce or separation in which one party has made a claim for permanent alimony. — Also termed *provisional alimony*; *alimony pendente lite*; *allowance pendente lite.*

transitional alimony. See *rehabilitative alimony.*

alimony trust. See TRUST.

aliquot (al-ə-kwot), *adj.* (16c) Contained in a larger whole an exact number of times; fractional <5 is an aliquot part of 30>.

aliquot-part rule. (1947) The principle that a person must intend to acquire a fractional part of the ownership of property before a court can declare a resulting trust in the person's favor.

ALI test. See SUBSTANTIAL-CAPACITY TEST.

aliunde (ay-lee-yən-dee), *adj.* [Latin] (17c) From another source; from elsewhere <evidence aliunde>. See *extrinsic evidence* under EVIDENCE.

aliunde rule. (1943) *Evidence.* The doctrine that a verdict may not be impeached by a juror's testimony unless a foundation for the testimony is first made by competent evidence from another source.

ALJ. *abbr.* ADMINISTRATIVE-LAW JUDGE.

all and singular. (16c) Collectively and individually.

all-claims rule. *Patents.* The now-abandoned doctrine that a patent is invalid unless every inventor named in the patent made an inventive contribution to every claim in the patent. • Section 116 of the Patent Act now expressly provides that inventors may apply for a patent jointly even though each did not make a contribution to the subject matter of every claim.

allegation, *n.* (15c) **1.** The act of declaring something to be true. **2.** Something declared or asserted as a matter of fact, esp. in a legal pleading; a party's formal statement of a factual matter as being true or provable, without its having yet been proved. — **allege,** *vb.*

defensive allegation. *Eccles. law.* A defendant's response in an ecclesiastical action; specif., a defendant's pleading of the facts relied upon that require the plaintiff's response under oath. Cf. *primary allegation* (2).

disjunctive allegation. (1814) A statement in a pleading or indictment that expresses something in the alternative, usu. with the conjunction "or" <a charge that the defendant murdered or caused to be murdered is a disjunctive allegation>.

material allegation. (18c) In a pleading, an assertion that is essential to the claim, charge, or defense <a material allegation in a battery case is harmful or offensive contact with a person>.

primary allegation. (1847) **1.** The principal charge made against an adversary in a legal proceeding. **2.** *Eccles. law.* The opening pleading in an action in ecclesiastical court. — Also termed *primary plea.* Cf. *defensive allegation.* **3.** *Eccles. law.* The entire statement of facts to be used in a contested suit.

allegation of faculties. *Family law. Archaic.* A statement detailing a husband's or wife's property, made by a spouse who seeks alimony. See FACULTIES.

allegation of use. See *amendment to allege use* under TRADEMARK APPLICATION AMENDMENT.

allegations-of-the-complaint rule. See EIGHT-CORNERS RULE.

alleged (ə-lejd), *adj.* (15c) **1.** Asserted to be true as described <alleged offenses>. **2.** Accused but not yet tried <alleged murderer>.

allegiance. 1. A citizen's or subject's obligation of fidelity and obedience to the government or sovereign in return for the benefits of the protection of the state. • Allegiance may be either an absolute and permanent obligation or a qualified and temporary one.

acquired allegiance. The allegiance owed by a naturalized citizen or subject.

actual allegiance. The obedience owed by one who resides temporarily in a foreign country to that country's government. • Foreign sovereigns, their representatives, and military personnel are typically excepted from this requirement. — Also termed *local allegiance.*

natural allegiance. The allegiance that native-born citizens or subjects owe to their nation.

permanent allegiance. The lasting allegiance owed to a state by its citizens or subjects.

temporary allegiance. The impermanent allegiance owed to a state by a resident alien during the period of residence.

2. *Hist.* A vassal's obligation to the liege lord. See LIEGE.

all-elements rule. *Patents.* The principle that under the doctrine of equivalents, there can be no patent infringement if even one element of a claim or its equivalent is not present in the accused device. • This rule acts to limit the doctrine of equivalents and prevent the doctrine's application to an entire claim, rather than the claim's constituent elements. — Also termed *all-limitations rule*; *rule* *against vitiation of a claim element.* Cf. ALL-STEPS RULE, INHERENCY DOCTRINE.

Allen charge. (1940) *Criminal procedure.* A supplemental jury instruction given by the court to encourage a deadlocked jury, after prolonged deliberations, to reach a verdict. *Allen v. United States,* 164 U.S. 492, 17 S.Ct. 154 (1896). — Also termed *dynamite charge; dynamite instruction; nitroglycerine charge; shotgun instruction; third-degree instruction.*

all-estate clause. See ALL-THE-ESTATE CLAUSE.

all-events test. (1954) *Tax.* A requirement that all events fixing an accrual-method taxpayer's right to receive income or incur expense must occur before the taxpayer can report an item of income or expense.

all faults, with. See AS IS.

all fours. See ON ALL FOURS.

all-holders rule. *Securities.* **1.** An SEC rule that prohibits a public offering by the issuer of shares to some, but not all, of the holders of a class of shares. **2.** An SEC rule requiring a tender offeror to make its offer to all the target company's shareholders.

alliance. 1. A bond or union between persons, families, states, or other parties. Cf. STRATEGIC ALLIANCE. **2.** *Int'l law.* A union or association of two or more states or nations, usu. formed by league or treaty, esp. for jointly waging war or mutually protecting against and repelling hostile attacks. • An example is the North Atlantic Treaty Organization (NATO). Cf. DÉTENTE; ENTENTE.

allied offense. See OFFENSE (1).

all-inclusive mortgage. See *wraparound mortgage* under MORTGAGE.

allision (ə-**lizh**-ən), *n. Maritime law.* The contact of a vessel with a stationary object such as an anchored vessel or a pier. • In modern practice, "collision" is often used where "allision" was once the preferred term. Cf. COLLISION. — **allide** (ə-**lɪd**), *vb.*

all-limitations rule. See ALL-ELEMENTS RULE.

allocable (**al**-ə-kə-bəl), *adj.* Capable of being allocated.

allocation, *n.* (16c) A designation or apportionment for a specific purpose; esp., the crediting of a receipt or the charging of a disbursement to an account <allocation of funds>. — **allocate,** *vb.* — **allocable,** *adj.* — **allocator,** *n.*

allocatur (al-ə-**kay**-tər). [Law Latin] It is allowed. • This word formerly indicated that a writ, bill, or other pleading was allowed. It is still used today in Pennsylvania to denote permission to appeal. — Also termed *allogatur.*

special allocatur. An allowance of a writ (such as a writ of error) that is legally required in certain cases.

allocute (**al**-ə-kyoot), *vb.* To deliver an allocution in court.

allocution (al-ə-**kyoo**-shən), *n. Criminal procedure.* **1.** A trial judge's formal address to a convicted defendant, asking him or her to speak in mitigation of the sentence to be imposed. • This address is required under Fed. R. Crim. P. 32(c)(3)(C). **2.** An unsworn statement from a convicted defendant to the sentencing judge or jury in which the defendant can ask for mercy, explain his or her conduct, apologize for the crime, or say anything else in an effort to lessen the impending sentence. • This statement is not subject to cross-examination.

victim allocution. A crime victim's address to the court before sentencing, usu. urging a harsher punishment.

allocutory (ə-**lok**-yə-tor-ee), *adj.* Of or relating to an allocution <allocutory pleas for mercy>.

allod (**al**-əd), *n. Hist.* The domain of a household.

allodial (ə-**loh**-dee-əl), *adj.* (17c) Held in absolute ownership; pertaining to an allodium. — Also spelled *alodial.* Cf. FEUDAL. — **allodially,** *adv.*

allodium (ə-**loh**-dee-əm), *n.* (17c) An estate held in fee simple absolute. — Also spelled *alodium.* — Also termed *alod; alode.*

allogatur. See ALLOCATUR.

allograph (**al**-ə-graf). (1954) An agent's writing or signature for the principal. • This is the antonym of *autograph.*

allonge (a-**lawnzh**). (1859) A slip of paper sometimes attached to a negotiable instrument for the purpose of receiving further indorsements when the original paper is filled with indorsements. • Former UCC § 3-202 required that indorsements be made on the instrument unless there was no space — and only then could an allonge be used. Current 3-3-204(a) eliminates that requirement and provides that "a paper affixed to the instrument is part of the instrument." The UCC comment makes it clear that the allonge is valid even if space is available on the instrument.

all-or-none offering. See OFFERING.

all-or-none order. See ORDER (8).

all-or-nothing rule. (1954) A gloss on the rule against perpetuities holding that a class gift is invalid in its entirety if it is invalid in part. • The effect is to invalidate a class member's interest even if it vests within the period of the rule because it may be subject to partial divestment by the remote interest of another class member.

allotment, *n.* (16c) **1.** A share or portion of something, such as property previously held in common or shares in a corporation, or time assigned to speakers or sides in a deliberative assembly. **2.** In American Indian law, the selection of specific land awarded to an individual allottee from a common holding. — **allot,** *vb.*

allotment certificate. *Securities.* A document that records the essential elements of a subscription of shares, such as how many shares are to be purchased, the price to be paid, and the payment and delivery schedule.

allottee. One to whom an allotment is made; a recipient of an allotment.

allowable state. *Patents.* Of a patent claim, the condition of containing patentable subject matter in an acceptable form.

allowance. (14c) **1.** A share or portion, esp. of money that is assigned or granted.

allowance pendente lite. See *temporary alimony* under ALIMONY.

backhaul allowance. A price discount given to customers who get their goods from a seller's warehouse as a reflection of the seller's freight-cost savings.

family allowance. (1869) A portion of a decedent's estate set aside by statute for a surviving spouse, children, or parents, regardless of any testamentary disposition or competing claims. ● Every state has a statute authorizing the probate court to award an amount for the temporary maintenance and support of the surviving spouse (and often for dependent children). The allowance may be limited for a fixed period (18 months under the Uniform Probate Code) or may continue until all contests are resolved and a decree of distribution is entered. This support, together with probate homesteads and personal-property allowances, is in addition to whatever interests pass by the will or by intestate succession. See *probate homestead* under HOMESTEAD. Cf. *spousal allowance.*

gratuitous allowance. A pension voluntarily granted by a public entity. ● The gratuitous (rather than contractual) nature of this type of allowance gives the pensioner no vested rights in the allowance.

spousal allowance. (1985) A portion of a decedent's estate set aside by statute for a surviving spouse, regardless of any testamentary disposition or competing claims. ● This allowance is superior to the claims of general creditors. In some states, it is even preferred to the expenses of administration, funeral, and last illness of the spouse. — Also termed *widow's allowance; widower's allowance.* See *probate homestead* under HOMESTEAD. Cf. *family allowance.*

widower's allowance. See *spousal allowance.*

widow's allowance. See *spousal allowance.*

2. The sum awarded by a court to a fiduciary as payment for services. **3.** A deduction.

depletion allowance. A tax deduction for the owners of oil, gas, mineral, or timber resources corresponding to the reduced value of the property resulting from the removal of the resource.

4. *Archaic.* A special sum that a court awards to the prevailing party in addition to the usual costs of court, esp. in a difficult case. — Also termed *extra allowance; special allowance.* **5.** *Patents.* The U.S. Patent and Trademark Office's decision to issue a patent to an applicant; specif., the patent examiner's approval of at least one of an application's claims. ● Once a Notice of Allowance is sent, the inventor must pay an issue fee before the PTO issues the patent. **6.** *Trademarks.* The U.S. Patent and Trademark Office's decision to approve a trademark for which the application was made under § 1(b) of the Lanham Act. ● If a trademark application made under § 1(b) is approved by the PTO, the Office publishes the mark and — unless it is successfully opposed — issues a certificate of registration and publishes notice of the registration in the Official Gazette.

allowed application. See PATENT APPLICATION.

allow the appeal. See REVERSE.

all-purpose public figure. See PUBLIC FIGURE.

all rights reserved. *Copyright.* A phrase required as part of a valid copyright notice under the Buenos Aires Convention. ● Because other international copyright treaties do not require the phrase, and all signatories to the Buenos Aires Convention are parties to other treaties, the phrase is now surplusage.

all-risk insurance. See INSURANCE.

all-steps rule. *Patents.* The doctrine that in order for a method or process claim to be literally infringed by an accused process, the accused process must have every step and limitation—or an equivalent—of the infringed claim. Cf. ALL-ELEMENTS RULE.

all substantial rights. *Patents.* Every right in a patent (whether or not held by the grantor) that is of value when the patent rights or an undivided interest in a patent is transferred. ● A transfer is not a transfer of all substantial rights to a patent if: (1) it is territorially restricted; (2) its term is less than the patent term; (3) it contains field-of-use limitations; or (4) it does not convey rights to all claims in the patent.

allurement. (1873) *Torts.* An attractive object that tempts a trespassing child to meddle when the child ought to abstain. See ATTRACTIVE-NUISANCE DOCTRINE. Cf. *attractive nuisance* under NUISANCE.

alluvial mining. (1894) The practice of removing sand and gravel from a riverbed.

alluvion (ə-**loo**-vee-ən). [fr. Latin *alluvio* "flood"] (16c) *Roman & civil law.* **1.** Strictly, the flow or wash of water against a shore or riverbank. **2.** An accumulation of soil, clay, or other material deposited by water; esp., in land law, an addition of land caused by the buildup of deposits from running water, the added land then belonging to the owner of the property to which it is added. — Also termed *alluvium.* **3.** *Louisiana law.* An accumulation of soil, clay, or other material deposited on the bank of a river. • In Louisiana, lands formed on a seashore or the bank of a navigable lake are not alluvion. They belong to the state rather than the riparian owners. Cf. ACCRETION (1); AVULSION (2); DELICTION; EROSION. — **alluvial,** *adj.* — **alluviate,** *vb.* — **alluviation,** *n.*

alluvium. See ALLUVION (2).

All Writs Act. A federal statute that gives the U.S. Supreme Court and all courts established by Congress the power to issue writs in aid of their jurisdiction and in conformity with the usages and principles of law. 28 USCA § 1651(a).

ally. *Int'l law.* **1.** A nation tied to another by treaty or alliance. **2.** A citizen or subject of an allied nation.

almoign (al-**moyn**). [Law French "alms"] **1.** Alms; a church treasury; an ecclesiastical possession. **2.** FRANKALMOIN.

almoin. See FRANKALMOIN.

almoner (al-mə-nər). A person charged with distributing the alms of a monarch, religious house, or other institution. • This office was first instituted in religious houses and although formerly one of importance is now almost a sinecure.

alms (ahmz *or* ahlmz). Charitable donations; any type of relief bestowed on the poor.

almshouse. *Archaic.* A dwelling for the publicly or privately supported poor of a city or county.

alod. See ALLODIUM.

alode. See ALLODIUM.

alodium. See ALLODIUM.

alpha subclass. *Patents.* In U.S. patent law, a patent classification that has an alphabetic suffix.

alpha testing. *Intellectual property.* The first phase of operational experimenting with a software program before the program's production release, usu. at the developer's site. • Often, alpha testing involves only modular or component testing and not system testing. Alpha testing is usu. followed by beta testing, in which the entire system is tested at a customer's site before the product is released to the general public. Cf. BETA TESTING.

ALTA. *abbr.* American Land Title Association.

altarage (**awl**-tər-ij). *Eccles. law.* **1.** The offerings made upon an altar or to a church. **2.** An endowment or honorarium received by a priest for services performed at the altar.

alteration. 1. *Property.* A substantial change to real estate, esp. to a structure, usu. not involving an addition to or removal of the exterior dimensions of a building's structural parts. • Although any addition to or improvement of real estate is by its very nature an alteration, real-estate lawyers habitually use *alteration* in reference to a lesser change. Still, to constitute an alteration, the change must be substantial — not simply a trifling modification.

    structural alteration. (1905) A significant change to a building or other structure, essentially creating a different building or structure.

2. An act done to an instrument, after its execution, whereby its meaning or language is changed; esp., the changing of a term in a negotiable instrument without the consent of all parties to it. • Material alterations void an instrument, but immaterial ones do not. An alteration is material if it (1) changes the burden of a party (as by changing the date, time, place, amount, or rate of interest), (2) changes the liabilities or duties of any party (as by adding or removing the name of a maker, drawer, indorser, payee, or cosurety), or (3) changes the operation of the instrument or its effect in evidence (as by adding words or negotiability, changing the form of an indorsement, or changing the liability from joint to several).

    material alteration. (17c) **1.** A significant change in something; esp., a change in a legal instrument sufficient to alter the instrument's legal meaning or effect. **2.** An unauthorized change in an instrument or an addition to an incomplete instrument resulting in the modification of a party's obligations. UCC § 3-407.

altercation. A vehement dispute; a noisy argument.

alter ego. (1879) A corporation used by an individual in conducting personal business, the result being that a court may impose liability on the individual by piercing the corporate veil when fraud has been perpetrated on someone dealing with the corporation. See PIERCING THE CORPORATE VEIL.

alter-ego rule. (1939) **1.** *Corporations.* The doctrine that shareholders will be treated as the owners of a corporation's property, or as the real parties in interest, whenever it is necessary to do so to prevent fraud or to do justice. **2.** *Criminal law.* The principle that one who defends another against attack stands in the position of that other person and can use only the amount of force that the other person could use under the circumstances.

altering or amending a judgment. A trial court's act of correcting a substantive mistake in a judgment, as by correcting a manifest error of law or fact. Fed. R. Civ. P. 59(e).

alternat (**awl**-tər-nit *or* al-ter-**nah**). [French] The rotation in precedence among states, diplomats, etc., esp. in the signing of treaties. • This practice gives each diplomat a copy of the treaty with the diplomat's signature appearing first.

alternate. *Parliamentary law.* A proxy for a delegate, usu. chosen in the same manner as the delegate rather than chosen by the delegate. See DELEGATE (2); PROXY (1).

alternate legacy. See LEGACY.

alternate valuation date. *Tax.* The date six months after a decedent's death. • Generally, the estate can elect to appraise the decedent's property either as of the date of the decedent's death or as of the alternate valuation date. See BASIS.

Alternative Agricultural Research and Commercialization Corporation. A federally chartered corporation in the U.S. Department of Agriculture responsible for funding the development and marketing of new nonfood products made from farm and forestry materials. — Abbr. AARCC.

alternative constituency. See NONSHAREHOLDER CONSTITUENCY.

alternative contract. See CONTRACT.

alternative devise. See DEVISE.

alternative dispute resolution. (1978) A procedure for settling a dispute by means other than litigation, such as arbitration or mediation. — Abbr. ADR. — Also termed *dispute resolution.* See ARBITRATION; MEDIATION.

alternative expression. *Patents.* In a patent claim, a recitation of two or more elements or limitations that perform the same function <iron, steel, or other magnetic material>. • Although once contrary to U.S. Patent and Trademark Office policy, alternative expressions are now permitted if they present no uncertainty or ambiguity about the scope or clarity of the claims. — Also termed *alternative language.*

alternative judgment. See JUDGMENT.

alternative liability. See LIABILITY.

alternative mandamus. See MANDAMUS.

alternative-means doctrine. (1968) *Criminal law.* The principle that when a crime may be committed in more than one way, the jury must be unanimous on the defendant's guilt but need not be unanimous on the possible different methods of committing the crime, as long as each possible method is supported by substantial evidence.

alternative-methods-of-performance contract. See *alternative contract* under CONTRACT.

alternative minimum tax. See TAX.

alternativeness rejection. See REJECTION.

alternative obligation. See OBLIGATION.

alternative order. 1. See ORDER (2). **2.** See ORDER (8).

alternative pleading. See PLEADING (2).

alternative promise. See PROMISE.

alternative relief. See RELIEF.

alternative remainder. See REMAINDER.

alternative sentence. See SENTENCE.

alternative writ. See WRIT.

always-speaking statute. See *speaking statute* under STATUTE.

ALWD (**ahl**-wəd *or* **al**-wəd). *abbr.* See ASSOCIATION OF LEGAL WRITING DIRECTORS.

ALWD Citation Manual. A guide to American legal citation written and edited by legal-writing professionals affiliated with the Association of Legal Writing Directors. • First published in 2000 as an alternative to the *Bluebook,* it contains one citation system for all legal documents and does not distinguish between citations in law-journal footnotes and those in other writings. The full name is the *ALWD Citation Manual: A Professional System of Citation.* — Often shortened to *ALWD Manual.* Cf. BLUEBOOK.

a.m. *abbr.* ANTE MERIDIEM.

AMA. *abbr.* (1911) **1.** American Medical Association. **2.** Against medical advice.

amalgamation (ə-mal-gə-**may**-shən), *n.* (17c) The act of combining or uniting; consolidation <amalgamation of two small companies to form a new corporation>. See MERGER (1). — **amalgamate,** *vb.* — **amalgamator,** *n.*

Amalphitan Code (ə-**mal**-fə-tən). *Hist.* A compilation of maritime law made late in the 11th century at the port of Amalfi near Naples. • The Code was regarded as a primary source of maritime law throughout the Mediterranean to the end of the 16th century. — Also termed *Amalphitan Table; Laws of Amalfi; Tablets of Amalfi.*

amanuensis (ə-man-yoo-**en**-sis), *n.* [fr. Latin *ab-* "from" + *manus* "hand"] **1.** One who takes dictation; a scribe or secretary. **2.** An assistant, esp. one with scribal responsibilities. **3.** A protégé. See PROTÉGÉ (1).

ambassador. 1. A diplomatic officer of the highest rank, usu. designated by a government as its resident representative in a foreign state. • Ambassadors represent the sovereign as well as the nation and enjoy many privileges while abroad in their official capacity, including immunity. Ambassadors are distinguished from ministers and envoys, who represent only the state where they are from and not the sovereign. Ambassadors are also generally distinguished from certain legates who have only ecclesiastical authority. But the papal nuncio and some legates, such as the *legate a latere*, bear the rank of ambassador. See NUNCIO; LEGATE. **2.** A representative appointed by another. **3.** An unofficial or nonappointed representative. — Also spelled (archaically) *embassador*. — **ambassadorial,** *adj.* — **ambassadorship,** *n.*

ambassador extraordinary. An ambassador who is employed for a particular purpose or occasion and has limited discretionary powers. Cf. *ambassador plenipotentiary.*

ambassador leger. See *resident ambassador.*

ambassador ordinary. See *resident ambassador.*

ambassador plenipotentiary. An ambassador who has unlimited discretionary powers to act as a sovereign's or government's deputy, esp. to carry out a particular task, such as treaty negotiations. — Also termed *minister plenipotentiary; envoy plenipotentiary.* Cf. *ambassador extraordinary.*

ordinary ambassador. See *resident ambassador.*

resident ambassador. An ambassador who resides in a foreign country as the permanent representative of a sovereign or nation. • A resident ambassador has the right to request a personal interview with the host nation's head of state. — Also termed *ambassador leger; ordinary ambassador; ambassador ordinary.*

AMBER. *abbr.* See AMBER ALERT.

Amber Alert. A system by which the police can rapidly broadcast to the general public a report of a missing or endangered child by means of radio and television announcements. • The alert is named for Amber Hagerman of Texas, a nine-year-old who was abducted and murdered in 1996 by an unknown person. The system has been adopted by many communities in the U.S. and Canada. Local variations exist. In Arkansas, for example, the system is called the Morgan Nick Alert after a child who was abducted by a stranger in 1995. When the first word is in all capital letters, AMBER is an acronym meaning America's Missing: Broadcast Emergency Response. — Also termed *Amber Plan.* See AMBER'S LAW. Cf. CODE ADAM.

Amber Hagerman Act. See AMBER'S LAW.

Amber's law. A federal law that requires, among other things, life in prison without parole for two-time sex offenders whose victims are children, and reports to Congress about judges whose sentences fall below federal guidelines. • The law was named for Amber Hagerman of Texas, a nine-year-old girl who was abducted and murdered by an unknown person in 1996. — Also termed *Amber Hagerman Act.* See AMBER ALERT.

A.M. Best Company. An investment-analysis and -advisory service. • A.M. Best rates the financial strength of businesses from A++ (strongest) to A+, A, A–, B++, and so on to C– and D. A grade of E means that the company is under state supervision, and an F indicates that the company is in liquidation.

ambidexter. 1. A judge or embracer who takes bribes from both sides in a dispute. **2.** A lawyer who abandons the party that he or she initially represented in a dispute to represent the opposing party in the same suit. **3.** A person who engages in double-dealing.

ambiguitas latens (am-bi-**gyoo**-ə-tas **lay**-tenz). See *latent ambiguity* under AMBIGUITY.

ambiguitas patens (am-bi-**gyoo**-ə-tas **pay**-tenz). See *patent ambiguity* under AMBIGUITY.

ambiguity (am-bi-**gyoo**-ə-tee), *n.* (15c) An uncertainty of meaning or intention, as in a contractual term or statutory provision. Cf. MEANING. — **ambiguous** (am-**big**-yoo-əs), *adj.*

ambiguity on the factum. An ambiguity relating to the foundation of an instrument, such as a question relating to whether a testator intended for a particular clause to be part of an agreement, whether a codicil was intended to republish a former will, or whether the residuary clause was accidentally omitted.

calculated ambiguity. A purposeful use of unclear language, usu. when two negotiating parties cannot agree on clear, precise language and therefore leave a decision-maker to sort out the meaning in case of a dispute. • Strictly speaking, this is a misnomer: the more precise term is vagueness, not ambiguity. See VAGUENESS (1).

extrinsic ambiguity. See *latent ambiguity.*

intrinsic ambiguity. See *patent ambiguity.*

latent ambiguity. (18c) An ambiguity that does not readily appear in the language of a document, but instead arises from a collateral matter when the document's terms are applied or executed <the contract contained a latent ambiguity: the shipping terms stated that the goods would arrive on the *Peerless*, but two ships have that name>. — Also termed *extrinsic ambiguity; equivocation; ambiguitas latens.*

patent ambiguity (**pay**-tənt). (18c) An ambiguity that clearly appears on the face of a document, arising from the language itself <the nonperformance was excused because the two different prices expressed in the contract created a patent ambiguity>. — Also termed *intrinsic ambiguity; ambiguitas patens.*

ambiguity doctrine. See CONTRA PROFERENTEM.

ambit (**am**-bit). (14c) **1.** A boundary line or limit; esp., the scope of a statute or regulation, or the sphere of influence and authority of an agency, committee, department, or the like. **2.** A space surrounding a house or town.

ambulance chaser. 1. A lawyer who approaches victims of accidents in hopes of persuading them to hire the lawyer and sue for damages. **2.** A lawyer's agent who engages in this activity. **3.** *Tendentious slang.* An attorney. — **ambulance-chasing,** *n.*

ambulance-chasing. A blatant form of solicitation in which the lawyer (either personally or through an agent) urges injured people to employ the lawyer to represent them.

ambulatory (am-byə-lə-tor-ee), *adj.* (16c) **1.** Able to walk <the accident victim is still ambulatory>. **2.** Capable of being altered or revised; not yet legally fixed <a will is ambulatory because it is revocable until the testator's death>.

ambulatory automatism. See AUTOMATISM.

ambulatory disposition. See DISPOSITION (2).

ambulatory will. See WILL.

ameliorate (ə-**meel**-yə-rayt), *vb.* (18c) **1.** To make better <the charity tries to ameliorate the conditions of the homeless>. **2.** To become better <with time, the situation ameliorated>.

ameliorating waste. See WASTE (1).

amelioration, *n.* **1.** The act of improving something; the state of being made better. **2.** An improvement. — **ameliorative,** *adj.*

ameliorative waste. See *ameliorating waste* under WASTE (1).

amenable (ə-**mee**-nə-bəl *or* -**men**-), *adj.* (16c) Legally answerable; liable to being brought to judgment <amenable to process>. — **amenability,** *n.*

amend, *vb.* (13c) **1.** To make right; to correct or rectify <amend the order to fix a clerical error>. **2.** To change the wording of; specif., to formally alter (a statute, constitution, motion, etc.) by striking out, inserting, or substituting words <amend the legislative bill>. See AMENDMENT (3). — **amendable,** *adj.* — **amendability,** *n.*

amend a previous action. See *amend something previously adopted.*

amend something previously adopted. *Parliamentary law.* (Of a deliberative assembly) to change an otherwise final text. — Also termed *amend a previous action.*

amendatory (ə-**men**-də-tor-ee), *adj.* Designed or serving to amend; corrective <an amendatory rider to an insurance policy>.

amended complaint. See COMPLAINT.

amended pleading. See PLEADING (1).

amended return. See TAX RETURN.

amender, *n.* One who amends (a document, etc.).

amendment. (17c) **1.** A formal revision or addition proposed or made to a statute, constitution, pleading, order, or other instrument; specif., a change made by addition, deletion, or correction; esp., an alteration in wording. **2.** The process of making such a revision.

amendment as of course. An amendment, usu. to pleadings, that a party has a statutory right to apply for without the court's permission.

amendment on court's own motion. A change to a pleading or other document by the judge without a motion from a party.

nunc pro tunc amendment (**nəngk** proh **təngk** *or* **nuungk** proh **tuungk**). An amendment that is given retroactive effect, usu. by court order.

3. *Parliamentary law.* A motion that changes another motion's wording by striking out text, inserting or adding text, or substituting text. See AMEND (2). Cf. BLANK (2).

amendment by adding. An amendment that places new wording at the end of a motion or of a paragraph or other readily divisible part within a motion. ● Some authorities treat amendment by adding as a form of amendment by inserting. Cf. *amendment by inserting.*

amendment by inserting. An amendment that places new wording within or around a motion's current wording. ● Some authorities distinguish amendment by adding, which places new wording after the current wording, from amendment by inserting. Cf. *amendment by adding.*

amendment by striking out. An amendment that removes wording from a motion's current wording.

amendment by striking out and inserting. An amendment that removes wording and replaces it with alternative wording. ● The motion can properly apply only to inserting wording in place of the wording being struck out; it cannot strike out some wording and insert new wording in a different place. See *amendment by substituting;* CREATE A BLANK.

amendment by substituting. **1.** A special type of amendment by striking out and inserting that replaces an entire main motion or a paragraph or other readily divisible part within a main motion; an amendment of greater scope than a perfecting amendment. Cf. *perfecting amendment.* **2.** An amendment by striking out and inserting. See *amendment by striking out and inserting.* — Also termed *amendment in the nature of a substitute* (in sense 1); *substitute; substitution; substitute amendment.* ● Parliamentary writers differ on when an amendment by striking out and inserting qualifies as an amendment by substituting. Some manuals treat the two as equivalent and apply the same rules to them.

Others maintain that an amendment is not a substitute unless it replaces the entire main motion — or at least a readily divisible part within the main motion — and apply different rules to an amendment by substituting than to a less drastic amendment.

amendment in the nature of a substitute. See *amendment by substituting* (1).

amendment of the first degree. See *primary amendment.*

amendment of the first rank. See *primary amendment.*

amendment of the second degree. See *secondary amendment.*

amendment of the second rank. See *secondary amendment.*

amendment to the amendment. See *secondary amendment.*

amendment to the main question. See *primary amendment.*

amendment to the text. See *primary amendment.*

committee amendment. An amendment to a motion reported by a committee to which the motion was referred.

first-degree amendment. See *primary amendment.*

floor amendment. An amendment offered from the floor by an individual member, as distinguished from a committee amendment. Cf. *committee amendment.*

friendly amendment. An amendment that the mover of the motion being amended supports, and to which no other member objects.

hostile amendment. An amendment that is opposed by the supporters of the main motion.

killer amendment. An amendment that has the effect, intended or not, of ensuring the defeat of the main motion.

nongermane amendment. An amendment that adds an unrelated rider. • A nongermane amendment is out of order in most ordinary assemblies and many legislative bodies. But some legislative bodies, in jurisdictions where legislation may embrace more than one subject, allow nongermane amendments to a bill. See RIDER.

perfecting amendment. An amendment that merely edits the form of a main motion or a primary amendment but does not substantially change its content; an amendment of lesser scope than an amendment by substituting. Cf. *amendment by substituting* (1).

primary amendment. An amendment that directly amends the main motion. Cf. *secondary amendment.*

pro forma amendment. An amendment moved solely for the purpose of obtaining the floor and treated as withdrawn once the mover has spoken. • The customary pro forma amendment in Congress is a motion "to strike the last word."

secondary amendment. An amendment that alters a pending primary amendment. Cf. *primary amendment.*

second-degree amendment. See *secondary amendment.*

substitute amendment. **1.** A secondary amendment that substantially replaces rather than edits a primary amendment. **2.** See *amendment by substituting.*

amendment after allowance. See PATENT-APPLICATION AMENDMENT.

amendment after appeal. See PATENT-APPLICATION AMENDMENT.

amendment after final action. See PATENT-APPLICATION AMENDMENT.

amendment after payment of issue fee. See PATENT-APPLICATION AMENDMENT.

amendment before first action. See *preliminary amendment* under PATENT-APPLICATION AMENDMENT.

amendment by implication. A rule of construction that allows a person to interpret a repugnant provision in a statute as an implicit modification or abrogation of a provision that appears before it. • Amendments by implication are not favored. *See United States v. Welden*, 377 U.S. 95, 102 n.12, 84 S.Ct. 1082, 1087 n.12 (1964).

amendment in excess of filing fee. See PATENT-APPLICATION AMENDMENT.

amendment of indictment. (1828) The alteration of the charging terms of an indictment, either literally or in effect, after the grand jury has made a decision on it. • The indictment usu. cannot be amended at trial in a way that would prejudice the defendant by having a trial on matters that were not contained in the indictment. To do so would violate the defendant's Fifth Amendment right to indictment by grand jury.

constructive amendment of indictment. The admission of evidence that modifies the indictment by modifying the elements of a charged offense or by establishing an offense different from or in addition to those in the indictment.

amendment of registration. See TRADEMARK-APPLICATION AMENDMENT.

amendment on court's own motion. See AMENDMENT (2).

amendment to allege use. See TRADEMARK-APPLICATION AMENDMENT.

amendment to different register. See TRADEMARK-APPLICATION AMENDMENT.

amends, *n.* Compensation given for a loss or injury; reparation.

amenity. [fr. Latin *amoenitas* "pleasantness"] Something tangible or intangible that increases the enjoyment of real property, such as location, view, landscaping, security, or access to recreational facilities.

a mensa et thoro (ay **men**-sə et **thor**-oh). [Latin "from board and hearth"] (17c) (Of a divorce decree) effecting a separation of the parties rather than a dissolution of the marriage <a separation *a mensa et thoro* was the usual way for a couple to separate under English law up until 1857>. • Not all states provide for such a proceeding. See *divorce a mensa et thoro* under DIVORCE; SEPARATION; A VINCULO MATRIMONII.

amerce (ə-**mərs**), *vb.* **1.** To impose a fine or penalty that is not fixed but is left to the court's discretion; to punish by amercement. **2.** To fine or punish in any manner. — **amerceable** (ə- **mər**-sə-bəl), **amerciable** (ə-**mər**-see-ə-bəl), *adj.*

amercement (ə-**mərs**-mənt), *n.* [fr. Law French *estre à merci* "to be at the mercy (of another)," fr. Latin *merces* "payment"] (14c) **1.** The imposition of a discretionary fine or penalty by a court, esp. on an official for misconduct <an amercement proceeding>. **2.** The fine or penalty so imposed <an amercement charged to the sheriff for failing to return the writ of execution>. — Also termed *cashlite*; (archaically) *amerciament*; *merciament*.

American Academy of Actuaries. A national organization of actuaries whose members must meet specified educational requirements and have at least three years of actuarial work experience. • Created in 1965, the Academy promotes public awareness of the actuarial profession, represents the profession before federal and state governments, and sponsors continuing-education conferences. — Abbr. AAA. See ACTUARY.

American Accounting Association. An organization of accounting practitioners, educators, and students, founded in 1916 to promote accounting as an academic discipline by sponsoring research projects and continuing-education seminars. — Abbr. AAA.

American Arbitration Association. A national organization that maintains a panel of arbitrators to hear labor and commercial disputes. — Abbr. AAA.

American Bankers Association. A voluntary trade association of banking institutions, including banks, trust companies, and savings banks and associations, whose members represent the vast majority of banking deposits in the United States.

• The association was founded in 1875. — Abbr. ABA.

American Bar Association. A voluntary national organization of lawyers organized in 1878. • Among other things, it participates in law reform, law-school accreditation, and continuing legal education in an effort to improve legal services and the administration of justice. — Abbr. ABA.

American Bar Foundation. An outgrowth of the American Bar Association involved with sponsoring and funding projects in law-related research, education, and social studies. — Abbr. ABF.

American Bureau of Shipping. An organization of marine underwriters, shipbuilders, and marine carriers charged with conducting research, technological development, officer training, and standards of building, maintaining, and operating seagoing vessels and stationary offshore facilities. • The organization was founded in 1862 as the American Shipbuilders' Association. Its name was changed in 1898, and it was formally recognized in the Merchant Marine Act of 1920. Its core mission is to promulgate rules for evaluating the design of new vessels and structures and for maintaining all existing vessels and structures. — Abbr. ABS. See ABS RULES.

American Civil Liberties Union. A national organization whose primary purpose is to help enforce and preserve individual rights and liberties guaranteed by federal and state constitutions. — Abbr. ACLU.

American clause. *Marine insurance.* A policy provision that prevents an insurer from claiming contribution from a policy later purchased by the insured.

American common law. See COMMON LAW (2).

American depositary receipt. A negotiable instrument issued by an American bank as a substitute for stock shares in a foreign-based corporation. • ADRs are the most common method by which foreign companies secure American shareholders. Companies that offer ADRs maintain a stock listing in their domestic market in their domestic currency, while the ADRs are held in U.S. dollars and listed on a U.S. stock exchange, usu. the New York Stock Exchange. The holder of the receipt is entitled to receive the specified securities upon presentation of the ADR to the depositary institution — Abbr. ADR. — Also termed *American depository receipt*. Cf. AMERICAN DEPOSITARY SHARE.

American depositary share. A foreign security that is exempt from reporting requirements and deposited in an American bank to be held for private sale. • American depositary receipts are used to transfer the securities. — Abbr. ADS. Cf. AMERICAN DEPOSITARY RECEIPT.

American depository receipt. See AMERICAN DEPOSITARY RECEIPT.

American Experience Table of Mortality. *Insurance.* A chart developed by insurers in the 1860s to predict mortality rates and thereby more accurately set insurance rates. • The Table was widely used by insurers to establish rates until the 1950s.

American Federation of Labor and Congress of Industrial Organizations. A voluntary affiliation of more than 100 labor unions that operate autonomously yet benefit from the affiliation's political activities and its establishment of broad policies for the national labor movement. — Abbr. AFL-CIO.

American Federation of Musicians. A labor union composed of musicians, orchestra leaders, contractors, copyists, orchestrators, composers, and arrangers. • In the recording industry, artists hired by record companies that have agreements with the union must be paid according to the union's set scale. — Abbr. AF of M.

American Federation of Television and Radio Artists. A labor union composed of actors, announcers, narrators, and vocalists. • In the entertainment industry, performers hired by producers that have agreements with the union must be paid according to the union's set scale. It is affiliated with the AFL-CIO. — Abbr. AFTRA.

American Forces Information Service. An agency in the U.S. Department of Defense responsible for operating the Armed Forces Radio and Television Service, the Armed Forces Press and Publications Service, and a Broadcast Center. • Established in 1977, the Service publishes various periodicals and pamphlets and the *Stars and Stripes* newspapers. — Abbr. AFIS.

American Guild of Variety Artists. A labor union composed of performers in nightclubs, cabarets, theaters, and other areas of live entertainment. • The Guild regulates its members' contracts with agents through an agreement with the Artists' Representatives Association. — Abbr. AGVA.

American Indian law. See NATIVE AMERICAN LAW.

American Inns of Court Foundation. See INN OF COURT (2).

American Institute of Parliamentarians. A national nonprofit educational organization founded in 1958 to improve and promote the rules of parliamentary procedure as a way of implementing sound democratic principles. — Abbr. AIP.

American Intellectual Property Law Association. A national bar association of lawyers who practice patent, trademark, copyright, trade-secret, and unfair-competition law. • The association was formerly known as the American Patent Law Association. Membership is also open to law students who are interested in intellectual-property law. — Abbr. AIPLA.

American Inventors Protection Act. *Patents.* A 1999 statute designed to (1) curb deceptive practices by invention-promotion companies, (2) reduce patent fees, (3) provide a defense against infringement for a party who in good faith reduced a patented invention to practice at least one year before a patent's effective filing date, (4) extend the patent term when the PTO is responsible for a delay in issuance, and (5) require publication of a patent application 18 months after its filing unless the applicant requests otherwise. Pub. L. No. 106-113, 113 Stat. 1537-544. — Abbr. AIPA.

American Judicature Society. An organization made up of judges, lawyers, and lay people for the purpose of improving the administration of justice. • The AJS was founded in 1913. Its interests include ensuring the judiciary's independence, improving judicial selection and the performance of juries, and educating the public about the justice system. — Abbr. AJS.

American Law Institute. An organization of lawyers, judges, and legal scholars who promote consistency and simplification of American law by publishing the Restatements of the Law, and other model codes and treatises, as well as promoting continuing legal education. — Abbr. ALI.

American Law Institute test. See SUBSTANTIAL-CAPACITY TEST.

American Lloyd's. See LLOYD'S UNDERWRITERS.

American National Standards Institute. A private nonprofit organization, founded in 1918, that administers the U.S. standardization- and conformity-assessment system and coordinates voluntary participants in the system. — Abbr. ANSI.

American option. See OPTION.

American Patent Law Association. See AMERICAN INTELLECTUAL PROPERTY LAW ASSOCIATION.

American Printing House for the Blind. A federally-aided institution that assists blind children by distributing Braille books, talking books, and educational aids without charge. • The printing house was incorporated in Kentucky in 1858. — Abbr. APH.

American rule. (1868) **1.** The general policy that all litigants, even the prevailing one, must bear their own attorney's fees. • The rule is subject to bad-faith and other statutory and contractual exceptions. Cf. ENGLISH RULE. **2.** The doctrine that a witness cannot be questioned on cross-examination about any fact or circumstance not connected with the matters brought out in the direct examination.

American share. See SHARE (2).

American Society of Composers, Authors & Publishers. *Copyright.* One of the U.S. performing-rights societies that licenses and polices the public performance of nondramatic musical works on behalf of the copyright owners. — Abbr. ASCAP.

American Society of Writers on Legal Subjects. The formal name for Scribes, an association of lawyers dedicated to the improvement of legal writing. ● Founded in 1953, it sponsors annual writing competitions and publishes *The Scribes Journal of Legal Writing*, the first journal devoted exclusively to legal writing.

American Stock Exchange. An organized stock exchange and self-regulating organization under the Securities Exchange Act of 1934, located in New York City and engaged in national trading of corporate stocks. ● It often trades in the securities of young or small companies because its listing requirements are less strict than those of the New York Stock Exchange. — Abbr. AMEX; ASE.

American-style option. See *American option* under OPTION.

Americans with Disabilities Act. A federal statute that prohibits discrimination in employment, public services, and public accommodations against any person because of the person's disability ("a physical or mental impairment that substantially limits one or more of the major life activities"). 42 USCA §§ 12101–12213. ● Under the ADA and related regulations and caselaw, major life activities include those that an average person in the general population can perform with little or no difficulty, such as seeing, hearing, sleeping, eating, walking, traveling, and working. The statute applies to both private and governmental entities but not to a private employer having fewer than 15 employees. 42 USCA § 12111(5)(A). — Abbr. ADA. See DISABILITY (2); MAJOR LIFE ACTIVITY.

AMEX (**am**-eks). *abbr.* (1961) AMERICAN STOCK EXCHANGE.

amiable compositor. *Int'l law.* An unbiased third party, often a head of state or high government official, who suggests a solution that disputing countries might accept of their own volition. — Also termed *aimable compositeur.*

amicable action. See *test case* (1) under CASE.

amicable compounder. See COMPOUNDER (1).

amicable scire facias to revive a judgment. See SCIRE FACIAS.

amicable suit. See *test case* (1) under CASE.

amicus. **1.** See AMICUS CURIAE. **2.** See *amicus brief* under BRIEF (1).

amicus brief. See BRIEF (1).

amicus curiae (ə-**mee**-kəs **kyoor**-ee-ɪ *or* ə-**mɪ**-kəs **kyoor**-ee-ee *also* **am**-i-kəs). [Latin "friend of the court"] (17c) A person who is not a party to a lawsuit but who petitions the court or is requested by the court to file a brief in the action because that person has a strong interest in the subject matter. — Often shortened to *amicus.* — Also termed *friend of the court.* Pl. **amici curiae** (ə-**mee**-kee *or* ə-**mɪ**-sɪ *or* ə-**mɪ**-kɪ).

Amish exception. An exemption of the Amish from compulsory-school-attendance laws under the Free Exercise Clause of the First Amendment. ● In *Wisconsin v. Yoder*, 406 U.S. 205, 92 S.Ct. 1526 (1972), the Supreme Court held that Amish children could not be compelled to attend high school even though they were within the age range of the state's compulsory-attendance law. The Court has very narrowly construed the Amish exception and has refused to extend it to non-Amish children. See COMPULSORY-ATTENDANCE LAW; FREE EXERCISE CLAUSE.

amittere liberam legem (ə-**mit**-ə-ree **lib**-ər-əm **lee**-jəm). See LIBERAM LEGEM AMITTERE.

amnesty, *n.* (16c) A pardon extended by the government to a group or class of persons, usu. for a political offense; the act of a sovereign power officially forgiving certain classes of persons who are subject to trial but have not yet been convicted <the 1986 Immigration Reform and Control Act provided amnesty for undocumented aliens already present in the country>. ● Unlike an ordinary pardon, amnesty is usu. addressed to crimes against state sovereignty — that is, to political offenses with respect to which forgiveness is deemed more expedient for the public welfare than prosecution and punishment. Amnesty is usu. general, addressed to classes or even communities. — Also termed *general pardon.* See PARDON. — **amnesty,** *vb.*

express amnesty. Amnesty granted in direct terms.

implied amnesty. Amnesty indirectly resulting from a peace treaty executed between contending parties.

amnesty clause. A clause, esp. one found in a peace treaty, that wipes out past offenses such as treason, sedition, rebellion, and even war crimes. ● A sovereign may grant amnesty to all guilty persons or only to certain categories of offenders.

Amnesty International. An international nongovernmental organization founded in the early 1960s to protect human rights throughout the world. ● Its mission is to "secure throughout the world the observance of the Universal Declaration of Human Rights." Amnesty Int'l Statute, art. 1.

amortization (am-ər-tə-**zay**-shən), *n.* (1851) **1.** The act or result of gradually extinguishing a debt, such as a mortgage, usu. by contributing payments of principal each time a periodic interest payment is due.

negative amortization. An increase in a loan's principal balance caused by monthly payments insufficient to pay accruing interest.

2. The act or result of apportioning the initial cost of a usu. intangible asset, such as a patent, over the asset's useful life. Cf. DEPRECIATION. — Sometimes also termed *amortizement.*

amortization reserve. See RESERVE.

amortization schedule. A schedule of periodic payments of interest and principal owed on a debt obligation; specif., a loan schedule showing both the amount of principal and interest that is due at regular intervals over the loan term and the remaining unpaid principal balance after each scheduled payment is made.

amortize, *vb.* (1867) **1.** To extinguish (a debt) gradually, often by means of a sinking fund. **2.** To arrange to extinguish (a debt) by gradual increments. **3.** *Hist.* To alienate or convey lands to a corporation (that is, in mortmain). — Also spelled *amortise.* See MORTMAIN.

amortized loan. See LOAN.

amortized mortgage. See MORTGAGE.

amotion. (17c) **1.** A turning out, as the eviction of a tenant or the removal of a person from office. **2.** The common-law procedure available to shareholders to remove a corporate director for cause. **3.** The wrongful moving or carrying away of another's personal property.

amount in controversy. (1809) The damages claimed or relief demanded by the injured party in a lawsuit. • For a federal court to have diversity jurisdiction, the amount in controversy must exceed $75,000. 28 USCA § 1332(a). — Also termed *jurisdictional amount; matter in controversy.* See DIVERSITY OF CITIZENSHIP; AGGREGATION DOCTRINE.

amount realized. *Tax.* The amount received by a taxpayer for the sale or exchange of an asset, such as cash, property, services received, or debts assumed by a buyer. Cf. GAIN (3); LOSS (2).

amove, *vb.* To remove (a person) from an office or position. — **amoval,** *n.*

AMS. *abbr.* AGRICULTURAL MARKETING SERVICE.

AMT. *abbr.* See *alternative minimum tax* under TAX.

Amtrak. See NATIONAL RAILROAD PASSENGER CORPORATION.

a multo fortiori (ay məl-toh for-shee-**or**-I). [Latin] By far the stronger reason. Cf. A FORTIORI.

amusement tax. See TAX.

anaconda clause. See MOTHER HUBBARD CLAUSE (1).

anacrisis (an-ə-**krI**-sis). *Civil law.* An investigation or inquiry, esp. one conducted by torture.

analog. *Patents.* A different material, usu. a chemical or DNA sequence, that produces the same result as the specified material when used in a certain way. • To prevent others from free-riding on their innovation without technically infringing their exclusive rights, patent applicants often include analogs in their claims. — Also spelled *analogue.* — Also termed *functional analog; equivalent.*

analogous art. See ART.

analogous use. 1. *Patents.* The application of a process already known in one field of art to produce a similar result in another field. • Unless the fields are so unrelated or the outcomes so different as to produce a novel, useful, and nonobvious result, an analogous use is not patentable. **2.** *Trademarks.* The use of a mark in marketing and advertising a product or service before the actual sale of the product or service, in order to establish the mark's use in commerce. • For the owner to take advantage of the analogous-use doctrine, the marketing campaign must be substantial and the product or service must be available soon after the campaign. An owner who files an intent-to-use application may tack on the period of analogous use for purposes of priority and incontestability.

analytical jurisprudence. See JURISPRUDENCE.

analytical memorandum. See *research memorandum* under MEMORANDUM.

anarchist, *n.* (17c) One who advocates the overthrow of organized government by force or who believes in the absence of government as a political ideal. — **anarchism** (the philosophy), *n.*

anarchy, *n.* (16c) **1.** Absence of government; lawlessness. **2.** A sociopolitical theory holding that the only legitimate form of government is one under which individuals govern themselves voluntarily, free from any collective power structure enforcing compliance with social order. — **anarchic,** *adj.*

criminal anarchy. (1831) A doctrine advocating the overthrow of organized government by force or violence, by assassinating a head of government, or by some other unlawful act. • Most states have laws limiting speech that incites criminal anarchy. The laws do not apply to abstract philosophical expressions or predictions or like expressions protected by the First and Fourteenth Amendments. Criminal-anarchy statutes (e.g., 18 USCA § 2385) apply only to speech that is calculated to induce forceful and violent activity, such as attempts to incite people to riot, or that otherwise generates some "clear and present danger" that the advocated violent overthrow may be attempted or accomplished. *See Gitlow v. New York*, 268 U.S. 652, 666, 45 S.Ct. 625, 630 (1925).

anathema (ə-**nath**-ə-mə), *n.* An ecclesiastical curse that prohibits a person from receiving communion (as in excommunication) and bars the person from contact with members of the church. — **anathematize**, *vb.*

anatocism (ə-**nat**-ə-siz-əm), *n.* [fr. Greek *anatokismos* "to lend on interest again"] *Rare.* **1.** Compound interest. See *compound interest* under INTEREST (3). **2.** The practice of compounding interest.

anatomical gift. See GIFT.

ancestor, *n.* A person from whom an estate has passed; ASCENDANT. • This word is the correlative of *heir*. Cf. HEIR (1).

   common ancestor. A person to whom the ancestry of two or more persons is traced.

ancestral debt. See DEBT.

ancestral estate. See ESTATE (1).

ancestry. (14c) A line of descent; lineage.

anchorage. *Maritime law.* **1.** An area where ships anchor. **2.** A duty paid by shipowners for the use of a port; a toll for anchoring.

ancient, *adj. Evidence.* (14c) Having existed for a long time without interruption, usu. at least 20 to 30 years <ancient deed> <ancient map>. • Ancient items are usu. presumed to be authentic even if proof of authenticity cannot be made. Fed. R. Evid. 901(b)(8).

ancient demesne. See DEMESNE.

ancient document. See DOCUMENT.

ancient fact. See FACT.

ancient house. See HOUSE.

ancient law. The law of antiquity, considered esp. either from an anthropological standpoint or from the standpoint of tracing precursors to modern law.

ancient-lights doctrine. The common-law principle by which a landowner acquired, after 20 years of uninterrupted use, an easement preventing a neighbor from building an obstruction that blocks light from passing through the landowner's window. • The window (or other opening) is termed an *ancient light.* This doctrine has rarely been applied in the United States. — Also termed *ancient-windows doctrine.*

ancient readings. *Hist.* Lectures on ancient English statutes, formerly having substantial legal authority.

ancient rent. *Hist.* The rent reserved at the time the lease is made, if the estate was not then under lease.

ancients. *Hist.* Certain members of seniority in the Inns of Court and Chancery. • In Gray's Inn, the society consisted of benchers, ancients, barristers, and students under the bar, with the ancients being the oldest barristers. In the Middle Temple, those who passed the readings were termed *ancients.* The Inns of Chancery consisted of both ancients and students or clerks. — Also termed (in singular) *ancient.*

ancient wall. See WALL.

ancient watercourse. See WATERCOURSE.

ancient-windows doctrine. See ANCIENT-LIGHTS DOCTRINE.

ancient writing. See *ancient document* under DOCUMENT.

ancillary (**an**-sə-ler-ee), *adj.* (17c) Supplementary; subordinate <ancillary claims>. — **ancillarity** (an-sə-**la**[i]r-ə-tee), *n.*

ancillary administration. See ADMINISTRATION.

ancillary administrator. See ADMINISTRATOR (2).

ancillary attachment. See ATTACHMENT (3).

ancillary bill. See *ancillary suit* under SUIT.

ancillary claim. See CLAIM (4).

ancillary guardianship. See GUARDIANSHIP.

ancillary jurisdiction. See JURISDICTION.

ancillary legislation. See LEGISLATION.

ancillary letters testamentary. See LETTERS TESTAMENTARY.

ancillary proceeding. See *ancillary suit* under SUIT.

ancillary process. See *ancillary suit* under SUIT.

ancillary receiver. See RECEIVER.

ancillary receivership. See RECEIVERSHIP.

ancillary suit. See SUIT.

ancillary to priority. *Patents.* (Of a legal issue) so logically related to the issue of priority of invention that it cannot be separated from the issue of priority. • The question whether an issue is ancillary to priority was once used to challenge the jurisdiction of the U.S. Patent and Trademark Office, but the Board of Patent Appeals and Interferences now has explicit jurisdiction over ancillary issues.

ancipitis usus. See *conditional contraband* under CONTRABAND.

***Anders* brief.** See BRIEF.

and his heirs. A term of art formerly required to transfer complete title (a fee simple absolute) to real estate <A conveys Blackacre to B and his heirs>. • This phrase originated in the translation of a Law French phrase used in medieval grants (*a lui et a ses heritiers pour toujours* "to him and his heirs forever"). See FEE SIMPLE.

and other good and valuable consideration. See *other consideration* under CONSIDERATION.

androlepsy (**an**-drə-lep-see). [fr. Greek "seizure of men"] *Hist.* The taking by one nation of citizens or subjects of another nation either in reprisal or to enforce some claim (as to surrender or punish a fugitive). — Also termed *androlepsia* (an-drə-**lep**-see-ə).

angary (**ang**-gə-ree). *Int'l law.* A country's right, in war or other urgent circumstances, to seize — for temporary use — neutral merchant ships in its inland or territorial waters as well as aircraft within its territory, with full indemnity by the country. — Also termed *right of angary*; *jus angariae*; *angaria*.

angel. *Mergers & acquisitions.* An investor who infuses enough cash to close a deal or who comes in at the last minute to save a deal that otherwise would not close.

angel investor. See INVESTOR.

Anglo-American common law. See *American common law* under COMMON LAW (2).

Anglo-Saxon law. The body of royal decrees and customary laws developed by the Germanic peoples who dominated England from the 5th century to 1066.

animal. Any living creature other than a human being. — Also termed *creature*.

    animal ferae naturae. See *wild animal*.

    animal mansuetae naturae. See *domestic animal*.

    dangerous animal. An animal that has harmed or has threatened to harm a person or another animal.

    domestic animal. **1.** An animal that is customarily devoted to the service of humankind at the time and in the place where it is helped. See DOMITAE NATURAE; MANSUETAE NATURAE. **2.** Any animal that is statutorily so designated. — Also termed *animal mansuetae naturae*.

    domesticated animal. **1.** A feral animal that has been tamed. **2.** An animal that has customarily lived peaceably with people, such as farm animals and pets.

    feral animal. A domestic animal that has returned to a wild state. ● Feral animals, unlike others of their species, are usu. unsocialized to people.

    vicious animal. **1.** An animal that has shown itself to be dangerous to humans. **2.** Loosely, one belonging to a breed or species that is known or reputed to be dangerous. ● A vicious animal may be domestic, feral, or wild. See VICIOUS PROPENSITY.

    wild animal. **1.** An animal that, as a matter of common knowledge, are naturally untamable, unpredictable, dangerous, or mischievous. **2.** Any animal not statutorily designated as a domestic animal. — Also termed *wild creature*; *animal ferae naturae*.

Animal and Plant Health Inspection Service. An agency in the U.S. Department of Agriculture responsible for controlling or eliminating pests and plant diseases by regulating the shipment of agricultural products within the United States ● Established in 1977, some of its functions were transferred to the U.S. Department of Homeland Security in 2003. — Abbr. APHIS.

animal ferae naturae. See *wild animal* under ANIMAL.

animal law, *n.* The field of law dealing with vertebrates other than humans. ● The field cuts across many traditional doctrinal areas (e.g., contracts, torts, administrative law) as well as jurisprudence. Topics include wildlife-management law, laws concerning treatment of laboratory animals, and laws relating to companion animals.

animal mansuetae naturae. See *domesticated animal* under ANIMAL.

animo (**an**-ə-moh). [Latin] See ANIMUS (2).

animo felonico (**an**-ə-moh fə-**lon**-ə-koh), *adv.* [Latin] With felonious intent; with the intention to commit a felony.

animus (**an**-ə-məs). [Latin] (1816) **1.** Ill will; animosity.

    class-based animus. A prejudicial disposition toward a discernible, usu. constitutionally protected, group of persons. ● A *class-based animus* is an essential element of a civil-rights conspiracy case.

2. Intention. ● All the following Latin "animus" phrases have analogous adverbial forms beginning with "animo" (the definition merely needing "with" at the outset). For example, *animo furandi* means "with the intention to steal," *animo testandi* means "with testamentary intention," etc.

animus adimendi (**an**-ə-məs ad-i-**men**-dI). [Latin] The intention to adeem.

animus belligerendi (**an**-ə-məs bə-lij-ə-**ren**-dI). [Latin] The intention to wage war.

animus cancellandi (**an**-ə-məs kan-sə-**lan**-dI). [Latin] The intention to cancel. ● This phrase usu. refers to a will.

animus capiendi (**an**-ə-məs kap-ee-**en**-dI). [Latin] The intention to take or capture.

animus contrahentium (**an**-ə-məs kon-trə-**hen**-shee-əm). [Latin] The intention of the contracting parties.

animus dedicandi (**an**-ə-məs ded-ə-**kan**-dI). [Latin] The intention to donate or dedicate.

animus defamandi (**an**-ə-məs def-ə-**man**-dı). [Latin] The intention to defame.

animus derelinquendi (**an**-ə-məs dee-rel-ing-**kwen**-dı). [Latin] The intention to abandon.

animus deserendi (**an**-ə-məs des-ə-**ren**-dı). [Latin] The intention to desert (usu. a spouse, child, etc.).

animus differendi (**an**-ə-məs dif-ə-**ren**-dı). [Latin] The intention to obtain a delay. ● The phrase *animo differendi* ("with the intention to obtain a delay") appeared in reference to a presumption that certain actions of a defendant were designed to obtain a delay.

animus domini (**an**-ə-məs **dom**-ə-nı). [Latin] *Roman law.* The intent to exercise dominion over a thing; the intent to own something. Cf. *animus possidendi.*

animus donandi (**an**-ə-moh doh-**nan**-dı). [Latin] The intention of donating; the intention to give.

animus et factum (**an**-ə-məs et **fak**-təm). [Latin "mind and deed"] The intention and the deed. ● This phrase can refer to a person's intent to reside in a given country permanently or for an indefinite period.

animus felonicus (**an**-ə-məs fe-**loh**-ni-kəs). [Latin] The intention to commit a felony.

animus furandi (**an**-ə-məs fyuu-**ran**-dı). [Latin] The intention to steal. ● In Roman law, the focus was on the unauthorized use of property rather than an intent to permanently deprive the owner of it.

animus gerendi (**an**-ə-məs jə-**ren**-dı). [Latin] The intention to act as heir.

animus immiscendi et adeundi hereditatem (**an**-ə-məs im-i-**sen**-dı et ad-ee-**ən**-dı hə-red-i-**tay**-təm). [Latin] The intention to meddle with and take up a succession.

animus indorsandi (**an**-ə-moh in-dor-**san**-dı). [Law Latin] *Hist.* The intention of indorsing. ● One who indorsed a check *animo indorsandi* would be liable for the amount if the check was dishonored.

animus injuriandi (**an**-ə-məs in-j[y]oor-ee-**an**-dı). [Latin] The intention to injure, esp. to insult.

animus lucrandi (**an**-ə-məs loo-**kran**-dı). [Latin] The intention to make a gain or profit.

animus malus (**an**-ə-məs **mal**-əs). [Latin] Evil intent.

animus manendi (**an**-ə-məs mə-**nen**-dı). [Latin "will to remain"] The intention to remain; the intention to establish a permanent residence. — Also termed *animus remandendi.*

animus morandi (**an**-ə-məs mə-**ran**-dı). [Latin "will to tarry"] The intention to remain. ● Although *animus morandi* is broadly synonymous with *animus manendi*, *morandi* suggests less permanency.

animus nocendi (**an**-ə-məs noh-**sen**-dı). [Latin] The intention to harm.

animus obligandi (**an**-ə-məs ahb-li-**gan**-dı). [Latin] The intention to enter into an obligation.

animus occidendi (**an**-ə-məs ahk-si-**den**-dı). [Latin] The intention to kill.

animus possidendi (**an**-ə-məs pah-sə-**den**-dı). [Latin] *Roman law.* The intent to possess a thing. Cf. *animus domini.*

animus quo (**an**-ə-məs **kwoh**). [Latin] The intent with which; motive.

animus recipiendi (**an**-ə-məs ri-sip-ee-**en**-dı). [Latin] The intention to receive.

animus recuperandi (**an**-ə-məs ri-k[y]oo-pə-**ran**-dı). [Latin] The intention to recover.

animus remanendi (**an**-ə-məs rem-ə-**nen**-dı). [Latin] See *animus manendi.*

animus republicandi (**an**-ə-məs ree-pub-lə-**kan**-dı). [Latin] The intention to republish.

animus restituendi (**an**-ə-məs rə-sti-tyoo-**en**-dı). [Latin] The intention to restore.

animus revertendi (**an**-ə-məs ree-vər-**ten**-dı). [Latin] The intention to return (to a place). ● In Roman law, this intent was a factor to deciding whether animals, such as doves and bees, remained in a person's ownership.

animus revocandi (**an**-ə-məs rev-oh-**kan**-dı). [Latin] The intention to revoke (a will) <her destruction of the will indicated that she had animus revocandi>.

animus signandi (**an**-ə-məs sig-**nan**-dı). [Latin] The intention to sign.

animus testandi (**an**-ə-məs tes-**tan**-dı). [Latin] Testamentary intention.

animus ulciscendi (**an**-ə-məs əl-si-**sen**-dı). [Latin] The intention to take revenge.

Annapolis. See UNITED STATES NAVAL ACADEMY.

annex, *n.* (16c) Something that is attached, such as a document to a report or an addition to a building.

annexation, *n.* (17c) **1.** The act of attaching; the state of being attached. **2.** *Property.* The point at which a fixture becomes a part of the realty to which it is attached. **3.** A formal act by which a nation, state, or municipality incorporates land within its dominion. ● In international law, the usual formalities of announcing annexation involve having specially commissioned officers hoist the national flag and read a proclamation.

4. The annexed land itself. Cf. ACCESSION (5). — **annex,** *vb.*

cherry-stem annexation. 1. Annexed land that resembles (on a map) a cherry because the annexed territory — the cherry — is not contiguous to the acquiring municipality, and the narrow corridor of annexed land leading to the targeted area resembles a stem. **2.** The process of annexing land with this configuration.

anniversary date. *Insurance.* The annually recurring date of the initial issuance of a policy. Cf. POLICY YEAR.

ann, jour, et wast (an, zhoor, ay wayst). [Law French] See YEAR, DAY, AND WASTE.

Anno Domini (**an**-oh **dom**-ə-nɪ *or* -nee). [Latin "in the year of the Lord"] Since the supposed year in which Jesus Christ was born; of the current era <A.D. 1776>. — Abbr. A.D. — Also termed *in the year of Our Lord.* Cf C.E.

Anno Regni (**an**-oh **reg**-nɪ). [Latin] In the year of the reign. • A.R.V.R. 22, for example, is an abbreviated reference to *Anno Regni Victoriae Reginae vicesimo secundo* ("in the twenty-second year of the reign of Queen Victoria"). — Abbr. A.R.

annotation (an-ə-**tay**-shən), *n.* (15c) **1.** A brief summary of the facts and decision in a case, esp. one involving statutory interpretation. **2.** A note that explains or criticizes a source of law, usu. a case. • Annotations appear, for example, in the *United States Code Annotated* (USCA). **3.** A volume containing such explanatory or critical notes. **4.** RESCRIPT (3). Cf. NOTE (2). — **annotate** (an-ə-tayt), *vb.* — **annotative** (an-ə-tay-tiv), *adj.* — **annotator** (an-ə-tay-tər), *n.*

announce, vb. To make publicly known; to proclaim formally <the judge announced her decision in open court>.

annoyance. See NUISANCE (1).

annual account. See *intermediate account* under ACCOUNT.

annual crops. See CROPS.

annual depreciation. See DEPRECIATION.

annual exclusion. See EXCLUSION (1).

annual gift-tax exclusion. See *annual exclusion* under EXCLUSION.

annual meeting. See MEETING.

annual message. See MESSAGE.

annual percentage rate. See INTEREST RATE.

annual permit. A permit, required by some states, that must be paid each year by a corporation that does business in the state. • In some states, the permit fee is set according to the corporation's capitalization.

annual report. A yearly corporate financial report for shareholders and other interested parties. •

The Securities Exchange Act of 1934 requires registered corporations to file an annual report on the SEC's Form 10-K. An annual report includes a balance sheet, income statement, statement of changes in financial position, reconciliation of changes in owners' equity accounts, a summary of significant accounting principles, other explanatory notes, the auditor's report, and comments from management about prospects for the coming year. — Also termed *annual statement; financial report.*

annual value. See VALUE (2).

annuitant (ə-**n**[**y**]**oo**-ə-tənt), *n.* (18c) A beneficiary of an annuity.

annuity (ə-**n**[**y**]**oo**-ə-tee). (15c) **1.** An obligation to pay a stated sum, usu. monthly or annually, to a stated recipient. • These payments terminate upon the death of the designated beneficiary. **2.** A fixed sum of money payable periodically. **3.** A right, often acquired under a life-insurance contract, to receive fixed payments periodically for a specified duration. Cf. PENSION. **4.** *Patents.* See MAINTENANCE FEE. **5.** A savings account with an insurance company or investment company, usu. established for retirement income. • Payments into the account accumulate tax-free, and the account is taxed only when the annuitant withdraws money in retirement.

annuity certain. An annuity payable over a specified period, regardless of whether the annuitant dies before the period ends. — Also termed *term annuity.*

annuity due. An annuity that makes payments at the beginning of each pay period. Cf. *ordinary annuity.*

cash-refund annuity. An annuity providing for a lump-sum payment after the annuitant's death of the difference between the total received and the price paid.

constituted annuity. *Louisiana law.* An annuity that has a maximum duration of 10 years and, under some circumstances, can be redeemed before the term's expiration. La. Civ. Code art. 2796.

contingent annuity. 1. An annuity that begins making payments when some future event occurs, such as the death of a person other than the annuitant. **2.** An annuity that makes an uncertain number of payments, depending on the outcome of a future event.

continuing annuity. See *survivorship annuity.*

deferred annuity. An annuity that begins making payments on a specified date if the annuitant is alive at that time. — Also termed *deferred-payment annuity.* Cf. *immediate annuity.*

fixed annuity. An annuity that guarantees fixed payments, either for life or for a specified period.

group annuity. An annuity payable to members of a group, esp. employees, who are covered by a single annuity contract, such as a group pension plan.

immediate annuity. An annuity paid for with a single premium and that begins to pay benefits within the first payment interval. Cf. *deferred annuity.*

joint annuity. An annuity payable to two annuitants until one of them dies, at which time the annuity terminates for the survivor (unless the annuity also provides for survivorship rights). See *survivorship annuity.*

life annuity. An annuity payable only during the annuitant's lifetime, even if the annuitant dies prematurely.

life-income period-certain annuity. An annuity that pays a specified number of payments even if the annuitant dies before the minimum amount has been paid.

nonrefund annuity. An annuity with guaranteed payments during the annuitant's life, but with no refund to anyone at death. — Also termed *straight life annuity; pure annuity.*

ordinary annuity. An annuity that makes payments at the end of each pay period. Cf. *annuity due.*

private annuity. An annuity from a private source rather than from a public or life-insurance company.

pure annuity. See *nonrefund annuity.*

refund annuity. An annuity that, upon the annuitant's death, pays to the annuitant's estate the difference between the purchase price and the total payments received during the annuitant's lifetime.

retirement annuity. An annuity that begins making payments only after the annuitant's retirement. ● If the annuitant dies before retirement, an agreed amount will usu. be refunded to the annuitant's estate.

single-premium deferred annuity. An annuity for which a party pays a lump-sum premium in exchange for receiving a specified sum at a future date. ● The income earned on the investment is tax-free until it is withdrawn. — Abbr. SPDA.

straight annuity. An annuity that makes payments in fixed amounts at periodic intervals. Cf. *variable annuity.*

straight life annuity. See *nonrefund annuity.*

survivorship annuity. An annuity providing for continued payments to a survivor, usu. a spouse, after the original annuitant dies. — Also termed *continuing annuity.*

tax-deferred annuity. See *403(b) plan* under EMPLOYEE BENEFIT PLAN.

tax-sheltered annuity. See *403(b) plan* under EMPLOYEE BENEFIT PLAN.

term annuity. See *annuity certain.*

variable annuity. An annuity that makes payments in varying amounts depending on the success of the underlying investment strategy. See *variable annuity contract* under CONTRACT. Cf. *straight annuity.*

annuity bond. See BOND (3).

annuity certain. See ANNUITY.

annuity depreciation method. See DEPRECIATION METHOD.

annuity insurance. See INSURANCE.

annuity policy. An insurance policy providing for monthly or periodic payments to the insured to begin at a fixed date and continue through the insured's life.

annuity trust. See TRUST.

annulment (ə-nəl-mənt), *n.* (15c) **1.** The act of nullifying or making void; VOIDANCE. **2.** A judicial or ecclesiastical declaration that a marriage is void. ● An annulment establishes that the marital status never existed. So annulment and dissolution of marriage (or divorce) are fundamentally different: an annulment renders a marriage void from the beginning, while dissolution of marriage terminates the marriage as of the date of the judgment of dissolution. Although a marriage terminated by annulment is considered never to have occurred, under modern ecclesiastical law and in most states today a child born during the marriage is not considered illegitimate after the annulment. Cf. DIVORCE. **3.** A rescission. See RESCIND (3). — **annul** (ə-nəl), *vb.*

annulment of adoption. See ABROGATION OF ADOPTION.

annulment of judgment. A retroactive obliteration of a judicial decision, having the effect of restoring the parties to their pretrial positions. ● Types of annulment include reversal and vacation. See REVERSE; VACATE (1).

anomalous indorsement. See *irregular indorsement* under INDORSEMENT.

anomalous jurisdiction. See JURISDICTION.

anomalous-jurisdiction rule (ə-nom-ə-ləs). The principle that a court of appeals has provisional jurisdiction to review the denial of a motion to intervene in a case, and if the court of appeals finds that the denial was correct, then its jurisdiction disappears — and it must dismiss the appeal for want of jurisdiction — because an order denying a motion to intervene is not a final, appealable order. • This rule has been criticized by courts and commentators. Many appellate courts, upon finding that the trial court properly denied a motion to intervene, will affirm the denial instead of dismissing the appeal for want of jurisdiction. — Sometimes shortened to *anomalous rule*.

anomalous plea. See PLEA (2).

anomalous pleading. See PLEADING (1).

anomalous rule. See ANOMALOUS-JURISDICTION RULE.

anonymous, *adj.* (17c) Not named or identified <the police arrested the defendant after a tip from an anonymous informant>. — **anonymity** (an-ə-**nim**-ə-tee), *n.*

anonymous case. A reported case in which the word "anonymous" is substituted for at least one party's name to conceal the party's identity. *See, e.g., Anonymous v. Anonymous*, 735 N.Y.S.2d 26 (App. Div. 2001).

anonymous work. See WORK (2).

ANSI. *abbr.* AMERICAN NATIONAL STANDARDS INSTITUTE.

answer, *n.* (bef. 12c) **1.** A defendant's first pleading that addresses the merits of the case, usu. by denying the plaintiff's allegations. • An answer usu. sets forth the defendant's defenses and counterclaims.

false answer. (18c) A sham answer in a pleading. See *sham pleading* under PLEADING (1).

2. A person's, esp. a witness's, response to a question posed.

evasive answer. (17c) A response that neither directly admits nor denies a question. • In discovery, this is considered a failure to answer. Fed. R. Civ. P. 37(a)(3).

unresponsive answer. (1891) *Evidence.* A response from a witness (usu. at a deposition or hearing) that is irrelevant to the question asked. — Also termed *nonresponsive answer.*

3. *Patents.* A patent applicant's response to an office action.

answer, *vb.* (12c) **1.** To respond to a question, a pleading, or a discovery request <the company failed to answer the interrogatories within 30 days>. **2.** To assume the liability of another <a guarantor answers for another person's debt>. **3.** To pay (a debt or other liability) <she promised to answer damages out of her own estate>.

answer date. See *answer day* under DAY.

answer day. See DAY.

ante (**an**-tee), *prep.* [Latin] Before. Cf. POST.

antea (an-**tee**-ə), *adv.* [Latin] Formerly; heretofore.

antecedent (an-tə-**see**-dənt), *adj.* (14c) Earlier; preexisting; previous. — **antecedent** (preceding thing), *n.* — **antecedence** (quality or fact of going before), *n.*

antecedent basis. *Patents.* A general word or phrase in a patent claim or description to which a later specific word or phrase must refer. • Claims will be rejected as impermissibly vague or indefinite if the latter word is not clearly connected to its antecedent, because the wording becomes ambiguous. In general, a term is first introduced with an indefinite article and is later referred to with the definite article (or *said*).

antecedent claim. A preexisting claim. • Under the UCC, a holder takes an instrument for value if it is taken for an antecedent claim. UCC § 3-303.

antecedent debt. See DEBT.

antedate (an-ti-dayt), *vb.* (16c) **1.** To affix with a date earlier than the true date; BACKDATE (1) <antedate a check>. **2.** To precede in time <the doctrine antedates the *Smith* case by many years>. — Also termed *predate.* Cf. POSTDATE. — **antedate,** *n.*

antedating of a prior-art reference. *Patents.* The removal of a publication, a U.S. patent, or a foreign patent cited as prior art against the application by filing an affidavit or declaration establishing the applicant's completion of the invention in this country, or in another NAFTA or WTO member country, before the effective date of the cited reference. • The term applies only to U.S. patent applications. An issued patent may also antedate a prior-art reference if the conception predates the prior art and the inventor used due diligence in reducing the concept to practice. — Also termed *antedating a reference; swearing behind a prior art reference; carrying back the date of invention.*

ante meridiem (**an**-tee mə-**rid**-ee-əm). [Latin] Before noon. — Abbr. a.m.; A.M.

ante mortem. [Latin] Before death.

antenuptial (an-ti-**nəp**-shəl), *adj.* See PRENUPTIAL.

antenuptial agreement. See PRENUPTIAL AGREEMENT.

antenuptial contract. See PRENUPTIAL AGREEMENT.

antenuptial gift. See *prenuptial gift* under GIFT.

antenuptial will. See *prenuptial will* under WILL.

anthropometry (an-thrə-**pom**-ə-tree). A system of measuring the human body, esp. the size relationships among the different parts. • Before the advent of fingerprinting, minute measurements of the human body — taken and compared to other persons' measurements — were used to identify criminals and deceased persons. Cf. BERTILLON SYSTEM. — **anthropometric,** *adj.*

Anti-Assignment Act. A federal statute prohibiting the assignment or transfer of claims against the United States. 31 USCA § 3727.

anti-assignment-in-gross rule. *Trademarks.* The doctrine that an assignment of a mark without the goodwill symbolized by the mark is invalid. • Although trademark rights are not destroyed when a mark is assigned in gross, the failure of the assignor to continue to use the mark, coupled with an ineffective transfer, may result in abandonment. — See *assignment in gross* under ASSIGNMENT.

antibootleg, *adj. Copyright.* Of or pertaining to an effort to combat or discourage illegal recording, distribution, and sale of unauthorized reproductions of live and broadcast performances. • The federal antibootleg statute, 18 USCA § 2319A, and the antibootleg statutes of several states criminalize bootlegging activities. See ANTIBOOTLEG STATUTE. — **antibootlegging,** *n.*

antibootleg statute. *Copyright.* A law, esp. a state law, that prohibits making, distributing, or selling an unauthorized recording of a live performance.

antichurning rule. *Tax.* A statutory or regulatory provision that denies certain tax advantages, esp. accelerated depreciation and amortization schedules, to taxpayers who acquire property in a transaction that does not result in a significant change in the property's ownership or use. See CHURNING (2).

anticipated, *adj. Patents.* (Of a patent claim) having all the same elements of a prior-art reference. • If a claim is anticipated by a previous invention or publication, that claim is not allowable; if a patent has already been issued it will be declared invalid. — Also termed *fully met.*

anticipation. 1. The distribution or receipt of trust income before it is due. **2.** *Patents.* The prior invention or disclosure of the claimed invention by another, or the inventor's own disclosure of the claimed invention by publication, sale, or offer to sell if that disclosure predates the date of the patent-application filing by more than one year. • By disproving the claim's novelty, anticipation bars the allowance of a claim and provides a defense to an action for infringement based on that claim. See NOVELTY; *prior art* under ART. — **anticipate,** *vb.*

anticipatory breach. See BREACH OF CONTRACT.

anticipatory filing. The bringing of a lawsuit or regulatory action against another with the expectation that the other party is preparing an action of its own. • If properly brought, an anticipatory filing may determine procedural matters such as jurisdiction and venue. See FIRST-TO-FILE RULE; RACE TO THE COURTHOUSE.

anticipatory nuisance. See NUISANCE.

anticipatory offense. See *inchoate offense* under OFFENSE (1).

anticipatory replication. See REPLICATION.

anticipatory repudiation. See REPUDIATION.

anticipatory search warrant. See SEARCH WARRANT.

anticircumvention device. *Copyright.* An apparatus designed to prevent bypassing, avoiding, removing, deactivating, or impairing a technological measure that controls access to a work protected by copyright; an apparatus in a media player or receiver, such as a DVD or a TV satellite dish, designed to prevent unauthorized use or duplication of copyrighted material.

anticompetitive, *adj.* Having a tendency to reduce or eliminate competition. • This term describes the type of conduct or circumstances generally targeted by antitrust laws. Cf. PROCOMPETITIVE.

anticompetitive conduct. *Antitrust.* An act that harms or seeks to harm the market or the process of competition among businesses, and that has no legitimate business purpose.

anticontest clause. See NO-CONTEST CLAUSE.

Anticounterfeiting Consumer Protection Act. *Trademarks & Copyright.* A federal law to discourage counterfeiting of trademarks and copyrighted merchandise such as computer programs, phonorecords, and motion pictures. • The law imposes criminal liability for trafficking in counterfeit goods and services (18 USCA § 2318), provides for the seizure of counterfeit goods (15 USCA § 1116 (d)(9)), and provides enhanced statutory civil penalties (15 USCA § 1117(c)). — Abbr. ACPA.

Anticybersquatting Consumer Protection Act. *Trademarks.* A 1999 federal law authorizing a trademark owner to obtain a federal-court order transferring ownership of a domain name from a cybersquatter to the trademark owner. • A mark's owner must show that (1) the mark and the domain name are identical or confusingly similar; (2) the mark was distinctive when the domain name was first registered; (3) the trademark's owner used the mark commercially before the domain name was registered; and (4) the domain registrant acted in bad faith and intended to profit from the trademark's use. Registering a domain name with the intent to sell it to the trademark owner is presumptively an act of bad faith. But if a defendant can prove a legitimate reason for the domain-name registration, the defendant may be allowed to keep the name. — Abbr. ACPA. — Also termed *Trademark Cyberpiracy Prevention Act.*

antideficiency legislation. See LEGISLATION.

antideficiency statute. See *antideficiency legislation* under LEGISLATION.

antidestructibility statute. See DESTRUCTIBILITY OF CONTINGENT REMAINDERS.

antidestruction clause. A provision in a security protecting a shareholder's conversion rights, in the event of a merger, by granting the shareholder a right to convert the securities into the securities that will replace the company's stock when the merger is complete. See *convertible security* under SECURITY.

antidilution act. *Trademarks.* A statute prohibiting actions that are likely to lessen, diminish, or erode a famous mark's capacity to identify and distinguish goods and services, without regard to whether the action creates a likelihood of confusion, mistake, or deception. ● The Federal Trademark Dilution Act provides relief against another's commercial use of a mark or tradename that dilutes the distinctive quality of a famous mark. More than half the states also have antidilution statutes, which are based on the International Trademark Association's 1964 Model State Trademark Bill. — Also termed *antidilution statute.*

antidilution provision. A convertible-security provision that safeguards the conversion privilege from share splits, share dividends, or other transactions that might affect the conversion ratio. See CONVERSION RATIO; DILUTION (2).

antidissection rule. *Trademarks.* A rule, applied in comparing potentially conflicting marks, that requires that the marks be compared as a whole or as they are viewed by consumers in the marketplace, not broken down into their component parts. ● The antidissection rule does not preclude an analysis of the dominant and subordinate features of a mark to determine which features of the mark make the most significant impression on consumers, but the mark must still be considered in its entirety.

antidumping duty. See *antidumping tariff* under TARIFF (3).

antidumping law. A statute designed to protect domestic companies by preventing the sale of foreign goods at less than fair value, as defined in the statute (for example, at a price below that of the domestic market). See DUMPING.

antidumping tariff. See TARIFF (2).

anti-evolution statute. *Hist.* A law that forbids the teaching of the theory of evolution in schools. ● Such statutes were held unconstitutional as violative of the Establishment Clause in *Epperson v. Arkansas*, 393 U.S. 97, 89 S.Ct. 266 (1968). — Also termed *evolution statute.* See CREATIONISM.

antifraud rule. See RULE 10B-5.

antigraph (**an**-ti-graf). *Archaic.* A copy or counterpart of an instrument.

antiharassment order. See ORDER (2).

antihazing statute. A (usu. criminal) law that prohibits an organization or members of an organization from requiring a prospective member, as a condition of membership, to do or submit to any act that presents a substantial risk of physical or mental harm. ● In 1874 Congress passed the first antihazing statute, directed at stopping hazing by midshipmen at the United States Naval Academy. Most states have passed their own antihazing statutes. — Also termed *hazing statute.*

anti-heartbalm statute. See HEARTBALM STATUTE.

Anti-Injunction Act. A federal statute providing that a federal court may not enjoin state-court proceedings unless an injunction is (1) expressly authorized by Congress, (2) necessary for the federal court's in rem jurisdiction, or (3) necessary to prevent relitigation of a judgment rendered by the federal court. 28 USCA § 2283. See NORRIS-LA GUARDIA ACT.

anti-john law. A criminal-law statute punishing prostitutes' customers.

antilapse statute. (1937) *Wills & estates.* A statute that substitutes certain heirs of some types of testamentary beneficiaries when the beneficiary has predeceased the testator and permits them to take the gift, which would otherwise fail and thus pass to the residuary beneficiary (if any) or to the intestate heirs. ● Under the common law and the laws of all states, a testamentary beneficiary must survive a testator or else the gift is said to lapse. Although most states have enacted antilapse statutes, their terms vary from state to state. — Also termed *lapse statute; nonlapse statute.*

antilynching law. A statute that criminalizes any unjustified act of violence by two or more people against another, regardless of race. ● Such laws were originally passed to stop all forms of extralegal violence aimed at black people. — Also termed *lynching law.*

antimanifesto. *Int'l law.* A proclamation in which a belligerent power asserts that the war is a defensive one for that power.

antimarital-facts privilege. See *marital privilege* (2) under PRIVILEGE (3).

antinomy (an-**tin**-ə-mee), *n.* (16c) A contradiction in law or logic; esp., a conflict of authority, as between two decisions <antinomies in the case-law>. — **antinomic** (an-ti-**nom**-ik), *adj.*

antipiracy, *adj. Copyright & Trademarks.* Of or pertaining to an effort to combat or discourage illegal reproduction, distribution, or use of copyrighted or trademarked products <an antipiracy group>.

antishelving clause. *Patents.* A provision in a patent-licensing contract, usu. one in which payment is based on royalties, requiring the licensee to put the patented article into commercial use within a specified time and to notify the patentee if the licensee decides to stop selling or manufacturing it. • The licensee generally agrees to commercially exploit the patent or else risk losing the license or exclusivity. Antishelving clauses are also used in trademark licenses. — Also termed *antishelving provision*; *shelving clause*; *shelving provision*.

antisocial behavior order. *English law.* A judicial order prohibiting a person from certain types of conduct, potentially including conduct that is otherwise legal, where the conduct is likely to cause harm or distress to a nonoccupant of the individual's household • ABSOs were introduced in Great Britain by the Crime and Disorder Act 1998. — Abbr. ABSO or ASBO.

antisocial personality disorder. See PSYCHOPATH.

antispamming law. A statute enacted to combat or criminalize the sending of unsolicited commercial e-mail. • Many states have such a law. See SPAM.

antistructuring statute. A federal law that forbids structuring monetary transactions with the intent to evade federal reporting requirements.

antisubrogation rule (an-tee-səb-roh-**gay**-shən). *Insurance.* The principle that an insurance carrier has no right of subrogation — that is, no right to assert a claim on behalf of the insured or for payments made under the policy — against its own insured for the risk covered by the policy. See SUBROGATION.

antisuit, *adj.* Of or relating to a court order forbidding the defendant in a lawsuit, pending or resolved, from filing a similar action against the same party in another jurisdiction. • The purpose of an antisuit order is usu. to prevent forum-shopping. See RES JUDICATA; COLLATERAL ESTOPPEL.

antisuit injunction. See INJUNCTION.

antitakeover measure. A provision in a company's organizational documents intended to discourage unwanted takeover bids by setting forth the actions the company may take, as a target, to avoid an involuntary takeover.

antitakeover statute. A state law designed to protect companies based in the state from hostile takeovers.

Antitrust Civil Process Act. A federal law prescribing the procedures for an antitrust action by way of a petition in U.S. District Court. 15 USCA §§ 1311 et seq.

Antitrust Guidelines for the Licensing of Intellectual Property. A set of criteria, jointly issued by the Antitrust Division of the U.S. Justice Department and the FTC, that those agencies apply in deciding whether to initiate an investigation or enforcement action as a result of restrictions in patent, copyright, trade-secret, and know-how licenses. 4 Trade Reg. Rep. (CCH) ¶ 13,132 (April 6, 1995).

antitrust law. 1. The body of law designed to protect trade and commerce from restraints, monopolies, price-fixing, and price discrimination. • The principal federal antitrust laws are the Sherman Act (15 USCA §§ 1–7) and the Clayton Act (15 USCA §§ 12–27). **2.** (*cap.*) SHERMAN ANTITRUST ACT.

antlike persistency. (1924) *Patents. Slang.* The steady tenacity of a patent practitioner or applicant who tries to wear down the U.S. Patent and Trademark Office by prosecuting patent claims in the hope that the Office will eventually relent. • Judge Learned Hand coined this pejorative expression in *Lyon v. Boh*, 1 F.2d 48, 49–50 (S.D.N.Y. 1924).

AO. *abbr.* ADMINISTRATIVE OFFICE OF THE UNITED STATES COURTS.

AOC. *abbr.* **1.** ANNO ORBIS CONDITI. **2.** And other consideration. See *other consideration* under CONSIDERATION.

AOD. *abbr.* ACTION ON DECISION.

AOGI. *abbr.* See *adjusted ordinary gross income* under INCOME.

AOUSC. *abbr.* ADMINISTRATIVE OFFICE OF THE UNITED STATES COURTS.

APA. *abbr.* **1.** ADMINISTRATIVE PROCEDURE ACT. **2.** ADVANCE PRICING AGREEMENT.

apartheid (ə-**pahrt**-hayt *or* ə-**pahr**-tɪt). Racial segregation; specif., a comprehensive governmental policy of racial discrimination and segregation, as it was practiced in South Africa.

apertum breve. See BREVE.

apex deposition. See DEPOSITION.

apex rule. *Mining law.* The principle that a vein of ore may be mined if it extends beyond the vertical boundaries of the surface claim on which the vein apexes. — Also termed *extralateral right*. Cf. INTRALIMINAL RIGHT.

APH. *abbr.* AMERICAN PRINTING HOUSE FOR THE BLIND.

APHIS. *abbr.* ANIMAL AND PLANT HEALTH INSPECTION SERVICE.

APJ. *abbr.* See *administrative patent judge* under JUDGE.

apocha (**ap**-ə-kə). *Roman & civil law.* A receipt acknowledging payment. • An apocha discharges only the obligation represented by the payment, in contrast to an acceptilation, which discharges an entire debt. — Also spelled *apoca*. Cf. ACCEPTILATION.

apostasy (ə-**pos**-tə-see). **1.** *Hist.* A crime against religion consisting in the total renunciation of Christianity by one who had previously embraced it. **2.** *Eccles. law.* Abandonment of religious vows without dispensation.

apostate (ə-**pos**-tayt). A person who has forsaken religion or a particular religion. — Also termed (archaically) *apostata* (ap-ə-**stay**-tə).

a posteriori (ay pos-teer-ee-**or**-ı *or* ah pos-teer-ee-**or**-ee), *adv.* [Latin "from what comes after"] (16c) Inductively; from the particular to the general, or from known effects to their inferred causes <as a legal analyst, she reasoned a posteriori — from countless individual cases to generalized rules that she finally applied>. Cf. A PRIORI. — **a posteriori,** *adj.*

apostille (ə-**pos**-til). [French "postscript, footnote"] *Int'l law.* A marginal note or observation; esp., a standard certification provided under the Hague Convention for authenticating documents used in foreign countries. — Also spelled *apostil.* See CERTIFICATE OF AUTHORITY (1).

apostle (ə-**pos**-əl), *n. Civil & maritime law.* **1.** A letter sent from a trial court to an appellate court, stating the case on appeal. **2.** The record or papers sent up on appeal. — Also termed *apostoli.* **3.** DIMISSORY LETTERS.

apparatus. See MACHINE.

apparatus claim. See PATENT CLAIM.

apparatus limitation. *Patents.* The inclusion of a structure or physical apparatus in a method or process claim. ● An apparatus limitation, while not objectionable, carries little weight toward establishing the patentability of a method or process claim.

apparent, *adj.* (14c) **1.** Visible; manifest; obvious. **2.** Ostensible; seeming.

apparent agency. See *agency by estoppel* under AGENCY (1).

apparent agent. See AGENT (2).

apparent assent. See ASSENT.

apparent authority. See AUTHORITY (1).

apparent danger. See DANGER.

apparent defect. See *patent defect* under DEFECT.

apparent easement. See EASEMENT.

apparent heir. See *heir apparent* under HEIR.

apparent principal. See PRINCIPAL (1).

apparent servitude. See SERVITUDE (2).

apparent title. See COLOR OF TITLE.

apparitor (ə-**par**-ə-tər *or* -tor). **1.** *Roman law.* (*ital.*) An officer who served a court, esp. as secretary, messenger (*viator*), or herald. — Also termed *viator.* **2.** *Civil law.* An officer who attends court to execute judicial orders. **3.** *Eccles. law.* An officer who executes orders and decrees, esp. by serving summonses.

appeal, *n.* (13c) **1.** A proceeding undertaken to have a decision reconsidered by a higher authority; esp., the submission of a lower court's or agency's decision to a higher court for review and possible reversal <the case is on appeal>. — Also termed *petition in error;* (in Scots law) *falsing of dooms.* See CERTIORARI.

appeal as of right. See *appeal by right.*

appeal by application. An appeal for which permission must first be obtained from the reviewing court. — Also termed *appeal by leave.*

appeal by right. An appeal to a higher court from which permission need not be first obtained. — Also termed *appeal as of right; appeal of right.*

appeal de novo. An appeal in which the appellate court uses the trial court's record but reviews the evidence and law without deference to the trial court's rulings. — Also termed *de novo review; de novo judicial review.*

appeal from the decision of the chair. *Parliamentary law.* A motion by which a member invokes the assembly's right of reviewing its chair's decision on a point of order. — Also termed *appeal from the ruling of the chair.*

appeal from the ruling of the chair. See *appeal from the decision of the chair.*

appeal in forma pauperis (in **for**-mə **paw**-pər-is). An appeal by an indigent party, for whom court costs are waived. Fed. R. App. P. 24. See IN FORMA PAUPERIS.

consolidated appeal. An appeal in which two or more parties, whose interests were similar enough to make a joinder practicable, proceed as a single appellant.

cross-appeal. An appeal by the appellee, usu. heard at the same time as the appellant's appeal.

delayed appeal. An appeal that takes place after the time for appealing has expired, but only when the reviewing court has granted permission because of special circumstances.

devolutive appeal (di-**vol**-yə-tiv). An appeal that does not suspend the execution of the underlying judgment.

direct appeal. An appeal from a trial court's decision directly to the jurisdiction's highest court, thus bypassing review by an intermediate appellate court. ● Such an appeal may be authorized, for example, when the case involves the constitutionality of a state law.

duplicitous appeal. An appeal from two separate judgments, from a judgment and an order, or from two orders.

federal appeal. An appeal to a federal appellate court usu. from (1) a federal district court to a United States circuit court, (2) a United States circuit court to the Supreme Court of the United States, or (3) a state supreme court to the Supreme Court of the United States.

frivolous appeal. (18c) An appeal having no legal basis, usu. filed for delay to induce a judgment creditor to settle or to avoid payment of a judgment. • Federal Rule of Appellate Procedure 38 provides for the award of damages and costs if the appellate court determines that an appeal is frivolous. Fed. R. App. P. 38.

interlocutory appeal. An appeal that occurs before the trial court's final ruling on the entire case. 28 USCA § 1292(b). • Some interlocutory appeals involve legal points necessary to the determination of the case, while others involve collateral orders that are wholly separate from the merits of the action. See INTERLOCUTORY APPEALS ACT; FINAL-JUDGMENT RULE.

judgment-roll appeal. An appeal based only on the pleadings, the findings of the court, and the judgment.

limited appeal. An appeal from only certain portions of a decision, usu. only the adverse or unfavorable portions.

precautionary appeal. See *protective appeal.*

protective appeal. A precautionary appeal filed by counsel when the client might otherwise lose an effective right to appeal. • A protective appeal is typically filed when (1) a client's motion to intervene has been denied, and the trial court is entering other orders that the client wants to appeal, (2) counsel has doubts about where to appeal, (3) counsel has doubts about the length of the appeal period, or (4) the client must preserve uncertain or contingent rights. — Also termed *precautionary appeal.*

state appeal. An appeal to a state appellate court, either from a court of first instance to any intermediate appellate court or from a lower court to the highest court in the state-court system.

suspensive appeal. An appeal that stays the execution of the underlying judgment.

2. *Hist.* The charging of someone with a crime; specif., an accusation of a crime, esp. treason or a felony.

appeal, *vb.* **1.** To seek review (from a lower court's decision) by a higher court <petitioner appeals the conviction>. **2.** *Hist.* To charge with a crime; accuse. — **appealability,** *n.*

appealable decision. See DECISION.

appeal as of right. See *appeal by right* under APPEAL.

appeal bond. See BOND (2).

appeal brief. See BRIEF.

appeal by leave. See *appeal by application* under APPEAL.

appeal by right. See APPEAL.

appeal court. See *appellate court* under COURT.

appeal de novo. See APPEAL.

appealer. *Archaic.* APPELLANT.

appeal from the chair. *Parliamentary law.* An assembly member's formal objection to a decision made by the chair. • If the appeal is seconded, the chair must state what question was answered and explain the reasons for the chair's decision, then allow the members present to vote in support of or against that decision.

appeal in forma pauperis. See APPEAL.

appeal of felony. *Hist.* A procedure by which a person accused another of a crime, demanded proof of innocence by wager of battle, or informed against an accomplice. — Also termed *appellum de felonia.*

appeal of right. See *appeal by right* under APPEAL.

appeals council. A commission that hears appeals of rulings by administrative-law judges in social-security matters.

appeals court. See *appellate court* under COURT.

appearance, *n.* (14c) *Procedure.* A coming into court as a party or interested person, or as a lawyer on behalf of a party or interested person; esp., a defendant's act of taking part in a lawsuit, whether by formally participating in it or by an answer, demurrer, or motion, or by taking post-judgment steps in the lawsuit in either the trial court or an appellate court. — **appear,** *vb.*

appearance de bene esse. See *special appearance.*

appearance pro hac vice (proh hak **vi**-see *or* proh hahk **vee**-chay). [Latin] An appearance made by an out-of-state lawyer for one particular case, usu. by leave of court. • For more on the pronunciation of this term, see PRO HAC VICE.

appearance under protest. *English & Canadian law.* See *special appearance.*

compulsory appearance. An appearance by one who is required to appear by having been served with process.

general appearance. A general-purpose appearance that waives a party's ability later to dispute the court's authority to enter a binding judgment against him or her.

initial appearance. A criminal defendant's first appearance in court to hear the charges read, to be advised of his or her rights, and to have bail determined. • The initial appearance is usu. required by statute to occur without undue delay. In a misdemeanor case, the initial appearance may be combined with the arraignment. See ARRAIGNMENT.

limited appearance. See *special appearance.*

special appearance. **1.** A defendant's pleading that either claims that the court lacks personal jurisdiction over the defendant or objects to improper service of process. **2.** A defendant's showing up in court for the sole purpose of contesting the court's assertion of personal jurisdiction over the defendant. ● Special appearances have been abolished in federal court. Fed. R. Civ. P. 12(b). — Also termed *limited appearance; appearance de bene esse;* (in English & Canadian law) *appearance under protest.*

voluntary appearance. An appearance entered by a party's own will, without the service of process.

appearance bond. See *bail bond* under BOND (2).

appearance date. See *answer day* under DAY.

appearance day. See *answer day* under DAY.

appearance de bene esse. See *special appearance* under APPEARANCE.

appearance docket. See DOCKET (1).

appearance doctrine. (1972) In the law of self-defense, the rule that a defendant's use of force is justified if the defendant reasonably believed it to be justified.

appearance pro hac vice. See APPEARANCE.

appearance term. See TERM (5).

appearance ticket. See CITATION (2).

appearance under protest. *English & Canadian law.* See *special appearance* under APPEARANCE.

appellant (ə-**pel**-ənt). (15c) A party who appeals a lower court's decision, usu. seeking reversal of that decision. — Also termed (archaically) *plaintiff in error;* (formerly) *appealer.* Cf. APPELLEE.

appellate (ə-**pel**-it), *adj.* (18c) Of or relating to an appeal or appeals generally.

appellate brief. See BRIEF (1).

appellate counsel. See COUNSEL.

appellate court. See COURT.

appellate division. A department of a superior court responsible for hearing appeals; an intermediate appellate court in some states, such as New York and New Jersey.

appellate jurisdiction. See JURISDICTION.

appellate record. See RECORD ON APPEAL.

appellate review. See REVIEW.

appellate rules. A body of rules governing appeals from lower courts.

Appellate Term. A division of the New York Supreme Court established to hear both appeals from decisions of the civil and criminal courts of New York City and appeals from district courts, town courts, and other lower courts. ● The Appellate Term's decisions are often unpublished but are binding authority on the lower courts.

appellation of origin. *Trademarks.* Representation of a product's geographic origin by use of a mark — such as symbol, word, phrase, or graphic element such as a map — whose use is regulated to ensure that the products so marked reflect some well-known feature peculiar to the region. ● This term usu. applies to a product whose quality or some characteristic feature has been gained by natural means, such as by the nature of the local climate or soil, or by the nature of the way it is made, such as by local customs of production. For example, the appellation *burgundy* can be used only for wines made from certain types of varietal grapes from particular regions of France.

appellee (ap-ə-**lee**). (16c) A party against whom an appeal is taken and whose role is to respond to that appeal, usu. seeking affirmance of the lower court's decision. See RESPONDENT. Cf. APPELLANT.

appendant (ə-**pen**-dənt), *adj.* (15c) Attached or belonging to property as an additional but subsidiary right. — **appendant,** *n.*

appendant claim. See *dependent claim* under PATENT CLAIM.

appendant easement. See *easement appurtenant* under EASEMENT.

appendant power. See POWER (5).

appendix, *n.* (16c) **1.** A supplementary document attached to the end of a writing <the brief includes an appendix of exhibits>. ● For the requirements of an appendix to a federal appellate brief, see Fed. R. App. P. 30. **2.** *English law.* A volume that contains material documents and other evidence presented in a lower court. ● The volume is used by the House of Lords or Privy Council when functioning as an appellate tribunal. Pl. **appendixes, appendices.**

applicable exclusion amount. *Tax.* The dollar value of an estate that is exempt from federal estate and gift taxes. See *unified estate-and-gift-tax credit* under TAX CREDIT.

applicable exclusion credit. See *unified estate-and-gift-tax credit* under TAX CREDIT.

applicant. (18c) **1.** One who requests something; a petitioner, such as a person who applies for letters of administration. **2.** ACCOUNT PARTY.

application. (15c) **1.** A request or petition. See COPYRIGHT APPLICATION; PATENT APPLICATION; TRADEMARK APPLICATION. **2.** MOTION.

ex parte application. See *ex parte motion* under MOTION (1).

interlocutory application. A motion for equitable or legal relief sought before a final decision.

3. *Bankruptcy.* A request for an order not requiring advance notice and an opportunity for a hearing before the order is issued.

Application Division. *Patents.* The part of the U.S. Patent and Trademark Office that is responsible for accepting patent applications, assigning them serial numbers, checking them for completeness and formalities, placing them in file wrappers, and assigning them to an appropriate art group based on the invention's class and subclass of technology.

application for a reissue patent. See PATENT APPLICATION.

application for leave to appeal. (1882) A motion asking an appellate court to hear a party's appeal from a judgment when the party has no appeal by right or when the party's time limit for an appeal by right has expired. • The reviewing court has discretion whether to grant or reject such a motion.

application for transfer. In some jurisdictions, a request to a state's highest court to hear an appeal from an intermediate court of appeal. • The appeal is heard as though it had been appealed to the highest court originally. The court may typically ignore the intermediate court's decision and may consider an error that was not raised in the intermediate court.

application number. *Patents & Trademarks.* The eight-digit sequential number assigned by the U.S. Patent and Trademark Office to a patent or trademark application. • Applications are typically referred to by an application number, which consists of a two-digit series code, a slash, and a six-digit serial number. References to patent applications also include the filing date <application no. 08/944,183, filed September 20, 1978>. — Also termed *serial number.*

application service provider. A business that hosts software on its computers and gives subscribers access as needed. • The subscriber does not need to purchase a license to use the software before the provider sends it to the subscriber's computer, usu. over the Internet or a private electronic network. — Abbr. ASP.

applied-art doctrine. *Copyright.* The rule that a pictorial, graphic, or sculptural work that has an inherent use apart from its appearance, and is also an expressive work apart from its utility, may qualify for copyright protection. • Examples have included bookends, lamps, and sundials. In contrast to applied art, industrial designs are not copyrightable, although they may be protected by design patents instead. — Also termed *useful-article doctrine.*

applied cost. See COST (1).

apply, *vb.* (14c) **1.** To make a formal request or motion <apply for a loan> <apply for injunctive relief>. **2.** To employ for a limited purpose <apply payments to a reduction in interest>. **3.** To put to use with a particular subject matter <apply the law to the facts> <apply the law only to transactions in interstate commerce>.

appointed counsel. See *assigned counsel* under COUNSEL.

appointee. (18c) **1.** One who is appointed. **2.** One who receives the benefit of a power of appointment. See POWER OF APPOINTMENT.

   permissible appointee. A person to whom appointive property may be assigned under a power of appointment. — Also termed *object of the power of appointment; object of the power; object of a power.*

appointive asset. See ASSET.

appointive property. See PROPERTY.

appointment, *n.* (15c) **1.** The designation of a person, such as a nonelected public official, for a job or duty; esp., the naming of someone to a nonelected public office <Article II of the U.S. Constitution grants the President the power of appointment for principal federal officials, subject to senatorial consent>.

   at-pleasure appointment. See *pleasure appointment.*

   pleasure appointment. The assignment of someone to employment that can be taken away at any time, with no requirement for cause, notice, or a hearing. — Also termed *at-pleasure appointment.*

   public appointment. An appointment to a public office.

   recess appointment. An appointment, including a judicial appointment, made by the President when the Senate is not in session, subject to the Senate's later ratification.

2. An office occupied by someone who has been appointed <a high appointment in the federal government>. **3.** *Parliamentary law.* The naming of an officer, the members of a committee, or the holder of any other title in an organization by means other than the organization's election. **4.** The act of disposing of property, in exercise of a power granted for that purpose <the tenant's appointment of lands>. See POWER OF APPOINTMENT. — **appoint,** *vb.* — **appointer** (for senses 1–3), *n.* — **appointor** (for sense 4), *n.*

   illusory appointment. A nominal, unduly restrictive, or conditional transfer of property under a power of appointment.

Appointments Clause. (1976) The clause of the U.S. Constitution giving the President the power to nominate federal judges and various other officials. U.S. Const. art. II, § 2.

apportionment, *n.* (16c) **1.** Division into proportionate shares; esp., the division of rights and liabilities between two or more persons or entities. **2.** *Tax.* The act of allocating or attributing moneys or expenses in a given way, as when a taxpayer allocates part of profits to a particular tax year or part of the use of a personal asset to a business. **3.** Distribution of legislative seats among districts; esp., the allocation of congressional representatives among the states based on population, as required by the 14th Amendment. ● The claim that a state is denying the right of representation to its citizens through improper apportionment presents a justiciable issue. — Also termed *legislative apportionment.* See REAPPORTIONMENT. **4.** The division (by statute or by the testator's instruction) of an estate-tax liability among persons interested in an estate. — **apportion,** *vb.*

apportionment clause. *Insurance.* A policy provision that distributes insurance proceeds in proportion to the total coverage.

apportionment of liability. (1855) *Torts.* The parceling out of liability for an injury among multiple tortfeasors, and possibly the plaintiff as well. ● Apportionment of liability encompasses such legal doctrines as joint and several liability, comparative responsibility, indemnity, and settlements. See Restatement (Third) of Torts: Apportionment of Liability (1999).

apportionment rule. *Oil & gas.* The minority doctrine that royalties accrued under an oil-and-gas lease on land that is subdivided during the lease term must be shared by the landowners in proportion to their interests in the land. ● For example, if Grey granted a lease to Simms, then sold one-half of the land to Metcalfe, Simms and Metcalfe would each be entitled to one-half of any royalty from the land, no matter where the producing well is located. Only California, Mississippi, and Pennsylvania follow this rule. Cf. NONAPPORTIONMENT RULE.

appose (ə-**pohz**), *vb. Hist.* **1.** To interrogate, esp. with difficult questions. **2.** To confront (someone) with objections to something. **3.** To examine the books and accounts of; audit.

apposer (ə-**pohz**-ər). *Hist.* **1.** A questioner; interrogator. **2.** An Exchequer officer who examined sheriffs' accounts; specif., an officer responsible for examining the sheriff's estreat (book of fines), comparing the entries with those in court records, and apposing (interrogating) the sheriff on each sum in the estreat. ● This office was abolished in England in 1833. — Also termed *foreign apposer.*

apposite (**ap**-ə-zit), *adj.* Suitable; appropriate.

appraisal, *n.* (1817) **1.** The determination of what constitutes a fair price; valuation; estimation of worth. **2.** The report of such a determination. — Also termed *appraisement.* Cf. ASSESSMENT (3). — **appraise,** *vb.*

appraisal clause. An insurance-policy provision allowing either the insurer or the insured to demand an independent estimation of a claimed loss.

appraisal remedy. The statutory right of corporate shareholders who oppose some extraordinary corporate action (such as a merger) to have their shares judicially appraised and to demand that the corporation buy back their shares at the appraised value. — Also termed *appraisal right; dissenters' right; right of dissent and appraisal.*

appraisal trinity. The three most commonly accepted methods of appraising real property: the market approach, the cost approach, and the income approach. See MARKET APPROACH; COST APPROACH; INCOME APPROACH.

appraisement. (17c) **1.** APPRAISAL. **2.** An ADR method used for resolving the amount or extent of liability on a contract when the issue of liability itself is not in dispute. ● Unlike arbitration, appraisement is not a quasi-judicial proceeding but instead an informal determination of the amount owed on a contract.

appraiser. An impartial person who estimates the value of something, such as real estate, jewelry, or rare books. — Also termed *valuer.*

   business appraiser. An appraiser who specializes in determining the value of commercial enterprises and property, including real estate and intellectual property.

   merchant appraiser. See MERCHANT APPRAISER.

appreciable, *adj.* Capable of being measured or perceived.

appreciate, *vb.* **1.** To understand the significance or meaning of. **2.** To increase in value.

appreciation, *n.* (18c) An increase in an asset's value, usu. because of inflation. Cf. DEPRECIATION. — **appreciate,** *vb.* — **appreciable,** *adj.*

appreciation surplus. See *revaluation surplus* under SURPLUS.

appreciation test. (1970) *Criminal law.* A test for the insanity defense requiring proof by clear and convincing evidence that at the time of the crime, the defendant suffered from a severe mental disease or defect preventing him or her from appreciating the wrongfulness of the conduct. ● This test, along with the accompanying plea of *not guilty by reason of insanity,* was established by the Insanity Defense Reform Act of 1984. 18 USCA § 17. — Also termed *Insanity Defense Reform Act of 1984 test.* See INSANITY DEFENSE.

apprehension, *n.* (14c) **1.** Seizure in the name of the law; arrest <apprehension of a criminal>. **2.** Perception; comprehension; belief <the tort of assault requires apprehension by the plaintiff of imminent contact>. **3.** Fear; anxiety <most people approach public speaking with some apprehension>. — **apprehend,** *vb.*

apprentice. 1. *Hist.* A person bound by an indenture to work for an employer for a specified period to learn a craft, trade, or profession. **2.** A learner in any field of employment or business, esp. one who learns by hands-on experience or technical on-the-job training by one experienced in the field.

apprentice of the law. *Hist.* **1.** A law student. **2.** A barrister of junior status. — Also termed *apprentice en la ley; apprenticius ad legem.*

apprize, *vb.* To appraise; to assign a value to.

approach, right of. See RIGHT OF APPROACH.

appropriated retained earnings. See EARNINGS.

appropriated surplus. See SURPLUS.

appropriation, *n.* (14c) **1.** The exercise of control over property; a taking of possession. Cf. EXPROPRIATION (1); MISAPPROPRIATION (1). **2.** A legislative body's act of setting aside a sum of money for a public purpose. • If the sum is earmarked for a precise or limited purpose, it is sometimes called a *specific appropriation.* **3.** The sum of money so voted. **4.** *Torts.* An invasion of privacy whereby one person takes the name or likeness of another for commercial gain. **5.** The transfer of a benefice, together with all its interests, to a spiritual corporation. See *spiritual corporation* under CORPORATION. Cf. IMPROPRIATION. **6.** The benefice so transferred. — **appropriate,** *vb.* — **appropriable,** *adj.* — **appropriator,** *n.*

appropriations bill. See BILL (3).

approval sale. See *sale on approval* under SALE.

approve, *vb.* **1.** To give formal sanction to; to confirm authoritatively. **2.** *Parliamentary law.* To adopt. See ADOPTION (5). — **approval,** *n.*

Approved Drug Products with Therapeutic Equivalence Evaluations. See ORANGE BOOK.

approved indorsed note. See NOTE (1).

approved list. See LEGAL LIST.

approver (ə-**proo**-vər), *n. Hist.* **1.** One who offers proof; esp., a criminal who confesses and testifies against one or more accomplices. See *relative confession* under CONFESSION. **2.** An agent or bailiff; esp., one who manages a farm or estate for another.

approximation, doctrine of. See DOCTRINE OF APPROXIMATION.

appurtenance (ə-**pərt**-[ə-]nənts), *n.* (14c) Something that belongs or is attached to something else <the garden is an appurtenance to the land>.

appurtenant, *adj.* (14c) Annexed to a more important thing. — Also termed (in Scots law) *part and pertinent.*

appurtenant easement. See *easement appurtenant* under EASEMENT.

APR. *abbr.* See *annual percentage rate* under INTEREST RATE.

à prendre (ah **prawn**-drə *or* -dər). [French] (17c) For taking; for seizure. See PROFIT À PRENDRE.

a priori (ay prɪ-**or**-ɪ *or* ah pree-**or**-ee), *adv.* [Latin "from what is before"] (17c) Deductively; from the general to the particular <as an analyst, he reasoned a priori — from seemingly self-evident propositions to particular conclusions>. Cf. A POSTERIORI. — **a priori,** *adj.*

APS. *abbr.* **1.** ADULT PROTECTIVE SERVICES. **2.** AUTOMATED PATENT SYSTEM.

APV. *abbr.* See *adjusted present value* under PRESENT VALUE.

aquatic right. See WATER RIGHT.

Aquilian law. See LEX AQUILIA.

a quo (ah *or* ay **kwoh**), *adv.* [Latin] From which. — Also termed *a qua.* See AD QUEM; *court a quo* under COURT.

A.R. *abbr.* ANNO REGNI.

arable land. See LAND.

ARB. *abbr.* ACCOUNTING RESEARCH BULLETIN.

arbiter (**ahr**-bə-tər). (14c) One with the power to decide disputes, such as a judge <the Supreme Court is the final arbiter of legal disputes in the United States>. Cf. ARBITRATOR.

arbitrage (**ahr**-bə-trahzh), *n.* The simultaneous buying and selling of identical securities in different markets, with the hope of profiting from the price difference between those markets. — Also termed *space arbitrage.* — **arbitrager** (**ahr**-bə-trahzh-ər), **arbitrageur** (ahr-bə-trah-**zhər**), *n.*

convertible arbitrage. See *kind arbitrage.*

covered-interest arbitrage. The simultaneous investment in a currency and execution of spot- and forward-rate foreign-exchange contracts to take advantage of exchange-rate and interest-rate differentials between currencies without assuming foreign-exchange risk.

currency arbitrage. The simultaneous purchase of a currency in one market and sale of it in another to take advantage of differences or fluctuations in exchange rates.

kind arbitrage. Purchase of a security that, having no restriction other than the payment of money, is exchangeable or convertible within a reasonable time to a second security, with a simultaneous offsetting sale of the second security. — Also termed *convertible arbitrage*.

risk arbitrage. Arbitrage of assets that are probably, but not necessarily, equivalent; esp., arbitrage of corporate stock in a potential merger or takeover, whereby the target company's stock is bought and the acquiring company's stock is sold simultaneously.

time arbitrage. Purchase of a commodity against a present sale of the identical commodity for a future delivery; esp., the simultaneous buying and selling of securities for immediate delivery and future delivery, with the hope of profiting from the difference in prices.

arbitrage bond. See BOND (3).

arbitrament (ahr-**bi**-trə-mənt). (15c) **1.** The power to decide for oneself or others; the power to decide finally and absolutely. **2.** The act of deciding or settling a dispute that has been referred to arbitration. **3.** AWARD. — Also spelled (archaically) *arbitrement*.

arbitrament and award. A plea that the same matter has already been decided in arbitration.

arbitrary, *adj.* (15c) **1.** Depending on individual discretion; specif., determined by a judge rather than by fixed rules, procedures, or law. **2.** (Of a judicial decision) founded on prejudice or preference rather than on reason or fact. ● This type of decision is often termed *arbitrary and capricious*. Cf. CAPRICIOUS.

arbitrary mark. See *arbitrary trademark* under TRADEMARK.

arbitrary name. See *arbitrary trademark* under TRADEMARK.

arbitrary trademark. See TRADEMARK.

arbitration, *n.* (15c) A method of dispute resolution involving one or more neutral third parties who are usu. agreed to by the disputing parties and whose decision is binding. — Also termed (redundantly) *binding arbitration*. Cf. MEDIATION (1). — **arbitrate,** *vb.* — **arbitral,** *adj.*

ad hoc arbitration. (1931) Arbitration of only one issue.

adjudicative-claims arbitration. (1972) Arbitration designed to resolve matters usu. handled by courts (such as a tort claim), in contrast to arbitration of labor issues, international trade, and other fields traditionally associated with arbitration.

compromissory arbitration. An international arbitration grounded on a mutual promise to define the scope of the dispute and abide by the arbitrator's decision. See COMPROMIS.

compulsory arbitration. (1813) Arbitration required by law or forced by law on the parties.

court-ordered arbitration. See *judicial arbitration*.

final-offer arbitration. (1971) Arbitration in which each party must submit a "final offer" to the arbitrator, who may choose only one. ● This device gives each party an incentive to make a reasonable offer or risk the arbitrator's accepting the other party's offer. The purpose of this type of arbitration is to counteract arbitrators' tendency to make compromise decisions halfway between the two parties' demands.

grievance arbitration. 1. Arbitration that involves the violation or interpretation of an existing contract. ● The arbitrator issues a final decision regarding the meaning of the contractual terms. **2.** *Labor law.* Arbitration of an employee's grievance, usu. relating to an alleged violation of the employee's rights under a collective-bargaining agreement. ● The arbitration procedure is set out in the collective-bargaining agreement. Grievance arbitration is the final step in grievance procedure. — Also termed *rights arbitration*. See GRIEVANCE PROCEDURE.

interest arbitration. Arbitration that involves settling the terms of a contract being negotiated between the parties; esp., in labor law, arbitration of a dispute concerning what provisions will be included in a new collective-bargaining agreement. ● When the parties cannot agree on contractual terms, an arbitrator decides. This type of arbitration is most common in public-sector collective bargaining.

judicial arbitration. Court-referred arbitration that is final unless a party objects to the award. — Also termed *court-ordered arbitration*.

rights arbitration. See *grievance arbitration*.

voluntary arbitration. (18c) Arbitration by the agreement of the parties.

arbitration act. (1807) A federal or state statute providing for the submission of disputes to arbitration.

arbitration and award. An affirmative defense asserting that the subject matter of the action has already been settled in arbitration.

arbitration board. A panel of arbitrators appointed to hear and decide a dispute according to the rules of arbitration.

arbitration bond. A performance bond executed by the parties in an arbitration. See PERFORMANCE BOND (1).

arbitration clause. (1828) A contractual provision mandating arbitration — and thereby avoiding litigation — of disputes about the contracting parties' rights, duties, and liabilities.

arbitration of exchange. The simultaneous buying and selling of bills of exchange in different international markets, with the hope of profiting from the price difference of the currencies in those markets. See ARBITRAGE; DRAFT (1).

arbitrator, *n.* (15c) A neutral person who resolves disputes between parties, esp. by means of formal arbitration. — Also termed *impartial chair*; (in Latin) *compromissarius.* Cf. MEDIATOR; ARBITER. — **arbitratorship,** *n.*

arbitrement. *Archaic.* See ARBITRAMENT.

Architect of the Capitol. The officer in the legislative branch of the federal government responsible for maintaining the buildings and grounds of the U.S. Capitol, the Supreme Court, and the Library of Congress. • The Architect also plans and supervises new building construction. The office was established in 1876. 2 USCA §§ 1801, 1811.

architect's lien. See LIEN.

architectural review. See DESIGN REVIEW.

architectural work. See WORK (2).

archival copy. *Copyright.* A copy of an original piece of software, made by the consumer for backup. • An owner may make archival copies of software without infringing its copyright. But if the owner transfers the original software, all archival copies must also be transferred or else destroyed. 17 USCA § 117.

archive, *n.* (*usu. pl.*) **1.** A place where public, historical, or institutional records are systematically preserved. **2.** Collected and preserved public, historical, or institutional papers and records. **3.** Any systematic compilation of materials, esp. writings, in physical or electronic form. — **archive,** *vb.*

Archivist of the United States. The federal officer in charge of the National Archives and Records Administration.

area bargaining. Negotiation of collective-bargaining agreements by a union with several employers in a particular geographic area.

area-rate clause. *Oil & gas.* A price-escalation provision in a long-term gas contract permitting an automatic increase in the contract price if any regulatory agency prescribes or allows a higher price on gas sold in the area. — Also termed *FPC clause.*

area-standards picketing. *Labor law.* The practice that a union undertakes to protect its members in a particular region by picketing employers that may undercut the market through the potentially lower labor costs of a nonunion workforce.

area variance. See VARIANCE (2).

Areeda-Turner test. *Antitrust.* An economic test for predatory pricing whereby a price below average variable cost is presumed to be predatory and therefore illegal. • This test is widely accepted by federal courts. Its name derives from the coauthors of an influential law-review article: Phillip Areeda & Donald F. Turner, *Predatory Pricing and Practices Under Section 2 of the Sherman Act,* 88 Harv. L. Rev. 692 (1975). They reformulated their test in 3 Phillip Areeda & Donald F. Turner, *Antitrust Law* ¶¶ 710–722 (1978). See PREDATORY PRICING.

A reorganization. See REORGANIZATION (2).

arg. *abbr.* ARGUENDO (2).

arguendo (ahr-gyoo-**en**-doh). [Latin "in arguing"] (1817) **1.** For the sake of argument <assuming arguendo that discovery procedures were correctly followed, the court still cannot grant the defendant's motion to dismiss>. **2.** During the course of argument <counsel mentioned arguendo that the case has been followed in three other decisions>. — Abbr. **arg.**

arguer. One who makes an oral argument; esp., an attorney, often one of several attorneys representing the same client, who presents an oral argument in court.

argument. (14c) **1.** A statement that attempts to persuade; esp., the remarks of counsel in analyzing and pointing out or repudiating a desired inference, for the assistance of a decision-maker. **2.** The act or process of attempting to persuade. See ORAL ARGUMENT; CLOSING ARGUMENT.

argumentative, *adj.* (15c) **1.** Of or relating to argument or persuasion <an argumentative tone of voice>. **2.** Expressing not only facts, but also inferences and conclusions drawn from facts <the judge sustained the prosecutor's objection to the argumentative question>.

argumentative instruction. See JURY INSTRUCTION.

argumentative pleading. See PLEADING (1).

argumentative question. A question in which the examiner interposes a viewpoint under the guise of asking a question. • This is considered an abuse of interrogation.

argumentum (ahr-gyoo-**men**-təm), *n.* [Latin] An argument. Pl. **argumenta.**

argumentum ab auctoritate (ahr-gyoo-**men**-təmab awk-tor-ə-**tay**-tee). [Latin] An argument from authority (of a statute or case).

argumentum ab impossibili (ahr-gyoo-**men**-təmab im-pah-**sib**-ə-lı). [Latin] An argument from impossibility.

argumentum ab inconvenienti (ahr-gyoo-**men**-təm ab in-kən-vee-nee-**en**-tı). [Latin] An argument from inconvenience; an argument that emphasizes the harmful consequences of failing to follow the position advocated.

argumentum a contrario (ahr-gyoo-**men**-təm ay kən-**trair**-ee-oh). [Latin] An argument for contrary treatment.

argumentum ad baculum (ahr-gyoo-**men**-təm ad **bak**-yə-ləm). [Latin] An argument depending on physical force to back it up.

argumentum ad captandum (ahr-gyoo-**men**-təm ad kap-**tan**-dəm). [Latin] An argument appealing to the emotions of a crowd.

argumentum ad crumenam (ahr-gyoo-**men**-təm ad kroo-**mee**-nəm). [fr. Latin *crumena* "purse"] An argument appealing to the purse (or one's desire to save money).

argumentum ad hominem (ahr-gyoo-**men**-təm ad **hom**-ə-nəm *or* -nem). [Latin "argument to the man"] An argument based on disparagement or praise of another in a way that obscures the real issue.

argumentum ad ignorantiam (ahr-gyoo-**men**-təmad ig-nə-**ran**-shee-əm). [Latin] An argument based on an adversary's ignorance of the matter in dispute.

argumentum ad invidiam (ahr-gyoo-**men**-təm ad in-**vid**-ee-əm). [Latin] An argument appealing to one's hatreds or prejudices.

argumentum ad judicium (ahr-gyoo-**men**-təm ad joo-**dish**-ee-əm). [Latin] An argument addressed to the judgment; a proof based on knowledge or probability.

argumentum ad misericordiam (ahr-gyoo-**men**-təm ad miz-ə-ri-**kor**-dee-əm). [Latin] An argument appealing to pity.

argumentum ad populum (ahr-gyoo-**men**-təmad **pop**-yə-ləm). [Latin] An argument appealing to the crowd.

argumentum ad rem (ahr-gyoo-**men**-təm ad **rem**). [Latin] An argument on the point at issue.

argumentum ad verecundiam (ahr-gyoo-**men**-təm ad ver-ə-**kən**-dee-əm). [Latin] An argument appealing to the listener's modesty; an argument based on the opinions of people who are considered authorities.

argumentum a simili (ahr-gyoo-**men**-təm ay **sim**-ə-lı). [Latin "argument from a like case"] An argument by analogy or similarity.

argumentum baculinum (ahr-gyoo-**men**-təm bak-yə-**lı**-nəm). [fr. Latin *baculus* "a rod or scepter"] An argument appealing to force.

argumentum ex concesso (ahr-gyoo-**men**-təm eks kən-**ses**-oh). [Latin] An argument based on an earlier admission by the adversary.

argumentum ex silentio (ahr-gyoo-**men**-təm eks si-**len**-shee-oh). [Latin] An argument from silence — i.e., based on the absence of express evidence to the contrary.

arise, *vb.* (bef. 12c) **1.** To originate; to stem (from) <a federal claim arising under the U.S. Constitution>. **2.** To result (from) <litigation routinely arises from such accidents>. **3.** To emerge in one's consciousness; to come to one's attention <the question of appealability then arose>. **4.** (Of a court) to adjourn; to suspend sitting.

arising-in jurisdiction. See JURISDICTION.

aristocracy. 1. A privileged class of persons, esp. the hereditary nobility. **2.** A government ruled by a privileged class.

aristodemocracy. A government consisting of both democratic and aristocratic elements; a government in which power is divided between the nobility (or more powerful group) and the rest of the people.

Arkansas rule. *Secured transactions.* The principle that the collateral securing a loan is presumed to be worth at least as much as the loan's balance, and that the creditor has the burden to prove that a sale of the collateral would not satisfy the loan amount. *Norton v. National Bank of Commerce,* 398 S.W.2d 538 (Ark. 1966).

ARM. *abbr.* See *adjustable-rate mortgage* under MORTGAGE.

armed, *adj.* **1.** Equipped with a weapon <an armed robber>. **2.** Involving the use of a weapon <armed robbery>.

armed conflict. *Int'l law.* **1.** A state of open hostility between two nations, or between a nation and an aggressive force. ● A state of armed conflict may exist without a formal declaration of war by either side. **2.** A military action taken under Article 42 of the United Nations Charter. — Also termed *police action.*

armed neutrality. See NEUTRALITY.

armed peace. See PEACE.

armed robbery. See ROBBERY.

Armed Services Board of Contract Appeals. A quasi-judicial board that reviews appeals from final decisions of contracting officers involving disputes relating to contracts made by elements of the Department of Defense and designated civilian agencies. ● Its decisions are subject to judicial review. — Abbr. ASBCA.

arm-in-arm, *adj.* (2000) Of, relating to, or involving a transaction between parties whose personal interests are involved. Cf. ARM'S-LENGTH.

armistice. See TRUCE.

arm of the court. An officer of the court who performs tasks or duties related to the court's functions.

arm of the sea. The portion of a river or bay in which the tide ebbs and flows. ● It may extend as far into the interior as the water of the river is propelled backward by the tide.

arm of the state. (1953) An entity created by a state and operating as an alter ego or instrumentality of the state, such as a state university or a state department of transportation. • The 11th Amendment of the U.S. Constitution generally bars suits in federal court by individuals against states. The Amendment has been interpreted as protecting arms of the state as well as the state itself. Cities and local school districts have been held not to be arms of the state.

arms, law of. 1. Rules concerning conditions of war, such as the treatment of prisoners. **2.** The law relating to the right to bear arms. **3.** The law relating to armorial bearings, i.e., coats of arms granted by the College of Heralds in England, Lord Lyon King of Arms in Scotland, and corresponding officers in some other countries.

arms, right to bear. See RIGHT TO BEAR ARMS.

arms control. *Int'l law.* A policy of minimizing instabilities in the military field by lessening the possibility of the outbreak of war while reducing in number a country's weapons of mass destruction. Cf. DISARMAMENT.

arm's-length, *adj.* Of or relating to dealings between two parties who are not related or not on close terms and who are presumed to have roughly equal bargaining power; not involving a confidential relationship <an arm's-length transaction does not create fiduciary duties between the parties>. Cf. ARM-IN-ARM.

arm's-length price. See PRICE.

arm's-length transaction. See TRANSACTION.

army. 1. A military force, esp. of ground troops. **2.** Any substantial group of individuals armed for combat. **3.** A vast, organized group.

> *regular army.* The permanent military establishment, maintained during both war and peacetime.

arraignment, *n.* (16c) The initial step in a criminal prosecution whereby the defendant is brought before the court to hear the charges and to enter a plea. Fed. R. Crim. P. 10. Cf. PRELIMINARY HEARING; *initial appearance* under APPEARANCE. — **arraign,** *vb.*

arrangement in order of breadth. *Patents.* The placement of claims in a patent application in order of scope so that the first claim in the application or patent is the broadest and later claims are progressively narrower.

arrangements committee. See COMMITTEE.

arrangement with creditors. *Bankruptcy.* A debtor's agreement with creditors for the settlement, satisfaction, or extension of time for payment of debts. See BANKRUPTCY PLAN.

arranger for disposal. *Environmental law.* An entity that owns or possesses hazardous substances, and either disposes of them or has an obligation to control them. • An arranger for disposal can be held liable for environmental cleanup costs under CERCLA.

array, *n.* (14c) **1.** A panel of potential jurors; VENIRE (1) <the array of mostly wealthy professionals seemed to favor the corporate defendant>. **2.** The jurors actually empaneled <the array hearing the case consisted of seven women and five men>. **3.** A list or roster of empaneled jurors <the plaintiff obtained a copy of the array to help prepare for voir dire>. **4.** Order; arrangement <the array of jurors from oldest to youngest>. **5.** A militia <the array organized antigovernment rallies>. **6.** A series of statistics or a group of elements <a mathematical array>.

array, *vb.* (16c) **1.** To empanel a jury for trial. **2.** To call out the names of jurors, one by one, as they are empaneled.

arrear, *n.* (*usu. pl.*) (17c) **1.** The state of being behind in the payment of a debt or the discharge of an obligation <the creditor filed a lawsuit against the debtor who was in arrears>. — Also termed *arrearage.* **2.** An unpaid or overdue debt <the creditor reached an agreement with the debtor on settling the arrears>. **3.** An unfinished duty <the arrears of work have accumulated>. See IN ARREARS.

arrearage. 1. See ARREAR (1). **2.** An unpaid dividend from a past period that is due to a holder of preferred stock. See *cumulative dividend* under DIVIDEND.

arrest, *n.* (14c) **1.** A seizure or forcible restraint. **2.** The taking or keeping of a person in custody by legal authority, esp. in response to a criminal charge; specif., the apprehension of someone for the purpose of securing the administration of the law, esp. of bringing that person before a court. — **arrest,** *vb.*

> *arrest by warrant.* See *lawful arrest* under ARREST.

> *arrest in execution.* See *arrest on final process.*

> *arrest in quarters.* *Military law.* A nonjudicial punishment that can be given to officers and warrant officers only by a general, a flag officer in command, or an officer exercising general court-martial jurisdiction. See BREACH OF ARREST.

> *arrest on final process.* *Hist.* Arrest in a civil case after the conclusion of a trial. — Also termed *arrest in execution.*

> *arrest on mesne process* (meen). *Hist.* Arrest in a civil case before trial takes place.

> *citizen's arrest.* (1941) An arrest of a private person by another private person on grounds that (1) a public offense was committed in the arrester's presence, or (2) the arrester has reasonable cause to believe that the arrestee has committed a felony.

civil arrest. *Hist.* An arrest and detention of a civil-suit defendant until bail is posted or a judgment is paid. • Civil arrest is prohibited in most states.

dragnet arrest. A sweeping arrest of people suspected of possible involvement in criminal activity or a civil disturbance. • This type of arrest is illegal because it is based not on probable cause but on unsupported suspicion or belief. — Also termed *round-up*; *wholesale arrest*.

false arrest. (18c) An arrest made without proper legal authority. Cf. FALSE IMPRISONMENT.

house arrest. See HOUSE ARREST.

lawful arrest. (18c) The taking of a person into legal custody either under a valid warrant or on probable cause that the person has committed a crime. — Also termed *arrest by warrant*; *warrant arrest*. Cf. *unlawful arrest*.

malicious arrest. (18c) An arrest made without probable cause and for an improper purpose; esp., an abuse of process by which a person procures the arrest (and often the imprisonment) of another by means of judicial process, without any reasonable cause. • Malicious arrest can be grounds for an action for abuse of process, false imprisonment, or malicious prosecution.

material-witness arrest. An arrest of a witness to a crime for the purpose of inducing the witness to talk to police. • This type of arrest requires a warrant based on probable cause.

parol arrest (pə-**rohl** *or* **par**-əl). (1904) An arrest ordered by a judge or magistrate from the bench, without written complaint, and executed immediately, such as an arrest of a person who breaches the peace in open court. See CONTEMPT.

pretextual arrest. (1968) An arrest of a person for a minor offense to create an opportunity to investigate the person's involvement in a more serious offense for which there is no lawful ground to make an arrest. — Also termed *pretext arrest*.

rearrest. A warrantless arrest of a person who has escaped from custody, violated parole or probation, or failed to appear in court as ordered.

subterfuge arrest. An arrest of a suspect for the stated purpose of obtaining evidence of one crime but with the underlying intent to search the suspect for evidence of a different crime.

unlawful arrest. The taking of a person into custody either without a valid warrant or without probable cause to believe that the person has committed a crime. Cf. *lawful arrest*.

warranted arrest. (1950) An arrest made under authority of a warrant.

warrantless arrest. (1958) A legal arrest, without a warrant, based on probable cause of a felony, or for a misdemeanor committed in a police officer's presence. — Also termed *arrest without a warrant*. See WARRANT.

wholesale arrest. See *dragnet arrest*.

3. *Maritime law.* The taking of a ship and sometimes its cargo into custody by virtue of a court's warrant.

arrestable offense. See OFFENSE (1).

arrest by warrant. See *lawful arrest* under ARREST.

arrestee. (1844) **1.** A person who has been taken into custody by legal authority; a person who has been arrested. **2.** *Scots law.* One who holds property attached by arrestment.

arrester. One who arrests. — Also spelled *arrestor*.

arrest in execution. See *arrest on final process* under ARREST.

arrest in quarters. See ARREST.

arrest of inquest. A plea that a matter proposed for inquiry has already been investigated and should therefore not be reexamined.

arrest of judgment. (17c) The staying of a judgment after its entry; esp., a court's refusal to render or enforce a judgment because of a defect apparent from the record. • At common law, courts have the power to arrest judgment for intrinsic causes appearing on the record, as when the verdict differs materially from the pleadings or when the case alleged in the pleadings is legally insufficient. Today, this type of defect must typically be objected to before trial or before judgment is entered, so that the motion in arrest of judgment has been largely superseded. — Also termed *allocutus*.

arrest on final process. See ARREST.

arrest on mesne process. See ARREST.

arrest record. (1930) **1.** A form completed by a police officer when a person is arrested. **2.** A cumulative list of the instances when a person has been arrested. — Also termed *police blotter*; (in sense 2) *bench blotter*; *blotter*; *log*.

arrest warrant. See WARRANT (1).

arrest without a warrant. See *warrantless arrest* under ARREST.

arrêt (ah-**ret** *or* -**ray**). [French] *Civil law.* **1.** A judgment, sentence, or decree of a court with competent jurisdiction. **2.** A sovereign's decree. Pl. **arrêts.**

arriere fee. See *arriere fee* under FEE (2).

arriere vassal. See VASSAL.

arrogation (ar-ə-**gay**-shən), *n.* (16c) **1.** The act of claiming or taking something without the right to do so <some commentators argue that limited

military actions unilaterally ordered by the President are an arrogation of Congress's power to declare war>. **2.** *Roman & civil law.* The adoption of an adult; specif., the adoption of a person sui juris, as a result of which the adoptee loses independence and comes within the paternal power (*patria potestas*) of the adopting father. — **arrogate,** *vb.*

ARS. *abbr.* AGRICULTURAL RESEARCH SERVICE.

arson, *n.* (17c) **1.** At common law, the malicious burning of someone else's dwelling house or outhouse that is either appurtenant to the dwelling house or within the curtilage. **2.** Under modern statutes, the intentional and wrongful burning of someone else's property (as to destroy a building) or one's own property (as to fraudulently collect insurance). See Model Penal Code § 220.1(1). — Also termed (in Latin) *crimen incendii*; (in sense 2) *statutory arson.* Cf. HOUSEBURNING; CRIMINAL DAMAGE TO PROPERTY.

> **aggravated arson.** Arson accompanied by some aggravating factor, as when the offender foresees or anticipates that one or more persons will be in or near the property being burned.

arsonable, *adj.* (1902) (Of property) of such a nature as to give rise to a charge of arson if maliciously burned <only real property, and not personal property, is arsonable>.

arson clause. *Insurance.* An insurance-policy provision that excludes coverage of a loss due to fire if the insured intentionally started the fire.

arsonist. (1864) One who commits arson; INCENDIARY (1).

arsonous, *adj.* Of, relating to, or involving arson <an arsonous purpose>.

ART. *abbr.* ASSISTED REPRODUCTIVE TECHNOLOGY.

art. (13c) **1.** Creative expression, or the product of creative expression. **2.** An occupation or business that requires skill; a craft. **3.** *Patents.* A field of useful endeavor; the methodical application of knowledge or skill in creating something new.

> **analogous art.** *Patents.* A technique, product, application, machine, or method that is reasonably related to the problem addressed by the invention, and with which the inventor is assumed to be familiar. — Also termed *pertinent art.* See NONOBVIOUSNESS.

> **nuisance prior art.** *Patents.* Information that appears to anticipate or obviate an invention, but does not actually do so because the earlier described invention was neither reduced to practice nor adequately disclosed in any documents. ● Nuisance prior art does not bar a patent's issuance, but it may prolong the prosecution. The term does not apply to efforts that are not prior art at all, such as descriptions of unsuccessful attempts to reduce an invention to practice, or

to writings that do not disclose real inventions or technology, such as science-fiction.

> **pertinent art. 1.** See *analogous art.* **2.** See *relevant art.*

> **prior art.** *Patents.* Knowledge that is publicly known, used by others, or available on the date of invention to a person of ordinary skill in an art, including what would be obvious from that knowledge. ● Prior art includes (1) information in applications for previously patented inventions; (2) information that was published more than one year before a patent application is filed; and (3) information in other patent applications and inventor's certificates filed more than a year before the application is filed. The U.S. Patent and Trademark Office and courts analyze prior art before deciding the patentability of a comparable invention. 35 USCA §§ 102.

> **relevant art.** *Patents.* Art to which one can reasonably be expected to look for a solution to the problem that a patented device tries to solve. ● The term includes not only knowledge about a problem in a particular industry, but also knowledge accumulated in scientific fields whose techniques have been commonly employed to solve similar problems. — Also termed *pertinent art.*

4. *Hist.* In a seduction case, the skillful and systematic coaxing of another to engage in sexual activity.

artful pleading. See PLEADING (2).

art group. *Patents.* A collection of art units in the U.S. Patent and Trademark Office, led by a group director.

article, *n.* (13c) **1.** Generally, a particular item or thing <article of clothing>.

> **proprietary article.** (*often pl.*) A product manufactured under an exclusive right to sell it.

2. A separate and distinct part (as a clause or stipulation) of a writing, esp. in a contract, statute, or constitution <Article III>. **3.** (*pl.*) An instrument containing a set of rules or stipulations <articles of war> <articles of incorporation>. **4.** A nonfictional literary composition forming an independent part of a publication, such as a law review or journal <a well-researched, timely article>. **5.** *Patents.* A workpiece, product, or thing that is operated on, modified, or changed by a machine or process. **6.** *Patents.* An article of manufacture. See MANUFACTURE. **7.** *Eccles. law.* In an ecclesiastical court, one of a plaintiff's complaints or charges against the defendant. ● The complaint or charge may be presented by oral declaration or by a written document.

article, *vb.* **1.** To bring charges against by an exhibition of articles. **2.** To be an articled clerk.

article of manufacture. See MANUFACTURE.

article of merchandise. 1. See MERCHANDISE (1). **2.** See MERCHANDISE (2).

Article I court. (1955) **1.** See *legislative court* under COURT. **2.** A type of federal legislative court that is not bound by the requirements of or protected under U.S. Const. art. III, § 2, and that performs functions similar to those of an administrative agency, such as issuing advisory opinions. U.S. Const. art. I, § 8. Cf. ARTICLE III COURT.

Article I judge. (1958) A U.S. bankruptcy judge, magistrate judge, or administrative-law judge appointed for a term of years as authorized by Congress under Article I of the U.S. Constitution. 28 USCA §§ 151 et seq., 631 et seq. **2.** A federal judge temporarily appointed by the President without prior Senate approval. ● The appointment power derives from the recess-appointment clause, which allows the President to appoint temporary government officers while Congress is not in session. U.S. Const. art. II, § 2, cl. 3. See *recess appointment* under APPOINTMENT (1).

Article III court. (1949) A federal court that, deriving its jurisdiction from U.S. Const. art. III, § 2, hears cases arising under the Constitution and the laws and treaties of the United States, cases in which the United States is a party, and cases between the states and between citizens of different states. — Also termed *constitutional court*. Cf. ARTICLE I COURT.

Article III judge. (1937) A U.S. Supreme Court, Court of Appeals, or District Court judge appointed for life under Article III of the U.S. Constitution.

Article 15. See *nonjudicial punishment* under PUNISHMENT.

article of manufacture. See MANUFACTURE.

articles of agreement. A writing that records matters that the parties agreed on when forming a partnership or business or transferring real property. ● Unlike a contract, articles of agreement usu. contain only agreements and not express promises of performance, e.g., "the parties agree that it isn't possible to guarantee delivery within 10 days." Articles of agreement often supplement a contract. They may be informal or detailed.

articles of amendment. (1891) A document filed to effectuate an amendment or change to a corporation's articles of incorporation.

articles of apprenticeship. *Hist.* A contract under which a minor agrees to work for a master for a specified time in exchange for learning a trade.

articles of association. (17c) **1.** ARTICLES OF INCORPORATION. **2.** A governing document — similar to articles of incorporation — that legally creates a nonstock or nonprofit organization. — Often shortened (informally) to *articles*. — Also termed

articles of organization. See *governing document* under DOCUMENT (1).

Articles of Confederation. The instrument that governed the association of the 13 original states from March 1, 1781 until the adoption of the U.S. Constitution (September 17, 1787). ● They were prepared by the Continental Congress, submitted to the states in 1777, and later ratified by representatives of the states empowered by their respective legislatures for that purpose.

articles of dissolution. (1802) A document that a dissolving corporation must file with the appropriate governmental agency, usu. the secretary of state, after the corporation has settled all its debts and distributed all its assets.

articles of impeachment. (17c) A formal document alleging the specific charges against a public official and the reasons for removing that official from office. ● It is similar to an indictment in a criminal proceeding. See IMPEACHMENT (1).

articles of incorporation. (18c) A governing document that sets forth the basic terms of a corporation's existence, including the number and classes of shares and the purposes and duration of the corporation. ● In most states, the articles of incorporation are filed with the secretary of state as part of the process of forming the corporation. In some states, the articles serve as a certificate of incorporation and are the official recognition of the corporation's existence. In other states, the government issues a certificate of incorporation after approving the articles and other required documents. — Often shortened (informally) to *articles.* — Also termed *articles of association; articles of organization; certificate of incorporation.* Cf. BYLAW (1); CHARTER. See *governing document* under DOCUMENT (1).

articles of organization. 1. See ARTICLES OF INCORPORATION. **2.** See ARTICLES OF ASSOCIATION (2).

articles of partnership. See PARTNERSHIP AGREEMENT.

articles of the peace. *English law.* A sworn complaint in which a person alleges that a named person poses a threat to the complainant's person, family, or property.

Articles of Union. *Hist.* The 25 articles agreed to by the English and Scottish parliaments in 1707 for the union of the two kingdoms.

articles of war. 1. The rules and regulations that govern the activities of an army and navy. **2.** (*cap.*) The body of laws and procedures that governed the U.S. military until replaced in 1951 by the Uniform Code of Military Justice.

articulated pleading. See PLEADING (1).

artifice (**ahr**-tə-fis). A clever plan or idea, esp. one intended to deceive.

artificer. 1. A skilled worker, such as a mechanic or craftsman; an artisan. **2.** One who builds or contrives; an inventor.

artificial, *adj.* **1.** Existing only by virtue of or in consideration of the law <artificial presumption>. • This term is often used in reference to a company or a corporation. See *artificial person* under PERSON (3). **2.** Made or produced by a human or human intervention rather than by nature <artificial condition>. **3.** Of or relating to artifice <an artificial demeanor>.

artificial condition. See CONDITION (5).

artificial day. See DAY.

artificial force. *Patents.* A natural force that is so transformed in character or energies by human power as to become something new.

artificial insemination. *Family law.* A process for achieving conception, whereby semen is inserted into a woman's vagina by some means other than intercourse. • If the woman is married when the artificial insemination and the birth occur, and her husband has consented to the insemination, and the insemination is performed by a licensed physician, the husband is considered the father of the child. If the woman is unmarried at the time of the insemination, several factors, varying from jurisdiction to jurisdiction, determine whether the donor is considered the father of the child. Cf. IN VITRO FERTILIZATION; GAMETE INTRAFALLOPIAN TRANSFER; ZYGOTE INTRAFALLOPIAN TRANSFER.

   artificial insemination by donor. Artificial insemination in which the semen donor is someone other than the recipient's husband. — Abbr. AID. — Also termed *heterologous artificial insemination; exogamous insemination.*

   artificial insemination by husband. Artificial insemination in which the semen donor is the recipient's husband. — Abbr. AIH. — Also termed *homologous insemination; endogenous insemination.*

   endogenous insemination. See *artificial insemination by husband.*

   exogamous insemination. See *artificial insemination by donor.*

   heterologous artificial insemination. See *artificial insemination by donor.*

   homologous artificial insemination. See *artificial insemination by husband.*

artificial person. See PERSON (3).

artificial presumption. See *presumption of law* under PRESUMPTION.

artificial succession. See SUCCESSION (4).

artificial watercourse. See WATERCOURSE.

artisan. 1. An artist; esp., a skilled crafter. **2.** *Patents.* A person of ordinary skill in an art, for purposes of determining whether a patent application meets the enablement requirement of 35 USCA § 112. • In patent-law terms, the disclosure in the application must teach the artisan how to practice the invention. — Also termed *skilled artisan.*

artisan's lien. See *mechanic's lien* under LIEN.

artistic license. See LICENSE.

artistic work. See WORK (2).

art unit. *Patents.* A group of patent examiners in the U.S. Patent and Trademark Office specializing in a particular field of technology. • Each art unit is led by a senior patent examiner.

as-applied challenge. See CHALLENGE (1).

ASBCA. *abbr.* See ARMED SERVICES BOARD OF CONTRACT APPEALS.

ASCAP. *abbr.* AMERICAN SOCIETY OF COMPOSERS, AUTHORS AND PUBLISHERS.

ascendant (ə-**sen**-dənt), *n.* (17c) One who precedes in lineage, such as a parent or grandparent. — Also termed *ancestor.* Cf. DESCENDANT. — **ascendant,** *adj.*

   collateral ascendant. (1832) Loosely, an aunt, uncle, or other relative who is not strictly an ancestor. — Also termed *collateral ancestor.*

   lineal ascendant. A blood relative in the direct line of ascent; ancestor. • Parents, grandparents, and great-grandparents are lineal ascendants.

ascent. (17c) The passing of an estate upwards to an heir in the ascending line. Cf. DESCENT.

ASE. *abbr.* AMERICAN STOCK EXCHANGE.

as-extracted collateral. See COLLATERAL.

asexualization. See STERILIZATION.

asexually reproducing plant. *Patents.* A plant that reproduces other than by seeds. • Examples of asexual reproduction include cutting, grafting, and budding. Only new, distinctive, and nonobvious species of asexually reproducing plants may be protected under the Plant Patent Act. 35 USCA § 161.

ASFA. *abbr.* ADOPTION AND SAFE FAMILIES ACT.

***Ashwander* rules.** (1953) A set of principles outlining the U.S. Supreme Court's policy of deciding constitutional questions only when necessary, and of avoiding a constitutional question if the case can be decided on the basis of another issue. • These rules were outlined in Justice Brandeis's concurring opinion in *Ashwander v. Tennessee Valley Authority*, 297 U.S. 288, 56 S.Ct. 466 (1936). They include the policy that the court should not decide a constitutional question in a friendly suit, should not anticipate a question of constitutional law, should not create a rule of constitutional law that is broader than that called for by the facts of the case, should not decide a constitutional issue if the case can be decided on another ground, should not rule on the constitutionality of a statute unless the plaintiff is harmed by the statute or if the plaintiff has accepted the benefits of the statute, and should not rule on the constitutionality of an act of Congress without first analyzing whether the act can be fairly construed in a way that would avoid the constitutional question. — Also termed *Brandeis rules*.

as is, *adv. & adj.* In the existing condition without modification <the customer bought the car as is>. • Under UCC § 2-316(3)(a), a seller can disclaim all implied warranties by stating that the goods are being sold "as is" or "with all faults." Generally, a sale of property "as is" means that the property is sold in its existing condition, and use of the phrase *as is* relieves the seller from liability for defects in that condition. — Also termed *with all faults*.

as-is warranty. See WARRANTY (2).

asked price. See PRICE.

asking price. See PRICE.

as of right. By virtue of a legal entitlement <the case is not one triable to a jury as of right>.

ASP. *abbr.* APPLICATION SERVICE PROVIDER.

as per. (18c) In accordance with; PER (3). • This phrase has traditionally been considered a barbarism, *per* being the preferred form in commercialese <per your request>. But even *per* can be improved on <as you requested>.

aspirin wars. *Slang.* A series of false-advertising lawsuits between makers of over-the-counter pain relievers in the 1980s, all centering on the boundaries of comparative advertising.

asportation (as-pər-**tay**-shən), *n.* (18c) The act of carrying away or removing (property or a person). • Asportation is a necessary element of larceny. — Also termed *carrying away*. See LARCENY. — **asport,** *vb.* — **asportative,** *adj.*

ASR. *abbr.* ACCOUNTING SERIES RELEASE.

assailant. (16c) **1.** One who physically attacks another; one who commits an assault. **2.** One who attacks another using nonphysical means; esp., one who attacks another's position or feelings, as by criticism, argument, or abusive language.

assassination, *n.* (17c) The act of deliberately killing someone, esp. a public figure, usu. for hire or for political reasons. — **assassinate,** *vb.* — **assassin,** *n.*

assault, *n.* (14c) **1.** *Criminal & tort law.* The threat or use of force on another that causes that person to have a reasonable apprehension of imminent harmful or offensive contact; the act of putting another person in reasonable fear or apprehension of an immediate battery by means of an act

amounting to an attempt or threat to commit a battery. **2.** *Criminal law.* An attempt to commit battery, requiring the specific intent to cause physical injury. — Also termed (in senses 1 and 2) *simple assault; common assault.* **3.** Loosely, a battery. **4.** Popularly, any attack. Cf. BATTERY. — **assault,** *vb.* — **assaultive,** *adj.*

aggravated assault. (18c) Criminal assault accompanied by circumstances that make it more severe, such as the intent to commit another crime or the intent to cause serious bodily injury, esp. by using a deadly weapon. See Model Penal Code § 211.1(2).

assault by contact. The offense of knowingly or intentionally touching another person when the actor knows or believes that the touch will offend or provoke the other person.

assault to rape. See *assault with intent to commit rape.*

assault with a dangerous weapon. See *assault with a deadly weapon.*

assault with a deadly weapon. (1803) An aggravated assault in which the defendant, using a deadly weapon, threatens the victim with death or serious bodily injury. — Also termed *assault with a dangerous weapon.*

assault with intent. (17c) Any of several assaults that are carried out with an additional criminal purpose in mind, such as assault with intent to murder, assault with intent to rob, assault with intent to rape, and assault with intent to inflict great bodily injury. • These are modern statutory inventions that are often found in state criminal codes.

assault with intent to commit rape. An assault carried out with the additional criminal purpose of raping the victim. — Also termed *assault to rape.*

atrocious assault. An assault that causes severe wounding or maiming.

attempted assault. (1870) An attempt to commit an assault; an attempted battery that has not progressed far enough to be an assault, as when a person intends to harm someone physically but is captured while or after trying to locate the intended victim in his or her place of employment. • Traditionally, most commentators held that an attempted assault could not exist because assault was in itself an attempt to commit a crime. Many modern authorities, however, assert that an attempted assault can occur, and that it should be punishable. — Also termed *attempt to assault.* See ATTEMPT TO ATTEMPT.

civil assault. (1892) An assault considered as a tort and not as a crime. • Although the same assaultive conduct can be both a tort and a crime, this term isolates the legal elements that give rise to civil liability.

conditional assault. (1971) An assault expressing a threat on condition, such as "your money or your life."

criminal assault. (1835) An assault considered as a crime and not as a tort. • This term isolates the legal elements that give rise to criminal liability even though the act might also have been tortious.

excusable assault. An assault committed by accident or while doing a lawful act by lawful means, with ordinary caution and without any unlawful intent.

felonious assault. An assault that is of sufficient severity to be classified and punished as a felony. See *aggravated assault*; *assault with a deadly weapon.*

indecent assault. See *sexual assault* (2).

indecent assault by contact. See *sexual assault* (2)

indecent assault by exposure. See INDECENT EXPOSURE.

intoxication assault. An assault that occurs when an inebriated person causes bodily injury to another person.

malicious assault with a deadly weapon. An aggravated assault in which the victim is threatened with death or serious bodily harm from the defendant's use of a deadly weapon. • Malice is inferred from both the nature of the assault and the weapon used.

sexual assault. (1880) **1.** Sexual intercourse with another person who does not consent. • Several state statutes have abolished the crime of rape and replaced it with the offense of sexual assault. **2.** Offensive sexual contact with another person, exclusive of rape. • The Model Penal Code lists eight circumstances under which sexual contact results in an assault, as when the offender knows that the victim is mentally incapable of appreciating the nature of the conduct, either because of a mental disease or defect or because the offender has drugged the victim to prevent resistance. Model Penal Code § 213.4. — Also termed (in sense 2) *indecent assault*; *sexual assault by contact*; *indecent assault by contact*. Cf. RAPE.

sexual assault by contact. See *sexual assault* (2).

simple assault. **1.** See ASSAULT (1). **2.** See ASSAULT (2).

assault and battery. (16c) Loosely, a criminal battery. See BATTERY.

assault by contact. See ASSAULT.

assaultee. A person who is assaulted.

assaulter. A person who assaults another.

assault with a dangerous weapon. See *assault with a deadly weapon* under ASSAULT.

assault with a deadly weapon. See ASSAULT.

assay, *n.* **1.** A proof or trial, by chemical experiments, of the purity of metals, esp. gold and silver. **2.** An examination of weights and measures.

assayer. One who makes assays of precious metals.

assembly. (14c) **1.** A group of persons organized and united for some common purpose.

delegate assembly. See CONVENTION (4).

deliberative assembly. Parliamentary law. A body that transacts business according to parliamentary law. • A deliberative assembly typically has several distinguishing characteristics: (1) it is a group of people who meet to propose, discuss, and possibly vote on courses of action to be undertaken in the group's name; (2) participants are free to use their own judgment; (3) enough people participate so that a certain degree of formality in the proceedings is desirable; (4) each participant has one vote and may dissent without fear of expulsion; and (5) when some members are absent, the members actually present have the authority to act for the entire group (subject to quorum and other requirements). *See* Henry M. Robert, *Robert's Rules of Order Newly Revised* § 1, at 2 (10th ed. 2000).

ordinary assembly. Parliamentary law. A deliberative assembly other than a legislative body.

riotous assembly. Hist. An unlawful assemblage of 12 or more persons causing a disturbance of the peace. See RIOT.

unlawful assembly. (16c) A meeting of three or more persons who intend either to commit a violent crime or to carry out some act, lawful or unlawful, that will constitute a breach of the peace. Cf. RIOT.

2. In many states, the lower house of a legislature. **3.** *Parliamentary law.* CONVENTION (4). **4.** *Patents.* In a patent claim, a collection of parts used to form a structure.

assembly, right of. See RIGHT OF ASSEMBLY.

assent, *n.* (14c) Agreement, approval, or permission; esp., verbal or nonverbal conduct reasonably interpreted as willingness. See CONSENT. — **assent,** *vb.*

actual assent. Assent given by words or conduct intended to express willingness.

apparent assent. Assent given by language or conduct that, while not necessarily intended to express willingness, would be understood by a reasonable person to be so intended and is actually so understood.

constructive assent. (1811) Assent imputed to someone based on conduct.

express assent. (16c) Assent clearly and unmistakably communicated.

implied assent. (18c) Assent inferred from one's conduct rather than from direct expression.

mutual assent. (17c) Agreement by both parties to a contract, usu. in the form of offer and acceptance. ● In modern contract law, mutual assent is determined by an objective standard — that is, by the apparent intention of the parties as manifested by their actions. Cf. MEETING OF THE MINDS.

assented stock. See STOCK.

assenting-silence doctrine. (1976) The principle that an accusation will be taken as true, despite silence by the accused, if the accusation was made under circumstances in which silence can be fairly said to be an agreement. ● This doctrine is usu. held to be invalid as a measure of a criminal defendant's guilt.

assert, *vb.* **1.** To state positively. **2.** To invoke or enforce a legal right. — **assertory, assertive,** *adj.* — **assertor,** *n.*

assertion, *n.* (15c) **1.** A declaration or allegation. **2.** A person's speaking, writing, acting, or failing to act with the intent of expressing a fact or opinion; the act or an instance of engaging in communicative behavior. See *assertive conduct* under CONDUCT. — **assert,** *vb.* — **assertor,** *n.*

assertive conduct. See CONDUCT.

assertive question. *Civil law.* A question asked of a witness at a criminal trial, by which inadmissible evidence is sought, to provide the jury with details regarding another crime. Cf. INTERROGATIVE QUESTION.

assertory covenant. See COVENANT (1).

assertory oath. See OATH.

assessable insurance. 1. See INSURANCE. **2.** See *assessable policy* (1) under INSURANCE POLICY.

assessable policy. 1. See INSURANCE POLICY. **2.** See *assessable insurance* (1) under INSURANCE.

assessable security. See SECURITY.

assessable stock. See STOCK.

assessed valuation. See VALUATION.

assessed value. See VALUE (2).

assessment, *n.* (16c) **1.** Determination of the rate or amount of something, such as a tax or damages <assessment of the losses covered by insurance>. **2.** Imposition of something, such as a tax or fine, according to an established rate; the tax or fine so imposed <assessment of a luxury tax>.

assessment for benefits. See *special assessment.*

deficiency assessment. An assessment by the IRS — after administrative review and tax-court

adjudication — of additional tax owed by a taxpayer who underpaid. See DEFICIENCY (2).

double assessment. The act of requiring that tax be paid twice for the same property. See *double taxation* under TAXATION.

erroneous assessment. An assessment that deviates from the law and creates a jurisdictional defect, and that is therefore invalid.

excessive assessment. A tax assessment that is grossly disproportionate as compared with other assessments.

frontage assessment. (1877) A municipal tax charged to a property owner for local improvements that abut a street or highway, such as sidewalks, pavements, or sewage lines.

jeopardy assessment. An assessment by the IRS — without the usual review procedures — of additional tax owed by a taxpayer who underpaid, based on the IRS's belief that collection of the deficiency would be jeopardized by delay. IRC (26 USCA) §§ 6811 et seq.

local assessment. A tax to pay for improvements (such as sewers and sidewalks) in a designated area, levied on property owners who will benefit from the improvements. — Also termed *local-improvement assessment.*

maintenance assessment. See MAINTENANCE FEE (2).

political assessment. *Hist.* A charge levied on officeholders and political candidates by a political party to defray the expenses for a political canvass.

special assessment. The assessment of a tax on property that benefits in some important way from a public improvement. — Also termed *assessment for benefits.*

3. Official valuation of property for purposes of taxation <assessment of the beach house>. — Also termed *tax assessment.* Cf. APPRAISAL. **4.** An audit or review <internal financial assessment> <environmental site assessment>. — **assess,** *vb.*

assessment bond. See BOND (3).

assessment company. An association that offers its members life insurance, and then pays for death losses by levying an assessment on the surviving members of the association.

assessment contract. See CONTRACT.

assessment district. See DISTRICT.

assessment for benefits. See *special assessment* under ASSESSMENT.

assessment fund. The balance of the assessments of a mutual benefit association, minus expenses, from which beneficiaries are paid.

assessment insurance. See INSURANCE.

assessment list. See ASSESSMENT ROLL.

assessment period. A taxable period.

assessment ratio. For property tax purposes, the ratio of assessed value to fair market value.

assessment roll. A record of taxable persons and property, prepared by a tax assessor. — Also termed *assessment list*; (in some New England states) *grand list*.

assessment work. *Mining law.* The annual labor (such as improvements) that must be performed on an unpatented mining claim to continue to hold the claim.

assessor. (14c) **1.** An official who evaluates or makes assessments, esp. for purposes of taxation. — Also termed (specif.) *tax assessor*. **2.** A person who advises a judge or magistrate about scientific or technical matters during a trial. See MASTER (2). **3.** ADSESSOR. — **assessorial** (as-ə-sor-ee-əl), *adj.* — **assessorship**, *n.*

asset. (16c) **1.** An item that is owned and has value. **2.** (*pl.*) The entries on a balance sheet showing the items of property owned, including cash, inventory, equipment, real estate, accounts receivable, and goodwill. **3.** (*pl.*) All the property of a person (esp. a bankrupt or deceased person) available for paying debts or for distribution.

accrued asset. An asset arising from revenues earned but not yet due.

admitted asset. An asset that by law may be included in evaluating the financial condition of an insurance company. Cf. *nonadmitted asset*.

appointive asset. An asset distributed under a power of appointment.

assets by descent. The portion of an estate that passes to an heir and is sufficient to charge the heir with the decedent's specialty debts. — Also termed *assets per descent*.

assets in hand. The portion of an estate held by an executor or administrator for the payment of debts chargeable to the executor or administrator. — Also termed *assets entre main*; *assets entre mains*.

assets per descent. See *assets by descent*.

asset under management. A securities portfolio for which an investment adviser provides ongoing, regular supervisory or management services.

capital asset. 1. A long-term asset used in the operation of a business or used to produce goods or services, such as equipment, land, or an industrial plant. — Also termed *fixed asset*. **2.** For income-tax purposes, any of most assets held by a taxpayer except those assets specifically excluded by the Internal Revenue Code. ● Excluded from the definition are, among other things, stock in trade, inventory, and property held by the taxpayer primarily for sale to customers in the ordinary course of trade or business.

commercial assets. The aggregate of available property, stock in trade, cash, and other assets belonging to a merchant.

current asset. An asset that is readily convertible into cash, such as a marketable security, a note, or an account receivable. — Also termed *liquid asset*; *quick asset*; *near money*; *financial asset*.

dead asset. A worthless asset; an asset that has no realizable value, such as an uncollectible account receivable.

earning asset. (*usu. pl.*) An asset (esp. of a bank) on which interest is received. ● Banks consider loans to be earning assets.

equitable asset. An asset that is subject to payment only in a court of equity.

financial asset. See *current asset*.

fixed asset. See *capital asset* (1).

frozen asset. An asset that is difficult to convert into cash because of court order or other legal process.

hard asset. See *real asset*.

hidden asset. An asset carried on the books at a substantially reduced or understated value that is considerably less than market value.

illiquid asset. An asset that is not readily convertible into cash, usu. because of (1) the lack of demand, (2) the absence of an established market, or (3) the substantial cost or time required for liquidation (such as for real property, even when it is desirable).

individual asset. (*usu. pl.*) Property belonging to a member of a partnership as personal property, separate from the partnership's property.

intangible asset. Any nonphysical asset or resource than can be amortized or converted to cash, such as patents, goodwill, and computer programs, or a right to something, such as services paid for in advance.

junk asset. See *troubled asset*.

legal asset. A decedent's asset that by law is subject to the claims of creditors or legacies. — Also termed *probate asset*.

liquid asset. See *current asset*.

mass asset. An intangible asset, such as a dominant market position, that is made up of several components but that is considered a single entity for purposes of depreciation, because the loss of any component of the asset is replaced by new components, so that the whole asset has little or no fluctuation in value. ● An entity with a dominant market position might lose a vendor but, because of its dominant market position, still be able to replace the loss with a new vendor. The market position is therefore considered a mass asset.

net assets. See *net worth* under WORTH.

net quick assets. The excess of quick assets less current liabilities. See QUICK-ASSET RATIO.

new asset. *Wills & estates.* In the administration of a decedent's estate, property that the administrator or executor receives after the time has expired to file claims against the estate.

nominal asset. An asset whose value is difficult to assess, such as a judgment or claim.

nonadmitted asset. An asset that by law may not be included in evaluating the financial condition of an insurance company because it cannot be converted quickly into cash without a financial loss. Cf. *admitted asset.*

nonprobate asset. Property that passes to a named beneficiary upon the owner's death according to the terms of some contract or arrangement other than a will. ● Such an asset is not a part of the probate estate and is not ordinarily subject to the probate court's jurisdiction (and fees), though it is part of the taxable estate. Examples include life-insurance contracts, joint property arrangements with right of survivorship, pay-on-death bank accounts, and inter vivos trusts. — Also termed *nonprobate property.* Cf. WILL SUBSTITUTE.

personal asset. An asset in the form of money or chattels.

premarital asset. Property that a spouse owned before marrying. ● In most jurisdictions, this is part of the spouse's separate property. See SEPARATE PROPERTY. Cf. COMMUNITY PROPERTY.

probate asset. See *legal asset.*

quick asset. **1.** Cash and other current assets other than inventory. **2.** See *current asset.*

real asset. **1.** An asset in the form of land. **2.** Loosely, any tangible asset. — Also termed *hard asset.*

tangible asset. An asset that has a physical existence and is capable of being assigned a value.

toxic asset. See *troubled asset.*

troubled asset. A debt-related asset, such as a mortgage loan, for which the debt has become or is likely to become uncollectable, resulting in a sudden, sharp decrease in the asset's value. — Also termed *toxic asset; junk asset.*

wasting asset. An asset exhausted through use or the loss of value, such as an oil well or a coal deposit.

asset acquisition. Acquisition of a corporation by purchasing all its assets directly from the corporation itself, rather than by purchasing shares from its shareholders. — Also termed *asset purchase.* Cf. SHARE ACQUISITION.

asset allocation. The spreading of funds between different types of investments with the intention of decreasing risk and increasing return.

asset-backed security. See SECURITY.

asset-based financing. See FINANCING.

asset-coverage test. *Accounting.* A bond-indenture restriction that permits additional borrowing only if the ratio of assets (typically net tangible assets) to debt (typically long-term debt) does not fall below a specified minimum.

asset-depreciation range. (1971) *Tax.* The IRS's range of depreciation lifetimes allowed for assets placed in service between 1970 and 1980 and for assets depreciated under the Modified Accelerated Cost Recovery System under the Tax Reform Act of 1986. — Abbr. ADR. See ACCELERATED COST RECOVERY SYSTEM.

asset dividend. See DIVIDEND.

asset-protection trust. See TRUST (3).

asset purchase. See ASSET ACQUISITION.

asset sale and liquidation. *Mergers & acquisitions.* A merger in which a corporation's board and a majority of the stockholders approve a sale of most or all of the corporation's assets to another corporation in exchange for cash or debt.

assets by descent. See ASSET.

assets entre main. See *assets in hand* under ASSET.

assets in hand. See ASSET.

assets per descent. See *assets by descent* under ASSET.

asset under management. See ASSET.

asset value. See NET ASSET VALUE.

asseverate (ə-**sev**-ə-rayt), *vb.* (1744) To state solemnly or positively; to aver. See AVERMENT. — **asseveration** (ə-sev-ə-**ray**-shən), *n.*

assign, *n.* (*usu. pl.*) See ASSIGNEE.

assign, *vb.* **1.** To convey; to transfer rights or property <the bank assigned the note to a thrift institution>. **2.** To assert; to point out <the appellant assigned as errors two of the trial court's rulings>. See ASSIGNMENT OF ERROR.

assignable, *adj.* (1809) Able to be assigned; transferable from one person to another, so that the transferee has the same rights as the transferor had <assignable right>. Cf. NEGOTIABLE.

assignable lease. See LEASE.

assignation (as-ig-**nay**-shən), *n.* **1.** *Archaic.* An appointment of a time and place to meet, esp. for engaging in illicit sex. **2.** *Eccles. law.* A specific allegation in a defendant's counterpleading.

3. *French law.* A plaintiff's complaint; a writ of summons.

assignation house. See DISORDERLY HOUSE.

assign dower. To set out the legal description of a widow's share of her deceased husband's estate. See DOWER.

assigned account. See ACCOUNT.

assigned counsel. See COUNSEL.

assigned error. See ERROR.

assigned risk. See RISK.

assignee (ə-sı-**nee** *or* as-ə-**nee**). (14c) One to whom property rights or powers are transferred by another. ● Use of the term is so widespread that it is difficult to ascribe positive meaning to it with any specificity. Courts recognize the protean nature of the term and are therefore often forced to look to the intent of the assignor and assignee in making the assignment — rather than to the formality of the use of the term *assignee* — in defining rights and responsibilities. — Also termed *assign.*

   absolute assignee. A person who is assigned an unqualified interest in property in a transfer of some or all of the incidents of ownership.

   assignee ad interim. An assignee appointed between the time of bankruptcy and the appointment of a regular assignee.

   assignee for value. An assignee who has paid for or otherwise given consideration for the assignment.

   collateral assignee. A lender who is assigned an interest in property (usu. real property) as security for a loan.

   gratuitous assignee. An assignee under an assignment not given for value.

   subassignee. A person to whom a right is assigned by one who is a previous assignee of the right.

assignee clause. (1925) A provision of the Judiciary Act of 1789 that prevented a litigant without diversity of citizenship from assigning a claim to another who did have the required diversity. ● In 1948 the assignee clause was replaced by 28 USCA § 1359, which denies federal jurisdiction when a party is improperly or collusively joined, by assignment or otherwise, merely to invoke jurisdiction.

assignee estoppel. See ESTOPPEL.

assigner. See ASSIGNOR.

assignment. (14c) **1.** The transfer of rights or property <assignment of stock options>. **2.** The rights or property so transferred <the aunt assigned those funds to her niece, who promptly invested the assignment in mutual funds>.

   absolute assignment. An assignment that leaves the assignor no interest in the assigned property or right.

   assignment by operation of law. A transfer of a right or obligation as a necessary consequence of a change in legal status, regardless of the affected party's intent. ● For example, a right and a corresponding obligation may disappear if they vest in the same person, as might happen in a merger or acquisition.

   assignment for value. An assignment given in exchange for consideration.

   assignment in gross. A transfer of a company's trademark separately from the goodwill of the business. ● Courts often hold that such an assignment passes nothing of value to the transferee. — Also termed *naked assignment.* See ANTI-ASSIGNMENT-IN-GROSS RULE.

   assignment of account. An assignment that gives the assignee the right to funds in an account, usu. to satisfy a debt.

   assignment of application. **1.** *Patents.* The U.S. Patent and Trademark Office's formal routing of a patent or trademark application to the examining group to which it appears to belong based on subject matter. **2.** The transfer of the right to prosecute a patent or register a trademark. ● The assignee must show ownership in the property to be patented or registered and, if less than absolute, the extent of ownership. See 37 CFR § 3.73.

   assignment of dower (**dow**-ər). The act of setting apart a widow's share of her deceased husband's real property.

   assignment of income. See *assignment of wages.*

   assignment of lease. An assignment in which a lessee transfers the entire unexpired remainder of the lease term, as distinguished from a sublease transferring only a portion of the remaining term.

   assignment of realty. A transfer of a real-property interest that is less than a freehold. ● The term includes debt-security interests in land.

   assignment of wages. A transfer of the right to collect wages from the wage earner to a creditor. — Also termed *assignment of income.*

   assignment pro tanto. An assignment that results when an order is drawn on a third party and made payable from a particular fund that belongs to the drawer. ● The drawee becomes an assignee with respect to the drawer's interest in that fund.

   collateral assignment. An assignment of property as collateral security for a loan.

   common-law assignment. An assignment for the benefit of creditors made under the common law, rather than by statute.

   conditional assignment. An assignment of income (such as rent payments or accounts receivable) to a lender, made to secure a loan. • The lender receives the assigned income only if the assignor defaults on the underlying loan.

effective assignment. An assignment that terminates the assignor's interest in the property and transfers it to the assignee.

equitable assignment. An assignment that, although not legally valid, will be recognized and enforced in equity — for example, an assignment of a chose in action or of future acquisitions of the assignor. • To accomplish an "equitable assignment," there must be an absolute appropriation by the assignor of the debt or fund sought to be assigned.

fly-power assignment. A blank written assignment that, when attached to a stock certificate, renders the stock transferable.

foreign assignment. An assignment made in a foreign country or in another jurisdiction.

general assignment. Assignment of a debtor's property for the benefit of all the assignor's creditors, instead of only a few. — Also termed *voluntary assignment.* See ASSIGNMENT FOR THE BENEFIT OF CREDITORS.

gratuitous assignment. An assignment not given for value; esp., an assignment given or taken as security for — or in total or partial satisfaction of — a preexisting obligation.

mesne assignment (meen). A middle or intermediate assignment; any assignment before the last one.

naked assignment. See *assignment-in-gross.*

partial assignment. The immediate transfer of part but not all of the assignor's right.

preferential assignment. See PREFERENTIAL TRANSFER.

total assignment. An assignment empowering the assignee to enforce the entire right for the benefit of the assignor or others. • Examples are assignment to secure an obligation and assignment to a trustee.

voluntary assignment. See *general assignment.*

wage assignment. An assignment by an employee of a portion of the employee's pay to another (such as a creditor).

3. The instrument of transfer <the assignment was appended to the contract>. **4.** A welfare recipient's surrender of his or her rights to child support (both current and past due) in favor of the state as a condition of receiving governmental financial assistance <the assignment made economic sense to her because her child support amounted to $200 a month, while she received $400 a month in welfare>. **5.** A task, job, or appointment <the student's math assignment> <assignment as ambassador to a foreign country>. **6.**

The act of assigning a task, job, or appointment <the assignment of various duties>.

assignment of the floor. *Parliamentary law.* The process by which the chair recognizes who is entitled to speak.

7. In litigation practice, a point that a litigant advances <the third assignment of error>.

new assignment. *Hist.* A plaintiff's restatement of a claim because the first complaint did not contain sufficient details. • The purpose was to allow a plaintiff to reply to a defendant's responsive plea that did not address the plaintiff's specific claim because the complaint was too general. New assignment has been replaced by amended pleadings. — Also termed *novel assignment.*

assignment clause. *Oil & gas.* See CHANGE-OF-OWNERSHIP CLAUSE.

Assignment Division. The section of the U.S. Patent and Trademark Office that is responsible for recording assignments and other documents affecting title to patent and trademark applications, patents, and registrations.

assignment for the benefit of creditors. (18c) Assignment of a debtor's property to another person in trust so as to consolidate and liquidate the debtor's assets for payment to creditors, any surplus being returned to the debtor. • This procedure serves as a state-law substitute for federal bankruptcy proceedings. The debtor is not discharged from unpaid debts by this procedure since creditors do not agree to any discharge.

assignment of dower (dow-ər). See ASSIGNMENT (2).

assignment of error. (17c) A specification of the trial court's alleged errors on which the appellant relies in seeking an appellate court's reversal, vacation, or modification of an adverse judgment. Pl. **assignments of error.** See ERROR. Cf. WRIT OF ERROR.

assignment of income. See *assignment of wages* under ASSIGNMENT (2).

assignment-of-income doctrine. *Family law.* The common-law principle that the person who has earned income is the person taxed on it, regardless of who receives the proceeds. • Under this doctrine, future income assigned to another is taxable to the assignor. For example, in *Lucas v. Earl*, 281 U.S. 111, 50 S.Ct. 241 (1930), the Court held that a husband who was the sole wage-earner could not assign to his wife half his income and then pay the federal income tax on only the unassigned part.

assignment of lease. See ASSIGNMENT (2).

assignment of property. See EQUITABLE DISTRIBUTION.

assignment of realty. See ASSIGNMENT (2).

assignment-of-rents clause. A mortgage provision or separate agreement that entitles the lender to collect rents from the mortgaged premises if the borrower defaults.

assignment of rights. (18c) *Contracts.* The transfer of rights, esp. contractual rights, from one party to another.

assignment of wages. See ASSIGNMENT (2).

assignment pro tanto. See ASSIGNMENT (2).

assignor (as-ə-**nor** *or* ə-**si**-nər *or* ə-si-**nor**). (17c) One who transfers property rights or powers to another. — Also spelled *assigner.*

assignor estoppel. See ESTOPPEL.

Assimilative Crimes Act. A federal statute providing that state law applies to a crime committed within a federal enclave in that state (such as a reservation or military installation) if the crime is not punishable under federal law. 18 USCA § 13. • This statute uses local laws as gap-fillers for federal criminal law.

assistance. *Civil law.* Compensation for an effort to save a threatened vessel, cargo, or ship personnel at sea. Cf. NO CURE, NO PAY.

assistance, writ of. See WRIT OF ASSISTANCE.

assistance of counsel. (17c) Representation by a lawyer, esp. in a criminal case. • The phrase in its modern uses derives from the Sixth Amendment: "In all criminal prosecutions, the accused shall enjoy the right . . . to have the assistance of counsel for his defense." U.S. Const. amend. VI. See RIGHT TO COUNSEL.

effective assistance of counsel. (1937) A conscientious, meaningful legal representation, whereby the defendant is advised of all rights and the lawyer performs all required tasks reasonably according to the prevailing professional standards in criminal cases. *See* Fed. R. Crim. P. 44; 18 USCA § 3006A.

inadequate assistance of counsel. See *ineffective assistance of counsel.*

ineffective assistance of counsel. (1957) A representation in which the defendant is deprived of a fair trial because the lawyer handles the case unreasonably, usu. either by performing incompetently or by not devoting full effort to the defendant, esp. because of a conflict of interest. • In determining whether a criminal defendant received ineffective assistance of counsel, courts generally consider several factors: (1) whether the lawyer had previously handled criminal cases; (2) whether strategic trial tactics were involved in the allegedly incompetent action; (3) whether, and to what extent, the defendant was prejudiced as a result of the lawyer's alleged ineffectiveness; and (4) whether the

ineffectiveness was due to matters beyond the lawyer's control. — Also termed *inadequate assistance of counsel.*

Assistant Commissioner for Patents. See *commissioner for patents* under COMMISSIONER.

Assistant Commissioner for Trademarks. See *commissioner for trademarks* under COMMISSIONER.

assistant jurisdiction. See JURISDICTION.

Assistant United States Attorney. See UNITED STATES ATTORNEY.

assisted conception. *Family law.* The fertilization of a woman's egg with a man's sperm by some means other than sexual intercourse. See ARTIFICIAL INSEMINATION; IN VITRO FERTILIZATION; GAMETE INTRAFALLOPIAN TRANSFER; ZYGOTE INTRAFALLOPIAN TRANSFER.

assisted reproductive technology. *Family law.* Any medical means of aiding human reproduction, esp. through laboratory procedures. — Abbr. ART. — Also termed *assisted reproduction*; *assisted-reproductive therapy.*

assisted self-determination. See *assisted suicide* under SUICIDE.

assisted suicide. See SUICIDE.

assize (ə-**siz**), *n.* (14c) **1.** A session of a court or council.

maiden assize. *Hist.* **1.** An assize in which no prisoner is sentenced to death. **2.** An assize in which the sheriff presents the judges with white gloves because there are no prisoners to try. • This practice stemmed from a custom in which a prisoner who was convicted of murder but pardoned by the Crown presented gloves to the judges as a fee.

2. A law enacted by such a body, usu. one setting the measure, weight, or price of a thing. **3.** The procedure provided for by such an enactment. **4.** The court that hears cases involving that procedure. **5.** A jury.

grand assize. (*often cap.*) A sworn panel summoned by judicial writ to resolve disputes concerning real property. • Henry II instituted the Grand Assize in the 12th century as an alternative to trial by battle. — Also termed *magna assisa.*

petite assize. A jury convened to decide questions of possession.

6. A jury trial.

assize of mort d'ancestor (**mor**[t] **dan**-ses-tər). An action for the recovery of land belonging to the claimant's ancestor. • Mort d'ancestor was abolished in the early 19th century. — Also termed *assisa mortis d'ancestoris*; *assisa de morte antecessoris.*

judicial assize. An assize begun by judicial writ and deriving from pleas of *gage, mort d'ancestor,* and *darrein presentment.*

petty assize. An assize begun by an original writ. • Petty assizes were characterized by the form of the writ, which specified the questions to be put to the panel, and ordered that a panel be assembled. The petty assizes were *novel disseisin, mort d'ancestor, utrum,* and *darrein presentment.*

7. A jury's finding. **8.** A writ. — Also spelled *assise; assisa.*

assizer, *n. Hist.* **1.** A member of a grand assize. See *grand assize* under ASSIZE (5). **2.** *Scots law.* A juror. **3.** One having custody of the standards of weight and measure; esp., one who fixes the assize of bread, ale, and other items of general consumption. — Also spelled *assizor; assiser; assisor.*

Assizes de Jerusalem (ə-**siz**-əz də jə-**roo**-sə-ləm). A code of feudal law intended to serve as the law of the lands conquered by the Crusaders. • The code was prepared in the 12th century after the 1099 conquest of Jerusalem.

assizor. See ASSIZER.

associate, *n.* (16c) **1.** A colleague or companion. **2.** A junior member of an organization or profession; esp., a lawyer in a law firm, usu. with fewer than a certain number of years in practice, who may, upon achieving the requisite seniority, receive an offer to become a partner or shareholder. — Also termed *associate attorney.* **3.** *Hist. English law.* An officer of a common-law court responsible for maintaining the court's records, attending jury trials, and entering verdicts. • In 1894, associates' duties were taken over by the staff of the Central Office. See CLERK OF ASSIZE; CENTRAL OFFICE.

associate agent. See AGENT (3).

associate attorney. See ATTORNEY.

associated person. *Securities.* **1.** A partner, officer, director, branch manager of a broker or dealer, or any person performing similar functions or occupying a similar status, any person directly or indirectly controlling, controlled by, or under common control with the broker or dealer, or any employee of the broker or dealer — with two exceptions: (1) those whose functions are solely clerical or ministerial, and (2) those required to register under state law as a broker or dealer solely because they are issuers of securities or associated with an issuer of securities. 15 USCA § 78(a) (21), (49). **2.** A natural person who is a partner, officer, director, or employee of: (1) the issuer; (2) a general partner of a limited partnership issuer; or (3) a company or partnership that controls, is controlled by, or is under common control with the issuer. Cf. AFFILIATE (2).

associate judge. See JUDGE.

associate justice. See JUSTICE (2).

association. (16c) **1.** The process of mentally collecting ideas, memories, or sensations. **2.** A gathering of people for a common purpose; the persons so joined. **3.** An unincorporated organization that is not a legal entity separate from the persons who compose it. • If an association has sufficient corporate attributes, such as centralized management, continuity of existence, and limited liability, it may be classified and taxed as a corporation. — Also termed *unincorporated association; voluntary association.*

beneficial association. See *benevolent association.*

benefit association. See *benevolent association.*

benevolent association. An unincorporated, nonprofit organization that has a philanthropic or charitable purpose. — Also termed *beneficial association; benefit association; benevolent society; fraternal society; friendly society.*

homeowners' association. **1.** An association of people who own homes in a given area and have united to improve or maintain the area's quality. **2.** An association formed by a land developer or homebuilder to manage and maintain property in which the developer or the builder owns an undivided common interest. • Homeowners' associations — which are regulated by statute in many states — are commonly formed by restrictive covenant or a declaration of restrictions. — Also spelled *homeowners association.* — Also termed *owners' association.*

nonprofit association. A group organized for a purpose other than to generate income or profit, such as a scientific, religious, or educational organization.

owners' association. **1.** See *homeowners' association.* **2.** See OWNERS' ASSOCIATION.

professional association. (1837) **1.** A group of professionals organized to practice their profession together, though not necessarily in corporate or partnership form. **2.** A group of professionals organized for education, social activity, or lobbying, such as a bar association. — Abbr. P.A.

trade association. (1909) An association of business organizations having similar concerns and engaged in similar fields, formed for mutual protection, the interchange of ideas and statistics, and the establishment and maintenance of industry standards. • A trade association may be composed of members of a single industry (e.g., the Chemical Manufacturers Association) or members having a common interest or purpose (e.g., the Consumer Mortgage Coalition). Among the joint actions that a trade association often takes are collecting industry data, advertising, marketing, and engaging in public relations and government relations.

association-in-fact enterprise. Under RICO, a group of people or entities that have not formed a legal entity, but that have a common or shared purpose, and maintain an ongoing organizational structure through which the associates function as a continuing unit. • A RICO violation is not shown merely by proving that an enterprise, including an association-in-fact, exists. A pattern of racketeering activity must also be proved. 18 USCA § 1961(4); *United States v. Turkette*, 452 U.S. 576, 101 S.Ct. 2524 (1981).

Association of American Law Schools. An organization of U.S. law schools that have each graduated at least three annual classes of students. — Abbr. AALS.

Association of Legal Writing Directors. A nonprofit corporation composed of the directors and former directors of law-school legal-writing programs, mostly in the United States. • Created in 1996 to improve those programs, it supports research and scholarship; holds a biennial conference; conducts (with the Legal Writing Institute) an annual survey of the programs; maintains a listserv; represents writing teachers before the American Bar Association; and publishes various resources, including the *ALWD Citation Manual.* — Abbr. ALWD (**al**-wid). See ALWD CITATION MANUAL.

assoil (ə-**soyl**), *vb.* [Law French] *Hist.* To acquit or absolve; to deliver from excommunication. — Also spelled *assoile.* — Also termed *absoile; assoilyie.*

assumed bond. See *guaranteed bond* (1) under BOND (3).

assumed name. (17c) **1.** ALIAS (1). **2.** The name under which a business operates or by which it is commonly known <Antex Corporation's assumed name is Computer Warehouse>. • Many states require an individual or business operating under an assumed name to file an assumed-name certificate, usu. in the secretary of state's office or the county clerk's office where the principal place of business is located. — Also termed *fictitious name.* See D/B/A. Cf. *corporate name* under NAME.

assume or reject. *Bankruptcy.* (Of a debtor-in-possession or a trustee) to make an election under the Bankruptcy Code concerning an executory contract or an unexpired lease within a prescribed period, depending on the chapter of the Code under which the case is proceeding and the subject matter of the contract. • The timing, procedure, and consequences of the election are described in 11 USCA § 365.

assumpsit (ə-**səm**[**p**]-sit). [Law Latin "he undertook"] (16c) **1.** An express or implied promise, not under seal, by which one person undertakes to do some act or pay something to another <an assumpsit to pay a debt>. **2.** A common-law action for breach of such a promise or for breach of a contract <the creditor's assumpsit against the debtor>.

> **general assumpsit.** (18c) An action based on the defendant's breach of an implied promise to pay a debt to the plaintiff. — Also termed *common assumpsit; indebitatus assumpsit.*

> **indebitatus assumpsit** (in-deb-i-**tay**-təs ə-**səm**[**p**]-sit). [Latin "being indebted, he undertook"] **1.** A form of action in which the plaintiff alleges that the defendant contracted a debt and, as consideration, had undertaken (i.e., promised) to pay. • The action was equivalent to the common-law action for debt (an action based on a sealed instrument), but could be used to enforce an oral debt. In England, *indebitatus assumpsit* was abolished in 1873 by the Judicature Act. But it is still used in several American states, such as California. See CONCESSIT SOLVERE. **2.** See *general assumpsit.*

> **special assumpsit.** An action based on the defendant's breach of an express contract. — Also termed *express assumpsit.*

assumption, *n.* (13c) **1.** A fact or statement taken as true or correct; a supposition <a logical assumption>. **2.** The act of taking (esp. someone else's debt or other obligation) for or on oneself; the agreement to so take <assumption of a debt>. — **assume,** *vb.*

> **assumption of mortgage or trust deed.** The acquisition of real property coupled with the assumption of personal liability for debt secured by that property.

> **implied assumption.** (1852) The imposition of personal liability on a land purchaser who buys subject to a mortgage and who deducts the mortgage amount from the purchase price, so that the purchaser is treated as having assumed the debt.

assumption clause. 1. A mortgage provision that prohibits another from assuming the mortgage without the permission of the mortgagee. **2.** A provision by which the transferee of an instrument agrees to assume an obligation of the transferor.

assumption fee. A lender's charge for processing records for a new buyer's assumption of an existing mortgage.

assumption of mortgage or trust deed. See ASSUMPTION.

assumption of the risk. (1824) *Torts.* **1.** The act or an instance of a prospective plaintiff's taking on the risk of loss, injury, or damage <the skydiver's assumption of the risk>. — Also termed *assumption of risk.* **2.** The principle that one who takes on the risk of loss, injury, or damage cannot maintain an action against a party that causes the loss, injury, or damage <assumption of the risk was not a valid defense>. ● Assumption of the risk was originally an affirmative defense, but in most jurisdictions it has now been wholly or largely subsumed by the doctrines of contributory or comparative negligence. The risk assumed by the person was often termed an *incurred risk.*

implied assumption of the risk. An assumption based on the plaintiff's conduct that seems to consent to relieve another of liability for negligence. ● For this defense to apply, the plaintiff's conduct must suggest (1) open consent to the risk, (2) voluntary participation in the activity, and (3) full understanding of the danger. See VOLENTI NON FIT INJURIA.

primary assumption of the risk. A legal conclusion that the defendant was not negligent because the defendant either did not owe a duty of care to the injured party or did not breach any duty owed. ● Courts decide questions of duty through policy judgments, which include the relative balance between risks and utilities.

secondary assumption of risk. 1. The act or an instance of voluntarily encountering a known unreasonable risk that is out of proportion to any advantage gained. ● With secondary assumption of the risk, the fact-finder considers the reasonableness of the plaintiff's conduct in the particular case, balancing the risks and utilities under the circumstances. **2.** An affirmative defense to an established breach of a duty, based on a claim that the plaintiff acted unreasonably in encountering a known risk. See *contributory negligence* under NEGLIGENCE.

voluntary assumption of the risk. An intentional and unreasonable exposure of oneself to danger created by another's negligence, when one knows or has reason to know of the danger.

assurance, *n.* (14c) **1.** Something that gives confidence; the state of being confident or secure <self-assurance>. **2.** *English law.* See *life insurance* under INSURANCE <she obtained assurance before traveling abroad, naming her husband as the beneficiary>. **3.** The act of transferring real property; the instrument by which it is transferred <the owner's assurance of the farm to his son>. **4.** A pledge or guarantee <adequate assurances of the borrower's solvency>. — **assure,** *vb.*

adequate assurance. 1. *Contracts.* A circumstance or a contractual obligor's act that gives an obligee reason to be confident that the contract will be duly performed. ● If the obligee has good reason to feel insecure and justifiably demands assurance, an obligor's failure to provide adequate assurance may constitute a repudiation

of the contract. UCC § 2-609. **2.** *Bankruptcy.* Evidence that a debtor will probably be able to perform its obligations under a contract, such as the posting of a bond or a showing that the debtor will generate sufficient income to pay any arrearages and future payment obligations.

collateral assurance. A pledge made in addition to the principal assurance of an agreement.

common assurance. See MUNIMENT OF TITLE.

further assurance. (17c) A covenant, usu. contained in a warranty deed, whereby the grantor promises to execute any document that might be needed in the future to perfect the title that the original instrument purported to transfer.

assured, *n.* *Insurance.* One who is indemnified against loss; INSURED.

assurer. See INSURER.

as their interests may appear. See ATIMA.

astipulation (as-tip-yə-**lay**-shən). *Archaic.* Agreement; assent.

astronomical day. See *solar day* (2) under DAY.

asylee (ə-sɪ-**lee**). A refugee applying for asylum; an asylum-seeker.

asylum. (15c) **1.** A sanctuary or shelter. **2.** Protection of usu. political refugees from arrest by a foreign jurisdiction; a nation or embassy that affords such protection. — Also termed *political asylum.* **3.** An institution for the protection and relief of the unfortunate, esp. the mentally ill. — Also termed (in sense 3, archaically) *insane asylum.*

at arm's length. See ARM'S-LENGTH.

at bar. (17c) Now before the court <the case at bar>. — Also termed *at bench; at the bar.*

at bench. See AT BAR.

at equity. According to equity; by, for, or in equity.

ATF. *abbr.* BUREAU OF ALCOHOL, TOBACCO, FIREARMS, AND EXPLOSIVES.

ATIMA (ə-**tee**-mə). *abbr.* As their interests may appear. ● The phrase is sometimes used in insurance policies to show that the named insured has an interest, usu. an unspecified one, in the property covered by the policy and is entitled to benefits to the extent of that interest. The phrase is also used in a policy's mortgage clause to protect the mortgagee's real-property interest. See INSURABLE INTEREST; MORTGAGE CLAUSE.

Atinian law. See LEX ATINIA.

at issue. (18c) Taking opposite sides; under dispute; in question <the federal appeals courts are at issue over a question of law>.

at-issue waiver. (1985) An exemption from the attorney–client privilege, whereby a litigant is considered to have waived the privilege by taking a position that cannot be effectively challenged without analyzing privileged information. Cf. OFFENSIVE-USE WAIVER.

Atlantic Reporter. A set of regional lawbooks, part of the West Group's National Reporter System, containing every published appellate decision from Connecticut, Delaware, Maine, Maryland, New Hampshire, New Jersey, Pennsylvania, Rhode Island, and Vermont, as well as the decisions of the District of Columbia Municipal Court of Appeals, from 1885 to date. ● The first series ran from 1885 to 1938; the second series is the current one. — Abbr. A.; A.2d.

at large. (14c) **1.** Free; unrestrained; not under control <the suspect is still at large>. **2.** Not limited to any particular place, person, matter, or question <at-large election>. **3.** Chosen by the voters of an entire political entity, such as a state, county, or city, rather than from separate districts within the entity <councilmember at large>. **4.** Not ordered in a topical way; at random <statutes at large>. **5.** Fully; in detail; in an extended form <there wasn't time to discuss the issue at large>.

at-large election. See *election at large* under ELECTION.

at law. (16c) According to law; by, for, or in law.

at maturity. See *date of maturity* under DATE.

at par, *adj.* (Of a stock or bond) issued or selling at face value.

at-pleasure appointment. See *pleasure appointment* under APPOINTMENT (1).

at-risk rules, *n. pl.* (1977) Statutory limitations of a taxpayer's deductible losses to the amount the taxpayer could actually lose, to prevent the taxpayer from sheltering income.

atrocious assault. See ASSAULT.

atrocious felony. See FELONY.

ATS. *abbr.* At the suit of.

ATSDR. *abbr.* AGENCY FOR TOXIC SUBSTANCES AND DISEASE REGISTRY.

attach, *vb.* (14c) **1.** To annex, bind, or fasten <attach the exhibit to the pleading>. **2.** To take or seize under legal authority <attach the debtor's assets>. **3.** To become attributed; to adhere <jeopardy attaches when the jury is sworn>.

attaché (at-ə-**shay** *or* a-ta-**shay**), *n.* A person who serves as a technical adviser to an embassy.

attaching creditor. See CREDITOR.

attachment. (14c) **1.** The seizing of a person's property to secure a judgment or to be sold in satisfaction of a judgment. — Also termed (in civil law) *provisional seizure.* Cf. GARNISHMENT; SEQUESTRATION (1).

    attachment of wages. The attachment by a plaintiff of a defendant's earnings as an employee. ●

In some jurisdictions, an attachment-of-earnings order requires the defendant's employer to deduct a specified sum or percentage of the defendant's wages or salary and to pay the money into court. The court then sends the money to the plaintiff. Federal law provides a garnishment statute for satisfaction of judgments for child support and alimony. Under this statute, up to 50% of a wage-earner's disposable income can be seized if the wage-earner has another family of dependents and up to 60% if there is only one family. If the obligor is more than three months in arrears, an additional 5% can be seized until the arrearage is paid. 15 USCA § 1673(b)(2). — Also termed *attachment of earnings; wage-withholding; automatic wage-withholding; wage assignment.* Cf. GARNISHMENT; INCOME-WITHHOLDING ORDER.

    prejudgment attachment. An attachment ordered before a case is decided. Cf. *provisional attachment.*

    provisional attachment. A prejudgment attachment in which the debtor's property is seized so that if the creditor ultimately prevails, the creditor will be assured of recovering on the judgment through the sale of the seized property. ● Ordinarily, a hearing must be held before the attachment takes place, and most courts require the creditor to post a bond for any damages that result from the seizure (esp. if the creditor ultimately loses in the lawsuit). Cf. *prejudgment attachment.*

2. The arrest of a person who either is in contempt of court or is to be held as security for the payment of a judgment. **3.** A writ ordering legal seizure of property (esp. to satisfy a creditor's claim) or of a person. — Also termed *writ of attachment.*

    ancillary attachment. An attachment that results in seizure and holding of property pending a resolution of the plaintiff's claim. — Also termed *attachment on mesne process.*

4. The creation of a security interest in property, occurring when the debtor agrees to the security, receives value from the secured party, and obtains rights in the collateral. UCC § 9-203. Cf. PERFECTION. **5.** The act of affixing or connecting; something (as a document) that is affixed or connected to something else.

attachment bond. See BOND (2).

attachment lien. See LIEN.

attachment of earnings. See *attachment of wages* under ATTACHMENT (1).

attachment of risk. (1900) The point when the risk of loss of purchased goods passes from the seller to the buyer. UCC § 2-509.

attachment of wages. See ATTACHMENT (1).

attachment on mesne process. See *ancillary attachment* under ATTACHMENT (3).

attainder (ə-**tayn**-dər), *n.* (15c) **1.** At common law, the act of extinguishing a person's civil rights when that person is sentenced to death or declared an outlaw for committing a felony or treason. **2.** *Hist.* A grand-jury proceeding to try whether a jury has given a false verdict. **3.** The conviction of a jury so tried. See BILL OF ATTAINDER. — **attaint** (ə-**taynt**), *vb.*

attaint (ə-**taynt**), *adj.* (14c) Maligned or tarnished reputationally; under an attainder for crime.

attaint, *n. Hist.* A writ to inquire whether a 12-member jury gave a false verdict. • If it was so found (by a 24-member jury), the judgment based on the verdict was overturned. The writ was abolished in England in 1826.

attempt, *n.* (16c) **1.** The act or an instance of making an effort to accomplish something, esp. without success. **2.** *Criminal law.* An overt act that is done with the intent to commit a crime but that falls short of completing the crime. • Attempt is an inchoate offense distinct from the intended crime. Under the Model Penal Code, an attempt includes any act that is a substantial step toward commission of a crime, such as enticing, lying in wait for, or following the intended victim or unlawfully entering a building where a crime is expected to be committed. Model Penal Code § 5.01. — Also termed *criminal attempt*; *offer.* See DANGEROUS-PROXIMITY TEST; INDISPENSABLE-ELEMENT TEST; LAST-PROXIMATE-ACT TEST; PHYSICAL-PROXIMITY TEST; PREPARATION; PROBABLE-DESISTANCE TEST; RES IPSA LOQUITUR TEST; PREPARATION; SUBSTANTIAL-STEP TEST. Cf. CONSPIRACY; SOLICITATION (2). — **attempt,** *vb.*

attempted assault. See ASSAULT.

attempted marriage. See *void marriage* under MARRIAGE (1).

attempted monopolization. See MONOPOLIZATION.

attempted suicide. See SUICIDE.

attempt to assault. See *attempted assault* under ASSAULT.

attempt to attempt. (1903) A first step made toward a criminal attempt of some sort, such as a failed effort to mail someone a note inciting that person to engage in criminal conduct. • As a general rule, courts do not recognize an attempt to commit a crime that is itself an attempt. But some jurisdictions recognize this offense, esp. when the attempted crime is defined to be an independent substantive crime. For example, some jurisdictions recognize an attempted assault if assault is defined as placing a person in apprehension of bodily injury (as opposed to being defined merely as an attempted battery). In this situation, courts

have been willing to punish conduct that falls short of the attempted crime but constitutes more than mere preparation to commit it. See *attempted assault* under ASSAULT.

attendance officer. See TRUANCY OFFICER.

attendant, *adj.* (15c) Accompanying; resulting <attendant circumstances>.

attendant circumstance. See CIRCUMSTANCE.

attendant term. See TERM (4).

attenuation doctrine (ə-ten-yə-**way**-shən). (1962) *Criminal procedure.* The rule providing that evidence obtained by illegal means may nonetheless be admissible if the connection between the evidence and the illegal means is sufficiently attenuated or remote. • This is an exception to the fruit-of-the-poisonous-tree doctrine. See FRUIT-OF-THE-POISONOUS-TREE DOCTRINE.

atterminement (ə-**tər**-min-mənt). **1.** The granting of a delay for some purpose; esp., the extension of time to pay a debt. **2.** The fixing of a time limit. — **attermine,** *vb.*

attest (ə-**test**), *vb.* (16c) **1.** To bear witness; testify <attest to the defendant's innocence>. **2.** To affirm to be true or genuine; to authenticate by signing as a witness <attest the will>. — **attestation** (a-te-**stay**-shən), *n.* — **attestative** (ə-**tes**-tə-tiv), *adj.*

attestation clause. (18c) A provision at the end of an instrument (esp. a will) that is signed by the instrument's witnesses and that recites the formalities required by the jurisdiction in which the instrument might take effect (such as where the will might be probated). • The attestation strengthens the presumption that all the statutory requirements for executing the will have been satisfied. — Also termed *witnessing part.* Cf. TESTIMONIUM CLAUSE.

attested copy. See *certified copy* under COPY.

attested will. See WILL.

attester (ə-**tes**-tər). One who attests or vouches for. — Also spelled *attestant; attestator; attestor.*

attesting witness. See WITNESS.

at the bar. See AT BAR.

at the courthouse door. (Of the posting of a notice of judicial sale, etc.) on the courthouse door, or in direct proximity to the door, as on a bulletin board that is located just outside the door and that is regularly used for the posting of legal notices. • Some statutes may specify that the notice be actually posted on the door. See POSTING (5).

at-the-market price. See PRICE.

attorn (ə-**tərn**), *vb.* (15c) **1.** To agree to be the tenant of a new landlord. — Also termed *attorn tenant.* **2.** To transfer (money, goods, etc.) to another.

attorney. (14c) **1.** Strictly, one who is designated to transact business for another; a legal agent. — Also termed *attorney-in-fact*; *private attorney*. **2.** A person who practices law; LAW-YER. — Also termed (in sense 2) *attorney-at-law*; *public attorney*. Cf. COUNSEL (2). — Abbr. att'y. Pl. **attorneys.**

associate attorney. 1. See ASSOCIATE (2). **2.** *Patents.* An attorney who is registered to practice before the U.S. Patent and Trademark Office, who has been appointed by a principal attorney, and who is authorized to prosecute a patent application through the filing of a power of attorney.

attorney ad litem (ad lı-tem *or* -təm). A court-appointed lawyer who represents a child during the course of a legal action, such as a divorce, termination, or child-abuse case. • The attorney owes to the child the duties of loyalty, confidentiality, and competent representation. A child's right to legal representation in a juvenile proceeding was mandated in *In re Gault*, 387 U.S. 1, 87 S.Ct. 1428 (1967). The appointment of an attorney ad litem is a limited one — only for a specific lawsuit. — Also termed *child's attorney*; *attorney for the child*. Cf. *guardian ad litem* under GUARDIAN.

attorney not of record. 1. A lawyer who is not recognized as a party's legal representative. Cf. *attorney of record* (1). **2.** *Patents & trademarks.* An attorney whose name is not included in a power of attorney on file with the U.S. Patent and Trademark Office for a patent or trademark application. • An attorney not of record may nevertheless prosecute a patent application if registered to practice before the U.S. Patent and Trademark Office and appointed by the principal attorney. 37 CFR 1.34(a). Cf. *attorney not recognized.*

attorney not recognized. *Patents.* An attorney appointed by a patent applicant but not registered to practice before the U.S. Patent and Trademark Office. • A power of attorney appointing an unregistered attorney is void. Cf. *attorney not of record.*

attorney of record. 1. The lawyer who appears for a party in a lawsuit and who is entitled to receive, on the party's behalf, all pleadings and other formal documents from the court and from other parties. — Also termed *counsel of record*. See OF RECORD (1). **2.** *Patents & Trademarks.* The attorney or agent whose name is included in the power of attorney filed by an applicant for a patent or a trademark registration. • For a patent application, the attorney of record must be a patent attorney or a patent agent.

briefing attorney. 1. An attorney who specializes in brief-writing, particularly appellate briefs and legal memoranda. **2.** CLERK (5).

panel attorney. (1951) A private attorney who represents an indigent defendant at the government's expense. • A panel attorney is usu. a member of an affiliated list and assigned by a court to a particular client.

research attorney. 1. An attorney who specializes in providing legal support by researching, by writing memoranda, and by preparing drafts of documents. **2.** CLERK (5). • In some jurisdictions, a research attorney is a midlevel law clerk, above a briefing attorney but below a staff attorney.

settlement attorney. An attorney who specializes in negotiating resolutions for disputes, such as pending lawsuits, or in finalizing negotiated transactions, such as real-property sales. — Sometimes also termed (in real-property sales) *settlement agent.*

special attorney. See *special counsel* under COUN-SEL.

staff attorney. (1934) **1.** A lawyer who works for a court, usu. in a permanent position, on matters such as reviewing motions, screening docketing statements, preparing scheduling orders, and examining habeas corpus petitions. • Staff attorneys do not rule on motions or decide cases, but they review and research factual and legal points, and recommend proposed rulings to judges, as well as drafting the orders implementing those rulings. See CLERK (5). **2.** An in-house lawyer for an organization, esp. a nonprofit organization but sometimes for a corporation. Cf. *in-house counsel* under COUNSEL. **3.** A lawyer who works for a law firm and performs the functions of an associate but who is not on a partnership track.

attorney, power of. See POWER OF ATTORNEY.

attorney-at-law. See ATTORNEY (2).

attorney–client privilege. See PRIVILEGE (3).

attorney–client relationship. See RELATIONSHIP.

attorney fees. See ATTORNEY'S FEES.

attorney for the child. See *attorney ad litem* under ATTORNEY.

attorney general. (16c) The chief law officer of a state or of the United States, responsible for advising the government on legal matters and representing it in litigation. • "General" is a postpositive adjective, not an honorific, so the title should not, strictly speaking, be shortened. — Abbr. AG. Pl. **attorneys general.**

attorney general's opinion. (1808) **1.** An opinion furnished by the U.S. Attorney General to the President or another executive official on a request concerning a question of law. **2.** A written opinion by a state attorney general, usu. given at the request of a public official, interpreting a legal provision.

attorney in charge. See *lead counsel* (1) under COUNSEL.

attorney-in-fact. See ATTORNEY (1).

attorney malpractice. See *legal malpractice* under MALPRACTICE.

attorney not of record. See ATTORNEY.

attorney not recognized. See ATTORNEY.

attorney of record. See ATTORNEY.

Attorneys and Agents Registered to Practice Before the U.S. Patent and Trademark Office. A PTO publication listing all registered patent attorneys and agents by name and location.

attorney's fees. (18c) The charge to a client for services performed for the client, such as an hourly fee, a flat fee, or a contingent fee. — Also spelled *attorneys' fees.* — Also termed *attorney fees.* Cf. RETAINER (2).

attorney's lien. See LIEN.

attorney-witness rule. See LAWYER-WITNESS RULE.

attorney work product. See WORK PRODUCT.

attorney-work-product privilege. See WORK-PRODUCT RULE.

attornment (ə-tərn-mənt), *n.* (16c) **1.** A tenant's agreement to hold the land as the tenant of a new landlord. **2.** A constructive delivery involving the transfer of mediate possession while a third person has immediate possession; esp., a bailee's acknowledgment that he or she will hold the goods on behalf of someone other than the bailor. ● For the other two types of constructive delivery, see CONSTITUTUM POSSESSORIUM; TRADITIO BREVI MANU. — **attorn,** *vb.*

attractive nuisance. See NUISANCE.

attractive-nuisance doctrine. (1903) *Torts.* The rule that a person who owns property on which there is a dangerous thing or condition that will foreseeably lure children to trespass has a duty to protect those children from the danger <the attractive-nuisance doctrine imposed a duty on the school to protect the children from the shallow, polluted pond on school property>. — Also termed *turntable doctrine; torpedo doctrine.* See ALLUREMENT; DANGEROUS INSTRUMENTALITY.

attribution, *n.* The process — outlined in the Internal Revenue Code — by which a person's or entity's stock ownership is assigned to a related family member or related entity for tax purposes. — Also termed *stock attribution.* — **attribute,** *vb.* — **attributive,** *adj.*

attribution right. *Copyright.* A person's right to be credited as a work's author, to have one's name appear in connection with a work, or to forbid the use of one's name in connection with a work that the person did not create. ● Attribution rights constitute one aspect of the moral rights recognized primarily in civil-law countries. Under the Visual Artists Rights Act of 1990, the creators of a very limited class of works—called works of visual art—have certain statutory attribution rights. 17 USCA § 106A. Under the Berne Convention Implementation Act, attribution rights afforded foreign copyright owners may be enforceable in the U.S. — Also termed *rights of attribution; paternity; maternity.* Cf. INTEGRITY RIGHT; MORAL RIGHT.

att'y. *abbr.* ATTORNEY.

ATVEF. *abbr.* ADVANCED TELEVISION ENHANCEMENT FORUM.

at will. (14c) Subject to one's discretion; as one wishes or chooses; esp. (of a legal relationship), able to be terminated or discharged by either party without cause <employment at will>.

at-will employment. See *employment at will* under EMPLOYMENT.

at-will tenancy. See *tenancy at will* under TENANCY.

Atwood **doctrine.** The principle that, to the extent an ERISA plan and its summary-plan description conflict regarding the circumstances under which benefits may be denied, the summary-plan description controls. *Atwood v. Newmont Gold Co.,* 45 F.3d 1317 (9th Cir. 1995); 29 USCA § 1022. See SUMMARY-PLAN DESCRIPTION.

au besoin (oh bə-zwan). [French "in case of need"] A designation in a bill of exchange stating who is responsible for payment if the drawee fails or refuses to pay. ● For example, *au besoin* is part of the phrase *au besoin, chez Messrs. Garnier et DuCloux* (meaning "in case of need, apply to Messrs. Garnier and DuCloux").

auction, *n.* (16c) A public sale of property to the highest bidder. ● Under UCC § 2-328, a sale at auction is ordinarily complete when the auctioneer so announces in a customary manner, as by pounding a hammer. — Also termed *auction sale.* — **auction,** *vb.*

auction without reserve. An auction in which the property will be sold to the highest bidder, no minimum price will limit bidding, the owner may not withdraw property after the first bid is received, the owner may not reject any bids, and the owner may not nullify the bidding by outbidding all other bidders. ● In an auction without reserve, the owner essentially becomes an offeror, and each successively higher bid creates a contingent acceptance, with the highest bid creating an enforceable contract. — Also termed *absolute auction.* See WITHOUT RESERVE.

auction with reserve. An auction in which the property will not be sold unless the highest bid exceeds a minimum price. See WITH RESERVE.

Dutch auction. 1. An auction in which property is initially offered at an excessive price that is gradually lowered until the property is sold. **2.** An auction in which several identical items are offered simultaneously, one to a bidder, and sold to the highest bidders for the amount of the lowest winning bid. **3.** *Securities.* A method of tendering stock shares whereby a corporation provides a price range, shareholders indicate how many shares they will sell and at what price, and the corporation buys however many shares it wants at the lowest prices offered. — Also termed *Dutch-auction tender method.* **4.** *Securities.* An auction of securities, usu. other than stock, in which a security's price is gradually lowered until it meets an acceptable bid and is sold. **5.** *Securities.* An auction of a new issue of stock in which there is a stated minimum price per share, but bidders may offer a higher price for any number of shares until the highest price offered becomes the final price at which all the shares issued will be sold. — Also termed (in sense 4) *offer for sale by tender.*

knock-out auction. An auction at which two or more bidders have agreed in advance not to bid against one another. ● At common law, knock-out auctions were not forbidden, on grounds that a person could not be constrained to make an offer. But most jurisdictions now have statutes that (1) forbid dealers (those who buy at auctions with the intention of reselling to others) from giving or offering an inducement to abstain from bidding at an auction, and (2) penalize the person who seeks such an inducement from a dealer.

auctioneer, *n.* A person legally authorized to sell goods or lands of other persons at public auction for a commission or fee. ● The auctioneer is the property owner's agent up to the moment when a purchaser's bid is accepted, when the auctioneer becomes the purchaser's agent. — Formerly also termed *vendue master.*

auction market. See MARKET.

auction sale. See AUCTION.

auctor (ahk-tor), *n.* [Latin "author"] **1.** The source of a right or title, such as a grantor; AUTHOR (2). **2.** A principal.

audience, *n.* A hearing before judges. See RIGHT OF AUDIENCE.

audience test. *Copyright.* A judicial analysis used to determine whether the lay observer or an ordinary, reasonable audience would conclude that the protectable expression in a copyrighted work is substantially similar to the expression in the accused work. — Also termed *ordinary-observer test*; *ordinary-lay-observer test.*

Audio Home Recording Act. *Copyright.* A 1992 federal law designed to prevent copyright-infringement suits based on the manufacture, importation, distribution, or sale of digital-audio technology. ● Manufacturers of digital recording devices must pay royalties on sales of the devices and related media, and build security mechanisms into each device. The security mechanisms allow the owner of a digital-recording device to make a copy from the original medium, but not to make a copy from the copy. 17 USCA §§ 1001–1010. — Abbr. AHRA.

audiovisual work. See WORK (2).

audit, *n.* (15c) A formal examination of an individual's or organization's accounting records, financial situation, or compliance with some other set of standards. See GENERALLY ACCEPTED AUDITING STANDARDS. — **audit,** *vb.* — **auditor,** *n.*

audit of return. See *tax audit.*

compliance audit. An audit conducted by a regulatory agency, an organization, or a third party to assess compliance with one or more sets of laws and regulations.

correspondence audit. An IRS audit of a taxpayer's return conducted by mail or telephone.

desk audit. A review of a civil-service position to determine whether its duties and responsibilities fit the prescribed job classification and pay scale.

double audit. An audit of the same subject performed separately by two independent auditors.

environmental audit. A company's voluntary self-audit to evaluate its environmental-management programs and to determine whether it is in compliance with environmental regulations.

event-driven audit. An audit that focuses on particular transactions or activities that may raise significant legal issues. ● Unlike routine periodic audits, an event-driven audit can focus substantial auditing resources on analyzing a particular event.

field audit. An IRS audit conducted at the taxpayer's business premises, accountant's offices, or lawyer's offices.

independent audit. An audit conducted by an outside person or firm not connected with the person or organization being audited.

internal audit. An audit performed by an organization's personnel to ensure that internal procedures, operations, and accounting practices are in proper order.

office audit. An IRS audit of a taxpayer's return conducted in the IRS agent's office.

periodic audit. An audit conducted at regular intervals to assess a company's current condition.

post audit. An audit of funds spent on a completed capital project, the purpose being to assess the efficiency with which the funds were spent and to compare expected cash-flow estimates with actual cash flows.

tax audit. The review of a taxpayer's return by the IRS, including an examination of the taxpayer's books, vouchers, and records supporting the return. — Also termed *audit of return*.

transactional audit. An audit performed for due-diligence purposes to determine whether there are potentially significant problems with a transaction. ● Transactional audits are often conducted in real-property transactions to identify any environmental problems. In that context, the audit is sometimes called a *site assessment*.

audit committee. See COMMITTEE.

audit letter. A written request for an attorney, banker, or someone else to give financial auditors information about a person or entity being audited, including information about pending or threatened litigation. ● The recipient of an audit letter usu. sends the response (called an *audit-letter response*) directly to the financial auditors. See AUDIT RESPONSE.

audit-letter response. See AUDIT RESPONSE.

audit of return. See *tax audit* under AUDIT.

audit opinion. See OPINION (2).

auditor. A person or firm, usu. an accountant or an accounting firm, that formally examines an individual's or entity's financial records or status.

city auditor. A municipal official responsible for examines a city's accounts and financial records.

county auditor. An official who examines a county's accounts and financial records.

state auditor. The appointed or elected official responsible for overseeing state fiscal transactions and auditing state-agency accounts. See AUDIT.

audit privilege. In an intellectual-property license agreement, the right of the licensor to inspect the licensee's books and records. — Also termed *audit rights*.

audit report. An independent auditor's written statement, usu. accompanying a company's financial statement, expressing the auditor's opinion of the accuracy of the company's financial condition as set forth in the financial statement.

audit response. A letter that an attorney provides to a client's financial auditors, usu. at the client's request, regarding matters such as pending or threatened litigation. ● Audit responses should comply with the American Bar Association's Statement of Policy Regarding Lawyer's Responses

to Auditors' Requests for Information, published in December 1975. — Also termed *audit-letter response*. See AUDIT LETTER.

audit rights. See AUDIT PRIVILEGE.

audit trail. (1954) The chain of evidence connecting account balances to original transactions and calculations.

augmented estate. See ESTATE (3).

***Aunt Jemima* doctrine.** *Trademarks.* The principle that a trademark is protected not only from use on a directly competing product, but also from use on a product so closely related in the marketplace that consumers would be confused into thinking that the products came from a single source. *Aunt Jemima Mills Co. v. Rigney & Co.,* 247 F. 407 (2d Cir. 1917); 15 USCA § 1114. ● In the namesake case, the name used on pancake flour was later used on syrup. The issue was not whether a competitor was trying to pass off goods, but whether it was fair to let the name's second user jeopardize the goodwill built up by the first user. See COMPLEMENTARY GOODS.

aural acquisition. (1968) *Criminal law.* Under the Federal Wiretapping Act, hearing or tape-recording a communication, as opposed to tracing its origin or destination. 18 USCA § 2510(4).

AUSA. *abbr.* See *assistant United States attorney* under UNITED STATES ATTORNEY.

Australian ballot. See BALLOT (4).

authentic act. *Civil law.* **1.** A writing signed before a notary public or other public officer. **2.** A certified copy of a writing.

authenticate, *vb.* **1.** To prove the genuineness of (a thing). **2.** To render authoritative or authentic, as by attestation or other legal formality. See UCC § 9-102(a)(7).

authentication, *n.* (18c) **1.** Broadly, the act of proving that something (as a document) is true or genuine, esp. so that it may be admitted as evidence; the condition of being so proved <authentication of the handwriting>. **2.** Specif., the assent to or adoption of a writing as one's own.

self-authentication. (1939) Authentication without extrinsic evidence of truth or genuineness. ● In federal courts, certain writings, such as notarized documents and certified copies of public records, may be admitted into evidence by self-authentication. Fed. R. Evid. 902.

authentic interpretation. See INTERPRETATION.

authenticum (aw-**then**-tə-kəm). *Roman & civil law.* **1.** An original instrument. **2.** (*cap.*) A Latin version of 134 Novels promulgated by Justinian mostly in Greek between A.D. 535 and 556. — Also termed *Authenticae*.

author. 1. *Copyright.* The person who creates an expressive work, or the person or business that hires another to create an expressive work. • In copyright law, "author" applies to a broad range of occupations, including writers, artists, programmers, choreographers, and translators. **2.** One from whom a right or title derives in some way other than by descent. See AUCTOR (1).

authoritative precedent. See *binding precedent* under PRECEDENT.

authority. (13c) **1.** The right or permission to act legally on another's behalf; esp., the power of one person to affect another's legal relations by acts done in accordance with the other's manifestations of assent; the power delegated by a principal to an agent <authority to sign the contract>. — Also termed *power over other persons.* See AGENCY.

actual authority. (18c) Authority that a principal intentionally confers on an agent or authority that the agent reasonably believes he or she has as a result of the agent's dealings with the principal. • Actual authority can be either express or implied. — Also termed *real authority.*

apparent authority. (1808) Authority that a third party reasonably believes an agent has, based on the third party's dealings with the principal, even though the principal did not confer or intend to confer the authority. • Apparent authority can be created by law even when no actual authority has been conferred. — Also termed *ostensible authority; authority by estoppel.*

authority coupled with an interest. (17c) Authority given to an agent for valuable consideration. • This authority cannot be unilaterally terminated by the principal. Cf. *naked authority.*

constructive authority. (1823) Authority that is inferred because of an earlier grant of authority.

express authority. (16c) Authority given to the agent by explicit agreement, either orally or in writing. — Also termed *stipulated authority.*

general authority. (17c) A general agent's authority, intended to apply to all matters arising in the course of the principal's business.

implied authority. (18c) Authority intentionally given by the principal to the agent as a result of the principal's conduct, such as the principal's earlier acquiescence to the agent's actions. — Also termed *presumptive authority.*

incidental authority. (18c) Authority needed to carry out actual or apparent authority. • For example, the actual authority to borrow money includes the incidental authority to sign commercial paper to bring about the loan. — Also termed *inferred authority.*

inherent authority. (17c) Authority of an agent arising from the agency relationship.

naked authority. (18c) Authority delegated to an agent solely for the principal's benefit, without a beneficial interest in the matter for the agent. • This authority can be revoked by the principal at any time. Cf. *authority coupled with an interest.*

ostensible authority. See *apparent authority.*

presumptive authority. See *implied authority.*

real authority. See *actual authority.*

special authority. (18c) Authority limited to an individual transaction.

stipulated authority. See *express authority.*

supervisory authority. See SUPERVISORY AUTHORITY.

2. Governmental power or jurisdiction <within the court's authority>. **3.** A governmental agency or corporation that administers a public enterprise <transit authority>. — Also termed *public authority.*

constituted authority. (*often pl.*) Each of the legislative, executive, and judicial departments officially and rightfully governing a nation, people, municipality, or other governmental unit; an authority properly appointed or elected under organic law, such as a constitution or charter.

examining authority. A self-regulatory organization registered with the Securities and Exchange Commission and vested with the authority to examine, inspect, and otherwise oversee the activities of a registered broker or dealer.

4. A legal writing taken as definitive or decisive; esp., a judicial or administrative decision cited as a precedent <that case is good authority in Massachusetts>. • The term includes not only the decisions of tribunals but also statutes, ordinances, and administrative rulings.

adverse authority. (18c) Authority that is unfavorable to an advocate's position. • Most ethical codes require counsel to disclose adverse authority in the controlling jurisdiction even if the opposing counsel has not cited it.

imperative authority. Authority that is absolutely binding on a court. — Also termed *binding authority.* Cf. *binding precedent* under PRECEDENT.

persuasive authority. (1842) Authority that carries some weight but is not binding on a court.

primary authority. (1826) Authority that issues directly from a law-making body; legislation and the reports of litigated cases.

secondary authority. (1826) Authority that explains the law but does not itself establish it, such as a treatise, annotation, or law-review article.

5. A source, such as a statute, case, or treatise, cited in support of a legal argument <the brief's table of authorities>.

authority by estoppel. See *apparent authority* under AUTHORITY (1).

authorization clause. *Patents.* A Patent Act provision directing that if a person uses or manufactures something protected by a valid U.S. patent, acts on behalf of the U.S. government, and acts with the government's authorization or consent, the U.S., not the person, is deemed the infringing user or manufacturer. • If an infringing act is done by a government contractor or subcontractor working for the U.S. and the act is covered by the authorization or consent clause, the patent owner's only recourse is a suit against the U.S. in the U.S. Claims Court for compensation. The authorization or consent clause is in the second paragraph of 28 USCA § 1498(a). — Also termed *consent clause.*

authorization to sell. See LISTING (1).

authorize, *vb.* (14c) **1.** To give legal authority; to empower <he authorized the employee to act for him>. **2.** To formally approve; to sanction <the city authorized the construction project>. — **authorization,** *n.*

authorized capital. See *nominal capital* under CAPITAL.

authorized capital stock. See *capital stock* (1) under STOCK.

authorized committee. See SPECIAL LITIGATION COMMITTEE.

authorized shares. See *capital stock* (1) under STOCK.

authorized stock. See *capital stock* (1) under STOCK.

authorship. See *work of authorship* under WORK (2).

author's right. *Copyright.* The system of protecting the moral and economic rights of the creator of a work, esp. in civil-law countries. — Also termed (in French) *droit d'auteur*; (in German) *Urheberrecht*; (in Italian) *diritto d' autore*; (in Spanish) *derecho de autor.*

author's share. *Copyright.* An author's portion of royalties, as determined by an agreement with the publisher.

autocracy (aw-**tok**-rə-see), *n.* (17c) Government by one person with unlimited power and authority; unlimited monarchy. — **autocratic** (aw-tə-**krat**-ik), *adj.* — **autocrat** (**aw**-tə-krat), *n.*

autograph, *n.* A person's own writing or signature; HOLOGRAPH. Cf. ALLOGRAPH.

autolimitation, *n.* An authority's establishment of rules that, in effect, limit the authority's own power. — **autolimit,** *vb.*

Automated Bond System. The New York Stock Exchange's computerized network that enables subscribers to electronically transmit quotations and execute orders for bond trades. — Abbr. ABS.

Automated Patent System. A computerized database of patents, maintained by the U.S. Patent and Trademark Office database. — Abbr. APS. — Also termed *automated patent search system.*

automated transaction. (1977) A contract formed or performed, in whole or in part, by electronic means or by electronic messages in which neither party's electronic actions or messages establishing the contract are intended to be reviewed by an individual in the ordinary course. UCITA §§ 2-102(a)(7), 102:10UC; UETA § 14.

automatic-adjustment clause. A provision in a utility-rate schedule that allows a public utility to increase its rates without a public hearing or state review, if certain operating costs, such as the price of fuel, increase. *Federal Energy Regulatory Comm'n v. Mississippi*, 456 U.S. 742, 102 S.Ct. 2126 (1982).

automatic-assignment doctrine. *Trademarks.* The rule that, absent evidence to the contrary, the sale of an entire business carries with it and transfers to the purchaser any common-law marks used in that business without the need for a written assignment. • For marks registered under the Lanham Act or under some state registration schemes, a written assignment is required to transfer an interest in a registered mark or in a pending application to register a mark.

automatic disclosure. See DISCLOSURE (2).

automatic perfection. See PERFECTION.

automatic stay. See STAY.

automatic suspension. See *automatic stay* under STAY.

automatic-transfer statute. See TRANSFER STATUTE.

automatic wage-withholding. See *attachment of wages* under ATTACHMENT (1).

automatism (aw-**tom**-ə-tiz-əm), *n.* (1838) **1.** Action or conduct occurring without will, purpose, or reasoned intention, such as sleepwalking; behavior carried out in a state of unconsciousness or mental dissociation without full awareness. • Automatism may be asserted as a defense to negate the requisite mental state of voluntariness for commission of a crime. **2.** The state of a person who, though capable of action, is not conscious of his or her actions. — **automaton,** *n.*

ambulatory automatism. Automatism that consists in irresponsible or purposeless wanderings.

automobile exception. (1970) The doctrine that when probable cause exists, a law-enforcement officer need not obtain a warrant before searching a movable vehicle (such as a car or boat) in which an individual has a lessened expectation of privacy. • This is an exception to the Fourth Amendment's warrant requirement for search and seizure; exigent circumstances are presumed to exist. Once the right to conduct a warrantless search arises, the actual search may take place at a later time. *Carroll v. United States*, 267 U.S. 132, 45 S.Ct. 280 (1925); *Cardwell v. Lewis*, 417 U.S. 583, 94 S.Ct. 2464 (1974); *California v. Acevedo*, 500 U.S. 565, 111 S.Ct. 1982 (1991). See *exigent circumstances* under CIRCUMSTANCE.

automobile exclusion. See EXCLUSION (3).

automobile-guest statute. See GUEST STATUTE.

automobile homicide. See *vehicular homicide* under HOMICIDE.

automobile insurance. See INSURANCE.

autonomic law (aw-tə-**no m**-ik). (1832) An internal regulation that has its source in various forms of subordinate and restricted legislative authority possessed by private persons and bodies of persons. • Examples are corporate bylaws, university regulations, and the rules of the International Monetary Fund.

autonomous tariff. See TARIFF (2).

autonomy (aw-**tahn**-ə-mee), *n.* (17c) **1.** The right of self-government. **2.** A self-governing nation. **3.** An individual's capacity for self-determination. — **autonomous** (aw-**tahn**-ə-məs), *adj.*

autonomy of the parties. See FREEDOM OF CONTRACT.

autonomy privacy. See PRIVACY.

autopsy (**aw**-top-see). (1678) **1.** A medical examination of a corpse to determine the cause of death, esp. in a criminal investigation. — Also termed *postmortem; necropsy.* **2.** The evidence of one's own senses.

autoptic evidence (aw-**top**-tik). See *demonstrative evidence* under EVIDENCE.

autoptic proference (proh-**fər**-ənts). **1.** The presentation of an item for inspection by the court. **2.** See *demonstrative evidence* under EVIDENCE.

autrefois (oh-trə-**fwah** *or* oh-**tər**-foyz). [Law French] On another occasion; formerly.

autrefois acquit (ə-**kwit** *or* a-**kee**). [Law French "previously acquitted"] A plea in bar of arraignment that the defendant has been acquitted of the offense. — Also termed *former acquittal.* See DOUBLE JEOPARDY.

autrefois attaint (ə-**taynt**). *Hist.* A plea in bar that the defendant has already been attainted for one felony and therefore cannot be prosecuted for another. • This plea was abolished in 1827.

autrefois convict. [Law French "previously convicted"] A plea in bar of arraignment that the defendant has been convicted of the offense. See DOUBLE JEOPARDY.

autre vie (**oh**-trə **vee**). [Law French "another's life"] **1.** See PUR AUTRE VIE. **2.** See VIE.

auxiliary (awg-**zil**-yə-ree), *adj.* **1.** Aiding or supporting. **2.** Subsidiary. **3.** Supplementary.

auxiliary covenant. See COVENANT (1).

auxiliary jurisdiction. See *assistant jurisdiction* under JURISDICTION.

auxilium (awg-**zil**-ee-əm), *n.* [Latin] *Hist.* Aid; esp., compulsory aid such as a tax or tribute to be paid by a vassal to a lord as an incident of the tenure by knight's service.

avail, *n.* (15c) **1.** Use or advantage <of little or no avail>. **2.** (*pl.*) Profits or proceeds, esp. from a sale of property <the avails of the trust fund>.

available, *adj.* Legally valid <available claims> <available defenses>.

available for work, *adj.* (Of a person) ready, willing, and able to accept temporary or permanent employment when offered.

availment, *n.* (17c) The act of making use or taking advantage of something for oneself <availment of the benefits of public office>. — **avail,** *vb.*

aver (ə-**vər**), *vb.* (15c) To assert positively, esp. in a pleading; to allege.

average, *n.* **1.** A single value that represents the midpoint of a broad sample of subjects; esp., in mathematics, the mean of a series. **2.** The ordinary or typical level; the norm. **3.** *Maritime law.* Accidental partial loss or damage to an insured ship or its cargo during a voyage. — **average,** *vb.* & *adj.*

extraordinary average. A contribution by all the parties concerned in a commercial voyage — whether for vessel or cargo — toward a loss sustained by some of the parties in interest for the benefit of all.

general average. Average resulting from an intentional partial sacrifice of ship or cargo to avoid total loss. • The liability is proportionately shared by all parties who had an interest in the voyage. — Abbr. GA. — Also termed *gross average; general-average contribution.*

particular average. Average resulting from an accidental partial loss or damage. • Any average that is not general is termed particular. The liability is borne solely by the person who suffered the loss. — Also termed *simple average; partial average; petty average.*

average adjuster. See ADJUSTER.

average bond. See *general-average bond* under BOND (2).

average cost. See COST (1).

average daily balance. See DAILY BALANCE.

average gross sales. See SALE.

average tax rate. See TAX RATE.

average variable cost. The average cost per unit of output, arrived at by dividing the total variable expenses of production by the total units of output. See COST (1). Cf. LONG-RUN INCREMENTAL COST.

averaging down. An investment strategy in which shares in the same company are purchased at successively lower prices to achieve a lower average cost basis than the first purchase. ● An investor may buy any number of shares in each transaction, not necessarily the same number each time. Cf. AVERAGING UP.

averaging up. An investment strategy in a rising market in which equal numbers of shares in the same company are purchased at successively higher prices to reduce the investment's average cost basis. ● For example, if an investor buys an equal number of shares at $10, $13, $15, and $18, the average cost basis per share is $14. Cf. AVERAGING DOWN.

averment (ə-**vər**-mənt), *n.* (15c) A positive declaration or affirmation of fact; esp., an assertion or allegation in a pleading <the plaintiff's averment that the defendant ran a red light>. Cf. ASSEVERATE.

> *immaterial averment.* (18c) An averment that alleges something in needless detail; a statement that goes far beyond what is in issue. ● This type of averment may be ordered struck from the pleading.

> *negative averment.* (18c) An averment that is negative in form but affirmative in substance and that must be proved by the alleging party. ● An example is the statement "she was not old enough to enter into the contract," which is more than just a simple denial. Cf. TRAVERSE.

averment of notice. A statement in a pleading that someone else has been properly notified about some fact, esp. in special actions of assumpsit. See NOTICE.

aviation easement. See *avigational easement* under EASEMENT.

aviation insurance. See INSURANCE.

avigational easement. See EASEMENT.

avigation easement. See *avigational easement* under EASEMENT.

a vinculo matrimonii (ay **ving**-kyə-loh ma-trə-**moh**-nee-ı). [Latin] From the bond of matrimony. — Often shortened to *a vinculo.* See *divorce a vinculo matrimonii* under DIVORCE.

avoid, *vb.* (14c) To render void <because the restrictive covenant was overbroad, the court avoided it>. ● Because this legal use of *avoid* can be easily confused with the ordinary sense of the word, the verb *to void* is preferable.

avoidable, *adj.* **1.** Not inevitable; subject to prevention <an avoidable accident>.

> *practically avoidable.* (Of harm) capable of being eliminated in whole or substantial part without incurring prohibitive expense or hardship.

2. Capable of being refrained from <avoidable habits>. **3.** Voidable.

avoidable-consequences doctrine. See MITIGATION-OF-DAMAGES DOCTRINE.

avoidable cost. See COST (1).

avoidance, *n.* (14c) **1.** The act of evading or escaping <avoidance of tax liability>. See TAX AVOIDANCE. **2.** The act of refraining from (something) <avoidance of an argument>. **3.** RESCISSION (1) <avoidance of the agreement>. **4.** VOIDANCE <avoidance of a penalty>. **5.** ANNULMENT (1) <avoidance of the marriage>. **6.** CONFESSION AND AVOIDANCE <the defendant filed an avoidance in an attempt to avert liability>. — **avoid,** *vb.*

avoiding power. See POWER (5).

avoision (ə-**voy**-zhən), *n.* An ambiguous act that falls between legal avoidance and illegal evasion of the law. ● The term, coined by Arthur Seldon, an economist, is a blend of *evasion* and *avoidance.* *Avoision* usu. refers to financial acts that are not clearly legal tax avoidance or illegal tax evasion, but it may appear in other contexts.

avowal (ə-**vow**-əl), *n.* **1.** An open declaration. **2.** OFFER OF PROOF. — **avow,** *vb.*

avowant (ə-**vow**-ənt), *n.* A person who makes avowry in an action of replevin.

avowry (ə-**vow**-ree), *n. Common-law pleading.* An acknowledgment — in an answer to a replevin action — that one has taken property, and a justification for that taking <the defendant's avowry was based on alleged damage to the property by the plaintiff>. Cf. COGNIZANCE (4). — **avow,** *vb.*

avulsion (ə-**vəl**-shən), *n.* (17c) **1.** A forcible detachment or separation. **2.** A sudden removal of land caused by change in a river's course or by flood. ● Land removed by avulsion remains the property of the original owner. Cf. ALLUVION; ACCRETION (1); DELICTION; EROSION. **3.** A tearing away of a body part surgically or accidentally. — **avulse,** *vb.*

award, *n.* (14c) A final judgment or decision, esp. one by an arbitrator or by a jury assessing damages. — Also termed *arbitrament.*

award, *vb.* (14c) To grant by formal process or by judicial decree <the company awarded the contract

to the low bidder> <the jury awarded punitive damages>.

award in interference. See PRIORITY AWARD.

AWOL. *abbr.* (1921) Absent without leave; missing without notice or permission.

axiom (**ak**-see-əm), *n.* (15c) An established principle that is universally accepted within a given framework of reasoning or thinking <"innocent until proven guilty" is an age-old axiom of criminal law>. — **axiomatic** (ak-see-ə-**mat**-ik), *adj.*

ayant cause (ay-ənt). *Civil law.* **1.** One to whom a right has been assigned by will, gift, sale, or exchange; an assignee. **2.** One who has a "cause" or standing in one's own right.

aye (ɪ), *n. Parliamentary law.* An affirmative vote.

ayel (**ay**-əl). See AIEL.

ayle (ayl). See AIEL.

B

B2B. *abbr.* BUSINESS-TO-BUSINESS <a B2B transaction>.

B2C. *abbr.* BUSINESS-TO-CONSUMER <a B2C transaction>.

BA. *abbr.* See *banker's acceptance* under ACCEPTANCE (4).

baby act, pleading the. *Slang.* The act of asserting a person's infancy as a defense to a contract claim.

baby-bartering. See BABY-SELLING.

baby bond. See BOND (3).

baby-brokering. See BABY-SELLING.

Baby Doe. (1974) A generic pseudonym for a very young child involved in litigation. • Today a gender designation is often added: *Baby Girl Doe* or *Baby Boy Doe.* The generic term is used to shield the child's identity.

Baby FTC Act. (1988) A state statute that, like the Federal Trade Commission Act, outlaws deceptive and unfair trade practices.

Baby Moses law. See SAFE-HAVEN LAW.

baby-selling. The exchange of money or something of value for a child. • All states have prohibitions against baby-selling. It is not considered baby-selling for prospective adoptive parents to pay money to a birth mother for pregnancy-related expenses. — Also termed *baby-brokering*; *baby-bartering*.

baby-snatching. See *child-kidnapping* under KIDNAPPING.

BAC. *abbr.* BLOOD ALCOHOL CONTENT.

bachelor. 1. An unmarried man. **2.** The usual title of the first degree that is conferred on a university graduate. **3.** *English law.* A member of one of the orders of chivalry, such as the Order of the Bath. — Also termed (in sense 3) *knight bachelor.*

bachelor of laws. See LL.B.

back, *vb.* (18c) **1.** To indorse; to sign the back of a negotiable instrument. **2.** To sign so as to show acceptance or approval. **3.** To sign so as to indicate financial responsibility for (someone or something). **4.** *Hist.* (Of a magistrate) to sign (a warrant issued in another county) to permit execution in the signing magistrate's county.

backadation. See BACKWARDATION.

backberend (bak-ber-ənd). [Old English] *Hist.* **1.** The bearing of stolen goods upon one's back or about one's person. • *Backberend* is sometimes modernized to *backbearing.* **2.** A person caught carrying stolen goods. — Also spelled *bacberende*; *backberinde.* Cf. HANDHABEND.

back carry. *Hist.* The crime of carrying, on one's back, unlawfully killed game.

backdate, *vb.* (1944) **1.** To put a date earlier than the actual date on (something, as an instrument). • Under UCC § 3-113(a), backdating does not affect an instrument's negotiability. Cf. POSTDATE; ANTEDATE (1). **2.** To make (something) retroactively valid.

back door to Berne. *Copyright.* A U.S. copyright owner's simultaneous publication of the copyrighted work in both the United States and in a Berne Convention country in order to obtain Berne Convention protection. • This backdoor method was used before March 1989, when the United States became a member of the Berne Convention.

back-end load. See *load fund* under MUTUAL FUND.

background of the invention. *Patents.* In a U.S. patent application and any resulting patent, the section that identifies the field of art to which the invention pertains, summarizes the state of the art, and describes the problem solved by the invention. • The Background of the Invention section usu. includes two subsections: "Field of the Invention" and "Description of the Related Art." A mistaken inclusion in this section of a reference that postdates the date of invention may be construed as an admission.

backhaul allowance. See ALLOWANCE (1).

backing. Endorsement, esp. of a warrant by a magistrate. See BACK (4).

back-in right. *Oil & gas.* A reversionary interest in an oil-and-gas lease entitling an assignor to a share of the working interest after the assignee has recovered specified costs from production.

back lands. (17c) Generally, lands lying away from — not next to — a highway or a watercourse.

backpay. The wages or salary that an employee should have received but did not because of an employer's unlawful action in setting or paying the wages or salary. — Also written *back pay.* Cf. FRONTPAY.

backpay award. A judicial or quasi-judicial body's decision that an employee or ex-employee is entitled to accrued but uncollected wages or benefits. — Sometimes shortened to *backpay.*

backspread. *Securities.* In arbitrage, a less than normal price difference in the price of a currency or commodity. See ARBITRAGE; SPREAD (3).

back taxes. See *back tax* under TAX.

back-title certificate. See BACK-TITLE LETTER.

back-title letter. An official letter from a title insurer advising about the condition of title to land as of a certain date. • With this information, the title can be examined from that date forward. — Also termed *back-title certificate.*

back-to-back loan. See LOAN.

back-to-work agreement. A contract between a union and an employer covering the terms under which the employees will return to work after a strike.

backwardation. *Securities.* A fee paid by the seller of securities so that the buyer will allow delivery after their original delivery date. — Also termed *backadation; inverted market.*

backward integration. See INTEGRATION (5).

backwater. See WATER.

bad, *adj.* Invalid or void; legally unsound <bad service of process> <bad law>.

bad actor. See ACTOR (1).

bad-boy disqualification. *Securities.* An issuer's disqualification from certain SEC-registration exemptions as a result of the issuer's securities-law violations.

bad-boy provision. *Securities.* A statutory or regulatory clause in a blue-sky law stating that certain persons, because of their past conduct, are not entitled to any type of exemption from registering their securities. • Such clauses typically prohibit issuers, officers, directors, control persons, or broker-dealers from being involved in a limited offering if they have been the subject of an adverse proceeding concerning securities, commodities, or postal fraud.

bad character. (17c) A person's propensity for or tendency toward unlawful or immoral behavior. • In limited circumstances, proof of bad character may be introduced into evidence to discredit a witness. Fed. R. Evid. 608, 609. See *character evidence* under EVIDENCE.

bad check. See CHECK.

bad-conduct discharge. See DISCHARGE (8).

bad debt. See DEBT.

bad-debt loss ratio. The proportion of a business's uncollectible debt to a business's total receivables.

bad-debt reserve. See RESERVE.

bad faith, *n.* (17c) **1.** Dishonesty of belief or purpose <the lawyer filed the pleading in bad faith>. — Also termed *mala fides* (**mal**-ə-**fı**-deez). **2.**

Insurance. An insurance company's unreasonable and unfounded (though not necessarily fraudulent) refusal to provide coverage in violation of the duties of good faith and fair dealing owed to an insured. • Bad faith often involves an insurer's failure to pay the insured's claim or a claim brought by a third party. **3.** *Insurance.* An insured's claim against an insurance company for an unreasonable and unfounded refusal to provide coverage. Cf. GOOD FAITH. — **bad-faith,** *adj.*

bad-faith enforcement. *Patents.* **1.** The filing of an infringement action by a patentee who knows that the accused product or process does not infringe or that the patent is invalid or unenforceable. **2.** In an infringement action, a counterclaim alleging that at the time of filing suit, the patentee knew that the accused product or process did not infringe or that the patent was invalid or unenforceable. • A counterclaim for bad-faith enforcement arises under § 2 of the Sherman Act and under the common law of unfair competition. Cf. PATENT-MISUSE DOCTRINE.

bad-faith filing, *n. Bankruptcy.* The act of submitting a bankruptcy petition that is inconsistent with the purposes of the Bankruptcy Code or is an abuse of the bankruptcy system (that is, by not being filed in good faith). • A court may dismiss a bankruptcy case if it finds that the petition was filed in bad faith.

badge of fraud. (18c) A circumstance generally considered by courts as an indicator that a party to a transaction intended to hinder or defraud the other party, such as a transfer in anticipation of litigation, a transaction outside the usual course of business, or a false statement. See FRAUD.

badge of slavery. (17c) **1.** Strictly, a legal disability suffered by a slave, such as the inability to vote or to own property. **2.** Broadly, any act of racial discrimination — public or private — that Congress can prohibit under the 13th Amendment.

badger game. (1858) A scheme to extort money or some other benefit by arranging to catch someone in a compromising position and then threatening to make that person's behavior public.

bad-man theory. (1938) The jurisprudential doctrine or belief that a bad person's view of the law represents the best test of what the law actually is because that person will carefully calculate precisely what the rules allow and will operate up to the rules' limits. • This theory was first expounded by Oliver Wendell Holmes in his essay *The Path of the Law,* 10 Harv. L. Rev. 457 (1897). In the essay, Holmes maintained that a society's legal system is defined by predicting how the law will affect a person, as opposed to considering the ethics or morals supposedly underlying the law. Under Holmes's theory, the prediction is best made by viewing the law as would a "bad man" who is unconcerned with morals. Such a person is not concerned with acting morally or in accord with a grand philosophical scheme. Rather, that person is concerned with whether and to what degree certain acts will incur punishment by the public force of the law. See LEGAL REALISM. — Also termed *prediction theory*.

bad motive. See MOTIVE.

bads, *n. Slang.* In economics, the counterpart of "goods," characterized by a negative correlation between the amount consumed and the consumer's wealth; specif., the kinds of products that tend to be bought only by poor people.

bad title. See TITLE (2).

bagman. *Slang.* (1928) A person who collects and distributes illegally obtained money; esp., an intermediary who collects a bribe for a public official.

bail, *n.* (15c) **1.** A security such as cash or a bond; esp., security required by a court for the release of a prisoner who must appear in court at a future time <bail is set at $500>. Cf. RECOGNIZANCE.

  bail absolute. A fiduciary bond conditioning a surety's liability on the failure of an estate administrator, executor, or guardian to properly account for estate funds. See *fiduciary bond* under BOND (2).

  cash bail. A sum of money (rather than a surety bond) posted to secure a prisoner's release from jail. — Also termed *stationhouse bail.*

  civil bail. A bond or deposit of money given to secure the release of a person arrested for failing to pay a court-ordered civil debt. ● The bail is conditioned on the payment of the debt.

  excessive bail. (17c) Bail that is unreasonably high considering both the offense with which the accused is charged and the risk that the accused will not appear for trial. ● The Eighth Amendment prohibits excessive bail.

  stationhouse bail. See *cash bail.*

2. The process by which a person is released from custody either on the undertaking of a surety or on his or her own recognizance. **3.** Release of a prisoner on security for a future court appearance; esp., the delivery of a person in custody to a surety <the court refused bail for the accused serial killer>. **4.** One or more sureties for a criminal defendant <the attorney stood as bail for her client>. See BAILER (1).

bail above. See *bail to the action.*

bail below. See *bail to the sheriff.*

bail common. *Hist.* A fictitious surety filed by a defendant in a (usu. minor) civil action. — Also termed *common bail; straw bail.*

  bail to the action. *Hist.* A surety for a civil defendant arrested by a mesne process (i.e., a process issued during the lawsuit). ● If the defendant lost the lawsuit, the *bail to the action* was bound either to pay the judgment or to surrender the defendant into custody. — Also termed *bail above; special bail.* Cf. *bail to the sheriff.*

  bail to the sheriff. *Hist.* A person who pledged to the sheriff that a defendant served with process during a civil action would appear on the writ's return day. — Also termed *bail below.* Cf. *bail to the action.*

  common bail. See *bail common.*

  discretionary bail. Bail set in an amount that is subject to judicial discretion.

  special bail. See *bail to the action.*

  straw bail. See *bail common.*

5. *Archaic.* Legal custody of a detainee or prisoner who obtains release by giving surety for a later appearance. **6.** *Canadian law.* A lease.

bail, *vb.* (16c) **1.** To obtain the release of (oneself or another) by providing security for a future appearance in court <his parents bailed him out of jail>. **2.** To release (a person) after receiving such security <the court bailed the prisoner>. **3.** To place (personal property) in someone else's charge or trust <bail the goods with the warehouse>.

bailable, *adj.* (Of an offense or person) eligible for bail.

bailable offense. See OFFENSE (1).

bailable process. See PROCESS.

bail above. See *bail to the action* under BAIL (4).

bail absolute. See BAIL (1).

bail below. See *bail to the sheriff* under BAIL (4).

bail bond. See BOND (2).

bail bondsman. See BAILER (1).

Bail Clause. The clause in the Eighth Amendment to the U.S. Constitution prohibiting excessive bail. ● This clause was derived from similar language in England's Bill of Rights (1689).

bail commissioner. 1. An adjudicator or official empowered to hold an emergency hearing to set bail when a hearing cannot be held during regular court hours. ● A bail commissioner does not review other judge's bail decisions. **2.** An officer appointed to take bail bonds. — Also termed *commissioner of bail.* **3.** *Hist.* A court-appointed officer who made a written acknowledgement of bail in civil cases.

bail common. See BAIL (4).

Bail Court. *Hist.* An ancillary court of Queen's Bench responsible for ensuring that bail sureties were worth the sums pledged (i.e., hearing *justifications*) and for handling other procedural matters. • The court was established in 1830 and abolished in 1854. — Also termed *Practice Court.*

bail dock. A small compartment in a courtroom used to hold a criminal defendant during trial. — Often shortened to *dock.* — Also spelled *bale dock.* See DOCK (3).

bailee. (16c) A person who receives personal property from another, and has possession of but not title to the property. • A bailee is responsible for keeping the property safe until it is returned to the owner. See BAILMENT.

bailee policy. See INSURANCE POLICY.

bail-enforcement agent. See BOUNTY HUNTER.

bailer. (16c) **1.** One who provides bail as a surety for a criminal defendant's release. — Also spelled *bailor.* — Also termed *bail bondsman; bailsman.* **2.** BAILOR (1).

bailiff. (14c) **1.** A court officer who maintains order during court proceedings. • In many courts today, the bailiff also acts as crier, among other responsibilities. See CRIER. — Also termed (in England and Wales) *usher;* (in Scotland) *macer.* **2.** A sheriff's officer who executes writs and serves processes.

bailiff-errant. Hist. A bailiff appointed by the sheriff to deliver writs and other process within a county. Cf. *bailiffs of franchises.*

bailiffs of franchises. Hist. Bailiffs who executed writs and performed other duties in privileged districts that were outside the Crown's (and therefore the sheriff's) jurisdiction. Cf. *bailiffs-errant.*

bailiffs of hundreds. Hist. Bailiffs appointed by a sheriff to collect fines, summon juries, attend court sessions, and execute writs and process in the county district known as a *hundred.* See HUNDRED.

bailiffs of manors. Hist. Persons appointed to superintend the estates of the nobility. • These bailiffs collected fines and rents, inspected buildings, and took account of waste, spoils, and misdemeanors in the forests and demesne lands.

bound bailiff. Hist. A deputy sheriff placed under bond to ensure the faithful performance of assigned duties. — Also termed *bumbailiff.*

high bailiff. Hist. A bailiff attached to a county court, responsible for attending court sessions, serving summonses, and executing orders, warrants, and writs.

special bailiff. Hist. A deputy sheriff appointed at a litigant's request to serve or execute some writ or process related to the lawsuit.

bail in error. Security given by a defendant who intends to bring a writ of error on a judgment and

desires a stay of execution in the meantime. See *appeal bond, supersedeas bond* under BOND (2).

bailiwick (**bay**-lə-wik). The office, jurisdiction, or district of a bailiff; esp., a bailiff's territorial jurisdiction.

bail-jumping, *n.* (1881) The criminal offense of failing to appear in court after having been released on bail. See Model Penal Code § 242.8. See JUMP BAIL. — **bail-jumper,** *n.*

bailment. (16c) **1.** A delivery of personal property by one person (the *bailor*) to another (the *bailee*) who holds the property for a certain purpose, usu. under an express or implied-in-fact contract. • Unlike a sale or gift of personal property, a bailment involves a change in possession but not in title. Cf. PAWN.

actual bailment. (1821) A bailment that arises from an actual or constructive delivery of property to the bailee.

bailment for hire. A bailment for which the bailee is compensated, as when one leaves a car with a parking attendant. — Also termed *lucrative bailment.* Cf. *bailment for mutual benefit.*

bailment for mutual benefit. (1868) A bailment for which the bailee is compensated and from which the bailor receives some additional benefit, as when one leaves a car with a parking attendant who will also wash the car while it is parked. Cf. *bailment for hire.*

bailment for sale. A bailment in which the bailee agrees to sell the goods on behalf of the bailor; a consignment.

bailment for sole benefit of bailor. See *gratuitous bailment.*

constructive bailment. (1843) A bailment that arises when the law imposes an obligation on a possessor of personal property to return the property to its rightful owner, as with an involuntary bailment. Cf. *involuntary bailment.*

gratuitous bailment. (1811) A bailment for which the bailee receives no compensation, as when one borrows a friend's car. • A gratuitous bailee is liable for loss of the property only if the loss is caused by the bailee's gross negligence. — Also termed *naked bailment; depositum; naked deposit; gratuitous deposit; deposit; bailment for sole benefit of bailor.*

involuntary bailment. (1840) A bailment that arises when a person accidentally, but without any negligence, leaves personal property in another's possession. • An involuntary bailee who refuses to return the property to the owner may be liable for conversion. — Also termed *involuntary deposit.* See *abandoned property, lost property, mislaid property* under PROPERTY. Cf. *constructive bailment.*

lucrative bailment. See *bailment for hire.*

naked bailment. See *gratuitous bailment.*

2. The personal property delivered by the bailor to the bailee. **3.** The contract or legal relation resulting from such a delivery. **4.** The act of posting bail for a criminal defendant. **5.** The documentation for the posting of bail for a criminal defendant.

bailor (bay-**lor** *or* bay-lər). (17c) **1.** A person who delivers personal property to another as a bailment. — Also spelled *bailer.* **2.** BAILER (1).

bailout, *n.* **1.** A rescue of an entity, usu. a corporation or an industry, from financial trouble. **2.** An attempt by a business to receive favorable tax treatment of its profits, as by withdrawing profits at capital-gain rates rather than distributing stock dividends that would be taxed at higher ordinary-income rates.

bailout stock. See STOCK.

bailpiece. **1.** *Hist.* A document recording the nature of the bail granted to a defendant in a civil action; specif., a surety issued to attest the act of offering bail **2.** More modernly, a warrant issued to a surety upon which the surety may arrest the person bailed by him. • The bailpiece was filed with the court and usu. was signed by the defendant's sureties. See BAIL (2); RECOGNIZANCE. — Sometimes written *bail piece.*

bail-point scale. A system for determining a criminal defendant's eligibility for bail, whereby the defendant either will be released on personal recognizance or will have a bail amount set according to the total number of points given, based on the defendant's background and behavior.

bail revocation. (1950) The court's cancellation of bail previously granted to a criminal defendant.

bailsman. See BAILER (1).

bail to the action. See BAIL (4).

bail to the sheriff. See BAIL (4).

bait advertising. See BAIT AND SWITCH.

bait and switch. (1967) **1.** A sales practice whereby a merchant advertises a low-priced product to lure customers into the store only to induce them to buy a higher-priced product. • Most states prohibit the bait and switch when the original product is not actually available as advertised. Cf. LOSS LEADER. — Also termed *bait advertising.* **2.** The unethical practice of offering an attractive rate or premium to induce a person to apply for a loan or contract, with approval contingent on some condition, and then telling the person that the offered rate is not available but that a higher one can be substituted.

Baker v. Selden **doctrine.** See MERGER DOCTRINE (1).

balance, *vb.* (16c) **1.** To compute the difference between the debits and credits of (an account) <the accountant balanced the company's books>. **2.**

To equalize in number, force, or effect; to bring into proportion <the company tried to balance the ratio of mid-level managers to assembly-line workers>. **3.** To measure competing interests and offset them appropriately <the judge balanced the equities before granting the motion>. — **balance,** *n.*

balance billing. A healthcare provider's practice of requiring a patient or other responsible party to pay any charges remaining after insurance and other payments and allowances have been applied to the total amount due for the provider's services.

balanced budget. See BUDGET.

balanced economy. See ECONOMY.

balanced fund. See MUTUAL FUND.

balance of convenience. A balancing test that courts use to decide whether to issue a preliminary injunction stopping the defendant's allegedly infringing or unfair practices, weighing the benefit to the plaintiff and the public against the burden on the defendant. — Also termed **balance of hardship.**

balance of power. *Int'l law.* A relative equality of force between countries or groups of countries, as a result of which peace is encouraged because no country or group is in a position to predominate.

balance of probability. See PREPONDERANCE OF THE EVIDENCE.

balance of sentence suspended. (1942) A sentencing disposition in which a criminal defendant is sentenced to jail but is credited with the time already served before sentencing, resulting in a suspension of the remaining sentence and release of the defendant from custody. Cf. SENTENCED TO TIME SERVED.

balance sheet. (18c) A statement of an entity's current financial position, disclosing the value of the entity's assets, liabilities, and owners' equity. — Also termed *statement of financial condition; statement of condition; statement of financial position.* Cf. INCOME STATEMENT.

balance-sheet insolvency. See INSOLVENCY.

balance-sheet test. See *balance-sheet insolvency* under INSOLVENCY.

balancing test. (1951) A judicial doctrine, used esp. in constitutional law, whereby a court measures competing interests — as between individual rights and governmental powers, or between state authority and federal supremacy — and decides which interest should prevail.

bale. A package of goods wrapped in cloth and marked so as to be identifiable on a bill of lading.

ballistics. (18c) **1.** The science of the motion of projectiles, such as bullets. **2.** The study of a weapon's firing characteristics, esp. as used in criminal cases to determine a gun's firing capacity and whether a particular gun fired a given bullet.

balloon loan. See LOAN.

balloon note. See NOTE (1).

balloon payment. See PAYMENT.

balloon-payment mortgage. See MORTGAGE.

ballot, *n.* **1.** An instrument, such as a paper or ball, used for casting a vote. **2.** The system of choosing officers by a recorded vote, such as by marking a paper.

     absentee ballot. A ballot that a voter submits, sometimes by mail, before an election. — Also termed *absentee vote.* See *absentee voting* under VOTING.

     bullet ballot. See *bullet vote* under VOTE (1).

     butterfly ballot. A punchcard ballot that opens like a book and usu. has arrows pointing to the punchhole beside a candidate's name. ● The butterfly ballots used in Florida during the 2000 presidential elections produced widespread controversy because the layout of the candidates' names on the ballots allegedly confused voters and caused them to cast votes mistakenly for candidates they did not support.

     exhausted ballot. See *exhausted vote* under VOTE (1).

     joint ballot. A vote by legislators of both houses sitting together as one body.

     preferential ballot. See *preferential vote* under VOTE (1).

     secret ballot. A vote cast in such a way that the person voting cannot be identified. Cf *Australian ballot.*

     spoiled ballot. A ballot reflecting a vote that cannot be counted because it was cast in a form or manner that does not comply with the applicable rules. See *illegal vote* under VOTE (1).

3. A vote in a series of votes that is not conclusive until one candidate attains the necessary majority or supermajority <the candidate was nominated on the 21st ballot>. **4.** A list of candidates running for office <four candidates are on the ballot>. — **ballot,** *vb.*

     Australian ballot. A uniform ballot printed by the government, listing all eligible candidates, and marked in secret. ● Before Australian ballots became standard, candidates often printed their own ballots with only their name, and watchers at polling places could see whose ballot a voter was casting. — Loosely termed *secret ballot.*

     Massachusetts ballot. A ballot in which, under each office, the candidates' names appear in alphabetical order alongside their party designations. ● This is a type of Australian ballot.

     office-block ballot. A ballot that lists the candidates' names under the title of the office sought without mentioning the candidates' party affiliations.

     party-column ballot. A ballot that lists the candidates' names in separate columns by political party regardless of the offices sought by the candidates.

     Texas ballot. A ballot that the voter marks for the candidates that he or she does not want elected. ● The Texas ballot is particularly useful when the number of candidates only slightly exceeds a large number of representatives being elected.

ballot box. A locked box into which ballots are deposited.

ban, *n.* **1.** *Hist.* A public proclamation or summons. ● *Bans* dealt with a variety of matters, such as the calling to arms of a lord's vassals or the proclamation that an offender was henceforth to be considered an outlaw. **2.** *Eccles. law.* An authoritative ecclesiastical prohibition; an interdict or excommunication. **3.** BANNS OF MATRIMONY. — Also spelled *bann.*

ban, *vb.* To prohibit, esp. by legal means.

banc (bangk *or* bongk). [French] A bench; esp., the bench on which one or more judges sit. — Also spelled *bank.* — Also termed *bancus.* See EN BANC.

banco (bang-koh). **1.** A seat or bench of justice. See EN BANC. **2.** A tract of land cut off by the shifting of a river's course; esp., land that has become cut off in such a manner from the country it originally belonged to. See AVULSION (2).

B and E. *abbr.* Breaking and entering. See BURGLARY (2).

banish, *vb.* See EXILE.

bank. (15c) **1.** A financial establishment for the deposit, loan, exchange, or issue of money and for the transmission of funds; esp., a member of the Federal Reserve System. ● Under securities law, a bank includes any financial institution, whether or not incorporated, doing business under federal or state law, if a substantial portion of the institution's business consists of receiving deposits or exercising fiduciary powers similar to those permitted to national banks and if the institution is supervised and examined by a state or federal banking authority; or a receiver, conservator, or other liquidating agent of any of the above institutions. 15 USCA § 78c(a)(6). **2.** The office in which such an establishment conducts transactions.

     bank for cooperatives. A bank within a system of banks established to provide a permanent source of credit to farmers' cooperatives and supervised by the Farm Credit Administration.

collecting bank. (1834) In the check-collection process, any bank handling an item for collection, except for the payor bank. UCC § 4-105(5).

commercial bank. (18c) A bank authorized to receive both demand and time deposits, to make loans, to engage in trust services, to issue letters of credit, to rent time-deposit boxes, and to provide similar services.

correspondent bank. A bank that acts as an agent for another bank, or engages in an exchange of services with that bank, in a geographical area to which the other bank does not have direct access.

custodian bank. A bank or trust company that acts as custodian for a clearing corporation and that is supervised and audited by a state or federal authority.

depository bank. (1848) The first bank to which an item is transferred for collection. UCC § 4-105(2).

drawee bank. See *payor bank.*

Federal Home Loan Bank. See FEDERAL HOME LOAN BANK.

federal intermediate credit bank. One of a system of twelve regional banks created in 1923 to discount obligations of agricultural credit corporations and similar institutions making short-term loans to farmers and ranchers. • The system is now merged with federal land banks to create the federal farm-credit system.

federal land bank. See FEDERAL LAND BANK.

intermediary bank. (1896) A bank to which an item is transferred in the course of collection, even though the bank is not the depositary or payor bank. UCC § 4-105(4).

investment bank. A bank whose primary purpose is to acquire financing for businesses, esp. through the sale of securities. • An investment bank does not accept deposits and, apart from selling securities, does not deal with the public at large. See INVESTMENT BANKER.

member bank. A bank that is a member of the Federal Reserve System. — Also termed *reserve bank.* See FEDERAL RESERVE SYSTEM.

mutual savings bank. A bank that has no capital stock and in which the depositors are the owners. See SAVINGS-AND-LOAN ASSOCIATION.

national bank. A bank incorporated under federal law and governed by a charter approved by the Comptroller of the Currency. • A national bank must use the term "national," "national bank," or "national association" as part of its name.

negotiating bank. A financial institution that discounts or purchases drafts drawn under a letter of credit issued by another bank.

nonbank bank. A financial institution that either accepts demand deposits or makes commercial loans, but, unlike traditional banks, does not do both at the same time and therefore can avoid federal regulations on bank ownership. • Nonbank banks were esp. prolific in the 1980s, but amendments to the definition of a bank under federal law have essentially closed this loophole.

nonmember bank. A bank that is not a member of the Federal Reserve System. See FEDERAL RESERVE SYSTEM.

payor bank. (1911) A bank that is asked to pay the amount of a negotiable instrument and, on the bank's acceptance, is obliged to pay that amount; a bank by which an item is payable as drawn or accepted. • Because the bank is the drawee of a draft, it is also termed a *drawee bank.* UCC § 4-105(3).

presenting bank. (1862) A nonpayor bank that presents a negotiable instrument for payment. UCC § 4-105(6).

private bank. An unincorporated banking institution owned by an individual or a partnership and, depending on state statutes, may or may not be subject to state regulation.

remitting bank. A payor or intermediary bank that pays or transfers an item.

reserve bank. See *member bank.*

respondent bank. A bank, association, or other entity that exercises fiduciary powers, that holds securities on behalf of beneficial owners, and that deposits the securities for safekeeping with another bank, association, or other entity exercising fiduciary powers. SEC Rule 14a-1(k) (17 CFR § 240.14a-1(k)).

savings-and-loan bank. See SAVINGS-AND-LOAN ASSOCIATION.

savings bank. (1817) A bank that makes primarily home mortgage and some other consumer loans, receives deposits and pays interest on them, and may offer checking accounts. • Historically, savings banks did not provide any checking services.

state bank. A bank chartered by a state and supervised by the state banking department. •A state bank must have FDIC insurance on deposits but need not become a member of the Federal Reserve System to obtain the insurance. A state bank that is a member of the Federal Reserve is regulated by the state banking department and by the Federal Reserve. Nonmember state banks are regulated by both the state banking department and the FDIC.

bank, *vb.* (18c) **1.** To keep money at <he banks at the downtown branch>. **2.** To deposit (funds) in a bank <she banked the prize money yesterday>. **3.** *Slang.* To lend money to facilitate (a transaction) <who banked the deal?>. • The lender's consideration usu. consists of a fee or an interest in the property involved in the transaction.

bankable paper. See PAPER.

bank acceptance. See *banker's acceptance* under ACCEPTANCE (4).

bank account. See ACCOUNT.

bank-account trust. See *Totten trust* under TRUST.

bank bill. See BANKNOTE.

bankbook. See PASSBOOK.

bank charter. See CHARTER (3).

bank credit. See CREDIT (4).

bank discount. The interest that a bank deducts in advance on a note. See DISCOUNT (2).

bank draft. See DRAFT.

banker. A person who engages in the business of banking.

banker's acceptance. See ACCEPTANCE (4).

banker's bill. See *finance bill* under BILL (6).

banker's lien. See LIEN.

banker's note. See NOTE (1).

bank examiner. A federal or state official who audits banks with respect to their financial condition, management, and policies. — Sometimes shortened to *examiner.*

bank for cooperatives. See BANK.

bank fraud. See FRAUD.

bank holding company. A company that owns or controls one or more banks. • Ownership or control of 25 percent is usu. enough for this purpose. — Abbr. BHC.

banking. The business carried on by or with a bank.

Banking Act of 1933. See GLASS–STEAGALL ACT.

banking day. (18c) **1.** Banking hours on a day when a bank is open to the public for carrying on substantially all its banking functions. • Typically, if the bookkeeping and loan departments are closed by a certain hour, the remainder of that day is not part of that bank's banking day. **2.** A day on which banks are open for banking business.

banking game. A gambling arrangement in which the house (i.e., the bank) accepts bets from all players and then pays out winning bets and takes other bettors' losses.

bank night. A lottery in which a prize is awarded to a person (often a theater patron) whose name is drawn randomly from a hopper.

banknote. A bank-issued promissory note that is payable to bearer on demand and that may circulate as money. — Also written *bank note.* — Also termed *bank bill.*

  spurious banknote. **1.** A banknote that is legitimately made from a genuine plate but that has forged signatures of the issuing officers, or the names of fictitious officers. **2.** A banknote that is not a legitimate impression from a genuine plate, or is made from a counterfeit plate, but that is signed by the persons shown on it as the issuing officers. — Also termed *spurious bank bill.*

bank rate. See INTEREST RATE.

Bankr. Rep. *abbr.* Bankruptcy Reporter. — Also abbreviated B.R.

bankrupt, *adj.* Indebted beyond the means of payment; insolvent. — Also spelled (archaically) *bankerout; bankrout.* — **bankrupt,** *vb.*

bankrupt, *n.* (16c) **1.** A person who cannot meet current financial obligations; an insolvent person. • This term was used in bankruptcy statutes until 1979, and is still commonly used by nonbankruptcy courts. But the Bankruptcy Code uses *debtor* instead of *bankrupt.* **2.** DEBTOR (2).

  cessionary bankrupt. *Archaic.* A person who forfeits all property so that it may be divided among creditors. • For the modern near-equivalent, see CHAPTER 7.

bankruptcy. (18c) **1.** A statutory procedure by which a (usu. insolvent) debtor obtains financial relief and undergoes a judicially supervised reorganization or liquidation of the debtor's assets for the benefit of creditors; a case under the Bankruptcy Code (Title 11 of the United States Code). • For various types of bankruptcy under federal law, see the entries at CHAPTER. — Also termed *bankruptcy proceeding; bankruptcy case.*

  family-farmer bankruptcy. See CHAPTER 12 (2).

  farmer bankruptcy. See CHAPTER 12 (2).

  involuntary bankruptcy. (1842) A bankruptcy case commenced by the debtor's creditors (usu. three or more), or, if the debtor is a partnership, by fewer than all the general partners. 11 USCA § 303(b). — Also termed *involuntary proceeding.*

  liquidation bankruptcy. See CHAPTER 7 (2).

  malicious bankruptcy. An abuse of process by which a person wrongfully petitions to have another person adjudicated a bankrupt or to have a company wound up as insolvent.

  straight bankruptcy. See CHAPTER 7 (2).

  voluntary bankruptcy. (18c) A bankruptcy case commenced by the debtor. 11 USCA § 301.

2. The field of law dealing with the rights of debtors who are financially unable to pay their debts and the rights of their creditors. — Also termed *bankruptcy law.* **3.** The status of a party who has declared bankruptcy under a bankruptcy statute. — Also termed *statutory insolvency.* **4.** Informally, the fact of being financially unable to pay one's debts and obligations as they become due; insolvency. ● The roots of *bankruptcy* are the Latin *bancus* (table) and *ruptus* (broken). The English word *bankruptcy* derives from the Italian *banca rotta,* referring to the medieval Italian custom of breaking the counter of a financially failed merchant. — Also termed (in sense 4) *failure to meet obligations.*

Bankruptcy Act. The Bankruptcy Act of 1898, which governed bankruptcy cases filed before October 1, 1979.

bankruptcy case. A proceeding commenced by filing a voluntary or involuntary petition under a bankruptcy statute. See BANKRUPTCY (1).

bankruptcy clause. See IPSO FACTO CLAUSE.

Bankruptcy Code. Title I of the Bankruptcy Reform Act of 1978 (as amended and codified in 11 USCA), which governs bankruptcy cases filed on or after October 1, 1979.

Bankruptcy Court. A U.S. district court subunit comprising the bankruptcy judges within the district and exclusively concerned with administering bankruptcy proceedings.

bankruptcy crime. A crime committed in connection with a bankruptcy case, such as a trustee's embezzling from the debtor's estate. 18 USCA §§ 152–57. See *bankruptcy fraud* under FRAUD.

bankruptcy estate. A debtor's legal and equitable interests in property at the beginning of a bankruptcy case where the property is subject to administration. See 11 USCA § 541.

bankruptcy fraud. See FRAUD.

bankruptcy judge. See JUDGE.

bankruptcy law. 1. INSOLVENCY LAW. **2.** Traditionally, a statute that provides some relief and protection to an insolvent debtor or to the debtor's creditors. Cf. INSOLVENCY LAW. **3.** BANKRUPTCY (2).

bankruptcy petition. See *voluntary petition* under PETITION.

bankruptcy plan. (1944) A detailed program of action formulated by a debtor or its creditors to govern the debtor's rehabilitation, continued operation or liquidation, and payment of debts. ● The bankruptcy court must approve the plan before it is implemented. — Often shortened to *plan.* — Also termed *plan of reorganization* (for Chapter 11); *plan of rehabilitation* (for Chapter 13). See ARRANGEMENT WITH CREDITORS.

bankruptcy proceeding. (1828) **1.** BANKRUPTCY (1). **2.** Any judicial or procedural action (such as a hearing) related to a bankruptcy.

bankruptcy-remote entity. A business entity formed in a manner designed to minimize the risk of becoming a debtor in a bankruptcy case. ● The entity's organizational charter usu. requires at least one independent director to be appointed, as well as a unanimous vote by the entity's directors, before a bankruptcy petition may be filed. The business is usu. a special-purpose entity established to perform limited functions, such as to purchase and hold accounts receivable or other financial assets that generate revenue. It also has only one or a few primary creditors, to reduce the likelihood of an involuntary bankruptcy. A bankruptcy-remote entity will sometimes issue securities instead of receiving a loan from a financial institution. See SINGLE-PURPOSE PROJECT; SPECIAL-PURPOSE ENTITY; *project financing* under FINANCING.

bankruptcy trustee. See TRUSTEE (2).

Bank Secrecy Act. A federal statute that requires banks and other financial institutions to maintain records of customers' transactions and to report certain domestic and foreign transactions. ● This act, passed by Congress in 1970, is designed to help the federal government in criminal, tax, and other regulatory investigations. 12 USCA § 1829b; 31 USCA § 5311.

bank statement. See STATEMENT OF ACCOUNT (1).

bank-statement rule. (1974) *Commercial law.* The principle that if a bank customer fails to examine a bank statement and any items returned with it, and report to the bank within a reasonable time any unauthorized payments because of a material alteration or forgery, the customer may be precluded from complaining about the alteration or forgery. UCC § 4-406.

bann, *n.* [Law Latin] **1.** BAN. **2.** *Hist.* The power of a court to issue an edict, esp. one relating to the public peace. **3.** *Hist.* The edict itself. — Also termed *bannum.*

banns of matrimony. *Family law.* Public notice of an intended marriage. ● The notice is given to ensure that objections to the marriage would be voiced before the wedding. Banns are still common in many churches. — Also spelled *bans of matrimony.* — Also termed *banns of marriage.*

bar, *n.* (14c) **1.** In a courtroom, the railing that separates the front area, where court business is conducted, from the back area, which provides seats for observers; by extension, a similar railing in a legislative assembly <the spectator stood behind the bar>. **2.** The whole body of lawyers qualified to practice in a given court or jurisdiction; the legal profession, or an organized subset of it <the

attorney's outrageous misconduct disgraced the bar>. See BAR ASSOCIATION.

integrated bar. A bar association in which membership is a statutory requirement for practicing law; a usu. statewide organization of lawyers in which membership is compulsory in order for a lawyer to have a law license. — Also termed *unified bar.*

specialty bar. A voluntary bar association for lawyers with special interests, specific backgrounds, or common practices.

voluntary bar. A bar association that lawyers need not join to practice law.

3. A particular court or system of courts <case at bar>. • Originally, *case at bar* referred to an important case tried "at bar" at the Royal Courts of Justice in London. **4.** BAR EXAMINATION <Pendarvis passed the bar>. **5.** A barrier to or the destruction of a legal action or claim; the effect of a judgment for the defendant <a bar to any new lawsuit>. Cf. MERGER (6). **6.** A plea arresting a lawsuit or legal claim <the defendant filed a bar>. See PLEA IN BAR. **7.** *Patents.* Statutory preclusion from patentability, based on publication, use, sale, or other anticipatory activity that occurred before an invention's critical date and thereby negated the invention's novelty. • Under § 102 of the Patent Act, a person is not entitled to a patent if (1) before the date of invention, the same invention was publicly known or used by others in this country or was patented or described in a printed publication anywhere in the world; (2) more than one year before the U.S. filing date, the invention was patented or described in a printed publication anywhere in the world or was in public use, on sale, or offered for sale in the U.S.; (3) the invention has been abandoned by the applicant; (4) the invention was first patented by the applicant or its representatives in a foreign country before the U.S. filing date, and the foreign application was filed more than 12 months before the U.S. filing; (5) before the date of invention, the invention was described in a patent granted on an application filed by someone else in the U.S.; (6) the inventor did not invent the subject matter of the application; or (7) the invention was previously made in this country by someone else who has not abandoned, suppressed, or concealed it. — Also termed *statutory bar.* **8.** *Trademarks.* Statutory preclusion of certain marks from listing on the Principal Register. • Under 15 USCA § 1052, a mark is not entitled to registration if: (1) it consists of immoral, deceptive, or scandalous matter; (2) it falsely suggests a connection with, or brings into contempt or disrepute, a living or dead person, an institution, a belief, or a nation's symbols; (3) it depicts or simulates the flag, coat of arms, or other insignia of the U.S., a state, a municipality, or a foreign nation; (4) it consists of a geographic

designation that, when used on wines or spirits, designates a place other than the goods' actual origin; (5) it consists of the name, signature, or portrait of a living person who has not consented to registration; (6) it is likely to deceive or to cause confusion or mistake because when applied to specific goods and services it resembles someone else's unabandoned mark registered in the U.S. Patent and Trademark Office, or an unabandoned mark or tradename previously used in the U.S.; (7) it is descriptive or deceptively misdescriptive of the goods or services; (8) it is primarily geographically descriptive or primarily geographically misdescriptive of the goods or services; (9) it is primarily a surname; or (10) it comprises matter that, as a whole, is functional.

bar, *vb.* (16c) To prevent, esp. by legal objection <the statute of limitations barred the plaintiff's wrongful-death claim>.

bar association. (1872) An organization of members of the legal profession <several state bar associations sponsor superb CLE programs>. See BAR (2).

local bar association. A bar association organized on a local level, such as an association within a county or city. • Local bar associations are voluntary in membership.

state bar association. (1883) An association or group of attorneys that have been admitted to practice law in a given state; a bar association organized on a statewide level, often with compulsory membership. • State bar associations are usu. created by statute, and membership is often mandatory for those who practice law in the state. Unlike voluntary, professional-development bar associations such as the American Bar Association, state bar associations often have the authority to regulate the legal profession, by undertaking such matters as disciplining attorneys and bringing lawsuits against those who engage in the unauthorized practice of law.

bar date. *Patents.* The date by which a U.S. patent application must be filed to avoid losing the right to receive a patent. • In the U.S., the bar date for a patent application is one year after the invention is disclosed in a publication or patented in another country, or put into public use, sold, or offered for sale in the U.S. <Since the invention was offered for domestic sale on January 1, 2000, the bar date for the U.S. patent application is January 1, 2001.> Cf. *absolute novelty* under NOVELTY.

bareboat charter. See CHARTER (8).

barebones indictment. See INDICTMENT.

bare-bones legislation. See *skeletal legislation* under LEGISLATION.

bare license. See LICENSE.

bare licensee. See LICENSEE.

bare ownership. See *trust ownership* under OWNERSHIP.

bare possibility. See *naked possibility* under POSSIBILITY.

bare promise. See *gratuitous promise* under PROMISE.

bare trustee. See TRUSTEE (1).

bar examination. (1875) A written test that a person must pass before being licensed to practice law. ● The exam varies from state to state. — Often shortened to *bar*.

> **Multistate Bar Examination.** A nationally standardized part of a state bar examination given as a multiple-choice test covering broad legal subjects, including constitutional law, contracts, criminal law, evidence, property, and torts. — Abbr. MBE.

bar examiner. (1902) One appointed by the state to test applicants (usu. law-school graduates) by preparing, administering, and grading the bar examination.

bargain, *n.* (14c) An agreement between parties for the exchange of promises or performances. ● A bargain is not necessarily a contract because the consideration may be insufficient or the transaction may be illegal. See BARGAIN SALE; *informal contract* under CONTRACT. — **bargain,** *vb.*

> **catching bargain.** An agreement on unconscionable terms to purchase real property from — or loan money secured by real property to — a person who has an expectant or reversionary interest in the property.

> **illegal bargain.** A bargain whose formation or performance is criminal, tortious, or otherwise contrary to public policy.

> **plea bargain.** See PLEA BARGAIN.

> **time-bargain.** See FUTURES CONTRACT.

> **unconscionable bargain.** See *unconscionable agreement* under AGREEMENT.

bargain and sale. (16c) **1.** A negotiated transaction, usu. for goods, services, or real property. **2.** *Hist.* A written agreement for the sale of land whereby the buyer would give valuable consideration (recited in the agreement) without having to enter the land and perform livery of seisin, so that the parties equitably "raised a use" in the buyer. ● The result of the transaction was to leave the legal estate in fee simple in the seller and to create an equitable estate in fee simple in the buyer until legal title was transferred to the buyer by delivery of a deed. In most jurisdictions, the bargain and sale has been replaced by the statutory deed of grant.

bargain-and-sale deed. See DEED.

bargained-for exchange. *Contracts.* A benefit or detriment that the parties to a contract agree to as the price of performance. ● The Restatement of Contracts (Second) defines *consideration* exclusively in terms of bargain, but it does not mention benefit or detriment.

bargainee. The buyer in a bargained-for exchange.

bargaining agent. See AGENT (2).

bargaining unit. A group of employees authorized to engage in collective bargaining on behalf of all the employees of a company or an industry sector.

bargain money. See EARNEST MONEY.

bargainor (bahr-gən-**or** *or* **bahr**-gə-nər). The seller in a bargained-for exchange.

bargain purchase. See BARGAIN SALE.

bargain sale. (1898) A sale of property for less than its fair market value. ● For tax purposes, the difference between the sale price and the fair market value must be taken into account. And bargain sales between family members may lead to gift-tax consequences. — Also termed *bargain purchase.*

bargain theory of consideration. (1927) The theory that a promise or performance that is bargained for in exchange for a promise is consideration for the promise. ● This theory underlies all bilateral contracts. See *bilateral contract* under CONTRACT.

barometer stock. See STOCK.

baronial court. See COURT.

Baron Parke's rule. See GOLDEN RULE.

Barons of the Exchequer. *Hist.* The six judges of the Court of Exchequer. ● After the 1873 transfer of the Court's jurisdiction to the High Court of Justice, the judges were known as *justices of the High Court.* — Also termed *barones scaccarii.* See COURT OF EXCHEQUER.

bar pilot. See *branch pilot* under PILOT.

barrator (bar-ə-tər), *n.* (15c) **1.** One who commits barratry (in any sense). **2.** A fomenter of quarrels and lawsuits; one who stirs up dissension and litigation among people. — Also spelled *barretor.* Cf. CHAMPERTOR.

barratry (**bar**-ə-tree *or* **bair**-), *n.* (15c) **1.** Vexatious incitement to litigation, esp. by soliciting potential legal clients. ● Barratry is a crime in most jurisdictions. A person who is hired by a lawyer to solicit business is called a *capper.* See CAPPER (1). **2.** *Maritime law.* Fraudulent or grossly negligent conduct (by a master or crew) that is prejudicial to a shipowner. **3.** The buying or selling of ecclesiastical or governmental positions. **4.** The crime committed by a judge who accepts a bribe in exchange for a favorable decision. Cf. BRIBE. — **barratrous** (**bar**-ə-trəs), *adj.*

barrier to entry. An economic factor that makes it difficult for a business to enter a market and compete with existing businesses.

barring of entail. (18c) The freeing of an estate from the limitations imposed by an entail and permitting its free disposition. • This was anciently done by means of a fine or common recovery, but later by a deed in which the tenant and next heir join. — Also termed *breaking of entail*; *disentailment*. See ENTAIL.

barrister (**bar**-is-tər), *n.* (15c) In England or Northern Ireland, a lawyer who is admitted to plead at the bar and who may argue cases in superior courts. • In many other Commonwealth nations, the legal profession is similarly divided into barristers and solicitors. Cf. SOLICITOR (4). — **barristerial** (bar-ə-**steer**-ee-əl), *adj.*

inner barrister. **1.** QUEEN'S COUNSEL. **2.** A student member of an Inn of Court.

outer barrister. A barrister called to the bar, but not called to plead from within it, as a Queen's Counsel or (formerly) serjeant-at-law is permitted to do; a barrister belonging to the outer bar. — Also termed *utter barrister*. See CALL TO THE BAR; OUTER BAR.

vacation barrister. A barrister who, being newly called to the bar, for at least three years must attend inn of court functions that are held during the long vacation.

barter, *n.* (15c) The exchange of one commodity for another without the use of money. — **barter,** *vb.*

base and meridian. *Property.* The east–west and north–south lines used by a surveyor to demarcate the position of the boundaries of real property. • A base line runs east to west. A meridian line runs north to south.

base court. See COURT.

based on. *Copyright.* Derived from, and therefore similar to, an earlier work. • If one work is "based on" an earlier work, it infringes the copyright in the earlier work. To be based on an earlier work, a later work must embody substantially similar expression, not just substantially similar ideas. See *derivative work* under WORK (2).

base estate. See ESTATE (1).

base fee. (1800) **1.** See FEE (2). **2.** See *fee simple determinable* under FEE SIMPLE.

baseline. *Int'l law.* The line that divides the land from the sea, by which the extent of a state's coastal jurisdiction is measured.

baseline documentation. The record of a parcel of real property's condition and conservation values at a specific time, signed by the landowner and the land trust when a conservation easement is created, and used to monitor and enforce the easement's terms. See IRS Reg. 1.170A-14(g)(5).

basement court. (1995) *Slang.* A low-level court of limited jurisdiction, such as a police court, traffic court, municipal court, or small-claims court.

base-point pricing. 1. A pricing method that adds the price at the factory to the freight charges, which are calculated as the cost of shipping from a set location to the buyer's location. • The chosen shipping base-point may be the same for all customers, or it may be a specific, established location, such as a manufacturing plant nearest to the buyer. **2.** A uniform pricing policy in which the cost of transportation to all locations is presumed to be the same.

base service. *Hist.* Agricultural work performed by a villein tenant in exchange for the lord's permission to hold the land. Cf. KNIGHT-SERVICE.

base tenure. See TENURE.

basic crops. See CROPS.

basic-form policy. See INSURANCE POLICY.

basic mistake. See MISTAKE.

basic norm. See NORM.

basic patent. See *pioneer patent* under PATENT (3).

basilica (bə-**sil**-i-kə). [Greek] *Hist.* **1.** (*cap.*) A 60-book Greek summary of Justinian's *Corpus Juris Civilis*, with comments (*scholia*). • The *Basilica* ("royal law") was begun by the Byzantine emperor Basil I, and it served as a major source of the law of the Eastern Empire from the early 10th century until Constantinople's fall in 1453. **2.** A colonnaded hall used as a law court or for trading; specif., in ancient Rome, a public building usu. used as a court of justice. • A basilica typically featured a nave with two aisles and an apse. Architects adopted the basilica's layout for the design of early Christian churches.

basis. (14c) **1.** A fundamental principle; an underlying fact or condition. **2.** *Tax.* The value assigned to a taxpayer's investment in property and used primarily for computing gain or loss from a transfer of the property. • Basis is usu. the total cost of acquiring the asset, including the purchase price plus commissions and other related expenses, less depreciation and other adjustments. When the assigned value represents the cost of acquiring the property, it is also called *cost basis.* — Also termed *tax basis.* Pl. **bases.**

adjusted basis. (1932) Basis increased by capital improvements and decreased by depreciation deductions.

adjusted cost basis. (1934) Basis resulting from the original cost of an item plus capital additions minus depreciation deductions.

carryover basis. (1952) The recipient's basis in property transferred by gift or in trust, equaling the transferor's basis. — Also termed *substituted basis*.

stepped-up basis. (1951) The beneficiary's basis in property transferred by inheritance, equaling the fair market value of the property on the date of the decedent's death or on the alternate valuation date.

substituted basis. (1932) **1.** The basis of property transferred in a tax-free exchange or other specified transaction. **2.** See *carryover basis*.

basis point. One-hundredth of 1%; .01%. ● Basis points are used in computing investment yields (esp. of bonds) and in apportioning costs and calculating interest rates in real-estate transactions. — Abbr. bp.

Basket Clause. See NECESSARY AND PROPER CLAUSE.

bastard. (14c) **1.** See *illegitimate child* under CHILD. **2.** A child born to a married woman whose husband could not be or is otherwise proved not to be the father. ● Because the word is most commonly used as a slur, its use in family-law contexts is much in decline.

adulterine bastard. A child born to a married woman whose husband is not the father of the child. ● The rebuttable presumption is generally that a child born of the marriage is the husband's child. A child born to a woman by means of artificial insemination may be termed an *adulterine bastard*, but most jurisdictions prohibit a husband who has consented to the artificial insemination from denying paternity and responsibility for the child. Cf. ARTIFICIAL INSEMINATION.

bastardy. See ILLEGITIMACY.

bastardy proceeding. See PATERNITY SUIT.

bastardy process. See PATERNITY SUIT.

batable ground (**bay**-tə-bəl). (16c) Land of uncertain ownership. ● *Batable* (or *debatable*) *ground* originally referred to certain lands on the border of England and Scotland before the 1603 union of the two kingdoms.

batch number. See SERIES CODE.

Bates number. See BATES-STAMP NUMBER.

Bates stamp, *n.* **1.** A self-advancing stamp machine used for affixing an identifying mark, usu. a number, to a document or to the individual pages of a document. **2.** BATES-STAMP NUMBER. — Sometimes (erroneously) written *Bate stamp*.

Bates-stamp, *vb.* To affix a mark, usu. a number, to a document or to the individual pages of a document for the purpose of identifying and distinguishing it in a series of documents <the paralegal is Bates-stamping the records described in the request for discovery>. — Sometimes (erroneously) written *Bate-stamp*.

Bates-stamp number. The identifying number that is affixed to a document or to the individual pages of a document. ● The term gets its name from a self-advancing stamp machine made by the Bates Manufacturing Company. The number is typically used to identify documents produced during discovery. — Often shortened to *Bates number*; *Bates stamp*.

bathtub conspiracy. See *intra-enterprise conspiracy* under CONSPIRACY.

Batson challenge. See CHALLENGE (1).

battered child. See CHILD.

battered-child syndrome. (1962) *Family law.* A constellation of medical and psychological conditions of a child who has suffered continuing injuries that could not be accidental and are therefore presumed to have been inflicted by someone close to the child, usu. a caregiver. ● Diagnosis typically results from a radiological finding of distinct bone trauma and persistent tissue damage caused by intentional injury, such as twisting or hitting with violence. The phrase was first used by Dr. Henry Kempe and his colleagues in a 1962 article entitled "The Battered Child Syndrome," which appeared in the *Journal of the American Medical Association.* As a result of research on battered-child syndrome, the Children's Bureau of the United States Department of Health, Education, and Welfare drafted a model statute requiring physicians to report serious cases of suspected child abuse. See CHILD-ABUSE AND -NEGLECT REPORTING STATUTE.

battered-person syndrome. See BATTERED-WOMAN SYNDROME.

battered-spouse syndrome. See BATTERED-WOMAN SYNDROME.

battered-wife syndrome. See BATTERED-WOMAN SYNDROME.

battered woman. *Family law.* A woman who is the victim of domestic violence; a woman who has suffered physical, emotional, or sexual abuse at the hands of a spouse or partner. See *domestic violence* under VIOLENCE.

battered-woman syndrome. (1984) *Family law.* A constellation of medical and psychological conditions of a woman who has suffered physical, sexual, or emotional abuse at the hands of a spouse or partner. ● Battered-woman syndrome was first described in the early 1970s by Dr. Lenore Walker. It consists of a three-stage cycle of violence: (1) the tension-building stage, which may include verbal and mild physical abuse; (2) the acute battering stage, which includes stronger verbal abuse, increased physical violence, and perhaps rape or other sexual abuse; and (3) the loving-contrition stage, which includes the abuser's apologies, attentiveness, kindness, and gift-giving. This syndrome is sometimes proposed as a defense to justify or mitigate a woman's killing of a man. — Sometimes (more specif.) termed *battered-wife syndrome*; (more broadly) *battered-spouse syndrome*; (broadly) *battered-person syndrome*.

battery, *n.* (16c) **1.** *Criminal law.* The use of force against another, resulting in harmful or offensive contact. — Also termed *criminal battery.*

aggravated battery. (1811) A criminal battery accompanied by circumstances that make it more severe, such as the use of a deadly weapon or the fact that the battery resulted in serious bodily harm. ● In most state statutes, aggravated battery is classified as both a misdemeanor and a felony.

sexual battery. (1974) The forced penetration of or contact with another's sexual organs or the perpetrator's sexual organs. ● In most state statutes, sexual battery is classified as both a misdemeanor and a felony. Cf. RAPE.

simple battery. (1877) A criminal battery not accompanied by aggravating circumstances and not resulting in serious bodily harm. ● Simple battery is usu. a misdemeanor but may rise to a felony if the victim is, for instance, a child or a senior citizen.

2. *Torts.* An intentional and offensive touching of another without lawful justification. — Also termed *tortious battery.* Cf. ASSAULT. — **batter,** *vb.*

battle of the forms. (1947) The conflict between the terms of standard forms exchanged between a buyer and a seller during contract negotiations. ● In its original version, UCC § 2-207 attempted to resolve battles of the forms by abandoning the common-law requirement of mirror-image acceptance and providing that a definite expression of acceptance may create a contract for the sale of goods even though it contains different or additional terms. — Also termed *UCC battle of the forms.* See MIRROR-IMAGE RULE.

Baumes Law. A statute that provides for stricter criminal prosecution and penalties up to life imprisonment for an offender who has four convictions for felonies or certain misdemeanors. ● The first Baumes Law, named for New York state Senator Caleb H. Baumes, was passed by the New York legislature in 1926. Cf. THREE-STRIKES LAW.

bawd. *Archaic.* A person, usu. a woman, who solicits customers for a prostitute; a madam. See DISORDERLY HOUSE (2). Cf. PIMP.

bawdy house. See DISORDERLY HOUSE (2).

bay. *Int'l law.* An inlet of the sea, over which the coastal country exercises jurisdiction to enforce its environmental, immigration, and customs laws.

historic bay. A bay that, because of its shape, would not be considered a bay subject to the coastal country's jurisdiction, except for that country's long-standing unilateral claim over it; a bay over which the coastal country has traditionally asserted and maintained dominion.

Bayh-Dole Act. *Patents.* A federal statute that permits the U.S. Government to take title to or require licensing of nongovernmental inventions made by small businesses and nonprofit organizations while participating in federally funded programs. ● Under the Act, an entity funded by the federal government must timely disclose any invention made in the course of a federally funded program. The entity may elect to retain title and to file and prosecute a patent application covering the invention. If the entity retains title to the invention, the government may still "march in" to force the entity to grant exclusive or nonexclusive licenses in appropriate circumstances. The Act is codified in 35 USCA §§ 200–212. — Also termed *Patent and Trademark Law Amendments Act.* See MARCH-IN RIGHTS.

BCA. *abbr.* See *business-continuation agreement* under AGREEMENT.

BCD. See *bad-conduct discharge* under DISCHARGE (8).

BCD special court-martial. See COURT-MARTIAL.

BCIA. *abbr.* BERNE CONVENTION IMPLEMENTATION ACT.

BEA. *abbr.* BUREAU OF ECONOMIC ANALYSIS.

bear, *vb.* **1.** To support or carry <bear a heavy load>. **2.** To produce as yield <bear interest>. **3.** To give as testimony <bear witness>.

bear drive. See BEAR RAID.

bearer. (13c) One who possesses a negotiable instrument marked "payable to bearer" or indorsed in blank.

bearer bill of lading. See BILL OF LADING.

bearer bond. See BOND (3).

bearer document. See *bearer paper* under PAPER.

bearer instrument. See *bearer paper* under PAPER.

bearer paper. See PAPER.

bearer security. See SECURITY.

bear hug. *Slang.* A (usu. hostile) takeover strategy in which the acquiring entity offers the target firm a price per share that is significantly higher than market value, intending to squeeze the target into accepting.

reverse bear hug. A maneuver by which a takeover target responds to a bidder's offer by showing a willingness to negotiate but demanding a much higher price than that offered. • This is usu. an antitakeover tactic.

bear market. See MARKET.

bear raid. *Slang.* High-volume stock selling by a large trader in an effort to drive down a stock price in a short time. • Bear raids are prohibited by federal law. — Also termed *bear drive.*

beat, *n.* **1.** A law-enforcement officer's patrol territory. **2.** A colloquial term for the principal county subdivision in some southern states, such as Alabama, Mississippi, and South Carolina. **3.** A voting precinct.

beauty contest. *Slang.* A meeting at which a major client interviews two or more law firms to decide which firm to hire.

before-and-after theory. *Antitrust.* A method of determining damages for lost profits (and sometimes overcharges), whereby the plaintiff's profits are examined before, during, and after the violation to estimate the reduction in profits due to the defendant's violation. — Also termed *before-and-after method.* Cf. YARDSTICK THEORY; MARKET-SHARE THEORY (1).

before first action, *adv. Patents.* After the filing of a patent application but before the mailing of any office action by the U.S. Patent and Trademark Office examiner. • For example, an applicant typically files an information disclosure statement before first action, and often files preliminary amendments as well.

before the fact. (17c) In advance of an event of legal significance.

beg, *vb.* **1.** To request earnestly; to beseech. **2.** *Hist.* To request to be appointed as guardian for (a person). **3.** *Hist.* To request that someone be appointed as guardian for. **4.** To ask for charity, esp. habitually or pitiably.

beggar, *n.* A person who communicates with people, often in public places, asking for money, food, or other necessities for personal use, often as a habitual means of making a living.

beggar-thy-neighbor policy. A government's protectionist course of action taken to discourage imports by raising tariffs and instituting nontariff barriers, usu. to reduce domestic unemployment and increase domestic output. • This term is sometimes applied to competitive currency devaluation.

behavioral science. The body of disciplines (psychology, sociology, anthropology) that study human behavior.

behoof, *n. Archaic.* A use, profit, or advantage that is part of a conveyance <to his use and behoof>. — **behoove,** *vb.*

beige book. *Slang.* The popular name of the Federal Reserve's *Summary of Commentary on Current Economic Conditions by Federal Reserve District,* a publication that summarizes the economic conditions in each of the 12 Federal Reserve Bank regions. • Each Federal Reserve Bank gathers information from reports submitted by bank and branch directors; through interviews with economists, market experts, and key business contacts; and from other sources. The beige book is published eight times each year.

belief, *n.* A state of mind that regards the existence of something as likely or relatively certain.

belief–action distinction. (1966) *Constitutional law.* In First Amendment law, the Supreme Court's distinction between allowing a person to follow any chosen belief and allowing the state to intervene if necessary to protect others from the practices of that belief.

belief-cluster. In critical legal studies, a group of unconnected ideas or opinions that appear to be related when considered together in reference to a specific subject, such as racism, sexism, or religious intolerance.

believe, *vb.* **1.** To feel certain about the truth of; to accept as true. Cf. SUSPECT, *vb.*

> ***reasonably believe.*** To believe (a given fact or combination of facts) under circumstances in which a reasonable person would believe.

2. To think or suppose.

belligerency. *Int'l law.* **1.** The status assumed by a nation that wages war against another nation. **2.** The quality of being belligerent; the act or state of waging war.

belligerent, *n.* A country involved in a war or other armed international conflict. Cf. NEUTRAL (1). — **belligerent,** *adj.*

bellum justum (**bel**-əm **jəs**-təm). [Latin] *Int'l law.* A just war; one that the proponent considers morally and legally justifiable, such as a war against an aggressive, totalitarian regime. • Under Roman law, before war could be declared, the *fetiales* (a group of priests who monitored international treaties) had to certify to the Senate that just cause for war existed. With the adoption of the U.N. Charter, the *bellum justum* concept has lost its legal significance. The Charter outlaws the use of force except in self-defense. U.N. Charter arts. 2(4), 51 (59 Stat. 1031). — Also termed *just war; justifiable war.*

bellwether stock. See *barometer stock* under STOCK.

belong, *vb.* **1.** To be the property of a person or thing <this book belongs to the judge>. See OWNERSHIP. **2.** To be connected with as a member <they belong to the state bar>.

belongings. 1. Personal property; EFFECTS. See *personal property* under PROPERTY. **2.** All property, including realty.

below, *prep., adv. & adj.* **1.** Beneath; under; underneath. **2.** (Of a lower court) having heard or having the power to hear the case at issue in the first instance <court below>; at a lower level <the motion was heard below>. Cf. ABOVE.

below-market loan. See *interest-free loan* under LOAN.

below-the-line, *adj.* (1970) (Of a deduction) taken after calculating adjusted gross income and before calculating taxable income. • Examples of below-the-line deductions are medical payments and local taxes. Cf. ABOVE-THE-LINE.

***Ben Avon* Doctrine.** The principle that due process entitles public utilities to judicial review of rates set by public-service commissions. *Ohio Valley Water Co. v. Ben Avon Borough*, 253 U.S. 287, 40 S.Ct. 527 (1920).

bench. (13c) **1.** The raised area occupied by the judge in a courtroom <approach the bench>. **2.** The court considered in its official capacity <remarks from the bench>. **3.** Judges collectively <bench and bar>. **4.** The judges of a particular court <the Fifth Circuit bench>.

   cold bench. A court, esp. an appellate court, in which the judges are largely unfamiliar with the facts and issues of a case, typically because they have not reviewed the briefs or the record before hearing oral arguments. Cf. *hot bench*; *lukewarm bench*.

   hot bench. A court, esp. an appellate court, in which, before oral argument, the judges thoroughly familiarize themselves with the facts and issues of the case, usu. by reading the briefs and the record, and often prepare questions for counsel. • In the United States today, courts are generally expected to be hot. Cf. *cold bench*; *lukewarm bench*.

   lukewarm bench. A court, esp. an appellate court, in which only some of the judges, before oral argument, have familiarized themselves with the facts and issues of the case. — Also termed *tepid bench*. Cf. *hot bench*; *cold bench*.

   tepid bench. See *lukewarm bench*.

bench blotter. See ARREST RECORD (2).

bench brief. See BRIEF.

bench conference. See SIDEBAR CONFERENCE (1).

bench docket. See DOCKET (1).

bencher. A governing officer of an English Inn of Court; one of the Masters of the Bench. See INN OF COURT (1).

bench legislation. See JUDGE-MADE LAW (2).

benchmark. 1. *Property.* A mark made on a permanent object by a surveyor to serve as a uniform reference point in making topographic surveys and tidal observations. — Formerly also written *bench mark*. **2.** A standard unit used as a basis for comparison.

bench memo. (1975) **1.** A short brief submitted by a lawyer to a trial judge, often at the judge's request. **2.** A legal memorandum prepared by an appellate judge's law clerk to help the judge in preparing for oral argument and perhaps in drafting an opinion. • A trial-court judge may similarly assign a bench memo to a law clerk, for use in preparing for hearing or trial or in drafting an opinion. **3.** A memo that summarizes the facts and issues in a case, usu. prepared for a judge by a law clerk.

bench parole. See *bench probation* under PROBATION.

bench probation. See PROBATION.

bench ruling. (1971) An oral ruling issued by a judge from the bench.

bench trial. See TRIAL.

bench warrant. See WARRANT (1).

benefice (ben-ə-fis). 1. *Hist.* A feudal estate in land, held during the life of the tenant. See BENEFICIUM (4). **2.** *Hist. Eccles. law.* An estate held by the Catholic Church in feudal tenure. See BENEFICIUM (1), (2). **3.** An ecclesiastical office such as a bishopric or parish; a preferment. **4.** BENEFICIUM (3).

bénéfice de discussion. [French] BENEFIT OF DISCUSSION.

bénéfice de division. [French] BENEFIT OF DIVISION.

bénéfice d'inventaire. [French] BENEFIT OF INVENTORY.

beneficial, *adj.* (15c) **1.** Favorable; producing benefits <beneficial ruling>. **2.** Consisting in a right that derives from something other than legal title <beneficial interest in a trust>.

beneficial association. See *benevolent association* under ASSOCIATION.

beneficial enjoyment. See ENJOYMENT.

beneficial holder of securities. A holder of equitable title to corporate stock. • The stock is not registered under the holder's name in the corporation's records.

beneficial improvement. See *valuable improvement* under IMPROVEMENT.

beneficial interest. See INTEREST (2).

beneficial owner. See OWNER.

beneficial ownership. See OWNERSHIP.

beneficial power. See POWER (5).

beneficial use. See USE (1).

beneficiary (ben-ə-**fish**-ee-er-ee *or* ben-ə-**fish**-ə-ree), *n.* (17c) **1.** A person for whose benefit property is held in trust; esp., one designated to benefit from an appointment, disposition, or assignment (as in a will, insurance policy, etc.), or to receive something as a result of a legal arrangement or instrument. **2.** A person to whom another is in a fiduciary relation, whether the relation is one of agency, guardianship, or trust. **3.** A person who is initially entitled to enforce a promise, whether that person is the promisee or a third party. — **beneficiary,** *adj.*

contingent beneficiary. (1867) **1.** A person designated by the testator to receive a gift if the primary beneficiary is unable or unwilling to take the gift. — Also termed *contingency beneficiary.* **2.** A person designated in a life-insurance policy to receive the proceeds if the primary beneficiary is unable to do so. — Also termed *secondary beneficiary.*

creditor beneficiary. (1894) A third-party beneficiary of a contract who is owed a debt that is to be satisfied by another party's performance under the contract.

direct beneficiary. See *intended beneficiary.*

donee beneficiary. (1925) A third-party beneficiary who is intended to receive the benefit of the contract's performance as a gift from the promisee.

expectant beneficiary. See *expectant distributee* under DISTRIBUTEE.

favored beneficiary. A beneficiary of a will who receives disproportionate amounts of the testator's property as compared with others having equal claims to the property, raising the specter of the beneficiary's undue influence over the testator. See UNDUE INFLUENCE.

incidental beneficiary. (1901) **1.** A third-party beneficiary who is not intended to benefit from a contract and thus does not acquire rights under the contract. Cf. *intended beneficiary.* **2.** A person to whom a settlor of a trust does not manifest an intention to give a beneficial interest but who may benefit from the trust's performance.

income beneficiary. (1945) A person entitled to income from property; esp., a person entitled to receive trust income.

intended beneficiary. (1845) A third-party beneficiary who is intended to benefit from a contract and thus acquires rights under the contract as well as the ability to enforce the contract once those rights have vested. — Also termed *direct beneficiary.* Cf. *incidental beneficiary.*

life beneficiary. (1953) One who receives payments or other benefits from a trust for life.

primary beneficiary. (1850) The person designated in a life-insurance policy to receive the proceeds when the insured dies.

secondary beneficiary. See *contingent beneficiary* (2).

third-party beneficiary. (1894) A person who, though not a party to a contract, stands to benefit from the contract's performance. • For example, if Ann and Bob agree to a contract under which Bob will render some performance to Chris, then Chris is a third-party beneficiary.

unborn beneficiary. A person who, though not yet born, is named in a general way as sharing in an estate or gift. • An example might be a grandchild not yet born when a grandparent specifies, in a will, that Blackacre is to go to "my grandchildren."

beneficiary heir. See HEIR.

beneficium (ben-ə-**fish**-ee-əm), *n.* [Latin "benefit"] **1.** *Roman law.* A privilege, remedy, or benefit granted by law, such as the *beneficium abstinendi* ("privilege of abstaining"), by which an heir could refuse to accept an inheritance (and thereby avoid the accompanying debt). **2.** *Hist.* A lease, generally for life, given by a ruler or lord to a freeman. • *Beneficium* in this sense arose on the continent among the German tribes after the collapse of the Roman Empire. **3.** *Hist. English law.* An estate in land granted by the king or a lord in exchange for services. • Originally, a *beneficium* could not be passed to the holder's heirs, in contrast to *feuds,* which were heritable from an early date. Tenants, however, persisted in attempting to pass the property to their heirs, and over time the *beneficium* became a heritable estate. As this process occurred, the meaning of *beneficium* narrowed to a holding of an ecclesiastical nature. See BENEFICE (2). **4.** *Hist. Eccles. law.* A feudal tenure for life in church-owned land, esp. land held by a layperson. • Over time, this sense of *beneficium* faded, and it came to be restricted to that of an ecclesiastical living, i.e., a benefice. See BENEFICE (2), (3). **5.** *Hist.* A benefit or favor; any particular privilege, such as benefit of clergy (*beneficium clericale*). **6.** BENEFICE (3). — Also termed (in senses 3–5) *benefice.*

benefit, *n.* (14c) **1.** Advantage; privilege <the benefit of owning a car>. **2.** Profit or gain; esp., the consideration that moves to the promisee <a benefit received from the sale>. — Also termed *legal benefit; legal value.* Cf. DETRIMENT (2).

death benefit. (*usu. pl.*) (1873) A sum or sums paid to a beneficiary from a life-insurance policy on the death of an insured.

fringe benefit. (1952) A benefit (other than direct salary or compensation) received by an employee from an employer, such as insurance, a company car, or a tuition allowance. — Often shortened (esp. in pl.) to *benefit*.

general benefit. (1925) *Eminent domain.* The whole community's benefit as a result of a taking. ● It cannot be considered to reduce the compensation that is due the condemnee.

peculiar benefit. See *special benefit*.

pecuniary benefit. (17c) A benefit capable of monetary valuation.

private benefit. See PRIVATE BENEFIT.

special benefit. (1857) *Eminent domain.* A benefit that accrues to the owner of the land in question and not to any others. ● Any special benefits justify a reduction in the damages payable to the owner of land that is partially taken by the government during a public project. — Also termed *peculiar benefit*.

3. Financial assistance that is received from an employer, insurance, or a public program (such as social security) in time of sickness, disability, or unemployment <a benefit from the welfare office>. — **benefit,** *vb.*

benefit association. See *benevolent association* under ASSOCIATION.

benefit certificate. A written obligation to pay a named person a specified amount upon stipulated conditions. ● Benefit certificates are often issued by fraternal and beneficial societies.

benefit of an earlier filing date. *Patents & Trademarks.* For a patent or trademark applicant, the advantage of being assigned the filing date of a related, earlier-filed application. ● Under 35 USCA § 119: (1) a U.S. patent application is given the filing date of an earlier foreign application filed in accordance with the Paris Convention as long as the U.S. filing occurs not more than one year after the foreign filing; and (2) a continuing application filed in accordance with 35 USCA § 120 is given the filing date of an earlier-filed U.S. application. Similarly, under 15 USCA § 1126(d), a U.S. trademark applicant receives the filing date of an earlier-filed foreign application if: (1) the foreign application was filed in a Paris Convention country; and (2) the U.S. application is filed within six months after the foreign application. — Also termed *benefit of priority filing date*; *claim of priority*.

benefit-of-bargain rule. See BENEFIT-OF-THE-BARGAIN RULE.

benefit of cession. *Civil law.* A debtor's immunity from imprisonment for debt. ● The immunity arises when the debtor's property is assigned to the debtor's creditors.

benefit of clergy. **1.** At common law, the privilege of a cleric not to be tried for a felony in the King's Court <in the Middle Ages, any man who could recite the "neck verse" was granted the benefit of clergy>. ● Although *clergy* includes monks and nuns as well as priests, there are no known cases of women claiming or being granted benefit of clergy. Congress outlawed benefit of clergy in federal courts in April 1790. It was abolished in England in 1827 but survived even longer in some American states, such as South Carolina, where it was successfully claimed in 1855. *State v. Bosse,* 42 S.C.L. (3 Rich.) 276 (1855). — Also termed *clergy privilege; clericale privilegium.* See NECK VERSE. **2.** Loosely, religious approval as solemnized by church ritual <the couple had several children without benefit of clergy>. ● This common use of the phrase is premised on a misunderstanding of its original meaning (sense 1).

benefit of counsel. See RIGHT TO COUNSEL (1).

benefit of discussion. *Civil law.* A guarantor's right to require a creditor to seek payment from the principal debtor before seeking payment from the guarantor. — Also termed (in French law) *bénéfice de discussion;* (in Scots law) *right of discussion.*

benefit of division. *Civil law.* A surety's right to be sued only for a part of the debt proportionate to the number of solvent cosureties. — Also termed (in Roman law) *beneficium divisionis;* (in French law) *bénéfice de division;* (in Scots law) *right of division.*

benefit of inventory. *Civil law.* The principle that an heir's liability for estate debts is limited to the value of what is inherited, if the heir so elects and files an inventory of the estate's assets. — Also termed *bénéfice d'inventaire.*

benefit of priority filing date. See BENEFIT OF AN EARLIER FILING DATE.

benefit-of-the-bargain damages. See DAMAGES.

benefit-of-the-bargain rule. (1913) **1.** The principle that a party who breaches a contract must pay the aggrieved party an amount that puts that person in the same financial position that would have resulted if the contract had been fully performed. **2.** The principle that a defrauded buyer may recover from the seller as damages the difference between the value of the property as represented and the actual value received. — Also termed *benefit-of-bargain rule.* Cf. OUT-OF-POCKET RULE.

benevolent association. See ASSOCIATION.

benevolent society. See *benevolent association* under ASSOCIATION.

Benthamism. See *hedonistic utilitarianism* under UTILITARIANISM.

Benthamite, *adj.* Of or relating to the utilitarian theory of Jeremy Bentham. See *hedonistic utilitarianism* under UTILITARIANISM.

BEP. *abbr.* BUREAU OF ENGRAVING AND PRINTING.

bequeath (bə-**kweeth**), *vb.* (12c) **1.** To give property (usu. personal property) by will. **2.** *Hist.* To assign or transfer real or personal property by formal declaration, either *inter vivos* or after death.

bequeathal. See BEQUEST.

bequest (bə-**kwest**), *n.* (14c) **1.** The act of giving property (usu. personal property) by will. **2.** Property (usu. personal property other than money) disposed of in a will. — Also termed *bequeathal* (bə-**kwee**-thəl). Cf. DEVISE; LEGACY.

   charitable bequest. (18c) A bequest given to a philanthropic organization. See CHARITABLE ORGANIZATION.

   conditional bequest. (18c) A bequest whose effectiveness or continuation depends on the occurrence or nonoccurrence of a particular event. • An example might be a testator's gift of "the income from the farm to my daughter, Betty, until she remarries." If a condition prohibits certain legal conduct, such as using tobacco or growing a beard, it is sometimes termed a *reformation condition* or *character-improvement condition.*

   demonstrative bequest. (1905) A bequest that, by its terms, must be paid out of a specific source, such as a stock fund.

   executory bequest. (18c) A bequest of a future, deferred, or contingent interest in personal property.

   general bequest. (18c) **1.** A bequest of a general benefit, rather than a particular asset, such as a gift of money or a gift of all the testator's stocks. **2.** A bequest payable out of the general assets of the estate.

   monetary bequest. See *pecuniary bequest.*

   money bequest. See *pecuniary bequest.*

   pecuniary bequest. (18c) A testamentary gift of money; a legacy. — Also termed *monetary bequest*; *money bequest.*

   remainder bequest. See *residuary bequest.*

   residuary bequest. (18c) A bequest of the remainder of the testator's estate, after the payment of the debts, legacies, and specific bequests. — Also termed *remainder bequest.*

   specific bequest. (18c) A bequest of a specific or unique item of property, such as any real estate or a particular piece of furniture.

Berlin Act. *Copyright.* A 1908 revision of the Berne Convention prohibiting formalities as a requirement for copyright protection, recommending (but not requiring) a term of protection equal to the life of the author plus 50 years, and expanding the types of works eligible for copyright protection. • Motion pictures were included in copyright protection for the first time. — Also termed *Berlin Act of 1908; 1908 Berlin Act.*

Berne Additional Protocol. *Copyright.* A 1914 amendment to the Berne Convention providing for reprisals against a foreign national who publishes simultaneously in both a member nation and the author's own nonmember and nonreciprocating country. • The reprisal was aimed at the United States, which until 1989 refused to join the Berne Convention but whose citizens could enjoy Berne protection by first publishing in a member nation. See BACK DOOR TO BERNE.

Berne Convention. *Copyright.* An international copyright treaty providing that works created by citizens of one signatory nation will be fully protected in other signatory nations, without the need for local formalities. • The treaty was drafted in Berne in 1886 and revised in Berlin in 1908. It is now administered by the World Intellectual Property Organization and prescribes minimum levels and terms of copyright protection. The United States ratified the Berne Convention in 1989 and changed several aspects of U.S. copyright law to comply with the treaty's terms. — Also termed *Berne Copyright Convention; Berne Convention for the Protection of Literary and Artistic Property.* See CONGRESS OF AUTHORS AND ARTISTS.

Berne Convention Implementation Act. *Copyright.* The 1988 federal law making the United States a signatory to the Berne Convention, 102 years after the convention was first opened for signatures. • The law ended rigid formalities for registration and marking, although registration is still required before United States-copyright owners can sue for infringement. Pub. L. No. 100-568, 102 Stat. 2853. — Abbr. BCIA.

Berne Copyright Convention. See BERNE CONVENTION.

Berne-minus, *adj. Copyright.* Of or relating to the second sentence of Art. 9(1) of the TRIPs Agreement, which provides that intellectual-property rights and duties under the Berne Convention will not be expressly enforced on noncomplying signators through the TRIPs Agreement. U.S. reluctance to expressly protect moral rights of authors and artists has been criticized as a "Berne-minus" attitude.

Berne Paris Act. *Copyright.* A 1971 revision of the Berne Convention reducing the obligations of nations that became members as colonies of signatories. — Also termed *1971 Paris Act of the Berne Convention.*

Berne-plus, *adj. Copyright.* Of or relating to a copyright-treaty provision that affords greater intellectual-property protection than the minimum required by the Berne Convention, either by granting stronger rights or by extending protection to new forms of subject matter. • The term arose during negotiations over the TRIPs Agreement, reflecting the principle that the treaty should incorporate and build on existing international law. The WIPO treaties are said to be "Berne-plus" treaties because they incorporate Berne protections and add additional protections of their own.

Berne Safeguard Clause. *Copyright.* A provision in the Universal Copyright Convention barring protection in Berne Union countries for the works of any country that withdraws from the Berne Union after January 1, 1951. • The purpose of the clause was to prevent countries from withdrawing from the Berne Union in favor of the more relaxed copyright-protection standards of the Convention. The clause was amended in 1971 to give developing countries the right to opt out of its mandate.

Berne Union. *Copyright.* The treaty alliance of Berne Convention member nations.

***Berry* rule.** (1956) The doctrine that a defendant seeking a new trial on grounds of newly discovered evidence must show that (1) the evidence is newly discovered and was unknown to the defendant at the time of trial; (2) the evidence is material rather than merely cumulative or impeaching; (3) the evidence will probably produce an acquittal; and (4) the failure to learn of the evidence was not due to the defendant's lack of diligence. *Berry v. State*, 10 Ga. 511 (1851).

Bertillon system (bər-tə-lon *or* bair-tee-**yaw***n*). A system of anthropometry once used to identify criminals by measuring and describing them. • The Bertillon system is named for Alphonse Bertillon, the French anthropologist who developed the technique early in the 20th century. It has been largely replaced by fingerprinting. Cf. ANTHROPOMETRY.

bespeaks-caution doctrine. *Securities.* The principle that if soft information in a prospectus is accompanied by cautionary language that adequately warns investors that actual results or events may affect performance, then the soft information may not be materially misleading to investors. • Soft information includes forecasts, estimates, opinions, and projections about future performance. The doctrine was codified in the Private Securities Litigation Reform Act of 1995.

best bid. See BID (1).

best edition. *Copyright.* A particular version of a copyrighted work that is published in the U.S. before the date of deposit and that is designated by the Library of Congress, in its discretion, as the most suitable for its purposes. • Two copies of a copyrighted work, in the selected best-edition form, must be deposited with the Library.

best efforts. (17c) Diligent attempts to carry out an obligation <the contractor must use best efforts to complete its work within the stated time>. • As a

standard, a best-efforts obligation is stronger than a good-faith obligation. Best efforts are measured by the measures that a reasonable person in the same circumstances and of the same nature as the acting party would take. — Also termed *best endeavors.* Cf. *due diligence* (1) under DILIGENCE; GOOD FAITH.

best-efforts contract. See CONTRACT.

best-efforts underwriting. See UNDERWRITING.

best embodiment. See BEST MODE.

best endeavors. See BEST EFFORTS.

best evidence. See EVIDENCE.

best-evidence rule. (1894) The evidentiary rule providing that, to prove the contents of a writing (or a recording or photograph), a party must produce the original writing (or a mechanical, electronic, or other familiar duplicate, such as a photocopy) unless it is unavailable, in which case secondary evidence — the testimony of the drafter or a person who read the document — may be admitted. Fed. R. Evid. 1001–1004. — Also termed *documentary-originals rule*; *original-writing rule*; *original-document rule*.

bestiality (bes-chee-**al**-ə-tee). (14c) Sexual activity between a human and an animal. • Some authorities restrict the term to copulation between a human and an animal of the opposite sex. See SODOMY.

best interests of creditors. *Bankruptcy.* A test for confirmation of a reorganization plan whereby the court inquires into whether the plan ensures that the value of property to be distributed to each creditor is at least the amount that the creditor would receive if the debtor's estate were liquidated in a Chapter 7 case. • A court may not confirm a plan in a Chapter 9, Chapter 12, or Chapter 13 case unless it is in the best interests of the creditors. In a Chapter 11 case, a court may confirm a plan even though some creditors do not vote to accept it if the court finds that the plan is in the creditors' best interest. 11 USCA §§ 944(7), 1129(a)(7), 1225(a)(4), 1325(a)(4). — Also written *best interest of creditors.*

best interests of the child. *Family law.* A standard by which a court determines what arrangements would be to a child's greatest benefit, often used in deciding child-custody and visitation matters and in deciding whether to approve an adoption or a guardianship. • A court may use many factors, including the emotional tie between the child and the parent or guardian, the ability of a parent or guardian to give the child love and guidance, the ability of a parent or guardian to provide necessaries, the established living arrangement between a parent or guardian and the child, the child's preference if the child is old enough that the court will consider that preference in making a custody award, and a parent's ability to foster a healthy relationship between the child and the other parent. — Abbr. BIC. — Also termed *best interest of the child*. Cf. PARENTAL-PREFERENCE DOCTRINE.

best-interests-of-the-child doctrine. *Family law.* The principle that courts should make custody decisions based on whatever best advances the child's welfare, regardless of a claimant's particular status or relationship with the child. ● One important factor entering into these decisions is the general belief that the child's best interests normally favor custody by parents, as opposed to grandparents or others less closely related. The doctrine is quite old, having been stated, for example, in the early 19th-century case of *Commonwealth v. Briggs*, 33 Mass. 203 (1834). — Sometimes shortened to *best-interests doctrine*; *best-interest doctrine*. See PARENTAL-PREFERENCE DOCTRINE.

best mode. *Patents.* The best way that the inventor knows to work the invention described and claimed in a patent or patent application. ● A patent application must disclose the best mode known to the inventor at the time of the filing. Failure to disclose the best mode can render a patent invalid. 35 USCA § 112, ¶ 1. — Also termed *best embodiment*. Cf. ENABLEMENT REQUIREMENT.

best-mode requirement. *Patents.* The requirement that a patent application show the best physical method known to the inventor for using the invention. Cf. ENABLEMENT REQUIREMENT.

bestow, *vb.* (14c) To convey as a gift <bestow an honor on another>. — **bestowal,** *n.*

best use. See *highest and best use* under USE (1).

bet, *n.* Something (esp. money) staked or pledged as a wager. — **bet,** *vb.* — **betting,** *n.* — **bettor,** *n.*

> **layoff bet.** A bet placed by a bookmaker to protect against excessive losses or to equalize the total amount placed on each side of the wager. See LAYOFF BETTOR.

beta. A statistical measure of a security's risk, based on how widely a particular security's return swings as compared to the overall return in the market for that security. ● The market's beta is set at 1.0; a security with a beta lower than 1.0 is less risky than the general market, while a security with a beta higher than 1.0 is more so.

beta-test agreement. *Intellectual property.* A software license agreement, usu. between a software developer and a customer, permitting the customer to use the software program in a "live" environment before its release to the general public. ● Beta-test agreements differ from more conventional software licenses in that they typically (1) have more significant limitations on liability; (2)

contain few, if any, warranties; and (3) require user evaluation and feedback. — Also termed *software beta-test agreement*.

beta testing. *Intellectual property.* The process of testing products and services, esp. software, under real-life conditions. ● Consumers often engage in beta testing at no cost in exchange for reporting to the developer how satisfied they are, any problems they encounter, and any suggested improvements. To protect a trade secret or to avoid a statutory bar, the developer may require the user to sign a nondisclosure agreement. Cf. ALPHA TESTING.

bet din. See BETH DIN.

beth din. *Family law.* A rabbinical tribunal empowered by Jewish law to decide and enforce matters of Jewish law and custom; esp., a tribunal consisting of three rabbis who decide questions of Jewish law. — Also spelled *bet din*. See BETH TORAH.

beth Torah. The judgment rendered by a panel of rabbis. See BETH DIN.

betrothal. 1. *Eccles. law.* A religious ceremony confirming an agreement to marry. ● Historically, a betrothal was performed months or years before the parties wedded. It was in theory as legally binding as a marriage and created an impediment to marriage with any other person, but not an insurmountable impediment. In modern form, the betrothal is usu. part of the marriage ceremony. — Also termed *betrothment*. See ENGAGEMENT (2). Cf. *precontract* under CONTRACT; ESPOUSALS. **2.** *Slang.* A corporate merger agreement.

betrothment. See BETROTHAL (1).

betterment. (18c) **1.** An improvement that increases the value of real property; esp., an enhancement in the nature of an alteration or addition that goes beyond repair or restoration to a former condition. **2.** An improvement of a highway, railroad, or building that goes beyond repair or restoration. **3.** An increase in value, esp. real-estate value, attributable to improvements. See IMPROVEMENT.

betterment act. (1819) A statute requiring a landowner to compensate an occupant who improves the land under a mistaken belief that the occupant is the real owner. ● The compensation usu. equals the increase in the land's value generated by the improvements. — Also termed *occupying-claimant act*; *occupant statute*.

betterment tax. A tax for the improvement of highways.

betting. See PARIMUTUEL BETTING.

beyond a reasonable doubt. See REASONABLE DOUBT.

beyond seas. (16c) *Hist.* **1.** (Of a person) being absent from a jurisdiction or nation; out of the country, esp. across the ocean. ● This term was used when a person could not be served with a summons, notice, etc. because the person was absent from the jurisdiction. Some jurisdictions toll the statute of limitations during a defendant's absence. **2.** Out-of-state. • Although originally *beyond seas* meant "out of the country," the U.S. Supreme Court declared that the term includes absence from a state. *Murray's Lessee v. Baker*, 16 U.S. 541, 545 (1818). — Also termed *beyond sea*; *beyond the seas*; *ultra mare*.

b.f. *abbr.* BONUM FACTUM.

BFOQ. *abbr.* BONA FIDE OCCUPATIONAL QUALIFICATION.

BFP. See *bona fide purchaser* under PURCHASER (1).

BHC. *abbr.* BANK HOLDING COMPANY.

BIA. *abbr.* **1.** BUREAU OF INDIAN AFFAIRS. **2.** BOARD OF IMMIGRATION APPEALS.

bias, *n.* (16c) Inclination; prejudice; predilection <the juror's bias prompted a challenge for cause>. — **bias,** *vb.* — **biased,** *adj.*

actual bias. Genuine prejudice that a judge, juror, witness, or other person has against some person or relevant subject. Cf. *implied bias.*

advocate's bias. The bias that attorneys often develop in favor of a client involved in a dispute and that may potentially cause such missteps as overlooking certain arguments or misjudging the way facts or cases may appear to a dispassionate outsider.

implied bias. Prejudice that is inferred from the experiences or relationships of a judge, juror, witness, or other person. — Also termed *presumed bias.* Cf. *actual bias.*

judicial bias. A judge's bias toward one or more of the parties to a case over which the judge presides. • Judicial bias is usu. not enough to disqualify a judge from presiding over a case unless the judge's bias is personal or based on some extrajudicial reason.

BIC. *abbr.* BEST INTERESTS OF THE CHILD.

bicameral, *adj.* (Of a legislature) having two legislative houses (usu. called the House of Representatives, or the Assembly, and the Senate). • The federal government and all states except Nebraska have bicameral legislatures. — **bicameralism,** *n.*

Bicameral Clause. The constitutional provision that creates the two legislative chambers of Congress. See U.S. Const. art. I, § I.

bid, *n.* (18c) **1.** A buyer's offer to pay a specified price for something that may or may not be for sale <a bid at an auction> <a takeover bid>.

best bid. The highest auction bid; in the letting of a contract, the lowest bid by a qualified bidder.

bid in. A bid made by the owner of auctioned property to ensure that the property is not sold below actual value.

bid off. To purchase by bid at auction or judicial sale.

upset bid. A bid in a judicial sale made for more than the purchaser's bid so that the sale will be set aside (i.e., upset).

2. A submitted price at which one will perform work or supply goods <the subcontractor's bid>. See BID-SHOPPING. — **bid,** *vb.* — **bidder,** *n.*

competitive bid. A bid submitted in response to public notice of an intended sale or purchase.

firm bid. (1907) A bid that, by its terms, remains open and binding until accepted or rejected. • A firm bid commonly contains no unusual conditions that might defeat acceptance.

open bid. (1849) A bid that the bidder may alter after submission so as to meet competing bids.

sealed bid. (1849) A bid that is not disclosed until all submitted bids are opened and considered simultaneously.

bid and asked. *Securities.* A notation describing the range of prices quoted for securities in an over-the-counter stock exchange. • *Bid* denotes the highest price the buyer is willing to pay, and *asked* denotes the lowest price the seller will accept. See SPREAD (2).

bid bond. See BOND (2).

bidding up. (1823) The act or practice of raising the price for an auction item by making a series of progressively higher bids. • Bidding up is unlawful if the bids are made collusively by persons with an interest in raising the bids. Cf. BY-BIDDING; SHILLING (1).

bid in. See BID (1).

bid off. See BID (1).

bid peddling. See BID-SHOPPING.

bid price. See PRICE.

bid quote. *Securities.* The price a broker will pay for a security or commodity.

bid-shopping. (1964) A general contractor's effort — after being awarded a contract — to reduce its own costs by finding a subcontractor that will submit a lower bid than the one used in calculating the total contract price. • If a lower bid is obtained, the general contractor will receive a windfall profit because the savings are usu. not passed on to the property owner. The subcontractor whose bid is used in the initial proposal can seek to avoid bid-shopping by insisting that it be irrevocably named in the contract as the project's subcontractor.

bid wanted. *Securities.* A dealer's notation that bids are being sought from anyone on a security for sale. • The notation appears in the pink sheets. — Abbr. BW. See PINK SHEET.

biennial session. See SESSION (1).

biennium (bī-**en**-ee-əm). **1.** A two-year period. **2.** The period for which many state legislatures make appropriations.

bifactoral obligation. See OBLIGATION.

bifurcated divorce. See *divisible divorce* under DIVORCE.

bifurcated trial. See TRIAL.

bigamous (**big**-ə-məs), *adj.* **1.** (Of a person) guilty of bigamy. **2.** (Of a marriage) involving bigamy.

bigamy, *n.* (13c) **1.** The act of marrying one person while legally married to another. • Bigamy is distinct from adultery. It is a criminal offense if it is committed knowingly. In 1878, the U.S. Supreme Court held that the government was not constitutionally prohibited from banning Mormon polygamy. *Reynolds v. United States*, 98 U.S. (8 Otto) 145 (1878). **2.** *Eccles. law.* The act of marrying a widow or widower, or a divorced person. • Somewhat surprisingly, sense 2 is valid even under modern ecclesiastical law, but it is not an offense, only a bar to entering holy orders. — Also termed *sequential marriage.* See DEUTEROGAMY. Cf. POLYGAMY; MONOGAMY; ADULTERY. — **bigamist,** *n.*

big bath. *Slang.* A write-off of significant costs, taken to shed an unprofitable business line or to remove the necessity for future write-offs.

Big Board. 1. The New York Stock Exchange. • This sense of *Big Board* may have derived from the former name of the NYSE — New York Stock and Exchange Board. **2.** A quotation display showing the current prices of securities listed on the New York Stock Exchange.

big pot. See MAIN POT.

bilateral, *adj.* (18c) Affecting or obligating both parties <a bilateral contract>.

bilateral act. See ACT.

bilateral advance pricing agreement. See ADVANCE PRICING AGREEMENT.

bilateral contract. See CONTRACT.

bilateral mistake. See *mutual mistake* (1) under MISTAKE.

bilateral monopoly. See MONOPOLY.

bill, *n.* (14c) **1.** A formal written complaint, such as a court paper requesting some specific action for reasons alleged. **2.** An equitable pleading by which a claimant brings a claim in a court of equity. • Before the merger of law and equity, the bill in equity was analogous to a declaration in law. The nine parts of every equitable bill are (1) the address to the person holding the great seal, (2) the introduction, which identifies the parties, (3) the premises, which state the plaintiff's case, (4) the confederating part, in which the defendants are charged with combination, (5) the charging part, in which the plaintiff may try to overcome defenses that the defendants may allege, (6) the jurisdictional clause, showing that the court has jurisdiction, (7) the interrogating part, inserted to try to compel a full and complete answer, (8) the prayer for relief, and (9) the prayer for process to compel the defendants to appear and answer. — Also termed *bill in equity.* See DECLARATION (7). — Also termed *bill in chancery; bill of chancery; bill of equity; bill for foreclosure.*

bill for a new trial. A bill in equity to enjoin a judgment and to obtain a new trial because of some fact that would render enforcement of the judgment inequitable. • The fact must have been either unavailable or unknown to the party at trial through fraud or accident. Cf. MOTION FOR NEW TRIAL.

bill for redemption. See *bill of redemption.*

bill in aid of execution. A bill filed by a judgment creditor to set aside a fraudulent encumbrance or conveyance.

bill in perpetuam rei memoriam. See *bill to perpetuate testimony.*

bill in the nature of a bill of review. A postjudgment bill of review filed by someone who was neither a party to the original suit nor bound by the decree sought to be reversed. — Also termed *supplemental bill in the nature of a bill of review.*

bill in the nature of a bill of revivor. A bill filed when a litigant dies or becomes incapacitated before the litigant's interest in property could be determined. • The purpose of the bill is to resolve who holds the right to revive the original litigation in the deceased's stead.

bill in the nature of a supplemental bill. A bill bringing to court new parties and interests arising from events that occur after the suit is filed. • A *supplemental bill,* in contrast, involves parties or interests already before the court.

bill in the nature of interpleader. A bill of interpleader filed by a person claiming an interest in interpleaded property.

bill of certiorari. (18c) A bill in equity seeking removal of an action to a higher court. See CERTIORARI.

bill of complaint. An original bill that begins an action in a court of equity. See COMPLAINT (1).

bill of conformity. A bill filed by an executor or administrator who seeks the court's guidance in administering an estate. • The bill is usu. filed to adjust creditors' claims.

bill of costs. (16c) A certified, itemized statement of the amount of costs owed by one litigant to another, prepared so that the prevailing party may recover the costs from the losing party. — Also termed *cost bill.*

bill of discovery. (17c) A bill in equity seeking disclosure of facts within the opposing party's knowledge. See DISCOVERY.

bill of evidence. A transcript of testimony heard at trial.

bill of exceptions. (17c) **1.** A formal written statement — signed by the trial judge and presented to the appellate court — of a party's objections or exceptions taken during trial and the grounds on which they are founded. • These bills have largely been replaced by straight appeals under the Federal Rules of Civil Procedure. See EXCEPTION (1). **2.** In some jurisdictions, a record made to preserve error after the judge has excluded evidence.

bill of foreclosure. A bill in equity filed by a lender to have mortgaged property sold to satisfy all or part of the secured, unpaid debt.

bill of interpleader. An original bill filed by a party against two or more persons who claim from that party the same debt or duty. • The requesting party asks the court to compel the contenders to litigate and establish their rights to the debt or the duty. See INTERPLEADER.

bill of peace. (18c) An equitable bill filed by one who is threatened with multiple suits involving the same right, or with recurrent suits on the same right, asking the court to determine the question once and for all, and to enjoin the plaintiffs from proceeding with the threatened litigation. • One situation involves many persons having a common claim but threatening to bring separate suits; another involves one person bringing a second action on the same claim.

bill of redemption. A bill in equity filed to enforce a right to redeem real property, usu. following a mortgage foreclosure or a delinquent-tax sale. — Also termed *bill for redemption.*

bill of review. (17c) A bill in equity requesting that a court reverse or revise a prior decree.

bill of revivor. (17c) A bill filed for the purpose of reviving and continuing a suit in equity when the suit has been abated before final consummation. • The most common cause of such an abatement is the death of either the plaintiff or the defendant.

bill of revivor and supplement. A compound of a supplemental bill and a bill of revivor, joined for convenience. • Its distinct parts must be framed and proceeded on separately.

bill quia timet. An equitable bill used to guard against possible or prospective injuries and to preserve the means by which existing rights are protected from future or contingent violations.

• It differs from an injunction, which corrects past and present — or imminent and certain — injuries. One example is a bill to perpetuate testimony. See QUIA TIMET.

bill to carry a decree into execution. A bill brought when a decree could not be enforced without further court order because of the parties' neglect or for some other reason. — Also termed *bill to enforce a decree.*

bill to perpetuate testimony. (18c) An original bill to preserve the testimony of a material witness who may die or leave the jurisdiction before a suit is commenced, or to prevent or avoid future litigation. — Also termed *bill in perpetuam rei memoriam.*

bill to suspend a decree. A bill brought to set aside a decree.

bill to take testimony de bene esse (dee *or* də **bee**-nee **es**-ee *also* day **ben**-ay es-ay). A bill brought to take testimony pertinent to pending litigation from a witness who may be unavailable at the time of trial.

cost bill. See *bill of costs.*

cross-bill. A bill brought by the defendant against the plaintiff in the same suit, or against other defendants in the same suit, relating to the matters alleged in the original bill.

nonoriginal bill. A bill relating to some matter already litigated by the same parties. • It is an addition to or a continuation of an original bill.

original bill. A bill relating to some matter that has never before been litigated by the same parties with the same interests.

skeleton bill of exceptions. A bill of exceptions that, in addition to the formal parts, contains only the court's directions to the clerk to copy or insert necessary documents into the record for appellate review, but does not contain the actual evidence or trial-court rulings. • For example, the statement "the clerk will insert the official transcript here" is typically a skeleton bill.

supplemental bill. A bill filed for the purpose of adding something to an original bill. • This addition usu. results from the discovery of new facts or from a new understanding of facts after the defendant has put on a defense.

supplemental bill in the nature of a bill of review. See *bill in the nature of a bill of review.*

3. A legislative proposal offered for debate before its enactment.

administration bill. A bill drafted and submitted by the executive branch.

appropriations bill. (18c) A bill that authorizes governmental expenditures. • The federal government cannot spend money unless Congress has appropriated the funds. U.S. Const. art. I,

§ 9, cl. 7. — Also termed *spending bill*. See AP-PROPRIATION (2), (3).

budget bill. A bill designating how money will be allocated for the following fiscal year.

clean bill. A bill that has been changed so much by a legislative committee that it is better to introduce a new bill (a "clean" one) than to explain the changes made. — Also termed *committee substitute*.

companion bill. A bill introduced in the other house of a bicameral legislature in a substantially identical form.

deficiency bill. An appropriations bill covering expenses omitted from the general appropriations bills, or for which insufficient appropriations were made. • An *urgent deficiency bill* covers immediate expenses usu. for one item, and a *general deficiency bill* covers a variety of items.

engrossed bill. (18c) **1.** A bill in a form ready for final passage by a legislative chamber. **2.** A bill in the form passed by one house of the legislature. See ENGROSS (3); ENGROSSMENT (2).

enrolled bill. (18c) A bill passed by both houses of the legislature and signed by their presiding officers. See ENROLL (2); ENROLLED-BILL RULE.

house bill. (*often cap.*) (1871) A legislative bill being considered by a house of representatives. — Abbr. H; H.B.

money bill. See *revenue bill*.

must-pass bill. Legislation of vital importance, such as an appropriation without which the government will shut down. • A must-pass bill will often attract unrelated riders. See RIDER.

omnibus bill. (1840) **1.** A single bill containing various distinct matters, usu. drafted in this way to force the executive either to accept all the unrelated minor provisions or to veto the major provision. **2.** A bill that deals with all proposals relating to a particular subject, such as an "omnibus judgeship bill" covering all proposals for new judgeships or an "omnibus crime bill" dealing with different subjects such as new crimes and grants to states for crime control.

prefiled bill. A bill that has been drafted and submitted before a legislative session begins.

private bill. A bill relating to a matter of personal or local interest only. Cf. *special law* under LAW.

public bill. (18c) A bill relating to public policy in the whole community.

revenue bill. (18c) A bill that levies or raises taxes. • Federal revenue bills must originate in the House of Representatives. U.S. Const. art. I, § 7, cl. 1. — Also termed *money bill*.

senate bill. (*often cap.*) (1857) A legislative bill being considered by a senate. — Abbr. S.B.

spending bill. See *appropriations bill*.

4. An enacted statute <the GI Bill>. **5.** An itemized list of charges; an invoice <hospital bill>. See FEE STATEMENT.

bill of parcels. **1.** A seller's itemized list of goods and prices, intended to assist a buyer in detecting any mistakes or omissions in a shipment of goods. **2.** INVOICE.

bill payable. See *account payable* under ACCOUNT.

bill receivable. See *account receivable* under ACCOUNT.

bill rendered. See *account rendered* under ACCOUNT.

6. A bill of exchange; a draft <the bank would not honor the unsigned bill>. See DRAFT (1).

advance bill. A bill of exchange drawn before the shipment of the goods.

banker's bill. See *finance bill*.

blank bill. A bill with the payee's name left blank. Cf. DRAFT (1).

domestic bill. **1.** A bill of exchange that is payable in the state or country where it is drawn. **2.** A bill on which both the drawer and drawee reside within the same state or country. — Also termed (in sense 2) *inland bill of exchange*. Cf. *foreign bill*.

finance bill. A bill of exchange drawn by a bank in one country on a bank in another country to raise short-term credit. • Finance bills are often issued in tight money periods, and usu. have maturity dates of more than 60 days. — Also termed *banker's bill*; *working capital acceptance*.

foreign bill. A bill of exchange drawn in one state or country and payable in another. Cf. *domestic bill*.

inland bill of exchange. See *domestic bill* (2).

investment bill. A bill of exchange purchased at a discount and intended to be held to maturity as an investment.

7. A formal document or note; an instrument <bill of sale>.

bill obligatory. A written promise to pay; a promissory note under seal. — Also termed *single bond*. See NOTE (1).

bill of debt. A debt instrument, such as a bill obligatory or promissory note.

bill of lading. See BILL OF LADING.

bill penal. A written promise to pay that carries a penalty in excess of the underlying debt for failure to pay. Cf. *bill single*.

bill single. A written promise to pay that is not under seal and has no penalty for failure to pay. — Also termed *single bill.* Cf. *bill penal.*

grand bill of sale. **1.** *Hist.* An instrument used to transfer title to a ship that is at sea. **2.** An instrument used to transfer title of a ship from the builder to the first purchaser.

single bill. See *bill single.*

skeleton bill. A bill drawn, indorsed, or accepted in blank.

8. A piece of paper money <a $10 bill>. **9.** A promissory note <the debtor signed a bill for $7,000>.

billable hour. (1968) A unit of time used by an attorney, law clerk, or paralegal to account for work performed and chargeable to a client. ● Billable hours are usu. divided into quarters or tenths of an hour.

billable time. (1966) An attorney's, law clerk's, or paralegal's time that is chargeable to a client. Cf. NONBILLABLE TIME.

billa vera (**bil**-ə **veer**-ə). [Latin] See TRUE BILL.

bill broker. A middleman who negotiates the purchase or sale of commercial paper.

billhead. A printed invoice containing a business's name and address.

bill in aid of execution. See BILL (2).

bill in equity. See BILL (2).

billing cycle. The period between billings for goods sold or services rendered.

bill *in perpetuam rei memoriam*. See *bill to perpetuate testimony* under BILL (2).

bill number. The number assigned to a proposed piece of legislation, typically designating the house in which it was introduced (S for senate or HR for house of representatives) followed by a sequential number.

bill of adventure. *Maritime law.* A shipper's written statement that the shipped property belongs to another and is conveyed at the owner's risk.

bill of attainder. (17c) **1.** *Archaic.* A special legislative act that imposes a death sentence on a person without a trial. **2.** A special legislative act prescribing punishment, without a trial, for a specific person or group. ● Bills of attainder are prohibited by the U.S. Constitution (art. I, § 9, cl. 3; art. I, § 10, cl. 1). — Also termed *act of attainder.* See ATTAINDER; BILL OF PAINS AND PENALTIES.

bill of credit. 1. Legal tender in the form of paper, issued by a state and involving the faith of the state, designed to circulate as money in the ordinary uses of business. U.S. Const. art. I, § 10. **2.** LETTER OF CREDIT.

bill of debt. See BILL (7).

bill of entry. *Maritime law.* A written description of goods filed by an importer with customs officials to obtain permission to unload a ship's goods.

bill of exchange. See DRAFT (1).

bill of health. *Maritime law.* A statement certifying the healthy condition of a ship's cargo and crew. ● The bill is issued by the port authority from which a vessel sails and is shown to the port authority at the ship's destination as proof that the ship's cargo and crew are disease-free. A "clean" bill states that no contagious or infectious diseases were present at the port; a "touched" or "foul" bill states that the named disease was suspected, anticipated, or actually present.

bill of indemnity. 1. *Hist.* An act of Parliament passed annually to protect officeholders who unwittingly fail to take a required oath from liability for acts done in an official capacity. ● A more general statute, the Promissory Oaths Act, replaced the bill of indemnity in 1868. **2.** A law protecting a public official from liability for official acts. **3.** An initial pleading by which a plaintiff seeks to require another (often an insurance company) to discharge the plaintiff's liability to a third person.

bill of indictment. (16c) An instrument presented to a grand jury and used by the jury to declare whether there is enough evidence to formally charge the accused with a crime. See INDICTMENT; NO BILL; TRUE BILL.

bill of information. 1. INFORMATION. **2.** *Hist.* A civil suit begun by the Crown or by those under its protection, such as a charity.

bill of interpleader. See BILL (2).

bill of lading (**layd**-ing). (16c) A document acknowledging the receipt of goods by a carrier or by the shipper's agent and the contract for the transportation of those goods; a document that indicates the receipt of goods for shipment and that is issued by a person engaged in the business of transporting or forwarding goods. UCC § 1-201(6). ● A negotiable bill of lading is a document of title. — Abbr. B/L. — Cf. WAYBILL; AIRBILL.

bearer bill of lading. A negotiable bill of lading that authorizes the carrier or holder of freight to deliver it to the bearer.

claused bill of lading. See *unclean bill of lading.*

clean bill of lading. A bill of lading containing no clause or notation qualifying the bill's terms. ● Possible clauses or notations could include a provision for deck storage or a recording of cargo damage. Cf. *unclean bill of lading.*

destination bill of lading. A bill procured to be issued at the destination point or any other place than the place of shipment. UCC § 7-305.

foul bill of lading. See *unclean bill of lading.*

long-form bill of lading. A bill of lading that expressly contains all the terms of the transportation contract. Cf. *short-form bill of lading.*

negotiable bill of lading. A bill of lading calling for the delivery of goods to the bearer or to a named person's order. UCC § 7-104.

nonnegotiable bill of lading. See *straight bill of lading.*

ocean bill of lading. A negotiable bill of lading used in shipment by water. — Often shortened to *ocean bill.*

onboard bill of lading. A bill of lading reflecting that goods have been loaded onto a ship. • In multimodal shipments, an onboard bill of lading may include goods loaded onto land vehicles also. — Often shortened to *onboard bill.*

order bill of lading. A negotiable bill of lading stating that the goods are consigned to the order of the person named in the bill.

overseas bill of lading. A bill of lading used for overseas shipment by water or air. UCC § 2-323. • In air freight, an overseas bill of lading is called an *air waybill.* — Often shortened to *overseas bill.*

short-form bill of lading. A bill of lading that does not expressly contain all the terms of the transportation contract, but incorporates them by reference to another document, usu. one at the office of the carrier.

spent bill of lading. A negotiable bill of lading that is not produced, canceled, or surrendered after the carrier has delivered the goods. — Often shortened to *spent bill.*

straight bill of lading. A nonnegotiable bill of lading that specifies a consignee to whom the carrier is contractually obligated to deliver the goods. • In some countries, including England, a document is not a bill of lading unless it is negotiable. — Also termed *nonnegotiable bill of lading.*

through bill of lading. A bill of lading by which a carrier agrees to transport goods to a designated destination, even though the carrier will have to use a connecting carrier for part of the passage. UCC § 7-302. — Often shortened to *through bill.*

unclean bill of lading. A bill of lading that shows on its face that the goods were damaged or that there was a shortage of goods at the time of shipment. — Also termed *claused bill of lading; foul bill of lading.* Cf. *clean bill of lading.*

bill of mortality. *Hist.* A record of the number of deaths occurring in a given district. • Bills of mortality were compiled — often week to week — in England from late in the 16th century to the 19th century as a way to keep track of the plague and other highly contagious diseases.

bill of pains and penalties. (18c) A legislative act that, though similar to a bill of attainder, prescribes punishment less severe than capital punishment. • Bills of pains and penalties are included within the U.S. Constitution's ban on bills of attainder. U.S. Const. art I, § 9.

bill of parcels. See BILL (5).

bill of particulars. (1831) A formal, detailed statement of the claims or charges brought by a plaintiff or a prosecutor, usu. filed in response to the defendant's request for a more specific complaint. • The bill of particulars has been abolished in federal civil actions and replaced by the motion for a more definite statement. See Fed. R. Civ. P. 12(e). But it is still used in some states (such as California) and in federal criminal cases. See Fed. R. Crim. P. 7(f). — Also termed *statement of particulars.* See MOTION FOR MORE DEFINITE STATEMENT.

bill of peace. See BILL (2).

bill of privilege. See BILL (2).

bill of redemption. See BILL (2).

bill of review. See BILL (2).

bill of revivor. See BILL (2).

bill of revivor and supplement. See BILL (2).

bill of rights. (18c) **1.** (*usu. cap.*) A section or addendum, usu. in a constitution, defining the situations in which a politically organized society will permit free, spontaneous, and individual activity, and guaranteeing that governmental powers will not be used in certain ways; esp., the first ten amendments to the U.S. Constitution. **2.** (*cap.*) One of the four great charters of English liberty (1 W. & M. (1689)), embodying in statutory form all the principles of the other three charters, namely, Magna Carta, the Petition of Right (3 Car. I, 1628), and the Habeas Corpus Act (31 Car. 2, 1679).

bill of sale. (16c) An instrument for conveying title to personal property, absolutely or by way of security. Cf. DEED.

bill of sight. *Maritime law.* A declaration made to a customs officer by an importer who is unsure about what is being shipped. • The bill of sight allows an importer to inspect the goods before paying duties.

bill payable. See *account payable* under ACCOUNT.

bill penal. See BILL (7).

bill quia timet. See BILL (2).

bill receivable. See *account receivable* under ACCOUNT.

bill rendered. See *account rendered* under ACCOUNT.

bills and notes. 1. See PAPER (1). **2.** See PAPER (2).

bills in a set. A bill of lading made up of a series of independent parts, each bearing a number and providing that goods delivered against any one part voids the other parts. • Traditionally, in overseas-goods shipments, the parts of this type of bill were sent under separate cover so that if one was lost, the buyer could take delivery of the goods with another one. UCC § 7-304.

bill single. See BILL (7).

bill status. The current state of a proposed law in the legislative process, such as its assignment to a committee, its schedule for a hearing or a vote, and its passage or defeat by one or both houses.

bill to carry a decree into execution. See BILL (2).

bill to enforce a decree. See *bill to carry a decree into execution* under BILL (2).

bill to perpetuate testimony. See BILL (2).

bill to suspend a decree. See BILL (2).

bill to take testimony *de bene esse.* See BILL (2).

bimetallism. A monetary system in which currency is defined in terms of two metals (usu. gold and silver), both being legal tender and with a fixed rate of exchange between them. • The American money system was based on a bimetallic standard from 1792 to 1873.

bind, *vb.* (15c) **1.** To impose one or more legal duties on (a person or institution) <the contract binds the parties> <courts are bound by precedent>. **2.** *Hist.* To indenture; to legally obligate to serve. — **binding,** *adj.* — **bindingness,** *n.*

binder. **1.** A document in which the buyer and the seller of real property declare their common intention to bring about a transfer of ownership, usu. accompanied by the buyer's initial payment. **2.** Loosely, the buyer's initial payment in the sale of real property. Cf. EARNEST MONEY. **3.** An insurer's memorandum giving the insured temporary coverage while the application for an insurance policy is being processed or while the formal policy is being prepared. — Also termed *binding receipt*; *binding slip*.

binding, *adj.* (14c) **1.** (Of an agreement) having legal force <a binding contract>. **2.** (Of an order) requiring obedience <the temporary injunction was binding on the parties>.

binding agreement. See AGREEMENT.

binding arbitration. See ARBITRATION.

binding authority. **1.** See *binding precedent* under PRECEDENT. **2.** See *imperative authority* under AUTHORITY.

binding instruction. See *mandatory instruction* under JURY INSTRUCTION.

binding precedent. See PRECEDENT.

binding receipt. See BINDER.

binding slip. See BINDER.

bind over, *vb.* (16c) **1.** To put (a person) under a bond or other legal obligation to do something, esp. to appear in court. **2.** To hold (a person) for trial; to turn (a defendant) over to a sheriff or warden for imprisonment pending further judicial action. • A court may bind over a defendant if it finds at a preliminary examination that there is enough evidence to require a trial on the charges against the defendant. — **binding over,** *n.* — **bindover,** *adj.*

bindover hearing. See PRELIMINARY HEARING.

biochemical warfare. See WARFARE.

biological, *adj.* **1.** Of or relating to biology or life <biological study>. **2.** Genetically related <biological parents>.

biological child. See *natural child* (1) under CHILD.

biological father. See FATHER.

biological material. *Patents.* Patentable microorganisms — such as bacteria, fungi, algae, protozoa, and viruses — that are capable of self-replication. • To satisfy the Patent Act's enablement requirement, biological material that is the subject of a U.S. patent application must be deposited in an appropriate cell depository before the patent is granted.

biological mother. See MOTHER.

biological parent. See PARENT.

biological terrorism. See *bioterrorism* under TERRORISM.

biological warfare. See WARFARE.

biotechnology. *Patents.* A branch of molecular biology dealing with the use of biological processes to produce useful medical and industrial materials. Cf. GENETIC ENGINEERING.

Biotechnology Patent Process Protection Act. *Patents.* A 1995 federal statute that made biotechnological processes per se patentable if either the process or the resulting material is novel and nonobvious. 35 USCA § 103(b). — Also termed *Biotechnology Act.*

bioterrorism. See TERRORISM.

bipartite, *adj.* (16c) (Of an instrument) executed in two parts by both parties.

bird-dog fee. *Slang.* **1.** Money paid by a business to a person who directs consumers to the business. **2.** An illegal payment to a person who arranges a business deal; KICKBACK.

BIRPI. See INTERNATIONAL BUREAU FOR THE PROTECTION OF INTELLECTUAL PROPERTY.

birth. The complete emergence of a newborn baby from the mother's body. • The quotation below states the traditional legal view of *birth*. In a few jurisdictions, the state of the law may be changing. In South Carolina, for example, a child does not have to be born alive to be a victim of murder; a woman can be convicted of fetal murder if her baby is stillborn because of the mother's prenatal drug abuse.

birth certificate. A formal document that records a person's birthdate, birthplace, and parentage. • In all 50 states, an adopted child receives a second birth certificate reflecting his or her adoptive parents. In such a case, the original birth certificate is usu. sealed and can be opened only by court order. Some states allow limited access, depending on the year when an adoptee was born and (sometimes) on whether the birth parents consent. The trend today is to open records if (1) both the child and the biological parent consent — for example, through an adoption registry, or (2) the child requests and, upon notification, the biological parent does not veto the request. Oregon enacted the first statute to permit access to birth records upon the unilateral demand of the adopted child, once the child reaches the age of majority. See ADOPTION-REGISTRY STATUTE.

birth control. 1. Any means of preventing conception and pregnancy, usu. by mechanical or chemical means, but also by abstaining from intercourse. **2.** More narrowly, contraception.

birthday club. See GIFTING CLUB.

birth father. See *biological father* under FATHER.

birth injury. Harm that occurs to a fetus during the birth process, esp. during labor and delivery. Cf. PRENATAL INJURY.

birth mother. See MOTHER.

birth parent. See PARENT.

birth records. (1854) Statistical data kept by a governmental entity concerning people's birthdates, birthplaces, and parentage.

BIS. *abbr.* BUREAU OF INDUSTRY AND SECURITY.

bishop. The chief superintendent and highest-ranking member of the clergy within a diocese. • The bishop is subject to the archbishop of a province.

bishopric (bish-ə-prik). **1.** DIOCESE. **2.** The office of a bishop.

bishop's court. 1. An ecclesiastical court usu. held in the diocese cathedral and presided over by the bishop's chancellor. **2.** *Hist. Eccles. law.* (*cap.*) A court (usu.) held in the cathedral of a diocese, the judge being the bishop's chancellor, who applied civil canon law. • The jurisdiction included appeals from the Court of Archdeacon. In a large diocese, the bishop's chancellor would have commissaries in remote parts who held consistory courts. See CONSISTORY COURT.

biting rule. A rule of construction that once a deed or will grants a fee simple, a later provision attempting to cut down, modify, or qualify the grant will be held void.

***Bivens* action.** (1972) A lawsuit brought to redress a federal official's violation of a constitutional right. *Bivens v. Six Unknown Named Agents of the Federal Bureau of Narcotics*, 403 U.S. 388, 91 S.Ct. 1999 (1971). • A *Bivens* action allows federal officials to be sued in a manner similar to that set forth at 42 USCA § 1983 for state officials who violate a person's constitutional rights under color of state law.

.biz. *Trademarks.* A top-level domain name assigned by ICANN for use by businesses as distinct from individual, personal, or noncommercial use. See DOMAIN NAME; INTERNET CORPORATION FOR ASSIGNED NAMES AND NUMBERS.

B/L. *abbr.* BILL OF LADING.

Blackacre. (17c) A fictitious tract of land used in legal discourse (esp. law-school hypotheticals) to discuss real-property issues. • When another tract of land is needed in a hypothetical, it is often termed "Whiteacre."

Black Act. *Hist.* An English statute (9 Geo. ch. 22) establishing the death penalty for the unlawful killing or maiming of animals. • The statute was passed in 1722 in the wake of crimes committed by persons with faces blackened or otherwise disguised. The statute was repealed in 1827. The classic study of this law is E.P. Thompson, *Whips and Hunters: The Origins of the Black Act* (1975).

Black Book of the Exchequer. *Hist.* A record book containing treaties, conventions, charters, papal bulls, and other English state documents. • It dates from the 13th century. — Also termed *Liber Niger Parvus.*

black cap. A square cap worn by English judges on certain state or solemn occasions. • The black cap was formerly worn by judges when handing down a death sentence.

black codes. (*usu. cap.*) *Hist.* **1.** Antebellum state laws enacted to regulate slavery. **2.** Laws enacted shortly after the Civil War in the ex-Confederate states to restrict the liberties of the newly freed slaves to ensure a supply of inexpensive agricultural labor and to maintain white supremacy.

black economy. See SHADOW ECONOMY.

black-leg labor. See SCAB.

blackletter law. (18c) One or more legal principles that are old, fundamental, and well settled. • The term refers to the law printed in books set in Gothic type, which is very bold and black. — Also termed *hornbook law.*

blacklist, *vb.* (18c) To put the name of (a person) on a list of those who are to be boycotted or punished <the firm blacklisted the former employee>. — **blacklist,** *n.*

black-lung disease. See PNEUMOCONIOSIS.

blackmail, *n.* (16c) **1.** A threatening demand made without justification; EXTORTION. Cf. FEEMAIL; GRAYMAIL; GREENMAIL (1), (2). — **blackmail,** *vb.* **2.** BLACK RENT.

blackmail suit. See SUIT.

black maria. *Slang.* A locked van used by the police to transport prisoners to and from jail.

black market. 1. See MARKET. **2.** See SHADOW ECONOMY.

black-market adoption. 1. See ADOPTION. **2.** See SHADOW ECONOMY.

blackout period. *Trademarks.* The time between the examining attorney's approval of an intent-to-use application for publication in the Official Gazette and the issuance of a notice of allowance after publication, during which the applicant may not file a statement of use or make any other substantive amendment to the application.

black-rage insanity defense. See INSANITY DEFENSE.

black rent. *Hist.* Feudal rents paid in work, grain, or money baser than silver. — Also termed *blackmail*. Cf. WHITE RENT.

Black-Scholes formula. A mathematical model used to estimate the present value of stock options or warrants based on the exercise price, the length of the option's or warrant's exercise period, and the fair market value and volatility of the underlying security. • The term derives from Fischer Black and Myron Scholes, the names of the economists who presented the formula in *The Pricing of Options and Corporate Liabilities*, 81 J. Pol. Econ. 637 (1973).

Blackstone lawyer. *Slang.* **1.** A lawyer with a broad knowledge of blackletter principles. **2.** A self-educated lawyer (esp. in antebellum America) whose legal training consists primarily of reading Blackstone's *Commentaries.*

black ward. *Hist.* A subvassal; a vassal of the king's vassal.

Blaine amendment. A provision in a state constitution for stricter separation of church and state than is required by the Establishment Clause. • In 1875, at the request of President Ulysses S. Grant, Senator James G. Blaine proposed an amendment to the U.S. Constitution, applying the Free Exercise and Establishment Clause to the states, and specifically prohibiting the use of any state funds to support any religious institutions, including private church-run schools (esp. Roman Catholic). The House of Representatives passed the amendment, but the Senate narrowly voted against it. Many states, however, amended their constitutions to include a "Blaine Amendment" strictly prohibiting the use of public money for the support of religious institutions.

blame, *n.* **1.** An act of attributing fault; an expression of disapproval <the judge said that all the plaintiff's attorneys were to blame>. **2.** Responsibility for something wrong <blame rested with all the defendants>. — **blame,** *vb.* — **blameworthy, blamable,** *adj.*

blank acceptance. See ACCEPTANCE (4).

blank bar. *Hist.* A plea in bar interposed by a defendant in a trespass action. • This type of plea was filed to compel the plaintiff to state exactly where the alleged trespass occurred. — Also termed *common bar.*

blank bill. See BILL (6).

blank bond. See BOND (2).

blank check. See CHECK.

blank consent. A general authorization from a natural parent who voluntarily relinquishes a child for private adoption and allows adoption proceedings without further consent. • Jurisdictions are divided over whether a blank consent is valid if the natural parents do not identify and approve the prospective adoptive parents. — Also termed *blanket consent; general consent.*

blanket agreement. *Labor law.* A collective-bargaining agreement that applies to workers throughout an organization, industry, or geographical area.

blanket bond. See BOND (2).

blanket contract. See CONTRACT.

blanket license. See LICENSE.

blanket lien. See LIEN.

blanket mortgage. See MORTGAGE.

blanket order. 1. A judicial order that covers a broad subject or class. — Also termed *umbrella order.* See ORDER (2). **2.** See *blanket protective order* under PROTECTIVE ORDER. **3.** An order negotiated by a customer with a supplier for multiple purchases and deliveries of specified goods over a stated period, as an alternative to placing a separate order for each transaction. — Also termed *blanket purchase agreement; blanket purchase order.* See PURCHASE AGREEMENT; PURCHASE ORDER.

blanket policy. See INSURANCE POLICY.

blanket protective order. See PROTECTIVE ORDER.

blanket purchase agreement. See BLANKET ORDER (3).

blanket purchase order. See BLANKET ORDER (3).

blanket search warrant. See SEARCH WARRANT.

blank form. *Copyright.* A form, usu. one for record keeping and business purposes, that does not convey information until it has been filled in. • Blank forms are not eligible for copyright protection. — Also termed *business form*. See BLANK-FORMS RULE.

blank-forms rule. *Copyright.* The principle that forms are not protectable by copyright if they are designed for recording information but do not themselves convey any information. • The rule, first promulgated by the U.S. Supreme Court in *Baker v. Selden*, 101 U.S. 99 (1880), is now a U.S. Copyright Office regulation, 37 CFR § 202.1(c). See MERGER DOCTRINE (1).

blank indorsement. See INDORSEMENT.

blank stock. See STOCK.

blasphemy (**blas**-fə-mee), *n.* (13c) Irreverence toward God, religion, a religious icon, or something else considered sacred. • Blasphemy was a crime at common law and remains so in some U.S. jurisdictions, but it is rarely if ever enforced because of its questionable constitutionality under the First Amendment. Cf. PROFANITY. — **blaspheme** (blas-**feem** *or* blas-feem), *vb.* — **blasphemous** (**blas**-fə-məs), *adj.* — **blasphemer** (**blas**-fee-mər), *n.*

blended family. See FAMILY.

blended fund. See FUND (1).

blended sentence. See SENTENCE.

blended trust. See TRUST.

blending clause. (1947) A provision in a will disposing of both the testator's own property and the property over which the testator has a power of appointment, so that the two types of property are treated as a unit.

blind bidding. *Copyright.* In the licensing of movies for first-run engagements, the practice by film distributors of requiring theater owners to bid for and book movies without having seen them. • By statute, some states prohibit blind bidding.

blind entry. See ENTRY (2).

blind pig. See BLIND TIGER.

blind plea. See PLEA (1).

blind selling. (1946) The sale of goods without giving a buyer the opportunity to examine them.

blind tiger. *Slang.* A place where intoxicants are illegally sold. • This term was commonly used during Prohibition. — Also termed *blind pig*. See PROHIBITION (3).

blind trust. See TRUST.

bloc. (1903) A group of persons or political units aligned with a common interest or purpose, even if only temporarily <voting bloc>.

block, *n.* (18c) **1.** A municipal area enclosed by streets <three blocks away>. See LOT (1). **2.** A quantity of things bought or sold as a unit <a block of preferred shares>. **3.** SQUARE (1).

blockade. *Int'l law.* A belligerent's prevention of access to or egress from an enemy's ports by

stationing ships to intercept vessels trying to enter or leave those ports. • To be binding, a blockade must be effective — that is, it must be maintained by a force sufficient to prevent access to ports. — Also termed *simple blockade*; *de facto blockade*.

blockage rule. *Tax.* The principle that a large block of stock shares may be valued at less than the total value of the individual shares because such a large block may be difficult to sell at full price.

block booking, *n.* *Copyright.* In the licensing or use of movies, the practice by film distributors of conditioning the license or use on the acceptance of an entire package or block of films, which typically includes unwanted or inferior films. • In *United States v. Loew's Inc.*, 371 U.S. 38, 83 S.Ct. 97 (1962), the U.S. Supreme Court condemned block booking as an illegal tying arrangement that violates the Sherman Act.

***Blockburger* test.** *Criminal law.* A test, for double-jeopardy purposes, of whether a defendant can be punished separately for convictions on two charges or prosecuted later on a different charge after being convicted or acquitted on a charge involving the same incident; a comparison of two charges to see if each contains at least one element that the other does not. • Although the test is frequently called the *same-evidence test*, that term is misleading since the analysis involves the elements of the charged offenses rather than the facts of the incident. *Blockburger v. U.S.*, 284 U.S. 299, 304, 52 S.Ct. 180, 192 (1932). — Also termed *same-elements test*; *actual-evidence test*. Cf. SAME-CONDUCT TEST; SAME-TRANSACTION TEST.

blockbusting. (1954) The act or practice, usu. by a real-estate broker, of persuading one or more property owners to sell their property quickly, and often at a loss, to avoid an imminent influx of minority groups. • Blockbusting is illegal in many states.

blocked account. See ACCOUNT.

blocked currency. See CURRENCY.

blocked income. See INCOME.

block grant. An unrestricted grant of federal funds.

blocking patent. See PATENT (3).

block interest. See *add-on interest* under INTEREST (3).

block policy. See INSURANCE POLICY.

block voting. A shareholders' agreement to cast their votes in a single block. See *voting trust* under TRUST.

***Blonder–Tongue* doctrine.** *Patents.* The rule that a patentee is barred by collateral estoppel from relitigating the validity of a patent that has been held invalid in an earlier proceeding in which the patentee had a full and fair opportunity to litigate the patent's validity. • The rule was adopted by the U.S. Supreme Court in *Blonder–Tongue Laboratory, Inc. v. University of Illinois*, 402 U.S. 313, 91 S.Ct. 1434 (1971). — Also termed *Blonder–Tongue rule.*

blood. (13c) A relationship between persons arising by descent from a common ancestor. See RELATIVE.

entire blood. See *full blood.*

full blood. (1812) The relationship existing between persons having the same two parents; unmixed ancestry. — Also termed *whole blood; entire blood.*

half blood. (17c) The relationship existing between persons having the same father or mother, but not both parents in common. — Sometimes written *half-blood.* See *relative of the half blood* under RELATIVE.

heritable blood. *Hist.* A relationship between an ancestor and an heir that the law recognizes for purposes of passing good title to property. — Also termed *inheritable blood.*

mixed blood. (1817) *Archaic.* The relationship between persons whose ancestors are of different races or nationalities.

whole blood. See *full blood.*

blood, corruption of the. See CORRUPTION OF BLOOD.

blood alcohol content. (1926) The concentration of alcohol in one's bloodstream, expressed as a percentage. • Blood alcohol content is used to determine whether a person is legally intoxicated, esp. under a driving-while-intoxicated law. In many states, a blood alcohol content of .08% is enough to charge a person with an offense. — Abbr. BAC. — Also termed *blood alcohol count; blood alcohol concentration.* See DRIVING UNDER THE INFLUENCE; DRIVING WHILE INTOXICATED.

blood border. *Slang.* The dividing line between adjoining states that have different minimum drinking ages. • The term derives from the fact that juveniles from the state with the higher minimum age drive to the state with a lower minimum age, purchase and consume alcohol, and drive home intoxicated.

blood diamond. See CONFLICT DIAMOND.

blood feud. See FEUD (4).

blood-grouping test. (1930) A test used in paternity and illegitimacy cases to determine whether a particular man could be the father of a child, examples being the genetic-marker test and the human-leukocyte antigen test. • The test does not establish paternity; rather, it eliminates men who could not be the father. See PATERNITY TEST; GENETIC-MARKER TEST; HUMAN-LEUKOCYTE ANTIGEN TEST.

blood money. **1.** *Hist.* A payment given by a murderer's family to the next of kin of the murder victim. — Also termed *wer.* **2.** A reward given for the apprehension of a person charged with a crime, esp. capital murder.

blood relative. See RELATIVE.

blood test. The medical analysis of blood, esp. to establish paternity or (as required in some states) to test for sexually transmitted diseases in marriage-license applicants. See SEROLOGICAL TEST.

blotter. **1.** See ARREST RECORD. **2.** See WASTE BOOK.

BLS. *abbr.* BUREAU OF LABOR STATISTICS.

blue-blue-ribbon jury. See *blue-ribbon jury* under JURY.

Blue Book. **1.** A compilation of session laws. See SESSION LAWS (2). **2.** A volume formerly published to give parallel citation tables for a volume in the National Reporter System. **3.** *English law.* A government publication, such as a Royal Commission report, issued in a blue paper cover.

Bluebook. The citation guide — formerly titled *A Uniform System of Citation* — that is generally considered the authoritative reference for American legal citations. • The book's complete title is *The Bluebook: A Uniform System of Citation.* Although it has been commonly called the *Bluebook* for decades, the editors officially included *Bluebook* in the title only in the mid-1990s. The book is compiled by the editors of the *Columbia Law Review*, the *Harvard Law Review*, the *University of Pennsylvania Law Review*, and *The Yale Law Journal.* Cf. ALWD CITATION MANUAL.

bluebook, *vb.* To ensure the conformity of citations with *The Bluebook: A Uniform System of Citation.*

blue books. See SESSION LAWS.

blue chip, *n.* A corporate stock that is considered a safe investment because the corporation has a history of stability, consistent growth, and reliable earnings. • The term is said to come from poker, in which the blue chips usu. have the highest value. — Also termed *blue-chip stock.* — **blue-chip,** *adj.*

blue law. (1762) A statute regulating or prohibiting commercial activity on Sundays. • Although blue laws were formerly common, they have declined since the 1980s, when many courts held them invalid because of their origin in religion (i.e., Sunday being the Christian Sabbath). Blue laws usu. pass constitutional challenge if they are enacted to support a nonreligious purpose, such as a day of rest for workers. — Also termed *Sunday law; Sunday-closing law; Sabbath law; Lord's Day Act.*

Blue List. *Securities.* A daily listing (on blue paper) of secondary-market offerings of municipal bonds.

blue note. See NOTE (1).

blue-pencil test. (1921) A judicial standard for deciding whether to invalidate the whole contract or only the offending words. • Under this standard, only the offending words are invalidated if it would be possible to delete them simply by running a blue pencil through them, as opposed to changing, adding, or rearranging words.

blue-ribbon jury. See JURY.

blue-sky, *vb.* (1931) To approve (the sale of securities) in accordance with blue-sky laws <the company's IPO has not yet been blue-skyed>.

blue-sky, *adj.* (1906) (Of a security) having little value. • The term was first used in reference to the assets at issue in *Lowell v. People*, 131 Ill. App. 137 (1907) ("hot air and blue sky").

blue-sky law. (1912) A state statute establishing standards for offering and selling securities, the purpose being to protect citizens from investing in fraudulent schemes or unsuitable companies. • Such a statute typically includes provisions for licensing brokers, registering securities, and formal approvals of the offerings by the appropriate government agencies.

bluewater seaman. See *able-bodied seaman* under SEAMAN.

blurring, *n. Trademarks.* A form of dilution in which goodwill in a famous mark is eroded through the mark's unauthorized use by others on or in connection with dissimilar products or services. • Blurring is one type of dilution that is actionable under the Federal Trademark Dilution Act, 15 USCA § 1125(c). <The court found that Nabisco's use of a fish shape in its animal crackers diluted Pepperidge Farm's famous Goldfish trademark.> — Also termed *dilution by blurring*; *diminution.* Cf. TARNISHMENT.

board. 1. A group of persons having managerial, supervisory, or advisory powers <board of directors>. • In parliamentary law, a board is a form of deliberative assembly and is distinct from a committee — which is usu. subordinate to a board or other deliberative assembly — in having greater autonomy and authority. 2. Daily meals furnished to a guest at an inn, boardinghouse, or other lodging <room and board>. 3. BOARD OF DIRECTORS.

board-certified, *adj.* (1938) (Of a professional) recognized by an official body as a specialist in a given field of law or medicine <board-certified in civil litigation>. See BOARD OF LEGAL SPECIALIZATION.

board lot. See *round lot* under LOT (3).

board of adjustment. See ADJUSTMENT BOARD.

board of aldermen. See CITY COUNCIL.

Board of Appeals. *Patents & Trademarks. Hist.* A quasi-judicial body within the U.S. Patent and Trademark Office that was empowered to hear appeals by applicants whose patent applications had been wholly or partially rejected by patent examiners. • Its work is now done by the Board of Patent Appeals and Interferences. See BOARD OF PATENT APPEALS AND INTERFERENCES.

board of directors. (18c) 1. The governing body of a corporation, elected by the shareholders to establish corporate policy, appoint executive officers, and make major business and financial decisions. — Also termed (esp. in charitable organizations) *board of trustees.* See DIRECTOR. 2. The governing body of a corporation, partnership, association, or other organization, elected by the shareholders or members to establish policy, elect or appoint officers and committees, and make other governing decisions. — Often shortened (informally) to *board.* — Also termed *board of governors*; *board of managers*; *board of trustees* (esp. in charitable and educational organizations); *executive board.* See DIRECTOR.

   staggered board of directors. A board of directors whose members' terms of service overlap so that only part of the board's makeup is voted on in any single election. • Typically, members serve terms of two or more years, with some members' terms expiring at each annual election. See Del. Code Ann. tit. 8, § 141 (1991) (authorizing classified boards with two or three classes having two- or three-year terms). — Also termed *classified board of directors.*

board of education. A state or local agency that governs and manages public schools within a state or local district. Cf. SCHOOL BOARD.

board of equalization. See EQUALIZATION BOARD.

board of examiners. See EXAMINING BOARD.

board of fire underwriters. *Insurance.* An unincorporated voluntary association made up of fire insurers.

board of governors. 1. See BOARD OF DIRECTORS. 2. (*cap.*) FEDERAL RESERVE BOARD OF GOVERNORS.

Board of Green Cloth. *Hist.* A group of persons responsible for governing the royal-household staff, esp. in financial matters such as accounting for expenses and paying servants' wages. • The Board consisted of the Lord Steward and inferior officers, and its name derived from the green cloth that covered the table used by the Board to conduct its duties. In more ancient times, it kept the peace and maintained courts of justice within the area around the royal household (i.e., the *verge*). — Also termed *Counting House of the King's Household*; *Green Cloth.*

board of health. A municipal or state agency charged with protecting the public health.

Board of Immigration Appeals. The highest administrative tribunal for interpreting and applying United States immigration law, esp. reviewing appeals from adverse decisions of immigration judges and district directors of the Department of Homeland Security. ● The Board may have up to 15 permanent members appointed by the Attorney General. — Abbr. BIA. — Also termed *Immigration Appeals Board*.

board of legal specialization. (1969) A body, usu. an arm of a state bar association, that certifies qualified lawyers as specialists within a given field. ● Typically, to qualify as a specialist, a lawyer must meet a specified level of experience, pass an examination, and provide favorable recommendations from peers.

board of managers. See BOARD OF DIRECTORS.

Board of Medical Examiners. See EXAMINING BOARD.

board of pardons. (1872) A state agency, of which the governor is usu. a member, authorized to pardon persons convicted of crimes.

board of parole. See PAROLE BOARD.

Board of Patent Appeals and Interferences. *Patents & Trademarks.* The quasi-judicial body in the U.S. Patent and Trademark Office that hears (1) appeals from patent applicants whose claims have been rejected by a patent examiner, and (2) interference contests between two or more applicants trying to patent the same invention. ● This tribunal assumed the work previously handled by the Board of Appeals and the Board of Patent Interferences. The U.S. Court of Appeals for the Federal Circuit hears appeals from this tribunal. See INTERFERENCE (3).

board of police commissioners. An administrative tribunal vested with disciplinary powers over law-enforcement personnel.

board of regents. A group of persons appointed to supervise an educational institution, esp. a university.

board of registration. A state agency authorized to license and discipline members of a trade or profession.

board of review. 1. A body that reviews administrative-agency decisions. 2. A body that reviews property-tax assessments. 3. In some cities, a board that reviews allegations of police misconduct.

Board of Tax Appeals. See TAX COURT, U.S.

board of trade. 1. A federation of business executives dedicated to advancing and protecting business interests. 2. An organization that runs a commodities exchange. See CHICAGO BOARD OF TRADE. 3. *Hist.* The Lords of the Committee of the Privy Council that had jurisdiction over trade and foreign plantations. ● Today, the responsibilities once assigned to this committee are carried out by the Ministry for Trade and Industry.

board of trustees. See BOARD OF DIRECTORS.

Board of Veterans' Appeals. The agency in the U.S. Department of Veterans' Appeals responsible for reviewing decisions on entitlements to veterans' benefits. ● The Board's decisions are subject to review by the U.S. Court of Appeals for Veterans Claims. — Abbr. BVA.

board of zoning appeals. See ADJUSTMENT BOARD.

boatable, *adj.* See NAVIGABLE.

boatable water. See NAVIGABLE WATER (1).

bodily harm. See HARM.

bodily heir. See *heir of the body* under HEIR.

bodily injury. See INJURY.

body. (15c) 1. The main part of a written instrument, such as the central part of a statute (after the title and preamble) or the middle part of a complainant's bill in equity. 2. A collection of laws. — Also termed *body of laws*. See CORPUS JURIS. 3. An artificial person created by a legal authority. See CORPORATION. 4. An aggregate of individuals or groups. See BODY POLITIC. 5. A deliberative assembly <legislative body>. See *deliberative assembly* under ASSEMBLY. 6. An aggregate of individuals or groups <student body>. 7. BODY OF A CLAIM.

body corporate. See CORPORATION.

body execution. 1. See CAPIAS. 2. See EXECUTION.

body of a claim. *Patents.* The portion of a patent claim that defines the elements or steps of the invention. ● The body of the claim follows the preamble and transition phrase. In a combination claim, the body of a claim sets forth the elements of a patentable combination. Cf. PREAMBLE (2); TRANSITION PHRASE.

body of a county. A county as a whole.

body of laws. See BODY (2).

body politic. (15c) A group of people regarded in a political (rather than private) sense and organized under a common governmental authority.

body-snatching, *n.* The unlawful removal of a corpse, esp. from a grave. — **body-snatcher,** *n.*

bogus (boh-gəs), *adj.* Not genuine; counterfeit; SPURIOUS (1). Cf. GENUINE.

bogus check. See *bad check* under CHECK.

bogus will. See WILL.

boilerplate, *n.* (1893) 1. Ready-made or all-purpose language that will fit in a variety of documents. ● Originally, the term may have denoted a steel plate affixed to a boiler. But the modern sense comes from copy and artwork etched on metal plates (or molds made from a master plate) and distributed to newspapers and printers. The copy could not be edited. **2.** Fixed or standardized contractual language that the proposing party often views as relatively nonnegotiable. — **boilerplate,** *adj.*

boiler-room transaction. (1988) *Slang.* A high-pressure telephone sales pitch, often of a fraudulent nature. Cf. PHISHING; TELESCAM.

Bolger test. The judicial test for determining whether a statement is commercial speech, by examining (1) whether it is an advertisement; (2) whether it refers to a specific product or service; and (3) whether the speaker has an economic motivation for making the statement. *Bolger v. Youngs Drug Prods. Corp.,* 463 U.S. 60, 66–67, 103 S.Ct. 2875, 2879–80 (1983). • An affirmative answer to all three questions is "strong support" that the speech is commercial, but it is not dispositive; rather, the decision should be based on common sense.

bolster, *vb.* To enhance (unimpeached evidence) with additional evidence. • This practice is often considered improper when lawyers seek to enhance the credibility of their own witnesses.

bolts. *Hist.* Student-argued cases in the Inns of Court. • These practice cases were held privately, in contrast to the more formal and public *moots.* — Also termed *boltings.*

bombardment. *Int'l law.* An attack from land, sea, or air with weapons that are capable of destroying enemy targets at a distance with bombs, missiles, or projectiles.

bona (**boh**-nə), *n.* [Latin "goods"] Chattels; personal property.

bona adventitia (**boh**-nə ad-ven-**tish**-ee-ə). [Latin] **1.** *Roman law.* Goods acquired by free persons in some way other than through their paterfamilias, or by slaves in a way other than through their owner. **2.** *Civil law.* Goods acquired fortuitously, but not by inheritance. — Also spelled *bona adventicia.* — Also termed *adventitia bona.*

bona confiscata (**boh**-nə kon-fi-**skay**-tə). Goods confiscated by — or forfeited to — the Crown.

bona felonum (**boh**-nə fə-**loh**-nəm). Personal property belonging to a convicted felon.

bona forisfacta (**boh**-nə for-is-**fak**-tə). Forfeited goods.

bona fugitivorum (**boh**-nə fyoo-jə-ti-**vor**-əm). Goods belonging to a fugitive. — Also termed *bona utlagatorum.*

bona immobilia (**boh**-nə i-moh-**bil**-ee-ə). Immovable property.

bona mobilia (**boh**-nə moh-**bil**-ee-ə). [Latin] Movable property. See MOVABLE.

bona notabilia (**boh**-nə noh-tə-**bil**-ee-ə). Notable goods; property worth accounting for in a decedent's estate.

bona paraphernalia (**boh**-nə par-ə-fər-**nay**-lee-ə). Clothes, jewelry, and ornaments not included in a married woman's dowry.

bona peritura (**boh**-nə per-ə-**t[y]uur**-ə). Perishable goods; goods that an executor or trustee must diligently convert into money.

bona utlagatorum (**boh**-nə ət-lay-gə-**tor**-əm). See *bona fugitivorum.*

bona vacantia (**boh**-nə və-**kan**-shee-ə). [Latin "vacant goods"] **1.** Property not disposed of by a decedent's will and to which no relative is entitled under intestacy laws. See ESCHEAT. **2.** Ownerless property; goods without an owner. • *Bona vacantia* often resulted when a deceased person died without an heir willing and able to make a claim. The property either belonged to the finder or escheated to the Crown. — Sometimes shortened to *vacantia.* — Also termed *vacantia bona.*

bona waviata (**boh**-nə way-vee-**ay**-tə). Stolen goods thrown away in flight by a thief. • The goods escheated to the Crown as a penalty to the owner for failing to pursue the thief and recover the goods.

vacantia bona. See *bona vacantia.*

bona activa (**boh**-nə ak-**tɪ**-və). [Latin "active goods"] **1.** Assets. See ASSET (1). **2.** The claims that a person has against others.

bona fide (**boh**-nə fɪd *or* **boh**-nə **fɪ**-dee), *adj.* [Latin "in good faith"] (17c) **1.** Made in good faith; without fraud or deceit. **2.** Sincere; genuine. See GOOD FAITH. — **bona fide,** *adv.*

bona fide contract. See CONTRACT.

bona fide emptor (**boh**-nə fɪd-ee emp-tər). [Latin] Good-faith purchaser. See *bona fide purchaser* under PURCHASER (1).

bona fide holder for value. See HOLDER FOR VALUE.

bona fide intent to use. *Trademarks.* A specific, good-faith intention to use a mark in the ordinary course of trade in interstate commerce and not merely to reserve it for later use, as determined by objective circumstantial evidence. • A federal registration obtained under Lanham Act § 1(b) requires a bona fide intent to use the mark. If the required intent is later determined to be lacking, the registration may be invalidated.

bona fide judgment creditor. See JUDGMENT CREDITOR.

bona fide occupational qualification. (1945) An employment qualification that, although it may discriminate against a protected class (such as sex, religion, or national origin), relates to an essential job duty and is considered reasonably necessary to the operation of the particular business. • Such a qualification is not illegal under federal employment-discrimination laws. — Abbr. BFOQ.

bona fide operation. A real, ongoing business.

bona fide possession. See POSSESSION.

bona fide purchaser. See PURCHASER (1).

bona fide purchaser for value. See *bona fide purchaser* under PURCHASER (1).

bona fides (boh-nə **fi**-deez), *n.* [Latin] **1.** GOOD FAITH. **2.** *Roman law.* The standard of conduct expected of a reasonable person, esp. in making contracts and similar actions; acting without fraudulent intent or malice.

bona fide sale. See SALE.

bond, *n.* (16c) **1.** An obligation; a promise. **2.** A written promise to pay money or do some act if certain circumstances occur or a certain time elapses; a promise that is defeasible upon a condition subsequent; esp., an instrument under seal by which (1) a public officer undertakes to pay a sum of money if he or she does not faithfully discharge the responsibilities of office, or (2) a surety undertakes that if the public officer does not do so, the surety will be liable in a penal sum.

administrator's bond. See *fiduciary bond.*

appeal bond. (18c) A bond that an appellate court may require from an appellant in a civil case to ensure payment of the costs of appeal; a bond required as a condition to bringing an appeal or staying execution of the judgment appealed from. Fed. R. App. P. 7. Cf. *supersedeas bond.*

appearance bond. See *bail bond.*

arbitration bond. See ARBITRATION BOND.

attachment bond. A bond that a defendant gives to recover attached property. • The plaintiff then looks to the bond issuer to satisfy a judgment against the defendant.

average bond. See *general average bond.*

bail bond. (17c) A bond given to a court by a criminal defendant's surety to guarantee that the defendant will duly appear in court in the future and, if the defendant is jailed, to obtain the defendant's release from confinement. • The effect of the release on bail bond is to transfer custody of the defendant from the officers of the law to the custody of the surety on the bail bond, whose undertaking is to redeliver the defendant to legal custody at the time and place appointed in the bond. — Also termed *appearance bond*; *recognizance.* See BAIL.

bid bond. A bond filed in public construction projects to ensure that the bidding contractor

will enter into the contract. • The *bid bond* is a type of performance bond.

blank bond. *Archaic.* A bond in which the space for the creditor's name is left blank.

blanket bond. **1.** A bond covering several persons or projects that require performance bonds. **2.** See *fidelity bond.*

bond for land. A bond given by the seller of land to a buyer, binding the seller to convey once the buyer tenders the agreed price. — Also termed *bond for a deed.* Cf. BINDER (1).

bond of corroboration. An additional obligation undertaken to corroborate the debtor's original obligation.

bond to keep the peace. See *peace bond.*

bottomry bond. A contract for the loan of money on a ship, usu. at extraordinary interest, for maritime risks encountered during a certain period or for a certain voyage. • The loan can be enforced only if the vessel survives the voyage. — Also termed *bottomage bond.* Cf. *respondentia bond.*

claim-property bond. See *replevin bond.*

common-defeasance bond. See *penal bond.*

common-law bond. A performance bond given by a construction contractor. • A common-law bond exceeds the requirements of a statutory performance bond because it provides additional coverage for construction projects. Cf. PERFORMANCE BOND.

common money bond. A promise to pay money as a penalty for failing to perform a duty or obligation.

contract bond. See PERFORMANCE BOND.

cost bond. A bond given by a litigant to secure the payment of court costs.

counterbond. A bond to indemnify a surety.

delivery bond. See *forthcoming bond.*

depository bond. A bond given by a bank to protect a public body's deposits should the bank become insolvent.

discharging bond. (18c) A bond that both permits a defendant to regain possession of attached property and releases the property from the attachment lien. — Also termed *dissolution bond.* See *forthcoming bond.*

executor's bond. A bond given to ensure the executor's faithful administration of the estate. See *fiduciary bond.*

fidelity bond. A bond to indemnify an employer or business for loss due to embezzlement, larceny, or gross negligence by an employee or other person holding a position of trust. — Also termed *blanket bond.*

fiduciary bond. (1831) A type of surety bond required of a trustee, administrator, executor, guardian, conservator, or other fiduciary to ensure the proper performance of duties. — Also termed *administrator's bond*.

forthcoming bond. **1.** A bond guaranteeing that something will be produced or forthcoming at a particular time, or when called for. **2.** A bond (usu. given to a sheriff) to permit a person to repossess attached property in exchange for that person's commitment to surrender the property in the event of an adverse judgment; specif., a bond required of a defendant as a condition of retaining or regaining possession of a chattel in an attachment or replevin action, whereby the surety agrees to surrender the chattel and to pay its value if the plaintiff wins the lawsuit. — Also termed *delivery bond*. Cf. *replevin bond*.

general-average bond. *Maritime law.* A bond given to the captain of a ship by consignees of cargo subject to general average, guaranteeing payment of their contribution once it is ascertained. • When the contribution amounts are disputed, the carrier requires this bond before agreeing to unload the ship. It may also be required when the amounts are undisputed, as security for payment. — Also termed *average bond*. See *general average* under AVERAGE (3).

guaranty bond. A bond combining the features of a fidelity and a surety bond, securing both payment and performance.

hypothecation bond. *Maritime law.* A bond given in the contract of bottomry or respondentia.

indemnity bond. A bond to reimburse the holder for any actual or claimed loss caused by the issuer's or some other person's conduct.

injunction bond. A bond required of an injunction applicant to cover the costs incurred by a wrongfully enjoined party; a bond required as a condition of the issuance or continuance of a bond. Fed. R. Civ. P. 65(c).

interim bond. **1.** A bond set by a police officer when a person is arrested for a minor offense, such as a misdemeanor, without a warrant. • Although the bond allows the arrestee to be released, it requires that the person be available for arraignment. **2.** A bond set by a judge or magistrate and attached to a misdemeanor warrant.

judicial bond. (18c) A bond to indemnify an adverse party in a lawsuit against loss occasioned by delay or by deprivation of property resulting from the lawsuit. • Judicial bonds are usu. classified according to the nature of the action in which they are required, as with appeal bonds, injunction bonds, attachment bonds, replevin bonds, forthcoming or redelivery bonds, and bail bonds. A bond of a fiduciary — such as

a receiver, administrator, executor, or guardian — is often required as a condition to appointment.

liability bond. A bond intended to protect the assured from a loss arising from some event specified in the bond.

license bond. A bond required of a person seeking a license to engage in a specified business or to receive a certain privilege. — Also termed *permit bond*.

maintenance bond. A bond guaranteeing against construction defects for a period after the completion of the contracted-for work.

negotiable bond. A bond that can be transferred from the original holder to another.

official bond. **1.** A bond given by a public officer requiring the faithful performance of the duties of office. **2.** A bond filed by an executor, guardian, trustee, or other fiduciary. See *fiduciary bond*.

payment bond. (1877) A bond given by a surety to cover any amounts that, because of the general contractor's default, are not paid to a subcontractor or materials supplier.

peace bond. (1846) A bond required by a court from a person who has breached or threatened to breach the peace. — Also termed *bond to keep the peace*. See BREACH OF THE PEACE.

penal bond. (17c) A bond requiring the obligor to pay a specified sum as a penalty if the underlying obligation is not performed. — Also termed *penal bill*; *common-defeasance bond*.

performance bond. See PERFORMANCE BOND.

permit bond. See *license bond*.

personal bond. **1.** See *bail bond*. **2.** A written document in which an obligor formally recognizes an obligation to pay money or to do a specified act. **3.** *Scots law.* A bond containing a promise without security.

probate bond. A bond, such as that filed by an executor, required by law to be given during a probate proceeding to ensure faithful performance by the person under bond.

redelivery bond. See *replevin bond*.

refunding bond. A bond given to assure an executor that a legatee will return an estate distribution should the remaining estate assets be insufficient to pay the other legacies.

registered bond. A governmental or corporate obligation to pay money, represented by a single certificate delivered to the creditor. • The obligation is registered in the holder's name on the books of the debtor.

removal bond. **1.** A bond to cover possible duties owed by a person who removes goods from a warehouse for export. **2.** A bond required in some states when a litigant seeks to remove an action to another court.

replevin bond (ri-**plev**-in). **1.** A bond given by a plaintiff to replevy or attach property in the defendant's possession before judgment is rendered in a replevin action. ● The bond protects the attaching officer and ensures the property's safekeeping until the court decides whether it should be returned to the defendant. — Also termed *replevy bond.* See REPLEVIN. **2.** A bond given by a defendant in a replevin action to regain attached property pending the outcome of litigation. ● The bond does not discharge the attachment lien. — Also termed *replevy bond; claim-property bond; redelivery bond.* Cf. *forthcoming bond.*

respondentia bond (re-spon-**den**-shee-ə *or* ree-). A contract containing the pledge of a ship's cargo; a mortgage of a ship's cargo. Cf. *bottomry bond.*

simple bond. 1. A bond without a penalty. **2.** A bond payable to a named obligee on demand or on a certain date.

statutory bond. A bond that literally or substantially meets the requirements of a statute.

straw bond. (1876) A bond, usu. a bail bond, that carries either a fictitious name or the name of a person who is unable to pay the sum guaranteed; a worthless or inadequate bond.

submission bond. A bond given by a litigant who agrees to submit a lawsuit to arbitration and to be bound by an arbitrator's award.

supersedeas bond (soo-pər-**see**-dee-əs). (18c) An appellant's bond to stay execution on a judgment during the pendency of the appeal. Fed. R. Civ. P. 62(d); Fed. R. App. P. 8(b). — Often shortened to *supersedeas.* See SUPERSEDE (2). Cf. *appeal bond.*

surety bond. See PERFORMANCE BOND.

ten-percent bond. A bail bond in the amount of 10% of the bond otherwise required for a defendant's release. ● This type of bond usu. allows a defendant to arrange a bond without the services of a bondsman or other surety.

unsecured bail bond. A bond that holds a defendant liable for a breach of the bond's conditions (such as failure to appear in court), but that is not secured by a deposit of or lien on property. See RECOGNIZANCE.

3. A long-term, interest-bearing debt instrument issued by a corporation or governmental entity, usu. to provide for a particular financial need; esp., such an instrument in which the debt is secured by a lien on the issuer's property. Cf. DEBENTURE.

accrual bond. A bond — usu. the last collateralized-mortgage-obligation issue — from which no principal or interest payment will be made until any bonds issued earlier have been fully paid. — Also termed *Z-bond.*

adjustment bond. A bond issued when a corporation is reorganized. — Also termed *reorganization bond.*

annuity bond. A bond that lacks a maturity date and that perpetually pays interest. — Also termed *consol; perpetual bond; continued bond; irredeemable bond.*

arbitrage bond. A municipal bond, the proceeds of which are invested in bonds paying a higher yield than that paid by the municipality on its own bonds. ● Under the Internal Revenue Code, the tax-free aspect of municipal-bond income may be lost if the bonds are classified as arbitrage bonds. See ARBITRAGE.

assessment bond. A municipal bond repaid from property assessment taxes.

assumed bond. See *guaranteed bond* (1).

baby bond. A bond usu. having a face value of $1,000 or less.

bearer bond. (1887) A bond payable to the person holding it. ● The transfer of possession transfers the bond's ownership. Cf. *registered bond.*

bond and mortgage. A bond that is backed by a mortgage on realty. — Also termed *mortgage bond.* Cf. DEBENTURE (3).

book-entry bond. A bond for which no written certificate is issued to reflect ownership.

callable bond. (1926) See *redeemable bond.*

chattel-mortgage bond. A bond secured by a mortgage on personal property.

closed-end mortgage bond. A mortgage bond with provisions prohibiting the debtor from issuing additional bonds against the bond's collateral.

collateral trust bond. 1. A bond representing a debt secured by the deposit of another security with a trustee. — Also termed *collateral trust certificate.* **2.** A long-term corporate bond that is secured by other companies' mortgage bonds held by the corporation, which pledges and deposits the mortgage bonds in trust. ● The interest on these collateral trust bonds is typically lower than that received on the bonds pledged; the surplus is used to form a sinking fund to redeem the collateral trust bonds. A holding company often issues these bonds by pledging the stock of a subsidiary.

commodity-backed bond. A bond with interest payments or principal repayment tied to the price of a specific commodity, such as gold. ● This type of bond, which has a low interest rate but provides a hedge against inflation because the commodity price will usu. rise, is often issued by a firm with a stake in the commodity.

consolidated bond. **1.** A railroad bond secured by a mortgage on the entire railroad line formed by several consolidated railroads. Cf. *divisional bond.* **2.** A single bond that replaces two or more outstanding issues.

construction bond. A bond issued by a governmental entity for a building project.

continued bond. See *annuity bond.*

convertible bond. (1857) A bond that can be exchanged for stock shares in the corporation that issued the bond.

corporate bond. **1.** An interest-bearing instrument containing a corporation's promise to pay a fixed sum of money at some future time. • A corporate bond may be secured or unsecured. **2.** A bond issued by a corporation, usu. having a maturity of ten years or longer.

county bond. A county-issued bond paid through a levy on a special taxing district, whether or not the district is coextensive with the county.

coupon bond. A bond with attached interest coupons that the holder may present to receive interest payments. See BOND COUPON.

cumulative income bond. See *income bond.*

cushion bond. A bond paying an uncommonly high interest rate.

debenture bond. See DEBENTURE (3).

deferred-interest bond. A bond whose interest payments are postponed for a time.

discount bond. (1918) A bond sold at its current market value, which is less than its face value. — Also termed *non-interest-bearing bond.*

divisional bond. A railroad bond secured by a mortgage on a specific segment of a consolidated railroad system. Cf. *consolidated bond* (1).

endorsed bond. See *guaranteed bond* (1).

equipment trust bond. A bond secured by tangible property, such as an airplane. • A trustee usu. holds title to the equipment, which is leased to the issuer. — Also termed *equipment trust certificate.*

ex coupon bond. A bond sold without coupons attached.

ex legal municipal bond. A municipal bond that does not have the legal opinion of a bond-law firm printed on it. Cf. *municipal bond.*

first-mortgage bond. A long-term bond that has the first claim on specified assets.

flat bond. A bond that trades without accrued interest.

floating-interest bond. A bond with an interest rate that moves up and down with changing economic conditions.

flower bond. A Treasury bond redeemable before maturity if used to settle federal estate taxes. • Flower bonds were issued before April 1971 and reached final maturity in 1998. Two etymological theories have been advanced to explain the term. The first, and more likely, is that the bonds had flowers engraved on their reverse side. The second is that they "blossomed" upon the death of their owner.

foreign bond. A bond issued in a currency different from that used where the issuer is located, such as a Canadian-government bond that is denominated in U.S. dollars and issued in the United States.

full-faith-and-credit bond. See *general-obligation bond.*

general-mortgage bond. A corporate bond secured by a blanket mortgage on property. • The general-mortgage bond, however, is often less valuable because it is subordinate to prior mortgages.

general-obligation bond. A municipal bond payable from general revenue rather than from a special fund. • Such a bond has no collateral to back it other than the issuer's taxing power. — Often shortened to *obligation bond.* — Also termed *full-faith-and-credit bond.*

gold bond. **1.** *Hist.* A bond payable in gold coin or U.S. currency at the election of the bondholder. • This type of bond existed until 1933, when the U.S. monetary system abandoned the gold standard. **2.** A commodity-backed bond that is secured by gold and issued by a gold-mining company.

government bond. **1.** See *savings bond.* **2.** See *government security* under SECURITY.

guaranteed bond. **1.** A bond issued by a corporation and guaranteed by a third party. • This type of bond is common among railroads. — Also termed *endorsed bond; assumed bond; joint bond.* **2.** A bond issued by a subsidiary corporation whose parent corporation guarantees the principal and interest payments.

high-yield bond. A high-risk, high-yield subordinated bond issued by a company with a credit rating below investment grade. — Also termed *junk bond; high-yield debt obligation.*

improvement bond. See *revenue bond.*

income bond. A corporate bond secured by the corporation's net income, after the payment of interest on senior debt. • Sometimes this type of bond is a *cumulative-income bond,* in which case, if the income in any year is insufficient to pay the full interest, the deficit is carried forward as a lien on any future income. — Also termed *cumulative income bond*.

indeterminate bond. A callable bond with no set maturity date.

industrial-development bond. 1. A type of revenue bond in which interest and principal payments are backed by a corporation rather than a municipality. • This type of bond usu. finances a private business facility. **2.** A tax-exempt municipal bond that finances a usu. local industry. — Also termed *industrial-revenue bond*.

interchangeable bond. A bond that can be exchanged for a different type of bond, such as a coupon bond that may be exchanged for a registered bond.

interest bond. A bond paid in lieu of interest due on other bonds.

investment-grade bond. A bond with a rating of BBB or better by the leading bond rating services. See INVESTMENT-GRADE RATING.

irredeemable bond. See *annuity bond*.

joint and several bond. A bond in which the principal and interest are guaranteed by two or more obligors.

joint bond. A bond signed by two or more obligors. • In contrast to a joint and several bond, all the obligors must be joined if an action is brought on the bond.

junior bond. A bond subordinate in priority to another bond.

junk bond. (1974) See *high-yield bond*.

leasehold-mortgage bond. A bond issued by a lessee and secured by the lessee's leasehold interest.

Lloyd's bond. *Hist. English law.* A corporate bond issued on work done or goods delivered. • A bond issued in this manner avoids any restriction on indebtedness existing either in law or in corporate bylaws. The term supposedly derives from an English lawyer named Lloyd, who is credited with devising the method.

mortgage bond. A bond secured by the issuer's real property.

multimaturity bond. See *put bond*.

municipal bond. (1858) A bond issued by a non-federal government or governmental unit, such as a state bond to finance local improvements. • The interest received from a municipal bond may be exempt from federal, state, and local taxes. — Often shortened (in plural) to *municipals*; *munies*. — Also termed *municipal security*. Cf. *ex legal municipal bond*.

noncallable bond. See *noncallable security* under SECURITY.

non-interest-bearing bond. See *discount bond*.

nonstatutory bond. See *voluntary bond*.

obligation bond. See *general obligation bond*.

open-end mortgage bond. A mortgage bond that can be used as security for another bond issue.

optional bond. A bond that the holder may redeem before its maturity date if the issuer agrees.

option tender bond. See *put bond*.

participating bond. A bond that entitles the holder to a share of corporate profits but does not have a fixed interest rate.

passive bond. A bond bearing no interest. See *passive debt* under DEBT.

perpetual bond. See *annuity bond*.

post-obit bond. An agreement by which a borrower promises to pay to the lender a lump sum (exceeding the amount advanced) upon the death of a person whose property the borrower expects to inherit. • Equity traditionally enforces such bonds only if the terms are just and reasonable. — Also termed *post-obit agreement*.

premium bond. (1871) A bond with a selling price above face or redemption value. See PREMIUM (3).

put bond. A bond that gives the holder the right to redeem it for full value at specified times before maturity. — Also termed *multimaturity bond*; *option tender bond*. Cf. *put option* under OPTION.

railroad-aid bond. A bond issued by a public body to fund railway construction.

redeemable bond. A bond that the issuer may call for payment. — Also termed *callable bond*.

re-funding bond. A bond that retires an outstanding bond.

registered bond. (1865) A bond that only the holder of record may redeem, enjoy benefits from, or transfer to another. Cf. *bearer bond*.

reorganization bond. See *adjustment bond*.

revenue bond. A government bond repayable from public funds. — Also termed *improvement bond*.

savings bond. (1948) A nontransferable bond issued by the U.S. government. — Also termed *government bond*.

school bond. A bond issued by a city or school district to fund school construction.

secured bond. (1849) A bond backed by some type of security. Cf. DEBENTURE (1), (3).

serial bond. (1889) A bond issued concurrently with other bonds having different maturity dates.

series bonds. (1920) A group of bonds issued under the authority of the same indenture, but offered publicly at different times and with different maturity dates and interest rates.

single bond. See *bill obligatory* under BILL (7).

sinking-fund bond. A bond backed by a sinking fund for bond redemption. See *sinking fund* under FUND (1).

special-tax bond. A municipal bond secured by taxes levied for a specific governmental purpose, usu. improvements. — Also termed *special-assessment bond.*

state bond. A bond issued by a state.

statutory bond. A bond given in accordance with a statute.

subordinated bond. See *junior bond.*

tax-exempt bond. A bond that pays tax-free interest.

term bond. A bond that matures concurrently with other bonds in that issue.

TIPS bond. See TREASURY BOND.

Treasury bond. See TREASURY BOND.

unsecured bond. See DEBENTURE (3).

voluntary bond. A bond not required by statute but given anyway. — Also termed *nonstatutory bond.*

Z-bond. See *accrual bond.*

zero-coupon bond. (1979) A bond paying no interest. • It is sold at a discount price and later redeemed at face value, the profit being the difference. — Also termed *passive bond.* See *zero-coupon security* under SECURITY.

bond, *vb.* (16c) **1.** To secure payment by providing a bond <at the creditor's insistence, Gabriel consolidated and bonded his various loans>. **2.** To provide a bond for (a person) <the company bonded its off-site workers>.

bondable, *adj.* Capable of obtaining a bond to protect another person; of or relating to a person whose record is sufficiently clear of criminal convictions or other evidence of questionable character that a bonding agency would be willing to guarantee the person's conduct. See BOND (2).

bond and mortgage. See BOND (3).

bond conversion. The exchange of a convertible bond for another asset, usu. stock.

bond coupon. The part of a coupon bond that is clipped by the holder and surrendered to obtain an interest payment. See *coupon bond* under BOND (3).

bond covenant. A bond-indenture provision that protects bondholders by specifying what the issuer may or may not do, as by prohibiting the issuer

from issuing more debt. See BOND INDENTURE (1).

bond creditor. See CREDITOR.

bond discount. See DISCOUNT (3).

bond dividend. See DIVIDEND.

bonded, *adj.* (1945) (Of a person or entity) acting under, or placed under, a bond <a bonded court official>.

bonded debt. See DEBT.

bonded warehouse. See WAREHOUSE.

bond for a deed. See *bond for land* under BOND (2).

bond for deed. 1. See CONVEYANCE (6). **2.** See BOND FOR TITLE.

bond for land. See BOND (2).

bond for title. *Real estate.* The seller's retention of legal title until the buyer pays the purchase price. — Also termed *bond for deed.* Cf. *contract for deed* under CONTRACT.

bond fund. See MUTUAL FUND.

bondholder. One who holds a government or business bond.

bond indenture. (1891) **1.** A contract between a bond issuer and a bondholder outlining a bond's face value, interest rate, maturity date, and other features. **2.** A mortgage held on specified corporate property to secure payment of the bond.

bonding company. See COMPANY.

bond issue. See ISSUE (2).

bondman. See BONDSMAN (2).

bond of corroboration. See BOND (2).

bond premium. See PREMIUM (3).

bond rating. A system of evaluating and appraising the investment value of a bond issue.

bond retirement. (1897) The cancellation of a bond that has been called or paid.

bondsman. (13c) **1.** One who guarantees a bond; a surety. **2.** *Hist.* A serf or peasant; VILLEIN. — Also termed (in sense 2) *bondman.*

bond table. A schedule used in determining a bond's current value by its coupon rate, its time to maturity, and its effective yield if held to maturity.

bond trust. See TRUST.

bonification (bahn-ə-fi-**kay**-shən). A tax remission, usu. on goods intended for export. • Bonification enables a commodity to be sold in a foreign market as if it had not been taxed.

bonitarian (bahn-ə-**tair**-ee-in), *adj. Roman law.* **1.** Equitable or beneficial. — Also termed *bonitary.* Cf. QUIRITARIAN. **2.** *Hist.* Pertaining to or designating a property interest governed by praetorian edict rather than civil law. See *edictum praetoris* under EDICTUM.

bonitary (bahn-ə-**tair**-ee-in), *adj.* Equitable; BONITARIAN (1).

bonitary ownership. See OWNERSHIP.

bonus. (18c) **1.** A premium paid in addition to what is due or expected <year-end bonus>. • In the employment context, workers' bonuses are not a gift or gratuity; they are paid for services or on consideration in addition to or in excess of the compensation that would ordinarily be given. **2.** BOUNTY (3). **3.** *Oil & gas.* A payment that is made in addition to royalties and rent as an incentive for a lessor to sign an oil-and-gas lease <the lessee received a large bonus at closing>.

  performance bonus. A bonus given as a reward for outstanding productivity.

bonus share. See *bonus stock* under STOCK.

bonus stock. See STOCK.

bonus zoning. See *incentive zoning* under ZONING.

boodle. *Slang.* Money paid as a bribe, usu. to a public official.

boodling. *Hist. Slang.* Bribery. — **boodle**, *vb.*

book, *vb.* (13c) **1.** To record in an accounting journal (as a sale or accounting item) <Jenkins booked three sales that day>. **2.** To record the name of (a person arrested) in a sequential list of police arrests, with details of the person's identity (usu. including a photograph and a fingerprint), particulars about the alleged offense, and the name of the arresting officer <the defendant was booked immediately after arrest>. **3.** To engage (someone) contractually as a performer or guest <although the group was booked for two full performances, the lead singer, Raven, canceled and this action ensued>. See BOOKING CONTRACT.

book account. See ACCOUNT.

book entry. (18c) **1.** A notation made in an accounting journal. **2.** The method of reflecting ownership of publicly traded securities whereby a customer of a brokerage firm receives confirmations of transactions and monthly statements, but not stock certificates. See CENTRAL CLEARING SYSTEM.

book-entry bond. See BOND (3).

book equity. The percentage of a corporation's book value allocated to a particular class of stock. Cf. BOOK VALUE; MARKET EQUITY.

bookie. See BOOKMAKER.

booking contract. An agreement by which an actor or other performer is engaged.

bookkeeping, *n.* (17c) The mechanical recording of debits and credits or the summarizing of financial information, usu. about a business enterprise. Cf. ACCOUNTING.

  double-entry bookkeeping. A method of bookkeeping in which every transaction recorded by a business involves one or more "debit" entries and one or more "credit" entries. • The debit entries must equal the credit entries for each transaction recorded.

  single-entry bookkeeping. A method of bookkeeping in which each transaction is recorded in a single record, such as a record of cash or credit accounts.

bookland (**buuk**-land). *Hist.* Land held under royal charter or deed; freehold land. • This was a privileged form of ownership (usu. free of the customary burdens on land) generally reserved for churches and leaders. — Also spelled *bocland; bockland.* — Also termed *charter-land.* Cf. LOANLAND; FOLKLAND.

bookmaker. A person who determines odds and receives bets on the outcome of events, esp. sports events. — Also termed *bookie.* See BOOKMAKING.

bookmaking. Gambling that entails the taking and recording of bets on an event, esp. a sporting event such as a horse race or football game.

book of original entry. A day-to-day record in which a business's transactions are first recorded.

books of account. See SHOP BOOKS.

book value. (1894) **1.** The value at which an asset is carried on a balance sheet. Cf. BOOK EQUITY. — Also termed *carrying value.* **2.** See OWNER'S EQUITY.

  adjusted book value. The current actual value of an asset or liability as compared to the value when it was first acquired or incurred or when changes were previously updated.

  net book value. See OWNER'S EQUITY.

book-value stock. See STOCK.

boomage. **1.** A fee charged by a company for collecting and distributing logs that have accumulated in its boom (i.e., a line of sawed logs collected and stored on a stream's surface). **2.** A right to enter on riparian lands to fasten booms. **3.** An anchorage fee charged by a canal proprietor.

boon day. (*usu. pl.*) *Hist.* One of several days in the year when copyhold tenants were obliged to perform base services for the lord (such as reaping corn) without pay. — Also termed *due day.* — Sometimes (erroneously) termed *bind day.*

boot, *n.* **1.** *Tax.* Supplemental money or property subject to tax in an otherwise tax-free exchange. **2.** *Corporations.* In a corporate reorganization, anything received other than the stock or securities of a controlled corporation. **3.** *Commercial* *law.* Cash or other consideration used to balance an otherwise unequal exchange. **4.** *Hist.* ESTOVERS (1). **5.** BOTE (1).

boot camp. (1916) **1.** A camp for basic training of Navy or Marine Corps recruits. **2.** A military-like facility esp. for juvenile offenders. ● Boot camps are specialized programs for offenders who are generally nonviolent males from 17 to 25 years old. While proponents applaud the success of these programs, others find their long-term success limited at best. See *shock incarceration* under INCARCERATION.

bootleg, *vb. Copyright.* To make, distribute, or traffic in unauthorized sound or video recordings of live, broadcast, or recorded performances that have not been commercially released by the copyright owner. ● The term strictly applies only to unauthorized copies of commercially unreleased performances. *Dowling v. United States,* 473 U.S. 207, 209 n. 2, 105 S.Ct. 3127, 3129 n. 2 (1985) (Blackmun, J.). See PIRACY (4). — **bootleg,** *vb.* — **bootleg; bootlegged,** *adj.*

bootleg copy. *Copyright.* See BOOTLEG RECORDING (1).

bootlegger, *n.* A person who manufactures, transports, or sells something illegally, esp. alcoholic beverages. See MOONSHINE.

bootleg recording, *n. Copyright.* **1.** An unauthorized fixation or copy of a live or broadcast performance in a tangible medium or digital duplication made available over the Internet. — Also termed *bootleg copy, underground recording, import recording.* **2.** See PIRATE RECORDING. **3.** COUNTERFEIT RECORDING.

bootstrap, *vb.* (1951) **1.** To succeed despite sparse resources. **2.** To reach an unsupported conclusion from questionable premises.

bootstrap doctrine. (1940) *Conflict of laws.* The doctrine that forecloses collateral attack on the jurisdiction of another state's court that has rendered final judgment. ● The doctrine applies when a court in an earlier case has taken jurisdiction over a person, over status, or over land. It is based on the principle that under res judicata, the parties are bound by the judgment, whether the issue was the court's jurisdiction or something else. The bootstrap doctrine, however, cannot give effectiveness to a judgment by a court that had no subject-matter jurisdiction. For example, parties cannot, by appearing before a state court, "bootstrap" that court into having jurisdiction over a federal matter.

bootstrap sale. See SALE.

booty. 1. *Int'l law.* Movables taken from the enemy as spoils in the course of warlike operations. — Also termed *spoils of war.* **2.** Property taken by force or piracy; prize or loot.

BOP. *abbr.* BUREAU OF PRISONS.

border. A boundary between one nation (or a political subdivision) and another.

Border and Transportation Security Directorate. The division of the U.S. Department of Homeland Security responsible for maintaining the safety of the nation's borders and transportation systems. ● The Directorate includes the Transportation Security Administration, the U.S. Customs Service, the border security functions of the U.S. Citizenship and Immigration Service, the Animal & Plant Health Inspection Service, and the Federal Law Enforcement Training Center. It is the Department's largest division. — Abbr. BTS.

border control. *Int'l law.* A country's physical manifestation of its territorial sovereignty, by which it regulates which people and goods may enter and leave. ● As a practical matter, border controls are often used to contain plant and animal diseases, fight terrorism, and detect the movement of criminals.

bordereau (bor-də-**roh**), *n.* **1.** A description of reinsured risks; esp., a periodic report provided by a cedent to a treaty reinsurer, consisting of basic information affecting the reinsurance treaty, such as the underlying insureds, the types of risks covered, policies, and dates of loss. See REINSURANCE TREATY. **2.** A detailed note of account. Pl. **bordereaux.** — **bordereau,** *vb.*

border search. See SEARCH.

border warrant. See WARRANT (1).

bork (bork), *vb.* (1987) *Slang.* **1.** (Of the U.S. Senate) to reject a nominee, esp. for the U.S. Supreme Court, on grounds of the nominee's political and legal philosophy. ● The term derives from the name of Robert Bork, President Ronald Reagan's unsuccessful nominee for the Supreme Court in 1987. **2.** (Of political and legal activists) to embark on a media campaign to pressure U.S. Senators into rejecting a President's nominee. **3.** Generally, to smear a political opponent.

born-alive test. 1. Under the common law, a showing that an infant was completely expelled from the mother's womb and possessed a separate and independent existence from the mother. **2.** A showing that an infant, at the time of birth, was capable of living a separate and independent existence (regardless of how long the infant actually lived). ● This test was first announced in *Bonbrest v. Kotz,* 65 F. Supp. 138 (D.D.C. 1946).

born valid. *Patents.* Presumed to be good; entitled to the legal presumption that a patent was justified when issued and that challengers bear the burden of proving by clear and convincing evidence that the patent should not have been granted. ● Defenses against infringement claims take three tacks: denying that the product infringes on the plaintiff's rights, challenging the validity of the patent itself, or challenging its enforceability. — Also termed *presumption of validity*.

borough (bər-ə), *n.* **1.** A town or township with a municipal charter, such as one of the five political divisions of New York City. **2.** *English law.* A chartered town that originally sent a member to Parliament. **3.** *Hist.* A fortified or important town. — Also spelled *burgh*.

borough court. *English law.* An inferior civil court of record, usu. presided over by the municipal recorder. • Most borough courts were abolished by Parliament in 1972. Cf. RECORDER (1).

borough English. *Hist.* A common-law rule of descent whereby the youngest son (or sometimes the youngest daughter or collateral heir) inherited all his father's lands. • If the landowner had no issue, his youngest brother inherited the land. This practice applied to socage tenures in some parts of England. It was abolished by statute in 1925. — Also termed *postremogeniture*; *ultimogeniture*. — Also termed *burgh English*; *burgh Engloys*. See PRIMOGENITURE.

borrow, *vb.* **1.** To take something for temporary use. **2.** To receive money with the understanding or agreement that it must be repaid, usu. with interest. See LOAN.

borrowed capital. Funds lent to a corporation or other entity to finance its operations, such as cash dividends that are declared by a corporation but temporarily retained (with stockholder approval) to provide operating funds.

borrowed employee. See EMPLOYEE.

borrowed servant. See *borrowed employee* under EMPLOYEE.

borrowed-statutes doctrine. The principle that if one state adopts a statute identical to that of another state, any settled judicial construction of that statute by the courts of the other state is binding on the courts of the state that later enacts the statute.

borrower. A person or entity to whom money or something else is lent.

borrowing statute. (1934) A legislative exception to the conflict-of-laws rule holding that a forum state must apply its own statute of limitations. • A borrowing statute specifies the circumstances in which a forum state will apply another state's statute of limitations.

borsholder (**bors**-hohl-dər). *Hist.* **1.** The chief of a tithing or frankpledge. **2.** A petty constable. — Also termed *borough-holder*; *borrowhead*; *headborough*.

Boston interest. See INTEREST (3).

bote (boht). [Anglo-Saxon] *Hist.* **1.** A compensation or profit; esp., an allowance of wood; ESTOVERS (1). — Also spelled *bot*; *boot*.

brigbote. See BRIGBOTE.

cartbote. See *plowbote*.

firebote. See *housebote*.

haybote. See HAYBOTE.

hedgebote. See HAYBOTE.

housebote. An allowance of wood from the estate used to repair a house or to burn in the fireplace. — Also termed *firebote*.

plowbote. An allowance of wood for the construction and repair of farm equipment. — Also termed *cartbote*.

wainbote. An allowance of wood for the repair of wagons.

2. A compensatory payment for causing an injury. Cf. BOTELESS.

Godbote. A church fine paid for offenses against God.

hadbote. *Hist.* Amends for an affront to or violence against a person in holy orders. — Also spelled *had-bot*.

kinbote. See *manbote*.

lowbote. See LOWBOTE.

maegbote (**mag**-boht). Bote paid to the relatives of an injured person.

manbote. Compensation for killing someone. — Also termed *kinbote*.

theftbote (**theft**-boht). The acceptance of a payment from a thief in exchange for an agreement not to prosecute; COMPOUNDING A CRIME. • The payment might be either a bribe or a return of the stolen goods themselves. This was a form of compounding a felony.

3. A tenant's right to use as much wood from the estate as necessary for fuel, fences, and other agricultural operations. • *Bote* in this sense is an earlier form of *estovers*. **4.** BRIGBOTE.

boteless (**boht**-ləs), *adj.* *Hist.* **1.** Of or relating to an offense that cannot be expiated or otherwise remedied by the payment of a fine, the offender being required to suffer loss of liberty or life. • Boteless offenses appeared in Anglo-Saxon Britain about A.D. 700. They appear to have involved treason or violence against the king. **2.** Without relief or remedy; without the privilege of making satisfaction for a crime by pecuniary payment. • The modern word *bootless* is derived from this term. Cf. BOTE (2).

bottomage bond. See *bottomry bond* under BOND (2).

bottom-hole agreement. *Oil & gas.* A support agreement in which the contributing party agrees to make a cash contribution to the drilling party in exchange for geological or drilling information if the well is drilled to the agreed depth. See SUPPORT AGREEMENT.

bottomland. (18c) Low-lying land, often located in a river's floodplain.

bottomry. *Maritime law.* A contract by which a shipowner pledges the ship as security for a loan to finance a voyage (as to equip or repair the ship), the lender losing the money if the ship is lost during the voyage. • The term refers to the idea that the shipowner pledges the ship's bottom, or keel. Cf. RESPONDENTIA.

bottomry bond. See BOND (2).

bought and sold notes. Two memoranda prepared by a broker to record the sale of a note. • The broker sends the *bought note* to the purchaser, and sends the *sold note* to the seller.

bought note. See NOTE (1).

boulevard rule. The principle that the driver of a vehicle approaching a highway from a smaller road must stop and yield the right-of-way to all highway traffic.

boulwarism. *Labor law.* A bargaining tactic in which an employer researches the probable outcome of collective bargaining and uses the information to make a firm settlement offer to a union on a take-it-or-leave-it basis, so that there is no real negotiation. • *Boulwarism* is now considered to be an unfair labor practice by the National Labor Relations Board. The practice takes its name from Lemuel Boulware, vice president for employee relations at General Electric Company, who used the technique during the mid-20th century.

bounced check. See *bad check* under CHECK.

bound, *adj.* (15c) **1.** Constrained by a contractual or other obligation <they are bound to make the payments by the first of each month>. **2.** (Of a court) constrained to follow a precedent <bound by a Supreme Court decision>.

bound, *n.* (usu. pl.) (13c) **1.** BOUNDARY <metes and bounds>. **2.** A limitation or restriction on action <within the bounds of the law>.

bound, *vb.* (14c) To delineate a property boundary <property bounded by the creek>. Cf. BIND.

boundary. (1598) **1.** A natural or artificial separation that delineates the confines of real property <the creek serves as a boundary between the two properties>. See METES AND BOUNDS.

agreed boundary. A negotiated boundary by which adjacent landowners resolve uncertainties over the extent of their land. — Also termed *boundary by agreement; boundary by acquiescence.* See DOCTRINE OF PRACTICAL LOCATION.

land boundary. (18c) The limit of a landholding, usu. described by linear measurements of the borders, by points of the compass, or by stationary markers. See FORTY; LEGAL DESCRIPTION.

lost boundary. A boundary whose markers have decayed, changed, or been removed or displaced in such a manner that the boundary's correct location can no longer be determined with confidence.

natural boundary. Any nonartificial thing (such as a river or ocean) that forms a boundary of a nation, a political subdivision, or a piece of property. — Also termed *natural object.*

private boundary. An artificial boundary marker.

public boundary. A natural formation that marks the beginning of a boundary line. — Also termed *natural boundary.*

2. *Int'l law.* A line marking the limit of the territorial jurisdiction of a state or other entity having an international status.

boundary by acquiescence. See *agreed boundary* under BOUNDARY.

boundary by agreement. See *agreed boundary* under BOUNDARY.

boundary traffic. The movement of persons or goods across an international boundary.

bound bailiff. See BAILIFF.

bounded tree. A tree that marks a corner of a property's boundary.

bounder. A visible mark that indicates a territorial limit in a land survey.

bounty. (13c) **1.** A premium or benefit offered or given, esp. by a government, to induce someone to take action or perform a service <a bounty for the killing of dangerous animals>. Cf. REWARD. **2.** A gift, esp. in a will; generosity in giving <the court will distribute the testator's bounty equally>. **3.** The portion of a salvage award exceeding what the salvor would be entitled to on the basis of quantum meruit. — Also termed *gratuity; bonus.*

bounty hunter. (1930) A person who for a fee pursues someone charged with or suspected of a crime; esp., a person hired by a bail-bond company to find and arrest a criminal defendant who has breached the bond agreement by failing to appear in court as ordered. — Also termed *bail-enforcement agent.*

bounty land. See LAND.

boutique (boo-*teek*). (1984) A small specialty business; esp., a small law firm specializing in one particular aspect of law practice <a tax boutique>.

box-top license. See *shrink-wrap license* under LICENSE.

boycott, *n.* (1880) **1.** An action designed to achieve the social or economic isolation of an adversary. • The term derives from Captain Charles C. Boycott, an English landowner in famine-plagued Ireland of the 1870s; because of his ruthless treatment of Irish tenant farmers, the Irish Land League ostracized him. **2.** A concerted refusal to do business with a party to express disapproval of that party's practices. **3.** A refusal to deal in one transaction in an effort to obtain terms desired in a second transaction. • Under the Sherman Antitrust Act, even peaceful persuasion of a person to refrain from dealing with another can amount to a boycott. *See* 15 USCA §§ 1–7. Cf. PICKETING; STRIKE. — **boycott,** *vb.*

   consumer boycott. (1941) A boycott by consumers of products or services to show displeasure with the manufacturer, seller, or provider.

   group boycott. *Antitrust.* **1.** CONCERTED REFUSAL TO DEAL. **2.** A type of secondary boycott by two or more competitors who refuse to do business with one firm unless it refrains from doing business with an actual or potential competitor of the boycotters. • A group boycott can violate the Sherman Act and is analyzed under either the per se rule or the rule of reason, depending on the nature of the boycott. See PER SE RULE; RULE OF REASON.

   primary boycott. (1903) A boycott by union members who stop dealing with a former employer.

   secondary boycott. (1903) A boycott of the customers or suppliers of a business so that they will withhold their patronage from that business. • For example, a group might boycott a manufacturer who advertises on a radio station that broadcasts messages considered objectionable by the group.

Boykin Act. *Hist. Patents.* A statute, passed after World War II, that extended the U.S. patenting deadlines for citizens of former enemy nations. • A similar measure, the Nolan Act, was passed after World War I.

Boyle defense. See GOVERNMENT-CONTRACTOR DEFENSE.

bp. *Abbr.* See BASIS POINT.

B.R. *abbr.* **1.** Bankruptcy Reporter. — Also abbreviated *Bankr. Rep.* **2.** *Bancus Regis* [Latin "King's Bench"]. **3.** *Bancus Reginae* [Latin "Queen's Bench"]. • This abbreviation has been replaced by the English initials of these courts, K.B. and Q.B.

bracery. *Hist.* **1.** The offense of selling pretended rights or title to land. • This practice was outlawed by statute of 32 Hen. 8, ch. 9. **2.** EMBRACERY.

bracket creep. (1978) The process by which inflation or increased income pushes individuals into higher tax brackets.

bracket system. *Tax.* A system for collecting a sales tax based on an index providing for a graduated payment depending on the purchase price of the item, the purpose being fourfold: (1) to avoid having the seller collect a tax less than one cent; (2) to avoid requiring the state to figure the exact amount of tax on each sale; (3) to allow the seller to have a ready means for fixing the tax to be collected; and (4) to allow the state to collect about the right amount of tax. • This system may be provided for either by statute or by administrative regulation.

Bracton. The common title of one of the earliest books of English law, *De Legibus et Consuetudinibus Angliae* (ca. 1250). • Henry of Bratton (also known as *Bracton*), a judge of the Court of King's Bench and of Assize, is credited with writing the work, though he may have merely revised an earlier version.

Brady Act. A federal law establishing a national system for quickly checking the background of a prospective handgun purchaser. • The formal name of the law is the Brady Handgun Violence Prevention Act. The U.S. Supreme Court held unconstitutional the law's interim provision, which required chief state law-enforcement officers (usu. sheriffs) to conduct background checks until the national system was in place. The act is named for James Brady, who, as a member of President Ronald Reagan's staff, was wounded by gunfire during an attempted presidential assassination in 1981. 18 USCA §§ 921–930. — Also termed (informally) *Brady Bill.*

Brady material. (1972) *Criminal procedure.* Information or evidence that is favorable to a criminal defendant's case and that the prosecution has a duty to disclose. • The prosecution's withholding of such information violates the defendant's due-process rights. *Brady v. Maryland,* 373 U.S. 83, 83 S.Ct. 1194 (1963). See *exculpatory evidence* under EVIDENCE. Cf. JENCKS MATERIAL.

Brady motion. A criminal defendant's request that a court order the prosecution to turn over evidence favorable to the defendant when the evidence is relevant to the defendant's guilt or punishment. *Brady v. Maryland,* 373 U.S., 83 S.Ct. 1194 (1963). See BRADY MATERIAL.

brain death. See DEATH.

branch. (13c) **1.** An offshoot, lateral extension, or division of an institution <the executive, legislative, and judicial branches of government>. **2.** A line of familial descent stemming from a common ancestor <the Taylor branch of the Bradshaw family>. — Also termed *stock.* **3.** A license held by a ship's pilot. See *branch pilot* under PILOT.

branch pilot. See PILOT.

brand. *Trademarks.* A name or symbol used by a seller or manufacturer to identify goods or services and to distinguish them from competitors' goods or services; the term used colloquially in business and industry to refer to a corporate or product name, a business image, or a mark, regardless of whether it may legally qualify as a trademark. • Branding is an ancient practice, evidenced by individual names and marks found on bricks, pots, etc. In the Middle Ages, guilds granted their members the right to use a guild-identifying symbol as a mark of quality and for legal protection. — Also termed *brand name.* Cf. TRADEMARK; TRADENAME.

> *private brand.* An identification mark placed on goods made by someone else under license or other arrangement and marketed as one's own. • The seller of private-brand goods sponsors those goods in the market, becomes responsible for their quality, and has rights to prevent others from using the same mark.

brand architecture. *Trademarks.* The strategic analysis and development of optimal relationships among the multiple levels of a company and its brands, products, features, technology, or ingredient names.

Brandeis brief (bran-DIS). (1930) A brief, usu. an appellate brief, that makes use of social and economic studies in addition to legal principles and citations. • The brief is named after Supreme Court Justice Louis D. Brandeis, who as an advocate filed the most famous such brief in *Muller v. Oregon,* 208 U.S. 412, 28 S.Ct. 324 (1908), in which he persuaded the Court to uphold a statute setting a maximum ten-hour workday for women.

Brandeis rules. See ASHWANDER RULES.

branding. 1. The act of marking cattle with a hot iron to identify their owner. **2.** Formerly, the punishment of marking an offender with a hot iron.

brand name. 1. See BRAND. **2.** See TRADENAME.

brawl, *n.* **1.** A noisy quarrel or fight. **2.** The offense of engaging in such a quarrel or fight. • In most jurisdictions, the offense is a statutory civil misdemeanor. **3.** *Hist. Eccles. law.* The offense of disturbing the peace of a consecrated building or area; specif., a disturbance, such as arguing, within the churchyard or church. • Until 1860, offenders faced trial in ecclesiastical courts. — Also termed *brawling.* — **brawl,** *vb.*

breach, *n.* (15c) A violation or infraction of a law or obligation <breach of warranty> <breach of duty>. — **breach,** *vb.*

breach of arrest. A military offense committed by an officer who, being under arrest in quarters, leaves those quarters without a superior officer's authorization. See *arrest in quarters* under ARREST.

breach of close. (18c) The unlawful or unauthorized entry on another person's land; a common-law trespass. — Also termed *breaking a close.* See CLOSE (1).

breach of contract. (17c) Violation of a contractual obligation by failing to perform one's own promise, by repudiating it, or by interfering with another party's performance.

> *active breach of contract.* Civil law. The negligent performance of a contractual obligation, to the point of acting outside the contract's terms. • Under Louisiana law before 1984, active breach of contract was contrasted with passive breach of contract, which was a failure to perform the obligations created by the contract. Unlike a passive breach, an active breach of contract could give rise to a claim in contract and in tort. The distinction was abolished in 1984. Cf. *passive breach of contract.*

> *anticipatory breach.* (1889) A breach of contract caused by a party's anticipatory repudiation, i.e., unequivocally indicating that the party will not perform when performance is due. • Under these circumstances, the nonbreaching party may elect to treat the repudiation as an immediate breach and sue for damages. — Also termed *breach by anticipatory repudiation; constructive breach.* See *anticipatory repudiation* under REPUDIATION.

> *constructive breach.* See *anticipatory breach.*

> *continuing breach.* (1817) A breach of contract that endures for a considerable time or is repeated at short intervals.

> *efficient breach.* (1977) An intentional breach of contract and payment of damages by a party who would incur greater economic loss by performing under the contract. See EFFICIENT-BREACH THEORY.

> *immediate breach.* (1820) A breach that entitles the nonbreaching party to sue for damages immediately.

> *material breach.* (1840) A breach of contract that is significant enough to permit the aggrieved party to elect to treat the breach as total (rather than partial), thus excusing that party from further performance and affording it the right to sue for damages.

> *partial breach.* (18c) A breach of contract that is less significant than a material breach and that gives the aggrieved party a right to damages, but does not excuse that party from performance; specif., a breach for which the injured party may substitute the remedial rights provided by law for only part of the existing contract rights.

> *passive breach of contract.* Civil law. A failure to perform the requirements of a contract. • Under Louisiana law up to 1984, passive breach of contract was contrasted with active breach of contract, which was negligence in performing a

contractual obligation. While an active breach of contract could give rise to claims in contract and in tort, a passive breach of contract usu. did not give rise to a tort claim. Cf. *active breach of contract*.

total breach. (18c) A breach of contract for which the remedial rights provided by law are substituted for all the existing contractual rights, or can be so substituted by the injured party; esp., a material breach that gives rise to a claim for damages based on the aggrieved party's remaining rights to performance under the contract.

breach of covenant. (16c) The violation of an express or implied promise, usu. in a contract, either to do or not to do an act. See COVENANT.

breach of duty. (16c) The violation of a legal or moral obligation; the failure to act as the law obligates one to act; esp., a fiduciary's violation of an obligation owed to another. See NEGLIGENCE.

breach of loyalty. An act that is detrimental to the interests of someone to whom a fiduciary duty is owed; esp., an act that furthers the actor's own interests or those of a competitor of the beneficiary.

breach of peace. See BREACH OF THE PEACE.

breach of prison. See PRISON BREACH.

breach of promise. The violation of one's word or undertaking, esp. a promise to marry. • Under English common law, an engagement to marry had the nature of a commercial contract, so if one party broke the engagement without justification, the innocent party was entitled to damages. See HEARTBALM STATUTE.

breach of the peace. (16c) The criminal offense of creating a public disturbance or engaging in disorderly conduct, particularly by making an unnecessary or distracting noise. — Also termed *breach of peace; disturbing the peace; disturbance of the peace; public disturbance*. See *disorderly conduct* under CONDUCT.

breach of trust. (17c) **1.** A trustee's violation of either the trust's terms or the trustee's general fiduciary obligations; the violation of a duty that equity imposes on a trustee, whether the violation was willful, fraudulent, negligent, or inadvertent. • A breach of trust subjects the trustee to removal and creates personal liability. **2.** See MALADMINISTRATION.

breach of warranty. (18c) **1.** A breach of an express or implied warranty relating to the title, quality, content, or condition of goods sold. UCC § 2-312. **2.** *Insurance.* A breach of the insured's pledge or stipulation that the facts relating to the insured person, thing, or risk are as stated. See WARRANTY (3).

bread acts. *Hist.* Laws providing for the sustenance of persons kept in prison for debt. • These laws were formerly on the books in both England and the United States.

bread-and-cheese ordeal. See *ordeal of the morsel* under ORDEAL.

breadth of a claim. *Patents.* The scope or extent to which a patent claim excludes others from infringing activity.

break, *vb.* (bef. 12c) **1.** To violate or disobey (a law) <to break the law>. **2.** To nullify (a will) by court proceeding <Samson, the disinherited son, successfully broke the will>. **3.** To escape from (a place of confinement) without permission <break out of prison>. **4.** To open (a door, gate, etc.) and step through illegally <break the close>.

breakage. (1848) **1.** An allowance given by a manufacturer to a buyer for goods damaged during transit or storage. **2.** Insignificant amounts of money retained by racetrack promoters from bets. • The retention of these small sums avoids the inconvenience of counting and paying out inconsequential winnings.

break a house. To violently and feloniously remove or sever any part of a house or its locks.

breakdown of the marriage. See IRRETRIEVABLE BREAKDOWN OF THE MARRIAGE.

breaking, *n. Criminal law.* (17c) In the law of burglary, the act of entering a building without permission. • It does not require damage to the property.

breaking a case. (1950) **1.** The voicing by one appellate judge to another judge on the same panel of a tentative view on how a case should be decided. • These informal expressions assist the judges in ascertaining how close they are to agreement. **2.** The solving of a case by the police.

breaking a close. See BREACH OF CLOSE.

breaking and entering. See BURGLARY (2).

breaking a patent. The act of demonstrating that a patent is invalid or unenforceable because it was used unlawfully by the patentee (esp. in violation of antitrust laws), or improperly issued by the U.S. Patent and Trademark Office because of fraud, the existence of prior art, or any other barrier to proper issuance. • Defendants in patent-infringement actions may overcome the infringement allegations by showing that the patent should not have been allowed in the first place (so it is invalid), or that the patentee has misused the patent (so the patent is unenforceable).

breaking bulk, *n.* (18c) **1.** The act of dividing a large shipment into smaller units. **2.** Larceny by a bailee, esp. a carrier, who opens containers, removes items from them, and converts the items to personal use. — Also termed *breaking bale*. — **break bulk,** *vb.*

breaking of entail. See BARRING OF ENTAIL.

break-up fee. See TERMINATION FEE.

Breathalyzer. (1960) A device used to measure a person's blood alcohol content from a sample of the person's breath, esp. when the police suspect that the person was driving while intoxicated. • The term is a trademarked name. Breathalyzer test results are admissible as evidence if the test was properly administered. — Also termed *alcoholometer*; *drunkometer*; *intoxilyzer*; *intoximeter*. See BLOOD ALCOHOL CONTENT. — **breathalyze,** *vb.*

breathing room. (1967) *Slang.* The postbankruptcy period during which a debtor may formulate a debt-repayment plan without harassment or interference by creditors.

B reorganization. See REORGANIZATION (2).

brethren (breth-rən), *n. pl.* Brothers, esp. those considered spiritual kin (such as male colleagues on a court) <my brethren argue in the dissent that my statutory interpretation is faulty>. • The use of this collegial term has naturally dwindled as more women have entered law and esp. into the judiciary. Cf. SISTREN.

breve (breev *or* **bree**-vee), *n.* [Law Latin] *Hist.* Writ. • The word *brevis* meant "short," and *brevia* were short writs, unlike charters. Pl. **brevia** (**bree**-vee-ə).

  album breve (**al**-bəm breev *or* **bree**-vee). A blank writ; a writ with a blank or omission in it.

  apertum breve (ə-**pər**-təm breev *or* **bree**-vee). [Latin "open writ"] An open, unsealed writ. See *patent writ* under WRIT. Cf. *close write* under WRIT; CLAUSUM.

  breve de bono et malo (breev *or* **bree**-vee dee **boh**-noh et **mal**-oh). See DE ODIO ET ATIA.

  breve de conventione (breev *or* **bree**-vee dee kən-ven-shee-**oh**-nee). See WRIT OF COVENANT.

  breve de cursu. See WRIT OF COURSE.

  breve de recto (breev *or* **bree**-vee dee **rek**-toh). See DE RECTO.

  breve de transgressione super casum (breev *or* **bree**-vee dee trans-gres[h]-ee-**oh**-nee s[y]**oo**-pər **kay**-səm). See TRESPASS ON THE CASE.

  breve innominatum (breev *or* bree-vee i-nom-ə-**nay**-təm). [Latin "innominate writ"] A writ that recites a cause of action only in general terms.

  breve magnum de recto (breev *or* bree-vee **mag**-nəm dee **rek**-toh). See DE RECTO PATENS.

  breve nominatum. A writ in which the complaint particularly states the time, place, and demand.

  breve perquirere (breev *or* bree-vee pər-**kwi**-rə-ree). [Latin "to obtain a writ"] To purchase a writ or license of trial in the king's courts.

breve rebellionis. See COMMISSION OF REBELLION.

breve testatum (breev *or* **bree**-vee tes-**tay**-təm). [Latin "a witnessed writ"] A written memorandum used to memorialize the terms of a conveyance and investiture of land. • Witnesses to the conveyance did not sign the document, but their names were recorded. *Brevia testata* were introduced to reduce disputes concerning the terms of oral grants.

brevia amicabilia (**bree**-vee-ə am-ə-kə-**bil**-ee-ə). [Latin "writs with agreement"] Writs obtained with the agreement or consent of the opposing party in an action.

brevia anticipantia (**bree**-vee-ə an-tis-ə-**pan**-shee-ə). [Latin "anticipatory writs"] Anticipatory or preventive writs. • Six were included in this category: writs of *mesne; warrantia chartae; monstraverunt; audita querela; curia claudenda;* and *ne injuste vexes.* See QUIA TIMET.

brevia formata (**bree**-vee-ə for-**may**-tə). [Latin "writs of approved form"] Writs of established and approved form, issued as a matter of course. Cf. *brevia magistralia.*

brevia judicialia (**bree**-vee-ə joo-dish-ee-**ay**-lee-ə). [Latin "judicial writs"] Writs that issue during an action or afterward in aid of judgment. • A court issued such a writ after an original writ had issued out of Chancery. Cf. *brevia originale.*

brevia magistralia (**bree**-vee-ə maj-i-**stray**-lee-ə). [Latin "masters' writs"] Writs issued by the masters or clerks of Chancery according to the circumstances of particular cases. • These writs, unlike some others, might be varied in accordance with the complainant's particular situation. Cf. *brevia formata.*

brevia originale (**bree**-vee-ə ə-rij-i-**nay**-lee). [Latin] Original writ. • This writ began a judicial action. Cf. *brevia judicialia.*

brevia selecta (**bree**-vee-ə sə-**lek**-tə). [Latin "selected writs"] Choice or selected writs or processes. — Abbr. *brev. sel.*

brevet (brə-**vet** *or* **brev**-it). [French] **1.** *Military law.* A commission promoting an officer to a higher rank, esp. during wartime, but without a corresponding pay increase. **2.** *French law.* A privilege or warrant granted by the government to a private person, authorizing a special benefit or the exercise of an exclusive privilege. • For example, a *brevet d'invention* is a patent for an invention. **3.** *Patents.* A patent. — Also termed (in sense 3) *brevet d'invention.*

brevet officer. See OFFICER (2).

brevia amicabilia. See BREVE.

brevia anticipantia. See BREVE.

brevia formata. See BREVE.

brevia judicialia. See BREVE.

brevia magistralia. See BREVE.

brevia originale. See BREVE.

Breviarium Alaricianum (bree-vee-**air**-ee-əm al-ə-ri-**kay**-nəm). [Latin] An abridgment (or *breviary*) of Roman law compiled by order of the Visigoth king Alaric II, published for the use of his Roman subjects in the year 506. • Revised versions were known as the *Lex Romana Visigothorum.* It was also termed the *Breviarium Aniani* after Alaric's chancellor, Anian, who edited and distributed the work. — Also termed *Breviary of Alaric* (**bree**-vee-er-ee əv **al**-ə-rik).

brevia selecta. See BREVE.

breviate (**bree**-vee-ət). [Latin] *Hist.* An abstract of a writing; esp., a short statement attached to a Parliamentary bill summarizing the contents of the bill.

brevia testata (**bree**-vee-ə tes-**tay**-tə). [Latin] *Hist.* See *breve testatum* under BREVE.

brevibus et rotulis liberandis (**bree**-və-bəs et **roch**-ə-ləs lib-ər-**an**-dis). [Latin "breves and rolls to be freed"] *Hist.* A writ ordering a sheriff to turn over to a successor all paraphernalia of office.

brevi manu (**bree**-vI **man**-yoo), *adv.* [Latin "with a short hand"] *Roman & civil law.* **1.** Directly; by the shortest route. **2.** Without a legal warrant; on one's own authority. • In Roman law, the term referred to the contractual transfer (*traditio*) of ownership of an item to one who already had physical control of the item. See TRADITIO BREVI MANU; CONSTITUTUM POSSESSORIUM. In Scotland, this phrase usu. signified the performance of an act without the necessity of resorting to the courts.

brevitatis causa (brev-i-**tay**-tis **kaw**-zə). [Latin] *Scots law.* For the sake of brevity. • The phrase was inserted in legal documents to show that another document had been incorporated by reference but not fully quoted.

brev. sel. See *brevia selecta* under BREVE.

bribe, *n.* (15c) A price, reward, gift or favor bestowed or promised with a view to pervert the judgment of or influence the action of a person in a position of trust. Cf. BARRATRY (4). — **bribe,** *vb.*

bribee. (19c) One who receives a bribe. — Also termed *bribe-taker.*

bribe-giver. See BRIBER.

briber. (17c) One who offers a bribe. — Also termed *bribe-giver.*

bribery, *n.* (16c) The corrupt payment, receipt, or solicitation of a private favor for official action. • Bribery is a felony in most jurisdictions. See

Model Penal Code § 240.1. Cf. KICKBACK. — **bribe,** *vb.*

commercial bribery. (1927) **1.** The knowing solicitation or acceptance of a benefit in exchange for violating an oath of fidelity, such as that owed by an employee, partner, trustee, or attorney. Model Penal Code § 224.8(1). **2.** A supposedly disinterested appraiser's acceptance of a benefit that influences the appraisal of goods or services. Model Penal Code § 224.8(2). **3.** Corrupt dealing with the agents or employees of prospective buyers to secure an advantage over business competitors.

bribe-taker. See BRIBEE.

bridge bank. A national bank chartered to operate an insolvent bank for up to three years or until the bank is sold.

bridge financing. See *bridge loan* under LOAN.

bridge loan. See LOAN.

bridge the gap. *Trademarks.* To capitalize on the goodwill associated with an existing trademark or tradename by using it or a similar mark on new lines of products or services, or on the same products or services in new marketing territories.

brief, *n.* (14c) **1.** A written statement setting out the legal contentions of a party in litigation, esp. on appeal; a document prepared by counsel as the basis for arguing a case, consisting of legal and factual arguments and the authorities in support of them. — Also termed *legal brief; brief of argument.*

amicus brief. A brief, usu. at the appellate level, prepared and filed by an amicus curiae with the court's permission. — Sometimes shortened to *amicus.* — Also termed *friend-of-the-court brief.*

Anders brief. (1969) *Criminal procedure.* A brief filed by a court-appointed defense attorney who wants to withdraw from the case on appeal based on a belief that the appeal is frivolous. • In an *Anders* brief, the attorney seeking to withdraw must identify anything in the record that might arguably support the appeal. The court then decides whether the appeal is frivolous and whether the attorney should be permitted to withdraw. *Anders v. California,* 386 U.S. 738, 87 S.Ct. 1396 (1967). — Also termed *no-merit brief.*

appeal brief. **1.** See *appellate brief.* **2.** *Patents.* A patent applicant's brief to the Board of Patent Appeals and Interferences, arguing that the patent examiner was incorrect in rejecting the application. Cf. EXAMINER'S ANSWER.

appellate brief. A brief submitted to an appeals court; specif., a brief filed by a party to an appeal pending in a court exercising appellate jurisdiction. • The brief may be filed for an individual party or on behalf of two or more parties. — Also termed *appeal brief.*

bench brief. An advocate's short brief, prepared for use by panelists in a moot-court competition or mock oral argument. • The brief summarizes the facts, law, and arguments for both sides on the issues.

Brandeis brief. See BRANDEIS BRIEF.

brief on the merits. A brief that sets out the issues to be decided, the party's position, and the arguments and authorities in support. — Also termed *points-and-authorities brief; merits brief.*

closed brief. In law school, an appellate brief prepared by a student using only a stipulated factual outline and research materials provided in a package. • Closed briefs are usu. assigned in first-year legal-writing classes, sometimes in preparation for moot court. They may also be used to select among candidates for law review.

merits brief. See *brief on the merits.*

no-merit brief. See *Anders brief.*

open brief. In law school, an appellate brief prepared by a student using a stipulated factual outline and open-ended research that the student independently finds, as opposed to sources supplied by a professor.

opening brief. A party's first brief at a given stage of a lawsuit. • Although this term is most often associated with a plaintiff or appellant, it is sometimes applied to a defendant or respondent. — Also termed *opening brief on the merits.*

points-and-authorities brief. See *brief on the merits.*

proof brief. (1997) A preliminary appellate brief to be reviewed by the clerk of the court for compliance with applicable rules. • Proof briefs are required by local rules of the U.S. Court of Appeals for the Sixth Circuit. A proof brief in full compliance will be accepted and filed. If not in compliance, it will be returned for corrections to be made, and a deadline will be set for refiling. After all proof briefs have been accepted in a case, a date is set for filing a final brief, which may be modified only to include joint-appendix references, repagination, or updated citations.

reply brief. (1872) A brief that responds to issues and arguments raised in the brief previously filed by one's opponent; esp., a movant's or appellant's brief filed to rebut a brief in opposition. See REBUTTAL (3).

trial brief. (1927) Counsel's written submission, usu. just before trial, outlining the legal issues before the court and arguing one side's position.

2. *English law.* A solicitor's document that abstracts the pleadings and facts to inform a barrister about the case. **3.** ABSTRACT OF TITLE. **4.** CASE NOTE. — **brief,** *vb.*

briefing attorney. See ATTORNEY.

briefmanship, *n.* The quality of the work done in producing a written legal argument.

brief of argument. See BRIEF (1).

brief of title. See ABSTRACT OF TITLE.

brief on the merits. See BRIEF.

brief-writing. (1891) The art or practice of preparing legal briefs. — Also termed *brief-making.* — **brief-writer,** *n.*

brigandage (**brig**-ən-dij). *Archaic.* Plundering and banditry carried out by bands of robbers. • Piracy is sometimes called "maritime brigandage."

brigbote (**brig**-boht), *n. Hist.* An obligation, often extracted as a tax or a charge on land, to contribute to the cost of maintaining castles, walls, and bridges. — Also spelled *bridgebote.* — Often termed *bote.* See BOTE (4).

Briggs Law. *Archaic.* A 1921 Massachusetts law that required all criminal defendants who had been repeatedly indicted, previously convicted of a felony, or charged with a capital offense to undergo psychiatric evaluation. • The purpose of the evaluation was "to determine [offenders'] mental condition and the existence of any mental disease or defect [that] would affect [their] criminal responsibility." Mass. Gen. Laws ch. 123, § 100A (1921). Although the term is no longer used in Massachusetts, an updated form of the law still exists, and every state has its own form of it.

bright-line rule. (1973) A legal rule of decision that tends to resolve issues, esp. ambiguities, simply and straightforwardly, sometimes sacrificing equity for certainty.

bring an action. To sue; institute legal proceedings.

bring-down provision. *Contracts.* A contractual covenant that all of a party's representations and warranties were true when the contract was executed and will be true on the closing date.

bring to book. (1865) To arrest and try (an offender) <the fugitives were brought to book and convicted>.

British subject. The status conferred on a citizen of the United Kingdom and the Commonwealth countries such as Canada, Australia, New Zealand, and India by the British Nationality Act of 1981. • Although this is the current sense, the phrase *British subject* has had many different meanings over the years, under different statutes.

broad constructionism. See *liberal constructionism* under CONSTRUCTIONISM.

broad constructionist. See *liberal constructionist* under CONSTRUCTIONIST.

broadened reissue patent. See PATENT (3).

broadening of a claim. *Patents.* The enlargement of the scope of a patent claim to expand its coverage. • The broader a patent claim, the greater the scope of protection because more methods or devices may potentially infringe the claim. But drafting a claim broadly increases the risk that an accused infringer may successfully invalidate the claim through prior art. See *prior art* under ART.

broadening statement. *Patents.* Wording in a claim to the effect that the invention includes forms other than the details shown in the application. • A broadening statement is usu. taken as boilerplate and given little or no effect. — Also termed *catch-all.*

broader than the invention, *adj.* (Of a patent claim) having a scope that exceeds the limits of the invention disclosed in the application or patent.

broad-form insurance. See INSURANCE.

broad-form policy. See INSURANCE POLICY.

broad interpretation. See *liberal construction* under CONSTRUCTION.

broadside objection. See *general objection* under OBJECTION.

brocard (**brahk**-ərd *or* **broh**-kərd). An elementary legal principle or maxim, esp. one deriving from Roman law or ancient custom.

broker, *n.* (14c) **1.** An agent who acts as an intermediary or negotiator, esp. between prospective buyers and sellers; a person employed to make bargains and contracts between other persons in matters of trade, commerce, or navigation. • A broker differs from a factor because the broker usu. does not have possession of the property. Cf. FACTOR. **2.** *Securities.* A person engaged in the business of conducting securities transactions for the accounts of others. — **broker,** *vb.*

broker-agent. 1. A person who acts as an intermediary between parties to a transaction, and as a representative of one of them. **2.** A person licensed both as a broker and as an agent.

broker-dealer. A brokerage firm that engages in the business of trading securities for its own account (i.e., as a principal) before selling them to customers. • Such a firm is usu. registered with the SEC and with the state in which it does business. See DEALER (2).

broker for sale. A broker retained to sell something, but having neither possession of the goods nor any right of action in the broker's own name on contracts that the broker enters into.

broker's broker. A municipal securities broker or dealer who routinely effects transactions for the account of other brokers, dealers, and municipal securities dealers.

commercial broker. A broker who negotiates the sale of goods without having possession of or control of the goods. Cf. FACTOR (2).

commission broker. A member of a stock or commodity exchange who executes buy and sell orders.

customhouse broker. A broker who prepares paperwork for the entry or clearance of ships, and for the import or export of goods. — Also termed *customs broker.*

discount broker. 1. A broker who discounts bills of exchange and promissory notes, and advances money on securities. **2.** A broker who executes buy and sell orders at commission rates lower than those of full-service brokers.

government-securities interdealer broker. A broker engaged exclusively in the business of transacting in government securities for parties who are themselves government brokers or dealers.

institutional broker. A broker who trades securities for institutional clients such as banks, mutual funds, pension funds, and insurance companies.

insurance broker. (18c) *Insurance.* A person who, for compensation, brings about or negotiates contracts of insurance as an agent for someone else, but not as an officer, salaried employee, or licensed agent of an insurance company. • The broker acts as an intermediary between the insured and the insurer. — Also termed *producer.*

loan broker. A person who is in the business of lending money, usu. to an individual, and taking as security an assignment of wages or a security interest in the debtor's personal property.

merchandise broker. One who negotiates the sale of merchandise without possessing it. • A merchandise broker is an agent with very limited powers.

money broker. A broker who negotiates the lending or raising of money for others.

mortgage broker. An individual or organization that markets mortgage loans and brings lenders and borrowers together. • A mortgage broker does not originate or service mortgage loans.

note broker. A broker who negotiates the discount or sale of commercial paper.

real-estate broker. A broker who negotiates contracts of sale and other agreements (such as mortgages or leases) between buyers and sellers of real property. • Real-estate brokers must be licensed in the states where they conduct business.

registered broker. A broker registered or required to be registered under the Securities Exchange Act of 1934.

responsible broker-dealer. A broker-dealer who communicates bids or offers on the floor of a stock exchange at the designated location for trading in a reported security or who, in an off-exchange transaction, communicates the bid or offer as either a principal or an agent, for its own or another's account. SEC Rule 11Ac1–1(a)(21) (17 CFR § 240.11Ac1–1(a)(21)).

securities broker. A broker employed to buy or sell securities for a customer, as opposed to a securities dealer, who trades as a principal before selling the securities to a customer. See DEALER (2).

brokerage. (15c) **1.** The business or office of a broker <a profitable stock brokerage>. **2.** A broker's fee <collect the brokerage after the house sells>.

brokerage contract. An agency agreement employing a broker to make contracts in the name of and on behalf of the principal and for which the broker receives a commission.

broker-agent. See BROKER.

brokerage-run dividend-reinvestment plan. See DIVIDEND-REINVESTMENT PLAN.

broker call loan. See *call loan* under LOAN.

broker-dealer. See BROKER.

broker for sale. See BROKER.

broker's broker. See BROKER.

broker's loan statement. *Property.* A document that details the costs of and deductions from a loan negotiated by a real-estate or mortgage broker on behalf of a borrower. • Deductions may be made for commissions and other costs. The borrower usu. signs the statement and retains a copy. The statement may be required by law. See Cal. Bus. & Prof. Code § 10240 (West 2008). Cf. CLOSING STATEMENT (2).

broker's note. See NOTE (3).

brothel. (16c) A building or business where prostitutes ply their trade; a whorehouse. — Also termed *house of ill fame.* See DISORDERLY HOUSE (2).

brother. (bef. 12c) A male who has one parent or both parents in common with another person.

brother-german. A full brother; the son of both of one's parents. See GERMAN.

consanguine brother (kahn-**sang**-gwin *or* kən-**san**-gwin). *Civil law.* A brother who has the same father, but a different mother.

half brother. A brother who has the same father or the same mother, but not both.

stepbrother. The son of one's stepparent.

uterine brother (**yoo**-tər-in). *Civil law.* A brother who has the same mother, but a different father.

brother-in-law. (14c) The brother of one's spouse or the husband of one's sister. • The husband of one's spouse's sister is also sometimes considered a brother-in-law. Pl. **brothers-in-law.**

brother-sister corporation. See *sister corporation* under CORPORATION.

brownfield site. An abandoned, idled, or underused industrial or commercial site that is difficult to expand or redevelop because of environmental contamination. Cf. GREENFIELD SITE (1).

Brussels Act. *Copyright.* A 1948 revision of the Berne Convention mandating the life-plus-50-years copyright term as a minimum standard, extending the moral rights of attribution and integrity in most member countries to the full copyright term, extending the broadcast right to television, strengthening protection of several forms of copyright protection, and extending some protection to industrial designs.

Brussels Convention. See BRUSSELS SATELLITE CONVENTION.

Brussels Satellite Convention. *Copyright.* A 1974 treaty standardizing the regulation of broadcasting and cable retransmission using satellites. • Since the Convention addresses regulation of the signal rather than copyright or neighboring rights, what is transmitted is protected even if the content is not protected by any intellectual-property right. The U.S. ratified the Brussels Satellite Convention in 1984. — Also termed *Brussels Convention*; *Convention Relating to the Distribution of Program-Carrying Signals Transmitted by Satellite.*

Bruton **error** (**broot**-ən). (1968) The violation of a criminal defendant's constitutional right of confrontation by admitting into evidence a nontestifying codefendant's confession that implicates both of them, where the statement is not admissible against the defendant under any exception to the hearsay rule. • The error is not cured by a limiting instruction to the jury to consider the confession only against the one who made it, because of the high risk that the jury will disregard the instruction. *Bruton v. United States*, 391 U.S. 123, 88 S.Ct. 1620 (1968).

Bryan treaties. *Int'l law.* Any of 48 treaties designed to avert war by requiring the signatories to submit disputes of any kind to standing peace commissions. • The first of these treaties, named after Secretary of State William Jennings Bryan, was signed between the United States and Great Britain in 1914.

BSD license. See LICENSE.

BSD-style license. See *BSD license* under LICENSE.

BTA. *abbr.* Board of Tax Appeals. See TAX COURT, U.S.

BTS. *abbr.* **1.** BORDER AND TRANSPORTATION SAFETY DIRECTORATE. **2.** BUREAU OF TRANSPORTATION STATISTICS.

bubble. (18c) *Slang.* A dishonest or insubstantial business project, generally founded on a fictitious or exaggerated prospectus, designed to ensnare unwary investors.

Bubble Act. An English statute passed in 1720 to prevent corporate fraud.

bucketing. *Securities.* The illegal practice of receiving an order to buy or sell stock but not immediately performing the order. ● The perpetrator profits by executing the order when the stock market goes down or up, respectively, but confirming the order to the customer at the original price.

bucket shop. *Securities.* An establishment that is nominally engaged in stock-exchange transactions or some similar business, but in fact engages in registering bets or wagers, usu. for small amounts, on the rise or fall of the prices of stocks and commodities. ● A bucket shop uses the terms and outward forms of the exchanges, but differs from exchanges because there is no delivery of — and no expectation or intention to deliver or receive — the securities or commodities nominally exchanged.

Buckley Amendment. See FAMILY EDUCATIONAL RIGHTS AND PRIVACY ACT.

Budapest Treaty on the International Recognition of the Deposit of Microorganisms for the Purpose of Patent Procedures. *Patents.* An international treaty promulgating standards and procedures for depositing microorganisms and requiring member countries to recognize a deposit of biological material made in any depository approved by the World Intellectual Property Organization. ● The purpose of the Budapest Treaty is to allow inventors to satisfy the enablement requirement of national patent laws by depositing in a convenient depository a sample of a microorganism to be patented. The U.S. is a signatory to the Budapest Treaty.

budget. (15c) **1.** A statement of an organization's estimated revenues and expenses for a specified period, usu. a year. **2.** A sum of money allocated to a particular purpose or project.

   balanced budget. A budget in which a period's total projected income equals the total estimated expenses.

budget bill. See BILL (3).

Buenos Aires Convention. *Copyright.* A 1910 treaty regulating copyright reciprocity among Latin American nations and the United States. ● Under this agreement, the phrase "all rights reserved" guaranteed copyright protection in member nations. Since all the Convention's signatories are now signatories to more recent and broader international-copyright treaties, this Convention now has little if any practical effect.

buffer zone. (1908) *Land-use planning.* An area of land separating two different zones or areas to help each blend more easily with the other, such as a strip of land between industrial and residential areas.

bug. 1. A flaw or mistake in a computer program that results in an error or undesired result. **2.** The printed mark of a labor union.

buggery, *n.* (14c) Sodomy or bestiality. See SODOMY. — **bugger,** *vb.* — **bugger,** *n.*

bugging, *n.* (1955) A form of electronic surveillance by which conversations may be electronically intercepted, overheard, or recorded, usu. covertly; eavesdropping by electronic means. See EAVESDROPPING; WIRETAPPING.

building. A structure with walls and a roof, esp. a permanent structure. ● For purposes of some criminal statutes, such as burglary and arson, the term *building* may include such things as motor vehicles and watercraft.

   accessory building. A building separate from but complementing the main structure on a lot, such as a garage. ● The question whether a structure is an "accessory building" is often litigated in zoning disputes.

building-and-loan association. (1857) A quasi-public corporation that accumulates funds through member contributions and lends money to the members buying or building homes. Cf. SAVINGS-AND-LOAN ASSOCIATION.

building code. A law or regulation setting forth standards for the construction, maintenance, occupancy, use, or appearance of buildings and dwelling units. — Also termed (for dwelling units) *housing code.* Cf. BUILDING RESTRICTIONS.

building lease. See LEASE.

building line. (1885) A boundary drawn along a curb or the edge of a municipality's sidewalks to establish how far a building must be set away from the street to maintain a uniform appearance. ● This is often referred to as a *setback requirement.*

building loan. See LOAN.

building permit. A license granted by a government agency (esp. a municipality) for the construction of a new building or the substantial alteration of an existing structure.

building restrictions. Regulations governing the type of structures that can be constructed on certain property. • The restrictions are usu. listed in zoning ordinances or restrictive covenants in deeds. Cf. BUILDING CODE; *restrictive covenant* under COVENANT (4). Cf. BUILDING CODE.

build-to-print contract. See CONTRACT.

built-in obsolescence. See *planned obsolescence* under OBSOLESCENCE.

bulk, *adj.* (Of goods) not divided into parts <a bulk shipment of grain>.

bulk discount. See *volume discount* under DISCOUNT.

bulk mortgage. See MORTGAGE.

bulk sale. (1902) A sale of a large quantity of inventory outside the ordinary course of the seller's business. • Bulk sales are regulated by Article 6 of the UCC, which is designed to prevent sellers from defrauding unsecured creditors by making these sales and then dissipating the sale proceeds. — Also termed *bulk transfer.*

bulk-sales law. A statute regulating the transfer of business assets, usu. by requiring public notice of any sale to prevent business owners from disposing of assets to the detriment of creditors and suppliers. *See* UCC §§ 6-101 et seq. See BULK SALE.

bulk transfer. See BULK SALE.

bulky goods. See GOODS.

bull. *Eccles. law.* **1.** A document issued by a pope, so called from the leaden seal (*bulla*) attached to it. **2.** A seal attached to an official document, esp. a papal edict.

bullet ballot. See *bullet vote* under VOTE (1).

bullet vote. See VOTE (1).

bullion (**buul**-yən). An uncoined solid mass of gold or silver.

bullion fund. Public money used by a mint to purchase precious metals for coinage and to pay bullion depositors.

bull market. See MARKET.

bullpen. (1809) *Slang.* **1.** An area in a prison where inmates are kept in close confinement. **2.** A detention cell where prisoners are held until they are brought into court.

bumbershoot insurance. See INSURANCE.

bum-marriage doctrine. *Evidence.* The principle that the marital-witness privilege may not be asserted by a partner in a marriage that is in fact moribund, though legally valid. See *marital privilege* (2) under PRIVILEGE (3).

bumping. (1937) **1.** Displacement of a junior employee's position by a senior employee. **2.** An airline-industry practice of denying seats to passengers because of overbooking.

bunco. (1872) A swindling game or scheme; any trick or ploy calculated to win a person's confidence in an attempt to deceive that person. — Also spelled *bunko.* — Also termed *bunco steering.* Cf. CONFIDENCE GAME.

bunco steerer. 1. One who uses tricks, schemes, or other illegal devices to obtain money or property from others; a swindler. **2.** One who acts as a decoy in bunco. — Also termed *bunco operator; bunco man.* See CONFIDENCE MAN.

bundle. See RECORD (4).

bundle, *vb.* To sell related products or services in one transaction at an all-inclusive price.

bundled software. Software that is sold together with hardware, other software, or services at a single price.

bundle of rights. See PROPERTY (1).

bundling, *n.* In the computer industry, the practice of charging a single price for a combination of hardware, software, or services. • Personal computers are typically sold with bundled software, such as an operating system and applications software that are preinstalled on the hardware.

bunkhouse rule. The principle that an employee's injury suffered while living in an employer's housing is compensable even if the injury occurs during off-duty hours.

burden, *n.* (bef. 12c) **1.** A duty or responsibility <the seller's burden to insure the shipped goods>. **2.** Something that hinders or oppresses <a burden on interstate commerce>. **3.** A restriction on the use or value of land; an encumbrance <the easement created a burden on the estate>. **4.** *Scots law.* An encumbrance, restriction, or obligation imposed on a person or on property <the burden of curatorship> <a servitude is a burden on land>. • When the burden is on real property, it is called a *real burden.* — **burden,** *vb.* — **burdensome,** *adj.*

undue burden. A substantial and unjust obstacle to the performance of a duty or enjoyment of a right. • For example, excessive discovery requests place an undue burden on the person who must produce the data requested. And a state law requiring a particular kind of mud flap on trucks may place an undue burden on the flow of interstate commerce.

burden of allegation. (1862) A party's duty to plead a matter in order for that matter to be heard in the lawsuit. — Also termed *burden of pleading.*

burden of going forward with evidence. See BURDEN OF PRODUCTION.

burden of persuasion. (1923) A party's duty to convince the fact-finder to view the facts in a way that favors that party. • In civil cases, the plaintiff's burden is usu. "by a preponderance of the evidence," while in criminal cases the prosecution's burden is "beyond a reasonable doubt." — Also termed *persuasion burden; risk of nonpersuasion;*

risk of jury doubt. — Also loosely termed *burden of proof.*

burden of pleading. See BURDEN OF ALLEGATION.

burden of production. (1893) A party's duty to introduce enough evidence on an issue to have the issue decided by the fact-finder, rather than decided against the party in a peremptory ruling such as a summary judgment or a directed verdict. — Also termed *burden of going forward with evidence*; *burden of producing evidence*; *production burden*; *degree of proof.*

burden of proof. (18c) **1.** A party's duty to prove a disputed assertion or charge. ● The burden of proof includes both the *burden of persuasion* and the *burden of production.* — Also termed *onus probandi.* See SHIFTING THE BURDEN OF PROOF. **2.** Loosely, BURDEN OF PERSUASION.

middle burden of proof. A party's duty to prove a fact by clear and convincing evidence. ● This standard lies between the preponderance-of-the-evidence standard and the beyond-a-reasonable-doubt standard. See *clear and convincing evidence* under EVIDENCE.

burden-shifting analysis. A court's scrutiny of a complainant's evidence to determine whether it is sufficient to require the opposing party to present contrary evidence. ● Burden shifting is most commonly applied in discrimination cases. If the plaintiff presents sufficient evidence of discrimination, the burden shifts to the defendant to show a legitimate, nondiscriminatory basis for its actions. The precise components of the analysis vary depending on the context of the claim. Cf. MCDONNELL DOUGLAS TEST.

Bureau of Alcohol, Tobacco, and Firearms. 1. See ALCOHOL AND TOBACCO TAX AND TRADE BUREAU. **2.** See BUREAU OF ALCOHOL, TOBACCO, FIREARMS, AND EXPLOSIVES.

Bureau of Alcohol, Tobacco, Firearms, and Explosives. A unit in the U.S. Department of Homeland Security responsible for enforcing laws relating to firearms and explosives and laws relating to the production, taxation, and distribution of alcohol and tobacco products. ● Formerly called the Bureau of Alcohol, Tobacco, and Firearms and a part of the Department of the Treasury, its law-enforcement functions were transferred in the Homeland Security Act of 2002. Pub. L. 107-296. — Abbr. ATF. Cf. ALCOHOL AND TOBACCO TAX AND TRADE BUREAU.

Bureau of Arms Control. A unit in the U.S. Department of State responsible for directing U.S. participation in multilateral arms-control negotiations and in the Organization for the Prohibition of Chemical Weapons. ● It also monitors developments relating to arms control and weapons development.

Bureau of Consular Affairs. A unit in the U.S. Department of State responsible for protecting U.S. citizens and interests abroad. ● Through its Office of Passport Services it issues over 7 million passports each year.

Bureau of Customs. See UNITED STATES CUSTOMS SERVICE.

Bureau of Democracy, Human Rights, and Labor. A unit in the U.S. Department of State responsible for developing policy on human rights and freedoms and for preparing the annual *Country Reports on Human Rights Practices.* — Abbr. DRL.

Bureau of Diplomatic Security. A unit of the U.S. Department of State responsible for protecting the Secretary of State and domestic and foreign dignitaries, for investigating criminal activities such as identity-document fraud involving U.S. passports and visas, and for developing security programs protecting diplomats and American interests worldwide. ● The Bureau employs special agents (members of the U.S. Foreign Service) who are located throughout the United States and in scores of embassies worldwide. It also operates the Diplomatic Courier Service and supervises the transportation of classified documents and materials. — Abbr. DS. — Also termed *Diplomatic Security Service.*

Bureau of Economic Analysis. A unit in the U.S. Department of Commerce responsible for compiling and analyzing data about the U.S. economy. ● It is a part of the Department's Economics and Statistics Administration. — Abbr. BEA.

Bureau of Economic and Business Affairs. A unit in the U.S. Department of State responsible for developing policy on international matters relating to food, communications, energy, air transportation, and maritime affairs. — Abbr. EB.

Bureau of Engraving and Printing. A unit in the U.S. Department of the Treasury responsible for designing and printing the nation's paper currency, postage stamps, Treasury securities, and other documents. — Abbr. BEP.

Bureau of Export Administration. The former name of a bureau in the U.S. Department of Commerce that issues export licenses and enforces export-control laws. ● The unit's name was changed in 2002 to the Bureau of Industry and Security. — Abbr. BXA.

Bureau of Indian Affairs. A unit in the U.S. Department of the Interior responsible for helping Indian and Alaskan native people manage their affairs under the trust relationship with the U.S., and for promoting programs for their benefit. ● Originally created as part of the War Department in 1824, the Bureau was transferred to the Interior Department in 1849. — Abbr. BIA.

Bureau of Industry and Security. A unit in the U.S. Department of Commerce responsible for issuing export licenses and enforcing export-control laws. • The Bureau is charged with furthering U.S. national-security, foreign-policy, and economic interests while furthering the growth of U.S. exports. It was named the Bureau of Export Administration until 2002. — Abbr. BIS.

Bureau of Intelligence and Research. A unit in the U.S. Department of State responsible for coordinating activities of U.S. intelligence agencies to ensure consistency with U.S. foreign policy. • The Bureau also monitors foreign public and media opinions. — Abbr. INR.

Bureau of International Labor Affairs. A unit in the U.S. Department of Labor responsible for helping formulate policy on international matters that affect American workers. • For example, the Bureau compiles and publishes worldwide data on child-labor practices and on foreign labor markets and programs. It also studies the labor consequences of immigration proposals and legislation.

Bureau of International Narcotics and Law Enforcement. A unit in the U.S. Department of State responsible for coordinating the narcotics and anticrime-assistance activities of the Department and for advising the President, the Secretary of State, and others on international narcotics matters. — Abbr. INL.

Bureau of International Organization Affairs. A unit in the U.S. Department of State responsible for coordinating U.S. diplomatic participation in the United Nations and other international organizations and conferences. — Abbr. IO.

Bureau of Labor Statistics. An independent agency in the U.S. Department of Labor responsible for compiling and analyzing statistical information on employment and the economy. • The Bureau reports on employment, unemployment, consumer and producer prices, consumer expenditures, import and export prices, wages and employee benefits, productivity and technological change, employment projections, and occupational illness and injury. — Abbr. BLS.

Bureau of Land Management. The unit within the U.S. Department of the Interior responsible for managing the national-resource lands (some 450 million acres) and their resources and for administering the mineral resources connected with acquired lands and the submerged lands of the Outer Continental Shelf (OCS). • The bureau was established on July 16, 1946, by consolidating the General Land Office (established in 1812) and the Grazing Service (established in 1934). *See* 35 USCA §§ 1731 et seq.

Bureau of Nonproliferation. A unit in the U.S. Department of State responsible for leading efforts to prevent the proliferation of weapons of mass destruction, delivery systems, and advanced conventional arms. — Also termed *Nonproliferation Bureau.*

Bureau of Oceans and International Environmental and Scientific Affairs. A unit in the U.S. Department of State responsible for coordinating U.S. ocean, environment, and health policies. — Abbr. OES.

Bureau of Political–Military Affairs. A unit in the U.S. Department of State responsible for analyzing defense-related policy issues, managing security-assistance funds, and coordinating peace-keeping and humanitarian operations. — Abbr. PM. — Also termed *Political–Military Affairs Bureau.*

Bureau of Population, Refugees, and Migration. A unit in the U.S. Department of State responsible for formulating policy and administering U.S. assistance and admissions programs for refugees and others. — Abbr. PRM.

Bureau of Prisons. The unit in the U.S. Department of Justice responsible for operating the federal prison system. • It oversees all federal penal and correctional facilities, assists states and local governments in improving their correctional facilities, and provides notice of prisoner releases. 18 USCA §§ 4041 et seq. See NATIONAL INSTITUTE OF CORRECTIONS. — Abbr. BOP.

Bureau of Reclamation. A unit in the U.S. Department of the Interior that built dams in 17 western states and is now responsible for selling hydroelectric power from those dams and water from the reservoirs. • Among the 600 dams constructed are Hoover Dam and Grand Coulee Dam.

Bureau of the Budget. See OFFICE OF MANAGEMENT AND BUDGET.

Bureau of the Census. A unit in the U.S. Department of Commerce responsible for conducting and publishing the census required by the U.S. Constitution to be taken every ten years. • Established in 1902, the Bureau also conducts other population surveys and estimates as required by law. It is a part of the Department's Economics and Statistics Administration. — Also termed *Census Bureau.*

Bureau of the Mint. See UNITED STATES MINT.

Bureau of the Public Debt. A unit in the U.S. Department of the Treasury responsible for issuing and redeeming Treasury bills, notes, and bonds, and for managing the U.S. Savings Bond Program.

Bureau of Transportation Statistics. A unit in the U.S. Department of Transportation responsible for compiling and publishing transportation statistics. — Abbr. BTS.

Bureaux Internationaux Reunis pour la Protection de la Propriete Intellectuelle. See INTERNATIONAL BUREAU FOR THE PROTECTION OF INTELLECTUAL PROPERTY.

Burford **abstention.** See ABSTENTION.

burgess (bər-jis). *Hist.* **1.** An inhabitant or freeman of a borough or town. **2.** A magistrate of a borough. **3.** A person entitled to vote at elections. **4.** A representative of a borough or town in Parliament.

burglar, *n.* (16c) One who commits burglary.

burglarious (bər-**glair**-ee-əs), *adj.* Of or relating to burglary <burglarious intent>. — **burglariously,** *adv.*

burglarize, *vb.* To commit a burglary <the defendant burglarized three houses>. — Also termed (esp. in BrE) *burgle.*

burglary, *n.* (16c) **1.** The common-law offense of breaking and entering another's dwelling at night with the intent to commit a felony. **2.** The modern statutory offense of breaking and entering any building — not just a dwelling, and not only at night — with the intent to commit a felony. • Some statutes make petit larceny an alternative to a felony for purposes of proving burglarious intent. — Also termed (in sense 2) *breaking and entering; statutory burglary.* Cf. ROBBERY.

> *generic burglary.* An unlawful or unprivileged entry into, or remaining in, a building or structure with intent to commit a crime. *Taylor v. United States,* 495 U.S. 575, 110 S.Ct. 2143 (1990).

burglary tool. (*often pl.*) (1903) An implement designed to help a person commit a burglary. • In many jurisdictions, it is illegal to possess such a tool if the possessor intends to commit a burglary.

burgle. See BURGLARIZE.

burial insurance. See INSURANCE.

buried-facts doctrine. *Securities.* The rule that a proxy-statement disclosure is inadequate if a reasonable shareholder could fail to understand the risks presented by facts scattered throughout the proxy. • In applying this rule, a court will consider a securities disclosure to be false and misleading if its overall significance is obscured because material information is buried in footnotes, appendixes, and the like.

burking, *n.* The crime of murdering someone, usu. by smothering, for the purpose of selling the corpse. • This term arose from the Scottish murder team of Burke and Hare, whose practice in 1828 of suffocating their victims while leaving few visible marks made the corpses more salable to medical schools. — **burke,** *vb.*

burnt-records act. A statute that enables a property owner to quiet title if the public records for the property have been lost or destroyed in a disaster.

bursting-bubble theory. (1941) *Evidence.* The principle that a presumption disappears once the presumed facts have been contradicted by credible evidence.

Bush doctrine. The policy announced by President George W. Bush after the September 11, 2001 attacks on the World Trade Center and the Pentagon, to the effect that nations harboring terrorists will be treated as terrorists themselves and may be subject to a first-strike strategy. Cf. SOVEREIGN EQUALITY.

business. 1. A commercial enterprise carried on for profit; a particular occupation or employment habitually engaged in for livelihood or gain. **2.** Commercial enterprises <business and academia often have congruent aims>. **3.** Commercial transactions <the company has never done business in Louisiana>. See DOING BUSINESS. **4.** By extension, transactions or matters of a noncommercial nature <the courts' criminal business occasionally overshadows its civil business>. **5.** *Parliamentary law.* The matters that come before a deliberative assembly for its consideration and action, or for its information with a view to possible action in the future. • In senses 2, 3, and 4, the word is used in a collective meaning.

> *new business.* An item of business introduced from the floor or taken from the table without having been scheduled for consideration. See TAKE FROM THE TABLE.

> *old business.* See *unfinished business.*

> *unfinished business.* A general order carried over from an earlier meeting in the same session because the meeting adjourned before or while considering it. • The term "unfinished business" is preferred to "old business," which may incorrectly imply renewed consideration of business that has been finally disposed of. See *general order* under ORDER (4); SESSION (2).

> *unfinished business and general orders.* A common category on an agenda. See *unfinished business; general order* under ORDER (4).

business agent. 1. See *managing agent* under AGENT. **2.** A labor-union representative selected to deal with employers.

business angel. See *angel investor* under INVESTOR.

business appraiser. See APPRAISER.

business associations. See BUSINESS ENTERPRISES.

business combination. 1. The consolidation, for accounting purposes, of a corporation and one or more incorporated or unincorporated businesses.

2. The two entities considered as one entity for accounting purposes.

business compulsion. See *economic duress* under DURESS.

business-continuation agreement. See AGREEMENT.

business corporation. See CORPORATION.

business court. See COURT.

business cycle. The recurrent expansion and contraction of economic activity.

business day. See DAY.

business enterprises. The field of law dealing with various forms of business, such as corporations, limited-liability companies, and partnerships. — Also termed *business entities*; *business associations*; *enterprise organizations*.

business entry. A writing admissible under the business-records exception to the hearsay rule. See BUSINESS-RECORDS EXCEPTION.

business-entry rule. See BUSINESS-RECORDS EXCEPTION.

business expense. See EXPENSE.

business guest. See BUSINESS VISITOR (1).

business homestead. See HOMESTEAD.

business-interruption insurance. See INSURANCE.

business invitee. 1. See INVITEE. **2.** See BUSINESS VISITOR (1).

business-judgment rule. (1946) *Corporations.* The presumption that in making business decisions not involving direct self-interest or self-dealing, corporate directors act on an informed basis, in good faith, and in the honest belief that their actions are in the corporation's best interest. • The rule shields directors and officers from liability for unprofitable or harmful corporate transactions if the transactions were made in good faith, with due care, and within the directors' or officers' authority.

business loss. See *ordinary loss* under LOSS.

business method. *Patents.* A way or an aspect of a way in which a commercial enterprise is operated.

business-method exception. *Intellectual property.* The traditional doctrine that business methods are not protected by intellectual-property laws. • Early caselaw established that "pure methods of doing business" were unpatentable. But in 1998, the Federal Circuit held in *State St. Bank & Trust Co. v. Signature Fin. Group* (149 F.3d 1368) that business methods are not per se unpatentable if they otherwise meet the requirements for a valid patent. The European Patent Convention expressly excludes business methods from patent protection.

business-method patent. See PATENT (3).

Business Methods Patent Initiative. A U.S. Patent and Trademark Office program that added a second level to business-method-patent reviews for the purpose of reducing the number of business-method patents issued. • The PTO created the initiative in response to complaints that examiners improperly approved many business-method patents. After an examiner approves the application and before a business-method patent is granted, a second examiner must completely review the application and either reject the application or affirm the issuance of the patent.

business opportunity. The chance to buy or lease either a going business, or a product, service, or equipment that will enable the buyer or lessee to profit.

business-partner insurance. See *partnership insurance* under INSURANCE.

business plan. (1890) A written proposal explaining a new business or business idea and usu. covering financial, marketing, and operational plans.

business-purpose doctrine. (1939) *Tax.* The principle that a transaction must serve a bona fide business purpose (i.e., not just for tax avoidance) to qualify for beneficial tax treatment.

business record. A report, memorandum, or other record made usu. in the ordinary course of business. • It may be ordered produced as part of discovery in a lawsuit.

business-records exception. (1939) *Evidence.* A hearsay exception allowing business records (such as reports or memoranda) to be admitted into evidence if they were prepared in the ordinary course of business. • If there is good reason to doubt a record's reliability (e.g., the record was prepared in anticipation of litigation), the exception will not apply. Fed. R. Evid. 803(6). — Also termed *business-entry rule*.

business-risk exclusion. See EXCLUSION (3).

Business Software Alliance. *Copyright.* An international trade organization representing leading software and e-commerce developers, formed to educate governments and the public about software issues and to fight software piracy and Internet theft. — Abbr. BSA.

business-to-business, *adj.* Of or relating to commerce between businesses, as distinguished from commerce between a business and consumers. — Abbr. B2B. Cf. BUSINESS-TO-CONSUMER.

business-to-business e-commerce. Electronic commerce between businesses over the Internet.

business-to-consumer, *adj.* Of or relating to commerce between a business and consumers, as distinguished from commerce between businesses. — Abbr. B2C. Cf. BUSINESS-TO-BUSI-NESS.

business-to-consumer e-commerce. Electronic commerce between a business and consumers over the Internet.

business tort. See TORT.

business transaction. An action that affects the actor's financial or economic interests, including the making of a contract.

business trust. See TRUST (4).

business visitor. 1. *Torts.* A person who is invited or permitted to enter or remain on another's land for a purpose directly or indirectly connected with the landowner's or possessor's business dealings. — Also termed *business invitee; business guest.* See INVITEE. **2.** *Immigration law.* A non-U.S. citizen who has a B-1 visa, which allows the person to be employed while in the United States.

bust-up merger. See MERGER.

but-for cause. See CAUSE (1).

but-for materiality. *Patents.* In an analysis of allegedly inequitable conduct, a test for determining the materiality of withheld information by assessing whether the withheld information, if disclosed, would have resulted in a finding of unpatentability. ● Under this test, the issue is whether the patent would have issued if not for the misconduct of the applicant. By contrast, under the subjective but-for test, the issue is whether the misrepresentation caused the examiner to issue the patent. Although both tests have been applied by the courts, the Federal Circuit has rejected the but-for materiality test in favor of the materiality test codified in 37 CFR 1.56. — Also termed *objective but-for test.* Cf. REASONABLE EXAMINER TEST.

but-for test. (1925) *Tort & criminal law.* The doctrine that causation exists only when the result would not have occurred without the party's conduct. — Also termed (in criminal law) *had-not test.* See *but-for cause* under CAUSE (1). Cf. SUBSTANTIAL-CAUSE TEST.

but so insane as not to be responsible. See GUILTY BUT MENTALLY ILL.

butterfly ballot. See BALLOT.

butts and bounds. See METES AND BOUNDS.

buy. See PURCHASE (1).

buy-and-sell agreement. See BUY–SELL AGREEMENT.

buy-back clause. 1. *Contracts.* A provision that requires a manufacturer or franchiser to buy back inventory and equipment if the distributor or franchisee's contract is terminated prematurely. **2.** *Contracts.* A clause allowing the seller of property the right or opportunity to repurchase

the property under stated conditions. **3.** *Insurance.* An insurance-policy clause that provides for the reinstatement of coverage that the insurer excludes or cancels if the insured meets certain conditions. ● For instance, buy-back clauses are often used to reinstate some of the coverage taken away under pollution-exclusion clauses.

buy-down, *n.* Money paid by the buyer of a house to reduce the mortgage-interest payments.

buyer. (12c) One who makes a purchase. See PURCHASER.

    buyer in due course. See *buyer in ordinary course of business.*

    buyer in ordinary course of business. (1915) A person who — in good faith and without knowledge that the sale violates a third party's ownership rights or security interest in the goods — buys from a person regularly engaged in the business of selling goods of that kind. ● Pawnbrokers are excluded from the definition. UCC § 1-201(9). — Also termed *buyer in due course.*

    qualified institutional buyer. *Securities.* An institution with more than $100 million in invested assets.

buyer's market. See MARKET.

buying in, *n.* (17c) The purchase of property by the original owner or an interested party at an auction or foreclosure sale. — **buy in,** *vb.*

buying on margin. See MARGIN TRANSACTION.

buying syndicate. See SYNDICATE.

buy order. See ORDER (8).

buyout, *n.* The purchase of all or a controlling percentage of the assets or shares of a business. Cf. MERGER (8). — **buy out,** *vb.*

    leveraged buyout. (1975) The purchase of a publicly held corporation's outstanding stock by its management or outside investors, financed mainly with funds borrowed from investment bankers or brokers and usu. secured by the corporation's assets. — Abbr. LBO.

    management buyout. (1976) **1.** A buyout of a corporation by its own directors and officers. **2.** A leveraged buyout of a corporation by an outside entity in which the corporation's management has a material financial interest. — Abbr. MBO. See GOING PRIVATE.

buy–sell agreement. (1956) **1.** An arrangement between owners of a business by which the surviving owners agree to purchase the interest of a withdrawing or deceased owner. — Also termed *cross-purchase buy–sell agreement.* Cf. CONTINUATION AGREEMENT. **2.** *Corporations.* A share-transfer restriction that commits the shareholder to sell, and the corporation or other shareholders to buy, the shareholder's shares at a fixed price when a specified event occurs. — Also termed *buy-and-sell agreement*. Cf. OPTION AGREEMENT.

BVA. *abbr.* BOARD OF VETERANS' APPEALS.

BW. *abbr.* BID WANTED.

BXA. *abbr.* BUREAU OF EXPORT ADMINISTRATION.

by-bidder. At an auction, a person employed by the seller to bid on property for the sole purpose of stimulating bidding by potential genuine buyers; SHILL (2). — Also termed *puffer*.

by-bidding. The illegal practice of employing a person to bid at an auction for the sole purpose of stimulating bidding on the seller's property. — Also termed *puffing*. Cf. BIDDING UP; SHILLING (1).

by-election. See ELECTION (3).

bylaw [fr. Danish *bye*, Old Norse *byr*, "town"] (14c) **1.** *Parliamentary law.* (*usu. pl.*) A rule or administrative provision adopted by an organization for its internal governance and its external dealings. ● Although the bylaws may be an organization's most authoritative governing document, they are subordinate to a charter or articles of incorporation or association or to a constitution. The "constitution and bylaws" are sometimes a single document. See *governing document* under DOCUMENT; ARTICLES OF INCORPORATION. Cf. CONSTITUTION. **2.** ORDINANCE. — Sometimes spelled *by-law*; *byelaw*.

by operation of law. See OPERATION OF LAW.

bypass trust. See TRUST.

bystander. (16c) One who is present when an event takes place, but who does not become directly involved in it.

C

c. *abbr.* (1947) **1.** CIRCA. **2.** COPYRIGHT.

ca. *abbr.* CIRCA.

CA. *abbr.* CERTIFICATION AUTHORITY.

cabal (kə-**bal** *or* kə-**bahl**). (17c) A small group of political schemers or conspirators. • The term is sometimes said to have originated as an acronym from a committee of five ministers of Charles II, whose surnames began with C, A, B, A, and L (Clifford, Arlington, Buckingham, Ashley, and Lauderdale). Though colorful, this etymology is false: the term came into English directly from the French *cabale* "intrigue," which derives ultimately from Hebrew *kabbalah* "received lore."

cabala (**kab**-ə-lə *or* kə-**bahl**-ə). An esoteric or obscure doctrine.

cabinet. (*often cap.*) (17c) The advisory council to an executive officer, esp. the President. • The President's cabinet is a creation of custom and tradition, dating back to the term of George Washington. The U.S. Constitution alludes to a group of presidential advisers — the President "may require the Opinion, in writing, of the principal Officer in each of the executive Departments, upon any Subject relating to the Duties of their respective Offices" (art. II, § 2, cl. 1) — but the term *cabinet* is not specifically mentioned. The cabinet today comprises the heads of the 15 executive departments: the Secretary of State, the Secretary of the Treasury, the Secretary of Defense, the Attorney General, the Secretary of the Interior, the Secretary of Agriculture, the Secretary of Commerce, the Secretary of Labor, the Secretary of Health and Human Services, the Secretary of Housing and Urban Development, the Secretary of Transportation, the Secretary of Energy, the Secretary of Education, the Secretary of Veterans Affairs, and the Secretary of Homeland Security. Other officials, such as the U.S. ambassador to the United Nations and the director of the Office of Management and the Budget, have been accorded cabinet rank.

> **inner cabinet.** The heads of the departments of State, Treasury, Defense, and Justice. • This group is so called because in most administrations it tends to be closer to the executive and more influential than the rest of the cabinet (the *outer cabinet*).

> **kitchen cabinet.** An unofficial and informal body of noncabinet advisers who often have more sway with the executive than the real cabinet does. • This term was first used derisively in reference to some of President Andrew Jackson's advisers, who, because of their reputation for unpolished manners, were supposedly not important enough to meet in the formal rooms of the White House.

Cable and Satellite Directive. See DIRECTIVE ON THE COORDINATION OF CERTAIN RULES CONCERNING COPYRIGHT AND NEIGHBOURING RIGHTS APPLICABLE TO SATELLITE BROADCASTING AND CABLE RETRANSMISSION.

cabotage (**kab**-ə-tij). *Int'l law.* **1.** The carrying on of trade along a country's coast; the transport of goods or passengers from one port or place to another in the same country. • The privilege to carry on this trade is usu. limited to vessels flying the flag of that country. **2.** The privilege of carrying traffic between two ports in the same country. **3.** The right of a foreign airline to carry passengers and cargo between airports in the same country.

ca'canny strike. See *slowdown strike* under STRIKE.

cadastre (kə-**das**-tər). A survey and valuation of real estate in a county or region compiled for tax purposes. — Also spelled *cadaster*. — **cadastral**, *adj.*

caducary (kə-**d[y]oo**-kə-ree), *adj.* (Of a bequest or estate) subject to, relating to, or by way of escheat, lapse, or forfeiture of property <the statute was intended to waive the rights of the caducary heirs>.

caduce (kə-**d[y]oos**), *vb.* To take by escheat or lapse <the government caduced the unclaimed mineral royalties>.

caducity (kə-**d[y]oo**-sə-tee), *n.* The lapse of a testamentary gift <the testator failed to provide a contingency for the caducity of the legacy>.

caeteris paribus. See CETERIS PARIBUS.

caeterorum administration. See ADMINISTRATION.

c.a.f. Cost, assurance, and freight. • This term is synonymous with C.I.F.

CAFC. *abbr.* UNITED STATES COURT OF APPEALS FOR THE FEDERAL CIRCUIT.

cafeteria plan. An employee fringe-benefit plan allowing a choice of basic benefits up to a certain dollar amount.

cahoots (kə-**hoots**). *Slang.* Partnership, esp. in an illegal act; collusion <the lawyer was in cahoots with her client>.

Cairns's Act (**kairn**-zəz). *Hist.* An 1858 statute that expanded the relief available in England's chancery courts to include monetary damages in addition to injunctive relief. • Cairns's Act was superseded by the Judicature Acts of 1873–1875. — Also spelled *Cairns' Act.* Cf. JUDICATURE ACTS.

Calandra rule (kə-**lan**-drə). The doctrine that a grand-jury witness may be compelled to answer questions about certain items, even though the items were obtained by the police illegally. *United States v. Calandra*, 414 U.S. 338, 94 S.Ct. 613 (1974).

calculated ambiguity. See AMBIGUITY.

Caldwell error. See ERROR (2).

calendar, *n.* (15c) **1.** A systematized ordering of time into years, months, weeks, and days; esp., the Gregorian calendar established by Pope Gregory XIII in 1582 and adopted in Great Britain in 1752. • The Gregorian calendar is used throughout the Western world.

Gregorian calendar. See NEW STYLE.

Julian calendar. See OLD STYLE.

2. (18c) A court's list of civil or criminal cases. See DOCKET (2).

court calendar. See COURT CALENDAR.

short-cause calendar. A trial calendar on which a short-cause trial may be scheduled for the 10th day after the opposing party is given notice. • The request for scheduling must include an affidavit that the trial will take no longer than a certain specified period (e.g., an hour).

special calendar. A calendar marked with court cases that have been specially set for hearing or trial. See *special setting* under SETTING.

trial calendar. See DOCKET (2).

3. A list of bills reported out of a legislative committee for consideration by the entire legislature. **4.** *Parliamentary law.* AGENDA. — Also termed *calendar of business.*

action calendar. The list of business awaiting a deliberative assembly's vote. — Also termed *action agenda.*

consent calendar. A list of business awaiting a deliberative assembly's vote that is not expected to be substantially opposed and is therefore scheduled for a vote without debate, or for automatic adoption unless a member objects. — Also termed *consent agenda; unanimous-consent agenda; unanimous-consent calendar.*

debate calendar. The list of business that is awaiting a deliberative assembly's vote and that is not on the consent calendar. — Also termed *debate agenda.*

report calendar. The list of business coming before a deliberative assembly for information only rather than for its vote. • An item on the report calendar may be the subject of a vote in the future. — Also termed *report agenda.*

special-order calendar. The list of business scheduled as special orders. — Also termed *special-order agenda.* See *special order* under ORDER (4).

unanimous-consent calendar. See *consent calendar.*

calendar, *vb.* **1.** To place an important event on a calendar, esp. so that the event will be remembered. **2.** To place a case on a calendar.

calendar call. (1918) A court session in which the judge calls each case awaiting trial, determines its status, and assigns a trial date.

calendar day. See DAY.

calendar month. See MONTH (1).

calendar motion. See MOTION (1).

calendar year. See YEAR (1).

call, *n.* (13c) **1.** A request, demand, or command, esp. to come or assemble; an invitation or summons.

call for the orders of the day. *Parliamentary law.* A demand that the meeting proceed according to its order of business. — Also termed *call for the regular order.*

call for the regular order. See *call for the orders of the day.*

call of a meeting. *Parliamentary law.* Formal written notice of a meeting's time and place, sometimes stating its business, sent to each member in advance.

call of the house. A legislative body's order compelling each absent member's attendance, usu. instructing that the sergeant at arms arrest and present each absentee.

call of the roll. See *roll call.*

call to order. *Parliamentary law.* **1.** The chair's declaration that a deliberative assembly has properly convened and is ready for business. — Also termed *convocation.* **2.** The chair's request that a member follow the applicable rules or observe appropriate decorum. See DECORUM.

quorum call. A roll call to determine whether a quorum is present. See QUORUM.

roll call. *Parliamentary law.* A calling of the roll to take attendance or a vote. See *roll-call vote* under VOTE (4). — Also termed *call of the roll.*

2. A demand for payment of money.

margin call. A securities broker's demand that a customer put up money or stock as collateral when the broker finances a purchase of securities. • A margin call usu. occurs when the market prices of the securities are falling. — Also termed *maintenance call.*

3. See *call option* under OPTION. **4.** A demand for the presentation of a security (esp. a bond) for redemption before the maturity date. **5.** A landmark designating a property boundary. • The landmarks are chosen by the surveyor and recorded in his field notes or in the accompanying deed. See DIRECTORY CALL; LOCATIVE CALL; METES AND BOUNDS.

call, *vb.* (bef. 12c) **1.** To summon. **2.** To demand payment of money. **3.** To redeem (a bond) before maturity.

callable, *adj.* (Of a security) redeemable by the issuing corporation before maturity. See REDEMPTION.

callable bond. See *redeemable bond* under BOND (3).

callable preferred stock. See STOCK.

callable security. See *redeemable security* under SECURITY.

called meeting. See *special meeting* under MEETING.

call equivalent position. *Securities.* A security position that increases in value as the value of the underlying equity increases. • It includes a long convertible security, a long call option, and a short put option. SEC Rule 16a-1(b) (17 CFR § 240.16a-1(b)).

call for the orders of the day. See CALL (1).

call for the regular order. See *call for the orders of the day* under CALL (1).

calling to the bar. See CALL TO THE BAR.

call loan. See LOAN.

call of a meeting. See CALL (1).

call of the house. See CALL (1).

call of the roll. See *roll call* under CALL (1).

call option. See OPTION.

call patent. See PATENT (2).

call premium. The percentage amount of a bond's face value that a company pays, along with the face value, to redeem a callable bond; the difference between a bond's call price and its par value.

call price. See PRICE.

call-protection clause. A clause in a bond issue or a callable preferred stock issue prohibiting the issuer from recalling the security during a specified period.

call the question. *Parliamentary law.* **1.** (Of a member) to move to close debate. **2.** (Of a deliberative assembly) to adopt a motion to close debate. See CLOSE DEBATE.

call to order. See CALL (1).

call to the bar, *n.* The admission of a person to practice law. • This common phrase is a loan translation of the Latin *ad barram evocatus* ("called to the bar"). — Also termed *calling to the bar.*

call up, *vb.* *Parliamentary law.* To bring before a deliberative assembly business that is ready for consideration <call up the motion to reconsider>.

calumniate (kə-**ləm**-nee-ayt), *vb.* To slander or make false charges against. — **calumniator,** *n.*

calumny (**kal**-əm-nee), *n.* (16c) *Archaic.* **1.** The act of maliciously misrepresenting someone's words or actions in a way that is calculated to injure that person's reputation. See OBLOQUY (1). **2.** A false charge or imputation. — **calumnious** (kə-**ləm**-nee-əs), *adj.* — **calumniator** (kə-**ləm**-nee-ay-tər), *n.*

Calvin's case. The decision establishing that persons born in Scotland after the 1603 accession of James I to the English throne were deemed natural-born subjects of the King of England and could inherit English land. *Calvin v. Smith,* 7 Eng. Rep. 1, 2 S.T. 559 (1608).

Calvo clause (**kahl**-voh). A contractual clause by which an alien waives the right to invoke diplomatic immunity. • Such a clause typically appears in a contract between a national government and an alien.

Calvo doctrine. *Int'l law.* The rule that resident aliens have the same rights to protection as citizens, but no more. • This doctrine, which sought to establish a minimum international standard for the treatment of aliens, was developed by the Argentinian jurist Carlos Calvo in his treatise *Le Droit International Théorique et Pratique* (5th ed. 1896). The doctrine was intended to prevent aliens from abusing their right of diplomatic protection. It was rejected by many states on the ground that the doctrine sought to deprive states of their right to protect their citizens in countries when the rights of the general population fell below the minimum international standards.

cambist (**kam**-bist). [fr. Latin *cambiare* "to exchange"] A broker who trades promissory notes or bills of exchange. — Also termed *cambiator.*

cambium (**kam**-bee-əm). [Law Latin "exchange"] *Hist.* **1.** An exchange of money, debt, or land.

    cambium locale. A contract of exchange in which a person agrees to pay a sum of money at one location in consideration of money received at another location. — Also termed *cambium mercantile; cambium trajectitium.*

    cambium reale. An exchange of land. — Also termed *cambium manuale.*

2. A mercantile contract in which the parties agree to exchange money for money; a bill of exchange. — Also termed *escambium.* **3.** *Eccles. law.* An exchange of money that potentially allows one party to profit. • Historically, most forms of cambium were forbidden under laws against usury but were gradually allowed as a fair recompense for trouble and risk. Cf. (in sense 3) USURY.

camera (**kam**-ə-rə). [Latin] Chamber; room. See IN CAMERA.

camera regis (**kam**-ə-rə **ree**-jis). [Latin "chambers of the king"] *Hist.* A locale that the king takes a particular interest in, usu. expressed as a royal privilege benefiting a city.

Camera Stellata (**kam**-ə-rə stə-**lay**-tə). [Law Latin] See STAR CHAMBER, COURT OF.

campers. *Hist.* The share of a lawsuit's proceeds payable to a champertor. See CHAMPERTY.

CAMs. *abbr.* See COMMON-AREA MAINTENANCE CHARGES.

can, *vb.* (bef. 12c) **1.** To be able to do something <you can lift 500 pounds>. **2.** To have permission (as often interpreted by courts); MAY <no appeal can be filed until the filing fee is paid>.

cancel, *vb.* **1.** To destroy a written instrument by defacing or obliterating it <she canceled her will by marking through it>. **2.** To terminate a promise, obligation, or right <the parties canceled the contract>.

canceled check. See CHECK.

cancellation, *n.* (16c) **1.** The act of defacing or obliterating a writing (as by marking lines across it) with the intention of rendering it void. **2.** An annulment or termination of a promise or an obligation.

 flat cancellation. The cancellation of an insurance policy without any charge to the insured.

3. An equitable remedy by which courts call in and annul outstanding void or rescinded instruments because they may either spawn vexatious litigation or cloud someone's title to property. **4.** *Trademarks.* The removal of a trademark from the Principal Register. • A trademark already on the Principal Register can be challenged by a person who claims to be damaged by the placement. For five years after a mark is allowed, it can be canceled for any reason that would have blocked allowance of the application. After that time, if the owner files a declaration under § 15, the grounds for cancellation are more restricted. See INCONTESTABILITY STATUS. Cf. OPPOSITION. — **cancel,** *vb.* — **cancelable,** *adj.*

cancellation clause. A contractual provision allowing one or both parties to annul their obligations under certain conditions. — Also termed *termination clause.*

cancelled check. See CHECK.

C & F. *abbr.* COST AND FREIGHT. — Also spelled *CandF.*

candidate, *n.* [fr. Latin *candidatus*, "clothed in white"; fr. *candidus*, "white," from the white toga worn by a candidate for public office in ancient Rome as a symbol of clean government] An individual seeking nomination, election, or appointment to an office, membership, award, or like title or status. • A candidate for election becomes a "nominee" after being formally nominated. Cf. NOMINEE (1).

candidate species. See SPECIES (1).

canon (**kan**-ən), *n.* (bef. 12c) **1.** A rule or principle, esp. one accepted as fundamental.

 canon of construction. A rule used in construing legal instruments, esp. contracts and statutes. • Although a few states have codified the canons of construction — examples of which are *contra proferentem* and *ejusdem generis* — most jurisdictions treat the canons as mere customs not having the force of law. — Often shortened to *canon.* — Also termed *rule of construction; rule of interpretation.*

 canon of descent. (*usu. pl.*) A common-law rule governing intestate succession. • In England, canons of descent tended to concentrate landholdings in the hands of a few people, an approach generally rejected in the United States. — Also termed *canon of inheritance.*

2. (*usu. cap.*) A maxim stating in general terms the standards of professional conduct expected of lawyers. • The Model Code of Judicial Conduct (1990) contains five canons and hundreds of specific rules. **3.** A rule of ecclesiastical law. **4.** A corpus of writings. **5.** A clergy member on the staff of a cathedral.

 honorary canon. A canon who serves without pay or other benefits.

6. A fixed regular payment or tribute made as a contribution payable to the church.

canonical (kə-**non**-ə-kəl), *adj.* **1.** (Of a rule or decree) prescribed by, in conformity with, or relating to canon law. **2.** Orthodox; conforming to accepted rules or conventions.

canonical disability. See DISABILITY (3).

canonical impediment. See IMPEDIMENT.

canonical law. See CANON LAW.

canonical purgation. See PURGATION.

canonist (**kan**-ən-ist), *n.* An expert in canon law; esp., a canon lawyer or professor of ecclesiastical law.

canon law. 1. A body of western ecclesiastical law that was first compiled from the 12th to 14th centuries. • It has grown steadily since that time, and is now codified in the *Codex Juris Canonici* of 1983, replacing that of 1918. — Also termed *corpus juris canonici; papal law; jus canonicum.* **2.** A body of law developed within a particular religious tradition. — Also termed *church law*; *canonical law*. Cf. ECCLESIASTICAL LAW.

canon of construction. See CANON (1).

canon of descent. See CANON (1).

canon of inheritance. See *canon of descent* under CANON (1).

cant (kant). *Civil law.* A method of dividing commonly held property by awarding it to the highest-bidding owner on condition that the successful bidder must buy out each coowner's interest. — Also termed *licitation*.

canvass, *vb.* (16c) **1.** To examine in detail; scrutinize <that issue has been repeatedly canvassed by our state's courts>. **2.** To formally count ballots and report the returns <canvass the votes>. **3.** To solicit political support from voters or a voting district; to take stock of public opinion <the candidate is actively canvassing the Western states>. — **canvass,** *n.*

cap, *n.* (1947) An upper limit, such as a statutory limit on the recovery in a tort action or on the interest a bank can charge. — **cap,** *vb.*

capacitate (kə-**pas**-ə-tayt), *vb.* (17c) To qualify; to make legally competent. — **capacitation** (kə-pas-ə-**tay**-shən), *n.*

capacity. (15c) **1.** The role in which one performs an act <in her corporate capacity>.

   proprietary capacity. The capacity of a city or town when it engages in a business-like venture rather than a governmental function. See PROPRIETARY FUNCTION.

   representative capacity. (17c) The position of one standing or acting for another, esp. through delegated authority <an agent acting in a representative capacity for the principal>.

2. The power to create or enter into a legal relation under the same circumstances in which a normal person would have the power to create or enter into such a relation; specif., the satisfaction of a legal qualification, such as legal age or soundness of mind, that determines one's ability to sue or be sued, to enter into a binding contract, and the like <she had full capacity to bind the corporation with her signature>. • Unless necessary to show the court's jurisdiction, a plaintiff's pleadings need not assert the legal capacity of any party. A party wishing to raise the issue of capacity must do so by specific negative pleading. Fed. R. Civ. P. 9(a). — Also termed (specif.) *capacity to sue; power over oneself.* See STANDING. Cf. LACK OF CAPACITY. **3.** The mental ability to understand the nature and effect of one's acts <his acute pain reduced his capacity to understand the hospital's admission form>. — Also termed *mental capacity; sane memory.* See COMPETENCY.

   criminal capacity. (1853) The mental ability that a person must possess to be held accountable for a crime; the ability to understand right from wrong. See INSANITY; INFANCY.

   diminished capacity. (1912) An impaired mental condition — short of insanity — that is caused by intoxication, trauma, or disease and that prevents a person from having the mental state necessary to be held responsible for a crime. • In some jurisdictions, a defendant's diminished capacity can be used to determine the degree of the offense or the severity of the punishment. — Also termed *diminished responsibility; partial insanity; partial responsibility.* Cf. INSANITY.

   disposing capacity. See *testamentary capacity.*

   testamentary capacity. (1819) The mental ability that a person must have to prepare a valid will. • This capacity is often described as the ability to recognize the natural objects of one's bounty, the nature and extent of one's estate, and the fact that one is making a plan to dispose of the estate after death. Traditionally, the phrase "of legal age and sound mind" refers to the testator's capacity. — Also termed *disposing capacity; disposing mind; sound mind.* See *age of capacity* under AGE.

4. The ability or power to do or experience something.

   decreased capacity. A diminution in a person's physical ability because of an illness, injury, or impairment.

capacity defense. See DEFENSE (1).

capacity to sue. See CAPACITY (2).

capax doli (**kay**-paks **doh**-lı). See DOLI CAPAX.

cape (**kay**-pee). *Hist.* [Latin "take"] A writ filed to recover possession of land.

capias (**kay**-pee-əs *or* **kap**-ee-əs). [Latin "that you take"] (15c) Any of various types of writs that require an officer to take a named defendant into custody. • A capias is often issued when a respondent fails to appear or when an obligor has failed to pay child support. — Also termed *writ of capias; body execution.*

capias ad audiendum judicium (ad aw-dee-**en**-dəm joo-**dish**-ee-əm). [Latin "that you take to hear the judgment"] In a misdemeanor case, a writ issued to bring the defendant to hear the judgment to be imposed after having failed to appear.

capias ad computandum (ad kom-pyoo-**tan**-dəm). [Latin "that you take for computation"] *Hist.* A writ issued when a debtor has failed to appear and make account after losing in an action of account render. See ACCOUNTING (3).

capias ad faciendum. *Hist.* A writ used to enforce a creditor's judgment against a debtor by authorizing the debtor's arrest and imprisonment.

capias ad respondendum (ad ree-spon-**den**-dəm). [Latin "that you take to answer"] A writ commanding the sheriff to take the defendant into custody to ensure that the defendant will appear in court. — Abbr. *ca. resp.*; *ca. re.*; *ca. ad re.*

capias ad satisfaciendum (ad sat-is-fay-shee-**en**-dəm). [Latin "that you take to satisfy"] *Hist.* A postjudgment writ commanding the sheriff to imprison the defendant until the judgment is satisfied. — Abbr. *ca. sa.*

capias extendi facias (ek-**sten**-dɪ fay-shee-əs). [Latin "take for extending"] *Hist.* A writ of execution issued against one who is indebted to the Crown, commanding the sheriff to arrest the debtor.

capias in withernam (**kay**-pee-əs in **with**-ər-nahm). [Law Latin "taking again"] A writ authorizing the sheriff to seize the goods or cattle of a wrongful distrainor. — Also termed *writ of withernam*. See WITHERNAM.

capias pro fine (**kay**-pee-əs proh **fɪ**-nee). [Latin "that you take for the fine"] A writ for the arrest of a person who had not paid an imposed fine. — Also termed *capiatur pro fine*.

capias utlagatum (**kay**-pee-əs ət-lə-**gay**-təm). [Latin "you take the outlaw"] A writ commanding the arrest of an outlawed person.

capita. See PER CAPITA.

capital, *adj.* (16c) **1.** Of or relating to economic or financial capital <capital market>. **2.** Punishable by execution; involving the death penalty <a capital offense>.

capital, *n.* (17c) **1.** Money or assets invested, or available for investment, in a business. **2.** The total assets of a business, esp. those that help generate profits. **3.** The total amount or value of a corporation's stock; corporate equity. See *capital stock* under STOCK.

actual capital. Funds generated by the sale of stock. See *capital stock* (1) under STOCK.

authorized capital. See *nominal capital.*

circulating capital. See *floating capital.*

debt capital. Funds raised by issuing bonds.

equity capital. Funds provided by a company's owners in exchange for evidence of ownership, such as stock.

fixed capital. **1.** The amount of money invested in fixed assets, such as land and machinery. **2.** Fixed assets.

floating capital. **1.** Funds not allocated to a particular class of the corporation's capital stock. **2.** Funds not presently invested or committed; esp., money retained for the purpose of meeting current expenditures. — Also termed *circulating capital.*

impaired capital. Corporate funds consisting of assets that are less than the sum of the corporation's legal capital and its liabilities.

legal capital. An amount equal to the aggregate "par" or stated value of all outstanding shares of a corporation, or, in the case of stock without par value, an amount set by the board of directors. ● A minority of states require this amount to remain in the corporation to protect creditors. — Also termed *stated capital.*

moneyed capital. Money that is invested with the intent of making a profit.

nominal capital. The minimum value of the shares that a company is authorized by its association documents to issue. — Also termed *authorized capital.*

paid-in capital. The money paid for the capital stock of a corporation.

proprietary capital. Money that represents the initial investment in a sole proprietorship.

risk capital. **1.** Money or property invested in a business venture, esp. one in which the investor has no managerial control. **2.** See *venture capital.*

stated capital. **1.** See *legal capital.* **2.** The total equity of a corporation as it appears on the balance sheet.

subscribed capital. The total value of stock for which there are subscriptions (contracts of purchase).

venture capital. Funds invested in a new enterprise that has high risk and the potential for a high return. — Also termed *risk capital.* See SEED MONEY.

working capital. Current assets (such as cash, inventory, and accounts receivable) less current liabilities. ● Working capital measures liquidity and the ability to discharge short-term obligations.

capital account. See ACCOUNT.

capital asset. See ASSET.

capital contribution. 1. Cash, property, or services contributed by partners to a partnership. **2.** Funds made available by a shareholder, usu. without an increase in stock holdings.

capital crime. See *capital offense* under OFFENSE (1).

capital expenditure. (1898) An outlay of funds to acquire or improve a fixed asset. — Also termed *capital improvement*; *capital outlay.*

capital expense. See EXPENSE.

capital flight. The sending of large amounts of investment money out of a country, usu. as a result of panic caused by political turmoil or a severe recession.

capital gain. (1921) The profit realized when a capital asset is sold or exchanged. — Also termed *capital gains.* Cf. *ordinary gain* under GAIN (3); *capital loss* under LOSS.

long-term capital gain. The profit realized from selling or exchanging a capital asset held for more than a specified period, usu. one year.

short-term capital gain. The profit realized from selling or exchanging a capital asset held for less than a specified period, usu. one year. • It is treated as ordinary income under current federal tax law.

capital-gain distribution. See *capital-gain dividend* under DIVIDEND.

capital-gain dividend. See DIVIDEND.

capital gains. See CAPITAL GAIN.

capital-gains tax. See TAX.

capital goods. See GOODS.

capital impairment. The financial condition of a corporation whose assets are less than the sum of its legal capital and its liabilities.

capital improvement. See CAPITAL EXPENDITURE.

capitalis justiciarius (kap-i-**tay**-lis jəs-tish-ee-**air**-ee-əs). [Latin "chief justiciary"] *Hist.* The principal minister of state who governed when the king traveled abroad. • By the 13th century the duties of office were more judicial than political. See JUSTICIARY (2).

capitalism, *n.* (1849) An economic system that depends on the private ownership of the means of production and on competitive forces to determine what is produced. Cf. COMMUNISM (1). — **capitalist,** *adj. & n.*

capitalization, *n.* **1.** The act or process of capitalizing or converting something into capital. **2.** The amount or sum resulting from this act or process. **3.** The total amount of long-term financing used by a business, including stocks, bonds, retained earnings, and other funds. **4.** The total par value or stated value of the authorized or outstanding stock of a corporation.

thin capitalization. The financial condition of a firm that has a high ratio of liabilities to capital.

undercapitalization. The financial condition of a firm that does not have enough capital to carry on its business.

capitalization accounting method. See ACCOUNTING METHOD.

capitalization rate. The interest rate used in calculating the present value of future periodic payments. — Also termed *cap rate; income yield.*

capitalization ratio. The ratio between the amount of capital raised and the total capitalization of the firm. — Also termed *capital ratio.*

capitalize, *vb.* **1.** To convert (earnings) into capital. **2.** To treat (a cost) as a capital expenditure rather than an ordinary and necessary expense. **3.** To determine the present value of (long-term income). **4.** To supply capital for (a business).

capitalized expense. See EXPENSE.

capital lease. See LEASE-PURCHASE AGREEMENT.

capital leverage. (1940) The use of borrowed funds in a business to obtain a return greater than the interest rate. See LEVERAGE.

capital loss. See LOSS.

capital market. See MARKET.

capital offense. See OFFENSE (1).

capital outlay. (1857) **1.** CAPITAL EXPENDITURE. **2.** Money expended in acquiring, equipping, and promoting a business.

capital punishment. The sentence of death for a serious crime. — Also termed *death penalty.* See DEATH PENALTY.

capital ratio. See CAPITALIZATION RATIO.

capital recovery. (1942) The collection of charged-off bad debt that has been previously written off against the allowance for doubtful accounts.

capital return. See RETURN.

capital-risk test. *Securities.* A method of determining whether a transaction constitutes an investment contract (subject to securities laws), whereby if a substantial portion of the capital used by a franchiser to start its operations is provided by a franchisee, then the transaction is treated as an investment contract. Cf. RISK-CAPITAL TEST.

capital stock. See STOCK.

capital-stock tax. See TAX.

capital structure. (1923) The mix of debt and equity by which a business finances its operations; the relative proportions of short-term debt, long-term debt, and capital stock.

capital surplus. See SURPLUS.

capital transaction. A purchase, sale, or exchange of a capital asset.

capitated, *adj. Insurance.* Of or relating to a health-care system that gives a medical-care provider a fixed fee per patient regardless of the treatment required.

capitation. **1.** See *poll tax* under TAX. **2.** A method of paying a healthcare provider based on the number of members in a health-benefit plan that the provider contracts to treat. • The health plan's sponsor agrees to pay a fixed amount per person each period, regardless of what services are provided.

capitation tax. See *poll tax* under TAX.

capitulary (kə-**pich**-ə-ler-ee). [Latin "chapter *or* section (of a code)"] **1.** Any orderly and systematic collection or code of laws. **2.** *Hist.* A law or series of laws enacted by a Frankish king, esp. Charlemagne, dealing esp. with ecclesiastical affairs.

capitulation (kə-pich-ə-**lay**-shən), *n.* (16c) **1.** The act of surrendering or giving in. **2.** *Int'l law.* An agreement to surrender a fortified place or a military or naval force. • A commander in control may generally make such an agreement for the place or force. **3.** *Hist.* An agreement between a Christian state and a non-Christian one (such as the Ottoman Empire) giving subjects of the former certain privileges in the territory of the latter. **4.** *Hist. International law.* A special, usu. nonreciprocal, right established by a treaty through which one nation could exercise jurisdiction over its citizens and their property within the territory of another nation. • Capitulations were a common feature of trade treaties in particular because merchants often accumulated wealth in foreign nations. Capitulations became disfavored before World War I and were gradually abolished during the 20th century. — **capitulate,** *vb.* — **capitulatory,** *adj.*

CAPJ. *abbr.* See *chief administrative patent judge* under JUDGE.

capper. 1. One who solicits business for an attorney. See BARRATRY (1); RUNNER (2). **2.** *Slang.* A person who acts as a lure for others (as in a gambling or confidence game). — Also termed (in sense 2) *stool pigeon.*

cap rate. See CAPITALIZATION RATE.

caprice (kə-**prees**), *n.* **1.** Arbitrary or unfounded motivation. **2.** The disposition to change one's mind impulsively.

capricious (kə-**prish**-əs), *adj.* (17c) **1.** (Of a person) characterized by or guided by unpredictable or impulsive behavior. **2.** (Of a decree) contrary to the evidence or established rules of law. Cf. ARBITRARY.

CAPTA. *abbr.* CHILD ABUSE PREVENTION AND TREATMENT ACT.

captain-of-the-ship doctrine. In medical-malpractice law, the doctrine imposing liability on a surgeon for the actions of assistants who are under the surgeon's control but who are employees of the hospital, not the surgeon.

captain's mast. See MAST (1).

captation (kap-**tay**-shən). *Civil law.* Coercion of a testator resulting in the substitution of another person's desires for those of the testator. • The term formerly applied to the first stage of a hypnotic trance. Cf. UNDUE INFLUENCE.

captator (kap-**tay**-tər). *Civil law.* A person who obtains or tries to obtain a gift or legacy through artifice. See UNDUE INFLUENCE.

caption. (17c) **1.** The introductory part of a court paper stating the names of the parties, the name of the court, the docket or file number, and a description of the paper. Fed. R. Civ. P. 10(a). Cf. STYLE (1). **2.** The arrest or seizure of a person by legal process. **3.** See HEADING.

captive, *n.* **1.** A person who is unlawfully seized and held by another. Cf. PRISONER. **2.** PRISONER OF WAR. **3.** An animal, esp. a wild one, that is caught and kept confined.

captive-audience doctrine. 1. *Constitutional law.* The principle that when the listener cannot, as a practical matter, escape from intrusive speech, the speech can be restricted. **2.** *Labor law.* The rule that prohibits either party to a union election from making a speech on company time to a mass assembly of employees within 24 hours of an election. — Also termed *captive-audience rule.*

captive insurance. See INSURANCE.

captive insurance company. See INSURANCE COMPANY.

captive insurer. See *captive insurance company* under INSURANCE COMPANY.

captive law firm. See LAW FIRM.

capture. See RULE OF CAPTURE.

capture-and-hold rule. *Oil & gas.* For royalty-calculation purposes, the doctrine that "production" occurs when oil or gas is pumped to the surface and stored, whether at the wellhead or elsewhere on the leased property. Cf. MARKETABLE-PRODUCT RULE.

cardinal-change doctrine. *Contracts.* The principle that if the government makes a fundamental, unilateral change to a contract beyond the scope of what was originally contemplated, the other party (usu. a contractor) will be released from the obligation to continue work under the contract. • A contractor's allegation of *cardinal change* is essentially an assertion that the government has breached the contract.

care, *n.* (bef. 12c) **1.** Serious attention; heed <written with care>. **2.** Under the law of negligence or of obligations, the conduct demanded of a person in a given situation. • Typically, this involves a person's giving attention both to possible dangers, mistakes, and pitfalls and to ways of minimizing those risks <standard of care>. See DEGREE OF CARE; REASONABLE PERSON.

adequate care. See *reasonable care.*

due care. See *reasonable care.*

extraordinary care. See *great care.*

great care. (15c) **1.** The degree of care that a prudent person exercises in dealing with very important personal affairs. **2.** The degree of care exercised in a given situation by someone in the business or profession of dealing with the situation. — Also termed *extraordinary care*; *high degree of care*; *utmost care*.

high degree of care. See *great care*.

highest degree of care. 1. The degree of care exercised commensurate with the danger involved. **2.** See *great care*.

ordinary care. See *reasonable care*.

proper care. See *reasonable care*.

reasonable care. (17c) As a test of liability for negligence, the degree of care that a prudent and competent person engaged in the same line of business or endeavor would exercise under similar circumstances. — Also termed *due care*; *ordinary care*; *adequate care*; *proper care*. See REASONABLE PERSON.

slight care. (17c) The degree of care a person gives to matters of minor importance; the degree of care given by a person of limited accountability.

utmost care. See *great care*.

3. *Family law.* The provision of physical or psychological comfort to another, esp. an ailing spouse, child, or parent.

career criminal. See RECIDIVIST.

career offender. See OFFENDER.

career vice-consul. See VICE-CONSUL.

caregiver. *Family law.* A person, usu. not a parent, who has and exercises custodial responsibility for a child or for an elderly or disabled person. — Also termed *caretaker*; *custodian*. See RESIDENTIAL RESPONSIBILITY.

careless, *adj.* (bef. 12c) **1.** (Of a person) not exercising reasonable care. **2.** (Of an action or behavior) engaged in without reasonable care. Cf. RECKLESS.

carelessness, *n.* (bef. 12c) **1.** The fact, condition, or instance of a person's either not having done what he or she ought to have done, or having done what he or she ought not to have done; heedless inattention. **2.** A person's general disposition not to do something that ought to be done.

ca. resp. See *capias ad respondendum* under CAPIAS.

caretaker. See CAREGIVER.

caretaking functions. *Family law.* A parent's or caregiver's task that either involves interaction with a child or directs others' interaction with a child. ● Some caretaking functions include feeding and bathing a child, guiding the child in language and motor-skills development, caring for a sick child, disciplining the child, being involved in the child's educational development,

and giving the child moral instruction and guidance. *Principles of the Law of Family Dissolution: Analysis and Recommendations* § 2.03 (ALI, Tentative Draft No. 3, pt. I, 1998). Cf. PARENTING FUNCTIONS.

cargo. Goods transported by a vessel, airplane, or vehicle; FREIGHT (1).

general cargo. Goods and materials of various types transported by carriers, often in a common load, with few or no restrictions.

hazardous cargo. Dangerous goods or materials whose carriage is usu. subject to stringent regulatory and statutory restrictions.

cargo insurance. See INSURANCE.

carjacking. The forcible theft of a vehicle from a motorist; the unlawful commandeering of an automobile. 18 USCA § 2119. — **carjack,** *vb.*

carnal abuse. See *sexual abuse* (1) under ABUSE.

carnal knowledge. (15c) *Archaic.* Sexual intercourse, esp. with an underage female. — Sometimes shortened to *knowledge*.

carnet (kahr-**nay**). A customs document allowing an item (esp. an automobile) to be exported temporarily from one country into another country.

carriage. Transport of freight or passengers.

carriage and insurance paid to. A mercantile-contract term allocating the rights and duties of the buyer and the seller of goods with respect to delivery, payment, and risk of loss, whereby the seller must (1) clear the goods for export, (2) procure and pay for insurance against the buyer's risk of damage while the goods are in carriage, (3) deliver the goods to the buyer's chosen carrier, and (4) bear the costs of carriage (apart from import duties) to the named destination. ● When the goods are delivered to the carrier, the seller's delivery is complete; the risk of loss then passes to the buyer. Any mode of transportation can be used to carry the goods. — Abbr. CIP. Cf. CARRIAGE PAID TO.

Carriage of Goods by Sea Act. *Maritime law.* A 1936 federal statute regulating a carrier's liability for the loss or damage, and sometimes the delay, of ocean cargo shipped under a bill of lading. 46 USCA §§ 1300–15. ● The Act defines many of the rights and responsibilities of both the issuers and the holders of ocean bills of lading. — Abbr. COGSA.

carriage paid to. A mercantile-contract term allocating the rights and duties of the buyer and the seller of goods with respect to delivery, payment, and risk of loss, whereby the seller must (1) clear the goods for export, (2) deliver them to the buyer's chosen carrier, and (3) pay the costs of carriage (apart from import duties) to the named destination. ● When the goods are delivered to the carrier, the seller's delivery is complete; the risk of loss then passes to the buyer. Any mode of transportation can be used to carry the goods. — Abbr. CPT. Cf. CARRIAGE AND INSURANCE PAID TO.

carried interest. See INTEREST (2).

carrier. 1. An individual or organization (such as a shipowner, a railroad, or an airline) that contracts to transport passengers or goods for a fee. Cf. SHIPPER.

   common carrier. (15c) A commercial enterprise that holds itself out to the public as offering to transport freight or passengers for a fee. • A common carrier is generally required by law to transport freight or passengers or freight, without refusal, if the approved fare or charge is paid. — Also termed *public carrier.*

   marine carrier. A carrier operating on navigable waters subject to the jurisdiction of the United States.

   non-vessel-operating common carrier. Maritime law. A freight forwarder that does not own the means of transportation, but that contracts with a shipper to transport freight, and with a carrier to perform the transportation. • The non-vessel-operating common carrier becomes the carrier in the contract with the original shipper, and the shipper in the contract with the eventual carrier. See FREIGHT FORWARDER. — Abbr. NVOCC.

   private carrier. (18c) Any carrier that is not a common carrier by law. • A private carrier is not bound to accept business from the general public. — Also termed *contract carrier.*

   2. INSURER.

carrier's lien. See LIEN.

Carroll **doctrine.** The principle that a broadcast licensee has standing to contest any grant of a competitive license by the Federal Communications Commission because the grant could lead to a diminution in broadcast service by causing economic injury to an existing licensee. *Carroll Broadcasting Co. v. FCC*, 258 F.2d 440 (D.C. Cir. 1958).

carry, *vb.* **1.** To sustain the weight or burden of; to hold or bear <more weight than a single person can carry>. **2.** To convey or transport <carrying the coal from one state to another>. **3.** To possess and convey (a firearm) in a vehicle, including the locked glove compartment or trunk of a car <he carried the guns in his trunk>. • The United States Supreme Court adopted this definition in interpreting the phrase *carries a firearm* as used in a statute imposing a mandatory prison term on a person who uses or carries a firearm while committing a drug-trafficking crime. *Muscarello v. U.S.*, 524 U.S. 125, 118 S.Ct. 1911 (1998). **4.** In

a figurative sense, to possess or hold (insurance, etc.) <the decedent did not carry life insurance>. **5.** *Parliamentary law.* To adopt. • In this sense, the verb may be either intransitive <the motion carries> or transitive (in a passive construction) <the motion is carried>. See ADOPTION (5). **6.** To provide funds or credit for the payment of (stock, etc.), often as an advance, for an agreed-on period <the investor carried the stock purchases for eight months>. **7.** To absorb the cost of holding or having, usu. temporarily <the business will carry the debt for another quarter>.

carry away, *vb.* To take or move (stolen property, etc.). • The traditional count for larceny was that the defendant "did steal, take, and carry away" the property. A "carrying away" can be a slight movement of the property. See ASPORTATION.

carryback. (1942) *Tax.* An income-tax deduction (esp. for a net operating loss) that cannot be taken entirely in a given period but may be taken in an earlier period (usu. the previous three years). — Also termed *loss carryback; tax-loss carryback.* Cf. CARRYOVER.

carryforward. See CARRYOVER.

carrying away. See ASPORTATION.

carrying back the date of invention. See ANTE-DATING OF A PRIOR-ART REFERENCE.

carrying charge. 1. A cost, in addition to interest, paid to a creditor for carrying installment credit. **2.** Expenses incident to property ownership, such as taxes and upkeep.

carrying cost. See COST (1).

carrying value. See BOOK VALUE (1).

carryover. (1925) *Tax.* An income-tax deduction (esp. for a net operating loss) that cannot be taken entirely in a given period but may be taken in a later period (usu. the next five years). — Also termed *loss carryover; tax-loss carryover; carryforward; loss carryforward; tax-loss carryforward.* Cf. CARRYBACK.

carryover basis. See BASIS.

Carta Mercatoria (**kahr**-tə mər-kə-**tor**-ee-ə). *Hist.* An English statute (enacted in 1303) establishing various rules that favored certain foreign merchants. • In exchange for paying customs duties, merchants received extensive trading rights throughout England, the power to export their merchandise, the liberty to dwell where they pleased, and certain legal rights. — Also termed *Statutum de Nova Custuma.*

carte blanche (kahrt **blah***n***sh**). [French "blank card"] **1.** A signed, blank instrument that is filled out at an agent's discretion. **2.** Full discretionary power; unlimited authority.

cartel (kahr-**tel**), *n.* (17c) **1.** A combination of producers or sellers that join together to control a product's production or price. **2.** An association of firms with common interests, seeking to prevent extreme or unfair competition, allocate markets, or share knowledge. **3.** *Int'l law.* An agreement between belligerents about the means of conducting whatever relations they allow during wartime; esp., such an agreement regarding the exchange of prisoners. — Also spelled *chartel.* — **cartelize** (**kahr**-tə-lɪz *or* kahr-**tel**-ɪz), *vb.*

car trust certificate. See EQUIPMENT TRUST CERTIFICATE.

cartulary (**kahr**-tyoo-lair-ee), *n.* A collection of legal documents, esp. charters and title deeds to property.

carve out, *vb.* **1.** To create an explicit exception to a broad rule. **2.** *Tax.* To separate from property the income derived from the property.

carveout, *n.* (1966) **1.** An explicit exception to a broad rule. **2.** *Tax.* For tax purposes, the separation from property of the income derived from the property.

ca. sa. See *capias ad satisfaciendum* under CAPIAS.

CASA. *abbr.* **1.** COURT-APPOINTED SPECIAL ADVOCATE. **2.** COURT APPOINTED SPECIAL ADVOCATES.

CASA volunteer. *Family law.* A specially screened and trained child-welfare volunteer appointed by the court to conduct an independent investigation of both the state agency and the family and to submit a report with findings and recommendations. ● In some jurisdictions such volunteers are provided for statutorily. They sometimes act as guardians ad litem. The CASA volunteer usu. (1) provides independent assessment of the child's needs, (2) acts as an advocate for the child, and (3) monitors agency decision-making and court proceedings. See COURT APPOINTED SPECIAL ADVOCATES.

case. (13c) **1.** A civil or criminal proceeding, action, suit, or controversy at law or in equity <the parties settled the case>.

active case. (1949) A case that is still pending.

case agreed on. See *case stated* (1).

case at bar. (16c) A case under the immediate consideration of the court. — Also termed *case at bench; instant case; present case.* See BAR (3).

case at bench. See *case at bar.*

case made. See *case reserved* (1).

case of first impression. (1806) A case that presents the court with an issue of law that has not previously been decided by any controlling legal authority in that jurisdiction.

case reserved. (18c) **1.** A written statement of the facts proved at trial and drawn up and stipulated to by the parties, so that certain legal issues can be decided by an appellate court. — Also termed *case made; special case.* **2.** *Hist.* An agreement between litigants to submit the case to a judge rather than to a jury.

case stated. (17c) **1.** A formal written statement of the facts in a case, submitted to the court jointly by the parties so that a decision may be rendered without trial. — Also termed *case agreed on.* **2.** *Hist.* A procedure used by the Court of Chancery to refer difficult legal questions to a common-law court. ● This procedure was abolished in 1852. **3.** *English law.* An appeal from a Magistrates' Court to the Divisional Court of Queen's Bench on a point of criminal law. ● After ruling, the magistrate states the facts for the appeal and the Queen's Bench rules on the question of law presented by the magistrate's ruling.

congressional-reference case. A request by Congress for the United States Court of Claims to give an advisory opinion on the merits of a non-pension claim against the United States. See 28 USCA §§ 1492, 2509.

inactive case. (1981) A pending case that is not proceeding toward resolution. ● This may occur for several reasons, such as nonservice, want of prosecution, or (in a criminal case) the defendant's having absconded.

instant case. See *case at bar.*

present case. See *case at bar.*

reference case. *Canadian law.* An advisory opinion issued by the Supreme Court of Canada at the request of the executive or legislative branch of the federal government. ● A reference is exceptional because the opinion interprets, and often resolves, a dispute even though no case or controversy is presented to the court. *See, e.g., Reference re Secession of Quebec,* [1998] 2 S.C.R. 217.

special case. See *case reserved* (1).

test case. (1894) **1.** A lawsuit brought to establish an important legal principle or right. ● Such an action is frequently brought by the parties' mutual consent on agreed facts — when that is so, a test case is also sometimes termed *amicable action* or *amicable suit.* **2.** An action selected from several suits that are based on the same facts and evidence, raise the same question of law, and have a common plaintiff or a common defendant. ● Sometimes, when all parties agree, the court orders a consolidation and all parties are bound by the decision in the test case. — Also termed *test action.*

2. A criminal investigation <the Manson case>. **3.** An individual suspect or convict in relation to any aspect of the criminal-justice system <the probation officer said he considers Mr. Jones a difficult case>. **4.** An argument <the debater made a

compelling case for gun control>. **5.** An instance, occurrence, or situation <a case of mistaken identity> <a terminal case of cancer>. **6.** See *trespass on the case* under TRESPASS <the actions of trover and case are not entirely defunct>.

case abstract. See CASE NOTE.

case agreed on. See *case stated* (1) under CASE.

casebook. (18c) A compilation of extracts from instructive cases on a particular subject, usu. with commentary and questions about the cases, designed as a teaching aid. See SOCRATIC METHOD. Cf. HORNBOOK.

casebook method. (1915) An inductive system of teaching law in which students study specific cases to learn general legal principles. • Professor Christopher C. Langdell introduced the technique at Harvard Law School in 1869. The casebook method is now the most widely used form of instruction in American law schools. — Also termed *case method*; *case system*; *Langdell method.* Cf. SOCRATIC METHOD; HORNBOOK METHOD.

case brief. See CASE NOTE.

case evaluation. 1. Assessment of a case's strengths and weaknesses, along with the cost of litigation and the amount of potential liability or recovery, typically done to decide whether to accept a case or to advise a client or potential client about how to proceed. **2.** MEDIATION (1).

caseflow. (1957) **1.** The movement of cases through the judicial system, from the initial filing to the final appeal. **2.** An analysis of that movement.

case-in-chief. (1853) **1.** The evidence presented at trial by a party between the time the party calls the first witness and the time the party rests. **2.** The part of a trial in which a party presents evidence to support the claim or defense. Cf. REBUTTAL (1), (2).

caselaw. (1861) The law to be found in the collection of reported cases that form all or part of the body of law within a given jurisdiction. — Also written *case law*; *case-law.* — Also termed *decisional law*; *adjudicative law*; *jurisprudence*; *organic law.*

case lawyer. An attorney whose knowledge is largely confined to a specific field of expertise.

caseload. (1938) The volume of cases assigned to a given court, agency, officer, judge, law firm, or lawyer.

case made. See *case reserved* (1) under CASE.

case-management order. A court order designed to control the procedure in a case on the court's docket, esp. by limiting pretrial discovery. — Abbr. CMO.

case method. See CASEBOOK METHOD.

case note. A short statement summarizing a case, esp. the relevant facts, the issues, the holding, and the court's reasoning. — Sometimes written *casenote.* — Also termed *brief*, *case brief*; *case statement*; *case abstract.*

case number. The number assigned to a lawsuit when it is filed with the clerk of the court. • Each case has a distinct number that distinguishes it from all other suits filed within the jurisdiction.

case of first impression. See CASE.

case-or-controversy requirement. (1937) The constitutional requirement that, for a federal court to hear a case, the case must involve an actual dispute. See CONTROVERSY (3); *advisory opinion* under OPINION (1).

case plan. A written procedure for the care and management of a child who has been removed from his or her home and placed in foster care or in an institution. • The case plan includes (1) a description of the place where the child has been placed, (2) a plan for providing the child with safe and proper care, and (3) a plan for services that will be provided to the child's parents. Each state must have a case-review system formulated to ensure that the child is placed in the least restrictive and most appropriate place and that the plan is in the best interests of the child; the plan must be reviewed every six months. See ADOPTION AND SAFE FAMILIES ACT.

case reserved. See CASE.

case stated. See CASE.

case statement. See CASE NOTE.

case system. See CASEBOOK METHOD.

case-within-a-case rule. *Torts.* The requirement that a legal-malpractice- action plaintiff show that, but for the attorney's negligence, the plaintiff would have won the case underlying the malpractice action.

cash, *n.* (16c) **1.** Money or its equivalent. **2.** Currency or coins, negotiable checks, and balances in bank accounts. — **cash,** *vb.*

petty cash. Currency kept on hand for incidental expenditures.

cash-against-documents sale. See *documentary sale* under SALE.

cash-and-carry clause. *Int'l law.* A regulation that, before U.S. involvement in World War II, allowed belligerent countries to pay cash for goods whose export was prohibited. • Formally, this regulation was entirely neutral, but in practice it favored Great Britain.

cash bail. See BAIL (1).

cash-basis accounting method. See ACCOUNTING METHOD.

cash book. An account book of all cash received and paid out by a business.

cash budget. A period-by-period schedule of a business's opening cash on hand, estimated cash receipts, cash disbursements, and cash balance. • A cash budget is used to project a business's cash receipts and disbursements over some future period.

cash collateral. See COLLATERAL.

cash cycle. The time it takes for cash to flow into and out of a business, such as the time between the purchase of raw materials for manufacture and the sale of the finished product.

cash discount. See DISCOUNT.

cash dividend. See DIVIDEND.

cash equivalent. A short-term security that is liquid enough to be considered equivalent to cash.

cash-equivalent doctrine. *Tax.* The doctrine requiring income to be reported even if it is not cash, as when the taxpayer barters to receive in-kind payments.

cash-expenditure method. *Tax.* A technique used by the IRS to reconstruct a taxpayer's unreported income by comparing the amount spent on goods and services during a given period with the income reported for that period. • If the expenditures exceed the reported revenue, the IRS treats the difference as taxable income.

cash flow. (1954) **1.** The movement of cash through a business, as a measure of profitability or liquidity. **2.** The cash generated from a business or transaction. **3.** Cash receipts minus cash disbursements for a given period. — Sometimes written *cashflow*.

cash flow per common share. The cash flow from operations minus preferred stock dividends, divided by the number of outstanding common shares.

discounted cash flow. A method of evaluating a capital investment by comparing its projected income and costs with its current value. • Discounted cash flow is used to determine the value of a company by calculating the present value of its future cash flows. In theory, the value of the corporation's assets equals the present value of the expected cash flow generated by those assets. — Also termed *discounted-cash-flow method.* — Abbr. DCF; DCF method.

incremental cash flow. The net increase in cash flow attributable to a particular capital investment.

negative cash flow. A financial situation in which cash outflow exceeds cash inflow. See INSOLVENCY.

net cash flow. Cash inflow minus cash outflow.

cashier, *n.* **1.** One who receives and records payments at a business. **2.** A bank's or trust com-

pany's executive officer, who is responsible for banking transactions.

cashier, *vb.* (16c) To dismiss from service dishonorably <after three such incidents, Jones was cashiered>.

cashier's check. See CHECK.

cashlite. See AMERCEMENT.

cash merger. See MERGER.

cash-option transaction. *Mergers & acquisitions.* A provision in a merger agreement giving the target company's stockholders a choice between receiving either a tax-free exchange of stock or a taxable cash buyout.

cash or deferred arrangement. A retirement-plan provision permitting an employee to have a certain amount of compensation paid in cash or contributed, on behalf of the employee, to a profit-sharing or stock-bonus plan. • A 401(k) plan is a type of cash or deferred arrangement. — Abbr. CODA.

cashout, *n.* (1971) An arrangement by a seller to receive the entire amount of equity in cash rather than retain an interest in the property. — **cash out,** *vb.*

cash-out merger. See *cash merger* under MERGER.

cash-refund annuity. See ANNUITY.

cash sale. See SALE.

cash surrender value. See VALUE (2).

cash tender offer. See TENDER OFFER.

cash-transaction report. IRS Form 4789, which requires banks and other financial institutions to report cash transactions above a certain amount.

cash value. 1. See *fair market value* under VALUE (2). **2.** See *full cash value* under VALUE (2).

cash-value option. See OPTION.

casing. *Oil & gas.* The pipe in a wellbore hole, cemented into place to prevent pollution and to protect the hole.

intermediate casing. Casing that protects deep formations against pollution from drilling and producing operations.

production casing. Wellbore pipe through which oil and gas is produced. • Production casing is the last pipe set in the hole.

surface casing. Casing that protects groundwater against pollution from drilling and producing operations. • Surface casing is the first pipe set in the hole.

casinghead gas. *Oil & gas.* Natural gas in a liquid solution with crude oil, produced at the casinghead (top) of a oil well. • Casinghead gas separates from the oil at the time of production or shortly afterward.

casing point. *Oil & gas.* The point at which a well has been drilled to the desired depth and the owners must decide whether to place production pipe ("casing") in the hole to complete and equip the well for production.

cassation (ka-**say**-shən), *n.* A quashing. See COURT OF CASSATION.

CASSIS/BIB. *Patents.* A U.S. Patent and Trademark Office database of bibliographies relating to patents, sorted by their classification. • CASSIS stands for Classification and Search Support Information System. Cf. CASSIS/CLASS.

CASSIS/CLASS. *Patents.* A U.S. Patent and Trademark Office database of patents sorted by classification, available at any PTO Depository Library. Cf. CASSIS/BIB.

cast, *vb.* To formally deposit (a ballot) or signal one's choice (in a vote) <most voters cast their ballots for write-in candidates>.

cast a cloud on, *vb. Patents.* Create doubt about (a patent, esp. its validity).

castigatory (**kas**-ti-gə-tor-ee). *Hist.* A device for punishing scolds by repeatedly plunging them underwater. • This device is mentioned by the ancient Saxons (*scealfing stole*) and in Domesday Book (*cathedra stercoralis*). It was also used to punish bakers and brewers by ducking them into "stinking water" (*stercore*), possibly into a midden. — Also termed *ducking stool*; *cucking stool*; *trebucket*. See SCOLD.

casting vote. See VOTE (1).

cast-iron-pipe doctrine. See DIVIDEND-CREDIT RULE.

castle doctrine. (1892) *Criminal law.* An exception to the retreat rule allowing the use of deadly force by a person who is protecting his or her home and its inhabitants from attack, esp. from a trespasser who intends to commit a felony or inflict serious bodily harm. — Also termed *dwelling defense*; *defense of habitation*. See RETREAT RULE.

castle-guard, *n. Hist.* **1.** The protection of a castle. **2.** A form of knight-service in which a tenant must protect the lord's castle. **3.** The tenure giving rise to this knight-service. **4.** A tax once imposed in lieu of this knight-service. **5.** The territory that is chargeable with the tax imposed in lieu of the knight-service. — Also termed (in senses 2–5) *ward*.

casual, *adj.* **1.** (Of employment) occurring without regularity; occasional <a casual employee>. See *casual employment* under EMPLOYMENT. **2.** (Of an event or occurrence) not expected, foreseen, or planned; fortuitous <a casual deficit>.

casual affray. See CHANCE-MEDLEY.

casual condition. See CONDITION (2).

casual deficit. An unforeseen shortfall of funds.

casual ejector. See EJECTOR.

casual employment. See EMPLOYMENT.

casual negligence. See NEGLIGENCE.

casualty. (15c) **1.** A serious or fatal accident. **2.** A person or thing injured, lost, or destroyed.

casualty gain. *Insurance.* The profit realized by an insured when the benefits paid exceed the insured property's adjusted value.

casualty insurance. See INSURANCE.

casualty loss. See LOSS.

casualty pot. *Tax.* A step in evaluating tax liability in which casualty gains and losses are compared to determine whether a net loss or gain has occurred. Cf. MAIN POT.

casu consimili (**kay**-s[y]oo kən-**sim**-ə-lī), *n.* [Latin "in a like case"] *Hist.* A writ of entry allowing the holder of a reversionary interest in land to sue for the return of land alienated by a life tenant or a tenant by the curtesy. • This writ originated in the second Statute of Westminster (13 Edw. I) ch. 24 (1285), which expanded the writs available to litigants by requiring the Chancery to issue a writ for any situation that called for a writ similar to one that had previously issued *consimili casu* ("in a like case"). Specifically, the statute provided (in Latin) that "as often as it shall happen in chancery that in one case a writ is found, and in a like case [*in consimili casu*], falling under the same right, and requiring like remedy, no writ is to be found, the clerks of chancery shall agree in making a writ . . . ." Many other writs were framed under Westminster 2, but this particular writ's close association with the statute led to its taking the generic name. — Also termed *consimili casu*; *entry in casu consimili.*

casus (**kay**-səs). [Latin] **1.** A chance accident; an event without human intervention or fault. Cf. CULPA (1); DOLUS (1). **2.** A situation actually contemplated by the legislature in enacting a statute that applies to the situation. • In this sense, the term is opposed to *casus omissus.* Cf. CASUS OMISSUS.

casus belli (**kay**-səs **bel**-ī). [Latin] An act or circumstance that provokes or justifies war.

casus foederis (**kay**-səs **fed**-ər-is). [Latin "the case of the treaty" *or* "the case of the agreement"] **1.** *Int'l law.* A provocative act by one nation toward another, entitling the latter to call upon an ally to fulfill the terms of an alliance. **2.** A clause within a treaty of alliance specifying such provocative acts. **3.** *Contracts.* A case or an event falling within the terms of a contract.

casus fortuitus (**kay**-səs for-**t**[y]**oo**-ə-təs). [Latin] **1.** A fortuitous event. **2.** A loss not attributable to human fault.

casus male inclusus (**kay**-səs **mal**-ee in-**kloo**-səs). [Latin "case wrongly included"] A situation literally provided for by a statute or contract, but wrongly so because the provision's literal application has unintended or absurd consequences.

casus omissus (**kay**-səs ə-**mis**-əs). [Latin "case omitted"] A situation not provided for by a statute or contract, and therefore governed by caselaw or new judge-made law. Cf. CASUS (2). Pl. *casus omissi.*

catch-all, *adj.* Broad; widely encompassing <the catch-all factor allows the jury to consider all circumstances extenuating the gravity of the crime>.

catch-all, *n.* See BROADENING STATEMENT.

catching bargain. See BARGAIN.

categorical question. See QUESTION (1).

cater cousin (**kay**-tər). A distant relative. • The term derives from the French *quatrecousin*, meaning a cousin in the fourth degree.

cathedral. *Eccles. law.* The principal church of a diocese, in which the bishop's throne, or *cathedra*, is situated.

catholic creditor. See CREDITOR.

cats and dogs. *Slang.* **1.** Nonperforming securities. **2.** Highly speculative securities.

cattle rustling. The stealing of cattle.

cattle-trespass. See TRESPASS.

caucus (**kaw**-kəs), *n.* (18c) **1.** Representatives from a political party who assemble to nominate candidates and decide party policy. **2.** A meeting of a group, usu. within a deliberative assembly, of people aligned by party or interest to formulate a policy or strategy. — **caucus,** *vb.*

separate caucus. A confidential mediation session that a mediator holds with an individual party to elicit settlement offers and demands. • When separate caucuses are used, the mediator typically shuttles between the two (or more) sides of a dispute to communicate offers and demands. Formerly, ABA Model Rule of Professional Responsibility 2.2 (governing when a lawyer could act for more than one client or as an intermediary between parties) applied when a lawyer acted as a mediator. Although the rule was deleted from the Model in 2002, many states have similar rules in effect. The rule requires a lawyer acting as an intermediary to inform the parties about mediation and the mediator's role, to act impartially, and to have a good-faith belief that the matter can be resolved in all parties' best interests.

causal (**kaw**-zəl), *adj.* (16c) **1.** Of, relating to, or involving causation <a causal link exists between the defendant's action and the plaintiff's injury>.

2. Arising from a cause <a causal symptom>. Cf. CAUSATIVE.

causal challenge. See *challenge for cause* under CHALLENGE (2).

causality (kaw-**zal**-ə-tee), *n.* (17c) The principle of causal relationship; the relation between cause and effect <the foreseeability test is one of duty and of causality>. — Also termed *causation.* — **causal,** *adj.*

causa mortis (**kaw**-zə **mor**-tis), *adj.* Done or made in contemplation of one's own death. See *gift causa mortis* under GIFT.

causation (kaw-**zay**-shən). (17c) **1.** The causing or producing of an effect <the plaintiff must prove causation>. **2.** CAUSALITY.

negative causation. Securities. The defense that part of the plaintiff's damages were caused by factors other than the depreciation in value of the securities resulting from registration-statement defects. • If negative causation is proved, the plaintiff's damages should be reduced. 15 USCA § 77k(e).

transaction causation. Securities. The fact that an investor would not have engaged in a given transaction if the other party had made truthful statements at the required time.

causative (**kaw**-zə-tiv), *adj.* **1.** Effective as a cause or producing a result <causative factor of the accident>. **2.** Expressive of causation <the causative relationship between drinking and assault>. Cf. CAUSAL.

cause, *n.* (13c) **1.** Something that produces an effect or result <the cause of the accident>.

but-for cause. (1924) The cause without which the event could not have occurred. — Also termed *actual cause; cause in fact; factual cause.*

concurrent cause. (17c) One of two or more causes that simultaneously produce a result.

contributing cause. A factor that — though not the primary cause — plays a part in producing a result.

cooperative cause. Archaic. A person who is contributorily or comparatively negligent.

direct and proximate cause. See *proximate cause.*

direct cause. See *proximate cause.*

efficient adequate cause. See *proximate cause.*

efficient cause. See *proximate cause.*

efficient intervening cause. See *intervening cause.*

efficient proximate cause. See *proximate cause.*

factual cause. See *but-for cause.*

first cause. See *proximate cause.*

immediate cause. (16c) The last event in a chain of events, though not necessarily the proximate cause of what follows. — Also termed *effective cause.*

initial cause. See *proximate cause.*

intervening cause. (17c) An event that comes between the initial event in a sequence and the end result, thereby altering the natural course of events that might have connected a wrongful act to an injury. • If the intervening cause is strong enough to relieve the wrongdoer of any liability, it becomes a *superseding cause.* A *dependent intervening cause* is one that is not an act and is never a superseding cause. An *independent intervening cause* is one that operates on a condition produced by an antecedent cause but in no way resulted from that cause. — Also termed *intervening act; intervening agency; intervening force; independent intervening cause; efficient intervening cause; supervening cause; novus actus interveniens; nova causa interveniens.* See *superseding cause.*

jural cause. See *proximate cause.*

legal cause. See *proximate cause.*

primary cause. See *proximate cause.*

procuring cause. 1. See *proximate cause* (2). 2. *Real estate.* The efforts of the agent or broker who effects the sale of realty and who is therefore entitled to a commission.

proximate cause. (17c) 1. A cause that is legally sufficient to result in liability; an act or omission that is considered in law to result in a consequence, so that liability can be imposed on the actor. 2. A cause that directly produces an event and without which the event would not have occurred. — Also termed (in both senses) *direct cause; direct and proximate cause; efficient proximate cause; efficient cause; efficient adequate cause; initial cause; first cause; legal cause; procuring cause; producing cause; primary cause; jural cause.* Cf. (in sense 2) *remote cause.*

remote cause. (16c) A cause that does not necessarily or immediately produce an event or injury. Cf. *proximate cause* (2).

sole cause. (16c) The only cause that, from a legal viewpoint, produces an event or injury. • If it comes between a defendant's action and the event or injury at issue, it is treated as a *superseding cause.*

superseding cause. (1891) An intervening act or force that the law considers sufficient to override the cause for which the original tortfeasor was responsible, thereby exonerating that tortfeasor from liability. — Also termed *sole cause.* Cf. *intervening cause.*

supervening cause. See *intervening cause.*

unavoidable cause. A cause that a reasonably prudent person would not anticipate or be expected to avoid.

2. A ground for legal action <the plaintiff does not have cause to file suit>.

good cause. (16c) A legally sufficient reason. • Good cause is often the burden placed on a litigant (usu. by court rule or order) to show why a request should be granted or an action excused. The term is often used in employment-termination cases. — Also termed *good cause shown; just cause; lawful cause; sufficient cause.*

probable cause. See PROBABLE CAUSE.

3. A lawsuit; a case <the court has 50 causes on the motion docket>.

preferred cause. A case that a court may for good reason accelerate and try ahead of other cases. — Also termed *preference case; preference cause.*

short cause. A case that requires little time to try, usu. half a day or less. — Also termed *short-cause trial.*

cause, *vb.* To bring about or effect <dry conditions caused the fire>.

cause-and-prejudice rule. (1977) *Criminal law.* The doctrine that a prisoner petitioning for a federal writ of habeas corpus on the basis of a constitutional challenge must first show that the claim rests on either a new rule of constitutional law (one that was unavailable while the case was heard in the state courts) or a fact that could not have been uncovered earlier despite due diligence, and then show by clear and convincing evidence that if the constitutional error had not occurred, the prisoner would not have been convicted. 28 USCA § 2254(e)(2). • This is an exception to the procedural-default doctrine. Before 1996, the cause-and-prejudice rule allowed federal courts to grant relief on the basis of a constitutional challenge that was not presented to the trial if the prisoner showed good cause for failing to make the challenge at trial, and also showed that the trial court's error actually prejudiced the prisoner.

cause célèbre (**kawz** sə-**leb** *or* **kawz** say-**leb**-rə). [French "celebrated case"] (18c) A trial or decision in which the subject matter or the characters are unusual or sensational <the O.J. Simpson trial was a cause célèbre in the 1990s>.

cause in fact. See *but-for cause* under CAUSE (1).

cause lawyering. The practice of a lawyer who advocates for social justice by combining the activities of litigation, community organizing, public education, and lobbying to advance a cause past its current legal limitations and boundaries. — Also termed *activist lawyering; progressive lawyering; radical lawyering.* See *social justice* under JUSTICE. Cf. PUBLIC-INTEREST LAW.

cause list. See DOCKET (2).

cause of action. (15c) **1.** A group of operative facts giving rise to one or more bases for suing; a factual situation that entitles one person to obtain a remedy in court from another person; CLAIM (4) <after the crash, Aronson had a cause of action>. **2.** A legal theory of a lawsuit <a malpractice cause of action>. Cf. RIGHT OF ACTION. — Also termed (in senses 1 & 2) *ground of action.*

> *new cause of action.* A claim not arising out of or relating to the conduct, occurrence, or transaction contained in the original pleading. • An amended pleading often relates back to the date on which the original pleading was filed. Thus, a plaintiff may add claims to a suit without facing a statute-of-limitations bar, as long as the original pleading was timely filed. But if the amended pleading adds a claim that arises out of a different transaction or occurrence, or out of different alleged conduct, the amendment does not relate back to the date on which the original pleading was filed. Fed. R. Civ. P. 15(c)).

3. Loosely, a lawsuit <there are four defendants in the pending cause of action>. — Abbr. COA.

cause-of-action estoppel. See COLLATERAL ESTOPPEL.

cautionary instruction. See JURY INSTRUCTION.

caution money. See EARNEST MONEY.

c.a.v. *abbr.* CURIA ADVISARI VULT.

caveat (**kav**-ee-aht *or* **kay**-vee-at *or* **kav**-ee-at). [Latin "let him or her beware"] (16c) **1.** A warning or proviso <he sold the car to his friend with the caveat that the brakes might need repairs>.

> *caveat actor* (**ak**-tor). [Latin] Let the doer, or actor, beware.

> *caveat emptor* (**emp**-tor). [Latin "let the buyer beware"] A doctrine holding that purchasers buy at their own risk. • Modern statutes and cases have greatly limited the importance of this doctrine.

> *caveat venditor* (**ven**-di-tor). [Latin] Let the seller beware.

> *caveat viator* (vi-**ay**-tor). [Latin "let the traveler beware"]. The duty of a traveler on a highway to use due care to detect and avoid defects in the way.

2. A formal notice or warning given by a party to a court or court officer requesting a suspension of proceedings <the decedent's daughter filed a caveat stating the facts on which her will contest is based>. **3.** Under the Torrens system of land titles, a formal notice of an unregistered interest in land. • Once lodged with the register of deeds, this notice prevents the register from recording any dealing affecting the estate or the interest claimed. See TORRENS SYSTEM. — **caveat,** *vb.*

caveatable (kay-vee-**at**-ə-bəl), *adj.* Of or relating to a legal or equitable interest that is protectable by a caveat. See CAVEAT (2), (3).

caveatee (kay-vee-at-**ee**). One whose interest is challenged by a caveat.

caveator (**kay**-vee-ay-tər). One who files a caveat, esp. to challenge the validity of a will; CONTESTANT (1).

C.B. *abbr.* **1.** COMMON BENCH. **2.** *Hist.* Chief Baron of the Exchequer.

CBA. *abbr.* COLLECTIVE-BARGAINING AGREEMENT.

CBO. *abbr.* CONGRESSIONAL BUDGET OFFICE.

CBOE. *abbr.* CHICAGO BOARD OPTIONS EXCHANGE.

CBOT. *abbr.* CHICAGO BOARD OF TRADE.

CBT. *abbr.* CHICAGO BOARD OF TRADE.

CC. *abbr.* **1.** Circuit, city, civil, or county court. **2.** Chancery, civil, criminal, or Crown cases. **3.** CIVIL CODE.

CCC. *abbr.* **1.** COMMODITY CREDIT CORPORATION. **2.** CUSTOMS COOPERATION COUNCIL.

C corporation. See CORPORATION.

CCPA. *abbr.* **1.** COURT OF CUSTOMS AND PATENT APPEALS. **2.** CONSUMER CREDIT PROTECTION ACT.

CCR. *abbr.* UNITED STATES COMMISSION ON CIVIL RIGHTS.

CD. *abbr.* CERTIFICATE OF DEPOSIT.

CDC. *abbr.* CENTERS FOR DISEASE CONTROL AND PREVENTION.

CDFI Fund. *abbr.* COMMUNITY DEVELOPMENT FINANCIAL INSTITUTION FUND.

CEA. *abbr.* COUNCIL OF ECONOMIC ADVISORS.

cease, *vb.* **1.** To stop, forfeit, suspend, or bring to an end. **2.** To become extinct; to pass away. — **cessation** (se-**say**-shən), *n.*

cease-and-desist letter. A cautionary notice sent to an alleged wrongdoer, describing the offensive activity and the complainant's remedies and demanding that the activity stop. • A cease-and-desist letter is commonly used to stop or block the suspected or actual infringement of an intellectual-property right before litigation. Ignoring a cease-and-desist letter may be used as evidence that the infringement was willful.

cease-and-desist order. (1918) A court's or agency's order prohibiting a person from continuing a particular course of conduct. See INJUNCTION; RESTRAINING ORDER.

ceasefire. See TRUCE.

cedant. See REINSURED.

cede (seed), *vb.* (18c) **1.** To surrender or relinquish. **2.** To assign or grant. — **cession** (sesh-ən), *n.* — **cessionary** (sesh-ən-er-ee), *adj.*

cedent. See REINSURED.

cédula (say-doo-lah). [Spanish] *Spanish law.* **1.** An official document used to identify someone; an identity card. **2.** A promissory note. **3.** A summons; specif., a citation requiring a fugitive to appear in court to face criminal charges. • The citation is usu. affixed to the fugitive's door. **4.** *Hist.* A decree of the Spanish Crown; esp., a royal enactment issued by the Council of Castile or of the Indies.

ceiling price. See PRICE.

ceiling rent. See RENT (1).

censor, *n.* **1.** *Roman law.* (*ital.*) A Roman officer who acted as a census taker, assessor, and reviewer of public morals. **2.** A person who inspects publications, films, and the like for objectionable content. **3.** In the armed forces, someone who reads letters and other communications and deletes material considered a security threat. — **censorial,** *adj.* — **censorship,** *n.*

censor (sen-sər), *vb.* (1882) To officially inspect (esp. a book or film) and delete material considered offensive.

censorial jurisprudence. See LAW REFORM.

censure (sen-shər), *n.* (14c) An official reprimand or condemnation; harsh criticism <the judge's careless statements subjected her to the judicial council's censure>. — **censorious,** *adj.*

censure, *vb.* To reprimand; to criticize harshly <the Senate censured the senator for his inflammatory remarks>.

census. (17c) An official count of people made for the purpose of compiling social and economic data for the political subdivision to which the people belong. Pl. **censuses.**

federal census. A census of a state or territory, or a portion of either, taken by the Census Bureau of the United States. • The Constitution (art. I, § 2) requires only a simple count of persons for purposes of apportioning congressional representation among the states. Under Congress's direction, however, the census has evolved to include a wide variety of information that is useful to businesses, historians, and others not affiliated with the federal government.

Census Bureau. See BUREAU OF THE CENSUS.

Center for Minority Veterans. A unit in the U.S. Department of Veterans Affairs responsible for promoting the use of VA services, benefits, and programs by minority veterans.

Center for Women Veterans. A unit in the U.S. Department of Veterans Affairs responsible for advising female veterans about VA programs and for evaluating VA programs to ensure access by women.

center-of-gravity doctrine. *Conflict of laws.* The rule that, in choice-of-law questions, the law of the jurisdiction with the most significant relationship to the transaction or event applies. — Also termed *significant-relationship theory*; *grouping-of-contacts theory.*

Centers for Disease Control and Prevention. An agency in the U.S. Department of Health and Human Services responsible for conducting medical research, promoting disease and injury prevention, and responding to public-health emergencies. • This agency was established in 1999 when the Department of Health and Human Services was reorganized. Its forerunner was the Communicable Diseases Center, established in 1964. — Abbr. CDC.

Central American Court of Justice. A court created in 1962 under the 1951 Charter of the Organization of Central American States between Costa Rica, El Salvador, Guatemala, Honduras, and Nicaragua, to guarantee the rights of the various republics to maintain peace and harmony in their relations and to prevent recourse to the use of force. • This court's predecessor of the same name was created by a 1908 convention between the same parties, and dissolved in 1918 when the convention expired. It was re-created in 1962 by the Organization of Central American States.

central clearing system. A method of facilitating securities transactions in which an agent or subsidiary of an exchange acts as a clearinghouse for member brokerage firms by clearing their checks, settling their accounts, and delivering their payments. • Most transactions are reflected solely by computerized book entries, and clearinghouse statements are submitted showing the net balance to be paid to reconcile the member firm's accounts.

Central Criminal Court. The Crown Court sitting in London, formerly known as the Old Bailey. • The Central Criminal Court, created in 1834, has jurisdiction to try all indictable offenses committed in London. See CROWN COURT.

central government. See *federal government* (1) under GOVERNMENT.

Central Intelligence Agency. An independent federal agency that compiles intelligence information, conducts counterintelligence activities outside the United States, and advises the President and the National Security Council on matters of foreign intelligence and national security. • It was created by the National Security Act of 1947. 50 USCA § 401 et seq. — Abbr. CIA. See NATIONAL SECURITY COUNCIL.

Central Office. *English law.* The primary office for most of England's courts. • The Central Office was established in 1879 to consolidate the masters and associates of the common-law courts, and the clerical functions of the Crown Office of the Queen's Bench Division, the Report and Enrollment offices of the Chancery Division, and several other offices.

CEO. *abbr.* CHIEF EXECUTIVE OFFICER.

ceorl (chorl). *Hist.* A Saxon freeman who either possessed no landed property or held land of a thane by paying rent or providing services. • After the Norman Conquest, ceorls were reduced to the status of unfree villeins. Under Norman rule, the variant form of the word, *churl*, became associated with a base peasant, and soon acquired the connotation of a surly, coarse person (hence the modern meaning). — Also termed *churl*; *cirliscus*.

CEQ. *abbr.* COUNCIL ON ENVIRONMENTAL QUALITY.

CERCLA (sər-klə). *abbr.* Comprehensive Environmental Response, Compensation, and Liability Act of 1980. • This statute holds responsible parties liable for the cost of cleaning up hazardous-waste sites. 42 USCA §§ 9601 et seq. See SUPERFUND.

ceremonial marriage. See MARRIAGE (3).

cert. *abbr.* CERTIORARI.

certain contract. See CONTRACT.

certificate, *n.* (15c) **1.** A document in which a fact is formally attested <death certificate>. See STOCK CERTIFICATE. **2.** A document certifying the bearer's status or authorization to act in a specified way <nursing certificate>. **3.** A notice by one court to another court of the action it has taken <when issuing its opinion, the Seventh Circuit sent a certificate to the Illinois Supreme Court>.

certificate creditor. See CREDITOR.

certificated security. See SECURITY.

certificate land. See LAND.

certificate of acknowledgment. See ACKNOWLEDGMENT (5).

certificate of amendment. A document filed with a state corporation authority, usu. the secretary of state, reflecting changes made to a corporation's articles of incorporation.

certificate of appealability. In an appeal from the denial of federal habeas corpus relief, a document issued by a United States circuit judge certifying that the prisoner showed that a constitutional right may have been denied. 28 USCA § 2253(c) (2). • The prisoner does not have to show that the case would succeed on the merits, only that reasonable jurists would find the claim at least debatable. *Miller-El v. Cockrell*, 537 U.S. 322, 123 S.Ct. 1029, 1039 (2003). If the certificate is not issued, no appeal is possible. 28 USCA § 2253 (c) (1); Fed. R. App. P. 22(b). — Abbr. COA. — Also

termed (before 1996) *certificate of probable cause* (Abbr. CPC); *certificate of reasonable doubt; writ of probable cause.*

certificate of assize. *Hist.* In England, a writ granting a retrial. • The certificate of assize has been replaced by a court order granting a new trial.

certificate of authority. (1808) **1.** A document authenticating a notarized document that is being sent to another jurisdiction. • The certificate assures the out-of-state or foreign recipient that the notary public has a valid commission. — Also termed *certificate of capacity; certificate of official character; certificate of authentication; certificate of prothonotary; certificate of magistracy; apostille; verification.* **2.** A document issued by a state agency, usu. the secretary of state, granting an out-of-state corporation the right to do business in the state. — Also termed (in some states) *certificate of qualification.*

certificate of bad faith. In a case in which a party has been allowed to proceed in a United States District Court *in forma pauperis*, a court-issued document attesting that an appeal by that party would be frivolous and therefore should not be allowed unless the party pays the ordinary filing fees and costs. 28 USCA § 1915 (a)(3). Cf. CERTIFICATE OF GOOD FAITH.

certificate of capacity. See CERTIFICATE OF AUTHORITY (1).

certificate of conference. (1979) A section of a pleading or motion filed with the court, usu. contained separately on a page near the end of the document, whereby the party filing the pleading or motion certifies to the court that the parties have attempted to resolve the matter, but that a judicial determination is needed because an agreement could not be reached. • Courts require some motions to have a certificate of conference attached to them. This compels the parties to try to resolve the issue themselves, without burdening the court unless necessary. Fed. R. Civ. P. 26(c), 37.

certificate of convenience and necessity. A certificate issued by an administrative agency granting operating authority to a utility or transportation company. — Also termed *certificate of public convenience and necessity.*

certificate of conviction. A signed and certified warrant authorizing a person's imprisonment after an adjudication of guilt.

certificate of correction. 1. A document that corrects an error in an official document, such as a certificate of incorporation. **2.** *Patents.* A document issued by the U.S. Patent and Trademark Office after a patentee or assignee rectifies a minor error unrelated to either questions of ownership or else defects in a patent application's specifications or drawings. • The certificate can correct only three types of errors: (1) mistakes made by the PTO, (2) minor clerical or typographical errors, and (3) the omission or misidentification of an inventor's name. 35 USCA §§ 254–256. Cf. *reissue patent* under PATENT (3).

certificate of deposit. (1846) **1.** A banker's certificate acknowledging the receipt of money and promising to repay the depositor. — Also termed *certificate of indebtedness.* **2.** A bank document showing the existence of a time deposit, usu. one that pays interest. — Abbr. CD.

> *negotiable certificate of deposit.* A security issued by a financial institution as a short-term source of funds, usu. with a fixed interest rate and maturity of one year or less.

certificate of discharge. See SATISFACTION PIECE.

certificate of dishonor. See NOTICE OF DISHONOR.

certificate of dissolution. A document issued by a state authority (usu. the secretary of state) certifying that a corporation has been dissolved.

certificate of election. A document issued by a governor, board of elections, or other competent authority certifying that the named person has been duly elected.

certificate of good faith. In a case in which a party has been allowed to proceed in a United States District Court *in forma pauperis*, a document issued by the court attesting that an appeal by the party would not be frivolous, so the party should not be required to pay costs or security. • District judges occasionally issue certificates of good faith even though they are never required: a party is allowed to appeal *in forma pauperis* unless the court issues a certificate of bad faith. 28 USCA § 1915(a)(3). Cf. CERTIFICATE OF BAD FAITH.

certificate of holder of attached property. A certificate given by a person who holds — but does not own — property attached by a sheriff. • The certificate sets forth the holder's interest in the property.

certificate of incorporation. (18c) **1.** A document issued by a state authority (usu. the secretary of state) granting a corporation its legal existence and the right to function as a corporation. — Also termed *charter; corporate charter.* **2.** ARTICLES OF INCORPORATION.

certificate of indebtedness. 1. See DEBENTURE. **2.** See TREASURY BILL. **3.** See CERTIFICATE OF DEPOSIT (1).

certificate of insurance. A document acknowledging that an insurance policy has been written, and setting forth in general terms what the policy covers.

certificate of interest. *Oil & gas.* A document evidencing a fractional or percentage ownership in oil-and-gas production.

certificate of magistracy. See CERTIFICATE OF AUTHORITY (1).

certificate of marriage. See MARRIAGE CERTIFICATE.

certificate of merit. A certificate, signed by the plaintiff's attorney and filed with the complaint in a civil suit, declaring that the plaintiff's attorney has conferred with at least one competent expert and afterward concluded that the suit has merit. • Many states have a law mandating certificates of merit in certain types of cases, such as professional malpractice. The law's purpose is to weed out frivolous claims as early as possible. In those states, if a certificate is not filed with the complaint, the action is usu. dismissed. If the law requires the certificate to be signed under oath or penalty of perjury, it is sometimes called an *affidavit of merit.*

certificate of occupancy. A document indicating that a building complies with zoning and building ordinances, and ready to be occupied. • A certificate of occupancy is often required before title can be transferred and the building occupied.

certificate of official character. See CERTIFICATE OF AUTHORITY (1).

certificate of probable cause. See CERTIFICATE OF APPEALABILITY.

certificate of proof. See PROOF OF ACKNOWLEDGMENT.

certificate of protest. See NOTICE OF DISHONOR.

certificate of prothonotary. See CERTIFICATE OF AUTHORITY (1).

certificate of public convenience and necessity. See CERTIFICATE OF CONVENIENCE AND NECESSITY.

certificate of purchase. A document reflecting a successful bid for property at a judicial sale. • The bidder receives a property deed if the land is not redeemed or if the sale is confirmed by court order. — Also termed *certificate of sale.*

certificate of qualification. See CERTIFICATE OF AUTHORITY (2).

certificate of reasonable doubt. See CERTIFICATE OF APPEALABILITY.

certificate of redemption. A document issued by a sheriff or other statutorily designated officer to a debtor whose property has been foreclosed as evidence that the debtor paid the redemption price for the foreclosed property. See *statutory redemption* under REDEMPTION.

certificate of registration. 1. *Copyright.* A U.S. Copyright Office document approving a copyright application and stating the approved work's registration date and copyright registration number. **2.** *Trademarks.* A document affirming that the U.S. Patent and Trademark Office has allowed and recorded a trademark or servicemark. • The certificate identifies (1) the registered mark, (2) the date of first use, (3) the type of product or service the mark applies to, (4) the registration number and date, (5) the registration's term, (6), the original application date, and (7) any conditions or limitations on registration.

certificate of registry. *Maritime law.* A document certifying that a ship has been registered as required by law. See REGISTRY (2).

certificate of rehabilitation. 1. A document issued in some states by a court or other authorized governmental agency, such as a parole board, as evidence that a convicted offender is entitled to recover at least some of the rights and privileges of citizenship. • The terms and conditions under which certificates of rehabilitation are issued vary widely among the states that use them. Some states, such as New York, issue different kinds of rehabilitation certificates based on the number or type of convictions. **2.** A document issued by a (usu. local) government on the renovation, restoration, preservation, or rehabilitation of a historic building. • The certificate usu. entitles the property owner to favorable tax treatment. **3.** A document attesting that substandard housing has been satisfactorily renovated and meets housing-code standards.

certificate of sale. See CERTIFICATE OF PURCHASE.

certificate of service. (1819) A section of a pleading or motion filed with the court, usu. contained separately on the last page, in which the filing party certifies to the court that a copy has been mailed to or otherwise served on all other parties. • A certificate of service is usu. not included with the initial pleading that the plaintiff files to begin a suit, because that pleading is usu. filed before it is served (although the plaintiff may be required to file proof of service). Other pleadings and motions are usu. required to have a certificate of service. Fed. R. Civ. P. 5(d). — Also termed *proof of service.*

certificate of stock. See STOCK CERTIFICATE.

certificate of title. (1831) A document indicating ownership of real or personal property. UCC § 9-102(a)(10). • This document usu. identifies any liens or other encumbrances.

certification, *n.* (15c) **1.** The act of attesting. **2.** The state of having been attested. **3.** An attested statement. **4.** The writing on the face of a check by which it is certified. **5.** A procedure by which a federal appellate court asks the U.S. Supreme Court or the highest state court to review a question of law arising in a case pending before the appellate court and on which it needs guidance. • Certification is commonly used with state courts, but the U.S. Supreme Court has steadily restricted the number of cases it reviews by certification. See 28 USCA § 1254(2). Cf. CERTIORARI.

certification authority. An organization that issues digital certificates and maintains a database of certificates available on the Internet. • Many states have licensing laws for certification authorities. — Also termed *certifying authority.* — Abbr. CA.

certification hearing. See *transfer hearing* under HEARING.

certification mark. See *certification trademark* under TRADEMARK.

certification of bargaining agent. See UNION CERTIFICATION.

certification of labor union. See UNION CERTIFICATION.

certification to state court. The procedure by which a federal court of appeals defers deciding a novel question of state law by certifying the question to the highest court of the state. See CERTIFICATION (5).

certification trademark. See TRADEMARK.

certified check. See CHECK.

certified copy. See COPY.

certified file history. *Patents.* A patent application together with records of all proceedings and correspondence related to its prosecution, as certified by the U.S. Patent and Trademark Office for appeals, arbitration, and other postprosecution proceedings. Cf. FILE WRAPPER.

certified financial planner. See FINANCIAL PLANNER.

certified financial statement. See FINANCIAL STATEMENT.

certified juvenile. See JUVENILE.

certified mail. See MAIL.

certified military lawyer. See LAWYER.

certified public accountant. See ACCOUNTANT.

certified question. (1835) A point of law on which a federal appellate court seeks guidance from either the U.S. Supreme Court or the highest state court by the procedure of certification.

certify, *vb.* (14c) **1.** To authenticate or verify in writing. **2.** To attest as being true or as meeting certain criteria. **3.** (Of a court) to issue an order allowing a class of litigants to maintain a class action; to create (a class) for purposes of a class action. See CERTIFICATION. Cf. DECERTIFY. — **certified,** *adj.*

certifying authority. See CERTIFICATION AUTHORITY.

certiorari (sər-shee-ə-**rair**-I *or* -**rair**-ee *or* -**rah**-ree). [Law Latin "to be more fully informed"]

(15c) An extraordinary writ issued by an appellate court, at its discretion, directing a lower court to deliver the record in the case for review. ● The writ evolved from one of the prerogative writs of the English Court of King's Bench, and in the United States it became a general appellate remedy. The U.S. Supreme Court uses certiorari to review most of the cases that it decides to hear. — Abbr. cert. — Also termed *writ of certiorari*. Cf. CERTIFICATION (5).

certiorari facias (sər-shee-ə-**rair**-ı **fay**-shee-əs). [Latin "a cause to be certified"] The command of a writ of certiorari, referring to certification of the court record for review.

limited certiorari. See *narrow certiorari*.

narrow certiorari. Certiorari limited to reviewing questions about jurisdiction, the regularity of the proceeding, the exercise of unauthorized powers, and constitutional rights. ● Narrow certiorari is usu. applied to appeals from arbitrators' awards or the decisions of state agencies. It is most common in Pennsylvania. — Also termed *limited certiorari*.

certiorari petition. See PETITION.

cert pool. A group of clerks in the U.S. Supreme Court who read petitions for certiorari and write memorandums for the justices with a synopsis of the facts and issues and often a recommendation of whether a grant of certiorari is warranted.

certworthy, *adj.* (1965) *Slang.*(Of a case or issue) deserving of review by writ of certiorari. — **certworthiness,** *n.*

cessation-of-production clause. *Oil & gas.* A lease provision that specifies what the lessee must do to maintain the lease if production stops. ● The purpose of the clause is to avoid the uncertainties of the temporary-cessation-of-production doctrine. Cf. TEMPORARY-CESSATION-OF-PRODUCTION DOCTRINE.

cesser (**ses**-ər). **1.** *Hist.* A tenant whose failure to pay rent or perform prescribed services gives the landowner the right to recover possession of the land. — Also spelled *cessor; cessure.* **2.** The termination of a right or interest.

cession (**sesh**-ən). (15c) **1.** The act of relinquishing property rights. **2.** *Int'l law.* The relinquishment or transfer of land from one nation to another, esp. after a war. as part of the price of peace. **3.** The land so relinquished or transferred.

cessionary bankrupt. See BANKRUPT.

cestui (**set**-ee *or* **ses**-twee). [French "he who"] (16c) A beneficiary. — Also spelled *cestuy.*

cestui que trust (**set**-ee [*or* **ses**-twee] kee [*or* kə] **trəst**). [Law French] (18c) *Archaic.* One who possesses equitable rights in property, usu. receiving the rents, issues, and profits from it; BENEFICIARY. — Also termed *fide-commissary;*

fidei-commissarius. Pl. **cestuis que trust** or (erroneously) **cestuis que trustent.**

cestui que use (**set**-ee [*or* **ses**-twee] kee [*or* kə] **yoos**). [Law French] (16c) *Archaic.* The person for whose use and benefit property is being held by another, who holds the legal title to the property. Pl. **cestuis que use** or (erroneously) **cestuis que usent.**

cestui que vie (**set**-ee [*or* **ses**-twee] kee [*or* kə] **vee**). [Law French] (17c) The person whose life measures the duration of a trust, gift, estate, or insurance contract. Cf. MEASURING LIFE.

ceteris paribus (**set**-ə-ris **par**-ə-bəs). [Latin] Other things being equal. — Also spelled *caeteris paribus.*

cf. *abbr.* [Latin *confer*] (1850) Compare. ● As a citation signal, *cf.* directs the reader's attention to another authority or section of the work in which contrasting, analogous, or explanatory statements may be found.

C.F. *abbr.* COST AND FREIGHT.

CFC. See *controlled foreign corporation* under CORPORATION.

CFO. *abbr.* CHIEF FINANCIAL OFFICER.

CFP. *abbr.* Certified financial planner. See FINANCIAL PLANNER.

CFR. *abbr.* **1.** CODE OF FEDERAL REGULATIONS. **2.** COST AND FREIGHT.

CFTC. *abbr.* COMMODITY FUTURES TRADING COMMISSION.

CGL insurance. See *comprehensive general-liability insurance* under INSURANCE.

CGL policy. 1. See *commercial general-liability policy* under INSURANCE POLICY. **2.** See *comprehensive general-liability policy* under INSURANCE POLICY.

ch. *abbr.* **1.** Chapter. **2.** Chancellor. **3.** Chancery. **4.** Chief.

Chace Act. *Hist. Copyright.* An 1891 statute giving U.S. copyright protection to the citizens of other nations that in turn gave a similar degree of reciprocal protection to U.S. citizens. ● The Act was invoked by presidential order or by treaty, primarily with European countries. Under the Act's manufacturing clause, English-language books and other printed matter had to be produced in the U.S. or Canada in order to qualify for domestic protection. — Also termed *1891 Copyright Amendment Act.*

chad. The small bit of precut paper that is attached to a punch-card ballot by several points and punched out by a voter to cast a vote. ● Because most punch-card ballots are machine-read, the chad must be completely separated from the ballot for the vote to be counted. The results of the closely contested 2000 presidential election were delayed for several weeks because more than 40,000 ballots with partially attached chads had to be hand-counted.

dimpled chad. A chad that is bulging but not pierced, with all its points attached to the ballot. — Sometimes termed *pregnant chad.*

hanging chad. A chad that is attached to the ballot by a single point.

pregnant chad. See *dimpled chad.*

swinging-door chad. A chad that is attached to the ballot by two points.

tri-chad. A chad that is attached to the ballot by three points.

chafewax (**chayf**-waks). *Hist.* A chancery officer who heated (or *chafed*) wax to seal writs, commissions, and other instruments. • The office was abolished in 1852. — Also spelled *chaffwax.*

chaffer (**chaf**-ər), *vb.* To bargain; negotiate; haggle; dicker. For *offer to chaffer,* see INVITATION TO NEGOTIATE.

chain-certificate method. (1966) The procedure for authenticating a foreign official record by the party seeking to admit the record as evidence at trial. *See* Fed. R. Civ. P. 44.

chain conspiracy. See CONSPIRACY.

chain gang. A group of prisoners chained together to prevent their escape while working outside a prison.

chain of causation. (18c) **1.** A series of events each caused by the previous one. **2.** The causal connection between a cause and its effects. Cf. CAUSATION.

chain-of-causation rule. *Workers' compensation.* The principle that an employee's suicide is compensable under workers' compensation statutes if the employee suffered an earlier work-related injury that led to a mental disorder resulting in the suicide.

chain of custody. (1947) **1.** The movement and location of real evidence, and the history of those persons who had it in their custody, from the time it is obtained to the time it is presented in court. **2.** The history of a chattel's possession. — Also termed *chain of possession.*

chain of title. (18c) **1.** The ownership history of a piece of land, from its first owner to the present one. — Also termed *line of title; string of title.* **2.** The ownership history of commercial paper, traceable through the indorsements. • For the holder to have good title, every prior negotiation must have been proper. If a necessary indorsement is missing or forged, the chain of title is broken and no later transferee can become a holder.

chain-referral scheme. See PYRAMID SCHEME.

chair. *Parliamentary law.* **1.** A deliberative assembly's presiding officer <the chair calls for order>. See PRESIDE. **2.** The presiding officer's seat <take the chair>. **3.** The officer who heads an organization <the treasurer reports directly to the chair>. — Also termed *chairman* (of a male chair, in senses 1 & 3); *chairwoman* (of a female chair, in senses 1 & 3); *chairperson* (in senses 1 & 3); *moderator* (in sense 1); *president* (in senses 1 & 3); *presiding officer* (in sense 1); *speaker* (in sense 1). — **chair,** *vb.*

chair by decree. A chair appointed by an outside authority rather than elected by the deliberative assembly being presided over.

chair pro tempore. A chair elected or appointed during or in anticipation of the regular presiding officer's (or officers') absence from the chair, and whose service ends when a regular presiding officer resumes the chair. — Often shortened to *chair pro tem.* See PRO TEMPORE.

chairman. See CHAIR.

Chairman of Committees of the Whole House. The member of Parliament who presides over the House of Commons when it is sitting in committee.

chairperson. See CHAIR.

chairwoman. See CHAIR.

challenge, *n.* (14c) **1.** An act or instance of formally questioning the legality or legal qualifications of a person, action, or thing <a challenge to the opposing party's expert witness>.

as-applied challenge. (1974) A claim that a law or governmental policy, though constitutional on its face, is unconstitutional as applied, usu. because of a discriminatory effect; a claim that a statute is unconstitutional on the facts of a particular case or in its application to a particular party.

Batson challenge. (1987) *Procedure.* An objection that an opposing party has used a peremptory challenge to exclude a potential juror on the basis of race, ethnicity, or sex. • It is named for *Batson v. Kentucky,* 476 U.S. 79, 106 S.Ct. 1712 (1986), a criminal case in which the prosecution struck potential jurors on the basis of race. The principle of Batson was extended in later Supreme Court cases to civil litigants (*Edmonson v. Leesville Concrete Co.,* 500 U.S. 614, 111 S.Ct. 2077 (1991)) and to criminal defense attorneys (*Georgia v. McCollum,* 505 U.S. 42, 112 S.Ct. 2348 (1992)). The Court also applied it to peremptory challenges based on a juror's sex (J.E.B. v. Alabama, 511 U.S. 127, 114 S.Ct. 1419 (1994)). *See* Fed. R. Civ. P. 47(b).

constitutional challenge. (1936) A claim that a law or governmental action is unconstitutional.

facial challenge. (1973) A claim that a statute is unconstitutional on its face — that is, that it always operates unconstitutionally.

2. A party's request that a judge disqualify a potential juror or an entire jury panel <the personal-injury plaintiff used his last challenge to disqualify a neurosurgeon>. — Also termed *jury challenge.*

causal challenge. See *challenge for cause.*

challenge for cause. (17c) A party's challenge supported by a specified reason, such as bias or prejudice, that would disqualify that potential juror. — Also termed *for-cause; causal challenge; general challenge; challenge to the poll.*

challenge propter affectum (**prop**-tər ə-**fek**-təm). A challenge because some circumstance, such as kinship with a party, renders the potential juror incompetent to serve in the particular case.

challenge propter defectum (**prop**-tər də-**fek**-təm). A challenge based on a claim that the juror is incompetent to serve on any jury for a reason such as alienage, infancy, or nonresidency.

challenge propter delictum (**prop**-tər də-**lik**-təm). A challenge based on a claim that the potential juror has lost citizenship rights, as by being convicted of an infamous crime. See *civil death* (1) under DEATH.

challenge to the array. (16c) A legal challenge to the manner in which the entire jury panel was selected, usu. for a failure to follow prescribed procedures designed to produce impartial juries drawn from a fair cross-section of the community. • Such a challenge is either a principal challenge (if some defect renders the jury prima facie incompetent, as where the officer selecting veniremembers is related to the prosecutor or defendant) or a challenge for favor (as where the defect does not amount to grounds for a principal challenge, but there is a probability of partiality). — Also termed *challenge to the jury array.*

challenge to the favor. A challenge for cause that arises when facts and circumstances tend to show that a juror is biased but do not warrant the juror's automatic disqualification. See *challenge for cause.*

challenge to the poll. See *challenge for cause.*

general challenge. See *challenge for cause.*

peremptory challenge. (16c) One of a party's limited number of challenges that do not need to be supported by a reason unless the opposing party makes a prima facie showing that the challenge was used to discriminate on the basis of race, ethnicity, or sex. • At one time, a peremptory challenge could not be attacked and did not have to be explained. But today if discrimination is charged, the party making the

peremptory challenge must give a nondiscriminatory reason for striking the juror. The court must consider several factors in deciding whether the proffered reason is merely a screen for illegal discrimination. *Batson v. Kentucky*, 476 U.S. 79, 106 S.Ct. 1712 (1986). — Often shortened to *peremptory.* — Also termed *peremptory strike; sight strike* under STRIKE (2). See STRIKE (2); *Batson challenge* under CHALLENGE (1).

principal challenge. A for-cause challenge that arises when facts and circumstances support a conclusive presumption of a juror's bias, resulting in automatic disqualification. See *challenge for cause.*

3. *Military law.* An objection to a member of the court serving in a court-martial case. • A military judge can be challenged only for cause.

challenge, *vb.* **1.** To dispute or call into question <the columnist challenged the wisdom of the court's ruling>.

challenge the vote. See DIVIDE THE ASSEMBLY.

2. To formally object to the legality or legal qualifications of <the defendant challenged the person's eligibility for jury service>.

chamber, *n.* (13c) **1.** A room or compartment <gas chamber>. **2.** A legislative or judicial body or other deliberative assembly <chamber of commerce>. **3.** The hall or room where such a body conducts business <the senate chamber>. — **chamber,** *adj.*

judge's chamber. (*usu. pl.*) (17c) **1.** The private room or office of a judge. **2.** Any place where a judge transacts official business when not holding a session of the court. See IN CAMERA.

lower chamber. (1885) In a bicameral legislature, the larger of the two legislative bodies, such as the House of Representatives or the House of Commons.

Star Chamber. See STAR CHAMBER.

upper chamber. (1850) In a bicameral legislature, the smaller of the two legislative bodies, such as the Senate or the House of Lords. • Before passage of the House of Lords Act in 1999, the House of Lords traditionally had more members than the House of Commons.

chamber, *vb. Slang.* (Of a judge) to sit in one's chambers at a given location <Chief Judge Kaye chambers sometimes in New York City and sometimes in Albany>.

chamber business. (1805) Official judicial business conducted outside the courtroom.

chamberlain (**chaym**-bər-lin). A treasurer; originally, the keeper of the royal treasure chamber. • The term has been used for several high offices in England, such as the Lord Great Chamberlain, Lord Chamberlain of the Household, and Chamberlain of the Exchequer.

chamber of commerce. An association of merchants and other business leaders who organize to promote the commercial interests in a given area and whose group is generally affiliated with the national organization of the same name.

champertor (**cham**-pər-tər), *n.* (16c) A person who engages in champerty; one who supports and promotes another person's lawsuit for pecuniary gain. — Also termed (archaically) *campiparticeps*. Cf. BARRATOR.

champertous (**cham**-pər-təs), *adj.* (17c) Of, relating to, or characterized by champerty; constituting champerty <a champertous contract>.

champerty (**cham**-pər-tee), *n.* [fr. French *champs parti* "split field"] (15c) **1.** An agreement between an officious intermeddler in a lawsuit and a litigant by which the intermeddler helps pursue the litigant's claim as consideration for receiving part of any judgment proceeds; specif., an agreement to divide litigation proceeds between the owner of the litigated claim and a party unrelated to the lawsuit who supports or helps enforce the claim. — Also termed (archaically) *campipartia*. Cf. BARRATRY; MAINTENANCE (6). **2.** *Hist.* A writ available to the party who is the target of a champertous action.

chance, *n.* (14c) **1.** A hazard or risk. **2.** The unforeseen, uncontrollable, or unintended consequences of an act. **3.** An accident. **4.** Opportunity; hope.

chance bargain. *Contracts.* A transaction in which the parties mutually agree to accept the risk that facts and circumstances assumed by the parties at the time of contracting may not actually be what the parties believe they are. ● If no fraud or misrepresentation is involved, a court will uphold a chance bargain. For instance, in a chance bargain involving a land swap, each deed may describe a tract as containing a number of acres "more or less." If the tract is actually larger than described, the seller cannot demand more money for the excess. And if the tract is actually smaller, the disappointed buyer cannot ask for a reduced price to make up for the deficiency.

chancellor, *n.* (14c) **1.** A judge serving on a court of chancery. **2.** A university president or CEO of an institution of higher education. **3.** In the U.S., a judge in some courts of chancery or equity. **4.** *Scots law.* The presiding juror. **5.** *Eccles. law.* A law officer who presides over the bishop's court. ● The chancellor advises and assists the bishop in all matters of canon law, both juridical and administrative. — **chancellorship,** *n.*

Chancellor, Lord. See LORD CHANCELLOR.

Chancellor of the Exchequer. In England, a government minister who controls revenue and expenditures. ● Formerly, the Chancellor sat in the Court of Exchequer.

chancellor's foot. A symbol of the variability of equitable justice. ● John Selden, the 17th-century jurist, is thought to have coined the phrase in this passage, from his best-known book: "Equity is a roguish thing. For law we have a measure, know what to trust to: equity is according to the conscience of him that is Chancellor, and as that is larger or narrower, so is equity. 'Tis all one as if they should make the standard for the measure the Chancellor's foot. What an uncertain measure would this be! One Chancellor has a long foot, another a short foot, a third an indifferent foot; 'tis the same thing in the Chancellor's conscience." *Table Talk* (1689).

chance-medley. [fr. Anglo-Norman *chance medlee* "chance scuffle"] A spontaneous fight during which one participant kills another in self-defense. — Also termed *chaud-medley*; *casual affray.* Cf. MEDLEY.

chance-of-survival doctrine. (1991) The principle that a wrongful-death plaintiff need only prove that the defendant's conduct was a substantial factor in causing the death — that is, that the victim might have survived but for the defendant's conduct.

chancer (**chan**-sər), *vb.* To adjust according to equitable principles, as a court of chancery would. ● The practice arose in parts of New England when the courts had no equity jurisdiction, and were compelled to act on equitable principles.

chancery (**chan**-sər-ee). (14c) **1.** A court of equity; collectively, the courts of equity. ● The term is derived from the court of the Lord Chancellor, the original English court of equity. — Also termed *court of chancery*; *chancery court.* **2.** The system of jurisprudence administered in courts of equity. See EQUITY. **3.** *Int'l law.* The place where the head of a diplomatic mission and staff have their offices, as distinguished from the embassy (where the ambassador lives).

Chancery Court of York. *Eccles. law.* The ecclesiastical court of the province of York, responsible for appeals from provincial diocesan courts. ● This court corresponds to the Court of Arches in the Province of Canterbury. Cf. COURT OF ARCHES.

chancery guardian. See GUARDIAN.

chance verdict. See VERDICT.

change in circumstances. (1899) *Family law.* A modification in the physical, emotional, or financial condition of one or both parents, used to show the need to modify a custody or support order; esp., an involuntary occurrence that, if it had been known at the time of the divorce decree, would have resulted in the court's issuing a different decree, as when an involuntary job loss creates a need to modify the decree to provide for reduced child-support payments. — Also termed *change of circumstances*; *changed circumstances*; *material change in circumstances*; *substantial change in circumstances*; *change of condition*. See MODIFICATION ORDER.

change of condition. 1. *Workers' compensation.* A substantial worsening of an employee's physical health occurring after an award, as a result of which the employee merits an increase in benefits. **2.** *Family law.* CHANGE IN CIRCUMSTANCES.

change-of-ownership clause. *Oil & gas.* A provision in an oil-and-gas lease specifying what notice must be given to a lessee about a change in the leased land's ownership before the lessee is obliged to recognize the new owner. — Also termed *assignment clause*.

change of venue. (18c) The transfer of a case from one locale to another court in the same judicial system to cure a defect in venue, either to minimize the prejudicial impact of local sentiment or to secure a more sensible location for trial. — Also termed *transfer of venue*. See VENUE.

change order. 1. A modification of a previously ordered item or service. See VALUE (2). **2.** A directive issued by the federal government to a contractor to alter the specifications of an item the contractor is producing for the government.

changing fund. See FUND (1).

channel. (14c) **1.** The bed of a stream of water; the groove through which a stream flows <digging a deeper channel was thought to help protect the river from flooding>.

   main channel. The bed over which the principal volume of water flows; the deepest and most navigable part of a channel.

   natural channel. The naturally formed bed and banks of a stream.

   natural flood channel. A channel through which floodwaters naturally accumulate and flow downstream.

2. The line of deep water that shipping vessels follow <a shipping channel>. **3.** A water route between two islands or an island and a continent <the English Channel>. **4.** A mode of transmitting something <the news channel>.

channel of distribution. See DISTRIBUTION CHANNEL.

channel of trade. See DISTRIBUTION CHANNEL.

Chapter 7. 1. The chapter of the United States Bankruptcy Code allowing a trustee to collect and liquidate a debtor's nonexempt property, either voluntarily or by court order, to satisfy creditors. **2.** A bankruptcy case filed under this chapter. • An individual debtor who undergoes this type of liquidation usu. gets a fresh financial start by receiving a discharge of all debts. — Also termed (in sense 2) *straight bankruptcy*; *liquidation bankruptcy*.

Chapter 9. 1. The chapter of the United States Bankruptcy Code governing the adjustment of a municipality's debts. **2.** A bankruptcy case filed under this chapter.

Chapter 11. (1970) **1.** The chapter of the United States Bankruptcy Code allowing an insolvent business, or one that is threatened with insolvency, to reorganize its capital structure under court supervision (and subject to creditor approval) while continuing its normal operations. • Although the Code permits individual nonbusiness debtors to use Chapter 11, the vast majority of Chapter 11 cases involve business debtors. **2.** A business reorganization conducted under this chapter; REORGANIZATION (1).

Chapter 12. 1. The chapter of the United States Bankruptcy Code providing for a court-approved debt-payment relief plan for family farmers with a regular income, allowing the farmer's net income to be collected by a trustee and paid to creditors. **2.** A bankruptcy case filed under this chapter. — Also termed (in sense 2) *family-farmer bankruptcy*; *farmer bankruptcy*.

Chapter 13. 1. The chapter of the United States Bankruptcy Code allowing a person's earnings to be collected by a trustee and paid to creditors by means of a court-approved debt-repayment plan if the person has a regular income. • A plan filed under Chapter 13 is sometimes called a *wage-earner's plan*, a *wage-earner plan*, or an *income-based plan*. Chapter 13 allows the debtor to propose a plan of rehabilitation to extend or reduce the balance of any obligations and to receive a discharge from unsecured debts upon completion of the payments under the plan. A plan made in good faith will be confirmed if the creditors receive what they would have received under Chapter 7, and if the plan pledges all of the debtor's disposable income for three years. **2.** A bankruptcy case filed under this chapter.

Chapter 20. *Slang. Bankruptcy.* A debtor who files a Chapter 7 petition and receives a discharge, and then immediately files a Chapter 13 petition to deal with remaining nondischargeable or secured debts.

Chapter 22. *Slang. Bankruptcy.* A debtor, usu. a corporation, that files a second Chapter 11 petition shortly after a previous Chapter 11 petition has failed, because the debtor has become insolvent again or is again threatened with insolvency.

chapter surfing. *Slang.* A debtor's movement from a filing under one United States Bankruptcy Code chapter to a filing under another.

character evidence. See EVIDENCE.

characterization. 1. *Conflict of laws.* The classification, qualification, and interpretation of laws that apply to the case. — Also termed *qualification*; *classification*; *interpretation.* **2.** *Family law.* The process of classifying property accumulated by spouses as either separate or marital property (or community property).

character loan. See LOAN.

character-reformation condition. See *conditional bequest* under BEQUEST.

character witness. See WITNESS.

charge, *n.* (13c) **1.** A formal accusation of an offense as a preliminary step to prosecution <a murder charge>. — Also termed *criminal charge.* **2.** An instruction or command <a mother's charge to her son>. **3.** JURY CHARGE <review the charge for appealable error>. **4.** An assigned duty or task; a responsibility <the manager's charge to open and close the office>. **5.** An encumbrance, lien, or claim <a charge on property>. **6.** A person or thing entrusted to another's care <a charge of the estate>. **7.** Price, cost, or expense <free of charge>.

    delinquency charge. A charge assessed against a borrower for failing to timely make a payment.

    finance charge. See FINANCE CHARGE.

    late charge. An additional fee assessed on a debt when a payment is not received by the due date.

    noncash charge. A cost (such as depreciation or amortization) that does not involve an outlay of cash.

    special charge. An ordinary cost of business excluded from income calculations. • The term is meaningless under generally accepted accounting principles because "special charge" expenses do not meet the GAAP test for extraordinary items. — Also termed *one-time charge*; *unusual charge*; *exceptional charge.* See *extraordinary expense* under EXPENSE; *operating earnings* under EARNINGS.

8. *Parliamentary law.* A deliberative assembly's mandate to a committee. — Also termed *committee jurisdiction.*

charge, *vb.* **1.** To accuse (a person) of an offense <the police charged him with murder>. **2.** To instruct or command <the dean charged the students to act ethically>. **3.** To instruct a jury on matters of law <the judge charged the jury on self-defense>. **4.** To impose a lien or claim; to encumber <charge the land with a tax lien>. **5.** To entrust with responsibilities or duties <charge the guardian with the ward's care>. **6.** To demand a fee; to bill <the clerk charged a small filing fee>.

chargeable, *adj.* (Of an act) capable or liable of being charged as a criminal offense <taking that money for personal use would be chargeable>.

charge account. A credit arrangement by which a customer purchases goods and services and pays for them periodically or within a specified time. See CREDIT (4).

charge and discharge. *Equity practice.* Court-ordered account filings by a plaintiff and a defendant. • The plaintiff's account (*charge*) and the defendant's response (*discharge*) were filed with a master in chancery.

charge and specification. *Military law.* A written description of an alleged offense.

charge-back, *n.* A bank's deducting of sums it had provisionally credited to a customer's account, occurring usu. when a check deposited in the account has been dishonored. UCC § 4-214.

charge bargain. See PLEA BARGAIN.

charge conference. (1972) A meeting between a trial judge and the parties' attorneys to develop a jury charge. — Also termed *prayer conference.*

chargé d'affaires (shahr-**zhay** də-**fair**). [French "one in charge of affairs"] A diplomat who is the second in command in a diplomatic mission (hence, subordinate to an ambassador or minister). — Also spelled *chargé des affaires.* Pl. **chargés d'affaires.**

    acting chargé d'affaires. A chargé d'affaires who performs mission functions when the leader of the mission is not available to do so or when the position is vacant. — Also termed *chargés d'affaires ad interim.*

    permanent chargé d'affaires. A chargé d'affaires with a high enough rank to head a mission (if there is no ambassador or minister). — Also termed *chargé d'affaires en pied*; *chargé d'affaires en titre.*

charged with notice. Imputed with knowledge or awareness that is legally binding <the defendant was charged with notice of the defect yet failed to act before the plaintiff was injured by it>. — Also termed *put on notice.*

chargee (chahr-**jee**). **1.** The holder of a charge on property or of a security on a loan. **2.** One charged with a crime.

charge off, *vb.* To treat (an account receivable) as a loss or expense because payment is unlikely; to treat as a bad debt. See *bad debt* under DEBT.

charge sheet. 1. A police record showing the name of each person brought into custody, the nature of the accusations, and the identity of the accusers. **2.** *Military law.* A four-part charging instrument containing (1) information about the accused and the witnesses, (2) the charges and specifications, (3) the preferring of charges and their referral to a summary, special, or general court-martial for trial, and (4) for a summary court-martial, the trial record.

charging instrument. (1951) A formal document — usu. either an indictment or an information — that sets forth an accusation of a crime. — Also termed *accusatory instrument*.

charging lien. See LIEN.

charging order. (1904) *Partnership.* A statutory procedure whereby an individual partner's creditor can satisfy its claim from the partner's interest in the partnership.

charitable, *adj.* **1.** Dedicated to a general public purpose, usu. for the benefit of needy people who cannot pay for benefits received <charitable contribution>. **2.** Involved in or otherwise relating to charity <charitable foundation>.

charitable bequest. See BEQUEST.

charitable contribution. (17c) A gratuitous transfer of property to a charitable social-welfare, religious, scientific, educational, or other qualified organization. • Such a contribution has tax value because it may result in a current income-tax deduction, may reduce federal estate taxes, and can be made free of any gift taxes.

charitable corporation. See CORPORATION.

charitable deduction. See DEDUCTION.

charitable gift. See GIFT.

charitable immunity. See IMMUNITY (2).

charitable lead trust. See TRUST.

charitable organization. (1897) *Tax.* A tax-exempt organization that (1) is organized and operated exclusively for religious, scientific, literary, educational, athletic, public-safety, or community-service purposes, (2) does not distribute earnings for the benefit of private individuals, and (3) does not participate in any way in political candidate campaigns, or engage in substantial lobbying. IRC (26 USCA) § 501(c)(3). — Also termed *charity*; *501(c)(3) organization*.

charitable purpose. (1877) *Tax.* The purpose for which an organization must be formed so that it qualifies as a charitable organization under the Internal Revenue Code. — Also termed *charitable use*.

charitable remainder. See REMAINDER.

charitable-remainder annuity trust. See TRUST.

charitable-remainder trust. See TRUST.

charitable-remainder-trust retirement fund. See *charitable-remainder annuity trust* under TRUST.

charitable trust. See TRUST.

charitable use. 1. See CHARITABLE PURPOSE. **2.** See *charitable trust* under TRUST.

charity, *n.* **1.** CHARITABLE ORGANIZATION. **2.** Aid given to the poor, the suffering, or the general community for religious, educational, economic, public-safety, or medical purposes. **3.** Goodwill.

charlatan (**shahr**-lə-tən), *n.* (17c) A person who pretends to have more knowledge or skill than he or she actually has; a quack or faker. — **charlatanism, charlatanry,** *n.*

charta (**kahr**-tə). (17c) [Law Latin] *Hist.* **1.** A charter or deed. **2.** A token by which an estate is held. **3.** A royal grant of privileges or liberties.

chartel. See CARTEL.

charter, *n.* (13c) **1.** An instrument that establishes a body politic or other organization, or that grants rights, liberties, or powers to its citizens or members <Charter of the United Nations>. **2.** An instrument by which a municipality is incorporated, specifying its organizational structure and its highest laws; specif., a written document making the persons residing within a fixed boundary, along with their successors, a corporation and body politic for and within that boundary, and prescribing the powers, privileges, and duties of the corporation. • A city charter trumps all conflicting ordinances. — Also termed *municipal charter*.

> *home-rule charter.* A local government's organizational plan or framework, analogous to a constitution, drawn by the municipality itself and adopted by popular vote of the citizenry. See HOME RULE.

3. A governmental act that creates a business or defines a corporate franchise; also, the document evidencing this act.

> *bank charter.* A document issued by a governmental authority permitting a bank to conduct business.

> *corporate charter.* **1.** CERTIFICATE OF INCORPORATION (1). **2.** A document that one files with the secretary of state upon incorporating a business. • The corporate charter is often the articles of incorporation.

> *special charter. Hist.* A legislative act creating a private corporation as opposed to a public, charitable, or educational corporation. • Special charters were common until the 19th century, when legislatures enacted general incorporation laws that allowed private corporations to be formed without legislative action.

4. The organic law of an organization; loosely, the highest law of any entity. Cf. ARTICLES OF INCORPORATION. **5.** A governing document granting authority or recognition from a parent organization to a subordinate or constituent organization, such as a local affiliate or chapter, organized under the first organization's authority; or the instrument granting such authority or recognition.

See *governing document* under DOCUMENT (1).
6. *Hist.* The writing that accompanies a livery of seisin. • Rather than being an operative element of transfer, the writing was merely evidence of it. **7.** The leasing or hiring of an airplane, ship, or other vessel. **8.** CHARTERPARTY.

bareboat charter. A charter under which the shipowner surrenders possession and control of the vessel to the charterer, who then succeeds to many of the shipowner's rights and obligations. • The charterer, who provides the personnel, insurance, and other materials necessary to operate the vessel, is known either as a *demise charterer* or as an *owner pro hac vice.* — Also termed *demise charter.*

demise charter. See *bareboat charter.*

gross charter. A charter under which the shipowner provides all personnel and pays all expenses.

slot charter. A charter for one or more slots on a container vessel. • Each slot accommodates a 20-foot container. A slot charter is a form of vessel-sharing agreement. Cf. *space charter.*

space charter. A charter for a part of a vessel's capacity, such as a specified hold or deck or a specified part of the vessel's carrying capacity. • A space charter is a form of vessel-sharing agreement. Cf. *slot charter.*

time charter. A charter for a specified period, rather than for a specific task or voyage; a charter under which the shipowner continues to manage and control the vessel, but the charterer designates the ports of call and the cargo carried. • Each party bears the expenses related to its functions and for any damage it causes. Cf. *voyage charter.*

voyage charter. A charter under which the shipowner provides a ship and crew, and places them at the disposal of the charterer for the carriage of cargo to a designated port. • The voyage charterer may lease the entire vessel for a voyage or series of voyages — or may (by "space charter") lease only part of the vessel. Cf. *time charter.*

charter, *vb.* **1.** To establish or grant by charter <charter a bank>. **2.** To hire or rent for temporary use <charter a boat>.

charter agreement. See CHARTERPARTY.

chartered life underwriter. See UNDERWRITER.

chartered ship. See SHIP.

charter-land. *Hist.* See BOOKLAND.

charter member. See MEMBER.

charter of affreightment. See AFFREIGHTMENT.

charterparty. (16c) A contract by which a ship, or a principal part of it, is leased by the owner, esp. to a merchant for the conveyance of goods on a

predetermined voyage to one or more places or for a specified period of time; a special contract between the shipowner and charterer, esp. for the carriage of goods by sea. — Also written *charter-party; charter party.* — Often shortened to *charter.* — Also termed *charter agreement.*

chase, *n. Hist.* A franchise granted by the Crown empowering the grantee to keep, within a certain district, animals for hunting, i.e., the objects of the chase. • This franchise was also known as a *free chase* to contrast it with a *chase royal* — a chase held by the Crown.

common chase. A chase in which everyone is entitled to hunt.

chattel (**chat**-əl). (*usu. pl.*) (14c) Movable or transferable property; personal property; esp., a physical object capable of manual delivery and not the subject matter of real property.

chattel personal. (16c) A tangible good or an intangible right (such as a patent). — Also termed *personal chattel.*

chattel real. (16c) A real-property interest that is less than a freehold or fee, such as a leasehold estate. • The most important chattel real is an estate for years in land, which is considered a chattel because it lacks the indefiniteness of time essential to real property. — Also termed *real chattel.*

chattel vegetable. A movable article of a vegetable origin, such as timber, undergrowth, corn, or fruit.

local chattel. Personal property that is affixed to land; FIXTURE.

personal chattel. See *chattel personal.*

real chattel. See *chattel real.*

unique chattel. A chattel that is absolutely irreplaceable because it is one of a kind.

chattel lien. See *mechanic's lien* under LIEN.

chattel mortgage. See MORTGAGE.

chattel-mortgage bond. See BOND (3).

chattel paper. (1935) A writing that shows both a monetary obligation and a security interest in or a lease of specific goods. UCC § 9-102(1)(11). • Chattel paper is generally used in a consumer transaction when the consumer buys goods on credit. The consumer typically promises to pay for the goods by executing a promissory note, and the seller retains a security interest in the goods. See SECURITY AGREEMENT.

electronic chattel paper. (1998) Chattel paper evidenced by a record or records consisting of information stored in an electronic medium and retrievable in perceivable form. UCC § 9-102(a) (31).

tangible chattel paper. Chattel paper evidenced by a record or records consisting of information inscribed on a tangible medium. UCC § 9-102(a) (78).

chattel personal. See CHATTEL.

chattel real. See CHATTEL.

chattel vegetable. See CHATTEL.

chaud-medley (**showd**-med-lee). See CHANCE-MEDLEY.

cheap stock. See STOCK.

cheat, *n.* **1.** CHEATING. **2.** A person who habitually cheats; a swindler.

cheat, *vb.* To defraud; to practice deception.

cheater. 1. A person who cheats. **2.** ESCHEATOR.

cheating. (16c) The fraudulent obtaining of another's property by means of a false symbol or token, or by other illegal practices. — Also termed *cheating at common law*; *common-law cheat*; *cheat*. See FRAUD.

    cheating by false pretenses. (1827) The intentional obtaining of both the possession and ownership of money, goods, wares, or merchandise by means of misrepresentations, with the intent to defraud. See FALSE PRETENSES. Cf. *larceny by trick* under LARCENY.

check, *n.* (18c) A draft signed by the maker or drawer, drawn on a bank, payable on demand, and unlimited in negotiability. ● Under UCC § 3-104(f), an instrument may be a check even though it is described on its face by another term, such as "money order." — Also spelled *cheque*. See DRAFT.

    bad check. (1856) A check that is not honored because the account either contains insufficient funds or does not exist. — Also termed *hot check*; *worthless check*; *rubber check*; *bounced check*; *cold check*; *bogus check*; *false check*; *dry check*.

    blank check. (1819) A check signed by the drawer but left blank as to the payee or the amount, or both.

    bogus check. See *bad check*.

    bounced check. See *bad check*.

    canceled check. (1839) A check bearing a notation that it has been paid by the bank on which it was drawn. ● A canceled check is often used as evidence of payment. — Also spelled *cancelled check*.

    cashier's check. (1846) A check drawn by a bank on itself, payable to another person, and evidencing the payee's authorization to receive from the bank the amount of money represented by the check; a draft for which the drawer and drawee are the same bank, or different branches of the same bank.

    certified check. (1841) A depositor's check drawn on a bank that guarantees the availability of funds for the check. ● The guarantee may be by the drawee's signed agreement to pay the draft or by a notation on the check that it is certified.

    cold check. See *bad check*.

    crossed check. A check that has lines drawn across its face and writing that specifies the bank to which the check must be presented for payment. ● The same effect is achieved by stamping the bank's name on the check. The check's negotiability at that bank is unaffected, but no other bank can honor it. Cf. *open check*.

    depository-transfer check. (1976) An unsigned, nonnegotiable check that is used by a bank to transfer funds from its branch to the collection bank.

    dry check. See *bad check*.

    e-check. A paper check that is supplied by a consumer to a payee (usu. a merchant) who uses the check to make an electronic funds transfer. ● The payee electronically scans the check's magnetic-ink character-recognition coding to obtain the bank-routing, account, and serial numbers, then enters the amount of the check. This is usu., but not always, done at a point-of-sale terminal. — Also termed *electronic check*. Cf. *e-money* under MONEY.

    electronic check. See *e-check*.

    false check. See *bad check*.

    hot check. See *bad check*.

    memorandum check. A check that a borrower gives to a lender for the amount of a short-term loan, with the understanding that it is not to be presented for payment but will be redeemed by the borrower when the loan falls due.

    open check. A check that may be cashed by any bank. Cf. *crossed check*.

    personal check. A check drawn on a person's own account.

    postdated check. A check that bears a date after the date of its issue and is payable on or after the stated date.

    raised check. (1867) A check whose face amount has been increased, usu. without the knowledge of the issuer — an act that under the UCC is considered an alteration. UCC § 3-407. See RAISING AN INSTRUMENT.

    registered check. A check purchased at a bank and drawn on bank funds that have been set aside to pay that check.

    rubber check. See *bad check*.

    stale check. (1899) A check that has been outstanding for an unreasonable time — more than six months under the UCC. • Banks in jurisdictions adopting the UCC may choose not to honor such a check. UCC § 4-404.

teller's check. A draft drawn by a bank on another bank or payable at or through a bank.

traveler's check. A cashier's check that must be signed by the purchaser at the time of purchase and countersigned when cashed; an instrument that (1) is payable on demand, (2) is drawn on or payable at or through a bank, (3) is designated by the term "traveler's check" or by a substantially similar term, and (4) requires, as a condition to payment, a countersignature by a person whose specimen signature appears on the instrument. UCC § 3-104(i). • Traveler's checks, which are available in various denominations, are typically purchased from a bank or financing company.

worthless check. See *bad check.*

check, *vb.* (14c) **1.** To control or restrain <handcuffs checked the defendant's movement>. **2.** To verify or audit <an accountant checked the invoices>. **3.** To investigate <the police checked the suspect's story>. • In this sense, *check* is typically used with *up, on,* or *out.* **4.** To leave for safekeeping with an attendant <the diner checked her coat at the door>.

check-kiting. (1892) The illegal practice of writing a check against a bank account with insufficient funds to cover the check, in the hope that the funds from a previously deposited check will reach the account before the bank debits the amount of the outstanding check. — Also termed *kiting*; *check-flashing.*

check-off system. The procedure by which an employer deducts union dues directly from the employees' wages and remits those dues to the union.

checkpoint search. See SEARCH.

checks and balances. (18c) The theory of governmental power and functions whereby each branch of government has the ability to counter the actions of any other branch, so that no single branch can control the entire government. • For example, the executive branch can check the legislature by exercising its veto power, but the legislature can, by a sufficient majority, override any veto. See SEPARATION OF POWERS.

chemical warfare. See WARFARE.

cheque. See CHECK.

cherry-stem annexation. See ANNEXATION.

Chevron **deference.** A two-part test under which a court will uphold a federal agency's construction of a federal statute if (1) the statute is ambiguous or does not address the question at issue, and (2) the agency's interpretation of the statute is reasonable. • If the court finds that the legislature's intent is clearly expressed in the statute, then that intent is upheld. The U.S. Supreme Court enunciated the rule in *Chevron U.S.A., Inc. v. Natural Res. Def. Council, Inc.,* 467 U.S. 837, 842–43, 104 S.Ct. 2778, 2781–82 (1984). — Also termed *Chevron rule.*

Chicago Board of Trade. The commodities exchange where futures contracts in a large number of agricultural products are made. — Abbr. CBT; CBOT.

Chicago Board Options Exchange. The predominant organized marketplace in the United States for trading options. — Abbr. CBOE.

chicanery (shi-**kay**-nər-ee), *n.* (17c) Trickery; deception. — Also termed *chicane.* — **chicanerous,** *adj.*

chief, *n.* **1.** A person who is put above the rest; the leader <chief of staff>. **2.** The principal or most important part or position <commander-in-chief>. — **chief,** *adj.*

chief administrative patent judge. See JUDGE.

chief executive. See EXECUTIVE.

chief executive officer. (1854) A corporation's highest-ranking administrator, who manages the firm day by day and reports to the board of directors. — Abbr. CEO.

chief financial officer. The executive in charge of making a company's accounting and fiscal decisions. — Abbr. CFO.

chief information officer. The executive who supervises a company's informational infrastructure, including the system for retaining and destroying records. — Abbr. CIO.

chief judge. See JUDGE.

chief justice. See JUSTICE (2).

Chief Justice of England. The former title of the Lord Chief Justice of England. See LORD CHIEF JUSTICE OF ENGLAND.

Chief Justice of the Common Pleas. *Hist.* Formerly, the presiding judge in the Court of Common Pleas. • The Judicature Act of 1875 reduced the Court of Common Pleas to the Common Pleas Division. In 1881 the last Chief Justice of the Common Pleas, Lord Coleridge, was appointed Lord Chief Justice of England, merging the Common Pleas Division and the Queen's Bench Division. The Lord Chief Justice of England now exercises the powers formerly belonging to the Chief Justice of the Common Pleas. Cf. LORD CHIEF JUSTICE OF ENGLAND.

Chief Justice of the United States. The formal title of the officer who is the Chief Justice of the Supreme Court of the United States. — Often shortened to *the Chief Justice.*

chief justiciar. See JUSTICIARY (2).

chief lease. See HEADLEASE.

chief lord. *Hist.* The immediate lord of a fee, to whom the tenants were directly and personally responsible.

chief magistrate. See MAGISTRATE (1).

Chief of Protocol. An officer in the U.S. Department of State responsible for managing the Office of Protocol and advising the President, Vice President, Secretary of State, and other U.S. officials on matters of diplomatic procedure governed by law or international custom and practice.

chief operating officer. A manager who supervises a company's day-to-day operations and who usu. reports to the chief executive officer. — Abbr. COO.

chief rents. *Hist.* A small, fixed, annual rent payable to the lord by a freeholder of a manor; annual quit rent. • Chief rents were abolished in 1922. See QUIT RENT.

chief use. A standard for determining a proper tariff classification in which a commodity's use is understood by examining the intended users as a whole, rather than individually.

child. (bef. 12c) **1.** A person under the age of majority. **2.** *Hist.* At common law, a person who has not reached the age of 14. **3.** A boy or girl; a young person. **4.** A son or daughter. **5.** A baby or fetus. See JUVENILE; MINOR. Pl. **children.**

abortive child. *Civil law.* A stillborn child or a child born so prematurely that it cannot and does not survive 24 hours.

abused child. A child who has been subjected to physical or mental neglect or harm. See *child abuse* under ABUSE.

adopted child. A child who has become the son or daughter of a parent or parents by virtue of legal or equitable adoption; ADOPTEE. See ADOPTION.

afterborn child. (18c) A child born after execution of a will or after the time in which a class gift closes. — Also spelled *after-born child.* See *afterborn heir* under HEIR. Cf. *posthumous child.*

battered child. A child upon whom physical or sexual abuse has been inflicted, usu. by a relative, caregiver, or close family friend. See *child abuse* under ABUSE; *domestic violence* under VIOLENCE; BATTERED-CHILD SYNDROME.

biological child. See *natural child* (1).

child in need of supervision. A child who has committed an offense that only children can commit, such as being ungovernable and disobedient to parents, running away from home, violating a curfew, being habitually truant from school, violating age restrictions on the purchase or possession of liquor or tobacco, or the like. —

Also termed *person in need of supervision; minor in need of supervision.* — Abbr. CHINS.

child out of wedlock. See *illegitimate child.*

child with disabilities. Under the Individuals with Disabilities Education Act, a child who needs special-education or related services because of (1) mental retardation, (2) a hearing, language, or visual impairment, (3) a serious emotional disturbance, or (4) another health impairment or specific learning disability. See INDIVIDUALS WITH DISABILITIES EDUCATION ACT.

delinquent child. (1902) A child who has committed an offense that would be a crime if committed by an adult. • A delinquent child may not be subject to the jurisdiction of the juvenile court if the child is under a statutory age. Cf. *child in need of supervision*; JUVENILE DELINQUENT.

dependent child. A needy child who has been deprived of parental support or care because of the parent's or other responsible person's death, absence from the home, physical or mental incapacity, or (in some cases) unemployment. • This definition was formerly found in Aid to Families with Dependent Children (AFDC), 42 USCA § 606(a). When that program was replaced with Temporary Assistance to Needy Families (TANF), the definition was eliminated although sections of TANF refer to it (*see, e.g.,* 42 USCA § 672(h)).

deprived child. A child who (1) lacks proper parental care or control, subsistence, education, or other care and control for his or her physical, mental, or emotional well-being, (2) has been placed for care or adoption in violation of the law, (3) has been abandoned, or (4) is without a parent, guardian, or legal custodian. Uniform Juvenile Delinquency Act, 18 USCA §§ 5031 et seq. Cf. *neglected child.*

disobedient child. See *incorrigible child.*

foster child. (12c) A child whose care and upbringing are entrusted to an adult other than the child's natural or adoptive parents, usu. by an agency. • A foster child may receive informal, voluntary care by someone (often a grandparent, other relative, or neighbor) who enters into an agreement with the parent or who simply substitutes for the parent as necessary to ensure the child's protection. More formally, the child may be part of the federal–state foster-care program that identifies, trains, and pays caregivers who will provide family care for children who lack parents or cannot safely remain with their biological or adoptive parents. — Also termed (archaically) *fosterling.* See *foster parent* under PARENT.

genetic child. See *natural child* (1).

handicapped child. A child who is mentally retarded, deaf or hearing-impaired, speech-impaired, blind or visually disabled, seriously emotionally disturbed, or orthopedically impaired, or who because of specific learning disabilities requires special education.

illegitimate child. (17c) A child who was not conceived or born in lawful wedlock, nor later legitimated. • At common law, such a child was considered the child of nobody (*nullius filius*) and had no name except one that was gained by reputation. Being no one's child, an illegitimate child could not inherit, even from the mother, but all states now allow maternal inheritance. In cases such as *Levy v. Louisiana*, 391 U.S. 68, 88 S.Ct. 1509 (1968), and *Glona v. American Guar. & Liab. Ins. Co.*, 391 U.S. 73, 88 S.Ct. 1515 (1968), the Supreme Court held that limitations on a child's right to inherit from his or her mother were unconstitutional. As a result, states changed their laws to permit full maternal inheritance. Full paternal inheritance is permitted if the child can prove paternity in accordance with state law (the proof varies from state to state). This burden of proof, uniquely imposed on an illegitimate child, is constitutionally permissible. *Lalli v. Lalli*, 439 U.S. 259, 99 S.Ct. 518 (1978). — Also termed *bastard*; *child out of wedlock*; *nonmarital child*; (archaically) *natural child*. Cf. BASTARD.

incorrigible child. (17c) A child who habitually refuses to obey his or her parents or guardians. — Also termed *disobedient child*.

intended child. The child who is intended to result from a surrogacy contract. See *surrogate parent* under PARENT; *surrogate mother* under MOTHER; *intentional parent* under PARENT; *legal father* under FATHER; SURROGACY CONTRACT.

legitimate child. (17c) **1.** At common law, a child conceived or born in lawful wedlock. **2.** Modernly, a child conceived or born in lawful wedlock, or legitimated either by the parents' later marriage or by a declaration or judgment of legitimation.

mantle child. *Hist.* A child born out of wedlock and later legitimated when the parents are married, traditionally by standing under a cloak with the parents during the marriage ceremony.

natural child. (16c) **1.** A child by birth, as distinguished from an adopted child. — Also termed *biological child*; *genetic child*. **2.** A child that is genetically related to the mother and father as opposed to a child conceived by donor insemination or by egg donation. **3.** *Archaic.* An illegitimate child, usu. one acknowledged by the father.

neglected child. (17c) **1.** A child whose parents or legal custodians are unfit to care for him or her because of cruelty, immorality, or incapacity. **2.** A child whose parents or legal custodians refuse to provide the necessary care and medical services for the child. Cf. *deprived child*.

nonmarital child. See *illegitimate child*.

posthumous child. (17c) A child born after a parent's death. • Ordinarily, the phrase *posthumous child* suggests one born after the father's death. But in at least one case, a legally dead pregnant woman was kept on life-support machines until the child could be safely delivered; so it is possible for a mother's posthumous child to be born. Cf. *afterborn child*.

prostituted child. See *child prostitute* under PROSTITUTE.

quasi-posthumous child. *Civil law.* A child who becomes a direct heir of a grandfather or other male ascendant because of the death of the child's father.

special-needs child. **1.** A child with medical problems or with a physical, mental, or emotional handicap. **2.** A child that is likely to be unadoptable because of medical problems or physical, mental, or emotional handicaps, or by reason of age or ethnic background. See ADOPTION ASSISTANCE AND CHILD WELFARE ACT.

stepchild. The child of one's spouse by a previous marriage. • A stepchild is generally not entitled to the same legal rights as a natural or adopted child. For example, a stepchild has no right to a share of an intestate stepparent's property.

unborn child. A child not yet born, esp. at the happening of some event.

child abuse. See ABUSE.

child-abuse and -neglect reporting statute. *Family law.* A state law requiring certain persons, among them healthcare providers, teachers, and childcare workers, to report suspected child abuse. • By 1967, every state had adopted some form of reporting statute. In the Child Abuse Prevention and Treatment Act (42 USCA §§ 5101–5157), Congress provided federal funding for all states that implement federal standards in their reporting statutes and defined child maltreatment broadly. See CHILD ABUSE PREVENTION AND TREATMENT ACT.

Child Abuse Prevention and Treatment Act. *Family law.* A federal statute that provides limited funding to states for preventing, identifying, and treating child abuse and neglect. • Enacted in 1974, the Act was amended in 1996 to reinforce an emphasis on child safety. The Act established the National Center on Child Abuse and Neglect in the Department of Health and Human Services. Its function is to study child abuse, conduct research into its causes, and make grants to agencies for the study, prevention, and treatment of child abuse. 42 USCA §§ 5101–5157. — Abbr. CAPTA. See CHILD-ABUSE AND -NEGLECT REPORTING STATUTE.

child-access prevention statute. See SAFE-STORAGE STATUTE.

child- and dependent-care tax credit. See TAX CREDIT.

child application. See PATENT APPLICATION.

child-benefit theory. See STUDENT-BENEFIT THEORY.

child-care fund. *Family law.* State-government funds set aside to reimburse counties for part of the payments for children's foster care and expenses.

child-care rules. *Family law.* State administrative rules for the care of foster children. ● In most states, departments concerned with social services establish and enforce the rules governing the welfare of foster children. A few states have created agencies expressly dedicated to services for children.

child custody. See CUSTODY (2).

child destruction. 1. See FETICIDE. 2. See INFANTICIDE (1).

child endangerment. (1981) The placing of a child in a place or position that exposes him or her to danger to life or health. — Also termed *endangering the welfare of a child.*

physical child endangerment. Reckless behavior toward a child that has caused or could cause serious physical injury. — Sometimes shortened to *physical endangerment.*

child in need of supervision. See CHILD.

child-kidnapping. See KIDNAPPING.

child labor. The employment of workers under the age of majority. ● This term typically focuses on abusive practices such as exploitative factory work; slavery, sale, and trafficking in children; forced or compulsory labor such as debt bondage and serfdom; and the use of children in prostitution, pornography, drug-trafficking, or anything else that might jeopardize their health, safety, or morals. Some writers restrict the term to activities forbidden by the International Labor Organization's minimum-age conventions. *See* ILO Minimum Age Convention ch. 138 (1973). See FAIR LABOR STANDARDS ACT. Cf. CHILD WORK.

oppressive child labor. Under the Fair Labor Standards Act, the employment of workers under the age of 16 in any occupation, or the employment of those 16 to 18 years old in particularly hazardous occupations. 29 USCA § 203(l); 29 CFR § 570.1(b). The Secretary of Labor may assess civil penalties of up to $10,000 per violation. 29

USCA § 216(e). — Also termed *harmful child labor.*

child-labor law. (1904) A state or federal statute that protects children by prescribing the necessary working conditions for children in a workplace. See FAIR LABOR STANDARDS ACT.

child maltreatment. See *child abuse* under ABUSE.

child molestation. See MOLESTATION.

childnapping. See *child-kidnapping* under KIDNAPPING.

child neglect. See NEGLECT.

Child Online Protection Act. A 1998 federal statute designed to control child pornography on the Internet by prohibiting Internet speech that is "harmful to minors." ● Unlike the Communications Decency Act, COPA does not apply to e-mail or chat-room communications. Among other things, COPA applies to sexually explicit material that appears to depict minors, even if the people are actually over 18 or the images are computer-generated and do not depict living people. After several court challenges, COPA was held unconstitutional and never became effective. — Abbr. COPA.

child out of wedlock. See *illegitimate child* under CHILD.

child pornography. See PORNOGRAPHY.

child prostitute. See PROSTITUTE.

child prostitution. See PROSTITUTION.

Child Protective Services. A governmental agency responsible for investigating allegations of child abuse and neglect, providing family services to the parent or guardian of a child who has been abused or neglected, and administering the foster-care program. — Abbr. CPS. — Also termed (in some states) *Department of Social Services*; (esp. in Michigan) *family independence agency*.

child-rearing. *Family law.* The practices and customs followed in the upbringing of children, whether in a particular family or in society generally. — Sometimes written *childrearing*.

children's court. See *juvenile court* under COURT.

child's attorney. See *attorney ad litem* under ATTORNEY.

child-sexual-abuse accommodation syndrome. The supposed medical and psychological condition of a child who has suffered repeated instances of sexual abuse, usu. from a relative or family friend. ● This so-called "syndrome" has been repudiated by the scientific community. It cannot be validated and thus cannot discriminate between abuse and nonabuse cases. — Abbr. CSAAS. — Also termed *child-sexual-abuse syndrome.*

child's income tax. See *kiddie tax* under TAX.

child-slaying. See INFANTICIDE.

child's part. An inheritance that, by statute in some states, a widow may claim in lieu of dower or what she would receive under her husband's will. • The amount is calculated by counting the widow as a child of the decedent, sharing equally any entitlement with any other child.

child-stealing. See *child-kidnapping* under KIDNAPPING.

child support. (1939) *Family law.* **1.** A parent's legal obligation to contribute to the economic maintenance and education of a child until the age of majority, the child's emancipation before reaching majority, or the child's completion of secondary education. • The obligation is enforceable both civilly and criminally. **2.** In a custody or divorce action, the money legally owed by one parent to the other for the expenses incurred for children of the marriage. • The right to child support is the child's right and cannot be waived, and any divorce-decree provision waiving child support is void. Cf. ALIMONY.

decretal child support. Child support provided for in a divorce decree or modification order.

child-support-enforcement agency. *Family law.* A governmental agency that helps custodial parents collect child support. • Under Title IV(D) of the Social Security Act (42 USCA § 654), states are required to establish child-support-enforcement agencies to collect support for obligee parents. Although the agencies are governed by a set of federal standards, each state has its own central registry. The CSE agency may operate through the state's Department of Human Services, its Department of Justice, its tax agency, or its Attorney General's office. The agency can help locate a missing parent and establish paternity. The agency works to establish and enforce support orders. — Abbr. CSE agency. — Also termed *IV-D agency.* See OFFICE OF CHILD-SUPPORT ENFORCEMENT.

child-support guidelines. *Family law.* Statutory provisions that govern the amount of child support that an obligor parent must pay. • Child-support guidelines have been developed in every state in response to the creation of the Temporary Assistance to Needy Families program. 42 USCA §§ 601–603a.

Child Support Recovery Act of 1994. A statute that made it a federal offense for a person to willfully fail to pay past-due child support for a child who lived in another state. • This Act has been replaced by the Deadbeat Parents Punishment Act. 42 USCA § 228. See DEADBEAT PARENTS PUNISHMENT ACT.

child with disabilities. See CHILD.

child work. A minor's salutary employment, esp. within the family. • This term is sometimes used in contrast to *child labor*, the idea being that child work within the family unit can be a positive experience. Some scholars and courts note that child work can facilitate vocational skills and social adaptation, and is often viewed as an expression of family solidarity. Cf. CHILD LABOR.

chill, *vb.* To inhibit or discourage <chill one's free-speech rights>.

chilling a sale. (1881) The act of bidders or others who combine or conspire to discourage others from attempting to buy an item so that they might buy the item themselves for a lower price.

chilling effect. (1952) **1.** *Constitutional law.* The result of a law or practice that seriously discourages the exercise of a constitutional right, such as the right to appeal or the right of free speech. **2.** Broadly, the result when any practice is discouraged. — Also termed *chilling bidding; chilling the bidding.*

chilling the bidding. 1. See CHILLING EFFECT. **2.** See CHILLING A SALE.

Chimel **search.** See *protective search* under SEARCH.

Chinese Wall. See ETHICAL WALL.

CHINS. *abbr.* See *child in need of supervision* under CHILD.

chirograph (kɪ-rə-**graf**), *n.* **1.** *Civil law.* A handwritten instrument. **2.** A written deed, subscribed and witnessed. — Also termed *cyrographum.* **3.** Such a deed in two parts from a single original document separated by an indented line through the word "chirographum," each party retaining one part. **4.** *Hist.* FOOT OF THE FINE. — Also termed (in sense 4) *cyrographarius.* — **chirographic,** *adj.*

chirographer of fines (kɪ-**rahg**-rə-fər). *Hist.* A Court of Common Pleas officer who engrossed court-ordered fines and delivered indentures of the fines to the parties. See INDENTURE OF A FINE.

chit. (18c) **1.** A signed voucher for money received or owed, usu. for food, drink, or the like. **2.** A slip of paper with writing on it.

chivalry (**shiv**-əl-ree). (14c) *Hist.* Tenure held by knight-service; tenure in which a person held land in exchange for military service of the highest order. See KNIGHT-SERVICE.

choate (**koh**-it *or* -ayt), *adj.* (1878) **1.** Complete in and of itself. **2.** Having ripened or become perfected. Cf. INCHOATE. — **choateness,** *n.*

choate lien. See LIEN.

choice. See FREEDOM OF CHOICE.

choice of evils. See NECESSITY (1).

choice-of-evils defense. See *lesser-evils defense* under DEFENSE (1).

choice-of-exclusive-forum clause. See FORUM-SELECTION CLAUSE.

choice of jurisdiction. *Conflict of laws.* The choice of the state (or country) that should exercise jurisdiction over a case.

choice of law. (1900) The question of which jurisdiction's law should apply in a given case. Cf. CONFLICT OF LAWS.

choice-of-law clause. (1957) A contractual provision by which the parties designate the jurisdiction whose law will govern any disputes that may arise between the parties. Cf. FORUM-SELECTION CLAUSE.

choice voting. See *single transferable vote* under VOTE (1).

chop-shop, *n. Criminal law.* A garage where stolen automobiles are dismantled so that their parts can be sold separately.

chose (shohz), *n.* [French] (17c) A thing, whether tangible or intangible; a personal article; a chattel. See THING.

    chose in action. (17c) **1.** A proprietary right in personam, such as a debt owed by another person, a share in a joint-stock company, or a claim for damages in tort. **2.** The right to bring an action to recover a debt, money, or thing. **3.** Personal property that one person owns but another person possesses, the owner being able to regain possession through a lawsuit. — Also termed *thing in action.*

    chose in possession. Personal property for which title and possession unite in the same person. — Also termed *thing in possession.*

    chose local. A fixed chattel.

    chose transitory. A movable chattel.

Christian name. See *personal name* under NAME.

church court. See *ecclesiastical court* under COURT.

church law. See CANON LAW (2).

churl (chərl). See CEORL.

churn, burn, and bury, *vb.* (Of a stockbroker) to make numerous risky trades in (an account) and, as a result, squander the customer's money. • The term denotes the action involved in particularly reckless churning.

churning, *n.* (1953) **1.** *Securities.* A stockbroker's excessive trading of a customer's account to earn more commissions rather than to further the customer's interests; an abuse of a customer's confidence for personal gain by frequent and numerous transactions, disproportionate to the size and nature of the customer's account. • Under securities laws, the practice is illegal — a violation of § 10(b) of the Exchange Act (15 USCA § 78j(b)). But because the fraud is the activity as a whole and there is no communication between the broker and the customer about a specific sale of securities, there is not normally a right of action for fraud based on churning. **2.** *Tax.* A transfer of property that does not result in a significant change of ownership or use of the property, usu. to make the property eligible for amortization or a more favorable method of depreciation. See ANTICHURNING RULE. — **churn,** *vb.*

CIA. *abbr.* (1951) CENTRAL INTELLIGENCE AGENCY.

CID. *abbr.* CIVIL INVESTIGATIVE DEMAND.

CIF. *abbr.* COST, INSURANCE, AND FREIGHT.

CIF destination. See COST, INSURANCE, AND FREIGHT.

CIF place of destination. See *CIF destination* under COST, INSURANCE, AND FREIGHT.

Cinque Ports (singk ports). (17c) [Fr. "five ports"] The five English ports — Hastings, Romney, Hythe, Dover, and Sandwich — that were important defenses against French invasion. • They received special privileges and were obliged to furnish a certain number of ships for use in war.

CIO. *abbr.* **1.** The Congress of Industrial Organizations, which merged with the AFL in 1955. See AMERICAN FEDERATION OF LABOR AND CONGRESS OF INDUSTRIAL ORGANIZATIONS. **2.** CHIEF INFORMATION OFFICER.

CIP. *abbr.* **1.** CONTINUATION-IN-PART. **2.** CARRIAGE AND INSURANCE PAID TO.

circa (sər-kə), *prep.* [Latin] (1861) About or around (a date, esp. an ancient one); approximately <the book was written circa 1938–1941>. — Abbr. ca.; c.

circle conspiracy. See *wheel conspiracy* under CONSPIRACY.

circuit, *n.* (15c) **1.** A judicial division in which hearings occur at several locations, as a result of which judges often travel to different locations. **2.** A judicial division of the United States — that is, one of the 13 circuits into which the U.S. courts of appeals are organized. 28 USCA § 41.

circuit court. See COURT.

circuit executive. The chief executive officer of a federal judicial circuit responsible for daily administration of the courts. • The circuit executive is the highest-ranking nonjudicial officer within a circuit.

circuit judge. See JUDGE.

circuit justice. See JUSTICE (2).

circuit mediator. An attorney-employee of a U.S. court of appeals who mediates civil cases, usu. before oral argument. — Also termed *preargument-conference attorney*; *settlement counsel*.

circuit-riding, *n. Hist.* The practice of a judge's traveling within a legislatively defined circuit to hear cases in one place for a time, then another, and so on. • The American practice of circuit-riding was based on the English eyre system, in which justices rode between the shire towns to hold assizes. See *circuit-riding justice* under JUS-TICE (2).

circuit-riding justice. See JUSTICE (2).

circuity of action. (17c) A procedure allowing duplicative lawsuits, leading to unnecessarily lengthy and indirect litigation, as when a defendant fails to bring a counterclaim, but later brings a separate action to recover what could have been awarded in the original lawsuit. • Civil-procedure rules have eliminated many problems associated with circuity of action.

circular letter of credit. See LETTER OF CREDIT.

circular note. See LETTER OF CREDIT.

circulating capital. See *floating capital* under CAPI-TAL.

circumstance, *n.* (*often pl.*) (13c) An accompanying or accessory fact, event, or condition, such as a piece of evidence that indicates the probability of an event. — **circumstantial,** *adj.*

   aggravating circumstance. (17c) **1.** A fact or situation that increases the degree of liability or culpability for a criminal act. **2.** A fact or situation that relates to a criminal offense or defendant and that is considered by the court in imposing punishment (esp. a death sentence). • Aggravating circumstances in death-penalty cases are usu. prescribed by statute. For a list of aggravating circumstances in a capital-murder case, see Model Penal Code § 210.6(3). — Also termed *aggravating element*; *aggravating factor*; *aggravator.* Cf. *mitigating circumstance*; MITIGATOR.

   attendant circumstance. A fact that is situationally relevant to a particular event or occurrence. • A fact-finder often reviews the attendant circumstances of a crime to learn, for example, the perpetrator's motive or intent.

   exigent circumstances. (1906) **1.** A situation that demands unusual or immediate action and that may allow people to circumvent usual procedures, as when a neighbor breaks through a window of a burning house to save someone inside. **2.** A situation in which a police officer must take immediate action to effectively make an arrest, search, or seizure for which probable cause exists, and thus may do so without first obtaining a warrant. • Exigent circumstances may exist if (1) a person's life or safety is threatened, (2) a suspect's escape is imminent, or (3) evidence is about to be removed or destroyed. — Also

termed *emergency circumstances*; *special circumstances.*

   extenuating circumstance. See *mitigating circumstance.*

   extraordinary circumstances. (17c) A highly unusual set of facts that are not commonly associated with a particular thing or event.

   incriminating circumstance. (1885) A fact or situation showing either that a crime was committed or that a particular person committed it.

   mitigating circumstance. (17c) **1.** A fact or situation that does not justify or excuse a wrongful act or offense but that reduces the degree of culpability and thus may reduce the damages (in a civil case) or the punishment (in a criminal case). **2.** A fact or situation that does not bear on the question of a defendant's guilt but that is considered by the court in imposing punishment and esp. in lessening the severity of a sentence. • A court's or jury's power to consider mitigating circumstances cannot be limited by statute. See *Lockett v. Ohio*, 438 U.S. 586, 606, 98 S.Ct. 2954, 2965 (1978). For a list of mitigating circumstances in a capital-murder case, see Model Penal Code § 210.6(4). **3.** *Contracts.* An unusual or unpredictable event that prevents performance, such as a labor strike. — Also termed *extenuating circumstance.* Cf. *aggravating circumstance.*

   special circumstances. See *exigent circumstances.*

circumstantial evidence. See EVIDENCE.

circumvention. 1. *Copyright.* The act of bypassing, avoiding, removing, deactivating, or impairing a technological measure or device that controls access to a work protected by U.S. copyright law. • Circumvention of technology that effectively controls access to a work protected by a U.S. copyright is prohibited under 17 USCA § 1201. **2.** *Scots law.* FACILITY AND CIRCUMVENTION.

CIT. *abbr.* Court of International Trade. See UNITED STATES COURT OF INTERNATIONAL TRADE.

citable, *adj.* Authorized by a court to be used as legal precedent. • In general, published opinions are citable, but unpublished ones are not. — Also written *citeable.* Cf. NONCITABLE.

citation, *n.* (13c) **1.** A court-issued writ that commands a person to appear at a certain time and place to do something demanded in the writ, or to show cause for not doing so. **2.** A police-issued order to appear before a judge on a given date to defend against a stated charge, such as a traffic violation. — Also termed *appearance ticket.* **3.** A reference to a legal precedent or authority, such as a case, statute, or treatise, that either substantiates or contradicts a given position. — Often shortened to (in sense 3) *cite.*

parallel citation. (1911) An additional reference to a case that has been reported in more than one reporter. • For example, whereas a *Bluebook* citation reads "*Morgan v. United States*, 304 U.S. 1 (1938)," the same reference including parallel citations reads "*Morgan v. United States*, 304 U.S. 1, 58 S.Ct. 773, 82 L.Ed. 1129 (1938)," in which the main citation is to the *U.S. Reports* and the parallel citations are to the *Supreme Court Reporter* and to the *Lawyer's Edition.*

pinpoint citation. (1961) The page on which a quotation or relevant passage appears, as opposed to the page on which a case or article begins. • For example, the number 217 is the pinpoint citation in *Baker v. Carr*, 369 U.S. 186, 217 (1962). — Also termed *jump citation; dictum page; pincite.*

4. A reference to another document in support of an argument, as in a patent prosecution in which a party trying to defeat a claim of patentability refers to a previous patent or a publication to show that the invention lacks novelty or nonobviousness. See REFERENCE (4).

front-page citation. Patents. A citation of prior art listed on the front page of a patent application and disclosing a patent or publication that is pertinent to the patentability of any of the application's claims.

textual citation. Patents. A reference to a work containing prior art listed in a patent application's body.

citational, *adj.* Of or relating to a citation (esp. a reference citation) <citational analysis>.

citation order. (1955) The appropriate ranking of the various authorities marshaled in support of a legal proposition.

citation signal. See SIGNAL (2).

citator (sɪ-tay-tər). A catalogued list of cases, statutes, and other legal sources showing the subsequent history and current precedential value of those sources. • Citators allow researchers to verify the authority of a precedent and to find additional sources relating to a given subject. Citators were originally printed on gummed paper and pasted next to the report of a cited case. Today, citators are published in volumes and are also available online; the two most popular are Shepard's and KeyCite.

citatory (sɪ-tə-tor-ee), *adj.* Of, relating to, or having the power of a citation or summons <letters citatory>.

cite, *n.* See CITATION (3).

cite, *vb.* (15c) **1.** To summon before a court of law <the witness was cited for contempt>. **2.** To refer to or adduce as precedent or authority <counsel then cited the appropriate statutory provision>.

3. To commend or honor <the soldier was cited for bravery>.

citeable. See CITABLE.

citizen, *n.* (14c) **1.** A person who, by either birth or naturalization, is a member of a political community, owing allegiance to the community and being entitled to enjoy all its civil rights and protections; a member of the civil state, entitled to all its privileges. Cf. RESIDENT; DOMICILIARY.

citizen by naturalization. See *naturalized citizen.*

federal citizen. A citizen of the United States.

natural-born citizen. A person born within the jurisdiction of a national government.

naturalized citizen. A foreign-born person who attains citizenship by law. — Also termed *citizen by naturalization.*

2. For diversity-jurisdiction purposes, a corporation that was incorporated within a state or has its principal place of business there. 28 USCA § 1332(c)(1).

citizen-informant. See INFORMANT.

citizen's arrest. See ARREST.

citizenship, *n.* **1.** The status of being a citizen. **2.** The quality of a person's conduct as a member of a community.

corporate citizenship. See CORPORATE CITIZENSHIP.

dual citizenship. See DUAL CITIZENSHIP.

Citizenship Clause. (1896) The clause of the U.S. Constitution providing that all persons born or naturalized in the United States are citizens of the United States and the state they reside in. U.S. Const. amend. XIV, § 1, cl. 1.

citizen suit. An action under a statute giving citizens the right to sue violators of the law (esp. environmental law) and to seek injunctive relief and penalties. • In the 1970s, during the heyday of antipollution statutes such as the Clean Water Act and the Clean Air Act, legislators believed that regulators sometimes become too close to the industries they oversee and, as a result, lack the aggressiveness that individual citizens bring to litigation. The statutes therefore authorize, among other things, "private attorneys general" (citizens) to protect the environment. This includes not only injunctions to stop pollution but also penalties to be paid to the U.S. Treasury. A federal plaintiff must sue under a statutory citizen-suit provision and also satisfy constitutional-standing requirements. See STANDING.

citology. See LEGAL CITOLOGY.

city. 1. A municipal corporation, usu. headed by a mayor and governed by a city council; a municipality of the highest grade. **2.** The territory within a city's corporate limits. **3.** Collectively, the people who live in this territory. Cf. TOWN.

city attorney. (1837) An attorney employed by a city to advise it and represent it in legal matters. — Also termed *municipal attorney*; *city counsel*; *corporation counsel*; *city solicitor*.

city auditor. See AUDITOR.

city clerk. See CLERK (1).

city council. A city's legislative body, usu. responsible for passing ordinances, levying taxes, appropriating funds, and generally administering city government. — Also termed (in some states) *board of aldermen*.

city counsel. See CITY ATTORNEY.

city court. See *municipal court* under COURT.

city manager. A local official appointed to manage and administer the executive affairs of a municipality in accordance with the policies established by the city council or other governing body.

city judge. See *municipal judge* under JUDGE.

city solicitor. See CITY ATTORNEY.

city treasurer. See TREASURER.

Civ. Ct. See *civil court* under COURT.

civic, *adj.* (1656) **1.** Of or relating to citizenship or a particular citizen <civic responsibilities>. **2.** Of or relating to a city <civic center>.

civil, *adj.* (14c) **1.** Of or relating to the state or its citizenry <civil rights>. **2.** Of or relating to private rights and remedies that are sought by action or suit, as distinct from criminal proceedings <civil litigation>. **3.** Of or relating to any of the modern legal systems derived from Roman law <Louisiana is a civil-law jurisdiction>.

civil action. See ACTION (4).

civil arrest. See ARREST.

civil assault. See ASSAULT.

civil-authority clause. *Insurance.* A clause, esp. in a fire-insurance policy, insuring against damages caused by firefighters, police, or other civil authority.

civil bail. See BAIL (1).

civil code. (18c) **1.** A comprehensive and systematic legislative pronouncement of the whole private, noncommercial law in a legal system of the continental civil-law tradition. **2.** *(caps.)* The code that embodies the law of France, from which a great part of the Louisiana civil code is derived. — Abbr. CC. — Also termed *Code Civil*. See NAPOLEONIC CODE. **3.** A codification of noncriminal statutes.

civil cognation. See COGNATION.

civil commitment. (1945) **1.** A commitment of a person who is ill, incompetent, drug-addicted, or the like, as contrasted with a criminal sentence.

● In contrast to a criminal commitment, the length of a civil commitment is indefinite because it depends on the person's recovery. **2.** A public demonstration by two people of their intent to be bound together in a marriage-like relationship. ● The demonstration is usu. in the form of a ceremony, often identical to a wedding, but the relationship is usu. not legally recognized and can be dissolved without legal formalities. See CIVIL UNION. **3.** A residential program characterized by intense and strict supervision of sex offenders who have completed their prison sentences but are found to be likely to commit more sex crimes.

civil-commitment statute. A law that provides for the confinement of a person who is mentally ill, incompetent, drug-addicted, or the like. ● Unlike criminal incarceration, civil commitment is for an indefinite period.

civil commotion. (16c) A public uprising by a large number of people who, acting together, cause harm to people or property. ● A civil commotion usu. involves many more people than a riot. — Sometimes shortened to *commotion*. Cf. RIOT.

civil conspiracy. See CONSPIRACY.

civil contempt. See CONTEMPT.

civil corporation. See CORPORATION.

civil court. See COURT.

civil-damage law. See DRAM-SHOP ACT.

civil day. See *artificial day* under DAY.

civil death. See DEATH.

civil defense. 1. The practice of protecting civilians from dangers caused by hostilities or disasters and helping them recover from the immediate effects of such events. **2.** The policies that underlie this practice.

civil disability. See DISABILITY (3).

civil disobedience. (1866) A deliberate but nonviolent act of lawbreaking to call attention to a particular law or set of laws believed by the actor to be of questionable legitimacy or morality.

civil disorder. (18c) A public disturbance involving three or more people who commit violent acts that cause immediate danger or injury to people or property. See RIOT.

civil embargo. See EMBARGO (2).

civil forfeiture. See FORFEITURE.

civil fraud. See FRAUD.

civil fruit. See FRUIT.

civilian, *n.* **1.** A person not serving in the military. **2.** A lawyer practicing in a civil-law jurisdiction. — Also termed *civilista*. **3.** A scholar in civil or Roman law. — **civilian,** *adj.*

civil impediment. See IMPEDIMENT.

civil imprisonment. *Hist.* See IMPRISONMENT FOR DEBT.

civil infraction. See INFRACTION.

civil injury. See INJURY.

civil investigative demand. 1. A request for information served by the U.S. Attorney General on any person who may have documents or information relevant to a civil antitrust investigation or to an investigation authorized by section 3 of the International Antitrust Enforcement Assistance Act (15 USCA § 6202). ● A civil investigative demand can be issued before a civil or criminal action is begun, and can be served on anyone — not just potential defendants — thought to possess information pertinent to the investigation. If the Attorney General begins a civil or criminal action, this demand may not be served on persons within the scope of the proceeding. **2.** A similar request for information served by a different governmental entity, esp. a state attorney general. — Abbr. CID.

civilization. (18c) The transformation of a criminal matter to a civil one by law or judgment. Cf. CRIMINALIZATION (1).

civil justice. (16c) The methods by which a society redresses civil wrongs. Cf. CRIMINAL JUSTICE (1).

civil law. (14c) **1.** (*usu. cap.*) One of the two prominent legal systems in the Western world, originally administered in the Roman Empire and still influential in continental Europe, Latin America, Scotland, and Louisiana, among other parts of the world; ROMAN LAW. ● In reference to Romans, *civil law* (commonly referred to as *jus civile*) denotes the whole body of Roman law, from whatever source derived. But it is also used to denote that part of Roman law peculiar to the Romans, as opposed to the common law of all peoples (*jus gentium*). — Also termed *jus civile*; *Romanesque law.* Cf. COMMON LAW (2). **2.** The body of law imposed by the state, as opposed to moral law. **3.** The law of civil or private rights, as opposed to criminal law or administrative law. — Abbr. CL.

civil liability. See LIABILITY.

civil-liability act. See DRAM-SHOP ACT.

civil liberty. (*usu. pl.*) (17c) Freedom from undue governmental interference or restraint. ● This term usu. refers to freedom of speech, freedom of the press, freedom of religion, freedom of association, and other liberties associated with the Bill of Rights. In American law, early civil liberties were promulgated in the Lawes and Libertyes of Massachusetts (1648) and the Bill of Rights (1791). In English law, examples are found in Magna Carta (1215), the Petition of Right (1628), and the Bill of Rights (1689). — Also termed *civil right.*

civil list. An annual sum granted by Parliament for the expenses of the royal household.

civil marriage. See MARRIAGE (3).

civil month. See MONTH (1).

civil obligation. 1. See *conventional obligation* under OBLIGATION (3). **2.** See OBLIGATION (2).

civil offense. See *public tort* under TORT.

civil partnership. See CIVIL UNION.

civil penalty. See PENALTY (1).

civil possession. See POSSESSION.

civil power. See POLITICAL POWER.

civil procedure. (18c) **1.** The body of law — usu. rules enacted by the legislature or courts — governing the methods and practices used in civil litigation. ● An example is the Federal Rules of Civil Procedure. **2.** A particular method or practice used in carrying on civil litigation in a particular jurisdiction.

civil process. See PROCESS.

civil remedy. See REMEDY (1).

civil right. (*usu. pl.*) (17c) **1.** The individual rights of personal liberty guaranteed by the Bill of Rights and by the 13th, 14th, 15th, and 19th Amendments, as well as by legislation such as the Voting Rights Act. ● Civil rights include esp. the right to vote, the right of due process, and the right of equal protection under the law. **2.** CIVIL LIBERTY.

civil-rights act. (1867) One of several federal statutes enacted after the Civil War (1861–1865) and, much later, during and after the civil-rights movement of the 1950s and 1960s, for the purpose of implementing and giving further force to the basic rights guaranteed by the Constitution, and esp. prohibiting discrimination in employment and education on the basis of race, sex, religion, color, or age.

civil-rights removal. See REMOVAL.

civil service, *n.* **1.** The administrative branches of a government. **2.** The group of people employed by these branches. — **civil servant,** *n.*

Civil Service Commission. A former independent federal agency that supervised the government's personnel system. ● The agency was created in 1883 and abolished by Reorganization Plan No. 2 of 1978. Its functions were transferred to the Merit Systems Protection Board and the Office of Personnel Management. See MERIT SYSTEMS PROTECTION BOARD; OFFICE OF PERSONNEL MANAGEMENT.

civil-service reform. The use of business principles and methods instead of the spoils system in the conduct of the civil service, esp. in awarding contracts and appointing officials.

civil society. See SOCIETY.

civil term. See TERM (5).

civil union. *Family law.* A marriage-like relationship, often between members of the same sex, recognized by civil authorities within a jurisdiction. ● Vermont was the first state to recognize civil unions. In December 1999, the Vermont Supreme Court ruled that denying gay couples the benefits of marriage amounted to unconstitutional discrimination. *Baker v. State*, 744 A.2d 864 (Vt. 1999). Several months later the legislature passed a civil-unions law, which took effect on July 1, 2000. — Also termed *civil partnership.* Cf. DOMESTIC PARTNERSHIP; *same-sex marriage* under MARRIAGE (1).

civil war. See WAR.

civil wrong. (17c) **1.** See WRONG. **2.** See TORT. **3.** See DELICT.

C.J. *abbr.* **1.** See *chief justice* under JUSTICE (2). **2.** See *chief judge* under JUDGE. **3.** See *circuit judge* under JUDGE. **4.** CORPUS JURIS.

CJC. *abbr.* CODE OF JUDICIAL CONDUCT.

CJE. *abbr.* CONTINUING JUDICIAL EDUCATION.

C.J.S. *abbr. Corpus Juris Secundum.* — Also written CJS.

CL. *abbr.* CIVIL LAW.

Claflin trust. See *indestructible trust* under TRUST.

Claflin-trust principle. The doctrine that a trust cannot be terminated by the beneficiaries if the termination would defeat one of the settlor's material purposes in establishing the trust, even if all the beneficiaries seek its termination. ● The *Claflin* principle, which derives from *Claflin v. Claflin*, 20 N.E. 454 (Mass. 1889), is often cited as the purest illustration of "deadhand control," in which the wishes of the now dead settlor prevail over the wishes and needs of living beneficiaries. If the settlor is alive and consents to the modification or termination of the trust, the trust may usu. be terminated, unless it is irrevocable. Trusts in the *Claflin* category are spendthrift trusts, support trusts, trusts in which the trustee has discretion to make distributions, and trusts in which the beneficiary is entitled to income until a certain age, at which point the beneficiary will receive the principal.

claim, *n.* (13c) **1.** The aggregate of operative facts giving rise to a right enforceable by a court <the plaintiff's short, plain statement about the crash established the claim>. — Also termed *claim for relief* (1808). **2.** The assertion of an existing right; any right to payment or to an equitable remedy, even if contingent or provisional <the spouse's claim to half of the lottery winnings>. **3.** A demand for money, property, or a legal remedy to which one asserts a right; esp., the part of a complaint in a civil action specifying what relief the plaintiff asks for.

donation claim. *Property law.* A claim for ownership of land under a donation act or bounty-land warrant. See DONATION ACT; BOUNTY-LAND WARRANT.

honest claim. A claim made by someone who believes, however unreasonably, that he or she has a right to something or that there is a chance that such a right exists.

liquidated claim. 1. A claim for an amount previously agreed on by the parties or that can be precisely determined by operation of law or by the terms of the parties' agreement. **2.** A claim that has been determined in a judicial proceeding. — Also termed *liquidated demand.*

matured claim. A claim based on a debt that is due for payment.

stale claim. (18c) A claim that is barred by the statute of limitations or the defense of laches. — Also termed *stale demand.*

unliquidated claim. A claim in which the amount owed has not been determined.

4. An interest or remedy recognized at law; the means by which a person can obtain a privilege, possession, or enjoyment of a right or thing; CAUSE OF ACTION (1) <claim against the employer for wrongful termination>.

ancillary claim. (1906) A claim that is collateral to, dependent on, or auxiliary to another claim, such as a state-law claim that is sufficiently related to a federal claim to permit federal jurisdiction over it. ● The concept of ancillary federal jurisdiction is now contained in the supplemental-jurisdiction statute, 28 USCA § 1367. See *ancillary jurisdiction* and *supplemental jurisdiction* under JURISDICTION.

colorable claim. 1. A claim that is legitimate and that may reasonably be asserted, given the facts presented and the current law (or a reasonable and logical extension or modification of the current law). **2.** A claim in which the debtor and property holder are, as a matter of law, not adverse. ● An example of a colorable claim is one made by a person holding property as an agent or bailee of the bankrupt.

contingent claim. A claim that has not yet accrued and is dependent on some future event that may never happen.

counterclaim. See COUNTERCLAIM.

cross-claim. See CROSS-CLAIM.

frivolous claim. A claim that has no legal basis or merit, esp. one brought for an unreasonable purpose such as harassment. Fed. R. Civ. P. 11(b).

supplemental claim. A claim for further relief based on events occurring after the original claim was made.

5. *Bankruptcy.* (1842) A right to payment or to an equitable remedy for breach of performance if the breach gives rise to a right to payment. • It does not matter whether the right has been reduced to judgment or whether it is liquidated or unliquidated, fixed or contingent, matured or unmatured, disputed or undisputed, or secured or unsecured.

creditor's claim. A claim that a creditor has against a debtor.

involuntary gap claim. A claim that accrues in the ordinary course of business after an involuntary bankruptcy petition has been filed but before the order for relief or the appointment of a trustee. • The Bankruptcy Code gives priority to creditors with claims of this type to encourage creditors to continue dealing with a debtor until the debtor has a chance to challenge the involuntary petition.

priority claim. An unsecured claim that, under bankruptcy law, must be paid before other unsecured claims. • The Bankruptcy Code sets forth nine classes of claims, to be paid in order of priority: (1) administrative expenses of the bankruptcy estate, (2) involuntary gap claims, (3) wage claims, (4) contributions to employee benefit plans, (5) claims of grain farmers and fishermen, (6) consumer deposits, (7) alimony, maintenance, and child-support claims, (8) tax claims, and (9) capital requirements of an insured depository institution.

secured claim. A claim held by a creditor who has a lien or a right of setoff against the debtor's property.

unsecured claim. **1.** A claim by a creditor who does not have a lien or a right of setoff against the debtor's property. **2.** A claim by a creditor to the extent that its lien on or right of setoff against the debtor's property is worth less than the amount of the debt.

6. *Patents.* PATENT CLAIM.

claim and delivery. (1842) A claim for the recovery of specific personal property wrongfully taken or detained, as well as for any damages caused by the taking or detention. • This claim derives from the common-law action of replevin. — Sometimes written *claim-and-delivery.* See REPLEVIN.

claimant, *n.* (15c) One who asserts a right or demand, esp. formally; esp., one who asserts a property interest in land, chattels, or tangible things.

occupying claimant. See OCCUPYING CLAIMANT.

claim check. A receipt obtained for bailed or checked property and surrendered by the holder when the bailee returns the property.

claim differentiation. *Patents.* A canon of construction presuming that each claim in a patent is different in scope and meaning from all other claims; the presumption that different terms in separate claims must have different meanings if one of the claims would otherwise be rendered superfluous. • The presumption cannot be used by the patentee to broaden claims, and a court will ignore it when convinced that its own interpretation of the claims is correct. The presumption is strongest when a different interpretation would be the only way to make a dependent claim more limiting than the independent claim it refers to. — Also termed *doctrine of claim differentiation.*

claim dilution. *Bankruptcy.* The reduction in the likelihood that a debtor's claimants will be fully repaid, including considerations of the time value of money.

claim for relief. (1808) See CLAIM (1).

claim in equity. *Hist.* A summary proceeding created to eliminate protracted pleading procedure in simple cases. • The claim in equity was established in England in 1850 and abolished in 1860.

claim-jumping. 1. The extension of the borders of a mining claim to infringe on other areas or claims. **2.** The filing of a duplicate claim to take advantage of a flaw in the original claim.

claim limitation. *Patents.* In a patent application, a statement that describes the means for performing a specified function without reciting the structure, materials, or acts that support that function. • Claim limitations define the invention by distinguishing it from prior art.

claim of appeal. See NOTICE OF APPEAL.

claim of cognizance. *Hist.* An intervention seeking the return of a case to the claimant's own court. • Cognizance may be claimed by a person, city, or public corporation granted the right to hold court. — Also termed *claim of conusance.* See COGNIZANCE; CONUSANCE.

claim of conusance. See CLAIM OF COGNIZANCE.

claim of liberty. *Hist.* A petition to the Crown, filed in the Court of Exchequer, seeking the Attorney General's confirmation of liberties and franchises.

claim of ownership. (1818) **1.** The possession of a piece of property with the intention of claiming it in hostility to the true owner. **2.** A party's manifest intention to take over land, regardless of title or right. — Also termed *claim of right*; *claim of title.*

claim of priority. See BENEFIT OF AN EARLIER FIL-ING DATE.

claim of right. 1. *Hist.* A criminal defendant's plea that the defendant committed the act in question under the mistaken but honest belief that it was legal. ● Defendants accused of theft often raised this plea, asserting an honest belief in a superior right to the property taken. The claim of right could also be raised as a defense against bigamy if the defendant honestly believed that an earlier marriage had been legally dissolved. The usual phrase today is *honesty defense.* Cf. *honesty defense* under DEFENSE (1). **2.** *Hist.* An owner's action to recover unjustly taken land in fee simple by employing a writ of course. See WRIT OF COURSE. **3.** CLAIM OF OWNERSHIP.

claim-of-right doctrine. *Tax.* The rule that any income constructively received must be reported as income, whether or not the taxpayer has an unrestricted claim to it.

claim of title. See CLAIM OF OWNERSHIP.

claim preclusion. See RES JUDICATA.

claim-property bond. See *replevin bond* under BOND (2).

claims adjuster. See ADJUSTER.

claims-consciousness, *n.* The quality characterizing a legal culture in which people have firm expectations of justice and are willing to take concrete steps to see that justice is done <claims-consciousness in the United States has resulted from certain social changes, not from any character deficiency>. — Also termed *rights-consciousness.* — **claims-conscious,** *adj.*

claims court. See *court of claims* under COURT.

Claims Court, U.S. See UNITED STATES COURT OF FEDERAL CLAIMS.

claims-made policy. See INSURANCE POLICY.

claim the floor. *Parliamentary law.* To address the chair for the purpose of being recognized as entitled to speak. See FLOOR (1).

clamor. 1. *Hist.* A lawsuit; a claim. **2.** HUE AND CRY (1). **3.** *Civil law.* A claimant. **4.** *Civil law.* The thing claimed from another.

clandestine (klan-**des**-tin), *adj.* (16c) Secret or concealed, esp. for illegal or concealed purposes.

clandestine marriage. See MARRIAGE (1).

Clarity. An international association of lawyers and other professionals who advocate plain language in legal and official documents. ● Founded in 1983, it has members in more than 25 countries and a system of country representatives. It publishes a journal called *Clarity.*

class, *n.* (17c) **1.** A group of people, things, qualities, or activities that have common characteristics or attributes <a class of common-stock shares> <the upper-middle class>.

 protected class. A class of people who benefit from protection by statute, such as Title VII of the Civil Rights Act of 1964, which prohibits discrimination based on race, sex, national origin, or religion.

2. The order or rank in which people or things are arranged <she flew first class to Chicago>. **3.** A group of people, uncertain in number <a class of beneficiaries>.

 testamentary class (tes-tə-**men**-tə-ree *or* -tree). (1865) A group of beneficiaries who are uncertain in number but whose number will be ascertainable in the future, when each will take an equal or other proportionate share of the gift.

4. *Civil procedure.* A group of people who have a common legal position, so that all their claims can be efficiently adjudicated in a single proceeding <a class of asbestos plaintiffs>.

 opt-out class. A plaintiff class, certified under Federal Rule of Civil Procedure 23(b)(3), from which class members may choose to exclude themselves if they do not want to be bound by the decisions or settlements reached in the case. ● Rule 23(e) permits courts to dismiss class members who request exclusion. Class members may wait until the settlement's terms are announced before choosing to opt out.

 settlement class. (1971) Numerous similarly situated people for whom a claimant's representative and an adversary propose a contract specifying the payment terms for the class members' claims in exchange for the release of all claims against the adversary. ● During the 1980s and 1990s, mass-tort defendants began using settlement classes as a means of foreclosing claims by some unknown number of existing and future claimants. See, e.g., *Amchem Prods. Inc. v. Windsor,* 521 U.S. 591, 117 S.Ct. 2231 (1997).

class action. (1909) A lawsuit in which the court authorizes a single person or a small group of people to represent the interests of a larger group; specif., a lawsuit in which the convenience either of the public or of the interested parties requires that the case be settled through litigation by or against only a part of the group of similarly situated persons and in which a person whose interests are or may be affected does not have an opportunity to protect his or her interests by appearing personally or through a personally selected representative, or through a person specially appointed to act as a trustee or guardian. ● Federal procedure has several prerequisites for maintaining a class action: (1) the class must be so large that individual suits would be impracticable, (2) there must be legal or factual questions common to the class, (3) the claims or defenses of the representative parties must be typical of those of the class, and (4) the representative parties must adequately protect the interests of the class. Fed. R. Civ. P. 23. — Also termed *class suit; representative action.*

hybrid class action. (1937) *Hist.* A type of action in which the rights to be enforced were several and varied, but the object was to adjudicate claims that affected or might have affected the specific property in the action.

spurious class action. *Hist.* A former category of class action in which the interests of class members are several, not interdependent, and joinder is allowed to avoid multiplicity of suits.

class-based animus. See ANIMUS (1).

class director. See DIRECTOR.

class gift. See GIFT.

classification. See CHARACTERIZATION (1).

classification of patents. *Patents.* **1.** The sorting of inventions by type into broad classes and narrow subclasses, as an aid in patent searches. **2.** Any one of the several classes into which the inventions are sorted. — Also termed (in both senses) *office classification;* (in sense 2) *field of invention;* (in sense 2) *field of search.*

classified board of directors. See *staggered board of directors* under BOARD OF DIRECTORS.

classified information. Data or material that, having been designated as secret or confidential, only a limited number of authorized persons may know about.

classified risk. See RISK.

classified tax. See TAX.

class legislation. See *local and special legislation* under LEGISLATION.

class lottery. See *Dutch lottery* under LOTTERY.

class of stock. A category of corporate shares used when more than one type of stock is issued. See *preferred stock* and *common stock* under STOCK.

class-one insured. See INSURED.

class rate. See RATE.

class representative. See REPRESENTATIVE.

class suit. See CLASS ACTION.

class-two insured. See INSURED.

class voting. See VOTING.

clausa rebus sic stantibus (**klawz**-ə **ree**-bəs sik **stan**-tə-bəs). [Law Latin] *Int'l law.* **1.** A treaty provision stating that the treaty is binding only as long as the circumstances in existence when the treaty was signed remain substantially the same. **2.** A doctrine by which the law supplies such a provision to a treaty that does not expressly contain one; REBUS SIC STANTIBUS. • The doctrine may be invoked when a fundamental change in circumstances (1) alters the essential basis for the

parties' consent to be bound by the treaty, and (2) radically transforms the extent of the parties' performances under the treaty. But the doctrine does not apply to treaties establishing geographic boundaries. Vienna Convention on the Law of Treaties art. 62 (1155 U.N.T.S. 331, 8 I.L.M. 679 (1969)). — Often shortened to *clausa.* — Also termed *clausula rebus sic stantibus; clausula.*

clause, *n.* (13c) **1.** A distinct section or provision of a legal document or instrument. **2.** ITEM (3). — **clausal,** *adj.*

confidentiality clause. A clause prohibiting the parties to an agreement from disclosing to nonparties the terms of the agreement and, often, anything related to the formation of the agreement. — Also termed *nondisclosure clause; no-talk provision.*

enabling clause. The part of a statute or constitution that gives governmental officials the power and authority to put the law into effect and to enforce it. Cf. *enacting clause.*

enacting clause. (17c) The part of a statute stating the legislative authority by which it is made and often the date when it will take effect. • A typical enacting clause begins with the words "Be it enacted that . . . ." The enacting clause of a federal statute is, "Be it enacted by the Senate and House of Representatives of the United States of America in Congress assembled." Some state constitutions specify the enacting clause for legislation, without which the legislation is void. In codifications of statutes, enacting clauses generally appear not in the text of the statutes but in historical or legislative notes. Cf. *enabling clause.*

introductory clause. See EXORDIUM.

nondisclosure clause. See *confidentiality clause.*

nondisparagement clause. **1.** A contractual provision prohibiting the parties from publicly communicating anything negative about each other. **2.** *Family law.* A provision in a divorce decree, marital settlement agreement, parenting agreement, or similar document prohibiting either parent from criticizing the other parent in the presence of their child or children.

operative clause. A provision under an enacting or resolving clause; a provision that is not a mere recital or preamble. See *resolving clause.*

partial-release clause. A provision in a mortgage or trust deed allowing a certain property or portions of a property to be removed from the effect of a lien in exchange for an agreed payment. • This clause is often found in mortgages or trust deeds for properties covered by blanket liens, such as subdivisions or condominiums.

pay-if-paid clause. In a construction contract, a provision that makes the general contractor's payment to the subcontractor for work performed contingent on whether the property owner pays the general contractor for the work. ● The subcontractor must assume the risk of nonpayment if the owner fails to pay the general contractor. Courts in some states have held that this risk-shifting violates public policy. Cf. *pay-when-paid clause.*

pay-when-paid clause. In a construction contract, a provision requiring a general contractor to pay a subcontractor within a specified period of time after the property owner pays the general contractor. ● A minority of courts have held that the subcontractor bears the risk of nonpayment if the owner becomes insolvent. But because the general contractor normally bears the risk of nonpayment, most courts hold that a subcontractor is entitled to payment for work done despite the owner's insolvency. Cf. *pay-if-paid clause.*

resolving clause. The clause that introduces a resolution's operative text, usu. beginning with "*Resolved*, That . . . ." ● A resolving clause is comparable to a statute's enacting clause.— Also termed *operative clause*. See *enacting clause*; RESOLUTION (1). Cf. PREAMBLE (1).

strong-arm clause. A provision of the Bankruptcy Code allowing a bankruptcy trustee to avoid a security interest that is not perfected when the bankruptcy case is filed. 11 USCA § 544(a)(1).

title-object clause. A provision in a state constitution rendering a statute unconstitutional if the contents of the statute are not reasonably reflected in the title or the statute has more than one object. ● The purpose of the clause is to ensure that the public and legislature have notice of the content of legislation.

whereas clause. 1. See RECITAL (2). 2. See PREAMBLE (1).

claused bill of lading. See BILL OF LADING.

clause of accrual. A provision, usu. found in a gift by will or in a deed between tenants in common, that grants a predeceasing beneficiary's shares to the surviving beneficiary. — Also termed *clause of accruer.*

clause paramount. *Maritime law.* A provision in a charterparty that specifies what jurisdiction's law will govern the agreement, typically incorporating the Carriage of Goods by Sea Act into the charter. See CHARTERPARTY; CARRIAGE OF GOODS BY SEA ACT.

clause rolls. *Hist.* Sealed rolls containing royal writs (*close writs*) and other documents that the sovereign deemed inappropriate for the public record. — Also termed *close rolls*. See *close writ* under WRIT.

clausum (**klawz-**əm). [Latin "close; closed"] *Hist.* **1.** CLOSE (1). — Also termed *clausura*. **2.** See *close writ* under WRIT.

clausum fregit (**klawz-**əm **free-**jit). [Latin "he broke the close"] See *trespass quare clausum fregit* under TRESPASS.

clawback, *n.* (1953) **1.** Money taken back. **2.** The retrieval or recovery of tax allowances by additional forms of taxation. — **claw back,** *vb.*

claw-back option. The right to require repayment of funds earmarked for a specific purpose if the funds are disbursed for another purpose or in a manner inconsistent with the document governing the specified purpose.

Clayton Act. A federal statute — enacted in 1914 to amend the Sherman Act — that prohibits price discrimination, tying arrangements, and exclusive-dealing contracts, as well as mergers and interlocking directorates, if their effect might substantially lessen competition or create a monopoly in any line of commerce. 15 USCA §§ 12–27.

Cl. Ct. *abbr.* Court of Claims. See UNITED STATES COURT OF FEDERAL CLAIMS.

CLE. *abbr.* CONTINUING LEGAL EDUCATION.

clean bill. See BILL (3).

clean bill of lading. See BILL OF LADING.

clean draft. See DRAFT.

clean-hands doctrine. (1914) The principle that a party cannot seek equitable relief or assert an equitable defense if that party has violated an equitable principle, such as good faith. ● Such a party is described as having "unclean hands." For example, section 8 of the Uniform Child Custody Jurisdiction Act contains an unclean-hands provision that forbids a court from exercising jurisdiction in a child-custody suit in certain situations, as when one party has wrongfully removed a child from another state, has improperly retained custody of a child after visitation, or has wrongfully removed a child from the person with custody. The clean-hands doctrine evolved from the discretionary nature of equitable relief in English courts of equity, such as Chancery. — Also termed *unclean-hands doctrine.*

clean house, *vb. Slang.* **1.** To discharge a considerable number of employees, usu. in management, so that new employees may be brought in. **2.** To sell securities not meeting an investor's requirements.

clean letter of credit. See LETTER OF CREDIT.

clean-slate rule. *Criminal procedure.* The doctrine that the double-jeopardy prohibition does not apply to the retrial of a defendant who appealed and obtained a reversal of an earlier conviction.

cleanup clause. In a loan agreement, a clause that calls for the loan to be repaid in full within a given period, after which no further loans will be afforded to the debtor for a specified "cleanup" period.

cleanup doctrine. The jurisdictional principle that once an equity court has acquired jurisdiction over a case, it may decide both equitable and legal issues as long as the legal issues are ancillary to the equitable ones.

clear, *adj.* **1.** Free from encumbrances or claims. **2.** Free from doubt; sure. **3.** Unambiguous.

clear, *vb.* (15c) **1.** To acquit or exonerate <she was cleared of all wrongdoing>. **2.** (Of a drawee bank) to pay (a check or draft) out of funds held on behalf of the maker <the bank cleared the employee's check>. **3.** (Of a check or draft) to be paid by the drawee bank out of funds held on behalf of the maker <the check cleared yesterday>. **4.** *Maritime law.* To settle (customs, harbor dues, etc.) and obtain official permission to leave the port.

clearance. **1.** *Maritime law.* The right of a ship to leave port, or the certificate issued by the port collector evidencing the ship's right to leave port. **2.** The time that must elapse between runs of the same movie within a particular area; a theater's exclusive right of exhibition over competing theaters.

clearance card. A letter given by an employer to a departing employee, stating the duration and nature of the employment and the reasons for leaving. • The clearance card is not necessarily a recommendation.

clear and convincing evidence. See EVIDENCE.

clear and convincing proof. See *clear and convincing evidence* under EVIDENCE.

clear-and-present-danger test. (1939) *Constitutional law.* The doctrine allowing the government to restrict the First Amendment freedoms of speech and press if necessary to prevent immediate and severe danger to interests that the government may lawfully protect. • This test was formulated by Justice Oliver Wendell Holmes in *Schenck v. United States*, 249 U.S. 47, 39 S.Ct. 247 (1919). — Also termed *clear-and-present-danger doctrine.*

clear and unmistakable error. See *clear error* under ERROR (2).

clear annual value. See VALUE (2).

clear chance. See LAST-CLEAR-CHANCE DOCTRINE.

clear day. See DAY.

clear error. See ERROR (2).

Clearfield Trust **doctrine.** (1957) The doctrine describing the federal courts' power to make federal common law when there is both federal lawmaking power to do so and a strong federal interest in a nationally uniform rule. *Clearfield Trust Co. v. United States*, 318 U.S. 363, 63 S.Ct. 573 (1943). Cf. ERIE DOCTRINE.

clearing. **1.** *Banking.* The exchanging of checks and balancing of accounts. **2.** *Maritime law.* The departure of a ship from port, after complying with customs, health laws, and other local regulations. See CLEARANCE (1).

clearing account. *Banking.* An account (usu. a temporary one) containing amounts to be transferred to another account before the end of an accounting period.

clearing agency. See *clearing agent* under AGENT (2).

clearing agent. See AGENT (2).

clearing agreement. A contract designed to facilitate the collective settlement of monetary claims between creditors and debtors in different currency areas, without resort to foreign-exchange reserves.

clearing corporation. See CORPORATION.

clearinghouse. (18c) **1.** A place where banks exchange checks and drafts and settle their daily balances; an association of banks or other payors regularly clearing items. See UCC § 4-104(a)(4). **2.** A stock-and-commodity exchange where the daily transactions of the brokers are cleared. **3.** Any place for the exchange of specialized information. — Also written *clearing house.*

clearing loan. See LOAN.

clearings. *Banking.* Checks or other items drawn on a local bank and presented for payment through a clearinghouse or directly to the drawee bank. See CLEARINGHOUSE (1).

clearly-erroneous standard. (1950) The standard of review that an appellate court usu. applies in judging a trial court's treatment of factual issues. • Under this standard, a judgment will be upheld unless the appellate court is left with the firm conviction that an error has been committed.

clear market value. See *fair market value* under VALUE (2).

clear-reflection-of-income standard. (1972) *Tax.* An income-accounting method that the IRS can force on a taxpayer if the method used does not clearly reflect income. IRC (26 USCA) § 446(b).

clear residue. The income deriving from funds used to pay a decedent's debts, administration expenses, and general legacies. — Also termed *true residue.*

clear title. See TITLE (2).

clear-to-use search. See INFRINGEMENT SEARCH.

clear value. See VALUE (2).

clear-view doctrine. See PLAIN-VIEW DOCTRINE.

clemency (**klem**-ən-see), *n.* (15c) Mercy or leniency; esp., the power of the President or a governor to pardon a criminal or commute a criminal sentence. — Also termed *executive clemency.* See PARDON; COMMUTATION. — **clement** (**klem**-ənt), *adj.*

Clementines (**klem**-ən-tinz *or* -tinz *or* -teenz). *Eccles. law.* A collection of decretals of Pope Clement V, published in 1317 by his successor, Pope John XXII, and forming the fourth of the six parts of the *Corpus Juris Canonici,* completed in 1502. — Also termed *Clementine Constitutions.*

clergy, benefit of. See BENEFIT OF CLERGY.

clergyable, *adj. Archaic.* **1.** (Of an offense) not triable if benefit of clergy is claimed. **2.** (Of a person) eligible to claim benefit of clergy.

clergyman–penitent privilege. See *priest–penitent privilege* under PRIVILEGE (3).

clergy privilege. See BENEFIT OF CLERGY (1).

clerical error. See ERROR (2).

clerical misprision. See MISPRISION.

clerk, *n.* (bef. 12c) **1.** A public official whose duties include keeping records or accounts.

  city clerk. A public official who records a city's official proceedings and vital statistics.

  town clerk. An officer who keeps the records, issues calls for town meetings, and performs the duties of a secretary to the town's political organization.

2. A court officer responsible for filing papers, issuing process, and keeping records of court proceedings as generally specified by rule or statute. — Also termed *clerk of court.*

  district clerk. The clerk of a district court within a state or federal system. See *district court* under COURT.

3. An employee who performs general office work. **4.** A law student or recent law-school graduate who helps a lawyer or judge with legal research, writing, and other tasks. — Also termed *law clerk; extern;* or (depending on the time of year) *summer clerk; summer associate.* See INTERN. **5.** A lawyer who assists a judge with research, writing, and case management. — Also termed *briefing attorney; research attorney; staff attorney.*

  elbow clerk. An individual judge's personal clerk; esp., one who works closely with the judge. • The name derives from the metaphoric expectation that the clerk is always at the judge's elbow.

  pool clerk. A clerk who does not work for only one judge but performs a range of duties for several judges or for the entire court.

6. *Hist.* A cleric. **7.** SECRETARY (3).

  reading clerk. A legislative officer charged with reading bills to the body.

clerk, *vb.* To work as a clerk <she clerked for a Chicago law firm last summer>.

clerk of arraigns (ə-**raynz**). *Hist.* A deputy of the clerk of assize responsible for arraigning defendants and putting the formal questions to the jurors as they deliver their verdict. • The office was abolished in England in 1946.

clerk of assize (ə-**sIz**). *Hist.* An assize associate responsible for record-keeping and other clerical and administrative functions. See ASSOCIATE (3).

clerk of court. See CLERK (2).

clerk of enrollments. *Hist.* The former chief of the Enrollment Office, which the British Parliament abolished in 1879, reassigning its duties to the Central Office. See ENROLLMENT OFFICE; CENTRAL OFFICE.

clerk of indictment. *Hist.* An officer of England's Central Criminal Court, responsible for preparing indictments and assisting the Clerk of Arraigns. • The office was abolished in 1946, when its duties were moved to the Central Office. See CENTRAL OFFICE.

clerk of records and writs. *Hist.* An officer of the English Court of Chancery responsible for filing documents and sealing bills of complaint and writs of execution. • The office was abolished in 1879, when its duties were moved to the Central Office. See CENTRAL OFFICE.

clerk of the corporation. See SECRETARY (2).

Clerk of the Crown in Chancery. The head of the permanent staff of the Crown Office in Chancery (of the Central Office), responsible for reading the title of Bills in the House of Lords, sending out writs of summons to peers, and issuing election writs.

Clerk of the House of Commons. An officer of the House of Commons who keeps the House journal, signs orders, indorses bills sent to the House of Lords, and has custody of all records. • The Clerk is appointed for life by the Crown.

clerk of the market. *Hist.* The overseer of a public market, responsible for witnessing oral contracts, inquiring into weights and measures, measuring land, and settling disputes between people dealing there. • The office has become obsolete as a result of various statutes regulating weights and measures.

Clerk of the Parliaments. The principal permanent official of the House of Lords, responsible for the House's minutes and documents, and for advising the members on procedure.

Clerk of the Peace. *Hist.* An officer of the Quarter Sessions responsible for maintaining the courts' records, preparing indictments, entering judgments, issuing process, and other clerical and administrative functions. • The office was abolished in England in 1971, when the Quarter Sessions' jurisdiction was transferred to the Crown Courts. See *quarter session* under SESSION (1).

Clerk of the Pells. *Hist.* An Exchequer officer who entered tellers' bills on the parchment rolls (*pells*), one for receipts and the other for disbursements. — Also termed *Master of the Pells.*

Clerk of the Pipe. *Hist.* An Exchequer officer responsible for the Pipe Rolls. • The office was abolished in 1833. — Also termed *Engrosser of the Great Roll.* See PIPE ROLLS.

Clerk of the Privy Seal (priv-ee **seel**).** *Hist.* An officer responsible for preparing documents for the Lord Privy Seal. • The use of the Privy Seal was abolished in 1884. See PRIVY SEAL.

Clerk of the Signet (sig-nit**).** *Hist.* An officer who kept the privy signet and attended the sovereign's principal secretary. • The signet was used to seal royal letters and other documents not requiring the Great Seal of the Realm. The office was abolished in England in 1851. See *great seal* (3) under SEAL; PRIVY SIGNET.

clerkship. (1836) **1.** An internship in which a law student or recent law-school graduate assists a lawyer or judge with legal writing, research, and other tasks. • In many common-law jurisdictions, recent law-school graduates are required to complete clerkships as a condition of admission to the bar. **2.** *Hist.* A law student's employment as an attorney's apprentice before gaining admission to the bar. • Until shortly before World War II, a person could be admitted to the bar in many states without attending law school merely by passing the bar exam.

clerk's record. See RECORD (4).

click fraud. See FRAUD.

click-wrap agreement. See POINT-AND-CLICK AGREEMENT.

click-wrap license. See POINT-AND-CLICK AGREEMENT.

client, *n.* (14c) A person or entity that employs a professional for advice or help in that professional's line of work. — **cliental,** *adj.*

client control. The influence that a lawyer has over his or her client, esp. in relation to positions taken, decisions made, and general conduct with other parties and their attorneys. • Lawyers whose clients behave irrationally, as by acting vindictively or refusing even generous settlement offers, are said to have little or no client control.

client-security fund. See FUND (1).

client's privilege. See *attorney–client privilege* under PRIVILEGE (3).

client state. See STATE.

client trust account. A bank account, usu. interest-bearing, in which a lawyer deposits money belonging to a client (e.g., money received from a client's debtor, from the settlement of a client's case, or from the client for later use in a business transaction). — Also termed *trust account.*

***Clifford* trust.** See TRUST.

clinical diagnosis. See DIAGNOSIS.

clinical legal studies. (1972) Law-school training in which students participate in actual cases under the supervision of a practicing attorney or law professor. • This training was first introduced in the late 1960s under the leadership of Gary Bellow and others. It provided law students with a substitute for traditional apprenticeship programs. — Often shortened to *clinical studies.* Cf. CLERKSHIP (1).

clog on the equity of redemption. An agreement or condition that prevents a defaulting mortgagor from getting back the property free from encumbrance upon paying the debt or performing the obligation for which the security was given. See EQUITY OF REDEMPTION.

close, *n.* (14c) **1.** An enclosed portion of land. **2.** The interest of a person in a particular piece of land, enclosed or not. **3.** The final price of a stock at the end of the exchange's trading day.

close, *vb.* (13c) **1.** To conclude; to bring to an end <the case was closed>. **2.** To conclude discussion or negotiation about <close on a house>. See CLOSING.

close-connectedness doctrine. A doctrine used by some courts to deny an assignee of a negotiable note holder-in-due-course status if the assignee is too closely connected to the original holder-mortgagee. — Also termed *close-connection doctrine.*

close corporation. See CORPORATION.

closed, *adj.* (13c) **1.** (Of a class or organization) confined to a limited number <a closed mass-tort class> <nonunion workers were excluded from the closed shop>. **2.** (Of a proceeding or gathering) conducted in secrecy <a closed hearing> <a closed shareholders' meeting>.

closed account. See ACCOUNT.

closed adoption. See ADOPTION.

closed brief. See BRIEF.

closed corporation. See *close corporation* under CORPORATION.

closed court. 1. *Hist.* The English Court of Common Pleas, open only to serjeants-at-law. • The monopoly of the serjeants-at-law was abolished in 1845. **2.** See *closed session* (2) under SESSION (1). **3.** See *closed session* (3) under SESSION (1).

close debate. *Parliamentary law.* To pass a motion that ends debate and amendment of a pending question or series of questions. • The synonymous shorthand "previous question," a somewhat archaic and misleading term that several parliamentary manuals still use for this motion, has evolved over time. Two centuries ago, the motion was invented for suppressing an undesirable debate: if the original form — "Shall the main question be put?" — passed in the negative, then the body immediately stopped considering the pending question. The motion's form later became "that the main question shall now be put," which if passed in the affirmative brought the pending question to an immediate vote, and if passed in the negative had no effect. — Also termed *vote immediately*. See CLOTURE. Cf. EXTEND DEBATE; LIMIT DEBATE.

closed-ended claim. See PATENT CLAIM.

closed-end fund. See MUTUAL FUND.

closed-end mortgage. See MORTGAGE.

closed-end mortgage bond. See BOND (3).

closed insurance contract. See *closed policy* under INSURANCE POLICY.

closed memorandum. See MEMORANDUM.

closed mortgage. See *closed-end mortgage* under MORTGAGE.

closed nonunion shop. See SHOP.

closed policy. See INSURANCE POLICY.

closed session. See SESSION (1).

closed shop. See SHOP.

closed-shop contract. A labor agreement requiring an employer to hire and retain only union members and to discharge nonunion members. See *closed shop* under SHOP.

closed source, *adj.* Of or related to software that does not include the source code and cannot be modified without either damaging the program or violating the software developer's ownership rights. ● Proprietary software is usu. closed source.

closed testament. See *mystic will* under WILL.

closed transaction. See TRANSACTION.

closed trial. See TRIAL.

closed union. See UNION.

closed union shop. See *closed shop* under SHOP.

closed-universe memo. See *closed memorandum* under MEMORANDUM.

closed will. See *mystic will* under WILL.

close-jail execution. See EXECUTION.

closely held corporation. See *close corporation* under CORPORATION.

close-nexus test. See NEXUS TEST.

close nominations. *Parliamentary law.* To end nominations from the floor by passage of a motion.

close rolls. See CLAUSE ROLLS.

close writ. See WRIT.

closing. The final meeting between the parties to a transaction, at which the transaction is consummated; esp., in real estate, the final transaction between the buyer and seller, whereby the conveyancing documents are concluded and the money and property transferred. — Also termed *settlement*. Cf. *settlement date* (3) under DATE.

closing agent. See *settlement agent* under AGENT (2).

closing agreement. See AGREEMENT.

closing argument. (1828) In a trial, a lawyer's final statement to the judge or jury before deliberation begins, in which the lawyer requests the judge or jury to consider the evidence and to apply the law in his or her client's favor. ● After the closing arguments in a jury trial, the judge ordinarily instructs the jury on the law that governs the case. — Also termed *closing statement*; *final argument*; *jury summation*; *summing up*; *summation*; *closing argument*; (in English law) *final submission*; (in English law) *final speech*.

closing costs. *Real estate.* The expenses that must be paid, usu. in a lump sum at closing, apart from the purchase price and interest. ● These may include taxes, title insurance, and attorney's fees.

closing of estate. (1843) *Wills & estates.* The completion of the administration of a decedent's estate, brought about by the administrator's distribution of estate assets, payment of taxes, and filing of necessary accounts with the probate court.

closing price. See PRICE.

closing statement. (1875) **1.** CLOSING ARGUMENT. **2.** A written breakdown of the costs involved in a particular real-estate transaction, usu. prepared by a lender or an escrow agent. — Also termed *settlement sheet*; *settlement statement*. Cf. BROKER'S LOAN STATEMENT.

closure. See CLOTURE.

cloture (kloh-chər), *n.* (1871) The procedure of ending debate in a legislative body and calling for an immediate vote. — Also spelled *closure*. — **cloture,** *vb.*

cloud on title. A defect or potential defect in the owner's title to a piece of land arising from some claim or encumbrance, such as a lien, an easement, or a court order. See *action to quiet title* under ACTION (4).

CLS. *abbr.* CRITICAL LEGAL STUDIES.

CLSer. See CRIT.

CLU. See *chartered life underwriter* under UNDERWRITER.

Club Fed. *Slang.* A low-security federal prison, usu. for white-collar criminals, that has a comparatively informal, relaxed atmosphere and, reputedly, luxury facilities. • Some sources claim that "Club Fed" prisons offer weight-lifting equipment, tennis courts, cable television, computers, musical instruments, and even miniature golf.

club-law. Government by clubs (big sticks) or violence; the use of illegal force in place of law.

cluster zoning. See ZONING.

CMO. *abbr.* **1.** CASE-MANAGEMENT ORDER. **2.** COLLATERALIZED MORTGAGE OBLIGATION.

CMR. *abbr.* **1.** Court of Military Review. See COURT OF CRIMINAL APPEALS (1). **2.** COURT-MARTIAL REPORTS.

CN. *abbr.* Code Napoléon. See NAPOLEONIC CODE (1).

co-. *prefix.* Jointly or together with <coowner> <codefendant>.

co. *abbr.* (*usu. cap.*) **1.** COMPANY. **2.** COUNTY.

c/o. *abbr.* Care of.

COA. *abbr.* **1.** CONTRACT OF AFFREIGHTMENT. **2.** CERTIFICATE OF APPEALABILITY. **3.** CAUSE OF ACTION.

coadjutor (koh-ə-**joo**-tər *or* koh-**aj**-ə-tər), *n.* (15c) A coworker or assistant, esp. one appointed to assist a bishop who, because of age or infirmity, is unable to perform all duties of the office. — **coadjutor,** *adj.*

co-administrator. *Wills & estates.* A person appointed to jointly administer an estate with one or more other administrators.

co-adventurer. See COVENTURER.

co-agent. See AGENT (2).

coal note. See NOTE (1).

coal notice. In Pennsylvania, a notice that must be included in deeds and other instruments relating to the sale of surface property (excepting mortgages or quitclaim deeds) detailing any severance of the ownership of coal under the land.

Coase Theorem (kohs). (1968) A proposition in economics describing the relationship between legal rules and economic efficiency. • The theorem, innovated by Ronald Coase, holds that if there are no transaction costs — such as the costs of bargaining or acquiring information — then any legal rule will produce an efficient result. Coase's seminal article was *The Problem of Social Cost*, 3 J. Law & Econ. 1 (1960).

co-assignee. A person who, along with one or more others, is an assignee of the same subject matter.

coastal-state control. *Maritime law.* The exercise of authority under international conventions for a state to stop, board, inspect, and when necessary detain vessels that are under foreign flags while they are navigating in the coastal state's territorial waters. • The purpose is to ensure the safety of the vessels and to enforce environmental regulations. Cf. FLAG STATE-CONTROL; PORT-STATE CONTROL.

Coast Guard jurisdiction. The law-enforcement authority of the United States Coast Guard over the high seas and navigable waters over which the United States has jurisdiction, including the powers of stopping, searching, and seizing property, and arresting persons. See UNITED STATES COAST GUARD.

coasting license. *Maritime law.* A federal permit to operate a commercial vessel in coastal waters. • The Coasting Act of 1793, which originally created the licensing requirement, was intended to exclude foreign vessels from interstate trade and encourage the growth of American shipping.

coasting trade. *Maritime law.* Commerce among different coastal ports or navigable rivers of the United States, in contrast to commerce carried on between nations. — Also termed *coastwise trade.*

coast water. See WATER.

coastwise trade. See COASTING TRADE.

COB clause. *Insurance.* A coordination-of-benefits clause, which provides that the total sums paid for medical and hospital care will not exceed the benefits receivable from all combined sources of insurance.

COBRA (koh-brə). *abbr.* CONSOLIDATED OMNIBUS BUDGET RECONCILIATION ACT OF 1985.

cockfighting. A traditional bloodsport in which specially bred and trained gamecocks are equipped with metal spurs and made to fight in a pen until at least one bird is killed or injured too seriously to continue fighting. • In the United States, cockfighting was once common in rural areas. Now considered a form of animal cruelty, it has been outlawed in every state.

coconspirator. (1837) A person who engages in a criminal conspiracy with another; a fellow conspirator. — Also spelled *co-conspirator.* See CONSPIRATOR.

unindicted coconspirator. (1936) A person who has been identified by law enforcement as a member of a conspiracy, but who has not been named in the fellow conspirator's indictment. • Prosecutors typically name someone an unindicted coconspirator because any statement that the unindicted coconspirator has made in the course and furtherance of the conspiracy is admissible against the indicted defendants. — Also termed *unindicted conspirator.*

coconspirator's exception. (1954) An exception to the hearsay rule whereby one conspirator's acts and statements, if made during and in furtherance of the conspiracy, are admissible against a codefendant even if the statements are made in the codefendant's absence. *See* Fed. R. Evid.

801(d)(2)(E). — Also termed *coconspirator's rule.* See HEARSAY.

C.O.D. *abbr.* (1859) **1.** Cash on delivery; collect on delivery. • By consenting to this delivery term, the buyer agrees to pay simultaneously with delivery and appoints the carrier as the buyer's agent to receive and transmit the payment to the seller. With C.O.D. contracts, the practice of carriers has traditionally been to disallow inspection before payment. **2.** Costs on delivery. **3.** Cash on demand. — Sometimes written *c.o.d.*

CODA. *abbr.* CASH OR DEFERRED ARRANGEMENT.

code. (18c) **1.** A complete system of positive law, carefully arranged and officially promulgated; a systematic collection or revision of laws, rules, or regulations <the Uniform Commercial Code>. • Strictly, a code is a compilation not just of existing statutes, but also of much of the unwritten law on a subject, which is newly enacted as a complete system of law. — Also termed *consolidated laws.* See CODIFICATION. **2.** (*usu. cap.*) The collection of laws and constitutions made by order of the Roman Emperor Justinian and first authoritatively published in A.D. 529 (with a second edition in 534). • Contained in 12 books, the Code is one of four works that make up what is now called the *Corpus Juris Civilis.* — Also termed (in sense 2) *Legal Code.* See CODEX; CORPUS JURIS CIVILIS.

Code Adam. A procedure used by offices, stores, and other places to alert people to look for a child who has become separated from a parent or guardian and has been reported as missing somewhere within the building. • Typically, a description of the missing child is broadcast over a paging system. All exits are locked or closely monitored. If the child is not found within a short time, the police are called. Many stores, museums, malls, and amusements parks have adopted some form of Code Adam. In 2003, Congress passed legislation requiring Code Adam programs in all federal office buildings. This term is a memorial to 6-year-old Adam Walsh of Florida, who in 1981 was abducted from a department store and murdered. Cf. AMBER ALERT.

Code Civil. The code embodying the civil law of France, dating from 1804. • It was first known as the *Code civil des français* to distinguish it from the other four codes promoted by Napoleon. From 1807 to 1816 it was called *Code Napoléon,* a title that was restored by a decree of Louis Napoleon. Since 1870, French statutes have consistently referred simply to the *code civil.* Cf. NAPOLEONIC CODE. See CIVIL CODE (1).

coded communications. Messages that are encoded or enciphered by some method of transposition or substitution so that they become unintelligible to anyone who does not have the key to the code or cipher.

Code de commerce (**kohd** də kaw-**mairs**). A codification of French commercial law, enacted in 1807, dealing with commercial transactions, bankruptcy, and the jurisdiction and procedure of the courts handling these subjects. • This code supplemented the *Code Napoléon.* See NAPOLEONIC CODE.

Code de procédure civil (**kohd** də praw-se-**door** see-**veel**). A French civil-procedure code, enacted in 1806 and appended to the *Code Napoléon.* See NAPOLEONIC CODE.

Code d'instruction criminelle (**kohd** dan-struuk-see-**awn** kri-mi-**nel**). A French criminal-procedure code, enacted in 1811 and appended to the *Code Napoléon.* See NAPOLEONIC CODE.

codefendant. (17c) One of two or more defendants sued in the same litigation or charged with the same crime. — Also termed *joint defendant.* Cf. COPLAINTIFF.

Code Napoléon (**kohd** na-poh-lay-**awn**). See NAPOLEONIC CODE.

code of conduct. (1919) A written set of rules governing the behavior of specified groups, such as lawyers, government employees, or corporate employees.

Code of Federal Regulations. The annual collection of executive-agency regulations published in the daily Federal Register, combined with previously issued regulations that are still in effect. — Abbr. CFR.

Code of Hammurabi (hah-mə-**rah**-bee *or* ham-ə-). The oldest known written legal code, produced in Mesopotamia during the rule of Hammurabi (who reigned from 1792 to 1750 B.C.). • The code consisted of nearly 300 provisions, arranged under headings such as family, trade, real property, personal property, and labor.

Code of Judicial Conduct. The body of standards governing the professional ethics and behavior of judges. • The American Bar Association drafted a Model Code of Judicial Conduct and formally adopted it in 1972. In 1973, the U.S. Judicial Conference used the code as the basis for the Code of Conduct for United States Judges. Portions of the code are also found in federal law (see, e.g. 28 USCA § 455). The 1972 ABA Code has been superseded by the 1990 ABA Model Code of Judicial Conduct. Each state has a code of judicial conduct, based on the 1972 or 1990 model codes or a blend of both. A state's highest court is responsible for drafting and enacting the code. — Abbr. CJC.

Code of Justinian. See JUSTINIAN CODE.

Code of Military Justice. The collection of substantive and procedural rules governing the discipline of members of the armed forces. 10 USCA §§ 801 et seq. — Also termed *Uniform Code of Military Justice* (UCMJ).

Code of Professional Responsibility. See MODEL CODE OF PROFESSIONAL RESPONSIBILITY.

code of war. Legal rules that regulate international armed conflict. • A code of war may arise from many sources, including custom, treaties, scholarly writings, and domestic legislation. One of the earliest known treatises on rules governing the conduct of war was written by Sun Tzu in the 4th century B.C.

Code pénal (**kohd** pay-**nal**). The fourth of five codes promoted by Napoleon, enacted in 1810, setting forth the penal code of France. See NAPOLEONIC CODE.

code pleading. See PLEADING (2).

code state. *Hist.* A state that, at a given time, had already procedurally merged law and equity, so that equity was no longer administered as a separate system; a state in which there is only one form of civil action. • This term was current primarily in the early to mid-20th century. Cf. NONCODE STATE.

codex (**koh**-deks). [Latin] *Archaic.* **1.** A code, esp. the Justinian Code. See JUSTINIAN CODE. **2.** A book written on paper or parchment; esp., a volume of an ancient text.

Codex Gregorianus (**koh**-deks gri-gor-ee-**ay**-nəs). [Latin] *Roman law.* A collection of imperial constitutions compiled by the Roman jurist Gregorius and published in A.D. 291. — Also termed *Gregorian Code.*

Codex Hermogenianus (**koh**-deks hər-mə-jee-nee-**ay**-nəs). [Latin] *Roman law.* A collection of imperial constitutions compiled by the Roman jurist Hermogenianus and published A.D. 295. • The *Codex Hermogenianus* supplemented the *Codex Gregorianus.* — Also termed *Hermogenian Code.*

Codex Justinianus. See JUSTINIAN CODE.

Codex Repetitae Praelectionis (**koh**-deks rep-ə-**tı**-tee pri-lek-shee-**oh**-nis). [Latin "code of the resumed reading"] *Roman law.* See JUSTINIAN CODE.

Codex Theodosianus (**koh**-deks thee-ə-doh-shee-**ay**-nəs). [Latin] See THEODOSIAN CODE.

codicil (**kod**-ə-səl *or* -sil). (15c) A supplement or addition to a will, not necessarily disposing of the entire estate but modifying, explaining, or otherwise qualifying the will in some way. • When admitted to probate, the codicil becomes a part of the will.

codicillary (kod-ə-**sil**-ə-ree), *adj.* Of or relating to a codicil.

codification (kod-ə-fi-**kay**-shən), *n.* (1817) **1.** The process of compiling, arranging, and

systematizing the laws of a given jurisdiction, or of a discrete branch of the law, into an ordered code. **2.** The code that results from this process. — **codify** (**kod**-ə-fı), *vb.* — **codifier** (**kod**-ə-fı-ər), *n.*

codifying statute. See STATUTE.

Coefficient Clause. See NECESSARY AND PROPER CLAUSE.

coemption (koh-**emp**-shən), *n.* (14c) **1.** The act of purchasing the entire quantity of any commodity. **2.** COEMPTIO. — **coemptional, coemptive,** *adj.*

coerce (koh-**ərs**), *vb.* To compel by force or threat <coerce a confession>.

coerced-compliant confession. See CONFESSION.

coerced-compliant false confession. See *coerced-compliant confession* under CONFESSION.

coerced confession. See CONFESSION.

coercion (koh-**ər**-zhən), *n.* (15c) **1.** Compulsion by physical force or threat of physical force. • An act that must be voluntary, such as signing a will, is not legally valid if done under coercion. And since a valid marriage requires voluntary consent, coercion or duress is grounds for invalidating a marriage.

criminal coercion. Coercion intended to restrict another's freedom of action by: (1) threatening to commit a criminal act against that person; (2) threatening to accuse that person of having committed a criminal act; (3) threatening to expose a secret that either would subject the victim to hatred, contempt, or ridicule or would impair the victim's credit or goodwill, or (4) taking or withholding official action or causing an official to take or withhold action.

implied coercion. See UNDUE INFLUENCE (1).

moral coercion. See UNDUE INFLUENCE (1).

2. Conduct that constitutes the improper use of economic power to compel another to submit to the wishes of one who wields it. — Also termed *economic coercion.* **3.** *Hist.* A husband's actual or supposed control or influence over his wife's actions. • Under the common-law doctrine of coercion, a wife who committed a crime in her husband's presence was presumed to have been coerced by him and thus had a complete defense. Courts have abolished this doctrine. — Also termed *doctrine of coercion.* — **coercive,** *adj.* — **coercer,** *n.*

coercive relief. See RELIEF.

coexecutor (koh-eg-**zek**-yə-tər). See *joint executor* under EXECUTOR.

coexistence. *Int'l law.* The peaceful continuation of nations, peoples, or other entities or groups within an effective political-military equilibrium.

coexisting motion. See MOTION (2).

cogent (**koh**-jənt), *adj.* (17c) Compelling or convincing <cogent reasoning>. — **cogency**, *n.*

cognate, *adj.* See COGNATIC.

cognate, *n.* (18c) One who is kin to another. • In Roman law, the term means a blood relationship and implies that the kinship derives from a lawful marriage. In Scots and later civil law, the term implies kinship from the mother's side. Cf. AGNATE.

cognate nuisance. See NUISANCE.

cognate offense. See OFFENSE (1).

cognatic (kog-**nat**-ik), *adj.* (18c) (Of a relationship) existing between cognates. — Also termed *cognate.*

cognation (kog-**nay**-shən), *n.* (14c) **1.** Relationship by blood rather than by marriage; relationship arising through common descent from the same man and woman, whether the descent is traced through males or females. **2.** *Civil law.* A relationship existing between two people by blood, by family, or by both.

> **civil cognation.** A relationship arising by law, such as that created by adoption.

> **mixed cognation.** A relationship that combines the ties of blood and family, such as that existing between brothers who are born of the same marriage.

> **natural cognation.** A blood relationship, usu. arising from an illicit connection.

3. Relationship between persons or things of the same or similar nature; likeness.

cognitive test. (1955) *Criminal law.* A test of the defendant's ability to know certain things, specifically the nature of his or her conduct and whether the conduct was right or wrong. • This test is used in assessing whether a defendant may rely on an insanity defense.

cognitor (**kog**-ni-tor), *n. Roman law.* A person formally appointed to represent another in a civil trial. Cf. PROCURATOR (1).

cognizable (**kog**-ni- *or* kog-**nɪ**-zə-bəl), *adj.* (17c) **1.** Capable of being known or recognized <for purposes of establishing standing, a plaintiff must allege a judicially cognizable injury>. **2.** Capable of being identified as a group because of a common characteristic or interest that cannot be represented by others <American Indians qualify as a cognizable group for jury-selection purposes>. **3.** Capable of being judicially tried or examined before a designated tribunal; within the court's jurisdiction <the tort claims are not cognizable under the consumer-protection statute>.

cognizance (**kog**-ni-zəns), *n.* (14c) **1.** A court's right and power to try and to determine cases; JURISDICTION. **2.** The taking of judicial or authoritative notice. **3.** Acknowledgment or admission of an alleged fact; esp. (*hist.*), acknowledgment of a fine. See FINE (1); FINE SUR COGNIZANCE DE DROIT. **4.** *Common-law pleading.* In a replevin action, a plea by the defendant that the goods are held in bailment for another. Cf. AVOWRY.

cognizee (kog-ni-**zee**). (16c) *Hist.* The grantee of land in a conveyance by fine. — Also termed *conusee; conuzee.* See FINE (1).

cognizor (**kog**-ni-zər *or* -zor). (16c) *Hist.* The grantor of land in a conveyance by fine. — Also termed *conusor; conuzor.* See FINE (1).

cognovit (kog-**noh**-vit). (18c) [Latin "he has conceded (a debt or an action)"] An acknowledgment of debt or liability in the form of a confessed judgment. • Formerly, credit contracts often included a cognovit clause in which the consumer relinquished, in advance, any right to be notified of court hearings in any suit for nonpayment — but such clauses are now generally illegal. See CONFESSION OF JUDGMENT. Cf. WARRANT OF ATTORNEY.

cognovit clause. (1925) A contractual provision by which a debtor agrees to jurisdiction in certain courts, waives notice requirements, and authorizes the entry of an adverse judgment in the event of a default or breach. • Cognovit clauses are outlawed or restricted in most states.

cognovit judgment. See JUDGMENT.

cognovit note. A promissory note containing a cognovit clause. — Also termed *judgment note.*

COGSA. **1.** *abbr.* CARRIAGE OF GOODS BY SEA ACT. **2.** *Maritime law.* A country's enactment of the international convention popularly known as the Hague Rules. • The acronym is used even when the country's statute has a different title; for example, the Canadian Carriage of Goods by Water Act is referred to as the "Canadian COGSA."

cohabitation (koh-hab-ə-**tay**-shən), *n.* (15c) The fact or state of living together, esp. as partners in life, usu. with the suggestion of sexual relations. — **cohabit** (koh-**hab**-it), *vb.* — **cohabitative** (koh-**hab**-ə-tay-tiv), *adj.* — **cohabitant** (koh-**hab**-ə-tənt), *n.* — **cohabitor** (koh-**hab**-ə-tər), *n.*

> **illicit cohabitation.** (18c) **1.** The offense committed by an unmarried man and woman who live together as husband and wife and engage in sexual intercourse. • This offense, where it still exists, is seldom prosecuted. **2.** The condition of a man and a woman who are not married to one another and live together in circumstances that make the arrangement questionable on grounds of social propriety, though not necessarily illegal. — Also termed *lascivious cohabitation; lewd and lascivious cohabitation.* Cf. FORNICATION.

> **lascivious cohabitation.** See *illicit cohabitation.*

> **matrimonial cohabitation.** The living together of husband and wife.

notorious cohabitation. (18c) *Archaic.* Illicit cohabitation in which the parties make no attempt to hide their living arrangements. — Also termed *open and notorious cohabitation.* See *illicit cohabition.*

cohabitation agreement. A contract outlining the property and financial arrangements between persons who live together. — Also termed *living-together agreement.* Cf. PRENUPTIAL AGREEMENT.

cohabiting unmarried person of the opposite sex. See CUPOS.

Cohan **rule** (**koh**-han). *Tax.* A former rule that a taxpayer may approximate travel and entertainment expenses when no records exist if the taxpayer has taken all possible steps to provide documentation. ● Since 1962, travel and entertainment expenses have been only partly deductible and must be carefully documented, but courts may apply the *Cohan* reasoning to other items. *Cohan v. Commissioner,* 39 F.2d 540 (2d Cir. 1930).

coheir (koh-**air**). See HEIR.

coheiress (koh-**air**-is). *Hist.* A female coheir.

Cohen **doctrine** (**koh**-ən). See COLLATERAL-ORDER DOCTRINE.

cohort analysis (**koh**-hort). (1954) A method of measuring discrimination in the workplace by comparing, at several points in time, the pay and promotions of employees of different cognizable groups. ● Cohort analyses are often used in employment-discrimination cases.

coif (koyf). (14c) *Hist.* **1.** A white linen headpiece formerly worn by serjeants at law (barristers of high standing) in common-law courts. **2.** The rank or order of serjeants at law. See ORDER OF THE COIF.

Coinage Clause. (1863) The provision in the U.S. Constitution (art. I, § 8, cl. 5) granting to Congress the power to coin money.

coincident indicator. See INDICATOR.

coindictee. One of two or more persons who have been jointly indicted. See *joint indictment* under INDICTMENT.

coined mark. See *fanciful trademark* under TRADEMARK.

coined-name claim. See PATENT CLAIM.

coined term. See *fanciful trademark* under TRADEMARK.

coined trademark. See *fanciful trademark* under TRADEMARK.

coinsurance. See INSURANCE.

coinsurance clause. A provision in an insurance policy requiring a property owner to carry separate insurance up to an amount stated in the policy to qualify for full coverage. — Also termed *contribution clause.*

coinsurer. An insurer who shares losses sustained under an insurance policy. See *coinsurance* under INSURANCE.

cojudices. *Archaic.* In England, associate judges.

COLA. *abbr.* COST-OF-LIVING ADJUSTMENT.

cold bench. See BENCH.

cold blood. (18c) A killer's state of mind when committing a willful and premeditated homicide <a shooting in cold blood>. See COOL BLOOD. Cf. HEAT OF PASSION.

cold check. See *bad check* under CHECK.

cold-comfort letter. See COMFORT LETTER (1).

cold-water ordeal. See *ordeal by water* (1) under ORDEAL.

colegatee (koh-le-gə-**tee**). A joint legatee; one of two or more persons who receive a legacy under a will. Cf. LEGATEE.

COLI. See *corporate-owned life insurance* under LIFE INSURANCE.

collaborative divorce. See DIVORCE.

collaborative law. A dispute-resolution method by which parties and their attorneys settle disputes using nonadversarial techniques to reach a binding agreement, with the understanding that if the parties cannot agree and choose to litigate instead, the attorneys involved in the negotiations will be disqualified from representing them any further. Cf. COOPERATIVE LAW; MEDIATION (1).

collapsible corporation. See CORPORATION.

collapsible partnership. See PARTNERSHIP.

collar, *n.* The minimum and maximum price or ratio for a transaction.

collate (kə-**layt**), *vb. Civil law.* To return (inherited property) to an estate for division <the grandchildren collated the property they had received>.

collateral (kə-**lat**-ər-əl), *adj.* **1.** Supplementary; accompanying, but secondary and subordinate to <whether the accident victim was wearing a seat belt is a collateral issue>. **2.** Not direct in line, but on a parallel or diverging line of descent; of or relating to persons who are related by blood but are neither ancestors nor descendants <an uncle is in a collateral, not a direct, line>. Cf. LINEAL. — **collaterality** (kə-lat-ər-al-ə-tee), *n.*

collateral (kə-**lat**-ər-əl), *n.* (17c) **1.** A person collaterally related to a decedent. **2.** Property that is pledged as security against a debt; the property subject to a security interest or agricultural lien. *See* UCC § 9-102(a)(12). — Also termed (in sense 2) *collateral security.*

as-extracted collateral. **1.** Oil, gas, or other minerals that are subject to a security interest that is created by a debtor having an interest in the minerals before extraction and that attaches to the minerals as they are extracted. UCC 9-102(a)(6)(A). **2.** An account arising out of the sale at the wellhead or minehead of oil, gas, or other minerals in which the debtor had an interest before extraction. UCC 9-102(a)(6)(B).

cash collateral. Collateral consisting of cash, negotiable instruments, documents of title, securities, deposit accounts, or other cash equivalents. 11 USCA § 363(a).

cross-collateral. **1.** Security given by all parties to a contract. **2.** *Bankruptcy.* Bargained-for security that in addition to protecting a creditor's postpetition extension of credit protects the creditor's prepetition unsecured claims, which, as a result of such security, obtain priority over other creditors' prepetition unsecured claims. ● Some courts allow this procedure, which is known as *cross-collateralization.*

collateral act. Any act (usu. excluding the payment of money) for which a bond or recognizance is given as security.

collateral affinity. See AFFINITY.

collateral-agreement doctrine. See COLLATERAL-CONTRACT DOCTRINE.

collateral ancestor. See *collateral ascendant* under ASCENDANT.

collateral ascendant. See ASCENDANT.

collateral assignee. See ASSIGNEE.

collateral assignment. See ASSIGNMENT (2).

collateral assurance. See ASSURANCE.

collateral attack. (1833) An attack on a judgment in a proceeding other than a direct appeal; esp., an attempt to undermine a judgment through a judicial proceeding in which the ground of the proceeding (or a defense in the proceeding) is that the judgment is ineffective. ● Typically a collateral attack is made against a point of procedure or another matter not necessarily apparent in the record, as opposed to a direct attack on the merits exclusively. A petition for a writ of habeas corpus is one type of collateral attack. — Also termed *indirect attack.* Cf. DIRECT ATTACK (1).

collateral-benefit rule. See COLLATERAL-SOURCE RULE.

collateral condition. See CONDITION (2).

collateral consanguinity. See CONSANGUINITY.

collateral consequence. A penalty for committing a crime, in addition to the penalties included in the criminal sentence. ● An example is the loss of a professional license. When a collateral consequence exists, a defendant's appeal of a conviction does not become moot when the criminal sentence is completed.

collateral contract. See CONTRACT.

collateral-contract doctrine. (1947) The principle that in a dispute concerning a written contract, proof of a second (usu. oral) agreement will not be excluded under the parol-evidence rule if the oral agreement is independent of and not inconsistent with the written contract, and if the information in the oral agreement would not ordinarily be expected to be included in the written contract. — Also termed *collateral-agreement doctrine.*

collateral covenant. See COVENANT (1).

collateral defense. See DEFENSE (1).

collateral descendant. See DESCENDANT.

collateral descent. See DESCENT.

collateral estoppel (e-**stop**-əl). (1941) **1.** The binding effect of a judgment as to matters actually litigated and determined in one action on later controversies between the parties involving a different claim from that on which the original judgment was based. **2.** A doctrine barring a party from relitigating an issue determined against that party in an earlier action, even if the second action differs significantly from the first one. — Also termed *issue preclusion; issue estoppel; direct estoppel; estoppel by judgment; estoppel by record; estoppel by verdict; cause-of-action estoppel; technical estoppel; estoppel per rem judicatam.* Cf. RES JUDICATA.

administrative collateral estoppel. Estoppel that arises from a decision made by an agency acting in a judicial capacity.

defensive collateral estoppel. (1968) Estoppel asserted by a defendant to prevent a plaintiff from relitigating an issue previously decided against the plaintiff.

nonmutual collateral estoppel. Estoppel asserted either offensively or defensively by a nonparty to an earlier action to prevent a party to that earlier action from relitigating an issue determined against it.

offensive collateral estoppel. (1964) Estoppel asserted by a plaintiff to prevent a defendant from relitigating an issue previously decided against the defendant.

collateral fact. See FACT.

collateral fraud. See *extrinsic fraud* (1) under FRAUD.

collateral heir. See HEIR.

collateral-inheritance tax. See TAX.

collateral issue. See ISSUE (1).

collateralize (kə-**lat**-ər-əl-ɪz), *vb.* (1941) **1.** To serve as collateral for <the purchased property collateralized the loan agreement>. **2.** To make (a loan) secure with collateral <the creditor insisted that

the loan be collateralized>. — **collateralization** (kə-lat-ər-əl-ə-**zay**-shən), *n.*

collateralized mortgage obligation. *Securities.* A bond secured by a group of mortgage obligations or pass-through securities and paid according to the payment schedule of its class (or *tranche*). ● CMOs are issued by the Federal Home Loan Mortgage Corporation, and benefit from predictable payments of interest and principal. — Abbr. CMO. See *pass-through security* under SECURITY; TRANCHE.

collateral limitation. See LIMITATION.

collateral line. See LINE.

collateral loan. See *secured loan* under LOAN.

collateral matter. (17c) *Evidence.* Any matter on which evidence could not have been introduced for a relevant purpose. ● If a witness has erred in testifying about a detail that is collateral to the relevant facts, then another party cannot call witnesses to contradict that point — cross-examination alone must suffice. Fed. R. Evid. 608(b).

collateral mistake. See *unessential mistake* under MISTAKE.

collateral mortgage. See MORTGAGE.

collateral negligence. See NEGLIGENCE.

collateral-negligence doctrine. (1941) The rule holding that one who engages an independent contractor is not liable for physical harm that the contractor causes if (1) the contractor's negligence consists solely of the improper manner in which the contractor's work is performed, (2) the risk of harm created is not normal to the work, and (3) the employer had no reason to contemplate the contractor's negligence when the contract was made.

collateral note. See *secured note* under NOTE (1).

collateral obligation. A liability undertaken by a person who becomes bound for another's debt. — Also termed *accessorial obligation.*

collateral-order doctrine. (1950) A doctrine allowing appeal from an interlocutory order that conclusively determines an issue wholly separate from the merits of the action and effectively unreviewable on appeal from a final judgment. — Also termed *Cohen doctrine* (fr. *Cohen v. Beneficial Indus. Loan Corp.*, 337 U.S. 541, 69 S.Ct. 1221 (1949)). See *appealable decision* under DECISION.

collateral power. See POWER (5).

collateral proceeding. See PROCEEDING.

collateral promise. See PROMISE.

collateral relative. See RELATIVE.

collateral security. See SECURITY.

collateral-source rule. (1951) *Torts.* The doctrine that if an injured party receives compensation for the injuries from a source independent of the tortfeasor, the payment should not be deducted from the damages that the tortfeasor must pay. ● Insurance proceeds are the most common collateral source. — Also termed *collateral-benefit rule.*

collateral trust bond. See BOND (3).

collateral trust certificate. See *collateral trust bond* (1) under BOND (3).

collateral use. See USE (1).

collateral warranty. See WARRANTY (1).

collation (kə-**lay**-shən), *n.* (14c) **1.** The comparison of a copy with its original to ascertain its correctness; the report of the officer who made the comparison. **2.** The taking into account of the value of advancements made by an intestate to his or her children so that the estate may be divided in accordance with the intestacy statute. Cf. HOTCHPOT. **3.** *Eccles. law.* The act (by a bishop) of conferring a benefice in which the bishop holds the right of advowson, thus combining the acts of *presentation* and *institution.* — Also termed *collation to a benefice.* See *advowson collative* under ADVOWSON. — **collate** (kə-**layt**), *vb.* — **collator** (kə-**lay**-tər), *n.*

collation to a benefice. See COLLATION.

collative fact. See *investitive fact* under FACT.

collectability. The ability of a judgment creditor to make a judgment debtor pay the amount of the judgment; the degree to which a judgment can be satisfied through collection efforts against the judgment debtor.

collecting bank. See BANK.

collection. *Banking.* The process through which an item (such as a check) passes in a payor bank. See *payor bank* under BANK.

collection indorsement. See *restrictive indorsement* under INDORSEMENT.

collection item. An item (such as a documentary draft) taken by a bank for a customer's account, but not credited until payment for the item has actually been received. See *documentary draft* under DRAFT.

collective bargaining. Negotiations between an employer and the representatives of organized employees to determine the conditions of employment, such as wages, hours, discipline, and fringe benefits. See CONCESSION BARGAINING.

collective-bargaining agreement. *Labor law.* A contract between an employer and a labor union regulating employment conditions, wages, benefits, and grievances. — Abbr. CBA. — Also termed *labor agreement; labor contract; union contract; collective-labor agreement; trade agreement.*

collective-knowledge rule. See FELLOW-OFFICER RULE.

collective-labor agreement. See COLLECTIVE-BAR-GAINING AGREEMENT.

collective mark. See *collective trademark* under TRADEMARK.

collective measure. *Int'l law.* An activity undertaken by more than one country to achieve an agreed-upon end. ● The countries involved may undertake a collective measure either in an ad hoc manner or through an institutionalized association.

collective punishment. (1872) A penalty inflicted on a group of persons without regard to individual responsibility for the conduct giving rise to the penalty. ● Collective punishment was outlawed in 1949 by the Geneva Convention.

collective trademark. See TRADEMARK.

collective work. See WORK (2).

collector of decedent's estate. A person temporarily appointed by a probate court to collect assets and payments due to a decedent's estate, and to settle other financial matters requiring immediate attention. ● A collector is often appointed to look after an estate when there is a will contest or a dispute about who should be appointed administrator. The collector's duties end when an executor or administrator is appointed.

collegatary (kə-**leg**-ə-ter-ee). A colegatee; a person who shares a common legacy with one or more other persons. — Also termed *collegatarius* (kə-leg-ə-**ter**-ee-əs).

college. 1. An institution of learning that offers instruction in the liberal arts, humanities, and sciences, but not in the technical arts or in studies preparatory to admission to a profession. **2.** An assembly of people, established by law or private agreement to perform some special function or to promote some common purpose, usu. of an educational, political, ecclesiastical, or scientific nature.

College of Arms. See HERALDS' COLLEGE.

collision. *Maritime law.* **1.** The contact of two or more moving vessels. **2.** ALLISION.

collision insurance. See INSURANCE.

colloquium (kə-**loh**-kwee-əm). (17c) **1.** The offer of extrinsic evidence to show that an allegedly defamatory statement referred to the plaintiff even though it did not explicitly mention the plaintiff. **2.** The introductory averments in a plaintiff's pleading setting out all the special circumstances that make the challenged words defamatory. Cf. INDUCEMENT (4); INNUENDO (2). Pl. **colloquiums, colloquia.**

colloquy (**kol**-ə-kwee). (15c) Any formal discussion, such as an oral exchange between a judge, the prosecutor, the defense counsel, and a criminal defendant in which the judge ascertains the defendant's understanding of the proceedings and of the defendant's rights. ● This discussion helps the court to determine the defendant's ability to continue in the proceedings (esp. important during a change-of-plea hearing).

collusion (kə-**loo**-zhən), *n.* (14c) **1.** An agreement to defraud another or to do or obtain something forbidden by law. **2.** As a defense to divorce, an agreement between a husband and wife to commit or to appear to commit an act that is grounds for divorce. ● For example, before the advent of no-fault divorce, a husband and wife might agree to make it appear that one of them had committed adultery. Cf. CONNIVANCE (2); CONDONATION (2); RECRIMINATION (1). — **collude,** *vb.* — **collusive,** *adj.* — **colluder,** *n.*

tacit collusion. *Antitrust.* See CONSCIOUS PARALLELISM.

collusive action. See ACTION.

collusive joinder. See JOINDER.

Collyer **doctrine** (**kol**-yər). *Labor law.* The principle under which the National Labor Relations Board will refer an issue brought before it to arbitration if the issue is arbitrable under the collective-bargaining agreement. *Collyer Insulated Wire,* 192 NLRB 837 (1971). Cf. SPIELBERG DOCTRINE.

colonial law. 1. Law governing a colony or colonies. **2.** The body of law in force in the 13 original U.S. colonies before the Declaration of Independence.

colon-semicolon form. *Patents.* A style of writing patent claims that uses a colon after the preamble and semicolons between every two elements. Cf. OUTLINE FORM, SINGLE-PARAGRAPH FORM; SUBPARAGRAPH FORM.

colony, *n.* *Int'l law.* **1.** A dependent territorial entity subject to the sovereignty of an independent country, but considered part of that country for purposes of relations with third countries. **2.** A group of people who live in a new territory but retain ties with their parent country. **3.** The territory inhabited by such a group. See MOTHER COUNTRY. — **colonize,** *vb.* — **colonial,** *adj.*

color, *n.* (13c) **1.** Appearance, guise, or semblance; esp., the appearance of a legal claim to a right, authority, or office <color of title> <under color of state law>. **2.** *Common-law pleading.* An apparent, but legally insufficient, right or ground of action, admitted in a defendant's pleading to exist for the plaintiff; esp., a plaintiff's apparent (and usu. false) right or title to property, the existence of which is pleaded by the defendant and then attacked as defective, as part of a confession and avoidance to remove the case from the jury by turning the issue from one of fact to one of law. See GIVE COLOR.

express color. Hist. A defendant's admission that the plaintiff has an apparent right to something coupled with an assertion that the plaintiff's right is legally inferior to the defendant's right to the same thing. • This pleading was typically used in cases of trespass to land by making fictitious allegations that put the plaintiff's ownership of the land in question. For instance, the defendant would admit that the plaintiff had shown apparent ownership of the land by possessing it but then claim that the plaintiff's title was somehow defective, so that the plaintiff did not actually own the land. This pleading was abolished by the Common-Law Procedure Act of 1852, 15 & 16 Vict., ch. 76, § 64.

implied color. **1.** A defendant's tacit admission of a plaintiff's prima facie case by failing to deny it. **2.** An apparent ground of action that arises from the nature of the defense, as when the defense consists of a confession and avoidance in which the defendant admits the facts but denies their legal sufficiency. • This is a quality inherent in all pleadings in confession and avoidance.

colorable, *adj.* (14c) **1.** (Of a claim or action) appearing to be true, valid, or right <the pleading did not state a colorable claim>. **2.** Intended to deceive; counterfeit <the court found the conveyance of exempt property to be a colorable transfer, and so set it aside>.

colorable alteration. *Intellectual property.* A modification that effects no real or substantial change, but is made only to distinguish an invention or work from an existing patent or copyright; a small change made in a product or process solely to avoid literal infringement of an earlier patent's claim. — Also termed *colorable deviation.*

colorable claim. See CLAIM (4).

colorable deviation. See COLORABLE ALTERATION.

colorable imitation. *Trademarks.* Any mark, whether or not created with an intent to deceive, whose resemblance to a registered mark is likely to cause confusion or mistake. See SIMILARITY.

colorable-imitation test. *Trademarks.* A test for a trademark violation in which a court determines whether an ordinary person who is not allowed to compare the two items side by side could recognize the difference between the two.

colorable transaction. See TRANSACTION.

colorable transfer. See TRANSFER.

Colorado Air Force School. See UNITED STATES AIR FORCE ACADEMY.

Colorado River **abstention.** See ABSTENTION.

color book. *Archaic. Int'l law.* An official compilation of diplomatic documents and internal papers and reports of a government, the purpose of which is to inform the legislature and the public about foreign policy, esp. during foreign crises. • Color books reached their height of popularity in the late 19th and early 20th centuries. They are now little used in most countries.

color of apparent organization. The appearance of corporate authority, including the assumption and exercise of corporate functions in good faith, even though the corporation's organizers did not fully or substantially comply with the terms of the corporate charter or the statutory requirements for incorporation. See *de facto corporation* under CORPORATION.

color of authority. The appearance or presumption of authority sanctioning a public officer's actions. • The authority derives from the officer's apparent title to the office or from a writ or other apparently valid process the officer bears.

color of law. (17c) The appearance or semblance, without the substance, of a legal right. • The term usu. implies a misuse of power made possible because the wrongdoer is clothed with the authority of the state. *State action* is synonymous with *color of [state] law* in the context of federal civil-rights statutes or criminal law. See STATE ACTION.

color of office. The authority or power that is inherent in an office, esp. a public office. • Acts taken under the color of an office are vested with, or appear to be vested with, the authority entrusted to that office.

color of process. The appearance of validity and sufficiency surrounding a legal proceeding that is later found to be invalid.

color of title. (18c) A written instrument or other evidence that appears to establish title but does not in fact do so. — Also termed *apparent title.*

com. *abbr.* COMPANY.

comaker. One who participates jointly in borrowing money on a promissory note; esp., one who acts as surety under a note if the maker defaults. — Also termed *cosigner.* Cf. MAKER (2).

combatant (kəm-**bat**-ənt *or* **kom**-bə-tənt). (15c) *Int'l law.* A person who participates directly in hostilities. • "Legitimate" combatants are members of the armed forces or uniformed members of a militia or volunteer corps, under military command and subject to the laws of war. Cf. NONCOMBANT.

enemy combatant (kəm-**bat**-ənt). A combatant captured and detained while serving in a hostile force during open warfare. • In general, the separation-of-powers doctrine prevents a United States civilian court from interfering with the military's handling of enemy combatants, at least as long as the hostilities continue. An enemy combatant may be detained without charges but has the right to contest the detention. *Rasul v. Bush,* 542 U.S. 466, 124 S.Ct. 2686

(2004). United States citizenship does not prevent a person from being designated an enemy combatant, but the government must give a citizen-detainee notice of the factual basis for the classification and a fair opportunity to rebut the factual assertions before a neutral decisionmaker. *Hamdi v. Rumsfeld*, 542 U.S. 507, 124 S.Ct. 2633 (2004).

combination. 1. An alliance of individuals or corporations working together to accomplish a common (usu. economic) goal. See COMBINATION IN RESTRAINT OF TRADE. **2.** CONSPIRACY. **3.** STRADDLE. **4.** *Patents.* A union of old and new elements in an invention. • The term encompasses not only a combination of mechanical elements but also a combination of substances in a composition claim or steps in a process claim. Cf. AGGREGATION. **5.** *Patents.* An invention that uses two or more patented inventions to make a distinct and useful third product. • In the past, an inventor seeking a combination patent had to show "synergism," a surprising result from the combination. But the U.S. Court of Appeals for the Federal Circuit ruled that the term "combination" has no legal effect, because most inventions combine and build on existing technology. Today there are no special rules for combination patents. **6.** *Patents.* A union of elements in an invention that work together cooperatively to perform a useful function; the opposite of an aggregation. Cf. AGGREGATION.

exhausted combination. See *old combination.*

old combination. A combination in which an element works in a different way but performs the same function as the corresponding element in a previously patented combination. • The new element may be patentable but the combination may not be. — Also termed *exhausted combination.*

combination in restraint of trade. *Antitrust.* An express or tacit agreement between two or more persons or entities designed to raise prices, reduce output, or create a monopoly. — Also termed *combine.*

combination patent. See PATENT (3).

combine (kom-**bin**), *n.* See COMBINATION IN RESTRAINT OF TRADE.

combined application. See TRADEMARK APPLICATION.

combined § 8 and § 15 affidavit. *Trademarks.* A sworn statement that satisfies the requirements of both § 8 and § 15 of the Lanham Act. — Sometimes shortened to *§ 8 and § 15 affidavit.* — Also termed *combined § 8 and § 15 declaration.* See DECLARATION OF INCONTESTABILITY; DECLARATION OF USE.

comes and defends. *Archaic.* Traditionally, the standard commencement of a defendant's plea

or demurrer. • The phrase, now rarely used, announces the defendant's appearance in court and intent to defend against the action.

comes now. *Archaic.* Traditionally, the standard commencement in pleadings <Comes now the plaintiff, Gilbert Lewis, by and through his attorneys of record, and would show unto the court the following>. • For a plural subject, the phrase is *come now* <Come now the plaintiffs, Bob and Louise Smith>. — Sometimes shortened to *comes* <Comes the State of Tennessee>. — Also termed *now comes.*

comfort letter. 1. *Securities.* A letter from a certified public accountant certifying that no false or misleading information has been used in preparing a financial statement accompanying a securities offering. • Such a letter usu. has limited effect because the CPA ordinarily attests to certain representations and warranties that the issuer has authorized the CPA to rely on. — Also termed *cold-comfort letter.* **2.** *Corporations.* A letter, esp. from a parent corporation on behalf of a subsidiary, stating its support (but short of a guarantee) for the activities and commitments of another corporation. — Also termed *letter of comfort.*

comfort opinion. See OPINION (2).

comingle, *vb.* See COMMINGLE.

comingling. See COMMINGLING.

coming-to-rest doctrine. *Insurance.* The principle that coverage of shipped goods ends when the goods are unloaded and any cables or other links to the transporting vehicle have been disconnected. • The coming-to-rest doctrine covers only the movement of goods from the shipping vehicle to a place of rest outside the vehicle, in contrast to the broader coverage of the complete-operation rule. Cf. COMPLETE-OPERATION RULE.

comitas (**kom**-ə-təs). [Latin "courtesy"] See COMITY.

comitas gentium. See COMITY.

comitatus (kom-ə-**tay**-təs). [Latin] *Hist.* **1.** A county or shire. See POSSE COMITATUS. **2.** The territorial jurisdiction of a count or earl. **3.** A county court. **4.** The retinue accompanying a prince or high government official.

comitia (kə-**mish**-ee-ə), *n.* [Latin "assembly"] *Roman law.* An assembly of the Roman people, gathered together for legislative or judicial purposes. • Women were excluded from participation.

comitia centuriata (kə-**mish**-ee-ə sen-tyoor-ee-**ay**-tə). (*often cap.*) An assembly of the entire populace, voting by centuries (that is, military units) empowered to elect magistrates and to act as a court of appeal in a capital matter.

comitia curiata (kə-**mish**-ee-ə kyoor-ee-**ay**-tə). (*often cap.*) An assembly of (originally) patricians whose chief function was to authorize private acts of citizens, such as declaring wills and adoptions. ● The *comitia curiata* engaged in little legislative activity.

comitia tributa (kə-**mish**-ee-ə tri-**byoo**-tə). (*often cap.*) An assembly of tribes convened to elect lower-ranking officials. ● The *comitia tributa* undertook a great deal of legislative activity in the later Roman republic.

comity (**kom**-ə-tee). (16c) **1.** A practice among political entities (as nations, states, or courts of different jurisdictions), involving esp. mutual recognition of legislative, executive, and judicial acts. — Also termed *comitas gentium; courtoisie internationale.* See FEDERAL-COMITY DOCTRINE; JUDICIAL COMITY. Cf. ABSTENTION. **2.** INTERNATIONAL LAW. ● This sense is considered a misusage: "[I]n Anglo-American jurisprudence, . . . the term is also misleadingly found to be used as a synonym for international law." Peter Macalister-Smith, "Comity," in 1 *Encyclopedia of Public International Law* 672 (1992).

Comity Clause. (1921) The clause of the U.S. Constitution giving citizens of one state the right to all privileges and immunities enjoyed by citizens of the other states. U.S. Const. art. IV, § 2, cl. 1. See PRIVILEGES AND IMMUNITIES CLAUSE.

comm. *abbr.* COMMONWEALTH.

command. (14c) **1.** An order; a directive. **2.** In legal positivism, the sovereign's express desire that a person act or refrain from acting a certain way, combined with the threat of punishment for failure to comply.

command, *vb.* To direct authoritatively; to order.

commander-in-chief. (17c) **1.** One who holds supreme or highest command of armed forces. **2.** (*cap.*) The title of the U.S. President when acting as the constitutionally designated leader of the nation's military. U.S. Const. art. II, § 2.

Commander in Chief Clause. The clause of the U.S. Constitution appointing the President as supreme commander of the military. U.S. Const. art. II, § 2, cl. 1.

commandment. *Hist.* **1.** An authoritative order of a judge or magisterial officer. **2.** The offense of inducing another to commit a crime.

command rape. See RAPE.

commencement. See INTRODUCTORY CLAUSE.

commencement of infringement. *Copyright.* The first of a series of discrete copyright violations, such as the first of many separate sales of infringing items. See INFRINGEMENT.

commenda (kə-**men**-də). A business association in which one person has responsibility for managing all business property.

commendam (kə-**men**-dam *or* -dəm). **1.** *Hist. Eccles. law.* A vacant benefice held by a clerk until a regular pastor could be appointed. ● Bishops and other dignitaries found commendams to be lucrative sources of income. Commendams were abolished in England in 1836. See BENEFICE. **2.** Partnership in commendam. See *limited partnership* under PARTNERSHIP.

commendation. *Hist.* The act of becoming a lord's feudal tenant to receive the lord's protection.

commendator (**kom**-ən-day-tər). *Eccles. law.* A person holding a commendam (a benefice) as a trustee. ● Commendators are so called because benefices are commended to their supervision. See COMMENDAM.

commendatus (kom-ən-**day**-təs). *Hist.* A person who, by voluntary oath of homage, was placed under a lord's protection.

comment, *n.* (14c) **1.** NOTE (2). **2.** An explanatory statement made by the drafters of a particular statute, code section, or rule. — **commentator,** *n.*

commentators. See POSTGLOSSATORS.

commenter. One who comments; esp., one who sends comments to an agency about a proposed administrative rule or regulation. See NOTICE-AND-COMMENT PERIOD.

comment letter. *Securities.* A letter prepared by an SEC examiner to request additional information or describe deficiencies in a filing, particularly a registration statement.

comment on the evidence. (18c) A statement made to the jury by the judge or by counsel on the probative value of certain evidence. Fed. R. Evid. 105. ● Lawyers typically make such comments in closing argument, and judges may make such comments in federal court. But most state-court judges are not permitted to do so when examining a witness, instructing the jury, and the like (in which case the comment is sometimes termed an *impermissible comment on the evidence*).

comment period. See NOTICE-AND-COMMENT PERIOD.

commerce. (16c) The exchange of goods and services, esp. on a large scale involving transportation between cities, states, and nations.

internal commerce. See *intrastate commerce.*

international commerce. Trade and other business activities between nations.

interstate commerce. (1843) Trade and other business activities between those located in different states; esp., traffic in goods and travel of people between states. ● For purposes of this phrase, most statutory definitions include a territory of the United States as a state. Some statutory definitions of *interstate commerce* include commerce between a foreign country and a state. — Also termed *interstate trade.*

intrastate commerce. (1887) Commerce that begins and ends entirely within the borders of a single state. — Also termed *internal commerce.*

Commerce Clause. (1868) U.S. Const. art. I, § 8, cl. 3, which gives Congress the exclusive power to regulate commerce among the states, with foreign nations, and with Indian tribes.

Dormant Commerce Clause. (1930) The constitutional principle that the Commerce Clause prevents state regulation of interstate commercial activity even when Congress has not acted under its Commerce Clause power to regulate that activity. — Also termed *Negative Commerce Clause.*

Commerce Court. See COURT.

commerce power. Congress's constitutionally conferred power to regulate trade between the states.

commercial acquiescence. See ACQUIESCENCE.

commercial acre. *Property.* The amount of land left in a subdivided acre after deducting the amount dedicated to streets, sidewalks, utilities, etc. • The area of a commercial acre is always less than an actual acre. Cf. ACRE.

commercial activity. See ACTIVITY (1).

commercial-activity exception. (1973) An exemption from the rule of sovereign immunity, permitting a claim against a foreign state to be adjudicated in the courts of another state if the claim arises from private acts undertaken by the foreign state, as opposed to the state's public acts. See RESTRICTIVE PRINCIPLE OF SOVEREIGN IMMUNITY; JURE GESTIONIS; JURE IMPERII.

commercial agent. See AGENT (2).

commercial assets. See ASSET.

commercial bank. See BANK.

commercial bribery. See BRIBERY.

commercial broker. See BROKER.

commercial court. See COURT.

commercial credit company. See *commercial finance company* under FINANCE COMPANY.

commercial crime. See CRIME.

commercial defamation. See *trade defamation* under DEFAMATION.

commercial disparagement. See TRADE DISPARAGEMENT.

commercial division. See *business court* under COURT.

commercial domicile. See DOMICILE.

commercial finance company. See FINANCE COMPANY.

commercial franchise. See FRANCHISE (4).

commercial frustration. See FRUSTRATION.

commercial general-liability policy. See INSURANCE POLICY.

commercial goodwill. See GOODWILL.

commercial impracticability. See IMPRACTICABILITY.

commercial insurance. See INSURANCE.

commercialized obscenity. See OBSCENITY.

commercial law. (18c) **1.** The substantive law dealing with the sale and distribution of goods, the financing of credit transactions on the security of the goods sold, and negotiable instruments. • Most American commercial law is governed by the Uniform Commercial Code. — Also termed *mercantile law.* **2.** LAW MERCHANT.

commercial-law notice. See NOTICE.

commercial lease. See LEASE.

commercial letter of credit. See LETTER OF CREDIT.

commercial loan. See LOAN.

commercially reasonable, *adj.* (1922) (Of a property sale) conducted in good faith and in accordance with commonly accepted commercial practice. • Under the UCC, a sale of collateral by a secured party must be done in a commercially reasonable manner, or the obligor's liability for any deficiency may be reduced or eliminated. See UCC § 9-610(b), 9-626.

commercially significant noninfringing use. *Intellectual property.* The routine use of a product in a way that does not infringe intellectual-property rights; the judicial test for determining whether the sale of a product amounts to contributory infringement. • If the product (such as a video recorder) can be used in a way that does not infringe those rights (such as recording a program in order to watch it at a later time), then its sale cannot be enjoined, or its manufacturer subjected to a court-imposed royalty. *See Sony Corp. of Am. v. Universal City Studios, Inc.,* 464 U.S. 417, 442, 104 S.Ct. 774 (1984) (Stevens, J.). — Also termed *Sony doctrine; substantial noninfringing use.* Cf. PRIMARY PURPOSE OR EFFECT.

commercial morality. Collectively, fair practices among competitors. • Commercial espionage is often cited by courts as being below accepted standards of commercial morality.

commercial name. See TRADENAME.

commercial paper. See PAPER.

commercial partnership. See *trading partnership* under PARTNERSHIP.

commercial set. 1. The primary documents covering shipment of goods, usu. including an invoice, bill of lading, bill of exchange, and certificate of insurance. **2.** The documents required under a letter of credit.

commercial signature. *Trademarks.* A trademark (as commonly described).

commercial speech. See SPEECH.

commercial surety. See *compensated surety* under SURETY.

commercial tort claim. (1994) A claim arising in tort when the claimant is either (1) an organization, or (2) an individual whose claim arose in the course of the claimant's business or profession, and the claim does not include damages arising out of personal injury or death. UCC § 9-102(a) (13). • Typical commercial tort claims are fraud and conversion.

commercial-traveler rule. *Workers' compensation.* The principle that an accident will be treated as occurring during the course of employment if it was caused by an employee whose job requires travel, and the employee was not on a personal errand. • The commercial-traveler rule is an exception to the going-and-coming rule. Cf. GOING-AND-COMING RULE.

commercial treaty. See TREATY (1).

commercial unit. (1960) A unit of goods that by commercial usage is a single whole for purposes of sale and whose division materially impairs its character or value in the relevant market or in use. UCC § 2-105(6). • Under the UCC, "a commercial unit may be a single article (as a machine) or a set of articles (as a suite of furniture or an assortment of sizes) or a quantity (as a bale, gross, or carload) or any other unit treated in use or in the relevant market as a single whole." *Id.*

commercial use. See USE (1).

commingle, *vb.* (kə-**ming**-gəl). (17c) **1.** To put together (as funds or property) into one mass, as by mixing together a spouse's separate property with marital or community property, or mixing together the separate property of both spouses. **2.** (Of a fiduciary) to mix personal funds with those of a beneficiary or client. — Also spelled *comingle.* See COMMINGLING. Cf. TRACING.

commingling (kə-**ming**-gling), *n.* A mixing together; esp., a fiduciary's mixing of personal funds with those of a beneficiary or client. • Commingling is usu. considered a breach of the fiduciary relationship. Under the Model Rules of Professional Conduct, a lawyer is prohibited from commingling personal funds with those of a client. Commingling also occurs when a spouse has mixed his or her separate property with community property to such an extent that they cannot be separated. — Also spelled *comingling.*

commissary (kom-i-ser-ee), *n.* (14c) **1.** A person who is delegated or commissioned to perform some duty, usu. as a representative of a superior.

2. A general store, esp. on a military base. **3.** A lunchroom. — **commissary,** *adj.*

commissary court. See COURT.

commission, *n.* (14c) **1.** A warrant or authority, from the government or a court, that empowers the person named to execute official acts <the student received his commission to the U.S. Navy after graduation>. **2.** The authority under which a person transacts business for another <the client gave her attorney express commission to sign the contract>. **3.** A body of persons acting under lawful authority to perform certain public services <the Federal Communications Commission>.

public-service commission. A commission created by a legislature to regulate public utilities or public-service corporations.

4. The act of doing or perpetrating (as a crime) <the perpetrator fled to Mexico after commission of the assault>. **5.** A fee paid to an agent or employee for a particular transaction, usu. as a percentage of the money received from the transaction <a real-estate agent's commission>.

double commission. A commission obtained by a person acting in dual roles, each of which generates a commission, such as a person serving as both executor and trustee in an estate matter. • Double commissions paid without proper authority or disclosure may raise fiduciary-duty issues. See FIDUCIARY; *fiduciary duty* under DUTY (2).

commissionaire. See AGENT.

commission broker. See BROKER.

commission del credere (del **kred**-ər-ay). (18c) The commission received by the seller's agent for guaranteeing a buyer's debt.

commissioned officer. See OFFICER (2).

commissioner. (15c) **1.** A person who directs a commission; a member of a commission. **2.** The administrative head of an organization, such as a professional sport. **3.** See *judicial officer* (3) under OFFICER.

bail commissioner. See BAIL COMMISSIONER.

Commissioner for Patents. The chief operating officer of the patents section of the U.S. Patent and Trademark Office. • The commissioner is appointed by the Secretary of Commerce.

Commissioner for Trademarks. The chief operating officer of the trademarks section of the U.S. Patent and Trademark Office. • The commissioner is appointed by the Secretary of Commerce.

commissioner in bankruptcy. *English law.* A commissioner who is appointed by the Lord Chancellor and empowered to proceed in corporate-bankruptcy cases.

commissioner of bail. See BAIL COMMISSIONER.

commissioner of circuit court. A court-appointed officer who helps the circuit and district courts by performing judicial and ministerial functions.

commissioner of deeds. An officer authorized by a state to take acknowledgments of deeds and other papers while residing in another state. • The acknowledgments are recognized in the state that licensed the commissioner. Cf. NOTARY PUBLIC.

commissioner of highways. A public officer responsible for overseeing the construction, alteration, and repair of highways.

commissioner of partition. An equity-court-appointed officer who is empowered to examine a request for partition and recommend an action to the court, or to make the partition and report the act to the court.

Commissioner of Patents and Trademarks. See DIRECTOR OF THE UNITED STATES PATENT AND TRADEMARK OFFICE.

commissioner of woods and forests. *Hist.* An officer who, by an 1817 Act of Parliament, assumed the jurisdiction of the Chief Justice of the Forest.

county commissioner. A county officer charged usu. with the management of the county's financial affairs, its police regulations, and its corporate business. — Also termed *county supervisor.*

court commissioner. An officer appointed by the court esp. to hear and report facts, or to conduct judicial sales.

jury commissioner. An officer responsible for drawing and summoning the panels of potential jurors in a given county.

public commissioner. See PROSECUTOR (1).

town commissioner. A member of the board of administrative officers charged with managing the town's business.

United States Commissioner. *Hist.* A judicial officer appointed by a U.S. district court to hear a variety of pretrial matters in criminal cases. • Commissioners' duties have been transferred to U.S. Magistrate Judges. Cf. UNITED STATES MAGISTRATE JUDGE.

commissioner's court. See COURT.

commission government. A type of municipal government in which the legislative power is in the hands of a few people.

commission merchant. See FACTOR (2).

commission of appraisement and sale. *Maritime law.* A court order requiring the sale of property in an in-rem admiralty action.

commission of assize. *Hist.* A royal authorization empowering a person to hold court and try cases arising while the justices in eyre held court elsewhere. Cf. EYRE.

commission of charitable uses. *Hist.* An authorization issuing out of the Court of Chancery to a bishop or other person authorizing the appointee to investigate allegations of fraud or other disputed matters concerning charitable land grants.

commission of delegates. *Hist.* A commission appointing a person (usu. a lord, bishop, or judge) to sit with several other appointees to hear an appeal of an ecclesiastical judgment in the Court of Chancery. • This commission was abolished in 1832, and its functions transferred to the Judicial Committee of the Privy Council.

Commission of Fine Arts. An independent federal commission that advises the President, Congress, and governmental agencies on the design of public buildings, memorials, and parks in the nation's capital so as to complement historic structures and districts. • The commission was created in 1910.

Commission of Gaol Delivery. *Hist.* A royal appointment authorizing a judge to go on the assize circuit and hear all criminal cases of those held in county jails. See JAIL DELIVERY. Cf. COMMISSION OF OYER AND TERMINER.

commission of lieutenancy. *Hist.* A commission issued to send officers into every county to establish military order over the inhabitants. • This commission superseded the former *commission of array*, which provided the same powers. The commissions became obsolete with the establishment of the militia system.

Commission of Oyer and Terminer (oy-ər an[d] tər-mə-nər). [Law French *oyer et terminer* "to hear and determine"] *Hist.* A royal appointment authorizing a judge (often a serjeant-at-law) to go on the assize circuit and hear felony and treason cases. Cf. COMMISSION OF GAOL DELIVERY; COURT OF OYER AND TERMINER.

commission of partition. An authorization appointing a person to sit with several other appointees for the purpose of dividing land held by tenants in common who desire a partition.

commission of rebellion. *Hist.* An attaching process that empowered a layperson to arrest and bring a defendant to Chancery to enforce obedience to a writ of subpoena or decree. • The commission of rebellion was abolished in 1841. — Also termed *writ of rebellion; commissio rebellionis; breve rebellionis.*

commission of review. *Hist.* In England, an authorization sometimes granted in an extraordinary case to review a judgment of the Court of Delegates. • The commission of review is no longer used because the Privy Council was substituted for the Court of Delegates as the appellate court in ecclesiastical cases in 1832. See COURT OF DELEGATES.

commission of the peace. *Hist.* An appointment of a person to keep the peace (i.e., provide police protection) on a local level. • Over time the recipients of these commissions began to acquire judicial responsibilities, and became known as justices of the peace.

Commission on Civil Rights. See UNITED STATES COMMISSION ON CIVIL RIGHTS.

commission plan. (1919) A form of municipal government whereby both legislative and executive power is vested in a small group of elected officials. • Today, commission plans are used in only a few cities.

commission to examine a witness. A judicial commission directing that a witness beyond the court's territorial jurisdiction be deposed. • The commission usu. identifies the person to be deposed, when and where the deposition will be taken, and any other information that will help the commissioner to perform. — Also termed *commission to take a deposition*; *commission to take testimony*. Cf. LETTER OF REQUEST.

commission to take a deposition. See COMMISSION TO EXAMINE A WITNESS.

commission to take testimony. See COMMISSION TO EXAMINE A WITNESS.

commissio rebellionis. See COMMISSION OF REBELLION.

commissive waste. See WASTE (1).

commit, *vb.* **1.** To perpetrate (a crime). **2.** To send (a person) to prison or to a mental health facility, esp. by court order. **3.** *Parliamentary law.* REFER.

commitment, *n.* (14c) **1.** An agreement to do something in the future, esp. to assume a financial obligation <the shipper made a firm commitment to deliver the goods>. **2.** The act of entrusting or giving in charge <commitment of money to the bank>. **3.** The act of confining a person in a prison, mental hospital, or other institution <commitment of the felon to prison>. **4.** The order directing an officer to take a person to a penal or mental institution; MITTIMUS (1) <the judge signed the commitment after ruling that it was in the best interest of the troubled teen>.

civil commitment. See CIVIL COMMITTMENT (1).

diagnostic commitment. Pretrial or presentencing confinement of an individual, usu. to determine the individual's competency to stand trial or to determine the appropriate sentence to be rendered.

discretionary commitment. A commitment that a judge may or may not grant, depending on whether the government has proved — usu. by clear and convincing evidence — that the commitment is necessary for the well-being of the defendant or society (as when the defendant is insane and dangerous). • Most states allow discretionary commitment.

mandatory commitment. (1985) An automatically required commitment for a defendant found not guilty by reason of insanity. • This type of commitment is required under federal law, but in only a minority of states.

new court commitment. The confinement in prison of a person who is being admitted on a new conviction — that is, someone who is not being returned to prison for a parole violation.

voluntary commitment. A commitment of a person who is ill, incompetent, drug-addicted, or the like, upon the request or with the consent of the person being committed.

commitment document. An order remanding a defendant to prison in order to carry out a judgment and sentence.

commitment fee. An amount paid to a lender by a potential borrower for the lender's promise to lend money at a stipulated rate and within a specified time. • Commitment fees are common in real estate transactions. See LOAN COMMITMENT.

commitment letter. 1. A lender's written offer to grant a mortgage loan. • The letter generally outlines the loan amount, the interest rate, and other terms. — Also termed *letter of commitment.* **2.** LETTER OF INTENT.

commitment warrant. See *warrant of commitment* under WARRANT (1).

committee. 1. (kə-**mit**-ee). A subordinate group to which a deliberative assembly or other organization refers business for consideration, investigation, oversight, or action <the bill was sent to legislative committee>.

ad hoc committee. See *special committee.*

arrangements committee. A committee charged with organizing the physical space in which a deliberative assembly meets.

audit committee. A committee appointed by the board of an organization, esp. a corporation, to oversee the financial reporting process, select an independent auditor, and receive the audit. • Ideally, a committee member is financially literate and wholly independent, having no financial interest (direct or indirect) in the company, no executive position, and no familial relationship with any member of the company's management or a major shareholder.

committee of one. A committee with only one member.

committee of the whole. A special committee that comprises all the deliberative assembly's members who are present. • A deliberative assembly may resolve itself into a committee of the whole so that it can take advantage of the greater procedural flexibility that a committee enjoys, usu. presided over by some chair other than the assembly's regular chair. Cf. *quasi committee of the whole.*

committee on conference. See *conference committee.*

committee with full power. See *committee with power.*

committee with power. A committee to whom the referring body has delegated the necessary authority for acting on the business referred, usu. without need for a prior report to the referring body. — Also termed *committee with full power.*

conference committee. A joint meeting of two legislative committees, one from each house of a bicameral legislature, usu. charged with adjusting differences in a bill passed by both houses in different versions. — Also termed *committee on conference.* See CONFERENCE (2).

congressional committee. A committee of the House of Representatives, a committee of the Senate, or a joint committee.

credentials committee. A committee charged with preparing a roster of delegates entitled to be seated, examining contested claims to such entitlement, and preparing and issuing credentials to the delegates who appear so entitled. See CREDENTIAL.

executive committee. The committee of principal officers and directors who directly manage an organization's affairs between board meetings.

joint committee. A legislative committee composed of members of both houses of a legislature.

legislative committee. A group of legislators appointed to help a legislature conduct its business, esp. by providing careful consideration of proposals for new legislation within a particular field so that the entire body can handle its work efficiently without wasting time and effort on unmeritorious submissions.

membership committee. A committee charged with recruiting and keeping members and getting them involved.

nominating committee. A committee charged with identifying (and perhaps recruiting) and recommending a suitable candidate or candidates for election by a deliberative assembly. — Also termed *screening committee.*

ordinary committee. A committee other than a committee of the whole.

parent committee. A committee that refers business to a subcommittee. • The parent committee is so called only when considered in relation to the subcommittee. See *subcommittee.*

permanent committee. See *standing committee.*

platform committee. A committee charged with developing a comprehensive statement of an organization's, usu. a political party's, public policies and principles.

program committee. The committee that plans a convention's program, usu. including both its formal business and its educational and social events.

quasi committee of the whole. A committee of the whole over which the deliberative assembly's regular chair presides.

reference committee. See *resolutions committee.*

resolutions committee. A committee charged with screening the original main motions offered for a convention's consideration. — Also termed *reference committee; screening committee.*

rules committee. A committee charged with drafting rules and an agenda for the orderly conduct of a deliberative assembly's business, particularly that of a legislative body or a convention.

screening committee. 1. See *nominating committee.* **2.** See *resolutions committee.*

search committee. A committee charged with finding a suitable choice from several options, such as candidates for employment or places for a meeting.

select committee. See *special committee.*

special committee. A committee established for a particular purpose or a limited time. • A legislature will ordinarily establish a special committee for a nonlegislative purpose, such as writing memorials, procuring chaplains, determining the qualifications of members, and settling election disputes. — Also termed *ad hoc committee; select committee; temporary committee.*

standing committee. A committee that is established for ongoing business, that continues to exist from session to session, and that is usu. charged with considering business of a certain recurring kind. • A legislature will ordinarily establish a standing committee concerned with a specific field of legislation. A legislative standing committee usu. considers basic questions of legislative policy, holds hearings on legislation, eliminates unwanted bills, and prepares favored measures for passage. — Also termed *permanent committee.*

subcommittee. A group within a committee to which the committee may refer business, standing in the same relation to its parent committee as the committee stands to the deliberative assembly. See *parent committee*.

tellers committee. A committee that helps the chair administer an election or other vote by handing out and picking up ballots if necessary, counting the votes or canvassing the ballots, and reporting the result to the chair for announcement. See CANVASS (2).

temporary committee. See *special committee*.

2. (kəm-i-**tee**) A person who is civilly committed, usu. to a psychiatric hospital <the board determined that the committee was dangerous and should not be released>. **3.** (kəm-i-**tee**) The guardian for the person so committed <the patient's lawyer objected to the appointment of the committee>.

committee amendment. See AMENDMENT (3).

committee jurisdiction. See CHARGE (8).

committee report. See REPORT (1).

committee substitute. See *clean bill* under BILL (3).

committing magistrate. See MAGISTRATE.

committitur (kə-**mit**-ə-tər). [Latin "he is committed"] *Archaic.* An order or minute stating that the person named in it is to be committed to the custody of the sheriff.

commodatum (kom-ə-**day**-təm), *n.* (17c) [Latin *commodare* "to lend"] *Roman & civil law.* The gratuitous lending of goods to be used by the borrower and then returned undamaged to the lender. ● This arrangement is for the sole benefit of the borrower. It is one of three types of contracts for permissive use, the other two being *locatio conductio* and *mutuum.* — Also termed *accommodatum*; *commodate.* Pl. **commodata.**

commodity. 1. An article of trade or commerce. ● The term embraces only tangible goods, such as products or merchandise, as distinguished from services. **2.** An economic good, esp. a raw material or an agricultural product.

commodity-backed bond. See BOND (3).

Commodity Credit Corporation. A federally chartered corporation responsible for extending credit in order to stabilize farm income and prices. ● Incorporated in Delaware in 1933 and operated in affiliation with the Reconstruction Finance Corporation, it was transferred to the U.S. Department of Agriculture in 1939 and chartered in 1948 as a federal corporation. 15 USCA § 714. — Abbr. CCC.

Commodity Futures Trading Commission. A five-member federal commission that regulates trading in futures and options contracts and monitors the activities of commodity-exchange members, brokerage houses, commission-registered salespeople, and others associated with the industry. ● The commission began operating in April 1975. 7 USCA § 2(a)(2). — Abbr. CFTC.

commodity loan. See LOAN.

commodity option. See OPTION.

commodity paper. See PAPER.

common, *n.* **1.** A legal right to use another person's property, such as an easement. See PROFIT À PRENDRE.

common appendant (ə-**pen**-dənt). *Hist.* A tenant's right to graze animals on the landowner's land as a result of longstanding practice. See *profit appendant* under PROFIT (2).

common appurtenant (ə-**pər**-tə-nənt). *Hist.* A landowner's right to graze animals on another's land as a result of a written grant relating to the ownership or occupancy of land. See *profit appurtenant* under PROFIT (2).

common in gross. *Hist.* A right to graze animals on another's land as a result of a written grant unrelated to ownership or occupancy of land. — Also termed *common at large.* See *profit in gross* under PROFIT (2).

common in the soil. *Hist.* The right to dig and take away earth from another's land. — Also termed *common of digging.*

common of estovers (e-**stoh**-vərz). *Hist.* A tenant's right to take necessary supplies, esp. wood, from the lord's estate; the right to estovers. See ESTOVERS (1).

common of fishery. See *common of piscary.*

common of pasture. *Hist.* A right to pasture one's cattle on another's land. ● The common of pasture may be appendant, appurtenant, or in gross.

common of piscary (**pis**-kə-ree). *Hist.* A right to fish in waters on another's land. — Often shortened to *piscary.* — Also termed *common of fishery.*

common of shack. *Hist.* The right of people occupying land in a common field to release their cattle to graze after harvest.

common of turbary (**tər**-bə-ree). *Hist.* The right to dig turf (for use as fuel in a house) from another's land.

common without stint. *Hist.* A right to graze an unlimited number of cattle.

2. A tract of land set aside for the general public's use.

commonable, *adj.* (17c) **1.** (Of an animal) allowed to graze on common land. **2.** (Of land) capable of being held in common.

common adventure. See ADVENTURE.

common agent. See AGENT (2).

commonality test. The requirement that members of a group certified as a class in a class-action suit share at least one issue of law or fact whose resolution will affect all or a significant number of the putative class members. Cf. COMMON-CHARACTER REQUIREMENT.

common ancestor. See ANCESTOR.

common and notorious thief. See *common thief* under THIEF.

common appendant. See COMMON.

common appurtenant. See COMMON.

common area. 1. *Landlord-tenant law.* The realty that all tenants may use though the landlord retains control over and responsibility for it. **2.** An area owned and used in common by the residents of a condominium, subdivision, or planned-unit development. — Also termed *common elements.*

common-area maintenance charges. Fees paid by tenants, usu. on a pro rata basis, to compensate the landlord for the costs of operating, repairing, and maintaining common areas. ● Such costs include those incurred for cleaning, lighting, and repairs. — Abbr. CAMs. — Also termed *common-area operating expenses.*

common-area operating expenses. See COMMON-AREA MAINTENANCE CHARGES.

common assault. 1. See ASSAULT (1). **2.** See ASSAULT (2).

common assumpsit. See *general assumpsit* under ASSUMPSIT.

common assurance. See MUNIMENT OF TITLE.

common at large. See *common in gross* under COMMON.

common-authority rule. The principle that a person may consent to a police officer's search of another person's property if both persons use, control, or have access to the property. ● Under this rule, the consenting person must have been legally able to permit the search in his or her own right, and the defendant must have assumed the risk that a fellow occupant might permit a search. *See U.S. v. Matlock*, 415 U.S. 164, 171 n.7, 94 S.Ct. 988, 993 n.7 (1974). See THIRD-PARTY CONSENT.

common bail. See *bail common* under BAIL (4).

common bar. See BLANK BAR.

Common Bench. *Hist.* The former name of the English Court of Common Pleas. ● The court was so called because it was the forum for the common people, that is, for cases between two or more subjects when the Crown had no interest. — Abbr. C.B.

common-bond doctrine. The rule that prospective members of a credit union must share some connection (such as common employment) other than a desire to create a credit union.

common business purpose. Related activity by two or more associated businesses. ● If one of the businesses comes within the jurisdiction of the Fair Labor Standards Act, then another business that shares a common business purpose will also.

common calling. 1. An ordinary occupation that a citizen has a right to pursue under the Privileges and Immunities Clause. **2.** A commercial enterprise that offers services to the general public, with a legal duty to serve anyone who requests the services. ● For example, an innkeeper or a common carrier engages in a common calling.

common carrier. See CARRIER.

common cause. See *common plea* (1) under PLEA (3).

common-character requirement. (1997) The rule that for a group of persons to qualify as a class in a class-action lawsuit, the appointment of the class must achieve economies of time, effort, and expense, and must promote uniformity of decision for persons similarly situated, in addition to sharing common questions of fact and law. Cf. COMMONALITY TEST.

common chase. See CHASE.

common cost. See *indirect cost* under COST (1).

common council. See COUNCIL.

common count. See COUNT.

common day. See DAY.

common debtor. See DEBTOR.

common-defeasance bond. See *penal bond* under BOND (2).

common descriptive name. See GENERIC NAME.

common design. (17c) **1.** The intention by two or more people to join in committing an unlawful act. **2.** An intention to commit more than one crime. **3.** The general design or layout of plots of land surrounding a particular tract. — Also termed *common scheme*; *common plan.* See ZONING.

common diligence. See *due diligence* (1) and *ordinary diligence* under DILIGENCE (2).

common disaster. (1878) An event that causes two or more persons with related property interests (such as an insured and the beneficiary) to die at very nearly the same time, with no way of determining who died first. See UNIFORM SIMULTANEOUS DEATH ACT; COMMORIENTES.

common-disaster clause. (1949) A provision in a dispositive instrument, such as an insurance policy or a will, that seeks to cover the situation in which the transferor and transferee die in a common disaster.

common duty of care. (1887) A landowner's obligation to take reasonable care under the circumstances to see that a lawful visitor will be reasonably safe in using the premises for the purposes for which the visitor is permitted to be there.

common easement. See EASEMENT.

common elements. See COMMON AREA (2).

common-employment doctrine. See FELLOW-SERVANT RULE.

common-enemy doctrine. (1905) *Property.* The rule that a landowner may repel surface waters as necessary (as during a flood), without having to consider the consequences to other landowners. ● The doctrine takes its name from the idea that the floodwater is every landowner's common enemy.

common enterprise. See JOINT ENTERPRISE.

commoner. (17c) **1.** *BrE.* An ordinary citizen; one not a peer. **2.** *Archaic.* A member of the House of Commons. **3.** *Archaic.* A common lawyer. **4.** *Archaic.* A person having a right of common — that is, a right to pasture on a lord's land. **5.** A person who shares a right in common.

common error. (1897) *Copyright.* A mistake found both in a copyrighted work and in an allegedly infringing work, the mistake being persuasive evidence of unauthorized copying.

common external tariff. See TARIFF (2).

common fine. See FINE (4).

common fishery. See FISHERY (2).

common-fund doctrine. The principle that a litigant who creates, discovers, increases, or preserves a fund to which others also have a claim is entitled to recover litigation costs and attorney's fees from that fund. — Also termed *equitable-fund doctrine.*

common gambler. 1. One who owns or is employed by a gambling establishment; a bookmaker. **2.** A professional gambler. ● A person who gambles but not customarily, habitually, or frequently, and who does not rely on gambling for a living, is considered a casual gambler, not a common gambler.

common heritage of mankind. *Int'l law.* The parts of the earth and cosmos that can be said to belong to all humanity, without regard for geographic location, and that should be protected and administered for its benefit. ● The term embraces the ocean floor and its subsoil, and outer space. — Also termed *common heritage of humankind.*

common highway. See HIGHWAY.

common informer. (18c) A person who sues to recover a penalty in a penal action. ● In some jurisdictions, such an action may be instituted either by the attorney general on behalf of the state or by a common informer. See INFORMER; *penal action* under ACTION (4).

common in gross. See COMMON.

common intendment. See INTENDMENT.

common-interest doctrine. See *joint-defense privilege* under PRIVILEGE (3).

common-interest exception. See *joint-defense privilege* under PRIVILEGE (3).

common-interest privilege. See *joint-defense privilege* under PRIVILEGE (3).

common in the soil. See COMMON.

common jury. See *petit jury* under JURY.

common knowledge. (17c) A fact that is so widely known that a court may accept it as true without proof. See JUDICIAL NOTICE.

common-knowledge exception. (1929) The principle that lay testimony concerning routine or simple medical procedures is admissible to establish negligence in a medical-malpractice action. ● This is a narrow exception in some jurisdictions to the rule that a medical-malpractice plaintiff must present expert testimony to establish negligence.

common law, *n.* [fr. Law French *commen ley* "common law"] (14c) **1.** The body of law derived from judicial decisions, rather than from statutes or constitutions; CASELAW <federal common law>. Cf. STATUTORY LAW.

  federal common law. (1855) The body of decisional law derived from federal courts when adjudicating federal questions and other matters of federal concern, such as disputes between the states and foreign relations, but excluding all cases governed by state law. ● An example is the nonstatutory law applying to interstate streams of commerce.

  general federal common law. (1890) *Hist.* In the period before *Erie v. Tompkins* (304 U.S. 64, 58 S.Ct. 817 (1938)), the judge-made law developed by federal courts in deciding disputes in diversity-of-citizenship cases. ● Since *Erie*, a federal court has been bound to apply the substantive law of the state in which it sits. So even though there is a "federal common law," there is no longer a *general* federal common law applicable to all disputes heard in federal court.

2. The body of law based on the English legal system, as distinct from a civil-law system; the general Anglo-American system of legal concepts, together with the techniques of applying them, that form the basis of the law in jurisdictions where the system applies <all states except Louisiana have the common law as their legal system>. Cf. CIVIL LAW (1).

  American common law. **1.** The body of English law that was adopted as the law of the American colonies and supplemented with local enactments and judgments. **2.** The body of judge-made law that developed during and after the United States' colonial period, esp. since independence. — Also termed *Anglo-American common law*. **3.** General law common to the country as a whole, as opposed to special law that has only local application <the issue is whether the common law trumps our jurisdiction's local rules>. — Also termed *jus commune*. **4.** The body of law deriving from law courts as opposed to those sitting in equity <a mortgage founded in common law>. ● The common law of England was one of the three main historical sources of English law. The other two were legislation and equity. The common law evolved from custom and was the body of law created by and administered by the king's courts. Equity developed to overcome the occasional rigidity and unfairness of the common law. Originally the king himself granted or denied petitions in equity; later the task fell to the chancellor, and later still to the Court of Chancery.

common-law action. See ACTION (4).

common-law assignment. See ASSIGNMENT (2).

common-law bond. See BOND (2).

common-law cheat. See CHEATING.

common-law contempt. See *criminal contempt* under CONTEMPT.

common-law copyright. See COPYRIGHT.

common-law corporation. See *corporation by prescription* under CORPORATION.

common-law crime. See CRIME.

common-law dedication. See DEDICATION.

common-law extortion. See EXTORTION (1).

common-law fraud. See *promissory fraud* under FRAUD.

common-law husband. See HUSBAND.

common-law jurisdiction. See JURISDICTION.

common-law lawyer. (19c) A lawyer who is versed in or practices under a common-law system. — Also termed *common lawyer* (16c).

common-law lien. See LIEN.

common-law malice. See *actual malice* (2) under MALICE.

common-law marriage. See MARRIAGE (1).

common-law mortgage. See *deed of trust* under DEED.

common-law pleading. See PLEADING (2).

common-law-property state. See COMMON-LAW STATE (2).

common-law rule. (17c) **1.** A judge-made rule as opposed to a statutory one. **2.** A legal as opposed to an equitable rule. **3.** A general rule as opposed to one deriving from special law (such as a local custom or a rule of foreign law that, based on

choice-of-law principles, is applied in place of domestic law). **4.** An old rule of English law.

common-law seal. See SEAL (1).

common-law specialty. See *contract under seal* under CONTRACT; SPECIALTY (1).

common-law state. (1848) **1.** NONCODE STATE. **2.** Any state that has not adopted a community-property regime. ● The chief difference today between a community-property state and a common-law state is that in a common-law state, a spouse's interest in property held by the other spouse does not vest until (1) a divorce action has been filed, or (2) the other spouse has died. Cf. COMMUNITY-PROPERTY STATE.

common-law trust. See *business trust* under TRUST (4).

common-law wife. See WIFE.

common lawyer. See COMMON-LAW LAWYER.

common market. See MARKET.

Common Market. The European Economic Community. ● *Common Market* is a colloquial term — not a formal designation. See EUROPEAN UNION.

common mistake. See *mutual mistake* (2) under MISTAKE.

common money bond. See BOND (2).

common-nucleus-of-operative-fact test. (1966) The doctrine that a federal court will have pendent jurisdiction over state-law claims that arise from the same facts as the federal claims providing a basis for subject-matter jurisdiction. ● One purpose of this test is to promote judicial economy.

common nuisance. See *public nuisance* under NUISANCE.

common occupant. See *general occupant* under OCCUPANT.

common of digging. See *common in the soil* under COMMON.

common of estovers. See COMMON.

common of fishery. See *common of piscary* under COMMON.

common of pasture. See COMMON.

common of piscary. See COMMON.

common of shack. See COMMON.

common of turbary. See COMMON.

common order. See *conditional judgment* under JUDGMENT.

common parliamentary law. See PARLIAMENTARY LAW.

common plan. See COMMON DESIGN.

common plea. See PLEA (3).

Common Pleas, Court of. See COURT OF COMMON PLEAS.

common property. See PROPERTY.

common recovery. *Hist.* An elaborate proceeding, full of legal fictions, by which a tenant in tail disentailed a fee-tail estate. • The action facilitated land transfer by allowing a potential transferee who was barred by law from receiving land to "recover" the land by suing the actual owner. Common recoveries, which were abolished early in the 19th century, were originally concocted by the clergy as a way to avoid the land-conveyance restrictions imposed by mortmain acts. — Also termed *feigned recovery*. See MORTMAIN STATUTE.

common-return days. See *dies communes in banco* (1) under DIES.

common scheme. See COMMON DESIGN.

common school. See *public school* under SCHOOL.

common scold. See SCOLD.

common-situs picketing. See PICKETING.

common-source doctrine. (1938) The principle that a defendant in a trespass-to-try-title action who claims under a source common to both the defendant and the plaintiff may not demonstrate title in a third source that is paramount to the common source because doing so amounts to an attack on the source under which the defendant claims title.

common stock. See STOCK.

common-stock equivalent. A security that is exchangeable for common stock, and thus is considered to be the same as common stock. • Common-stock equivalents include certain types of convertible securities, stock options, and warrants.

common-stock fund. See MUTUAL FUND.

common-stock ratio. The relationship of outstanding common stock to the corporation's total capitalization. • The common-stock ratio measures the relative claims of stockholders to earnings (earnings per share and payout ratio), cash flow (cash flow per share), and equity (book value per share). Cf. PAYOUT RATIO.

common substitution. See SUBSTITUTION (4).

common suit. See *common plea* (1) under PLEA (3).

common tenancy. See *tenancy in common* under TENANCY.

common thief. See THIEF.

common traverse. See TRAVERSE.

common trust fund. See TRUST FUND.

common venture. See *common adventure* under ADVENTURE.

common wall. See *party wall* under WALL.

commonweal (kom-ən-weel). The general welfare; the common good.

commonwealth. (15c) **1.** A nation, state, or other political unit <the Commonwealth of Pennsylvania>. **2.** A political unit that has local autonomy but is voluntarily united with the United States <Puerto Rico and the Northern Mariana Islands are commonwealths>. Cf. DEPENDENCY (1); INSULAR AREA; TERRITORY (2). **3.** A loose association of countries that recognize one sovereign <the British Commonwealth>. • In this context, in Great Britain, the term *British* has been dropped from *British Commonwealth*; BrE speakers refer simply to *the Commonwealth*. — Abbr. Commw.; comm. **4.** The central (federal) power in Australia. — Abbr. (in sense 4) Cwth.

commonwealth attorney. A prosecutor in some jurisdictions, such as Virginia.

commonwealth court. See COURT.

common without stint. See COMMON.

commorancy (kom-ə-rən-see). **1.** Temporary residency. **2.** *English law.* Permanent residency in a certain place.

commorant (kom-ə-rənt). **1.** A person who dwells in a place temporarily. **2.** *English law.* A person who resides permanently in a certain place.

commorientes (kə-mor-ee-en-teez). (18c) [fr. Latin *commorior* "to die together"] **1.** (*pl.*) Persons who die at the same time, often of the same cause, such as spouses who die in an accident. **2.** *Civil law.* The rule establishing presumptions of survivorship for purposes of succession regarding such persons. See *simultaneous death* under DEATH; UNIFORM SIMULTANEOUS DEATH ACT.

commotion. See CIVIL COMMOTION.

commune (kom-yoon), *n.* (17c) A community of people who share property and responsibilities.

communication. (14c) **1.** The expression or exchange of information by speech, writing, gestures, or conduct; the process of bringing an idea to another's perception. **2.** The information so expressed or exchanged.

conditionally privileged communication. (1889) A defamatory statement made in good faith by a person with an interest in a subject to someone who also has an interest in the subject, as an employer giving a negative but accurate job review of a former employee to a potential future employer. • The privilege may be lost upon a showing of malice or bad faith.

confidential communication. (18c) A communication made within a certain protected relationship and legally protected from compelled disclosure in a legal proceeding. • Among confidential communications are those between husband and wife, attorney and client, and priest and penitent. See PRIVILEGE (3).

ex parte communication. (1804) A communication between counsel and the court when opposing counsel is not present. • Such communications are ordinarily prohibited.

privileged communication. (1809) A communication that is protected by law from compelled disclosure in a legal proceeding, or that cannot be used against the person who made it. • Examples include an informant's communication to a government agency and statements made in a legislative session by a legislator. See PRIVILEGE (3).

communication right. *Copyright.* The power of a copyright owner to authorize or prohibit the transmission of a work to the public by way of interactive on-demand systems such as the Internet. • This right is included in the WIPO Copyright Treaty and the European Commission's Directive on the Information Society.

communicative evidence. See *testimonial evidence* under EVIDENCE.

communism. (19c) **1.** A political doctrine, based on Marxism, advocating the abolition of capitalism by ground-roots revolution; specif., a social and political doctrine advocating the abolition of private ownership in favor of common ownership of the means of production and the goods produced, each person contributing as able and receiving as needed. Cf. CAPITALISM. **2.** Totalitarian government.

communitization (kə-myoo-nə-tə-**zay**-shən), *n. Oil & gas.* The aggregating of small tracts sufficient for the granting of a well permit under applicable well-spacing rules; POOLING. Cf. UNITIZATION. — **communitize** (kə-**myoo**-nə-tız), *vb.*

community. (14c) **1.** A neighborhood, vicinity, or locality. **2.** A society or group of people with similar rights or interests. **3.** Joint ownership, possession, or participation.

community account. See ACCOUNT.

community control. A criminal sentence whose terms include intensive and strict supervision of an offender in the community, as by restricting the offender's movements and activities and conducting electronic surveillance, and providing severe sanctions for violations of any of the sentence's terms.

community correctional center. See JAIL.

community debt. See DEBT.

Community Development Financial Institution Fund. A fund in the U.S. Department of the Treasury created to expand available credit, investment capital, and financial services in distressed urban and rural communities. — Abbr. CDFI Fund.

community estate. In a community-property state, the total of the assets and debts making up

a married couple's property owned in common. Cf. COMMUNITY PROPERTY.

community grant. See GRANT.

community lease. See LEASE.

Community mark. See *Community trademark* under TRADEMARK.

community-notification law. See MEGAN'S LAW.

community obligation. See OBLIGATION.

community of interest. (17c) **1.** Participation in a joint venture characterized by shared liability and shared opportunity for profit. See JOINT VENTURE. **2.** A common grievance that must be shared by all class members to maintain the class action. See CLASS ACTION. **3.** *Labor law.* A criterion used by the National Labor Relations Board in deciding whether a group of employees should be allowed to act as a bargaining unit. • The Board considers whether the employees have similar duties, wages, hours, benefits, skills, training, supervision, and working conditions. See BARGAINING UNIT.

community of profits. The right of partners to share in the partnership's profits.

Community patent. See PATENT (3).

Community Patent Convention. A 1975 treaty that, for patent purposes, treats the European Union as a single state and allows a patent applicant to obtain patent protection in all European Union nations through a single blanket filing and examination procedure. • If the application is approved, the European Patent Office issues a single Community patent. The treaty's full name is the Convention for the European Patent for the Common Market.

community policing. (1969) A law-enforcement technique in which police officers are assigned to a particular neighborhood or area to develop relationships with the residents for the purpose of enhancing the chances of detecting and thwarting criminal activity.

community property. (1820) Assets owned in common by husband and wife as a result of its having been acquired during the marriage by means other than an inheritance or a gift to one spouse, each spouse generally holding a one-half interest in the property. • Only nine states have community-property systems: Arizona, California, Idaho, Louisiana, Nevada, New Mexico, Texas, Washington, and Wisconsin. See *marital property* under PROPERTY; TITLE DIVISION. Cf. COMMUNITY ESTATE; SEPARATE PROPERTY.

quasi-community property. Personal property that, having been acquired in a non-community-property state, would have been community property if acquired in a community-property state. • If a community-property state is the forum for a divorce or administration of a decedent's estate, state law may allow the court to treat quasi-community property as if it were community property when it determines the spouses' interests.

community-property state. (1907) A state in which spouses hold property that is acquired during marriage (other than property acquired by inheritance or individual gift) as community property. See COMMUNITY PROPERTY. Cf. COMMON-LAW STATE (2).

community service. Socially valuable work performed without pay. • Community service is often required as part of a criminal sentence, esp. one that does not include incarceration.

Community trademark. See TRADEMARK.

Community Trademark Treaty. A 1996 agreement allowing a trademark registrant to file a single application with the European Trademark Office for trademark protection in all European Union nations instead of filing a separate application in each country. • The trademark registrant does not have to be a citizen of a member nation to file an application.

community trust. An agency organized to administer funds placed in trust for public-health, educational, and other charitable purposes in perpetuity.

commutation (kom-yə-**tay**-shən), *n.* (15c) **1.** An exchange or replacement. **2.** *Criminal law.* The executive's substitution in a particular case of a less severe punishment for a more severe one that has already been judicially imposed on the defendant. Cf. PARDON; REPRIEVE. • Commutation may be based on the discovery of pertinent facts that were not known or available when the sentenced was decided, or that arose and were developed afterward. It may also be based on the executive's statutorily or constitutionally granted discretion, regardless of the facts. Under § 1–2.113 of the US DOJ Manual, commutation is rarely granted but may be considered for old age, illness, disparity, or undue severity of sentence. **3.** *Commercial & civil law.* The substitution of one form of payment for another. — **commute,** *vb.* — **commutative,** *adj.*

commutation of payments. *Workers' compensation.* A substitution of lump-sum compensation for periodic payments. • The lump sum is equal to the present value of the future periodic payments.

commutation of taxes. A tax exemption resulting from a taxpayer's paying either a lump sum or a specific sum in lieu of an ad valorem tax.

commutation tax. See TAX.

commutative contract. See CONTRACT.

commutative justice. See JUSTICE (1).

commuted value. See VALUE (2).

Commw. *abbr.* COMMONWEALTH.

compact (**kom**-pakt), *n.* (14c) An agreement or covenant between two or more parties, esp. between governments or states.

family compact. An agreement to further common interests made between related people or within a group that behaves as a family. • Historically, some international treaties among nations ruled by monarchs have been called family compacts because of intermarriage among the royal houses.

interstate compact. (1903) A voluntary agreement between states enacted into law in the participating states upon federal congressional approval. Cf. INTERSTATE AGREEMENT.

Compact Clause. (1925) U.S. Const. art. I, § 10, cl. 3, which forbids a state from entering into a contract with another state or a foreign country without congressional approval.

companion bill. See BILL (3).

companionship services. Assistance provided to someone who needs help with personal matters such as bathing and dressing. • This type of service (in contrast to housecleaning) is exempt from the Federal Labor Standards Act's minimum-wage and overtime requirements.

company. (13c) **1.** A corporation — or, less commonly, an association, partnership, or union — that carries on a commercial or industrial enterprise. **2.** A corporation, partnership, association, joint-stock company, trust, fund, or organized group of persons, whether incorporated or not, and (in an official capacity) any receiver, trustee in bankruptcy, or similar official, or liquidating agent, for any of the foregoing. Investment Company Act § 2(a)(8) (15 USCA § 80a-2(a)(8)). — Abbr. co.; com.

bonding company. A company that insures a party against a loss caused by a third party.

controlled company. A company that is under the control of an individual, group, or corporation that owns most of the company's voting stock. Cf. *subsidiary corporation* under CORPORATION.

dead-and-buried company. A business that has dissolved, leaving no assets.

deposit company. An institution whose business is the safekeeping of securities or other valuables deposited in boxes or safes leased to the depositors. See DEPOSITARY; DEPOSITORY.

development-stage company. *Securities.* A company that devotes substantially all of its efforts to establishing a new business in which the principal operations either have not yet begun or have begun but are not generating significant revenue.

diversified holding company. A holding company that controls several unrelated companies or businesses.

diversified investment company. An investment company that by law must invest 75% of its assets, but may not invest more than 5% of its assets in any one company or hold more than 10% of the voting shares in any one company.

face-amount certificate company. An investment company that is engaged or proposes to engage in the business of issuing face-amount certificates of the installment type, or that has been engaged in this business and has such a certificate outstanding. See *investment company.*

growth company. A company whose earnings have increased at a rapid pace and that usu. directs a high proportion of income back into the business.

guaranty company. See *surety company.*

holding company. (1906) A company formed to control other companies, usu. confining its role to owning stock and supervising management. • It does not participate in making day-to-day business decisions in those companies.

investment company. A company formed to acquire and manage a portfolio of diverse assets by investing money collected from different sources. • The Investment Company Act of 1940 defines the term as an issuer of securities that (1) is, holds itself out to be, or proposes to be engaged primarily in the business of investing, reinvesting, or trading in securities; (2) is engaged or proposes to engage in the business of issuing face-amount certificates of the installment type, or has been engaged in this business and has such a certificate outstanding; or (3) is engaged or proposes to engage in the business of investing, reinvesting, owning, holding, or trading in securities, and owns or proposes to acquire investment securities having a value exceeding 40% of the value of the issuer's total assets (exclusive of government securities and cash items) on an unconsolidated basis. 15 USCA § 80a-2(a)(16). — Also termed *investment trust.* See REAL-ESTATE INVESTMENT TRUST; MUTUAL FUND.

joint-stock company. (18c) **1.** An unincorporated association of individuals possessing common capital, the capital being contributed by the members and divided into shares, of which each member possesses a number of shares proportionate to the member's investment. **2.** A partnership in which the capital is divided into shares that are transferable without the express consent of the partners. — Also termed *joint-stock association; stock association.*

limited company. (1862) A company in which the liability of each shareholder is limited to the amount individually invested. • A corporation is the most common example of a limited company.

limited-liability company. (1856) A company — statutorily authorized in certain states — that is characterized by limited liability, management by members or managers, and limitations on ownership transfer. — Abbr. L.L.C. — Also termed *limited-liability corporation.*

management company. Any investment company that is neither a face-amount certificate company nor a unit-investment trust. See *investment company; face-amount certificate company; unit-investment trust* under TRUST.

mutual company. A company that is owned by its customers rather than by a separate group of stockholders. • Many insurance companies are mutual companies, as are many federal savings-and-loan associations. See MUTUAL INSURANCE COMPANY.

parent company. See *parent corporation* under CORPORATION.

personal holding company. (1924) A holding company that is subject to special taxes and that usu. has a limited number of shareholders, with most of its revenue originating from passive income such as dividends, interest, rent, and royalties.

railroad company. See *railroad corporation* under CORPORATION.

reporting company. A company that, because it issues publicly traded securities, must comply with the reporting requirements of the Securities Exchange Act of 1934.

safe-deposit company. See DEPOSITARY (1).

shelf company. A company that is formed without a particular purpose and may not actually operate until some purpose for its existence arises, usu. when sold to a buyer. • After being formed, shelf companies are usu. allowed to age before being offered for sale. The benefits of a shelf company to a buyer include time saved by not having to form a company, the appearance of longevity, and easier access to credit. If the company is incorporated, it is also termed a *shelf corporation.*

small-business investment company. See SMALL-BUSINESS INVESTMENT COMPANY.

surety company. A company authorized to engage in the business of entering into guaranty and suretyship contracts and acting as a surety on bonds, esp. bail, fidelity, and judicial bonds. — Also termed *guaranty company.*

title company. (1892) A company that examines real-estate titles for any encumbrances, claims, or other flaws, and issues title insurance. —

Also termed *title-guaranty company*. See TITLE SEARCH.

trust company. (1834) A company that acts as a trustee for people and entities and that sometimes also operates as a commercial bank. — Also termed (if incorporated) *trust corporation*. See TITLE (1), (2).

company-run dividend-reinvestment plan. See DIVIDEND-REINVESTMENT PLAN.

company's paper. See *commercial paper* under PAPER.

company union. See UNION.

comparable (kom-pər-ə-bəl), *n.* (19c) (*usu. pl.*) A piece of property used as a comparison to determine the value of a similar piece of property. — **comparable,** *adj.*

comparable accommodation. A standard used for determining the maximum allowable rent in rent-regulated housing. • In applying this standard, a court reviews the prevailing rent for substantially similar housing units in the same area.

comparable-sales approach. See MARKET APPROACH.

comparables analysis. See MARKET APPROACH.

comparable worth. (1983) **1.** The analogous value that two or more employees bring to a business through their work. **2.** The idea that employees who perform identical work should receive identical pay, regardless of their sex; the doctrine that men and women who perform work of equal value should receive comparable pay.

comparatist. A comparative-law scholar.

comparative advertising. See ADVERTISING.

comparative criminology. See CRIMINOLOGY.

comparative disparity. (1977) *Constitutional law.* The percentage of underrepresentation of a particular group among potential jurors on a venire, in comparison with the group's percentage of the general population. • Comparative disparity is calculated by subtracting a group's percentage of representation on the venire from the group's percentage of the population — that is, calculating the group's absolute-disparity representation — then dividing that percentage by the group's percentage-representation in the population, and multiplying the result by 100. For example, if African-Americans make up 12% of a county's population, and 8% of the potential jurors on the venire, the absolute disparity of African-Americans is 4%. And the comparative disparity is 33%, because 4 divided by 12 is .33, or 33%. Many courts criticize the comparative-disparity analysis, and favor an absolute-disparity analysis, because the comparative-disparity analysis is said to exaggerate the deviation. The reason for calculating the disparity is to analyze a claim that the jury

was not impartial because it was not selected from a pool of jurors that fairly represented the makeup of the jurisdiction. See DUREN TEST; FAIR-CROSS-SECTION REQUIREMENT; STATISTICAL-DECISION THEORY. Cf. ABSOLUTE DISPARITY.

comparative fault. See *comparative negligence* under NEGLIGENCE.

comparative history of law. See *descriptive comparative law* under COMPARATIVE LAW.

comparative-impairment test. (1974) *Conflict of laws.* A test that asks which of two or more forums would have its policies most impaired by not having its law applied in the case.

comparative interpretation. See INTERPRETATION.

comparative jurisprudence. See COMPARATIVE LAW.

comparative law. The scholarly study of the similarities and differences between the legal systems of different jurisdictions, such as between civil-law and common-law countries. — Also termed *comparative jurisprudence*. See INTERNATIONAL LAW.

    descriptive comparative law. The inventory of legal systems (past and present) as a whole, as well as of individual rules that these systems establish for several categories of legal relations. • Descriptive comparative law is sometimes considered one of three subsets of comparative law, the other two being comparative legislation and comparative history of law. See COMPARATIVE LEGISLATION; COMPARATIVE LEGAL HISTORY.

comparative legal history. A species of comparative law seeking to establish a universal history of law, so that the succession of social phenomena influencing the evolution of the legal world might be better understood. • This field is closely allied to ethnological jurisprudence, folklore, legal sociology, and jurisprudence. — Also termed *comparative history of law*. Cf. *descriptive comparative law* under COMPARATIVE LAW; COMPARATIVE LEGISLATION.

comparative legislation. A species of comparative law seeking to define the common link for modern statutory doctrines, concerned with the development of legal study as a social science and with awakening an international legal consciousness. Cf. *descriptive comparative law* under COMPARATIVE LAW; COMPARATIVE LEGAL HISTORY.

comparative negligence. See NEGLIGENCE.

comparative-negligence doctrine. (1904) *Torts.* The principle that reduces a plaintiff's recovery proportionally to the plaintiff's degree of fault in causing the damage, rather than barring recovery completely. • Most states have statutorily adopted the comparative-negligence doctrine. See

NEGLIGENCE. Cf. CONTRIBUTORY-NEGLIGENCE DOCTRINE.

comparative nomogenetics. The study of the development of the world's legal ideas and systems. • This term, like *comparative nomoscopy* and *comparative nomothetics*, was devised by John Henry Wigmore. *See* John Henry Wigmore, *A Panorama of the World's Legal Systems* 1121 (libr. ed. 1936).

comparative nomoscopy. The description of the world's legal systems.

comparative nomothetics. The analysis of the merits of legal systems.

comparative rectitude. (1913) *Archaic. Family law.* The degree to which one spouse is less culpable than the other in damaging the marriage, so that even though both spouses are at fault, the less culpable spouse may successfully petition for a separation or divorce. • Comparative rectitude tempers the doctrine of recrimination by making a divorce possible even though both parties are at fault. Comparative rectitude is now virtually obsolete because of the prevalence of no-fault divorce. See RECRIMINATION (1).

comparative-sales approach. See MARKET APPROACH.

comparator (kəm-**par**-ə-tər *or* kom-pə-**ray**-tər). Something with which something else is compared <the female plaintiffs alleged illegal wage discrimination and contrasted their pay with that of male comparators>.

compassing (**kəm**-pə-sing). *Hist.* The act of contriving or plotting, esp. of something underhanded. • The Treason Act of 1351 criminalized the act of compassing the sovereign's death. — Also termed *imagining*.

compel, *vb.* (14c) **1.** To cause or bring about by force, threats, or overwhelming pressure <a lawyer cannot be compelled to testify about a privileged communication>. **2.** (Of a legislative mandate or judicial precedent) to convince (a court) that there is only one possible resolution of a legal dispute <the wording of the statute compels us to affirm>.

compellable, *adj.* Capable of or subject to being compelled, esp. to testify <an accused person's spouse is not a compellable witness for the prosecution>.

compelling need. A need so great that irreparable harm or injustice would result if it is not met. • Generally, courts decide whether a compelling need is present based on the unique facts of each case. In some jurisdictions, however, statutes define "compelling need" or provide guidelines for determining whether one exists. See, e.g., 5 USCA § 552(a)(6)(E)(v) (defining "compelling need" for an expedited response to a Freedom of Information Act request).

compelling-state-interest test. (1966) *Constitutional law.* A method for determining the constitutional validity of a law, whereby the government's interest in the law and its purpose is balanced against an individual's constitutional right that is affected by the law. • Only if the government's interest is strong enough will the law be upheld. The compelling-state-interest test is used, e.g., in equal-protection analysis when the disputed law requires strict scrutiny. See STRICT SCRUTINY.

compensable (kəm-**pen**-sə-bəl), *adj.* (17c) Able or entitled to be compensated for <a compensable injury>. — Also termed *recompensable*.

compensable death. See DEATH.

compensable injury. See INJURY.

compensate (**kom**-pən-sayt), *vb.* **1.** To pay (another) for services rendered <the lawyer was fairly compensated for her time and effort>. **2.** To make an amendatory payment to; to recompense (for an injury) <the court ordered the defendant to compensate the injured plaintiff>.

compensated surety. See SURETY.

compensating balance. The amount of money a borrower from a bank is required to keep on deposit as a condition for a loan or a line of credit.

compensation (kom-pən-**say**-shən), *n.* (14c) **1.** Remuneration and other benefits received in return for services rendered; esp., salary or wages. **2.** Payment of damages, or any other act that a court orders to be done by a person who has caused injury to another. • In theory, compensation makes the injured person whole. **3.** SETOFF (2). — **compensatory,** (kəm-**pen**-sə-tor-ee), **compensational** (kom-pən-**say**-shə-nəl), *adj.*

accrued compensation. (1919) Remuneration that has been earned but not yet paid.

adequate compensation. See *just compensation.*

deferred compensation. (1926) **1.** Payment for work performed, to be paid in the future or when some future event occurs. **2.** An employee's earnings that are taxed when received or distributed rather than when earned, such as contributions to a qualified pension or profit-sharing plan.

just compensation. (16c) Under the Fifth Amendment, a payment by the government for property it has taken under eminent domain — usu. the property's fair market value, so that the owner is theoretically no worse off after the taking. — Also termed *adequate compensation; due compensation; land damages.*

unemployment compensation. Compensation paid at regular intervals by a state agency to an unemployed person, esp. one who has been laid off. — Also termed *unemployment insurance.*

unreasonable compensation. (1946) *Tax.* Compensation that is not deductible as a business expense because the compensation is out of proportion to the services actually rendered or because it exceeds statutorily defined limits. IRC (26 USCA) § 162.

Compensation Clause. The clause of the U.S. Constitution providing for federal judges to be paid. U.S. Const. art. III, § 1, cl. 2.

compensation period. The time fixed by unemployment or workers'-compensation law during which an unemployed or injured worker is entitled to receive compensation.

compensatories. See *compensatory damages* (1) under DAMAGES.

compensatory damages. See DAMAGES.

compensatory payment. *Family law.* A postmarital spousal payment made by the richer ex-spouse to the poorer one and treated as an entitlement rather than as a discretionary award. ● Compensatory payments are set by statute and are based on a formula using the length of the marriage, differences in postdivorce income, role as primary caregiver, and other factors. The purpose is to compensate somewhat for disparate income levels after a failed marriage. Cf. ALIMONY.

compensatory time. See COMP TIME.

competence, *n.* (17c) **1.** A basic or minimal ability to do something; qualification, esp. to testify <competence of a witness>. **2.** The capacity of an official body to do something <the court's competence to enter a valid judgment>. **3.** Authenticity <the documents were supported by a business-records affidavit, leaving their competence as evidence beyond doubt>. Cf. COMPETENCY. — **competent,** *adj.*

competency, *n.* (16c) **1.** The mental ability to understand problems and make decisions. **2.** A criminal defendant's ability to stand trial, measured by the capacity to understand the proceedings, to consult meaningfully with counsel, and to assist in the defense. — Also termed *competency to stand trial.* Cf. COMPETENCE. — **competent,** *adj.*

competency hearing. See PATE HEARING.

competency proceeding. See PROCEEDING.

competency to stand trial. See COMPETENCY.

competent contractor. See CONTRACTOR.

competent court. See *court of competent jurisdiction* under COURT.

competent evidence. See EVIDENCE.

competent jurisdiction. See JURISDICTION (2).

competent witness. See WITNESS.

competition. (16c) The struggle for commercial advantage; the effort or action of two or more commercial interests to obtain the same business from third parties.

fair competition. (17c) Open, equitable, and just competition between business competitors.

horizontal competition. (1930) Competition between a seller and its competitors. ● The Sherman Antitrust Act prohibits unreasonable restraints on horizontal competition, such as price-fixing agreements between competitors. — Also termed *primary-line competition.*

perfect competition. A completely efficient market situation characterized by numerous buyers and sellers, a homogeneous product, perfect information for all parties, and complete freedom to move in and out of the market. ● Perfect competition rarely if ever exists, but antitrust scholars often use the theory as a standard for measuring market performance.

primary-line competition. See *horizontal competition.*

vertical competition. (1954) Competition between participants at different levels of distribution, such as manufacturer and distributor. — Also termed *secondary-line competition.*

competitive advantage. The potential benefit from information, ideas, or devices that, if kept secret by a business, might be economically exploited to improve the business's market share or to increase its income.

competitive advertising. See ADVERTISING.

competitive bid. See BID (2).

competitive civil-service examination. A test designed to evaluate a person's qualifications for a civil-service position. ● This type of examination may be open to all those seeking civil-service employment, or it may be restricted to those civil servants seeking a promotion. See CIVIL SERVICE.

competitive injury. A wrongful economic loss caused by a commercial rival, such as the loss of sales due to unfair competition; a disadvantage in a plaintiff's ability to compete with a defendant, caused by the defendant's unfair competition. ● Most courts require the plaintiff to show a competitive injury as an element of a misappropriation action, or to have standing to prosecute a false-advertising action under 15 USCA § 1125(a) (1)(B). — Also termed *competitive harm.*

competitor click fraud. See FRAUD.

compilation (kom-pə-**lay**-shən), *n.* (15c) **1.** *Copyright.* A collection of literary works arranged in an original way; esp., a work formed by collecting and assembling preexisting materials or data that are selected, coordinated, or arranged in such a way that the resulting product constitutes an original work of authorship. ● An author who creates a compilation owns the copyright of the compilation but not of the component parts. See

17 USCA § 101. Cf. *collective work, derivative work* under WORK (2). **2.** A collection of statutes, updated and arranged to facilitate their use. — Also termed *compiled statutes.* **3.** A financial statement that does not have an accountant's assurance of conformity with generally accepted accounting principles. • In preparing a compilation, an accountant does not gather evidence or verify the accuracy of the information provided by the client; rather, the accountant reviews the compiled reports to ensure that they are in the appropriate form and are free of obvious errors. — **compile,** *vb.*

compiled statutes. 1. See COMPILATION (2). **2.** See STATUTE.

complainant (kəm-**playn**-ənt). (15c) **1.** The party who brings a legal complaint against another; esp., the plaintiff in a court of equity or, more modernly, a civil suit. **2.** A person who, under oath, signs a statement (called a "complaint") establishing reasonable grounds to believe that some named person has committed a crime. — Also termed *affiant.*

complainantless crime. See *victimless crime* under CRIME.

complaint. (14c) **1.** The initial pleading that starts a civil action and states the basis for the court's jurisdiction, the basis for the plaintiff's claim, and the demand for relief. • In some states, this pleading is called a *petition.* **2.** *Criminal law.* A formal charge accusing a person of an offense. Fed. R. Crim. P. 3. Cf. INDICTMENT; INFORMATION.

> **amended complaint.** (1822) A complaint that modifies and replaces the original complaint by adding relevant matters that occurred before or at the time the action began. Fed. R. Civ. P. 15(d). • In some circumstances, a party must obtain the court's permission to amend its complaint. Fed. R. Civ. Pro. 15(a). — Also termed *substituted complaint.* Cf. *supplemental complaint.*

> **complaint for modification.** See *motion to modify* under MOTION.

> **counter-complaint.** A complaint filed by a defendant against the plaintiff, alleging that the plaintiff has committed a breach and is liable to the defendant for damages.

> **fresh complaint.** See FRESH COMPLAINT.

> **preliminary complaint.** (1833) A complaint issued by a court to obtain jurisdiction over a criminal suspect for a hearing on probable cause or on whether to bind the suspect over for trial.

> **substituted complaint.** See *amended complaint.*

> **supplemental complaint.** (1821) An additional complaint that either corrects a defect in the original complaint or adds relevant matters that occurred after the action began. • Generally, a party must obtain the court's permission to file a supplemental complaint. Fed. R. Civ. Pro. 15(d). Cf. *amended complaint.*

> **third-party complaint.** (1938) A complaint filed by the defendant against a third party, alleging that the third party may be liable for some or all of the damages that the plaintiff is trying to recover from the defendant. Fed. R. Civ. P. 14.

> **well-pleaded complaint.** (1954) An original or initial pleading that sufficiently sets forth a claim for relief — by including the grounds for the court's jurisdiction, the basis for the relief claimed, and a demand for judgment — so that a defendant may draft an answer that is responsive to the issues presented. • In federal court, a well-pleaded complaint must raise a controlling issue of federal law, or else the court will not have federal-question jurisdiction over the lawsuit.

complementarity, *n.* **1.** The state or quality of being complementary. **2.** *International law.* See COMPLEMENTARITY PRINCIPLE.

complementarity principle. *International law.* The doctrine that a country with control of a person accused of violating international criminal law has the jurisdiction to charge and try a person. • Because the jurisdiction of the International Criminal Court is complementary to the criminal jurisdiction of countries, that tribunal can assert jurisdiction over the accused person only if the country is unable or unwilling to undertake a genuine investigation and prosecution. — Sometimes shortened to *complementarity.*

complementary goods. *Trademarks.* Products that are typically used together, such as pancake syrup and pancake mix, or motion-picture projectors and film. • Trademark law may prevent the use of a similar mark on complementary goods because consumers may be confused into thinking the goods come from a common source. The patent-misuse doctrine may provide a defense in an infringement suit if the plaintiff has used its patent rights to gain market control over unpatented complementary goods. — Also termed *complementary products.* See AUNT JEMIMA DOCTRINE; PATENT-MISUSE DOCTRINE.

complementary products. See COMPLEMENTARY GOODS.

complete conception of invention. See CONCEPTION OF INVENTION.

completed-contract accounting method. See ACCOUNTING METHOD.

completed gift. See GIFT.

complete diversity. See DIVERSITY OF CITIZENSHIP.

completed-operations policy. See INSURANCE POLICY.

complete in itself, *adj.* (18c) (Of a legislative act) fully covering an entire subject.

complete integration. See INTEGRATION (2).

complete interdiction. See *full interdiction* under INTERDICTION (3).

complete jurisdiction. See JURISDICTION.

completely integrated contract. See INTEGRATED CONTRACT.

completeness doctrine. See RULE OF OPTIONAL COMPLETENESS.

complete-operation rule. *Insurance.* The principle that goods are covered against damage at any time during the shipping process, including the loading and unloading of the goods. • Under some circumstances, the rule has been extended to cover personal injuries that occur during the shipping process. See WAREHOUSE-TO-WAREHOUSE COVER. Cf. COMING-TO-REST DOCTRINE.

complete ownership. See *perfect ownership* under OWNERSHIP.

complete-preemption doctrine. (1987) The rule that a federal statute's preemptive force may be so extraordinary and all-encompassing that it converts an ordinary state-common-law complaint into one stating a federal claim for purposes of the well-pleaded-complaint rule. See *well-pleaded complaint* under COMPLAINT.

complete property. See PROPERTY.

complete voluntary trust. See *executed trust* under TRUST.

completion bond. See PERFORMANCE BOND.

complex litigation. See LITIGATION.

complex trust. See TRUST.

compliance audit. See AUDIT.

complicated larceny. See *mixed larceny* under LARCENY.

complice (**kom**-plis). *Archaic.* An accomplice or accessory to a crime or immoral behavior.

complicity (kəm-**plis**-ə-tee), *n.* (17c) Association or participation in a criminal act; the act or state of being an accomplice. • Under the Model Penal Code, a person can be an accomplice as a result of either that person's own conduct or the conduct of another (such as an innocent agent) for which that person is legally accountable. Model Penal Code § 2.06. See ACCOMPLICE; *innocent agent* under AGENT. — **complicitous** (kəm-**plis**-ə-təs), *adj.*

composite mark. See *composite trademark* under TRADEMARK.

composite state. See STATE.

composite trademark. See TRADEMARK.

composite work. See WORK (2).

composition, *n.* (14c) **1.** An agreement between a debtor and two or more creditors for the adjustment or discharge of an obligation for some lesser amount; an agreement among the debtor and two or more creditors that the debtor will pay the creditors less than their full claims in full satisfaction of their claims. • The preexisting-duty rule is not a defense to this type of agreement because consideration arises from the agreement by each creditor with each other to take less than full payment. Through the performance of this agreement, the debtor is discharged in full for the debts of the participating creditors. — Also termed *composition with creditors*; *creditors' composition*; *attermoiement.* **2.** The compensation paid as part of such an agreement. **3.** *Hist.* A payment of money or chattels as satisfaction for an injury. • In Anglo-Saxon and other early societies, a *composition* with the injured party was recognized as a way to deter acts of revenge by the injured party. — **compose,** *vb.*

composition deed. See DEED.

composition of matter. *Patents.* One of the five types of patentable statutory subject matter, consisting of combinations of natural elements whether resulting from chemical union or from mechanical mixture, and whether the substances are gases, fluids, powders, or solids. • This classification includes chemical compounds such as drugs and fuels, physical products such as plastics and particleboard, and new life forms made by genetic engineering. Its subject matter is always the substance itself, rather than the form or shape. — Often shortened to *composition.*

composition with creditors. See COMPOSITION (1).

compos mentis (**kom**-pəs **men**-tis), *adj.* [Latin "master of one's mind"] (17c) Of sound mind; having use of and control over one's own mental faculties. Cf. NON COMPOS MENTIS.

compound (**kom**- *or* kəm-**pownd**), *vb.* (14c) **1.** To put together, combine, or construct. **2.** To compute (interest) on the principal and the accrued interest. **3.** To settle (a matter, esp. a debt) by a money payment, in lieu of other liability; to adjust by agreement. **4.** To agree for consideration not to prosecute (a crime). • Compounding a felony in this way is itself a felony. **5.** Loosely, to aggravate; to make (a crime, etc.) more serious by further bad conduct.

compound duty. See DUTY (4).

compounder (**kom**- *or* kəm-**pown**-dər). (16c) **1.** One who settles a dispute; the maker of a composition. — Also termed *amicable compounder.* See COMPOSITION (1). **2.** One who knows of a crime by another and agrees, for a promised or received reward, not to prosecute.

compounding a crime. (17c) The offense of either agreeing not to prosecute a crime that one knows has been committed or agreeing to hamper the prosecution. — Also termed *compounding a felony*; (archaically) *theftbote*. See STIFLING OF A PROSECUTION.

compounding a felony. See COMPOUNDING A CRIME.

compound interest. See INTEREST (3).

compound journal entry. See ENTRY (2).

compound larceny. 1. See *mixed larceny* under LARCENY. **2.** See *aggravated larceny* under LARCENY.

compound offense. See OFFENSE (1).

compound policy. See *blanket policy* under INSURANCE POLICY.

comprehensive general-liability insurance. See INSURANCE.

comprehensive general-liability policy. See INSURANCE POLICY.

comprehensive insurance. See INSURANCE.

comprehensive nonliteral similarity. See SIMILARITY.

comprehensive zoning plan. (1925) A general plan to control and direct the use and development of a large piece of property. See ZONING.

comprint (**kom**-print). *Hist. Copyright.* The surreptitious and supposedly illegal printing of another bookseller's copy of a work. ● Despite the word's appearance as a legal term in dictionaries since 1706, no such offense ever existed. The term, which is properly a verb meaning "to share in printing (a book)," was first given this erroneous definition by John Kersey when he produced a new edition of Edward Phillips's *New World of English Words*. It has occasionally been copied by legal lexicographers ever since.

comprising, *adj. Patents.* (In the transition between the preamble and the body of a patent claim) including; having. ● This term does not limit the claim to the specified elements, so a later patent applicant's product or process cannot avoid infringement by merely adding another claim element. See *closed-ended claim* under PATENT CLAIM.

compromis (kom-prə-**mee**). [French] *Int'l law.* **1.** An agreement between two or more countries to submit an existing dispute to the jurisdiction of an arbitrator, an arbitral tribunal, or an international court. See *compromissory arbitration* under ARBITRATION.

ad hoc compromis (ad hok kom-prə-**mee**). An agreement in which countries submit a particular dispute that has arisen between them to an ad hoc or institutionalized arbitral tribunal or to an international court. — Also termed *compromis proper*; *special agreement*.

general compromis. An agreement in which countries submit all or a definite class of disputes that may arise between them to an arbitral institution, a court, or an ad hoc arbitral tribunal by concluding a general arbitration treaty or by including an arbitration clause in a treaty. — Also termed *abstract compromis*; *anticipated compromis*.

2. In international-law moot-court competitions, the record upon which the arguments are based.

compromise, *n.* (15c) **1.** An agreement between two or more persons to settle matters in dispute between them; an agreement for the settlement of a real or supposed claim in which each party surrenders something in concession to the other. — Also termed *compromise and settlement*; (erroneously) *compromise settlement*. **2.** A debtor's partial payment coupled with the creditor's promise not to claim the rest of the amount due or claimed. Cf. ACCORD; ACCORD AND SATISFACTION. — **compromise,** *vb.*

compromise and settlement. See COMPROMISE (1).

compromise verdict. See VERDICT.

compromis proper. See *ad hoc compromis* under COMPROMIS.

compromissory arbitration. See ARBITRATION.

comp time. Time that an employee is allowed to take off from work instead of being paid for overtime already worked. — Also termed *compensatory time*.

comptroller (kən-**troh**-lər). (15c) An officer of a business or a private, state, or municipal corporation who is charged with duties usu. relating to fiscal affairs, including auditing and examining accounts and reporting the financial status periodically. — Also spelled *controller*.

Comptroller General of the United States. The officer in the legislative branch of the federal government who heads the General Accountability Office. ● The Comptroller General is appointed by the President with the advice and consent of the Senate. See GENERAL ACCOUNTABILITY OFFICE.

Comptroller of the Currency. See OFFICE OF THE COMPTROLLER OF THE CURRENCY.

compulsion, *n.* (15c) **1.** The act of compelling; the state of being compelled. **2.** An uncontrollable inclination to do something. **3.** Objective necessity; duress. — **compel,** *vb.*

compulsory (kəm-**pəl**-sə-ree), *adj.* (16c) Compelled; mandated by legal process or by statute <compulsory counterclaim>.

compulsory, *n. Eccles. law.* An order that compels the attendance of a witness.

compulsory appearance. See APPEARANCE.

compulsory arbitration. See ARBITRATION.

compulsory-attendance law. A statute requiring minors of a specified age to attend school. ● Compulsory-attendance laws do not apply to married persons. — Also termed *compulsory-school-attendance law.* See AMISH EXCEPTION.

compulsory condition. See CONDITION (2).

compulsory counterclaim. See COUNTERCLAIM.

compulsory-counterclaim rule. The rule requiring a defending party to present every counterclaim arising out of the same transaction or occurrence that is the basis of the plaintiff's claim. Fed. R. Civ. P. 13(a). ● Most courts hold that if a party does not timely bring a compulsory counterclaim, the party is estopped from asserting the claim.

compulsory disclosure. See DISCLOSURE (2).

compulsory insurance. See INSURANCE.

compulsory joinder. See JOINDER.

compulsory labor. See FORCED LABOR.

compulsory license. See LICENSE.

compulsory nonsuit. See NONSUIT (2).

compulsory pilot. See PILOT.

compulsory pilotage. See PILOTAGE.

compulsory pooling. See POOLING.

compulsory process. See PROCESS.

Compulsory Process Clause. (1957) The clause of the Sixth Amendment to the U.S. Constitution giving criminal defendants the subpoena power for obtaining witnesses in their favor.

compulsory purchase. *Rare.* **1.** See EMINENT DOMAIN. **2.** See EXPROPRIATION (1).

compulsory retirement. See RETIREMENT.

compulsory sale. See SALE.

compulsory-school-attendance law. See COMPULSORY-ATTENDANCE LAW.

compulsory surrender. 1. See EMINENT DOMAIN. **2.** See EXPROPRIATION (1).

compulsory unitization. See UNITIZATION.

compurgation (kom-pər-**gay**-shən), *n.* (17c) [Latin *con-* "together" + *purgare* "to clear or purge"] *Hist.* A trial by which a defendant could have supporters (called *compurgators*), frequently 11 in number, testify that they believed the defendant was telling the truth. — Also termed *wager of law; trial by oath.* — **compurgatory,** *adj.*

compurgator (kom-pər-gay-tər). (16c) *Hist.* A person who appeared in court and made an oath in support of a civil or criminal defendant. — Also termed *oath-helper.* See COMPURGATION.

computer crime. See CRIME.

computer-information transaction. *Copyright.* An agreement whose primary purpose is to create, modify, transfer, or license computer information or rights in computer information.

computer matching. The comparing of computer records in two separate systems to determine whether the same record exists in both systems. ● The government, for example, uses computer matching to find persons who are both employed and receiving welfare payments and to find instances in which both divorced parents are claiming the same child on their income-tax returns. See COMPUTER MATCHING AND PRIVACY PROTECTION ACT OF 1988.

Computer Matching and Privacy Protection Act of 1988. An act that allows governmental agencies, with certain limitations, to compare computerized records to establish or verify eligibility for benefits or to recoup payments on benefits. 5 USCA § 552a. See COMPUTER MATCHING.

Computer Programs Directive. See DIRECTIVE ON THE LEGAL PROTECTION OF COMPUTER PROGRAMS.

Computer Software Protection Act of 1980. *Copyright.* An amendment to the Copyright Act of 1976, defining "computer program" as a literary work for copyright purposes and qualifying the exclusive rights of copyrighted-software owners. 17 USCA §§ 117.

Computer Software Protection Act of 1984. *Copyright.* An amendment to the Copyright Act of 1976, enacted to protect copyrighted computer programs against illegal copying. 17 USCA § 109.

Computer Software Rental Amendments Act. *Copyright.* A 1990 statute prohibiting computer-program purchasers from leasing, renting, or lending the software for commercial gain. 17 USCA §§ 801–805.

Comstock Act. See COMSTOCK LAW.

comstockery (kom-stok-ər-ee). (*often cap.*) Censorship or attempted censorship of art or literature that is supposedly immoral or obscene.

Comstock law (kom-stok). (1878) An 1873 federal statute that prohibited mailing "obscene, lewd, or lascivious" books or pictures, as well as "any article or thing designed for the prevention of conception or procuring of abortions." ● Because of the intolerance that led to this statute, the law gave rise to an English word roughly equivalent to *prudery* — namely, *comstockery.* — Also termed *Comstock Act.*

con. *abbr.* **1.** Confidence <con game>. **2.** Convict <ex-con>. **3.** Contra <pros and cons>. **4.** (*cap.*) Constitutional <Con. law>.

con, *n.* See CONFIDENCE GAME.

concealed debtor. See DEBTOR.

concealed weapon. See WEAPON.

concealment, *n.* (14c) **1.** The act of refraining from disclosure; esp., an act by which one prevents or hinders the discovery of something; a cover-up. **2.** The act of removing from sight or notice; hiding. **3.** *Insurance.* The insured's intentional withholding from the insurer material facts that increase the insurer's risk and that in good faith ought to be disclosed. Cf. NONDISCLOSURE. — **conceal,** *vb.*

  active concealment. (1865) The concealment by words or acts of something that one has a duty to reveal.

  fraudulent concealment. (1801) The affirmative suppression or hiding, with the intent to deceive or defraud, of a material fact or circumstance that one is legally (or, sometimes, morally) bound to reveal. — Also termed *hidden fraud.*

  passive concealment. (1882) The act of maintaining silence when one has a duty to speak.

concealment rule. (1950) The principle that a defendant's conduct that hinders or prevents a plaintiff from discovering the existence of a claim tolls the statute of limitations until the plaintiff discovers or should have discovered the claim. — Also termed *fraudulent-concealment rule.*

concentration account. A single centralized bank account into which funds deposited at or collected at out-of-area locations are periodically transferred.

conception of invention. (1859) *Patents.* The formation in the inventor's mind of a definite and permanent idea of a complete invention that is thereafter applied in practice. ● Courts usu. consider conception when determining priority of invention.

  complete conception of invention. *Patents.* The point at which an inventor knows every feature of the process or device to be patented, such that a person with ordinary skill in the art could reproduce it without extensive research or experimentation. — Often shortened to *complete conception.*

concerted action. (18c) An action that has been planned, arranged, and agreed on by parties acting together to further some scheme or cause, so that all involved are liable for the actions of one another. — Also termed *concert of action.*

concerted activity. *Labor law.* Action by employees concerning wages or working conditions. ● Concerted activity is protected by the National Labor Relations Act and cannot be used as a basis for disciplining or discharging an employee.

concerted refusal to deal. *Antitrust.* An agreement between two or more persons or firms to not do business with a third party. ● The parties to the agreement may or may not be competitors. Concerted refusals to deal may violate § 1 of the Sherman Act and are analyzed under either the per se rule or the rule of reason, depending on the nature of the agreement. See BOYCOTT; PER SE RULE; RULE OF REASON.

concert of action. See CONCERTED ACTION.

concert-of-action rule. See WHARTON'S RULE.

concession, *n.* (15c) **1.** A government grant for specific privileges. **2.** The voluntary yielding to a demand for the sake of a settlement. **3.** A rebate or abatement. **4.** *Int'l law.* A contract in which a country transfers some rights to a foreign enterprise which then engages in an activity (such as mining) contingent on state approval and subject to the terms of the contract. — **concede,** *vb.* — **concessive,** *adj.*

concession bargaining. *Labor law.* A type of collective bargaining in which the parties negotiate the employees' giving back previously gained improvements in wages, benefits, or working conditions in exchange for some form of job security, such as protection against layoffs. — Also termed *employee givebacks*; *union givebacks.* See COLLECTIVE BARGAINING.

conciliation, *n.* (1803) **1.** A settlement of a dispute in an agreeable manner. **2.** A process in which a neutral person meets with the parties to a dispute and explores how the dispute might be resolved; esp., a relatively unstructured method of dispute resolution in which a third party facilitates communication between parties in an attempt to help them settle their differences. ● Some jurisdictions, such as California, have Family Conciliation Courts to help resolve problems within the family. — Also termed (in sense 2) *facilitation*; *conciliation procedure.* Cf. MEDIATION; ARBITRATION. — **conciliate,** *vb.* — **conciliative, conciliatory,** *adj.* — **conciliator,** *n.*

conciliation court. See *small-claims court* under COURT.

conciliation procedure. See CONCILIATION (2).

conclude, *vb.* (16c) **1.** To ratify or formalize (a treaty, convention, or contract) <it can be difficult to amend a contract that the parties have already concluded>. **2.** To bind; estop <the admissions concluded the party as a matter of law>. **3.** *Scots law.* To sign (a contract, letter, etc.) for the sale of real property. ● This term most commonly appears in the phrase *conclude missives.*

conclusion, *n.* (14c) **1.** The final part of a speech or writing (such as a jury argument or a pleading). **2.** A judgment arrived at by reasoning; an inferential statement. **3.** The closing, settling, or final arranging of a treaty, contract, deal, etc. See OPINION (2). **4.** *Archaic.* An act by which one estops oneself from doing anything inconsistent with the act. **5.** See OPINION (3).

conclusional, *adj.* See CONCLUSORY.

conclusionary, *adj.* See CONCLUSORY.

conclusion of fact. (18c) A factual deduction drawn from observed or proven facts; an evidentiary inference. Cf. FINDING OF FACT.

conclusion of law. (17c) An inference on a question of law, made as a result of a factual showing, no further evidence being required; a legal inference. Cf. FINDING OF FACT; LEGAL CONCLUSION.

conclusion to the country. *Archaic.* The closing part of a pleading that requests the trial of an issue by a jury. Cf. GOING TO THE COUNTRY.

conclusive, *adj.* (17c) Authoritative; decisive; convincing <her conclusive argument ended the debate>. Cf. CONCLUSORY.

conclusive evidence. See EVIDENCE.

conclusive presumption. See PRESUMPTION.

conclusive proof. See *conclusive evidence* (1) under EVIDENCE.

conclusory (kən-**kloo**-zə-ree *or* -sə-ree), *adj.* (1923) Expressing a factual inference without stating the underlying facts on which the inference is based <because the plaintiff's allegations lacked any supporting evidence, they were merely conclusory>. — Also termed *conclusional; conclusionary.* Cf. CONCLUSIVE.

concomitant (kən-**kom**-ə-tənt), *adj.* (17c) Accompanying; incidental <concomitant actions>. — **concomitant,** *n.*

concomitant evidence. See EVIDENCE.

concord (**kon**-kord *or* **kong**-), *n.* (14c) **1.** An amicable arrangement between parties, esp. between peoples or nations; a compact or treaty. **2.** *Archaic.* An agreement to compromise and settle an action in trespass. **3.** *Archaic.* An in-court agreement in which a person who acquired land by force acknowledges that the land in question belongs to the complainant. See DEFORCE. **4.** *Hist.* The settlement of a dispute.

   final concord. A written agreement between the parties to an action by which they settle the action in court, with the court's permission. — Also termed *finalis concordia; final peace.*

concordat (**kon**- *or* kən-**kor**-dat). **1.** An agreement between a government and a church, esp. the Roman Catholic Church. **2.** *Hist. Eccles. law.* An agreement between ecclesiastical persons concerning a benefice, such as a resignation or promotion. See BENEFICE. **3.** An agreement between secular persons or entities.

concordatory (kən-**kor**-də-tor-ee), *adj.* Of or relating to a concordat, esp. one between church and state in France.

concubinage (kon-**kyoo**-bə-nij), *n.* (14c) **1.** The relationship of a man and woman who cohabit without the benefit of marriage. **2.** The state of being a concubine. **3.** *Hist.* A plea in a dower action made by a defendant who asserts that the plaintiff is the defendant's concubine rather than wife.

concubinatus (kon-kyoo-bi-**nay**-təs), *n.* [Latin "concubinage"] *Roman law.* A permanent, monogamous union of a man and a woman who are not legally married. • *Concubinatus* was not prohibited by law, but carried fewer benefits than a legal marriage.

concubine (**kong**-kyə-bin). **1.** *Archaic.* A woman who cohabits with a man to whom she is not married. • A concubine is often considered a wife without title. A concubine's status arises from the permanent cohabitation of a man and a woman as husband and wife although without the benefit of marriage. Cf. *common-law wife* under WIFE; COURTESAN. **2.** *Hist. Eccles. law.* A secondary or inferior wife, usu. in a polygamous marriage, who lacks the full rights and privileges of the first wife. • Although a concubine was expected to serve all the functions of a legitimate wife, she had no authority in the family or household, and was denied certain legal protections. For instance, her husband could easily disown her, she had no dower rights, and her children could not inherit from their father if he had children by his first wife. A concubine was also barred from certain spiritual comforts, such as churching after the birth of a child.

concur (kən-**kər**), *vb.* (15c) **1.** To agree; to consent. **2.** In a judicial opinion, to agree with the judgment in the case (usu. as expressed in the opinion of another judge), or the opinion of another judge, but often for different reasons or through a different line of reasoning. **3.** (Of a house in a bicameral legislature) to accept an amendment passed by the other house. **4.** *Civil law.* To join with other claimants in presenting a demand against an insolvent estate.

concurator (kon- *or* kən-**kyuur**-ə-tər). *Civil law.* A joint guardian or co-curator. See CURATOR.

concurrence. (15c) **1.** Agreement; assent. **2.** A vote cast by a judge in favor of the judgment reached, often on grounds differing from those expressed in the opinion or opinions explaining the judgment. **3.** A separate written opinion explaining such a vote. — Also termed (in sense 3) *concurring opinion.* **4.** Acceptance by one house in a bicameral legislature of an amendment passed by the other house.

concurrency, *n.* **1.** *Archaic.* The quality or fact of being concurrent in jurisdiction; joint right or authority. **2.** *Criminal procedure.* An identical duration for two or more criminal sentences assessed against the same defendant.

concurrent, *adj.* (14c) **1.** Operating at the same time; covering the same matters <concurrent interests>. **2.** Having authority on the same matters <concurrent jurisdiction>.

concurrent cause. See CAUSE (1).

concurrent condition. See CONDITION (2).

concurrent consideration. See CONSIDERATION (1).

concurrent covenant. See COVENANT (1).

concurrent estate. See ESTATE (1).

concurrent finding. See FINDING OF FACT.

concurrent interest. See *concurrent estate* under ESTATE (1).

concurrent jurisdiction. See JURISDICTION.

concurrent lease. See LEASE.

concurrent lien. See LIEN.

concurrent negligence. See NEGLIGENCE.

concurrent policy. See INSURANCE POLICY.

concurrent power. See POWER (3).

concurrent registration. *Trademarks.* The approved recording of identical or similar marks by multiple owners if each mark was commercially used before the owners applied for registration and the risk of consumer confusion is slight. • The U.S. Patent and Trademark Office may impose restrictions on each mark's use to prevent consumer confusion.

concurrent remedy. See REMEDY.

concurrent representation. See REPRESENTATION (2).

concurrent resolution. See RESOLUTION (1).

concurrent-sentence doctrine. (1969) The principle that an appellate court affirming a conviction and sentence need not hear a challenge to a conviction on another count if the conviction on the other count carries a sentence that is equal to or less than the affirmed conviction.

concurrent sentences. See SENTENCE.

concurrent tortfeasors. See TORTFEASOR.

concurrent writ. See WRIT.

concurring opinion. See CONCURRENCE (3).

concurso (kon- *or* kən-**kər**-soh), *n.* [Latin lit. "to run hither and thither"] *Civil law.* An action in which a creditor seeks to enforce a claim against an insolvent debtor.

condedit (kən-**dee**-dit *or* -**ded**-it). [Latin "he made (a will)"] *Eccles. law.* A defensive plea filed by a party in response to an ecclesiastical- court libel (i.e., complaint) questioning the veracity of a will or the competency of the testator. — Also spelled *condidit.*

condemn, *vb.* (14c) **1.** To judicially pronounce (someone) guilty. **2.** To determine and declare (property) to be assigned to public use. See EMINENT DOMAIN. **3.** To adjudge (a building) as being unfit for habitation. **4.** To adjudge (food or drink) as being unfit for human consumption. **5.**

Maritime law. To declare (a vessel) to be forfeited to the government, to be a prize, or to be unfit for service.

condemnation (kon-dem-**nay**-shən), *n.* (14c) **1.** The act of judicially pronouncing someone guilty; conviction. **2.** The determination and declaration that certain property (esp. land) is assigned to public use, subject to reasonable compensation; the exercise of eminent domain by a governmental entity. See EMINENT DOMAIN.

   excess condemnation. (1921) A taking of land in excess of the boundaries of the public project as designed by the condemnor.

   inverse condemnation. (1932) An action brought by a property owner for compensation from a governmental entity that has taken the owner's property without bringing formal condemnation proceedings. — Also termed *constructive condemnation; reverse condemnation.*

   quick condemnation. (1918) The immediate taking of possession of private property for public use, whereby the estimated compensation is deposited in court or paid to the condemnee until the actual amount of compensation can be established. — Also termed *quick-take.*

3. An official pronouncement that a building is unfit for habitation; the act of making such a pronouncement. **4.** The official pronouncement that a thing (such as food or drink) is unfit for use or consumption; the act of making such a pronouncement. **5.** *Maritime law.* The declaration that a vessel is forfeited to the government, is a prize, or is unfit for service.

condemnation blight. 1. The reduction in value that the property targeted for condemnation suffers in anticipation of the taking. **2.** The physical deterioration of property targeted for condemnation in anticipation of the taking.

condemnation money. (18c) **1.** Damages that a losing party in a lawsuit is condemned to pay. **2.** Compensation paid by an expropriator of land to the landowner for taking the property.

condemnatory (kən-**dem**-nə-tor-ee), *adj.* (16c) **1.** Condemning; expressing condemnation or censure. **2.** Of or relating to the use of eminent domain or expropriation.

condemnee (kon-dem-**nee**). (1890) One whose property is expropriated for public use or taken by a public-works project.

condemnor (kon-dem-**nor** *or* kən-**dem**-nər). (1890) A person or entity that expropriates property for public use. — Also spelled *condemner* (kən-**dem**-nər).

condensate. See DISTILLATE (1).

condictio (kən-**dik**-shee-oh), *n.* [fr. Latin *condicere* "to demand back"] *Roman & civil law.* A personal action in the nature of demanding something back; an action of debt. • In the sense here used, *debt* must be understood broadly to cover not only contractual but also quasi-contractual or tort claims. *Condictio* is usu. founded on an obligation to give or do a certain thing or service. — Also termed *condiction; action of debt.* Pl. **condictiones** (kən-dik-shee-**oh**-neez). — **condictitious, condictious** *adj.*

condictio certi (kən-**dik**-shee-oh sər-tɪ). [Latin "claim for recovery of a certain sum or thing"] An action based on a promise to do a thing, where the promise is certain.

condictio ex causa furtiva (kən-**dik**-shee-oh eks **kaw**-zə fər-**tɪ**-və). See *condictio rei furtivae.*

condictio ex lege (kən-**dik**-shee-oh eks **lee**-jee). [Latin "claim for recovery under a statute"] An action arising where a statute creates an obligation but provides no remedy.

condictio furtiva (kən-**dik**-shee-oh fər-**tɪ**-və). See *condictio rei furtivae.*

condictio incerti (kən-**dik**-shee-oh in-**sər**-tɪ). [Latin "claim for recovery of an uncertain amount"] An action to recover an uncertain amount.

condictio indebiti (kən-**dik**-shee-oh in-**deb**-ə-tɪ). [Latin "claim for recovery of something not due"] An action to prevent the unjust enrichment of a defendant who had received money or property from the plaintiff by mistake. — Also termed *actio condictio indebiti* (though strictly speaking this is a solecism).

condictio rei furtivae (kən-**dik**-shee-oh **ree**-ɪ fər-**tɪ**-vee). [Latin "claim for recovery of a stolen thing"] An action to recover a stolen thing or its value if the thing could not be returned. • A *condictio rei furtivae* could be brought by an owner or pledgee against the thief or the thief's heirs. — Also termed *condictio furtiva; condictio ex causa furtiva.*

condictio sine causa (kən-**dik**-shee-oh **sɪ**-nee **kaw**-zə). [Latin "claim for recovery of money or a thing given without consideration"] An action for the recovery of property transferred without consideration and in contemplation of a specific event that did not occur, such as a dowry made in view of a marriage that does not take place.

condictio triticaria (kən-**dik**-shee-oh trɪ-ti-**kair**-ee-ə). [Latin "claim for recovery of wheat"] An action for the recovery of a specified quantity of a named commodity.

condidit. See CONDEDIT.

condign justice. See JUSTICE (1).

condition, *n.* (14c) **1.** A future and uncertain event on which the existence or extent of an obligation or liability depends; an uncertain act or event that triggers or negates a duty to render a promised performance. • For example, if Jones promises to pay Smith $500 for repairing a car, Smith's failure to repair the car (an implied or constructive condition) relieves Jones of the promise to pay. **2.** A stipulation or prerequisite in a contract, will, or other instrument, constituting the essence of the instrument. • If a court construes a contractual term to be a condition, then its untruth or breach will entitle the party to whom it is made to be discharged from all liabilities under the contract.

affirmative condition. See *positive condition.*

casual condition. *Civil law.* A condition that depends on chance; one that is not within the power of either party to an agreement.

collateral condition. A condition that requires the performance of an act having no relation to an agreement's main purpose.

compulsory condition. (1876) A condition expressly requiring that a thing be done, such as a tenant's paying rent on a certain day.

concurrent condition. (1840) A condition that must occur or be performed at the same time as another condition, the performance by each party separately operating as a condition precedent; a condition that is mutually dependent on another, arising when the parties to a contract agree to exchange performances simultaneously. — Also termed *condition concurrent.*

condition implied by law. See *constructive condition.*

condition implied in law. See *constructive condition.*

condition precedent (prə-**seed**-ənt *also* pres-ə-dənt). (1818) An act or event, other than a lapse of time, that must exist or occur before a duty to perform something promised arises. • If the condition does not occur and is not excused, the promised performance need not be rendered. The most common condition contemplated by this phrase is the immediate or unconditional duty of performance by a promisor.

condition subsequent. (1818) A condition that, if it occurs, will bring something else to an end; an event the existence of which, by agreement of the parties, discharges a duty of performance that has arisen.

constructive condition. A condition contained in an essential contractual term that, though omitted by the parties from their agreement, a court has supplied as being reasonable in the circumstances; a condition imposed by law to do justice. • The cooperation of the parties to a contract, for example, is a constructive condition. — Also termed *implied-in-law condition; condition implied by law; condition implied in law.* Cf. *implied-in-fact condition.*

copulative condition (**kop**-yə-lə-tiv *or* -lay-tiv). A condition requiring the performance of more than one act. Cf. *disjunctive condition*; *single condition*.

dependent condition. A mutual covenant that goes to the consideration on both sides of a contract.

disjunctive condition. A condition requiring the performance of one of several acts. Cf. *copulative condition*; *single condition*.

dissolving condition. See *resolutory condition*.

express condition. (16c) **1.** A condition that is the manifested intention of the parties.

precondition. A stipulated act or event that must occur before either party to a contract will be bound by the contract; a prerequisite.

2. A condition that is explicitly stated in an instrument; esp., a contractual condition that the parties have reduced to writing.

implied condition. (17c) A condition that is not expressly mentioned, but is imputed by law from the nature of the transaction or the conduct of the parties to have been tacitly understood between them as a part of the agreement. See *constructive condition*; *implied-in-fact condition*.

implied-in-fact condition. A contractual condition that the parties have implicitly agreed to by their conduct or by the nature of the transaction. Cf. *constructive condition*.

implied-in-law condition. See *constructive condition*.

inherent condition. A condition that is an intrinsic part of an agreement; a condition that is not newly imposed but is already present in an agreement.

lawful condition. A condition that can be fulfilled without violating the law.

mixed condition. *Civil law.* A condition that depends either on the will of one party and the will of a third person, or on the will of one party and the happening of a causal event.

negative condition. (17c) A condition forbidding a party from doing a certain thing, such as prohibiting a tenant from subletting leased property; a promise not to do something, usu. as part of a larger agreement. See *negative easement* under EASEMENT. — Also termed *restrictive condition*.

positive condition. A condition that requires some act, such as paying rent. — Also termed *affirmative condition*.

potestative condition (**poh**-tes-tə-tiv). *Civil law.* A condition that will be fulfilled only if the obligated party chooses to do so. ● Louisiana no longer uses this term, instead providing that this type of condition will render the obligation null. La. Civ. Code art. 1770. Cf. *suspensive condition*; *resolutory condition*.

preexisting condition. *Insurance.* A physical or mental condition evident during the period before the effective date of a medical-insurance policy. ● Typically, coverage for later treatment for such a condition is excluded if symptoms of the condition were present during the period before the policy was effective.

promissory condition. A condition that is also a promise.

resolutory condition (rə-**zol**-yə-tor-ee). *Civil law.* A condition that upon fulfillment terminates an already enforceable obligation and entitles the parties to be restored to their original positions. — Also termed *resolutive condition*; *dissolving condition*. Cf. *potestative condition*.

restrictive condition. See *negative condition*.

single condition. A condition requiring the performance of a specified thing. Cf. *copulative condition*; *disjunctive condition*.

suspensive condition. *Civil law.* A condition that makes an obligation mandatory only if a specified but uncertain event occurs. Cf. *potestative condition*.

testamentary condition. A condition that must be satisfied before a gift made in a will becomes effective.

triggering condition. A circumstance that must exist before a legal doctrine applies; esp., in criminal law, a circumstance that must exist before an actor will be entitled to a justification defense.

unlawful condition. A condition that cannot be fulfilled without violating the law.

3. Loosely, a term, provision, or clause in a contract. **4.** A qualification attached to the conveyance of property providing that if a particular event does or does not take place, the estate will be created, enlarged, defeated, or transferred. **5.** A state of being; an essential quality or status. — **condition,** *vb.*

artificial condition. A physical characteristic of real property, brought about by a person's affirmative act instead of by natural forces.

dangerous condition. (1850) **1.** A property defect creating a substantial risk of injury when the property is used in a reasonably foreseeable manner. ● A dangerous condition may result in waiver of sovereign immunity. **2.** A property risk that children, because of their immaturity, cannot appreciate or avoid. Cf. *attractive nuisance* under NUISANCE.

conditional, *adj.* Subject to or dependent on a condition <a conditional sale>.

conditional acceptance. See ACCEPTANCE (4).

conditional adjournment. See ADJOURNMENT.

conditional admissibility. See ADMISSIBILITY.

conditional assault. See ASSAULT.

conditional assignment. See ASSIGNMENT (2).

conditional bequest. See BEQUEST.

conditional contraband. See CONTRABAND.

conditional contract. See CONTRACT.

conditional conveyance. See CONVEYANCE.

conditional covenant. See COVENANT (1).

conditional creditor. See CREDITOR.

conditional delivery. See DELIVERY.

conditional devise. See DEVISE.

conditional divorce. See *conversion divorce* under DIVORCE.

conditional duty. See DUTY (1).

conditional estate. See *estate on condition* under ESTATE (1).

conditional fee. 1. See *fee simple conditional* under FEE SIMPLE. 2. See CONTINGENT FEE.

conditional fee agreement. *English law.* A contract between a lawyer and a client that provides for the lawyer to receive a fee only if the client wins the case. ● Unlike American contingent-fee arrangements, the lawyer does not receive a percentage of the damages awarded but instead charges the client a base fee plus a success fee, which is usu. calculated as a percentage of up to 100% of the base fee. See *success fee* under FEE (1).

conditional guaranty. See GUARANTY.

conditional indorsement. See INDORSEMENT.

conditional judgment. See JUDGMENT.

conditional legacy. See LEGACY.

conditional limitation. See LIMITATION.

conditionally privileged communication. See COMMUNICATION.

conditional obligation. See OBLIGATION.

conditional pardon. See PARDON.

conditional payment. See PAYMENT.

conditional plea. See PLEA (1).

conditional presumption. See *rebuttable presumption* under PRESUMPTION.

conditional privilege. See *qualified privilege* under PRIVILEGE (1).

conditional promise. See PROMISE.

conditional proof. See PROOF.

conditional purpose. (16c) 1. An intention to do something, conditions permitting. 2. *Criminal law.* A possible defense against a crime if the conditions make committing the crime impossible (e.g., "I will steal the money if it's there," and the money is not there).

conditional release. See RELEASE.

conditional revocation. See DEPENDENT RELATIVE REVOCATION.

conditional right. See RIGHT.

conditional sale. See SALE.

conditional sales contract. See *retail installment contract* under CONTRACT.

conditional sentence. See SENTENCE.

conditional use. See USE (1).

conditional-use permit. See SPECIAL-USE PERMIT.

conditional will. See WILL.

conditional zoning. See ZONING.

condition concurrent. See *concurrent condition* under CONDITION (2).

condition implied by law. See *constructive condition* under CONDITION (2).

condition implied in law. See *constructive condition* under CONDITION (2).

conditioning the market. See GUN-JUMPING.

condition of employment. (1875) A qualification or circumstance required for obtaining or keeping a job.

condition precedent. See CONDITION (2).

conditions of sale. (16c) The terms under which an auction will be conducted. ● The conditions of sale are usu. placed in the auction room for public viewing before the sale.

condition subsequent. See CONDITION (2).

condominia (kon-də-**min**-ee-ə). *Civil law.* Coownerships or limited ownerships. ● *Condominia* are considered part of the *dominium* of the property, and thus are more than mere rights in the property (i.e., *jure in re aliena*); examples of *condominia* include *emphyteusis, superficies, pignus, hypotheca, usufructus, usus,* and *habitatio.*

condominium (kon-də-**min**-ee-əm). (1962) 1. Ownership in common with others. 2. A single real-estate unit in a multi-unit development in which a person has both separate ownership of a unit and a common interest, along with the development's other owners, in the common areas. Cf. COOPERATIVE (2). Pl. (for sense 2) **condominiums**. 3. Joint sovereignty by two or more nations. 4. A politically dependent territory under such sovereignty. Pl. **condominia** (senses 3 & 4).

condonation (kon-də-**nay**-shən), *n.* (17c) 1. A victim's express or (esp.) implied forgiveness of an offense, esp. by treating the offender as if there had been no offense. ● Condonation is not usu. a valid defense to a crime. 2. One spouse's express or implied forgiveness of a marital offense by resuming marital life and sexual intimacy. ● For example, one spouse might impliedly forgive the other spouse's infidelity by continuing to live with him or her. If adultery is charged as a ground for divorce and condonation is proved, the forgiving spouse is barred from proof of that offense. Cf. COLLUSION (2); CONNIVANCE (2); RECRIMINATION (1); RECONCILIATION.

condone (kən-**dohn**), *vb.* To voluntarily pardon or overlook (esp. an act of adultery). — **condonable** (kən-**dohn**-ə-bəl), *adj.*

conduct, *n.* (15c) Personal behavior, whether by action or inaction; the manner in which a person behaves. ● Conduct does not include the actor's natural death or a death that results from behavior consciously engaged in but not reasonably expected to have this result. — **conduct,** *vb.*

active conduct. Behavior that involves a person doing something by exerting will on the external world. Cf. *passive conduct.*

assertive conduct. (1968) *Evidence.* Nonverbal behavior that is intended to be a statement, such as pointing one's finger to identify a suspect in a police lineup. ● Assertive conduct is a statement under the hearsay rule, and thus it is not admissible unless a hearsay exception applies. Fed. R. Evid. 801(a)(2). — Also termed *implied assertion.*

contumacious conduct (kon-t[y]oo-**may**-shəs). A willful disobedience of a court order. See CONTUMACY.

disorderly conduct. (17c) Behavior that tends to disturb the public peace, offend public morals, or undermine public safety. See BREACH OF THE PEACE.

disruptive conduct. (1959) Disorderly conduct in the context of a governmental proceeding. See CONTEMPT.

nonassertive conduct. (1965) *Evidence.* Nonverbal behavior that is not intended to be a statement, such as fainting while being questioned as a suspect by a police officer. ● Nonassertive conduct is not a statement under the hearsay rule, and thus it is admissible. Fed. R. Evid. 801.

outrageous conduct. (18c) Conduct so extreme that it exceeds all reasonable bounds of human decency. See EMOTIONAL DISTRESS.

passive conduct. Behavior that does not involve exerting will on the external world. Cf. *active conduct.*

tortious conduct. An act or omission that subjects the actor to liability under the principles of tort law.

unduly dangerous conduct. See *unreasonably dangerous conduct.*

unprofessional conduct. (1836) Behavior that is immoral, unethical, or dishonorable, esp. when judged by the standards of the actor's profession.

unreasonably dangerous conduct. Conduct that involves undue risk under the circumstances. — Sometimes shortened to *dangerous conduct.* — Also termed *unduly dangerous conduct.*

wrongful conduct. (1807) An act taken in violation of a legal duty; an act that unjustly infringes on another's rights. — Also termed *wrongful act.*

conduct money. See *witness fee* under FEE (1).

conduit taxation. See *pass-through taxation* under TAXATION.

confederacy, *n.* (14c) **1.** A league of states or countries that have joined for mutual support or joint action; an alliance. **2.** An association of two or more persons, usu. for unlawful purposes; CONSPIRACY. **3.** The fact or condition of being allied or associated.

confederacy clause. *Archaic.* A clause in a complaint charging that the defendant or defendants have combined with others (who may yet be named as defendants) to defraud or deprive the plaintiff of personal rights.

confederate, *n.* An ally; esp., a coconspirator or accomplice.

confederation. (15c) **1.** A league or union of states or nations, each of which retains its sovereignty but also delegates some rights and powers to a central authority. ● The United States, for example, was first organized under the Articles of Confederation. Cf. FEDERATION.

confederation of states. A confederation involving a central government that exists and exercises certain powers but does not control all the external relations of the member states. ● For international purposes there exists not one but a number of states. Cf. *federal state* under STATE.

2. An alliance; esp., in a negative sense, a conspiracy.

conferee (kon-fər-**ee**). See MANAGER (2).

conference. 1. CONVENTION (3). **2.** A meeting between the two houses of a bicameral legislature. See *conference committee* under COMMITTEE.

conference committee. See COMMITTEE.

Conference of Chief Justices. An organization consisting of the highest judicial officers of all the states in the United States, the District of Columbia, the Commonwealth of Puerto Rico, the Commonwealth of the Northern Mariana Islands, and the territories of American Samoa, Guam, and the Virgin Islands. ● Established in 1949, the organization seeks to improve the administration of justice in various ways, as by supporting adequate judicial funding, promoting the independence and effectiveness of state judicial systems, and advancing professionalism and lawyer competence.

Since 1983, the organization has operated as a nonprofit corporation. — Abbr. CCJ.

confess, *vb.* To admit (an allegation) as true; to make a confession. — **confessor,** *n.*

confessed judgment. See CONFESSION OF JUDGMENT.

confessing error. A plea admitting to an assignment of error. See ASSIGNMENT OF ERROR.

confession, *n.* (14c) A criminal suspect's oral or written acknowledgment of guilt, often including details about the crime. Cf. ADMISSION; STATEMENT (3).

  coerced-compliant confession. A confession by a suspect who knows that he or she is innocent but is overcome by fatigue, the questioner's tactics, or a desire for some potential benefit. — Also termed *coerced-compliant false confession.*

  coerced confession. (1937) A confession that is obtained by threats or force.

  direct confession. (17c) A statement in which an accused person acknowledges having committed the crime.

  extrajudicial confession. (1813) A confession made out of court, and not as a part of a judicial examination or investigation. • Such a confession must be corroborated by some other proof of the corpus delicti, or else it is insufficient to warrant a conviction. Cf. *judicial confession.*

  implied confession. A confession in which the person does not plead guilty but invokes the mercy of the court and asks for a light sentence.

  indirect confession. A confession that is inferred from the defendant's conduct.

  interlocking confessions. (1973) Confessions by two or more suspects whose statements are substantially the same and consistent concerning the elements of the crime.

  involuntary confession. (1830) A confession induced by the police or other law-enforcement authorities who make promises to, coerce, or deceive the suspect.

  judicial confession. (16c) A plea of guilty or some other direct manifestation of guilt in court or in a judicial proceeding. Cf. *extrajudicial confession.*

  naked confession. (18c) A confession unsupported by any evidence that a crime has been committed, and therefore usu. highly suspect.

  oral confession. A confession that is not made in writing. • Oral confessions are admissible, though as a practical matter police interrogators prefer to take written or recorded confessions since juries typically view these as being more reliable.

  persuaded confession. A false confession by a suspect who has no knowledge of a crime but adopts a belief in his or her guilt.

  plenary confession (**plee**-nə-ree *or* **plen**-ə). (1907) A complete confession; one that is believed to be conclusive against the person who made it.

  relative confession. *Hist.* A confession of guilt coupled with an accusation against another person as a participant in the crime. • If the accusation against the other person was proved, the accusing defendant was pardoned. If not, the defendant was convicted on the confession. See *State v. Willis,* 41 A. 820, 825 (Conn. 1898). See APPROVER (1).

  threshold confession. (1962) A spontaneous confession made promptly after arrest and without interrogation by the police. • The issue whether the defendant's statement is a threshold confession usu. arises when the defendant challenges the admissibility of the confession on grounds that he or she suffered an impermissibly long delay before being brought before a magistrate. Courts generally admit this type of confession into evidence if the confession was given before the delay occurred.

  voluntary confession. A confession given freely, without any benefit or punishment promised, threatened, or expected.

confession and avoidance. (17c) A plea in which a defendant admits allegations but pleads additional facts that deprive the admitted facts of an adverse legal effect. • For example, a plea of contributory negligence (before the advent of comparative negligence) was a confession and avoidance. — Also termed *avoidance; plea in confession and avoidance; plea of confession and avoidance.* Cf. *affirmative defense* under DEFENSE (1).

confession of judgment. (18c) **1.** A person's agreeing to the entry of judgment upon the occurrence or nonoccurrence of an event, such as making a payment. **2.** A judgment taken against a debtor by the creditor, based on the debtor's written consent. **3.** The paper on which the person so agrees, before it is entered. — Also termed *confessed judgment; cognovit judgment; statement of confession; warrant of confession; judgment by confession.* See COGNOVIT. Cf. WARRANT OF ATTORNEY.

confidence. (14c) **1.** Assured expectation; firm trust; faith <the partner has confidence in the associate's work>. **2.** Reliance on another's discretion; a relation of trust <she took her coworker into her confidence>. **3.** A communication made in trust and not intended for public disclosure; specif., a communication protected by the attorney–client or similar privilege <the confidences between lawyer and client>. • Under the ABA Code of Professional Responsibility, a lawyer cannot reveal a client's confidence unless the client consents after full disclosure. DR 4-101. Cf. SE-CRET (2). — **confide,** *vb.*

confidence game. (1856) A means of obtaining money or property whereby a person intentionally misrepresents facts to gain the victim's trust so that the victim will transfer money or property to the person. — Also termed *con game; con.* Cf. BUNCO.

confidence man. One who defrauds a victim by first gaining the victim's confidence and then, through trickery, obtaining money or property; a swindler. • The equivalent term *confidence woman* is exceptionally rare, even though women are often involved in confidence games. — Often shortened to *con man.* See CONFIDENCE GAME. Cf. BUNCO-STEERER.

confidential, *adj.* **1.** (Of information) meant to be kept secret <confidential settlement terms>. **2.** (Of a relationship) characterized by trust and a willingness to confide in the other <a confidential relationship between attorney and client>.

confidential adoption. See *closed adoption* under ADOPTION.

confidential communication. See COMMUNICATION.

confidentiality, *n.* (1834) **1.** Secrecy; the state of having the dissemination of certain information restricted. **2.** The relation between lawyer and client or guardian and ward, or between spouses, with regard to the trust that is placed in the one by the other.

confidentiality agreement. *Trade secrets.* A promise not to disclose trade secrets or other proprietary information learned in the course of the parties' relationship. • Confidentiality agreements are often required as a condition of employment. — Also termed *nondisclosure agreement.*

confidentiality clause. See CLAUSE.

confidentiality statute. A law that seals adoption records and prevents an adopted child from learning the identity of his or her biological parent and prevents the biological parent from learning the identity of the adoptive parents. — Also termed *sealed-record statute.*

confidential marriage. See MARRIAGE (1).

confidential relationship. See RELATIONSHIP.

confidential source. A person who provides information to a law-enforcement agency or to a journalist on the express or implied guarantee of anonymity. • Confidentiality is protected both under the Federal Freedom of Information Act (for disclosures to law enforcement) and under the First Amendment (for disclosures to journalists).

confinee. A person held in confinement.

confinement, *n.* (16c) The act of imprisoning or restraining someone; the state of being imprisoned or restrained <solitary confinement>. See SOLITARY CONFINEMENT. — **confine,** *vb.*

confirm, *vb.* **1.** To give formal approval to <confirm the bankruptcy plan>. **2.** To verify or corroborate <confirm that the order was signed>. **3.** To make firm or certain <the judgment confirmed the plaintiff's right to possession>.

Confirmatio Chartarum (kon-fər-**may**-shee-oh kahr-**tair**-əm). [Latin "confirmation of the charters"] *Hist.* A declaration first made by Henry III in 1225 confirming the guarantees of Magna Carta and the Charter of the Forest. • It was not enrolled until 1297, when, during the reign of Edward I, it was enacted, thus introducing these charters into the common law. — Also spelled *Confirmatio Cartarum.*

confirmation, *n.* (14c) **1.** The act of giving formal approval <Senate confirmation hearings>. **2.** The act of verifying or corroborating; a statement that verifies or corroborates <the journalist sought confirmation of the district attorney's remarks>. **3.** The act of ratifying a voidable estate; a type of conveyance in which a voidable estate is made certain or a particular estate is increased <deed of confirmation>. **4.** *Civil law.* A declaration that corrects a null provision of an obligation in order to make the provision enforceable. **5.** *Commercial law.* A bank's agreement to honor a letter of credit issued by another bank. Cf. RATIFICATION. — **confirmatory** (kən-**fər**-mə-tor-ee), *adj.*

silent confirmation. A bank's confirmation of a letter of credit based on the request of the letter's beneficiary rather than the issuing bank.

confirmation of sale. A court's approval — usu. in the form of a docket entry or order — of the terms of a court-ordered sale.

confirmation slip. The form verifying a purchase or sale of a security, usu. mailed by the broker to the investor. — Also termed *transaction slip; sold note.*

confirmed letter of credit. See LETTER OF CREDIT.

confirmee (kon-fər-**mee**). *Hist.* The grantee of a deed of confirmation. See CONFIRMATION (3).

confirmor (kən-**fər**-mər *or* -mor). *Hist.* The grantor of a deed of confirmation. See CONFIRMATION (3).

confiscable (kən-**fis**-kə-bəl *or* kon-fə-skə-bəl), *adj.* (Of property) liable to confiscation; subject to forfeiture <confiscable contraband>.

confiscate (**kon**-fə-skayt), *vb.* **1.** To appropriate (property) as forfeited to the government. **2.** To seize (property) by authority of law.

confiscation (kon-fi-**skay**-shən), *n.* (16c) **1.** Seizure of property for the public treasury. **2.** Seizure of property by actual or supposed authority. — **con-fiscatory** (kən-**fis**-kə-tor-ee), *adj.* — **confiscator** (**kon**-fə-skay-tər), *n.*

confiscatory rate. See RATE.

conflict. See CONFLICT OF LAWS.

conflict diamond. A diamond that originated in an area controlled by forces or factions opposed to a legitimate, internationally recognized government, and is used to fund military action against that government. • Congress enacted the Clean Diamond Trade Act in 2003 to stop trade in conflict diamonds. 19 USCA §§ 3901 et seq. — Also termed *blood diamond.*

conflicting evidence. See EVIDENCE.

conflicting presumption. See PRESUMPTION.

conflict of authority. (1822) **1.** A disagreement between two or more courts, often courts of coordinate jurisdiction, on a point of law. **2.** A disagreement between two or more treatise authors or other scholars, esp. in an area in which scholarly authority is paramount, such as public or private international law.

conflict of interest. (1843) **1.** A real or seeming incompatibility between one's private interests and one's public or fiduciary duties. **2.** A real or seeming incompatibility between the interests of two of a lawyer's clients, such that the lawyer is disqualified from representing both clients if the dual representation adversely affects either client or if the clients do not consent. *See* Model Rules of Prof'l Conduct 1.7(a).

thrust-upon conflict. A conflict of interest that arises during an attorney's representation of two clients but did not exist and was not reasonably foreseeable when each client's representation began, and arises through no fault of the attorney's. • Some states may require that the conflict be of a type that clients may waive under the rules of professional responsibility. This situation may create an exception to the hot-potato rule. See HOT-POTATO RULE.

conflict of laws. (1827) **1.** A difference between the laws of different states or countries in a case in which a transaction or occurrence central to the case has a connection to two or more jurisdictions. — Often shortened to *conflict.* Cf. CHOICE OF LAW.

conflict of personal laws. **1.** A difference of laws between a jurisdiction's general laws and the laws of a racial or religious group, such as a conflict between federal law and American Indian tribal law. **2.** A difference between personal laws. See PERSONAL LAW.

false conflict of laws. **1.** A situation resembling but not embodying an actual conflict because the potentially applicable laws do not differ, because the laws' underlying policies have the same objective, or because one of the laws is not meant to apply to the case before the court. **2.** The situation in which, although a case has a territorial connection to two or more states whose laws conflict with one another, there is no real conflict because one state has a dominant interest in having its law chosen to govern the case — hence there is no real conflict. **3.** The situation in which the laws of all states that are relevant to the facts in dispute either are the same or would produce the same decision in the case. — Often shortened to *false conflict.*

2. The body of jurisprudence that undertakes to reconcile such differences or to decide what law is to govern in these situations; the principles of choice of law. — Often shortened (in sense 2) to *conflicts.* — Also termed (in international contexts) *private international law; international private law.*

conflict out, *vb.* (1981) To disqualify (a lawyer or judge) on the basis of a conflict of interest <the judge was conflicted out of the case by his earlier representation of one of the litigants>.

conflict preemption. See *obstacle preemption* under PREEMPTION.

conflicts. See CONFLICT OF LAW (2).

conformed copy. See COPY.

conforming, *adj.* (1956) Being in accordance with contractual obligations <conforming goods> <conforming conduct>. UCC § 2-102(a)(8).

conforming use. See USE (1).

Conformity Act. *Hist.* An 1872 federal statute providing that the practice and procedure in federal district courts (other than in equity and admiralty matters) must conform to the practice and procedure used by the state courts for like cases. • The Federal Rules of Civil Procedure (effective in 1938) superseded the Conformity Act.

conformity hearing. (1970) **1.** A court-ordered hearing to determine whether the judgment or decree prepared by the prevailing party conforms to the decision of the court. **2.** A hearing before a federal agency or department to determine whether a state-submitted plan complies with the requirements of federal law. • This type of hearing is common in cases involving social services.

Confrontation Clause. (1913) The Sixth Amendment provision generally guaranteeing a criminal defendant's right to confront an accusing witness face-to-face and to cross-examine that witness. • This right may be overridden if the witness is esp. vulnerable, as with a child who is an alleged victim of sexual abuse. Even then, the defendant's attorney must have an opportunity to examine the witness while the defendant observes by means of closed-circuit television or the like. See *Maryland v. Craig*, 497 U.S. 836, 110 S.Ct. 3157 (1990).

confusion. 1. CONFUSION OF GOODS. **2.** MERGER (9). **3.** *Trademarks.* A consumer's mistaken belief about the origin of goods or services. See LIKELI-HOOD-OF-CONFUSION TEST.

direct confusion. See *forward confusion.*

forward confusion. Confusion occurring when consumers are likely to believe mistakenly that the infringing company's products are from the same source as the trademark owner's. • In forward-confusion cases, the infringing company is usu. smaller than the owner. Thus, consumers may believe the infringer to be an affiliate of the owner. — Also termed *direct confusion.*

reverse confusion. Confusion occurring when consumers are likely to believe mistakenly — usu. through widespread advertising and promotion by the infringing company — that the trademark owner's products are actually those of the infringer. • Reverse confusion often injures the owner's reputation and goodwill. In an action for reverse confusion, the trademark owner is typically the smaller company.

confusion of boundaries. The branch of equity that deals with the settlement of disputed or uncertain real-property boundaries.

confusion of debts. See MERGER (9).

confusion of goods. (18c) The mixture of things of the same nature but belonging to different owners so that the identification of the things is no longer possible. • If this occurs by common consent of the owners, they are owners in common, but if the mixture is done willfully by one person alone, that person loses all right in the property unless (1) the goods can be distinguished and separated among owners, or (2) the mixing person's goods are equal in value to the goods with which they were intermingled. *Confusion of goods* combines the civil-law concepts of *confusio* (a mixture of liquids) and *commixtio* (a mixture of dry items). — Also termed *intermixture of goods*; *confusio bonorum.*

confusion of rights. See MERGER (9).

confusion of titles. *Civil law.* The merger of two titles to the same land in the same person. Cf. MERGER (9).

con game. See CONFIDENCE GAME.

congeable (**kon**-jee-ə-bəl), *adj.* [fr. French *congé* "permission"] *Hist.* Lawful; permissible.

congeries (kon-**jeer**-eez *or* **kon**-jə-reez). (17c) A collection or aggregation <a congeries of rights>.

conglomerate (kən-**glom**-ər-it), *n.* (1967) A corporation that owns unrelated enterprises in a wide variety of industries. — Also termed *conglomerate*

corporation. — **conglomerate** (kən-**glom**-ə-rayt), *vb.* — **conglomerate** (kən-**glom**-ər-it), *adj.*

conglomerate merger. See MERGER.

congress, *n.* (16c) **1.** A formal meeting of delegates or representatives; CONVENTION (4). **2.** (*cap.*) The legislative body of the federal government, created under U.S. Const. art. I, § 1 and consisting of the Senate and the House of Representatives. — **congressional,** *adj.*

Congressional Budget Office. An office in the legislative branch of the federal government responsible for forecasting economic trends, making cost estimates, conducting special studies in budget-related areas, and issuing annual reports that discuss federal spending and revenue levels and the allocation of funds. • It was established by the Congressional Budget and Impoundment Control Act of 1974. — Abbr. CBO

congressional committee. See COMMITTEE.

congressional district. See DISTRICT.

Congressional Globe. A privately issued record of the proceedings in Congress. • The *Globe* was the sole record of congressional speeches and statements from 1833 until the publicly printed *Congressional Record* appeared in 1873. It contains the congressional debates of the 23d through the 42d Congress.

congressional immunity. See IMMUNITY (1).

congressional intent. See LEGISLATIVE INTENT.

congressional power. See POWER (3).

Congressional Record. The official record of the daily proceedings in the U.S. Senate and House of Representatives. • Members of Congress are allowed to edit their speeches before printing, and they may insert material never actually spoken by obtaining permission from their respective houses to revise or extend their remarks.

congressional-reference case. See CASE.

Congressional Research Service. A nonpartisan agency in the Library of Congress that researches and analyzes legislative issues for congressional committees and individual members of Congress. • Congress created the agency in 1914 as the Legislative Reference Service. It was renamed in 1970. — Abbr. CRS.

congressional survey. See *government survey* under SURVEY.

Congress of Authors and Artists. *Copyright.* A 19th-century convention of writers, artists, librarians, and others promoting universal copyright protection. • The Congress, which met in 1858, 1861, and 1877, passed resolutions that helped lay the groundwork for the Berne Convention. See BERNE CONVENTION.

conjectural choice, rule of. (1956) The principle that no basis for recovery is presented when all theories of causation rest only on conjecture. See CONJECTURE.

conjecture (kən-**jek**-chər), *n.* (14c) A guess; supposition; surmise. — **conjecture** (kən-**jek**-chər), *vb.* — **conjectural** (kən-**jek**-chər-əl), *adj.*

conjoint (kən-**joynt**), *n.* A person connected with another in a joint interest, obligation, or undertaking, such as a cotenant or spouse. — **conjoint,** *adj.*

conjoint robbery. See ROBBERY.

conjoint will. See *joint will* under WILL.

conjugal (**kon**-jə-gəl), *adj.* (16c) Of or relating to the married state, often with an implied emphasis on sexual relations between spouses <the prisoner was allowed a private bed for conjugal visits>.

conjugal rights. (18c) The rights and privileges arising from the marriage relationship, including the mutual rights of companionship, support, and sexual relations. • Loss of conjugal rights amounts to loss of consortium. See CONSORTIUM.

conjugal union. See MARRIAGE (1).

conjugal visit. An opportunity for physical contact granted to a prisoner and the prisoner's spouse, usu. in the form of an overnight stay at the prison. • Some jurisdictions allow conjugal visits between unmarried partners.

conjunct (kən-**jəngkt** or **kon**-jəngkt), *adj. Civil law.* (Of persons) so closely related to a person (such as an insolvent) as to be disqualified from acting as a judge or witness in a case involving that person.

conjunctive denial. See DENIAL.

conjunctive obligation. See OBLIGATION.

conjuration (kon-jə-**ray**-shən). *Hist.* **1.** A plot or compact made by persons who swear to each other to do something that will result in public harm. **2.** The offense of attempting a conference with evil spirits to discover some secret or effect some purpose; witchcraft; sorcery.

conjurator (**kon**-jə-ray-tər). *Hist.* A person who swears an oath with others; a coconspirator.

con man. See CONFIDENCE MAN.

connecting factor. (1950) *Conflict of laws.* A factual or legal circumstance that helps determine the choice of law by linking an action or individual with a state or jurisdiction. • An example of a connecting factor is a party's domicile within a state. See POINT OF ATTACHMENT.

connecting-up doctrine. (1986) The rule allowing evidence to be conditionally admitted if the offering party promises to show relevance by adducing other evidence.

connexity (kə-**nek**-sə-tee). Connectedness; the quality of being connected. • In some states, *connexity* expresses the relationship that must exist

between a foreign party (such as a corporation) and the state for a plaintiff to maintain personal jurisdiction over the party; generally, the claim must arise from a transaction connected with the activities of the party in the state.

connivance (kə-**nı**-vənts), *n.* (16c) **1.** The act of indulging or ignoring another's wrongdoing, esp. when action should be taken to prevent it. **2.** *Family law.* As a defense to divorce, one spouse's corrupt consent, express or implied, to have the other commit adultery or some other act of sexual misconduct. • Consent is an essential element of connivance. The complaining spouse must have consented to the act complained of. Cf. COLLUSION (2); CONDONATION (2); RECRIMINATION. — **connive** (kə-**nıv**), *vb.*

connive (kə-**nıv**), *vb.* **1.** To knowingly overlook another's wrongdoing. **2.** Loosely, to conspire.

connubium. See CONUBIUM.

conqueror, *n.* [fr. Law French *conquerir* "to acquire"] *Hist.* **1.** One who acquires territory by force during war with the intention of exercising sovereignty. See CONQUEST (1). **2.** The first person who acquired land by purchase; one who first brought an estate into a family. See CONQUEST (2); PURCHASE (2).

conquest. 1. *Int'l law.* An act of force by which, during a war, a belligerent occupies territory within an enemy country with the intention of extending its sovereignty over that territory. • That intention is usu. explained in a proclamation or some other legal act. **2.** *Hist.* The acquisition of land by any method other than descent, esp. by purchase. **3.** *Hist.* The land so acquired. Cf. PURCHASE (2).

consanguine brother. See BROTHER.

consanguine sister. See SISTER.

consanguinity (kon-sang-**gwin**-ə-tee), *n.* (14c) The relationship of persons of the same blood or origin. See *prohibited degree* under DEGREE. Cf. AFFINITY. — **consanguineous,** *adj.*

collateral consanguinity. (16c) The relationship between persons who have the same ancestor but do not descend or ascend from one another (for example, uncle and nephew, cousins, etc.).

lineal consanguinity. The relationship between persons who are directly descended or ascended from one another (for example, mother and daughter, great-grandfather and grandson, etc.).

conscience. (13c) **1.** The moral sense of right or wrong; esp., a moral sense applied to one's own judgment and actions. **2.** In law, the moral rule that requires justice and honest dealings between people.

conscience clause. A legislative provision that allows a person to claim an exemption from compliance, usu. on religious-freedom grounds.

conscience of the court. (17c) **1.** The court's equitable power to decide issues based on notions of fairness and justice. See EQUITY (4). **2.** A standard applied by the court in deciding whether a party or a jury has acted within acceptable limits. • Thus, in some cases, a jury's award of damages is upset because it is said to "shock the conscience of the court." See SHOCK THE CONSCIENCE.

conscientious objector. A person who for moral or religious reasons is opposed to participating in any war, and who may be excused from military conscription but remains subject to serving in civil work for the nation's health, safety, or interest. See 50 USCA § 456. Cf. PACIFIST.

conscionable (kon-shə-nə-bəl), *adj.* (16c) Conforming with good conscience; just and reasonable <a conscionable bargain>. Cf. UNCONSCIONABLE. — **conscionableness, conscionability,** *n.*

conscious avoidance. See *deliberate indifference* under INDIFFERENCE.

conscious-avoidance instruction. See *willful-blindness instruction* under JURY INSTRUCTION.

conscious indifference. See INDIFFERENCE.

consciously parallel. *Antitrust.* Of, relating to, or characterizing the conduct of a party who has knowledge of a competitor's action (such as raising prices) and who makes an independent decision to take the same action. • In some cases this is viewed as evidence of a conspiracy.

conscious parallelism. *Antitrust.* An act of two or more businesses in a concentrated market intentionally engaging in monopolistic conduct. — Also termed *tacit collusion; oligopolistic price coordination.*

conscious-presence test. A method for judging whether a testator is in the presence of a witness to a will, whereby if the testator can sense the presence of the witness — even if the witness cannot be seen — the witness is present. Restatement (Third) of Property: Wills and Other Donative Transfers § 3.1. — Also termed *conscious presence.* See PRESENCE-OF-THE-TESTATOR RULE.

conscription. See DRAFT (2).

consecutive sentences. See SENTENCE.

consecutive tortfeasors. See TORTFEASOR.

consensual (kən-sen-shoo-əl), *adj.* **1.** Having, expressing, or occurring with full consent <consensual relations>. **2.** Created or existing by mutual consent without formalities such as a written document or ceremony <consensual marriage>. — Also termed *consentaneous; consentient.*

consensual contract. See CONTRACT.

consensual crime. See *victimless crime* under CRIME.

consensual marriage. See MARRIAGE (1).

consensual search. See *consent search* under SEARCH.

consensus. A general agreement; collective opinion. See *general consent* under CONSENT (2).

consensus ad idem (kən-**sen**-səs ad I-dem). [Latin] An agreement of parties to the same thing; a meeting of minds. — Also termed *consensus in idem; consensus in idem, placitum et conventio.*

consent, *n.* (14c) **1.** Agreement, approval, or permission as to some act or purpose, esp. given voluntarily by a competent person; legally effective assent. • Consent is an affirmative defense to assault, battery, and related torts, as well as such torts as defamation, invasion of privacy, conversion, and trespass. Consent may be a defense to a crime if the victim has the capacity to consent and if the consent negates an element of the crime or thwarts the harm that the law seeks to prevent. See Model Penal Code § 2.11.

blank consent. See BLANK CONSENT.

express consent. (16c) Consent that is clearly and unmistakably stated.

implied consent. (17c) **1.** Consent inferred from one's conduct rather than from one's direct expression. — Also termed *implied permission.* **2.** Consent imputed as a result of circumstances that arise, as when a surgeon removing a gall bladder discovers and removes colon cancer.

informed consent. (1938) **1.** A person's agreement to allow something to happen, made with full knowledge of the risks involved and the alternatives. • For the legal profession, informed consent is defined in Model Rule of Professional Conduct 1.0(e). **2.** A patient's knowing choice about a medical treatment or procedure, made after a physician or other healthcare provider discloses whatever information a reasonably prudent provider in the medical community would give to a patient regarding the risks involved in the proposed treatment or procedure. — Also termed *knowing consent.*

knowing consent. See *informed consent.*

parental consent. Consent given on a minor's behalf by at least one parent, or a legal guardian, or by another person properly authorized to act for the minor, for the minor to engage in or submit to a specified activity.

voluntary consent. Consent that is given freely and that has not been coerced.

2. *Parliamentary law.* ADOPTION (5). — **consent,** *vb.* — **consensual,** *adj.*

general consent. **1.** Adoption without objection, regardless of whether every voter affirmatively approves. **2.** See *unanimous consent* (1).

unanimous consent. **1.** Adoption with every voter's approval. **2.** See *general consent* (1). • The terms "general consent" and "unanimous consent" have distinct but interchangeable meanings. Some parliamentary manuals treat them as synonymous; others distinguish them; and still others distinguish them, but in exactly the opposite way.

consent agenda. See *consent calendar* under CALENDAR (4).

consentaneous, *adj.* See CONSENSUAL.

consent calendar. 1. *Family law.* A schedule of informal hearings involving a child, usu. arranged when it appears that the child's best interests will be served if the case is heard informally. ● The child and all interested parties must first consent before the case goes on the consent calendar. **2.** For the parliamentary sense relating to a deliberative assembly's business, see *consent calendar* under CALENDAR (4).

consent clause. See AUTHORIZATION CLAUSE.

consent decree. See DECREE.

consent dividend. See DIVIDEND.

consentient, *adj.* See CONSENSUAL.

consent judgment. See *agreed judgment* under JUDGMENT.

consent jurisdiction. See JURISDICTION.

consent order. See *consent decree* under DECREE.

consent search. See SEARCH.

consent to be sued. (1872) Agreement in advance to be sued in a particular forum. See COGNOVIT CLAUSE.

consent to notice. (1996) A provision stating that notice required by a document may be given beforehand or to a designated person.

consequential contempt. See CONTEMPT.

consequential damages. See DAMAGES.

consequential economic loss. See ECONOMIC LOSS.

consequential injury. See *consequential loss* under LOSS.

consequentialism. *Ethics.* An ethical theory that judges the rightness or wrongness of actions according to their consequences. ● One of the best-known types of consequentialism is utilitarianism. See UTILITARIANISM. Cf. VIRTUE ETHICS.

consequential loss. See LOSS.

conservation. *Environmental law.* The supervision, management, and maintenance of natural resources; the protection, improvement, and use of natural resources in a way that ensures the highest social as well as economic benefits.

conservation easement. See EASEMENT.

conservation restriction. See *conservation easement* under EASEMENT.

conservation servitude. See *conservation easement* under EASEMENT.

conservator (kən-**sər**-və-tər *or* **kon**-sər-vay-tər), *n.* (15c) A guardian, protector, or preserver. ● *Conservator* is the modern equivalent of the common-law *guardian*. Judicial appointment and supervision are still required, but a conservator has far more flexible authority than a guardian, including the same investment powers that a trustee enjoys. The Uniform Probate Code uses the term *conservator*, and Article 5 is representative of modern conservatorship laws. — **conservatorship,** *n.*

managing conservator. (1974) **1.** A person appointed by a court to manage the estate or affairs of someone who is legally incapable of doing so; GUARDIAN (1). **2.** In the child-custody laws of some states, the parent who has primary custody of a child, with the right to establish the child's primary domicile. See CUSTODY.

possessory conservator. (1974) See *noncustodial parent* under PARENT.

conservator of the peace. See PEACE OFFICER.

conserve, *vb.* **1.** To take care of; to care for. **2.** To protect from change, destruction, or depletion. **3.** To reduce or minimize the use of.

consideration, *n.* (16c) **1.** Something (such as an act, a forbearance, or a return promise) bargained for and received by a promisor from a promisee; that which motivates a person to do something, esp. to engage in a legal act. ● Consideration, or a substitute such as promissory estoppel, is necessary for an agreement to be enforceable. See Restatement (Second) of Contracts § 81 (1979).

adequate consideration. (17c) Consideration that is fair and reasonable under the circumstances of the agreement. Cf. *sufficient consideration.*

and other good and valuable consideration. See *other consideration.*

concurrent consideration. Consideration arising at the same time as other consideration, or where the promises are simultaneous.

continuing consideration. An act or performance extending over time.

due consideration. See *sufficient consideration.*

executed consideration. A consideration that has been wholly given; past consideration as opposed to present or future consideration.

executory consideration (eg-**zek**-yə-tor-ee). A consideration that is to be given only after formation of the contract; present or future consideration as opposed to past consideration.

express consideration. Consideration that is specifically stated in an instrument.

fair consideration. (18c) **1.** Consideration that is roughly equal in value to the thing being exchanged; consideration given for property or for an obligation in either of the following circumstances: (1) when given in good faith as an exchange for the property or obligation, or (2) when the property or obligation is received in good faith to secure a present advance or prior debt in an amount not disproportionately small as compared with the value of the property or obligation obtained. — Also termed *fair and valuable consideration*. **2.** Consideration that is honest, reasonable, and free from suspicion, but not strictly adequate or full.

future consideration. (1979) **1.** Consideration to be given in the future; esp., consideration that is due after the other party's performance. **2.** Consideration that is a series of performances, some of which will occur after the other party's performance. **3.** Consideration the specifics of which have not been agreed on between the parties. Cf. *past consideration*.

good and valuable consideration. See *valuable consideration*.

good consideration. (18c) **1.** Consideration based on natural love or affection or on moral duty <good consideration, being based purely on affection, does not amount to valuable consideration>. • Such consideration is usu. not valid for the enforcement of a contract. — Also termed *meritorious consideration*; *moral consideration*. **2.** Loosely, valuable consideration; consideration that is adequate to support the bargained-for exchange between the parties <his agreement to pay the offering price was good consideration for the sale>.

gratuitous consideration (grǝ-t[y]oo-i-tǝs). (1880) Consideration that, not being founded on any detriment to the party who gives it, will not support a contract; a performance for which a party was already obligated.

grossly inadequate consideration. Consideration whose value is so much less than the fair value of the object acquired that it may not support finding that the transaction is a valid exchange. • Depending on the surrounding circumstances, the transaction may actually be fraud, a gift, or something else other than a sale and purchase.

illegal consideration. (18c) Consideration that is contrary to the law or public policy, or prejudicial to the public interest. • Such consideration does not support a contract.

immoral consideration. A consideration that so offends societal norms as to be invalid. • A contract supported by immoral consideration is usu. voidable or unenforceable. — Also termed *turpis causa*.

implied consideration. (18c) Consideration that is inferred by law from the parties' actions.

impossible consideration. Consideration stemming from a promise or performance that cannot be fulfilled.

inadequate consideration. (18c) Consideration that is not fair or reasonable under the circumstances of the agreement. Cf. *adequate consideration*.

invented consideration. (1977) Fictional consideration created by a court to prevent the invalidation of a contract that lacks consideration.

legal consideration. See VALUABLE CONSIDERATION.

legally sufficient consideration. See *sufficient consideration*.

meritorious consideration. See *good consideration*.

moral consideration. See *good consideration*.

nominal consideration. (18c) Consideration that is so insignificant as to bear no relationship to the value of what is being exchanged (e.g., $10 for a piece of real estate). • Such consideration can be valid, since courts do not ordinarily examine the adequacy of consideration (although they do often inquire into such issues as fraud and duress). — Also termed *peppercorn*.

other consideration. (18c) Additional things of value to be provided under the terms of a contract, usu. unspecified in the contract, deed, or bill of sale, because they are too numerous to conveniently list, or to avoid public knowledge of the total amount of consideration. — Also termed *other good and valuable consideration*.

past consideration. (18c) An act done or a promise given by a promisee before making a promise sought to be enforced. • Past consideration is not consideration for the new promise because it has not been given in exchange for this promise (although exceptions exist for new promises to pay debts barred by limitations or debts discharged in bankruptcy). See PREEXISTING-DUTY RULE. Cf. *future consideration*.

sufficient consideration. (17c) Enough consideration as a matter of law to support a contract. — Also termed *due consideration*; *legally sufficient consideration*. Cf. *adequate consideration*.

valuable consideration. (17c) Consideration that is valid under the law; consideration that either confers a pecuniarily measurable benefit on one party or imposes a pecuniarily measurable detriment on the other. — Also termed *good and valuable consideration*; *legal consideration*.

2. *Parliamentary law.* The process by which a deliberative assembly disposes of a motion; DELIBERATION. • Consideration begins with a member making a motion and the chair stating the question on the motion; it ends with the chair putting the question on the motion (or on a subsidiary motion that disposes of the first motion). It also includes debate and may also include (among other things) amendment and referral to a committee.

consideration by paragraph. See *consideration seriatim.*

consideration seriatim. Consideration serially, whereby a deliberative assembly considers a long or complex motion in a series of readily divisible parts before voting on the entire motion. — Also termed *consideration by paragraph* (in which case a "paragraph" means not a literary paragraph but any readily divisible part of a motion, which may include more than one literary paragraph); *serial consideration.*

informal consideration. Consideration without limit on how often a member may speak to the same question. • Informal consideration is substantially equivalent to consideration in committee of the whole or quasi committee of the whole, without the fiction of the assembly resolving itself into a committee. See *committee of the whole* under COMMITTEE.

serial consideration. See *consideration seriatim.*

3. *Hist.* A court's judgment. — Also termed (in Roman law) *consideratio.*

consideration, failure of. See FAILURE OF CONSIDERATION.

consideration, want of. See WANT OF CONSIDERATION.

consign (kən-**sin**), *vb.* (16c) **1.** To transfer to another's custody or charge. **2.** To give (goods) to a carrier for delivery to a designated recipient. **3.** To give (merchandise or the like) to another to sell, usu. with the understanding that the seller will pay the owner for the goods from the proceeds.

consignation (kon-sig-**nay**-shən), *n.* **1.** A debtor's delivery of money to an authorized third party after the creditor refuses to accept the payment. • Unlike a tender, a valid consignation discharges the debtor. Cf. TENDER (1). **2.** CONSIGNMENT (1).

consignator (kən-**sig**-nə-tor), *n.* A person authorized to accept delivery of money from a debtor if a creditor refuses to accept it. See CONSIGNATION.

consignee (kon-sɪ-**nee** *or* kən-). (18c) One to whom goods are consigned. Cf. CONSIGNOR.

consignment (kən-**sin**-mənt). (17c) **1.** The act of consigning goods for custody or sale. — Also termed (archaically) *consignation.* **2.** A quantity of goods delivered by this act, esp. in a single shipment. **3.** Under the UCC, a transaction in which a person delivers goods to a merchant for the purpose of sale, and (1) the merchant deals in goods of that kind under a name other than the name of the person making delivery, is not an auctioneer,

and is not generally known by its creditor to be substantially engaged in selling others' goods, (2) with respect to each delivery, the aggregate value of the goods is $1,000 or more at the time of delivery, (3) the goods are not consumer goods immediately before delivery, and (4) the transaction does not create a security interest that secures an obligation. UCC § 9-102(a)(20). **4.** See *bailment for sale* under BAILMENT.

consignment sale. See SALE.

consignor (kən-**sɪ**-nər *or* kon-sɪ-**nor**). (18c) One who dispatches goods to another on consignment. Cf. CONSIGNEE.

consimili casu. See CASU CONSIMILI.

consistory court (kən-**sis**-tər-ee). *Eccles. law.* In England, a diocesan court exercising jurisdiction over the clergy and church property, such as a cemetery, and other ecclesiastical matters. • Consistory courts are presided over by the bishop's chancellor or the chancellor's commissary. — Also termed *consistorial court.* Cf. BISHOP'S COURT.

consol (**kon**-sol *or* kən-**sol**). See *annuity bond* under BOND (3).

consolidate, *vb.* **1.** To combine or unify into one mass or body. **2.** *Civil procedure.* To combine, through court order, two or more actions involving the same parties or issues into a single action ending in a single judgment or, sometimes, in separate judgments. **3.** *Corporations.* To unite (two or more corporations or other organizations) to create one new corporation or other organization.

consolidated appeal. See APPEAL.

consolidated bond. See BOND (3).

consolidated financial statement. See FINANCIAL STATEMENT.

consolidated laws. See CODE (1).

consolidated mortgage. See MORTGAGE.

Consolidated Omnibus Budget Reconciliation Act of 1985. A federal statute requiring employers that offer group health coverage to their employees to continue to do so for a prescribed period (usu. 18 to 36 months) after employment has terminated so that the former employee can continue to benefit from group-health rates until becoming a member of another health-insurance plan. • The statute temporarily continues group-health coverage for a person no longer entitled to receive it, such as a terminated employee or an overage dependent. "Qualifying events" justifying the continuation of group-health-insurance benefits include divorce, legal separation, or the death of a spouse. So COBRA often provides critical transitional coverage until a separated, divorced, or surviving spouse and children can arrange for new health insurance. The period of transitional coverage is up to 36 months, and an applicant spouse of the employee must make written application to the employer within 60 days of the separation or divorce. — Abbr. COBRA.

consolidated return. See TAX RETURN.

consolidated school district. See SCHOOL DISTRICT.

consolidated security. See SECURITY.

consolidated sentence. See *general sentence* under SENTENCE.

consolidating statute. See STATUTE.

consolidation, *n.* (15c) **1.** The act or process of uniting; the state of being united. **2.** *Legislation.* The combination into a single statutory measure of various legislative provisions that have previously been scattered in different statutes. **3.** *Civil procedure.* The court-ordered unification of two or more actions, involving the same parties and issues, into a single action resulting in a single judgment or, sometimes, in separate judgments. Fed. R. Civ. P. 42(a). — Also termed *consolidation of actions.* Cf. JOINDER; SEVERANCE (2).

> *procedural consolidation.* See JOINT ADMINISTRATION.

> *substantive consolidation.* *Bankruptcy.* The merger of two or more bankruptcy cases, usu. pending against the same debtor or related debtors, into one estate for purposes of distributing the assets, usu. resulting in the two estates sharing assets and liabilities, and in the extinguishment of duplicate claims and claims between the debtors.

4. *Corporations.* The unification of two or more corporations or other organizations by dissolving the existing ones and creating a single new corporation or organization. — Also termed (with respect to corporations) *consolidation of corporations.* Cf. MERGER (8). **5.** *Corporations. Archaic.* A union of the stock, property, or franchises of two or more companies whereby the conduct of their affairs is permanently — or for a long period — put under one management, whether the agreement between them is by lease, sale, or other form of contract, and whether the effect is the dissolution of one, both, or neither of the companies. — **consolidate,** *vb.* — **consolidatory** (kən-sol-ə-**day**-tər-ee), *adj.*

consolidation loan. See LOAN.

consolidation of actions. See CONSOLIDATION (3).

consolidation of corporations. See CONSOLIDATION (4).

consolidation of mortgages. *Hist.* The equitable right of a mortgagee who holds multiple mortgages on real property owned by the same person to refuse to release one mortgage unless all the mortgages are redeemed.

consonant statement. See STATEMENT.

consortium (kən-**sor**-shee-əm). (1836) **1.** The benefits that one person, esp. a spouse, is entitled to receive from another, including companionship, cooperation, affection, aid, financial support, and (between spouses) sexual relations <a claim for loss of consortium>. See LOSS OF CONSORTIUM; CONJUGAL RIGHTS.

> *filial consortium* (**fil**-ee-əl). A child's society, affection, and companionship given to a parent.

> *parental consortium.* A parent's society, affection, and companionship given to a child.

> *spousal consortium.* A spouse's society, affection, and companionship given to the other spouse.

2. *Hist.* The services of a wife or daughter, the loss of which gives rise to a cause of action. • A husband could, for example, bring an action against a person who had injured his wife, "whereby he lost the help or companionship (of his wife)" (*per quod consortium amisit*). **3.** A group of companies that join or associate in an enterprise <several high-tech businesses formed a consortium to create a new supercomputer>. **4.** *Roman law.* A community of undivided goods existing among coheirs after the death of the head of their family (*paterfamilias*). Pl. **consortiums, consortia.**

consortship (**kon**-sort-ship). *Maritime law.* An agreement by which salvors agree to work together to salvage wrecks, the recovery being apportioned among the salvors. • Consortships reduce interference among competing salvors and help prevent collisions at sea between operators attempting to salvage the same wreck.

conspicuous, *adj.* (1534) (Of a term or clause) clearly visible or obvious. • Whether a printed clause is conspicuous as a matter of law usu. depends on the size and style of the typeface. Under the UCC, a term or clause is conspicuous if it is written in a way that a reasonable person against whom it is to operate ought to notice it. UCC § 1-201(10). See FINE PRINT.

conspicuous place. (18c) For purposes of posting notices, a location that is reasonably likely to be seen.

conspiracy, *n.* (14c) An agreement by two or more persons to commit an unlawful act, coupled with an intent to achieve the agreement's objective, and (in most states) action or conduct that furthers the agreement; a combination for an unlawful purpose. 18 USCA § 371. • Conspiracy is a separate offense from the crime that is the object of the conspiracy. A conspiracy ends when the unlawful act has been committed or (in some states) when the agreement has been abandoned. A conspiracy does not automatically end if the conspiracy's object is defeated. *See* Model Penal Code § 5.03(7); *United States v. Jiminez Recio*, 537 U.S. 270, 123 S.Ct. 819 (2003). — Also termed *criminal conspiracy*. Cf. ATTEMPT (2); SOLICITATION (2). — **conspiratorial,** *adj.*

bathtub conspiracy. See *intra-enterprise conspiracy*.

chain conspiracy. (1959) A single conspiracy in which each person is responsible for a distinct act within the overall plan, such as an agreement to produce, import, and distribute narcotics in which each person performs only one function. • All participants are interested in the overall scheme and liable for all other participants' acts in furtherance of that scheme.

circle conspiracy. See *wheel conspiracy*.

civil conspiracy. (1901) An agreement between two or more persons to commit an unlawful act that causes damage to a person or property.

conspiracy in restraint of trade. See RESTRAINT OF TRADE.

conspiracy to infringe. *Intellectual property.* An agreement by two or more persons to commit an act that would interfere with the exclusive rights of a patent, copyright, or trademark owner. • This action is commonly recognized in trademark law. 18 USCA § 371; 17 USCA § 506(a)(1). The Copyright Act does not provide a basis for alleging a conspiracy to infringe, but an action is recognized by some states. The Patent Act provides no basis for an action asserting conspiracy to infringe because patent law covers only acts, not threats of acts.

conspiracy to monopolize. *Antitrust.* A conspiracy to take exclusive control of a commercial market. • Under § 2 of the Sherman Act, a conspiracy to monopolize exists if there is a conspiracy or concerted action directed at a substantial part of interstate commerce with the intent to acquire monopoly power.

hub-and-spoke conspiracy. See *wheel conspiracy*.

intracorporate conspiracy. A conspiracy existing between a corporation and its own officers, agents, or employees. • To be prosecutable under federal law, the conspiracy must involve at least two persons (i.e., not just the corporation and one person). 18 USCA § 371. A corporation cannot conspire with its employees, and its employees, acting in the scope of their employment, conspire among themselves. *McAndrew v. Lockheed Martin Corp.*, 206 F.3d 1031, 1035 (11th Cir. 2000).

intra-enterprise conspiracy. *Antitrust.* A conspiracy existing between two subsidiaries, divisions, or other parts of the same firm. — Also termed *bathtub conspiracy*.

seditious conspiracy. (1893) A criminal conspiracy to forcibly (1) overthrow or destroy the U.S. government, (2) oppose its authority, (3) prevent the execution of its laws, or (4) seize or possess its property. 18 USCA § 2384.

wheel conspiracy. (1959) A conspiracy in which a single member or group (the "hub") separately agrees with two or more other members or groups (the "spokes"). • The person or group at the hub is the only party liable for all the conspiracies. — Also termed *circle conspiracy*; *hub-and-spoke conspiracy*.

conspirator, *n.* (15c) A person who takes part in a conspiracy.

unindicted conspirator. See *unindicted coconspirator* under COCONSPIRATOR.

conspire, *vb.* To engage in conspiracy; to join in a conspiracy.

constable (**kon**-stə-bəl), *n.* (13c) **1.** A peace officer responsible for minor judicial duties, such as serving writs and warrants, but with less authority and smaller jurisdiction than a sheriff. **2.** In the United Kingdom, a police officer; also, the title of a police officer. — **constabulary** (kən-**stab**-yə-ler-ee), *adj.* — **constabulary** (police station or force), *n.*

constablewick (**kon**-stə-bəl-wik). *Hist.* In the United Kingdom, the territorial jurisdiction of a constable. Cf. BAILIWICK.

constant dollars. The value of current money expressed as a percentage of its buying power in a previous year as determined by the consumer price index. • This value is used as a measure of inflation.

constate (kən-**stayt**), *vb.* To establish, constitute, or ordain. • *Constate* usu. appears in relation to corporate documents; for example, a corporation is constated by its charter, organic law, or grant of powers to it.

constituency. 1. The body of citizens dwelling in a defined area and entitled to elect a representative. **2.** The residents of an electoral district.

constituency-based quorum. See *interest-based quorum* under QUORUM.

constituent, *adj.* **1.** (Of a component) that helps make up or complete a unit or a whole <a constituent element of the criminal offense>. **2.** (Of an assembly) able to frame or amend a constitution <a constituent council>.

constituent, *n.* (17c) **1.** A person who gives another the authority to act as a representative; a principal who appoints an agent. **2.** Someone who is represented by a legislator or other elected official. **3.** One part of something that makes up a whole; an element. — **constituency,** *n.*

constituent element. An essential component of a crime or cause of action.

constituted annuity. See ANNUITY.

constituted authority. See AUTHORITY (3).

constitution. (18c) **1.** The fundamental and organic law of a nation or state that establishes the institutions and apparatus of government, defines the scope of governmental sovereign powers, and guarantees individual civil rights and civil liberties. **2.** The written instrument embodying this fundamental law, together with any formal amendments.

flexible constitution. A constitution that has few or no special amending procedures. • The British Constitution is an example. Parliament can alter constitutional principles and define new baselines for government action through ordinary legislative processes. The Canadian Constitution also grants its legislature some limited ability to amend the Constitution by legislation.

rigid constitution. A constitution whose terms cannot be altered by ordinary forms of legislation, only by special amending procedures. • The U.S. Constitution is an example. It cannot be changed without the consent of three-fourths of the state legislatures or through a constitutional convention. U.S. Const. art. V.

unwritten constitution. **1.** The customs and values, some of which are expressed in statutes, that provide the organic and fundamental law of a state or country that does not have a single written document functioning as a constitution. • In British constitutional law, the constitution is a collection of historical documents, statutes, decrees, conventions, traditions, and royal prerogatives. Documents and statutes include Magna Carta (1215), the Bill of Rights (1689), and the European Communities Act (1972). **2.** The implied parts of a written constitution, encompassing the rights, freedoms, and processes considered to be essential, but not explicitly defined in the written document. • Many aspects of an unwritten constitution are based on custom and precedent. The U.S. Constitution does not, for example, give the Supreme Court the power to declare laws unconstitutional but the Court does so without question. Nor does the Constitution expressly guarantee a right of privacy, but the Supreme Court has declared that the right exists and is protected. See PENUMBRA; RIGHT OF PRIVACY.

3. A nation's history of government and institutional development. • This was the standard definition before the United States produced the first written constitution. It remains current in Great Britain and other nations that have unwritten constitutions. **4.** *Parliamentary law.* A

governing document adopted by an organization for its internal governance and its external dealings. • The constitution may be an organization's most authoritative governing document, but if the organization has also received a charter or adopted articles of incorporation or association, then the constitution is subordinate to them. If the organization has also adopted bylaws, then the bylaws are subordinate to (and usu. more easily amended than) the constitution. The constitution and bylaws are sometimes contained in a single document. See *governing document* under DOCUMENT. Cf. BYLAW (1).

constitutional, *adj.* (18c) **1.** Of or relating to a constitution <constitutional rights>. **2.** Proper and valid under a constitution <constitutional actions>.

constitutional challenge. See CHALLENGE (1).

constitutional convention. See CONVENTION (2).

constitutional court. See COURT.

constitutional-fact doctrine. 1. The rule that federal courts are not bound by an administrative agency's findings of fact when the facts involve whether the agency has exceeded constitutional limitations on its power, esp. regarding personal rights. • The courts reviewed the facts de novo to afford protection of constitutional rights. Although it has not been overruled or wholly discredited, this rule has fallen out of favor. **2.** The rule that a federal appellate court is not bound by a trial court's findings of fact when constitutional rights are implicated, specifically in citizenship-determination and First Amendment cases. *See, e.g., Bose Corp. v. Consumers Union,* 466 U.S. 485, 104 S.Ct. 1949 (1984). Cf. JURISDICTIONAL-FACT DOCTRINE.

constitutional freedom. (1822) A basic liberty guaranteed by the Constitution or Bill of Rights, such as the freedom of speech. — Also termed *constitutional protection; constitutional liberty.*

constitutional guarantee. A promise contained in the United States Constitution that supports or establishes an inalienable right, such as the right to due process.

constitutional homestead. See HOMESTEAD.

constitutional immunity. See IMMUNITY (1).

constitutionality, *n.* The quality or state of being constitutional <the constitutionality of the senator's bill is questionable>.

constitutionalize, *vb.* (1831) **1.** To provide with a constitution <constitutionalize the new government>. **2.** To make constitutional; to bring in line with a constitution <the court plans to constitutionalize the segregated school district>. **3.** To make a constitutional question out of (a question of law); to subject (issue, etc.) to the burden of passing constitutional muster <the dissenter

accused the majority of unnecessarily constitutionalizing its issue>.

constitutional law. (18c) **1.** The body of law deriving from the U.S. Constitution and dealing primarily with governmental powers, civil rights, and civil liberties. **2.** The body of legal rules that determine the constitution of a state or country with an unwritten constitution. Cf. STATUTORY LAW; COMMON LAW. **3.** The field of law dealing with aspects of constitutional provisions, such as restrictions on government powers and guarantees of rights.

constitutional liberty. See CONSTITUTIONAL FREEDOM.

constitutional limitation. (18c) A constitutional provision that restricts the powers of a governmental branch, department, agency, or officer.

constitutional majority. See *majority of all the members* under MAJORITY.

constitutional malice. See *actual malice* (2) under MALICE.

constitutional monarchy. See *limited monarchy* under MONARCHY.

constitutional office. A public position that is created by a constitution, rather than by a statute.

constitutional officer. See OFFICER (1).

constitutional protection. See CONSTITUTIONAL FREEDOM.

constitutional question. (18c) A legal issue resolvable by the interpretation of a constitution, rather than a statute.

constitutional right. (18c) A right guaranteed by a constitution; esp., one guaranteed by the U.S. Constitution or by a state constitution.

constitutional taking. See TAKING (2).

constitutional tort. See TORT.

Constitutions of Clarendon. *Hist.* A 12th-century statement of customary law, produced during the reign of Henry II, intended to limit the jurisdiction of the ecclesiastical courts and narrow the clergy's exemption from secular justice.

constitutum possessorium (kon-sti-t[y]oo-təm pah-ses-**sor**-ee-əm). [Latin "possessory agreement"] *Roman law.* **1.** A type of constructive delivery in which mediate possession is transferred while the immediate control or custody remains in the transferor. **2.** The agreement by which this transfer is brought about. ● In the context of a security interest, the pledged property may remain in the possession of the debtor, but as bailee of the creditor. For the other two types of constructive delivery, see ATTORNMENT; BREVI MANU. — Also termed *traditio longa manu* (trə-**dish**-ee-oh **long**-gə **man**-yoo).

construction, *n.* (14c) **1.** The act of building by combining or arranging parts or elements; the thing so built. **2.** The act or process of interpreting or explaining the sense or intention of a writing (usu. a constitution, statute, or instrument); the ascertainment of a document's meaning in accordance with judicial standards. — **construct** (for sense 1), *vb.* — **construe** (for sense 2), *vb.*

construction ut res magis valeat quam pereat (kən-**strək**-shən ət rays [*or* reez *or* rez] **may**-jis **vay**-lee-at kwam **peer**-ee-at). [Latin "a construction that gives effect to the matter rather than having it fail"] A construction arrived at when alternative readings are possible, one of which (usu. the broader reading) would achieve the manifest purpose of the document and one of which (usu. the narrower reading) would reduce it to futility or absurdity, whereby the interpreter chooses the one that gives effect to the document's purpose.

contemporaneous construction. An interpretation given at or near the time when a writing was prepared, usu. by one or more persons involved in its preparation. — Also termed *practical construction; practical interpretation; contemporaneous and practical interpretation.* See CONTEMPORANEOUS-CONSTRUCTION DOCTRINE.

liberal construction. (17c) An interpretation that applies to a writing in light of the situation presented and that tends to effectuate the spirit and purpose of the writing. — Also termed *equitable construction; loose construction; broad interpretation.* Cf. *strict construction.*

literal construction. See *strict construction.*

loose construction. See *liberal construction.*

practical construction. See *contemporaneous construction.*

purposive construction (pər-pə-siv). An interpretation that looks to the "evil" that the statute is trying to correct (i.e., the statute's purpose). — Also termed *teleological interpretation.* See *liberal construction.*

statutory construction. See STATUTORY CONSTRUCTION.

strict construction. (16c) **1.** An interpretation that considers only the literal words of a writing. — Also termed *literal construction; literal interpretation.* See STRICT CONSTRUCTIONISM. **2.** A construction that considers words narrowly, usu. in their historical context. ● This type of construction treats statutory and contractual words with highly restrictive readings. — Also termed *strict interpretation.* **3.** The philosophy underlying strict interpretation of statutes. See *strict constructionism* under CONSTRUCTIONISM.

construction bond. See BOND (3).

construction contract. See CONTRACT.

construction financing. See *interim financing* under FINANCING.

constructionism. A judicial approach to interpreting the text of statutes, regulations, constitutions, and the like.

> **broad constructionism.** See *liberal constructionism*.

> **liberal constructionism.** Broad interpretation of a text's language, including the use of related writings to clarify the meanings of the words, and possibly also a consideration of meaning in both contemporary and current lights. — Also termed *broad constructionism*; *loose constructionism*.

> **loose constructionism.** See *liberal constructionism*.

> **strict constructionism,** *n.* (1892) The doctrinal view of judicial construction holding that judges should interpret a document or statute (esp. one involving penal sanctions) according to its literal terms, without looking to other sources to ascertain the meaning. — Also termed *strict construction*; *literal canon*; *literal rule*; *textualism*. — **strict constructionist,** *n.*

constructionist. One who interprets a controlling text, such as a statute, constitution, or the like.

> **broad constructionist.** See *liberal constructionist*.

> **liberal constructionist.** A decision-maker who derives the meaning of a text's language not only from the words but from reasonable inferences drawn from the words and from other sources, such as a statute's legislative history. • A liberal constructionist may also consider the reasonableness of an interpretation under modern social mores. — Also termed *broad constructionist, loose constructionist*. See *liberal constructionism* under CONSTRUCTIONISM. Cf. *strict constructionist*.

> **loose constructionist.** See *liberal constructionist*.

> **strict constructionist.** A decision-maker who derives a text's meaning narrowly, using tools such as originalism or textualism, and applies the text according to that meaning. See ORIGINALISM; *strict constructionism* under CONSTRUCTIONISM. Cf. *liberal constructionist*.

construction lien. See *mechanic's lien* under LIEN.

construction loan. See *building loan* under LOAN.

construction mortgage. See MORTGAGE.

construction statute. See STATUTE.

construction warranty. See WARRANTY (2).

constructive, *adj.* (17c) Legally imputed; existing by virtue of legal fiction though not existing in fact. • Courts usu. give something a constructive effect for equitable reasons <the court held that the shift supervisor had constructive knowledge of the machine's failure even though he did not actually know until two days later>. See LEGAL FICTION. Cf. ACTUAL.

constructive abandonment. 1. *Family law.* See *constructive desertion* under DESERTION. 2. *Intellectual property.* ABANDONMENT (10).

constructive adverse possession. See ADVERSE POSSESSION.

constructive amendment of indictment. See AMENDMENT OF INDICTMENT.

constructive assent. See ASSENT.

constructive authority. See AUTHORITY (1).

constructive bailment. See BAILMENT.

constructive breach. See *anticipatory breach* under BREACH OF CONTRACT.

constructive breaking into a house. See *constructive housebreaking* under HOUSEBREAKING.

constructive condemnation. See *inverse condemnation* under CONDEMNATION.

constructive condition. See CONDITION (2).

constructive contempt. See *indirect contempt* under CONTEMPT.

constructive contract. See *implied-in-law contract* under CONTRACT.

constructive conversion. See CONVERSION (2).

constructive crime. See CRIME.

constructive custody. See CUSTODY (1).

constructive delivery. See DELIVERY.

constructive desertion. See DESERTION.

constructive discharge. See DISCHARGE (7).

constructive dividend. See DIVIDEND.

constructive emancipation. See EMANCIPATION.

constructive escape. See ESCAPE (2).

constructive eviction. See EVICTION.

constructive force. See FORCE.

constructive fraud. See FRAUD.

constructive housebreaking. See HOUSEBREAKING.

constructive intent. See INTENT (1).

constructive knowledge. See KNOWLEDGE.

constructive larceny. See LARCENY.

constructive loss. See *constructive total loss* (1) under LOSS.

constructive malice. See *implied malice* under MALICE.

constructive murder. See *felony murder* under MURDER.

constructive notice. See NOTICE.

constructive occupancy. See OCCUPANCY.

constructive parent. See *equitable parent* under PARENT.

constructive payment. See PAYMENT.

constructive possession. See POSSESSION.

constructive presence. See PRESENCE.

constructive-receipt doctrine. (1936) The rule that gross income under a taxpayer's control before it is actually received (such as accumulated interest income that has not been withdrawn) must be included by the taxpayer in gross income, unless the actual receipt is subject to significant constraints. IRC (26 USCA) § 451.

constructive reduction to practice. See REDUCTION TO PRACTICE.

constructive search. See SEARCH.

constructive seisin. See *seisin in law* under SEISIN.

constructive seizure. See SEIZURE.

constructive service. 1. See SERVICE (2). **2.** See DOCTRINE OF CONSTRUCTIVE SERVICE (2).

constructive taking. See TAKING (1).

constructive total loss. See LOSS.

constructive transfer. See TRANSFER.

constructive treason. See TREASON.

constructive trespass. See *trespass to chattels* under TRESPASS.

constructive trust. See TRUST.

construe (kən-**stroo**), *vb.* (14c) To analyze and explain the meaning of (a sentence or passage) <the court construed the language of the statute>.

constuprate (**kon**-st[y]ə-prayt), *vb. Archaic.* To rape or violate (a person).

consuetudinary law. See LAW.

consul (**kon**-səl), *n.* **1.** A governmental representative living in a foreign country to oversee commercial and other matters involving the representative's home country and its citizens in that foreign country. • Consuls are not diplomatic agents, so unless a treaty provides otherwise, they do not enjoy diplomatic privileges and immunities. But consuls are entitled to consular immunities, which protect them from local law and jurisdiction in the exercise of their consular functions. — **consular** (**kon**-sə-lər), *adj.* — **consulship** (**kon**-səl-ship), *n.*

consul general. A high-ranking consul appointed to a strategically important region and often having supervisory powers over other regions or other consuls.

2. *Roman law.* One of two chief magistrates elected annually during the Republic to exercise supreme authority. • Under the Empire, the consulship was reduced to a sinecure, held by appointees of the emperor or the emperor himself.

consular court. See COURT.

consular invoice. See INVOICE.

consular jurisdiction. The exercise of a judicial function by a consul in a foreign territory, as by performing a wedding ceremony between nationals of the country represented by the consul.

consular law. The law relating to consuls, developed through custom and multitudes of bilateral consular agreements.

consular marriage. See MARRIAGE (1).

consular relations. *Int'l law.* The aggregate of relations established between two countries through the exercise of consuls' functions on behalf of a sending state within the territory of a receiving state. See *sending state* and *receiving state* under STATE.

consulate (**kon**-sə-lit). **1.** The office or jurisdiction of a consul <the senator advised the businessman to notify the U.S. consulate in Kuwait before visiting the country>. **2.** The location of a consul's office or residence <the family was staying on the second floor, just above the Turkish consulate>.

foreign consulate. The consulate of a foreign country in the receiving state.

3. Government by consuls <after the French Revolution, the Directory was overthrown and the Consulate was created>. • This sense of *consulate* is based on the original Roman meaning ("chief magistrate") — not on the modern sense of an overseas representative of a country.

consul general. See CONSUL.

consultation, *n.* (15c) **1.** The act of asking the advice or opinion of someone (such as a lawyer). **2.** A meeting in which parties consult or confer. **3.** *Int'l law.* The interactive methods by which states seek to prevent or resolve disputes. — **consult,** *vb.* — **consulting, consultative,** *adj.*

consultative exam. As a foundation for an expert opinion, a check-up performed by a qualified medical professional to determine whether a person has a mental or physical disability, and, if so, the extent of the disability and expectations for improvement.

consulting expert. See EXPERT.

consumable, *n.* (1802) A thing (such as food) that cannot be used without changing or extinguishing its substance. Cf. NONCONSUMABLE. — **consumable,** *adj.*

consumer. (15c) A person who buys goods or services for personal, family, or household use, with no intention of resale; a natural person who uses products for personal rather than business purposes.

consumer boycott. See BOYCOTT.

consumer confusion. *Trademarks.* The incorrect perception formed by a purchaser or user about a product's or service's manufacturer or origin. • The mistake usu. occurs when a product or service is marketed in a way that makes it appear to be affiliated with a well-known product, service, or provider. — Also termed *actual consumer confusion; user confusion; actual user confusion.*

consumer-contemplation test. (1979) A method of imposing product liability on a manufacturer if the evidence shows that a product's danger is greater than that which a reasonable consumer would expect. — Also termed *consumer-user-contemplation test; consumer-expectation test.* Cf. RISK-UTILITY TEST.

consumer credit. See CREDIT (4).

Consumer Credit Code. See UNIFORM CONSUMER CREDIT CODE.

Consumer Credit Protection Act. A federal statute that safeguards consumers in the use of credit by (1) requiring full disclosure of the terms of loan agreements, including finance charges, (2) restricting the garnishment of wages, and (3) regulating the use of credit cards. 15 USCA §§ 1601–1693. • Many states have also adopted consumer-credit-protection acts. — Abbr. CCPA. — Also termed *Truth in Lending Act* (abbr. TILA). See UNIFORM CONSUMER CREDIT CODE.

consumer-credit sale. See SALE.

consumer-credit transaction. (1954) A transaction by which a person receives a loan to buy consumer goods or services. • Consumer-credit transactions are usu. subject to regulations enacted for the consumer's protection.

consumer debt. See DEBT.

consumer-expectation test. See CONSUMER-CONTEMPLATION TEST.

consumer finance company. See FINANCE COMPANY.

consumer goods. See GOODS.

consumer-goods transaction. *Secured transactions.* A transaction in which (1) an individual incurs an obligation primarily for a personal, family, or household purpose, and (2) a security interest in consumer goods secures the obligation. UCC § 9-102(a)(24).

consumer law. (1966) The area of law dealing with consumer transactions — that is, a person's obtaining credit, goods, real property, or services for personal, family, or household purposes. — Also termed *consumer-transactions law.*

consumer lease. See LEASE.

consumer loan. See LOAN.

consumer price index. An index that tracks the price of goods and services purchased by the average consumer and that is published monthly by the U.S. Bureau of Labor Statistics. • The consumer price index is used to monitor periodic changes in the rate of inflation. — Abbr. CPI. — Also termed *cost-of-living index.* Cf. PRODUCER PRICE INDEX.

consumer product. (1949) An item of personal property that is distributed in commerce and is normally used for personal, family, or household purposes. 15 USCA § 2301(1).

Consumer Product Safety Commission. An independent federal regulatory commission that develops safety standards for consumer products and promotes research into the causes and prevention of product-related deaths, illnesses, and injuries. • It was established in 1972. 15 USCA §§ 2051 et seq. — Abbr. CPSC.

consumer-protection law. (1954) A state or federal statute designed to protect consumers against unfair trade and credit practices involving consumer goods, as well as to protect consumers against faulty and dangerous goods.

consumer transaction. A bargain or deal in which a party acquires property or services primarily for a personal, family, or household purpose.

consumer-transactions law. See CONSUMER LAW.

consumer-user-contemplation test. See CONSUMER-CONTEMPLATION TEST.

consummate (kən-**səm**-it *or* **kahn**-sə-mit), *adj.* Completed; fully accomplished. • *Consummate* was often used at common law to describe the status of a contract or an estate, such as the transformation of a husband's interest in his wife's inheritance from that of a tenant by the curtesy *initiate* to a tenant by curtesy *consummate* upon the wife's death (assuming that a child had been born during the marriage). See *curtesy consummate* under CURTESY. — **consummation,** *n.*

consummate (**kon**-sə-mayt), *vb.* (16c) **1.** To bring to completion; esp., to make (a marriage) complete by sexual intercourse. **2.** To achieve; to fulfill. **3.** To perfect; to carry to the highest degree.

consummate dower. See DOWER.

consummate lien. See LIEN.

consummation of marriage. *Family law.* The first postmarital act of sexual intercourse between a husband and wife. • Under canon law, a refusal to consummate the marriage may be grounds for an annulment or for divorce. But this is not so at common law or under modern state law.

consumption. (14c) The act of destroying a thing by using it; the use of a thing in a way that exhausts it.

consumption tax. See TAX.

contagion. *Int'l law.* A discredited doctrine holding that revolution or abhorrent practices in a neighboring state justify its invasion and the overthrow of its government on the grounds of national security. • The doctrine was employed by the Holy Alliance (1815–1848) in Europe to invade countries where revolutions were brewing. — Also termed *doctrine of contagion.*

containment. *Int'l law.* A policy of restricting the ideological or territorial expansion of one's enemy. • This was the basic policy of the United States during the Cold War.

contango (kən-**tang**-goh), *n. Securities.* **1.** A market in which long-term futures or options contracts sell at a premium over short-term contracts. — Also termed *normal market.* **2.** The premium so paid. • The premium paid for securities with longer maturities reflects the cost of holding the commodity for future delivery.

contemn (kən-**tem**), *vb.* To treat (as laws or court orders) with contemptuous disregard. See CONTEMPT.

contemnor (kən-**tem**-ər *or* -nər *or* -nor). (16c) A person who is guilty of contempt before a governmental body, such as a court or legislature. — Also spelled *contemner.*

contemplation of bankruptcy. The thought of declaring bankruptcy because of the inability to continue current financial operations, often coupled with action designed to thwart the distribution of assets in a bankruptcy proceeding. — Also termed *contemplation of insolvency.*

contemplation of death. (18c) The thought of dying, not necessarily from imminent danger, but as the compelling reason to transfer property to another. See *gift causa mortis* under GIFT.

contemplation of insolvency. See CONTEMPLATION OF BANKRUPTCY.

contemporaneous and practical interpretation. See *contemporaneous construction* under CONSTRUCTION.

contemporaneous construction. See CONSTRUCTION.

contemporaneous-construction doctrine. (1956) The rule that the initial interpretation of an ambiguous statute by an administrative agency or lower court is entitled to great deference if the interpretation has been used over a long period.

contemporaneous-objection rule. (1965) The doctrine that a timely and proper objection to the admission of evidence must be made at trial for the issue of admissibility to be considered on appeal. • An objection is timely if it is made as soon as practicable and is proper if made formally on the record. These requirements afford the trial court an opportunity to correct the alleged error, and they preserve the issue for appeal.

contemporary community standards. (1957) The gauge by which a fact-finder decides whether material is obscene, judging by its patent offensiveness and its prurience in the locale at a given time. See OBSCENITY (1).

contempt, *n.* (14c) **1.** The act or state of despising; the condition of being despised. **2.** Conduct that defies the authority or dignity of a court or legislature. • Because such conduct interferes with the administration of justice, it is punishable, usu. by fine or imprisonment. Fed. R. Civ. P. 45(e); Fed. R. Crim. P. 42; 18 USCA § 401. See CONTUMACY. — Also termed *contempt of court; judicial contempt.* — **contemptuous,** *adj.*

civil contempt. (1884) The failure to obey a court order that was issued for another party's benefit. • A civil-contempt proceeding is coercive or remedial in nature. The usual sanction is to confine the contemnor until he or she complies with the court order. The act (or failure to act) complained of must be within the defendant's power to perform, and the contempt order must state how the contempt may be purged. Imprisonment for civil contempt is indefinite and for a term that lasts until the defendant complies with the decree.

common-law contempt. See *criminal contempt.*

consequential contempt. **1.** Contempt that, although not amounting to gross insolence or direct opposition, tends to create a universal disregard of the power and authority of courts and judges. **2.** See *indirect contempt.*

constructive contempt. See *indirect contempt.*

contempt of Congress. Deliberate interference with the duties and powers of Congress, such as a witness's refusal to answer a question from a congressional committee. • Contempt of Congress is a criminal offense. 2 USCA § 192.

contempt of sovereignty. *Int'l law.* The minor diplomatic offense of interference in domestic affairs by a foreign representative, esp. by making a public statement about an issue currently being debated in the legislature.

criminal contempt. (1841) An act that obstructs justice or attacks the integrity of the court. • A criminal-contempt proceeding is punitive in nature. The purpose of criminal-contempt proceedings is to punish repeated or aggravated failure to comply with a court order. All the protections of criminal law and procedure apply, and the commitment must be for a definite period. — Also termed *common-law contempt.*

direct contempt. (1863) A contempt (such as an assault of a testifying witness) committed in the immediate vicinity of a court; esp., a contempt committed in a judge's presence. • A direct contempt is usu. immediately punishable when the transgression occurs.

indirect contempt. (1896) Contempt that is committed outside of court, as when a party disobeys a court order. • Indirect contempt is punishable only after proper notice to the contemnor and a hearing. — Also termed *constructive contempt*; *consequential contempt*.

contempt of court. See CONTEMPT (2).

contempt power. (1885) The power of a governmental body (such as Congress or a court) to punish someone who shows contempt for the process, orders, or proceedings of that body.

contempt proceeding. See PROCEEDING.

contemptuous damages. See *nominal damages* under DAMAGES.

contenement (kən-**ten**-ə-mənt). *Hist.* **1.** Freehold land held by a feudal tenant, esp. land used to support the tenant. • Magna Carta (1215) exempted this property from seizure. **2.** A person's reputation or standing in the community. • Though *contenement* as used in this sense is also rooted in the ownership of land, it may stem from the Law French *contenance* ("countenance") rather than the Law Latin *contenementum* ("with tenement"), as used in sense (1).

content, *n. Maritime law.* A written declaration of a departing vessel's destination, the kind and quantity of cargo it is carrying, and other particulars, submitted to a customs inspector for approval and permission for the vessel to leave port. Cf. MANIFEST.

content-based discrimination. See DISCRIMINATION.

content-based restriction. (1973) *Constitutional law.* A restraint on the substance of a particular type of speech. • This type of restriction is presumptively invalid but can survive a constitutional challenge if it is based on a compelling state interest and its measures are narrowly drawn to accomplish that end. *Boos v. Barry*, 485 U.S. 312, 108 S.Ct. 1157 (1998). See SPEECH (1).

contention interrogatory. See INTERROGATORY.

contentious jurisdiction. See JURISDICTION.

contentious possession. See *hostile possession* under POSSESSION.

content-neutral. See NEUTRAL.

contents unknown. A statement placed on a bill of lading to show that the carrier does not know what is inside shipped containers. • Carriers use this phrase in an attempt to limit their liability for damage to the goods shipped. *Shipper's load and count* is also used.

content-valid test. A job-applicant examination that bears a close relationship to the skills required by the job. • Content-validation studies are often performed in employment-discrimination cases that contest the validity of an examination.

conterminous, *adj.* **1.** Sharing a common boundary <the surveyor set a new line between the conterminous counties>. — Also termed *coterminous*. **2.** Enclosed within a common boundary <all 48 conterminous states of this country>. **3.** See COTERMINOUS.

contest (kən-**test**), *vb.* (17c) **1.** To strive to win or hold; contend <he chose to contest for the prize>. **2.** To litigate or call into question; challenge <they want to contest the will>. **3.** To deny an adverse claim or assert a defense to it in a court proceeding <she contests that charge>. — **contest** (**kon**-test), *n.*

contestability clause (kən-tes-tə-**bil**-ə-tee). *Insurance.* A policy provision setting forth when and under what conditions the insurer may contest a claim or void the policy based on a representation or omission made when the policy was issued. • Contestability clauses usu. lapse after two years. — Also termed *contestable clause*. Cf. INCONTESTABILITY CLAUSE.

contestant. (17c) **1.** One who contests the validity of a will, trust, or other legal instrument. — Also termed *objectant*; *caveator*. **2.** *Trademarks.* One who challenges the placement of a trademark on the Principal Register. • The term refers to a challenger in (1) an interference proceeding, (2) an opposition proceeding before a mark is placed on the Principal Register, or (3) a cancellation proceeding after the mark is placed on the Principal Register. **3.** *Patents.* A party to an interference proceeding in the U.S. Patent and Trademark Office. — Also termed (in sense 3) *interferant*.

contestation of suit (kon-tes-**tay**-shən). *Eccles. law.* The point in an action when the defendant answers the plaintiff's libel (i.e., complaint); the plea and joinder of an issue. — Also termed *litis contestatio*.

contested divorce. See DIVORCE.

contested hearing. See HEARING.

context, *n.* (16c) **1.** The surrounding text of a word or passage, used to determine the meaning of that word or passage <his remarks were taken out of context>. **2.** Setting or environment <in the context of foreign relations>. — **contextual,** *adj.*

context rule. *Contracts.* The principle that a court may look to extrinsic evidence to determine the intended meaning of a contract, even though the language itself is clear and unambiguous. • The court may consider (1) the subject matter and purpose of the contract, (2) the circumstances surrounding the making of the contract, (3) the subsequent conduct of the parties to the contract, (4) the reasonableness of the parties' respective interpretations, (5) statements made by the parties in preliminary negotiations, (6) usages of trade, and (7) the course of dealing between the parties. This rule does not make extrinsic evidence admissible for other purposes, such as adding to, modifying, or contradicting the contract's terms, unless a party can show that the actual language resulted from fraud, accident, or mistake. Restatement (Second) of Contracts §§ 212, 214(c) (1981).

contextual zoning. See ZONING.

contiguity (kon-ti-**gyoo**-ə-tee), *n.* The state or condition of being contiguous <contiguity existed between the two adjoining tracts of land>.

contiguous (kən-**tig**-yoo-əs), *adj.* (17c) **1.** Touching at a point or along a boundary; ADJOINING <Texas and Oklahoma are contiguous>. **2.** Near in time or sequence; successive <contiguous thunder and lightning>.

contiguous zone. *Int'l law.* An area abutting and extending beyond the territorial sea, in which countries have limited powers to enforce customs as well as fiscal, sanitary, and immigration laws.

Continental Congress. The first national governmental assembly in the United States, formed in 1774 to protest British treatment of the colonies. ● The Second Continental Congress, commencing in 1775, adopted the Declaration of Independence and served as the national government until the Articles of Confederation were ratified in 1781.

contingency (kən-**tin**-jən-see). (16c) **1.** An event that may or may not occur; a possibility. **2.** The condition of being dependent on chance; uncertainty. **3.** CONTINGENT FEE.

contingency beneficiary. See *contingent beneficiary* (1) under BENEFICIARY.

contingency fee. See CONTINGENT FEE.

contingency reserve. See *contingent fund* under FUND (1).

contingency with a double aspect. A contingent remainder existing along with a second remainder, the latter remainder taking effect only if the first fails. ● In the following example, this type of remainder would arise if A never has children: "to A for life, and if A has children, then to the children and their heirs forever; and if A dies without children, then to B and B's heirs forever." See *contingent remainder* under REMAINDER.

contingent (kən-**tin**-jənt), *adj.* **1.** Possible; uncertain; unpredictable <the trust was contingent, and the contingency never occurred>. **2.** Dependent on something else; conditional <her acceptance of the position was contingent upon the firm's agreeing to guarantee her husband a position as well>.

contingent annuity. See ANNUITY.

contingent beneficiary. See BENEFICIARY.

contingent claim. See CLAIM (4).

contingent debt. See DEBT.

contingent demand. See DEMAND (1).

contingent estate. See ESTATE (1).

contingent fee. (17c) A fee charged for a lawyer's services only if the lawsuit is successful or is favorably settled out of court. ● Contingent fees are usu. calculated as a percentage of the client's net recovery (such as 25% of the recovery if the case is settled, and 33% if the case is won at trial). — Also termed *contingency fee; contingency; conditional fee.*

reverse contingent fee. A fee in which a defense lawyer's compensation depends in whole or in part on how much money the lawyer saves the client, given the client's potential liability — so that the lower the settlement or judgment, the higher the lawyer's fee. ● For example, if a client might be liable for up to $2 million, and agrees to pay the lawyer 40% of the difference between $1 million and the amount of the settlement or judgment, then a settlement of $800,000 would result in a fee of $80,000 (40% of the $200,000 under the threshold amount of $1 million). — Also termed *negative contingent fee; defense contingent fee; reverse bonus.*

contingent fund. See FUND (1).

contingent guaranty. See GUARANTY.

contingent interest. See INTEREST (2).

contingent-interest mortgage. See MORTGAGE.

contingent legacy. See LEGACY.

contingent liability. See LIABILITY.

contingent ownership. See OWNERSHIP.

contingent remainder. See REMAINDER.

contingent trust. See TRUST.

contingent use. See USE (4).

contingent will. See WILL.

continual claim. *Hist.* A formal claim to a tract of land made by an out-of-possession owner who is deterred from taking possession by a menace of some type. ● The claim — called *continual* because it had to be renewed annually — preserved the claimant's right to the land. The owner had to make the claim as near to the land as could be done safely. This procedure gave the disseised person the same benefits (such as the right to devise the land) as a legal entry. The continual claim was abolished early in the 19th century.

continual injury. See INJURY.

continuance, *n.* (14c) **1.** The act of keeping up, maintaining, or prolonging <continuance of the formal tradition>. **2.** Duration; time of continuing <the senator's continuance in office>. **3.**

Procedure. The adjournment or postponement of a trial or other proceeding to a future date <motion for continuance>. Cf. RECESS (1). — **continue,** *vb.*

continuation. *Patents.* A patent application that is based on the same disclosure and claiming the same invention as a rejected parent application but containing some change in the scope of the claims. • A continuation application maintains the original filing date for prior-art and interference purposes, as long as it is filed while the parent application is still pending, has at least one inventor in common with the parent application, and refers to the parent application. — Also termed *continuation application; continuation-in-whole application; continuing application; file-wrapper continuing application.* Cf. CONTINUATION-IN-PART; *continued-prosecution application* under PATENT APPLICATION; REQUEST FOR CONTINUED EXAMINATION.

continuation agreement. (1942) *Partnership.* An agreement among the partners that, in the event of dissolution, the business of the partnership can be continued without the necessity of liquidation. Cf. BUY–SELL AGREEMENT (1).

continuation application. 1. See CONTINUATION. **2.** See CONTINUATION-IN-PART.

continuation-application laches doctrine. *Patents.* An equitable defense to patent infringement, based on an assertion that the patentee deliberately delayed the issuance of the patent-in-suit by filing multiple continuing applications that added new patent claims to cover products marketed or processes used after the original application was filed. — Also termed *prosecution laches doctrine.* See SUBMARINE PATENT.

continuation-in-part. *Patents.* A patent application filed by the same applicant during the pendency of an earlier application, repeating a substantial part of the earlier application but adding to or subtracting from the claims. 35 USCA § 120. • This type of application contains new technical descriptions from the inventor or reflects improvements made since the parent application was filed. A claim in a continuation-in-part application is entitled to the benefit of the parent application's filing date if the claimed subject matter is the same, but the new matter takes the filing date of the continuation-in-part application. Continuation-in-part applications are usu. filed to describe and claim later-discovered improvements to an invention, or to distinguish the invention from some prior-art reference. — Abbr. CIP. — Also termed *continuation-in-part application; continuation application; continuing application; file-wrapper continuation application.* Cf. CONTINUATION.

continuation-in-part application. See CONTINUATION-IN-PART.

continuation-in-whole application. See CONTINUATION (2).

continued bond. See *annuity bond* under BOND (3).

continued-custody hearing. See *shelter hearing* under HEARING.

continued meeting. See MEETING.

continued-prosecution application. See PATENT APPLICATION.

continuing, *adj.* (14c) **1.** Uninterrupted; persisting <a continuing offense>. **2.** Not requiring renewal; enduring <continuing stockholders> <continuing jurisdiction>.

continuing annuity. See *survivorship annuity* under ANNUITY.

continuing application. See PATENT APPLICATION.

continuing breach. See BREACH OF CONTRACT.

continuing consideration. See CONSIDERATION (1).

continuing contract. See CONTRACT.

continuing covenant. See COVENANT (1).

continuing damages. See DAMAGES.

continuing guaranty. See GUARANTY.

continuing harm. See *continuing injury* under INJURY.

continuing injury. See INJURY.

continuing judicial education. (1964) Continuing legal education for judges, usu. organized and sponsored by a governmentally subsidized body and often involving topics such as judicial writing, efficient decision-making, caseload management, and the like. — Abbr. CJE.

continuing jurisdiction. See JURISDICTION.

continuing-jurisdiction doctrine. (1966) **1.** The rule that a court retains power to enter and enforce a judgment over a party even though that party is no longer subject to a new action. **2.** *Family law.* The rule that once a court has acquired jurisdiction over a child-custody or support case, that court continues to have jurisdiction to modify orders, even if the child or a parent moves to another state.

continuing legal education. (1948) **1.** The process or system through which lawyers extend their learning beyond their law-school studies, usu. by attending seminars designed to sharpen lawyering skills or to provide updates on legal developments within particular practice areas. • In many jurisdictions, lawyers have annual or biennial requirements to devote a given number of hours (usu. 12–15) to continuing legal education. **2.** The enhanced skills or knowledge derived from this process. **3.** The business field in which educational providers supply the demand for legal seminars, books, audiotapes, and videotapes designed to further the education of lawyers. — Abbr. CLE.

continuing nuisance. See NUISANCE.

continuing objection. See OBJECTION.

continuing offense. See OFFENSE (1).

continuing part-time judge. See JUDGE.

continuing threat of harm. A condition or situation that presents a high risk of injury at intervals or over an extended period, whether or not an injury has actually occurred. • The condition or situation can be a behavior that is subject to repetition, as with unfair-competition practices or stalking, or an enduring state, such as environmental contamination. — Also termed *threat of continuing harm*; *continuing threat of injury*; *threat of continuing injury*. Cf. *continuing injury* under INJURY.

continuing trespass. See TRESPASS.

continuing-violation doctrine. *Employment law.* The judge-made rule that if an employer's discriminatory acts are of an ongoing nature, the statute of limitations will be extended to allow the plaintiff to recover even when a claim based on those acts would otherwise be time-barred.

continuing warranty. See *promissory warranty* under WARRANTY (3).

continuing wrong. See WRONG.

continuity (kon-ti-**n**[y]**oo**-ə-tee). **1.** *Int'l law.* The principle that upheavals and revolutions within a country — as well as changes in governmental forms, the extent of a country's territory, and measures taken during a military occupation — do not affect the existence of the country and therefore cannot lead to its extinction. **2.** *Patents.* The rule that a continuation or divisional patent application carries the effective filing date of its parent application if (1) the parent application fully discloses the same invention, (2) there is at least one common inventor, and (3) the parent application was still pending when the latter application was filed. • A continuation-in-part application carries the effective filing date for everything disclosed in the parent application, but not for new material. 35 USCA § 120. — Also termed *doctrine of continuity*. Cf. HIATUS.

continuity of business enterprise. (1980) *Tax.* A doctrine covering acquisitive reorganizations whereby the acquiring corporation must continue the target corporation's historical business or must use a significant portion of the target's business assets in a new business to qualify the acquisition as a tax-deferred transaction.

continuity-of-enterprise doctrine. See SUBSTANTIAL-CONTINUITY DOCTRINE.

continuity-of-entity doctrine. See MERE-CONTINUATION DOCTRINE.

continuity of existence. See CONTINUITY-OF-LIFE DOCTRINE.

continuity of interest. (1974) **1.** *Tax.* A doctrine covering acquisitive reorganizations whereby a target corporation's shareholders must retain a share in the acquiring corporation to qualify the acquisition as a tax-deferred transaction. **2.** A judicial requirement for divisive reorganizations whereby a target corporation's shareholders must retain an interest in both the distributing and the controlled corporations to qualify the exchange as a tax-deferred transaction.

continuity-of-life doctrine. The principle that the withdrawal, incapacity, bankruptcy, or death of the owner of an entity (esp. a corporation) does not end the entity's existence. — Also termed *continuity of existence*.

continuous-adverse-use principle. The rule that the uninterrupted use of land — along with the other elements of adverse possession — will result in a successful claim for adverse possession. — Also termed *uninterrupted-adverse-use principle*. See ADVERSE POSSESSION.

continuous crime. See CRIME.

continuous easement. See EASEMENT.

continuous injury. See *continual injury* under INJURY.

continuous-operations clause. *Oil & gas.* A provision in an oil-and-gas lease giving the lessee the right to continue any drilling well that was begun before the lease expired and to begin drilling more wells. See OPERATIONS CLAUSE.

continuous policy. See INSURANCE POLICY.

continuous-representation doctrine. The principle that the limitations period for bringing a legal-malpractice action is tolled as long as the lawyer against whom the action is brought continues the representation that is related to the negligent act or omission.

continuous servitude. See *continuous easement* under EASEMENT.

continuous-treatment doctrine. (1962) The principle that the limitations period for bringing a medical-malpractice action is tolled while the patient continues treatment that is related to the negligent act or omission.

continuous trigger. See TRIPLE TRIGGER.

contort (kon-tort), *n.* **1.** (*usu. pl.*) The overlapping domain of contract law and tort law. **2.** A specific wrong that falls within that domain. **3.** *Informal.* A constitutional tort. See *constitutional tort* under TORT.

contra (kon-trə), *prep.* (15c) Against or contrary to. • As a citation signal, *contra* denotes that the cited authority supports a contrary view. In old law reports, *contra* often identifies the defendant's attorney (*pro querente* refers to the plaintiff's).

contra account. See ACCOUNT.

contraband (kon-trə-band), *n.* (16c) **1.** Illegal or prohibited trade; smuggling. **2.** Goods that are unlawful to import, export, produce, or possess. — **contraband,** *adj.*

 absolute contraband. Goods used primarily for war, such as arms and ammunition, as well as clothing and equipment of a military character.

 conditional contraband. Goods susceptible of being used for warlike and peaceful purposes, such as coal and food. — Also termed *ancipitis usus* (an-**sip**-i-təs **yoo**-səs).

 contraband per se. Property whose possession is unlawful regardless of how it is used. Cf. *derivative contraband.*

 derivative contraband. Property whose possession becomes unlawful when it is used in committing an illegal act. Cf. *contraband per se.*

contra bonos mores (kon-trə **boh**-nohs **mor**-eez). [Latin "against good morals"] Offensive to the conscience and to a sense of justice. ● Contracts *contra bonos mores* are voidable. — Also termed *contra bonos mores et decorum; adversus bonos mores.*

contraceptivism. *Hist.* The criminal offense of distributing or prescribing contraceptives.

contract, *n.* (14c) **1.** An agreement between two or more parties creating obligations that are enforceable or otherwise recognizable at law <a binding contract>. **2.** The writing that sets forth such an agreement <a contract is valid if valid under the law of the residence of the party wishing to enforce the contract>. **3.** A promise or set of promises by a party to a transaction, enforceable or otherwise recognizable at law; the writing expressing that promise or set of promises <when the lessor learned that the rooms were to be used for the delivery of blasphemous lectures, he declined to perform his contract>. See Restatement (Second) of Contracts § 2 (1979). **4.** Broadly, any legal duty or set of duties not imposed by the law of tort; esp., a duty created by a decree or declaration of a court <an obligation of record, as a judgment, recognizance, or the like, is included within the term "contract">. **5.** The body of law dealing with agreements and exchange <the general theory of contract>. **6.** The terms of an agreement, or any particular term <there was no express contract about when the money was payable>. **7.** Loosely, a sale or conveyance. **8.** Loosely, an enforceable agreement between two or more parties to do or not to do a thing or set of things;

a compact <when they finally agreed, they had a contract>. — **contract,** *vb.* — **contractual,** *adj.*

 absolute simulated contract. Civil law. A simulated contract that the parties intend to be wholly ineffective. La. Civ. Code art. 2026. See *simulated contract.*

 accessory contract. A contract entered into primarily for the purpose of carrying out a principal contract. ● The principal types are suretyship, indemnity, pledge, warranty, and ratification. Cf. *principal contract.*

 adhesion contract. (1949) A standard-form contract prepared by one party, to be signed by another party in a weaker position, usu. a consumer, who adheres to the contract with little choice about the terms. — Also termed *contract of adhesion; adhesive contract; adhesory contract; adhesionary contract; take-it-or-leave-it contract; leonine contract.*

 aleatory contract (**ay**-lee-ə-tor-ee). [fr. Latin *aleator* "gambler," fr. *alea* "the throwing of dice"] (1891) A contract in which at least one party's performance depends on some uncertain event that is beyond the control of the parties involved. ● Most insurance contracts and life annuities are of this type. — Also termed *hazardous contract; wagering contract.* Cf. *certain contract.*

 alternative contract. (1871) A contract in which the performing party may elect to perform one of two or more specified acts to satisfy the obligation; a contract that provides more than one way for a party to complete performance, usu. permitting that party to choose the manner of performance. — Also termed *alternative-methods-of-performance contract.*

 assessment contract. A contract in which the payment of a benefit is dependent on the collection of an assessment levied on persons holding similar contracts. See *assessment insurance* under INSURANCE.

 best-efforts contract. A contract in which a party undertakes to use best efforts to fulfill the promises made rather than to achieve a specific result; a contract in which the adequacy of a party's performance is measured by the party's ability to fulfill the specified obligations. ● Although the obligor must use best efforts, the risk of failure lies with the obligee. To be enforceable, a best-efforts term must generally set some kind of goal or guideline against which the efforts may be measured. See BEST EFFORTS.

 bilateral contract. (1866) A contract in which each party promises a performance, so that each party is an obligor on that party's own promise and an obligee on the other's promise; a contract in which the parties obligate themselves reciprocally, so that the obligation of one party is correlative to the obligation of the other. — Also termed *mutual contract*; *reciprocal contract*; (in civil law) *synallagmatic contract*. See COUNTERPROMISE.

blanket contract. A contract covering a group of products, goods, or services for a fixed period.

bona fide contract (**boh**-nə f ɪd *or* **fɪ**-dee). A contract in which equity may intervene to correct inequalities and to adjust matters according to the parties' intentions.

build-to-print contract. A contract requiring the contractor to build a product according to exact technical specifications provided by the customer. ● The design specifications are explicit and are often coupled with performance specifications, so the contractor has little discretion in how to perform. Much governmental contracting is build-to-print. — Also termed *design-specification contract*. Cf. *performance contract* (1).

certain contract. (17c) A contract that will be performed in a stipulated manner. Cf. *aleatory contract*.

collateral contract. (1809) A side agreement that relates to a contract, which, if unintegrated, can be supplemented by evidence of the side agreement; an agreement made before or at the same time as, but separately from, another contract. See COLLATERAL-CONTRACT DOCTRINE.

commutative contract (kə-**myoo**-tə-tiv *or* **kom**-yə-tay-tiv). **1.** *Civil law.* A contract in which, at the time it is formed, the parties' obligations and advantages are certain and determinate. ● This definition applied in Louisiana law before the civil code was revised in 1984. **2.** *Louisiana law.* A contract in which one party's performance is correlative to the performance of the other, so that nonperformance by either affords a defense to the other. La. Civ. Code art. 1911. Cf. *independent contract*; *synallagmatic contract*.

conditional contract. An agreement that is enforceable only if another agreement is performed or if another particular prerequisite or condition is satisfied. — Also termed *hypothetical contract*.

conditional sales contract. See *retail installment contract*.

consensual contract. *Hist.* A contract arising from the mere consensus of the parties, without any formal or symbolic acts performed to fix the obligation. ● Although the consensual contract was known to the common law, it originated in Roman law, where it embraced four types of contracts in which informal consent alone was sufficient: (1) an agency agreement (*mandatum*), (2) a partnership agreement (*societas*), (3)

a sale (*emptio venditio*), or (4) a letting or hiring (*locatio conductio*). Cf. *real contract*.

construction contract. A contract setting forth the specifications for a building project's construction. ● This type of contract is usu. secured by performance and payment bonds to protect both the owner and the subcontractors.

constructive contract. See *implied-in-law contract*.

continuing contract. A contract calling for periodic performances.

contract for deed. (1825) A conditional sales contract for the sale of real property. — Also termed *installment land contract*; *land sales contract*; *land contract*.

contract for sale. (1808) **1.** A contract for the present transfer of property for a price. — Also termed *contract of sale*. **2.** A contract to sell goods at a future time. — Also termed (in sense 2) *contract to sell*.

contract implied in fact. See *implied-in-fact contract*.

contract implied in law. See *implied-in-law contract*.

contract of adhesion. See *adhesion contract*.

contract of affreightment. See CONTRACT OF AFFREIGHTMENT.

contract of beneficence. See *gratuitous contract*.

contract of benevolence. See *gratuitous contract*.

contract of carriage. See CONTRACT OF AFFREIGHTMENT.

contract of indemnity. See *indemnity contract*.

contract of insurance. See INSURANCE POLICY.

contract of marriage. See *marriage contract*.

contract of record. A contract that is declared by a court and entered into the court's record. ● Contracts of record include judgments, recognizances, and (in England) statutes staple.

contract of sale. See *contract for sale* (1).

contract to pledge. **1.** An agreement purporting to create a present pledge without a bailment. **2.** An agreement to make a future bailment for the purpose of security. See PLEDGE (3).

contract to satisfaction. See *satisfaction contract*.

contract to sell. See *contract for sale* (2).

contract uberrimae fidei (yoo-**ber**-ə-mee **fɪ**-dee-ɪ). A contract in which the parties owe each other duties with the utmost good faith.

contract under seal. A formal contract that requires no consideration and has the seal of the signer attached. ● A contract under seal must be in writing or printed on paper or parchment and is conclusive between the parties when signed, sealed, and delivered. Delivery is made either by actually handing it to the other party (or party's representative) or by stating an intention that the deed be operative even though it is retained in the possession of the party executing it. Modern statutes have mostly eliminated the special effects of a sealed contract. — Also termed *sealed contract*; *special contract*; *deed*; *covenant*; *specialty*; *specialty contract*; *common-law specialty*. See SEAL. Cf. *sealed instrument* under INSTRUMENT (3).

cost-plus contract. (1920) A contract in which payment is based on a fixed fee or a percentage added to the actual cost incurred.

de facto contract of sale. A contract that purports to pass property but is defective in some element.

dependent contract. A contract conditioned or dependent on another contract.

deposit contract. An agreement between a financial institution and its customer governing the treatment of deposited funds and the payment of checks and other demands against the customer's account.

design-specification contract. See *build-to-print contract*.

destination contract. (1958) A contract in which a seller bears the risk of loss until the goods arrive at the destination. UCC § 2-509. Cf. *shipment contract*.

discharged contract. See *void contract* (2).

divisible contract. See *severable contract*.

dual contract. A contract between parties who have made two contracts for the same transaction, sometimes so that one may be used to defraud a person or entity (such as a lender) as to the terms of the parties' actual agreement.

employment contract. (1927) A contract between an employer and employee in which the terms and conditions of employment are stated.

engineering, procurement, and construction contract. A fixed-price, schedule-intensive construction contract — typical in the construction of single-purpose projects, such as energy plants — in which the contractor agrees to a wide variety of responsibilities, including the duties to provide for the design, engineering, procurement, and construction of the facility; to prepare start-up procedures; to conduct performance tests; to create operating manuals; and to train people to operate the facility. — Abbr. EPC contract. — Also termed *turnkey contract*. See SINGLE-PURPOSE PROJECT.

entire-output contract. See *output contract*.

escrow contract. The contract among buyer, seller, and escrow holder, setting forth the rights and responsibilities of each. See ESCROW.

evergreen contract. A contract that renews itself from one term to the next in the absence of contrary notice by one of the parties.

exclusive contract. See EXCLUSIVE-DEALING ARRANGEMENT.

executed contract. (18c) **1.** A contract that has been fully performed by both parties. **2.** A signed contract.

executory contract (eg-**zek**-yə-tor-ee). (18c) **1.** A contract that remains wholly unperformed or for which there remains something still to be done on both sides, often as a component of a larger transaction and sometimes memorialized by an informal letter agreement, by a memorandum, or by oral agreement. **2.** *Bankruptcy.* A contract under which debtor and nondebtor each have unperformed obligations and the debtor, if it ceased further performance, would have no right to the other party's continued performance.

express contract. (17c) A contract whose terms the parties have explicitly set out. — Also termed *special contract*. Cf. *implied contract*.

financial contract. *Securities.* An arrangement that (1) takes the form of an individually negotiated contract, agreement, or option to buy, sell, lend, swap, or repurchase, or other similar individually negotiated transaction commonly entered into by participants in the financial markets; (2) involves securities, commodities, currencies, interest or other rates, other measures of value, or any other financial or economic interest similar in purpose or function; and (3) is entered into in response to a request from a counterparty for a quotation, or is otherwise entered into and structured to accommodate the objectives of the counterparty to such an arrangement.

fixed-price contract. A contract in which the buyer agrees to pay the seller a definite and predetermined price regardless of increases in the seller's cost or the buyer's ability to acquire the same goods in the market at a lower price.

formal contract. A contract made through the observance of certain prescribed formalities. ● Among the formal contracts are the contract under seal, the recognizance, the negotiable instrument, and the letter of credit. Cf. *informal contract*; *formal agreement* under AGREEMENT.

forward contract. An agreement to buy or sell a particular nonstandardized asset (usu. currencies) at a fixed price on a future date. ● Unlike a futures contract, a forward contract is not traded on a formal exchange. — Also termed *forward agreement*. Cf. FUTURES CONTRACT.

futures contract. See FUTURES CONTRACT.

gambling contract. An agreement to engage in a gamble; a contract in which two parties wager something, esp. money, for a chance to win a prize. ● Where gambling is legal, contracts related to legal gambling activities are enforceable. — Also termed *gaming contract*. See *wagering contract*.

government contract. A contract to which a government or government agency is a party, esp. for the purchase of goods and services. See *procurement contract*.

gratuitous contract (grə-t[y]oo-i-təs). **1.** A contract made for the benefit of a promisee who does not give consideration to the promisor. — Also termed *contract of beneficence*; *contract of benevolence*. Cf. *onerous contract*. **2.** *Civil law.* A contract in which one party promises to give a benefit to the other party without expecting or gaining any benefit in return. — Also termed *voluntary contract*.

grubstake contract. A contract between two parties in which one party provides the grubstake — money and supplies — and the other party prospects for and locates minerals on public land. ● Each party acquires an interest in the minerals as agreed to in the contract. Grubstake contracts are used chiefly in the western United States. In some states, such as Alaska, a request for grubstake money is considered the offer of a security and must be registered. — Also termed *grubstaking contract*.

guaranteed-sale contract. A contract between a real-estate agency and a property owner in which the agency agrees to buy the property at a guaranteed price after a specified length of time if it has not been sold under the listing agreement. ● The guaranteed price is usu. a substantial discount from the listed price. — Also termed *guaranteed-purchase contract*.

guaranty contract. See GUARANTY (1).

hazardous contract. See *aleatory contract*.

hypothetical contract. See *conditional contract*.

illegal contract. (18c) A promise that is prohibited because the performance, formation, or object of the agreement is against the law. ● Technically speaking, an illegal contract is not a contract at all because it cannot be enforced, so the phrase is a misnomer. Cf. *unenforceable contract*; *void contract*.

illusory contract. (18c) An agreement in which one party gives as consideration a promise that is so insubstantial as to impose no obligation. ● The insubstantial promise renders the agreement unenforceable.

immoral contract. An agreement that so flagrantly violates societal norms as to be unenforceable.

implied contract. (17c) **1.** An implied-in-law contract. **2.** An implied-in-fact contract. Cf. *express contract*.

implied-in-fact contract. A contract that the parties presumably intended as their tacit understanding, as inferred from their conduct and other circumstances. — Also termed *contract implied in fact*.

implied-in-law contract. An obligation created by law for the sake of justice; specif., an obligation imposed by law because of some special relationship between the parties or because one of them would otherwise be unjustly enriched. ● An implied-in-law contract is not actually a contract, but instead is a remedy that allows the plaintiff to recover a benefit conferred on the defendant. — Also termed *contract implied in law*; *quasi-contract*; *constructive contract*. See UNJUST ENRICHMENT.

impossible contract. An agreement that the law will not enforce because there is no feasible way for one of the parties to perform. See IMPOSSIBILITY (3).

indemnity contract. A contract by which the promisor agrees to reimburse a promisee for some loss irrespective of a third person's liability. — Also termed *contract of indemnity*.

independent contract. A contract in which the mutual acts or promises of the parties have no relation to each other, either as equivalents or as considerations. Cf. *commutative contract*.

informal contract. **1.** A contract other than one under seal, a recognizance, or a negotiable instrument; specif., that derives its force not from the observance of formalities but because of the presence in the transaction of certain elements that are usu. present when people make promises with binding intent — namely mutual assent and consideration (or a device other than consideration). ● An informal contract may be made with or without a writing. Most modern contracts are informal. — Also termed *bargain*; *simple contract*. **2.** See *parol contract*.

innominate contract (i-nom-ə-nit). *Roman & civil law.* A contract not classifiable under any particular name; a contract for which the law supplies nothing in addition to the express agreement of the parties. La. Civ. Code art. 1914. ● This type of contract was developed late in classical Roman law. Although the agreements were reciprocal, they did not become operational without at least part performance. — Also termed *innominate real contract*. Cf. *nominate contract*.

installment contract. (1896) A contract requiring or authorizing the delivery of goods in separate lots, or payments in separate increments, to be separately accepted. • Under the UCC, this type of agreement will be considered one contract even if it has a clause stating that each delivery is a separate contract. UCC § 2-612.

installment land contract. See *contract for deed.*

integrated contract. See INTEGRATED CONTRACT.

invalid contract. An agreement that is either void or voidable. — Also termed *invalid agreement.*

investment contract. See INVESTMENT CONTRACT.

joint contract. A contract in which two or more promisors are together bound to fulfill its obligations, or one in which two or more promisees are together entitled to performance. Cf. *severable contract.*

land contract. See *contract for deed.*

land sales contract. See *contract for deed.*

leonine contract. See *adhesion contract.*

letter contract. In federal contract law, a written contract with sufficient provisions to permit the contractor to begin performance.

leverage contract. See LEVERAGE CONTRACT.

literal contract. 1. *Roman law.* A type of written contract originally created by — and later evidenced by — an entry of the sum due on the debit side of a ledger, binding a signatory even though the signatory receives no consideration. • Literal contracts were often used for novations. 2. *Civil law.* A contract fully evidenced by a writing and binding on the signatory.

marine contract. See *maritime contract.*

maritime contract. A contract that is recognized in admiralty jurisdiction. • In general, a maritime contract relates to a vessel in its use as such, to navigation on navigable waters, to transportation by sea, or to maritime employment. — Also termed *marine contract.*

marketing contract. 1. A business's agreement with an agency or other association for the promotion of sales of the business's goods or services. 2. An agreement between a cooperative and its members, by which the members agree to sell through the cooperative, and the cooperative agrees to obtain an agreed price.

marriage contract. A form of mutual consent required for a matrimonial relationship to exist according to the law of the place where the consent takes place. — Also termed *contract of marriage.*

mixed contract. 1. *Civil law.* A contract in which the respective benefits conferred are unequal. 2. A contract for both the sale of goods and services. • The UCC may apply to a mixed contract if the predominant purpose is for the sale of goods.

mutual contract. See *bilateral contract.*

naked contract. See NUDUM PACTUM.

nominate contract (**nom**-ə-nit). *Civil law.* A contract distinguished by a particular name, such as sale, insurance, or lease, the very use of which determines some of the rules governing the contract and the contractual rights of the parties, without the need for special stipulations. • The contracts are generally divided into four types: (1) real (arising from something done), (2) oral (arising from something said), (3) literal (arising from something written), and (4) consensual (arising from something agreed to). La. Civ. Code art. 1914. Cf. *innominate contract.*

nude contract. See NUDUM PACTUM.

onerous contract. *Civil law.* A contract in which each party is obligated to perform in exchange for each party's promise of performance. La. Civ. Code art. 1909. Cf. *gratuitous contract.*

option contract. See OPTION (2).

oral contract. See *parol contract* (1).

output contract. (1904) A contract in which a seller promises to supply and a buyer to buy all the goods or services that a seller produces during a specified period and at a set price. • The quantity term is measured by the seller's output. An output contract assures the seller of a market or outlet for the period of the contract. — Also termed *entire-output contract.* Cf. *requirements contract.*

parol contract (pə-**rohl** or **par**-əl). (18c) 1. A contract or modification of a contract that is not in writing or is only partially in writing. — Also termed *oral contract; parol agreement;* (loosely) *verbal contract.* 2. At common law, a contract not under seal, although it could be in writing. — Also termed *informal contract; simple contract.* See PAROL-EVIDENCE RULE.

pay-or-play contract. A contract in which one party agrees to perform and the other agrees to pay for the promised performance even if performance is never demanded. • Pay-or-play contracts are usu. made in the entertainment industry.

performance contract. 1. A contract that requires a party to act personally and does not allow substitution. • People who provide unique personal services often make performance contracts. 2. A contract that allows the contractor to choose the means to achieve the end result. • The product's specifications may be loose and allow the contractor latitude in deciding how to perform. Cf. *build-to-print contract.*

personal contract. 1. A contract that binds a person but not that person's heirs or assignees because the contract requires a personal performance for which there is no adequate substitute. **2.** A contract that binds a representative as an individual rather than binding the person or entity represented. • For instance, contracts made by a decedent's personal representative traditionally bind the representative, not the estate, unless expressly agreed otherwise. **3.** A real-property-related contract that is treated as personal property, not as a substitute for the real property. • Examples include oil-and-gas royalty contracts and property-insurance policies.

pignorative contract (**pig**-nə-ray-tiv). *Civil law.* A contract in which the seller of real property, instead of relinquishing possession of the property that is theoretically sold, gives the buyer a lien; a contract of pledge, hypothecation, or mortgage of realty.

precontract. (15c) A contract that precludes a party from entering into a comparable agreement with someone else. • Historically, a precontract was usu. a promise to marry. It formed an impediment to marriage with any person other than the promisee. The legal impediment was extinguished and revived several times until it was finally abolished in 1752 by 26 Geo. 2, ch. 33, § 13. Cf. LETTER OF INTENT.

principal contract. A contract giving rise to an accessory contract, as an agreement from which a secured obligation originates. Cf. *accessory contract.*

private contract. An agreement between private parties affecting only private rights.

procurement contract. A contract in which a government receives goods or services. • A procurement contract, including the bidding process, is usu. subject to government regulation. — Also termed *government contract.* See FEDERAL ACQUISITION REGULATION.

public contract. A contract that, although it involves public funds, may be performed by private persons and may benefit them.

quasi-contract. See *implied-in-law contract.*

real contract. *Hist.* A contract in which money or other property passes from one party to another; a contract requiring something more than mere consent, such as the lending of money or handing over of a thing. • This term, derived from Roman law, referred to contracts concerning both personal and real property. Real contracts included transactions in the form of *commodatum, depositum, mutuum,* and *pignus.* Cf. *consensual contract.*

reciprocal contract. See *bilateral contract.*

referral sales contract. See REFERRAL SALES CONTRACT.

relative simulated contract. *Civil law.* A simulated contract that the parties intend to have some effects, but not necessarily those recited in the contract. La. Civ. Code art. 2027. See *simulated contract.*

requirements contract. (1932) A contract in which a buyer promises to buy and a seller to supply all the goods or services that a buyer needs during a specified period. • The quantity term is measured by the buyer's requirements. A requirements contract assures the buyer of a source for the period of the contract. Cf. *output contract.*

retail installment contract. A contract for the sale of goods under which the buyer makes periodic payments and the seller retains title to or a security interest in the goods. — Also termed *retail installment contract and security agreement; conditional sales contract.* Cf. *chattel mortgage* under MORTGAGE.

satisfaction contract. A contract by which one party agrees to perform to the satisfaction of the other. — Also termed *contract to satisfaction.*

sealed contract. See *contract under seal.*

self-determination contract. Under the Indian Self-Determination and Education Assistance Act, an agreement under which the federal government provides funds to an Indian tribe and allows the tribe to plan and administer a program that would otherwise be administered by the federal government. 25 USCA § 450b(j).

service contract. A contract to perform a service; esp., a written agreement to provide maintenance or repairs on a consumer product for a specified term.

severable contract. (1854) A contract that includes two or more promises each of which can be enforced separately, so that failure to perform one of the promises does not necessarily put the promisor in breach of the entire contract. — Also termed *divisible contract; several contract.* See SEVERABILITY CLAUSE. Cf. *joint contract.*

shipment contract. (1893) A contract in which a seller bears the risk of damage to the items sold only until they are brought to the place of shipment. • If a contract for the sale of goods does not address the terms of delivery, it is presumed to be a shipment contract. UCC §§ 2-319, 2-504, 2-509. Cf. *destination contract.*

simple contract. 1. See *informal contract* (1). **2.** See *parol contract* (2).

simulated contract. *Civil law.* A contract that, by mutual agreement, does not express the true intent of the parties. La. Civ. Code art. 2025. • A simulated contract is absolute when the parties intend that the contract will impose no obligations; no obligations are enforceable on the parties by such a contract. A simulated contract is relative if the parties intend it to impose obligations different from those recited in the contract; the intended obligations are enforceable if all relevant conditions are met. A simulated contract may affect the rights of third parties. See *action en declaration de simulation* under ACTION (4). — Also termed *simulation*.

special contract. 1. See *contract under seal*. **2.** A contract with peculiar provisions that are not ordinarily found in contracts relating to the same subject matter. **3.** See *express contract*.

specialty contract. See *contract under seal*.

standard-form contract. (1923) A usu. preprinted contract containing set clauses, used repeatedly by a business or within a particular industry with only slight additions or modifications to meet the specific situation. • Because standard-form contracts usu. favor the drafting party, they can amount to adhesion contracts. Courts offset the drafting party's advantage by construing the contract in the light least favorable to the drafting party. — Also termed *standardized contract*. See *adhesion contract*.

statutory contract. A contract for which a statute prescribes certain terms. • Statutes often govern the contracts made by public entities, but also some by private persons. For example, a statute may define and set minimum standards for terms in home-improvement contracts.

stock-option contract. A negotiable instrument that gives the holder the right to buy or sell — for a specified price within a fixed time limit — a certain number of shares of the corporation's stock. See STOCK OPTION.

subcontract. (18c) A secondary contract made by a party to the primary contract for carrying out the primary contract, or a part of it.

subscription contract. See SUBSCRIPTION (3).

substituted contract. A contract made between parties to an earlier contract so that the new one takes the place of and discharges the earlier one. • A substituted contract differs from a novation (as "novation" is traditionally defined) in that the latter requires the substitution for the original obligor of a third person not a party to the original agreement; when the obligee accepts the third party, the agreement is immediately discharged. In contrast to both substituted contract and novation, an executory accord does not immediately discharge an obligation; rather, the obligation is discharged on performance, often by a third person, rather than the original obligor. Cf. NOVATION; ACCORD (2).

synallagmatic contract (sin-ə-lag-**mat**-ik). [fr. Greek *synallagma* "mutual agreement"] *Civil law.* A contract in which the parties obligate themselves reciprocally, so that the obligation of each party is correlative to the obligation of the other. La. Civ. Code arts. 1908, 1911. • A synallagmatic contract is characterized by correlative obligations, whereas a commutative contract is characterized by correlative performances. The term *synallagmatic contract* is essentially the civil-law equivalent of the common law's *bilateral contract*. Cf. *commutative contract*.

tacit contract. A contract in which conduct takes the place of written or spoken words in the offer or acceptance (or both).

take-it-or-leave-it contract. See *adhesion contract*.

take-or-pay contract. A contract requiring the buyer to either purchase and receive a minimum amount of a product ("take") or pay for this minimum without taking immediate delivery ("pay"). • These contracts are often used in the energy and oil-and-gas businesses.

task-order contract. A contract under which a vendor agrees to render services or deliver products as ordered from time to time. • Governments use this type of contract when the quantities that will be needed or the times for performance are uncertain. The contract may describe the services or products generally, but it must specify the period of performance, the number of option periods, and the total minimum and maximum quantity of products or services that the government will acquire under the contract. When exercising its contractual rights, the government issues task orders to specify the product or service requirements, which may vary with each order. — Sometimes shortened to *task order*.

third-party-beneficiary contract. A contract that directly benefits a third party and that gives the third party a right to sue any of the original contracting parties for breach.

turnkey contract. See *engineering, procurement, and construction contract*.

unconscionable contract. See *unconscionable agreement* under AGREEMENT.

unenforceable contract. A valid contract that, because of some technical defect, cannot be fully enforced; a contract that has some legal consequences but that may not be enforced in an action for damages or specific performance in the face of certain defenses, such as the statute of frauds. — Also termed *agreement of imperfect obligation*. Cf. *illegal contract*; *void contract*.

unilateral contract. (1855) A contract in which only one party makes a promise or undertakes a performance; a contract in which no promisor receives a promise as consideration for the promise given.

valid contract. A contract that is fully operative in accordance with the parties' intent. — Also termed *valid agreement.*

variable annuity contract. *Securities.* An annuity whose payments vary according to how well the fund (usu. made up of common stocks) that backs it is performing. SEC Rule 0-1(e)(1) (17 CFR § 270.0-1(e)(1)). See *variable annuity* under ANNUITY.

verbal contract. See *parol contract* (1).

voidable contract. (18c) A contract that can be affirmed or rejected at the option of one of the parties; a contract that is void as to the wrongdoer but not void as to the party wronged, unless that party elects to treat it as void.

void contract. (17c) **1.** A contract that is of no legal effect, so that there is really no contract in existence at all. • A contract may be void because it is technically defective, contrary to public policy, or illegal. Cf. *illegal contract; unenforceable contract.* **2.** A contract that has been fully performed. — Also termed *discharged contract.* **3.** Loosely, a voidable contract.

voluntary contract. See *gratuitous contract* (2).

wagering contract. 1. A contract the performance of which depends on the happening of an uncertain event, made entirely for sport. See *gambling contract.* Cf. *aleatory contract.* **2.** A contract in which an uncertain event affects or results from a business transaction. • With this type of wagering contract, a business person is protected from a trade risk.

written contract. A contract whose terms have been reduced to writing.

yellow-dog contract. See YELLOW-DOG CONTRACT.

contract, freedom of. See FREEDOM OF CONTRACT.

contract bond. See PERFORMANCE BOND.

contract carrier. See *private carrier* under CARRIER.

Contract Clause. See CONTRACTS CLAUSE.

contract demurrage. See DEMURRAGE.

contractee. *Rare.* A person with whom a contract is made.

contract labor. See INDEPENDENT CONTRACTOR.

contract loan. See *add-on loan* under LOAN.

contract not to compete. See *noncompetition covenant* under COVENANT (1).

contract not to sue. See *covenant not to sue* under COVENANT (1).

contract of affreightment (ə-**frayt**-mənt). *Maritime law.* An agreement for the carriage of goods by water. • A contract of affreightment may

employ a bill of lading, a charterparty, or both to ship the goods. — Abbr. COA. — Also termed *contract of carriage.* See CHARTERPARTY.

contractor. (16c) **1.** A party to a contract. **2.** More specif., one who contracts to do work or provide supplies for another.

competent contractor. A contractor who has the knowledge, skill, experience, and available equipment to do the work that he or she is employed to do without creating an unreasonable risk of injury to others and who has the personal characteristics necessary to carry out the work.

general contractor. One who contracts for the completion of an entire project, including purchasing all materials, hiring and paying subcontractors, and coordinating all the work. — Also termed *original contractor; prime contractor.*

independent contractor. See INDEPENDENT CONTRACTOR.

subcontractor. See SUBCONTRACTOR.

contract rate. See INTEREST RATE.

Contracts Clause. (1875) The clause of the U.S. Constitution prohibiting states from passing any law that would impair private contractual obligations. • The Supreme Court has generally interpreted this clause so that states can regulate private contractual obligations if the regulation is reasonable and necessary to serve an important public purpose. U.S. Const. art. I, § 10, cl. 1. — Also termed *Contract Clause; Obligation of Contracts Clause.*

contract-specification defense. An affirmative defense that immunizes a contractor from liability for a defect in a product when the contractor has manufactured or performed according to detailed contractual orders. • The defense applies to specialized, single-use components and protects a component supplier from claims of negligent design if the component conforms to the contractual specifications — unless the specifications are obviously dangerous. Under modern notions of strict liability, courts have increasingly rejected this defense. Cf. GOVERNMENT-CONTRACTOR DEFENSE; GOVERNMENT-AGENCY DEFENSE.

contract system. *Hist.* The practice of leasing prisoners out to private individuals for the prisoners' labor.

contract to pledge. See CONTRACT.

contract to satisfaction. See *satisfaction contract* under CONTRACT.

contract to sell. See *contract for sale* (2) under CONTRACT.

contractual duty. See DUTY (1).

contractual fault. See FAULT.

contractual indemnity. See INDEMNITY.

contractual obligation. See OBLIGATION.

contract *uberrimae fidei*. See CONTRACT.

contract under seal. See CONTRACT.

contractus (kən-**trak**-təs). [Latin] *Roman law.* A contract; an agreement between two or more parties, usu. to create an actionable bond between them.

contract zoning. See ZONING.

contradictory judgment. See JUDGMENT.

contradictory motion. See MOTION (1).

contra formam statuti (**kon**-trə **for**-məm stə-**tyoo**-tı). [Law Latin] Contrary to the form of the statute. See AGAINST THE FORM OF THE STATUTE.

contra proferentem (**kon**-trə prof-ə-**ren**-təm). [Latin "against the offeror"] The doctrine that, in interpreting documents, ambiguities are to be construed unfavorably to the drafter. — Also spelled *contra proferentes*. — Also termed *ambiguity doctrine*.

contrary to law. (16c) Illegal; unlawful; conflicting with established law.

contrary to the evidence. (16c) (Of an argument, finding, etc.) conflicting with the weight of the evidence presented at a contested hearing.

contravene (kon-trə-**veen**), *vb.* **1.** To violate or infringe; to defy <the soldier contravened the officer's order, and then went AWOL>. **2.** To come into conflict with; to be contrary to <the court held that the regulation contravenes public policy>.

contravening equity. See EQUITY.

contravention (kon-trə-**ven**-shən). **1.** An act violating a legal condition or obligation; esp., an entail heir's act that conflicts with the entail provision. **2.** *French law.* A criminal breach of a law, treaty, or agreement; a minor violation of the law. • A contravention is traditionally punishable by *peines de police*, usu. a fine not exceeding 15 francs and imprisonment not exceeding three days. See *public-welfare offense* under OFFENSE (1). **3.** *Scots law.* An action brought for breach of a peace bond. **4.** *Hist. Scots law.* An act committed in violation of a legal condition or obligation, esp. one done contrary to a deed by an heir to an entailment.

contributing cause. See CAUSE (1).

contributing to the delinquency of a minor. (1913) The offense of an adult's engaging in conduct involving a minor — or in the presence of a minor — likely to result in delinquent conduct. • Examples include encouraging a minor to shoplift, enabling underage drinking, and soliciting sex for money. — Often shortened to *contributing to delinquency*. See JUVENILE DELINQUENCY. Cf. IMPAIRING THE MORALS OF A MINOR.

contribution. (14c) **1.** The right that gives one of several persons who are liable on a common debt the ability to recover proportionately from each of the others when that one person discharges the debt for the benefit of all; the right to demand that another who is jointly responsible for a third party's injury supply part of what is required to compensate the third party. — Also termed *right of contribution.* **2.** One tortfeasor's right to collect from joint tortfeasors when — and to the extent that — the tortfeasor has paid more than his or her proportionate share to the injured party, the shares being determined as percentages of causal fault. **3.** The actual payment by a joint tortfeasor of a proportionate share of what is due. Cf. INDEMNITY. **4.** *Maritime law.* A share of the loss resulting from a ship's sacrifice of cargo, payable by each party whose property was spared to the party whose property was sacrificed. **5.** WAR CONTRIBUTION.

contribution agreement. See SUPPORT AGREEMENT.

contribution bar. Preclusion of a defendant having contribution rights against other defendants, who have settled their dispute with the plaintiff, from seeking contribution from them. • The bar is usu. allowed in exchange for a credit against any judgment the plaintiff obtains against the nonsettling defendant.

contribution clause. See COINSURANCE CLAUSE.

contribution margin. The difference between a product's selling price and its variable production costs. • The contribution margin measures the amount of funds available for profit and payment of fixed costs.

contributory (kən-**trib**-yə-tor-ee), *adj.* (15c) **1.** Tending to bring about a result. **2.** (Of a pension fund) receiving contributions from both the employer and the employees.

contributory, *n.* (15c) **1.** One who contributes or who has a duty to contribute. **2.** A contributing factor. **3.** *Hist.* A person who, as a result of being or representing a past or present member of a corporation, is liable to contribute to the corporation's debts upon its winding up.

contributory infringement. See INFRINGEMENT.

contributory negligence. See NEGLIGENCE.

contributory-negligence doctrine. (1911) *Torts.* The principle that completely bars a plaintiff's recovery if the damage suffered is partly the plaintiff's own fault. • Most states have abolished this doctrine and have adopted instead a comparative-negligence analysis. See FAULT; NEGLIGENCE. Cf. COMPARATIVE-NEGLIGENCE DOCTRINE.

contributory pension plan. See PENSION PLAN.

control, *n.* (16c) The direct or indirect power to govern the management and policies of a person or entity, whether through ownership of voting securities, by contract, or otherwise; the power or authority to manage, direct, or oversee <the principal exercised control over the agent>.

superintending control. The general supervisory control that a higher court in a jurisdiction has over the administrative affairs of a lower court within that jurisdiction.

working control. The effective control of a corporation by a person or group who owns less than 50% of the stock.

control, *vb.* (15c) **1.** To exercise power or influence over <the judge controlled the proceedings>. **2.** To regulate or govern <by law, the budget office controls expenditures>. **3.** To have a controlling interest in <the five shareholders controlled the company>.

control group. (1937) The persons with authority to make decisions on a corporation's behalf.

control-group test. (1969) A method of determining whether the attorney–client privilege protects communications made by corporate employees, by providing that those communications are protected only if made by an employee who is a member of the group with authority to direct the corporation's actions as a result of that communication. • The U.S. Supreme Court rejected the control-group test in *Upjohn Co. v. United States*, 449 U.S. 383, 101 S.Ct. 677 (1981). Cf. SUBJECT-MATTER TEST.

controlled company. See COMPANY.

controlled corporate groups. See CONTROLLED GROUP.

controlled corporation. See CORPORATION.

controlled debate. See DEBATE.

controlled foreign corporation. See CORPORATION.

controlled group. *Tax.* Two or more corporations whose stock is substantially held by five or fewer persons. • The Internal Revenue Code subjects these entities (such as parent-subsidiary or brother-sister groups) to special rules for computing tax liability. IRC (26 USCA) §§ 851(c)(3), 1563(a). — Also termed *controlled corporate groups.*

controlled-securities-offering distribution. See *securities-offering distribution* (1) under DISTRIBUTION.

controlled substance. (1970) Any type of drug whose possession and use is regulated by law, including a narcotic, a stimulant, or a hallucinogen. See DRUG.

controlled-substance act. (1970) A federal or state statute that is designed to control the distribution, classification, sale, and use of certain drugs. • Most states have enacted these laws, which are usu. modeled on the Uniform Controlled Substances Act.

controlled time. See *controlled debate* under DEBATE.

controller. See COMPTROLLER.

controlling interest. See INTEREST (2).

controlling person. See CONTROL PERSON.

controlling shareholder. See SHAREHOLDER.

control person. *Securities.* A person who has actual control or significant influence over the issuer of securities, as by directing corporate policy. • The control person is subject to many of the same requirements applicable to the sale of securities by the issuer. — Also termed *controlling person.*

control premium. See PREMIUM (3).

control stock. Stock belonging to a control person at the time of a given transaction. — Also termed *control shares.*

control test. See IRRESISTIBLE-IMPULSE TEST.

control theory. (1949) The theory that people will engage in criminal behavior unless certain personally held social controls (such as a strong investment in conventional, legitimate activities or a belief that criminal behavior is morally wrong) are in place to prevent them from doing so. Cf. ROUTINE-ACTIVITIES THEORY; RATIONAL-CHOICE THEORY; STRAIN THEORY.

control-your-kid law. See PARENTAL-RESPONSIBILITY STATUTE.

controversy. (14c) **1.** A disagreement or a dispute, esp. in public. **2.** A justiciable dispute.

public controversy. A controversy involving issues that are debated publicly and that have substantial ramifications for persons other than those engaged in it. • A participant in a public controversy may be deemed a public figure for purposes of a defamation suit arising from the controversy. See PUBLIC FIGURE.

separable controversy. (1881) A claim that is separate and independent from the other claims being asserted in a suit. • This term is most often associated with the statute that permits an entire case to be removed to federal court if one of the claims, being separate and independent from the others, presents a federal question that is within the jurisdiction of the federal courts. 28 USCA § 1441(c).

3. *Constitutional law.* A case that requires a definitive determination of the law on the facts alleged for the adjudication of an actual dispute, and not merely a hypothetical, theoretical, or speculative legal issue. — Also termed (in senses 2 & 3) *actual controversy.* See CASE-OR-CONTROVERSY REQUIREMENT.

controvert (**kon**-trə-vərt *or* kon-trə-**vərt**), *vb.* (16c) To dispute or contest; esp., to deny (as an allegation in a pleading) or oppose in argument

<the allegations in Peck's pleadings were never adequately controverted>.

contumacious conduct. See CONDUCT.

contumacy (kon-t[y]uu-mə-see), *n.* (15c) Contempt of court; the refusal of a person to follow a court's order or direction. See CONTEMPT. — **contumacious,** *adj.*

contumelious (kon-t[y]oo-**mee**-lee-əs), *adj.* Insolent, abusive, spiteful, or humiliating.

contumely (**kon**-t[y]uu-mə-lee *or* kən-**t[y]oo**-mə-lee), *n.* Insulting language or treatment; scornful rudeness.

conubium (kə-**n[y]oo**-bee-əm), *n.* [fr. Latin *con* "together" + *nubere* "to marry"] *Roman law.* **1.** The legal capacity to wed. **2.** The collection of rights that accompany a marriage between persons who have the capacity to marry. — Also spelled *connubium.* — Also termed *jus connubii.* See CONCUBINATUS.

conusance (**kon**-yə-zənts). *Hist.* **1.** Cognizance; jurisdiction. • The word *conusance* is actually an archaic form of *cognizance.* See COGNIZANCE (1); CLAIM OF COGNIZANCE. **2.** JUDICIAL NOTICE. **3.** An acknowledgment (of a debt, act, or opposing claim). • Examples of *conusance* include an acknowledgment in replevin that the defendant took the sued-for goods, or an acknowledgment in a land transfer (by *fine*) that the grantee is entitled to the land. See FINE (1).

conusant (**kon**-yə-zənt), *adj.* (Of a person) having cognizance or knowledge. See COGNIZANCE.

conusee (kon-yə-**zee**). See COGNIZEE.

conusor (kon-yə-zər *or* -zor). See COGNIZOR.

convene, *vb.* (15c) **1.** To call together; to cause to assemble. **2.** *Eccles. law.* To summon to respond to an action. See CONVENTIO (1). **3.** *Civil law.* To bring an action.

convenience account. See ACCOUNT.

convening authority. *Military law.* An officer (usu. a commanding officer) with the power to convene, or who has convened, a court-martial.

convening order. *Military law.* An instrument that creates a court-martial. • The convening order specifies (1) the type of court-martial and its time and place, (2) the names of the members and the trial and defense counsel, (3) the name of the military judge, if one has been detailed, and (4) if necessary, the authority by which the court-martial has been convened.

conventicle (kən-**ven**-tə-kəl). [fr. Latin *conventiculum* "small assembly"] **1.** An assembly of a clandestine or unlawful character. **2.** An assembly for religious worship; esp., a secret meeting for worship not sanctioned by law. **3.** A place where such meetings are held.

convention. (15c) **1.** An agreement or compact, esp. one among nations; a multilateral treaty <the Geneva Convention>. See TREATY. **2.** A special deliberative assembly elected for the purpose of framing, revising, or amending a constitution. — Also termed *constitutional convention.* See CONSTITUTION (1). **3.** An assembly or meeting of members belonging to an organization or having a common objective <an ABA convention>. — Also termed *conference.* **4.** *Parliamentary law.* A deliberative assembly that consists of delegates elected or appointed from subordinate or constituent organizations within a state or national organization, or elected directly from the organization's membership or from defined geographic or other constituencies into which the membership is grouped, and that usu. exercises the organization's highest policymaking authority <a national political convention>. — Also termed *assembly; congress; convocation; delegate assembly; general assembly.* See HOUSE OF DELEGATES. **5.** *Parliamentary law.* A session of a convention (sense 4), consisting of a series of consecutive meetings separated by short recesses or adjournments, often during a convention (sense 3) that includes educational and social programs for the benefit of delegates and other members. **6.** A generally accepted rule or practice; usage or custom <the court dispensed with the convention of having counsel approach the bench>.

conventional, *adj.* **1.** Customary; orthodox; traditional <conventional motion practice>. **2.** Depending on, or arising from, the agreement of the parties, as distinguished from something arising by law <conventional subrogation>. **3.** Arising by treaty or convention <conventional international law>.

conventional custom. See CUSTOM.

conventional interest. See INTEREST (3).

conventionalism. (1837) A jurisprudential conception of legal practice and tradition holding that law is a matter of respecting and enforcing legal and social rules.

conventional law. (17c) A rule or system of rules agreed on by persons for the regulation of their conduct toward one another; law constituted by agreement as having the force of special law between the parties, by either supplementing or replacing the general law of the land. • The most important example is conventional international law, but there are many lesser examples such as rules and regulations of a country club or professional association, or the rules of golf, basketball, or any other game. — Also termed (in international law) *treaty-made law; treaty-created law; treaty law.* See CONVENTION (1).

conventional lien. See LIEN.

conventional loan. See *conventional mortgage* under MORTGAGE.

conventional mortgage. See MORTGAGE.

conventional obligation. See OBLIGATION.

conventional remission. See REMISSION.

conventional sequestration. See SEQUESTRATION.

conventional servitude. See SERVITUDE (2).

conventional subrogation. See SUBROGATION.

Convention application. See PATENT APPLICATION.

Convention for the European Patent for the Common Market. See COMMUNITY PATENT CONVENTION.

Convention for the Protection of Performers, Producers of Phonograms, and Broadcasting Organizations. See ROME CONVENTION ON RELATED RIGHTS.

Convention for the Protection of Producers of Phonograms Against Unauthorized Duplication of Their Phonograms. See GENEVA PHONOGRAMS CONVENTION.

Convention on the Grant of European Patent. See EUROPEAN PATENT CONVENTION.

Convention Relating to the Distribution of Program-Carrying Signals Transmitted by Satellite. See BRUSSELS SATELLITE CONVENTION.

converse-Erie doctrine. See REVERSE-ERIE DOCTRINE.

conversion, *n.* (14c) **1.** The act of changing from one form to another; the process of being exchanged.

   equitable conversion. A change in the nature of property so that real property is treated as personal property, or vice versa, in certain circumstances. ● Equitable conversion is based on the maxim that equity regards as done that which ought to be done. The most common situation involves transferring real property as the parties to a contract intended before the seller experienced a change in circumstances, such as marriage or death, that could affect the property's ownership. When a contract is made, the buyer acquires equitable title to the property, and the seller retains legal title. But the seller's interest is treated as one in personal property rather than in real property because the seller's true interest is in the proceeds (usu. personal property such as cash); the legal title is security for the buyer's payment. Courts usu. apply the doctrine of equitable conversion to recognize the transfer of equitable title, including the right of possession, to the buyer when the contract was signed. The buyer then acquires legal title by performing under the contract.

   forced conversion. The conversion of a convertible security, after a call for redemption, when the value of the security that it may be converted to is greater than the amount that will be received if the holder permits the security to be redeemed.

2. *Tort & criminal law.* The wrongful possession or disposition of another's property as if it were one's own; an act or series of acts of willful interference, without lawful justification, with an item of property in a manner inconsistent with another's right, whereby that other person is deprived of the use and possession of the property. — **convert,** *vb.* — **conversionary,** *adj.*

   constructive conversion. Conversion consisting of an action that in law amounts to the appropriation of property. ● Constructive conversion could be, for example, an appropriation that was initially lawful.

   conversion by detention. Conversion by detaining property in a way that is adverse to the owner or other lawful possessor. ● The mere possession of property without title is not conversion. The defendant must have shown an intention to keep it in defiance of the owner or lawful possessor.

   conversion by estoppel. A judicial determination that a conversion has taken place — though in truth one has not — because a defendant is estopped from offering a defense. ● This occurs, for example, under the traditional rule that a bailee is estopped from denying the bailor's title even if the bailor has no title to the chattel.

   conversion by taking. Conversion by taking a chattel out of the possession of another with the intention of exercising a permanent or temporary dominion over it, despite the owner's entitlement to use it at all times.

   conversion by wrongful delivery. Conversion by depriving an owner of goods by delivering them to someone else so as to change the possession.

   conversion by wrongful destruction. Conversion by willfully consuming or otherwise destroying a chattel belonging to another person.

   conversion by wrongful disposition. Conversion by depriving an owner of goods by giving some other person a lawful title to them.

   direct conversion. The act of appropriating the property of another to one's own benefit, or to the benefit of a third person. ● A direct conversion is per se unlawful, and the traditional requirements of demand and refusal of the property do not apply.

   fraudulent conversion. Conversion that is committed by the use of fraud, either in obtaining the property or in withholding it.

   innocent conversion. See *technical conversion.*

involuntary conversion. The loss or destruction of property through theft, casualty, or condemnation.

negligent conversion. See *technical conversion.*

technical conversion. The taking of another's personal property by one who acts in good faith and mistakenly believes that he or she is lawfully entitled to the property. — Also termed *innocent conversion; negligent conversion.*

conversionary act. See ACT.

conversion divorce. See DIVORCE.

conversion premium. *Securities.* The surplus at which a security sells above its conversion price.

conversion price. *Securities.* The contractually specified price per share at which a convertible security can be converted into shares of common stock.

conversion ratio. 1. The number of common shares into which a convertible security may be converted. **2.** The ratio of the face amount of the convertible security to the conversion price.

conversion rule. See SPECIFIC-PURPOSE RULE.

conversion security. See SECURITY.

conversion statute. A law under which a state official or court oversees the sale or transfer of control of an organization in order to protect public assets.

conversion value. A convertible security's value as common stock. ● For example, a bond that can be converted into ten shares of stock worth $40 each has a conversion value of $400. See BOND CONVERSION.

converter, *n.* One who wrongfully possesses or disposes of another's property; esp., one who engages in a series of acts of willful interference, without lawful justification, with an item of property in a manner inconsistent with another's right, whereby that other person is deprived of the use and possession of the property.

innocent converter. A person who takes another's chattel tortiously but in good faith and without knowledge that he or she has no entitlement to it.

convertible arbitrage. See *kind arbitrage* under ARBITRAGE.

convertible bond. See BOND (3).

convertible collision insurance. See INSURANCE.

convertible debenture. See DEBENTURE.

convertible debt. 1. See DEBT. **2.** See *convertible security* under SECURITY.

convertible divorce. See *conversion divorce* under DIVORCE.

convertible insurance. See INSURANCE.

convertible security. See SECURITY.

convertible stock. See *convertible security* under SECURITY.

convertible subordinated debenture. See DEBENTURE.

convey, *vb.* (14c) To transfer or deliver (something, such as a right or property) to another, esp. by deed or other writing; esp., to perform an act that is intended to create one or more property interests, regardless of whether the act is actually effective to create those interests.

conveyance (kən-**vay**-ənts), *n.* (15c) **1.** The voluntary transfer of a right or of property.

absolute conveyance. A conveyance in which a right or property is transferred to another free of conditions or qualifications (i.e., not as a security). Cf. *conditional conveyance.*

conditional conveyance. A conveyance that is based on the happening of an event, usu. payment for the property; a mortgage. Cf. *absolute conveyance.*

derivative conveyance. See *secondary conveyance.*

innocent conveyance. *Hist.* A leaseholder's conveyance of the leaseholder's property interest — that is, something less than a fee simple. ● The conveyance is of an equitable interest.

mesne conveyance (meen). An intermediate conveyance; one occupying an intermediate position in the chain of title between the first grantee and the present holder.

original conveyance. See *primary conveyance.*

present conveyance. A conveyance made with the intent that it take effect at once rather than in the future.

primary conveyance. A conveyance that creates an estate. ● Examples of primary conveyances include feoffment, gift, grant, lease, exchange, and partition. — Also termed *original conveyance.* Cf. *secondary conveyance.*

secondary conveyance. A conveyance that follows an earlier conveyance and that serves only to enlarge, confirm, alter, restrain, restore, or transfer the interest created by the primary conveyance. — Also termed *derivative conveyance; derivative deed.* Cf. *primary conveyance.*

voluntary conveyance. A conveyance made without valuable consideration, such as a deed in favor of a relative.

2. The transfer of a property right that does not pass by delivery of a thing or merely by agreement. **3.** The transfer of an interest in real property from one living person to another, by means of an instrument such as a deed. **4.** The document (usu. a deed) by which such a transfer occurs. **5.** A means of transport; a vehicle. **6.** *Bankruptcy.* A transfer of an interest in real or personal property, including an assignment, a release, a monetary payment, or the creation of a lien or encumbrance. — Also termed (in sense 6) *bond for deed*. See FRAUDULENT CONVEYANCE; PREFERENTIAL TRANSFER.

conveyancer (kən-**vay**-ən-sər). (17c) A lawyer who specializes in real-estate transactions. ● In England, a *conveyancer* is a solicitor or licensed conveyancer who examines title to real estate, prepares deeds and mortgages, and performs other functions relating to the transfer of real property.

conveyancing (kən-**vay**-ən-sing). (17c) The act or business of drafting and preparing legal instruments, esp. those (such as deeds or leases) that transfer an interest in real property.

conveyancing counsel. *English law.* Three to six lawyers who are appointed by the Lord Chancellor to assist the High Court of Justice with opinions in matters of property titles and conveyancing. — Also termed *conveyancing counsel of the Supreme Court*; (formerly) *conveyancing counsel to the Court of Chancery.*

conveyee (kən-vay-**ee**). (18c) One to whom property is conveyed.

conveyor (kən-**vay**-ər *or* -or). (16c) One who transfers or delivers title to another.

convict (**kon**-vikt), *n.* (15c) A person who has been found guilty of a crime and is serving a sentence of confinement for that crime; a prison inmate.

convict (kən-**vikt**), *vb.* (15c) To find (a person) guilty of a criminal offense upon a criminal trial, a plea of guilty, or a plea of nolo contendere (no contest).

convicted felon. See FELON.

conviction (kən-**vik**-shən), *n.* **1.** The act or process of judicially finding someone guilty of a crime; the state of having been proved guilty. **2.** The judgment (as by a jury verdict) that a person is guilty of a crime. **3.** A strong belief or opinion.

　　abiding conviction. A settled conviction; a definite conviction based on a thorough examination of the case.

　　summary conviction. A conviction of a person for a violation or minor misdemeanor as the result of a trial before a magistrate sitting without a jury.

conviction rate. (1928) Within a given area or for a given time, the number of convictions (including plea bargains) as a percentage of the total number of prosecutions undertaken.

convocation. **1.** CONVENTION (4). **2.** See *call to order* under CALL (1). **3.** See *provincial synod* under SYNOD.

convoy, *n.* A group of vehicles or vessels traveling together for safety, esp. with armed escorts. ● The

term also applies figuratively to groups traveling together for convenience. — **convoy,** *vb.*

COO. *abbr.* CHIEF OPERATING OFFICER.

co-obligee. One of two or more persons to whom an obligation is owed. See OBLIGEE.

co-obligor. 1. One of two or more persons who have undertaken an obligation. See OBLIGOR. **2.** A person who is under a duty of contribution. See CONTRIBUTION (1).

cool blood. (17c) *Criminal law.* In the law of homicide, a condition in which the defendant's emotions are not in such an excited state that they interfere with his or her faculties and reason. — Also termed *cool state of blood.* See COLD BLOOD. Cf. HEAT OF PASSION.

***Cooley* doctrine.** (1936) *Constitutional law.* The principle that Congress has exclusive power under the Commerce Clause to regulate the national as well as the local aspects of national commercial matters, and that the states may regulate those aspects of interstate commerce so local in character as to require diverse treatment. ● The Supreme Court has abandoned the *Cooley* doctrine in favor of a balancing test for Commerce Clause cases. *Cooley v. Port Bd. of Wardens,* 53 U.S. (12 How.) 299 (1851).

cooling-off period. (1913) **1.** An automatic delay between a person's taking some legal action and the consequence of that action. **2.** A period during which a buyer may cancel a purchase. **3.** An automatic delay in some states between the filing of divorce papers and the divorce hearing. **4.** *Securities.* A period (usu. at least 20 days) between the filing of a registration and the effective registration. **5.** During a dispute, a period during which no action may be taken by either side. ● In labor disputes, a statutory cooling-off period forbids employee strikes and employer lockouts.

cooling time. (1874) *Criminal law.* Time to recover cool blood after great excitement, stress, or provocation, so that one is considered able to contemplate, comprehend, and act with reference to the consequences that are likely to follow. See COOL BLOOD.

cool state of blood. See COOL BLOOD.

co-op. See COOPERATIVE.

cooperation. 1. An association of individuals who join together for a common benefit. **2.** *Patents.* A unity of action to a common end or result, not merely joint or simultaneous action. **3.** *Int'l law.* The voluntary coordinated action of two or more countries occurring under a legal régime and serving a specific objective.

cooperation clause. *Insurance.* A policy provision requiring that the insured assist the insurer in investigating and defending a claim.

cooperative, *n.* (1883) **1.** An organization or enterprise (as a store) owned by those who use its services. **2.** A dwelling (as an apartment building) owned by its residents, to whom the apartments are leased. — Often shortened to *coop; co-op.* Cf. CONDOMINIUM (2).

cooperative adoption. See ADOPTION.

cooperative cause. See CAUSE (1).

cooperative corporation. See CORPORATION.

cooperative federalism. See FEDERALISM.

cooperative law. A dispute-resolution method by which the parties and their attorneys agree first to use nonadversarial strategies in an attempt to reach a binding agreement, with the possibility of litigation if a settlement fails, typically with the same attorneys involved in the litigation. Cf. COLLABORATIVE LAW; MEDIATION (1).

Cooperative State Research, Education, and Extension Service. An agency in the U.S. Department of Agriculture responsible for coordinating departmental research activities with those of academic and land-grant institutions. — Abbr. CSREES.

co-opt, *vb.* **1.** To add as a member. **2.** To assimilate; absorb.

co-optation (koh-ahp-**tay**-shən), *n.* The act of selecting a person to fill a vacancy (usu. in a close corporation). — **co-optative,** *adj.*

coordinate jurisdiction. See *concurrent jurisdiction* under JURISDICTION.

coordination-of-benefits clause. See COB CLAUSE.

coowner, *n.* (1858) A person who is in concurrent ownership, possession, and enjoyment of property with one or more others; a tenant in common, a joint tenant, or a tenant by the entirety. — **coown,** *vb.* — **coownership,** *n.*

COPA. *abbr.* CHILD ONLINE PROTECTION ACT.

cop a plea, *vb.* (1914) *Slang.*(Of a criminal defendant) to plead guilty to a lesser charge as a means to avoid standing trial for a more serious offense. See PLEA BARGAIN.

coparcenary (koh-**pahr**-sə-ner-ee), *n.* (16c) An estate that arises when two or more persons jointly inherit from one ancestor, the title and right of possession being shared equally by all. ● Coparcenary was a form of coownership created by common-law rules of descent upon intestacy when two or more persons together constituted the decedent's heirs. Typically, this situation arose when the decedent was survived by no sons but by two or more daughters, so that the daughters took as coparceners. — Also termed *parcenary; tenancy in coparcenary.* — **coparcenary,** *adj.*

coparcener (koh-**pahr**-sə-nər). A person to whom an estate descends jointly, and who holds it as an entire estate; a person who has become a concurrent owner as a result of descent. — Also termed *parcener;* (archaically) *coparticeps.*

copartner. A member of a partnership; PARTNER.

copartnership. See PARTNERSHIP. ● The terms *copartnership* and *partnership* are equally old — each having first appeared in the 1570s.

coparty. (1906) A litigant or participant in a legal transaction who has a like status with another party; a party on the same side of a lawsuit. — Also termed *joint party.* See CODEFENDANT; COPLAINTIFF.

copayment. A fixed amount that a patient pays to a healthcare provider according to the terms of the patient's health plan. — Often shortened to *copay.*

copending, *adj. Patents.* (Of serial applications filed in the same patent prosecution) before the U.S. Patent and Trademark Office at or near the same time and concerning the same invention. ● A continuation or divisional application that is copending with its parent application benefits from the parent's earlier filing date.

copending patent. See PATENT (3).

coplaintiff. (18c) One of two or more plaintiffs in the same litigation. — Also termed *joint plaintiff.* Cf. CODEFENDANT.

coprincipal. (17c) **1.** One of two or more participants in a criminal offense who either perpetrate the crime or aid a person who does so. **2.** One of two or more persons who have appointed an agent whom they both have the right to control.

copulative condition. See CONDITION (2).

copy, *n.* (14c) **1.** An imitation or reproduction of an original. ● In the law of evidence, a copy is generally admissible to prove the contents of a writing. Fed. R. Evid. 1003. See BEST-EVIDENCE RULE.

archival copy. See ARCHIVAL COPY.

attested copy. See *certified copy.*

certified copy. (18c) A duplicate of an original (usu. official) document, certified as an exact reproduction usu. by the officer responsible for issuing or keeping the original. — Also termed *attested copy; exemplified copy; verified copy.*

conformed copy. (1937) An exact copy of a document bearing written explanations of things that were not or could not be copied, such as a note on the document indicating that it was signed by a person whose signature appears on the original.

examined copy. A copy (usu. of a record, public book, or register) that has been compared with the original or with an official record of an original.

exemplified copy. See *certified copy.*

true copy. A copy that, while not necessarily exact, is sufficiently close to the original that anyone can understand it.

verified copy. See *certified copy.*

2. *Copyright.* The physical form in which a creative work is fixed and from which the work can be reproduced or perceived, with or without the aid of a special device. 17 USCA § 101. **3.** *Copyright.* An expressive work that is substantially similar to a copyrighted work and not produced coincidentally and independently from the same source as the copyrighted work. ● Proof of copying in an infringement action requires evidence of the defendant's access to the original work and substantial similarity of the defendant's work to the original. See *substantial similarity* under SIMILARITY.

copycat drug. See *generic drug* under DRUG.

copyhold. *Hist.* A base tenure requiring the tenant to provide the customary services of the manor, as reflected in the manor's court rolls. ● Copyhold tenure descended from pure villeinage; over time, the customs of the manor, as reflected on the manor's rolls, dictated what services a lord could demand from a copyholder. This type of tenure was abolished by the Law of Property Act of 1922, which converted copyhold land into freehold or leasehold land. — Also termed *copyhold tenure*; *customary estate*; *customary freehold*; *tenancy by the verge*; *tenancy par la verge*; *tenancy by the rod.* See *base tenure* under TENURE; VILLEINAGE.

copyholder. *Hist.* A tenant by copyhold tenure. — Also termed *tenant by the verge*; *tenant par la verge.*

copyhold tenant. See *customary tenant* under TENANT.

copyleft. *Slang.* A software license that allows users to modify or incorporate open-source code into larger programs on the condition that the software containing the source code is publicly distributed without restrictions.

copylefted software. *Slang.* Free software whose distribution terms forbid the addition of restrictions if the software is redistributed in its original or a modified form. ● Not actually a legal term, this phrase is popularly used as the antithesis of copyright by Internet free-software promoters. See FREEWARE.

copyright, *n.* (18c) **1.** The right to copy; specifically, a property right in an original work of authorship (including literary, musical, dramatic, choreographic, pictorial, graphic, sculptural, and architectural works; motion pictures and other audiovisual works; and sound recordings) fixed in any tangible medium of expression, giving the holder the exclusive right to reproduce, adapt, distribute, perform, and display the work. **2.** The

body of law relating to such works. ● Copyright law is governed by the Copyright Act of 1976. 17 USCA §§ 101–1332. — Abbr. c. — **copyright,** *vb.* — **copyrighted,** *adj.*

ad interim copyright. *Hist.* A limited five-year U.S. copyright granted to the author of a foreign edition of an English- language book or periodical if, within six months after its publication abroad, the author deposited one complete copy of that edition in the U.S. Copyright Office and requested ad interim copyright protection. ● An ad interim copyright was granted as an exception to the 1909 Copyright Act's manufacturing clause, which limited copyright protection for English-language books and periodicals to those printed in the U.S. If the copyright owner published the work in the U.S. during the period of ad interim protection and complied with the Act's manufacturing requirements, full copyright protection related back to the date of first publication. Otherwise, the work went into the public domain at the end of five years.

common-law copyright. A property right that arose when the work was created, rather than when it was published. ● Under the Copyright Act of 1976, which took effect on January 1, 1978, common-law copyright was largely abolished for works created after the statute's effective date. But the statute retained the common law's recognition that the property right arose when the work was created rather than when it was published. The common-law copyright still applies in a few areas: notably, a common-law copyright received before January 1, 1978 remains entitled to protection. 17 USCA § 301. — Also termed *right of first publication.*

copyrightability test. A judicial test for determining whether a contributor to a joint work is an author for legal purposes, based on whether the contributor's effort is an original expression that could qualify for copyright protection on its own. ● This test has been adopted by a majority of courts. Cf. DE MINIMIS TEST.

Copyright Act of 1790. The first U.S. copyright law, which, like England's Statute of Anne, gave authors copyright protection for 14 years, renewable for another 14 years, after which time the work then entered the public domain.

Copyright Act of 1909. A major revision of U.S. copyright law, extending the term of protection from 14 to 28 years (renewable for a second 28-year term); measuring the copyright term from the time of publication rather than the time of registration with the Copyright Office; and expanding coverage to all writings. ● The Act retained the formalities for securing a copyright and required that a copyright mark appear on the work. It governed U.S. copyrights issued between July 1, 1909 and December 31, 1977. Although the

1976 Copyright Act supplanted the 1909 Act, the 1909 Act still applies to some pre-1978 claims and affects certain other rights of copyright owners. — Also termed *1909 Copyright Act*.

Copyright Act of 1976. A major revision of U.S. copyright law, extending the term of protection to the life of the author plus 50 years, measured from the date of creation; greatly expanding the types of works that qualify for protection; dropping the requirement that the work be published before it can be protected; making fair use a statutory defense to a claim in infringement; and preempting state common-law copyright. 17 USCA §§ 101 et seq. • This is the current federal statute that governs copyright registrations and rights. — Also termed *1976 Copyright Act*.

Copyright and the Challenge of Technology. See GREEN PAPER ON COPYRIGHT AND THE CHALLENGE OF TECHNOLOGY.

copyright application. A written request for copyright protection made by a work's creator, filed with the U.S. Copyright Office and accompanied by a filing fee and either a deposit copy of the work or approved identifying material. • A registrant who does not meet the deposit requirement of the Copyright Act of 1976 risks losing copyright protection. *See, e.g., Coles v. Wonder,* 283 F.3d 798 (6th Cir. 2002).

copyright bug. See COPYRIGHT NOTICE.

Copyright Clause. (1940) U.S. Const. art. I, § 8, cl. 8, which gives Congress the power to secure to authors the exclusive rights to their writings for a limited time.

copyright clearinghouse. An organization that licenses members' works to applicants for specific purposes. • A clearinghouse usu. licenses only one type or class of works, such as songs, photographs, cartoons, or written materials.

copyright infringement. See INFRINGEMENT.

copyright legend. See COPYRIGHT NOTICE.

copyright-management information. The name and other identifying information about the creator, performer, or copyright owner of a creative work. See DIGITAL MILLENNIUM COPYRIGHT ACT.

copyright misuse. In an infringement action, an affirmative defense based on the copyright owner's use of a license to restrain trade or in any other manner that is against public policy. • The defense, roughly parallel to the declining patent-misuse defense, was invoked, for example, to prevent the American Medical Association from enforcing its copyright in its medical-procedure codes after licensing them to the U.S. Government for use in the Medicaid program. See *Practice Mgmt. Info. Corp. v. Am. Med. Ass'n,* 121 F.3d 516 (9th Cir. 1997).

copyright notice. (1889) A notice that a work is copyright-protected, usu. placed in each published copy of the work. • A copyright notice takes the form © (year of publication) (name of basic copyright owner). Since March 1, 1989, such notice is not required for a copyright to be valid (although the notice continues to provide certain procedural advantages). The phrase "all rights reserved" is usu. no longer required. — Sometimes termed *copyright bug; copyright legend; notice of copyright.* See ALL RIGHTS RESERVED; BUENOS AIRES CONVENTION.

copyright owner. (1886) **1.** One who holds an exclusive right or rights to copyrighted material. 17 USCA § 101. **2.** One who is named as the owner on any copyright notice attached to a work and who is registered with the U.S. Copyright Office as the owner.

Copyright Royalty Tribunal. A former board in the legislative branch of the federal government responsible for establishing and monitoring copyright royalty rates for published and recorded materials. • Its functions are now performed by copyright arbitration royalty panels.

coram (**kor**-əm), *prep.* [Latin] (Of a person) before; in the presence of.

coram nobis (**kor**-əm **noh**-bis). [Latin "before us"] **1.** *Hist.* A writ of error taken from a judgment of the King's Bench. • "Before us" refers to the sovereign, in contrast to the writ *coram vobis* ("before you"), which refers to any court other than King's Bench, esp. the Court of Common Pleas. **2.** A writ of error directed to a court for review of its own judgment and predicated on alleged errors of fact. — Also termed *writ of error coram nobis; writ of coram nobis;* (misspelled) *quorum nobis.*

coram non judice (**kor**-əm non **joo**-di-see). [Latin "not before a judge"] **1.** Outside the presence of a judge. **2.** Before a judge or court that is not the proper one or that cannot take legal cognizance of the matter.

Coram Rege Court. See KING'S BENCH.

coram vobis (**kor**-əm **voh**-bis), *n.* [Latin "before you"] *Hist.* **1.** A writ of error directed to a court other than the King's Bench, esp. the Court of Common Pleas, to review its judgment. **2.** A writ of error sent by an appellate court to a trial court to review the trial court's judgment based on an error of fact. — Also termed *writ of error coram vobis; writ of coram vobis.*

Cordon rule. A rule of the U.S. Senate requiring any committee that is reporting a bill amending current law to show in its report what wording the bill would strike from or insert into the current statute. • The rule is named for Senator Guy Cordon (1890–1969) of Oregon, who proposed it. The analogous rule in the U.S. House of Representatives is the Ramseyer rule. See RAMSEYER RULE.

core earnings. See *operating earnings* under EARN-INGS.

core proceeding. *Bankruptcy.* **1.** A proceeding involving claims that substantially affect the debtor-creditor relationship, such as an action to recover a preferential transfer. • In such a proceeding, the bankruptcy court, as opposed to the district court, conducts the trial or hearing and enters a final judgment. Cf. RELATED PROCEEDING. **2.** In federal courts, an action involving subject matter that is clearly within the confines of federal bankruptcy law and the management of the bankrupt's estate. • A federal bankruptcy court may also hear noncore matters that have an independent basis for subject-matter jurisdiction, such as a federal question. For a nonexclusive list of core proceedings, see 28 USCA § 157(b)(2).

core rights. **1.** Human rights that are generally recognized and accepted throughout the world. • These rights include freedom from extrajudicial execution, torture, and arbitrary arrest and detention. Core rights are embodied in many human rights conventions, including the Universal Declaration of Human Rights, the International Covenant on Civil and Political Rights, and the International Covenant on Economic, Social and Cultural Rights. **2.** Fundamental rights claimed within a social, cultural, or other context. • These are not universally recognized rights. For example, the ability to vote may be a fundamental right of citizens in one country but only a privilege limited to selected people in another.

corespondent. (1857) **1.** A coparty who responds to a petition, such as a petition for a writ of certiorari. **2.** In some states, a coparty who responds to an appeal. **3.** *Family law.* In a divorce suit based on adultery, the person with whom the spouse is accused of having committed adultery. See RE-SPONDENT.

core work product. See *opinion work product* under WORK PRODUCT.

cornage (**kor**-nij). [fr. Anglo-French *corne* "horn"] *Hist.* **1.** A type of grand-sergeanty military tenure in which the tenant was bound to blow a horn to alert others whenever an enemy approached. **2.** A form of tenure entitling a landowner to rent based on the number of horned cattle owned by the tenant. • Cornage may have developed into a type of serjeanty or knight-service tenure that obligated the tenant to blow a horn to warn of invaders, esp. along the border with Scotland. — Also termed (in senses 1 & 2) *horn tenure.* See KNIGHT-SERVICE; SERJEANTY. **3.** A tribute of corn due only on special occasions, as distinguished from a regularly provided service. • This term has often been spelled *coraage* or *coraagium*, stemming perhaps from a spelling error in the 1569 edition of Bracton's *De Legibus et Consuetudinibus Angliae.*

corner, *n.* **1.** The common end of two survey lines; an angle made by two boundary lines.

existent corner. A corner whose location can be verified by an original landmark, a surveyor's field notes, or other reliable evidence.

lost corner. A point in a land description, such as a landmark or natural object, whose position cannot be reasonably determined from traces of the original marks or other acceptable evidence. • The location can be determined by reference to one or more independent points remaining in the description.

obliterated corner. A corner that can be located only with evidence other than that put in place by the original surveyor.

2. The acquisition of control over all or a dominant quantity of a commodity with the purpose of artificially enhancing the price, carried out by purchases and sales of the commodity — and of options and futures — in a way that depresses the market price so that the participants are enabled to purchase the commodity at satisfactory prices and withhold it from the market for a time, thereby inflating its price. • A corner accomplished by confederation, with the purpose of raising or depressing prices and operating on the market, is a criminal conspiracy if the means are unlawful.

corner influence. *Property.* In an appraisal, the additional value of a corner lot, esp. one zoned for commercial purposes, attributable to factors such as increased light and air, easier ingress and egress, greater accessibility by pedestrian and automotive traffic, and more space for displays and advertisements.

cornering the market. The act or process of acquiring ownership or control of a large portion of the available supply of a commodity or security, permitting manipulation of the commodity's or security's price.

Corn Products **doctrine.** *Tax.* The principle that a capital asset should be narrowly defined to exclude inventory-related property that is integrally tied to the day-to-day operations of a business. *Corn Prods. Refining Co. v. C.I.R.,* 350 U.S. 46, 76 S.Ct. 20 (1955).

corollary (**kor-** or **kahr-**ə-ler-ee), *n.* (14c) A proposition that follows from a proven proposition with little or no additional proof; something that naturally follows.

coronation case. *Hist.* Any of the many lawsuits for breach of contract resulting from the postponement of the coronation of Edward VII because of his illness. • In one case, for example, the defendant had agreed to hire a ship for watching the naval review by King Edward VII and for a day's cruise around the fleet. The court held that the contract was not frustrated by the cancellation of the naval review — the day's cruise around the fleet was still possible, and indeed, the ship could have been used for many other purposes.

coroner (**kor-** *or* **kahr-**ə-nər). (14c) **1.** A public official whose duty is to investigate the causes and circumstances of any death that occurs suddenly, suspiciously, or violently. See MEDICAL EXAMINER. **2.** *Hist.* A royal official with countywide jurisdiction to investigate deaths, to hold inquests, and to assume the duties of the sheriff if need be. ● The coroner acted as a check on the sheriff, a local officer whose growing power threatened royal control over the counties. The coroner reported criminal activity to the king's justices in eyre. When the eyre court arrived in a county, it collected the coroner's roll to learn what had occurred in the county during the eyre's absence. The justices fined the coroner if he failed to produce the roll, or if they learned of criminal activity in the county from a source other than the roll.

coroner's court. See COURT.

coroner's inquest. See INQUEST (1).

coroner's jury. See JURY.

corpnership. [Portmanteau word probably formed fr. *corporation* + *partnership*] A limited partnership (usu. having many public investors as limited partners) whose general partner is a corporation.

corporale sacramentum (kor-pə-**ray**-lee sak-rə-**men**-təm). See *corporal oath* under OATH.

corporal oath. See OATH.

corporal punishment. See PUNISHMENT.

corporate, *adj.* (16c) Of or relating to a corporation, esp. a business corporation <corporate bonds>.

corporate acquisition. (1911) The takeover of one corporation by another if both parties retain their legal existence after the transaction. Cf. MERGER (8).

corporate agent. See AGENT (2).

corporate authority. (1817) **1.** The power rightfully wielded by officers of a corporation. **2.** In some jurisdictions, a municipal officer, esp. one empowered to represent the municipality in certain statutory matters.

corporate body. See CORPORATION.

corporate bond. See BOND (3).

corporate books. (1846) Written records of a corporation's activities and business transactions.

corporate charter. See CHARTER (3).

corporate citizenship. (1889) Corporate status in the state of incorporation, though a corporation is not a constitutional citizen for the purposes of the Privileges and Immunities Clauses in Article IV § 2 and in the 14th Amendment to the U.S. Constitution.

corporate counsel. See COUNSEL.

corporate crime. See CRIME.

corporate distribution. See DISTRIBUTION.

corporate domicile. See DOMICILE.

corporate entity. See ENTITY.

corporate franchise. See FRANCHISE (2).

corporate immunity. See IMMUNITY (2).

corporate indenture. See INDENTURE.

corporate merger. See MERGER (8).

corporate-mortgage trust. A financing device in which debentures are issued and secured by property held in trust. ● An independent trustee protects the interests of those who purchase the debentures.

corporate name. See NAME.

corporate officer. See OFFICER (1).

corporate-opportunity doctrine. (1942) The rule that a corporation's directors, officers, and employees are precluded from using information gained as such to take personal advantage of any business opportunities that the corporation has an expectancy right or property interest in, or that in fairness should otherwise belong to the corporation. ● In a partnership, the analogous principle is termed the *firm-opportunity doctrine*.

corporate-owned life insurance. See LIFE INSURANCE.

corporate purpose. (18c) The general scope of the business objective for which a corporation was created. ● A statement of corporate purpose is commonly required in the articles of incorporation.

corporate raider. A person or business that attempts to take control of a corporation, against its wishes, by buying its stock and replacing its management. — Often shortened to *raider*. — Also termed *hostile bidder*; *unfriendly suitor*. Cf. WHITE KNIGHT.

corporate resolution. See RESOLUTION (2).

corporate seal. See SEAL.

corporate speech. See SPEECH.

corporate stock. See STOCK.

corporate trustee. See TRUSTEE (1).

corporate veil. (1927) The legal assumption that the acts of a corporation are not the actions of its shareholders, so that the shareholders are exempt from liability for the corporation's actions. See PIERCING THE CORPORATE VEIL.

corporate welfare. See WELFARE (2).

corporation, *n.* (15c) An entity (usu. a business) having authority under law to act as a single person distinct from the shareholders who own it and having rights to issue stock and exist indefinitely; a group or succession of persons established in accordance with legal rules into a legal or juristic person that has a legal personality distinct from the natural persons who make it up, exists indefinitely apart from them, and has the legal powers that its constitution gives it. — Also termed *corporation aggregate*; *aggregate corporation*; *body corporate*; *corporate body*. See COMPANY. — **incorporate**, *vb.* — **corporate**, *adj.*

acquired corporation. The corporation that no longer exists after a merger or acquisition.

admitted corporation. A corporation licensed or authorized to do business within a particular state. — Also termed *qualified corporation*; *corporation qualified to do business*.

aggressor corporation. A corporation that attempts to obtain control of a publicly held corporation by (1) a direct cash tender, (2) a public exchange offer to shareholders, or (3) a merger, which requires the agreement of the target's management.

alien corporation. See *foreign corporation*.

brother-sister corporation. See *sister corporation*.

business corporation. A corporation formed to engage in commercial activity for profit. Cf. *nonprofit corporation*.

C corporation. A corporation whose income is taxed through it rather than through its shareholders. • Any corporation not electing S-corporation tax status under the Internal Revenue Code is a C corporation by default. — Also termed *subchapter-C corporation*. Cf. *S corporation*.

charitable corporation. (17c) A nonprofit corporation that is dedicated to benevolent purposes and thus entitled to special tax status under the Internal Revenue Code. — Also termed *eleemosynary corporation*. See CHARITABLE ORGANIZATION.

civil corporation. Any corporation other than a charitable or religious corporation.

clearing corporation. A corporation whose capital stock is held by or for a national security exchange or association registered under federal law such as the Securities Exchange Act of 1934.

close corporation. (1840) A corporation whose stock is not freely traded and is held by only a few shareholders (often within the same family). • The requirements and privileges of close corporations vary by jurisdiction. — Also termed *closely held corporation*; *closed corporation*; (when family owned) *family corporation*.

collapsible corporation. (1955) A corporation formed to give a short-term venture the appearance of a long-term investment in order to portray income as capital gain, rather than profit. • The corporation is typically formed for the sole purpose of purchasing property. The corporation is usu. dissolved before the property has generated substantial income. The Internal Revenue Service treats the income earned through a collapsible corporation as ordinary income rather than as capital gain. IRC (26 USCA) § 341(a). Cf. *collapsible partnership* under PARTNERSHIP.

common-law corporation. See *corporation by prescription*.

conglomerate corporation. See CONGLOMERATE.

controlled corporation. **1.** A corporation in which the majority of the stock is held by one individual or firm. **2.** A corporation in which a substantial amount (but less than a majority) of the stock is held by one individual or firm. • Some states presume control with as little as 10%.

controlled foreign corporation. *Tax.* A foreign corporation in which more than 50% of the stock is owned by U.S. citizens who each own 10% or more of the voting stock. • These shareholders (known as *U.S. shareholders*) are required to report their pro rata share of certain passive income of the corporation. IRC (26 USCA) §§ 951–964. — Abbr. CFC.

cooperative corporation. An entity that has a corporate existence, but is primarily organized for the purpose of providing services and profits to its members and not for corporate profit. • The most common kind of cooperative corporation is formed to purchase real property, such as an apartment building, so that its shareholders may lease the apartments. See COOPERATIVE (1).

corporation aggregate. **1.** See CORPORATION. **2.** *Hist.* A corporation made up of a number of individuals. Cf. *corporation sole*.

corporation by estoppel. A business that is deemed, by operation of law, to be a corporation because a third party dealt with the business as if it were a corporation, thus preventing the third party from holding a shareholder or officer of the corporation individually liable. See ESTOPPEL.

corporation by prescription. A corporation that, though lacking a charter, has acquired its corporate status through a long period of operating as a corporation. • Such an entity may engage in any enterprises that are not manifestly inconsistent with the purposes for which it is assumed to have been created. — Also termed *common-law corporation*.

corporation de facto. See *de facto corporation*.

corporation de jure. See *de jure corporation*.

corporation for profit. See *for-profit corporation*.

corporation qualified to do business. See *admitted corporation*.

corporation sole. A series of successive persons holding an office; a continuous legal personality that is attributed to successive holders of certain monarchical or ecclesiastical positions, such as kings, bishops, rectors, vicars, and the like. • This continuous personality is viewed, by legal fiction, as having the qualities of a corporation. Cf. *corporation aggregate* (2).

dead corporation. See *dissolved corporation*.

de facto corporation (di **fak**-toh). An incompletely formed corporation whose existence operates as a defense to personal liability of the directors, officers, and shareholders who in good faith thought they were operating the business as a duly formed corporation. — Also termed *corporation de facto*.

de jure corporation (di **juur**-ee). A corporation formed in accordance with all applicable laws and recognized as a corporation for liability purposes. — Also termed *corporation de jure*.

dissolved corporation. A corporation whose charter has expired or been revoked, relinquished, or voluntarily terminated. — Also termed *dead corporation*.

domestic corporation. (1819) **1.** A corporation that is organized and chartered under the laws of a state. • The corporation is considered *domestic* by the chartering state. Cf. *foreign corporation*. **2.** *Tax.* A corporation created or organized in the United States or under federal or state law. IRC (26 USCA) § 7701(a)(4).

dormant corporation. 1. An inactive corporation; a legal corporation that is presently not operating. **2.** A corporation whose authority to do business has been revoked or suspended either by operation of law (as by failure to pay franchise taxes) or by an act of the government official responsible for the corporation's authority.

dummy corporation. (1899) A corporation whose only function is to hide the principal's identity and to protect the principal from liability.

ecclesiastical corporation (i-klee-zee-**as**-tə-kəl). *English law.* A corporation that is organized for spiritual purposes or for the administration of property held for religious uses. — Also termed *religious corporation*. Cf. *lay corporation*.

eleemosynary corporation. See *charitable corporation*.

foreign corporation. (18c) A corporation that was organized and chartered under the laws of another state, government, or country <in Arizona, a California corporation is said to be a foreign corporation>. — Also termed *alien corporation*. Cf. *domestic corporation*.

for-profit corporation. A corporation organized for the purpose of making a profit; a business corporation. — Also termed *corporation for profit*; *moneyed corporation*.

government corporation. See *public corporation* (3).

joint-venture corporation. A corporation that has joined with one or more individuals or corporations to accomplish some specified project.

lay corporation. *English law.* A corporation made up of laypersons, and existing for a business or charitable purpose. Cf. *ecclesiastical corporation*.

limited-liability corporation. See *limited-liability company* under COMPANY.

migratory corporation. A corporation formed under the laws of another state than that of the incorporators' residence for the purpose of carrying on a significant portion of its business in the state of the incorporators' residence or in a state other than where it was incorporated.

moneyed corporation. 1. A corporation that uses money capital in its business, esp. one (such as a bank) that engages in the exchange or lending of money. **2.** See *for-profit corporation*.

multinational corporation. A company with operations in two or more countries, generally allowing it to transfer funds and products according to price and demand conditions, subject to risks such as changes in exchange rates or political instability. — Also termed *transnational corporation*.

multistate corporation. A corporation incorporated under the laws of two or more states.

municipal corporation. See MUNICIPAL CORPORATION.

municipal corporation de facto. See MUNICIPAL CORPORATION.

nonprofit corporation. (1908) A corporation organized for some purpose other than making a profit, and usu. afforded special tax treatment. — Also termed *not-for-profit corporation*. Cf. *business corporation*.

nonstock corporation. A corporation that does not issue shares of stock as evidence of ownership but instead is owned by its members in accordance with a charter or agreement. • Examples are mutual insurance companies, charitable organizations, and private clubs.

not-for-profit corporation. See *nonprofit corporation*.

parent corporation. (1893) A corporation that has a controlling interest in another corporation (called a *subsidiary corporation*), usu. through ownership of more than one-half the voting stock. — Often shortened to *parent*. — Also termed *parent company*.

political corporation. See *public corporation* (2).

private corporation. (17c) A corporation founded by and composed of private individuals principally for a nonpublic purpose, such as manufacturing, banking, and railroad corporations (including charitable and religious corporations). — Also termed *quasi-individual*.

professional corporation. (1958) A corporation providing services of a type requiring a professional license. • A professional corporation may be made up of architects, accountants, lawyers, physicians, veterinarians, or the like. — Abbr. P.C.

public corporation. (17c) **1.** A corporation whose shares are traded to and among the general public. — Also termed *publicly held corporation*. **2.** A corporation that is created by the state as an agency in the administration of civil government. — Also termed *political corporation*. **3.** A government-owned corporation that engages in activities that benefit the general public, usu. while remaining financially independent. • Such a corporation is managed by a publicly appointed board. — Also termed (in sense 3) *government corporation*; *public-benefit corporation*.

publicly held corporation. See *public corporation* (1).

public-service corporation. (1894) A corporation whose operations serve a need of the general public, such as public transportation, communications, gas, water, or electricity. • This type of corporation is usu. subject to extensive governmental regulation.

qualified corporation. See *admitted corporation*.

quasi-corporation. An entity that exercises some of the functions of a corporation but that has not been granted corporate status by statute; esp., a public corporation with limited authority and powers (such as a county or school district). — Also sometimes termed *quasi-municipal corporation*. Cf. MUNICIPAL CORPORATION.

quasi-public corporation. A for-profit corporation providing an essential public service. • An example is an electric company or other utility.

railroad corporation. A corporation organized to construct, maintain, and operate railroads. — Also termed *railroad company*.

registered corporation. (1928) A publicly held corporation, a security of which is registered under § 12 of the Securities Exchange Act of 1934. • The corporation is subject to the Act's periodic disclosure requirements and proxy regulations. 15 USCA § 78*l*.

religious corporation. A corporation created to carry out some ecclesiastical or religious purpose. See *ecclesiastical corporation*.

S corporation. (1961) A corporation whose income is taxed through its shareholders rather than through the corporation itself. • Only corporations with a limited number of shareholders can elect S-corporation tax status under Subchapter S of the Internal Revenue Code. — Also termed *subchapter-S corporation*; *tax-option corporation*. Cf. C corporation.

shelf corporation. See *shelf company* under COMPANY.

shell corporation. (1969) A corporation that has no active business and usu. exists only in name as a vehicle for another company's business operations.

sister corporation. One of two or more corporations controlled by the same, or substantially the same, owners. — Also termed *brother-sister corporation*.

small-business corporation. (1898) **1.** A corporation having no more than 75 shareholders and otherwise satisfying the requirements of the Internal Revenue Code provisions permitting a subchapter S election. IRC (26 USCA) § 1361. See *S corporation*. **2.** A corporation receiving money for stock (as a contribution to capital and paid-in surplus) totaling not more than $1,000,000, and otherwise satisfying the requirements of the Internal Revenue Code section 1244(c) thereby enabling the shareholders to claim an ordinary loss on worthless stock. IRC (26 USCA) § 1244(c).

sole corporation. A corporation having or acting through only a single member.

spiritual corporation. A corporation whose members are spiritual persons, such as bishops, rectors, and abbots.

stock corporation. A corporation in which the capital is contributed by the shareholders and divided into shares represented by certificates.

subchapter-C corporation. See *C corporation*.

subchapter-S corporation. See *S corporation*.

subsidiary corporation. (1882) A corporation in which a parent corporation has a controlling share. — Often shortened to *subsidiary*; *sub*.

surviving corporation. A corporation that acquires the assets and liabilities of another corporation by a merger or takeover.

target corporation. A corporation over which control is being sought by another party. See TAKEOVER.

tax-option corporation. See *S corporation*.

thin corporation. A corporation with an excessive amount of debt in its capitalization. See *thin capitalization* under CAPITALIZATION.

trading corporation. A corporation whose business involves the buying and selling of goods.

tramp corporation. A corporation chartered in a state where it does not conduct business.

transnational corporation. See *multinational corporation*.

trust corporation. See *trust company* under COMPANY.

U.S.-owned foreign corporation. A foreign corporation in which 50% or more of the total combined voting power or total value of the stock is held directly or indirectly by U.S. citizens. IRC (26 USCA) § 904(g)(6). ● If the dividend or interest income paid by a U.S. corporation is classified as a foreign source, the U.S. corporation is treated as a U.S.-owned foreign corporation. IRC (26 USCA) § 861.

Corporation Act. *Hist.* A 1661 English statute (13 Car. 2, St. 2, ch. 1) prohibiting the holding of public office by anyone who would not take the Anglican sacrament and the oaths of supremacy and allegiance. ● The Act was repealed by the Promissory Oaths Act of 1871.

corporation counsel. See COUNSEL.

corporation court. See COURT.

Corporation for National and Community Service. A federal corporation that fosters civic responsibility, provides educational opportunity for those who contribute services, and oversees AmeriCorps (the domestic Peace Corps), Learn and Serve America, and the National Senior Service Corps. ● It was established in 1993. 42 USCA § 12651.

corporator (kor-pə-ray-tər). (18c) **1.** A member of a corporation. **2.** INCORPORATOR.

corporeal (kor-**por**-ee-əl), *adj.* (15c) Having a physical, material existence; TANGIBLE <land and fixtures are corporeal property>. Cf. INCORPOREAL. — **corporeality,** *n.*

corporeal hereditament. See HEREDITAMENT.

corporeal ownership. See OWNERSHIP.

corporeal possession. See POSSESSION.

corporeal property. See PROPERTY.

corporeal thing. See THING.

corpus (**kor**-pəs), *n.* [Latin "body"] **1.** The property for which a trustee is responsible; the trust principal. — Also termed *res; trust estate; trust fund;*

trust property; trust res; trust. **2.** PRINCIPAL (4). Pl. **corpora** (kor-pə-rə), **corpuses** (kor-pə-səz).

corpus delicti (kor-pəs də-**lik**-tɪ *or* -tee). [Latin "body of the crime"] (1818) **1.** The fact of a transgression; ACTUS REUS. **2.** Loosely, the material substance on which a crime has been committed; the physical evidence of a crime, such as the corpse of a murdered person. ● Despite the common misunderstanding, a victim's body could be evidence of a homicide but the prosecutor does not have to locate or present the body to meet the corpus delicti requirement.

corpus delicti rule. (1926) *Criminal law.* The doctrine that prohibits a prosecutor from proving the corpus delicti based solely on a defendant's extrajudicial statements. ● The prosecution must establish the *corpus delicti* with corroborating evidence to secure a conviction.

corpus juris (kor-pəs **joor**-is). [Latin "body of law"] (1832) The law as the sum or collection of laws <*Corpus Juris Secundum*>. — Abbr. C.J.

corpus juris Angliae (kor-pəs **joor**-is **ang**-glee-ee). The entire body of English law, comprising the common law, statutory law, equity, and special law in its various forms.

Corpus Juris Canonici (kor-pəs **joor**-is kə-**non**-ə-sɪ). [Latin] *Hist.* The body of the canon law, compiled from the decrees and canons of the Roman Catholic Church. ● The *Corpus Juris Canonici* emerged during the 12th century, beginning with the publication of Gratian's *Decretum* (c. 1140). In addition to the *Decretum*, it includes Raymond of Peñaforte's *Liber Extra* (1234), the *Liber Sextus* of Pope Boniface VIII (1298), the *Clementines* of Pope Clement V (1313), the *Extravagantes Joannis* of Pope John XXII (1325), and *Extravagantes Communes* published by Pope John's successors (1499-1502). In 1582, the entire collection was edited by a commission of church dignitaries and officially named the *Corpus Juris Canonici*. It remained the Catholic Church's primary body of law until the promulgation of the Code of Canon Law in 1917, now replaced by that of 1983.

Corpus Juris Civilis (kor-pəs **joor**-is sə-**vil**-is *or* sə-**vɪ**-lis). The body of the civil law, compiled and codified under the direction of the Roman emperor Justinian in A.D. 528–556. ● The collection includes four works — the Institutes, the Digest (or Pandects), the Code, and the Novels. The title *Corpus Juris Civilis* was not original, or even early, but was modeled on the *Corpus Juris Canonici* and given in the 16th century and later to editions of the texts of the four component parts of the Roman law. See ROMAN LAW. Cf. JUSTINIAN CODE.

correal (**kor**-ee-əl *or* kə-**ree**-əl), *adj.* [fr. Latin *correus* "codebtor"] *Roman law.* Of or relating to liability that is joint and several. ● A *correal* debtor who paid an entire obligation had no right of action against a codebtor. See SOLIDARY.

correality (kor-ee-**al**-ə-tee), *n.* The quality or state of being correal; the relationship between parties to an obligation that terminates when an entire payment is made by one of two or more debtors to a creditor, or a payment is made by a debtor to one of two or more creditors.

correal obligation. See OBLIGATION.

corrected policy. See INSURANCE POLICY.

correction, *n.* (14c) **1.** Generally, the act or an instance of making right what is wrong <mark your corrections in red ink>. **2.** A change in business activity or market price following and counteracting an increase or decrease in the activity or price <the broker advised investors to sell before the inevitable stock-market correction>. See DOWN REVERSAL. **3.** (*usu. pl.*) The punishment and treatment of a criminal offender through a program of imprisonment, parole, and probation <Department of Corrections>. — **correct,** *vb.* — **corrective** (for senses 1 & 2), **correctional** (for sense 3), *adj.*

correction, house of. See *house of correction* under HOUSE.

correctional institution. See PRISON.

correctional system. A network of governmental agencies that administer a jurisdiction's prisons and parole system.

corrective advertising. Advertising that informs consumers that earlier advertisements contained a deceptive claim, and that provides consumers with corrected information. • This type of advertising may be ordered by the Federal Trade Commission.

correlative (kə-**rel**-ə-tiv), *adj.* (16c) **1.** Related or corresponding; analogous. **2.** Having or involving a reciprocal or mutually interdependent relationship <the term *right* is correlative with *duty*>.

correlative-rights doctrine. (1938) **1.** *Water law.* The principle that adjoining landowners must limit their use of a common water source to a reasonable amount. **2.** *Oil & gas.* The rule that a lessee's or landowner's right to capture oil and gas from the property is restricted by the duty to exercise that right without waste or negligence. • This is a corollary to the rule of capture. Cf. RULE OF CAPTURE (4).

correspondence audit. See AUDIT.

correspondent, *n.* (17c) **1.** The writer of a letter or letters. **2.** A person employed by the media to report on events. **3.** A securities firm or financial institution that performs services for another in a place or market that the other does not have direct access to. — **correspond,** *vb.*

correspondent bank. See BANK.

corresponding promise. See PROMISE.

corresponding secretary. See SECRETARY.

corrigendum (kor-ə-**jen**-dəm), *n.* [Latin "correction"] An error in a printed work discovered after the work has gone to press. — Also termed *erratum*. Pl. **corrigenda** (kor-ə-**jen**-də).

corroborate (kə-**rob**-ə-rayt), *vb.* To strengthen or confirm; to make more certain <the witness corroborated the plaintiff's testimony>.

corroborating evidence. See EVIDENCE.

corroborating witness. See WITNESS.

corroboration (kə-rob-ə-**ray**-shən), *n.* (16c) **1.** Confirmation or support by additional evidence or authority <corroboration of the witness's testimony>. **2.** Formal confirmation or ratification <corroboration of the treaty>. — **corroborate,** *vb.* — **corroborative** (kə-**rob**-ə-rə-tiv), *adj.* — **corroborator** (kə-**rob**-ə-ray-tər), *n.*

corroborative evidence. See *corroborating evidence* under EVIDENCE.

corrupt, *adj.* **1.** Having an unlawful or depraved motive; esp., influenced by bribery. **2.** *Archaic.* (Of a person) subject to corruption of blood.

corrupt, *vb.* **1.** To change (a person's morals or principles) from good to bad. **2.** To destroy or diminish the quality and usefulness of an electronic or mechanical device or its components. **3.** *Archaic.* To impose corruption of blood on (a person).

corrupting, *n.* See IMPAIRING THE MORALS OF A MINOR.

corruption. (14c) **1.** Depravity, perversion, or taint; an impairment of integrity, virtue, or moral principle; esp., the impairment of a public official's duties by bribery. **2.** The act of doing something with an intent to give some advantage inconsistent with official duty and the rights of others; a fiduciary's or official's use of a station or office to procure some benefit either personally or for someone else, contrary to the rights of others.

corruption in office. See *official misconduct* under MISCONDUCT.

corruption of a minor. See IMPAIRING THE MORALS OF A MINOR.

corruption of blood. A defunct doctrine, now considered unconstitutional, under which a person loses the ability to inherit or pass property as a result of an attainder or of being declared civilly dead. — Also termed *corruption of the blood*. See ATTAINDER; *civil death* (1) under DEATH.

corruptly, *adv.* (16c) In a corrupt or depraved manner; by means of corruption or bribery. • As used in criminal-law statutes, *corruptly* usu. indicates a wrongful desire for pecuniary gain or other advantage.

corrupt-motive doctrine. (1962) *Criminal law.* The rule that conspiracy is punishable only if the agreement was entered into with an evil purpose, not merely with an intent to do the illegal act. • This doctrine — which originated in *People v. Powell,* 63 N.Y. 88 (1875) — has been rejected by the Model Penal Code. — Also termed *Powell doctrine.*

corrupt-practices act. (1897) A federal or state statute that regulates campaign contributions and expenditures as well as their disclosure.

cosen, *vb.* See COZEN.

cosening, *n.* See COZENING.

cosign, *vb.* (1967) To sign a document along with another person, usu. to assume obligations and to supply credit to the principal obligor. — **cosignature,** *n.*

cosigner. See COMAKER.

cosinage (kəz-ən-ij). *Hist.* A writ used by an heir to secure the right to land held by a great-great-grandfather or certain collateral relatives. — Also spelled *cosenage; cousinage.* — Also termed *consanguineo; de consanguineo; de consanguinitate.* Cf. AIEL.

cosmetic damages. See DAMAGES.

cost, *n.* (13c) **1.** The amount paid or charged for something; price or expenditure. Cf. EXPENSE.

aboriginal cost. The cost of an asset incurred by the first company to use it for public utilities.

acquisition cost. (1926) **1.** An asset's net price; the original cost of an asset. — Also termed *historical cost; original cost.* **2.** See LOAD.

after cost. A delayed expense; an expense, such as one for repair under a warranty, incurred after the principal transaction.

applied cost. A cost appropriated to a project before it has been incurred.

average cost. The sum of the costs of beginning inventory and the costs of later additions divided by the total number of available units.

average variable cost. The average cost per unit of output, arrived at by dividing the total variable expenses of production by the total units of output. Cf. LONG-RUN INCREMENTAL COST.

avoidable cost. A cost that can be averted if production is held below a certain level so that additional expenses will not be incurred.

carrying cost. **1.** *Accounting.* The variable cost of stocking one unit of inventory for one year. • Carrying cost includes the opportunity cost of the capital invested in the inventory. — Also termed *cost of carrying.* **2.** A current charge or noncapital expenditure made to prevent the causing or accelerating of the termination of a defeasible estate, as well as the sums spent on

repairs required by the duty to avoid permissive waste.

common cost. See *indirect cost.*

cost of completion. (1852) *Contracts.* An element of damages based on the expense that would be incurred by the nonbreaching party to finish the promised performance.

direct cost. (1818) The amount of money for material, labor, and overhead to produce a product.

distribution cost. Any cost incurred in marketing a product or service, such as advertising, storage, and shipping.

fixed cost. (1894) A cost whose value does not fluctuate with changes in output or business activity; esp., overhead expenses such as rent, salaries, and depreciation. — Also termed *fixed charge; fixed expense.*

flotation cost. (*usu. pl.*) A cost incurred in issuing additional stock.

historical cost. See *acquisition cost.*

implicit cost. See *opportunity cost.*

indirect cost. (1884) A cost that is not specific to the production of a particular good or service but that arises from production activity in general, such as overhead allocations for general and administrative activities. — Also termed *common cost.*

manufacturing cost. The cost incurred in the production of goods, including direct and indirect costs.

marginal cost. (1891) The additional cost incurred in producing one more unit of output.

mitigation cost. A party's expenditures to reduce an existing harm so that further damage might be halted, slowed, or diminished.

mixed cost. A cost that includes fixed and variable costs.

net book cost. The cost of property when it was first acquired or devoted to public use, minus accumulated depreciation. — Also termed *rate-base value.*

net cost. The cost of an item, arrived at by subtracting any financial gain from the total cost.

opportunity cost. (1894) The cost of acquiring an asset measured by the value of an alternative investment that is forgone <her opportunity cost of $1,000 in equipment was her consequent inability to invest that money in bonds>. — Also termed *implicit cost.*

original cost. See *acquisition cost* (1).

prime cost. The true price paid for goods on a bona fide purchase.

prophylactic cost. A party's expenditures to prepare property to withstand or prevent potential future harm. • These costs are not related to any existing property damage and are usu. not recoverable under insurance contracts.

replacement cost. (1928) The cost of a substitute asset that is equivalent to an asset currently held. • The new asset has the same utility but may or may not be identical to the one replaced.

social cost. The cost to society of any particular practice or rule <although automobiles are undeniably beneficial to society, they carry a certain social cost in the lives that are lost every year on the road>.

sunk cost. (1916) A cost that has already been incurred and that cannot be recovered.

tangible cost. *Oil & gas.* A particular expense associated with drilling, such as the costs incurred for materials and land. • Drilling and testing costs are considered intangible.

transaction cost. (*usu. pl.*) A cost connected with a process transaction, such as a broker's commission, the time and effort expended to arrange a deal, or the cost involved in litigating a dispute.

unit cost. The cost of a single unit of a product or service; the total manufacturing cost divided by the number of units.

variable cost. (1953) The cost that varies in the short run in close relationship with changes in output.

2. (*pl.*) The charges or fees taxed by the court, such as filing fees, jury fees, courthouse fees, and reporter fees. — Also termed *court costs.* **3.** (*pl.*) The expenses of litigation, prosecution, or other legal transaction, esp. those allowed in favor of one party against the other. • Some but not all states allow parties to claim attorney's fees as a litigation cost. — Also termed (in sense 3) *litigation costs.*

accruing costs. Costs and expenses incurred after judgment.

costs of increase. See COSTS OF INCREASE.

costs of the day. Costs incurred in preparing for trial.

costs to abide event. Costs incurred by a successful party who is entitled to an award of those costs incurred at the conclusion of the matter; esp., appellate court's order for payment of costs to the party who finally prevails in a proceeding that has been returned to a lower court.

interlocutory costs. Costs incurred during the pendency of an appeal.

taxable cost. A litigation-related expense that the prevailing party is entitled to as part of the court's award.

cost accounting. See *cost accounting method* under ACCOUNTING METHOD.

cost accounting method. See ACCOUNTING METHOD.

cost and freight. A mercantile-contract term allocating the rights and duties of the buyer and the seller of goods with respect to delivery, payment, and risk of loss, whereby the seller must (1) clear the goods for export, (2) arrange for transportation by water, and (3) pay the costs of shipping to the port of destination. • When the goods are safely stowed on the receiving ship while docked, the seller's delivery is complete; the risk of loss then passes to the buyer. This term is used only when goods are transported by sea or inland waterway. — Abbr. CF; CFR; C&F; CandF. Cf. COST, INSURANCE, AND FREIGHT; FREE ON BOARD.

cost approach. (1949) A method of appraising real property, based on the cost of building a new structure with the same utility, assuming that an informed buyer would pay no more for the property than it would cost to build a new structure having the same usefulness. Cf. MARKET APPROACH; INCOME APPROACH.

cost basis. See BASIS (2).

cost-benefit analysis. (1963) An analytical technique that weighs the costs of a proposed decision, holding, or project against the expected advantages, economic or otherwise.

cost bill. See *bill of costs* under BILL (2).

cost bond. See BOND (2).

cost-book mining company. An association of persons organized for the purpose of working mines or lodes, whose capital stock is divided into shares that are transferable without the consent of other members. • The management of the mine is entrusted to an agent called a purser.

cost depletion. *Oil & gas.* The recovery of an oil-and-gas producer's basis (i.e., investment) in a producing well by deducting the basis proportionately over the producing life of the well. Treas. Reg. § 1.611-2. Cf. PERCENTAGE DEPLETION.

cost, insurance, and freight. A mercantile-contract term allocating the rights and duties of the buyer and the seller of goods with respect to delivery, payment, and risk of loss, whereby the seller must (1) clear the goods for export, (2) arrange for transportation by water, (3) procure insurance against the buyer's risk of damage during carriage, and (4) pay the costs of shipping to the port of destination. • The seller's delivery is complete (and the risk of loss passes to the buyer) when the goods are loaded on the receiving ship while docked in the port of shipment. This term is used only when goods are transported by sea or inland waterway. — Abbr. CIF. Cf. COST AND FREIGHT; FREE ON BOARD.

CIF destination. A contractual term denoting that the price includes in a lump sum the cost of the goods and the insurance and freight to the named destination. — Also termed *CIF place of destination.*

cost justification. (1938) Under the Robinson-Patman Act, an affirmative defense against a charge of price discrimination dependent on the seller's showing that it incurs lower costs in serving those customers who are paying less. 15 USCA § 13(a).

cost-of-capital method. A means of measuring a utility's cost of acquiring debt and equity capital. • Regulatory commissions often use this method to determine a fair rate of return for the utility's investors.

cost of carrying. See *carrying cost* under COST (1).

cost of completion. See COST (1).

cost-of-living adjustment. An automatic increase or decrease in the amount of money, usu. support or maintenance, to be paid by one party to another, the adjustment being tied to the cost-of-living-adjustment figures maintained and updated by the federal government. — Abbr. COLA.

cost-of-living clause. (1953) A provision (as in a contract or lease) that gives an automatic wage, rent, or benefit increase tied in some way to cost-of-living rises in the economy. • A cost-of-living clause may also cover a decrease, though this is rare. See INFLATION.

cost-of-living index. See CONSUMER PRICE INDEX.

cost-plus contract. See CONTRACT.

cost-push inflation. See INFLATION.

costs of collection. (1833) Expenses incurred in receiving payment of a note; esp., attorney's fees incurred in the effort to collect a note.

costs of increase. Costs of court awarded in addition to what a jury awards. • Juries usu. awarded the successful party only a small sum for costs. A party wishing to recoup the additional costs had to file an affidavit of increase setting forth what further costs were incurred by taking the matter through trial. — Also termed *costs de incremento.* See *affidavit of increase* under AFFIDAVIT.

costs of the day. See COST (3).

costs to abide event. See COST (3).

cosurety. A surety who shares the cost of performing suretyship obligations with another. See SURETY.

cosuretyship. The relation between two or more sureties who are bound to answer for the same duty of the principal, and who are jointly responsible for any loss resulting from the principal's default.

cotenancy. See TENANCY.

coterminous (koh-**tər**-mə-nəs), *adj.* (18c) **1.** (Of ideas or events) coextensive in time or meaning <Judge Smith's tenure was coterminous with Judge Jasper's>. **2.** CONTERMINOUS (1).

cotortfeasor (koh-**tort**-fee-zər). One who, together with another, has committed a tort. See TORTFEASOR.

cotrustee. One of two or more persons in whom the administration of a trust is vested. • The cotrustees form a collective trustee and exercise their powers jointly. — Also termed *joint trustee.* See TRUSTEE.

council. (12c) **1.** A deliberative assembly <the U.N. Security Council>.

   common council. **1.** In some cities, the lower branch of a city council. **2.** In some cities, the city's governing board.

   general council. A body of elected persons who represent all the citizens of a territory or members of an organization.

   select council. In some cities, the upper branch of a city council.

2. An administrative or executive body <a parish council>.

councillor. See COUNCILOR.

Council of Economic Advisers. A three-member council in the Executive Office of the President responsible for analyzing the national economy and advising the President on economic matters. • Created by the Employment Act of 1946, it now functions under Reorganization Plan No. 9 of 1953. Its members are appointed by the President with the advice and consent of the Senate. — Abbr. CEA.

Council of the North. *Hist.* A body used by the Tudors to administer the northern parts of England (esp. Yorkshire) during the 16th and 17th centuries. • The council probably predated the Tudors, but Henry VIII revived it. In addition to enforcing Crown policy in the northern territories, the appointees (many of whom were lawyers) exercised wide criminal and civil jurisdiction. The Council disbanded ca. 1640.

Council on Environmental Quality. A three-member council in the Executive Office of the President responsible for developing and recommending national policy on environmental quality. • The council was created by the National Environmental Policy Act of 1969. Its members are appointed by the President with the advice and consent of the Senate. 42 USCA § 4321 et seq. & § 4371 et seq. — Abbr. CEQ.

councilor, *n.* (15c) A person who serves on a council, esp. at the local level. — Also spelled *councillor.* — **councillorship,** *n.*

counsel, *n.* (13c) **1.** Advice or assistance <the lawyer's counsel was to petition immediately for a change of immigration status>. **2.** One or more lawyers who represent a client <the client acted on advice of counsel>. — In the singular, also termed *counselor; counselor-at-law*. Cf. ATTORNEY; LAWYER. **3.** *English law.* A member of the bar; BARRISTER.

advisory counsel. 1. An attorney retained merely to give advice on a particular matter, as distinguished from one (such as trial counsel) actively participating in a case. **2.** See *standby counsel*.

appellate counsel. (1921) A lawyer who represents a party on appeal. ● The term is often used in contrast with *trial counsel*.

appointed counsel. See *assigned counsel*.

assigned counsel. (17c) An attorney appointed by the court to represent a person, usu. an indigent person. — Also termed *court-appointed attorney; court-appointed counsel; appointed counsel; appointed counsel*.

corporate counsel. An in-house attorney for a corporation. Cf. *in-house counsel*.

corporation counsel. A city attorney in an incorporated municipality. See CITY ATTORNEY.

counsel of record. See *attorney of record* under ATTORNEY.

court-appointed counsel. See *assigned counsel*.

Cumis counsel. An independent attorney hired by a defendant in a lawsuit in which the damages may be covered by the defendant's insurer but a conflict of interest between the defendant and the insurer makes it unreasonable for an attorney selected by the insurer to represent the defendant. ● The term derives from *San Diego Federal Credit Union v. Cumis Ins. Society, Inc.,* 162 Cal. App. 3d 358 (1984), in which the concept was first clearly articulated.

general counsel. (1848) **1.** A lawyer or law firm that represents a client in all or most of the client's legal matters, but that sometimes refers extraordinary matters — such as litigation and intellectual-property cases — to other lawyers. **2.** The most senior lawyer in a corporation's legal department, usu. also a corporate officer.

house counsel. See *in-house counsel*.

independent counsel. (1920) An attorney hired to provide an unbiased opinion about a case or to conduct an impartial investigation; esp., an attorney appointed by a governmental branch or agency to investigate alleged misconduct within that branch or agency. See *special prosecutor* under PROSECUTOR. Cf. *special counsel*.

in-house counsel. (1974) One or more lawyers employed by a company. — Also termed *house counsel*; (when employed by a corporation) *corporate counsel*. Cf. *corporate counsel*.

junior counsel. 1. The younger or lower-ranking of two or more attorneys employed on the same side of a case, esp. someone charged with the less important aspects of the case. **2.** *English law.* The barrister who assists Queen's Counsel.

King's Counsel. See KING'S COUNSEL.

lead counsel. (1956) **1.** The more highly ranked lawyer if two or more are retained; the lawyer who manages or controls the case or cases, esp. in class actions or multidistrict litigation. — Also termed *senior counsel; attorney in charge.* **2.** QUEEN'S COUNSEL; KING'S COUNSEL. — Also termed *leading counsel.*

local counsel. One or more lawyers who practice in a particular jurisdiction and are retained by nonresident counsel to help prepare and try a case or to complete a transaction in accordance with that jurisdiction's law, rules, and customs.

of counsel. 1. A lawyer employed by a party in a case; esp., one who — although not the principal attorney of record — is employed to assist in the preparation or management of the case or in its presentation on appeal. **2.** A lawyer who is affiliated with a law firm, though not as a member, partner, or associate.

Queen's Counsel. See QUEEN'S COUNSEL.

senior counsel. 1. See *lead counsel.* **2.** See KING'S COUNSEL; QUEEN'S COUNSEL.

settlement counsel. See CIRCUIT MEDIATOR.

special counsel. (1854) An attorney employed by the state or a political subdivision to assist in a particular case when the public interest so requires. — Also termed *special attorney.* Cf. *independent counsel.*

standby counsel. An attorney who is appointed to be prepared to represent a pro se criminal defendant if the defendant's self-representation ends. ● The standby counsel may also provide some advice and guidance to the defendant during the self-representation. — Also termed *advisory counsel.*

trial counsel. (1928) **1.** A lawyer who represents a party at trial. ● The term is often used in contrast with *appellate counsel.* **2.** *Military law.* The person who prosecutes a case on the government's behalf.

counsel, assistance of. See ASSISTANCE OF COUNSEL.

counsel, right to. See RIGHT TO COUNSEL.

counsel and procure. See AID AND ABET.

counselor. See COUNSEL (2).

counselor-at-law. See COUNSEL (2).

count, *n.* (14c) *Procedure.* **1.** The part of an indictment charging the suspect with a distinct offense. **2.** In a complaint or similar pleading, the statement of a distinct claim. Cf. DECLARATION (7).

common count. *Hist.* In a plaintiff's pleading in an action for debt, boilerplate language that is not founded on the circumstances of the individual case but is intended to guard against a possible variance and to enable the plaintiff to take advantage of any ground of liability that the proof may disclose. • In the action for indebitatus assumpsit, the common count stated that the defendant had failed to pay a debt as promised. See *indebitatus assumpsit* under AS-SUMPSIT.

general count. A count that states the plaintiff's claim without undue particularity.

money count. *Hist.* A count, usu. founded on a simple contract, giving rise to a claim for payment of money.

multiple counts. (1941) Several separate causes of action or charged offenses contained in a single pleading or indictment.

omnibus count (**ahm**-ni-bəs). A count that combines into one count all money claims, claims for goods sold and delivered, claims for work and labor, and claims for an account stated.

separate count. (18c) One of two or more criminal charges contained in one indictment, each charge constituting a separate indictment for which the accused may be tried.

several count. One of two or more counts in a pleading, each of which states a different cause of action.

special count. (18c) A section of a pleading in which the plaintiff's claim is stated with great particularity — usu. employed only when the pleading rules require specificity.

3. A canvassing. See CANVASS (2). **4.** *Hist.* The plaintiff's declaration, or initial pleading, in a real action. See DECLARATION (7). **5.** *Patents.* The part of a patent application that defines the subject matter in a priority contest (i.e., an *interference*) between two or more applications or between one or more applications and one or more patents. See INTERFERENCE (3).

count, *vb.* (17c) **1.** In pleading, to declare or state; to narrate the facts that state a claim. **2.** *Hist.* To plead orally; to plead or argue a case in court.

counted vote. See VOTE (4).

counter. *Hist.* An advocate or professional pleader; one who counts (i.e., orally recites) for a client. • Counters had coalesced into an identifiable group practicing before the Common Bench by the beginning of the 13th century. They were the leaders of the medieval legal profession, and over time came to be known as *serjeants at law.* — Also spelled *countor; contor; counteur.* See SERJEANT-AT-LAW.

counteraction. See COUNTERCLAIM.

counteraffidavit. See AFFIDAVIT.

counterbond. See BOND (2).

counterclaim, *n.* (18c) A claim for relief asserted against an opposing party after an original claim has been made; esp., a defendant's claim in opposition to or as a setoff against the plaintiff's claim. — Also termed *counteraction; countersuit; cross-demand.* Cf. CROSS-CLAIM. — **counterclaim,** *vb.* — **counterclaimant,** *n.*

compulsory counterclaim. (1938) A counterclaim that must be asserted to be cognizable, usu. because it relates to the opposing party's claim and arises out of the same subject matter. • If a defendant fails to assert a compulsory counterclaim in the original action, that claim may not be brought in a later, separate action (with some exceptions). See Fed. R. Civ. P. 13(a).

permissive counterclaim. (1924) A counterclaim that need not be asserted to be cognizable, usu. because it does not arise out of the same subject matter as the opposing party's claim or involves third parties over which the court does not have jurisdiction. • Permissive counterclaims may be brought in a later, separate action. See Fed. R. Civ. P. 13(b).

counter-complaint. See COMPLAINT.

counterdeed. See DEED.

counterfeisance (**kown**-tər-fee-zənts). *Archaic.* The act of counterfeiting.

counterfeit, *vb.* (14c) To unlawfully forge, copy, or imitate an item, esp. money or a negotiable instrument (such as a security or promissory note) or other officially issued item of value (such as a postage stamp or a food stamp), or to possess such an item without authorization and with the intent to deceive or defraud by presenting the item as genuine. • Counterfeiting includes producing or selling an item that displays a reproduction of a genuine trademark, usu. to deceive buyers into thinking they are purchasing genuine merchandise. See 18 USCA §§ 470 et seq. — **counterfeiting,** *n.* — **counterfeit,** *n.* — **counterfeit,** *adj.*

Counterfeit Access Device and Computer Fraud and Abuse Act of 1984. A federal statute that criminalizes various computer-related activities such as accessing without permission a computer system belonging to a bank or the federal government, or using that access to improperly obtain anything of value. 18 USCA § 1030.

counterfeiter. A person who forges or otherwise makes a copy or an unauthorized imitation of something (esp. a document, currency, or another's signature) with the intent to deceive or defraud.

counterfeiting, *n.* The unlawful forgery, copying, or imitation of an item, esp. money or a negotiable instrument (such as a security or promissory note) or other officially issued item of value (such as a postage stamp), or the unauthorized possession of such an item, with the intent to deceive or defraud by claiming or passing the item as genuine. *See* 18 USCA §§ 470 et seq. — **counterfeit,** *vb.* — **counterfeit,** *n.* — **counterfeit,** *adj.*

counterfeit mark. See *counterfeit trademark* under TRADEMARK.

counterfeit recording. *Copyright.* An unauthorized copy of a copyright-protected recording's sounds, artwork, label, trademark, or packaging. — Also termed *bootleg recording.*

counterfeit trademark. See TRADEMARK.

counterfoil (**kown**-tər-foyl), *n.* A detachable part of a writing on which the particulars of the main part are summarized. ● The most common example is a check stub, on which the date, the payee, and the amount are typically noted.

counterletter. *Civil law.* A document in which the parties to a simulated contract record their true intentions. La. Civ. Code art. 2025. ● For example, the record owner of real property may acknowledge in a counterletter that another person actually owns the property; the counterletter may then be used when the property is to be reconveyed after a period. A counterletter can have no effect against a third party acting in good faith. See *simulated contract* under CONTRACT.

countermand (**kown**-tər-mand), *n.* (16c) **1.** A contradictory command that overrides or annuls a previous one. **2.** An action that has the effect of voiding something previously ordered; a revocation. — **countermand** (kown-tər-**mand** *or* **kown**-), *vb.*

counteroffer, *n.* (18c) *Contracts.* An offeree's new offer that varies the terms of the original offer and that ordinarily rejects and terminates the original offer. ● A late or defective acceptance is considered a counteroffer. See MIRROR-IMAGE RULE. — **counteroffer,** *vb.* — **counterofferor,** *n.*

counterpart. (15c) **1.** In conveyancing, a corresponding part of an instrument <the other half of the indenture — the counterpart — could not be found>. **2.** One of two or more copies or duplicates of a legal instrument <this lease may be executed in any number of counterparts, each of which is considered an original>.

counterpart writ. See WRIT.

counterpromise, *n.* (18c) A promise made in exchange for another party's promise <a promise supported by a counterpromise is binding in its inception>. See *bilateral contract* under CONTRACT. — **counterpromise,** *vb.*

countersign, *vb.* (16c) To write one's own name next to someone else's to verify the other signer's identity. — **countersignature,** *n.*

countersuit. See COUNTERCLAIM.

countertrade. A type of international trade in which purchases made by an importing nation are linked to offsetting purchases made by the exporting nation.

countervailable subsidy. See SUBSIDY.

countervailing duty. See DUTY (4).

countervailing equity. See EQUITY.

counter will. See *mutual will* under WILL.

Counting House of the King's Household. See BOARD OF GREEN CLOTH.

country. 1. A nation or political state; STATE (1). **2.** The territory of such a nation or state.

county. (14c) The largest territorial division for local government within a state, generally considered to be a political subdivision and a quasi-corporation. ● Every county exists as a result of a sovereign act of legislation, either constitutional or statutory, separating it from the rest of the state as an integral part of its territory and establishing it as one of the primary divisions of the state for purposes of civil administration. — Abbr. co.

> *foreign county.* Any county separate from that of a county where matters arising in the former county are called into question, though both may lie within the same state or country.

county agent. See *juvenile officer* under OFFICER (1).

county attorney. An attorney who represents a county in civil matters and, in some jurisdictions, prosecutes criminal offenders.

county auditor. See AUDITOR.

county bond. See BOND (3).

county commissioner. See COMMISSIONER.

county court. See COURT.

county judge. See JUDGE.

county officer. See OFFICER (1).

county palatine (**pal**-ə-tin *or* -tin). *Hist.* A county in which the lord held certain royal privileges, such as the right to pardon a felon or to have indictments recite that offenses were committed against the lord's — rather than the king's — peace. ● In England, there were three such counties: Chester, Durham, and Lancaster. The separate legal systems in these counties were slowly eliminated; the last vestiges of a separate system were abolished by the Courts Act (1971). Cf. *proprietary government* under GOVERNMENT.

county property. Property that a county is authorized to acquire, hold, or sell.

county purpose. An objective pursued by a county; esp., one that a county levies taxes for.

county seat. The municipality where a county's principal offices are located. — Also termed *county town.*

county supervisor. See *county commissioner* under COMMISSIONER.

county town. See COUNTY SEAT.

county warrant. See WARRANT (3).

coup d'état (koo day-**tah**). [French "stroke of state"] A sudden, usu. violent, change of government through seizure of power.

coupon (**koo**-pon). An interest or dividend certificate that is attached to another instrument, such as a bond, and that may be detached and separately presented for payment of a definite sum at a specified time. — Also termed *interest coupon*.

coupon bond. See BOND (3).

coupon interest rate. See *coupon rate* under INTEREST RATE.

coupon note. See NOTE (1).

coupon rate. See INTEREST RATE.

coupon security. See SECURITY.

coupon yield. See YIELD.

Cour de Cassation. See COURT OF CASSATION.

courier. A messenger, esp. one who delivers parcels, packages, and the like. • In international law, the term denotes a messenger duly authorized by a sending state to deliver a diplomatic pouch.

course of business. (17c) The normal routine in managing a trade or business. — Also termed *ordinary course of business*; *regular course of business*; *ordinary course*; *regular course*.

course of dealing. (16c) An established pattern of conduct between parties in a series of transactions (e.g., multiple sales of goods over a period of years). • If a dispute arises, the parties' course of dealing can be used as evidence of how they intended to carry out the transaction. Cf. COURSE OF PERFORMANCE; *trade usage* under USAGE.

course of employment. (17c) Events that occur or circumstances that exist as a part of one's employment; esp., the time during which an employee furthers an employer's goals through employer-mandated directives. Cf. SCOPE OF EMPLOYMENT; ZONE OF EMPLOYMENT.

course of performance. (18c) A sequence of previous performance by either party after an agreement has been entered into, when a contract involves repeated occasions for performance and both parties know the nature of the performance and have an opportunity to object to it. • A course of performance accepted or acquiesced in without objection is relevant to determining the meaning of the agreement. Cf. COURSE OF DEALING; *trade usage* under USAGE.

course of trade. See *trade usage* under USAGE.

court, *n.* (12c) **1.** A governmental body consisting of one or more judges who sit to adjudicate disputes and administer justice <a question of law for the court to decide>. **2.** The judge or judges who sit on such a governmental body <the court asked the parties to approach the bench>. **3.** A legislative assembly <in Massachusetts, the General Court is the legislature>. **4.** The locale for a legal proceeding <an out-of-court statement>. **5.** The building where the judge or judges convene to adjudicate disputes and administer justice <the lawyers agreed to meet at the court at 8:00 a.m.>. — Also termed (in sense 5) *courthouse*.

admiralty court. See ADMIRALTY (1).

appeals court. See *appellate court*.

appellate court. (18c) A court with jurisdiction to review decisions of lower courts or administrative agencies. — Also termed *appeals court*; *appeal court*; *court of appeals*; *court of appeal*; *court of review*.

Article I Court. See *legislative court*.

Article III Court. See ARTICLE III COURT.

Bankruptcy Court. See BANKRUPTCY COURT.

baronial court. *Hist.* A feudal court established by the owner of extensive lands held directly of the king under military tenure.

base court. *Archaic.* An inferior court.

basement court. See BASEMENT COURT.

business court. (1914) A court that handles exclusively commercial litigation. • In the late 20th century, business courts emerged as a way to unclog the general dockets and to dispose of commercial cases more efficiently and consistently. — Also termed *commercial court*; *commercial division*.

Central Criminal Court. See CENTRAL CRIMINAL COURT.

children's court. See *juvenile court* (1).

church court. See *ecclesiastical court*.

circuit court. (17c) **1.** A court usu. having jurisdiction over several counties, districts, or states, and holding sessions in all those areas. See CIRCUIT; CIRCUIT-RIDING. **2.** UNITED STATES COURT OF APPEALS.

city court. See *municipal court*.

civil court. (16c) A court with jurisdiction over noncriminal cases. — Abbr. Civ. Ct.

claims court. See *court of claims*.

closed court. See CLOSED COURT.

Commerce Court. *Hist.* A federal court that had the power to review and enforce determinations of the Interstate Commerce Commission. • The Commerce Court existed from 1910 to 1913.

commercial court. **1.** See *business court*. **2.** *English law.* A court that hears business disputes under simplified procedures designed to expedite the trials. • This court was created in 1971 as part of the Queen's Bench Division of the High Court of Justice.

commissioner's court. In certain states, a court having jurisdiction over county affairs and often functioning more as a managerial group than as a judicial tribunal.

common pleas court. See COURT OF COMMON PLEAS.

commonwealth court. 1. In some states, a court of general jurisdiction. **2.** In Pennsylvania, a court that hears suits against the state and reviews decisions of state agencies and officials.

competent court. See *court of competent jurisdiction.*

conciliation court. See *small-claims court.*

consistory court. See CONSISTORY COURT.

constitutional court. (1823) **1.** A court named or described and expressly protected in a constitution; esp., ARTICLE III COURT. **2.** A court whose jurisdiction is solely or primarily over claims that legislation (and sometimes executive action) is inconsistent with a nation's constitution. • Germany, for example, has state constitutional courts and a Federal Constitutional Court.

consular court (**kon**-sə-lər). A court held by the consul of one country within the territory of another. • Consular courts are created by treaty, and their jurisdiction is usu. limited to civil cases. The last of the U.S. consular courts (Morocco) was abolished in 1956.

coroner's court. *English law.* A common-law court that holds an inquisition if a person died a violent or unnatural death, died in prison, or died suddenly when the cause is not known. • The court also has jurisdiction over treasure trove.

corporation court. In some jurisdictions, a court that serves an incorporated municipality. See *municipal court.*

county court. (16c) **1.** A court with powers and jurisdiction dictated by a state constitution or statute. • The county court may govern administrative or judicial matters, depending on state law. — Also termed *parish court*; (in Latin) *curia comitatus*. **2.** See *probate court.*

court above. (17c) A court to which a case is appealed. — Also termed *higher court*; *upper court.*

court a quo (ay **kwoh**). A court from which a case has been removed or appealed.

court below. (17c) A trial court or intermediate appellate court from which a case is appealed. — Also termed *lower court.*

court christian. See *ecclesiastical court.*

court de facto. See *de facto court.*

court merchant. *Hist.* A court of limited jurisdiction that decided controversies arising between merchants, dealers, shipmasters, supercargoes, and other, usu. transient, people connected with trade. • Cases were usu. tried before a jury of merchants.

court not of record. An inferior court that is not required to routinely make a record of each proceeding and usu. does not.

court of appeals. (17c) **1.** An intermediate appellate court. — Also termed (as in California and England) *court of appeal*. See *appellate court.* **2.** In New York and Maryland, the highest appellate court within the jurisdiction.

court of chivalry. See HIGH COURT OF CHIVALRY.

court of claims. A court with the authority to hear claims made against a state (or its political subdivision) for cases in which the state has waived sovereign immunity. — Also termed *claims court*. See UNITED STATES COURT OF FEDERAL CLAIMS.

court of competent jurisdiction. A court that has the power and authority to do a particular act; one recognized by law as possessing the right to adjudicate a controversy. — Also termed *competent court.*

court of domestic relations. See *family court.*

court of equity. (16c) A court that (1) has jurisdiction in equity, (2) administers and decides controversies in accordance with the rules, principles, and precedents of equity, and (3) follows the forms and procedures of chancery. Cf. *court of law.*

court of final appeal. 1. See *court of last resort.* **2.** *Eccles. law.* (*cap.*) JUDICIAL COMMITTEE OF THE PRIVY COUNCIL.

court of first instance. See *trial court.*

court of general jurisdiction. (18c) A court having unlimited or nearly unlimited trial jurisdiction in both civil and criminal cases. — Also termed *general-jurisdiction court.*

court of impeachment. See COURT FOR THE TRIAL OF IMPEACHMENTS.

court of inquiry. 1. *Hist.* In English law, a court appointed by the monarch to ascertain whether it was proper to use extreme measures against someone who had been court-martialed. **2.** *Hist.* In American law, an agency created under articles of war and vested with the power to investigate the nature of a transaction or accusation of an officer or soldier. **3.** In some jurisdictions, a procedure that allows a magistrate to examine witnesses in relation to any offense that the magistrate has a good-faith reason to believe was committed.

court of instance. See *trial court.*

court of last resort. (17c) The court having the authority to handle the final appeal of a case, such as the U.S. Supreme Court.

court of law. (16c) **1.** Broadly, any judicial tribunal that administers the laws of a state or nation. **2.** A court that proceeds according to the course of the common law, and that is governed by its rules and principles. Cf. *court of equity.*

court of limited jurisdiction. A court with jurisdiction over only certain types of cases, or cases in which the amount in controversy is limited.

court of ordinary. See *probate court.*

court of original jurisdiction. (18c) A court where an action is initiated and first heard.

court of record. (18c) **1.** A court that is required to keep a record of its proceedings. • The court's records are presumed accurate and cannot be collaterally impeached. See OF RECORD (2). **2.** A court that may fine and imprison people for contempt.

court of review. See *appellate court.*

court of special jurisdiction. See *limited court.*

court of special session. (1813) A court that has no stated term and is not continuous, but is organized only for hearing a particular case.

court of summary jurisdiction. See *magistrate's court.*

criminal court. A court with jurisdiction over criminal matters.

Crown Court. See CROWN COURT.

Dean of Guild Court. See DEAN OF GUILD COURT.

de facto court (di **fak**-toh). **1.** A court functioning under the authority of a statute that is later adjudged to be invalid. — Also termed *court de facto.* **2.** A court established and acting under the authority of a *de facto* government.

dependency court. A court having jurisdiction over matters involving abused and neglected children, foster care, the termination of parental rights, and (sometimes) adoption.

diocesan court (dı-**ahs**-i-sin). *Eccles. law.* A court exercising general or limited jurisdiction (as determined by patent, local custom, or legislation) of matters arising within a bishop's diocese. • Diocesan courts include the consistory court, the courts of the commissaries, and the courts of archdeacons.

district court. (18c) **1.** A trial court having general jurisdiction within its judicial district. — Abbr. D.C. **2.** *Scots law.* A local court, usu. staffed by lay magistrates, with jurisdiction over petty crimes.

divided court. See DIVIDED COURT.

divisional court. An English court made up of two or more judges from the High Court of Justice sitting in special cases that cannot be disposed of by one judge. • Each division of the High Court has a divisional court, e.g., the Divisional Court of the Family Division. With the exception of the Divisional Court of the Chancery Division, which has jurisdiction to review land-registration appeals from the county court, almost all judicial appeals are from decisions of a magistrates' court. The Divisional Court of the Queen's Bench Division hears appeals from the Crown Court or the magistrates' court by way of case stated in criminal prosecutions, which is the most frequent use of a divisional court.

domestic court. (1801) **1.** A court having jurisdiction at the place of a party's residence or domicile. **2.** See *family court.*

domestic-relations court. See *family court.*

drug court. A court that hears cases against non-violent adults and juveniles, who are often first-time offenders and who are usu. charged with possession of a controlled substance or with committing a minor drug-related crime. • Drug courts focus on treatment rather than on incarceration. Cf. *problem-solving court.*

ecclesiastical court (i-klee-zee-**as**-ti-kəl). **1.** A religious court that hears matters concerning a particular religion. **2.** In England, a court having jurisdiction over matters concerning the Church of England (the established church) as well as the duties and rights of the people serving it, but whose modern jurisdiction is limited to matters of ecclesiastical discipline and church property. — Also termed *church court; court christian; spiritual court;* (in Latin) *christianitatis curia; curia christianitatis.*

examining court. (18c) A lower court (usu. presided over by a magistrate) that determines probable cause and sets bail at a preliminary hearing in a criminal case.

family court. (1923) A court having jurisdiction over matters involving divorce, child custody and support, paternity, domestic violence, and other family-law issues. — Also termed *domestic-relations court; court of domestic relations; domestic court.*

federal court. (18c) A court having federal jurisdiction, including the U.S. Supreme Court, circuit courts of appeals, district courts, bankruptcy courts, and tax courts. — Also termed *United States court.*

foreign court. (16c) **1.** The court of a foreign nation. **2.** The court of another state.

forty-days court. See COURT OF ATTACHMENTS.

full court. (16c) A court session that is attended by all the court's judges; an en banc court. — Also termed *full bench.*

General Court. See GENERAL COURT.

general-jurisdiction court. See *court of general jurisdiction.*

High Commission Court. See COURT OF HIGH COMMISSION.

High Court. 1. See HIGH COURT OF JUSTICE. 2. See HIGH COURT OF JUSTICIARY.

High Court of Admiralty. See HIGH COURT OF ADMIRALTY.

High Court of Chivalry. See HIGH COURT OF CHIVALRY.

High Court of Delegates. See COURT OF DELEGATES.

High Court of Errors and Appeals. See COURT OF ERRORS AND APPEALS.

High Court of Justice. See HIGH COURT OF JUSTICE.

High Court of Justiciary. See HIGH COURT OF JUSTICIARY.

higher court. See *court above.*

highest court. (16c) The court of last resort in a particular jurisdiction; a court whose decision is final and cannot be appealed because no higher court exists to consider the matter. • The U.S. Supreme Court, for example, is the highest federal court.

hot court. (1972) A court, esp. an appellate court, that is familiar with the briefs filed in the case, and therefore with the issues, before oral argument. • Typically, a hot court controls the oral argument with its questioning, as opposed to listening passively to set presentations of counsel.

housing court. A court dealing primarily with landlord-and-tenant matters, including disputes over maintenance, lease terms, and building and fire codes.

hundred court. *Hist.* In England, a larger court baron, held for all inhabitants of a particular hundred rather than a manor, in which the free suitors were the judges (jurors) and the steward the register. • A hundred court was not a court of record, and it resembled a court-baron in all respects except for its larger territorial jurisdiction. The last hundred court was abolished in 1971. — Also termed *hundred moot.* See COURT BARON.

impeachment court. See COURT FOR THE TRIAL OF IMPEACHMENTS.

inferior court. (17c) 1. Any court that is subordinate to the chief appellate tribunal within a judicial system. 2. A court of special, limited, or statutory jurisdiction, whose record must show the existence of jurisdiction in any given case to give its ruling presumptive validity. — Also termed *lower court.*

inquisitorial court. A court in which the inquisitorial system prevails.

instance court. 1. See *trial court.* 2. *Hist.* The admiralty court in England that exercised original jurisdiction in all cases except those involving prizes.

insular court. A federal court with jurisdiction over U.S. island territories, such as the Virgin Islands.

intermediate court. An appellate court that is below a court of last resort.

International Court of Justice. See INTERNATIONAL COURT OF JUSTICE.

International Criminal Court. See INTERNATIONAL CRIMINAL COURT.

International Trade Court. See UNITED STATES COURT OF INTERNATIONAL TRADE.

J.P. court. See *justice court.*

justice court. (16c) A court, presided over by a justice of the peace, that has jurisdiction to hear minor criminal cases, matters involving small amounts of money, or certain specified claims (such as forcible-entry-and-detainer suits). — Also termed *justice-of-the-peace court*; *J.P. court.*

juvenile court. (1903) 1. A court having jurisdiction over cases involving children under a specified age, usu. 18. • Illinois enacted the first statewide juvenile-court act in 1899. Today every state has a specialized juvenile or family court with exclusive original delinquency jurisdiction. — Also termed *children's court.* 2. A court having special jurisdiction over orphaned, delinquent, dependent, and neglected children. • This type of juvenile court is created by statute and derives its power from the specific wording of the statute, usu. having exclusive original jurisdiction over matters involving abuse and neglect, adoption, status offenses, and delinquency. Generally, juvenile courts are special courts of a paternal nature that have jurisdiction over the care, custody, and control of children (as defined by the statute). The jurisdiction of the juvenile court is exercised as between the state (for the child) and the parents of the child and is not concerned with a custody controversy that does not affect the morale, health, or welfare of the child. A juvenile court is not a criminal court. The primary concern of a juvenile court is the child's immediate welfare. See UNIFORM JUVENILE COURT ACT.

kangaroo court. (1849) 1. A self-appointed tribunal or mock court in which the principles of law and justice are disregarded, perverted, or parodied. • Kangaroo courts may be assembled by various groups, such as prisoners in a jail (to settle disputes between inmates) and players on a baseball team (to "punish" teammates who commit fielding errors). **2.** A court or tribunal characterized by unauthorized or irregular procedures, esp. so as to render a fair proceeding impossible. **3.** A sham legal proceeding. • The term's origin is uncertain, but it appears to be an Americanism. It has been traced to 1853 in the American West. "Kangaroo" might refer to the illogical leaps between "facts" and conclusions, or to the hapless defendant's quick bounce from court to gallows.

King's Court. See CURIA REGIS.

land court. A court having jurisdiction over land-related matters including: (1) exclusive original jurisdiction of applications for registration of land titles and related questions, writs of entry and petitions to clear title to real estate, petitions to determine the validity and extent of municipal zoning ordinances, bylaws, and regulations, and proceedings for foreclosure and redemption from tax titles; (2) original concurrent jurisdiction of declaratory judgment proceedings, shared with the supreme judicial, superior, and probate courts; and (3) original concurrent equity jurisdiction in land-related matters, except for cases of specific performance of land contracts. • Land courts today exist in the United States only in Massachusetts and Hawaii.

legatine court. A court held by a papal legate and having ecclesiastical jurisdiction.

legislative court. (1828) A court created by a statute, as opposed to one created by a constitution. — Also termed (in federal law) *Article I court.*

levy court. *Hist.* A court in the District of Columbia that exercised many of the functions typical of county commissioners or county supervisors in the states, such as constructing and repairing roads and bridges.

limited court. A court having special jurisdiction conferred by statute, such as a probate court. — Also termed *court of special jurisdiction.*

liquidation court. Any court in which a liquidation proceeding takes place.

local court. A court whose jurisdiction is limited to a particular territory, such as a state, municipal, or county court.

lord mayor's court. *Hist.* A court of law and equity that had jurisdiction in civil cases arising within the city of London and acted as the appellate court from the Chamberlain Court. • It was abolished by the Court Act of 1971.

lower court. **1.** See *court below.* **2.** See *inferior court.*

magistrate's court (**maj**-i-strayts *or* -strits). (1904) **1.** A court with jurisdiction over minor criminal offenses. • Such a court also has the power to bind over for trial persons accused of more serious offenses. — Also termed *police court.* **2.** A court with limited jurisdiction over minor criminal and civil matters. — Sometimes spelled (esp. in England) *magistrates' court.* — Also termed (in England) *court of petty sessions; court of summary jurisdiction.*

maritime court. See ADMIRALTY (1).

mayor's court. A municipal court in which the mayor presides as the judge, with jurisdiction over minor criminal (and sometimes civil) matters, traffic offenses, and the like.

military court. A court that has jurisdiction over members of the armed forces and that enforces the Code of Military Justice. See CODE OF MILITARY JUSTICE.

military court of inquiry. A military court that has special and limited jurisdiction and that is convened to investigate specific matters and, traditionally, to determine whether further procedures are warranted. 10 USCA § 935.

moot court. See MOOT COURT.

municipal court. (17c) A court having jurisdiction (usu. civil and criminal) over cases arising within the municipality in which it sits. • A municipal court's civil jurisdiction to issue a judgment is often limited to a small amount, and its criminal jurisdiction is limited to petty offenses. — Also termed *city court.*

naturalization court. See NATURALIZATION COURT.

nisi prius court. See NISI PRIUS.

open court. See OPEN COURT.

ordinary's court. See *probate court.*

orphan's court. See *probate court.*

Palace Court. See PALACE COURT.

parish court. See *county court.*

peacemaker's court. *Native American law.* A tribal court that adjudicates, arbitrates, or mediates some disputes, usu. according to traditional and statutory tribal law.

people's court. See PEOPLE'S COURT.

police court. See *magistrate's court* (1).

policy court. An appellate court, usu. a court of last resort, that must consider a decision's effects not only on the litigants but also on public policy.

practice court. 1. See MOOT COURT. **2.** (*cap.*) See BAIL COURT.

prerogative court. In New Jersey, a probate court. See *probate court.*

pretorial court. Hist. A 17th-century Maryland court that had jurisdiction over capital and other serious crimes. ● It consisted of three judges: the colony's lord proprietor or his lieutenant-general, the Secretary or Register of the Council of State, and one other member of the Council.

prize court. A court having jurisdiction to adjudicate the captures made at sea in time of war. See PRIZE (2). Cf. COURT OF APPEALS IN CASES OF CAPTURE.

probate court. (18c) A court with the power to declare wills valid or invalid, to oversee the administration of estates and (in some states) to appoint guardians and approve the adoption of minors. — Also termed *surrogate's court; surrogate court; court of ordinary; ordinary's court; county court; orphan's court* (abbr. o.c.). See PROBATE.

problem-solving court. A specialized court that matches community resources to litigants whose problems or cases may benefit from those resources. ● In criminal cases, a problem-solving court endeavors to promote solutions to underlying behavior problems that may lead to misconduct by providing treatment rather than imprisonment. For example, it may match offenders with resources for drug-abuse or mental-health treatment, often with close court supervision. In civil cases, a problem-solving court may help the parties try to resolve disputes through counseling or mediation rather than litigation. Cf. *drug court.*

provisional court. A federal court with jurisdiction and powers governed by the order granting its authority, such as a temporary court established in a conquered or occupied territory.

recorder's court. A court having jurisdiction over felony cases. ● This court exists in only a few jurisdictions, such as Michigan, where the recorder's court hears felony cases arising within the Detroit city limits.

register's court. Hist. A probate court in Pennsylvania or Delaware. See *probate court.*

rogue court. A court that fails to apply controlling law in making its decisions.

small-claims court. (1923) A court that informally and expeditiously adjudicates claims that seek damages below a specified monetary amount, usu. claims to collect small accounts or debts. — Also termed *small-debts court; conciliation court.*

spiritual court. See *ecclesiastical court.*

state court. (18c) A court of the state judicial system, as opposed to a federal court.

superior court. (18c) **1.** In some states, a trial court of general jurisdiction. **2.** In Pennsylvania, an intermediate court between the trial court and the chief appellate court.

supreme court. See SUPREME COURT.

Supreme Court of the United States. See SUPREME COURT OF THE UNITED STATES.

Supreme Judicial Court. (18c) The highest appellate court in Maine and Massachusetts.

surrogate's court. See *probate court.*

tax court. See TAX COURT.

teen court. A group of teenagers who (1) hear cases involving juveniles, usu. first-time offenders, who have acknowledged their guilt or responsibility, and (2) impose sanctions within a fixed range, usu. involving counseling, community service, or restitution. ● Some local jurisdictions in more than half the states have provided for this type of tribunal. The juvenile offender consents to the assessment of punishment by this jury of peers. The American Bar Association encourages the formation of these kinds of courts. — Also termed *youth court.*

territorial court. A U.S. court established in a U.S. territory (such as the Virgin Islands) and serving as both a federal and state court. ● The Constitution authorizes Congress to create such court. U.S. Const. art. IV, § 3, cl. 2.

three-judge court. A court made up of three judges; esp., a panel of three federal judges convened to hear a trial in which a statute is challenged on constitutional grounds. ● Three-judge courts were virtually abolished in 1976 when Congress restricted their jurisdiction to constitutional challenges to congressional reapportionments. Occasionally, Congress creates three-judge courts in special legislation, as with the 2002 campaign-finance law. Appeals from a three-judge court go directly to the Supreme Court. See 28 USCA § 2284.

traffic court. A court with jurisdiction over prosecutions for parking violations and infractions of road law.

trial court. (18c) A court of original jurisdiction where the evidence is first received and considered. — Also termed *court of first instance; instance court; court of instance.*

Tribal Court. See TRIBAL COURT.

unified family court. In some jurisdictions, a court that hears all family matters, including matters of divorce, juvenile delinquency, adoption, abuse and neglect, and criminal abuse. ● A unified family court also hears matters typically heard in family court (in jurisdictions that have statutory family courts) or in courts of general jurisdiction, such as divorce, paternity, and emancipation proceedings. Proponents of unified family courts cite the benefits of having all family-related matters heard by one court — for instance, the benefit of having a child testify only once rather than forcing the child to testify in one court in a divorce proceeding, in a different court in criminal proceedings against an abuser, and in yet another in a civil proceeding initiated by Child Protective Services.

United States Claims Court. See UNITED STATES COURT OF FEDERAL CLAIMS.

United States court. See *federal court.*

United States Court of International Trade. See UNITED STATES COURT OF INTERNATIONAL TRADE.

United States Customs Court. See UNITED STATES CUSTOMS COURT.

United States District Court. See UNITED STATES DISTRICT COURT.

United States Supreme Court. See SUPREME COURT OF THE UNITED STATES.

United States Tax Court. See TAX COURT, U.S.

upper court. See *court above.*

vice-admiralty court. See VICE-ADMIRALTY COURT.

World Court. See INTERNATIONAL COURT OF JUSTICE.

youth court. See *teen court.*

court administrator. See ADMINISTRATOR (1).

court-appointed attorney. See *assigned counsel* under COUNSEL.

court-appointed counsel. See *assigned counsel* under COUNSEL.

court-appointed expert. See *impartial expert* under EXPERT.

court-appointed special advocate. A trained volunteer appointed by a court to represent the interests of a child in an abuse or neglect case. — Abbr. CASA. Cf. *guardian ad litem* under GUARDIAN.

Court Appointed Special Advocates. A federally funded program in which trained laypersons act on behalf of children in abuse and neglect cases. ● The CASA program began in 1977 in Seattle, Washington. In 1989, the American Bar Association endorsed using a combination of CASA volunteers and attorneys in abuse and neglect cases. CASA volunteers are sanctioned by the ABA as permissible guardians ad litem. — Abbr. CASA.

court a quo. See COURT.

court baron. *Hist.* A manorial court that had jurisdiction over amounts in controversy of 40 shillings or less. ● According to some authorities, the court baron developed into two courts: the customary court baron for disputes involving copyholders, and the court baron proper (also known as the freeholders' court baron), in which freeholders were allowed to hold court concerning minor disputes. — Also termed *freeholder's court baron.*

court below. See COURT.

court calendar. (1852) A list of matters scheduled for trial or hearing; DOCKET (2).

court christian. See *ecclesiastical court* under COURT.

court clinic. A medical clinic, established for the benefit of the courts, to which a judge may send a defendant for psychiatric evaluation or, esp. in the case of a juvenile, to explore why the defendant committed the offense and what treatment is appropriate.

court commissioner. See COMMISSIONER.

court costs. See COST (2).

court crier. See CRIER (1).

court day. See DAY.

court de facto. See *de facto court* under COURT.

courtesy supervision. (1970) Oversight of a parolee by a correctional agency located in a jurisdiction other than where the parolee was sentenced. ● Courtesy supervision is usu. arranged informally between correctional authorities in cases in which the offense is not serious and the parolee's rehabilitative needs are better served in another jurisdiction.

Court for Consideration of Crown Cases Reserved. *Hist.* A court established in 1848 to review questions of law arising in criminal cases. ● Trial judges posed the postverdict questions of law to the Court, which decided whether error had been committed. The Court was abolished in 1907, and its jurisdiction was transferred to the Court of Criminal Appeal. — Also termed *Court for Crown Cases Reserved.*

Court for Divorce and Matrimonial Causes. *Hist.* A court that exercised jurisdiction over family issues, such as legitimacy and divorce. ● The Court, which was established in 1857, acquired the matrimonial jurisdiction previously exercised by the ecclesiastical courts. It consisted of the Lord Chancellor, the Chief Justices of the Queen's Bench and Common Pleas, the Chief Baron of Exchequer, the senior puisne judges of the last three courts, and the Judge Ordinary. In most instances, the Judge Ordinary heard the cases. The Judicature Act of 1873 abolished the Court and transferred its jurisdiction to the Probate Divorce and Admiralty Division (now Family Division) of the High Court of Justice.

Court for the Correction of Errors. A court having jurisdiction to review a lower court. ● The name was formerly used in New York and South Carolina.

Court for the Relief of Insolvent Debtors. *Hist.* A court located in London that had jurisdiction over bankruptcy matters. • The Bankruptcy Act of 1861 abolished the Court.

court for the trial of impeachments. (18c) A tribunal empowered to try a government officer or other person brought before it by the process of impeachment. • The U.S. Senate and the British House of Lords have this authority, as do the upper houses of most state legislatures. — Also termed *impeachment court*; *court of impeachment*.

court hand. *Hist.* A script style used by English court clerks, the words being abbreviated and contracted according to a set of common principles for maintaining brevity and uniformity. • This type of writing, along with the use of Latin (except for technical or untranslatable phrases), was banned early in the 18th century in an effort to make court records more accessible to non-lawyers.

courthouse. See COURT (5).

courthouse steps. The figurative location of settlement negotiations that occur shortly before trial commences, regardless of the literal location of the negotiations <the parties settled the lawsuit on the courthouse steps>.

court leet (kort leet). *Hist.* A feudal court responsible for receiving frankpledges and notices of criminal accusations. • Courts leet exercised both governmental and judicial powers, but they declined in the 14th century after the justices in eyre began to take over serious criminal cases. The court met once or twice a year, and was presided over by the lord's steward, a lawyer who acted as judge.

court-martial, *n.* (18c) An ad hoc military court convened under military authority to try someone, particularly a member of the armed forces, accused of violating the Uniform Code of Military Justice. Pl. **courts-martial.** — **court-martial,** *vb.*

BCD special court-martial. A special court-martial in which a possible punishment is a bad-conduct discharge (a "BCD").

general court-martial. A proceeding that is presided over by a military judge, and no fewer than five members (who serve as jurors), and that has jurisdiction over all the members of the armed forces. • It is the highest military trial court.

special court-martial. A proceeding that is presided over by a military judge and no fewer than three members (who serve as jurors) to hear noncapital offenses and prescribe a sanction of hard labor, dismissal, or extended confinement (up to one year). • It is the intermediate level of courts-martial.

summary court-martial. A proceeding presided over by a single commissioned officer who is jurisdictionally limited in what sanctions can be imposed. • It is the lowest level of courts-martial.

court-martial order. A written order containing the result of a court-martial trial.

Court-Martial Reports. A publication containing the opinions of the U.S. Court of Military Appeals and select decisions of the Courts of Military Review. • This publication appeared during the years 1951–1975. — Abbr. CMR.

court merchant. See COURT.

court not of record. See COURT.

Court of Admiralty. See HIGH COURT OF ADMIRALTY.

court of ancient demesne. *Hist.* A court made up of freeholders of land held by the Crown (i.e., an *ancient demesne*). • The freeholders acted as judges much the same way that freeholders of an ordinary manor would in a court baron. See *ancient demesne* under DEMESNE; COURT BARON.

Court of Appeal. An English court of civil and criminal appellate jurisdiction established by the Judicature Acts of 1873 and 1875. • The court is made up of the Lord Chancellor, Lord Chief Justice, Master of the Rolls, President of the Family Division, Vice-Chancellor of the Chancery Division, former Lord Chancellors, Lords of Appeal in Ordinary, and Lords Justices of Appeal. In practice it is made up of the Master of Rolls and the Lords Justices. It sits in several divisions, each having three members.

Court of Appeal in Chancery. *Hist.* An English court of intermediate appeal in equity cases, established in 1851 and abolished in 1873–1875, when its jurisdiction was transferred to the Court of Appeal.

court of appeals. See COURT.

Court of Appeals, U.S. See UNITED STATES COURT OF APPEALS.

Court of Appeals for the Armed Forces. See UNITED STATES COURT OF APPEALS FOR THE ARMED FORCES.

Court of Appeals for the Federal Circuit. See UNITED STATES COURT OF APPEALS FOR THE FEDERAL CIRCUIT.

Court of Appeals for Veterans Claims. The federal court that reviews decisions of the Board of Veterans Appeals.

Court of Appeals in Cases of Capture. *Hist.* A court responsible for reviewing state-court decisions concerning British ships captured by American privateers during the Revolution. • Congress established the court under the Articles of Confederation. It was the first federal court in the

United States and the chief United States court from 1780 to 1787. Cf. *prize court* under COURT.

Court of Archdeacon (ahrch-**dee**-kən). *Hist. Eccles. law.* An inferior ecclesiastical court that had jurisdiction over cases arising within the archdeaconry and probate matters. ● Appeal was to the Bishop's Court. The Court of Archdeacon was abolished in 1967. — Also termed *Archdeacon's Court*; *Archdiaconal Court* (ahr-kə-dɪ-**ak**-ən-əl).

Court of Arches. *Eccles. law.* The ecclesiastical court of the province of Canterbury, responsible for appeals from provincial diocesan courts. ● The Pope heard appeals from the Court of Arches until the break with Rome prompted a transfer of the appellate jurisdiction to the Court of Delegates. The Judicial Committee of the Privy Council now hears certain appeals from the Court of Arches. — Also termed *Arches Court of Canterbury*; *Court of Canterbury*; *Court of the Official Principal.* Cf. CHANCERY COURT OF YORK.

Court of Assistants. *Hist.* A colonial body organized in Massachusetts Bay Colony in 1630 to act as a legislature and court for the colony. Cf. GENERAL COURT.

Court of Attachments. *Hist.* An inferior forest court with jurisdiction over trespasses of the royal forests. ● The judges of this court (the *verderers*) met every 40 days to hear charges made by the royal foresters. Major trespass cases were heard by the justices in eyre. — Also termed *wood-mote*; *forty-days court.*

Court of Audience. *Hist. Eccles. law.* A court in which the Archbishop of York or Canterbury exercised personal jurisdiction. ● This court was abolished in 1963.

Court of Augmentations. *Hist.* A court established in 1536 by Henry VIII to determine controversies arising from the royal policy of taking over property owned by monasteries. ● The court was merged into the Court of Exchequer in 1554.

Court of Canterbury. See COURT OF ARCHES.

Court of Cassation (ka-**say**-shən). The highest court of France. ● The court's name derives from its power to quash (*casser*) the decrees of inferior courts. — Also termed (more formally) *Cour de Cassation.*

court of chancery. See CHANCERY (1).

court of chivalry. See HIGH COURT OF CHIVALRY.

Court of Civil Appeals. (1892) An intermediate appellate court in some states, such as Alabama and (formerly) Texas.

court of claims. 1. See COURT. **2.** (*cap.*) See UNITED STATES COURT OF FEDERAL CLAIMS.

Court of Common Pleas. (16c) **1.** *Hist.* A superior court having jurisdiction of all real actions and common pleas (i.e., actions between subjects). ●

The Court was presided over by a chief justice with four (later five) puisne judges. In 1873 it became the Common Pleas Division of the High Court of Justice. In 1881 it merged into the Queen's Bench Division. **2.** An intermediate-level court in some states, such as Arkansas. **3.** A trial court of general jurisdiction in some states, such as Ohio, Pennsylvania, and South Carolina. — Also termed *Court of Common Bench.* — Abbr. C.P.

court of competent jurisdiction. See COURT.

court of conscience. *Hist.* A local English court that had jurisdiction over small-debt cases. ● The court was so called because its judgments were supposed to reflect equity and good conscience. County courts assumed the jurisdiction of the courts of conscience in 1846.

Court of Convocation. *Eccles. law.* An assembly of high-ranking provincial officials and representatives of the lower clergy having jurisdiction over cases of heresy, schism, and other ecclesiastical matters.

Court of Criminal Appeals. (1856) **1.** For each armed service, an intermediate appellate court that reviews court-martial decisions. ● The court was established by the Military Justice Act of 1968. 10 USCA §§ 859–876. — Formerly termed *Court of Military Review* (abbr. CMR). **2.** In some jurisdictions, such as Texas and Oklahoma, the highest appellate court that hears criminal cases.

Court of Customs and Patent Appeals. *Hist.* An Article III court created in 1929 to hear appeals in customs and patent cases. ● This court was abolished in 1982 and was superseded by the U.S. Court of Appeals for the Federal Circuit. — Abbr. CCPA. See UNITED STATES COURT OF APPEALS FOR THE FEDERAL CIRCUIT.

Court of Delegates. *Hist. Eccles. law.* A court serving as the final court of appeal for admiralty and ecclesiastical matters. ● The Court was established in 1534 to serve in the stead of the Papal Curia when the English Church severed its ties with the Papacy. Six delegates, appointed to hear only one case, made up the Court, usu. three persons trained in common law and three in civil law. This mixture led to confused rulings and unreliable precedents that hindered the Court's credibility and ultimately led to its dissolution. The Court was abolished in 1833 and its jurisdiction transferred to the Judicial Committee of the Privy Council. — Also termed *High Court of Delegates.*

court of domestic relations. See *family court* under COURT.

Court of Earl Marshal. 1. See COURT OF THE LORD HIGH CONSTABLE AND EARL MARSHAL. **2.** See HIGH COURT OF CHIVALRY.

court of equity. See COURT.

court of error. **1.** *Hist.* Formerly, the Court of Exchequer Chamber and the House of Lords. • Appeals from common-law courts lay to the Court of Exchequer Chamber, and then to the House of Lords until 1873, when the Judicature Act gave jurisdiction of superior-court appeals to the Court of Appeal. Cf. COURT OF EXCHEQUER CHAMBER. **2.** Generally, a court having jurisdiction to review a lower court's rulings.

Court of Errors and Appeals. *Hist.* Formerly, the court of last resort in New Jersey and New York. — Also termed *High Court of Errors and Appeals.*

Court of Exchequer (eks-**chek**-ər *or* eks-chek-ər). *Hist.* A former English superior court responsible primarily for adjudicating disputes about the collection of public revenue. • In 1873 it became the Exchequer Division of the High Court of Justice. In 1881 that Division was merged into the Queen's Bench Division. See QUEEN'S BENCH DIVISION.

Court of Exchequer Chamber. *Hist.* **1.** An informal assembly of common-law judges who (sometimes with the Lord Chancellor) gathered to discuss important cases that had adjourned pending an opinion from the Court. • This body never became a court of law in a technical sense, but judges gave great weight to its decisions. The last reported decision of this body is from 1738. **2.** A court created by statute in 1357 to hear appeals from the Court of Exchequer. **3.** A court created by statute in 1585 to hear appeals from the King's Bench. • This court consisted of all the justices of the Common Pleas and the Barons of Exchequer who were serjeants. At least six judges were necessary to render a judgment. **4.** A court charged with hearing appeals from the common-law courts of record. • This court was created in 1830 by combining the courts created by the statutes of 1357 and 1585. Appeals from one common-law court were heard by judges from the other two courts.

Court of Faculties. *Eccles. law.* An archbishop's tribunal that grants special dispensations (such as a marriage license) and decides questions relating to monuments and mortuary matters.

Court of Federal Claims, U.S. See UNITED STATES COURT OF FEDERAL CLAIMS.

court officer. See OFFICER OF THE COURT.

court of final appeal. See COURT.

court of first instance. See *trial court* under COURT.

court of general jurisdiction. See COURT.

court of impeachment. See COURT FOR THE TRIAL OF IMPEACHMENTS.

court of inquiry. See COURT.

court of instance. See *trial court* under COURT.

Court of International Trade, U.S. See UNITED STATES COURT OF INTERNATIONAL TRADE.

Court of Justice Seat. See COURT OF THE CHIEF JUSTICE IN EYRE.

Court of Justiciary, High. See HIGH COURT OF JUSTICIARY.

Court of King's Bench. See KING'S BENCH.

court of last resort. See COURT.

court of law. See COURT.

court of limited jurisdiction. See COURT.

Court of Military Appeals. See UNITED STATES COURT OF APPEALS FOR THE ARMED FORCES.

Court of Military Review. See COURT OF CRIMINAL APPEALS (1).

court of nisi prius. See NISI PRIUS.

court of ordinary. See *probate court* under COURT.

court of original jurisdiction. See COURT.

Court of Orphans. *Hist.* In Maryland and Pennsylvania, a court that exercised probate jurisdiction.

Court of Oyer and Terminer (**oy**-ər an[d] **tər**-mə-nər). (17c) **1.** *Hist.* An assize court commissioned by the Crown to pass through the counties two or more times a year and hear felonies and treason cases. • The judges sat by virtue of several commissions, each of which, strictly speaking, created a separate and distinct court. A judge with an *oyer and terminer* commission, for example, was allowed to hear only cases of felony and treason; he could not try persons charged with other criminal offenses. But if the judge also carried a commission of *gaol delivery* (as most did), he could try all prisoners held in gaol for any offense; in this way most Courts of Oyer and Terminer gathered full criminal jurisdiction. The jurisdiction of the assize courts was taken over by the Crown Court in 1971. See ASSIZE (1); COMMISSION OF OYER AND TERMINER; COMMISSION OF GAOL DELIVERY. **2.** In some states, a court of higher criminal jurisdiction.

Court of Oyer and Terminer and General Gaol Delivery. *Hist.* **1.** A court that carries the commissions of *oyer and terminer* and *gaol delivery*. See COMMISSION OF OYER AND TERMINER; COMMISSION OF GAOL DELIVERY. **2.** In Pennsylvania, a court of criminal jurisdiction.

Court of Peculiars. *Hist. Eccles. law.* A branch of the Court of Arches that had jurisdiction over the provincial parishes of Canterbury that were exempt from the jurisdiction of the diocesan bishop and responsible to the metropolitan only. • The Court of Peculiars was abolished in the 19th century. See COURT OF ARCHES; PECULIAR.

court of petty sessions. See *magistrate's court* under COURT.

Court of Probate. 1. *Hist.* A court established in 1857 to receive the testamentary jurisdiction formerly held by the ecclesiastical courts. • In 1873 the Court was merged into the High Court of Justice, where its jurisdiction was exercised by the Probate Divorce and Admiralty (now Family) Division. **2.** See *probate court* under COURT.

Court of Queen's Bench. See QUEEN'S BENCH.

court of record. See COURT.

court of review. See *appellate court* under COURT.

court of special jurisdiction. See *limited court* under COURT.

court of special session. See COURT.

Court of Star Chamber. See STAR CHAMBER (1).

court of summary jurisdiction. See *magistrate's court* under COURT.

Court of the Chief Justice in Eyre (air). *Hist.* An eyre court responsible for trying offenses against the forest laws. • The jurisdiction of this Court was similar to that of the Court of Sweinmote. — Also termed *Court of Justice Seat.*

Court of the Earl Marshal. HIGH COURT OF CHIVALRY.

Court of the Lord High Admiral. See HIGH COURT OF ADMIRALTY.

Court of the Official Principal. See COURT OF ARCHES.

Court of Verge. 1. See VERGE (1). **2.** See VERGE (2).

Court of Veterans Appeals, U.S. See UNITED STATES COURT OF VETERANS APPEALS.

Court of Wards and Liveries. *Hist.* A court created in 1540 to assert the Crown's right to income from a variety of feudal tenures. • The Court's unpopularity led to its abolition in 1660.

courtoisie internationale. See COMITY.

court order. See ORDER (2).

court-ordered arbitration. See *judicial arbitration* under ARBITRATION.

court-packing plan. A unsuccessful proposal — made in 1937 by President Franklin D. Roosevelt — to increase the number of U.S. Supreme Court justices from nine to fifteen. • The ostensible purpose of the proposal was to increase the court's efficiency, but President Roosevelt wanted to appoint justices who would not block his administration's New Deal programs.

court papers. (17c) All documents that a party files with the court, including pleadings, motions, notices, and the like. — Often shortened to *papers.* — Also termed *suit papers.*

court probation. See *bench probation* under PROBATION.

court recorder. See RECORDER.

court reporter. (1894) **1.** A person who records testimony, stenographically or by electronic or other means, and when requested, prepares a transcript <the deposition could not start until the court reporter arrived>. — Also termed (in BrE) *official shorthand writer.* Cf. *court recorder* under RECORDER. **2.** REPORTER OF DECISIONS.

court roll. *Hist.* A record of a manor's tenures; esp., a record of the terms by which the various tenants held their estates. • Copyhold tenure, for example, developed from the practice of maintaining court rolls. See COPYHOLD.

courtroom. The part of a courthouse where trials and hearings take place. Cf. *judge's chamber* under CHAMBER.

courtroom deputy. See DEPUTY.

courtroom privilege. See *judicial privilege* under PRIVILEGE (1).

court rules. (17c) Regulations having the force of law and governing practice and procedure in the various courts, such as the Federal Rules of Civil Procedure, the Federal Rules of Criminal Procedure, the U.S. Supreme Court Rules, and the Federal Rules of Evidence, as well as any local rules that a court promulgates. — Also termed *rules of court.*

court system. The network of courts in a jurisdiction.

court trial. See *bench trial* under TRIAL.

court witness. See WITNESS.

cousin. 1. A child of one's aunt or uncle. — Also termed *first cousin; full cousin; cousin-german.* **2.** A relative descended from one's ancestor (such as a grandparent) by two or more steps in a diverging line. **3.** Any distant relative by blood or marriage; a kinsman or kinswoman.

cousin-german. A first cousin; a child of a full sibling of one's mother or father. See GERMAN.

cousin-in-law. **1.** The husband or wife of one's cousin. **2.** A cousin of one's husband or one's wife.

cousin once removed. **1.** A child of one's cousin. **2.** A cousin of one's parent.

cousin twice removed. **1.** A grandchild of one's cousin. **2.** A cousin of one's grandparent.

first cousin. See COUSIN (1).

second cousin. A person related to another by descending from the same great-grandfather or great-grandmother.

third cousin. A person related to another by descending from the same great-great-grandfather or great-great-grandmother.

covenant (kəv-ə-nənt), *n.* (14c) **1.** A formal agreement or promise, usu. in a contract or deed, to do or not do a particular act.

absolute covenant. (17c) A covenant that is not qualified or limited by any condition. Cf. *conditional covenant.*

affirmative covenant. A covenant that obligates a party to do some act; esp., an agreement that real property will be used in a certain way. ● An affirmative covenant is more than a restriction on the use of property. For the real-property sense, see *affirmative covenant* under COVENANT (4). Cf. *negative covenant.*

assertory covenant (ə-sər-tə-ree). One that affirmatively states certain facts; an affirming promise under seal.

auxiliary covenant (awg-**zil**-yə-ree). A covenant that does not relate directly to the primary subject of the agreement, but to something connected to it. Cf. *principal covenant.*

collateral covenant (kə-**lat**-ə-rəl). A covenant entered into in connection with the grant of something, but that does not relate immediately to the thing granted; esp., a covenant in a deed or other sealed instrument not pertaining to the conveyed property. Cf. *inherent covenant.*

concurrent covenant. (1819) A covenant that requires performance by one party at the same time as another's performance.

conditional covenant. (17c) A covenant that is qualified by a condition. Cf. *absolute covenant.*

continuing covenant. A covenant that requires the successive performance of acts, such as an agreement to pay rent in installments.

covenant in deed. See *express covenant.*

covenant in law. See *implied covenant.*

covenant not to compete. See *noncompetition covenant.*

covenant not to execute. A covenant in which a party who has won a judgment agrees not to enforce it. ● This covenant is most common in insurance law.

covenant not to sue. (18c) A covenant in which a party having a right of action agrees not to assert that right in litigation. — Also termed *contract not to sue.*

dependent covenant. A covenant that imposes a duty that depends on the other party's prior performance. ● Until the performance, the other party does not have to perform. Cf. *concurrent covenant*; *independent covenant.*

executed covenant. A covenant that has been fully performed.

executory covenant (eg-**zek**-yə-tor-ee). A covenant that remains unperformed in whole or in part.

express covenant. (17c) A covenant created by the words of the parties. — Also termed *covenant in deed.* Cf. *implied covenant.*

implied covenant. (17c) A covenant that can be inferred from the whole agreement and the conduct of the parties. — Also termed *covenant in law.* See *implied term* under TERM (2). Cf. *express covenant.*

implied covenant of good faith and fair dealing. (1924) An implied covenant to cooperate with the other party to an agreement so that both parties may obtain the full benefits of the agreement; an implied covenant to refrain from any act that would injure a contracting party's right to receive the benefit of the contract. ● Breach of this covenant is often termed *bad faith.* See BAD FAITH (2).

implied negative covenant. (1890) A covenant binding a grantor not to permit use of any reserved right in a manner that might destroy the benefits that would otherwise inure to the grantee.

independent covenant. A covenant that imposes a duty that does not depend on the other party's prior performance. Cf. *dependent covenant.*

inherent covenant. A covenant that relates directly to land, such as a covenant of quiet enjoyment. Cf. *collateral covenant.*

intransitive covenant. A covenant whose performance does not pass from the original covenantor to the covenantor's representatives. Cf. *transitive covenant.*

joint covenant. A covenant that binds two or more covenantors together. Cf. *several covenant.*

negative covenant. (18c) A covenant that requires a party to refrain from doing something; esp., in a real-estate financing transaction, the borrower's promise to the lender not to encumber or transfer the real estate as long as the loan remains unpaid. Cf. *affirmative covenant.*

noncompetition covenant. A promise, usu. in a sale-of-business, partnership, or employment contract, not to engage in the same type of business for a stated time in the same market as the buyer, partner, or employer. ● Noncompetition covenants are valid to protect business goodwill in the sale of a company. In other contexts, they are generally disfavored as restraints of trade: courts generally enforce them for the duration of the business relationship, but provisions that extend beyond the termination of that relationship must be reasonable in scope, time, and territory. — Also termed *noncompetition agreement*; *noncompete covenant*; *covenant not* to compete; *restrictive covenant; promise not to compete; contract not to compete.*

positive covenant. A covenant that requires a party to do something (such as to erect a fence within a specified time).

principal covenant. A covenant that relates directly to the principal matter of an agreement. Cf. *auxiliary covenant.*

protection covenant. See PROTECTION COVENANT.

restrictive covenant. See *noncompetition covenant.* (For the real-property sense, see *restrictive covenant* under COVENANT (4).)

several covenant. A covenant that binds two or more covenantors separately. — Also termed *separate covenant.* Cf. *joint covenant.*

transitive covenant. A covenant whose duty of performance passes from the original covenantor to the covenantor's representatives. Cf. *intransitive covenant.*

2. TREATY. **3.** A common-law action to recover damages for breach of contract under seal. **4.** A promise made in a deed or implied by law; esp., an obligation in a deed burdening or favoring a landowner. See *contract under seal* under CONTRACT. — **covenantal,** *adj.*

affirmative covenant. An agreement that real property will be used in a certain way. ● An affirmative covenant is more than a restriction on the use of property. It requires the owner to undertake certain acts on the property. For a more general definition of this term, see *affirmative covenant* under COVENANT (1).

covenant against encumbrances. (1807) A grantor's promise that the property has no visible or invisible encumbrances. ● In a special warranty deed, the covenant is limited to encumbrances made by the grantor. — Also termed *general covenant against encumbrances.* Cf. *special covenant against encumbrances.*

covenant appurtenant (ə-**pər**-tə-nənt). (1899) A covenant that is connected with the grantor's land; a covenant running with the land. Cf. *covenant in gross.*

covenant for further assurances. (18c) A covenant to do whatever is reasonably necessary to perfect the title conveyed if it turns out to be imperfect. See *further assurance* under ASSURANCE.

covenant for possession. A covenant giving a grantee or lessee possession of land.

covenant for quiet enjoyment. (17c) **1.** A covenant insuring against the consequences of a defective title or any other disturbance of the title. **2.** A covenant ensuring that the tenant will not be evicted or disturbed by the grantor or a person having a lien or superior title. ● This covenant is sometimes treated as being synonymous with *covenant of warranty.* — Also termed *covenant of quiet enjoyment.*

covenant for title. (18c) A covenant that binds the grantor to ensure the completeness, security, and continuance of the title transferred. ● This covenant usu. includes the covenants for seisin, against encumbrances, for the right to convey, for quiet enjoyment, and of warranty.

covenant in gross. (17c) A covenant that does not run with the land. Cf. *covenant appurtenant.*

covenant of good right to convey. See *covenant of seisin.*

covenant of habitability (hab-ə-tə-**bil**-ə-tee). See *implied warranty of habitability* under WARRANTY (2).

covenant of nonclaim. (1848) A covenant barring a grantor or the grantor's heirs from claiming title in the conveyed land.

covenant of quiet enjoyment. See *covenant for quiet enjoyment.*

covenant of seisin (**see**-zin). (18c) A covenant, usu. appearing in a warranty deed, stating that the grantor has an estate, or the right to convey an estate, of the quality and size that the grantor purports to convey. ● For the covenant to be valid, the grantor must have both title and possession at the time of the grant. — Also termed *covenant of good right to convey; right-to-convey covenant.*

covenant of warranty. (18c) A covenant by which the grantor agrees to defend the grantee against any lawful or reasonable claim of superior title by a third party and to indemnify the grantee for any loss sustained by the claim. ● This covenant is sometimes treated as being synonymous with *covenant for quiet enjoyment.* The covenant is not breached if the grantor fails to defend the grantee against an invalid claim. See WARRANTY (1).

covenant running with the land. (18c) A covenant intimately and inherently involved with the land and therefore binding subsequent owners and successor grantees indefinitely. — Also termed *real covenant.*

covenant running with the title. 1. A covenant that relates to the land but has a specific or reasonably determinable expiration time. **2.** See *covenant running with the land.*

covenant to convey. A covenant in which the covenantor agrees to transfer an estate's title to the covenantee.

covenant to renew. An executory contract that gives a lessee the right to renew the lease.

covenant to stand seised (seezd). *Archaic.* A covenant to convey land to a relative. ● This covenant could not be used to convey land to a stranger; the only consideration that supports the covenant is the relationship by blood or marriage.

future covenant. A covenant that can be breached only upon interference with the possession of the grantee or the grantee's successors. ● The covenants in this class are the covenant for further assurances, the covenant for quiet enjoyment, and the covenant of warranty. The distinction between future and present covenants becomes important in determining when the statute of limitations begins to run. Cf. *present covenant.*

general covenant against encumbrances. See *covenant against encumbrances.*

implied reciprocal covenant. A presumption that a promisee has, in return for a promise made respecting land, impliedly made a promise to the promisor respecting other land. — Also termed *implied reciprocal servitude.*

personal covenant. A covenant that creates a personal right or obligation enforceable only between the covenanting parties and that is not binding on the heirs or assigns of the parties. Cf. *covenant running with the land.*

present covenant. A covenant that can be breached only at the time of conveyance. ● The three covenants in this class are the covenant against encumbrances, the covenant of right to convey, and the covenant of seisin. Cf. *future covenant.*

protection covenant. See PROTECTION COVENANT.

real covenant. See *covenant running with the land.*

restrictive covenant. (1811) **1.** A private agreement, usu. in a deed or lease, that restricts the use or occupancy of real property, esp. by specifying lot sizes, building lines, architectural styles, and the uses to which the property may be put. ● Some restrictive covenants, such as race-based restrictions on transfers, are unenforceable but do not necessarily void the deed. — Also termed *restrictive covenant in equity*; *equitable easement*; *equitable servitude.* **2.** See *noncompetition covenant* under COVENANT (1).

right-to-convey covenant. See *covenant of seisin.*

special covenant against encumbrances. (1860) A grantor's promise that the property is free of encumbrances created by the grantor only, not the grantor's predecessors. See *special warranty deed* under DEED. Cf. *covenant against encumbrances.*

covenant, *vb.* (14c) To promise or undertake in a covenant; to agree formally.

covenantee (kəv-ə-nən-**tee**). (17c) The person to whom a promise by covenant is made; one entitled to the benefit of a covenant.

covenanter. See COVENANTOR.

covenant marriage. See MARRIAGE (1).

covenant of good right to convey. See *covenant of seisin* under COVENANT (4).

covenant of seisin. See COVENANT (4).

covenantor (kəv-ə-nən-tər *or* kəv-ə-nən-**tor**). (17c) The person who makes a promise by covenant; one subject to the burden of a covenant. — Also spelled *covenanter.*

covenant running with the land. See COVENANT (4).

covenant to protect against drainage. See PROTECTION COVENANT.

coventurer (koh-**ven**-chər-ər). (1913) A person who undertakes a joint venture with one or more persons. — Also termed *co-adventurer.* Cf. JOINT VENTURE.

cover, *n.* The purchase on the open market, by the buyer in a breach-of-contract dispute, of goods to substitute for those promised but never delivered by the seller. ● Under UCC § 2-712, the buyer can recover from the seller the difference between the cost of the substituted goods and the original contract price.

coverage, *n.* (1912) **1.** Inclusion of a risk under an insurance policy; the risks within the scope of an insurance policy. — **cover,** *vb.*

dependent coverage. An insurance provision for protection of an insured's dependents.

full coverage. Insurance protection that pays for the full amount of a loss with no deduction.

2. The ratio between corporate pretax income and corporate liability for bond interest payments.

coverage opinion. See OPINION (2).

coverage ratio. (1975) A measurement of a firm's ability to cover its financing charges.

cover-all clause. See MOTHER HUBBARD CLAUSE (2).

cover-baron. See COVERT BARON.

covered-interest arbitrage. See ARBITRAGE.

covered wages. See WAGE.

cover letter. See TRANSMITTAL LETTER.

cover note. A written statement by an insurance agent confirming that coverage is in effect. ● The cover note is distinguished from a binder, which is prepared by the insurance company.

covert baron (kəv-ərt **bar**-ən). [Law French] *Hist.* The condition or status of a married woman at common law. — Also written *cover-baron*. — Also termed *covert de baron*.

covert-entry search warrant. See SEARCH WARRANT.

coverture (kəv-ər-chər *also* -tyoor), *n. Archaic.* The condition of being a married woman <under former law, a woman under coverture was allowed to sue only through the personality of her husband>. See *feme covert* under FEME. — **covert** (kəv-ərt), *adj.*

cover-up, *n.* Concealment of wrongdoing, esp. by a conspiracy of deception, nondisclosure, and destruction of evidence, usu. combined with a refusal to cooperate with investigators. ● A cover-up often involves obstruction of justice. — **cover up,** *vb.*

covin (kəv-ən). *Hist.* A secret conspiracy or agreement between two or more persons to injure or defraud another. — Also spelled *covine*.

covinous (kəv-ə-nəs), *adj. Hist.* Of a deceitful or fraudulent nature.

cozen (kəz-ən), *vb. Hist.* To cheat or defraud. — Also spelled *cosen*.

cozening (kəz-ən-ing). *Hist.* A deceitful practice; the offense of cheating, or fraudulent dealing. — Also spelled *cosening*.

C.P. *abbr.* COURT OF COMMON PLEAS.

CPA. *abbr.* **1.** See *certified public accountant* under ACCOUNTANT. **2.** See *continued-prosecution application* under PATENT APPLICATION.

CPC. *abbr.* Certificate of probable cause. See CERTIFICATE OF APPEALABILITY.

CPD. *abbr.* OFFICE OF COMMUNITY PLANNING AND DEVELOPMENT.

CPI. *abbr.* CONSUMER PRICE INDEX.

CPS. *abbr.* CHILD PROTECTIVE SERVICES.

CPSC. *abbr.* CONSUMER PRODUCT SAFETY COMMISSION.

CPT. *abbr.* CARRIAGE PAID TO.

C.R. *abbr.* CURIA REGIS.

crack. *vb. Slang.* **1.** To open (a lock). **2.** To decode (security information); esp., to decipher or discover (a code, a password, etc. needed to break into a computer, network, server, or database). Cf. HACK. **3.** To bypass (an encryption or a security device, esp. one designed to prevent unauthorized access, as in a cable television box, or copying, as in a DVD player). **4.** To hack (a computer, network, server, or database) with the intention of causing damage or disruption.

cracking, *n.* A gerrymandering technique in which a geographically concentrated political or racial group that is large enough to constitute a district's dominant force is broken up by district lines and dispersed throughout two or more districts. Cf. PACKING; STACKING (2).

craft union. See UNION.

cramdown, *n.* (1954) Court confirmation of a Chapter 11 bankruptcy plan despite the opposition of certain creditors. ● Under the Bankruptcy Code, a court may confirm a plan — even if it has not been accepted by all classes of creditors — if the plan (1) has been accepted by at least one impaired class, (2) does not discriminate unfairly, and (3) is fair and equitable. 11 USCA § 1129(b). — **cram down,** *vb.*

crash-and-dash. See RAM RAID.

crashworthiness doctrine. (1969) *Products liability.* The principle that the manufacturer of a product will be held strictly liable for injuries occurring in a collision, even if the collision results from an independent cause, to the extent that a defect in the product causes injuries above and beyond those that would have occurred in the collision itself. — Also termed *second-collision doctrine*; *second-impact doctrine*.

CRAT. *abbr.* Charitable-remainder annuity trust. See *charitable remainder annuity trust* under TRUST.

create a blank. *Parliamentary law.* To amend a motion by striking out one or more terms and replacing them with blanks rather than different terms. See *amendment by striking out and inserting* under AMENDMENT (3). ● This form allows a vote on several competing proposals at one time, rather than the usual process of voting separately upon each proposal. See BLANK (2).

creationism. The teaching of the biblical version of the creation of the universe. ● The United States Supreme Court held unconstitutional a Louisiana law that forbade the teaching of the theory of evolution unless biblical creation was also taught. The Court found the law violated the Establishment Clause of the First Amendment because it lacked a "clear secular purpose." *Edwards v. Aguillard*, 482 U.S. 578, 107 S.Ct. 2573 (1987). See ANTI-EVOLUTION STATUTE.

    scientific creationism. A doctrine holding that the biblical account of creation is supported by scientific evidence.

creation science. The interpretation of scientific evidence, arguments, and knowledge to support creationism. See CREATIONISM.

creative sentence. See *alternative sentence* under SENTENCE.

creative work. See *work of authorship* under WORK (2).

creativity. *Copyright.* The degree to which a work displays imaginativeness beyond what a person of very ordinary talents might create. ● Labor and expense are not elements of creativity; for that reason, they are not protected by copyright. *Feist Pubs. Inc. v. Rural Tel. Serv. Co.*, 499 U.S. 340, 111 S.Ct. 1282 (1991). Cf. ORIGINALITY, SWEAT-OF-THE-BROW DOCTRINE.

creator. See SETTLOR (1).

creature. See ANIMAL.

creature of statute. (1854) A doctrine, governmental agency, etc. that would not exist but for a legislative act that brought it into being.

credential. (*usu. pl.*) **1.** A document or other evidence that proves one's authority or expertise. **2.** A testimonial that a person is entitled to credit or to the right to exercise official power. **3.** The letter of credence given to an ambassador or other representative of a foreign country. **4.** *Parliamentary law.* Evidence of a delegate's entitlement to be seated and vote in a convention or other deliberative assembly. ● Before the meeting begins, the evidence usu. takes the form of a certificate or proof of election or appointment, which the delegate presents to a credentials committee so that the committee can list the delegate on its roster. During the meeting, the evidence usu. takes the form of a badge or card that the credentials committee issues to each delegate on its roster. See *credentials committee* under COMMITTEE. — **credential,** *vb.*

credentials committee. See COMMITTEE.

credibility, *n.* (16c) The quality that makes something (as a witness or some evidence) worthy of belief. — **credible,** *adj.*

credible evidence. See EVIDENCE.

credible witness. See WITNESS.

credit, *n.* (16c) **1.** Belief; trust <the jury gave credit to Benson's version>. **2.** One's ability to borrow money; the faith in one's ability to pay debts <a customer with good credit>. **3.** The time that a seller gives the buyer to make the payment that is due <30 days' credit>. **4.** The availability of funds either from a financial institution or under a letter of credit <the bank extended a line of credit to the customer>.

> *bank credit.* Credit that a bank makes available to a borrower.

> *consumer credit.* Credit extended to an individual to facilitate the purchase of consumer goods and services.

> *installment credit.* Consumer credit scheduled to be repaid in two or more payments, usu. at regular intervals. ● The seller ordinarily exacts finance charges.

> *noninstallment credit.* Consumer credit arranged to be repaid in a single payment. ● Examples include doctors' and plumbers' bills.

> *revolving credit.* A consumer-credit arrangement that allows the borrower to buy goods or

secure loans on a continuing basis as long as the outstanding balance does not exceed a specified limit. — Also termed *open credit; revolving charge account.* Cf. *revolver loan* under LOAN.

5. LETTER OF CREDIT <the bank issued a credit in favor of the exporter>. **6.** A deduction from an amount due; an accounting entry reflecting an addition to revenue or net worth <confirm that the credit was properly applied to my account>. Cf. DEBIT. **7.** TAX CREDIT <the $500 credit reduced their income-tax liability by $500>.

> *accumulated-earnings credit.* *Tax.* A deduction allowed in arriving at a corporation's accumulated taxable income. ● It offsets the base on which the tax is assessed by reducing the taxable base by the greater of $250,000 or the accumulated earnings retained for the reasonable needs of the corporation, reduced by the net capital gain. IRC (26 USCA) § 535. See *accumulated-earnings tax* under TAX.

credit, *vb.* (17c) **1.** To believe <the jury did not credit this testimony>. **2.** To enter (as an amount) on the credit side of an account <the account was credited with $500>.

creditable. 1. Worthy of being believed; credible <creditable evidence>. **2.** Capable of being ascribed or credited <creditable service time>. **3.** Reputable; respectable <creditable witness>.

credit balance. *Accounting.* The status of an account when the sum of the credit entries exceeds the sum of the debit entries.

credit bureau. (1874) An organization that compiles information on people's creditworthiness and publishes it in the form of reports that are used chiefly by merchants and service-providers who deal directly with customers. ● The practices of credit bureaus are regulated by federal (and often state) law. Most bureaus are members of the Associated Credit Bureaus of America. Cf. CREDIT-REPORTING BUREAU.

credit card. An identification card used to obtain items on credit, usu. on a revolving basis. See *revolving credit* under CREDIT. Cf. DEBIT CARD.

credit-card cramming. 1. A credit-card issuer's practice of charging consumers for optional goods or services that the consumers have not agreed to pay or do not understand. ● For example, the credit-card crammer may offer the consumer a free service for a limited period without making it clear that if the service is not canceled when the period ends, it will be automatically renewed for a fee. **2.** A single act of charging a consumer's credit card without authorization, particularly for goods or services that the consumer did not agree to or receive.

credit-card crime. (1970) The offense of using a credit card to purchase something with knowledge that (1) the card is stolen or forged, (2) the card has been revoked or canceled, or (3) the card's use is unauthorized.

credit freeze. See FREEZE.

credit insurance. See INSURANCE.

credit life insurance. See LIFE INSURANCE.

credit line. See LINE OF CREDIT.

credit memorandum. A document issued by a seller to a buyer confirming that the seller has credited (i.e., reduced) the buyer's account because of an error, return, or allowance.

credit mobilier. A company or association that carries on a banking business by making loans on the security of personal property.

creditor. (15c) **1.** One to whom a debt is owed; one who gives credit for money or goods. — Also termed *debtee.* **2.** A person or entity with a definite claim against another, esp. a claim that is capable of adjustment and liquidation. **3.** *Bankruptcy.* A person or entity having a claim against the debtor predating the order for relief concerning the debtor. **4.** *Roman law.* One to whom any obligation is owed, whether contractual or otherwise. Cf. DEBTOR.

attaching creditor. A creditor who has caused an attachment to be issued and levied on the debtor's property.

bond creditor. A creditor whose debt is secured by a bond.

certificate creditor. A creditor of a municipal corporation who receives a certificate of indebtedness rather than payment because the municipality cannot pay the debt. Cf. *warrant creditor.*

conditional creditor. *Civil law.* A creditor who has either a future right of action or a right of action in expectancy.

creditor at large. A creditor who has not established the debt by reducing it to judgment, or who has not otherwise secured a lien on any of the debtor's property. See *unsecured creditor.*

domestic creditor. A creditor who resides in the same state or country as the debtor or the debtor's property.

double creditor. A creditor who has a lien on two funds. Cf. *single creditor.*

execution creditor. A judgment creditor who has caused an execution to issue on the judgment.

foreign creditor. A creditor who resides in a different state or country from that of the debtor or the debtor's property.

gap creditor. *Bankruptcy.* A creditor who extends credit to, lends money to, or has a claim arise against the debtor in the period between the filing of an involuntary bankruptcy petition and the entry of the order for relief. ● Under the Bankruptcy Code, a gap creditor's claim receives second priority, immediately below administrative claims. 11 USCA §§ 502(f), 507(a)(2).

general creditor. See *unsecured creditor.*

hypothetical creditor. *Bankruptcy.* An actual or code-created judicial-lien creditor or bona fide purchaser who establishes a bankruptcy trustee's status under the Bankruptcy Code's priority scheme, claiming property through the debtor at the time of the bankruptcy filing. 11 USCA § 544. — Also termed *hypothetical lien creditor.*

joint creditor. A creditor who is entitled, along with another creditor, to demand payment from a debtor.

judgment creditor. See JUDGMENT CREDITOR.

junior creditor. A creditor whose claim accrued after that of another creditor; a creditor who holds a debt that is subordinate to another's.

known creditor. A creditor whose identity or claim is either known or reasonably ascertainable by the debtor. ● Known creditors are entitled to notice of the debtor's bankruptcy or corporate dissolution, as well as notice of any deadline for filing proofs of claim.

lien creditor. A creditor whose claim is secured by a lien on the debtor's property. UCC § 9-102(a)(52).

preferred creditor. A creditor with a superior right to payment, such as a holder of a perfected security interest as compared to a holder of an unsecured claim.

principal creditor. A creditor whose claim or demand greatly exceeds the claims of other creditors.

prior creditor. A creditor who is given priority in payment from the debtor's assets.

secondary creditor. A creditor whose claim is subordinate to a preferred creditor's.

secured creditor. A creditor who has the right, on the debtor's default, to proceed against collateral and apply it to the payment of the debt. UCC § 9-102-(a)(72). — Also termed *secured party.*

single creditor. In the marshaling of assets, a creditor with a lien on one fund. See RULE OF MARSHALING ASSETS. Cf. *double creditor.*

specialty creditor. A creditor to whom an heir is liable for a decedent's debts to the extent of the land inherited. ● Historically, unless the creditor obtained a judgment against the debtor before the debtor's death, the creditor's right of action on the debt was limited to the decedent's lawful heir. If the debtor devised the land to a stranger, the creditor's claim was defeated. See HEIR (1).

subsequent creditor. A creditor whose claim comes into existence after a given fact or transaction, such as the recording of a deed or the execution of a voluntary conveyance.

unsecured creditor. A creditor who, upon giving credit, takes no rights against specific property of the debtor. — Also termed *general creditor.* See *creditor at large.*

warrant creditor. A creditor of a municipal corporation who is given a municipal warrant for the amount of the claim because the municipality lacks the funds to pay the debt. Cf. *certificate creditor.*

creditor beneficiary. See BENEFICIARY.

creditor's bill. (1826) An equitable suit in which a judgment creditor seeks to reach property that cannot be reached by the process available to enforce a judgment. — Also termed *creditor's suit.*

creditor's claim. See CLAIM (5).

creditors' committee. (1874) *Bankruptcy.* A committee comprising representatives of the creditors in a Chapter 11 proceeding, formed to negotiate the debtor's plan of reorganization. ● Generally, a committee has no fewer than 3 and no more than 11 members and serves as an advisory body. 11 USCA § 1102.

creditors' composition. See COMPOSITION (1).

creditors' meeting. See MEETING.

creditor's suit. See CREDITOR'S BILL.

credit plan. A financing arrangement under which a borrower and a lender agree to terms for a loan's repayment with interest, usu. in installments.

open-end credit plan. A plan under which a creditor reasonably expects repeated transactions, prescribes terms for those transactions, and includes a finance charge that may be periodically computed on the outstanding balance. 15 USCA § 1602(i).

credit rating. An evaluation of a potential borrower's ability to repay debt, prepared by a credit bureau at the request of a lender.

credit report. 1. A credit bureau's report on a person's financial status, usu. including the approximate amounts and locations of a person's bank accounts, charge accounts, loans, and other debts, bill-paying habits, defaults, bankruptcies, foreclosures, marital status, occupation, income, and lawsuits. See CREDIT BUREAU. **2.** The report of a credit-reporting bureau, usu. including highly personal information gathered through interviews with a person's friends, neighbors, and coworkers. See CREDIT-REPORTING BUREAU.

credit-reporting bureau. (1904) An organization that, on request, prepares investigative reports not just on people's creditworthiness but also on personal information gathered from various sources, including interviews with neighbors, friends, and coworkers. ● These reports are used chiefly by employers (for prospective employees), insurance companies (for applicants), and landlords (for prospective tenants). — Also termed *investigating bureau.* Cf. CREDIT BUREAU.

credit sale. See SALE.

credit service charge. See SERVICE CHARGE (2).

credit-shelter trust. See *bypass trust* under TRUST.

credit slip. A document that allows a store customer to either purchase another item or receive cash or credit for merchandise the customer has returned to the store.

credit union. A cooperative association that offers low-interest loans and other consumer banking services to persons sharing a common bond — often fellow employees and their family members. ● Most credit unions are regulated by the National Credit Union Administration. State-chartered credit unions are also subject to regulation by the chartering state, and they may be regulated by state banking boards.

creditworthy, *adj.* (1924) (Of a borrower) financially sound enough that a lender will extend credit in the belief default is unlikely; fiscally healthy. — **creditworthiness,** *n.*

creeping acquisition. See ACQUISITION.

creeping tender offer. See *creeping acquisition* under ACQUISITION.

C reorganization. See REORGANIZATION (2).

crescendo rental. See RENTAL.

cretion (**kree**-shən), *n.* [fr. Latin *cernere* "to decide"] *Roman law.* **1.** A method or form of accepting an inheritance by an heir who is appointed in a testament. ● Cretion usu. had to be declared within 100 days from the date an heir received notice of the appointment. **2.** The period within which an heir might decide whether to accept an inheritance. — Also termed (in Latin) *cretio* (**kree**-shee-oh). — **cretionary** (**kree**-shən-er-ee), *adj.*

crew member. See SEAMAN.

CRF. *abbr.* CRIMINAL-REFERRAL FORM.

crier (**krI**-ər). (15c) **1.** An officer of the court who makes public pronouncements as required by the court. Cf. BAILIFF (1). — Also termed *court crier.* **2.** An auctioneer. — Also spelled *cryer.*

crim. con. *abbr.* CRIMINAL CONVERSATION.

crime. (14c) An act that the law makes punishable; the breach of a legal duty treated as the subject-matter of a criminal proceeding. — Also termed *criminal wrong.* See OFFENSE (1).

administrative crime. (1943) An offense consisting of a violation of an administrative rule or regulation that carries with it a criminal sanction.

capital crime. See *capital offense* under OFFENSE (1).

commercial crime. (1900) A crime that affects commerce; esp., a crime directed toward the property or revenues of a commercial establishment. • Examples include robbery of a business, embezzlement, counterfeiting, forgery, prostitution, illegal gambling, and extortion. See 26 CFR § 403.38.

common-law crime. (1827) A crime that is punishable under the common law, rather than by force of statute. Cf. *statutory crime.*

complainantless crime. See *victimless crime.*

computer crime. (1971) A crime involving the use of a computer, such as sabotaging or stealing electronically stored data. — Also termed *cybercrime.*

consensual crime. See *victimless crime.*

constructive crime. A crime that is built up or created when a court enlarges a statute by altering or straining the statute's language, esp. to drawing unreasonable implications and inferences from it. — Also termed *implied crime; presumed crime.*

continuous crime. (1907) **1.** A crime that continues after an initial illegal act has been consummated; a crime that involves ongoing elements. • An example is illegal U.S. drug importation. The criminal act is completed not when the drugs enter the country, but when the drugs reach their final destination. **2.** A crime (such as driving a stolen vehicle) that continues over an extended period. Cf. *instantaneous crime.*

corporate crime. (1934) A crime committed by a corporation's representatives acting on its behalf. • Examples include price-fixing and consumer fraud. Although a corporation as an entity cannot commit a crime other than through its representatives, it can be named as a criminal defendant — Also termed *organizational crime.* Cf. *occupational crime.*

credit-card crime. See CREDIT-CARD CRIME.

crime against nature. See SODOMY.

crime against the environment. See ENVIRONMENTAL CRIME.

crime malum in se. See MALUM IN SE.

crime malum prohibitum. See MALUM PROHIBITUM.

crime of omission. (18c) An offense that carries as its material component the failure to act.

crime of passion. (18c) A crime committed in the heat of an emotionally charged moment, with no opportunity to reflect on what is happening. See HEAT OF PASSION.

crime of violence. See *violent crime.*

crime without victims. See *victimless crime.*

cybercrime. See *computer crime.*

economic crime. A nonphysical crime committed to obtain a financial gain or a professional advantage.

environmental crime. See ENVIRONMENTAL CRIME.

expressive crime. A crime committed for the sake of the crime itself, esp. out of frustration, rage, or other emotion rather than for financial gain. Cf. *instrumental crime.*

federal crime. See FEDERAL CRIME.

general-intent crime. A crime that involves performing a particular act without intending a further act or a further result.

hate crime. (1984) A crime motivated by the victim's race, color, ethnicity, religion, or national origin. • Certain groups have lobbied to expand the definition by statute to include a crime motivated by the victim's disability, gender, or sexual orientation. Cf. *hate speech* under SPEECH.

high crime. (17c) A crime that is very serious, though not necessarily a felony. • Under the U.S. Constitution, a government officer's commission of a "high crime" is, along with treason and bribery, grounds for removal from office. U.S. Const. art. II, § 4. See IMPEACHABLE OFFENSE.

honor crime. A crime motivated by a desire to punish a person who the perpetrator believes has injured a person's or group's sense of honor. • The term is most often applied to crimes committed against Muslim women by members of their own families for behavior that leads to perceived social harm, esp. loss of family honor. The term also extends to non-Muslims and covers many acts of violence, including assault, rape, infanticide, and murder. When the crime involves a death, it is also termed *honor killing.*

implied crime. See *constructive crime.*

inchoate crime. See *inchoate offense* under OFFENSE (1).

index crime. See *index offense* under OFFENSE (1).

infamous crime (**in**-fə-məs). (16c) **1.** At common law, a crime for which part of the punishment was infamy, so that one who committed it would be declared ineligible to serve on a jury, hold public office, or testify. • Examples are perjury, treason, and fraud. **2.** A crime punishable by imprisonment in a penitentiary. • The Fifth Amendment requires a grand-jury indictment for the prosecution of infamous (or capital) crimes, which include all federal felony offenses. See *indictable offense* under OFFENSE (1). Cf. *noninfamous crime.*

instantaneous crime. (1887) A crime that is fully completed by a single act, as arson or murder, rather than a series of acts. ● The statute of limitations for an instantaneous crime begins to run with its completion. Cf. *continuous crime.*

instrumental crime. A crime committed to further another end or result; esp., a crime committed to obtain money to purchase a good or service. Cf. *expressive crime.*

international crime. See INTERNATIONAL CRIME.

major crime. See FELONY (1).

noninfamous crime. A crime that does not qualify as an infamous crime. Cf. *infamous crime.*

occupational crime. A crime that a person commits for personal gain while on the job. Cf. *corporate crime.*

organizational crime. See *corporate crime.*

organized crime. See ORGANIZED CRIME.

personal-condition crime. See *status crime.*

personal crime. A crime (such as rape, robbery, or pickpocketing) that is committed against an individual's person.

political crime. See POLITICAL OFFENSE.

predatory crime. A crime that involves preying upon and victimizing individuals. ● Examples include robbery, rape, and carjacking.

preliminary crime. See *inchoate offense* under OFFENSE (1).

presumed crime. See *constructive crime.*

quasi-crime. (18c) *Hist.* **1.** An offense not subject to criminal prosecution (such as contempt or violation of a municipal ordinance) but for which penalties or forfeitures can be imposed. ● The term includes offenses that give rise to *qui tam* actions and forfeitures for the violation of a public duty. **2.** An offense for which someone other than the actual perpetrator is held liable, the perpetrator being presumed to act on the command of the responsible party. See *quasi-delict* (1) under DELICT.

serious crime. **1.** See *serious offense* under OFFENSE (1). **2.** See FELONY (1).

signature crime. (1974) A distinctive crime so similar in pattern, scheme, or modus operandi to previous crimes that it identifies a particular defendant as the perpetrator.

spontaneous crime. A criminal act that occurs suddenly and without premeditation in response to an unforeseen stimulus. ● For example, a husband who discovers his wife in bed with another man and shoots him could be said to have committed an effectively spontaneous crime.

status crime. (1961) A crime of which a person is guilty by being in a certain condition or of a specific character. ● An example of a status crime is vagrancy. — Also termed *status offense*; *personal-condition crime.*

statutory crime. (1940) A crime punishable by statute. Cf. *common-law crime.*

street crime. (1966) A crime generally directed against a person in public, such as mugging, theft, or robbery. — Also termed *visible crime.*

strict-liability crime. A crime that does not require a *mens rea* element, such as traffic offenses and illegal sales of intoxicating liquor.

substantive crime. See *substantive offense* under OFFENSE (1).

vice crime. A crime of immoral conduct, such as gambling or prostitution.

victimless crime. (1964) A crime that is considered to have no direct victim, usu. because only consenting adults are involved. ● Examples are possession of illicit drugs and deviant sexual intercourse between consenting adults. — Also termed *consensual crime*; *crime without victims*; *complainantless crime.*

violent crime. (18c) A crime that has as an element the use, attempted use, threatened use, or substantial risk of use of physical force against the person or property of another. 18 USCA § 16; USSG § 2E1.3. — Also termed *crime of violence.*

visible crime. See *street crime.*

war crime. See WAR CRIME.

white-collar crime. See WHITE-COLLAR CRIME.

crime against humanity. *Int'l law.* A brutal crime that is not an isolated incident but that involves large and systematic actions, often cloaked with official authority, and that shocks the conscience of humankind. ● Among the specific crimes that fall within this category are mass murder, extermination, enslavement, deportation, and other inhumane acts perpetrated against a population, whether in wartime or not. *See* Statute of the International Criminal Court, art. 3 (37 ILM 999).

crime against international law. See CRIME AGAINST THE LAW OF NATIONS.

crime against peace. *Int'l law.* An international crime in which the offenders plan, prepare, initiate, or wage a war of aggression or a war in violation of international peace treaties, agreements, or assurances.

crime against the law of nations. *Int'l law.* **1.** A crime punishable under internationally prescribed criminal law or defined by an international convention and required to be made punishable under the criminal law of the member states. **2.** A crime punishable under international law; an act that is internationally agreed to be of a criminal nature, such as genocide, piracy, or engaging in the slave trade. — Also termed *crime against international law*.

crime against the person. See CRIMES AGAINST PERSONS.

crime-fraud exception. (1973) The doctrine that neither the attorney–client privilege nor the attorney-work-product privilege protects attorney–client communications that are in furtherance of a current or planned crime or fraud. *Clark v. United States,* 289 U.S. 1, 53 S.Ct. 465 (1933); *In re Grand Jury Subpoena Duces Tecum,* 731 F.2d 1032 (2d Cir. 1984).

crime insurance. See INSURANCE.

crime malum in se. See MALUM IN SE.

crime malum prohibitum. See MALUM PROHIBI-TUM.

crimen (krī-mən), *n.* [Latin] **1.** An accusation or charge of a crime. **2.** A crime. Pl. *crimina* (krim-ə-nə).

crimen expilatae hereditatis (krī-mən eks-pə-**lay**-tee hə-red-i-**tay**-tis). *Roman law.* A false claimant's willful spoliation of an inheritance.

crimen falsi (krī-mən **fal**-sī *or* **fawl**-sī). [Latin "the crime of falsifying"] **1.** A crime in the nature of perjury. — Also termed *falsum.* **2.** Any other offense that involves some element of dishonesty or false statement. *See* Fed. R. Evid. 609(a)(2).

crimen feloniae imposuit (krī-mən fə-**loh**-nee-ee im-**poz**-yə-wit). To accuse or charge with a felony.

crimen furti (krī-mən **fər**-tī). [Latin "the crime of stealing"] See THEFT.

crimen incendii (krī-mən in-**sen**-dee-ī). [Latin "the crime of burning"] See ARSON.

crimen innominatum (krī-mən i-nom-ə-**nay**-təm). [Latin "the nameless crime"] See SOD-OMY.

crimen majestatis (krī-mən maj-ə-**stay**-tis). [Latin "crime against majesty"] *Hist.* High treason; any crime against the king's person or dignity; LESE MAJESTY. ● Under Roman law, *crimen majestatis* denoted any enterprise by a Roman citizen or other person against the republic or the emperor. — Also termed *crimen laesae majestatis.* See LESE MAJESTY.

crimen plagii (krī-mən **play**-jee-ī). [Latin] *Roman law.* See PLAGIUM.

crimen raptus (krī-mən **rap**-təs). [Latin "the crime of rape"] See RAPE.

crimen repetundarum (krī-mən rep-ə-tən-**dair**-əm). [Latin "accusation of (money) to be repaid"] *Roman law.* **1.** A charge of extortion brought against a Roman provincial governor. **2.** Any act of misgovernment or oppression on the part of a magistrate or official.

crimen roberiae (krī-mən rə-**beer**-ee-ee). [Latin "the crime of robbery"] ROBBERY.

crime of omission. See CRIME.

crime of passion. See CRIME.

crime of violence. See *violent crime* under CRIME.

crimes against persons. (1827) A category of criminal offenses in which the perpetrator uses or threatens to use force. ● Examples include murder, rape, aggravated assault, and robbery. — Also termed *crimes against the person.* Cf. *offense against the person* under OFFENSE (1).

crimes against property. (1827) A category of criminal offenses in which the perpetrator seeks to derive an unlawful benefit from — or do damage to — another's property without the use or threat of force. ● Examples include burglary, theft, and arson (even though arson may result in injury or death). — Also termed *property crimes.* Cf. *offense against property* under OFFENSE (1).

crimes against the person. See CRIMES AGAINST PERSONS.

crime score. (1952) A number assigned from an established scale, indicating the relative seriousness of an offense based on the nature of the injury or the extent of property damage. ● Prosecutors use crime scores and defendant scores to promote uniform treatment of similar cases and to assess which cases need extensive pretrial preparation. Cf. DEFENDANT SCORE.

crime statistics. Figures compiled by a governmental agency to show the incidence of various types of crime within a defined geographic area during a specified time.

crime without victims. See *victimless crime* under CRIME.

criminal, *adj.* (15c) **1.** Having the character of a crime; in the nature of a crime <criminal mischief>. **2.** Connected with the administration of penal justice <the criminal courts>.

criminal, *n.* (17c) **1.** One who has committed a criminal offense. **2.** One who has been convicted of a crime.

career criminal. See RECIDIVIST.

dangerous criminal. (18c) A criminal who has either committed a violent crime or used force in trying to escape from custody.

episodic criminal. (1976) **1.** A person who commits crimes sporadically. **2.** A person who commits crimes only during periods of intense stress, as in the heat of passion.

habitual criminal. See RECIDIVIST.

state criminal. **1.** A person who has committed a crime against the state (such as treason); a political criminal. **2.** A person who has committed a crime under state law.

criminal action. See ACTION (4).

criminal anarchy. See ANARCHY.

criminal anthropology. See CRIMINOLOGY.

criminal assault. See ASSAULT.

criminal attempt. See ATTEMPT.

criminal bankruptcy. See *bankruptcy fraud* under FRAUD.

criminal battery. See BATTERY (1).

criminal behavior. Conduct that causes social harm and is defined and punished by law.

criminal capacity. See CAPACITY (3).

criminal charge. See CHARGE (1).

criminal code. See PENAL CODE.

criminal coercion. See COERCION.

criminal conspiracy. See CONSPIRACY.

criminal contempt. See CONTEMPT.

criminal conversation. *Archaic.* A tort action for adultery, brought by a husband against a third party who engaged in sexual intercourse with his wife. ● Criminal conversation has been abolished in most jurisdictions. — Abbr. crim. con. See HEARTBALM STATUTE.

criminal court. See COURT.

criminal-court judge. See JUDGE.

criminal damage to property. (1946) **1.** Injury, destruction, or substantial impairment to the use of property (other than by fire or explosion) without the consent of a person having an interest in the property. **2.** Injury, destruction, or substantial impairment to the use of property (other than by fire or explosion) with the intent to injure or defraud an insurer or lienholder. Cf. ARSON.

criminal defendant. One who is accused in a criminal proceeding.

criminal desertion. See DESERTION.

criminal forfeiture. See FORFEITURE.

criminal fraud. See FRAUD.

criminal homicide. See HOMICIDE.

criminal infringement. See INFRINGEMENT.

criminal instrument. (1901) **1.** Something made or adapted for criminal use. Model Penal Code § 5.06(1)(a). **2.** Something commonly used for criminal purposes and possessed under circumstances showing an unlawful purpose. Model Penal Code § 5.06(1)(b). — Also termed *instrument of crime.*

criminal-instrumentality rule. (1942) The principle that when a criminal act is committed, that act — rather than the victim's negligence that made the crime possible — will be considered to be the crime's proximate cause.

criminal intent. 1. See INTENT (1). **2.** MENS REA.

criminalism. 1. A pathological tendency toward criminality. **2.** *Archaic.* The branch of psychiatry dealing with habitual criminals.

criminalist (**krim**-ə-nəl-ist). **1.** A person who practices criminalistics as a profession. **2.** *Archaic.* One versed in criminal law. **3.** *Archaic.* A psychiatrist who treats criminals. **4.** *Archaic.* A habitual criminal.

criminalistics (krim-ə-nə-**lis**-tiks), *n.* (1943) The science of crime detection, usu. involving the subjection of physical evidence to laboratory analysis, including ballistic testing, blood-fluid and tissue analysis, and other tests. Cf. CRIMINOLOGY. — **criminalistic,** *adj.*

criminality (krim-ə-**nal**-ə-tee). (17c) **1.** The state or quality of being criminal. **2.** An act or practice that constitutes a crime. See DOUBLE CRIMINALITY.

criminalization (**krim**-ə-nəl-ə-**zay**-shən), *n.* (1945) **1.** The act or an instance of making a previously lawful act criminal, usu. by passing a statute. Cf. DECRIMINALIZATION; CIVILIZATION. **2.** The process by which a person develops into a criminal.

criminalize (**krim**-ə-nəl-iz), *vb.* To make illegal; to outlaw.

criminal jurisdiction. See JURISDICTION.

criminal justice. (16c) **1.** The methods by which a society deals with those who are accused of having committed crimes. See LAW ENFORCEMENT (1). Cf. CIVIL JUSTICE. **2.** The field of study pursued by those seeking to enter law enforcement as a profession. ● Many colleges offer degrees in criminal justice, typically after two to four years of study. — Also termed (in sense 2) *police science; law enforcement.*

criminal-justice system. (1929) The collective institutions through which an accused offender passes until the accusations have been disposed of or the assessed punishment concluded. ● The system typically has three components: law enforcement (police, sheriffs, marshals), the judicial process (judges, prosecutors, defense lawyers), and corrections (prison officials, probation officers, and parole officers). — Also termed *law-enforcement system.*

criminal law. (18c) The body of law defining offenses against the community at large, regulating how suspects are investigated, charged, and tried, and establishing punishments for convicted offenders. — Also termed *penal law.*

criminal lawyer. See LAWYER.

criminal libel. See LIBEL.

criminally negligent homicide. See *negligent homicide* under HOMICIDE.

criminal mischief. See MALICIOUS MISCHIEF.

criminal neglect of family. See NONSUPPORT.

criminal negligence. See NEGLIGENCE.

criminal nonsupport. See NONSUPPORT.

criminal offense. See OFFENSE (1).

criminal plea. See PLEA (1).

criminal policy. (1893) The branch of criminal science concerned with protecting against crime. • It draws on information provided by criminology, and its subjects for investigation are (1) the appropriate measures of social organization for preventing harmful activities, and (2) the treatment to be accorded to those who have caused harm, i.e., whether the offenders should receive warnings, supervised probation, or medical treatment, or whether they should suffer serious deprivations of life or liberty such as imprisonment or capital punishment.

criminal possession. See POSSESSION.

criminal procedure. (18c) The rules governing the mechanisms under which crimes are investigated, prosecuted, adjudicated, and punished. • It includes the protection of accused persons' constitutional rights.

criminal proceeding. See PROCEEDING.

criminal process. See PROCESS.

criminal prosecution. See PROSECUTION (2).

criminal protector. (1978) An accessory after the fact to a felony; one who aids or harbors a wrongdoer after the commission of a crime.

criminal-referral form. A form once required by federal regulatory authorities (from 1988 to 1996) for reporting every instance when a bank employee or affiliate committed or aided in committing a crime such as credit-card fraud, employee theft, or check-kiting. • This form, like the suspicious-transaction report, has since been superseded by the suspicious-activity report. — Abbr. CRF. See SUSPICIOUS-ACTIVITY REPORT.

criminal registration. See REGISTRATION (1).

criminal responsibility. 1. See RESPONSIBILITY (2). 2. See RESPONSIBILITY (3).

criminal sanction. See SANCTION.

criminal science. (1891) The study of crime with a view to discovering the causes of criminality, devising the most effective methods of reducing crime, and perfecting the means for dealing with those who have committed crimes. • The three main branches of criminal science are criminology, criminal policy, and criminal law.

criminal sexual conduct in the first degree. See FIRST-DEGREE SEXUAL CONDUCT.

criminal solicitation. See SOLICITATION (2).

criminal statute. See STATUTE.

criminal syndicalism. See SYNDICALISM.

criminal term. See TERM (5).

criminal trespass. See TRESPASS.

criminal wrong. See CRIME.

criminate, *vb.* See INCRIMINATE.

crimination (krim-ə-**nay**-shən), *n.* **1.** INCRIMINATION. **2.** An accusation or strong censure.

criminative (**krim**-ə-nay-tiv), *adj.* Of, relating to, or involving incrimination or accusation. Cf. INFIRMATIVE.

criminogenic (krim-ə-nə-**jen**-ik), *adj.* Tending to cause crime or criminality. — **criminogenesis,** *n.*

criminology (krim-ə-**nol**-ə-jee), *n.* (1872) The study of crime and criminal punishment as social phenomena; the study of the causes of crime and the treatment of offenders, comprising (1) criminal biology, which examines causes that may be found in the mental and physical constitution of an offender (such as hereditary tendencies and physical defects), and (2) criminal sociology, which deals with inquiries into the effects of environment as a cause of criminality. — Also termed *criminal anthropology.* Cf. CRIMINALISTICS; PENOLOGY. — **criminological** (krim-ə-nə-**loj**-ə-kəl), *adj.* — **criminologist,** *n.*

   comparative criminology. The scholarly study of the similarities and differences between the criminal-justice systems of different nations.

   environmental criminology. The scholarly study of areas where crime occurs and of why offenders are active in those areas. — Also termed *geography of crime; ecology of crime.*

criss-cross agreement. See *cross-purchase agreement* under AGREEMENT.

crit. (1985) An adherent to the critical-legal-studies school of thought. — Also termed *CLSer; Critic; critter.*

   fem-crit. A feminist adherent of critical legal studies.

critical evidence. See EVIDENCE.

Critical Legal Studies. (1978) **1.** A school of thought advancing the idea that the legal system perpetuates the status quo in terms of economics, race, and gender by using manipulable concepts and by creating an imaginary world of social harmony regulated by law. • The Marxist wing of this school focuses on socioeconomic issues. Fem-crits emphasize gender hierarchy, whereas critical race theorists focus on racial subordination. See *fem-crit* under CRIT; CRITICAL RACE THEORY.

2. The body of work produced by adherents to this school of thought. — Abbr. CLS.

critical limitation. *Patents.* A limitation essential either to the operativeness of an invention or to the patentability of a patent claim for the invention.

Critical Race Theory. (1989) **1.** A reform movement within the legal profession, particularly within academia, whose adherents believe that the legal system has disempowered racial minorities. ● The term first appeared in 1989. Critical race theorists observe that even if the law is couched in neutral language, it cannot be neutral because those who fashioned it had their own subjective perspectives that, once enshrined in law, have disadvantaged minorities and even perpetuated racism. **2.** The body of work produced by adherents to this theory. — Abbr. CRT.

critical stage. (1962) *Criminal procedure.* A point in a criminal prosecution when the accused's rights or defenses might be affected by the absence of legal representation. ● Under the Sixth Amendment, a critical stage triggers the accused's right to appointed counsel. Examples of critical stages include preliminary hearings, jury selection, and (of course) trial. Cf. ACCUSATORY STAGE.

critter. See CRIT.

crop insurance. See INSURANCE.

crop rent. See RENT (1).

crops. Products that are grown, raised, and harvested. ● Crops usu. are from the soil, but fruit grown on trees are also considered crops.

   annual crops. **1.** Crops that must be planted each year, such as cotton, wheat, barley, corn, carrots, potatoes, and melons. **2.** Crops for which the produce in any single year is mainly the result of attention and care exerted in the same agricultural year, such as hops and sugar cane.

   away-going crops. A tenant's crops that were sown and will not be ready to harvest before the tenancy expires. ● The tenant retains the ownership of the crop after the tenancy expires.

   basic crops. Crops (such as wheat and corn) that are usu. subject to government-price supports.

   growing crops. Crops that are in the process of growth. ● Growing crops are goods under UCC § 2-105(1). Judicial decisions vary on the growth stage at which a crop becomes a growing crop and on whether pasturage grass is a growing crop. Cf. FARM PRODUCT.

   standing crops. Crops that have not been harvested or otherwise severed from the land.

cross, *n.* **1.** CROSS-EXAMINATION. **2.** A sale of a large amount of publicly traded stock between two private parties. ● Although the transaction does not happen on the exchange floor, it typically requires exchange permission.

cross-action. **1.** See ACTION (4). **2.** See CROSS-CLAIM.

cross-appeal. See APPEAL.

cross-bill. See BILL (2).

cross-claim, *n.* (1825) A claim asserted between co-defendants or coplaintiffs in a case and that relates to the subject of the original claim or counterclaim. *See* Fed. R. Civ. P. 13(g). — Also termed *cross-action; cross-suit.* Cf. COUNTERCLAIM. — **cross-claim,** *vb.* — **cross-claimant,** *n.*

cross-collateral. See COLLATERAL.

cross-collateral clause. (1965) An installment-contract provision allowing the seller, if the buyer defaults, to repossess not only the particular item sold but also every other item bought from the seller on which a balance remained due when the last purchase was made. — Also termed *dragnet clause.*

cross-collateralization. See *cross-collateral* under COLLATERAL.

cross-complaint. (1854) **1.** A claim asserted by a defendant against another party to the action. — Also termed (in some jurisdictions) *cross-petition.* **2.** A claim asserted by a defendant against a person not a party to the action for a matter relating to the subject of the action.

cross-default clause. (1979) A contractual provision under which default on one debt obligation triggers default on another obligation.

cross-defendant. The party against whom a cross-claim is asserted. Cf. CROSS-PLAINTIFF.

cross-demand. See DEMAND (1).

crossed check. See CHECK.

cross-elasticity of demand. *Antitrust.* A relationship between two products, usu. substitutes for each other, in which a price change for one product affects the price of the other.

cross-error. See ERROR (2).

cross-examination, *n.* (18c) The questioning of a witness at a trial or hearing by the party opposed to the party who called the witness to testify. ● The purpose of cross-examination is to discredit a witness before the fact-finder in any of several ways, as by bringing out contradictions and improbabilities in earlier testimony, by suggesting doubts to the witness, and by trapping the witness into admissions that weaken the testimony. The cross-examiner is typically allowed to ask leading questions but is traditionally limited to matters covered on direct examination and to credibility issues. — Also termed *cross-interrogation.* Cf. DIRECT EXAMINATION; RECROSS-EXAMINATION. — **cross-examine,** *vb.*

cross-interrogatory. See INTERROGATORY.

cross-license. See LICENSE.

cross-marriage. See MARRIAGE (1).

cross-motion. See MOTION (1).

cross-offer, *n.* (1931) *Contracts.* An offer made to another in ignorance that the offeree has made the same offer to the offeror. — **cross-offer,** *vb.* — **cross-offeror,** *n.*

cross-petition. See CROSS-COMPLAINT.

cross-plaintiff. The party asserting a cross-claim. Cf. CROSS-DEFENDANT.

cross-purchase agreement. See AGREEMENT.

cross-purchase buy-sell agreement. 1. BUY–SELL AGREEMENT (1). **2.** A partnership insurance plan in which each partner individually buys and maintains enough insurance on the life or lives of other partners to purchase a deceased or expelled partner's equity.

cross-question. See QUESTION (1).

cross-rate. The exchange rate between two currencies expressed as the ratio of two foreign exchange rates in terms of a common third currency (usu. the U.S. dollar). ● Foreign-exchange-rate dealers use cross-rate tables to look for arbitrage opportunities. See ARBITRAGE.

cross-reference, *n.* An explicit citation to a related provision within the same or a closely related document; esp., in a patent application the explicit citation in a continuing patent application to all interrelated applications, back to the original filing. ● A cross-reference alone does not incorporate the disclosure of the parent application. Cf. INCORPORATION BY REFERENCE (1), (2). — **cross-reference,** *vb.*

cross-remainder. See REMAINDER.

cross-stream guaranty. See GUARANTY.

cross-suit. See CROSS-CLAIM.

Crown. *English law.* The sovereign in his or her official capacity as a governing power. See KING; QUEEN (1).

Crown case. *English law.* A criminal action.

Crown Court. An English court having jurisdiction over major criminal cases. ● Crown Courts date from 1971, when they assumed the criminal jurisdiction of the Assize Courts and all the jurisdiction of the Courts of Quarter Sessions.

crown jewel. A company's most valuable asset, esp. as valued when the company is the subject of a hostile takeover. ● A common antitakeover device is for the target company to sell its crown jewel to a third party so that the company will be less attractive to an unfriendly suitor.

crown-jewel defense. An antitakeover device in which the target company agrees to sell its most valuable assets to a third party if a hostile bid is tendered, so that the company will be less attractive to an unfriendly suitor. Cf. SCORCHED-EARTH DEFENSE; PAC-MAN DEFENSE.

Crown land. See LAND.

Crown loan. See LOAN.

CRS. *abbr.* See CONGRESSIONAL RESEARCH SERVICE.

CRT. *abbr.* **1.** CRITICAL RACE THEORY. **2.** See *charitable-remainder trust* under TRUST.

crucial evidence. See *critical evidence* under EVIDENCE.

cruel and abusive treatment. See ABUSE (2).

cruel and inhumane treatment. See *extreme cruelty* under CRUELTY.

cruel and unusual punishment. See PUNISHMENT.

cruelty. (13c) The intentional and malicious infliction of mental or physical suffering on a living creature, esp. a human; abusive treatment; outrage. Cf. ABUSE; INHUMAN TREATMENT; INDIGNITY.

cruelty to a child. See *child abuse* under ABUSE.

cruelty to animals. A malicious or criminally negligent act that causes an animal to suffer pain or death.

extreme cruelty. (17c) As a ground for divorce, one spouse's physical violence toward the other spouse, or conduct that destroys or severely impairs the other spouse's mental health. — Also termed *cruel and inhumane treatment.* Cf. ABUSE (2).

legal cruelty. (18c) Cruelty that will justify granting a divorce to the injured party; specif. conduct by one spouse that endangers the life, person, or health of the other spouse, or creates a reasonable apprehension of bodily or mental harm.

mental cruelty. (1898) As a ground for divorce, one spouse's course of conduct (not involving actual violence) that creates such anguish that it endangers the life, physical health, or mental health of the other spouse. See EMOTIONAL DISTRESS.

physical cruelty. (1874) As a ground for divorce, actual personal violence committed by one spouse against the other.

cruelty to a child. See *child abuse* under ABUSE.

cruelty to children. See *child abuse* under ABUSE.

Crummey power. The right of a beneficiary of a Crummey trust to withdraw gifts made to the trust up to a maximum amount (often the lesser of the annual exclusion or the value of the gift made to the trust) for a certain period after the gift is made. ● The precise characteristics of a

Crummey power are established by the settlor of a Crummey trust. Typically, the power is exercisable for 30 days after the gift is made and permits withdrawals up to $5,000 or 5% of the value of the trust. A beneficiary may allow the power to lapse without making any demand for distribution. See *Crummey trust* under TRUST; *annual exclusion* under EXCLUSION.

Crummey trust. See TRUST.

cryer. See CRIER.

CSAAS. *abbr.* CHILD-SEXUAL-ABUSE-ACCOMMODATION SYNDROME.

CSE agency. *abbr.* CHILD-SUPPORT-ENFORCEMENT AGENCY.

CSREES. *abbr.* COOPERATIVE STATE RESEARCH, EDUCATION, AND EXTENSION SERVICE.

CSV. See *cash surrender value* under VALUE (2).

c.t.a. *abbr.* See *administration cum testamento annexo* under ADMINISTRATION.

Ct. Cl. *abbr.* Court of Claims. See UNITED STATES COURT OF FEDERAL CLAIMS.

cucking stool. See CASTIGATORY.

cui in vita (kɪ [*or* kwɪ *or* kwee] in-**vɪ**-tə). [Law Latin "to whom in the life"] *Hist.* A writ of entry enabling a woman to recover land that she had held in fee but that her deceased husband had sold without her permission. • It is so called from the words of the writ: *cui ipsa in vita sua contradicere non potuit* ("whom she, in his lifetime, could not gainsay"). — Also termed *sur cui in vita*.

cujus contrarium est verum (k[y]oo-jəs kən-**trair**-ee-əm est **veer**-əm). [Latin] *Hist.* The contrary of which is the truth.

culpa (**kəl**-pə). [Latin] **1.** *Roman & civil law.* Fault, neglect, or negligence; unintentional wrong. See NEGLIGENCE. (1); DOLUS (1). **2.** *Roman law.* Conduct that made a party to a contract, or quasi-contract, liable to the other party.

lata culpa (**lay**-tə **kəl**-pə). [Latin "grave fault"] Gross negligence amounting to bad faith (*dolus*). • This phrase occurs most commonly in bailment law and in the law of the transport of persons. — Also termed *culpa lata*. See *gross negligence* under NEGLIGENCE.

levis culpa (**lee**-vis **kəl**-pə). [Latin "slight fault"] **1.** Ordinary negligence. **2.** Failure to act as the ideal *paterfamilias* should. — Also termed *culpa levis; culpa levis in concreto*. See *ordinary negligence* under NEGLIGENCE.

levissima culpa (lə-**vis**-ə-mə **kəl**-pə). [Latin "the slightest fault"] Slight negligence. — Also termed *culpa levissima*. See *slight negligence* under NEGLIGENCE.

culpability (kəl-pə-**bil**-ə-tee), *n.* Blameworthiness; the quality of being culpable. • Except in cases of absolute liability, criminal culpability requires a showing that the person acted purposely, knowingly, recklessly, or negligently with respect to each material element of the offense. See Model Penal Code § 2.02.

culpable (**kəl**-pə-bəl), *adj.* (14c) **1.** Guilty; blameworthy. **2.** Involving the breach of a duty.

culpable accident. See ACCIDENT.

culpable homicide. 1. See HOMICIDE. **2.** See MANSLAUGHTER.

culpable intoxication. See *voluntary intoxication* under INTOXICATION.

culpable neglect. See NEGLECT.

culpable negligence. See NEGLIGENCE.

culpa lata. See *lata culpa* under CULPA.

culpa levis. See *levis culpa* under CULPA.

culpa levis in concreto. See *levis culpa* under CULPA.

culpa levissima. See *levissima culpa* under CULPA.

culprit. (17c) **1.** A person accused or charged with the commission of a crime. **2.** A person who is guilty of a crime. • *Culprit* may be a running together of *cul*, shortened from the Latin *culpabilis* ("guilty"), and *prit*, from Old French *prest* ("ready"), two words formerly used to orally plead at the outset of a criminal case.

cultural agreement. *Int'l law.* A bilateral or multilateral agreement between nations for the purpose of furthering cultural or intellectual relations.

cultural property. *Int'l law.* Movable and immovable property that has cultural significance, whether in the nature of antiquities and monuments of a classical age or important modern items of fine arts, decorative arts, and architecture. • Some writers prefer the term *cultural heritage*, which more broadly includes intangible cultural things such as folklore, crafts, and skills.

cum dividend. With dividend. • Stocks purchased cum dividend entitle the buyer to any pending declared dividends. Cf. EX DIVIDEND.

Cumis counsel. See COUNSEL.

cum rights. With rights. • A *cum rights* purchaser of stock is entitled to rights that have been declared but not distributed, such as the right to purchase additional shares at a stated price. — Also termed *rights on*.

cum testamento annexo (kəm tes-tə-**men**-toh ə-**nek**-soh). See *administration cum testamento annexo* under ADMINISTRATION.

cumulative approach. See UNITY OF ART.

cumulative dividend. See DIVIDEND.

cumulative-effects doctrine. (1987) The rule that a transaction affecting interstate commerce in a trivial way may be taken together with other similar transactions to establish that the combined effect on interstate commerce is not trivial and can therefore be regulated under the Commerce Clause.

cumulative error. See ERROR (2).

cumulative-error analysis. Appellate scrutiny of whether all of the individual harmless errors made in a trial had the cumulative effect of prejudicing the outcome. ● If they did, the harmless errors taken together may amount to reversible error.

cumulative evidence. See EVIDENCE.

cumulative income bond. See *income bond* under BOND (3).

cumulative legacy. 1. See *accumulative legacy* under LEGACY. **2.** See *additional legacy* under LEGACY.

cumulatively harmful behavior. See HARMFUL BEHAVIOR.

cumulative offense. See OFFENSE (1).

cumulative preference share. See *cumulative preferred stock* under STOCK.

cumulative preferred stock. See STOCK.

cumulative punishment. See PUNISHMENT.

cumulative remedy. See REMEDY.

cumulative sentences. See *consecutive sentences* under SENTENCE.

cumulative stock. See *cumulative preferred stock* under STOCK.

cumulative supplement. See POCKET PART.

cumulative testimony. See TESTIMONY.

cumulative traverse. See TRAVERSE.

cumulative voting. See VOTING.

cumulative zoning. See ZONING.

CUPOS. *abbr.* A cohabiting unmarried person of the opposite sex. ● Although this term is intended to be synonymous with "POSSLQ" (a person of the opposite sex sharing living quarters), it is more literally precise because it excludes married persons. See POSSLQ.

cur. abbr. CURIA (3).

cura (**kyoor**-ə), *n.* [Latin] *Roman law.* A guardianship that protects the interests of minors who are between puberty and the age of 25, or incapacitated persons. Pl. *curae.*

cura furiosi (**kyoor**-ə fyoor-ee-**oh**-sɪ). A guardianship for an insane person who was mentally incapacitated.

cura minoris (**kyoor**-ə mi-**nor**-is). A form of guardianship for a minor under 25 whose capacity of action was complete, but whose judgment might be defective. Pl. *cura minorum.*

cura prodigi (**kyoor**-ə **prah**-də-jɪ). A form of guardianship for a spendthrift, usu. at the request of the person's agnatic family.

curate (**kyuur**-it). *Eccles. law.* **1.** A person in charge of a parish; a pastor. **2.** A member of the clergy who receives a stipend or salary to assist a vicar, rector, or pastor; an assistant to a parish priest.

curative admissibility. See ADMISSIBILITY.

curative-admissibility doctrine. (1975) The rule that otherwise inadmissible evidence will be admitted to rebut inadmissible evidence placed before the fact-finder by the adverse party. ● The doctrine applies when a motion to strike cannot cure the prejudice created by the adverse party.

curative instruction. See JURY INSTRUCTION.

curative statute. See STATUTE.

curator (**kyuur**-ə-tər *or* **kyuur**-ay-tər *or* kyuu-**ray**-tor), *n.* **1.** *Roman law.* (*ital*). A person who manages the affairs of another; a guardian. Pl. *curatores* (kyər-ə-**tor**-eez). See CURA.

curator ad litem (kyuu-**ray**-tor ad **lɪ**-təm). A curator appointed by a court to represent the interests of a youth, or an incapacitated or unborn person, during the proceedings before the court.

curator bonis (kyuu-**ray**-tor **boh**-nis). [Latin "a guardian of property"] **1.** *Roman law.* A guardian appointed to care for property, esp. for the benefit of creditors. **2.** *Scots law.* A person appointed by a court to manage an estate, esp. of a minor or an insane person. — Also termed *curator ad bona.*

curator bonorum (kyuu-**ray**-tor bə-**nor**-əm). A person appointed by a court to administer the estate of an insolvent person.

2. A temporary guardian or conservator appointed by a court to care for the property or person of a minor or incapacitated person.

interim curator. *Archaic.* A person appointed by a justice of the peace to hold a felon's property until a royal administrator could be assigned the task.

3. *Civil law.* A guardian who manages the estate of a minor, an absent person, or an incapacitated person. Pl. *curatores.*

curator ad hoc (kyuu-**ray**-tor ad **hok**). A court-appointed curator who manages a single matter or transaction. See *special guardian* under GUARDIAN.

4. *Parliamentary law.* An officer charged with custody of an organization's valuable property.

curator ad bona (kyuu-**ray**-tor ad **boh**-nə). See *curator bonis* under CURATOR (1).

curatorship. (16c) The office of a curator or guardian.

dative curatorship. See *dative tutorship* under TUTORSHIP.

curatrix (kyuu-**ray**-triks). *Archaic.* A female curator.

curb. See TRADING CURB.

cure, *n.* **1.** A seller's right under the UCC to correct a nonconforming delivery of goods, usu. within the contract period. **2.** *Maritime law.* Restoration to health after disease or injury; medical attention and nursing care during a period of convalescence. See MAINTENANCE AND CURE; MAXIMUM CURE. — **curative,** *adj.*

cure, *vb.* (14c) To remove legal defects or correct legal errors. • For example, curing title involves removing defects from title to unmarketable land so that title becomes marketable.

cure by verdict. See AIDER BY VERDICT.

curfew (**kər**-fyoo). **1.** *Hist.* A law requiring that all fires be extinguished at a certain time in the evening, usu. announced by the ringing of a bell. **2.** A regulation that forbids people (or certain classes of them, such as minors) from being outdoors or in vehicles during specified hours.

curia (**kyoor**-ee-ə), *n.* [Latin] **1.** *Roman law.* One of 30 divisions (three tribes of ten *curiae*) into which the Roman people were said to be divided by Romulus. See *comitia curiata* under COMITIA. **2.** *Roman law.* A legislative gathering, esp. of the Roman Senate; the building used for the gathering. **3.** *Hist.* A judicial tribunal held in the sovereign's palace; a royal court. — Abbr. *cur.* **4.** *Hist.* A court. **5.** The papal court, including its functionaries and officials.

curia advisari vult (**kyoor**-ee-ə ad-və-**sair**-ɪ **vəlt**). [Latin] The court will be advised; the court will consider. • This phrase signaled a court's decision to delay judgment pending further consideration. In England, the phrase is still used in all Court of Appeal decisions when the judgment is reserved; that is, not delivered after the hearing. — Abbr. *cur. adv. vult*; *c.a.v.*

Curia Regis (**kyoor**-ee-ə **ree**-jis). [Latin "king's court"] *Hist.* (*sometimes not cap.*) **1.** The chief court in early Norman England, established by William the Conqueror, • The *curia regis* was a body of advisers who traveled with the king, advising him on political matters and acting as an appellate court in important or complicated cases. Over time the functions of the *curia regis* became exclusively judicial in nature. — Also termed *King's Court*; *aula regis*. — Abbr. C.R. **2.** The sessions of this court.

curing title. The act of removing defects from a land title to make it marketable.

currency. (17c) An item (such as a coin, government note, or banknote) that circulates as a medium of exchange. See LEGAL TENDER.

blocked currency. Currency or bank deposits that, by government restriction, may be used only within the country where they are located.

fractional currency. Paper money worth less than one dollar; esp., the currency issued by the federal government from 1863 to 1876.

hard currency. Currency backed by reserves, esp. gold and silver reserves.

national currency. Currency approved by a national government and placed in circulation as a medium of exchange. See LEGAL TENDER.

postal currency. *Hist.* A fractional currency bearing a facsimile of postage stamps. • The United States Post Office issued these miniature notes in the 19th century until 1876. They were exchangeable for postage stamps, accepted for payments to the government in amounts up to $5, and could be exchanged for federal currency in multiples of $5. They were also used as small change when people hoarded coins during the Civil War. — Also termed *postage currency*.

soft currency. Currency not backed by reserves and therefore subject to sharp fluctuations in value.

United States currency. Currency issued under the authority of the federal government.

currency swap. See SWAP.

currency-transaction report. A deposit report that must be signed by a person who deposits $10,000 or more in a bank account. • The report is on blue paper, much like the skin color of the cartoon characters called Smurfs, so it is also termed (in slang) a *smurf.*

current account. See ACCOUNT.

current asset. See ASSET.

current-cost accounting. (1938) A method of measuring assets in terms of replacement cost. • This approach accounts for inflation by recognizing price changes in a company's assets and restating the assets in terms of their current cost.

current expense. See *operating expense* under EXPENSE.

current funds. See FUNDS (2).

current income. See INCOME.

current liability. 1. See *short-term debt* under DEBT. **2.** See LIABILITY.

current market value. (18c) The price at which an asset can be sold within the present accounting period.

current money. See MONEY.

current obligation. See OBLIGATION.

current revenue. See *current income* under INCOME.

current wages. See WAGE.

current yield. See YIELD.

curtesy (kər-tə-see). (16c) At common law, a husband's right, upon his wife's death, to a life estate in the land that his wife owned during their marriage, assuming that a child was born alive to the couple. • This right has been largely abolished. Traditionally, the full phrase was *estate by the curtesy of England* (or *Scotland*). — Also spelled (esp. in Scots law) *courtesy*. — Also termed *tenancy by the curtesy*. Cf. DOWER.

   curtesy consummate (kər-tə-see kən-**səm**-it *or* **kahn**-sə-mit). The interest the husband has in his wife's estate after her death.

   curtesy initiate (kər-tə-see i-**nish**-ee-it). The interest the husband has in his wife's estate after the birth of issue capable of inheriting, and before the death of the wife.

curtilage (kər-tə-lij). (14c) The land or yard adjoining a house, usu. within an enclosure. • Under the Fourth Amendment, the curtilage is an area usu. protected from warrantless searches. — Also termed (in Latin) *curtillium*. See OPEN-FIELDS DOCTRINE. Cf. MESSUAGE.

cushion. See EQUITY (7).

cushion bond. See BOND (3).

custodes pacis (kə-**stoh**-deez **pay**-sis). [Latin] *Hist.* Guardians (or *conservators*) of the peace. See PEACE OFFICER.

custodial account. See ACCOUNT.

custodial interference. *Family law.* **1.** The abduction of a child or the inducement of a minor child to leave the parent legally entitled to custody or not to return to the parent entitled to legal custody. **2.** Any hindrance to a parent's rightful access to a child. • The Restatement (Second) of Torts § 700 (1977) provides for an action in tort by the parent entitled to custody against one who, with knowledge that the parent does not consent, either takes the child or compels or induces the child to leave or not to return to the parent legally entitled to custody. — Also termed *custody interference*.

custodial interrogation. See INTERROGATION.

custodial parent. See PARENT.

custodial responsibility. *Family law.* Physical child custody and supervision, usu. including overnight responsibility for the child. • This term encompasses visitation and sole, joint, and shared custody. Both parents share responsibility for the child regardless of the amount of time they spend with the child. See CUSTODY.

custodial trust. See TRUST.

custodian, *n.* **1.** A person or institution that has charge or custody (of a child, property, papers, or other valuables); GUARDIAN. • In reference to a child, a custodian has either legal or physical custody. See CAREGIVER. **2.** *Bankruptcy.* A prepetition agent who has taken charge of any asset belonging to the debtor. 11 USCA § 101(11). — **custodianship,** *n.*

custodian bank. See BANK.

custody, *n.* (15c) **1.** The care and control of a thing or person for inspection, preservation, or security.

   constructive custody. (1822) Custody of a person (such as a parolee or probationer) whose freedom is controlled by legal authority but who is not under direct physical control.

   penal custody. Custody intended to punish a criminal offender.

   physical custody. See PHYSICAL CUSTODY (1).

   preventive custody. (1976) Custody intended to prevent further dangerous or criminal behavior.

   protective custody. (1929) **1.** The government's confinement of a person for that person's own security or well-being, such as a witness whose safety is in jeopardy or an incompetent person who may harm him- or herself or others. **2.** *Family law.* An arrangement intended to protect a child from abuse, neglect, or danger whereby the child is placed in the safety of a foster family after being removed from a home or from the custody of the person previously responsible for the child's care. **3.** An arrangement made by law-enforcement authorities to safeguard a person in a place other than the person's home because of criminal threats to harm the person.

2. *Family law.* The care, control, and maintenance of a child awarded by a court to a responsible adult. • Custody involves legal custody (decision-making authority) and physical custody (caregiving authority), and an award of custody usu. grants both rights. In a divorce or separation proceeding between the parents, the court usu. awards custody to one of them, unless both are found to be unfit, in which case the court may award custody to a third party, typically a relative. In a case involving parental dereliction, such as abuse or neglect, the court may award custody to the state for placing the child in foster care if no responsible relative or family friend is willing and able to care for the child. — Also termed *child custody; legal custody; managing conservatorship; parental functions.* See *managing conservator* (2) under CONSERVATOR; PARENTING PLAN.

   divided custody. (1905) An arrangement by which each parent has exclusive physical custody and full control of and responsibility for the child part of the time, with visitation rights in the other parent. • For example, a mother might have custody during the school year, and the father might have custody during the summer vacation.

joint custody. (1870) An arrangement by which both parents share the responsibility for and authority over the child at all times, although one parent may exercise primary physical custody. ● In most jurisdictions, there is a rebuttable presumption that joint custody is in the child's best interests. Joint-custody arrangements are favored unless there is so much animosity between the parents that the child or children will be adversely affected by a joint-custody arrangement. An award of joint custody does not necessarily mean an equal sharing of time; it does, however, mean that the parents will consult and share equally in the child's upbringing and in decision-making about upbringing. In a joint-custody arrangement, the rights, privileges, and responsibilities are shared, though not necessarily the physical custody. In a joint-custody arrangement, physical custody is usu. given to one parent. In fact, awards of joint physical custody, in the absence of extraordinary circumstances, are usu. found not to be in the best interests of the child. — Also termed *shared custody*; *joint managing conservatorship*.

legal custody. 1. CUSTODY (2). 2. CUSTODY (3). 3. The authority to make significant decisions on a child's behalf, including decisions about education, religious training, and healthcare.

physical custody. 1. PHYSICAL CUSTODY (2). 2. PHYSICAL CUSTODY (3).

residential custody. See PHYSICAL CUSTODY (2).

shared custody. See *joint custody*.

sole custody. (1870) An arrangement by which one parent has full control and sole decision-making responsibility — to the exclusion of the other parent — on matters such as health, education, religion, and living arrangements.

split custody. An arrangement in which one parent has custody of one or more children, while the other parent has custody of the remaining children. ● Split custody is fairly uncommon, since most jurisdictions favor keeping siblings together.

3. The detention of a person by virtue of lawful process or authority. — Also termed *legal custody*. — **custodial,** *adj.*

custody decree. See DECREE.

custody determination. *Family law.* A court order determining custody and visitation rights. ● The order typically does not include any instructions on child support or other monetary obligations.

custody evaluation. See HOME-STUDY REPORT.

custody hearing. See HEARING.

custody interference. See CUSTODIAL INTERFERENCE.

custody of the law. (17c) The condition of property or a person being under the control of legal authority (as a court or law officer). See IN CUSTODIA LEGIS.

custody proceeding. *Family law.* An action to determine who is entitled to legal or physical custody of a child. ● Legal custody gives one the right to make significant decisions regarding the child, and physical custody gives one the right to physical care and control of the child. See CUSTODY; *custody hearing* under HEARING.

custom, *n.* (13c) 1. A practice that by its common adoption and long, unvarying habit has come to have the force of law. See USAGE. — **customary,** *adj.*

conventional custom. A custom that operates only indirectly through the medium of agreements, so that it is accepted and adopted in individual instances as conventional law between the parties to those agreements. — Also termed *usage.* See USAGE.

general custom. 1. A custom that prevails throughout a country and constitutes one of the sources of the law of the land. 2. A custom that businesses recognize and follow. See *trade usage* under USAGE.

legal custom. A custom that operates as a binding rule of law, independently of any agreement on the part of those subject to it. — Often shortened to *custom.*

local custom. A custom that prevails in some defined locality only, such as a city or county, and constitutes a source of law for that place only. — Also termed *particular custom*; *special custom.*

2. (*pl.*) Duties imposed on imports or exports. 3. (*pl.*) The agency or procedure for collecting such duties.

custom and usage. General rules and practices that have become the norm through unvarying habit and common use. Cf. CUSTOM (1); USAGE.

customary, *n.* (16c) A record of all the established legal and quasi-legal practices within a community. — Also termed *custumal*; *customal.*

customary dispatch. See DISPATCH.

customary estate. See COPYHOLD.

customary freehold. See COPYHOLD.

customary international law. See INTERNATIONAL LAW.

customary interpretation. See INTERPRETATION.

customary law. (16c) Law consisting of customs that are accepted as legal requirements or obligatory rules of conduct; practices and beliefs that are so vital and intrinsic a part of a social and economic system that they are treated as if they were laws. — Also termed *consuetudinary law*.

customary seisin. See *quasi-seisin* under SEISIN.

customary tenant. See TENANT.

customers' goods. See GOODS.

customer's man. See *registered representative* under REPRESENTATIVE.

customer's person. See *registered representative* under REPRESENTATIVE.

customhouse. A building or office, esp. at a port, where duties or customs are collected and where ships are cleared for entering or leaving the port. — Also spelled *customshouse*.

customhouse broker. See BROKER.

Customs and Patent Appeals, Court of. See COURT OF CUSTOMS AND PATENT APPEALS.

customs broker. See *customhouse broker* under BROKER.

Customs Cooperation Council. A specialized intergovernmental organization for the study of customs questions. • Established in 1952, the Council has its headquarters in Brussels. — Abbr. CCC.

Customs Court, U.S. See UNITED STATES CUSTOMS COURT.

customs duty. See DUTY (4).

customs frontier. *Int'l law.* The territorial boundary at which a country imposes customs duties.

customshouse. See CUSTOMHOUSE.

customs union. *Int'l law.* A combination of two or more countries within a single customs area with a common external tariff, though each participating country remains politically independent. • The effect is that tariffs originally levied on the traffic of goods between those countries are abolished or else successively dismantled according to an agreed-upon scheme, and that common tariffs are imposed on imports from nonmembers.

custos (kəs-tahs *also* kəs-təs). [Latin] *Hist.* A keeper, protector, or guardian.

custos morum (kəs-tahs mor-əm). [Law Latin] Custodian of morals <H.L.A. Hart believed that courts should not be seen as the *custos morum*>. • This name was sometimes used in reference to the Court of King's Bench.

Custos Rotulorum (kəs-tahs roch-yə-**lor**-əm *or* rot-yə-**lor**-əm). [Law Latin "keeper of the pleas of the Crown"] *Hist.* The principal justice of the peace in a county, responsible for the rolls of the county sessions of the peace. — Also termed *Keeper of the Rolls*.

Custos Sigilli. See KEEPER OF THE GREAT SEAL.

cutoff date. See DATE.

cutpurse. *Hist.* A person who steals by cutting purses; a pickpocket.

CVA. *abbr.* United States Court of Veterans Appeals. See UNITED STATES COURT OF APPEALS FOR VETERANS CLAIMS.

CVSG. *abbr.* A call for the view of the Solicitor General — an invitation from the U.S. Supreme Court for the Solicitor General's views on a pending petition for writ of certiorari in a case in which, though the government is not a party, governmental interests are involved.

Cwth. *abbr.* COMMONWEALTH (4).

CXT. *abbr.* See *common external tariff* under TARIFF (2).

cybercrime. See *computer crime* under CRIME.

cyberlaw (**sɪ**-bər-law). (1994) The field of law dealing with the Internet, encompassing cases, statutes, regulations, and disputes that affect people and businesses interacting through computers. • Cyberlaw addresses issues of online speech and business that arise because of the nature of the medium, including intellectual property rights, free speech, privacy, e-commerce, and safety, as well as questions of jurisdiction. — Also termed *cyberspace law*.

cyberpatent. See *business-method patent* and *Internet patent* under PATENT (3).

cyberpayment. A transfer of money over the Internet, usu. through a payment service. — Also termed *Internet payment*.

cyberpiracy. *Trademarks.* The act of registering a well-known name or mark (or one that is confusingly similar) as a website's domain name, usu. for the purpose of deriving revenue. • One form of cyberpiracy is cybersquatting. Another is using a similar name or mark to mislead consumers. For example, a site called Nikee.com that sells Nikee branded athletic shoes and sporting goods would draw customers away the famous Nike brand. — **cyberpirate,** *n.*

cyberspace law. See CYBERLAW.

cybersquatting. (1997) The act of reserving a domain name on the Internet, esp. a name that would be associated with a company's trademark, and then seeking to profit by selling or licensing the name to the company that has an interest in being identified with it. • The practice was banned by federal law in 1999. See ANTICYBERSQUATTING CONSUMER PROTECTION ACT.

cyberstalking. (1995) The act of threatening, harassing, or annoying someone through multiple e-mail messages, as through the Internet, esp. with the intent of placing the recipient in fear that an illegal act or an injury will be inflicted on the recipient or a member of the recipient's family or household.

cyberterrorism. See TERRORISM.

cybertheft. (1994) The act of using an online computer service, such as one on the Internet, to steal someone else's property or to interfere with someone else's use and enjoyment of property. ● Examples of cybertheft are hacking into a bank's computer records to wrongfully credit one account and debit another, and interfering with a copyright by wrongfully sending protected material over the Internet.

cyclical (sɪ-klə-kəl *or* sik-lə-kəl), *adj.* (Of a stock or an industry) characterized by large price swings that occur because of government policy, economic conditions, and seasonal changes.

cy pres (see **pray** *or* sɪ). [Law French "as near as"] (1885) **1.** The equitable doctrine under which a court reforms a written instrument with a gift to charity as closely to the donor's intention as possible, so that the gift does not fail. ● Courts use *cy pres* esp. in construing charitable gifts when the donor's original charitable purpose cannot be fulfilled. It is also used to distribute unclaimed portions of a class-action judgment or settlement funds to a charity that will advance the interests of the class. More recently, courts have used cy pres to distribute class-action-settlement funds not amenable to individual claims or to a meaningful pro rata distribution to a nonprofit charitable organization whose work indirectly benefits the class members and advances the public interest. Cf. DOCTRINE OF APPROXIMATION. **2.** A statutory provision that allows a court to reform a will, deed, or other instrument to avoid violating the rule against perpetuities. See RULE AGAINST PERPETUITIES.

D

D. *abbr.* **1.** DISTRICT. **2.** DEFENDANT. **3.** DIGEST.

D.A. *abbr.* **1.** DISTRICT ATTORNEY. **2.** See *deposit account* under ACCOUNT.

dactylography (dak-tə-**log**-rə-fee), *n.* The scientific study of fingerprints as a method of identification. — Also termed *dactyloscopy.* — **dactylographic** (dak-til-ə-**graf**-ik), *adj.*

DAF. *abbr.* DELIVERED AT FRONTIER.

daily balance. (1859) The final daily accounting for a day on which interest is to be accrued or paid.

   average daily balance. The average amount of money in an account (such as a bank account or credit-card account) during a given period. • This amount serves as the basis for computing interest or a finance charge for the period.

daily newspaper. See NEWSPAPER.

daisy chain. A series of purchases and sales of the same stock by a small group of securities dealers attempting to drive up the stock's price to attract unsuspecting buyers' interest. • Once the buyers have invested (i.e., are caught up in the chain), the traders sell for a quick profit, leaving the buyers with overpriced stock. This practice is illegal.

damage, *adj.* Of or relating to monetary compensation for loss or injury to a person or property <a damage claim> <a damage award>. — Also termed *damages* <a damages claim>. Cf. DAMAGES.

damage, *n.* (14c) Loss or injury to person or property <actionable damage resulting from negligence>.

damage rule. See LEGAL-INJURY RULE.

damages, *n. pl.* (16c) Money claimed by, or ordered to be paid to, a person as compensation for loss or injury <the plaintiff seeks $8,000 in damages from the defendant>. — **damage,** *adj.*

   accumulative damages. Statutory damages allowed in addition to amounts available under the common law. — Also termed *enhanced damages.*

   actual damages. (18c) An amount awarded to a complainant to compensate for a proven injury or loss; damages that repay actual losses. — Also termed *compensatory damages; tangible damages; real damages.*

   added damages. See *punitive damages.*

   additional damages. Damages usu. provided by statute in addition to direct damages. • Additional damages can include expenses resulting from the injury, consequential damages, or punitive damages.

   benefit-of-the-bargain damages. (1955) Damages that a breaching party to a contract must pay to the aggrieved party, equal to the amounts that the aggrieved party would have received, including profits, if the contract had been fully performed. — Also termed *loss-of-bargain damages.*

   compensatory damages (kəm-**pen**-sə-tor-ee). (1817) **1.** Damages sufficient in amount to indemnify the injured person for the loss suffered. — Often shortened to *compensatories.* **2.** See *actual damages.*

   consequential damages. (17c) Losses that do not flow directly and immediately from an injurious act but that result indirectly from the act. — Also termed *indirect damages.*

   contemptuous damages. See *nominal damages.*

   continuing damages. **1.** Ongoing damages arising from the same injury. **2.** Damages arising from the repetition of similar acts within a definite period.

   cosmetic damages. The amount awarded to compensate for personal disfigurement.

   damages for lost expectations. See *expectation damages.*

   damages ultra (əl-trə). Additional damages claimed by a plaintiff who is not satisfied with the amounts the defendant paid into court.

   direct damages. See *general damages.*

   discretionary damages. Damages (such as mental anguish or pain and suffering) that are not precisely measurable but are determined by the subjective judgment of a jury. — Also termed *indeterminate damages.*

   double damages. Damages that, by statute, are twice the amount that the fact-finder determines is owed or twice the amount of actual damages awarded. • In some cases, double damages are awarded in addition to actual damages, so the effect is the same as treble damages.

   enhanced damages. **1.** See *accumulative damages.* **2.** *Patents.* Damages for patent infringement in an amount up to three times that of compensatory damages, at the discretion of the court, based on the egregiousness of the defendant's conduct, including the willfulness of the infringement. 35 USCA § 284.

   estimated damages. See *liquidated damages.*

   excess damages. Damages awarded to an insured — beyond the coverage provided by an insurance policy — because the insurer did not settle the claim within policy limits. • If the insurer acted in bad faith in not settling, the insured may have a claim to recover the excess damages from the insurer. — Also termed *excess-liability damages.*

excessive damages. A jury award that grossly exceeds the amount warranted by law based on the facts and circumstances of the case; unreasonable or outrageous damages, which are subject to reduction by remittitur. See REMITTITUR.

exemplary damages. See *punitive damages.*

expectation damages. (1939) Compensation awarded for the loss of what a person reasonably anticipated from a transaction that was not completed. — Also termed *expectancy damages; lost-expectation damages; damages for lost expectations.*

fee damages. Damages awarded to the owner of property abutting an elevated railroad for injury caused by the railroad's construction and operation. • The term is used because the damage is to the property owner's easements of light, air, and access, which are parts of the fee.

foreseeable damages. Damages that a breaching party knew or should have known when the contract was made would be likely to result from a breach.

future damages. (17c) Money awarded to an injured party for an injury's residual or projected effects, such as those that reduce the person's ability to function. • Examples are expected pain and suffering, loss or impairment of earning capacity, and projected medical expenses.

general damages. (18c) Damages that the law presumes follow from the type of wrong complained of; specif., compensatory damages for harm that so frequently results from the tort for which a party has sued that the harm is reasonably expected and need not be alleged or proved. • General damages do not need to be specifically claimed. — Also termed *direct damages; necessary damages.*

gross damages. The total damages found before adjustments and offsets.

hedonic damages (hi-**don**-ik). (1985) Damages that attempt to compensate for the loss of the pleasure of being alive. • Such damages are not allowed in most jurisdictions. — Also termed (erroneously) *hedonistic damages.*

imaginary damages. See *punitive damages.*

inadequate damages. Damages insufficient to fully and fairly compensate the parties; damages bearing no reasonable relation to the plaintiff's injuries, indicating prejudice, mistake, or other fact to support setting aside a jury's verdict.

incidental damages. (18c) **1.** Losses reasonably associated with or related to actual damages.

2. A seller's commercially reasonable expenses incurred in stopping delivery or in transporting and caring for goods after a buyer's breach. UCC § 2-710. **3.** A buyer's expenses reasonably incurred in caring for goods after a seller's breach. UCC § 2-715(1).

indeterminate damages. See *discretionary damages.*

indirect damages. See *consequential damages.*

intervening damages. Continuing damages that accrue during the pendency and prosecution of an unsuccessful appeal. • A lower court may include intervening damages in an award.

irreparable damages (i-**rep**-ə-rə-bəl). Damages that cannot be easily ascertained because there is no fixed pecuniary standard of measurement, e.g., damages for a repeated public nuisance. — Also termed *nonpecuniary damages.*

land damages. See *just compensation* under COMPENSATION.

lawful damages. Those damages fixed by law and ascertained in a court of law.

liquidated damages. (18c) An amount contractually stipulated as a reasonable estimation of actual damages to be recovered by one party if the other party breaches. • If the parties to a contract have properly agreed on liquidated damages, the sum fixed is the measure of damages for a breach, whether it exceeds or falls short of the actual damages. — Also termed *stipulated damages; estimated damages.* See LIQUIDATED-DAMAGES CLAUSE. Cf. *unliquidated damages;* PENALTY CLAUSE.

loss-of-bargain damages. See *benefit-of-the-bargain damages.*

lost-expectation damages. See *expectation damages.*

lost-profits damages. See LOST-PROFITS (1).

moratory damages (**mor**-ə-tor-ee or **mahr**-). *Civil law.* Damages for a delay in performing an obligation. La. Civ. Code arts. 1989, 1994. • There must be a default before these damages can be recovered, while compensatory damages are recoverable for both a failure of performance and for a defective performance.

multiple damages. Statutory damages (such as double or treble damages) that are a multiple of the amount that the fact-finder determines to be owed. — Also termed *multiplied damages.* See *double damages; treble damages.*

necessary damages. See *general damages.*

nominal damages. (18c) **1.** A trifling sum awarded when a legal injury is suffered but there is no substantial loss or injury to be compensated. **2.** A small amount fixed as damages for breach of contract without regard to the amount of harm. — Also termed *contemptuous damages.* Cf. *substantial damages.*

nonpecuniary damages. Damages that cannot be measured in money. See *irreparable damages.*

particular damages. See *special damages.*

pecuniary damages (pə-**kyoo**-nee-er-ee). (17c) Damages that can be estimated and monetarily compensated. • Although this phrase appears in many old cases, it is now widely considered a redundancy — since damages are always pecuniary.

permanent damages. Damages for past, present, and future harm that cannot be avoided or remedied.

presumptive damages. See *punitive damages.*

prospective damages. Future damages that, based on the facts pleaded and proved by the plaintiff, can reasonably be expected to occur.

proximate damages. Damages directly, immediately, and naturally flowing from the act complained of. Cf. *speculative damages* (1).

punitive damages. (1848) Damages awarded in addition to actual damages when the defendant acted with recklessness, malice, or deceit; specif., damages assessed by way of penalizing the wrongdoer or making an example to others. • Punitive damages, which are intended to punish and thereby deter blameworthy conduct, are generally not recoverable for breach of contract. The Supreme Court has held that three guidelines help determine whether a punitive-damages award violates constitutional due process: (1) the reprehensibility of the conduct being punished; (2) the reasonableness of the relationship between the harm and the award; and (3) the difference between the award and the civil penalties authorized in comparable cases. *BMW of North America, Inc. v. Gore*, 517 U.S. 559, 116 S.Ct. 1589 (1996). — Also termed *exemplary damages*; *vindictive damages*; *punitory damages*; *presumptive damages*; *added damages*; *aggravated damages*; *speculative damages*; *imaginary damages*; *smart money*; *punies.*

putative damages. Damages that are alleged; claimed but unproved damages.

real damages. See *actual damages.*

reliance damages. (1938) Damages awarded for losses incurred by the plaintiff in reliance on the contract. • Reliance damages restore the plaintiff to the economic condition the plaintiff enjoyed before the contract was formed.

reliance-loss damages. A reimbursement for losses or expenses that the plaintiff suffers in reliance on the defendant's contractual promise that has been breached.

remote damages. See *speculative damages* (1).

rescissory damages (ri-**sis**-ə-ree *or* ri-**siz**-). Damages awarded to restore a plaintiff to the position occupied before the defendant's wrongful acts.

restitution damages. (1939) Damages awarded to a plaintiff when the defendant has been unjustly enriched at the plaintiff's expense.

severance damages. In a condemnation case, damages awarded to a property owner for diminution in the fair market value of land as a result of severance from the land of the property actually condemned; compensation awarded to a landowner for the loss in value of the tract that remains after a partial taking of the land.

special damages. Damages that are alleged to have been sustained in the circumstances of a particular wrong. • To be awardable, special damages must be specifically claimed and proved. *See* Fed. R. Civ. P. 9(g). — Often shortened to *specials.* — Also termed *particular damages.*

speculative damages. (1804) **1.** Damages that are so uncertain to occur that they will not be awarded. — Also termed *remote damages.* **2.** See *punitive damages.*

statutory damages. Damages provided by statute (such as a wrongful death and survival statute), as distinguished from damages provided under the common law.

stipulated damages. See *liquidated damages.*

substantial damages. A considerable sum awarded to compensate for a significant loss or injury. Cf. *nominal damages.*

tangible damages. See *actual damages.*

temperate damages. *Rare.* Reasonable damages.

temporary damages. Damages allowed for an intermittent or occasional wrong, such as a real-property injury whose cause can be removed or abated.

treble damages. (18c) Damages that, by statute, are three times the amount of actual damages that the fact-finder determines is owed. — Also termed *triple damages.*

uncertain damages. Damages that are not clearly the result of a wrong. • The rule against allowing recovery of uncertain damages refers to these damages, not damages that are uncertain only in amount.

unliquidated damages. (18c) Damages that cannot be determined by a fixed formula and must be established by a judge or jury. Cf. *liquidated damages.*

vindictive damages. See *punitive damages.*

damages, mitigation of. See MITIGATION-OF-DAMAGES DOCTRINE.

damages clause. See SURFACE-DAMAGE CLAUSE.

damages for detention. See *noncontract demurrage* under DEMURRAGE.

dame. **1.** The legal title of the wife of a knight or baronet. **2.** The female equivalent of a knight. **3.** A form of address to a woman of high rank. **4.** A matron. **5.** *Slang.* A woman. — Also termed (in senses 1 & 2) *domina*.

damn-fool doctrine. *Insurance.* The principle that an insurer may deny (esp. liability) coverage when an insured engages in behavior that is so ill-conceived that the insurer should not be compelled to bear the loss resulting from the insured's actions. — Also termed *damned-fool doctrine*.

damnification, *n.* Something that causes damage <damnification in the form of a penalty>.

damnify, *vb.* To cause loss or damage to; to injure <the surety was damnified by the judgment obtained against it>.

damnum (**dam**-nəm), *n.* [Latin] (1828) A loss; damage suffered. See AD DAMNUM. Pl. **damna.**

damnum absque injuria (**dam**-nəm ab-skwee in-**joor**-ee-ə). See DAMNUM SINE INJURIA.

damnum sine injuria (**dam**-nəm **sɪ**-nee in-**joor**-ee-ə *or* **sin**-ay). [Latin "damage without wrongful act"] Loss or harm that is incurred from something other than a wrongful act and occasions no legal remedy. • An example is a loss from fair trade competition. — Also termed *damnum absque injuria; absque injuria damnum; absque injuria.* Cf. INJURIA ABSQUE DAMNO.

D&O liability insurance. See *directors' and officers' liability insurance* under INSURANCE.

danger. (13c) **1.** Peril; exposure to harm, loss, pain, or other negative result. **2.** A cause of peril; a menace.

apparent danger. (16c) **1.** Obvious danger; real danger. — Also termed *patent danger.* **2.** *Criminal law.* The perceived danger in one person's actions toward another, as a result of which it seems necessary for the threatened person to use force in self-defense. See SELF-DEFENSE.

deterrent danger. (1959) An obvious danger that an occupier of land creates to discourage trespassers, such as a barbed-wire fence or spikes on the top of a wall.

imminent danger. (16c) **1.** An immediate, real threat to one's safety that justifies the use of force in self-defense. **2.** *Criminal law.* The danger resulting from an immediate threatened injury sufficient to cause a reasonable and prudent person to defend himself or herself.

patent danger. See *apparent danger* (1).

retributive danger. A concealed danger that an occupier of land creates to injure trespassers. • A retributive danger is lawful only to the extent that it could be justified if the occupier had

inflicted the injury personally or directly to the trespasser. Thus, a spring gun or a land mine is an unlawful means of defending land against a trespasser.

seeming danger. Danger that a reasonable person would perceive to be real, even if it is not.

unavoidable danger. (16c) **1.** Inescapable danger. **2.** A danger that is unpreventable, esp. by a person operating a vessel.

danger-creation doctrine. (2000) The theory that if a state's affirmative conduct places a person in jeopardy, then the state may be liable for the harm inflicted on that person by a third party. • This is an exception to the general principle that the state is not liable for an injury that a third party inflicts on a member of the public. — Also termed *danger-creation exception.* Cf. SPECIAL-RELATIONSHIP DOCTRINE.

danger-invites-rescue doctrine. See RESCUE DOCTRINE.

danger of navigation. See PERIL OF THE SEA.

danger of river. See PERIL OF THE SEA.

danger of the sea. See PERIL OF THE SEA.

dangerous, *adj.* (15c) **1.** (Of a condition, situation, etc.) perilous; hazardous; unsafe <a dangerous intersection>. **2.** (Of a person, an object, etc.) likely to cause serious bodily harm <a dangerous weapon> <a dangerous criminal>.

imminently dangerous. (1834) (Of a person, behavior, activity, or thing) reasonably certain to place life and limb in peril. • This term is relevant in several legal contexts. For example, if a mental condition renders a person imminently dangerous to self or others, he or she may be committed to a mental hospital. And the imminently dangerous behavior of pointing a gun at someone's head could subject the actor to criminal and tort liability. Further, the manufacturer of an imminently dangerous product may be held to a strict-liability standard in tort.

inherently dangerous. (1887) (Of an activity or thing) requiring special precautions at all times to avoid injury; dangerous per se. See DANGEROUS INSTRUMENTALITY; INHERENTLY DANGEROUS ACTIVITY.

dangerous animal. See ANIMAL.

dangerous condition. See CONDITION (5).

dangerous conduct. See *unreasonably dangerous conduct* under CONDUCT.

dangerous criminal. See CRIMINAL.

dangerous drug. See DRUG.

dangerous exposure. See EXPOSURE.

dangerous instrumentality. (1857) An instrument, substance, or condition so inherently dangerous that it may cause serious bodily injury or death without human use or interference. • It may serve as the basis for strict liability. See ATTRACTIVE-NUISANCE DOCTRINE. Cf. *deadly weapon* under WEAPON.

dangerous lunatic. See LUNATIC.

dangerous occupation. See OCCUPATION.

dangerous-propensity test. See DANGEROUS-TENDENCY TEST.

dangerous-proximity test. (1973) *Criminal law.* A common-law test for the crime of attempt, focusing on whether the defendant is dangerously close to completing the offense. • Factors include the gravity of the potential crime, the apprehension of the victim, and the uncertainty of the crime's occurrence. See ATTEMPT (2).

dangerous situation. (1898) Under the last-clear-chance doctrine, the circumstance in which a plaintiff operating a motor vehicle has reached a position (as on the path of an oncoming train) that cannot be escaped by the exercise of ordinary care. — Also termed *situation of danger.* See LAST-CLEAR-CHANCE DOCTRINE.

dangerous-tendency test. (1938) A propensity of a person or animal to inflict injury. • The test is used, esp. in dog-bite cases, to determine whether an owner will be held liable for injuries caused by the owner's animal. — Also termed *dangerous-propensity test.*

dangerous weapon. See WEAPON.

danger-utility test. See RISK-UTILITY TEST.

***Darden* hearing.** (1979) *Criminal procedure.* An ex parte proceeding to determine whether disclosure of an informant's identity is pertinent to establishing probable cause when there is otherwise insufficient evidence to establish probable cause apart from the arresting officer's testimony about an informant's communications. • The defense attorney may be excluded from the hearing but can usu. submit questions to be used by the judge in the examination. *People v. Darden*, 313 N.E.2d 49 (N.Y. 1974).

DARPA. *abbr.* DEFENSE ADVANCED RESEARCH PROJECTS AGENCY.

database. A compilation of information arranged in a systematic way and offering a means of finding specific elements it contains, often today by electronic means. • Unless the information itself is original, a database is not protected by U.S. copyright law. Elsewhere, it may be protected as a distinct class of "literary works," or it may be the subject of *sui generis* intellectual-property laws. See SWEAT-OF-THE-BROW DOCTRINE.

Database Directive. See DIRECTIVE ON THE LEGAL PROTECTION OF DATABASES.

data protection. Any method of securing information, esp. information stored on a computer, from being either physically lost or seen by an unauthorized person.

date. **1.** The day when an event happened or will happen <date of trial>. **2.** A period of time in general <at a later date>. **3.** An appointment at a specified time <no dates are available>.

answer date. See *answer day* under DAY.

appearance date. See *answer day* under DAY.

cutoff date. A deadline; esp., in the sale of a note or other interest-paying asset, the last date on which the seller is entitled to any interest due on the note or asset.

date of bankruptcy. (1809) *Bankruptcy.* The date when a court declares a person to be bankrupt; the date of bankruptcy adjudication. • This date may coincide with the voluntary-filing date.

date of cleavage. *Bankruptcy.* The filing date of a voluntary-bankruptcy petition. • With a few exceptions, only the debts existing at this time are dischargeable.

date of injury. (1831) *Torts.* The inception date of an injury; the date of an accident causing an injury.

date of invention. *Patents.* For purposes of a patent application, the date when the creation was reduced to practice. • If the invention has not been built, the date of invention is the date when the patent application is filed, since that is a constructive reduction to practice.

date of issue. **1.** *Commercial law.* An arbitrary date (for notes, bonds, and other documents in a series) fixed as the beginning of the term for which they run; the date that a stock or bond bears on its face, not the date on which it is actually signed, delivered, or put into circulation. • When a bond is delivered to a purchaser, it is considered "issued." But this concept is distinguishable from the "date of issue," which remains fixed, regardless of the date of sale or delivery. **2.** *Insurance.* The date specified in the policy as the "date of issue," not the date on which the policy is executed or delivered, and regardless of other dates that may be specified in the policy or elsewhere, such as the date that the policy is to "take effect."

date of maturity. *Commercial law.* The date when a debt falls due, such as a debt on a promissory note or bond. — Also termed *maturity date.*

date of record. See *record date* (1).

declaration date. *Corporations.* The date when corporate directors declare a dividend. Cf. DIVIDEND DATE; EX-DIVIDEND DATE.

dividend date. See DIVIDEND DATE.

effective filing date. *Patents.* The date that a patent application is considered to have been filed. • The actual filing date may be later, as for a continuing application. But under the doctrine of continuity, the child application is usu. entitled to the filing date of the parent application to prove priority. — Also termed *parent filing date*. See DOCTRINE OF CONTINUITY.

filing date. 1. Generally, the date when any document is delivered to the appropriate authority. 2. *Patents.* The date when a patent application is filed. ● The filing date closes the door on prior art; starts the clock on the period of eligibility to file in other countries; sets the priority date for public use, disclosure, or sale; and (absent other evidence) establishes the date of constructive reduction to practice. 3. *Trademarks.* The date when a trademark application is filed.

maturity date. See *date of maturity*.

parent filing date. See *effective filing date*.

payable date. Corporations. The official date on which shareholder dividends or distributions become payable. — Also termed *record date*.

payment date. Corporations. The date on which stock dividends or interest checks are paid to shareholders.

priority date. Patents. The date that will determine which applicant will get a patent in an interference proceeding. ● The priority date is also the cut-off date for prior art. In the United States the priority date is the date of invention; in the rest of the world it is the date the patent application was filed. Cf. FIRST-TO-FILE, FIRST-TO-INVENT.

record date. Corporations. 1. The date on which a stockholder must own shares to be entitled to vote or receive a dividend. — Also termed *date of record*. See EX-DIVIDEND DATE. 2. See *payable date*.

settlement date. Securities. 1. The date on which an investor must pay the broker for securities purchased. 2. The date on which a seller must deliver negotiable certificates for securities sold. 3. The date on which a real-estate purchaser pays for and takes title to the real estate. Cf. CLOSING.

submission date. 1. The date that a case is to be submitted to a court for determination. 2. The date on which an investor must pay the broker for securities purchased. 3. The date on which a seller must deliver negotiable certificates for securities sold.

date certain. A fixed or appointed day; a specified day, esp. a date fixed by an instrument such as a deed. Cf. TIME CERTAIN (1). — Also termed (in French law) *date certaine* (**dat** sair-**tayn**).

date of record. See *record date* under DATE.

date rape. See RAPE.

datum (**day**-təm), *n.* [fr. Latin *dare* "to give"] 1. A piece of information. Pl. **data.** 2. *Hist.* Something given or executed. 3. A date.

***Daubert* hearing** (**dah**-bərt or **doh**-behr). A hearing conducted by federal district courts, usu. before trial, to determine whether proposed expert testimony meets the federal requirements for relevance and reliability, as clarified by the Supreme Court in *Daubert v. Merrell Dow Pharms., Inc.*, 509 U.S. 579, 113 S.Ct. 2786 (1993).

***Daubert* test.** (1993) *Evidence.* A method that federal district courts use to determine whether expert testimony is admissible under Federal Rule of Evidence 702, which generally requires that expert testimony consist of scientific, technical, or other specialized knowledge that will assist the fact-finder in understanding the evidence or determining a fact in issue. ● In its role as "gatekeeper" of the evidence, the trial court must decide whether the proposed expert testimony meets the requirements of relevance and reliability. The court applies the test outside the jury's presence, usu. during a pretrial *Daubert* hearing. At the hearing, the proponent must show that the expert's underlying reasoning or methodology, and its application to the facts, are scientifically valid. In ruling on admissibility, the court considers a flexible list of factors, including (1) whether the theory can be or has been tested, (2) whether the theory has been subjected to peer review or publication, (3) the theory's known or potential rate of error and whether there are standards that control its operation, and (4) the degree to which the relevant scientific community has accepted the theory. *Daubert v. Merrell Dow Pharms., Inc.*, 509 U.S. 579, 113 S.Ct. 2786 (1993). Similar scrutiny must be applied to nonscientific expert testimony. *Kumho Tire Co. v. Carmichael*, 526 U.S. 137, 119 S.Ct. 1167 (1999). Variations of the *Daubert* test are applied in the trial courts of most states.

daughter. A parent's female child; a female child in a parent–child relationship.

daughter-in-law. The wife of one's son.

Davis-Bacon Act. A federal law originally enacted in 1931 to regulate the minimum-wage rates payable to employees of federal public-works projects. 40 USCA § 276a.

day. (bef. 12c) 1. Any 24-hour period; the time it takes the earth to revolve once on its axis <we have a day to prepare a mandamus petition>. 2. The period between the rising and the setting of the sun <day or night>. — Also termed *natural day*. 3. Sunlight <we can see it in the day>. 4. The period when the sun is above the horizon, along with the period in the early morning and late evening when a person's face is discernible. 5. Any specified time period, esp. as distinguished from other periods <the good old days> <a day's work>. — Also termed (in senses 2–4) *daytime*. Cf. NIGHT.

adjournment day. 1. The day on which an organization, such as a court or legislature, adjourns. **2.** *Hist.* A later day appointed by the judges at regular sittings at *nisi prius* to try an issue of fact not then ready for trial.

adjournment day in error. *Hist.* A day scheduled for completion of matters not finished on the affirmance day of the term.

affirmance day general. *Hist.* In the Court of Exchequer, a day appointed after the beginning of every term to affirm or reverse judgments.

answer day. (1859) *Civil procedure.* The last day for a defendant to file and serve a responsive pleading in a lawsuit. ● Under the Federal Rules of Civil Procedure, a defendant generally must serve an answer (1) within 20 days after being served with the summons and complaint, or (2) if a defendant timely waives service at the plaintiff's request, within 60 days after the request for waiver was sent. Fed. R. Civ. P. 4(d), 12(a). — Also termed *answer date; appearance date; appearance day.*

artificial day. The period from the rising to the setting of the sun. — Also termed *solar day; civil day; dies solaris.*

astronomical day. See *solar day* (2).

banking day. See BANKING DAY.

business day. A day that most institutions are open for business, usu. a day on which banks and major stock exchanges are open, excluding Saturdays, Sundays, and certain major holidays.

calendar day. A consecutive 24-hour day running from midnight to midnight. — Also termed *natural day.*

civil day. See *artificial day.*

clear day. One of many full, consecutive days between (1) the date when a period, measured in days, begins and (2) the date when an event that ends the period occurs. ● For example, if a statute or contract requires a party to give another party five clear days of notice of a hearing, and the hearing is scheduled to be held on the 31st day of the month, the party giving notice must do so by the 25th day of the month so that five full (clear) days elapse between but not including the 25th and 31st.

common day. In England, an ordinary court day.

court day. A day on which a particular court is open for court business. *See* Fed. R. Civ. P. 6(a); Fed. R. Crim. P. 45(a).

day of demurrage. *Maritime law.* A day beyond the days allowed for loading or unloading cargo. ● A fine is usu. assessed for each day of delay. *See* DEMURRAGE. Cf. LAYDAY.

dedication day. *Hist.* A day on which people from several villages gathered in one place to celebrate the feast day of the saint and patron of a church.

entire day. An undivided day, rather than parts of two or more days aggregated to form a 24-hour period. ● An entire day must have a legal, fixed, precise time to begin and end. A statute referring to an *entire day* contemplates a 24-hour period beginning and ending at midnight.

juridical day (juu-**rid**-i-kəl). (17c) A day on which legal proceedings can be held. — Also termed *judicial day.* Cf. *nonjudicial day;* NONJURIDICAL.

law day. See LAW DAY.

lay day. See LAYDAY.

legislative day. A day that begins when a legislative body reconvenes after a recess or adjournment, and ends when the body next recesses or adjourns until a different calendar day. ● A legislative day may extend over several calendar days.

love day. *Hist.* **1.** A day when neighbors amicably settled a dispute. **2.** A day when one neighbor helped another without payment.

natural day. 1. The 24-hour period from midnight to midnight. — Also termed *calendar day.* **2.** The period between sunrise and sunset. — Also termed *artificial day.*

nonjudicial day. (18c) A day when courts do not sit or when legal proceedings cannot be conducted, such as a Sunday or legal holiday. *See* LEGAL HOLIDAY; NON JURIDICUS. Cf. *juridical day.*

peremptory day. (16c) A day assigned for trial or hearing, without further opportunity for postponement.

quarter day. *Hist.* One of four days during a year that money owed (such as rent) was legally or customarily payable. ● In England and Wales the quarter days are Lady Day, March 25; Midsummer Day, June 24; Michaelmas Day, September 29; and Christmas Day, December 25. In Scotland the traditional quarter or term days are Candlemas, February 2; Whitsunday (or Whitsuntide), May 15; Lammas, August 1; and Martinmas, November 11. Scotland's statutory quarter or term days are the 28th of February, May, August, and November. If a document specifies a different date for a quarter day, then the specified date controls. — Also termed (in Scots law) *term day.*

return day. (17c) **1.** A day on which a defendant must appear in court (as for an arraignment). **2.** A day on which a defendant must file an answer. **3.** A day on which a proof of service must be returned to court. — Also termed *rule day.* **4.** A day on which a writ of execution must be returned to court. **5.** A day specified by law for counting votes in an election. — Also termed *return date.*

solar day. **1.** See *artificial day.* **2.** The 24-hour period from noon to noon. — Also termed *astronomical day.*

term day. Scots law. See *quarter day.*

daybook. A merchant's original record of daily transactions.

day fine. See FINE (5).

day in court. (16c) **1.** The right and opportunity, in a judicial tribunal, to litigate a claim, seek relief, or defend one's rights. **2.** The right to be notified and given an opportunity to appear and to be heard when one's case is called.

day loan. See LOAN.

day order. See ORDER (8).

day rule. See DAY WRIT.

days in bank. Particular days set aside by the Court of Common Pleas for specific matters, including the appearance of parties and service of process. — Also termed *dies in banco.*

daysman (**dayz**-mən). *Hist.* **1.** An arbitrator; an elected judge; an umpire. **2.** A day laborer. — Also spelled *deiesman.*

days of grace. **1.** GRACE PERIOD (1). **2.** *Int'l law.* A timed exemption from prize law that is granted to enemy merchant ships when they are caught unawares by the outbreak of war.

daytime. **1.** See DAY (2). **2.** See DAY (3). **3.** See DAY (4).

day trading. See TRADING.

daywork. **1.** Short-term employment that is intended to last only for a day, or for a few days. **2.** *Hist.* In England, a measure of land being the amount of arable land that can be plowed in a day. — Also termed *daywere.*

daywork drilling contract. *Oil & gas.* A contract under which the lease operator hires a drilling rig and oilfield workers, pays an amount based on the time spent in drilling operations, and retains the right to direct drilling operations. ● This type of contract gives the lease operator broad control over the drilling contractor, so courts in turn impose broad liability on the lease operator for any damages that result from the drilling. Cf. FOOTAGE DRILLING CONTRACT; TURNKEY DRILLING CONTRACT.

D.B. *abbr.* DOMESDAY BOOK.

d/b/a. *abbr.* Doing business as. ● The abbreviation usu. precedes a person's or business's assumed name <Paul Smith d/b/a Paul's Dry Cleaners>. It signals that the business may be licensed or incorporated under a different name. Cf. TRADENAME.

d.b.e. *abbr.* DE BENE ESSE.

d.b.n. *abbr.* See *administration de bonis non* under ADMINISTRATION.

d.b.n.c.t.a. *abbr.* See *administration de bonis non cum testamento annexo* under ADMINISTRATION.

DBO. *abbr.* Death benefit only. See *survivor's income benefit plan* under EMPLOYEE BENEFIT PLAN.

D.C. *abbr.* **1.** DISTRICT OF COLUMBIA. **2.** See *district court* (1) under COURT.

DCAA. *abbr.* DEFENSE CONTRACT AUDIT AGENCY.

DCF. See *discounted cash flow* under CASH FLOW.

DCMA. *abbr.* DEFENSE CONTRACT MANAGEMENT AGENCY.

DDoS. *abbr.* DISTRIBUTED DENIAL-OF-SERVICE ATTACK.

DDP. *abbr.* **1.** DELIVERED DUTY PAID. **2.** DISCLOSURE DOCUMENT PROGRAM.

DDU. *abbr.* DELIVERED DUTY UNPAID.

de (də *or* duu). [French] Of; about. ● This is a French preposition often used to show the genitive case, as in *brefe de droit* ("writ of right").

de (dee *or* day). [Latin] Of; about; concerning; respecting; by; from; out of; affecting. ● This preposition is used in the titles of English statutes, of original and judicial writs, and of court proceedings.

deacon. *Eccles. law.* **1.** In certain churches, a member of the clerical order who assists the priest in various duties, including the presentation of the sacrament. ● It is the third order below bishops and priests. A deacon is not allowed to consecrate the Holy Communion or pronounce absolution but can perform most of the other priestly duties. **2.** An elected or appointed officer of a church who assists a minister or priest in various duties.

dead-and-buried company. See COMPANY.

dead asset. See ASSET.

deadbeat. (1863) *Slang.* A person who does not pay debts or financial obligations (such as child-support payments, fines, and legal judgments), usu. with the suggestion that the person is also adept or experienced at evading creditors.

deadbeat dad. (1983) *Slang.* A father who has not paid or who is behind in making child-support payments.

deadbeat mom. (1987) *Slang.* **1.** A mother who has not paid or who is behind in making child-support payments. • This term is used far less frequently than either *deadbeat dad* or *deadbeat parent*, probably because nearly ten times as many men as women fail to support (or are ordered to support) their children financially after divorce. **2.** An able-bodied mother whose income is derived from welfare payments, not from gainful employment.

Deadbeat Parents Punishment Act. A 1998 federal statute that makes it a felony, punishable by up to two years in prison, for failure to pay child support if the obligor has crossed state lines in an attempt to avoid paying the support. • The Act provides felony penalties if (1) a person travels across state lines intending to evade a child-support obligation that is over $5,000 or that has remained unpaid longer than one year, or (2) a person willfully fails to pay support for a child living in a different state if that obligation is greater than $10,000 or if it remains unpaid for more than two years. The Act supersedes the Child Support Recovery Act of 1994. The greatest change in the new statute is the provision regarding the obligor's crossing of state lines in an effort to evade the support obligation. 42 USCA § 228. — Abbr. DPPA. See CHILD SUPPORT RECOVERY ACT OF 1994.

deadborn. See STILLBORN.

dead corporation. See *dissolved corporation* under CORPORATION.

dead freight. See FREIGHT.

deadhand control. (1952) The convergence of various legal doctrines that allow a decedent's control of wealth to influence the conduct of a living beneficiary; esp., the use of executory interests that vest at some indefinite and remote time in the future to restrict alienability and to ensure that property remains in the hands of a particular family or organization. • Examples include the lawful use of conditional gifts, contingent future interests, and the *Claflin*-trust principle. The rule against perpetuities restricts certain types of deadhand control, which is sometimes referred to either as the power of the *mortua manus* (dead hand) or as trying to retain property *in mortua manu*. See RULE AGAINST PERPETUITIES.

dead letter. 1. A law or practice that, although not formally abolished, is no longer used, observed, or enforced. **2.** A piece of mail that can be neither delivered nor returned because it lacks correct addresses for both the intended recipient and the sender.

deadlock, *n.* **1.** A state of inaction resulting from opposition, a lack of compromise or resolution, or a failure of election. See *tie vote* under VOTE (2). **2.** *Corporations.* The blocking of corporate action by one or more factions of shareholders or directors who disagree about a significant aspect of corporate policy. — **deadlock,** *vb.*

deadlocked jury. See *hung jury* under JURY.

deadly force. See FORCE.

deadly weapon. See WEAPON.

deadly weapon per se. See WEAPON.

dead man's part. *Archaic.* **1.** *Archaic.* By custom in certain places, the portion of a dead man's estate set aside for mass services; later, that portion set aside as payment for the administrator. • That portion ranged from one-third (if the deceased had a wife and children) to the entire estate (if the deceased had no wife or children). **2.** *Scots law.* The part of the movable estate that may be disposed of by will in any way the testator wishes; specif., the part of a dead man's personal estate not legally reserved for his spouse or children and capable of being bequeathed by will or falling upon intestacy to his next-of-kin. — Also termed *dead's part.*

dead man's statute. (1879) A law prohibiting the admission of a decedent's statement as evidence in certain circumstances, as when an opposing party or witness seeks to use the statement to support a claim against the decedent's estate. — Also termed *dead person's statute.*

dead marriage. See MARRIAGE (1).

dead person's statute. See DEAD MAN'S STATUTE.

dead pledge. *Archaic.* See MORTGAGE (1).

dead rent. A mining-lease payment, either in addition to or as part of the royalty, that must be made whether or not the mine is working. • The purpose of the provision is to secure the working of the mine. See *delay rental* under RENTAL.

dead-ship doctrine. *Maritime law.* The rule that admiralty law no longer applies to a ship when its purpose has been so changed that it is no longer a vessel because it has no further navigation function.

dead's part. See DEAD MAN'S PART.

dead stock. Goods that remain in inventory because there is no market for them.

dead storage. The stowage of goods, esp. motor vehicles, for a long time in a public storage area, as opposed to the daily or regular stowage of goods in active use. Cf. LIVE STORAGE.

dead time. See TIME.

dead use. A future use.

deal, *n.* (15c) **1.** An act of buying and selling; the purchase and exchange of something for profit <a business deal>. **2.** An arrangement for mutual advantage <the witness accepted the prosecutor's deal to testify in exchange for immunity>. **3.** An indefinite quantity <a great deal of money>.

deal, *vb.* (bef. 12c) **1.** To distribute (something) <to deal drugs>. **2.** To transact business with (a person or entity) <to deal with the competitor>. **3.** To conspire with (a person or entity) <to deal for the account>.

dealer, *n.* (17c) **1.** A person who purchases goods or property for sale to others; a retailer. **2.** A person or firm that buys and sells securities for its own account as a principal, and then sells to a customer. See DEAL, *n.* & *vb.*

> **broker-dealer.** See *broker-dealer* under BROKER.

> **registered dealer.** A dealer registered or required to be registered under the Securities Exchange Act of 1934.

dealer's talk. See PUFFING (1).

dean. 1. *Eccles. law.* An officer who leads a chapter, parish, or other subdivision of a diocese, usu. upon a bishop's request or appointment. **2.** In a school, college, or university, the administrative or academic head. • In larger schools, there may be several kinds of deans, such as a dean of admissions and a dean of student affairs. Within a university, there may be deans of specific schools. **3.** The head or commander of a group of ten, such as ten soldiers or ten monks.

death. (bef. 12c) The ending of life; the cessation of all vital functions and signs. — Also termed *decease; demise.*

> **accidental death.** A death that results from an unusual event, one that was not voluntary, intended, expected, or foreseeable. — Also termed *death by misadventure.*

> **brain death.** (1964) The bodily condition of showing no response to external stimuli, no spontaneous movements, no breathing, no reflexes, and a flat reading (usu. for a full day) on a machine that measures the brain's electrical activity. • In 1971, Kansas became the first state to enact a statutory definition of the term. Before that, heart transplants raised the question of when — and whether — death had occurred. Early cases dealing with this problem include a tort case (wrongful death), *Tucker v. Lower,* No. 2831 (Richmond, Va., L. & Eq. Ct., May 23, 1972) (jury accepted the defendants' definition of brain death); a criminal case (vehicular homicide), *People v. Flores,* No. 20190 (Sonoma Co. Mun. Ct. Dec. 19, 1973), No. N746-C (Sonoma Co. Super. Ct. July 23, 1974) (defendant acquitted because no statute defined brain death); and a criminal case (murder), *People v. Lyons,* 15 Crim. L. Rep. 2240, No. 56072 (Alameda Co. Super. Ct. May 21, 1974) (court accepted prosecutor's definition of brain death and convicted defendant). — Also termed *legal death.*

> **civil death. 1.** *Archaic.* At common law, the loss of rights — such as the rights to vote, make contracts, inherit, and sue — by a person who has been outlawed or convicted of a serious crime, or who is considered to have left the temporal world for the spiritual by entering a monastery. **2.** In some states, the loss of rights — such as the rights to vote and hold public office — by a person serving a life sentence. Cf. *civil disability* under DISABILITY (3). **3.** The state of a corporation that has formally dissolved or become bankrupt, leaving an estate to be administered for the benefit of shareholders and creditors. — Also termed (in senses 2 & 3) *legal death.*

> **compensable death.** *Workers' compensation.* A death that, because it occurred in the course of employment, entitles the employee's heirs to compensation.

> **death by one's own hand.** See SUICIDE (1).

> **immediate death.** (16c) **1.** See *instantaneous death.* **2.** A death occurring within a short time after an injury or seizure, but not instantaneously.

> **instantaneous death.** (18c) Death occurring in an instant or within an extremely short time after an injury or seizure. • It is a factor in determining an award of damages for the victim's pain and suffering. — Sometimes also termed *immediate death.*

> **legal death. 1.** See *brain death.* **2.** See *civil death* (2). **3.** See *civil death* (3).

> **natural death.** (15c) **1.** Bodily death, as opposed to civil death. **2.** Death from causes other than accident or violence; death from natural causes. — Also termed *mors naturalis.* See NATURAL-DEATH ACT. Cf. *violent death.*

> **presumptive death.** (1856) Death inferred from proof of the person's long, unexplained absence, usu. after seven years. See ENOCH ARDEN LAW.

> **simultaneous death.** (1878) The death of two or more persons in the same mishap, under circumstances that make it impossible to determine who died first. See UNIFORM SIMULTANEOUS DEATH ACT; COMMON DISASTER; COMMORIENTES.

> **violent death.** (16c) Death accelerated by human intervention and resulting from a sharp blow, explosion, gunfire, or the like. Cf. *natural death.*

death, contemplation of. See CONTEMPLATION OF DEATH.

death action. See WRONGFUL-DEATH ACTION.

deathbed declaration. See *dying declaration* under DECLARATION (6).

deathbed deed. See DEED.

death benefit. See BENEFIT.

death-benefit-only plan. See *survivor's income benefit plan* under EMPLOYEE BENEFIT PLAN.

death by misadventure. 1. See ACCIDENTAL KILLING. **2.** See *accidental death* under DEATH. **3.** *Archaic.* A defense to a murder charge on the ground that the defendant lacked the requisite mental state for murder. • The defense was abolished as redundant because the prosecution had to prove state of mind anyway as an essential element of murder.

death by one's own hand. See SUICIDE (1).

death case. (1907) **1.** A criminal case in which the death penalty may be or has been imposed. **2.** WRONGFUL-DEATH ACTION.

death certificate. (1888) An official document issued by a public registry verifying that a person has died, with information such as the date and time of death, the cause of death, and the signature of the attending or examining physician.

death-damage statute. *Archaic.* See WRONGFUL-DEATH STATUTE.

death duty. 1. See DUTY (4). **2.** See *estate tax* under TAX.

death-knell doctrine. (1972) A rule allowing an interlocutory appeal if precluding an appeal until final judgment would moot the issue on appeal and irreparably injure the appellant's rights. • Once recognized as an exception to the final-judgment rule, the doctrine was limited by the U.S. Supreme Court in *Coopers & Lybrand v. Livesay*, 437 U.S. 463, 98 S.Ct. 2454 (1978). There, the Court held that the death-knell doctrine does not permit an immediate appeal of an order denying class certification. But the doctrine still applies in some contexts. For example, the doctrine allows an immediate appeal of the denial of a temporary restraining order when the lack of an appeal would leave nothing to be considered in the trial court. *Woratzeck v. Arizona Bd. of Executive Clemency*, 117 F.3d 400 (9th Cir. 1997). — Also termed *death-knell exception*. Cf. FINAL-JUDGMENT RULE.

Death on the High Seas Act. A federal law, enacted in 1920, permitting a wrongful-death action to be filed in U.S. district court for a death occurring on the high seas. 46 USCA app. §§ 761–67. — Abbr. DOHSA.

death penalty. (1848) **1.** CAPITAL PUNISHMENT. **2.** A penalty that makes a person or entity ineligible to participate in an activity that the person or entity previously participated in. • The penalty is usu. imposed because of some type of gross misconduct. **3.** See *death-penalty sanction* under SANCTION.

death-penalty sanction. See SANCTION.

death-qualified jury. See JURY.

death row. (1950) The area of a prison where those who have been sentenced to death are confined.

death sentence. See SENTENCE.

deathsman. An executioner; a hangman.

death-spiral deal. A convertible security for which the conversion price depends on the market price less a percentage discount on the date of conversion. — Also termed *toxic convert*.

death statute. (1910) A law that protects the interests of a decedent's family and other dependents, who may recover in damages what they would reasonably have received from the decedent if the death had not occurred. Cf. SURVIVAL STATUTE.

death tax. 1. See *estate tax* under TAX. **2.** See *inheritance tax* under TAX.

death trap. (1835) **1.** A structure or situation involving an imminent risk of death. **2.** A situation that, although seemingly safe, is actually quite dangerous.

death warrant. See WARRANT (1).

debarment, *n.* The act of precluding someone from having or doing something; exclusion or hindrance. — **debar,** *vb.*

debasement. (17c) **1.** The act of reducing the value, quality, or purity of something; esp., the act of lowering the value of coins by either reducing the weight of gold and silver in the coins or increasing the coins' alloy amounts. **2.** Degradation. **3.** The state of being degraded.

debate. *Parliamentary law.* Formal consideration of a motion's merits in the form of speeches for, against, or otherwise addressing the motion. See CONSIDERATION (2). — **debatable,** *adj.* — **debatability,** *n.*

controlled debate. Debate in which designated managers, usu. a partisan leader, lead each side and allot time for speeches. — Also termed *controlled time.*

extended debate. Debate that continues beyond an otherwise applicable limit. See EXTEND DEBATE.

floor debate. (1884) The legislative process of debating a proposed bill before an entire chamber rather than before a committee.

limited debate. Debate with restrictions. See LIMIT DEBATE.

pro–con debate. A debate that adheres to the parliamentary principle that speeches should alternate between opposing viewpoints. • Sometimes those seeking the floor on one side outnumber those on the other side, in which case the chair may allow two (or more) speeches in a row on the same side of the question.

debate agenda. See *debate calendar* under CALENDAR (4).

debate calendar. See CALENDAR (4).

debauch (di-**bawch**), *vb.* **1.** *Archaic.* To draw (a person) away from duty; to lead (a person) astray. **2.** To corrupt (a person) with lewdness; to seduce (someone). **3.** To mar or spoil (a person or thing).

debauchery (di-**bawch**-ə-ree), *n.* Excessive indulgence in sensual pleasures; sexual immorality or excesses. — **debauch**, *vb.*

de bene esse (dee **bee**-nee **es**-ee *also* day **ben**-ay **es**-ay), *adv.* [Law Latin "of well-being"] (17c) As conditionally allowed for the present; in anticipation of a future need <Willis's deposition was taken *de bene esse*>. — Abbr. *d.b.e.* — *de bene esse*, *adj.*

debenture (di-**ben**-chər). [fr. L. *debentur* "there are owed"] (15c) **1.** A debt secured only by the debtor's earning power, not by a lien on any specific asset. ● Originally, this was the first word of a deed detailing sums acknowledged to be owed. **2.** An instrument acknowledging such a debt. **3.** A bond that is backed only by the general credit and financial reputation of the corporate issuer, not by a lien on corporate assets. — Also termed *debenture bond*; *unsecured bond*; *naked debenture*; *plain bond*. Cf. BOND (3).

  convertible debenture. (1908) A debenture that the holder may change or convert into some other security, such as stock.

  convertible subordinated debenture. (1961) A debenture that is subordinate to another debt but can be converted into a different security.

  sinking-fund debenture. (1893) A debenture that is secured by periodic payments into a fund established to retire long-term debt.

  subordinate debenture. (1929) A debenture that is subject to the prior payment of ordinary debentures and other indebtedness.

4. *English law.* A company's security for a monetary loan. ● The security usu. creates a charge on company stock or property. **5.** A customhouse certificate providing for a refund of the duties on imported goods when the importer reexports the goods rather than selling them in the country where they were imported.

debenture bond. See DEBENTURE (3).

debenture indenture. See INDENTURE.

debenture stock. 1. Stock that is issued under a contract providing for periodic, fixed payments. **2.** *English law.* A type of bond representing money borrowed by a company using its property or other fixed assets as security.

debit. (15c) **1.** A sum charged as due or owing. **2.** In bookkeeping, an entry made on the left side of a ledger or account, noting an increase in assets or a decrease in liabilities. **3.** An account balance showing that something remains due to the holder of the account. Cf. CREDIT (6).

debit card. A card used to pay for purchases by electronic transfer from the purchaser's bank account. Cf. CREDIT CARD.

debitor (**deb**-i-tor), *n. Roman law.* Someone who has a legal obligation to someone else. Cf. CREDITOR (1). Pl. *debitores.*

de bonis asportatis (dee **boh**-nis as-pər-**tay**-tis). See *trespass de bonis asportatis* under TRESPASS.

debt. (13c) **1.** Liability on a claim; a specific sum of money due by agreement or otherwise <the debt amounted to $2,500>. **2.** The aggregate of all existing claims against a person, entity, or state <the bank denied the loan application after analyzing the applicant's outstanding debt>. **3.** A nonmonetary thing that one person owes another, such as goods or services <her debt was to supply him with 20 international first-class tickets on the airline of his choice>. **4.** A common-law writ by which a court adjudicates claims involving fixed sums of money <he brought suit in debt>. — Also termed (in sense 4) *writ of debt*.

  active debt. *Civil law.* A debt due to another person.

  ancestral debt. An ancestor's debt that an heir can be compelled to pay.

  antecedent debt. **1.** *Contracts.* An old debt that may serve as consideration for a new promise if the statute of limitations has run on the old debt. See PREEXISTING-DUTY RULE. **2.** *Bankruptcy.* A debtor's prepetition obligation that existed before a debtor's transfer of an interest in property. ● For a transfer to be preferential, it must be for or on account of an antecedent debt. See PREFERENTIAL TRANSFER.

  bad debt. A debt that is uncollectible and that may be deductible for tax purposes.

  bonded debt. A debt secured by a bond; a business or government debt represented by issued bonds.

  community debt. A debt that is chargeable to the community of husband and wife. See COMMUNITY PROPERTY.

  consumer debt. A debt incurred by someone primarily for a personal, family, or household purpose.

  contingent debt. A debt that is not presently fixed but that may become fixed in the future with the occurrence of some event.

  convertible debt. A debt whose security may be changed by a creditor into another form of security.

  debt by simple contract. See *simple-contract debt.*

debt by special contract. See *special-contract debt.*

debt by specialty contract. See *special-contract debt.*

debt of record. A debt evidenced by a court record, such as a judgment.

desperate debt. 1. Uncollectable debt. **2.** A debt taken on by one who is either insolvent or on the verge of insolvency.

distressed debt. A debt instrument issued by a company that is financially troubled and in danger of defaulting on the debt, or in bankruptcy, or likely to default or declare bankruptcy in the near future.

exigible debt. A liquidated and demandable debt; a matured claim.

fixed debt. Generally, a permanent form of debt commonly evidenced by a bond or debenture; long-term debt. — Also termed *fixed liability.*

floating debt. Short-term debt that is continuously renewed to finance the ongoing operations of a business or government.

fraudulent debt. A debt created by fraudulent practices.

funded debt. 1. A state or municipal debt to be paid out of an accumulation of money or by future taxation. **2.** Secured long-term corporate debt meant to replace short-term, floating, or unsecured debt.

general debt. A governmental body's debt that is legally payable from general revenues and is backed by the full faith and credit of the governmental body.

hypothecary debt. A lien on an estate.

individual debt. (*usu. pl.*) Debt personally owed by a partner, rather than by the partnership.

installment debt. A debt that is to be repaid in a series of payments at regular times over a specified period.

judgment debt. A debt that is evidenced by a legal judgment or brought about by a successful lawsuit against the debtor.

junior debt. See *subordinate debt.*

legal debt. A debt recoverable in a court of law.

liquidated debt. A debt whose amount has been determined by agreement of the parties or by operation of law.

liquid debt. A debt that is due immediately and unconditionally.

long-term debt. Generally, a debt that will not come due within the next year.

mutual debts. Cross-debts of the same kind and quality between two persons. Cf. SETOFF (2).

national debt. See NATIONAL DEBT.

nondischargeable debt. (1908) A debt (such as one for delinquent taxes) that is not released through bankruptcy.

passive debt. A debt that, by agreement between the debtor and creditor, is interest-free.

preferential debt. A debt that is legally payable before others, such as an employee's wages.

privileged debt. A debt that has priority over other debts if a debtor becomes insolvent; a secured debt.

public debt. A debt owed by a municipal, state, or national government.

pure debt. See *pure obligation* under OBLIGATION.

secured debt. A debt backed by collateral.

senior debt. A debt that takes priority over other debts. • Senior debts are often secured by collateral.

short-term debt. Collectively, all debts and other liabilities that are payable within one year. — Also termed *current liability.*

simple-contract debt. A debt that is either oral or written but is not of record and not under seal. — Also termed *debt by simple contract.*

special-contract debt. A debt due, or acknowledged to be due, by an instrument under seal, such as a deed of covenant or sale, a lease reserving rent, or a bond. — Also termed *debt by special contract*; *debt by specialty contract*; *specialty debt.*

subordinate debt. A debt that is junior or inferior to other types or classes of debt. • Subordinate debt may be unsecured or have a low-priority claim against property secured by other debt instruments. — Also termed *junior debt.*

unliquidated debt. A debt that has not been reduced to a specific amount, and about which there may be a dispute.

unsecured debt. A debt not supported by collateral or other security.

debt adjustment. See DEBT POOLING.

debt capital. See CAPITAL.

debt consolidation. 1. See DEBT POOLING. **2.** The replacement of multiple loans from one or more lenders with a single loan from one lender, usu. with a lower monthly payment and a longer repayment period.

debtee. *Archaic.* See CREDITOR (1).

debt-equity ratio. See DEBT-TO-EQUITY RATIO.

debt financing. See FINANCING.

debt instrument. (1953) A written promise to repay a debt, such as a promissory note, bill, bond, or commercial paper.

debt limitation. A ceiling placed on borrowing by an individual, business, or government. • The constitutions of many states prohibit the states from incurring debt in excess of a stated amount. Other state constitutions allow states to incur debt above a stated amount only through a vote of the people. — Also termed *limitation on indebtedness.*

debt of record. See DEBT.

debtor. (13c) **1.** One who owes an obligation to another, esp. an obligation to pay money. **2.** *Bankruptcy.* A person who files a voluntary petition or against whom an involuntary petition is filed. — Also termed *bankrupt.* **3.** *Secured transactions.* A person who either (1) has a property interest — other than a security interest or other lien — in collateral, even if the person is not an obligor, or (2) is a seller of accounts, chattel paper, payment intangibles, or promissory notes. UCC § 9-102(a) (28). — Abbr. Dr. Cf. CREDITOR.

absconding debtor. (18c) A debtor who flees from creditors to avoid having to pay a debt. • Absconding from a debt was formerly considered an act of bankruptcy. See ACT OF BANKRUPTCY.

absent debtor. A debtor who lacks the intent to defraud creditors but is beyond the geographic reach of ordinary service of process.

account debtor. A person obligated on an account, chattel paper, or general intangible. • The UCC exempts from the definition of *account debtor* a person obligated to pay a negotiable instrument, even if the instrument constitutes chattel paper. UCC § 9-102(a)(3).

common debtor. *Scots law.* A debtor whose property has been arrested by more than one creditor.

concealed debtor. A debtor who hides from creditors, usu. with the intent to defraud the creditors or to avoid service of process, but does not leave the community or move out of state.

joint debtor. One of two or more debtors jointly liable for the same debt.

judgment debtor. See JUDGMENT DEBTOR.

new debtor. (18c) *Secured transactions.* A person who becomes bound as debtor under a security agreement previously entered into by another person. UCC §§ 9-102(a)(56), 9-203(c).

solvent debtor. A debtor who owns enough property to cover all outstanding debts and against whom a creditor can enforce a judgment.

debtor-in-possession. (1806) *Bankruptcy.* A Chapter 11 or 12 debtor that continues to operate its business as a fiduciary to the bankruptcy estate. • With certain exceptions, the debtor-in-possession has all the rights, powers, and duties of a Chapter 11 trustee. — Abbr. DIP.

debtor rehabilitation. See REHABILITATION (3).

Debtor's Act of 1869. An English statute that, among other things, (1) abolished imprisonment for debt except in certain cases, as when a debtor owed a debt to the Crown or a debtor had money but refused to pay a debt, (2) abolished arrest by mesne process, that is, by compelling the defendant to appear and give bail unless it was believed that the defendant would leave the country, (3) made it a misdemeanor to obtain credit under false pretenses or to defraud creditors, and (4) defined how warrants and judgment orders would be executed.

debtor's examination. *Bankruptcy.* A meeting between a debtor and his or her creditors during which the creditors ask the debtor questions designed to uncover information about the location and extent of the debtor's assets and the dischargeability of debts. • The examination may be conducted under § 343 of the Bankruptcy Code or Rule 2004 of the Federal Rules of Bankruptcy Procedure. The bankruptcy trustee may be present and preside over the initial § 343 examination, which is held shortly after the bankruptcy filing. But the party (usu. a creditor) who requests a Rule 2004 examination presides over the meeting, which can be held at any time. See 11 USCA § 343; Fed. R. Bankr. P. 2004.

debtor's petition. See *voluntary petition* under PETITION.

debtor's property. See PROPERTY OF THE DEBTOR.

debt pooling. (1957) **1.** *Bankruptcy.* An arrangement by which a person's debts are consolidated and creditors agree to accept lower monthly payments or to take less money. — Also termed *debt consolidation; debt adjustment.* **2.** An arrangement under which a debtor agrees to pay (1) a sum of money periodically or otherwise to a third person who will then distribute the money among certain specified creditors in accordance with a plan, and (2) a fee to the third person for his or her services as distributor. • Debt-pooling in this manner is generally illegal if the arrangement is not made with a bank, attorney, judicial officer, retail-merchants' association, or nonprofit organization that provides debt-counseling services.

debt ratio. (1932) A corporation's total long-term and short-term liabilities divided by the firm's total assets. • A low debt ratio indicates conservative financing and thus usu. an enhanced ability to borrow in the future. — Also termed *debt-to-total-assets ratio.*

debt retirement. (1928) Repayment of debt; RETIREMENT (3).

debt security. See SECURITY.

debt service. (1930) **1.** The funds needed to meet a long-term debt's annual interest expenses, principal payments, and sinking-fund contributions. **2.** Payments due on a debt, including interest and principal.

debt-to-equity ratio. (1954) A corporation's long-term debt divided by its owners' equity, calculated to assess its capitalization. — Also termed *debt-equity ratio*; *debt-to-net-worth ratio*.

debt-to-total-assets ratio. See DEBT RATIO.

DeCA. *abbr.* DEFENSE COMMISSARY AGENCY.

decapitation (dee-kap-ə-**tay**-shən). *Hist.* The act of cutting off a head; a beheading. • This was once a common method of capital punishment.

decarceration. See DISIMPRISONMENT.

decease, *n.* See DEATH.

decease, *vb.* To die; to depart from life.

deceased, *n.* See DECEDENT.

decedent (di-**see**-dənt), *n.* (16c) A dead person, esp. one who has died recently. • This term is little used outside law. It typically appears in legal proceedings or administrative inquiries. — Also termed *deceased*.

> **nonresident decedent.** A decedent who was domiciled outside the jurisdiction in question (such as probate jurisdiction) at the time of death.

decedent's estate. See ESTATE (3).

deceit, *n.* (14c) **1.** The act of intentionally giving a false impression <the juror's deceit led the lawyer to believe that she was not biased>. **2.** A false statement of fact made by a person knowingly or recklessly (i.e., not caring whether it is true or false) with the intent that someone else will act upon it. See *fraudulent misrepresentation* under MISREPRESENTATION. **3.** A tort arising from a false representation made knowingly or recklessly with the intent that another person should detrimentally rely on it <the new homeowner sued both the seller and the realtor for deceit after discovering termites>. See FRAUD; MISREPRESENTATION. — **deceive,** *vb.*

deceitful plea. See *sham pleading* under PLEADING (1).

decenary. [fr. Latin *decena* "a tithing"] *Hist.* A town or district consisting of ten freeholding families. • A freeholder of the decenary (a *decennarius*) was bound by frankpledge to produce any wrongdoer living in the decenary. — Also spelled (incorrectly) *decennary.* — Also termed *decenna*; *tithing.* Cf. FRANKPLEDGE.

decency. The state of being proper, as in speech or dress; the quality of being seemly.

decennary. See DECENARY.

deceptive act. (1939) As defined by the Federal Trade Commission and most state statutes, conduct that is likely to deceive a consumer acting reasonably under similar circumstances. — Also

termed *deceptive practice*; *deceptive sales practice*.

deceptive advertising. See FALSE ADVERTISING.

deceptive practice. See DECEPTIVE ACT.

deceptive sales practice. See DECEPTIVE ACT.

deceptive warranty. See WARRANTY (2).

decertify, *vb.* (1918) **1.** To revoke the certification of. **2.** To remove the official status of (a labor union) by withdrawing the right to act as a collective-bargaining agent. **3.** (Of a court) to overrule a previous order that created a class for purposes of a class action; to officially undo (a class). Cf. CERTIFY. — **decertification,** *n.*

decimation (des-ə-**may**-shən). **1.** A major destruction of people; a great loss of life. **2.** *Hist.* A tithing; a payment of the tenth part. **3.** *Hist.* A punishment, esp. by death, of every tenth person by lot. • Under Roman law, *decimatio* referred to the punishment by lot of every tenth soldier in a legion for mutiny or cowardice.

decision, *n.* (16c) **1.** A judicial or agency determination after consideration of the facts and the law; esp., a ruling, order, or judgment pronounced by a court when considering or disposing of a case. See JUDGMENT (1); OPINION (1). — **decisional,** *adj.*

> **appealable decision.** (1870) A decree or order that is sufficiently final to receive appellate review (such as an order granting summary judgment), or an interlocutory decree or order that is immediately appealable, usu. by statute (such as an order denying immunity to a police officer in a civil-rights suit). — Also termed *reviewable issue.* See COLLATERAL-ORDER DOCTRINE.

> **final decision.** See *final judgment* under JUDGMENT.

> **interlocutory decision.** See *interlocutory order* under ORDER (2).

> **unreasonable decision.** (1962) An administrative agency's decision that is so obviously wrong that there can be no difference of opinion among reasonable minds about its erroneous nature.

2. *Parliamentary law.* VOTE (4). **3.** *Parliamentary law.* The chair's ruling on a point of order. See *appeal from the decision of the chair* under APPEAL.

decisional law. See CASELAW.

decision-making responsibility. The authority to come to a binding resolution of an issue. • For example, in child-rearing, decision-making responsibility involves the authority to make significant decisions on a child's behalf, including decisions about education, religious training, and healthcare.

decision on the merits. See *judgment on the merits* under JUDGMENT.

decisive oath. See OATH.

decisory oath. See *decisive oath* under OATH.

Decker test. See SUBJECT-MATTER TEST.

declarant (di-**klair**-ənt), *n.* (17c) **1.** One who has made a statement <in accordance with the rules of evidence, the statement was offered to prove the declarant's state of mind>. **2.** One who has signed a declaration, esp. one stating an intent to become a U.S. citizen <the declarant grew up in Italy>. — **declarant**, *adj.*

declaration, *n.* (15c) **1.** A formal statement, proclamation, or announcement, esp. one embodied in an instrument. Cf. AFFIDAVIT.

  declaration of alienage. A declaration by a person with dual citizenship of a wish to renounce the citizenship of one state. • For the declaration to be effective, the person making it must be of full age and not under any disability.

  declaration of default. A creditor's notice to a debtor regarding the debtor's failure to perform an obligation, such as making a payment.

  declaration of dividend. (1837) A company's setting aside of a portion of its earnings or profits for distribution to its shareholders. See DIVIDEND.

  declaration of homestead. (1856) A statement required to be filed with a state or local authority to prove property ownership in order to claim homestead-exemption rights. See HOMESTEAD.

  declaration of intention. (1812) An alien's formal statement resolving to become a U.S. citizen and to renounce allegiance to any other government or country.

  declaration of legitimacy. (1861) A formal or legal pronouncement that a child is legitimate.

  declaration of trust. (17c) **1.** The act by which the person who holds legal title to property or an estate acknowledges that the property is being held in trust for another person or for certain specified purposes. **2.** The instrument that creates a trust. — Also termed (in sense 2) *trust instrument; trust deed; trust agreement.*

2. *Int'l law.* The part of a treaty containing the stipulations under which the parties agree to conduct their actions; TREATY (1). **3.** *Int'l law.* A country's unilateral pronouncement that affects the rights and duties of other countries.

  declaration of war. A country's announcement that it is officially engaged in war against another country.

4. A document that governs legal rights to certain types of real property, such as a condominium or a residential subdivision. **5.** A listing of the merchandise that a person intends to bring into the United States. • This listing is given to U.S. Customs when one enters the country. **6.** *Evidence.* An unsworn statement made by someone having knowledge of facts relating to an event in dispute.

  deathbed declaration. See *dying declaration.*

  declaration against interest. (1940) A statement by a person who is not a party to a suit and is not available to testify at trial, discussing a matter that is within the declarant's personal knowledge and is adverse to the declarant's interest. • Such a statement is admissible into evidence as an exception to the hearsay rule. Fed. R. Evid. 804(b)(3). — Also termed *self-disserving declaration.* See *admission against interest* under ADMISSION (1).

  declaration of pain. (1891) A person's exclamation of present pain, which operates as an exception to the hearsay rule. Fed. R. Evid. 803(3).

  declaration of state of mind. (1843) A person's state-of-mind statement that operates as an exception to the hearsay rule. Fed. R. Evid. 803(3).

  dying declaration. (18c) A statement by a person who believes that death is imminent, relating to the cause or circumstances of the person's impending death. • The statement is admissible in evidence as an exception to the hearsay rule. — Also termed *deathbed declaration; ante mortem statement.*

  self-disserving declaration. See *declaration against interest.*

  self-serving declaration. (1881) An out-of-court statement made to benefit one's own interest.

7. *Common-law pleading.* The plaintiff's first pleading in a civil action. • It is an amplification of the original writ on which the action is founded, with the additional circumstances of the time and place of injury. In a real action, the declaration is called a *count.* Today the equivalent term in English law is *statement of claim*; in most American jurisdictions, it is called a *petition* or *complaint.* — Also termed *narratio.* See COUNT (2), (3). Cf. PLEA (2).

  declaration in chief. A declaration for the principal cause of action.

8. A formal, written statement — resembling an affidavit but not notarized or sworn to — that attests, under penalty of perjury, to facts known by the declarant. • Such a declaration, if properly prepared, is admissible in federal court with the same effect as an affidavit. 28 USCA § 1746. — Also termed *declaration under penalty of perjury; unsworn declaration under penalty of perjury.* Cf. AFFIDAVIT; *sworn statement* under STATEMENT. **9.** *Int'l law.* An oral or written statement, unilaterally made, by which a state expresses its will, intent, or opinion when acting in the field of international relations. **10.** See *declaratory judgment* under JUDGMENT. **11.** DECLARATION OF RIGHTS. — **declare,** *vb.* — **declaratory,** *adj.*

declaration after final rejection. See *affidavit after final rejection* under AFFIDAVIT.

declaration date. See DATE.

declaration of a desire for a natural death. See LIVING WILL.

declaration of alienage. See DECLARATION (1).

declaration of continued use. See DECLARATION OF USE.

declaration of estimated tax. (1946) A required IRS filing by certain individuals and businesses of current estimated tax owed, accompanied by periodic payments of that amount. • The requirement ensures current collection of taxes from taxpayers (such as self-employed persons) whose incomes are not fully taxed by payroll withholding. IRC (26 USCA) §§ 6315, 6654.

declaration of incontestability. *Trademarks.* A sworn statement submitted by the owner of a registered mark after five years of registration, averring that the mark has been in continuous use in commerce for at least five consecutive years since registration, that the mark has not become generic, that there has been no final adverse decision to ownership in the mark, and that there is no pending proceeding in the U.S. Patent and Trademark Office or courts involving the mark. • The statement entitles the mark to immunity from some legal challenges under § 15 of the Lanham Act. — Also termed *affidavit of incontestability*; *affidavit under § 15*; *declaration under § 15*; *Section 15 affidavit*; *Section 15 declaration*.

Declaration of Independence. The formal proclamation of July 4, 1776, in the name of the people of the American colonies, asserting their independence from the British Crown and announcing themselves to the world as an independent nation.

declaration of legitimacy. See DECLARATION (1).

declaration of no defenses. See WAIVER OF DEFENSES.

declaration of pain. See DECLARATION (6).

Declaration of Paris. An international agreement, signed by Great Britain, France, Turkey, Sardinia, Austria, Prussia, and Russia in 1856 (at the end of the Crimean War), providing that (1) privateering is illegal, (2) with the exception of contraband, a neutral flag covers an enemy's goods, (3) with the exception of contraband, neutral goods cannot be confiscated under a hostile flag, and (4) a blockade must work to be binding. • The agreement was later adopted by most other maritime powers, except the United States and a few others.

declaration of restrictions. *Property.* A statement of all the covenants, conditions, and restrictions affecting a parcel of land, usu. imposed and recorded by a developer of a subdivision. • The restrictions usu. promote a general plan of development by requiring all lot owners to comply with the specified standards, esp. for buildings. The restrictions run with the land. — Sometimes also written *declarations of restrictions*.

declaration of rights. 1. An action in which a litigant requests a court's assistance not because any rights have been violated but because those rights are uncertain. • Examples include suits for a declaration of legitimacy, for declaration of nullity of marriage, and for the authoritative interpretation of a will. **2.** See *declaratory judgment* under JUDGMENT. — Often shortened to *declaration*.

declaration of state of mind. See DECLARATION (6).

Declaration of Taking Act. The federal law regulating the government's taking of private property for public use under eminent domain. 40 USCA § 3114 et seq. • Fair compensation must be paid for the property.

declaration of trust. See DECLARATION (1).

declaration of use. *Trademarks.* A sworn statement submitted by a registered mark's owner averring that the registered mark is currently in use in commerce, and providing a specimen or facsimile of the mark's use. • The § 8 affidavit must be filed (1) between the fifth and sixth year following registration, and (2) within the year before the end of every ten-year period after the date of registration. If a registered mark's owner fails to file a § 8 affidavit within the required time, the U.S. Patent and Trademark Office may cancel the registration. The term comes from § 8 of the Lanham Act. — Also termed *affidavit of continued use*; *affidavit of use*; *affidavit under § 8*; *declaration of continued use*; *declaration under § 8*; *Section 8 declaration*; *statement of use*. Cf. INCONTESTABILITY STATUS; CANCELLATION.

declaration of war. See DECLARATION (3).

declaration under penalty of perjury. See DECLARATION (8).

declaration under § 8. See DECLARATION OF USE.

declaration under § 15. See DECLARATION OF INCONTESTABILITY.

declarator. See *action of declarator* under ACTION (4).

declarator of trust (di-**klar**-ə-tər *or* di-**klair**-ə-tər *or* -tor). A common-law action against a trustee who holds property under a title *ex facie* for the trustee's own benefit.

declaratory (di-**klar**-ə-tor-ee *or* di-**klair**-), *adj.* **1.** Clear; manifest <a declaratory statute>. **2.** Explanatory <a declaratory judgment>.

declaratory, *n.* See *action of declarator* under AC-
TION.

declaratory act. See *declaratory statute* under STAT-
UTE.

declaratory decree. See *declaratory judgment*
under JUDGMENT.

declaratory judgment. See JUDGMENT.

declaratory-judgment act. (1921) A federal or state
law permitting parties to bring an action to determine their legal rights and positions regarding a controversy not yet ripe for adjudication, as
when an insurance company seeks a determination of coverage before deciding whether to cover
a claim. 28 USCA §§ 2201, 2202. See *declaratory
judgment* under JUDGMENT.

declaratory part of a law. A portion of a law clearly
defining rights to be observed or wrongs to be
avoided.

declaratory precedent. See PRECEDENT.

declaratory relief. See RELIEF.

declaratory statute. See STATUTE.

declaratory theory. (1895) The belief that judges'
decisions never make law but instead merely constitute evidence of what the law is. • This antiquated view — held by such figures as Coke and
Blackstone — is no longer accepted.

declared trust. See *express trust* under TRUST.

declination (dek-lə-**nay**-shən). (14c) **1.** A deviation from proper course <declination of duty>.
2. An act of refusal <declination of a gift>. **3.** A
document filed by a fiduciary who chooses not
to serve. **4.** At common law, a plea to the court's
jurisdiction by reason of the judge's personal interest in the lawsuit. — Also termed (esp. in sense
2) *declinature.*

declinatory exception (di-**klin**-ə-tor-ee). See EX-
CEPTION (1).

declinatory plea. *Hist.* A pretrial plea claiming
benefit of clergy. — Also termed *plea of sanctuary.* See BENEFIT OF CLERGY.

declining-balance depreciation method. See DE-
PRECIATION METHOD.

decolonization. *Int'l law.* The process by which a
colonial power divests itself of sovereignty over a
colony — whether a territory, a protectorate, or
a trust territory — so that the colony is granted
autonomy and eventually attains independence.

deconstruction, *n.* (1969) In critical legal studies,
a method of analyzing legal principles or rules by
breaking down the supporting premises to show
that these premises might also advance the opposite rule or result. — Also termed *trashing.* —
deconstructionist, *adj.* & *n.*

decorum. *Parliamentary law.* The customs of formality and courtesy observed by the members
and chair in conducting business.

decoy, *n.* An undercover law-enforcement officer
or agent who acts as the willing subject of an attempted or completed crime in an attempt to lure
a potential criminal defendant into a situation
that establishes the grounds for a prosecution.

decoy, *vb.* *Slang.* To entice (a person) without force;
to inveigle <the victim was decoyed out of her
home> <the defendant was decoyed into the
county and then served with process>. See EN-
TRAPMENT.

decoy letter. A letter prepared and mailed to detect
a criminal who has violated the postal or revenue
laws.

decreased capacity. See CAPACITY (4).

decreasing term insurance. See INSURANCE.

decreasing-term life insurance. See *decreasing
term insurance* under INSURANCE.

decree, *n.* (14c) **1.** Traditionally, a judicial decision
in a court of equity, admiralty, divorce, or probate — similar to a judgment of a court of law
<the judge's decree in favor of the will's benefi-
ciary>. **2.** A court's final judgment. **3.** Any court
order, but esp. one in a matrimonial case <divorce
decree>. See JUDGMENT; ORDER (2); DECISION.

agreed decree. A final judgment, the terms of
which are agreed to by the parties.

consent decree. (1831) A court decree that all parties agree to. — Also termed *consent order.*

custody decree. A decree awarding or modifying
child custody. • The decree may be included in
the decree for a related proceeding — such as a
divorce — or it may be a separate order.

decree absolute. (1826) A ripened decree nisi; a
court's decree that has become unconditional
because the time specified in the decree nisi
has passed. — Also termed *order absolute; rule
absolute.*

decree nisi (**ni**-sɪ). (18c) A court's decree that will
become absolute unless the adversely affected
party shows the court, within a specified time,
why it should be set aside. — Also termed *nisi
decree; order nisi; rule nisi.* See NISI.

decree of distribution. (1841) An instrument by
which heirs receive the property of a deceased
person.

decree of insolvency. (18c) A probate-court decree
declaring an estate's insolvency.

decree of nullity. (17c) A decree declaring a marriage to be void *ab initio.* See ANNULMENT; NUL-
LITY OF MARRIAGE.

decree of registration. 1. A court order that quiets title to land and directs recording of the title. **2.** *Scots law.* CONFESSION OF JUDGMENT.

decree pro confesso (proh kən-**fes**-oh). (1821) *Equity practice.* A decree entered in favor of the plaintiff as a result of the defendant's failure to timely respond to the allegations in the plaintiff's bill; esp., a decree entered when the defendant has defaulted by not appearing in court at the prescribed time. — Also termed *decree taken pro confesso.*

deficiency decree. See *deficiency judgment* under JUDGMENT.

divorce decree. A final judgment in a suit for divorce. ● A divorce decree dissolves the marriage and usu. resolves all matters concerning property and children. Generally, matters concerning children can be modified in a post-divorce action if there has been a substantial change in circumstances.

final decree. See *final judgment* under JUDGMENT.

interlocutory decree. See *interlocutory judgment* under JUDGMENT.

decree nunc pro tunc. See *judgment nunc pro tunc* under JUDGMENT.

decree of furthcuming. See *decree of forthcoming* under DECREE.

decree taken pro confesso. See *decree pro confesso* under DECREE.

decrepit (di-**krep**-it), *adj.* (15c) (Of a person) disabled; physically or mentally incompetent to such an extent that the individual would be helpless in a personal conflict with a person of ordinary health and strength.

decretal (di-**kree**-təl), *adj.* Of or relating to a decree.

decretal child support. See CHILD SUPPORT.

decretal interdict. See INTERDICT (1).

decretal order. See ORDER (2).

decretals (di-**kree**-təlz), *n. Eccles. law.* Canonical epistles written either by the Pope or by the Pope and his cardinals to settle controversial matters; esp., the second part of the *Corpus Juris Canonici,* canonical epistles consisting mainly of: (1) *Decretales Gregorii Noni,* a collection by Raymundus Barcinius, chaplain to Gregory IX, dating from about 1227; (2) *Decretales Bonifacii Octavi,* a collection by Boniface VIII in the year 1298; (3) *Clementinae,* a collection of Clement V, published in the year 1308; and (4) the *Extravagantes,* a collection by John XXII and other bishops. — Also termed (in Law Latin) *Decretales.* See CANON LAW.

decretist (di-**kree**-tist), *n.* In medieval universities, a law student; esp., a student or commentator on Gratian's *Decretum.*

decriminalization, *n.* (1945) The legislative act or process of legalizing an illegal act <many doctors seek the decriminalization of euthanasia>. Cf. CRIMINALIZATION (1). — **decriminalize,** *vb.*

decrowning. The act of depriving someone of a crown.

decry (di-**krı**), *vb.* (17c) To speak disparagingly about (someone or something).

dedication, *n.* (1809) *Property.* The donation of land or creation of an easement for public use. — **dedicate,** *vb.* — **dedicatory,** *adj.*

> **common-law dedication.** (1858) A dedication made without a statute, consisting in the owner's appropriation of land, or an easement in it, for the benefit or use of the public, and the acceptance, by or on behalf of the land or easement. — Often shortened to *dedication.*

> **dedication by adverse user.** (1895) A dedication arising from the adverse, exclusive use by the public with the actual or imputed knowledge and acquiescence of the owner.

> **express dedication.** (1836) A dedication explicitly manifested by the owner.

> **implied dedication.** (1837) A dedication presumed by reasonable inference from the owner's conduct.

> **statutory dedication.** (1852) A dedication for which the necessary steps are statutorily prescribed, all of which must be substantially followed for an effective dedication.

> **tacit dedication.** (1926) A dedication of property for public use arising from silence or inactivity and without an express agreement.

dedication and reservation. A dedication made with reasonable conditions, restrictions, and limitations.

dedication day. See DAY.

dedition (di-**dish**-ən), *n.* [fr. Latin *deditio* "give up"] (16c) A surrender of something, such as property.

deductible, *adj.* Capable of being subtracted, esp. from taxable income. See DEDUCTION (2).

deductible, *n.* (1929) **1.** Under an insurance policy, the portion of the loss to be borne by the insured before the insurer becomes liable for payment. Cf. SELF-INSURED RETENTION.

> **straight deductible.** A deductible that is a specified, fixed amount.

2. The insurance-policy clause specifying the amount of this portion.

deduction, *n.* (15c) **1.** The act or process of subtracting or taking away. **2.** *Tax.* An amount subtracted from gross income when calculating adjusted gross income, or from adjusted gross income when calculating taxable income. — Also termed *tax deduction*. Cf. EXEMPTION (3); TAX CREDIT.

additional standard deduction. (1956) The sum of the additional amounts that a taxpayer who turns 65 or becomes blind before the close of the taxable year is entitled to deduct.

charitable deduction. (1925) A deduction for a contribution to a charitable enterprise that has qualified for tax-exempt status in accordance with IRC (26 USCA) § 501(c)(3) and is entitled to be deducted in full by the donor from the taxable estate or from gross income. See CHARITABLE CONTRIBUTION (2); CHARITABLE ORGANIZATION.

deduction in respect of a decedent. (1949) A deduction that accrues to the point of death but is not recognizable on the decedent's final income-tax return because of the accounting method used, such as an accrued-interest expense of a cash-basis debtor.

itemized deduction. (1943) An expense (such as a medical expense, home-mortgage interest, or a charitable contribution) that can be subtracted from adjusted gross income to determine taxable income.

marital deduction. (1949) A federal tax deduction allowed for lifetime and testamentary transfers from one spouse to another. IRC (26 USCA) §§ 2056, 2523.

miscellaneous itemized deduction. (1955) Generally, an itemized deduction of job or investment expenses; a deduction other than those allowable in computing adjusted gross income, those enumerated in IRC (26 USCA) § 67(b), and personal exemptions. • This type of deduction is allowed only to an itemizing taxpayer whose total miscellaneous itemized deductions exceed a statutory percentage of adjusted gross income.

standard deduction. (1944) A specified dollar amount that a taxpayer can deduct from adjusted gross income, instead of itemizing deductions, to determine taxable income.

3. The portion of a succession to which an heir is entitled before a partition. **4.** The act or process of reasoning from general propositions to a specific application or conclusion. Cf. INDUCTION (2). — **deduct** (for senses 1–3), *vb.* — **deduce** (for sense 4), *vb.*

deduction for new. See NEW-FOR-OLD (1).

deduction in respect of a decedent. See DEDUCTION.

deed, *n.* (bef. 12c) **1.** Something that is done or carried out; an act or action. **2.** A written instrument by which land is conveyed. **3.** At common law, any written instrument that is signed, sealed, and delivered and that conveys some interest in property. See *special contract* & *contract under seal* under CONTRACT. — Also termed (in senses 2 & 3) *evidence of title.* Cf. CONVEYANCE; BILL OF SALE. — **deed,** *vb.*

absolute deed. (17c) A deed that conveys title without condition or encumbrance. — Also termed *deed absolute.*

administrator's deed. A document that conveys property owned by a person who has died intestate.

bargain-and-sale deed. (1972) A deed that conveys property to a buyer for valuable consideration but that lacks any guarantee from the seller about the validity of the title. See BARGAIN AND SALE.

composition deed. A deed reflecting the terms of an agreement between a debtor and a creditor to discharge or adjust a debt.

counterdeed. A secret deed, executed either before a notary or under a private seal, that voids, invalidates, or alters a public deed.

deathbed deed. *Rare.* A deed executed by a grantor shortly before death. • The grantor need not be aware that he or she is near death when the deed is executed.

deed absolute. See *absolute deed.*

deed in fee. (18c) A deed conveying the title to land in fee simple, usu. with covenants.

deed in lieu of foreclosure. (1934) A deed by which a borrower conveys fee-simple title to a lender in satisfaction of a mortgage debt and as a substitute for foreclosure. • This deed is often referred to simply as "deed in lieu."

deed of covenant. (17c) A deed to do something, such as a document providing for periodic payments by one party to another (usu. a charity) for tax-saving purposes. • The transferor can deduct taxes from the payment and, in some cases, the recipient can reclaim the deducted tax.

deed of distribution. A fiduciary's deed conveying a decedent's real estate.

deed of gift. (16c) A deed executed and delivered without consideration. — Also termed *gratuitous deed.*

deed of inspectorship. *Hist.* An instrument reflecting an agreement between a debtor and a creditor to appoint a receiver to oversee the winding up of the debtor's affairs on behalf of the creditor.

deed of partition. (18c) A deed that divides land held by joint tenants, tenants in common, or coparceners.

deed of reconveyance. A deed conveying title to real property from a trustee to a grantor when a loan is repaid. Cf. *deed of trust.*

deed of release. A deed that surrenders full title to a piece of property upon payment or performance of specified conditions.

deed of separation. An instrument governing a spouse's separation and maintenance.

deed of settlement. 1. A deed to settle something, such as the distribution of property in a marriage. **2.** *English law.* A deed formerly used to form a joint-stock company.

deed of trust. (17c) A deed conveying title to real property to a trustee as security until the grantor repays a loan. • This type of deed resembles a mortgage. — Also termed *trust deed; trust indenture; indemnity mortgage; common-law mortgage.* Cf. *deed of reconveyance.*

deed poll. (16c) A deed made by and binding on only one party, or on two or more parties having similar interests. • It is so called because, traditionally, the parchment was "polled" (that is, shaved) so that it would be even at the top (unlike an indenture). — Also spelled *deed-poll.* Cf. INDENTURE.

deed to lead uses. A common-law deed prepared before an action for a fine or common recovery to show the object of those actions.

deed without covenants. See *quitclaim deed.*

defeasible deed. (1802) A deed containing a condition subsequent causing title to the property to revert to the grantor or pass to a third party.

derivative deed. See *secondary conveyance* under CONVEYANCE.

disentailing deed. *Hist.* A tenant-in-tail's assurance that the estate tail will be barred and converted into an estate in fee. • The Fines and Recoveries Act (3 & 4 Will. 4 ch. 74) introduced this way of barring an entail. It authorized nearly every tenant in tail, if certain conditions were met, to dispose of the land in fee simple absolute and thus to defeat the rights of all persons claiming under the tenant.

donation deed. A deed granted by the government to a person who either satisfies the statutory conditions in a donation act or redeems a bounty-land warrant. See DONATION ACT; BOUNTY-LAND WARRANT.

full-covenant-and-warranty deed. See *warranty deed.*

general warranty deed. See *warranty deed.*

gift deed. (1864) A deed given for a nominal sum or for love and affection.

good deed. A deed that conveys good title as opposed to a deed that is merely good in form. — Also termed *lawful deed.*

grant deed. (1891) A deed containing, or having implied by law, some but not all of the usual covenants of title; esp., a deed in which the grantor warrants that he or she (1) has not previously conveyed the estate being granted, (2) has not encumbered the property except as noted in the deed, and (3) will convey to the grantee any title to the property acquired after the date of the deed.

gratuitous deed. See *deed of gift.*

inclusive deed. See *inclusive grant* under GRANT.

indented deed. See INDENTURE (2).

latent deed. A deed kept in a strongbox or other secret place, usu. for 20 years or more.

lawful deed. See *good deed.*

mineral deed. A conveyance of an interest in the minerals in or under the land.

mortgage deed. The instrument creating a mortgage. • A mortgage deed typically must contain (1) the name of the mortgagor, (2) words of grant or conveyance, (3) the name of the mortgagee, (4) a property description sufficient to identify the mortgaged premises, (5) the mortgagor's signature, and (6) an acknowledgment. To be effective and binding, a mortgage deed must also be delivered.

onerous deed. *Scots law.* A deed given in exchange for a valuable consideration, often as part of a marriage settlement.

quitclaim deed. (18c) A deed that conveys a grantor's complete interest or claim in certain real property but that neither warrants nor professes that the title is valid. — Often shortened to *quitclaim.* — Also termed *deed without covenants.* Cf. *warranty deed.*

release deed. A deed that is issued once a mortgage has been discharged, explicitly releasing and reconveying to the mortgagor the entire interest conveyed by an earlier deed of trust. — Also termed *reconveyance; satisfaction; release.*

sheriff's deed. A deed that gives ownership rights in property bought at a sheriff's sale.

special warranty deed. (1808) **1.** A deed in which the grantor covenants to defend the title against only those claims and demands of the grantor and those claiming by and under the grantor. **2.** In a few jurisdictions, a quitclaim deed. Cf. *warranty deed.*

statutory deed. (1832) A warranty-deed form prescribed by state law and containing certain warranties and covenants even though they are not included in the printed form.

support deed. A deed by which a person (usu. a parent) conveys land to another (usu. a son or daughter) with the understanding that the grantee will support the grantor for life. • Support deeds often result in litigation.

tax deed. A deed showing the transfer of title to real property sold for the nonpayment of taxes. See *office grant* under GRANT; *tax sale* under SALE. Cf. TAX CERTIFICATE.

title deed. (18c) A deed that evidences a person's legal ownership of property. See TITLE.

trust deed. See *deed of trust.*

warranty deed. (1802) A deed containing one or more covenants of title; esp., a deed that expressly guarantees the grantor's good, clear title and that contains covenants concerning the quality of title, including warranties of seisin, quiet enjoyment, right to convey, freedom from encumbrances, and defense of title against all claims. — Also termed *general warranty deed*; *full-covenant-and-warranty deed.* See WARRANTY (1). Cf. *quitclaim deed*; *special warranty deed.*

wild deed. (1914) A recorded deed that is not in the chain of title, usu. because a previous instrument connected to the chain of title has not been recorded.

deed box. *Archaic.* A box in which deeds of land title are traditionally kept. • Such a box is considered an heirloom in the strict sense. See HEIRLOOM (1).

deed of agency. A revocable, voluntary trust for payment of a debt.

deed of crime. See ACTUS REUS.

deed of feoffment. See FEOFFMENT (3).

deed of inspectorship. See DEED.

deed of reconveyance. See DEED.

deed of trust. See DEED.

deem, *vb.* (bef. 12c) **1.** To treat (something) as if (1) it were really something else, or (2) it has qualities that it does not have <although the document was not in fact signed until April 21, it explicitly states that it must be deemed to have been signed on April 14>. **2.** To consider, think, or judge <she deemed it necessary>.

deemed transferor. (1988) *Tax.* A person who holds an interest in a generation-skipping trust on behalf of a beneficiary, and whose death will trigger the imposition of a generation-skipping transfer tax. • A *deemed transferor* is often a child of the settlor. For example, a grandfather could establish a trust with income payable for life to his son (who, because he is only one generation away from his father, is also known as a *nonskip person*) with the remainder to his grandson, a beneficiary also known as the *skip person.* When the son dies, the trust will be included in his gross estate for determining the generation-skipping transfer tax.

IRC (26 USCA) §§ 2601–2663. See GENERATION-SKIPPING TRANSFER; *generation-skipping transfer tax* under TAX; *generation-skipping trust* under TRUST; SKIP PERSON; NONSKIP PERSON.

deep issue. See ISSUE (1).

deep link. *Intellectual property.* A Web-page hyperlink that, when clicked, opens a page on another website other than that site's home page. • Some plaintiffs have argued, with mixed success, that bypassing their home page in this manner deprives them of advertising revenue. Deep linking does not violate copyright if the portal provided does not copy any of the linked page's content. And if there is no confusion about the source of the information, deep linking does not constitute unfair competition.

deep pocket. (1975) **1.** (*pl.*) Substantial wealth and resources <the plaintiff nonsuited the individuals and targeted the corporation with deep pockets>. **2.** A person or entity with substantial wealth and resources against which a claim may be made or a judgment may be taken <that national insurance company is a favorite deep pocket among plaintiff's lawyers>.

Deep Rock doctrine. *Bankruptcy.* The principle by which unfair or inequitable claims presented by controlling shareholders of bankrupt corporations may be subordinated to claims of general or trade creditors. • The doctrine is named for a corporation that made fraudulent transfers to its parent corporation in *Taylor v. Standard Gas & Elec. Co.*, 306 U.S. 307, 59 S.Ct. 543 (1939).

de-escalation clause. A contractual provision to decrease the price of something if specified costs decrease. Cf. ESCALATOR CLAUSE (1).

deface (di-**fays**), *vb.* (14c) **1.** To mar or destroy (a written instrument, signature, or inscription) by obliteration, erasure, or superinscription. **2.** To detract from the value of (a coin) by punching, clipping, cutting, or shaving. **3.** To mar or injure (a building, monument, or other structure). — **defacement,** *n.*

de facto (di **fak**-toh *also* dee *or* day), *adj.* [Law Latin "in point of fact"] (17c) **1.** Actual; existing in fact; having effect even though not formally or legally recognized <a de facto contract> **2.** Illegitimate but in effect <a de facto government>. Cf. DE JURE.

de facto adoption. See ADOPTION.

de facto blockade. See BLOCKADE.

de facto contract of sale. See CONTRACT.

de facto corporation. See CORPORATION.

de facto court. See COURT.

de facto dissolution. See DISSOLUTION.

de facto father. See *de facto parent* under PARENT.

de facto government. See GOVERNMENT.

de facto judge. See JUDGE.

de facto marriage. See MARRIAGE (1).

de facto merger. See MERGER.

de facto mother. See *de facto parent* under PARENT.

de facto officer. See *officer de facto* under OFFICER (1).

de facto parent. See PARENT.

de facto segregation. See SEGREGATION.

de facto stepparent adoption. See *second-parent adoption* under ADOPTION.

de facto taking. See TAKING (2).

defalcation (dee-fal-**kay**-shən), *n.* (15c) **1.** EMBEZZLEMENT. **2.** Loosely, the failure to meet an obligation; a nonfraudulent default. **3.** *Archaic.* A deduction; a setoff. — **defalcate** (di-**fal**-kayt *or* dee-), *vb.* — **defalcator,** *n.*

defalk (di-**fawlk**), *vb. Archaic.* To deduct (a debt); to set off (a claim).

defamacast (di-**fam**-ə-kast). (1997) Defamation by television or radio broadcast. • The word was first used in *American Broadcasting-Paramount Theatres, Inc. v. Simpson,* 126 S.E.2d 873, 879 (Ga. Ct. App. 1962). Although Prosser called it "a barbarous word" (William Prosser, *The Law of Torts* 753 [4th ed. 1971]), another authority has said that "[t]he word seems to be quite apt" (Laurence H. Eldredge, *The Law of Defamation* § 12, at 77 [1978]). See DEFAMATION.

defamation, *n.* (14c) **1.** The act of harming the reputation of another by making a false statement to a third person. • If the alleged defamation involves a matter of public concern, the plaintiff is constitutionally required to prove both the statement's falsity and the defendant's fault. **2.** A false written or oral statement that damages another's reputation. See LIBEL; SLANDER. Cf. DISPARAGEMENT. — **defame,** *vb.*

defamation per quod. (1915) Defamation that either (1) is not apparent but is proved by extrinsic evidence showing its injurious meaning or (2) is apparent but is not a statement that is actionable per se.

defamation per se. (1928) A statement that is defamatory in and of itself and is not capable of an innocent meaning.

trade defamation. The damaging of a business by a false statement that tends to diminish the reputation of that business. • Trade defamation may be trade libel if it is recorded, or trade slander if it is not. — Also termed *commercial defamation.* Cf. TRADE DISPARAGEMENT.

defamation privilege. See *litigation privilege* under PRIVILEGE (1).

defamatory, *adj.* (16c) (Of a statement or communication) tending to harm a person's reputation, usu. by subjecting the person to public contempt, disgrace, or ridicule, or by adversely affecting the person's business.

defamatory communication. See DEFAMATORY STATEMENT.

defamatory libel. See LIBEL (1).

defamatory propaganda. See PROPAGANDA.

defamatory statement. A statement that tends to injure the reputation of a person referred to in it. • The statement is likely to lower that person in the estimation of reasonable people and in particular to cause that person to be regarded with feelings of hatred, contempt, ridicule, fear, or dislike. — Also termed *defamatory communication.*

default (di-**fawlt** *also* dee-fawlt), *n.* (13c) The omission or failure to perform a legal or contractual duty; esp., the failure to pay a debt when due.

default (di-**fawlt**), *vb.* **1.** To be neglectful; esp., to fail to perform a contractual obligation. **2.** To fail to appear or answer. **3.** To enter a default judgment against (a litigant).

defaultant (di-**fawl**-tənt), *adj.* In default; having defaulted. See DEFAULTER.

defaulter. 1. A person who is in default. **2.** A person who misappropriates or fails to account for money held in the person's official or fiduciary capacity. — Also termed *defaultant.*

default judgment. (16c) **1.** A judgment entered against a defendant who has failed to plead or otherwise defend against the plaintiff's claim. **2.** A judgment entered as a penalty against a party who does not comply with an order, esp. an order to comply with a discovery request. *See* Fed. R. Civ. P. 55(b). — Also termed *judgment by default.* See JUDGMENT.

nil-dicit default judgment (nil **dī**-sit). [Latin "he says nothing"] (2002) A judgment for the plaintiff entered after the defendant fails to file a timely answer, often after the defendant appeared in the case by filing a preliminary motion. — Often shortened to *nihil dicit.* — Also termed *nihil-dicit default judgment; judgment by nil dicit.*

no-answer default judgment. (1979) A judgment for the plaintiff entered after the defendant fails to timely answer or otherwise appear.

post-answer default judgment. (1979) A judgment for the plaintiff entered after the defendant files an answer, but fails to appear at trial or otherwise provide a defense on the merits.

default jurisdiction. See JURISDICTION.

default of issue. See FAILURE OF ISSUE.

default rule. See RULE (1).

defeasance (di-**feez**-ənts), *n.* (15c) **1.** An annulment or abrogation; VOIDANCE. **2.** The fact or an instance of bringing an estate or status to an end, esp. by conditional limitation. **3.** A condition upon the fulfillment of which a deed or other instrument is defeated or made void; a contractual provision containing such a condition. — Also termed *defeasance clause.* **4.** *Hist.* A collateral deed made simultaneously with a conveyance and containing a condition by which the main deed might be defeated or made void. — Also spelled *defeazance.* — **defease,** *vb.*

defeasance clause. A mortgage provision stating that the conveyance to the mortgagee will be ineffective if the mortgagor pays the debt on time. See DEFEASANCE (3).

defeasible, *adj.* (16c) (Of an act, right, agreement, or position) capable of being annulled or avoided <defeasible deed>. See *fee simple defeasible* under FEE SIMPLE. — **defeasibility,** *n.*

defeasible deed. See DEED.

defeasible estate. See ESTATE (1).

defeasible fee simple. See *fee simple defeasible* under FEE SIMPLE.

defeasible interest. See INTEREST (2).

defeasible remainder. See REMAINDER.

defeasible title. See TITLE (2).

defeasive, *adj. Rare.* Capable of defeating <a counterclaim defeasive of the plaintiff's right to recovery>.

defeat, *vb.* **1.** To deprive (someone) of something expected, usu. by an antagonistic act <to defeat the opponent in an election>. **2.** To annul or render (something) void <to defeat title>. **3.** To vanquish; to conquer (someone or something) <to defeat the armies>. **4.** To frustrate (someone or something) <the expenditures defeat the bill's purpose>.

defect, *n.* (15c) An imperfection or shortcoming, esp. in a part that is essential to the operation or safety of a product. — **defective,** *adj.*

apparent defect. See *patent defect.*

design defect. (1954) An imperfection occurring when the seller or distributor could have reduced or avoided a foreseeable risk of harm by adopting a reasonable alternative design, and when, as a result of not using the alternative, the product or property is not reasonably safe. Cf. *manufacturing defect.*

fatal defect. (18c) A serious defect capable of nullifying a contract.

hidden defect. (1896) A product imperfection that is not discoverable by reasonable inspection and for which a seller or lessor is generally liable if the flaw causes harm. ● Upon discovering a hidden defect, a purchaser may revoke a prior

acceptance. UCC § 2-608(1)(b). — Also termed *latent defect; inherent defect.*

latent defect. See *hidden defect.*

manufacturing defect. (1925) An imperfection in a product that departs from its intended design even though all possible care was exercised in its assembly. Cf. *design defect.*

marketing defect. (1980) **1.** The failure to adequately warn of a potential risk of harm that is known or should have been known about a product or its foreseeable use. **2.** The failure to adequately instruct the user about how to use a product safely.

patent defect. (1827) A defect that is apparent to a normally observant person, esp. a buyer on a reasonable inspection. — Also termed *apparent defect.*

product defect. (1967) An imperfection in a product that has a manufacturing defect or design defect, or is faulty because of inadequate instructions or warnings. See *manufacturing defect; design defect; marketing defect.*

defective, *adj.* (14c) **1.** (Of a position, right, act, or process) lacking in legal sufficiency <defective execution of documents> <defective service of process>. **2.** (Of a product) containing an imperfection or shortcoming in a part essential to the product's safe operation <defective wiring caused the accident>.

defective condition. (1823) An unreasonably dangerous state that might well cause physical harm beyond that contemplated by the ordinary user or consumer who purchases the product. See PRODUCTS LIABILITY.

defective performance. See PERFORMANCE.

defective pleading. See PLEADING (1).

defective process. See PROCESS.

defective product. See PRODUCT.

defective record. See RECORD.

defective title. See TITLE (2).

defective trust. See TRUST.

defective verdict. See VERDICT.

defect of form. (17c) An imperfection in the style, manner, arrangement, or nonessential parts of a legal document, as distinguished from a substantive defect. Cf. DEFECT OF SUBSTANCE.

defect of parties. (18c) A failure to include all indispensable parties in a lawsuit.

defect of reason. *Archaic.* **1.** Mental illness. **2.** Mental retardation.

defect of substance. (18c) An imperfection in the substantive part of a legal document, as by omitting an essential term. Cf. DEFECT OF FORM.

defence. See DEFENSE.

defend, *vb.* (14c) **1.** To deny, contest, or oppose (an allegation or claim) <the corporation vigorously defended against the shareholder's lawsuit>. **2.** To represent (someone) as an attorney <the accused retained a well-known lawyer to defend him>.

defendant (di-**fen**-dənt). (14c) A person sued in a civil proceeding or accused in a criminal proceeding. — Abbr. D. Cf. PLAINTIFF.

> **John Doe defendant.** An anonymous defendant labeled "John Doe" because the plaintiff does not, at the time of filing suit, know the person's name. • John Doe defendants are common in several situations, such as police-brutality lawsuits in which the plaintiff does not know the names of the officers allegedly at fault, and in some copyright-infringement lawsuits where defendants are identified only by Internet addresses. See JOHN DOE.

> **target defendant.** In a case with multiple defendants, the one whom the plaintiff considers the primary source for any recovery of damages. • Among several defendants, one is usu. the most blameworthy or has the most insurance or greatest assets, or both.

defendant in error. (18c) *Archaic.* In a case on appeal, the prevailing party in the court below. See APPELLEE; RESPONDENT (1).

defendant score. (1982) A number taken from an established scale, indicating the relative seriousness of the defendant's criminal history. Cf. CRIME SCORE.

defendant's gain. (1882) The amount of money or the value of property that a criminal defendant has obtained by committing a crime. • Some states, such as New York, consider the defendant's gain when assessing a criminal fine or ordering restitution.

defender. **1.** One who defends, such as the defendant in a lawsuit, a person using self-defense, or defense counsel. **2.** PUBLIC DEFENDER.

defenestration (dee-fen-ə-**stray**-shən). (17c) The act of throwing someone or something out a window. — **defenestrate,** *vb.*

defense (di-**fen**[t]s). (16c) **1.** A defendant's stated reason why the plaintiff or prosecutor has no valid case; esp., a defendant's answer, denial, or plea <her defense was that she was 25 miles from the building at the time of the robbery>.

> **affirmative defense.** (1837) A defendant's assertion of facts and arguments that, if true, will defeat the plaintiff's or prosecution's claim, even if all the allegations in the complaint are true. • The defendant bears the burden of proving an affirmative defense. Examples of affirmative defenses are duress (in a civil case) and insanity and self-defense (in a criminal case). — Also termed *plea in avoidance*; *plea in justification*.

Cf. *negative defense*; CONFESSION AND AVOIDANCE.

> **capacity defense.** (1967) A defense based on the defendant's inability to be held accountable for an illegal act or the plaintiff's inability to prosecute a lawsuit (as when the plaintiff was a corporation, but has lost its corporate charter). See CAPACITY.

> **choice-of-evils defense.** See *lesser-evils defense.*

> **collateral defense** (kə-**lat**-ə-rəl). *Criminal law.* A defense of justification or excuse not involving a rebuttal of the allegation and therefore collateral to the elements that the prosecutor must prove. See EXCUSE (2); JUSTIFICATION (2).

> **cultural defense.** **1.** A criminal defendant's assertion that because an admitted act is not a crime in the perpetrator's culture or native land, it should not be judged by the laws of the place where it was committed. • This cultural defense is asserted as an affirmative defense to a criminal charge. **2.** The defense that the actor's mental state at the time the alleged crime was committed was heavily influenced by cultural factors. • This is not a complete defense but a mitigating one, pleaded to reduce the charges, the sentence, or both. See FEMALE GENITAL MUTILATION.

> **defense of habitation.** The defense that conduct constituting a criminal offense is justified if an aggressor unjustifiably threatens the defendant's place of abode or premises and the defendant engages in conduct that is (1) harmful to the aggressor, (2) sufficient to protect that place of abode or premises, and (3) reasonable in relation to the harm threatened. — Also termed *defense of premises.* See CASTLE DOCTRINE.

> **defense of honesty.** See *honesty defense.*

> **defense of inequitable conduct.** *Patents.* A defense to an action for patent infringement, made by charging the plaintiff with breaching the duty of candor and good faith. • To succeed, the defendant must show that, in the patent prosecution, the plaintiff intentionally withheld material information from or misled the examiner. Inequitable conduct is a combination of two former defenses: unclean hands and fraud on the Patent Office.

> **derivative defense.** (1972) A defense that rebuts the criminal elements that a prosecutor must establish to justify the submission of a criminal case to a jury.

> **designer defense.** A novel defense based on diminished capacity attributed to stress or impairment. • The phrase derives from the fact that the defense is tailored to the defendant and the circumstances of the crime. Examples include extraordinary reactions to snack food (the Twinkie defense), unconsciousness or

sleepwalking, and postpartum psychosis. See AUTOMATISM.

dilatory defense (dil-ə-tor-ee). (1845) A defense that temporarily obstructs or delays a lawsuit but does not address the merits. • Examples of dilatory defenses include misjoinder, nonjoinder, res judicata, misnomer, lack of capacity to sue, another action pending, statute of limitations, prematurity, unripeness, release, and settlement.

dwelling defense. See CASTLE DOCTRINE.

eleemosynary defense. See *charitable immunity* under IMMUNITY (2).

empty-suit defense. A defense in which a high-ranking officer or director in an organization claims ignorance of any wrongdoing by subordinates.

equitable defense. (18c) A defense formerly available only in a court of equity but now maintainable in a court of law. • Examples include mistake, fraud, illegality, failure of consideration, forum non conveniens, laches, estoppel, and unclean hands.

frivolous defense. (18c) A defense that has no basis in fact or law.

full defense. A technical common-law defensive plea, stated at length and without abbreviation. • This plea is obsolete because of the pleading requirements in federal and state rules of civil procedure.

general-justification defense. See *lesser-evils defense*.

honesty defense. *Rare.* An assertion that the defendant acted honestly and in good faith. • This defense, almost unique to civil suits, is rarely raised. For example, a defendant may assert honesty as a defense to a charge of fraudulent misrepresentation. — Also termed *defense of honesty.* Cf. CLAIM OF RIGHT (1).

imperfect defense. (1835) A defense that fails to meet all legal requirements and usu. results only in a reduction in grade or sentence rather than an acquittal, as when a defendant is charged with manslaughter rather than murder because the defendant, while defending another, used unreasonable force to repel the attack. See *imperfect self-defense* under SELF-DEFENSE. Cf. *perfect defense.*

inconsistent defense. (1852) A defense so contrary to another defense that the acceptance of one requires abandonment of the other. • A person accused of murder, for example, cannot claim both self-defense and the alibi of having been in a different city when the murder took place.

innocent-owner defense. In forfeiture action, an affirmative defense in which the owner of property (such as real estate or money) asserts

that another person committed the wrongful act or omission while using the property without the owner's knowledge or consent. *See* 18 USCA § 983(d). See *civil forfeiture* under FORFEITURE.

insanity defense. See INSANITY DEFENSE.

issuable defense. (1847) *Common-law pleading.* A plea on the merits setting forth a legal defense. Cf. *issuable plea* under PLEA (3).

justification defense. See JUSTIFICATION DEFENSE.

legal defense. (17c) A complete and adequate defense in a court of law.

lesser-evils defense. (1982) The defense that, while the defendant may have caused the harm or evil that would ordinarily constitute a criminal offense, in the present case the defendant has not caused a net harm or evil because of justifying circumstances and therefore should be exculpated. — Also termed *choice-of-evils defense; necessity; general-justification defense.*

meritorious defense (mer-ə-tor-ee-əs). (18c) **1.** A defense that addresses the substance or essentials of a case rather than dilatory or technical objections. **2.** A defense that appears likely to succeed or has already succeeded.

necessity defense. See JUSTIFICATION (2).

negative defense. A defendant's outright denial of the plaintiff's allegations without additional facts pleaded by way of avoidance. Cf. *affirmative defense.*

new-value defense. *Bankruptcy.* A defense to a suit to recover preferential payments whereby the transferee of the payments can reduce liability by the amount of consideration or value that the transferee provided to the transferor after a suspect transfer.

ostrich defense. A criminal defendant's claim not to have known of the criminal activities of an associate.

partial defense. (1818) A defense going either to part of the action or toward mitigation of damages.

pass-on defense. An antitrust defense that a member of the distributive chain who was overcharged or undercharged passed on the price adjustment to reflect the charge and thereby suffered no damage. — Also termed *passing on.*

peremptory defense (pər-emp-tər-ee). (1860) A defense that questions the plaintiff's legal right to sue or contends that the right to sue has been extinguished.

perfect defense. (1817) A defense that meets all legal requirements and results in the defendant's acquittal. See *perfect self-defense* under SELF-DEFENSE. Cf. *imperfect defense.*

pretermitted defense (pree-tər-**mit**-id). (1947) A defense available to a party that must be pleaded at the right time or be waived.

sham defense. (1853) A fictitious, untrue defense, made in bad faith.

sleepwalking defense. See AUTOMATISM.

SODDI. See SODDI DEFENSE.

true defense. A defense admitting that a defendant committed the charged offense, but seeking to avoid punishment based on a legal excuse (such as insanity) or justification (such as self-defense).

unconsciousness defense. See AUTOMATISM.

XYY-chromosome defense. See XYY-CHROMO-SOME DEFENSE.

2. A defendant's method and strategy in opposing the plaintiff or the prosecution; a doctrine giving rise to such a method or strategy <the lawyer advised her client to adopt a passive defense and to avoid taking the witness stand>.

empty-chair defense. (1981) A trial tactic in a multiparty case whereby one defendant attempts to put all the fault on a defendant who plea-bargained or settled before trial or on a person who was neither charged nor named as a party.

malicious defense. *Torts.* A defendant's use of unfair, harassing, or illegal tactics to advance a frivolous or unmeritorious defense. ● The elements of the tort are (1) the defendant's initiation, continuation, or procurement of proceedings; (2) knowledge that the defense lacks merit; (3) the assertion of the defense for a purpose other than to properly adjudicate the claim, such as to harass, annoy, or injure, or to cause unnecessary delay or needless increase in the cost of litigation; (4) termination of the suit in the plaintiff's favor; and (5) harm to the plaintiff resulting from the proceeding. Damages are the same as in an action for malicious prosecution. A minority of states recognize the tort. Cf. MALICIOUS PROSECUTION.

Stalingrad defense. The strategy of wearing down the plaintiff by tenaciously fighting by whatever means anything the plaintiff presents and appealing every ruling favorable to the plaintiff, rather than presenting a meritorious case. ● The tactic is named for the Russian city besieged by the Germans in World War II. The defenders refused to surrender and used every available tactic and tool to hold the attackers at bay until winter cut the enemy's supply lines, leaving the attackers with inadequate resources with which to continue the siege.

3. One or more defendants in a trial, as well as their counsel <the defense rests>. **4.** *Commercial law.* A basis for avoiding liability on a negotiable instrument <the drawer asserted a real defense against the holder in due course>.

absolute defense. See *real defense.*

personal defense. (1950) An ordinary defense in a contract action — such as failure of consideration or nonperformance of a condition — that the maker or drawer of a negotiable instrument is precluded from raising against a person who has the rights of a holder in due course. See UCC § 3-305(b). ● A personal defense can be asserted only against a transferee who is not a holder in due course. — Also termed *limited defense.*

real defense. A type of defense that is good against any possible claimant, so that the maker or drawer of a negotiable instrument can raise it even against a holder in due course. ● The ten real defenses are (1) fraud in the factum, (2) forgery of a necessary signature, (3) adjudicated insanity that, under state law, renders the contract void from its inception, (4) material alteration of the instrument, (5) infancy, which renders the contract voidable under state law, (6) illegality that renders the underlying contract void, (7) duress, (8) discharge in bankruptcy, or any discharge known to the holder in due course, (9) a suretyship defense (for example, if the holder knew that one indorser was signing as a surety or accommodation party), and (10) a statute of limitations (generally three years after dishonor or acceptance on a draft and six years after demand or other due date on a note). — Also termed *absolute defense; universal defense.*

5. Measures taken by a country or individual to protect against an attack. See SELF-DEFENSE; NATIONAL DEFENSE (1).

self-defense. See SELF-DEFENSE.

6. A country's military establishment. See NATIONAL DEFENSE (2). — Also spelled in all senses (esp. in BrE) *defence.* **7.** TAKEOVER DEFENSE.

Defense Advanced Research Projects Agency. An agency in the U.S. Department of Defense responsible for military research and development. — Abbr. DARPA.

defense attorney. A lawyer who represents a defendant in a civil or criminal case. — Also termed *defense counsel; defense lawyer.*

Defense Commissary Agency. An agency in the U.S. Department of Defense responsible for providing goods and services to members of the armed forces at reduced prices. — Abbr. DeCA.

defense contingent fee. See *reverse contingent fee* under CONTINGENT FEE.

Defense Contract Audit Agency. An agency in the U.S. Department of Defense responsible for conducting contract audits and for providing accounting and financial advice to all Department components responsible for procurement and contract administration. — Abbr. DCAA.

Defense Contract Management Agency. A unit in the U.S. Department of Defense responsible for managing contracts to ensure that supplies and services are delivered on time and within cost and that they meet performance requirements. — Abbr. DCMA.

defense counsel. See DEFENSE ATTORNEY.

Defense Department. An executive department of the federal government, responsible for coordinating and overseeing military affairs and the agencies responsible for national security. • The Department was established as the National Military Establishment in 1947, by combining the War and the Navy Departments. Its name was changed to Department of Defense in 1949. The Department's components include the Army, the Air Force, the Navy, the Marine Corps, and the Joint Chiefs of Staff. It is headed by the Secretary of Defense, who is answerable to the President as Commander-in-Chief. — Also termed *Department of Defense* (abbr. DOD).

Defense Finance and Accounting Service. A unit in the U.S. Department of Defense responsible for providing professional finance and accounting services and for overseeing the Department's day-to-day finance and accounting activities. — Abbr. DFAS.

Defense Information Systems Agency. An agency in the U.S. Department of Defense responsible for developing and operating information systems to provide combat support for the armed forces. — Abbr. DISA.

Defense Intelligence Agency. A combat-support unit in the U.S. Department of Defense responsible for developing and managing foreign military intelligence in support of military planning and operations and of weapons-systems acquisition. — Abbr. DIA.

Defense Investigative Services. See DEFENSE SECURITY SERVICE.

defense lawyer. See DEFENSE ATTORNEY.

Defense Legal Services Agency. An agency in the U.S. Department of Defense responsible for providing legal services to all agencies in the Department. • The General Counsel of the Department directs its operations. — Abbr. DLSA.

Defense Logistics Agency. A unit in the U.S. Department of Defense responsible for providing worldwide logistics support for military missions both in peace and in war. • The Agency also supports nonmilitary agencies overseas. — Abbr. DLA.

Defense Nuclear Facilities Safety Board. An independent federal board that sets standards for the design, construction, operation, and decommissioning of defense nuclear facilities of the U.S. Department of Energy. • It was established in 1988. 42 USCA §§ 2286–2286i.

defense of habitation. See DEFENSE (1).

defense of honesty. See DEFENSE (1).

Defense of Marriage Act. A federal statute that (1) provides that no state can be required to recognize or give effect to same-sex marriages, (2) defines the term "marriage" for purposes of federal law as the union of a man and a woman as husband and wife, and (3) defines "spouse" for purposes of federal law as being only a person of the opposite sex. 1 USCA § 7; 28 USCA 1738C. • The Defense of Marriage Act was enacted in response to the fear that if one state sanctioned same-sex marriages, other states might then have to give full faith and credit to those marriages. — Abbr. DOMA.

defense of others. (1942) A justification defense available if one harms or threatens another when defending a third person. See JUSTIFICATION (2).

defense of premises. See *defense of habitation* under DEFENSE (1).

defense of property. (1918) A justification defense available if one harms or threatens another when defending one's property. See JUSTIFICATION (2).

defense of self. See SELF-DEFENSE.

Defense Security Cooperation Agency. A unit in the U.S. Department of Defense responsible for fostering and overseeing security-cooperation arrangements and for promoting security relationships with U.S. friends and allies. — Abbr. DSCA.

Defense Security Service. A unit in the U.S. Department of Defense responsible for conducting personnel investigations and providing industrial-security products and services to the Department and other agencies. • The agency was formerly known as the Defense Investigative Service. — Abbr. DSS.

Defense Threat Reduction Agency. A unit in the U.S. Department of Defense responsible for reducing the risk of and defending against attacks that involve nuclear, chemical, biological, or other weapons of mass destruction. • The Agency was created in 1998. — Abbr. DTRA.

defensive allegation. See ALLEGATION.

defensive collateral estoppel. See COLLATERAL ESTOPPEL.

defensive disclosure. *Patents.* The deliberate publication of details about an invention in order to render it prior art and preclude others from getting a patent on the same invention. • This can be done formally, by filing for public disclosure through the Statutory Invention Registration and publishing the abstract in the Official

Gazette of the U.S. Patent and Trademark Office, or privately, by publishing it in an independent journal that will probably be consulted by a patent examiner. — Also termed *defensive publication.* See STATUTORY INVENTION REGISTRATION.

defensive-force justification. See JUSTIFICATION.

defensive lockout. See LOCKOUT.

defensive-posture memorandum. See DEFENSIVE PROFILE.

defensive profile. The set of strategies devised by a company to discourage others from attempting a hostile takeover.

defensive-profile memorandum. *Corporations.* An outline of a company's strategy against a hostile takeover. — Also termed *defensive-posture memorandum.*

defensive publication. See DEFENSIVE DISCLOSURE.

defensive treaty. See TREATY (1).

defer, *vb.* (17c) **1.** To postpone; to delay <to defer taxes to another year>. **2.** To show deference to (another); to yield to the opinion of <because it was a political question, the courts deferred to the legislature>.

deferment, *n.* **1.** The act of delaying; postponement <deferment of a judicial decision>. **2.** *Military law.* A delay in serving in the military. **3.** *Military law.* A delay in serving confinement that results from a court-martial until the sentence has been approved and its execution has been ordered. • The convening authority may grant a deferment. — **defer,** *vb.*

deferral of taxes. The postponement of paying a tax from one year to another, as by contributing money to an IRA, for which earnings and contributions will be taxed only when the money is withdrawn.

deferral state. (1977) Under the Age Discrimination in Employment Act (ADEA), a state that has its own anti-discrimination legislation and enforcement mechanism, so that the time to file a federal lawsuit under the ADEA is postponed until state remedies have been exhausted.

deferred adjudication. See *deferred judgment* under JUDGMENT.

deferred-adjudication probation. See *deferred judgment* under JUDGMENT.

deferred annuity. See ANNUITY.

deferred charge. (1917) An expense not currently recognized on an income statement but carried forward on the balance sheet as an asset to be written off in the future <insurance premiums are a deferred charge>.

deferred claim. (1900) A claim postponed to a future accounting period.

deferred compensation. See COMPENSATION.

deferred credit. A credit (such as a premium on an issued bond) that is required to be spread over later accounting periods.

deferred dividend. See DIVIDEND.

deferred-dividend insurance policy. See INSURANCE POLICY.

deferred expense. See EXPENSE.

deferred income. See INCOME.

deferred-interest bond. See BOND (3).

deferred judgment. See JUDGMENT.

deferred lien. See LIEN.

deferred payment. (1831) A principal-and-interest payment that is postponed; an installment payment.

deferred-payment annuity. See *deferred annuity* under ANNUITY.

deferred prosecution. See *deferred judgment* under JUDGMENT.

deferred revenue. See *prepaid income* under INCOME.

deferred sentence. See SENTENCE.

deferred stock. See STOCK.

deficiency, *n.* (17c) **1.** A lack, shortage, or insufficiency. **2.** A shortfall in paying taxes; the amount by which the tax properly due exceeds the sum of the amount of tax shown on a taxpayer's return. — Also termed *tax deficiency; income-tax deficiency; deficiency in tax.* **3.** The amount still owed when the property secured by a mortgage is sold at a foreclosure sale for less than the outstanding debt; esp., the shortfall between the proceeds from a foreclosure sale and an amount consisting of the principal debt plus interest plus the foreclosure costs. See *deficiency judgment* under JUDGMENT.

deficiency assessment. See ASSESSMENT.

deficiency bill. See BILL (3).

deficiency decree. See *deficiency judgment* under JUDGMENT.

deficiency dividend. See DIVIDEND.

deficiency in tax. See DEFICIENCY (2).

deficiency judgment. See JUDGMENT.

deficiency letter. 1. An IRS letter to a taxpayer, detailing the ways in which a tax return seems to be deficient. **2.** An SEC letter to a registrant of a securities offering, detailing the ways in which the registration statement seems not to conform to federal disclosure requirements. — Also termed *letter of comment; letter of comments.* See NINETY-DAY LETTER; THIRTY-DAY LETTER.

deficiency notice. See NINETY-DAY LETTER.

deficiency suit. (1927) An action to recover the difference between a mortgage debt and the amount realized on foreclosure. See *deficiency judgment* under JUDGMENT.

deficit. (18c) **1.** A deficiency or disadvantage; a deficiency in the amount or quality of something.

> **trade deficit.** In economics, the excess of merchandise imports over merchandise exports during a specific period. — Also termed *trade gap.* Cf. *trade surplus* under SURPLUS.

2. An excess of expenditures or liabilities over revenues or assets.

deficit spending. (1938) The practice of making expenditures in excess of income, usu. from borrowed funds rather than actual revenues or surplus.

defile (di-**fɪl**), *vb.* (14c) **1.** To make dirty; to physically soil. **2.** To figuratively tarnish; to dishonor. **3.** To make ceremonially unclean; to desecrate. **4.** To morally corrupt (someone). **5.** *Archaic.* To debauch (a person); to deprive (a person) of chastity.

defilement (di-**fɪl**-mənt), *n.* **1.** An act of defiling. **2.** A condition of being defiled.

define, *vb.* **1.** To state or explain explicitly. **2.** To fix or establish (boundaries or limits). **3.** To set forth the meaning of (a word or phrase).

defined-benefit pension plan. See PENSION PLAN.

defined-benefit plan. See EMPLOYEE BENEFIT PLAN.

defined-contribution pension plan. See *defined-contribution plan* under EMPLOYEE BENEFIT PLAN.

defined-contribution plan. See EMPLOYEE BENEFIT PLAN.

defined pension plan. See PENSION PLAN.

defined term. In legal drafting, a word or phrase given a specific meaning for purposes of the document in which it appears; a definiendum.

definite failure of issue. See FAILURE OF ISSUE.

definite sentence. See *determinate sentence* under SENTENCE.

definition. (14c) The meaning of a term as explicitly stated in a drafted document such as a contract, a corporate bylaw, an ordinance, or a statute; a definiens.

> **lexical definition.** (1875) A dictionary-style definition of a word, purporting to give the full meaning of a term.

> **stipulative definition.** (1989) A definition that, for purposes of the document in which it appears, arbitrarily clarifies a term with uncertain boundaries or that includes or excludes specified items from the ambit of the term.

definitive judgment. See *final judgment* under JUDGMENT.

definitive partition. See PARTITION.

definitive sentence. See *determinate sentence* under SENTENCE.

deflation, *n.* A general decline in the price of goods and services. Cf. INFLATION; DISINFLATION. — **deflate,** *vb.* — **deflationary,** *adj.*

deforce, *vb.* (15c) **1.** To keep (lands) from the true owner by means of force. **2.** To oust another from possession by means of force. **3.** To detain (a creditor's money) unjustly and forcibly. — **deforciant,** *n.*

deforcement. **1.** An act of keeping lands from the true owner by force. **2.** An act of ousting another from possession by means of force. **3.** An act of detaining a creditor's money unjustly and forcibly.

deforciant (di-**for**-shənt), *n.* [fr. Law Latin *deforcians* "a deforcer"] **1.** A person who prevents another from taking possession of property. **2.** The defendant in an action of fine. See FINE (1).

defraud, *vb.* (14c) To cause injury or loss to (a person) by deceit. See FRAUD.

defraudation. The perpetration of a fraud; the act of committing fraud.

defrauder. See FRAUDFEASOR.

defunct, *adj.* Dead; extinct <defunct corporation>.

defunct marriage. See MARRIAGE (1).

degradation (deg-rə-**day**-shən). (16c) **1.** A reduction in rank, degree, or dignity; specif., censure of a clergy member by divestiture of holy orders, either by word or by a solemn divestiture of robes and other insignia. Cf. DEPOSITION (4); DEPRIVATION (4). **2.** A moral or intellectual decadence or degeneration; a lessening of a person's or thing's character or quality <degradation of resources>. **3.** A wearing down of something, as by erosion.

degree. (13c) **1.** Generally, a classification or specification <degrees of proof>. **2.** An incremental measure of guilt or negligence; a level based on the seriousness of an offense <murder in the first degree>. **3.** A stage in a process; a step in a series of steps toward an end <the statute went through several degrees of development>. **4.** A stage in intensity <a high degree of legal skill is required>. **5.** In the line of descent, a measure of removal determining the proximity of a blood or marital relationship <the council member did not participate in the vote because he was related to one of the bidders within the first degree of consanguinity>. ● In the civil law, and in the degree-of-relationship system used by many American jurisdictions, an intestate estate passes to the closest of kin, counting degrees of kinship. To calculate the degree of relationship of the decedent to the claimant, one counts the steps (one for each generation) up from the decedent to the nearest common ancestor of the decedent and the claimant, and on down to the claimant from the common ancestor. The total number of steps is the degree of relationship. For example, a decedent's cousin stands in the fourth degree of relationship. Degrees of relationship are used not only to determine who is the closest heir but also to establish the incest prohibition in marriage requirements. — Also termed *degree of kin*; *degree of relationship*; *degree of descent*. See AFFINITY (2); CONSANGUINITY.

equal degree. (16c) A relationship between two or more relatives who are the same number of steps away from a common ancestor.

prohibited degree. (17c) A degree of relationship so close (as between brother and sister) that marriage between the persons is forbidden by law. • Generally, with slight variations from jurisdiction to jurisdiction, the law forbids marriages between all persons lineally related and within the third civil-law degree of relationship. That is, aunt–nephew and uncle–niece relations are prohibited. Prohibited degrees are also known as *Levitical degrees*, since the incest prohibition is pronounced in the Bible in Leviticus 18:6–18. — Also termed *forbidden degree*.

6. A title conferred on a graduate of a school, college, or university, either after the completion of required studies or in honor of special achievements <she began studying for the bar exam the day after receiving her law degree>. Cf. DIPLOMA (3).

degree of care. (17c) A standard of care to be exercised in a given situation. See CARE.

degree of crime. (1826) **1.** A division or classification of a single crime into several grades of guilt, according to the circumstances surrounding the crime's commission, such as aggravating factors present or the type of injury suffered. **2.** A division of crimes generally, such as felonies or misdemeanors.

degree of descent. See DEGREE (5).

degree of kin. See DEGREE (5).

degree of negligence. (18c) One of the varying levels of negligence typically designated as slight negligence, ordinary negligence, and gross negligence. See NEGLIGENCE.

degree of proof. 1. See BURDEN OF PROOF. **2.** BURDEN OF PRODUCTION.

degree of relationship. See DEGREE (5).

dehors (də-**hor** *or* də-**horz**). [Law French] (18c) Outside; beyond the scope of <the court cannot consider the document because it is dehors the record>.

dejeration (dej-ə-**ray**-shən). The act of taking a solemn oath.

de jure (di **juur**-ee *also* dee *or* day), *adj.* [Law Latin "as a matter of law"] (17c) Existing by right or according to law <de jure segregation during the pre-*Brown* era>. Cf. DE FACTO.

de jure corporation. See CORPORATION.

de jure government. See GOVERNMENT.

de jure officer. See *officer de jure* under OFFICER (1).

de jure segregation. See SEGREGATION (2).

delator (di-**lay**-tər), *n.* [Latin] *Roman law.* **1.** An informer. **2.** An accuser; esp., a person who made a practice of informing on and prosecuting others, esp. for fiscal offenses. • This was at first encouraged, but later the informer became subject to the death penalty. Pl. *delatores.*

Delaware trust. See *asset-protection trust* under TRUST (3).

delay, *n.* (13c) **1.** The act of postponing or slowing <the continuance was sought for no purpose other than delay>. Cf. VEXATIOUS DELAY. **2.** An instance at which something is postponed or slowed <the delay in starting the trial made it difficult for all of the witnesses to attend>. **3.** The period during which something is postponed or slowed <during the delay, the case settled>. **4.** *Civil law.* The period within which a party to a suit must take some action, such as perfecting an appeal or responding to a written-discovery request <the delay for responding to written interrogatories is 15 days after the date they are served on the responding party>.

delayed appeal. See APPEAL.

delayed-compliance order. *Environmental law.* An order issued by the Environmental Protection Agency or by a state agency to an existing source of pollutants, whereby the deadline for complying with an implementation plan is postponed. See IMPLEMENTATION PLAN.

delayed funds availability. A hold that a bank places on uncollected funds that are represented by a deposited check. — Abbr. DFA.

delayed rental. See RENTAL.

delayed sentence. See SENTENCE.

delay rental. *Oil & gas.* A payment from the lessee to the lessor made to maintain the mineral lease from period to period during the primary term without an obligation to drill. See DRILLING-DELAY RENTAL CLAUSE; *"or" lease, paid-up lease, "until" lease* under LEASE.

del credere (del **kred**-ə-ray *or* **kray**-də-ray), *adj.* [Italian] (18c) Of belief or trust.

del credere **agent.** See AGENT (2).

del credere **bailiff.** See FACTOR (2).

del credere **commission.** A factor's commission that is increased because the factor guarantees the payment to the principal of all debts that become due through the agency relationship.

del credere **factor.** See *del credere agent* under AGENT.

delegable duty. See DUTY (1).

delegate (del-ə-git), *n.* (15c) **1.** One who represents or acts for another person or a group. **2.** *Parliamentary law.* A voting member of a convention, whether entitled to vote as an elected or appointed delegate (sense 1), as an upgraded alternate, or ex officio. See CONVENTION (4); ALTERNATE; EX OFFICIO.

> **instructed delegate.** A delegate bound to vote according to a constituency's expressed wishes. Cf. *uninstructed delegate*; UNIT RULE (2).

> **uninstructed delegate.** A delegate who is not instructed and may therefore vote according to his or her conscience. Cf. *instructed delegate*.

delegate assembly. See CONVENTION (4).

delegated legislation. See REGULATION (3).

delegated power. See POWER (3).

delegatee (del-ə-gə-**tee**). (1875) An agent or representative to whom a matter is delegated.

delegation, *n.* (1612) **1.** The act of entrusting another with authority or empowering another to act as an agent or representative <delegation of contractual duties>. **2.** A group of representatives <a large delegation from Texas>. — **delegate** (del-ə-gayt) (for sense 1), *vb.* — **delegable** (del-ə-gə-bəl) (for sense 1), *adj.*

delegation doctrine. (1883) *Constitutional law.* The principle (based on the separation-of-powers concept) limiting Congress's ability to transfer its legislative power to another governmental branch, esp. the executive branch. ● Delegation is permitted only if Congress prescribes an intelligible principle to guide an executive agency in making policy. — Also termed *nondelegation doctrine*.

delegation of duties. (1893) *Contracts.* A transaction by which a party to a contract arranges to have a third party perform the party's contractual duties.

delegation of powers. (1854) A transfer of authority by one branch of government to another branch or to an administrative agency. See DELEGATION DOCTRINE.

delegator (del-i-gay-tər or -tor). One who delegates (a responsibility, etc.) to another.

deleterious (del-ə-**teer**-ee-əs), *adj.* (1643) **1.** Poisonous <deleterious toxins>. **2.** Unwholesome; psychologically or physically harmful <deleterious influence>.

deliberate (di-**lib**-[ə]-rit), *adj.* (15c) **1.** Intentional; premeditated; fully considered. **2.** Unimpulsive; slow in deciding.

deliberate (di-**lib**-ə-rate), *vb.* (Of a court, jury, etc.) to weigh and analyze all the evidence after closing arguments <the jury deliberated for 12 hours before reaching a verdict>.

deliberate elicitation. (1966) *Criminal procedure.* The purposeful yet covert drawing forth of an incriminating response (usu. not during a formal interrogation) from a suspect whose Sixth Amendment right to counsel has attached but who has not waived that right. ● Deliberate elicitation may occur, for example, when a police officer engages an arrested suspect in conversation on the way to the police station. Deliberate elicitation violates the Sixth Amendment. *Massiah v. United States*, 377 U.S. 201, 84 S.Ct. 1199 (1964). See MASSIAH RULE.

deliberate indifference. See INDIFFERENCE.

deliberate-indifference instruction. See JEWELL INSTRUCTION.

deliberate speed, with all. (1817) As quickly as the maintenance of law and order and the welfare of the people will allow, esp. with respect to the desegregation of public schools. *Brown v. Board of Educ.*, 347 U.S. 483, 74 S.Ct. 686 (1954).

deliberation, *n.* (14c) The act of carefully considering issues and options before making a decision or taking some action; esp., the process by which a jury reaches a verdict, as by analyzing, discussing, and weighing the evidence. See CONSIDERATION (3). — **deliberate** (di-**lib**-ə-rayt), *vb.*

deliberative assembly. See ASSEMBLY.

deliberative-process privilege. (1977) The principle that a decision-maker's thoughts and how they led to a decision are not subject to revelation or scrutiny. See *U.S. v. Morgan*, 313 U.S. 409, 61 S.Ct. 999 (1941). ● An exception to the rule may be allowed if a party can clearly show that the decision resulted from bias, bad faith, misconduct, or illegal or unlawful action. The privilege is meant to encourage open and independent discussion among those who develop government policy. — Also termed *mental-process privilege*.

delict (di-**likt**), *n.* [Latin *delictum* "an offense"] (16c) *Roman & civil law.* A violation of the law; esp., a wrongful act or omission giving rise to a claim for compensation; TORT. — Also termed (in Roman law) *delictum*; (in French law) *délit*.

> **private delict.** A wrong regarded primarily as a matter of compensation between individuals.

> **public delict.** A wrong for which the community as a whole takes steps to punish the offender. Cf. *public tort* under TORT.

> **quasi-delict. 1.** *Roman law.* A residuary category of private wrongs, characterized by either

vicarious or strict liability. **2.** See *quasi-offense* under OFFENSE (2). **3.** *Scots law.* Tortious conduct that is negligent, as opposed to intentional.

delictal. See DELICTUAL.

deliction (di-**lik**-shən). (1966) The loss of land by gradual, natural changes, such as erosion resulting from a change in the course of a river or stream. Cf. ACCRETION (1); ALLUVION; AVULSION (2); EROSION.

delictual (di-**lik**-chə-wəl), *adj.* Of, relating to, or involving a delict; TORTIOUS. — Also termed *delictal.*

delictual fault. See FAULT.

delictum. See DELICT.

delimination. The act of marking a boundary or fixing a limit.

delimit (di-**lim**-it), *vb.* (1852) To mark (a boundary); to fix (a limit).

delimitation. A fixing of limits or boundaries.

delineational gerrymandering. See GERRYMANDERING.

delinquency, *n.* (17c) **1.** A failure or omission; a violation of a law or duty. See JUVENILE DELINQUENCY. **2.** A debt that is overdue in payment.

delinquency charge. See CHARGE.

delinquency jurisdiction. See JURISDICTION.

delinquent, *adj.* (17c) **1.** (Of a person) failing to perform an obligation. **2.** (Of a person) guilty of serious antisocial or criminal conduct. **3.** (Of an obligation) past due or unperformed.

delinquent, *n.* (15c) **1.** A person who fails to perform an obligation. **2.** A person guilty of serious antisocial or criminal conduct. **3.** JUVENILE DELINQUENT.

delinquent child. See CHILD.

delinquent minor. See JUVENILE DELINQUENT.

delinquent tax. See TAX.

delirium. (16c) **1.** A disordered mental state, often occurring during illness. **2.** Exaggerated excitement. **3.** A delusion; a hallucination.

delirium tremens. An illness characterized by hallucinations and violent trembling, induced by excessive consumption of alcohol over a long period. — Also termed *mania a potu; settled insanity.* — Abbr. d.t.'s.

delisting, *n.* The suspension of the privilege of having a security listed on an exchange. • Delisting results from failing to meet the exchange's listing requirements, as by not complying with the minimum net-asset requirement. Cf. DEREGISTRATION. — **delist,** *vb.*

délit. See DELICT.

deliverance. (14c) **1.** A jury's verdict. **2.** A judicial opinion or judgment. **3.** A court's order directing that a person in custody be released; esp., such an order by an ecclesiastical court. — Also termed *writ of deliverance.* **4.** *Archaic.* In a replevin action, a writ ordering the redelivery of goods to the owner.

> *second deliverance. Hist.* A second replevin remedy after the plaintiff has been nonsuited and the distrained property has been returned to the defendant. — Also termed *writ of second deliverance.*

5. Such a release (as in sense 3) or redelivery (as in sense 4).

delivered at frontier. A mercantile-contract term allocating the rights and duties of the buyer and the seller of goods with respect to delivery, payment, and risk of loss, whereby the seller must (1) clear the goods for export, (2) arrange and pay for transportation, and (3) deliver the goods to a specified place on the importing nation's border. • The seller's delivery is complete (and the risk of loss passes to the buyer) when the goods arrive at the designated point and are placed at the disposal of the buyer. This term is generally used when the delivery place is on land, but it places no explicit restrictions on the mode of carriage. If the delivery place is a border port and delivery is complete either onboard or alongside the vessel, the term *delivered ex ship* or *delivered ex quay* is preferred. — Abbr. DAF. Cf. DELIVERED EX SHIP; DELIVERED EX QUAY.

delivered duty paid. A mercantile-contract term allocating the rights and duties of the buyer and the seller of goods with respect to delivery, payment, and risk of loss, whereby the seller must (1) clear the goods for export, (2) bear the costs of carriage, (3) pay the buyer's import duties, and (4) make the goods available to the buyer on board the carrier at the destination. • The seller's delivery is complete (and the risk of loss passes to the buyer) when the seller's carrier arrives at the agreed destination. This term is generally used when the delivery place is on land, but it places no explicit restrictions on the mode of carriage. If the delivery point is a port and delivery is complete either onboard or alongside the vessel, the term *delivered ex ship* or *delivered ex quay* is preferred. — Abbr. DDP. Cf. DELIVERED DUTY UNPAID; DELIVERED EX SHIP; DELIVERED EX QUAY.

delivered duty unpaid. A mercantile-contract term allocating the rights and duties of the buyer and the seller of goods with respect to delivery, payment, and risk of loss, whereby the seller must (1) clear the goods for export, (2) bear the costs of carriage (apart from unloading charges and import duties), and (3) make the goods available to the buyer on board the carrier at the destination. • The seller's delivery is complete (and the risk of loss passes to the buyer) when the seller's carrier arrives at the agreed destination. The buyer is responsible for all import duties. This term is generally used when the delivery place is on land, but it places no explicit restrictions on the mode of carriage. If the delivery point is a port and delivery is complete either onboard or alongside the vessel, the term *delivered ex ship* or *delivered ex quay* is preferred. — Abbr. DDU. Cf. DELIVERED DUTY PAID; DELIVERED EX SHIP; DELIVERED EX QUAY.

delivered ex quay. A mercantile-contract term allocating the rights and duties of the buyer and the seller of goods with respect to delivery, payment, and risk of loss, whereby the seller must (1) clear the goods for export, (2) bear the costs of transportation to the port named by the importing buyer, and (3) place the goods alongside the ship in the port of destination. • The seller's delivery is complete (and the risk of loss passes to the buyer) when the goods are unloaded in the destination port. This term is used only when goods are transported by sea or inland waterway. — Abbr. DEQ. Cf. DELIVERED EX SHIP; FREE ALONGSIDE SHIP.

delivered ex ship. A mercantile-contract term allocating the rights and duties of the buyer and the seller of goods with respect to delivery, payment, and risk of loss, whereby the seller must clear the goods for export and bear the costs of transportation (apart from unloading charges and import duties) to the importing nation's port of destination. • The seller's delivery is complete (and the risk of loss passes to the buyer) when the seller's carrier arrives at the destination port. This term is used only when goods are transported by sea or inland waterway. — Abbr. DES. Cf. DELIVERED EX QUAY; FREE ON BOARD.

delivery, *n.* (15c) **1.** The formal act of transferring something, such as a deed; the giving or yielding possession or control of something to another. **2.** The thing so transferred or conveyed. Cf. LIVERY. — **deliver,** *vb.*

   absolute delivery. (1808) A delivery that is complete upon the actual transfer of the instrument from the grantor's possession. • Such a delivery does not usu. depend on recordation.

   actual delivery. (17c) The act of giving real and immediate possession to the buyer or the buyer's agent.

   conditional delivery. (18c) A delivery that passes possession subject to the happening of a specified event. • Possession passes immediately; title remains conditional.

   constructive delivery. (18c) An act that amounts to a transfer of title by operation of law when actual transfer is impractical or impossible. • For example, the delivery of a deposit-box key by someone who is ill and immobile may amount to a constructive delivery of the box's contents even though the box may be miles away. For the three traditional types of constructive delivery, see ATTORNMENT; CONSTITUTUM POSSESSORIUM; TRADITIO BREVI MANU.

   good delivery. *Securities.* A security's delivery when the certificate (1) is in good condition, (2) belongs to the person transferring it, (3) is properly indorsed, and (4) is accompanied by any legal documents necessary for its negotiability.

   jail delivery. See JAIL DELIVERY.

   second delivery. (17c) A legal delivery by the depositary of a deed placed in escrow.

   symbolic delivery. (18c) The constructive delivery of the subject matter of a sale or gift by the actual delivery of an article that represents the item, that renders access to it possible, or that provides evidence of the title to it, such as the key to a warehouse or a bill of lading for goods on shipboard.

   unconditional delivery. (18c) A delivery that immediately passes both possession and title and that takes effect immediately.

delivery bond. See *forthcoming bond* under BOND (2).

delivery in escrow. (1842) The physical transfer of something to an escrow agent to be held until some condition is met, at which time the agent will release it. • An example of such a delivery is a stock buyer's transfer of cash to a bank that will give the seller the cash upon receiving the stock certificates. This type of delivery creates immediate conditional rights in the promisee. The device may be used to create an option contract in which the promisee has the option. See ESCROW.

delivery of deed. (18c) The placing of a deed in the grantee's hands or within the grantee's control. • By this act, the grantor shows an intention that the deed operates immediately as a conveyance. A deed may also be held to be delivered when the grantor manifests the intention to complete the conveyance, regardless of actual delivery.

delivery order. A written order to deliver goods, directed to a warehouseman, carrier, or other person who ordinarily issues warehouse receipts or bills of lading. UCC § 7-102(1)(d).

dem. *abbr.* DEMISE.

demain. See DEMESNE.

demand, *n.* (13c) **1.** The assertion of a legal or procedural right.

   contingent demand. A demand that cannot be fixed because it depends on the occurrence of a contingency.

   cross-demand. (18c) A party's demand opposing an adverse party's demand. See COUNTERCLAIM; CROSS-CLAIM.

   demand in reconvention. See *reconventional demand.*

incidental demand. Civil law. A plea by which a party other than the plaintiff asserts a claim that is related to the plaintiff's suit. • Examples include a cross-claim, a demand against a third party, an intervention, and a reconventional demand. La. Code Civ. Proc. art. 1031.

legal demand. A lawful demand made by an authorized person.

main demand. Civil law. A plaintiff's principal or primary claim against one or more defendants, contained in an original or validly amended pleading. — Also termed *principal demand*; *principal action*.

reconventional demand. Civil law. A plea by which a defendant asserts any claim that it has against the plaintiff, or any offset against the plaintiff's claim. • This plea is similar to the common-law counterclaim. La. Code Civ. Proc. 1061 et seq. — Also termed *demand in reconvention*.

2. Parliamentary law. A request, usu. invoking a right, that must be granted on a single member's motion. See REQUEST. **3.** A request for payment of a debt or an amount due. **4.** In economics, the intensity of buyer pressure on the availability and cost of a commodity or service. **3.** A request for payment of a debt or an amount due.

personal demand. An in-person demand for payment upon the drawer, maker, or acceptor of a bill or note.

4. In economics, the intensity of buyer pressure on the availability and cost of a commodity or service.

aggregate demand. **1.** The total amount spent on goods and services in an economy during a specific period. **2.** The total demand for a firm's products and services during a specific period.

derived demand. Product demand that is related to another product's demand.

demand, vb. (14c) **1.** To claim as one's due; to require; to seek relief. **2.** To summon; to call into court.

demandant. Archaic. The plaintiff in a real action (the defendant being called a *tenant*). See *real action* under ACTION.

demand clause. (1919) A provision in a note allowing the holder to compel full payment if the maker fails to meet an installment. Cf. ACCELERATION CLAUSE.

demand deposit. See DEPOSIT (2).

demand draft. See *sight draft* under DRAFT.

demand for document inspection. See REQUEST FOR PRODUCTION.

demand for relief. See PRAYER FOR RELIEF.

demand in reconvention. See *reconventional demand* under DEMAND.

demand instrument. (1924) An instrument payable on demand, at sight, or on presentation, as opposed to an instrument that is payable at a set future date. — Also termed *demand note*.

demand letter. (1911) A letter by which one party explains its legal position in a dispute and requests that the recipient take some action (such as paying money owed), or else risk being sued. • Under some statutes (esp. consumer-protection laws), a demand letter is a prerequisite for filing a lawsuit.

demand loan. See *call loan* under LOAN.

demand note. 1. See NOTE (1). **2.** See DEMAND INSTRUMENT.

demand of oyer. Hist. The assertion of a party's right to hear, read, or inspect a deed of which profert is made by the opposing party in a pleading. See OYER (3); PROFERT.

demand of view. Hist. In a real action, a request by a defendant (called a *tenant*) to see the thing at issue to ascertain its identity and the circumstances of the claim. • If a real action was brought against a tenant who did not know what land was at issue, the tenant might demand a view. See VIEW (4).

demand-pull inflation. See INFLATION.

demand registration rights. See REGISTRATION RIGHTS.

demarcation line. Int'l law. A provisional border having the function of separating territories under different jurisdictions, usu. established when the political situation does not admit a final boundary arrangement. — Also termed *line of demarcation*.

démarche (day-**mahrsh**). [French "gait; walk"] An oral or written diplomatic statement, esp. one containing a demand, offer, protest, threat, or the like. — Also spelled *demarche*. See AIDE-MÉMOIRE.

demeanor. (15c) Outward appearance or behavior, such as facial expressions, tone of voice, gestures, and the hesitation or readiness to answer questions. • In evaluating credibility, the jury may consider the witness's demeanor.

demeanor evidence. See EVIDENCE.

demented, adj. Not of sound mind; insane.

demesne (di-**mayn** or di-**meen**), n. [French] (14c) **1.** At common law, land held in one's own right, and not through a superior; esp., land attached to a manor and reserved for the court's own use. **2.** Domain; realm. — Also spelled *demain*.

ancient demesne. Hist. A manor that was held by the Crown at the time of William the Conqueror and was recorded in the Domesday Book.

demesne as of fee. Hist. Complete ownership of something.

demesne land. See LAND.

demesne land of the Crown. See *Crown land* under LAND.

demesnial (di-**may**-nee-əl *or* di-**meen**-ee-əl), *adj.* Of or relating to a demesne.

demilitarization. *Int'l law.* The process by which a country obligates itself not to station military forces — or to maintain military installations — in specified areas or zones within its territory.

demilitarized zone. *Int'l law.* A territorial area in a country or between countries in which no military forces or military installations are stationed or maintained.

de minimis (də **min**-ə-mis), *adj.* [Latin "of the least"] (1952) **1.** Trifling; minimal. **2.** (Of a fact or thing) so insignificant that a court may overlook it in deciding an issue or case. **3.** DE MINIMIS NON CURAT LEX.

de minimis non curat lex (də **min**-ə-mis non **kyoor**-at **leks**). [Latin] The law does not concern itself with trifles. — Often shortened to *de minimis.*

de minimis **test.** *Copyright.* A judicial test for determining whether a contributor to a joint work is an author for legal purposes, based on whether the joint effort itself is an original expression that qualifies for copyright protection. ● This test has been rejected in favor of the copyrightability test by most courts that have addressed the issue. Cf. COPYRIGHTABILITY TEST.

demise (di-**mIz**), *n.* (15c) **1.** The conveyance of an estate usu. for a term of years, a lease <the demise of the land for one year>. **2.** The instrument by which such a conveyance is accomplished <the demise set forth the terms of the transfer>. **3.** The passing of property by descent or bequest <a testator's demise of $100,000 to charity>. **4.** The death of a person or (figuratively) of a thing <the corporation's untimely demise>. — Abbr. dem. See DEATH. — **demise,** *vb.*

joint demise. In an ejectment action, a demise made by two or more persons in one declaration.

separate demise. In an ejectment action, a demise made solely by the lessor.

several demise. (*often pl.*) *Hist.* In an ejectment action, a list of demises by all people potentially owning the property at issue, used to ensure that the plaintiff had proved a lease from the person actually having title. See EJECTMENT.

single demise. In an ejectment action, a declaration containing one demise. See EJECTMENT.

demise charter. See *bareboat charter* under CHARTER (8).

demise charterer. See *bareboat charter* under CHARTER (8).

demised premises. See PREMISES.

demobilization. A dismissal of troops from active service.

democracy, *n.* Government by the people, either directly or through representatives elected by the people. Cf. REPUBLIC. — **democratic,** *adj.*

demonetization. A disuse of a metal in coinage; a withdrawal of the value of a metal as money <the demonetization of gold in the United States>.

demonstrative bequest. See BEQUEST.

demonstrative devise. See DEVISE.

demonstrative evidence. See EVIDENCE.

demonstrative legacy. See LEGACY.

demote, *vb.* To lower (usu. a person) in rank, position, pay, or other status. See DEGRADATION (1).

demur (di-**mər**), *vb.* (17c) **1.** To file a demurrer. See DEMURRER. **2.** To object to the legal sufficiency of a claim alleged in a pleading without admitting or denying the truth of the facts stated. **3.** To object to the legal sufficiency of a claim alleged in a pleading while admitting the truth of the facts stated.

demurrable (di-**mər**-ə-bəl), *adj.* (1827) (Of a claim, pleading, etc.) subject to a demurrer <a demurrable pleading>. See DEMURRER.

demurrage (di-**mər**-ij). (*usu. pl.*) *Maritime law.* **1.** Liquidated damages owed by a charterer to a shipowner for the charterer's failure to load or unload cargo by the agreed time.

contract demurrage. Demurrage paid by a vessel's charterer if the time to load or unload the vessel at port takes longer than that agreed on in the charterer's contract with the shipowner. Cf. DISPATCH MONEY.

noncontract demurrage. Demurrage not provided by contract, but ordered by a court. — Also termed *damages for detention.*

2. A charge due for the late return of ocean containers or other equipment.

demurrage lien. See LIEN.

demurrant (di-**mər**-ant). One who demurs; esp., a litigant who files a demurrer.

demurrer (di-**mər**-ər). [Law French *demorer* "to wait or stay"] (16c) A pleading stating that although the facts alleged in a complaint may be true, they are insufficient for the plaintiff to state a claim for relief and for the defendant to frame an answer. ● In most jurisdictions, such a pleading is now termed a *motion to dismiss,* but *demurrer* is still used in a few states, including California, Nebraska, and Pennsylvania. Cf. DENIAL (1).

demurrer ore tenus. An oral demurrer. See ORE TENUS.

general demurrer. See *general exception* (1) under EXCEPTION (1).

parol demurrer. *Hist.* A suspension of proceedings during the minority of an infant.

speaking demurrer. (18c) A demurrer that cannot be sustained because it introduces new facts not contained in the complaint.

special demurrer. (17c) A demurrer that states grounds for an objection and specifically identifies the nature of the defect, such as that the pleading violates the rules of pleading or practice. ● If a pleading is defective in form but not substance, the defect must be pointed out by a special demurrer.

demurrer book. *Hist.* A record of the demurrer issue used by the court and counsel in argument.

demurrer to evidence. (17c) A party's objection or exception that the evidence is legally insufficient to make a case. ● Its effect, upon joinder in the demurrer by the opposite party, is that the jury is discharged and the demurrer is entered on record and decided by the court. A demurrer to evidence admits the truth of all the evidence and the legal deductions from that evidence.

demurrer to interrogatories. (18c) The objection or reason given by a witness for failing to answer an interrogatory.

demutualization, *n.* The process of converting a mutual insurance company (which is owned by its policyholders) to a stock insurance company (which is owned by outside shareholders), usu. as a means of increasing the insurer's capital by allowing the insurer to issue shares. ● About half the states have demutualization statutes authorizing such a conversion. — **demutualize,** *vb.*

denationalization. 1. *Int'l law.* The unilateral act of a country in depriving a person of nationality, whether by administrative decision or by operation of law. ● Strictly, the term does not cover a person's renunciation of citizenship. **2.** The act of returning government ownership and control of an industry or function to private ownership and control. Cf. PRIVATIZATION. — **denationalize,** *vb.*

denaturalization. The process by which a government deprives a naturalized citizen of all rights, duties, and protections of citizenship. *See* 8 USCA § 1451. — **denaturalize,** *vb.*

denial, *n.* (16c) **1.** A refusal or rejection; esp., a court's refusal to grant a request presented in a motion or petition <denial of the motion for summary judgment>. **2.** A defendant's response controverting the facts that a plaintiff has alleged in a complaint; a repudiation <the worker filed

a denial alleging that physical contact never occurred>. Cf. DEMURRER.

conjunctive denial. (1860) A response that controverts all the material facts alleged in a complaint.

disjunctive denial. (1920) A response that controverts the truthfulness of two or more factual allegations of a complaint in the alternative.

general denial. (16c) A response that puts in issue all the material assertions of a complaint or petition. — Also termed *general plea.*

qualified general denial. (1844) A general denial of all the allegations except the allegations that the pleader expressly admits.

specific denial. (1850) A separate response applicable to one or more particular allegations in a complaint.

3. A refusal or rejection <denial of an employment application>. **4.** A deprivation or withholding <denial of due process>. — **deny,** *vb.*

denial of justice. *Int'l law.* A defect in a country's organization of courts or administration of justice, resulting in the country's violating its international legal duties to protect aliens. ● A denial of justice is a wrongful act under international law. — Also termed *justitia denegata; déni de justice; refus de justice.*

denial-of-service attack. A malicious strike against a computer, website, network, server, or database designed to render it inaccessible, usu. by overwhelming it with activity or by forcing it to malfunction. — Also termed *nuke.* — Abbr. DoS attack.

distributed denial-of-service attack. A denial-of-service attack carried out by distributing a virus that causes infected computers to try to access the target computer at the same time. — Abbr. DDoS attack.

denization (den-ə-**zay**-shən). The act of making a person a denizen. See DENIZEN. — Also termed *indenization.*

denize (**den**-ɪz *or* di-**nɪz**), *vb.* To make (a person) a denizen. See DENIZEN.

denizen (**den**-ə-zən).(15c) **1.** A person given certain rights in a foreign nation or living habitually in a foreign nation. **2.** *English law.* A person whose status is midway between being an alien and a natural-born or naturalized subject.

Denman's Act. *Hist.* **1.** The (English) Evidence Act of 1843, providing that no person offered as a witness can be excluded because of incapacity due to a past crime or an interest in the proceedings. — Also termed *Lord Denman's Act.* **2.** The (English) Criminal Procedure Act of 1865 that allowed defense counsel to sum up evidence as allowed in a civil trial, to prove contradictory statements made by an adverse witness, to prove a previous criminal conviction of an adverse witness, and to compare samples of disputed handwriting. — Also termed *Mr. Denman's Act.*

denomination. (15c) **1.** An act of naming. **2.** A collective designation, esp. of a religious sect.

denotative fact. See FACT.

denounce, *vb.* (13c) **1.** To condemn openly, esp. publicly. **2.** To declare (an act or thing) to be a crime and prescribe a punishment for it. **3.** To accuse or inform against. **4.** To give formal notice to a foreign country of the termination of (a treaty).

denouncement. 1. An act of accusation or condemnation <denouncement of a thief>. **2.** A declaration of a threatened action <denouncement of war> <denouncement of a treaty>. **3.** An application for a grant to work a mine that is either newly discovered or forfeited <the denouncement was granted>. • Historically, denouncements were also granted under Spanish-American law. **4.** *Archaic.* A formal announcement; a declaration <a denouncement of a doctrine>. — Also termed *denunciation.* — **denunciatory, denunciative,** *adj.*

de novo (di **noh**-voh *or* dee), *adj.* (1536) Anew.

hearing de novo. See HEARING.

trial de novo. See TRIAL.

venire facias de novo (və-**nı**-ree **fay**-shee-əs dee **noh**-voh). See VENIRE FACIAS.

de novo judicial review. See JUDICIAL REVIEW.

de novo review. 1. See *appeal de novo* under AP-PEAL. **2.** See *de novo judicial review* under JUDI-CIAL REVIEW.

density zoning. See *cluster zoning* under ZONING.

denumeration. (18c) An act of making a present payment.

denunciation. See DENOUNCEMENT.

deny the appeal. See AFFIRM (1).

deodand (**dee**-ə-dand). *Hist.* Something (such as an animal) that has done wrong and must therefore be forfeited to the Crown. • Deodand was abolished in 1846.

de odio et atia (dee **oh**-dee-oh et **ay**-shee-ə), *n.* [Law Latin "of hatred and malice"] *Hist.* A writ ordering a sheriff to summon a 12-member jury to inquire whether a prisoner jailed for murder was charged for a good reason or only because of ill-will and to determine whether bail should be set. • If the prisoner was accused out of spite or had committed the crime in self-defense, then another writ called *tradas in ballim* would have been issued ordering the sheriff to release the prisoner on bail if the sheriff could find 12 good citizens of the county to vouch for the prisoner. This writ, similar to *habeas corpus*, was first mentioned in

Magna Carta. — Also termed *breve de bono et malo.*

deontology. The philosophy of ethics, rights, and duties as a matter of natural law. • Moral rights in one's one intellectual property are often considered deontological issues. — **deontological,** *adj.*

department, *n.* (18c) **1.** A division of a greater whole; a subdivision <a legal department>. **2.** A country's division of territory, usu. for governmental and administrative purposes, as in the division of a state into counties <France has regional departments similar to states>. **3.** A principal branch or division of government <legislative department>; specif., a division of the executive branch of the U.S. government, headed by a secretary who is a member of the President's cabinet <Department of Labor>. — **departmental,** *adj.*

Department of Agriculture. The cabinet-level department of the federal government responsible for improving farm income, developing foreign markets for U.S. farm products, conducting agricultural research, and inspecting and grading food products. • Created in 1862, it is headed by the Secretary of Agriculture. — Abbr. USDA.

Department of Commerce. The cabinet-level department of the federal government responsible for promoting the nation's international trade, economic growth, and technical advancement. • Designated as a department in 1913, it is headed by the Secretary of Commerce. — Abbr. DOC.

Department of Defense. See DEFENSE DEPART-MENT.

Department of Defense Dependents Schools. A unit in the U.S. Department of Defense responsible for operating schools from kindergarten through grade 12 for the dependents of military and civilian personnel stationed overseas. — Abbr. DoDDS.

Department of Education. The cabinet-level department of the federal government responsible for advising the President on federal education policy, and administering and coordinating most federal programs of assistance to education. • Headed by the Secretary of Education, the Department includes the Office of Bilingual Education and Minority Languages Affairs (OBEMLA), the Office of Educational Research and Improvement (OERI), the Office of Elementary and Secondary Education (OESE), the Office of Postsecondary Education (OPE), the Office of Special Education and Rehabilitative Services (OSERS), the Office of Student Financial (OSF), the Office of Vocational and Adult Education (OVAE), and ten regional offices. — Abbr. DOE.

Department of Energy. The cabinet-level department of the federal government responsible for advising the President on energy policies, plans, and programs, and for providing leadership in achieving efficient energy use, diversity in energy sources, and improved environmental quality.● Headed by the Secretary of Energy, it oversees a comprehensive national energy plan, including the research, development, and demonstration of energy technology; energy conservation; the nuclear-weapons program; and pricing and allocation. — Abbr. DOE.

Department of Health and Human Services. The cabinet-level department of the federal government responsible for matters of health, welfare, and income security. ● It was originally established by Reorganization Plan No. 1 of 1953 under the title Department of Health, Education, and Welfare. The Department is headed by the Secretary of Health and Human Services. — Abbr. HHS.

Department of Homeland Security. The cabinet-level department of the federal government responsible for ensuring security within the U.S. borders and in its territories and possessions. ● The Department has five major divisions: Border and Transportation Security, Emergency Preparedness and Response, Science and Technology, Information Analysis and Infrastructure, and Management. It was established in 2002 and began operating in 2003. — Abbr. DHS.

Department of Housing and Urban Development. The cabinet-level department of the federal government responsible for overseeing programs that are concerned with housing needs and fair-housing opportunities, and with improving and developing the nation's communities. ● It was established in 1965 by the Department of Housing and Urban Development Act. 42 USCA §§ 3532–37. It is headed by the Secretary of Housing and Urban Development. — Abbr. HUD.

department of human services. See DEPARTMENT OF PUBLIC WELFARE. — Abbr. DHS.

Department of Justice. The federal executive division that is responsible for federal law enforcement and related programs and services. ● The U.S. Attorney General heads this department, which has separate divisions for prosecuting cases under federal antitrust laws, tax laws, environmental laws, and criminal laws. The department also has a civil division that represents the U.S. government in cases involving tort claims and commercial litigation. — Abbr. DOJ.

Department of Labor. The cabinet-level department of the federal government responsible for promoting the welfare of wage earners and for improving working conditions and opportunities for profitable employment. ● Headed by the Secretary of Labor, it was created in 1913. 29 USCA § 551. — Abbr. DOL.

department of public welfare. A state-government agency that administers public-assistance programs of all types, such as food stamps and housing vouchers. ● In many communities, this department is now called the Department of Human Services or Department of Social Services. — Abbr. DPW.

Department of Social Services. See CHILD PROTECTIVE SERVICES. — Abbr. DSS.

Department of State. The cabinet-level department of the federal government responsible for advising the President in formulating and executing foreign policy. ● Headed by the Secretary of State, the Department negotiates treaties and other agreements with foreign nations; speaks for the United States before the United Nations and other international organizations; and represents the United States at international conferences. It was established in 1789 as the Department of Foreign Affairs and was renamed the Department of State later the same year. 22 USCA 2651–2728. Foreign affairs are handled through six bureaus: African Affairs, European Affairs, East Asian and Pacific Affairs, Near East Affairs, South Asian Affairs, and Western Hemisphere Affairs. — Also termed *State Department.*

Department of the Interior. The cabinet-level department of the federal government responsible for managing the nation's public lands and minerals, national parks, national wildlife refuges, and western water resources, and for upholding federal trust responsibilities to Indian tribes. ● The Department also has responsibility for migratory-wildlife conservation; historical preservation; endangered species; surface-mined-lands preservation and restoration; mapping; and geological, hydrological, and biological science. It was created in 1849 and reorganized in 1950. Headed by the Secretary of the Interior, it administers several agencies, including the Bureau of Land Management, the Bureau of Indian Affairs, the U.S. Fish and Wildlife Service, and the U.S. Geological Survey. — Also termed *Interior Department.*

Department of the Navy. See NAVY DEPARTMENT.

Department of the Treasury. The cabinet-level department of the federal government responsible for recommending tax and fiscal policies, collecting taxes, disbursing U.S. government funds, enforcing tax laws, and manufacturing coins and currency. ● Created by Congress in 1789, it is headed by the Secretary of the Treasury. — Also termed *Treasury Department.*

Department of Transportation. The federal executive division responsible for programs and policies concerning transportation. ● Through a series of specialized agencies, this department oversees aviation, highways, railroads, mass transit, the U.S. merchant marine, and other programs. — Abbr. DOT.

Department of Veterans Affairs. The cabinet-level department of the federal government responsible for operating programs that benefit veterans of military service and their families. ● It is headed by the Secretary of Veterans Affairs. — Abbr. VA. — Formerly termed *Veterans Administration.*

departure, *n.* (15c) **1.** A deviation or divergence from a standard rule, regulation, measurement, or course of conduct <an impermissible departure from sentencing guidelines>.

downward departure. (1982) In the federal sentencing guidelines, a court's imposition of a sentence more lenient than the standard guidelines propose, as when the court concludes that a criminal's history is less serious than it appears.

forbidden departure. (1996) An impermissible deviation from the federal sentencing guidelines based on race, sex, national origin, creed, religion, or socioeconomic status.

lateral departure. (1993) In the federal sentencing guidelines, a sentence allowing a defendant to avoid incarceration through community or home confinement. — Also termed *lateral sentencing.*

upward departure. (1982) In the federal sentencing guidelines, a court's imposition of a sentence harsher than the standard guidelines propose, as when the court concludes that a criminal's history did not take into account additional offenses committed by the prisoner.

2. A variance between a pleading and a later pleading or proof <the departure between the plaintiff's pleadings and the actual evidence was significant>. **3.** A party's desertion of the ground (either legal or factual) taken in the immediately preceding pleading and resort to another ground <the defendant's departure from the asserted alibi necessitated a guilty plea>. — **depart,** *vb.*

departure in despite of court. *Hist.* A failure of a defendant (called a tenant) in a real action to appear on demand. ● A tenant, having once appeared in a real action, was considered to be constructively present until again called. So if the tenant failed to appear when demanded, the tenant was said to have departed in despite (in contempt) of court.

dépeçage (dep-ə-**sahzh**). [French "dismemberment"] A court's application of different state laws to different issues in a legal dispute; choice of law on an issue-by-issue basis.

depeculation (dee-pek-yə-**lay**-shən). *Hist.* Embezzlement from the public treasury. Cf. PECULATION. — **depeculate,** *vb.*

dependency. (16c) **1.** A land or territory geographically distinct from the country governing it, but belonging to the country and governed by its laws. ● The Philippines was formerly a dependency of the United States. Cf. COMMONWEALTH (2); TERRITORY (1). **2.** A relationship between two persons or things whereby one is sustained by the other or relies on the other for support or necessities.

dependency court. See COURT.

dependency exemption. See EXEMPTION.

dependency hearing. See *shelter hearing* under HEARING.

dependent, *n.* (16c) **1.** One who relies on another for support; one not able to exist or sustain oneself without the power or aid of someone else.

lawful dependent. (1908) **1.** One who receives an allowance or benefits from the public, such as social security. **2.** One who qualifies to receive a benefit from private funds as determined by the laws governing the distribution.

legal dependent. (1909) A person who is dependent according to the law; a person who derives principal support from another and usu. may invoke laws to enforce that support.

partial dependent. Workers' compensation. A person whose partial reliance on an employee covered under workers'-compensation law for support entitles him or her to receive death benefits if the employee is killed on the job.

2. *Tax.* A person, such as a child or parent, for whom a taxpayer may be able to claim a personal exemption if the taxpayer provides more than half of the person's support during the taxable year. ● Besides support, other criteria must be met as well. IRC (26 USCA) § 152. — **dependent,** *adj.*

dependent child. See CHILD.

dependent claim. See PATENT CLAIM.

dependent condition. See CONDITION (2).

dependent contract. See CONTRACT.

dependent covenant. See COVENANT (1).

dependent coverage. See COVERAGE.

dependent intervening cause. A cause of an accident or injury that occurs between the defendant's behavior and the injurious result, but that does not change the defendant's liability. See *intervening cause* under CAUSE (1).

dependent promise. See PROMISE.

dependent relative revocation. (1855) A common-law doctrine that operates to undo an otherwise sufficient revocation of a will when there is evidence that the testator's revocation was conditional rather than absolute. ● Typically, the doctrine applies when a testator has physically revoked the will and believes that a new will is valid, although this belief is mistaken. The doctrine undoes only the revocation; it does not always accomplish the testator's intent or validate an otherwise invalid will. — Also termed *dependent-relative-revoca-tion doctrine*; *conditional revocation*; *mistakenly induced revocation*; *ineffective revocation*; *doc-trine of ineffective revocation*.

dependent state. See *nonsovereign state* under STATE.

depletable economic interest. A mineral-land interest subject to depletion by the removal (by drilling or mining) of the mineral that is the sub-ject of the interest.

depletion, *n.* (17c) An emptying, exhausting, or wasting of an asset, esp. of a finite natural re-source such as oil. — **deplete,** *vb.* — **depletive,** *adj.*

depletion allowance. See ALLOWANCE (3).

depletion reserve. *Accounting.* A charge to income reflecting the decrease in the value of a wasting asset, such as an oil reserve.

deponent (di-**poh**-nənt), *n.* (16c) **1.** One who testi-fies by deposition. **2.** A witness who gives written testimony for later use in court; AFFIANT. — **de-pone,** *vb.*

depopulation. 1. A substantial reduction in popu-lation. **2.** *Hist.* A species of waste by which the kingdom's population was diminished. See DE-POPULATIO AGRORUM.

deportable, *adj.* (Of an alien) subject to removal from a country after an illegal entry.

deportable alien. See ALIEN.

deportation (dee-por-**tay**-shən), *n.* The act or an in-stance of removing a person to another country; esp., the expulsion or transfer of an alien from a country. — **deport,** *vb.*

depose (di-**pohz**), *vb.* (14c) **1.** To examine (a wit-ness) in a deposition <the defendant's attorney will depose the plaintiff on Tuesday>. **2.** To testi-fy; to bear witness <the affiant deposes and states that he is at least 18 years old>. **3.** To remove from office or from a position of power; dethrone <reb-els sought to depose the dictator>.

deposit, *n.* (17c) **1.** The act of giving money or other property to another who promises to preserve it or to use it and return it in kind; esp., the act of placing money in a bank for safety and conve-nience. **2.** The money or property so given.

demand deposit. A bank deposit that the deposi-tor may withdraw at any time without prior no-tice to the bank.

direct deposit. The payment of money by transfer-ring the payment directly into the payee's bank account, usu. by electronic transfer.

frozen deposit. A bank deposit that cannot be withdrawn, as when the financial institution is insolvent or an account is restricted.

general deposit. **1.** A bank deposit of money that is commingled with other depositors' money. **2.** A bank deposit that is to the depositor's credit, thus giving the depositor a right to the money and creating a debtor–creditor relationship be-tween the bank and the depositor. • A bank is not required to return the actual money de-posited as a general deposit, as it must with a special deposit; the bank need return only an equivalent sum.

special deposit. A bank deposit that is made for a specific purpose, that is kept separately, and that is to be returned to the depositor. • The bank serves as a bailee or trustee for a special deposit. — Also termed *specific deposit.*

time deposit. A bank deposit that is to remain for a specified period or for which notice must be given to the bank before withdrawal. — Also termed *term deposit.*

3. Money placed with a person as earnest money or security for the performance of a contract. • The money will be forfeited if the depositor fails to perform. — Also termed *security deposit.* **4.** *Copy-right.* The placing of two copies of a published work with the Library of Congress within three months of publication. • This requirement is in-dependent of copyright registration. **5.** *Civil law.* A contract by which a depositor delivers a thing to a depositary for safekeeping. La. Civ. Code arts. 2926, 2929. • A deposit may be either an onerous or a gratuitous contract. — Also termed *deposi-tum*; *naked deposit*; *gratuitous deposit.* See *gratu-itous bailment* under BAILMENT.

involuntary deposit. A deposit made by acci-dentally leaving or placing personal property in another's possession. See *involuntary bail-ment* under BAILMENT.

necessary deposit. A bailment, usu. made by reason of emergency or other necessity, that prevents the depositor from freely choosing the depositary. • A necessary deposit occurs, for example, when a person entrusts goods to a stranger during a fire.

quasi-deposit. An involuntary deposit made when one party lawfully possesses property merely by finding it.

voluntary deposit. A deposit made by the mutual consent of the bailor and bailee.

6. *Patents.* The placing of a sample of microor-ganisms or cell lines with the U.S. Patent and Trademark Office to satisfy the enablement re-quirement. • The practice is not statutory but has been established by regulation and caselaw. 37 CFR §§ 1.801–809. — Also termed *enablement by deposit.*

deposit account. See ACCOUNT.

depositary. (17c) **1.** A person or institution that one leaves money or valuables with for safekeeping <a title-insurance officer is the depositary of the funds>. ● When a depositary is a company, it is often termed a *safe-deposit company.* Cf. DEPOSITORY. **2.** A gratuitous bailee. See DEPOSIT (5).

depositary bank. See BANK.

deposit box. See SAFE-DEPOSIT BOX.

deposit company. See COMPANY.

deposit contract. See CONTRACT.

deposit in court. The placing of money or other property that represents a person's potential liability in the court's temporary custody, pending the outcome of a lawsuit. — Also termed *deposit into the registry of the court.*

deposit insurance. See INSURANCE.

deposit into the registry of the court. See DEPOSIT IN COURT.

deposition (dep-ə-**zish**-ən). (14c) **1.** A witness's out-of-court testimony that is reduced to writing (usu. by a court reporter) for later use in court or for discovery purposes. *See* Fed. R. Civ. P. 30; Fed. R. Crim. P. 15. — Also termed *examination before trial.* **2.** The session at which such testimony is recorded.

   apex deposition. (1992) The deposition of a person whose position is at the highest level of a company's hierarchy. ● Courts often preclude an apex deposition unless (1) the person to be deposed has particular knowledge regarding the claim, and (2) the requesting party cannot obtain the requested — and discoverable — information through less intrusive means.

   deposition de bene esse (dee **bee**-nee **es**-ee *also* day **ben**-ay **es**-ay). (18c) A deposition taken from a witness who will likely be unable to attend a scheduled trial or hearing. ● If the witness is not available to attend trial, the testimony is read at trial as if the witness were present in court. See *testimony de bene esse* under TESTIMONY.

   deposition on written questions. (1970) A deposition given in response to a prepared set of written questions, as opposed to a typical oral deposition. *See* Fed. R. Civ. P. 31. — Formerly also termed *deposition on written interrogatories.*

   oral deposition. (1910) A deposition given in response to oral questioning by a lawyer.

   30(b)(6) deposition. (1979) Under the Federal Rules of Civil Procedure, the deposition of an organization, through the organization's designated representative. ● Under Rule 30(b)(6), a party may take the deposition of an organization, such as a corporation. The notice of deposition (or subpoena) may name the organization and may specify the matters to be covered in the deposition. The organization must then designate a person to testify about those matters on its behalf. Fed. R. Civ. P. 30(b)(6). Most states authorize a similar procedure under state-court procedural rules.

3. The written record of a witness's out-of-court testimony. **4.** *Eccles. law.* The involuntary release of a clergyman from the exercise of his office. Cf. DEGRADATION (1); DEPRIVATION (4).

deposition on written interrogatories. See *deposition on written questions* under DEPOSITION.

deposition subpoena. See SUBPOENA.

deposition subpoena duces tecum. See *subpoena duces tecum* under SUBPOENA.

deposit of title deeds. A pledge of real property as security for a loan, by placing with the lender, as pledgee, the title-deed to the land.

depositor, *n.* One who makes a deposit. See DEPOSIT.

depository (di-**poz**-ə-tor-ee), *n.* (17c) A place where one leaves money or valuables for safekeeping <the grade school's depository for used books>. Cf. DEPOSITARY.

depository bond. See BOND (2).

depository institution. 1. An organization formed under state or federal law, authorized by law to receive deposits, and supervised and examined by a government agency for the protection of depositors. **2.** A trust company or other institution authorized by law to exercise fiduciary powers similar to those of a national bank. ● The term does not include an insurance company, a Morris Plan bank, an industrial loan company, or similar bank unless its deposits are insured by a federal agency.

depository-transfer check. See CHECK.

Depository Trust Corporation. The principal central clearing agency for securities transactions on the public markets. — Abbr. DTC.

deposit premium. The initial premium paid by an insured pending the final premium adjustment.

deposit ratio. The ratio of total deposits to total capital.

deposit slip. A bank's written acknowledgment of an amount received on a certain date from a depositor.

depositum (di-**poz**-i-təm), *n. Roman law.* The gratuitous deposit of goods for the benefit of the depositor. ● The depositee was liable only for *dolus.* See DOLUS. Cf. *gratuitous bailment* under BAILMENT; DEPOSIT (5).

deposit warrant. See WARRANT (2).

depraved, *adj.* (14c) **1.** (Of a person or crime) corrupt; perverted. **2.** (Of a crime) heinous; morally horrendous. — **depravity,** *n.*

depraved-heart murder. See MURDER.

depraved-indifference murder. See *depraved-heart murder* under MURDER.

depreciable life. See USEFUL LIFE.

depreciation (di-pree-shee-**ay**-shən), *n.* (1862) A decline in an asset's value because of use, wear, obsolescence, or age. Cf. APPRECIATION; AMORTIZATION (2). — **depreciate,** *vb.* — **depreciable,** *adj.*

> **accelerated depreciation.** Depreciation recorded using a method that writes off the cost of an asset more rapidly than the straight-line method.

> **accumulated depreciation.** (1916) The total depreciation currently recorded on an asset. ● On the balance sheet, an asset's total cost less accumulated depreciation reflects the asset's book value. — Also termed *accrued depreciation.*

> **annual depreciation.** (1862) The yearly decrease in a property's value due to regular wear and tear.

> **economic depreciation.** A reduction in the value of an asset due to a shortening of the asset's economic life.

> **functional depreciation.** (1910) Depreciation that results from the replacement of equipment that is not yet worn out but that is obsolete in light of new technology or improved methodology allowing more efficient and satisfactory production.

depreciation method. (1915) A set formula used in estimating an asset's use, wear, or obsolescence over the asset's useful life or some portion thereof. ● This method is useful in calculating the allowable annual tax deduction for depreciation. See USEFUL LIFE.

> **accelerated depreciation method.** (1964) A depreciation method that yields larger deductions in the earlier years of an asset's life and smaller deductions in the later years.

> **annuity depreciation method.** A depreciation method that allows for a return of imputed interest on the undepreciated balance of an asset's value. ● The imputed interest is subtracted from the current depreciation amount before it is credited to the accumulated depreciation accounts.

> **declining-balance depreciation method.** (1947) A method of computing the annual depreciation allowance by multiplying the asset's undepreciated cost each year by a uniform rate that may not exceed double the straight-line rate or 150 percent.

> **double-declining depreciation method.** (1996) A depreciation method that spreads over time the initial cost of a capital asset by deducting in each period twice the percentage recognized by the straight-line method and applying that double percentage to the undepreciated balance existing at the start of each period.

> **replacement-cost depreciation method.** A depreciation method that fixes an asset's value by the price of its substitute.

> **sinking-fund depreciation method.** A depreciation method that accounts for the time value of money by setting up a depreciation-reserve account that earns interest, resulting in a gradual yearly increase in the depreciation deduction.

> **straight-line depreciation method.** (1930) A depreciation method that writes off the cost or other basis of the asset by deducting the expected salvage value from the initial cost of the capital asset, and dividing the difference by the asset's estimated useful life.

> **sum-of-the-years'-digits depreciation method.** A method of calculating the annual depreciation allowance by multiplying the depreciable cost basis (cost minus salvage value) by a constantly decreasing fraction, which is represented by the remaining years of useful life at the beginning of each year divided by the total number of years of useful life at the time of acquisition. — Sometimes shortened to *SYD method.*

> **unit depreciation method.** A depreciation method — directly related to the productivity of the asset — that divides the asset's value by the estimated total number of units to be produced, and then multiplies the unit cost by the number of units sold during the year, representing the depreciation expense for the year.

> **units-of-output depreciation method.** A method by which the cost of a depreciable asset, minus salvage value, is allocated to the accounting periods benefited based on output (as miles, hours, number of times used, and the like).

depreciation reserve. An account built up to offset the depreciation of property because of time and use, so that at the end of the property's service there is enough money to replace the property.

depredation. (15c) The act of plundering; pillaging.

depression. (18c) A period of economic stress that persists over an extended period, accompanied by poor business conditions and high unemployment. Cf. RECESSION.

deprivation. (15c) **1.** An act of taking away <deprivation of property>. **2.** A withholding of something <deprivation of food>. **3.** The state of being without something; wanting <sleep deprivation>. **4.** A removal or degradation from office, esp. an ecclesiastical office <deprivation of the bishop>. Cf. DEPOSITION (4); DEGRADATION (1).

deprived child. See CHILD.

Deprizio doctrine. (1990) *Bankruptcy.* The rule that a debtor's payment to an outside creditor more than 90 days before a bankruptcy filing is voidable as a preferential transfer if the payment also benefits an inside creditor. *Levit v. Ingersoll Rand Fin. Corp. (In re V.N. Deprizio Constr. Co.),* 874 F.2d 1186 (7th Cir. 1989).

depublished opinion. See OPINION (1).

deputy, *n.* (15c) A person appointed or delegated to act as a substitute for another, esp. for an official. — **deputize, depute,** *vb.*

   courtroom deputy. The deputy clerk assigned to a particular courtroom or a particular judge.

   general deputy. **1.** A deputy appointed to act in another officer's place and execute all ordinary functions of the office. **2.** See *deputy sheriff* under SHERIFF.

   special deputy. A deputy specially appointed to serve a particular purpose, such as keeping the peace during a riot.

deputy sheriff. See SHERIFF.

de recto (dee **rek**-toh), *n.* [Law Latin] A writ of right to recover both the seisin and the property. — Also termed *breve de recto.* See WRIT OF COURSE.

de recto patens (dee **rek**-toh **pay**-tenz), *n.* [Law Latin "of right patent"] *Hist.* The highest writ of right under the law given to an owner in fee simple to recover the possession and use of land from the freehold tenant. — Also termed *breve magnum de recto.*

deregistration, *n.* The point at which an issuer's registration under section 12 of the Securities Exchange Act of 1934 is no longer required because of a decline in the number of holders of the issuer's securities. 15 USCA § 78*l.* ● Deregistration is triggered when the number of holders falls below a certain number or when required by an administrative order. Cf. DELISTING. — **deregister,** *vb.*

deregulation, *n.* (1963) The reduction or elimination of governmental control of business, esp. to permit free markets and competition. — **deregulate,** *vb.*

   financial deregulation. The lessening of governmental oversight and intervention in the business of financial institutions. ● Among other effects, regulation of financial contracts is relaxed and competition for depositors and borrowers increases.

deregulation clause. *Oil & gas.* A gas-contract provision specifying how the price of gas will be calculated and what the buyer's and seller's obligations will be if regulated natural gas becomes deregulated.

derelict (**der**-ə-likt), *adj.* (17c) **1.** Forsaken; abandoned; cast away <derelict property>. See *quasi-*

derelict under DERELICT. **2.** Lacking a sense of duty; in breach of a legal or moral obligation <the managers were derelict in their duties>. **3.** Dilapidated; run-down.

derelict, *n.* (17c) **1.** Personal property abandoned or thrown away by the owner with no intent to claim it any longer, such as a ship deserted at sea.

   quasi-derelict. A ship that has been deserted or abandoned temporarily or involuntarily, as when the crew is dead or otherwise incapable of navigating the ship.

2. Land uncovered by water receding from its former bed. **3.** A street person or vagrant; a hobo.

dereliction (der-ə-**lik**-shən), *n.* (16c) **1.** The forsaking of a legal or moral obligation with no intent to reassume it; abandonment <dereliction of duty>.

   dereliction in the performance of duties. *Military law.* Willful or negligent failure to perform assigned duties; culpable inefficiency in performing assigned duties.

2. An increase of land caused by the receding of a sea, river, or stream from its usual watermark. See RELICTION.

derelict-official act. A statute that mandates forfeiture of office if the holder willfully neglects or fraudulently fails to perform official duties.

derivation clause. A deed-of-trust provision that provides information about the transfer of a property, esp. the source of the title, such as the name of the previous grantor and the recording date of the deed. See *deed of trust* under DEED.

derivative, *adj. Copyright.* Of, relating to, or constituting a work that is taken from, translated from, adapted from, or in some way further develops a previous work. ● Copyright protection includes the exclusive right in derivative works, such as a screenplay adapted from a book, or a variant musical arrangement.

derivative, *n.* **1.** A financial instrument whose value depends on or is derived from the performance of a secondary source such as an underlying bond, currency, or commodity. — Also termed *derivative instrument; derivative security.* **2.** See *derivative work* under WORK (2).

derivative acquisition. See ACQUISITION.

derivative action. (18c) **1.** A suit by a beneficiary of a fiduciary to enforce a right belonging to the fiduciary; esp., a suit asserted by a shareholder on the corporation's behalf against a third party (usu. a corporate officer) because of the corporation's failure to take some action against the third party. *See* Fed. R. Civ. P. 23.1. — Also termed *derivative suit; shareholder derivative suit; stockholder derivative suit; representative action.* Cf. DIRECT ACTION (3). **2.** A lawsuit arising from an injury to another person, such as a husband's action for loss of consortium arising from an injury to his wife caused by a third person.

derivative contraband. See CONTRABAND.

derivative conveyance. See *secondary conveyance* under CONVEYANCE.

derivative deed. See *secondary conveyance* under CONVEYANCE.

derivative defense. See DEFENSE (1).

derivative entrapment. See ENTRAPMENT.

derivative estate. See ESTATE (1).

derivative evidence. See EVIDENCE.

derivative instrument. See DERIVATIVE (1).

derivative-jurisdiction doctrine. (1964) The principle that a case is not properly removable unless it is within the subject-matter jurisdiction of the state court from which it is removed.

derivative lease. See SUBLEASE.

derivative liability. See LIABILITY.

derivative market. See MARKET.

derivative possession. See POSSESSION.

derivative power. See POWER (3).

derivative security. See DERIVATIVE (1).

derivative settlement. See SETTLEMENT (2).

derivative suit. See DERIVATIVE ACTION (1).

derivative title. See TITLE (2).

derivative-use immunity. See *use immunity* under IMMUNITY (3).

derivative work. See WORK (2).

derived demand. See DEMAND (4).

derogation (der-ə-**gay**-shən), *n.* (15c) **1.** The partial repeal or abrogation of a law by a later act that limits its scope or impairs its utility and force <statutes in derogation of the common law>. **2.** Disparagement; depreciation in value or estimation <some argue that the derogation of family values has caused an increase in crime>. **3.** Detraction, prejudice, or destruction (of a grant or right) <an attorney may be punished for derogation from professional integrity>. — **derogate** (**der**-ə-gayt), *vb.*

derogation clause. *Int'l law.* A reservation in a treaty allowing a signator to refuse to comply with certain provisions. ● For example, a signator may be allowed to suspend some or all of its treaty obligations during a war or other national emergency. If a treaty lacks an express derogation clause, then general principles governing suspension or termination of treaties govern.

derogation from grant. A provision in an instrument of transfer (such as a deed) that diminishes, avoids, or otherwise limits the grant itself.

derogatory clause. (16c) **1.** A statutory or contractual provision proclaiming that the document in which it appears, or a part of the document, cannot be repealed or amended. ● Such provisions are considered ineffective. **2.** A clause that a testator inserts secretly in a will, containing a provision that any later will not having that precise clause is invalid. ● A derogatory clause seeks to protect against a later will extorted by undue influence, duress, or violence. — Also termed *clausula derogativa*; *clausula derogatoria*.

DES. *abbr.* DELIVERED EX SHIP.

descend, *vb.* To pass (a decedent's property) by intestate succession.

descendant (di-**sen**-dənt), *n.* (17c) One who follows in the bloodline of an ancestor, either lineally or collaterally. ● Examples are children and grandchildren. Cf. ASCENDANT. — **descendant,** *adj.*

   collateral descendant. Loosely, a blood relative who is not strictly a descendant, such as a niece or nephew.

   lineal descendant. A blood relative in the direct line of descent. ● Children, grandchildren, and great-grandchildren are lineal descendants.

descendibility of future interests. (1936) The legal possibility that a future interest (such as a remainder or an executory interest) can legally pass by inheritance.

descendible, *adj.* (15c) (Of property) capable of passing by descent or being inherited. See HERITABLE.

descent, *n.* (15c) **1.** The acquisition of real property by law, as by inheritance; the passing of intestate real property to heirs. See SUCCESSION (2). Cf. DISTRIBUTION (1); PURCHASE (2). **2.** The fact or process of originating from a common ancestor. Cf. ASCENT. — **descend,** *vb.*

   collateral descent. Descent in a collateral or oblique line, from brother to brother or cousin to cousin. ● With collateral descent, the donor and donee are related through a common ancestor. Cf. *collateral descendant* under DESCENDANT.

   direct-line descent. See *lineal descent.*

   immediate descent. **1.** A descent directly to an heir, as from a grandmother to granddaughter, brought about by the earlier death of the mother. **2.** A direct descent without an intervening link in consanguinity, as from mother to daughter.

   lineal descent. Descent in a direct or straight line, as from father or grandfather to son or grandson. — Also termed *direct-line descent.*

   maternal-line descent. Descent between two persons, traced through the mother of the younger.

   mediate descent. **1.** A descent not occurring immediately, as when a granddaughter receives land from her grandmother, which first passed to the mother. **2.** A direct descent occurring through a link in consanguinity, as when a granddaughter receives land from her grandfather directly.

paternal-line descent. Descent between two persons, traced through the father of the younger.

descent and distribution. 1. See *intestate succession* under SUCCESSION (2). **2.** Broadly, the rules by which a decedent's property is passed, whether by intestate succession or by will. See DISTRIBUTION.

descent cast. *Hist.* The devolution of realty that has been acquired by disseisin, abatement, or intrusion, upon an heir whose ancestor died intestate. • This tolled the real owner's right of entry until the owner brought a legal action. — Also termed *descent that tolls entry.*

description. (14c) **1.** A delineation or explanation of something by an account setting forth the subject's characteristics or qualities <description of a patentable process>. **2.** A representation by words or drawing of something seen or heard or otherwise experienced <description of the criminal> <description of the accident>. **3.** An enumeration or specific identification of something <description of items in the estate>. **4.** LEGAL DESCRIPTION. **5.** *Patents.* In a U.S. patent application, the section that (1) comprehensively characterizes the invention in language that is clear and complete enough to enable anyone of ordinary skill in the relevant art to make and use the invention; (2) explains the best mode for using the invention; and (3) usu. includes an explanation of drawings that are part of the application. • The detailed description typically makes up the largest portion of the application's specification. — Also termed (in sense 5) *enabling disclosure; written description.*

descriptive comparative law. See COMPARATIVE LAW.

descriptive mark. See *descriptive trademark* under TRADEMARK.

descriptive trademark. See TRADEMARK.

descriptive word. *Trademarks.* A term that portrays a general characteristic or function of a product or service. • A descriptive word may not be registered as a trademark unless it has acquired secondary meaning in the minds of consumers such that it is directly associated with one brand.

desecrate, *vb.* (17c) To divest (a thing) of its sacred character; to defile or profane (a sacred thing).

desegregation, *n.* (1951) **1.** The abrogation of policies that separate people of different races into different institutions and facilities (such as public schools). **2.** The state of having had such policies abrogated. Cf. INTEGRATION (4). — **desegregate,** *vb.*

deserter. *Int'l law.* A member of the armed forces who leaves national military service with the intention of reneging on military obligations either permanently or for the duration of a military operation; a member of the armed forces who illegally abandons a military force, often by seeking refuge in a foreign territory or by joining enemy forces.

desertion, *n.* (16c) The willful and unjustified abandonment of a person's duties or obligations, esp. to military service or to a spouse or family. • In family law, the five elements of spousal desertion are (1) a cessation of cohabitation, (2) the lapse of a statutory period, (3) an intention to abandon, (4) a lack of consent from the abandoned spouse, and (5) a lack of spousal misconduct that might justify the abandonment. — Also termed *gross neglect of duty.* Cf. ABANDONMENT. — **desert,** *vb.*

constructive desertion. (1894) One spouse's misconduct that forces the other spouse to leave the marital abode. • The actions of the offending spouse must be serious enough that the spouse who is forced from the home finds the continuation of the marriage to be unendurable or dangerous to his or her safety and well-being, and finds it necessary to seek safety outside the marital domicile. — Also termed *constructive abandonment.*

criminal desertion. (18c) One spouse's willful failure without just cause to provide for the care, protection, or support of the other spouse who is in ill health or needy circumstances.

obstinate desertion. Desertion by a spouse who persistently refuses to return to the marital home, so that the other spouse has grounds for divorce. • Before the advent of no-fault divorce, this term was commonly used in divorce statutes. The term was often part of the longer phrase *willful, continued, and obstinate desertion.*

willful, continued, and obstinate desertion. See *obstinate desertion.*

deserts. See JUST DESERTS.

design, *n.* (16c) **1.** A plan or scheme. **2.** Purpose or intention combined with a plan.

formed design. *Criminal law.* The deliberate and fixed intention to kill, though not necessarily a particular person. See PREMEDITATION.

3. The pattern or configuration of elements in something, such as a work of art. **4.** *Patents.* The drawing or the depiction of an original plan for a novel pattern, model, shape, or configuration that is chiefly decorative or ornamental. • If it meets other criteria, a design may also be protectable as a trademark. — **design,** *vb.*

design around, *vb. Patents.* To make something that performs the same function or has the same physical properties as (a patented product or process) but in a way different enough from the original that it does not infringe the patent. Cf. DOCTRINE OF EQUIVALENTS.

designate, *n.* See DESIGNEE.

designated public forum. See PUBLIC FORUM.

designating petition. A document used to designate a candidate for a political-party nomination at a primary election or for election to a party position.

design claim. See PATENT CLAIM.

design defect. See DEFECT.

design-defect exclusion. See EXCLUSION (3).

designedly, *adv.* (17c) Willfully; intentionally.

designee. A person who has been designated to perform some duty or carry out some specific role. — Also termed *designate* (**dez**-ig-nət), *n.*

designer defense. See DEFENSE (1).

designer drug. See DRUG.

design patent. See PATENT (3).

design review. A process by which a building permit is withheld until the proposed building meets the architectural standards established by land-use regulations. — Also termed *architectural review.*

design specification. See STATEMENT OF WORK.

design-specification contract. See *build-to-print contract* under CONTRACT.

desist. To stop or leave off. See CEASE-AND-DESIST ORDER.

desk audit. See AUDIT.

de son tort (də sawn [*or* son] **tor**[t]). [Law French "by his own wrongdoing"] Wrongful.

   executor de son tort. See EXECUTOR.

   trustee de son tort. See TRUSTEE.

desperate debt. See DEBT.

despoil (di-**spoil**), *vb.* (14c) To deprive (a person) of possessions illegally by violence or by clandestine means; to rob. — **despoliation** (di-spoh-lee-**ay**-shən), **despoilment**, *n.*

desponsation (dee-spon-**say**-shən). *Archaic.* The act of betrothal; the act of contracting for marriage.

despot (**des**-pət), *n.* (16c) **1.** A ruler with absolute power and authority. **2.** A tyrant. — **despotic** (di-**spot**-ik), *adj.*

despotism (**des**-pə-tiz-əm). (18c) **1.** A government by a ruler with absolute, unchecked power. **2.** Total power or controlling influence.

destination. 1. The predetermined end of a course, as of a voyage or package. **2.** The act of appointment, esp. in a will; a designation. **3.** *Scots law.* The nomination of heirs — esp. in a certain

order — by law or under a will. **4.** *Scots law.* The line of successors so appointed.

destination bill of lading. See BILL OF LADING.

destination contract. See CONTRACT.

destitute (**des**-ti-t[y]oot), *adj.* (14c) **1.** Deprived; bereft. **2.** Not possessing the necessaries of life; lacking possessions and resources; indigent.

destructibility, *n.* (18c) The capability of being destroyed by some action, turn of events, or operation of law. — **destructible**, *adj.*

destructibility of contingent remainders. (1918) *Property.* The common-law doctrine requiring a future interest to vest by the time it is to become possessory or else be totally destroyed, the interest then reverting to the grantor. ● The doctrine could be avoided by the use of trustees to preserve contingent remainders. This doctrine has been abolished in all but a few American jurisdictions; the abolishing statutes are commonly termed *anti-destructibility statutes.* — Also termed *destructibility rule.*

destructible trust. See TRUST.

destruction. 1. The act of destroying or demolishing; the ruining of something. **2.** Harm that substantially detracts from the value of property, esp. personal property. **3.** The state of having been destroyed.

desuetude (**des**-wə-t[y]ood). (15c) **1.** Lack of use; obsolescence through disuse. **2.** The doctrine holding that if a statute or treaty is left unenforced long enough, the courts will no longer regard it as having any legal effect even though it has not been repealed.

detainee. A person held in custody, confined, or delayed by an authority, such as law enforcement or a government.

   ghost detainee. See *secret detainee.*

   secret detainee. A person who is held, usu. without being formally charged with a crime or facing any other legal proceedings, in an undisclosed place, and whose detention is unknown to anyone other than the detaining authority. — Also termed *ghost detainee.* See *secret detention* under DETENTION.

detainer. (17c) **1.** The action of detaining, withholding, or keeping something in one's custody.

   forcible detainer. See FORCIBLE DETAINER.

   unlawful detainer. (18c) The unjustifiable retention of the possession of real property by one whose original entry was lawful, as when a tenant holds over after lease termination despite the landlord's demand for possession.

2. The confinement of a person in custody. **3.** A writ authorizing a prison official to continue holding a prisoner in custody. **4.** A person who detains someone or something.

detection. The act of discovering or revealing something that was hidden, esp. to solve a crime.

détente (day-**tahnt**). [French] **1.** The relaxation of tensions between two or more parties, esp. nations. **2.** A policy promoting such a relaxation of tensions. **3.** A period during which such tensions are relaxed. Cf. ENTENTE; ALLIANCE.

detention, *n.* (15c) **1.** The act or fact of holding a person in custody; confinement or compulsory delay. — **detain,** *vb.*

investigative detention. (1968) The holding of a suspect without formal arrest during the investigation of the suspect's participation in a crime. • Detention of this kind is constitutional only if probable cause exists.

pretrial detention. (1962) **1.** The holding of a defendant before trial on criminal charges either because the established bail could not be posted or because release was denied. **2.** In a juvenile-delinquency case, the court's authority to hold in custody, from the initial hearing until the probable-cause hearing, any juvenile charged with an act that, if committed by an adult, would be a crime. • If the court finds that releasing the juvenile would create a serious risk that before the return date the juvenile might commit a criminal act, it may order the juvenile detained pending a probable-cause hearing. Juveniles do not have a constitutional right to bail. The Supreme Court upheld the constitutionality of such statutes in *Schall v. Martin*, 467 U.S. 253, 104 S.Ct. 2403 (1984). — Also termed *temporary detention.*

preventive detention. (1952) Confinement imposed usu. on a criminal defendant who has threatened to escape, poses a risk of harm, or has otherwise violated the law while awaiting trial, or on a mentally ill person who may cause harm.

secret detention. The holding of a suspect in an undisclosed place, without formal charges, a legal hearing, or access to legal counsel, and without the knowledge of anyone other than the detaining authority. See *secret detainee* under DETAINEE.

2. Custody of property; esp., an employee's custody of the employer's property without being considered as having legal possession of it.

detention hearing. See HEARING.

detention in a reformatory. A juvenile offender's sentence of being sent to a reformatory school for some period.

determinable, *adj.* (15c) **1.** Liable to end upon the happening of a contingency; terminable <fee simple determinable>. **2.** Able to be determined or ascertained <the delivery date is determinable because she kept the written invoice>.

determinable easement. See EASEMENT.

determinable estate. See ESTATE (1).

determinable fee. 1. See *fee simple determinable* under FEE SIMPLE. **2.** See *base fee* under FEE (2).

determinable freehold. See *determinable estate* under ESTATE (1).

determinate hospitalization. A fixed period of hospitalization, usu. by civil commitment.

determinate obligation. See OBLIGATION.

determinate sentence. See SENTENCE.

determinate sentencing. See *mandatory sentencing* under SENTENCING.

determination, *n.* (14c) **1.** A final decision by a court or administrative agency <the court's determination of the issue>.

initial determination. The first determination made by the Social Security Administration of a person's eligibility for benefits.

2. The ending or expiration of an estate or interest in property, or of a right, power, or authority <the easement's determination after four years>. — **determine,** *vb.*

determination letter. (1929) A letter issued by the Internal Revenue Service in response to a taxpayer's request, giving an opinion about the tax significance of a transaction, such as whether a nonprofit corporation is entitled to tax-exempt status. — Also termed *ruling letter.*

determinative judgment. See *final judgment* under JUDGMENT.

determinism. (*sometimes cap.*) A philosophy that human behavior is governed primarily by preexisting conditions, such as family or environmental factors, and is not influenced by will. — **deterministic,** *adj.*

deterrence, *n.* (1861) The act or process of discouraging certain behavior, particularly by fear; esp., as a goal of criminal law, the prevention of criminal behavior by fear of punishment. Cf. REHABILITATION (1); RETRIBUTION (1). — **deter,** *vb.* — **deterrent,** *adj.*

general deterrence. (1949) A goal of criminal law generally, or of a specific conviction and sentence, to discourage people from committing crimes.

special deterrence. (1955) A goal of a specific conviction and sentence to dissuade the offender from committing crimes in the future.

deterrent, *n.* (1824) Something that impedes; something that prevents <a deterrent to crime>.

deterrent danger. See DANGER.

deterrent punishment. See PUNISHMENT.

detinet (**det**-i-net). [Latin "he detains"] A holding back; detention. • An action in debt may be in detinet when the plaintiff alleges that the defendant wrongfully kept goods, as distinguished from wrongfully taking them. An action in debt may also be in *detinet* when it is brought by or against someone other than an original party to the debt, such as an executor. An action of replevin is in *detinet* when the defendant retains possession of the property until after the judgment.

detinue (**det**-i-nyoo *or* -noo). (15c) A common-law action to recover personal property wrongfully taken or withheld by another. Cf. REPLEVIN; TROVER.

> *detinue of goods in frankmarriage. Hist.* A writ allowing a divorced wife to obtain the goods given to her during the marriage.

> *detinue sur bailment* (**det**-i-nyoo sər **bayl**-mənt) [Law French] *Hist.* An action to recover property that the defendant acquired by bailment but refuses to return.

detinuit (di-**tin**-yoo-it). [Latin "he has detained"] (Of property) the former condition of being withheld. • An action is said to be *in the detinuit* when the plaintiff finally recovers possession of the property claimed under a writ of replevin.

detour, *n. Torts.* An employee's minor deviation from the employer's business for personal reasons. • Because a detour falls within the scope of employment, the employer is still vicariously liable for the employee's actions. Cf. FROLIC.

detournement (di-**tuurn**-mənt), *n.* An employee's misappropriation of the employer's funds.

detraction, *n.* (14c) The removal of personal property from one state to another after transfer of title by a will or inheritance.

detriment. (15c) **1.** Any loss or harm suffered by a person or property. **2.** *Contracts.* The relinquishment of some legal right that a promisee would have otherwise been entitled to exercise. — Also termed *legal detriment.* Cf. BENEFIT (2).

> *detriment to a promisee. Contracts.* Consideration offered by a promisee to a promisor, esp. in a unilateral contract.

detrimental reliance. See RELIANCE.

deuterogamy (d[y]oo-tər-**og**-ə-mee), *n.* [fr. Greek *deuterogamia* "second marriage"] A second marriage after the death of or divorce from the first spouse, or after an annulment of a first marriage. — Also termed *digama*; *digamy.*

devaluation, *n.* The reduction in the value of one currency in relation to another currency. Cf. REVALUATION. — **devalue**, *vb.*

devastation. (17c) **1.** An executor's squandering or mismanagement of the deceased's estate. **2.** An act of destruction. **3.** WASTE (1).

devastavit (dev-ə-**stay**-vit), *n.* [Latin "he (or she) has wasted"] A fiduciary's failure to administer an estate or trust promptly and properly, esp. by spending extravagantly or misapplying assets. • A fiduciary who commits waste in this way becomes personally liable to those having claims on the assets, such as creditors and beneficiaries.

developed water. See WATER.

developing country. *Int'l law.* A country that is not as economically or politically advanced as the main industrial powers. • Developing countries are located mostly in Africa, Asia, Eastern Europe, the Middle East, and Latin and South America. — Also termed *developing state*; *underdeveloped country*; *less-developed country*; *Third World country.*

development. (1885) **1.** A substantial human-created change to improved or unimproved real estate, including the construction of buildings or other structures. **2.** An activity, action, or alteration that changes undeveloped property into developed property.

developmental disability. See DISABILITY (2).

developmental neglect. See NEGLECT.

development-stage company. See COMPANY.

devest (di-**vest**), *vb.* **1.** *Hist.* To deprive (a person) of possession, title, or property. **2.** To take; to draw away. — Also spelled *divest.*

deviance, *n.* (1941) The quality or state of departing from established norms, esp. in social customs. — **deviate** (dee-vee-ayt), *vb.* — **deviant**, *adj. & n.* — **deviate** (dee-vee-ət), *n.*

deviation. **1.** Generally, a change from a customary or agreed-on course of action. **2.** *Employment law.* A departure from one's course of employment to tend to a personal matter. • A deviation from the course of employment may be an issue in disputes about workers' compensation or about the employer's tort liability to third parties based on the employee's actions. See COURSE OF EMPLOYMENT. Cf. FROLIC. **3.** *Insurance.* A departure by an insured party from a routine course of action, resulting in increased risk of some loss that the insured is indemnified against. **4.** *Maritime law.* A departure from the terms expressed in a bill of lading or other transportation contract.

> *quasi-deviation.* A deviation from an agreed-on shipping term other than a deviation in course or destination (e.g., an unreasonable delay or the unauthorized carriage of cargo on deck).

> *reasonable deviation.* A deviation that is justified by circumstances. • If a deviation is reasonable, the carrier does not lose its usual limitations and exemptions under the Carriage of Goods by Sea Act.

> *unreasonable deviation.* A deviation that is not justified by circumstances. • An unreasonable deviation causes the carrier to lose the benefit

of its usual limitations and exemptions under the Carriage of Goods by Sea Act.

deviation doctrine. (1948) **1.** A principle allowing variation from a term of a will or trust to avoid defeating the document's purpose. **2.** A principle allowing an agent's activity to vary slightly from the scope of the principal's permission. **3.** *Maritime law.* The rule that a carrier loses the benefit of its limitations and exemptions under the Carriage of Goods by Sea Act if a deviation from the terms of the bill of lading is unreasonable, but does not if it is reasonable.

deviation-well survey. An examination to determine whether a well is bottomed under another person's land.

device. (14c) **1.** *Patents.* A mechanical invention, as differentiated in patent law from a chemical discovery. • A device may be an apparatus or an article of manufacture. — Also termed *machine*. **2.** A scheme to trick or deceive; a stratagem or artifice, as in the law relating to fraud.

deviling (**dev-ə-ling**). **1.** The act of a barrister's handing a brief over to another to handle a case. **2.** The practice of a junior barrister (known as a "devil") who drafts pleadings or other documents for a senior barrister who approves them, signs them, and is ultimately responsible for the work. — Also spelled *devilling*.

devisable, *adj.* (16c) **1.** Capable of being bequeathed by a will. **2.** Capable of being invented. **3.** Feigned.

devise (di-**vIz**), *n.* (15c) **1.** The act of giving property by will. • Although this term traditionally referred to gifts of real property — and in British usage the term is still confined to real property — in American usage the term has been considerably broadened. In both the Restatement of Property and the Uniform Probate Code, a disposition of any property by will is a devise. In the United States today, it is pedantry to insist that the noun *devise* be restricted to real property. **2.** The provision in a will containing such a gift. **3.** Property disposed of in a will. **4.** A will disposing of property. Cf. TESTAMENT (1); BEQUEST; LEGACY. — **devise,** *vb.*

alternative devise. A devise that, under the terms of the will, is designed to displace another devise if one or more specified events occur. — Also termed *secondary devise*.

conditional devise. (18c) A devise that depends on the occurrence of some uncertain event.

demonstrative devise. A devise, usu. of a specific amount of money or quantity of property, that is primarily payable from a designated source, but that may be payable from the estate's general assets if the designated property is insufficient. See Restatement (Third) of Property: Wills and

Other Donative Transfers § 5.1 (1999). Cf. *pecuniary devise.*

executory devise. (17c) An interest in land, created by will, that takes effect in the future and depends on a future contingency; a limitation, by will, of a future estate or interest in land when the limitation cannot, consistently with legal rules, take effect as a remainder. • An executory devise, which is a type of conditional limitation, differs from a remainder in three ways: (1) it needs no particular estate to support it, (2) with it a fee simple or lesser estate can be limited after a fee simple, and (3) with it a remainder can be limited in a chattel interest after a particular estate for life is created in that interest. See *conditional limitation* under LIMITATION.

failed devise. See *lapsed devise.*

general devise. (18c) **1.** A devise, usu. of a specific amount of money or quantity of property, that is payable from the estate's general assets. See Restatement (Third) of Property: Wills and Other Donative Transfers § 5.1 (1999). **2.** A devise that passes the testator's lands without specifically enumerating or describing them.

lapsed devise. (18c) A devise that fails because the testator outlives the named recipient. — Also termed *failed devise*; *failed gift*.

pecuniary devise. A demonstrative devise consisting of money. Cf. *demonstrative devise.*

primary devise. A devise to the first person named as taker. • For example, a devise of "Blackacre to A, but if A does not survive me then to B" names A as the recipient of the primary devise and B as the recipient of the secondary or alternative devise.

residuary devise. (18c) A devise of the remainder of the testator's property left after other specific devises are taken.

secondary devise. See *alternative devise.*

specific devise. (18c) A devise that passes a particular piece of property.

younger-generation devise. An alternative devise to a descendant of the recipient of a primary devise. Unif. Probate Code § 2-603. • A devise of "Blackacre to A, but if A does not survive me then to A's child B" creates a younger-generation devise in A's descendant, B. See *alternative devise.*

devise, *vb.* To give (property) by will.

devisee (dev-ə-**zee** *or* di-vi-**zee**). (16c) A recipient of property by will. Cf. LEGATEE.

first devisee. The first devisee designated to receive an estate under a will.

next devisee. The devisee who receives the remainder of an estate in tail, as distinguished from the first devisee. See FEE TAIL.

residuary devisee. The person named in a will to receive the testator's remaining property after the other devises are distributed.

deviser. (16c) One who invents or contrives <the deviser of these patents>.

devisor. (16c) One who disposes of property (usu. real property) in a will.

devolution (dev-ə-**loo**-shən), *n.* (16c) The act or an instance of transferring one's rights, duties, or powers to another; the passing of such rights, duties, or powers by transfer or succession <the federal government's devolution of police power to the states>. — **devolutionary,** *adj.* — **devolutionist,** *n.*

devolve (di-**vahlv**), *vb.* (16c) **1.** To transfer (rights, duties, or powers) to another. **2.** To pass (rights, duties, or powers) by transmission or succession. See DEVOLUTION.

DFA. *abbr.* DELAYED FUNDS AVAILABILITY.

DFAS. *abbr.* DEFENSE FINANCE AND ACCOUNTING SERVICE.

DHS. *abbr.* **1.** DEPARTMENT OF HOMELAND SECURITY. **2.** Department of human services. See DEPARTMENT OF PUBLIC WELFARE.

DIA. *abbr.* DEFENSE INTELLIGENCE AGENCY.

diagnosis (dɪ-əg-**noh**-sis). (17c) **1.** The determination of a medical condition (such as a disease) by physical examination or by study of its symptoms. **2.** The result of such an examination or study. Cf. PROGNOSIS.

clinical diagnosis. A diagnosis from a study of symptoms only.

physical diagnosis. A diagnosis from physical examination only.

diagnostic commitment. See COMMITMENT.

dialectic (dɪ-ə-**lek**-tik), *n.* (16c) **1.** A school of logic that teaches critical examination of the truth of an opinion, esp. by discussion or debate. • The method was applied by ancient philosophers, such as Plato and Socrates, primarily in the context of conversational discussions involving questions and answers, and also by more modern philosophers, such as Immanuel Kant, who viewed it as a theory of fallacies, and G.W.F. Hegel, who applied the term to his philosophy proceeding from thesis, to antithesis, to synthesis. **2.** An argument made by critically examining logical consequences. **3.** A logical debate. **4.** A disputant; a debater. Pl. **dialectics.**

diarchy. See DYARCHY.

dictate, *vb.* **1.** To pronounce orally for transcription. **2.** To order; to command authoritatively.

dictation. 1. The act of speaking words to be transcribed. **2.** The words so transcribed.

dictator. 1. *Roman law.* An absolute ruler appointed in an emergency for a term of six months and subject to reappointment. **2.** A person, esp. a ruler, with absolute authority.

dictum (**dik**-təm), *n.*(16c) **1.** A statement of opinion or belief considered authoritative because of the dignity of the person making it. **2.** A familiar rule; a maxim. **3.** OBITER DICTUM. Pl. **dicta.**

dictum proprium (**dik**-təm **proh**-pree-əm). A personal or individual dictum that is given by the judge who delivers an opinion but that is not necessarily concurred in by the whole court and is not essential to the disposition of the case. — Also termed (loosely) *dictum propria.*

gratis dictum (**gray**-tis **dik**-təm). **1.** A voluntary statement; an assertion that a person makes without being obligated to do so. **2.** A court's stating of a legal principle more broadly than is necessary to decide the case. **3.** A court's discussion of points or questions not raised by the record or its suggestion of rules not applicable in the case at bar.

judicial dictum. An opinion by a court on a question that is directly involved, briefed, and argued by counsel, and even passed on by the court, but that is not essential to the decision. Cf. OBITER DICTUM.

obiter dictum. See OBITER DICTUM.

simplex dictum (**sim**-pleks **dik**-təm). An unproved or dogmatic statement. See IPSE DIXIT.

dictum page. See *pinpoint citation* under CITATION (3).

dictum propria. See *dictum proprium* under DICTUM.

dies (**dɪ**-eez), *n.* [Latin] A day; days. Pl. *dies.*

dies ad quem (**dɪ**-eez ad **kwem**), *n.* [Latin "the day to which"] *Civil law.* An ending date for a transaction; the ending date for computing time, such as the day on which interest no longer accrues.

dies amoris (**dɪ**-eez ə-**mor**-is), *n.* [Law Latin] *Hist.* A day of favor; esp., a day set by the court for the defendant to make an appearance. • This was usu. the fourth day of the term, which was the first day the court normally sat for business. In addition, the defendant usu. had three days of grace from the summons to appear, but an appearance on the fourth day *quarto die post* ("on the fourth day thereafter") was usu. sufficient.

dies a quo (**dɪ**-eez ay **kwoh**), *n.* [Latin "the day from which"] *Civil law.* A transaction's commencement date; the date from which to compute time, such as a day when interest begins to accrue. La. Civ. Code art. 1784.

dies cedit (**dɪ**-eez **see**-dit). [Latin "the time begins to run"] *Roman & Scots law.* The day on which an interest, esp. a legacy, vests; the day on which a conditional obligation becomes due. • An interest usu., but not always, vested on the day of the testator's death. — Also termed *dies cedens*. Cf. *dies venit*.

dies comitiales (dɪ-eez kə-mish-ee-**ay**-leez). [Latin] *Roman law*. The 190 days in the year when an election could be held or the people could assemble as a legislative body. • The praetors could not hold court while a legislative assembly was in session.

dies communes in banco (dɪ-eez kə-**myoo**-neez in **bang**-koh), *n*. [Law Latin "common days before the bench"] **1.** Regular appearance dates in court. — Also termed *common-return days*. **2.** An enactment printed under the Statutes of Henry III, regulating continuances and writ return dates.

dies datus (dɪ-eez **day**-təs), *n*. [Law Latin "a given day"] A continuance, esp. for a defendant before a declaration is filed; a time of respite in a case. • A continuance granted after the filing of the declaration is called an *imparlance*. See IMPARLANCE.

dies datus in banco (dɪ-eez **day**-təs in **bang**-koh), *n*. [Law Latin] A day given before the bench, as distinguished from a day at *nisi prius*.

dies datus partibus (dɪ-eez **day**-təs **pahr**-tə-bəs), *n*. [Law Latin "a day given to the parties"] A continuance; an adjournment.

dies datus prece partium (dɪ-eez **day**-təs pree-see **pahr**-shee-əm), *n*. [Law Latin "a day given at the prayer of the parties"] A day given at the parties' request.

dies Dominicus (dɪ-eez də-**min**-i-kəs), *n*. [Latin] The Lord's day; Sunday.

dies excrescens (dɪ-eez ek-**skree**-sənz), *n*. [Law Latin "the increasing day"] The additional day in a leap year.

dies fasti (dɪ-eez **fas**-tɪ). [Latin] *Roman law*. A day when justice could be administered; a day when the praetor could officially pronounce the three words "*do*," "*dico*," and "*addico*." — Also called *triverbial days*.

dies feriati (dɪ-eez fer-ee-**ay**-tɪ), *n*. [Latin] *Roman & civil law*. A holiday; holidays.

dies gratiae (dɪ-eez **gray**-shee-ee), *n*. [fr. Law French *jour de grace*] *Hist*. A day of grace, usu. granted to the plaintiff.

dies in banco. See DAYS IN BANK.

dies intercisi (dɪ-eez in-tər-**sɪ**-zɪ). [Latin "divided days"] *Roman law*. A day when the courts were open for only part of the day.

dies juridicus (dɪ-eez juu-**rid**-i-kəs), *n*. [Latin] A day when justice can be administered. • This term was derived from the civil-law term *dies fasti*. See *dies fasti*.

dies legitimus (dɪ-eez lə-**jit**-i-məs). [Latin] *Roman law*. A lawful day; a law day.

dies marchiae (dɪ-eez **mahr**-kee-ee), *n*. [Law Latin "a day of the march"] *Hist*. In the reign of Richard II, the annual day set aside for the wardens of the English and Scottish borders to hold peace talks and resolve differences.

dies nefasti (dɪ-eez nee-**fas**-tɪ), *n*. See *dies non juridicus*.

dies non (dɪ-eez non). See *dies non juridicus*.

dies non juridicus (dɪ-eez non juu-**rid**-i-kəs), *n*. [Law Latin "a day not juridical"] A day exempt from court proceedings, such as a holiday or a Sunday. — Often shortened to *dies non*.

dies pacis (dɪ-eez **pay**-sis), *n*. [Law Latin "day of peace"] *Hist*. A day of peace. • The days were originally divided into two categories: *dies pacis ecclesiae* ("a day of the peace of the church") and *dies pacis regis* ("a day of the Crown's peace").

dies religiosi (dɪ-eez ri-lij-ee-**oh**-sɪ). [Latin] *Roman law*. Religious days on which it was unlawful to transact legal or political business.

dies solaris (dɪ-eez sə-**lair**-is), *n*. [Law Latin "a solar day"] See *solar day* under DAY.

dies solis (dɪ-eez **soh**-lis). [Latin "day of the sun"] *Roman law*. Sunday.

dies utiles (dɪ-eez **yoo**-tə-leez). [Latin "available days"] *Roman law*. A day when something can be legally done, such as an application to the praetor to claim an inheritance.

dies venit (dɪ-eez **vee**-nit). [Latin "the day has come"] *Roman & Scots law*. The date when an interest is both vested and actionable. • It is usu. the day when the heir accepts the inheritance and a legatee can claim payment of a legacy. — Also termed *dies veniens*. Cf. *dies cedit*.

dies votorum (dɪ-eez voh-**tor**-əm), *n*. [Latin "a day of vows"] A wedding day.

diet. 1. A regimen, esp. of food. **2.** (*cap*.) A nation's parliamentary assembly, as in Israel, Japan, or some eastern European nations. **3.** A governing body's meeting day for legislative, political, or religious purposes; specif., a national assembly of various European countries, such as the diet of the German empire, which was summoned by the emperor regularly to perform various functions, including levying taxes, enacting laws, and declaring war. **4.** *Scots law*. A day to perform a duty, such as a court sitting day, an appearance day, and a criminal pleading or trial day. — Also spelled *dyet*.

dietary law. Any of the body of laws observed by members of various faiths regulating what foods may be eaten, how the foods must be prepared and served, and what combinations and contacts (e.g., between meat and milk) are prohibited.

different-department rule. A doctrine holding that people who work for the same employer are not fellow servants if they do not do the same work or do not work in the same department. ● This rule, which creates an exception to the fellow-servant doctrine, has been rejected by many jurisdictions. See FELLOW-SERVANT DOCTRINE; *fellow servant* under SERVANT.

differential pricing. (1946) The setting of the price of a product or service differently for different customers. See PRICE DISCRIMINATION.

diffused surface water. See WATER.

DIF system. See DISCRIMINANT FUNCTION.

digama (dig-ə-mə). See DEUTEROGAMY.

digamy (dig-ə-mee). See DEUTEROGAMY.

digest, *n.* (14c) **1.** An index of legal propositions showing which cases support each proposition; a collection of summaries of reported cases, arranged by subject and subdivided by jurisdiction and court. ● The chief purpose of a digest is to make the contents of reports available and to group together those cases bearing on some specific point. The American Digest System covers the decisions of all American courts of last resort, state and federal, from 1658 to present. — Abbr. D.; Dig. **2.** *Civil law.* (*cap.*) A compilation and systematic statement of the various areas of law; chiefly, the Pandects of Justinian in 50 books, known as the *Digest.* — Also termed *digesta; digests.* See PANDECT (2).

digital agenda. *Copyright.* A series of 10 proposed changes to copyright law announced by WIPO in 1999 and designed to protect intellectual-property rights on the Internet while promoting e-commerce. — Also termed *WIPO digital agenda.*

digital cash. See *e-money* under MONEY.

digital certificate. A publicly available computer-based record that identifies the certifying authority and the subscriber who was issued a digital signature for electronically transmitted documents and that also provides the person's public key for decrypting the digital signature. ● Subscribers register with certification authorities to obtain digital signatures. Certificates may include additional information, including issuance and expiration dates, and recommended reliance limits for transactions relying on the certificate. The certificate also serves as an electronic notarization when attached to an electronic document by the sender.

digital fingerprinting. See STEGANOGRAPHY.

Digital Millennium Copyright Act. A 1998 federal law harmonizing United States copyright protection with international law, limiting copyright liability for Internet service providers, and expanding software owners' ability to copy programs. ● Among many other provisions, the statute extends copyright protection to computer programs, movies, and other audiovisual works worldwide; attempts to regulate cyberspace; forbids devices whose purpose is to evade digital antipiracy tools; and bars the production or distribution of falsified copyright-management information. 17 USCA §§ 1301–1332. — Abbr. DMCA.

digital sampling. See SAMPLING.

digital signature. See SIGNATURE.

digital watermarking. See STEGANOGRAPHY.

dignitary, *adj.* Of or relating to one's interest in personal dignity, as contrasted with one's interest in freedom from physical injury and property damage. ● Tort actions that compensate a plaintiff for a dignitary insult rather than physical injury or property damage include false-light privacy and negligent infliction of emotional distress.

dignitary, *n.* **1.** A person who holds a high rank or honor. **2.** *Eccles. law.* A person who, by virtue of holding a superior office stands above ordinary priests and canons.

dignitary tort. See TORT.

dignity, *n.* **1.** The state of being noble; the state of being dignified. **2.** An elevated title or position. **3.** A person holding an elevated title; a dignitary. **4.** A right to hold a title of nobility, which may be hereditary or for life.

dijudication (dı-joo-də-**kay**-shən). *Archaic.* A judicial determination.

dilapidation. (*often pl.*) Damage to a building resulting from acts of either commission or omission. ● A dilapidation may give rise to liability if it constitutes an act of waste, a breach of contract, or a statutory violation.

dilatory (**dil**-ə-tor-ee), *adj.* (15c) Tending to cause delay <the judge's opinion criticized the lawyer's persistent dilatory tactics>.

dilatory defense. See DEFENSE (1).

dilatory exception. See EXCEPTION (1).

dilatory fiduciary. See FIDUCIARY.

dilatory motion. 1. See MOTION (1). **2.** See MOTION (2).

dilatory plea. See PLEA (3).

diligence. (14c) **1.** A continual effort to accomplish something. **2.** Care; caution; the attention and care required from a person in a given situation. ● The Roman-law equivalent is *dilegentia.* See DILEGENTIA.

    common diligence. **1.** See *due diligence* (1). **2.** See *ordinary diligence.*

    due diligence. (18c) **1.** The diligence reasonably expected from, and ordinarily exercised by, a person who seeks to satisfy a legal requirement or to discharge an obligation. — Also termed *reasonable diligence*; *common diligence*. **2.** *Corporations & securities.* A prospective buyer's or broker's investigation and analysis of a target company, a piece of property, or a newly issued security. • A failure to exercise due diligence may sometimes result in liability, as when a broker recommends a security without first investigating it adequately.

extraordinary diligence. Extreme care that a person of unusual prudence exercises to secure rights or property.

great diligence. The diligence that a very prudent person exercises in handling his or her own property like that at issue. — Also termed *high diligence.*

low diligence. See *slight diligence.*

necessary diligence. The diligence that a person is required to exercise to be legally protected.

ordinary diligence. (18c) The diligence that a person of average prudence would exercise in handling his or her own property like that at issue. — Also termed *common diligence.*

reasonable diligence. (18c) **1.** A fair degree of diligence expected from someone of ordinary prudence under circumstances like those at issue. **2.** See *due diligence* (1).

slight diligence. (1836) The diligence that a person of less than common prudence takes with his or her own concerns. — Also termed *low diligence.*

special diligence. The diligence expected from a person practicing in a particular field of specialty under circumstances like those at issue.

3. *Patents.* Speed and perseverance in perfecting an invention. • Diligence is one factor in deciding which of two or more independent inventors will be granted a patent: if the first inventor cannot prove reasonable diligence in reducing the invention to practice, a later inventor may take priority. **4.** *Scots law.* A court-issued warrant to compel something, such as the attendance of a witness or the enforcement of an unpaid judgment debt. **5.** *Scots law.* Any legal process available to a creditor to seize a debtor's property to compel the debtor to answer an action for debt, to preserve the property as security for a judgment that the creditor may obtain, or to liquidate the property in satisfaction of a judgment already obtained. • Forms of diligence include adjudication, arrestment, inhibition, poinding, and sequestration for rent. Until the mid-20th century, a debtor could also be imprisoned. The term *diligence* is also sometimes used to denote a warrant that may be granted to compel a witness's attendance or to compel production of documents. See EXECUTION (3).

diligent, *adj.* Careful; attentive; persistent in doing something.

diligent inquiry. A careful and good-faith probing to ascertain the truth of something.

Dillon's rule. The doctrine that a unit of local government may exercise only those powers that the state expressly grants to it, the powers necessarily and fairly implied from that grant, and the powers that are indispensable to the existence of the unit of local government. • For the origins of this rule, see 1 John F. Dillon, *The Law of Municipal Corporations* § 89, at 115 (3d ed. 1881).

dilution. (17c) **1.** The act or an instance of diminishing a thing's strength or lessening its value. **2.** *Corporations.* The reduction in the monetary value or voting power of stock by increasing the total number of outstanding shares. **3.** *Constitutional law.* The limitation of the effectiveness of a particular group's vote by legislative reapportionment or political gerrymandering. • Such dilution violates the Equal Protection Clause. — Also termed *vote dilution.* **4.** *Trademarks.* The impairment of a famous trademark's strength, effectiveness, or distinctiveness through the use of the mark on an unrelated product, usu. blurring the trademark's distinctive character or tarnishing it with an unsavory association. • Trademark dilution may occur even when the use is not competitive and when it creates no likelihood of confusion. The elements of trademark dilution are (1) ownership of a famous mark and (2) actual dilution. But a plaintiff does not have to prove actual loss of sales or profits. *Moseley v. V Secret Catalogue, Inc.,* 537 U.S. 418, 123 S.Ct. 1115 (2003). See BLURRING; TARNISHMENT.

Dilution Act. See FEDERAL TRADEMARK DILUTION ACT.

dilution doctrine. *Trademarks.* The rule protecting a trademark from a deterioration in strength, as when a person seeks to use the mark for an unrelated product.

diminished capacity. See CAPACITY (3).

diminished responsibility. See *diminished capacity* under CAPACITY (3).

diminution (dim-ə-n[y]**oo**-shən), *n.* (14c) **1.** The act or process of decreasing, lessening, or taking away. **2.** An incompleteness or lack of certification in a court record sent from a lower court to a higher one for review. **3.** *Trademarks.* BLURRING. — **diminish** (for sense 1), *vb.*

diminution-in-value method. (1980) A way of calculating damages for breach of contract based on a reduction in market value that is caused by the breach.

dimpled chad. See CHAD.

diocesan (dı-**os**-ə-sən), *adj.* Of or belonging to a diocese; of or relating to the relationship between a bishop and the clergy within the diocese.

diocesan court. See COURT.

diocesan mission. A mission performing its work in a single diocese.

diocesan synod. See SYNOD.

diocese (**dı**-ə-sees *or* -sis). **1.** *Roman law.* A division of the later Roman empire into groups of provinces. **2.** *Eccles. law.* A territorial unit of the church, governed by a bishop, and further divided into parishes. **3.** *Eccles. law.* A bishop's jurisdiction. • Several dioceses together are governed by an archbishop.

DIP. *abbr.* DEBTOR-IN-POSSESSION.

diploma. 1. *Roman law.* A letter giving permission to use the imperial post. **2.** *Hist.* A royal charter; letters patent. **3.** A document that evidences or memorializes graduation from a school or society. Cf. DEGREE (6). **4.** A document that evidences a license or privilege to practice a profession, such as medicine.

diplomacy, *n. Int'l law.* **1.** The art and practice of conducting negotiations between national governments.

   open diplomacy. Diplomacy carried on with free access to interested observers and members of the press.

   parliamentary diplomacy. The negotiations and discussions carried out in international organizations according to their rules of procedure.

   secret diplomacy. Diplomacy carried on behind closed doors. — Also termed *quiet diplomacy.*

   shuttle diplomacy. Diplomatic negotiations assisted by emissaries, who travel back and forth between negotiating countries. • In legal contexts, the term usu. refers to a similar approach used by a mediator in negotiating the settlement of a lawsuit. The mediator travels back and forth between different rooms, one of which is assigned to each side's decision-makers and counsel. The mediator relays offers and demands between the rooms and, by conferring with the parties about their positions and about the uncertainty of litigation, seeks to reach an agreed resolution of the case. The mediator does not bring the parties together in the same room.

2. Loosely, foreign policy. **3.** The collective functions performed by a diplomat. — **diplomatic,** *adj.* — **diplomat,** *n.*

diplomatic, *n.* See DIPLOMATICS.

diplomatic agent. See AGENT (2).

diplomatic bag. See DIPLOMATIC POUCH.

diplomatic corps. *Int'l law.* The ambassador and other diplomatic personnel assigned by their government to a foreign capital.

diplomatic immunity. See IMMUNITY (1).

diplomatic pouch. 1. A bag containing official correspondence, documents, or articles intended exclusively for official communications of a nation with its missions, consular posts, or delegations. **2.** The contents of the bag. — Also termed *diplomatic bag; valise diplomatique.*

diplomatic protection. Protection given by one country's representatives to a person, usu. its citizen, against another country's alleged violation of international law.

diplomatic relations. *Int'l law.* The customary form of permanent contact and communication between sovereign countries.

diplomatic representation. See REPRESENTATION (5).

diplomatics. The science of deciphering and authenticating ancient writings. • The principles were largely developed by the Benedictine Dom Mabillon in his 1681 work entitled *De re diplomatica.* — Also termed *diplomatic (n.).*

Diplomatic Security Service. See BUREAU OF DIPLOMATIC SECURITY.

diptych (**dip**-tik), *n.* [fr. Latin *diptycha* fr. Greek *diptycha* "two-leaved"] **1.** *Roman law.* Two tablets usu. made of wood or metal and tied with string through holes at the edges so that they could fold over (like a book with two leaves). • Diptychs were often used to send letters, and the text was sometimes written using a stylus, once on the inside waxed leaves and again on the outside, so that it could be read without opening the tablets. **2.** *Hist. Eccles. law.* Tablets used by the church, esp. to register names of those making supplication, and to record births, marriages, and deaths. **3.** *Hist. Eccles. law.* The registry of those names.

direct (di-**rekt**), *adj.* **1.** (Of a thing) straight; undeviating <a direct line>. **2.** (Of a thing or a person) straightforward <a direct manner> <direct instructions>. **3.** Free from extraneous influence; immediate <direct injury>. **4.** Of or relating to passing in a straight line of descent, as distinguished from a collateral line <a direct descendant> <a direct ancestor>. **5.** (Of a political action) effected by the public immediately, not through representatives <direct resolution> <direct nomination>.

direct, *n.* See DIRECT EXAMINATION.

direct, *vb.* (14c) **1.** To aim (something or someone). **2.** To cause (something or someone) to move on a particular course. **3.** To guide (something or someone); to govern. **4.** To instruct (someone) with authority. **5.** To address (something or someone).

direct action. (1912) **1.** A lawsuit by an insured against his or her own insurance company rather than against the tortfeasor and the tortfeasor's insurer. **2.** A lawsuit by a person claiming against an insured but suing the insurer directly instead of pursuing compensation indirectly through the insured. **3.** A lawsuit to enforce a shareholder's rights against a corporation. Cf. DERIVATIVE ACTION (1).

direct-action statute. A statute that grants an injured party direct standing to sue an insurer instead of the insured tortfeasor. • Under Rhode Island's direct-action statute, for example, an injured party may bring a direct action against an insurer when good-faith efforts to serve process on the insured are unsuccessful. These statutes exist in several states, including Alabama, Arkansas, Louisiana, Minnesota, New York, Pennsylvania, and Wisconsin.

direct adoption. See *private adoption* under ADOPTION.

direct affinity. See AFFINITY.

direct aggression. See AGGRESSION.

direct and proximate cause. See *proximate cause* under CAUSE (1).

direct appeal. See APPEAL.

direct attack. **1.** An attack on a judgment made in the same proceeding as the one in which the judgment was entered; specif., seeking to have the judgment vacated or reversed or modified by appropriate proceedings in either the trial court or an appellate court. • Examples of direct attacks are motions for new trial and appeals. Cf. COLLATERAL ATTACK. **2.** The taking of independent proceedings in equity to prevent the enforcement of a judgment.

direct beneficiary. See *intended beneficiary* under BENEFICIARY.

direct cause. See *proximate cause* under CAUSE (1).

direct charge-off accounting method. See ACCOUNTING METHOD.

direct confession. See CONFESSION.

direct confusion. See CONFUSION.

direct contempt. See CONTEMPT.

direct conversion. See CONVERSION (2).

direct cost. See COST (1).

direct damages. See *general damages* under DAMAGES.

direct deposit. See DEPOSIT (2).

direct economic loss. See ECONOMIC LOSS.

directed verdict. See VERDICT.

direct estoppel. See COLLATERAL ESTOPPEL.

direct evidence. See EVIDENCE.

direct examination. (1859) The first questioning of a witness in a trial or other proceeding, conducted by the party who called the witness to testify. — Often shortened to *direct*. — Also termed *examination-in-chief*. Cf. CROSS-EXAMINATION; REDIRECT EXAMINATION.

direct infringement. See INFRINGEMENT.

direct injury. See INJURY.

direct interest. See INTEREST (2).

direction (di-rek-shən). **1.** The course taken in relation to the point toward or away from which something or someone is moving; a point to or from which a person or thing moves <the storm moved in a northerly direction>. **2.** The course on which something is aimed <the direction of the trial>. **3.** An act of guidance <under the chair's direction>. **4.** An order; an instruction on how to proceed <the judge's direction to the jury>. See JURY INSTRUCTION. **5.** The address to the court contained on a bill of equity <the direction on the bill>. **6.** A board of directors; a board of managers <the direction met on Wednesday>.

directive. See ADVANCE DIRECTIVE.

Directive Harmonizing the Term of Copyright and Certain Related Rights. *Copyright.* A 1993 European Commission initiative setting the term of most copyright protection at the life of the author plus 70 years. • The directive extended coverage in most member countries to match that of Germany, whose term was the longest on the Continent. In 2006, it was repealed. Its provisions were incorporated into the Directive on the Term of Protection of Copyright and Certain Related Rights. — Also termed *Duration Directive*.

Directive on Certain Aspects of Electronic Commerce in the Internal Market. *Copyright.* A 2000 European Commission initiative that harmonizes members' laws governing commercial use of the Internet, including electronic contracts, the liability of service providers, unsolicited commercial e-mail, and related issues. — Also termed *Electronic Commerce Directive*; *E-Commerce Directive*.

Directive on Rental, Lending and Certain Neighboring Rights. *Copyright.* A 1992 European Commission initiative setting rules for reimbursing copyright owners for home rental and public lending of videotapes and other copies of works, and establishing the rights of performers, producers, broadcasters, and cable distributors. — Also termed *Rental and Related Rights Directive*; *Rental Directive*.

Directive on the Coordination of Certain Rules Concerning Copyright and Neighbouring Rights Applicable to Satellite Broadcasting and Cable Retransmission. *Copyright.* A 1993 European Commission initiative requiring members, among other things, to (1) recognize the right of a copyright owner to decide whether the work may be relayed by either cable or satellite, and (2) define the "place" of a satellite broadcast as the location where the signal originates. — Also termed *Cable and Satellite Directive*.

Directive on the Legal Protection of Computer Programs. *Copyright.* A 1991 European Commission initiative requiring members to protect computer software by copyright rather than by patent or some *sui generis* set of legal rights. • The purpose of the Directive was to harmonize copyright laws among the members of the European Commission. It standardized the degree of originality required for software to qualify for copyright protections. — Also termed *Computer Programs Directive*; *Software Directive*.

Directive on the Legal Protection of Databases. *Copyright.* A 1996 European Commission initiative that sets uniform copyright protection among members for databases of original content and requires a *sui generis* system of protection for databases that do not qualify for copyright protection because their content is not original. — Also termed *Database Directive*.

Directive on the Term of Protection of Copyright and Certain Related Rights. See DIRECTIVE HARMONIZING THE TERM OF COPYRIGHT AND CERTAIN RELATED RIGHTS.

directive to physicians. See LIVING WILL.

direct line. See LINE.

direct-line descent. See *lineal descent* under DESCENT.

direct loss. See LOSS.

directly, *adv.* **1.** In a straightforward manner. **2.** In a straight line or course. **3.** Immediately.

direct notice. See NOTICE.

director (di-**rek**-tər). (15c) **1.** One who manages, guides, or orders; a chief administrator. **2.** A person appointed or elected to sit on a board that manages the affairs of a corporation or other organization by electing and exercising control over its officers. — Also termed *trustee*. See BOARD OF DIRECTORS. Cf. OFFICER (1).

affiliated director. See *outside director*.

class director. **1.** A director whose term on a corporate board is staggered with those of the other directors to make a hostile takeover more difficult. **2.** A director elected or appointed to a corporate board to represent a special interest group, e.g., the preferred stockholders.

dummy director. A board member who is a mere figurehead and exercises no real control over the corporation's business. — Also termed *accommodation director*; *nominal director*.

inside director. A director who is also an employee, officer, or major shareholder of the corporation.

interlocking director. A director who simultaneously serves on the boards of two or more corporations that deal with each other or have allied interests.

outside director. A nonemployee director with little or no direct interest in the corporation. — Also termed *affiliated director*.

provisional director. A director appointed by a court to serve on a close corporation's deadlocked board of directors.

public director. A director elected from outside a corporation's shareholders or an organization's membership to represent the public interest.

direct order of alienation. (1852) *Real estate.* The principle that a grantee who assumes the debt on a mortgaged property is required to pay the mortgage debt if the original mortgagor defaults.

Director of Public Prosecutions. An officer (usu. a barrister or solicitor of ten years' standing) who advises the police and prosecutes criminal cases in England, Wales, and Northern Ireland under the supervision of the Attorney General. • This title, or a similar one, is used in various countries, including Australia, Canada, China, Northern Ireland, the Republic of Ireland, and South Africa. In Scotland, the equivalent officer is the *procurator fiscal*.

Director of the Mint. An officer appointed by the President, with the advice and consent of the Senate, to control and manage the U.S. Mint and its branches.

Director of the United States Patent and Trademark Office. The presidential appointee in charge of the U.S. Patent and Trademark Office. • Until a 2000 reorganization, the PTO chief was the Commissioner of Patents and Trademarks. The Director is also the Under Secretary of Commerce for Intellectual Property. — Formerly termed *Commissioner of Patents and Trademarks*.

directors' and officers' liability insurance. See INSURANCE.

directory, *n.* **1.** A book containing an alphabetical list of names, addresses, and telephone numbers, esp. those of a city's or area's residents and businesses. **2.** Any organization's publication containing information on its members or business, such as a legal directory. **3.** *Eccles. law.* A church's book of directions for conducting worship. • One of the primary directories is the Directory for the Public Worship of God, prepared by the Assembly of Divines in England in 1644 to replace the Book of Common Prayer, which had been abolished by Parliament (and was later reinstated). The Directory was ratified by Parliament in 1645 and adopted by the Scottish Parliament and General Assembly of the Church of Scotland that same year. A directory in the Roman Catholic Church contains instructions for saying the mass and offices each day of the year. **4.** A small governing body; specif., the five-member executive body that governed France from 1795–1799 during the French Revolution until it was overthrown by Napoleon and succeeded by the consulate.

directory call. (1812) *Property.* In a land description, a general description of the areas in which landmarks or other calls are found. See CALL (5); LOCATIVE CALLS.

directory provision. A statutory or contractual sentence or paragraph in which a directory requirement appears.

directory requirement. (1865) A statutory or contractual instruction to act in a way that is advisable, but not absolutely essential — in contrast to a mandatory requirement. ● A directory requirement is frequently introduced by the word *should* or, less frequently, *shall* (which is more typically a mandatory word).

directory statute. See STATUTE.

directory trust. See TRUST.

direct-participation program. An investment vehicle that is financed through the sale of securities not traded on an exchange or quoted on NASDAQ and that provides flow-through tax consequences to the investors.

direct payment. See PAYMENT.

direct placement. 1. The sale by a company, such as an industrial or utility company, of an entire issue of securities directly to a lender (such as an insurance company or group of investors), instead of through an underwriter. ● This type of offering is exempt from SEC filing requirements. **2.** PRIVATE PLACEMENT (1).

direct-placement adoption. See *private adoption* under ADOPTION.

direct possession. See *immediate possession* under POSSESSION.

direct question. See QUESTION (1).

direct-reduction mortgage. See MORTGAGE.

direct selling. 1. Selling to a customer without going through a dealer. **2.** Selling to a retailer without going through a wholesaler.

direct skip. (1988) *Tax.* A generation-skipping transfer of assets, either directly or through a trust. ● A direct skip may be subject to a generation-skipping transfer tax — either a gift tax or an estate tax. IRC (26 USCA) §§ 2601–2602. See GENERATION-SKIPPING TRANSFER; *generation-skipping transfer tax* under TAX; SKIP PERSON.

direct tax. See TAX.

Direct Tax Clauses. The provisions in the U.S. Constitution requiring direct taxes to be apportioned among the states according to their respective numbers (U.S. Const. art. I, § 2, cl. 3) and prohibiting capitation or other direct taxes except in proportion to the census (U.S. Const. art. I, § 9, cl. 4). ● An additional provision of Article I, § 2 concerning computation of taxes is affected by § 2 of the Fourteenth Amendment, and both clauses are affected by the Sixteenth Amendment concerning income taxes.

direct trust. See *express trust* under TRUST.

dirt-for-debt transfer. A transaction in which a bankrupt debtor satisfies all or part of a secured debt by transferring the collateral to the creditor.

DISA. *abbr.* DEFENSE INFORMATION SYSTEMS AGENCY.

disability. (16c) **1.** The inability to perform some function; esp., the inability of one person to alter a given relation with another person. **2.** An objectively measurable condition of impairment, physical or mental <his disability entitled him to workers'-compensation benefits>. — Also termed *handicap*; *incapacity.*

   developmental disability. (1973) An impairment of general intellectual functioning or adaptive behavior.

   partial disability. A worker's inability to perform all the duties that he or she could do before an accident or illness, even though the worker can still engage in some gainful activity on the job.

   permanent disability. (1804) A disability that will indefinitely prevent a worker from performing some or all of the duties that he or she could do before an accident or illness.

   physical disability. (1826) An incapacity caused by a physical defect or infirmity, or by bodily imperfection or mental weakness.

   temporary disability. (18c) A disability that exists until an injured worker is as far restored as the nature of the injury will permit.

   temporary total disability. Total disability that is not permanent.

   total disability. (18c) A worker's inability to perform employment-related duties because of a physical or mental impairment.

3. Incapacity in the eyes of the law <most of a minor's disabilities are removed when he or she turns 18>. — Also termed *incapacity.*

   canonical disability. A canonical impediment (usu. impotence). See *canonical impediment* under IMPEDIMENT.

   civil disability. (18c) The condition of a person who has had a legal right or privilege revoked as a result of a criminal conviction, as when a person's driver's license is revoked after a DWI conviction. Cf. *civil death* (2) under DEATH.

disability benefits. See DISABILITY COMPENSATION.

disability clause. *Insurance.* A life-insurance-policy provision providing for a waiver of premiums during the policyholder's period of disability, and sometimes providing for monthly payments equal to a percentage of the policy's face value.

disability compensation. Payments from public or private funds to a disabled person who cannot work, such as social-security or workers'-compensation benefits. — Also termed *disability benefits.*

disability insurance. See INSURANCE.

disability retirement plan. See EMPLOYEE BENEFIT PLAN.

disable, *vb.* **1.** To deprive (someone or something) of the ability to function; to weaken the capability of (someone or something). **2.** To impair; to diminish. **3.** To legally disqualify (someone); to render (someone) legally incapable.

disabled person. See PERSON (1).

disablement, *n.* (15c) **1.** The act of incapacitating or immobilizing. **2.** The imposition of a legal disability.

disabling restraints. (1963) Limits on the alienation of property. • These restraints are sometimes void as being against public policy.

disabling statute. See STATUTE.

disaffirm (dis-ə-fərm), *vb.* (16c) **1.** To repudiate; to revoke consent; to disclaim the intent to be bound by an earlier transaction. **2.** To declare (a voidable contract) to be void.

disaffirmance (dis-ə-fərm-ənts). **1.** An act of denial; a repudiation, as of an earlier transaction. **2.** A declaration that a voidable contract (such as one entered into by a minor) is void. — Also termed *disaffirmation.*

disagreement. 1. A difference of opinion; a lack of agreement. **2.** A quarrel. **3.** An annulment; a refusal to accept something, such as an interest in an estate.

disallow, *vb.* (14c) **1.** To refuse to allow (something). **2.** To reject (something).

disappeared person. (1944) **1.** A person who has been absent from home for a specified number of continuous years (often five or seven) and who, during that period, has not communicated with the person most likely to know his or her whereabouts. See SEVEN-YEARS'-ABSENCE RULE; MISSING PERSON. **2.** *Human-rights law.* A person who has been illegally detained or kidnapped, often by governmental authorities or soldiers, and whose current whereabouts and condition are unknown and undiscoverable.

disappearing quorum. See QUORUM.

disappropriation. 1. *Eccles. law.* The alienation of church property from its original use; the severance of property from church ownership or possession. **2.** The release of property from individual ownership or possession.

disapprove, *vb.* **1.** To pass unfavorable judgment on (something). **2.** To decline to sanction (something).

disarmament. *Int'l law.* The negotiated or voluntary reduction of military arms, esp. nuclear weapons, to a greatly reduced level or to nil. Cf. ARMS CONTROL.

disaster. A calamity; a catastrophic emergency.

disaster area. (1953) A region officially declared to have suffered a catastrophic emergency, such as a flood or hurricane, and therefore eligible for government aid.

disaster loss. See LOSS.

Disaster Relief Act. A federal statute that provides a means by which the federal government can help state and local governments to relieve suffering and damage resulting from disasters such as hurricanes, tornadoes, floods, earthquakes, volcanic eruptions, landslides, mudslides, drought, fire, and explosions. • A 1974 amendment established a process for the President to declare affected communities disaster areas.

disavow (dis-ə-vow), *vb.* To disown; to disclaim knowledge of; to repudiate <the company disavowed the acts of its agent>. — **disavowal,** *n.*

disbarment, *n.* (1862) The action of expelling a lawyer from the bar or from the practice of law, usu. because of some disciplinary violation. • One who has *passed the bar*, been *called to the bar*, or been *admitted to the bar* is privileged to stand inside the wooden barrier that separates the gallery from the actual courtroom, particularly the judge's bench, and conduct business with the court. So this term literally describes the loss of the privilege. Although disbarment is typically a permanent removal from the practice of law, in some jurisdictions a disbarred attorney may (after a certain period) petition for readmission. In England and Wales, only a barrister is disbarred; a solicitor is struck off the roll, so the expulsion of a solicitor is termed *striking off the roll.* See STRUCK OFF. — **disbar,** *vb.*

disbursement (dis-bərs-mənt), *n.* The act of paying out money, commonly from a fund or in settlement of a debt or account payable <dividend disbursement>. — **disburse,** *vb.*

DISC. *abbr.* DOMESTIC INTERNATIONAL SALES CORPORATION.

discharge (dis-chahrj), *n.* (15c) **1.** Any method by which a legal duty is extinguished; esp., the payment of a debt or satisfaction of some other obligation. **2.** *Bankruptcy.* The release of a debtor from monetary obligations upon adjudication of bankruptcy; DISCHARGE IN BANKRUPTCY. Cf. RELEASE (1). **3.** The dismissal of a case. **4.** The canceling or vacating of a court order. **5.** The release of a prisoner from confinement.

> ***unconditional discharge.*** (18c) **1.** A release from an obligation without any conditions attached. **2.** A release from confinement without any parole requirements to fulfill.

6. The relieving of a witness, juror, or jury from further responsibilities in a case. **7.** The firing of an employee.

> ***constructive discharge.*** (1830) A termination of employment brought about by making the employee's working conditions so intolerable that the employee feels compelled to leave.

> ***retaliatory discharge.*** (1967) A discharge that is made in retaliation for the employee's conduct (such as reporting unlawful activity by the employer to the government) and that clearly violates public policy. • Federal and state statutes may entitle an employee who is dismissed by retaliatory discharge to recover damages.

> ***wrongful discharge.*** (1825) A discharge for reasons that are illegal or that violate public policy.

8. The dismissal of a member of the armed services from military service <the sergeant was honorably discharged>.

> ***administrative discharge.*** A military-service discharge given by administrative means and not by court-martial.

> ***bad-conduct discharge.*** A punitive discharge that a court-martial can give a member of the military, usu. as punishment for repeated minor offenses. — Abbr. BCD.

> ***dishonorable discharge.*** The most severe punitive discharge that a court-martial can give to a member of the military. • A dishonorable discharge may result from conviction for an offense recognized in civilian law as a felony or of a military offense requiring severe punishment. Only a general court-martial can give a dishonorable discharge.

> ***general discharge.*** One of the administrative discharges given to a member of the military who does not qualify for an honorable discharge.

> ***honorable discharge.*** A formal final judgment passed by the government on a soldier's entire military record, and an authoritative declaration that he or she has left the service in a status of honor. • Full veterans' benefits are given only to a person honorably discharged.

> ***undesirable discharge.*** One of the administrative discharges given to a member of the mili-

tary who does not qualify for an honorable discharge.

9. *Parliamentary law.* A motion by which a deliberative assembly, having referred a matter to a committee, takes the matter's further consideration out of the committee and back into its own hands. — Also termed *discharge a committee*; *withdrawal.* — **discharge** (dis-**chahrj**), *vb.*

dischargeability proceeding. *Bankruptcy.* A hearing to determine whether a debt is dischargeable or is subject to an exception to discharge. 11 USCA § 523.

dischargeable claim. *Bankruptcy.* A claim that can be discharged in bankruptcy.

discharged contract. See *void contract* (2) under CONTRACT.

discharge hearing. *Bankruptcy.* A hearing at which the court informs the debtor either that a discharge has been granted or the reasons why a discharge has not been granted. See REAFFIRMATION HEARING.

discharge in bankruptcy. (1820) **1.** The release of a debtor from personal liability for prebankruptcy debts; specif., discharge under the United States Bankruptcy Code. **2.** A bankruptcy court's decree releasing a debtor from that liability.

discharging bond. See BOND (2).

disciplinary proceeding. (1900) An action brought to reprimand, suspend, or expel a licensed professional or other person from a profession or other group because of unprofessional, unethical, improper, or illegal conduct. • A disciplinary proceeding against a lawyer may result in the lawyer's being suspended or disbarred from practice.

disciplinary rule. (*often cap.*) (1890) A mandatory regulation stating the minimum level of professional conduct that a professional must sustain to avoid being subject to disciplinary action. • For lawyers, the disciplinary rules are found chiefly in the Model Code of Professional Responsibility. — Abbr. DR. Cf. ETHICAL CONSIDERATION.

discipline, *n.* **1.** Punishment intended to correct or instruct; esp., a sanction or penalty imposed after an official finding of misconduct. **2.** The punishment or penalties (often termed "sanctions") imposed by a disciplining agency on an attorney who has breached a rule of professional ethics. • Three types of discipline are common: disbarment, suspension, and reprimand (public or private). **3.** Control gained by enforcing compliance or order. **4.** *Military law.* A state of mind inducing instant obedience to a lawful order, no matter how unpleasant or dangerous such compliance might be. — **discipline,** *vb.* — **disciplinary,** *adj.*

disclaimer, *n.* (15c) **1.** A renunciation of one's legal right or claim; esp., a renunciation of a patent claim, usu. to save the remainder of the application from being rejected. **2.** A repudiation of another's legal right or claim. **3.** A writing that contains such a renunciation or repudiation. **4.** RENUNCIATION (2). — **disclaim,** *vb.*

disclaimer of warranty. (1881) An oral or written statement intended to limit a seller's liability for defects in the goods sold. • In some circumstances, printed words must be specific and conspicuous to be effective.

patent disclaimer. See *statutory disclaimer.*

qualified disclaimer. (1889) **1.** A disclaimer with a restriction or condition attached. • In this sense it is *qualified* because it carries the restriction or condition. **2.** A person's refusal to accept an interest in property so that he or she can avoid having to pay estate or gift taxes. • To be effective under federal tax law, the refusal must be in writing and must be executed no later than nine months from the time when the interest was created. In this sense, it is *qualified* in the sense of being within the lawful exemption. IRC (26 USCA) § 2518.

statutory disclaimer. *Patents.* A patent applicant's amendment of a specification to relinquish one or more claims to the invention. 35 USCA § 253. • Before the statute was enacted, a single invalid claim was grounds for denying a patent. — Also termed *patent disclaimer.* See SPECIFICATION (3).

terminal disclaimer. A patent applicant's statement shortening the term of the patent. • To revive an abandoned application for a design application or for a utility or plant application filed before June 8, 1995, the applicant must disclaim a period equal to the duration of abandonment. A terminal disclaimer may also be required in an application for an obvious variation on an existing patent with a common inventor or owner: to avoid a double-patenting rejection the inventor agrees that both patents will expire on the same day. 37 CFR 1.321.

disclosed principal. See PRINCIPAL (1).

disclosure, *n.* (16c) **1.** The act or process of making known something that was previously unknown; a revelation of facts <a lawyer's disclosure of a conflict of interest>. See DISCOVERY.

defensive disclosure. See DEFENSIVE DISCLOSURE.

full disclosure. A complete revelation of all material facts.

public disclosure of private facts. (1964) The public revelation of some aspect of a person's private life without a legitimate public purpose. • The disclosure is actionable in tort if the disclosure would be highly objectionable to a reasonable person. See INVASION OF PRIVACY.

voluntary disclosure of offense. A person's uncoerced admission to an undiscovered crime. • Under the federal sentencing guidelines, a lighter sentence may be allowed. See USSG 5K2.16. **2.** The mandatory divulging of information to a litigation opponent according to procedural rules. — Also termed *compulsory disclosure*; *automatic disclosure.* See DISCOVERY (2). — **disclose,** *vb.* — **disclosural,** *adj.*

accelerated disclosure. See *accelerated discovery* under DISCOVERY.

initial disclosure. *Civil procedure.* In federal practice, the requirement that parties make available to each other the following information without first receiving a discovery request: (1) the names, addresses, and telephone numbers of persons likely to have relevant, discoverable information, (2) a copy or description of all relevant documents, data compilations, and tangible items in the party's possession, custody, or control, (3) a damages computation, and (4) any relevant insurance agreements. Fed. R. Civ. P. 26(a)(1)(A)–(D).

3. *Patents.* A document explaining how an invention works in sufficient detail for one skilled in the art to be able to understand and duplicate the invention; everything revealed about an invention in the patent application, including drawings, descriptions, specifications, references to prior art, and claims. • An invention disclosure statement is sometimes attested by a knowledgeable witness, who signs and dates the disclosure document to establish the inventor's identity and the date of the invention before the patent application is prepared. An inventor can file a disclosure document with the U.S. Patent and Trademark Office before submitting a patent application, but the document's date has no relationship to the later application's effective filing date. See ENABLEMENT REQUIREMENT. Cf. ENABLING SOURCE; DEFENSIVE DISCLOSURE. **4.** *Patents.* PUBLICATION (1).

Disclosure Document Program. *Patents.* A U.S. Patent and Trademark Office program allowing an inventor to file a preliminary description of an invention and establish its date of conception before applying for a patent. • The document can help establish a date of inventive effort for use in a later interference. — Abbr. DDP. Cf. PROVISIONAL PATENT APPLICATION.

discommon (dis-**kom**-ən), *vb.* **1.** To deprive of the right of common (e.g., the right to pasture). **2.** To deprive (something, esp. land) of commonable character. • A person could discommon land by separating or enclosing it. **3.** To deprive (someone) of the privileges of a place, such as the right to use common land or to enjoy a church fellowship.

disconformity. See NEW MATTER.

discontinuance (dis-kən-**tin**-yoo-ənts), *n.* (14c) **1.** The termination of a lawsuit by the plaintiff; a voluntary dismissal or nonsuit. See DISMISSAL; NONSUIT (1); *judgment of discontinuance* under JUDGMENT. **2.** The termination of an estate-tail by a tenant in tail who conveys a larger estate in the land than is legally allowed.

discontinuee, *n.* A person whose acquisition of an entailed estate causes a discontinuance of the fee tail heirs' right to the estate.

discontinuing easement. See *discontinuous easement* under EASEMENT.

discontinuous easement. See EASEMENT.

discontinuous servitude. See *discontinuous easement* under EASEMENT.

discount, *n.* (17c) **1.** A reduction from the full amount or value of something, esp. a price. **2.** An advance deduction of interest when a person lends money on a note, bill of exchange, or other commercial paper, resulting in its present value. See PRESENT VALUE. **3.** The amount by which a security's market value is below its face value. — Also termed *bond discount*. Cf. PREMIUM (3). — **discount,** *vb.*

bulk discount. See *volume discount*.

cash discount. (1889) **1.** A seller's price reduction in exchange for an immediate cash payment. **2.** A reduction from the stated price if the bill is paid on or before a specified date.

functional discount. **1.** A supplier's price discount given to a purchaser based on the purchaser's role (such as warehousing or advertising) in the supplier's distributive system. • This type of discount typically reflects the value of services performed by the purchaser for the supplier. If a functional discount constitutes a reasonable reimbursement for the purchaser's actual marketing functions, it does not constitute unlawful price discrimination and does not violate antitrust laws. **2.** A supplier's price discount based on the purchaser's relative distance from the supplier in the chain of distribution. • For example, a wholesaler or distributor usu. receives a greater discount than a retailer.

quantity discount. See *volume discount*.

trade discount. (1889) **1.** A discount from list price offered to all customers of a given type — for example, a discount offered by a lumber dealer to building contractors. **2.** The difference between a seller's list price and the price at which the dealer actually sells goods to the trade.

volume discount. (1939) A price decrease based on a large-quantity purchase. — Also termed *bulk discount*; *quantity discount*.

discount bond. See BOND (3).

discount broker. See BROKER.

discounted cash flow. See CASH FLOW.

discounted-cash-flow method. See *discounted cash flow* under CASH FLOW.

discount interest. See INTEREST (3).

discount loan. See LOAN.

discount market. See MARKET.

discount rate. See INTEREST RATE.

discount share. See *discount stock* under STOCK.

discount stock. See STOCK.

discount yield. See YIELD.

discoverable, *adj.* Subject to pretrial discovery <the defendant's attorney argued that the defendant's income-tax returns were not discoverable during the liability phase of the trial>.

discovered-peril doctrine. See LAST-CLEAR-CHANCE DOCTRINE.

discoveree. A party who is required to respond to a litigant's discovery request or order. Cf. DISCOVERER (1).

discoverer. **1.** A litigant who seeks information or materials from another party by means of a discovery request. — Also termed *discovering party*. Cf. DISCOVEREE. **2.** *Patent law.* See INVENTOR. See 35 USCA § 101.

discovering party. See DISCOVERER (1).

discovert (dis-**kəv**-ərt), *adj.* **1.** *Archaic.* Uncovered; exposed. **2.** Not married, esp. a widow or a woman who has never married.

discovery, *n.* (16c) **1.** The act or process of finding or learning something that was previously unknown <after making the discovery, the inventor immediately applied for a patent>. **2.** Compulsory disclosure, at a party's request, of information that relates to the litigation <the plaintiff filed a motion to compel discovery>. See Fed. R. Civ. P. 26–37; Fed. R. Crim. P. 16. • The primary discovery devices are interrogatories, depositions, requests for admissions, and requests for production. Although discovery typically comes from parties, courts also allow limited discovery from nonparties. **3.** The facts or documents disclosed <the new associate spent all her time reviewing discovery>. **4.** The pretrial phase of a lawsuit during which depositions, interrogatories, and other forms of discovery are conducted. — **discover,** *vb.* — **discoverable,** *adj.*

accelerated discovery. A party's production of relevant evidence to an opponent at a time earlier than would otherwise be required by rule or standing order of the court. • The accelerated discovery is usu. carried out in compliance with a specific court order or the parties' agreement. — Also termed *accelerated disclosure*.

jurisdictional discovery. Discovery that is limited to finding facts relevant to whether the court has jurisdiction. • A court may allow limited jurisdictional discovery before it rules on a motion to dismiss for lack of jurisdiction.

merits discovery. Discovery to uncover facts that support the claim or defense, or that might lead to other facts that will support the allegations of a legal proceeding.

postjudgment discovery. (1967) Discovery conducted after judgment has been rendered, usu. to determine the nature of the judgment debtor's assets or to obtain testimony for use in future proceedings. — Also termed *posttrial discovery.*

pretrial discovery. (1939) Discovery conducted before trial to reveal facts and develop evidence. • Modern procedural rules have broadened the scope of pretrial discovery to prevent the parties from surprising each other with evidence at trial.

reciprocal discovery. See *reverse Jencks material* under JENCKS MATERIAL.

reverse discovery. See *reverse Jencks material* under JENCKS MATERIAL.

discovery abuse. (1975) **1.** The misuse of the discovery process, esp. by making overbroad requests for information that is unnecessary or beyond the scope of permissible disclosure or by conducting discovery for an improper purpose. **2.** The failure to respond adequately to proper discovery requests. — Also termed *abuse of discovery.*

discovery immunity. (1975) An exemption provided by statute, caselaw, or court rules to exclude certain documents and information from being disclosed during discovery.

discovery policy. See *claims-made policy* under INSURANCE POLICY.

discovery rule. (1916) *Civil procedure.* The rule that a limitations period does not begin to run until the plaintiff discovers (or reasonably should have discovered) the injury giving rise to the claim. • The discovery rule usu. applies to injuries that are inherently difficult to detect, such as those resulting from medical malpractice. See STATUTE OF LIMITATIONS. Cf. OCCURRENCE RULE.

discovery vein. See VEIN.

discredit, *vb.* To destroy or impair the credibility of (a witness, a piece of evidence, or a theory); to lessen the degree of trust to be accorded to (a witness or document). — **discredit,** *n.*

discreet (di-**skreet**), *adj.* Exercising discretion; prudent; judicious; discerning.

discrete (di-**skreet**), *adj.* Individual; separate; distinct.

discretion (di-**skresh**-ən). (14c) **1.** Wise conduct and management; cautious discernment; prudence. **2.** Individual judgment; the power of free decision-making.

sole discretion. An individual's power to make decisions without anyone else's advice or consent.

3. *Criminal & tort law.* The capacity to distinguish between right and wrong, sufficient to make a person responsible for his or her own actions. **4.** A public official's power or right to act in certain circumstances according to personal judgment and conscience, often in an official or representative capacity. — Also termed *discretionary power.*

administrative discretion. A public official's or agency's power to exercise judgment in the discharge of its duties.

judicial discretion. (17c) The exercise of judgment by a judge or court based on what is fair under the circumstances and guided by the rules and principles of law; a court's power to act or not act when a litigant is not entitled to demand the act as a matter of right. — Also termed *legal discretion.*

prosecutorial discretion. (1966) A prosecutor's power to choose from the options available in a criminal case, such as filing charges, prosecuting, not prosecuting, plea-bargaining, and recommending a sentence to the court.

discretion, abuse of. See ABUSE OF DISCRETION.

discretionary (di-**skresh**-ə-ner-ee), *adj.* (18c) (Of an act or duty) involving an exercise of judgment and choice, not an implementation of a hard-and-fast rule. • Such an act by a court may be overturned only after a showing of abuse of discretion.

discretionary account. An account that allows a broker access to a customer's funds to purchase and sell securities or commodities for the customer based on the broker's judgment and without first having to obtain the customer's consent to the purchase or sale.

discretionary act. A deed involving an exercise of personal judgment and conscience. — Also termed *discretionary function.* See DISCRETION; ABUSE OF DISCRETION.

discretionary bail. See BAIL (3).

discretionary commitment. See COMMITMENT.

discretionary damages. See DAMAGES.

discretionary duty. See DUTY (2).

discretionary function. See DISCRETIONARY ACT.

discretionary immunity. See IMMUNITY (1).

discretionary order. See ORDER (8).

discretionary power. 1. See POWER (3). **2.** See DISCRETION (4).

discretionary review. See REVIEW.

discretionary sentencing. See *indeterminate sentencing* under SENTENCING.

discretionary-transfer statute. See TRANSFER STATUTE.

discretionary trust. See TRUST.

discriminant function (di-**skrim**-ə-nənt). An IRS method of selecting tax returns to be audited. ● The method consists of (1) using a computer program to identify returns with a high probability of error (such as those showing a disproportionate amount of deductible expenses), and (2) having examiners manually review the selected returns to determine which ones should be audited. — Also termed *DIF system.*

discriminatee (di-skrim-ə-nə-**tee**). A person unlawfully discriminated against.

discrimination, *n.* (1866) **1.** The effect of a law or established practice that confers privileges on a certain class or that denies privileges to a certain class because of race, age, sex, nationality, religion, or disability. ● Federal law, including Title VII of the Civil Rights Act, prohibits employment discrimination based on any one of those characteristics. Other federal statutes, supplemented by court decisions, prohibit discrimination in voting rights, housing, credit extension, public education, and access to public facilities. State laws provide further protections against discrimination. **2.** Differential treatment; esp., a failure to treat all persons equally when no reasonable distinction can be found between those favored and those not favored.

age discrimination. Discrimination based on age. ● Federal law prohibits discrimination in employment against people who are age 40 or older.

content-based discrimination. A state-imposed restriction on the content of speech, esp. when the speech concerns something of slight social value and is vastly outweighed by the public interest in morality and order. ● Types of speech subject to content-based discrimination include obscenity, fighting words, and defamation. *R.A.V. v. City of St. Paul,* 505 U.S. 377, 383–84, 112 S.Ct. 2538, 2543 (1992).

gender discrimination. See *sex discrimination.*

invidious discrimination (in-**vid**-ee-əs). (1856) Discrimination that is offensive or objectionable, esp. because it involves prejudice or stereotyping.

racial discrimination. Discrimination based on race.

reverse discrimination. (1964) Preferential treatment of minorities, usu. through affirmative-action programs, in a way that adversely affects members of a majority group. See AFFIRMATIVE ACTION.

sex discrimination. Discrimination based on gender, esp. against women. ● The Supreme Court has established an intermediate-scrutiny standard of review for gender-based classifications, which must serve an important governmental interest and be substantially related to the achievement of that objective. *Craig v. Boren,* 429 U.S. 190, 97 S.Ct. 451 (1976). — Also termed *gender discrimination.*

viewpoint discrimination. Content-based discrimination in which the government targets not a particular subject, but instead certain views that speakers might express on the subject; discrimination based on the content of a communication. ● If restrictions on the content of speech are reasonable and not calculated to suppress a particular set of views or ideas, a governmental body may limit speech in a nonpublic forum to expressions that serve a specific purpose. For example, an agency holding a workshop to inform state employees of laws related to the agency's functions may reasonably prohibit the expression of opinions regarding the motives of the legislators. But if speech favorable to the legislators' intent is allowed and opponents are denied the opportunity to respond, the restriction would constitute viewpoint discrimination. — Also termed *viewpoint-based discrimination.*

3. The effect of state laws that favor local interests over out-of-state interests. ● Such a discriminatory state law may still be upheld if it is narrowly tailored to achieve an important state interest. Cf. FAVORITISM. — **discriminate,** *vb.* — **discriminatory,** *adj.*

discriminatory tariff. See TARIFF (2).

discussion. **1.** The act of exchanging views on something; a debate. **2.** *Civil law.* A creditor's act of exhausting all remedies against the principal debtor before proceeding with a lawsuit against the guarantor. See BENEFIT OF DISCUSSION.

disease. **1.** A deviation from the healthy and normal functioning of the body <the drug could not be linked to his disease>. **2.** (*pl.*) Special classes of pathological conditions with similar traits, such as having similar causes and affecting similar organs <respiratory diseases> <occupational diseases>. **3.** Any disorder; any depraved condition.

functional disease. A disease that prevents, obstructs, or interferes with an organ's special function, without anatomical defect or abnormality in the organ itself.

industrial disease. See OCCUPATIONAL DISEASE.

occupational disease. See OCCUPATIONAL DISEASE.

organic disease. A disease that is caused by an injury to, or lesion or malfunction in, an organ.

disembarrass, *vb.* To free from embarrassment; to extricate or disentangle one thing from another.

disembodied technology. *Intellectual property.* Know-how or knowledge that is in the form of information only. ● Disembodied technology includes proprietary technology and information in the public domain. Cf. EMBODIED TECHNOLOGY.

disenfranchise (dis-ən-**fran**-chīz), *vb.* (17c) To deprive (a person) of the right to exercise a franchise or privilege, esp. to vote. — Also termed *disfranchise.*

disenfranchisement (dis-ən-**fran**-chīz-mənt *or* -**fran**-chīz-mənt). **1.** The act of depriving a member of a corporation or other organization of a right, as by expulsion. **2.** The act of taking away the right to vote in public elections from a citizen or class of citizens. — Also termed *disfranchisement.*

disentailing assurance. See DISENTAILMENT.

disentailing deed. See DEED.

disentailing statute (dis-ən-**tayl**-ing). A statute regulating or prohibiting disentailing deeds. See *disentailing deed* under DEED.

disentailment (dis-ən-**tayl**-mənt), *n.* (1886) The act or process by which a tenant in tail bars the entail on an estate and converts it into a fee simple, thereby nullifying the rights of any later claimant to the fee tail. — Also termed *disentailing assurance.* See BARRING OF ENTAIL. — **disentail,** *vb.*

disentitle (dis-ən-**tīt**-əl), *vb.* (17c) To deprive (someone) of a title or claim <the plaintiffs' actions disentitled them to recover damages>.

disfigurement (dis-**fig**-yər-mənt). An impairment or injury to the appearance of a person or thing.

disfranchise. See DISENFRANCHISE.

disfranchisement. See DISENFRANCHISEMENT.

disgavel (dis-**gav**-əl), *vb.* *Hist.* To convert (gavelkind land) into ordinary freehold land. See GAVELKIND.

disgorgement, *n.* (15c) The act of giving up something (such as profits illegally obtained) on demand or by legal compulsion. — **disgorge,** *vb.*

disgrading. *Hist.* **1.** The act of degrading. **2.** The depriving of an order; the depriving of a dignity.

disguised dividend. See *informal dividend* under DIVIDEND.

disguised installment sale. See INSTALLMENT SALE.

disherison (dis-**her**-ə-zən). See DISINHERITANCE.

disheritor (dis-**her**-ə-tər *or* -tor). *Archaic.* A person who deprives someone of an inheritance.

dishonest act. See FRAUDULENT ACT.

dishonor, *vb.* (1814c) **1.** To refuse to accept or pay (a negotiable instrument) when presented. See NOTICE OF DISHONOR; WRONGFUL DISHONOR. **2.** To deface or defile (something, such as a flag). — **dishonor,** *n.*

dishonorable discharge. See DISCHARGE (8).

disimprisonment. The release of a prisoner; the removal of a prisoner from confinement. — Also termed *disincarceration; decarceration.* Cf. INCARCERATION.

disincarcerate, *vb.* To release (a person) from jail; to set free.—Also termed *disimprison.*

disincarceration. See DISIMPRISONMENT.

disincentive, *n.* (1946) A deterrent (to a particular type of conduct), often created, intentionally or unintentionally, through legislation <federal tax law creates a disincentive to marriage> <sales taxes provide a disincentive to excessive consumer spending>.

disinflation. A period or process of slowing down the rate of inflation. Cf. DEFLATION.

disinherison (dis-in-**her**-ə-zən), *n.* See DISINHERITANCE.

disinheritance, *n.* (16c) **1.** The act by which an owner of an estate deprives a would-be heir of the expectancy to inherit the estate. ● A testator may expressly exclude or limit the right of a person or a class to inherit property that the person or class would have inherited through intestate succession, but only if the testator devises all the property to another. **2.** The state of being disinherited. See *forced heir* under HEIR. — Also termed *disherison; disinherison; deherison.* — **disinherit,** *vb.*

negative disinheritance. The act by which a testator attempts to exclude a person from inheritance without disposing of the property to another. ● Negative disinheritance is ineffective at common law, although today it may be permitted by statute.

disinter (dis-in-**tər**), *vb.* (17c) **1.** To exhume (a corpse). **2.** To remove (something) from obscurity. — **disinterment** (dis-in-**tər**-mənt), *n.*

disinterested, *adj.* (17c) Free from bias, prejudice, or partiality; not having a pecuniary interest <a disinterested witness>. — **disinterest, disinterestedness,** *n.*

disinterested witness. See WITNESS.

disintermediation. The process of bank depositors' withdrawing their funds from accounts with low interest rates to put them into investments that pay higher returns.

disinvestment, *n.* (1936) **1.** The consumption of capital. **2.** The withdrawal of investments, esp. on political grounds. — Also termed (in sense 2) *divestment.* — **disinvest,** *vb.*

disjoinder (dis-**joyn**-dər). (1936) The undoing of the joinder of parties or claims. See JOINDER. Cf. MISJOINDER (1); NONJOINDER (1).

disjunctive allegation. See ALLEGATION.

disjunctive condition. See CONDITION (2).

disjunctive denial. See DENIAL.

disjunctive obligation. See *alternative obligation* under OBLIGATION.

dismemberment. 1. The cutting off of a limb or body part. **2.** *Int'l law.* The disappearance of a country as a result of a treaty or an annexation, whereby it becomes part of one or more other countries. **3.** *Int'l law.* The reduction of a country's territory by annexation or cession, or the secession of one part. **4.** *Int'l law.* The extinguishment of a country and the creation of two or more new countries from the former country's territory.

dismiss, *vb.* **1.** To send (something) away; specif., to terminate (an action or claim) without further hearing, esp. before the trial of the issues involved. **2.** To release or discharge (a person) from employment. See DISMISSAL.

dismissal, *n.* (1885) **1.** Termination of an action or claim without further hearing, esp. before the trial of the issues involved.

　dismissal agreed. A court's dismissal of a lawsuit with the acquiescence of all parties. ● Among other possibilities, the parties may have settled out of court or chosen to have their dispute arbitrated or mediated. — Also termed *agreed dismissal*.

　dismissal for failure to prosecute. See *dismissal for want of prosecution*.

　dismissal for lack of prosecution. See *dismissal for want of prosecution*.

　dismissal for want of equity. (1859) A court's dismissal of a lawsuit on substantive, rather than procedural, grounds, usu. because the plaintiff's allegations are found to be untrue or because the plaintiff's pleading does not state an adequate claim.

　dismissal for want of prosecution. (1831) A court's dismissal of a lawsuit because the plaintiff has failed to pursue the case diligently toward completion. — Abbr. DWOP. — Also termed *dismissal for failure to prosecute; dismissal for lack of prosecution*.

　dismissal without prejudice. (1831) A dismissal that does not bar the plaintiff from refiling the lawsuit within the applicable limitations period. See WITHOUT PREJUDICE.

　dismissal with prejudice. (1898) A dismissal, usu. after an adjudication on the merits, barring the plaintiff from prosecuting any later lawsuit on the same claim. ● If, after a dismissal with prejudice, the plaintiff files a later suit on the same

claim, the defendant in the later suit can assert the defense of res judicata (claim preclusion). See RES JUDICATA; WITH PREJUDICE.

　involuntary dismissal. (1911) A court's dismissal of a lawsuit because the plaintiff failed to prosecute or failed to comply with a procedural rule or court order. Fed. R. Civ. P. 41(b).

　voluntary dismissal. (1834) A plaintiff's dismissal of a lawsuit at the plaintiff's own request or by stipulation of all the parties. Fed. R. Civ. P. 41(a).

2. A release or discharge from employment. See DISCHARGE (7).

　dismissal for cause. (1877) A dismissal of a contract employee for a reason that the law or public policy has recognized as sufficient to warrant the employee's removal.

3. *Military law.* A court-martial punishment for an officer, commissioned warrant officer, cadet, or midshipman, consisting of separation from the armed services with dishonor. ● A dismissal can be given only by a general court-martial and is considered the equivalent of a dishonorable discharge. — **dismiss,** *vb.*

dismissal compensation. See SEVERANCE PAY.

dismissal order. See ORDER (2).

dismissed for want of equity. (Of a case) removed from the court's docket for substantive reasons, usu. because the plaintiff's allegations are found to be untrue or because the plaintiff's pleading does not state an adequate claim. See *dismissal for want of equity* under DISMISSAL (1).

dismissed for want of prosecution. (Of a case) removed from the court's docket because the plaintiff has failed to pursue the case diligently toward completion. See *dismissal for want of prosecution* under DISMISSAL (1).

dismissed without prejudice. (Of a case) removed from the court's docket in such a way that the plaintiff may refile the same suit on the same claim. See *dismissal without prejudice* under DISMISSAL (1); WITHOUT PREJUDICE.

dismissed with prejudice. (Of a case) removed from the court's docket in such a way that the plaintiff is foreclosed from filing a suit again on the same claim or claims. See *dismissal with prejudice* under DISMISSAL (1); WITH PREJUDICE.

dismission. *Archaic.* **1.** An act of dismissing <dismission of the jury>. **2.** A removal, esp. from office or position <dismission of the employee>. **3.** A decision that a suit cannot be maintained <dismission of the case>.

dismortgage. See REDEMPTION (4).

Disneyland parent. See PARENT.

disobedient child. See *incorrigible child* under CHILD.

disorder. (1877) **1.** A lack of proper arrangement <disorder of the files>. **2.** An irregularity <a disorder in the proceedings>. **3.** A public disturbance; a riot <civil disorder>. **4.** A disturbance in mental or physical health <an emotional disorder> <a liver disorder>.

disorderly conduct. See CONDUCT.

disorderly house. (16c) **1.** A dwelling where people carry on activities that are a nuisance to the neighborhood. **2.** A dwelling where people conduct criminal or immoral activities. ● Examples are brothels and drug houses. — Also termed (more narrowly) *bawdy house; house of prostitution; house of ill fame; house of ill repute; lewd house; assignation house; house of assignation.*

disorderly person. (18c) **1.** A person guilty of disorderly conduct. **2.** A person who breaches the peace, order, decency, or safety of the public, as defined by statute. ● The offense of being a disorderly person is usu. a misdemeanor.

disparagement (di-**spar**-ij-mənt), *n.* (16c) **1.** A derogatory comparison of one thing with another <the disparagement consisted in comparing the acknowledged liar to a murderer>. **2.** The act or an instance of castigating or detracting from the reputation of, esp. unfairly or untruthfully <when she told the press the details of her husband's philandering, her statements amounted to disparagement>. **3.** A false and injurious statement that discredits or detracts from the reputation of another's character, property, product, or business. ● To recover in tort for disparagement, the plaintiff must prove that the statement caused a third party to take some action resulting in specific pecuniary loss to the plaintiff. — Also termed *injurious falsehood.* — More narrowly termed *slander of title; trade libel; slander of goods.* See TRADE DISPARAGEMENT. Cf. *commercial defamation* under DEFAMATION. **4.** Reproach, disgrace, or indignity <self-importance is a disparagement of greatness>. **5.** *Hist.* The act or an instance of pairing an heir in marriage with someone of an inferior social rank <the guardian's arranging for the heir's marriage to a chimney sweep amounted to disparagement>. — **disparage,** *vb.*

disparaging instruction. See JURY INSTRUCTION.

disparaging mark. See *disparaging trademark* under TRADEMARK.

disparaging trademark. See TRADEMARK.

disparate impact (**dis**-pə-rit). (1973) The adverse effect of a facially neutral practice (esp. an employment practice) that nonetheless discriminates against persons because of their race, sex, national origin, age, or disability and that is not justified by business necessity. ● Discriminatory intent is irrelevant in a disparate-impact claim. — Also termed *adverse impact.*

disparate treatment. The practice, esp. in employment, of intentionally dealing with persons differently because of their race, sex, national origin, age, or disability. ● To succeed on a disparate-treatment claim, the plaintiff must prove that the defendant acted with discriminatory intent or motive.

disparity (di-**spar**-ə-tee). (16c) Inequality; a difference in quantity or quality between two or more things.

dispatch (di-**spach** *also* **dis**-pach), *n.* **1.** A prompt sending off of something <a dispatch of the letter agreement>. **2.** A prompt completion of something <dispatch of a business transaction>. **3.** Something quickly sent <the dispatch was mailed>. **4.** *Maritime law.* The required diligence in discharging cargo <dispatch is required on all charters>.

   customary dispatch. Dispatch that follows the rules, customs, and usages of the port where cargo is discharged.

   quick dispatch. A speedy dispatch that does not strictly follow the customs of the port, esp. to avoid delays resulting from a crowded wharf.

5. *Maritime law.* DISPATCH MONEY.

dispatch money. *Maritime law.* An amount paid by a shipowner to a vessel's charterer if the vessel's cargo is unloaded at the port sooner than provided for in the agreement between the charterer and the shipowner. — Also termed *dispatch.* Cf. *contract demurrage* under DEMURRAGE.

dispatch rule. See MAILBOX RULE.

dispauper (dis-**paw**-pər), *vb.* To disqualify from being a pauper; to deprive (a person) of the ability to sue *in forma pauperis.* See IN FORMA PAUPERIS.

dispensary (di-**spen**-sər-ee), *n.* **1.** A place where drugs are prepared or distributed. **2.** An institution, usu. for the poor, where medical advice and medicines are distributed for free or at a discounted rate.

dispensation (dis-pen-**say**-shən). An exemption from a law, duty, or penalty; permission to do something that is ordinarily forbidden.

dispense with the reading of the minutes. *Parliamentary law.* To forgo reciting the secretary's proposed minutes at the regular time. ● The reading is not foregone altogether, but simply postponed. If the proposed minutes have been printed and circulated, then their correction and approval is in order without reading them aloud, and a motion to dispense with reading them is superfluous.

displaced person. See PERSON (1).

displaced-persons camp. *Int'l. law.* In a nation in the throes of war, natural disaster, ethnic cleansing, or some similar extraordinary event, a temporary settlement where citizens who have become homeless are temporarily provided with the basic necessities of life and given assistance in resetttling or emigrating.

displacement. 1. Removal from a proper place or position <displacement of a file> <displacement of an officer>. **2.** A replacement; a substitution <displacement of one lawyer with another>. **3.** A forced removal of a person from the person's home or country, esp. because of war <displacement of refugees>. **4.** A shifting of emotional emphasis from one thing to another, esp. to avoid unpleasant or unacceptable thoughts or tendencies <emotional displacement>.

display right. (1944) *Copyright.* A copyright owner's exclusive right to show or exhibit a copy of the protected work publicly, whether directly or by technological means. • For example, this right makes it illegal to transmit a copyrighted work over the Internet without permission.

disposable earnings. See *disposable income* under INCOME.

disposable income. See INCOME.

disposable portion. The portion of property that can be willed to anyone the testator chooses.

disposal. *Patents.* A patent application's termination by withdrawal, rejection, or grant. • In some countries, the meaning is limited to rejection.

disposing capacity. See *testamentary capacity* under CAPACITY (3).

Disposing Clause. The clause of the U.S. Constitution giving Congress the power to dispose of property belonging to the federal government. U.S. Const. art. IV, § 3, cl. 2.

disposing mind. See *testamentary capacity* under CAPACITY (3).

disposition (dis-pə-**zish**-ən), *n.* (14c) **1.** The act of transferring something to another's care or possession, esp. by deed or will; the relinquishing of property <a testamentary disposition of all the assets>.

testamentary disposition. A disposition to take effect upon the death of the person making it, who retains substantially entire control of the property until death.

2. A final settlement or determination <the court's disposition of the case>.

ambulatory disposition. **1.** A judgment or sentence that is subject to amendment or revocation. **2.** A testamentary provision that is subject to change because the testator is still alive and capable of making a new will. • Sense 2 corresponds to the first sense of *disposition* above. See AMBULATORY.

informal disposition. The termination of a case by means other than trial; any action that leads to disposition without conviction and without a judicial determination of guilt, such as guilty pleas and decisions not to prosecute.

3. Temperament or character; personal makeup <a surly disposition>. — **dispose,** *vb.* — **dispositive,** *adj.*

dispositional hearing. See *disposition hearing* and *permanency hearing* under HEARING.

disposition hearing. See HEARING.

disposition without a trial. (1888) The final determination of a criminal case without a trial on the merits, as when a defendant pleads guilty or admits sufficient facts to support a guilty finding without a trial.

dispositive (dis-**poz**-ə-tiv), *adj.* (17c) **1.** Being a deciding factor; (of a fact or factor) bringing about a final determination. **2.** Of, relating to, or effecting the disposition of property by will or deed.

dispositive fact. See FACT.

dispositive treaty. See TREATY (1).

dispossess (dis-pə-**zes**), *vb.* To oust or evict (someone) from property. See DISPOSSESSION.

dispossession (dis-pə-**zesh**-ən), *n.* Deprivation of, or eviction from, rightful possession of property; the wrongful taking or withholding of possession of land from the person lawfully entitled to it; OUSTER (1).

dispossessor. A person who dispossesses.

dispossess proceeding. (1888) A summary procedure initiated by a landlord to oust a defaulting tenant and regain possession of the premises. See FORCIBLE ENTRY AND DETAINER.

disprove, *vb.* To refute (an assertion); to prove (an allegation) false.

dispunishable, *adj. Hist.* (Of an offense) not punishable; not answerable.

disputable presumption. See *rebuttable presumption* under PRESUMPTION.

dispute, *n.* (16c) A conflict or controversy, esp. one that has given rise to a particular lawsuit. — **dispute,** *vb.*

major dispute. *Labor law.* Under the Railway Labor Act, a disagreement about basic working conditions, often resulting in a new collective-bargaining agreement or a change in the existing agreement. • Under the Act, two classes of disputes — major and minor — are subject to mandatory arbitration. 45 USCA § 155. — Also termed *new-contract dispute.*

minor dispute. *Labor law.* Under the Railway Labor Act, a disagreement about the interpretation or application of a collective-bargaining agreement, as opposed to a disagreement over the formation of a new agreement. 45 USCA § 155.

dispute resolution. See ALTERNATIVE DISPUTE RESOLUTION.

dispute-resolution procedure. *Intellectual property.* A mechanism for resolving international grievances over intellectual-property protection, conducted by the World Trade Organization under the TRIPs agreement. ● The procedure begins with a complaint by one nation against another, followed by consultations between the nations, a WTO panel report on the issue, and (potentially) trade sanctions against one of the nations.

disqualification, *n.* (18c) **1.** Something that makes one ineligible; esp., a bias or conflict of interest that prevents a judge or juror from impartially hearing a case, or that prevents a lawyer from representing a party.

> **vicarious disqualification.** (1949) Disqualification of all the lawyers in a firm or in an office because one of the lawyers is ethically disqualified from representing the client at issue. — Also termed *imputed disqualification.*

2. The act of making ineligible; the fact or condition of being ineligible. Cf. RECUSAL. — **disqualify,** *vb.*

disrate, *vb.* To reduce to a lower rank, esp. to reduce a ship or petty officer's rank.

disregard, *n.* **1.** The action of ignoring or treating without proper respect or consideration. **2.** The state of being ignored or treated without proper respect or consideration. — **disregard,** *vb.*

> **reckless disregard.** (1820) **1.** Conscious indifference to the consequences of an act. **2.** *Defamation.* Serious indifference to truth or accuracy of a publication. ● "Reckless disregard for the truth" is the standard in proving the defendant's actual malice toward the plaintiff in a libel action. **3.** The intentional commission of a harmful act or failure to do a required act when the actor knows or has reason to know of facts that would lead a reasonable person to realize that the actor's conduct both creates an unreasonable risk of harm to someone and involves a high degree of probability that substantial harm will result.

disregarding the corporate entity. See PIERCING THE CORPORATE VEIL.

disrepair. A state of being in need of restoration after deterioration or damage.

disrepute. A loss of reputation; dishonor.

disruptive conduct. See CONDUCT.

disseise (dis-**seez**), *vb.* To wrongfully deprive (a person) of the freehold possession of property. — Also spelled *disseize.*

disseisee (dis-see-**zee**). A person who is wrongfully deprived of the freehold possession of property. — Also spelled *disseizee.* — Also termed *disseisitus.*

disseisin (dis-**see**-zin), *n.* (14c) The act of wrongfully depriving someone of the freehold possession of property; DISPOSSESSION. — Also spelled *disseizin.*

> **disseisin by election.** A legal fiction by which a property owner is allowed to claim that he or she has been disseised, regardless of whether this is actually true, in order to have a remedy against an adverse claimant.

> **equitable disseisin.** The wrongful deprivation of the equitable ownership, possession, or the fruits of ownership or possession.

> **fresh disseisin.** The right at common law of a person disseised of land to forcefully eject the disseisor from the land without resort to law, as long as the ejection occurred soon after the disseisin.

disseisor (dis-**see**-zər *or* -zor). A person who wrongfully deprives another of the freehold possession of property. — Also spelled *disseizor.*

dissemble (di-**sem**-bəl), *vb.* **1.** *Archaic.* To physically disguise <to dissemble by wearing a mask>. **2.** To give a false impression about (something); to cover up (something) by deception <to dissemble the facts>.

dissemination (di-sem-i-**nay**-shən), *n.* **1.** The act of spreading, diffusing, or dispersing; esp., the circulation of defamatory matter. **2.** The extension of the influence or establishment of a thing, such as an idea, book, or document.

dissent (di-**sent**), *n.* (16c) **1.** A disagreement with a majority opinion, esp. among judges. **2.** See *dissenting opinion* under OPINION (1). **3.** A withholding of assent or approval. **4.** The act of a surviving spouse who, as statutorily authorized in many states, refuses a devise and elects instead a statutory share. See ELECTIVE SHARE. — **dissent** (di-**sent**), *vb.*

dissent and appraisal, right of. See APPRAISAL REMEDY.

dissenters' right. See APPRAISAL REMEDY.

dissenting opinion. See OPINION (1).

dissipation, *n.* (17c) The use of an asset for an illegal or inequitable purpose, such as a spouse's use of community property for personal benefit when a divorce is imminent. — **dissipate,** *vb.*

dissociative amnesia. See REPRESSED-MEMORY SYNDROME.

dissolute, *adj.* (Of a person or thing) lacking restraint; wanton; devoted to pleasure <dissolute person> <a dissolute lifestyle>.

dissolution (dis-ə-**loo**-shən), *n.* (14c) **1.** The act of bringing to an end; termination. **2.** The cancellation or abrogation of a contract, with the effect of annulling the contract's binding force and restoring the parties to their original positions. See RESCISSION. **3.** The termination of a corporation's legal existence by expiration of its charter, by legislative act, by bankruptcy, or by other means; the event immediately preceding the liquidation or winding-up process.

de facto dissolution. The termination and liquidation of a corporation's business, esp. because of an inability to pay its debts.

involuntary dissolution. The termination of a corporation administratively (for failure to file reports or pay taxes), judicially (for abuse of corporate authority, management deadlock, or failure to pay creditors), or through involuntary bankruptcy.

voluntary dissolution. A corporation's termination initiated by the board of directors and approved by the shareholders.

4. The termination of a previously existing partnership upon the occurrence of an event specified in the partnership agreement, such as a partner's withdrawal from the partnership, or as specified by law. Cf. WINDING UP. **5.** *Patents.* The dismissal of an interference contest before a final judgment and an express award of priority. • The effect of dissolving an interference is that junior parties fail to meet their burden of proof, so the senior party retains priority. **5.** *Parliamentary law.* An adjournment sine die without any provision for reconvening the same deliberative assembly, even if another assembly of the same kind (such as a legislative body or a convention) will eventually convene. — **dissolve,** *vb.*

dissolution bond. See *discharging bond* under BOND (2).

dissolution of marriage. 1. DIVORCE. **2.** *Archaic.* A divorce-like remedy available when both spouses have signed a separation agreement that deals with (1) the issue of alimony (providing either some or none), and (2) if there are children, the issues of support, custody, and visitation. • Under a dissolution of marriage in this sense, the court is bound by the separation agreement and cannot later modify alimony payments. Courts in jurisdictions where the term has been used in this specific sense traditionally distinguish it from *divorce,* which was formerly available only on certain grounds and which allowed the court to modify alimony payments.

dissolved corporation. See CORPORATION.

dissolving condition. See *resolutory condition* under CONDITION (2).

dissuade, *vb.* To persuade (someone) not to do something <to dissuade the expert from testifying>.

distaff right. *Hist.* A woman's legal right.

distillate. *Oil & gas.* **1.** The "wet" element of natural gas that may be removed as a liquid. — Also termed *condensate; natural gas.* **2.** Any product of the process of distillation.

distinct invention. See INVENTION.

distinctive mark. See *distinctive trademark* under TRADEMARK.

distinctive name. See NAME.

distinctiveness, *n.* *Trademarks.* The quality of a trademarked word, symbol, or device that identifies the goods of a particular merchant and distinguishes them from the goods of others. — Also termed *acquired distinctiveness.* — **distinctive,** *adj.*

distinctive trademark. See TRADEMARK.

distinguish, *vb.* (15c) **1.** To note a significant factual, procedural, or legal difference in (an earlier case), usu. to minimize the case's precedential effect or to show that it is inapplicable <the lawyer distinguished the cited case from the case at bar>. **2.** To make a distinction <the court distinguished between willful and reckless conduct>. — **distinction,** *n.*

distinguishable, *adj.* (Of a case or law) different from, and thereby not controlling or applicable in, a given case or situation.

distinguishable variation. *Copyright.* A detectable difference between two works. • Distinguishable variation is the standard for determining whether a work that is based on a work in the public domain can itself be copyrighted. Examples include translations of books and mezzotints of paintings. Some nontrivial originality is also required: exact copies are not protectable.

distinguishing mark. A physical indication or feature that identifies or delineates one person or thing from another <the voting ballots contained distinguishing marks so that they could not be counted>. See DISTINCTIVENESS.

distracted, *adj.* **1.** (Of a person) not concentrating. **2.** (Of a person) disordered.

distraction doctrine. (1999) The rule that a plaintiff may not be guilty of contributory negligence if the plaintiff's attention was diverted from a known danger by a sufficient cause. See *contributory negligence* under NEGLIGENCE.

distrain, *vb.* (13c) **1.** To force (a person, usu. a tenant), by the seizure and detention of personal property, to perform an obligation (such as paying overdue rent). **2.** To seize (goods) by distress, a legal remedy entitling the rightful owner to recover property wrongfully taken. — Also spelled *distrein.* — **distraint,** *n.*

distrainee. One who is, or whose property is, distrained.

distrainer. Someone who seizes property under a distress. — Also spelled *distrainor; distreinor.*

distraint. See DISTRESS.

distress, *n.* (13c) **1.** The seizure of another's property to secure the performance of a duty, such as the payment of overdue rent. **2.** The legal remedy authorizing such a seizure; the procedure by which the seizure is carried out.

distress damage feasant. The right to seize animals or inanimate chattels that are damaging or encumbering land and to keep them as security until the owner pays compensation.

distress infinite. A distress that the sheriff can repeat from time to time to enforce the performance of something, as in summoning a juror or compelling a party to appear in court. • The goods must be returned after the delinquent person performs his or her duty.

grand distress. Hist. In a *quare impedit* action in which the defendant has failed to appear, a distress of the defendant's goods and lands to compel the defendant's appearance.

second distress. A supplementary distress allowed when goods seized under the first distress are insufficient to satisfy the claim.

3. The property seized. — Also termed *distraint.*

distressed debt. See DEBT.

distressed goods. See GOODS.

distressed property. See PROPERTY.

distress sale. See SALE.

distress warrant. See WARRANT (1).

distributable net income. See INCOME.

distribute (di-**strib**-yoot), *vb.* **1.** To apportion; to divide among several. **2.** To arrange by class or order. **3.** To deliver. **4.** To spread out; to disperse.

distributed denial-of-service attack. See DENIAL-OF-SERVICE ATTACK.

distributee (di-strib-yoo-**tee**), *n.* (1870) **1.** A beneficiary entitled to payment. **2.** An heir, esp. one who obtains personal property from the estate of an intestate decedent.

expectant distributee. A prospective heir whose interest depends on a contingency; an expectant heir. — Also termed *expectant beneficiary.* See *prospective heir* under HEIR.

legal distributee. A person whom the law would entitle to take property under a will.

distribution, *n.* (14c) **1.** The passing of personal property to an intestate decedent's heirs; specif.,

the process of dividing an estate after realizing its movable assets and paying out of them its debts and other claims against the estate. Cf. DESCENT (1). **2.** The act or process of apportioning or giving out. — **distribute,** *vb.*

controlled-securities-offering distribution. See *securities-offering distribution* (1).

corporate distribution. A corporation's direct or indirect transfer of money or other property, or incurring of indebtedness to or for the benefit of its shareholders, such as a dividend payment out of current or past earnings.

liquidating distribution. A distribution of trade or business assets by a dissolving corporation or partnership. — Also termed *distribution in liquidation.*

nonliquidating distribution. A distribution of assets by a corporation or partnership that is not going out of business, such as a distribution of excess capital not necessary for current operations.

partnership distribution. A partnership's payment of cash or property to a partner out of earnings or as an advance against future earnings, or a payment of the partners' capital in partial or complete liquidation of the partner's interest.

probate distribution. The judicially supervised apportionment and division — usu. after the payment of debts and charges — of assets of an estate among those legally entitled to share.

secondary distribution. **1.** The public sale of a large block of previously issued stock. — Also termed *secondary offering.* See OFFERING. **2.** The sale of a large block of stock after the close of the exchange.

securities-offering distribution. **1.** An issuer's public offering of securities through a formal underwriting agreement with a broker-dealer. — Also termed *controlled-securities-offering distribution.* **2.** An issuer's public offering of securities on an informal basis, with or without brokers. — Also termed (in both senses) *uncontrolled-securities-offering distribution.*

trust distribution. The cash or other property paid or credited to a trust beneficiary.

uncontrolled-securities-offering distribution. See *securities-offering distribution* (2).

distribution channel. One of several routes through which a manufacturer's or distributor's goods are marketed. • In trademark law, identical or similar marks that are used in the same channel may lead to consumer confusion. — Also termed *channel of trade; channel of distribution.*

distribution cost. See COST (1).

distribution in kind. (1819) A transfer of property in its original state, such as a distribution of land instead of the proceeds of its sale.

distribution in liquidation. See *liquidating distribution* under DISTRIBUTION.

distribution license. See LICENSE.

distribution right. (1936) *Copyright.* A copyright holder's exclusive right to sell, lease, or otherwise transfer copies of the protected work to the public. Cf. FIRST-SALE DOCTRINE.

distributive (di-**strib**-yə-tiv), *adj.* Of or relating to apportioning, dividing, and assigning in separate items or shares; of or relating to distributing.

distributive clause. (1821) A will or trust provision governing the distribution of income and gifts.

distributive deviation. A trustee's authorized or unauthorized departure from the express distributional terms of a trust. ● A trustee must apply to the court for authority to deviate from the terms of a trust. In American law, courts rarely authorize deviation unless all the beneficiaries consent and there is no material purpose of the settlor yet to be served. Some state statutes provide that deviation is permitted if the court finds that deviation would effectuate the settlor's intention, though the modification is not expressly authorized by the trust's provisions. The Pulitzer trust illustrates the possibility that extraordinary circumstances not anticipated by the settlor may justify deviation, despite an express prohibition within the trust. Joseph Pulitzer set up a testamentary trust with shares of *World* newspaper stock; his will directed that the sale of these shares was not authorized under any circumstances. Nonetheless, the court later approved the stock sale when given evidence that because of hemorrhaging losses, the trust's continuation was jeopardized. *In re Pulitzer's Estate*, 249 N.Y.S. 87 (Sur. Ct. 1931).

distributive finding. A jury's decision partly in favor of one party and partly in favor of another.

distributive justice. See JUSTICE (1).

distributive share. (18c) **1.** The share that an heir or beneficiary receives from the legal distribution of an estate. **2.** The portion (as determined in the partnership agreement) of a partnership's income, gain, loss, or deduction that is passed through to a partner and reported on the partner's tax return. **3.** The share of assets or liabilities that a partner or partner's estate acquires after the partnership has been dissolved.

distributor. (1884) A wholesaler, jobber, or other manufacturer or supplier that sells chiefly to retailers and commercial users.

distributorship. A franchise held by a person or company who sells merchandise, usu. in a specific area to individual customers <a car distributorship>.

dual distributorship. A business structure in which one party operates a branch or dealership on the same market level as one or more of its customers.

district. (17c) **1.** A territorial area into which a country, state, county, municipality, or other political subdivision is divided for judicial, political, electoral, or administrative purposes. **2.** A territorial area in which similar local businesses or entities are concentrated, such as a theater district or an arts district. — Abbr. D.

assessment district. *Tax.* A usu. municipal subdivision in which separate assessments of taxable property are made.

congressional district. (1804) A geographical unit of a state from which one member of the U.S. House of Representatives is elected.

consolidated school district. See SCHOOL DISTRICT.

election district. A subdivision of a state, county, or city that is established to facilitate an election or to elect governmental representatives for that subdivision.

floterial district (floh-**teer**-ee-əl). A legislative district that includes several separate districts or political subdivisions that independently would not be entitled to additional representation, but whose conglomerate population entitles the district to another seat in the legislative body being apportioned.

influence district. A voting district in which a racial or ethnic minority group does not constitute a majority of the voters, but does make up a sufficient proportion of the voters to constitute an influential minority, thus being able to elect its preferred candidate with a reasonable number of crossover votes from other groups. Cf. *majority-minority district.*

land district. A federally created state or territorial division containing a U.S. land office that manages the disposition of the district's public lands.

legislative district. (1840) A geographical subdivision of a state for the purpose of electing legislative representatives.

levee district. A local or regional political subdivision organized to construct and maintain levees within its territory at public expense.

majority-minority district. A voting district in which a racial or ethnic minority group makes up a majority of the voting citizens.

metropolitan district. A special district, embracing parts of or entire cities and towns in a metropolitan area, created by a state to provide unified administration of one or more common services, such as water supply or public transportation.

mineral district. (1812) A particular region of the country where valuable minerals are typically found and mined.

municipal utility district. (1921) A publicly owned corporation, or a political subdivision, that provides the public with a service or services, such as water, electricity, gas, transportation, or telecommunications. — Abbr. MUD. — Also termed *public utility district* (PUD).

school district. See SCHOOL DISTRICT.

special district. A political subdivision that is created to bypass normal borrowing limitations, to insulate certain activities from traditional political influence, to allocate functions to entities reflecting particular expertise, and to provide a single service within a specified area <a transit authority is a special district>.

stock-law district. A district in which cattle or other stock are prohibited from running free.

taxing district. A district — constituting the whole state, a county, a city, or other smaller unit — throughout which a particular tax or assessment is ratably apportioned and levied on the district's inhabitants.

water district. A geographical subdivision created by a state or local government entity to provide the public with a water supply.

district attorney. (18c) A public official appointed or elected to represent the state in criminal cases in a particular judicial district; PROSECUTOR (1). — Abbr. D.A. — Also termed *public prosecutor*; *state's attorney*; *prosecuting attorney*. Cf. UNITED STATES ATTORNEY.

district clerk. See CLERK (2).

district court. See COURT.

district-court magistrate. See MAGISTRATE.

districting. The act of drawing lines or establishing boundaries between geographic areas to create voting districts. See APPORTIONMENT (3); GERRYMANDERING.

district judge. See JUDGE.

District of Columbia. The seat of the U.S. government, situated on the Potomac River between Maryland and Virginia. • Neither a state nor a territory, it is constitutionally subject to the exclusive jurisdiction of Congress. — Abbr. D.C.

district parish. See PARISH.

district school. See SCHOOL.

distringas (di-**string**-gas), *n.* [Law Latin "you are to distrain"] **1.** A writ ordering a sheriff to distrain a defendant's property to compel the defendant to perform an obligation, such as appearing in court or giving up a chattel to a plaintiff awarded judgment in a detinue action. **2.** A writ ordering the sheriff to seize jurors' goods to compel them to appear for jury service. **3.** An equitable process of execution against a corporation that has refused to obey a summons. **4.** *Hist.* An order, issued initially from the Court of Exchequer, then the Court of Chancery, and finally the High Court of Justice, for someone interested in purchasing Bank of England stock, temporarily restraining the bank officers from transferring the stock or paying a dividend on it. • This proceeding was used to prevent fraudulent dealing by a trustee or other stockholder. The relief was only temporary, and if the bank received a request from the stockholder to permit a stock deal, the bank had to warn the distringing party to promptly obtain a restraining order or a writ of injunction, or else the stock deal would go through.

disturbance, *n.* (13c) **1.** An act causing annoyance or disquiet, or interfering with a person's pursuit of a lawful occupation or the peace and order of a neighborhood, community, or meeting. **2.** At common law, a wrong done to an incorporeal hereditament by hindering the owner's enjoyment of it.

disturbance of a public meeting. The unlawful interference with the proceedings of a public assembly.

disturbance of common. At common law, a wrongful interference with, or impediment to, another's right to commonable property, such as a wrongful fencing or surcharge on the common.

disturbance of franchise. At common law, a wrongful interference with a liberty or privilege.

disturbance of patronage. A wrongful obstruction of a patron from presenting a clerk to a benefice.

disturbance of public worship. Any conduct that interferes with the peaceful, lawful assembly of people for religious exercises.

disturbance of tenure. A stranger's ouster of a tenant from a tenancy. • The tenant's lord could recover damages for the ouster.

disturbance of the peace. See BREACH OF THE PEACE.

disturbance of ways. An impediment to a person's lawful right-of-way, as by an obstruction.

disturbing the peace. See BREACH OF THE PEACE.

diverse, *adj.* **1.** Of or relating to different types <the attorney handles diverse cases ranging from probate matters to criminal law>. **2.** (Of a person or entity) having a different citizenship from the party or parties on the other side of the lawsuit <the parties are diverse because the plaintiffs are citizens of Illinois and the defendant is a New York citizen>. See *diversity jurisdiction* under

JURISDICTION. **3.** (Of a group of people) including people of different races, sexes, nationalities, and cultural backgrounds <the school has a diverse student body>.

diversification, *n.* **1.** A company's movement into a broader range of products, usu. by buying firms already serving the market or by expanding existing operations <the soft-drink company's diversification into the potato-chip market has increased its profits>. **2.** The act of investing in a wide range of companies to reduce the risk if one sector of the market suffers losses <the prudent investor's diversification of the portfolio among 12 companies>. — **diversify,** *vb.*

diversified holding company. See COMPANY.

diversified investment company. See COMPANY.

diversion, *n.* (17c) **1.** A deviation or alteration from the natural course of things; esp., the unauthorized alteration of a watercourse to the detriment of a lower riparian owner, or the unauthorized use of funds. **2.** A distraction or pastime. — **divert,** *vb.*

diversion program. (1972) **1.** *Criminal law.* A program that refers certain criminal defendants before trial to community programs on job training, education, and the like, which if successfully completed may lead to the dismissal of the charges. — Also termed *pretrial diversion; pretrial intervention.* Cf. *deferred judgment* under JUDGMENT. **2.** A community-based program or set of services designed to prevent the need for court intervention in matters of child neglect, minor juvenile delinquency, truancy, or incorrigibility. • Sustained by government funding, the program provides services quickly and in a nonadversarial manner so that there is no need for a formal court trial.

diversity, *n.* **1.** DIVERSITY OF CITIZENSHIP. **2.** Ethnic, socioeconomic, and gender heterogeneity within a group; the combination within a population of people with different backgrounds. • The Supreme Court has found diversity in education to be a compelling government interest that can support a narrowly tailored affirmative-action plan. *Grutter v. Bollinger,* 123 S.Ct. 2325 (2003). **3.** *Hist.* A plea that a prisoner to be executed is not the one that was accused and found guilty, at which point a jury is immediately impaneled to try the issue of the prisoner's identity.

diversity, *adj.* Of, relating to, or involving diversity jurisdiction <a diversity case>.

diversity jurisdiction. See JURISDICTION.

diversity of citizenship. (1876) A basis for federal-court jurisdiction that exists when (1) a case is between citizens of different states, or between a citizen of a state and an alien, and (2) the matter in controversy exceeds a specific value (now $75,000). 28 USCA § 1332. • For purposes of diversity jurisdiction, a corporation is considered a citizen of both the state of incorporation and the state of its principal place of business. An unincorporated association, such as a partnership, is considered a citizen of each state where at least one of its members is a citizen. — Often shortened to *diversity.* See *diversity jurisdiction* under JURISDICTION.

complete diversity. (1925) In a multiparty case, diversity between both sides to the lawsuit so that all plaintiffs have different citizenship from all defendants. • Complete diversity must exist for a federal court to have diversity jurisdiction over the matter. The rule of complete diversity was first laid down by Chief Justice Marshall in *Strawbridge v. Curtiss,* 7 U.S. (3 Cranch) 267 (1806).

manufactured diversity. (1968) Improper or collusively created diversity of citizenship for the sole or primary purpose of creating federal jurisdiction. • Manufactured diversity is prohibited by 28 USCA § 1359.

divertee. A defendant who participates in a diversion program. See DIVERSION PROGRAM.

dives costs (dɪ-veez), *n.* Ordinary court costs granted to a successful party, as distinguished from limited costs (such as out-of-pocket costs) allowed to a successful pauper who sued or defended *in forma pauperis.* • The term derives from the name of Dives, the supposed name of the rich man in the parable of the rich man and Lazarus (*Luke* 16:19–31). *Dives* is a Latin word meaning "rich."

divestitive fact. See FACT.

divestitive publication. See PUBLICATION.

divestiture (di-**ves**-tə-chər *or* dɪ-), *n.*(17c) **1.** The loss or surrender of an asset or interest. **2.** A court order to a party to dispose of assets or property. **3.** *Antitrust.* A court order to a defendant to rid itself of property, securities, or other assets to prevent a monopoly or restraint of trade. — **divest,** *vb.*

divestment, *n.* (1844) **1.** *Property.* The cutting short of an interest in property before its normal termination. **2.** The complete or partial loss of an interest in an asset, such as land or stock. **3.** DISINVESTMENT (2). — **divest,** *vb.*

divide-and-pay-over rule. (1916) *Wills & estates.* The principle that if the only provisions in a testamentary disposition are words ordering that payment be made at some time after the testator's death, time will be of the essence and the interest is future and contingent rather than vested and immediate.

divided court. (18c) An appellate court whose opinion or decision in a particular case is not unanimous, esp. when the majority is slim, as in a 5-to-4 decision of the U.S. Supreme Court.

divided custody. See CUSTODY (2).

divided-damages rule. *Maritime law.* The obsolete principle that when two parties are jointly liable to a third party for a tort, each party is liable for only half the damages. • The courts now apply a comparative-negligence standard.

dividend. (17c) A portion of a company's earnings or profits distributed pro rata to its shareholders, usu. in the form of cash or additional shares.

    accumulated dividend. A dividend that has been declared but not yet paid. — Also termed *accrued dividend.*

    accumulative dividend. See *cumulative dividend.*

    asset dividend. A dividend paid in the form of property, usu. the company's product, rather than in cash or stock. — Also termed *property dividend.*

    bond dividend. A dividend in which a shareholder receives a bond instead of scrip, property, or money.

    capital-gain dividend. A taxable payment to a mutual-fund shareholder. • The payment is the shareholder's proportional share of the net capital gains realized by securities sales from the mutual fund's portfolio. — Also termed *capital-gain distribution.*

    cash dividend. A dividend paid to shareholders in the form of money.

    consent dividend. A dividend that is not actually paid to the shareholders, but is taxed to the shareholders and increases the basis in their stock investment. • A corporation declares a consent dividend to avoid or reduce an accumulated-earnings or personal-holding-company penalty tax.

    constructive dividend. A taxable benefit derived by a shareholder from the corporation even though the benefit was not designated a dividend. • Examples include excessive compensation, bargain purchases of corporate property, or shareholder use of corporate property for personal reasons.

    cumulative dividend. A dividend that grows from year to year when not paid. • A cumulative dividend is usu. on preferred shares, and it must be paid in full before common shareholders may receive any dividend. If the corporation does not pay a dividend in a particular year or period, it is carried over to the next year or period and must be paid before the common shareholders receive any payment. — Also termed *accumulative dividend.* Cf. *noncumulative dividend.*

    deferred dividend. A dividend that is declared, but is payable at a future date.

    deficiency dividend. A dividend paid to reduce or avoid personal-holding-company tax in a prior year.

    disguised dividend. See *informal dividend.*

    extraordinary dividend. A dividend paid in addition to a regular dividend, usu. because of exceptional corporate profits during the dividend period. — Also termed *extra dividend; nonrecurring dividend; special dividend.*

    fixed-return dividend. A dividend that is constant throughout the investment's life.

    informal dividend. A payment of salary, rent, interest, or the like to or for a shareholder as a substitute for a dividend. — Also termed *disguised dividend.*

    liability dividend. See *scrip dividend.*

    liquidation dividend. A dividend paid to a dissolving corporation's shareholders, usu. from the capital of the corporation, upon the decision to suspend all or part of its business operations. — Also termed *liquidating dividend.*

    nimble dividend. A dividend paid out of current earnings when there is a deficit in the account from which dividends may be paid. • Some state statutes prohibit nimble dividends.

    noncumulative dividend. A dividend that does not accrue for the benefit of a preferred shareholder if there is a passed dividend in a particular year or period. Cf. *cumulative dividend.*

    nonrecurring dividend. See *extraordinary dividend.*

    passed dividend. A dividend that is not paid when due by a company that has a history of paying regular dividends.

    preferred dividend. A dividend paid to preferred shareholders, who are generally paid a fixed amount and take priority over common shareholders.

    property dividend. See *asset dividend.*

    reinvested dividend. A dividend that is used to purchase additional shares in the corporation, instead of being taken in cash by the shareholder. See DIVIDEND-REINVESTMENT PLAN.

    scrip dividend. A dividend paid in certificates entitling the holder to ownership of capital stock to be issued in the future. • This type of dividend may signal that the corporation's cash flow is poor. — Also termed *liability dividend.*

    special dividend. See *extraordinary dividend.*

    stock dividend. A dividend paid in stock expressed as a percentage of the number of shares already held by a shareholder.

    unpaid dividend. A declared but unpaid dividend.

year-end dividend. An extra dividend paid at the end of the fiscal year depending on the amount of the profits.

dividend addition. An amount added to the face value of a life-insurance policy and purchased by using a dividend as a single premium payment.

dividend-credit rule. The principle that a corporate reserve fund amassed from unpaid dividends on preferred stock must be used to pay subsequent dividends on preferred stock before dividend payments on common stock. — Also termed *cast-iron-pipe doctrine.*

dividend date. The date on which a corporation distributes dividends to record owners of stock shares. See *record date* under DATE. Cf. EX-DIVIDEND DATE.

dividend income. See INCOME.

dividend-payout ratio. A profitability ratio computed by dividing annual dividends per share by earnings per share.

dividend preference. The right of a holder of preferred shares to receive a dividend before the company pays dividends to holders of common shares. See *preferred stock* under STOCK.

dividend-received deduction. (1957) A deduction allowed to a corporate shareholder for dividends received from a domestic corporation. IRC (26 USCA) §§ 243–247.

dividend-reinvestment plan. (1969) A stock-purchase program that allows investors to reinvest their dividends, and perhaps convert additional voluntary payments, into shares of the entity's common stock, usu. with no sales charge, and sometimes at a discount from the stock's market price. • Although the investor never receives the cash, it is still treated as income to the investor. An investor may be allowed to make optional cash purchases of additional stock. — Abbr. DRIP; DRP.

brokerage-run dividend-reinvestment plan. A formal or informal program managed by a brokerage and allowing shareholders to reinvest dividends in a portfolio, often at no cost. • Brokerage-run plans are usu. limited to dividend reinvestment.

company-run dividend-reinvestment plan. A program operated by a corporation for its own shareholders. • Company-run plans may offer additional features such as IRAs.

transfer-agent-run dividend-reinvestment plan. A program administered by a financial institution for several companies. • An investor can participate in more than one DRIP program simultaneously and also make additional cash investments in multiple companies.

dividend yield. The current annual dividend divided by the market price per share.

divide the assembly. *Parliamentary law.* To order that votes in a meeting be counted. — Also termed *challenge the vote; divide the house; doubt the vote.* See *counted vote* under VOTE (4).

divide the house. See DIVIDE THE ASSEMBLY.

divide the question. *Parliamentary law.* To break a long or complex motion, usu. one covering more than one subject, into shorter motions that the assembly considers independently.

divine law. Law that emanates from a supernatural source, such as a deity. Cf. NATURAL LAW.

divine right of kings. The political theory that the sovereign is a direct representative of God and has the right to rule absolutely by virtue of royal birth.

divine service. 1. *Hist.* A feudal tenure in which the tenants were obligated to perform special divine functions, such as singing at a certain number of masses or distributing a specified amount in alms. 2. A public worship service.

divisible contract. See *severable contract* under CONTRACT.

divisible divorce. See DIVORCE.

divisible offense. See OFFENSE (1).

divisible promises. See PROMISE.

division. 1. *Parliamentary law.* A counted vote. See *counted vote* under VOTE (4); DIVIDE THE ASSEMBLY. — Also termed *division of the assembly; division of the house; division vote.* 2. *Parliamentary law.* The separation of a long or complex motion, usu. one covering more than one subject, into shorter motions that the assembly considers independently. — Also termed *division of the question.* See DIVIDE THE QUESTION.

standing division. See *standing vote* under VOTE (4).

3. RESTRICTION (4).

divisional application. See PATENT APPLICATION.

divisional bond. See BOND (3).

divisional court. See COURT.

divisional security. See SECURITY.

division of fees. See FEE-SPLITTING.

division of powers. (18c) The allocation of power between the national government and the states. • Under the Tenth Amendment, powers not delegated to the federal government are reserved to the states or to the people. But today the Tenth Amendment provides only a limited check on Congress's power to regulate the states. Cf. SEPARATION OF POWERS.

division of property. See PROPERTY SETTLEMENT (1).

division of the assembly. See DIVISION (1).

division of the house. See DIVISION (1).

division of the question. See DIVISION (2).

division order. *Oil & gas.* A contract for the sale of oil or gas, specifying how the payments are to be distributed. • Royalty owners enter into division orders to sell minerals and to instruct how payments are to be made under a mineral lease. Working-interest owners also commonly sign division orders to instruct purchasers how payments are to be divided.

division vote. See DIVISION (1).

divorce. (14c) The legal dissolution of a marriage by a court. — Also termed *marital dissolution*; *dissolution of marriage.* Cf. ANNULMENT. — **divorce,** *vb.*

absolute divorce. See *divorce a vinculo matrimonii.*

bifurcated divorce. See *divisible divorce.*

collaborative divorce. A divorce negotiated in a nonadversarial forum, usu. between spouses who, with or without a lawyer, are assisted as needed by a team of experts in law, mental health, and financial matters (such as taxes and real estate).

conditional divorce. See *conversion divorce.*

contested divorce. 1. A divorce that one spouse opposes in court. 2. A divorce in which the spouses litigate. • In this sense, although both spouses may want the divorce, they disagree on the terms of the divorce decree. Cf. *uncontested divorce.*

conversion divorce. A divorce granted after (1) a legal separation has been granted or the parties have signed a separation agreement, and (2) the parties have lived separately for a statutorily prescribed period. — Also termed *convertible divorce*; *conditional divorce.*

divisible divorce. (1943) A divorce whereby the marriage itself is dissolved but the issues incident to the divorce, such as alimony, child custody, and visitation, are reserved until a later proceeding. • This type of divorce can be granted when the court has subject-matter jurisdiction but lacks personal jurisdiction over the defendant-spouse. The doctrine of divisible divorce was recognized by the Supreme Court in *Estin v. Estin,* 334 U.S. 541, 68 S.Ct. 1213 (1948), and *Vanderbilt v. Vanderbilt,* 354 U.S. 416, 77 S.Ct. 1360 (1957). — Also termed *bifurcated divorce.*

divorce a mensa et thoro (ay **men**-sə et **thor**-oh). [Latin "(divorce) from board and hearth"] (18c) *Hist.* A partial or qualified divorce by which the parties were separated and allowed or ordered to live apart, but remained technically married. • This type of divorce, abolished in England in 1857, was the forerunner of modern judicial separation. — Also termed *separation a mensa*

et thoro; separation from bed and board; limited divorce; legal separation; judicial separation.

divorce a vinculo matrimonii (ay **ving**-kyə-loh ma-trə-**moh**-nee-ɪ). [Latin "(divorce) from the chains of marriage"] (17c) A total divorce of husband and wife, dissolving the marriage tie and releasing the parties wholly from their matrimonial obligations. • At common law, but not always in canon law, this type of divorce bastardized any children from the marriage and was granted on grounds that existed before the marriage. In England, the Matrimonial Causes Act of 1857 introduced statutory divorce *a vinculo matrimonii.* — Usu. shortened to *divorce.* — Also termed *absolute divorce.* Cf. *limited divorce.*

Dominican divorce. See *Mexican divorce.*

ex parte divorce (eks **pahr**-tee). (1870) A divorce proceeding in which only one spouse participates or appears in court.

fault divorce. A divorce granted to one spouse on the basis of some proven wrongful act (grounds for divorce) by the other spouse. • Although all states now have some form of no-fault divorce, some jurisdictions still consider a spouse's fault in precipitating the divorce, esp. when dividing marital property or when awarding alimony. Traditionally, the common grounds for a fault divorce were adultery, abandonment, imprisonment, and physical or mental cruelty; the defenses to alleged fault in a petition for divorce were condonation, connivance, collusion, recrimination, and insanity. Section 303(e) of the Uniform Marriage and Divorce Act has abolished the defenses to divorce. Cf. *no-fault divorce.*

foreign divorce. (1831) A divorce obtained outside the state or country in which one spouse resides.

Haitian divorce. See *Mexican divorce.*

hotel divorce. *Slang.* A form of collusive divorce — occurring before widespread passage of no-fault divorce laws — in which the spouses agree to fake an adultery scene to create "fault." Cf. *no-fault divorce.*

legislative divorce. *Hist.* The legal termination of a particular marriage, through a statute enacted by the legislature rather than by a court's decree. • In the 18th century, Colonial American legislatures granted these special statutes. In 1816, the House of Burgesses of Virginia granted a divorce to Rachel Robards Jackson, the wife of then President Andrew Jackson, from a former spouse. Mrs. Jackson's untimely death was attributed to her reaction to the scandal that she had married Jackson before the divorce was procured. Now only state courts have authority to grant decrees of divorce. — Also termed *parliamentary divorce*.

limited divorce. (1831) **1.** A divorce that ends the legal relationship of marriage by court order but does not address financial support, property distribution, or care and custody of children. • In the days before no-fault divorce, a spouse might seek a quick divorce in a state with a short residency requirement (such as Nevada). Then courts in the home state would give full faith and credit only to the dissolution of the marital res, while maintaining sole jurisdiction over property-division, support, and custody issues. **2.** Loosely, a legal separation. **3.** See *divorce a mensa et thoro*. Cf. *divorce a vinculo matrimonii*.

mail-order divorce. (1922) *Slang.* A divorce obtained by parties who are not physically present or domiciled in the jurisdiction purporting to grant the divorce. • Such a divorce is not recognized in the United States because of the absence of the usual bases for jurisdiction.

Mexican divorce. A divorce obtained in Mexico by mail order or by the appearance of one spouse who does not have a Mexican domicile. • Neither type is recognized in the United States. — Also termed *Dominican divorce* (if granted in the Dominican Republic); *Haitian divorce* (if granted in Haiti).

migratory divorce. (1911) A divorce obtained in a jurisdiction other than the marital domicile; esp., a divorce obtained by a spouse who moves to, or temporarily resides in, another state or country to get the divorce.

no-fault divorce. (1969) A divorce in which the parties are not required to prove fault or grounds beyond a showing of the irretrievable breakdown of the marriage or irreconcilable differences. • The system of no- fault divorce has been adopted throughout the United States. By 1974, 45 states had adopted no-fault divorce; by 1985, every state but New York had adopted some form of it. In New York — one of the last bastions of fault grounds for divorce — the closest equivalent is a conversion divorce one year after legal separation or a legal-separation agreement. Cf. *fault divorce*; *hotel divorce*.

parliamentary divorce. See *legislative divorce*.

pro-con divorce. *Slang.* An uncontested divorce granted after only the plaintiff appears at the proceeding (since the defendant contests nothing).

quickie divorce. *Slang.* A fast divorce granted with minimal paperwork. — Also termed *quick divorce*.

rabbinical divorce. A divorce granted under the authority of a rabbi. • This type of divorce affects the relationship of the parties under the tenets of Judaism. It affects particularly a Jewish woman's ability to remarry in accordance with Judaic law. In the United States, it is not generally a divorce recognized in civil courts. — Also termed *get*.

uncontested divorce. A divorce that is unopposed by the spouse who did not initiate it. Cf. *contested divorce*.

divorce agreement. A contractual agreement that sets out divorcing spouses' rights and responsibilities regarding property, alimony, custody, visitation, and child support. • The divorce agreement usu. becomes incorporated by court order as a part of the divorce decree and thus is enforceable by contempt, among other remedies. — Also termed *agreement incident to divorce*; *marital settlement agreement*; *separation agreement*. Cf. PROPERTY SETTLEMENT.

divorce decree. See DECREE.

divorce proctor. A person (such as a guardian) who is appointed to protect the interest of the state or children in a divorce action. — Sometimes shortened to *proctor*.

D.J. See *district judge* under JUDGE.

DJIA. *abbr.* DOW JONES INDUSTRIAL AVERAGE.

DLA. *abbr.* DEFENSE LOGISTICS AGENCY.

DL/C. See *documentary letter of credit* under LETTER OF CREDIT.

DLOP. *abbr.* Dismissal for lack of prosecution. See *dismissal for want of prosecution* under DISMISSAL (1).

DLOP docket. See *DWOP docket* under DOCKET (2).

DLSA. *abbr.* DEFENSE LEGAL SERVICES AGENCY.

DMCA. *abbr.* DIGITAL MILLENNIUM COPYRIGHT ACT.

DNA. *abbr.* Deoxyribonucleic acid; the double-helix structure in cell nuclei that carries the genetic information of most living organisms.

DNA identification. (1987) A method of scientific identification based on a person's unique genetic makeup; specif., the comparison of a person's deoxyribonucleic acid (DNA) — a patterned chemical structure of genetic information — with the DNA in a biological specimen (such as blood, tissue, or hair) to determine whether the person is the source of the specimen. • DNA evidence is used in criminal cases for purposes such as identifying a victim's remains, linking a suspect to a crime, and exonerating an innocent suspect. — Also termed *DNA fingerprinting*; *genetic fingerprinting*; *DNA profiling*; *DNA typing*. Cf. HUMAN-LEUKOCYTE ANTIGEN TEST.

DNR order. *abbr.* DO-NOT-RESUSCITATE ORDER.

DOC. *abbr.* DEPARTMENT OF COMMERCE.

dock, *n.* **1.** A structure that encloses water, often between two piers, in which ships are received for loading, unloading, safekeeping, or repair. **2.** The part of a warehouse or other building (usu. elevated with oversized doors) at which trucks are received for loading and unloading. **3.** *English law.* In a criminal court, the enclosure in which the prisoner is placed during trial <it was through his own deliberate choice that Mr. Bourne found himself in the dock at the Old Bailey, charged with a felony>. See BAIL DOCK.

dockage. A charge for the use of a dock, esp. while a vessel is undergoing repairs.

docket, *n.* (15c) **1.** A formal record in which a judge or court clerk briefly notes all the proceedings and filings in a court case <review the docket to determine the filing date>. — Also termed *judicial record*; *bench docket*; *docket sheet*.

    appearance docket. (18c) A list of the parties and lawyers participating in an action, together with a brief abstract of the successive steps in the action.

    judgment docket. (1826) A book that a court clerk keeps for the entry or recordation of judgments, giving official notice of existing judgment liens to interested parties. — Also termed *judgment book*; *judgment file*; *judgment record*; *judgment roll*.

2. A schedule of pending cases <the case is third on Monday's trial docket>. — Also termed *court calendar*; *cause list*; *trial calendar*.

    DWOP docket. A list of cases that the court has set for possible dismissal for want of prosecution. — Also termed *doowop docket*; *DLOP docket*. See *dismissal for want of prosecution* under DISMISSAL (1).

    preferred docket. (1993) A list of cases set for trial, arranged in order of priority. • Criminal cases are, for example, generally given precedence over civil cases on the preferred docket because of the constitutional right to a speedy trial.

3. DOCKET CALL <the agreed judgment was signed at the court's uncontested docket call on May 24>. **4.** *Parliamentary law.* A list of each motion, report, election, and other business that awaits a deliberative assembly's consideration, from which a board or officer prepares and circulates an agenda for each meeting or for a series of upcoming meetings <in planning the meeting, the chair worked from an exhaustive docket>. See AGENDA. **5.** A written abstract that provides specific information (usu. about something attached); esp., a label <check the docket to determine the goods' destination and value>. **6.** *Hist.* A notary's attestation at the end of a deed or other instrument; esp., the attestation at the end of an instrument of seisin. — Also spelled *docquet*.

docket, *vb.* (17c) **1.** To make a brief entry in the docket of the proceedings and filings in a court case <to docket the filing date>. **2.** To abstract and enter in a book <to docket a judgment>. **3.** To schedule (a case) for trial or some other event <the case was docketed for a May trial>.

docket call. (1899) A court session in which attorneys (and sometimes parties) appear in court to report the status of their cases. • For example, they may announce readiness for trial or report the suit's settlement. — Often shortened to *docket*.

docket entry. A note made in the court's formal record of proceedings and filings. See DOCKET (1).

docket fee. See FEE (1).

docket number. (1866) A number that the court clerk assigns to a case on the court's docket.

docket order. See ORDER (2).

docket sheet. See DOCKET (1).

dock receipt. *Maritime law.* An interim document issued by a maritime carrier to evidence the delivery of goods at the dock. • Generally, a dock receipt entitles the designated person to receive a bill of lading, waybill, or other transport document. — Also termed *dock warrant*. See DOCUMENT OF TITLE.

dock sale. See SALE.

dock warrant. See DOCK RECEIPT.

doctor. **1.** *Hist.* In Roman Catholic canon law, an honorary title for a scholar. **2.** A title of a person who has acquired an advanced degree in academics, or has achieved an honorable distinction. **3.** A physician. — Abbr. Dr.

Doctor of Juridical Science. A graduate law degree, beyond the J.D. and the LL.M. — Abbr. S.J.D.; J.S.D. — Also termed *Doctor of Judicial Science*; *Doctor of the Science of Jurisprudence*; *Doctor of the Science of Law.*

Doctor of Jurisprudence. See JURIS DOCTOR.

Doctor of Law. See JURIS DOCTOR.

Doctor of Laws. An honorary degree bestowed on one who has achieved great distinction. — Abbr. LL.D. Cf. JURIS DOCTOR; MASTER OF LAWS.

Doctor of the Science of Jurisprudence. See DOCTOR OF JURIDICAL SCIENCE.

Doctor of the Science of Law. See DOCTOR OF JURIDICAL SCIENCE.

doctor–patient privilege. See PRIVILEGE (3).

doctor–patient relationship. See RELATIONSHIP.

doctrine. (14c) **1.** A principle, esp. a legal principle, that is widely adhered to. **2.** *Archaic.* HOLDING (1).

doctrine of acquired rights. See ACQUIRED-RIGHTS DOCTRINE.

doctrine of adverse domination. See ADVERSE-DOMINATION DOCTRINE.

doctrine of approximation. (1845) A doctrine that authorizes a court to vary the details of a trust's administration to preserve the trust and to carry out the donor's intentions. — Also termed *equitable doctrine of approximation*. Cf. CY PRES.

doctrine of capture. See RULE OF CAPTURE.

doctrine of claim differentiation. See CLAIM DIFFERENTIATION.

doctrine of coercion. See COERCION (3).

doctrine of completeness. See RULE OF OPTIONAL COMPLETENESS.

doctrine of constructive service. 1. See *constructive service* under SERVICE (2). **2.** *Employment law.* The principle that a person who contracts to work for a definite period and is wrongfully discharged after beginning work may wait until the contract period expires and then sue on the contract for the wages that the person would have earned between the time of the discharge and the expiration of the contract. ● In a jurisdiction that has adopted this principle, it is an exception to the mitigation-of-damages doctrine. — Often shortened to *constructive service*. Cf. MITIGATION-OF-DAMAGES DOCTRINE.

doctrine of contagion. See CONTAGION.

doctrine of continuity. See CONTINUITY (2).

doctrine of *contra non valentem* (kon-trə non və-len-təm). (1938) The rule that a limitations or prescriptive period does not begin to run against a plaintiff who is unable to act, usu. because of the defendant's culpable act, such as concealing material information that would give rise to the plaintiff's claim. — Often shortened to *contra non valentem*.

doctrine of contra proferentem. See CONTRA PROFERENTEM.

doctrine of curative admissibility. A rule allowing a party to introduce otherwise inadmissible evidence to remove the prejudice caused by the improper admission of evidence that was offered by the opposing party. ● The doctrine applies when a motion to strike cannot cure the prejudice created by the adverse party. — Also termed *curative-admissibility doctrine*.

doctrine of discovered peril. See LAST-CLEAR-CHANCE DOCTRINE.

doctrine of election (18c). A doctrine holding that when a person has contracted with an agent without knowing of the agency and later learns the principal's identity, the person may enforce the contract against either the agent or the principal, but not both. See ELECTION (1); ELECTION OF REMEDIES.

doctrine of entireties (en-tɪ-ər-teez). In customs law, the rule that when an entry consists of parts that assemble to form an article different from any of the parts, the proper classification will be of the whole article, rather than the individual components. ● For example, an unassembled product consisting of an empty decorative glass, powdered wax in a cellophane bag, wicks, and fragrance, boxed together and sold as one product may be properly classified as a candle.

doctrine of equitable indemnity. See *equitable indemnity* under INDEMNITY.

doctrine of equivalents. (1856) *Patents.* A judicially created theory for finding patent infringement when the accused process or product falls outside the literal scope of the patent claims. ● The doctrine evolved to prevent parties from evading liability for patent infringement by making trivial changes to avoid the literal language of the patent claims. *Graver Tank & Mfg. Co. v. Linde Air Prods. Co.*, 339 U.S. 605, 70 S.Ct. 854 (1950). In determining whether infringement exists under the doctrine, the court must first determine whether "the accused product or process contain[s] an element identical or equivalent to each claimed element of the patented invention." *Warner-Jenkinson Co. v. Hilton Davis Chem. Co.*, 520 U.S. 17, 39–40, 117 S.Ct. 1040, 1054 (1997). If it does, it infringes on the patent if the differing element performs substantially the same function in substantially the same way to get the same result as the patented product or process. Prosecution-history estoppel is not an absolute bar to a patentee who seeks to invoke the doctrine of equivalents to prove infringement on a claim that was voluntarily amended. *Festo v. Shoketsu Kinzoku Kogyo Kabushiki Co.*, 535 U.S. 722, 122 S.Ct. 1831 (2002). — Also termed *equivalents doctrine*; *doctrine of equivalence*; *doctrine of equivalency*; *doctrine of substantial equivalents*; *nonliteral infringement*. Cf. *literal infringement* under INFRINGEMENT.

reverse doctrine of equivalents. The doctrine preventing infringement liability when the invention is substantially described by the claims of another's patent but performs the same or a similar function in a substantially different way.

doctrine of finality. See FINALITY DOCTRINE.

doctrine of general average. *Maritime law.* A rule allowing a carrier to require cargo owners and the shipowner to contribute pro rata to the cost of protecting the ship and its cargo.

doctrine of illusory coverage. A rule requiring an insurance policy to be interpreted so that it is not merely a delusion to the insured. ● Courts avoid interpreting insurance policies in such a way that an insured's coverage is never triggered and the insurer bears no risk.

doctrine of incontrovertible physical facts. See PHYSICAL-FACTS RULE.

doctrine of ineffective revocation. See DEPENDENT RELATIVE REVOCATION.

doctrine of inherency. See INHERENCY DOCTRINE.

doctrine of intervening rights. See INTERVENING RIGHTS.

doctrine of legal unities. See LEGAL-UNITIES DOCTRINE.

doctrine of marital privacy. See MARITAL-PRIVACY DOCTRINE.

doctrine of necessaries. (1870) **1.** The rule holding a parent or spouse liable to anyone who sells goods or provides medical services to that person's child or spouse if the goods or services are required for sustenance, support, or healthcare. **2.** *Archaic.* The common-law rule holding a husband or father liable to anyone who sells goods to his wife or child if the goods are required for sustenance or support. See NECESSARIES.

doctrine of notice. See NOTICE DOCTRINE.

doctrine of optional completeness. See RULE OF OPTIONAL COMPLETENESS.

doctrine of *parens patriae*. See PARENS PATRIAE (2).

doctrine of practical location. See AGREED-BOUNDARY DOCTRINE.

doctrine of precedent. (18c) **1.** The rule that precedents not only have persuasive authority but also must be followed when similar circumstances arise. ● This rule developed in the 19th century and prevails today. See STARE DECISIS. **2.** A rule that precedents are reported, may be cited, and will probably be followed by courts. ● This is the rule that prevailed in England until the 19th century.

doctrine of preclusion of inconsistent positions. See *judicial estoppel* under ESTOPPEL.

doctrine of relation back. See RELATION BACK.

doctrine of res judicata. See RES JUDICATA.

doctrine of revestment. A rule by which a court regains jurisdiction after the entry of final judgment when the former opposing parties have actively participated in proceedings inconsistent with the court's judgment.

doctrine of scrivener's error. (1992) A rule permitting a typographical error in a document to be reformed by parol evidence, if the evidence is precise, clear, and convincing. See *clerical error* under ERROR (2).

doctrine of separate spheres. See SEPARATE-SPHERES DOCTRINE.

doctrine of specialty. *Int'l law.* The principle, included as a provision in most extradition treaties, under which a person who is extradited to a country to stand trial for certain criminal offenses may be tried only for those offenses and not for any other pre-extradition offenses. — Also termed *specialty doctrine.* See EXTRADITION.

doctrine of spousal unity. See SPOUSAL-UNITY DOCTRINE (1).

doctrine of subsequent negligence. See LAST-CLEAR-CHANCE DOCTRINE.

doctrine of substantial equivalents. See DOCTRINE OF EQUIVALENTS.

doctrine of substituted judgment. See SUBSTITUTED-JUDGMENT DOCTRINE.

doctrine of superior equities. *Insurance.* A rule by which an insurer is unable to recover from anyone whose equities are equal or superior to the insurer's; esp., a rule that a right of subrogation may be invoked against another party only if that party's guilty conduct renders the party's equity inferior to that of the insured. — Also termed *risk-stops-here rule.*

doctrine of the conclusiveness of the judgment. See *judicial estoppel* under ESTOPPEL.

doctrine of the last antecedent. See RULE OF THE LAST ANTECEDENT.

doctrine of the last preceding antecedent. RULE OF THE LAST ANTECEDENT.

doctrine of ultimate negligence. See LAST-CLEAR-CHANCE DOCTRINE.

doctrine of unconstitutional conditions. See UNCONSTITUTIONAL-CONDITIONS DOCTRINE.

doctrine of vested rights. See VESTED-RIGHTS DOCTRINE.

doctrine of worthier title. See WORTHIER-TITLE DOCTRINE.

document, *n.* (15c) **1.** Something tangible on which words, symbols, or marks are recorded. *See* Fed. R. Civ. P. 34(a). **2.** (*pl.*) The deeds, agreements, title papers, letters, receipts, and other written instruments used to prove a fact.

ancient document. (1846) *Evidence.* A document that is presumed to be authentic because its physical condition strongly suggests authenticity, it has existed for 20 or more years, and it has been maintained in proper custody (as by coming from a place where it is reasonably expected to be found). Fed. R. Evid. 901(b)(8). — Also termed *ancient writing.*

document of authority. See *governing document.*

foreign document. (1816) A document that originated in, or was prepared or executed in, a foreign state or country.

governing document. *Parliamentary law.* A document that defines or organizes an organization, or grants or establishes its authority and governance. • An organization's governing documents may include a charter, articles of incorporation or association, a constitution, bylaws, and rules. A charter or articles of incorporation or association, if they have been granted or adopted, are an organization's most authoritative governing document, followed by the constitution, bylaws, and rules, in that order. — Also termed *document of authority.* See CHARTER (4), (5); ARTICLES OF INCORPORATION; ARTICLES OF ASSOCIATION (2); CONSTITUTION (4); BYLAW (1); SUBORDINATION (2).

hot document. (1995) A document that directly supports a litigant's allegation.

public document. (17c) A document of public interest issued or published by a political body or otherwise connected with public business. Cf. *public record* under RECORD.

3. *Evidence.* Under the best-evidence rule, a physical embodiment of information or ideas, such as a letter, contract, receipt, account book, blueprint, or X-ray plate; esp., the original of such an embodiment. *See* Fed. R. Evid. 1001 et seq.

document, *vb.* (18c) **1.** To support with records, instruments, or other evidentiary authorities <document the chain of custody>. **2.** To record; to create a written record of <document a file>.

documentary credit. 1. Credit extended on a document of title or any other legal document. **2.** A financing arrangement in which a financial institution authorizes or makes a payment to a third party (usu. an exporter) at a customer's request. • This financing method facilitates international transactions by providing the importer with necessary credit and the exporter with an expedited cash payment.

documentary draft. See DRAFT.

documentary evidence. See EVIDENCE.

documentary instruction. A written agreement between an importer and exporter covering the relegation of various documents relating to the shipment and disposition of goods.

documentary letter of credit. See LETTER OF CREDIT.

documentary-originals rule. See BEST-EVIDENCE RULE.

documentary sale. See SALE.

documentary stamp. A stamp required to be affixed to a deed or other instrument before it is recorded.

documentary-stamp transfer tax. See *stamp tax* under TAX.

document of title. (18c) A written description, identification, or declaration of goods authorizing the holder (usu. a bailee) to receive, hold, and dispose of the document and the goods it covers. • Documents of title, such as bills of lading, warehouse receipts, and delivery orders, are generally governed by Article 7 of the UCC. See BAILMENT (1)–(3).

negotiable document of title. A document of title that actually stands for the goods it covers, so that any transfer of the goods requires a surrender of the document. UCC § 7-104(1).

nonnegotiable document of title. A document of title that merely serves as evidence of the goods it covers. UCC § 7-104(2).

document request. See REQUEST FOR PRODUCTION.

DOD. *abbr.* Department of Defense. See DEFENSE DEPARTMENT.

DoDDS. *abbr.* DEPARTMENT OF DEFENSE DEPENDENTS SCHOOLS.

DOE. *abbr.* **1.** DEPARTMENT OF EDUCATION. **2.** DEPARTMENT OF ENERGY.

Doe, Jane. See JANE DOE.

Doe, John. See JOHN DOE.

***D'Oench Duhme* doctrine** (dench **doom**). The rule that estops a borrower from asserting a claim or defense against a federal successor to a failed financial institution — if the claim or defense is based on a side or secret agreement or representation — unless the agreements or representations have been (1) put into writing, (2) executed by the financial institution and borrower when the loan was issued, (3) approved by the financial institution's board of directors or loan committee, and (4) made a permanent part of the financial institution's records. *D'Oench, Duhme & Co. v. FDIC*, 315 U.S. 447, 62 S.Ct. 676 (1942) (now partially codified at 12 USCA § 1823(e), and otherwise of questionable standing in light of *O'Melveny & Myers v. FDIC*, 512 U.S. 79, 114 S.Ct. 2048 (1994)).

do equity. (Of one who seeks an equitable remedy) to treat or offer to treat the other party as fairly as is necessary, short of abandoning one's own legal rights, to bring about a fair result. • The phrase derives from the maxim, "One who seeks equity must do equity." See UNCLEAN-HANDS DOCTRINE.

dog. *Slang.* **1.** Something undesirable, esp. a lawsuit <the cases assigned to the new lawyer were all dogs>. **2.** *Securities.* A stock or other investment that suffers public disdain and repeated price declines or poor performance.

dog-draw. *Hist.* The apprehension of someone chasing a deer in a forest with a dog.

dogma (dawg-mə *or* dahg-), *n.* A philosophy, opinion, or tenet that is strongly held, is believed to be authoritative, and is followed steadfastly, usu. to the exclusion of other approaches to the same subject matter; a formally stated and proclaimed doctrine of faith. Pl. **dogmas, dogmata** (-mə-tə).

DOHSA (doh-shə). *abbr.* DEATH ON THE HIGH SEAS ACT.

doing business. The act of engaging in business activities; specif., the carrying out of a series of similar acts for the purpose of realizing a pecuniary benefit, or otherwise accomplishing a goal, or doing a single act with the intention of starting a series of such acts; esp., a nonresident's participation in sufficient business activities in a foreign state to allow the state's courts to exercise personal jurisdiction over the nonresident. See BUSINESS (1); D/B/A/; DOING-BUSINESS STATUTE; LONG-ARM STATUTE; MINIMUM CONTACTS.

doing-business statute. A state law defining the acts that constitute undertaking business there, usu. for the purpose of establishing the circumstances under which the state's courts may exercise personal jurisdiction over a nonresident. See MINIMUM CONTACTS; LONG-ARM STATUTE.

DOJ. *abbr.* DEPARTMENT OF JUSTICE.

DOL. *abbr.* DEPARTMENT OF LABOR.

dole, *n.* **1.** A share of something that is jointly owned but divisible. **2.** *Slang.* Welfare benefits received from a governmental agency. **3.** *Scots law.* Criminal intent; the equivalent of *mens rea.*

Dole **test.** A four-part test used to determine the constitutionality of a condition attached by Congress under its Spending Clause power to the receipt of federal money. • The spending must be in pursuit of the general welfare, and the condition must be unambiguous, related to some federal interest, and not barred by any other provision of the Constitution. *South Dakota v. Dole,* 483 U.S. 203, 107 S.Ct. 2793 (1987).

doli capax (doh-lɪ **kay**-paks), *adj.* [Latin "capable of wrong"] *Roman law.* Capable of committing a crime or tort; esp., old enough to determine right from wrong. — Also termed *capax doli.* Cf. DOLI INCAPAX.

doli incapax (doh-lɪ in-**kay**-paks), *adj.* [Latin "incapable of wrong"] *Roman law.* Incapable of committing a crime or tort. — Also termed *incapax doli.* Cf. DOLI CAPAX.

dollar-cost averaging, *n.* The investment practice of purchasing a fixed dollar amount of a type of security at regular intervals.

dolose (də-**lohs** *or* doh-lohs). [Latin] *Hist.* Fraudulent; deceitful; malicious.

dolus (doh-ləs). [Latin "device; artifice"] *Roman & civil law.* **1.** Fraud or deceit; conduct intended to deceive someone; bad faith. • Although there may be *dolus* without fraud, fraud always includes *dolus.* Cf. CASUS (1); CULPA (1). **2.** Intentional aggression; willful injury, esp. to another's property. — Also termed *dolus malus; fraus.*

dolus bonus (doh-ləs **boh**-nəs). [Latin "good deceit"] Shrewdness or justifiable deceit, as when a person lies to an attacker to prevent an assault. • *Dolus bonus* does not produce any legal consequences.

dolus malus (doh-ləs **mal**-əs). [Latin "bad *or* evil deceit"] Evil or fraudulent design or intent; an unjustifiable deceit.

DOMA. *abbr.* DEFENSE OF MARRIAGE ACT.

domain (doh-**mayn**), *n.* (15c) **1.** The territory over which sovereignty is exercised <the 19th-century domains of the British Empire>. **2.** An estate in land <the family domain is more than 6,000 acres>. **3.** The complete and absolute ownership of land <his domain over this land has now been settled>. See EMINENT DOMAIN; PUBLIC DOMAIN.

domain name. The words and characters that website owners designate for their registered Internet addresses. • All domain names have at least two levels. The first-level domain name identifies the registrant's category as, e.g., a commercial site (.com), a governmental institution (.gov), an educational institution (.edu), a nonprofit group (.org), or a discussion group (.net). The second-level domain name is the unique identifier for the user in a particular category <rhapsangel.com> <rhapsangel.org>. A second-level domain name may be protected under trademark law but first-level domain names are not. In some circumstances, the entire domain name may be validly registered as a trademark. But trademark rights are not automatically created by registering a domain name. See INTERNET-PROTOCOL ADDRESS.

domain-name infringement. See INFRINGE-MENT.

Dombrowski **doctrine.** (1965) A short-lived rule that entitled a person to seek a federal-court injunction to prevent prosecution under a broad or vague state statute that affects rights guaranteed by the First Amendment. *Dombrowski v. Pfister,* 380 U.S. 479, 85 S.Ct. 1116 (1965). • The doctrine was greatly cut back six years after it was announced, when the Supreme Court ruled that a speculative First Amendment chilling effect does not justify federal-court intervention in state affairs. *Younger v. Harris,* 401 U.S. 37, 91 S.Ct. 746 (1971).

domebook. See DOOMBOOK.

Domesday Book (doomz-day). The census or survey, ordered by William the Conqueror and substantially completed in 1086, of England's landholdings, buildings, people, and livestock. — Abbr. D.B. — Also spelled *Doomsday Book*.

domestic, *adj.* (15c) **1.** Of or relating to one's own country <domestic affairs>. **2.** Of or relating to one's own jurisdiction <in Alaska, a domestic corporation is an Alaskan one>. **3.** Of or relating to the family or the household <a domestic dispute>.

domestic abuse. See *domestic violence* under VIOLENCE.

domestic animal. See ANIMAL.

domestic asset-protection trust. See *asset-protection trust* under TRUST (3).

domesticated animal. See ANIMAL.

domestic authority. (1833) **1.** The legal power to use nondeadly force when reasonably necessary to protect a person for whom one is responsible. **2.** A defense allowing a person responsible for another (such as a parent responsible for a child) to use nondeadly force when reasonably necessary to protect the person being cared for.

domestic bill. See BILL (6).

domestic corporation. See CORPORATION.

domestic court. See COURT.

domestic creditor. See CREDITOR.

domestic dispute. (1890) A disturbance, usu. at a residence and usu. within a family, involving violence and often resulting in a call to a law-enforcement agency. — Also termed *domestic disturbance*; *family disturbance*. See *domestic violence* under VIOLENCE.

domestic disturbance. See DOMESTIC DISPUTE.

domestic export. See EXPORT (1).

domestic fixture. See FIXTURE.

domestic guardian. See GUARDIAN.

Domestic International Sales Corporation. A U.S. corporation, esp. a subsidiary whose income is primarily attributable to exports. ● Income tax on part of a DISC's income is usu. deferred, resulting in a lower overall corporate tax for the parent than it would otherwise incur. IRC (26 USCA) §§ 991–997. — Abbr. DISC.

domestic judgment. See JUDGMENT.

domestic partnership. 1. A nonmarital relationship between two persons of the same or opposite sex who live together as a couple for a significant period of time. **2.** A relationship that an employer or governmental entity recognizes as equivalent to marriage for the purpose of extending employee-partner benefits otherwise reserved for the spouses of employees. Cf. CIVIL UNION; *same-sex marriage* under MARRIAGE (1). — **domestic partner,** *n.*

domestic-partnership law. A legislative enactment, often a municipal ordinance, that grants unmarried adults living in economically or emotionally based relationships, regardless of their sexual preference, some of the rights of a civil marriage without attempting to change the traditional definition of marriage.

domestic-partnership period. The period beginning when domestic partners begin living together and ending when the partners stop sharing a primary residence. See DOMESTIC PARTNERSHIP.

domestic-partnership property. See PROPERTY.

Domestic Policy Council. See OFFICE OF POLICY DEVELOPMENT.

domestic relations. See FAMILY LAW (1).

domestic-relations court. See *family court* under COURT.

domestic-relations exception. The exclusion of suits regarding the granting of divorce, alimony, and child custody from federal diversity jurisdiction. ● The domestic-relations exemption to federal diversity jurisdiction originated as dictum in *Barber v. Barber*, 62 U.S. (21 How.) 582 (1858). Federal courts do not have jurisdiction to grant divorces, award alimony, or determine child custody. In general, matters of domestic relations are left to the states. But the federal courts may hear other diversity matters involving family members, such as tort claims or suits seeking to enforce alimony orders. *Ankenbrandt v. Richards*, 504 U.S. 689, 112 S.Ct. 2206 (1992).

domestic-relations law. See FAMILY LAW (1).

domestic servant. A household servant. — Often shortened to *domestic*.

domestic terrorism. See TERRORISM.

domestic tort. See *marital tort* under TORT.

domestic violence. See VIOLENCE.

domicile (**dom**-ə-sɪl), *n.* (15c) **1.** The place at which a person has been physically present and that the person regards as home; a person's true, fixed, principal, and permanent home, to which that person intends to return and remain even though currently residing elsewhere. ● A person has a settled connection with his or her domicile for legal purposes, either because that place is home or because the law has so designated that place. — Also termed *permanent abode*; *habitancy*. **2.** The residence of a person or corporation for legal purposes. — Also termed (in sense 2) *legal residence*; *domicile by operation of law*. Cf. RESIDENCE; PLACE OF BUSINESS. — Also spelled (in BrE) *domicil*.

after-acquired domicile. (1858) A domicile established after the facts relevant to an issue arose. ● An after-acquired domicile cannot be used to establish jurisdiction or choice of law.

commercial domicile. (1839) **1.** A domicile acquired by a nonresident corporation conducting enough activities to permit taxation of the corporation's property or activities located outside the bounds of the taxing state. **2.** A domicile acquired by a person or company freely residing or carrying on business in enemy territory or enemy-occupied territory. — Also termed *quasi-domicile.*

corporate domicile. (1890) The place considered by law as the center of corporate affairs, where the corporation's functions are discharged; the legal home of a corporation, usu. its state of incorporation or the state in which it maintains its principal place of business. • For purposes of determining whether diversity jurisdiction exists in federal court, a corporation is considered a citizen of both its state of incorporation and the state of its principal place of business. See DIVERSITY OF CITIZENSHIP.

domicile of birth. See *domicile of origin.*

domicile of choice. (1878) **1.** A domicile established by physical presence within a state or territory, coupled with the intention to make it home. **2.** The domicile that a person chooses after reaching majority or being emancipated.

domicile of origin. (1831) The domicile of a person at birth, derived from the custodial parent or imposed by law. — Also termed *natural domicile; domicile of birth; original domicile.* See *necessary domicile.*

domicile of succession. (1874) The domicile that determines the succession of a person's estate.

domicile of trustee. The domicile where a trustee is appointed.

elected domicile. A contractually agreed domicile between parties for purposes of the contract.

foreign domicile. A domicile established by a citizen or subject of one sovereignty within the territory of another.

matrimonial domicile. A domicile that a husband and wife, as a married couple, have established as their home. — Also termed *marital domicile; matrimonial home.*

municipal domicile. A person's residence in a county or municipality, as distinguished from the person's state or national domicile.

national domicile. A domicile considered in terms of a particular nation rather than a locality or subdivision of a nation.

natural domicile. See *domicile of origin.*

necessary domicile. A domicile legally fixed and independent of choice, as in the domicile of origin. See *domicile of origin.*

original domicile. See *domicile of origin.*

quasi-domicile. See *commercial domicile.*

quasi-national domicile. A person's state of residence, as distinguished from the person's national or local domicile.

domiciliary (dom-ə-**sil**-ee-er-ee), *adj.* (18c) Of or relating to domicile <domiciliary jurisdiction>.

domiciliary (dom-ə-**sil**-ee-er-ee), *n.* (1845) A person who resides in a particular place with the intention of making it a principal place of abode; one who is domiciled in a particular jurisdiction. Cf. RESIDENT; CITIZEN (1).

domiciliary administration. See ADMINISTRATION.

domiciliary administrator. See ADMINISTRATOR (2).

domiciliary letters testamentary. See LETTERS TESTAMENTARY.

domiciliary parent. See PARENT.

domiciliate (dom-ə-**sil**-ee-ayt), *vb.* To establish a domicile; to fix a place of residence.

domiciliation (dom-i-sil-ee-**ay**-shən), *n.* The act of establishing a domicile.

dominant estate. See ESTATE (4).

dominant-jurisdiction principle. (1995) The rule that the court in which a case is first filed maintains the suit, to the exclusion of all other courts that would also have jurisdiction.

dominant property. See *dominant estate* under ESTATE (4).

dominant tenant. See TENANT.

dominant tenement. See *dominant estate* under ESTATE (4).

dominate, *vb.* (17c) **1.** To master (someone or something); to control (someone or something). **2.** Predominate.

dominating patent. See *fencing patent* under PATENT (3).

domination. *Patents.* The effect that an earlier patent (usu. a basic one) has on a later patent (esp. one for improvements on the patented device) because the earlier patent's claims are so broad or generic that the later patent's invention will always read on the earlier patent's claims, resulting in infringement. • Because the patent system is based on exclusion of others from an invention's subject matter, the earlier, basic patent's claims "dominate" the later-invented improvement. If the improvement is patented and worked, it infringes the basic patent. But the basic patent's owner cannot practice the improvement without infringing on the improvement's patent. This stand-off effect encourages improvement and basic-patentees to seek licenses or cross-licenses with each other. See BLOCKING PATENT.

dominical (də-**min**-ə-kəl), *adj.* Of or relating to a Sunday; of or relating to the Lord's day.

Dominican divorce. See *Mexican divorce* under DIVORCE.

dominicide (də-**min**-ə-sɪd), *n.* [fr. Latin *dominus* "master" + *caedo* "to kill"] *Hist.* **1.** The crime of killing one's master. **2.** A person who kills his or her master.

dominion. (14c) **1.** Control; possession <dominion over the car>. **2.** Sovereignty <dominion over the nation>. **3.** FOREIGN DOMINION.

dominium (də-**min**-ee-əm), *n.* [fr. Latin *dominus* "lord"] **1.** *Roman & civil law.* Absolute ownership including the right to possession and use; a right of control over property that the holder might retain or transfer at pleasure. • *Dominium* was subject to any servitudes, planning restrictions, etc. This term gradually came to also mean merely ownership of property, as distinguished from the right to possession or use.

donate, *vb.* (18c) To give (property or money) without receiving consideration for the transfer. — **donation,** *n.* — **donative** (**doh**-nə-tiv), *adj.*

donated stock. See STOCK.

donated surplus. See SURPLUS.

donatio (doh-**nay**-shee-oh). [Latin] A gift.

donatio causa mortis (doh-**nay**-shee-oh **kaw**-zə **mor**-tis), *n.* See *gift causa mortis* under GIFT. Pl. **donationes causa mortis.**

donatio inter vivos (doh-**nay**-shee-oh in-tər **vi**-vohs). See *inter vivos gift* under GIFT.

donatio mortis causa, *n.* See *gift causa mortis* under GIFT. Pl. **donationes mortis causa.**

donation. 1. A gift, esp. to a charity. **2.** *Eccles. law.* A method of acquiring a benefice by deed of gift alone, without presentation, institution, or induction.

donation claim. See CLAIM (3).

donation deed. See DEED.

donation land. See LAND.

donative (**don**-ə-tiv *or* **doh**-nə-tiv), *adj.* **1.** Of, relating to, or characterized by a donation <a donative transfer>. **2.** Subject to a donation <an advowson donative>.

donative advowson. See *advowson donative* under ADVOWSON.

donative intent. See INTENT (1).

donative trust. See TRUST.

donee (doh-**nee**). (16c) **1.** One to whom a gift is made; the recipient of a gift. **2.** The person in whose favor a power of appointment is created or reserved. See DONEE OF POWER.

donee beneficiary. See BENEFICIARY.

donee of power. (18c) A person who has been given a power of appointment, i.e., the power to dispose of someone else's property. — Often shortened to *donee.* See DONEE (2). Cf. DONOR (3).

donor. (15c) **1.** One who gives something without receiving consideration for the transfer. **2.** SETTLOR (1). **3.** The person who creates or reserves a power of appointment. Cf. DONEE OF POWER.

donor-advised fund. See *donor-advised trust* under TRUST (3).

donor-advised trust. See TRUST (3).

do-not-resuscitate order. A document, executed by a competent person, directing that if the person's heartbeat and breathing both cease while in a hospital, nursing home, or similar facility, no attempts to restore heartbeat or breathing should be made. — Abbr. DNR order. — Also termed *advance directive.*

> **out-of-hospital do-not-resuscitate order.** A do-not-resuscitate order, executed by a person who has been diagnosed by a physician as having a terminal condition, directing healthcare professionals to withhold certain life-sustaining treatments when acting outside a hospital or similar facility. — Abbr. OOH-DNR order.

donum (**doh**-nəm), *n.* [Latin "a gift"] *Roman law.* A gift.

donum gratuitum. See *gratuitous gift* under GIFT.

doom, *n. Hist.* **1.** A statute or law. **2.** A judgment; esp., a sentence in a criminal matter. **3.** Justice; fairness. **4.** A trial; the process of adjudicating.

doombook, *n.* [fr. Saxon *dombec*] *Hist.* A code, compiled under Alfred, containing maxims of common law, judicial forms, and criminal penalties. • The code existed until the reign of Edward IV, when it was lost. — Also termed *domebook* (**doom** buuk); *domboc*; *liber judicialis of Alfred.*

Doomsday book. See DOMESDAY BOOK.

door-closing statute. (1960) A state law closing or denying access to local courts unless a plaintiff meets specified conditions; esp., a statute requiring a foreign corporation to "qualify" before doing business in the state, including registering with the secretary of state, paying a fee or tax, and appointing an agent to receive service of process.

doorkeeper. *Parliamentary law.* An officer charged with regulating access to the chamber or hall where a deliberative assembly meets. — Also termed *guard.*

doorstep loan. See LOAN.

doowop docket. *Slang.* See *DWOP docket* under DOCKET (2).

dope. 1. A thick liquid used esp. for medicinal purposes. **2.** *Slang.* A drug, esp. a narcotic.

dormant (**dor**-mənt), *adj.* (15c) Inactive; suspended; latent <a dormant judgment>. — **dormancy,** *n.*

dormant claim. (18c) A claim that is in abeyance.

Dormant Commerce Clause. See COMMERCE CLAUSE.

dormant corporation. See CORPORATION.

dormant execution. See EXECUTION.

dormant judgment. See JUDGMENT.

dormant legislative intent. See LEGISLATIVE INTENT.

dormant partner. See *silent partner* under PARTNER.

dormant title. See TITLE (2).

DoS attack. See DENIAL-OF-SERVICE ATTACK.

dossier (**dos**-ee-ay), *n.* [French] A file or brief; a bundle of papers pertaining to a particular matter.

DOT. *abbr.* DEPARTMENT OF TRANSPORTATION.

dotage (**doh**-tij). **1.** Senility; feebleness of a person's mind in old age. **2.** Foolish affection; excessive fondness.

dotal (**doht**-əl), *adj.* Of or relating to dowry. See DOWRY.

dotal property. See PROPERTY.

dotation (doh-**tay**-shən), *n.* **1.** The act of giving a dowry. **2.** An endowment, esp. of funds for a charitable institution such as a hospital.

dote (doht), *vb.* **1.** To be silly due to old age. **2.** To bestow excessive fondness.

double agent. See *dual agent* under AGENT (2).

double adultery. See ADULTERY.

double assessment. See ASSESSMENT.

double audit. See AUDIT.

double-bill, *vb.* To charge two different clients or customers the same charge; to charge two different customers for services rendered to each customer at the same time.

double-breasted operation. An arrangement in which a business owner operates both a union business and a similar nonunion business, to compete for both types of business contracts. — Also termed *open-shop–closed-shop operation*.

double-breasting. *Labor law.* The practice by a common owner of dividing its employees between two companies, one that is unionized and is party to a collective-bargaining agreement, and one that is nonunion. — Also termed *dual-shop operation*.

double commission. See COMMISSION (5).

double complaint. See DUPLEX QUERELA.

double creditor. See CREDITOR.

double criminality. *Int'l law.* The punishability of a crime in both the country where a suspect is being held and a country asking for the suspect to be handed over to stand trial. • Double criminality is a requirement for extradition.

double damages. See DAMAGES.

double-declining depreciation method. See DEPRECIATION METHOD.

double-dipping, *n.* (1975) An act of seeking or accepting essentially the same benefit twice, either from the same source or from two different sources, as in simultaneously accepting retirement and unemployment benefits. — **double-dipper,** *n.*

double-entry bookkeeping. See BOOKKEEPING.

double forgery. See FORGERY.

double-fraction problem. *Oil & gas.* A common ambiguity that arises when the owner of a fractional interest conveys or reserves a fractional interest. • For example, if the owner of an undivided half interest in minerals conveys "an undivided half interest in the minerals," it is unclear whether the intention is to convey the owner's entire half interest or half of the owner's half interest.

double gibbet. See GIBBET.

double hearsay. See HEARSAY.

double indemnity. See INDEMNITY.

double insurance. See INSURANCE.

double jeopardy. (1847) The fact of being prosecuted or sentenced twice for substantially the same offense. • Double jeopardy is prohibited by the Fifth Amendment. In 2005, the United Kingdom abolished the rule for certain serious offenses, such as murder and hijacking. A court may quash an acquittal and order a retrial if new and compelling evidence of the defendant's guilt is discovered, and the evidence was not available before the acquittal. Only one retrial is allowed. Cf. FORMER JEOPARDY.

Double Jeopardy Clause. (1928) The Fifth Amendment provision stating, "nor shall any person be subject for the same offence to be twice put in jeopardy of life or limb." • The clause, which was ratified in 1791, does not prevent postacquittal appeals by the government if those appeals could not result in the defendant's being subjected to a second trial for substantially the same offense before a second fact-trier. *See United States v. Wilson*, 420 U.S. 332, 95 S.Ct. 1013 (1975).

double patenting. 1. Obtaining two patents covering the same invention. • An inventor is not allowed to receive more than one patent on one invention. 37 CFR 1.56. — Also termed *same-invention double patenting*. **2.** The issuance or obtaining of a patent for an invention that differs from an already patented invention only in some unpatentable detail. — Also termed *obviousness double patenting*.

judicially created double patenting. Attempting to patent an invention that is an obvious variation of another invention by the same inventor when the first invention has already been patented or has a pending application. • Double patenting is grounds for rejecting a patent application, limiting the term of a patent through a terminal disclaimer, or invalidating a patent. *In re Longi*, 225 U.S.P.Q. 645 (Fed. Cir. 1985). A double-patenting challenge can be overcome by filing a terminal disclaimer. 37 CFR 1.321. — Also termed *obviousness-type double patenting.*

obviousness-type double patenting. 1. DOUBLE PATENTING (2). 2. See *judicially created double patenting.*

same-invention double patenting. See *statutory double patenting.*

statutory double patenting. Attempting to patent an invention that is the same subject matter as another invention by the same inventor, when the first invention has already been patented or has a pending patent application. • Any double patenting is grounds for invalidating a patent claim or rejecting a claim in a patent application. 35 USCA § 101. — Also termed *same-invention double patenting.*

double plea. See PLEA (3).

double pleading. See DUPLICITY (2).

double possession. See POSSESSION.

double proof. See PROOF.

double-proxy marriage. See MARRIAGE (3).

double quarrel. See DUPLEX QUERELA.

double recovery. See RECOVERY.

double rent. See RENT (1).

double standard. (1900) A set of principles permitting greater opportunity or greater lenience for one class of people than for another, usu. based on a difference such as gender or race. See DISCRIMINATION.

double taxation. See TAXATION.

double-taxation treaty. *Int'l law.* An international agreement designed to ameliorate the legal and financial consequences to taxpayers who have income that is taxable by two nations.

double use. See USE (1).

double value. Twice the value of something; specif., a penalty payable by a tenant to a landlord of twice the yearly value of lands held by the tenant, who refused to leave when the landlord provided written notice of intent to possess the property. • The penalty was provided under the Landlord and Tenant Act (1730). St. 4 Geo. 2. ch. 28, s. 1.

double voucher. In a common-recovery suit, a voucher first by the fictitious tenant to the real tenant, and then by the real tenant to the common vouchee. • The use of a fictitious tenant was necessary because if the recovery had been obtained directly against the real tenant, it would be effective only to the limited extent that the real tenant actually possessed an interest in the estate. But if recovery was obtained against another party, it would be effective against any latent interest that the real tenant might assert in the estate. See COMMON RECOVERY.

double waste. See WASTE (1).

double will. See *mutual will* under WILL.

doubt, reasonable. See REASONABLE DOUBT.

doubtful title. See TITLE (2).

doubt the vote. See DIVIDE THE ASSEMBLY.

doulocracy. See DULOCRACY.

dovetail seniority. The combination of seniority lists from merging companies into one list that allows employees to keep their premerger seniority.

Dow (dow). See DOW JONES INDUSTRIAL AVERAGE.

dowable (dow-ə-bəl), *adj.* **1.** Capable of being endowed <the widow received the dowable estate>. **2.** Capable of receiving dower <the woman was dowable of the estate>.

dowager (dow-ə-jər). A widow holding property or title — esp. a life estate in real property — received from her deceased husband.

dowager-queen. The widow of the king of England.• If she is also the mother of the reigning monarch, she may also by known as the *queen mother.* — Also written *dowager queen.* — Also termed *queen dowager; queen mother.*

dower (dow-ər). (14c) At common law, a wife's right, upon her husband's death, to a life estate in one-third of the land that he owned in fee. • With few exceptions, the wife could not be deprived of dower by any transfer made by her husband during his lifetime. Although most states have abolished dower, many states retaining the concept have expanded the wife's share to a life estate in all the land that her husband owned in fee. — Also termed *dowment; maritagium.* Cf. CURTESY.

consummate dower (kən-**səm**-it *or* **kahn**-sə-mit). A widow's interest in her deceased husband's estate until that interest is legally assigned to her. — Also termed *dower consummate.*

dower by custom. *Hist.* Dower that is determined by custom rather than the general law. — Also termed *dower by particular custom.*

dower by particular custom. See *dower by custom.*

dower by the common law. The regular dower, consisting of a life interest in one-third of the lands that the husband held in fee. — Also termed *dos rationabilis* (dos rash-[ee]-ə-**nab**-ə-ləs).

dower inchoate. See *inchoate dower.*

election dower. (1883) A widow's right to take a statutory share of her deceased husband's estate if she chooses to reject her share under a will. See RIGHT OF ELECTION.

equitable dower. See *equitable jointure* under JOINTURE (1).

inchoate dower (in-**koh**-it). A wife's interest in her husband's estate while both are living. — Also termed *dower inchoate.*

doweress. See DOWRESS.

Dow Jones Industrial Average. A stock-market-performance indicator that consists of the price movements in the stocks of 30 leading industrial companies in the United States. — Abbr. DJIA. — Often shortened to *Dow.* — Also termed *Dow Jones Average.*

dowle stones (dohl). Rocks used as land boundaries. See CALL (5); LOCATIVE CALLS.

dowment. See DOWER.

down market. See *bear market* under MARKET.

down payment. See PAYMENT.

down reversal. *Securities.* A sudden market-price decline after a rising trend. • The term applies to the early stage of the decline; if the decline continues for several months, it is termed a *bear market.* — Also termed *correction; market correction.*

downright evidence. *Rare.* A preponderance of evidence.

downside. *Securities.* **1.** A downward movement of stock prices. **2.** The potential of a downward movement in stock prices. Cf. UPSIDE.

downside risk. *Securities.* A likely risk that stock prices will drop.

downside trend. *Securities.* The portion of the market cycle that shows declining stock prices. — Also termed *down trend.*

downsizing. (1975) Reducing the number of employees, usu. to decrease labor costs and to increase efficiency.

downstream guaranty. See GUARANTY.

downstream merger. See MERGER.

down trend. See DOWNSIDE TREND.

downward departure. See DEPARTURE.

dowress (dow-ris). *Archaic.* **1.** A woman legally entitled to dower. **2.** A tenant in dower. — Also spelled *doweress.*

dowry (**dow**-ree). *Archaic.* The money, goods, or property that a woman brings to her husband in marriage. — Also termed *marriage portion; maritagium* (mair-ə-**tay**-jee-əm); *maritage* (**mair**-i-tij).

DPPA. *abbr.* DEADBEAT PARENTS PUNISHMENT ACT.

DPW. *abbr.* DEPARTMENT OF PUBLIC SERVICES.

Dr. *abbr.* **1.** DEBTOR. **2.** DOCTOR.

DR. *abbr.* DISCIPLINARY RULE.

draconian (dray- *or* drə-**koh**-nee-in), *adj.* (18c) (Of a law) harsh; severe. • This term derives from *Draco,* the name of the ancient Athenian lawgiver. — Also termed *draconic.*

draff (draf). Refuse; dregs; sweepings of dust and dirt. • In weighing commodities, it is excluded from the waste allowance for goods sold by weight.

draft, *n.* (17c) **1.** An unconditional written order signed by one person (the *drawer*) directing another person (the *drawee* or *payor*) to pay a certain sum of money on demand or at a definite time to a third person (the *payee*) or to bearer. • A check is the most common example of a draft. — Also termed *bill of exchange; letter of exchange.* Cf. NOTE (1).

bank draft. (1835) A draft drawn by one financial institution on another.

clean draft. A draft with no shipping documents attached.

demand draft. See *sight draft.*

documentary draft. (1922) A payment demand conditioned on the presentation of a document, such as a document of title, invoice, certificate, or notice of default.

export draft. A draft drawn by a domestic seller on a foreign buyer, directing the buyer to pay the trade amount to the seller or the seller's bank.

foreign draft. A draft drawn in one country or state but payable in another. — Also termed *foreign bill of exchange; international bill of exchange.*

inland draft. A draft drawn and payable in the same state or country.

overdraft. See OVERDRAFT.

share draft. (1978) A demand that a member draws against a credit-union share account, payable to a third party. • A share draft is similar to a check that is written to draw funds out of a checking account at a bank.

sight draft. (1842) A draft that is payable on the bearer's demand or on proper presentment to the drawer. — Also termed *demand draft.*

time draft. A draft that contains a specified payment date. UCC § 3-108. — Also termed *time bill.*

trade draft. A draft that instructs a commercial enterprise or its agent to pay the amount specified.

2. The compulsory enlistment of persons into military service <his illness disqualified him from the draft>. — Also termed *conscription; military draft.* **3.** An initial or preliminary version <the second draft of the contract>.

draft, *vb.* (18c) **1.** To write or compose <to draft a contract>. **2.** To recruit or select (someone) <to draft someone to run for political office> <to draft someone into the armed services>.

draft board. A civilian board that registers and selects persons for mandatory military service. See SELECTIVE SERVICE SYSTEM.

drafter. (1884) A person who draws or frames a legal document, such as a will, contract, or legislative bill. — Also termed *draftsman.*

drafting. (1878) The practice, technique, or skill involved in preparing legal documents — such as statutes, rules, regulations, contracts, and wills — that set forth the rights, duties, liabilities, and entitlements of persons and legal entities. — Also termed *legal drafting.*

draftsman. See DRAFTER.

dragnet arrest. See ARREST.

dragnet clause. 1. See MOTHER HUBBARD CLAUSE (1). **2.** See CROSS-COLLATERAL CLAUSE.

dragnet lien. See LIEN.

Drago doctrine. The principle asserted by Luis Drago, Minister of Foreign Affairs of the Argentine Republic, in a December 29, 1902 letter to the Argentine Minister in Washington, in which Drago, responding to the forcible coercion of Venezuela's unpaid loans by Great Britain and others, argued that no public debt should be collected from a sovereign state by force or through the occupation of American territory by a foreign power. ● The subject was presented at the Hague Conference of 1907, when a modified version of the Drago doctrine was adopted.

drain, *n.* **1.** The act of drawing a liquid off gradually; the act of emptying. **2.** The act of gradually exhausting. **3.** A conduit for draining liquid, as a ditch or a pipe.

drain, *vb.* **1.** To draw (a liquid) off gradually <the farmer drained water from the property>. **2.** To exhaust gradually <the facility has drained the area's natural resources>. **3.** To empty gradually <the water drained>.

drainage district. A political subdivision authorized to levy assessments for making drainage improvements within its area.

drainage rights. The interest that a property owner has in the natural drainage and flow of water on the land.

dram (dram). **1.** An apothecary measurement of fluid equal to an eighth of an ounce. **2.** A small amount of anything, esp. liquor.

drama, *n.* **1.** A presentation of a story portrayed by words and actions or actions alone; a play. Cf. DRAMATIC COMPOSITION. **2.** An event or series of events having conflicting and exciting elements that capture people's attention.

drama-pricing. A seller's tactic of dramatically dropping the price of something, esp. real estate, to attract a buyer. — Also termed *trauma-pricing.*

dramatic composition. *Copyright.* A literary work setting forth a story, incident, or scene intended to be performed by actors, often with a musical accompaniment. Cf. DRAMA (1).

dramatic work. See WORK (2).

dram shop. *Archaic.* A place where alcoholic beverages are sold; a bar or saloon. — Also spelled *dram-shop; dramshop.* — Also termed *grog-shop; drinking shop.*

dram-shop act. (1859) A statute allowing a plaintiff to recover damages from a commercial seller of alcoholic beverages for the plaintiff's injuries caused by a customer's intoxication. — Also termed *civil-liability act; civil-damage law.*

dram-shop liability. (1995) Civil liability of a commercial seller of alcoholic beverages for personal injury caused by an intoxicated customer. ● Claims based on a similar type of liability have been brought against private citizens for personal injury caused by an intoxicated social guest.

draw, *vb.* (13c) **1.** To create and sign (a draft) <draw a check to purchase goods>. **2.** To prepare or frame (a legal document) <draw up a will>. **3.** To take out (money) from a bank, treasury, or depository <she drew $6,000 from her account>. **4.** To select (a jury) <the lawyers began voir dire and had soon drawn a jury>.

drawback. A government allowance or refund on import duties when the importer reexports imported products rather than selling them domestically. 19 USCA § 1313.

drawee (draw-ee). (18c) The person or entity that a draft is directed to and that is requested to pay the amount stated on it. ● The drawee is usu. a bank that is directed to pay a sum of money on an instrument. — Also termed *payor.*

drawee bank. See *payor bank* under BANK.

drawer. (17c) One who directs a person or entity, usu. a bank, to pay a sum of money stated in an instrument — for example, a person who writes a check; the maker of a note or draft. See MAKER.

drawing. 1. *Patents.* A specially prepared figure included with a patent application to explain and describe the invention. • A drawing is required when necessary to understand the invention. 35 USCA § 113. **2.** *Trademarks.* A graphic or textual depiction of a trademark, filed as part of an application for the mark to be placed on the primary register. • The drawing serves as the element that is published in the *Official Gazette*. It must include the applicant's name and address, the type of goods or services it will identify, and the date of first use or a statement of intent to use it in commerce.

> *formal drawing.* A drawing that complies with the formatting requirements of the U.S. Patent and Trademark Office, as set forth in 37 CFR 1.84, and is stamped "Approved" by the PTO Drafter. Cf. *informal drawing.*

> *front-page drawing.* A drawing submitted with the patent application and selected by the examiner as the application's representative drawing. • The drawing is reproduced on the front page of the published application or patent.

> *informal drawing.* A drawing that does not comply with the formatting requirements of the U.S. Patent and Trademark Office. • A drawing may be submitted as informal by the patent applicant, or declared informal by the PTO Drafter. Cf. *formal drawing.*

> *original drawing.* A drawing submitted with the original application.

> *special-form drawing.* A drawing of a trademark that contains some graphical element, such as a logo, a picture, or a special type style. • A stylized or special-form drawing must be submitted in black-and-white, with a description of the colors to be used on the final mark. — Also termed *stylized drawing.*

> *substitute drawing.* A drawing submitted after the original application has been filed. • A substitute drawing is often a formal drawing filed to replace an informal drawing.

> *typed drawing.* A drawing of a trademark that is purely textual, with no graphical component. • A typed drawing consists solely of the words, letters, and numbers that make up the mark, typed in all-capitals. — Also termed *typed-form drawing.*

drawing account. See ACCOUNT.

drawing lots. (13c) An act of selection or decision-making based on pure chance, with the result depending on the particular lot drawn. • Jurors are usu. instructed by the court not to base their verdict on drawing lots or similar methods of chance.

drayage. A charge for transporting property.

DRE. *abbr.* DRUG-RECOGNITION EXPERT.

dread-disease insurance. See INSURANCE.

D reorganization. See REORGANIZATION (2).

drift-stuff. Any material floating at random in water without a discoverable source. • Drift-stuff is usu. the property of the riparian owner.

drilling contract. *Oil & gas.* A well-drilling agreement between a drilling contractor, who owns drilling rigs and associated equipment, and the owner or lessor of the mineral rights. • The contract spells out the rights and duties of the parties. In general, the more control the interest-owner retains over the contractor, the more liability the owner is exposed to for damages the drilling causes. See DAYWORK DRILLING CONTRACT; FOOTAGE DRILLING CONTRACT.

> *turnkey drilling contract.* *Oil & gas.* A drilling contract under which the drilling contractor promises to perform specified functions for an agreed price. • The lease operator has little or no discretion to control the drilling contractor, and so assumes little or no liability for damages the drilling may cause.

drilling-delay rental clause. *Oil & gas.* A provision in an oil-and-gas lease giving the lessee the right to maintain the lease from period to period during the primary term by paying delay rentals instead of starting drilling operations. • Lessees use drilling-delay rental clauses because courts have said that they obviate any implied covenant to drill a test well on the premises. They are accepted by lessors because they provide for periodic income from the lease. See *"or" lease, "unless" lease* under LEASE.

drinking age. See AGE.

drinking shop. See DRAM SHOP.

DRIP. *abbr.* DIVIDEND-REINVESTMENT PLAN.

drip rights. A servitude allowing water dripping off a person's roof to fall on a neighbor's land.

driver. 1. A person who steers and propels a vehicle. **2.** A person who herds animals; a drover.

driver's license. The state-issued certificate authorizing a person to operate a motor vehicle. • It is also often used as a form of identification.

driving, *n.* The act of directing the course of something, such as an automobile or a herd of animals.

driving under the influence. (1924) The offense of operating a motor vehicle in a physically or mentally impaired condition, esp. after consuming alcohol or drugs. • Generally, this is a lesser offense than driving while intoxicated. But in a few jurisdictions the two are synonymous. — Abbr. DUI. — Also termed *driving while ability-impaired* (DWAI); *driving under the influence of liquor* (DUIL); *driving while intoxicated* (DWI); *operating under the influence* (OUI); *operating* *while intoxicated* (OWI); *operating a motor vehicle while intoxicated* (OMVI); *operating a motor vehicle under the influence* (OMVUI). Cf. DRIVING WHILE INTOXICATED.

driving while ability-impaired. See DRIVING UNDER THE INFLUENCE.

driving while intoxicated. (1913) **1.** The offense of operating a motor vehicle in a physically or mentally impaired condition after consuming enough alcohol to raise one's blood alcohol content above the statutory limit (.08% in many states), or after consuming drugs. ● Penalties vary widely; for example, the maximum penalty in Missouri and Louisiana is a $500 fine and six months in jail, while the penalties in New York range from $500 to $5,000 in fines and up to four years in jail. **2.** DRIVING UNDER THE INFLUENCE. — Abbr. DWI. — Also termed *drunk driving.* Cf. DRIVING UNDER THE INFLUENCE.

DRL. *abbr.* BUREAU OF DEMOCRACY, HUMAN RIGHTS, AND LABOR.

DRM. See *direct-reduction mortgage* under MORTGAGE.

droit (drwah *or* droyt). [French "right"] **1.** A legal right or claim. **2.** The whole body of law.

droit common (droyt **kom**-ən), *n.* [Law French] The common law. — Also termed *droit coutumier.* See COMMON LAW (2).

droit de suite (drwah də **sweet**), *n.* [French "right to follow"] **1.** A creditor's right to recover a debtor's property after it passes to a third party. **2.** *Copyright.* An artist's resale royalty; the right of a work's creator to benefit from appreciation in the value of the work by receiving a portion of the profit from its later resales. ● A *droit de suite* is recognized in some European nations.

droit moral (drwah maw-**ral**). [French] The doctrine of moral right, which entitles artists to prevent others from altering their works. ● The basic rights protected by this doctrine are (1) the right to create, (2) the right to disclose or publish, (3) the right to withdraw from publication, (4) the right to be identified with the work, and (5) the right to ensure the integrity of the work, including the right to object to any mutilation or distortion of the work. These rights are sometimes called *moral rights.* See MORAL RIGHT.

Droop quota. In some proportional-representation elections, the minimum number of votes needed to win a legislative seat. ● The quota is determined by a formula based on the reciprocal of the number of representatives plus one — or $1/(n + 1)$, where "n" is the number of representatives being elected. The term is named for the developer of the election format, Henry Richmond Droop (1831–1884).

drop-dead date. The date by which performance is required as a condition. Cf. TIME-IS-OF-THE-ESSENCE CLAUSE.

drop-dead provision. *Contracts.* A clause in an agreement or order allowing a party to take action without notice if the other party fails to perform certain acts.

drop-down clause. *Insurance.* An insurance-policy provision requiring an excess insurer to provide coverage to the insured even though the underlying coverage has not been exhausted, usu. because the underlying insurers are insolvent.

drop letter. A letter addressed to someone in the delivery area of the post office where the letter was posted.

drop-shipment delivery. A manufacturer's shipment of goods directly to the consumer rather than initially to a wholesaler. ● If the wholesaler takes the order, it may receive part of the profit from the sale.

drop shipper. A wholesaler who arranges to have goods shipped directly from a manufacturer to a consumer. See DROP-SHIPMENT DELIVERY.

dropsy testimony. See TESTIMONY.

drove, *n.* **1.** A group of animals driven in a herd. **2.** A large group of people in motion.

drover's pass. A free pass issued by a railroad company to the cattle's drover, who accompanies the cattle on the train.

DRP. *abbr.* DIVIDEND-REINVESTMENT PLAN.

drug, *n.* (14c) **1.** A substance intended for use in the diagnosis, cure, treatment, or prevention of disease. **2.** A natural or synthetic substance that alters one's perception or consciousness. See CONTROLLED SUBSTANCE.

   addictive drug. A drug (such as heroin or nicotine) that, usu. after repeated consumption, causes physical dependence and results in well-defined physiological symptoms upon withdrawal.

   adulterated drug. A drug that does not have the strength, quality, or purity represented or expected.

   copycat drug. See *generic drug.*

   dangerous drug. A drug that has potential for abuse or injury, usu. requiring a label warning that it cannot be dispensed without a prescription.

   designer drug. A chemical substance that is created to duplicate the pharmacological effects of controlled substances, often by using the same chemicals contained in controlled substances, but manipulating their formulas.

ethical drug. A drug that can be dispensed only with a doctor's prescription. Cf. *proprietary drug.*

generic drug. A drug containing the active ingredients but not necessarily the same excipient substances (such as binders or capsules) as the pioneer drug marketed under a brand name. — Also termed *copycat drug.* See *pioneer drug.*

new drug. A drug that experts have not recognized as safe and effective for use under the conditions prescribed. 21 USCA § 321(p)(1). • The Food and Drug Administration must approve all new drugs before they can be marketed.

orphan drug. A prescription drug developed to treat diseases affecting fewer than 200,000 people in the United States (such as a rare cancer) or whose developmental costs are not reasonably expected to be recovered from the drug's sales. 21 USCA § 360bb.

pioneer drug. The first drug that contains a particular active ingredient that is approved by the FDA for a specified use.

precompounded prescription drug. A drug that is distributed from the manufacturer, to the pharmacist, and then to the consumer without a change in form.

proprietary drug. A drug that is prepared and packaged for the public's immediate use. • Proprietary drugs may be sold over the counter. Cf. *ethical drug.*

drug abuse. The detrimental state produced by the repeated consumption of a narcotic or other potentially dangerous drug, other than as prescribed by a doctor to treat an illness or other medical condition.

drug addict. See ADDICT.

drug-assistance program. 1. A governmental program to ensure access to necessary prescription medicines for needy people who are uninsured or underinsured or who otherwise lack health coverage. **2.** Rehabilitative counseling, and monitoring, usu. in a nonresidential setting, for detecting and treating users of illegal drugs.

drug court. See COURT.

drug dependence. The psychological or physiological need for a drug.

drug-free zone. (1986) An area in which the possession or distribution of a controlled substance results in an increased penalty. • Drug-free zones are often established, for example, around public schools.

druggist. A person who mixes, compounds, dispenses, or otherwise deals in drugs and medicines, usu. either as a proprietor of a drugstore or as a pharmacist.

drug kingpin. An organizer, leader, manager, financier, or supervisor of a drug conspiracy; a person who has great authority in running an illegal drug operation.

drug paraphernalia. (1920) *Criminal law.* Any type of equipment, product, or material that is primarily designed or intended for the unlawful manufacture, processing, or hiding of a controlled substance, or for the introduction of a controlled substance into the human body, when possession of the substance is unlawful. 21 USCA § 863(d).

Drug Price Competition and Patent Term Restoration Act of 1984. See HATCH–WAXMAN ACT.

drug-recognition expert. A person trained to identify various types of drugs and alcohol, to understand the effects that drugs and alcohol have on people, and to recognize the signs and symptoms of drug and alcohol intoxication. — Abbr. DRE.

drug trafficking. See TRAFFICKING.

drummer. 1. A commercial agent who travels around taking orders for goods to be shipped from wholesale merchants to retail dealers; a traveling sales representative. **2.** A traveling salesperson.

drummer floater policy. See INSURANCE POLICY.

drunk, *adj.* Intoxicated; (of a person) under the influence of intoxicating liquor to such a degree that the normal capacity for rational thought and conduct is impaired. — **drunk,** *n.*

drunkard. 1. A person who consumes intoxicating substances frequently and excessively; esp., one who is habitually or often intoxicated. **2.** An alcoholic. • This term may also be used to refer to a drug addict. — Also termed *habitual drunkard.*

drunk driving. See DRIVING WHILE INTOXICATED.

drunkenness. 1. A state of intoxication; inebriation; the condition resulting from a person's ingestion of excessive amounts of intoxicating liquors sufficient to affect the person's normal capacity for rational thought and conduct. **2.** A habitual state of intoxication.

excessive drunkenness. A state of drunkenness in which a person is so far deprived of reason and understanding that he or she is incapable of understanding the character and consequences of an act.

drunkometer (drəng-kom-ə-tər). See BREATHALYZER.

dry, *adj.* (bef. 12c) **1.** Free from moisture; desiccated <dry land>. **2.** Unfruitful; destitute of profitable interest; nominal <a dry trust>. **3.** (Of a jurisdiction) prohibiting the sale or use of alcoholic beverages <a dry county>.

dry check. See *bad check* under CHECK.

dry exchange. Something that pretends to pass on both sides of a transaction, but passes on only one side.

dry hole. *Oil & gas.* An oil or gas well that is incapable of producing enough minerals to justify the cost of completing it and putting it into production.

dry-hole agreement. *Oil & gas.* A support agreement in which the contributing party agrees to make a cash contribution to the drilling party in exchange for geological or drilling information if the well drilled is unproductive. See SUPPORT AGREEMENT.

dry-hole clause. *Oil & gas.* A provision in an oil-and-gas lease specifying what a lessee must do to maintain the lease for the remainder of the primary term after drilling an unproductive well. • A dry-hole clause is intended to make clear that the lessee may maintain the lease by paying delay rentals for the remainder of the primary term.

dry mortgage. See MORTGAGE.

dry presumption. See PRESUMPTION.

dry receivership. See RECEIVERSHIP.

dry rent. See RENT (1).

dry trust. See TRUST.

DS. *abbr.* BUREAU OF DIPLOMATIC SECURITY.

d.s.b. *abbr.* DEBET SINE BREVE.

DSCA. *abbr.* DEFENSE SECURITY COOPERATION AGENCY.

DSS. *abbr.* **1.** DEPARTMENT OF SOCIAL SERVICES. **2.** DEFENSE SECURITY SERVICE.

DTC. *abbr.* DEPOSITORY TRUST CORPORATION.

DTRA. *abbr.* DEFENSE THREAT REDUCTION AGENCY.

d.t.'s. *abbr.* DELIRIUM TREMENS.

dual agent. See AGENT (2).

dual-capacity doctrine. (1914) The principle that makes an employer — who is normally shielded from tort liability by workers'-compensation laws — liable in tort to an employee if the employer and employee stand in a secondary relationship that confers independent obligations on the employer. — Also termed *dual-persona doctrine.* Cf. DUAL-PURPOSE DOCTRINE.

dual citizenship. 1. A person's status as a citizen of two countries, as when the person is born in the United States to parents who are citizens of another country, or one country still recognizes a person as a citizen even though that person has acquired citizenship in another country. **2.** The status of a person who is a citizen of both the United States and the person's country of residence.

dual contract. See CONTRACT.

dual-criminality principle. The rule prohibiting the international extradition of a fugitive unless the offense involves conduct that is criminal in both countries.

dual distributor. (1945) A firm that sells goods simultaneously to buyers on two different levels of the distribution chain; esp., a manufacturer that sells directly to both wholesalers and retailers.

dual distributorship. See DISTRIBUTORSHIP.

dual employment. See MOONLIGHTING.

dual fund. See MUTUAL FUND.

dual inheritance. See INHERITANCE.

duality of art. *Copyright.* The twofold nature of applied art as both functional and aesthetic. • The United States takes a duality-of-art approach to copyright, protecting applied art only when the item could stand alone as an identifiable work of art even if it did not perform the function it was designed to do. — Also termed *noncumulative approach.* Cf. UNITY OF ART.

dual listing. See LISTING (2).

dual-persona doctrine (d[y]oo-əl pər-**soh**-nə). (1982) See DUAL-CAPACITY DOCTRINE.

dual-priorities rule. The principle that partnership creditors have priority for partnership assets and that individual creditors have priority for a partner's personal assets. • This rule has been abandoned by the bankruptcy laws and the Revised Uniform Partnership Act. The bankruptcy code now allows partnership creditors access to all assets of bankrupt partners, not just those remaining after payment to individual creditors. — Also termed *jingle rule.*

dual-prosecution rule. (1981) The principle that the federal government and a state government may both prosecute a defendant for the same offense because both governments are separate and distinct entities. See DUAL-SOVEREIGNTY DOCTRINE.

dual-purpose doctrine. (1953) The principle that an employer is liable for an employee's injury that occurs during a business trip even though the trip also serves a personal purpose. Cf. DUAL-CAPACITY DOCTRINE.

dual-purpose fund. See *dual fund* under MUTUAL FUND.

dual-residential parent. See PARENT.

dual-shop operation. See DOUBLE-BREASTING.

dual-sovereignty doctrine. (1957) The rule that the federal and state governments may both prosecute a person for a crime without violating the constitutional protection against double jeopardy, if the person's act violated both jurisdictions' laws. See DUAL-PROSECUTION RULE.

duarchy (**d[y]oo**-ahr-kee), *n.* [fr. Greek *duo* "two" + *archia* "rule"] See DYARCHY.

dubitante (d[y]oo-bi-**tan**-tee). [Latin] Doubting. • This term was usu. placed in a law report next to a judge's name, indicating that the judge doubted a legal point but was unwilling to state that it was wrong. — Also termed *dubitans.*

ducat (**dək**-it). A gold coin used as currency, primarily in Europe and first appearing in Venice in the early 1100s, with the motto *sit tibi, Christe, dato, quem tu regis, iste Ducatus* ("let this duchy which thou rulest be dedicated to thee, O Christ"). • It survived into the 20th century in several countries, including Austria and the Netherlands.

duces tecum (**d[y]oo**-səs **tee**-kəm *also* **tay**-kəm). [Latin] (17c) Bring with you. See *subpoena duces tecum* under SUBPOENA.

ducking stool. See CASTIGATORY.

due, *adj.* (14c) **1.** Just, proper, regular, and reasonable <due care> <due notice>. **2.** Immediately enforceable <payment is due on delivery>. **3.** Owing or payable; constituting a debt <the tax refund is due from the IRS>.

due-bill. See IOU.

due care. See *reasonable care* under CARE.

due compensation. See *just compensation* under COMPENSATION.

due consideration. 1. The degree of attention properly paid to something, as the circumstances merit. **2.** See *sufficient consideration* under CONSIDERATION (1).

due course, payment in. See PAYMENT IN DUE COURSE.

due-course holder. See HOLDER IN DUE COURSE.

due course of law. See DUE PROCESS.

due day. See BOON DAY.

due deference. The appropriate degree of respect with which a reviewing authority must consider the decision of a primary decision-maker.

due diligence. See DILIGENCE.

due-diligence information. *Securities.* Information that a broker-dealer is required to have on file and make available to potential customers before submitting quotations for over-the-counter securities. • The informational requirements are set out in SEC Rule 15c2-11 (17 CFR § 240.15c2-11).

due influence. (17c) The sway that one person has over another, esp. as a result of temperate persuasion, argument, or appeal to the person's affections. Cf. UNDUE INFLUENCE.

duel. (15c) **1.** TRIAL BY COMBAT. **2.** A single combat; specif., a prearranged combat with deadly weapons fought between two or more persons under prescribed rules, usu. in the presence of at least two witnesses, to resolve a previous quarrel or avenge a deed. • In England and the United States, death resulting from a duel is treated as murder, and seconds may be liable as accessories. — Also termed *monomachy; single combat.* Cf. MUTUAL COMBAT.

dueling, *n.* The common-law offense of fighting at an appointed time and place after an earlier disagreement. • If one of the participants is killed, the other is guilty of murder, and all who are present, abetting the crime, are guilty as principals in the second degree.

duellum (d[y]oo-**el**-əm), *n.* [fr. Latin *duo* "two"] *Hist.* See TRIAL BY COMBAT.

due negotiation. See NEGOTIATION.

due notice. See NOTICE.

due-on-encumbrance clause. (1971) A mortgage provision giving the lender the option to accelerate the debt if the borrower further mortgages the real estate without the lender's consent. • All state laws on the enforcement of due-on-sale clauses have been preempted, and the subject is now governed exclusively by the Garn Act. 12 USCA § 1701j-3.

due-on-sale clause. (1967) A mortgage provision that gives the lender the option to accelerate the debt if the borrower transfers or conveys any part of the mortgaged real estate without the lender's consent.

due posting. (1893) **1.** The stamping and placing of letters or packages in the U.S. mail. **2.** The proper entry of an item into a ledger. **3.** Proper publication; proper placement of an item (such as an announcement) in a particular place, as on a particular wall.

due process. (16c) The conduct of legal proceedings according to established rules and principles for the protection and enforcement of private rights, including notice and the right to a fair hearing before a tribunal with the power to decide the case. — Also termed *due process of law; due course of law.* See FUNDAMENTAL-FAIRNESS DOCTRINE.

economic substantive due process. (1957) The doctrine that certain social policies, such as the freedom of contract or the right to enjoy property without interference by government regulation, exist in the Due Process Clause of the 14th Amendment, particularly in the words "liberty" and "property."

procedural due process. (1934) The minimal requirements of notice and a hearing guaranteed by the Due Process Clauses of the 5th and 14th Amendments, esp. if the deprivation of a significant life, liberty, or property interest may occur. • The Supreme Court has ruled that the fundamental guarantees of due process apply to children as well as to adults and that they apply in situations in which a juvenile may be deprived of liberty even though the juvenile proceedings may be labeled civil rather than criminal. *In re Gault*, 387 U.S. 1, 87 S.Ct. 1428 (1967). In that case, the Court held that an accused child was entitled to notice of the charges, the privilege against self-incrimination, the right to confront witnesses, and the right to summon witnesses on his or her own behalf. Justice Abe Fortas wrote the majority opinion in *Gault*, and Chief Justice Earl Warren predicted that it would come to be called the "Magna Carta for juveniles."

substantive due process. (1933) The doctrine that the Due Process Clauses of the 5th and 14th Amendments require legislation to be fair and reasonable in content and to further a legitimate governmental objective.

Due Process Clause. (1890) The constitutional provision that prohibits the government from unfairly or arbitrarily depriving a person of life, liberty, or property. ● There are two Due Process Clauses in the U.S. Constitution, one in the 5th Amendment applying to the federal government, and one in the 14th Amendment applying to the states (although the 5th Amendment's Due Process Clause also applies to the states under the incorporation doctrine). Cf. EQUAL PROTECTION CLAUSE.

due process of law. See DUE PROCESS.

due-process rights. (1930) The rights (as to life, liberty, and property) so fundamentally important as to require compliance with due-process standards of fairness and justice. See DUE PROCESS; DUE PROCESS CLAUSE; FUNDAMENTAL-FAIRNESS DOCTRINE.

due proof. Sufficient and properly submitted evidence to produce a result or support a conclusion, such as an entitlement to benefits supported by an insurance policy. ● The evidence need not be the best proof possible. *Metropolitan Life Ins. Co. v. Frisch*, 65 N.E. 2d 852, 855 (Ind. App. 1946).

Duhig rule. *Oil & gas.* A rule of title interpretation developed to deal with the common problem of overconveyance of fractional interests by giving priority to the granted interest over the reserved interest. *Duhig v. Peavy Moore Lumber Co., Inc.*, 144 S.W.2d 878 (Tex. 1940). ● The rule is not accepted in all states and is generally limited to conveyances by warranty deed.

DUI. *abbr.* DRIVING UNDER THE INFLUENCE.

DUIL. *abbr.* Driving under the influence of liquor. See DRIVING UNDER THE INFLUENCE.

duke. 1. A sovereign prince; a ruler of a duchy. **2.** The first order of nobility in Great Britain below the royal family.

Duke of York's Laws. A body of laws compiled in 1665 by Governor Nicholls for the more orderly government of the New York colony. ● The laws were gradually extended to the entire province.

dulocracy (d[y]oo-**lok**-rə-see), *n.* [fr. Greek *doulos* "servant" + *kratein* "to rule"] A government in which servants or slaves have so many privileges that they essentially rule. — Also spelled *doulocracy.*

duly, *adv.* In a proper manner; in accordance with legal requirements.

dum (dəm). [Latin] While; provided that.

dumb bidding. An auction bidding process in which the minimum acceptance price is placed under the object for sale — unbeknownst to the bidders — and no bids are accepted until they meet that price. ● Dumb bidding was initially intended to avoid the taxes imposed on auction sales by the statute of 1779, 19 Geo. 3, ch. 56, §§ 5–6, but the courts determined that the practice was fraudulent.

dummy, *adj.* (1846) Sham; make-believe; pretend <dummy corporation>.

dummy, *n.* (1866) **1.** A party who has no interest in a transaction, but participates to help achieve a legal goal. **2.** A party who purchases property and holds legal title for another. Cf. STRAW MAN (3).

dummy corporation. See CORPORATION.

dummy director. See DIRECTOR.

dummy shareholder. See SHAREHOLDER.

dump, *vb.* **1.** To drop (something) down, esp. in a heap; to unload. **2.** To sell (products) at an extremely low price; specif., to sell (products) in a foreign market at a lower price than at home.

dumping. (1857) **1.** The act of selling a large quantity of goods at less than fair value. **2.** Selling goods abroad at less than the market price at home. See ANTIDUMPING LAW. **3.** The disposal of waste matter into the environment.

Dumping Act. A federal antidumping law requiring the Secretary of the Treasury to notify the U.S. International Trade Commission (USITC) whenever the Secretary determines that goods are likely to be sold abroad at less than their fair value, so that the USITC can take appropriate action. 19 USCA § 1673.

dump-truck lawyer. *Slang.* A public defender who spends little time or effort and exhibits little skill mounting a defense on behalf of an indigent defendant. ● This derogatory term arises from criminal defendants' common perception (typically a misperception) that public defenders prefer to dump cases by making plea bargains rather than spend time preparing for trial. *People v. Clark*, 833 P.2d 561, 590 (Cal. 1992); *People v. Huffman*, 139 Cal. Rptr. 264, 267 n.2 (Cal. App. 1977).

dun (dən), *vb.* (17c) To demand payment from (a delinquent debtor) <his creditors are dunning him daily>. — **dun**, *n.*

Dunaway **hearing.** (1983) *Criminal law.* A pretrial hearing to determine whether evidence was obtained in violation of Fourth Amendment protections against unreasonable search and seizure. • The name derives from *Dunaway v. New York*, 442 U.S. 200, 99 S.Ct. 2249 (1979).

dungeon. 1. The bottom part of a fortress or tower, often used as a prison. — Also termed *dungeon-keep.* **2.** A dark underground prison.

dunnage (dən-ij). Anything, esp. pieces of wood, that are put underneath or between cargo on a vessel to prevent the cargo from bruising or getting wet from water leaking into the hold.

duodena (d[y]oo-ə-**dee**-nə). [Latin] **1.** A jury of twelve. **2.** A dozen of anything.

duopoly (d[y]oo-**op**-ə-lee). A market in which there are only two sellers of a product.

duopsony (d[y]oo-**op**-sə-nee). A market in which there are only two buyers of a product.

duplex querela (**d**[y]**oo**-pleks kwə-**ree**-lə). **1.** *Hist. Eccles. law.* An appeal by a clerk to the archbishop in response to the bishop's delaying or wrongfully refusing to do justice. **2.** *Eccles. law.* An appeal to a person's immediate superior, as when a bishop appeals to an archbishop. — Also termed *double quarrel; double complaint.*

duplicate (**d**[y]**oo**-pli-kit), *n.* (16c) **1.** A reproduction of an original document having the same particulars and effect as the original. *See* Fed. R. Evid. 101(4). **2.** A new original, made to replace an instrument that has been lost or destroyed. — Also termed (in sense 2) *duplicate original.* — **duplicate** (**d**[y]**oo**-pli-kit), *adj.*

duplicate (**d**[y]**oo**-pli-kayt), *vb.* **1.** To copy exactly <he duplicated the original document>. **2.** To double; to repeat <she duplicated the performance>.

duplicate-claiming rejection. See REJECTION.

duplicate taxation. See *double taxation* under TAXATION.

duplicate will. See WILL.

duplicative (doo-**plik**-ə-tiv *also* **doo**-pli-kay-tiv), *adj.* **1.** Having or characterized by having overlapping content, intentions, or effect <duplicative sources> <duplicative evidence> <duplicative regulations>. **2.** Duplicate; having or characterized by having identical content <duplicative database> <duplicative backup>.

duplicitous (d[y]oo-**plis**-i-təs), *adj.* **1.** (Of a person) deceitful; double-dealing. **2.** (Of a pleading, esp. an indictment) alleging two or more matters in one plea; characterized by double pleading.

duplicitous appeal. See APPEAL.

duplicitous indictment. See INDICTMENT.

duplicitous information. See INFORMATION.

duplicity (d[y]oo-**plis**-i-tee), *n.* (15c) **1.** Deceitfulness; double-dealing. **2.** The charging of the same offense in more than one count of an indictment. **3.** The pleading of two or more distinct grounds of complaint or defense for the same issue. • In criminal procedure, this takes the form of joining two or more offenses in the same count of an indictment. — Also termed *double pleading.* Cf. *alternative pleading* under PLEADING (2); *double plea* under PLEA (3).

durable goods. See GOODS.

durable lease. See LEASE.

durable power of attorney. See POWER OF ATTORNEY.

durables. See *durable goods* under GOODS.

duration. (14c) **1.** The length of time something lasts <the duration of the lawsuit>.

   duration of interest. The length of time a property interest lasts.

   duration of trust. The length of time a trust exists.

2. A length of time; a continuance in time <an hour's duration>.

durational-residency requirement. (1970) The requirement that one be a state resident for a certain time, such as one year, as a precondition to the exercise of a specified right or privilege. • When applied to voting, this requirement has been held to be an unconstitutional denial of equal protection because it burdens voting rights and impairs the fundamental personal right of travel.

Duration Directive. See DIRECTIVE HARMONIZING THE TERM OF COPYRIGHT AND CERTAIN RELATED RIGHTS.

Duren **test.** (1980) *Constitutional law.* A test to determine whether a jury's composition violates the fair-cross-section requirement and a criminal defendant's Sixth Amendment right to an impartial jury. • Under the test, a constitutional violation occurs if (1) a distinctive group is not fairly and reasonably represented in the jury pool in relation to its population in the community, (2) the underrepresentation is the result of a systematic exclusion of the group from the jury-selection process, and (3) the government cannot reasonably justify the discrepancy. *Duren v. Missouri*, 439 U.S. 357, 99 S.Ct. 664 (1979). See FAIR-CROSS-SECTION REQUIREMENT; STATISTICAL-DECISION THEORY; ABSOLUTE DISPARITY; COMPARATIVE DISPARITY.

duress (d[y]uu-**res**). (13c) **1.** Strictly, the physical confinement of a person or the detention of a contracting party's property. • In the field of torts, duress is considered a species of fraud in which compulsion takes the place of deceit in causing injury. **2.** Broadly, a threat of harm made to compel a person to do something against his or her will or judgment; esp., a wrongful threat made by one person to compel a manifestation of seeming assent by another person to a transaction without real volition. • A marriage that is induced by duress is generally voidable. **3.** The use or threatened use of unlawful force — usu. that a reasonable person cannot resist — to compel someone to commit an unlawful act. • Duress is a recognized defense to a crime, contractual breach, or tort. See Model Penal Code § 2.09. See COERCION.

duress of circumstances. See NECESSITY (1).

duress of goods. **1.** The act of seizing personal property by force, or withholding it from an entitled party, and then extorting something as the condition for its release. **2.** Demanding and taking personal property under color of legal authority that either is void or for some other reason does not justify the demand.

duress of imprisonment. The wrongful confining of a person to force the person to do something.

duress of the person. Compulsion of a person by imprisonment, by threat, or by a show of force that cannot be resisted.

duress per minas (pər **mɪ**-nəs). [Law Latin] Duress by threat of loss of life, loss of limb, mayhem, or other harm to a person.

economic duress. (1929) An unlawful coercion to perform by threatening financial injury at a time when one cannot exercise free will. — Also termed *business compulsion.*

moral duress. An unlawful coercion to perform by unduly influencing or taking advantage of the weak financial position of another. • Moral duress focuses on the inequities of a situation while economic duress focuses on the lack of will or capacity of the person being influenced.

Durham (dər-əm). One of the three remaining county palatines in England, the others being Chester and Lancaster. • Its jurisdiction was vested in the Bishop of Durham until the statute 6 & 7 Will. 4, ch. 19 vested it as a separate franchise and royalty in the Crown. The jurisdiction of the Durham Court of Pleas was transferred to the Supreme Court of Judicature by the Judicature Act of 1873, but Durham continued to maintain a Chancery Court according to the Palatine Court of Durham Act of 1889. See COUNTY PALATINE.

Durham rule. *Criminal law.* A test for the insanity defense, holding that a defendant is not criminally responsible for an act that was the product of mental disease or defect (*Durham v. United States,* 214 F.2d 862 (D.C. Cir. 1954)). • Formerly used in New Hampshire and the District of Columbia, the *Durham* rule has been criticized as being too broad and is no longer accepted in any American jurisdiction. — Also termed *product test.* See INSANITY DEFENSE.

Durrett rule. *Bankruptcy.* The principle that a transfer of property in exchange for less than 70% of the property's value should be invalidated as a preferential transfer. *Durrett v. Washington Nat'l Ins. Co.,* 621 F.2d 201 (5th Cir. 1980); 11 USCA § 548. • This rule has been applied most frequently to foreclosure sales. But it has essentially been overruled by the U.S. Supreme Court, which has held that, at least for mortgage foreclosure sales, the price received at a regularly conducted, noncollusive sale represents a reasonably equivalent value of the property, and the transfer is presumed valid. *BFP v. Resolution Trust Corp.,* 511 U.S. 531, 114 S.Ct. 1757 (1994).

Dutch auction. See AUCTION.

Dutch-auction tender method. See *Dutch auction* (3) under AUCTION.

Dutch lottery. See LOTTERY.

dutiable (d[y]oo-tee-ə-bəl), *adj.* Subject to a duty <dutiable goods>.

duty. (13c) **1.** A legal obligation that is owed or due to another and that needs to be satisfied; an obligation for which somebody else has a corresponding right.

absolute duty. **1.** A duty to which no corresponding right attaches. • According to John Austin's legal philosophy, there are four kinds of absolute duties: (1) duties not regarding persons (such as those owed to God and to lower animals), (2) duties owed to persons indefinitely (i.e., to the community as a whole), (3) self-regarding duties (such as the duty not to commit suicide), and (4) duties owed to the sovereign. 1 John Austin, *The Providence of Jurisprudence Determined* 400 (Sarah Austin ed., 2d ed. 1861). **2.** A duty as to which nothing but lapse of time remains necessary to make immediate performance by the promisor obligatory.

active duty. See *positive duty.*

affirmative duty. A duty to take a positive step to do something.

conditional duty. A duty that is conditioned on the occurrence of an event other than the lapse of time.

contractual duty. **1.** A duty arising under a particular contract. **2.** A duty imposed by the law of contracts.

delegable duty. (1908) A duty that may be transferred to another to perform. See ASSIGNMENT.

duty to act. (17c) A duty to take some action to prevent harm to another, and for the failure of which one may be liable depending on the relationship of the parties and the circumstances.

duty to defend. *Insurance.* The obligation of an insurer to provide an insured with a legal defense against claims of liability, within the terms of the policy. • The duty to defend applies if the terms of the policy and the facts of the claim allow an ambiguity about whether the insurer will have a duty to indemnify the insured. It does not apply if no such ambiguity exists.

duty to indemnify. An obligation to compensate another for the other's loss. • The duty arises under the terms of an agreement, which governs the extent of the duty. An insurance policy is fundamentally an indemnification agreement, but the duty is often made a part of other contracts as well.

duty to settle. *Insurance.* The obligation of an insurer to negotiate and settle third-party claims against an insured in good faith.

duty to speak. (16c) A requirement (not strictly a duty) to say something to correct another's false impression. • For example, a duty to speak may arise when a person has, during the course of negotiations, said something that was true at the time but that has ceased to be true before the contract is signed.

equitable duty. A duty enforceable in a court of chancery or in a court having the powers of a court in chancery.

imperfect duty. 1. A duty that, though recognized by law, is not enforceable against the person who owes it. 2. A duty that is not fit for enforcement but should be left to the discretion and conscience of the person whose duty it is.

implied duty of cooperation. A duty existing in every contract, obligating each party to cooperate with, or at least not to wrongfully hinder, the other party's performance. • Breach of this implied duty excuses performance.

legal duty. (17c) A duty arising by contract or by operation of law; an obligation the breach of which would give a legal remedy <the legal duty of parents to support their children>.

moral duty. A duty the breach of which would be a moral wrong. — Also termed *natural duty.*

negative duty. A duty that forbids someone to do something; a duty that requires someone to abstain from something. — Also termed *passive duty.*

noncontractual duty. A duty that arises independently of any contract.

nondelegable duty (non-**del**-ə-gə-bəl). (1902) **1.** *Contracts.* A duty that cannot be delegated by a contracting party to a third party. • If a contracting party purports to delegate the duty, the other party can rightfully refuse to accept performance by the third party. **2.** *Torts.* A duty that may be delegated to an independent contractor by a principal, who retains primary (as opposed to vicarious) responsibility if the duty is not properly performed. • For example, a landlord's duty to maintain common areas, though delegated to a service contractor, remains the landlord's responsibility if someone is injured by improper maintenance.

passive duty. See *negative duty.*

perfect duty. A duty that is not merely recognized by the law but is actually enforceable.

positive duty. A duty that requires a person either to do some definite action or to engage in a continued course of action. — Also termed *active duty.*

preexisting duty. (1823) A duty that one is already legally bound to perform. See PREEXISTING-DUTY RULE.

quasi-judicial duty. A discretionary judicial duty that a nonjudicial officer may perform under some circumstances.

2. Any action, performance, task, or observance owed by a person in an official or fiduciary capacity.

discretionary duty. A duty that allows a person to exercise judgment and choose to perform or not perform. Cf. *ministerial duty.*

duty of candor (**kan**-dər). A duty to disclose material facts; esp., a duty of a director seeking shareholder approval of a transaction to disclose to the shareholders all known material facts about the transaction.

duty of candor and good faith. *Patents.* A patent applicant's responsibility to disclose to the U.S. Patent and Trademark Office all known information relevant to the invention's patentability, esp. prior art, novelty, and embodiment. • If an applicant fails to be candid in disclosing all relevant information, the PTO may reject the application. If the patent is issued and undisclosed but relevant information is discovered later, the patent may be invalidated, and the applicant charged with fraud on the PTO, even if the undisclosed information might not have barred the patent's issuance. 37 CFR 1.56.

duty of fair representation. A labor union's duty to represent its member employees fairly, honestly, and in good faith.

duty of good faith and fair dealing. A duty that is implied in some contractual relationships, requiring the parties to deal with each other fairly, so that neither prohibits the other from realizing the agreement's benefits. See GOOD FAITH; BAD FAITH.

duty of loyalty. A person's duty not to engage in self-dealing or otherwise use his or her position to further personal interests rather than those of the beneficiary. • For example, directors have a duty not to engage in self-dealing to further their own personal interests rather than the interests of the corporation.

fiduciary duty (fi-d[y]oo-shee-er-ee). A duty of utmost good faith, trust, confidence, and candor owed by a fiduciary (such as a lawyer or corporate officer) to the beneficiary (such as a lawyer's client or a shareholder); a duty to act with the highest degree of honesty and loyalty toward another person and in the best interests of the other person (such as the duty that one partner owes to another). See FIDUCIARY; *fiduciary relationship* under RELATIONSHIP.

ministerial duty. A duty that requires neither the exercise of official discretion nor judgment. Cf. *discretionary duty.*

proprietary duty. A duty owed by a governmental entity while engaged in a proprietary, rather than governmental, activity.

3. *Torts.* A legal relationship arising from a standard of care, the violation of which subjects the actor to liability. — Also termed *duty of care.* **4.** A tax imposed on a commodity or transaction, esp. on imports; IMPOST. • A duty in this sense is imposed on things, not persons.

account duty. An inheritance tax payable by a decedent's beneficiary.

ad valorem duty. A tax calculated as a percentage of an imported product's value. Cf. *compound duty; specific duty.*

antidumping duty. See *antidumping tariff* under TARIFF (3).

compound duty. A tax based on a combination of imported goods' weight, volume, or item count, plus a percentage of their value. Cf. *ad valorem duty; specific duty.*

countervailing duty. A tax imposed on manufacturers of imported goods to protect domestic industry by offsetting subsidies given by foreign governments to those manufacturers.

customs duty. A tax levied on an imported or exported commodity; esp., the federal tax levied on goods shipped into the United States.

death duty. An estate tax or inheritance tax. — Also termed *estate duty.*

duty of detraction. A tax on property acquired by succession or will and then removed from one state to another.

estate duty. *Hist. English law.* A tax imposed on the principal value of all property that passed on death. • Estate duties were first imposed in 1889. A capital transfer tax replaced it in 1975. Since 1986, an inheritance tax has applied instead, with exceptions for certain transactions entered into before then. See *death duty.*

import duty. A tax on the importation of a product. — Also termed *duty on import.*

legacy duty. See *legacy tax* under TAX.

probate duty. A tax assessed by the government either on every will admitted to probate or on the gross value of the decedent's personal property.

specific duty. A tax calculated on an import's weight, volume, or item count. Cf. *ad valorem duty; compound duty.*

succession duty. A tax payable by the successor to real property, esp. when the successor has not purchased the property for value but has succeeded to the property in some other way.

tonnage duty. A charge imposed on a commercial vessel for entering, remaining in, or leaving a port., usu. assessed on the basis of the ship's weight. • U.S. Const. art. I, § 10, cl. 3 prohibits the states from levying tonnage duties. — Also termed *tonnage tax; tonnage.*

unascertained duty. A preliminary, estimated payment to a customs collector of the duty that will be due on final accounting. • An importer pays this duty to receive permission to land and sell the goods.

duty-bound, *adj.* Required by legal or moral obligation to do something <Jones is duty-bound to deliver the goods by Friday>.

duty-free, *adj.* Of or relating to products of foreign origin that are not subject to import or export taxes.

duty judge. See JUDGE.

duty of care. See DUTY (3).

duty of the flag. *Hist.* A maritime ceremony by which a foreign vessel struck her flag and lowered her topsail upon meeting the British flag. • The ceremony was an acknowledgment of British sovereignty over the British seas.

duty of tonnage (tən-ij). See *tonnage duty* under DUTY (4).

duty of water. The amount of water necessary to irrigate a given tract.

duty on import. See *import duty* under DUTY (4).

duty-to-defend clause. *Insurance.* A liability-insurance provision obligating the insurer to take over the defense of any lawsuit brought by a third party against the insured on a claim that falls within the policy's coverage. See *duty to defend* under DUTY (1).

duty to mitigate (mit-i-gayt). (1891) A nonbreaching party's or tort victim's duty to make reasonable efforts to limit losses resulting from the other party's breach or tort. • Not doing so precludes the party from collecting damages that might have been avoided. See MITIGATION-OF-DAMAGES DOCTRINE.

DWAI. *abbr.* Driving while ability-impaired. See DRIVING UNDER THE INFLUENCE.

dwell, *vb.* (13c) **1.** To remain; to linger <the case dwelled in her memory>. **2.** To reside in a place permanently or for some period <he dwelled in California for nine years>.

dwelling defense. See CASTLE DOCTRINE.

dwelling-house. (15c) **1.** The house or other structure in which a person lives; a residence or abode. **2.** *Real estate.* The house and all buildings attached to or connected with the house. **3.** *Criminal law.* A building, a part of a building, a tent, a mobile home, or another enclosed space that is used or intended for use as a human habitation. • The term has referred to connected buildings in the same curtilage but now typically includes only the structures connected either directly with the house or by an enclosed passageway. — Often shortened to *dwelling.* — Also termed (archaically) *mansion house;* (more broadly) *dwelling place.*

    quasi-dwelling-house. Hist. Any outbuilding, such as a barn, that is in proximity to the building used as a residence. See BURGLARY (1).

DWI. *abbr.* DRIVING WHILE INTOXICATED.

DWOP (**dee**-wop *or* **doo**-wop). *abbr.* See *dismissal for want of prosecution* under DISMISSAL (1).

DWOP docket. See DOCKET (2).

dyarchy (**dɪ**-ahr-kee), *n.* [fr. Greek *dy* "two" + *archein* "rule"] A government jointly ruled by two people, such as William and Mary of England. — Also termed *diarchy.*

dyathanasia, (dɪ-ath-ə-**nay**-zhə), *n.* The act of permitting death to occur naturally by withholding, terminating, or not offering life-prolonging treatments or intervention. — Also termed *passive mercy killing.* See EUTHANASIA.

Dyer Act. A federal law, enacted in 1919, making it unlawful either (1) to transport a stolen motor vehicle across state lines, knowing it to be stolen, or (2) to receive, conceal, or sell such a vehicle, knowing it to be stolen. 18 USCA §§ 2311–2313. — Also termed *National Motor Vehicle Theft Act.*

dyet. See DIET.

dying declaration. See DECLARATION (6).

dying without issue. See FAILURE OF ISSUE.

dynamite charge. See ALLEN CHARGE.

dynamite instruction. See ALLEN CHARGE.

dynasty. 1. A powerful family line that continues for a long time <an Egyptian dynasty>. **2.** A powerful group of individuals who control a particular industry or field and who control their successors <a literary dynasty> <a banking dynasty>.

dynasty trust. See TRUST.

dysnomy (**dis**-nə-mee), *n.* [fr. Greek *dys* "bad" + *nomos* "law"] The enactment of bad legislation.

E

EAJA. *abbr.* EQUAL ACCESS TO JUSTICE ACT.

E&O insurance. See *errors-and-omissions insurance* under INSURANCE.

earl. (12c) A title of nobility, formerly the highest in England but now the third highest, ranking between a marquis and a viscount. • This title corresponds with the French *comte* and the German *graf.* Originating with the Saxons, this title is the most ancient of the English peerage. William the Conqueror first made the title hereditary, giving it in fee to his nobles. No territorial, private, or judicial rights now accompany the title; it merely confers nobility and a hereditary seat in the House of Lords.

earldom. The dignity or jurisdiction of an earl. • Only the dignity remains now, the jurisdiction having been given over to the sheriff. See DIGNITY.

Earl Marshal of England. A great officer of state, who historically had jurisdiction over several courts, including the court of chivalry and the court of honor. • Under this office is the herald's office, or college of arms. The Earl Marshal was also a judge of the Marshalsea court, now abolished. This office is quite ancient. Since 1672, it has been hereditary in the family of Howards, Dukes of Norfolk. — Often shortened to *Earl Marshal.*

early voting. See VOTING.

earmark, *n.* (16c) **1.** Originally, a mark upon the ear — a mode of marking sheep and other animals. **2.** A mark put on something (such as a coin) to distinguish it from another.

earmark, *vb.* **1.** To mark with an earmark. **2.** To set aside for a specific purpose or recipient.

earmarking doctrine. *Bankruptcy.* An equitable principle that when a new lender makes a loan to enable a debtor to pay off a specified creditor, the funds are specifically set aside for that creditor so that, if the debtor lacks control over the disposition of the funds, they do not become part of the debtor's estate and thus subject to a preference.

earn, *vb.* (bef. 12c) **1.** To acquire by labor, service, or performance. **2.** To do something that entitles one to a reward or result, whether it is received or not.

earned income. See INCOME.

earned-income credit. See TAX CREDIT.

earned land. See LAND.

earned premium. See PREMIUM (1).

earned surplus. See *retained earnings* under EARNINGS.

earned time. See TIME.

earner. 1. One who produces income through personal efforts or property or both. **2.** Property or an asset that produces income for its owner.

earnest, *n.* (13c) **1.** A nominal payment or token act that serves as a pledge or a sign of good faith, esp. as the partial purchase price of property. • Though not legally necessary, an earnest may help the parties come to an agreement. **2.** EARNEST MONEY.

earnest money. (16c) A deposit paid (often in escrow) by a prospective buyer (esp. of real estate) to show a good-faith intention to complete the transaction, and ordinarily forfeited if the buyer defaults. • Although earnest money has traditionally been a nominal sum (such as a nickel or a dollar) used in the sale of goods, it is not a mere token in the real-estate context: it is generally a percentage of the purchase price and may be a substantial sum. — Also termed *earnest*; *bargain money*; *caution money*; *hand money*. Cf. BINDER (2); *down payment* under PAYMENT.

earning asset. See ASSET.

earning capacity. (1872) A person's ability or power to earn money, given the person's talent, skills, training, and experience. • Earning capacity is one element considered when measuring the damages recoverable in a personal-injury lawsuit. And in family law, earning capacity is considered when awarding child support and spousal maintenance (or alimony) and in dividing property between spouses upon divorce. — Also termed *earning power.* See LOST EARNING CAPACITY.

earnings. (16c) Revenue gained from labor or services, from the investment of capital, or from assets. See INCOME.

appropriated retained earnings. Retained earnings that a company's board designates for a distinct use, and that are therefore unavailable to pay dividends or for other uses. — Also termed *appropriated surplus*; *surplus revenue*; *suspense reserve.*

earnings before interest and taxes. Corporations. A company's income calculated without deductions for interest expenses and taxes, used as a measure of the company's ability to generate cash flow from ongoing operations.— Abbr. EBIT.

earnings before interest, taxes, and depreciation. Corporations. A company's income without deductions for interest expenses, taxes, depreciation expenses, or amortization expenses, used as an indicator of a company's profitabilty and ability to service its debt. — Abbr. EBITDA.

future earnings. See *lost earnings.*

gross earnings. See *gross income* under INCOME.

lost earnings. Wages, salary, or other income that a person could have earned if he or she had not lost a job, suffered a disabling injury, or died. • Lost earnings are typically awarded as damages in personal-injury and wrongful-termination cases. There can be past lost earnings and future lost earnings. Both are subsets of this category, though legal writers sometimes loosely use *future earnings* as a synonym for *lost earnings.* Cf. LOST EARNING CAPACITY.

net earnings. See *net income* under INCOME.

normalized earnings. *Corporations.* Earnings adjusted for inflation and to remove elements that are extraordinary, nonrecurring, nonoperating, or otherwise unusual.

ongoing earnings. See *operating earnings.*

operating earnings. Business income calculated in violation of generally accepted accounting principles by including income items and excluding various business expenses. • Many companies use operating earnings to favorably skew their price-earnings (P/E) ratios. Because the rationales for the underlying calculations vary from company to company, and from period to period within a company, operating earnings are almost always artificially inflated and unreliable. The term *operating earnings* is meaningless under generally accepted accounting principles. — Also termed *pro forma earnings*; *economic earnings*; *core earnings*; *ongoing earnings*; *earnings excluding special items.* See PRICE-EARNINGS RATIO.

pretax earnings. Net earnings before income taxes.

pro forma earnings. See *operating earnings.*

real earnings. Earnings that are adjusted for inflation so that they reflect actual purchasing power.

retained earnings. A corporation's accumulated income after dividends have been distributed. — Also termed *earned surplus*; *undistributed profit.*

surplus earnings. The excess of corporate assets over liabilities within a given period, usu. a year.

earnings and profits. *Corporations.* In corporate taxation, the measure of a corporation's economic capacity to make a shareholder distribution that is not a return of capital. • The distribution will be dividend income to the shareholders to the extent of the corporation's current and accumulated earnings and profits. Cf. *accumulated-earnings tax* under TAX; *accumulated taxable income* under INCOME.

earnings before interest and taxes. See EARNINGS.

earnings before interest, taxes, and depreciation. See EARNINGS.

earnings excluding special items. See *operating earnings* under EARNINGS.

earnings per share. *Corporations.* A measure of corporate value by which the corporation's net income is divided by the number of outstanding shares of common stock. • Investors benefit from calculating a corporation's earnings per share, because it helps the investors determine the fair market value of the corporation's stock. — Abbr. EPS.

fully diluted earnings per share. A corporation's net income — assuming that all convertible securities had been transferred to common equity and all stock options had been exercised — divided by the number of shares of the corporation's outstanding common stock.

earnings-price ratio. See *earnings yield* under YIELD.

earnings report. See INCOME STATEMENT.

earnings yield. See YIELD.

earnout agreement. (1977) An agreement for the sale of a business whereby the buyer first pays an agreed amount up front, leaving the final purchase price to be determined by the business's future profits. • The seller usu. helps manage the business for a period after the sale. — Sometimes shortened to *earnout.*

earwitness. (16c) A witness who testifies about something that he or she heard but did not see. Cf. EYEWITNESS.

easement (eez-mənt). (14c) An interest in land owned by another person, consisting in the right to use or control the land, or an area above or below it, for a specific limited purpose (such as to cross it for access to a public road). • The land benefiting from an easement is called the *dominant estate*; the land burdened by an easement is called the *servient estate.* Unlike a lease or license, an easement may last forever, but it does not give the holder the right to possess, take from, improve, or sell the land. The primary recognized easements are (1) a right-of-way, (2) a right of entry for any purpose relating to the dominant estate, (3) a right to the support of land and buildings, (4) a right of light and air, (5) a right to water, (6) a right to do some act that would otherwise amount to a nuisance, and (7) a right to place or keep something on the servient estate. See SERVI-

TUDE (1). Cf. PROFIT À PRENDRE. — Also termed *private right-of-way.*

access easement. (1933) An easement allowing one or more persons to travel across another's land to get to a nearby location, such as a road. • The access easement is a common type of easement by necessity. — Also termed *easement of access; easement of way; easement of passage.*

adverse easement. See *prescriptive easement.*

affirmative easement. (1881) An easement that forces the servient-estate owner to permit certain actions by the easement holder, such as discharging water onto the servient estate. — Also termed *positive easement.* Cf. *negative easement.*

apparent easement. (1851) A visually evident easement, such as a paved trail or a sidewalk.

appendant easement. See *easement appurtenant.*

appurtenant easement. See *easement appurtenant.*

avigational easement. An easement permitting unimpeded aircraft flights over the servient estate. — Also termed *avigation easement; aviation easement; flight easement; navigation easement.*

common easement. (18c) An easement allowing the servient landowner to share in the benefit of the easement. — Also termed *nonexclusive easement.*

continuous easement. (1863) An easement that may be enjoyed without a deliberate act by the party claiming it, such as an easement for drains, sewer pipes, lateral support of a wall, or light and air. — Also termed (in Louisiana) *continuous servitude.* Cf. *discontinuous easement.*

conservation easement. *Property.* A recorded, perpetual, nonpossessory interest in real property held by a government entity or by a qualified nonprofit entity that imposes restrictions or affirmative obligations on the property's owner or lessee to retain or protect natural, scenic, or open-space values of real property, ensure its availability for agricultural, forest, recreational, or open-space use, protect natural resources and habitat, maintain or enhance air or water quality, or preserve the historical, architectural, archeological, or cultural aspects of the real property. — Also termed *conservation restriction; conservation servitude.*

determinable easement. An easement that terminates on the happening of a specific event.

discontinuous easement. (1867) An easement that can be enjoyed only if the party claiming it deliberately acts in some way with regard to the servient estate. • Examples are a right-of-way and the right to draw water. — Also termed *discontinuing easement; noncontinuous easement;*

nonapparent easement; (in Louisiana) *discontinuous servitude.* Cf. *continuous easement.*

easement appurtenant. (1810) An easement created to benefit another tract of land, the use of easement being incident to the ownership of that other tract. — Also termed *appurtenant easement; appendant easement; pure easement; easement proper.* Cf. *easement in gross.*

easement by estoppel. (1907) A court-ordered easement created from a voluntary servitude after a person, mistakenly believing the servitude to be permanent, acted in reasonable reliance on the mistaken belief.

easement by implication. See *implied easement.*

easement by necessity. (1865) An easement created by operation of law because the easement is indispensable to the reasonable use of nearby property, such as an easement connecting a parcel of land to a road. — Also termed *easement of necessity; necessary way.*

easement by prescription. See *prescriptive easement.*

easement in gross. (1866) An easement benefiting a particular person and not a particular piece of land. • The beneficiary need not, and usu. does not, own any land adjoining the servient estate. Cf. *easement appurtenant.*

easement of access. See *access easement.*

easement of convenience. An easement that increases the facility, comfort, or convenience of enjoying the dominant estate or some right connected with it.

easement of natural support. See *lateral support* under SUPPORT (4).

easement of necessity. See *easement by necessity.*

easement of passage. See *access easement.*

easement of way. See *access easement.*

easement proper. See *easement appurtenant.*

equitable easement. (1869) 1. An implied easement created by equity when adjacent lands have been created out of a larger tract. • Such an easement is usu. created to allow implied privileges to continue. 2. See *restrictive covenant* (1) under COVENANT (4).

exclusive easement. An easement that the holder has the sole right to use. Cf. *common easement.*

flight easement. See *avigational easement.*

floating easement. An easement that, when created, is not limited to any specific part of the servient estate.

flowage easement. A common-law easement that gives the dominant-estate owner the right to flood a servient estate, as when land near a dam is flooded to maintain the dam or to control the water level in a reservoir.

implied easement. (1867) An easement created by law after an owner of two parcels of land uses one parcel to benefit the other to such a degree that, upon the sale of the benefited parcel, the purchaser could reasonably expect the use to be included in the sale. — Also termed *easement by implication, way of necessity.*

intermittent easement. An easement that is usable or used only from time to time, not regularly or continuously.

land-conservation easement. *Property.* An easement arising from an agreement between a landowner and a land trust to provide for the protection of the land in its natural state while perhaps also allowing the property to be used for agricultural or low-impact recreational activities. • The easement runs with the land. — Also termed *land-conservation agreement; land-preservation easement.*

light-and-air easement. (1940) A negative easement preventing an adjoining landowner from constructing a building that would prevent light or air from reaching the dominant estate. See *negative easement.* Cf. *solar easement.*

mineral easement. An easement that permits the holder to enter the property to remove minerals from it.

navigation easement. 1. An easement giving the federal government the right to regulate navigable waters, even when the regulation interferes with private water rights. 2. See *avigational easement.*

negative easement. (1861) An easement that prohibits the servient-estate owner from doing something, such as building an obstruction. Cf. *affirmative easement.*

nonapparent easement. See *discontinuous easement.*

noncontinuous easement. See *discontinuous easement.*

nonexclusive easement. See *common easement.*

positive easement. See *affirmative easement.*

prescriptive easement. (1838) An easement created from an open, adverse, and continuous use over a statutory period. — Also termed *easement by prescription; adverse easement.* See AD-VERSE POSSESSION.

private easement. An easement whose enjoyment is restricted to one specific person or a few specific people.

public easement. An easement for the benefit of an entire community, such as the right to travel down a street or a sidewalk.

pure easement. See *easement appurtenant.*

quasi-easement. 1. An easement-like right occurring when both tracts of land are owned by the same person. • A quasi-easement may become a true easement if the landowner sells one of the tracts. 2. An obligation or license that relates to land but that is not a true easement — for example, a landowner's obligation to maintain the fence between the landowner's tract and someone else's tract.

reciprocal negative easement. An easement created when a landowner sells part of the land and restricts the buyer's use of that part, and, in turn, that same restriction is placed on the part kept by the landowner. • Such an easement usu. arises when the original landowner creates a common scheme of development for smaller tracts that are carved out of the original tract.

reserved easement. An easement created by the grantor of real property to benefit the grantor's retained property and to burden the granted property.

secondary easement. An easement that is appurtenant to the primary or actual easement; the right to do things that are necessary to fully enjoy the easement itself.

solar easement. (1982) An easement created to protect the dominant estate's exposure to direct sunlight. • A solar easement is often created to prevent the servient-estate owner from constructing any building that would cause shadows on the dominant estate, thus interfering with the use of a solar-energy system. Cf. *light-and-air easement.*

timber easement. An easement that permits the holder to cut and remove timber from another's property. — Also termed *timber rights.*

Easter-offerings. *Eccles. law.* Small sums of money paid as personal tithes to the parochial clergy by the parishioners at Easter. • Under the Recovery of Small Tithes Act (1695), Easter-offerings were recoverable before justices of the peace. St. 7 & 8 Will. 3, ch. 6. — Also termed *Easter-dues.*

Easter sittings. *English law.* A term of court beginning on April 15 of each year and usu. ending on May 8, but sometimes extended to May 13. • This was known until 1875 as *Easter term.* Cf. HILARY SITTINGS; MICHAELMAS SITTINGS; TRINITY SITTINGS.

EAT. *abbr.* Earnings after taxes.

eaves-drip. 1. The dripping of water from the eaves of a house onto adjacent land. 2. An easement permitting the holder to allow water to drip onto the servient estate. See DRIP RIGHTS; STILLICIDIUM.

eavesdropping. (17c) The act of secretly listening to the private conversation of others without their consent. Cf. BUGGING; WIRETAPPING.

EB. *abbr.* BUREAU OF ECONOMIC AND BUSINESS AFFAIRS.

ebb and flow. (bef. 12c) The coming and going of the tides. • This expression was formerly used to denote the limits of admiralty jurisdiction. The tidewater limitation was abandoned in *The Genesee Chief v. Fitzhugh*, 53 U.S. (12 How.) 443 (1851).

EBIT. *abbr.* See *earnings before interest and taxes* under EARNINGS.

EBITDA. *abbr.* See EARNINGS.

EC. *abbr.* **1.** ETHICAL CONSIDERATION. **2.** European Community. See EUROPEAN UNION.

ecclesia (i-**klee**-z[h]ee-ə), *n.* [Latin fr. Greek *ekklesia* "assembly"] **1.** A place of religious worship. **2.** A Christian assembly; a church.

ecclesiarch (i-**klee**-zee-ahrk), *n.* The ruler of a church.

ecclesiastic (i-klee-zee-**as**-tik), *n.* (17c) A clergyman; a priest; one consecrated to the service of the church.

ecclesiastical (i-klee-zee-**as**-ti-kəl), *adj.* (15c) Of or relating to the church, esp. as an institution. — Also termed *ecclesiastic.*

ecclesiastical authorities. The church's hierarchy, answerable to the Crown, but set apart from the rest of the citizens, responsible for superintending public worship and other religious ceremonies and for administering spiritual counsel and instruction. • In England, the several levels of the clergy are (1) archbishops and bishops, (2) deans and chapters, (3) archdeacons, (4) rural deans, (5) parsons (under whom are included appropriators) and vicars, and (6) curates. Church-wardens, sidesmen, parish clerks, and sextons are also considered types of ecclesiastical authorities because their duties are connected with the church. Cf. *ecclesiastical court* under COURT.

ecclesiastical controversy. A civil claim based on the decision of a religious association's tribunal against one or more members of the association. • If the decision relates solely to matters within the church, such as church governance or questions of faith, secular courts have no jurisdiction to hear what is effectively an appeal. *See Watson v. Jones*, 80 U.S. 679, 728–29 (1871).

ecclesiastical court. See COURT.

ecclesiastical jurisdiction. Jurisdiction over ecclesiastical cases and controversies, such as that exercised by ecclesiastical courts.

ecclesiastical law. 1. The body of law derived largely from canon and civil law and administered by the ecclesiastical courts. **2.** The law governing the doctrine and discipline of a particular church; esp., Anglican canon law. — Also termed *jus ecclesiasticum; law spiritual.* Cf. CANON LAW.

ecclesiastical matter. A matter that concerns church doctrine, creed, or form of worship, or the adoption and enforcement, within a religious association, of laws and regulations to govern the membership, including the power to exclude from such an association those deemed unworthy of membership.

ecclesiastical sentence. The judgment in an ecclesiastical case.

ecclesiastical things. Property (such as buildings and cemeteries) given to a church to support the poor or for any other pious use.

e-check. See CHECK.

ECJ. *abbr.* European Court of Justice.

ECOA. *abbr.* EQUAL CREDIT OPPORTUNITY ACT.

ecological terrorism. See *ecoterrorism* under TERRORISM.

ecology of crime. See *environmental criminology* under CRIMINOLOGY.

e-commerce. (1993) The practice of buying and selling goods and services through online consumer services on the Internet. • The *e*, a shortened form of *electronic*, has become a popular prefix for other terms associated with electronic transactions. See ELECTRONIC TRANSACTION.

E-Commerce Directive. See DIRECTIVE ON CERTAIN ASPECTS OF ELECTRONIC COMMERCE IN THE INTERNAL MARKET.

e-commerce insurance. See INSURANCE.

econometrics (ee-kon-ə-**me**-triks). The branch of economics that expresses economic theory in mathematical terms and that seeks to verify theory through statistical methods.

economic coercion. See COERCION (2).

economic crime. See CRIME.

economic-cure trade embargo. See EMBARGO (3).

economic depreciation. See DEPRECIATION.

Economic Development Administration. A unit in the U.S. Department of Commerce responsible for helping to develop local economies and distressed areas by making grants for public works and development facilities that are designed to reduce persistent unemployment in economically distressed areas. • The agency was created in 1965 by the Public Works and Economic Development Act. — Abbr. EDA.

economic discrimination. (1919) Any form of discrimination within the field of commerce, such as boycotting a particular product or price-fixing. See BOYCOTT; PRICE DISCRIMINATION; PRICE-FIXING.

economic duress. See DURESS.

economic earnings. See *operating earnings* under EARNINGS.

Economic Espionage Act. *Trade secrets.* A 1996 federal statute criminalizing the misappropriation of trade secrets and providing criminal penalties for industrial espionage by or for a foreign entity. ● The Act also applies to one who knowingly receives, purchases, or possesses stolen trade-secret information. 18 USCA §§ 1831–1839. — Sometimes termed *Industrial Espionage Act.*

economic frustration. See *commercial frustration* under FRUSTRATION.

economic goodwill. See GOODWILL.

economic-harm rule. See ECONOMIC-LOSS RULE.

economic indicator. (1903) A statistical measure (such as housing starts) used to describe the state of the economy or to predict its direction. See INDICATOR.

> *lagging economic indicator.* An economic indicator (such as new-home sales) that tends to respond to the direction of the economy. — Often shortened to *lagging indicator.*

> *leading economic indicator.* An economic indicator (such as interest rates) that tends to predict the future direction of the economy. — Often shortened to *leading indicator.*

economic life. The duration of an asset's profitability, usu. shorter than its physical life.

economic loss. (1905) A monetary loss such as lost wages or lost profits. ● The term usu. refers to a type of damages recoverable in a lawsuit. For example, in a products-liability suit, economic loss includes the cost of repair or replacement of defective property, as well as commercial loss for the property's inadequate value and consequent loss of profits or use.

> *consequential economic loss.* Economic loss that proximately results from a defective product and that is beyond direct economic loss. ● Examples include lost profits and loss of goodwill or business reputation.

> *direct economic loss.* Economic loss flowing directly from insufficient product quality. ● The most common type is loss-of-bargain damages — the difference between the actual value of goods accepted and the value they would have had if they had been delivered as promised or warranted.

economic-loss rule. (1976) *Torts.* The principle that a plaintiff cannot sue in tort to recover for purely monetary loss — as opposed to physical injury or property damage — caused by the defendant. ● Many states recognize an exception to this rule when the defendant commits fraud or negligent misrepresentation, or when a special relationship exists between the parties (such as an attorney–client relationship). — Also termed *economic-harm rule; economic-loss doctrine.*

economic obsolescence. See OBSOLESCENCE.

economic-out clause. See MARKET-OUT CLAUSE.

economic-realities test. (1956) A method by which a court determines the true nature of a business transaction or situation by examining the totality of the commercial circumstances. ● Courts often use this test to determine whether a person is an employee or an independent contractor. Factors include whether the alleged employer controls the details of the work and whether taxes are withheld from payments made to the worker.

economic rent. 1. The return gained from an economic resource (such as a worker or land) above the minimum cost of keeping the resource in service. **2.** Rent that yields a fair return on capital and expenses.

Economic Research Service. An agency in the U.S. Department of Agriculture responsible for compiling and analyzing information about domestic and international agricultural developments. — Abbr. ERS.

economic right. (*usu. pl.*) *Copyright.* A legal interest and power that concerns a financial benefit from a work, as distinguished from a moral interest that a creator has in a creation. ● The term is mostly used in civil-law countries that recognize creators' moral rights.

economics. The social science dealing with the production, distribution, and consumption of goods and services.

Economics and Statistics Administration. A unit in the U.S. Department of Commerce responsible for maintaining high-quality standards of statistical reporting in the federal government and for responding to the needs of the Department of Commerce and the rest of the executive branch for statistical information and analysis. ● The unit comprises the Bureau of the Census, the Bureau of Economic Analysis, and STAT-USA. — Abbr. ESA.

economic strike. See STRIKE.

economic-substance doctrine. *Tax.* The principle that a transaction must be treated as a sham for tax purposes if (1) the transaction has no genuine business purpose, and (2) there is no reasonable possibility that it will generate a profit in the absence of tax benefits.

economic substantive due process. See DUE PROCESS.

economic warfare. See WARFARE.

economic unit. *Eminent domain.* In a partial-condemnation case, the property that is used to determine the fair-market value of the portion that is taken by eminent domain. ● The land taken may be a large or small portion of the entire property. To determine how much property to include in an economic unit, three factors are weighed: (1) unity of use, (2) unity of ownership, and (3) contiguity. Of these, the most important is unity of use. See LARGER PARCEL.

economic waste. Overproduction or excessive drilling of oil or gas.

economist. (16c) A professional who studies economics and the economy; a specialist in economics.

economy. (15c) **1.** The management or administration of the wealth and resources of a community (such as a city, state, or country). **2.** The sociopolitical organization of a community's wealth and resources. **3.** Restrained, thrifty, or sparing use of resources; efficiency.

balanced economy. An economy in which the monetary values of imports and exports are equal.

black economy. See SHADOW ECONOMY.

judicial economy. See JUDICIAL ECONOMY.

overheated economy. An economy that, although it has a high level of economic activity, has the capacity to cause interest rates and inflation to rise.

political economy. A social science dealing with the economic problems of government and the relationship between political policies and economic processes.

shadow economy. See SHADOW ECONOMY.

underground economy. See SHADOW ECONOMY.

economy of scale. (*usu. pl.*) A decline in a product's per-unit production cost resulting from increased output, usu. due to increased production facilities; savings resulting from the greater efficiency of large-scale processes.

e contra (ee **kon**-trə). [Latin] On the contrary.

e-contract, *n.* **1.** POINT-AND-CLICK AGREEMENT. **2.** Any type of contract formed in the course of e-commerce by (1) the interaction of two or more individuals using electronic means, such as e-mail, (2) the interaction of an individual with an electronic agent, such as a computer program, or (3) the interaction of at least two electronic agents that are programmed to recognize the existence of a contract. ● Sections 202–17 of the Uniform Computer Information Transactions Act provide rules for the formation, governance, and basic terms of an e-contract. Traditional contract principles and remedies usu. apply to e-contracts. — Also termed *electronic contract.* See ELECTRONIC AGENT.

e-contract, *vb.* To form a binding agreement by means of a computer or other electronic or automated technology.

e converso (ee kən-**vər**-soh). [Latin] Conversely; on the other hand; on the contrary.

ecosabotage. See *ecoterrorism* under TERRORISM.

ecoterrorism. See TERRORISM.

ecovandalism. See *ecoterrorism* under TERRORISM.

ECU. *abbr.* EUROPEAN CURRENCY UNIT.

ecumenical (ek-yə-**men**-ə-kəl), *adj.* (16c) **1.** General; universal. **2.** Interreligious; interdenominational.

E.D. *abbr.* Eastern District, in reference to U.S. judicial districts.

EDA. *abbr.* ECONOMIC DEVELOPMENT ADMINISTRATION.

edge lease. See LEASE.

EDI agreement. *abbr.* Electronic Data Interchange agreement; an agreement that governs the transfer or exchange of data, such as purchase orders, between parties by computer. ● Electronic data transmitted under an EDI agreement is usu. formatted according to an agreed standard, such as the American National Standards Institute ANSI X12 standard or the U.N. EDIFACT standard.

edict (**ee**-dikt), *n.* [fr. Latin *edictum*] (14c) A formal decree, demand, or proclamation issued by the sovereign of a country. ● In some countries, an edict has legal force equivalent to that of a statute. For Roman law edicts, see EDICTUM.

perpetual edict. See *edictum perpetuum* under EDICTUM.

praetorian edict (pri-**tor**-ee-ən). See *edictum praetoris* under EDICTUM.

edictal (ee-**dik**-təl), *adj.* (17c) Of, relating to, consisting of, or pronounced in one or more edicts. — **edictally,** *adv.*

edictal interdict. See INTERDICT (1).

Edicts of Justinian. *Roman law.* Thirteen constitutions or laws of Justinian, appended to the Greek collection of the Novels in the Venetian manuscript. ● The Edicts were confined to administrative matters in the provinces of the Roman Empire. They were not known to the glossators.

edictum (ə-**dik**-təm), *n.* [Latin] *Roman law.* **1.** In imperial Rome, an edict or mandate; an ordinance or law proclaimed by the emperor. ● An edict was a constitution of the emperor acting on his own initiative, differing from a rescript in not being returned in the way of answer; from a decree in not being given in judgment; and from both in not being founded upon solicitation. As an imperial constitution, it had the force of law. **2.** A declaration by a magistrate relevant to his jurisdiction or area of competence; esp., the pronouncement of a magistrate of the principles by which he proposed to act in office. See *edictum annuum;* FORMULA (1). Pl. *edicta.*

edictum aedilicium (ee-**dik**-təm ee-də-**lish**-ee-əm). A curule aedile's edict regarding sales in the public market; esp., an edict giving remedies for sales of defective goods, animals, or slaves. • An aedile could, for instance, declare that sellers would be strictly liable for latent defects in goods, and dictate how dogs and wild animals for sale should be confined to protect the public. — Also written *aedilitium edictum*. Pl. *edicta aedilicia.*

edictum annuum (**an**-yoo-əm). An edict issued by a praetor at the beginning of the one-year term of office. Pl. *edicta annua.*

edictum perpetuum (pər-**pech**-oo-əm). The urban praetor's edict in its permanent form, edited by Julian in A.D. 131 and given legislative force. • This term originally had the narrower sense of the praetors' general edicts as opposed to edicts issued in specific cases. — Also termed *perpetual edict*. Pl. *edicta perpetua.*

edictum praetoris (pri-**tor**-əs). The proclamation issued by a praetor at the start of the year's term, explaining the grounds on which a formula would be granted. — Also termed *praetorian edict*. See *edictum annuum*; FORMULA (1).

edictum provinciale (prə-vin-shee-**ay**-lee). An edict or system of rules for the administration of justice, modeled on edictum praetoris, issued by the provincial governors in the Roman Empire. Pl. *edicta provincialia.*

edictum repentinum (rep-ən-**tı**-nəm). [Latin] *Roman law.* A supplementary edict issued to deal with some emergency. • This term was contrasted with *edictum perpetuum*. Pl. *edicta repentina.*

Edictum Theodorici (thee-ə-də-**rı**-sı). A collection of laws applicable to both Romans and Goths, issued by Theodoric, king of the Ostrogoths, at Rome about A.D. 500, or perhaps by Theodoric III, king of the Visigoths in Gaul about A.D. 460.

edictum tralatitium (tral-ə-**tish**-ee-əm). A praetor's edict that retained all or a principal part of the predecessor's edict, with only such additions as appeared necessary to adapt it to changing social conditions or juristic ideas. • This had become standard practice by the end of the Republic. — Also spelled *edictum tralacticium* (tral-ək-**tish**-ee-əm). Pl. *edicta tralatitia.*

edile (**ee**-dɪl). See AEDILE.

editorial privilege. See *journalist's privilege* (2) under PRIVILEGE (3).

editus (**ed**-ə-təs), *adj. Hist.* **1.** (Of a statute or rule) enacted; promulgated. **2.** (Of a child) born; brought forth.

Edmunds–Tucker Act. An 1882 federal law enacted to punish polygamy. 48 USCA § 1480a. — Sometimes shortened to *Edmunds Act.*

educational expense. See EXPENSE.

educational institution. 1. A school, seminary, college, university, or other educational facility, though not necessarily a chartered institution. **2.** As used in a zoning ordinance, all buildings and grounds necessary to accomplish the full scope of educational instruction, including those things essential to mental, moral, and physical development.

educational neglect. See NEGLECT.

educational trust. See TRUST.

education individual retirement account. See INDIVIDUAL RETIREMENT ACCOUNT.

EEC. *abbr.* European Economic Community. See EUROPEAN UNION.

EEOC. *abbr.* EQUAL EMPLOYMENT OPPORTUNITY COMMISSION.

EEZ. *abbr.* EXCLUSIVE ECONOMIC ZONE.

effect, *n.* (14c) **1.** Something produced by an agent or cause; a result, outcome, or consequence. **2.** The result that an instrument between parties will produce on their relative rights, or that a statute will produce on existing law, as discovered from the language used, the forms employed, or other materials for construing it.

effect, *vb.* (16c) To bring about; to make happen <the improper notice did not effect a timely appeal>.

effective, *adj.* (14c) **1.** (Of a statute, order, contract, etc.) in operation at a given time <effective June 1>. • A statute, order, or contract is often said to be effective beginning (and perhaps ending) at a designated time. **2.** Performing within the range of normal and expected standards <effective counsel>. **3.** Productive; achieving a result <effective cause>.

effective assignment. See ASSIGNMENT (2).

effective assistance of counsel. See ASSISTANCE OF COUNSEL.

effective cause. See *immediate cause* under CAUSE (1).

effective date. (1909) The date on which a statute, contract, insurance policy, or other such instrument becomes enforceable or otherwise takes effect. • This date sometimes differs from the date on which the instrument was enacted or signed.

effective filing date. See DATE.

effective possession. See *constructive possession* under POSSESSION.

effective rate. See INTEREST RATE.

effective tax rate. See *average tax rate* under TAX RATE.

effective vote. See VOTE (1).

effects, *n. pl.* (17c) Movable property; goods <personal effects>.

personal effects. (1818) Items of a personal character; esp., personal property owned by a decedent at the time of death.

effects doctrine. See AFFECTS DOCTRINE.

efficient adequate cause. See *proximate cause* under CAUSE (1).

efficient breach. See BREACH OF CONTRACT.

efficient-breach theory. (1980) *Contracts.* The view that a party should be allowed to breach a contract and pay damages, if doing so would be more economically efficient than performing under the contract. • This relatively modern theory stems from the law-and-economics movement. See BREACH OF CONTRACT.

efficient cause. See *proximate cause* under CAUSE (1).

efficient intervening cause. See *intervening cause* under CAUSE (1).

efficient proximate cause. See *proximate cause* under CAUSE (1).

effigy (**ef**-ə-jee), *n.* (16c) A figure, image, or other representation; esp., a crude representation of someone who is disliked. • Effigies are sometimes hanged, burned, or otherwise abused to express public disapproval or ridicule.

effluent (**ef**-loo-ənt), *n.* (1859) Liquid waste that is discharged into a river, lake, or other body of water.

effluxion of time (i-**fluk**-shən). (17c) The expiration of a lease term resulting from the passage of time rather than from a specific action or event. — Also termed *efflux of time.*

effraction (ə-**frak**-shən). (19c) *Archaic.* A breach made by the use of force; BURGLARY (1).

effractor (i-**frak**-tər). [Latin] *Hist.* One who breaks through; a burglar. Pl. **effractors,** *effractores* (ef-rak-**tor**-eez). See HOUSEBREAKING.

EFT. *abbr.* Electronic funds transfer. See FUNDS TRANSFER.

e.g. *abbr.* [Latin *exempli gratia*] (17c) For example <an intentional tort, e.g., battery or false imprisonment>. Cf. I.E.

egg donation. *Family law.* A type of assisted-reproductive therapy in which eggs are removed from one woman and transplanted into the uterus of another woman who carries and delivers the child. • In egg donation, the egg is usu. fertilized in vitro. See IN VITRO FERTILIZATION; ASSISTED-REPRODUCTIVE TECHNOLOGY.

eggshell-skull rule. (1961) *Torts.* The principle that a defendant is liable for a plaintiff's unforeseeable and uncommon reactions to the defendant's negligent or intentional act. • Under this rule, for example, if one person negligently scrapes another who turns out to be a hemophiliac, the negligent defendant is liable for the full extent of the plaintiff's injuries even though the harm to another plaintiff would have been minor. — Also termed *eggshell-plaintiff rule; thin-skull rule; special-sensitivity rule; old-soldier's rule.*

egregious (i-**gree**-jəs), *adj.* (16c) Extremely or remarkably bad; flagrant <the defendant's egregious behavior>.

egress (**ee**-gres). (16c) **1.** The act of going out or leaving. **2.** The right or ability to leave; a way of exit. Cf. INGRESS.

EIC. *abbr.* See *earned-income credit* under TAX CREDIT.

eight-corners rule. *Insurance.* The principle that a liability insurer's duty to defend its insured — generally triggered if the plaintiff's claims against the insured are within the policy's coverage — is assessed by reviewing the claims asserted in the plaintiff's complaint, without reference to matters outside the four corners of the complaint plus the four corners of the policy. — Also termed *allegations-of-the-complaint rule.* Cf. FOUR-CORNERS RULE.

1891 Copyright Amendment Act. See CHACE ACT.

Eighteenth Amendment. The constitutional amendment — ratified in 1919 and repealed by the 21st Amendment in 1933 — that prohibited the manufacture, sale, transportation, and possession of alcoholic beverages in the United States. See PROHIBITION (3).

Eighth Amendment. The constitutional amendment, ratified as part of the Bill of Rights in 1791, prohibiting excessive bail, excessive fines, and cruel and unusual punishment.

eight-hour law. A law that sets eight hours as the standard workday for some jobs and that usu. requires a higher pay rate for work beyond eight hours. • One example is the federal Fair Labor Standards Act. See WAGE-AND-HOUR LAW.

8-K. An SEC form that a registered corporation must file if a material event affecting its financial condition occurs between the due dates for regular SEC filings. — Also termed *Form 8-K.* Cf. 10-K.

83(b) election. *Tax.* An employee's choice to treat an employer's grant of unvested property, usu. stock, as being vested immediately and as currently taxable on the amount the employer paid for it. • The alternative is for the employee to wait until the property vests and pay taxes on its value at that time. An 83(b) election is typically used when the property is expected to have a dramatic increase in value before the employee's interest in it vests. IRC (26 USCA) § 83(b).

EIN. *abbr.* See TAX-IDENTIFICATION NUMBER.

einetia. See EISNETIA.

EIR. *abbr.* Environmental-impact report. See ENVIRONMENTAL-IMPACT STATEMENT.

eire (air), *n. Hist.* A journey; route; circuit. See EYRE.

EIS. *abbr.* ENVIRONMENTAL-IMPACT STATEMENT.

eisnetia (ɪz-**nee**-shee-ə), *n.* [Law Latin] The share of the oldest son; the portion of an estate acquired by primogeniture. — Also spelled *einetia.* Cf. ESNECY.

either-or order. See *alternative order* under ORDER (8).

eiusdem generis. See EJUSDEM GENERIS.

eject, *vb.* (15c) **1.** To cast or throw out. **2.** To oust or dispossess; to put or turn out of possession. **3.** To expel or thrust out forcibly (e.g., disorderly patrons). — **ejector,** *vb.*

ejection, *n.* (16c) **1.** An expulsion by action of law or by actual or threatened physical force. See OUSTER. **2.** EJECTMENT (2).

ejectment. (16c) **1.** The ejection of an owner or occupier from property. **2.** A legal action by which a person wrongfully ejected from property seeks to recover possession, damages, and costs. **3.** The writ by which such an action is begun. ● The essential allegations in an action for ejectment are that (1) the plaintiff has title to the land, (2) the plaintiff has been wrongfully dispossessed or ousted, and (3) the plaintiff has suffered damages. — Also termed *action of ejectment*; *action for the recovery of land*; *ejection.* See FORCIBLE ENTRY AND DETAINER. Cf. EVICTION; OUSTER.

    equitable ejectment. (1820) A proceeding brought to enforce specific performance of a contract for the sale of land and for other purposes. ● Though in the form of an ejectment action, this proceeding is in reality a substitute for a bill in equity.

    justice ejectment. (1900) A statutory proceeding to evict a tenant who has held over after termination of the lease or breach of its conditions.

ejectment bill. (18c) *Equity practice.* A bill in equity brought to recover real property and an accounting of rents and profits, without setting out a distinct ground of equity jurisdiction (and thus demurrable).

ejector, *n.* (17c) One who ejects, puts out, or dispossesses another.

    casual ejector. The nominal defendant in an ejectment action who, under a legal fiction, is supposed to come casually or by accident upon the premises and to eject the lawful possessor.

ejectum (i-**jek**-təm), *n.* Something that is cast out, esp. by the sea. See FLOTSAM. Cf. JETSAM; LAGAN (1); WAVESON.

ejuration (ej-ə-**ray**-shən). The renouncing or resigning of one's place.

ejusdem generis (ee-**jəs**-dəm **jen**-ə-ris *also* ee-**joos**- *or* ee-**yoos**-). [Latin "of the same kind or class"] (17c) **1.** A canon of construction holding that when a general word or phrase follows a list of specifics, the general word or phrase will be interpreted to include only items of the same class as those listed. ● For example, in the phrase *horses, cattle, sheep, pigs, goats, or any other farm animals*, the general language *or any other farm animals* — despite its seeming breadth — would probably be held to include only four-legged, hoofed mammals typically found on farms, and thus would exclude chickens. — Also termed *Lord Tenterden's rule.* Cf. EXPRESSIO UNIUS EST EXCLUSIO ALTERIUS; NOSCITUR A SOCIIS; RULE OF RANK. **2.** Loosely, NOSCITUR A SOCIIS.

Elastic Clause. See NECESSARY AND PROPER CLAUSE.

elbow clerk. See CLERK (5).

elder abuse. See *abuse of the elderly* under ABUSE.

Elder Brethren. A distinguished body of men elected as masters of Trinity House, an institution incorporated in the reign of Henry VIII and charged with many duties in marine affairs, such as superintending lighthouses. ● The full title of the corporation is Elder Brethren of the Holy and Undivided Trinity.

elder law. (1986) The field of law dealing with the elderly, including such issues as estate planning, retirement benefits, social security, age discrimination, and healthcare.

elder title. A title of earlier date but one that becomes operative simultaneously with, and prevails over, a title of newer origin.

elected domicile. See DOMICILE.

electee. 1. A person chosen or elected. **2.** A person to whom the law gives a choice about status.

electing small-business trust. See TRUST (3).

election, *n.* (13c) **1.** The exercise of a choice; esp., the act of choosing from several possible rights or remedies in a way that precludes the use of other rights or remedies <the taxpayers' election to file jointly instead of separately>. See ELECTION OF REMEDIES. **2.** The doctrine by which a person is compelled to choose between accepting a benefit under a legal instrument and retaining some property right to which the person is already entitled; an obligation imposed on a party to choose between alternative rights or claims, so that the party is entitled to enjoy only one <the prevailing plaintiff was put to an election between out-of-pocket damages and lost profits>. — Also termed *equitable election.* See RIGHT OF ELECTION. **3.** The process of selecting a person to occupy an office (usu. a public office), membership, award, or other title or status <the 2004 congressional election>.

Cf. *two-round voting* under VOTING. — **elect,** *vb.* — **elective,** *adj.*

by-election. An election specially held to fill a vacant post. — Also spelled *bye-election*. Cf. *general election.*

election at large. An election in which a public official is selected from a major election district rather than from a subdivision of the larger unit. — Also termed *at-large election.*

free election. An election in which the political system and processes guarantee that each voter will be allowed to vote according to conscience.

general election. 1. An election that occurs at a regular interval of time. — Also termed *regular election.* **2.** An election for all seats, as contrasted with a by-election. Cf. *by-election.*

municipal election. The election of municipal officers.

off-year election. An election conducted at a time other than the presidential election year.

popular election. An election by people as a whole, rather than by a select group.

primary election. A preliminary election in which a political party's registered voters nominate the candidate who will run in the general election. — Often shortened to *primary.*

recall election. An election in which voters have the opportunity to remove a public official from office.

regular election. See *general election.*

representation election. An election held by the National Labor Relations Board to decide whether a certain union will represent employees in a bargaining unit. See BARGAINING UNIT.

runoff election. An election held after a general election, in which the two candidates who received the most votes — neither of whom received a majority — run against each other so that the winner can be determined. Cf. *two-round voting* under VOTING.

special election. An election that occurs in an interim between general elections, usu. to fill a sudden vacancy in office. Cf. *by-election.*

4. *Patents.* A patent applicant's choice of a single invention to continue prosecuting under the original application, after an examiner has required a restriction. See RESTRICTION (4).

election of species. A patent applicant's choice of one alternative over others after an examiner determines that a generic claim is not allowable.

election, doctrine of. A doctrine holding that when a person has contracted with an agent without knowing of the agency and later learns of the principal's identity, the person may enforce the contract against either the agent or the principal, but not both. See ELECTION (1).

election, estoppel by. See *estoppel by election* under ESTOPPEL.

election board. 1. A board of inspectors or commissioners appointed for each election precinct to determine voter qualification, to supervise the polling, and often to ascertain and report the results. **2.** A local agency charged with the conduct of elections.

election by spouse. See RIGHT OF ELECTION.

election contest. A challenge by an election's loser against the winner, calling for an analysis of the election returns, which may include reviewing voter qualifications or re-counting the ballots.

election district. See DISTRICT.

election dower. See DOWER.

election fraud. (18c) Illegal conduct committed in an election, usu. in the form of fraudulent voting. • Examples include voting twice, voting under another person's name (usu. a deceased person), or voting while ineligible.

election judge. 1. A person appointed to supervise an election at the precinct level; a local representative of an election board. **2.** *English law.* One of two puisne judges of the Queen's Bench Division of the High Court selected to try election petitions.

election of remedies. (18c) **1.** A claimant's act of choosing between two or more concurrent but inconsistent remedies based on a single set of facts. **2.** The affirmative defense barring a litigant from pursuing a remedy inconsistent with another remedy already pursued, when that other remedy has given the litigant an advantage over, or has damaged, the opposing party. • This doctrine has largely fallen into disrepute and is now rarely applied. **3.** The affirmative defense that a claimant cannot simultaneously recover damages based on two different liability findings if the injury is the same for both claims, thus creating a double recovery. Cf. *alternative relief* under RELIEF (3).

election of species. See ELECTION (4).

election returns. The report made to the board of canvassers or the election board, by those charged with tallying votes, of the number of votes cast for a particular candidate or proposition.

elective franchise. See FRANCHISE (1).

elective office. An office that is filled by popular election rather than by appointment.

elective share. (1931) *Wills & estates.* The percentage of a deceased spouse's estate, set by statute, that a surviving spouse (or sometimes a child) may choose to receive instead of taking under a will or in the event of being unjustifiably disinherited. — Also termed *forced share*; *statutory share*; *statutory forced share*. See RIGHT OF ELECTION.

elector. (15c) **1.** A member of the electoral college chosen to elect the U.S. President and Vice President. — Also termed *presidential elector*. **2.** A voter.

qualified elector. A legal voter; a person who meets the voting requirements for age, residency, and registration and who has the present right to vote in an election. See VOTER.

3. A person who chooses between alternative rights or claims. **4.** *Hist.* The title of certain German princes who had a voice in electing the Holy Roman Emperors. • This office sometimes became hereditary and was connected with territorial possessions.

electoral college. (*often cap.*) (17c) The body of electors chosen from each state to formally elect the U.S. President and Vice President by casting votes based on the popular vote.

electoral process. (1851) **1.** The method by which a person is elected to public office in a democratic society. **2.** The taking and counting of votes.

electric chair. (1889) A chair that is wired so that electrodes can be fastened to a condemned person's body and a lethal charge passed through the body for the purpose of carrying out a death penalty. • The electric chair was first used in 1890 at the Auburn State Prison in New York.

electronic agent. Any electronic or automated means, such as a computer program, that can independently initiate or respond to an action or message without a human's review.

electronic cash. See *e-money* under MONEY.

electronic chattel paper. See CHATTEL PAPER.

electronic check. See *e-check* under CHECK.

electronic-check conversion. In a discrete electronic-funds transfer, the process by which a paper check is used as the source of information for the check number, account number, and bank-routing number. • The check itself is not considered the method of payment. See *e-check* under CHECK.

Electronic Commerce Directive. See DIRECTIVE ON CERTAIN ASPECTS OF ELECTRONIC COMMERCE IN THE INTERNAL MARKET.

Electronic Communications Privacy Act. A federal statute that limits the circumstances under which the federal and state government may gain access to oral, wire, and electronic communications. 18 USCA § 2510.

electronic contract. See E-CONTRACT.

Electronic Data Interchange agreement. See EDI AGREEMENT.

electronic funds transfer. See FUNDS TRANSFER.

electronic currency. See *e-money* under MONEY.

electronic signature. See SIGNATURE.

Electronic Signatures in Global and National Commerce Act. See E-SIGN ACT.

electronic surveillance. 1. See EAVESDROPPING. **2.** See WIRETAPPING.

electronic transaction. (1975) A transaction formed by electronic messages in which the messages of one or both parties will not be reviewed by an individual as an expected step in forming a contract. UCC § 2A-102(a)(16).

eleemosynae (el-ə-**mos**-ə-nee), *n. pl. Eccles. law.* Possessions belonging to the church.

eleemosynaria (el-ə-mos-ə-**nair**-ee-ə), *n. Hist.* **1.** The place in a religious house or church where the common alms were deposited, to be distributed to the poor by the almoner. **2.** The office of almoner.

eleemosynarius (el-ə-mos-ə-**nair**-ee-əs), *n.* [Law Latin] *Hist.* **1.** An almoner, or chief officer, who received the eleemosynary rents and gifts and distributed them to pious and charitable uses. **2.** The name of an officer (Lord Almoner) of the English kings, in former times, who distributed the royal alms or bounty.

eleemosynary (el-ə-**mos**-ə-ner-ee), *adj.* (17c) Of, relating to, or assisted by charity; not-for-profit <an eleemosynary institution>.

eleemosynary corporation. See *charitable corporation* under CORPORATION.

eleemosynary defense. See *charitable immunity* under IMMUNITY (2).

elegit (ə-**lee**-jit). [Latin "he has chosen"] (16c) *Hist.* A writ of execution (first given by 13 Edw., ch. 18) either upon a judgment for a debt or damages or upon the forfeiture of a recognizance taken in the king's court. • Under it, the defendant's goods and chattels were appraised and, except for plow beasts, delivered to the plaintiff to satisfy the debt. If the goods were not sufficient to pay the debt, then the portion of the defendant's freehold lands held at the time of judgment was also delivered to the plaintiff, to hold until the debt was satisfied out of rents and profits or until the defendant's interest expired. During this period the plaintiff was called *tenant by elegit*, and the estate an *estate by elegit*. The writ was abolished in England in 1956, and it is no longer used anywhere in the United States.

element. (13c) **1.** A constituent part of a claim that must be proved for the claim to succeed <Burke failed to prove the element of proximate cause in prosecuting his negligence claim>. **2.** *Patents.* A discretely claimed component of a patent claim. • For a prior-art reference to anticipate a claim, it must teach each and every claim element. To recover for patent infringement, the plaintiff must prove that the accused product infringes every element of at least one claim, either literally or under the doctrine of equivalents. — Also termed (in sense 2) *limitation*. See DOCTRINE OF EQUIVALENTS.

elemental fact. See *ultimate fact* under FACT.

elements of crime. (1909) The constituent parts of a crime — usu. consisting of the actus reus, mens rea, and causation — that the prosecution must prove to sustain a conviction. • The term is more broadly defined by the Model Penal Code in § 1.13(9) to refer to each component of the actus reus, causation, the mens rea, any grading factors, and the negative of any defense.

Eleventh Amendment. The constitutional amendment, ratified in 1795, prohibiting a federal court from hearing an action against a state by a person who is not a citizen of that state. See *sovereign immunity* under IMMUNITY (1).

eligible, *adj.* (15c) Fit and proper to be selected or to receive a benefit; legally qualified for an office, privilege, or status. — **eligibility,** *n.*

elimination. *Hist.* The act of banishing or turning out of doors; rejection.

elinguation (ee-ling-**gway**-shən). *Hist.* The punishment of cutting out a person's tongue. — **elinguate,** *vb.*

elisor (i-**lɪ**-zər). (17c) A person appointed by a court to assemble a jury, serve a writ, or perform other duties of the sheriff or coroner if either is disqualified. — Also spelled *eslisor.*

Elkins Act. A 1903 federal law that strengthened the Interstate Commerce Act by prohibiting rebates and other forms of preferential treatment to large carriers. 49 USCA §§ 41–43 (superseded).

elogium (i-**loh**-jee-əm), *n. Civil law.* **1.** A will or testament. **2.** A clause or provision in a will or testament.

eloign (i-**loyn**), *vb.* (15c) **1.** To remove (a person or property) from a court's or sheriff's jurisdiction. **2.** To remove to a distance; conceal. — Also spelled *eloin.* — **eloigner,** *n.*

eloignment (i-**loyn**-mənt), *n.* (17c) The getting of a thing or person out of the way, or removing it to a distance, so as to be out of reach.

elope, *vb.* (17c) **1.** *Archaic.* To run away; escape. **2.** *Archaic.* To abandon one's husband and run away with a lover. **3.** To run away secretly for the purpose of getting married, often without parental consent. — **elopement,** *n.*

elsewhere, *adv.* (bef. 12c) In another place. • In shipping articles, this term, following the designation of the port of destination, must be construed either as void for uncertainty or as subordinate to the principal voyage stated in the preceding words.

eluviation (i-loo-vee-**ay**-shən). (1899) Movement of soil caused by excessive water in the soil.

e-mail, *n.* (1982) A communication exchanged between people by computer, through either a local area network or the Internet. — Also spelled *email.* — **e-mail,** *vb.*

emanation. (16c) **1.** The act of coming or flowing forth from something. **2.** That which flows or comes forth from something; an effluence.

emancipate, *vb.* (17c) **1.** To set free from legal, social, or political restraint; esp., to free from slavery or bondage. **2.** To release (a child) from the control, support, and responsibility of a parent or guardian. — **emancipative, emancipatory,** *adj.* — **emancipator,** *n.*

emancipated minor. See MINOR.

emancipation. (17c) **1.** The act by which one who was under another's power and control is freed. **2.** A surrender and renunciation of the correlative rights and duties concerning the care, custody, and earnings of a child; the act by which a parent (historically a father) frees a child and gives the child the right to his or her own earnings. • This act also frees the parent from all legal obligations of support. Emancipation may take place by agreement between the parent and child, by operation of law (as when the parent abandons or fails to support the child), or when the child gets legally married or enters the armed forces. **3.** *Roman law.* The enfranchisement of a son by his father, accomplished through the formality of an imaginary sale. • Justinian substituted the simpler proceeding of a manumission before a magistrate. — Also termed (in sense 3) *emancipatio.* Cf. MANCIPATION.

> *constructive emancipation.* Emancipation by law, as opposed to a voluntary act of the parent. • Constructive emancipation may occur in several ways, as by (1) conduct of the parent that is inconsistent with the performance of parental duties, (2) marriage of the child, or (3) child's service in the armed forces.

> *partial emancipation.* Emancipation that frees a child for only a part of the period of minority, or from only a part of the parent's rights, or for only some purposes.

emancipation act. See MARRIED WOMEN'S PROPERTY ACTS.

Emancipation Proclamation. An executive proclamation, issued by President Abraham Lincoln on January 1, 1863, declaring that all persons held in slavery in designated states and districts were freed.

embargo, *n.* (16c) **1.** A government's wartime or peacetime detention of an offending nation's private ships found in the ports of the aggrieved nation <the President called off the embargo of Iraq's ships after the war ended>. — Also spelled *imbargo*. — Also termed *hostile embargo*. **2.** A nation's detention of all ships in its own ports, including its own, to promote safety and to preclude transportation to an offending nation <the embargo of all U.S. ships traveling to Iraq remained in effect until hostilities subsided>. — Also termed *civil embargo*. **3.** The unilateral or collective restrictions on the import or export of goods, materials, capital, or services into or from a specific country or group of countries for political or security reasons <for a time, the industrialized nations placed an embargo on all goods from Libya>. — Also termed *trade embargo*; *economic-cure trade embargo*. **4.** The conscription of private property for governmental use, such as to transport troops <the Army's embargo of the company jet to fly General White to Washington>. **5.** A temporary prohibition on disclosure <the embargo on the press release expired at 11:59 p.m.>. — **embargo,** *vb.*

embassador. See AMBASSADOR.

embassy. (1534) **1.** The building in which a diplomatic body is located; esp., the residence of the ambassador. **2.** A body of diplomatic representatives headed by an ambassador; a diplomatic mission on the ambassadorial level. **3.** The mission, business, and function of an ambassador. Cf. LEGATION.

Ember Days. *Eccles. law.* The days — which the ancient church fathers called *quatuor tempora jejunii* — that are observed on the Wednesday, Friday, and Saturday following (1) Quadragesima Sunday (the first Sunday in Lent), (2) Whitsuntide, or Holyrood Day, in September, and (3) St. Lucy's day, about the middle of December. ● Almanacs refer to the weeks in which these days fall as *Ember Weeks*; they are now chiefly noticed because, by tradition, the Sundays following Ember Days are used to ordain priests and deacons, although the canon law allows bishops to ordain on any Sunday or holiday.

embezzlement, *n.* (15c) The fraudulent taking of personal property with which one has been entrusted, esp. as a fiduciary. ● The criminal intent for embezzlement — unlike larceny and false pretenses — arises after taking possession (not before or during the taking). — Also termed *defalcation*; *peculation*. See LARCENY; FALSE PRETENSES. — **embezzle,** *vb.* — **embezzler,** *n.*

emblem. (15c) **1.** A flag, armorial bearing, or other symbol of a country, organization, or movement. **2.** Loosely, something that is used to symbolize something else.

emblements (**em**-blə-mənts). (15c) **1.** The growing crop annually produced by labor, as opposed to a crop occurring naturally. ● Emblements are considered personal property that the executor or administrator of a deceased tenant may harvest and take regardless of who may have since occupied the land. — Also termed *fructus industriales*. **2.** The tenant's right to harvest and take away such crops after the tenancy has ended.

embodied technology. *Intellectual property.* Know-how or knowledge that is manifest in products and equipment, including software. Cf. DISEMBODIED TECHNOLOGY.

embodiment. *Patents.* **1.** The tangible manifestation of an invention. **2.** The method for using this tangible form. **3.** The part of a patent application or patent that describes a concrete manifestation of the invention. ● Embodiments are less common in software or process patents than in manufacturing-related patents.

embossed seal. See NOTARY SEAL.

embrace, *vb.* To attempt to influence (a judge or juror) by corruption, or to behave in a way that might have a corrupting influence; to engage in embracery.

embracee (em-bray-**see**). The bribe-taker in the offense of embracery.

embracer (im-**brays**-ər). [fr. Old French *embraseor* "one who kindles or instigates," fr. *embraser* "to set fire to"] (15c) The bribe-giver in the offense of embracery; one who attempts to influence a judge or a juror by means of corruption. — Also spelled *embraceor*.

embracery (im-**brays**-ə-ree), *n.* (15c) The attempt to corrupt or wrongfully influence a judge or juror, esp. by threats or bribery. — Also spelled *imbracery*. — Also termed *jury-tampering*; *laboring a jury*. Cf. JURY-FIXING; JURY-PACKING.

embryo (**em**-bree-oh). A developing but unborn or unhatched animal; esp., an unborn human from conception until the development of organs (i.e., until about the eighth week of pregnancy). Cf. FETUS; ZYGOTE.

embryo formatus (for-**may**-təs). *Eccles. law.* A human embryo organized into human shape and endowed with a soul. ● Though rejected in the early doctrine of the Christian church, the distinction between the embryo *formatus* and *informatus* was accepted by Gratian (regarded as the founder of canon law) in his *Decretum* (ca. 1140), in which he said that abortion is not murder if the fetus has not yet been infused with a soul. Though he did not specify the time of formation or animation, by the 16th century canonists accepted that the time of formation and animation was the 40th day after conception for the male fetus and the 80th day for the female. — Also termed *embryo animatus*.

embryo informatus (in-for-**may**-təs). *Eccles. law.* A human embryo before it has been endowed with a soul. — Also termed *embryo inanimatus.*

embryo adoption. See ADOPTION.

emend (i-**mend**), *vb.* (15c) To correct or revise; esp., to edit or change (a text).

emendation (ee-men-**day**-shən). (16c) **1.** Correction or revision, esp. of a text. **2.** *Hist.* The correction of an error or wrongdoing; atonement for a criminal offense, esp. by the payment of money. ● As criminal law developed over time, emendation by payment of *wer* or *wite* gradually faded away and was replaced by harsher punishments.

emergency circumstances. See *exigent circumstances* under CIRCUMSTANCE.

Emergency Court of Appeals. *Hist.* A temporary court, established during World War II, whose purpose was to review wage- and price-control matters. ● The court was created in 1942 and abolished in 1962. Cf. TEMPORARY EMERGENCY COURT OF APPEALS.

emergency doctrine. (1929) **1.** A legal principle exempting a person from the ordinary standard of reasonable care if that person acted instinctively to meet a sudden and urgent need for aid. — Also termed *imminent-peril doctrine*; *sudden-emergency doctrine*; *sudden-peril doctrine*; *sudden-peril rule.* **2.** A legal principle by which consent to medical treatment in a dire situation is inferred when neither the patient nor a responsible party can consent but a reasonable person would do so. — Also termed (in sense 2) *emergency-treatment doctrine.* Cf. GOOD SAMARITAN DOCTRINE; RESCUE DOCTRINE. **3.** The principle that a police officer may conduct a search without a warrant if the officer has probable cause and reasonably believes that immediate action is needed to protect life or property. — Also termed *emergency exception.* See *exigent circumstances* under CIRCUMSTANCE.

emergency-employment doctrine. The principle that an employee may enlist another's help in dealing with an emergency that falls within the scope of the employee's duties and that could not be overcome without the assistance of the other person.

emergency exception. See EMERGENCY DOCTRINE (3).

emergency jurisdiction. See JURISDICTION.

Emergency Preparedness and Response Directorate. The former division of the U.S. Department of Homeland Security responsible for coordinating relief and recovery efforts and for developing and coordinating plans to prevent terrorism and to minimize risks of danger from natural disasters. ● The Directorate included the Federal Emergency Management Agency and also coordinated efforts with the Strategic National Stockpile and the National Disaster Medical System from the Department of Health and Human Services, the Nuclear Incident Response Team from the Department of Energy, the Domestic Emergency Support Teams from the Department of Justice, the National Domestic Preparedness Office of the Federal Bureau of Investigation, and state and local emergency responders. It was abolished in July 2005.— Abbr. EPR.

emergency protective order. See PROTECTIVE ORDER.

emergency search. See SEARCH.

emergency-treatment doctrine. See EMERGENCY DOCTRINE (2).

emerita. See EMERITUS.

emeritus. (18c) An honorary title conferred on a former officer or professor who has honorably retired, usu. after serving for an extended period well beyond the norm. ● The term is loosely used as an adjective meaning "honored," but it is not a synonym for "former," "retired," or "immediate past" (as in "immediate past president"). See HONORARY. Pl. **emeriti.** Fem. **emerita.** Fem. pl. **emeritae.**

emigrant (**em**-ə-grənt), *n.* (18c) One who leaves his or her country for any reason with the intent to establish a permanent residence elsewhere. Cf. IMMIGRANT.

emigrant agent. See AGENT (2).

emigration (em-ə-**gray**-shən), *n.* (17c) The act of leaving a country with the intent not to return and to reside elsewhere. Cf. IMMIGRATION. — **emigrate,** *vb.*

emigré (**em**-ə-gray *or* em-ə-**gray**), *n.* [French] (18c) One who is forced to leave his or her country for political reasons. — Also spelled *émigré.*

eminence (**em**-ə-nənts). (17c) (*usu. cap.*) *Eccles. law.* An honorary title given to cardinals of the Roman Catholic Church. ● Until the pontificate of Urban VIII, cardinals were called *illustrissimi* and *reverendissimi.*

eminent domain. (18c) The inherent power of a governmental entity to take privately owned property, esp. land, and convert it to public use, subject to reasonable compensation for the taking. — Also (rarely) termed *compulsory purchase*; (in Scots law) *compulsory surrender.* See CONDEMNATION (2); EXPROPRIATION; TAKING (2).

Eminent Domain Clause. The Fifth Amendment provision providing that private property cannot be taken for public use without just compensation. See TAKINGS CLAUSE.

emissary. (17c) One sent on a special mission as another's agent or representative, esp. to promote a cause or to gain information.

emit, *vb.* (16c) **1.** To give off or discharge into the air <emit light>. **2.** To issue with authority <emit a new series of currency>. — **emission,** *n.*

emolument (i-**mol**-yə-mənt), *n.* (15c) (*usu. pl.*) Any advantage, profit, or gain received as a result of one's employment or one's holding of office.

Emoluments Clause. (1991) **1.** The clause of the United States Constitution preventing members of Congress from continuing to serve in Congress after accepting an appointment to another federal office, and also prohibiting such an appointment if the office was created or its emoluments increased while the Senator or Representative served in Congress. U.S. Const. art. I, § 6, cl. 2. — Also written *Emolument Clause.* **2.** FOREIGN EMOLUMENTS CLAUSE.

e-money. See MONEY.

emotional abuse. See ABUSE.

emotional distress. (1933) A highly unpleasant mental reaction (such as anguish, grief, fright, humiliation, or fury) that results from another person's conduct; emotional pain and suffering. • Emotional distress, when severe enough, can form a basis for the recovery of tort damages. — Also termed *emotional harm; mental anguish; mental distress; mental suffering.* See INTENTIONAL INFLICTION OF EMOTIONAL DISTRESS; NEGLIGENT INFLICTION OF EMOTIONAL DISTRESS. Cf. *mental cruelty* under CRUELTY.

emotional harm. See EMOTIONAL DISTRESS.

emotional incapacity. 1. The inability to control one's emotions or express appropriate emotions because of a mental disorder. **2.** *Hist. Evidence.* (Of a witness) hostility or partiality rooted in bias, corruption, or interest. • At common law, an interested witness was not competent to testify on grounds of emotional incapacity. See *State v. Craft,* 41 So. 550, 551 (La. 1906).

emotional insanity. See INSANITY.

empanel, *vb.* (15c) To swear in (a jury) to try an issue or case. — Also spelled *impanel.* — **empanelment, empaneling,** *n.*

empaneled jury. See JURY

emperor. (13c) **1.** The title of the sovereign ruler of an empire. **2.** The chief of a confederation of states of which kings are members. • The rulers of the Roman world adopted the designation *emperor* after the fall of the republic. The title was later assumed by those — including Napoleon — who claimed to be their successors in the Holy Roman Empire. The sovereigns of Japan and Morocco are often called *emperors,* as were, in Western speech, the former sovereigns of Turkey and China. The title denotes a power and dignity superior to that of a king. It appears to be the appropriate style of the executive head of a federal government constructed on the monarchial principle and comprising several distinct kingdoms or other quasi-sovereign states, as with the German empire from 1871 to 1918.

emphasis added. (1945) A citation signal indicating that the writer quoting another's words has italicized or otherwise emphasized some of them. — Also termed *emphasis supplied.*

emphyteusis (em-fi-**t[y]oo**-sis), *n.* [Greek "implanting"] (16c) *Greek, Roman & civil law.* A contract by which one person delivered to another (the *emphyteuta*) a tract of land, either in perpetuity or for a long period of time, in exchange for the obligation to cultivate the land and to pay annual rental. • In Roman law, the land was state-owned (*ager vectigalis*). In the 5th century, *emphyteusis* was officially recognized as distinct from ownership or a lease. The land's lessee or tenant, called an *emphyteuta,* had to bear any burdens imposed on the land. Although the *emphyteusis* was alienable, the owner had to consent to the sale. Unlike a usufruct, *emphyteusis* did not terminate with the death of the *emphyteuta.* Perpetual *emphyteusis* was abolished in the 18th century.

emphyteutic (em-fi-**t[y]oo**-tik), *adj.* [Latin] (17c) *Civil law.* Founded on, growing out of, or having the character of an *emphyteusis;* held under an *emphyteusis.*

empire. (14c) The jurisdiction of an emperor; the region over which an emperor's dominion extends.

empirical (em-**pir**-i-kəl), *adj.* (16c) Of, relating to, or based on experience, experiment, or observation <the expert's theory was not supported by empirical data>. — Also termed *empiric.*

emplead. See IMPLEAD.

employ, *vb.* (15c) **1.** To make use of. **2.** To hire. **3.** To use as an agent or substitute in transacting business. **4.** To commission and entrust with the performance of certain acts or functions or with the management of one's affairs.

employee. (1822) A person who works in the service of another person (the employer) under an express or implied contract of hire, under which the employer has the right to control the details of work performance. — Also spelled *employe.* Cf. AGENT (1); INDEPENDENT CONTRACTOR.

borrowed employee. (1932) An employee whose services are, with the employee's consent, lent to another employer who temporarily assumes control over the employee's work. • Under the doctrine of respondeat superior, the borrowing employer is vicariously liable for the borrowed employee's acts. But the borrowing employer may also be entitled to assert immunity under workers'-compensation laws. — Also termed *borrowed servant*; *loaned employee*; *loaned servant*; *employee pro hac vice*; *special employee*. See RESPONDEAT SUPERIOR.

probationary employee. A recently hired employee whose ability and performance are being evaluated during a trial period of employment.

statutory employee. *Workers' compensation.* An employee who is covered, or required to be covered, by the employer's workers'- compensation insurance and who therefore has no independent tort claim against the employer for unintentional injuries suffered on the job. See *statutory employer* under EMPLOYER.

employee benefit plan. (1942) A written stock-purchase, savings, option, bonus, stock-appreciation, profit-sharing, thrift, incentive, pension, or similar plan solely for employees, officers, and advisers of a company. • The term includes an employee-welfare benefit plan, an employee-pension benefit plan, or a combination of those two. See 29 USCA § 1002(3). But the term excludes any plan, fund, or program (other than an apprenticeship or training program) in which no employees are plan participants. — Often shortened to *plan*. Cf. PENSION PLAN.

defined-benefit plan. A plan established and maintained by an employer primarily to provide systematically for the payment of definitely determinable benefits to employees over a period of years, usu. for life, after retirement; any pension plan that is not a defined-contribution plan. • Retirement benefits under a defined benefit plan generally are based on a formula that included such factors as years of service and compensation. If the trust funding the plan lacks sufficient assets to pay the promised benefits, ERISA requires the employer to cover the shortfall. 29 USCA § 1002(35). Cf. *defined contribution plan*.

defined-contribution plan. Under ERISA, an employee retirement plan in which each participant has a separate account — funded by the employee's contributions and the employer's contributions (usu. in a preset amount) — and each participant's benefits are based solely on what has accumulated in the participant's account. 29 USCA § 1002(34). — Also termed *defined-contribution pension plan*; *individual account plan*. Cf. *defined-benefit plan*.

disability retirement plan. **1.** A plan that is invoked when a covered person is disabled from working to normal retirement age. **2.** A plan that provides increased benefits if a person retires because of a disability.

employee-stock-ownership plan. A type of profit-sharing plan that invests primarily in the employer's stock. • Employee-stock-ownership plans receive special tax benefits and can borrow money to fund employee stock purchases, which makes them a useful corporate finance tool. IRC (26 USCA) § 4975(e)(7). — Abbr. ESOP.

excess-benefit plan. An employee benefit plan maintained by an employer solely for the purpose of providing benefits for certain employees in excess of limitations on contributions and benefits imposed by the Internal Revenue Code. 29 USCA § 1002(36).

401(k) plan. A retirement and savings plan that allows an employee to elect to have a portion of his or her pretax salary contributed to a defined contribution plan. • Employers often match all or part of the employee's contributions. Employees usu. can choose investments from a list of options. IRC (26 USCA) § 401(k).

403(b) plan. A retirement plan for employees of public educational systems and certain tax-exempt organizations that is funded by pretax employee contributions much like a 401(k) plan, but may also provide for employer contributions. IRC (26 USCA) § 403(b). — Also termed *tax-sheltered annuity*; *tax-deferred annuity*.

457 plan. A type of deferred-compensation plan for employees of state and local governments and tax-exempt organizations that operates much like a 401(k) plan, but (except for governmental plans) is unfunded. IRC (26 USCA) § 457.

governmental plan. Under ERISA, an employee benefit plan established or maintained for its employees by the federal government, state or local governments, or their agencies or instrumentalities. 29 USCA § 1002(32). • If a collective-bargaining agreement between a labor union and a governmental entity includes a benefit plan, that plan may be a governmental plan if it is funded by and covers only employees of the governmental entity. — Also termed *governmental employee benefit plan*; *government plan*.

individual account plan. See *defined-contribution plan*.

Keogh plan. See KEOGH PLAN.

medical-expense reimbursement plan. An arrangement provided by an employer to reimburse employees for medical expenses, including vision and dental expenses, that are not covered under a medical plan available to all employees. • Some plans may also be used to substitute for health insurance, or to pay for medical expenses in excess of insurance-policy limits. IRC (26 USCA) 105. — Abbr. MERP.

money-purchase plan. A defined-contribution plan that provides for mandatory employer contributions without regard to employer profits. • Contributions are frequently stated as a percentage of employee compensation.

nonqualified deferred-compensation plan. An unfunded compensation arrangement, frequently offered to executives, that defers compensation and the recognition of its accompanying taxable income to a later date. • It is termed "nonqualified" because it does not qualify for favorable tax treatment under IRC (26 USCA) § 401(a). The plan avoids the restrictions on qualified plans, esp. the limits on contributions and benefits and rules against discrimination in favor of highly compensated employees. — Abbr. NQDC. — Also termed *nonqualified executive-compensation plan; unfunded deferred-compensation plan.*

pension plan. See PENSION PLAN.

profit-sharing plan. See PROFIT-SHARING PLAN.

qualified plan. 1. See *qualified pension plan* under PENSION PLAN. **2.** See *qualified profit-sharing plan* under PROFIT-SHARING PLAN.

retirement plan. An employee benefit plan — such as a pension plan or Keogh plan — provided by an employer (or a self-employed person) for an employee's retirement.

SIMPLE plan. An arrangement under which an individual retirement account or annuity is established for each eligible employee and funded by elective pretax employee contributions, much as with a 401(k) plan, and certain matching or minimum employer contributions. • The plan can be attractive to employers because it is easier to administer than a 401(k) plan. The name is a loose acronym for "Savings Incentive Match Plan for Employees." IRC (26 USCA) § 408(p).

simplified employee pension plan. An arrangement under which an individual retirement account or annuity is established for each eligible employee and funded by discretionary employer contributions. IRC (26 USCA) § 408(k). • A simplified employee pension plan operates much like a 401(k) plan, in that the employee contributions can be made by deferred compensation and the employer can contribute. But the plan is attractive to small employers because it is much easier to administer than a 401(k) plan and gives the employer complete discretion on whether to make an annual contribution. IRC (26 USCA) § 408(k). — Abbr. SEP; SEP-IRA.

split-funded plan. A retirement plan combining elements of both life-insurance and investment plans.

survivor-income benefit plan. An agreement between an employer and an employee whereby the employer agrees that if the employee dies before retirement, the employer will pay a specified or determinable amount to the employee's spouse or other designated beneficiary. • Typically, a formula is used, so the benefit amount may be a multiple of the employee's salary (e.g., two times the average base pay in the three years preceding death) or based on the length of employment. — Abbr. SIB. — Also written *survivor's-income benefit plan.* — Also termed *death-benefit-only plan* (abbr. DBO).

target benefit plan. A money-purchase plan that sets a "target" benefit for each participant and mandates employer contributions determined by an actuarial cost method designed to fund the target benefit.

unfunded deferred-compensation plan. See *nonqualified deferred-compensation plan.*

welfare plan. Under ERISA, any plan, fund, or program established or maintained by an employer or an employee organization for the purpose of providing to participants or their beneficiaries any number of potential benefits: medical, surgical, or hospital care or benefits; benefits in the event of sickness, accident, disability, death or unemployment; vacation benefits; apprenticeship or other training programs; daycare centers; scholarship funds; prepaid legal services; or holiday and severance benefits. 29 USCA § 1002(1).

employee givebacks. See CONCESSION BARGAINING.

employee-liability exclusion. See EXCLUSION (3).

employee pro hac vice. See *borrowed employee* under EMPLOYEE.

Employee Retirement Income Security Act. A federal statute that regulates private pension plans and employee benefit plans and that established the Pension Benefit Guaranty Corporation. 29 USCA §§ 1001 et seq. — Abbr. ERISA.

employee stock option. See STOCK OPTION (2).

employee-stock-ownership plan. See EMPLOYEE BENEFIT PLAN.

Employee's Withholding Allowance Certificate. See W-4 FORM.

employer. (16c) A person who controls and directs a worker under an express or implied contract of hire and who pays the worker's salary or wages. Cf. PRINCIPAL (1).

equal-opportunity employer. An employer who agrees not to discriminate against any job applicant or employee on the basis of race, color, religion, sex, natural origin, age, or disability. — Abbr. EOE.

general employer. An employer who transfers an employee to another employer for a limited period. See *borrowed employee* under EMPLOYEE.

special employer. An employer who has borrowed an employee for a limited period and has temporary responsibility for and control over the employee's work.

statutory employer. *Workers' compensation.* One who employs a statutory employee. See *statutory employee* under EMPLOYEE.

employer–employee relationship. See RELATIONSHIP.

employer-identification number. See TAX-IDENTIFICATION NUMBER.

employers' liability. See WORKERS' COMPENSATION.

employers'-liability insurance. See INSURANCE.

employment. (15c) **1.** The relationship between master and servant. See MASTER AND SERVANT. **2.** The act of employing. **3.** The state of being employed. **4.** Work for which one has been hired and is being paid by an employer.

casual employment. Work that is occasional, irregular, or for a short time — often associated with day labor.

employment at will. Employment that is usu. undertaken without a contract and that may be terminated at any time, by either the employer or the employee, without cause. — Also termed *at-will employment*; *hiring at will.*

gainful employment. Work that a person can pursue and perform for money.

hazardous employment. High-risk work; work involving extra peril. ● In the context of workers' compensation, hazardous employment often requires an employer to carry workers'-compensation coverage or its equivalent, regardless of the number of employees.

joint employment. A job in which the essential terms and conditions of the employee's work are controlled by two or more entities, as when a company hires a contractor to perform a task and retains control over the contractor's employees in matters such as hiring, firing, discipline, conditions of employment, promulgation of work rules, assignment of day-to-day job duties, and issuance of operating instructions.

permanent employment. Work that, under a contract, is to continue indefinitely until either party wishes to terminate it for some legitimate reason.

seasonal employment. An occupation possible only during limited parts of the year, such as a summer-camp counselor, a baseball-park vendor, or a shopping-mall Santa.

temporary employment. Work for a specific need or fixed duration, usu. agreed upon beforehand.

employment agency. (19c) A business that procures, for a fee, employment for others and employees for employers. ● Whether the employer or the employee pays the fee depends on the terms of the agreement. See FINDER (1).

Employment and Training Administration. A unit in the U.S. Department of Labor responsible for developing plans for training dislocated and unemployed workers, including young people and those who are disabled; and for interpreting federal workforce-security laws as they apply to the states.

employment contract. See CONTRACT.

employment-practices-liability insurance. See INSURANCE.

employment-related-practices exclusion. See EXCLUSION (3).

Employment Standards Administration. A unit in the U.S. Department of Labor responsible for enforcing various laws and administering programs pertaining to minimum-wage and overtime standards, registration of farm-labor contractors, wage rates to be paid and the nondiscrimination and affirmative-action programs to be followed by government contractors and subcontractors, workers'-compensation programs for federal and certain private employers, financial integrity and the internal organizational practices of labor unions, and certification of employee protection for federally sponsored transportation programs. ● The Administration operates through four divisions that have regional offices or administrators in various cities: the Office of Federal Contract Compliance Programs, the Wage and Hour Division, the Office of Labor-Management Standards, and the Office of Workers' Compensation Programs. — Abbr. ESA.

emporium (em-**por**-ee-əm), *n.* (16c) **1.** A place for wholesale trade in commodities carried by sea. ● The term is sometimes applied to a seaport town, but properly signifies only a particular place in such a town. **2.** An important marketplace. **3.** A large retail store that sells a wide variety of goods.

empresario (em-pre-**sahr**-ee-oh), *n.* [Spanish] **1.** *Spanish law.* A businessperson; one who invests in or manages a business; esp., a land developer. **2.** *Hist.* A person receiving extensive land grants as consideration for bringing people into Mexico (esp. into what would become Texas) and settling them on the land for the purpose of increasing the population, developing the country's resources, and controlling the aboriginal peoples.

emptio (**emp**-shee-oh), *n.* [Latin "purchase"] *Roman & civil law.* The act of buying; a purchase. — Also spelled *emtio.* Pl. **emptiones.**

emptio bonorum (bə-**nor**-əm). [Latin "purchase of goods"] A type of forced assignment for the benefit of creditors, involving a public sale of an insolvent debtor's estate whereby the purchaser succeeded to all the debtor's property, rights, and claims, and became responsible for the debtor's debts and liabilities to an extent fixed before the transfer.

emptio et venditio (et ven-**dish**-ee-oh). [Latin "purchase and sale"] A contract of sale. • The double name reflects that both the buyer and seller had duties and rights in the transaction. In Roman law, agreement on the thing to be sold and its price were essential. The buyer could enforce the contract by *actio empti*, and the seller could enforce by *actio venditi*. — Also termed *emptio venditio*.

emptio rei facta a pluribus ementibus (**emp**-shee-oh **ree**-ɪ **fak**-tə ay **pluur**-ə-bəs i-**men**-tə-bəs). [Latin] *Hist.* A purchase made by many buyers. La. Civ. Code art. 2450. • An *emptio rei facta a pluribus ementibus* did not automatically create a partnership among the purchasers.

emptio rei speratae (**ree**-ɪ spə-**ray**-tee). [Latin "purchase of a hoped-for thing"] The purchase of a thing not yet in existence or not yet in the seller's possession; e.g., a future crop. La. Civ. Code art. 2451. • The price of such a purchase typically depended on the actual yield and thus could fluctuate.

emptio spei (**spee**-ɪ). [Latin "purchase of a hope"] An *emptio rei speratae* in which the price is fixed, regardless of actual gain. • Even if the future event, such as the casting of a net, produced nothing, the buyer had to pay.

emptio venditio. See *emptio et venditio*.

emptor (**emp**-tor *or* -tər), *n.* [Latin] *Civil law.* A buyer; purchaser. — Also spelled *emtor*. See *caveat emptor* under CAVEAT. Pl. **emptores.**

empty-chair defense. See DEFENSE (2).

empty-chair doctrine. See ADVERSE-INTEREST RULE.

empty-suit defense. See DEFENSE (1).

emtio. See EMPTIO.

emtor. See EMPTOR.

enable, *vb.* To give power to do something; to make able.

enablement. *Patents.* The disclosure in a patent application; specif. the description of the subject matter clear and complete enough to teach a person of ordinary skill in the art how to make and use the invention. • If the artisan would still be unable to work the invention without undue experimentation after reading the description — in light of the information known in the art as of the filing date of the patent application — the patent application will be rejected for lack of enablement. 35 USCA § 112. Cf. NONENABLEMENT.

enablement by deposit. See DEPOSIT (6).

enablement requirement. *Patents.* The rule that the specification of a patent application must describe the invention so that a person with ordinary skill in the art could make and use the invention without undue experimentation. • A specification that meets this requirement is referred to as *enabling*. Cf. ENABLING SOURCE.

enabling act. See *enabling statute* under STATUTE.

enabling clause. See CLAUSE.

enabling disclosure. See DESCRIPTION (5).

enabling power. See POWER OF APPOINTMENT.

enabling source. *Patents.* A document that defeats the patentability of an invention because the information provided made it possible — before the patent application was filed — for a person skilled in the art to make the invention. Cf. ENABLEMENT REQUIREMENT.

enabling statute. 1. See STATUTE. **2.** *Hist.* (*cap.*) The Lease Act (1540), by which tenants in tail, husbands seised in right of their wives, and others were empowered to make leases for their lives or for 21 years. St. 32 Hen. 8, ch. 28.

enact, *vb.* (15c) **1.** To make into law by authoritative act; to pass <the statute was enacted shortly before the announced deadline>. **2.** (Of a statute) to provide <the statute of frauds enacts that no action may be brought on certain types of contracts unless the plaintiff has a signed writing to prove the agreement>. — **enactor,** *n.*

enacted law. See LAW.

enacting clause. See CLAUSE.

enacting words. The statutory phrasing denoting that an act is taking effect as law. • The most common enacting words are *Be it enacted that . . . .*

enactment, *n.* (18c) **1.** The action or process of making into law <enactment of a legislative bill>. **2.** A statute <a recent enactment>.

en banc (en **bangk** *or* on **bongk**). [Law French "on the bench"] *adv. & adj.* (1863) With all judges present and participating; in full court <the court heard the case en banc> <an en banc rehearing>. — Also spelled *in banc*; *in bank*. — Also termed *in banco*.

en banc sitting. See SITTING.

enbancworthy, *adj. Slang.* Worthy of being considered en banc <the Fifth Circuit concluded that two of the four issues are truly enbancworthy>. — **enbancworthiness,** *n.*

en bloc (on **blok** *or* en **blok**), *adj. & adv.* [French] As a whole; as a unit. • In parliamentary law, this term can refer to a series of resolutions or other motions that are disposed of with a single vote. — Also termed *en grosse*.

enclave (en-**klayv** *or* on-). (19c) *Int'l law.* An isolated part of a country's territory entirely surrounded by the territory of one foreign country, so that any communication with the main part of the country must pass through the territory of the foreign country. • Although international enclaves were once common, they are now relatively rare; examples include Baarle-Hertog, a Belgian enclave in the Netherlands, and Kaliningrad, a Russian enclave between Lithuania and Poland. — Also termed *international enclave*.

federal enclave. Territory or land that a state has ceded to the United States. • Examples of federal enclaves are military bases, national parks, federally administered highways, and federal Indian reservations. The U.S. government has exclusive authority and jurisdiction over federal enclaves.

quasi-enclave. An isolated part of a country's territory that, though not entirely surrounded by the territory of a foreign country, is inaccessible by way of the country's own territory because of topographical features such as impassable mountains.

enclose, *vb.* (14c) **1.** To surround or encompass; to fence or hem in on all sides. **2.** To place (something) in a parcel or envelope. — Also spelled *inclose.*

enclosed land. See LAND.

enclosed please find. See TRANSMITTAL LETTER.

enclosure. (15c) **1.** Something enclosed in a parcel or envelope. **2.** Land surrounded by some visible obstruction; CLOSE (1). **3.** An artificial fence around one's estate. — Also spelled *inclosure.*

encourage, *vb.* (15c) *Criminal law.* To instigate; to incite to action; to embolden; to help. See AID AND ABET.

encroach, *vb.* (16c) **1.** To enter by gradual steps or stealth into the possessions or rights of another; to trespass or intrude. **2.** To gain or intrude unlawfully upon another's lands, property, or authority. — Formerly also spelled *incroach.*

encroachment, *n.* (16c) **1.** An infringement of another's rights. **2.** An interference with or intrusion onto another's property <the court remedied the encroachment by ordering the defendant to cut down the tree limb hanging over the plaintiff's yard>. — Formerly also spelled *incroachment.* See TRESPASS.

encumbrance, *n.* (16c) A claim or liability that is attached to property or some other right and that may lessen its value, such as a lien or mortgage; any property right that is not an ownership interest. • An encumbrance cannot defeat the transfer of possession, but it remains after the property or right is transferred. — Also spelled *incumbrance.* — **encumber,** *vb.*

mesne encumbrance (meen). An intermediate encumbrance; an encumbrance that first occurred both earlier and later than other encumbrances.

encumbrancer. (1858)·One having a legal claim, such as a lien or mortgage, against property.

end, *n.* **1.** An object, goal, or purpose. **2.** A result; a termination point.

endangered species. See SPECIES (1).

endangering the welfare of a child. See CHILD ENDANGERMENT.

endangerment, *n.* (17c) The act or an instance of putting someone or something in danger; exposure to peril or harm. See CHILD ENDANGERMENT; RECKLESS ENDANGERMENT. — **endanger,** *vb.*

endeavor, *n.* (15c) A systematic or continuous effort to attain some goal; any effort or assay to accomplish some goal or purpose.

endeavor, *vb.* (15c) To exert physical or intellectual strength toward the attainment of an object or goal.

endenizen (en-**den**-ə-zən), *vb.* (16c) To recognize as a legal resident; to naturalize. — Also spelled *endenize; indenizen; indenize.* — **endenization,** *n.*

endless-chain scheme. See PYRAMID SCHEME.

end lines. *Mining law.* A claim's lines, as platted or laid down on the ground, that mark its boundaries on the shorter dimension, where the claim crosses the vein, in contrast to side lines, which mark the longer dimension and follow the course of the vein. • With reference to the apex rule, if the claim as a whole crosses the vein instead of following its course, the end lines will become the side lines and vice versa. See APEX RULE. Cf. SIDE LINES; APEX RULE.

endnote. (1926) A note that, instead of appearing at the bottom of the page (as a footnote does), appears at the end of the book, chapter, or paper.

endogenous insemination. See *artificial insemination by husband* under ARTIFICIAL INSEMINATION.

endorse, *vb.* See INDORSE.

endorsed bond. See *guaranteed bond* (1) under BOND (3).

endorsee. See INDORSEE.

endorsement, *n.* (16c) **1.** INDORSEMENT. **2.** An amendment to an insurance policy; a rider. — **endorse,** *vb.* — **endorseable,** *adj.*

endorser. See INDORSER.

endow, *vb.* (14c) **1.** To give money or property to, esp. as a source of continuing or permanent income. **2.** *Hist.* To provide (a woman) with a dower.

endowment. (15c) **1.** A gift of money or property to an institution (such as a university) for a specific purpose, esp. one in which the principal is kept intact indefinitely and only the interest income from that principal is used. **2.** *Hist.* The assigning or giving of a dower to a woman.

endowment insurance. 1. See INSURANCE. **2.** See *endowment life insurance* under LIFE INSURANCE.

endowment life insurance. See LIFE INSURANCE.

endowment policy. See INSURANCE POLICY.

end position. (1964) One's legal and financial position on the signing of a contract, including the choices now available, such as renewal and renegotiation.

end user. See USER (2).

Enelow–Ettelson **rule** (en-ə-loh–**et**-əl-sən). The defunct doctrine that an order staying federal-court proceedings pending the determination of an equitable defense (such as arbitration) is an injunction appealable under 28 USCA § 1292(a)(1) if the proceeding stayed was an action that could have been maintained as an action at law before the merger of law and equity. *Enelow v. New York Life Ins. Co.*, 293 U.S. 379, 55 S.Ct. 310 (1935); *Ettelson v. Metropolitan Life Ins. Co.*, 317 U.S. 188, 63 S.Ct. 163 (1942).

enemy. (13c) **1.** One who opposes or inflicts injury on another; an antagonist. **2.** An opposing military force. **3.** A state with which another state is at war. — Also termed *public enemy*. **4.** A person possessing the nationality of the state with which one is at war. — Also termed *enemy subject*. **5.** A foreign state that is openly hostile to another whose position is being considered.

alien enemy. See ALIEN.

public enemy. (16c) **1.** A notorious criminal who is a menace to society; esp., one who seems more or less immune from successful prosecution. **2.** ENEMY (3). **3.** A social, health, or economic condition or problem that affects the public at large and is difficult to control <teenage smoking has been declared a public enemy in this country>.

enemy alien. See *alien enemy* under ALIEN.

enemy combatant. See COMBATANT.

enemy's property. *Int'l law.* Property used in illegal commerce or trading with a public enemy, whether that property belongs to an ally or a citizen. ● This term is esp. common in prize courts. The illegal traffic makes the property hostile, and allows penal consequences to attach to the property itself.

enemy subject. See ENEMY (4).

Energy, Department of. See DEPARTMENT OF ENERGY.

en fait (on **fay**), *adv.* [French] In fact; actually.

enfeoff (en-**fef** *or* en-**feef**), *vb.* (15c) To put (a person) in legal possession of a freehold interest; to trans-

fer a fief to. — Formerly spelled *infeoff*. — Also termed *feoff*; *infeudate*; (in Law Latin) *feoffare*.

enfeoffment (en-**fef**-mənt *or* en-**feef**-), *n.* (15c) **1.** At common law, the act or process of transferring possession and ownership of an estate in land. — Also termed *infeudation*; *infeudatio*. **2.** The property or estate so transferred. **3.** The instrument or deed by which one obtains such property or estate. — Also spelled *infeoffment*. — Also termed *feoffment*; (in Scots law) *infeftment*.

enforce, *vb.* (14c) **1.** To give force or effect to (a law, etc.); to compel obedience to. **2.** Loosely, to compel a person to pay damages for not complying with (a contract).

enforcement, *n.* (15c) The act or process of compelling compliance with a law, mandate, command, decree, or agreement.

extrajudicial enforcement. See SELF-HELP.

law enforcement. See LAW ENFORCEMENT.

remedial enforcement. See *secondary right* under RIGHT.

sanctional enforcement. See *secondary right* under RIGHT.

secondary enforcement. See *secondary right* under RIGHT.

selective enforcement. See SELECTIVE ENFORCEMENT.

specific enforcement. See *primary right* under RIGHT.

Enforcement of Foreign Judgments Act. A uniform law, adopted by most states, that gives the holder of a foreign judgment essentially the same rights to levy and execute on the judgment as the holder of a domestic judgment. ● The Act defines a *foreign judgment* as any judgment, decree, or order (of a court in the United States or of any other court) that is entitled to full faith and credit in the state. See FULL FAITH AND CREDIT.

enforcement power. (1939) The authority by which Congress may enforce a particular constitutional amendment's provisions by appropriate legislation. ● Enforcement power is granted to Congress under the 13th, 14th, 15th, 19th, 23rd, 24th, and 26th Amendments.

enfranchise, *vb.* (15c) **1.** To grant voting rights or other rights of citizenship to (a person or class). **2.** To set free, as from slavery.

enfranchisement (en-**fran**-chiz-mənt *or* -chiz-mənt), *n.* (16c) **1.** The granting of voting rights or other rights of citizenship to a class of persons. **2.** The act of making free, as from slavery.

engage, *vb.* (15c) To employ or involve oneself; to take part in; to embark on.

engagement, *n.* (17c) **1.** A contract or agreement involving mutual promises. **2.** An agreement to marry; the period after which a couple has agreed to marry but before they do so. — Also termed (in sense 2) *betrothal; betrothment.*

engagement fee. See RETAINER (3).

engagement letter. A document identifying the scope of a professional's services to a client and outlining the respective duties and responsibilities of both.

engagement slip. (1933) A note sent by a lawyer to a court informing the court that the lawyer is professionally engaged in a second court on a given day and thus cannot appear before the first court on that day as scheduled. ● The term is used in Pennsylvania.

engender, *vb.* To cause; to bring about; to occasion.

engineering, procurement, and construction contract. See CONTRACT.

England **procedure.** A procedure by which — after a federal court has referred a case back to state court under the *Pullman* abstention doctrine, and the state court has adjudicated the state-court issues — a litigant may return to federal court to have the federal claims adjudicated. *England v. Louisiana State Bd. of Med. Examiners,* 375 U.S. 411, 84 S.Ct. 461 (1964). See *Pullman abstention* under ABSTENTION.

English rule. The requirement that a losing litigant must pay the winner's costs and attorney's fees. — Also termed *loser-pays rule.* Cf. AMERICAN RULE (1).

en gros (on groh). [French] (18c) Total; by wholesale; IN GROSS. — Also spelled *en grosse.* Cf. EN BLOC.

engross, *vb.* (15c) **1.** *Hist.* To handwrite (a document, esp. a deed) in a style characterized by large letters. ● This method of writing, which was derived from ancient court hand, was also used in transcribing wills well into the 19th century. See COURT HAND. **2.** To prepare a copy of (a legal document, such as a deed) for execution. **3.** To prepare a copy of (a bill or mandate) before a final legislative vote. **4.** *Hist.* To buy large quantities of (a stock or commodity) in an effort to corner the market and control the price. **5.** To absorb or fully occupy. — Formerly also spelled *ingross.* Cf. ENROLL (2). — **engrossment,** *n.*

engrossed bill. See BILL (3).

engrosser, *n.* **1.** A person who engrosses legal documents. **2.** *Hist.* A person who buys large quantities of a commodity in an effort to control the price.

Engrosser of the Great Roll. See CLERK OF THE PIPE.

engrossing, *n. Hist.* The practice of buying large quantities of commodities or merchandise with the intent of gaining a monopoly and selling them at a very high price. ● Engrossing was a misdemeanor in England until 1834. — Also termed *engrossment.* See CORNERING THE MARKET.

engrossment, *n.* (16c) **1.** The preparation of a legal document (such as a deed) for execution. **2.** The drafting of a resolution or bill just before a final vote on the matter in the legislature. **3.** ENGROSSING.

enhanced, *adj.* Made greater; increased <because of his recidivism, Monte was subject to an enhanced sentence after his latest conviction>.

enhanced damages. See DAMAGES.

enhancement. The act of augmenting; the state of being enhanced <the use of a deadly weapon led to an enhancement of the sentence>.

enjoin, *vb.* (13c) **1.** To legally prohibit or restrain by injunction <the company was enjoined from selling its stock>. **2.** To prescribe, mandate, or strongly encourage <the graduating class was enjoined to uphold the highest professional standards>. — Also spelled *injoin.* — **enjoinment** (for sense 1), *n.* — **enjoinder** (for sense 2), *n.*

enjoinable, *adj.* Capable of being prohibited by injunction <an enjoinable nuisance>.

enjoy, *vb.* (15c) To have, possess, and use (something) with satisfaction; to occupy or have the benefit of (property).

enjoyment, *n.* (16c) **1.** Possession and use, esp. of rights or property. **2.** The exercise of a right.

adverse enjoyment. (18c) The possession or use of land under a claim of right against the property owner.

beneficial enjoyment. (18c) The possession and benefit of land or other property, but without legal title.

present enjoyment. (18c) The immediate possession and use of land or other property.

quiet enjoyment. (18c) The possession of land with the assurance that the possession will not be disturbed by a superior title. See *covenant for quiet enjoyment* under COVENANT (4).

enlarge, *vb.* (14c) **1.** To increase in size or extend in scope or duration <the court enlarged the time allotted for closing arguments>. **2.** To free from custody or imprisonment <at common law, an action for escape lay when a prisoner was wrongly enlarged>. Cf. AT LARGE. — **enlargement,** *n.*

enlargement of time. (18c) A usu. court-ordered extension of the time allowed to perform an action, esp. a procedural one.

enlisted member. *Military law.* A person in an enlisted grade; a person in military service below the grade of officer or warrant officer. — Also termed *enlisted man.*

enlistment, *n.* (18c) Voluntary entry into a branch of the armed services. — **enlist,** *vb.*

en masse (en **mas**). [French] (18c) In a mass; in a large group all at once; all together.

Enoch Arden law (ee-nək **ahrd**-ən). (1923) A statute that grants a divorce or an exemption from liability so that a person can remarry when his or her spouse has been absent without explanation for a specified number of years (usu. five or seven). • This type of law is named after a Tennyson poem, in which the eponymous hero, having been shipwrecked for years on a desert island, returns home to find that his wife has remarried. He selflessly conceals his identity from her so that she can remain with her new husband. — Also spelled *Enoc Arden law.* See *presumptive death* under DEATH; ABANDONMENT (3). Cf. SEVEN-YEARS' ABSENCE RULE.

enormous, *adj.* Aggravated; excessively large <enormous crimes>.

enrichment. (17c) The receipt of a benefit. Cf. UNJUST ENRICHMENT.

enroll, *vb.* (14c) **1.** To register or transcribe (a legal document, as a deed) into an official record on execution. — Formerly also spelled *inroll.* **2.** To prepare (a bill passed by the legislature) for the executive's signature. Cf. ENGROSS.

enrolled, *adj.* Registered; recorded.

enrolled agent. One who, though neither a certified public accountant nor an attorney, has been admitted to practice before the IRS, either by passing an examination or by working for the IRS in a technical area for at least five years. • The enrolled agent is one of four types of persons who are allowed to practice before the IRS, the other three being attorneys, certified public accountants, and persons who are admitted to represent either themselves or others in a particular case.

enrolled bill. See BILL (3).

enrolled-bill rule. (1914) The conclusive presumption that a statute, once formalized, appears precisely as the legislature intended, thereby preventing any challenge to the drafting of the bill.

enrollment, *n.* The act of recording or registering. — Also spelled (archaically) *inrollment.*

enrollment of vessels. Maritime law. The recording and certification of vessels used in coastal or inland navigation, as distinguished from the "registration" of vessels used in foreign commerce. • *Enrollment* and *registry* are used to distinguish certificates granted to two classes of vessels. Enrollment evidences the national character of a vessel engaged in coasting trade or home traffic; registry is used to declare the nationality of a vessel engaged in foreign trade. Cf. REGISTRY (2).

Enrollment Office. *Hist.* A department of the Court of Chancery responsible for storing enrolled deeds and judgments. • The Enrollment Office was abolished in 1879; its duties were transferred to the Central Office.

en route (en *or* on **root**). [French] On the way; in the course of transportation or travel.

enschedule, *vb. Archaic.* To insert in a list, account, or writing.

enseal, *vb. Archaic.* To seal (a document).

entail, *n.* (14c) A fee abridged or limited to the owner's issue or class of issue rather than descending to all the heirs. See BARRING OF ENTAIL; FEE TAIL. — Also termed (in Scots law) *tailzie.* — **entailable,** *adj.*

quasi-entail. An estate *pur autre vie* that is granted to a person and the heirs of the person's body. • The interest so granted is not properly an estate-tail (because it is not granted by inheritance), but it is similar enough that the interest will go to the heir of the body as special occupant during the life of the *cestui que vie,* in the same manner as an estate of inheritance would descend if limited to the grantee and the heirs of his body.

entail, *vb.* (14c) **1.** To make necessary; to involve <responding to this onerous discovery will entail countless hours of work>. **2.** To limit the inheritance of (an estate) to only the owner's issue or class of issue, so that none of the heirs can transfer the estate <the grantor entailed the property through a so-called "tail female">. See FEE TAIL. — **entailable,** *adj.*

entailed, *adj.* Settled or limited to specified heirs or in tail <entailed gifts>.

entailed estate. See FEE TAIL.

entailed interest. See INTEREST (2).

entailment, *n.* **1.** The act of entailing an estate. **2.** An estate so entailed.

entendment. *Archaic.* See INTENDMENT.

entente (ahn-**tahnt**). [French "intent, understanding"] (19c) *Int'l law.* **1.** An understanding that two or more nations have for carrying out a common policy or course of action. • An *entente* is looser than an alliance but stronger than the nations' merely having good relations. **2.** The nations having such an understanding. Cf. ALLIANCE; DÉTENTE.

enter, *vb.* (13c) **1.** To come or go into; esp., to go onto (real property) by right of entry so as to take possession <the landlord entered the defaulting tenant's premises>. **2.** To put formally before a court or on the record <the defendant entered a plea of no contest>. **3.** To become a party to <they entered into an agreement>. See ENTRY.

enterprise, *n.* (15c) **1.** An organization or venture, esp. for business purposes.

> **governmental enterprise.** An enterprise undertaken by a governmental body, such as a parks department that creates a public park. — Also termed *government enterprise.*

2. Under federal anti-racketeering law, an individual, partnership, corporation, association, union, other legal entity, or group of individuals associated in fact, although not a legal entity. ● The enterprise must be ongoing and must exist as an entity separate from the allegedly illegal activity that it engages in. 18 USCA § 1961(4). See RACKETEER INFLUENCED AND CORRUPT ORGANIZATIONS ACT. **3.** One or more persons or organizations that have related activities, unified operation or common control, and a common business purpose. ● Under the Fair Labor Standards Act, an employee who is employed by an enterprise is entitled to minimum-wage and overtime benefits. 29 USCA §§ 201 et seq.

enterprise goodwill. See GOODWILL.

enterprise liability. See LIABILITY.

enterprise organization. See BUSINESS ENTERPRISES.

enterprise value. See VALUE (2)

entertain, *vb.* (15c) **1.** To bear in mind or consider; esp., to give judicial consideration to <the court then entertained motions for continuance>. **2.** To amuse or please. **3.** To receive (a person) as a guest or provide hospitality to (a person). **4.** *Parliamentary law.* To recognize and state (a motion); to receive and take into consideration <the chair will entertain the motion>.

entertainment expense. See EXPENSE.

entertainment law. (1953) The field of law dealing with the legal and business issues in the entertainment industry (such as film, music, and theater), and involving the representation of artists and producers, the negotiation of contracts, and the protection of intellectual-property rights.

entice, *vb.* (14c) To lure or induce; esp., to wrongfully solicit (a person) to do something.

enticement, *n.* (14c) **1.** The act or an instance of wrongfully soliciting or luring a person to do something. **2.** *Hist.* The tort of inducing a man's wife to leave him or to remain away from him against his will.

> **enticement of a child.** *Criminal law.* The act or offense of inviting, persuading, or attempting to persuade a child to enter a vehicle, building, room, or secluded place with the intent of committing an unlawful sexual act against the child. — Often shortened to *enticement.*

> **enticement of a parent.** *Rare. Torts.* The tortious interference with a child's rights and interests in maintaining the parent–child relationship, usu. caused by a third person who induces a parent to abandon the child. ● Actions based on enticement, where they are recognized, are rarely successful because many states do not recognize a child's legal right to a parent's consortium or affection.

entire, *adj.* **1.** Whole; complete in all its parts. **2.** Not divisible into parts.

entire-agreement clause. (1960) **1.** INTEGRATION CLAUSE. **2.** A provision in an insurance contract stating that the entire agreement between the insured and insurer is contained in the contract, often including the application (if attached), declarations, insuring agreement, exclusions, conditions, and endorsements. — Also termed *entire-contract clause.*

entire benefit. See *entire use* under USE (4).

entire blood. See *full blood* under BLOOD.

entire-contract clause. See ENTIRE-AGREEMENT CLAUSE.

entire-controversy doctrine. (1970) The principle that a plaintiff or defendant who does not assert all claims or defenses related to the controversy in a legal proceeding is not entitled to assert those claims or defenses in a later proceeding. — Also termed *single-controversy doctrine.* Cf. *compulsory counterclaim* under COUNTERCLAIM; RES JUDICATA (2).

entire day. See DAY.

entire interest. See INTEREST (2).

entire-output contract. See *output contract* under CONTRACT.

entire tenancy. See TENANCY.

entirety (en-tɪ-ər-tee). (16c) **1.** The whole, as opposed to a moiety or part. **2.** Something (such as certain judgments and contracts) that the law considers incapable of being divided into parts.

entirety, tenancy by the. See *estate by entirety* under ESTATE (1).

entirety clause. *Oil & gas.* A mineral-lease or deed provision specifying that royalties must be apportioned if the property is subdivided after the lease is granted. ● For the lessee, the clause makes it clear that the lessee's duties will increase if the lessor transfers a part of the leased premises. For the lessor, the clause avoids the nonapportionment rule.

entire use. See USE (4).

entitle, *vb.* (14c) **1.** To grant a legal right to or qualify for. **2.** *Eccles. law.* To ordain as a minister. — Formerly also spelled *intitle.*

entitlement. (19c) An absolute right to a (usu. monetary) benefit, such as social security, granted immediately upon meeting a legal requirement.

entitlement program. A government program guaranteeing certain benefits, such as financial aid or government-provided services, to people or entities that meet the criteria set by law. • Some examples of entitlement programs are unemployment benefits, Social Security, food stamps, and agricultural price-support plans. Qualified beneficiaries have an enforceable right to participate in the programs.

entity. An organization (such as a business or a governmental unit) that has a legal identity apart from its members or owners.

corporate entity. A corporation's status as an organization existing independently of its shareholders. • As a separate entity, a corporation can, in its own name, sue and be sued, lend and borrow money, and buy, sell, lease, and mortgage property.

public entity. A governmental entity, such as a state government or one of its political subdivisions.

entity assumption. (1972) The presumption that a business is a unit separate from its owners and from other firms.

entity theory of partnership. (1916) The theory that a partnership is an entity with a legal existence apart from the partners who make it up. • Under the Uniform Partnership Act, "[a] partnership is an entity distinct from its partners." UPA § 201 (1994). Cf. AGGREGATE THEORY OF PARTNERSHIP.

entrapment, *n.* (1899) **1.** A law-enforcement officer's or government agent's inducement of a person to commit a crime, by means of fraud or undue persuasion, in an attempt to later bring a criminal prosecution against that person. **2.** The affirmative defense of having been so induced. • To establish entrapment (in most states), the defendant must show that he or she would not have committed the crime but for the fraud or undue persuasion. — **entrap,** *vb.*

derivative entrapment. Entrapment in which the government uses a private person, acting either as an agent of the government or as an unwitting participant, to induce the subject of the entrapment to commit a crime.

objective entrapment. Entrapment as judged by focusing on egregious law-enforcement conduct, not on the defendant's predisposition.

sentencing entrapment. Entrapment of a defendant who is predisposed to commit a lesser offense but who is unlawfully induced to commit a more serious offense that carries a more severe sentence. — Also termed *sentence-factor manipulation.*

entrepreneur (on-trə-prə-**nər** *or* -**noor**), *n.* (19c) One who initiates and assumes the financial risks of a new enterprise and who usu. undertakes its management.

entrepreneurial rights. See NEIGHBORING RIGHTS.

entrust, *vb.* (16c) To give (a person) the responsibility for something, usu. after establishing a confidential relationship. — Also spelled (archaically) *intrust.* See NEGLIGENT ENTRUSTMENT. — **entrustment,** *n.*

entrusting, *n. Commercial law.* The transfer of possession of goods to a merchant who deals in goods of that type and who may in turn transfer the goods and all rights to them to a purchaser in the ordinary course of business. UCC § 2-403(2).

entry, *n.* (13c) **1.** The act, right, or privilege of entering real property <they were given entry into the stadium>.

forcible entry. See FORCIBLE ENTRY.

lawful entry. (17c) **1.** The entry onto real property by a person not in possession, under a claim or color of right, and without force or fraud. **2.** The entry of premises under a search warrant. See SEARCH WARRANT.

open entry. (18c) A conspicuous entry onto real property to take possession; an entry that is neither clandestine nor carried out by secret artifice or stratagem and that (by law in some states) is accomplished in the presence of two witnesses.

reentry. See REENTRY.

unlawful entry. (17c) **1.** The crime of entering another's real property, by fraud or other illegal means, without the owner's consent. Cf. TRESPASS (1). **2.** An alien's crossing of a border into a country without proper documents.

2. An item written in a record; a notation <Forney made a false entry in the books on March 3>.

blind entry. An accounting entry that indicates only the debited and credited amounts without any explanation.

compound journal entry. A journal entry requiring more than one debit and credit (as when revenue is received partly in cash and partly in securities).

journal entry. An entry in an accounting journal of equal debits and credits, with occasional explanations of the recorded transactions.

3. The placement of something before the court or on the record. **4.** *Copyright.* The deposit of a title of work with the Register of Copyrights to secure its protection. **5.** *Immigration.* Any entrance of an alien into the United States, whether voluntary or involuntary. **6.** *Criminal law.* The unlawful coming into a building to commit a crime.

entry, right of. See POWER OF TERMINATION.

entry, writ of. See WRIT OF ENTRY.

entry fiction. The assumption, for purposes of immigration and deportation proceedings, that an excludable alien is to be treated as if detained at the border despite his or her physical presence in the United States.

entry *in casu consimili* (en-tree in **kay-**s[y]oo kən-**sim-**ə-lı). [Latin] See CASU CONSIMILI.

entry of judgment. (17c) The ministerial recording of a court's final decision, usu. by noting it in a judgment book or civil docket. Cf. RENDITION OF JUDGMENT.

entry on the roll. *Hist.* **1.** A clerk's notation on a parchment roll of the proceedings and issues in a particular case. ● Before parties began submitting written pleadings, they would appear (in person or through counsel) in open court and state their respective contentions orally until they settled on the issue or precise point in dispute. During the progress of these oral statements, an appointed officer of the court would make minutes of the various proceedings on a parchment roll that then became the official record of the suit. Even after the practice of oral pleadings had fallen into disuse, proceedings continued to be entered "on the roll." This practice was abolished early in the 19th century. **2.** A future interest created in a transferor who conveys an estate on condition subsequent.

enumerate (i-n[y]oo-mə-rayt), *vb.* To count off or designate one by one; to list. — **enumeration**, *n.*

enumerated motion. See MOTION (1).

enumerated power. See POWER (3).

enumerator. A person appointed to collect census papers or schedules.

enunciate (i-nən-see-ayt), *vb.* (17c) **1.** To state publicly; to announce or proclaim <the court enunciated a new doctrine yesterday>. **2.** To articulate or pronounce <enunciate your syllables more clearly when you speak>. — **enunciation**, *n.* — **enunciable**, *adj.* — **enunciator**, *n.*

enure. See INURE.

en ventre sa mere (on **von**-trə sa **mair**). [Law French "in utero"] (18c)(Of a fetus) in the mother's womb <child *en ventre sa mere*>. ● This phrase refers to an unborn child, usu. in the context of a discussion of that child's rights. If the child is *en ventre sa mere* at the time of a decedent's death and is subsequently born alive, the child is treated as having been in existence at the time of the decedent's death for purposes of inheritance. — Also spelled *in ventre sa mere*. See VENTER.

en vie (on vee). [Law French "in life"] Alive.

environmental audit. See AUDIT.

environmental crime. (1972) *Environmental law.* A statutory offense involving harm to the environment, such as a violation of the criminal

provisions in the Clean Air Act Amendments of 1970, the Federal Water Pollution Control Act of 1972 (commonly called the Clean Water Act), or the Endangered Species Act of 1973. ● Although the most significant environmental-crime statutes were passed in the 1970s, they date back to the late 19th century, with statutes such as the Pure Food and Drug Act of 1896 and the assorted statutes that ultimately became the Rivers and Harbors Act of 1899. — Also termed *crime against the environment.*

environmental criminology. See CRIMINOLOGY.

environmental effect. (1967) *Environmental law.* A natural or artificial disturbance of the physical, chemical, or biological components that make up the environment.

environmental-impact statement. (1971) *Environmental law.* **1.** A document that the National Environmental Policy Act (42 USCA § 4332(2)(c)) requires a federal agency to produce for a major project or legislative proposal so that better decisions can be made about the positive and negative environmental effects of an undertaking. **2.** In some states, a public document used by a government agency to analyze the significant environmental effects of a proposed project, to identify alternatives, and to disclose possible ways to reduce or avoid possible environmental damage. — Abbr. EIS. — Also termed *environmental-impact report* (EIR).

environmental law. (1971) The field of law dealing with the maintenance and protection of the environment, including preventive measures such as the requirements of environmental-impact statements, as well as measures to assign liability and provide cleanup for incidents that harm the environment. ● Because most environmental litigation involves disputes with governmental agencies, environmental law is heavily intertwined with administrative law.

Environmental Protection Agency. An independent federal agency in the executive branch responsible for setting pollution-control standards in the areas of air, water, solid waste, pesticides, radiation, and toxic materials; enforcing laws enacted to protect the environment; and coordinating the antipollution efforts of state and local governments. ● The commission was created by Reorganization Plan No. 3 of 1970. — Abbr. EPA.

environmental terrorism. See *ecoterrorism* under TERRORISM.

environmental tort. See TORT.

enviroterrorism. See *ecoterrorism* under TERRORISM.

envoy (en-voy). (17c) **1.** A high-ranking diplomat sent to a foreign country to execute a special mission or to serve as a permanent diplomatic representative. — Formerly also termed *envoy extraordinary.* **2.** A messenger or representative.

envoy extraordinary. *Int'l law.* **1.** A person who heads a legation rather than an embassy. ● In current usage, the term is honorific and has no special significance. **2.** *Hist.* ENVOY (1).

envoy plenipotentiary. See *ambassador plenipotentiary* under AMBASSADOR.

EOE. *abbr.* **1.** See *equal-opportunity employer* under EMPLOYER. **2.** Errors and omissions excepted. ● This phrase is sometimes appended to an account stated to allow for slight errors. See *errors-and-omissions insurance* under INSURANCE.

eo instante (ee-oh in-**stan**-tee). [Latin] At that very instant. — Also spelled *eo instanti.*

E.O.M. *abbr.* End of month. ● This appears as a payment term in some sales contracts.

eo nomine (ee-oh **nahm**-ə-nee). [Latin] (17c) By or in that name <interest *eo nomine*>.

EPA. *abbr.* ENVIRONMENTAL PROTECTION AGENCY.

EPC. *abbr.* **1.** EUROPEAN PATENT CONVENTION. **2.** Engineering, procurement, and construction. See *engineering, procurement, and construction contract* under CONTRACT.

EPC contract. See *engineering, procurement, and construction contract* under CONTRACT.

ephemeral recording. *Copyright.* A temporary copy of a work that may be created and used by a broadcaster under a license or under a statutory exemption that waives the need to obtain the copyright owner's permission. ● A broadcaster must still pay royalties, and usu. must destroy the ephemeral recording within a statutorily defined time after creation or use.

episcopacy (i-**pis**-kə-pə-see), *n.* (17c) *Eccles. law.* **1.** The office of a bishop. **2.** A form of church government by bishops. **3.** An office of overlooking or overseeing.

episcopalia (i-pis-kə-**pay**-lee-ə), *n. pl.* (19c) *Eccles. law.* Synodals, pentecostals, and other customary payments from the clergy to their diocesan bishop, collected by rural deans and forwarded to the bishop.

episcopate (i-**pis**-kə-pit), *n.* (17c) *Eccles. law.* **1.** A bishopric. **2.** The dignity or office of a bishop.

episodic criminal. See CRIMINAL.

EPL insurance. See *employment-practices liability insurance* under INSURANCE.

e pluribus unum (ee **ploor**-ə-bəs [y]**oo**-nəm). [Latin] One out of many. ● This is the motto on the official seal of the United States and on several U.S. coins.

EPO. *abbr.* **1.** See *emergency protective order* under PROTECTIVE ORDER. **2.** EUROPEAN PATENT OFFICE.

epoch (**ep**-ək), *n.* **1.** A period of time marked by distinctive features or noteworthy events. **2.** A time when a new computation is begun; a time from which memorable dates are counted. — **epochal** (**ep**-ə-kəl), *adj.*

EPR. *abbr.* EMERGENCY PREPAREDNESS AND RESPONSE DIRECTORATE.

EPS. *abbr.* EARNINGS PER SHARE.

Equal Access Act of 1984. A federal law that prohibits school districts receiving federal funds and allowing extracurricular activities to be held in its facilities from denying secondary-school students the right to meet for religious and other purposes in public-school facilities. 20 USCA § 4071. ● The constitutionality of the Act was upheld in *Board of Education of Westside Community Schools v. Mergens,* 496 U.S. 226, 110 S.Ct. 2356 (1990).

equal-access rule. (1989) *Criminal law.* The doctrine that contraband found on a defendant's premises will not support a conviction if other persons have the same access to the premises as the defendant. ● To invoke this defense successfully, the defendant must show that other persons did in fact have equal access to the premises; speculative evidence that trespassers might have come onto the premises will not bar a conviction.

Equal Access to Justice Act. A 1980 federal statute that allows a prevailing party in certain actions against the government to recover attorney's fees and expert-witness fees. Pub. L. No. 96-481, title II, 94 Stat. 2325 (codified as amended in scattered sections of 5, 15, and 28 USCA). — Abbr. EAJA.

equal and uniform taxation. See TAXATION.

Equal Credit Opportunity Act. A federal statute that prohibits creditors from discriminating against credit applicants on the basis of race, color, religion, national origin, age, sex, or marital status with respect to any aspect of a credit transaction. 15 USCA §§ 1691(a)–(f). — Abbr. ECOA.

equal degree. See DEGREE.

equal-dignities rule. *Agency.* The doctrine that an agent can perform all acts requiring a writing signed by the principal only if the agent's authority is set forth in a writing. ● This rule is an adjunct to the statute of frauds and applies when one or more of the signatories to a contract acted through an agent.

Equal Employment Opportunity Commission. An independent federal commission that investigates claims of employment discrimination based on race, color, religion, sex, national origin, or age and enforces antidiscrimination statutes through lawsuits. ● It was created by Title VII of the Civil Rights Act of 1964. The EEOC encourages mediation and other nonlitigious means of resolving employment disputes. A claimant must file a charge of discrimination with the EEOC before pursuing a claim under Title VII of the Civil Rights Act and certain other employment-related statutes. — Abbr. EEOC.

equal-footing doctrine. (1949) The principle that a state admitted to the Union after 1789 enters with the same rights, sovereignty, and jurisdiction within its borders as did the original 13 states.

equality. (15c) The quality or state of being equal; esp., likeness in power or political status. See EQUAL PROTECTION.

political equality. The sharing of governmental decisions in such a way that, in the setting of governmental policies, the preference of each citizen is assigned an equal value.

equality before the law. (18c) The status or condition of being treated fairly according to regularly established norms of justice; esp., in British constitutional law, the notion that all persons are subject to the ordinary law of the land administered by the ordinary law courts, that officials and others are not exempt from the general duty of obedience to the law, that discretionary governmental powers must not be abused, and that the task of superintending the operation of law rests with an impartial, independent judiciary.

equality of states. *Int'l law.* The doctrine that all fully independent nations are equal under international law. • This doctrine does not, of course, mean that all nations are equal in power or influence, but merely that, as nations, they all have the same legal rights.

equalization, *n.* (18c) **1.** The raising or lowering of assessed values to achieve conformity with values in surrounding areas. **2.** *Tax.* The adjustment of an assessment or tax to create a rate uniform with another. — Also termed *equalization of taxes*; *fair and proper legal assessment*.

equalization board. (1875) A local governmental agency responsible for adjusting the tax rates in different districts to ensure an equitable distribution of the tax burden. — Also termed *board of equalization*.

equalization of taxes. See EQUALIZATION (2).

equalize, *vb.* To make equal; to cause to correspond or be the same in amount or degree.

equally divided. (16c) **1.** (Of property) apportioned per capita — not per stirpes — among heirs on the testator's death. • A provision in a will calling for property to be divided "share and share alike" has the same effect. **2.** (Of a court, legislature, or other group) having the same number of votes on each side of an issue or dispute.

equal-management rule. The doctrine that each spouse alone may manage community property

unless the law provides otherwise. Cf. HEAD-AND-MASTER RULE.

equal-opportunity employer. See EMPLOYER.

equal-or-superior-knowledge rule. See SUPERIOR-KNOWLEDGE RULE.

Equal Pay Act. A federal law mandating that all who perform substantially the same work must be paid equally. 29 USCA § 206.

equal protection. (1866) The 14th Amendment guarantee that the government must treat a person or class of persons the same as it treats other persons or classes in like circumstances. • In today's constitutional jurisprudence, equal protection means that legislation that discriminates must have a rational basis for doing so. And if the legislation affects a fundamental right (such as the right to vote) or involves a suspect classification (such as race), it is unconstitutional unless it can withstand strict scrutiny. — Also termed *equal protection of the laws*; *equal protection under the law*. See RATIONAL-BASIS TEST; STRICT SCRUTINY.

Equal Protection Clause. (1899) The 14th Amendment provision requiring the states to give similarly situated persons or classes similar treatment under the law. Cf. DUE PROCESS CLAUSE.

equal protection of the laws. See EQUAL PROTECTION.

equal protection under the law. See EQUAL PROTECTION.

Equal Rights Amendment. A failed constitutional amendment that, had it been ratified, would have constitutionally prohibited sex-based discrimination. • Congress passed the Amendment in 1972, but it failed in 1982, having been ratified by only 35 of the required 38 states. — Abbr. ERA.

equal-shares clause. *Insurance.* A clause requiring an insurer to pay its proportionate share of a claimed loss.

Equal Time Act. A federal law requiring that a broadcasting-facility licensee who permits a legally qualified candidate for public office to use the facility for broadcasting must afford an equal opportunity to all other candidates for the office. 47 USCA § 315.

equal-time doctrine. See FAIRNESS DOCTRINE.

equinox (**ee**-kwə-noks *or* **ek**-wə-noks), *n.* (14c) One of the two periods of the year when the time from the sun's rising to its setting is equal to that from its setting to its rising. • The *vernal equinox* is about March 21, and the *autumnal equinox* is about September 22.

equip, *vb.* (16c) To furnish for service or against a need or exigency; to fit out; to supply with whatever is necessary for efficient action.

equipment, *n.* (17c) The articles or implements used for a specific purpose or activity (esp. a business operation). • Under the UCC, *equipment* includes goods if (1) the goods are used in or bought for a business enterprise (including farming or a profession) or by a debtor that is a nonprofit organization or a governmental subdivision or agency, and (2) the goods are not inventory, farm products, or consumer goods. UCC § 9-102(a)(33).

equipment trust. A financing device commonly used by railroads in which a trustee and the railroad together buy equipment from a manufacturer, with the trustee providing most of the purchase price, and the trustee then leases the equipment to the railroad, which pays a rental fee comprising interest, amortization for serial retirement, and the trustee's fee. See EQUIPMENT TRUST CERTIFICATE; *equipment trust bond* under BOND (3).

equipment trust bond. See BOND (3).

equipment trust certificate. A security, usu. issued by a railroad, to pay for new equipment. • Title to the equipment is held by a trustee until the note has been paid off. — Also termed *car trust certificate; trust certificate.* See EQUIPMENT TRUST.

equitable (ek-wi-tə-bəl), *adj.* (16c) **1.** Just; consistent with principles of justice and right. **2.** Existing in equity; available or sustainable by an action in equity, or under the rules and principles of equity.

equitable abstention. See ABSTENTION.

equitable action. See *action in equity* under ACTION (4).

equitable-adjustment theory. (1979) The doctrine that in settling a federal contract dispute, the contracting officer should make a fair adjustment within a reasonable time before the contractor has to settle with its subcontractors, suppliers, and other creditors.

equitable adoption. See *adoption by estoppel* under ADOPTION (1).

equitable asset. See ASSET.

equitable assignment. See ASSIGNMENT (2).

equitable-benefit doctrine. *Bankruptcy.* The principle that allows a bankruptcy court to grant preferred status to claims for service rendered by persons other than bankruptcy officers, to the extent that the service benefited the estate, when the person filing the claim acted primarily for the benefit of the estate as a whole.

equitable construction. See *liberal construction* under CONSTRUCTION.

equitable conversion. See CONVERSION (1).

equitable defense. See DEFENSE (1).

equitable disseisin. See DISSEISIN.

equitable distribution. (1893) *Family law.* The division of marital property by a court in a divorce proceeding, under statutory guidelines that provide for a fair, but not necessarily equal, allocation of the property between the spouses. • With equitable distribution, when a marriage ends in divorce, property acquired during the marriage is divided equitably between the spouses regardless of who holds title to the property. The courts consider many factors in awarding property, including a spouse's monetary contributions, nonmonetary assistance to a spouse's career or earning potential, the efforts of each spouse during the marriage, and the length of the marriage. The court may take into account the relative earning capacity of the spouses and the fault of either spouse. Equitable distribution is applied in 47 states (i.e., all the states except California, Louisiana, and New Mexico, which are "equal division" community-property states). — Also termed *equitable division; assignment of property.* Cf. TITLE DIVISION; COMMUNITY PROPERTY.

equitable division. See EQUITABLE DISTRIBUTION.

equitable doctrine of approximation. See DOCTRINE OF APPROXIMATION.

equitable dower. See *equitable jointure* under JOINTURE.

equitable duty. See DUTY (1).

equitable easement. See EASEMENT.

equitable ejectment. See EJECTMENT.

equitable election. See ELECTION (2).

equitable estate. See ESTATE (1).

equitable estoppel. See ESTOPPEL.

equitable foreclosure. See FORECLOSURE.

equitable fraud. See *constructive fraud* (1) under FRAUD.

equitable-fund doctrine. See COMMON-FUND DOCTRINE.

equitable indemnity. See INDEMNITY.

equitable interest. See INTEREST (2).

equitable jettison. See JETTISON.

equitable jointure. See JOINTURE.

equitable levy. See *equitable lien* under LIEN.

equitable lien. See LIEN.

equitable life estate. See ESTATE (1).

equitable life tenant. See LIFE TENANT.

equitable mortgage. See MORTGAGE.

equitable owner. See *beneficial owner* (1) under OWNER.

equitable ownership. See *beneficial ownership* (1) under OWNERSHIP.

equitable parent. See PARENT.

equitable-parent doctrine. *Family law.* The principle that a spouse who is not the biological parent of a child born or conceived during the marriage may, in a divorce action, be considered the child's natural father or mother if (1) the other spouse and the child both acknowledge a parent–child relationship, esp. when that other spouse has co-operated in the development of this relationship before the divorce action, (2) the nonbiologically related spouse wants parental rights, and (3) he or she is willing to take on the responsibility of paying support. ● The doctrine sometimes applies to nonspousal partners as well. Very few jurisdictions apply the doctrine. *See* Carolee Kvoriak Lezuch, *Michigan's Doctrine of Equitable Parenthood*, 45 Wayne L. Rev. 1529 (1999). — Also termed *equitable-parenthood doctrine.*

equitable recoupment. (1878) **1.** *Tax.* A doctrine allowing a taxpayer to offset previously overpaid taxes against current taxes due, even though the taxpayer is time-barred from claiming a refund on the previous taxes. **2.** *Tax.* A doctrine allowing the government to offset taxes previously uncollected from a taxpayer against the taxpayer's current claim for a refund, even though the government is time-barred from collecting the previous taxes. ● In both senses, this type of recoupment can be asserted only if the statute of limitations has created an inequitable result. See RECOUPMENT (2). **3.** A principle that diminishes a party's right to recover a debt to the extent that the party holds money or property of the debtor to which the party has no right. ● This doctrine is ordinarily a defensive remedy going only to mitigation of damages. The doctrine is sometimes applied so that a claim for a tax refund that is barred by limitations may nonetheless be recouped against a tax claim of the government. — Also termed *equitable-recoupment doctrine.* See SET-OFF; RECOUPMENT (3).

equitable relief. See *equitable remedy* under REMEDY.

equitable remedy. See REMEDY.

equitable remuneration. See *compulsory license* (1) under LICENSE.

equitable rescission. See RESCISSION.

equitable-restraint doctrine. See *Younger abstention* (1) under ABSTENTION.

equitable reversion. See REVERSION (1).

equitable right. See RIGHT.

equitable right to setoff. (1895) The right to cancel cross-demands, usu. used by a bank to take from a customer's deposit accounts the amount equal to the customer's debts that have matured and that are owed to that bank. See SETOFF.

equitable seisin. See SEISIN.

equitable servitude. See *restrictive covenant* under COVENANT (4).

equitable subrogation. See *legal subrogation* under SUBROGATION.

equitable title. See TITLE (2).

equitable tolling. (1967) **1.** The doctrine that the statute of limitations will not bar a claim if the plaintiff, despite diligent efforts, did not discover the injury until after the limitations period had expired. ● Equitable tolling does not require misconduct by the defendant. **2.** The doctrine that if a plaintiff files a suit first in one court and then refiles in another, the statute of limitations does not run while the litigation is pending in the first court if various requirements are met. ● Among those requirements are (1) timely notice to the defendant; (2) no prejudice to the defendant; and (3) reasonable and good-faith conduct on the part of the plaintiff.

equitable waste. See WASTE (1).

equity, *n.* (14c) **1.** Fairness; impartiality; evenhanded dealing <the company's policies require managers to use equity in dealing with subordinate employees>. **2.** The body of principles constituting what is fair and right; natural law <the concept of "inalienable rights" reflects the influence of equity on the Declaration of Independence>. **3.** The recourse to principles of justice to correct or supplement the law as applied to particular circumstances <the judge decided the case by equity because the statute did not fully address the issue>. — Also termed *natural equity.* **4.** The system of law or body of principles originating in the English Court of Chancery and superseding the common and statute law (together called "law" in the narrower sense) when the two conflict <in appealing to the equity of the court, she was appealing to the "king's conscience">; CHANCERY (2). **5.** A right, interest, or remedy recognizable by a court of equity <there was no formal contract formation, so they sued for breach in equity>.

> *contravening equity* (kon-trə-**veen**-ing). (1888) A right or interest that is inconsistent with or contrary to a right sought to be enforced.

> *countervailing equity* (kown-tər-**vayl**-ing). (1824) A contrary and balancing equity, equally deserving of consideration.

> *latent equity* (**lay**-tənt). (18c) An equitable claim or right known only by the parties for and against whom it exists, or that has been concealed from one who is interested in the subject matter. — Also termed *secret equity.*

> *perfect equity.* (1821) An equitable title or right that, to be a legal title, lacks only the formal conveyance or other investiture that would make it cognizable at law; esp., the equity of a real-estate

purchaser who has paid the full amount due but has not yet received a deed.

secret equity. See *latent equity*.

6. The right to decide matters in equity; equity jurisdiction <the court decided that the wrong was egregious enough to ignore the statute of limitations and decide the case in equity>. **7.** The amount by which the value of or an interest in property exceeds secured claims or liens; the difference between the value of the property and all encumbrances upon it <thanks to the real-estate boom, the mortgaged house still had high equity>. — Also termed *cushion*.

negative equity. The difference between the value of an asset and the outstanding amount of the loan secured by the asset when the asset's current value is less than the loan's balance.

8. An ownership interest in property, esp. in a business <the founders gave her equity in the business in return for all her help>. See OWNERS' EQUITY; BOOK EQUITY; MARKET EQUITY. **9.** A share in a publicly traded company <he did not want to cash in his equity>.

equity, bill in. See BILL (2).

equity, court of. See COURT.

equity accounting method. See ACCOUNTING METHOD.

equity capital. See CAPITAL.

equity contra legem (kon-trə lee-jəm). *Int'l law.* The use of equity in derogation of the law, where, under the circumstances of the case, an exception to the law is needed to achieve an equitable and just result. — Sometimes shortened to *contra legem*. See EX AEQUO ET BONO. Cf. EQUITY INTRA LEGEM.

equity financing. See FINANCING.

equity insolvency. See INSOLVENCY.

equity intra legem (in-trə lee-jəm). A court's power to interpret and apply the law to achieve the most equitable result. — Sometimes shortened to *intra legem*. — Also written *equity infra legem*. Cf. EQUITY CONTRA LEGEM.

equity jurisdiction. See JURISDICTION.

equity jurisprudence. See JURISPRUDENCE.

equity kicker. See EQUITY PARTICIPATION.

equity loan. See *home equity loan* under LOAN.

equity of exoneration (eg-zon-ə-ray-shən). The right of a person who is secondarily liable on a debt to make the primarily liable party discharge the debt or reimburse any payment that the secondarily liable person has made. • One example is the right of a surety to call on the principal for reimbursement after the surety has paid the debt. Unlike contribution, which exists when the parties are equally liable, the equity of exoneration

exists when parties are successively liable. — Also termed *right of exoneration*. See EXONERATION.

equity of partners. The right of each partner to have the firm's property applied to the firm's debts.

equity of redemption. *Real estate.* The right of a mortgagor in default to recover property before a foreclosure sale by paying the principal, interest, and other costs that are due. • A defaulting mortgagor with an equity of redemption has the right, until the foreclosure sale, to reimburse the mortgagee and cure the default. In many jurisdictions, the mortgagor also has a statutory right to redeem within six months after the foreclosure sale, and the mortgagor becomes entitled to any surplus from the sale proceeds above the amount of the outstanding mortgage. — Also termed *right of redemption*. See CLOG ON THE EQUITY OF REDEMPTION; REDEMPTION (4); STATUTORY RIGHT OF REDEMPTION.

equity of subrogation. (1850) The right of a person who is secondarily liable on a debt, and who pays the debt, to personally enforce any right that the original creditor could have pursued against the debtor, including the right to foreclose on any security held by the creditor and any right that the creditor may have to contribution from others who are liable for the debt. — Also termed *right of subrogation*; (in Scots law) *right of relief*. See SUBROGATION.

equity-of-the-statute rule. (1959) In statutory construction, the principle that a statute should be interpreted according to the legislators' purpose and intent, even if this interpretation goes beyond the literal meaning of the text. • Under this little-used rule, for example, if a statute defines jury-tampering to include a party's "giving a juror food or drink," the giving of cigars to a juror would also fall within that definition. Cf. GOLDEN RULE; MISCHIEF RULE; PLAIN-MEANING RULE.

equity participation. (1947) The inclusion of a lender in the equity ownership of a project as a condition of the lender's granting a loan. — Also termed *equity kicker*.

equity pleading. See PLEADING (2).

equity praeter legem (pree-tər lee-jəm) The use of equity to fill a gap in the law. — Sometimes shortened to *praeter legem*.

equity ratio. 1. The percentage relationship between a purchaser's equity value (esp. the amount of a down payment) and the property value. **2.** The measure of a shareholder's equity divided by total equity.

equity security. See SECURITY.

equity stock. See STOCK.

equity term. See TERM (5).

equity to a settlement. (1838) A wife's equitable right, arising when her husband sues in equity for the reduction of her equitable estate to his own possession, to have all or part of that estate settled upon herself and her children. — Also termed *wife's equity*; *wife's settlement*.

equivalence of advantages. See RECIPROCITY (2).

equivalent, *adj.* (15c) **1.** Equal in value, force, amount, effect, or significance. **2.** Corresponding in effect or function; nearly equal; virtually identical.

equivalent, *n. Patents.* An element that (1) existed before another element; (2) can perform the same function as the other element; and (3) is recognizable as a substitute for the other element. ● For instance, mechanical devices are equivalents when one skilled in the art would have recognized that each device would produce the same result. If the equivalent is known at the time an invention is conceived, the invention's patentability may be questioned. See ANALOG.

equivalents doctrine. See DOCTRINE OF EQUIVALENTS.

equivocal (i-**kwiv**-ə-kəl), *adj.* (17c) **1.** Of doubtful character; questionable. **2.** Having more than one meaning or sense; ambiguous.

equivocality test (i-kwiv-ə-**kal**-ə-tee). See RES IPSA LOQUITUR TEST.

equivocation (i-kwiv-ə-**kay**-shən). See *latent ambiguity* under AMBIGUITY.

ERA. *abbr.* EQUAL RIGHTS AMENDMENT.

erase, *vb.* (14c) **1.** To rub or scrape out (something written); to obliterate. **2.** To obliterate (recorded material). **3.** To seal (criminal records) from disclosure. — **erasure,** *n.*

Erastian (i-**ras**-chən *or* i-**ras**-tee-ən). (17c) *Hist.* A follower of Thomas Erastus (1524–1583), who thought that offenses against religion and morality should be punished by the civil power and not by the censures of the church. ● As a sect, Erastians had great influence in England, particularly among 17th-century common-law lawyers.

erasure of record. See EXPUNGEMENT OF RECORD.

erect, *vb.* (15c) **1.** To construct. **2.** To establish. ● In England, *erect* is one of the formal words of incorporation in a royal charter, being part of the phrase, "We do incorporate, erect, ordain, name, constitute, and establish."

erectile dysfunction. See IMPOTENCE.

E reorganization. See REORGANIZATION (2).

ergo (**ər**-goh *or* **air**-goh), *adv.* [Latin] Therefore; thus.

Erie-bound, *adj.* (Of a federal court) required to apply the *Erie* doctrine.

Erie doctrine (**eer**-ee). (1943) The principle that a federal court exercising diversity jurisdiction over a case that does not involve a federal question must apply the substantive law of the state where the court sits. *Erie R.R. v. Tompkins*, 304 U.S. 64, 58 S.Ct. 817 (1938). Cf. REVERSE ERIE DOCTRINE.

Erie/Klaxon doctrine. See KLAXON DOCTRINE.

ERISA (ee- *or* ə-**ris**-ə). *abbr.* EMPLOYEE RETIREMENT INCOME SECURITY ACT.

eristic (e-**ris**-tik), *adj.* Of or relating to controversy or disputation. — Also termed *eristical.*

ermine (**ər**-min), *n.* (18c) The station of a judge; judgeship. ● The term refers to the fur trimmings (made from the coats of white weasels called "ermine") adorning official robes of English judges. — **ermined,** *adj.*

erosion. (1841) The wearing away of something by action of the elements; esp., the gradual eating away of soil by the operation of currents or tides. Cf. ACCRETION (1); DELICTION; AVULSION (2); ALLUVION.

err (ər), *vb.* (14c) To make an error; to be incorrect or mistaken <the court erred in denying the motion for summary judgment>.

errant (**er**-ənt), *adj.* (14c) **1.** Fallible; incorrect; straying from what is proper <an errant judicial holding>. **2.** Traveling <a knight errant>.

errata sheet. (1932) An attachment to a deposition transcript containing the deponent's corrections upon reading the transcript and the reasons for those corrections. — Also termed *errata page.*

erratum (i-**ray**-təm *or* i-**rah**-təm), *n.* [Latin "error"] (16c) An error that needs correction. Pl. **errata** (i-**ray**-tə *or* i-**rah**-tə). See CORRIGENDUM.

erroneous (i-**roh**-nee-əs), *adj.* (15c) Incorrect; inconsistent with the law or the facts.

erroneous assessment. See ASSESSMENT.

erroneous extradition. See *extraordinary rendition* under RENDITION.

erroneous judgment. See JUDGMENT.

erroneous rendition. See RENDITION.

erroneous tax. See TAX.

error, *n.* (13c) **1.** An assertion or belief that does not conform to objective reality; a belief that what is false is true or that what is true is false; MISTAKE.

    error in corpore (**kor**-pə-ree). (18c) A mistake involving the identity of a particular object, as when a party buys a horse believing it to be the one that the party had already examined and ridden, when in fact it is a different horse.

    error in negotio (ni-**goh**-shee-oh). (1944) A mistake about the type of contract that the parties actually wanted to enter.

error in qualitate (kwah-lə-**tay**-tee). A mistake affecting the quality of the contractual object.

error in quantitate (kwahn-tə-**tay**-tee). A mistake affecting the amount of the contractual object.

reissuable error. See REISSUABLE ERROR.

2. A mistake of law or of fact in a tribunal's judgment, opinion, or order.

assigned error. An alleged error that occurred in a lower court and is pointed out in an appellate brief as grounds for reversal <appellants' two assigned errors appeared to the court to be harmless errors>. See ASSIGNMENT OF ERROR.

Caldwell error. The constitutionally impermissible error of resting a death sentence on a determination made by a sentencer who has been led to believe that the responsibility for determining the appropriateness of the defendant's death sentence lies elsewhere. *Caldwell v. Mississippi*, 472 U.S. 320, 105 S.Ct. 2633 (1985). ● The error most often occurs when the prosecutor or the judge tells the jury that the death sentence, if inappropriate, may be overturned on appeal.

clear error. (18c) A trial judge's decision or action that appears to a reviewing court to have been unquestionably erroneous. ● Even though a clear error occurred, it may not warrant reversal. — Also termed *clear and unmistakable error.*

clerical error. (18c) An error resulting from a minor mistake or inadvertence, esp. in writing or copying something on the record, and not from judicial reasoning or determination. ● Among the boundless examples of clerical errors are omitting an appendix from a document; typing an incorrect number; mistranscribing a word; and failing to log a call. A court can correct a clerical error at any time, even after judgment has been entered. *See* Fed. R. Civ. P. 60(a); Fed. R. Crim. P. 36. — Also termed *scrivener's error; vitium clerici.*

cross-error. (1838) An error brought by the party responding to a writ of error.

cumulative error. The prejudicial effect of two or more trial errors that may have been harmless individually. ● The cumulative effect of multiple harmless errors may amount to reversible error. See CUMULATIVE-ERROR ANALYSIS.

error apparent of record. See *plain error.*

error in vacuo. See *harmless error.*

fatal error. See *reversible error.*

fundamental error. See *plain error.*

harmful error. See *reversible error.*

harmless error. (1851) An error that does not affect a party's substantive rights or the case's outcome. ● A harmless error is not grounds for reversal. *See* Fed. R. Civ. P. 61; Fed. R. Crim.

P. 52. — Also termed *technical error; error in vacuo.* Cf. *substantial error.*

invited error. (1893) An error that a party cannot complain of on appeal because the party, through conduct, encouraged or prompted the trial court to make the erroneous ruling.

manifest constitutional error. (1985) An error by the trial court that has an identifiably negative impact on the trial to such a degree that the constitutional rights of a party are compromised. ● A manifest constitutional error can be reviewed by a court of appeals even if the appellant did not object at trial.

manifest error. (18c) An error that is plain and indisputable, and that amounts to a complete disregard of the controlling law or the credible evidence in the record.

obvious error. See OBVIOUS ERROR.

plain error. (1801) An error that is so obvious and prejudicial that an appellate court should address it despite the parties' failure to raise a proper objection at trial. ● A plain error is often said to be so obvious and substantial that failure to correct it would infringe a party's due-process rights and damage the integrity of the judicial process. *See* Fed. R. Evid. 103(d). — Also termed *fundamental error; error apparent of record.*

reissuable error. See REISSUABLE ERROR.

reversible error. (1855) An error that affects a party's substantive rights or the case's outcome, and thus is grounds for reversal if the party properly objected at trial. — Also termed *harmful error; prejudicial error; fatal error.*

scrivener's error. See *clerical error.*

substantial error. An error that affects a party's substantive rights or the outcome of the case. ● A substantial error may require reversal on appeal. Cf. *harmless error.*

technical error. See *harmless error.*

3. An appeal <a proceeding in error>.

error, assignment of. See ASSIGNMENT OF ERROR.

error, writ of. See WRIT OF ERROR.

error in fact. See *mistake of fact* (1) under MISTAKE.

error in law. See *mistake of law* (1) under MISTAKE.

error *in vacuo* (in **vak**-yoo-oh). [Latin "error in a void"] See *harmless error* under ERROR.

error of fact. See *mistake of fact* (1) under MISTAKE.

error-of-judgment rule. The doctrine that a professional is not liable to a client for advice or an opinion given in good faith and with an honest belief that the advice was in the client's best interests, but that was based on a mistake either in judgment or in analyzing an unsettled area of the professional's business. ● For example, an attorney who makes an error in trial tactics involving an unsettled area of the law may, under certain circumstances, defeat a malpractice claim arising from the tactical error. — Also termed *judgmental immunity.*

error of law. See *mistake of law* (1) under MISTAKE.

errors, assignment of. See ASSIGNMENT OF ERRORS.

errors-and-omissions insurance. See INSURANCE.

ERS. *abbr.* ECONOMIC RESEARCH SERVICE.

ESA. *abbr.* **1.** ECONOMICS AND STATISTICS ADMINISTRATION. **2.** EMPLOYMENT STANDARDS ADMINISTRATION.

ESBT. *abbr.* See *electing small-business trust* under TRUST (3).

escalation clause. See ESCALATOR CLAUSE.

escalator clause. (1930) **1.** A contractual provision that makes pricing flexible by increasing or decreasing the contract price according to changing market conditions, such as higher or lower taxes or operating costs. Cf. DE-ESCALATION CLAUSE. **2.** A provision in a divorce decree or divorce agreement providing for the automatic increase of alimony payments upon the occurrence of any of various triggering events, such as cost-of-living increases or an increase in the obligor's salary. ● Escalation clauses for child support are often unenforceable. **3.** *Oil & gas.* A provision in a long-term gas contract allowing the base price of the gas to be adjusted as the market changes. ● The actual adjustment may be up or down. — Also termed *escalation clause; fluctuating clause.*

escambium. See CAMBIUM (2).

escape, *n.* (14c) **1.** The act or an instance of breaking free from confinement, restraint, or an obligation. **2.** An unlawful departure from legal custody without the use of force. — Also termed *actual escape.* Cf. PRISON BREACH.

    constructive escape. A prisoner's obtaining more liberty than the law allows, while not fully regaining freedom.

3. At common law, a criminal offense committed by a peace officer who allows a prisoner to depart unlawfully from legal custody. — Also termed *voluntary escape.* — **escape,** *vb.*

    negligent escape. The offense committed by a peace officer who negligently allows a prisoner to depart from legal custody.

escape clause. (1945) A contractual provision that allows a party to avoid performance under specified conditions; specif., an insurance-policy provision — usu. contained in the "other insurance" section of the policy — requiring the insurer to provide coverage only if no other coverage is available. Cf. EXCESS CLAUSE; PRO RATA CLAUSE.

escapee. (19c) A prisoner or other inmate who has escaped from lawful custody.

escape period. *Labor law.* A time agreed upon in some union contracts during which workers may withdraw from the union near the end of one term covered by the contract and before the start of the next.

escape warrant. See WARRANT (1).

escheat (es-**cheet**), *n.* (14c) **1.** *Hist.* The reversion of land ownership back to the lord when the immediate tenant dies without heirs. See WRIT OF ESCHEAT. **2.** Reversion of property (esp. real property) to the state upon the death of an owner who has neither a will nor any legal heirs. **3.** Property that has so reverted. See *heirless estate* under ESTATE (3). — **escheat,** *vb.* — **escheatable,** *adj.*

escheat grant. See GRANT.

escheator (es-**cheet**-ər). *Hist.* A royal officer appointed to assess the value of property escheating to the Crown. ● Corrupt officers led many to associate the escheator with fraudulent conduct, giving rise to the word *cheat* as used in the modern sense. — Also termed *cheater.*

escheat patent. See *escheat grant* under GRANT.

Escobedo rule (es-kə-**bee**-doh). *Criminal procedure.* The principle that a statement by an unindicted, targeted suspect in police custody is inadmissible at trial unless the police warn the suspect of the right to remain silent and provide an opportunity for the suspect to consult with retained or appointed counsel. ● This rule was a precursor to the *Miranda* rule. *Escobedo v. Illinois,* 378 U.S. 478, 84 S.Ct. 1758 (1964). See MIRANDA RULE.

escrow (es-**kroh**), *n.* (16c) **1.** A legal document or property delivered by a promisor to a third party to be held by the third party for a given amount of time or until the occurrence of a condition, at which time the third party is to hand over the document or property to the promisee <the agent received the escrow two weeks before the closing date>. **2.** An account held in trust or as security <the earnest money is in escrow>. — Also termed *escrow account; impound account; reserve account.* See *escrow account* under ACCOUNT. **3.** The holder of such a document, property, or deposit <the attorney performed the function of escrow>. — Also termed *escrow agent.* **4.** The general arrangement under which a legal document or property is delivered to a third person until the occurrence of a condition <creating an escrow>. — **escrow,** *vb.*

escrow account. See ACCOUNT.

escrow agent. See AGENT (2).

escrow agreement. (1882) The instructions given to the third-party depositary of an escrow.

escrow contract. See CONTRACT.

escrow deposit. See *escrow account* under AC-COUNT.

escrowee. See *escrow agent* under AGENT (2).

escrow holder. See *escrow agent* under AGENT (2).

escrow officer. See *escrow agent* under AGENT (2).

E-Sign Act. The short name for the Electronic Signatures in Global and National Commerce Act, a 2000 federal statute that establishes the legal equivalency of electronic contracts, electronic signatures, and other electronic records with their paper counterparts. • The E-Sign Act applies to all types of transactions, whether in interstate or foreign commerce, unless a specific exception applies. Among the few exceptions are documents related to family law and probate law, most documents required by the Uniform Commercial Code, court documents, and a list of notices that directly impact the lives of consumers (e.g., a notice of termination of utility services or a notice of eviction).

eskipper (ə-**skip**-ər), *vb.* To ship. — Also termed *eskippare* (es-kə-**pair**-ee).

eskippeson (ə-**skip**-[ə]-sən), *n.* Shippage; passage by sea. — Also termed *skippeson*.

eslisor (es-**lī**-zər). See ELISOR.

esnecy (**es**-ni-see), *n. Hist.* Seniority; the condition, right, or privilege of the eldest-born. • The term esp. applied to the privilege of the eldest among coparceners to make a first choice of shares upon a voluntary partition. — Also termed *aesnecia*.

ESOP (**ee**-sop). *abbr.* See *employee-stock-ownership plan* under EMPLOYEE BENEFIT PLAN.

espera (**es**-pə-rə), *n.* A period fixed by law or by a court within which certain acts are to be performed (such as payment of a debt).

espionage (**es**-pee-ə-nahzh). (18c) The practice of using spies to collect information about what another government or company is doing or plans to do.

industrial espionage. (1962) *Intellectual property.* One company's spying on another to steal trade secrets or other proprietary information.

Espionage Act. A federal law that criminalizes and punishes espionage, spying, and related crimes. 18 USCA §§ 793 et seq. • Two Espionage Acts were passed. The 1917 act criminalized false statements intended to interfere with the war effort; to willfully cause or attempt to cause dissension in the armed forces; or to willfully obstruct national recruiting and enlistment activities. This act remains enforceable "when the United States is at war." The 1918 act criminalized speech intended to obstruct war-bond sales; to generate scorn or contempt for democratic government, the flag, or the uniform of the Army or Navy; to urge reduced production of war materials with the intent to hinder the war effort; or to express support for a national enemy or opposition to the United States' cause. The act's constitutionality was upheld by the U.S. Supreme Court before it was repealed in 1921.

esplees (es-**pleez**), *n. pl.* (17c) *Archaic.* **1.** Products yielded from land. **2.** Rents or other payments derived from land. **3.** Land itself. — Also termed *explees.*

espousals (ə-**spow**-zəlz), *n.* (14c) Mutual promises between a man and a woman to marry one another.

espouse, *vb.* (15c) **1.** To marry. **2.** To dedicate oneself to and advocate for (a cause).

esquire (**es**-kwir *or* e-**skwir**). (15c) **1.** *Hist.* A candidate for knighthood who assisted knights in martial endeavors. **2.** *Hist.* A member of the gentry whose rank was inferior to that of a knight. **3.** *Archaic.* A landed gentleman; a member of the landed gentry. **4.** (*usu. cap. as an honorific*) A title of courtesy commonly appended after the name of a lawyer. — Abbr. Esq.

essence, of the. See OF THE ESSENCE.

essence test. *Labor law.* A test under which an arbitrator's interpretation of a collective-bargaining agreement must be upheld if it derives in any rational way from the agreement, viewed in light of the agreement's language, its context, and any other evidence of the parties' intention.

essential finding. See FINDING OF FACT.

essential mistake. See MISTAKE.

essential term. See *fundamental term* under TERM (2).

essoin (e-**soyn**), *n.* [fr. Old French *essoi(g)ne* "excuse"] (14c) *Hist.* **1.** An excuse for not appearing in court on an appointed day in obedience to a summons. **2.** The offering or presentation of such an excuse. — Also spelled *essoign.*

essoin, *vb.* [fr. Old French *essoi(g)nier* "to excuse"] (14c) *Hist.* To present an excuse for not appearing in court as ordered.

essoiner (e-**soyn**-ər), *n. Hist.* A person making an essoin. — Also termed *essoiniator* (e-**soyn**-ee-ay-tər).

essoin roll. *Hist.* A roll upon which essoins were entered, together with the day to which they were adjourned.

establish, *vb.* (14c) **1.** To settle, make, or fix firmly; to enact permanently <one object of the Constitution was to establish justice>. **2.** To make or form; to bring about or into existence <Congress has the power to establish Article III courts>. **3.** To prove; to convince <the House managers tried to establish the President's guilt>.

establishment, *n.* (15c) **1.** The act of establishing; the state or condition of being established. **2.** An institution or place of business. **3.** A group of people who are in power or who control or exercise great influence over something.

Establishment Clause. (1959) The First Amendment provision that prohibits the federal and state governments from establishing an official religion, or from favoring or disfavoring one view of religion over another. U.S. Const. amend. I. Cf. FREE EXERCISE CLAUSE.

estate. (15c) **1.** The amount, degree, nature, and quality of a person's interest in land or other property; esp., a real-estate interest that may become possessory, the ownership being measured in terms of duration. See *periodic tenancy* under TENANCY.

absolute estate. A full and complete estate that cannot be defeated.

base estate. Hist. An estate held at the will of the lord, as distinguished from a freehold.

concurrent estate. (18c) Ownership or possession of property by two or more persons at the same time. • In modern practice, there are three types of concurrent estates: tenancy in common, joint tenancy, and tenancy by the entirety. — Also termed *concurrent interest.*

conditional estate. See estate on condition.

contingent estate. (17c) An estate that vests only if a specified event does or does not happen. Cf. *estate on condition.*

defeasible estate. (17c) An estate that may come to an end before its maximum duration has run because of the operation of a special limitation, a condition subsequent, or an executory limitation. • If an estate is defeasible by operation of a special limitation, it is called a *determinable estate.*

derivative estate. (18c) A particular interest that has been carved out of another, larger estate. Cf. *original estate.*

determinable estate. (17c) An estate that is defeasible by operation of a special limitation. — Also termed *determinable freehold.*

equitable estate. (17c) An estate recognized in equity, such as a trust beneficiary's interest. See EQUITY.

equitable life estate. An interest in real or personal property that lasts for the life of the holder of the estate and that is equitable as opposed to legal in its creation. • An example is a life estate held by a trust beneficiary.

estate ad remanentiam (ad rem-ə-**nen**-shee-əm). An estate in fee simple.

estate at sufferance. See tenancy at sufferance under TENANCY.

estate at will. See tenancy at will under TENANCY.

estate by curtesy. An estate owned by a wife, to which the husband is entitled upon her death. See CURTESY.

estate by elegit. An estate held by a judgment creditor, entitling the creditor to the rents and profits from land owned by the debtor until the debt is paid. See ELEGIT.

estate by entirety. A common-law estate in which each spouse is seised of the whole of the property. • An estate by entirety is based on the legal fiction that a husband and wife are a single unit. The estate consists of five unities: time, title, interest, possession, and marriage. The last of these unities distinguishes the estate by entirety from the joint tenancy. A joint tenancy can exist with any number of persons, while an estate by entirety can be held only by a husband and wife and is not available to any other persons. And it can be acquired only during the marriage. This estate has a right of survivorship, but upon the death of one spouse, the surviving spouse retains the entire interest rather than acquiring the decedent's interest. Most jurisdictions have abolished this estate. — Also termed *estate by the entirety; estate by entireties; estate by the entireties; tenancy by the entirety; tenancy by the entireties.* Cf. *joint tenancy* and *tenancy in common* under TENANCY.

estate by purchase. An estate acquired in any manner other than by descent. See PURCHASE.

estate by statute staple. An estate in a defendant's land held by a creditor under the statute staple until the debt was paid. See STATUTE STAPLE.

estate by the curtesy of England. See CURTESY.

estate for a term. See tenancy for a term under TENANCY.

estate for life. See life estate.

estate for years. See tenancy for a term under TENANCY.

estate in common. See tenancy in common under TENANCY.

estate in fee simple. See FEE SIMPLE.

estate in fee tail. See FEE TAIL.

estate in gage. An estate that has been pledged as security for a debt. See MORTGAGE.

estate in partnership. A joint estate that is vested in the members of a partnership when real estate is purchased with partnership funds and for partnership purposes.

estate in possession. An estate in which a present interest passes to the tenant; an estate in which the tenant is entitled to receive the rents and other profits arising from the estate.

estate in remainder. See REMAINDER (1).

estate in reversion. See REVERSION (1).

estate in severalty (sev-ə-rəl-tee). An estate held by a tenant separately, without any other person being joined or connected in interest.

estate in tail. See FEE TAIL.

estate in vadio (in **vad**-ee-oh). An estate in gage or pledge. See MORTGAGE.

estate less than freehold. An estate for years, an estate at will, or an estate at sufferance.

estate on condition. (18c) An estate that vests, is modified, or is defeated upon the occurrence or nonoccurrence of some specified event. • While an estate on limitation can revert without any action by the grantor or the grantor's heirs, an estate on condition requires the entry of the grantor or the grantor's heirs to end the estate whenever the condition occurs. — Also termed *estate on conditional limitation*; *conditional estate*. Cf. *estate on limitation*.

estate on conditional limitation. See *estate on condition*.

estate on condition expressed. (18c) A contingent estate in which the condition upon which the estate will fail is stated explicitly in the granting instrument.

estate on condition implied. (18c) A contingent estate having some condition that is so inseparable from the estate's essence that it need not be expressed in words.

estate on limitation. (18c) An estate that automatically reverts back to the grantor according to a provision, usu. regarding the passage of a determined time period, designated by words such as "during," "while," and "as long as." See *fee simple determinable* under FEE SIMPLE. Cf. *estate on condition*.

estate pur autre vie. See *life estate pur autre vie*.

estate tail. See FEE TAIL.

estate tail quasi. An estate granted by a life tenant, who, despite using language of conveyance that is otherwise sufficient to create an estate tail, is unable to grant in perpetuity.

executed estate. See REMAINDER (1).

expectant estate. See FUTURE INTEREST.

fast estate. See *real property* under PROPERTY.

freehold estate. See FREEHOLD.

future estate. See FUTURE INTEREST.

joint estate. (15c) Any of the following five types of estates: (1) a joint tenancy, (2) a tenancy in common, (3) an estate in coparcenary (a common-law estate in which coheirs hold as tenants in common), (4) a tenancy by the entirety, or (5) an estate in partnership.

landed estate. An interest in real property, esp. suburban or rural land, as distinguished from real estate situated in a city. — Also termed *landed property*.

leasehold estate. See LEASEHOLD.

legal estate. An interest enforced in law rather than in equity.

legal life estate. See *life estate*.

life estate. (18c) An estate held only for the duration of a specified person's life, usu. the possessor's. • Most life estates — created, for example, by a grant "to Jane for life" — are beneficial interests under trusts, the corpus often being personal property, not real property. — Also termed *estate for life*; *legal life estate*; *life tenancy*. See LIFE TENANT.

life estate pur autre vie (pər **oh**-trə vee). (1888) A life estate for which the measuring life — the life whose duration determines the duration of the estate — is someone's other than the possessor's. — Also spelled *life estate per autre vie*.

marital estate. See *marital property* under PROPERTY.

next eventual estate. (1836) An estate taking effect upon an event that terminates the accumulation of undisposed rents and profits; an estate taking effect when the existing estate terminates.

nonancestral estate. An estate from any source other than the owner's ancestors. — Also termed *nonancestral property*.

nonfreehold estate. Any estate in real property without seisin, such as an estate for years, from period to period, at will, or at sufferance; any estate except a fee simple, fee tail, or life estate.

original estate. An estate that is the first of one or more derivative estates, bearing to each other the relation of a particular estate and a reversion.

particular estate. An estate or interest less than a fee simple, such as a fee tail, a life estate, or a term for years. • It is so called because the estate is a mere part (*particula*) of the fee simple.

periodic estate. See *periodic tenancy* under TENANCY.

possessory estate. (18c) An estate giving the holder the right to possess the property, with or without an ownership interest in the property.

present estate. An estate in immediate possession; one vested at the present time, as distinguished from a future estate. See *present interest* under INTEREST (2).

qualified estate. Any estate that is not absolute and unconditional; a limited or conditional estate.

reversionary estate. See REVERSION.

separate estate. The individual property of one of two persons who stand in a marital or business relationship. See SEPARATE PROPERTY.

settled estate. An estate created or limited under a settlement; an estate in which the powers of alienation, devising, and transmission according to the ordinary rules of descent are restrained by the settlement's terms.

stipendiary estate (stī-**pen**-dee-er-ee). *Hist.* An estate granted in return for services, usu. of a military kind.

vested estate. (18c) An estate with a present right of enjoyment or a present fixed right of future enjoyment.

2. All that a person or entity owns, including both real and personal property.

bankruptcy estate. See BANKRUPTCY ESTATE.

3. The property that one leaves after death; the collective assets and liabilities of a dead person.

adjusted gross estate. 1. The total value of a decedent's property after subtracting administration expenses, funeral expenses, creditors' claims, and casualty losses. ● The value of the adjusted gross estate is used in computing the federal estate tax. Cf. *net probate estate* under PROBATE ESTATE. **2.** See *gross estate* (1).

ancestral estate. An estate that is acquired by descent or by operation of law with no other consideration than that of blood.

augmented estate. A refinement of the elective share to which a surviving spouse is entitled, whereby the "fair share" is identified as something other than the traditional one-third of the probate estate. ● The current version of the Uniform Probate Code uses a sliding scale that increases with each year of marriage. Under the UPC, a surviving spouse has accrued full marital-property rights after 15 years of marriage. This percentage of spousal entitlement is applied to a reconceptualization of the decedent's estate to take into account more than just the assets remaining in the probate estate at death. Also added into the calculation are the value of certain inter vivos transfers that the decedent made to others in a way that depleted the probate estate; the value of similar transfers made to others by the spouse as well as the value of the marital property owned by the spouse at the decedent's death; and the value of inter vivos transfers of property made by the decedent to the spouse. The Uniform Probate Code adopted this version of the augmented-estate concept in an attempt to equalize the treatment of surviving spouses in non-community-property states vis-à-vis community- property states. Unif. Probate Code § 2-202. See ELECTIVE SHARE.

decedent's estate. (18c) The real and personal property that a person possesses at the time of death and that passes to the heirs or testamentary beneficiaries.

estate of inheritance. An estate that may descend to heirs.

gross estate. 1. The total value of a decedent's property without any deductions. **2.** Loosely, adjusted gross estate.

heirless estate. The property of a person who dies intestate and without heirs. See ESCHEAT.

net estate. See *net probate estate* under PROBATE ESTATE.

net probate estate. See PROBATE ESTATE.

probate estate. See PROBATE ESTATE.

residuary estate. (18c) The part of a decedent's estate remaining after payment of all debts, expenses, statutory claims, taxes, and testamentary gifts (special, general, and demonstrative) have been made. — Also termed *residual estate*; *residue*; *residuary*; *residuum*.

taxable estate. (18c) A decedent's gross estate reduced by allowable deductions (such as administration costs and ESOP deductions). IRC (26 USCA) § 2051. ● The taxable estate is the amount that is subject to the federal unified transfer tax at death.

4. A tract of land, esp. one affected by an easement.

dominant estate. (18c) An estate that benefits from an easement. — Also termed *dominant tenement*; *dominant property*; *upper estate*. Cf. *servient estate*.

lower estate. See *servient estate*.

real estate. See *real property* under PROPERTY.

servient estate (sər-vee-ənt). (18c) An estate burdened by an easement. — Also termed *servient tenement*; *servient property*; *lower estate*. Cf. *dominant estate*.

upper estate. See *dominant estate*.

estate duty. See DUTY (4).

estate freeze. (1986) An estate-planning maneuver whereby an owner of a closely held business exchanges common stock for dividend-paying preferred stock and gives the common stock to his or her children, thus seeking to guarantee an income in retirement and to avoid estate tax on future appreciation in the business's value.

estate from period to period. See *periodic tenancy* under TENANCY.

estate in expectancy. See FUTURE INTEREST.

estate in freehold. See FREEHOLD.

estate in lands. (16c) **1.** Property that one has in lands, tenements, or hereditaments. **2.** The conditions or circumstances under which a tenant stands in relation to the leased property.

estate in remainder. See REMAINDER (1).

estate planning. (1938) **1.** The preparation for the distribution and management of a person's estate at death through the use of wills, trusts, insurance policies, and other arrangements, esp. to reduce administration costs and transfer-tax liability. **2.** A branch of law that involves the arrangement of a person's estate, taking into account the laws of wills, taxes, insurance, property, and trusts.

estates of the realm. 1. The lords spiritual, the lords temporal, and the commons of Great Britain. — Also termed *the three estates*. **2.** In feudal Europe, the clergy, nobles, and commons. • Because the lords spiritual had no separate assembly or negative in their political capacity, some authorities reduce the estates in Great Britain to two, the lords and commons. In England (until about the 14th century), the three estates of the realm were the clergy, barons, and knights. In legal practice, the lords spiritual and lords temporal are usu. collectively designated simply as *lords*.

estate's property. See PROPERTY OF THE ESTATE.

estate tax. See TAX.

estate trust. See TRUST.

estimated damages. See *liquidated damages* under DAMAGES.

estimated tax. See TAX.

estimated useful life. See USEFUL LIFE.

estop (e-**stop**), *vb.* (15c) To bar or prevent by estoppel.

estoppage (e-**stop**-ij), *n.* (18c) The state or condition of being estopped.

estoppel (e-**stop**-əl), *n.* (16c) **1.** A bar that prevents one from asserting a claim or right that contradicts what one has said or done before or what has been legally established as true. **2.** A bar that prevents the relitigation of issues. **3.** An affirmative defense alleging good-faith reliance on a misleading representation and an injury or detrimental change in position resulting from that reliance. Cf. WAIVER (1). — **estop,** *vb.*

administrative collateral estoppel. See COLLATERAL ESTOPPEL.

assignee estoppel. *Patents.* The equitable doctrine that bars the assignee of a patent from contesting the patent's validity under some circumstances, as when the assignee seeks to avoid royalty payments, to void an assignment contract, or to mitigate damages related to the assignee's fraudulent acquisition of the patent. • The doctrine prevents an assignee from simultaneously attacking and defending the validity of the same patent.

assignor estoppel. *Patents.* Estoppel barring someone who has assigned the rights to a patent from later attacking the patent's validity. *Westinghouse Elec. & Mfg. Co. v. Formica Insulation Co.*, 266 U.S. 342, 45 S.Ct. 117 (1924). • The doctrine was narrowed by *Diamond Scientific Co. v. Ambico, Inc.*, 848 F.2d 1220 (Fed. Cir. 1988), in which the court held that in some circumstances equity may outweigh the public-policy reasons behind the estoppel doctrine.

collateral estoppel. See COLLATERAL ESTOPPEL.

equitable estoppel. (18c) **1.** A defensive doctrine preventing one party from taking unfair advantage of another when, through false language or conduct, the person to be estopped has induced another person to act in a certain way, with the result that the other person has been injured in some way. • This doctrine is founded on principles of fraud. The five essential elements of this type of estoppel are that (1) there was a false representation or concealment of material facts, (2) the representation was known to be false by the party making it, or the party was negligent in not knowing its falsity, (3) it was believed to be true by the person to whom it was made, (4) the party making the representation intended that it be acted on, or the person acting on it was justified in assuming this intent, and (5) the party asserting estoppel acted on the representation in a way that will result in substantial prejudice unless the claim of estoppel succeeds. — Also termed *estoppel by conduct*; *estoppel in pais*. **2.** See *promissory estoppel*.

estoppel by conduct. See *equitable estoppel*.

estoppel by contract. A bar that prevents a person from denying a term, fact, or performance arising from a contract that the person has entered into.

estoppel by deed. Estoppel that prevents a party to a deed from denying anything recited in that deed if the party has induced another to accept or act under the deed; esp., estoppel that prevents a grantor of a warranty deed, who does not have title at the time of the conveyance but who later acquires title, from denying that he or she had title at the time of the transfer. See AFTER-ACQUIRED-TITLE DOCTRINE. — Also termed *estoppel by warranty*.

estoppel by election. The intentional exercise of a choice between inconsistent alternatives that bars the person making the choice from the benefits of the one not selected.

estoppel by inaction. See *estoppel by silence*.

estoppel by judgment. See COLLATERAL ESTOPPEL.

estoppel by laches. (1894) An equitable doctrine by which some courts deny relief to a claimant who has unreasonably delayed or been negligent in asserting a claim.

estoppel by misrepresentation. An estoppel that arises when one makes a false statement that induces another person to believe something and that results in that person's reasonable and detrimental reliance on the belief.

estoppel by negligence. An estoppel arising when a negligent person induces someone to believe certain facts, and then the other person reasonably and detrimentally relies on that belief.

estoppel by record. See COLLATERAL ESTOPPEL.

estoppel by representation. An estoppel that arises when one makes a statement or admission that induces another person to believe something and that results in that person's reasonable and detrimental reliance on the belief; esp., equitable estoppel.

estoppel by silence. (1872) Estoppel that arises when a party is under a duty to speak but fails to do so. — Also termed *estoppel by standing by*; *estoppel by inaction.*

estoppel by standing by. See *estoppel by silence.*

estoppel by verdict. See COLLATERAL ESTOPPEL.

estoppel by warranty. See *estoppel by deed.*

estoppel in pais. See *equitable estoppel.*

estoppel on the record. See *prosecution-history estoppel.*

file-wrapper estoppel. See *prosecution-history estoppel.*

judicial estoppel. (1886) Estoppel that prevents a party from contradicting previous declarations made during the same or an earlier proceeding if the change in position would adversely affect the proceeding or constitute a fraud on the court. — Also termed *doctrine of preclusion of inconsistent positions*; *doctrine of the conclusiveness of the judgment.*

legal estoppel. Estoppel recognized in law (as distinguished from equitable estoppel or estoppel in pais), such as an estoppel resulting from a recital or other statement in a deed or official record, and precluding any denial or assertion concerning a fact.

marking estoppel. Patents. Estoppel that prevents a party from asserting that a product is not covered by a patent if that party has marked the product with a patent number. ● This type of estoppel has been questioned in recent years, and has been sharply limited by some courts.

promissory estoppel. (1924) The principle that a promise made without consideration may nonetheless be enforced to prevent injustice if the promisor should have reasonably expected the promisee to rely on the promise and if the promisee did actually rely on the promise to his

or her detriment. — Also termed (inaccurately) *equitable estoppel.*

prosecution-history estoppel. Patents. The doctrine limiting a patent-holder's invocation of the doctrine of equivalents by eliminating from the claims those elements that the holder surrendered or abandoned during the prosecution of the patent. — Also termed *estoppel on the record*; *file-wrapper estoppel.* See DOCTRINE OF EQUIVALENTS.

quasi-estoppel. (1823) An equitable doctrine preventing one from repudiating an act or assertion if it would harm another who reasonably relied on the act or assertion.

technical estoppel. **1.** An estoppel arising from a matter of record or from a deed made by the party who is claimed to be estopped. ● Estoppels by deed or by record are called "technical" because the rules of estoppel apply with certainty in appropriate cases. **2.** COLLATERAL ESTOPPEL. See *estoppel by deed.*

estoppel certificate. (1897) **1.** A signed statement by a party (such as a tenant or a mortgagee) certifying for another's benefit that certain facts are correct, such as that a lease exists, that there are no defaults, and that rent is paid to a certain date. ● A party's delivery of this statement estops that party from later claiming a different state of facts. **2.** See WAIVER OF CLAIMS AND DEFENSES.

estoppel per rem judicatam (pər rem joo-di-**kay**-təm). See COLLATERAL ESTOPPEL.

estover (e-**stoh**-vər). (*usu. pl.*) **1.** Wood that a tenant is allowed to take for fuel, the manufacture or repair of agricultural instruments, and the erection and maintenance of fences and hedges; necessary supplies. — Also termed *botes.* See BOTE (1); *common of estovers* under COMMON. **2.** The tenant's right to obtain that wood. **3.** ALIMONY.

estrange, *vb.* **1.** To separate, to keep away (a person or thing), or to keep away from (a person or thing). **2.** To destroy or divert affection, trust, and loyalty. — **estrangement,** *n.*

estray (e-**stray**), *n.* **1.** A valuable tame animal found wandering and ownerless; an animal that has escaped from its owner and wanders about. ● At common law, an estray belonged to the Crown or to the lord of the manor, but today the general rule is that it passes to the state in trust for the true owner, who may regain it by proving ownership. An animal cannot be an estray when on the range where it was raised and where its owner permits it to run, and esp. when the owner is known to the party who takes the animal. **2.** FLOTSAM.

estreat (e-**street**), *n.* (15c) A copy or duplicate of some original writing or record, esp. of a fine or amercement imposed by a court, extracted from the record, and certified to one who is authorized and required to collect it. — Also termed (in Scots law) *extract*.

estreat, *vb.* (16c) To take out a forfeited recognizance from the recordings of a court and return it to the court to be prosecuted.

estrepe (e-**streep**), *vb.* (17c) **1.** To strip; to despoil; to commit waste upon an estate, as by cutting down trees or removing buildings. **2.** To injure the value of a reversionary interest by stripping or spoiling the estate. See WASTE (1).

estrepement (e-**streep**-mənt), *n.* (16c) A species of aggravated waste, by stripping or devastating land to the injury of the reversioner, esp. pending a suit for possession.

et, *conj.* [Latin] And. • This conjunction was the introductory word of several Latin and Law French phrases that were once common.

et al. (et **al** *or* **ahl**). *abbr.* **1.** [Latin *et alii or et alia*] And other persons <the office of Thomas Webb et al.>. **2.** [Latin *et alibi*] And elsewhere.

et alius (et **ay**-lee-əs). [Latin] And another.

et allocatur (et al-ə-**kay**-tər). [Latin] And it is allowed.

etc. *abbr.* ET CETERA.

et cetera (et **set**-ər-ə). [Latin "and others"] (12c) And other things. • The term usu. indicates additional, unspecified items in a series. — Abbr. etc.

eternal law. See NATURAL LAW.

ethical, *adj.* (16c) **1.** Of or relating to moral obligations that one person owes another; esp., in law, of or relating to legal ethics <the ethical rules regarding confidences>. See LEGAL ETHICS. **2.** In conformity with moral norms or standards of professional conduct <refusing to identify the informant was a perfectly ethical act>.

ethical absolutism. See MORAL ABSOLUTISM.

ethical consideration. (*often cap.*) A structural component of the ethical canons set forth in the legal profession's Model Code of Professional Responsibility, containing a goal or ethical principle intended to guide a lawyer's professional conduct. • Ethical considerations are often used in the interpretation and application of the Model Rules of Professional Conduct. — Abbr. EC. Cf. DISCIPLINARY RULE.

ethical drug. See DRUG.

ethical jurisprudence. See JURISPRUDENCE.

ethical relativism. See MORAL RELATIVISM.

ethical wall. (1988) A screening mechanism maintained by an organization, esp. a law firm, to protect client confidences from improper disclosure to lawyers or staff who are not involved in a particular representation. • The screening mechanism is designed to prevent lawyer or law-firm disqualification from certain representations because of conflicts of interest. — Also termed *screening mechanism*; *Chinese wall*.

ethics. See LEGAL ETHICS.

ethnic cleansing. (1991) The officially sanctioned forcible and systematic diminution or elimination of targeted ethnic minorities from a geographic area, usu. by confiscating real and personal property, ordering or condoning mass murders and mass rapes, and expelling the survivors. • In theory, the purpose of ethnic cleansing is to drive all members of the victimized group out of a territory. In practice, ethnic cleansing is nearly synonymous with genocide as mass murder is a characteristic of both. Ethnic cleansing additionally includes mass rapes for two cultural reasons: (1) the victims are often put to death by their relatives or commit suicide, and (2) any children born are regarded as belonging to the father's ethnic group, not the mother's. Both acts — murder and rape — are intended to diminish or extinguish the victimized minority. Cf. GENOCIDE.

ethnic profiling. See RACIAL PROFILING.

etiquette of the profession. See LEGAL ETIQUETTE.

et seq. (et **sek**). *abbr.* [Latin *et sequens* "and the following one," *et sequentes* (masc.) "and the following ones," or *et sequentia* (neuter) "and the following ones"] (18c) And those (pages or sections) that follow <11 USCA §§ 101 et seq.>.

et uxor (et **ək**-sor). [Latin] *Archaic.* And wife. • This phrase was formerly common in case names and legal documents (esp. abstracts of title) involving a husband and wife jointly. It usu. appears in its abbreviated form, *et ux.* <conveyed the land to Donald Baird et ux.>. See UXOR.

EU. *abbr.* EUROPEAN UNION.

Euclidean zoning. See ZONING.

eunomy (**yoo**-nə-mee), *n.* (19c) A system of good laws that lead to civil order and justice. — Also termed *eunomia.* Cf. DYSNOMY. — **eunomic,** *adj.*

eureka model. *Patents.* The view that the inventive process is the product of a stroke of luck rather than labor. • The notion is used to counter labor-based theories justifying intellectual-property rights, since no labor is involved in a "eureka" discovery. Cf. LABOR-DESERT MODEL; VALUE-ADDED MODEL.

eureka moment. *Slang.* The instant when an inventor realizes the answer to a question or the significance of a discovery. — Also termed *flash of genius.*

euro (**yuur**-oh). (1981) The official currency of most countries in the European Union. • On January 1, 1999, the euro became the single currency of the participating countries. Euro notes and coins began circulating on January 1, 2002.

Eurodollar. (1960) United States currency held in a bank outside the U.S., usu. in Europe, and used to settle international transactions.

Euro Interbank Offered Rate. A measure of what major international banks charge each other for large-volume, short-term loans of euros, based on interest-rate data provided daily by a panel of representative banks across Europe. — Abbr. Euribor. Cf. LONDON INTERBANK OFFERED RATE.

European Commission of Human Rights. A body of the Council of Europe charged with overseeing the operation of the European Convention on Human Rights. • The commission was abolished in 1998. The European Court of Human Rights absorbed its functions. See EUROPEAN COURT OF HUMAN RIGHTS.

European Community. See EUROPEAN UNION.

European Convention on Human Rights and Fundamental Freedoms. A 1950 international agreement to protect human rights. • The European Commission for Human Rights and the European Court for Human Rights were created under the convention's terms.

European Copyright Directive. An official instruction of the European Union designed to promote uniformity in certain aspects of copyright law and related rights, esp. on the Internet. • Officially titled Directive 2001/29 on the Harmonisation of Certain Aspects of Copyright and Related Rights in the Information Society, this is the European Union equivalent of the Digital Millennium Copyright Act. Among other provisions, the directive provides broad exclusive rights of reproduction and distribution to copyright holders, and requires E.U. member nations to prohibit the circumvention of technical measures and devices intended to prevent the alteration or reproduction of copyrighted works.

European Court of Human Rights. The judicial body of the Council of Europe. • The court was set up in 1959 and was substantially changed in 1994–1998. As of 2008, the court had 47 judges, each elected by the Council of Europe's Parliamentary Assembly. The court adjudicates alleged violations of the civil and political rights enumerated in the Convention for the Protection of Human Rights and Fundamental Freedoms.

European Currency Unit. A monetary unit that was the precursor of the euro. • Created in 1979, it was an artificial currency used by the members of the European Union as their internal accounting unit. It ceased to exist in January 1999, when it was replaced by the euro. — Abbr. ECU; ecu. See EURO.

European Economic Community. See EUROPEAN UNION.

European law. (1844) **1.** The law of the European Union. **2.** More broadly, the law of the European Union, together with the conventions of the Council of Europe, including the European Convention on Human Rights. **3.** More broadly still, all the law current in Europe, including the law of European organizations, the North Atlantic Treaty Organization, and all the bilateral and multilateral conventions in effect, as well as European customary law.

European option. See OPTION.

European Patent Convention. A 1973 treaty allowing a patent applicant to obtain patent protection in all signatory nations, mostly European Union members, through a single blanket filing and examination procedure. • The Community patent is valid in any member nation in which it is registered. The procedure is administered through the European Patent Office in Munich, Germany and The Hague, Netherlands. — Abbr. EPC. — Also termed *Convention on the Grant of European Patent.*

European Patent Office. The office that receives filings, conducts examinations, and issues Community patents applied for under the European Patent Convention. • The office is located in Munich, Germany, and The Hague, Netherlands.

European Patent Organization. A centralized patent-grant system, established in 1978, comprising a legislative body (the Administrative Council) and an executive body (the European Patent Office).

European-style option. See *European option* under OPTION.

European Union. An association of European nations whose purpose is to achieve full economic unity (and eventual political union) by agreeing to eliminate barriers to the free movement of capital, goods, and labor among the member-nations. • The European Union was formed as the European Economic Community (EEC) by the Treaty of Rome in 1957, and later renamed the European Community (EC). The European Community became the European Union when the Maastricht Treaty on European Union took effect in November 1993. — Abbr. EU.

euthanasia (yoo-thə-**nay**-zhə), *n.* (1869) The act or practice of causing or hastening the death of a person who suffers from an incurable or terminal disease or condition, esp. a painful one, for reasons of mercy. • Euthanasia is sometimes regarded by the law as second-degree murder, manslaughter, or criminally negligent homicide. In 2001, the Netherlands became the first nation to legalize euthanasia. — Also termed *mercy killing.* See LIVING WILL; ADVANCE DIRECTIVE. Cf. *assisted suicide* under SUICIDE; DYATHANASIA. — **euthanasic** (yoo-thə-**nay**-zik), *adj.*

active euthanasia. Euthanasia performed by a facilitator (such as a healthcare practitioner) who not only provides the means of death but also carries out the final death-causing act.

involuntary euthanasia. Euthanasia of a competent, nonconsenting person.

nonvoluntary euthanasia. Euthanasia of an incompetent, and therefore nonconsenting, person.

passive euthanasia. The act of allowing a terminally ill person to die by either withholding or withdrawing life-sustaining support such as a respirator or feeding tube.

voluntary euthanasia. Euthanasia performed with the terminally ill person's consent.

euthanize (**yoo**-thə-nɪz), *vb.* (1873) To put to death by euthanasia. ● This term is used chiefly in reference to animals. — Also termed *euthanatize.*

evacuee. A person who has been evacuated, esp. because of a natural disaster or an imminent man-made danger, such as war. ● This loanword from French dates from World War I. Cf. *displaced person* under PERSON (1); REFUGEE.

evaluative fact. See FACT.

Evarts Act (**ev**-ərts). An 1891 federal statute that established the circuit courts of appeals (now U.S. courts of appeals) and fixed the contemporary method of federal appellate review.

evasion. See TAX EVASION.

evasive, *adj.* (17c) Tending or seeking to evade; elusive; shifting. ● If a pleading requiring a response is evasive, the responding party may move for a more definite statement. Fed. R. Civ. P. 12(e).

evasive answer. See ANSWER (2).

even date. The same date. ● This jargonistic phrase is sometimes used in one instrument to refer to another instrument with the same date, esp. when both relate to the same transaction (as a deed and a mortgage).

even lot. See *round lot* under LOT (3).

event-driven audit. See AUDIT.

evergreen contract. See CONTRACT.

evict, *vb.* (15c) 1. To expel (a person, esp. a tenant), from real property, usu. by legal process. — Also termed *put out.* 2. *Archaic.* To recover (property or title) from a person by legal process. — **evictor,** *n.*

eviction. (16c) The act or process of legally dispossessing a person of land or rental property. See FORCIBLE ENTRY AND DETAINER. Cf. EJECTMENT.

actual eviction. (18c) A physical expulsion of a person from land or rental property.

constructive eviction. (1826) 1. A landlord's act of making premises unfit for occupancy, often with the result that the tenant is compelled to leave. 2. The inability of a land purchaser to obtain possession because of paramount outstanding title. ● Such an eviction usu. constitutes a breach of the covenants of warranty and quiet enjoyment.

eviction by paramount title. An eviction by judicially establishing title superior to that under which the possessor claims. — Also termed *eviction by title paramount.*

eviction by title paramount. See *eviction by paramount title.*

partial eviction. An eviction, either constructive or actual, from a portion of a tenant's premises.

retaliatory eviction. (1966) An eviction — nearly always illegal — commenced in response to a tenant's complaints or involvement in activities with which the landlord does not agree.

summary eviction. (1907) An eviction accomplished through a simplified legal procedure, without the formalities of a full trial.

total eviction. (1832) An eviction that wholly deprives the tenant of any right in the premises.

evidence, *n.* (14c) 1. Something (including testimony, documents and tangible objects) that tends to prove or disprove the existence of an alleged fact <the bloody glove is the key piece of evidence for the prosecution>. 2. See *fact in evidence* under FACT. 3. The collective mass of things, esp. testimony and exhibits, presented before a tribunal in a given dispute <the evidence will show that the defendant breached the contract>. 4. The body of law regulating the admissibility of what is offered as proof into the record of a legal proceeding <under the rules of evidence, the witness's statement is inadmissible hearsay that is not subject to any exception>. — Also termed (in sense 4) *rules of evidence.* — **evidence,** *vb.*

adminicular evidence. *Rare.* Corroborating or auxiliary evidence presented for the purpose of explaining or completing other evidence.

admissible evidence. (18c) Evidence that is relevant and is of such a character (e.g., not unfairly prejudicial, based on hearsay, or privileged) that the court should receive it. — Also termed *competent evidence; proper evidence; legal evidence.*

autoptic evidence. See *demonstrative evidence.*

best evidence. (17c) Evidence of the highest quality available, as measured by the nature of the case rather than the thing being offered as evidence. ● The term is usu. applied to writings and recordings. If the original is available, it must be offered rather than a copy or oral rendition. Fed. R. Evid. 1002. — Also termed *primary evidence;*

original evidence. See BEST-EVIDENCE RULE. Cf. *secondary evidence.*

character evidence. (1949) Evidence regarding someone's general personality traits or propensities, of a praiseworthy or blameworthy nature; evidence of a person's moral standing in a community. Fed. R. Evid. 404, 405, 608. ● Character evidence is usu., but not always, prohibited if offered to show that the person acted in conformity with that character. Cf. *reputation evidence.*

circumstantial evidence. (18c) **1.** Evidence based on inference and not on personal knowledge or observation. — Also termed *indirect evidence; oblique evidence.* Cf. *direct evidence* (1). **2.** All evidence that is not given by eyewitness testimony.

clear and convincing evidence. (17c) Evidence indicating that the thing to be proved is highly probable or reasonably certain. ● This is a greater burden than preponderance of the evidence, the standard applied in most civil trials, but less than evidence beyond a reasonable doubt, the norm for criminal trials. — Also termed *clear and convincing proof.* See REASONABLE DOUBT. Cf. PREPONDERANCE OF THE EVIDENCE.

communicative evidence. See *testimonial evidence.*

competent evidence. **1.** See *admissible evidence.* **2.** See *relevant evidence.*

conclusive evidence. (17c) **1.** Evidence so strong as to overbear any other evidence to the contrary. — Also termed *conclusive proof.* **2.** Evidence that so preponderates as to oblige a fact-finder to come to a certain conclusion.

concomitant evidence. (17c) Evidence that, at the time of the act, the alleged doer of the act was present and actually did it.

conflicting evidence. (1803) Evidence that comes from different sources and is often irreconcilable.

corroborating evidence. (17c) Evidence that differs from but strengthens or confirms what other evidence shows (esp. that which needs support). — Also termed *corroborative evidence.* Cf. *cumulative evidence.*

credible evidence. (17c) Evidence that is worthy of belief; trustworthy evidence.

critical evidence. (18c) Evidence strong enough that its presence could tilt a juror's mind. ● Under the Due Process Clause, an indigent criminal defendant is usu. entitled to an expert opinion of the merits of critical evidence. — Also termed *crucial evidence.*

crucial evidence. See *critical evidence.*

cumulative evidence. (18c) Additional evidence that supports a fact established by the existing evidence (esp. that which does not need further support). Cf. *corroborating evidence.*

demeanor evidence. (1909) The behavior and appearance of a witness on the witness stand, to be considered by the fact-finder on the issue of credibility.

demonstrative evidence (di-**mon**-strə-tiv). (17c) Physical evidence that one can see and inspect (i.e. an explanatory aid, such as a chart, map, and some computer simulations) and that, while of probative value and usu. offered to clarify testimony, does not play a direct part in the incident in question. ● This term sometimes overlaps with and is used as a synonym of real evidence. — Also termed *illustrative evidence; autoptic evidence; autoptic proference; real evidence; tangible evidence.* See *nonverbal testimony* under TESTIMONY. Cf. *real evidence; testimonial evidence.*

derivative evidence. (1961) Evidence that is discovered as a result of illegally obtained evidence and is therefore inadmissible because of the primary taint. See EXCLUSIONARY RULE; FRUIT-OF-THE-POISONOUS-TREE DOCTRINE.

direct evidence. (16c) **1.** Evidence that is based on personal knowledge or observation and that, if true, proves a fact without inference or presumption. — Also termed *positive evidence.* Cf. *circumstantial evidence; negative evidence.* **2.** See *original evidence* (1).

documentary evidence. (18c) Evidence supplied by a writing or other document, which must be authenticated before the evidence is admissible.

downright evidence. See DOWNRIGHT EVIDENCE.

evidence aliunde. See *extrinsic evidence* (1).

evidence-in-chief. (18c) Evidence used by a party in making its case-in-chief.

exclusive evidence. (18c) The only facts that have, or are allowed by law to have, any probative force at all on a particular matter in issue.

exculpatory evidence (ek-**skəl**-pə-tor-ee). (18c) Evidence tending to establish a criminal defendant's innocence. Fed. R. Crim. P. 16. ● The prosecution has a duty to disclose exculpatory evidence in its possession or control when the evidence may be material to the outcome of the case. See BRADY MATERIAL.

expert evidence. (16c) Evidence about a scientific, technical, professional, or other specialized issue given by a person qualified to testify because of familiarity with the subject or special training in the field. — Also termed *expert testimony.* Fed. R. Evid. 702–705. See DAUBERT TEST.

extrajudicial evidence. (18c) Evidence that does not come directly under judicial cognizance but nevertheless constitutes an intermediate link between judicial evidence and the fact requiring proof. ● It includes all facts that are known to the tribunal only by way of inference from some form of judicial evidence. See JUDICIAL NOTICE. Cf. *judicial evidence.*

extrinsic evidence. (17c) **1.** Evidence relating to a contract but not appearing on the face of the contract because it comes from other sources, such as statements between the parties or the circumstances surrounding the agreement. ● Extrinsic evidence is usu. not admissible to contradict or add to the terms of an unambiguous document. — Also termed *extraneous evidence*; *parol evidence*; *evidence aliunde.* **2.** Evidence that is not legitimately before the court. Cf. *intrinsic evidence.* **3.** Evidence that is calculated to impeach a witness's credibility, adduced by means other than cross-examination of the witness. ● The means may include evidence in documents and recordings and the testimony of other witnesses. *See* Fed. R. Evid. 608(b) & note.

fabricated evidence. (18c) False or deceitful evidence that is unlawfully created, usu. after the relevant event, in an attempt to achieve or avoid liability or conviction. — Also termed *fabricated fact.*

false evidence. See *false testimony* under TESTIMONY.

forensic evidence. (18c) Evidence used in court; esp., evidence arrived at by scientific or technical means, such as ballistic or medical evidence.

foundational evidence. (1946) Evidence that determines the admissibility of other evidence.

habit evidence. (1921) Evidence of one's regular response to a repeated specific situation. Fed. R. Evid. 406.

hearsay evidence. See HEARSAY.

illegally obtained evidence. (1924) Evidence obtained by violating a statute or a person's constitutional or other right, esp. the Fourth Amendment guarantee against unreasonable searches, the Fifth Amendment right to remain silent, or the Sixth Amendment right to counsel.

illustrative evidence. See *demonstrative evidence.*

immaterial evidence. (18c) **1.** Evidence lacking in probative value. **2.** Evidence offered to prove a matter that is not in issue.

impeachment evidence. (1861) Evidence used to undermine a witness's credibility. Fed. R. Evid. 607–610.

impertinent evidence. See *irrelevant evidence.*

incompetent evidence. (18c) Evidence that is for any reason inadmissible.

incriminating evidence. (1878) Evidence tending to establish guilt or from which a fact-trier can infer guilt.

inculpatory evidence (in-kəl-pə-tor-ee). (1849) Evidence showing or tending to show one's involvement in a crime or wrong.

indirect evidence. See *circumstantial evidence* (1).

indispensable evidence. (18c) Evidence without which a particular fact cannot be proved.

insufficient evidence. (17c) Evidence that is inadequate to prove or support a finding of something. ● This term usu. describes a case that is not strong enough to even get to the fact-finder.

intrinsic evidence. (17c) **1.** Evidence brought out by the examination of the witness testifying. **2.** Evidence existing within a writing. Cf. *extrinsic evidence* (2).

irrelevant evidence. Evidence not tending to prove or disprove a matter in issue. Fed. R. Evid. 401–403. — Also termed *impertinent evidence.* See IRRELEVANT.

judicial evidence. (17c) Evidence produced in court, consisting of all facts brought to the attention of or admitted into evidence before the tribunal. Cf. *extrajudicial evidence.*

legal evidence. (17c) **1.** See *admissible evidence.* **2.** All admissible evidence, both oral and documentary, of such a character that it reasonably and substantially proves the point rather than merely raising suspicion or conjecture.

material evidence. (17c) Evidence having some logical connection with the facts of consequence or the issues. Cf. *relevant evidence*; *immaterial evidence.*

mathematical evidence. (18c) **1.** Loosely, evidence that establishes its conclusions with absolute certainty. **2.** Evidence pertaining to mathematical or statistical matters, or probabilities.

mediate evidence. See *secondary evidence.*

medical evidence. (18c) Evidence furnished by a doctor, nurse, or other qualified medical person testifying in a professional capacity as an expert, or by a standard treatise on medicine or surgery.

moral evidence. (17c) Loosely, evidence that depends on a belief, rather than complete and absolute proof. ● Generally, moral evidence is testimonial.

multiple evidence. (1926) Evidence with probative or other value on more than one issue but usu. admitted into evidence for one specific purpose. ● Impeachment evidence, for example, may not be probative on a particular issue but may nonetheless affect the jury's perceptions of several issues.

negative evidence. (17c) Evidence suggesting that an alleged fact does not exist, such as a witness's testifying that he or she did not see an event occur. • Negative evidence is generally regarded as weaker than positive evidence because a positive assertion that a witness saw an event is a stronger statement than an assertion that a witness did not see it. But a negative assertion will sometimes be considered positive evidence, depending on the witness's opportunity to see the event. For instance, testimony that the witness watched the entire game and saw no riot in the stands is stronger than testimony stating only that the witness did not see a riot. — Also termed *negative testimony*. Cf. *direct evidence* (1).

newly discovered evidence. (18c) Evidence existing at the time of a motion or trial but then unknown to a party, who, upon later discovering it, may assert it as grounds for reconsideration or a new trial. *See* Fed. R. Civ. P. 60(b).

no evidence. See NO EVIDENCE.

oblique evidence. See *circumstantial evidence* (1).

opinion evidence. (1955) A witness's belief, thought, inference, or conclusion concerning a fact or facts. Fed. R. Evid. 701–705. See OPINION (3); OPINION RULE.

oral evidence. See *testimonial evidence*.

original evidence. (18c) **1.** A witness's statement that he or she perceived a fact in issue by one of the five senses, or that the witness was in a particular physical or mental state. — Also termed *direct evidence*. Cf. HEARSAY. **2.** See *best evidence*.

parol evidence (pə-**rohl** *or* **par**-əl). (18c) **1.** Evidence of oral statements. **2.** See *extrinsic evidence* (1). See PAROL-EVIDENCE RULE.

partial evidence. (17c) Evidence that establishes one of a series of facts.

personal evidence. See TESTIMONY.

positive evidence. See *direct evidence* (1).

preappointed evidence. (1850) Evidence prescribed in advance (as by statute) for the proof of certain facts.

preliminary evidence. (18c) Evidence that is necessary to begin a hearing or trial and that may be received conditionally in anticipation of other evidence linking it to issues in the case. Fed. R. Evid. 104.

presumptive evidence. (17c) **1.** Evidence deemed sufficient to establish another fact unless discredited by other evidence. **2.** *Archaic.* Circumstantial evidence as distinct from testimonial evidence. — Also termed *probable evidence*.

prima facie evidence (**prı**-mə **fay**-shə). (18c) Evidence that will establish a fact or sustain a judgment unless contradictory evidence is produced.

primary evidence. See *best evidence*.

privileged evidence. (1897) Evidence that is exempt from production to an opposing party or tribunal (with certain, limited exceptions) because it is covered by one or more statutory or common-law protections, such as the attorney–client privilege. See *privileged communication* under COMMUNICATION.

probable evidence. See *presumptive evidence*.

probative evidence (**proh**-bə-tiv). (1877) Evidence that tends to prove or disprove a point in issue. Cf. *relevant evidence*.

proffered evidence (**prof**-ərd). (1904) **1.** Evidence that is offered to the court to obtain a ruling on its admissibility. **2.** Evidence whose admissibility depends on the existence or nonexistence of a preliminary fact.

proper evidence. See *admissible evidence*.

prospectant evidence (prə-**spek**-tənt). (1924) Evidence that, before someone does an act, suggests that the person might or might not do the act. • This evidence typically falls into any of five categories: (1) moral character or disposition, (2) physical and mental capacity, (3) habit or custom, (4) emotion or motive, and (5) plan, design, or intention.

real evidence. (17c) **1.** Physical evidence (such as clothing or a knife wound) that itself plays a direct part in the incident in question. — Also termed *physical evidence*. **2.** See *demonstrative evidence*.

rebuttal evidence. (1859) Evidence offered to disprove or contradict the evidence presented by an opposing party. • Rebuttal evidence is introduced in the rebutting party's answering case; it is not adduced, e.g., through cross-examination during the case-in-chief of the party to be rebutted. — Also termed *rebutting evidence*.

relevant evidence. (18c) Evidence tending to prove or disprove a matter in issue. • Relevant evidence is both probative and material and is admissible unless excluded by a specific statute or rule. Fed. R. Evid. 401–403. — Also termed *competent evidence*. Cf. *material evidence*; *probative evidence*.

reputation evidence. (1888) Evidence of what one is thought by others to be. • Reputation evidence may be introduced as proof of character when character is in issue or is used circumstantially. Fed. R. Evid. 405(a). — Also termed *reputational evidence*. Cf. *character evidence*.

retrospectant evidence (re-trə-**spek**-tənt). (1929) Evidence that, although it occurs after an act has been done, suggests that the alleged doer of the act actually did it <when goods have been stolen, and the thief is sought, a person's later possession of those goods amounts to retrospectant evidence that this person took them>. — Also termed *traces*.

satisfactory evidence. (17c) Evidence that is sufficient to satisfy an unprejudiced mind seeking the truth. — Also termed *sufficient evidence*; *satisfactory proof*.

scientific evidence. (17c) Fact or opinion evidence that purports to draw on specialized knowledge of a science or to rely on scientific principles for its evidentiary value. See DAUBERT TEST.

secondary evidence. (17c) Evidence that is inferior to the primary or best evidence and that becomes admissible when the primary or best evidence is lost or inaccessible. • Examples include a copy of a lost instrument or testimony regarding a lost instrument's contents. — Also termed *mediate evidence*; *mediate testimony*; *substitutionary evidence*. See Fed. R. Evid. 1004. Cf. *best evidence*.

secondhand evidence. See HEARSAY.

secret evidence. (1983) Classified information that may be used against a defendant in an immigration proceeding but withheld from the defendant, the defendant's lawyer, and the public on national-security grounds. • The use of secret evidence was made easier under the Anti-Terrorism and Effective Death Penalty Act of 1996.

signature evidence. Highly distinctive evidence of a person's prior bad acts. • While ordinarily inadmissible, signature evidence will be admitted if it shows, for example, that two crimes were committed through the same planning, design, scheme, or modus operandi, and in such a way that the prior act and the current act are uniquely identifiable as those of the defendant. *See* Fed. R. Evid. 404(b).

slight evidence. (18c) A small quantity of evidence; esp., the small amount of evidence sufficient to remove a presumption from a case or for a rational fact-finder to conclude that something essential has not been established beyond a reasonable doubt. See SLIGHT-EVIDENCE RULE.

state's evidence. (1886) Testimony provided by one criminal defendant — under a promise of immunity or reduced sentence — against another criminal defendant. See TURN STATE'S EVIDENCE.

substantial evidence. (17c) **1.** Evidence that a reasonable mind could accept as adequate to support a conclusion; evidence beyond a scintilla. See SUBSTANTIAL-EVIDENCE RULE. **2.** The product of adequately controlled investigations, including clinical studies, carried out by qualified experts that establish the effectiveness of a drug under FSA regulations. 21 USCA § 355(e).

substantive evidence (səb-stən-tiv). Evidence offered to help establish a fact in issue, as opposed to evidence directed to impeach or to support a witness's credibility.

substitutionary evidence. See *secondary evidence*.

sufficient evidence. See *satisfactory evidence*.

tainted evidence. (1876) Evidence that is inadmissible because it was directly or indirectly obtained by illegal means. See FRUIT-OF-THE-POISONOUS-TREE DOCTRINE.

tangible evidence. Physical evidence that is either real or demonstrative. See *demonstrative evidence*; *real evidence*.

testimonial evidence. (1831) A person's testimony offered to prove the truth of the matter asserted; esp., evidence elicited from a witness. — Also termed *communicative evidence*; *oral evidence*. Cf. *demonstrative evidence*.

traditionary evidence. (18c) Evidence derived from a deceased person's former statements or reputation. • Traditionary evidence is admissible to prove ancestry, ancient boundaries, or similar facts, usu. when no living witnesses are available to testify.

unwritten evidence. (18c) Evidence given orally, in court or by deposition.

evidence by inspection. See *demonstrative evidence* under EVIDENCE.

evidence code. A relatively comprehensive set of statutory provisions or rules governing the admissibility of evidence at hearings and trials.

evidence of debt. See SECURITY (4).

evidence of indebtedness. See SECURITY (4).

evidence of insurability. Information — such as medical records or a medical examination — that an insurer may require to establish a potential insured's qualification for a particular insurance policy.

evidence of title. (17c) The means by which the ownership of land is satisfactorily demonstrated within a given jurisdiction. See DEED (2), (3).

evidence rules. See EVIDENCE (4).

evidencing feature. *Evidence.* A group of circumstances that, when taken as a whole, form a composite feature that can be reliably associated with a single object. • This term appears more frequently in criminal cases than in civil. In criminal cases, it usu. refers to evidence that establishes a perpetrator's identity, but in civil cases it often refers to evidence that an event did or did not occur. — Also termed *evidencing mark*; *evidential mark.*

evidencing mark. See EVIDENCING FEATURE.

evidential, *adj.* Of, relating to, relying on, or constituting evidence; EVIDENTIARY (1).

evidential fact. See *evidentiary fact* (2) under FACT.

evidential mark. See EVIDENCING FEATURE.

evidentiary (ev-i-**den**-shə-ree), *adj.* (1810) **1.** Having the quality of evidence; constituting evidence; evidencing. **2.** Pertaining to the rules of evidence or the evidence in a particular case.

evidentiary fact. See FACT.

evidentiary hearing. See HEARING.

evince, *vb.* (17c) To show, indicate, or reveal <in abstaining from the vote, Hariden evinced misgivings about the nomination>.

evocative trademark. See *suggestive trademark* under TRADEMARK.

evolution statute. See ANTI-EVOLUTION STATUTE.

ex. (18c) **1.** Former <ex-wife>. **2.** Without <ex rights>. **3.** From <*ex cathedra*>. **4.** (*usu. cap.*) *abbr.* Exhibit <Ex. 4>. **5.** *abbr.* Example <this is but one ex. of several that might be cited>. **6.** (*cap.*) *abbr.* EXCHEQUER.

ex abundanti cautela (eks ab-ən-**dan**-tɪ kaw-**tee**-lə). [Latin] *Archaic.* Out of abundant caution; to be on the safe side.

exaction, *n.* (15c) **1.** The act of demanding more money than is due; extortion. **2.** A fee, reward, or other compensation arbitrarily or wrongfully demanded. — **exact,** *vb.*

exactor. 1. *Civil law.* A tax collector; a gatherer or receiver of money. **2.** *Hist.* A collector of public funds; a tax collector.

ex aequo et bono (eks **ee**-kwoh et **boh**-noh). [Latin] According to what is equitable and good. • A decision-maker (esp. in international law) who is authorized to decide *ex aequo et bono* is not bound by legal rules and may instead follow equitable principles. For example, article 38(2) of the Statute of the International Court of Justice provides that the Court may "decide a case *ex aequo et bono* if the parties agree thereto." 37 ILM 999.

examination. (14c) **1.** The questioning of a witness under oath. See DIRECT EXAMINATION; CROSS-EXAMINATION. **2.** *Bankruptcy.* The questioning of a debtor, esp. at the first meeting of creditors, concerning such matters as the bankrupt's debts and assets. **3.** An inquiry made at the U.S. Patent and Trademark Office, upon application for a patent, into the alleged invention's novelty and utility, and whether it interferes with any other pending application or in-force patent. **4.** *Banking.* The government's fact-finding mechanism for determining the soundness of a bank's finances and management. **5.** *Insurance.* A periodic investigation by a state insurance commission into the affairs and soundness of an insurance company licensed in that state.

preliminary examination. *Patents.* A patent office's initial review of an application, usu. to see whether the specification is properly set out and to prepare a search report.

4. PRELIMINARY HEARING. **5.** A test, such as a bar examination.

examination before trial. See DEPOSITION (1).

examination-in-chief. See DIRECT EXAMINATION.

examination on the voir dire. See VOIR DIRE.

examination system. *Patents.* A patent system in which an invention is subjected to official scrutiny to determine whether it qualifies for patent protection. Cf. REGISTRATION SYSTEM.

examined copy. See COPY.

examiner. (16c) **1.** One authorized to conduct an examination; esp., a person appointed by the court, esp. a court of equity, to administer an oath and take testimony. — Also formerly termed *examiner in chancery.* See MASTER (2). **2.** A patent officer responsible for determining the patentability of an invention submitted to the patent office. **3.** MEDICAL EXAMINER. **4.** BANK EXAMINER.

examiner-in-chief. *Hist. Patents.* **1.** A member of the quasi-judicial body in the U.S. Patent and Trademark Office that formerly heard appeals of interference decisions and patent-application rejections. **2.** (*pl. cap.*) The body comprising those members; the predecessor of the Board of Appeals, the Board of Patent Interferences, and the present-day Board of Patent Appeals and Interferences.

examiner's amendment. *Patents & Trademarks.* Minor changes in the form of a patent or trademark application, made by the examiner rather than the applicant. • For example, the examiner may correct spelling and grammar rather than wait for the applicant to respond. A patent examiner may also amend or cancel claims if authorized by the applicant.

examiner's answer. *Patents.* The brief filed by a patent examiner with the Board of Patent Appeals and Interferences to rebut the arguments in an appeal brief and to defend the examiner's decision to reject the application. Cf. *appeal brief* under BRIEF.

examining authority. See AUTHORITY (3).

examining board. (1851) An appointed group of public officials responsible for conducting the tests required by those applying for occupational and professional licenses. — Also termed *board of examiners.*

examining court. See COURT.

examining group. *Patents.* A subunit of the Patent Office consisting of patent examiners who specialize in a particular area of technology.

examining trial. See PRELIMINARY HEARING.

example. *Patents.* A detailed description of an invention's embodiment. • Alternatives without detail may be referred to as *by example.* — Also termed *specific example; working example.*

exannual roll (eks-**an**-yoo-əl). *Hist.* In England, a roll into which illeviable fines and desperate debts were transcribed and that was annually read to the sheriff upon his accounting to see what might be gotten.

ex ante (eks **an**-tee), *adj. & adv.* [Latin "from before"] (1937) Based on assumption and prediction, on how things appeared beforehand, rather than in hindsight; subjective; prospective <from an *ex ante* perspective>. Cf. EX POST.

excambium (eks-**kam**-bee-əm), *n.* [Latin] **1.** An exchange; a place where merchants meet to transact their business. — Also termed (in Scots law) *excambion.* **2.** An equivalent in recompense; a recompense in lieu of dower *ad ostium ecclesiae.*

ex cathedra (eks kə-**thee**-drə *or* **kath**-ə-drə), *adv. & adj.* [Latin "from the chair"] (17c) By virtue of one's high office or position; with authority <ex cathedra pronouncements>.

excellency. (*usu. cap.*) (16c) A title of honor given to certain high officials or dignitaries, such as governors, ambassadors, and Roman Catholic bishops or archbishops.

Excelsior list. *Labor law.* A roster of the names and addresses of employees who are eligible to vote in a union election. • The NLRB requires an employer to file the list within seven days after the employer and a union reach a consent-election agreement. *Excelsior Underwear, Inc.,* 156 N.L.R.B. 1236 (1966).

exception, *n.* (14c) **1.** A formal objection to a court's ruling by a party who wants to preserve an overruled objection or rejected proffer for appeal <the prosecutor stated her exception to the court's ruling disallowing the witness's testimony>. • To make an exception or objection, attorneys sometimes say, "I except" or "I object." *Exception* properly refers only to an objection made after an initial objection or proffer is made and overruled. In most courts, an exception is no longer required to preserve the initial objection.

declinatory exception (di-**klin**-ə-tor-ee). *Louisiana law.* An exception to a court's jurisdiction. • Grounds for refusing to submit to a court's jurisdiction include lack of personal jurisdiction and insufficient service of process.

dilatory exception (**dil**-ə-tor-ee). (1822) *Louisiana law.* An exception intended to delay but not dismiss an action.

general exception. (16c) **1.** An objection pointing out a substantive defect in an opponent's pleading, such as the insufficiency of the claim or the court's lack of subject-matter jurisdiction; an objection to a pleading for want of substance. — Also termed *general demurrer.* Cf. SPECIAL EXCEPTION (1). **2.** An objection in which the excepting party does not specify the grounds of the objection.

peremptory exception. (16c) *Louisiana law.* A defensive pleading asserting that no legal remedy exists for the plaintiff's alleged injury, that res judicata or prescription bars the claim, or that an indispensable party has not been included in the litigation.

special exception. See SPECIAL EXCEPTION.

2. Something that is excluded from a rule's operation <employers with fewer than five employees are an exception to the rule>.

statutory exception. (18c) A provision in a statute exempting certain persons or conduct from the statute's operation.

3. The retention of an existing right or interest, by and for the grantor, in real property being granted to another. Cf. RESERVATION (1). — **except,** *vb.*

exceptionable (ek-**sep**-shən-ə-bəl), *adj.* (17c) Liable to objection; OBJECTIONABLE.

exceptional charge. See *special charge* under CHARGE.

exception clause. A clause that attempts to modify or exclude the prima facie obligations that arise when a document is signed. — Also termed *exemption clause.*

excess-benefit plan. See EMPLOYEE BENEFIT PLAN.

excess clause. An insurance-policy provision — usu. contained in the "other insurance" section of the policy — that limits the insurer's liability to the amount exceeding other available coverage. • This clause essentially requires other insurers to pay first. Cf. ESCAPE CLAUSE; PRO RATA CLAUSE.

excess condemnation. See CONDEMNATION.

excess damages. See DAMAGES.

excess insurance. See INSURANCE.

excess insurer. See INSURER.

excessive assessment. See ASSESSMENT.

excessive bail. See BAIL (1).

excessive damages. See DAMAGES.

excessive drunkenness. See DRUNKENNESS.

excessive execution. An exercise of a power of appointment exceeding the limits (express or statutory) set on the use of the power.

excessive fine. See FINE (5).

Excessive Fines Clause. (1986)The clause of the Eighth Amendment to the U.S. Constitution prohibiting the imposition of excessive fines.

excessive force. See FORCE.

excessive punishment. See PUNISHMENT.

excessive sentence. See SENTENCE.

excessive verdict. See VERDICT.

excess judgment. See JUDGMENT.

excess jurisdiction. See EXCESS OF JURISDICTION (1).

excess-liability damages. See *excess damages* under DAMAGES.

excess limits. Insurance coverage against losses in excess of a specified limit.

excess-lines insurance. See *surplus-lines insurance* under INSURANCE.

excess margin. Equity in a brokerage firm's customer account that exceeds either the legal-minimum dollar amount for a margin account or the maintenance requirement.

excess of jurisdiction. (17c) **1.** A court's acting beyond the limits of its power, usu. in one of three ways: (1) when the court has no power to deal with the kind of matter at issue, (2) when the court has no power to deal with the particular person concerned, or (3) when the judgment or order issued is of a kind that the court has no power to issue. **2.** A court's departure from recognized and established requirements of law, despite apparent adherence to procedural form, the effect of which is a deprivation of one's constitutional right. — Also termed *excess jurisdiction*.

excess of privilege. (1889) **1.** An excessive publication of a privileged statement — that is, beyond the limits of the privilege. **2.** The improper and malicious use of the privilege to publish a statement.

excess policy. See *excess insurance* under INSURANCE.

excess-profits tax. See TAX.

excess reinsurance. See REINSURANCE.

excess reserve. See RESERVE.

excess theory. *Insurance.* The principle that a tortfeasor will be considered underinsured if the injured party's damages exceed the tortfeasor's liability-insurance coverage. • This principle allows an injured party to invoke underinsured-motorist coverage. Cf. GAP THEORY.

excess vote. See VOTE (1).

excess water. See WATER.

exchange, *n.* (14c) *Commercial law.* **1.** The act of transferring interests, each in consideration for the other.

bargained-for exchange. See BARGAINED-FOR EXCHANGE.

like-kind exchange. See LIKE-KIND EXCHANGE.

tax-free exchange. See TAX-FREE EXCHANGE.

1031 exchange. See 1031 EXCHANGE.

2. Money or negotiable instruments presented as payment; CURRENCY. See MEDIUM OF EXCHANGE. **3.** The interchange or conversion of money. See FOREIGN EXCHANGE. **4.** The payment of a debt using a bill of exchange or credit rather than money. **5.** An organization that brings together buyers and sellers of securities, commodities, and the like to promote uniformity in the customs and usages of merchants, to facilitate the speedy adjustment of business disputes, to gather and disseminate valuable commercial and economic information, and to secure to its members the benefits of cooperation in the furtherance of their legitimate pursuits. • The best-known exchanges are stock, produce, livestock, cotton, and grain exchanges. See RECIPROCAL EXCHANGE. **6.** The building or hall where members of an exchange meet every business day to buy and sell for themselves, or as brokers for their customers, for present and future delivery. See SECURITIES EXCHANGE (1). — **exchange,** *vb.*

Exchange Act. See SECURITIES EXCHANGE ACT OF 1934.

exchange agreement. See AGREEMENT.

exchange broker. One who negotiates money or merchandise transactions for others.

exchange rate. The ratio for converting one country's money into another country's money. See FOREIGN EXCHANGE.

exchange ratio. The number of shares that an acquiring company must give for each share of an acquired company.

exchange value. See VALUE (2).

Exchequer (eks-**chek**-ər *or* eks-chek-ər). (14c) **1.** *English law.* The government department charged with collecting and administering the national revenue; the treasury department. • The name is said to have derived from the checkered cloth, resembling a chessboard, that anciently covered the table on which certain of the king's accounts were tallied, the sums being marked and scored with counters. **2.** COURT OF EXCHEQUER. — Abbr. Ex.

Exchequer bill. A bill of credit issued in England by the authority of Parliament; an instrument issued at the Exchequer, usu. under the authority of an act of Parliament passed for that specific purpose, containing an engagement on the part of the government to repay, with interest, the principal sums advanced.

Exchequer Chamber. An English court of intermediate appeal from the common-law courts, namely, the Court of King's Bench, the Court of Common Pleas, and the Court of Exchequer. • It was established in 1822. — Also termed *Camera Scaccarii*.

Exchequer Division. *Hist. English law.* A division of the High Court of Justice, to which the business of the Court of Exchequer was specially assigned by section 34 of the Judicature Act of 1873, and later merged into the Queen's Bench Division in 1881.

excise, *n.* (15c) A tax imposed on the manufacture, sale, or use of goods (such as a cigarette tax), or on an occupation or activity (such as a license tax or an attorney occupation fee). — Also termed *excise tax*. Cf. *income tax* and *property tax* under TAX.

excise lieu property tax. See TAX.

excise tax. See EXCISE.

excision. See FEMALE GENITAL MUTILATION.

excited utterance. (1800) A statement about a startling event made under the stress and excitement of the event. • An excited utterance may be admissible as a hearsay exception. Fed. R. Evid. 803(2). Cf. PRESENT SENSE IMPRESSION.

excludable, *adj.* (1916) **1.** (Of evidence) subject to exclusion <excludable hearsay>. **2.** (Of an alien) ineligible for admission or entry into a country.

excludable alien. See ALIEN.

exclude. See RIGHT TO EXCLUDE.

exclusion, *n.* **1.** *Tax.* An item of income excluded from gross income. — Also termed *income exclusion*.

   annual exclusion. (1940) The amount allowed as nontaxable gift income during the calendar year. • The purpose of the annual exclusion is both to serve as an estate-planning mechanism (so that gifts made during the donor's lifetime remain nontestamentary and nontaxable) and to eliminate the administrative inconvenience of taxing relatively small gifts. In 2009, for an individual, the first $13,000 in gifts can be excluded; for married persons, the exclusion is $26,000 per couple for joint gifts, regardless of which spouse supplied the donated property. IRC (26 USCA) § 2503. — Also termed *annual gift-tax exclusion*.

2. *Evidence.* A trial judge's determination that an item offered as evidence may not be presented to the trier of fact (esp. the jury). **3.** *Insurance.* An insurance-policy provision that excepts certain events or conditions from coverage. — **exclude,** *vb.* — **exclusionary,** *adj.*

   automobile exclusion. A provision in some commercial general liability policies, excluding coverage for damages arising from the use (including loading and unloading) of an automobile, aircraft, or other motor vehicle owned, operated, rented, or borrowed by the insured.

   business-risk exclusion. An exclusion in some commercial general liability policies, excluding coverage for common risks of doing business, including harm to the insured's product or work, damages arising from a product recall, damages arising from the insured's failure to perform under a contract, or damages arising from a failure of the insured's product to perform as intended.

   design-defect exclusion. A provision in some umbrella policies and some older commercial general liability policies, excluding coverage for bodily injury arising from the failure of the insured's product to perform its intended function because of a defect or deficiency in its design, formula, specifications, instructions, or advertising materials.

   employee-liability exclusion. A provision in some commercial general liability policies, excluding coverage for injury to an employee (or a member of the employee's family), arising from and in the course of employment with the insured. • This exclusion is generally intended to exclude from coverage all injuries covered by the workers'-compensation laws.

   employment-related-practices exclusion. A provision in some commercial general liability policies, excluding coverage for damages arising from an insured's employment practices, including any policy, action, or omission — such as coercion, demotion, evaluation, reassignment, discipline, defamation, harassment, humiliation, or discrimination — that is directed at the person injured.

   expected/intended exclusion. A provision in some commercial general liability policies, excluding coverage for property damage or bodily injury that is expected or intended by the insured, except any harm arising from the use of reasonable force to protect a person or property. • This exclusion is sometimes referred to as "exclusion a" because it is the first exclusion listed on most policies. — Also termed *exclusion a*; *intentional-injury exclusion*.

   failure-to-perform exclusion. A provision in some commercial general liability policies, excluding coverage for (1) the loss of use of undamaged property resulting from the insured's delay or failure in performing an obligation, or (2) a design defect or failure in the insured's product. — Also termed *loss-of-use exclusion*.

   knowledge-of-falsity exclusion. A provision in some commercial general liability policies, excluding coverage for damages arising from an oral or written communication made by the insured with knowledge that it is false.

named-insured exclusion. An exclusion limiting liability-insurance coverage to a named insured whose injuries were caused by another named insured under the same insurance policy.

owned-property exclusion. *Insurance.* A provision in a comprehensive general-liability insurance policy allowing only third parties who are injured on or by the insured's property to make liability claims against the insurer. • The provision ordinarily excludes coverage for (1) property owned, rented, occupied, sold, given away, or abandoned by the insured, (2) personal property in the care, custody, or control of the insured, and (3) property located where the insured and its employees work.

own-product exclusion. A provision in some commercial general liability policies, excluding coverage for property damage to a product that is manufactured, sold, handled, distributed, or disposed of by the insured.

own-work exclusion. A provision in some commercial general liability policies, excluding coverage for damage to the work or services performed by the insured.

pollution exclusion. A provision in some commercial general liability policies, excluding coverage for bodily injury or property damages arising from the discharge, dispersal, release, or escape of chemicals, waste, acid, and other pollutants. • Pollution-exclusion clauses may take one of two forms: (1) sudden and accidental, and (2) absolute. The sudden-and-accidental clause, usu. limited to policies issued before 1985, contains an exception under which the damages are covered (i.e., exempted from the exclusion) if the discharge or other release was sudden and accidental. The absolute pollution exclusion, in most policies issued since 1985, does not contain this exception.

sistership exclusion. A provision in some commercial general liability policies, excluding coverage for damages arising from the withdrawal, inspection, repair, replacement, or loss of use of the insured's product or work, to the extent that the product or work is withdrawn or recalled from the market because of a known or suspected defect or deficiency. — Also termed *recall exclusion.*

exclusion a. See *expected/intended exclusion* under EXCLUSION (3).

exclusionary hearing. See HEARING.

exclusionary practice. *Antitrust.* A method by which a firm can gain or maintain monopoly power without the express or tacit cooperation of competing or potentially competing firms.

exclusionary rule. (1855) **1.** *Evidence.* Any rule that excludes or suppresses evidence <despite many exceptions, hearsay has long been inadmissible under an exclusionary rule>. — Also termed *exclusionary evidence rule.* **2.** *Criminal procedure.* A rule that excludes or suppresses evidence obtained in violation of an accused person's constitutional rights <in accordance with the exclusionary rule, the court did not admit the drugs into evidence because they had been obtained during a warrantless search of the defendant's home>. See FRUIT-OF-THE-POISONOUS-TREE DOCTRINE; GOOD-FAITH EXCEPTION.

exclusionary zoning. See ZONING.

exclusive agency. See AGENCY (1).

exclusive-agency listing. See LISTING (1).

exclusive authorization-to-sell listing. See *exclusive-agency listing* under LISTING (1).

exclusive contract. See EXCLUSIVE-DEALING ARRANGEMENT.

exclusive control. (1890) Under the doctrine of res ipsa loquitur, a defendant's sole management of and responsibility for the instrumentality causing harm. • Exclusive control is a prerequisite to the doctrine's applicability. See RES IPSA LOQUITUR.

exclusive-dealing arrangement. (1943) An agreement requiring a buyer to purchase all needed goods or services from one seller. — Often shortened to *exclusive dealing.* — Also termed *exclusive contract.* See *requirements contract* under CONTRACT.

exclusive easement. See EASEMENT.

exclusive economic zone. *Int'l law.* An area just beyond the territorial sea, extending up to 200 nautical miles from the baseline of the territorial sea, in which the coastal country enjoys special authority for economic purposes. — Abbr. EEZ.

exclusive evidence. See EVIDENCE.

exclusive franchise. See *exclusive agency* under AGENCY (1).

exclusive jurisdiction. See JURISDICTION.

exclusive license. See LICENSE.

exclusive listing. See *exclusive-agency listing* under LISTING (1).

exclusive ownership. See FEE SIMPLE.

exclusive possession. See POSSESSION.

exclusive right of sale. The right to sell a principal's products or to act as the seller's real-estate agent to the exclusion of all others, including the owner. — Also termed *exclusive right to sell.* Cf. *exclusive agency* under AGENCY (1).

exclusive sale. See SALE.

exclusive use. See USE (1).

exclusive-use clause. A lease provision enumerating conditions for a lessee's use of the leased property.

excommunicant (eks-kə-**myoo**-ni-kənt), *n.* (16c) *Eccles. law.* **1.** An excommunicated person. **2.** *Rare.* An excommunicator.

excommunication, *n.* (15c) *Eccles. law.* A sentence of censure pronounced by a spiritual court for an offense falling under ecclesiastical cognizance; expulsion from religious society or community. • In England, an excommunicated person was formerly subject to various civil disabilities, such as an inability to be a juror, to be a witness in any court, or to sue to recover lands or money due. These penalties were abolished by the Ecclesiastical Courts Act (1813). St. 53 Geo. 3, ch. 127. — Also termed *excommengement.* — **excommunicate,** *vb.*

excommunicator. (17c) A person who excommunicates.

ex contractu (eks kən-**trak**-t[y]oo). [Latin "from a contract"] Arising from a contract <action *ex contractu*>. Cf. EX DELICTO (1).

ex-coupon bond. See BOND (2).

exculpate (**ek**-skəl-payt *or* ek-**skəl**-payt), *vb.* (17c) To free from blame or accusation. Cf. EXONERATE (1). — **exculpation** (ek- skəl-**pay**-shən), *n.* — **exculpatory** (ek-**skəl**-pə-tor-ee), *adj.*

exculpatory clause. (1891) A contractual provision relieving a party from liability resulting from a negligent or wrongful act. • A will or a trust may contain an exculpatory clause purporting to immunize a fiduciary from a breach of duty; the clause may reduce the degree of care and prudence required of the fiduciary. But courts generally find that if an exculpatory clause in a will or trust seeks to confer absolute immunity, it is void as being against public policy. See EXEMPTION CLAUSE.

exculpatory evidence. See EVIDENCE.

exculpatory-no doctrine. (1977) *Criminal law.* The principle that a person cannot be charged with making a false statement for falsely denying guilt in response to an investigator's question. • This doctrine is based on the Fifth Amendment right against self-incrimination. But the U.S. Supreme Court has overruled this doctrine in federal law. *Brogan v. United States*, 522 U.S. 398, 118 S.Ct. 805 (1998).

ex curia (eks **kyoor**-ee-ə). [Latin] Out of court; away from the court.

excusable, *adj.* (14c) (Of an illegal act or omission) not punishable under the specific circumstances <excusable neglect>.

excusable assault. See ASSAULT.

excusable homicide. See HOMICIDE.

excusable neglect. See NEGLECT.

excuse (ek-**skyoos**), *n.* (14c) **1.** A reason that justifies an act or omission or that relieves a person of a duty. **2.** *Criminal law.* A defense that arises because the defendant is not blameworthy for having acted in a way that would otherwise be criminal. • The following defenses are the traditional excuses: duress, entrapment, infancy, insanity, and involuntary intoxication. — Also termed *legal excuse.* Cf. JUSTIFICATION (2). — **excuse** (ek-**skyooz**), *vb.* — **excusatory** (ek-**skyooz**-ə-tor-ee), *adj.*

excuse by failure of presupposed conditions. See *commercial impracticability* under IMPRACTICABILITY.

excuss (ek-**skəs**), *vb.* (18c) To seize and detain by law.

ex-date. See EX-DIVIDEND DATE.

ex delicto (eks də-**lik**-toh), *adj. & adv.* [Latin "from a wrong"] **1.** Arising from a crime or tort <action ex delicto>. • Although *ex delicto* refers most commonly to a tort in modern usage, it referred historically to both torts and crimes. Cf. IN DELICTO; EX CONTRACTU. **2.** *Int'l law. Rare.* As a consequence of a crime or tort <because they were counterfeit, the goods were seized and condemned ex delicto>.

ex delicto trust. See TRUST.

ex distribution. Without distribution. • Shares are traded ex distribution when they no longer carry the right to receive a distribution to be made to holders. — Abbr. X; XDIS.

ex dividend. Without dividend. • Shares are traded ex dividend when the seller, not the purchaser, is entitled to the next dividend payment because it will be made before the stock transfer is completed. The first day on which shares are traded ex dividend, the stock price will drop by an amount usu. approximating the amount of the dividend. — Abbr. XD.; X. Cf. CUM DIVIDEND.

ex-dividend date. The date on or after which the buyer of a security does not acquire the right to receive a recently declared dividend. — Also termed *ex-date.* Cf. DIVIDEND DATE.

exeat (**ek**-see-ət), *n.* (18c) **1.** Generally, permission to go outside (a place). **2.** Permission that a bishop grants to a priest to go out of his diocese. Cf. NE EXEAT (1).

execute, *vb.* (14c) **1.** To perform or complete (a contract or duty) <once the contract was fully executed, the parties owed no further contractual duties to each other>. **2.** To change (as a legal interest) from one form to another <the shifting use was executed into a valid legal estate>. **3.** To make (a legal document) valid by signing; to bring (a legal document) into its final, legally enforceable form <each party executed the contract without a signature witness>. **4.** To put to death, esp. by legal sentence <Johnson was executed shortly after midnight>. **5.** To enforce and collect on (a money judgment) <Williams asked the sheriff to execute on the judgment>.

executed, *adj.* (16c) **1.** (Of a document) that has been signed <an executed will>. **2.** That has been done, given, or performed <executed consideration>.

executed consideration. See CONSIDERATION (1).

executed contract. See CONTRACT.

executed covenant. See COVENANT (1).

executed estate. See REMAINDER (1).

executed fine. See FINE (1).

executed note. See NOTE (1).

executed remainder. See *vested remainder* under REMAINDER.

executed trust. See TRUST.

executed use. See USE (4).

execution, *n.* (14c) **1.** The act of carrying out or putting into effect (as a court order or a securities transaction) <execution of the court's decree> <execution of the stop-loss order>. **2.** Validation of a written instrument, such as a contract or will, by fulfilling the necessary legal requirements <delivery of the goods completed the contract's execution>. **3.** Judicial enforcement of a money judgment, usu. by seizing and selling the judgment debtor's property <even if the plaintiff receives a judgment against the foreign debtor, execution is unlikely>. — Also termed (in Scots law) *diligence.* **4.** A court order directing a sheriff or other officer to enforce a judgment, usu. by seizing and selling the judgment debtor's property <the court issued the execution authorizing seizure of the car>. — Also termed *writ of execution; judgment execution; general execution.*

alias execution. A second execution issued to enforce a judgment not fully satisfied by the original writ. Cf. *alias writ* under WRIT.

body execution. A court order requiring an officer to take a named person into custody, usu. to bring the person before the court to pay a debt; CAPIAS.

close-jail execution. A body execution stating that the person to be arrested should be confined in jail without the privilege of movement about the jailyard.

dormant execution. An execution authorizing an officer to seize and hold property rather than sell it, until further notice.

junior execution. An execution that is subordinate to another execution issued from an earlier judgment against the same debtor.

malicious execution. An abuse of process by which a person, maliciously and without reasonable cause, issues an execution against the property of a judgment debtor.

special execution. An execution authorizing a judgment to be satisfied from specified property.

speedy execution. An execution issuing quickly (esp. by judges at nisi prius) after a trial.

5. *Criminal law.* The carrying out of a death sentence <the Supreme Court stayed the execution>. — **execute,** *vb.*

execution clause. The part of a deed containing the date, seal (if required), and signatures of the grantor, grantor's spouse, and witnesses.

execution creditor. See CREDITOR.

executioner. (16c) A person who puts another person to death to carry out a death sentence; a person who carries out capital punishment on the state's behalf.

execution lien. See LIEN.

execution-proof. See JUDGMENT-PROOF.

execution sale. See SALE.

executive, *n.* (18c) **1.** The branch of government responsible for effecting and enforcing laws; the person or persons who constitute this branch. ● The executive branch is sometimes said to be the residue of all government after subtracting the judicial and legislative branches. — Sometimes also termed *executive department.* Cf. LEGISLATURE; JUDICIARY (1).

chief executive. (1876) The head of the executive branch of a government, such as the President of the United States.

2. A corporate officer at the upper levels of management. — Also termed *executive officer; executive employee.* — **executive,** *adj.*

executive administration. Collectively, high public officials who administer the chief departments of the government.

executive agency. An executive-branch department whose activities are subject to statute and whose contracts are subject to judicial review. ● One example is the National Aeronautics and Space Agency.

executive agreement. (1942) An international agreement entered into by the President, without approval by the Senate, and usu. involving routine diplomatic or military matters. Cf. TREATY (1).

executive board. See BOARD OF DIRECTORS.

executive branch. (18c) The branch of government charged with administering and carrying out the law; EXECUTIVE (1). Cf. JUDICIAL BRANCH; LEGISLATIVE BRANCH.

executive clemency. See CLEMENCY.

executive committee. See COMMITTEE.

executive department. See EXECUTIVE (1).

executive director. A salaried employee who serves as an organization's chief administrative and operating officer and heads its professional staff. — Also termed *executive secretary; staff director.*

executive employee. An employee whose duties include some form of managerial authority and active participation in the control, supervision, and management of the business. — Often shortened to *executive.*

executive immunity. See IMMUNITY (1).

executive officer. See EXECUTIVE (2).

executive order. (1862) An order issued by or on behalf of the President, usu. intended to direct or instruct the actions of executive agencies or government officials, or to set policies for the executive branch to follow. — Abbr. ex. ord.

executive pardon. See PARDON.

executive power. (17c) *Constitutional law.* The power to see that the laws are duly executed and enforced. ● Under federal law, this power is vested in the President; in the states, it is vested in the governors. The President's enumerated powers are found in the U.S. Constitution, art. II, § 2; governors' executive powers are provided for in state constitutions. The other two great powers of government are the legislative power and the judicial power.

executive privilege. See PRIVILEGE (3).

executive right. *Oil & gas.* The exclusive right to lease specified land or mineral rights. ● The executive right is one of the incidents of the mineral interest.

executive secretary. See EXECUTIVE DIRECTOR.

executive session. See SESSION (1).

executor, *n.* (13c) **1.** (**ek**-sə-kyoo-tər) One who performs or carries out some act. **2.** (eg-**zek**-yə-tər) A person named by a testator to carry out the provisions in the testator's will. Cf. ADMINISTRATOR (2). — Abbr. *exor.*

   acting executor. (18c) One who assumes the role of executor — usu. temporarily — but is not the legally appointed executor or the executor-in-fact. — Also termed *temporary executor.*

   coexecutor. See *joint executor.*

   executor ab episcopo constitutus (ab ə-**pis**-kə-poh kon-sti-**t[y]oo**-təs). [Law Latin] *Eccles. law.* An executor appointed by a bishop; an administrator to an intestate. — Also termed *executor dativus.*

   executor a lege constitutus (ay [*or* ah] **lee**-jee kon-sti-**t[y]oo**-təs). [Law Latin] *Eccles. law.* One authorized by law to be an executor; the ordinary of the diocese.

   executor a testatore constitutus (ay [*or* ah] tes-tə-**tor**-ee kon-sti-**t[y]oo**-təs). [Law Latin] *Eccles.*

law. An executor appointed by a testator. — Also termed *executor testamentarius.*

   executor dative. See DATIVE (1).

   executor dativus. See *executor ab episcopo constitutus.*

   executor de son tort (də sawn [*or* son] **tor**[t]). [Law French "executor of his own wrong"] (17c) A person who, without legal authority, takes on the responsibility to act as an executor or administrator of a decedent's property, usu. to the detriment of the estate's beneficiaries or creditors.

   executor lucratus (loo-**kray**-təs). An executor who has assets of the testator, the latter having become liable by wrongfully interfering with another's property.

   executor testamentarius. See *executor a testatore constitutus.*

   executor to the tenor. Eccles. law. A person who is not named executor in the will but who performs duties similar to those of an executor.

   general executor. (18c) An executor who has the power to administer a decedent's entire estate until its final settlement.

   independent executor. (1877) An executor who, unlike an ordinary executor, can administer the estate with very little supervision by the probate court. ● Only a few states — mostly in the West and Southwest — allow testators to designate independent executors. But lawyers routinely write wills that relieve a trusted executor from obtaining appraisals, from providing inventories and surety bonds, and from obtaining court approval "to the maximum extent permitted by law." The Uniform Probate Code endorses independent administration, and it is the usual process unless a party demands court-supervised administration. — Also termed *nonintervention executor.*

   joint executor. (17c) One of two or more persons named in a will as executor of an estate. — Also termed *coexecutor.*

   limited executor. (18c) An executor whose appointment is restricted in some way, such as time, place, or subject matter.

   literary executor. Copyright. A limited-purpose executor appointed to manage copyrighted materials in an estate.

   nonintervention executor. See *independent executor.*

   special executor. (18c) An executor whose power is limited to a portion of the decedent's estate.

   substituted executor. (18c) An executor appointed to act in the place of an executor who cannot or will not perform the required duties.

   temporary executor. See *acting executor.*

3. (eg-**zek**-yə-tər) *Patents.* One who represents a legally incapacitated inventor. — **executorial,** *adj.* — **executorship,** *n.*

executor fund. See FUND (1).

executor's bond. See BOND (2).

executory (eg-**zek**-yə-tor-ee), *adj.* (16c) **1.** Taking full effect at a future time <executory judgment>. **2.** To be performed at a future time; yet to be completed <executory contract>.

executory accord. See ACCORD (2).

executory bequest. See BEQUEST.

executory consideration. See CONSIDERATION (1).

executory contract. See CONTRACT.

executory covenant. See COVENANT (1).

executory devise. See DEVISE.

executory interest. (1833) A future interest, held by a third person, that either cuts off another's interest or begins after the natural termination of a preceding estate. Cf. REMAINDER.

> *shifting executory interest.* An executory interest that operates in defeasance of an interest created simultaneously in a third person.

> *springing executory interest.* An executory interest that operates in defeasance of an interest left in the transferor.

executory judgment. See JUDGMENT.

executory limitation. See LIMITATION.

executory process. *Civil law.* **1.** A process that can be resorted to either (1) when the right of a creditor arises from an act importing a confession of judgment, and that contains a privilege or mortgage in the creditor's favor, or (2) when the creditor demands the execution of a judgment that has been rendered by a different tribunal. **2.** An accelerated procedure, summary in nature, by which the holder of a mortgage or privilege evidenced by a confession of judgment seeks to effect an ex parte seizure and sale of the subject property.

executory remainder. See *contingent remainder* under REMAINDER.

executory sale. See SALE.

executory trust. See TRUST.

executory unilateral accord. (1940) An offer to enter a contract; OFFER (2).

executory use. See *springing use* under USE (4).

executory warranty. See WARRANTY (3).

executress. See EXECUTRIX.

executrix (eg-**zek**-yə-triks), *n. Archaic.* A female executor. — Abbr. exrx. — Also termed *executress.* Pl. **executrixes** (eg-**zek**-yə-trik-səz), **executrices** (eg-zek-yə-**trı**-seez). See EXECUTOR.

exemplar (eg-**zem**-plər *or* -plahr), *n.* (15c) **1.** An ideal or typical example; a standard specimen <handwriting exemplars>. **2.** Nontestimonial identification evidence, such as fingerprints, voiceprints, and DNA samples. See VOICE EXEMPLAR.

exemplary, *adj.* (16c) **1.** Serving as an ideal example; commendable <exemplary behavior>. **2.** Serving as a warning or deterrent; admonitory <exemplary damages>.

exemplary damages. See *punitive damages* under DAMAGES.

exemplary substitution. See SUBSTITUTION (5).

exemplification, *n.* (16c) An official transcript of a public record, authenticated as a true copy for use as evidence. — **exemplify,** *vb.*

exemplified copy. See *certified copy* under COPY.

exempli gratia (eg-**zem**-plı **gray**-shee-ə *or* ek-**sem**-plee **grah**-tee-ə). [Latin] (17c) For example; for instance. — Abbr. e.g. or (rarely) ex. gr.

exemplum (eg-**zem**-pləm), *n.* [Latin] (19c) *Civil law.* A copy; a written authorized copy.

exempt, *adj.* (14c) Free or released from a duty or liability to which others are held <persons exempt from military service> <property exempt from sequestration>. — **exempt,** *vb.* — **exemptive,** *adj.*

exempt income. See INCOME.

exemption. (14c) **1.** Freedom from a duty, liability, or other requirement; an exception. See IMMUNITY; EXCEPTION (2). **2.** A privilege given to a judgment debtor by law, allowing the debtor to retain certain property without liability. **3.** *Tax.* An amount allowed as a deduction from adjusted gross income, used to determine taxable income. Cf. DEDUCTION (2).

> *dependency exemption.* (1920) A tax exemption granted to an individual taxpayer for each dependent whose gross income is less than the exemption amount and for each child who is younger than 19 or, if a student, younger than 24.

> *personal exemption.* (1920) An amount allowed as a deduction from an individual taxpayer's adjusted gross income.

exemption clause. (1840) A contractual provision providing that a party will not be liable for damages for which that party would otherwise have ordinarily been liable. Cf. EXCEPTION CLAUSE; EXCULPATORY CLAUSE; INDEMNITY CLAUSE.

exemption equivalent. The maximum value of assets that one can transfer to another before incurring a federal gift and estate tax.

exemption law. (1839) A law describing what property of a debtor cannot be attached by a judgment creditor or trustee in bankruptcy to satisfy a debt. See EXEMPT PROPERTY (1).

exempt organization. An organization that is either partially or completely exempt from federal income taxation. See CHARITABLE ORGANIZATION.

exempt property. (1839) **1.** A debtor's holdings and possessions that, by law, a creditor cannot attach to satisfy a debt. • All the property that creditors may lawfully reach is known as *nonexempt property.* Many states provide a homestead exemption that excludes a person's house and household items, up to a certain amount, from the liens of most creditors. The purpose of the exemption is to prevent debtors from becoming destitute. See HOMESTEAD. Cf. NONEXEMPT PROPERTY. **2.** Personal property that a surviving spouse is automatically entitled to receive from the decedent's estate.

exempt security. See SECURITY.

exempt transaction. A sale that falls outside the scope of a certain statute, such as the Securities Act of 1933 or the Securities Exchange Act of 1934.

exequatur (ek-sə-**kway**-tər). [Latin "let it be executed"] (17c) A written official recognition and authorization of a consular officer, issued by the government to which the officer is accredited.

exercise, *vb.* (14c) **1.** To make use of; to put into action <exercise the right to vote>. **2.** To implement the terms of; to execute <exercise the option to buy the commodities>. — **exercise,** *n.*

Exercise Clause. See FREE EXERCISE CLAUSE.

exercise of judgment. (17c) The use of sound discretion — that is, discretion exercised with regard to what is right and equitable rather than arbitrarily or willfully.

exercise price. See *strike price* under PRICE.

exercise value. The value to an optionholder of using the option.

exercitor (eg-**zər**-si-tor), *n.* [Latin "an exercisor"] (17c) *Civil law.* The person to whom the profits of a ship temporarily belong, whether that person is the owner, charterer, or mortgagee. — Also termed *exercitor maris; exercitor navis.* Cf. SHIP'S HUSBAND.

exercitorial power (eg-zər-si-**tor**-ee-əl). The trust given to a shipmaster.

ex facie (eks **fay**-shee-ee *or* -shee *or* -shə). [Latin] (1861) *Archaic.* On the face of it; evidently; apparently. • The phrase typically referred to a defect appearing from the document itself, without further inquiry.

ex facto (eks **fak**-toh). [Latin "from a fact"] From or in consequence of a fact or action; actually; DE FACTO.

ex. gr. abbr. EXEMPLI GRATIA.

ex gratia (eks **gray**-shee-ə *or* **grah**-tee-ə). [Latin "by favor"] (18c) As a favor; not legally necessary. — Also termed *a gratia.*

ex gratia payment. (1916) A payment not legally required; esp., an insurance payment not required to be made under an insurance policy.

exhausted ballot. See *exhausted vote* under VOTE (1).

exhausted combination. See *old combination* under COMBINATION.

exhausted-combination rejection. See *old-combination rejection* under REJECTION.

exhausted vote. See VOTE (1).

exhaustion of remedies. (1876) The doctrine that, if an administrative remedy is provided by statute, a claimant must seek relief first from the administrative body before judicial relief is available. • The doctrine's purpose is to maintain comity between the courts and administrative agencies and to ensure that courts will not be burdened by cases in which judicial relief is unnecessary. — Also termed *exhaustion of administrative remedies.*

> *vicarious exhaustion of remedies.* The rule that if one member of a class satisfies a requirement to exhaust administrative remedies, that is enough for all others similarly situated to be considered as having exhausted the remedies. — Often shortened to *vicarious exhaustion.*

exhaustion-of-rights doctrine. *Int'l law.* The principle that once the owner of an intellectual-property right has placed a product covered by that right into the marketplace, the right to control how the product is resold within that internal market is lost. • Within a common market, such as the European Union, the doctrine also applies to the import and export of the goods between member nations. Cf. PATENT-EXHAUSTION DOCTRINE.

exhaustion of state remedies. (1944) The doctrine that an available state remedy must be exhausted in certain types of cases before a party can gain access to a federal court. • For example, a state prisoner must exhaust all state remedies before a federal court will hear a petition for habeas corpus.

exhibit, *n.* (17c) **1.** A document, record, or other tangible object formally introduced as evidence in court. **2.** A document attached to and made part of a pleading, motion, contract, or other instrument.

exhibit, *vb. Archaic.* To bring a lawsuit by filing (a bill).

exhibitionism, *n.* (1893) The indecent display of one's body. — **exhibitionist,** *adj. & n.*

exhibition value. In the motion-picture industry, the minimum receipts that distributors expect to realize from showing a particular film. — Also termed *minimum sale*; *price expectancy*.

exhibit list. (1929) **1.** A pretrial filing that identifies by number and description the exhibits a party intends to offer into evidence at trial. ● Courts often require the exchange of exhibit lists before trial so that evidentiary disputes can be resolved with minimal disruption in the course of a jury trial. **2.** A document prepared during a trial by the clerk or a courtroom deputy to identify by number and description the exhibits that the parties have entered into evidence.

exhibitory interdict. See INTERDICT (1).

exhumation (eks-hyoo-**may**-shən *or* eg-zyoo-), *n.* (18c) The removal from the earth of something buried, esp. a human corpse; disinterment.

ex hypothesi (eks hɪ-**poth**-ə-sɪ). [Latin] Hypothetically; by hypothesis; on the assumption <conviction for a felony is *ex hypothesi* impossible in the case of suicide>.

exigency (**ek**-sə-jən-see), *n.* (16c) A state of urgency; a situation requiring immediate action. — Also termed *exigence*.

exigendary (ek-sə-**jen**-də-ree), *n.* See EXIGENTER.

exigent, *adj.* (17c) Requiring immediate action or aid; urgent <exigent circumstances>.

exigent (**ek**-sə-jənt), *n. Hist.* A judicial writ employed in the process of outlawry, commanding the sheriff to demand the defendant's appearance, from county court to county court, until he was outlawed — or, if the defendant appeared, to take him before the court to answer the plaintiff's action.

exigent circumstances. See CIRCUMSTANCE.

exigenter (**ek**-sə-jen-tər), *n.* (16c) *Hist.* An officer of the court of common pleas responsible for preparing exigents and proclamations in the process of outlawry. ● This office was abolished in 1837 by the Superior Courts (Officers) Act, St. 7 Will. 4, and 1 Vict., ch. 30. — Also termed *exigendary*.

exigent list. A list of cases set down for hearing upon various incidental and ancillary motions and rules.

exigent search. See SEARCH.

exigible debt. See DEBT.

exile, *n.* (14c) **1.** Expulsion from a country, esp. from the country of one's origin or longtime residence; banishment.

forced exile. Compelled removal or banishment from one's native country.

2. A person who has been banished. **3.** A prolonged voluntary absence from one's home country. — **exile,** *vb.*

Ex-Im Bank. See EXPORT-IMPORT BANK OF THE UNITED STATES.

existent corner. See CORNER.

exit, *n.* (16c) **1.** A way out. See EGRESS. **2.** In a docket entry, an issuance of something (as a writ or process). ● For example, *exit attachment* denotes that a writ of attachment has been issued in the case. — **exit,** *vb.*

ex jure (eks **juur**-ee). [Latin] Of or by legal right.

ex justa causa (eks jəs-tə **kaw**-zə). [Latin] From a just or lawful cause; by a just or legal title.

ex justitia (eks jəs-**tish**-ee-ə). [Latin] From justice; as a matter of justice.

ex legal municipal bond. See BOND (3).

ex lege (eks **lee**-jee *or* **lay**-gay). [Latin] By virtue of law; as a matter of law <property forfeited *ex lege*>.

ex maleficio (eks mal-ə-**fish**-ee-oh), *adv.* [Latin] By malfeasance.

ex maleficio, *adj.* [Latin] Tortious.

ex natura (eks nə-**t**[**y**]**oor**-ə). [Latin] *Hist.* Naturally; according to nature.

ex necessitate (eks nə-ses-i-**tay**-tee). [Latin] Of or from necessity.

ex necessitate legis (eks nə-ses-i-**tay**-tee **lee**-jis). From or by necessity of law.

ex necessitate rei (eks nə-ses-i-**tay**-tee **ree**-ɪ). From the necessity or urgency of the thing or case.

ex nihilo (eks **nɪ**-hi-loh). [Latin] From nothing.

ex officio (eks ə-**fish**-ee-oh), *adv. & adj.* [Latin] (16c) By virtue or because of an office; by virtue of the authority implied by office. ● The term is often misused as a synonym for "nonvoting." Some meetings mistakenly label their regularly invited guests as "ex officio members" when in fact they are not members at all; others mistakenly refer to the nonvoting members as "ex officio members" even though some nonvoting members are present only in an individual capacity and not by virtue of office, or even though some voting members also serve ex officio. But an ex officio member is a voting member unless the applicable governing document provides otherwise.

ex officio justice. (1855) A judge who serves on a commission or board only because the law requires the presence of a judge rather than because the judge was selected for the position.

ex officio member. See *member ex officio* under MEMBER.

ex officio service (eks ə-**fish**-ee-oh). (1845) A service that the law imposes on an official by virtue of the office held, such as that of a local justice of the peace to perform marriage ceremonies.

exogamous insemination. See *artificial insemination by donor* under ARTIFICIAL INSEMINATION.

exonerate (eg-**zon**-ə-rayt), *vb.* (16c) **1.** To free from responsibility <exonerate from the payment of the debt>. Cf. EXCULPATE. **2.** To free from encumbrances <exonerate the property from the mortgage lien>. — **exonerative** (eg-**zon**-ər-ay-tiv *or* -ə-tiv), *adj.*

exoneration (eg-zon-ə-**ray**-shən). (16c) **1.** The removal of a burden, charge, responsibility, or duty. **2.** The right to be reimbursed by reason of having paid money that another person should have paid. **3.** The equitable right of a surety — confirmed by statute in many states — to proceed to compel the principal debtor to satisfy the obligation, as when, even though the surety would have a right of reimbursement, it would be inequitable for the surety to be compelled to perform if the principal debtor can satisfy the obligation. • When a testator leaves a gift of property encumbered by a mortgage or lien, the doctrine of exoneration operates to satisfy the encumbrance from the general assets of the estate. Many states have abandoned the common-law rule in favor of exoneration. See EQUITY OF EXONERATION; QUIA TIMET.

exoneration, suit for. See SUIT FOR EXONERATION.

exonerative fact. See FACT.

ex. ord. (*often cap.*) *abbr.* EXECUTIVE ORDER.

exordium (eg-**zor**-dee-əm). [Latin] (16c) An introduction in a discourse or writing, esp. in a will. • In a will, the exordium usu. contains statements of the testator's name and capacity to make the will. — Also termed *exordium clause; introductory clause*.

ex parte (eks **pahr**-tee), *adv.* [Latin "from the part"] (18c) On or from one party only, usu. without notice to or argument from the adverse party <the judge conducted the hearing ex parte>.

ex parte, *adj.* (17c) Done or made at the instance and for the benefit of one party only, and without notice to, or argument by, any person adversely interested; of or relating to court action taken by one party without notice to the other, usu. for temporary or emergency relief <an ex parte hearing> <an ex parte injunction>. • Despite the traditional one-sidedness of ex parte matters, some courts now require notice to the opposition before what they call an "ex parte hearing." — Sometimes spelled *exparte.* — **ex parte,** *adv.*

ex parte application. See *ex parte motion* under MOTION (1).

ex parte communication. See COMMUNICATION.

ex parte divorce. See DIVORCE.

ex parte hearing. See *ex parte proceeding* under PROCEEDING.

ex parte injunction. See INJUNCTION.

ex parte motion. See MOTION (1).

ex parte order. See ORDER (2).

ex parte proceeding. See PROCEEDING.

Ex Parte Quayle **action.** See QUAYLE ACTION.

ex parte reexamination. See REEXAMINATION.

expatriate (ek-**spay**-tree-it), *n.* (18c) An expatriated person; esp., a person who lives permanently in a foreign country.

expatriate (ek-**spay**-tree-ayt), *vb.* (1812) **1.** To withdraw (oneself) from residence in or allegiance to one's native country; to leave one's home country to live elsewhere. **2.** To banish or exile (a person). — **expatriation,** *n.*

expectancy, *n.* (1811) **1.** *Property.* An estate with a reversion, a remainder, or an executory interest. **2.** *Wills & estates.* The possibility that an heir apparent, an heir presumptive, or a presumptive next of kin will acquire property by devolution on intestacy, or the possibility that a presumptive beneficiary will acquire property by will. **3.** *Insurance.* The probable number of years in one's life. See LIFE EXPECTANCY.

expectancy damages. See *expectation damages* under DAMAGES.

expectancy table. See ACTUARIAL TABLE.

expectant, *adj.* (14c) Having a relation to, or being dependent on, a contingency; CONTINGENT.

expectant beneficiary. See *expectant distributee* under DISTRIBUTEE.

expectant distributee. See DISTRIBUTEE.

expectant estate. See FUTURE INTEREST.

expectant heir. See HEIR.

expectant right. See RIGHT.

expectation, *n.* (16c) **1.** The act of looking forward; anticipation. **2.** A basis on which something is expected to happen; esp., the prospect of receiving wealth, honors, or the like.

expectation damages. See DAMAGES.

expectation interest. See INTEREST (2).

expectation of life. See LIFE EXPECTANCY.

expectation of privacy. (1965) A belief in the existence of the right to be free of governmental intrusion in regard to a particular place or thing. • To suppress a search on privacy grounds, a defendant must show the existence of the expectation and that the expectation was reasonable.

expected/intended exclusion. See EXCLUSION (3).

expediment (ek-**sped**-ə-mənt), *n.* (1848) The whole of one's goods and chattels.

expedited proceeding. See SHOW-CAUSE PROCEEDING.

expel, *vb.* (15c) To drive out or away; to eject, esp. with force. See EJECT; EVICT.

expenditor (ek-**spen**-də-tər). (15c) One who expends or disburses certain taxes; a paymaster.

expenditure. (18c) **1.** The act or process of paying out; disbursement. **2.** A sum paid out.

expense, *n.* (14c) An expenditure of money, time, labor, or resources to accomplish a result; esp., a business expenditure chargeable against revenue for a specific period. Cf. COST (1). — **expense,** *vb.*

accrued expense. (1880) An expense incurred but not yet paid.

administrative expense. See *general administrative expense.*

business expense. (1858) An expense incurred to operate and promote a business; esp., an expenditure made to further the business in the taxable year in which the expense is incurred. ● Most business expenses — unlike personal expenses — are tax-deductible.

capital expense. (1913) An expense made by a business to provide a long-term benefit; a capital expenditure. ● A capital expense is not deductible, but it can be used for depreciation or amortization.

capitalized expense. An amortized expense.

current expense. See *operating expense.*

deferred expense. (1925) A cost incurred by a business when the business expects to benefit from that cost over a period beyond the current year. ● An example is a prepaid subscription to a business periodical the cost of which will be recognized as an expense over a multiyear subscription period.

educational expense. (1882) A deductible expense incurred either to maintain or improve an existing job skill or to meet a legally imposed job requirement.

entertainment expense. An expense incurred while providing entertainment relating directly to or associated with a business purpose. ● Entertainment expenses are partially tax-deductible.

extraordinary expense. (16c) An unusual or infrequent expense, such as a write-off of goodwill or a large judgment. ● As used in a constitutional provision authorizing a state to incur extraordinary expenses, the term denotes an expense for the general welfare compelled by an unforeseen condition such as a natural disaster or war. — Also termed *extraordinary item.*

fixed expense. See *fixed cost* under COST.

funeral expense. (*usu. pl.*) (18c) An expense necessarily and reasonably incurred in procuring the burial, cremation, or other disposition of a corpse, including the funeral or other ceremonial rite, a casket and vault, a monument or tombstone, a burial plot and its care, and a visitation (or wake).

general administrative expense. (*usu. pl.*) (1907) An expense incurred in running a business, as distinguished from an expense incurred in manufacturing or selling; overhead. ● Examples include executive and clerical salaries, rent, utilities, and legal and accounting services. — Also termed *administrative expense; general expense.* — Abbr. G & A.

medical expense. (1853) **1.** An expense for medical treatment or healthcare, such as drug costs and health-insurance premiums. ● Medical expenses are tax-deductible to the extent that the amounts (less insurance reimbursements) exceed a certain percentage of adjusted gross income. **2.** (*usu. pl.*) In civil litigation, any one of many possible medical costs that the plaintiff has sustained or reasonably expects to incur because of the defendant's allegedly wrongful act, including charges for visits to physicians' offices, medical procedures, hospital bills, medicine, and recuperative therapy needed in the past and in the future. — Often shortened (in pl.) to *medicals.*

moving expense. (1903) An expense incurred in changing one's residence. ● If incurred for business reasons (as when one's job requires relocation), most moving expenses are tax-deductible.

operating expense. (1861) An expense incurred in running a business and producing output. — Also termed *current expense.*

ordinary and necessary expense. (1826) An expense that is normal or usual and helpful or appropriate for the operation of a particular trade or business and that is paid or incurred during the taxable year. ● Ordinary and necessary expenses are tax-deductible. — Also termed *ordinary and necessary business expense.*

organizational expense. (1941) An expense incurred while setting up a corporation or other entity.

out-of-pocket expense. (1905) An expense paid from one's own funds.

prepaid expense. (1919) An expense (such as rent, interest, or insurance) that is paid before the due date or before a service is rendered.

travel expense. (1905) An expense (such as for meals, lodging, and transportation) incurred while away from home in the pursuit of a trade or business. See TAX HOME.

expense loading. See LOADING.

expense ratio. *Accounting.* The proportion or ratio of expenses to income.

expenses of administration. (18c) Expenses incurred by a decedent's representatives in administering the estate.

expenses of receivership. (18c) Expenses incurred by a receiver in conducting the business, including rent and fees incurred by the receiver's counsel and by any master, appraiser, and auditor.

expense stop. (1990) A lease provision establishing the maximum expenses to be paid by the landlord, beyond which the tenant must bear all remaining expenses.

experience rating. *Insurance.* A method of determining the amount of the premium by analyzing the insured's loss record over time to assess (1) the risk that covered events will occur, and (2) the amount of probable damages if they do.

experimental use. See USE (1).

experimental-use defense. *Patents.* A defense to a claim of patent infringement raised when the construction and use of the patented invention was for scientific purposes only. ● While still recognized, this defense is narrowly construed and today may apply only to research that tests the inventor's claims. 35 USCA § 271(e)(1).

experimental-use exception. *Patents.* An exception to the public-use statutory bar, whereby an inventor is allowed to make public use of an invention for more than one year when that use is necessary to test and improve the invention.

expert, *n.* (16c) A person who, through education or experience, has developed skill or knowledge in a particular subject, so that he or she may form an opinion that will assist the fact-finder. Fed. R. Evid. 702. See DAUBERT TEST. — **expertise** (ek-spər-**teez**), *n.*

   consulting expert. (1897) An expert who, though retained by a party, is not expected to be called as a witness at trial. ● A consulting expert's opinions are generally exempt from the scope of discovery. Fed. R. Civ. P. 26(b)(4)(B). — Also termed *nontestifying expert.*

   impartial expert. (1870) An expert who is appointed by the court to present an unbiased opinion. — Also termed *court-appointed expert.* Fed. R. Evid. 706.

   testifying expert. (1952) An expert who is identified by a party as a potential witness at trial. ● As a part of initial disclosures in federal court, a party must provide to all other parties a wide range of information about a testifying expert's qualifications and opinion, including all information that the witness considered in forming the opinion. Fed. R. Civ. P. 26(a)(2)(b).

expert evidence. See EVIDENCE.

expert opinion. See OPINION (3).

expert-reliance materials. Facts, documents, and other sources that provide data or information to an expert witness. ● Often shortened to *reliance materials.*

expert testimony. See *expert evidence* under EVIDENCE.

expert witness. See WITNESS.

expert-witness fee. See FEE (1).

expiration, *n.* A coming to an end; esp., a formal termination on a closing date <expiration of the insurance policy>. — **expire,** *vb.*

expiration date. (1803) The date on which an offer, option, or the like ceases to exist. — Also termed *expiry date.*

expiry date. See EXPIRATION DATE.

explanatory-phrase rule. *Trademarks.* The principle that a senior user of a family-name trademark is entitled to a judicial remedy for unfair competition if the same family name appears on competing goods or services, the remedy being that the junior user must include on signs, labels, and advertisements an explanation that the company is not affiliated with the senior user's company. ● The rule resolves two conflicting principles: (1) everyone has the right to use a family name in business, and (2) no one may use a family name in a way that unfairly hurts someone else's business.

explees (ek-**spleez**). See ESPLEES.

exploding adjustable-rate mortgage. See MORTGAGE.

exploitation, *n.* (19c) The act of taking advantage of something; esp., the act of taking unjust advantage of another for one's own benefit. See SEXUAL EXPLOITATION. — **exploit,** *vb.* — **exploitative,** *adj.*

exploration manager. See LAND MANAGER.

export, *n.* (17c) **1.** A product or service created in one country and transported to another.

   domestic export. A product originally grown or manufactured in the United States, as distinguished from a product originally imported into the United States and then exported.

2. The process of transporting products or services to another country. Cf. IMPORT (1), (2).

export, *vb.* (15c) **1.** To send or carry abroad. **2.** To send, take, or carry (a good or commodity) out of the country; to transport (merchandise) from one country to another in the course of trade. **3.** To carry out or convey (goods) by sea.

exportation. (17c) The act of sending or carrying goods and merchandise from one country to another.

Export Clause. See IMPORT-EXPORT CLAUSE.

export declaration. (1920) A document — required by federal law — containing details of an export shipment.

export draft. See DRAFT.

Export-Import Bank of the United States. A federally chartered bank that finances the export of goods and services by direct lending or by issuing guarantees and insurance so that private banks can extend credit. ● The bank was organized by Executive Order 6581 of 2 Feb. 1934. It became independent in 1945. 12 USCA §§ 635 et seq. — Often shortened to *Ex-Im Bank.*

export letter of credit. See LETTER OF CREDIT.

export quota. See QUOTA.

export tax. See TAX.

exposé (ek-spoh-**zay**), *n.* [French] (1803) **1.** A statement or account; an explanation. • In diplomatic language, the term describes a written explanation of the reasons for a certain act or course of conduct. **2.** Exposure of discreditable matter.

expository jurisprudence. See JURISPRUDENCE.

expository statute. See *declaratory statute* under STATUTE.

ex post, *adj.* [Latin "from after"] (1937) Based on knowledge and fact; viewed after the fact, in hindsight; objective; retrospective. Cf. EX ANTE.

ex post facto (eks pohst **fak**-toh), *adj.* (18c) Done or made after the fact; having retroactive force or effect.

ex post facto, *adv.* [Latin "from a thing done afterward"] (17c) After the fact; retroactively.

Ex Post Facto Clause. (1848) One of two clauses in the U.S. Constitution forbidding the enactment of ex post facto laws. U.S. Const. art. I, § 9, cl. 3; art. I, § 10, cl. 1.

ex post facto law. (18c) A law that impermissibly applies retroactively, esp. in a way that negatively affects a person's rights, as by criminalizing an action that was legal when it was committed. • Ex post facto criminal laws are prohibited by the U.S. Constitution. But retrospective civil laws may be allowed. See RETROACTIVE LAW.

exposure. (17c) The amount of liability or other risk to which a person is subject <the client wanted to know its exposure before it made a settlement offer>.

dangerous exposure. *Maritime law.* Exposure that is reasonably foreseeable in the ordinary chances, mistakes, or hazards of navigation.

exposure of person. See INDECENT EXPOSURE.

exposure theory. *Insurance.* A theory of coverage providing that an insurer must cover a loss if the insurance was in effect when the claimant was exposed to the product that caused the injury. Cf. MANIFESTATION THEORY; ACTUAL-INJURY TRIGGER; TRIPLE TRIGGER.

express, *adj.* (14c) Clearly and unmistakably communicated; directly stated. Cf. IMPLIED. — **expressly,** *adv.*

express abandonment. See ABANDONMENT (10).

express abrogation. (1857) The repeal of a law or provision by a later one that refers directly to it; abrogation by express provision or enactment.

express acceptance. See ACCEPTANCE (4).

express active trust. See *active trust* under TRUST.

express actual knowledge. See *actual knowledge* (1) under KNOWLEDGE.

express agency. See AGENCY (1).

express aider. See AIDER BY SUBSEQUENT PLEADING.

express amnesty. See AMNESTY.

express assent. See ASSENT.

express assumpsit. See *special assumpsit* under ASSUMPSIT.

express authority. See AUTHORITY (1).

express color. See COLOR.

express condition. See CONDITION (2).

express consent. See CONSENT (1).

express consideration. See CONSIDERATION (1).

express contract. See CONTRACT.

express covenant. See COVENANT (1).

express dedication. See DEDICATION.

express dissatisfaction. *Wills & estates.* A beneficiary's contesting of a will or objecting to any provision of the will in a probate proceeding.

expressed, *adj.* (16c) Declared in direct terms; stated in words; not left to inference or implication.

expression, freedom of. See FREEDOM OF EXPRESSION.

expressio unius est exclusio alterius (ek-**spres**[h]-ee-oh yoo-**ni**-əs est ek-**skloo**-zhee-oh al-tə-**ri**-əs). [Law Latin] A canon of construction holding that to express or include one thing implies the exclusion of the other, or of the alternative. • For example, the rule that "each citizen is entitled to vote" implies that noncitizens are not entitled to vote. — Also termed *inclusio unius est exclusio alterius; expressum facit cessare tacitum.* Cf. EJUSDEM GENERIS; NOSCITUR A SOCIIS; RULE OF RANK.

expressive association, freedom of. See FREEDOM OF ASSOCIATION.

expressive crime. See CRIME.

express malice. See MALICE.

express notice. See NOTICE.

express obligation. See *conventional obligation* under OBLIGATION.

express permission. See PERMISSION.

express power. See *enumerated power* under POWER (3).

express private passive trust. See TRUST.

express repeal. See REPEAL.

express republication. (18c) A testator's repeating of the acts essential to a will's valid execution, with the avowed intent of republishing the will. See REPUBLICATION (2).

express trust. See TRUST.

expressum facit cessare tacitum. See EXPRESSIO UNIUS EST EXCLUSIO ALTERIUS.

express waiver. See WAIVER (1).

express warranty. See WARRANTY (2).

expromissio (eks-prə-**mis**[h]-ee-oh), *n. Roman law.* A type of novation by which a creditor accepts a new debtor in place of a former one, who is then released.

expromissor (eks-prə-**mis**-ər), *n. Roman law.* One who assumes another's debt and becomes solely liable for it, by a stipulation with the creditor.

expromittere (eks-prə-**mit**-ə-ree), *vb. Roman law.* To undertake for another with the view of becoming liable in the other's place.

expropriation, *n.* (15c) **1.** A governmental taking or modification of an individual's property rights, esp. by eminent domain; CONDEMNATION (2). — Also termed (in England) *compulsory purchase*; (in Scotland) *compulsory surrender.* Cf. APPROPRIATION. **2.** A voluntary surrender of rights or claims; the act of renouncing or divesting oneself of something previously claimed as one's own. — **expropriate,** *vb.* — **expropriator,** *n.*

expulsion, *n.* (15c) An ejectment or banishment, either through depriving a person of a benefit or by forcibly evicting a person. — **expulsive,** *adj.*

expunction of record. See EXPUNGEMENT OF RECORD.

expunge (ek-**spənj**), *vb.* (17c) **1.** To erase or destroy <the trustee wrongfully expunged the creditor's claim against the debtor>. **2.** *Parliamentary law.* To declare (a vote or other action) null and outside the record, so that it is noted in the original record as expunged, and redacted from all future copies. — Also termed *rescind and expunge; rescind and expunge from the minutes; rescind and expunge from the record.* — **expungement** (ek-**spənj**-mənt), **expunction** (ek-**spəngk**-shən), *n.*

expungement of record. (1966) The removal of a conviction (esp. for a first offense) from a person's criminal record. — Also termed *expunction of record; erasure of record.*

expurgation (ek-spər-**gay**-shən), *n.* (15c) The act or practice of purging or cleansing, as by publishing a book without its obscene passages. — **expurgate** (**eks**-pər-gayt), *vb.* — **expurgator** (**eks**-pər-gay-tər), *n.*

ex quasi contractu (eks **kway**-zı kən-**trak**-t[y]oo). [Latin] From quasi-contract.

ex rel. *abbr.* [Latin *ex relatione* "by or on the relation of"] (1838) On the relation or information of. ● A suit *ex rel.* is typically brought by the government upon the application of a private party (called a *relator*) who is interested in the matter. See RELATOR (1).

ex rights, *adv.* Without rights. ● Shares are traded ex rights when the value of the subscription privilege has been deducted, giving the purchaser no right to buy shares of a new stock issue. — Abbr. X; XR. — Also termed *rights off.*

ex-rights date. The date on which a share of common stock no longer offers privilege subscription rights.

exrx. *abbr.* EXECUTRIX.

ex ship. Of or referring to a shipment of goods for which the liability or risk of loss passes to the buyer once the goods leave the ship.

ex-stock dividend. Without stock dividend. ● The phrase often denotes the interval between the announcement and payment of a stock dividend. A purchaser of shares during this interval is not entitled to the dividend, which goes to the seller.

extend debate. *Parliamentary law.* To cancel or relax an otherwise applicable limit on debate. — Also termed *extend the limits of debate.* See DEBATE. Cf. CLOSE DEBATE; LIMIT DEBATE.

extended-coverage clause. *Insurance.* A policy provision that insures against hazards beyond those covered (or excluded) in the basic policy.

extended debate. See DEBATE.

extended family. See FAMILY.

extended first mortgage. See *wraparound mortgage* under MORTGAGE.

extended insurance. See INSURANCE.

extended policy. See INSURANCE POLICY.

extended-reporting-period endorsement. See TAIL COVERAGE.

extended service contract. See *extended warranty* under WARRANTY (2).

extended service warranty. See *extended warranty* under WARRANTY (2).

extended-term insurance. See INSURANCE.

extended warranty. See WARRANTY (2).

extend the limits of debate. See EXTEND DEBATE.

extension, *n.* (17c) **1.** The continuation of the same contract for a specified period. Cf. RENEWAL (3). **2.** *Patents.* A continuation of the life of a patent for an additional statutorily allowed period. **3.** *Tax.* A period of additional time to file an income-tax return beyond its due date. **4.** A period of additional time to take an action, make a decision, accept an offer, or complete a task. — **extend,** *vb.*

extension agreement. (1869) An agreement providing additional time for the basic agreement to be performed.

extensive interpretation. See INTERPRETATION.

extent. *Hist.* **1.** A seizure of property in execution of a writ. **2.** A writ issued by the Exchequer to recover a debt owed to the Crown, under which the debtor's lands, goods, or body could all be seized to secure payment. — Also termed *writ of extent*; *extent in chief*. **3.** A writ giving a creditor temporary possession of the debtor's property (esp. land). — Also termed *extendi facias*.

extent in aid. *Hist.* A writ that a Crown debtor could obtain against a person indebted to the Crown debtor so that the Crown debtor could satisfy the debt to the Crown. ● This writ, having been much abused because of some peculiar privileges that Crown debtors enjoyed, was abolished in 1947 by the Crown Proceedings Act.

extent in chief. See EXTENT (2).

extenuate (ek-**sten**-yoo-ayt), *vb.* (16c) To make less severe; to mitigate.

extenuating circumstance. See *mitigating circumstance* under CIRCUMSTANCE.

extenuation (ek-sten-yoo-**ay**-shən), *n.* The act or fact of making the commission of a crime or tort less severe.

extern. See CLERK (4).

external act. See ACT.

externality. (*usu. pl.*) (1957) A consequence or side effect of one's economic activity, causing another to benefit without paying or to suffer without compensation. — Also termed *spillover*; *neighborhood effect*.

   negative externality. (1970) An externality that is detrimental to another, such as water pollution created by a nearby factory.

   positive externality. (1970) An externality that benefits another, such as the advantage received by a neighborhood when a homeowner attractively landscapes the property.

external obsolescence. See *economic obsolescence* under OBSOLESCENCE.

external sovereignty. See SOVEREIGNTY (3).

exterritorial. See EXTRATERRITORIAL.

exterritoriality. See EXTRATERRITORIALITY.

extinct, *adj.* (15c) **1.** No longer in existence or use. **2.** (Of a debt) lacking a claimant.

extinctive fact. See *divestitive fact* under FACT.

extinctive prescription. See PRESCRIPTION (4).

extinguish, *vb.* **1.** To bring to an end; to put an end to. **2.** To terminate or cancel. **3.** To put out or stifle.

extinguishment, *n.* (16c) The cessation or cancellation of some right or interest. ● For example, the extinguishment of a legacy occurs when the item bequeathed no longer exists or no longer belongs to the testator's estate.

extinguishment of copyhold. The destruction of copyhold by a uniting of freehold and copyhold interests in the same person and in the same right. ● In England, under the 1922 Law of Property Act, copyholds were enfranchised and became either leasehold or, more often, freehold. See COPYHOLD.

extinguishment of legacy. See ADEMPTION.

extinguishment of lien. (1800) A lien's discharge by operation of law.

extirpation (ek-stər-**pay**-shən), *n.* (16c) **1.** The act of completely removing or destroying something. **2.** Damage to land intentionally done by a person who has lost the right to the land.

extort, *vb.* (15c) **1.** To compel or coerce (a confession, etc.) by means that overcome one's power to resist. **2.** To gain by wrongful methods; to obtain in an unlawful manner; to exact wrongfully by threat or intimidation. — **extortive,** *adj.*

extortion, *n.* (14c) **1.** The offense committed by a public official who illegally obtains property under the color of office; esp., an official's collection of an unlawful fee. — Also termed *common-law extortion*. **2.** The act or practice of obtaining something or compelling some action by illegal means, as by force or coercion. — Also termed *statutory extortion*. — **extortionate,** *adj.*

extortionate credit transaction. See LOANSHARKING.

extra (ek-strə), *prep.* [Latin] (1852) Beyond; except; without; out of; additional.

extra allowance. In New York practice, a sum in addition to costs that may, in the court's discretion, be awarded to the successful party in an unusually difficult case. See ALLOWANCE (5).

extract (ek-strakt), *n.* **1.** A portion or segment, as of a writing. **2.** *Scots law.* See ESTREAT.

extract (ek-**strakt**), *vb.* To draw out or forth; to pull out from a fixed position.

extraction. *Intellectual property.* The transfer of data from a database from the server where the database resides to a different computer or medium.

extradite (ek-strə-dɪt), *vb.* (1864) **1.** To surrender or deliver (a fugitive) to another jurisdiction. **2.** To obtain the surrender of (a fugitive) from another jurisdiction.

extradition (ek-strə-**dish**-ən). (18c) The official surrender of an alleged criminal by one state or nation to another having jurisdiction over the crime charged; the return of a fugitive from justice, regardless of consent, by the authorities where the fugitive is found. Cf. RENDITION (2).

   international extradition. Extradition in response to a demand made by the executive of one nation on the executive of another nation. ● This procedure is generally regulated by treaties.

interstate extradition. Extradition in response to a demand made by the governor of one state on the governor of another state. • This procedure is provided for by the U.S. Constitution, by federal statute, and by state statutes.

Extradition Clause. (1878) The clause of the U.S. Constitution providing that any accused person who flees to another state must, on request of the executive authority of the state where the crime was committed, be returned to that state. U.S. Const. art. IV, § 2, cl. 2.

extradition treaty. (1847) A treaty governing the preconditions for, and exceptions to, the surrender of a fugitive from justice by the country where the fugitive is found to another country claiming criminal jurisdiction over the fugitive.

extradition warrant. See WARRANT (1).

extra dividend. See *extraordinary dividend* under DIVIDEND.

extradotal property. See PROPERTY.

extra-elements test. *Intellectual property.* A judicial test for determining whether a state-law claim is preempted by federal intellectual-property statutes under the *Sears–Compco* doctrine, the criterion being that if the claim requires proof of an extra element that makes the action qualitatively different from an infringement action based on federal law, the state action is not preempted.

extrahazardous, *adj.* (1831) Especially or unusually dangerous. • This term is often applied to exceptionally dangerous railroad crossings. — Also termed *ultrahazardous.*

extrahazardous activity. See ABNORMALLY DANGEROUS ACTIVITY.

extrajudicial, *adj.* (17c) Outside court; outside the functioning of the court system <extrajudicial confessions>. — Also termed *out-of-court.*

extrajudicial admission. See ADMISSION (1).

extrajudicial confession. See CONFESSION.

extrajudicial enforcement. See SELF-HELP.

extrajudicial evidence. See EVIDENCE.

extrajudicial oath. See OATH.

extrajudicial opinion. See OPINION (1).

extrajudicial remedy. See REMEDY.

extrajudicial statement. (1838) Any utterance made outside of court. • It is usu. treated as hearsay under the rules of evidence.

extralateral right. See APEX RULE.

extralegal, *adj.* (17c) Beyond the province of law.

extramural powers (ek-strə-**myuur**-əl). Powers exercised by a municipality outside its corporate limits.

extranational, *adj.* Beyond the territorial and governing limits of a country.

extraneous (ek-**stray**-nee-əs), *adj.* See EXTRINSIC.

extraneous evidence. See *extrinsic evidence* (1) under EVIDENCE.

extraneous offense. See OFFENSE (1).

extraneous question. (1808) A question that is beyond or beside the point to be decided.

extraordinary average. See AVERAGE.

extraordinary care. See *great care* under CARE.

extraordinary circumstances. See CIRCUMSTANCE.

extraordinary danger. See *extraordinary hazard* under HAZARD (1).

extraordinary diligence. See DILIGENCE.

extraordinary dividend. See DIVIDEND.

extraordinary expense. See EXPENSE.

extraordinary flood. A flood whose occurrence is not predictable and whose magnitude and destructiveness could not have been anticipated or provided against by the exercise of ordinary foresight; a flood so unusual that a person of ordinary prudence and experience could not have foreseen it. See ACT OF GOD.

extraordinary gain. See GAIN (3).

extraordinary grand jury. See *special grand jury* under GRAND JURY.

extraordinary hazard. See HAZARD (1).

extraordinary item. See *extraordinary expense* under EXPENSE.

extraordinary loss. See LOSS.

extraordinary majority. See *supermajority* under MAJORITY.

extraordinary relief. See RELIEF.

extraordinary remedy. See REMEDY.

extraordinary rendition. See RENDITION.

extraordinary repair. (1828) As used in a lease, a repair that is made necessary by some unusual or unforeseen occurrence that does not destroy the building but merely renders it less suited to its intended use; a repair that is beyond the usual, customary, or regular kind.

extraordinary risk. See *extraordinary hazard* under HAZARD (1).

extraordinary session. See *special session* under SESSION (1).

extraordinary writ. See WRIT.

extraparochial (ek-strə-pə-**roh**-kee-əl), *adj.* Out of a parish; not within the bounds or limits of any parish.

extrapolate (ek-**strap**-ə-layt), *vb.* (19c) **1.** To estimate an unknown value or quantity on the basis of the known range, esp. by statistical methods. **2.** To deduce an unknown legal principle from a known case. **3.** To speculate about possible results, based on known facts. — **extrapolative** (-lay-tiv *or* -lə-tiv), **extrapolatory** (-lə-tor-ee), *adj.* — **extrapolator** (-lay-tər), *n.*

extrapolation (ek-strap-ə-**lay**-shən), *n.* (19c) **1.** The process of estimating an unknown value or quantity on the basis of the known range of variables. **2.** The process by which a court deduces a legal principle from another case. **3.** The process of speculating about possible results, based on known facts.

extras. *Construction law.* Contractual amendments in the nature of additions that were not originally part of the contract, requested by an owner of a building under construction. Cf. CHANGE ORDER (1).

extra session. See *special session* under SESSION (1).

extraterritorial, *adj.* (19c) Beyond the geographic limits of a particular jurisdiction. — Also termed *exterritorial.*

extraterritoriality. (19c) The freedom of diplomats, foreign ministers, and royalty from the jurisdiction of the country in which they temporarily reside. — Also termed *exterritoriality.* See *diplomatic immunity* under IMMUNITY (1).

extraterritorial jurisdiction. See JURISDICTION.

extraterritorial recognition of rights. See *private international law* under INTERNATIONAL LAW.

extra vires (eks-trə **vI**-reez *or* **veer**-eez). See ULTRA VIRES.

extra work. See WORK (1).

extreme cruelty. See CRUELTY.

extreme force. See *deadly force* under FORCE.

extrinsic, *adj.* (17c) From outside sources; of or relating to outside matters. — Also termed *extraneous.*

extrinsic ambiguity. See *latent ambiguity* under AMBIGUITY.

extrinsic evidence. See EVIDENCE.

extrinsic fraud. See FRAUD.

extrinsic test. *Copyright.* A test for determining whether two ideas or works are substantially similar by listing and analyzing like and unlike elements. ● The test may be applied and decided by the trier of law rather than the trier of fact. Cf. INTRINSIC TEST.

EXW. *abbr.* EX WORKS.

ex warrants, *adv.* Without warrants. ● Shares are traded ex warrants when they no longer carry the right to receive declared warrants that have been distributed to holders. — Abbr. X; XW.

ex works. From the factory. ● This trade term defines the obligations of a buyer and a seller of goods with respect to delivery, payment, and risk of loss. The seller's delivery is complete (and the risk of loss passes to the buyer) when the goods are made available to the buyer at a location of the seller's choice without requiring a collecting vehicle to be loaded, as at the seller's showroom, factory, or warehouse. — Abbr. EXW.

ex-works price. See PRICE.

eye for an eye. See LEX TALIONIS.

eye of the law. (16c) The law as a personified thinker; legal contemplation <dead people are no longer persons in the eye of the law>.

eyewitness. (16c) One who personally observes an event. Cf. EARWITNESS.

eyewitness identification. (1939) A naming or description by which one who has seen an event testifies from memory about the person or persons involved.

eyre (air). [Old French *eire* "journey, march"] (12c) *Hist.* A system of royal courts sent out into the counties by the Crown to investigate allegations of wrongdoing, to try cases, and to raise revenue for the Crown through the levy of fines. ● The eyre system was abolished in the 13th century. See JUSTICE IN EYRE.

F

F. 1. *abbr.* The first series of the *Federal Reporter*, which includes federal decisions (trial and appellate) from 1880 to 1924. **2.** *Hist.* A letter branded on a felon who claimed benefit of clergy so that the felon could claim the benefit only once. ● Additionally, those convicted for an affray (fray) or falsity were so branded.

F.2d. *abbr.* The second series of the *Federal Reporter*, which includes federal appellate decisions from 1924 to 1993.

F.3d. *abbr.* The third series of the *Federal Reporter*, which includes federal appellate decisions from 1993.

FAA. *abbr.* **1.** FEDERAL AVIATION ADMINISTRATION. **2.** FEDERAL ARBITRATION ACT. **3.** FREE OF ALL AVERAGE.

fabricate, *vb.* (15c) To invent, forge, or devise falsely. ● To fabricate a story is to create a plausible version of events that is advantageous to the person relating those events. The term is softer than *lie.* See LIE (1).

fabricated evidence. See EVIDENCE.

fabricated fact. See *fabricated evidence* under EVIDENCE.

fabric land. See LAND.

FAC. *abbr.* Failure to answer a (traffic) citation. ● In some jurisdictions, if someone fails to respond after receiving a ticket, the court notifies the relevant administrative agency, which records this information and suspends the defendant's driver's license until the FAC is vacated and any fines or fees are paid.

FACE. *abbr.* FREEDOM OF ACCESS TO CLINIC ENTRANCES ACT.

face, *n.* (13c) **1.** The surface of anything, esp. the front, upper, or outer part <the face of a clock>. **2.** By extension, the apparent or explicit part of a writing or record <the fraud must appear on the face of the record>. **3.** The inscribed side of a document, instrument, or judgment <although the contract appeared valid on its face, the buyer did not have the legal capacity to enter into it>.

face amount. 1. PAR VALUE. **2.** *Insurance.* The amount payable under an insurance policy. — Also termed *face value; face amount insured by the policy; face of policy.*

face-amount certificate. See STOCK CERTIFICATE (1).

face-amount certificate company. See COMPANY.

face-amount certificate of the installment type. See *face-amount certificate* (1) under STOCK CERTIFICATE (1).

face amount insured by the policy. See FACE AMOUNT.

face of policy. See FACE AMOUNT.

face rate. See *nominal rate* under INTEREST RATE.

face value. 1. FACE AMOUNT. **2.** PAR VALUE.

facial, *adj.* (19c) Apparent; of or relating to the face of things; prima facie <a facial challenge to the statute>.

facial attack. (1966) A challenge to the sufficiency of a complaint, such as a motion to dismiss in federal practice.

facial challenge. See CHALLENGE (1).

facially sufficient, *adj.* (1972) (Of a document) appearing valid on its face. ● A search-warrant affidavit's facial sufficiency will not protect it from attack if the affidavit is based on false testimony by the officer making the affidavit. See FRANKS HEARING.

facially void. See VOID.

facias (**fay**-shee-əs). [Law Latin] That you cause. ● *Facias* is used in writs as an emphatic word. See FIERI FACIAS; LEVARI FACIAS; SCIRE FACIAS. It also appears in the phrase *ut facias* ("so that you do").

facies (**fay**-shee-eez). (17c) [Latin] The outward appearance or surface of a thing.

facilitate, *vb.* (17c) *Criminal law.* To make the commission of a crime easier. ● Property (such as a vehicle or home) that facilitates the commission of certain offenses may be forfeited. — **facilitator,** *n.*

facilitated negotiation. See MEDIATION.

facilitation, *n.* (17c) **1.** The act or an instance of aiding or helping; esp., in criminal law, the act of making it easier for another person to commit a crime. **2.** CONCILIATION.

facility-of-payment clause. 1. *Insurance.* An insurance-policy provision allowing the appointment of a person to receive payment from the insurer on the beneficiary's behalf. **2.** *Trusts.* A trust provision that allows anyone who owes money to an incapacitated trust beneficiary to discharge the debt by paying the money owed to the custodial trustee.

facsimile (fak-**sim**-ə-lee). (17c) **1.** An exact copy. **2.** FAX.

facsimile signature. See SIGNATURE.

facsimile transmission. 1. See FAX (1). **2.** See FAX (3).

fact. (15c) **1.** Something that actually exists; an aspect of reality <it is a fact that all people are mortal>. • Facts include not just tangible things, actual occurrences, and relationships, but also states of mind such as intentions and opinions. **2.** An actual or alleged event or circumstance, as distinguished from its legal effect, consequence, or interpretation <the jury made a finding of fact>. **3.** An evil deed; a crime <an accessory after the fact>.

ablative fact. See *divestitive fact.*

adjudicative fact (ə-**joo**-di-kay-tiv *or* -kə-tiv). (1959) A controlling or operative fact, rather than a background fact; a fact that concerns the parties to a judicial or administrative proceeding and that helps the court or agency determine how the law applies to those parties. • For example, adjudicative facts include those that the jury weighs. Cf. *legislative fact.*

alienative fact (**ay**-lee-ə-nay-tiv *or* **ay**-lee-ə-nə-tiv). A fact that divests a person of a right by transferring it to another.

ancient fact. A fact about a person, thing, or event that existed or occurred a very long time ago, and about which no living person has firsthand knowledge. — Also termed *fact in pais.*

collateral fact. A fact not directly connected to the issue in dispute, esp. because it involves a different transaction from the one at issue.

collative fact. See *investitive fact.*

denotative fact (**dee**-noh-tay-tiv *or* di-**noh**-tə-tiv). A fact relevant to the use of a nonlegal term in a legal rule.

destitutive fact. See *divestitive fact.*

dispositive fact (dis-**poz**-ə-tiv). (1946) **1.** A fact that confers rights or causes the loss of rights. • A dispositive fact may be either an investitive or a divestitive fact. — Also termed *vestitive fact* (**ves**-tə-tiv). **2.** A fact that is decisive of a legal matter; evidence that definitively resolves a legal issue or controversy. See DISPOSITION.

divestitive fact (di-**ves**-tə-tiv *or* dī-). (1973) A fact that causes the loss of rights; an act or event modifying or extinguishing a legal relation. — Also termed *extinctive fact*; *destitutive fact*; *ablative fact.*

elemental fact. See *ultimate fact.*

evaluative fact. (1986) A fact used to assess an action as being reasonable or negligent.

evidentiary fact (ev-i-**den**-shə-ree) (1855) **1.** A fact that is necessary for or leads to the determination of an ultimate fact. — Also termed *predicate fact.* **2.** A fact that furnishes evidence of

the existence of some other fact. — Also termed *evidential fact.* **3.** See *fact in evidence.*

exonerative fact (eg-**zon**-ər-ə-tiv *or* -ay-tiv). (1980) A divestitive fact that extinguishes a duty.

extinctive fact. See *divestitive fact.*

fabricated fact. See *fabricated evidence* under EVIDENCE.

fact in evidence. (18c) A fact that a tribunal considers in reaching a conclusion; a fact that has been admitted into evidence in a trial or hearing. — Also written *fact-in-evidence.* — Also termed *evidentiary fact.*

fact in issue. (*usu. pl.*) (17c) **1.** *Hist.* A fact that one party alleges and that the other controverts. **2.** A fact to be determined by a fact-finder; PROBANDUM. — Also written *fact-in-issue.* — Also termed *principal fact.*

fact in pais. See *ancient fact.*

fact material to risk. *Insurance.* A fact that may increase the risk and that, if disclosed, might induce the insurer either to decline to insure or to require a higher premium.

foundational fact. See *predicate fact.*

immaterial fact. A fact that is not relevant to a matter in issue.

impositive fact. An investitive fact that imposes duties.

inferential fact. (1858) A fact established by conclusions drawn from other evidence rather than from direct testimony or evidence; a fact derived logically from other facts.

investitive fact (in-**ves**-tə-tiv). (1939) A fact that confers rights. — Also termed *collative fact* (kə-**lay**-tiv).

judicial fact. (1862) See *judicially noticed fact.*

judicially noticed fact. A fact that is not established by admissible evidence but may be accepted by the court because the fact is generally known within the trial court's territorial jurisdiction, or because its validity can be determined from sources whose accuracy cannot be reasonably questioned. See Fed. R. Evid. 201(b). — Also termed *judicial fact.* See JUDICIAL NOTICE.

jurisdictional fact. (*usu. pl.*) (1837) A fact that must exist for a court to properly exercise its jurisdiction over a case, party, or thing. See JURISDICTIONAL-FACT DOCTRINE.

legal fact. (18c) A fact that triggers a particular legal consequence.

legislative fact. (1828) A fact that explains a particular law's rationality and that helps a court or agency determine the law's content and application. • Legislative facts are not ordinarily specific to the parties in a proceeding. Cf. *adjudicative fact.*

material fact. (1848) A fact that is significant or essential to the issue or matter at hand.

minor fact. A subordinate fact or circumstance.

operative fact. (1857) **1.** A fact that affects an existing legal relation, esp. a legal claim. • When applying the hearsay rule, this term distinguishes between out-of-court statements that are operative facts (e.g., a party's saying "I agree to reimburse you" in a case for breach of oral contract), and hearsay, out-of-court statements that only relate to operative facts (e.g., "Joel told me Mike said he would reimburse me"). **2.** A fact that constitutes the transaction or event on which a claim or defense is based.

physical fact. (1857) A fact having a physical existence, such as a fingerprint left at a crime scene.

predicate fact (**pred**-ə-kit). (1899) **1.** A fact from which a presumption or inference arises. **2.** A fact necessary to the operation of an evidentiary rule. • For example, there must actually be a conspiracy for the co-conspirator exception to the hearsay rule to apply. — Also termed *foundational fact*; *evidentiary fact.*

presumed fact. A fact whose existence can be justifiably inferred from facts established by evidence.

primary fact. (18c) A fact that can be established by direct testimony and from which inferences are made leading to ultimate facts. See *ultimate fact.*

principal fact. **1.** See *fact in issue.* **2.** See *ultimate fact.*

private fact. (16c) A fact that has not been made public. • Whether a fact is private often arises in invasion-of-privacy claims. Cf. *public fact.*

probative fact (**proh**-bə-tiv). (1858) A fact in evidence used to prove an ultimate fact, such as skid marks used to show speed as a predicate to a finding of negligence.

psychological fact. A fact that is related to mental state, such as motive or knowledge.

public fact. (1955) For the purpose of an invasion-of-privacy claim, a fact that is in a public record or in the public domain. Cf. *private fact.*

relative fact. A fact incidental to another fact; a minor fact.

simulated fact. (1943) A fabricated fact intended to mislead; a lie.

translative fact (trans- or tranz-**lay**-tiv). A fact by means of which a right is transferred from one person to another; a fact that fulfills the double function of terminating one person's right to an object and of originating another's right to it.

transvestitive fact. A fact that is simultaneously investitive and divestitive.

ultimate fact. (18c) A fact essential to the claim or the defense. — Also termed *elemental fact*; *principal fact.*

undisputed fact. (18c) An uncontested or admitted fact.

vestitive fact. See *dispositive fact* (1).

fact-finder. (1926) One or more persons — such as jurors in a trial or administrative-law judges in a hearing — who hear testimony and review evidence to rule on a factual issue. — Also termed *finder of fact*; *fact-trier* or *trier of fact* (in a judicial proceeding); *fact-finding board* (for a group or committee). See FINDING OF FACT.

fact-finding. (1909) **1.** The process of taking evidence to determine the truth about a disputed point of fact. **2.** *Int'l law.* The gathering of information for purposes of international relations, including the peaceful settlement of disputes and the supervision of international agreements. • Examples of fact-finding include legislative tours to acquire information needed for making decisions at an international level. — Also termed *inquiry.* **3.** A method of alternative dispute resolution in which an impartial third party determines and studies the facts and positions of disputing parties that have reached an impasse, with a view toward clarifying the issues and helping the parties work through their dispute.

fact-finding board. See FACT-FINDER.

fact interrogatory. See *identification interrogatory* under INTERROGATORY.

faction. (16c) A number of citizens, whether a majority or a minority, who are united and motivated by a common impulse or interest that is adverse to the rights of others or to the permanent or aggregate interests of the community. • This definition is adapted from *The Federalist*, No. 10.

fact issue. See *issue of fact* under ISSUE (1).

facto (**fak**-toh), *adj.* In or by the fact. See DE FACTO; IPSO FACTO.

factor, *n.* (15c) **1.** An agent or cause that contributes to a particular result <punishment was a factor in the court's decision>. **2.** An agent who is employed to sell property for the principal and who possesses or controls the property; a person who receives and sells goods for a commission <a factor was employed to sell goods for the company>. • A factor differs from a broker because the factor possesses or controls the property. — Also termed *commission merchant*; *del credere bailiff.* Cf. BROKER. **3.** One who buys accounts receivable at a discount <the company sold its receivables to a factor at only 5% of their stated value>. **4.** A garnishee <the factor held $400 of the debtor's property when the writ of garnishment was served>.

5. A person in charge of managing property, esp. real property.

factorage. (17c) **1.** The compensation paid to a factor for his or her services. **2.** The business of a factor.

factoring, *n.* The buying of accounts receivable at a discount. • The price is discounted because the factor (who buys them) assumes the risk of delay in collection and loss on the accounts receivable.

factorize (**fak**-tə-rɪz), *vb.* (19c) **1.** GARNISH (2). **2.** GARNISH (3). — **factorization,** *n.*

factorizing process. (1837) A procedure or legal process by which a third party, rather than the creditor, attaches a debtor's property; GARNISHMENT. — Also termed *trustee process*; *process by foreign attachment.*

factor's act. A statute protecting one who buys goods from a factor or agent by creating the presumption that the agent was acting on the owner's behalf and with the owner's approval.

factor's lien. See LIEN.

factory act. A statute that regulates workers' hours, health, and safety. See FAIR LABOR STANDARDS ACT.

fact pleading. See *code pleading* under PLEADING (2).

fact question. See QUESTION OF FACT.

fact-trier. See FACT-FINDER.

factual cause. See *but-for cause* under CAUSE (1).

factual impossibility. See IMPOSSIBILITY.

factual presumption. See *presumption of fact* under PRESUMPTION.

factum (**fak**-təm), *n.* [Latin] (18c) **1.** A fact, such as a person's physical presence in a new domicile. **2.** An act or deed, such as the due execution of a will. • Over time, *factum* in this sense came to mean "charter" — that is, the act or deed of conveying land, reduced to written form. See *fraud in the factum* under FRAUD.

factum juridicum (**fak**-təm juu-**rid**-i-kəm). [Latin] A juridical fact.

factum probandum (**fak**-təm prə-**ban**-dəm). [Latin] A fact to be proved.

factum probans (**fak**-təm **proh**-banz). [Latin] A probative or evidentiary fact; a subsidiary fact tending to prove a principal fact in issue.

3. A statement of facts. **4.** BRIEF (1). Pl. **facta.**

factum of a will. The formal ceremony of making a will; a will's execution by the testator and attestation by the witnesses.

fact work product. See WORK PRODUCT.

facultative certificate (**fak**-əl-tay-tiv). *Insurance.* A contract of reinsurance separately negotiated

to cover risks under a single insurance policy. • Facultative reinsurance allows the reinsurer the "faculty" of assessing and possibly rejecting a particular risk (esp. if underwriting information is inadequate).

facultative reinsurance. See REINSURANCE.

faculties. (16c) *Hist. Eccles. law.* **1.** An authorization granted to a person to do what otherwise would not be allowed. **2.** The extent of a husband's estate; esp., the ability to pay alimony. See ALLEGATION OF FACULTIES.

Faculties, Court of. See COURT OF FACULTIES.

Faculties, Master of the. See MASTER OF THE FACULTIES.

faggot. *Hist.* **1.** A piece of firewood used to burn a heretic alive. **2.** An embroidered figure of a faggot, required to be worn by heretics who had recanted.

fail, *n.* A transaction between securities brokers in which delivery and payment do not occur at the prescribed time, usu. on the settlement date. — Also termed *fail contract.*

fail to deliver. The nondelivery of securities from a selling broker to a buying broker by the settlement date.

fail to receive. The failure of a buying broker to receive delivery of securities from the selling broker by the settlement date.

fail, *vb.* (13c) **1.** To be deficient or unsuccessful; to fall short <they failed to settle the dispute>. **2.** To become insolvent or bankrupt <two banks failed last week>. **3.** To lapse <the bequest failed as a result of ademption>.

fail contract. See FAIL.

failed devise. See *lapsed devise* under DEVISE.

failed gift. 1. See *lapsed devise* under DEVISE. **2.** See *lapsed legacy* under LEGACY.

failed legacy. See *lapsed legacy* under LEGACY.

failing circumstances. See INSOLVENCY.

failing-company doctrine. *Antitrust.* The rule that allows an otherwise proscribed merger or acquisition between competitors when one is bankrupt or near failure. 15 USCA §§ 12–27. — Also termed *failing-firm defense.*

fail position. A situation existing when, after all transactions in a security have been netted out, a broker owes another broker more securities than it has coming in from other firms.

failure. (17c) **1.** Deficiency; lack; want. **2.** An omission of an expected action, occurrence, or performance. See LAPSE (2).

failure of a condition. The nonoccurrence of an event that has been made a condition of the contract. • The usual result is that one or both of the parties do not have to perform because of the failure of the condition.

failure of consideration. See FAILURE OF CONSIDERATION.

failure of good behavior. A civil servant's act that is ground for removal.

failure of issue. See FAILURE OF ISSUE.

failure of justice. See MISCARRIAGE OF JUSTICE.

failure of proof. A party's not having produced evidence establishing a fact essential to a claim or defense.

failure of title. A seller's inability to establish a good claim to the property contracted for sale. Cf. *clear title* under TITLE (2).

failure of trust. The invalidity of a trust because the instrument creating it has a defect or because of its illegality or other legal impediment.

failure of will. The invalidity of a will that was not executed with necessary statutory formalities.

failure otherwise than on the merits. The defeat of a plaintiff's claim by a procedural device without a decision on the existence of the claim's elements.

failure to bargain collectively. An employer's refusal to discuss labor issues with a union.

failure to claim. *Patents.* A finding by the U.S. Patent and Trademark Office or by a court that a patent applicant or patentee has forfeited the right to broader protection by not seeking protection for some disclosed subject matter. • Any art outside the explicit claims, including foreseeable alteration of the claimed structure, is considered dedicated to the public domain.

failure to make delivery. Nondelivery or misdelivery.

failure to meet obligations. **1.** See BANKRUPTCY (4). **2.** See INSOLVENCY.

failure to perform. A party's not meeting its obligations under a contract. See CONTRACT (4).

failure to state a cause of action. A plaintiff's not having alleged facts in the complaint sufficient to maintain a claim. • This failure warrants dismissal of the complaint.

failure to testify. A party's — esp. a criminal defendant's — decision not to testify. • Under the Fifth Amendment, the prosecutor and the judge cannot comment to the jury on a criminal defendant's failure to testify. But comments on the failure are usu. permissible in a civil case.

failure of consideration. (1803) A seriously deficient contractual performance that causes a contract's basis or inducement to cease to exist or to become worthless. • Scholars disapprove of this term as misleading, since *failure of performance* is more accurate. Unlike *consideration*, the phrase

failure of consideration relates not to the formation of a contract but to its performance. See CONSIDERATION (1). Cf. WANT OF CONSIDERATION.

partial failure of consideration. (1808) A party's incomplete performance of a contract with multiple, severable performances, so that if some of the performances are not accomplished, the appropriate part of the agreement can be apportioned to whatever has been completed.

total failure of consideration. (1809) A situation in which the contract is indivisible so that a complete lack of consideration voids the contract.

failure of good behavior. See FAILURE.

failure of issue. (17c) *Archaic.* The fact of a person's dying when the person has no surviving children or other descendants who are eligible to inherit the person's estate. — Also termed *dying without issue*; *definite failure of issue*; *default of issue*. See ISSUE (3).

indefinite failure of issue. (18c) A failure of issue whenever it happens, without any certain period within which it must happen.

failure of justice. See MISCARRIAGE OF JUSTICE.

failure of proof. See FAILURE.

failure-of-proof defense. (1982) The defense that a party's proof does not establish a fact essential to a claim or defense.

failure of title. See FAILURE.

failure of trust. See FAILURE.

failure of will. See FAILURE.

failure otherwise than on the merits. See FAILURE.

failure to bargain collectively. See FAILURE.

failure to claim. See FAILURE.

failure-to-disclose-best-mode rejection. See REJECTION.

failure to make delivery. See FAILURE.

failure to meet obligations. **1.** See BANKRUPTCY (4). **2.** See INSOLVENCY.

failure to perform. See FAILURE.

failure-to-perform exclusion. See EXCLUSION (3).

failure to protect. *Family law.* The refusal or inability of a parent or guardian to prevent abuse of a child under his or her care.

failure to state a cause of action. See FAILURE.

failure-to-supervise statute. See PARENTAL-LIABILITY STATUTE.

failure to testify. See FAILURE.

failure to thrive. (1967) *Family law.* **1.** A medical and psychological condition in which a child's height, weight, and motor development fall significantly below average growth rates. • Failure to thrive is sometimes asserted as a ground for alleging abuse or neglect by a parent or caregiver. **2.** A condition, occurring during the first three years of a child's life, in which the child suffers marked retardation or ceases to grow. — Abbr. FTT.

faint action. See FEIGNED ACTION.

faint pleader. (17c) A false, fraudulent, or collusive manner of pleading.

fair, *adj.* (bef. 12c) **1.** Impartial; just; equitable; disinterested <everyone thought that Judge Jones was fair>. **2.** Free of bias or prejudice <in jury selection, the lawyers tried to select a fair and impartial jury>.

fair, *n.* (13c) *Hist.* A privileged market for the buying and selling of goods. • A fair was an incorporeal hereditament granted to a town by royal patent or franchise or established by prescription. The franchise to hold a fair conferred important privileges, and a fair, as a legally recognized institution, possessed distinctive legal characteristics, most of which are now obsolete. Cf. *market overt* under MARKET.

fair-and-equitable requirement. (17c) *Bankruptcy.* A Bankruptcy Code standard requiring a forced, nonconsensual Chapter 11 plan (a "cramdown" plan) to provide adequately for each class of interests that has not accepted the plan. • In determining whether a cramdown plan is fair and equitable and thus can be confirmed, a bankruptcy court must apply the Code's detailed statutory criteria, consider the plan as a whole, and weigh all the circumstances surrounding the treatment of each impaired class of interests. In addition to the fair-and-equitable requirement, the Chapter 11 cramdown plan must (1) be accepted by at least one impaired class of claims, and (2) not discriminate unfairly among impaired classes that have not accepted the plan. 11 USCA § 1129(b). See CRAMDOWN.

fair and impartial jury. See *impartial jury* under JURY.

fair and impartial trial. See FAIR TRIAL.

fair and proper legal assessment. See EQUALIZATION (2).

fair and reasonable value. See *fair market value* under VALUE (2).

fair and valuable consideration. See *fair consideration* (1) under CONSIDERATION (1).

fair averaging. The process of assessing taxes by using the average of the amount and price of goods acquired over a 12-month period rather than the amount and price at a particular time of the year.

fair cash market value. See *fair market value* under VALUE (2).

fair cash value. See *fair market value* under VALUE (2).

fair comment. (18c) A statement based on the writer's or speaker's honest opinion about a matter of public concern. • Fair comment is a defense to libel or slander.

fair competition. See COMPETITION.

fair consideration. See CONSIDERATION (1).

Fair Credit Billing Act. A federal law that facilitates the correction of billing errors by credit-card companies and makes those companies more responsible for the quality of goods purchased by cardholders. 15 USCA §§ 1666–1666j.

fair-credit-reporting act. (1971) A federal or state law that regulates disclosure and use of consumer-credit information and ensures the right of consumers to have access to and to correct their credit reports. • The federal Fair Credit Reporting Act was enacted in 1970. 15 USCA §§ 1681–1681u. — Abbr. FCRA.

fair-cross-section requirement. (1975) *Constitutional law.* The principle that a person's right to an impartial jury, guaranteed by the Sixth Amendment, includes a requirement that the pool of potential jurors fairly represent the composition of the jurisdiction's population. • The pool of potential jurors need not precisely match the composition of the jurisdiction. But the representation of each group must be fair — no group should be systematically excluded or underrepresented. A minimal disparity in a particular group's representation, such as an absolute disparity of 10%, will not ordinarily violate this principle unless some aggravating factor exists. See DUREN TEST; ABSOLUTE DISPARITY; COMPARATIVE DISPARITY; STATISTICAL-DECISION THEORY.

fair dealing, *n.* (17c) **1.** The conduct of business with full disclosure, usu. by a corporate officer with the corporation. **2.** A fiduciary's transacting of business so that, although the fiduciary might derive a personal benefit, all interested persons are fully apprised of that potential and of all other material information about the transaction. Cf. SELF-DEALING. **3.** *Canadian law.* FAIR USE.

Fair Debt Collection Practices Act. A federal statute that regulates debt-collection practices, and defines the rights of consumers who are contacted by debt collectors. 15 USCA §§ 1692–1692p. — Abbr. FDCPA.

fair hearing. See HEARING.

Fair Labor Standards Act. A federal law, enacted in 1938, that regulates minimum wages, overtime pay, and the employment of minors. 29 USCA §§ 201–219. — Abbr. FLSA.

fairly-debatable rule. 1. *Insurance.* In some states, a test that requires an insurer to have a plausible basis for denying a claim to avoid bad-faith liability. **2.** *Zoning.* A doctrine that bars a court from interfering with a zoning decision that is supported by substantial evidence, although it is one on which reasonable minds can differ. • A court will not interfere with a decision supported by substantial evidence.

fair market price. See *fair market value* under VALUE (2).

fair market value. See VALUE (2).

fairness doctrine. (1965) *Hist.* A federal law, based on an FCC rule, requiring the broadcast media to furnish a reasonable opportunity for the discussion of conflicting views on issues of public importance. • The FCC abandoned the fairness doctrine in 1987. — Also termed *equal-time doctrine.* Cf. EQUAL TIME ACT.

fair notice. See NOTICE.

fair on its face. (18c) (Of a document) having the appearance of being regular or legal and not capable of being shown to be defective without extraneous evidence.

fair persuasion. See PERSUASION.

fair play. Equity, candor, and fidelity in dealings with another.

fair play and substantial justice. (1945) The fairness requirement that a court must meet in its assertion of personal jurisdiction over a nonresident defendant to comport with due process. *International Shoe Co. v. Washington,* 326 U.S. 310, 66 S.Ct. 154 (1945). See MINIMUM CONTACTS.

fair preponderance of the evidence. See PREPONDERANCE OF THE EVIDENCE.

fair presentation. 1. *Commercial law.* A materially accurate disclosure of a company's financial condition, achieved by selecting and using appropriate accounting policies, reasonably reflecting transactions that underlie the financial data, and making any additional necessary disclosures. **2.** *Criminal law.* The requirement that an applicant for a writ of habeas corpus in a state's custody must show (1) he or she has exhausted all available remedies in the state courts, (2) the state has offered no corrective process, or (3) circumstances exist that render a state's corrective process insufficient to protect the applicant's rights.

fair rate of return. See RATE OF RETURN.

fair-report privilege. (1980) A defense to liability for publishing defamatory matter from a report of an official or judicial proceeding, when the report is a full, fair, and accurate account of the proceeding.

fair representation. *Labor law.* Union representation that adequately covers all union members in collective bargaining and in the lodging of grievances.

fair return on investment. See RETURN.

fair sale. See SALE.

fair-share membership. See FINANCIAL-CORE MEMBERSHIP.

fair trade, *n.* Commerce conducted under a fair-trade agreement.

fair-trade agreement. (1937) A commercial agreement that a seller will sell all of a producer's goods at or above a specified minimum price. • Fair-trade agreements were valid until 1975, when the Consumer Goods Pricing Act made them illegal. 15 USCA §§ 1, 45.

fair-trade law. A state statute that protects and enforces fair-trade agreements. • At one time, many states had fair-trade laws. But when applied to interstate commerce, the laws may violate the Sherman Antitrust Act, so most states have repealed them.

fair trial. (17c) A trial by an impartial and disinterested tribunal in accordance with regular procedures; esp., a criminal trial in which the defendant's constitutional and legal rights are respected. — Also termed *fair and impartial trial.*

fair use. (1869) *Copyright.* A reasonable and limited use of a copyrighted work without the author's permission, such as quoting from a book in a book review or using parts of it in a parody. • Fair use is a defense to an infringement claim, depending on the following statutory factors: (1) the purpose and character of the use, (2) the nature of the copyrighted work, (3) the amount of the work used, and (4) the economic impact of the use. 17 USCA § 107. — Also termed (in Canadian law) *fair dealing.*

fair value. See *fair market value* under VALUE (2).

fair-value accounting method. See ACCOUNTING METHOD.

fair-value law. A statute allowing a credit against a deficiency for the amount that the fair market value of land exceeds the price at foreclosure. — Also termed *fair-value legislation.*

fair warning. (1931) *Criminal law.* The requirement that a criminal statute define an offense with enough precision so that a reasonable person can know what conduct is prohibited and so that a reasonably skilled lawyer can predict what conduct falls within the statute's scope. — Also termed *fair notice.*

fair wear and tear. See WEAR AND TEAR.

faith and trust. See FLIM FLAM.

Faithfully Executed Clause. (1967) The clause of the U.S. Constitution providing that the President must take care that the laws are carried out faithfully. U.S. Const. art. II, § 3.

faith-healing exemption. *Family law.* In a child-abuse or child-neglect statute, a provision that a parent who provides a child with faith healing (in place of standard medical treatment) will not, for that reason alone, be charged with abuse or neglect. ● Nearly all states have enacted some form of faith-healing exemption. But the statutes differ greatly. For example, they differ on whether the exemption is available as a defense to manslaughter or murder charges brought against a parent whose child dies as a result of the parent's having refused to consent to medical treatment. — Also termed *religious-exemption statute*; *spiritual-treatment exemption*. Cf. *medical neglect* under NEGLECT.

fake, *n.* (19c) Something that is not what it purports to be. See FORGERY (2); IMPOSTOR.

fake, *vb.* (19c) To make or construct falsely. See COUNTERFEIT.

Falcidian law (fal-**sid**-ee-ən). (17c) *Roman law.* A law prescribing that one could give no more than three-fourths of one's property in legacies and that the heirs should receive at least one-fourth (the Falcidian portion). ● If the testator violated this law, the heir had the right to deduct proportionally from each legatee as necessary. The law, proposed by the Roman tribune Falcidius, was enacted in 40 B.C. — Also termed *lex Falcidia.* See LEGITIME.

Falcidian portion. *Roman law.* The one-fourth part of an estate that one or more instituted heirs are entitled to retain. La. Civ. Code art. 1494. — Also termed *quarta Falcidiana.* See *forced heir* under HEIR; LEGITIME.

Falconer **error.** A trial court's failure to instruct the jury that a guilty finding on a manslaughter charge requires acquittal on a murder charge. *Falconer v. Lane,* 905 F.2d 1129 (7th Cir. 1990).

fallacy. Any unsound, and usu. deceptive, argument or inference. ● Both "formal" and "material" fallacies occur in a variety of recognized categories, knowledge of which is fundamental in the analysis of the validity of legal reasoning employed in any legal argument, esp. in judicial opinions. The presence of a fallacy in a legal argument is a defect — often fatal and usu. deceptive — in the legal reasoning.

formal fallacy. A fallacy involving flaws in the form of the argument, such as a violation of the formal rules of syllogistic reasoning.

material fallacy. A fallacy involving flaws in the factual content of a logical argument.

fall of the hammer. An auctioneer's closing of bidding <the bureau will be sold at the fall of the hammer>. ● Traditionally, an auctioneer bangs a hammer, gavel, or other object when bidding is closed. In some circumstances, such as online auctions, a verbal announcement that bidding is closed substitutes.

falsa demonstratio (**fal**-sə *or* **fawl**-sə dem-ən-**stray**-shee-oh). *Roman law.* A false designation; an erroneous description of a person or thing in a legal instrument. ● Generally, a simple error in description, grammar, or spelling will not void an instrument or even a single provision in it (such as a bequest by will). — Also termed *false demonstration.*

false, *adj.* (12c) **1.** Untrue <a false statement>. **2.** Deceitful; lying <a false witness>. **3.** Not genuine; inauthentic <false coinage>. ● What is false can be so by intent, by accident, or by mistake.

false action. See FEIGNED ACTION.

false advertising, *n.* (1911) **1.** The tortious and sometimes criminal act of distributing an advertisement that is untrue, deceptive, or misleading; esp., under the Lanham Trademark Act, an advertising statement that tends to mislead consumers about the characteristics, quality, or geographic origin of one's own or someone else's goods, services, or commercial activity. ● Under § 43(a) of the Lanham Act, false advertising is actionable by anyone who reasonably believes that he or she has been or is likely to be damaged by the statement. An exaggerated opinion ("puffing") is an immaterial statement and therefore not actionable. **2.** At common law, a statement in a defendant's advertising about its own goods or services intended to deceive or confuse customers into buying those goods or services instead of the plaintiff's, and causing actual damage to the plaintiff, esp. the loss of sales. — Also termed (in both senses) *deceptive advertising.*

false answer. See ANSWER (1).

false arrest. See ARREST.

false-association claim. *Intellectual property.* A claim based on the wrongful use of a distinctive name, mark, trade dress, or other device to misrepresent sponsorship, origin of goods or services, or affiliation. ● The power to assert a false-association claim is not limited to trademark registrants. Any person who claims an injury caused by deceptive use of a trademark or its equivalent may have standing to bring suit. See 15 USCA § 1125(a)(1)(A).

false character. *Hist.* The crime of impersonating a servant's master or mistress. See IMPOSTOR.

false check. See *bad check* under CHECK.

false claim. An assertion or statement that is untrue; esp., overbilling.

False Claims Act. A federal statute establishing civil and criminal penalties against persons who bill the government falsely, deliver less to the government than represented, or use a fake record to decrease an obligation to the government. 18 USCA §§ 286–287; 31 USCA §§ 3729–3733. ● The Act may be enforced either by the attorney general or by a private person in a qui tam action. See QUI TAM ACTION.

false conflict of laws. See CONFLICT OF LAWS.

false demonstration. See FALSA DEMONSTRATIO.

false designation of origin. *Trademarks.* A mark, design, or similar element that creates a misleading or erroneous impression of a good or product's source.

false evidence. See *false testimony* under TESTIMONY.

falsehood. 1. See LIE. 2. See PERJURY.

false impersonation. See IMPERSONATION.

false-implication libel. See LIBEL.

false imprisonment. (14c) A restraint of a person in a bounded area without justification or consent. • False imprisonment is a common-law misdemeanor and a tort. It applies to private as well as governmental detention. Cf. *false arrest* under ARREST.

false judgment. *Hist.* A writ filed to obtain review of a judgment of a court not of record.

false light. (1962) 1. *Torts.* In an invasion-of-privacy action, a plaintiff's allegation that the defendant attributed to the plaintiff views that he or she does not hold and placed the plaintiff before the public in a highly offensive and untrue manner. • If the matter involves the public interest, the plaintiff must prove the defendant's malice. See *invasion of privacy by false light* under INVASION OF PRIVACY. 2. (*usu. pl.*) *Maritime law.* A signal displayed intentionally to lure a vessel into danger. 18 USCA § 1658(b). — Also termed *false light or signal.*

false making. See FORGERY (1).

false-memory syndrome. The supposed recovery of memories of traumatic or stressful episodes that did not actually occur, often in session with a mental-health therapist. • This term is most frequently applied to claims by adult children that repressed memories of prolonged and repeated child sexual abuse, usu. by parents, have surfaced, even though there is no independent evidence to substantiate the claims. Cf. REPRESSED-MEMORY SYNDROME.

False Memory Syndrome Foundation. An organization of parents who claim that their adult children have falsely accused them of childhood sexual abuse. • The organization was formed for the purpose of aiding persons who claim to have been wrongly accused as a result of the recovery of repressed memories. — Abbr. FMSF. Cf. VICTIMS OF CHILD ABUSE LAWS.

false misrepresentation. See MISREPRESENTATION. • This phrase is redundant because *misrepresentation* includes the idea of falsity.

false news. *Hist.* The misdemeanor of spreading false information that causes discord between the monarch and the people or between important people in the realm. 3 Edw., ch. 34.

false oath. See PERJURY.

false personation. See *false impersonation* under IMPERSONATION.

false plea. See *sham pleading* under PLEADING (1).

false pretenses. (18c) The crime of knowingly obtaining title to another's personal property by misrepresenting a fact with the intent to defraud. • Although unknown to English common law, false pretenses became a misdemeanor under a statute old enough to make it common law in the United States. Modern American statutes make it either a felony or a misdemeanor, depending on the property's value. — Also termed *obtaining property by false pretenses*; *fraudulent pretenses.* Cf. *larceny by trick* under LARCENY; EMBEZZLEMENT.

false promise. See PROMISE.

false report. (1827) *Criminal law.* The criminal offense of informing law enforcement about a crime that did not occur.

false representation. See MISREPRESENTATION.

false return. (16c) 1. A process server's or other court official's recorded misrepresentation that process was served, that some other action was taken, or that something is true. See RETURN (2). 2. A tax return on which taxable income is incorrectly reported or the tax is incorrectly computed. See TAX RETURN.

false statement. See STATEMENT.

false swearing. See PERJURY.

false testimony. See TESTIMONY.

false token. See TOKEN.

false verdict. See VERDICT.

false weight. (*usu. pl.*) A weight or measure that does not comply with governmentally prescribed standards or with the prevailing custom in the place and business in which the weight or measure is used.

falsi crimen. See *crimen falsi* under CRIMEN.

falsify, *vb.* (15c) 1. To make something false; to counterfeit or forge <the chiropractor falsified his records to help the plaintiff>. — Also termed (archaically) *false.* See COUNTERFEIT; FORGERY. 2. *Rare.* To prove something to be false or erroneous <their goal in the appeal was to falsify the jury's verdict>. — **falsification,** *n.*

falsifying a record. (18c) The crime of making false entries or otherwise tampering with a public record with the intent to deceive or injure, or to conceal wrongdoing. 18 USCA §§ 1506, 2071, 2073; Model Penal Code § 224.4.

falsity, *n.* (13c) **1.** Something (such as a statement) that is false. See LIE. **2.** The quality of being false. See FALSE.

falsus in uno **doctrine (fal-**səs [*or* **fawl-**səs] in **yoo-**noh). [fr. Latin *falsus in uno, falsus in omnibus* "false in one thing, false in all"] The principle that if the jury believes that a witness's testimony on a material issue is intentionally deceitful, the jury may disregard all of that witness's testimony.

faltering-company exception. A provision in the Worker Adjustment and Retraining Notification Act exempting an employer from giving the required 60-day notice for a plant shutdown if (1) at the time notice was due, the employer was seeking capital or resources that would have allowed the employer to avoid a shutdown, and (2) the employer reasonably believed that providing the notice would have precluded the employer from obtaining the necessary capital or other resources. 29 USCA § 2102(b)(1). See WORKER ADJUSTMENT AND RETRAINING NOTIFICATION ACT.

familiae erciscundae (fə-**mil**-ee-ee ər-sis-**kən**-dee). See *actio familiae erciscundae* under ACTIO.

family, *n.* (14c) **1.** A group of persons connected by blood, by affinity, or by law, esp. within two or three generations. **2.** A group consisting of parents and their children. **3.** A group of persons who live together and have a shared commitment to a domestic relationship. See RELATIVE. — **familial,** *adj.*

blended family. (1985) The combined families of persons with children from earlier marriages or relationships.

extended family. (1942) **1.** The immediate family together with the collateral relatives who make up a clan; GENS. **2.** The immediate family together with collateral relatives and close family friends.

immediate family. (18c) **1.** A person's parents, spouse, children, and siblings. **2.** A person's parents, spouse, children, and siblings, as well as those of the person's spouse. • Stepchildren and adopted children are usu. immediate family members. For some purposes, such as taxes, a person's immediate family may also include the spouses of children and siblings.

intact family. A family in which both parents live together with their children.

family allowance. See ALLOWANCE (1).

Family and Medical Leave Act. A 1993 federal statute providing that employees may take unpaid, job-protected leave for certain family reasons, as when a family member is sick or when a child is born. 29 USCA §§ 2601 et seq. • The statute applies to businesses with 50 or more employees. An employee may take up to 12 weeks of unpaid leave per year under the FMLA. — Abbr. FMLA. Cf. FAMILY LEAVE.

family arrangement. (1817) An informal agreement among family members, usu. to distribute property in a manner other than what the law provides for. — Also termed *family settlement.*

family-automobile doctrine. See FAMILY-PURPOSE RULE.

family-autonomy doctrine. See PARENTAL-AUTONOMY DOCTRINE.

family-car doctrine. See FAMILY-PURPOSE RULE.

family compact. See COMPACT.

family corporation. See *close corporation* under CORPORATION.

family council. See FAMILY MEETING.

family court. See COURT.

family-court judge. See JUDGE.

family disturbance. See DOMESTIC DISPUTE.

Family Division. *English law.* A section of the High Court that has jurisdiction over family matters such as divorce and custody and over uncontested probate matters.

Family Educational Rights and Privacy Act. An act that prescribes minimum standards for the maintenance and dissemination of student records by educational institutions. 20 USCA § 1232g. • It applies only to schools that receive federal funding. — Abbr. FERPA. — Also termed *Buckley Amendment.*

family-expense statute. (1901) **1.** A state law that permits a charge against the property of a spouse for family debts such as rent, food, clothing, and tuition. **2.** A section of the federal tax code providing that a person may not deduct expenses incurred for family, living, or personal purposes. IRC (26 USCA) § 262. See NECESSARIES.

family farmer. See FARMER.

family-farmer bankruptcy. See CHAPTER 12 (2).

family home. A house that was purchased during marriage and that the family has resided in, esp. before a divorce. • In some jurisdictions, the court may award the family home to the custodial parent until (1) the youngest child reaches the age of 18 or is otherwise emancipated, (2) the custodial parent moves, or (3) the custodial parent remarries. In making such an award, the court reasons that it is in the best interests of the child to remain in the family home. — Also termed *marital home; marital residence.*

family-income insurance. See INSURANCE.

family law. (1919) **1.** The body of law dealing with marriage, divorce, adoption, child custody and support, child abuse and neglect, paternity, juvenile delinquency, and other domestic-relations issues. — Also termed *domestic relations;*

domestic-relations law. **2.** (More broadly) the bodies of law dealing with wills and estates, property, constitutional rights, contracts, employment, and finance as they relate to families.

family leave. (1981) An unpaid leave of absence from work taken to have or care for a baby or to care for a sick family member. See FAMILY AND MEDICAL LEAVE ACT.

family meeting. *Hist. Civil law.* **1.** An advisory council called to aid the court in a family-law matter, such as arrangement of a guardianship for a minor or an incompetent adult. ● If a person had no relatives, the court could summon friends of the person instead. **2.** A council of relatives of a minor assembled to advise the minor in his or her affairs and to help administer the minor's property. — Also termed *family council.*

family of marks. *Trademarks.* A group of trademarks that share a recognizable characteristic so that they are recognized by consumers as identifying a single source. ● An example of a family of marks is the variety of marks beginning with *Mc-* and identifying items served at McDonald's restaurants.

family of nations. *Int'l law.* The community of countries to which international law applies. ● This term is now obsolescent. It is increasingly rejected as Eurocentric.

family partnership. See PARTNERSHIP.

family-partnership rules. (1946) Laws or regulations designed to prevent the shifting of income among partners, esp. family members, who may not be dealing at arm's length.

family-pot trust. See TRUST.

family-purpose rule. (1927) *Torts.* The principle that a vehicle's owner is liable for injuries or damage caused by a family member's negligent driving. ● Many states have abolished this rule. — Also termed *family-purpose doctrine; family-automobile doctrine; family-car doctrine.* Cf. GUEST STATUTE.

family reunification. See REUNIFICATION.

family settlement. See FAMILY ARRANGEMENT.

family shelter. See *women's shelter* under SHELTER.

family support. A combined award of child support and alimony that does not apportion the amount of each.

Family Support Act of 1988. A federal statute requiring states to develop and implement child-support guidelines. 42 USCA § 667. See CHILD-SUPPORT GUIDELINES.

family trust. See TRUST.

family violence. See *domestic violence* under VIOLENCE.

famous mark. See *famous mark* under TRADEMARK.

famous trademark. See TRADEMARK.

fanciful mark. See *fanciful trademark* under TRADEMARK.

fanciful term. See *fanciful trademark* under TRADEMARK.

fanciful trademark. See TRADEMARK.

Fannie Mae (fan-ee may). See FEDERAL NATIONAL MORTGAGE ASSOCIATION.

FAPE. *abbr.* Free appropriate public education. ● This is a right of children with disabilities to have access to free education, guaranteed by the Rehabilitation Act of 1973 and the Individuals with Disabilities Education Act. See 34 C.F.R. § 100.33; 34 C.F.R. § 300.13.

FAR. (*often pl.*) *abbr.* FEDERAL AVIATION REGULATION <the pilot violated several FARs before the crash>.

farm, *n.* (14c) **1.** Land and connected buildings used for agricultural purposes. **2.** *Hist.* Rent. ● By extension, the term came to mean the land for which the rent was paid. — Also termed and spelled *ferm; fearm; firme.*

farm, *vb.* (15c) **1.** To cultivate land; to conduct the business of farming. **2.** To lease. See FARM OUT.

Farm Credit Administration. An independent federal agency that regulates and examines the borrower-owned banks and cooperative associations that make up the Federal Farm Credit System. ● The agency was created in 1929 under the title "Federal Farm Board," became an agency in the Department of Agriculture in 1933, and again became independent in 1971. — Abbr. FCA. See FEDERAL FARM CREDIT SYSTEM.

farmee. See FARMOUTEE.

farmer. (14c) A person whose business is farming.

family farmer. A person or entity whose income and debts primarily arise from a family-owned and -operated farm; esp., a person who received more than 80% of gross income from a farm in the taxable year immediately preceding a Chapter 12 filing. ● Only a family farmer can file for Chapter 12 bankruptcy. 11 USCA § 101(18). See CHAPTER 12.

farmer bankruptcy. See CHAPTER 12 (2).

Farmers' Home Administration. An agency, formerly in the U.S. Department of Agriculture, responsible for making mortgages and insuring loans to farmers and for funding rural public-works projects. ● The agency was abolished in 1994, and its functions were assumed by other agencies in the Department — Abbr. FmHA; FHA.

farminee. See FARMOUTEE.

farming operation. (1859) *Bankruptcy.* A business engaged in farming, tillage of soil, dairy farming, ranching, raising of crops, poultry, or livestock, and production of poultry or livestock products in an unmanufactured state. 11 USCA § 101(21). See CHAPTER 12.

farminor. See FARMOUTOR.

farm let, *vb. Hist.* To lease; to let land for rent. • *To farm let* is a phrasal verb that commonly appeared in real-property leases; it corresponds with its Latin root, *ad firmam tradidi.*

farmor. See FARMOUTOR.

farm out, *vb.* (17c) **1.** To turn over something (such as an oil-and-gas lease) for performance by another. • The term evolved from the Roman practice of transferring the right to collect taxes to a third party for a fee. That practice continued in England, Scotland, and France, but it has been long abolished. **2.** *Hist.* To lease for a term. **3.** To exhaust farmland, esp. by continuously raising a single crop.

farmout agreement. *Oil & gas.* An agreement by which one who owns an oil-and-gas lease (the *farmoutor* or *farmor*) agrees to assign to another (the *farmoutee* or *farmee*) an interest in the lease in return for drilling and testing operations on the lease. • For the farmor, the agreement either (1) maintains the lease by securing production or complying with the implied covenant to develop or offset, or (2) obtains an interest in production without costs. For the farmee, the agreement obtains acreage that is not otherwise available or at lower cost than would otherwise be possible. A farmout agreement may also serve as a device to keep people and equipment gainfully employed. — Often shortened to *farmout.* — Also written *farm out agreement; farm-out agreement.* See ASSIGNMENT.

farmoutee (fahrm-ow-**tee**). An oil-and-gas sublessee to whom the lease is assigned for purposes of drilling a well. — Also termed *farmee; farminee.*

farmoutor (**fahrm**-ow-tor *or* -tər). An oil-and-gas lessee who assigns the lease to another, who agrees to drill a well. — Also spelled *farmouter.* — Also termed *farmor; farminor.*

farm products. Crops, livestock, and supplies used or produced in farming or products of crops or livestock in their unmanufactured states, if they are in the possession of a debtor engaged in farming. UCC § 9-102(a)(34). Cf. *growing crops* under CROPS.

Farm Service Agency. An agency in the U.S. Department of Agriculture responsible for administering farm-commodity, crop-insurance, and resource-conservation programs for farmers and ranchers and for making or guaranteeing farm emergency and operating loans through a network of state and county offices. — Abbr. FSA.

farvand (**fahr**-vənd). *Hist. Maritime law.* Voyage or passage by water under a charterparty.

FAS. *abbr.* **1.** FREE ALONGSIDE SHIP. **2.** FETAL ALCOHOL SYNDROME. **3.** FOREIGN AGRICULTURAL SERVICE.

FASB (**faz**-bee). *abbr.* FINANCIAL ACCOUNTING STANDARDS BOARD.

FASB statement. An official pronouncement from the Financial Accounting Standards Board establishing a given financial-accounting practice as acceptable.

fascism. A totalitarian political ideology under which all economic and social aspects of life come under rigid government control or direction, and the state's interests supersede individual interests.

fast estate. See *real property* under PROPERTY.

fast land. See LAND.

fast-tracking, *n.* (1996) A court's method of accelerating the disposition of cases in an effort to clear its docket. • For example, a judge might order that all discovery must be finished within 90 days and that trial is set for 30 days later. See ROCKET DOCKET. — **fast-track,** *vb.*

fatal, *adj.* (14c) **1.** Of or relating to death; producing death <the decision had fatal consequences> <fatal blow>. **2.** Providing grounds for legal invalidity <a fatal defect in the contract>.

fatal defect. See DEFECT.

fatal error. See *reversible error* under ERROR (2).

fatal variance. See VARIANCE (1).

fate and transport. *Environmental law.* The physical condition and migration of contaminants and hazardous materials along environmental pathways such as air, water, and soil.

father. (bef. 12c) A male parent. See PARENT.

acknowledged father. The admitted biological father of a child born to unmarried parents. See ACKNOWLEDGMENT (1).

adoptive father. See *adoptive parent* under PARENT.

biological father. (1951) The man whose sperm impregnated the child's biological mother. — Also termed *natural father; birth father; genetic father.*

birth father. See *biological father.*

de facto father. See *de facto parent* under PARENT.

filiated father. The proven biological father of a child born to unmarried parents. See FILIATION.

foster father. See *foster parent* under PARENT.

genetic father. See *biological father.*

godfather. See GODPARENT.

intentional father. See *intentional parent* under PARENT.

legal father. (16c) The man recognized by law as the male parent of a child. • A man is the legal father of a child if he was married to the child's natural mother when the child was born, if he has recognized or acknowledged the child, or if he has been declared the child's natural father in a paternity action. If a man consents to the artificial insemination of his wife, he is the legal father of the child that is born as a result of the artificial insemination even though he may not be the genetic father of the child.

natural father. See *biological father.*

presumed father. (1937) The man presumed to be the father of a child for any of several reasons: (1) because he was married to the child's natural mother when the child was conceived or born (even though the marriage may have been invalid), (2) because the man married the mother after the child's birth and agreed either to have his name on the birth certificate or to support the child, or (3) because the man welcomed the child into his home and held out the child as his own. • This term represents a complicated category, and state laws vary in their requirements. See PRESUMPTION OF PATERNITY.

psychological father. See *psychological parent* under PARENT.

putative father (**pyoo**-tə-tiv). (16c) The alleged biological father of a child born out of wedlock.

stepfather. (bef. 12c) The husband of one's mother by a later marriage. — Formerly also termed *vitricus.*

Fatico hearing (**fat**-ə-koh). (1979) *Criminal procedure.* A sentencing hearing at which the prosecution and the defense may present evidence about what the defendant's sentence should be. *United States v. Fatico*, 603 F.2d 1053 (2d Cir. 1979).

fault. (13c) **1.** An error or defect of judgment or of conduct; any deviation from prudence or duty resulting from inattention, incapacity, perversity, bad faith, or mismanagement. See NEGLIGENCE. Cf. LIABILITY. **2.** *Civil law.* The intentional or negligent failure to maintain some standard of conduct when that failure results in harm to another person.

contractual fault. *Civil law.* Fault resulting from the intentional or negligent failure to perform an enforceable obligation in a contract.

delictual fault. *Civil law.* Fault resulting from intentional or negligent misconduct that violates a legal duty.

inscrutable fault. *Maritime law.* Fault ascribed solely to human error but for which no responsible party or parties can be identified.

fault-based liability. See *fault liability* under FAULT.

fault divorce. See DIVORCE.

fault-first method. (1996) A means by which to apply a settlement credit to a jury verdict, by first reducing the amount of the verdict by the percentage of the plaintiff's comparative fault, then subtracting from the remainder the amount of any settlements the plaintiff has received on the claim. See SETTLEMENT CREDIT. Cf. SETTLEMENT-FIRST METHOD.

faultless pardon. See PARDON.

fault liability. See LIABILITY.

fault of omission. (17c) Negligence resulting from a negative act. See *negative act* under ACT; NONFEASANCE.

Fauntleroy **doctrine.** The principle that a state must give full faith and credit to another state's judgment, if the other state had proper jurisdiction, even though the judgment is based on a claim that is illegal in the state in which enforcement is sought. *Fauntleroy v. Lum*, 210 U.S. 230, 28 S.Ct. 641 (1908).

faux (foh), *adj.* [Law French] *Hist.* False or counterfeit.

faux (foh), *n.* [French "false"] *Civil law.* The fraudulent alteration of the truth. See CRIMEN FALSI.

faux action. A false action. See PLEADING.

faux money. Counterfeit money.

faux peys (foh **pay**). [French] False weights. See FALSE WEIGHT.

faux serement (foh ser-**mahn**). [French] A false oath.

favor, *n.* See BIAS.

favored beneficiary. See BENEFICIARY.

favored nation. See MOST FAVORED NATION.

favored-nation clause. See MOST-FAVORED-NATION CLAUSE.

favorite of the law. (18c) A person or status entitled to generous and preferential treatment in legal doctrine.

favoritism. (18c) Preference or selection, usu. invidious, based on factors other than merit. See NEPOTISM; PATRONAGE. Cf. DISCRIMINATION.

fax, *n.* (1948) **1.** A method of transmitting over telephone lines an exact copy of a printing. **2.** A machine used for such transmission. — Also termed *telecopier.* **3.** The communication sent or received by such a machine. — Also termed *facsimile*; (in senses 1 & 3) *facsimile transmission.* — **fax,** *vb.*

FBI. *abbr.* FEDERAL BUREAU OF INVESTIGATION.

FCA. *abbr.* **1.** FARM CREDIT ADMINISTRATION. **2.** FREE CARRIER.

F. Cas. *abbr.* *Federal Cases*, a series of reported decisions (1789–1880) predating the *Federal Reporter*.

FCC. *abbr.* FEDERAL COMMUNICATIONS COMMISSION.

FCFAA. *abbr.* FEDERAL COMPUTER FRAUD AND ABUSE ACT.

FCIC. *abbr.* FEDERAL CROP INSURANCE CORPORATION.

FCJ. *abbr.* Failure to comply with a judgment imposed for a traffic violation. ● The defendant's driver's license is suspended until the FCJ is remedied and the fines and fees are paid.

FCPV. *abbr.* Failure to comply with parking-violation tickets. ● If a person has a certain number of unpaid parking tickets (often six) within a jurisdiction, the person will be barred from obtaining or renewing a driver's license.

FDA. *abbr.* FOOD AND DRUG ADMINISTRATION.

f/d/b/a. *abbr.* Formerly doing business as.

FDCA. *abbr.* FOOD, DRUG, AND COSMETIC ACT.

FDCPA. *abbr.* See FAIR DEBT COLLECTION PRACTICES ACT.

FDIC. *abbr.* FEDERAL DEPOSIT INSURANCE CORPORATION.

feal (fee-əl), *adj.* *Archaic.* Faithful; truthful. — Also termed *fele*.

fealty (**feel**-tee *or* fee-əl-tee). (14c) *Hist.* In feudal law, the allegiance that a tenant or vassal owes to a lord. — Also termed *feodality*.

fear-of-cancer claim. *Torts.* A tort claim founded on a plaintiff's mental anguish or emotional distress arising from the fear of developing cancer, where either (1) the plaintiff was exposed to asbestos or other carcinogenic agents, or (2) a physician's negligence gave rise to a potentially cancerous condition or permitted a cancer to develop unchecked. ● The plaintiff must demonstrate (1) actual exposure to a disease-causing agent, and (2) the reasonableness of the emotional distress. See *Winik v. Jewish Hosp. of Brooklyn*, 293 N.E.2d 95 (N.Y. 1972); *Ferrara v. Galluchio*, 152 N.E.2d 249 (N.Y. 1958). — Also termed *cancerphobia claim*.

feasance (fee-zənts), *n.* (16c) The doing or execution of an act, condition, or obligation. Cf. MALFEASANCE; MISFEASANCE; NONFEASANCE. — **feasor**, *n.*

feasant (fez-ənt *or* fee-zənt). *Archaic.* Doing or causing. See DAMAGE FEASANT.

feasibility standard. (1978) *Bankruptcy.* The requirement that, to obtain bankruptcy-court approval, a Chapter 11 reorganization plan must

be workable and have a reasonable likelihood of success.

feasor (fee-zər), *n.* (1808) An actor; a person who commits an act. See TORTFEASOR.

feast, *n.* (13c) **1.** *Roman law.* An established holiday or festival in the ecclesiastical calendar, used as a date in a legal instrument. **2.** *Hist.* One of four principal days (feasts) of the year: March 25, the annunciation of the Virgin Mary; June 24, the birth of John the Baptist; September 28, the feast of St. Michael the Archangel; and December 21, the feast of St. Thomas the Apostle. ● The four feast days were used as fixed dates (called "quarter-days") for paying rent; before 1875, they were used as a reference point to set terms of courts. — Also termed *feast day*; *feast-day*.

featherbedding. (1921) A union practice designed to increase employment and guarantee job security by requiring employers to hire or retain more employees than are needed. ● The practice stems from employees' desire for job security in the face of technological improvement. Featherbedding is restricted by federal law but is an unfair labor practice only if, for example, a union exacts pay from an employer for services not performed or not to be performed.

FEC. *abbr.* FEDERAL ELECTION COMMISSION.

FECA. *abbr.* FEDERAL EMPLOYEES' COMPENSATION ACT.

feciales, *n.* See FETIALES.

fecial law. See FETIAL LAW.

Fed. *abbr.* **1.** FEDERAL. **2.** FEDERAL RESERVE SYSTEM.

Fed. Appx. *abbr.* FEDERAL APPENDIX.

Fed. Cir. *abbr.* UNITED STATES COURT OF APPEALS FOR THE FEDERAL CIRCUIT.

federal, *adj.* (18c) Of or relating to a system of associated governments with a vertical division of governments into national and regional components having different responsibilities; esp., of or relating to the national government of the United States. — Abbr. Fed.

Federal Acquisition Regulation. (*usu. pl.*) A federal regulation that governs contracting methods, requirements, and procedures with the federal government. 48 CFR ch. 1. — Also termed *Federal Procurement Regulation*.

federal act. A statute enacted by the U.S. Congress. See FEDERAL LAW.

federal agency. See AGENCY (3).

federal appeal. See APPEAL.

Federal Appendix. A set of reports containing all the full-text "unpublished" opinions that West receives from the federal circuit courts of appeals. ● These are the opinions not designated for publication in the *Federal Reporter*. Coverage began January 1, 2001. — Abbr. Fed. Appx.

Federal Arbitration Act. A federal statute providing for the enforcement of private agreements to arbitrate disputes related to interstate commercial and maritime matters. • Under the Act, arbitration agreements are enforced in accordance with their terms, just as other contracts are. The Act supersedes substantive state laws that frustrate enforcement of arbitration agreements but does not apply to matters of procedure. 9 USCA §§ 1–16. — Abbr. FAA. — Also termed *United States Arbitration Act.*

Federal Aviation Act. A federal law establishing the Federal Aviation Administration (FAA) to be responsible for regulation of aircraft and air travel, including aircraft safety, certification of aircraft personnel, and airport development. 49 USCA §§ 44720 et seq.

Federal Aviation Administration. The federal agency charged with regulating air commerce, promoting civil aviation and a national system of airports, achieving efficient use of navigable airspace, developing and operating a common system of air-traffic control and air navigation, and developing and implementing programs and regulations relating to environmental effects of civil aviation. • The Federal Aviation Agency was established in 1958. 49 USCA § 106. Its name was changed when it became a part of the Department of Transportation in 1967. The FAA was formerly charged with promoting safety in air transportation, but that task was transferred to the Transportation Security Administration after the terrorist attacks of 11 Sept. 2001. Abbr. FAA. — Formerly also termed *Federal Aviation Agency.*

Federal Aviation Regulation. (*usu. pl.*) A federal regulation governing the safety, maintenance, and piloting of civil aircraft. 14 CFR ch. 1. — Abbr. FAR.

Federal Bureau of Investigation. A division of the U.S. Department of Justice charged with investigating all violations of federal laws except those specifically assigned to another federal agency. — Abbr. FBI.

Federal Bureau of Prisons. The U.S. government unit responsible for the custody and care of federal offenders, whether incarcerated in federal correctional and detention centers or in state-run or privately operated facilities. • The Bureau was established in 1930 to centralize federal-prison administration and ensure consistency in prison operations.

federal census. See CENSUS.

Federal Circuit. See COURT OF APPEALS FOR THE FEDERAL CIRCUIT.

federal citizen. See CITIZEN.

Federal Claims, U.S. Court of. See UNITED STATES COURT OF FEDERAL CLAIMS.

federal-comity doctrine. (1976) The principle requiring federal district courts to refrain from interfering in each other's affairs.

federal common law. See COMMON LAW (1).

Federal Communications Commission. An independent federal commission that regulates interstate and foreign communications by radio, television, wire, satellite, and cable. • The commission was created by the Communications Act of 1934. 47 USCA §§ 151 et seq. — Abbr. FCC.

Federal Computer Fraud and Abuse Act. A law establishing civil liability for gaining unauthorized access to a computer and causing damage to that computer. • Damage is statutorily defined to include harm to the computer's data, programs, systems, and information either by compromising integrity or by impairing availability. — Abbr. FCFAA.

federal court. See COURT.

federal crime. (1860) A criminal offense under a federal statute. • Most federal crimes are codified in Title 18 of the U.S. Code.

Federal Crop Insurance Corporation. A federally chartered corporation that protects farmers against financial losses from crop failure due to adverse weather conditions, insect infestation, plant disease, floods, fires, and earthquakes by encouraging the sale of insurance through licensed agents and brokers and by reinsuring private companies that issue insurance under brand names. • Created by the Agricultural Adjustment Act of 1938, the Corporation operates under the general supervision of the Secretary of Agriculture. — Abbr. FCIC.

Federal Deposit Insurance Corporation. A federal corporation that protects bank and thrift deposits by insuring accounts up to $100,000, examining banks that are not members of the Federal Reserve System, and liquidating failed institutions. • It was established in 1933 and began insuring banks in 1934. — Abbr. FDIC.

Federal Election Commission. A ten-member independent federal commission that certifies payments to qualifying presidential campaigns in primary and general elections and to national-nominating conventions, audits campaign expenditures, and enforces laws requiring public disclosure of financial activities of presidential campaigns and political parties. • It was established by the Federal Election Campaign Act of 1971. 2 USCA § 437c. — Abbr. FEC.

Federal Emergency Management Agency. A unit in the Department of Homeland Security responsible for coordinating all emergency-preparedness activities of the federal government through its ten regional offices. • FEMA also operates the National Flood Insurance Program and is responsible for fire protection and arson control. It was established as an independent agency by Executive Order 12127 of 31 Mar. 1979 and became a unit in the Department of Homeland Security in 2003. — Abbr. FEMA.

Federal Employees' Compensation Act. A workers'-compensation law for federal employees. 5 USCA §§ 8101–8152 — Abbr. FECA. See WORKERS' COMPENSATION.

federal-employer-identification number. See TAX-IDENTIFICATION NUMBER.

Federal Employers' Liability Act. A workers'-compensation law that provides death and disability benefits for employees of railroads engaged in interstate and foreign commerce. 45 USCA §§ 51–60 — Abbr. FELA.

federal enclave. See ENCLAVE.

Federal Energy Regulatory Commission. An independent five-member commission in the U.S. Department of Energy responsible for licensing hydroelectric-power projects and for setting interstate rates on (1) transporting and selling natural gas for resale, (2) transporting and selling electricity at wholesale, and (3) transporting oil by pipeline. • It was created by the Department of Energy Organization Act of 1977. As enforcer of the Natural Gas Act, it succeeded the Federal Power Commission. — Abbr. FERC.

Federal Farm Credit Bank. One of a system of federally chartered institutions created to provide credit to farm-related enterprises. • The banks resulted from a merger of federal land banks and federal intermediate credit banks. They are supervised by the Farm Credit Administration.

Federal Farm Credit Banks Funding Corporation. A federal corporation that manages the sale of Federal Farm Credit System securities in the money and capital markets and also provides advisory services to banks in the Federal Farm Credit System.

Federal Farm Credit System. The national cooperative system of banks and associations providing credit to farmers, agricultural concerns, and related businesses. • The system consists of the banks for cooperatives, the farm credit banks, and the Federal Farm Credit Banks Funding Corporation. It is supervised by the Farm Credit Administration and was originally capitalized by the federal government. The system is now self-funding and owned by its member-borrowers.

Federal Food Stamp Act. A federally funded program that provides needy families with financial assistance in obtaining a nutritionally adequate diet. • The Secretary of Agriculture administers the Act.

federal-funds rate. The interest rate at which banks lend to each other overnight. • The loans are usu. made by banks with excess reserves to those with temporarily insufficient reserves. — Often shortened to *fed funds*. — Also termed *fed-funds rate*.

federal government. See GOVERNMENT.

Federal Highway Administration. An agency in the U.S. Department of Transportation responsible for granting aid to states for highway construction and improvement; providing matching grants to states for highway-safety programs; seeking uniformity among the states in commercial motor-carrier registration and taxation; regulating the safety of motor carriers operating in interstate commerce; and training employees of state and local agencies engaged in highway work backed by federal aid. — Abbr. FHWA.

Federal Home Loan Bank. One of 12 federally chartered banks created in 1932 to extend secured loans (advances) to savings institutions that are members of the system and to community financial institutions that finance small businesses, small farms, and small agribusinesses. • The banks are supervised by the Federal Housing Finance Board. — Abbr. FHLB. — Sometimes shortened to *home loan bank*.

Federal Home Loan Bank Board. See FEDERAL HOUSING FINANCE BOARD.

Federal Home Loan Mortgage Corporation. A corporation that purchases both conventional and federally insured first mortgages from members of the Federal Reserve System and other approved banks. — Abbr. FHLMC. — Also termed *Freddie Mac*.

Federal Housing Administration. The HUD division that encourages mortgage lending by insuring mortgage loans on homes meeting the agency's standards. — Abbr. FHA. See DEPARTMENT OF HOUSING AND URBAN DEVELOPMENT.

Federal Housing Finance Board. A five-member independent federal board that supervises the 12 Federal Home Loan Banks. • Formerly known as the Federal Home Loan Bank Board, it was established by the Federal Home Loan Bank Act of 1932. That Act was amended by the Financial Institutions Reform, Recovery, and Enforcement Act of 1989. 12 USCA §§ 1421 et seq.

federal instrumentality, *n.* **1.** A means or agency used by the national government. **2.** A national agency or other entity immune from state control.

Federal Insurance Contributions Act. The federal act imposing the social-security tax on employers and employees. IRC (26 USCA) §§ 3101–3127. — Abbr. FICA.

federal intermediate credit bank. See BANK.

federalism. (1787) The legal relationship and distribution of power between the national and regional governments within a federal system of government.

> *cooperative federalism.* (1947) Distribution of power between the federal government and the states in which each recognizes the powers of the other while jointly engaging in certain governmental functions.

> *our federalism.* See OUR FEDERALISM.

Federalist Papers. A series of 85 essays written by Alexander Hamilton, John Jay, and James Madison (under the pseudonym Publius) expounding on and advocating the adoption of the U.S. Constitution. • Most of the essays were published in 1787 and 1788. — Also termed *The Federalist.*

Federalist Society. A national association of lawyers, law students, and others committed to conservative and libertarian viewpoints on political and social matters. • The group is based in Washington, D.C. Cf. NATIONAL LAWYERS GUILD.

Federal Judicial Center. An agency in the judicial branch of the federal government responsible for researching judicial administration and for training judges and employees of the federal judiciary. • Its director is appointed by a seven-member board presided over by the Chief Justice of the United States. 28 USCA § 620. — Abbr. FJC.

Federal Judicial Code. The portion (Title 28) of the U.S. Code dealing with the organization, jurisdiction, venue, and procedures of the federal court system, as well as court officers, personnel, and the Department of Justice.

federal jurisdiction. See JURISDICTION.

federal-juvenile-delinquency jurisdiction. See JURISDICTION.

Federal Kidnapping Act. A federal law punishing kidnapping for ransom or reward when the victim is transported interstate or internationally. • The law presumes that a victim has been transported in violation of the law if the victim is not released within 24 hours. The Federal Kidnapping Act, by express provision, does not apply to the kidnapping of a minor by either parent. The law was enacted in 1932 after the son of aviator Charles Lindbergh was kidnapped and murdered. For this reason, it is also termed the *Lindbergh Act.* 18 USCA § 1201. — Also termed *Lindbergh Act.* Cf. PARENTAL KIDNAPPING PREVENTION ACT.

Federal Labor Relations Authority. An agency that protects the right of federal employees to organize, engage in collective bargaining, and select their own union representatives. • It was established under Reorganization Plan No. 2 of 1978 and began operating in 1979. 5 USCA §§ 7101–35. — Abbr. FLRA.

federal labor union. See UNION.

federal land. See LAND.

Federal Land Bank. (1914) One of a system of 12 regional banks created in 1916 to provide mortgage loans to farmers. • The system is now merged with federal intermediate credit banks to create the Federal Farm Credit System.

federal law. (18c) The body of law consisting of the U.S. Constitution, federal statutes and regulations, U.S. treaties, and federal common law. Cf. STATE LAW.

Federal Law Enforcement Training Center. An interagency law-enforcement training facility responsible for serving over 70 law-enforcement organizations in the federal government. • The Center was transferred from the Department of the Treasury to the Department of Homeland Security in 2003. — Abbr. FLETC.

federal magistrate. UNITED STATES MAGISTRATE JUDGE.

Federal Maritime Commission. An independent federal agency that regulates the waterborne foreign and domestic commerce of the United States by (1) ensuring that U.S. international trade is open to all countries on fair and equitable terms, (2) guarding against unauthorized monopolies in U.S. waterborne commerce, and (3) ensuring that financial responsibility is maintained to clean up oil spills and indemnify injured passengers. • The Agency was established in 1961. Its five commissioners are appointed by the President with the advice and consent of the Senate. — Abbr. FMC.

Federal Maritime Lien Act. A statute that confers an automatic lien on anyone who provides a vessel with any of a wide range of goods and services. 46 USCA §§ 31341–43. — Abbr. FMLA.

Federal Mediation and Conciliation Service. An independent federal agency that tries to prevent the interruption of interstate commerce that could result from a labor–management dispute by helping the parties reach a settlement without resorting to a job action or strike. • The Service can intervene on its own authority or at the request of a party to the dispute. It also helps employers and unions select qualified arbitrators. The Service was established by the Labor Management Relations Act of 1947. 29 USCA § 172. — Abbr. FMCS. Cf. NATIONAL MEDIATION BOARD.

Federal Mine Safety and Health Review Commission. An independent five-member commission that (1) monitors compliance with occupational safety and health standards in the nation's surface and underground coal, metal, and nonmetal mines, and (2) adjudicates disputes that arise under the Federal Mine Safety and Health

Amendments Act of 1977. • It was established in 1977. 30 USCA §§ 801 et seq. —Abbr. FMSHRC.

Federal Motor Carrier Safety Administration. A unit in the U.S. Department of Transportation responsible for regulating the operation of large trucks and buses. — Abbr. FMCSA.

Federal National Mortgage Association. A privately owned and managed corporation chartered by the U.S. government that provides a secondary mortgage market for the purchase and sale of mortgages guaranteed by the Veterans Administration and those insured under the Federal Housing Administration. — Abbr. FNMA. — Also termed *Fannie Mae.*

Federal Parent Locator Service. A federal program created to help enforce child-support obligations. • In an effort to increase the collection of child support, Congress authorized the use of all information contained in the various federal databases to help locate absent, delinquent child-support obligors. Although initially information could be released only if the family was receiving public assistance, any judgment obligee can now apply to receive the last known address of a delinquent child-support obligor. 42 USCA § 653. Abbr. FPLS.

Federal Power Commission. See FEDERAL ENERGY REGULATORY COMMISSION.

federal preemption. See PREEMPTION (5).

federal prison camp. A federal minimum-security detention facility. • Federal prison camps, which often do not have walls or fences, usu. house nonviolent inmates who are serving sentences shorter than a year plus one day and who are not considered escape risks.

Federal Procurement Regulation. See FEDERAL ACQUISITION REGULATION.

Federal Protective Service. A law-enforcement agency in the U.S. Department of Homeland Security responsible for protecting ambassadors, diplomatic staffs, and embassy property. • It was transferred from the General Services Administration in 2003.

federal question. In litigation, a legal issue involving the interpretation and application of the U.S. Constitution, an act of Congress, or a treaty. • Jurisdiction over federal questions rests with the federal courts. 28 USCA § 1331.

federal-question jurisdiction. See JURISDICTION.

Federal Railroad Administration. A unit in the U.S. Department of Transportation responsible for promulgating and enforcing rail-safety regulations; administering rail-related financial-aid programs; conducting research on rail safety; and rehabilitating rail passenger service for the Northeast corridor. — Abbr. FRA.

Federal Register. A daily publication containing presidential proclamations and executive orders, federal-agency regulations of general applicability and legal effect, proposed agency rules, and documents required by law to be published. • The *Federal Register* is published by the National Archives and Records Administration. — Abbr. Fed. Reg.

federal regulations. See CODE OF FEDERAL REGULATIONS.

Federal Reporter. See F. (1).

Federal Reporter Second Series. See F.2D.

Federal Reporter Third Series. See F.3D.

Federal Reserve Board of Governors. The board that supervises the Federal Reserve System and sets national monetary and credit policy. • The board consists of seven members nominated by the President and confirmed by the Senate for 14-year terms. — Often shortened to *Federal Reserve Board.* — Abbr. FRB.

federal reserve note. (1913) The paper currency in circulation in the United States. • Non-interest-bearing promissory notes are payable to their bearer on demand. The Federal Reserve Banks issue the notes in denominations of $1, $2, $5, $10, $20, $50, and $100. Until 1945, the United States Mint also printed $500, $1,000, $5,000, and $10,000 bills. Although the Federal Reserve System discontinued using bills larger than $100 in 1969, the outstanding bills remain legal tender. 31 USCA § 5103. Cf. GOLD CERTIFICATE; SILVER CERTIFICATE.

Federal Reserve System. The central bank that sets credit and monetary policy by fixing the reserves to be maintained by depository institutions, determining the discount rate charged by Federal Reserve Banks, and regulating the amount of credit that may be extended on any security. • The Federal Reserve System was established by the Federal Reserve Act of 1913. 12 USCA § 221. It comprises 12 central banks supervised by a Board of Governors whose members are appointed by the President and confirmed by the Senate. — Abbr. FRS; Fed.

Federal Retirement Thrift Investment Board. A board that administers the Thrift Savings Plan that allows federal employees to save additional funds for retirement. • It was established in 1986. 5 USCA § 8472. — Abbr. FRTIB.

Federal Rules Decisions. See F.R.D.

Federal Rules Enabling Act. A 1934 statute granting the U.S. Supreme Court the authority to adopt rules of civil procedure for federal courts. • For the rulemaking power of federal courts today, see 28 USCA §§ 2071, 2072. See also Fed. R. Civ. P. 83; Fed. R. Crim. P. 57.

Federal Rules of Appellate Procedure. The rules governing appeals to the U.S. courts of appeals from lower courts, some federal-agency proceedings, and applications for writs. — Abbr. Fed. R. App. P.; FRAP.

Federal Rules of Bankruptcy Procedure. The rules governing proceedings instituted under the Bankruptcy Code. — Abbr. Fed. R. Bankr. P.

Federal Rules of Civil Procedure. The rules governing civil actions in the U.S. district courts. — Abbr. Fed. R. Civ. P.; FRCP.

Federal Rules of Criminal Procedure. The rules governing criminal proceedings in the U.S. district courts. — Abbr. Fed. R. Crim. P.

Federal Rules of Evidence. The rules governing the admissibility of evidence at trials in federal courts. — Abbr. Fed. R. Evid.; FRE.

Federal Savings and Loan Insurance Corporation. A federal agency created in 1934 to insure deposits in savings-and-loan associations and savings banks. • When this agency became insolvent in 1989, its assets and liabilities were transferred to an insurance fund managed by the FDIC. — Abbr. FSLIC. See RESOLUTION TRUST CORPORATION.

federal sentencing guidelines. See UNITED STATES SENTENCING GUIDELINES.

federal state. See STATE.

federal statute. See FEDERAL ACT.

Federal Supplement. See F.SUPP.

Federal Supplement 2d. See F.SUPP.2D.

Federal Supply Service. A unit in the General Services Administration responsible for providing supplies to federal agencies worldwide. • In procuring supplies the agency takes advantage of the government's aggregate buying power. Abbr. FSS.

Federal Technology Service. A unit in the General Services Administration that provides communications services worldwide to other federal departments and agencies. — Abbr. FTS.

Federal Tort Claims Act. A statute that limits federal sovereign immunity and allows recovery in federal court for tort damages caused by federal employees, but only if the law of the state where the injury occurred would hold a private person liable for the injury. 28 USCA §§ 2671–2680 — Abbr. FTCA. See *sovereign immunity* under IMMUNITY (1).

Federal Trade Commission. An independent five-member federal commission that administers various laws against business monopolies, restraint of trade, and deceptive trade practices. • It was established by the Federal Trade Commission Act of 1914. 15 USCA §§ 41–58. The Commission's body of rulings reaches into many state-law actions because many so-called "Little FTC Acts" of the states specify that FTC interpretations should provide a model for state-court decisions. — Abbr. FTC.

Federal Trademark Act. See LANHAM ACT.

Federal Trademark Dilution Act. A 1995 amendment to the Lanham Act (Trademark Act of 1946) that provides additional remedies against the dilution of famous trademarks. 15 USCA § 1125(c). — Sometimes shortened to *Dilution Act.* — Abbr. FTDA.

federal transfer. The federal district court's right to move a civil action filed there to any other district or division where the plaintiff could have brought the action originally. 28 USCA § 1404(a). See CHANGE OF VENUE.

Federal Transit Administration. A unit in the U.S. Department of Transportation responsible for increasing public-transit ridership through demonstration projects and financial assistance. — Abbr. FTA.

Federal Unemployment Tax Act. The federal statute requiring employers to remit taxes based on employees' wages and salaries. 18 USCA § 1201 et seq. — Abbr. FUTA.

federation. (18c) A league or union of states, groups, or peoples united under a strong central authority but retaining limited regional sovereignty, esp. over local affairs. Cf. CONFEDERATION.

fed funds. See FEDERAL FUNDS RATE.

fed-funds rate. See FEDERAL FUNDS RATE.

Fed. R. App. P. *abbr.* FEDERAL RULES OF APPELLATE PROCEDURE.

Fed. R. Bankr. P. *abbr.* FEDERAL RULES OF BANKRUPTCY PROCEDURE.

Fed. R. Civ. P. *abbr.* FEDERAL RULES OF CIVIL PROCEDURE.

Fed. R. Crim. P. *abbr.* FEDERAL RULES OF CRIMINAL PROCEDURE.

Fed. Reg. *abbr.* FEDERAL REGISTER.

Fed. R. Evid. *abbr.* FEDERAL RULES OF EVIDENCE.

Fed Wire. The Federal Reserve's computer network that allows nearly instantaneous domestic money and securities transfers among the Federal Reserve's offices, depository institutions, the U.S. Treasury, and other government agencies.

fee. (14c) **1.** A charge for labor or services, esp. professional services.

   attorney's fees. See ATTORNEY'S FEES.

   contingent fee. See CONTINGENT FEE.

   docket fee. (1836) A fee charged by a court for filing a claim.

   expert-witness fee. A fee paid for the professional services of an expert witness.

fixed fee. (18c) **1.** A flat charge for a service; a charge that does not vary with the amount of time or effort required to complete the service. **2.** In a construction contract, a predetermined amount that is added to costs for calculating payments due under the contract.

franchise fee. (1894) **1.** A fee paid by a franchisee to a franchisor for franchise rights. ● Franchise fees are regulated by state laws. **2.** A fee paid to the government for a government grant of a franchise, such as the one required for operating a radio or television station.

jury fee. (1806) A fee, usu. a minimal one, that a party to a civil suit must pay the court clerk to be entitled to a jury trial.

loan-origination fee. A fee charged by a lender to cover the administrative costs of making a loan.

maintenance fee. See MAINTENANCE FEE.

management fee. A fee charged by an investment manager for supervisory services.

origination fee. (1921) A fee charged by a lender for preparing and processing a loan.

probate fee. Compensation paid with a probate court's approval to an attorney who performs probate-related services to the estate.

success fee. A bonus paid to a representative who performs exceptionally well in gaining favorable results; esp., a bonus that a client pays to an attorney if the attorney obtains something of value to the client. ● For instance, a client might agree to pay a success fee for success in litigation, for favorable negotiations in a transaction, or for the successful conclusion of a corporate merger, acquisition, or loan. See CONDITIONAL FEE AGREEMENT.

witness fee. **1.** A statutory fee that must be tendered with a subpoena for the subpoena to be binding. **2.** A fee paid by a party to a witness as reimbursement for reasonable expenses (such as travel, meals, lodging, and loss of time) incurred as a result of the witness's having to attend and testify at a deposition or trial. ● Any other payment to a nonexpert witness is considered unethical. — Also termed (in English law) *conduct money.* Cf. *expert-witness fee.*

2. A heritable interest in land; esp., a fee simple absolute. — Also termed *fee estate; feod; feodum; feud; feudum; fief.* See FEE SIMPLE.

arriere fee (**ar**-ee-air *or* **ar**-ee-ər). *Hist.* A fee dependent on a superior one; a subfief. — Also termed *arriere fief.*

base fee. (16c) A fee that has some qualification connected to it and that terminates whenever the qualification terminates. ● An example of the words creating a base fee are "to A and his heirs, tenants of the manor of Tinsleydale,"

which would terminate when A or his heirs are no longer tenants of the manor of Tinsleydale. Among the base fees at common law are the fee simple subject to a condition subsequent and the conditional fee. — Also termed *determinable fee; qualified fee; limited fee.* See *fee simple determinable* under FEE SIMPLE.

determinable fee. See *base fee.*

fee expectant. *Rare.* A fee tail created when land is given to a man and wife and the heirs of their bodies. See FRANKMARRIAGE.

fee simple. See FEE SIMPLE.

fee tail. See FEE TAIL.

great fee. *Hist.* In feudal law, a fee received directly from the Crown.

knight's fee. See KNIGHT'S FEE.

lay fee. *Hist.* A fee interest in land held by ordinary feudal tenure, such as socage, rather than by ecclesiastical tenure through frankalmoin. See FRANKALMOIN; SOCAGE.

limited fee. See *base fee.*

plowman's fee. *Hist.* A species of tenure for peasants or small farmers by which the land descended in equal shares to all the tenant's sons.

qualified fee. See *base fee.*

quasi-fee. *Hist.* An estate in fee acquired wrongfully.

fee damages. See DAMAGES.

feeder organization. *Tax.* An entity that conducts a business or trade for the benefit of a tax-exempt organization. ● The feeder organization is not tax-exempt. IRC (26 USCA) § 502.

fee estate. See FEE (2).

fee farm. *Hist.* A species of tenure in which land is held in perpetuity at a yearly rent (fee-farm rent), without fealty, homage, or other services than those in the feoffment. — Also termed *feodi firma; firma feodi.* See EMPHYTEUSIS.

fee-farm rent. See RENTCHARGE.

fee interest. **1.** See FEE. **2.** See FEE SIMPLE. **3.** See FEE TAIL. **4.** *Oil & gas.* Ownership of both the surface interest and the mineral interest.

feemail (**fee**-mayl). (1994) *Slang.* **1.** An attorney's fee extorted by intimidation, threats, or pressure. **2.** The act or process of extorting such a fee. Cf. BLACKMAIL (1); GRAYMAIL; GREENMAIL (1), (2).

fee-sharing. See FEE SPLITTING.

fee-shifting, *n.* The transfer of responsibility for paying fees, esp. attorney's fees, from one party to another. See AMERICAN RULE (1); ENGLISH RULE.

fee simple. (15c) An interest in land that, being the broadest property interest allowed by law, endures until the current holder dies without heirs; esp., a fee simple absolute. — Often shortened to *fee.* — Also termed *estate in fee simple; tenancy in fee; fee-simple title; exclusive ownership; feudum simplex.* See AND HIS HEIRS.

fee simple absolute. (18c) An estate of indefinite or potentially infinite duration (e.g., "to Albert and his heirs"). — Often shortened to *fee simple* or *fee.* — Also termed *fee simple absolute in possession.*

fee simple conditional. (17c) An estate restricted to some specified heirs, exclusive of others (e.g., "to Albert and his female heirs"). • The fee simple conditional is obsolete except in Iowa, Oregon, and South Carolina. — Also termed *general fee conditional; conditional fee.*

fee simple defeasible (di-**fee**-zə-bəl). (18c) An estate that ends either because there are no more heirs of the person to whom it is granted or because a special limitation, condition subsequent, or executory limitation takes effect before the line of heirs runs out. — Also termed *defeasible fee simple; qualified fee.*

fee simple determinable. (18c) An estate that will automatically end and revert to the grantor if some specified event occurs (e.g., "to Albert and his heirs while the property is used for charitable purposes"); an estate in fee simple subject to a special limitation. • The future interest retained by the grantor is called a *possibility of reverter.* — Also termed *determinable fee; qualified fee; fee simple subject to common-law limitation; fee simple subject to special limitation; fee simple subject to special interest; base fee; estate on limitation.*

fee simple subject to a condition subsequent. (1874) An estate subject to the grantor's power to end the estate if some specified event happens (e.g., "to Albert and his heirs, upon condition that no alcohol is sold on the premises"). • The future interest retained by the grantor is called a *power of termination* (or a *right of entry*). — Also termed *fee simple on a condition subsequent; fee simple subject to a power of termination; fee simple upon condition.*

fee simple subject to an executory limitation. (1856) A fee simple defeasible that is subject to divestment in favor of someone other than the grantor if a specified event happens (e.g., "to Albert and his heirs, but if the property is ever used as a parking lot, then to Bob"). — Also termed *fee simple subject to an executory interest.*

fee simple subject to a power of termination. See *fee simple subject to a condition subsequent.*

fee simple subject to common-law limitation. See *fee simple determinable.*

fee simple subject to special interest. See *fee simple determinable.*

fee simple subject to special limitation. See *fee simple determinable.*

fee simple upon condition. See *fee simple subject to a condition subsequent.*

fee-simple title. See FEE SIMPLE.

fee-splitting. 1. The division of attorney's fees between two or more lawyers, esp. between the lawyer who handled a matter and the lawyer who referred the matter. • Some states consider this practice unethical. **2.** The division of attorney's fees between two or more lawyers who represent a client jointly but are not in the same firm. • Under most states' ethics rules, an attorney is prohibited from splitting a fee with a nonlawyer. — Also termed *fee-sharing; division of fees.*

fee statement. A lawyer's bill for services either already rendered or to be rendered, usu. including itemized expenses.

fee tail. (15c) An estate that is heritable only by specified descendants of the original grantee, and that endures until its current holder dies without issue (e.g., "to Albert and the heirs of his body"). • Most jurisdictions — except Delaware, Maine, Massachusetts, and Rhode Island — have abolished the fee tail. — Also termed *entailed estate; estate tail; estate in tail; estate in fee tail; tenancy in tail; entail; feodum talliatum.* See ENTAIL; TAIL.

fee tail general. A fee tail that is heritable by all of the property owner's issue by any spouse. • Formerly, a grant "to A and the heirs of his body" created a fee tail general.

fee tail special. A fee tail that restricts the eligibility of claimants by requiring a claimant to prove direct descent from the grantee and meet the special condition in the grant. • For example, the words "to A and the heirs of his body begotten on his wife Mary" meant that only descendants of A and Mary could inherit; A's children by any other wife were excluded. An estate tail special could also be restricted to only male or only female descendants, as in "to A and the heirs male of his body."

feign (fayn), *vb.* (13c) To make up or fabricate; to make a false show of <he feigned an illness>.

feigned, *adj.* Pretended; simulated; fictitious.

feigned accomplice. See INFORMANT.

feigned action. *Hist.* An action brought for an illegal purpose on a pretended right. — Also termed *faint action; false action.*

feigned issue. *Hist.* A proceeding in which the parties, by consent, have an issue tried by a jury without actually bringing a formal action. • The proceeding was done when a court either lacked jurisdiction or was unwilling to decide the issue. — Also termed *fictitious issue.*

feigned recovery. See COMMON RECOVERY.

FEIN. *abbr.* See TAX-IDENTIFICATION NUMBER.

***Feist* doctrine.** (1991) *Copyright.* The rule that "sweat of the brow" will not support U.S. copyright protection in an unoriginal collection of facts. *Feist Pubs. v. Rural Tel. Serv. Co.,* 499 U.S. 340, 111 S. Ct. 1282 (1991). Cf. SWEAT-OF-THE-BROW DOCTRINE.

FELA (fee-lə). *abbr.* FEDERAL EMPLOYERS' LIABILITY ACT.

fele (feel). [Law French] See FEAL.

fellow, *n.* **1.** One joined with another in some legal status or relation. **2.** A member of a college, board, corporate body, or other organization.

fellow-officer rule. (1971) *Criminal procedure.* The principle that an investigative stop or an arrest is valid even if the law-enforcement officer lacks personal knowledge to establish reasonable suspicion or probable cause as long as the officer is acting on the knowledge of another officer and the collective knowledge of the law-enforcement office. — Also termed *Whiteley rule; collective-knowledge rule.*

fellow servant. A coworker having the same employer; esp., an employee who is so closely related to another employee's work that there is a special risk of harm if either one is negligent. See FELLOW-SERVANT RULE; DIFFERENT-DEPARTMENT RULE.

> **superior fellow servant.** A worker that has the power of control or direction over a coworker. — Also termed *superior servant.*

fellow-servant rule. (1905) A common-law doctrine holding that an employer is not liable for an employee's injuries caused by a negligent coworker. • This doctrine has generally been abrogated by workers'-compensation statutes. In some jurisdictions, employees were considered fellow servants when they were working with one aim or result in view. In others, the relation of fellow servant was tested by the "doctrine of vice principal" or the "superior-servant rule," meaning that an employer is liable for injuries to an employee if they result from the negligence of another employee who is given power of control or direction over the injured employee. — Also termed *common-employment doctrine.* Cf. DIFFERENT-DEPARTMENT RULE.

felo-de-se (fee-loh *or* fel-oh dee **see**), *n.* (17c) See SUICIDE (2). Pl. **felones de se.**

felon, *n.* (13c) A person who has been convicted of a felony. — Also termed (redundantly) *convicted felon.*

felon-de-se. See SUICIDE (2).

felonious (fə-**loh**-nee-əs), *adj.* (16c) **1.** Of, relating to, or involving a felony. **2.** Constituting or having the character of a felony. **3.** Proceeding from an evil heart or purpose; malicious; villainous.

4. Wrongful; (of an act) done without excuse or color of right.

felonious assault. See ASSAULT.

felonious homicide. See HOMICIDE.

felonious intent. See *criminal intent* under INTENT (1).

felonious restraint. (1971) **1.** The offense of knowingly and unlawfully restraining a person under circumstances that expose the person to serious bodily harm. Model Penal Code § 212.2(a). **2.** The offense of holding a person in involuntary servitude. Model Penal Code § 212.2(b).

felon of oneself. See SUICIDE (2).

felony, *n.* (14c) **1.** A serious crime usu. punishable by imprisonment for more than one year or by death. • Examples include burglary, arson, rape, and murder. — Also termed *major crime; serious crime.* Cf. MISDEMEANOR.

> **atrocious felony.** (1814) *Archaic.* A serious, usu. cruel felony involving personal violence. • The common practice today is to refer to the specific type of crime alleged (e.g., first-degree murder or aggravated sexual assault).

> **serious felony.** (1874) A major felony, such as burglary of a residence or an assault that causes great bodily injury. • In many jurisdictions, a defendant's prior serious-felony convictions can be used to enhance another criminal charge.

> **substantive felony.** See *substantive offense* under OFFENSE (1).

> **treason felony.** See TREASON FELONY.

> **violent felony.** See *violent offense* under OFFENSE (1).

2. *Hist.* At common law, an offense for which conviction results in forfeiture of the defendant's lands or goods (or both) to the Crown, regardless of whether any capital or other punishment is mandated. • At early common law, the term *felony* included any offense for which a defendant who fled before trial could be summarily convicted, attainted, and outlawed, or that carried a right of appeal after conviction. Although treason carried the same penalties as a common-law felony, it was usu. defined as a separate class of crime. **3.** *Hist. Feudal law.* A grave act that resulted in the forfeiture of land granted by a superior.

felony-de-se. See SUICIDE (1).

felony injury to a child. The act of causing or allowing a child to suffer in circumstances likely to produce great bodily harm or death, or inflicting unjustifiable pain or mental suffering in those circumstances.

felony murder. See MURDER.

felony-murder rule. (1943) The doctrine holding that any death resulting from the commission or attempted commission of a felony is murder. • Most states restrict this rule to inherently dangerous felonies such as rape, arson, robbery, and burglary. Cf. MISDEMEANOR-MANSLAUGHTER RULE.

FEMA. *abbr.* FEDERAL EMERGENCY MANAGEMENT AGENCY.

female genital mutilation. (1979) **1.** Female circumcision. **2.** The act of cutting, or cutting off, one or more female sexual organs. • Female genital mutilation is practiced primarily among certain tribes in Africa, but it also occurs among some immigrant populations in the United States and in other Western nations. There are three commonly identified types: *sunna*, in which the hood of the clitoris is cut off; *excision*, in which the entire clitoris is cut off; and *infibulation*, in which the clitoris, the labia minora, and much of the labia majora are cut off. In the United States, Congress has outlawed female genital mutilation, specifically prohibiting the use of a cultural defense for persons accused of performing the act. 18 USCA § 16. — Abbr. FGM. See CULTURAL DEFENSE.

fem-crit. See CRIT.

feme (fem), *n.* (16c) [Law French] *Archaic.* **1.** A woman. **2.** A wife. — Also spelled *femme.*

feme covert (fem **kəv**-ərt). [Law French "covered woman"] *Archaic.* A married woman. • The notion, as Blackstone put it, was that the husband was the one "under whose wing, protection, and cover, she performs every thing." 1 William Blackstone, *Commentaries on the Law of England* 430 (1766). See COVERTURE.

feme sole (fem **sohl**). [Law French] *Archaic.* **1.** An unmarried woman. **2.** A married woman handling the affairs of her separate estate. — Also termed (in sense 2) *feme sole trader; feme sole merchant.*

femicide (fem-ə-sɪd). (19c) **1.** The killing of a woman. **2.** One who kills a woman.

feminist jurisprudence. See JURISPRUDENCE.

femme. See FEME.

fence, *n.* (14c) **1.** A person who receives stolen goods, usu. with the intent to sell them in a legitimate market. **2.** A place where stolen goods are sold. See RECEIVING STOLEN PROPERTY. **3.** LAWFUL FENCE. **4.** *Scots law.* The formal warning to not interrupt or obstruct judicial or legislative proceedings. **5.** *Scots law.* A penalty of forfeiture prescribed in a statute or a contract.

fence, *vb.* **1.** To sell (stolen property) to a fence. **2.** *Scots law.* To open (a legislative or judicial sitting) by warning persons against obstructing or interrupting the legislature or court. **3.** *Scots law.* To threaten with forfeiture as a consequence of violating a law or breaching a contractual promise.

fencing patent. See PATENT (3).

feneration (fen-ə-**ray**-shən). (16c) *Hist.* **1.** The act or practice of lending money with interest. **2.** USURY.

feod (fyood). **1.** See FEE (2). **2.** See FEUD.

feodal (**fyoo**-dəl), *adj.* See FEUDAL.

feodal action. See FEUDAL ACTION.

feodality (fyoo-**dal**-ə-tee). See FEALTY.

feodal system. See FEUDALISM.

feodary (**fyoo**-də-ree). (15c) *Hist.* An officer of the Court of Wards who traveled with the escheator from county to county in order to receive royal rents and estimate the value of land tenures for the Crown. See COURT OF WARDS AND LIVERIES.

feodatory (**fyoo**-də-tor-ee). See FEUDATORY.

feodi firma (**fee**-ə-dɪ *or* **fyoo**-dɪ fər-mə). See FEE FARM.

feoff (fef *or* feef), *vb.* See ENFEOFF.

feoffee (fef-ee *or* feef-ee). (15c) The transferee of an estate in fee simple; the recipient of a fief.

feoffee to uses. *Hist.* A person to whom land is conveyed for the use of a third party (called a *cestui que use*); one who holds legal title to land for the benefit of another. See CESTUI QUE USE; GRANT TO USES. Cf. TRUSTEE (1).

feoffer. See FEOFFOR.

feoffment (fef-mənt *or* feef-mənt). (14c) *Hist.* **1.** The act of conveying a freehold estate; a grant of land in fee simple. — Also termed *feoffment with livery of seisin.* **2.** The land so granted. **3.** The charter that transfers the land. — Also termed *deed of feoffment.*

feoffment to uses. An enfeoffment of land to one person for the use of a third party. • The feoffee was bound in conscience to hold the land according to the prescribed use and could derive no benefit from the holding.

feoffment with livery of seisin. See FEOFFMENT (1).

feoffor (fef- *or* feef-ər *or* -or). The transferor of an estate in fee simple. — Also spelled *feoffer.*

ferae bestiae (**feer**-ee bes-tee-ee). [Latin] *Roman law.* Wild beasts. • Since a wild animal belonged to no one (*res nullius*), its captor acquired ownership by *occupatio*. See OCCUPATIO.

ferae naturae (**feer**-ee nə-**tyoor**-ee). [Latin "of a wild nature"] **1.** *adj.* (Of animals) wild; untamed; undomesticated. **2.** *n.* Wild animals. See RULE OF CAPTURE (2).

feral animal. See ANIMAL.

FERC (fərk). *abbr.* FEDERAL ENERGY REGULATORY COMMISSION.

FERC-out clause. *Oil & gas.* A provision in a contract to sell natural gas specifying that if a regulatory agency does not allow the price paid to the producer to be passed on to consumers, either the contract price will be reduced accordingly or the contract will be terminated. — Also termed *regulatory-out clause.*

Feres doctrine (**feer**-is *or* feer-eez *or* fer-ez). *Torts.* The rule that a member of the military is barred from recovering damages from the United States on a claim brought under the Federal Tort Claims Act for injuries sustained in military service. *Feres v. United States*, 340 U.S. 135, 71 S.Ct. 153 (1950). — Also termed *Feres rule.* See ACTIVITY INCIDENT TO SERVICE.

ferial day. See DAY.

fermer. [Law French] *Hist.* **1.** A lessee, esp. one who holds lands for agricultural purposes. **2.** One who holds something (such as land or an incorporeal right) by the term.

FERPA. *abbr.* FAMILY EDUCATIONAL RIGHTS AND PRIVACY ACT.

ferry, *n.* (bef. 12c) **1.** A boat or vessel used to carry persons or property across water, usu. with fixed terminals and short distances. **2.** The commercial transportation of persons or property across water. **3.** The place where a ferry passes across water, including the continuation of the highway on both sides of the water. **4.** The right, usu. exclusive, given by government franchise, to carry persons or property across water for a fee. — Also termed *ferry franchise.*

ferry, *vb.* To carry persons or property, usu. across water, for a fee.

ferry franchise. See FERRY (4).

fertile-octogenarian rule. (1856) The legal fiction, assumed under the rule against perpetuities, that a woman can become pregnant as long as she is alive. ● The case that gave rise to this fiction was *Jee v. Audley*, 1 Cox 324, 29 Eng. Rep. 1186 (ch. 1787). *See* W. Barton Leach, *Perpetuities: New Hampshire Defertilizes Octogenarians,* 77 Harv. L. Rev. 729 (1963). — Also termed *presumption-of-fertility rule.*

Festo doctrine. (2003) *Patents.* The rule that the voluntary narrowing of a patent claim may give rise to prosecution-history estoppel. *Festo Corp. v. Shoketsu Kinzoku Kogyo Kabushiki Co.*, 304 F.3d 1289 (Fed. Cir. 2003).

festuca (fes-**tyoo**-kə). *Hist.* A rod, staff, or stick used as a pledge (or *gage*) of good faith by a party to a contract or as a token of conveyance of land. ● In Roman law, a festuca was a symbol of ownership. — Also termed *fistuca; vindicta.* See LIVERY OF SEISIN.

festum (**fes**-təm). [Latin] A feast-day, holiday, or festival.

fetal alcohol syndrome. A variety of birth defects caused by the mother's alcohol consumption during pregnancy. ● The birth defects include facial abnormalities, mental retardation, and growth deficiencies. — Abbr. FAS.

fetiales (fee-shee-**ay**-leez), *n. pl. Roman law.* The order of priests whose duties concerned international relations and treaties, including the declaration of war and peace. — Also spelled *feciales.*

fetial law (fee-shəl). (16c) *Roman law.* A branch of law concerned with matters (such as treaties, embassies, and war declarations) affecting relations between peoples or nations. — Also spelled *fecial law.* — Also termed *jus fetiale.*

feticide (fee-tə-sīd). (1842) **1.** The act or an instance of killing a fetus, usu. by assaulting and battering the mother; esp., the act of unlawfully causing the death of a fetus. **2.** An intentionally induced miscarriage. — Also spelled *foeticide.* — Also termed *child destruction.* Cf. INFANTICIDE (1). — **feticidal,** *adj.*

fetter, *n.* (*usu. pl.*) (bef. 12c) A chain or shackle for the feet. — **fetter,** *vb.*

fettering of property. The act of making the disposition or ownership of property more complex so that those with separate interests must cooperate if they are to handle their interests reasonably. ● Fettering of property occurs whenever ownership is split into two or more interests, as when present and future interests are divided or when a tenancy in common is created.

fetus. (14c) A developing but unborn mammal, esp. in the latter stages of development. — Also spelled *foetus.* Cf. EMBRYO; ZYGOTE.

feud, *n.* (15c) *Hist.* **1.** A heritable estate in land conveyed from a feudal superior to a grantee or tenant, held on the condition of rendering services to the superior.

   impartible feud. An indivisible feud; a feud not subject to partition.

   improper feud. A nonmilitary feud; a feud that is base or servile in nature.

   proper feud. A feud based on military service.

2. The interest of the tenant in the land conveyed. **3.** The land itself conveyed. — Also termed (in senses 1, 2 & 3) *fee; fief; feod; feude; feudum.* **4.** An enmity or private war existing between families or clans, esp. as a result of a murder.

   blood feud. A state of hostility between families in which one family seeks to avenge the killing of one of its members by killing a member of the other family. See VENDETTA.

feudal, *adj.* (17c) **1.** Of, relating to, or growing out of feudalism <feudal law>. **2.** Of or relating to a feud <feudal tenure>. — Also spelled (archaically) *feodal.* Cf. ALLODIAL.

feudal action. *Hist.* A real action; an action that concerned only real property.

feudalism (**fyood**-əl-iz-əm). (19c) **1.** A landholding system, particularly applying to medieval Europe, in which all are bound by their status in a hierarchy of reciprocal obligations of service and defense. • The lord was obligated to give the vassal (1) some land, (2) protection, and (3) justice. The lord guaranteed the quiet occupation of the land by the vassal and guaranteed to do right if the vassal became involved in a dispute. In return, the vassal owed the lord some type of service, called "tenure" (literally "means of holding"), because the different types of service were the methods by which the vassals held the property. **2.** The social, political, and economic system of medieval Europe. — Also termed *feudal system; feodal system.* — **feudalistic,** *adj.*

feudal law. *Hist.* The real-property law of land tenures that prevailed in England, esp. after the Norman Conquest.

feudal system. See FEUDALISM.

feudary. See FEUDATORY.

feudatory, *adj.* (16c) *Hist.* (Of a vassal) owing feudal allegiance to a lord.

feudatory, *n.* (17c) *Hist.* The grantee of a feud; the vassal or tenant who held an estate by feudal service. — Also termed *feudary; feodatory.*

feude. See FEUD.

feudist. (17c) A writer on feuds (for example, Cujacius, Spelman, Craig).

feuholding (**fyoo**-hohl-ding). *Hist.* A tenancy held by rendering produce or money instead of military service. — Also written *feu holding.*

ff. *abbr.* **1.** And the pages following. **2.** (*often cap.*) FRAGMENTA.

FGA. *abbr.* **1.** Free from general average. **2.** Foreign general average.

FGM. *abbr.* FEMALE GENITAL MUTILATION.

FHA. *abbr.* **1.** FARMERS HOME ADMINISTRATION. **2.** FEDERAL HOUSING ADMINISTRATION.

FHA mortgage. See MORTGAGE.

FHEO. *abbr.* OFFICE OF FAIR HOUSING AND EQUAL OPPORTUNITY.

FHLB. *abbr.* FEDERAL HOME LOAN BANK.

FHLBB. *abbr.* FEDERAL HOME LOAN BANK BOARD.

FHLMC. *abbr.* FEDERAL HOME LOAN MORTGAGE CORPORATION.

FHWA. *abbr.* FEDERAL HIGHWAY ADMINISTRATION.

fiancer (fyah*n*-**say**), *vb.* [Law French] To pledge one's faith.

fiat (**fee**-aht *or* **fee**-at *or* **fI**-at *or* **fI**-ət), *n.* [Latin "let it be done"] (17c) **1.** An order or decree, esp. an arbitrary one <judicial fiat>. **2.** A court decree, esp.

one relating to a routine matter such as scheduling <the court requires all motions to contain a fiat — to be filled in by the court — setting the hearing date>. — Also termed *fiaunt.*

fiat justitia (**fI**-at jəs-**tish**-ee-ə). [Latin] *Hist.* Let justice be done. • This phrase signaled the Crown's commission to the House of Lords to hear an appeal.

fiat money. See MONEY.

FICA (**fI**-kə). *abbr.* FEDERAL INSURANCE CONTRIBUTIONS ACT.

fickle-fiduciary rule. The principle that a partner or employee who breaches a fiduciary duty should forfeit all compensation, bonuses, and other benefits received for as long as the breach continues. • The rule usu. applies to a person who engages in or assists a competing business, or resigns from employment to set up or work for a competing business. Traditionally, mitigating factors, including the absence of harm to the employer or partnership, are not considered in applying the rule. But some courts have found that if a strict application would produce unjustly harsh results, mitigating factors must be weighed.

fictio juris. See LEGAL FICTION.

fiction. See LEGAL FICTION.

fictional action. See *collusive action* under ACTION (4).

fiction of law. See LEGAL FICTION.

fictitious, *adj.* (17c) Of or relating to a fiction, esp. a legal fiction.

fictitious action. See ACTION (4).

fictitious issue. See FEIGNED ISSUE.

fictitious name. 1. See ASSUMED NAME. **2.** See ALIAS (1). **3.** See JOHN DOE.

fictitious party. See PARTY (2).

fictitious-payee rule. *Commercial law.* The principle that if a drawer or maker issues commercial paper to a payee whom the drawer or maker does not actually intend to have any interest in the instrument, an ensuing forgery of the payee's name will be effective to pass good title to later transferees. — Also termed *padded-payroll rule.*

fictitious person. See *artificial person* under PERSON (3).

fictitious promise. See *implied promise* under PROMISE.

fictitious seisin. See *seisin in law* under SEISIN.

fide-committee. A beneficiary; CESTUI QUE TRUST. — Also termed *fidei-commissarius.*

fidei-commissarius. See CESTUI QUE TRUST.

fidei-commissary (fI-dee-I **kom**-ə-ser-ee). See CESTUI QUE TRUST.

fideicommissary heir. See HEIR.

fideicommissary substitution. 1. SUBSTITUTION (6). 2. SUBSTITUTION (7).

fideicommissum (fı-dee-ı-kə-**mis**-əm). [Latin] (18c) 1. *Roman law.* A direction to an heir asking the heir as a matter of good faith to give some part of the inheritance, such as a particular object, or all the inheritance, to a third party. • A *fideicommissum* was a device to overcome some of the technicalities of the Roman will. Originally it created a mere moral obligation, but Augustus made it enforceable by legal process. 2. *Roman & civil law.* An arrangement similar to a trust by which a testator gave property to a person for the benefit of another who could not, by law, inherit property. • Over time, this device was used to tie up property for generations, and most civil jurisdictions now prohibit or limit it. For example, in Louisiana, an arrangement in which one person bequeaths property to a second with a charge to preserve it and, at death, to restore it to a third person is a prohibited *fideicommissum.* — Sometimes spelled *fidei-commissum.* Pl. *fideicommissa.*

fidejussion (fı-di-**jəsh**-ən). [fr. Latin *fidejussio*] (16c) *Roman law.* An act by which a person becomes an additional security for another. • The act does not remove the principal's liability but only adds to the surety's security. Fidejussion was one of the three types of adpromission, and the only type remaining in Justinian's law. — Also spelled *fidejussio; fideiussio.* See ADPROMISSION (1). — **fidejussionary,** *adj.*

fidejussor (fı-dee-**jəs**-or *or* -**jəs**-ər). (16c) 1. *Roman law.* (ital.) A guarantor; a person who binds himself to pay another's debt. 2. *Hist. Maritime law.* A person who acts as bail for a defendant in the Court of Admiralty. — Also spelled *fideiussor.* Cf. ADPROMISSOR. — **fidejussory,** *adj.*

fidelity and guaranty insurance. See *fidelity insurance* under INSURANCE.

fidelity bond. See BOND (2).

fidelity guaranty insurance. See *fidelity insurance* under INSURANCE.

fidelity insurance. See INSURANCE.

fidepromission (fı-dee-proh-**mish**-ən), *n.* [Latin "faith-promise"] (19c) *Roman law.* A contract of guaranty by stipulation. • Fidepromission was one of the three types of adpromission. See ADPROMISSION (1); STIPULATION (3). — **fidepromissor,** *n.*

fides (**fı**-deez). [Latin] Faith.

fiducia (fı-**d[y]oo**-shee-ə), *n.* [Latin "an entrusting"] *Roman law.* An early form of transfer of title by way of mortgage, deposit, etc., with a provision for reconveyance upon payment of the debt, termination of the deposit, etc.

fiducial, *adj.* (16c) Of, relating to, or characterized by confidence in and reliance on another person or thing <there must be a fiducial bond between a patient and a doctor>.

fiducial relationship. See *trust relationship* under RELATIONSHIP.

fiduciarius heres (fı-d[y]oo-shee-**air**-ee-əs **heer**-eez). [Latin "fiduciary heir"] *Roman law.* A person formally named an heir in a testament, but in a fiduciary capacity, and charged to deliver the succession to the person designated by the testament.

fiduciarius tutor (fı-d[y]oo-shee-**air**-ee-əs t[y]oo-tər). *Roman law.* A fiduciary guardian; a person who by fulfilling a trust to free someone in power became his or her guardian.

fiduciary (fı-**d[y]oo**-shee-er-ee), *n.* (17c) 1. A person who is required to act for the benefit of another person on all matters within the scope of their relationship; one who owes to another the duties of good faith, trust, confidence, and candor <the corporate officer is a fiduciary to the corporation>. 2. One who must exercise a high standard of care in managing another's money or property <the beneficiary sued the fiduciary for investing in speculative securities>. — **fiduciary,** *adj.*

> *dilatory fiduciary* (**dil**-ə-tor-ee). A trustee or other fiduciary who is unreasonably slow in administering an estate.

> *successor fiduciary.* A fiduciary who is appointed to succeed or replace a prior one.

> *temporary fiduciary.* An interim fiduciary appointed by the court until a regular fiduciary can be appointed.

fiduciary bond. See BOND (2).

fiduciary contract. *Hist.* An agreement by which one party delivers something to another on condition that the second party will return the thing to the first.

fiduciary debt. A debt founded on or arising from a fiduciary relationship, rather than from a solely contractual relationship.

fiduciary duty. See DUTY (2).

fiduciary heir. See HEIR.

fiduciary-out clause. *Mergers & acquisitions.* A merger-agreement provision that allows the target corporation to terminate the agreement without committing a breach if a specified condition occurs. • The most common condition is the receipt of a more favorable offer, but other conditions may also be specified.

fiduciary relationship. See RELATIONSHIP.

fiduciary-shield doctrine. *Corporations.* The principle that a corporate officer's act cannot be the basis for jurisdiction over the officer in an individual capacity.

fief (feef), *n.* **1.** See FEE. **2.** See FEUD. • Metaphorically, the term refers to an area of dominion, esp. in a corporate or governmental bureaucracy.

fief-tenant. *Hist.* The holder of a fief or fee; a feeholder or freeholder.

field audit. See AUDIT.

field book. A log or book containing a surveyor's notes that are made on-site and that describe by course and distance the running of the property lines and the establishment of the corners of a parcel of land.

Field Code. The New York Code of Procedure of 1848, which was the first comprehensive Anglo-American code of civil procedure and served as a model for the Federal Rules of Civil Procedure. • It was drafted by David Dudley Field (1805–1894), a major law-reformer. See *code pleading* under PLEADING (2).

field notes. The notes in a surveyor's field book.

field of invention. See CLASSIFICATION OF PATENTS (2).

field of search. See CLASSIFICATION OF PATENTS (2).

field-of-use restriction. *Intellectual property.* A license provision restricting the licensee's use of the licensed property to a defined product or service market or to a designated geographical area.

field sobriety test. See SOBRIETY TEST.

field stop. See STOP AND FRISK.

field-warehouse financing agreement. The loan agreement in a field-warehousing arrangement.

field warehousing. An inventory-financing method by which a merchant pledges its inventory, which is in the possession of a third person (a warehouser). • This is a method of financing an inventory that cannot economically be delivered to the creditor or third party. The borrower segregates part of the inventory and places it under the nominal control of a lender or third party, so that the lender has a possessory interest. Cf. *floor-plan financing* under FINANCING; PLEDGE.

fieri facias (fī-ə-rī fay-shee-əs). [Latin "that you cause to be done"] (15c) A writ of execution that directs a marshal or sheriff to seize and sell a defendant's property to satisfy a money judgment. — Abbr. *fi. fa.*; *Fi. Fa.* Cf. LEVARI FACIAS.

fieri facias de bonis ecclesiasticis (fī-ə-rī fay-shee-əs dee boh-nis e-klee-z[h]ee-as-tə-sis). [Latin "that you cause to be made of the ecclesiastical goods"] *Hist.* A writ of execution — used when the defendant was a beneficed clerk who had no lay fee — that commanded the bishop to satisfy the judgment from the ecclesiastical goods and chattels of the defendant within the diocese. • This was accomplished by issuing a sequestration to levy the debt out of the defendant's benefice. This writ was issued after a *fieri facias* had been returned *nulla bona.*

fieri facias de bonis propriis (fī-ə-rī fay-shee-əs dee boh-nis proh-pree-is). [Latin "that you cause to be made of his own goods"] *Hist.* A writ that executes on an executor's property when a writ *fieri facias de bonis testatoris* is returned by the sheriff *nulla bona* or *devastavit* (a wasting of the testator's goods by the executor).

fieri facias de bonis testatoris (fī-ə-rī fay-shee-əs dee boh-nis tes-tə-tor-is). [Latin "that you cause to be made of the testator's goods"] *Hist.* A writ of execution served on an executor for a debt incurred by the testator.

fieri feci (fī-ə-rī fee-sī). [Latin "I have caused to be made"] *Hist.* A sheriff's return on a *fieri facias* where the sheriff has collected, in whole or in part, the sum to be levied on. • The return is usu. expressed by the word "satisfied."

fi. fa. (*sometimes cap.*) *abbr.* FIERI FACIAS.

FIFO (fī-foh). *abbr.* FIRST-IN, FIRST-OUT.

FIFRA. *abbr.* Federal Insecticide, Fungicide, and Rodenticide Act. 7 USCA §§ 136–136y.

Fifteenth Amendment. The constitutional amendment, ratified in 1870, guaranteeing all citizens the right to vote regardless of race, color, or prior condition of servitude.

Fifth Amendment. The constitutional amendment, ratified with the Bill of Rights in 1791, providing that a person cannot be (1) required to answer for a capital or otherwise infamous offense unless a grand jury issues an indictment or presentment, (2) subjected to double jeopardy, (3) compelled to engage in self-incrimination on a criminal matter, (4) deprived of life, liberty, or property without due process of law, or (5) deprived of private property for public use without just compensation.

Fifth Amendment, pleading the. See TAKE THE FIFTH.

Fifty Decisions. Justinian's rulings that settled controversies and eliminated obsolete rules in the law. • The decisions were made in preparation for *Justinian's Digest.* — Also termed (in Latin) *Quinquaginta Decisiones.*

50 percent plus one. See HALF PLUS ONE.

50-percent rule. (1975) The principle that liability for negligence is apportioned in accordance with the percentage of fault that the fact-finder assigns to each party, that the plaintiff's recovery will be reduced by the percentage of negligence assigned to the plaintiff, and that the plaintiff's recovery is barred if the plaintiff's percentage of fault is 50% or more. — Also termed *modified-comparative-negligence doctrine.* Cf. PURE-COMPARATIVE-NEGLIGENCE DOCTRINE. See *comparative negligence* under NEGLIGENCE; APPORTIONMENT OF LIABILITY.

fighting age. See AGE.

fighting words. (1917) **1.** Inflammatory speech that might not be protected by the First Amendment's free-speech guarantee because it might incite a violent response. **2.** Inflammatory speech that is pleadable in mitigation — but not in defense — of a suit for assault. — Also termed *fighting talk.*

file, *n.* (17c) **1.** A court's complete and official record of a case <the associate went to the courthouse to verify that the motion is in the file>. **2.** A lawyer's complete record of a case <the paralegal stored the file in three drawers in her office>. **3.** A portion or section of a lawyer's case record <the janitor found the correspondence file behind the copy machine>. **4.** A case <Jonah was assigned the Watson file after Amy left the firm>.

file, *vb.* (16c) **1.** To deliver a legal document to the court clerk or record custodian for placement into the official record <Tuesday is the deadline for filing a reply brief>. — Also termed (in BrE) *lodge.* **2.** To commence a lawsuit <the seller threatened to file against the buyer>. **3.** To record or deposit something in an organized retention system or container for preservation and future reference <please file my notes under the heading "research">. **4.** *Parliamentary law.* To acknowledge and deposit (a report, communication, or other document) for information and reference only without necessarily taking any substantive action.

filed-rate doctrine. A common-law rule forbidding a regulated entity, usu. a common carrier, to charge a rate other than the one on file with the appropriate federal regulatory authority, such as (formerly) the Interstate Commerce Commission. — Also termed *filed-tariff doctrine.* See TARIFF (3).

file history. See FILE WRAPPER.

file-transport protocol. A set of programmed rules enabling computers to exchange files over the Internet. — Abbr. FTP.

file wrapper. *Patents & Trademarks.* The complete record of proceedings in the Patent and Trademark Office from the initial application to the issued patent or trademark; specif., a patent or trademark-registration application together with all documentation, correspondence, and any other record of proceedings before the PTO concerning that application. — Also termed *file history*; *prosecution history.* Cf. CERTIFIED FILE HISTORY.

file-wrapper continuation. 1. See CONTINUATION. **2.** See CONTINUATION-IN-PART. — Abbr. FWC.

file-wrapper continuation application. 1. See CONTINUATION. **2.** See CONTINUATION-IN-PART.

file-wrapper estoppel. See *prosecution-history estoppel* under ESTOPPEL.

filial consortium. See CONSORTIUM.

filiality. See FILIATION (1).

filiated father. See FATHER.

filiation (fil-ee-**ay**-shən). (15c) **1.** The fact or condition of being a son or daughter; relationship of a child to a parent. • Despite Bentham's protest (see below), *filiation* is usual in this sense. — Also termed *filiality.* **2.** Judicial determination of paternity. See PATERNITY; *filiated father* under FATHER.

filiation order. See ORDER (2).

filibuster (**fil**-ə-bəs-tər), *n.* (18c) **1.** A dilatory tactic, esp. prolonged and often irrelevant speechmaking, employed in an attempt to obstruct legislative action. • The filibuster is common in the U.S. Senate, where the right to debate is usu. unlimited and where a filibuster can be terminated only by a cloture vote of two-thirds of all members. **2.** In a deliberative body, a member in the minority who resorts to obstructive tactics to prevent the adoption of a measure or procedure that is favored by the majority. — Also termed *filibusterer.* **3.** *Hist.* A person who, together with others, works to invade and revolutionize a foreign state in disregard of international law. See CLOTURE. — **filibuster,** *vb.*

filicide (**fil**-i-sɪd). (17c) **1.** A person who kills his or her own child. **2.** The act of killing one's own child. Cf. INFANTICIDE.

filing, *n.* (18c) A particular document (such as a pleading) in the file of a court clerk or record custodian <the lawyer argued that the plaintiff's most recent filing was not germane to the issue before the court>.

filing date. See DATE.

filing fee. (1864) A sum of money required to be paid to the court clerk before a proceeding can start.

filing status. *Tax.* One of the four categories under which a person files an income tax return. • Under federal law, the four categories are: (1) single; (2) head of household; (3) married filing a joint return; and (4) married filing separate returns.

fill a blank. *Parliamentary law.* To replace a blank in a motion with one or more proposals from the floor. See BLANK.

fill-or-kill order. See ORDER (8).

finable (**fɪ**-nə-bəl), *adj.* (15c) Liable to a fine; subject to having to pay a fine. — Also spelled *fineable.*

final, *adj.* (14c) **1.** (Of a judgment at law) not requiring any further judicial action by the court that rendered judgment to determine the matter litigated; concluded. **2.** (Of an equitable decree) not requiring any further judicial action beyond supervising how the decree is carried out. • Once an order, judgment, or decree is final, it may be appealed on the merits. Cf. INTERLOCUTORY.

final and conclusive. Terminal and unappealable, except on grounds of procedural error, fraud, or mistake.

final agenda. See AGENDA.

final alimony. See *permanent alimony* under ALIMONY.

final and conclusive. See FINAL.

final appealable judgment. See *final judgment* under JUDGMENT.

final appealable order. See *final judgment* under JUDGMENT.

final argument. See CLOSING ARGUMENT.

final concord. See CONCORD.

final decision. See *final judgment* under JUDGMENT.

final-decision rule. See FINAL-JUDGMENT RULE.

final decree. See *final judgment* under JUDGMENT.

final injunction. See *permanent injunction* under INJUNCTION.

finalis concordia (fi-**nay**-lis kən-**kor**-dee-ə). [Latin] A final or conclusive agreement. See *final concord* under CONCORD; FINE (1).

finality doctrine. (1942) The rule that a court will not judicially review an administrative agency's action until it is final. — Also termed *final-order doctrine*; *doctrine of finality*; *principle of finality.* Cf. FINAL-JUDGMENT RULE; INTERLOCUTORY APPEALS ACT.

finality rule. See FINAL-JUDGMENT RULE.

final judgment. See JUDGMENT.

final-judgment rule. (1931) The principle that a party may appeal only from a district court's final decision that ends the litigation on the merits. • Under this rule, a party must raise all claims of error in a single appeal. — Also termed *final-decision rule*; *finality rule.* 28 USCA § 1291. See DEATH-KNELL DOCTRINE. Cf. FINALITY DOCTRINE; INTERLOCUTORY APPEALS ACT; DEATH-KNELL DOCTRINE.

final-offer arbitration. See ARBITRATION.

final office action. See OFFICE ACTION.

final order. See ORDER (2).

final-order doctrine. See FINALITY DOCTRINE.

final peace. See *final concord* under CONCORD.

final process. See PROCESS.

final receiver's receipt. The government's acknowledgment that it has received full payment from a person for public land, that it holds the legal title in trust for the person, and that it will in due course issue the person a land patent.

final rejection. See REJECTION.

final settlement. See SETTLEMENT (2).

final speech. See CLOSING ARGUMENT.

final submission. See CLOSING ARGUMENT.

finance, *n.* (18c) **1.** That aspect of business concerned with the management of money, credit, banking, and investments <after a brief career in finance, Andrea decided to go to law school>. **2.** The science or study of the management of money, etc. <Bill sought a degree in finance because he wanted to be an investment banker>.

finance, *vb.* (19c) To raise or provide funds.

finance bill. See BILL (6).

finance charge. An additional payment, usu. in the form of interest, paid by a retail buyer for the privilege of purchasing goods or services in installments. • This phrase is increasingly used as a euphemism for *interest.* See INTEREST (3).

finance company. (20c) A nonbank company that deals in loans either by making them or by purchasing notes from another company that makes the loans directly to borrowers.

commercial finance company. A finance company that makes loans to manufacturers and wholesalers. — Also termed *commercial credit company.*

consumer finance company. A finance company that deals directly with consumers in extending credit. — Also termed *small-loan company.*

sales finance company. A finance company that does not deal directly with consumers but instead purchases consumer installment paper arising from the sale of consumer durables "on time." — Also termed *acceptance company.*

finance lease. See LEASE.

finance officer. See TREASURER.

financial accounting. See ACCOUNTING (1).

Financial Accounting Standards Board. The independent body of accountants responsible for establishing, interpreting, and improving standards for financial accounting and reporting. — Abbr. FASB.

financial asset. See *current asset* under ASSET.

financial contract. See CONTRACT.

financial-core membership. Union membership in which a private-company employee pays the union's initiation fees and periodic dues but is not a full union member. • Financial-core membership is allowed only in states without a right-to-work law, where a union-security contract clause can require employees to pay financial-core membership dues but cannot require full union membership. The dues are limited to the amount required to support the union's representational activities, such as collective bargaining.

See Communications Workers of Am. v. Beck, 487 U.S. 735, 744, 108 S.Ct. 2641, 2648 (1988). — Also termed (in public-employment sector) *fair-share membership; agency-shop membership.* See UNION-SECURITY CLAUSE.

Financial Crimes Enforcement Network. A unit in the U.S. Department of the Treasury responsible for supporting law-enforcement efforts against domestic and international financial crimes. — Abbr. FinCEN.

financial deregulation. See DEREGULATION.

financial futures. See FUTURES (1).

financial institution. (1821) A business, organization, or other entity that manages money, credit, or capital, such as a bank, credit union, savings-and-loan association, securities broker or dealer, pawnbroker, or investment company.

financial interest. See INTEREST (2).

financial intermediary. (1873) A financial entity — usu. a commercial bank — that advances the transfer of funds between borrowers and lenders, buyers and sellers, and investors and savers.

Financial Management Service. A unit in the U.S. Department of the Treasury responsible for developing and managing systems for moving the U.S. government's cash by assisting other agencies in collecting and disbursing funds; collecting and publishing financial information; and collecting delinquent debts. — Abbr. FMS.

financial market. See MARKET.

financial planner. A person whose business is advising clients about personal finances and investments. • Upon completing a certification program, such a person is called a *certified financial planner.* — Abbr. CFP.

financial report. See FINANCIAL STATEMENT.

financial-responsibility act. (1930) A state statute conditioning license and registration of motor vehicles on proof of insurance or other financial accountability.

financial-responsibility clause. (1946) *Insurance.* A provision in an automobile insurance policy stating that the insured has at least the minimum amount of liability insurance coverage required by a state's financial-responsibility law.

financial restatement. A report correcting material errors in a financial statement, esp. to adjust profits and losses after an accounting procedure has been disallowed.

financials. *Slang.* Financial statements.

financial secretary. 1. See SECRETARY. **2.** See TREASURER.

Financial Services Agency. The regulatory body that oversees the United Kingdom's financial-services industry, including exchanges and related entities. — Formerly termed *Securities and Investment Board.*

financial statement. 1. A balance sheet, income statement, or annual report that summarizes an individual's or organization's financial condition on a specified date or for a specified period by reporting assets and liabilities. — Also termed *financial report.* Cf. FINANCING STATEMENT.

certified financial statement. A financial statement examined and reported by an independent public or certified public accountant. SEC Rule 12b-2 (17 CFR § 240.12b-2).

consolidated financial statement. The financial report of a company and all its subsidiaries combined as if they were a single entity.

normalized financial statement. A statement in which some components have been adjusted to exclude anomalies, such as unusual and nonrecurring elements, and nonoperating assets or liabilities, so the statement may be compared with others.

2. INCOME-AND-EXPENSE DECLARATION.

financing, *n.* (19c) **1.** The act or process of raising or providing funds. **2.** Funds that are raised or provided. — **finance,** *vb.*

asset-based financing. A method of lending in which lenders and investors look primarily to the cash flow from a particular asset for repayment.

construction financing. See *interim financing.*

debt financing. The raising of funds by issuing bonds or notes or by borrowing from a financial institution.

equity financing. **1.** The raising of funds by issuing capital securities (shares in the business) rather than making loans or selling bonds. **2.** The capital so raised.

floor-plan financing. A loan that is secured by merchandise and paid off as the goods are sold. • Usu. such a loan is given by a manufacturer to a retailer or other dealer (as a car dealer). — Also termed *floor planning.* Cf. FIELD WAREHOUSING.

gap financing. Interim financing used to fund the difference between a current loan and a loan to be received in the future, esp. between two long-term loans. See *bridge loan* under LOAN.

interim financing. A short-term loan secured to cover certain major expenditures, such as construction costs, until permanent financing is obtained. — Also termed *construction financing.*

internal financing. A funding method using funds generated through the company's operations rather than from stock issues or bank loans.

link financing. The obtaining of credit by depositing funds in another's bank account to aid the other in obtaining a loan.

outside financing. The raising of funds by selling stocks (equity financing) or bonds (debt financing).

permanent financing. A long-term loan obtained to repay an interim loan, such as a mortgage loan that is used to repay a construction loan.

project financing. A method of funding in which the lender looks primarily to the money generated by a single project as security for the loan. • This type of financing is usu. used for large, complex, and expensive single-purpose projects such as power plants, chemical-processing plants, mines, and toll roads. The lender is usu. paid solely or primarily from the money generated by the contracts for the facility's output (sometimes paid by customers directly into an account maintained by the lender), such as the electricity sold by a power plant. The lender usu. requires the facility to be developed and owned by a special-purpose entity (sometimes called a bankruptcy-remote entity), which can be a corporation, limited partnership, or other legal entity, that is permitted to perform no function other than developing, owning, and operating the facility. See SINGLE-PURPOSE PROJECT; SPECIAL-PURPOSE ENTITY; BANKRUPTCY-REMOTE ENTITY.

financing agency. See AGENCY (1).

financing statement. (1954) A document filed in the public records to notify third parties, usu. prospective buyers and lenders, of a secured party's security interest in goods or real property. See UCC § 9-102(a)(39). Cf. FINANCIAL STATEMENT.

FinCEN. *abbr.* FINANCIAL CRIMES ENFORCEMENT NETWORK.

find, *vb.* (bef. 12c) To determine a fact in dispute by verdict or decision <find guilty> <found that no duty existed>. Cf. HOLD (2).

finder. (13c) **1.** An intermediary who brings together parties for a business opportunity, such as two companies for a merger, a borrower and a financial institution, an issuer and an underwriter of securities, or a seller and a buyer of real estate. • A finder differs from a broker-dealer because the finder merely brings two parties together to make their own contract, while a broker-dealer usu. participates in the negotiations. See INTERMEDIARY. **2.** A person who discovers an object, often a lost or mislaid chattel.

finder of fact. See FACT-FINDER.

finder's fee. (1937) **1.** The amount charged by one who brings together parties for a business opportunity. **2.** The amount charged by a person who locates a lost or missing item and returns it to its owner.

finder's-fee contract. (1959) An agreement between a finder and one of the parties to a business opportunity.

finding. See FINDING OF FACT.

finding of fact. (18c) A determination by a judge, jury, or administrative agency of a fact supported by the evidence in the record, usu. presented at the trial or hearing <he agreed with the jury's finding of fact that the driver did not stop before proceeding into the intersection>. — Often shortened to *finding.* See FACT-FINDER. Cf. CONCLUSION OF FACT; CONCLUSION OF LAW.

concurrent finding. (*usu. pl.*) Identical factual findings by two different tribunals on a specific issue of fact.

essential finding. *Military law.* A military tribunal's determination of a collateral pretrial motion.

general finding. An undifferentiated finding in favor of one party.

special finding. 1. (*usu. pl.*) A finding of the necessary and ultimate facts to support a judgment in favor of one party. **2.** *Military law.* A military tribunal's finding that directly relates to the determination of guilt or innocence.

fine, *n.* (13c) **1.** An amicable final agreement or compromise of a fictitious or actual suit to determine the true possessor of land. • The fine was formerly used as a form of conveyance to disentail an estate. — Also termed *final concord*; *finalis concordia.* See FOOT OF THE FINE.

executed fine. *Hist.* A fine made on acknowledgment of the right of the grantee to land given to him as a gift from the grantor. • This was abolished in England in 1833. 3 & 4 Will. 4, ch. 74.

2. FINE FOR ALIENATION. **3.** A fee paid by a tenant to the landlord at the commencement of the tenancy to reduce the rent payments. **4.** *Hist.* A money payment from a tenant to the tenant's lord.

common fine. A sum of money due from a tenant to a lord to defray the cost of a court leet or to allow the litigants to try the action closer to home. — Also termed *head-silver.*

5. A pecuniary criminal punishment or civil penalty payable to the public treasury. — **fine,** *vb.*

day fine. A fine payable over time, usu. as a percentage of the defendant's earnings on a weekly or monthly basis.

excessive fine. (16c) **1.** *Criminal law.* A fine that is unreasonably high and disproportionate to the offense committed. • The Eighth Amendment proscribes excessive fines. An example of an excessive fine is a civil forfeiture in which the property was not an instrumentality of the crime and the worth of the property was not proportional to the owner's culpability. **2.** A fine or penalty that seriously impairs one's earning capacity, esp. from a business.

fresh fine. *Hist.* A fine levied within the past year.

fineable. See FINABLE.

Fine and Recovery Act. *Hist.* An English statute, enacted in 1833, that abolished the use of fines as a method of conveying title to land. 3 & 4 Will. 4, ch. 74. See FINE (1).

fine print. (1951) The part of an agreement or document — usu. in small, light print that is not easily noticeable — referring to disclaimers, restrictions, or limitations.

finger, *vb.* (1930) *Slang.* To identify (a person) as a perpetrator, usu. of a crime <in his grand-jury testimony, Vinson fingered Bauer as the gunman>.

finger pillory. See PILLORY.

fingerprint, *n.* (1859) **1.** The distinctive pattern of lines on a human fingertip <no two fingerprints are identical>. **2.** The impression of a fingertip made on any surface <the detective found several fingerprints on the knife>. **3.** An ink impression of the pattern of lines on a fingertip, usu. taken during the booking procedure after an arrest <after Dick had his fingerprints taken, he was put in the drunk tank>. — Also termed *print*; *thumbprint*. Cf. DNA IDENTIFICATION. — **fingerprint,** *vb.* — **fingerprinting,** *n.*

fingerprint claim. See PATENT CLAIM.

finis (fī-nis *or* fin-is). [Latin] (15c) *Hist.* **1.** Boundary or limit. **2.** The compromise of a fine of conveyance. See FINE (1). **3.** A fine, or payment of money made to satisfy a claim of criminal penalty.

FIO. *abbr.* Free in and out. • This bill-of-lading term means that the shipper supervises and pays for loading and unloading of cargo.

FIOS. *abbr.* Free in and out stowed. • This bill-of-lading term means that the shipper supervises and pays for loading, unloading, and stowing.

fire, *vb.* (1885) To discharge or dismiss a person from employment; to terminate as an employee.

firearm. (17c) A weapon that expels a projectile (such as a bullet or pellets) by the combustion of gunpowder or other explosive.

firebote. See *housebote* under BOTE (1).

firebug. See INCENDIARY (1).

firefighter's rule. A doctrine holding that a firefighter, police officer, or other emergency professional may not hold a person, usu. a property owner, liable for unintentional injuries suffered by the professional in responding to the situation created or caused by the person. — Also termed *fireman's rule.*

fire insurance. See INSURANCE.

fireman's rule. See FIREFIGHTER'S RULE.

fire ordeal. See *ordeal by fire* under ORDEAL.

fire sale. See SALE.

firing squad. (19c) **1.** A group of persons assembled to carry out a capital-punishment sentence by shooting the prisoner with high-powered rifles at the same time from a short distance. **2.** A military detachment that fires a salute, usu. during the burial ceremony for the person being honored.

firm, *n.* (18c) **1.** The title under which one or more persons conduct business jointly. **2.** The association by which persons are united for business purposes. • Traditionally, this term has referred to a partnership, as opposed to a company. But today it frequently refers to a company. See LAW FIRM.

firm bid. See BID (2).

firm-commitment underwriting. See UNDERWRITING.

firm offer. See *irrevocable offer* under OFFER.

firm opportunity. A law-firm lawyer's opportunity to profit individually from a venture from which the firm might benefit, as opposed to the individual lawyer, and as to which the lawyer must therefore defer to the firm and turn over any income to the firm.

firm-opportunity doctrine. See CORPORATE-OPPORTUNITY DOCTRINE.

First Amendment. The constitutional amendment, ratified with the Bill of Rights in 1791, guaranteeing the freedoms of speech, religion, press, assembly, and petition.

first-blush rule. The common-law principle that allows a court to set aside a verdict as excessive because the verdict causes the mind to immediately conclude that it resulted from passion or prejudice on the part of the jury.

first cause. See *proximate cause* under CAUSE (1).

first chair, *n.* (1952) *Slang.* The lead attorney in court for a given case <despite having worked at the firm for six years, the associate had yet to be first chair in a jury trial>. — **first-chair,** *vb.*

first cousin. See COUSIN (1).

first-degree, *adj.* See DEGREE (2).

first-degree amendment. See *primary amendment* under AMENDMENT (3).

first-degree manslaughter. See MANSLAUGHTER.

first-degree murder. See MURDER.

first-degree principal. See *principal in the first degree* under PRINCIPAL (2).

first-degree sexual conduct. (1979) Sexual battery that involves an aggravating factor, as when the perpetrator commits the offense against a minor or when the perpetrator commits the offense in the course of committing another crime, such as a burglary. — Also termed *criminal sexual conduct in the first degree*.

first devisee. See DEVISEE.

first-filed rule. See FIRST-TO-FILE RULE.

first-filing rule. See FIRST-TO-FILE RULE.

first fruits. 1. *Hist.* One year's profits from the land of a tenant *in capite*, payable to the Crown after the tenant's death. — Also termed *primer seisin*. **2.** *Hist. Eccles. law.* The first year's whole profits of a clergyman's benefice, paid by the incumbent to the Pope, or (after the break with Rome) to the Crown. ● This revenue was later termed "Queen Anne's Bounty" when it was converted to a fund to benefit the poor. — Sometimes written *first-fruits*. — Also termed *primitiae*; *primitive*; *annates*; *annats*; *Queen Anne's Bounty*.

firsthand knowledge. See *personal knowledge* under KNOWLEDGE.

first impression, case of. See CASE.

first-in, first-out. An accounting method that assumes that goods are sold in the order in which they were purchased — that is, the oldest items are sold first. — Abbr. FIFO. Cf. LAST-IN, FIRST-OUT; NEXT-IN, FIRST-OUT.

first instance, court of. See *trial court* under COURT.

first-inventor defense. *Patents.* In a suit alleging infringement of a business-method patent, a statutory affirmative defense made out by showing that the defendant was using the business method commercially for at least a year before the plaintiff filed the patent application. ● The First Inventor Defense Act of 1999 is codified at 35 USCA § 273.

first lien. See LIEN.

First Lord of the Admiralty. *Hist.* In Britain, a minister and one of the lord commissioners who presided over the navy. ● The First Lord was assisted by other lords, called Sea Lords, and various secretaries.

First Lord of the Treasury. *English law.* The chief officer in charge of the treasury. ● Today, this position is held by the Prime Minister.

first magistrate. See MAGISTRATE (1).

first meeting. *Archaic. Criminal law.* The first contact between a killer and a victim after the killer has been informed of the victim's insulting words or conduct that provoked the killing. ● If the killing occurred during the first meeting, a murder charge could be reduced to manslaughter. See HEAT OF PASSION.

first meeting of creditors. See *creditors' meeting* under MEETING.

first mortgage. See MORTGAGE.

first-mortgage bond. See BOND (3).

first name. See *personal name* under NAME.

first-named insured. See *primary insured* under INSURED.

first offender. See OFFENDER.

first office action. See OFFICE ACTION.

first option to buy. See RIGHT OF PREEMPTION.

first-party insurance. See INSURANCE.

first-past-the-post voting. See *plurality voting* under VOTING.

first policy year. *Insurance.* The first year of a life-insurance policy that is to be automatically renewed annually. ● This statutory phrase prohibits an insurer from using the policy's suicide exclusion as a defense — and refusing payment on the policy — when an insured commits suicide after the first year of the policy. The insurer can invoke the suicide exclusion as a defense to payment only if the insured commits suicide in the first policy year.

first purchaser. See PURCHASER (2).

first refusal, right of. See RIGHT OF FIRST REFUSAL.

first-sale doctrine. (1963) **1.** *Copyright.* The rule that the purchaser of a physical copy of a copyrighted work, such as a book or CD, may give or sell that copy to someone else without infringing the copyright owner's exclusive distribution rights. ● With regard to that physical copy, the copyright owner's distribution right is said to be exhausted. 17 USCA § 109(a). **2.** *Patents.* The principle that the buyer of a patented article has the right to use, repair, and resell the article without interference from the patentee. ● The patentee may still retain control of the article through terms in the license or sale contract. See PATENT-EXHAUSTION DOCTRINE.

first taker. See TAKER.

first-to-file rule. (1969) *Civil procedure.* **1.** The principle that, when two suits are brought by the same parties, regarding the same issues, in two courts of proper jurisdiction, the court that first acquires jurisdiction usu. retains the suit, to the exclusion of the other court. ● The court with the second-filed suit ordinarily stays proceedings or abstains. But an exception exists if the first-filed suit is brought merely in anticipation of the true plaintiff's suit and amounts to an improper attempt at forum-shopping. See ANTICIPATORY FILING. **2.** The doctrine allowing a party to a previously filed lawsuit to enjoin another from pursuing a later-filed action. — Also termed *first-filing rule*; *first-filed rule*; *priority-jurisdiction rule*.

first-to-file system. *Patents.* The practice of granting priority to the first person to file a patent application. • Most of the world uses a first-to-file patent system; the only major exception is the United States, which grants priority to the first inventor. Cf. FIRST-TO-INVENT SYSTEM.

first-to-invent system. *Patents.* The practice of awarding a patent to the first person to create an invention, rather than the first to file a patent application. • Because the first inventor is not necessarily the first person to file for a patent, an interference hearing is held to decide who is entitled to the patent. This system is used only in the United States. See CONCEPTION OF INVENTION; PRIORITY OF INVENTION. Cf. FIRST-TO-FILE SYSTEM.

first user. See SENIOR USER.

FISA. *abbr.* FOREIGN INTELLIGENCE SURVEILLANCE ACT.

FISC. *abbr.* UNITED STATES FOREIGN INTELLIGENCE SURVEILLANCE COURT.

fisc (fisk), *n.* [Latin *fiscus*] The public treasury. — Also spelled *fisk.*

fiscal (fis-kəl), *adj.* (16c) **1.** Of or relating to financial matters <fiscal year>. **2.** Of or relating to public finances or taxation <the city's sound fiscal policy>.

fiscal agent. See AGENT (2).

fiscal officer. See OFFICER (1).

fiscal period. See *fiscal year* under YEAR.

fiscal year. See YEAR.

fiscus (fis-kəs), *n.* [Latin "the basket" *or* "money-bag"] **1.** *Roman law.* The emperor's treasury. • In later Roman times, the term also included the treasury of the state. **2.** *Hist.* The treasury of a monarch (as the repository of forfeited property), a noble, or any private person. **3.** The treasury or property of the state as distinguished from the private property of the monarch.

fishery. (16c) **1.** A right or liberty of taking fish. • Fishery was an incorporeal hereditament under old English law. — Also termed *piscary.*

free fishery. An exclusive right of fishery, existing by grant or prescription from the monarch, to take fish in public water such as a river or an arm of the sea. — Also termed *libera piscaria.*

right of fishery. The right of persons to fish in public waters, subject to federal and state restrictions and regulations, such as fishing seasons, licensing, and catch limits.

several fishery. A right to fish in waters that are neither on one's own land nor on the land of a person who granted the right to fish.

2. A fishing ground.

common fishery. A fishing ground where all persons have a right to take fish. Cf. *common of piscary* under COMMON.

fishing expedition. An attempt, through broad discovery requests or random questions, to elicit information from another party in the hope that something relevant might be found; esp., such an attempt that exceeds the scope of discovery allowed by procedural rules. — Also termed *fishing trip.*

fish royal. *Hist.* Whales, sturgeon, and porpoises that, when thrown ashore or caught near the English coast, become Crown property.

fisk. See FISC.

fistuca. See FESTUCA.

fitness for a particular purpose. See *implied warranty of fitness for a particular purpose* under WARRANTY (2).

fitness hearing. See *transfer hearing* under HEARING.

Five Mile Act. *Hist.* A 1665 English act prohibiting Puritan ministers from teaching or coming within five miles of any town where they had held office if they refused to pledge that they would not seek to overturn the Church of England. • The Act was repealed in 1689.

501(c)(3) organization. See CHARITABLE ORGANIZATION.

529 plan. A state-sponsored plan administered by certain investment companies to allow parents and others to accumulate pretax income to pay for a beneficiary's (usu. a child's) college education. • Anyone can contribute to an account set up under 529 plan guidelines. Withdrawals made for educational purposes are taxed at the beneficiary's tax rate; other withdrawals trigger an additional 10% penalty. IRC (26 USCA) § 529.

fix, *n.* (1816) **1.** A dose of an illegal drug <the defendant testified that he robbed the store because he needed to buy a fix>. **2.** A navigational reading.

fix, *vb.* (14c) **1.** To announce (an exchange price, interest rate, etc.) <interest was fixed at 6%>. **2.** To establish (a person's liability or responsibility) <you cannot fix liability on the defendant without evidence>. **3.** To agree with another to establish (a price for goods or services), often illegally <representatives of Acme and Widget secretly met to fix prices for their companies' products>. See PRICE-FIXING. **4.** To influence (an action or outcome, esp. a sports event) by improper or illegal means <after losing the election, the challenger claimed that the incumbent had fixed the election>.

fix a day to which to adjourn. See *adjourn to a day certain* under ADJOURN.

fixation. *Copyright.* The process or result of recording a work of authorship in tangible form so that it can be copyrighted under federal law. • Fixation occurs, for instance, when a live television broadcast is transmitted and simultaneously recorded on videotape.

fix bail, *vb.* (18c) To set the amount and terms of bail <after hearing the officer's testimony, the judge fixed bail for the defendant at $100,000>. See BAIL.

fixed annuity. See ANNUITY.

fixed asset. See *capital asset* (1) under ASSET.

fixed-benefit plan. See *defined pension plan* under PENSION PLAN.

fixed capital. See CAPITAL.

fixed charge. See *fixed cost* under COST (1).

fixed cost. See COST (1).

fixed debt. See DEBT.

fixed-dollar investment. See INVESTMENT.

fixed expense. See *fixed cost* under COST (1).

fixed fee. See FEE (1).

fixed in a tangible medium of expression. *Copyright.* (Of a work) embodied in a physical form that is made by the author or under the author's authority and that is either permanent or stable enough to be perceived, reproduced, or otherwise communicated. ● A work consisting of sounds, images, or both that is being transmitted is "fixed" if it is recorded at the same time that it is transmitted.

fixed income. See INCOME.

fixed-income investment. See INVESTMENT.

fixed-income security. See SECURITY.

fixed liability. See *fixed debt* under DEBT.

fixed opinion. See OPINION (3).

fixed price. See PRICE.

fixed-price contract. See CONTRACT.

fixed-rate mortgage. See MORTGAGE.

fixed-return dividend. See DIVIDEND.

fixed sentence. See SENTENCE.

fixed sentencing. See *mandatory sentencing* under SENTENCING.

fixed-term lease. *Oil & gas.* An oil-and-gas lease for a fixed period of time, lacking the indefinite "so long thereafter" provision commonly found in such leases. Cf. HABENDUM CLAUSE.

fixed trust. See TRUST.

fixing a jury. See JURY-FIXING.

fixture. (18c) Personal property that is attached to land or a building and that is regarded as an irremovable part of the real property, such as a fireplace built into a home. See UCC § 9-102(a)(41). ● Historically, personal property becomes a fixture when it is physically fastened to or connected with the land or building and the fastening or connection was done to enhance the utility of the land or building. If personal property has been attached to the land or building and enhances only

the chattel's utility, it is not a fixture. For example, if bricks are purposely stacked to form a wall, a fixture results. But if the bricks are merely stacked for convenience until used for some purpose, they do not form a fixture. — Also termed *permanent fixture; immovable fixture.* Cf. IMPROVEMENT.

   agricultural fixture. A fixture erected on leased land for use in agricultural pursuits, such as tilling the land or keeping farm animals. ● These fixtures may or may not be removable at the end of the lease.

   domestic fixture. Removable personal property provided by a tenant for the tenant's personal comfort and convenience while occupying leased premises. ● This term frequently applies to items such as large kitchen appliances. See *tenant's fixture.* Cf. *ornamental fixture.*

   ornamental fixture. Removable personal property that a tenant attaches to leased premises to make them more attractive and comfortable. ● This term sometimes overlaps with *domestic fixture* when an object is decorative as well as functional. See *tenant's fixture.* Cf. *domestic fixture.*

   tenant's fixture. (1832) Removable personal property that a tenant affixes to the leased property but that the tenant can detach and take away. — Also termed *movable fixture.* See *domestic fixture; ornamental fixture.*

   trade fixture. (1839) Removable personal property that a tenant attaches to leased land for business purposes, such as a display counter. ● Despite its name, a trade fixture is not usu. treated as a fixture — that is, as irremovable.

fixture filing. (1972) The act or an instance of recording, in public real-estate records, a security interest in personal property that is intended to become a fixture. See UCC § 9-102(a)(40). ● The creditor files a financing statement in the real-property records of the county where a mortgage on the real estate would be filed. A fixture-filing financing statement must contain a description of the real estate.

FJC. *abbr.* FEDERAL JUDICIAL CENTER.

FKA. *abbr.* Formerly known as. — Also rendered *F/K/A; fka; f/k/a.*

flag, *n.* (14c) **1.** A usu. rectangular piece of cloth, bunting, or other material decorated with a distinctive design and used as a symbol or signal. **2.** Something symbolized by the display of a flag, such as a ship or nationality. See DUTY OF THE FLAG; LAW OF THE FLAG.

   flag of convenience. *Int'l law.* A national flag flown by a ship not because the ship or its crew has an affiliation with the nation, but because the lax controls and modest fees and taxes imposed by that nation have attracted the owner to register it there. • After World War II, shipowners began registering their ships in countries such as Panama, Liberia, and Honduras to avoid expensive and restrictive national regulation of labor, safety, and other matters. Since the late 1950s, there has been increasing international pressure to require a "genuine link" between a ship and its flag state, but this reform has been slow in coming. — Abbr. FOC.

flag of truce. *Int'l law.* A white flag used as a signal when one belligerent wishes to communicate with the other in the field. • The bearers of such a flag may not be fired on, injured, or taken prisoner, as long as they carry out their mission in good faith.

flag desecration. The act of mutilating, defacing, burning, or flagrantly misusing a flag. • Flag desecration is constitutionally protected as a form of free speech. *United States v. Eichman,* 496 U.S. 310, 110 S.Ct. 2404 (1990).

flag mast. See MAST (1).

flagrans bellum (**flay**-granz **bel**-əm). [Latin "raging war"] A war currently being waged.

flagrans crimen (**flay**-granz **crı**-mən). [Latin] A crime in the very act of its commission or of recent occurrence; a fresh crime.

flagrante bello (flə-**gran**-tee **bel**-oh). [Latin] During an actual state of war.

flagrante delicto. See IN FLAGRANTE DELICTO.

flag state. *Maritime law.* The state under whose flag a ship is registered. • A ship may fly the flag of one state only.

flag-state control. *Maritime law.* The exercise of authority by a state over vessels that fly under its flag to ensure compliance with domestic and international safety and environmental laws and regulations. Cf. COASTAL-STATE CONTROL; PORT-STATE CONTROL.

flash-of-genius rule. *Patents.* The now-defunct principle that a device is not patentable if it was invented as the result of trial and error rather than as a "flash of creative genius." • The rule, which takes its name from language in *Cuno Engineering Corp. v. Automatic Devices Corp.,* 314 U.S. 84, 91, 62 S.Ct. 37, 41 (1941), was legislatively overturned in 1952. 35 USCA § 103.

flat, *adv.* Without an allowance or charge for accrued interest <the stock was sold flat>.

flat, *n.* A house in a larger block; an apartment.

flat bond. See BOND (3).

flat cancellation. See CANCELLATION.

flat money. See *fiat money* under MONEY.

flat reinsurance. See REINSURANCE.

flat sentence. See *determinate sentence* under SENTENCE.

flat tax. See TAX.

flat time. See TIME.

flee from justice. See FLIGHT.

fleet insurance. See INSURANCE.

Fleet marriage. See MARRIAGE (1).

Fleet Prison. *Hist.* A large London jail best known for holding debtors and bankrupts in the 18th and 19th centuries. • Formerly standing beside the Fleet River, it was opened in 1197 and operated almost continuously until it was closed and demolished in 1846.

FLETC. *abbr.* FEDERAL LAW ENFORCEMENT TRAINING CENTER.

flexdollars. Money that an employer pays an employee, who can apply it to a choice of employee benefits.

flexible constitution. See CONSTITUTION.

flexible-rate mortgage. **1.** See *adjustable-rate mortgage* under MORTGAGE. **2.** See *renegotiable-rate mortgage* under MORTGAGE.

flextime. (1972) A work schedule that employees have discretion to alter as long as they work their required number of hours over a specified period (usu. a week).

flexweek. A four-day workweek, usu. consisting of four 10-hour days.

flier policy. See INSURANCE POLICY.

flight. (bef. 12c) The act or an instance of fleeing, esp. to evade arrest or prosecution <the judge denied bail because the defendant is a flight risk>. — Also termed *flight from prosecution; flee from justice.*

flight easement. See *avigational easement* under EASEMENT.

flight from prosecution. See FLIGHT.

flim flam. (16c) A scheme by which a person is tricked out of money; CONFIDENCE GAME. • The term originated as the name of a machine at the heart of a mid-19th-century patent case, *Sloat v. Spring,* 22 F. Cas. 330 (C.C.E.D. Pa. 1850). — Also termed *faith and trust.*

flip, *vb.* *Slang.* **1.** To buy and then immediately resell securities or real estate in an attempt to turn a profit. **2.** To refinance consumer loans. **3.** To turn state's evidence. See TURN STATE'S EVIDENCE.

flip mortgage. See MORTGAGE.

flipping. *Slang.* **1.** The legitimate practice of buying something, such as goods, real estate, or securities, at a low price and quickly reselling at a higher price. **2.** The fraudulent practice of buying property at a low price, preparing a false appraisal or other documentation showing that property has a much greater value, and quickly reselling the property for an inflated price based on the false document.

float, *n.* (1915) **1.** The sum of money represented by outstanding or uncollected checks. **2.** The delay between a transaction and the withdrawal of funds to cover the transaction. **3.** The amount of a corporation's shares that are available for trading on the securities market.

float, *vb.* (1833) **1.** (Of a currency) to attain a value in the international exchange market solely on the basis of supply and demand <the IMF allowed the peso to float>. **2.** To issue (a security) for sale on the market <PDQ Corp. floated a new series of preferred shares>. **3.** To arrange or negotiate (a loan) <the bank floated a car loan to Alice despite her poor credit history>.

floatage. See FLOTSAM.

floater. See *floating-rate note* under NOTE (1).

floater insurance. See INSURANCE.

floating, *adj.* Not fixed or settled; fluctuating; variable.

floating capital. See CAPITAL.

floating charge. See *floating lien* under LIEN.

floating debt. See DEBT.

floating easement. See EASEMENT.

floating-interest bond. See BOND (3).

floating lien. See LIEN.

floating policy. See INSURANCE POLICY.

floating rate. See INTEREST RATE.

floating-rate note. See NOTE (1).

floating stock. See STOCK.

floating zone. See ZONE.

floating zoning. See ZONING.

floodgate. (*usu. pl.*) (13c) A restraint that prevents a release of a usu. undesirable result <the new law opened the floodgates of litigation>.

flood insurance. See INSURANCE.

floodplain. (19c) Land that is subject to floodwaters because of its level topography and proximity to a river or arroyo; esp., level land that, extending from a riverbank, is inundated when the flow of water exceeds the channel's capacity.

floodwater. See WATER.

floor. (18c) **1.** *Parliamentary law.* The part of the hall where the members of a deliberative body meet to debate issues and conduct business; esp., a legislature's central meeting place where the members sit and conduct business, as distinguished from the galleries, corridors, or lobbies <the Senate floor> <nominations from the floor>. See *assignment of the floor* under ASSIGNMENT (6); CLAIM THE FLOOR; HAVE THE FLOOR; OBTAIN THE FLOOR; ON THE FLOOR; *privilege of the floor* under

PRIVILEGE (6). **2.** The trading area where stocks and commodities are bought and sold on an exchange <the broker placed his buy order with the trader on the floor of the NYSE>. **3.** The lowest limit <the floor for that position is $25,000 per year>.

floor amendment. See AMENDMENT (3).

floor debate. See DEBATE.

floor-plan financing. See FINANCING.

floor planning. See *floor-plan financing* under FINANCING.

floor-plan rule. The principle by which a vehicle owner who has placed for sale a vehicle in a retail dealer's showroom is estopped to deny the title of an innocent purchaser from the dealer in the ordinary course of retail dealing.

floor price. See PRICE.

floor tax. See TAX.

flotage. See FLOTSAM.

flotation. See OFFERING.

flotation cost. See COST (1).

floterial district. See DISTRICT.

flotsam (flot-səm). (17c) Goods and debris, esp. those from a shipwreck, that float on the surface of a body of water. — Also termed *floatage; flotage.* Cf. JETSAM; LAGAN (1); WAVESON.

flowage. (19c) The natural movement of water from a dominant estate to a servient estate. • It is a privilege or easement of the owner of the upper estate and a servitude of the lower estate.

flowage easement. See EASEMENT.

flower bond. See BOND (3).

FLRA. *abbr.* FEDERAL LABOR RELATIONS AUTHORITY.

FLSA. *abbr.* FAIR LABOR STANDARDS ACT.

fluctuating clause. See ESCALATOR CLAUSE.

flyer policy. See *flier policy* under INSURANCE POLICY.

fly for it. *Hist.* To flee after allegedly committing a crime. • The ancient custom in criminal trials was to ask the jury after its verdict — even a not-guilty verdict — "Did he fly for it?" The purpose was to enable the jury to find whether the defendant had fled from justice. A defendant who had fled would forfeit personal property, even though found not guilty on the underlying charge.

fly-power assignment. See ASSIGNMENT (2).

flyspeck, *n. Insurance.* A potential trivial defect in title to real property, as a result of which a title-insurance company is likely to exclude any risk from that defect before issuing a policy. — **flyspeck,** *vb.*

FMC. *abbr.* FEDERAL MARITIME COMMISSION.

FMCS. *abbr.* FEDERAL MEDIATION AND CONCILI-ATION SERVICE.

FMCSA. *abbr.* FEDERAL MOTOR CARRIER SAFETY ADMINISTRATION.

FmHA. *abbr.* FARMERS' HOME ADMINISTRATION.

FMLA. *abbr.* **1.** FAMILY AND MEDICAL LEAVE ACT. **2.** FEDERAL MARITIME LIEN ACT.

FMS. *abbr.* FINANCIAL MANAGEMENT SERVICE.

FMSF. *abbr.* FALSE MEMORY SYNDROME FOUNDA-TION.

FMSHRC. *abbr.* FEDERAL MINE SAFETY AND HEALTH REVIEW COMMISSION.

FMV. See *fair market value* under VALUE (2).

FNMA. *abbr.* FEDERAL NATIONAL MORTGAGE AS-SOCIATION.

FNS. *abbr.* FOOD, NUTRITION, AND CONSUMER SER-VICE.

FOB. *abbr.* FREE ON BOARD.

FOB destination. See FREE ON BOARD.

FOB shipping. See FREE ON BOARD.

FOC. See *flag of convenience* under FLAG.

foeticide. See FETICIDE.

foetus. See FETUS.

FOIA (foy-ə). *abbr.* FREEDOM OF INFORMATION ACT.

foiable (foy-ə-bəl), *adj.* (1981) *Slang.* (Of docu-ments) subject to disclosure under the Freedom of Information Act (FOIA).

folcland. See FOLKLAND.

folio (foh-lee-oh). [fr. Latin *folium* "leaf"] (15c) **1.** *Hist.* A leaf of a paper or parchment, numbered only on the front. ● A folio includes both sides of the leaf, or two pages, with the letters "a" and "b" (or "r" and "v," signifying *recto* and *verso*) added to show which of the two pages was intended. **2.** *Hist.* A certain number of words in a legal docu-ment, used as a method of measurement. ● In England, 72 or 90 words formed a folio; in the United States, 100 words. — **folio,** *vb.* **3.** A page number on a printed book. **4.** A large book the pages of which are formed by folding a sheet of paper only once in the binding to form two leaves, making available four pages (both sides of each leaf).

folkland. *Hist.* Land held by customary law, with-out written title. — Also spelled *folcland.* Cf. BOOKLAND; LOANLAND.

folk laws. See LEGES BARBARORUM.

folkmote. See HALLMOTE (3).

follow, *vb.* (bef. 12c) To conform to or comply with; to accept as authority <the lawyer assumed that the Supreme Court would follow its own prec-edent>.

following-form policy. See INSURANCE POLICY.

follow-the-fortunes doctrine. *Insurance.* The prin-ciple that a reinsurer must reimburse the rein-sured for its payment of settled claims as long as the reinsured's payments were reasonable and in good faith. ● This rule prevents a reinsurer from second-guessing a reinsured's good-faith decision to pay a claim arguably not covered under the original insurance policy. — Often shortened to *follow the fortunes.*

follow-the-settlements doctrine. *Insurance.* The principle that an indemnitor must accede to the actions of the indemnitee in adjusting and set-tling claims; esp., the principle that a reinsurer must follow the actions of the reinsured.

fons juris. See SOURCE OF LAW.

Food and Drug Administration. A division of the U.S. Public Health Service in the Department of Health and Human Services responsible for en-suring that food is safe, pure, and wholesome; that human and animal drugs, biological prod-ucts, and medical devices are safe and effective; and that certain other products, such as electronic products that emit radiation, are safe. ● Created by the Pure Food and Drug Act of 1906, the agen-cy today enforces the Food, Drug, and Cosmetic Act of 1938 and related statutes and regulations. 21 USCA §§ 301 et seq. — Abbr. FDA.

food-disparagement law. See AGRICULTURAL-DIS-PARAGEMENT LAW.

Food, Drug, and Cosmetic Act. A 1938 federal law prohibiting the transportation in interstate com-merce of adulterated or misbranded food, drugs, or cosmetics. ● The Act superseded the Pure Food and Drug Act of 1906. — Abbr. FDCA.

Food, Nutrition, and Consumer Service. An agen-cy in the U.S. Department of Agriculture respon-sible for reducing hunger by educating children and needy people about healthy diets and by providing them access to food through the food-stamp and other programs. — Abbr. FNS.

Food Safety and Inspection Service. An agency in the U.S. Department of Agriculture responsible for inspecting all types of meat, poultry, eggs, and related products to ensure safety and accurate la-beling. — Abbr. FSIS.

fool's test. The test formerly used by federal courts and by the Federal Trade Commission to deter-mine whether an advertisement is deceptive, by asking whether even a fool might believe it. ● The name comes from Isaiah: "wayfaring men, though fools, shall not err therein." The test was announced in *Charles of the Ritz Distrib. Corp. v. Fed. Trade Comm'n,* 143 F.2d 676 (2d Cir. 1944). It was replaced by a "reasonable consumer" test by the FTC in 1984. Cf. REASONABLE-CONSUMER TEST.

foot acre. See ACRE.

footage drilling contract. *Oil & gas.* A drilling contract under which the drilling contractor is paid to drill to a specified formation or depth, is paid a set amount per foot drilled, and is given broad control over how to do the work. ● The risk of unexpected delays, as well as most liabilities, is on the contractor rather than the lease operator under this type of contract. Cf. DAYWORK DRILL-ING CONTRACT; *turnkey drilling contract* DRILL-ING CONTRACT.

foot-frontage rule. *Tax.* A method of property-tax assessment — used esp. to pay for improvements such as sidewalks and sewers — that considers only the lot's actual frontage on the line of im-provement and ignores the depth of the lot and the number and character of other improvements or their value.

foot of the fine. *Hist.* At common law, the fifth and last part of a fine of conveyance. ● This part in-cluded the entire matter, reciting the names of the parties and the date, place, and before whom it was acknowledged or levied. — Also termed *chirograph*. See FINE (1).

footprint. (16c) **1.** *Evidence.* The impression made on a surface of soil, snow, etc., by a human foot or a shoe, boot, or any other foot covering. **2.** *Real estate.* The shape of a building's base.

for account of. (1826) A form of indorsement on a note or draft introducing the name of the person entitled to receive the proceeds.

Foraker Act (for-ə-kər). The original (1900) fed-eral law providing Puerto Rico with a civil gov-ernment, but keeping it outside the U.S. customs area. See 48 USCA §§ 731–752.

forbearance, *n.* (16c) **1.** The act of refraining from enforcing a right, obligation, or debt. ● Strictly speaking, *forbearance* denotes an intentional negative act, while *omission* or *neglect* is an un-intentional negative act. **2.** The act of tolerating or abstaining. — **forbear,** *vb.*

forbidden degree. See *prohibited degree* under DE-GREE.

forbidden departure. See DEPARTURE.

for cause. For a legal reason or ground. ● The phrase expresses a common standard govern-ing the removal of a civil servant or an employee under contract. — **for-cause,** *adj.*

for-cause, *n.* See *challenge for cause* under CHAL-LENGE (2).

force, *n.* (14c) Power, violence, or pressure directed against a person or thing.

   actual force. (16c) Force consisting in a physical act, esp. a violent act directed against a robbery victim. — Also termed *physical force.*

   constructive force. (1802) Threats and intimida-tion to gain control or prevent resistance; esp., threatening words or gestures directed against a robbery victim.

   deadly force. (16c) Violent action known to cre-ate a substantial risk of causing death or seri-ous bodily harm. ●Generally, a person may use deadly force in self-defense or in defense of another only if retaliating against another's deadly force. — Also termed *extreme force.* Cf. *nondeadly force.*

   excessive force. (16c) Unreasonable or unneces-sary force under the circumstances.

   extreme force. See *deadly force.*

   independent force. Force not stimulated by a situ-ation created by the actor's conduct.

   intervening force. Force that actively produces harm to another after the actor's negligent act or omission has been committed.

   irresistible force. (16c) Force that cannot be fore-seen or controlled, esp. that which prevents the performance of a contractual obligation; FORCE MAJEURE.

   legal force. See *reasonable force.*

   nondeadly force. (1961) **1.** Force that is neither intended nor likely to cause death or serious bodily harm; force intended to cause only minor bodily harm. **2.** A threat of deadly force, such as displaying a knife. — Also termed *moderate force.* Cf. *deadly force.*

   physical force. See *actual force.*

   reasonable force. (17c) Force that is not excessive and that is appropriate for protecting oneself or one's property. ● The use of reasonable force will not render a person criminally or tortiously li-able. — Also termed *legal force.*

   unlawful force. (16c) Force that is directed against a person without that person's consent, and that is a criminal offense or an actionable tort. Model Penal Code § 3.11.

force, *vb.* (14c) To compel by physical means or by legal requirement <Barnes used a gun to force Jillian to use her ATM card> <under the malprac-tice policy, the insurance company was forced to defend the doctor>.

force and arms. *Hist.* Violence. ● The phrase was used in common-law pleading in declarations of trespass and in indictments to denote that the of-fending act was committed violently. See VI ET ARMIS.

force and effect, *n.* (16c) Legal efficacy <mailing the brief had the force and effect of filing it with the clerk>. ● The term is now generally regarded as a redundant legalism.

forced abortion. See ABORTION.

forced conversion. See CONVERSION (1).

forced exile. See EXILE.

forced heir. See HEIR.

forced labor. *Int'l law.* Work exacted from a person under threat of penalty; work for which a person has not offered himself or herself voluntarily. ● Under the U.N. Convention on Civil and Political Rights (article 8), exemptions from this definition include (1) penalties imposed by a court, (2) compulsory military service, (3) action taken in an emergency, (4) normal civil obligations, and (5) minor communal services. — Also termed *compulsory labor.*

forced pooling. See *compulsory pooling* under POOLING.

forced portion. See LEGITIME.

forced resettlement. *Int'l law.* The involuntary transfer of individuals or groups within the jurisdiction of a country whether inside its own territory or into or out of occupied territory.

forced respite. See RESPITE.

forced sale. See SALE.

forced share. See ELECTIVE SHARE.

forced unitization. See *compulsory unitization* under UNITIZATION.

force majeure (**fors** ma-**zhər**). [Law French "a superior force"] (1883) An event or effect that can be neither anticipated nor controlled. ● The term includes both acts of nature (e.g., floods and hurricanes) and acts of people (e.g., riots, strikes, and wars). — Also termed *force majesture; vis major; superior force.* Cf. ACT OF GOD; VIS MAJOR (1).

force-majeure clause. (1916) A contractual provision allocating the risk of loss if performance becomes impossible or impracticable, esp. as a result of an event or effect that the parties could not have anticipated or controlled.

force-the-vote provision. *Mergers & acquisitions.* A contractual clause requiring a company's board of directors to approve a merger transaction and submit it to the shareholders, who then vote on the merger regardless of whether the board recommends that the shareholders approve it when the vote is held.

forcible, *adj.* (15c) Effected by force or threat of force against opposition or resistance.

forcible detainer. 1. The wrongful retention of possession of property by one originally in lawful possession, often with threats or actual use of violence. 2. FORCIBLE ENTRY AND DETAINER (2).

forcible entry. (17c) 1. The act or an instance of violently and unlawfully taking possession of lands and tenements against the will of those in lawful possession. 2. The act of entering land in another's possession by the use of force against another or by breaking into the premises.

forcible entry and detainer. (17c) 1. The act of violently taking and keeping possession of lands and tenements without legal authority. 2. A quick and simple legal proceeding for regaining possession of real property from someone who has wrongfully taken, or refused to surrender, possession. — Also termed *forcible detainer.* See EVICTION; EJECTMENT.

foreclose, *vb.* (15c) To terminate a mortgagor's interest in property; to subject (property) to foreclosure proceedings.

foreclosure (for-**kloh**-zhər). (18c) A legal proceeding to terminate a mortgagor's interest in property, instituted by the lender (the mortgagee) either to gain title or to force a sale in order to satisfy the unpaid debt secured by the property. Cf. REPOSSESSION.

> **equitable foreclosure.** (1876) A foreclosure method in which the court orders the property sold, and the proceeds are applied first to pay the costs of the lawsuit and sale and then to the mortgage debt. ● Any surplus is paid to the mortgagor.

> **judicial foreclosure.** (1839) A costly and time-consuming foreclosure method by which the mortgaged property is sold through a court proceeding requiring many standard legal steps such as the filing of a complaint, service of process, notice, and a hearing. ● Judicial foreclosure is available in all jurisdictions and is the exclusive or most common method of foreclosure in at least 20 states.

> **mortgage foreclosure.** (1842) A foreclosure of the mortgaged property upon the mortgagor's default.

> **nonjudicial foreclosure.** (1916) 1. See *power-of-sale foreclosure.* 2. A foreclosure method that does not require court involvement.

> **power-of-sale foreclosure.** (1946) A foreclosure process by which, according to the mortgage instrument and a state statute, the mortgaged property is sold at a nonjudicial public sale by a public official, the mortgagee, or a trustee, without the stringent notice requirements, procedural burdens, or delays of a judicial foreclosure. ● Power-of-sale foreclosure is authorized and used in more than half the states. — Also termed *nonjudicial foreclosure; statutory foreclosure.*

> **strict foreclosure.** (1823) A rare procedure that gives the mortgagee title to the mortgaged property — without first conducting a sale — after a defaulting mortgagor fails to pay the mortgage debt within a court-specified period. ● The use of strict foreclosure is limited to special situa-

tions except in those few states that permit this remedy generally.

tax foreclosure. (1869) A public authority's seizure and sale of property for nonpayment of taxes.

foreclosure decree. (1847) **1.** Generally, a decree ordering a judicial foreclosure sale. **2.** A decree ordering the strict foreclosure of a mortgage.

foreclosure sale. See SALE.

foreign, *adj.* (13c) **1.** Of or relating to another country <foreign affairs>. **2.** Of or relating to another jurisdiction <the Arizona court gave full faith and credit to the foreign judgment from Mississippi>. — **foreigner,** *n.*

foreign administration. See *ancillary administration* under ADMINISTRATION.

foreign administrator. See ADMINISTRATOR (2).

foreign agent. See AGENT (2).

Foreign Agricultural Service. An agency in the U.S. Department of Agriculture responsible for maintaining a worldwide agricultural intelligence and reporting system. — Abbr. FAS.

foreign apposer. See APPOSER.

foreign assignment. See ASSIGNMENT (2).

foreign bill. See BILL (6).

foreign bill of exchange. See *foreign draft* under DRAFT.

foreign bond. See BOND (3).

foreign consulate. See CONSULATE.

foreign corporation. See CORPORATION.

Foreign Corrupt Practices Act. A 1977 federal statute that prohibits United States citizens from offering or paying bribes to foreign officials in order to obtain or maintain a commercial interest, and requires companies whose securities are listed in the United States to comply with certain accounting practices. 15 USCA § 78dd-1, et. seq.

foreign county. See COUNTY.

foreign court. See COURT.

foreign creditor. See CREDITOR.

foreign divorce. See DIVORCE.

foreign document. See DOCUMENT.

foreign domicile. See DOMICILE.

foreign dominion. *Hist.* A country that at one time was a foreign state but that by conquest or cession has come under the British Crown.

foreign draft. See DRAFT.

foreign-earned-income exclusion. (1964) The Internal Revenue Code provision that excludes from taxation a limited amount of income earned by nonresident taxpayers outside the United States. • The taxpayer must elect between this exclusion

and the foreign tax credit. IRC (26 USCA) § 911(a), (b). See *foreign tax credit* under TAX CREDIT.

Foreign Emoluments Clause. The clause of the U.S. Constitution prohibiting titles of nobility and the acceptance of a gift, title, or other benefit from a foreign power. U.S. Const. art. I, § 9, cl. 8. — Sometimes shortened to *Emoluments Clause.*

foreigner. (15c) **1.** *Hist.* A person not an inhabitant of a particular city under discussion. **2.** A citizen of another country.

foreign exchange. (17c) **1.** The process of making international monetary transactions; esp., the conversion of one currency to that of a different country. **2.** Foreign currency or negotiable instruments payable in foreign currency, such as traveler's checks.

foreign-exchange market. See MARKET.

foreign-exchange rate. The rate at which the currency of one country is exchanged for the currency of another country.

foreign guardian. See GUARDIAN.

foreign immunity. See IMMUNITY (1).

Foreign Intelligence Surveillance Act. A 1978 federal statute that established new procedures and courts to authorize electronic surveillance of foreign intelligence operations in the United States. • The Act established the Foreign Intelligence Surveillance Court and the Foreign Intelligence Court of Review. It allows the Attorney General to obtain warrants that authorize electronic surveillance of suspected foreign-intelligence operatives without public disclosure and without a showing of probable cause that criminal activity is involved. — Abbr. FISA.

Foreign Intelligence Surveillance Court. See UNITED STATES FOREIGN INTELLIGENCE SURVEILLANCE COURT.

Foreign Intelligence Surveillance Court of Review. See UNITED STATES FOREIGN INTELLIGENCE SURVEILLANCE COURT OF REVIEW.

foreign judgment. See JUDGMENT.

foreign jurisdiction. See JURISDICTION.

foreign jury. See JURY.

foreign law. 1. Generally, the law of another country. **2.** *Conflict of laws.* The law of another state or of a foreign country.

foreign minister. See MINISTER.

foreign object. (17c) An item that appears where it does not belong; esp., an item introduced into a living body, such as a sponge that is left in a patient's body during surgery. • The discovery rule usu. tolls the statute of limitations for a medical-malpractice claim based on a foreign object. — Also termed *foreign substance.* See FOREIGN SUBSTANCE.

foreign port. See PORT.

foreign-relations law. See INTERNATIONAL LAW.

foreign service. (19c) **1.** UNITED STATES FOREIGN SERVICE. **2.** FORINSEC SERVICE. **3.** *Hist.* A feudal service performed by a tenant outside of the fee.

Foreign Service Institute. A unit in the U.S. Department of State responsible for training officers and employees of the Foreign Service as well as personnel in other agencies. — Abbr. FSI.

foreign situs trust. See TRUST.

Foreign Sovereign Immunities Act. A federal statute providing individuals with a right of action against foreign governments, under certain circumstances, to the extent the claim arises from the private, as opposed to the public, acts of the foreign state. 28 USCA §§ 1602–1611. — Abbr. FSIA. See RESTRICTIVE PRINCIPLE OF SOVEREIGN IMMUNITY.

foreign state. 1. A foreign country. **2.** An American state different from the one under discussion.

foreign substance. (17c) A substance found in a body, organism, or thing where it is not supposed to be found <the plaintiff sued because she thought she saw — and later confirmed that she had found — a foreign substance (namely, a piece of glass) in her hamburger>.

foreign support order. See SUPPORT ORDER.

foreign tax credit. See TAX CREDIT.

foreign trade zone. See FREE-TRADE ZONE.

foreign trust. See *foreign-situs trust* under TRUST.

foreign vessel. See VESSEL.

foreign voyage. See VOYAGE.

foreign water. See WATER.

forejudge, *vb.* **1.** To prejudge; to judge beforehand. **2.** Loosely, FORJUDGE.

foreman. (15c) **1.** See *presiding juror* under JUROR. **2.** A person who directs the work of employees; an overseer, crew chief, or superintendent. — **foremanship,** *n.*

forematron. *Hist.* The presiding juror in an all-woman jury.

forensic (fə-**ren**-sik *also* -zik), *adj.* [fr. Latin *forensis* "public," fr. Latin *forum* "court"] (17c) **1.** Used in or suitable to courts of law or public debate <forensic psychiatry>. **2.** Rhetorical; argumentative <Tietjen's considerable forensic skills>. **3.** *Hist.* Exterior; foreign.

forensic engineering. (1976) The use of engineering principles or analysis in a lawsuit, usu. through an expert witness's testimony.

forensic evidence. See EVIDENCE.

forensic linguistics. (1973) The science or technique that evaluates the linguistic characteris-

tics of written or oral communications, usu. to determine identity or authorship.

forensic medicine. (1845) The branch of medicine that establishes or interprets evidence using scientific or technical facts, such as ballistics. — Also termed *medical jurisprudence.*

forensic pathology. (1959) The specific branch of medicine that establishes or interprets evidence dealing with diseases and disorders of the body, esp. those that cause death.

forensics (fə-**ren**-siks *also* -ziks). (1963) **1.** The art of argumentative discourse. **2.** The branch of law enforcement dealing with legal evidence relating to firearms and ballistics.

forensic services. *Hist.* In feudal law, the payment of extraordinary aids or the rendition of extraordinary military services.

foreperson. See *presiding juror* under JUROR.

foreseeability, *n.* (1928) The quality of being reasonably anticipatable. ● Foreseeability, along with actual causation, is an element of proximate cause in tort law. — **foreseeable,** *adj.*

foreseeable damages. See DAMAGES.

forest, *n.* (13c) *Hist.* A tract of land, not necessarily wooded, reserved to the king or a grantee, for hunting deer and other game.

forestall (for-**stawl**), *vb.* (bef. 12c) **1.** To prevent (an event, result, etc.). **2.** *Hist.* To intercept or obstruct (as a person on a royal highway). **3.** *Hist.* To prevent (a tenant) from coming on the premises. **4.** *Hist.* To intercept (as a deer reentering a forest). **5.** *Hist.* To buy (goods) for the purpose of reselling at a higher price. ● At common law, this was an indictable offense. See FORESTALLING THE MARKET. — Also spelled *forstall.*

forestaller, *n.* **1.** A person who forestalls. **2.** *Hist.* One guilty of the offense of forestalling. See FORESTALL (5).

forestalling the market. *Hist.* **1.** The taking possession of commodities on their way to the market. **2.** The purchase of goods on their way to the market, with the intention of reselling them at a higher price. **3.** The deterrence of having sellers offer their goods at market at a reasonable price; specif., the crime of inhibiting normal trading by persuading sellers to raise their prices on goods or dissuading them from offering the goods in a particular market, or by purchasing as much as possible of certain goods before they reach the market to drive up prices.

forest law. *Hist.* The body of law protecting game and preserving timber.

forestry right. A land interest under which a person has the right to enter the land, establish and maintain a crop of trees, harvest them, and construct works for that purpose.

Forest Service. An agency in the U.S. Department of Agriculture responsible for managing the nation's national forests. ● The Forest Service also operates the Youth Conservation Corps and the Volunteers in the National Forest programs.

forfeiture (**for**-fi-chər), *n.* (14c) **1.** The divestiture of property without compensation. **2.** The loss of a right, privilege, or property because of a crime, breach of obligation, or neglect of duty. ● Title is instantaneously transferred to another, such as the government, a corporation, or a private person. **3.** Something (esp. money or property) lost or confiscated by this process; a penalty. — **forfeit,** *vb.* — **forfeitable,** *adj.*

civil forfeiture. (1867) An in rem proceeding brought by the government against property that either facilitated a crime or was acquired as a result of criminal activity.

criminal forfeiture. (1866) A governmental proceeding brought against a person to seize property as punishment for the person's criminal behavior.

forfeiture of marriage. *Hist.* A penalty exacted by a lord from a ward who married without the lord's consent. ● The penalty was a money payment double the value that the marriage would otherwise have been worth to the lord.

forfeiture of pay. *Military law.* A punishment depriving the guilty party of all or part of his or her military pay.

4. A destruction or deprivation of some estate or right because of the failure to perform some contractual obligation or condition.

forfeiture clause. (1804) **1.** A contractual provision stating that, under certain circumstances, one party must forfeit something to the other. ● Forfeiture clauses are often held to be void, although they are similar to conditions and other qualifications of estates in land. **2.** NO-CONTEST CLAUSE.

forfeiture restraint. An attempt by an otherwise effective conveyance or contract to cause a later conveyance to terminate or to make some or all of the later conveyance subject to termination. — Sometimes shortened to *restraint.*

forgery, *n.* (16c) **1.** The act of fraudulently making a false document or altering a real one to be used as if genuine <the contract was void because of the seller's forgery>. ● Though forgery was a misdemeanor at common law, modern statutes typically make it a felony. — Also termed *false making.* **2.** A false or altered document made to look genuine by someone with the intent to deceive <he was not the true property owner because the deed was a forgery>. — Also termed *fake.* **3.** Under the Model Penal Code, the act of fraudulently altering, authenticating, issuing, or transferring a writing

without appropriate authorization. ● Under the explicit terms of the Code, *writing* can include items such as coins and credit cards. Model Penal Code § 224.1(1). — **forge,** *vb.* — **forger,** *n.*

double forgery. A draft having a forged payor signature and a forged indorsement.

foris (**for**-is), *adj.* [Latin] Abroad; outdoors; without.

forjudge, *vb.* (15c) **1.** *Hist.* To expel a person, esp. an officer or attorney, from court for some offense or misconduct. **2.** To deprive (a person) of a thing by a judgment; to condemn (a person) to lose a thing. — Also spelled (loosely) *forejudge.*

forjudger (for-**jəj**-ər), *n.* (15c) *Hist.* **1.** A judgment that deprives a person of a thing. **2.** A judgment of expulsion or banishment. — Also termed *forisjudicatio; forisjudicatus.*

form, *n.* (13c) **1.** The outer shape or structure of something, as distinguished from its substance or matter <courts are generally less concerned about defects in form than defects in substance>. **2.** Established behavior or procedure, usu. according to custom or rule <the prosecutor followed the established form in her closing argument>. **3.** A model; a sample; an example <attorneys often draft pleadings by using a form instead of starting from scratch>. **4.** The customary method of drafting legal documents, usu. with fixed words, phrases, and sentences <Jones prepared the contract merely by following the state bar's form>. **5.** A legal document with blank spaces to be filled in by the drafter <the divorce lawyer used printed forms that a secretary could fill in>.

Form 8-K. See 8-K.

Form 10-K. See 10-K.

Form 10-Q. See 10-Q.

forma (**for**-mə). [Latin "form"] *Hist.* The prescribed form of judicial proceedings.

formal, *adj.* (14c) **1.** Pertaining to or following established procedural rules, customs, and practices. **2.** Ceremonial. — **formality,** *n.*

formal abandonment. See *express abandonment* under ABANDONMENT (10).

formal acknowledgment. See ACKNOWLEDGMENT.

formal agreement. See AGREEMENT.

formal contract. See CONTRACT.

formal drawing. See DRAWING.

formal fallacy. See FALLACY.

formal impeachment. 1. See IMPEACHMENT (1). **2.** See IMPEACHMENT (2).

formality. (16c) **1.** A small point of practice that, though seemingly unimportant, must usu. be observed to achieve a particular legal result. **2.** *Hist.* (*pl.*) Robes worn by magistrates on solemn occasions. **3.** *Copyright.* (*usu. pl.*) A procedural requirement formerly required before receiving U.S. copyright protection. • Formalities included (1) a copyright notice appearing on the work, (2) actual publication, (3) registration with the Copyright Office, and (4) deposit of the work with the Library of Congress. The formality requirements eroded during the 20th century. Today, none are required, although registration remains a prerequisite for an infringement suit by U.S. authors in the United States.

formal law. (17c) Procedural law.

formal party. See *nominal party* under PARTY (2).

formal rejection. See REJECTION.

formal rulemaking. See RULEMAKING.

forma pauperis. See IN FORMA PAUPERIS.

formbook. A book that contains sample legal documents, esp. transaction-related documents such as contracts, deeds, leases, wills, trusts, and securities disclosure documents.

formed design. See DESIGN.

formedon (for-mə-don). [fr. Latin *forma doni* "form of the gift"] (15c) *Hist.* A writ of right for claiming entailed property held by another. • A writ of formedon was the highest remedy available to a tenant in tail. — Also termed *writ of formedon.*

> **formedon in the descender.** A writ of formedon brought by the issue in tail to recover possession of the land.

> **formedon in the remainder.** A writ of formedon brought by a remainderman under a grant or gift in tail to recover possession of the land.

> **formedon in the reverter.** A writ of formedon brought by a reversioner or donor of the grant or gift in tail to recover possession of the land.

former acquittal. See *autrefois acquit* under AUTREFOIS.

former adjudication. (18c) A judgment in a prior action that resulted in a final determination of the rights of the parties or essential fact questions and serves to bar relitigation of the issues relevant to that determination. • Collateral estoppel and res judicata are the two types of former adjudication. See COLLATERAL ESTOPPEL; RES JUDICATA.

former jeopardy. (1870) The fact of having previously been prosecuted for the same offense. • A defendant enters a plea of former jeopardy to inform the court that a second prosecution is improper. Cf. DOUBLE JEOPARDY.

former punishment. *Military law.* The rule that nonjudicial punishment for a minor offense may bar trial by court-martial for the same offense.

form of action. The common-law legal and procedural device associated with a particular writ, each of which had specific forms of process, pleading, trial, and judgment. • The 11 common-law forms of action were trespass, trespass on the case, trover, ejectment, detinue, replevin, debt, covenant, account, special assumpsit, and general assumpsit.

Form S-1. See S-1.

formula. [Latin "set form of words"] (17c) **1.** *Roman law.* A written document, prepared by a praetor and forwarded to a judex, identifying the issue to be tried and the judgment to be given by the judex. • It was based on model pleas formulated by the praetor in his edict and adapted by him or other magistrates in civil suits for the benefit of the judex who had to try the issue. These pleas were adapted to the circumstances of the case. The usual parts of a formula were (1) the *demonstratio,* in which the plaintiff stated the facts of the claim; (2) the *intentio,* in which the plaintiff specified the relief sought against the defendant; and (3) the *condemnatio,* in which the judex condemned (usu. to pay the plaintiff a sum) or acquitted the defendant. Pl. *formulae* (for-myə-lee). — Also termed *verba concepta* (vər-bə kən-sep-tə). **2.** *Common-law pleading.* A set form of words (such as those appearing in writs) used in judicial proceedings.

formula deal. An agreement between a movie distributor and an independent or affiliated circuit to exhibit a feature movie in all theaters at a specified percentage of the national gross receipts realized by the theaters.

formula instruction. See JURY INSTRUCTION.

formulary. (16c) **1.** *Hist.* A collection of the forms of proceedings (*formulae*) used in litigation, such as the writ forms kept by the Chancery. See WRIT SYSTEM. **2.** A list of drugs that Medicare or a health-maintenance organization will pay for.

formulary procedure. *Hist.* The common-law method of pleading and practice, which required formulaic compliance with the accepted forms of action even if through elaborate fictions. • In the 19th century, this type of procedure was replaced both in the United States and in England. See *code pleading* under PLEADING (2).

fornication, *n.* (14c) **1.** Voluntary sexual intercourse between two unmarried persons. • Fornication is still a crime in some states, such as Virginia. **2.** *Hist.* Voluntary sexual intercourse with an unmarried woman. • At common law, the status of the woman determined whether the offense was adultery or fornication — *adultery* was sexual intercourse between a man, single or married, and a married woman not his wife; *fornication* was sexual intercourse between a man, single or married, and a single woman. Cf. ADULTERY. — **fornicate,** *vb.* — **fornicator,** *n.*

forprise (for-**prīz**). *Hist.* **1.** An exception or reservation. • The term was frequently used in leases and conveyances. **2.** An exaction. — **forprise,** *vb.*

for-profit corporation. See CORPORATION.

forstall. See FORESTALL.

forswearing (for-**swair**-ing), *n.* (14c) **1.** The act of repudiating or renouncing under oath. **2.** PERJURY. — **forswear,** *vb.*

forthcoming bond. See BOND (2).

forthwith, *adv.* (14c) **1.** Immediately; without delay. **2.** Directly; promptly; within a reasonable time under the circumstances.

fortuitous (for-**t[y]oo**-ə-təs), *adj.* (17c) Occurring by chance. • A fortuitous event may be highly unfortunate. Literally, the term is neutral, despite its common misuse as a synonym for *fortunate.*

fortuitous collision. See COLLISION.

fortuitous event. (1856) **1.** A happening that, because it occurs only by chance or accident, the parties could not reasonably have foreseen. **2.** An event that, so far as contracting parties are aware, depends on chance. **3.** *Louisiana law.* An event that could not have been reasonably foreseen at the time a contract was made. La. Civ. Code art. 1875. — Also termed *cas fortuit.* See FORCE MAJEURE; UNAVOIDABLE-ACCIDENT DOCTRINE.

Fortune 500. An annual compilation of the 500 largest U.S. corporations as ranked by gross revenues. • It is published in, and gets its name from, *Fortune* magazine.

forty, *n. Archaic.* Forty acres of land in the form of a square <the south forty>. • To determine a forty, a section of land (640 acres) was quartered, and one of those quarters was again quartered.

forum, *n.* (15c) **1.** A public place, esp. one devoted to assembly or debate. See PUBLIC FORUM; NONPUBLIC FORUM. **2.** A court or other judicial body; a place of jurisdiction. Pl. **forums, fora.**

forum competens (**for**-əm **kom**-pə-tenz). [Latin] *Hist.* A competent court; a court that has jurisdiction over a case.

forum conveniens (**for**-əm kən-**vee**-nee-enz). [Latin "a suitable forum"] The court in which an action is most appropriately brought, considering the best interests and convenience of the parties and witnesses. Cf. FORUM NON CONVENIENS.

forum inconveniens. See FORUM NON CONVENIENS.

forum non conveniens (**for**-əm non kən-**vee**-nee-enz). [Latin "an unsuitable court"] *Civil procedure.* The doctrine that an appropriate forum — even though competent under the law — may divest itself of jurisdiction if, for the convenience of the litigants and the witnesses, it appears that the action should proceed in another forum in which the action might also have been properly brought in the first place. — Also termed *forum inconveniens.*

forum-selection clause. (1970) A contractual provision in which the parties establish the place (such as the country, state, or type of court) for specified litigation between them. — Also termed *choice-of-exclusive-forum clause.* Cf. CHOICE-OF-LAW CLAUSE.

forum-shopping. (1954) The practice of choosing the most favorable jurisdiction or court in which a claim might be heard. • A plaintiff might engage in forum-shopping, for example, by filing suit in a jurisdiction with a reputation for high jury awards or by filing several similar suits and keeping the one with the preferred judge. Cf. JUDGE-SHOPPING.

forum state. *Conflict of laws.* The state in which a suit is filed.

for use. For the benefit or advantage of another. See USE.

forward agreement. See *forward contract* under CONTRACT.

forward and backward at sea. *Marine insurance.* From port to port in the course of a voyage, and not merely from one terminus to the other and back.

forward confusion. See CONFUSION.

forward contract. See CONTRACT.

forward cover. The purchase of a cash commodity to meet the obligation of a forward contract. See *forward contract* under CONTRACT.

forwarding agent. See AGENT (2).

forward market. See *futures market* under MARKET.

forward-rate agreement. A contract that specifies what the interest rate on an obligation will be on some future date. — Abbr. FRA.

forward triangular merger. See *triangular merger* under MERGER.

foster, *adj.* (bef. 12c) **1.** (Of a relationship) involving parental care given by someone not related by blood or legal adoption <foster home>. **2.** (Of a person) giving or receiving parental care to or from someone not related by blood or legal adoption <foster parent> <foster child>.

foster, *vb.* (12c) To give care to (something or someone); esp., to give parental care to (a child who is not one's natural or legally adopted child).

fosterage, *n.* (17c) **1.** The act of caring for another's child. **2.** The entrusting of a child to another. **3.** The condition of being in the care of another. **4.** The act of encouraging or promoting.

foster care. (1876) **1.** A federally funded child-welfare program providing substitute care for abused and neglected children who have been removed by court order from their parents' or guardians' care or for children voluntarily placed by their parents in the temporary care of the state because of a family crisis. 42 USCA §§ 670–679a. • The state welfare agency selects, trains, supervises, and pays those who serve as foster parents. Cf. ADOPTION (1).

long-term foster care. The placing of a child in foster care for extended periods, perhaps even for the child's entire minority, in lieu of family reunification, termination and adoption, or guardianship. • Although most courts do not generally find this arrangement to be in a child's best interests, sometimes it is the only possibility, as when the child, because of age or disability, is unlikely to be adopted or when, although the parent cannot be permanently reunited with the child, limited contact with the parent would serve the child's best interests. Under the Adoption and Safe Families Act, long-term foster care is the permanent placement of last resort.

2. The area of social services concerned with meeting the needs of children who participate in these types of programs.

foster-care drift. The phenomenon that occurs when children placed in foster care remain in that system, in legal limbo, for too many years of their developmental life before they are reunited with their parents or freed for adoption and placed in permanent homes. • The Adoption and Safe Families Act was passed in 1997 to help rectify this problem. See ADOPTION AND SAFE FAMILIES ACT.

foster-care placement. (1968) The (usu. temporary) act of placing a child in a home with a person or persons who provide parental care for the child. Cf. OUT-OF-HOME PLACEMENT.

foster-care review board. A panel of screened and trained volunteers who routinely review cases of children placed in foster care, examine efforts at permanency planning, and report to the court.

foster child. See CHILD.

foster father. See *foster parent* under PARENT.

foster home. (19c) A household in which foster care is provided to a child who has been removed from his or her birth or adoptive parents, usu. for abuse or neglect. • A foster home is usu. an individual home, but it can also be a group home.

fosterling. (bef. 12c) See *foster child* under CHILD.

foster mother. See *foster parent* under PARENT.

foster parent. See PARENT.

foul bill of lading. See BILL OF LADING.

foundation. (14c) **1.** The basis on which something is supported; esp., evidence or testimony that establishes the admissibility of other evidence <laying the foundation>. **2.** A fund established for charitable, educational, religious, research, or other benevolent purposes; an endowment <the Foundation for the Arts>.

private foundation. A charitable organization that is funded by a single source, derives its income from investments rather than contributions, and makes grants to other charitable organizations. • A private foundation is generally exempt from taxation. IRC (26 USCA) § 509. — Also termed *private nonoperating foundation.*

private nonoperating foundation. See *private foundation.*

private operating foundation. A private foundation that conducts its own charitable program rather than making grants to other charitable organizations. • Most of the foundation's earnings and assets must be used to further its particular charitable purpose.

foundational evidence. See EVIDENCE.

foundational fact. See *predicate fact* under FACT.

founded on, *adj.* (16c) Having as a basis <the suit was founded on the defendant's breach of contract>.

founder, *n.* (14c) **1.** A person who founds or establishes; esp., a person who supplies funds for an institution's future needs. **2.** SETTLOR (1).

founder's share. (*usu. pl.*) In England, a share issued to the founder of a company as a part of the consideration for the business. • Now rare, a founder's share participates in profits only if the dividend on ordinary shares has been paid to a specified amount.

founding father. (1914) A prominent figure in the founding of an institution or esp. a country; specif., one who played a leading role in founding the United States of America, esp. in the Revolutionary War and the making of the U.S. Constitution.

foundling. (14c) A deserted or abandoned infant.

foundling hospital. A charitable institution, found esp. in Europe, the purpose of which is to care for abandoned children.

four, rule of. See RULE OF FOUR.

four corners. (1874) The face of a written instrument. • The phrase derives from the ancient custom of putting all instruments (such as contracts) on a single sheet of parchment, as opposed to multiple pages, no matter how long the sheet might be. At common law, this custom prevented people from fraudulently inserting materials into a fully signed agreement. The requirement was that every contract could have only four corners.

four-corners rule. (1948) **1.** The principle that a document's meaning is to be gathered from the entire document and not from its isolated parts. **2.**

The principle that no extraneous evidence should be used to interpret an unambiguous document. Cf. PAROL-EVIDENCE RULE.

IV-D agency. See CHILD-SUPPORT-ENFORCEMENT AGENCY.

401(k) plan. See EMPLOYEE BENEFIT PLAN.

403(b) plan. See EMPLOYEE BENEFIT PLAN.

419 fraud. See *advance-fee fraud* under FRAUD.

457 plan. See EMPLOYEE BENEFIT PLAN.

Fourteenth Amendment. The constitutional amendment, ratified in 1868, whose primary provisions effectively apply the Bill of Rights to the states by prohibiting states from denying due process and equal protection and from abridging the privileges and immunities of U.S. citizenship. • The amendment also gave Congress the power to enforce these provisions, leading to legislation such as the civil-rights acts.

Fourth Amendment. The constitutional amendment, ratified with the Bill of Rights in 1791, prohibiting unreasonable searches and seizures and the issuance of warrants without probable cause. See PROBABLE CAUSE.

fourth estate. (1821) The journalistic profession; the news media. • The term comes from the British Parliament's reporters' gallery, whose influence was said to equal Parliament's three traditional estates: the Lords Spiritual, the Lords Temporal, and the Commons. (In France, the three estates were the clergy, the nobility, and the commons.)

fourth-sentence remand. See REMAND.

four unities. (1852) The four qualities needed to create a joint tenancy at common law — interest, possession, time, and title. See UNITY (2).

Fox's Libel Act. *Hist.* A 1792 statute that gave the jury in a libel prosecution the right of rendering a guilty or not-guilty verdict on the whole matter in issue. • The jury was no longer bound to find the defendant guilty if it found that the defendant had in fact published the allegedly libelous statement. The Act empowered juries to decide whether the defendant's statement conformed to the legal standard for libel.

FPA. *abbr.* Free from particular average.

FPC clause. See AREA-RATE CLAUSE.

FPLS. *abbr.* FEDERAL PARENT LOCATOR SERVICE.

Fr. *abbr.* **1.** French. **2.** FRAGMENTA.

FRA. *abbr.* **1.** FEDERAL RAILROAD ADMINISTRATION. **2.** FORWARD-RATE AGREEMENT.

fractional, *adj.* (1815) (Of a tract of land) covering an area less than the acreage reflected on a survey; pertaining to any irregular division of land containing either more or less than the conventional amount of acreage.

fractional currency. See CURRENCY.

fractional interest. See *undivided interest* under INTEREST (2).

fragmented literal similarity. See SIMILARITY.

frame, *vb.* (14c) **1.** To plan, shape, or construct; esp., to draft or otherwise draw up (a document). **2.** To incriminate (an innocent person) with false evidence, esp. fabricated. — **framable, frameable,** *adj.*

frame-up, *n.* A plot to make an innocent person appear guilty.

framing. On the Internet, a website's display of another entity's Web page inside a bordered area, often without displaying the page's URL or domain name. • Framing may constitute a derivative work and may infringe on a copyright or trademark if done without giving credit to or obtaining permission from the other website's owner.

francbordus. See FREE-BORD.

franchise (fran-chIz), *n.* (14c) **1.** The right to vote. — Also termed *elective franchise.* **2.** The government-conferred right to engage in a specific business or to exercise corporate powers. — Also termed *corporate franchise; general franchise.*

> **franchise appurtenant to land.** *Rare.* A franchise that is used in connection with real property and thus is sometimes characterized as real property.

> **general franchise.** A corporation's charter.

> **special franchise.** A right conferred by the government, esp. one given to a public utility, to use property for a public use but for private profit.

3. The sole right granted by the owner of a trademark or tradename to engage in business or to sell a good or service in a certain area. **4.** The business or territory controlled by the person or entity that has been granted such a right.

> **commercial franchise.** A franchise using local capital and management by contracting with third parties to operate a facility identified as offering a particular brand of goods or services.

> **sports franchise. 1.** A franchise granted by a professional sports league to field a team in that league. **2.** The team itself.

> **trial franchise.** A franchise having an initial term of limited duration, such as one year.

franchise, *vb.* (14c) To grant (to another) the sole right of engaging in a certain business or in a business using a particular trademark in a certain area.

franchise agreement. (1905) The contract between a franchisor and franchisee establishing the terms and conditions of the franchise relationship. • State and federal laws regulate franchise agreements.

franchise appurtenant to land. See FRANCHISE (2).

franchise clause. *Insurance.* A provision in a casualty insurance policy stating that the insurer will pay a claim only if it is more than a stated amount, and that the insured is responsible for all damages if the claim is under that amount. • Unlike a deductible, which the insured always has to pay, with a franchise clause, once the claim exceeds the stated amount, the insurer pays the entire claim.

franchisee. One who is granted a franchise.

franchise fee. See FEE (1).

franchiser. See FRANCHISOR.

franchise tax. See TAX.

franchisor. (19c) One who grants a franchise. — Also spelled *franchiser*.

francus bancus. See FREE BENCH.

frank, *adj.* [Law French] *Hist.* Free. — Also spelled *fraunc*; *fraunche*; *fraunke*.

frank, *n.* **1.** (*cap.*) A member of the Germanic people who conquered Gaul in the 6th century. • France received its name from the Franks. **2.** A signature, stamp, or mark affixed to mail as a substitute for postage. **3.** The privilege of sending certain mail free of charge, accorded to certain government officials, such as members of Congress and federal courts. — Also termed (in sense 3) *franking privilege*. — **frank,** *vb.*

frankalmoin (**frangk**-al-moyn). [Law French "free alms"] (16c) *Hist.* A spiritual tenure by which a religious institution held land, usu. with a general duty to pray for the donor. • This tenure differed from the tenure by *divine service*, which required specific church services, such as a certain number of masses or alms distributions. — Also spelled *frankalmoign*; *frankalmoigne*. — Also termed *almoign*; *almoin*; *free alms*; *libera eleemosyna*. See *spiritual tenure* under TENURE.

frank bank. See FREE BENCH.

frank-fee. (15c) *Hist.* Freehold land — land that one held to oneself and one's heirs — exempted from all services except homage; land held other than by ancient demesne or copyhold.

franking privilege. See FRANK (3).

frank-law. *Hist.* The rights and privileges of a citizen or freeman; specif., the condition of being legally capable of giving an oath (esp. as a juror or witness).

franklin (**frangk**-lin). (14c) *Hist.* A freeman; a freeholder; a gentleman. — Also spelled *francling*; *frankleyn*; *frankleyne*.

frankmarriage. (14c) *Hist.* An entailed estate in which the donor retains control of the land by refusing to accept feudal services from the donee

(usu. the donor's daughter) for three generations. • If the donee's issue fail in that time, the land returns to the donor. A donor who accepted homage (and the corresponding services arising from it) from the donee risked losing control of the land to a collateral heir. After three generations — a time considered sufficient to demonstrate that the line was well established — the donee's heir could insist on paying homage; doing so transformed the estate into a fee simple. — Also termed *liberum maritagium.* See MARITAGIUM.

frankpledge. (bef. 12c) *Hist.* A promise given to the sovereign by a group of ten freeholders (a *tithing*) ensuring the group's good conduct. • The frankpledge was of Saxon origin, but continued after the Norman Conquest. The members of the group were not liable for an injury caused by an offending member, but they did act as bail to ensure that the culprit would appear in court. They were bound to produce a wrongdoer for trial. — Also termed *borrow*; *laughe*. Cf. DECENARY.

Franks hearing. (1979) A hearing to determine whether a police officer's affidavit used to obtain a search warrant that yields incriminating evidence was based on false statements by the police officer. *Franks v. Delaware*, 438 U.S. 154, 98 S.Ct. 2674 (1978).

frank-tenant. *Hist.* A freeholder. — Also termed *francus tenens*. See FREEHOLD.

frank-tenement. *Hist.* A free tenement; a freehold. • This term described both the tenure and the estate.

FRAP (frap). *abbr.* FEDERAL RULES OF APPELLATE PROCEDURE.

fraternal, *adj.* (15c) **1.** Of or relating to the relationship of brothers. **2.** Of or relating to a fraternity or a fraternal benefit association.

fraternal benefit association. A voluntary organization or society created for its members' mutual aid and benefit rather than for profit, and whose members have a common and worthy cause, objective, or interest. • These associations usu. have a lodge system, a governing body, rituals, and a benefits system for their members. — Also termed *fraternal benefit society*; *fraternity*; *fraternal lodge*; *fraternal order*. Cf. FRIENDLY SOCIETY.

fraternal insurance. See INSURANCE.

fraternal lodge. See FRATERNAL BENEFIT ASSOCIATION.

fraternal order. See FRATERNAL BENEFIT ASSOCIATION.

fraternal society. See *benevolent association* under ASSOCIATION.

fraternity. See FRATERNAL BENEFIT ASSOCIATION.

fratricide (fra-trə-sɪd *or* fray-). (15c) **1.** The killing of one's brother or sister. **2.** One who has killed one's brother or sister. Cf. SORORICIDE. — **fratricidal**, *adj.*

fraud, *n.* (14c) **1.** A knowing misrepresentation of the truth or concealment of a material fact to induce another to act to his or her detriment. • Fraud is usu. a tort, but in some cases (esp. when the conduct is willful) it may be a crime. — Also termed *intentional fraud*. **2.** A misrepresentation made recklessly without belief in its truth to induce another person to act. **3.** A tort arising from a knowing misrepresentation, concealment of material fact, or reckless misrepresentation made to induce another to act to his or her detriment. **4.** Unconscionable dealing; esp., in contract law, the unfair use of the power arising out of the parties' relative positions and resulting in an unconscionable bargain. — **fraudulent**, *adj.*

actual fraud. (17c) A concealment or false representation through a statement or conduct that injures another who relies on it in acting. — Also termed *fraud in fact*; *positive fraud*; *moral fraud*.

advance-fee fraud. A criminal fraud in which the victim is persuaded by the perpetrator to pay "fees" in anticipation of receiving a much larger benefit that is ultimately never delivered. • The perpetrator usu. claims to have, or to represent someone with, a large sum of money that must be immediately transferred out of a foreign country for some compelling reason, such as to avoid seizure by a government. The criminal promises the victim a portion of the money in return for the victim's agreement to open a bank account in the victim's name. The victim then must pay "upfront fees" to the designated "bank" and others. Although the Internet has become a favorite tool for this fraud, it has been around for years, beginning with handwritten or typed letters and later faxes. Because advance-fee fraud is believed to have originated in Nigeria, it is also termed *419 fraud* after the section of the Nigerian penal code designed to punish those who defraud by this method.

affiliate click fraud. Click fraud committed by a third party who agrees to host the ad in exchange for payment based on the number of clicks. See *click fraud*.

affinity fraud. A fraud in which the perpetrator tailors the fraud to target members of a particular group united by common traits or interests that produce inherent trust. • The perpetrator often is or pretends to be a member of the group. Investment scams such as Ponzi or pyramid schemes are common forms of affinity fraud. When a religious group is targeted, it is usu. called *religious-affinity fraud*.

bank fraud. The criminal offense of knowingly executing, or attempting to execute, a scheme or artifice to defraud a financial institution, or to obtain property owned by or under the control of a financial institution, by means of false or fraudulent pretenses, representations, or promises. 18 USCA § 1344.

bankruptcy fraud. (1815) A fraudulent act connected to a bankruptcy case; esp., any of several proscribed acts performed knowingly and fraudulently in a bankruptcy case, such as concealing assets or destroying, withholding, or falsifying documents in an effort to defeat bankruptcy-code provisions. See 18 USCA § 152. — Also termed *criminal bankruptcy*; *bankruptcy crime*.

civil fraud. (18c) **1.** FRAUD (3). **2.** *Tax.* An intentional — but not willful — evasion of taxes. • The distinction between an intentional (i.e., *civil*) and willful (i.e., *criminal*) fraud is not always clear, but *civil fraud* carries only a monetary, noncriminal penalty. Cf. *criminal fraud*; TAX EVASION.

click fraud. A scheme in which a person or robot repeatedly clicks on a merchant's pay-per-click advertisement on a website for purposes other than viewing the website or making a purchase.

collateral fraud. See *extrinsic fraud* (1).

common-law fraud. See *promissory fraud*.

competitor click fraud. Click fraud committed by a business's competitor in order to increase the amount of money the advertising merchant must pay to the site hosting the ad. See *click fraud*.

constructive fraud. (18c) **1.** Unintentional deception or misrepresentation that causes injury to another. — Also termed *legal fraud*; *fraud in contemplation of law*; *equitable fraud*; *fraud in equity*. **2.** See *fraud in law*.

criminal fraud. (18c) Fraud that has been made illegal by statute and that subjects the offender to criminal penalties such as fines and imprisonment. • An example is the willful evasion of taxes accomplished by filing a fraudulent tax return. Cf. *civil fraud*; *larceny by trick* under LARCENY.

election fraud. See ELECTION FRAUD.

equitable fraud. See *constructive fraud* (1).

extrinsic fraud. (1851) **1.** Deception that is collateral to the issues being considered in the case; intentional misrepresentation or deceptive behavior outside the transaction itself (whether a contract or a lawsuit), depriving one party of informed consent or full participation. • For example, a person might engage in extrinsic fraud by convincing a litigant not to hire counsel or answer by dishonestly saying the matter will not be pursued. — Also termed *collateral fraud*. **2.** Deception that prevents a person from knowing about or asserting certain rights.

419 fraud. See *advance-fee fraud*.

fraud in contemplation of law. See *constructive fraud* (1).

fraud in equity. See *constructive fraud* (1).

fraud in fact. See *actual fraud*.

fraud in law. (17c) Fraud that is presumed under the circumstances, as when a debtor transfers assets and thereby impairs creditors' efforts to collect sums due. — Also termed *constructive fraud*.

fraud in the execution. See *fraud in the factum*.

fraud in the factum. (1848) Fraud occurring when a legal instrument as actually executed differs from the one intended for execution by the person who executes it, or when the instrument may have had no legal existence. • Compared to fraud in the inducement, fraud in the factum occurs only rarely, as when a blind person signs a mortgage when misleadingly told that the paper is just a letter. — Also termed *fraud in the execution*; *fraud in the making*. Cf. *fraud in the inducement*.

fraud in the inducement. (1831) Fraud occurring when a misrepresentation leads another to enter into a transaction with a false impression of the risks, duties, or obligations involved; an intentional misrepresentation of a material risk or duty reasonably relied on, thereby injuring the other party without vitiating the contract itself, esp. about a fact relating to value. — Also termed *fraud in the procurement*. Cf. *fraud in the factum*.

fraud in the making. See *fraud in the factum*.

fraud in the procurement. See *fraud in the inducement*.

fraud on the community. *Family law.* In a community-property state, the deliberate hiding or fraudulent transfer of community assets before a divorce or death for the purpose of preventing the other spouse from claiming a half-interest ownership in the property.

fraud on the court. (1810) In a judicial proceeding, a lawyer's or party's misconduct so serious that it undermines or is intended to undermine the integrity of the proceeding. • Examples are bribery of a juror and introduction of fabricated evidence.

fraud on the market. 1. Fraud occurring when an issuer of securities gives out misinformation that affects the market price of stock, the result being that people who buy or sell are effectively misled even though they did not rely on the statement itself or anything derived from it other than the market price. **2.** The securities-law claim based on such fraud. See FRAUD-ON-THE-MARKET PRINCIPLE.

fraud on the Patent Office. *Patents.* A defense in a patent-infringement action, attacking the validity of the patent on the grounds that the patentee gave the examiner false or misleading information or withheld relevant information that the examiner would have considered important in considering patentability. • The scope of prohibited acts is wider than that covered by common-law fraud, and today the defense is generally called "inequitable conduct before the PTO." If the defense is established, the entire patent is rendered unenforceable. See *defense of inequitable conduct* under DEFENSE (1).

hidden fraud. See *fraudulent concealment* under CONCEALMENT.

insurance fraud. Fraud committed against an insurer, as when an insured lies on a policy application or fabricates a claim.

intrinsic fraud. (1832) Deception that pertains to an issue involved in an original action. • Examples include the use of fabricated evidence, a false return of service, perjured testimony, and false receipts or other commercial documents.

legal fraud. See *constructive fraud* (1).

long-firm fraud. The act of obtaining goods or money on credit by falsely posing as an established business and having no intent to pay for the goods or repay the loan.

mail fraud. (1918) An act of fraud using the U.S. Postal Service, as in making false representations through the mail to obtain an economic advantage. 18 USCA §§ 1341–1347.

moral fraud. See *actual fraud*.

positive fraud. See *actual fraud*.

promissory fraud. (1934) A promise to perform made when the promisor had no intention of performing the promise. — Also termed *common-law fraud*.

religious-affinity fraud. See *affinity fraud*.

tax fraud. See TAX EVASION.

wire fraud. (1955) An act of fraud using electronic communications, as by making false representations on the telephone to obtain money. • The federal Wire Fraud Act provides that any artifice to defraud by means of wire or other electronic communications (such as radio or television) in foreign or interstate commerce is a crime. 18 USCA § 1343.

fraud, badge of. See BADGE OF FRAUD.

fraud by hindsight. *Hist. Securities.* A claim of fraud based on the assumption that a corporation deliberately misled investors by issuing optimistic financial statements or forecasts and later reporting worse-than-expected results. Suits for fraud by hindsight were common in the early 1990s. Congress eliminated this claim in the Private Securities Litigation Reform Act of 1995. 15 USCA §§ 78u-4(b).

fraudfeasor (**frawd**-fee-zər). A person who has committed fraud. — Also termed *defrauder*.

fraud in the execution. See *fraud in the factum* under FRAUD.

fraud on creditors. See FRAUDULENT CONVEYANCE (1).

fraud on the community. In a community-property state, the deliberate hiding or fraudulent transfer of community assets before a divorce or death for the purpose of preventing the other spouse from claiming a half-interest ownership in the property.

fraud-on-the-market principle. *Securities.* The doctrine that, in a claim under the antifraud provisions of the federal securities laws, a plaintiff may presumptively establish reliance on a misstatement about a security's value — without proving actual knowledge of the fraudulent statement — if the stock is purchased in an open and developed securities market. ● This doctrine recognizes that the market price of an issuer's stock reflects all available public information. The presumption is rebuttable. — Also termed *fraud-on-the-market theory.* See *fraud on the market* under FRAUD.

frauds, statute of. See STATUTE OF FRAUDS.

fraudulent act. Conduct involving bad faith, dishonesty, a lack of integrity, or moral turpitude. — Also termed *dishonest act*; *fraudulent or dishonest act.*

fraudulent alienation. 1. The transfer of property with an intent to defraud others, esp. creditors and lienholders. **2.** The transfer of an estate asset by the estate's administrator for little or no consideration.

fraudulent alienee. See ALIENEE.

fraudulent banking. The receipt of a deposit by a banker who knew that the bank was insolvent at the time of the deposit.

fraudulent claim. A false insurance claim. See FRAUD.

fraudulent concealment. See CONCEALMENT.

fraudulent-concealment rule. See CONCEALMENT RULE.

fraudulent conversion. See CONVERSION (2).

fraudulent conveyance. (17c) **1.** A transfer of property for little or no consideration, made for the purpose of hindering or delaying a creditor by putting the property beyond the creditor's reach; a transaction by which the owner of real or personal property seeks to place the property beyond the reach of creditors. — Also termed *fraud on creditors.* **2.** *Bankruptcy.* A prebankruptcy transfer or obligation made or incurred by a debtor for little or no consideration or with the actual intent to hinder, delay, or defraud a creditor. ● A bankruptcy trustee may recover such a conveyance from the transferee if the requirements of 11 USCA § 548 are met. — Also termed *fraudulent transfer.* Cf. PREFERENTIAL TRANSFER.

fraudulent debt. See DEBT.

fraudulent joinder. See JOINDER.

fraudulent marriage. See MARRIAGE (1).

fraudulent misrepresentation. See MISREPRESENTATION.

fraudulent or dishonest act. See FRAUDULENT ACT.

fraudulent pretenses. See FALSE PRETENSES.

fraudulent representation. See *fraudulent misrepresentation* under MISREPRESENTATION.

fraudulent sale. See SALE.

fraudulent transfer. See FRAUDULENT CONVEYANCE (2).

fray. See AFFRAY.

FRB. *abbr.* FEDERAL RESERVE BOARD OF GOVERNORS.

FRCA. *abbr.* See FAIR-CREDIT-REPORTING ACT.

FRCP. *abbr.* FEDERAL RULES OF CIVIL PROCEDURE.

F.R.D. *abbr.* Federal Rules Decisions; a series of reported federal court decisions (beginning in 1938) that construe or apply the Federal Rules of Civil and Criminal Procedure. ● Also included are rule changes, ceremonial proceedings of federal courts, and articles on federal-court practice and procedure. — Often written *FRD.*

FRE. *abbr.* FEDERAL RULES OF EVIDENCE.

Freddie Mac. See FEDERAL HOME LOAN MORTGAGE CORPORATION.

free, *adj.* (bef. 12c) **1.** Having legal and political rights; enjoying political and civil liberty <a free citizen> <a free populace>. **2.** Not subject to the constraint or domination of another; enjoying personal freedom; emancipated <a free person>. **3.** Characterized by choice, rather than by compulsion or constraint <free will>. **4.** Unburdened <the land was free of any encumbrances>. **5.** Not confined by force or restraint <free from prison>. **6.** Unrestricted and unregulated <free trade>. **7.** Costing nothing; gratuitous <free tickets to the game>. — **freely,** *adv.*

free, *vb.* **1.** To liberate. **2.** To remove (a person, animal, or thing) from a constraint or burden.

free agency, *n.* (ca. 1955) A professional athlete's ability to negotiate an employment contract with any team in the league, rather than being confined to the league's collective-bargaining system. • Free agency is usu. granted to veteran players who have been in the league for a certain number of years. Cf. RESERVE CLAUSE. — **free agent,** *n.*

free alms. See FRANKALMOIN.

free alongside ship. A mercantile-contract term allocating the rights and duties of the buyer and the seller of goods with respect to delivery, payment, and risk of loss, whereby the seller must clear the goods for export, and deliver the goods to the wharf beside the buyer's chosen vessel. • The seller's delivery is complete (and the risk of loss passes to the buyer) when the goods are placed on the wharf beside the vessel. The buyer is responsible for all costs of carriage. This term is used only when goods are transported by sea or inland waterway. UCC § 2-319. — Abbr. FAS. Cf. FREE ON BOARD; DELIVERED EX QUAY.

free and clear, *adj.* Unencumbered by any liens; marketable <free and clear title>.

free and common socage. See *free socage* under SOCAGE.

free and equal, *adj.* (Of an election) conducted so that the electorate has a reasonable opportunity to vote, with each vote given the same effect.

free bench. *Hist.* A widow's (and occasionally a widower's) interest in the deceased spouse's estate. • *Free bench* gave the surviving spouse a half interest in the estate until death or remarriage. — Also termed *francus bancus*; *frank bank*; *liber bancus*.

free-bord. (17c) *Hist.* **1.** A small strip of land (usu. 2½ feet wide and lying just outside a fence) that the owner of the fenced property was allowed to claim and use. **2.** The right of claiming that quantity of land. — Also spelled *freebord*; *free bord*; *freeboard*. — Also termed *francbordus*.

free carrier. A mercantile-contract term allocating the rights and duties of the buyer and the seller of goods with respect to delivery, payment, and risk of loss, whereby the seller must clear the goods for export and deliver them to the buyer's chosen carrier at a named place. • The seller's delivery is complete (and the risk of loss passes to the buyer) when the goods are loaded on the collecting vehicle or otherwise placed at the carrier's disposal. The buyer is responsible for all costs of carriage. There are no restrictions on the buyer's choice of carrier. — Abbr. FCA.

free chapel. *Hist. Eccles. law.* A church founded by the Crown (or by a person under royal grant) and not subject to the bishop's jurisdiction.

free chase. See CHASE.

free city. *Int'l law.* A country-like political and territorial entity that, although independent in principle, does not have the full capacity to act according to general international law but is nevertheless a subject of international law.

freedman (freed-mən). (16c) *Hist.* An emancipated slave.

freedom. (bef. 12c) **1.** The state of being free or liberated. **2.** A political right.

Freedom of Access to Clinic Entrances Act. A 1994 federal statute that provides for criminal sanctions, private civil causes of action, and civil action by the U.S. Attorney General against a person who uses force, threat of force, or physical obstruction to injure, intimidate, or interfere with a provider or patient of reproductive services or who damages a reproductive-services facility. — Abbr. FACE.

freedom of assembly. See RIGHT OF ASSEMBLY.

freedom of association. (1889) The right to join with others in a common undertaking that would be lawful if pursued individually. • This right is protected by the First Amendment to the U.S. Constitution. The government may not prohibit outsiders from joining an association, but the insiders do not necessarily have a right to exclude others. Cf. RIGHT OF ASSEMBLY.

freedom of expressive association. The constitutional right of an individual to associate with others, without undue government interference, for the purpose of engaging in activities protected by the First Amendment, such as speech, assembly, and the exercise of religion.

freedom of intimate association. The constitutional right of privacy to form and preserve certain intimate human relationships without intrusion by the state because the relationships safeguard individual freedom. • The group relationships protected by the right to freedom of intimate association are familial in nature and are characterized by deep attachments, a high degree of commitment, and the sharing of distinctly personal aspects of life. The exclusion of others is an essential characteristic of these relationships.

freedom of choice. (1817) **1.** The liberty embodied in the exercise of one's rights. **2.** The parents' opportunity to select a school for their child in a unitary, integrated school system that is devoid of de jure segregation. **3.** The liberty to exercise one's right of privacy, esp. the right to have an abortion. — Also termed *right to choose*; *choice*.

freedom of contract. (1879) The doctrine that people have the right to bind themselves legally; a judicial concept that contracts are based on mutual agreement and free choice, and thus should not be hampered by external control such as governmental interference. • This is the principle that people are able to fashion their relations by private agreements, esp. as opposed to the assigned roles of the feudal system. As Maine famously said, "[T]he movement of progressive societies has been a movement from *Status* to *Contract*." Henry Sumner Maine, *Ancient Law* 165 (1864). — Also termed *liberty of contract*; *autonomy of the parties.*

freedom of expression. (1877) The freedom of speech, press, assembly, or religion as guaranteed by the First Amendment; the prohibition of governmental interference with those freedoms. Cf. FREEDOM OF SPEECH.

Freedom of Information Act. The federal statute that establishes guidelines for public disclosure of documents and materials created and held by federal agencies. 5 USCA § 552. • The basic purpose of the statute, or of a state statute modeled after it, is to give the public access to official information so that the public will be better informed and the government will be more accountable for its actions. — Abbr. FOIA. See REVERSE FOIA SUIT.

freedom of intimate association. See FREEDOM OF ASSOCIATION.

freedom of petition. See RIGHT TO PETITION.

freedom of religion. (16c) The right to adhere to any form of religion or none, to practice or abstain from practicing religious beliefs, and to be free from governmental interference with or promotion of religion, as guaranteed by the First Amendment and Article VI, § 3 of the U.S. Constitution.

freedom of speech. (17c) The right to express one's thoughts and opinions without governmental restriction, as guaranteed by the First Amendment. — Also termed *liberty of speech*. Cf. FREEDOM OF EXPRESSION.

Freedom of Speech Clause. See SPEECH CLAUSE.

freedom of the city. *Hist.* An immunity or privilege from some burden, esp. from county jurisdiction and its privilege of municipal taxation and self-government, held under a royal charter.

freedom of the press. (17c) The right to print and publish materials without governmental intervention, as guaranteed by the First Amendment. — Also termed *liberty of the press.*

freedom of the seas. *Int'l law.* The principle that the seas beyond territorial waters are not subject to any country's control. • Ships on the high seas are subject only to the jurisdiction of the country whose flag they fly, except in cases of piracy, hijacking, hot pursuit from territorial waters, slave trading, and certain rights of approach by warships. — Also termed *mare liberum.*

freedom-to-create statute. *Patents.* A law restricting an employer's ability to require employees to assign to the employer all rights to their inventions, even those independently developed.

freedom-to-operate search. See INFRINGEMENT SEARCH.

free election. See ELECTION (3).

free enterprise. (1890) A private and consensual system of production and distribution, usu. conducted for a profit in a competitive environment that is relatively free of governmental interference. See CAPITALISM.

free entry, egress, and regress (ee-gres / ree-gres). *Hist.* A person's right to go on land as often as reasonably necessary. • A tenant could go on land to gather crops still growing after the tenancy expired.

Free Exercise Clause. (1950) The constitutional provision (U.S. Const. amend. I) prohibiting the government from interfering in people's religious practices or forms of worship. — Also termed *Exercise Clause.* Cf. ESTABLISHMENT CLAUSE.

free fishery. See FISHERY (1).

free-gas clause. *Oil & gas.* A provision in an oil-and-gas lease entitling the lessor or the surface owner to use gas produced from the leased property without charge. • Used commonly in colder states, free-gas clauses usu. limit how the gas may be used (e.g., domestic heating and light), how much gas may be used (e.g., not more than 300 MCF per year), or both.

freehold, *n.* (15c) **1.** An estate in land held in fee simple, in fee tail, or for term of life; any real-property interest that is or may become possessory. • At common law, these estates were all created by enfeoffment with livery of seisin. **2.** The tenure by which such an estate is held. — Also termed *freehold estate*; *estate in freehold*; *freehold interest*; *franktenement*; *liberum tenementum.* Cf. LEASEHOLD.

   determinable freehold. See *determinable estate* under ESTATE (4).

   movable freehold. (18c) The land a seashore owner acquires or loses as water recedes or approaches.

   perpetual freehold. An estate given to a grantee for life, and then successively to the grantee's heirs for life. • The effect of this type of freehold was to keep land within a family in perpetuity, much like a fee tail.

freeholder. (15c) *Hist.* One who possesses a freehold.

freeholder's court baron. See COURT BARON.

freehold estate. See FREEHOLD.

freehold interest. See FREEHOLD.

freehold land society. (*usu. pl.*) *Hist.* A society in England created to enable mechanics, artisans, and other workers to buy at the lowest possible price freehold land with a sufficient yearly value to entitle the owner to the right to vote in the county in which the land was located.

free ice. *Hist.* Ice in navigable streams that does not belong to the adjacent riparian owner or to another with the right to appropriate it, but that belongs to the person who first appropriates it.

free law. *Hist.* The civil rights enjoyed by a free-man (as opposed to a serf). • Free law could be forfeited if the freeman was convicted of treason or an infamous crime.

freeman. (bef. 12c) **1.** A person who possesses and enjoys all the civil and political rights belonging to the people under a free government. **2.** A person who is not a slave. **3.** *Hist.* A member of a municipal corporation (a city or borough) who possesses full civic rights, esp. the right to vote. **4.** *Hist.* A freeholder. Cf. VILLEIN. **5.** *Hist.* An allodial landowner. Cf. VASSAL. — Also written *free man.*

Freeman–Walter–Abele test. *Patents.* An outmoded two-step judicial test for determining whether a claimed invention is an unpatentable mathematical algorithm. • The test looks first to whether an algorithm is explicit or inherent in the claim, and second to whether a patent would wholly preempt others from using the algorithm. *In re Freeman,* 573 F.2d 1237 (CCPA 1978); *In re Walter,* 618 F.2d 758 (CCPA 1980); *In re Abele,* 684 F.2d 902 (CCPA 1982). The Federal Circuit has said the test has "little, if any, applicability" after *State St. Bank & Trust Co. v. Signature Fin. Group,* 149 F.3d 1368 (Fed. Cir. 1998).

free market. See *open market* under MARKET.

free of all average. *Maritime law.* Insurance that covers a total loss only. — Abbr. FAA.

free on board. (ca. 1924) A mercantile-contract term allocating the rights and duties of the buyer and the seller of goods with respect to delivery, payment, and risk of loss, whereby the seller must clear the goods for export, and the buyer must arrange for transportation. • The seller's delivery is complete (and the risk of loss passes to the buyer) when the goods pass the transporter's rail. The buyer is responsible for all costs of carriage. UCC § 2.319. — Abbr. FOB. Cf. FREE ALONGSIDE SHIP; DELIVERED EX SHIP.

> **FOB destination.** A mercantile term denoting that the seller is required to pay the freight charges as far as the buyer's named destination.

> **FOB shipping.** A mercantile term denoting that the seller is required to bear the risk of placing the goods on a carrier.

free port. See PORT.

free ride. (19c) A benefit obtained without paying a fair price. • For example, a competitor who used aerial photographs of a plant-construction site to discover secret manufacturing techniques was judicially criticized for getting a free ride, in contrast to others who might spend time and effort legally reverse-engineering the same techniques.

free rider. One who obtains an economic benefit at another's expense without contributing to it. — Also written *freerider.*

free seas. See SEA.

free socage. See SOCAGE.

Freestone rider. See PUGH CLAUSE.

free trade, *n.* (17c) The open and unrestricted import and export of goods without barriers, such as quotas or tariffs, other than those charged only as a revenue source, as opposed to those designed to protect domestic businesses. Cf. *protective tariff* under TARIFF (2).

free-trade zone. A duty-free area within a country to promote commerce, esp. transshipment and processing, without entering into the country's market. — Also termed *foreign trade zone; free port.*

freeware. (ca. 1983) Software, esp. open-source code, that is made generally available with express or implicit permission for anyone to use, copy, modify, and distribute for any purpose, including financial gain. • The term "free" refers to usage rights rather than price — a distinction important in two respects. First, a user may purchase the initial copy of freeware. Second, software available at no cost may not include permission for the software's user to copy, modify, or give away the software. — Also termed *free software.* Cf. PROPRIETARY SOFTWARE; SEMI-FREE SOFTWARE; SHAREWARE.

free warren. See WARREN.

freeze, *n.* (1942) **1.** A period when the government restricts or immobilizes certain commercial activity.

> **credit freeze.** (1922)A period when the government restricts bank-lending.

> **wage-and-price freeze.** (1943) A period when the government forbids the increase of wages and prices.

2. A recapitalization of a closed corporation so that the value of its existing capital is concentrated primarily in preferred stock rather than in common stock. • By freezing capital, the owner can transfer the common stock to heirs without taxation while continuing to enjoy preferred-stock income during the owner's lifetime, while the common stock grows.

freeze, *vb.* **1.** To cause to become fixed and unable to increase <to freeze interest rates> <to freeze prices>. **2.** To make immobile by government mandate or banking action <to freeze assets>. **3.** To cease physical movement, esp. when ordered by a law enforcement officer <the police officer shouted at the suspect to freeze>.

freezee, *n.* A person or entity subjected to a freeze-out.

freezeout, *n. Corporations.* A transaction in which a shareholder or group of shareholders obtains the entire common-equity interest in a company while the other shareholders receive cash, debt, or preferred stock in exchange for their common-equity shares. — Also termed *going-private transaction.* Cf. SQUEEZE-OUT.

> **parent–subsidiary freezeout.** A transaction in which a parent company uses its majority ownership in a subsidiary to acquire the minority shareholders' interest.

> **pure freezeout.** A transaction in which company insiders or employees acquire all the public shares of the company, often with the help of lenders. — Also termed *management buyout.* See *management buyout* under BUYOUT.

> **second-step freezeout.** A freezeout that takes place as the final phase of a two-step takeover, after the initial phase in which a majority interest is acquired by the purchase of shares in a tender offer, on the open market, from the issuer, from a control group, or from an issuer–control-group combination.

freeze out, *vb.* **1.** To subject one to a freeze-out. **2.** To exclude a business competitor <freezing out the competition>.

freeze-out merger. See *cash merger* under MERGER.

freight. (15c) **1.** Goods transported by water, land, or air; CARGO. **2.** The compensation paid to a carrier for transporting goods.

> **dead freight.** The amount paid by a shipper to a shipowner for the ship's unused cargo space.

freight absorption. See ABSORPTION (5).

freight forwarder. *Maritime law.* A person or company whose business is to receive and ship goods for others. ● A freight forwarder may be an agent of the cargo's owner or of the carrier, or may be an independent contractor acting as a principal and assuming the carrier's responsibility for delivering the cargo. — Also termed *third-party logistical service provider; forwarding agent.*

freighting voyage. See VOYAGE.

freight rate. See RATE.

F reorganization. See REORGANIZATION (2).

fresh, *adj.* (13c) Recent; not stale; characterized by newness without any material interval.

fresh complaint. (1853) A reasonably prompt lodging of a grievance; esp., a victim's prompt report of a sexual assault to someone trustworthy.

fresh-complaint rule. The theory that a sexual-assault victim's credibility is bolstered if the victim reports the assault soon after it occurs. ● Most courts no longer recognize this theory.

fresh disseisin. See DISSEISIN.

fresh fine. See FINE (5).

fresh force. *Hist.* Force, such as disseisin or deforcement, newly done. ● This term refers to force used in a town, and for which a remedy (the Assize of Fresh Force) existed. See *assize of fresh force* under ASSIZE (8).

fresh pursuit. (17c) **1.** The right of a police officer to make a warrantless search of a fleeing suspect or to cross jurisdictional lines to arrest a fleeing suspect. **2.** The right of a person to use reasonable force to retake property that has just been taken. — Also termed *hot pursuit.*

fresh start. (1857) *Bankruptcy.* The favorable financial status obtained by a debtor who receives a release from personal liability on prepetition debts or who reorganizes debt obligations through the confirmation and completion of a bankruptcy plan.

Friday market. See MARKET.

friendly amendment. See AMENDMENT (3).

friendly fire. (1976) **1.** A fire burning where it is intended to burn, yet capable of causing unintended damage. **2.** Military or police gunfire that injures one's own side.

friendly-parent law. A statute that requires or allows a judge to consider as a factor in awarding custody the extent to which one parent encourages or thwarts the child's relationship with the other parent.

friendly-parent principle. *Family law.* The theory that if one parent is more likely to support the child's relationship with the other parent after a divorce is granted, then that more supportive parent should be awarded custody. ● This theory has been criticized as fundamentally flawed because (1) a court may not consider the legitimate fears and concerns that motivate a parent's "unfriendly" behavior, and (2) the theory's simplicity discourages a parent from revealing anything negative about the other parent to the child, even if relevant to the child's safety, for fear of being viewed as too hostile. — Also termed *friendly-parent doctrine; friendly-parent paradigm.*

friendly society. (18c) In Britain, a voluntary association, supported by subscriptions or contributions, for the purpose of providing financial relief to ill members and to their widows and children upon death. ● Friendly societies are regulated by statute. See *benevolent association* under ASSOCIATION. Cf. FRATERNAL BENEFIT ASSOCIATION.

friendly subpoena. See SUBPOENA.

friendly suit. (18c) A lawsuit in which all the parties have agreed beforehand to allow a court to resolve the issues. ● Friendly suits are often filed by settling parties who wish to have a judgment entered.

friendly suitor. See WHITE KNIGHT.

friendly takeover. See TAKEOVER.

friend of the court. (1816) **1.** AMICUS CURIAE. **2.** In some jurisdictions, an official who investigates and advises the court in domestic-relations cases involving minors. ● The friend of the court may also help enforce court orders in those cases.

friend-of-the-court brief. See *amicus brief* under BRIEF.

fringe benefit. See BENEFIT.

frisk, *n.* (18c) A pat-down search to discover a concealed weapon. — Also termed *pat-down.* See STOP AND FRISK. Cf. SEARCH (1).

frivolous, *adj.* (15c) Lacking a legal basis or legal merit; not serious; not reasonably purposeful <a frivolous claim>.

frivolous appeal. See APPEAL.

frivolous claim. See CLAIM (4).

frivolous defense. See DEFENSE (1).

frivolous suit. See SUIT.

FRM. See *fixed-rate mortgage* under MORTGAGE.

frolic (frol-ik), *n. Torts.* An employee's significant deviation from the employer's business for personal reasons. ● A frolic is outside the scope of employment, and thus the employer is not vicariously liable for the employee's actions. Cf. DETOUR.

front, *n.* (14c) **1.** The side or part of a building or lot that is open to view, that is the principal entrance, or that faces out to the open (as to a lake or ocean); the foremost part of something <the property's front was its most valuable attribute>. **2.** A person or group that serves to conceal the true identity or activity of the person or group in control <the political party was a front for the terrorist group>. **3.** A political association similar to a party <popular front>.

frontage (frən-tij). (17c) **1.** The part of land abutting a street or highway or lying between a building's front and a street or highway <the property's value was so low because of its narrow frontage>. **2.** The linear distance of a frontage <the lot's frontage was 90 feet>.

frontage assessment. See ASSESSMENT.

frontager (frən-tij-ər), *n.* (17c) A person owning or occupying land that abuts a highway, river, seashore, or the like.

front-end load. See *loan fund* under MUTUAL FUND.

front-end money. See SEED MONEY.

front foot. (1863) A measurement used to calculate a frontage assessment. — Also termed *abutting foot.*

front-foot rule. (1872) The principle that an improvement cost is to be apportioned among several properties in proportion to their frontage, without regard to the benefits conferred on each property. — Also termed *front-foot plan.*

frontier. For trade purposes, an international boundary.

front money. See SEED MONEY.

front-page citation. See CITATION (4).

front-page drawing. See DRAWING.

frontpay. *Labor law.* Court-awarded compensation for the post-judgment effects of continuing employment discrimination. Cf. BACKPAY.

front-running, *n. Securities.* A broker's or analyst's use of nonpublic information to acquire securities or enter into options or futures contracts for his or her own benefit, knowing that when the information becomes public, the price of the securities will change in a predictable manner. ● This practice is illegal. Front-running can occur in many ways. For example, a broker or analyst who works for a brokerage firm may buy shares in a company that the firm is about to recommend as a strong buy or in which the firm is planning to buy a large block of shares. See INSIDER TRADING.

front wages. See WAGE.

frottage. (ca. 1935) Sexual stimulation by rubbing the genitals against another person. ● This may be accomplished without removing clothing. When a child is involved, it is a form of sexual abuse.

frozen account. See *blocked account* under ACCOUNT.

frozen asset. See ASSET.

frozen deposit. See DEPOSIT (2).

FRS. *abbr.* FEDERAL RESERVE SYSTEM.

FRTIB. *abbr.* FEDERAL RETIREMENT THRIFT INVESTMENT BOARD.

fructus (frək-təs). [Latin "fruits"] **1.** *Roman & civil law.* The natural produce of land and animals; the profit or increase from land and animals. ● The owner of the land or animals acquired ownership by *separatio,* the separation of the fruit from the parent body. A *bona fide possessor* or an *emphyteuta* also acquired ownership by *separatio,* which allowed a nonowner to claim title from a thief. But in Justinian's law, a bona fide possessor had to account to a successful claimant for ownership for the principal thing and any unconsumed fruits. A tenant or usufructuary acquired title only by *perceptio*, and cannot claim title from a thief. See PERCEPTION. Cf. FRUCTUS CIVILES. **2.** USUFRUCT. Pl. *fructus.*

fructus civiles (frək-təs sə-**vī**-leez). [Latin "civil fruits"] *Roman & civil law.* Income (such as rent or interest) that one receives from another for the use or enjoyment of a thing, esp. real property or loaned money. • In Roman law, *fructus civiles* included both minerals and the earnings of slaves.

fructus fundi (frək-təs fən-dı). [Latin "land fruits"] The fruits or produce of land.

fructus industriales (frək-təs in-dəs-tree-**ay**-leez). [Latin "industrial fruits"] See EMBLEMENTS (1).

fructus legis (frək-təs lee-jis). [Latin "fruits of the law"] The proceeds of judgment or execution.

fructus naturales (frək-təs nach-ə-**ray**-leez). [Latin "natural fruits"] The natural produce of land or plants and the offspring of animals. • *Fructus naturales* are considered part of the real property.

fructus pecudum (frək-təs **pek**-yə-dəm). [Latin "fruits of the herd"] The produce or increase of flocks or herds.

fructus pendentes (frək-təs pen-**den**-teez). [Latin "hanging fruits"] Fruits not yet severed or gathered; fruits united with that which produces them.

fructus percepti (frək-təs pər-**sep**-tı). [Latin "gathered fruits"] *Roman & civil law.* Fruits that have been gathered.

fructus rei alienae (frək-təs ree-ı ay-lee-**ee**-nee *or* al-ee-). [Latin "fruits of another's property"] The fruits of another's property; fruits taken from another's estate.

fructus separati (frək-təs sep-ə-**ray**-tı). [Latin "separated fruits"] *Roman & civil law.* The produce of a thing after being separated from it, and so becoming in law "fruits."

fructus stantes (frək-təs **stan**-teez). [Latin "standing fruits"] Fruits that have not yet been severed from the stalk or stem.

fruit. (14c) **1.** The produce or product of something (as of land or property). **2.** *Civil law.* Income or goods derived or produced from property without a diminution of the property's inherent value.

civil fruit. Civil law. Revenue derived from a thing by operation of law or by reason of a juridical act, such as lease or interest payments, or certain corporate distributions. La. Civ. Code art. 551. See FRUCTUS CIVILES.

natural fruit. Civil law. A product of the land or of animals. • Examples are crops and eggs. La. Civ. Code art. 2317. See FRUCTUS NATURALES.

3. Something (such as evidence) obtained during an activity or operation <the fruit of the officer's search>. See FRUIT-OF-THE-POISONOUS-TREE DOCTRINE.

fruit-and-the-tree doctrine. (1979) *Tax.* The rule that an individual who earns income cannot assign that income to another person to avoid taxation.

fruit-of-the-poisonous-tree doctrine. (1948) *Criminal procedure.* The rule that evidence derived from an illegal search, arrest, or interrogation is inadmissible because the evidence (the "fruit") was tainted by the illegality (the "poisonous tree"). • Under this doctrine, for example, a murder weapon is inadmissible if the map showing its location and used to find it was seized during an illegal search. — Also termed *fruits doctrine.* See EXCLUSIONARY RULE; ATTENUATION DOCTRINE; INDEPENDENT-SOURCE RULE; INEVITABLE-DISCOVERY RULE.

fruits of a crime. The proceeds acquired through criminal acts.

frustration, *n.* (16c) **1.** The prevention or hindering of the attainment of a goal, such as contractual performance.

commercial frustration. (1918) An excuse for a party's nonperformance because of some unforeseeable and uncontrollable circumstance. — Also termed *economic frustration.*

self-induced frustration. (1926) A breach of contract caused by one party's action that prevents the performance. • The phrase is something of a misnomer, since *self-induced frustration* is not really a type of frustration at all but is instead a breach of contract.

temporary frustration. (1950) An occurrence that prevents performance and legally suspends the duty to perform for the duration of the event. • If the burden or circumstance is substantially different after the event, then the duty may be discharged.

2. *Contracts.* The doctrine that if a party's principal purpose is substantially frustrated by unanticipated changed circumstances, that party's duties are discharged and the contract is considered terminated. — Also termed *frustration of purpose.* Cf. IMPOSSIBILITY (4); IMPRACTICABILITY; MISTAKE. — **frustrate,** *vb.*

Frye test. The defunct federal common-law rule of evidence on the admissibility of scientific evidence. • It required that the tests or procedures must have gained general acceptance in their particular field. *Frye v. United States*, 293 F. 1013 (D.C. Cir. 1923). In *Daubert v. Merrell Dow Pharms., Inc.*, 509 U.S. 579, 113 S.Ct. 2786 (1993), the Supreme Court held that scientific evidence must meet the requirements of the Federal Rules of Evidence, not the *Frye* test, to be admissible. See DAUBERT TEST.

FSA. *abbr.* FARM SERVICE AGENCY.

FSI. *abbr.* FOREIGN SERVICE INSTITUTE.

FSIA. *abbr.* FOREIGN SOVEREIGN IMMUNITIES ACT.

FSIS. *abbr.* FOOD SAFETY AND INSPECTION SERVICE.

FSLIC. *abbr.* FEDERAL SAVINGS AND LOAN INSURANCE CORPORATION.

FSS. *abbr.* FEDERAL SUPPLY SERVICE.

FST. See *field sobriety test* under SOBRIETY TEST.

F.Supp. *abbr.* Federal Supplement, a series of reported decisions of the federal district courts (from 1932 to 1998), the U.S. Court of Claims (1932 to 1960), and the U.S. Customs Court (from 1949 to 1998, but renamed the Court of International Trade in 1980). • It is the first of the Federal Supplement series.

F.Supp.2d. *abbr.* The second series of the Federal Supplement, which includes decisions of federal district courts and the Court of International Trade from 1997 to the present. • Some of the F.Supp. volumes contain cases from 1998 and some of the F.Supp.2d volumes contain cases decided in 1997.

FTA. *abbr.* FEDERAL TRANSIT ADMINISTRATION.

FTC. *abbr.* FEDERAL TRADE COMMISSION.

FTCA. *abbr.* FEDERAL TORT CLAIMS ACT.

FTDA. *abbr.* FEDERAL TRADEMARK DILUTION ACT.

FTO search. See INFRINGEMENT SEARCH.

FTP. See FILE-TRANSFER PROTOCOL.

FTS. *abbr.* FEDERAL TECHNOLOGY SERVICE.

FTT. *abbr.* FAILURE TO THRIVE.

fugitation (fyoo-jə-**tay**-shən). (18c) *Hist.* A sentence or declaration of fugitive status that was pronounced against an accused person for failing to answer a citation and appear. • The effect was that the person forfeited his or her goods and chattels. — **fugitate,** *vb.*

fugitive. (14c) **1.** A person who flees or escapes; a refugee. **2.** A criminal suspect or a witness in a criminal case who flees, evades, or escapes arrest, prosecution, imprisonment, service of process, or the giving of testimony, esp. by fleeing the jurisdiction or by hiding. See 18 USCA § 1073. — Also termed (in sense 2) *fugitive from justice.*

fugitive-disentitlement doctrine. An equitable rule that allows a trial or appellate court to limit a fugitive's access to civil and criminal courts in the United States.

fugitive-dismissal rule. The principle that an appellate court may dismiss a criminal defendant's appeal if the defendant is a fugitive.

Fugitive Felon Act. A federal statute that makes it a felony to flee across state lines to avoid state-felony prosecution or confinement, or to avoid giving testimony in a state-felony case. 18 USCA § 1073.

fugitive from justice. See FUGITIVE.

fugitive's goods. *Hist.* The goods that a person forfeited as a result of fleeing.

fugitive-slave laws. *Hist.* Federal statutes passed in 1793 and 1850 providing for the surrender and return of slaves who had escaped and fled to a free territory or a free state.

fugitive warrant. See WARRANT (1).

fugue (fyoog). (16c) An abnormal state of consciousness in which one appears to function normally but on recovery has no memory of what one did while in that condition.

full adversary hearing. See *adjudication hearing* under HEARING.

full age. See *age of majority* (1) under AGE.

full bench. See *full court* under COURT.

full blood. See BLOOD.

full cash value. See VALUE (2).

full copy. *Equity practice.* A complete transcript of a bill or other pleading, with all indorsements and a copy of all exhibits.

full court. See COURT.

full cousin. See COUSIN (1).

full-covenant-and-warranty deed. See *warranty deed* under DEED.

full coverage. See COVERAGE.

full-crew law. A law that regulates the number of railroad employees required to operate a train, or airline employees required to operate an airplane.

full defense. See DEFENSE (1).

full disclosure. See DISCLOSURE (1).

full faith and credit. The recognition, acceptance, and enforcement of the laws, orders, and judgments of another jurisdiction; specif., the recognition by one state of another state's legal decisions.

Full Faith and Credit Act. A federal statute requiring federal courts to give a state court's judgment the same preclusive effect as the judgment would have under state law. 28 USCA § 1738. *See Migra v. Warren City School Dist. Bd. of Educ.,* 465 U.S. 75, 81, 104 S.Ct. 892, 896 (1984).

full-faith-and-credit bond. See *general-obligation bond* under BOND (3).

Full Faith and Credit Clause. (1896) U.S. Const. art. IV, § 1, which requires states to give effect to the acts, public records, and judicial decisions of other states.

Full Faith and Credit for Child-Support Orders Act. A 1994 federal statute designed to facilitate interstate child-support collection. • Under the Act, the state first issuing a child-support order maintains continuing, exclusive jurisdiction to modify the order as long as the child or one or both of the litigants continue to reside there, unless all the contestants agree in writing to change jurisdiction. An order from one state may be registered for enforcement in another state. 28 USCA § 1738B.

full hearing. See HEARING.

full indorsement. **1.** See *irregular indorsement* under INDORSEMENT. **2.** See *special indorsement* under INDORSEMENT.

full interdiction. See INTERDICTION (3).

full member. See *voting member* under MEMBER.

full name. See NAME.

full ownership. See *perfect ownership* under OWNERSHIP.

full-paid stock. See STOCK.

full pardon. See *absolute pardon* under PARDON.

full partner. See *general partner* under PARTNER.

full payout lease. See *finance lease* under LEASE.

full performance. See PERFORMANCE.

full powers. *Int'l law.* An official document designating a person to represent a country for (1) negotiating, adopting, or authenticating the text of a treaty, (2) expressing the consent of the country to be bound by a treaty, or (3) accomplishing any act with respect to the treaty.

full proof. See PROOF.

full-reporting clause. 1. *Insurance.* An insurance-policy clause that requires the insured to reveal values and that penalizes the insured if the insured revealed less than required in the policy application. — Also termed *honesty clause.* **2.** An insurance-policy clause providing that the indemnity will not exceed the proportion of the loss that the last reported value bears to the actual value.

full right. (18c) The union of good title with actual possession.

full-service lease. See LEASE.

full settlement. See SETTLEMENT (2).

full value. See *fair market value* under VALUE (2).

full warranty. See WARRANTY (2).

fully administered. (17c) A plea by an executor or administrator that he or she has completely and legally disposed of all the assets of the estate and that the estate has no remaining assets from which a new claim could be satisfied.

fully diluted earnings per share. See EARNINGS PER SHARE.

fully funded, *adj.* **1.** Having sufficient financial resources to meet current payments, even upon bankruptcy <the company's pension plan was fully funded>. **2.** Having completely satisfied a funding requirement; paid <the construction loan was fully funded>. — Also termed *funded.*

fully managed fund. See MUTUAL FUND.

fully met. See ANTICIPATED.

fully paid face-amount certificate. See *face-amount certificate* (2) under CERTIFICATE.

function, *n.* (16c) **1.** Activity that is appropriate to a particular business or profession <a court's function is to administer justice>. **2.** Office; duty; the occupation of an office <presidential function>.

functional analog. See ANALOG.

functional depreciation. See DEPRECIATION.

functional discount. See DISCOUNT.

functional disease. See DISEASE.

functional feature. *Trademarks.* A design element that is either physically necessary to construct an article or commercially necessary to manufacture and sell it; a product's attribute that is essential to its use, necessary for its proper and successful operation, and utilitarian rather than ornamental in every detail. • A functional feature is not eligible for trademark protection.

functionality. (19c) *Trademarks.* The quality of having a shape, configuration, design, or color that is so superior to available alternatives that giving the first user exclusive trademark rights would hinder competition.

aesthetic functionality. A doctrine that denies protection to the design of a product or its container when the design is necessary to enable the product to function as intended.

functional limitation. *Patents.* In a patent application, the definition of an invention by what it does rather than what it is. • A functional limitation is not inherently invalid, but it is examined closely because it tends to be too broad, claiming every possible way of doing the same thing. MPEP 2173.05(g).

functional obsolescence. See OBSOLESCENCE.

functional rejection. See REJECTION.

functionary. A public officer or employee.

functus officio (fǝngk-tǝs ǝ-**fish**-ee-oh). [Latin "having performed his or her office"] (19c) (Of an officer or official body) without further authority or legal competence because the duties and functions of the original commission have been fully accomplished. • The term is sometimes abbreviated to *functus* <the court was *functus*>.

fund, *n.* (17c) **1.** A sum of money or other liquid assets established for a specific purpose <a fund reserved for unanticipated expenses>.

blended fund. A fund created by income from more than one source, usu. from the sale of a testator's real and personal property.

changing fund. A fund, esp. a trust fund, that changes its form periodically as it is invested and reinvested.

client-security fund. A fund established usu. by a state or a state bar association to compensate persons for losses that they suffered because of their attorneys' misappropriation of funds or other misconduct.

contingent fund. (18c) **1.** A fund created by a municipality for expenses that will necessarily arise during the year but that cannot be appropriately classified under any of the specific purposes for which taxes are collected. **2.** A fund segregated by a business to pay unknown costs that may arise in the future. — Also termed *contingency reserve.*

executor fund. A fund established for an executor to pay an estate's final expenses.

fund in court. (18c) **1.** Contested money deposited with the court. See INTERPLEADER. **2.** Money deposited to pay a contingent liability.

general fund. (17c) **1.** A government's primary operating fund; a state's assets furnishing the means for the support of government and for defraying the legislature's discretionary appropriations. • A general fund is distinguished from assets of a special character, such as trust, escrow, and special-purpose funds. **2.** A nonprofit entity's assets that are not earmarked for a specific purpose.

general revenue fund. (1855) The fund out of which a municipality pays its ordinary and incidental expenses.

guaranty fund. A private deposit-insurance fund, raised primarily by assessments on banks, and used to pay the depositors of an insolvent bank. • Guaranty funds preceded the FDIC's federal-deposit insurance, which began in 1933, though many funds continued until the savings-and-loan crisis in the 1980s. Massachusetts has a guaranty fund for uninsured deposits (deposits above $100,000) that are not covered by federal-deposit insurance.

imprest fund (**im**-prest). A fund used by a business for small, routine expenses.

joint-welfare fund. A fund that is established in collective bargaining to provide health and welfare benefits to union employees. • The fund is jointly managed by labor and management

representatives. — Also termed *Taft–Hartley fund.*

paid-in fund. A reserve cash fund established by a mutual insurance company to pay unforeseen losses. • The fund is in lieu of a capital stock account.

pooled-income fund. See POOLED-INCOME FUND.

public fund. (*usu. pl.*) **1.** The revenue or money of a governmental body. • The term includes not only coins and paper but also bank deposits and instruments representing investments of public money. **2.** The securities of a state or national government.

revolving fund. (1928) A fund whose moneys are continually expended and then replenished, such as a petty-cash fund.

sinking fund. (18c) A fund consisting of regular deposits that are accumulated with interest to pay off a long-term corporate or public debt. — Abbr. SF.

strike fund. See STRIKE FUND.

Taft–Hartley fund. See *joint-welfare fund.*

trust fund. See TRUST FUND.

unsatisfied-judgment fund. (1953) A fund established by a state to compensate persons for losses stemming from an automobile accident caused by an uninsured or underinsured motorist.

2. (*usu. pl.*) Money or other assets, such as stocks, bonds, or working capital, available to pay debts, expenses, and the like <Sue invested her funds in her sister's business>.

current funds. Assets that can be readily converted into cash.

3. A pool of investments owned in common and managed for a fee; MUTUAL FUND <a diverse portfolio of funds>.

fund, *vb.* (18c) **1.** To furnish money to (an individual, entity, or venture), esp. to finance a particular project. **2.** To use resources in a manner that produces interest. **3.** To convert (a debt, esp. an open account) into a long-term debt that bears interest at a fixed rate.

fundamental error. See *plain error* under ERROR (2).

fundamental-fairness doctrine. (1969) The rule that applies the principles of due process to a judicial proceeding. • The term is commonly considered synonymous with *due process.*

fundamental interest. See FUNDAMENTAL RIGHT.

fundamental law. (17c) The organic law that establishes the governing principles of a nation or state; esp., CONSTITUTIONAL LAW. — Also termed *organic law*; *ground-law.* Cf. NATURAL LAW.

fundamental-miscarriage-of-justice exception.
The doctrine allowing a federal court in a habeas corpus proceeding to address a claim of constitutional error that, although ordinarily unreviewable, is subject to review because of a state-court procedural default that rendered the proceedings basically unfair. • For the exception to apply, among other things, the petitioner must show by a preponderance of the evidence that constitutional error resulted in the conviction of one who is actually innocent. If the defaulted claim applies only to sentencing, the exception permits review of the claim if the petitioner shows by clear and convincing evidence that, but for the constitutional error, no reasonable judge or jury would have imposed the sentence that the petitioner received.

fundamental right. (17c) **1.** A right derived from natural or fundamental law. **2.** *Constitutional law.* A significant component of liberty, encroachments of which are rigorously tested by courts to ascertain the soundness of purported governmental justifications. • A fundamental right triggers strict scrutiny to determine whether the law violates the Due Process Clause or the Equal Protection Clause of the 14th Amendment. As enunciated by the Supreme Court, fundamental rights include voting, interstate travel, and various aspects of privacy (such as marriage and contraception rights). — Also termed *fundamental interest.* See STRICT SCRUTINY. Cf. SUSPECT CLASSIFICATION.

fundamental term. See TERM (2).

fundamental trend. See *major trend* under TREND.

funded. See FULLY FUNDED.

funded debt. See DEBT.

fund in court. See FUND (1).

funding, *n.* (18c) **1.** The process of financing capital expenditures by issuing long-term debt obligations or by converting short-term obligations into long-term obligations to finance current expenses; the process of creating a funded debt. **2.** The refinancing of a debt before its maturity. — Also termed *refunding.* **3.** The provision or allocation of money for a specific purpose, such as for a pension plan, by putting the money into a reserve fund or investments. **4.** The provision of financial resources to finance a particular activity or project, such as a research study. **5.** The transfer of property to a trust.

funds transfer. A payment of money from one person or entity to another; esp., the process by which payment is made through a series of transactions between computerized banking systems, beginning with an originator's payment order and ending when a final payment order is received by the beneficiary's bank. • Commercial or wholesale funds transfers are governed by Article 4A of the UCC. Consumer funds transfers are regulated by the federal Electronic Fund Transfer Act (15 USCA §§ 1693 et seq.). — Also termed (specif.) *electronic funds transfer* (EFT).

funeral expense. See EXPENSE.

fungible (fən-jə-bəl), *adj.* (18c) Commercially interchangeable with other property of the same kind <corn and wheat are fungible goods, whereas land is not>. — **fungible,** *n.*

fungible goods. See GOODS.

furandi animus (fyuu-**ran**-dɪ an-ə-məs). See *animus furandi* under ANIMUS.

furlough (fər-loh). (17c) **1.** A leave of absence from military or other employment duty. **2.** A brief release from prison. See *study release* under RELEASE. — **furlough,** *vb.*

furor brevis. See HEAT OF PASSION.

further advance. 1. A second or later loan to a mortgagor by a mortgagee, either on the same security as the original loan or on an additional security. **2.** *Equity practice.* The agreed conversion of arrears of interest on a mortgage security into principal.

further assurance. See ASSURANCE.

further-exploration covenant. *Oil & gas.* In an oil-and-gas lease, an implied promise that once production has been obtained from the leased property, the lessee will continue to explore other parts of the property and other formations under it. • Some jurisdictions hold that the covenant for further exploration does not exist independently of the covenant for reasonable development. See also REASONABLE-DEVELOPMENT COVENANT; REASONABLY-PRUDENT-OPERATOR STANDARD.

further instruction. See *additional instruction* under JURY INSTRUCTION.

furtum (fər-təm), *n.* [Latin "theft"] *Roman law.* **1.** The offense of stealing movable property. • Under Roman law, *furtum* included not only the taking of another's property, but any handling of the property done with the intent of profiting by it. *Furtum* was not only a private wrong (*delictum*) prosecuted by the person suffering the loss. **2.** The thing stolen.

furtum conceptum (fər-təm kən-**sep**-təm). [Latin] *Roman law.* A theft in which someone is discovered in possession of stolen property after a search with witnesses. • The possessor was liable to pay the owner three times the value of the stolen property. The possessor could bring an action against the thief and recover triple damages.

fustigation (fəs-ti-**gay**-shən), *n.* (16c) **1.** *Hist.* The beating of someone with a stick or club. **2.** Harsh criticism. — **fustigate,** *vb.*

FUTA. *abbr.* See FEDERAL UNEMPLOYMENT TAX ACT.

future-acquired property. See AFTER-ACQUIRED PROPERTY (1).

future advance. (1805) Money secured by an original security agreement even though it is lent after the security interest has attached.

future-advance clause. (1911) A contractual term in a security agreement covering additional loaned amounts on present collateral or collateral to be acquired in the future, regardless of whether the secured party is obliged to make the advances; esp., a provision in an open-end mortgage or deed of trust allowing the borrower to borrow additional sums in the future, secured under the same instrument and by the same security. • This type of clause makes a new security agreement unnecessary when the secured creditor makes a future loan to the debtor.

future-advances mortgage. See MORTGAGE.

future consideration. See CONSIDERATION (1).

future covenant. See COVENANT (4).

future damages. See DAMAGES.

future earnings. See *lost earnings* under EARNINGS.

future estate. See *future interest* under INTEREST (2).

future goods. See GOODS.

future interest. See INTEREST (2).

future performance. See PERFORMANCE.

futures, *n.* **1.** Standardized assets (such as commodities, stocks, or foreign currencies) bought or sold for future acceptance or delivery. — Also termed *financial futures.* **2.** FUTURES CONTRACT. **3.** Future claimants, esp. those who would become members of a class of persons injured by a defendant and thus included in a class action.

futures-commission merchant. An individual or firm that executes orders to buy and sell futures or futures options.

futures contract. An agreement to buy or sell a standardized asset (such as a commodity, stock, or foreign currency) at a fixed price at a future time, usu. during a particular time of a month. • Futures contracts are traded on exchanges such as the Chicago Board of Trade or the Chicago Mercantile Exchange. — Often shortened to *futures.* — Also termed *futures agreement; time-bargain.* Cf. *forward contract* under CONTRACT; LEVERAGE CONTRACT; OPTION.

futures market. See MARKET.

futures option. See OPTION.

futures trading. The buying and selling of futures contracts, usu. on formal exchanges.

future use. See *contingent use* under USE (4).

future value. See VALUE (2).

FWC. *abbr.* File wrapper continuation. See CONTINUATION; CONTINUATION-IN-PART.

FWS. *abbr.* UNITED STATES FISH AND WILDLIFE SERVICE.

G

GA. *abbr.* See *general average* under AVERAGE.

GAAP (gap). *abbr.* GENERALLY ACCEPTED AC-COUNTING PRINCIPLES.

GAAS (gas). *abbr.* GENERALLY ACCEPTED AUDITING STANDARDS.

gage (gayj), *n.* (14c) A pledge, pawn, or other thing deposited as security for performance. • An archaic use of this word corresponded to the way *wage* was formerly used in legal contexts: a *gager del ley*, for example, was an earlier form of *wager of law*, while *gager de deliverance* had the same meaning as *wager of deliverance*. Cf. WAGE (2).

gage, *vb.* (14c) To pawn or pledge; to give as security for.

gager (gay-jər), *n.* The giving of security; the transaction in which one gives a gage. See GAGE.

gager del ley. See WAGER OF LAW.

gag order. (1952) **1.** A judge's order directing parties, attorneys, witnesses, or journalists to refrain from publicly discussing the facts of a case. • When directed to the press, such an order is generally unconstitutional under the First Amendment. **2.** A judge's order that an unruly defendant be bound and gagged during trial to prevent further interruptions.

gain, *n.* (14c) **1.** An increase in amount, degree, or value.

pecuniary gain. (18c) **1.** A gain of money or of something having monetary value. **2.** *Criminal law.* Any monetary or economic gain that serves as an impetus for the commission of an offense. • In most states, an offense and its punishment are aggravated if the offense was committed for pecuniary gain. Murder, for example, is often aggravated to capital murder if the murderer is paid to commit the crime. See SOLICITATION (2).

2. Excess of receipts over expenditures or of sale price over cost. See PROFIT (1). **3.** *Tax.* The excess of the amount realized from a sale or other disposition of property over the property's adjusted value. IRC (26 USCA) § 1001. — Also termed *realized gain*; *net gain*; (in senses 2 & 3) *business gain*.

capital gain. See CAPITAL GAIN.

extraordinary gain. (16c) A gain that is both unusual and infrequent, such as the gain realized from selling a large segment of a business.

ordinary gain. (1945) A gain from the sale or exchange of a noncapital asset. Cf. CAPITAL GAIN.

recognized gain. (1951) The portion of a gain that is subject to income taxation. IRC (26 USCA) § 1001(c). See BOOT (1).

4. (*pl.*) *Civil law.* A type of community property that reflects the increase in property value brought about by the spouses' common skill or labor. See COMMUNITY PROPERTY; ACQUET.

gainful employment. See EMPLOYMENT.

gains, *n.* See GAIN.

GAL. *abbr.* See *guardian ad litem* under GUARDIAN.

***Gallagher* agreement.** (1977) A contract that gives one codefendant the right to settle with the plaintiff for a fixed sum at any time during trial and that guarantees payment of the sum regardless of the trial's outcome. *City of Tucson v. Gallagher,* 493 P.2d 1197 (Ariz. 1972). Cf. MARY CARTER AGREEMENT.

gallows. (bef. 12c) A wooden frame consisting of two upright posts and a crossbeam, from which condemned criminals are hanged by a rope.

gambler. See COMMON GAMBLER.

gambling, *n.* (18c) The act of risking something of value, esp. money, for a chance to win a prize. • Gambling is regulated by state and federal law. 18 USCA §§ 1081 et seq. — Also termed *gaming.* See COMMON GAMBLER.

Indian gambling. Gambling conducted by a federally recognized Indian tribe and regulated by federal law.

gambling contract. See CONTRACT.

gambling device. Any thing, such as cards, dice, or an electronic or mechanical contrivance, that allows a person to play a game of chance in which money may be won or lost. • Gambling devices are regulated by law, and the use or possession of a gambling device can be illegal. — Also termed *gaming device.*

gambling place. Any location where gambling occurs. 18 USCA § 1081. — Also termed *gaming house*; *gaming room.*

gambling policy. See *wager policy* under INSURANCE POLICY.

gambling verdict. See *chance verdict* under VERDICT.

game, *n.* (13c) **1.** Wild animals and birds considered as objects of pursuit, for food or sport; esp., animals for which one must have a license to hunt. **2.** A contest, for amusement or for a prize, whose outcome depends on the skill, strength, or luck of the players.

game of chance. A game whose outcome is determined by luck rather than skill. See GAMBLING DEVICE.

game of skill. A game in which the outcome is determined by a player's superior knowledge or ability, not chance.

percentage game. A game of chance from which the house collects an amount calculated as a percentage of the wagers made or the sums won. • Percentage games are illegal in many states.

game, *vb.* To gamble; to play for a stake.

game law. (18c) A federal or state law that regulates the hunting of game, esp. one that forbids the capturing or killing of specified game either entirely or seasonally, describes the means for killing or capturing game in season, or restricts the number and type of game animals that may be killed or captured in season. 16 USCA §§ 661–667; 18 USCA §§ 41–47.

gamete intrafallopian transfer. (ca. 1984) A procedure in which mature eggs are implanted in a woman's fallopian tubes and fertilized with semen. — Abbr. GIFT. — Also termed *gamete intrafallopian-tube transfer*. Cf. ZYGOTE INTRAFALLOPIAN TRANSFER; ARTIFICIAL INSEMINATION; IN VITRO FERTILIZATION.

gaming. See GAMBLING.

gaming contract. See *gambling contract* under CONTRACT.

gaming device. See GAMBLING DEVICE.

gaming house. See GAMBLING PLACE.

gaming room. See GAMBLING PLACE.

ganancial (gə-**nan**-shəl), *adj.* (1843) Of, relating to, or consisting of community property <a spouse's ganancial rights>. See COMMUNITY PROPERTY.

G & A. *abbr.* See *general administrative expense* under EXPENSE.

gang. (15c) A group of persons who go about together or act in concert, esp. for antisocial or criminal purposes. • Many gangs have common identifying signs and symbols, such as hand signals and distinctive colors. — Also termed *street gang.*

gangland. (ca. 1912) The world of criminal gangs and organized crime.

gangster. A member of a criminal gang or an organized-crime syndicate.

Ganser's syndrome (**gahn**-zər *or* **gan**-sər). (1968) An abnormality characterized by the giving of irrelevant and nonsensical answers to questions. • Prisoners have been known to feign this syndrome in an attempt to obtain leniency.

gantlet (**gawnt**-lit). [fr. Swedish *gata* "lane" + *lopp* "course"] (15c) **1.** *Hist.* A former military punishment in which the offender was stripped to the waist and forced to run between two rows of soldiers who gave him lashes as he passed. **2.** A series of severe troubles or difficulties; an ordeal. — Also spelled *gauntlet*; (archaically) *gantlope*.

GAO. *abbr.* GENERAL ACCOUNTABILITY OFFICE.

gaol. See JAIL.

gaol delivery. See JAIL DELIVERY.

gaoler. See JAILER.

gaol liberties. See JAIL LIBERTIES.

gap. See GAP PERIOD.

gap creditor. See CREDITOR.

gap-filler. (15c) A rule that supplies a contractual term that the parties failed to include in the contract. • For example, if the contract does not contain a sales price, UCC § 2-305(1) establishes the price as being a reasonable one at the time of delivery. Cf. DEFAULT RULE.

gap financing. See FINANCING.

gap period. (1978) *Bankruptcy.* The duration of time between the filing of an involuntary bankruptcy petition and the entry of the order for relief. — Often shortened to *gap.*

gap report. (1984) In the making of federal court rules, a report that explains any changes made by an advisory committee in the language of a proposed amendment to a procedural rule after its publication for comment. • Before advisory committees began issuing gap reports in the early 1980s, there were complaints that the public record did not show why changes were made after the public-comment period. The five advisory committees — for appellate, bankruptcy, civil, criminal, and evidence rules — therefore began filing the reports to fill in the "gaps" in the record. Although the phrase is sometimes written in capital letters (*GAP report*), it is not an acronym.

gap theory. *Insurance.* The principle that a tortfeasor will be considered underinsured if his or her liability-insurance coverage — although legally adequate — is less than the injured party's underinsured-motorist coverage. • This principle allows an injured party to invoke underinsured-motorist coverage. Cf. EXCESS THEORY.

garageman's lien. See *mechanic's lien* under LIEN.

***Garcia* hearing** (gahr-**see**-ə). (1981) *Criminal procedure.* A hearing held to ensure that a defendant who is one of two or more defendants represented by the same attorney understands (1) the risk of a conflict of interest inherent in this type of representation, and (2) that he or she is entitled to the services of an attorney who does not represent anyone else in the defendant's case. *United States v. Garcia*, 517 F.2d 272 (5th Cir. 1975). See CONFLICT OF INTEREST (2).

garde (gahrd). [French] **1.** *Civil law.* A relationship that gives rise to a person's liability when an injury is caused by a thing, whether animate or inanimate, that is considered by law to be that person's responsibility or to be in that person's custody. **2.** See GARD.

Garmon doctrine. See *Garmon preemption* under PREEMPTION.

Garmon preemption. See PREEMPTION.

Garner doctrine. (1970) The rule that allows shareholder plaintiffs in a corporate derivative action to discover confidential communications between a corporate officer and the corporation's attorney. • The *Garner* doctrine does not apply to attorney work product, and the movant must show good cause. *Garner v. Wolfinbarger*, 430 F.2d 1093 (5th Cir. 1970). See DERIVATIVE ACTION (1).

garnish, *n.* (16c) *Hist.* Money exacted from a new prisoner by other prisoners or as a jailer's fee. • This practice was banned in England in 1815.

garnish, *vb.* [Old French *garnir* "to warn" "to prepare"] (16c) **1.** *Hist.* To notify or warn (a person) of certain debts that must be paid before the person is entitled to receive property as an heir. **2.** To subject (property) to garnishment; to attach (property held by a third party) in order to satisfy a debt. **3.** To notify (a person, bank, etc.) that a garnishment proceeding has been undertaken and that the one receiving notice may be liable as stakeholder or custodian of the defendant's property. — Also termed *garnishee*; (in senses 2 & 3) *factorize.* — **garnishable,** *adj.*

garnishee (gahr-ni-**shee**), *n.* (17c) A person or institution (such as a bank) that is indebted to or is bailee for another whose property has been subjected to garnishment. — Also termed *garnishee-defendant* (as opposed to the "principal defendant," i.e., the primary debtor).

garnishee (gahr-ni-**shee**), *vb.* See GARNISH.

garnisher. (16c) A creditor who initiates a garnishment action to reach the debtor's property that is thought to be held or owed by a third party (the *garnishee*). — Also spelled *garnishor.*

garnishment, *n.* (16c) **1.** A judicial proceeding in which a creditor (or potential creditor) asks the court to order a third party who is indebted to or is bailee for the debtor to turn over to the creditor any of the debtor's property (such as wages or bank accounts) held by that third party. • A plaintiff initiates a garnishment action as a means of either prejudgment seizure or postjudgment collection.

   wrongful garnishment. (1896) **1.** An improper or tortious garnishment. **2.** A cause of action against a garnisher for improperly or tortiously filing a garnishment proceeding.

2. The judicial order by which such a turnover is effected. Cf. ATTACHMENT (1); SEQUESTRATION (1).

garnishment lien. See LIEN.

garnishor. See GARNISHER.

***Garrity* statement** (**gar**-ə-tee). (1967) A public employee's oral or written report (as of an incident) obtained under a threat of termination of employment. • A public employee usu. makes a *Garrity* statement in the course of an internal investigation (as by a police department). Because a *Garrity* statement is coerced, the statement and any evidence obtained as a result of it cannot be used in a later criminal prosecution against the public employee. The statement and evidence may be used only to evaluate the employee's performance. *Garrity v. New Jersey*, 385 U.S. 493, 87 S.Ct. 616 (1967).

gas-balancing agreement. *Oil & gas.* A contract among owners of the production of a gas well to balance production if one owner sells more of the gas stream than the other owners do.

gas chamber. (ca. 1945) A small, sealed room in which a capital punishment is carried out by strapping the prisoner into a chair and releasing poisonous fumes.

gas contract. *Oil & gas.* An agreement for the sale of natural gas.

gas sold. *Oil & gas.* Natural gas that is actually sold but not necessarily all that a well produces. • The term is used in natural-gas leases.

gastonette. (1988) A dilatory "dance" in which each of the two responsible parties waits until the other party acts — so that the delay seems interminable; esp., a standoff occurring when two courts simultaneously hear related claims arising from the same bases and delay acting while each court waits for the other to act first. • The term was coined by Judge Jon O. Newman in *In re McLean Industries, Inc.*, 857 F.2d 88, 90 (2d Cir. 1988), on the model of "After you, my dear Alphonse." "No, after you, Gaston."

gas used. *Oil & gas.* Natural gas that is consumed while a well is in operation but that is not necessarily sold.

GATT (gat). *abbr.* GENERAL AGREEMENT ON TARIFFS AND TRADE. See TRIPS.

gauger (**gay**-jər). (15c) A surveying officer who examines containers of liquids to give them a mark of allowance, as containing the lawful measure.

gauntlet. See GANTLET.

gavel (**gav**-əl). (bef. 12c) **1.** *Hist.* A tribute, toll, or custom paid to a superior. **2.** *Hist.* An annual payment of rent or revenue, esp. payment in kind, such as gavel-corn, gavel-malt, or oat-gavel. — Sometimes spelled *gabel.* **3.** A mallet used by a presiding officer, often a judge, to bring a meeting or court to order.

gavelkind (**gav**-əl-kɪnd). (14c) *Hist.* **1.** A species of socage tenure arising in land that has descended equally to the decedent's sons. • It was widespread before 1066, when it was mainly superseded by primogeniture. This property-division technique was then largely limited to Kent. The person holding land in this manner enjoyed several advantages not available under the common law: the land could be disposed of by will, did not escheat for felony other than treason or for want of heirs, and was alienable by an heir at age 15. Gavelkind was abolished in 1925. Although the etymology of this term was much debated in the 19th century, the explanation given in the first quotation below appears to be the true one. **2.** Land that yields gavel service.

gavel through. *Parliamentary law.* To put (a question) to a vote before any member can obtain the floor. ● The practice of "gaveling through" a motion is improper under parliamentary law.

gay marriage. See *same-sex marriage* under MARRIAGE (1).

Gazette (gə-**zet**). (17c) An official newspaper of the British government in which acts of State, Crown appointments, notices of bankruptcy, and other legal matters are reported. ● Although the *London Gazette* is the most famous, there are also publications called the *Edinburgh Gazette* and the *Belfast Gazette* with similar purposes.

gazumping (gə-**zəmp**-ing). (20c) *BrE Slang.* The improper sale of a house, usu. by raising the price after accepting an offer. ● Gazumping can take different forms, the usual one being when a seller raises the price after accepting the buyer's offer. But it may also occur when a competing buyer makes a higher bid than the one already accepted, thus encouraging the seller to back out of the earlier contract.

g.b.h. *abbr.* Grievous bodily harm. See *serious bodily injury* under INJURY.

GBMI. *abbr.* GUILTY BUT MENTALLY ILL.

gdn. *abbr.* GUARDIAN.

Gebrauchsmuster. [German] *Patents.* UTILITY MODEL. — Abbr. GM.

GEM. See *growing-equity mortgage* under MORTGAGE.

gender discrimination. See *sex discrimination* under DISCRIMINATION.

General Accounting Office. See GENERAL ACCOUNTABILITY OFFICE.

General Accountability Office. An office in the legislative branch of the federal government responsible for auditing the receipt and disbursement of U.S. government funds and conducting investigations for members of Congress and congressional committees. ● Headed by the Comptroller General of the United States, it was formerly called the General Accounting Office, established by the Budget and Accounting Act of 1921. It was renamed in 2004. 31 USCA § 702. — Abbr. GAO.

general act. See PUBLIC LAW (2).

general administration. See ADMINISTRATION.

general administrative expense. See EXPENSE.

general administrator. See ADMINISTRATOR (2).

general agency. See AGENCY (1).

general agent. 1. See AGENT (2). **2.** See INSURANCE AGENT.

General Agreement on Tariffs and Trade. A multiparty international agreement — signed originally in 1948 — that promotes international trade by lowering import duties and providing equal access to markets. ● More than 150 nations are parties to the agreement. — Abbr. GATT.

general appearance. See APPEARANCE.

general assembly. 1. The name of the legislative body in many states. **2.** (*cap.*) The deliberative body of the United Nations. **3.** CONVENTION (4).

general assignment. See ASSIGNMENT (2).

general assumpsit. See ASSUMPSIT.

general authority. See AUTHORITY (1).

general average. See AVERAGE.

general-average bond. See BOND (2).

general-average contribution. See *general average* under AVERAGE.

general average loss. See LOSS.

general-average statement. *Maritime law.* A statement containing an exact calculation of the general average and each party's contributory share. See AVERAGE (3).

general benefit. See BENEFIT.

general bequest. See BEQUEST.

general cargo. See CARGO.

general challenge. See *challenge for cause* under CHALLENGE (2).

general compromis. See COMPROMIS.

general consent. 1. See BLANK CONSENT. **2.** See CONSENT (2).

general contractor. See CONTRACTOR.

general council. See COUNCIL.

general counsel. See COUNSEL.

General Counsel's Memorandum. *Tax.* **1.** A written discussion, issued by the office of the Chief Counsel of the IRS, on the merits of a legal issue involving tax law. **2.** A written explanation, issued by the office of the Chief Counsel of the IRS, explaining the IRS's positions in revenue rulings and technical advice memorandums.

general count. See COUNT.

General Court. The name of the legislatures of Massachusetts and New Hampshire. ● "General Court" was a common colonial-era term for a body that exercised judicial and legislative functions. Cf. COURT OF ASSISTANTS.

general court-martial. See COURT-MARTIAL.

general covenant against encumbrances. See *covenant against encumbrances* under COVENANT (4).

general creditor. See *unsecured creditor* under CREDITOR.

general criminal intent. See *general intent* under INTENT (1).

general custom. See CUSTOM.

general damages. See DAMAGES.

general debt. See DEBT.

general deficiency bill. See *deficiency bill* under BILL (3).

general demurrer. See *general exception* (1) under EXCEPTION (1).

general denial. See DENIAL.

general deposit. See DEPOSIT (2).

general deputy. **1.** See DEPUTY (2). **2.** See *deputy sheriff* under SHERIFF.

general deterrence. See DETERRENCE.

general devise. See DEVISE.

general-disability insurance. See INSURANCE.

general discharge. See DISCHARGE (8).

general election. See ELECTION (3).

general employer. See EMPLOYER.

general exception. See EXCEPTION (1).

general execution. See EXECUTION (4).

general executor. See EXECUTOR.

general expense. See *general administrative expense* under EXPENSE.

general federal common law. See COMMON LAW (1).

general fee conditional. See *fee simple conditional* under FEE SIMPLE.

general finding. See FINDING OF FACT.

general franchise. See FRANCHISE (2).

general fund. See FUND (1).

general good and welfare. See GOOD OF THE ORDER.

general guaranty. See GUARANTY.

general guardian. See GUARDIAN.

general hypothecation. See HYPOTHECATION.

generalia specialibus non derogant (jen-ə-**ray**-lee-ə spesh-ee-**ay**-lə-bəs non der-ə-gənt). [Latin "general things do not derogate from specific things"] The doctrine holding that general words in a later statute do not repeal an earlier statutory provision dealing with a special subject. • This principle illustrates the cautious approach that some courts have adopted in interpreting broad provisions, but there are many exceptions.

general imparlance. See IMPARLANCE.

general improvement. See IMPROVEMENT.

general indorsement. See *blank indorsement* under INDORSEMENT.

general instruction. See JURY INSTRUCTION.

general intangible. See INTANGIBLE.

general intent. See INTENT (1).

general-intent crime. See CRIME.

general issue. See ISSUE (1).

general jail delivery. See JAIL DELIVERY.

general jurisdiction. See JURISDICTION.

general-jurisdiction court. See *court of general jurisdiction* under COURT.

general jurisprudence. See JURISPRUDENCE.

general-justification defense. See *lesser-evils defense* under DEFENSE (1).

General Land Office. A former U.S. Interior Department division that exercised executive power relating to the public lands, including their survey, patenting, and sale or other disposition. • The General Land Office and the U.S. Grazing Service were consolidated into the Bureau of Land Management in 1946. See BUREAU OF LAND MANAGEMENT.

general law. See LAW.

general ledger. See LEDGER (1).

general legacy. See LEGACY.

general legal principle. See GENERAL PRINCIPLE OF LAW.

general legatee. See LEGATEE.

general legislation. See LEGISLATION.

general letter of credit. See LETTER OF CREDIT.

general-liability policy. See *comprehensive general-liability policy* under INSURANCE POLICY.

general lien. See LIEN.

general listing. See *open listing* under LISTING (1).

generally accepted accounting principles. (1930) The conventions, rules, and procedures that define approved accounting practices at a particular time. • These principles are issued by the Financial Accounting Standards Board for use by accountants in preparing financial statements. The principles include not only broad guidelines of general application but also detailed practices and procedures. — Abbr. GAAP. — Also termed *generally accepted accountancy principles*.

generally accepted auditing standards. The guidelines issued by the American Institute of Certified Public Accountants establishing an auditor's professional qualities and the criteria for the auditor's examination and required reports. — Abbr. GAAS.

general malice. See MALICE.

general manager. See MANAGER.

general maritime law. The body of U.S. legal precedents and doctrines developed through caselaw in maritime and admiralty litigation. • General maritime law is a branch of federal common law. It is distinguished from statutory law. Cf. MARITIME LAW; LAW OF THE SEA.

general mens rea. See *general intent* under INTENT (1).

general mortgage. See MORTGAGE.

general-mortgage bond. See BOND (3).

general objection. See OBJECTION.

general-obligation bond. See BOND (3).

general occupant. See OCCUPANT.

general officer. See OFFICER (2).

general order. See ORDER (4).

general owner. See OWNER.

general parliamentary law. See PARLIAMENTARY LAW.

general pardon. See AMNESTY.

general partner. See PARTNER.

general partnership. See PARTNERSHIP.

general personal jurisdiction. See JURISDICTION.

general plea. See *general denial* under DENIAL.

general plea in bar. See PLEA IN BAR.

general power. See POWER OF APPOINTMENT.

general power of appointment. See POWER OF APPOINTMENT.

general power of attorney. See POWER OF ATTORNEY.

general prayer. See PRAYER FOR RELIEF.

general principle of law. 1. A principle widely recognized by peoples whose legal order has attained a certain level of sophistication. **2.** *Int'l law.* A principle that gives rise to international legal obligations. **3.** A principle recognized in all kinds of legal relations, regardless of the legal system to which it belongs (state law, federal law, international law, etc.). — Also termed *general legal principle.*

general privilege. See PRIVILEGE (5).

general property. See PROPERTY.

general publication. See PUBLICATION.

general-public license. See *open-source license* under LICENSE.

general receiver. See *principal receiver* under RECEIVER.

general reference. See REFERENCE.

general replication. See REPLICATION.

general reprisal. See REPRISAL.

general retainer. See RETAINER.

general retention. See RETENTION.

general revenue. See REVENUE.

general revenue fund. See FUND (1).

general rule. See RULE.

general sentence. See SENTENCE.

General Services Administration. The independent federal agency that constructs and operates buildings; manages government property and records; procures and distributes supplies; and provides management services in communications, traffic, and automatic data processing. • Its Office of Enterprise Development assists small businesses in dealing with the agency through GSA's 12 regional offices. The agency was created by the Federal Property and Administrative Services Act of 1949. 40 USCA § 751. — Abbr. GSA.

general ship. See SHIP.

general special imparlance. See IMPARLANCE.

general statute. 1. See STATUTE. **2.** See PUBLIC LAW (2).

general strike. See STRIKE.

general synod. See SYNOD.

general tail. See *tail general* (1) under TAIL.

general tax. See TAX.

general tenancy. See TENANCY.

general term. See TERM (5).

general title. See TITLE (3).

general traverse. See TRAVERSE.

general truce. See TRUCE.

general trust. See *passive trust* under TRUST.

general usage. See USAGE.

general verdict. See VERDICT.

general-verdict rule. (1930) The principle that when a jury returns a general verdict on multiple causes of action (or theories of recovery), it is presumed on appeal that the jury found in the prevailing party's favor on each cause of action.

general verdict subject to a special case. See VERDICT.

general verdict with interrogatories. See VERDICT.

general warrant. See WARRANT (1).

general warranty. See WARRANTY (1).

general warranty deed. See *warranty deed* under DEED.

general welfare. See WELFARE (1).

General Welfare Clause. (1898) U.S. Const. art. I, § 8, cl. 1, which empowers Congress to levy taxes and pay debts in order to provide for the country's general welfare. • The Supreme Court has broadly interpreted this clause to allow Congress to create, for example, the social-security system. — Also termed *Welfare Clause.*

general words. (18c) Semantically broad expression; esp., language used in deeds to convey not only the specific property described in the conveyance but also all easements, privileges, and appurtenances that may belong to the property.

generation. (14c) **1.** A single degree or stage in the succession of persons in natural descent. **2.** The average time span between the birth of parents and the birth of their children.

generation-skipping tax. See TAX.

generation-skipping transfer. (1979) *Wills & trusts.* A conveyance of assets to a "skip person," that is, a person more than one generation removed from the transferor. ● For example, a conveyance either directly or in trust from a grandparent to a grandchild is a generation-skipping transfer subject to a generation-skipping transfer tax. IRC (26 USCA) §§ 2601–2663. See *generation-skipping transfer tax* under TAX; *generation-skipping trust* under TRUST; SKIP PERSON.

generation-skipping transfer tax. See TAX.

generation-skipping trust. See TRUST.

generic, *adj.* (1846) *Trademarks.* **1.** Common or descriptive, and thus not eligible for trademark protection; nonproprietary <a generic name>. **2.** Not having a trademark or brand name <generic drugs>.

genericalness. See GENERICNESS.

generic burglary. See BURGLARY.

generic claim. See PATENT CLAIM.

generic drug. See DRUG.

generic-drug law. (1977) A statute that allows pharmacists to substitute a generic drug for a brand-name drug under specified conditions. ● Most states have enacted generic-drug laws to ensure that less-expensive generic drugs are available to consumers.

genericide (jə-**ner**-ə-sīd). *Trademarks.* The loss or cancellation of a trademark that no longer distinguishes the owner's product from others' products. ● Genericide occurs when a trademark becomes such a household name that the consuming public begins to think of the mark not as a brand name but as a synonym for the product itself. Examples of trademarks that have been "killed" by genericide include *aspirin* and *escalator.*

genericism (jə-**ner**-ə-siz-əm). See GENERICNESS.

generic name. (1872) *Trademarks.* A term that describes something generally without designating the thing's source or creator, such as the word *car* or *sink.* ● A generic name cannot be protected as a trademark for the thing it denotes; e.g., *Apple* can be a trademark for computers but not for apples. — Also termed *generic term*; *generic mark*; *common descriptive name.*

genericness, *n.* (20c) The state or condition of being generic <an affirmative defense of genericness in a trademark suit>. — Also termed *genericalness*; *genericism.*

generic swap. See *plain-vanilla swap* under INTEREST-RATE SWAP. ●

generic term. See GENERIC NAME. ●

genetic child. See *natural child* (1) under CHILD.

genetic engineering. (ca. 1951) A method of creating new life forms and organic matter by gene-splicing and other techniques. ● The Supreme Court has ruled that those creations are patentable. *Diamond v. Chakrabarty,* 447 U.S. 303, 100 S.Ct. 2204 (1980).

genetic father. See *biological father* under FATHER.

genetic fingerprinting. See DNA IDENTIFICATION.

genetic-marker test. A medical method of testing tissue samples used in paternity and illegitimacy cases to determine whether a particular man could be the father of a child. ● This test represents a medical advance over blood-grouping tests. It analyzes DNA and is much more precise in assessing the probability of paternity. — Abbr. GMT. See PATERNITY TEST. Cf. BLOOD-GROUPING TEST; HUMAN-LEUKOCYTE ANTIGEN TEST.

genetic mother. See *biological mother* under MOTHER.

genetic parent. See *biological parent* under PARENT.

Geneva Conventions of 1949 (jə-**nee**-və). Four international agreements dealing with the protection of wounded members of the armed forces, the treatment of prisoners of war, and the protection of civilians during international armed conflicts. ● Common Article 3 of the Conventions proclaims certain minimum standards of treatment that are applicable to noninternational armed conflicts. The humanitarian-law protection established in these four agreements was amplified in 1977 by the two Protocols Additional to the Geneva Conventions. In common parlance, people refer to the *Geneva Convention* as if there were just one agreement. Cf. LAWS OF WAR.

Geneva Phonograms Convention. A 1971 treaty requiring signatories to protect phonorecord producers against piracy and the importation of pirated copies, by copyright protection, unfair-competition law, or criminal sanctions. ● The treaty was drafted by representatives from WIPO and UNESCO to correct weaknesses in the Rome Convention. — Also termed *Convention for the Protection of Producers of Phonograms Against Unauthorized Duplication of Their Phonograms*; *Phonograms Convention.*

genocide (**jen**-ə-sīd). (ca. 1944) *Int'l law.* An international crime involving acts causing serious physical and mental harm with the intent to destroy, partially or entirely, a national, ethnic, racial, or religious group. • The widely ratified Genocide Convention of 1948 defines the crime. The International Criminal Court has jurisdiction to try those accused of genocide. Many nations also have criminal laws providing punishment for individuals convicted of genocide. Cf. ETHNIC CLEANSING.

Genoese lottery (jen-oh-**eez** or -**ees**). See LOTTERY.

genotype. (19c) *Patents.* The genetic makeup of a living organism. • A patent on living matter must disclose its genotype rather than just describe its physical characteristics (phenotype) or behavior. Cf. PHENOTYPE. — **genotypic,** *adj.*

gens (jenz), *n.* [Latin] (19c) *Roman law.* A clan or group of families who share the same name and (supposedly) a common ancestor; extended family. • Members of a *gens* are freeborn and possess full civic rights. Pl. *gentes.*

gentes (**jen**-teez), *n.* [Latin] (19c) *Roman law.* The peoples or nations of the world, particularly the civilized peoples.

gentile (**jen**-tIl). [fr. Latin *gentilis*] *Roman law.* A member of a *gens.* See GENS.

gentleman. (12c) *Hist.* **1.** A man of noble or gentle birth or rank; a man above the rank of yeoman. **2.** A man belonging to the landed gentry. • Today the term has no precise legal meaning.

gentleman's agreement. See GENTLEMEN'S AGREEMENT.

Gentleman Usher of the Black Rod. *English law.* An officer of the House of Lords who has various ceremonial duties, including the summoning of the members of the House of Commons to the House of Lords when a bill is to receive royal approval. • The office dates from the 14th century.

gentlemen's agreement. (1886) An unwritten agreement that, while not legally enforceable, is secured by the good faith and honor of the parties. — Also spelled *gentleman's agreement.*

gentrification, *n.* (1973) The restoration and upgrading of a deteriorated or aging urban neighborhood by middle-class or affluent persons, resulting in increased property values and often in displacement of lower-income residents. — **gentrify,** *vb.*

genuine, *adj.* (17c) **1.** (Of a thing) authentic or real; having the quality of what a given thing purports to be or to have <the plaintiff failed to question whether the exhibits were genuine>. **2.** (Of an instrument) free of forgery or counterfeiting <the bank teller could not determine whether the signature on the check was genuine>. UCC § 1-201(18).

genuine issue of material fact. (1938) *Civil procedure.* In the law of summary judgments, a triable, substantial, or real question of fact supported by substantial evidence. • An issue of this kind precludes entry of summary judgment.

genus (**jee**-nəs or **jen**-əs). (16c) A general class comprising several species or divisions. • In legal usage, the terms *genus* and (sometimes) *species* invoke the taxonomic classification of life forms in biological science. For example, patent law is a species within the genus of intellectual property; burglary is a species within the genus of crime. In the law of sales, *genus* referred to fungibles, while *species* referred to specific, individual items. Cf. SPECIES (2).

genus claim. See *generic claim* under PATENT CLAIM.

geodetic-survey system (jee-ə-**det**-ik). (1990) A federally created land-description method consisting of nationwide marks (or *benches*) made at longitude and latitude points. • The geodetic-survey system integrates most of the real property in the United States into one unified form of measurement.

geographically descriptive trademark. See TRADEMARK.

geographic market. See MARKET.

geographic name. See NAME.

geography of crime. See *environmental criminology* under CRIMINOLOGY.

Georgia-Pacific **analysis.** *Patents.* A 15-factor test for setting a reasonable royalty in infringement suits. • Among other factors, the test considers what a prudent licensee would have paid while still being able to earn a profit. *Georgia-Pacific Corp. v. U.S. Plywood Corp.*, 318 F. Supp. 1116 (S.D.N.Y. 1970).

german (jər-mən), *adj.* (14c) Having the same parents or grandparents; closely related.

brother-german. See BROTHER.

cousin-german. See COUSIN (1).

sister-german. See SISTER.

germane (jər-**mayn**), *adj.* (14c) Relevant; pertinent <the caselaw cited in the brief was not germane to the legal issue pending before the court>. • Under parliamentary law, debate and amendments are in order only if they are germane to the motion under consideration.

gerrymandering (**jer**-ee-man-dər-ing or **ger**-ee-), *n.* (1812) **1.** The practice of dividing a geographical area into electoral districts, often of highly irregular shape, to give one political party an unfair advantage by diluting the opposition's voting strength. • When Massachusetts Governor Elbridge Gerry ran for reelection in 1812, members of his political party, the Anti-Federalists, altered the state's voting districts to benefit the party. One newly created district resembled a salamander, inspiring a critic to coin the word *gerrymander* by combining the governor's name,

Gerry, with the ending of *salamander*. Gerry was not reelected governor, but was elected as James Madison's vice president. — Also termed *political gerrymandering*. **2.** The practice of dividing any geographical or jurisdictional area into political units (such as school districts) to give some group a special advantage. — Also termed *jurisdictional gerrymandering*. Cf. REAPPORTIONMENT. — **gerrymander,** *vb.*

> *delineational gerrymandering.* Gerrymandering by varying the districts' shape. • There are three kinds of delineational gerrymandering: cracking (or fracturing), packing, and stacking. See CRACKING; PACKING; STACKING (2).

> *institutional gerrymandering.* Gerrymandering by means of varying the number of representatives per district.

Geschmacksmuster. *Patents.* [German] See *design patent* under PATENT.

Gestalt factors. The criteria that a court uses in a minimum-contacts analysis to determine the reasonableness of subjecting a nonresident to personal jurisdiction. • These fairness criteria include (1) the defendant's burden of making a personal appearance, (2) the forum state's interest in adjudicating the dispute, (3) the plaintiff's interest in obtaining convenient and effective relief, (4) the judicial system's interest in arriving at the most effective resolution of the controversy, and (5) the common interests of all sovereigns in promoting substantive social policies. These factors were articulated by the United States Supreme Court in *Burger King Corp. v. Rudzewicz*, 471 U.S. 462, 478, 105 S.Ct. 2174, 2185 (1985), but the Court has never used the term *Gestalt factors*; it was coined in *Donatelli v. National Hockey League*, 893 F.2d 459, 465 (1st Cir. 1990). See MINIMUM CONTACTS.

gestational carrier. See *surrogate mother* (1) under MOTHER.

gestational mother. See *birth mother* under MOTHER.

gestational surrogacy. See SURROGACY.

gestational surrogate. See *surrogate mother* (1) under MOTHER.

gestio (**jes**-chee-oh), *n.* [Latin] (16c) *Roman law.* **1.** Behavior or conduct. **2.** The management of a thing, esp. a transaction. See NEGOTIORUM GESTIO. — Also termed GESTION.

> *negotiorum gestio* (ni-goh-shee-**or**-əm **jes**-chee-oh). See NEGOTIORUM GESTIO.

gesture. (15c) A motion of the body calculated to express a thought or emphasize a certain point <the prosecutor was known for her dramatic gestures during closing argument>.

get-up. See TRADE DRESS.

ghost detainee. See *secret detainee* under DETAINEE.

ghosting. The assumption of the identity of a deceased person to conceal one's true identity. Cf. IDENTITY THEFT.

gibbet (**jib**-it), *n.* (13c) *Hist.* A post with one arm extending from the top, from which criminals are either executed by hanging or suspended after death as a warning to other potential offenders; a type of gallows.

> *double gibbet.* A gibbet with two arms extending from its top so that it resembles a capital "T."

gibbet law. See HALIFAX LAW.

GIC. See *guaranteed investment contract* under INVESTMENT CONTRACT.

GIFT. *abbr.* GAMETE INTRAFALLOPIAN TRANSFER.

gift, *n.* (12c) **1.** The voluntary transfer of property to another without compensation. **2.** A thing so transferred. — **gift,** *vb.*

> *absolute gift.* See *inter vivos gift.*

> *anatomical gift.* (1971) A testamentary donation of a bodily organ or organs, esp. for transplant or for medical research. • The procedures for making an anatomical gift are set forth in the Uniform Anatomical Gift Act, which has been adopted in every state.

> *antenuptial gift.* See *prenuptial gift.*

> *charitable gift.* An inter vivos or testamentary donation to a nonprofit organization for the relief of poverty, the advancement of education, the advancement of religion, the promotion of health, governmental, or municipal purposes, and other purposes the accomplishment of which is beneficial to the community. Restatement (Second) of Trusts § 368 (1959). • When the beneficiary is a religious organization or the gift is intended for a religious purpose, it is sometimes also termed a *pious gift.*

> *class gift.* (1949) A gift to a group of persons, uncertain in number at the time of the gift but to be ascertained at a future time, who are all to take in definite proportions, the share of each being dependent on the ultimate number in the group.

> *completed gift.* (1952) A gift that is no longer in the donor's possession and control. • Only a completed gift is taxable under the gift tax.

> *gift causa mortis* (**kaw**-zə **mor**-tis). (18c) A gift made in contemplation of the donor's imminent death. • The three essentials are that (1) the gift must be made with a view to the donor's present illness or peril, (2) the donor must actually die from that illness or peril, without ever recovering, and (3) there must be a delivery. Even though *causa mortis* is the more usual word order in modern law, the correct Latin phrasing is *mortis causa* — hence *gift mortis*

causa. — Also termed *donatio causa mortis; donatio mortis causa; gift in contemplation of death; transfer in contemplation of death.* See CONTEMPLATION OF DEATH.

gift in contemplation of death. See *gift causa mortis.*

gift inter vivos. See *inter vivos gift.*

gift in trust. (18c) A gift of legal title to property to someone who will act as trustee for the benefit of a beneficiary.

gift over. (18c) A property gift (esp. by will) that takes effect after the expiration of a preceding estate in the property (such as a life estate or fee simple determinable) <to Sarah for life, with gift over to Don in fee>.

gift splitting. See *split gift.*

gratuitous gift. A gift made without consideration, as most gifts are. ● Strictly speaking, the term looks redundant, but it answers to the *donum gratuitum* of Roman law.

inter vivos gift (**in**-tər **vi**-vohs *or* **vee**-vohs). (1848) A gift of personal property made during the donor's lifetime and delivered to the donee with the intention of irrevocably surrendering control over the property. — Also termed *gift inter vivos; lifetime gift; absolute gift.*

lifetime gift. See *inter vivos gift.*

manual gift. *Civil law.* A gift of movable, tangible property, made by delivery without any formalities. La. Civ. Code art. 1539.

onerous gift (**ohn**-ə-rəs *or* **on**-ə-rəs). A gift made subject to certain conditions imposed on the recipient.

pious gift. See *charitable gift.*

prenuptial gift (pree-**nəp**-shəl). (1921) A gift of property from one spouse to another before marriage. ● In community-property states, prenuptial gifts are often made to preserve the property's classification as separate property. — Also termed *antenuptial gift.*

split gift. (1957) *Tax.* A gift that is made by one spouse to a third person and that, for gift-tax purposes, both spouses treat as being made one-half by each spouse; a gift in which the spouses combine their annual gift-tax exclusions. ● A split gift, for example, is eligible for two annual exclusions of $10,000 each, or a total of $20,000 for one gift. — Also termed *gift-splitting; gift-splitting election.* See *annual exclusion* under EXCLUSION (1).

substitute gift. (1934) A testamentary gift to one person in place of another who is unable to take under the will for some reason. — Also termed *substitutional gift.*

taxable gift. (1922) A gift that, after adjusting for the annual exclusion and applicable deductions, is subject to the federal unified transfer tax. IRC (26 USCA) § 2503.

testamentary gift (tes-tə-**men**-tə-ree *or* -tree). (18c) A gift made in a will.

vested gift. (1820) An absolute gift, being neither conditional nor contingent, though its use or enjoyment might not occur until sometime in the future.

gift deed. See DEED.

gift enterprise. (1858) **1.** A scheme for the distribution of items by chance among those who have purchased shares in the scheme. **2.** A merchant's scheme to increase sales without lowering prices by giving buyers tickets that carry a chance to win a prize. ● Gift enterprises are regulated by state law. See LOTTERY.

gifting circle. See GIFTING CLUB.

gifting club. A type of pyramid scheme or Ponzi scheme in which recruits make "gifts" of money to other club members with the expectation that future recruits will make "gifts" to the present recruits. ● Many gifting clubs limit membership to women. Club leaders usu. try to evade income-tax laws by claiming that the money paid in by a recruit is a tax-free "gift" to a club member and warning new recruits not to expect "gifts" in the future. Some states forbid gifting clubs as illegal pyramid schemes. Other states hold that the clubs are illegal lotteries. — Also termed *gifting circle; sisterhood; birthday club.* See PONZI SCHEME.

gift inter vivos. See *inter vivos gift* under GIFT.

gift in trust. See GIFT.

gift over. See GIFT.

gift splitting. See *split gift* under GIFT.

gift-splitting election. See *split gift* under GIFT.

Gifts to Minors Act. See UNIFORM TRANSFERS TO MINORS ACT.

gift tax. See TAX.

gift-tax exclusion. See *annual exclusion* under EXCLUSION.

gildhall. See GUILDHALL (1).

GI loan. See *veteran's loan* under LOAN.

gilt-edged, *adj.* (Of a security) having the highest rating for safety of investment; exceptionally safe as an investment.

Ginnie Mae (**jin**-ee **may**). See GOVERNMENT NATIONAL MORTGAGE ASSOCIATION.

GIPSA. *abbr.* GRAIN INSPECTION, PACKERS, AND STOCKYARD ADMINISTRATION.

girth (gərth). [Old English] (13c) **1.** A measure of length, equal to a yard. ● This term, which was used in Saxon and early English law, was taken from the circumference of a man's body. **2.** The area surrounding a church. **3.** A place of sanctuary. **4.** A band or strap that encircles the body of an animal to fasten something (usu. a saddle) to its back.

gist (jist). (18c) **1.** The ground or essence (of a legal action) <the gist of the crime>. **2.** The main point <she skimmed the brief to get the gist of it>. • This noun derives from the Law French verb *giser* "to lie."

gist-of-the-action doctrine. The principle that a plaintiff who brings a tort claim arising from a contractual relationship must show that the contract and any contractual claim are collateral to the tort claim. • The doctrine prevents plaintiffs from recasting contract claims as tort claims. This term is most common in Pennsylvania but also appears in New Jersey, Delaware, the Virgin Islands, and elsewhere.

give, *vb.* (13c) **1.** To voluntarily transfer (property) to another without compensation <Jack gave his daughter a car on her birthday>. **2.** To confer by a formal act <the First Amendment gives all citizens the right to free speech>. **3.** To present for another to consider <the witness gave compelling testimony before the jury>. **4.** (Of a jury) to impose or award by verdict <the jury gave the defendant the death penalty> <the jury gave the plaintiff $1,000 in damages>.

give bail, *vb.* To post security for one's appearance in court <the court ordered the accused to give bail in the amount of $10,000>. — Also termed *post bail.*

give color, *vb. Hist.* To admit, either expressly or impliedly by silence, that an opponent's allegations appear to be meritorious. • In common-law pleading, a defendant's plea of confession and avoidance had to give color to the plaintiff's allegations in the complaint or the plea would be fatally defective. See COLOR (2).

give, devise, and bequeath, *vb.* (17c) To transfer property by will <I give, devise, and bequeath all the rest, residue, and remainder of my estate to my beloved daughter Sarah>. • This wording has long been criticized as redundant. In modern usage, *give* ordinarily suffices. See BEQUEST.

given name. See *personal name* under NAME.

give way, *vb. Maritime law.* (Of a vessel) to deviate from a course, or to slow down, in accordance with navigation rules, so that a second vessel may pass without altering its course.

giving in payment. *Civil law.* The act of discharging a debt by giving something to the creditor (with the creditor's consent) other than what was originally called for. La. Civ. Code art. 2655. • The phrase is a translation of the French *dation en paiement* and derives from the Roman *datio in solutum.* Cf. ACCORD AND SATISFACTION.

glamour stock. See *growth stock* under STOCK.

glass ceiling. (1984) An actual or supposed upper limit of professional advancement, esp. for women, as a result of discriminatory practices.

Glass–Steagall Act. A federal statute that protects bank depositors by restricting the securities-related business of commercial banks, specif. by prohibiting banks from owning brokerage firms or engaging in the brokerage business. 12 USCA § 378. — Also termed *Banking Act of 1933.*

glebe (gleeb). [fr. Latin *gleba* "clod of earth"] (15c) **1.** *Roman law.* The soil of an inheritance; an agrarian estate. • *Servi addicti glebae* ("slaves bound to the land") were serfs attached to and passing with the estate. **2.** *Eccles. law.* Land possessed as part of the endowment or revenue of a church or ecclesiastical benefice.

global fund. See MUTUAL FUND.

***Globe* election.** *Labor law.* The procedure by which a group of employees is given the opportunity to decide whether to be represented as a distinct group or to be represented as a part of a larger, existing unit. *Globe Machine & Stamping Co.,* 3 NLRB 294 (1937). — Also termed *self-determination election.*

gloss, *n.* (16c) **1.** A note inserted between the lines or in the margin of a text to explain a difficult or obscure word in the text <this edition of Shakespeare's works is bolstered by its many glosses on Elizabethan English>. **2.** A collection of explanations; a glossary <the hornbook's copious gloss>. **3.** (*usu. pl.*) A pronouncement about meaning; an interpretation <the statutory language needs no gloss>.

glossators (glah-**say**-tərz). (15c) (*usu. cap.*) A group of Italian jurisconsults who, from the 11th to the 13th centuries, were primarily responsible for the revival of the study of Roman law. • They originally worked by glossing (that is, explaining in the margin) difficult or unclear passages, and gradually their writings blossomed into full-blown commentaries and discussions. See POSTGLOSSATORS. — **glossatorial,** *adj.*

GMI. *abbr.* GUILTY BUT MENTALLY ILL.

GMT. *abbr.* GENETIC-MARKER TEST.

GNMA. *abbr.* GOVERNMENT NATIONAL MORTGAGE ASSOCIATION.

GNP. *abbr.* GROSS NATIONAL PRODUCT.

go bail, *vb. Archaic.* To act as a surety on a bail bond.

Godbote. See BOTE (2).

godparent. (1865) *Eccles. law.* A person, usu. a close family friend or relative, who accepts a parent's invitation to assume part of the responsibility for the religious education of a newly baptized child. • Often, too, there is an understanding that the godparent would help support and rear the child if the parents were to die or become incapacitated. The spiritual parent–child relationship creates a canonical impediment to marriage. — Also termed (more specifically) *godmother*; *godfather*; (in *eccles. law*) *sponsor*.

God's penny. *Hist.* Earnest money; a small sum paid on the striking of a bargain. — Also termed *denarius Dei*; *earnest-penny*; *godpenny*.

go forward, *vb.* (1964) To commence or carry on with the presentation of a case in court <after the lunch recess, the judge instructed the plaintiff to go forward with its case>.

go hence without day. (18c) (Of a defendant to a lawsuit) to be finished with legal proceedings without any further settings on the court's calendar. ● Thus, a defendant who "goes hence without day" succeeds in getting a case finally resolved, usu. by dismissal. The phrase derives from the Law French phrase *aller sans jour*, and over time defendants came to use it to request that the case against them be dismissed without the necessity of a day in court. — Sometimes shortened to *go without day*; *without day*. See SINE DIE.

going-and-coming rule. (1927) **1.** The principle that torts committed by an employee while commuting to or from work are generally outside the scope of employment. **2.** The principle that denies workers'-compensation benefits to an employee injured while commuting to or from work. Cf. COMMERCIAL-TRAVELER RULE.

going concern. (1881) A commercial enterprise actively engaging in business with the expectation of indefinite continuance. — Also termed *going business*.

going-concern value. See VALUE (2).

going price, *n.* (18c) The prevailing or current market value of something. See *fair market value* under VALUE (2).

going private. The process of changing a public corporation into a close corporation by terminating the corporation's status with the SEC as a publicly held corporation and by having its outstanding publicly held shares acquired by a single shareholder or a small group.

going-private transaction. See FREEZEOUT.

going public. The process of a company's selling stock to the investing public for the first time (after filing a registration statement under applicable securities laws), thereby becoming a public corporation.

going through the bar. *Hist.* A daily process in which the court would ask all barristers present whether they had motions to present. ● This practice, which ended in 1873, was conducted according to seniority, except for the last day of a term, when the junior barristers were asked first.

going to the country. *Hist.* The act of requesting a jury trial. ● A defendant was said to be "going to the country" by concluding a pleading with the phrase "and of this he puts himself upon the country." Similarly, a plaintiff would conclude a pleading with the phrase "and this the plaintiff prays may be enquired of by the country." — Also termed *go to the country*. Cf. CONCLUSION TO THE COUNTRY.

going value. See *going-concern value* under VALUE (2).

going witness. See WITNESS.

gold bond. See BOND (3).

gold certificate. *Hist.* A banknote issued by the United States Treasury from 1863 to 1934 and redeemable in gold. ● When the United States abandoned the gold standard in 1933, Congress declared ownership of gold certificates illegal even though the Treasury continued to issue them until mid-1934. The certificates were legalized again in 1964, but they can no longer be redeemed for gold. They now have the same status as Federal Reserve notes, which are not redeemable for precious metal. Cf. FEDERAL RESERVE NOTE; SILVER CERTIFICATE.

gold clause. A provision calling for payment in gold. ● Gold clauses, which are now void, were once used in contracts, bonds, and mortgages.

golden handcuffs. Remuneration set at such a high level that the employee earning it cannot leave the firm or company and receive commensurate pay elsewhere. ● As a result, the employee often stays in the position even if it is otherwise unrewarding or unpleasant.

golden handshake. *Corporations.* A generous compensation package offered to an employee, usu. as an inducement to retire or upon dismissal.

golden parachute. (1981) *Corporations.* An employment-contract provision that grants an upper-level executive lucrative severance benefits — including long-term salary guarantees or bonuses — if control of the company changes hands (as by a merger). Cf. TIN PARACHUTE.

golden rule. The principle that, in construing written instruments, a court should adhere to the grammatical and ordinary sense of the words unless that adherence would lead to some manifest absurdity; esp., in statutory construction, the principle that if a statute's literal meaning would lead to an absurd or unjust result, or even to an inconsistency within the statute itself, the statute should be interpreted in a way that avoids such a result or inconsistency. — Also termed *Baron Parke's rule*. Cf. ABSURDITY; MISCHIEF RULE; PLAIN-MEANING RULE; EQUITY-OF-THE-STATUTE RULE.

golden-rule argument. A jury argument in which a lawyer asks the jurors to reach a verdict by imagining themselves or someone they care about in the place of the injured plaintiff or crime victim. ● Because golden-rule arguments ask the jurors to become advocates for the plaintiff or victim and to ignore their obligation to exercise calm and reasonable judgment, these arguments are widely condemned and are considered improper in most states.

gold standard. (19c) A monetary system in which currency is convertible into its legal equivalent in gold or gold coin. ● The United States adopted the gold standard in 1900 and abandoned it in 1934. Cf. PAPER STANDARD.

good, *adj.* (bef. 12c) **1.** Sound or reliable <a good investment>. **2.** Valid, effectual, and enforceable; sufficient under the law <good title>.

good, *n.* See GOODS.

good and lawful fence. See LAWFUL FENCE.

good and merchantable abstract of title. See ABSTRACT OF TITLE.

good and valuable consideration. See *valuable consideration* under CONSIDERATION (1).

good and workmanlike. (18c) (Of a product or service) characterized by quality craftsmanship; constructed or performed in a skillful way or method <the house was built in a good and workmanlike manner>.

good behavior. (16c) **1.** A standard by which judges are considered fit to continue their tenure, consisting in the avoidance of criminal behavior. **2.** Orderly conduct, which in the context of penal law allows a prisoner to reduce the time spent in prison. Cf. *good time* under TIME.

good cause. See CAUSE (2).

good cause shown. See *good cause* under CAUSE (2).

good consideration. See CONSIDERATION (1).

good deed. See DEED.

good delivery. See DELIVERY.

good faith, *n.* (18c) A state of mind consisting in (1) honesty in belief or purpose, (2) faithfulness to one's duty or obligation, (3) observance of reasonable commercial standards of fair dealing in a given trade or business, or (4) absence of intent to defraud or to seek unconscionable advantage. — Also termed *bona fides.* Cf. BAD FAITH. — **good-faith,** *adj.*

good-faith bargaining. *Labor law.* Negotiations between an employer and a representative of employees, usu. a union, in which both parties meet and confer at reasonable times with open minds and with a view to reaching an agreement. ● The National Labor Relations Act requires good-faith bargaining, and failure to bargain in good faith is considered an unfair labor practice. 29 USCA §§ 151–169. See UNFAIR LABOR PRACTICE.

good-faith exception. (1980) *Criminal procedure.* An exception to the exclusionary rule whereby evidence obtained under a warrant later found to be invalid (esp. because it is not supported by probable cause) is nonetheless admissible if the police reasonably relied on the notion that the warrant was valid. ● The Supreme Court adopted the good-faith exception in *United States v. Leon,* 468 U.S. 897, 104 S.Ct. 3405 (1984).

good-faith improver. A person who makes improvements to real property while actually and reasonably believing himself or herself to be the owner or lawful occupant. ● The improver may be entitled to recover the value of the improvements from the true owner or to remove them. See IMPROVEMENT.

good-faith margin. See MARGIN.

good-faith purchaser. See *bona fide purchaser* under PURCHASER (1).

good-guy clause. See *good-guy guaranty* under GUARANTY.

good-guy guaranty. See GUARANTY.

good health. *Insurance.* A state of reasonable healthiness; a state of health free from serious disease. ● Good health, a phrase often appearing in life-insurance policies, does not mean perfect health. — Also termed *sound health.*

good jury. See *special jury* under JURY.

good moral character, *n.* (18c) **1.** A pattern of behavior that is consistent with the community's current ethical standards and that shows an absence of deceit or morally reprehensible conduct. ● An alien seeking to be naturalized must show good moral character in the five years preceding the petition for naturalization. **2.** A pattern of behavior conforming to a profession's ethical standards and showing an absence of moral turpitude. ● Good moral character is usu. a requirement of persons applying to practice a profession such as law or medicine.

good offices. *Int'l law.* The involvement of one or more countries or an international organization in a dispute between other countries with the aim of contributing to its settlement or at least easing relations between the disputing countries.

good of the order. *Parliamentary law.* A time scheduled, usu. late in a meeting, for informal announcements, comments, and suggestions that do not seek the meeting's immediate action. — Also termed *general good and welfare; open forum; open microphone.*

Goodright. *Hist.* A name sometimes used as a fictitious plaintiff in an ejectment action. ● "John Doe" was used more frequently. — Also termed *Goodtitle.* Cf. JOHN DOE.

goods. (bef. 12c) **1.** Tangible or movable personal property other than money; esp., articles of trade or items of merchandise <goods and services>. ● The sale of goods is governed by Article 2 of the UCC. **2.** Things that have value, whether tangible or not <the importance of social goods varies from society to society>.

> **bulky goods.** Goods that are obviously difficult to move because of their nature, their number, or their location.

> **capital goods.** Goods (such as equipment and machinery) used for the production of other goods or services. — Also termed *industrial goods.*

> **consumer goods.** Goods bought or used primarily for personal, family, or household purposes, and not for resale or for producing other goods. UCC § 9-102(23).

> **customers' goods.** *Insurance.* Goods belonging to the customers of a casualty-insurance policyholder; goods held by a policyholder as a bailee.

> **distressed goods.** Goods sold at unusually low prices or at a loss.

> **durable goods.** Consumer goods that are designed to be used repeatedly over a long period, such as automobiles or refrigerators. — Also termed *durables*; *hard goods.*

> **fungible goods** (fən-jə-bəl). Goods that are interchangeable with one another; goods that, by nature or trade usage, are the equivalent of any other like unit, such as coffee or grain. UCC § 1-201(b)(18).

> **future goods.** Goods that will come into being, such as those yet to be manufactured; goods that are not both existing and identified. ● A purported present sale of future goods or any interest in them operates as a contract to sell. UCC § 2-105(2).

> **gray-market goods.** See PARALLEL IMPORTS.

> **hard goods.** See *durable goods.*

> **household goods.** Goods that are used in connection with a home. ● This term usu. arises when a warehouser claims a lien on what he or she asserts are "household" goods. According to the UCC, a warehouser may claim a lien on a depositor's furniture, furnishings, and personal effects that are used in a dwelling. UCC § 7-209(d).

> **industrial goods.** See *capital goods.*

> **mobile goods.** Goods that are normally used in more than one jurisdiction (such as shipping containers and road-construction machinery) and that are held by the debtor as equipment or leased by the debtor to others. ● Under previous drafts of the Uniform Commercial Code, the procedure for perfecting a security interest in

mobile goods was generally defined by the law of the state where the debtor is located. The current UCC does not distinguish mobile goods. See *ordinary goods.* UCC § 9-103(3).

> **nonconforming goods.** Goods that fail to meet contractual specifications, allowing the buyer to reject the tender of the goods or to revoke their acceptance. UCC §§ 2-601, 2-608. See PERFECT-TENDER RULE.

> **ordinary goods.** Goods that are anything other than mobile goods, minerals, or goods covered by a certificate of title. UCC § 9-103(1)(a). ● The current UCC does not distinguish between ordinary and mobile goods.

> **prize goods.** Goods captured at sea during wartime.

> **soft goods.** Consumer goods (such as clothing) that are not durable goods.

Good Samaritan action. 1. A deed performed gratuitously by a person to help another who is in peril. — Also termed *Good Samaritan act.* See GOOD SAMARITAN DOCTRINE; GOOD SAMARITAN LAW. **2.** A lawsuit brought by a person or group for the benefit of all or part of a community.

Good Samaritan doctrine (sə-**mar**-i-tən). (1952) *Torts.* The principle that a person who is injured while attempting to aid another in imminent danger, and who then sues the one whose negligence created the danger, will not be charged with contributory negligence unless the rescue attempt is an unreasonable one or the rescuer acts unreasonably in performing the attempted rescue. Cf. EMERGENCY DOCTRINE; RESCUE DOCTRINE; LOST-CHANCE DOCTRINE.

good-samaritan law. (1965) A statute that exempts from liability a person (such as an off-duty physician) who voluntarily renders aid to another in imminent danger but negligently causes injury while rendering the aid. ● Some form of good-samaritan legislation has been enacted in all 50 states and in the District of Columbia. — Also written *Good Samaritan law.* — Also termed *good-samaritan statute.* Cf. GOOD SAMARITAN DOCTRINE.

goods and chattels (**chat**-əlz), *n.* (16c) Loosely, personal property of any kind; occasionally, tangible personal property only. — Also termed *goods and effects*; *goods and merchandise.*

good-soldier defense. An excuse theory based on the assertion that a defendant was following orders, esp. of a military or corporate superior. ● The term is a derisive label rather than a valid defense. Following an order does not relieve a defendant of responsibility for wrongful acts unless there are circumstances that would amount to coercion.

good time. See TIME.

good-time law. A statute allowing a prisoner's sentence to be reduced by a stated number of days for each month or year of good behavior while incarcerated. — Also termed *good-time statute.*

good title. See TITLE (2).

goodwill. (bef. 12c) A business's reputation, patronage, and other intangible assets that are considered when appraising the business, esp. for purchase; the ability to earn income in excess of the income that would be expected from the business viewed as a mere collection of assets. ● Because an established business's trademark or servicemark is a symbol of goodwill, trademark infringement is a form of theft of goodwill. By the same token, when a trademark is assigned, the goodwill that it carries is also assigned. — Also written *good will.* — Also termed *enterprise goodwill; commercial goodwill; practice goodwill; economic goodwill.* Cf. *going-concern value* under VALUE (2).

individual goodwill. See *personal goodwill.*

personal goodwill. Goodwill attributable to an individual's skills, knowledge, efforts, training, or reputation in making a business successful. — Also termed *professional goodwill; separate goodwill; individual goodwill.*

professional goodwill. See *personal goodwill.*

separate goodwill. See *personal goodwill.*

goose case. See WHITEHORSE CASE.

goosehorn, *n. Slang.* A bawdy house; a house of prostitution. See DISORDERLY HOUSE.

gore (gor), *n.* (bef. 12c) **1.** *Hist.* A small, narrow slip of land. **2.** A small (often triangular) piece of land, such as may be left between surveys that do not close. **3.** In some New England states (such as Maine and Vermont), a county's subdivision that has little population and thus is not organized as a town.

Gothland sea laws. See LAWS OF VISBY.

go to protest. (Of commercial paper) to be dishonored by nonpayment or nonacceptance <the draft will go to protest>. See DISHONOR (1); PROTEST (2).

go to the country. See GOING TO THE COUNTRY.

govern, *vb.* (14c) (Of a precedent) to control a point in issue <the *Smith* case will govern the outcome of the appeal>.

governing body. 1. GOVERNMENT (2). **2.** A group of (esp. corporate) officers or persons having ultimate control <the board of directors is the governing body of XYZ, Inc.>.

governing document. See DOCUMENT.

government. (14c) **1.** The structure of principles and rules determining how a state or organization is regulated. **2.** The sovereign power in a nation or state. **3.** An organization through which a body of people exercises political authority; the machinery by which sovereign power is expressed <the Canadian government>. ● In this sense, the term refers collectively to the political organs of a country regardless of their function or level, and regardless of the subject matter they deal with. Cf. NATION; STATE.

central government. See *federal government* (1).

de facto government (di **fak**-toh). **1.** A government that has taken over the regular government and exercises sovereignty over a nation. **2.** An independent government established and exercised by a group of a country's inhabitants who have separated themselves from the parent state. — Also termed *government de facto.*

de jure government. A functioning government that is legally established. — Also termed *government de jure.*

federal government. **1.** A national government that exercises some degree of control over smaller political units that have surrendered some degree of power in exchange for the right to participate in national political matters. — Also termed (in federal states) *central government.* **2.** The U.S. government. — Also termed *national government.*

government de facto. See *de facto government.*

government de jure. See *de jure government.*

local government. The government of a particular locality, such as a city, county, or parish; a governing body at a lower level than the state government. ● The term includes a school district, fire district, transportation authority, and any other special-purpose district or authority. — Also termed *municipal government.*

mixed government. A government containing a blend of forms, as in democracy and monarchy.

municipal government. See *local government.*

national government. **1.** See NATIONAL GOVERNMENT. **2.** See *federal government* (2).

proprietary government. *Hist.* A government granted by the Crown to an individual, in the nature of a feudatory principality, with powers of legislation formerly belonging to the owner of a county palatine. Cf. COUNTY PALATINE.

provisional government. A government temporarily established to govern until a permanent one is organized to replace it.

republican government. A government in the republican form; specif., a government by representatives chosen by the people.

state government. The government of a state of the United States.

4. The executive branch of the U.S. government. **5.** The prosecutors in a given criminal case <the government has objected to the introduction of that evidence>. **6.** An academic course devoted to the study of government; political science <Bridges is enrolled in Government 101>.

government agency. See AGENCY (3).

government-agency defense. *Torts.* An affirmative defense that immunizes a contractor from liability upon proof that the contractor acted on the government's behalf as an agent or as a government officer. ● This defense is extremely limited because of the difficulty of establishing the government–agent relationship. *See Yearsley v. W.A. Ross Constr. Co.*, 309 U.S. 18, 20–22, 60 S. Ct. 413, 414–15 (1940). Cf. GOVERNMENT-CONTRACTOR DEFENSE; CONTRACT-SPECIFICATION DEFENSE.

government-agency security. See *government security* under SECURITY.

government agent. See AGENT (2).

governmental act. See GOVERNMENTAL FUNCTION.

governmental activity. See GOVERNMENTAL FUNCTION.

governmental employee benefit plan. See *governmental plan* under EMPLOYEE BENEFIT PLAN.

governmental enterprise. See ENTERPRISE.

governmental function. (1817) *Torts.* A government agency's conduct that is expressly or impliedly mandated or authorized by constitution, statute, or other law and that is carried out for the benefit of the general public. ● Generally, a governmental entity is immune from tort liability for governmental acts. — Also termed *governmental act*; *governmental activity*. See PUBLIC-FUNCTION TEST. Cf. PROPRIETARY FUNCTION.

governmental-function theory. (1936) *Constitutional law.* A principle by which private conduct is characterized as state action, esp. for due-process and equal-protection purposes, when a private party is exercising a public function. ● Under this theory, for example, a political party (which is a private entity) cannot exclude voters from primary elections on the basis of race. — Also termed *public-function rationale*.

governmental immunity. See *sovereign immunity* under IMMUNITY (1).

governmental instrumentality. (1854) A constitutionally or legislatively created agency that is immune from certain kinds of liability, as for taxes or punitive damages.

governmental-interest-analysis technique. See INTEREST-ANALYSIS TECHNIQUE.

governmental plan. See EMPLOYEE BENEFIT PLAN.

governmental secret. See STATE SECRET.

governmental trust. See TRUST.

governmental unit. A subdivision, agency, department, county, parish, municipality, or other unit of the government of a country or a state. ● The term includes an organization with a separate corporate existence only if the organization can legally issue debt obligations on which interest is exempt from income taxation under national law. UCC § 9-102(a)(45).

government-annuity society. *Hist.* One of several organizations formed in England to enable the working class to provide for themselves by purchasing, on advantageous terms, a government annuity for life or for a term of years.

government bond. 1. See *savings bond* under BOND (3). **2.** See *government security* under SECURITY.

government contract. See CONTRACT.

government-contractor defense. An affirmative defense that immunizes a government contractor from civil liability under state law when the contractor complies with government specifications. ● Immunization is extended when two conditions are satisfied: (1) the supplier warned the government about any dangers presented by the goods about which the supplier had knowledge but the government did not, and (2) the government itself is immune from liability under the *Feres* doctrine. Essentially, this federal common-law defense, which has been applied in cases of negligence, strict liability, and breach of warranty, extends sovereign immunity over the contractor. The leading case on this defense is *Boyle v. United Techs. Corp.*, 487 U.S. 500, 108 S.Ct. 2510 (1988). — Also termed *Boyle defense*; *government-contract defense*; *government-contract-specification defense*; (in military context) *military-contractor defense*. See FERES DOCTRINE. Cf. GOVERNMENT-AGENCY DEFENSE.

government-contract-specification defense. See GOVERNMENT-CONTRACTOR DEFENSE.

government-controlled corporation. See *quasi-governmental agency* under AGENCY (3).

government corporation. See *public corporation* (3) under CORPORATION.

government de facto. See *de facto government* under GOVERNMENT.

government de jure. See *de jure government* under GOVERNMENT.

government enterprise. See *governmental enterprise* under ENTERPRISE.

government immunity. See *sovereign immunity* under IMMUNITY (1).

government-in-exile. An individual or group of individuals residing in a foreign country while (1) claiming supreme authority over a country, (2) being recognized by the hosting country as the supreme authority over that other country, and (3) being organized to perform and actually performing some acts of state on behalf of the home country.

government insurance. See INSURANCE.

government land. See *public land* under LAND.

Government National Mortgage Association. A federally owned corporation in the U.S. Department of Housing and Urban Development responsible for guaranteeing mortgage-backed securities composed of FHA-insured or VA-guaranteed mortgage loans. • The Association purchases, on the secondary market, residential mortgages originated by local lenders; it then issues federally insured securities backed by these mortgages. — Abbr. GNMA. — Also termed *Ginnie Mae.*

government of laws. The doctrine that government must operate according to established, consistent legal principles and not according to the interests of those who happen to be in power at a given time; esp., the doctrine that judicial decisions must be based on the law, regardless of the character of the litigants or the personal predilections of the judge.

government plan. See *governmental plan* under EMPLOYEE BENEFIT PLAN.

Government Printing Office. An office in the legislative branch of the federal government responsible for printing and distributing congressional publications and publications of other agencies of the United States government. • The Office is supervised by the Congressional Joint Committee on Printing. It began operating in 1860. — Abbr. GPO.

government secret. See STATE SECRET.

government-securities interdealer broker. See BROKER.

government security. See SECURITY.

government survey. See SURVEY.

government-survey system. A land-description method that divides the United States into checks or tracts of ground, which are further broken down into smaller descriptions, such as metes and bounds.

government tort. See TORT.

governor. (14c) The chief executive official of a U.S. state. • Governors are elected and usu. serve a two- or four-year term.

go without day. See GO HENCE WITHOUT DAY.

GPARM. See *graduated-payment adjustable-rate mortgage* under MORTGAGE.

GPO. *abbr.* GOVERNMENT PRINTING OFFICE.

grab law. (1884) The various means of debt collection involving remedies outside the scope of federal bankruptcy law, such as attachment and garnishment; aggressive collection practices.

grace period. (1945) **1.** A period of extra time allowed for taking some required action (such as making payment) without incurring the usual penalty for being late. • Insurance policies typically provide for a grace period of 30 days beyond the premium's due date, during which the premium may be paid without the policy being canceled. And Article 9 of the UCC provides for a 10-day grace period, after the collateral is received, during which a purchase-money security interest must be perfected to have priority over any conflicting security interests. — Also termed *days of grace*; *grace days*. **2.** *Patents.* The one-year interval allowed by the U.S. Patent Act between the time an invention is used in public, sold, offered for sale, or disclosed in a publication and the time the inventor applies for a patent. • Most countries follow the doctrine of absolute priority and do not allow a grace period. — Sometimes shortened to *grace*. Cf. STATUTORY BAR; *absolute novelty* under NOVELTY.

grade, *n.* *Criminal law.* An incremental step in the scale of punishments for offenses, based on a particular offense's seriousness <several grades of murder>. See DEGREE (2).

graded offense. See OFFENSE (1).

grading. The fixing of a criminal offense at a level of seriousness, such as first degree, second degree, or third degree (in reference to a felony), or Class A, Class B, or Class C (in reference to a misdemeanor). See DEGREE OF CRIME.

gradual method. An intestate-inheritance scheme that gives priority to relatives who are nearest in degree of consanguinity. • This method dates back to the English Statute of Distributions (1670). Cf. PARENTELIC METHOD; UNIVERSAL INHERITANCE RULE.

graduated lease. See LEASE.

graduated mortgage. See *graduated-payment mortgage* under MORTGAGE.

graduated-payment adjustable-rate mortgage. See MORTGAGE.

graduated-payment mortgage. See MORTGAGE.

graduated tax. See TAX.

graffer (graf-ər). (15c) *Hist.* A notary or scrivener. — Also termed *graffarius.*

graft, *n.* (14c) **1.** The act of using a position of trust to gain money or property dishonestly; esp., a public official's fraudulent acquisition of public funds. **2.** Money or property gained illegally or unfairly.

***Graham* factors.** (1966) *Patents.* A three-part test for determining obviousness under § 103 of the Patent Act of 1952, looking at (1) the scope and content of the prior art, (2) the differences between the prior art and the patent claims, and (3) the level of ordinary skill in the pertinent art. *Graham v. John Deere Co. of Kansas City*, 383 U.S. 1, 86 S.Ct. 684 (1966). See NONOBVIOUSNESS.

Grain Inspection, Packers, and Stockyards Administration. An agency in the U.S. Department of Agriculture responsible for helping to market meat, cereals, and related agricultural products, and for promoting fair trade practices. — Abbr. GIPSA.

grain rent. See *crop rent* under RENT (1).

grammatical interpretation. See INTERPRETATION.

grand, *adj.* (17c) Of or relating to a crime involving the theft of money or property valued more than a statutorily established amount, and therefore considered more serious than those involving a lesser amount <grand theft>. See *grand larceny* under LARCENY. Cf. PETTY.

grand assize. See ASSIZE (5).

grand bill of sale. See BILL (7).

grand distress. See DISTRESS.

grandfather, *vb.* (1953) To cover (a person) with the benefits of a grandfather clause <the statute sets the drinking age at 21 but grandfathers those who are 18 or older on the statute's effective date>.

grandfather clause. (1900) **1.** *Hist.* A clause in the constitutions of some Southern states exempting from suffrage restrictions the descendants of men who could vote before the Civil War. • The U.S. Supreme Court held that a clause of this kind in the Oklahoma Constitution violated the 15th Amendment. *Guinn v. United States*, 238 U.S. 347, 35 S.Ct. 926 (1915). **2.** A provision that creates an exemption from the law's effect for something that existed before the law's effective date; specif., a statutory or regulatory clause that exempts a class of persons or transactions because of circumstances existing before the new rule or regulation takes effect. **3.** In a government contract, a provision that immunizes the contractor against any changes in federal law that would otherwise adversely affect the contract. • For example, the government may promise to cover any increased costs that arise from a change in the law, even though the contractor would bear them for any other reason. **4.** In a construction contract, a general and inclusive provision that makes a party responsible for dealing with risks, whether expected or unexpected.

grand inquest. See INQUEST.

grand juror. See JUROR.

grand jury. (15c) A body of (usu. 16 to 23) people who are chosen to sit permanently for at least a month — and sometimes a year — and who, in ex parte proceedings, decide whether to issue indictments. *See* Fed. R. Crim. P. 6. • If the grand jury decides that evidence is strong enough to hold a suspect for trial, it returns a bill of indictment (a *true bill*) charging the suspect with a specific crime. — Also termed *accusing jury*; *presenting jury*; *jury of indictment*. Cf. *petit jury* under JURY.

additional grand jury. See *special grand jury*.

investigative grand jury. (1960) A grand jury whose primary function is to examine possible crimes and develop evidence not currently available to the prosecution. — Also termed *investigatory grand jury*.

runaway grand jury. (1959) A grand jury that acts essentially in opposition to the prosecution, as by calling its own witnesses, perversely failing to return an indictment that the prosecution has requested, or returning an indictment that the prosecution did not request.

screening grand jury. (1990) A grand jury whose primary function is to decide whether to issue an indictment.

special grand jury. (1854) A grand jury specially summoned, usu. when the regular grand jury either has already been discharged or has not been drawn; a grand jury with limited authority. — Also termed *additional grand jury*; *extraordinary grand jury*.

Grand Jury Clause. (1949) The clause of the Fifth Amendment to the U.S. Constitution requiring an indictment by a grand jury before a person can be tried for serious offenses.

grand-jury witness. See WITNESS.

grand larceny. See LARCENY.

grand list. See ASSESSMENT ROLL.

grandparent application. See PATENT APPLICATION.

grandparent rights. A grandfather's or grandmother's rights in seeking visitation with a grandchild. • By statute in most states, in certain circumstances a grandparent may seek court-ordered visitation with a grandchild. Typically these circumstances include the death of the grandparents' child (the child's parent) and the divorce of the child's parents. But the United States Supreme Court has held that the primary, constitutionally protected right of decision-making regarding association with a child lies with the child's parents. As a general rule, if the parent is a fit and proper guardian and objects to visitation, the parent's will prevails. *Troxel v. Granville*, 530 U.S. 57, 120 S.Ct. 2054 (2000).

grandparent visitation. See VISITATION.

grand serjeanty. See SERJEANTY.

Grand Survey. See *grand inquest* (2) under INQUEST.

grange (graynj). (14c) **1.** *Hist.* A farm furnished with all the necessities for husbandry, such as a barn, granary, and stables; esp., an outlying farm that belonged to a religious establishment or a feudal lord. **2.** (*cap.*) A social, educational, and political organization, formally called the National Grange of the Patrons of Husbandry, that informs its members about agriculture-related legislation and proposals, and represents farm interests in lobbying government. • The Grange was formed in 1867 and soon became the foundation of the Granger Movement, a 19th-century political force that protested economic abuses that increased farmers' costs while forcing down prices for agricultural products. Movement followers (called Grangers) controlled several Midwest state legislatures and passed Granger laws that set maximum rates for railroads, warehouses, and grain elevators. Railroads and other interested parties challenged the constitutionality of these laws in what have become known as the Granger Cases.

Granger Cases (**grayn**-jər). Six U.S. Supreme Court decisions holding that the police power of the states enabled them, through legislation, to regulate fees charged by common carriers, warehouses, and grain elevators. • The cases, decided in 1876, arose out of grangers' (i.e., farmers') frustration with the inflated prices they were paying to store and transport their agricultural products. When several state legislatures passed laws regulating those prices, the affected businesses sued to have the laws overturned on grounds that they violated the Commerce Clause and the Due Process Clause of the 14th Amendment. The Court rejected these claims, holding that the activities involved affected the public interest and were therefore subject to the government's regulatory authority. See GRANGE (2).

Granger Movement. See GRANGE (2).

grant, *n.* (13c) **1.** An agreement that creates a right or interest in favor of a person or that effects a transfer of a right or interest from one person to another. • Examples include leases, easements, charges, patents, franchises, powers, and licenses. **2.** The formal transfer of real property. **3.** The document by which a transfer is effected; esp., DEED. **4.** The property or property right so transferred.

community grant. A grant of real property made by a government (or sometimes by an individual) for communal use, to be held in common with no right to sell. • A community grant may set out specific, communal uses for the property, such as for grazing animals or maintaining a playground. Cf. *private grant.*

escheat grant. A government's grant of escheated land to a new owner. — Also termed *escheat patent.*

imperfect grant. **1.** A grant that requires the grantor to do something before the title passes to another. Cf. *perfect grant.* **2.** A grant that does not convey all rights and complete title against both private persons and government, so that the granting person or political authority may later disavow the grant. See *Paschal v. Perex,* 7 Tex. 368 (1851).

inclusive grant. A deed or grant that describes the boundaries of the land conveyed and excepts certain parcels within those boundaries from the conveyance, usu. because those parcels of land are owned or claimed by others. — Also termed *inclusive deed.*

office grant. A grant made by a legal officer because the owner is either unwilling or unable to execute a deed to pass title, as in the case of a tax deed. See *tax deed* under DEED.

perfect grant. A grant for which the grantor has done everything required to pass a complete title, and the grantee has done everything required to receive and enjoy the property in fee. Cf. *imperfect grant* (1).

private grant. A grant of real property made to an individual for his or her private use, including the right to sell it. • Private grants made by a government are often found in the chains of title for land outside the original 13 states, esp. in former Spanish and Mexican possessions. Cf. *community grant.*

5. SUBSIDY (1).

grant, *vb.* (13c) **1.** To give or confer (something), with or without compensation <the parents granted the car to their daughter on her 16th birthday>. **2.** To formally transfer (real property) by deed or other writing <the Lewisons granted the townhouse to the Bufords>. **3.** To permit or agree to <the press secretary granted the reporter access to the Oval Office>. **4.** To approve, warrant, or order (a request, motion, etc.) <the court granted the continuance>. **5.** *Int'l law.* See SUBSIDY (3).

grantback, *n.* (1956) A license-agreement provision requiring the licensee to assign or license back to the licensor any improvements that the licensee might make to a patent or other proprietary right.

grant deed. See DEED.

grantee. (15c) One to whom property is conveyed.

grantee–grantor index. See INDEX (1).

grant-in-aid. (19c) **1.** A sum of money given by a governmental agency to a person or institution for a specific purpose; esp., federal funding for a state public program. **2.** *Hist.* AID (1).

granting clause. (18c) The words that transfer an interest in a deed or other instrument, esp. an oil-and-gas lease. • In an oil-and-gas lease, the granting clause typically specifies the rights transferred, the uses permitted, and the substances covered by the lease.

grant of rights. *Copyright.* A copyright owner's prepublication assignment to the publisher of all rights in exchange for a payment or an advance on royalties.

grantor. (17c) **1.** One who conveys property to another. **2.** SETTLOR (1).

grantor–grantee index. See INDEX (1).

grantor-retained annuity trust. See TRUST.

grantor-retained income trust. See TRUST.

grantor-retained unitrust. See TRUST.

grantor's lien. See *vendor's lien* under LIEN.

grantor trust. See TRUST.

grant to uses. *Hist.* A conveyance of legal title to real property to one person for the benefit of another. • If, for example, A conveyed land to B and his heirs to the use of C and his heirs, B — the feoffee to uses — acquired seisin in and had possession of the land and was considered the legal owner. C — the cestui que use — was considered the equitable owner of the land and was entitled to the land's rents, profits, and benefits. Because the cestui que use did not have seisin in the land, he was not subject to feudal payments. From the 13th century forward, the grant to uses was an increasingly popular mode of conveyance. See CESTUI QUE USE; STATUTE OF USES; USE (4).

GRAT. *abbr.* GRANTOR-RETAINED ANNUITY TRUST.

gratification. (16c) *Archaic.* A voluntarily given reward or recompense for a service or benefit; a gratuity.

gratis (**grat**-is *or* **gray**-tis), *adj.* Free; without compensation.

gratis dictum. See DICTUM.

gratuitous (grə-t[y]oo-ə-təs), *adj.* (17c) **1.** Done or performed without obligation to do so; given without consideration in circumstances that do not otherwise impose a duty <gratuitous promise>. Cf. ONEROUS (3). **2.** Done unnecessarily <gratuitous obscenities>. — **gratuity,** *n.*

gratuitous allowance. See ALLOWANCE (1).

gratuitous assignee. See ASSIGNEE.

gratuitous assignment. See ASSIGNMENT (2).

gratuitous bailment. See BAILMENT.

gratuitous consideration. See CONSIDERATION (1).

gratuitous contract. See CONTRACT.

gratuitous deed. See *deed of gift* under DEED.

gratuitous deposit. 1. See *gratuitous bailment* under BAILMENT. **2.** See DEPOSIT (5).

gratuitous gift. See GIFT.

gratuitous promise. See PROMISE.

gratuitous surety. See SURETY.

gratuitous trust. See *donative trust* under TRUST.

gratuity. See BOUNTY.

gravamen (grə-**vay**-mən). (17c) The substantial point or essence of a claim, grievance, or complaint.

graveyard insurance. See *wager policy* under INSURANCE POLICY.

gravity. (16c) Seriousness of harm, an offense, etc., as judged from an objective, legal standpoint.

graymail. (1978) A criminal defendant's threat to reveal classified information during the trial in the hope of forcing the government to drop the criminal charge. Cf. BLACKMAIL (1); GREENMAIL (1), (2); FEEMAIL.

gray market. See MARKET.

gray-market adoption. See *private adoption* under ADOPTION.

gray-market goods. See PARALLEL IMPORTS.

gray mule case. See WHITEHORSE CASE.

Greaser Law. *Hist. Slang.* An anti-vagrancy statute that gave law-enforcement authorities broad discretion to arrest, fine, and jail people of Hispanic appearance who had no visible means of support. • This statute was enacted in California in 1855 and repealed in the mid-20th century. The term *greaser* is racially derogatory. — Also termed *Greaser Act.*

great bodily injury. See *serious bodily injury* under INJURY.

great care. See CARE.

great diligence. See DILIGENCE.

great fee. See FEE (2).

Great Inquest. See *grand inquest* (2) under INQUEST.

Great Lakes rule. *Maritime law.* The statutory provision that an admiralty litigant is entitled to a jury trial in a contract or tort action if the lawsuit arises from the operation of a commercial vessel on the Great Lakes or the navigable waters connecting them. See 28 USCA § 1873.

Great Law, The. *Hist.* The first code of laws enacted in Pennsylvania. • The Great Law was passed in 1682 by an assembly that had been called by William Penn.

great pond. A body of water larger than ten acres, and thus subject to public ownership. • This term applies in Maine, New Hampshire, and Massachusetts. — Also termed *public pond.*

great seal. See SEAL.

Great Survey. See *grand inquest* (2) under IN-QUEST.

great tithe. See TITHE.

Great Waters Program. A scheme created by Congress in 1990 to make the Environmental Protection Agency more directly responsible for protecting large bodies of fresh water and coastal waters from environmental harm caused by air pollution. Clean Air Act Amendments of 1990, 42 USCA § 7412(m).

Great Writ. See HABEAS CORPUS.

greenback, *n.* (ca. 1862) *Slang.* A legal-tender note of the United States; any note issued by a federal reserve bank. ● The term was coined in 1862 when the backs of American paper currency were first printed in green ink.

green card. (1969) A registration card evidencing a resident alien's status as a permanent U.S. resident.

green-card marriage. See MARRIAGE (1).

Green Cloth. See BOARD OF GREEN CLOTH.

greenfield site. (ca. 1962) **1.** Land that has never been developed. ● Such land is presumably uncontaminated. Cf. BROWNFIELD SITE. **2.** Property acquired as an investment, esp. for establishing a new business.

green goods. *Slang.* Counterfeit money.

greenmail. (1983) **1.** The act or practice of buying enough stock in a company to threaten a hostile takeover and then selling the stock back to the corporation at an inflated price. **2.** The money paid for stock in the corporation's buyback. Cf. BLACKMAIL (1); FEEMAIL; GRAYMAIL. **3.** A shareholder's act of filing or threatening to file a derivative action and then seeking a disproportionate settlement.

Green Paper on Copyright and the Challenge of Technology. *Copyright.* A 1988 European Commission publication that laid out a plan to harmonize the copyright laws of member nations, esp. laws relating to information technology. ● The Green Paper was followed by a series of directives that mandated uniform policies regarding copyright and new technologies. — Usu. shortened to *Green Paper.*

Green River ordinance. A local licensing law that protects residents from unwanted peddlers and salespersons, typically by prohibiting door-to-door solicitations without prior consent. ● The ordinance takes its name from Green River, Wyoming, which enacted the first such law in the early 20th century before others came into vogue during the 1930s and 1940s throughout the United States.

Gregorian calendar. See NEW STYLE.

Gregorian Code. See CODEX GREGORIANUS.

G reorganization. See REORGANIZATION (2).

Gresham's law. (19c) The principle a debased currency will drive out valuable currency. ● This economic principle is popularly attributed to Sir Thomas Gresham (1519–1579), even though earlier writers such as Oresme and Copernicus discussed it.

Gretna-Green marriage. See MARRIAGE (1).

greve. See REEVE.

grievance, *n.* (14c) **1.** An injury, injustice, or wrong that gives ground for a complaint <a petition for a redress of grievances>. **2.** The complaint itself <the client filed a grievance with the state-bar committee>. **3.** *Labor law.* A complaint that is filed by an employee or the employee's union representative and that usu. concerns working conditions, esp. an alleged violation of a collective-bargaining agreement. See *grievance arbitration* under ARBITRATION; GRIEVANCE PROCEDURE.

grievance arbitration. See ARBITRATION.

grievance procedure. *Labor law.* A process, consisting of several steps, for the resolution of an employee's complaint. ● The first step usu. occurs at the shop level and is handled by a supervisor. If the grievance is not resolved at the first step, the grievance is appealed in successive steps that vary among collective-bargaining agreements. The final step of the procedure is grievance arbitration. See *grievance arbitration* under ARBITRATION; GRIEVANCE (3).

grievant, *n.* (1958) *Labor law.* An employee who files a grievance and submits it to the grievance procedure outlined in a collective-bargaining agreement.

grieve, *vb.* To contest under a grievance procedure <the union urged the employee to grieve the suspension>. — **grievable,** *adj.*

grievous bodily harm. See *serious bodily injury* under INJURY.

grift, *vb.* (1915) *Slang.* To obtain money or other property illicitly by adroit use of a scam, confidence game, or other fraudulent means. — **grifter,** *n.*

GRIT. *abbr.* GRANTOR-RETAINED INCOME TRUST.

GRM. *abbr.* GROSS-RENT MULTIPLIER.

grog-shop. See DRAM SHOP.

groin-grabbing. The act of fondling or touching a person's genitals through the person's clothing, esp. in a crowded space or while walking along a sidewalk in the opposite direction from the person. — Also termed *groin-groping.*

gross, easement in. See *easement in gross* under EASEMENT.

gross adventure. See ADVENTURE.

gross average. See *general average* under AVERAGE.

gross charter. See CHARTER (8).

gross damages. See DAMAGES.

gross earnings. See *gross income* under INCOME.

gross estate. See ESTATE (3).

gross income. See INCOME.

gross-income multiplier. See GROSS-RENT MULTI-PLIER.

gross-income tax. See TAX.

gross interest. See INTEREST (3).

gross lease. See LEASE.

grossly inadequate consideration. See CONSIDER-ATION (1).

gross misdemeanor. See MISDEMEANOR.

gross national product. (1947) The market value of all goods and services produced in a country within a year, used to measure a country's economic development and wealth. — Abbr. GNP.

gross neglect of duty. See DESERTION.

gross negligence. See NEGLIGENCE.

gross premium. See PREMIUM (1).

gross profit. See PROFIT (1).

gross receipts. *Tax.* The total amount of money or other consideration received by a business taxpayer for goods sold or services performed in a taxable year, before deductions. IRC (26 USCA) § 448; 26 C.F.R. § 1.448-1T (f)(2)(iv).

gross-receipts tax. See TAX.

gross-rent multiplier. The ratio between the market value of rent-producing property and its annual gross rental income. ● The gross-rent multiplier is used as a method to estimate a property's market value. — Abbr. GRM. — Also termed *gross-income multiplier*.

gross sales. See SALE.

gross spread. See SPREAD (4).

gross up, *vb.* (1987) *Slang. Tax.* To add back to a decedent's gross estate the gift taxes paid by the decedent or the decedent's estate on gifts made by the decedent or the decedent's spouse during the three-year period preceding the decedent's death. IRC (26 USCA) § 2035.

gross weight. See WEIGHT.

ground, *n.* (*usu. pl.*) (13c) The reason or point that something (as a legal claim or argument) relies on for validity <grounds for divorce> <several grounds for appeal>.

ground, *vb.* (14c) **1.** To provide a basis for (something, such as a legal claim or argument) <the decision was grounded on public policy>. **2.** To base (something, such as a legal principle or judicial decision) on <the court grounded the decision on common law> <strict liability is grounded on public policy>.

groundage (**grown**-dij), *n.* (15c) *Hist. Maritime law.* A tax or toll levied on a vessel lying in port; the tax or toll so paid.

ground landlord. *Hist.* The grantor of an estate on which ground rent is reserved. See *ground rent* under RENT (1).

ground-law. A fundamental law. See FUNDAMENTAL LAW.

ground lease. See LEASE.

groundless, *adj.* (17c) (Of a legal claim or argument) lacking a basis or a rationale <groundless cause of action>. See FRIVOLOUS.

ground of action. 1. CAUSE OF ACTION (1). **2.** CAUSE OF ACTION (2).

ground rent. See RENT (1).

ground-rent lease. See *ground lease* under LEASE.

groundwater. See WATER (1).

ground writ. See WRIT.

group annuity. See ANNUITY.

group art unit. *Patents.* A U.S. Patent and Trademark Office division consisting of patent examiners who specialize in a particular invention's subject matter.

group boycott. See BOYCOTT.

group director. *Patents.* The person responsible for directing the operations of an examining group within the U.S. Patent and Trademark Office.

grouping-of-contacts theory. See CENTER-OF-GRAVITY DOCTRINE.

group insurance. See INSURANCE.

group libel. See LIBEL.

group litigation. (1936) A set of lawsuits on behalf of or against numerous persons recognized as one litigating entity, such as a civil-rights group.

group policy. See *master policy* under INSURANCE POLICY.

growing crops. See CROPS.

growing-equity mortgage. See MORTGAGE.

growth. The gain, increase, or expansion in value of securities or of a business.

growth company. See COMPANY.

growth fund. See MUTUAL FUND.

growth industry. (1954) An industry or business sector whose revenues and earnings are rising at a faster rate than average.

growth management. (1974) *Land-use planning.* The regulation of a community's rate of growth through zoning ordinances, impact fees, and other measures. See ZONING.

growth stock. See STOCK.

grubstake contract. See CONTRACT.

grubstaking contract. See *grubstake contract* under CONTRACT.

grundnorm. See *basic norm* under NORM.

Grundy Tariff. See SMOOT–HAWLEY TARIFF ACT.

GRUT. *abbr.* GRANTOR-RETAINED UNITRUST.

GSA. *abbr.* GENERAL SERVICES ADMINISTRATION.

GST supertrust. See *dynasty trust* under TRUST.

guarantee (gar-ən-**tee**), *n.* (17c) **1.** The assurance that a contract or legal act will be duly carried out. **2.** GUARANTY (1). **3.** Something given or existing as security, such as to fulfill a future engagement or a condition subsequent. **4.** One to whom a guaranty is made. — Also spelled *guaranty.*

guarantee, *vb.* (18c) **1.** To assume a suretyship obligation; to agree to answer for a debt or default. **2.** To promise that a contract or legal act will be duly carried out. **3.** To give security to.

guarantee clause. (1887) **1.** A provision in a contract, deed, or mortgage by which one person promises to pay the obligation of another. **2.** (*cap.*) U.S. Const. art. IV, § 4, under which the federal government ensures for the states both a republican form of government and protection from invasion or internal insurrection. • The U.S. Supreme Court has consistently treated claims under the Guarantee Clause as nonjusticiable political questions. *See Pacific States Tel. & Tel. Co. v. Oregon,* 223 U.S. 118, 82 S.Ct. 224 (1912).

guaranteed annual wage plan. *Labor law.* A wage-payment method in which the employer agrees either to pay employees a predetermined minimum sum each year or to provide a minimum number of hours of employment each year. • A wide variety of guaranteed annual wage plans are used. For example, an employer may agree to pay employees wages for each week in the year, even though work may not be available at certain times of the year. The purpose of such a plan is to provide a stable labor force year-round.

guaranteed bond. See BOND (3).

guaranteed investment contract. See INVESTMENT CONTRACT.

guaranteed-purchase contract. See *guaranteed-sale contract* under CONTRACT.

guaranteed-sale contract. See CONTRACT.

guaranteed stock. See STOCK.

guarantee of title. *Property.* A warranty that the title to a piece of real property is vested in a particular person, given by a title company or abstract company, and based on a title searcher's opinion of the status of the property's title. The guarantee is usu. backed by insurance to cover damages resulting from the title searcher's oversight or negligence in finding recorded legal instruments. Cf. *title insurance* under INSURANCE.

guarantee stock. See STOCK.

guarantee treaty. See TREATY (1).

guarantor. (19c) One who makes a guaranty or gives security for a debt. • While a surety's liability begins with that of the principal, a guarantor's liability does not begin until the principal debtor is in default. Cf. SURETY (1).

guarantor of collectibility. (1881) One who guarantees a debtor's solvency and is under a duty to pay only if the creditor is unable to collect from the principal debtor after exhausting all legal remedies, including demand, suit, judgment, and any supplementary proceedings.

guarantor of payment. (1814) One who guarantees payment of a negotiable instrument when it is due without the holder first seeking payment from another party. • A guarantor of payment is liable only if "payment guaranteed" or equivalent words are added to the guarantor's indorsement.

guarantor trust. See TRUST.

guaranty (gar-ən-tee), *n.* (16c) **1.** A promise to answer for the payment of some debt, or the performance of some duty, in case of the failure of another who is liable in the first instance. • The term is most common in finance and banking contexts. While a warranty relates to things (not persons), is not collateral, and need not be in writing, a guaranty is an undertaking that a person will pay or do some act, is collateral to the duty of the primary obligor, and must be in writing. — Also termed *guaranty contract.*

absolute guaranty. (18c) **1.** An unqualified promise that the principal will pay or perform. **2.** A guarantor's contractual promise to perform some act for the creditor — such as paying money or delivering property — if the principal debtor defaults.

conditional guaranty. (1813) A guaranty that requires the performance of some condition by the creditor before the guarantor will become liable.

contingent guaranty. (1843) A guaranty in which the guarantor will not be liable unless a specified event occurs.

continuing guaranty. (1817) A guaranty that governs a course of dealing for an indefinite time or by a succession of credits. — Also termed *open guaranty.*

cross-stream guaranty. A guaranty made by a company for the obligation of another company when both are owned by the same parent company or individual.

downstream guaranty. **1.** A parent corporation's guaranty of a subsidiary's obligations. **2.** A guaranty made for a company by a guarantor who is also a partner, member, or stockholder of the company.

general guaranty. (17c) **1.** A guaranty addressed to no specific person, so that anyone who acts on it can enforce it. **2.** A guaranty for the principal's default on obligations that the principal undertakes with anyone.

good-guy guaranty. A limited guaranty by a third-person that leased property or collateral will be kept in good condition and returned to the lessor or lender if a default occurs. • Good-guy guaranties are most commonly associated with real-property leases. — Also written *good-guy guarantee.* — Also termed *good-guy clause.*

guaranty of collection. (1843) A guaranty that is conditioned on the creditor's having first exhausted legal remedies against the principal debtor before suing the guarantor. See *guarantor of collectibility* under GUARANTOR.

guaranty of payment. (1811) A guaranty that is not conditioned on the creditor's exhausting legal remedies against the principal debtor before suing the guarantor. See *guarantor of payment* under GUARANTOR.

irrevocable guaranty (i-**rev**-ə-kə-bəl). (1898) A guaranty that cannot be terminated unless the other parties consent.

limited guaranty. (1831) An agreement to answer for a debt arising from a single transaction. — Also termed *noncontinuing guaranty.*

open guaranty. See *continuing guaranty*

revocable guaranty. (1936) A guaranty that the guarantor may terminate without any other party's consent.

special guaranty. (18c) **1.** A guaranty addressed to a particular person or group of persons, who are the only ones who can enforce it. **2.** A guaranty that names a definite person as obligee and that can be accepted only by the person named.

specific guaranty. (18c) A guaranty of a single debt or obligation.

upstream guaranty. A guaranty made by a corporate subsidiary for the parent corporation's obligations.

2. GUARANTEE (1).

guaranty bond. See BOND (2).

guaranty company. See *surety company* under COMPANY.

guaranty contract. See GUARANTY (1).

guaranty fund. See FUND (1).

guaranty insurance. See INSURANCE.

guaranty letter of credit. See *standby letter of credit* under LETTER OF CREDIT.

guaranty stock. See STOCK.

guaranty treaty. See *guarantee treaty* under TREATY (1).

guard. See DOORKEEPER.

guardhouse lawyer. See JAILHOUSE LAWYER.

guardian, *n.* (15c) **1.** One who has the legal authority and duty to care for another's person or property, esp. because of the other's infancy, incapacity, or disability. • A guardian may be appointed either for all purposes or for a specific purpose. — Abbr. gdn. — Also termed *custodian.* See CONSERVATOR. Cf. WARD (1).

chancery guardian (**chan**-sər-ee). A guardian appointed by a court of chancery to manage both the person and the estate of the ward.

domestic guardian. A guardian appointed in the state in which the ward is domiciled.

foreign guardian. A guardian appointed by a court in a state other than the one in which the ward is domiciled. • A foreign guardian cares for the ward's property that is located in the state of appointment.

general guardian. A guardian who has general care and control of the ward's person and estate.

guardian ad litem (ad **li**-tem *or* -təm). (18c) A guardian, usu. a lawyer, appointed by the court to appear in a lawsuit on behalf of an incompetent or minor party. — Abbr. GAL. — Also termed *special advocate; special guardian; law guardian.* Cf. NEXT FRIEND; *attorney ad litem* under ATTORNEY.

guardian by custom. *Hist.* A person who, under local custom, had the right to act as a minor's guardian.

guardian by election. A guardian chosen by a ward who would otherwise be without one.

guardian by estoppel. See *quasi-guardian.*

guardian by nature. *Hist.* The parental guardian of an heir apparent who has not yet reached the age of 21. • Although the common law recognized the father as a guardian by nature and the mother as one only after the father's death, most states have given both parents equal rights of guardianship over their children (see, e.g., N.Y. Dom. Rel. Law § 81). — Also termed *natural guardian.*

guardian by nurture. *Hist.* The parental guardian of a child who is not the heir apparent, lasting until the child reaches the age of 14. — Also termed *guardian for nurture.*

guardian by statute. See *statutory guardian.*

guardian de son tort (də sawn [*or* son] **tor**[t]). See *quasi-guardian.*

guardian for nurture. See *guardian by nurture.*

guardian in chivalry. *Hist.* A guardian who, by virtue of knight's service, had custody of the body and lands of a male heir under 21 or a female heir under 14. • This type of guardian had no accountability for profits.

guardian in socage. *New York law.* A guardian for a child who has acquired lands by descent. • A guardian is usu. a relative who could not possibly inherit from the child. This type of guardianship applies to both the person and the property of the child and, historically, lasted only until the child was 14, when the child was allowed to select a guardian; now it lasts until the child reaches age 18 or is emancipated.

guardian of property. See *guardian of the estate.*

guardian of the estate. A guardian responsible for taking care of the property of someone who is incapable of caring for his or her own property because of infancy, incapacity, or disability. — Also termed *guardian of property.*

guardian of the person. A guardian responsible for taking care of someone who is incapable of caring for himself or herself because of infancy, incapacity, or disability.

law guardian. See *guardian ad litem.*

natural guardian. 1. *Hist.* The eldest son's father, until the son turned 21. **2.** In the absence of statute, the father of a legitimate child until the child reaches the age of 21. • A father of illegitimate children may be appointed as their guardian upon the mother's death. **3.** Most commonly and by statute, either the father or the mother of a minor child — each bearing the title simultaneously. • If one parent dies, the other is the natural guardian. See *guardian by nature.*

partial guardian. A guardian whose rights, duties, and powers are strictly limited to those specified in a court order.

quasi-guardian. A guardian who assumes that role without any authority. • Such a person may be made to account as guardian. — Also termed *guardian by estoppel; guardian de son tort.*

special guardian. (17c) **1.** A guardian who has special or limited powers over the ward's person or estate. • Examples are guardians who have custody of the estate but not of the person, those who have custody of the person but not of the estate, and guardians ad litem. — Also termed (in civil law) *curator ad hoc.* See CURATOR (2). **2.** See *guardian ad litem.*

standby guardian. A parent-designated guardian appointed to assume responsibility for a child at a future date if the child's parent becomes incapable of caring for the child but who does not divest the parent of custodial rights. • Several states have enacted statutes providing for a standby guardian in the case of a terminally ill single parent. A standby guardian assumes responsibility for a child during the parent's incapacity and upon the parent's death.

statutory guardian. A guardian appointed by a court having special statutory jurisdiction. — Also termed *guardian by statute.*

successor guardian. An alternate guardian named in a parent's will against the possibility that the first nominee cannot or will not serve as guardian.

testamentary guardian. A guardian nominated by a parent's will for the person and property of a child until the child reaches the age of majority.

2. *Hist.* A mesne lord who was entitled to treat an infant heir's lands for all practical purposes as the lord's own, enjoying fully their use and whatever profits they yielded. • At the end of the guardianship, when the heir reached majority, no accounting was owed by the mesne lord.

guardian of the poor. *Hist.* A person in charge of the relief and maintenance of the poor in a parish. • Guardians of the poor administered poor-relief funds raised under the Poor Relief Act of 1601. • The function is now performed by local authorities.

guardian of the spiritualities. *Eccles. law.* A person who exercises the spiritual and ecclesiastical jurisdiction of a diocese during a vacancy in the see or the absence of the bishop.

guardian of the temporalities. *Eccles. law.* The person to whom custody of the secular possessions of a vacant see or abbey is committed by the Crown. • Temporalities (secular possessions) are the land, revenue, and tenements that archbishops and bishops have had annexed to their sees.

guardianship. (15c) **1.** The fiduciary relationship between a guardian and a ward or other incapacitated person, whereby the guardian assumes the power to make decisions about the ward's person or property. • A guardianship is almost always an involuntary procedure imposed by the state on the ward. Cf. CONSERVATORSHIP; INTERDICTION. **2.** The duties and responsibilities of a guardian. — Also termed GUARDAGE.

ancillary guardianship. A subservient and subsidiary guardianship in a state other than that in which guardianship is originally granted.

guardianship of the estate. A guardianship in which the guardian can make decisions only about matters regarding the ward's assets and property.

guardianship of the person. A guardianship in which the guardian is authorized to make all significant decisions affecting the ward's well-being, including the ward's physical custody, education, health, activities, personal relationships, and general welfare.

plenary guardianship. A guardianship in which the guardian can make decisions about both the ward's estate and the ward's person.

standby guardianship. A guardianship in which a parent designates a guardian to assume responsibility for a child at a future date, if the child's parent becomes incapable of caring for the child, but without divesting the parent of custodial rights.

guerrilla warfare. See WARFARE.

guest. (13c) **1.** A person who is entertained or to whom hospitality is extended. **2.** A person who pays for services at an establishment, esp. a hotel or restaurant. **3.** A nonpaying passenger in a motor vehicle.

business guest. (1942) *Torts.* See BUSINESS VISITOR (1).

social guest. *Torts.* A guest who is invited to enter or remain on another person's property primarily for private entertainment as opposed to entertainment open to the general public. See LICENSEE (2).

guest statute. (1914) A law that bars a nonpaying passenger in a noncommercial vehicle from suing the host-driver for damages resulting from the driver's ordinary negligence. • Though once common, guest statutes remain in force in only a few states. — Also termed *automobile-guest statute.* Cf. FAMILY-PURPOSE RULE.

guild. (14c) **1.** A group of persons sharing a common vocation who unite to regulate the affairs of their trade in order to protect and promote their common vocation; specif., a voluntary society or fraternity of persons employed in the same trade or craft, formed for the mutual benefit and protection of its members, who pay a fee (a *geld* or *gild*) for its general expenses. — Also termed (in senses 1 and 2) *trade guild.* **2.** *Hist.* A company or corporation.

guildhall. (14c) *Hist.* **1.** The meeting place of a guild. — Also spelled *gildhall.* **2.** The chief hall of a city, used for holding court and the meetings of the municipal corporation.

guild rent. See RENT (1).

guilt, *n.* (bef. 12c) The fact or state of having committed a wrong, esp. a crime <the state's burden was to prove guilt beyond a reasonable doubt>. Cf. INNOCENCE.

guiltless, *adj.* (14c) **1.** Free from guilt; not having committed a wrong. **2.** Having the quality or appearance of innocence.

guilt phase. (1960) The part of a criminal trial during which the fact-finder determines whether the defendant committed a crime. Cf. PENALTY PHASE.

guilty, *adj.* (bef. 12c) **1.** Having committed a crime; responsible for a crime <guilty of armed robbery>. **2.** Responsible for a civil wrong, such as a tort or breach of contract <guilty of fraudulent misrepresentation>. — **guiltily,** *adv.*

guilty, *n.* **1.** A plea of a criminal defendant who does not contest the charges. **2.** A jury verdict convicting the defendant of the crime charged.

guilty but mentally ill. (1977) A form of verdict in a criminal case whereby the jury rejects the defendant's insanity defense but still recommends psychiatric treatment because the defendant is mentally ill. — Abbr. GBMI; GMI. — Also termed *guilty but insane; guilty of the act, but so insane as not to be responsible.* See INSANITY DEFENSE.

guilty mind. See MENS REA.

guilty plea. See PLEA (1).

guilty verdict. See VERDICT.

gun-control law. (1968) A statute or ordinance that regulates the sale, possession, or use of firearms. • Gun-control laws vary widely among the states, and many cities have gun-control ordinances. Federal law restricts and regulates the illegal sale, possession, and use of firearms. 18 USCA §§ 921–930. See BRADY ACT.

Gun-Free Schools Act. A federal law designed to eliminate weapons in schools. 20 USCA § 7151. • The Gun-Free Schools Act provides that each state receiving federal funds for elementary and secondary schools must require school districts to expel for one year any student found to have brought a weapon to school. The Act does, however, provide for a case-by-case modification of the expulsion requirement.

gun-jumping. *Slang.* The act of unlawfully soliciting the public's purchase of securities before the SEC approves a registration statement; the making of offers after the filing of a registration statement, but before its effective date, when such offers violate the Securities Act. — Also termed *conditioning the market.* See REGISTRATION STATEMENT.

gynecocracy (gı-nə-**kok**-rə-see *also* jin-ə *or* jı-nə-). (17c) Government by a woman or by women. — Also spelled *gynaecocracy.*

H

H. *abbr.* **1.** HOUSE OF REPRESENTATIVES. **2.** House report. **3.** See *house bill* under BILL (3). **4.** In the citation of English statutes, a king named Henry. **5.** In the Year Books, the Hilary term. See YEAR BOOKS (3); HILARY SITTINGS. **6.** In tax assessments and other such official reports, a house.

habeas corpora juratorum (**hay**-bee-əs **kor**-pər-ə juur-ə-**tor**-əm). [Law Latin "that you have the bodies of the jurors"] *Hist.* A writ commanding the sheriff to bring in jurors and, if necessary, to take their lands and goods as security to ensure their attendance in court for a trial setting. • This writ issued from the Court of Common Pleas and served the same purpose as a *distringas juratores* in the King's Bench. The writ was abolished in 1852.

habeas corpus (**hay**-bee-əs **kor**-pəs). [Law Latin "that you have the body"] (18c) A writ employed to bring a person before a court, most frequently to ensure that the person's imprisonment or detention is not illegal (*habeas corpus ad subjiciendum*). • In addition to being used to test the legality of an arrest or commitment, the writ may be used to obtain judicial review of (1) the regularity of the extradition process, (2) the right to or amount of bail, or (3) the jurisdiction of a court that has imposed a criminal sentence. — Abbr. H.C. — Sometimes shortened to *habeas*. — Also termed *writ of habeas corpus*; *Great Writ*.

habeas corpus ad deliberandum et recipiendum (**hay**-bee-əs **kor**-pəs ad di-lib-ə-**ran**-dəm et ri-sip-ee-**en**-dəm). [Law Latin "that you have the body to consider and receive"] *Hist.* A writ used to remove a person for trial from one county to the county where the person allegedly committed the offense. Cf. EXTRADITION.

habeas corpus ad faciendum et recipiendum (**hay**-bee-əs **kor**-pəs ad fay-shee-**en**-dəm et ri-sip-ee-**en**-dəm). [Law Latin "that you have the body to do and receive"] *Hist.* A writ used in civil cases to remove the case, and also the body of the defendant, from an inferior court to a superior court. — Also termed *habeas corpus cum causa*. See CERTIORARI.

habeas corpus ad prosequendum (**hay**-bee-əs **kor**-pəs ad prahs-ə-**kwen**-dəm). [Law Latin "that you have the body to prosecute"]. A writ used in criminal cases to bring before a court a prisoner to be tried on charges other than those for which the prisoner is currently being confined.

habeas corpus ad respondendum (**hay**-bee-əs **kor**-pəs ad ree-spon-**den**-dəm). [Law Latin "that you have the body to respond"] *Hist.* A writ used in civil cases to remove a person from one court's custody into that of another court, in which the person may then be sued.

habeas corpus ad satisfaciendum (**hay**-bee-əs **kor**-pəs ad sat-is-fay-shee-**en**-dəm). [Law Latin "that you have the body to make amends"] In England, a writ used to bring a prisoner against whom a judgment has been entered to some superior court so that the plaintiff can proceed to execute that judgment.

habeas corpus ad subjiciendum (**hay**-bee-əs **kor**-pəs ad səb-jis-ee-**en**-dəm). [Law Latin "that you have the body to submit to"] A writ directed to someone detaining another person and commanding that the detainee be brought to court. — Usu. shortened to *habeas corpus.*

habeas corpus ad testificandum (**hay**-bee-əs **kor**-pəs ad tes-ti-fi-**kan**-dəm). [Law Latin "that you have the body to testify"] *Hist.* A writ used in civil and criminal cases to bring a prisoner to court to testify.

habeas corpus cum causa. See *habeas corpus ad faciendum et recipiendum.*

Habeas Corpus Act. 1. One of the four great charters of English liberty (31 Car. 2, 1679), securing to English subjects speedy relief from all unlawful imprisonments. • The other three great charters are Magna Carta, the Petition of Right (3 Car. 1, 1628), and the Bill of Rights (1 Wm. & M. 1689). The Habeas Corpus Act does not apply in Scotland; the corresponding statute is the Criminal Procedure Act of 1701, ch. 6. **2.** A statute deriving ultimately from the English statute and enacted in the United States as a constitutional guarantee of personal liberty.

habendum clause (hə-**ben**-dəm). (1829) **1.** The part of an instrument, such as a deed or will, that defines the extent of the interest being granted and any conditions affecting the grant. • The introductory words to the clause are ordinarily *to have and to hold.* — Also termed *to-have-and-to-hold clause.* **2.** *Oil & gas.* The provision in an oil-and-gas lease defining how long the interest granted to the lessee will extend. • Modern oil-and-gas leases typically provide for a primary term — a fixed number of years during which the lessee has no obligation to develop the premises — and a secondary term (for "so long thereafter as oil and gas produced") once development takes place. Most jurisdictions require production of paying quantities to keep the lease in effect. — Often shortened to *habendum.* — Also termed *term clause.*

habendum et tenendum (hə-**ben**-dəm et tə-**nen**-dəm). [Law Latin] *Hist.* To have and to hold. • This formal phrase appeared in land deeds and defined the estate or interest being transferred. See HABENDUM CLAUSE; TENENDUM; TO HAVE AND TO HOLD.

habitability. (1890) The condition of a building in which inhabitants can live free of serious defects that might harm health and safety <lack of running water adversely affects the apartment's habitability>.

habitability, implied warranty of. See *implied warranty of habitability* under WARRANTY (2).

habitancy (**hab**-ə-tən-see). (18c) **1.** DOMICILE (1). **2.** RESIDENCE.

habitation. (14c) **1.** The act of inhabiting; occupancy. **2.** A dwelling place; a domicile. **3.** *Civil law.* A nontransferable and nonheritable right to dwell in the house of another. La. Civ. Code art. 630. See RESIDENCE; DOMICILE. Cf. USUFRUCT.

habit evidence. See EVIDENCE.

habitual, *adj.* (17c) **1.** Customary; usual <habitual late sleeper>. **2.** Recidivist <habitual offender>.

habitual criminal. See RECIDIVIST.

habitual drunkard. See DRUNKARD.

habitual offender. 1. See RECIDIVIST. **2.** See OFFENDER.

habitual residence. See RESIDENCE.

hack, *vb.* To surreptitiously break into the computer, network, servers, or database of another person or organization. Cf. CRACK. — **hacker,** *n.*

had. Commenced or begun, as used in a statute providing that no legal proceeding may be *had* (usu. followed by the words *or maintained*) <no action for foreclosure may be had or maintained until the debtor has been given at least 30 days' notice>.

hadbote. See BOTE (2).

Hadley v. Baxendale **rule.** (1930) *Contracts.* The principle that consequential damages will be awarded for breach of contract only if it was foreseeable at the time of contracting that this type of damage would result from the breach. *Hadley v. Baxendale,* 9 Exch. 341 (1854). • *Hadley v. Baxendale* is best known for its impact on a nonbreaching party's ability to recover consequential damages, but the case also confirmed the principle that the nonbreaching party may recover damages that arise naturally from the breach. See *foreseeable damages* under DAMAGES.

had-not test. See BUT-FOR TEST.

haereditas. See HEREDITAS.

haeres. See HERES.

Hague Academy of International Law (hayg). A center for advanced studies in international law, both public and private, aimed at facilitating the comprehensive and impartial examination of problems of international legal relations. • It was founded in the Netherlands in 1923 on the initiative of the Carnegie Endowment for International Peace and the Institut de Droit International. — Also termed *Académie de Droit International de La Haye.*

Hague Convention. The short name for any one of the many numerous international conventions that address different legal issues and attempt to standardize procedures between nations.

Hague Convention on Protection of Children and Cooperation in Respect of Intercountry Adoption. A 1993 international agreement to establish uniform procedures governing intercountry adoptions. • The Convention has not been widely adopted. The U.S. has signed but not ratified it.

Hague Convention on the Civil Aspects of International Child Abduction. An international convention (concluded in 1980) that seeks to counteract cross-border child-snatching by noncustodial parents. • This convention created a legal mechanism available to parents seeking the return of, or access to, their children. Its purposes are to secure the prompt return of children who have been wrongfully taken from one country to another and to enforce custody and visitation rights in the contracting countries. The procedure is summary in nature and does not contemplate continuing hearings on the merits of a dispute. More than 80 countries are parties to the Convention, including the United States. 42 USCA §§ 11601–11610.

Hague Convention on the Service Abroad of Judicial and Extrajudicial Documents. An international convention, concluded on November 15, 1965, governing procedures for effecting service of process in a foreign country. • More than 35 countries are parties to the Convention, including the United States.

Hague Convention on the Taking of Evidence Abroad in Civil or Commercial Matters. An international convention, concluded on October 26, 1968, that establishes procedures for obtaining evidence in a foreign country, such as taking a deposition abroad. • More than 27 countries are parties, including the United States.

Hague Rules. *Maritime law.* An international agreement adopted at the International Convention for the Unification of Certain Rules of Law Relating to Bills of Lading in 1924. • Under the Hague Rules, a carrier is not liable for losses.

Hague Tribunal. *Int'l law.* A permanent court of arbitration established by the Hague Peace Conference of 1899 to facilitate immediate recourse to arbitration to settle international differences. • The court was given jurisdiction over all arbitration cases, unless the parties agreed to institute a special tribunal. An international bureau was likewise established to serve as a registry for the court and to issue communications about the court's meetings. The court is "permanent" only in the sense that there is a permanent list of members from whom arbitrators in a given case are selected. Apart from making minor changes in the court, the Second Hague Conference of 1907 provided that, of the two arbitrators appointed by each party, only one should be a national of the appointing state.

haircut. 1. *Securities.* The discount required by the National Association of Securities Dealers on the value of stock that a brokerage firm holds in its own account at the time of filing a monthly report about the firm's net capital condition. **2.** The difference between the amount of a loan and the market value of the collateral securing the loan.

haircut reorganization. See REORGANIZATION (1).

Haitian divorce. See *Mexican divorce* under DIVORCE.

hale, *v.* To compel (a person) to go, esp. to court <hale a party into court>.

half, *n.* (bef. 12c) One of two equal parts into which a thing can be divided; MOIETY.

half blood. See BLOOD.

half brother. See BROTHER.

half nephew. See NEPHEW (1).

half niece. See NIECE.

half orphan. See ORPHAN (2).

half-pilotage. See PILOTAGE.

half plus one. *Parliamentary law.* A common but inexact (and often inaccurate) approximation for a majority. ● For a body with 100 members, a majority is indeed half plus one, or 51. But for a body with an odd number of members, "half plus one" would not be a whole number. So "a simple majority" is a better choice for designating majority rule. — Also termed *50 percent plus one.* See MAJORITY (2).

half-proof. *Civil law.* **1.** Proof established by one witness, or by a private instrument. See UNUS NULLUS RULE. **2.** Prima facie proof that is nonetheless insufficient to support a sentence or decree.

half-seal. *Hist.* A seal used in the Court of Chancery to mark commissions to the Court of Delegates on the appeal of an ecclesiastical or maritime case. ● The use of the seal ended when the Court of Delegates was abolished in 1832. See COURT OF DELEGATES.

half section. See SECTION.

half sister. See SISTER.

half-timer. *Hist.* In England, a child excused from full-time attendance at school under the Factory and Workshop Act of 1908 so that the child could work part-time in a factory or workshop. ● The Factory and Workshop Acts from 1901 to 1911 were repealed by the Factory and Workshop (Cotton Cloth Factories) Act of 1929 and the Factories Act of 1937.

half-tongue. *Hist.* In England, a jury empaneled to try an alien, and composed half of one nationality and half of another. ● The use of this type of jury ended in 1914 with the passage of the Status of Aliens Act.

halfway house. (1970) A transitional housing facility designed to rehabilitate people who have recently left a prison or medical-care facility, or who otherwise need help in adjusting to a normal life. — Also termed *residential community treatment center.*

half-year. See YEAR.

Halifax law. 1. LYNCH LAW; more broadly, an irrevocable punishment carried out after a summary trial. **2.** The summary and unauthorized trial and execution (usu. by decapitation) of a person accused of a crime. ● This term comes from the parish of Halifax, in England, where — according to custom in the forest of Hardwick — this form of private justice was anciently practiced by the free burghers against people accused of stealing. Thieves could be condemned to death by beheading on market day. The last such case is said to have occurred in 1650. — Also termed *gibbet law; Halifax inquest.*

haligemot. See HALLMOTE.

hall. (bef. 12c) **1.** A building or room of considerable size, used for meetings of bodies such as public assemblies, conventions, and courts. **2.** *Parliamentary law.* The room or other space in which a deliberative assembly meets. **3.** *Hist.* A manor house or chief mansion house. ● It was called a *hall* because the magistrate's court was typically held there.

hallage (hawl-ij), *n.* (17c) *Hist.* A fee or toll due for goods or merchandise sold in a hall used as a market; a toll payable to the lord of a fair or market for commodities sold in the common hall.

hallmark. (18c) **1.** An official stamp affixed by goldsmiths and silversmiths on articles made of gold or silver to show genuineness. **2.** A mark of genuineness.

hallmote (hahl-moht), *n.* (bef. 12c) **1.** *Hist.* A court baron; specif., an annual court, presided over by the lord of the manor, to decide civil disputes between feudal tenants. ● The court was usu. held in the manor's great hall. See COURT BARON. **2.** A trade-guild's commercial court, in which guild members were tried for trade-related offenses against the guild. **3.** A convention of citizens in their public hall. — Also termed *folkmote*. **4.** (Erroneously) an ecclesiastical court. • Although this definition appears in many secular legal dictionaries, it is unheard of in canon law. In sense 4, it is often (erroneously) spelled *holymote*. — Also spelled (in senses 1–3) *hallmoot*; *halmote*; *halymote*; *halle-gemot*; *haligemote*.

ham (ham *or* am). (bef. 12c) **1.** A place of dwelling; a village. • This word now usu. appears in compound form at the end of place names, such as *Buckingham*. **2.** A small (esp. enclosed) pasture; a piece of land. — Also spelled *hamm*. Cf. HAMLET.

hamel. See HAMLET.

hameleta. See HAMLET.

hamlet. (bef. 12c) A small village; a part or member of a vill. • A hamlet in a rural community might consist of no more than a store, a church, and a few residences. — Also termed *hamel*; *hameleta*; *hamleta*. See VILL. Cf. HAM.

hamleta. See HAMLET.

hammer, *n. Slang.* A forced sale; a sale at public auction <her jewelry was brought to the hammer>. See *forced sale* under SALE.

Hammurabi, Code of. See CODE OF HAMMURABI.

Hanaper Office. *Hist.* An office formerly belonging to the common-law jurisdiction of the Chancery Court. • The term derives from the storage of writs in a hamper (*in hanaperio*). Crown writs, on the other hand, were stored in the Petty Bag Office. The Hanaper Office was abolished in 1842.

hand, *n.* **1.** A person's handwriting <a holographic will must be in the testator's hand>. **2.** An instrumental part <he had a hand in the crime>. **3.** One who performs some work or labor <Hickory was one of the Gales' hired hands>. **4.** (*usu. pl.*) Possession <the cocaine was now in the hands of the police>. **5.** Assistance <the carpenter lent a hand to the project>. **6.** A measure of length equal to four inches, used in measuring the height of equines, esp. horses <the pony stood ten hands tall>. **7.** *Hist.* An oath <he gave his hand on the matter>. **8.** One of two sides or aspects of an issue or argument <on the one hand we can argue for imprisonment, on the other for leniency>.

hand, *vb.* To give; to deliver <he handed over the documents>.

handbill. (18c) A written or printed notice displayed, handed out, or posted, usu. to inform interested people of an event or of something to be done. • Posting and distribution of handbills is regulated by ordinance or statute in most localities.

hand down, *vb.* (17c) To announce or file (a judgment) in a case. • The term was originally used in connection with an appellate-court opinion

sent to the court below; it was later expanded to include any decision by a court on a case or point under consideration.

handfasting. 1. See *handfast marriage* (3) under MARRIAGE (1). **2.** See *handfast marriage* (4) under MARRIAGE (1).

handfast marriage. See MARRIAGE (1).

Hand formula. (1972) A balancing test for determining whether conduct has created an unreasonable risk of harm, first formulated by Judge Learned Hand in *United States v. Carroll Towing Co.*, 159 F.2d 169 (2d Cir. 1947). • Under this test, an actor is negligent if the burden of taking adequate precautions against the harm is outweighed by the probable gravity of the harm multiplied by the probability that the harm will occur.

handhabend (**hand**-hab-ənd), *adj.* (14c) *Hist.* (Of a thief) caught in possession of a stolen item.

handhabend, *n.* [fr. Old English *aet haebbendre handa* "at or with a having hand"] *Hist.* **1.** The bearing of stolen goods in hand or about the person. Cf. BACKBEREND. **2.** A thief or another person caught carrying stolen goods. **3.** Jurisdiction to try a person caught carrying stolen goods. — Also spelled *hand-habende*.

handicap. See DISABILITY (2).

handicapped child. See CHILD.

hand money. Money paid in hand to bind a bargain; earnest money paid in cash. See EARNEST MONEY.

hand note. See NOTE (1).

handsale. *Hist.* A sale memorialized by shaking hands. • Over time, *handsale* also came to refer to the earnest money given immediately after the handshake. In some northern European countries, shaking hands was necessary to bind a bargain. This custom sometimes persists for oral contracts. The Latin phrase for *handsale* was *venditio per mutuam manuum complexionem* ("a sale by the mutual joining of hands"). — Also spelled *handsel*.

hands-off agreement. (1986) A noncompete contractual provision between an employer and a former employee prohibiting the employee from using information learned during his or her employment to divert or to steal customers from the former employer.

hand up, *vb.* (1930) (Of a grand jury) to deliver (an indictment) to a criminal court.

handwriting. (15c) *Evidence.* **1.** A person's chirography; the cast or form of writing peculiar to a person, including the size, shape, and style of letters, and whatever gives individuality to one's writing. **2.** Something written by hand; a writing specimen. • Nonexpert opinion about the genuineness of handwriting, based on familiarity not acquired for litigation purposes, can authenticate a document. Fed. R. Evid. 901(b)(2).

hang, *vb.* (1848) **1.** (Of a jury) to be unable to reach a verdict <the jury was hung after 12 hours of continuous deliberation>. See *hung jury* under JURY. **2.** To suspend a person above the ground by a rope tied around the person's neck in order to cause the person's death. • The standard past tense of the verb in sense 2 is *hanged*, not *hung* — the latter being the standard past tense in all other uses of the verb. See HANGING.

hanged, drawn, and quartered. *Hist.* An ancient sentence for high treason, consisting of the prisoner's being drawn on a hurdle to the place of execution, hanged by the neck (but not until dead), disemboweled, and beheaded, and the body then divided into four pieces for the king's disposal. • The sentence was abolished in England in 1870. See TREASON.

hanging, *n.* The killing of someone by suspending the person above the ground by a rope around the person's neck. • Death is caused by asphyxiation (by being hoisted from the ground) or by a sudden breaking of the cervical vertebrae (by being dropped from a height). Hanging was a common form of capital punishment in the United States until the 1930s. See HANG.

hanging chad. See CHAD.

hanging in chains. *Hist. English law.* As the punishment in an atrocious case, the suspending of an executed murderer's body by chains near where the crime was committed. • Hanging in chains was abolished in 1834.

hanging judge. See JUDGE.

hangman. *Archaic.* An executioner, esp. one who executes condemned criminals by hanging.

Hansard (**han**-sərd). The official reports of debates in the British Parliament. • The name derives from Luke Hansard (1752–1828), printer of the *Journal of the House of Commons* from 1774 to 1828. The name has varied at different times. In 1892 it became the *Authorised Edition*; in 1909 the title was changed to the *Official Report*; and since 1943 the name *Hansard* has been added to *Official Report*. — Also termed *Hansard Official Report*; *Hansard's Debates*.

hanse (hans), *n.* [German] (14c) *Hist.* **1.** A merchant guild, esp. one engaging in trade abroad. **2.** A fee for entrance to the guild; an impost levied on merchants not belonging to the guild.

Hanseatic (han-see-**at**-ik), *adj.* (17c) *Hist.* **1.** Of or relating to the union of the Hanse Towns, usu. referred to as the *Hanseatic League*. **2.** Of or relating to a hanse or commercial alliance.

Hanse Towns (hans). *Hist.* The collective name of certain German cities — including Lübeck, Hamburg, and Bremen — that allied in the 12th century to protect and further their mutual commercial interests. • This alliance was usu. called the *Hanseatic League*. The League framed and promulgated a code of maritime law known as the *Laws of the Hanse Towns*, or *Jus Hanseaticum Maritimum*. The League's power peaked in the 14th century, then gradually declined until 1669, when the last general assembly was held.

Hanse Towns, laws of the. *Hist.* A uniform maritime code drawn from the laws of the Hanse towns, esp. that of Lübeck, published in German at Lübeck in 1597 and revised and enlarged in 1614.

happiness, right to pursue. (1829) The constitutional right to pursue any lawful business or activity — in any manner not inconsistent with the equal rights of others — that might yield the highest enjoyment, increase one's prosperity, or allow the development of one's faculties. • This is a penumbral rather than explicit right under the U.S. Constitution. *See* the Declaration of Independence ¶ 2 (1776).

happy-slapping. *Slang.* An assault on a randomly chosen victim by a person or group while another person films the assault with the intention of later broadcasting or selling copies of the recording. • Happy-slapping began in the early 2000s as a fad in London, in which a teenage victim was merely slapped or struck with an object such as a rolled-up newspaper while the assault was recorded on a cellphone camera. As the fad spread across England and into Europe, the perpetrators attacked victims of all ages, and the assaults escalated from mere slaps to serious bodily injury, rape, and murder.

harassment (hə-**ras**-mənt *or* **har**-əs-mənt). (18c) Words, conduct, or action (usu. repeated or persistent) that, being directed at a specific person, annoys, alarms, or causes substantial emotional distress in that person and serves no legitimate purpose. • Harassment is actionable in some circumstances, as when a creditor uses threatening or abusive tactics to collect a debt. — **harass** (hə-**ras** *or* **har**-əs), *vb.*

same-sex harassment. See *same-sex sexual harassment* under SEXUAL HARASSMENT.

sexual harassment. See SEXUAL HARASSMENT.

harbinger (**hahr**-bin-jər), *n.* (14c) **1.** *Hist.* In England, a royal officer who went ahead and was responsible for securing lodging for troops or for a traveling royal entourage. **2.** A person or thing that predicts what is to come <a harbinger of bad news>.

harbor, safe. See SAFE HARBOR.

harboring, *n.* (14c) The act of affording lodging, shelter, or refuge to a person, esp. a criminal or illegal alien.

harboring an illegal alien. The act of providing concealment from detection by law-enforcement authorities or shelter, employment, or transportation to help a noncitizen remain in the United States unlawfully, while knowing about or recklessly disregarding the noncitizen's illegal immigration status. • The crime of harboring an illegal alien does not require that the offender be involved in the smuggling of illegal aliens into the country. 8 USCA § 1324.

harbor line. A line marking the boundary of a certain part of public water that is reserved for a harbor; esp., the line beyond which wharves and other structures may not extend.

hard asset. See *real asset* under ASSET.

hard case. (1836) A lawsuit involving equities that tempt a judge to stretch or even disregard a principle of law at issue. • Hence the expression, "Hard cases make bad law."

hard currency. See CURRENCY.

hard dollars. 1. Cash proceeds given to a seller. **2.** The part of an equity investment that is not deductible in the first year. Cf. SOFT DOLLARS.

hard goods. See *durable goods* under GOODS.

hard labor. (18c) Work imposed on prisoners as additional punishment, usu. for misconduct while in prison. • Several states (such as Louisiana, Maine, and New Jersey) impose hard labor as a sentence for a variety of crimes. Hard labor is also imposed in military sentencing. See PENAL SERVITUDE.

hard-look doctrine. (1979) *Administrative law.* The principle that a court should carefully review an administrative-agency decision to ensure that the decision did not result from expediency, pressure, or whim.

hard money. See MONEY.

hard sell. A sales practice characterized by slogans, aggressiveness, intimidation, and urgent decision-making. Cf. SOFT SELL.

hardship. (13c) **1.** Privation; suffering or adversity. **2.** The asperity with which a proposed construction of law would bear on a particular case, sometimes forming a basis (also known as an argument *ab inconvenienti*) against the construction. See HARD CASE. **3.** *Family law.* A condition that makes it onerous or impossible for a child-support obligor to make the required child-support payment. **4.** *Zoning.* A ground for a variance under some zoning statutes if the zoning ordinance as applied to a particular property is unduly oppressive, arbitrary, or confiscatory; esp., a ground for granting a variance, based on the impossibility or prohibitive expense of conforming the property or its use to the zoning regulation. — Also termed *unnecessary hardship.* See VARIANCE (2).

Hare–Ware voting. See *instant-runoff voting* under VOTING.

harm, *n.* (bef. 12c) Injury, loss, damage; material or tangible detriment.

    accidental harm. 1. Harm not caused by a purposeful act. **2.** Harm not caused by a tortious act.

    bodily harm. (16c) Physical pain, illness, or impairment of the body.

    grievous bodily harm. See *serious bodily injury* under INJURY.

    physical harm. (18c) Any physical injury or impairment of land, chattels, or the human body.

    serious bodily harm. See *serious bodily injury* under INJURY.

    social harm. (1933) An adverse effect on any social interest that is protected by the criminal law.

harmful behavior. Conduct that could injure another person, esp. a child.

    cumulatively harmful behavior. *Family law.* Seriously harmful parental (or caregiver) behavior that, if continued for a significant period, will over time cause serious harm to a child.

    immediately harmful behavior. *Family law.* Seriously harmful parental (or caregiver) behavior that could have caused serious injury to a child but that, because of the intervention of an outside force or a fortuitous event, did not result in any injury.

    seriously harmful behavior. *Family law.* Parental (or caregiver) behavior that could cause serious injury to a child in the person's care. • Some examples of seriously harmful behavior are physical battering, physical neglect, sexual abuse, and abandonment.

harmful child labor. See *oppressive child labor* under CHILD LABOR.

harmful error. See *reversible error* under ERROR (2).

harmless error. See ERROR (2).

harmony. (14c) Agreement or accord; conformity <the decision in *Jones* is in harmony with earlier Supreme Court precedent>. — **harmonize,** *vb.*

Harter Act. *Maritime law.* An 1893 federal statute regulating a carrier's liability for the loss or damage of ocean cargo shipped under bills of lading. 46 USCA app. §§ 190–96. • The Act was the primary model for the Carriage of Goods by Sea Act, which has largely superseded it in practice. See CARRIAGE OF GOODS BY SEA ACT.

Hart–Scott–Rodino Antitrust Improvement Act. A federal statute, enacted in 1976, that generally strengthens the Justice Department's antitrust enforcement powers, esp. by requiring firms to give notice to the Federal Trade Commission and the Justice Department of an intent to merge if one of the firms has annual revenues or assets exceeding $100 million, and the acquisition price or value of the acquired firm exceeds $50 million. 15 USCA § 18(a). — Often shortened to *Hart-Scott-Rodino Act* (abbr. HSR Act).

hash, *vb.* To run (a document) through an encryption algorithm, usu. to secure the contents or to derive a number unique to the document. • The product of hashing is either run through the encryption algorithm in reverse to verify that the transmitted message has not been altered or combined with the sender's private-encryption key to produce a digital signature for the document.

hash number. A unique numerical code generated by encryption software for use in creating a digital signature. — Also termed *hashed number.* See DIGITAL SIGNATURE; HASH; KEY ENCRYPTION.

Hatch Act. A federal statute, enacted in 1939, that restricts political-campaign activities by federal employees and limits contributions by individuals to political campaigns. 5 USCA §§ 1501–1508. • Senator Carl Hatch sponsored the Act following disclosures that Works Progress Administration officials were using their positions to campaign for the Democratic Party.

Hatch–Waxman Act. The popular name of the 1984 federal law that provides incentives for the development of generic drugs and allows drug-patent owners to regain the time lost on a patent's term while awaiting approval of the drug from the Food and Drug Administration. — Also termed *Drug Price Competition and Patent Term Restoration Act of 1984.*

hate crime. See CRIME.

hate speech. See SPEECH.

hat money. *Maritime law.* A small gratuity traditionally paid to the master (and sometimes the crew) of a ship for the care of the cargo. — Also termed *pocket money; primage.*

Hatsell's Precedents. *Parliamentary law.* A compilation of points of order decided in the House of Commons, published by the House's clerk, John Hatsell, in two volumes, the first in 1776 and the second in 1781. • Hatsell's compilation was a primary source for the manual that Thomas Jefferson compiled while presiding over the United States Senate.

haulage royalty. See ROYALTY (2).

have and hold. See HABENDUM CLAUSE (1).

have the floor. *Parliamentary law.* To be entitled to speak after being recognized by the chair.

hawker. (16c) An itinerant or traveling salesperson who sells goods in a public street, esp. one who, in a loud voice, cries out the benefits of the items offered for sale; a peddler. • A hawker is usu. required to have a license.

hawking. The act of offering, by outcry, goods for sale from door to door or on a public street.

haybote (**hay**-boht), *n.* [fr. French *haye* "a hedge" + Saxon *bote* "an allowance"] *Hist.* The right or privilege of a tenant for life or years to have material to repair the hedges or fences, or to make farming implements. — Also termed *hedgebote.* See BOTE.

hayward. *Hist.* **1.** An officer of a town or manor responsible for maintaining fences and hedges, esp. to prevent cattle from breaking through to an enclosed pasture. **2.** A cattle herder.

Hazantown agreement (**hay**-zən-town). A type of collective-bargaining agreement used in the garment industry, governing the relationship between a jobber and the contractors that produce the jobber's garments. • The agreement does not govern the relationship between the jobber and its own employees. It governs the relationship between the jobber and the contractors that manufacture the garments that the jobber sells, including covenants that the jobber will use only unionized contractors, will ensure that salaries and bonuses are appropriately paid, and will contribute to employee-benefit funds maintained on behalf of the contractor's employees. This term gets its name from Hazantown, Inc., the jobber involved in *Danielson v. Joint Bd. of Coat, Suit & Allied Garment Workers' Union,* 494 F.2d 1230 (2d Cir. 1974). — Also termed *jobber's agreement.*

hazard, *n.* (14c) **1.** Danger or peril; esp., a contributing factor to a peril. See PERIL.

extraordinary hazard. *Workers' compensation.* An unusual occupational danger that is increased by the acts of employees other than the injured worker. — Also termed *extraordinary danger; extraordinary risk.*

imminent hazard. An immediate danger; esp., in environmental law, a situation in which the continued use of a pesticide will probably result in unreasonable adverse effects on the environment or will involve an unreasonable danger to the survival of an endangered species. 7 USCA § 136(1).

occupational hazard. (1917) A danger or risk that is peculiar to a particular calling or occupation. • Occupational hazards include both accidental injuries and occupational diseases.

2. *Insurance.* The risk or probability of loss or injury, esp. a loss or injury covered by an insurance policy.

moral hazard. A hazard that has its inception in mental attitudes, such as dishonesty, carelessness, and insanity. • The risk that an insured will destroy property or allow it to be destroyed (usu. by burning) in order to collect the insurance proceeds is a moral hazard. Also, an insured's potential interest, if any, in the burning of the property is sometimes called a moral hazard.

physical hazard. A hazard that has its inception in the material world, such as location, structure, occupancy, exposure, and the like.

3. *Hist.* An unlawful dice game in which the chances of winning are complicated by arbitrary rules.

hazarder (**haz**-ər-dər), *n. Hist.* A player in an unlawful game of dice. — Also spelled *hazardor.*

hazardous, *adj.* Risky; dangerous.

hazardous cargo. See CARGO.

hazardous contract. See *aleatory contract* under CONTRACT.

hazardous employment. See EMPLOYMENT.

hazardous negligence. See NEGLIGENCE.

hazardous substance. (1882) **1.** A toxic pollutant; an imminently dangerous chemical or mixture. **2.** See *hazardous waste* under WASTE (2).

hazardous waste. See WASTE (2).

hazard pay. (1956) Special compensation for work done under unpleasant or unsafe conditions.

hazing, *n.* (1850) The practice of physically or emotionally abusing newcomers to an organization as a means of initiation. • In the early 19th century, *hazing* referred to beating. Hazing was a well-established custom in fraternities at Ivy League universities by the mid-19th century. (One college magazine referred to "the absurd and barbarous custom of hazing, which has long prevailed in the college." 1 Harvard Mag. 413 (1860)). The first death from hazing was reported at Yale in 1892 (*N.Y. Daily News*, June 28, 1892). In the late 20th century, many colleges and universities banned hazing and many states passed antihazing statutes establishing criminal penalties. See ANTIHAZING STATUTE.

hazing statute. See ANTIHAZING STATUTE.

H.B. See *house bill* under BILL (3).

H.C. *abbr.* **1.** HOUSE OF COMMONS. **2.** HABEAS CORPUS.

HDC. *abbr.* HOLDER IN DUE COURSE.

he. (bef. 12c) A pronoun of the masculine gender, traditionally used and construed in statutes to include both sexes, as well as corporations. • It may also be read as *they.* Because of the trend toward nonsexist language, fastidious drafters avoid using the generic pronouns *he, him,* and *his* unless the reference is only to a male person.

head-and-master rule. *Hist.* The doctrine that the husband alone is authorized to manage community property. • Some courts have held that the

rule is unconstitutional gender-based discrimination. — Also termed *lord-and-master rule.* Cf. EQUAL-MANAGEMENT RULE.

headborough. See BORSHOLDER.

heading. (17c) A brief title or caption of a section of a statute, contract, or other writing.

headlease. (1909) A primary lease under which a sublease has been granted. — Also spelled *head lease.* — Also termed *primary lease; chief lease.*

headlessor. (1933) A lessor on a lease of property that has been subleased.

head money. (16c) **1.** A tax on people who fit within a designated class; a poll tax. See *capitation tax* and *poll tax* under TAX. **2.** A bounty offered by a government for a prisoner taken at sea during a naval engagement. • This bounty is divided among the officers and crew in the same manner as prize money. See PRIZE MONEY. **3.** A tax or duty on shipowners, imposed by an 1882 federal statute, for every immigrant brought into the United States. — Also termed *head tax.* **4.** *Hist.* A bounty or reward paid to a person who killed a bandit or outlaw and produced the head as evidence. See BOUNTY (1); REWARD.

headnote. (1855) A case summary that appears before the printed judicial opinion in a law report, addresses a point of law, and usu. includes the relevant facts bearing on that point of law. — Also termed *syllabus; synopsis; reporter's syllabus.* Cf. SYLLABUS.

headnote lawyer. See LAWYER.

head of family. A person who supports one or more people related by birth, adoption, or marriage and with whom those persons maintain their permanent domicile. • The phrase *head of family* appears most commonly in homestead law. For a person to have the status of head of family, there must, of necessity, be at least two people in the family. — Also termed *head of a family.* Cf. HEAD OF HOUSEHOLD.

head of household. (1847) **1.** The primary income-provider within a family. **2.** For income-tax purposes, an unmarried or separated person (other than a surviving spouse) who provides a home for dependents for more than one-half of the taxable year. • A head of household is taxed at a lower rate than a single person who is not head of a household. Cf. HEAD OF FAMILY; HOUSEHOLDER.

headright. (1930) In American Indian law, a tribe-member's right to a pro rata portion of income from a tribal trust fund set up under the Allotment Act of 1906. • This type of trust fund is funded largely by mineral royalties arising from land held or once held by the tribemember's tribe.

headright certificate. *Hist.* A certificate issued under authority of a Republic of Texas law of 1839 providing that a person was entitled to a grant of 640 acres if the person (1) had immigrated to the Republic between 1 October 1837 and 1 January 1840, (2) was a head of household, and (3) actually resided within the Republic with his or her family. • The grant was to be held under the certificate for three years and then conveyed by absolute deed to the settler.

head shop. A retail establishment that sells items intended for use with illegal drugs.

head-silver. See *common fine* under FINE (4).

head-start injunction. See INJUNCTION.

headstream. The source of a river.

head tax. 1. See *poll tax* under TAX. **2.** HEAD MONEY (3).

headwater. (18c) **1.** (*usu. pl.*) The part of a river or stream that is closest to its source. **2.** HEAD-STREAM.

health. (bef. 12c) **1.** The state of being sound or whole in body, mind, or soul. **2.** Freedom from pain or sickness.

good health. See GOOD HEALTH.

public health. (17c) **1.** The health of the community at large. **2.** The healthful or sanitary condition of the general body of people or the community en masse; esp., the methods of maintaining the health of the community, as by preventive medicine and organized care for the sick. • Many cities have a "public health department" or other agency responsible for maintaining the public health; federal laws dealing with health are administered by the Department of Health and Human Services.

sound health. See SOUND HEALTH.

healthcare-insurance receivable. An interest in or claim under an insurance policy, being a right to payment of a monetary obligation for healthcare goods or services provided. UCC § 9-104(c).

healthcare lien. See LIEN.

healthcare proxy. See ADVANCE DIRECTIVE (1).

health insurance. See INSURANCE.

health-insurance order. *Family law.* An order requiring a parent either to obtain health insurance for a child or to add a child to an existing health-insurance policy. • Health-insurance orders often include dental insurance.

Health Insurance Portability and Accountability Act. A 1996 federal law that provides additional health-insurance protections to employees by limiting the effect of preexisting conditions on an employee's ability to obtain insurance; permitting an employee to enroll a new dependent acquired by birth, adoption, or marriage; making it easier for people to maintain insurance coverage while changing jobs; and helping businesses employing fewer than 50 workers to obtain group insurance plans. • The Act is codified in various sections of 18 USCA, 26 USCA, 29 USCA, and 42 USCA. — Abbr. HIPAA.

health law. (18c) A statute, ordinance, or code that prescribes sanitary standards and regulations for the purpose of promoting and preserving the community's health.

health-maintenance organization. (1973) A group of participating healthcare providers that furnish medical services to enrolled members of a group health-insurance plan. — Abbr. HMO. Cf. MANAGED-CARE ORGANIZATION; PREFERRED-PROVIDER ORGANIZATION.

health officer. A government official charged with executing and enforcing health laws. • The powers of a health officer (such as the Surgeon General) are regulated by law.

hearing. (13c) **1.** A judicial session, usu. open to the public, held for the purpose of deciding issues of fact or of law, sometimes with witnesses testifying <the court held a hearing on the admissibility of DNA evidence in the murder case>. **2.** *Administrative law.* Any setting in which an affected person presents arguments to a decision-maker <a hearing on zoning variations>. **3.** In legislative practice, any proceeding in which legislators or their designees receive testimony about legislation that might be enacted <the shooting victim spoke at the Senate's hearing on gun control>. See PRELIMINARY HEARING. **4.** *Equity practice.* A trial. **5.** *English law.* ORAL ARGUMENT.

adjudication hearing. (1947) **1.** *Administrative law.* An agency proceeding in which a person's rights and duties are decided after notice and an opportunity to be heard. See *procedural due process* under DUE PROCESS. Cf. *disposition hearing.* **2.** In child-abuse and neglect proceedings, the trial stage at which the court hears the state's allegations and evidence and decides whether the state has the right to intervene on behalf of the child. **3.** In a juvenile-delinquency case, a hearing at which the court hears evidence of the charges and makes a finding of whether the charges are true or not true. — Also termed *adjudicatory hearing*; *adjudicatory proceeding.*

adjudicatory hearing (ə-joo-di-kə-tor-ee). See *adjudication hearing.*

certification hearing. See *transfer hearing.*

conformity hearing. See CONFORMITY HEARING.

contested hearing. A hearing in which at least one of the parties has objections regarding one or more matters before the court.

continued-custody hearing. See *shelter hearing.*

custody hearing. (1935) *Family law.* A judicial examination of the facts relating to child custody, typically in a divorce or separation proceeding. • Child-neglect and dependency matters are also often dealt with in custody hearings. — Also termed *custody proceeding*.

Daubert hearing. See DAUBERT HEARING.

dependency hearing. See *shelter hearing*.

detention hearing. (1959) **1.** *Criminal law.* A hearing to determine whether an accused should be released pending trial. See *pretrial detention* under DETENTION. **2.** *Family law.* A hearing held by a juvenile court to determine whether a juvenile accused of delinquent conduct should be detained, continued in confinement, or released pending an adjudicatory hearing. Cf. *adjudication hearing*; *disposition hearing*. **3.** See *shelter hearing*.

discharge hearing. See DISCHARGE HEARING.

dispositional hearing. See *disposition hearing*.

disposition hearing. (1960) *Family law.* **1.** In child-abuse and neglect proceedings, after an adjudication hearing at which the state proves its allegations, a hearing at which the court hears evidence and enters orders for the child's care, custody, and control. • Typically, the judge determines a plan for services aimed at reunifying or rehabilitating the family. **2.** In a juvenile-delinquency case, after an adjudication hearing at which the state proves its case against the juvenile or after a juvenile's pleading true to the charges against him, a hearing at which the court determines what sanctions, if any, will be imposed on the juvenile. • At a disposition hearing, the court balances the best interests of the child against the need to sanction the child for his or her actions. If the juvenile is adjudicated a delinquent, the probation staff prepares a social history of the youth and his family and recommends a disposition. After reviewing the social history and various recommendations, the court enters a disposition. Among the possible juvenile sanctions are a warning, probation, restitution, counseling, or placement in a juvenile-detention facility. Probation is the most common sanction. — Also termed *dispositional hearing*. Cf. *adjudication hearing*. **3.** See *permanency hearing*.

evidentiary hearing. (1952) **1.** A hearing at which evidence is presented, as opposed to a hearing at which only legal argument is presented. **2.** See ADMINISTRATIVE PROCEEDING.

exclusionary hearing. (1963) A pretrial hearing conducted to review and determine the admissibility of alleged illegally obtained evidence.

fair hearing. (1831) A judicial or administrative hearing conducted in accordance with due process.

Fatico hearing. See FATICO HEARING.

fitness hearing. See *transfer hearing*.

Franks hearing. See FRANKS HEARING.

full adversary hearing. See *adjudication hearing*.

full hearing. (17c) **1.** A hearing at which the parties are allowed notice of each other's claims and are given ample opportunity to present their positions with evidence and argument. **2.** See ADMINISTRATIVE PROCEEDING.

Garcia hearing. See GARCIA HEARING.

hearing de novo (dee *or* di **noh**-voh). (18c) **1.** A reviewing court's decision of a matter anew, giving no deference to a lower court's findings. **2.** A new hearing of a matter, conducted as if the original hearing had not taken place.

independent-source hearing. *Criminal procedure.* A hearing to determine whether evidence was obtained illegally, and if so, whether the evidence is admissible. See INDEPENDENT-SOURCE RULE.

Jackson–Denno hearing. See JACKSON–DENNO HEARING.

Mapp hearing. See MAPP HEARING.

neglect hearing. (1952) *Family law.* A judicial hearing involving alleged child abuse or some other situation in which a child has not been properly cared for by a parent or person legally responsible for the child's care. • At issue is the civil culpability of the parent or responsible party and the possible loss of children into foster care or — in extreme cases — the termination of parental rights.

omnibus hearing. (1969) *Criminal procedure.* A hearing designed to bring judicial oversight to a criminal case at an early stage to make certain that the case is being handled expeditiously and properly. • At an omnibus hearing, the court is primarily interested in ensuring that discovery is being conducted properly, that any necessary evidentiary hearings have been scheduled, and that all issues ripe for decision have been decided.

permanency hearing. (1832) *Family law.* Under the Adoption and Safe Families Act, a judicial proceeding to determine the future, permanent status of a child in foster care. • Under the Act, the term *permanency hearing* replaces the term *disposition hearing*. The permanency hearing must occur within 12 months of a child's being placed in foster care. The purpose of the hearing is to determine the final direction of the case, whether that means going forward with termination proceedings or continuing plans for family reunification. — Also termed *permanency-planning hearing*.

preliminary hearing. See PRELIMINARY HEARING.

preliminary protective hearing. See *shelter hearing.*

presentence hearing. See PRESENTENCE HEARING.

pretrial hearing. See PRETRIAL CONFERENCE.

probable-cause hearing. See *shelter hearing.*

public hearing. (18c) A hearing that, within reasonable limits, is open to anyone who wishes to observe. • Such a hearing is often characterized by the right to appear and present evidence in a case before an impartial tribunal.

reaffirmation hearing. See REAFFIRMATION HEARING.

review hearing. *Family law.* After a finding of child abuse or neglect, a hearing to assess the progress in the case plan. See CASE PLAN.

revocation hearing. (1928) *Criminal procedure.* A hearing held to determine whether a parolee should be returned to prison for violating the terms of parole.

sentencing hearing. See PRESENTENCE HEARING.

shelter hearing. *Family law.* A hearing shortly after the state's removal of a child for suspected abuse or neglect. • The hearing, generally held within 24 to 72 hours after the removal, is for the purpose of determining whether the state has adequate cause to maintain the children in protective care. — Also termed *shelter-care hearing; continued- custody hearing; preliminary protective hearing; probable-cause hearing; detention hearing; dependency hearing.*

suppression hearing. (1955) *Criminal procedure.* A pretrial hearing in which a criminal defendant seeks to prevent the introduction of evidence alleged to have been seized illegally.

termination-of-parental-rights hearing. *Family law.* A trial or court proceeding, usu. initiated by a state agency, that seeks to sever the legal ties between a parent and child, usu. so that the child can be adopted. • The standard of proof in a termination-of-parental-rights hearing is clear and convincing evidence. *Santosky v. Kramer,* 455 U.S. 745, 102 S.Ct. 1388 (1982). — Often shortened to *termination hearing.*

transfer hearing. (1968) *Criminal procedure.* In a juvenile-court case, a hearing to determine whether the case should be transferred to adult criminal court so that the juvenile may be tried as an adult. • Every state, as well as the District of Columbia, has a transfer statute. The United States Supreme Court defined the due-process requirements for transfer hearings in *Kent v. United States,* 383 U.S. 541, 86 S.Ct. 1045 (1966). — Also termed *certification hearing; waiver hearing; fitness hearing.* See TRANSFER STATUTE; MANDATORY WAIVER; STATUTORY EXCLUSION.

trial-type hearing. See ADMINISTRATIVE PROCEEDING.

uncontested hearing. A hearing in which either (1) the parties are in agreement as to all matters before the court, or (2) one of the parties has failed to appear despite notice.

unfair hearing. (1915) A hearing that is not conducted in accordance with due process, as when the defendant is denied the opportunity to prepare or consult with counsel.

Wade hearing. See WADE HEARING.

waiver hearing. See *transfer hearing.*

hearing examiner. See ADMINISTRATIVE-LAW JUDGE.

hearing officer. 1. ADMINISTRATIVE-LAW JUDGE. **2.** See *judicial officer* (3) under OFFICER (1).

hearsay. (16c) **1.** Traditionally, testimony that is given by a witness who relates not what he or she knows personally, but what others have said, and that is therefore dependent on the credibility of someone other than the witness. • Such testimony is generally inadmissible under the rules of evidence. **2.** In federal law, a statement (either a verbal assertion or nonverbal assertive conduct), other than one made by the declarant while testifying at the trial or hearing, offered in evidence to prove the truth of the matter asserted. Fed. R. Evid. 801(c). — Also termed *hearsay evidence; secondhand evidence.* Cf. *original evidence* under EVIDENCE.

double hearsay. (1921) A hearsay statement that contains further hearsay statements within it, none of which is admissible unless exceptions to the rule against hearsay can be applied to each level <the double hearsay was the report's statement that Amy had heard Joe admit running the red light>. Fed. R. Evid. 805. — Also termed *multiple hearsay; hearsay within hearsay.*

hearsay exception. Any of several deviations from the hearsay rule, allowing the admission of otherwise inadmissible statements because the circumstances surrounding the statements provide a basis for considering the statements reliable.

tender-years hearsay exception. A hearsay exception for an out-of-court statement by a child ten years of age or younger, usu. describing an act of physical or sexual abuse, when the child is unavailable to testify and the court determines that the time, content, and circumstances of the statement make it reliable.

hearsay rule. (1896) The rule that no assertion offered as testimony can be received unless it is or has been open to test by cross-examination or an opportunity for cross-examination, except as provided otherwise by the rules of evidence, by court rules, or by statute. • The chief reasons for the rule are that out-of-court statements amounting to hearsay are not made under oath and are not subject to cross-examination. Fed. R. Evid. 802. Rule 803 provides 23 explicit exceptions to the hearsay rule, regardless of whether the out-of-court declarant is available to testify, and Rule 804 provides five more exceptions for situations in which the declarant is unavailable to testify.

hearsay within hearsay. See *double hearsay* under HEARSAY.

heartbalm statute. A state law that abolishes the rights of action for monetary damages as solace for the emotional trauma occasioned by a loss of love and relationship. • The abolished rights of action include alienation of affections, breach of promise to marry, criminal conversation, and seduction of a person over the legal age of consent. Many states today have enacted heartbalm statutes primarily because of the highly speculative nature of the injury and the potential for abusive prosecution, as well as the difficulties of determining the cause of a loss. The terminology in this field is somewhat confusing, since a *heartbalm statute* abolishes lawsuits that were known as *heartbalm suits*; some scholars therefore call the abolitionary statutes *anti-heartbalm statutes*. But the prevailing term is *heartbalm statute*. — Also written *heart-balm statute*. — Also termed *heartbalm act; anti-heartbalm statute; anti-heartbalm act.*

heat of passion. (bef. 12c) Rage, terror, or furious hatred suddenly aroused by some immediate provocation, usu. another person's words or actions. • At common law, the heat of passion could serve as a mitigating circumstance that would reduce a murder charge to manslaughter. — Also termed *sudden heat of passion; sudden heat; sudden passion; hot blood; sudden heat and passion; furor brevis.* Cf. COLD BLOOD; COOL BLOOD.

heavy work. See WORK (1).

hedge, *vb.* (17c) To use two compensating or offsetting transactions to ensure a position of breaking even; esp., to make advance arrangements to safeguard oneself from loss on an investment, speculation, or bet, as when a buyer of commodities insures against unfavorable price changes by buying in advance at a fixed rate for later delivery. — **hedging,** *n.*

hedgebote. See HAYBOTE.

hedge fund. (1967) A specialized investment group — usu. organized as a limited partnership or offshore investment company — that offers the possibility of high returns through risky techniques such as selling short or buying derivatives. • Most hedge funds are not registered with the SEC and are therefore restricted in marketing their services to the public.

hedonic damages. See DAMAGES.

hedonistic damages. See *hedonic damages* under DAMAGES.

hedonistic utilitarianism. See UTILITARIANISM.

heeding presumption. See PRESUMPTION.

heedlessness, *n.* (16c) The quality of being thoughtless and inconsiderate; esp., conduct involving the disregard of others' rights or safety. • Heedlessness is often construed to involve the same degree of fault as recklessness. See RECKLESSNESS. — **heedless,** *adj.*

hegemonism (hi-**jem**-ə-niz-əm). (19c) **1.** A philosophical position advocating hegemony. **2.** All forms of political extension by means of hegemony.

hegemony (hi-**jem**-ə-nee), *n.* (16c) **1.** Influence, authority, or supremacy over others <the hegemony of capitalism>. **2.** The striving for leadership or predominant authority of one state of a confederacy or union over the others; political domination <the former Soviet Union's hegemony over Eastern Europe>. — **hegemonic** (hej-ə-**mon**-ik), *adj.*

heightened scrutiny. See INTERMEDIATE SCRUTINY.

heinous (**hay**-nəs), *adj.* (14c) (Of a crime or its perpetrator) shockingly atrocious or odious. — **heinousness,** *n.*

heir (air). (13c) **1.** A person who, under the laws of intestacy, is entitled to receive an intestate decedent's property. — Also termed *legal heir; heir at law; lawful heir; heir general; legitimate heir.* Cf. ANCESTOR.

2. Loosely (in common-law jurisdictions), a person who inherits real or personal property, whether by will or by intestate succession. **3.** Popularly, a person who has inherited or is in line to inherit great wealth. **4.** *Civil law.* A person who succeeds to the rights and occupies the place of, or is entitled to succeed to the estate of, a decedent, whether by an act of the decedent or by operation of law. • The term *heir* under the civil law has a more expansive meaning than under the common law.

afterborn heir. (18c) One born after the death of an intestate from whom the heir is entitled to inherit. See *afterborn child* under CHILD.

apparent heir. See *heir apparent.*

beneficiary heir (ben-ə-**fish**-ee-er-ee). *Civil law.* An heir who accepts an inheritance but whose liability for estate debts is limited to the value of the inheritance. — Also termed *heir beneficiary.* See BENEFIT OF INVENTORY. Cf. *unconditional heir.*

bodily heir. See *heir of the body.*

coheir (koh-**air**). One of two or more persons to whom an inheritance descends.

collateral heir. (17c) One who is neither a direct descendant nor an ancestor of the decedent, but whose kinship is through a collateral line, such as a brother, sister, uncle, aunt, nephew, niece, or cousin. Cf. *lineal heir.*

expectant heir. (17c) An heir who has a reversionary or future interest in property, or a chance of succeeding to it. — Also termed *heir expectant.* See REVERSION (1); REMAINDER (1). Cf. *prospective heir.*

fideicommissary heir (fī-dee-ı **kom**-i-sair-ee). *Roman & civil law.* A beneficiary of property who succeeds the direct (original) heir. See FIDEICOMMISSUM.

fiduciary heir. Roman & civil law. An heir who takes property as a trustee on behalf of a person who is not eligible to receive the property immediately. See FIDEICOMMISSUM.

forced heir. Civil law. (1813) A person whom the testator or donor cannot disinherit because the law reserves part of the estate for that person. • In Louisiana, only descendants are forced heirs. La. Civ. Code art. 1493. See LEGITIME.

heir apparent. (14c) An heir who is certain to inherit unless he or she dies first or is excluded by a valid will. — Also termed *apparent heir.* Cf. *heir presumptive.*

heir beneficiary. See *beneficiary heir.*

heir by adoption. A person who has been adopted by (and thus has become an heir to) the deceased. • By statute in most jurisdictions, an adopted child has the same right of succession to intestate property as a biological child unless the deceased clearly expresses a contrary intention. Jurisdictions differ on whether an adopted child may also inherit from his or her biological parents or family. The clear majority view, however, is that upon adoption, a complete severance of rights and obligations occurs and the child forfeits inheritance from all biological relatives.

heir by custom. Hist. In England, a person whose right of inheritance depends on a particular and local custom, such as gavelkind and borough English. See GAVELKIND; BOROUGH ENGLISH.

heir by devise. (1842) One to whom lands are given by will.

heir conventional. Civil law. One who takes a succession because of a contract or settlement entitling him or her to it.

heir expectant. See *expectant heir.*

heir in tail. See *heir special.*

heir male. Hist. The nearest male blood-relation of a decedent.

heir of the blood. (16c) An heir who succeeds to an estate because of consanguinity with the decedent, in either the ascending or descending line.

heir of the body. Archaic. A lineal descendant of the decedent, excluding a surviving spouse, adopted children, and collateral relations. • The term of art *heirs of the body* was formerly used to create a fee tail <A conveys Blackacre to B and the heirs of his body>. — Also termed *bodily heir.*

heir presumptive. (17c) An heir who will inherit if the potential intestate dies immediately, but who may be excluded if another, more closely related heir is born. — Also termed *presumptive heir.* Cf. *heir apparent.*

heirs and assigns. (16c) A term of art formerly required to create a fee simple <A conveys Blackacre to B and his heirs and assigns>.

heir special. Hist. An heir who receives property according to the nature of the estate held in fee tail. • Heirs special were said to receive property *per formam doni* ("by the form of the gift"). — Also termed *heir in tail.*

instituted heir. See *testamentary heir.*

irregular heir. Hist. Louisiana law. A person or entity who has a statutory right to take property from an estate in default of the testamentary or legal heirs.

joint heir. (16c) **1.** A coheir. **2.** A person who is or will be an heir to both of two designated persons at the death of the survivor of them, the word *joint* being here applied to the ancestors rather than the heirs.

known heir. (16c) An heir who is present to claim an inheritance, the extent of which depends on there being no closer relative.

laughing heir. (1943) *Slang.* An heir distant enough to feel no grief when a relative dies and leaves an inheritance (generally viewed as a windfall) to the heir.

lineal heir. (16c) A person who is either an ancestor or a descendant of the decedent, such as a parent or a child. Cf. *collateral heir.*

natural heir. (16c) An heir by consanguinity as distinguished from an heir by adoption or a statutory heir (such as a person's spouse).

presumptive heir. See *heir presumptive.*

pretermitted heir (pree-tər-**mit**-id). (1841) A child or spouse who has been omitted from a will, as when a testator makes a will naming his or her two children and then, sometime later, has two more children who are not mentioned in the will. — Also termed (more specif.) *pretermitted child; pretermitted spouse.* See PRETERMITTED-HEIR STATUTE.

prospective heir. (1855) An heir who may inherit but may be excluded; an heir apparent or an heir presumptive. Cf. *expectant heir.*

right heir. **1.** *Hist.* The preferred heir to an estate tail, as distinguished from a general heir. ● An estate tail would pass to a general heir only on the failure of the preferred heir and his line. **2.** HEIR (1).

testamentary heir (tes-tə-**men**-tə-ree *or* -tree). *Civil law.* A person who is appointed as an heir in the decedent's will. — Also termed *instituted heir.*

unconditional heir. Civil law. A person who chooses — expressly or tacitly — to inherit without any reservation or without making an inventory. Cf. *beneficiary heir.*

heirdom. (13c) The state of being an heir; succession by inheritance.

heiress. (17c) **1.** *Archaic.* A female heir. See HEIR (1). **2.** A woman or girl who has inherited or is in line to inherit great wealth.

heir general. See HEIR (1).

heir-hunter. A person whose business is to track down missing heirs.

heirless estate. See ESTATE (3).

heirloom. (15c) **1.** An item of personal property that by local custom, contrary to the usual legal rule, descends to the heir along with the inheritance, instead of passing to the executor or administrator of the last owner. ● Traditional examples are an ancestor's coat of arms, family portraits, title deeds, and keys. Blackstone gave a false etymology that many have copied: "The termination, *loom*, is of Saxon origin; in which language it signifies a limb or member; so that an heirloom is nothing else, but a limb or member of the inheritance." 2 William Blackstone, *Commentaries on the Law of England* 427 (1766). In fact, *loom* derives from Old English *geloma* "utensil," and *loom* meant "implement, tool." **2.** Popularly, a treasured possession of great sentimental value passed down through generations within a family.

heirship. (13c) **1.** The quality or condition of being an heir. **2.** The relation between an ancestor and an heir.

hell-or-high-water clause. (1980) A clause in a personal-property lease requiring the lessee to continue to make full rent payments to the lessor even if the thing leased is unsuitable, defective, or destroyed.

hell-or-high-water rule. (1960) **1.** The principle that a personal-property lessee must pay the full rent due, regardless of any claim against the lessor, unless the lessee proves unequal bargaining power or unconscionability. **2.** *Insurance.* The principle that an insured's automobile-liability policy will cover the insured while using a vehicle owned by another if the insured uses the vehicle in a manner within the scope of the permission granted.

henceforth, *adv.* (14c) From now on <the newly enacted rule will apply henceforth>.

Hepburn Act. A 1906 federal statute that amended the Interstate Commerce Act to (1) increase the (now defunct) Interstate Commerce Commission's jurisdiction to include pipelines, (2) prohibit free passes except to employees, (3) prohibit common carriers from transporting any products (except timber) in which they had an interest, and (4) require joint tariffs and a uniform system of accounts.

heptarchy (**hep**-tahr-kee). **1.** A government by seven rulers. **2.** A nation divided into seven governments, specif. the seven Anglo-Saxon kingdoms of Kent, Sussex, Essex, Wessex, East Anglia, Mercia, and Northumbria existing before the Norman Conquest.

herald, *n.* (13c) **1.** In England and Scotland, one of several officers responsible for keeping genealogical lists and tables, adjusting armorial bearings, and regulating the ceremonies at royal coronations and funerals. ● There are six in England and three in Scotland. **2.** *Hist.* A messenger who announces royal or state proclamations, and who carries diplomatic messages (esp. proclamations of war, peace, or truce) between kings or countries.

Heralds' College. A royal corporation responsible in England for granting and recording armorial insignia and genealogies, and for dealing with matters of precedence. ● The College was founded by Richard III in 1484, is governed by the Earl Marshal, and consists of three kings of arms, six heralds, and four pursuivants. The heralds' books, based on family-lineage inquiries made throughout England, are considered good evidence of pedigrees. The heralds' office is still allowed to make grants of arms and to grant name changes. — Also termed *College of Arms.*

hereafter, *adv.* (bef. 12c) **1.** From now on; henceforth <because of the highway construction, she will hereafter take the bus to work>. **2.** At some future time <the court will hereafter issue a ruling on the gun's admissibility>. **3.** HEREINAFTER <the exhibits hereafter referred to as Exhibit A and Exhibit B>.

here and there. See VALUE DATE.

hereby, *adv.* (13c) By this document; by these very words <I hereby declare my intention to run for public office>.

heredes. See HERES.

hereditament (her-ə-**dit**-ə-mənt *or* hə-**red**-i-tə-mənt). (15c) **1.** Any property that can be inherited;

anything that passes by intestacy. **2.** Real property; land.

corporeal hereditament (kor-**por**-ee-əl). A tangible item of property, such as land, a building, or a fixture.

incorporeal hereditament (in-kor-**por**-ee-əl). An intangible right in land, such as an easement. • The various types at common law were advowsons, annuities, commons, dignities, franchises, offices, pensions, rents, tithes, and ways.

hereditary, *adj.* (15c) Of or relating to inheritance; that descends from an ancestor to an heir.

hereditary succession. See *intestate succession* under SUCCESSION (2).

hereditas (hə-**red**-i-tas), *n.* [Latin] **1.** *Roman law.* An inheritance by universal succession to a decedent. • This succession applied whether the decedent died testate or intestate, and whether in trust (*ex fideicommisso*) for another or not. The comparable right under Praetorian law was *bonorum possessio,* possession of an inheritance that could be the basis of a right to succeed. **2.** *Hist.* An estate transmissible by descent; an inheritance. — Also spelled *haereditas.*

hereditas damnosa (hə-**red**-i-tas dam-**noh**-sə). A burdensome inheritance; an inheritance whose debts exceed its assets.

hereditas jacens (hə-**red**-i-tas **jay**-senz). [Latin *iaceo* "to lie"] **1.** Property belonging to an estate before an heir accepts it. • This term had a similar meaning at common law. See ABEYANCE (2). **2.** *Hist.* A decedent's estate that has no heir or legatee to take it; an escheated estate. — Also termed *caduca.* See ESCHEAT. **3.** *Hist.* An inheritance without legal owner and thus open to the first occupant.

hereditas legitima (hə-**red**-i-tas lə-**jit**-i-mə). A succession or inheritance devolving by operation of law rather than by will. See INTESTACY.

hereditas luctuosa (hə-**red**-i-tas lək-choo-**oh**-sə). A sad or mournful inheritance; one that disturbs the natural order of mortality (*turbato ordine mortalitatis*), as that of a parent inheriting a child's estate. • This term is more literary than legal. — Also termed *tristis successio.*

hereditas paterna (hə-**red**-i-tas pə-**tər**-nə). [Latin] *Hist.* A succession that descends through the father.

hereditas testamentaria (hə-**red**-i-tas tes-tə-men-**tair**-ee-ə). Testamentary inheritance; succession to an estate under a decedent's will.

heredity. (16c) **1.** *Archaic.* Intestate succession; the taking of an inheritance by common-law succession. **2.** The genetic transmission of characteristics from a parent to a child; the biological law by which characteristics of a living being tend to repeat themselves in the being's descendants.

herein, *adv.* (bef. 12c) In this thing (such as a document, section, or paragraph) <the due-process arguments stated herein should convince the court to reverse the judgment>. • This term is inherently ambiguous.

hereinafter, *adv.* (16c) Later in this document <the buyer agrees to purchase the property described hereinafter>. — Also loosely termed *hereafter.*

herenach (**her**-ə-nak), *n.* [fr. Old Irish *airchinnich* "chief man"] An archdeacon. — Also spelled *erenach.*

hereof, *adv.* (bef. 12c) Of this thing (such as a provision or document) <the conditions hereof are stated in section 3>.

heres (**heer**-eez), *n.* [Latin] *Roman law.* A successor to the rights and liabilities of a deceased person; an heir. • Because the *heres* succeeded to both the rights and the debts of the decedent, the office combined that of a modern executor with that of an heir at law. The institution of the *heres* was the essential characteristic of a testament; if this was not done, the instrument was called a *codicillus.* — Also spelled (in Law Latin) *haeres.* Pl. **heredes** (hə-**ree**-deez) or (for *haeres*) **haeredes.**

heres actu (**heer**-eez **ak**-t[y]oo). [Law Latin] *Hist.* Heir by appointment.

heres astrarius (as-**trair**-ee-əs). [Law Latin "heir of the hearth"] An heir who has received, by conveyance, an ancestor's estate during the ancestor's lifetime.

heres de facto (di **fak**-toh). [Law Latin "heir from fact"] *Hist.* **1.** An heir whose status arises from the disseisin or other wrongful act of the heir's ancestor. See DISSEISIN. **2.** An heir in fact, as distinguished from an heir by law (*de jure*).

heres ex asse (**as**-ee). [Latin "sole heir"] *Roman law.* An heir to the whole estate.

heres ex testamento (eks tes-tə-**men**-to). See *heres factus.*

heres extraneus (ek-**stray**-nee-əs). [Latin "extraneous heir"] *Roman law.* An external heir; one who had not been subject to the testator's power (*potestas*) and hence not bound to accept the inheritance. Pl. **heredes extranei** (hə-**ree**-deez ek-**stray**-nee-ɪ).

heres factus (**fak**-təs). [Latin "made heir"] An heir appointed by will; a testamentary heir. — Also termed *heres ex testamento; heres institutus.* Cf. *heres natus.*

heres fideicommissarius (fɪ-dee-ɪ-kom-ə-**sair**-ee-əs). [Latin] *Roman law.* The person for whose benefit an estate was given by will to a fiduciary heir. • This office corresponds loosely to the *cestui que trust* of the common law. Cf. *heres fiduciarius.*

heres fiduciarius (fi-d[y]oo-shee-**air**-ee-əs). [Latin "fiduciary heir"] *Roman law*. A person made heir by will, in trust for the benefit of another; an heir subject to a trust. Cf. *heres fidei-commissarius*.

heres in mobilibus (**heer**-eez in moh-**bil**-i-bəs). [Law Latin] *Hist*. Heir in movables.

heres institutus (in-sti-t[y]oo-təs). See *heres factus*.

heres legitimus (lə-**jit**-i-məs). [Latin "lawful heir"] *Roman law*. An heir entitled to succeed (on intestacy) by the laws of the Twelve Tables.

heres natus (**nay**-təs). [Latin "heir by birth"] An heir by reason of birth; an heir at law or by intestacy. Cf. *heres factus*.

heres necessarius (nes-ə-**sair**-ee-əs). [Latin "necessary heir"] *Roman law*. A slave freed on the testator's death and thus compelled to accept the inheritance.

heres rectus (**rek**-təs). [Law Latin] *Hist*. A right or proper heir.

heres suus (s[y]**oo**-əs). [Latin "one's own heir"] **1.** A decedent's proper or natural heir; a lineal descendant of the deceased. **2.** *Roman law*. A free person who was subject to the testator's power (*potestas*) but who could exercise full legal rights upon the testator's death.

heres suus et necessarius (s[y]**oo**-əs et nes-ə-**sair**-ee-əs). [Latin "one's own and necessary heir"] A free person subject to the decedent's *potestas*. • These heirs were called *necessary* because they became heirs by law, not by the decedent's choice. But since this was also true of slaves, when named heirs in a will, the former class was designated *suus et necessarius* by way of distinction, the word *suus* denoting that the necessity arose from the relationship to the decedent.

ultimus heres (əl-ti-məs). The last or remote heir; the lord.

heresy (**her**-ə-see), *n*. (13c) **1.** Opinion or doctrine contrary to (usu. Roman Catholic) church dogma. **2.** *Hist*. In England, an offense against religion, consisting not in totally denying Christianity, but in publicly denying some of its essential doctrines; an opinion on divine subjects devised solely by human reason, openly taught, and obstinately maintained. • This offense is now subject only to ecclesiastical correction and is no longer punishable by the secular law. — **heretical**, *adj*.

hereto, *adv*. (12c) To this document <the exhibits are attached hereto>.

heretofore, *adv*. (13c) Up to now; before this time <a question that has not heretofore been decided>.

hereunder, *adv*. (15c) **1.** Later in this document <review the provisions hereunder before signing the consent form>. **2.** In accordance with this document <notice hereunder must be provided within 30 days after the loss>.

herewith, *adv*. (bef. 12c) With or in this document <enclosed herewith are three copies>.

heriot (**her**-ee-ət), *n*. [fr. Old English *here* "army" + *geatwa* "trappings"] *Hist*. A customary tribute of goods and chattels, payable to the lord of the fee on the tenant's death. • *Heriot* derives from an earlier feudal service consisting of military equipment returned to the lord on the tenant's death; over time it came to refer only to the chattel payment due at the tenant's death.

heriot custom. A heriot due by custom. • This term is used primarily to distinguish a *heriot service* from an ordinary heriot.

heriot service. A tribute arising from special reservation in a grant or lease of lands, and thus amounting to little more than rent.

heritable (**her**-i-tə-bəl), *adj*. (14c) **1.** (Of property) capable of being inherited. **2.** (Of a person) capable of inheriting. — Also termed *inheritable*.

heritable blood. See BLOOD.

heritable bond. See BOND (2).

heritable obligation. See OBLIGATION.

heritable property. *Scots law*. See HERITAGE.

heritable security. See SECURITY.

hermeneutics (hər-mə-**n[y]oo**-tiks), *n*. (18c) The art of interpreting texts, esp. as a technique used in critical legal studies. — **hermeneutical, hermeneutic,** *adj*.

Hermogenian Code. See CODEX HERMOGENIANUS.

heterologous, *adj*. *Patents*. Of, relating to, or constituting the DNA of a foreign organism.

heterologous artificial insemination. See *artificial insemination by donor* under ARTIFICIAL INSEMINATION.

heuristic (hyuu-**ris**-tik), *adj*. (1821) Of or relating to a method of learning or problem-solving by using trial-and-error and other experimental techniques <heuristic discovery methods>.

HEW. *abbr*. The Department of Health, Education, and Welfare, a former agency of the U.S. government created in 1953. • When the Department of Education was created in 1979, the name of HEW was changed to the Department of Health and Human Services (HHS).

Heydon's case, rule in. See MISCHIEF RULE.

HGN test. *abbr*. HORIZONTAL-GAZE NYSTAGMUS TEST.

HHS. *abbr*. DEPARTMENT OF HEALTH AND HUMAN SERVICES.

hiatus. *Patents.* A gap between the time when a parent application ceases to be pending (by abandonment or issuance) and the time a continuing application is filed. • A hiatus breaks the chain of continuity, so that later applications are not entitled to the effective filing date of the parent application. Cf. CONTINUITY (2).

HIDC. *abbr.* HOLDER IN DUE COURSE.

hidden asset. See ASSET.

hidden defect. See DEFECT.

hidden fraud. See *fraudulent concealment* under CONCEALMENT.

hidden tax. See TAX.

high bailiff. See BAILIFF.

High Court. 1. See HIGH COURT OF JUSTICE. **2.** See HIGH COURT OF JUSTICIARY.

High Court of Admiralty. In England, a court exercising jurisdiction in matters relating to shipping, collision, and salvage cases. • The court dates from the 14th century, and much of its early history concerns prize and piracy cases. Its jurisdiction varied through the centuries, sometimes extending into criminal matters and other areas of law not related directly to maritime issues. The Judicature Acts of 1873–1875 merged the Court into the High Court as part of the Probate, Divorce, and Admiralty Division. The Administration of Justice Act of 1970 established a new Admiralty Court as part of the Queen's Bench Division of the High Court. It is regulated by the Supreme Court Act of 1981. — Also termed *Court of the Lord High Admiral*; *Court of Admiralty*. Cf. ADMIRALTY (1).

High Court of Chivalry. *Hist.* A court of honor having jurisdiction over matters relating to deeds of arms and war, armorial insignia, and precedence. — Also termed *Court of Chivalry*; *Court of Earl Marshal*. See COURT OF HONOR.

High Court of Delegates. See COURT OF DELEGATES.

High Court of Errors and Appeals. See COURT OF ERRORS AND APPEALS.

High Court of Justice. The superior civil court of England and Wales. — Often shortened to *High Court*.

High Court of Justiciary (jə-**stish**-ee-er-ee). *Scots law.* The superior criminal court of Scotland, acting both as a trial court and as a court of final criminal appeal. • Its judges are Lords Commissioners of Justiciary. — Often shortened to *High Court*.

high crime. See CRIME.

high degree of care. See *great care* under CARE.

high diligence. See *great diligence* under DILIGENCE.

higher court. See *court above* under COURT.

higher scale. See SCALE (4).

highest and best use. See USE (1).

highest court. See COURT.

highest degree of care. See CARE.

highest proved value. See VALUE (2).

high flier. *Slang.* A security that has strongly attracted public interest so that investors pay an unusually high price.

highgrade, *vb.* **1.** To steal rich ore, as from a mine by a miner. **2.** To mine only esp. valuable ore (such as gold).

high-grade security. See SECURITY.

high justice. See JUSTICE (3).

high–low agreement. (1980) A settlement in which a defendant agrees to pay the plaintiff a minimum recovery in return for the plaintiff's agreement to accept a maximum amount regardless of the outcome of the trial. — Also termed *hilo settlement*.

highly prudent person. See REASONABLE PERSON.

high-managerial agent. See AGENT (2).

high misdemeanor. See MISDEMEANOR.

high-probability rule. *Marine insurance.* The principle that an insured may abandon a vessel if it appears extremely likely that a total loss is imminent.

high seas. See SEA.

high sheriff. See SHERIFF (1).

high-test marriage. See *covenant marriage* under MARRIAGE (1).

high treason. See TREASON.

high-water line. See *high-water mark* under WATERMARK.

high-water mark. See WATER MARK.

highway. (bef. 12c) **1.** Broadly, any main route on land, on water, or in the air. **2.** A free and public roadway or street that every person may use. **3.** The main public road connecting towns or cities. **4.** The entire width between boundaries of every publicly maintained way when part is open to public use for purposes of vehicular traffic.

> **common highway.** A highway for use by the public for any purpose of transit or traffic.

> **public highway.** A highway controlled and maintained by governmental authorities for general use.

highway act. (*usu. pl.*) One of a body of statutes governing the laying out, construction, repair, and use of highways. — Also termed *highway law.*

highwayman. (17c) A highway robber; a person who robs on a public road.

highway rate. *Hist.* In England, a tax for the maintenance and repair of highways.

highway robbery. See ROBBERY.

highway tax. See TAX.

high-yield bond. See BOND (3).

high-yield debt obligation. See *high-yield bond* under BOND (3).

hijack, *vb.* (1923) **1.** To commandeer (a vehicle or airplane), esp. at gunpoint. See CARJACK; SKYJACK. **2.** To steal or rob from (a vehicle or airplane in transit). **3.** *Hist.* To rob by trickery or violence; esp., to rob (a smuggler or bootlegger) and take illegal goods.

Hilary Rules. (19c) *Hist.* A collection of English pleading rules designed to ease the strict pleading requirements of the special-pleading system, esp. by limiting the scope of the general issue in the formed actions and by forcing the defendant to set up affirmatively all matters other than a denial of the breach of duty or of the wrongful act. • Promulgated in England in the 1834 Hilary Term, these rules followed an 1828 initiative to examine procedural laws and other subjects and to report to Parliament changes that might be enacted. The rules had the unintended effect of extending the reach of strict-pleading requirements into new areas of law. Widespread dissatisfaction with the Hilary Rules led to the liberalization of the pleading system under the 1873–1875 Judicature Acts. — Formerly also termed *New Rules.*

Hilary sittings. In England, a term of court beginning on January 11 of each year and ending on the Wednesday before Easter. • The Hilary sittings were known as *Hilary term* until 1875. Cf. EASTER SITTINGS; MICHAELMAS SITTINGS; TRINITY SITTINGS.

hilo settlement. See HIGH-LOW AGREEMENT.

***Hilton* doctrine.** *Civil procedure.* The rule that in a dispute between parties to an oil-and-gas lease, royalty owners who would lose their rights if the defendant's lease were terminated are regarded as indispensable parties to a proceeding challenging the lease. *Hilton v. Atlantic Refining Co.,* 327 F.2d 217 (5th Cir. 1964).

Himalaya clause. *Maritime law.* A provision in a bill of lading extending the carrier's defenses and limitations under the Carriage of Goods by Sea Act to third parties, typically employees, agents, and independent contractors. • The Supreme Court has held that this type of clause must be strictly construed. *Robert C. Herd & Co. v. Krawill Machinery Corp.,* 359 U.S. 297, 79 S.Ct. 766 (1959). See CARRIAGE OF GOODS BY SEA ACT.

HIPAA (hip-ə). *abbr.* HEALTH INSURANCE PORTABILITY AND ACCOUNTABILITY ACT.

hire, *vb.* (bef. 12c) **1.** To engage the labor or services of another for wages or other payment. **2.** To procure the temporary use of property, usu. at a set price. **3.** To grant the temporary use of services <hire themselves out>.

hired gun. (1971) *Slang.* **1.** An expert witness who testifies favorably for the party paying his or her fee, often because of that financial relationship rather than because of the facts. **2.** A lawyer who stops at nothing to accomplish the client's goals, regardless of moral consequences.

hireling, *n.* A person who is hired or serves for wages, esp. one who works only for the sake of payments.

hire-purchase agreement. See LEASE-PURCHASE AGREEMENT.

hiring. See LOCATIO.

hiring at will. See *employment at will* under EMPLOYMENT.

his. (bef. 12c) A possessive pronoun of the masculine gender but traditionally used and construed to include both sexes. • Because of the trend toward nonsexist language, careful drafters now tend to avoid the generic use of *his* (and the personal pronouns *he* and *him*) unless the reference is only to a male person.

His Honor; Her Honor. (1827) **1.** A third-person title customarily given to a judge. **2.** A third-person title customarily given to the mayor of a city. **3.** A third-person title given by the Massachusetts Constitution to the lieutenant governor of the commonwealth. Cf. YOUR HONOR.

historian. *Parliamentary law.* An officer charged with compiling or contributing to an organization's official history.

historical cost. See *acquisition cost* (1) under COST (1).

historical jurisprudence. See JURISPRUDENCE.

historic-preservation law. An ordinance prohibiting the demolition or exterior alteration of certain historic buildings or of all buildings in a historic district.

historic site. A building, structure, area, or property that is significant in the history, architecture, archaeology, or culture of a country, state, or city, and has been so designated by statute. • A historic site usu. cannot be altered without the permission of the appropriate authorities.

hit, *n.* (bef. 12c) **1.** A physical strike. **2.** *Criminal law.* A murder committed for money or on orders from a gang leader. **3.** *Criminal law.* An instance of the taking of a drug. **3.** *Intellectual property.* A single instance of a computer's connection to a Web page. • Counters keep track of how many visitors a Web page attracts, and a large number of hits is a major selling point for advertising. **4.**

Intellectual property. A Web page identified by an Internet search engine as containing words matching a user's query. **5.** A creative work that is a popular or a commercial success.

hit-and-run statute. A law requiring a motorist involved in an accident to remain at the scene and to give certain information to the police and others involved.

hitherto, *adv.* (13c) Until now; heretofore.

H.L. *abbr.* HOUSE OF LORDS.

HLA test. See HUMAN-LEUKOCYTE ANTIGEN TEST.

HMO. *abbr.* HEALTH-MAINTENANCE ORGANIZATION.

hoard, *vb.* (bef. 12c) To acquire and hold (goods) beyond one's reasonable needs, usu. because of an actual or anticipated shortage or price increase <hoarding food and medical supplies during wartime>.

Hobbs Act. A federal anti-racketeering act making it a crime to interfere with interstate commerce by extortion, robbery, or physical violence. 18 USCA § 1951. See RACKETEER INFLUENCED AND CORRUPT ORGANIZATIONS ACT.

hobby loss. See LOSS.

hoc. [Latin] This; with; by; in.

hoc loco (**hok loh**-koh). [Law Latin] *Hist.* In this place.

hoc nomine (**hok nahm**-ə-nee). [Law Latin] *Hist.* In this name.

hoc ordine (**hok or**-di-nee). [Law Latin] *Hist.* In this order.

hoc titulo (**hok tit**-yə-loh *or* **tich**-ə-loh). [Law Latin] *Hist.* Under this title.

hodgepodge. (15c) **1.** HOTCHPOT (1). **2.** An unorganized mixture.

hodgepodge act. (1883) A statute that deals with incongruous subjects.

hold, *n.* **1.** An order to preserve something or to delay or postpone an action.

litigation hold. A notice issued in anticipation of a lawsuit or investigation, ordering employees to preserve documents and other materials relevant to that lawsuit or investigation.

2. *Archaic.* In England, tenure. ● This word occurs most often in conjunction with others — for example, *freehold, leasehold* — and rarely in its separate form. See HOLDING (4).

hold, *vb.* (bef. 12c) **1.** To possess by a lawful title <Sarah holds the account as her separate property>. **2.** (Of a court) to adjudge or decide as a matter of law (as opposed to fact) <this court thus holds the statute to be unconstitutional>. Cf. FIND. **3.** To direct and bring about officially;

to conduct according to law <we must hold an election every two years>. **4.** To keep in custody or under an obligation <I will ask the judge to hold you accountable>. **5.** To take or have an estate from another; to have an estate on condition of paying rent or performing service <James holds Hungerstream Manor under lease>. **6.** To conduct or preside at; to convoke, open, and direct the operations of <Judge Brown holds court four days a week>. **7.** To possess or occupy; to be in possession and administration of <Jones holds the office of treasurer>.

holdback, *n.* An amount withheld from the full payment of a contract pending the other party's completion of some obligation, esp. to ensure that a contractor finishes the work agreed on beforehand. ● The terms of a holdback are typically expressed in the contract. The device gives the contractor an incentive to finish the work, and the other party security that the work will be finished. — **hold back,** *vb.*

holder. (14c) **1.** A person who has legal possession of a negotiable instrument and is entitled to receive payment on it. **2.** A person with legal possession of a document of title or an investment security. **3.** A person who possesses or uses property.

holder for value. (18c) A person who has given value in exchange for a negotiable instrument. ● Under the UCC, examples of "giving value" include acquiring a security interest in the instrument and accepting the instrument in payment of an antecedent claim. UCC § 3-303(a). — Also termed *bona fide holder for value.*

holder in due course. (1882) A person who in good faith has given value for a negotiable instrument that is complete and regular on its face, is not overdue, and, to the possessor's knowledge, has not been dishonored. ● Under UCC § 3-305, a holder in due course takes the instrument free of all claims and personal defenses, but subject to real defenses. — Abbr. HDC; HIDC. — Also termed *due-course holder.*

holder in good faith. (18c) One who takes property or an instrument without knowledge of any defect in its title.

holder of record. See STOCKHOLDER OF RECORD.

hold harmless, *vb.* (18c) To absolve (another party) from any responsibility for damage or other liability arising from the transaction; INDEMNIFY. — Also termed *save harmless.*

hold-harmless agreement. (1939) A contract in which one party agrees to indemnify the other. — Also termed *save-harmless agreement.* See INDEMNITY.

hold-harmless clause. See INDEMNITY CLAUSE.

holding, *n.* (15c) **1.** A court's determination of a matter of law pivotal to its decision; a principle

drawn from such a decision. Cf. OBITER DICTUM.
2. A ruling on evidence or other questions presented at trial. **3.** (*usu. pl.*) Legally owned property, esp. land or securities. **4.** *Hist.* In feudal law, tenure.

holding cell. See JAIL.

holding charge. (1949) A criminal charge of some minor offense filed to keep the accused in custody while prosecutors take time to build a bigger case and prepare more serious charges.

holding company. See COMPANY.

holding-company tax. See TAX.

holding over. 1. A tenant's action in continuing to occupy the leased premises after the lease term has expired. ● Holding over creates a tenancy at sufferance, with the tenant being referred to as a *holdover*. See *tenancy at sufferance* under TENANCY. **2.** *Parliamentary law.* An officer's continued tenure beyond the term for which he or she was elected, usu. because a successor has not been elected or cannot yet assume the office.

holding period. (1935) *Tax.* The time during which a capital asset must be held to determine whether gain or loss from its sale or exchange is long-term or short-term.

holding zone. See ZONE.

hold order. (1945) A notation in a prisoner's file stating that another jurisdiction has charges pending against the prisoner and instructing prison officials to alert authorities in that other jurisdiction instead of releasing the prisoner.

hold out, *vb.* (16c) **1.** To represent (oneself or another) as having a certain legal status, as by claiming to be an agent or partner with authority to enter into transactions <even though he was only a promoter, Schwartz held himself out as the principal>. **2.** To refuse to yield or submit; to stand firm <Womack held out for a higher salary and better benefits>.

holdover clause. See TRAILER CLAUSE.

holdover tenancy. See *tenancy at sufferance* under TENANCY.

holdover tenant. See TENANT.

holdup. See STICKUP.

holiday. See LEGAL HOLIDAY.

holograph (**hol**-ə-graf), *n.* (17c) A document (such as a will or deed) that is handwritten by its author. ● The majority rule is that a holographic will need not be entirely handwritten — only the "material provisions" — to take into account the popular use of fill-in-the-blank will forms. This is also the position of the Uniform Probate Code. — Also termed *olograph; autograph.* Cf. ONOMASTIC; SYMBOLIC. — **holographic,** *adj.*

holographic will. See WILL.

holymote. See HALLMOTE (4).

homage (**hom**-ij). (14c) In feudal times, a ceremony that a new tenant performed for the lord to acknowledge the tenure. ● This was the most honorable service that a free tenant might do for a lord. In the ceremony, kneeling before the lord, the tenant placed his hands between the lord's hands while saying, "I become your man from this day forward, of life and limb and earthly honor, and to you will be faithful and loyal, and bear you faith, for the tenements that I claim to hold of you, saving the faith that I owe unto our sovereign lord the king, so help me God."

homage ancestral (**hom**-ij an-**ses**-trəl). [Law French] A type of homage in which a tenant and the tenant's ancestors have held immemorially of another by the service of homage. ● This long-standing relationship bound the lord to warrant the title and to hold the tenant clear of all services to superior lords. — Also spelled *homage auncestral* (aw-**mahzh** on-se-**stral**).

homage liege (**hom**-ij **leej**). Homage due the sovereign alone as supreme lord, done without any saving or exception of the rights of other lords. — Also termed *homagium ligium* (hə-**may**-jee-əm lı-jee-əm).

homage jury. See JURY.

homagium (hə-**may**-jee-əm), *n.* [Law Latin] A formal ceremony in which a feudal tenant acknowledged the tenure granted by a lord; HOMAGE.

home. (bef. 12c) A dwelling place. See FAMILY HOME.

manufactured home. *Secured transactions.* A structure, transportable in one or more sections, that when traveling is 8 body feet or more in width or 40 body feet or more in length, or, when erected on site, is 320 or more square feet, and that is built on a permanent chassis and designed to be used as a dwelling with or without a permanent foundation when connected to the required utilities, and that has within it plumbing, heating, air-conditioning, and electrical systems. UCC § 9-102(a)(36).

matrimonial home. See *matrimonial domicile* under DOMICILE.

tax home. See TAX HOME.

home-equity line of credit. See *home-equity loan* under LOAN.

home equity loan. See LOAN.

homeless shelter. See SHELTER.

home loan bank. See FEDERAL HOME LOAN BANK.

home office. 1. A corporation's principal office or headquarters. **2.** (*cap.*) In England, the Department of the Secretary of State for Home Affairs, responsible for overseeing the internal affairs of the country.

homeowners' association. See ASSOCIATION.

homeowner's equity loan. See LOAN.

homeowner's insurance. See INSURANCE.

homeowner's policy. See INSURANCE POLICY.

Home Owners Warranty. A warranty and insurance program that, among other coverage, insures a new home for ten years against major structural defects. • The program was developed by the Home Owners Warranty Corporation, a subsidiary of the National Association of Home Builders. Builders often provide this type of coverage, and many states provide similar warranty protection by statute. — Also spelled *Home Owners' Warranty*. — Abbr. HOW.

home port. See PORT.

home-port doctrine. *Maritime law.* The rule mandating that a vessel engaged in interstate and foreign commerce is taxable only at its home port, usu. where the vessel is registered.

home rule. (1860) A state legislative provision or action allocating a measure of autonomy to a local government, conditional on its acceptance of certain terms. Cf. LOCAL OPTION.

home-rule charter. See CHARTER (2).

homestall. *Hist.* Homestead.

home state. *Family law.* **1.** The state where a person is domiciled. **2.** In an interstate child-custody dispute governed by the Uniform Child Custody Jurisdiction and Enforcement Act, the state where a child has lived with a parent or a person acting as a parent for at least six consecutive months immediately before the proceeding.

home-state jurisdiction. See JURISDICTION.

homestead. (bef. 12c) **1.** The house, outbuildings, and adjoining land owned and occupied by a person or family as a residence. • As long as the homestead does not exceed in area or value the limits fixed by law, in most states it is exempt from forced sale for collection of a debt. — Also termed *homestead estate.* See HOMESTEAD LAW.

business homestead. (1882) The premises on which a family's business is located. • In some states, business homesteads are exempt from execution or judicial sale for most kinds of debt.

constitutional homestead. (1851) A homestead, along with its exemption from forced sale, conferred on the head of a household by a state constitution. — Also termed *statutory homestead; pony homestead.*

pony homestead. See *constitutional homestead.*

probate homestead. (1881) A homestead created by a probate court from a decedent's estate for the benefit of the decedent's surviving spouse

and minor children. • Under most statutes providing for the creation of a probate homestead, it is exempt from forced sale for the collection of decedent's debts. The family can remain in the home at least until the youngest child reaches the age of majority. Many states allow the surviving spouse to live in the home for life. In a few states, such as Texas, the right to a probate homestead is constitutional. See *family allowance, spousal allowance* under ALLOWANCE; HOMESTEAD LAW. Cf. *life estate* under ESTATE (4).

statutory homestead. See *constitutional homestead.*

2. A surviving spouse's right of occupying the family home for life. • In some states, the right is extended to other dependents of a decedent.

homesteader. (1872) One who acquires or occupies a homestead.

homestead estate. See HOMESTEAD.

homestead exemption. See HOMESTEAD LAW.

homestead-exemption statute. See HOMESTEAD LAW.

homestead law. (1847) A statute exempting a homestead from execution or judicial sale for debt, unless all owners, usu. a husband and wife, have jointly mortgaged the property or otherwise subjected it to creditors' claims. — Also termed *homestead exemption; homestead-exemption statute; homestead right.*

homestead right. See HOMESTEAD LAW.

home-study report. *Family law.* A summary of an investigation into a child's home, family environment, and background, usu. prepared by a social worker when a child has been removed from his or her home because of abuse or neglect, but also prepared after a similar investigation of the home of potential adoptive parents. — Often shortened to *home study.* — Also termed *custody evaluation; social study.*

home-style exemption. *Copyright.* A provision in the U.S. Copyright Act allowing for the public airing of radio and television broadcasts in public-accommodation establishments, such as bars and restaurants, with immunity from liability for infringement. • The exemption is so named because the equipment used for the airing must be a single receiver of the type typically found in homes. 17 USCA § 110(5).

homicide (hom-ə-sId), *n.* (14c) **1.** The killing of one person by another. **2.** A person who kills another. — **homicidal,** *adj.*

criminal homicide. (1850) **1.** Homicide prohibited and punishable by law, such as murder or manslaughter. **2.** The act of purposely, knowingly, recklessly, or negligently causing the death of another human being. Model Penal Code § 210.1.

criminally negligent homicide. See *negligent homicide*.

culpable homicide. *Scots law.* A wrongful act that results in a person's death but does not amount to murder. Cf. MANSLAUGHTER.

excusable homicide. (18c) **1.** Homicide resulting from a person's lawful act, committed without intention to harm another. **2.** See *justifiable homicide* (1).

felonious homicide. (18c) Homicide committed unlawfully, without legal justification or excuse. • This is the category into which murder and manslaughter fall.

homicide by abuse. (1989) Homicide in which the perpetrator, under circumstances showing an extreme indifference to human life, causes the death of the perpetrator's dependent — usu. a child or mentally retarded person.

homicide by misadventure. See ACCIDENTAL KILLING.

homicide per infortunium (pər in-for-**t**[y]**oo**-nee-əm). [Latin "homicide by misfortune"] (1856) The unintentional killing of another while engaged in a lawful act; ACCIDENTAL KILLING.

innocent homicide. (1884) Homicide that does not involve criminal guilt.

justifiable homicide. (18c) **1.** The killing of another in self-defense when faced with the danger of death or serious bodily injury. — Also termed *excusable homicide*. See SELF-DEFENSE (1). **2.** A killing mandated or permitted by the law, such as execution for a capital crime or killing to prevent a crime or a criminal's escape.

negligent homicide. (1859) Homicide resulting from the careless performance of a legal or illegal act in which the danger of death is apparent; the killing of a human being by criminal negligence. — Also termed *criminally negligent homicide*. See *criminal negligence* under NEGLIGENCE.

nonfelonious homicide. A killing that is legally either excusable or justifiable. See *excusable homicide*; *justifiable homicide*.

reckless homicide. (1866) The unlawful killing of another person with conscious indifference toward that person's life. Cf. MANSLAUGHTER.

vehicular homicide. (1952) The killing of a person as a result of the unlawful or negligent operation of a motor vehicle. — Also termed *automobile homicide*.

victim-precipitated homicide. 1. See *suicide-by-cop* under SUICIDE. **2.** A killing provoked by the victim who consciously intended to die at the hands of another person. • This term applies loosely to any assisted suicide. Unlike most types of homicide, the victim bears some of the responsibility for causing his or her own death.

willful homicide. (1860) The act of intentionally causing a person's death, with or without legal justification.

homo (**hoh**-moh), *n.* [Latin] *Hist.* **1.** A male human. **2.** A homo sapiens; a human being of either sex. **3.** A slave. **4.** A vassal; a feudal tenant. **5.** A retainer, dependent, or servant. Pl. **homines.**

homo chartularius (kahr-chə-**lair**-ee-əs). A slave manumitted by charter.

homo commendatus (kom-ən-**day**-təs). A man who commends himself into another's power for protection or support.

homo ecclesiasticus (e-klee-z[h]ee-**as**-ti-kəs). A church vassal; one bound to serve a church, esp. in an agricultural capacity.

homo exercitalis (eg-zər-shə-**tay**-lis). A man of the army; a soldier.

homo feodalis (fyoo-**day**-lis). A fee man; a vassal or tenant who holds a fee.

homo fiscalis (fis-**kay**-lis). A servant or vassal belonging to the treasury (*fiscus*). — Also termed *homo fiscalinus*.

homo francus (**frangk**-əs). **1.** In England, a freeman. **2.** A Frenchman.

homo ingenuus (in-**jen**-yoo-əs). A free and lawful man; a yeoman.

homo liber (**lɪ**-bər). **1.** A free man. **2.** A freeman lawfully competent to be a juror. **3.** An allodial proprietor, as distinguished from a feudal tenant. See ALLODIAL.

homo ligius (**lɪ**-jee-əs). A liege man, esp. the vassal of a king.

homo novus (**noh**-vəs). **1.** A new tenant or vassal; one invested with a new fee. **2.** A tenant pardoned after being convicted of a crime.

homo pertinens (**pər**-tə-nenz). A feudal bondman or vassal; one belonging to the soil.

homo regius (**ree**-jee-əs). A king's vassal.

homo Romanus (rə-**may**-nəs). A Roman. • A term used in Germanic law codes to describe the Roman inhabitants of Gaul and other former Roman provinces.

homo sui juris (s[y]**oo**-ɪ joor-is). See PATERFAMILIAS.

homo trium litterarum (**trɪ**-əm lit-ə-**rair**-əm). [Latin "a man of three letters"] A thief. • The "three letters" refers to *f*, *u*, and *r*, for the Latin word *fur* ("thief").

homologate (hə-**mol**-ə-gayt), *vb. Civil law.* To approve or confirm officially <the court homologated the sale>.

homologation (hə-mol-ə-**gay**-shən). *Civil law.* **1.** Confirmation, esp. of a court granting its approval to some action. **2.** The consent inferred by law from a party's failure, for a ten-day period, to complain of an arbitrator's sentence, of an appointment of a syndic (or assignee) of an insolvent, or of a settlement of successions. **3.** A judge's approval of certain acts and agreements to render them more readily enforceable. — Also termed (in Spanish law) *homologación* (oh-moh-loh-gah-**syohn**). See *judgment homologating the tableau* under JUDGMENT.

homologous artificial insemination. See *artificial insemination by husband* under ARTIFICIAL INSEMINATION.

homosexual marriage. See *same-sex marriage* under MARRIAGE (1).

Hon. *abbr.* HONORABLE.

honest claim. See CLAIM (3).

honest-services doctrine. See INTANGIBLE-RIGHTS DOCTRINE.

honesty clause. See FULL-REPORTING CLAUSE (1).

honesty defense. See DEFENSE (1).

honor, *n.* (13c) **1.** In the United States, a courtesy title given to judges and certain other public officials. **2.** (*usu. pl.*) In England, those dignities or privileges, degrees of nobility, knighthood, and other titles that flow from the Crown. **3.** *Hist.* In England, a seigniory of several manors held under one baron or lord paramount.

honor, *vb.* (13c) **1.** To accept or pay (a negotiable instrument) when presented. **2.** To recognize, salute, or praise.

Honorable. (15c) A title of respect given to judges, members of the U.S. Congress, ambassadors, and the like <The Honorable Ruth Bader Ginsburg>. — Abbr. Hon.

honorable discharge. See DISCHARGE (8).

honorable-engagement clause. *Reinsurance.* An arbitration provision in a reinsurance contract allowing the arbitrators to view the reinsurance arrangement reasonably — in line with the agreement's general purposes — rather than strictly according to the rules of law or an unduly technical interpretation of contractual language.

honorarium (on-ə-**rair**-ee-əm), *n.* (17c) **1.** A payment of money or anything else of value made to a person for services rendered for which fees cannot legally be or are not traditionally paid. **2.** A voluntary reward for that for which no remuneration could be collected by law; a voluntary donation in consideration of services that admit of no compensation in money. **3.** *Roman law.* A gratuitous payment, esp. for professional services, as distinguished from compensation for physical labor. Pl. **honoraria; honorariums.**

honorary, *adj.* (16c) (Of a title or status) conferred in recognition of merit or service, but without the attendant rights, powers, or duties; nominal <honorary member>. • An honorary title or status may be granted without regard to whether the honoree ever held the title or status in fact. The honorary title conferred on a former officer who has honorably retired from office is often "emeritus" or "emerita." See EMERITUS.

honorary canon. See CANON (5).

honorary trust. See TRUST.

honor crime. See CRIME.

honor killing. See *honor crime* under CRIME.

hooligan. 1. An unruly or mischievous person who causes trouble; a street-gang member. • This term is often associated with boisterous fans of British sporting events. **2.** See HOOLIGAN TOOL.

hooligan tool. A steel bar used by police officers and firefighters to break open doors or windows. — Sometimes shortened to *hooligan.* — Also termed *halligan tool.*

horizontal agreement. See *horizontal restraint* under RESTRAINT OF TRADE.

horizontal competition. See COMPETITION.

horizontal equality. In per capita distribution of an estate, parity of distribution among members of the same generation. See PER CAPITA. Cf. VERTICAL EQUALITY.

horizontal-gaze nystagmus test (nis-**tag**-məs). (1985) *Criminal law.* A field-sobriety test for intoxication, in which the suspect is told to focus on an object (such as a pencil) and to track its movement, usu. from side to side, by moving only the eyes. • Intoxication is indicated if the eyes jerk or twitch while tracking the object. — Abbr. HGN test.

horizontal integration. See *horizontal merger* under MERGER.

horizontal merger. See MERGER.

horizontal nonprivity. See NONPRIVITY.

horizontal price-fixing. See PRICE-FIXING.

horizontal privity. See PRIVITY.

horizontal-property act. A statute dealing with cooperatives and condominiums.

horizontal restraint. See RESTRAINT OF TRADE.

horizontal stare decisis. See STARE DECISIS.

horizontal union. See *craft union* under UNION.

hornbook. (16c) **1.** A book explaining the basics of a given subject. **2.** A textbook containing the rudimentary principles of an area of law. Cf. CASEBOOK.

hornbook law. See BLACKLETTER LAW.

hornbook method. (1895) A method of legal instruction characterized by a straightforward presentation of legal doctrine, occasionally interspersed with questions. ● The hornbook method predominates in civil-law countries, and in certain fields of law, such as procedure and evidence. — Also termed *lecture method.* Cf. CASEBOOK METHOD; SOCRATIC METHOD.

horn tenure. **1.** See CORNAGE (1). **2.** See CORNAGE (2).

hors (or). [French] **1.** Out or out of. **2.** Outside or outside of.

horse case. See WHITEHORSE CASE.

horsehead. See PUMPING UNIT.

horseshedding, *n.* (1931) The instructing of a witness favorable to one's case (esp. a client) about the proper method of responding to questions while giving testimony. — Also termed *woodshedding.* Cf. SANDPAPERING. — **horseshed,** *vb.*

Hospitallers (**hos**-pi-təl-ərz). A military and religious order founded in the 11th century and so called because it built a hospital at Jerusalem to care for pilgrims. ● The Crown seized all its lands and goods in England under the Grantees of Reversions Act (1540). The Hospitallers still functions in several countries as a humanitarian society.

hospital lien. See LIEN.

hospiticide (hah-**spit**-ə-sɪd), *n.* (17c) **1.** The murder of a host by a guest. **2.** A host who murders a guest.

hostage. (13c) **1.** An innocent person held captive by another who threatens to kill or harm that person if one or more demands are not met. ● Hostage-taking is a federal crime. 18 USCA § 1203. Cf. KIDNAPPING. **2.** *Int'l law.* A person who is given or taken into an enemy's custody, in time of war, with his or her freedom or life to stand as security for the performance of some agreement made to the enemy by the belligerent power giving the hostage.

hosteler (**hos**-tə-lər). (14c) **1.** A person who stays in a youth hostel. **2.** A stableman. **3.** *Archaic.* A person who receives and entertains guests, esp. at a monastery. **4.** *Archaic.* An innkeeper. See HOSTLER.

hostes (**hos**-teez), *n. pl.* [Latin] Enemies. Sing. *hostis* (**hos**-tis).

hostes humani generis (hyoo-**may**-nɪ jen-ə-ris). Enemies of the human race; specif., pirates.

hosticide (**hos**-tə-sɪd), *n.* (1848) **1.** The killing of an enemy. **2.** A person who kills an enemy.

hostile, *adj.* (16c) **1.** ADVERSE. **2.** Showing ill will or a desire to harm. **3.** Antagonistic; unfriendly.

hostile act. See ACT OF HOSTILITY.

hostile amendment. See AMENDMENT (3).

hostile bidder. See CORPORATE RAIDER.

hostile embargo. See EMBARGO (1).

hostile-environment sexual harassment. See SEXUAL HARASSMENT.

hostile possession. See POSSESSION.

hostile propaganda. See PROPAGANDA.

hostile takeover. See TAKEOVER.

hostile witness. See WITNESS.

hostility. (15c) **1.** A state of enmity between individuals or nations. **2.** An act or series of acts displaying antagonism. **3.** (*usu. pl.*) Acts of war.

hostler ([h]os-lər). [fr. *hosteler*] (14c) *Archaic.* **1.** A stableman; an ostler. **2.** An innkeeper. ● By the 16th century, this term had lost its "innkeeper" sense, and referred exclusively to a stableman.

hot bench. See BENCH.

hot blood. See HEAT OF PASSION.

hot cargo. (1938) *Labor law.* Goods produced or handled by an employer with whom a union has a dispute.

hot-cargo agreement. (1957) *Labor law.* A voluntary agreement between a union and a neutral employer by which the latter agrees to exert pressure on another employer with whom the union has a dispute, as by ceasing or refraining from handling, using, selling, transporting, or otherwise dealing in any of the products of an employer that the union has labeled as unfair. ● Most agreements of this type were prohibited by the Landrum–Griffin Act of 1959. See LANDRUM–GRIFFIN ACT.

hot check. See *bad check* under CHECK.

hotchpot (**hoch**-pot), *n.* (16c) **1.** The blending of items of property to secure equality of division, esp. as practiced either in cases of divorce or in cases in which advancements of an intestate's property must be made up to the estate by a contribution or by an accounting. — Also termed *hotchpotch; hotchpot rule.* **2.** In a community-property state, the property that falls within the community estate. **3.** MAIN POT.

hot court. See COURT.

hot document. See DOCUMENT.

hotel divorce. See DIVORCE.

hotelkeeper. See INNKEEPER.

hotelkeeper's lien. See LIEN.

hot issue. See ISSUE (2).

hot news. *Intellectual property.* Extremely time-sensitive or transient information that is usu. reliable for very brief periods, such as stock quotations.

hot-news test. *Intellectual property.* A judicial test for determining whether a misappropriation claim is preempted by the *Sears–Compco* doctrine, consisting in analyzing whether, in addition to the elements of copyright infringement, the claim also requires proof of (1) time-sensitive information collected at a cost to the plaintiff, (2) unfair use of that information by a directly competing defendant who has made no similar investment, and (3) a consequent threat to the plaintiff's commercial existence.

hot-potato rule. The principle that a lawyer may not unreasonably withdraw from representing a client. • The term comes from the rule's classic formulation: "a firm may not drop a client like a 'hot potato,' especially if it is in order to keep happy a far more lucrative client." *Picker Int'l, Inc. v. Varian Assocs., Inc.,* 670 F. Supp. 1363, 1365 (N.D. Ohio 1987). An exception may be allowed for a conflict of interest arising from circumstances beyond the control of the lawyer or the law firm. See *thrust-upon conflict* under CONFLICT OF INTEREST.

hot pursuit. (18c) **1.** See FRESH PURSUIT. **2.** *Int'l law.* The legitimate chase of a foreign vessel on the high seas just after that vessel has violated the law of the pursuing country while within that country's jurisdiction.

hot stock. See *hot issue* under ISSUE (2).

hot-water ordeal. See *ordeal by water* (2) under ORDEAL.

house. (bef. 12c) **1.** A home, dwelling, or residence.

   ancient house. *Hist.* In England, a house that has stood long enough to acquire an easement of support against the adjoining land or building.

   bawdy house. See DISORDERLY HOUSE (2).

   disorderly house. See DISORDERLY HOUSE.

   dwelling-house. See DWELLING-HOUSE.

   house of correction. **1.** A reformatory. **2.** A place for the confinement of juvenile offenders or those who have committed crimes of lesser magnitude. — Also termed *house of refuge.*

   house of detention. See JAIL.

   house of ill fame. **1.** See BROTHEL. **2.** See DISORDERLY HOUSE (2).

   house of prostitution. See DISORDERLY HOUSE (2).

   house of refuge. See *house of correction.*

   house of worship. A building or place set apart for and devoted to the holding of religious services or exercises or public worship; a church or chapel, or a place similarly used.

   public house. See PUBLIC HOUSE.

2. A branch of a legislature or a quorum of such a branch; esp., the lower chamber of a bicameral legislature. **3.** HOUSE OF REPRESENTATIVES. **4.** HOUSE OF DELEGATES (1).

houseage (howz-ij). A fee paid for housing goods, as by a carrier or at a wharf.

house arrest. (1936) The confinement of a person who has been accused or convicted of a crime to his or her home, usu. by attaching an electronically monitored bracelet to the person. • Most house-arrest programs require the offender to work and permit leaving the home only for reasons such as work, medical needs, or community-service obligations.

house bill. See BILL (3).

housebote. See BOTE (1).

housebreaking. (17c) The crime of breaking into a dwelling or other secured building, with the intent to commit a felony inside; BURGLARY. • *Burglary* is now used more frequently than *housebreaking.* In England, for example, *housebreaking* was replaced in 1968 with statutory burglary, though the term is still used in Scots law. In some jurisdictions, *housebreaking* includes "breaking out" of a house that was entered without a breaking. — **housebreaker,** *n.*

   constructive housebreaking. A breaking made out by construction of law, as when a burglar gains entry by threat or fraud. — Also termed *constructive breaking into a house.*

houseburning. The common-law misdemeanor of intentionally burning one's own house that is within city limits or that is close enough to other houses that they might be in danger of catching fire (even though no actual damage to them may result). — Also termed *combustio domorum.* Cf. ARSON.

house counsel. See *in-house counsel* under COUNSEL.

household, *adj.* Belonging to the house and family; domestic.

household, *n.* (14c) **1.** A family living together. **2.** A group of people who dwell under the same roof. Cf. FAMILY. **3.** The contents of a house.

householder. (14c) **1.** A person who keeps house with his or her family; the head or master of a family. **2.** A person who has a household. **3.** An occupier of a house. Cf. HEAD OF HOUSEHOLD. — **householdership,** *n.*

household goods. See GOODS.

house law. *Hist.* A regulatory code promulgated by the head of a royal or noble family, or of a prominent private family, governing intrafamily relationships and acts concerning events such as marriage, disposition of property, and inheritance. • Such a code had no legal authority but was enforced within the family by personal and economic sanctions.

house mark. See *house trademark* under TRADE-MARK.

house of assignation. See DISORDERLY HOUSE (2).

House of Commons. The lower chamber of the British and Canadian parliaments. — Abbr. H.C.

house of correction. See HOUSE.

house of delegates. (18c) **1.** (*often cap.*) The convention of many learned or professional associations, including the American Bar Association <the ABA House of Delegates>. — Often shortened to *House.* — Also termed *house of representatives.* See CONVENTION (4). **2.** (*cap.*) The lower chamber of the state legislature in Maryland, Virginia, and West Virginia.

house of detention. See JAIL.

house of ill fame. 1. See BROTHEL. **2.** See DISORDERLY HOUSE (2).

house of ill repute. See DISORDERLY HOUSE.

House of Lords. (17c) The upper chamber of the British Parliament, of which the 11-member judicial committee provides judges who serve as the final court of appeal in most civil cases. • In practice, the Lords sit as committees, usu. of five but occasionally of seven. Two committees may sit simultaneously. — Abbr. H.L. — Also termed *Lords.*

house of prostitution. See DISORDERLY HOUSE (2).

house of refuge. See *house of correction* under HOUSE.

House of Representatives. (18c) **1.** The lower chamber of the U.S. Congress, composed of 435 members — apportioned among the states on the basis of population — who are elected to two-year terms. **2.** The lower house of a state legislature. — Abbr. H.R.; (in senses 1 & 2) H. — Often shortened to *House.* **3.** HOUSE OF DELEGATES (1). — Often shortened (in all senses) to *House.* — Abbr. H.R.

house of worship. See HOUSE.

house trademark. See TRADEMARK.

housing code. See BUILDING CODE.

housing court. See COURT.

hovering act. *Int'l law.* A statute applying to a coastal country's criminal jurisdiction over ships, and persons aboard those ships, when the ships are outside the country's territory.

HOW. *abbr.* HOME OWNERS WARRANTY.

How say you? *Archaic.* (Asked of a jury) how do you find?

howsoever, *adv.* (14c) In whatever way; however.

H.R. *abbr.* HOUSE OF REPRESENTATIVES.

H.R. 10 plan. See KEOGH PLAN.

HSR Act. See HART–SCOTT–RODINO ANTITRUST IMPROVEMENT ACT.

HTML. *abbr.* HYPERTEXT MARKUP LANGUAGE.

http. *abbr.* HYPERTEXT TRANSFER PROTOCOL.

hub-and-spoke conspiracy. See *wheel conspiracy* under CONSPIRACY.

HUD. *abbr.* DEPARTMENT OF HOUSING AND URBAN DEVELOPMENT.

hue and cry. (15c) *Hist.* **1.** The public uproar that, at common law, a citizen was expected to initiate after discovering a crime. — Also termed *vociferatio; clamor.* **2.** The pursuit of a felon accompanying such an uproar. **3.** A written proclamation for the capture of a felon.

hui (hoo-ee), *n.* In Hawaiian law, an association of persons who own land together, usu. as tenants in common.

huissier (wee-syay), *n.* [French fr. *huis* "door"] **1.** *French law.* An usher of a court; an officer (such as a marshal) who serves process. **2.** *Hist.* In England, a ministerial officer attached to a court, responsible for service of process, issuing executions, and maintaining order during court sessions.

hulk, *n.* (17c) *Hist.* In England, a dismantled ship used as a prison. • Living conditions in hulks were notoriously poor, and their use as prisons ended as part of the broad prison-reform movements of the mid-19th century.

humanitarian doctrine. See LAST-CLEAR-CHANCE DOCTRINE.

humanitarian intervention. See INTERVENTION.

humanitarian law. *Int'l law.* Law dealing with such matters as the permissible use of weapons and other means of warfare, the treatment of prisoners of war and civilian populations in armed conflicts, and generally the direct impact of war on human life and liberty. • Most existing rules composing humanitarian law are codified in the Geneva Conventions and their protocols.

human-leukocyte antigen test. A medical process of analyzing the blood sample of a man in a paternity or legitimacy case by comparing certain indicators with the child's blood. — Abbr. HLA test. See BLOOD-GROUPING TEST. Cf. GENETIC-MARKER TEST.

human rights. (18c) The freedoms, immunities, and benefits that, according to modern values (esp. at an international level), all human beings should be able to claim as a matter of right in the society in which they live. See UNIVERSAL DECLARATION OF HUMAN RIGHTS.

human trafficking. See TRAFFICKING.

hundred. (bef. 12c) **1.** Formerly, a county subdivision that had its own local court. **2.** The populace of such a subdivision. **3.** See *hundred court* under COURT. **4.** In the United States, a political division derived from the English county division. • Hundreds existed in colonial Delaware, Maryland, Pennsylvania, and Virginia. Today, they exist only in Delaware. — **hundredal** (hundri-dəl), *adj.*

hundredary (hən-dri-der-ee), *n.* [Law Latin] *Hist.* The chief or presiding officer of a hundred. — Also termed *hundredarius.*

hundred court. See COURT.

hundred moot. See *hundred court* under COURT.

hundredor (hən-dri-dər), *n. Hist.* **1.** A freeholder of a hundred who can sue in, or act as judge of, a hundred court. **2.** A person who has been empaneled (or is fit to be empaneled) on a hundred-court jury, and who dwells within the hundred where the cause of action arose. **3.** An officer who has jurisdiction of a hundred and who holds the hundred court. **4.** The bailiff of a hundred.

hundred rolls. *Hist.* Records that list the various feudal tenancies and feudal obligations existing among English lords and tenants. • The *hundred rolls* were compiled in 1274–1275 by royal commissioners from inquiries put to hundred-court juries in order to alert the Crown to the existence of feudal relationships that infringed on royal prerogatives (and thereby royal revenue).

hung jury. See JURY.

Huntley **hearing.** In New York practice, a pretrial hearing in a criminal case to determine the admissibility of a defendant's statement. The hearing usu. follows a defendant's motion to suppress an involuntary statement. The name derives from *People v. Huntley*, 204 N.E.2d 179 (N.Y. 1965), in which the court held that a judge in a criminal trial must conduct a preliminary hearing to determine whether, beyond a reasonable doubt, a defendant's confession was made voluntarily.

husband. (13c) A married man; a man who has a lawful spouse living. • Etymologically, the word signified the *house bond*, the man who, according to Saxon ideas and institutions, held around him the family, for which he was legally responsible.

common-law husband. The husband in a common-law marriage; a man who contracts an informal marriage with a woman and then holds himself out to the community as being married to her. See *common-law marriage* under MARRIAGE (1).

husbandlike and proper. (Of land cultivation or management) according to the locale's usual practices.

husbandman. *Archaic.* A farmer.

husbandry. (14c) **1.** Agriculture or farming; cultivation of the soil for food. • In some states, tools and equipment used in farming are exempt from forced sale for collection of a debt. **2.** Generally, care of a household; careful management of resources.

husband–wife immunity. See IMMUNITY (2).

husband–wife privilege. See *marital privilege* under PRIVILEGE (3).

hush money. (18c) *Slang.* A bribe to suppress the dissemination of certain information; a payment to secure silence.

husting. (*usu. pl.*) [Old English] (bef. 12c) **1.** *Hist.* A deliberative assembly, esp. one called by the king or other leader. **2.** *Hist.* COURT OF HUSTINGS. **3.** *Hist.* The raised platform used by officials of the Court of Hustings. **4.** *Hist.* The raised platform used to nominate candidates for Parliament. • This practice ended after passage of the Ballot Act in 1872. **5.** Any place where political campaign speeches are made.

hybrid action. *Labor law.* A lawsuit in which a union member asserts claims against the employer for breach of a collective bargaining agreement, and against the union for breach of the duty of fair representation.

hybrid class action. See CLASS ACTION.

hybrid mark. See *composite trademark* under TRADEMARK.

hybrid security. See SECURITY.

hybrid trademark. See *composite trademark* under TRADEMARK.

Hyde Amendment. A federal law that prohibits the use of Medicaid funds for abortions except when necessary to save the mother's life, and that prohibits federally funded family-planning programs from providing abortion counseling. • The bill was sponsored by Representative Henry Hyde of Illinois.

Hydraflow **test.** (1996) A principle for deciding when an inadvertent disclosure of a privileged document is a waiver of the attorney–client privilege, whereby the court considers the reasonableness of the precautions taken to prevent the inadvertent disclosure, the number of disclosures involved, the extent of the disclosure, the promptness of any efforts to remedy the disclosure, and whether justice would be best served by permitting the disclosing party to retrieve the document. *Hydraflow, Inc. v. Enidine, Inc.*, 145 F.R.D. 626 (W.D.N.Y. 1993). — Also termed *middle-of-the-road test.* Cf. *lenient test; strict test.*

hyperlink. (1988) *Intellectual property.* An element on a Web page — usu. a word, phrase, or graphic, but sometimes a single pixel — that, when clicked on, takes the user to another part of the same website or to a different website. • A copyright violation occurs if a person knows or has reason to know that a link will be used for unauthorized copying, and creates a link to encourage or contribute to wrongful copying. — Often shortened to *link*. — **hyperlink,** *vb.*

hypertext markup language. The programming code used on websites to format text and provide links between resources. — Abbr. HTML.

hypertext transfer protocol. The set of programmed rules that enable computers to exchange information over the Internet. • Browsers use http to contact other computers. — Abbr. http.

hypothec (hɪ-**poth**-ek *or* hi-). (16c) *Civil law.* A mortgage given to a creditor on property to secure a debt; HYPOTHECA.

　mariner's hypothec. **1.** A lien that a seaman, freighter, or repairer can assert against a ship for payment of wages or other sums due. **2.** A shipowner's lien against the ship's cargo for the freight costs.

　solicitor's hypothec. A legal agent's lien for costs in excess of the costs recovered from an opposing party. • The lien may also apply to the retention of some documents, such as title deeds, as security for a client's outstanding account.

hypotheca (hɪ-pə-**thee**-kə *or* hip-ə-), *n.* [Latin fr. Greek] *Roman law.* A mortgage of property in which the debtor was allowed to keep, but not alienate, the property.

hypothecary (hɪ-**poth**-ə-ker-ee), *adj.* (17c) Of, relating to, or involving a hypothec or hypothecation.

hypothecary action. See ACTION (4).

hypothecary debt. See DEBT.

hypothecate (hɪ-**poth**-ə-kayt), *vb.* (17c) To pledge (property) as security or collateral for a debt, without delivery of title or possession.

hypothecation (hɪ-poth-ə-**kay**-shən), *n.* (17c) The pledging of something as security without delivery of title or possession. — **hypothecator** (hɪ-poth-ə-kay-tər), *n.*

　general hypothecation. **1.** A debtor's pledge to allow all the property named in the security instrument to serve as collateral and to be used to satisfy the outstanding debt. **2.** See *tacit hypothecation* (1), (2).

　tacit hypothecation. **1.** *Civil law.* A type of lien or mortgage that is created by operation of law and without the parties' express agreement. —

Also termed *tacit mortgage.* **2.** See *maritime lien* under LIEN.

hypothecation bond. See BOND (2).

hypothesis (hɪ-**poth**-ə-səs). (16c) **1.** A supposition based on evidence but not proven; a proposed explanation, supported by evidence, that serves as a starting point for investigation. **2.** A theory or supposition proposed for the sake of debate.

hypothetical, *adj.* (16c) **1.** Involving tentative theory or supposition adopted provisionally; assumed or postulated merely for the sake of argument.

hypothetical, *n.* (17c) A proposition or statement that is presumed true for the sake of logical analysis or debate. • Hypotheticals are often used as teaching tools to illustrate the application of legal principles or to explore the potential consequences of words and actions. See HYPOTHETICAL QUESTION.

hypothetical contract. See *conditional contract* under CONTRACT.

hypothetical creditor. See CREDITOR.

hypothetical lien creditor. See *hypothetical creditor* under CREDITOR.

hypothetical negotiation. A judicial construct used to calculate damages in a patent-infringement suit by arriving at a figure that would have been reasonable royalty acceptable to both parties.

hypothetical-person defense. (1979) An entrapment defense in which the defendant asserts that an undercover law-enforcement officer (or person acting at the law-enforcement officer's direction) encouraged the defendant to engage in the criminal conduct either by making false representations designed to convince the defendant that the conduct was not prohibited, or by using persuasive methods that created a substantial risk that the charged offense would be committed by a person who was not otherwise inclined to commit it. • This defense has been adopted by a minority of states and by the Model Penal Code. — Also termed *objective method.* See Model Penal Code § 2.13. Cf. SHERMAN–SORRELLS DOCTRINE.

hypothetical pleading. See PLEADING (1).

hypothetical question. (1826) A trial device that solicits an expert witness's opinion based on assumptions treated as facts established by evidence. — Also termed *abstract question.*

hypothetical tenant. *Hist.* A fictional person used for assessing property taxes, which are based on what the person would pay to lease the property.

I

IABA. *abbr.* INTER-AMERICAN BAR ASSOCIATION.

IAF. *abbr.* INTER-AMERICAN FOUNDATION.

IAIP. *abbr.* INFORMATION ANALYSIS AND INFRA-STRUCTURE PROTECTION DIRECTORATE.

ibi. [Latin] There and then.

ibid. (**ib**-id). *abbr.* [Latin *ibidem*] (17c) In the same place. ● This abbreviation, used in citations (mostly outside law), denotes that the reference is to a work cited immediately before, and that the cited matter appears on the same page of the same book (unless a different page is specified). — Also termed *ib*. Cf. ID.

ICANN. *abbr.* INTERNET CORPORATION FOR AS-SIGNED NAMES AND NUMBERS.

ICC. *abbr.* **1.** INTERSTATE COMMERCE COMMISSION. **2.** INTERNATIONAL CRIMINAL COURT.

ICJ. *abbr.* INTERNATIONAL COURT OF JUSTICE.

ICPC. *abbr.* INTERSTATE COMPACT ON THE PLACE-MENT OF CHILDREN.

ICSID (**ik**-sid). *abbr.* INTERNATIONAL CENTRE FOR SETTLEMENT OF INVESTMENT DISPUTES.

ICWA. *abbr.* INDIAN CHILD WELFARE ACT.

id. (id). *abbr.* [Latin *idem*] (17c) The same. ● *Id.* is used in a legal citation to refer to the authority cited immediately before <*id.* at 55>. Cf. IBID.

IDA. *abbr.* INVESTMENT-DIRECTION AGREEMENT.

IDEA. *abbr.* INDIVIDUALS WITH DISABILITIES EDU-CATION ACT.

idea–expression dichotomy. *Copyright.* The funda-mental rule that copyright law protects only spe-cific expressions of an idea, not the idea itself.

idem per idem (**ı**-dem pər **ı**-dem). [Latin] The same for the same. ● This phrase refers to an illustra-tion that adds nothing to a matter under consid-eration.

idem sonans (**ı**-dem **soh**-nanz), *adj.* [Latin] (1856) (Of words or names) sounding the same, re-gardless of spelling <the names Gene and Jean are *idem sonans*>. ● In trademark law, the term designates a name that sounds close enough to a registered trademark to create confusion among consumers and infringe that mark, so the Stein-way company was able to prevent a competitor from registering "Steinberg" for the name of its pianos.

idem sonans (**ı**-dem **soh**-nanz), *n.* [Latin] (1848) A legal doctrine preventing a variant spelling of a name in a document from voiding the document if the misspelling is pronounced the same way as the true spelling.

identification interrogatory. See INTERROGA-TORY.

identification of goods. (1887) A process that enables a buyer to obtain an identifiable (and therefore insurable) interest in goods before tak-ing possession from the seller. ● The goods are identified in any manner agreed to by the parties. UCC § 2-501.

identification parade. See LINEUP.

identified adoption. See *private adoption* under ADOPTION.

identify, *vb.* (18c) **1.** To prove the identity of (a per-son or thing) <the witness identified the weapon>. **2.** To look upon as being associated (with) <the plaintiff was identified with the environmental movement>. **3.** To specify (certain goods) as the object of a contract <identify the appliances to the contract>. See IDENTIFICATION OF GOODS.

identifying material. *Copyright.* A portion or rep-resentation of an entire work deposited with the U.S. Copyright Office. ● A copyright registrant is required to deposit at least one complete copy of the work, and often two. If a trade secret would be disclosed by a deposit or the work's nature (e.g., a holograph) makes deposit difficult, a substitu-tion is acceptable. Common forms of identifying material are drawings, photocopies, and selected pages of software code and databases.

identikit. A collection of pictures of facial features, used by police to create a composite image of a suspect from witnesses' descriptions. ● In Great Britain, the resulting image is called a *photofit*.

identity. (16c) **1.** The identical nature of two or more things; esp., in patent law, the sameness in two devices of the function performed, the way it is performed, and the result achieved. ● Under the doctrine of equivalents, infringement may be found even if the accused device is not identi-cal to the claimed invention. See DOCTRINE OF EQUIVALENTS. **2.** *Evidence.* The authenticity of a person or thing.

identity of interests. (18c) *Civil procedure.* A re-lationship between two parties who are so close that suing one serves as notice to the other, so that the other may be joined in the suit. Fed. R. Civ. P. 15(c)(1)(c).

identity of parties. (1803) *Civil procedure.* A re-lationship between two parties who are so close that a judgment against one prevents later action against the other because of res judicata.

identity theft. The unlawful taking and use of another person's identifying information for fraudulent purposes. Cf. GHOSTING.

ideo (I-dee-oh), *adv.* [Latin] Therefore; for that reason.

ideo consideratum est (I-dee-oh kən-sid-ə-**ray**-təm est). [Latin] *Hist.* Therefore it is considered. ● These words often prefaced a judgment at common law, and came to refer to the judgment itself.

ideological aggression. 1. See *hostile propaganda* under PROPAGANDA. **2.** See *subversive propaganda* under PROPAGANDA.

idiocy. *Archaic.* The condition of a person who, from birth, has never had any glimmering of reasoning or intellectual faculties. — Also termed *idiopathic insanity.*

idiot. A person afflicted with profound mental retardation. ● This term has largely fallen out of use in modern legal and medical contexts. Cf. IMBECILE.

IDP. *abbr.* INTERNALLY DISPLACED PERSON.

IDS. *abbr.* INFORMATION-DISCLOSURE STATEMENT.

i.e. *abbr.* [Latin *id est*] (17c) That is <the federal government's highest judicial body, i.e., the Supreme Court>. Cf. E.G.

IEP. *abbr.* See INDIVIDUALIZED EDUCATION PROGRAM.

IFP. *abbr.* IN FORMA PAUPERIS.

IFP affidavit. See *poverty affidavit* under AFFIDAVIT.

ignominy (**ig**-nə-min-ee). Public disgrace or dishonor. — **ignominious,** *adj.*

ignoramus (ig-nə-**ray**-məs). [Law Latin] *Hist.* We do not know. ● This notation, when written on a bill of indictment, indicated the grand jury's rejection of the bill. See NOT FOUND; NO BILL. Cf. TRUE BILL.

ignorantia (ig-nə-**ran**-shee-ə). [Latin] Ignorance; esp., ignorance of the law.

ignorantia facti (ig-nə-**ran**-shee-ə **fak**-tI). [Latin] Ignorance of fact.

ignorantia facti excusat (ig-nə-**ran**-shee-ə **fak**-tI ek-**skyoo**-sat *or* -zat). [Latin] Ignorance of fact is an excuse; whatever is done under a mistaken impression of a material fact is excused or provides grounds for relief. ● This maxim refers to the principle that acts done and contracts made under mistake or ignorance of a material fact are voidable.

ignorantia juris (ig-nə-**ran**-shee-ə **joor**-is). [Latin] **1.** Ignorance of law. ● Under Roman law, this type of ignorance was less likely than *ignorantia facti* to excuse mistaken conduct, except in the case of minors and people, such as women, under some

legal disability. **2.** IGNORANTIA JURIS NON EXCUSAT.

ignorantia juris non excusat (ig-nə-**ran**-shee-ə **joor**-is non ek-**skyoo**-sat *or* -zat). [Latin] Lack of knowledge about a legal requirement or prohibition is never an excuse to a criminal charge. ● In English, the idea is commonly rendered *ignorance of the law is no excuse.* — Often shortened to *ignorantia juris.* — Also termed *ignorantia juris neminem excusat* (ignorance of the law excuses no one); *ignorantia legis non excusat; ignorantia juris haud excusat.*

ignoratio elenchi (ig-nə-**ray**-shee-oh e-**leng**-kI *or* ig-nə-**rah**-tee-oh i-**leng**-kee). [Law Latin "ignorance of the conclusion to be proved"] (16c) An advocate's misunderstanding of an opponent's position, manifested by an argument that fails to address the opponent's point; the overlooking of an opponent's counterargument. ● This fallacy of logic often involves an advocate's trying to prove something that is immaterial to the point to be decided.

ignore, *vb.* (1801) **1.** To refuse to notice, recognize, or consider. **2.** (Of a grand jury) to reject (an indictment) as groundless; to no-bill (a charge).

ignoring, *n.* *Family law.* A parent's or caregiver's pattern of depriving a child of essential intellectual or emotional stimulation or of otherwise stifling a child's emotional growth and intellectual development, essentially by being unavailable. Cf. ISOLATING; REJECTING.

IIED. *abbr.* INTENTIONAL INFLICTION OF EMOTIONAL DISTRESS.

ill, *adj.* (Of a pleading) defective, bad, or null.

illation (i-**lay**-shən). (16c) **1.** The act or process of inferring. **2.** An inference; that which is inferred.

illegal, *adj.* Forbidden by law; unlawful <illegal dumping> <an illegal drug>.

illegal alien. See ALIEN.

illegal bargain. See BARGAIN.

illegal consideration. See CONSIDERATION (1).

illegal contract. See CONTRACT.

illegal entry. (18c) **1.** *Criminal law.* The unlawful act of going into a building with the intent to commit a crime. ● In some jurisdictions, illegal entry is a lesser included offense of burglary. **2.** *Immigration.* The unauthorized entrance of an alien into the United States by arriving at the wrong time or place, by evading inspection, or by fraud.

illegal interest. See USURY.

illegality, *n.* (17c) **1.** An act that is not authorized by law. **2.** The state of not being legally authorized. **3.** The state or condition of being unlawful. ● The affirmative defense of illegality must be expressly set forth in the response to the opponent's pleading. Fed. R. Civ. P. 8(c).

illegally obtained evidence. See EVIDENCE.

illegal per se. Unlawful in and of itself.

illegal rate. See INTEREST RATE.

illegal search. See *unreasonable search* under SEARCH.

illegal strike. See STRIKE.

illegal subdivision. See SUBDIVISION.

illegal tax. See TAX.

illegal tax protester. See TAX PROTESTER.

illegal vote. See VOTE (1).

illegitimacy. (17c) **1.** Unlawfulness. **2.** The status of a person who is born outside a lawful marriage and who is not later legitimated by the parents. — Also termed *bastardy*. Cf. LEGITIMACY.

illegitimate, *adj.* (16c) **1.** (Of a child) born out of lawful wedlock and never having been legitimated <illegitimate son>. ● Under modern ecclesiastical law, a child born out of wedlock may be automatically legitimated if the parents later marry. A child conceived while the mother is married but born after she is divorced or widowed is considered legitimate. **2.** Against the law; unlawful <illegitimate contract for the sale of contraband>. **3.** Improper <illegitimate conduct>. **4.** Incorrectly inferred <illegitimate conclusion>. **5.** *Ecclesiastical law.* (Of a child) born within a marriage that is regarded as an invalid sacrament from its inception.

illegitimate child. See CHILD.

ill fame. Evil repute; notorious bad character.

illicit (i[l]-**lis**-ət), *adj.* (16c) Illegal or improper <illicit relations>.

illicit cohabitation. See COHABITATION.

Illinois land trust. See *land trust* under TRUST.

illiquid asset. See ASSET.

illusory (i-**loo**-sə-ree), *adj.* (17c) Deceptive; based on a false impression.

illusory appointment. See APPOINTMENT (4).

Illusory Appointment Act. An 1830 English statute providing that no appointment of property is to be declared invalid on grounds that it is illusory. ● This statute was repealed and reissued in 1925 as part of the Law of Property Act.

illusory contract. See CONTRACT.

illusory promise. See PROMISE.

illusory tenant. See TENANT.

illusory-transfer doctrine. The rule that the law disregards an inter vivos gift over which the donor retains so much control that there is no good-faith intent to relinquish the transferred property. ● The illusory-transfer doctrine is usu.

applied to inter vivos trusts in which the settlor retains an excessive control or an interest — for instance, one in which the settlor retains the income for life, the power to revoke, and substantial managerial powers. The leading case on this doctrine is *Newman v. Dore*, 9 N.E.2d 966 (N.Y. 1937). See *colorable transfer* under TRANSFER.

illusory trust. See TRUST.

illustrative evidence. See *demonstrative evidence* under EVIDENCE.

imaginary damages. See *punitive damages* under DAMAGES.

imagining. See COMPASSING.

imbargo. *Archaic.* See EMBARGO (1).

imbecile (**im**-bə-səl *or* -sil). A person afflicted with severe mental retardation. Cf. IDIOT.

imbezzle. *Archaic.* See EMBEZZLE.

imbracery. See EMBRACERY.

IMCO. *abbr.* INTERGOVERNMENTAL MARITIME CONSULTATIVE ORGANIZATION.

IME. *abbr.* **1.** INDEPENDENT MEDICAL EXAMINATION. **2.** INDEPENDENT MENTAL EVALUATION.

IMF. *abbr.* INTERNATIONAL MONETARY FUND.

imitation. *Trademarks.* An item that so resembles a trademarked item as to be likely to induce the belief that it is genuine. See SIMILARITY.

IMLS. *abbr.* INSTITUTE OF MUSEUM AND LIBRARY SERVICES.

immaterial, *adj.* (1893) (Of evidence) tending to prove some fact that is not properly at issue; lacking any logical connection with the consequential facts. Cf. IRRELEVANT. — **immateriality,** *n.*

immaterial averment. See AVERMENT.

immaterial evidence. See EVIDENCE.

immaterial fact. See FACT.

immaterial issue. See ISSUE (1).

immaterial variance. See VARIANCE (1).

immatriculation. *Int'l law.* The grant of nationality to and enrollment on the national registry of a merchant ship, thereby giving the ship the right to fly the registering nation's flag.

immaturity. See MINORITY (1).

immediate, *adj.* (15c) **1.** Occurring without delay; instant <an immediate acceptance>. **2.** Not separated by other persons or things <her immediate neighbor>. **3.** Having a direct impact; without an intervening agency <the immediate cause of the accident>. Cf. PROXIMATE. — **immediacy, immediateness,** *n.*

immediate annuity. See ANNUITY.

immediate breach. See BREACH OF CONTRACT.

immediate cause. See CAUSE (1).

immediate control. (1962) *Criminal procedure.* **1.** The area within an arrestee's reach. ● A police officer may conduct a warrantless search of this area to ensure the officer's safety and to prevent the arrestee from destroying evidence. **2.** Vehicular control that is close enough to allow the driver to instantly govern the vehicle's movements. ● A driver's failure to maintain immediate control over the vehicle could be evidence of negligence.

immediate death. See DEATH.

immediate descent. See DESCENT.

immediate family. See FAMILY.

immediate intent. See INTENT (1).

immediately-apparent requirement. (1978) *Criminal procedure.* The principle that a police officer must have probable cause to believe that an item is contraband before seizing it. ● This plain-view exception to the warrant requirement was first announced in *Coolidge v. New Hampshire*, 403 U.S. 443, 91 S.Ct. 2022 (1971).

immediately harmful behavior. See HARMFUL BEHAVIOR.

immediately pending motion. See MOTION (2).

immediate notice. See NOTICE.

immediate-notice clause. *Insurance.* A provision in many insurance policies obligating the insured to notify the insurer as soon as possible after a claim arises. ● A requirement in a policy for "prompt" or "immediate" notice — or that notice must be given "immediately," "at once," "forthwith," "as soon as practicable," or "as soon as possible" — generally means that the notice must be given within a reasonable time under the circumstances.

immediate past president. **1.** See PRESIDENT. **2.** See EMERITUS.

immediate possession. See POSSESSION.

immemorial (im-ə-**mor**-ee-əl), *adj.* (17c) Beyond memory or record; very old. See TIME IMMEMORIAL.

immemorial possession. See POSSESSION.

immemorial usage. See USAGE.

immigrant. (18c) A person who enters a country to settle there permanently; a person who immigrates. Cf. EMIGRANT.

   alien immigrant. An immigrant who has not yet been naturalized.

immigration, *n.* (17c) The act of entering a country with the intention of settling there permanently. Cf. EMIGRATION. — **immigrate,** *vb.* — **immigrant,** *n.*

Immigration and Nationality Act. A comprehensive federal law regulating immigration, naturalization, and the exclusion of aliens. 8 USCA §§ 1101–1537. — Also termed *Nationality Act.*

Immigration and Naturalization Service. A former U.S. Department of Justice agency that administered the Immigration and Nationality Act and operates the U.S. Border Patrol. — Abbr. INS. See UNITED STATES CITIZENSHIP AND IMMIGRATION SERVICES.

Immigration Appeals Board. See BOARD OF IMMIGRATION APPEALS.

imminent danger. See DANGER.

imminent hazard. See HAZARD (1).

imminently dangerous. See DANGEROUS.

imminent-peril doctrine. See EMERGENCY DOCTRINE (1).

immobilize, *vb.* (1871) To make immobile; esp., to turn (movable property) into immovable property or to turn (circulating capital) into fixed capital.

immoral consideration. See CONSIDERATION (1).

immoral contract. See CONTRACT.

immoral subject matter. **1.** *Patents.* Inventions that do not have a socially beneficial use. ● In the past, patents were denied for some categories of inventions, such as gambling devices and fraudulent products, esp. medicines. The doctrine is rarely used today. **2.** *Trademarks.* SCANDALOUS SUBJECT MATTER.

immovable, *n.* (*usu. pl.*) (16c) Property that cannot be moved; an object so firmly attached to land that it is regarded as part of the land. — Also termed *immovable thing.* See FIXTURE. Cf. MOVABLE. — **immovable,** *adj.*

immovable fixture. See FIXTURE.

immune, *adj.* Having immunity; exempt from a duty or liability.

immunity. (14c) **1.** Any exemption from a duty, liability, or service of process; esp., such an exemption granted to a public official or governmental unit. Cf. IMPUNITY.

   absolute immunity. (17c) A complete exemption from civil liability, usu. afforded to officials while performing particularly important functions, such as a representative enacting legislation and a judge presiding over a lawsuit. Cf. *qualified immunity.*

   congressional immunity. (1969) Either of two special immunities given to members of Congress: (1) the exemption from arrest while attending a session of the body to which the member belongs, excluding an arrest for treason, breach of the peace, or a felony, or (2) the exemption from arrest or questioning for any speech or debate entered into during a legislative session. U.S. Const. art. I, § 6, cl. 1. See SPEECH AND DEBATE CLAUSE.

   constitutional immunity. (1852) Immunity created by a constitution.

diplomatic immunity. (1911) The general exemption of diplomatic ministers from the operation of local law, the exception being that a minister who is plotting against the security of the host nation may be arrested and sent out of the country. • A minister's family shares in diplomatic immunity to a great, though ill-defined, degree.

discretionary immunity. (1965) A qualified immunity for a public official's acts, granted when the act in question required the exercise of judgment in carrying out official duties (such as planning and policy-making). 28 USCA § 2680(a).

executive immunity. (1941) **1.** The absolute immunity of the U.S. President or a state governor from civil damages for actions that are within the scope of official responsibilities. **2.** The qualified immunity from civil claims against lesser executive officials, who are liable only if their conduct violates clearly established constitutional or statutory rights. • Executive immunity generally protects an official while carrying out clearly established responsibilities about which a reasonable person would know. Cf. *executive privilege* under PRIVILEGE (3).

foreign immunity. The immunity of a foreign sovereign, its agents, and its instrumentalities from litigation in U.S. courts.

government immunity. See *sovereign immunity.*

intergovernmental immunity. (1935) The immunity between the federal and state governments based on their independent sovereignty. See INTERGOVERNMENTAL-IMMUNITY DOCTRINE.

judicial immunity. (1850) The immunity of a judge from civil liability arising from the performance of judicial duties.

legislative immunity. (1890) The immunity of a legislator from civil liability arising from the performance of legislative duties. See *congressional immunity.*

prosecutorial immunity. The absolute immunity of a prosecutor from civil liability for decisions made and actions taken in a criminal prosecution.

qualified immunity. (1877) Immunity from civil liability for a public official who is performing a discretionary function, as long as the conduct does not violate clearly established constitutional or statutory rights. — Also termed *prima facie privilege.* Cf. *absolute immunity.*

sovereign immunity. (1857) **1.** A government's immunity from being sued in its own courts without its consent. • Congress has waived most of the federal government's sovereign immunity. See FEDERAL TORT CLAIMS ACT. **2.** A state's immunity from being sued in federal court by the state's own citizens. — Also termed *government immunity*; *governmental immunity.*

work-product immunity. See WORK-PRODUCT RULE.

2. *Torts.* A doctrine providing a complete defense to a tort action. • Unlike a privilege, immunity does not negate the tort, and it must be raised affirmatively or it will be waived. Cf. PRIVILEGE (2).

charitable immunity. (1935) The immunity of a charitable organization from tort liability. • This immunity has been eliminated or restricted in most states. — Also termed *eleemosynary defense.*

corporate immunity. A corporate officer's immunity from personal liability for a tortious act committed while acting in good faith and within the course of corporate duties.

husband–wife immunity. (1951) The immunity of one spouse from a tort action by the other spouse for personal injury. • The immunity arose from the age-old notion that a husband and wife were one in the eyes of the law, so that one could not injure the other — there being no "other." Most states and the District of Columbia have abolished interspousal tort immunity either by judicial opinion or by statute. Some states have abolished the rule only in specific instances such as intentional or vehicular torts. — Also termed *interspousal immunity*; *interspousal tort immunity*; *marital immunity.*

interspousal immunity. See *husband–wife immunity*

judgmental immunity. See ERROR-OF-JUDGMENT RULE.

marital immunity. See *husband–wife immunity.*

parental immunity. (1930) **1.** The principle that children cannot sue their parents, and that parents cannot sue their children, for tort claims. • This tort immunity did not exist at English common law; it was created by American courts, first appearing in *Hewellette v. George*, 9 So. 885 (Miss. 1891). Many courts have abolished the doctrine for some purposes, such as actions by unemancipated minors against parents to recover for injuries sustained in motor-vehicle accidents. *See, e.g., Merrick v. Sutterlin*, 610 P.2d 891 (Wash. 1980) (en banc). Nor does the immunity apply when an injury is inflicted by the parent or child through willful, wanton, or criminal conduct. *See, e.g., Nudd v. Matsoukas*, 131 N.E.2d 525 (Ill. 1956). — Also termed *parent–child immunity*; *parental-immunity doctrine.* **2.** The principle that parents are not liable for damages caused by the ordinary negligence of their minor child. Cf. PARENTAL-LIABILITY STATUTE.

3. *Criminal law.* Freedom from prosecution granted by the government in exchange for the person's testimony. • By granting immunity, the government can compel testimony — despite the Fifth Amendment right against self-incrimination — because that testimony can no longer incriminate the witness.

> **pocket immunity.** (1983) Immunity that results from the prosecutor's decision not to prosecute, instead of from a formal grant of immunity. — Also termed *informal immunity.*

> **testimonial immunity.** (1938) Immunity from the use of the compelled testimony against the witness. • Any information derived from that testimony, however, is generally admissible against the witness.

> **transactional immunity.** (1966) Immunity from prosecution for any event or transaction described in the compelled testimony. • This is the broadest form of immunity.

> **use immunity.** (1970) Immunity from the use of the compelled testimony (or any information derived from that testimony) in a future prosecution against the witness. • After granting use immunity, the government can still prosecute if it shows that its evidence comes from a legitimate independent source. — Also termed *use/derivative-use immunity; derivative-use immunity.*

4. Freedom of a person against having a given legal relation altered by someone else's act or omission.

immunize, *vb.* (1892) To grant immunity to <the new legislation immunized the police officers from liability>.

impacted area. A region that is affected by some event; esp., a region in which the school population increases due to an influx of federal employees who are working on a federal project or activity, but the tax revenue declines due to the U.S. government's immunity from local taxes.

impact rule. (1865) *Torts.* The common-law requirement that physical contact must have occurred to allow damages for negligent infliction of emotional distress. • This rule has been abandoned in most jurisdictions. — Also termed *physical-impact rule.*

impair, *vb.* (17c) To diminish the value of (property or a property right). • This term is commonly used in reference to diminishing the value of a contractual obligation to the point that the contract becomes invalid or a party loses the benefit of the contract. See CONTRACTS CLAUSE.

impaired capital. See CAPITAL.

impairing the morals of a minor. (1931) The offense of an adult's engaging in sex-related acts, short of intercourse, with a minor. • Examples of this conduct are fondling, taking obscene photographs, and showing pornographic materials. — Also termed *unlawful sexual conduct with a minor; corrupting; corruption of a minor.* Cf. CONTRIBUTING TO THE DELINQUENCY OF A MINOR.

impairment, *n.* (14c) The fact or state of being damaged, weakened, or diminished <impairment of collateral>. — **impair,** *vb.*

> **severe impairment.** In social-security or disability law, a physical or mental impairment that greatly restricts a person's ability to perform ordinary, necessary tasks of daily life. See DISABILITY (2); MAJOR LIFE ACTIVITY.

impalement, *n.* (17c) *Hist.* An ancient mode of inflicting punishment by thrusting a sharp pole through the body. — Formerly also spelled *empalement.* — **impale,** *vb.*

impanel, *vb.* See EMPANEL.

impaneled jury. See JURY.

imparl (im-**pahrl**), *vb.* **1.** *Hist.* To request or obtain an imparlance. **2.** To confer with the opposing party in an effort to settle a dispute amicably; to discuss settlement.

imparlance (im-**pahr**-lənts). *Hist.* **1.** A continuance granted for the purpose of giving the requesting party (usu. the defendant) further time to answer the adversary's last pleading (esp. the plaintiff's writ, bill, or count), often so that the parties will have time to settle the dispute. • Imparlances were abolished in England in 1853. **2.** A petition for such a continuance. **3.** The permission granting such a continuance. — Formerly also spelled *emparlance.* — Also termed *licentia loquendi.*

> **general imparlance.** The allowance of time until the court's next term, without reserving to the defendant the benefit of any exception. • With this type of imparlance, the requesting defendant cannot later object to the jurisdiction of the court or plead any matter in abatement.

> **general special imparlance.** The allowance of time with a saving of all exceptions, so that a defendant might later plead not only in abatement but also to the jurisdiction.

> **special imparlance.** The allowance of time with a saving only of exceptions to the writ, bill, or count, but not to the court's jurisdiction.

impartial, *adj.* (16c) Unbiased; disinterested.

impartial chair. (1993) **1.** ARBITRATOR. **2.** MEDIATOR. — Also termed *impartial chairman.*

impartial expert. See EXPERT.

impartial jury. See JURY.

impartible (im-**pahr**-tə-bəl), *adj.* (14c) Indivisible <an impartible estate>.

impartible feud. See FEUD (1).

impasse (**im**-pas). A point in negotiations at which agreement cannot be reached. • A neutral third party (such as a mediator) is often called in to help resolve an impasse.

impeach, *vb.* (14c) **1.** To charge with a crime or misconduct; esp., to formally charge (a public official) with a violation of the public trust <President Nixon resigned from office to avoid being impeached>. • Impeaching a federal official, such as the President, the Vice President, or a judge, requires that a majority of the U.S. House of Representatives vote to return at least one article of impeachment to the U.S. Senate, itemizing the charges and explaining their factual grounds. Even if an official is impeached, removal from office does not occur unless two-thirds of the senators who are present vote for conviction. **2.** To discredit the veracity of (a witness) <the lawyer hoped that her star witness wouldn't be impeached on cross-examination>. **3.** To challenge the accuracy or authenticity of (a document) <the handwriting expert impeached the holographic will>.

impeachable offense. An offense for which a public official may legally be impeached, during the first step in a two-step process that may, depending on the vote in the U.S. Senate, lead to the official's removal from office. • The U.S. Constitution states that "[t]he President, Vice President and all civil Officers of the United States, shall be removed from Office on Impeachment for, and Conviction of, Treason, Bribery, or other high Crimes and Misdemeanors." The meaning of this language was much debated during the impeachment and trial of President Bill Clinton, against whom two articles of impeachment were returned by the House of Representatives. The question arose concerning what type of misdemeanor will suffice, and whether the *high* in *high crimes* modifies *misdemeanors* as well. No definitive answer resulted from the proceedings.

impeachment. (16c) **1.** The act (by a legislature) of calling for the removal from office of a public official, accomplished by presenting a written charge of the official's alleged misconduct; esp., the initiation of a proceeding in the U.S. House of Representatives against a federal official, such as the President or a judge. — Also termed *formal impeachment.* • Congress's authority to remove a federal official stems from Article II, Section 4 of the Constitution, which authorizes the removal of an official for "Treason, Bribery, or other high Crimes and Misdemeanors." The grounds upon which an official can be removed do not, however, have to be criminal in nature. They usu. involve some type of abuse of power or breach of the public trust. Articles of impeachment — which can be approved by a simple majority in the House — serve as the charging instrument for the later trial in the Senate. If the President is impeached, the Chief Justice of the Supreme Court presides over the Senate trial. The defendant can be removed from office by the vote of a two-thirds majority of the senators who are present. In the United Kingdom, impeachment is by the House of Commons and trial by the House of Lords. But no case has arisen there since 1801, and many British scholars consider impeachment obsolete. **2.** The act of discrediting a witness, as by catching the witness in a lie or by demonstrating that the witness has been convicted of a criminal offense. **3.** The act of challenging the accuracy or authenticity of evidence.

formal impeachment. **1.** The discrediting of a witness's testimony by confronting the witness with his or her specific untruthful acts, prior convictions, prior inconsistent statements, or the like. **2.** See IMPEACHMENT (1).

impeachment court. See COURT FOR THE TRIALS OF IMPEACHMENT.

impeachment evidence. See EVIDENCE.

impeachment of verdict. (1821) A party's attack on a verdict, alleging impropriety by a member of the jury.

impeachment of waste. *Hist.* An action for waste against the tenant of the harmed property.

impediment (im-**ped**-ə-mənt). (14c) A hindrance or obstruction; esp., some fact (such as legal minority) that bars a marriage if known beforehand and, if discovered after the ceremony, renders the marriage void or voidable.

canonical impediment. A ground for annulment recognized by canon law and developed by the ecclesiastical courts of the Roman Catholic Church. • Canonical impediments include affinity, impotence, disparity of worship, and previous religious profession.

civil impediment. A ground for annulment recognized by civil law of contracts, such as minority, unsoundness of mind, fraud, and duress. • The defects of fraud and duress may be waived, and the parties may confirm the marriage.

diriment impediment (**dir**-ə-mənt im-**ped**-ə-mənt), *n.* [fr. Latin *dirimens impedimentum* "nullifying impediment"] A fact that raises an absolute bar to marriage and renders a contracted marriage void. • Diriment impediments include consanguinity within a prohibited degree and a prior undissolved marriage. — Also termed *impedimenta dirimentia.*

imperative authority. See AUTHORITY (4).

imperative law. See LAW.

imperative theory of law. (1909) The theory that law consists of the general commands issued by a country or other political community to its subjects and enforced by courts with the sanction of physical force. ● Imperative theorists believe that if there are rules predating or independent of the country, those rules may closely resemble law or even substitute for it, but they are not law. See POSITIVE LAW. Cf. NATURAL LAW.

imperfect defense. See DEFENSE (1).

imperfect duty. See DUTY (1).

imperfect grant. See GRANT.

imperfect justification. See JUSTIFICATION.

imperfect obligation. See *moral obligation* under OBLIGATION.

imperfect ownership. See OWNERSHIP.

imperfect right. See RIGHT.

imperfect self-defense. See SELF-DEFENSE.

imperfect statute. See STATUTE.

imperfect title. See TITLE (2).

imperfect trust. See *executory trust* under TRUST.

imperfect usufruct. See *quasi-usufruct* (1) under USUFRUCT.

imperfect war. See WAR.

imperial state. See STATE.

imperium (im-**peer**-ee-əm), *n*. [Latin] *Roman law*. Power or dominion; esp., the legal authority wielded by superior magistrates under the Republic, and later by the emperor under the Empire. ● *Imperium* implied the right of military command, and the powers of corporal punishment, and of life and death over citizens. It was symbolized by the lictors who carried the *fasces* and an ax, which symbolized those powers. *Imperium* was also used less technically; it applied to lesser types of authority under Roman law, and thus had different meanings. For example, *imperium domesticum* described the power of the head of a household.

impermissible comment on the evidence. See COMMENT ON THE EVIDENCE.

impersonal. See IN REM.

impersonation. (18c) The act of impersonating someone. — Also termed *personation*.

false impersonation. (1878) The crime of falsely representing oneself as another person, usu. a law-enforcement officer, for the purpose of deceiving someone. See 18 USCA §§ 912–917. — Also termed *false personation*.

impertinent, *adj*. See IRRELEVANT.

impertinent evidence. See EVIDENCE.

impertinent matter. (18c) *Procedure*. In pleading, matter that is not relevant to the action or defense. ● A federal court may strike any impertinent matter from a pleading. Fed. R. Civ. P. 12(f). Cf. SCANDALOUS MATTER.

impinge, *vb*. (17c) To encroach or infringe (*on* or *upon*) <impinge on the defendant's rights>.

implead, *vb*. (14c) **1.** To bring (someone) into a lawsuit; esp., to bring (a new party) into the action. Cf. INTERPLEAD. **2.** *Hist*. To bring an action against; to accuse. — Formerly also spelled *emplead*; *empleet*.

impleader, *n*. (1918) A procedure by which a third party is brought into a lawsuit, esp. by a defendant who seeks to shift liability to someone not sued by the plaintiff. Fed. R. Civ. P. 14. — Also termed *third-party practice*; *vouching-in*. Cf. INTERPLEADER; INTERVENTION (1).

implementation plan. *Environmental law*. A detailed outline of steps needed to meet environmental-quality standards by an established time.

implicate, *vb*. (15c) **1.** To show (a person) to be involved in (a crime, misfeasance, etc.) <when he turned state's evidence, he implicated three other suspects>. **2.** To be involved or affected <three judges were implicated in the bribery>.

implication. (15c) **1.** The act of showing involvement in something, esp. a crime or misfeasance <the implication of the judges in the bribery scheme>. **2.** An inference drawn from something said or observed <the implication was that the scheme involved several persons>.

necessary implication. (18c) An implication so strong in its probability that anything to the contrary would be unreasonable.

implicit cost. See *opportunity cost* under COST (1).

implied, *adj*. (16c) Not directly expressed; recognized by law as existing inferentially <implied agreement>. See IMPLY (1). Cf. EXPRESS.

implied abandonment. See ABANDONMENT (10).

implied acceptance. See ACCEPTANCE (4).

implied acquittal. See ACQUITTAL.

implied actual knowledge. See *actual knowledge* (2) under KNOWLEDGE.

implied admission. See ADMISSION (1).

implied agency. See AGENCY (1).

implied amnesty. See AMNESTY.

implied assent. See ASSENT.

implied assertion. See *assertive conduct* under CONDUCT.

implied assumption. See ASSUMPTION.

implied assumption of the risk. See ASSUMPTION OF THE RISK.

implied authority. See AUTHORITY (1).

implied bias. See BIAS.

implied coercion. See UNDUE INFLUENCE (1).

implied color. See COLOR.

implied condition. See CONDITION (2).

implied confession. See CONFESSION.

implied consent. See CONSENT (1).

implied consideration. See CONSIDERATION (1).

implied contract. See CONTRACT.

implied contractual indemnity. See INDEMNITY.

implied covenant. See COVENANT (1).

implied covenant of good faith and fair dealing. See COVENANT (1).

implied crime. See *constructive crime* under CRIME.

implied dedication. See DEDICATION.

implied duty of cooperation. See DUTY (1).

implied easement. See EASEMENT.

implied indemnity. See INDEMNITY.

implied in fact, *adj.* Inferable from the facts of the case.

implied-in-fact condition. See CONDITION (2).

implied-in-fact contract. See CONTRACT.

implied in law, *n.* (1806) Imposed by operation of law and not because of any inferences that can be drawn from the facts of the case.

implied-in-law condition. See *constructive condition* under CONDITION (2).

implied-in-law contract. See CONTRACT.

implied intent. See INTENT (1).

implied license. See LICENSE.

implied license by acquiescence. See LICENSE.

implied license by conduct. See LICENSE.

implied license by equitable estoppel. See LICENSE.

implied license by legal estoppel. See LICENSE.

implied-license doctrine. 1. The principle that a person's specific conduct may be tantamount to a grant of permission to do something. **2.** The principle that in some specified circumstances a statute can be construed as supplying a necessary authority by operation of law.

implied malice. See MALICE.

implied negative covenant. See COVENANT (1).

implied notice. See NOTICE.

implied obligation. See *obediential obligation* under OBLIGATION.

implied partnership. See *partnership by estoppel* under PARTNERSHIP.

implied permission. See PERMISSION.

implied power. See POWER (3).

implied promise. See PROMISE.

implied reciprocal covenant. See COVENANT (4).

implied reciprocal servitude. See *implied reciprocal covenant* under COVENANT (4).

implied repeal. See REPEAL.

implied reservation. See RESERVATION.

implied-reservation-of-water doctrine. A legal doctrine permitting the federal government to use and control, for public purposes, water appurtenant to federal lands. See EMINENT DOMAIN.

implied term. See TERM (2).

implied trust. 1. See *constructive trust* under TRUST. **2.** See *resulting trust* under TRUST.

implied waiver. See WAIVER (1).

implied warranty. See WARRANTY (2).

implied warranty of fitness for a particular purpose. See WARRANTY (2).

implied warranty of habitability. See WARRANTY (2).

implied warranty of merchantability. See WARRANTY (2).

imply, *vb.* (14c) **1.** To express or involve indirectly; to suggest <the opinion implies that the court has adopted a stricter standard for upholding punitive-damages awards>. Cf. INFER. **2.** (Of a court) to impute or impose on equitable or legal grounds <the court implied a contract between the parties>. **3.** To read into (a document) <citing grounds of fairness, the court implied a condition that the parties had not expressed>. See *implied term* under TERM (2). — **implication,** *n.*

import, *n.* (16c) **1.** A product brought into a country from a foreign country where it originated <imports declined in the third quarter>. See PARALLEL IMPORTS. **2.** The process of bringing foreign goods into a country <the import of products affects the domestic economy in significant ways>. Cf. EXPORT (1), (2). **3.** The meaning; esp., the implied meaning <the court must decide the import of that obscure provision>. **4.** Importance; significance <time will tell the relative import of Judge Posner's decisions in American law>.

importation. (17c) The bringing of goods into a country from another country.

import duty. See DUTY (4).

imported litigation. (1927) One or more lawsuits brought in a state that has no interest in the dispute.

importer. (15c) A person or entity that brings goods into a country from a foreign country and pays customs duties.

Import–Export Clause. (1945) U.S. Const. art. I, § 10, cl. 2, which prohibits states from taxing imports or exports. • The Supreme Court has liberally interpreted this clause, allowing states to tax imports as long as the tax does not discriminate in favor of domestic goods. — Also termed *Export Clause*.

import letter of credit. See LETTER OF CREDIT.

import quota. See QUOTA.

import recording. See BOOTLEG RECORDING (1).

importune (im-por-t[y]oon), *vb.* (16c) To solicit forcefully; to request persistently, and sometimes irksomely.

impose, *vb.* (17c) To levy or exact (a tax or duty).

imposition. (14c) An impost or tax.

impositive fact. See FACT.

impossibility. (14c) **1.** The fact or condition of not being able to occur, exist, or be done. **2.** A fact or circumstance that cannot occur, exist, or be done. **3.** *Contracts.* A fact or circumstance that excuses performance because (1) the subject or means of performance has deteriorated, has been destroyed, or is no longer available, (2) the method of delivery or payment has failed, (3) a law now prevents performance, or (4) death or illness prevents performance. ● Increased or unexpected difficulty and expense do not usu. qualify as an impossibility and thus do not excuse performance. — Also termed *impossibility of performance*. **4.** The doctrine by which such a fact or circumstance excuses contractual performance. Cf. FRUSTRATION (2); IMPRACTICABILITY. **5.** *Criminal law.* A fact or circumstance preventing the commission of a crime.

factual impossibility. (1932) Impossibility due to the fact that the illegal act cannot physically be accomplished, such as trying to pick an empty pocket. ● Factual impossibility is not a defense to the crime of attempt. — Also termed *physical impossibility*; *impossibility of fact*.

legal impossibility. (1831) **1.** Impossibility due to the fact that what the defendant intended to do is not illegal even though the defendant might have believed that he or she was committing a crime. ● A legal impossibility might occur, for example, if a person goes hunting while erroneously believing that it is not hunting season. This type of legal impossibility is a defense to the crimes of attempt, conspiracy, and solicitation. — Also termed *impossibility of law*; *true legal impossibility*. **2.** Impossibility due to the fact that an element required for an attempt has not been satisfied. ● This type of legal impossibility might occur, for example, if a person pulls the trigger of an unloaded gun pointed at another when the crime of attempt requires that the gun be loaded. This is a defense to the crime of attempt.

objective impossibility. Impossibility due to the nature of the performance and not to the inability of the individual promisor.

subjective impossibility. Impossibility due wholly to the inability of the individual promisor and not to the nature of the performance.

supervening impossibility. Impossibility arising after the formation of a contract but before the time when the promisor's performance is due, and arising because of facts that the promisor had no reason to anticipate and did not contribute to the occurrence of.

impossibility-of-performance doctrine. (1960) The principle that a party may be released from a contract on the ground that uncontrollable circumstances have rendered performance impossible. Cf. FRUSTRATION (2); IMPRACTICABILITY.

impossible consideration. See CONSIDERATION (1).

impossible contract. See CONTRACT.

impost (**im**-pohst). (16c) A tax or duty, esp. a customs duty <the impost was assessed when the ship reached the mainland>. See DUTY (4).

impostor (im-**pos**-tər). (16c) One who pretends to be someone else to deceive others, esp. to receive the benefits of a negotiable instrument. — Also spelled *imposter*.

impostor rule. *Commercial law.* The principle that an impostor's indorsement of a negotiable instrument is not a forgery, and that the drawer or maker who issues the instrument to the impostor is negligent and therefore liable to the holder for payment. ● If a drawer or maker issues an instrument to an impostor, any resulting forgery of the payee's name will be effective in favor of a person paying on the instrument in good faith or taking it for value or collection. UCC § 3-404.

impotence (**im**-pə-tənts). (15c) **1.** A man's inability to achieve an erection and therefore to have sexual intercourse. ● Because an impotent husband cannot consummate a marriage, impotence has often been cited as a ground for annulment. — Also termed *impotency*; *physical incapacity*; *erectile dysfunction.* **2.** *Hist.* Sterility. **3.** *Rare.* A woman's physical inability to engage in sexual intercourse.

impound, *n.* The portion of a monthly mortgage payment that is earmarked to pay property taxes and the property-insurance premiums. See *impound account* under ACCOUNT.

impound, *vb.* (15c) **1.** To place (something, such as a car or other personal property) in the custody of the police or the court, often with the understanding that it will be returned intact at the end of the proceeding. **2.** To take and retain possession of (something, such as a forged document to be produced as evidence) in preparation for a criminal prosecution.

impound account. See ACCOUNT.

impoundment. (17c) **1.** The action of impounding; the state of being impounded. See IMPOUND. **2.** *Constitutional law.* The President's refusal to spend funds appropriated by Congress. • Although not authorized by the Constitution and seldom used, impoundment effectively gives the executive branch a line-item veto over legislative spending.

impracticability (im-prak-ti-kə-**bil**-ə-tee). (17c) *Contracts.* **1.** A fact or circumstance that excuses a party from performing an act, esp. a contractual duty, because (though possible) it would cause extreme and unreasonable difficulty. • For performance to be truly impracticable, the duty must become much more difficult or much more expensive to perform, and this difficulty or expense must have been unanticipated. **2.** The doctrine by which such a fact or circumstance excuses performance. Cf. FRUSTRATION (2); IMPOSSIBILITY (4).

commercial impracticability. (1913) The occurrence of a contingency whose nonoccurrence was an assumption in the contract, as a result of which one party cannot perform. — Also termed (in the UCC) *excuse by failure of presupposed conditions.*

imprescriptible (im-prə-**skrip**-tə-bəl), *adj.* (16c) Not subject to prescription; not capable of being acquired by prescription.

imprescriptible right. See RIGHT.

impressment (im-**pres**-mənt), *n.* (18c) **1.** The act of forcibly taking (something) for public service. **2.** A court's imposition of a constructive trust on equitable grounds. See *constructive trust* under TRUST. **3.** *Archaic.* The method by which armed forces were formerly expanded, when so-called press-gangs seized men off the streets and forced them to join the army or navy. — **impress,** *vb.*

imprest fund. See FUND (1).

imprest money (**im**-prest). A payment made to a soldier or sailor upon enlistment or impressment.

imprimatur (im-pri-**may**-tər *or* -**mah**-tər). [Latin "let it be printed"] (17c) **1.** A license required to publish a book. • Once required in England, the imprimatur is now encountered only rarely in countries that censor the press. **2.** A general grant of approval; commendatory license or sanction.

imprimis (im-**prI**-mis), *adv.* [fr. Latin *in primis* "in the first"] (15c) In the first place. — Also termed *in primis.*

imprison, *vb.* (14c) To confine (a person) in prison.

imprisonment, *n.* (14c) **1.** The act of confining a person, esp. in a prison <the imprisonment of Jackson was entirely justified>. **2.** The state of being confined; a period of confinement <Jackson's imprisonment lasted 14 years>. See FALSE IMPRISONMENT.

imprisonment for debt. *Hist.* Detention of a debtor by court order to force the debtor to pay certain civil obligations. • The remedy was usu. available only when the debt arose from nonpayment of taxes or fines owed to the Crown, or from the debtor's failure to pay court-ordered support or alimony, or from the debtor's failure to obey a decree *ad factum praestandum.* — Also termed *civil imprisonment.* See *decree ad factum praestandum* under DECREE.

improper, *adj.* (15c) **1.** Incorrect; unsuitable or irregular. **2.** Fraudulent or otherwise wrongful.

improper cumulation of actions. *Hist.* Under the common-law pleading system, the joining of inconsistent causes of action in one proceeding. • This is permitted under most modern pleading systems.

improper feud. See FEUD (1).

improper influence. See UNDUE INFLUENCE (2).

improper means of discovery. *Trade secrets.* A wrongful way of figuring out a competitor's trade secret, as by misrepresentation, eavesdropping, or stealing.

improper motion. See MOTION (2).

impropriation (im-proh-pree-**ay**-shən). *Eccles. law.* The grant of an ecclesiastical benefice to the use of a lay person, whether individual or corporate. Cf. APPROPRIATION (5).

improve, *vb.* (16c) **1.** To increase the value or enhance the appearance of something. **2.** To develop (land), whether or not the development results in an increase or a decrease in value. — **improver,** *n.*

improved land. See LAND.

improved value. (1834) *Real estate.* In the appraisal of property, the value of the land plus the value of any improvements.

improvement. (16c) An addition to real property, whether permanent or not; esp., one that increases its value or utility or that enhances its appearance. — Also termed *land improvement.* Cf. FIXTURE.

beneficial improvement. See *valuable improvement.*

general improvement. (17c) An improvement whose primary purpose or effect is to benefit the public generally, though it may incidentally benefit property owners in its vicinity.

local improvement. (1831) A real-property improvement, such as a sewer or sidewalk, financed by special assessment, and specially benefiting adjacent property.

necessary improvement. (17c) An improvement made to prevent the deterioration of property.

public improvement. An improvement made to property owned by the state or any other political entity, such as a municipality.

valuable improvement. (18c) An improvement that adds permanent value to the freehold. • Because of its nature, a valuable improvement would not typically be made by anyone other than the owner. A valuable improvement may be slight and of small value, as long as it is both permanent and beneficial to the property. — Also termed *beneficial improvement.*

voluntary improvement. An improvement whose only purpose is ornamental.

improvement bond. See *revenue bond* under BOND (3).

improvement claim. See *Jepson claim* under PATENT CLAIM.

improvement invention. See INVENTION.

improvement patent. See PATENT (3).

improvidence (im-**prahv**-ə-dənts). (15c) A lack of foresight and care in the management of property, esp. as grounds for removing an estate administrator.

improvident (im-**prahv**-ə-dənt), *adj.* (16c) 1. Lacking foresight and care in the management of property. 2. Of or relating to a judgment arrived at by using misleading information or a mistaken assumption.

impugn (im-**pyoon**), *vb.* (14c) To challenge or call into question (a person's character, the truth of a statement, etc.). — **impugnment,** *n.*

impulse, *n.* (17c) A sudden urge or inclination that prompts an unplanned action.

uncontrollable impulse. (1844) An impulse so overwhelming that it cannot be resisted. • In some jurisdictions, an uncontrollable impulse serves as a defense to criminal conduct committed while in the grip of the impulse. See IRRESISTIBLE-IMPULSE TEST.

impunity (im-**pyoo**-nə-tee). (16c) Exemption from punishment; immunity from the detrimental effects of one's actions <because she was a foreign diplomat, she was able to park illegally with impunity>. Cf. IMMUNITY (1).

imputation, *n.* (16c) The act or an instance of imputing something, esp. fault or crime, to a person; an accusation or charge <an imputation of negligence>.

imputation of payment. *Civil law.* The act of applying or directing a payment to principal or interest on a debt, or to a particular debt when there are two or more. La. Civ. Code arts. 1864, 1866.

impute (im-**pyoot**), *vb.* (14c) To ascribe or attribute; to regard (usu. something undesirable) as being done, caused, or possessed by <the court imputed malice to the defamatory statement>. — **imputation,** *n.* — **imputable,** *adj.*

imputed disqualification. See *vicarious disqualification* under DISQUALIFICATION.

imputed income. See INCOME.

imputed interest. See INTEREST (3).

imputed knowledge. See KNOWLEDGE.

imputed negligence. See NEGLIGENCE.

imputed notice. See NOTICE.

in, *prep.* Under or based on the law of <to bring an action in contract>.

in absentia (in ab-**sen**-shee-ə *or* ab-**sen**-shə). [Latin] (1886) In the absence of (someone); in (someone's) absence <tried in absentia>.

inaccuracy rejection. See REJECTION.

in action. (18c) (Of property) attainable or recoverable through litigation. See *chose in action* under CHOSE.

inactive case. See CASE.

inactive stock. See STOCK.

inadequate assistance of counsel. See *ineffective assistance of counsel* under ASSISTANCE OF COUNSEL.

inadequate consideration. See CONSIDERATION (1).

inadequate damages. See DAMAGES.

inadequate remedy at law. (1817) A remedy (such as money damages) that does not sufficiently correct the wrong, as a result of which an injunction may be available to the disadvantaged party. See IRREPARABLE-INJURY RULE.

inadmissible, *adj.* (18c) 1. (Of a thing) not allowable or worthy of being admitted. 2. (Of evidence) excludable by some rule of evidence. 3. (Of an alien) ineligible for admission into a country or (if the alien has already entered illegally) subject to removal.

inadmissible alien. See ALIEN.

inadvertence, *n.* (15c) An accidental oversight; a result of carelessness.

inadvertent discovery. (1971) *Criminal procedure.* A law-enforcement officer's unexpected finding of incriminating evidence in plain view. • Even though this type of evidence is obtained without a warrant, it can be used against the accused under the plain-view exception to the warrant requirement.

inadvertent negligence. See NEGLIGENCE.

inalienable, *adj.* (17c) Not transferable or assignable <inalienable property interests>. — Also termed *unalienable.*

inalienable interest. See INTEREST (2).

inalienable right. See RIGHT.

inarbitrable, *adj.* (18c) **1.** (Of a dispute) not capable of being arbitrated; not subject to arbitration. **2.** Not subject to being decided.

in arrears (in ə-**reerz**), *adj.* & *adv.* (17c) **1.** Behind in the discharging of a debt or other obligation <the tenants were in arrears with the rent>. **2.** At the end of a term or period instead of the beginning <the interests, fees, and costs are payable in arrears>.

inauguration (i-naw-gyə-**ray**-shən), *n.* (16c) **1.** A formal ceremony inducting someone into office. **2.** A formal ceremony introducing something into public use. **3.** The formal commencement of a period of time or course of action. — **inaugurate** (i-**naw**-gyə-rayt), *vb.* — **inauguratory** (i-**naw**-gyə-rə-tor-ee), *adj.* — **inaugurator** (i-**naw**-gyə-ray-tər), *n.*

in banc. See EN BANC.

in banco. See EN BANC.

in bank. See EN BANC.

in being. (17c) Existing in life <life in being plus 21 years>. ● In property law, this term includes children conceived but not yet born. — Also termed *in esse.* See LIFE IN BEING.

in blank. (1836) (Of an indorsement) not restricted to a particular indorsee. See *blank indorsement* under INDORSEMENT.

inboard, *adj. Maritime law.* (Of cargo) stowed between the boards (i.e., sides) of the vessel; esp., stowed inside or near the vessel's centerline.

Inc. *abbr.* Incorporated.

in cahoots. See CAHOOTS.

in camera (in kam-ə-rə), *adv.* & *adj.* [Law Latin "in a chamber"] (1872) **1.** In the judge's private chambers. **2.** In the courtroom with all spectators excluded. **3.** (Of a judicial action) taken when court is not in session. — Also termed (in reference to the opinion of one judge) *in chambers.*

in camera inspection. (1953) A trial judge's private consideration of evidence.

in camera proceeding. See PROCEEDING.

in camera sitting. See SITTING.

incapacitated person. (1834) A person who is impaired by an intoxicant, by mental illness or deficiency, or by physical illness or disability to the extent that personal decision-making is impossible.

incapacitation, *n.* (18c) **1.** The action of disabling or depriving of legal capacity. **2.** The state of being disabled or lacking legal capacity. — **incapacitate,** *vb.*

incapacity. (17c) **1.** Lack of physical or mental capabilities. **2.** Lack of ability to have certain legal consequences attach to one's actions. ● For example, a five-year-old has an incapacity to make a

binding contract. **3.** DISABILITY (2). **4.** DISABILITY (3). Cf. INCOMPETENCY.

testimonial incapacity. (1867) The lack of capacity to testify.

in capita. Individually. See PER CAPITA.

in capite (in kap-ə-tee). [Law Latin "in chief"] *Hist.* A type of tenure in which a person held land directly of the Crown. — Also termed *tenure in capite.*

incarceration, *n.* (16c) The act or process of confining someone; IMPRISONMENT. Cf. DISIMPRISONMENT; DECARCERATION. — **incarcerate,** *vb.* — **incarcerator,** *n.*

shock incarceration. (1985) Incarceration in a military-type setting, usu. for three to six months, during which the offender is subjected to strict discipline, physical exercise, and hard labor. *See* 18 USCA § 4046. ● After successfully completing the program, the offender is usu. placed on probation. See BOOT CAMP. Cf. *shock probation* under PROBATION.

incendiary (in-**sen**-dee-er-ee), *n.* (15c) **1.** One who deliberately and unlawfully sets fire to property. — Also termed *arsonist; firebug.* **2.** An instrument (such as a bomb) or chemical agent designed to start a fire. — **incendiary,** *adj.*

incentive pay plan. (1948) A compensation plan in which increased productivity is rewarded with higher pay.

incentive stock option. See STOCK OPTION (2).

incentive theory. *Intellectual property.* The proposition that society grants creators exclusive rights to their intellectual property in order to stimulate further creativity. ● The Patent and Copyright Clause of the U.S. Constitution declares that the purpose of exclusive-right protection is "to Promote the Progress of Science and useful Arts." U.S. Const. art. I, § 8, cl. 8.

incentive-to-commercialize theory. *Patents.* The economic theory justifying the grant of patent rights based on how efficient the patent system is at bringing together diverse resources such as commercial backing, manufacturing capacity, marketing know-how, and other skills that the inventor alone would be unable to handle. — Also termed *incentive-to-invest theory; incentive-to-innovate theory; prospect theory.* Cf. INCENTIVE-TO-DESIGN-AROUND THEORY; INCENTIVE-TO-DISCLOSE THEORY; INCENTIVE-TO-INVENT THEORY.

incentive-to-design-around theory. *Patents.* The economic theory justifying the grant of patent rights based on their tendency to encourage others to design substitutes and improvements that are better or cheaper. Cf. INCENTIVE-TO-COMMERCIALIZE THEORY; INCENTIVE-TO-DISCLOSE THEORY; INCENTIVE-TO-INVENT THEORY.

incentive-to-disclose theory. *Patents.* The economic theory justifying the grant of patent rights based on the social benefit of having the information enter the public domain. • Without the incentive, the argument goes, the technical advancements would remain trade secrets and the duplication of research efforts would be a waste to society. Cf. INCENTIVE-TO- COMMERCIALIZE THEORY; INCENTIVE-TO-DESIGN-AROUND THEORY; INCENTIVE-TO-INVENT THEORY.

incentive-to-innovate theory. See INCENTIVE-TO-COMMERCIALIZE THEORY.

incentive-to-invent theory. *Patents.* The economic theory justifying the grant of patent rights based on their tendency to encourage new inventions that benefit society and that may not otherwise be developed. Cf. INCENTIVE-TO-COMMERCIALIZE THEORY; INCENTIVE-TO-DESIGN-AROUND THEORY; INCENTIVE-TO-DISCLOSE THEORY.

incentive-to-invest theory. See INCENTIVE-TO-COMMERCIALIZE THEORY.

incentive zoning. See ZONING.

incest, *n.* (13c) **1.** Sexual relations between family members or close relatives, including children related by adoption. • Incest was not a crime under English common law but was punished as an ecclesiastical offense. Modern statutes make it a felony. **2.** Intermarriage between persons related in any degree of consanguinity or affinity within which marriage is prohibited — for example, through the uncle–niece or aunt–nephew relationship. — **incestuous,** *adj.*

incestuous adultery. See ADULTERY.

in chambers. See IN CAMERA.

in chief. (17c) **1.** Principal, as opposed to collateral or incidental. **2.** Denoting the part of a trial in which the main body of evidence is presented. See CASE-IN-CHIEF.

***Inchmaree* clause** (**inch**-mə-ree). *Maritime law.* An insurance-policy provision that protects against risks not caused by nature, such as a sailor's negligence or a latent defect in machinery. • This term is taken from a British ship, the *Inchmaree*, whose sinking in 1884 gave rise to litigation that led to the clause bearing its name. *See Thames & Mersey Marine Ins. Co. v. Hamilton, Fraser & Co.,* [1887] L.R. 12 App. Cas. 484. — Also termed *additional-perils clause.*

inchoate (in-**koh**-it), *adj.* (16c) Partially completed or imperfectly formed; just begun. Cf. CHOATE. — **inchoateness,** *n.*

inchoate crime. See *inchoate offense* under OFFENSE (1).

inchoate dower. See DOWER.

inchoate instrument. See INSTRUMENT (3).

inchoate interest. See INTEREST (2).

inchoate lien. See LIEN.

inchoate offense. See OFFENSE (1).

inchoate right. 1. A right that has not fully developed, matured, or vested. **2.** *Patents.* An inventor's right that has not yet vested into a property right because the patent application is pending.

incident, *adj.* (15c) Dependent upon, subordinate to, arising out of, or otherwise connected with (something else, usu. of greater importance) <the utility easement is incident to the ownership of the tract>.

incident, *n.* (15c) **1.** A discrete occurrence or happening <an incident of copyright infringement> **2.** A dependent, subordinate, or consequential part (of something else) <child support is a typical incident of divorce>.

incidental, *adj.* (17c) Subordinate to something of greater importance; having a minor role <the FAA determined that the wind played only an incidental part in the plane crash>.

incidental admission. See ADMISSION (1).

incidental authority. See AUTHORITY (1).

incidental beneficiary. See BENEFICIARY.

incidental damages. See DAMAGES.

incidental demand. See DEMAND (1).

incidental main motion. See MOTION (2).

incidental motion. See MOTION (2).

incidental power. See *incident power* under POWER (3).

incidental use. See USE (1).

incident of ownership. (*usu. pl.*) (1821) Any right of control that may be exercised over a transferred life-insurance policy so that the policy's proceeds will be included in a decedent's gross estate for estate-tax purposes <because Douglas still retained the incidents of ownership after giving his life-insurance policy to his daughter, the policy proceeds were taxed against his estate>. • The incidents of ownership include the rights to change the policy's beneficiaries and to borrow against, assign, and cancel the policy.

incident power. See POWER (3).

incident to employment. *Workers' compensation.* A risk that is related to or connected with a worker's job duties.

incite, *vb.* (15c) To provoke or stir up (someone to commit a criminal act, or the criminal act itself). Cf. ABET.

incitee. A person who has been incited, esp. to commit a crime.

inciteful, *adj.* Tending to incite <inciteful speech>.

incitement, *n.* (15c) **1.** The act or an instance of provoking, urging on, or stirring up. **2.** *Criminal law.*

The act of persuading another person to commit a crime; SOLICITATION (2). — **inciteful,** *adj.*

inciter. (15c) A person who incites another to commit a crime; an aider or abettor.

inciting revolt. See MUTINY.

incivism (**in**-si-viz-əm). (18c) Unfriendliness toward one's own country or its government; lack of good citizenship.

inclose, *vb.* See ENCLOSE.

inclosure. See ENCLOSURE.

include, *vb.* (15c) To contain as a part of something. • The participle *including* typically indicates a partial list <the plaintiff asserted five tort claims, including slander and libel>. But some drafters use phrases such as *including without limitation* and *including but not limited to* — which mean the same thing. See NAMELY.

included offense. See *lesser included offense* under OFFENSE (1).

inclusionary-approach rule. (1981) The principle that evidence of a prior crime, wrong, or act is admissible for any purpose other than to show a defendant's criminal propensity as long as it is relevant to some disputed issue and its probative value outweighs its prejudicial effect.

inclusio unius est exclusio alterius. See EXPRESSIO UNIUS EST EXCLUSIO ALTERIUS.

inclusive deed. See *inclusive grant* under GRANT.

inclusive grant. See GRANT.

inclusive legal positivism. See INCORPORATIONISM.

inclusive survey. See SURVEY.

incognito (in-kog-**nee**-toh *or* in-**kog**-ni-toh), *adj.* or *adv.* [Latin "unknown"] (17c) Without making one's name or identity known <Binkley flew incognito to France>.

income. (16c) The money or other form of payment that one receives, usu. periodically, from employment, business, investments, royalties, gifts, and the like. See EARNINGS. Cf. PROFIT.

accrued income. (1869) Money earned but not yet received.

accumulated income. Income that is retained in an account; esp., income that a trust has generated, but that has not yet been reinvested or distributed by the trustee.

accumulated taxable income. The income of a corporation as adjusted for certain items (such as excess charitable contributions), less the dividends-paid deduction and the accumulated-earnings credit. • It serves as the base upon which the accumulated-earnings tax is imposed. See *accumulated-earnings tax* under TAX.

active income. (1972) **1.** Wages; salary. **2.** Income from a trade or business.

adjusted gross income. (1940) Gross income minus allowable deductions specified in the tax code. — Abbr. AGI.

adjusted ordinary gross income. A corporation's gross income less capital gains and certain expenses. • The IRS uses this calculation to determine whether a corporation is a personal holding company. If 60% or more of a corporation's AOGI consists of certain passive investment income, the company has met the test for personal-holding-company classification. IRC (26 USCA) § 543(b). — Abbr. AOGI. See *personal holding company* under COMPANY.

aggregate income. (1926) The combined income of a husband and wife who file a joint tax return.

blocked income. Money earned by a foreign taxpayer but not subject to U.S. taxation because the foreign country prohibits changing the income into dollars.

current income. Income that is due within the present accounting period. — Also termed *current revenue.*

deferred income. (1918) Money received at a time later than when it was earned, such as a check received in January for commissions earned in November.

disposable income. (1960) Income that may be spent or invested after payment of taxes and other primary obligations. — Also termed *disposable earnings.*

distributable net income. (1918) The amount of distributions from estates and trusts that the beneficiaries will have to include in income.

dividend income. (1930) The income resulting from a dividend distribution and subject to tax.

earned income. (1894) Money derived from one's own labor or active participation; earnings from services. Cf. *unearned income* (2).

exempt income. (1947) Income that is not subject to income tax.

fixed income. Money received at a constant rate, such as a payment from a pension or annuity.

gross income. (1843) Total income from all sources before deductions, exemptions, or other tax reductions. See IRC (26 USCA) § 61. — Also termed *gross earnings.*

imputed income. (1948) The benefit one receives from the use of one's own property, the performance of one's services, or the consumption of self-produced goods and services.

income in respect of a decedent. (1945) Income earned by a person, but not collected before death. • This income is included in the decedent's gross estate for estate-tax purposes. For income-tax purposes, it is taxed to the estate or, if the estate does not collect the income, it is taxed to the eventual recipient. — Abbr. IRD.

investment income. See *unearned income* (1).

net income. (18c) Total income from all sources minus deductions, exemptions, and other tax reductions. • Income tax is computed on net income. — Also termed *net earnings.*

net operating income. Income derived from operating a business, after subtracting operating costs.

nonoperating income. Business income derived from investments rather than operations.

operating income. See *ordinary income* (1).

ordinary income. (1860) **1.** For business-tax purposes, earnings from the normal operations or activities of a business. — Also termed *operating income.* **2.** For individual income-tax purposes, income that is derived from sources such as wages, commissions, and interest (as opposed to income from capital gains).

other income. Income not derived from an entity's principal business, such as earnings from dividends and interest.

passive income. (1958) Income derived from a business, rental, or other income-producing activity that the earner does not directly participate in or has no immediate control over. See PASSIVE ACTIVITY. Cf. *portfolio income.*

passive investment income. Investment income that does not involve or require active participation, such as gross receipts from royalties, rental income, dividends, interest, annuities, and gains from the sale or exchange of securities. IRC (26 USCA) § 1362(d).

personal income. (1851) The total income received by an individual from all sources.

portfolio income. (1978) Income not derived in the ordinary course of a trade or business, such as interest earned on savings, dividends, royalties, capital gains, or other investment sources. • For tax purposes, losses on passive activities cannot be used to offset net portfolio income. Cf. *passive income.*

prepaid income. (1935) Income received but not yet earned. — Also termed *deferred revenue.*

previously taxed income. An S corporation's undistributed taxable income taxed to the shareholders as of the last day of the corporation's tax year. • This income could usu. be withdrawn later by the shareholders without tax consequences. PTI has been replaced by the accumulated adjustments account. — Abbr. PTI.

real income. Income adjusted to allow for inflation or deflation so that it reflects true purchasing power.

regular income. Income that is received at fixed or specified intervals.

split income. (1949) An equal division between spouses of earnings reported on a joint tax return, allowing for equal tax treatment in community-property and common-law states.

taxable income. (1856) Gross income minus all allowable deductions and exemptions. • Taxable income is multiplied by the applicable tax rate to compute one's tax liability.

unearned income. (1921) **1.** Earnings from investments rather than labor. — Also termed *investment income.* **2.** Income received but not yet earned; money paid in advance. Cf. *earned income.*

unrelated-business income. (1952) *Tax.* Gross income earned by a nonprofit corporation from activities unrelated to its nonprofit functions. • A nonprofit corporation's income is tax-exempt only to the extent that it is produced by activities directly related to its nonprofit purpose. — Also termed *unrelated-business taxable income.* IRC (26 USCA) § 512(a)(3)(A).

income-and-expense declaration. *Family law.* In child-support litigation, a document that contains information on a parent's income, assets, expenses, and liabilities. — Also termed *financial statement.*

income approach. (1951) A method of appraising real property based on capitalization of the income that the property is expected to generate. — Also termed *income-capitalization approach.* Cf. MARKET APPROACH; COST APPROACH.

income averaging. *Tax.* A method of computing tax by averaging a person's current income with that of preceding years.

income-based plan. See CHAPTER 13.

income-basis method. A method of computing the rate of return on a security using the interest and price paid rather than the face value.

income beneficiary. See BENEFICIARY.

income bond. See BOND (3).

income-capitalization approach. See INCOME APPROACH.

income exclusion. See EXCLUSION (1).

income fund. See MUTUAL FUND.

income in respect of a decedent. See INCOME.

income property. See PROPERTY.

income-shifting. (1957) The practice of transferring income to a taxpayer in a lower tax bracket, such as a child, to reduce tax liability. • Often this is accomplished by forming a Clifford trust.

See *Clifford trust* under TRUST; *kiddie tax* under TAX.

income statement. (1863) A statement of all the revenues, expenses, gains, and losses that a business incurred during a given period. — Also termed *statement of income; profit-and-loss statement; earnings report.* Cf. BALANCE SHEET.

income stock. See STOCK.

income tax. See TAX.

income-tax deficiency. See DEFICIENCY (2).

income-tax return. See TAX RETURN.

income-tax withholding. See WITHHOLDING.

income-withholding order. (1986) A court order providing for the withholding of a person's income by an employer, usu. to enforce a child-support order. — Also termed *wage-withholding order; wage-assignment order; wage assignment.* Cf. ATTACHMENT OF WAGES.

income yield. See CAPITALIZATION RATE.

in common. (16c) Shared equally with others, undivided into separately owned parts. — Also termed *in communi.* See *tenancy in common* under TENANCY.

incommunicado (in-kə-myoo-ni-**kah**-doh), *adj.* [Spanish] (1844) **1.** Without any means of communication. **2.** (Of a prisoner) having the right to communicate with only a few designated people.

incommutable (in-kə-**myoot**-ə-bəl), *adj.* (18c) (Of an offense) not capable of being commuted. See COMMUTATION.

incompatibility, *n.* (1875) Conflict in personality and disposition, usu. leading to the breakup of a marriage. ● Every state now recognizes some form of incompatibility as a no-fault ground for divorce. See *no-fault divorce* under DIVORCE. Cf. IRRECONCILABLE DIFFERENCES; IRRETRIEVABLE BREAKDOWN OF THE MARRIAGE.

Incompatibility Clause. The clause of the U.S. Constitution prohibiting a person from simultaneously holding offices in both the executive and legislative branches of the federal government. U.S. Const. art. I, § 6, par. 2, cl. 2.

incompetence, *n.* (17c) **1.** The state or fact of being unable or unqualified to do something <the dispute was over her alleged incompetence as a legal assistant>. **2.** INCOMPETENCY <the court held that the affidavit was inadmissible because of the affiant's incompetence>.

incompetency, *n.* (17c) Lack of legal ability in some respect, esp. to stand trial or to testify <once the defense lawyer established her client's incompetency, the client did not have to stand trial>. — Also termed *incompetence; mental incompetence.* Cf. INCAPACITY. — **incompetent,** *adj.*

incompetency hearing. See PATE HEARING.

incompetent, *adj.* (16c) **1.** (Of a witness) unqualified to testify. **2.** (Of evidence) inadmissible. ● This sense is often criticized, as in the quotation below.

incompetent evidence. See EVIDENCE.

incomplete instrument. See INSTRUMENT (3).

incompleteness rejection. See REJECTION.

incomplete transfer. See TRANSFER.

inconclusive, *adj.* (18c) (Of evidence) not leading to a conclusion or definite result.

in consimili casu (in kən-**sim**-ə-lı **kay**-s[y]oo). See CASU CONSIMILI.

inconsistent, *adj.* (17c) Lacking agreement among parts; not compatible with another fact or claim <inconsistent statements>.

inconsistent defense. See DEFENSE (1).

inconsistent presumption. See *conflicting presumption* under PRESUMPTION.

inconsistent statement. See *prior inconsistent statement* under STATEMENT.

in contemplation of death. See CONTEMPLATION OF DEATH.

incontestability clause. *Insurance.* An insurance-policy provision (esp. found in a life-insurance policy) that prevents the insurer, after a specified period (usu. one or two years), from disputing the policy's validity on the basis of fraud or mistake; a clause that bars all defenses except those reserved (usu. conditions and the payment of premiums). ● Most states require that a life-insurance policy contain a clause making the policy incontestable after it has been in effect for a specified period, unless the insured does not pay premiums or violates policy conditions relating to military service. Some states also require similar provisions in accident and sickness policies. — Also termed *noncontestability clause; incontestable clause; uncontestable clause.* Cf. CONTESTABILITY CLAUSE.

incontestability status. *Trademarks.* A classification of a trademark that meets certain criteria — including commercial use for five years after being placed on the Principal Register — as immune from legal challenge. ● Although incontestability does not confer absolute immunity, it makes a challenge much more difficult. 15 USCA § 1065.

incontestable policy. See INSURANCE POLICY.

incontrovertible-physical-facts doctrine. See PHYSICAL-FACTS RULE.

inconvenience. See RULE OF INCONVENIENCE.

inconvenient forum. See FORUM NON CONVENIENS.

incorporate, *vb.* (14c) **1.** To form a legal corporation <she incorporated the family business>. **2.** To combine with something else <incorporate the exhibits into the agreement>. **3.** To make the terms of another (esp. earlier) document part of a document by specific reference <the codicil incorporated the terms of the will>; esp., to apply the provisions of the Bill of Rights to the states by interpreting the 14th Amendment's Due Process Clause as encompassing those provisions.

incorporation, *n.* (15c) **1.** The formation of a legal corporation. See ARTICLES OF INCORPORATION. **2.** *Constitutional law.* The process of applying the provisions of the Bill of Rights to the states by interpreting the 14th Amendment's Due Process Clause as encompassing those provisions. • In a variety of opinions since 1897, the Supreme Court has incorporated the First, Fourth, Sixth, and Ninth Amendments into the Fourteenth Amendment's Due Process Clause.

> **selective incorporation.** Incorporation of certain provisions of the Bill of Rights. • Justice Benjamin Cardozo, who served from 1932 to 1938, first advocated this approach.

> **total incorporation.** Incorporation of all of the Bill of Rights. • Justice Hugo Black, who served on the U.S. Supreme Court from 1937 to 1971, first advocated this approach.

3. INCORPORATION BY REFERENCE. — **incorporate,** *vb.*

incorporation by reference. (1886) **1.** A method of making a secondary document part of a primary document by including in the primary document a statement that the secondary document should be treated as if it were contained within the primary one. • With a contract, the document to be incorporated must be referred to and described in the contract in such a way that the document's identity is clear beyond doubt. With a will, the rule applies only to clearly identified writings that existed when the testator signed the will. Unif. Probate Code § 2-510. Not all jurisdictions follow this rule for either contracts or wills. — Often shortened to *incorporation.* — Also termed *adoption by reference.* **2.** *Patents.* The explicit inclusion in one patent application of information already contained in another document, such as another patent or patent application. • Generally, the reference must be to a U.S. patent or application if the information is essential (i.e., the description, enabling disclosure, or best mode), but otherwise it may be to a foreign patent or a nonpatent publication. Incorporation by reference is often used in a continuing application to cite the disclosure contained in a parent application. Cf. CROSS-REFERENCE. **3.** *Patents.* The inclusion in a patent claim of information from an external drawing or table. • Incorporation by reference is a necessity doctrine, available when there is no

other practical way to convey the information in words, and when it is more concise and clear to refer the examiner to the graphic element.

incorporationism. The philosophical view that (1) law is made possible by an interdependent convergence of behavior and attitude, esp. in agreements that take the form of social conventions or rules; (2) authoritative legal pronouncements must distinguish some situations from others; and (3) the legality of norms can depend on their substantive moral merit, not just on their pedigree or social source. See Jules Coleman, *The Practice of Principle* (2001); W.J. Waluchow, *Inclusive Legal Positivism* (1994). — Also termed *soft positivism; inclusive legal positivism.*

incorporator. (1883) A person who takes part in the formation of a corporation, usu. by executing the articles of incorporation. — Also termed *corporator.*

in corpore (in **kor**-pə-ree). [Latin] In body or substance; in a material thing or object.

incorporeal (in-kor-**por**-ee-əl), *adj.* (15c) Having a conceptual existence but no physical existence; INTANGIBLE <copyrights and patents are incorporeal property>. Cf. CORPOREAL. — **incorporeality,** *n.*

incorporeal chattel. See *incorporeal property* under PROPERTY.

incorporeal hereditament. See HEREDITAMENT.

incorporeal ownership. See OWNERSHIP.

incorporeal possession. See POSSESSION.

incorporeal property. See PROPERTY.

incorporeal right. See RIGHT.

incorporeal thing. 1. See *incorporeal property* under PROPERTY. **2.** See THING.

incorrigibility (in-kor-ə-jə-**bil**-ə-tee *or* in-kahr-), *n.* (14c) Serious or persistent misbehavior by a child, making reformation by parental control impossible or unlikely. Cf. JUVENILE DELINQUENCY. — **incorrigible,** *adj.*

incorrigible (in-**kor**-ə-jə-bəl *or* in-**kahr**-), *adj.* (14c) Incapable of being reformed; delinquent.

incorrigible child. See CHILD.

Incoterm (**in**[g]-koh-tərm). A standardized shipping term, defined by the International Chamber of Commerce, that apportions the costs and liabilities of international shipping between buyers and sellers. See EX WORKS; COST, INSURANCE, AND FREIGHT; COST AND FREIGHT; FREE ALONGSIDE SHIP; FREE ON BOARD.

increase (in-krees), *n.* (14c) **1.** The extent of growth or enlargement. **2.** *Archaic.* The produce of land or the offspring of human beings or animals. — **increase** (in-**krees**), *vb.*

increase, costs of. See COSTS OF INCREASE.

increased-risk-of-harm doctrine. See LOSS-OF-CHANCE DOCTRINE.

increment (in[g]-krə-mənt), *n.* (15c) A unit of increase in quantity or value. — **incremental,** *adj.*

unearned increment. An increase in the value of real property due to population growth.

incremental cash flow. See CASH FLOW.

increscitur (in-**kres**-i-tər). See ADDITUR.

incriminate (in-**krim**-ə-nayt), *vb.* (18c) **1.** To charge (someone) with a crime <the witness incriminated the murder suspect>. **2.** To identify (oneself or another) as being involved in the commission of a crime or other wrongdoing <the defendant incriminated an accomplice>. — Also termed *criminate.* — **incriminatory,** *adj.*

incriminating, *adj.* (18c) Demonstrating or indicating involvement in criminal activity <incriminating evidence>.

incriminating admission. See ADMISSION (1).

incriminating circumstance. See CIRCUMSTANCE.

incriminating evidence. See EVIDENCE.

incriminating statement. See STATEMENT.

incrimination. (18c) **1.** The act of charging someone with a crime. **2.** The act of involving someone in a crime. — Also termed *crimination.* See SELF-INCRIMINATION.

incroach, *vb. Archaic.* See ENCROACH.

incroachment. *Archaic.* See ENCROACHMENT.

inculpate (in-**kəl**-payt *or* in-kəl-payt), *vb.* (18c) **1.** To accuse. **2.** To implicate (oneself or another) in a crime or other wrongdoing; INCRIMINATE. — **inculpation,** *n.* — **inculpatory** (in-**kəl**-pə-tor-ee), *adj.*

inculpatory evidence. See EVIDENCE.

incumbent (in-**kəm**-bənt), *n.* (15c) One who holds an official post, esp. a political one. — **incumbency,** *n.* — **incumbent,** *adj.*

incumbrance. See ENCUMBRANCE.

incur, *vb.* (15c) To suffer or bring on oneself (a liability or expense). — **incurrence,** *n.* — **incurrable,** *adj.*

incurred risk. See ASSUMPTION OF THE RISK (2).

in custodia legis (in kə-**stoh**-dee-ə **lee**-jis). [Latin] In the custody of the law <the debtor's automobile was *in custodia legis* after being seized by the sheriff>. ● The phrase is traditionally used in reference to property taken into the court's charge during pending litigation over it. — Also termed *in legal custody.*

inde (**in**-dee), *adv.* [Latin] *Hist.* Thence; thereof. ● This word appeared in several Latin phrases, such as *quod eat inde sine die* ("that he go thence without day").

indebitatus assumpsit (in-deb-i-**tay**-təs ə-**səm**[p]-sit). See ASSUMPSIT.

indebitum (in-**deb**-i-təm), *n. & adj. Roman law.* A debt that in fact is not owed. ● Money paid for a nonexistent debt could be recovered by the action *condictio indebiti.*

indebtedness (in-**det**-id-nis). (17c) **1.** The condition or state of owing money. **2.** Something owed; a debt.

indecency, *n.* (16c) The state or condition of being outrageously offensive, esp. in a vulgar or sexual way. ● Unlike obscene material, indecent speech is protected under the First Amendment. Cf. OBSCENITY. — **indecent,** *adj.*

indecent advertising. 1. Signs, broadcasts, or other forms of communication that use grossly objectionable words, symbols, pictures, or the like to sell or promote goods, services, events, etc. **2.** *Archaic.* In some jurisdictions, the statutory offense of advertising the sale of abortifacients and (formerly) contraceptives.

indecent assault. See *sexual assault* (2) under ASSAULT.

indecent assault by contact. See *sexual assault* (2) under ASSAULT.

indecent assault by exposure. See INDECENT EXPOSURE.

indecent exhibition. The act of publicly displaying or offering for sale something (such as a photograph or book) that is outrageously offensive, esp. in a vulgar or sexual way.

indecent exposure. (1828) An offensive display of one's body in public, esp. of the genitals. — Also termed *indecent assault by exposure*; *exposure of person.* Cf. LEWDNESS; OBSCENITY.

indecent liberties. (18c) Improper behavior, usu. toward another person, esp. of a sexual nature.

indefeasible (in-də-**feez**-ə-bəl), *adj.* (16c) (Of a claim or right) not vulnerable to being defeated, revoked, or lost <an indefeasible estate>.

indefeasible remainder. See REMAINDER.

indefeasibly vested remainder. See *indefeasible remainder* under REMAINDER.

indefinite detainee. See NONREMOVABLE INMATE.

indefinite failure of issue. See FAILURE OF ISSUE.

indefinite payment. See PAYMENT.

indefinite postponement. See *postpone indefinitely* under POSTPONE.

indefinite sentence. See *indeterminate sentence* under SENTENCE.

indefinite sentencing. See INDETERMINATE SENTENCING.

in delicto (in də-**lik**-toh). [Latin] In fault. See IN PARI DELICTO. Cf. EX DELICTO (1).

indemnification (in-dem-nə-fi-**kay**-shən), *n.* (18c) **1.** The action of compensating for loss or damage sustained. **2.** The compensation so made. — **indemnificatory,** *adj.*

indemnifier. See INDEMNITOR.

indemnify (in-**dem**-nə-fi), *vb.* (17c) **1.** To reimburse (another) for a loss suffered because of a third party's or one's own act or default; HOLD HARMLESS. **2.** To promise to reimburse (another) for such a loss. **3.** To give (another) security against such a loss. — **indemnifiable,** *adj.*

indemnis (in-**dem**-nis), *adj.* [Latin] *Hist.* Free from loss or damage; harmless.

indemnitee (in-dem-nə-**tee**). (1884) One who receives indemnity from another.

indemnitor (in-**dem**-nə-tər *or* -tor). (1827) One who indemnifies another. — Also termed *indemnifier.*

indemnity (in-**dem**-nə-tee), *n.* (15c) **1.** A duty to make good any loss, damage, or liability incurred by another. **2.** The right of an injured party to claim reimbursement for its loss, damage, or liability from a person who has such a duty. **3.** Reimbursement or compensation for loss, damage, or liability in tort; esp., the right of a party who is secondarily liable to recover from the party who is primarily liable for reimbursement of expenditures paid to a third party for injuries resulting from a violation of a common-law duty. Cf. CONTRIBUTION. — **indemnitory,** *adj.*

contractual indemnity. Indemnity that is expressly provided for in an agreement.

double indemnity. (1859) The payment of twice the basic benefit in the event of a specified loss, esp. as in an insurance contract requiring the insurer to pay twice the policy's face amount in the case of accidental death.

equitable indemnity. **1.** A doctrine allowing a defendant in a tort action to allocate blame to a codefendant or cross-defendant, and thereby to proportionally reduce legal responsibility, even in the absence of contractual indemnity. — Also termed *implied indemnity; doctrine of equitable indemnity.* **2.** See *implied contractual indemnity.* **3.** See *implied indemnity.*

implied contractual indemnity. Indemnity that is not expressly provided for by an indemnity clause in an agreement but is nevertheless determined to be reasonably intended by the parties, based on equitable considerations. — Also termed *equitable indemnity.*

implied indemnity. Indemnity arising from equitable considerations and based on the parties' relationship, as when a guarantor pays a debt to a creditor that the principal debtor should have paid. — Also termed *equitable indemnity.*

indemnity against liability. (1838) A right to indemnity that arises on the indemnitor's default, regardless of whether the indemnitee has suffered a loss.

indemnity bond. See BOND (2).

indemnity clause. (1860) A contractual provision in which one party agrees to answer for any specified or unspecified liability or harm that the other party might incur. — Also termed *hold-harmless clause; save-harmless clause.* Cf. EXEMPTION CLAUSE.

indemnity contract. See CONTRACT.

indemnity insurance. See *first-party insurance* under INSURANCE.

indemnity land. 1. Public land granted to a railroad company to help defray the cost of constructing a right-of-way. • This land indemnifies a railroad company for land given in a previous grant but later rendered unavailable for railroad use by a disposition or reservation made after the original grant. **2.** Federally owned land granted to a state to replace previously granted land that has since been rendered unavailable for the state's use. — Also termed *place land.*

indemnity mortgage. See *deed of trust* under DEED.

indemnity principle. *Insurance.* The doctrine that an insurance policy should not confer a benefit greater in value than the loss suffered by the insured.

indenization (in-den-i-**zay**-shən), *n.* See DENIZATION.

indenizen. See ENDENIZEN.

indent, *n.* **1.** *Hist.* An indented certificate of indebtedness issued by the U.S. government or a state government in the late 18th or early 19th century. **2.** A contract or deed in writing.

indent (in-**dent**), *vb. Hist.* **1.** To cut in a serrated or wavy line; esp., to sever (an instrument) along a serrated line to create multiple copies, each fitting into the angles of the other. See CHIROGRAPH; INDENTURE (1). **2.** To agree by contract; to bind oneself. **3.** To bind (a person) by contract.

indented deed. See INDENTURE (1).

indenture (in-**den**-chər), *n.* (14c) **1.** A formal written instrument made by two or more parties with different interests, traditionally having the edges serrated, or indented, in a zigzag fashion to reduce the possibility of forgery and to distinguish it from a deed poll. — Also termed *indented deed.* Cf. *deed poll* under DEED. **2.** A deed or elaborate contract signed by two or more parties.

corporate indenture. A document containing the terms and conditions governing the issuance of debt securities, such as bonds or debentures.

debenture indenture. (1938) An indenture containing obligations not secured by a mortgage or other collateral. • It is a long-term financing vehicle that places the debenture holder in substantially the same position as a bondholder secured by a first mortgage.

trust indenture. **1.** A document containing the terms and conditions governing a trustee's conduct and the trust beneficiaries' rights. — Also termed *indenture of trust.* **2.** See *deed of trust* under DEED.

3. *Hist.* A contract by which an apprentice or other person, such as a servant, is bound to a master, usu. for a term of years or other limited period. — **indentured,** *adj.*

indentured servant. See SERVANT.

indenture of a fine. *Hist.* A document engrossed by the chirographer of fines to reflect penalties assessed by the court. • The chirographer prepared indentures in duplicate on the same piece of parchment, then split the parchment along an indented line through a word, sentence, or drawing placed on the parchment to help ensure its authenticity. See CHIROGRAPHER OF FINES.

indenture of trust. See *trust indenture* under INDENTURE.

indenture trustee. See TRUSTEE (1).

independence, *n.* (17c) The state or quality of being independent; esp., a country's freedom to manage all its affairs, whether external or internal, without control by other countries.

independent, *adj.* (17c) **1.** Not subject to the control or influence of another <independent investigation>. **2.** Not associated with another (often larger) entity <an independent subsidiary>. **3.** Not dependent or contingent on something else <an independent person>.

independent adjuster. See ADJUSTER.

independent adoption. See *private adoption* under ADOPTION.

independent advice. (1871) Counsel that is impartial and not given to further the interests of the person giving it. • Whether a testator or donor received independent advice before making a disposition is often an important issue in an undue-influence challenge to the property disposition. — Also termed *proper independent advice.*

independent agency. See AGENCY (3).

independent agent. See AGENT (2).

independent audit. See AUDIT.

independent claim. See PATENT CLAIM.

independent conception. See INDEPENDENT DEVELOPMENT.

independent contract. See CONTRACT.

independent contractor. (1841) One who is entrusted to undertake a specific project but who is left free to do the assigned work and to choose the method for accomplishing it. • It does not matter whether the work is done for pay or gratuitously. Unlike an employee, an independent contractor who commits a wrong while carrying out the work usu. does not create liability for the one who did the hiring. — Also termed *contract labor.* Cf. EMPLOYEE.

independent counsel. See COUNSEL.

independent covenant. See COVENANT (1).

independent creation. *Copyright.* A defense asserting that a later work is not a derivative of an allegedly infringed work, but is a product of coincidentally parallel labor.

independent development. *Intellectual property.* A defense against an industrial-espionage charge wherein the user shows that the property was independently discovered or conceived. • Trademarks, symbols, inventions, and other types of intellectual property are all subject to independent development. — Also termed *independent conception.*

independent executor. See EXECUTOR.

independent force. See FORCE.

independent intervening cause. See *intervening cause* under CAUSE (1).

independent invention. See INVENTION.

independent investigation committee. See SPECIAL LITIGATION COMMITTEE.

independent-living program. *Family law.* A training course designed to enable foster children who are near the age of majority to leave the foster-care system and manage their own affairs as adults. • Independent living programs provide education, training, and financial and employment counseling. They also help many foster youth in locating suitable post-foster-care housing. Permanency planning orders or case plans can — but are not required to — provide for independent living as a goal for a child in long-term foster care and describe how it is to be accomplished. See AGING-OUT; PERMANENCY PLAN.

independent medical examination. An assessment of a person's physical condition and health that is made by an impartial healthcare professional, usu. a physician. — Abbr. IME.

independent mental evaluation. An assessment of a person's mental and emotional condition that is made by an impartial mental-health professional, such as a psychologist or psychiatrist. Cf. PSYCHIATRIC EXAMINATION. — Abbr. IME.

independent personal representative. See *personal representative* under REPRESENTATIVE.

independent-practice association. A network of independent healthcare providers who contract with a health-maintenance organization (HMO) to provide services to the HMO's subscribers at negotiated rates. • Independent-practice associations generally remain free to accept patients who subscribe to other HMOs or who are not members of an HMO. — Abbr. IPA.

independent probate. See *informal probate* under PROBATE.

independent promise. See *unconditional promise* under PROMISE.

independent regulatory agency. See *independent agency* under AGENCY (3).

independent regulatory commission. See *independent agency* under AGENCY (3).

independent retirement account. See INDIVIDUAL RETIREMENT ACCOUNT.

independent-significance doctrine. (1968) *Wills & estates.* The principle that effect will be given to a testator's disposition that is not done solely to avoid the requirements of a will. • An example is a will provision that gives the contents of the testator's safe-deposit box to his niece. Because the safe-deposit box has utility ("significance") independent of the will, the gift of its contents at the testator's death is valid.

independent-source hearing. See HEARING.

independent-source rule. (1968) *Criminal procedure.* The rule providing — as an exception to the fruit-of-the-poisonous-tree doctrine — that evidence obtained by illegal means may nonetheless be admissible if that evidence is also obtained by legal means unrelated to the original illegal conduct. See FRUIT-OF-THE-POISONOUS-TREE DOCTRINE. Cf. INEVITABLE-DISCOVERY RULE.

independent state. See SOVEREIGN STATE.

independent union. See UNION.

indestructible trust. See TRUST.

indeterminate, *adj.* (14c) Not definite; not distinct or precise.

indeterminate bond. See BOND (3).

indeterminate conditional release. A release from prison granted once the prisoner fulfills certain conditions. • The release can be revoked if the prisoner breaches other conditions.

indeterminate damages. See *discretionary damages* under DAMAGES.

indeterminate obligation. See OBLIGATION.

indeterminate sentence. See SENTENCE.

indeterminate sentencing. (1941) **1.** The practice of not imposing a definite term of confinement, but instead prescribing a range for the minimum and maximum term, leaving the precise term to be fixed in some other way, usu. based on the prisoner's conduct and apparent rehabilitation while incarcerated. — Also termed *indefinite sentencing.* **2.** See *indeterminate sentencing* under SENTENCING.

index, *n.* (14c) **1.** An alphabetized listing of the topics or other items included in a single book or document, or in a series of volumes, usu. found at the end of the book, document, or series <index of authorities>.

grantee–grantor index. (1961) An index, usu. kept in the county clerk's or recorder's office, alphabetically listing by grantee the volume and page number of the grantee's recorded property transactions. • In some jurisdictions, the grantee–grantor index is combined with the grantor–grantee index.

grantor–grantee index. (1944) An index, usu. kept in the county clerk's or recorder's office, alphabetically listing by grantor the volume and page number of the grantor's recorded property transactions.

tract index. (1858) An index, usu. kept in the county clerk's or recorder's office, listing, by location of each parcel of land, the volume and page number of the recorded property transactions affecting the parcel.

2. A number, usu. expressed in the form of a percentage or ratio, that indicates or measures a series of observations, esp. those involving a market or the economy <cost-of-living index> <stock index>.

advance-decline index. A stock-market indicator showing the cumulative net difference between stock-price advances and declines.

indexation. See INDEXING.

index crime. See *index offense* under OFFENSE (1).

index fund. See MUTUAL FUND.

indexing. 1. The practice or method of adjusting wages, pension benefits, insurance, or other types of payments to compensate for inflation. **2.** The practice of investing funds to track or mirror an index of securities. — Also termed *indexation.*

index lease. See LEASE.

index of authorities. (1881) An alphabetical list of authorities cited in a book or brief, usu. with subcategories for cases, statutes, and treatises. — Also termed *table of authorities; table of cases.*

index offense. See OFFENSE (1).

Index of Patents. An annual two-part publication of the U.S. Patent and Trademark Office, containing the year's List of Patentees (Part I) and Index to Subjects of Inventions (Part II), arranged by class and subclass.

Index of Trademarks. An annual publication of the U.S. Patent and Trademark Office, listing all trademarks registered in a given year.

Index to the U.S. Patent Classification System. An entry-level aid to using the Patent Office's classification system, comprising an estimated 65,000 common terms and phrases and referring each entry to a class and subclass within the system.

Indian child. Under the Indian Child Welfare Act, any unmarried person under the age of 18 who either is a member of an Indian tribe or is both eligible for membership in an Indian tribe and the biological child of a member of an Indian tribe. See INDIAN CHILD WELFARE ACT.

Indian Child Welfare Act. A federal act that governs child-custody proceedings — including foster-care placement, preadoptive placement, adoptive placement, and termination of parental rights — in cases involving a child of American Indian descent. 25 USCA §§ 1911 et seq. ● Congress enacted the Act to help protect the best interests of Indian children, to promote the stability and security of Indian tribes and families, and to counteract the disproportionate foster-care placement and adoption of Indian children by non-Indians. The Act provides minimum federal standards for removing Indian children from their families and for placing them in foster or adoptive homes that will provide an environment reflecting the values of the Indian culture. The Act has an important jurisdictional feature: in a custody dispute involving an Indian child who resides in or is domiciled within an Indian reservation, the tribe and its tribal courts have exclusive jurisdiction. And in a custody dispute involving an Indian child who lives off a reservation, upon petition, any state court should usu. defer and transfer the case to the tribal court unless a party demonstrates good cause to the contrary. — Abbr. ICWA.

Indian Claims Commission. A federal agency — dissolved in 1978 — that adjudicated claims brought by American Indians, a tribe, or another identifiable group of Indians against the United States. ● The U.S. Court of Federal Claims currently hears these claims.

Indian country. 1. The land within the borders of all Indian reservations, the land occupied by an Indian community (whether or not located within a recognized reservation), and any land held in trust by the United States but beneficially owned by an Indian or tribe. **2.** *Hist.* Any region (esp. during the U.S. westward migration) where a person was likely to encounter Indians.

Indian gambling. See GAMBLING.

Indian land. Land owned by the United States but held in trust for and used by American In-

dians. — Also termed *Indian tribal property.* Cf. TRIBAL LAND.

Indian law. See NATIVE AMERICAN LAW.

Indian reservation. An area that the federal government has designated for use by an American Indian tribe, where the tribe generally settles and establishes a tribal government.

Indian Territory. A former U.S. territory — now a part of the state of Oklahoma — to which the Cherokee, Choctaw, Chickasaw, Creek, and Seminole tribes were forcibly removed between 1830 and 1843. ● In the late 19th century, most of this territory was ceded to the United States, and in 1907 the greater part of it became the State of Oklahoma.

Indian title. A right of occupancy that the federal government grants to an American Indian tribe based on the tribe's immemorial possession of the area. ● Congress does not recognize tribal ownership of the land, only possession. A tribe or nation must actually, exclusively, and continuously use the property to establish that it is the ancestral home. An individual may claim Indian title by showing that the individual or his or her lineal ancestors continuously occupied a parcel of land, as individuals, before the land was closed to settlers. — Also termed *aboriginal title; right of occupancy.* Cf. *aboriginal title* (1) under TITLE (2).

Indian tribal property. See INDIAN LAND.

Indian tribe. A group, band, nation, or other organized group of indigenous American people, including any Alaskan native village, that is recognized as eligible for the special programs and services provided by the U.S. government because of Indian status (42 USCA § 9601(36)); esp., any such group having a federally recognized governing body that carries out substantial governmental duties and powers over an area (42 USCA § 300f(14); 40 CFR § 146.3). ● A tribe may be identified in various ways, esp. by past dealings with other tribes or with the federal, state, or local government, or by recognition in historical records.

indicator. (17c) *Securities.* An average or index that shows enough of a correlation to market trends or economic conditions that it can help analyze market performance.

coincident indicator. An economic or market-activity index or indicator that shows changing trends near the same time that overall conditions begin to change.

economic indicator. See ECONOMIC INDICATOR.

lagging indicator. **1.** An index that indicates a major stock-market change sometime after the change occurs. **2.** See *lagging economic indicator* under ECONOMIC INDICATOR.

leading indicator. **1.** A quantifiable index that predicts a major stock-market change. **2.** See *leading economic indicator* under ECONOMIC INDICATOR.

indicia (in-**dish**-ee-ə), *n. pl.* (17c) **1.** *Roman law.* Evidence. **2.** (*pl.*) Signs; indications <the purchase receipts are indicia of ownership>.

indicia of title. A document that evidences ownership of personal or real property.

indicium (in-**dish**-ee-əm), *n.* [Latin] *Roman law.* **1.** The act of providing evidence against an accused. **2.** The act of promising recompense for a certain service. **3.** A sign or mark; esp., something used as a type of proof.

indict (in-**dIt**), *vb.* (17c) To charge (a person) with a crime by formal legal process, esp. by grand-jury presentation. — Also formerly spelled *endite*; *indite*.

indictable misdemeanor. See *serious misdemeanor* under MISDEMEANOR.

indictable offense. See OFFENSE (1).

indictee (in-dI-**tee**). (16c) A person who has been indicted; one officially charged with a crime.

indictment (in-**dIt**-mənt), *n.* (14c) **1.** The formal written accusation of a crime, made by a grand jury and presented to a court for prosecution against the accused person. *See* Fed. R. Crim. P. 7. **2.** The act or process of preparing or bringing forward such a formal written accusation. Cf. IN-FORMATION; PRESENTMENT (2).

    barebones indictment. (1963) An indictment that cites only the language of the statute allegedly violated; an indictment that does not provide a factual statement.

    duplicitous indictment (d[y]oo-**plis**-ə-təs). (1914) **1.** An indictment containing two or more offenses in the same count. **2.** An indictment charging the same offense in more than one count.

    joint indictment. (17c) An indictment that charges two or more people with an offense.

indictor (in-**dIt**-ər *or* in-**dI**-tor). (17c) A person who causes another to be indicted.

indifference. (15c) A lack of interest in or concern about something; apathy.

    conscious indifference. **1.** *Criminal law.* See *deliberate indifference* (2). **2.** *Torts.* See *deliberate indifference* (3).

    deliberate indifference. **1.** *Criminal law.* (1951) The careful preservation of one's ignorance despite awareness of circumstances that would put a reasonable person on notice of a fact essential to a crime. See JEWELL INSTRUCTION. **2.** *Criminal law.* Awareness of and disregard for the risk of harm to another person's life, body, or property. **3.** *Torts.* Conscious disregard of the harm that one's actions could do to the interests or rights of another. — Also termed *reckless*

indifference; *conscious avoidance*; *conscious indifference.*

    reckless indifference. See *deliberate indifference.*

indigency, *n.* (17c) The state or condition of a person who lacks the means of subsistence; extreme hardship or neediness; poverty. ● For purposes of the Sixth Amendment right to appointed counsel, *indigency* refers to a defendant's inability to afford an attorney. — Also termed *indigence.* — **indigent,** *adj. & n.*

indigent (in-di-jənt), *n.* (15c) **1.** A poor person. **2.** A person who is found to be financially unable to pay filing fees and court costs and so is allowed to proceed *in forma pauperis.* ● The Supreme Court has recognized an indigent petitioner's right to have certain fees and costs waived in divorce and termination-of-parental-rights cases. *Boddie v. Connecticut,* 401 U.S. 371, 91 S.Ct. 780 (1971); *M.L.B. v. S.L.J.,* 519 U.S. 102, 117 S.Ct. 555 (1996). See PAUPER; IN FORMA PAUPERIS. — **indigent,** *adj.*

indigent defendant. (1882) A person who is too poor to hire a lawyer and who, upon indictment, becomes eligible to receive aid from a court-appointed attorney and a waiver of court costs. See IN FORMA PAUPERIS. Cf. PAUPER.

indignity (in-**dig**-ni-tee), *n.* (16c) *Family law.* A ground for divorce consisting in one spouse's pattern of behavior calculated to humiliate the other. — Also termed *personal indignity.* Cf. CRUELTY.

indirect aggression. See AGGRESSION.

indirect attack. See COLLATERAL ATTACK.

indirect confession. See CONFESSION.

indirect contempt. See CONTEMPT.

indirect cost. See COST (1).

indirect damages. See *consequential damages* under DAMAGES.

indirect evidence. See *circumstantial evidence* (1) under EVIDENCE.

indirect loss. See *consequential loss* under LOSS.

indirect notice. See *implied notice* under NOTICE.

indirect possession. See *mediate possession* under POSSESSION.

indirect-purchaser doctrine. (1976) *Antitrust.* The principle that in litigation for price discrimination, the court will ignore sham middle parties in determining whether different prices were paid by different customers for the same goods. ● This doctrine gives standing to bring an antitrust action to a party who is not an immediate purchaser of a product. Thus, if a manufacturer sells a product to a retailer, but dictates the terms by which the retailer must sell the product to a consumer, a court will ignore the retailer and treat the consumer as the direct purchaser of the product.

indirect tax. See TAX.

indiscriminate attack. *Int'l law.* An aggressive act that (1) is not carried out for a specific military objective, (2) employs a means of combat not directed at a specific military objective, or (3) employs a means of combat the effects of which cannot be limited in accordance with an international protocol such as the Geneva Conventions of 1949 and their protocols or the Hague Conventions of 1899 and 1907.

indispensable-element test. *Criminal law.* A common-law test for the crime of attempt, based on whether the defendant acquires control over any thing that is essential to the crime. • Under this test, for example, a person commits a crime by buying the explosives with which to detonate a bomb. See ATTEMPT (2).

indispensable evidence. See EVIDENCE.

indispensable instrument. See INSTRUMENT (3).

indispensable party. See PARTY (2).

indistanter (in-di-**stan**-tər), *adv.* [Law Latin "immediately"] Forthwith; without delay.

indite. See INDICT.

individual, *adj.* (15c) **1.** Existing as an indivisible entity. **2.** Of or relating to a single person or thing, as opposed to a group.

individual account plan. See *defined-contribution plan* under EMPLOYEE BENEFIT PLAN.

individual asset. See ASSET.

individual contract. See CONTRACT.

individual debt. See DEBT.

individual goodwill. See *personal goodwill* under GOODWILL.

individualized educational placement. See INDIVIDUALIZED EDUCATION PROGRAM.

individualized education program. *Family law.* A specially designed plan of educational instruction for a child with disabilities. • The individualized education program is a written plan that details the particular child's abilities, the child's educational goals, and the services to be provided. — Abbr. IEP. — Also termed *individualized educational placement.* See *child with disabilities* under CHILD; INDIVIDUALS WITH DISABILITIES EDUCATION ACT.

individual liberty. See *personal liberty* under LIBERTY.

individual property. See SEPARATE PROPERTY (1).

individual proprietorship. See SOLE PROPRIETORSHIP.

individual retirement account. (1974) A savings or brokerage account to which a person may contribute up to a specified amount of earned income each year. • The contributions, along with any interest earned in the account, are not taxed until the money is withdrawn after a participant reaches 59½ (or before then, if a 10% penalty is paid). — Abbr. IRA. — Also termed *independent retirement account.* Cf. KEOGH PLAN.

> *education individual retirement account.* An individual retirement account from which withdrawals may be made tax-free if the withdrawn funds are used for education costs. • Before 2002, annual contributions were limited to $500. In 2002, the contribution limit increased to $2,000 per year for families with incomes under $190,000.

> *Roth IRA.* (1991) An IRA in which contributions are nondeductible when they are made. • No further taxes are assessed on the contributions (or accrued interest) when the money is withdrawn (if all applicable rules are followed). This term takes its name from Senator William Roth, who sponsored the legislation creating this type of IRA.

Individuals with Disabilities Education Act. A federal statute that governs the public education of children with physical or mental handicaps and attempts to ensure that these children receive a free public education that meets their unique needs. • The Education of All Handicapped Children Act (enacted in 1975) was renamed the Individuals with Disabilities Education Act in 1990, and this Act was substantially amended in 1997. All states currently participate in this joint federal–state initiative. 20 USCA §§ 1400–1485. — Abbr. IDEA.

indivisible, *adj.* (14c) Not separable into parts; held by two or more people in undivided shares <an indivisible debt>.

indivision. *Civil law.* Undivided ownership of property; the condition of being owned by coowners each having an undivided interest in the property.

indorse, *vb.* (16c) To sign (a negotiable instrument), usu. on the back, either to accept responsibility for paying an obligation memorialized by the instrument or to make the instrument payable to someone other than the payee. — Also spelled *endorse.*

indorsee (in-dor-**see**). (18c) A person to whom a negotiable instrument is transferred by indorsement. — Also spelled *endorsee.*

> *indorsee in due course.* An indorsee who, in the ordinary course of business, acquires a negotiable instrument in good faith for value, before its maturity, and without knowledge of its dishonor.

indorsement, *n.* (16c) **1.** The placing of a signature, sometimes with an additional notation, on the back of a negotiable instrument to transfer or guarantee the instrument or to acknowledge payment. **2.** The signature or notation itself. — Also spelled *endorsement.* — **indorse,** *vb.*

accommodation indorsement. (1888) An indorsement to an instrument by a third party who acts as surety for another party who remains primarily liable. See ACCOMMODATION PAPER.

anomalous indorsement. See *irregular indorsement.*

blank indorsement. An indorsement that names no specific payee, thus making the instrument payable to the bearer and negotiable by delivery only. UCC § 3-205(b). — Also termed *indorsement in blank; general indorsement.*

collection indorsement. See *restrictive indorsement.*

conditional indorsement. (1894) An indorsement that restricts the instrument in some way, as by limiting how the instrument can be paid or transferred; an indorsement giving possession of the instrument to the indorsee, but retaining title until the occurrence of some condition named in the indorsement. ● Wordings that indicate this type of indorsement are "Pay to Brad Jones when he becomes 18 years of age" and "Pay to Brigitte Turner, or order, unless before payment I give you notice to the contrary." — Also termed *restricted indorsement; restrictive indorsement.* Cf. *special indorsement.*

full indorsement. 1. See *irregular indorsement.* **2.** See *special indorsement.*

general indorsement. See *blank indorsement.*

indorsement in blank. See *blank indorsement.*

indorsement in full. See *special indorsement.*

indorsement without recourse. See *qualified indorsement.*

irregular indorsement. (1842) An indorsement by a person who signs outside the chain of title and who therefore is neither a holder nor a transferor of the instrument. ● An irregular indorser is generally treated as an accommodation party. — Also termed *anomalous indorsement; full indorsement.* See ACCOMMODATION PARTY.

qualified indorsement. (1806) An indorsement that passes title to the instrument but limits the indorser's liability to later holders if the instrument is later dishonored. ● Typically, a qualified indorsement is made by writing "without recourse" or "sans recourse" over the signature. UCC § 3-415(b). — Also termed *indorsement without recourse.* See WITHOUT RECOURSE.

restricted indorsement. See *conditional indorsement.*

restrictive indorsement. (18c) An indorsement that includes a condition (e.g., "pay Josefina Cardoza only if she has worked 8 full hours on April 13") or any other language restricting further negotiation (e.g., "for deposit only"). — Also termed *collection indorsement.* See *conditional indorsement.*

special indorsement. (18c) An indorsement that specifies the person to receive payment or to whom the goods named by the document must be delivered. UCC § 3-205(a). — Also termed *indorsement in full; full indorsement.* Cf. *conditional indorsement.*

trust indorsement. (1945) An indorsement stating that the payee becomes a trustee for a third person (e.g., "pay Erin Ray in trust for Kaitlin Ray"); a restrictive indorsement that limits the instrument to the use of the indorser or another person.

unauthorized indorsement. (1840) An indorsement made without authority, such as a forged indorsement.

unqualified indorsement. (1839) An indorsement that does not limit the indorser's liability on the paper. ● It does not, for example, include the phrase "without recourse."

unrestrictive indorsement. (1844) An indorsement that includes no condition or language restricting negotiation. — Also termed *unrestricted indorsement.*

indorser. (18c) A person who transfers a negotiable instrument by indorsement; specif., one who signs a negotiable instrument other than as maker, drawer, or acceptor. — Also spelled *endorser.*

accommodation indorser. (1820) An indorser who acts as surety for another person.

induced abortion. See ABORTION.

inducement, *n.* (15c) **1.** The act or process of enticing or persuading another person to take a certain course of action. See *fraud in the inducement* under FRAUD.

active inducement. The act of intentionally causing a third party to infringe a valid patent. ● Active inducement requires proof of (1) an actual intent to cause the patent infringement and (2) knowledge of the patent.

2. *Contracts.* The benefit or advantage that causes a promisor to enter into a contract. **3.** *Criminal law.* An enticement or urging of another person to commit a crime. **4.** The preliminary statement in a pleading; esp., in an action for defamation, the plaintiff's allegation that extrinsic facts gave a defamatory meaning to a statement that is not defamatory on its face, or, in a criminal indictment, a statement of preliminary facts necessary to show the criminal character of the alleged offense. Cf. INNUENDO (2); COLLOQUIUM. — **induce,** *vb.*

inducement of breach of contract. See TORTIOUS INTERFERENCE WITH CONTRACTUAL RELATIONS.

inducing infringement. See *infringement in the inducement* under INFRINGEMENT.

induct, *vb.* (14c) **1.** To put into possession of (something, such as an office or benefice). **2.** To admit as a member. **3.** To enroll (a person) for military service.

induction. (14c) **1.** The act or process of initiating <the induction of three new members into the legal fraternity>. **2.** The act or process of reasoning from specific instances to general propositions <after looking at several examples, the group reasoned by induction that it is a very poor practice to begin a new paragraph by abruptly bringing up a new case>. Cf. DEDUCTION (4).

indult (in-dəlt). *Eccles. law.* A dispensation granted by the Pope to do or obtain something contrary to canon law. • Historically, indults were often used for political ends. An indult granted to a sovereign empowered the recipient to present an ecclesiastical benefice, usu. without papal interference. Less exalted bodies, such as the parliament of Paris and the college of cardinals, were sometimes granted similar privileges. — Also termed *indulto*.

industrial design. *Patents.* The shape, configuration, pattern, or ornament applied to a finished article of manufacture, often to distinguish the product's appearance. • A design patent may be issued to protect the product's characteristic appearance.

industrial-development bond. See BOND (3).

industrial disease. See OCCUPATIONAL DISEASE.

industrial espionage. See ESPIONAGE.

Industrial Espionage Act. See ECONOMIC ESPIONAGE ACT.

industrial goods. See *capital goods* under GOODS.

industrial insurance. See *industrial life insurance* under LIFE INSURANCE.

industrial law. See LABOR LAW.

industrial life insurance. See LIFE INSURANCE.

industrial property. *Intellectual property.* Patented goods, industrial designs, trademarks, and copyrights that a business owns and may exclude others from using. • Employed in the Paris Convention, the term was not defined, but the treaty states that it is to be construed broadly.

industrial relations. All dealings and relationships between an employer and its employees, including collective bargaining about issues such as safety and benefits.

industrial-revenue bond. See *industrial-development bond* under BOND (3).

industrial union. See UNION.

industry. (15c) **1.** Diligence in the performance of a task. **2.** Systematic labor for some useful purpose; esp., work in manufacturing or production. **3.** A particular form or branch of productive labor; an aggregate of enterprises employing similar production and marketing facilities to produce items having markedly similar characteristics.

industry-wide liability. See *enterprise liability* (1) under LIABILITY.

inebriate (in-ee-bree-ət), *n.* (18c) *Archaic.* An intoxicated person; esp., a habitual drunkard.

inebriated (in-ee-bree-ay-tid), *adj.* (15c) Drunk; intoxicated.

ineffective assistance of counsel. See ASSISTANCE OF COUNSEL.

ineffective revocation. See DEPENDENT RELATIVE REVOCATION.

Ineligibility Clause. The clause of the U.S. Constitution that prohibits a member of Congress from accepting an appointment to an executive office that was created, or the compensation for which was increased, during the member's service in Congress. U.S. Const. art. I, § 6.

ineligible, *adj.* (18c) (Of a person) legally disqualified to serve in office. — **ineligibility,** *n.*

inequitable (in-ek-wi-tə-bəl), *adj.* (17c) Not fair; opposed to principles of equity <an inequitable ruling>.

inequitable conduct. See *defense of inequitable conduct* under DEFENSE (1).

in equity. (15c) In a chancery court rather than a court of law; before a court exercising equitable jurisdiction.

inequity (in-ek-wi-tee), *n.* (16c) **1.** Unfairness; a lack of equity. **2.** An instance of injustice.

inescapable peril. See PERIL.

in esse (in es-ee *also* es-ay). [Latin "in being"] (16c) In actual existence; IN BEING <the court was concerned only with the rights of the children *in esse*>. Cf. IN POSSE.

inessential mistake. See *unessential mistake* under MISTAKE.

in evidence. Having been admitted into evidence <the photograph was already in evidence when the defense first raised an objection to it>.

inevitability doctrine. See INEVITABLE-DISCLOSURE DOCTRINE.

inevitable accident. See *unavoidable accident* under ACCIDENT.

inevitable-accident doctrine. See UNAVOIDABLE-ACCIDENT DOCTRINE.

inevitable-disclosure doctrine. *Trade secrets.* The legal theory that a key employee, once hired by a competitor, cannot avoid misappropriating the former employer's trade secrets. ● To justify an injunction, the plaintiff must prove that the former employee has confidential information and will not be able to avoid using that knowledge to unfairly compete against the plaintiff. Most courts have rejected this controversial doctrine on grounds that it effectively turns a nondisclosure agreement into a disfavored noncompetition agreement. The leading case upholding the doctrine is *PepsiCo, Inc. v. Redmond*, 54 F.3d 1262 (7th Cir. 1995), where the court quipped: "PepsiCo finds itself in the position of a coach, one of whose players has left, playbook in hand, to join the opposing team before the big game." — Also termed *inevitable disclosure rule*; *inevitability doctrine*; *inevitable misappropriation doctrine.*

inevitable-discovery rule. (1873) *Criminal procedure.* The rule providing — as an exception to the fruit-of-the-poisonous-tree doctrine — that evidence obtained by illegal means may nonetheless be admissible if the prosecution can show that the evidence would eventually have been legally obtained anyway. See FRUIT-OF-THE-POISONOUS-TREE DOCTRINE. Cf. INDEPENDENT-SOURCE RULE.

inevitable-misappropriation doctrine. See INEVITABLE-DISCLOSURE DOCTRINE.

inexcusable neglect. See NEGLECT.

in extenso (in ek-**sten**-soh). [Latin] In full; unabridged <set forth *in extenso*>.

in extremis (in ek-**stree**-mis). [Latin "in extremity"] (16c) **1.** In extreme circumstances. **2.** Near the point of death; on one's deathbed. ● Unlike *in articulo mortis*, the phrase *in extremis* does not always mean at the point of death.

in fact. (18c) Actual or real; resulting from the acts of parties rather than by operation of law. Cf. IN LAW.

infamous (in-fə-məs), *adj.* (14c) **1.** (Of a person) having a bad reputation. **2.** (Of a person) deprived of some or all rights of citizenship after conviction for a serious crime. ● Historically, a person convicted of almost any crime became infamous. **3.** (Of conduct) that is punishable by imprisonment.

infamous crime. See CRIME.

infamous punishment. See PUNISHMENT.

infamy (in-fə-mee), *n.* (18c) **1.** Disgraceful repute. **2.** The loss of reputation or position resulting from a person's being convicted of an infamous crime. See *infamous crime* under CRIME.

infancy. (14c) **1.** MINORITY (1). **2.** Early childhood.

natural infancy. At common law, the period ending at age seven, during which a child was presumed to be without criminal capacity.

3. The beginning stages of anything.

infant, *n.* (14c) **1.** A newborn baby. **2.** MINOR (1).

infantia (in-**fan**-shee-ə), *n.* [Latin] *Roman law.* The period of a person's life from birth to seven years; early childhood.

infanticide (in-**fant**-ə-sɪd). (17c) **1.** The act of killing a newborn child, esp. by the parents or with their consent. ● In archaic usage, the word referred also to the killing of an unborn child. — Also termed *child destruction*; *neonaticide.* Cf. FETICIDE; FILICIDE (2). **2.** The practice of killing newborn children. **3.** One who kills a newborn child. — Also termed *child-slaying.* Cf. PROLICIDE. — **infanticidal,** *adj.*

infect, *vb.* (14c) **1.** To contaminate <the virus infected the entire network>. **2.** To taint with crime <one part of the city has long been infected with illegal drug-dealing>. **3.** To make (a ship or cargo) liable in the seizure of contraband, which is only a part of its cargo <claiming that the single package of marijuana had infected the ship, the Coast Guard seized the entire vessel>. — **infection,** *n.* — **infectious,** *adj.*

infection, doctrine of. *Int'l law.* The principle that any goods belonging to an owner of contraband and carried on the same ship as the contraband may be seized or otherwise treated in the same manner as the contraband itself.

infeoff, *vb.* See ENFEOFF.

infeoffment. See ENFEOFFMENT.

infer, *vb.* (16c) To conclude from facts or from factual reasoning; to draw as a conclusion or inference. Cf. IMPLY (1).

inference (in-fər-ənts), *n.* (16c) **1.** A conclusion reached by considering other facts and deducing a logical consequence from them.

adverse inference. A detrimental conclusion drawn by the fact-finder from a party's failure to produce evidence that is within the party's control. ● Some courts allow the inference only if the party's failure is attributable to bad faith. — Also termed *adverse presumption.* Cf. SPOLIATION (1).

2. The process by which such a conclusion is reached; the process of thought by which one moves from evidence to proof. — **infer,** *vb.* — **inferential,** *adj.* — **inferrer,** *n.*

inference-on-inference rule. (1940) The principle that a presumption based on another presumption cannot serve as a basis for determining an ultimate fact.

inference-stacking. The practice or an instance of piling one or more inferences on each other to arrive at a legal conclusion. — Also termed *pyramiding inferences.* See INFERENCE-ON-INFERENCE RULE.

inferential fact. See FACT.

inferential pleading. See *argumentative pleading* under PLEADING (1).

inferior court. See COURT.

inferior judge. See JUDGE.

inferior officer. See OFFICER (1).

inferred authority. See *incidental authority* under AUTHORITY (1).

infertile, *adj.* Unable to conceive or bear offspring; sterile. — **infertility,** *n.*

infeudate. See ENFEOFF.

infeudation (in-fyoo-**day**-shən), *n.* Under the feudal system of landholding, the process of giving a person legal possession of land; ENFEOFFMENT (1). — **infeudate,** *vb.*

infibulation. See FEMALE GENITAL MUTILATION.

infidel (**in**-fə-dəl). (15c) **1.** A person who does not believe in something specified, esp. a particular religion. **2.** *Hist.* A person who violates a feudal oath of fealty.

infidelity. (15c) Unfaithfulness to an obligation; esp., marital unfaithfulness. Cf. ADULTERY.

in fine (in **fı**-nee *or* **fın**), *adv.* [Latin] **1.** In short; in summary. **2.** At the end (of a book, chapter, section, etc.).

infirmative, *adj. Rare.* (Of evidence) tending to weaken or invalidate a criminal accusation <an infirmative fact>. Cf. CRIMINATIVE.

infirmative hypothesis. *Criminal law.* An approach to a criminal case in which the defendant's innocence is assumed, and incriminating evidence is explained in a manner consistent with that assumption.

infirmity (in-**fər**-mə-tee), *n.* (14c) Physical weakness caused by age or disease; esp., in insurance law, an applicant's ill health that is poor enough to deter an insurance company from insuring the applicant. — **infirm,** *adj.*

in flagrante delicto (in flə-**gran**-tee də-**lik**-toh). [Latin "while the crime is ablaze"] (18c) In the very act of committing a crime or other wrong; red-handed <the sheriff caught them *in flagrante delicto*>.

inflammatory (in-**flam**-ə-tor-ee), *adj.* (18c) Tending to cause strong feelings of anger, indignation, or other type of upset; tending to stir the passions. • Evidence can be excluded if its inflammatory nature outweighs its probative value.

inflation, *n.* (14c) A general increase in prices coinciding with a fall in the real value of money. Cf. DEFLATION. — **inflationary,** *adj.*

cost-push inflation. Inflation caused by a rise in production costs.

demand-pull inflation. Inflation caused by an excess of demand over supply.

inflation rate. The pace of change in the prices of goods and services in a particular period. • The primary indexes for measuring the rate are the Consumer Price Index and the Producer Price Index.

infliction of emotional distress. 1. See INTENTIONAL INFLICTION OF EMOTIONAL DISTRESS. **2.** See NEGLIGENT INFLICTION OF EMOTIONAL DISTRESS.

influence district. See DISTRICT.

in force, *adj.* In effect; operative; binding.

in-force patent. See PATENT (3).

informal, *adj.* (16c) Not done or performed in accordance with normal forms or procedures <an informal proceeding>.

informal acknowledgment. See ACKNOWLEDGMENT.

informal agency action. Administrative-agency activity other than adjudication or rulemaking, such as investigation, publicity, or supervision. Cf. RULEMAKING.

informal application. See PATENT APPLICATION.

informal consideration. See CONSIDERATION (2).

informal contract. See CONTRACT.

informal disposition. See DISPOSITION (2).

informal dividend. See DIVIDEND.

informal drawing. See DRAWING.

informal immunity. See *pocket immunity* under IMMUNITY (3).

informal issue. See ISSUE (1).

informal marriage. See *common-law marriage* under MARRIAGE (1).

informal probate. See PROBATE.

informal proceeding. See PROCEEDING.

informal proof of claim. See PROOF OF CLAIM.

informal rulemaking. See RULEMAKING.

informant. (17c) One who informs against another; esp., one who confidentially supplies information to the police about a crime, sometimes in exchange for a reward or special treatment. — Also termed *informer; feigned accomplice.*

citizen-informant. A witness who, without expecting payment and with the public good in mind, comes forward and volunteers information to the police or other authorities.

informant's privilege. See PRIVILEGE (3).

in forma pauperis (in **for**-mə **paw**-pə-ris), *adv.* [Latin "in the manner of a pauper"] (16c) In the manner of an indigent who is permitted to disregard filing fees and court costs <when suing, a poor person is generally entitled to proceed *in*

forma pauperis>. See 28 USCA § 1915; Fed. R. App. P. 24. ● For instance, in many jurisdictions, an indigent divorce petitioner's filing fees and court costs are waived. — Abbr. IFP.

in forma pauperis affidavit. See *poverty affidavit* under AFFIDAVIT.

information. (15c) A formal criminal charge made by a prosecutor without a grand-jury indictment. *See* Fed. R. Crim. P. 7. ● The information is used to prosecute misdemeanors in most states, and about half the states allow its use in felony prosecutions as well. — Also termed *bill of information.* Cf. INDICTMENT.

    duplicitous information. An information that charges two or more offenses as one count.

    substitute information in lieu of indictment. An information that the prosecutor files to take the place of a previously returned indictment, usu. because the indictment is defective or because the prosecutor has added, altered, or deleted facts and allegations.

informational member. See *nonvoting member* under MEMBER.

informational picketing. See PICKETING.

informational privacy. See PRIVACY.

informational report. See REPORT (1).

Information Analysis and Infrastructure Protection Directorate. The division of the U.S. Department of Homeland Security responsible for analyzing intelligence information gathered from the Central Intelligence Agency, the Defense Intelligence Agency, the Federal Bureau of Investigation, the National Security Administration, and other sources, and for issuing warnings about threats of terrorist attack. ● The unit is also charged with evaluating weaknesses in the nation's infrastructure and recommending ways to reduce vulnerability to attacks. — Abbr. IAIP.

information and belief, on. (1827) (Of an allegation or assertion) based on secondhand information that the declarant believes to be true. ● For the historical precursor to this phrase, see INSINUATIO.

information-disclosure statement. *Patents.* A document submitted in the patent-application process in which the inventor reveals all known relevant prior art during the patentability search. ● The statement must disclose all known patents, publications, and other references of prior art. The U.S. Patent and Trademark Office provides a form, "Information Disclosure Citation," for this purpose. — Abbr. IDS. — Also termed *statement of prior-art references.*

information in equity. An equitable action brought by a sovereign or a governmental unit to preserve or protect the public interest through a public remedy. ● When the action is to abate a nuisance

that affects public property, it is an equitable action for purpresture. See PURPRESTURE. Cf. INFORMATION OF INTRUSION.

information letter. A written statement issued by the Department of Labor — in particular, by the Pension and Welfare Benefits Administration — that calls attention to a well-established interpretation or principle of ERISA, without applying it to a specific factual situation.

information return. See TAX RETURN.

Information Society Directive. *Copyright.* An initiative of the European Commission implementing the standards set by the WIPO Copyright Treaty, setting reproduction rights and establishing a "making-available" right.

informative advertising. See ADVERTISING.

informed consent. See CONSENT (1).

informed intermediary. See INTERMEDIARY.

informer. (14c) **1.** INFORMANT. **2.** A private citizen who brings a penal action to recover a penalty. ● Under some statutes, a private citizen is required to sue the offender for a penalty before any criminal liability can attach. — Also termed *common informer.* See COMMON INFORMER.

informer's privilege. See *informant's privilege* under PRIVILEGE (3).

in foro (in **for**-oh), *adv.* [Latin] In a forum, court, or tribunal; in the forum.

in foro conscientiae (in **for**-oh kon-shee-**en**-shee-ee), *adv.* [Latin "in the forum of conscience"] Privately or morally rather than legally <this moral problem cannot be dealt with by this court, but only *in foro conscientiae*>.

in foro contentioso (in **for**-oh kən-ten-shee-**oh**-soh), *adv.* [Latin] *Hist.* In the forum of contention or litigation; in a contested action. — Also termed *in foro contradictorio.*

in foro ecclesiastico (in **for**-oh e-klee-z[h]ee-**as**-ti-koh), *adv.* [Law Latin] In an ecclesiastical court.

in foro saeculari (in **for**-oh sek-yə-**lair**-I), *adv.* [Law Latin] In a secular court.

infra (**in**-frə), *adv. & adj.* [Latin "below"] (18c) Later in this text. ● *Infra* is used as a citational signal to refer to a later-cited authority. In medieval Latin, *infra* also acquired the sense "within." Cf. INTRA; SUPRA.

infraction, *n.* (17c) A violation, usu. of a rule or local ordinance and usu. not punishable by incarceration. See VIOLATION (1). — **infract,** *vb.*

    civil infraction. An act or omission that, though not a crime, is prohibited by law and is punishable. ● In some states, many traffic violations are classified as civil infractions.

infrastructure. The underlying framework of a system; esp., public services and facilities (such as highways, schools, bridges, sewers, and water systems) needed to support commerce as well as economic and residential development.

infringement, *n.* (1861) *Intellectual property.* An act that interferes with one of the exclusive rights of a patent, copyright, or trademark owner. See INTELLECTUAL PROPERTY. Cf. PLAGIARISM. — **infringe,** *vb.*

contributory infringement. **1.** The act of participating in, or contributing to, the infringing acts of another person. • The law imposes vicarious liability for contributory infringement. **2.** *Patents.* The act of aiding or abetting another person's patent infringement by knowingly selling a nonstaple item that has no substantial noninfringing use and is esp. adapted for use in a patented combination or process. • In the patent context, contributory infringement is statutorily defined in the Patent Act. 35 USCA § 271(c). **3.** *Copyright.* The act of either (1) actively inducing, causing, or materially contributing to the infringing conduct of another person, or (2) providing the goods or means necessary to help another person infringe (as by making facilities available for an infringing performance). • In the copyright context, contributory infringement is a common-law doctrine. **4.** *Trademarks.* A manufacturer's or distributor's conduct in knowingly supplying, for resale, goods bearing an infringing mark.

copyright infringement. The act of violating any of a copyright owner's exclusive rights granted by the federal Copyright Act, 17 USCA §§ 106, 602. • A copyright owner has several exclusive rights in copyrighted works, including the rights (1) to reproduce the work, (2) to prepare derivative works based on the work, (3) to distribute copies of the work, (4) for certain kinds of works, to perform the work publicly, (5) for certain kinds of works, to display the work publicly, (6) for sound recordings, to perform the work publicly, and (7) to import into the United States copies acquired elsewhere.

criminal infringement. The statutory criminal offense of either (1) willfully infringing a copyright to obtain a commercial advantage or financial gain (17 USCA § 506; 18 USCA § 2319), or (2) trafficking in goods or services that bear a counterfeit mark (18 USCA § 2320). • Under the second category, the law imposes criminal penalties if the counterfeit mark is (1) identical with, or substantially indistinguishable from, a mark registered on the Principal Register of the U.S. Patent and Trademark Office, and (2) likely to confuse or deceive the public.

direct infringement. **1.** *Patents.* The act of making, using, selling, offering for sale, or importing into the United States, without the patentee's permission, a product that is covered by the claims of a valid patent. 35 USCA § 271(a). **2.** *Trademarks.* The use of a mark in trade when that use causes a likelihood of confusion about the source of goods or services already identified by a similar mark. **3.** *Copyright.* The unauthorized copying, distributing, or displaying of — or the adapting of a derivative work from — a copyrighted work. Cf. *contributory infringement*; *infringement in the inducement.*

domain-name infringement. Infringement of another's trademark or servicemark by the use of a confusingly similar Internet domain name.

infringement by sale. *Patents.* The unauthorized sale, resale, or offer of a possessory interest in a patented invention. — Also termed *infringement through sale.*

infringement in the inducement. *Patents.* The act of actively and knowingly aiding and abetting direct infringement by another person. • Although sometimes used in copyright and trademark law to mean contributory infringement, the term is usu. reserved for the patent context. — Also termed *inducing infringement.* Cf. *direct infringement.*

innocent infringement. The act of violating an intellectual-property right without knowledge or awareness that the act constitutes infringement. • An innocent infringer may, in limited circumstances, escape liability for some or all of the damages. In the copyright context, damages may be limited if (1) the infringer was misled by the lack of a copyright notice on an authorized copy of the copyrighted work, distributed under the owner's authority before March 1989 (the effective date of the Berne Convention Implementation Act of 1988), and (2) the infringing act occurred before the infringer received actual notice of the copyright. 17 USCA § 405(b). In the trademark context, publishers and distributors of paid advertisements who innocently infringe a mark have no liability for damages. 15 USCA § 1114. In both contexts, the innocent infringer is immunized only from an award of monetary damages, not from injunctive relief. Cf. *willful infringement.*

literal infringement. *Patents.* Infringement in which every element and every limitation of a patent claim is present, exactly, in the accused product or process. Cf. DOCTRINE OF EQUIVALENTS.

nonliteral infringement. See DOCTRINE OF EQUIVALENTS.

patent infringement. The unauthorized making, using, offering to sell, selling, or importing into the United States of any patented invention. 35 USCA § 271(a).

trademark infringement. The unauthorized use of a trademark — or of a confusingly similar name, word, symbol, or any combination of these — in connection with the same or related goods or services and in a manner that is likely to cause confusion, deception, or mistake about the source of the goods or services. See LIKELI-HOOD-OF-CONFUSION TEST.

vicarious infringement. A person's liability for an infringing act of someone else, even though the person has not directly committed an act of infringement. • For example, a concert theater can be vicariously liable for an infringing performance of a hired band.

willful infringement. An intentional and deliberate infringement of another person's intellectual property. Cf. *innocent infringement*.

infringement by sale. See INFRINGEMENT.

infringement search. *Patents.* A patent search aimed at discovering whether a product or method infringes any in-force patent. • An infringement search is usu. limited to the political territory where the patent is to be relied on. — Also termed *clear-to-use search*; *freedom-to-operate search*; *FTO search.* Cf. PATENTABILITY SEARCH; VALIDITY SEARCH.

infringement test. *Patents.* A means of determining whether a patent claim is dependent by asking if the claim would always be infringed if the independent claim on which it rests were infringed. • Since a dependent claim must incorporate all the elements of the independent claim, an infringement of the independent claim must also be an infringement of the dependent claim.

infringement through sale. See *infringement by sale* under INFRINGEMENT.

infringer. (16c) A person who interferes with one of the exclusive rights of a patent, copyright, or trademark owner. See INFRINGEMENT.

in full. Constituting the whole or complete amount <payment in full>.

in full life. (Of a person) alive in fact and in law; neither naturally nor civilly dead.

in futuro (in fyə-**tyoor**-oh), *adv.* [Latin] In the future. Cf. IN PRAESENTI.

in genere (in **jen**-ər-ee). [Latin "in kind"] Belonging to the same class, but not identical.

ingratitude, *n.* Civil law. Lack of appreciation for a generous or kind act, esp. for a gift received. • Under Louisiana law, a gift may be reclaimed on grounds of ingratitude if the recipient mistreats the giver by, for example, attempting to murder the giver or refusing to provide the giver with needed food. La. Civ. Code art. 1560.

ingress (in-gres). (15c) **1.** The act of entering. **2.** The right or ability to enter; access. Cf. EGRESS.

ingress, egress, and regress. (17c) The right of a lessee to enter, leave, and reenter the land in question.

in gross. 1. Undivided; still in one large mass. — Also termed *en gros; en grosse.* **2.** (Of a servitude) personal as distinguished from appurtenant to land. See *easement in gross* under EASEMENT.

ingross, *vb.* See ENGROSS.

inhabit, *vb.* (14c) To dwell in; to occupy permanently or habitually as a residence.

inhere (in-**heer**), *vb.* (15c) To exist as a permanent, inseparable, or essential attribute or quality of a thing; to be intrinsic to something.

inherency doctrine. *Patents.* The rule that anticipation can be inferred despite a missing element in a prior-art reference if the missing element is either necessarily present in or a natural result of the product or process and a person of ordinary skill in the art would know it. • On one hand, the doctrine precludes patenting an existing invention by merely claiming an inherent element. On the other hand, it allows the later patentability of a substance, usu. a chemical compound, that was inadvertently created but not recognized or appreciated. See INHERENT ANTICIPATION.

inherent anticipation. *Patents.* An invention's lack of novelty arising from the existence of prior-art products or processes that necessarily possess the same characteristics. • Inherency differs from obviousness in that a lack of novelty must be based on fact, not mere possibility or probability. See DOCTRINE OF INHERENCY.

inherent authority. See AUTHORITY (1).

inherent condition. See CONDITION (2).

inherent covenant. See COVENANT (1).

inherent defect. See *hidden defect* under DEFECT.

inherently dangerous. See DANGEROUS.

inherently dangerous activity. An activity that can be carried out only by the exercise of special skill and care and that involves a grave risk of serious harm if done unskillfully or carelessly.

inherently dangerous work. See WORK (1).

inherent power. See POWER (3).

inherent-powers doctrine. The principle that allows courts to deal with diverse matters over which they are thought to have intrinsic authority, such as (1) procedural rulemaking, (2) internal budgeting of the courts, (3) regulating the practice of law; and (4) general judicial housekeeping. • The power is based on interpretations of art. I, § 8, cl. 18 of the Constitution.

inherent right. See *inalienable right* under RIGHT.

inherit, *vb.* (14c) **1.** To receive (property) from an ancestor under the laws of intestate succession upon the ancestor's death. **2.** To receive (property) as a bequest or devise.

inheritable, *adj.* See HERITABLE.

inheritable blood. See *heritable blood* under BLOOD.

inheritable obligation. See *heritable obligation* under OBLIGATION.

inheritable security. See *heritable security* under SECURITY.

inheritance. (14c) **1.** Property received from an ancestor under the laws of intestacy. **2.** Property that a person receives by bequest or devise.

    dual inheritance. An adopted child's intestate inheritance through both his adopted family and his natural parent. • The problem of dual inheritance occurs only if a relative of the birth parent adopts the child. For instance, if a child's mother dies and the maternal grandparents adopt the grandchild, and if a grandparent then dies intestate, the child qualifies for two separate shares — one as a child and the other as a grandchild. In some jurisdictions, by statute, such a child is allowed to inherit only the adopted child's share. Under the Uniform Probate Code, the child takes the larger of the two shares.

    several inheritance. An inheritance that descends to two persons severally, as by moieties.

    shifting inheritance. Under intestacy laws, an inheritance that is transferred from an heir who was living when the intestate died to an afterborn heir who is more closely related to the intestate.

    universal inheritance. A system by which an intestate's estate escheats to the state only if the decedent leaves no surviving relatives, no matter how distant. • Universal inheritance has been almost universally abandoned in Anglo-American jurisdictions. See UNIVERSAL-INHERITANCE RULE.

inheritance tax. See TAX.

inheritor (in-**hair**-i-tər), *n.* (15c) A person who inherits; HEIR.

inheritrix (in-**hair**-i-triks), *n. Archaic.* A female heir; HEIRESS.

inhibition (in-hi-**bish**-ən), *n.* **1.** *Eccles. law.* A writ issued by a superior ecclesiastical court, forbidding a judge from proceeding in a pending case. **2.** *Eccles. law.* An order issuing from an ecclesiastical court, prohibiting a member of the clergy from taking office or performing an unlawful action. **3.** *Hist.* A writ of prohibition. **4.** *Scots law.* An order issued by the Court of Session to prohibit a debtor from encumbering or alienating the debtor's heritable property to the prejudice of a creditor. See (in senses 3 & 4) PROHIBITION (2).

in hoc (in **hok**), *adv.* [Latin] In this; in respect to this.

in hoc statu (in hok **stay**-t[y]oo). [Latin] *Hist.* In this position.

in-house counsel. See COUNSEL.

inhuman treatment. *Family law.* Physical or mental cruelty so severe that it endangers life or health. • Inhuman treatment is usu. grounds for divorce. See CRUELTY.

initial appearance. See APPEARANCE.

initial cause. See *proximate cause* under CAUSE (1).

initial determination. See DETERMINATION.

initial disclosure. See DISCLOSURE (2).

initial margin requirement. See MARGIN REQUIREMENT.

initial protest. See PROTEST (2).

initial public offering. See OFFERING.

initial surplus. See SURPLUS.

initiation of charges. *Military law.* The first report to the proper military authority of an alleged commission of an offense by a person subject to the Uniform Code of Military Justice. Cf. PREFERRING OF CHARGES.

initiative (i-**nish**-ə-tiv *or* i-**nish**-ee-ə-tiv). (1889) An electoral process by which a percentage of voters can propose legislation and compel a vote on it by the legislature or by the full electorate. • Recognized in some state constitutions, the initiative is one of the few methods of direct democracy in an otherwise representative system. Cf. PLEBISCITE; REFERENDUM.

injoin, *vb. Archaic.* See ENJOIN.

injunction (in-**jəngk**-shən), *n.* (16c) A court order commanding or preventing an action. • To get an injunction, the complainant must show that there is no plain, adequate, and complete remedy at law and that an irreparable injury will result unless the relief is granted. — Also termed *writ of injunction.* See IRREPARABLE-INJURY RULE.

    affirmative injunction. See *mandatory injunction.*

    antisuit injunction. An injunction prohibiting a litigant from instituting other, related litigation, usu. between the same parties on the same issues.

    ex parte injunction. (1854) A preliminary injunction issued after the court has heard from only the moving party. — Also termed *temporary restraining order.*

    final injunction. See *permanent injunction.*

    head-start injunction. *Trade secrets.* An injunction prohibiting the defendant from using a trade secret for a period of time equal to the time between the date of the secret's theft and the date when the secret became public. • So named since that period is the "head start" the defendant unfairly gained over the rest of the industry.

injunction pendente lite. See *preliminary injunction*.

interlocutory injunction. See *preliminary injunction*.

mandatory injunction. (1843) An injunction that orders an affirmative act or mandates a specified course of conduct. — Also termed *affirmative injunction*. Cf. *prohibitory injunction*.

permanent injunction. (1846) An injunction granted after a final hearing on the merits. • Despite its name, a permanent injunction does not necessarily last forever. — Also termed *perpetual injunction*; *final injunction*.

perpetual injunction. See *permanent injunction*.

preliminary injunction. (1828) A temporary injunction issued before or during trial to prevent an irreparable injury from occurring before the court has a chance to decide the case. • A preliminary injunction will be issued only after the defendant receives notice and an opportunity to be heard. — Also termed *interlocutory injunction*; *temporary injunction*; *provisional injunction*; *injunction pendente lite*. Cf. *ex parte injunction*; TEMPORARY RESTRAINING ORDER.

preventive injunction. (1882) An injunction designed to prevent a loss or injury in the future. Cf. *reparative injunction*.

prohibitory injunction. (1843) An injunction that forbids or restrains an act. • This is the most common type of injunction. Cf. *mandatory injunction*.

provisional injunction. See *preliminary injunction*.

quia-timet injunction (kwɪ-ə tɪ-mət *or* kwee-ə tim-et). [Latin "because he fears"] (1913) An injunction granted to prevent an action that has been threatened but has not yet violated the plaintiff's rights. See QUIA TIMET.

reparative injunction (ri-par-ə-tiv). (1955) An injunction requiring the defendant to restore the plaintiff to the position that the plaintiff occupied before the defendant committed a wrong. Cf. *preventive injunction*.

special injunction. *Hist.* An injunction in which the prohibition of an act is the only relief ultimately sought, as in prevention of waste or nuisance.

temporary injunction. See *preliminary injunction*.

injunction bond. See BOND (2).

injunctive, *adj.* (15c) That has the quality of directing or ordering; of or relating to an injunction. — Also termed *injunctional*.

in jure (in **joor**-ee). [Latin "in law"] **1.** According to the law. **2.** *Roman law.* Before the praetor or other magistrate. • *In jure* referred to the first stage of a Roman formulary trial, held before the praetor or other judicial magistrate for the purpose of establishing the legal issues and their competence. Evidence was taken in the second stage, which was held before a judex. See FORMULA (1).

in jure alterius (in **joor**-ee al-**teer**-ee-əs), *adv.* [Latin] In another's right.

in jure cessio (in **joor**-ee **sesh**-ee-oh). [Latin "a surrender in law"] *Roman law.* A fictitious trial held to transfer ownership of property; a collusive claim to formally convey property, esp. incorporeal property, by a court's assignment of ownership. • At trial, the transferee appeared before a praetor and asserted ownership of the property. The actual owner also appeared, but did not contest the assertion, and so allowed the transfer of the property to the plaintiff. *In jure cessio* was most often used to convey incorporeal property. — Also spelled *in iure cessio*.

in jure proprio (in **joor**-ee **proh**-pree-oh), *adv.* [Latin] In one's own right.

injuria (in-**joor**-ee-ə), *n.* [Latin] *Roman law.* **1.** See WRONG. **2.** An assault on a person's reputation or body. Pl. **injuriae** (in-**joor**-ee-ee).

injuria absque damno (in-**joor**-ee-ə **abs**-kwee **dam**-noh). [Latin "injury without damage"] A legal wrong that will not sustain a lawsuit because no harm resulted from it. — Also termed *injuria sine damno*. Cf. DAMNUM SINE INJURIA.

injurious, *adj.* (15c) Harmful; tending to injure.

injurious exposure. *Workers' compensation.* Contact with a substance that would cause injury if the person were repeatedly exposed to it over time. • An employer may be found liable for harm resulting from injurious exposure.

injurious falsehood. 1. See DISPARAGEMENT (3). **2.** See TRADE DISPARAGEMENT.

injurious words. *Louisiana law.* Slanderous or libelous language. See SLANDER; LIBEL (1), (2).

injury, *n.* (14c) **1.** The violation of another's legal right, for which the law provides a remedy; a wrong or injustice. See WRONG. **2.** *Scots law.* Anything said or done in breach of a duty not to do it, if harm results to another in person, character, or property. • Injuries are divided into real injuries (such as wounding) and verbal injuries (such as slander). They may be criminal wrongs (as with assault) or civil wrongs (as with defamation). **3.** Any harm or damage. • Some authorities distinguish *harm* from *injury*, holding that while *harm* denotes any personal loss or detriment, *injury* involves an actionable invasion of a legally protected interest. See Restatement (Second) of Torts § 7, cmt. a (1965). — **injure**, *vb.* — **injurious**, *adj.*

accidental injury. (1800) An injury resulting from external, violent, and unanticipated causes; esp., a bodily injury caused by some external force or agency operating contrary to a person's intentions, unexpectedly, and not according to the usual order of events.

advertising injury. Harm resulting from (1) oral or written speech that slanders or libels a person, or disparages a person's goods, products, or services; (2) oral or written speech that violates a person's right of privacy; (3) misappropriation of advertising ideas or style of doing business; or (4) infringement of copyright, esp. in a name or slogan.

bodily injury. (16c) Physical damage to a person's body. — Also termed *physical injury*. See *serious bodily injury.*

civil injury. (17c) Physical harm or property damage caused by breach of a contract or by a criminal offense redressable through a civil action.

compensable injury (kəm-**pen**-sə-bəl). *Workers' compensation.* An injury caused by an accident arising from the employment and in the course of the employee's work, and for which the employee is statutorily entitled to receive compensation.

consequential injury. See *consequential loss* under LOSS.

continual injury. An injury that recurs at repeated intervals. — Also termed (but improperly) *continuous injury.*

continuing injury. (1824) An injury that is still in the process of being committed. • An example is the constant smoke or noise of a factory. — Also termed *continuing harm.*

direct injury. (17c) **1.** An injury resulting directly from violation of a legal right. **2.** An injury resulting directly from a particular cause, without any intervening causes.

great bodily injury. See *serious bodily injury.*

injury in fact. (1809) An actual or imminent invasion of a legally protected interest, in contrast to an invasion that is conjectural or hypothetical. • An injury in fact gives the victim standing to bring an action for damages.

irreparable injury (i-**rep**-ər-ə-bəl). (17c) An injury that cannot be adequately measured or compensated by money and is therefore often considered remediable by injunction. — Also termed *irreparable harm*; *nonpecuniary injury.* See IRREPARABLE-INJURY RULE.

legal injury. (18c) Violation of a legal right.

malicious injury. (16c) **1.** An injury resulting from a willful act committed with knowledge that it is likely to injure another or with reckless disregard of the consequences. **2.** MALICIOUS MISCHIEF.

nonpecuniary injury. See *irreparable injury.*

pecuniary injury. An injury that can be adequately measured or compensated by money.

permanent injury. (17c) **1.** A completed wrong whose consequences cannot be remedied for an indefinite period. **2.** *Property.* A lasting injury to land that causes it to revert to the grantor or vests immediate right of possession in a remainderman. Cf. *temporary injury.*

personal injury. (16c) *Torts.* **1.** In a negligence action, any harm caused to a person, such as a broken bone, a cut, or a bruise; bodily injury. **2.** Any invasion of a personal right, including mental suffering and false imprisonment. — Also termed *private injury.* **3.** For purposes of workers' compensation, any harm (including a worsened preexisting condition) that arises in the scope of employment. — Abbr. PI.

physical injury. See *bodily injury.*

private injury. See *personal injury* (2).

public injury. A loss or an injury stemming from a breach of a duty or violation of a right that affects the community as a whole.

reparable injury (**rep**-ər-ə-bəl). (1832) An injury that can be adequately compensated by money.

scheduled injury. A partially disabling injury for which a predetermined amount of compensation is allowed under a workers'-compensation statute.

serious bodily injury. (1843) Serious physical impairment of the human body; esp., bodily injury that creates a substantial risk of death or that causes serious, permanent disfigurement or protracted loss or impairment of the function of any body part or organ. Model Penal Code § 210.0(3). • Typically, the fact-finder must decide in any given case whether the injury meets this general standard. Generally, an injury meets this standard if it creates a substantial risk of fatal consequences or, when inflicted, constitutes mayhem. Cf. MAYHEM (1). — Also termed *serious bodily harm*; *grievous bodily harm*; *great bodily injury.*

temporary injury. An injury that may be abated or discontinued at any time by either the injured party or the wrongdoer. Cf. *permanent injury.*

willful and malicious injury. *Bankruptcy.* Under the statutory exception to discharge, damage to another entity (such as a creditor) caused by a debtor intentionally performing a wrongful act — without just cause or excuse — that the debtor knew was certain or substantially certain to cause injury. 11 USCA § 523(a)(6).

injury-in-fact trigger. See ACTUAL-INJURY TRIGGER.

injustice. (15c) **1.** An unjust state of affairs; unfairness. **2.** An unjust act.

in kind, *adv.* (17c) **1.** In goods or services rather than money <payment in cash or in kind>. **2.** In a similar way; with an equivalent of what has been offered or received <returned the favor in kind>. — **in-kind,** *adj.* <in-kind repayment>.

INL. *abbr.* BUREAU OF INTERNATIONAL NARCOTICS AND LAW ENFORCEMENT.

inland. (15c) **1.** The interior part of a country or region, away from the coast or border. **2.** *Hist.* The portion of a feudal estate lying closest to the lord's manor and dedicated to the support of the lord's family. — Also termed (in sense 2) *inlantal*.

inland bill of exchange. See *domestic bill* (2) under BILL (6).

inland draft. See DRAFT.

inland marine insurance. See INSURANCE.

inland revenue. See INTERNAL REVENUE.

inland trade. See TRADE.

inland waters. See INTERNAL WATERS.

in law. (15c) Existing in law or by force of law; in the contemplation of the law. Cf. IN FACT.

in-law, *n.* (1894) A relative by marriage.

inlaw, *vb. Archaic.* To place (an offender) under the protection of the law. Cf. OUTLAW (1).

inlawry. The restoration of an outlawed person's rights and protections under the law.

in legal custody. See IN CUSTODIA LEGIS.

in lieu of. (13c) Instead of or in place of; in exchange or return for <the creditor took a note in lieu of cash> <the defendant was released in lieu of $5,000 bond>.

in lieu tax. See TAX.

in limine (in **lim**-ə-nee), *adv.* [Latin "at the outset"] (18c) Preliminarily; presented to only the judge, before or during trial <a question to be decided in limine>. See MOTION IN LIMINE.

in-limine, *adj.* (Of a motion or order) raised preliminarily, esp. because of an issue about the admissibility of evidence believed by the movant to be prejudicial <in-limine motion>.

in litem (in **lɪ**-tem *or* -təm), *adv.* [Latin] For a suit; to the suit. See AD LITEM.

in loco (in **loh**-koh). [Latin] In the place of.

in loco parentis (in **loh**-koh pə-**ren**-tis), *adv.* & *adj.* [Latin "in the place of a parent"] (1818) Of, relating to, or acting as a temporary guardian or caretaker of a child, taking on all or some of the responsibilities of a parent. • The Supreme Court has recognized that during the school day, a teacher or administrator may act *in loco parentis. See Vernonia Sch. Dist. v. Acton*, 515 U.S. 646, 115 S.Ct. 2386 (1995). See PERSON IN LOCO PARENTIS.

in loco parentis, *n.* Supervision of a young adult by an administrative body such as a university.

in manu mortua. See IN MORTUA MANU.

in-marriage. See MARRIAGE (1).

inmate. (16c) **1.** A person confined in a prison, hospital, or similar institution. **2.** *Archaic.* A person living inside a place; one who lives with others in a dwelling.

in medias res (in **mee**-dee-əs **reez** *or* in **me**-dee-ahs **rays**), *adv.* [Latin] Into the middle of things; without preface or introduction.

in mercy, *adv.* (17c) At a judge's discretion concerning punishment. • A judgment formerly noted (using the Law Latin phrase *in misericordia*) which litigant lost by stating that the unsuccessful party was in the court's mercy. A plaintiff held in mercy for a false claim, for example, was said to be *in misericordia pro falso clamore suo*.

in mortua manu (in **mor**-choo-ə **man**-yoo), *adj.* & *adv.* [Law Latin "in a dead hand"] *Hist.* (Of property) perpetually controlled according to a decedent's directions. • Land held by a religious society was described this way because the church could hold property perpetually without rendering feudal service. — Also termed *in manu mortua.* See DEADHAND CONTROL; MORTMAIN.

innavigable (in-**nav**-i-gə-bəl), *adj.* **1.** (Of a body of water) not capable of, or unsuitable for, navigation. **2.** *Marine insurance.* (Of a vessel) unfit for service. — Also termed *unnavigable.*

inner bar. *English law.* The group of senior barristers, called the Queen's Counsel or King's Counsel, who are admitted to plead within the bar of the court. Cf. OUTER BAR.

inner barrister. See BARRISTER.

inner cabinet. See CABINET.

inner-city post-traumatic-stress defense. See URBAN-SURVIVAL SYNDROME.

inning. *(pl.)* Land reclaimed from the sea.

innkeeper. (15c) A person who, for compensation, keeps open a public house for the lodging and entertainment of travelers. • A keeper of a boarding house is usu. not considered an innkeeper. — Also termed *hotelkeeper.*

innkeeper's lien. See *hotelkeeper's lien* under LIEN.

innocence, *n.* (14c) The absence of guilt; esp., freedom from guilt for a particular offense. Cf. GUILT.

actual innocence. (1839) *Criminal law.* The absence of facts that are prerequisites for the sentence given to a defendant. • In death-penalty cases, actual innocence is an exception to the cause-and-prejudice rule, and can result in a successful challenge to the death sentence on the basis of a defense that was not presented to the trial court. The prisoner must show by clear and convincing evidence that, but for constitutional error in the trial court, no reasonable judge or juror would find the defendant eligible for the death penalty. See *Sawyer v. Whitley*, 505 U.S. 333, 112 S.Ct. 2514 (1992). Cf. CAUSE-AND-PREJUDICE RULE.

legal innocence. (1813) *Criminal law.* The absence of one or more procedural or legal bases to support the sentence given to a defendant. • In the context of a petition for writ of habeas corpus or other attack on the sentence, legal innocence is often contrasted with actual innocence. Actual innocence, which focuses on the facts underlying the sentence, can sometimes be used to obtain relief from the death penalty based on trial-court errors that were not objected to at trial, even if the petitioner cannot meet the elements of the cause-and-prejudice rule. But legal innocence, which focuses on the applicable law and procedure, is not as readily available. Inadvertence or a poor trial strategy resulting in the defendant's failure to assert an established legal principle will not ordinarily be sufficient to satisfy the cause-and-prejudice rule or to establish the right to an exception from that rule. See CAUSE-AND-PREJUDICE RULE.

innocent, *adj.* (14c) Free from guilt; free from legal fault. See NOT GUILTY (2).

innocent agent. See AGENT (2).

innocent-construction rule. The doctrine that an allegedly libelous statement will be given an innocuous interpretation if the statement is either ambiguous or harmless.

innocent conversion. See *technical conversion* under CONVERSION (2).

innocent converter. See CONVERTER.

innocent conveyance. See CONVEYANCE.

innocent homicide. See HOMICIDE.

innocent infringement. See INFRINGEMENT.

innocent junior user. See JUNIOR USER.

innocent misrepresentation. See MISREPRESENTATION.

innocent-owner defense. See DEFENSE (1).

innocent party. See PARTY (2).

innocent passage. *Int'l law.* The right of a foreign ship to pass through a country's territorial waters; the right of a foreign vessel to travel through a country's maritime belt without paying a toll. •

The right of innocent passage is guaranteed in Article 17 of the United Nations Convention on the Law of the Sea. Passage is considered innocent as long as it is not prejudicial to the peace, good order, and security of the coastal country. — Also termed *right of innocent passage.* Cf. TRANSIT PASSAGE.

innocent purchaser. See *bona fide purchaser* under PURCHASER (1).

innocent purchaser for value. See *bona fide purchaser* under PURCHASER (1).

innocent spouse. See SPOUSE.

innocent trespass. See TRESPASS.

innocent trespasser. See TRESPASSER.

Inn of Chancery. *Hist.* Any of nine collegiate houses where students studied either to gain entry into an Inn of Court or to learn how to frame writs in order to serve in the chancery courts. • Over time, the Inns — Clement's, Clifford's, Lyon's, Furnival's, Thavies', Symond's, Barnard's, Staples', and the New Inn — became little more than dining clubs, and never exercised control over their members as the Inns of Court did. The Inns of Chancery were all dissolved in the 19th century. Cf. INN OF COURT.

Inn of Court. 1. Any of four autonomous institutions, one or more of which English barristers must join to receive their training and of which they remain members for life: The Honourable Societies of Lincoln's Inn, the Middle Temple, the Inner Temple, and Gray's Inn. • These powerful bodies examine candidates for the Bar, "call" them to the Bar, and award the degree of barrister. **2.** (*pl.*) In the United States, an organization (formally named the *American Inns of Court Foundation*) with more than 100 local chapters, whose members include judges, practicing attorneys, law professors, and law students. • Through monthly meetings, the chapters emphasize practice skills, professionalism, and ethics, and provide mentors to train students and young lawyers in the finer points of good legal practice.

innominate (i-**nom**-ə-nət), *adj.* (17c) *Civil law.* Unclassified; having no special name or designation. See *innominate contract* under CONTRACT.

innominate action. See ACTION (4).

innominate contract. See CONTRACT.

innominate obligations. (1949) Obligations having no specific classification or name because they are not strictly contractual, delictual, or quasi-contractual. • An example is the obligation of a trustee to a beneficiary. — Also termed *obligationes innominati.*

innominate real contract. See *innominate contract* under CONTRACT.

innuendo (in-yoo-**en**-doh). [Latin "by hinting"] (17c) **1.** An oblique remark or indirect suggestion, usu. of a derogatory nature. **2.** An explanatory word or passage inserted parenthetically into a legal document. • In criminal law, an innuendo is a statement in an indictment showing the application or meaning of matter previously expressed, the meaning of which would not otherwise be clear. In the law of defamation, an innuendo is the plaintiff's explanation of a statement's defamatory meaning when that meaning is not apparent from the statement's face. For example, the innuendo of the statement "David burned down his house" can be shown by pleading that the statement was understood to mean that David was defrauding his insurance company (the fact that he had insured his house is pleaded and proved by *inducement*). Cf. INDUCEMENT (4); COLLOQUIUM.

inofficious testament. See TESTAMENT.

inofficious will. See *inofficious testament* under TESTAMENT.

inoperable mode. *Patents.* In a patent application, a disclosed way of working an invention that is not the best mode. • The term usu. designates a mode that is intended to misrepresent or deliberately conceal the best mode. That misrepresentation or concealment is inequitable conduct that will bar patentability or render an issued patent unenforceable.

inoperative, *adj.* (17c) **1.** Having no force or effect; not operative <an inoperative statute>. **2.** *Patents.* (Of an invention), the condition of not being capable of functioning as described in the patent application.

in order. 1. Ready for business <the meeting is in order>. **2.** Available and appropriate for consideration under the applicable rules <the motion is in order>. Cf. OUT OF ORDER (1).

in pais (in **pay** *or* **pays**). [Law French "in the country"] Outside court or legal proceedings. See *equitable estoppel* (1) under ESTOPPEL.

in paper. *Hist.* Of a proceeding that is within the jurisdiction of the trial court; that is, before the record is prepared for an appeal.

in pari delicto (in **par**-ı də-**lik**-toh), *adv.* [Latin "in equal fault"] Equally at fault <the court denied relief because both parties stood *in pari delicto*>.

in pari delicto doctrine, *n.* [Latin] (1917) The principle that a plaintiff who has participated in wrongdoing may not recover damages resulting from the wrongdoing.

in pari materia (in **par**-ı mə-**teer**-ee-ə). [Latin "in the same matter"] **1.** *adj.* On the same subject; relating to the same matter. • It is a canon of construction that statutes that are *in pari materia* may be construed together, so that inconsistencies in one statute may be resolved by looking at another statute on the same subject. **2.** *adv.* Loosely, in conjunction with <the Maryland constitutional provision is construed *in pari materia* with the Fourth Amendment>.

in perpetuity (in pər-pə-**t[y]oo**-ə-tee). (14c) Forever. See PERPETUITY.

in personam (in pər-**soh**-nəm), *adj.* [Latin "against a person"] (18c) **1.** Involving or determining the personal rights and obligations of the parties. **2.** (Of a legal action) brought against a person rather than property. — Also termed *personal.* See *action in personam* under ACTION (4). Cf. IN REM. — **in personam,** *adv.*

in personam judgment. See *personal judgment* under JUDGMENT.

in personam jurisdiction. See *personal jurisdiction* under JURISDICTION.

in pleno lumine (in **plee**-noh **loo**-mə-nee), *adv.* & *adj.* [Law Latin] In the light of day; in common knowledge; in public.

in poenam (in **pee**-nəm). [Latin] *Hist.* As a penalty; as a punishment.

in point. See ON POINT.

in posse (in **pos**-ee). [Latin] Not currently existing, but ready to come into existence under certain conditions in the future; potential <the will contemplated both living children and children *in posse*>. Cf. IN ESSE.

in praesenti (in pri-**zen**-tı *or* pree-). [Latin] At present; right now. Cf. IN FUTURO.

in prender (in **pren**-dər), *adj.* [Law French "in taking"] *Hist.* (Of a right) consisting in property taken to fulfill a claim to it, such as an incorporeal hereditament (as a *heriot custom*) that a lord had to seize in order to exercise the right to it.

in-presence rule. The principle that a police officer may make a warrantless arrest of a person who commits a misdemeanor offense not only in the officer's actual presence but also within the officer's immediate vicinity.

in primis (in **prı**-mis). See IMPRIMIS.

in propria persona (in **proh**-pree-ə pər-**soh**-nə). [Latin "in one's own person"] See PRO SE.

inquest. (13c) **1.** An inquiry by a coroner or medical examiner, sometimes with the aid of a jury, into the manner of death of a person who has died under suspicious circumstances, or who has died in prison. — Also termed *coroner's inquest; inquisition after death.* **2.** An inquiry into a certain matter by a jury empaneled for that purpose. **3.** The finding of such a specially empaneled jury. **4.** A proceeding, usu. ex parte, to determine, after the defendant has defaulted, the amount of the plaintiff's damages. Cf. INQUISITION.

grand inquest. 1. An impeachment proceeding. **2.** *Hist.* (*cap.*) The survey of the lands of England in 1085–1086, by order of William the Conqueror, and resulting in the Domesday Book — Also termed *Great Inquest*; *Grand Survey*; *Great Survey*. See DOMESDAY BOOK. **3.** *Hist.* Grand jury.

inquest of office. *Hist.* An inquest conducted by a coroner, sheriff, or other royal officer into the Crown's right to property by reason of escheat, treason, or other ground of forfeiture.

5. WARDMOTE.

inquest jury. See JURY.

inquiry. (15c) **1.** *Int'l law.* FACT-FINDING (2). **2.** *Parliamentary law.* A request for information, either procedural or substantive. See REQUEST; POINT (2).

parliamentary inquiry. An inquiry that asks a question about procedure.

3. *Hist.* A writ to assess damages by the sheriff or sheriff's deputies.

inquiry notice. See NOTICE.

inquisition. (14c) **1.** The record of the finding of the jury sworn by the coroner to inquire into a person's death. **2.** A judicial inquiry, esp. in a derogatory sense. **3.** A persistent, grueling examination conducted without regard for the examinee's dignity or civil rights. Cf. INQUEST.

inquisition after death. See INQUEST (1).

inquisitor. (16c) **1.** An officer who examines and inquires, such as a coroner or sheriff. **2.** A person who inquires; esp., one who examines another in a harsh or hostile manner. **3.** *Hist. Eccles. law.* An officer authorized to inquire into heresies; esp., an officer of the Spanish Inquisition.

inquisitorial court. See COURT.

inquisitorial system. (1846) A system of proof-taking used in civil law, whereby the judge conducts the trial, determines what questions to ask, and defines the scope and the extent of the inquiry. • This system prevails in most of continental Europe, in Japan, and in Central and South America. Cf. ADVERSARY SYSTEM.

INR. *abbr.* BUREAU OF INTELLIGENCE AND RESEARCH.

in re (in **ree** *or* **ray**). [Latin "in the matter of"] (1877) (Of a judicial proceeding) not formally including adverse parties, but rather involving something (such as an estate). • The term is often used in case citations, esp. in uncontested proceedings <*In re Butler's Estate*>. — Also termed *matter of* <*Matter of Butler's Estate*>.

in rem (in **rem**), *adj.* [Latin "against a thing"] (18c) Involving or determining the status of a thing, and therefore the rights of persons generally with respect to that thing. — Also termed (archaically) *impersonal*. See *action in rem* under ACTION (4). Cf. IN PERSONAM. — **in rem,** *adv.*

quasi in rem (**kway**-SI in **rem** *or* **kway**-ZI). [Latin "as if against a thing"] (1804) Involving or determining the rights of a person having an interest in property located within the court's jurisdiction. See *action quasi in rem* under ACTION (4).

in rem judgment. See *judgment in rem* under JUDGMENT.

in rem jurisdiction. See JURISDICTION.

inroll, *vb.* See ENROLL (1).

inrollment. See ENROLLMENT.

INS. *abbr.* IMMIGRATION AND NATURALIZATION SERVICE.

insane, *adj.* (16c) Mentally deranged; suffering from one or more delusions or false beliefs that (1) have no foundation in reason or reality, (2) are not credible to any reasonable person of sound mind, and (3) cannot be overcome in a sufferer's mind by any amount of evidence or argument. See INSANITY.

insane asylum. See ASYLUM (3).

insane delusion. (1838) An irrational, persistent belief in an imaginary state of facts resulting in a lack of capacity to undertake acts of legal consequence, such as making a will. See CAPACITY (2).

insanity, *n.* (16c) Any mental disorder severe enough that it prevents a person from having legal capacity and excuses the person from criminal or civil responsibility. • Insanity is a legal, not a medical, standard. — Also termed *legal insanity*; *lunacy*. Cf. SANITY.

emotional insanity. (1872) Insanity produced by a violent excitement of the emotions or passions, although reasoning faculties may remain unimpaired; a passion that for a period creates complete derangement of intellect. • Emotional insanity is sometimes described as an irresistible impulse to do an act. See IRRESISTIBLE-IMPULSE TEST.

partial insanity. See *diminished capacity* under CAPACITY (3).

temporary insanity. (18c) Insanity that exists only at the time of a criminal act.

insanity defense. *Criminal law.* (1912) An affirmative defense alleging that a mental disorder caused the accused to commit the crime. See 18 USCA § 17; Fed. R. Crim. P. 12.2. • Unlike other defenses, a successful insanity defense may not result in an acquittal but instead in a special verdict ("not guilty by reason of insanity") that usu. leads to the defendant's commitment to a mental institution. — Also termed *insanity plea*. See MCNAGHTEN RULES; SUBSTANTIAL-CAPACITY TEST; IRRESISTIBLE-IMPULSE TEST; DURHAM RULE; APPRECIATION TEST.

black-rage insanity defense. An insanity defense based on an African-American's violent eruption of anger induced at least partly by racial tensions. • This defense was first used in the mid-1990s.

Insanity Defense Reform Act of 1984 test. See APPRECIATION TEST.

insanity plea. See INSANITY DEFENSE.

inscription, *n.* (14c) **1.** The act of entering a fact or name on a list, register, or other record. **2.** An entry so recorded. **3.** *Civil law.* An agreement whereby an accuser must, if the accusation is false, receive the same punishment that the accused would have been given if found guilty. — **inscribe,** *vb.* — **inscriptive,** *adj.*

inscrutable fault. See FAULT.

insecure, *adj.* (17c) Having a good-faith belief that the possibility of receiving payment or performance from another party to a contract is unlikely.

insecurity clause. (1872) A loan-agreement provision that allows the creditor to demand immediate and full payment of the loan balance if the creditor has reason to believe that the debtor is about to default, as when the debtor suddenly loses a significant source of income. Cf. ACCELERATION CLAUSE.

insert, *vb. Parliamentary law.* To amend (a motion) by placing new wording within or around the current wording. • Some authorities distinguish amendment by adding, which places new wording after the current wording, from amendment by inserting. See ADD; AMENDMENT (3).

inside director. See DIRECTOR.

inside information. Information about a company's financial or market situation obtained not from public disclosure, but from a source within the company or a source that owes the company a duty to keep the information confidential. — Also termed *insider information.* See INSIDER TRADING.

insider. (1848) **1.** *Securities.* A person who has knowledge of facts not available to the general public.

temporary insider. A person or firm that receives inside information in the course of performing professional duties for a client. • Generally, that person or firm is subject to the same proscriptions as an insider.

2. One who takes part in the control of a corporation, such as an officer or director, or one who owns 10% or more of the corporation's stock. **3.** *Bankruptcy.* An entity or person who is so closely related to a debtor that any deal between them will not be considered an arm's-length transaction and will be subject to close scrutiny.

insider dealing. See INSIDER TRADING.

insider information. See INSIDE INFORMATION.

insider preference. See PREFERENCE.

insider report. See REPORT (1).

insider trading. The use of material, nonpublic information in trading the shares of a company by a corporate insider or other person who owes a fiduciary duty to the company. • This is the classic definition. The Supreme Court has also approved a broader definition, known as the "misappropriation theory": the deceitful acquisition and misuse of information that properly belongs to persons to whom one owes a duty. Thus, under the misappropriation theory, it is insider trading for a lawyer to trade in the stock of XYZ Corp. after learning that a client of the lawyer's firm is planning a takeover of XYZ. But under the classic definition, that is not insider trading because the lawyer owed no duty to XYZ itself. — Also termed *insider dealing.*

insimul (in-**sim**-əl *or* in-si-məl), *adv.* [Latin] Together, jointly.

insinuation (in-sin-yoo-**ay**-shən). *Civil law.* **1.** The act of depositing (an instrument) with a public registry for recording. **2.** A document that evidences a donation of property.

insinuation of a will. *Civil law.* The first production of a will for probate.

insist, *vb.* (Of a house in a bicameral legislature) to reaffirm (an amendment) that the other house has considered but in which it has not concurred, or to reaffirm nonconcurrence in an amendment from which the other house has not receded. • An insistence often results in a request for a conference. See CONCUR (4); CONFERENCE (2); RECEDE. — **insistence,** *n.*

in solido (in **sol**-ə-doh). [Latin "as a whole"] (Of an obligation) creating joint and several liability. • The term is used in most civil-law jurisdictions, but no longer in Louisiana. — Also termed *in solidum.* See SOLIDARY.

insolvency, *n.* (17c) **1.** The condition of being unable to pay debts as they fall due or in the usual course of business. **2.** The inability to pay debts as they mature. — Also termed *failure to meet obligations; failing circumstances.* See BANKRUPTCY (2). Cf. SOLVENCY.

balance-sheet insolvency. Insolvency created when the debtor's liabilities exceed its assets. • Under some state laws, balance-sheet insolvency prevents a corporation from making a distribution to its shareholders. — Also termed *balance-sheet test.*

equity insolvency. Insolvency created when the debtor cannot meet its obligations as they fall due. • Under most state laws, equity insolvency prevents a corporation from making a distribution to its shareholders.

insolvency law. A statute that provides relief to a debtor who lacks the means to pay creditors. • The term is sometimes used interchangeably with *bankruptcy law* because legislative drafting may not produce a bright-line distinction. — Also termed *insolvent law.* Cf. BANKRUPTCY LAW (2).

insolvency proceeding. *Archaic.* A bankruptcy proceeding to liquidate or rehabilitate an estate. See BANKRUPTCY (1).

insolvent, *adj.* (16c) (Of a debtor) having liabilities that exceed the value of assets; having stopped paying debts in the ordinary course of business or being unable to pay them as they fall due. — **insolvent,** *n.*

insolvent law. See INSOLVENCY LAW.

in specie (in **spee**-shee-ee *or* **spee**-shee). [Latin "in kind"] In the same or like form; IN KIND <the partners were prepared to return the borrowed items *in specie*>.

inspection. (14c) A careful examination of something, such as goods (to determine their fitness for purchase) or items produced in response to a discovery request (to determine their relevance to a lawsuit).

inspection right. (1898) The legal entitlement in certain circumstances to examine articles or documents, such as a consumer's right to inspect goods before paying for them.

inspection search. See *administrative search* under SEARCH.

inspector. (17c) **1.** A person authorized to inspect something. **2.** A police officer who ranks below a superintendent or deputy superintendent, and who is in charge of several precincts.

inspector general. (*often cap.*) **1.** One of several federal officials charged with supervising a particular agency's audits or investigations. **2.** A governor-appointed state official who oversees internal review within executive agencies to ensure that there is no waste or abuse of resources.

install, *vb.* (16c) To induct (a person) into an office or a rank <the newly elected governor was soon installed in office>.

installment, *n.* (18c) A periodic partial payment of a debt.

installment accounting method. See ACCOUNTING METHOD.

installment contract. See *retail installment contract* under CONTRACT.

installment credit. See CREDIT (4).

installment debt. See DEBT.

installment land contract. See *contract for deed* under CONTRACT.

installment loan. See LOAN.

installment note. See NOTE (1).

installment payment. See PAYMENT.

installment plan. See INSTALLMENT SALE.

installment sale. (1893) A conditional sale in which the buyer makes a down payment followed by periodic payments and the seller retains title or a security interest until all payments have been received. — Also termed *installment plan*; *retail installment sale.*

> *disguised installment sale.* *Bankruptcy.* A debtor's leasing ploy to try to keep property outside the bankruptcy estate, whereby a lease either presents the lessee-debtor with a bargain purchase option or transfers title to the lessee-debtor at the end of the lease term. • When such a lease is discovered, the property is treated as part of the bankruptcy estate, meaning that to defeat competing creditors, the lessor must have perfected a security interest.

instance, *n.* (14c) **1.** An example or occurrence <there were 55 instances of reported auto theft in this small community last year>. **2.** The act of instituting legal proceedings <court of first instance>. **3.** Urgent solicitation or insistence <she applied for the job at the instance of her friend>.

instance, *vb.* (17c) To illustrate by example; to cite <counsel instanced three cases for the court to consider>.

instance court. See COURT.

instant, *adj.* This; the present (case, judgment, order, etc.); now being discussed <the instant order is not appealable>.

instantaneous crime. See CRIME.

instantaneous death. See DEATH.

instant case. See *case at bar* under CASE.

instanter (in-**stan**-tər), *adv.* (17c) Instantly; at once <the defendant was ordered to file its motion instanter>.

instant-runoff voting. See VOTING.

in statu quo (in **stay**-t[y]oo **kwoh**). [Latin "in the state in which"] In the same condition as previously <Johnson, as a minor, can recover the whole of what he paid if he puts the other party *in statu quo* by returning all the value received>. — Also termed *in statu quo ante.* See STATUS QUO.

instigate, *vb.* (16c) To goad or incite (someone) to take some action or course.

instinct, *adj.* *Archaic.* Imbued or charged <the contract is instinct with an obligation of good faith>.

in stirpes (in **stər**-peez). See PER STIRPES.

institorial power. See POWER (3).

institute, *n.* **1.** A legal treatise or commentary, such as Coke's *Institutes* in four volumes (published in 1628). **2.** (*cap. & pl.*) An elementary treatise on Roman law in four books. • This treatise is one of the four component parts of the *Corpus Juris Civilis.* — Also termed *Institutes of Justinian; Justinian's Institutes.* See CORPUS JURIS CIVILIS. **3.** (*cap. & pl.*) An elementary treatise written by the Roman jurist Gaius. • The *Institutes*, written in the second century A.D., served as a foundation for the *Institutes of Justinian.* — Also termed *Institutes of Gaius.* **4.** (*cap. & pl.*) A paraphrase of Justinian's *Institutes* written in Greek by Theophilus, a law professor at Constantinople who helped prepare the *Institutes of Justinian.* • This work was prepared in the sixth century A.D. — Also termed *Paraphrase of Theophilus; Institutes of Theophilus.* **5.** *Civil law.* A person named in a will as heir, but under directions to pass the estate on to some other specified person (called the *substitute*). See SUBSTITUTE (2). **6.** An organization devoted to the study and improvement of the law. See AMERICAN LAW INSTITUTE.

institute, *vb.* (14c) To begin or start; commence <institute legal proceedings against the manufacturer>.

instituted heir. See *testamentary heir* under HEIR.

Institute for Telecommunication Sciences. See NATIONAL TELECOMMUNICATIONS AND INFORMATION ADMINISTRATION. — Abbr. ITS.

Institute of Museum and Library Services. An independent federal agency that makes grants to support libraries and museums. • It was established within the National Foundation on the Arts and the Humanities in 1996. — Abbr. IMLS. See NATIONAL FOUNDATION ON THE ARTS AND THE HUMANITIES.

Institutes of Gaius. See INSTITUTE (3).

Institutes of Justinian. See INSTITUTE (2).

Institutes of Theophilus. See INSTITUTE (4).

institution. (14c) **1.** The commencement of something, such as a civil or criminal action. **2.** An elementary rule, principle, or practice. **3.** An established organization, esp. one of a public character, such as a facility for the treatment of mentally disabled persons. — Also termed *public institution.* **4.** *Civil law.* A testator's appointment of an heir; the designation of an institute. See INSTITUTE (5). **5.** *Eccles. law.* The investiture of a cleric with a benefice, by which the cleric becomes responsible for the spiritual needs of the members of a parish. Cf. PRESENTATION (2); ADVOWSON.

institutional broker. See BROKER.

institutional gerrymandering. See GERRYMANDERING.

institutional investor. See INVESTOR.

institutionalize, *vb.* (1865) **1.** To place (a person) in an institution. **2.** To give (a rule or practice) official sanction.

institutional lender. A business, esp. a bank, that routinely makes loans to the general public.

institutional litigant. (1858) An organized group that brings lawsuits not merely to win but also to bring about a change in the law or to defend an existing law.

institutional market. See MARKET.

instruct, *vb.* See JURY CHARGE (3).

instruct down. *Missouri law.* (Of a court) to give jurors an instruction on a lesser included offense. • A court must instruct down only if the jury could find the defendant not guilty of the higher offense but guilty of the lesser one.

instructed delegate. See DELEGATE.

instructed verdict. See *directed verdict* under VERDICT.

instruction. See JURY INSTRUCTION.

instructional text. *Copyright.* A literary, graphic, or pictorial work designed and prepared for use in ordinary teaching activities. See 17 USCA § 101.

instruction directive. A document that contains specific directions concerning the declarant's wishes for healthcare decisions. Cf. ADVANCE DIRECTIVE; LIVING WILL; PROXY DIRECTIVE.

instrument. (15c) **1.** A written legal document that defines rights, duties, entitlements, or liabilities, such as a contract, will, promissory note, or share certificate. — Also termed *legal instrument.*

statutory instrument. See STATUTORY INSTRUMENT.

testamentary instrument. See WILL.

2. *Commercial law.* An unconditional promise or order to pay a fixed amount of money, with or without interest or other fixed charges described in the promise or order. • Under the UCC, a promise or order must meet several other specifically listed requirements to qualify as an instrument. UCC § 3-104(a). See NEGOTIABLE INSTRUMENT. **3.** A means by which something is achieved, performed, or furthered <an instrument of social equality>.

inchoate instrument. (1834) An unrecorded instrument that must, by law, be recorded to serve as effective notice to third parties. • Until the instrument is recorded, it is effective only between the parties to the instrument.

incomplete instrument. (1822) A paper that, although intended to be a negotiable instrument, lacks an essential element. • An incomplete instrument may be enforced if it is subsequently completed. UCC § 3-115.

indispensable instrument. The formal written evidence of an interest in intangibles, so necessary to represent the intangible that the enjoyment, transfer, or enforcement of the intangible depends on possession of the instrument.

perfect instrument. (18c) An instrument (such as a deed or mortgage) that is executed and filed with a public registry.

sealed instrument. At common law and under some statutes, an instrument to which the bound party has affixed a personal seal, usu. recognized as providing indisputable evidence of the validity of the underlying obligations. ● Many states have abolished the common-law distinction between sealed and unsealed instruments. The UCC provides that the laws applicable to sealed instruments do not apply to negotiable instruments or contracts for the sale of goods. UCC § 2-203. Cf. *contract under seal* under CONTRACT.

instrumental crime. See CRIME.

instrumentality, *n.* **1.** A thing used to achieve an end or purpose. **2.** A means or agency through which a function of another entity is accomplished, such as a branch of a governing body.

instrumentality rule. The principle that a corporation is treated as a subsidiary if it is controlled to a great extent by another corporation. — Also termed *instrumentality theory.*

instrument of accession. *Int'l law.* A document formally acknowledging the issuing state's consent to an existing treaty, and exchanged with the treaty parties or deposited with a designated state or international organization. See ACCESSION (3).

instrument of crime. See CRIMINAL INSTRUMENT.

instrument of ratification. *Int'l law.* A document formally acknowledging the issuing state's confirmation and acceptance of a treaty, and exchanged by the treaty parties or deposited with a designated state or international organization. See RATIFICATION (4).

insubordination. (18c) **1.** A willful disregard of an employer's instructions, esp. behavior that gives the employer cause to terminate a worker's employment. **2.** An act of disobedience to proper authority; esp., a refusal to obey an order that a superior officer is authorized to give.

insufficient evidence. See EVIDENCE.

insufficient funds. See NOT SUFFICIENT FUNDS.

insular, *adj.* (17c) **1.** Of, relating to, from, or constituting an island <insular origin>. **2.** Isolated from, uninterested in, or ignorant of things outside a limited scope <insular viewpoint>.

insular area. A territory or commonwealth. ● This phrase is used by some writers to denote the genus of which the terms *territory* and *commonwealth* are species. See COMMONWEALTH (2); TERRITORY (1).

insular court. See COURT.

insular possession. See POSSESSION.

insurable, *adj.* Able to be insured <an insurable risk>. — **insurability,** *n.*

insurable interest. See INTEREST (2).

insurable value. The worth of the subject of an insurance contract, usu. expressed as a monetary amount.

insurance. (17c) **1.** A contract by which one party (the *insurer*) undertakes to indemnify another party (the *insured*) against risk of loss, damage, or liability arising from the occurrence of some specified contingency, and usu. to defend the insured or to pay for a defense regardless of whether the insured is ultimately found liable. ● An insured party usu. pays a premium to the insurer in exchange for the insurer's assumption of the insured's risk. Although indemnification provisions are most common in insurance policies, parties to any type of contract may agree on indemnification arrangements. **2.** The amount for which someone or something is covered by such an agreement. — **insure,** *vb.*

accident and health insurance. See *health insurance.*

accident insurance. Insurance that indemnifies against bodily injury caused by an accident. ● Covered losses may include expenses, time, suffering, or death. Cf. *casualty insurance.*

accounts-receivable insurance. **1.** Insurance against losses resulting from the insured's inability to collect outstanding accounts receivable because of damage to or destruction of records. **2.** See *credit insurance.*

additional insurance. Insurance added to an existing policy.

all-risk insurance. Insurance that covers every kind of insurable loss except what is specifically excluded.

annuity insurance. An agreement to pay the insured (or *annuitant*) for a stated period or for life.

assessable insurance. **1.** Insurance in which the insured is liable for additional premiums if a loss is unusually large. **2.** See *assessable policy* (1) under INSURANCE POLICY.

assessment insurance. A type of mutual insurance in which the policyholders are assessed as losses are incurred; a policy in which payments to an insured are not unalterably fixed, but are dependent on the collection of assessments necessary to pay the amount insured.

automobile insurance. An agreement to indemnify against one or more kinds of loss associated with the use of an automobile, including damage to a vehicle and liability for personal injury.

aviation insurance. Insurance that protects the insured against a loss connected with the use of an aircraft. • This type of insurance can be written to cover a variety of risks, including bodily injury, property damage, and hangarkeepers' liability.

broad-form insurance. (1959) Comprehensive insurance. • This type of insurance usu. takes the form of an endorsement to a liability or property policy, broadening the coverage that is typically available.

bumbershoot insurance. **1.** Marine insurance that provides broad coverage for ocean marine risks. **2.** See *umbrella insurance.* • This term derives from the British slang term for *umbrella.* The term applies esp. to a policy insured through the London insurance market. See *umbrella policy* under INSURANCE POLICY.

burial insurance. Insurance that pays for the holder's burial and funeral expenses.

business-interruption insurance. An agreement to protect against one or more kinds of loss from the interruption of an ongoing business, such as a loss of profits while the business is shut down to repair fire damage.

business-partner insurance. See *partnership insurance.*

captive insurance. **1.** Insurance that provides coverage for the group or business that established it. **2.** Insurance that a subsidiary provides to its parent company, usu. so that the parent company can deduct the premiums set aside as loss reserves.

cargo insurance. An agreement to pay for damage to freight damaged in transit.

casualty insurance. An agreement to indemnify against loss resulting from a broad group of causes such as legal liability, theft, accident, property damage, and workers' compensation. • The meaning of casualty insurance has become blurred because of the rapid increase in different types of insurance coverage. Cf. *accident insurance.*

coinsurance. (1889) **1.** Insurance provided jointly by two or more insurers. **2.** Insurance under which the insurer and insured jointly bear responsibility. • An example is commercial insurance under which only a portion of a property's value is covered, and the property

owner assumes liability for any loss in excess of the policy limits.

collision insurance. (1921) Automobile insurance that covers damage to the insured's vehicle resulting from a rollover or collision with any object, but does not cover a personal injury or damage to other property.

commercial insurance. **1.** An indemnity agreement in the form of a deed or bond to protect against a loss caused by a party's breach of contract. **2.** A form of coverage that allows an insurer to adjust the premium rates at will, and doesn't require the insured to accept the premium or renew the coverage from period to period.

comprehensive general-liability insurance. Insurance that broadly covers an insured's liability exposure, including product liability, contractual liability, and premises liability. — Abbr. CGL insurance.

comprehensive insurance. (1924) Insurance that combines coverage against many kinds of losses that may also be insured separately. • This is commonly used, for example, in an automobile-insurance policy.

compulsory insurance. (1887) Statutorily required insurance; esp., motor-vehicle liability insurance that a state requires as a condition to register the vehicle.

convertible collision insurance. Collision insurance that carries a low premium until a claim is made against the policy.

convertible insurance. (1926) Insurance that can be changed to another form without further evidence of insurability, usu. referring to a term-life-insurance policy that can be changed to permanent insurance without a medical examination.

credit insurance. An agreement to indemnify against loss that may result from the death, disability, or insolvency of someone to whom credit is extended. • A debtor typically purchases this type of insurance to ensure the repayment of the loan. — Also termed *accounts-receivable insurance.*

credit life insurance. See LIFE INSURANCE.

crime insurance. Insurance covering losses occasioned by a crime committed by someone other than the insured.

crop insurance. Insurance that protects against loss to growing crops from natural perils such as hail and fire.

D&O insurance. See *directors' and officers' liability insurance.*

decreasing term insurance. Insurance that declines in value during the term; esp., life insurance that lessens in value to zero by the end of the term.

deposit insurance. (1933) A federally sponsored indemnification program to protect depositors against the loss of their money, up to a specified maximum, if the bank or savings-and-loan association fails or defaults.

directors and officers' liability insurance. An agreement to indemnify corporate directors and officers against judgments, settlements, and fines arising from negligence suits, shareholder actions, and other business-related suits. — Often shortened to *D&O liability insurance*; *D&O insurance*.

disability insurance. Coverage purchased to protect a person from a loss of income during a period of incapacity for work. See *general-disability insurance*; *occupational-disability insurance*.

double insurance. (18c) Insurance coverage by more than one insurer for the same interest and for the same insured. • Except with life insurance, the insured is entitled to only a single indemnity from a loss, and to recover this, the insured may either (1) sue each insurer for its share of the loss, or (2) sue one or more of the insurers for the entire amount, leaving any paying insurers to recover from the others their respective shares of the loss.

dread-disease insurance. Health insurance that covers medical expenses arising from the treatment of any of several specified diseases.

e-commerce insurance. Insurance that covers a business's computer-related damages and losses caused by computer hackers and Internet viruses. • Covered damages usu. include physical destruction or harm to computer circuitry, loss of access, loss of use, loss of functionality, and business interruption.

employers'-liability insurance. 1. An agreement to indemnify an employer against an employee's claim not covered under the workers'-compensation system. **2.** An agreement to indemnify against liability imposed on an employer for an employee's negligence that injures a third party.

employment-practices liability insurance. Insurance that provides coverage for claims arising from an insured's injury-causing employment practice, such as discrimination, defamation, or sexual harassment. — Abbr. *EPL insurance*.

endowment insurance. A type of life insurance that is payable either to the insured at the end of the policy period or to the insured's beneficiary if the insured dies before the period ends. See *endowment life insurance* under LIFE INSURANCE.

errors-and-omissions insurance. An agreement to indemnify for loss sustained because of a mistake or oversight by the insured — though not for loss due to the insured's intentional wrongdoing. • For example, lawyers often carry this insurance as part of their malpractice coverage to protect them in suits for damages resulting from inadvertent mistakes (such as missing a procedural deadline). While this insurance does not cover the insured's intentional wrongdoing, it may cover an employee's intentional, but unauthorized, wrongdoing. — Often shortened to *E&O insurance*.

excess insurance. (1916) An agreement to indemnify against any loss that exceeds the amount of coverage under another policy. — Also termed *excess policy*. Cf. *primary insurance*. See EXCESS CLAUSE.

excess-lines insurance. See *surplus-lines insurance*.

extended insurance. Insurance that continues in force beyond the date that the last premium was paid by drawing on its cash value.

extended-term insurance. (1925) Insurance that remains in effect after a default in paying premiums, as long as the policy has cash value to pay premiums. • Many life-insurance policies provide this feature to protect against forfeiture of the policy if the insured falls behind in premium payments.

family-income insurance. An agreement to pay benefits for a stated period following the death of the insured. • At the end of the payment period, the face value is paid to the designated beneficiary.

fidelity insurance. An agreement to indemnify an employer against a loss arising from the lack of integrity or honesty of an employee or of a person holding a position of trust, such as a loss from embezzlement. — Also termed *fidelity guaranty insurance*; *fidelity and guaranty insurance*; *surety and fidelity insurance*.

fire insurance. An agreement to indemnify against property damage caused by fire, wind, rain, or other similar disaster.

first-party insurance. (1953) A policy that applies to an insured or the insured's own property, such as life insurance, health insurance, disability insurance, and fire insurance. — Also termed *indemnity insurance*; *self-insurance*.

fleet insurance. Insurance that covers a number of vehicles owned by the same entity.

floater insurance. An agreement to indemnify against a loss sustained to movable property, wherever its location within the territorial limit set by the policy.

flood insurance. Insurance that indemnifies against a loss caused by a flood. • This type of insurance is often sold privately but subsidized by the federal government.

fraternal insurance. Life or health insurance issued by a fraternal benefit society to its members.

general-disability insurance. Disability insurance that provides benefits to a person who cannot perform any job that the person is qualified for. — Also termed *total-disability insurance.* Cf. *occupational-disability insurance.*

government insurance. Life insurance underwritten by the federal government to military personnel, veterans, and government employees.

group insurance. A form of insurance offered to a member of a group, such as the employees of a business, as long as that person remains a member of the group. • Group insurance is typically health or life (usu. term life) insurance issued under a master policy between the insurer and the employer, who usu. pays all or part of the premium for the insured person. Other groups, such as unions and associations, often offer group insurance to their members.

guaranty insurance (**gar**-ən-tee). An agreement to cover a loss resulting from another's default, insolvency, or specified misconduct. — Also termed *surety insurance.*

health insurance. Insurance covering medical expenses resulting from sickness or injury. — Also termed *accident and health insurance; sickness and accident insurance.*

homeowner's insurance. Insurance that covers both damage to the insured's residence and liability claims made against the insured (esp. those arising from the insured's negligence).

indemnity insurance. See *first-party insurance.*

industrial life insurance. See LIFE INSURANCE.

inland marine insurance. An agreement to indemnify against losses arising from the transport of goods on domestic waters (i.e., rivers, canals, and lakes). Cf. *ocean marine insurance.*

insurance of the person. Insurance intended to protect the person, such as life, accident, and disability insurance.

interinsurance. See *reciprocal insurance.*

joint life insurance. See LIFE INSURANCE.

judicial insurance. Insurance intended to protect litigants and others involved in the court system.

key-employee insurance. See *key-employee life insurance* under LIFE INSURANCE.

last-survivor insurance. See *last-survivor life insurance* under LIFE INSURANCE.

lease insurance. An agreement to indemnify a leaseholder for the loss of a favorable lease terminated by damage to the property from a peril covered by the policy. • The amount payable is the difference between the rent and the actual rental value of the property, multiplied by the remaining term of the lease.

level-premium insurance. Insurance whose premiums remain constant throughout the life of the agreement. • Most whole life policies are set up this way.

liability insurance. An agreement to cover a loss resulting from the insured's liability to a third party, such as a loss incurred by a driver who injures a pedestrian. • The insured's claim under the policy arises once the insured's liability to a third party has been asserted. — Also termed *third-party insurance; public-liability insurance.*

life insurance. See LIFE INSURANCE.

limited-policy insurance. Insurance that covers only specified perils; esp., health insurance that covers a specific type of illness (such as dread-disease insurance) or a risk relating to a stated activity (such as travel-accident insurance).

Lloyd's insurance. (1897) Insurance provided by insurers as individuals, rather than as a corporation. • The insurers' liability is several but not joint. Most states either prohibit or strictly regulate this type of insurance. See LLOYD'S OF LONDON.

loss insurance. Insurance purchased by a person who may suffer a loss at the hands of another. • This is the converse of *liability insurance,* which is purchased by potential defendants.

malpractice insurance (mal-**prak**-tis). (1943) An agreement to indemnify a professional person, such as a doctor or lawyer, against negligence claims. See *errors-and-omissions insurance.*

manual-rating insurance. A type of insurance whereby the premium is set using a book that classifies certain risks on a general basis, rather than evaluating each individual case.

marine insurance. An agreement to indemnify against injury to a ship, cargo, or profits involved in a certain voyage or for a specific vessel during a fixed period, or to protect other marine interests.

medigap insurance. See MEDIGAP INSURANCE.

mortgage insurance. 1. An agreement to pay off a mortgage if the insured dies or becomes disabled. 2. An agreement to provide money to the lender if the mortgagor defaults on the mortgage payments. — Also termed *private mortgage insurance* (abbr. PMI).

mutual insurance. A system of insurance (esp. life insurance) whereby the policyholders become members of the insurance company, each paying premiums into a common fund from which each can draw in the event of a loss.

national-service life insurance. See LIFE INSURANCE.

no-fault auto insurance. An agreement to indemnify for a loss due to personal injury or property damage arising from the use of an automobile, regardless of who caused the accident.

nonassessable insurance. Insurance in which the premium is set and the insurer is barred from demanding additional payments from the insured.

occupational-disability insurance. Disability insurance that provides benefits to a person who cannot perform his or her regular job.

occurrence-based liability insurance. Insurance that covers bodily injuries or property damage suffered during the policy period. • Each instance of injury or damage is an "occurrence" that may trigger an insured's entitlement to benefits. The terms of occurrence-based liability insurance policies are usu. broad, limited only by specific exclusions. — Also termed *accident-based insurance.*

ocean marine insurance. Insurance that covers risks arising from the transport of goods by sea. Cf. *inland marine insurance.*

old-age and survivors' insurance. See OLD-AGE AND SURVIVORS' INSURANCE.

ordinary insurance. See *ordinary life insurance* under LIFE INSURANCE.

ordinary life insurance. See LIFE INSURANCE.

overinsurance. See OVERINSURANCE.

paid-up insurance. (1871) Insurance that remains in effect even though no more premiums are due.

participating insurance. A type of insurance that allows a policyholder to receive dividends. • This insurance is invariably issued by a mutual company.

partnership insurance. **1.** Life insurance on the life of a partner, purchased to ensure the remaining partners' ability to buy out a deceased partner's interest. — Also termed *partnership life insurance.* **2.** Health insurance for a partner, payable to the partnership to allow it to continue to operate while the partner is unable to work due to illness or injury. — Also termed (in both senses) *business-partner insurance.*

patent insurance (**pat**-ənt). **1.** Insurance against loss from an infringement of the insured's patent. **2.** Insurance against a claim that the insured has infringed another's patent. **3.** Insurance that funds a claim against a third party for infringing the insured's patent.

port-risk insurance. Insurance on a vessel lying in port. Cf. *time insurance; voyage insurance.*

primary insurance. Insurance that attaches immediately on the happening of a loss; insurance that is not contingent on the exhaustion of an underlying policy. Cf. *excess insurance.*

private mortgage insurance. See *mortgage insurance.*

products-liability insurance. An agreement to indemnify a manufacturer, supplier, or retailer for a loss arising from the insured's liability to a user who is harmed by any product manufactured or sold by the insured.

profit insurance. Insurance that reimburses the insured for profits lost because of a specified peril.

property insurance. An agreement to indemnify against property damage or destruction. — Also termed *property-damage insurance.*

public-liability insurance. See *liability insurance.*

reciprocal insurance. A system whereby several individuals or businesses act through an agent to underwrite one another's risks, making each insured an insurer of the other members of the group. — Also termed *interinsurance.*

reinsurance. See REINSURANCE.

renewable term insurance. Insurance that the insured may continue at the end of a term, but generally at a higher premium. • The insured usu. has the right to renew for additional terms without a medical examination.

replacement insurance. (1938) Insurance under which the value of the loss is measured by the current cost of replacing the insured property. See *replacement cost* under COST.

retirement-income insurance. An agreement whereby the insurance company agrees to pay an annuity beginning at a certain age if the insured survives beyond that age, or the value of the policy if the insured dies before reaching that age.

self-insurance. A plan under which a business maintains its own special fund to cover any loss. • Unlike other forms of insurance, there is no contract with an insurance company. — Also termed *first-party insurance.*

sickness and accident insurance. See *health insurance.*

single-premium insurance. See *single-premium life insurance* under LIFE INSURANCE.

social insurance. Insurance provided by a government to persons facing particular perils (such as unemployment or disability) or to persons who have a certain status (such as the elderly or the blind). ● Social insurance — such as that created by the Social Security Act of 1935 — is usu. part of a government's broader social policy. See WELFARE STATE.

split-dollar insurance. See *split-dollar life insurance* under LIFE INSURANCE.

step-rate-premium insurance. Insurance whose premiums increase at times specified in the policy.

stop-loss insurance. Insurance that protects a self-insured employer from catastrophic losses or unusually large health costs of covered employees. ● Stop-loss insurance essentially provides excess coverage for a self-insured employer. The employer and the insurance carrier agree to the amount the employer will cover, and the stop-loss insurance will cover claims exceeding that amount.

straight life insurance. See *whole life insurance* under LIFE INSURANCE.

surety and fidelity insurance. See *fidelity insurance.*

surety insurance. See *guaranty insurance.*

surplus-lines insurance. Insurance with an insurer that is not licensed to transact business within the state where the risk is located. — Also termed *excess-lines insurance.*

term life insurance. See LIFE INSURANCE.

terrorism insurance. Insurance that indemnifies against losses sustained because of an act of terrorism. ● Terrorism insurance has been available since the 1970s; it was (and is) required for U.S. airports of almost all sizes. In the mid-1980s, terrorism insurance was offered to individuals, originally as a form of travel insurance that provided compensation for terrorism-related cancellations or changes in itinerary when traveling to or in certain countries. See TERRORISM.

third-party insurance. See *liability insurance.*

time insurance. *Marine insurance.* Insurance covering the insured for a specified period. Cf. *voyage insurance.*

title insurance. (1889) An agreement to indemnify against loss arising from a defect in title to real property, usu. issued to the buyer of the property by the title company that conducted the title search. Cf. GUARANTEE OF TITLE.

total-disability insurance. See *general-disability insurance.*

travel-accident insurance. Health insurance limited to injuries sustained while traveling.

umbrella insurance. Insurance that is supplemental, providing coverage that exceeds the basic or usual limits of liability. — Also termed *bumbershoot insurance.*

underinsurance. See UNDERINSURANCE.

unemployment insurance. (1897) A type of social insurance that pays money to workers who are unemployed for reasons unrelated to job performance. ● Individual states administer unemployment insurance, which is funded by payroll taxes. — Also termed *unemployment compensation.*

universal life insurance. See LIFE INSURANCE.

variable life insurance. See LIFE INSURANCE.

valuable-papers insurance. Insurance covering the cost of research, labor, and materials necessary to reconstruct damaged or lost documents and records — written, printed, or otherwise inscribed — including books, maps, manuscripts, legal documents, drawings, and films. ● This insurance does not cover cash or securities.

voyage insurance. *Marine insurance.* Insurance covering the insured between destinations. Cf. *time insurance.*

war-risk insurance. 1. Insurance covering damage caused by war. ● Ocean marine policies are often written to cover this type of risk. 2. Life and accident insurance provided by the federal government to members of the armed forces. ● This type of insurance is offered because the hazardous nature of military service often prevents military personnel from obtaining private insurance.

whole life insurance. See LIFE INSURANCE.

insurance adjuster. (1934) A person who determines the value of a loss to the insured and settles the claim against the insurer. — Also termed *claims adjuster.* See ADJUSTER.

insurance agent. (1866) A person authorized by an insurance company to sell its insurance policies. — Also termed *producer*; (in property insurance) *recording agent*; *record agent*.

general agent. An agent with the general power of making insurance contracts on behalf of an insurer.

special agent. An agent whose powers are usu. confined to soliciting applications for insurance, taking initial premiums, and delivering policies when issued. — Also termed *local agent*; *solicitor.*

insurance broker. See BROKER.

insurance certificate. (1865) 1. A document issued by an insurer as evidence of insurance or membership in an insurance or pension plan. 2. A document issued by an insurer to a shipper as evidence that a shipment of goods is covered by a marine insurance policy.

insurance commissioner. (1889) A public official who supervises the insurance business conducted in a state.

insurance company. (18c) A corporation or association that issues insurance policies.

    captive insurance company. A company that insures the liabilities of its owner. ● The insured is usu. the sole shareholder and the only customer of the captive insurer. — Also termed *captive insurer.*

    mixed insurance company. An insurance company having characteristics of both stock and mutual companies in that it distributes part of the profits to stockholders and also makes distributions to the insureds.

    mutual insurance company. An insurance company whose policyholders are both insurers and insureds because they pay premiums into a common fund, from which claims are paid; an insurer whose policyholders are its owners, as opposed to a stock insurance company owned by outside shareholders. Cf. *stock insurance company.*

    stock insurance company. An insurance company operated as a private corporation and owned by stockholders who share in the company's profits and losses.

    stock life-insurance company. A stock insurance company that does life-insurance business.

insurance fraud. See FRAUD.

insurance of the person. See INSURANCE.

insurance policy. (1869) **1.** A contract of insurance. **2.** A document detailing such a contract. — Often shortened to *policy.* — Also termed *policy of insurance; contract of insurance.*

    accident policy. A type of business or personal policy that insures against loss resulting directly from accidental bodily injuries sustained during the policy term.

    assessable policy. **1.** A policy under which a policyholder may be held liable for losses of the insurance company beyond its reserves. — Also termed *assessable insurance.* **2.** See *assessable insurance* (1) under INSURANCE.

    bailee policy. A floating policy that covers goods in a bailee's possession but does not particularly describe the covered goods.

    basic-form policy. (1997) A policy that offers limited coverage against loss. ● A basic-form policy generally covers damages from fire, windstorm, explosion, riot, aircraft, vehicles, theft, or vandalism. — Also termed *limited policy; specific policy.*

    blanket policy. (1894) An agreement to indemnify all property, regardless of location. — Also termed *compound policy; floating policy.*

    block policy. An all-risk policy that covers groups of property (such as property held in bailment or a business's merchandise) against most perils. See *all-risk insurance* under INSURANCE.

    broad-form policy. (1950) A policy that offers broad protection with few limitations. ● This policy offers greater coverage than a basic-form policy, but less than an open-perils policy.

    claims-made policy. (1974) An agreement to indemnify against all claims made during a specified period, regardless of when the incidents that gave rise to the claims occurred. — Also termed *discovery policy.*

    closed policy. An insurance policy whose terms cannot be changed. ● A fraternal benefit society is not permitted to write closed policies. — Also termed *closed insurance contract.*

    commercial general-liability policy. A comprehensive policy that covers most commercial risks, liabilities, and causes of loss. ● This type of policy covers both business losses and situations in which a business is liable to a third party for personal injury or property damage. First introduced in 1986, this policy has largely replaced comprehensive general-liability policies. — Abbr. CGL policy. Cf. *comprehensive general-liability policy.*

    completed-operations policy. A policy usu. purchased by a building contractor to cover accidents arising out of a job or an operation that the contractor has completed.

    compound policy. See *blanket policy.*

    comprehensive general-liability policy. (1943) A broad-coverage commercial insurance policy covering a variety of general risks, esp. bodily injury and property damage to a third party for which the business entity is liable. ● This policy was first offered in 1940. It has largely been replaced by the commercial-general liability policy. — Also termed *CGL policy; general-liability policy.* Cf. *commercial general-liability policy.*

    concurrent policy. (1937) One of two or more insurance policies that cover the same risk. ● Concurrent insurance policies are stated in almost identical terms so that liability can be apportioned between the insurers.

    continuous policy. See *perpetual policy.*

    corrected policy. A policy issued after a redetermination of risk to correct a misstatement in the original policy.

    deferred-dividend insurance policy. Hist. A life insurance policy that accumulated a fixed percentage of the insurer's surplus profits, payable as a lump sum on a certain date or at the insured's death, whichever came first.

    discovery policy. See *claims-made policy.*

drummer floater policy. Hist. A policy that covered the goods carried by a commercial salesperson while traveling.

endowment policy. A life-insurance policy payable at the end of a specified period, if the insured survives that period, or upon the insured's death if death occurs before the end of the period.

excess policy. See *excess insurance* under INSURANCE.

extended policy. A policy that remains in effect beyond the time when premiums are no longer paid.

floating policy. An insurance policy covering property that frequently changes in quantity or location, such as jewelry. — Also termed *running policy; blanket policy.*

following-form policy. An insurance policy that adopts the terms and conditions of another insurance policy.

gambling policy. See *wager policy.*

graveyard insurance. See *wager policy.*

group policy. See *master policy.*

homeowner's policy. A multiperil policy providing coverage for a variety of risks, including loss by fire, water, burglary, and the homeowner's negligent conduct.

incontestable policy. (1897) A policy containing a provision that prohibits the insurer from contesting or canceling the policy on the basis of statements made in the application.

interest policy. A policy whose terms indicate that the insured has an interest in the subject matter of the insurance. Cf. *wager policy.*

joint life policy. (1927) A life-insurance policy that matures and becomes due upon the death of any of those jointly insured.

lapsed policy. (1873) **1.** An insurance policy on which there has been a default in premium payments. **2.** An insurance policy that, because of statutory provisions, remains in force after a default in premium payments. • Statutes normally provide a 30- or 31-day grace period after nonpayment of premiums.

level-rate legal-reserve policy. A policy that seeks to build a reserve equal to the policy's face value by the end of the insured's life.

life policy. A life-insurance policy that requires lifetime annual fixed premiums and that becomes payable only on the death of the insured. — Also termed *regular life policy.*

limited policy. (1884) **1.** An insurance policy that specifically excludes certain classes or types of loss. **2.** See *basic-form policy.*

manuscript policy. (1962) An insurance policy containing nonstandard provisions that have been negotiated between the insurer and the insured.

master policy. (1926) An insurance policy that covers multiple insureds under a group-insurance plan. — Also termed *group policy.* See *group insurance* under INSURANCE.

mixed policy. Marine insurance. A policy combining aspects of both a voyage policy and a time policy.

multiperil policy. (1951) An insurance policy that covers several types of losses, such as a homeowner's policy that covers losses from fire, theft, and personal injury. — Also termed *named-perils policy.*

nonmedical policy. An insurance policy issued without a prior medical examination of the applicant.

occurrence policy. An agreement to indemnify for any loss from an event that occurs within the policy period, regardless of when the claim is made.

open-perils policy. (1997) A property insurance policy covering all risks against loss except those specifically excluded from coverage.

open policy. See *unvalued policy.*

package policy. An insurance policy providing protection against multiple perils and losses of both the insured and third parties. • A homeowner's policy is usu. a package policy.

paid-up policy. A policy that remains in effect after premiums are no longer due.

participating policy. A policy that allows the holder a right to dividends or rebates from future premiums. • This type of policy is issued by a mutual company.

permanent policy. A renewable policy that is effective for a specified period and is terminable by either the insurer or the insured after giving express notice.

perpetual policy. An insurance policy that remains effective without renewal until one of the parties terminates it according to its terms. — Also termed *continuous policy.*

regular life policy. See *life policy.*

running policy. See *floating policy.*

specific policy. See *basic-form policy.*

standard policy. (1893) **1.** An insurance policy providing insurance that is recommended or required by state law, usu. regulated by a state agency. **2.** An insurance policy that contains standard terms used for similar insurance policies nationwide, usu. drafted by an insurance industrial association such as Insurance Services Office.

survivorship policy. A joint life policy that is payable after all the insureds have died.

term policy. A life-insurance policy that gives protection for a specified period, but that does not have a cash value or reserve value.

time policy. (1852) An insurance policy that is effective only during a specified period.

tontine policy (**tahn**-teen or tahn-**teen**). An insurance policy in which a group of participants share advantages so that upon the default or death of any participant, his or her advantages are distributed among the remaining participants until only one remains, whereupon the whole goes to that sole participant. • Under the tontine plan of insurance, no accumulation or earnings are credited to the policy unless it remains in force for the tontine period of a specified number of years. Thus, those who survive the period and keep their policies in force share in the accumulated funds, and those who die or permit their policies to lapse during the period do not. This type of policy takes its name from Lorenzo Tonti, an Italian who invented it in the 17th century. Today, newer and more ingenious forms of insurance have largely made tontine policies defunct. See TONTINE.

umbrella policy. An insurance policy covering losses that exceed the basic or usual limits of liability provided by other policies. See umbrella insurance under INSURANCE.

unvalued policy. A policy that does not state a value of the insured property but that, upon loss, requires proof of the property's worth. — Also termed open policy.

valued policy. An insurance policy in which the sum to be paid when a loss occurs is fixed by the terms of the contract. • The value agreed on is conclusive for a total loss and provides a basis for determining recovery in cases of partial loss. This value is in the nature of liquidated damages.

voyage policy. A marine-insurance policy that insures a vessel or its cargo during a specified voyage.

wager policy. An insurance policy issued to a person who is shown to have no insurable interest in the person or property covered by the policy. • Wager policies are illegal in most states. — Also termed gambling policy; graveyard insurance. See insurable interest under INTEREST (2). Cf. interest policy.

insurance pool. (1935) A group of several insurers that, to spread the risk, combine and share premiums and losses.

insurance premium. See PREMIUM (1).

insurance rating. (1905) The process by which an insurer arrives at a policy premium for a particular risk. — Often shortened to rating.

Insurance Services Office. A nonprofit organization that provides analytical and decision-support services and tools to the insurance industry, including statistical, actuarial, underwriting, and claims data, and drafts of model insurance policy forms and coverage provisions. • The organization is composed of member insurers. It provides data and information to its members and also to nonmember subscribers, such as risk managers, insurance regulators, and self-insureds. — Abbr. ISO.

insurance trust. See TRUST.

insurance underwriter. See UNDERWRITER.

insurant, n. A person who obtains insurance or to whom an insurance policy is issued. • This term is much less common than the attributive noun insured.

insure, vb. (17c) **1.** To secure, by payment of a premium, the payment of a sum of money in the event of a loss. **2.** To issue or procure an insurance policy on or for (someone or something).

insured, n. (17c) A person who is covered or protected by an insurance policy. — Also termed assured.

additional insured. (1929) A person who is covered by an insurance policy but who is not the primary insured. • An additional insured may, or may not, be specifically named in the policy. If the person is named, then the term is sometimes named additional insured. — Also termed secondary insured.

class-one insured. (1982) In a motor-vehicle policy, the named insured and any relative residing with the named insured.

class-two insured. (1985) In a motor-vehicle policy, a person lawfully occupying a vehicle at the time of an accident.

first-named insured. See primary insured.

named insured. (1899) A person designated in an insurance policy as the one covered by the policy.

primary insured. The individual or entity whose name appears first in the declarations of an insurance policy. — Also termed first-named insured.

insurer. (17c) One who agrees, by contract, to assume the risk of another's loss and to compensate for that loss. — Also termed underwriter; insurance underwriter; carrier; assurer (for life insurance).

excess insurer. An insurer who is liable for settling any part of a claim not covered by an insured's primary insurer. — Also termed *secondary insurer*. See *primary insurer*.

primary insurer. An insurer who is contractually committed to settling a claim up to the applicable policy limit before any other insurer becomes liable for any part of the same claim. See *excess insurer*.

quasi-insurer. (1830) A service provider who is held to strict liability in the provision of services, such as an innkeeper or a common carrier.

secondary insurer. See *excess insurer*.

insurgent, *n.* (18c) A person who, for political purposes, engages in armed hostility against an established government. — **insurgent,** *adj.* — **insurgency,** *n.*

insuring agreement. See INSURING CLAUSE.

insuring clause. A provision in an insurance policy or bond reciting the risk assumed by the insurer or establishing the scope of the coverage. — Also termed *insuring agreement*.

insurrection. (15c) A violent revolt against an oppressive authority, usu. a government.

intact family. See FAMILY.

in tail. See TAIL.

intake, *n.* (1943) **1.** The official screening of a juvenile charged with an offense in order to determine where to determine where to place the juvenile pending formal adjudication or informal disposition. **2.** The body of officers who conduct this screening. **3.** *Hist. English law.* A piece of land temporarily taken from a common or moorland by a tenant to raise a crop.

intake day. (1985) The day on which new cases are assigned to the courts.

intangible, *adj.* (17c) Not capable of being touched; impalpable; INCORPOREAL.

intangible, *n.* (1914) Something that lacks a physical form; an abstraction, such as responsibility; esp., an asset that is not corporeal, such as intellectual property.

general intangible. (1935) Any personal property other than goods, accounts, chattel paper, documents, instruments, investment property, rights to proceeds of written letters of credit, and money. ● Some examples are goodwill, things in action, and literary rights. UCC § 9-102(a)(42). See *intangible property* under PROPERTY.

payment intangible. (1996) A general intangible under which the account debtor's principal obligation is a monetary obligation. UCC § 9-102(a)(61).

intangible asset. **1.** See ASSET. **2.** See INTANGIBLE TRADE VALUE.

intangible drilling cost. *Oil & gas.* An expense that is incident to and necessary for drilling and completing an oil or gas well and that has no salvage value. ● Intangible drilling costs may be deducted in the year they are incurred rather than capitalized and depreciated. 26 USCA § 612.

intangible movable. See MOVABLE.

intangible property. See PROPERTY.

intangible-rights doctrine. The rule that a person is entitled to receive honest services from those in the public sector or in the private sector who have fiduciary duties to the person. ● Public-sector intangible rights derive from public officials' implied fiduciary duty to make governmental decisions in the public interest. Private-sector intangible rights arise out of fiduciary relationships. The intangible-rights doctrine is codified at 18 USCA § 1346. — Also termed *honest-services doctrine*.

intangible tax. See TAX.

intangible thing. See *incorporeal thing* under THING.

intangible trade property. See INTANGIBLE TRADE VALUE.

intangible trade value. *Intellectual property.* The measure of an enterprise's proprietary information, ideas, goodwill, and other nonphysical commercial assets. ● The law of misappropriation provides some protection against the taking of intangible trade values to compete unfairly with their original owner. — Also termed *intangible asset*; *intangible trade property*.

integrated agreement. See INTEGRATED CONTRACT.

integrated bar. See BAR.

integrated contract. (1930) One or more writings constituting a final expression of one or more terms of an agreement. — Also termed *integrated agreement*; *integrated writing*. See INTEGRATION (2).

completely integrated contract. (1950) An integrated agreement adopted by the parties as a full and exclusive statement of the terms of the agreement. ● The parties are therefore prohibited from varying or supplementing the contractual terms through parol (extrinsic) evidence.

partially integrated contract. (1958) An agreement in which some, but not all, of the terms are integrated; any agreement other than a completely integrated agreement.

integrated property settlement. See PROPERTY SETTLEMENT (2).

integrated writing. See INTEGRATED CONTRACT.

integration. (17c) **1.** The process of making whole or combining into one. **2.** *Contracts.* The full expression of the parties' agreement, so that all earlier agreements are superseded, the effect being that neither party may later contradict or add to

the contractual terms. — Also termed *merger*. See
PAROL-EVIDENCE RULE.

complete integration. (1930) The fact or state of
fully expressing the intent of the parties. • Parol
evidence is therefore inadmissible.

partial integration. (1910) The fact or state of not
fully expressing the parties' intent. • Parol (extrinsic) evidence is admissible to clear up ambiguities with respect to the terms that are not
integrated.

3. *Wills & estates.* The combining of more than
one writing into a single document to form the
testator's last will and testament. • The other
writing must be present at the time of execution
and intended to be included in the will. The issue
of integration is more complicated when it concerns a holographic will, which may be composed
of more than one document written at different
times. **4.** The incorporation of different races into
existing institutions (such as public schools) for
the purpose of reversing the historical effects of
racial discrimination. Cf. DESEGREGATION. **5.** *Antitrust.* A firm's performance of a function that
it could have obtained on the open market. • A
firm can achieve integration by entering a new
market on its own, by acquiring a firm that operates in a secondary market, or by entering into a
contract with a firm that operates in a secondary
market. — Also termed *vertical integration.* See
vertical merger under MERGER.

backward integration. A firm's acquisition of
ownership of facilities that produce raw materials or parts for the firm's products.

6. *Securities.* The requirement that all security offerings over a given period are to be considered
a single offering for purposes of determining an
exemption from registration. • The Securities and
Exchange Commission and the courts apply five
criteria to determine whether two or more transactions are part of the same offering of securities:
(1) whether the offerings are part of a single plan
of financing, (2) whether the offerings involve issuance of the same class of securities, (3) whether
the offerings are made at or about the same time,
(4) whether the same type of consideration is received, and (5) whether the offerings are made for
the same general purpose. 17 CFR § 230.502.

integration clause. (1941) A contractual provision
stating that the contract represents the parties'
complete and final agreement and supersedes all
informal understandings and oral agreements
relating to the subject matter of the contract. —
Also termed *merger clause*; *entire-agreement
clause.* See INTEGRATION (2); PAROL-EVIDENCE
RULE.

integration rule. (1899) The rule that if the parties
to a contract have embodied their agreement in a
final document, any other action or statement is
without effect and is immaterial in determining
the terms of the contract. See PAROL EVIDENCE
RULE.

integrity right. *Copyright.* The right of authors and
artists to insist that their creative works not be
changed without their authorization. • Integrity
is one of the moral rights of the moral rights of
artists recognized in civil-law countries, including much of Europe, but largely unavailable in
the United States. Cf. MORAL RIGHT; ATTRIBU-
TION RIGHT.

intellectual property. (1808) **1.** A category of intangible rights protecting commercially valuable
products of the human intellect. • The category
comprises primarily trademark, copyright, and
patent rights, but also includes trade-secret rights,
publicity rights, moral rights, and rights against
unfair competition. **2.** A commercially valuable
product of the human intellect, in a concrete or
abstract form, such as a copyrightable work, a
protectable trademark, a patentable invention,
or a trade secret. — Abbr. IP.

intemperance. (15c) A lack of moderation or temperance; esp., habitual or excessive drinking of
alcoholic beverages.

intend, *vb.* (14c) **1.** To have in mind a fixed purpose to reach a desired objective; to have as one's
purpose <Daniel intended to become a lawyer>.
2. To contemplate that the usual consequences of
one's act will probably or necessarily follow from
the act, whether or not those consequences are
desired for their own sake <although he activated
the theater's fire alarm only on a dare, the jury
found that Wilbur intended to cause a panic>.
3. To signify or mean <the parties intended for
the writing to supersede their earlier handshake
deal>.

intendant (in-ten-dənt). A director of a government agency, esp. (as used in 17th- and 18th-
century France) a royal official charged with the
administration of justice or finance.

intended beneficiary. See BENEFICIARY.

intended child. See CHILD.

intended parent. See *intentional parent* under PAR-
ENT.

intended to be recorded. (18c) (Of a deed or other
instrument) not yet filed with a public registry,
but forming a link in a chain of title.

intended-use doctrine. (1967) *Products liability.*
The rule imposing a duty on a manufacturer to
develop a product so that it is reasonably safe for
its intended or foreseeable users. • In determining the scope of responsibility, the court considers
the defendant's marketing scheme and the foreseeability of the harm.

intendment (in-**tend**-mənt). (14c) **1.** The sense
in which the law understands something <the

intendment of a contract is that the contract is legally enforceable>. — Also termed *intendment of law*. **2.** A decision-maker's inference about the true meaning or intention of a legal instrument <there is no need for intendment, the court reasoned, when the text of the statute is clear>. — Formerly also spelled *entendment*.

common intendment. The natural or common meaning in legal interpretation.

3. A person's expectations when interacting with others within the legal sphere.

intent. (13c) **1.** The state of mind accompanying an act, esp. a forbidden act. ● While motive is the inducement to do some act, intent is the mental resolution or determination to do it. When the intent to do an act that violates the law exists, motive becomes immaterial. Cf. MOTIVE; SCIENTER.

constructive intent. (1864) A legal principle that actual intent will be presumed when an act leading to the result could have been reasonably expected to cause that result.

criminal intent. (17c) **1.** MENS REA. **2.** An intent to commit an actus reus without any justification, excuse, or other defense. — Also termed *felonious intent*. See *specific intent*.

donative intent. The intent to surrender dominion and control over the gift that is being made.

felonious intent. See *criminal intent*.

general intent. (17c) The intent to perform an act even though the actor does not desire the consequences that result. ● This is the state of mind required for the commission of certain common-law crimes not requiring a specific intent or not imposing strict liability. General intent usu. takes the form of recklessness (involving actual awareness of a risk and the culpable taking of that risk) or negligence (involving blameworthy inadvertence). — Also termed *general criminal intent*; *general mens rea*.

immediate intent. (18c) The intent relating to a wrongful act; the part of the total intent coincident with the wrongful act itself.

implied intent. (18c) A person's state of mind that can be inferred from speech or conduct, or from language used in an instrument to which the person is a party.

intent to kill. (16c) An intent to cause the death of another; esp., a state of mind that, if found to exist during an assault, can serve as the basis for an aggravated-assault charge.

larcenous intent. (1832) A state of mind existing when a person (1) knowingly takes away the goods of another without any claim or pretense of a right to do so, and (2) intends to permanently deprive the owner of them or to convert the goods to personal use. See LARCENY.

manifest intent. (17c) Intent that is apparent or obvious based on the available circumstantial evidence, even if direct evidence of intent is not available. ● For example, some fidelity bonds cover an employer's losses caused by an employee's dishonest or fraudulent acts committed with a manifest intent to cause a loss to the employer and to obtain a benefit for the employee. Establishing manifest intent sufficient to trigger coverage does not require direct evidence that the employee intended the employer's loss. Even if the employee did not actively want that result, but the result was substantially certain to follow from the employee's conduct, the requisite intent will be inferred.

predatory intent. *Antitrust*. A business's intent to injure a competitor by unfair means, esp. by sacrificing revenues to drive a competitor out of business.

specific intent. (18c) The intent to accomplish the precise criminal act that one is later charged with. ● At common law, the specific-intent crimes were robbery, assault, larceny, burglary, forgery, false pretenses, embezzlement, attempt, solicitation, and conspiracy. — Also termed *criminal intent*. See SPECIFIC-INTENT DEFENSE.

testamentary intent. (1830) A testator's intent that a particular instrument function as his or her last will and testament. ● Testamentary intent is required for a will to be valid.

transferred intent. (1932) Intent that the law may shift from an originally intended wrongful act to a wrongful act actually committed. ● For example, if a person intends to kill one person but kills another inadvertently, the intent may be transferred to the actual act. See TRANSFERRED-INTENT DOCTRINE.

ulterior intent. (1848) The intent that passes beyond a wrongful act and relates to the objective for the sake of which the act is done; MOTIVE. ● For example, a thief's immediate intent may be to steal another's money, but the ulterior intent may be to buy food with that money.

2. A lawmaker's state of mind and purpose in drafting or voting for a measure.

legislative intent. See LEGISLATIVE INTENT.

original intent. (17c) The mental state of the drafters or enactors of the U.S. Constitution, a statute, or another document.

intention, *n.* (14c) The willingness to bring about something planned or foreseen; the state of being set to do something. — **intentional,** *adj.*

intentional, *adj.* (17c) Done with the aim of carrying out the act.

intentional act. See ACT.

intentional father. See *intentional parent* under PARENT.

intentional fraud. See FRAUD (1).

intentional infliction of emotional distress. (1958) The tort of intentionally or recklessly causing another person severe emotional distress through one's extreme or outrageous acts. • In a few jurisdictions, a physical manifestation of the mental suffering is required for the plaintiff to recover. — Abbr. IIED. — Also termed (in some states) *outrage*. See EMOTIONAL DISTRESS. Cf. NEGLIGENT INFLICTION OF EMOTIONAL DISTRESS.

intentional-injury exclusion. See *expected/intended exclusion* under EXCLUSION (3).

intentional invasion. See INVASION.

intentional manslaughter. See *voluntary manslaughter* under MANSLAUGHTER.

intentional mother. See *intentional parent* under PARENT.

intentional parent. See PARENT.

intentional tort. See TORT.

intentional wrong. See WRONG.

intent of the legislature. See LEGISLATIVE INTENT.

intent to kill. See INTENT (1).

intent to publish. *Defamation.* The intent to communicate (defamatory words, etc.) to a third person or with knowledge that the communication will probably reach third persons. See PUBLISH (2).

intent to use. See BONA FIDE INTENT TO USE.

intent-to-use application. See TRADEMARK APPLICATION.

inter (in-tər), *prep.* [Latin] Among.

inter alia (in-tər ay-lee-ə *or* ah-lee-ə), *adv.* [Latin] (17c) Among other things.

inter alios (in-tər ay-lee-əs *or* ah-lee-əs), *adv.* [Latin] (17c) Among other persons.

Inter-American Bar Association. An organization of lawyers from North America, Central America, and South America whose purpose is to promote education, cooperation, and professional exchanges among lawyers from different American countries. — Abbr. IABA.

Inter-American Foundation. An independent federal foundation that supports social and economic development in Latin America and the Caribbean by making grants to private, indigenous organizations that carry out self-help projects benefiting poor people. • The agency is governed by a nine-member board — six from the private sector and three from the government. It was created in 1969 as an experimental foreign-assistance program. 22 USCA § 290f. — Abbr. IAF.

intercept, *n. Family law.* A mechanism by which a portion of an obligor's unemployment benefits, disability income, income-tax refund, or lottery winnings is automatically diverted to a child-support-enforcement agency to satisfy past-due support obligations.

intercept, *vb.* (15c) **1.** To divert (money) from a payee to satisfy a financial obligation of the payee. **2.** To covertly receive or listen to (a communication). • The term usu. refers to covert reception by a law-enforcement agency. See WIRETAPPING.

interchangeable bond. See BOND (3).

intercountry adoption. See *international adoption* under ADOPTION.

intercourse. (15c) **1.** Dealings or communications, esp. between businesses, governmental entities, or the like. **2.** Physical sexual contact, esp. involving the penetration of the vagina by the penis.

interdependence. *Int'l law.* The reliance of countries on each other to ensure their mutual subsistence and advancement.

interdict (in-tər-dikt), *n.* (15c) *Roman & civil law.* **1.** An injunction or other prohibitory, exhibitory, or restitutory decree.

  decretal interdict (di-**kreet**-əl). An interdict that signified the praetor's order or decree by applying the remedy in a pending case.

  edictal interdict (ee-**dik**-təl). An interdict that declared the praetor's intention to give a remedy in certain cases, usu. in a way that preserves or restores possession.

  exhibitory interdict. An interdict by which a praetor compelled a person or thing to be produced.

  possessory interdict. An interdict that protected a person whose possession was disturbed without due process. • A possessor in bad faith could obtain a possessory interdict because the interdict did not depend on title. It would, however, establish whether the possessor would be the defendant or the plaintiff in any subsequent claim.

  prohibitory interdict. An interdict by which a praetor forbade something to be done.

  restitutory interdict (ri-**stich**-ə-tor-ee *or* res-ti-t[y]oo-tə-ree). An interdict by which a praetor directed something to be restored to someone who had been dispossessed of it.

2. *Civil law.* A person who has been interdicted; a natural person who, because of an infirmity, cannot make reasoned decisions about personal care or property or communicate those decisions; a person deprived of the capacity to make juridical acts. La. Civ. Code arts. 389, 390, 394.

  limited interdict. A person whose right to care for himself or herself is restricted by a court decision because of mental incapacity; a person subject to limited interdiction. La. Civ. Code art. 390.

interdict (in-tər-**dikt**), *vb.* (15c) **1.** To forbid or restrain. **2.** To intercept and seize (contraband, etc.). **3.** *Civil law.* To remove a person's right to handle personal affairs because of mental incapacity.

interdiction. 1. The act of forbidding or restraining.

> *interdiction of commercial intercourse. Int'l law.* A governmental prohibition of commercial trade.

2. The interception and seizure of something, esp. contraband. **3.** *Civil law.* The act of depriving a person of the right to handle his or her own affairs because of mental incapacity. Cf. GUARDIANSHIP (1); CURATORSHIP; CURATOR (2).

> *complete interdiction. See full interdiction.*

> *full interdiction.* The complete removal of one's right to care for oneself and one's affairs or estate because of mental incapacity. La. Civ. Code art. 389. — Also termed *complete interdiction.*

> *limited interdiction. See partial interdiction.*

> *partial interdiction.* The partial removal of one's right to care for oneself and one's affairs or estate because of mental incapacity. — Also termed *limited interdiction.*

interdictory (in-tər-**dik**-tər-ee), *adj.* **1.** Of or relating to an interdiction. **2.** Having the power to interdict. — Also termed *interdictive.*

interessee (in-tə-re-**see**). See *real party in interest* under PARTY (2).

interest, *n.* (15c) **1.** The object of any human desire; esp., advantage or profit of a financial nature <conflict of interest>. **2.** A legal share in something; all or part of a legal or equitable claim to or right in property <right, title, and interest>. ● Collectively, the word includes any aggregation of rights, privileges, powers, and immunities; distributively, it refers to any one right, privilege, power, or immunity.

> *absolute interest.* (18c) An interest that is not subject to any condition.

> *beneficial interest.* (18c) A right or expectancy in something (such as a trust or an estate), as opposed to legal title to that thing. ● For example, a person with a beneficial interest in a trust receives income from the trust but does not hold legal title to the trust property.

> *carried interest.* **1.** The share of any profits produced by a partnership's investment, paid to the general partner as compensation for managing the investment. ● The general partner often contributes little or no capital to acquire the investment but gains an interest in it by providing time and skill. The general partner's interest in the property is "carried" with the property until

it is liquidated. **2.** *Oil & gas.* In an oil-and-gas lease, a fractional interest that is free of some or all costs of exploring, drilling, and completing the well. ● The owner of a carried lease may earn royalties on production but does not have a working interest, at least until all costs are recouped by the working-interest owner or owners, and often until some multiple of those costs are paid.

> *concurrent interest. See concurrent estate* under ESTATE (1).

> *contingent interest.* (18c) An interest that the holder may enjoy only upon the occurrence of a condition precedent.

> *controlling interest.* Sufficient ownership of stock in a company to control policy and management; esp., a greater-than-50% ownership interest in an enterprise.

> *defeasible interest.* An interest that the holder may enjoy until the occurrence of a condition.

> *direct interest.* (17c) A certain, absolute interest <the juror was disqualified because she had a direct interest in the lawsuit>.

> *entailed interest.* An interest that devolves through lineal descendants only as a result of a fee tail.

> *entire interest.* (17c) A whole interest or right, without diminution. See FEE SIMPLE.

> *equitable interest.* (17c) An interest held by virtue of an equitable title or claimed on equitable grounds, such as the interest held by a trust beneficiary.

> *executory interest. See EXECUTORY INTEREST.*

> *expectation interest.* (1836) The interest of a nonbreaching party in being put in the position that would have resulted if the contract had been performed. See *expectation damages* under DAMAGES; BENEFIT-OF-THE-BARGAIN RULE.

> *financial interest.* An interest involving money or its equivalent; esp., an interest in the nature of an investment. — Also termed *pecuniary interest.*

> *fractional interest. See undivided interest.*

> *future interest.* (17c) A property interest in which the privilege of possession or of other enjoyment is future and not present. ● A future interest can exist in either the grantor (as with a reversion) or the grantee (as with a remainder or executory interest). Today, most future interests are equitable interests in stocks and debt securities, with power of sale in a trustee. — Also termed *future estate; expectant estate; estate in expectancy.* Cf. *present interest* under INTEREST (2).

> *inalienable interest.* (1848) An interest that cannot be sold or traded.

inchoate interest. (1800) A property interest that has not yet vested.

insurable interest. (18c) A legal interest in another person's life or health or in the protection of property from injury, loss, destruction, or pecuniary damage. • To take out an insurance policy, the purchaser or the potential insured's beneficiary must have an insurable interest. If a policy does not have an insurable interest as its basis, it will usu. be considered a form of wagering and thus be held unenforceable. See *wager policy* under INSURANCE POLICY.

interest in the use and enjoyment of land. The pleasure, comfort, and advantage that a person may derive from the occupancy of land. • The term includes not only the interests that a person may have for residential, agricultural, commercial, industrial, and other purposes, but also interests in having the present-use value of the land unimpaired by changes in its physical condition.

joint interest. An interest that is acquired at the same time and by the same title as another person's. See *joint tenancy* under TENANCY.

junior interest. An interest that is subordinate to a senior interest.

legal interest. (17c) **1.** An interest that has its origin in the principles, standards, and rules developed by courts of law as opposed to courts of chancery. **2.** An interest recognized by law, such as legal title.

legally protected interest. A property interest that the law will protect against impairment or destruction, whether in law or in equity.

liberty interest. (1960) An interest protected by the due-process clauses of state and federal constitutions. See FUNDAMENTAL RIGHT (2).

multiple interest. A property interest that is good against an indefinitely large number of people.

pecuniary interest. See *financial interest.*

possessory interest. See POSSESSORY INTEREST.

present interest. (17c) **1.** A property interest in which the privilege of possession or enjoyment is present and not merely future; an interest entitling the holder to immediate possession. — Also termed *present estate.* Cf. FUTURE INTEREST. **2.** A trust interest in which the beneficiary has the immediate beneficial enjoyment of the trust's proceeds. **3.** A trust interest in which the trustee has the immediate right to control and manage the property in trust.

proprietary interest. (17c) A property right; specif., the interest held by a property owner together with all appurtenant rights, such as a stockholder's right to vote the shares.

reliance interest. (1936) The interest of a nonbreaching party in being put in the position that would have resulted if the contract had not been made, including out-of-pocket costs.

restitution interest. A nonbreaching party's interest in preventing the breaching party from retaining a benefit received under the contract and thus being unjustly enriched. • The benefit may have been received from the nonbreaching party or from a third party.

reversionary interest. A future interest left in the transferor or successor in interest. See REVERSION.

senior interest. An interest that takes precedence over others; esp., a debt security or preferred share that has a higher claim on a corporation's assets and earnings than that of a junior obligation or common share.

terminable interest. (1883) An interest that may be terminated upon the lapse of time or upon the occurrence of some condition.

undivided interest. (18c) An interest held under the same title by two or more persons, whether their rights are equal or unequal in value or quantity. — Also termed *undivided right; undivided title; fractional interest.* See *joint tenancy* and *tenancy in common* under TENANCY.

vested interest. (18c) An interest for which the right to its enjoyment, either present or future, is not subject to the happening of a condition precedent.

working interest. See WORKING INTEREST.

3. The compensation fixed by agreement or allowed by law for the use or detention of money, or for the loss of money by one who is entitled to its use; esp., the amount owed to a lender in return for the use of borrowed money. — Also termed *finance charge.* See USURY.

accrued interest. (18c) Interest that is earned but not yet paid, such as interest that accrues on real estate and that will be paid when the property is sold if, in the meantime, the rental income does not cover the mortgage payments.

add-on interest. (1952) Interest that is computed on the original face amount of a loan and that remains the same even as the principal declines. • A $10,000 loan with add-on interest at 8% payable over three years would require equal annual interest payments of $800 for three years, regardless of the unpaid principal amount. With add-on interest, the effective rate of interest is typically about twice the stated add-on interest rate. In the example just cited, then, the effective rate of interest would be about 16%. — Also termed *block interest.* See *add-on loan* under LOAN.

Boston interest. Interest computed by using a 30-day month rather than the exact number of days in the month. — Also termed *New York interest.*

compound interest. (17c) Interest paid on both the principal and the previously accumulated interest. Cf. *simple interest.*

conventional interest. (1878) Interest at a rate agreed to by the parties themselves, as distinguished from that prescribed by law. Cf. *interest as damages.*

discount interest. The interest that accrues on a discounted investment instrument (such as a government bond) as it matures. ● The investor receives the interest when the instrument is redeemed.

gross interest. (1884) A borrower's interest payment that includes administrative, service, and insurance charges.

imputed interest. (1968) Interest income that the IRS attributes to a lender regardless of whether the lender actually receives interest from the borrower. ● This is common esp. in loans between family members.

interest as damages. (1841) Interest allowed by law in the absence of a promise to pay it, as compensation for a delay in paying a fixed sum or a delay in assessing and paying damages. Cf. *conventional interest.*

lawful interest. **1.** A rate of interest that is less than or equal to the statutory maximum. **2.** See *legal interest.*

legal interest. **1.** Interest at a rate usu. prescribed by statute. ● Courts often order monetary judgments to accumulate legal interest until paid. Cf. *legal rate* under INTEREST RATE. **2.** See *lawful interest.*

illegal interest. See USURY.

moratory interest. See *prejudgment interest.*

New York interest. See *Boston interest.*

prejudgment interest. Statutorily prescribed interest accrued either from the date of the loss or from the date when the complaint was filed up to the date the final judgment is entered. ● Prejudgment interest is usu. calculated only for liquidated sums. Depending on the statute, it may or may not be an element of damages. — Also termed *moratory interest.*

prepaid interest. (1887) Interest paid before it is earned.

qualified residence interest. (1993) *Tax.* Interest paid on debt that is secured by one's home and that was incurred to purchase, build, improve, or refinance the home. ● This type of interest is deductible from adjusted gross income.

simple interest. (17c) Interest paid on the principal only and not on accumulated interest. ● Interest accrues only on the principal balance regardless of how often interest is paid. — Also termed *straight-line interest.* Cf. *compound interest.*

straight-line interest. See *simple interest.*

unearned interest. (1880) Interest received by a financial institution before it is earned.

unlawful interest. See USURY.

interest-analysis technique. (1964) *Conflict of laws.* A method of resolving choice-of-law questions by reviewing a state's laws and the state's interests in enforcing those laws to determine whether that state's laws or those of another state should apply. — Also termed *governmental-interest-analysis technique.*

interest arbitration. See ARBITRATION.

interest as damages. See INTEREST (3).

interest-based quorum. See QUORUM.

interest bond. See BOND (3).

interest coupon. See COUPON.

interest-coverage ratio. The ratio between a company's pretax earnings and the annual interest payable on bonds and loans.

interested party. See PARTY (2).

interested person. See PERSON (1).

interested shareholder. See SHAREHOLDER.

interested stockholder. See *interested shareholder* under SHAREHOLDER.

interested witness. See WITNESS.

interest-equalization tax. See TAX.

interest factor. *Insurance.* In life-insurance ratemaking, an estimate of the interest or rate of return that the insurer will earn on premium payments over the life of a policy. ● The interest factor is one element that a life insurer uses to calculate premium rates. See PREMIUM RATE; *gross premium* (1) under PREMIUM (1). Cf. MORTALITY FACTOR; RISK FACTOR.

interest-free loan. See LOAN.

Interest on Lawyers' Trust Accounts. A program that allows a lawyer or law firm to deposit a client's retained funds into an interest-bearing account that designates the interest payments to charitable, law-related purposes, such as providing legal aid to the poor. ● Almost all states have either a voluntary or mandatory IOLTA program. — Abbr. IOLTA.

interest-only loan. See LOAN.

interest-only mortgage. See MORTGAGE.

interest policy. See INSURANCE POLICY.

interest rate. (1886) The percentage that a borrower of money must pay to the lender in return for the use of the money, usu. expressed as a percentage of the principal payable for a one-year period. — Often shortened to *rate*. — Also termed *rate of interest*.

annual percentage rate. (1941) The actual cost of borrowing money, expressed in the form of an annualized interest rate. — Abbr. APR.

bank rate. The rate of interest at which the Federal Reserve lends funds to member banks.

contract rate. (1856) The interest rate printed on the face of a bond certificate.

coupon rate. 1. The specific interest rate for a coupon bond. — Also termed *coupon interest rate*. See *coupon bond* under BOND (3). **2.** See *nominal rate*.

discount rate. (1913) **1.** The interest rate at which a member bank may borrow money from the Federal Reserve. • This rate controls the supply of money available to banks for lending. Cf. *rediscount rate*. **2.** The percentage of a commercial paper's face value paid by an issuer who sells the instrument to a financial institution. **3.** The interest rate used in calculating present value.

effective rate. (1912) The actual annual interest rate, which incorporates compounding when calculating interest, rather than the stated rate or coupon rate.

face rate. See *nominal rate*.

floating rate. (1921) A varying interest rate that is tied to a financial index such as the prime rate.

illegal rate. (1867) An interest rate higher than the rate allowed by law. See USURY.

legal rate. (1857) **1.** The interest rate imposed as a matter of law when none is provided by contract. **2.** The maximum interest rate, set by statute, that may be charged on a loan. See *legal interest* under INTEREST (3). Cf. USURY.

lock rate. (2000) A mortgage-application interest rate that is established and guaranteed for a specified period. — Also termed *locked-in rate*.

nominal rate. (1872) The interest rate stated in a loan agreement or on a bond, with no adjustment made for inflation. — Also termed *coupon rate*; *face rate*; *stated rate*; *stated interest rate*.

prime rate. (1952) The interest rate that a commercial bank holds out as its lowest rate for a short-term loan to its most creditworthy borrowers, usu. large corporations. • This rate, which can vary slightly from bank to bank, often dictates other interest rates for various personal and commercial loans. — Often shortened to *prime*. — Also termed *prime lending rate*.

real rate. (1895) An interest rate that has been adjusted for inflation over time.

rediscount rate. The interest rate at which a member bank may borrow from the Federal Reserve on a loan secured by commercial paper that has already been resold by the bank.

stated rate. See *nominal rate*.

variable rate. (1970) An interest rate that varies at preset intervals in relation to the current market rate (usu. the prime rate).

interest-rate swap. An agreement to exchange interest receipts or interest-payment obligations, usu. to adjust one's risk exposure, to speculate on interest-rate changes, or to convert an instrument or obligation from a fixed to a floating rate — or from a floating to a fixed rate. • The parties to such an agreement are termed "counterparties."

generic swap. See *plain-vanilla swap*.

plain-vanilla swap. A typical interest-rate swap that involves one counterparty's paying a fixed interest rate while the other assumes a floating interest rate based on the amount of the principal of the underlying debt. • The underlying debt, called the "notional" amount of the swap, does not change hands — only the interest payments are exchanged. — Also termed *generic swap*.

interest unity. See *unity of interest* under UNITY.

interest warrant. See WARRANT (2).

interferant. 1. Something that interferes with the proper function of a chemical analysis; specif., a chemical contaminant that renders the results of a blood, breath, or urine test unreliable. **2.** *Patents.* A party to an interference proceeding in the U.S. Patent and Trademark Office. • This term declined in use after the 1960s; today the PTO and courts use the term "contestant." — Also termed (in sense 2) *contestant*. See CONTESTANT (3).

interference, *n.* (18c) **1.** The act of meddling in another's affairs. **2.** An obstruction or hindrance. **3.** *Patents.* An administrative proceeding in the U.S. Patent and Trademark Office to determine who is entitled to the patent when two or more applicants claim the same invention, or when an application interferes with an existing patent. • This proceeding occurs when the same invention is claimed (1) in two pending applications, or (2) in one pending application and a patent issued within a year of the pending application's filing date. — Also termed *priority contest*. **4.** *Trademarks.* An administrative proceeding in the U.S. Patent and Trademark Office to determine whether a mark one party wants to register will cause confusion among consumers with another party's mark. • An administrative hearing may be held to determine whose mark prevails, but applicants usu. withdraw their applications and devise new marks instead. — **interfere,** *vb.*

interference-estoppel rejection. See REJECTION.

interference with a business relationship. See TORTIOUS INTERFERENCE WITH PROSPECTIVE ADVANTAGE.

interference with a contractual relationship. See TORTIOUS INTERFERENCE WITH CONTRACTUAL RELATIONS.

interference with contract. See TORTIOUS INTERFERENCE WITH CONTRACTUAL RELATIONS.

intergenerational love. 1. Affection between adults and children. ● This sense usu. refers to interfamilial affection, as between grandparents and grandchildren, and does not include sexual feelings. **2.** Romance or sexual contact between a child below the age of consent and an adult. ● Pedophiles use the term as a euphemism to assert that sexual contact between adults and children is consensual.

intergovernmental immunity. See IMMUNITY (1).

intergovernmental-immunity doctrine. (1939) *Constitutional law.* The principle that both the federal government and the states are independent sovereigns, and that neither sovereign may intrude on the other in certain political spheres. Cf. PREEMPTION (5).

Intergovernmental Maritime Consultative Organization. A unit of the United Nations charged with setting international standards for vessel safety and personnel training for shipping on the open seas. — Abbr. IMCO.

interim, *adj.* (16c) Done, made, or occurring for an intervening time; temporary or provisional <an interim director>.

interim bond. See BOND (2).

interim curator. See CURATOR (2).

interim financing. See FINANCING.

interim measure of protection. *Int'l law.* An international tribunal's order to prevent a litigant from prejudicing the final outcome of a lawsuit by arbitrary action before a judgment has been reached. ● This measure is comparable to a temporary injunction in national law.

interim-occupancy agreement. (1962) A contract governing an arrangement (called a *leaseback*) whereby the seller rents back property from the buyer. See LEASEBACK.

interim order. See ORDER (2).

interim receipt. See RECEIPT.

interim relief. See RELIEF.

interim statement. *Accounting.* A periodic financial report issued during the fiscal year (usu. quarterly) that indicates the company's current

performance. ● The SEC requires the company to file such a statement if it is distributed to the company's shareholders. — Also termed *interim report.*

interim trustee. See TRUSTEE (2).

interim zoning. See ZONING.

interinsurance. See *reciprocal insurance* under INSURANCE.

interinsurance exchange. See RECIPROCAL EXCHANGE.

Interior Department. See DEPARTMENT OF THE INTERIOR.

interlineation (in-tər-lin-ee-**ay**-shən), *n.* (15c) **1.** The act of writing something between the lines of an earlier writing. **2.** Something written between the lines of an earlier writing. Cf. INTERPOLATION (1). — **interline,** *vb.*

interlining. A carrier's practice of transferring a shipment to another carrier to reach a destination not served by the transferring carrier.

interlocking confessions. See CONFESSION.

interlocking director. See DIRECTOR.

interlocutory (in-tər-**lok**-yə-tor-ee), *adj.* (15c) (Of an order, judgment, appeal, etc.) interim or temporary; not constituting a final resolution of the whole controversy. — Also termed *medial.*

interlocutory appeal. See APPEAL.

Interlocutory Appeals Act. A federal statute, enacted in 1958, that grants discretion to a U.S. court of appeals to review an interlocutory order in a civil case if the trial judge states in writing that the order involves a controlling question of law on which there is substantial ground for difference of opinion, and that an immediate appeal from the order may materially advance the termination of the litigation. 28 USCA § 1292(b). Cf. FINALITY DOCTRINE; FINAL-JUDGMENT RULE.

interlocutory application. See APPLICATION.

interlocutory costs. See COSTS (3).

interlocutory decision. See *interlocutory order* under ORDER (2).

interlocutory decree. See *interlocutory judgment* under JUDGMENT.

interlocutory injunction. See *preliminary injunction* under INJUNCTION.

interlocutory judgment. See JUDGMENT.

interlocutory order. See ORDER (2).

interloper, *n.* (16c) **1.** One who interferes without justification. **2.** One who trades illegally. — **interlope,** *vb.*

intermeddler. See OFFICIOUS INTERMEDDLER.

intermediary (in-tər-**mee**-dee-er-ee), *n.* (18c) A mediator or go-between; a third-party negotiator. Cf. FINDER (1). — **intermediate** (in-tər-**mee**-dee-ayt), *vb.*

informed intermediary. *Products liability.* A person who is in the chain of distribution from the manufacturer to the consumer and who knows the risks of the product. — Also termed *learned intermediary.*

intermediary bank. See BANK.

intermediate account. See ACCOUNT.

intermediate casing. See CASING.

intermediate court. See COURT.

intermediate order. See *interlocutory order* under ORDER (2).

intermediate scrutiny. (1974) *Constitutional law.* A standard lying between the extremes of rational-basis review and strict scrutiny. • Under the standard, if a statute contains a quasi-suspect classification (such as gender or legitimacy), the classification must be substantially related to the achievement of an important governmental objective. — Also termed *middle-level scrutiny*; *mid-level scrutiny*; *heightened scrutiny.* Cf. STRICT SCRUTINY; RATIONAL-BASIS TEST.

intermediation. (17c) **1.** Any process involving an intermediary. **2.** The placing of funds with a financial intermediary that reinvests the funds, such as a bank that lends the funds to others or a mutual fund that invests the funds in stocks, bonds, or other instruments.

intermittent easement. See EASEMENT.

intermittent sentence. See SENTENCE.

intermixture of goods. See CONFUSION OF GOODS.

intermodal transport. See MULTIMODAL SHIPPING.

intermunicipal law. See *private international law* under INTERNATIONAL LAW.

intern, *n.* (1889) An advanced student or recent graduate who is apprenticing to gain practical experience before entering a specific profession. See CLERK (4). — **internship,** *n.*

intern, *vb.* (1866) **1.** To segregate and confine a person or group, esp. those suspected of hostile sympathies in time of war. See INTERNMENT. **2.** To work in an internship.

internal act. See ACT.

internal-affairs doctrine. *Conflict of laws.* The rule that in disputes involving a corporation and its relationships with its shareholders, directors, officers, or agents, the law to be applied is the law of the state of incorporation. • This doctrine applies in the majority of states. In a few states, notably California and New York, foreign corporations must meet state-law requirements in specified circumstances.

internal affairs of a foreign corporation. *Conflict of laws.* Matters that involve only the inner workings of a corporation, such as dividend declarations and the selection of officers.

internal attack. A beneficiary's questioning of the propriety of a trust's continuance, the purpose being to terminate the trust and receive from the trustee the interests held for the beneficiary's benefit.

internal audit. See AUDIT.

internal commerce. See *intrastate commerce* under COMMERCE.

internal financing. See FINANCING.

internal law. See LAW.

internal litigation-hold letter. See LITIGATION-HOLD LETTER.

internally displaced person. See *displaced person* under PERSON (1).

internal rate of return. See RATE OF RETURN.

internal revenue. Governmental revenue derived from domestic taxes rather than from customs or import duties. — Also termed (outside the United States) *inland revenue.*

Internal Revenue Code. Title 26 of the U.S. Code, containing all current federal tax laws. — Abbr. IRC. — Also termed *tax law.*

Internal Revenue Service. A unit in the U.S. Department of the Treasury responsible for enforcing and administering the internal-revenue laws and other tax laws except those relating to alcohol, tobacco, firearms, and explosives. — Abbr. IRS.

internal security. The field of law dealing with measures taken to protect a country from subversive activities.

internal-security act. (1950) A statute illegalizing and controlling subversive activities of organizations whose purpose is believed to be to overthrow or disrupt the government. • In the United States, many provisions in such statutes have been declared unconstitutional. One such law was repealed in 1993. See 50 USCA § 781.

internal sovereignty. See SOVEREIGNTY (3).

internal waters. Any natural or artificial body or stream of water within the territorial limits of a country, such as a bay, gulf, river mouth, creek, harbor, port, lake, or canal. — Also termed *inland waters.*

international administrative law. See ADMINISTRATIVE LAW.

international agreement. (1871) A treaty or other contract between different countries, such as GATT or NAFTA. See GENERAL AGREEMENT ON TARIFFS AND TRADE; NORTH AMERICAN FREE TRADE AGREEMENT.

international application. See PATENT APPLICA-
TION.

**international application designating the United
States.** See PATENT APPLICATION.

**international application originating in the Unit-
ed States.** See PATENT APPLICATION.

International Association. See L'ASSOCIATION LIT-
TERAIRE ET ARTISTIQUE INTERNATIONALE.

**International Bank for Reconstruction and De-
velopment.** See WORLD BANK.

international bill of exchange. See *foreign draft*
under DRAFT.

**International Bureau for the Protection of Intel-
lectual Property.** *Copyright.* A predecessor of the
World Intellectual Property Organization. • The
bureau was created by combining the Paris Convention's Secretariat (the International Bureau
for the Paris Convention) with the Berne Copyright Convention of 1886. It was supervised by the
Swiss government until 1970, when the bureau
became part of WIPO. — Also termed *Bureaux
Internationaux Reunis pour la Protection de la
Propriete Intellectuelle*; *BIRPI*.

**International Centre for Settlement of Invest-
ment Disputes.** An autonomous division of the
World Bank consisting of an international three-
member tribunal that presides over arbitrations
affecting the rights of foreign investors. • The
center was created in 1966 under the Convention on the Settlement of Investment Disputes
Between States and Nationals of Other States.
It provides services for the conciliation and arbitration of international investment and trade
disputes. — Abbr. ICSID.

international commerce. See COMMERCE.

international control. *Int'l law.* The supervision
over countries and their subdivisions for the purpose of ensuring the conformity of their conduct
with international law.

**International Convention for the Protection of
Performers, Producers of Phonograms and
Broadcasting Organizations.** See ROME CON-
VENTION.

International Court of Justice. The 15-member
permanent tribunal that is the principal judicial
organ of the United Nations. • The Court sits in
the Hague, Netherlands. It has jurisdiction to
decide disputes submitted to it by nations, and
to render advisory opinions requested by the
United Nations and its specialized agencies. The
U.N. Security Council has the express power to
enforce the Court's judgments. — Abbr. ICJ. —
Also termed *World Court*.

international crime. *Int'l law.* A grave breach of
international law, such as genocide or a crime
against humanity, made a punishable offense
by treaties or applicable rules of customary

international law. • An international crime occurs when three conditions are satisfied: (1) the
criminal norm must derive either from a treaty
concluded under international law or from customary international law, and must have direct
binding force on individuals without intermediate provisions of municipal law, (2) the provision
must be made for the prosecution of acts penalized by international law in accordance with the
principle of universal jurisdiction, so that the
international character of the crime might show
in the mode of prosecution itself (e.g., before the
International Criminal Court), and (3) a treaty
establishing liability for the act must bind the
great majority of countries. — Also termed *international offense.*

International Criminal Court. A court established
by a treaty known as the Statute of the International Criminal Court (effective 2002), with jurisdiction over genocides, crimes against humanity,
war crimes, and aggression. It sits in The Hague,
Netherlands. — Abbr. ICC.

International Criminal Police Organization. An
international law-enforcement group founded in
1923 and headquartered in Lyons, France. • The
organization gathers and shares information on
transnational criminals for more than 180 member nations. — Also termed *Interpol.*

international economic law. (1939) International
law relating to investment, economic relations,
economic development, economic institutions,
and regional economic integration.

international enclave. See ENCLAVE.

international extradition. See EXTRADITION.

international filing date. See PCT FILING DATE.

international fund. See MUTUAL FUND.

internationalization. The act or process of bringing a territory of one country under the protection
or control of another or of several countries.

international jurisdiction. See JURISDICTION.

international law. (18c) The legal system governing
the relationships between nations; more modernly, the law of international relations, embracing
not only nations but also such participants as international organizations and individuals (such as
those who invoke their human rights or commit
war crimes). — Also termed *public international
law*; *law of nations*; *law of nature and nations*; *jus
gentium*; *jus gentium publicum*; *jus inter gentes*;
foreign-relations law; *interstate law*; *law between
states* (the word *state*, in the latter two phrases,
being equivalent to *nation* or *country*). Cf. TRANS-
NATIONAL LAW.

   customary international law. International law
   that derives from the practice of states and is
   accepted by them as legally binding. • This is

one of the principal sources or building blocks of the international legal system.

private international law. International conflict of laws. • Legal scholars frequently lament the name "private international law" because it misleadingly suggests a body of law somehow parallel to public international law, when in fact it is merely a part of each legal system's private law. — Also termed *international private law*; *jus gentium privatum*; *intermunicipal law*; *comity*; *extraterritorial recognition of rights*. See CONFLICT OF LAWS (2).

International Law Commission. A body created in 1947 by the United Nations for the purpose of encouraging the progressive development and codification of international law. • The Commission is composed of experts in international law. It has drafted many important treaties that have become binding treaty law, including the Vienna Convention on the Law on Treaties.

international legal community. (1928) **1.** The collective body of countries whose mutual legal relations are based on sovereign equality. **2.** More broadly, all organized entities having the capacity to take part in international legal relations. **3.** An integrated organization on which a group of countries, by international treaty, confer part of their powers for amalgamated enterprise. • In this sense, the European Union is a prime example.

international legislation. *Int'l law.* **1.** Law-making among countries or intergovernmental organizations, displaying structural and procedural characteristics that are the same as national legislation. **2.** The product of any concerted effort to change international law by statute. **3.** The process of trying to change international law by statute. **4.** Loosely, the adoption by international bodies of binding decisions, other than judicial and arbitral decisions, concerning specific situations or disputes.

International Monetary Fund. A U.N. specialized agency established to stabilize international exchange rates and promote balanced trade. — Abbr. IMF.

international offense. See INTERNATIONAL CRIME.

international organization. (1907) *Int'l law.* **1.** An intergovernmental association of countries, established by and operated according to multilateral treaty, whose purpose is to pursue the common aims of those countries. • Examples include the World Health Organization, the International Civil Aviation Organization, and the Organization of Petroleum Exporting Countries. **2.** Loosely, an intergovernmental or nongovernmental international association.

International Parental Kidnapping Crime Act of 1993. A federal statute that implemented the Hague Convention on the Civil Aspects of International Child Abduction. 18 USCA § 1204. See HAGUE CONVENTION ON THE CIVIL ASPECTS OF INTERNATIONAL CHILD ABDUCTION.

international person. *Int'l law.* An entity having a legal personality in international law; one who, being a subject of international law, enjoys rights, duties, and powers established in international law and has the ability to act on the international plane.

international private law. 1. See *private international law* under INTERNATIONAL LAW. **2.** See CONFLICT OF LAWS (2).

international regime. See REGIME.

International Regulations for Preventing Collisions at Sea. See INTERNATIONAL RULES OF THE ROAD.

international relations. (1880) **1.** World politics. **2.** Global political interaction, primarily among sovereign nations. **3.** The academic discipline devoted to studying world politics, embracing international law, international economics, and the history and art of diplomacy.

international river. See RIVER.

International Rules of the Road. *Maritime law.* A set of statutes designed to promote navigational safety. • The International Rules were formalized at the convention on the International Regulations for Preventing Collisions at Sea, 1972. The rules set requirements for navigation lights, day shapes, steering and sailing rules, sound signals in good and restricted visibility condition, and distress signals, among other things. Congress adopted the rules and enacted them in statutory form. 33 USCA § 1602. — Also termed *72 COLREGS*; *International Regulations for Preventing Collisions at Sea, 1972*.

International Schedule of Classes of Goods and Services. *Trademarks.* A nearly worldwide classification system that enhances organization and retrieval of registered marks within a category of goods or services. — Abbr. ISCGS.

international seabed. The seabed and ocean floor, as well as the subsoil, lying beyond the territorial limits of nations. — Also termed *international seabed area*.

international terrorism. See TERRORISM.

International Trade Administration. A unit in the U.S. Department of Commerce responsible for promoting world trade and strengthening the international trade and investment position of the United States. • Created in 1980, the agency operates through three offices: the Office of the Assistant Secretary for Import Services, the Office of the Assistant Secretary for Market Access and

Compliance, and the Office of the Assistant Secretary for Trade Development. — Abbr. ITA.

International Trade Commission. See UNITED STATES INTERNATIONAL TRADE COMMISSION.

International Trade Court. See UNITED STATES COURT OF INTERNATIONAL TRADE.

international union. See UNION.

international will. See WILL.

internecine (in-tər-**nee**-sin *or* in-tər-**nee**-sin *or* in-tər-**nes**-een), *adj.* (17c) **1.** Deadly; characterized by mass slaughter. **2.** Mutually deadly; destructive of both parties <an internecine civil war>. **3.** Loosely, of or relating to conflict within a group <internecine faculty politics>.

Internet Corporation for Assigned Names and Numbers. A nonprofit corporation established in 1998 to assign and manage the system of Internet domain names and to allocate Internet-protocol (IP) address space. — Abbr. ICANN.

Internet patent. See PATENT (3).

Internet payment. See CYBERPAYMENT.

Internet payment service. An enterprise that offers electronic transfers of money.

Internet-protocol address. The 10-digit identification tag used by computers to locate specific websites.

Internet scrip. See SCRIP.

Internet service provider. A business or other organization that offers Internet access, typically for a fee. — Abbr. ISP.

internment (in-**tərn**-mənt), *n.* The government-ordered detention of people suspected of disloyalty to the government, such as the confinement of Japanese Americans during World War II. — **intern,** *vb.*

internuncio (in-tər-**nən**-shee-oh), *n.* [fr. Latin *internuntius*] **1.** A messenger between two parties. **2.** A broker who serves as agent of both parties to a transaction. — Also termed *internuncius.* **3.** A papal representative at a foreign court, ranking below a nuncio. Cf. NUNCIO (1); LEGATE (3). — **internuncial,** *adj.*

inter pares (**in**-tər **pair**-eez), *adv. & adj.* [Latin] Between peers; between people in an equal position.

inter partes (in-tər **pahr**-teez), *adv.* [Latin "between parties"] (1816) Between two or more parties; with two or more parties in a transaction. — *inter partes, adj.*

inter partes **reexamination.** See REEXAMINATION.

interpellate (in-tər-**pel**-ayt), *vb.* **1.** (Of a judge) to interrupt, with a question, a lawyer's argument. **2.** (Of a legislator) to interrupt a legislature's calendar by bringing into question a ministerial

policy, esp. in the legislature of France, Italy, or Germany. — Also termed (in Scots law) *interpel* (in-tər-**pel**). — **interpellation,** *n.*

interplea. (17c) A pleading by which a stakeholder places the disputed property into the court's registry; the plea made by an interpleader. See INTERPLEADER.

interplead, *vb.* (16c) **1.** (Of a claimant) to assert one's own claim regarding property or an issue already before the court. **2.** (Of a stakeholder) to institute an interpleader action, usu. by depositing disputed property into the court's registry to abide the court's decision about who is entitled to the property. Cf. IMPLEAD.

interpleader, *n.* (16c) **1.** A suit to determine a right to property held by a usu. disinterested third party (called a *stakeholder*) who is in doubt about ownership and who therefore deposits the property with the court to permit interested parties to litigate ownership. ● Typically, a stakeholder initiates an interpleader both to determine who should receive the property and to avoid multiple liability. Fed. R. Civ. P. 22. See STAKEHOLDER (1). Cf. IMPLEADER; INTERVENTION (1). **2.** Loosely, a party who interpleads. — Also termed (in civil law) *concursus.*

Interpol (**in**-tər-pohl). See INTERNATIONAL CRIMINAL POLICE ORGANIZATION.

interpolation (in-tər-pə-**lay**-shən), *n.* (17c) **1.** The act of inserting words into a document to change or clarify the meaning. ● In a negative sense, interpolation can refer to putting extraneous or false words into a document to change its meaning. Cf. INTERLINEATION. **2.** (often pl.) *Roman law.* An editorial change made by one of the compilers of the Digests and the Justinian Code. ● The compilers made insertions, deletions, and juxtapositions in the texts, but made few real changes to the substantive law. — **interpolate,** *vb.* — **interpolative,** *adj.* — **interpolator,** *n.*

interposition, *n.* (14c) **1.** The act of submitting something (such as a pleading or motion) as a defense to an opponent's claim. **2.** *Archaic.* The action of a state, while exercising its sovereignty, in rejecting a federal mandate that it believes is unconstitutional or overreaching. ● The Supreme Court has declared that interposition is an illegal defiance of constitutional authority. — **interpose,** *vb.*

interpretation, *n.* (14c) **1.** The process of determining what something, esp. the law or a legal document, means; the ascertainment of meaning to be given to words or other manifestations of intention.

administrative interpretation. An interpretation given to a law or regulation by an administrative agency.

authentic interpretation. (1967) An interpretation arrived at by asking the drafter or drafting body what the intended meaning was.

comparative interpretation. (1933) A method of statutory construction by which parts of the statute are compared to each other, and the statute as a whole is compared to other documents from the same source on a similar subject.

customary interpretation. (1902) Interpretation based on earlier rulings on the same subject.

extensive interpretation. (17c) A liberal interpretation that applies a statutory provision to a case not falling within its literal words.

grammatical interpretation. (1830) Interpretation that is based exclusively on the words themselves.

liberal interpretation. (18c) Interpretation according to what the reader believes the author reasonably intended, even if, through inadvertence, the author failed to think of it. — Also termed *mixed interpretation.*

limited interpretation. See *restrictive interpretation.*

logical interpretation. (1870) Interpretation that departs from the literal words on the ground that there may be other, more satisfactory evidence of the author's true intention. — Also termed *rational interpretation.*

mixed interpretation. See *liberal interpretation.*

practical interpretation. See *contemporaneous construction* under CONSTRUCTION.

rational interpretation. See *logical interpretation.*

restrictive interpretation. (17c) An interpretation that is bound by a principle or principles existing outside the interpreted text. — Also termed *restricted interpretation; limited interpretation; interpretatio limitata.* Cf. *unrestrictive interpretation.*

statutory interpretation. See STATUTORY CONSTRUCTION.

strict interpretation. (16c) Interpretation according to what the reader believes the author must have been thinking at the time of the writing, and no more. • Typically, this type of reading gives a text a narrow meaning.

unrestrictive interpretation. (1968) Interpretation in good faith, without reference to any specific principle. Cf. *restrictive interpretation.*

2. The understanding one has about the meaning of something. **3.** A translation, esp. oral, from one language to another. **4.** CHARACTERIZATION (1). See CONSTRUCTION (2). — **interpret,** *vb.* — **interpretative, interpretive,** *adj.*

interpretation clause. (1827) A legislative or contractual provision giving the meaning of frequently used words or explaining how the document as a whole is to be construed.

interpretative rule. *Administrative law.* **1.** The requirement that an administrative agency explain the statutes under which it operates. **2.** An administrative rule explaining an agency's interpretation of a statute. — Also termed *interpretive rule.* Cf. LEGISLATIVE RULE.

interpreted testimony. See TESTIMONY.

interpreter. (14c) A person who translates, esp. orally, from one language to another; esp., a person who is sworn at a trial to accurately translate the testimony of a witness who is deaf or who speaks a foreign language.

interpretive rule. See INTERPRETATIVE RULE.

interpretivism. (1978) A doctrine of constitutional interpretation holding that judges must follow norms or values expressly stated or implied in the language of the Constitution. Cf. NONINTERPRETIVISM; ORIGINALISM.

interracial adoption. See *transracial adoption* under ADOPTION.

interracial marriage. See MISCEGENATION.

interregnum (in-tə-**reg**-nəm). (16c) **1.** An interval between reigns; the time when a throne is vacant between the reign of a sovereign and the accession of a successor. **2.** *Archaic.* Authority exercised during a temporary vacancy of the throne or a suspension of the regular government. **3.** A break or pause in a continuous event.

interrogatee (in-ter-ə-gə-**tee**). A person who is interrogated. — Also termed *interrogee* (in-ter-ə-**gee**).

interrogation, *n.* (15c) The formal or systematic questioning of a person; esp., intensive questioning by the police, usu. of a person arrested for or suspected of committing a crime. • The Supreme Court has held that, for purposes of the Fifth Amendment right against self-incrimination, interrogation includes not only express questioning but also words or actions that the police should know are reasonably likely to elicit an incriminating response. *Rhode Island v. Innis,* 446 U.S. 291, 100 S.Ct. 1082 (1980). — **interrogate,** *vb.* — **interrogative,** *adj.*

custodial interrogation. (1966) Police questioning of a detained person about the crime that he or she is suspected of having committed. • Miranda warnings must be given before a custodial interrogation.

investigatory interrogation. (1962) Routine, nonaccusatory questioning by the police of a person who is not in custody.

noncustodial interrogation. (1966) Police questioning of a suspect who has not been detained and can leave at will. ● Miranda warnings are usu. not given before a noncustodial interrogation.

interrogative question. *Civil law.* In a criminal trial, a question asked of a witness to elicit inadmissible evidence relating to the crime at issue in the case. Cf. ASSERTIVE QUESTION.

interrogator (in-ter-ə-gay-tər). (18c) One who poses questions to another.

interrogatory (in-tə-**rog**-ə-tor-ee), *n.* (16c) A written question (usu. in a set of questions) submitted to an opposing party in a lawsuit as part of discovery. *See* Fed. R. Civ. P. 33.

contention interrogatory. An interrogatory designed to discover the factual basis of the allegations in a complaint, answer, or counterclaim, or to determine the theory of the opposing party's case.

cross-interrogatory. (17c) An interrogatory from a party who has received a set of interrogatories.

fact interrogatory. See *identification interrogatory.*

identification interrogatory. A request for the responding party to identify relevant documents, tangible objects, or individuals who have knowledge of facts relating to the lawsuit. — Also termed *fact interrogatory; state-all-facts interrogatory.*

special interrogatory. (18c) A written jury question whose answer is required to supplement a general verdict. ● This term is not properly used in federal practice, which authorizes interrogatories and special verdicts, but not special interrogatories. Fed. R. Civ. P. 49. The term is properly used, however, in the courts of some states. — Also termed *special issue.*

state-all-facts interrogatory. See *identification interrogatory.*

interrogee. See INTERROGATEE.

in terrorem (in te-**ror**-əm), *adv. & adj.* [Latin "in order to frighten"] (17c) By way of threat; as a warning <the demand letter was sent *in terrorem*; the client has no intention of actually suing>.

in terrorem **clause.** See NO-CONTEST CLAUSE.

interruption. (15c) A break in the period of possession of land, possibly ending a claim to ownership by prescriptive right.

legal interruption. Louisiana law. A break in the running of prescription that occurs when the property's possessor acknowledges another person's ownership rights, or the owner (or obligor) sues the possessor (or obligor). La. Civ.

Code arts. 3462, 3464. — Also termed *legal interruption of prescription.*

natural interruption. Louisiana law. A break of more than one year in a possessor's period of possession after a rightful owner or a third person seizes the real property. La. Civ. Code art. 3465. — Also termed *natural interruption of prescription.*

inter se (**in**-tər see *or* say). [Latin "between or among themselves"] (1845) (Of a right or duty) owed between the parties rather than to others. — Also termed *inter sese* (**in**-tər **see**-see).

intersection. (16c) A place where two roads meet or form a junction.

inter se **doctrine.** *Int'l law.* The now-defunct doctrine that relations between members of the British Commonwealth were in no circumstances international and were incapable of giving rights and duties under international law.

inter sese. See INTER SE.

interspousal, *adj.* (1906) Between husband and wife.

interspousal immunity. See *husband–wife immunity* under IMMUNITY (2).

interspousal tort immunity. See *husband–wife immunity* under IMMUNITY (2).

interstate, *adj.* (1844) Between two or more states or residents of different states.

interstate adoption. See ADOPTION.

interstate agreement. (1876) An agreement between states. Cf. *interstate compact* under COMPACT.

Interstate Agreement on Detainers Act. A law, originally enacted in 1956, that allows the federal government, certain states, and the District of Columbia to temporarily obtain custody of a prisoner for trial even though the prisoner is already incarcerated elsewhere. ● Under the Act, if a prisoner makes a written request for a disposition of the untried charges in the second forum, the government obtaining custody must try the prisoner within 180 days of the request. 18 USCA App. arts. 1–9. See UNIFORM MANDATORY DISPOSITION OF DETAINERS ACT.

interstate commerce. See COMMERCE.

Interstate Commerce Commission. The now-defunct federal agency established by the Interstate Commerce Act in 1887 to regulate surface transportation between states by certifying carriers and pipelines and by monitoring quality and pricing. ● In December 1995, when Congress eliminated this agency, the Surface Transportation Board (STB) — a three-member board that is a division of the Department of Transportation — assumed most of the agency's duties. — Abbr. ICC. See SURFACE TRANSPORTATION BOARD.

interstate compact. See COMPACT.

Interstate Compact on the Placement of Children. An agreement whose purpose is to ensure that when states are involved in the placement or adoption of children across state lines, the states cooperate with each other to facilitate the process and to protect the children. • This compact is intended to secure states' cooperation in investigating the suitability of proposed adoptive homes in an interstate adoption and also to alleviate conflicts that often occur when the agencies and courts of more than one state are involved. The compact has been enacted in almost identical form in all 50 states as well as in the District of Columbia and the Virgin Islands. — Abbr. ICPC. — Often shortened to *Interstate Compact.*

interstate extradition. See EXTRADITION.

interstate income-withholding order. (1994) A court order entered to enforce a support order of a court of another state by withholding income of the defaulting person.

interstate law. (1866) **1.** INTERNATIONAL LAW. **2.** The rules and principles used to determine controversies between residents of different states.

interstate rendition. See RENDITION (2).

interstate trade. See *interstate commerce* under COMMERCE.

intersubjective zap. In critical legal studies, a so-called spontaneous moment of shared intuition. — Also termed *zap.*

intertwining doctrine. The principle that if arbitrable and nonarbitrable claims arise from a single transaction and the claims are factually and legally mingled, a court can refuse to compel arbitration of any claims. • This doctrine is of limited effect because the Federal Arbitration Act usu. preempts it.

intervener. See INTERVENOR.

intervening act. See *intervening cause* under CAUSE (1).

intervening agency. See *intervening cause* under CAUSE (1).

intervening cause. See CAUSE (1).

intervening damages. See DAMAGES.

intervening force. 1. See FORCE. **2.** See *intervening cause* under CAUSE (1).

intervening rights. *Patents.* An infringement defense based on the right of a person who practiced a patent's broadened claims to continue practicing an invention, even though the invention's patent was reissued because of inadvertent claim errors in the original patent. 35 USCA § 252, second paragraph. — Also termed *doctrine of intervening rights.*

intervenor. (17c) One who voluntarily enters a pending lawsuit because of a personal stake in it. — Also spelled *intervener.*

intervention, *n.* (1860) **1.** The entry into a lawsuit by a third party who, despite not being named a party to the action, has a personal stake in the outcome. See Fed. R. Civ. P. 24. • The intervenor sometimes joins the plaintiff in claiming what is sought, sometimes joins the defendant in resisting what is sought, and sometimes takes a position adverse to both the plaintiff and the defendant. Cf. IMPLEADER; INTERPLEADER. **2.** The legal procedure by which such a third party is allowed to become a party to the litigation. — Formerly also termed (in senses 1 & 2) *trial of right of property.* **3.** *Int'l law.* One nation's interference by force, or threat of force, in another nation's internal affairs or in questions arising between other nations. — **intervene,** *vb.* — **interventionary,** *adj.*

   humanitarian intervention. An intervention by the international community to curb abuses of human rights within a country, even if the intervention infringes the country's sovereignty.

intervention duty. *Maritime law.* A shipowner's obligation to remedy hazardous working conditions for longshore workers, even though the shipowner did not create the condition, when the shipowner knows of a nonobvious condition arising in an area that cannot be avoided by the longshore workers in performing their duties. Cf. ACTIVE-OPERATIONS DUTY; TURNOVER DUTY.

interview-summary form. *Patents.* A U.S. Patent and Trademark Office form for noting in the record the contents of a conversation, by phone or in person, between a patent examiner and an applicant.

inter virum et uxorem (in-tər **vI**-rəm et ək-**sor**-əm), *adv. & adj.* [Latin] Between husband and wife.

inter vivos (in-tər **vI**-vohs *or* **vee**-vohs), *adj.* [Latin "between the living"] (1837) Of or relating to property conveyed not by will or in contemplation of an imminent death, but during the conveyor's lifetime. — *inter vivos, adv.*

inter vivos **gift.** See GIFT.

inter vivos **transfer.** See TRANSFER.

inter vivos **trust.** See TRUST.

intestable, *adj.* **1.** Not capable of being tested <an intestable DNA sample>. **2.** Legally incapable of making a will or of benefitting under a will <an insane person is intestable in all states> <the slaying-statute makes killers intestable in relation to their victims>. **3.** Disqualified from giving evidence, esp. testifying <the witness is intestable because of extreme youth>.

intestacy (in-**tes**-tə-see). (18c) The state or condition of a person's having died without a valid will. Cf. TESTACY.

intestate (in-**tes**-tayt), *adj.* (14c) **1.** Of or relating to a person who has died without a valid will <having revoked her will without making a new one, she was intestate when she died>. **2.** Of or relating to the property owned by a person who died without a valid will <an intestate estate>. **3.** Of or relating to intestacy <a spouse's intestate share>. Cf. TESTATE. **4.** *Archaic.* (Of a person) not qualified to testify <the witness could not testify after being found intestate>.

intestate, *n.* (17c) One who has died without a valid will. Cf. TESTATOR.

> **partial intestate.** One who has died with a valid will that does not dispose of all of his or her net probate estate.

intestate law. (18c) The relevant statute governing succession to estates of those who die without a valid will.

intestate share. See SHARE.

intestate succession. See SUCCESSION (2).

in testimonium (in tes-tə-**moh**-nee-əm), *adv.* & *adj.* [Latin] In witness; in evidence of which. • This phrase sometimes opens attestation clauses.

in the course of employment. (1911) *Workers' compensation.* (Of an accident) having happened to an on-the-job employee within the scope of employment.

intimate association, freedom of. See FREEDOM OF ASSOCIATION.

intimidation, *n.* (17c) Unlawful coercion; extortion. • In England, intimidation was established as a tort in the 1964 case of *Rookes v. Barnard*, 1964 App. Cas. 1129 (P.C. 1964) (appeal taken from B.C.). — **intimidate,** *vb.* — **intimidatory,** *adj.* — **intimidator,** *n.*

intitle, *vb. Archaic.* See ENTITLE.

in toto (in **toh**-toh), *adv.* [Latin "in whole"] (18c) Completely; as a whole <the company rejected the offer *in toto*>.

intoxicant, *n.* (1863) A substance (esp. liquor) that deprives a person of the ordinary use of the senses or of reason.

intoxication, *n.* (15c) A diminished ability to act with full mental and physical capabilities because of alcohol or drug consumption; drunkenness. See Model Penal Code § 2.08. — **intoxicate,** *vb.*

> *culpable intoxication.* See *voluntary intoxication.*

> *involuntary intoxication.* (1870) The ingestion of alcohol or drugs against one's will or without one's knowledge. • Involuntary intoxication is an affirmative defense to a criminal or negligence charge.

> *pathological intoxication.* (1947) An extremely exaggerated response to an intoxicant. • This

may be treated as involuntary intoxication if it is unforeseeable.

> *public intoxication.* (1885) The condition of a person who is under the influence of drugs or alcohol in a place open to the general public. • In most American jurisdictions, public intoxication is considered a misdemeanor. In some states, alcoholism is a defense if the offender agrees to attend a treatment program.

> *self-induced intoxication.* See *voluntary intoxication.*

> *voluntary intoxication.* (18c) A willing ingestion of alcohol or drugs to the point of impairment done with the knowledge that one's physical and mental capabilities would be impaired. • Voluntary intoxication is not a defense to a general-intent crime, but may be admitted to refute the existence of a particular state of mind for a specific-intent crime. — Also termed *culpable intoxication; self-induced intoxication.*

intoxication assault. See ASSAULT.

intoxication manslaughter. See MANSLAUGHTER.

intoxilyzer (in-**tok**-si-lı-zər). See BREATHALYZER.

intoximeter (in-tok-**sim**-ə-tər). See BREATHALYZER.

intra (**in**-trə), *adv.* & *adj.* [Latin] Within. Cf. INFRA.

intracorporate conspiracy. See CONSPIRACY.

intraday (**in**-trə-day), *adj.* Occurring within a single day.

intra-enterprise conspiracy. See CONSPIRACY.

intragovernmental, *adj.* Within a government; between a single government's departments or officials.

intraliminal right (in-trə-**lim**-ə-nəl). *Mining law.* The privilege to mine ore in areas within the boundaries of a mineral claim. • In contrast to an extralateral right, an intraliminal right does not give the holder the right to mine a vein of ore outside the lease even if the vein lies mostly within the lease. Cf. APEX RULE.

intransitive covenant. See COVENANT (1).

in transitu (in **tran**-si-t[y]oo *or* **tranz**-i-t[y]oo). [Latin "in transit; on the journey"] *Archaic.* Being conveyed from one place to another.

intrastate commerce. See COMMERCE.

intra vires (**in**-trə **vı**-reez), *adj.* [Latin "within the powers (of)"] (1877) Of or referring to an action taken within a corporation's or person's scope of authority <calling a shareholders' meeting is an *intra vires* function of the board of directors>. Cf. ULTRA VIRES. — **intra vires,** *adv.*

intrinsec service (in-**trin**-zik *or* -sik). *Hist.* The feudal services owed by a tenant to an immediate lord; the services arising from an agreement between the tenant and the lord. — Also termed *intrinsecum servitium* (in-**trin**-si-kəm sər-**vish**-ee-əm).

intrinsic (in-**trin**-zik *or* -sik), *adj.* Belonging to a thing by its very nature; not dependent on external circumstances; inherent; essential.

intrinsic ambiguity. See *patent ambiguity* under AMBIGUITY.

intrinsic evidence. See EVIDENCE.

intrinsic fraud. See FRAUD.

intrinsic test. *Copyright.* A subjective, fact-driven test for infringement whereby the fact-trier gauges whether a reasonable person would perceive substantial similarities between two expressions. Cf. EXTRINSIC TEST.

intrinsic value. See VALUE (2).

introduce into evidence. (18c) To have (a fact or object) admitted into the trial record, allowing it to be considered by the jury or the court in reaching a decision.

introductory clause. The first paragraph of a contract, which typically begins with words such as "This Agreement is made on [date] between [parties' names]." — Also termed *commencement*; *exordium*.

introductory recital. See RECITAL.

intromission (in-trə-**mish**-ən). (16c) **1.** The transactions of an employee or agent with funds provided by an employer or principal; loosely, dealing in the funds of another. **2.** *Scots law.* The act of handling or dealing with the affairs or property of another; the possession of another's property, with or without legal authority.

   legal intromission. Scots law. An authorized intromission, such as a creditor's enforcement of a debt.

   necessary intromission. Scots law. The intromission occurring when a spouse continues in possession of the deceased spouse's goods, for preservation.

   vitious intromission (**vish**-əs). *Scots law.* Unauthorized dealing with the property of another person, esp. a deceased person. — Also spelled *vicious intromission.*

3. Penile penetration into the vagina. See PENETRATION (1).

intruder. (15c) A person who enters, remains on, uses, or touches land or chattels in another's possession without the possessor's consent.

intrusion, *n.* (15c) **1.** A person's entering without permission. See TRESPASS. **2.** In an action for invasion of privacy, a highly offensive invasion of another person's seclusion or private life.— **intrude,** *vb.* — **intrusive,** *adj.*

inundate. (16c) To overflow or overwhelm; esp., to flood with water.

inure (in-**yoor**), *vb.* (15c) **1.** To take effect; to come into use <the settlement proceeds must inure to the benefit of the widow and children>. **2.** To make accustomed to something unpleasant; to habituate <abused children become inured to violence>. — Also spelled *enure.* — **inurement,** *n.*

inurement. A benefit; something that is useful or beneficial <a taxable inurement to the benefit of a private person>.

   private inurement. Tax. An inurement consisting in the use by a private shareholder or an individual who has an insider relationship with a tax-exempt organization of the organization's earnings or assets for personal gain other than reasonable and adequate compensation. • Such a benefit is prohibited. See IRC (26 USCA) § 501(c)(3).

in utero (in yoo-tə-roh). [Latin "in the uterus"] In the womb; during gestation or before birth <child *in utero*>.

invalid (in-**val**-id), *adj.* (17c) **1.** Not legally binding <an invalid contract>. **2.** Without basis in fact <invalid allegations>.

invalid (in-və-lid), *n.* (18c) A person who, because of serious illness or other disability, lacks the physical or mental capability of managing his or her day-to-day life.

invalid agreement. See *invalid contract* under CONTRACT.

invalid contract. See CONTRACT.

invalid will. See WILL.

invasion. (17c) **1.** A hostile or forcible encroachment on the rights of another.

   intentional invasion. A hostile or forcible encroachment on another's interest in the use or enjoyment of property, esp. real property, though not necessarily inspired by malice or ill will.

2. The incursion of an army for conquest or plunder. **3.** *Trusts.* A withdrawal from principal. • In the third sense, the term is used as a metaphor. — **invade,** *vb.*

invasion of privacy. (1862) An unjustified exploitation of one's personality or intrusion into one's personal activities, actionable under tort law and sometimes under constitutional law. See RIGHT OF PRIVACY.

   invasion of privacy by appropriation. The use of another's name or likeness for one's own benefit, esp. commercial gain. • This misappropriation tort protects one's property right to the economic benefits flowing from the commercial use of one's face or name.

invasion of privacy by false light. The use of publicity to place another in a false light in the public eye. • The false light may or may not be defamatory or fictional but the public use must be one that a reasonable person would object to under the circumstances. See FALSE LIGHT (1).

invasion of privacy by intrusion. An offensive, intentional interference with a person's seclusion or private affairs.

invasion of privacy by public disclosure of private facts. The public revelation of private information about another in an objectionable manner. • Even if the information is true and nondefamatory, a cause of action may arise.

inveigle (in-**vay**-gəl), *vb.* (16c) To lure or entice through deceit or insincerity <she blamed her friend for inveigling her into making the investment>. — **inveiglement,** *n.*

invent, *vb.* (15c) To create (something) for the first time.

invented consideration. See CONSIDERATION (1).

invention, *n.* (14c) *Patents.* **1.** A patentable device or process created through independent effort and characterized by an extraordinary degree of skill or ingenuity; a newly discovered art or operation. • *Invention* embraces the concept of nonobviousness. **2.** The act or process of creating such a device or process. **3.** Generally, anything that is created or devised. — **invent,** *vb.*

abandoned invention. An invention that an inventor has either deliberately stopped trying to exploit, or has otherwise treated in a way that precludes claiming the invention in a later patent. • Under § 102(c) of the Patent Act, abandonment bars a patent on that invention. But abandonment of an imperfect form of an invention does not bar a patent on a later-perfected form. Unless publicly known, an abandoned invention is not prior art to a later inventor. Under § 102(g) of the Patent Act, abandonment of the same invention by a first inventor also prevents the first inventor from blocking the second inventor's patent application in an interference. Cf. ABANDONED APPLICATION.

distinct invention. One part of an invention that can be used on its own, and the absence of which will not prevent the remainder of the invention from working. • When the subject matter of a patent application is found to be multiple distinct inventions, the examiner requires the inventor to restrict the application to a single invention. See RESTRICTION (4). Cf. *independent invention.*

improvement invention. A nontrivial and nonobvious betterment of an existing device or process. • The improvement may be patented, but the protection applies only to the improvement, not to the invention improved on.

independent invention. An invention that bears no relation to another invention, esp. to another invention covered in the same patent application. • A single patent may not cover multiple independent inventions; the applicant must elect one and drop any others from the application. See RESTRICTION (4). Cf. *distinct invention.*

new-use invention. Discovery of a new use for an existing invention. • As long as the new use is nonobvious — and actually useful — it may be patented. 35 USCA §§ 101–03.

small invention. See UTILITY MODEL.

software-based invention. A device or machine that uses innovative software to achieve results. • A software-based invention, process, or method may qualify for a patent, but the physical components and the underlying software are usu. not separately patentable.

inventively new. *Patents.* Original in any way. • The phrase is sometimes used to distinguish "new" in the usual sense from the term of art in patent law.

inventive step. *Patents.* In an invention, some advancement that is not obvious to a person reasonably skilled in the art. • The European Patent Convention requires an inventive step to qualify for a patent. The term is roughly equivalent to *nonobviousness* in American patent practice.

inventory, *n.* (15c) **1.** A detailed list of assets; esp., an executor's or administrator's detailed list of the probate-estate assets <make an inventory of the estate>. • The term also sometimes denotes a divorcing spouse's detailed list of all his or her marital and separate assets and liabilities. — Also termed *inventory and appraisement.* See PROBATE ESTATE; ACCOUNTING. **2.** *Accounting.* The portion of a financial statement reflecting the value of a business's raw materials, works-in-progress, and finished products <the company's reported inventory was suspiciously low>. **3.** Raw materials or goods in stock <the dealership held a sale to clear out its October inventory>. **4.** *Bankruptcy.* Personal property leased or furnished, held for sale or lease, or to be furnished under a contract for service; raw materials, work in process, or materials used or consumed in a business, including farm products such as crops or livestock <the debtor was found to have inventory that was valued at $300,000>. — **inventory,** *vb.*

inventory fee. A probate court's fee for services rendered to a decedent's estate.

inventory search. See SEARCH.

inventory-turnover ratio. *Accounting.* The result of dividing the cost of goods sold by the average value of inventory. • This calculation is used to determine the effectiveness of the company's inventory-management policy.

in ventre sa mere (in **ven**-tree sa **mer**). See EN VENTRE SA MERE.

inverse condemnation. See CONDEMNATION.

inverse-Erie doctrine. See REVERSE-ERIE DOCTRINE.

inverse floater. See *inverse-floating-rate note* under NOTE (1).

inverse-floating-rate note. See NOTE (1).

inverse-order-of-alienation doctrine. The principle that if a secured creditor has not collected on the mortgage or lien on a property sold off in successive parcels, the purchaser of the encumbered property may require the creditor to collect first from any parcel still held by the original owner, then from the parcel sold last, then next to last, and so on until the amount has been satisfied. • The creditor must exhaust an asset before attempting to recover the balance of the mortgage or lien from the next most recently transferred asset. — Also termed *rule of marshaling liens.*

inverse zoning. See ZONING.

inverted market. See BACKWARDATION.

invest, *vb.* (17c) **1.** To supply with authority or power <the U.S. Constitution invests the President with the power to conduct foreign affairs>. See INVESTITURE (1). **2.** To apply (money) for profit <Jillson invested her entire savings in the mutual fund>. **3.** To make an outlay of money for profit <Baird invested in stocks>.

investigate, *vb.* (16c) **1.** To inquire into (a matter) systematically; to make (a suspect) the subject of a criminal inquiry <the police investigated the suspect's involvement in the murder>. **2.** To make an official inquiry <after the judge dismissed the case, the police refused to investigate further>.

investigating bureau. See CREDIT-REPORTING BUREAU.

investigating magistrate. See MAGISTRATE.

investigative detention. See DETENTION.

investigative grand jury. See GRAND JURY.

investigatory detention. See STOP AND FRISK.

investigatory interrogation. See INTERROGATION.

investigatory power. See POWER (3).

investigatory stop. See STOP AND FRISK.

investitive fact. See FACT.

investitive publication. See PUBLICATION.

investiture (in-**ves**-tə-chuur). (14c) **1.** The act of formally installing a person in a ceremony in which the person is clothed in the insignia of the office's position or rank; esp., the installation of

a cleric in office. — Also termed *investment.* **2.** LIVERY OF SEISIN.

investment. (16c) **1.** An expenditure to acquire property or assets to produce revenue; a capital outlay.

fixed-dollar investment. An investment whose value is the same when sold as it was when purchased. • Examples are bonds held to maturity, certain government securities, and savings accounts.

fixed-income investment. An investment (including preferred stock) that pays a fixed dividend throughout its life and is not redeemable unless the corporation makes a special call.

net investment. **1.** The net cash required to start a new project. **2.** The gross investment in capital goods less capital consumption, including depreciation.

2. The asset acquired or the sum invested. **3.** INVESTITURE (1). **4.** LIVERY OF SEISIN.

investment adviser. A person who, for pay, advises others, either directly or through publications or writings, about the value of securities or the advisability of investing in, purchasing, or selling securities, or who is in the business of issuing reports on securities. • The term generally excludes an employee of an investment adviser; a depository institution, such as a bank; lawyers, accountants, engineers, and teachers whose investment advice is solely incidental to the practice of their profession; a broker-dealer whose advice is incidental to the conduct of business and who receives no special compensation for that advice; and publishers of bona fide newspapers, newsmagazines, or business or financial publications of general, regular, or paid circulation.

Investment Advisers Act. A 1940 federal statute — administered by the Securities and Exchange Commission — that regulates investment advisers. 15 USCA §§ 80b-1 et seq.

investment bank. See BANK.

investment banker. A person or institution that underwrites, sells, or assists in raising capital for businesses, esp. for new issues of stocks or bonds; a trader at an investment bank. See *investment bank* under BANK.

investment banking. The business of underwriting or selling securities; esp., the marketing of new stocks or bonds.

investment bill. See BILL (6).

investment company. See COMPANY.

Investment Company Act. A 1940 federal statute enacted to curb financial malpractices and abuses by regulating investment-company activities and transactions — specifically, by requiring registration of investment companies and prohibiting transactions by unregistered companies; by making certain persons ineligible as affiliated persons or underwriters; by regulating affiliations of directors, officers, and employees; by barring changes in investment policy without shareholder approval; and by regulating contracts of advisers and underwriters. 15 USCA §§ 80a-1 et seq.

investment contract. 1. A contract in which money is invested in a common enterprise with profits to come solely from the efforts of others; an agreement or transaction in which a party invests money in expectation of profits derived from the efforts of a promoter or other third party. **2.** A transaction in which an investor furnishes initial value or risk capital to an enterprise, a portion of that amount being subjected to the risks of the enterprise. ● In such an arrangement, the investor typically does not receive the right to exercise control over the managerial decisions of the enterprise.

guaranteed investment contract. An investment contract under which an institutional investor invests a lump sum (such as a pension fund) with an insurer that promises to return the principal (the lump sum) and a certain amount of interest at the contract's end. — Abbr. GIC.

investment-direction agreement. A contract by which a trustee agrees not to diversify the trust's assets, even though the trustee has the legal right to do so, and the beneficiary agrees to hold the trustee harmless for any losses resulting from not diversifying. — Abbr. IDA.

investment discretion. The ability of a person to (1) determine what will be purchased or sold by or for another person's account, (2) decide what will be purchased or sold by or for the account even though another may have the responsibility, or (3) influence the purchase or sale of securities or property in a way that, according to an administrative agency such as the Securities and Exchange Commission, should be subject to the agency's governing rules and regulations.

investment-grade bond. See BOND (8).

investment-grade rating. Any of the top four symbols given to a bond after an appraisal of its quality by a securities-evaluation agency such as Moody's. ● The rating indicates the degree of risk in an investment in the bond. See A (8).

investment income. See *unearned income* (1) under INCOME.

investment indebtedness. *Tax.* Debt incurred by a taxpayer to acquire or carry assets that may produce income. ● The Internal Revenue Code limits the amount of deductible interest on this type of debt.

investment property. Any asset purchased to produce a profit, whether from income or resale.

investment security. See SECURITY.

investment tax credit. See TAX CREDIT.

investment trust. See *investment company* under COMPANY.

investor. (17c) **1.** A buyer of a security or other property who seeks to profit from it without exhausting the principal. **2.** Broadly, a person who spends money with an expectation of earning a profit.

accredited investor. An investor treated under the Securities Act of 1933 as being knowledgeable and sophisticated about financial matters, esp. because of the investor's large net worth. ● In a securities offering that is exempt from registration, an accredited investor (either a person or an entity) is not entitled to protection under the Act's disclosure provisions, although the investor does keep its remedies for fraud.

angel investor. A person — usu. an experienced and successful entrepreneur, professional, or entity — that provides start-up or growth financing to a promising company, often together with advice and contacts. — Also termed *business angel*.

institutional investor. One who trades large volumes of securities, usu. by investing other people's money into large managed funds. ● Institutional investors are often pension funds, investment companies, trust managers, or insurance companies. See MUTUAL FUND.

qualified investor. *Securities.* An investor who is an individual and has an investment portfolio worth at least $5 million, or a company that owns or manages investments worth at least $25 million.

sophisticated investor. *Securities.* An investor who has sufficient knowledge and experience of financial matters to be capable of evaluating a security's qualities. ● Sophisticated investors do not require the full protection of securities laws.

invidious discrimination (in-**vid**-ee-əs di-skrim-ə-**nay**-shən). See DISCRIMINATION.

inviolability (in-vɪ-ə-lə-**bil**-ə-tee), *n.* The quality or fact of being safe from violation.

inviolable (in-**vɪ**-lə-bəl), *adj.* (15c) Safe from violation; incapable of being violated. — **inviolability**, *n.*

inviolate (in-**vɪ**-ə-lit), *adj.* (15c) Free from violation; not broken, infringed, or impaired.

invisible, *adj. Accounting.* Not reported in a financial statement <invisible earnings>.

invitation, *n. Torts.* In the law of negligence, the enticement of others to enter, remain on, or use property or its structures; conduct that justifies others in believing that the possessor wants them to enter. Cf. PERMISSION (3). — **invite,** *vb.*

invitation to negotiate. (1902) *Contracts.* A solicitation for one or more offers, usu. as a preliminary step to forming a contract. — Also termed *invitation seeking offers; invitation to bid; invitation to treat; solicitation for bids; preliminary letter; offer to chaffer.* Cf. OFFER.

invited error. See ERROR (2).

invitee (in-vi-**tee**). (1837) A person who has an express or implied invitation to enter or use another's premises, such as a business visitor or a member of the public to whom the premises are held open. ● The occupier has a duty to inspect the premises and to warn the invitee of dangerous conditions. — Also termed *licensee with an interest.* Cf. LICENSEE (2); TRESPASSER; BUSINESS VISITOR (1).

   public invitee. (1937) An invitee who is invited to enter and remain on property for a purpose for which the property is held open to the public.

inviter. (16c) One who expressly or impliedly invites another onto the premises for business purposes. — Also spelled *invitor.* Cf. INVITEE.

in vitro fertilization. A procedure by which an egg is fertilized outside a woman's body and then inserted into the womb for gestation. — Abbr. IVF. Cf. ARTIFICIAL INSEMINATION; ZYGOTE INTRAFALLOPIAN TRANSFER; GAMETE INTRAFALLOPIAN TRANSFER.

in vivo fertilization. The process in which an egg is fertilized inside a woman's body. Cf. ARTIFICIAL INSEMINATION; ZYGOTE INTRAFALLOPIAN TRANSFER; GAMETE INTRAFALLOPIAN TRANSFER.

invocation. (14c) **1.** The act of calling upon for authority or justification. **2.** The act of enforcing or using a legal right <an invocation of the contract clause>.

invoice, *n.* (16c) An itemized list of goods or services furnished by a seller to a buyer, usu. specifying the price and terms of sale; a bill of costs. — **invoice,** *vb.*

   consular invoice. An invoice used to hasten the entry of goods into a country by bearing the signature of the country's consul as assurance that the shipment's contents have been preverified for quantity and value.

   sales invoice. A document showing details of a purchase or sale, including price and quantity of merchandise.

invoice book. A journal into which invoices are copied.

involuntary, *adj.* (15c) Not resulting from a free and unrestrained choice; not subject to control by the will. — **involuntariness,** *n.*

involuntary alienation. See ALIENATION.

involuntary bailment. See BAILMENT.

involuntary bankruptcy. See BANKRUPTCY.

involuntary confession. See CONFESSION.

involuntary conversion. See CONVERSION (2).

involuntary conveyance. See *involuntary alienation* under ALIENATION.

involuntary deposit. 1. See DEPOSIT (5). **2.** See *involuntary bailment* under BAILMENT.

involuntary dismissal. See DISMISSAL (1).

involuntary dissolution. See DISSOLUTION.

involuntary euthanasia. See EUTHANASIA.

involuntary gap claim. See CLAIM (5).

involuntary intoxication. See INTOXICATION.

involuntary lien. See LIEN.

involuntary manslaughter. See MANSLAUGHTER.

involuntary nonsuit. See NONSUIT (2).

involuntary payment. See PAYMENT.

involuntary petition. See PETITION.

involuntary plaintiff. See PLAINTIFF.

involuntary proceeding. See *involuntary bankruptcy* under BANKRUPTCY.

involuntary servitude. See SERVITUDE (4).

involuntary stranding. See *accidental stranding* under STRANDING.

involuntary suretyship. See SURETYSHIP.

involuntary trust. See *constructive trust* under TRUST.

in witness whereof. (16c) The traditional beginning of the concluding clause (termed the *testimonium clause*) of a will or contract, esp. a deed. See TESTIMONIUM CLAUSE.

IO. *abbr.* BUREAU OF INTERNATIONAL ORGANIZATION AFFAIRS.

IOLTA (ı-**ohl**-tə). *abbr.* INTEREST ON LAWYERS' TRUST ACCOUNTS.

IO mortgage. See *interest-only mortgage* under MORTGAGE.

IOU (ı-oh-**yoo**). [abbr. "I owe you"] (17c) **1.** A memorandum acknowledging a debt. **2.** The debt itself. — Also termed *due-bill.*

IP. *abbr.* **1.** INTELLECTUAL PROPERTY. **2.** See *interested party* under PARTY (2). **3.** See *interested person* under PERSON (1).

IPA. *abbr.* See INDEPENDENT-PRACTICE ASSOCIATION.

IPD. *abbr.* IN PRAESENTIA DOMINORUM.

IPO. See *initial public offering* under OFFERING.

ipse (**ip**-see). [Latin "he himself"] The same; the very person.

ipse dixit (**ip**-see **dik**-sit). [Latin "he himself said it"] (15c) Something asserted but not proved <his

testimony that she was a liar was nothing more than an *ipse dixit*>.

ipsissima verba (ip-**sis**-ə-mə **vər**-bə). [Latin "the very (same) words"] (1807) The exact words used by somebody being quoted <on its face, the *ipsissima verba* of the statute supports the plaintiff's position on the ownership issue>.

ipso facto (ip-soh **fak**-toh). [Latin "by the fact itself"] (16c) By the very nature of the situation <if 25% of all contractual litigation is caused by faulty drafting, then, *ipso facto*, the profession needs to improve its drafting skills>.

ipso facto clause. *Bankruptcy.* A contract clause that specifies the consequences of a party's bankruptcy. ● The Bankruptcy Code prohibits enforcement of such clauses. — Also termed *bankruptcy clause.*

ipso jure (**ip**-soh **joor**-ee). [Latin "by the law itself"] By the operation of the law itself <despite the parties' actions, the property will revert to the state, *ipso jure*, on May 1>.

IRA (I-ahr-**ay** *or* I-rə). *abbr.* INDIVIDUAL RETIREMENT ACCOUNT.

IRAC (I-rak). A mnemonic acronym used mostly by law students and their writing instructors, esp. as a method of answering essay questions on law exams. ● The acronym is commonly said to stand for either (1) issue, rule, application, conclusion, or (2) issue, rule, analysis, conclusion.

IRC. *abbr.* INTERNAL REVENUE CODE.

IRD. See *income in respect of a decedent* under INCOME.

iron-safe clause. A provision in a fire-insurance policy requiring the insured to preserve the books and inventory records of a business in a fireproof safe.

IRR. See *internal rate of return* under RATE OF RETURN.

irrational, *adj.* Not guided by reason or by a fair consideration of the facts <an irrational ruling>. See ARBITRARY.

irrebuttable presumption. See *conclusive presumption* under PRESUMPTION.

irreconcilable differences. (1975) Persistent and unresolvable disagreements between spouses, leading to the breakdown of the marriage. ● These differences may be cited — without specifics — as grounds for no-fault divorce. At least 33 states have provided that irreconcilable differences are a basis for divorce. Cf. IRRETRIEVABLE BREAKDOWN OF THE MARRIAGE; INCOMPATIBILITY.

irrecusable, *adj.* (18c) (Of an obligation) that cannot be avoided, although made without one's consent, such as the obligation to not strike another without some lawful excuse. Cf. RECUSABLE (1).

irredeemable bond. See *annuity bond* under BOND (3).

irredeemable ground rent. See *ground rent* (2) under RENT (1).

irrefragable (i-**ref**-rə-gə-bəl), *adj.* (16c) Unanswerable; not to be controverted; impossible to refute <the defense feebly responded to the prosecution's irrefragable arguments>.

irregular, *adj.* (14c) Not in accordance with law, method, or usage; not regular.

irregular heir. See HEIR.

irregular indorsement. See INDORSEMENT.

irregularity. (14c) **1.** Something irregular; esp., an act or practice that varies from the normal conduct of an action. **2.** *Eccles. law.* An impediment to clerical office.

irregular judgment. See JUDGMENT.

irregular process. See PROCESS.

irregular succession. See SUCCESSION (2).

irrelevance, *n.* (1847) **1.** The quality or state of being inapplicable to a matter under consideration. — Also termed *irrelevancy.* **2.** IRRELEVANCY (1).

irrelevancy, *n.* **1.** Something not relevant. — Also termed *irrelevance.* **2.** IRRELEVANCE (1).

irrelevant (i-**rel**-ə-vənt), *adj.* (16c) **1.** (Of evidence) having no probative value; not tending to prove or disprove a matter in issue. — Also termed *impertinent.* Cf. IMMATERIAL. **2.** (Of a pleaded allegation) having no substantial relation to the action, and will not affect the court's decision. — **irrelevance,** *n.*

irrelevant evidence. See EVIDENCE.

irremediable breakdown of the marriage. See IRRETRIEVABLE BREAKDOWN OF THE MARRIAGE.

irreparable damages. See DAMAGES.

irreparable harm. See *irreparable injury* under INJURY.

irreparable injury. See INJURY.

irreparable-injury rule (i-**rep**-ə-rə-bəl). (1969) The principle that equitable relief (such as an injunction) is available only when no adequate legal remedy (such as monetary damages) exists. ● Although courts continue to cite this rule, they do not usu. follow it literally in practice. — Also termed *adequacy test.*

irrepleviable (i-rə-**plev**-ee-ə-bəl), *adj.* (Of property) not capable of being replevied. — Formerly also spelled *irreplevisable.* Cf. REPLEVIABLE.

irresistible force. See FORCE.

irresistible-impulse test. (1892) *Criminal law.* A test for insanity, holding that a person is not criminally responsible for an act if mental disease prevented that person from controlling potentially criminal conduct. ● The few jurisdictions that have adopted this test have combined it with the *McNaghten* rules. — Also termed *control test*; *volitional test*. See INSANITY DEFENSE; MCNAGHTEN RULES.

irresistible superhuman cause. See ACT OF GOD.

irresistible violence. *Archaic.* See VIS MAJOR.

irretrievable breakdown of the marriage. (1973) *Family law.* A ground for divorce that is based on incompatibility between marriage partners and in many states is the sole ground for no-fault divorce. — Also termed *irretrievable breakdown*; *irremediable breakdown of the marriage*; *irremediable breakdown*. Cf. IRRECONCILABLE DIFFERENCES; INCOMPATIBILITY.

irrevocable (i-**rev**-ə-kə-bəl), *adj.* (14c) Unalterable; committed beyond recall. — **irrevocability,** *n.*

irrevocable guaranty. See GUARANTY.

irrevocable letter of credit. See LETTER OF CREDIT.

irrevocable offer. See OFFER.

irrevocable power of attorney. See POWER OF ATTORNEY.

irrevocable trust. See TRUST.

irrigation district. *Water law.* A quasi-political subdivision or agency established to develop, preserve, and conserve water for the benefit and use of the district's residents.

irritant clause. *Civil law.* A deed term providing that if the deed's holder performs an act specifically prohibited by the deed, the act or deed is automatically nullified.

IRS. *abbr.* INTERNAL REVENUE SERVICE.

IRV. See *instant-runoff voting* under VOTING.

ISCGS. *abbr.* INTERNATIONAL SCHEDULE OF CLASSES OF GOODS AND SERVICES.

island. (bef. 12c) A tract of land surrounded by water but smaller than a continent; esp., land that is continually surrounded by water and not submerged except during abnormal circumstances.

ISO. *abbr.* **1.** Incentive stock option. See STOCK OPTION (2). **2.** INSURANCE SERVICES OFFICE.

isolated sale. See SALE.

isolating, *n. Family law.* A parent's or caregiver's pattern of cutting a child off from normal social experiences, preventing the child from forming friendships, or making the child believe that he or she is alone in the world. Cf. IGNORING; REJECTING.

ISP. *abbr.* INTERNET SERVICE PROVIDER.

issuable, *adj.* **1.** Capable of being issued <an issuable writ>. **2.** Open to dispute or contention <an issuable argument>. **3.** Possible as an outcome <an award as high as $5 million is issuable in this case>.

issuable defense. See DEFENSE (1).

issuable plea. See PLEA (3).

issue, *n.* (16c) **1.** A point in dispute between two or more parties. • In an appeal, an issue may take the form of a separate and discrete question of law or fact, or a combination of both.

   collateral issue. (18c) A question or issue not directly connected with the matter in dispute.

   deep issue. (1944) The fundamental issue to be decided by a court in ruling on a point of law. • A deep issue is usu. briefly phrased in separate sentences, with facts interwoven (in chronological order) to show precisely what problem is to be addressed. Cf. *surface issue*.

   fact issue. See *issue of fact*.

   general issue. (16c) **1.** A plea (often a general denial) by which a party denies the truth of every material allegation in an opposing party's pleading. **2.** The issue arising from such a plea.

   immaterial issue. (18c) An issue not necessary to decide the point of law. Cf. *material issue*.

   informal issue. *Rare.* An issue that arises when a defendant does not properly or fully plead in answer to a material allegation.

   issue of fact. (17c) A point supported by one party's evidence and controverted by another's. — Also termed *fact issue*.

   issue of law. (18c) A point on which the evidence is undisputed, the outcome depending on the court's interpretation of the law. — Also termed *legal issue*.

   legal issue. (17c) **1.** A legal question, usu. at the foundation of a case and requiring a court's decision. **2.** See *issue of law*.

   material issue. An issue that must be decided in order to resolve a controversy. • The existence of a material issue of disputed fact precludes summary judgment. Cf. *immaterial issue*.

   multifarious issue. An issue that inquires about several different points (esp. facts) when each one should be inquired about in a separate issue.

   special issue. (17c) **1.** At common law, an issue arising from a specific allegation in a pleading. • Special issues are no longer used in most jurisdictions. **2.** See *special interrogatory* under INTERROGATORY.

   surface issue. A superficially stated issue phrased in a single sentence, without many facts, and usu. beginning with the word *whether*. Cf. *deep issue*.

   ultimate issue. (17c) A not-yet-decided point that is sufficient either in itself or in connection with other points to resolve the entire case. — Also termed *ultimate question*.

2. A class or series of securities that are simultaneously offered for sale. — Also termed *bond issue*; *stock issue*. See OFFERING.

hot issue. A security that, after an initial or secondary offering, is traded in the open market at a substantially higher price. — Also termed *hot stock*.

new issue. A stock or bond sold by a corporation for the first time, often to raise working capital. See BLUE-SKY LAW.

original issue. The first issue of securities of a particular type or series.

shelf issue. An issue of securities that were previously registered but not released at the time of registration.

3. *Wills & estates.* Lineal descendants; offspring.

issue female. **1.** Female descendants. **2.** A female whose descent from a specified ancestor is traceable through the direct female line. See *tail female* under TAIL.

issue male. **1.** Male descendants. **2.** A male whose descent from a specified ancestor is traceable through the direct male line. See *tail male* under TAIL.

lawful issue. (16c) Descendants, including descendants more remote than children. • At common law, the term included only those who were children of legally recognized subsisting marriages. See DESCENDANT; HEIR.

4. *Commercial law.* The first delivery of a negotiable instrument by its maker or holder.

issue, *vb.* (14c) **1.** To accrue <rents issuing from land> **2.** To be put forth officially <without probable cause, the search warrant will not issue> **3.** To send out or distribute officially <issue process> <issue stock>. — **issuance,** *n.*

issued stock. See STOCK.

issue estoppel. See COLLATERAL ESTOPPEL.

issue fee. *Patents.* The charge that an inventor must pay the U.S. Patent and Trademark Office before an allowed patent application can be issued as a patent.

issue pleading. See PLEADING (2).

issue preclusion. See COLLATERAL ESTOPPEL.

issuer. **1.** A person or entity (such as a corporation or bank) that issues securities, negotiable instru-

ments, or letters of credit. **2.** A bailee that issues negotiable or nonnegotiable documents of title.

nonreporting issuer. An issuer not subject to the reporting requirements of the Exchange Act because it (1) has not voluntarily become subject to the reporting requirements, (2) has not had an effective registration statement under the Securities Act within the fiscal year, and (3) did not, at the end of its last fiscal year, meet the shareholder or asset tests under the Exchange Act registration requirements.

ITA. *abbr.* INTERNATIONAL TRADE ADMINISTRATION.

ITC. See *investment tax credit* under TAX CREDIT.

item. (16c) **1.** A piece of a whole, not necessarily separated. **2.** *Commercial law.* A negotiable instrument or a promise or order to pay money handled by a bank for collection or payment. • The term does not include a payment order governed by division 11 of the UCC or a credit- or debit-card slip. UCC 4-104(a)(9).

par item. An item that a drawee bank will remit to another bank without charge.

line item. *Accounting.* In a financial statement, a single entry or notation to which a particular dollar amount is attached.

3. In drafting, a subpart of text that is the next smaller unit than a subparagraph. • In federal drafting, for example, "(4)" is the item in the following citation: Rule 19(a)(1)(B)(4). — Also termed (in sense 3) *clause.*

itemize, *vb.* To list in detail; to state by items <an itemized bill>.

itemized deduction. See DEDUCTION.

item veto. See *line-item veto* under VETO.

itinerant vendor. See VENDOR.

itinerate (I-**tin**-ə-rayt), *vb.* (Of a judge) to travel on a circuit for the purpose of holding court. See CIRCUIT. — **itineration,** *n.* — **itinerant,** *adj. & n.*

ITS. *abbr.* Institute for Telecommunication Sciences. See NATIONAL TELECOMMUNICATIONS AND INFORMATION ADMINISTRATION.

iudex (**yoo**-deks). [Latin] See JUDEX.

ius (yəs *or* yoos). [Latin "law, right"] See JUS.

IVA. *abbr.* See INDIVIDUAL VOLUNTARY ARRANGEMENT.

IVF. *abbr.* IN VITRO FERTILIZATION.

J

J. *abbr.* **1.** JUDGE. **2.** JUSTICE (2). **3.** JUDGMENT. **4.** JUS. **5.** JOURNAL.

JA. *abbr.* **1.** JUDGE ADVOCATE. **2.** See *joint account* under ACCOUNT.

jackpot justice. *Slang.* The awarding of enormous and apparently arbitrary damages to plaintiffs, thereby making the plaintiffs wealthy and encouraging others to file lawsuits seeking excessive damages for even minor actual harm.

***Jackson–Denno* hearing.** (1965) A court proceeding, held outside the jury's presence to determine whether the defendant's confession was voluntary and therefore admissible as evidence. *Jackson v. Denno*, 378 U.S. 368, 84 S.Ct. 1774 (1964). — Also termed *Jackson v. Denno hearing.*

***Jackson* standard.** (1980) *Criminal law.* The principle that the standard of review on appeal — when a criminal defendant claims that there is insufficient evidence to support the conviction — is to determine whether, after considering the evidence in the light most favorable to the prosecution, any rational trier of fact could have found the essential elements of the crime beyond a reasonable doubt. *Jackson v. Virginia*, 443 U.S. 307, 99 S.Ct. 2781 (1979).

***Jackson v. Denno* hearing.** See JACKSON–DENNO HEARING.

Jacob Wetterling Crimes Against Children and Sexually Violent Offender Registration Act. A 1989 federal statute requiring each state to create a sex-offender registry of sexually violent offenders, particularly those who have been convicted of sex crimes against minors, and to disclose information about registered sex offenders for public-safety purposes. • The Act mandates a minimum registration period of 10 years, beginning on the offender's date of release from custody or supervision. It was amended in 1996 by Megan's Law, which added the disclosure requirement. See 42 USCA § 14071. The Act was named for 11-year-old Jacob Wetterling of Minnesota, who was abducted by a stranger in 1989. During the immediate search for Jacob, law-enforcement officers discovered that many of the county's halfway houses sheltered sex offenders from another county. Jacob was never found. — Often shortened to *Jacob Wetterling Act* or *Wetterling Act.* Cf. MEGAN'S LAW.

jactitation (jak-ti-**tay**-shən). (17c) **1.** A false boasting or claim that causes injury to another. **2.** *Civil law.* SLANDER OF TITLE.

jactitation of marriage. *Hist.* **1.** False and actionable boasting or claiming that one is married to another. **2.** An action against a person who falsely boasts of being married to the complainant.

jactitation of title. See SLANDER OF TITLE.

jactura (jak-t[y]**oor**-ə), *n.* [Latin] *Civil law.* **1.** A throwing of goods overboard to lighten or save a vessel; JETTISON. **2.** A loss incurred from this; general average. See *general average* under AVERAGE. — Also termed *jactus.*

JAG. *abbr.* JUDGE ADVOCATE GENERAL.

JAG Department. See JUDGE ADVOCATE GENERAL'S DEPARTMENT.

JAG Manual. See MANUAL OF THE JUDGE ADVOCATE GENERAL.

jail, *n.* (13c) A local government's detention center where persons awaiting trial or those convicted of misdemeanors are confined. — Also spelled (esp. in BrE) *gaol.* — Also termed *holding cell; lockup; jailhouse; house of detention; community correctional center.* Cf. PRISON. — **jail,** *vb.*

jail credit. (1950) Time spent by a criminal defendant in confinement while awaiting trial. • This time is usu. deducted from the defendant's final sentence (if convicted). — Also termed *jail-credit time.*

jail delivery. 1. An escape by several prisoners from a jail. **2.** *Archaic.* A clearing procedure by which all prisoners at a given jail are tried for the offenses that they are accused of having committed.

general jail delivery. Collectively, acquittals in high numbers as a result of either lax or reckless administration of the law or defects in the law.

3. *Archaic.* The commission issued to judges of assize, directing them to clear a jail by trying — and either acquitting or condemning — all the inmates. **4.** *Archaic.* The court charged with the trial of all ordinary criminal cases. — Also written *gaol delivery.* See COMMISSION OF GAOL DELIVERY.

jailer. A keeper, guard, or warden of a prison or jail. — Also spelled (esp. in BrE) *gaoler.*

jailhouse. See JAIL.

jailhouse lawyer. A prison inmate who seeks release through legal procedures or who gives legal advice to other inmates. — Also termed *guardhouse lawyer.*

jail liberties. Bounds within which a jail or prison lies and throughout which certain prisoners are allowed to move freely, usu. after giving bond for the liberties. • The bounds are considered an extension of the prison walls. Historically, jail liberties were given in England to those imprisoned for debt. The prisoners were allowed to move freely within the city in which the prison was located. — Also spelled (esp. in BrE) *gaol liberties*. — Also termed *jail limits*. See BOUND (2).

jail mail. *Slang.* Correspondence sent by or to an incarcerated person. • It is often screened by prison personnel.

Jamaican switch. An illegal scheme whereby one conspirator convinces the victim of a need for help in handling a large sum of money, usu. by claiming to have found the money or by claiming to be an unsophisticated foreigner, and promises to share part of the money with the victim or asks the victim for help in finding a suitable charity to donate to, at which time the other conspirator appears and promises to assist if both the victim and first conspirator provide good-faith money, the intent being for the two conspirators to leave with all the money, including the victim's. • The name given to this scheme is likely to be considered offensive by some. — Also termed *pigeon drop*.

***James* hearing.** (1981) A court proceeding held to determine whether the out-of-court statements of a coconspirator should be admitted into evidence, by analyzing whether there was a conspiracy, whether the declarant and the defendant were part of the conspiracy, and whether the statement was made in furtherance of the conspiracy. *United States v. James*, 590 F.2d 575 (5th Cir. 1979); Fed. R. Evid. 801(d)(2)(E).

Jane Doe. A fictitious name for a female party to a legal proceeding, used because the party's true identity is unknown or because her real name is being withheld. — Also termed *Jane Roe*; *Mary Major*. Cf. JOHN DOE.

Janus-faced (jay-nəs fayst), *adj.* (17c) Having two contrasting or contradictory aspects; two-faced <a Janus-faced plea>.

***Jason* clause.** *Maritime law.* A bill-of-lading clause requiring contribution in general average even when the peril that justified the sacrifice was the result of the carrier's negligence, for which the carrier is otherwise exempt from liability by statute. • The clause is named after the Supreme Court case that upheld its enforceability, *The Jason*, 225 U.S. 32, 32 S.Ct. 560 (1912). See *general average* under AVERAGE.

jaywalking, *n.* (1919) The act or instance of crossing a street without heeding traffic regulations, as by crossing between intersections or at a place other than a crosswalk. — **jaywalk,** *vb.*

JCP. *abbr.* Justice of the Common Pleas. See COURT OF COMMON PLEAS.

J.D. *abbr.* JURIS DOCTOR.

Jedburgh justice (jed-bər-ə). See JUSTICE (1).

Jeddart justice (jed-ərt). See *Jedburgh justice* under JUSTICE (1).

Jedwood justice (jed-wəd). See *Jedburgh justice* under JUSTICE (1).

***Jencks* material.** (1961) *Criminal procedure.* A prosecution witness's written or recorded pretrial statement that a criminal defendant, upon filing a motion after the witness has testified, is entitled to have in preparing to cross-examine the witness. • The defense may use a statement of this kind for impeachment purposes. *Jencks v. United States*, 353 U.S. 657, 77 S.Ct. 1007 (1957); Jencks Act, 18 USCA § 3500. Cf. BRADY MATERIAL.

reverse *Jencks* material. *Criminal procedure.* A defense witness's written or recorded pretrial statement that a prosecutor is entitled to have in preparing to cross-examine the witness. • Reverse *Jencks* material may be obtained during pretrial discovery. Discoverable statements include a witness's signed or adopted written statement, and transcripts or recordings of the witness's oral statements, including grand-jury testimony. *United States v. Nobles*, 422 U.S. 225, 231–34, 95 S. Ct. 2160, 2166–68 (1975); Fed. R. Crim. P. 26.2. — Also termed *reverse Jencks*; *reverse discovery*; *reciprocal discovery*.

***Jensen* doctrine.** *Maritime law.* The principle that a state statute may not apply in a maritime case if to do so would "work material prejudice to the characteristic features of the general maritime law or interfere with the proper harmony and uniformity of that law." *Southern Pac. Co. v. Jensen*, 244 U.S. 205, 37 S.Ct. 524 (1917).

jeofail (jef-ayl), *n.* [fr. French *j'ay faillé*] *Archaic.* **1.** A pleading error or oversight that results in a misjoined issue and requires a repleader. **2.** The acknowledgment of such an error. — Also spelled *jeofaile.*

jeopardy. (14c) The risk of conviction and punishment that a criminal defendant faces at trial. • Jeopardy attaches in a jury trial when the jury is empaneled, and in a bench trial when the first witness is sworn. — Also termed *legal jeopardy.* See DOUBLE JEOPARDY.

jeopardy assessment. See ASSESSMENT.

***Jepson* claim.** See PATENT CLAIM.

jerk note. *Hist. Maritime law.* A permit, issued by a customs collector to the ship's master, authorizing the master to receive cargo for an outbound voyage.

jetsam (jet-səm). (16c) The portion of a ship's cargo and equipment that is (1) thrown overboard in an effort to save the ship from a perilous condition, and that (2) either sinks beneath the surface or is washed ashore. — Also termed *jettison.* Cf. FLOTSAM; LAGAN (1); WAVESON.

jettison (jet-ə-sən), *n.* (15c) *Maritime law.* **1.** The act of voluntarily throwing cargo overboard to lighten or stabilize a ship that is in immediate danger. — Also termed *equitable jettison*; *jactura*; *jactus mercium navis levandae causa*. See *general average* under AVERAGE. **2.** JETSAM. — **jettison,** *vb.*

***Jewell* instruction** (**joo**-wəl). (1977) *Criminal procedure.* A court's instruction to the jury that the defendant can be found to have the requisite criminal mental state despite being deliberately ignorant of some of the facts surrounding the crime. ● If a defendant claims ignorance of some fact essential to the crime, such as not knowing that a particular bag contained drugs, but the surrounding circumstances would put a reasonable person on notice that there was a high probability of illegality, as when the defendant has taken the bag from a known drug-dealer and has noticed the smell of marijuana coming from the bag, then the court may instruct the jury that it is entitled to infer the defendant's guilty knowledge if the defendant deliberately avoided knowledge of the critical facts. *United States v. Jewell*, 532 F.2d 697 (9th Cir. 1976). — Also termed *deliberate-indifference instruction*. Cf. *ostrich instruction* under JURY INSTRUCTION.

Jim Crow law. (1891) *Hist.* A law enacted or purposely interpreted to discriminate against blacks, such as a law requiring separate restrooms for blacks and whites. ● Jim Crow laws are unconstitutional under the 14th Amendment.

jingle rule. See DUAL-PRIORITIES RULE.

JJ. *abbr.* **1.** Judges. **2.** Justices.

JNOV. *abbr.* Judgment *non obstante veredicto*. See *judgment notwithstanding the verdict* under JUDGMENT.

job action. *Labor law.* A concerted, temporary action by employees (such as a sickout or work slowdown), intended to pressure management to concede to the employees' demands without resorting to a strike. See STRIKE (1).

jobber, *n.* (17c) **1.** One who buys from a manufacturer and sells to a retailer; a wholesaler or middleman. **2.** A middleman in the exchange of securities among brokers. — Also termed *stock-jobber*; *stock-jobber*. **3.** One who works by the job; a contractor. — **job,** *vb.*

jobber's agreement. See HAZANTOWN AGREEMENT.

jobbery, *n.* (1837) The practice or act of perverting a public service in a way that serves private ends; unfair means to serve private interests.

job security. Protection of an employee's job, often through a union contract.

job-targeting program. An initiative by a labor union to maintain or improve its share of the labor in a particular market by financing or backing contractors who bid on targeted projects. — Also termed *market-recovery program*.

John Doe. A fictitious name used in a legal proceeding to designate a person whose identity is unknown, to protect a person's known identity, or to indicate that a true defendant does not exist. ● In England, "William Styles" was also used. Cf. JANE DOE; RICHARD ROE.

John Doe defendant. See DEFENDANT.

John Doe summons. See SUMMONS.

John Doe warrant. See WARRANT (1).

joinder, *n.* (17c) The uniting of parties or claims in a single lawsuit. Cf. CONSOLIDATION (3). — **join,** *vb.*

   collusive joinder. (1883) Joinder of a defendant, usu. a nonresident, in order to have a case removed to federal court. See *manufactured diversity* under DIVERSITY OF CITIZENSHIP.

   compulsory joinder. (1901) The necessary joinder of a party if either of the following is true: (1) in that party's absence, those already involved in the lawsuit cannot receive complete relief; or (2) the absent party claims an interest in the subject of an action, so that party's absence might either impair the protection of that interest or leave some other party subject to multiple or inconsistent obligations. Fed. R. Civ. P. 19(a). — Also termed *mandatory joinder.*

   fraudulent joinder. (1836) The bad-faith joinder of a party, usu. a resident of the state, to prevent removal of a case to federal court.

   joinder in demurrer. *Common-law pleading.* A set form of words by which either party accepts or joins in a legal issue; esp., the plaintiff's acceptance of the defendant's issue of law.

   joinder in issue. See *joinder of issue.*

   joinder in pleading. *Common-law pleading.* One party's acceptance of the opposing party's proposed issue and mode of trial.

   joinder of error. A written denial of the errors alleged in an assignment of errors in a criminal case.

   joinder of issue. **1.** The submission of an issue jointly for decision. **2.** The acceptance or adoption of a disputed point as the basis of argument in a controversy. — Also termed *joinder in issue*; *similiter.* **3.** The taking up of the opposite side of a case, or of the contrary view on a question.

   joinder of offenses. The charging of an accused with two or more crimes as multiple counts in a single indictment or information. ● Unless later severed, joined offenses are tried together at a single trial. Fed. R. Crim. P. 8(a).

   joinder of remedies. The joinder of alternative claims, such as breach of contract and quantum meruit, or of one claim with another prospective claim, such as a creditor's claim against a debtor to recover on a loan and the creditor's claim against a third party to set aside the transfer of the loan's collateral.

mandatory joinder. See *compulsory joinder.*

misjoinder. See MISJOINDER.

nonjoinder. See NONJOINDER.

permissive joinder. (1903) The optional joinder of parties if (1) their claims or the claims asserted against them are asserted jointly, severally, or in respect of the same transaction or occurrence, and (2) any legal or factual question common to all of them will arise. Fed. R. Civ. P. 20.

pretensive joinder. Joinder of defendants solely to obtain venue in a jurisdiction in which the action could not otherwise be tried.

joint, *adj.* (14c) **1.** (Of a thing) common to or shared by two or more persons or entities <joint bank account>. **2.** (Of a person or entity) combined, united, or sharing with another <joint heirs>.

joint account. See ACCOUNT.

joint action. See ACTION (4).

joint activity. See JOINT PARTICIPATION.

joint administration. *Bankruptcy.* The management of two or more bankruptcy estates, usu. involving related debtors, under one docket for purposes of handling various administrative matters, including notices to creditors, to conclude the cases more efficiently. ● A bankruptcy court can order a joint administration when there are two or more cases pending involving a husband and wife, a partnership and at least one partner, two or more business partners, or a business and an affiliate. The intent should be to increase the administrative efficiency of administering the two cases; the substantive rights of creditors should not ordinarily be affected. Fed. R. Bankr. P. 1015. — Also termed *procedural consolidation.* See ADMINISTRATION (3). Cf. *substantive consolidation* under CONSOLIDATION.

joint adoption. See ADOPTION.

joint adventure. 1. See *common adventure* under ADVENTURE. **2.** See JOINT VENTURE.

joint and mutual will. See WILL.

joint and reciprocal will. See *joint and mutual will* under WILL.

joint and several, *adj.* (17c) (Of liability, responsibility, etc.) apportionable at an adversary's discretion either among two or more parties or to only one or a few select members of the group; together and in separation. See JOINT; SEVERAL.

joint and several bond. See BOND (3).

joint and several liability. See LIABILITY.

joint and several note. See NOTE (1).

joint-and-survivorship account. See *joint account* under ACCOUNT.

joint annuity. See ANNUITY.

joint authors. *Copyright.* Two or more authors who collaborate in producing a copyrightable work, each author intending to merge his or her respective contributions into a single work, and each being able to exploit the work as desired while remaining accountable for a pro rata share of the profits to the coauthor or coauthors.

joint ballot. See BALLOT (2).

joint board. *Labor law.* A committee — usu. made up of an equal number of representatives from management and the union — established to conduct grievance proceedings or resolve grievances.

joint bond. See BOND (3).

joint-check rule. The principle that when an owner or general contractor issues a check that is made jointly payable to a subcontractor and the subcontractor's materialman supplier, the materialman's indorsement on the check certifies that all amounts due to the materialman. up to the amount of the check, have been paid. ● This rule protects the owner or general contractor from lien foreclosure by a materialman who was not paid by the subcontractor. By issuing a joint check, the owner or general contractor is not left merely to hope that the subcontractor pays all the materialmen. And the materialman is protected because it can refuse to indorse the check until it is satisfied that the subcontractor will pay it the appropriate amount.

joint committee. See COMMITTEE.

joint contract. See CONTRACT.

joint covenant. See COVENANT (1).

joint creditor. See CREDITOR.

joint custody. See CUSTODY (2).

joint debtor. See DEBTOR.

joint defendant. See CODEFENDANT.

joint-defense privilege. See PRIVILEGE (3).

joint demise. See DEMISE.

joint employment. See EMPLOYMENT.

joint enterprise. (17c) **1.** *Criminal law.* An undertaking by two or more persons who set out to commit an offense they have conspired to. See CONSPIRACY. **2.** *Torts.* An undertaking by two or more persons with an equal right to direct and benefit from the endeavor, as a result of which one participant's negligence may be imputed to the others. — Also termed (in senses 1 & 2) *common enterprise.* **3.** JOINT VENTURE. **4.** A joint venture for noncommercial purposes.

joint estate. See ESTATE (1).

joint executor. See EXECUTOR.

joint heir. See HEIR.

joint indictment. See INDICTMENT.

joint interest. See INTEREST (2).

joint-interest purchase. See SPLIT-INTEREST PURCHASE OF PROPERTY.

joint inventor. *Patents.* A person who collaborates with another or others in developing an invention. ● All joint inventors must be identified on a patent application.

joint legal custody. See *joint custody* under CUSTODY (2).

joint liability. See LIABILITY.

joint life insurance. See LIFE INSURANCE.

joint life policy. See INSURANCE POLICY.

joint managing conservatorship. See *joint custody* under CUSTODY (2).

joint mortgage. See MORTGAGE.

joint negligence. See NEGLIGENCE.

joint note. See NOTE (1).

joint obligation. See OBLIGATION.

joint offense. See OFFENSE (1).

joint ownership. See OWNERSHIP.

joint participation. (1971) *Civil-rights law.* A pursuit undertaken by a private person in concert with a governmental entity or state official, resulting in the private person's performing public functions and thereby being subject to claims under the civil-rights laws. — Also termed *joint activity.* See SYMBIOTIC-RELATIONSHIP TEST; NEXUS TEST.

joint party. See COPARTY.

joint physical custody. See *joint custody* under CUSTODY (2).

joint plaintiff. See COPLAINTIFF.

joint possession. See POSSESSION.

joint property. See PROPERTY.

joint rate. See RATE.

joint resolution. See RESOLUTION (1).

joint return. See TAX RETURN.

joint rule. See RULE (2).

joint session. See SESSION (1).

joint stock. See STOCK.

joint-stock association. See *joint-stock company* under COMPANY.

joint-stock company. See COMPANY.

joint tariff. See TARIFF (5).

joint tenancy. See TENANCY.

joint tenant. See *joint tenancy* under TENANCY.

joint tortfeasors. See TORTFEASOR.

joint trespass. See TRESPASS.

joint trial. See TRIAL.

joint trustee. See COTRUSTEE.

jointure (**joyn**-chər). (15c) **1.** *Archaic.* A woman's freehold life estate in land, made in consideration of marriage in lieu of dower and to be enjoyed by her only after her husband's death; a settlement under which a wife receives such an estate. ● The four essential elements are that (1) the jointure must take effect immediately upon the husband's death, (2) it must be for the wife's own life, and not for another's life or for a term of years, (3) it must be held by her in her own right and not in trust for her, and (4) it must be in lieu of her entire dower. See DOWER.

> **equitable jointure.** A premarital arrangement for a woman to enjoy a jointure, accepted by the woman in lieu of dower. — Also termed *equitable dower.*

2. A settlement under which a wife receives such an estate. — Also termed *legal jointure.* **3.** An estate in lands given jointly to a husband and wife before they marry. See JOINTRESS.

joint venture. (18c) A business undertaking by two or more persons engaged in a single defined project. ● The necessary elements are: (1) an express or implied agreement; (2) a common purpose that the group intends to carry out; (3) shared profits and losses; and (4) each member's equal voice in controlling the project. — Also termed *joint adventure; joint enterprise.* Cf. PARTNERSHIP; STRATEGIC ALLIANCE; VENTURE

joint-venture corporation. See CORPORATION.

joint verdict. See VERDICT.

joint welfare fund. See FUND (1).

joint will. See WILL.

joint work. See WORK (2).

joker. (1904) **1.** An ambiguous clause inserted in a legislative bill to render it inoperative or uncertain in some respect without arousing opposition at the time of passage. **2.** A rider or amendment that is extraneous to the subject of the bill.

Jones Act. *Maritime law.* A federal statute that allows a seaman injured during the course of employment to recover damages for the injuries in a negligence action against the employer. ● If a seaman dies from such injuries, the seaman's personal representative may maintain an action against the employer. 46 USCA app. § 688.

Jones Act vessel. See VESSEL.

journal. (15c) **1.** A book or record kept, usu. daily, as of the proceedings of a legislature or the events of a ship's voyage. — Also termed *log; logbook.* See MINUTES (2). **2.** *Accounting.* In double-entry bookkeeping, a book in which original entries are recorded before being transferred to a ledger. **3.** A periodical or magazine, esp. one published for a scholarly or professional group. — Abbr. J.

journal entry. See ENTRY (2).

journalist's privilege. See PRIVILEGE (3).

journal of notarial acts (noh-**tair**-ee-əl). The notary public's sequential record of notarial transactions, usu. a bound book listing the date, time, and type of each official act, the type of instrument acknowledged or verified before the notary, the signature of each person whose signature is notarized, the type of information used to verify the identity of parties whose signatures are notarized, and the fee charged. • This journal, required by law in many states, provides a record that may be used as evidence in court. — Also termed *notarial record*; *notarial register*; *notary record book*; *sequential journal*.

journeys accounts. *Hist.* The number of days (usu. 15) after the abatement of a writ within which a new writ could be obtained. • This number was based on how many days it took for the plaintiff to travel (or *journey*) to the court.

joyriding, *n.* (1909) The illegal driving of someone else's automobile without permission, but with no intent to deprive the owner of it permanently. • Under the Model Penal Code, the offender's reasonable belief that the owner would have consented is an affirmative defense. See Model Penal Code § 223.9. — Also termed *unauthorized use of a vehicle.* — **joyride,** *vb.* — **joyrider,** *n.*

J.P. *abbr.* JUSTICE OF THE PEACE.

J.P. court. See *justice court* under COURT.

JPML. *abbr.* JUDICIAL PANEL ON MULTIDISTRICT LITIGATION.

JPO. *abbr.* Japanese Patent Office.

J.P. Stevens test. *Patents.* A two-part test to determine whether a patent-applicant's conduct amounted to inequitable conduct before the Patent and Trademark Office, by deciding (1) whether the threshold levels of materiality and intent are met, and (2) whether, on balance, the facts show inequitable conduct as a matter of law. *J.P. Stevens v. Lex Tex Ltd.*, 747 F.2d 1553 (Fed. Cir. 1984). • In the balance, information that is clearly material or conduct that is clearly deceptive can decide the outcome.

JSC. *abbr.* Justice of Supreme Court.

J.S.D. [Law Latin *juris scientiae doctor*] *abbr.* DOCTOR OF JURIDICAL SCIENCE.

J.U.D. [Law Latin *juris utriusque doctor* "doctor of both laws"] *abbr.* A doctor of both civil and canon law.

judex (**joo**-deks), *n.* [Latin] **1.** *Roman law.* A private person appointed by a praetor or other magistrate to hear and decide a case. • The Roman judex was originally drawn from a panel of qualified persons of standing but was later himself a magistrate. **2.** *Roman & civil law.* A judge. **3.** *Hist.* A

juror. — Also spelled *iudex.* Pl. **judices** (**joo**-di-seez).

judex ad quem (ad **kwem**). *Civil law.* A judge to whom an appeal is taken.

judex a quo (ay **kwoh**). *Civil law.* A judge from whom an appeal is taken.

judex datus (**day**-təs). *Roman law.* A judex assigned by a magistrate or provincial governor to try a case under *cognitio extraordinaria.*

judex delegatus (del-ə-**gay**-təs). *Roman & civil law.* A delegated judge under *cognitio extraordinaria*; a special judge.

judex fiscalis (fis-**kay**-lis). *Roman law.* A judex having jurisdiction of matters relating to the *fiscus.* See FISCUS (1).

judex ordinarius (or-də-**nair**-ee-əs). *Civil law.* A judge having jurisdiction in his own right rather than by delegated authority. • The judge was typically a provincial governor.

judex pedaneus (pə-**day**-nee-əs). *Roman law.* A judex to whom petty cases are delegated; an inferior or deputy judge under *cognitio extraordinaria.* — Also termed *judex specialis.*

judex quaestionis (kwes-chee-**oh**-nis *or* kwes-tee-). *Roman law.* The chairman of the jury in a criminal case, either a praetor or a magistrate of lower rank.

judex selectus (sə-**lek**-təs). *Civil law.* A judge selected to hear the facts in a criminal case.

judex specialis (spesh-ee-**ay**-lis). *Roman law.* See *judex pedaneus.*

judge, *n.* (14c) A public official appointed or elected to hear and decide legal matters in court. • The term is sometimes held to include all officers appointed to decide litigated questions, including a justice of the peace and even jurors (who are judges of the facts). But in ordinary legal usage, the term is limited to the sense of an officer who (1) is so named in his or her commission, and (2) presides in a court. *Judge* is often used interchangeably with *court.* See COURT (2). — Abbr. J. (and, in plural, JJ.

administrative-law judge. See ADMINISTRATIVE-LAW JUDGE.

administrative patent judge. *Patents.* A U.S. Patent and Trademark Office adjudicator charged with conducting interference and appeal proceedings. — Abbr. APJ.

associate judge. (18c) An appellate judge who is neither a chief judge nor a presiding judge. — Also termed *puisne judge.*

bankruptcy judge. (1873) A judicial officer appointed by a U.S. Court of Appeals to preside over cases filed under the Bankruptcy Code and proceedings related to bankruptcy cases that are referred by the U.S. district court. •

A bankruptcy judge is appointed for a term of 14 years. 28 USCA §§ 151 et seq. See ARTICLE I JUDGE.

chief administrative patent judge. *Patents.* The supervisor of administrative patent judges at the U.S. Patent and Trademark Office. — Abbr. CAPJ.

chief judge. (15c) The judge who presides over the sessions and deliberations of a court, while also overseeing the administration of the court. — Abbr. C.J.

circuit judge. (18c) **1.** A judge who sits on a circuit court; esp., a federal judge who sits on a U.S. court of appeals. **2.** *Hist.* A special judge added to a court for the purpose of holding trials, but without being a regular member of the court. — Abbr. C.J.

city judge. See *municipal judge.*

continuing part-time judge. A judge who serves repeatedly on a part-time basis by election or under a continuing appointment.

county judge. (18c) A local judge having criminal or civil jurisdiction, or sometimes both, within a county.

criminal-court judge. A judge who sits on a court with jurisdiction only over criminal matters.

de facto judge (di **fak**-toh). (1829) A judge operating under color of law but whose authority is procedurally defective, such as a judge appointed under an unconstitutional statute. — Also termed *judge de facto.*

district judge. (18c) **1.** A judge in a federal or state judicial district. **2.** See *metropolitan stipendiary magistrate* under MAGISTRATE. — Abbr. D.J.

duty judge. A judge responsible for setting an arrestee's bail, usu. by telephone or videoconference.

family-court judge. A judge who sits on a court that has jurisdiction exclusively over matters involving domestic relations, such as divorce and child-custody matters.

hanging judge. (18c) *Slang.* A judge who is harsh (sometimes corruptly so) with defendants, esp. those accused of capital crimes.

inferior judge. A judge who sits on a lower court.

judge de facto. See *de facto judge.*

judge delegate. A judge who acts under delegated authority.

judge of probate. See *probate judge.*

judge ordinary. *Hist.* The judge of the English Court for Divorce and Matrimonial Causes from 1857-1875.

judge pro tempore (proh **tem**-pə-ree). See *visiting judge.*

juvenile-court judge. A judge who sits on a court that has jurisdiction exclusively over matters involving juveniles, such as suits involving child abuse and neglect, matters involving status offenses, and, sometimes, suits to terminate parental rights.

lay judge. (16c) A judge who is not a lawyer.

mentor judge. An experienced judge who helps a new judge by sharing knowledge and offering guidance.

military judge. A commissioned officer of the armed forces who is on active duty and is a member of a bar of a federal court or of the highest court of a state. • The Judge Advocate General of the particular service must certify a military judge as qualified for duty. A military judge of a general court-martial must also be a member of an independent judiciary. A military judge is detailed to every general court-martial and usu. to a special court-martial.

municipal judge. (18c) A local judge having criminal or civil jurisdiction, or sometimes both, within a city. — Also termed *city judge.*

presiding judge. (18c) **1.** A judge in charge of a particular court or judicial district; esp., the senior active judge on a three-member panel that hears and decides cases. **2.** A chief judge. — Abbr. P.J. — Also termed *president judge.*

probate judge. (18c) A judge having jurisdiction over probate, inheritance, guardianships, and the like. — Also termed *judge of probate; surrogate; register; registry.*

puisne judge (**pyoo**-nee). [Law French *puisné* "later born"] **1.** A junior judge; a judge without distinction or title. • This was the title formerly used in English common-law courts for a judge other than the chief judge. Today *puisne judge* refers to any judge of the English High Court, apart from the Chief Justice. **2.** See *associate judge.*

senior administrative patent judge. *Patents.* A semiretired administrative patent judge who remains active in hearing interferences in the U.S. Patent and Trademark Office. — Abbr. SAPJ.

senior judge. (18c) **1.** The judge who has served for the longest time on a given court. **2.** A federal or state judge who qualifies for senior status and chooses this status over retirement. See SENIOR STATUS.

side judge. *Archaic.* A judge — or one of two judges — of inferior rank, associated with a judge of a higher rank for the purpose of constituting a court.

special judge. (17c) A judge appointed or selected to sit, usu. in a specific case, in the absence or disqualification of the regular judge or otherwise as provided by statute.

temporary judge. See *visiting judge.*

trial judge. (17c) The judge before whom a case is tried. • This term is used most commonly on appeal from the judge's rulings.

United States Magistrate Judge. See UNITED STATES MAGISTRATE JUDGE.

visiting judge. (1888) A judge appointed by the presiding judge of an administrative region to sit temporarily on a given court, usu. in the regular judge's absence. — Also termed *temporary judge*; *judge pro tempore.*

judge advocate. (17c) *Military law.* **1.** An officer of a court-martial who acts as a prosecutor. **2.** A legal adviser on a military commander's staff. **3.** Any officer in the Judge Advocate General's Corps or in a department of a U.S. military branch. — Abbr. JA.

staff judge advocate. A certified military lawyer with the staff of a convening or supervisory authority that exercises general court-martial jurisdiction.

Judge Advocate General. *Military law.* The senior legal officer and chief legal adviser of the Army, Navy, or Air Force. — Abbr. JAG.

Judge Lynch. See LYNCH LAW.

judge-made law. (1817) **1.** The law established by judicial precedent rather than by statute. See COMMON LAW. **2.** The law that results when judges construe statutes contrary to legislative intent. — Also termed (in sense 2) *judicial legislation*; *bench legislation*; *judicial law.* See JUDICIAL ACTIVISM.

judgement. See JUDGMENT.

judge's chamber. See CHAMBER.

judgeship. (17c) **1.** The office or authority of a judge. **2.** The period of a judge's incumbency.

judge-shopping. (1962) The practice of filing several lawsuits asserting the same claims — in a court or a district with multiple judges — with the hope of having one of the lawsuits assigned to a favorable judge and of nonsuiting or voluntarily dismissing the others. Cf. FORUM-SHOPPING.

judge trial. See *bench trial* under TRIAL.

judgment. (13c) **1.** A court's final determination of the rights and obligations of the parties in a case. • The term *judgment* includes an equitable decree and any order from which an appeal lies. Fed. R. Civ. P. 54. — Also spelled (esp. in BrE) *judgement.* — Abbr. J. — Also termed (historically) *judgment ex cathedra.* Cf. RULING (1); OPINION (1). **2.** *English law.* An opinion delivered by a member of the appellate committee of the House of Lords; a Law Lord's judicial opinion. — Also termed (in sense 2) *speech.*

accumulative judgment. (1921) A second or additional judgment against a person who has already been convicted, the execution of which is postponed until the completion of any prior sentence.

agreed judgment. (1945) A settlement that becomes a court judgment when the judge sanctions it. • In effect, an agreed judgment is merely a contract acknowledged in open court and ordered to be recorded, but it binds the parties as fully as other judgments. — Also termed *consent judgment*; *stipulated judgment*; *judgment by consent.*

alternative judgment. A determination that gives the losing party options for satisfying that party's duties.

cognovit judgment (kog-**noh**-vit). A debtor's confession of judgment; judgment entered in accordance with a cognovit. See CONFESSION OF JUDGMENT; COGNOVIT.

conditional judgment. A judgment whose force depends on the performance of certain acts to be done in the future by one of the parties. • For example, a conditional judgment may order the sale of mortgaged property in a foreclosure proceeding unless the mortgagor pays the amount decreed within the time specified. — Also termed *common order.*

confession of judgment. See CONFESSION OF JUDGMENT.

consent judgment. See *agreed judgment.*

contradictory judgment. *Civil law.* A judgment that has been given after the court has heard the parties make their claims and defenses. • In Louisiana, this term is opposed to *default judgment.* Cf. *contradictory motion* under MOTION.

declaratory judgment. (1886) A binding adjudication that establishes the rights and other legal relations of the parties without providing for or ordering enforcement. • Declaratory judgments are often sought, for example, by insurance companies in determining whether a policy covers a given insured or peril. — Also termed *declaratory decree*; *declaration.*

default judgment. See DEFAULT JUDGMENT.

deferred judgment. (1896) A judgment placing a convicted defendant on probation, the successful completion of which will prevent entry of the underlying judgment of conviction. • This type of probation is common with minor traffic offenses. — Also termed *deferred adjudication*; *deferred-adjudication probation*; *deferred prosecution*; *probation before judgment*; *probation without judgment*; *pretrial intervention*; *adjudication withheld.*

deficiency judgment. (1865) A judgment against a debtor for the unpaid balance of the debt if a foreclosure sale or a sale of repossessed personal property fails to yield the full amount of the debt due. — Also termed *deficiency decree.*

definitive judgment. See *final judgment.*

determinative judgment. See *final judgment.*

domestic judgment. A judgment rendered by the courts of the state or country where the judgment or its effect is at issue.

dormant judgment. (18c) A judgment that has not been executed or enforced within the statutory time limit. • As a result, any judgment lien may have been lost and execution cannot be issued unless the judgment creditor first revives the judgment. See REVIVAL (1).

erroneous judgment. (17c) A judgment issued by a court with jurisdiction to issue it, but containing an improper application of law. • This type of judgment is not void, but can be corrected by a trial court while the court retains plenary jurisdiction, or in a direct appeal. — Also termed *judgment in error.* See ERROR (2).

excess judgment. *Insurance.* A judgment that exceeds all of the defendant's insurance coverage.

executory judgment (eg-**zek**-yə-tor-ee). (18c) A judgment that has not been carried out, such as a yet-to-be fulfilled order for the defendant to pay the plaintiff.

final appealable judgment. See *final judgment.*

final judgment. (18c) A court's last action that settles the rights of the parties and disposes of all issues in controversy, except for the award of costs (and, sometimes, attorney's fees) and enforcement of the judgment. — Also termed *final appealable judgment; final decision; final decree; definitive judgment; determinative judgment; final appealable order.* See FINAL-JUDGMENT RULE.

foreign judgment. A decree, judgment, or order of a court in a state, country, or judicial system different from that where the judgment or its effect is at issue.

in personam judgment. See *personal judgment.*

in rem judgment. See *judgment in rem.*

interlocutory judgment (in-tər-**lok**-[y]ə-tor-ee). (17c) An intermediate judgment that determines a preliminary or subordinate point or plea but does not finally decide the case. • A judgment or order given on a provisional or accessory claim or contention is generally interlocutory. — Also termed *interlocutory decree.*

irregular judgment. A judgment that may be set aside because of some irregularity in the way it was rendered, such as a clerk's failure to send a defendant notice that a default judgment has been rendered.

judgment as a matter of law. (1873) A judgment rendered during a jury trial — either before or after the jury's verdict — against a party on a given issue when there is no legally sufficient basis for a jury to find for that party on that issue. • In federal practice, the term *judgment as a matter of law* has replaced both the directed verdict and the judgment notwithstanding the verdict. Fed. R. Civ. P. 50. Cf. SUMMARY JUDGMENT.

judgment by confession. See CONFESSION OF JUDGMENT.

judgment by consent. See *agreed judgment.*

judgment by default. See DEFAULT JUDGMENT.

judgment by nil dicit. See *nil-dicit default judgment* under DEFAULT JUDGMENT.

judgment for money. See *money judgment.*

judgment homologating the tableau (hə-**mahl**-ə-gay-ting / ta-**bloh** *or* **tab**-loh). *Civil law.* A judgment approving a plan for distributing property of a decedent's estate. • The distribution plan is known as the tableau of distribution. La. Code Civ. Proc. art. 3307. See HOMOLOGATION.

judgment in error. See *erroneous judgment.*

judgment in personam. See *personal judgment.*

judgment in rem (in **rem**). (18c) A judgment that determines the status or condition of property and that operates directly on the property itself. • The phrase denotes a judgment that affects not only interests in a thing but also all persons' interest in the thing. — Also termed *in rem judgment.*

judgment in retraxit. See *judgment of retraxit.*

judgment inter partes. See *personal judgment.*

judgment nil capiat per billa (nil **kap**-ee-ət pər **bil**-ə). (1816) Judgment that the plaintiff take nothing by the bill; a take-nothing judgment in a case instituted by a bill.

judgment nil capiat per breve (nil **kap**-ee-ət pər **breev** *or* **bree**-vee). (1916) Judgment that the plaintiff take nothing by the writ; a take-nothing judgment in a case instituted by a writ.

judgment nisi (**nI**-sI). (18c) A provisional judgment that, while not final or absolute, may become final on a party's motion. See NISI.

judgment notwithstanding the verdict. (18c) A judgment entered for one party even though a jury verdict has been rendered for the opposing party. — Also termed *judgment non obstante veredicto* (non ahb-**stan**-tee ver-ə-**dik**-toh). — Abbr. JNOV; judgment N.O.V. See *judgment as a matter of law.*

judgment nunc pro tunc. A judgment entered on a day after the time when it should have been entered, as of the earlier date. — Also termed *decree nunc pro tunc.* See NUNC PRO TUNC.

judgment of acquittal. (17c) A judgment, rendered on the defendant's motion or court's own motion, that acquits the defendant of the offense charged when the evidence is insufficient. Fed. R. Crim. P. 29. See *directed verdict* under VERDICT.

judgment of blood. See *death sentence* under SENTENCE.

judgment of conviction. (1806) **1.** The written record of a criminal judgment, consisting of the plea, the verdict or findings, the adjudication, and the sentence. Fed. R. Crim. P. 32(d)(1). **2.** A sentence in a criminal case. See SENTENCE.

judgment of discontinuance. 1. A judgment dismissing a plaintiff's action based on interruption in the proceedings occasioned by the plaintiff's failure to continue the suit at the appointed time or times. **2.** NONSUIT (1). — Often shortened to *discontinuance*. See DISCONTINUANCE.

judgment of dismissal. (1809) A final determination of a case (against the plaintiff in a civil action or the government in a criminal action) without a trial on its merits. See DISMISSAL.

judgment of nolle prosequi (nahl-ee **prahs**-ə-kwɪ). (1869) A judgment entered against a plaintiff who, after appearance but before judgment on the merits, has decided to abandon prosecution of the lawsuit. See NOLLE PROSEQUI.

judgment of nonsuit. 1. *Hist.* The judgment given against a plaintiff who fails to be present in court to hear the jury render its verdict or who, after issue is joined, fails to bring the issue to be tried in due time. ● This judgment does not prevent the plaintiff from filing the same case again. **2.** NONSUIT (2).

judgment of repleader. See REPLEADER.

judgment of retraxit (ri-**trak**-sit). *Hist.* A judgment against a plaintiff who has voluntarily retracted the claim. ● Such a judgment bars the plaintiff from relitigating the claim. — Also termed *judgment in retraxit.* See RETRAXIT.

judgment on the merits. (18c) A judgment based on the evidence rather than on technical or procedural grounds. — Also termed *decision on the merits.*

judgment on the pleadings. (18c) A judgment based solely on the allegations and information contained in the pleadings, and not on any outside matters. Fed. R. Civ. P. 12(c). Cf. SUMMARY JUDGMENT.

judgment on the verdict. (17c) A judgment for the party receiving a favorable jury verdict.

judgment quasi in rem (**kway**-sɪ [*or* -zɪ] in **rem**). (1905) A judgment based on the court's jurisdiction over the defendant's interest in property rather than on its jurisdiction over the defendant or the property. ● Such a judgment affects only particular persons' interests in a thing —

that is, only the persons who are named or described in the proceeding.

judgment quod recuperet (kwod ri-**kyoo**-pər-it). Judgment that the plaintiff recover.

judgment respondeat ouster (ri-**spon**-dee-at **ows**-tər). *Hist.* An interlocutory judgment requiring the defendant who has made a dilatory plea to give a more substantial defense.

junior judgment. A judgment rendered or entered after the rendition or entry of another judgment, on a different claim, against the same defendant.

money judgment. (1869) A judgment for damages subject to immediate execution, as distinguished from equitable or injunctive relief. — Also termed *judgment for money.*

nunc pro tunc judgment (nəngk proh **təngk**). (1828) A procedural device by which the record of a judgment is amended to accord with what the judge actually said and did, so that the record will be accurate. ● This device is often used to correct defects in real-estate titles.

personal judgment. (1829) **1.** A judgment that imposes personal liability on a defendant and that may therefore be satisfied out of any of the defendant's property within judicial reach. **2.** A judgment resulting from an action in which a court has personal jurisdiction over the parties. **3.** A judgment against a person as distinguished from a judgment against a thing, right, or status. — Also termed *judgment in personam* (in pər-**soh**-nəm); *in personam judgment*; *judgment inter partes* (**in**-tər **pahr**-teez).

simulated judgment. *Civil law.* A judgment that, although founded on an actual debt and intended for collection by the usual legal processes, is actually entered into by the parties to give one of them an undeserving advantage or to defraud third parties.

stipulated judgment. See *agreed judgment.*

summary judgment. See SUMMARY JUDGMENT.

suspension of judgment. See STAY.

take-nothing judgment. (1938) A judgment for the defendant providing that the plaintiff recover nothing in damages or other relief. — Also termed (in some states) *no cause of action.*

valid judgment. 1. A judgment that will be recognized by common-law states as long as it is in force in the state where the judgment was rendered. **2.** A judicial act rendered by a court having jurisdiction over the parties and over the subject matter in a proceeding in which the parties have had a reasonable opportunity to be heard.

voidable judgment. (17c) A judgment that, although seemingly valid, is defective in some material way; esp., a judgment that, although rendered by a court having jurisdiction, is irregular or erroneous.

void judgment. (18c) A judgment that has no legal force or effect, the invalidity of which may be asserted by any party whose rights are affected at any time and any place, whether directly or collaterally. ● From its inception, a void judgment continues to be absolutely null. It is incapable of being confirmed, ratified, or enforced in any manner or to any degree. One source of a void judgment is the lack of subject-matter jurisdiction.

judgmental immunity. See ERROR-OF-JUDGMENT RULE.

judgment book. See *judgment docket* under DOCKET (1).

judgment by comparison. *Patents.* Allowance of a patent claim because a similar claim has been allowed before. ● There is no stare decisis doctrine in patent prosecutions, but examiners may consider allowance of similar claims as a decision-making aid.

judgment creditor. (18c) A person having a legal right to enforce execution of a judgment for a specific sum of money.

bona fide judgment creditor. One who recovers a judgment without engaging in fraud or collusion.

judgment debt. See DEBT.

judgment debtor. (18c) A person against whom a money judgment has been entered but not yet satisfied.

judgment docket. See DOCKET (1).

judgment ex cathedra. 1. See EX CATHEDRA. **2.** See JUDGMENT (1).

judgment execution. 1. See EXECUTION (3). **2.** See EXECUTION (4).

judgment file. See *judgment docket* under DOCKET (1).

judgment lien. See LIEN.

judgment *non obstante veredicto*. See *judgment notwithstanding the verdict* under JUDGMENT.

judgment note. 1. A nonnegotiable promissory note, illegal in most states, containing a power of attorney to appear and confess judgment for a specified sum. **2.** COGNOVIT NOTE.

judgment N.O.V. See *judgment notwithstanding the verdict* under JUDGMENT.

judgment of blood. See *death sentence* under SENTENCE.

judgment of repleader. See REPLEADER.

judgment-proof, *adj.* (18c) (Of an actual or potential judgment debtor) unable to satisfy a judgment for money damages because the person has no property, does not own enough property within the court's jurisdiction to satisfy the judgment, or claims the benefit of statutorily exempt property. — Also termed *execution-proof.*

judgment receiver. See RECEIVER.

judgment record. See *judgment docket* under DOCKET (1).

judgment roll. See *judgment docket* under DOCKET (1).

judgment-roll appeal. See APPEAL.

judgment sale. See *execution sale* under SALE.

judgment seat. 1. The bench on which a judge sits. **2.** By extension, a court or tribunal.

judgment summons. See SUMMONS.

judicable (**joo**-di-kə-bəl), *adj.* (17c) *Rare.* Capable of being adjudicated; triable; justiciable. — Also termed *judiciable* (joo-**dish**-ə-bəl).

judicative (**joo**-di-kay-tiv *or* -kə-tiv), *adj. Rare.* See ADJUDICATIVE.

judicator (**joo**-di-kay-tər), *n.* (18c) A person authorized to act or serve as a judge.

judicatory (**joo**-di-kə-tor-ee), *adj.* (17c) **1.** Of or relating to judgment. **2.** Allowing a judgment to be made; giving a decisive indication.

judicatory (**joo**-di-kə-tor-ee), *n.* (16c) **1.** A court; any tribunal with judicial authority <a church judicatory>. **2.** The administration of justice <working toward a more efficient judicatory>.

judicature (**joo**-di-kə-chər). (16c) **1.** The action of judging or of administering justice through duly constituted courts. **2.** JUDICIARY (3). **3.** A judge's office, function, or authority.

Judicature Acts. A series of statutes that reorganized the superior courts of England in 1875. ● The Judicature Acts were superseded by the Supreme Court Act of 1981.

judices (**joo**-di-seez). [Latin] *pl.* JUDEX.

judicia (joo-**dish**-ee-ə). [Latin] *pl.* JUDICIUM.

judicial (joo-**dish**-əl), *adj.* (14c) **1.** Of, relating to, or by the court or a judge <judicial duty> <judicial demeanor>. **2.** In court <the witness's judicial confession>. **3.** Legal <the Attorney General took no judicial action>. **4.** Of or relating to a judgment <an award of judicial interest at the legal rate>. Cf. JUDICIOUS.

quasi-judicial. See QUASI-JUDICIAL.

judicial act. See ACT (2).

judicial activism, *n.* (1949) A philosophy of judicial decision-making whereby judges allow their personal views about public policy, among other factors, to guide their decisions, usu. with the suggestion that adherents of this philosophy tend to find constitutional violations and are willing to ignore precedent. Cf. JUDICIAL RESTRAINT (3). — **judicial activist,** *n.*

judicial activity report. A regular report, usu. monthly or quarterly, on caseload and caseflow within a given court or court system.

judicial administration. The process of doing justice through a system of courts.

judicial admission. See ADMISSION (1).

judicial arbitration. See ARBITRATION.

Judicial Article. (1881) Article III of the U.S. Constitution, which creates the Supreme Court, vests in Congress the right to create inferior courts, provides for life tenure for federal judges, and specifies the powers and jurisdiction of the federal courts.

judicial assize. See ASSIZE (6).

judicial-authority justification. See JUSTIFICATION.

judicial bias. See BIAS.

judicial bond. See BOND (2).

judicial branch. (18c) The branch of government consisting of the courts, whose function is to ensure justice by interpreting, applying, and generally administering the laws; JUDICIARY (1). Cf. LEGISLATIVE BRANCH; EXECUTIVE BRANCH.

judicial bypass. (1977) A procedure permitting a person to obtain a court's approval for an act that would ordinarily require the approval of someone else, such as a law that requires a minor to notify a parent before obtaining an abortion but allows an appropriately qualified minor to obtain a court order permitting the abortion without parental notice.

judicial-bypass provision. *Family law.* **1.** A statutory provision that allows a court to assume a parental role when the parent or guardian cannot or will not act on behalf of a minor or an incompetent. **2.** A statutory provision that allows a minor to circumvent the necessity of obtaining parental consent by obtaining judicial consent.

judicial cognizance. See JUDICIAL NOTICE.

judicial combat. See TRIAL BY COMBAT.

judicial comity. See COMITY.

Judicial Committee of the Privy Council. A United Kingdom tribunal, created in 1833, with jurisdiction to hear certain admiralty and ecclesiastical appeals, and certain appeals from the Commonwealth. ● From the 16th century until the 19th, the Court of Delegates was the final court of appeal in England for ecclesiastical suits. During the reign of William IV, the power to hear final appeals was transferred to the Privy Council, and then to the Judicial Committee of the Privy Council. The committee consists entirely of lay people; ecclesiastics become members of the court only if an appeal is brought under the Church Discipline Act. Even then the ecclesiastics must be episcopal privy counselors. The Judicial Committee's decisions are not treated as binding precedent in the United Kingdom, but they are influential because of the overlapping composition of members of the Privy Council and the House of Lords in its judicial capacity. — Also termed *Court of Final Appeal.*

judicial compensation. 1. The remuneration that judges receive for their work. **2.** *Civil law.* A court's judgment finding that two parties are mutually obligated to one another and crafting the amount of the judgment in accordance with the amount that each party owes. ● A claim for compensation is usu. contained in a reconventional demand. La. Code Civ. Proc. 1902. See *reconventional demand* under DEMAND (1).

Judicial Conference of the United States. The policy-making body of the federal judiciary, responsible for surveying the business of the federal courts, making recommendations to Congress on matters affecting the judiciary, and supervising the work of the Administrative Office of the United States Courts. ● The Conference was originally established in 1923 as the Conference of Senior Circuit Judges. 28 USCA § 331. See ADMINISTRATIVE OFFICE OF THE UNITED STATES COURTS.

judicial confession. See CONFESSION.

judicial contempt. See CONTEMPT (2).

judicial control. *Civil law.* A doctrine by which a court can deny cancellation of a lease if the lessee's breach is of minor importance, is not caused by the lessee, or is based on a good-faith mistake of fact.

judicial council. (1925) A regularly assembled group of judges whose mission is to increase the efficiency and effectiveness of the courts on which they sit; esp., a semiannual assembly of a federal circuit's judges called by the circuit's chief judge. 28 USCA § 332.

judicial day. See *juridical day* under DAY.

judicial declaration. See DECLARATION (1).

judicial dictum. See DICTUM.

judicial discretion. See DISCRETION (4).

judicial document. A court-filed paper that is subject to the right of public access because it is or has been both relevant to the judicial function and useful in the judicial process. *See Lugosch v. Pyramid Co. of Onandaga,* 435 F.3d 110, 119 (2d Cir. 2006).

judicial economy. (1942) Efficiency in the operation of the courts and the judicial system; esp., the efficient management of litigation so as to minimize duplication of effort and to avoid wasting the judiciary's time and resources. ● A court can enter a variety of orders to promote judicial economy. For instance, a court may consolidate two cases for trial to save the court and the parties from having two trials, or it may order a separate trial on certain issues if doing so would provide the opportunity to avoid a later trial that would be more complex and time-consuming.

judicial-economy exception. (1981) An exemption from the final-judgment rule, by which a party may seek immediate appellate review of a nonfinal order if doing so might establish a final or nearly final disposition of the entire suit. See FINAL-JUDGMENT RULE.

judicial estoppel. See ESTOPPEL.

judicial evidence. See EVIDENCE.

judicial fact. See *judicially noticed fact* under FACT.

judicial factor. See FACTOR.

judicial foreclosure. See FORECLOSURE.

judicial immunity. See IMMUNITY (1).

judicial insurance. See INSURANCE.

judicialize, *vb.* **1.** To pattern (procedures, etc.) after a court of law <these administrative hearings have been judicialized>. **2.** To bring (something not traditionally within the judicial system) into the judicial system <political questions are gradually becoming judicialized>. — **judicialization,** *n.*

judicial jurisdiction. See JURISDICTION.

judicial knowledge. See JUDICIAL NOTICE.

judicial law. See JUDGE-MADE LAW.

judicial legislation. 1. See JUDGE-MADE LAW (2). **2.** See LEGISLATION.

judicial lien. See LIEN.

judicially created double patenting. See DOUBLE PATENTING.

judicially created double-patenting rejection. See REJECTION.

judicial morsel. See *ordeal of the morsel* under ORDEAL.

judicial mortgage. See MORTGAGE.

judicial notice. (17c) A court's acceptance, for purposes of convenience and without requiring a party's proof, of a well-known and indisputable fact; the court's power to accept such a fact <the trial court took judicial notice of the fact that water freezes at 32 degrees Fahrenheit>. Fed R. Evid. 201. — Also termed *judicial cognizance; judicial knowledge.* See *judicially noticed fact* under FACT.

judicial notice of prior art. *Patents.* Acknowledgment by the U.S. Patent and Trademark Office of all materials in its possession as prior art, for settling questions of novelty and priority. • Patents, applications, and records of interfer-

ences and appeals may be submitted by citation alone.

judicially noticed fact. See FACT.

judicial oath. See OATH.

judicial officer. See OFFICER (1).

judicial opinion. See OPINION (1).

judicial order. See ORDER (2).

Judicial Panel on Multidistrict Litigation. A panel of federal judges responsible for transferring civil actions having common questions of fact from one district court to another to consolidate pretrial proceedings. • The panel was created in 1968. The Chief Justice appoints its members. 28 USCA § 1407. — Abbr. JPML.

judicial power. (16c) **1.** The authority vested in courts and judges to hear and decide cases and to make binding judgments on them; the power to construe and apply the law when controversies arise over what has been done or not done under it. • Under federal law, this power is vested in the U.S. Supreme Court and in whatever inferior courts Congress establishes. The other two great powers of government are the legislative power and the executive power. **2.** A power conferred on a public officer involving the exercise of judgment and discretion in deciding questions of right in specific cases affecting personal and proprietary interests. • In this sense, the phrase is contrasted with *ministerial power.*

judicial privilege. 1. See PRIVILEGE (1). **2.** See *litigation privilege* under PRIVILEGE (1).

judicial proceeding. See PROCEEDING.

judicial-proceedings privilege. See *litigation privilege* under PRIVILEGE (1).

judicial process. See PROCESS.

judicial question. (18c) A question that is proper for determination by the courts, as opposed to a moot question or one properly decided by the executive or legislative branch. Cf. POLITICAL QUESTION.

judicial record. See DOCKET (1).

judicial remedy. See REMEDY.

judicial restraint. (18c) **1.** A restraint imposed by a court, as by a restraining order, injunction, or judgment. **2.** The principle that, when a court can resolve a case based on a particular issue, it should do so, without reaching unnecessary issues. **3.** A philosophy of judicial decision-making whereby judges avoid indulging their personal beliefs about the public good and instead try merely to interpret the law as legislated and according to precedent. — Also termed (in senses 2 & 3) *judicial self-restraint.* Cf. JUDICIAL ACTIVISM.

judicial review. (1851) **1.** A court's power to review the actions of other branches or levels of government; esp., the courts' power to invalidate legislative and executive actions as being unconstitutional. **2.** The constitutional doctrine providing for this power. **3.** A court's review of a lower court's or an administrative body's factual or legal findings.

> *de novo judicial review.* (1955) A court's nondeferential review of an administrative decision, usu. through a review of the administrative record plus any additional evidence the parties present. — Also termed *de novo review.*

> *plenary review.* Appellate review by all the members of a court rather than a panel.

judicial robe. See ROBE (1).

judicial sale. See SALE.

judicial self-restraint. 1. See JUDICIAL RESTRAINT (2). **2.** See JUDICIAL RESTRAINT (3).

judicial separation. 1. See SEPARATION (1). **2.** See SEPARATION (2). **3.** See *divorce a mensa et thoro* under DIVORCE.

judicial sequestration. See SEQUESTRATION.

judicial settlement. See SETTLEMENT (2).

judicial stacking. See STACKING.

judicial-tenure commission. A commission that reviews complaints against judges, investigates those complaints, and makes recommendations about appropriate measures to the highest court in the jurisdiction.

judicial trustee. See TRUSTEE (1).

judicial writ. See WRIT.

judiciary (joo-**dish**-ee-er-ee *or* joo-**dish**-ə-ree), *n.* (18c) **1.** The branch of government responsible for interpreting the laws and administering justice. Cf. EXECUTIVE (1); LEGISLATURE. **2.** A system of courts. **3.** A body of judges. — Also termed (in sense 3) *judicature.* — **judiciary,** *adj.*

judicious (joo-**dish**-əs), *adj.* (16c) Well-considered; discreet; wisely circumspect <the court's judicious application of the rules of evidence>. Cf. JUDICIAL. — **judiciousness,** *n.*

judicium (joo-**dish**-ee-əm), *n.* [Latin] *Hist.* **1.** A judgment. **2.** A judicial proceeding; a trial. **3.** A court or tribunal. • In Roman law, the plural *judicia* refers to criminal courts. Pl. *judicia.*

> *judicium capitale* (kap-i-**tay**-lee). [Latin] *Hist.* A judgment of death; a capital sentence.

> *judicium parium* (**par**-ee-əm). [Latin] *Hist.* A judgment of one's peers; a jury trial or verdict.

> *judicium publicum* (pəb-li-kəm). [Latin "public trial"] A criminal proceeding under a public statute. • The term derived from the Roman rule allowing any member of the public to initiate a prosecution. See COMITIA.

judicium Dei (joo-**dish**-ee-əm **dee**-ı). *Hist.* God's supposed judgment on the merits of the case, made manifest by the outcome of an observable event. • Examples dating from Norman times were the trial by combat and the ordeal. See ORDEAL; TRIAL BY COMBAT.

Julian calendar. See OLD STYLE.

jumbo certificate. A certificate of deposit of $100,000 or more. — Also termed *jumbo.*

jumbo mortgage. See MORTGAGE.

jump bail, *vb.* (1889) (Of an accused) to fail to appear in court at the appointed time after promising to appear and posting a bail bond. — Also termed *skip bail.* See BAIL-JUMPING.

jump citation. See *pinpoint citation* under CITATION (3).

jumping a claim. *Hist.* The act of taking possession of public land to which another has previously acquired a claim. • The first occupant has the right to the land both under squatter law and custom and under preemption laws of the United States.

junior, *adj.* (13c) Lower in rank or standing; subordinate <a junior interest>.

junior bond. See BOND (3).

junior counsel. See COUNSEL.

junior creditor. See CREDITOR.

junior debt. See *subordinate debt* under DEBT.

junior execution. See EXECUTION.

junior interest. See INTEREST (2).

junior judgment. See JUDGMENT.

junior lien. See LIEN.

junior mortgage. See MORTGAGE.

junior partner. See PARTNER.

junior party. *Patents.* In an interference proceeding, the party or parties who did not file the patent application first. • A junior party has the burden of proving that he or she is the first inventor. Cf. SENIOR PARTY.

junior security. See SECURITY.

junior user. *Trademarks.* A person other than the first person to use a trademark. • A junior user may be permitted to continue using a mark in areas where the senior user's mark is not used, if the junior user did not know about the other user, and was the first user to register the mark. — Also termed *second user; latecomer.* See INNOCENT JUNIOR USER. Cf. SENIOR USER.

> *innocent junior user.* *Trademarks.* A person who, without actual or constructive knowledge, uses a trademark that has previously been used in a geographically distant market, and who may continue to use the trademark in a limited geographic area as long as the senior user does not use the mark there.

junior writ. See WRIT.

junk asset. See *troubled asset* under ASSET.

junk bond. See BOND (3).

jura (joor-ə), *n. pl.* [Latin] Rights. See JUS.

jura fiscalia (fis-**kay**-lee-ə). *Hist.* Fiscal rights; rights of the Exchequer.

jura fixa (**joor**-ə fik-sə). *Hist.* Immovable rights.

jura in personam. A right to enforce a particular person's obligation to another. See JUS IN PERSONAM.

jura in rem. See JUS IN RE.

jura majestatis (maj-ə-**stay**-tis). *Hist.* Rights of sovereignty or majesty.

jura mixti dominii (**miks**-tɪ də-**min**-ee-ɪ). *Hist.* Rights of mixed dominion; the king's or queen's right or power of jurisdiction.

jura personarum (pər-sə-**nair**-əm). Rights of persons. See JUS PERSONARUM.

jura praediorum (pree-dee-**or**-əm). *Hist.* The rights of estates.

jura regalia (ri-**gay**-lee-ə). *Hist.* Royal rights; the prerogatives of the Crown. See REGALIA (1).

jura rerum (**reer**-əm). Rights of things. See JUS RERUM.

jura summi imperii (**səm**-ɪ im-**peer**-ee-ɪ). *Hist.* Rights of supreme dominion; rights of sovereignty.

jural (**joor**-əl), *adj.* (17c) **1.** Of or relating to law or jurisprudence; legal <jural and equitable rules>. **2.** Of or relating to rights and obligations <jural relations>.

jural act. See ACT.

jural activity. See *jural act* under ACT.

jural agent. (2004) An official — someone who has the appropriate authoritative status in society to enforce or affect the society's legal system — who engages in a jural act. • Common examples include judges, legislators, and police officers acting in their official capacities. See *jural act* under ACT.

jural cause. See *proximate cause* under CAUSE (1).

juramentum (joor-ə-**men**-təm), *n.* [Latin] *Civil law.* An oath. Pl. **juramenta** (joor-ə-**men**-tə).

juramentum calumniae (kə-**ləm**-nee-ee). An oath of calumny. See *oath of calumny* under OATH.

juramentum corporalis (kor-pə-**ray**-lis). A corporal oath. See *corporal oath* under OATH.

juramentum in litem (in lɪ-tem *or* -təm). An oath in litem. See *oath in litem* under OATH.

juramentum judiciale (joo-dish-ee-**ay**-lee). An oath by which the judge defers the decision of the case to either of the parties.

juramentum necessarium (nes-ə-**sair**-ee-əm). A necessary or compulsory oath.

juramentum voluntarium (vol-ən-**tair**-ee-əm). A voluntary oath.

jura mixti dominii. See JURA.

jurant (**joor**-ənt), *n. Archaic.* One who takes an oath. — **jurant,** *n.*

jura personarum. See JURA.

jura praediorum. See JURA.

jura regalia. See JURA.

jura rerum. See JURA.

jura summi imperii. See JURA.

jurat (**joor**-at). (18c) **1.** [fr. Latin *jurare* "to swear"] A certification added to an affidavit or deposition stating when and before what authority the affidavit or deposition was made. • A jurat typically says "Subscribed and sworn to before me this _____ day of [month], [year]," and the officer (usu. a notary public) thereby certifies three things: (1) that the person signing the document did so in the officer's presence, (2) that the signer appeared before the officer on the date indicated, and (3) that the officer administered an oath or affirmation to the signer, who swore to or affirmed the contents of the document. — Also termed *jurata*. Cf. VERIFICATION.

witness jurat. A subscribing witness's certificate acknowledging the act of witnessing. • Even though this certificate is technically an acknowledgment and not a true jurat, the phrase *witness jurat* is commonly used. See ACKNOWLEDGMENT.

2. [fr. Latin *juratus* "one sworn"] In France and the Channel Islands, a municipal officer or magistrate.

jurata (juu-**ray**-tə), *n.* **1.** *Hist.* A jury of 12 persons; esp., a jury existing at common law. **2.** JURAT (1).

juration (juu-**ray**-shən). *Archaic.* **1.** The act of administering an oath. **2.** The act of swearing on oath.

jurative. See JURATORY.

jurator (juu-**ray**-tər). *Archaic.* See JUROR.

juratorial (joor-ə-**toh**-ri-əl) *adj.* Of or pertaining to a jury.

juratory (**joor**-ə-tor-ee), *adj.* Of, relating to, or containing an oath. — Also termed *jurative.*

juratory caution. 1. *Maritime law.* A court's permission for an indigent to disregard filing fees and court costs. • A suit upon a juratory caution is the equivalent of a suit in forma pauperis. The right was first recognized in United States admiralty courts in *Bradford v. Bradford*, 3 F. Cas. 1129 (1878). See IN FORMA PAUPERIS. **2.** *Scots law.* A security given on oath, such as a bond.

jure (**joor**-ee), *adv.* [Latin] **1.** By right; in right. **2.** By law. See DE JURE.

juridical (juu-**rid**-i-kəl), *adj.* (16c) **1.** Of or relating to judicial proceedings or to the administration of justice. **2.** Of or relating to law; legal. — Also termed *juridic.* Cf. NONJURIDICAL.

juridical act. See ACT.

juridical day. See DAY.

juridical double taxation. See *double taxation* (3) under TAXATION.

juridical link. (1947) A legal relationship between members of a group, such as those in a potential class action, sufficient to make a single suit more efficient or effective than multiple suits. — Also termed *juridical relationship.*

juridical person. See *artificial person* under PERSON (3).

jurimetrics (joor-ə-**me**-triks), *n.* (1949) The use of scientific or empirical methods, including measurement, in the study or analysis of legal matters. — **jurimetrician** (joor-ə-me-**trish**-ən), **jurimetricist** (joor-ə-me-**trə**-sist), *n.*

juris (**joor**-is), *adj.* [Latin] **1.** Of law. **2.** Of right.

juris divini (di-**vɪ**-nɪ). *Roman law.* Of divine right; subject to divine law. • The phrase appeared in reference to churches or to religious items that could not be privately sold.

juris positivii. Of positive law.

juris privati (pri-**vay**-tɪ). Of private right; relating to private property or private law.

juris publici (**pəb**-li-sɪ). Of public right; relating to common or public use, or to public law.

juriscenter (**joor**-ə-sen-tər *or* joor-ə-**sen**-tər), *n. Conflict of laws.* The jurisdiction that is most appropriately considered a couple's domestic center of gravity for matrimonial purposes.

jurisconsult (joor-is-**kon**-səlt *or* -kən-**səlt**). One who is learned in the law, esp. in civil or international law; JURIST.

jurisdiction, *n.* (14c) **1.** A government's general power to exercise authority over all persons and things within its territory; esp., a state's power to create interests that will be recognized under common-law principles as valid in other states <New Jersey's jurisdiction>. **2.** A court's power to decide a case or issue a decree <the constitutional grant of federal-question jurisdiction>. — Also termed (in sense 2) *competent jurisdiction.*; (in both senses) *coram judice.* **3.** A geographic area within which political or judicial authority may be exercised <the accused fled to another jurisdiction>. **4.** A political or judicial subdivision within such an area <other jurisdictions have decided the issue differently>. Cf. VENUE. — **jurisdictional,** *adj.*

agency jurisdiction. The regulatory or adjudicative power of a government administrative agency over a subject matter or matters.

ancillary jurisdiction. (1835) A court's jurisdiction to adjudicate claims and proceedings related to a claim that is properly before the court. • For example, if a plaintiff brings a lawsuit in federal court based on a federal question (such as a claim under Title VII), the defendant may assert a counterclaim over which the court would not otherwise have jurisdiction (such as a state-law claim of stealing company property). The concept of ancillary jurisdiction has now been codified, along with the concept of pendent jurisdiction, in the supplemental-jurisdiction statute. 28 USCA § 1367. See *supplemental jurisdiction.* Cf. *pendent jurisdiction.*

anomalous jurisdiction. (1864) **1.** Jurisdiction that is not granted to a court by statute, but that is inherent in the court's authority to govern lawyers and other officers of the court, such as the power to issue a preindictment order suppressing illegally seized property. **2.** An appellate court's provisional jurisdiction to review the denial of a motion to intervene in a lower-court case, so that if the court finds that the denial was correct, then its jurisdiction disappears — and it must dismiss the appeal for want of jurisdiction — because an order denying a motion to intervene is not a final, appealable order. See ANOMALOUS-JURISDICTION RULE.

appellate jurisdiction. (18c) The power of a court to review and revise a lower court's decision. • For example, U.S. Const. art. III, § 2 vests appellate jurisdiction in the Supreme Court, while 28 USCA §§ 1291–1295 grant appellate jurisdiction to lower federal courts of appeals. Cf. *original jurisdiction.*

arising-in jurisdiction. A bankruptcy court's jurisdiction over issues relating to the administration of the bankruptcy estate, and matters that occur only in a bankruptcy case. 28 USCA §§ 157, 1334.

assistant jurisdiction. The incidental aid provided by an equity court to a court of law when justice requires both legal and equitable processes and remedies. — Also termed *auxiliary jurisdiction.*

common-law jurisdiction. 1. A place where the legal system derives fundamentally from the English common-law system <England, the United States, Australia, and other common-law jurisdictions>. **2.** A court's jurisdiction to try such cases as were cognizable under the English common law <in the absence of a controlling statute, the court exercised common-law jurisdiction over those claims>.

complete jurisdiction. A court's power to decide matters presented to it and to enforce its decisions.

concurrent jurisdiction. (17c) **1.** Jurisdiction that might be exercised simultaneously by more than one court over the same subject matter and within the same territory, a litigant having the right to choose the court in which to file the action. **2.** Jurisdiction shared by two or more states, esp. over the physical boundaries (such as rivers or other bodies of water) between them. — Also termed *coordinate jurisdiction*; *overlapping jurisdiction*. Cf. *exclusive jurisdiction*.

consent jurisdiction. (1855) Jurisdiction that parties have agreed to, either by accord, by contract, or by general appearance. ● Parties may not, by agreement, confer subject-matter jurisdiction on a federal court that would not otherwise have it.

contentious jurisdiction. **1.** A court's jurisdiction exercised over disputed matters. **2.** *Eccles. law.* The branch of ecclesiastical-court jurisdiction that deals with contested proceedings.

continuing jurisdiction. (1855) A court's power to retain jurisdiction over a matter after entering a judgment, allowing the court to modify its previous rulings or orders. See CONTINUING-JURISDICTION DOCTRINE.

coordinate jurisdiction. See *concurrent jurisdiction*.

criminal jurisdiction. (16c) A court's power to hear criminal cases.

default jurisdiction. *Family law.* In a child-custody matter, jurisdiction conferred when it is in the best interests of the child and either (1) there is no other basis for jurisdiction under the Uniform Child Custody Jurisdiction Act or the Parental Kidnapping Prevention Act, or (2) when another state has declined jurisdiction in favor of default jurisdiction. ● Jurisdiction is rarely based on default because either home-state jurisdiction or significant-connection jurisdiction almost always applies, or else emergency jurisdiction is invoked. Default jurisdiction arises only if none of those three applies, or a state with jurisdiction on any of those bases declines to exercise it and default jurisdiction serves the best interests of the child.

delinquency jurisdiction. The power of the court to hear matters regarding juvenile acts that, if committed by an adult, would be criminal. Cf. *status-offense jurisdiction*.

diversity jurisdiction. (1927) A federal court's exercise of authority over a case involving parties who are citizens of different states and an amount in controversy greater than a statutory minimum. 28 USCA § 1332. See DIVERSITY OF CITIZENSHIP; AMOUNT IN CONTROVERSY.

emergency jurisdiction. *Family law.* A court's ability to take jurisdiction of a child who is physically present in the state when that child has been abandoned or when necessary to protect the child from abuse. ● Section 3(a)(3) of the Uniform Child Custody Jurisdiction Act allows for emergency jurisdiction. It is usu. temporary, lasting only as long as is necessary to protect the child.

equity jurisdiction. (18c) In a common-law judicial system, the power to hear certain civil actions according to the procedure of the court of chancery, and to resolve them according to equitable rules.

exclusive jurisdiction. (18c) A court's power to adjudicate an action or class of actions to the exclusion of all other courts <federal district courts have exclusive jurisdiction over actions brought under the Securities Exchange Act>. Cf. *concurrent jurisdiction*.

extraterritorial jurisdiction. (1818) A court's ability to exercise power beyond its territorial limits. See LONG-ARM STATUTE.

federal jurisdiction. (1800) **1.** The exercise of federal-court authority. **2.** The area of study dealing with the jurisdiction of federal courts.

federal-juvenile-delinquency jurisdiction. A federal court's power to hear a case in which a person under the age of 18 violates federal law. ● In such a case, the federal court derives its jurisdictional power from 18 USCA §§ 5031 et seq. The Act severely limits the scope of federal-juvenile-delinquency jurisdiction because Congress recognizes that juvenile delinquency is essentially a state issue. The acts that typically invoke federal jurisdiction are (1) acts committed on federal lands (military bases, national parks, Indian reservations), and (2) acts that violate federal drug laws or other federal criminal statutes.

federal-question jurisdiction. (1941) The exercise of federal-court power over claims arising under the U.S. Constitution, an act of Congress, or a treaty. 28 USCA § 1331.

foreign jurisdiction. (16c) **1.** The powers of a court of a sister state or foreign country. **2.** Extraterritorial process, such as long-arm service of process.

general jurisdiction. (16c) **1.** A court's authority to hear a wide range of cases, civil or criminal, that arise within its geographic area. **2.** A court's authority to hear all claims against a defendant, at the place of the defendant's domicile or the place of service, without any showing that a connection exists between the claims and the forum state. Cf. *limited jurisdiction; specific jurisdiction.*

general personal jurisdiction. Jurisdiction arising when a person's continuous and systematic contacts with a forum state enable the forum state's courts to adjudicate a claim against the person, even when the claim is not related to the person's contacts with the forum state. Cf. *personal jurisdiction; specific personal jurisdiction.*

home-state jurisdiction. *Family law.* In interstate child-custody disputes governed by the Uniform Child Custody Jurisdiction and Enforcement Act, jurisdiction based on the child's having been a resident of the state for at least six consecutive months immediately before the commencement of the suit. See HOME STATE.

in personam jurisdiction. See *personal jurisdiction.*

in rem jurisdiction (in **rem**). (1930) A court's power to adjudicate the rights to a given piece of property, including the power to seize and hold it. — Also termed *jurisdiction in rem.* See IN REM. Cf. *personal jurisdiction; subject-matter jurisdiction.*

international jurisdiction. A court's power to hear and determine matters between different countries or persons of different countries.

judicial jurisdiction. The legal power and authority of a court to make a decision that binds the parties to any matter properly brought before it.

jurisdiction in personam. See *personal jurisdiction.*

jurisdiction in rem. See *in rem jurisdiction.*

jurisdiction loci. See *spatial jurisdiction.*

jurisdiction of the person. See *personal jurisdiction.*

jurisdiction over the person. See *personal jurisdiction.*

jurisdiction quasi in rem. See *quasi-in-rem jurisdiction.*

jurisdiction ratione materiae. See *subject-matter jurisdiction.*

jurisdiction ratione personae. See *personal jurisdiction.*

jurisdiction ratione temporis. See *temporal jurisdiction.*

legislative jurisdiction. A legislature's general sphere of authority to enact laws and conduct all business related to that authority, such as holding hearings.

limited jurisdiction. (16c) Jurisdiction that is confined to a particular type of case or that may be exercised only under statutory limits and prescriptions. — Also termed *special jurisdiction.* Cf. *general jurisdiction.*

long-arm jurisdiction. Jurisdiction over a nonresident defendant who has had some contact with the jurisdiction in which the petition is filed.

original jurisdiction. (17c) A court's power to hear and decide a matter before any other court can review the matter. Cf. *appellate jurisdiction.*

overlapping jurisdiction. See *concurrent jurisdiction.*

pendent jurisdiction (pen-dənt). (1942) A court's jurisdiction to hear and determine a claim over which it would not otherwise have jurisdiction, because the claim arises from the same transaction or occurrence as another claim that is properly before the court. • For example, if a plaintiff brings suit in federal court claiming that the defendant, in one transaction, violated both a federal and a state law, the federal court has jurisdiction over the federal claim (under federal-question jurisdiction) and also has jurisdiction over the state claim that is pendent to the federal claim. Pendent jurisdiction has now been codified as supplemental jurisdiction. 28 USCA § 1367. — Also termed *pendent-claim jurisdiction.* See *supplemental jurisdiction.* Cf. *ancillary jurisdiction.*

pendent-party jurisdiction. (1973) A court's jurisdiction to adjudicate a claim against a party who is not otherwise subject to the court's jurisdiction, because the claim by or against that party arises from the same transaction or occurrence as another claim that is properly before the court. • Pendent-party jurisdiction has been a hotly debated subject, and was severely limited by the U.S. Supreme Court in *Finley v. United States,* 490 U.S. 545, 109 S.Ct. 2003 (1990). The concept is now codified in the supplemental-jurisdiction statute, and it applies to federal-question cases but not to diversity-jurisdiction cases. 28 USCA § 1367. Neither pendent-party jurisdiction nor supplemental jurisdiction may be used to circumvent the complete-diversity requirement in cases founded on diversity jurisdiction. See *supplemental jurisdiction.*

personal jurisdiction. A court's power to bring a person into its adjudicative process; jurisdiction over a defendant's personal rights, rather than merely over property interests. — Also termed *in personam jurisdiction; jurisdiction in personam; jurisdiction of the person; jurisdiction over the person; jurisdiction ratione personae.* See IN PERSONAM. Cf. *in rem jurisdiction; general personal jurisdiction; specific personal jurisdiction.*

plenary jurisdiction (**plee**-nə-ree *or* **plen**-ə-ree). A court's full and absolute power over the subject matter and the parties in a case.

primary jurisdiction. The power of an agency to decide an issue in the first instance when a court, having concurrent jurisdiction with the agency, determines that it would be more pragmatic for the agency to handle the case initially. See PRIMARY-JURISDICTION DOCTRINE.

probate jurisdiction. Jurisdiction over matters relating to wills, settlement of decedents' estates, and (in some states) guardianship and the adoption of minors.

prorogated jurisdiction. Civil law. Jurisdiction conferred by the express consent of all the parties on a judge who would otherwise be disqualified. Cf. *tacit prorogation* under PROROGATION.

quasi-in-rem jurisdiction (**kway**-si in **rem** *or* **kway**-zi). (1918) Jurisdiction over a person but based on that person's interest in property located within the court's territory. — Also termed *jurisdiction quasi in rem.* See *quasi in rem* under IN REM.

significant-connection jurisdiction. Family law. In a child-custody matter, jurisdiction based on (1) the best interests of the child, (2) at least one parent's (or litigant's) significant connection to the state, and (3) the presence in the state of substantial evidence about the child's present or future care, protection, training, and personal relationships. • This type of jurisdiction is conferred by both the Uniform Child Custody Jurisdiction Act and the Parental Kidnapping Prevention Act. Generally, the home state will also be the state with significant connections and substantial evidence. Jurisdiction based on a significant connection or substantial evidence alone is conferred only when the child has no home state. — Also termed *significant-connection/substantial-evidence jurisdiction; significant connection-substantial evidence jurisdiction; substantial-evidence jurisdiction.* See HOME STATE.

spatial jurisdiction. Jurisdiction based on the physical territory that an entity's authority covers. — Also termed *jurisdiction loci.*

special jurisdiction. See *limited jurisdiction.*

specific jurisdiction. (1828) Jurisdiction that stems from the defendant's having certain minimum contacts with the forum state so that the court may hear a case whose issues arise from those minimum contacts. Cf. *general jurisdiction.*

specific personal jurisdiction. Jurisdiction based on a person's minimum contacts with the forum state when the claim arises out of or is related to those contacts. See MINIMUM CONTACTS. Cf. *personal jurisdiction; general personal jurisdiction.*

state jurisdiction. **1.** The exercise of state-court authority. **2.** A court's power to hear all matters, both civil and criminal, arising within its territorial boundaries.

status-offense jurisdiction. The power of the court to hear matters regarding noncriminal conduct committed by a juvenile. See *status offense* under OFFENSE (1). Cf. *delinquency jurisdiction.*

subject-matter jurisdiction. (1936) Jurisdiction over the nature of the case and the type of relief sought; the extent to which a court can rule on the conduct of persons or the status of things. — Also termed *jurisdiction of the subject matter; jurisdiction of the cause; jurisdiction over the action; jurisdiction ratione materiae.* Cf. *personal jurisdiction.*

summary jurisdiction. (18c) **1.** A court's jurisdiction in a summary proceeding. **2.** The court's authority to issue a judgment or order (such as a finding of contempt) without the necessity of a trial or other process. **3.** *English law.* A court's power to make an order immediately, without obtaining authority or referral, as in a magistrate's power to dispose of a criminal case without referring it to the Crown Court for a formal trial or without drawing a jury.

supplemental jurisdiction. (1836) Jurisdiction over a claim that is part of the same case or controversy as another claim over which the court has original jurisdiction. • Since 1990, federal district courts have had supplemental jurisdiction which includes jurisdiction over both ancillary and pendent claims. 28 USCA § 1367. See *ancillary jurisdiction; pendent jurisdiction.*

temporal jurisdiction. Jurisdiction based on the court's having authority to adjudicate a matter when the underlying event occurred. — Also termed *jurisdiction ratione temporis.*

territorial jurisdiction. **1.** Jurisdiction over cases arising in or involving persons residing within a defined territory. **2.** Territory over which a government, one of its courts, or one of its subdivisions has jurisdiction.

transient jurisdiction (**tran**-shənt). Personal jurisdiction over a defendant who is served with process while in the forum state only temporarily (such as during travel).

voluntary jurisdiction. **1.** Jurisdiction exercised over unopposed matters. **2.** *Eccles. law.* Jurisdiction that does not require a judicial proceeding, as with granting a license or installing a nominee to a benefice.

jurisdictional amount. See AMOUNT IN CONTRO-VERSY.

jurisdictional discovery. See DISCOVERY.

jurisdictional fact. See FACT.

jurisdictional-fact doctrine. *Administrative law.* The principle that if evidence is presented challenging the factual findings that triggered an agency's action, then a court will review the facts to determine whether the agency had authority to act in the first place. • This doctrine is generally no longer applied. Cf. CONSTITUTIONAL-FACT DOCTRINE.

jurisdictional gerrymandering. See GERRYMAN-DERING (2).

jurisdictional limits. (1800) The geographic boundaries or the constitutional or statutory limits within which a court's authority may be exercised.

jurisdiction *loci.* See *spatial jurisdiction* under JU-RISDICTION.

jurisdictional plea. See PLEA (3).

jurisdictional statement. See JURISDICTION CLAUSE (1).

jurisdictional strike. See STRIKE.

jurisdiction clause. (1861) **1.** At law, a statement in a pleading that sets forth the court's jurisdiction to act in the case. — Also termed *jurisdictional statement.* **2.** *Equity practice.* The part of the bill intended to show that the court has jurisdiction, usu. by an averment that adequate relief is unavailable outside equitable channels.

jurisdiction in personam. See *personal jurisdiction* under JURISDICTION.

jurisdiction in rem. See *in rem jurisdiction* under JURISDICTION.

jurisdiction of the cause. See *subject-matter jurisdiction* under JURISDICTION.

jurisdiction of the person. See *personal jurisdiction* under JURISDICTION.

jurisdiction of the subject matter. See *subject-matter jurisdiction* under JURISDICTION.

jurisdiction over the action. See *subject-matter jurisdiction* under JURISDICTION.

jurisdiction over the person. See *personal jurisdiction* under JURISDICTION.

jurisdiction quasi in rem. See *quasi-in-rem jurisdiction* under JURISDICTION.

jurisdiction *ratione materiae.* See *subject-matter jurisdiction* under JURISDICTION.

jurisdiction *ratione personae.* See *personal jurisdiction* under JURISDICTION.

jurisdiction *ratione temporis.* See *temporal jurisdiction* under JURISDICTION.

Juris Doctor (joor-is **dok**-tər). (1895) Doctor of law — the law degree most commonly conferred by an American law school. — Abbr. J.D. — Also termed *Doctor of Jurisprudence; Doctor of Law.* Cf. MASTER OF LAWS; LL.B.; LL.D.; DOCTOR OF LAWS.

jurisprude (**joor**-is-prood), *n.* (1937) **1.** A person who makes a pretentious display of legal knowledge or who is overzealous about the importance of legal doctrine. **2.** JURISPRUDENT.

jurisprudence (joor-is-**prood**-ənts), *n.* (17c) **1.** Originally (in the 18th century), the study of the first principles of the law of nature, the civil law, and the law of nations. — Also termed *jurisprudentia naturalis* (joor-is-proo-**den**-shee-ə nach-ə-**ray**-lis). **2.** More modernly, the study of the general or fundamental elements of a particular legal system, as opposed to its practical and concrete details. **3.** The study of legal systems in general. **4.** Judicial precedents considered collectively. **5.** In German literature, the whole of legal knowledge. **6.** A system, body, or division of law. **7.** CASELAW.

analytical jurisprudence. (1876) A method of legal study that concentrates on the logical structure of law, the meanings and uses of its concepts, and the formal terms and the modes of its operation.

censorial jurisprudence. See LAW REFORM.

comparative jurisprudence. See COMPARATIVE LAW.

equity jurisprudence. (1826) **1.** The legal science treating the rules, principles, and maxims that govern the decisions of a court of equity. **2.** The cases and controversies that are considered proper subjects of equity. **3.** The nature and form of the remedies that equity grants.

ethical jurisprudence. (1826) The branch of legal philosophy concerned with the law from the viewpoint of its ethical significance and adequacy. • This area of study brings together moral and legal philosophy. — Also termed (in German) *Rechtsphilosophie*; (in French) *philosophie du droit.*

expository jurisprudence. (18c) The scholarly exposition of the contents of an actual legal system as it now exists or once existed. — Also termed *systematic jurisprudence.*

feminist jurisprudence. (1978) A branch of jurisprudence that examines the relationship between women and law, including the history of legal and social biases against women, the elimination of those biases in modern law, and the enhancement of women's legal rights and recognition in society.

general jurisprudence. (18c) **1.** The scholarly study of the fundamental elements of a given legal system. — Also termed *jurisprudentia* *generalis.* **2.** The scholarly study of the law, legal theory, and legal systems generally. — Also termed *jurisprudentia universalis*; *philosophy of law*; *legal philosophy.*

historical jurisprudence. (1823) The branch of legal philosophy concerned with the history of the first principles and conceptions of a legal system, dealing with (1) the general principles governing the origin and development of law, and (2) the origin and development of the legal system's first principles.

jurisprudence constante (kən-**stan**-tee). *Civil law.* The doctrine that a court should give great weight to a rule of law that is accepted and applied in a long line of cases, and should not overrule or modify its own decisions unless clear error is shown and injustice will arise from continuation of a particular rule of law. ● Civil-law courts are not bound by the common-law doctrine of stare decisis. But they do recognize the doctrine of *jurisprudence constante*, which is similar to stare decisis, one exception being that *jurisprudence constante* does not command strict adherence to a legal principle applied on one occasion in the past. Cf. STARE DECISIS.

jurisprudence of conceptions. (1908) The extension of a maxim or definition, usu. to a logical extreme, with relentless disregard for the consequences. ● The phrase appears to have been invented by Roscoe Pound. See *Mechanical Jurisprudence*, 8 Colum. L. Rev. 605, 608 (1908).

normative jurisprudence. See NATURAL LAW (2).

particular jurisprudence. (18c) The scholarly study of the legal system within a particular jurisdiction, the focus being on the fundamental assumptions of that system only.

positivist jurisprudence. (1931) A theory that denies validity to any law that is not derived from or sanctioned by a sovereign or some other determinate source. — Also termed *positivistic jurisprudence.*

sociological jurisprudence. (1907) A philosophical approach to law stressing the actual social effects of legal institutions, doctrines, and practices. ● This influential approach was started by Roscoe Pound in 1906 and became a precursor to legal realism. — Also termed *sociology of law.* See LEGAL REALISM.

systematic jurisprudence. See *expository jurisprudence.*

therapeutic jurisprudence. The study of the effects of law and the legal system on the behavior, emotions, and mental health of people; esp., a multidisciplinary examination of how law and mental health interact. ● This discipline originated in the late 1980s as an academic approach to mental-health law.

jurisprudent, *n.* (17c) A person learned in the law; a specialist in jurisprudence. — Also termed *jurisprude.*

jurisprudentia generalis. See *general jurisprudence* (1) under JURISPRUDENCE.

jurisprudential (joor-is-proo-**den**-shəl), *adj.* Of or relating to jurisprudence.

jurisprudentia naturalis. See JURISPRUDENCE (1).

jurisprudentia universalis. See *general jurisprudence* (2) under JURISPRUDENCE.

jurist. (15c) **1.** A person who has thorough knowledge of the law; esp., a judge or an eminent legal scholar. — Also termed *legist.* **2.** JURISPRUDENT.

juristic, *adj.* (1831) **1.** Of or relating to a jurist <juristic literature>. **2.** Of or relating to law <a corporation is a typical example of a juristic person>. — Also termed *juristical.*

juristic act. See *act in the law* under ACT.

juristic person. See *artificial person* under PERSON (3).

Juris utriusque Doctor. See J.U.D.

juror (**joor**-ər *also* **joor**-or). (14c) A person serving on a jury panel. — Also formerly termed *layperson.*

grand juror. A person serving on a grand jury.

petit juror (**pet**-ee). A trial juror, as opposed to a grand juror.

presiding juror. The juror who chairs the jury during deliberations and speaks for the jury in court by announcing the verdict. ● The presiding juror is usu. elected by the jury at the start of deliberations. — Also termed *foreman*; *foreperson*; (in Scots law) *jury chancellor.*

stealth juror. A juror, esp. one in a high-profile case, who deliberately fails to disclose a relevant bias in order to qualify as a juror and bases a decision on that bias rather than on the facts and law. ● Although a stealth juror may be fined or prosecuted for perjury based on a lie or omission, the usual penalty is only removal from the jury.

tales-juror (**tay**-leez- *or* **taylz**-joor-ər). See TALESMAN.

juror misconduct. See MISCONDUCT.

jury, *n.* (15c) A group of persons selected according to law and given the power to decide questions of fact and return a verdict in the case submitted to them. ● In certain contexts, *jury* embraces any fact-trier, including an arbitrator or a trial judge sitting in a nonjury proceeding. — Also termed *empaneled jury*; *impaneled jury.*

advisory jury. (1892) A jury empaneled to hear a case when the parties have no right to a jury trial. *See* Fed. R. Civ. P. 39(c). ● The judge may accept or reject the advisory jury's verdict.

blue-ribbon jury. (1940) A jury consisting of jurors who are selected for their special qualities, such as advanced education or special training, sometimes used in a complex civil case (usu. by stipulation of the parties) and sometimes also for a grand jury (esp. one investigating governmental corruption). ● A blue-ribbon jury is not allowed in criminal trials because it would violate the defendant's right to trial by a jury of peers. An even more elite group of jurors, involving specialists in a technical field, is called a *blue-blue-ribbon jury*.

common jury. See *petit jury.*

coroner's jury. (17c) A jury summoned by a coroner to investigate the cause of death.

deadlocked jury. See *hung jury.*

death-qualified jury. *Criminal law.* A jury that is fit to decide a case involving the death penalty because the jurors have no absolute ideological bias against capital punishment. Cf. *life-qualified jury.*

fair and impartial jury. See *impartial jury.*

foreign jury. A jury obtained from a jurisdiction other than that in which the case is brought.

good jury. See *special jury.*

grand jury. See GRAND JURY.

homage jury. *Hist.* A jury in a court baron, consisting of tenants who made homage to the lord. See COURT BARON.

hung jury. (1854) A jury that cannot reach a verdict by the required voting margin. — Also termed *deadlocked jury.*

impartial jury. (17c) A jury that has no opinion about the case at the start of the trial and that bases its verdict on competent legal evidence. — Also termed *fair and impartial jury.*

inquest jury. (1873) A jury summoned from a particular district to appear before a sheriff, coroner, or other ministerial officer and inquire about the facts concerning a death. See INQUEST. — Also termed *jury of inquest.*

jury of indictment. See GRAND JURY.

jury of inquest. See *inquest jury.*

jury of matrons. *Hist.* A jury of "discreet and lawful women" impaneled to try a question of pregnancy, as when a woman sentenced to death pleads, in stay of execution, that she is pregnant.

jury of the vicinage (vis-ə-nij). **1.** At common law, a jury from the county where the crime

occurred. **2.** A jury from the county where the court is held. See VICINAGE.

life-qualified jury. *Criminal law.* In a case involving a capital crime, a jury selected from a venire from which the judge has excluded anyone unable or unwilling to consider a sentence of life imprisonment, instead of the death penalty, if the defendant is found guilty. Cf. *death-qualified jury.*

mixed jury. (1878) A jury composed of both men and women or persons of different races.

petit jury (pet-ee). (15c) A jury (usu. consisting of 6 or 12 persons) summoned and empaneled in the trial of a specific case. — Also termed *petty jury*; *trial jury*; *common jury*; *traverse jury.* Cf. GRAND JURY.

police jury. See POLICE JURY.

presenting jury. See GRAND JURY.

rogue jury. A jury that ignores the law and evidence in reaching a capricious verdict. ● Rogue juries include those that base their verdicts on unrevealed, deeply held prejudices; on undue sympathy or antipathy toward a party; or on chance (as by tossing a coin). The verdicts often result in inappropriate awards, punishments, convictions, or acquittals. Unlike jury nullification, a rogue jury's verdict is not based on a desire to achieve a just, fair, or moral outcome. Cf. JURY NULLIFICATION.

shadow jury. (1974) A group of mock jurors paid to observe a trial and report their reactions to a jury consultant hired by one of the litigants. ● The shadow jurors, who are matched as closely as possible to the real jurors, provide counsel with information about the jury's likely reactions to the trial. — Also termed *phantom jury.*

sheriff's jury. *Hist.* A jury selected and summoned by a sheriff to hold inquests for various purposes, such as assessing damages in an action in which the defendant makes no defense or ascertaining the mental condition of an alleged lunatic.

special jury. (17c) **1.** A jury chosen from a panel that is drawn specifically for that case. ● Such a jury is usu. empaneled at a party's request in an unusually important or complicated case. — Also termed *struck jury.* See STRIKING A JURY. **2.** At common law, a jury composed of persons above the rank of ordinary freeholders, usu. summoned to try more important questions than those heard by ordinary juries. — Also termed *good jury.*

struck jury. (18c) **1.** A jury selected by allowing the parties to alternate in striking from a list any person whom a given party does not wish to have on the jury, until the number is reduced to the appropriate number (traditionally 12). See STRIKING A JURY. **2.** See *special jury* (1).

traverse jury. See *petit jury.*

trial jury. See *petit jury.*

jury box. The enclosed part of a courtroom where the jury sits. — Also spelled *jury-box.*

jury challenge. See CHALLENGE (2).

jury chancellor. See *presiding juror* under JUROR.

jury charge. (1883) **1.** JURY INSTRUCTION. **2.** A set of jury instructions. — Often shortened to *charge.*

jury commissioner. See COMMISSIONER.

jury direction. See JURY INSTRUCTION.

jury duty. (1829) **1.** The obligation to serve on a jury. **2.** Actual service on a jury. — Also termed *jury service.*

jury fee. See FEE (1).

jury-fixing. (1887) The act or an instance of illegally procuring the cooperation of one or more jurors who actually influence the outcome of the trial. — Also termed *fixing a jury.* Cf. EMBRACERY; JURY-PACKING. — **jury-fixer,** *n.*

jury instruction. (*usu. pl.*) (1943) A direction or guideline that a judge gives a jury concerning the law of the case. — Often shortened to *instruction.* — Also termed *jury charge; charge; jury direction; direction.*

   additional instruction. (1821) A jury charge, beyond the original instructions, that is usu. given in response to the jury's question about the evidence or some point of law. — Also termed *further instruction.*

   affirmative converse instruction. (1966) An instruction presenting a hypothetical that, if true, commands a verdict in favor of the defendant. ● An affirmative converse instruction usu. begins with language such as "your verdict must be for the defendant if you believe . . . ."

   affirmative instruction. (1835) An instruction that removes an issue from the jury's consideration, such as an instruction that whatever the evidence, the defendant cannot be convicted under the indictment count to which the charge is directed. — Also termed *affirmative charge.*

   argumentative instruction. (1888) An instruction that assumes facts not in evidence, that singles out or unduly emphasizes a particular issue, theory, or defense, or that otherwise invades the jury's province regarding the weight, probative value, or sufficiency of the evidence.

   binding instruction. See *mandatory instruction.*

   cautionary instruction. (1881) **1.** A judge's instruction to the jurors to disregard certain evidence or consider it for specific purposes only. **2.** A judge's instruction for the jury not to be influenced by outside factors and not to talk to anyone about the case while the trial is in progress.

   conscious-avoidance instruction. See *willful-blindness instruction.*

   curative instruction. (1890) A judge's instruction that is intended to correct an erroneous instruction.

   deliberate-indifference instruction. See JEWELL INSTRUCTION.

   disparaging instruction. A jury charge that discredits or defames a party to a lawsuit.

   formula instruction. (1927) A jury charge derived from a standardized statement of the law on which the jury must base its verdict.

   further instruction. See *additional instruction.*

   general instruction. Any jury instruction that does not present a question or issue to be answered.

   Jewell instruction. See JEWELL INSTRUCTION.

   mandatory instruction. (1895) An instruction requiring a jury to find for one party and against the other if the jury determines that, based on a preponderance of the evidence, a given set of facts exists. — Also termed *binding instruction.*

   model jury instruction. (1964) A form jury charge usu. approved by a state bar association or similar group regarding matters arising in a typical case. ● Courts usu. accept model jury instructions as authoritative. — Also termed *pattern jury instruction; pattern jury charge; model jury charge.*

   ostrich instruction. (1966) *Criminal procedure. Slang.* An instruction stating that a defendant who deliberately avoided acquiring actual knowledge can be found to have acted knowingly. Cf. JEWELL INSTRUCTION.

   pattern jury instruction. See *model jury instruction.*

   peremptory instruction. (1829) A court's explicit direction that a jury must obey, such as an instruction to return a verdict for a particular party. See *directed verdict* under VERDICT.

   single-juror instruction. (1980) An instruction stating that if any juror is not reasonably satisfied with the plaintiff's evidence, then the jury cannot render a verdict for the plaintiff.

   special instruction. (1807) An instruction on some particular point or question involved in the case, usu. in response to counsel's request for such an instruction. — Also termed *special charge.*

   standard instruction. (1914) A jury instruction that has been regularly used in a given jurisdiction.

willful-blindness instruction. An instruction that an otherwise culpable defendant may be held accountable for a crime if the defendant deliberately avoided finding out about the crime. — Also termed *conscious-avoidance instruction.*

jury list. A list of persons who may be summoned to serve as jurors.

jury nullification. (1982) A jury's knowing and deliberate rejection of the evidence or refusal to apply the law either because the jury wants to send a message about some social issue that is larger than the case itself or because the result dictated by law is contrary to the jury's sense of justice, morality, or fairness. Cf. *verdict contrary to law* under VERDICT; *rogue jury* under JURY.

jury of indictment. See GRAND JURY.

jury-packing. (1887) The act or an instance of contriving to have a jury composed of persons who are predisposed toward one side or the other. — Also termed *packing a jury.* Cf. EMBRACERY; JURY-FIXING.

jury panel. See VENIRE (1).

jury pardon. (1974) A rule that permits a jury to convict a defendant of a lesser offense than the offense charged if sufficient evidence exists to convict the defendant of either offense.

jury pool. See VENIRE (1).

jury process. (18c) **1.** The procedure by which jurors are summoned and their attendance is enforced. **2.** The papers served on or mailed to potential jurors to compel their attendance.

jury question. (18c) **1.** An issue of fact that a jury decides. See QUESTION OF FACT. **2.** A special question that a court may ask a jury that will deliver a special verdict. See *special interrogatory* under INTERROGATORY.

jury sequestration. See SEQUESTRATION (8).

jury service. See JURY DUTY.

jury shuffle. *Texas law.* A process for rearranging a venire whereby the cards with the veniremembers' names on them are shuffled so that the veniremembers will be seated in a different order. • The prosecution and the defense may each request a jury shuffle once before voir dire begins. No reason for the request need be given. After voir dire begins, neither party may request a shuffle.

jury summation. See CLOSING ARGUMENT.

jury-tampering. See EMBRACERY.

jury trial. See TRIAL.

jury waiver. See WAIVER (2).

jury wheel. (1873) A physical device or electronic system used for storing and randomly selecting names of potential jurors.

jus (jəs *also* joos *or* yoos), *n.* [Latin "law, right"] **1.** Law in the abstract. **2.** A system of law. **3.** A legal right, power, or principle. **4.** *Roman law.* Manmade law. • The term usu. refers to a right rather than a statute. — Abbr. J. — Also spelled *ius.* Pl. *jura* (**joor**-ə *also* **yoor**-ə).

jus abstinendi (jəs ab-stə-**nen**-dɪ), *n.* [Law Latin "right of abstaining"] *Roman & civil law.* The right of an heir to renounce or decline an inheritance, as when it would require taking on debt.

jus abutendi (jəs ab-yə-**ten**-dɪ), *n.* [Latin "right of abusing"] *Roman & civil law.* The right to make full use of property, even to the extent of wasting or destroying it.

jus accrescendi (jəs ak-rə-**sen**-dɪ), *n.* [Latin "right of accretion"] A right of accrual; esp., the right of survivorship that a joint tenant enjoys. See RIGHT OF SURVIVORSHIP.

jus ad rem (jəs ad rem), *n.* [Law Latin "right to a thing"] A right in specific property arising from another person's duty and valid only against that person; an inchoate or incomplete right to a thing. Cf. JUS IN RE.

jus aedilium (jəs ee-**dil**-ee-əm). [Latin "law of the aediles"] *Roman law.* The body of law developed through the edicts of aediles. — Also termed *jus aedilicium* (jəs ee-dɪ-**lish**-ee-əm). See AEDILE; JUS HONORARIUM.

jus aesneciae (jəs ees-**neesh**-ee-ee). [Latin] *Hist.* The right of primogeniture. — Also spelled *esneciae.*

jus albanagii (jəs al-bə-**nay**-jee-ɪ), *n.* [Law Latin "confiscating the goods of aliens"].

jus albinatus (jəs al-bi-**nay**-təs), *n.* [Law Latin "right of alien confiscation"] See DROIT D'AUBAINE.

jus angariae (jəs ang-**gair**-ee-ee), *n.* [Latin "right of angary"] See ANGARY.

jus aquaeductus (jəs ak-wə-**dək**-təs), *n.* [Latin] *Roman & civil law.* A servitude that gives a landowner the right to conduct water from another's land through pipes or channels.

jus banci (jəs **ban**-sɪ), *n.* [Law Latin "right of bench"] *Hist.* The right or privilege of having an elevated and separate seat of judgment, formerly allowed only to the king's judges, who administered what was from then on called "high justice."

jus belli (jəs **bel**-ɪ), *n.* [Latin "law of war"] The law of nations as applied during wartime, defining in particular the rights and duties of the belligerent powers and of neutral nations.

jus bellum dicendi (jəs **bel**-əm di-**sen**-dɪ), *n.* [Latin] The right of proclaiming war.

jus canonicum (jəs kə-**non**-i-kəm), *n.* [Law Latin] See CANON LAW (1).

jus capiendi (jəs kap-ee-**en**-dɪ). [Latin "the right to take or receive"] *Roman law.* The right of taking property under a will.

jus cloacae (jəs kloh-**ay**-see), *n.* [Latin "right of sewer or drain"] *Civil law.* An easement consisting in the right of having a sewer or conducting surface water over or through the land of one's neighbor.

jus cogens (jəs **koh**-jenz), *n.* [Latin "compelling law"] **1.** *Int'l law.* A mandatory or peremptory norm of general international law accepted and recognized by the international community as a norm from which no derogation is permitted. • A peremptory norm can be modified only by a later norm that has the same character. Cf. JUS DISPOSITIVUM. **2.** *Civil law.* A mandatory rule of law that is not subject to the disposition of the parties, such as an absolute limitation on the legal capacity of minors below a certain age. — Also termed (in sense 2) *peremptory norm.*

jus commercii (jəs kə-**mər**-shee-ɪ), *n.* [Latin "right of commerce"] *Roman & civil law.* The right to make contracts, acquire and transfer property, and conduct business transactions.

jus commune (jəs kə-**myoo**-nee), *n.* **1.** *Roman & civil law.* The common or public law or right, as opposed to a law or right established for special purposes. Cf. JUS SINGULARE. **2.** The common law of England. See COMMON LAW (3). **3.** The shared law of much of continental Western Europe during the Middle Ages, consisting of a blend of canon law and rediscovered Roman law.

jus connubii (jəs kə-**n[y]oo**-bee-ɪ), *n.* [Latin "right of marriage"] See CONUBIUM.

jus coronae (jəs kə-**roh**-nee), *n.* [Latin "right of the Crown"] The right of succession to the English throne.

jus crediti (jəs **kred**-i-tɪ). [Latin "the right of credit"] *Roman & Scots law.* A creditor's right to a debt; a creditor's right to recover a debt through legal process.

jus dare (jəs **dair**-ee), *vb.* [Latin] To give or make the law. • This is the function and prerogative of the legislature. Cf. JUS DICERE.

jus deliberandi (jəs di-lib-ə-**ran**-dɪ), *n.* [Latin "right of deliberating"] *Roman & civil law.* A right granted to an heir to take time to consider whether to accept or reject an inheritance.

jus de non appellando (jəs dee non ap-ə-**lan**-doh). [Latin] *Hist.* The supreme judicial power.

jus dicere (jəs **dɪ**-sər-ee), *vb.* [Latin] *Hist.* To declare or decide the law. • This is the function and prerogative of the judiciary. Cf. JUS DARE.

jus disponendi (jəs dis-pə-**nen**-dɪ), *n.* [Latin "right of disposing"] The right to dispose of property; the power of alienation.

jus dispositivum (jəs dis-poz-ə-**tɪ**-vəm), *n.* [Latin "law subject to the disposition of the parties"] *Int'l law.* A norm that is created by the consent of participating nations, as by an international agreement, and is binding only on the nations that agree to be bound by it. Cf. JUS COGENS (1).

jus distrahendi (jəs dis-trə-**hen**-dɪ), *n.* [Latin "right of distraining"] The right to sell pledged goods upon default.

jus dividendi (jəs div-i-**den**-dɪ), *n.* [Latin "right of dividing"] The right to dispose of real property by will.

jus divinum (jəs di-**vɪ**-nəm). **1.** See DIVINE LAW. **2.** See NATURAL LAW.

jus ecclesiasticum (jəs e-klee-z[h]ee-**as**-ti-kəm). [Law Latin] See ECCLESIASTICAL LAW.

jus et norma loquendi (jəs et **nor**-mə loh-**kwen**-dɪ). [Latin "the law and rule of speech"] Idiomatic language, including speech and pronunciation, as established by the custom of a particular nation.

jus ex non scripto (jəs eks non **skrip**-toh). See *unwritten law* under LAW.

jus fetiale (jəs fee-shee-**ay**-lee), *n.* [Latin] **1.** FETIAL LAW. **2.** The law of negotiation and diplomacy. • This phrase captured the classical notion of international law. — Also spelled *jus feciale.*

jus fiduciarium (jəs fi-d[y]oo-shee-**air**-əm), *n.* [Latin] *Civil law.* A right in trust. Cf. JUS LEGITIMUM.

jus fluminum (jəs **floo**-mə-nəm), *n.* [Latin] *Civil law.* The right to use rivers.

jus fodiendi (jəs foh-dee-**en**-dɪ), *n.* [Latin] *Civil law.* The right to dig on another's land.

jus fruendi (jəs froo-**en**-dɪ), *n.* [Latin "right of enjoying"] *Roman & civil law.* The right to use and enjoy another's property without damaging or diminishing it. See USUFRUCT.

jus futurum (jəs fyoo-t[y]**oor**-əm), *n.* [Latin "future right"] *Civil law.* A right that has not fully vested; an inchoate or expectant right.

jus gentium (jəs **jen**-shee-əm). [Latin "law of nations"] **1.** INTERNATIONAL LAW. **2.** *Roman law.* The body of law, taken to be common to all civilized peoples, and applied in dealing with the relations between Roman citizens and foreigners. — Also termed *jus inter gentes.*

jus gentium privatum (jəs **jen**-shee-əm prɪ-**vay**-təm). See *private international law* under INTERNATIONAL LAW.

jus gentium publicum (jəs **jen**-shee-əm **pəb**-li-kəm). See INTERNATIONAL LAW.

jus habendi (jəs hə-**ben**-dɪ), *n.* [Latin] *Civil law.* The right to have a thing; the right to be put in actual possession of property.

jus haereditatis (jəs hə-red-ə-**tay**-tis), *n.* [Latin] *Civil law.* The right of inheritance.

jus hauriendi (jəs haw-ree-**en**-dɪ), *n.* [Latin] *Civil law.* The right of drawing water.

jus immunitatis (jəs i-myoo-nə-**tay**-tis), *n.* [Latin "law of immunity"] *Civil law.* Exemption from the burden of public office.

jus incognitum (jəs in-**kog**-nə-təm), *n.* [Latin] *Civil law.* An unknown or obsolete law.

jus incorporale (jəs in-kor-pə-**ray**-lee). [Latin] *Hist.* An incorporeal right. See INCORPOREAL.

jus individuum (jəs in-də-**vij**-oo-əm), *n.* [Latin] An individual or indivisible right; a right that cannot be divided.

jus in personam (jəs in pər-**soh**-nəm), *n.* [Latin "right against a person"] A right of action against a particular person to enforce that person's obligation. — Also termed *jura in personam.* See *right in personam* under RIGHT.

jus in re (jəs in ree), *n.* [Law Latin "right in or over a thing"] A right in property valid against anyone in the world; a complete and perfect right to a thing. — Also termed *jus in rem; jura in rem.* Cf. JUS AD REM.

jus in re aliena (jəs in ree ay-lee-**ee**-nə *or* al-ee-), *n.* [Latin] An easement or right in or over another's property; ENCUMBRANCE. — Also termed *right in re aliena.*

jus in rem (jəs in rem), *n.* [Latin "right to a thing"] See JUS IN RE.

jus in re propria (jəs in ree **proh**-pree-ə), *n.* [Latin] The right of enjoyment that is incident to full ownership of property; full ownership itself. — Also termed *right in re propria.*

jus inter gentes (jəs **in**-tər **jen**-teez), *n.* [Latin "law among nations"] See JUS GENTIUM.

jusjurandum (jəs-juu-**ran**-dəm), *n.* [Latin] An oath. See JURAMENTUM.

jus legitimum (jəs lə-**jit**-ə-məm), *n.* [Latin] *Civil law.* A right enforceable in law. Cf. JUS FIDUCIARIUM.

jus liquidissimum (jəs lik-wi-**dis**-i-məm). [Latin] *Maritime law.* The principle that a salvager is entitled to a reward for saving life or property imperiled at sea.

jus merae facultatis (jəs **meer**-ee fak-əl-**tay**-tis). [Law Latin] *Hist.* A right of mere power; a right of power merely to act.

jus merum (jəs **meer**-əm). See MERE RIGHT.

jus moribus constitutum (jəs **mor**-ə-bəs kon-stə-t[y]**oo**-təm). [Latin] See *unwritten law* under LAW.

jus naturae (jəs nə-t[y]**oor**-ee). [Latin] See NATURAL LAW.

jus naturale (jəs nach-ə-**ray**-lee). [Latin] See NATURAL LAW.

jus navigandi (jəs nav-ə-**gan**-dɪ), *n.* [Latin] *Civil law.* The right of navigation; the right of commerce by sea.

jus necessitatis (jəs nə-ses-i-**tay**-tis), *n.* [Latin] A person's right to do what is required for which no threat of legal punishment is a dissuasion. • This idea implicates the proverb that necessity knows no law (*necessitas non habet legem*), so that an act that would be objectively understood as necessary is not wrongful even if done with full and deliberate intention.

jus nobilius (jəs noh-**bil**-ee-əs). [Law Latin] *Hist.* A superior right.

jus non scriptum (jəs non **skrip**-təm). See *unwritten law* under LAW.

jus obligationis (jəs ob-li-gay-shee-**oh**-nis). [Law Latin "a right of obligation"] *Hist.* A personal right. See JUS AD REM.

jus personarum (jəs pər-sə-**nair**-əm), *n.* [Latin "law of persons"] *Civil law.* The law governing the rights of persons having special relations with one another (such as parents and children or guardians and wards) or having limited rights (such as aliens or incompetent persons). See LAW OF PERSONS. Cf. JUS RERUM.

jus poenitendi (jəs pen-i-**ten**-dɪ), *n.* [Latin] The right to rescind or revoke an executory contract when the other party defaults.

jus portus (jəs **por**-təs), *n.* [Latin] *Civil & maritime law.* The right of port or harbor.

jus positivum (jəs poz-i-**tiv**-əm). See POSITIVE LAW.

jus possessionis (jəs pə-zes[h]-ee-**oh**-nis), *n.* [Latin] *Civil law.* A right of which possession is the source or title; a possessor's right to continue in possession. Cf. JUS PROPRIETATIS.

jus possidendi (jəs pos-ə-**den**-dɪ), *n.* [Latin] *Civil law.* A person's right to acquire or to retain possession; an owner's right to possess.

jus postliminii (jəs pohst-lə-**min**-ee-ɪ). [Latin] See POSTLIMINIUM.

jus praesens (jəs **pree**-senz *or* -zenz), *n.* [Latin "present right"] *Civil law.* A right that has been completely acquired; a vested right.

jus precarium (jəs pri-**kair**-ee-əm), *n.* [Latin] *Civil law.* A right to a thing held for another, for which there was no remedy by legal action but only by entreaty or request.

jus presentationis (jəs prez-ən-tay-shee-**oh**-nis), *n.* [Latin] *Civil law.* The right to present a clerk to a church.

jus primae noctis (jəs **prɪ**-mee **nok**-tis). [Latin "right of first night"].

jus privatum (jəs prɪ-**vay**-təm), *n.* [Latin "private law"] **1.** *Roman & civil law.* Private law, consisting of all the branches of law that regulate the relations of citizens to one another, including family law, property, obligations, and testate and intestate succession. **2.** The right, title, or dominion of private ownership. See PRIVATE LAW. Cf. JUS PUBLICUM.

jus projiciendi (jəs prə-jish-ee-**en**-dɪ), *n.* [Latin] *Civil law.* A servitude granting the right to build a projection (such as a balcony) from one's house in the open space belonging to a neighbor.

jus proprietatis (jəs prə-prɪ-ə-**tay**-tis), *n.* [Latin] *Civil law.* A right in property based on ownership rather than actual possession. Cf. JUS POSSESSIONIS.

jus protegendi (jəs proh-tə-**jen**-dɪ), *n.* [Latin] *Civil law.* A servitude granting the right to make the roof or tiling of one's house extend over a neighbor's house.

jus publicum (jəs **pəb**-li-kəm), *n.* [Latin "public law"] **1.** *Roman & civil law.* Public law, consisting of constitutional law, administrative law, criminal law and procedure, and the law relating to sacred rites (*jus sacrum*). **2.** The right, title, or dominion of public ownership; esp., the government's right to own real property in trust for the public benefit. See PUBLIC LAW. Cf. JUS PRIVATUM.

jus quaesitum (jəs kwi-**sɪ**-təm *or* -**zɪ**-təm), *n.* [Latin] *Civil law.* **1.** A right to ask or recover, as from one who is under an obligation. **2.** An acquired right.

jus quiritium (jəs kwi-**rɪ**-shee-əm). [Latin] *Roman law.* The ancient, primitive law of the Romans before the development of the *jus praetorium* and the *jus gentium*; the original *jus civile.*

jus recuperandi (jəs ri-k[y]oo-pə-**ran**-dɪ), *n.* [Latin] *Civil law.* The right of recovering, esp. lands.

jus regendi (jəs ri-**jen**-dɪ), *n.* [Law Latin] A proprietary right vested in a sovereign.

jus relictae (jəs ri-**lik**-tee), *n.* [Law Latin "right of a widow"] *Civil & Scots law.* A widow's claim to her share of her deceased husband's movable estate. • If the widow has children, her share is one-third; if not, her share is one-half.

jus relicti (jəs ri-**lik**-tɪ), *n.* [Law Latin "right of a widower"] *Civil & Scots law.* A widower's right in his deceased wife's separate movable estate, historically two-thirds if there were surviving children, and otherwise one-half. Under the Married Women's Property Act of 1881, the amount became one-third in the case of surviving children, and otherwise one-half.

jus repraesentationis (jəs rep-ri-zen-tay-shee-**oh**-nis), *n.* [Latin] *Civil law.* The right to represent or be represented by another.

jus rerum (jəs **reer**-əm), *n.* [Latin "law of things"] *Civil law.* The law regulating the rights and powers of persons over things, as how property is acquired, enjoyed, and transferred. See LAW OF THINGS. Cf. JUS PERSONARUM.

jus retentionis (jəs ri-ten-shee-**oh**-nis), *n.* [Latin] *Civil law.* The right to retain a thing until the delivery of something else that the person retaining the thing is entitled to.

jus retractus (jəs ri-**trak**-təs), *n.* [Latin "the right of retraction"] *Civil law.* **1.** The right of certain relatives of one who has sold immovable property to repurchase it. **2.** A debtor's right, upon sale of the debt by the creditor, to have a third person redeem it within a year for the price paid by the purchaser.

jus rusticorum praediorum. See *rural servitude* under SERVITUDE (2).

jus sanguinis (jəs **sang**-gwə-nis), *n.* [Latin "right of blood"] The rule that a child's citizenship is determined by the parents' citizenship. • Most nations follow this rule. Cf. JUS SOLI.

jus scriptum (jəs **skrip**-təm). [Latin] See *written law* under LAW.

jus sibi dicere (jəs **sib**-ɪ **dɪ**-sər-ee). [Latin] *Hist.* To declare the law for oneself; to take the law into one's own hand.

jus singulare (jəs sing-gyə-**lair**-ee), *n.* [Latin "individual law"] *Roman & civil law.* A law or right established for special purposes, as opposed to the common or public law or right. Cf. JUS COMMUNE (1).

jus soli (jəs **soh**-lɪ), *n.* [Latin "right of the soil"] The rule that a child's citizenship is determined by place of birth. • This is the U.S. rule, as affirmed by the 14th Amendment to the Constitution. Cf. JUS SANGUINIS.

jus spatiandi (jəs spay-shee-**an**-dɪ), *n.* [Latin "right of walking about"] *Civil law.* The public's right-of-way over specific land for purposes of recreation and instruction.

jus stapulae (jəs **stay**-pyə-lee), *n.* [Law Latin "right of staple"] *Civil law.* A town's right or privilege of stopping imported merchandise and forcing it to be offered for sale in its own market. See STAPLE.

jus suffragii (jəs sə-**fray**-jee-ɪ). [Latin] *Roman law.* The right of a citizen to vote.

just, *adj.* (14c) Legally right; lawful; equitable.

justa causa (jəs-tə **kaw**-zə), *n.* [Latin] *Civil law.* A just cause; a lawful ground. See *good cause* under CAUSE (2).

jus talionis. See LEX TALIONIS.

just-as-probable rule. *Workers' compensation.* A doctrine whereby a workers'-compensation claim will be denied if it is equally likely that the injury resulted from a non-work-related cause as from a work-related cause.

just cause. See *good cause* under CAUSE (2).

just compensation. See COMPENSATION.

Just Compensation Clause. See TAKINGS CLAUSE.

just deserts (di-**zərts**). (16c) What one really deserves; esp., the punishment that a person deserves for having committed a crime. — Also termed *deserts*.

jus tertii (jəs **tər**-shee-ı), *n*. [Latin] **1.** The right of a third party. **2.** The doctrine that, particularly in constitutional law, courts do not decide what they do not need to decide.

justice. (17c) **1.** The fair and proper administration of laws.

    commutative justice (kə-**myoo**-tə-tiv *or* **kom**-yə-tay-tiv). (1856) Justice concerned with the relations between persons and esp. with fairness in the exchange of goods and the fulfillment of contractual obligations.

    condign justice. An outcome according to what the litigants deserve; esp., justice based on the kind and degree of punishment that is appropriate for a given offense.

    distributive justice. (16c) Justice owed by a community to its members, including the fair allocation of common advantages and sharing of common burdens.

    Jedburgh justice (**jed**-bər-ə). A brand of justice involving punishment (esp. execution) first and trial afterwards. • The term alludes to Jedburgh, a Scottish border town where in the 17th century raiders were said to have been hanged without the formality of a trial. Jedburgh justice differs from lynch law in that the former was administered by an established court (albeit after the fact). — Also termed *Jeddart justice*; *Jedwood justice.* Cf. LIDFORD LAW; LYNCH LAW.

    justice in personam. See *personal justice.*

    justice in rem. See *social justice.*

    natural justice. Justice as defined in a moral, as opposed to a legal, sense. — Also termed *justitia naturalis.* Cf. NATURAL LAW.

    personal justice. (16c) Justice between parties to a dispute, regardless of any larger principles that might be involved. — Also termed *justice in personam*; *popular justice*; *social justice.*

    popular justice. (17c) Demotic justice, which is usu. considered less than fully fair and proper even though it satisfies prevailing public opinion in a particular case. Cf. *social justice.*

    positive justice. (17c) Justice as it is conceived, recognized, and incompletely expressed by the civil law or some other form of human law. Cf. POSITIVE LAW.

    preventive justice. Justice intended to protect against probable future misbehavior. • Specific types of preventive justice include appointing a receiver or administrator, issuing a restraining order or injunction, and binding over to keep the peace.

    social justice. (1902) **1.** Justice that conforms to a moral principle, such as that all people are equal. **2.** One or more equitable resolutions sought on behalf of individuals and communities who are disenfranchised, underrepresented, or otherwise excluded from meaningful participation in legal, economic, cultural, and social structures, with the ultimate goal of removing barriers to participation and effecting social change. — Also termed *justice in rem.* Cf. *personal justice*; CAUSE LAWYERING.

    substantial justice. (17c) Justice fairly administered according to rules of substantive law, regardless of any procedural errors not affecting the litigant's substantive rights; a fair trial on the merits.

2. A judge, esp. of an appellate court or a court of last resort. — Abbr. J. (and, in plural, JJ.)

    associate justice. (18c) An appellate-court justice other than the chief justice.

    chief justice. (15c) The presiding justice of an appellate court, usu. the highest appellate court in a jurisdiction and esp. the U.S. Supreme Court. — Abbr. C.J.

    circuit justice. (18c) **1.** A justice who sits on a circuit court. **2.** A U.S. Supreme Court justice who has jurisdiction over one or more of the federal circuits, with power to issue injunctions, grant bail, or stay execution in those circuits.

    circuit-riding justice. *Hist.* A U.S. Supreme Court justice who, under the Judiciary Act of 1789, was required to travel within a circuit to preside over trials. • In each of three circuits that then existed, two justices sat with one district judge. See CIRCUIT-RIDING.

3. *Hist.* Judicial cognizance of causes or offenses; jurisdiction.

    high justice. *Hist.* Jurisdiction over crimes of every kind, including high crimes.

    low justice. *Hist.* Jurisdiction over petty offenses.

justice-broker. *Archaic.* A judge who sells judicial decisions.

justice court. See COURT.

justice ejectment. See EJECTMENT.

justice in eyre (air). *Hist.* One of the itinerant judges who, in medieval times, investigated allegations of wrongdoing, tried cases, and levied fines. — Also termed *justicia errante*; *justiciar in itinere.* See EYRE.

justice of the peace. (15c) A local judicial officer having jurisdiction over minor criminal offenses and minor civil disputes, and authority to perform routine civil functions (such as administering oaths and performing marriage ceremonies). — Abbr. J.P. Cf. MAGISTRATE (3).

justice-of-the-peace court. See *justice court* under COURT.

justice of the quorum. 1. A judge on a panel designated to hear appeals. • In Massachusetts, the panel is sometimes called a *quorum*. **2.** *Hist.* A county justice or justice of the peace, designated by the governor in a commission of peace, who had to be present or else a court could not sit. **3.** *Hist.* A distinction conferred on a justice of the peace by directing — in the commission authorizing the holding of quarter sessions — that from among those holding court must be two or more specially so named. • The distinction was conferred on some, or occasionally all, of the justices of the peace of a county in England.

justicer, *n. Archaic.* One who administers justice; a judge.

justiceship. 1. The office or authority of a justice. **2.** The period of a justice's incumbency.

justice's warrant. See *peace warrant* under WARRANT (1).

justiciability (jə-stish-ee-ə-**bil**-ə-tee *or* jə-stish-ə-**bil**-ə-tee), *n.* (15c) The quality or state of being appropriate or suitable for adjudication by a court. See MOOTNESS DOCTRINE; RIPENESS. Cf. STANDING.

justiciable (jə-**stish**-ee-ə-bəl *or* jəs-**tish**-ə-bəl), *adj.* (Of a case or dispute) properly brought before a court of justice; capable of being disposed of judicially <a justiciable controversy>.

justicia errante. See JUSTICE IN EYRE.

justiciar (jə-**stish**-ee-ər), *n.* **1.** *Hist.* A royal judicial officer in medieval England; esp., a justice presiding over a superior court. **2.** JUSTICIARY (2). — Also spelled *justicier.*

justiciarii itinerantes (jəs-tish-ee-**air**-ee-ı ı-tin-ə-**ran**-teez), *n.* [Latin "itinerant justices"] Justices in eyre. See JUSTICE IN EYRE.

justiciar in itinere. See JUSTICE IN EYRE.

justiciary (jə-**stish**-ee-er-ee), *adj.* Of or relating to the administration of justice; pertaining to the law. See HIGH COURT OF JUSTICIARY.

justiciary (jə-**stish**-ee-er-ee), *n.* **1.** A justice or judge. **2.** *Hist.* The chief administrator of both government and justice. • From the time of the Norman Conquest in 1066 until the reign of Henry III (1216–1272), the justiciary presided in the King's Court and in the Exchequer, supervising all governmental departments and serving as regent in the king's absence. These functions were later divided among several officials such as the Lord Chancellor, the Chief Justice, and the Lord High Treasurer. — Also termed *justiciar; chief justiciar; capitalis justiciarius.* **3.** *Scots law.* The administration of justice, esp. of criminal law.

justicier. See JUSTICIAR.

justicies (jə-**stish**-ee-eez). *Hist.* A writ empowering the sheriff to allow certain debt cases in a county court. • The writ was so called because of the significant word in the writ's opening clause, which stated in Latin, "We command you that you do justice to [a person named]."

justicing room. *Hist.* A room in which cases are heard and justice is administered; esp., such a room in the house of a justice of the peace.

justifiable, *adj.* Capable of being legally or morally justified; excusable; defensible.

justifiable homicide. See HOMICIDE.

justifiable war. See BELLUM JUSTUM.

justification, *n.* (14c) **1.** A lawful or sufficient reason for one's acts or omissions; any fact that prevents an act from being wrongful. **2.** A showing, in court, of a sufficient reason why a defendant acted in a way that, in the absence of the reason, would constitute the offense with which the defendant is charged. • Under the Model Penal Code, the defendant must show that the harm or evil that resulted from taking the action was less than the harm or evil that the law creating the offense charged was seeking to prevent. Model Penal Code § 3.02. — Also termed *justification defense; necessity defense.* — See *lesser-evils defense* under DEFENSE (1). **3.** A surety's proof of having enough money or credit to provide security for the party for whom it is required. — **justify,** *vb.* — **justificatory** (jəs-**ti**-fi-kə-tor-ee), *adj.*

defensive-force justification. A justification defense available when an aggressor has threatened harm to the particular interest that is the subject of the defense — usu. to the actor (self-defense), to other persons (defense of others), or to property (defense of property).

imperfect justification. (1853) A reason or cause that is insufficient to completely justify a defendant's behavior but that can be used to mitigate criminal punishment.

judicial-authority justification. A justification defense available when an actor has engaged in conduct constituting an offense in order to comply with a court order.

public-authority justification. A justification defense available when an actor has been specifically authorized to engage in the conduct constituting an offense in order to protect or further a public interest.

justification defense. *Criminal & tort law.* A defense that arises when the defendant has acted in a way that the law does not seek to prevent. • Traditionally, the following defenses were justifications: consent, self-defense, defense of others, defense of property, necessity (choice of evils), the use of force to make an arrest, and the use of force by public authority. — Sometimes shortened to *justification.* Cf. EXCUSE (2).

justificator (jəs-tə-fi-kay-tər). *Hist.* **1.** A compurgator; a person who testifies under oath in defense of an accused person. **2.** A juror.

Justinian Code (jəs-tin-ee-ən). *Roman law.* A collection of imperial constitutions drawn up by a commission of ten persons appointed by the Roman emperor Justinian, and published in A.D. 529. •Ten jurists, headed by Tribonian, carried out the project beginning in February A.D. 528 and ending in April 529. It replaced all prior imperial law, but was in force only until A.D. 534, when it was supplanted by a revision, the *Codex Repetitae Praelectionis.* The precise contents of the first work are unknown. But the second work, containing the 12 books of the revised code, includes the imperial constitutions of the Gregorian, Hermogenian, and Theodosian Codes, together with later legislation, revised and harmonized into one systematic whole. It deals with ecclesiastical law, criminal law, administrative law, and private law. In modern writings, the A.D. 534 version is the work referred to as the Justinian Code. — Also termed *Justinianean Code* (jəs-tin-ee-**an**-ee-ən); *Code of Justinian; Codex Justinianus* (**koh**-deks-jəs-tin-ee-**ay**-nəs); *Codex Vetus* ("Old Code"); *Codex Iustinianus Repetitae Praelectionis.*

Justinianist (jə-**stin**-ee-ə-nist), *n.* **1.** One who is knowledgeable about the Institutes of Justinian. **2.** One who has been trained in civil law.

Justinian's Institutes. See INSTITUTE.

justitia denegata (jəs-**tish**-ee-ə dee-nə-**gay**-tə). See DENIAL OF JUSTICE.

justitia naturalis (jəs-**tish**-ee-ə nach-ə-**ray**-lis). See *natural justice* under JUSTICE (1).

just title. See TITLE (2).

just value. See *fair market value* under VALUE (2).

just war. 1. BELLUM JUSTUM. **2.** See JUST-WAR DOCTRINE.

just-war doctrine. *Int'l law.* The principle that a war should have a morally and legally sufficient cause, and must be conducted with restraint. • Precisely what is morally or legally sufficient depends on the norms of a time and place. Over the centuries the doctrine has been invoked to justify wars waged in self- defense, to avenge injuries and punish wrongs, and over religious differences. Restraint means that the least amount of force possible under the circumstances should be used and only when necessary. — Also termed *just-war theory.* See BELLUM JUSTUM.

juvenile (**joo**-və-nəl *or* -nil), *n.* (18c) A person who has not reached the age (usu. 18) at which one should be treated as an adult by the criminal-justice system; MINOR. — **juvenile,** *adj.* — **juvenility** (joo-və-**nil**-ə-tee), *n.*

> *certified juvenile.* (1971) A juvenile who has been certified to be tried as an adult.

juvenile court. See COURT.

juvenile-court judge. See JUDGE.

juvenile delinquency. (1816) Antisocial behavior by a minor; esp., behavior that would be criminally punishable if the actor were an adult, but instead is usu. punished by special laws pertaining only to minors. Cf. INCORRIGIBILITY.

Juvenile Delinquency Prevention Act. A federal statute whose purpose is (1) to help states and local communities provide preventive services to youths who are in danger of becoming delinquent, (2) to help in training personnel employed in or preparing for employment in occupations that involve the provision of those services, and (3) to give technical assistance in this field. 42 USCA §§ 3801 et seq.

juvenile delinquent. (1816) A minor who is guilty of criminal behavior, usu. punishable by special laws not pertaining to adults. — Sometimes shortened to *delinquent.* — Also termed *juvenile offender; youthful offender; delinquent minor.* See OFFENDER. Cf. *delinquent child* under CHILD.

Juvenile Justice and Delinquency Prevention Act. A federal statute that provides funding, assistance, training, and support to state-operated juvenile-justice programs, initiatives, and court systems. 42 USCA §§ 5601–5785.

juvenile-justice system. The collective institutions through which a youthful offender passes until any charges have been disposed of or the assessed punishment has been concluded. • The system comprises juvenile courts (judges and lawyers), law enforcement (police), and corrections (probation officers and social workers).

juvenile offender. See JUVENILE DELINQUENT.

juvenile officer. See OFFICER (1).

juvenile parole. See PAROLE.

juvenile petition. See PETITION.

juxtaposition (jəks-tə-pə-**zish**-ən), *n.* (17c) **1.** The act or an instance of placing two or more things side by side or near one another. **2.** *Patents.* See AGGREGATION. — **juxtapose** (jəks-tə-**pohz**), *vb.* — **juxtapositional,** *adj.*

K

K. *abbr.* Contract.

k/a. *abbr.* Known as.

Kaldor-Hicks efficiency. See WEALTH MAXIMIZA-TION.

kalendarium (kal-ən-**dair**-ee-əm). [Latin] *Roman law.* **1.** A book of accounts in which a money-lender recorded the names of debtors and the principal and interest due. **2.** A written register of births, recorded daily.

kangaroo court. See COURT.

K.B. *abbr.* KING'S BENCH.

K.C. *abbr.* KING'S COUNSEL.

k.d., *adj. abbr.* (In a bill of lading) knocked down; not assembled or set up. ● When goods, equipment, or the like are shipped in disassembled form, the bill of lading is marked "k.d."

keelage (**keel**-ij). *Hist.* **1.** The right to demand payment of a toll by a ship entering or anchoring in a harbor. **2.** The toll so paid.

keelhaul (**keel**-hawl), *vb.* (17c) **1.** *Hist.* To drag (a person) through the water under the bottom of a ship as punishment or torture. **2.** To rebuke or reprimand harshly.

keeper. (15c) One who has the care, custody, or management of something and who usu. is legally responsible for it <a dog's keeper> <a keeper of lost property>.

Keeper of the Broad Seal. See KEEPER OF THE GREAT SEAL.

Keeper of the Great Seal. In England and Scotland, an officer who has custody of the Great Seal and who authenticates state documents of the highest importance. ● In England, the duties of the Keeper of the Great Seal are now discharged by the Lord Chancellor. — Also termed *Lord Keeper of the Great Seal*; *Lord Keeper*; *Keeper of the Broad Seal*; *Custos Sigilli*.

Keeper of the King's Conscience. See LORD CHANCELLOR.

Keeper of the Privy Seal (**priv**-ee). **1.** LORD PRIVY SEAL. **2.** In Scotland and Cornwall, an officer similar to the English Lord Privy Seal.

Keeper of the Rolls. See CUSTOS ROTULORUM.

Kellogg–Briand Pact. *Int'l law.* A 1928 treaty under which the United States, France, and (by 1933) 63 other nations purported to outlaw war and pledged to settle future differences through diplomacy. ● Among the signatories were Germany, Japan, and Italy — nations whose acts of aggression lead to World War II. 46 Stat. 2343, T.S. No. 796. — Also termed *Pact of Paris*.

Keogh plan (**kee**-oh). (1952) A tax-deferred retirement program developed for the self-employed. ● This plan is also known as an *H.R. 10 plan*, after the House of Representatives bill that established the plan. — Also termed *self-employed retirement plan*. Cf. INDIVIDUAL RETIREMENT ACCOUNT.

Ker–Frisbie rule. (1974) The principle that the government's power to try a criminal defendant is not impaired by the defendant's having been brought back illegally to the United States from a foreign country. *Ker v. Illinois*, 119 U.S. 436, 7 S.Ct. 225 (1886); *Frisbie v. Collins*, 342 U.S. 519, 72 S.Ct. 509 (1952).

Ketubah (ke-**too**-vah), *n. Jewish law.* A prenuptial agreement, signed by at least two independent witnesses, in which a husband promises to support his wife and to pay her a certain sum of money if the couple divorces. ● If the couple is still married when the husband dies, the sum promised upon divorce becomes the primary debt to be paid out of the husband's estate. The terms of a Ketubah are often enforceable in secular courts under general contract-law principles.

KeyCite, *vb.* (1997) To determine the subsequent history of (a case, statute, etc.) by using the online citator of the same name to establish that the point being researched is still good law. — **Key-Citing,** *n.*

key-employee life insurance. See LIFE INSURANCE.

key encryption. A software-cryptography system that generates and employs a secure key pair, one public key and one private key, to verify a digital signature and decipher a secure, coded document. ● The public key is known to all possible receivers of a message. The private key is known only to the message's sender. Key encryption transforms the message's characters into an indecipherable "hash." A person who has the signer's public key can decipher the message and detect whether it has been altered and whether it was transmitted using the sender's private key. It does not necessarily identify the sender; identity is verified using a digital certificate. — Also termed *public-key encryption.* — Abbr. PKE. See DIGITAL CERTIFICATE; HASH.

key-executive insurance. See *key-employee insurance* under INSURANCE.

key man. See KEY PERSON.

key-man insurance. See *key-employee life insurance* under LIFE INSURANCE.

key money. (1948) **1.** Payment (as rent or security) required from a new tenant in exchange for a key to the leased property. **2.** Payment made (usu. secretly) by a prospective tenant to a landlord or current tenant to increase the chance of obtaining a lease in an area where there is a housing shortage. ● Key money in the first sense is a legal transaction; key money in the second sense is usu. an illegal bribe that violates housing laws.

key-number system. (1909) A legal-research indexing system developed by West Publishing Company (now the West Group) to catalogue American caselaw with headnotes. ● In this system, a number designates a point of law, allowing a researcher to find all reported cases addressing a particular point by referring to its number.

key person. An important officer or employee; a person primarily responsible for a business's success. — Also termed *key man.*

key-person insurance. See *key-employee insurance* under INSURANCE.

kickback, *n.* (1920) A return of a portion of a monetary sum received, esp. as a result of coercion or a secret agreement <the contractor paid the city official a 5% kickback on the government contract>. — Also termed *payoff.* Cf. BRIBERY.

kicker. 1. An extra charge or penalty, esp. a charge added to a loan in addition to interest. **2.** An equity participation that a lender seeks as a condition for lending money, so that the lender may participate in rentals, profits, or extra interest.

kickout clause. (1983) A contractual provision allowing a party to end or modify the contract if a specified event occurs <under the kickout clause, the company could refuse to sell the land if it were unable to complete its acquisition of the new headquarters>.

kiddie tax. See TAX.

kidnap, *vb.* (17c) To seize and take away (a person) by force or fraud, often with a demand for ransom.

kidnapping. (17c) **1.** At common law, the crime of forcibly abducting a person from his or her own country and sending the person to another. ● This offense amounted to false imprisonment aggravated by moving the victim to another country. **2.** The crime of seizing and taking away a person by force or fraud. — Also termed *simple kidnapping;* (loosely) *abduction;* (archaically) *manstealing.* See ABDUCTION.

   aggravated kidnapping. (1943) Kidnapping accompanied by some aggravating factor (such as a demand for ransom or injury of the victim).

   child-kidnapping. (1978) The kidnapping of a minor, often without the element of force or fraud (as when someone walks off with another's baby). — Also termed *child-stealing; baby-snatching; childnapping.*

   kidnapping by cesarean. The kidnapping of a newborn baby by a person who causes the unlawful and forcible delivery of the baby by cesarean section without the mother's consent. ● The kidnapper is usu. a woman of childbearing age who has lost a baby or is unable to bear one. — Also termed *newborn kidnapping by cesarean section.*

   kidnapping for ransom. (1909) The offense of unlawfully seizing a person and then confining the person, usu. in a secret place, while attempting to extort ransom. ● This grave crime is sometimes made a capital offense. In addition to the abductor, a person who acts as a go-between to collect the ransom is generally considered guilty of the crime.

   newborn-kidnapping by cesarean section. See *kidnapping by cesarean.*

   parental kidnapping. (1984) The kidnapping of a child by one parent in violation of the other parent's custody or visitation rights. See PARENTAL KIDNAPPING PREVENTION ACT.

   simple kidnapping. (1943) Kidnapping not accompanied by an aggravating factor.

kidnapping by cesarean. See KIDNAPPING.

kill, *vb.* (14c) To end life; to cause physical death. ● The word is also used figuratively in putting an end to something <opponents were able to kill the proposed amendment>.

killer amendment. See AMENDMENT (3).

killing by misadventure. See ACCIDENTAL KILLING.

killing with malice. See MALICIOUS KILLING.

kin, *n.* (bef. 12c) **1.** One's relatives; family. — Also termed *kindred.* **2.** A relative by blood, marriage, or adoption, though usu. by blood only; a kinsman or kinswoman. See NEXT OF KIN.

kind arbitrage. See ARBITRAGE.

kindred. 1. See KIN. **2.** See KINSHIP.

king. 1. A man who possesses, in his own right, the sovereignty and royal power in a monarchy. Cf. QUEEN (1). **2.** (*cap.*) *English law.* The British government; the Crown. See CROWN.

King's Bench. Historically, the highest common-law court in England, presided over by the reigning monarch. ● When a queen begins to reign, the name automatically changes to *Queen's Bench.* In 1873, during Queen Victoria's reign, the court's jurisdiction was transferred to the Queen's Bench Division of the High Court of Justice. — Abbr. K.B. — Also termed *Court of King's Bench; Coram Rege Court.* Cf. QUEEN'S BENCH; QUEEN'S BENCH DIVISION.

King's Chambers. In the United Kingdom, waters lying within an imaginary line drawn from headland to headland around the coast of Great Britain.

King's Counsel. In the United Kingdom, Canada, and territories that have retained the rank, an elite, senior-level barrister or advocate. • Originally, a King's Counsel was appointed to serve as counsel to the reigning monarch. — Also termed *senior counsel.* — Abbr. K.C. Cf. QUEEN'S COUNSEL.

King's Court. See CURIA REGIS.

King's peace. *Hist.* A royal subject's right to be protected from crime (to "have peace") in certain areas subject to the king's immediate control, such as the king's palace or highway. • A breach of the peace in one of these areas subjected the offender to punishment in the King's Court. Over time, the area subject to the King's peace grew, which in turn increased the jurisdiction of the royal courts. — Also written *King's Peace.* Cf. AGAINST THE PEACE AND DIGNITY OF THE STATE.

King's proctor. See QUEEN'S PROCTOR.

kinship. Relationship by blood, marriage, or adoption. — Also termed *kindred.*

kinsman. See RELATIVE.

kintal. See QUINTAL.

kissing the Book. *Hist.* The practice of touching one's lips to a copy of the Bible (esp. the New Testament) after taking an oath in court. • This practice — formerly used in England — was replaced by the practice of placing one's hand on the Bible while swearing.

kitchen cabinet. See CABINET.

kiting. 1. CHECK-KITING. **2.** *Slang. Commercial law.* Raising money on credit, often by using accommodation paper.

Klaxon **doctrine (klak**-sən). (1966) *Conflict of laws.* The principle that a federal court exercising diversity jurisdiction must apply the choice-of-law rules of the state where the court sits. • In *Klaxon Co. v. Stentor Elec. Mfg. Co.,* the Supreme Court extended the rule of *Erie v. Tompkins* to choice-of-law issues. 313 U.S. 487, 61 S.Ct. 1020 (1941). — Also termed *Erie/Klaxon doctrine.* See ERIE DOCTRINE.

kleptomania (klep-tə-**may**-nee-ə), *n.* (1830) A compulsive urge to steal, esp. without economic motive. — **kleptomaniac,** *n. & adj.*

knight. (bef. 12c) **1.** *Hist.* In the Middle Ages, a person of noble birth who, having been trained in arms and chivalry, was bound to follow an earl, baron, or other superior lord into battle. **2.** In modern Britain, a man upon whom the monarch has bestowed an honorary dignity (knighthood) as a reward for personal merit of some

kind. • The status of knighthood no longer relates to birth or possessions and does not involve military service.

knight bachelor. See BACHELOR (3).

knight-service. *Hist.* A type of lay tenure in which a knight held land of another person or the Crown in exchange for a pledge of military service. — Also termed *knight's service;* (Scots law) *ward holding.* Cf. BASE SERVICE; SOCAGE; VILLEINAGE.

knight's fee. *Hist.* The amount of land that gave rise to the obligation of knight-service. • The amount varied from less than a hide to more than six hides. See HIDE.

knight's service. See KNIGHT-SERVICE.

knock-and-announce rule. (1969) *Criminal procedure.* The requirement that the police knock at the door and announce their identity, authority, and purpose before entering a residence to execute an arrest or search warrant. — Also termed *knock-and-notice rule.* Cf. *no-knock search warrant* under SEARCH WARRANT; *no-knock search* under SEARCH.

knock-for-knock agreement. (1949) An arrangement between insurers whereby each will pay the claim of its insured without claiming against the other party's insurance.

knock in, *vb.* To rap on the courtroom door to announce the entry of (one or more judges) <the law clerk, acting as bailiff, knocked in the judges>.

knock off, *vb.* (1879) **1.** To make an unauthorized copy of (another's product), usu. for sale at a substantially lower price than the original <the infringer knocked off popular dress designs>. **2.** *Slang.* To murder <the gang leader was knocked off by one of his lieutenants>. **3.** *Slang.* To rob or burglarize <the thieves knocked off the jewelry store in broad daylight>.

knockoff, *n.* (1966) *Intellectual property.* An unauthorized counterfeit and usu. inferior copy of another's product, esp. one protected by patent, trademark, trade dress, or copyright, usu. passed off at a substantially lower price than the original.

knock-out auction. See AUCTION.

know all men by these presents. (16c) Take note. • This archaic form of address — a loan translation of the Latin *noverint universi per praesentes* — was traditionally used to begin certain legal documents such as bonds and powers of attorney, but in modern drafting style the phrase is generally considered deadwood.

know-how. (1838) The information, practical knowledge, techniques, and skill required to achieve some practical end, esp. in industry or technology. • Know-how is considered intangible property in which rights may be bought and sold. See TRADE SECRET.

knowing, *adj.* (14c) **1.** Having or showing awareness or understanding; well-informed <a knowing waiver of the right to counsel>. **2.** Deliberate; conscious <a knowing attempt to commit fraud>. — **knowingly,** *adv.*

knowing consent. See *informed consent* under CONSENT (1).

knowledge. (14c) **1.** An awareness or understanding of a fact or circumstance; a state of mind in which a person has no substantial doubt about the existence of a fact. Cf. INTENT (1); NOTICE (1), (2); SCIENTER.

   actual knowledge. (16c) **1.** Direct and clear knowledge, as distinguished from constructive knowledge <the employer, having witnessed the accident, had actual knowledge of the worker's injury>. — Also termed *express actual knowledge.* **2.** Knowledge of information that would lead a reasonable person to inquire further <under the discovery rule, the limitations period begins to run once the plaintiff has actual knowledge of the injury>. — Also termed (in sense 2) *implied actual knowledge.*

   common knowledge. See COMMON KNOWLEDGE.

   constructive knowledge. (18c) Knowledge that one using reasonable care or diligence should have, and therefore that is attributed by law to a given person <the court held that the partners had constructive knowledge of the partnership agreement even though none of them had read it>.

   express actual knowledge. See *actual knowledge* (1).

   firsthand knowledge. See *personal knowledge.*

   implied actual knowledge. See *actual knowledge* (2).

   imputed knowledge. (18c) Knowledge attributed to a given person, esp. because of the person's legal responsibility for another's conduct <the principal's imputed knowledge of its agent's dealings>.

   personal knowledge. (17c) Knowledge gained through firsthand observation or experience, as distinguished from a belief based on what someone else has said. • Rule 602 of the Federal Rules of Evidence requires lay witnesses to have personal knowledge of the matters they testify about. An affidavit must also be based on personal knowledge, unless the affiant makes it clear that a statement relies on "information and belief." — Also termed *firsthand knowledge.*

   reckless knowledge. (1911) A person's awareness that a prohibited circumstance may exist, regardless of which the person accepts the risk and goes on to act.

   scientific knowledge. (17c) *Evidence.* Knowledge that is grounded on scientific methods that have been supported by adequate validation. • Four primary factors are used to determine whether evidence amounts to scientific knowledge: (1) whether it has been tested; (2) whether it has been subjected to peer review and publication; (3) the known or potential rate of error; and (4) the degree of acceptance within the scientific community. See DAUBERT TEST; SCIENTIFIC METHOD.

   superior knowledge. (17c) Knowledge greater than that of another person, esp. so as to adversely affect that person <in its fraud claim, the subcontractor alleged that the general contractor had superior knowledge of the equipment shortage>.

2. *Archaic.* CARNAL KNOWLEDGE.

knowledge-of-falsity exclusion. See EXCLUSION (3).

known creditor. See CREDITOR.

known heir. See HEIR.

known-loss doctrine. *Insurance.* A principle denying insurance coverage when the insured knows before the policy takes effect that a specific loss has already happened or is substantially certain to happen. — Also termed *known-risk doctrine.*

L

L. *abbr.* **1.** LAW (5). **2.** LORD (1). **3.** LOCUS. **4.** LATIN.

L. A measure of the money supply, including M3 items plus banker's acceptances, T-bills, and similar long-term investments. See M3.

label, *n.* (17c) **1.** *Trademarks.* An informative display of written or graphic matter, such as a logo, title, or similar marking, affixed to goods or services to identify their source. ● A label may be put on the packaging or container of a manufactured product, or on the packaging or surface of a natural substance. **2.** Any writing (such as a codicil) attached to a larger writing. **3.** A narrow slip of paper or parchment attached to a deed or writ in order to hold a seal.

label-and-significant-characteristics test. *Securities.* The rule that an instrument will be governed by the securities laws if it is labeled a stock and has the significant characteristics typically associated with shares of stock.

labeling. Under the Federal Food, Drug, and Cosmetic Act, any label or other written, printed, or graphic matter that is on a product or its container, or that accompanies the product. ● To come within the Act, the labeling does not need to accompany the product. It may be sent before or after delivery of the product, as long as delivery of the product and the written material are part of the same distribution program.

label license. See LICENSE.

labina (lə-**bɪ**-nə), *n. Archaic.* Land covered by water; swampland.

la bomba (lə **bom**-bə). (*sometimes cap.*) An incendiary device consisting of a plastic bag filled with fuel and placed inside a paper bag stuffed with tissue and rigged with a fuse. ● A person who uses such a device to start a fire violates the federal arson statute. See 18 USCA § 844(j).

labor, *n.* **1.** Work of any type, including mental exertion <the fruits of one's labor>. ● The term usu. refers to work for wages as opposed to profits.

child labor. See CHILD LABOR.

spousal labor. See SPOUSAL LABOR.

2. Workers considered as an economic unit or a political element <a dispute between management and labor over retirement benefits>. **3.** A Spanish land measure equal to 177¹/₇ acres. ● This measure has been used in Mexico and was once used in Texas.

labor, *vb.* (14c) **1.** To work, esp. with great exertion <David labored long and hard to finish the brief on time>. **2.** *Archaic.* To tamper with or improperly attempt to influence (a jury). ● This sense derives from the idea that the tamperer "endeavors" to influence the jury's verdict. See EMBRACERY. — **laborer,** *n.*

labor agreement. See COLLECTIVE-BARGAINING AGREEMENT.

laboratory conditions. *Labor law.* The ideal conditions for a union election, in which the employees may exercise free choice without interference from the employer, the union, or anyone else.

labor contract. See COLLECTIVE-BARGAINING AGREEMENT.

labor–desert model. The view that the inventive process results from the inventor's labor to create something of added value to society, and that this added value justifies some social reward ("just deserts") to the inventor. — Also termed *value-added model.* Cf. EUREKA MODEL; LABOR MODEL.

labor dispute. (1907) A controversy between an employer and its employees concerning the terms or conditions of employment, or concerning the association or representation of those who negotiate or seek to negotiate the terms or conditions of employment.

Labor Disputes Act. See NORRIS–LAGUARDIA ACT.

laborer. (14c) **1.** A person who makes a living by physical labor. **2.** WORKER.

laborer's lien. See *mechanic's lien* under LIEN.

laboring a jury. See EMBRACERY.

labor law. The field of law governing the relationship between employers and employees, esp. law governing the dealings of employers and the unions that represent employees. — Also termed *industrial law.* See NATIONAL LABOR RELATIONS ACT.

labor–management relations. (1947) The broad spectrum of activities concerning the relationship between employers and employees, both union and nonunion. See FAIR LABOR STANDARDS ACT; NATIONAL LABOR RELATIONS ACT; NATIONAL LABOR RELATIONS BOARD.

Labor–Management Relations Act. A federal statute, enacted in 1947, that regulates certain union activities, permits suits against unions for proscribed acts, prohibits certain strikes and boycotts, and provides steps for settling strikes involving national emergencies. 29 USCA §§ 141 et seq. — Also termed *Taft-Hartley Act.* See NATIONAL LABOR RELATIONS BOARD.

labor model. The view that the inventive process is the product of the inventor's labor, and the invention is therefore the property of the inventor by natural right. See LOCKEAN LABOR THEORY. Cf. EUREKA MODEL, LABOR-DESERT MODEL.

labor organization. See UNION.

labor-relations act. (1935) A statute regulating relations between employers and employees. • Although the Labor–Management Relations Act is the chief federal labor-relations act, various states have enacted these statutes as well.

Labor Relations Board. See NATIONAL LABOR RELATIONS BOARD.

labor theory. See LOCKEAN LABOR THEORY.

labor union. See UNION.

Lacey Act. A federal law, originally enacted in 1900, that permits states to enforce their own game laws prohibiting the importation of animals from other states or countries. 16 USCA §§ 661 et seq. See GAME LAW.

laches (**lach**-iz). [Law French "remissness; slackness"] (14c) **1.** Unreasonable delay in pursuing a right or claim — almost always an equitable one — in a way that prejudices the party against whom relief is sought. — Also termed *sleeping on rights.*

    prosecution laches. Patents. In a claim for patent-infringement, the equitable defense that the patentee did not timely enforce the patent rights.

2. The equitable doctrine by which a court denies relief to a claimant who has unreasonably delayed in asserting the claim, when that delay has prejudiced the party against whom relief is sought. Cf. LIMITATION (3).

laches, estoppel by. See *estoppel by laches* under ESTOPPEL.

Lackey **claim.** A prisoner's assertion that incarceration on death row for a protracted period is cruel and unusual punishment. *Lackey v. Texas,* 514 U.S. 1045, 115 S.Ct. 1421 (1995) (denying cert.).

lack-of-antecedent-basis rejection. See REJECTION.

lack of capacity. The disability of a person to create or enter into a legal relation because of some special characteristic. See CAPACITY (2).

lack of enablement. See NONENABLEMENT.

lack-of-enablement rejection. See *nonenablement rejection* under REJECTION (3).

lack of jurisdiction. See WANT OF JURISDICTION.

lack of prosecution. See WANT OF PROSECUTION.

lack-of-utility rejection. See REJECTION.

lade (layd), *n. Hist.* The mouth of a river. — Also spelled *lode.*

laden in bulk, *adj. Maritime law.* (Of a vessel) loaded with a cargo that lies loose in the hold instead of packaged. • Cargoes of corn, salt, and similar items are usu. shipped in bulk.

lading, bill of. See BILL OF LADING.

lady. (bef. 12c) In Britain, a title belonging to the wife of a peer, (by courtesy) the wife of a baronet or knight, or any single or married woman whose father was a nobleman carrying a rank of earl or higher.

laenland. See LOANLAND.

laesa majestas (**lee**-zə mə-**jes**-tas). See LESE MAJESTY.

laesio enormis (**lee**-shee-oh i-**nor**-mis). [Law Latin "excessive loss" or "abnormal loss of more than half"] *Roman & civil law.* **1.** The sale of a thing for which the buyer paid less than half of its real value. • The seller could rescind the sale, but the buyer could keep the item purchased by paying the full value. Generally, this doctrine was limited to land sales. **2.** The injury sustained by one party to an onerous contract when the overreaching party receives twice the value of that party's money or property, such as a purchaser who pays less than half of the value of the property sold, or a seller who receives more than double the property's value. • If coowner coheirs partition or sell property, *laesio enormis* may exist when the purchaser pays less than one-fourth of the value rather than one-half. See La. Civ. Code arts. 824, 1406. — Also spelled *lesio enormis.* — Also termed *lesion; enorm lesion;* (in full) *laesio enormis vel ultra dimidium* (**lee**-shee-oh i-**nor**-mis vel əl-trə di-**mid**-ee-əm); (in Louisiana) *lesion beyond moiety.*

lagan (**lag**-ən), *n.* (17c) **1.** Goods that are abandoned at sea but attached to a buoy so that they may be recovered. — Also termed *lagend; lagon; ligan; ligen; logan.* Cf. FLOTSAM; JETSAM; WAVESON. **2.** *Archaic.* Wreckage or cargo lying on the seabed.

lage (law *or* lay), *n.* [fr. Saxon *lag* "law"] *Hist.* **1.** Law. **2.** The territory in which certain law was in force, such as danelage, mercenlage, and West-Saxon lage. • This term is essentially an obsolete form of the word *law.* — Also termed *lagh; laga; lagu.* See MERCENLAGE; WEST-SAXON LAW.

lage day (**law** day). A law day; a juridical day; a day of open court. — Also termed *lagh day.*

lagging economic indicator. See ECONOMIC INDICATOR.

lagging indicator. See INDICATOR.

lagh day. See LAGE DAY.

lahman (**law**-mən *or* **lay**-mən), *n.* [Saxon fr. *lah* "law"] *Archaic.* A lawyer. — Also termed *lagemannus.*

Laidlaw vacancy. Under the National Labor Relations Act, a genuine opening in an employer's workforce, resulting from the employer's expanding its workforce or discharging a particular employee, or from an employee's resigning or otherwise leaving the employment. • The opening must be offered to striking workers, in order of seniority, after a strike has been resolved. *Laidlaw Corp. v. NLRB*, 414 F.2d 99 (7th Cir. 1969).

laissez-faire (les-ay-**fair**), *n.* [French "let (people) do (as they choose)"] (1825) **1.** Governmental abstention from interfering in economic or commercial affairs. **2.** The doctrine favoring such abstention. — **laissez-faire,** *adj.*

laity (**lay**-ə-tee). (15c) Collectively, persons who are not members of the clergy.

lake, *n.* (12c) **1.** A large body of standing water in a depression of land or basin supplied from the drainage of an extended area; esp., a natural depression in the surface of the earth containing a reasonably permanent body of water that is substantially at rest. **2.** A widened or expanded part of a river.

Lambeth degree (**lam**-bəth). *Hist.* A degree conferred by the Archbishop of Canterbury, rather than by a university, as authorized under the Ecclesiastical Licenses Act of 1533 (25 Hen. 8, ch. 21). • The degrees were conferred in music, theology, law, and medicine.

Lamb-Weston rule. *Insurance.* The doctrine that, when two insurance policies provide coverage for a loss, and each of them contains an other-insurance clause — creating a conflict in the order or apportionment of coverage — both of the other-insurance clauses will be disregarded and liability will be prorated between the insurers. *Lamb-Weston, Inc. v. Oregon Auto. Ins. Co.,* 341 P.2d 110 (Or. 1959).

lame duck. (1910) An elected official serving out a term after a successor has been elected.

lame-duck amendment. See TWENTIETH AMENDMENT.

lame-duck session. See SESSION (1).

lammas land. See LAND.

land, *n.* (bef. 12c) **1.** An immovable and indestructible three-dimensional area consisting of a portion of the earth's surface, the space above and below the surface, and everything growing on or permanently affixed to it. **2.** An estate or interest in real property.

accommodation land. (1843) Land that is bought by a builder or speculator who erects houses or improvements on it and then leases it at an increased rent.

acquired federal land. (*usu. pl.*) Federal land that was never in the public domain. See *federal land.*

acquired land. Land acquired by the government from private hands or from another governmental entity; esp., property acquired by the federal government from private or state ownership. • This term is frequently contrasted with *public domain.* — Also termed *acquired lands.* See PUBLIC DOMAIN (1).

arable land (ar-ə-bəl). (16c) Land fit for cultivation. — Formerly also termed *araturia; aralia; aratia.*

bounty land. A portion of public land given or donated as a reward, esp. for military service. See MILITARY BOUNTY LAND.

certificate land. Land in the western part of Pennsylvania set apart after the American Revolution to be bought with certificates that the soldiers received in lieu of pay. Cf. *donation land.*

Crown land. Demesne land of the Crown; esp., in England and Canada, land belonging to the sovereign personally, or to the government, as distinguished from land held under private ownership. — Also termed *demesne land of the Crown.* See *demesne land.*

demesne land (di-**mayn** or di-**meen**). *Hist.* Land reserved by a lord for personal use.

donation land. Land granted from the public domain to an individual as a gift, usu. as a reward for services or to encourage settlement in a remote area. • The term was initially used in Pennsylvania to reward Revolutionary War soldiers. Cf. *certificate land.*

earned land. Public land that is conveyed by a land patent to a private person who has performed a certain condition, usu. one spelled out in an earlier grant. See PATENT (2).

enclosed land. (17c) Land that is actually enclosed and surrounded with fences.

fabric land. *Hist.* Land given toward the maintenance, repair, or rebuilding of a cathedral or other church. • This term derives from funds given *ad fabricam ecclesiae reparandam* ("to repair the fabric of the church").

fast land. (*often pl.*) (16c) Land that is above the high-water mark and that, when flooded by a government project, is subjected to a governmental taking. • Owners of fast lands are entitled to just compensation for the taking. See TAKING (2).

federal land. (*usu. pl.*) Land owned by the United States government. • Federal lands are classified as public lands (also termed "lands in the public domain") or acquired federal lands, depending on how the land was obtained. See *acquired federal land.*

government land. See *public land.*

hide land. *Hist.* See HIDE.

improved land. (17c) Land that has been developed; esp., land occupied by buildings and structures. • The improvements may or may not enhance the value of the land.

indemnity land. See INDEMNITY LAND.

lammas land (lam-əs). *Hist.* Land over which persons other than the owner have the right of pasturage during winter, from lammas (reaping time) until sowing time.

lieu land (loo). Public land within indemnity limits granted in lieu of those lost within place limits.

life land. *Hist.* Land leased for a term measured by the life of one or more persons. — Also termed *life-hold.*

made land. Artificially formed land, usu. land that has been reclaimed by filling or created by dredging.

mineral land. (18c) Land that contains deposits of valuable minerals in quantities justifying the costs of extraction and using the land for mining, rather than agricultural or other purposes.

place land. See INDEMNITY LAND.

public land. (17c) Lands or land interests held by the government, without regard to how the government acquired ownership; unappropriated land belonging to the federal or state government. — Also termed *public lands; government land; public ground.*

reserved land. See RESERVATION (3).

riparian land. 1. Land that includes part of the bed of a watercourse or lake. 2. Land that borders on a public watercourse or public lake whose bed is owned by the public.

school land. (18c) Public real estate set apart for sale or exploitation by a state to establish and fund public schools.

seated land. (1822) Land that is occupied, cultivated, improved, reclaimed, farmed, or used as a place of residence, with or without cultivation.

settled land. Any land — or any interest in it — that is the subject of any document that limited it to, or put it into trust for, a person by way of succession.

swamp and overflowed land. (1853) Land that, because of its boggy, marshy, fenlike character, is unfit for cultivation, requiring drainage or reclamation to render it available for beneficial use. • Such lands were granted out of the U.S. public domain to the littoral states by acts of Congress in 1850 and thereafter. 43 USCA §§ 981 et seq.

tideland. See TIDELAND.

unimproved land. 1. Raw land that has never been developed, and usu. that lacks utilities. 2. Land that was formerly developed but has now been cleared of all buildings and structures.

withdrawn land. See RESERVATION (3).

land, law of. See LAW OF THE LAND.

land agent. See LAND MANAGER.

land bank. (1921) 1. A bank created under the Federal Farm Loan Act to make loans at low interest rates secured by farmland. 2. A program in which land is retired from agricultural production for conservation or tree-cultivation purposes. — Also termed *soil bank.* See FEDERAL HOME LOAN BANK.

land boundary. See BOUNDARY.

land certificate. A document entitling a person to receive from the government a certain amount of land by following prescribed legal steps. • It contains an official description of the land, as well as the name and address of the person receiving the entitlement, and is prima facie evidence of the truth of the matters it contains. — Also termed *land warrant.*

land-conservation agreement. See *land-conservation easement* under EASEMENT.

land-conservation easement. See EASEMENT.

land contract. See *contract for deed* under CONTRACT.

land court. See COURT.

land damages. See *just compensation* under COMPENSATION.

land department. A federal or state bureau that determines factual matters regarding the control and transfer of public land. • The federal land department includes the General Land Office headed by the Secretary of the Interior. See DEPARTMENT OF THE INTERIOR.

land description. See LEGAL DESCRIPTION.

land district. See DISTRICT.

landed, *adj.* (15c) 1. (Of a person) having an estate in land. 2. (Of an estate, etc.) consisting of land.

landed estate. See ESTATE (1).

landed-estates court. See COURT.

landed property. See *landed estate* under ESTATE (1).

landed security. See SECURITY.

landed servitude. See *servitude appurtenant* under SERVITUDE (2).

land flip. (1988) *Real estate.* A transaction in which a piece of property is purchased for one price and immediately sold, usu. to a fictitious entity, for a much higher price, to dupe a lender or later purchaser into thinking that the property is more valuable than it actually is.

land forces. See UNITED STATES ARMY.

land grant. (1862) A donation of public land to an individual, a corporation, or a subordinate government.

>   ***private land grant.*** (1861) A land grant to a natural person. See *land patent* under PATENT (2).

landholder. (17c) One who possesses or owns land.

land improvement. See IMPROVEMENT.

landing. (15c) **1.** A place on a river or other navigable water for loading and unloading goods, or receiving and delivering passengers and watercraft. **2.** The termination point on a river or other navigable water for these purposes. **3.** The act or process of coming back to land after a voyage or flight.

landing law. A law prohibiting the possession or sale of fish or game that have been taken illegally.

land lease. See *ground lease* under LEASE.

landlocked, *adj.* (17c) **1.** Surrounded by land, with no way to get in or out except by crossing the land of another <because the tract was landlocked, the buyer claimed an easement of necessity across the seller's property>. **2.** (Of a country) surrounded by other nations, with no access to major navigable waterways <the landlocked nation had always been at a mercantile disadvantage to its seafaring neighbors>.

landlord. (bef. 12c) **1.** At common law, the feudal lord who retained the fee of the land. — Sometimes shortened to *lord*. **2.** One who leases real property to another. — Also termed (in sense 2) *lessor*.

>   ***absentee landlord.*** A landlord who does not live on the leased premises; usu., one who lives far away. — Also termed *absentee management*.

landlord-and-tenant relationship. See LANDLORD–TENANT RELATIONSHIP.

landlord's lien. See LIEN.

landlord's warrant. See WARRANT (1).

landlord–tenant relationship. (1921) The legal relationship between the lessor and lessee of real estate. ● The relationship is contractual, created by a lease (or agreement for lease) for a term of years, from year to year, for life, or at will, and exists when one person occupies the premises of another with the lessor's permission or consent, subordinated to the lessor's title or rights. There must be a landlord's reversion, a tenant's estate, transfer of possession and control of the premises, and (generally) an express or implied contract. — Also termed *landlord-and-tenant relationship.* See LEASE.

landman. (1923) *Oil & gas.* A person responsible for acquiring oil and gas leases, negotiating arrangements for development of leases, and managing leased properties. ● In this field, both men and women are commonly known as *landmen.*

land manager. *Oil & gas.* A person who, usu. on behalf of an oil company, contracts with landowners for the mineral rights to their land. — Also termed *exploration manager; land agent; landman.*

landmark. (bef. 12c) **1.** A feature of land (such as a natural object, or a monument or marker) that demarcates the boundary of the land <according to the 1891 survey, the crooked oak tree is the correct landmark at the property's northeast corner>. **2.** A historically significant building or site <the schoolhouse built in 1898 is the county's most famous landmark>. See MONUMENT.

landmark decision. (1913) A judicial decision that significantly changes existing law. ● Examples are *Brown v. Board of Educ.*, 347 U.S. 483, 74 S.Ct. 686 (1954) (holding that segregation in public schools violates the Equal Protection Clause), and *Palsgraf v. Long Island R.R.*, 162 N.E. 99 (N.Y. 1928) (establishing that a defendant's duty in a negligence action is limited to plaintiffs within the apparent zone of danger — that is, plaintiffs to whom damage could be reasonably foreseen). — Also termed *landmark case.* Cf. LEADING CASE.

land office. (17c) A government office in which sales of public land are recorded.

landowner. One who owns land.

landowner's royalty. See ROYALTY (2).

land patent. See PATENT (2).

land-poor, *adj.* (1873) (Of a person) owning a substantial amount of unprofitable or encumbered land, but lacking the money to improve or maintain the land or to pay the charges due on it.

land-preservation agreement. See *land-conservation easement* under EASEMENT.

land revenue. See REVENUE.

Landrum–Griffin Act. A federal law, originally enacted in 1959 as the Labor–Management Reporting and Disclosure Act, designed to (1) curb corruption in union leadership and undemocratic conduct in internal union affairs, (2) outlaw certain types of secondary boycotts, and (3) prevent so-called hot-cargo provisions in collective-bargaining agreements. See HOT CARGO.

lands, *n. pl.* (14c) **1.** At common law, property less extensive than either tenements or hereditaments. **2.** By statute in some states, land including tenements and hereditaments. See HEREDITAMENTS; TENEMENT.

land sales contract. See *contract for deed* under CONTRACT.

land scrip. A negotiable instrument entitling the holder, usu. a person or company engaged in public service, to possess specified areas of public land. See SCRIP (1).

lands, tenements, and hereditaments. (16c) Real property. • The term was traditionally used in wills, deeds, and other instruments.

land tax. See *property tax* under TAX.

land-tenant. See TERRE-TENANT.

Land Titles and Transfer Act. *Hist.* An 1875 statute establishing a registry for titles to real property, and providing for the transfer of lands and recording of those transfers. 38 & 39 Vict., ch. 87. • The act is analogous in some respects to American recording laws, such as those providing for a registry of deeds. A system of title registration superseded this registry system in 1925.

land trust. See TRUST.

land trust certificate. An instrument granting the holder a share of the benefits of property ownership, while the trustee retains legal title. See *land trust* under TRUST.

land-use planning. (1939) The deliberate, systematic development of real estate through methods such as zoning, environmental-impact studies, and the like. — Also spelled *landuse planning.* — Also termed *urban planning.*

land-use regulation. An ordinance or other legislative enactment governing the development or use of real estate. — Also spelled *landuse regulation.*

land warfare. See WARFARE.

land warrant. See LAND CERTIFICATE.

Langdell system. See CASEBOOK METHOD.

language. (14c) **1.** Any organized means of conveying or communicating ideas, esp. by human speech, written characters, or sign language <what language did they speak?>. **2.** The letter or grammatical import of a document or instrument, as distinguished from its spirit <the language of the statute>.

Lanham Act (lan-əm). A federal trademark statute, enacted in 1946, that provides for a national system of trademark registration and protects the owner of a federally registered mark against the use of similar marks if any confusion might result or if the strength of a strong mark would be diluted. • The Lanham Act's scope is independent of and concurrent with state common law. 15 USCA §§ 1051 et seq. — Also termed *Federal Trademark Act; Trademark Act of 1946.*

lapidation (lap-ə-**day**-shən), *n.* An execution by stoning a person to death. — **lapidate** (**lap**-ə-dayt), *vb.*

lappage (**lap**-ij). Interference; lap and overlap; conflict. • Lappage applies when two different owners claim under deeds or grants that, in part, cover the same land.

lapping. (1939) An embezzlement technique by which an employee takes funds from one customer's accounts receivable and covers it by using a second customer's payment to pay the first account, then a third customer's payment to pay the second account, and so on.

lapse, *n.* (16c) **1.** The termination of a right or privilege because of a failure to exercise it within some time limit or because a contingency has occurred or not occurred. **2.** *Wills & estates.* The failure of a testamentary gift, esp. when the beneficiary dies before the testator. See ANTILAPSE STATUTE. Cf. ADEMPTION.

lapse, *vb.* (18c) **1.** (Of an estate or right) to pass away or revert to someone else because conditions have not been fulfilled or because a person entitled to possession has failed in some duty. See *lapsed policy* under INSURANCE POLICY. **2.** (Of a devise, grant, etc.) to become void.

lapsed devise. See DEVISE.

lapsed legacy. See LEGACY.

lapsed policy. See INSURANCE POLICY.

lapse patent. See PATENT (2).

lapse statute. See ANTILAPSE STATUTE.

larcenable (**lahr**-sə-nə-bəl), *adj.* (1920) Subject to larceny <because it cannot be carried away, real estate is not larcenable>.

larcenist, *n.* (1803) One who commits larceny. See LARCENY.

larcenous (**lahr**-sə-nəs), *adj.* (18c) **1.** Of, relating to, or characterized by larceny <a larcenous taking>. **2.** (Of a person) contemplating or tainted with larceny; thievish <a larcenous purpose>.

larcenous intent. See INTENT (1).

larceny (**lahr**-sə-nee), *n.* (15c) The unlawful taking and carrying away of someone else's personal property with the intent to deprive the possessor of it permanently. • Common-law larceny has been broadened by some statutes to include embezzlement and false pretenses, all three of which are often subsumed under the statutory crime of "theft. Cf. ROBBERY.

    aggravated larceny. (1831) Larceny accompanied by some aggravating factor (as when the theft is from a person). — Also termed *compound larceny.*

    complicated larceny. See *mixed larceny.*

    compound larceny. 1. See *aggravated larceny.* **2.** See *mixed larceny.*

    constructive larceny. (1827) Larceny in which the perpetrator's felonious intent to appropriate the goods is construed from the defendant's conduct at the time of asportation, although a felonious intent was not present before that time.

grand larceny. (1828) Larceny of property worth more than a statutory cutoff amount, usu. $100. Cf. *petit larceny.*

larceny by a constructive trespass. Larceny that occurs when a property owner mistakenly gives another person more property than is due, and the recipient knows about the error but does not disclose it before taking the excess property with the intent of converting it to his or her own use.

larceny by bailee. Larceny committed by a bailee who converts the property to personal use or to the use of a third party.

larceny by extortion. See *theft by extortion* under THEFT.

larceny by fraud and deception. See *larceny by trick.*

larceny by trick. (1898) Larceny in which the taker misleads the rightful possessor, by misrepresentation of fact, into giving up possession of (but not title to) the goods. — Also termed *larceny by trick and deception; larceny by trick and device; larceny by fraud and deception.* Cf. FALSE PRETENSES; *cheating by false pretenses* under CHEATING.

larceny from the person. (18c) Larceny in which the goods are taken directly from the person, but without violence or intimidation, the victim usu. being unaware of the taking. • Pickpocketing is a typical example. This offense is similar to robbery except that violence or intimidation is not involved. Cf. ROBBERY.

larceny of property lost, mislaid, or delivered by mistake. See *theft of property lost, mislaid, or delivered by mistake* under THEFT.

mixed larceny. (18c) **1.** Larceny accompanied by aggravation or violence to the person. Cf. *simple larceny.* **2.** Larceny involving a taking from a house. — Also termed *compound larceny; complicated larceny.*

petit larceny. (16c) Larceny of property worth less than an amount fixed by statute, usu. $100. — Also spelled *petty larceny.* Cf. *grand larceny.*

simple larceny. (18c) Larceny unaccompanied by aggravating factors; larceny of personal goods unattended by an act of violence. Cf. *mixed larceny* (1).

larger parcel. (1895) *Eminent domain.* A portion of land that is not a complete parcel, but is the greater part of a bigger tract, entitling the owner to damages both for the parcel taken and for its severance from the larger tract. • To grant both kinds of damages, a court generally requires the owner to show unity of ownership, unity of use, and contiguity of the land. But some states and the federal courts do not require contiguity when there is strong evidence of unity of use. See ECONOMIC UNIT.

Larrison rule (lar-ə-sən). (1952) *Criminal law.* The doctrine that a defendant may be entitled to a new trial on the basis of newly discovered evidence of false testimony by a government witness if the jury might have reached a different conclusion without the evidence and it unfairly surprised the defendant at trial. *Larrison v. United States,* 24 F.2d 82 (7th Cir. 1928).

lascivious (lə-siv-ee-əs), *adj.* (15c) (Of conduct) tending to excite lust; lewd; indecent; obscene.

lascivious cohabitation. See *illicit cohabitation* under COHABITATION.

L'Association Litteraire et Artistique Internationale. *Copyright.* An organization of authors, artists, and other supporters of international copyright protection. • In 1878, the Association drafted five resolutions that would become the starting point for the Berne Convention. In 1883, the organization called the first meeting in Berne, Switzerland for the purpose of creating a union to enforce international copyrights. — Often shortened to the *International Association.* — Abbr. ALAI.

last, *n. Hist.* **1.** A burden. **2.** A measure of weight used for bulky commodities.

last antecedent, rule of the. See RULE OF THE LAST ANTECEDENT.

last-clear-chance doctrine. (1904) *Torts.* The rule that a plaintiff who was contributorily negligent may nonetheless recover from the defendant if the defendant had the last opportunity to prevent the harm but failed to use reasonable care to do so (in other words, if the defendant's negligence is later in time than the plaintiff's). • This doctrine allows the plaintiff to rebut the contributory-negligence defense in the few jurisdictions where contributory negligence completely bars recovery. — Also termed *discovered-peril doctrine; humanitarian doctrine; last-opportunity doctrine; subsequent-negligence doctrine; supervening-negligence doctrine; doctrine of ultimate negligence; doctrine of discovered peril; doctrine of subsequent negligence.*

last-employer rule. The doctrine that liability for an occupational injury or illness falls to the employer who exposed the worker to the injurious substance just before the first onset of the disease or injury. — Also termed *last-injurious-exposure rule.*

last heir. *Hist.* The person — either the lord of the manor or the sovereign — to whom lands come by escheat when there is no lawful heir.

last illness. (1904) The sickness ending in the person's death. — Also termed *last sickness.*

last-in, first-out. (1934) An accounting method that assumes that the most recent purchases are sold or used first, matching current costs against current revenues. — Abbr. LIFO. Cf. FIRST-IN, FIRST-OUT; NEXT-IN, FIRST-OUT.

last-injurious-exposure rule. See LAST-EMPLOYER RULE.

last-in-time-marriage presumption. *Family law.* A presumption that the most recently contracted marriage is valid. • This presumption generally arises in a situation similar to this: A person, believing himself or herself to be divorced, remarries. This person dies, and the new spouse makes a claim for the decedent's pension benefits. Then a former spouse, claiming that there was never a valid divorce, also claims the right to receive the benefits. The last-in-time-marriage presumption operates so that the former spouse bears the burden of proving that there was no valid divorce.

last-link doctrine. (1985) The rule that an attorney need not divulge nonprivileged information if doing so would reveal information protected by the attorney–client privilege, particularly if the information would provide essential evidence to support indicting or convicting the client of a crime. • This doctrine is often relied on as an exception to the rule that a client's identity is not privileged. For example, if divulging the client's name would supply the last link of evidence to indict or convict that client, the attorney need not disclose the client's name.

last-opportunity doctrine. See LAST-CLEAR-CHANCE DOCTRINE.

last-proximate-act test. (1961) *Criminal law.* A common-law test for the crime of attempt, based on whether the defendant does the final act necessary to commit an offense (such as pulling the trigger of a gun, not merely aiming it). • Most courts have rejected this test as being too lenient. See ATTEMPT (2).

last resort, court of. See *court of last resort* under COURT.

last sickness. See LAST ILLNESS.

last-straw doctrine. *Employment law.* The rule that the termination of employment may be justified by a series of incidents of poor performance, not one of which alone would justify termination, followed by a final incident showing a blatant disregard for the employer's interests.

last-survivor life insurance. See LIFE INSURANCE.

last-treatment rule. The doctrine that, for an ongoing physician–patient relationship, the statute of limitations on a medical-malpractice claim begins to run when the treatment stops or the relationship ends.

last will. See WILL.

last will and testament. See *last will* under WILL.

lata culpa. See CULPA.

lata neglegentia (**lay**-tə neg-lə-**jen**-shee-ə). See NEGLEGENTIA.

latching. A survey of a mine; an underground survey.

late, *adj.* (bef. 12c) **1.** Tardy; coming after an appointed or expected time <a late filing>. **2.** (Of a person) only recently having died <the late Secretary of State>.

late charge. See CHARGE.

latecomer. See JUNIOR USER.

latent (**lay**-tənt), *adj.* (15c) Concealed; dormant <a latent defect>. Cf. PATENT.

latent ambiguity. See AMBIGUITY.

latent deed. See DEED.

latent defect. See *hidden defect* under DEFECT.

latent equity. See EQUITY.

latent intent. See *dormant legislative intent* under LEGISLATIVE INTENT.

latent intention. See *dormant legislative intent* under LEGISLATIVE INTENT.

lateral departure. See DEPARTURE.

lateral sentencing. See *lateral departure* under DEPARTURE.

lateral support. See SUPPORT (4).

late-term abortion. See ABORTION.

latrocination (la-trə-sə-**nay**-shən). [fr. Latin *latrocinium* "highway robbery"] *Archaic.* The act of robbing; a depredation; a theft. — Also termed *latrociny; latrocinium.* See LARCENY; THEFT.

latrocinium (la-trə-**sin**-ee-əm), *n.* [Latin fr. *latro* "a robber"] *Hist.* **1.** LATROCINATION. **2.** Something stolen. **3.** The right to judge and execute thieves.

latrociny (**la**-trə-sə-nee). See LATROCINATION.

laughe, *n.* See FRANKPLEDGE.

laughing heir. See HEIR.

launch, *n.* (18c) **1.** The movement of a vessel from the land into the water, esp. by sliding along ways from the stocks on which the vessel was built. **2.** A large open boat used in any service; LIGHTER.

laundering, *n.* See MONEY-LAUNDERING.

laundry list. (1958) *Slang.* An enumeration of items, as in a statute or court opinion <Texas's consumer-protection law contains a laundry list of deceptive trade practices>.

laureate (**lor**-ee-it), *n.* (16c) **1.** *Hist.* An officer of the sovereign's household, who composed odes annually on the sovereign's birthday, on the new year, and occasionally on the occurrence of a remarkable victory. **2.** A person honored for great achievement in the arts and sciences, and esp. in poetry.

law. (bef. 12c) **1.** The regime that orders human activities and relations through systematic application of the force of politically organized society, or through social pressure, backed by force, in such a society; the legal system <respect and obey the law>. **2.** The aggregate of legislation, judicial precedents, and accepted legal principles; the body of authoritative grounds of judicial and administrative action; esp., the body of rules, standards, and principles that the courts of a particular jurisdiction apply in deciding controversies brought before them <the law of the land>. **3.** The set of rules or principles dealing with a specific area of a legal system <copyright law>. **4.** The judicial and administrative process; legal action and proceedings <when settlement negotiations failed, they submitted their dispute to the law>. **5.** A statute <Congress passed a law>. — Abbr. L. **6.** COMMON LAW <law but not equity>. **7.** The legal profession <she spent her entire career in law>.

adjective law. See ADJECTIVE LAW.

canon law. See CANON LAW.

caselaw. See CASELAW.

civil law. See CIVIL LAW.

common law. See COMMON LAW.

consuetudinary law (kon-swə-**t[y]oo**-də-ner-ee). [fr. Latin *consuetudo* "custom"] *Hist.* Ancient customary law that is based on an oral tradition.

conventional law. See CONVENTIONAL LAW.

customary law. See CUSTOMARY LAW.

divine law. See DIVINE LAW.

enacted law. Law that has its source in legislation; WRITTEN LAW.

federal law. See FEDERAL LAW.

general law. **1.** Law that is neither local nor confined in application to particular persons. • Even if there is only one person or entity to which a given law applies when enacted, it is general law if it purports to apply to all persons or places of a specified class throughout the jurisdiction. — Also termed *general statute*; *law of a general nature.* Cf. *special law.* **2.** A statute that relates to a subject of a broad nature.

imperative law. A rule in the form of a command; a rule of action imposed on people by some authority that enforces obedience.

internal law. **1.** Law that regulates the domestic affairs of a country. Cf. INTERNATIONAL LAW. **2.** LOCAL LAW (3).

local law. See LOCAL LAW.

moral law. See MORAL LAW.

natural law. See NATURAL LAW.

partial law. A statute designed (usu. intentionally) to affect the rights of only one particular person or only certain classes of people, rather than all people.

permanent law. A statute that continues in force for an indefinite time.

positive law. See POSITIVE LAW.

procedural law. See PROCEDURAL LAW.

prospective law. See *prospective statute* under STATUTE.

special law. A law that pertains to and affects a particular case, person, place, or thing, as opposed to the general public. — Also termed *special act*; *private law.* Cf. *general law* (1).

state law. See STATE LAW.

sumptuary law. See SUMPTUARY LAW.

tacit law. A law that derives its authority from the people's consent, without a positive enactment.

unenacted law. Law that does not have its source in legislation; UNWRITTEN LAW (1).

unwritten law. A rule, custom, or practice that has not been enacted in the form of a statute or ordinance. • The term traditionally includes caselaw. — Also termed *jus non scriptum*; *jus ex non scripto*; *lex non scripta*; *jus moribus constitutum.* See CASELAW. Cf. *written law.*

written law. Statutory law, together with constitutions and treaties, as opposed to judge-made law. — Also termed *jus scriptum*; *lex scripta.* Cf. *unwritten law.*

law and economics. (*often cap.*) (1979) **1.** A discipline advocating the economic analysis of the law, whereby legal rules are subjected to a cost-benefit analysis to determine whether a change from one legal rule to another will increase or decrease allocative efficiency and social wealth. • Originally developed as an approach to antitrust policy, law and economics is today used by its proponents to explain and interpret a variety of legal subjects. **2.** The field or movement in which scholars devote themselves to this discipline. **3.** The body of work produced by these scholars.

law and literature. (*often cap.*) (1997) **1.** Traditionally, the study of how lawyers and legal institutions are depicted in literature; esp., the examination of law-related fiction as sociological evidence of how a given culture, at a given time, views law. — Also termed *law in literature.* **2.** More modernly, the application of literary theory to legal texts, focusing esp. on lawyers' rhetoric, logic, and style, as well as legal syntax and semantics. — Also termed *law as literature.* **3.** The field or movement in which scholars devote themselves to this study or application. **4.** The body of work produced by these scholars.

law arbitrary. A law not found in the nature of things, but imposed by the legislature's mere will; a bill not immutable.

law as literature. See LAW AND LITERATURE (2).

law between states. See INTERNATIONAL LAW.

lawbook. (16c) A book, usu. a technical one, about the law; esp., a primary legal text such as a statute book or book that reports caselaw. — Also written *law book*.

lawbreaker, *n.* (15c) A person who violates or has violated the law.

law clerk. **1.** See CLERK (4). **2.** See PARALEGAL (2).

law commission. (*often cap.*) An official or quasi-official body of people formed to propose legal reforms intended to improve the administration of justice. • Such a body is often charged with the task of reviewing the law with an eye toward systematic development and reform, esp. through codification.

law court. **1.** See COURT (1). **2.** See COURT (2). — Also written *law-court*.

law court of appeals. *Hist.* An appellate tribunal, formerly existing in South Carolina, for hearing appeals from the courts of law.

law-craft, *n.* (16c) The practice of law.

law day. **1.** *Archaic.* The yearly or twice-yearly meeting of one of the early common-law courts. **2.** *Archaic.* The day appointed for a debtor to discharge a mortgage or else forfeit the property to the lender. **3.** (*cap.*) A day on which American schools, public assemblies, and courts draw attention to the importance of law in modern society. • Since 1958, the ABA has sponsored Law Day on May 1 of each year.

law department. A branch of a corporation, government agency, university, or the like charged with handling the entity's legal affairs.

law enforcement. (1895) **1.** The detection and punishment of violations of the law. • This term is not limited to the enforcement of criminal laws. For example, the Freedom of Information Act contains an exemption from disclosure for information compiled for law-enforcement purposes and furnished in confidence. That exemption is valid for the enforcement of a variety of noncriminal laws (such as national-security laws) as well as criminal laws. See 5 USCA § 552(b)(7). **2.** CRIMINAL JUSTICE (2). **3.** Police officers and other members of the executive branch of government charged with carrying out and enforcing the criminal law.

Law Enforcement Assistance Administration. A former federal agency (part of the Department of Justice) that was responsible for administering law-enforcement grants under the Omnibus Crime Control and Safe Streets Act of 1968. • It has been replaced by a variety of federal agencies, including the National Institute of Corrections and National Institute of Justice. — Abbr. LEAA.

Law Enforcement Information Network. A computerized communications system that some states use to document driver's-license records, automobile registrations, wanted-persons' files, and the like. — Abbr. LEIN.

law-enforcement officer. A person whose duty is to enforce the laws and preserve the peace. See PEACE OFFICER; SHERIFF.

law-enforcement system. See CRIMINAL-JUSTICE SYSTEM.

law firm. (1852) An association of lawyers who practice law together, usu. sharing clients and profits, in a business organized traditionally as a partnership but often today as either a professional corporation or a limited-liability company. • Many law firms have a hierarchical structure in which the partners (or shareholders) supervise junior lawyers known as "associates," who are usu. employed on a track to partnership.

captive law firm. A law firm staffed by employees of an insurance company. • These lawyers typically defend insureds in lawsuits covered under the insurer's liability policies. The insurer's use of a captive firm to defend an insured raises ethical questions about whether the lawyers will act in the insured's best interests. — Often shortened to *captive firm.*

Law French. (17c) The corrupted form of the Norman French language that arose in England in the centuries after William the Conqueror invaded England in 1066 and that was used for several centuries as the primary language of the English legal system; the Anglo-French used in medieval England in judicial proceedings, pleadings, and lawbooks. — Also written *law French.* — Abbr. L.F. See NORMAN FRENCH.

lawful, *adj.* (13c) Not contrary to law; permitted by law <the police officer conducted a lawful search of the premises>. See LEGAL.

lawful admission. (1899) *Immigration.* Legal entry into the country, including under a valid immigrant visa. • Lawful admission is one of the requirements for an immigrant to receive a naturalization order and certificate. 8 USCA §§ 1101(a)(20), 1427(a)(1), 1429.

lawful age. (16c) **1.** See *age of capacity* under AGE. **2.** See *age of majority* (1) under AGE.

lawful arrest. See ARREST.

lawful authorities. (16c) Those persons (such as the police) with the right to exercise public power, to require obedience to their lawful commands, and to command or act in the public name.

lawful cause. See *good cause* under CAUSE (2).

lawful condition. See CONDITION (2).

lawful damages. See DAMAGES.

lawful deed. See *good deed* under DEED.

lawful dependent. See DEPENDENT.

lawful entry. See ENTRY (1).

lawful fence. (17c) A strong, substantial, and well-suited barrier that is sufficient to prevent animals from escaping property and to protect the property from trespassers. — Also termed *legal fence*; *good and lawful fence*. Cf. SPITE FENCE.

lawful goods. (16c) Property that one may legally hold, sell, or export; property that is not contraband.

lawful heir. See HEIR (1).

lawful interest. See INTEREST (3).

lawful issue. See ISSUE (3).

lawful money. See MONEY.

lawful process. See *legal process* under PROCESS.

lawful representative. See REPRESENTATIVE.

lawgiver. (14c) **1.** A legislator, esp. one who promulgates an entire code of laws. **2.** A judge with the power to interpret law. — **lawgiving,** *adj. & n.*

law guardian. See *guardian ad litem* under GUARDIAN.

law-hand. *Hist.* An outmoded rococo method of handwriting once used by scribes in preparing legal documents.

law in action. The law as applied in the day-to-day workings of the legal system, as opposed to the law found in books. — Sometimes written *law-in-action*. See LEGAL REALISM. Cf. LAW IN BOOKS.

law in books. The legal rules to be found in texts; esp., sterile, oft-repeated rules that seem to depart from the way in which the law actually operates in the day-to-day workings of the legal system. — Sometimes written *law-in-books*. Cf. LAW IN ACTION.

law in literature. See LAW AND LITERATURE (1).

law journal. 1. A legal periodical or magazine, esp. one published by a bar association. — Abbr. L.J. **2.** LAW REVIEW (1).

Law Latin. (16c) A corrupted form of Latin formerly used in law and legal documents, including judicial writs, royal charters, and private deeds. • It primarily consists of a mixture of Latin, French, and English words used in English sentence structures. — Abbr. L.L.; L. Lat. — Also written *law Latin*.

law list. (18c) **1.** A published compilation of the names and addresses of practicing lawyers and other information of interest to the profession, such as legal organizations, court calendars, rosters of specialists, court reporters, and the like. **2.** A legal directory that provides biographical information about lawyers, such as Martindale-Hubbell. • Many states and large cities have law lists or directories. See MARTINDALE-HUBBELL LAW DIRECTORY.

Law Lord. (18c) A member of the appellate committee of the House of Lords, consisting of the Lord Chancellor, the salaried Lords of Appeal in Ordinary, and any peer who holds or has held high judicial office. — Also written *law lord*.

lawmaker. See LEGISLATOR.

lawmaking. See LEGISLATION (1).

law martial. See MARTIAL LAW.

law merchant. A system of customary law that developed in Europe during the Middle Ages and regulated the dealings of mariners and merchants in all the commercial countries of the world until the 17th century. • Many of the law merchant's principles came to be incorporated into the common law, which in turn formed the basis of the Uniform Commercial Code. — Also termed *commercial law*; *lex mercatoria*.

lawnote. See NOTE (2).

law of a general nature. See *general law* under LAW.

law of arms. See ARMS, LAW OF.

law of capture. See RULE OF CAPTURE.

law of Citations. See CITATIONS, LAW OF.

law of competence. A law establishing and defining the powers of a government official, including the circumstances under which the official's pronouncements constitute laws. — Also termed *power-delegating law*. See *jural act* under ACT; JURAL AGENT.

law of deceit. *Hist.* The body of 19th-century common-law torts that developed into the modern laws of trademark, securities fraud, deceptive trade practices, and unfair competition.

law of evidence. See EVIDENCE (4).

law of marque (mahrk). A rule of reprisal allowing one who has been wronged but cannot obtain justice to take the goods of the wrongdoer found within the wronged person's precinct, in satisfaction of the wrong.

law of nations. See INTERNATIONAL LAW.

law of nature. See NATURAL LAW.

law of nature and nations. See INTERNATIONAL LAW.

law of obligations. The category of law dealing with proprietary rights in personam — namely, the relations between obligor and obligee. • It is one of the three departments into which civil law was traditionally divided. See IN PERSONAM. Cf. LAW OF PROPERTY; LAW OF STATUS.

law of persons. (17c) The law relating to persons; the law that pertains to the different statuses of persons. • This is also commonly known as the *jus personarum*, a shortened form of *jus quod ad personas pertinet* ("the law that pertains to persons"). See JUS PERSONARUM.

law of property. The category of law dealing with proprietary rights in rem, such as personal servitudes, predial servitudes, and rights of real security. • It is one of the three departments into which civil law was traditionally divided: persons, property, and modes of acquiring property (obligations). In modern civil codes that follow the model of the German Civil Code, civil law is divided into five books: general principles, obligations, family law, property, and succession. See IN REM. Cf. LAW OF OBLIGATIONS; LAW OF STATUS.

law of remedy. See REMEDY.

law of shipping. The part of maritime law relating to the building, equipping, registering, owning, inspecting, transporting, and employing of ships, along with the laws applicable to shipmasters, agents, crews, and cargoes; the maritime law relating to ships. — Also termed *shipping law*. See MARITIME LAW; JONES ACT.

law of status. The category of law dealing with personal or nonproprietary rights, whether in rem or in personam. • It is one of the three departments into which civil law is divided. Cf. LAW OF OBLIGATIONS; LAW OF PROPERTY.

law of the apex. *Mining law.* The principle that title to a given tract of mineral land, with defined mining rights, goes to the person who locates the surface covering the outcrop or apex.

law of the case. (18c) **1.** The doctrine holding that a decision rendered in a former appeal of a case is binding in a later appeal. **2.** An earlier decision giving rise to the application of this doctrine. Cf. LAW OF THE TRIAL; RES JUDICATA; STARE DECISIS.

law of the circuit. (1861) **1.** The law as announced and followed by a U.S. Circuit Court of Appeals. **2.** The rule that one panel of judges on a U.S. Circuit Court of Appeals should not overrule a decision of another panel of judges on the same court. **3.** The rule that an opinion of one U.S. Circuit Court of Appeals is not binding on another circuit but may be considered persuasive.

law of the flag. *Maritime law.* The law of the nation whose flag is flown by a particular vessel where it is registered. • That nation's laws govern the ship's internal affairs. See *McCulloch v. Sociedad de Marineros de Honduras*, 372 U.S. 10 (1963).

law of the forum. See LEX FORI.

Law of The Hague. The first widely accepted body of international law of war, as approved by conventions in The Hague in 1899 and 1907. • The Law of The Hague set up procedures for mediation and arbitration of disputes to avoid war, and attempted to regulate the type and use of weapons in warfare. See LIEBER CODE.

law of the land. (15c) **1.** The law in effect in a country and applicable to its members, whether the law is statutory, administrative, or case-made. **2.** Due process of law. See DUE PROCESS. — Also termed *lex terrae*; *ley de terre*.

law of the partnership. The rule that the parties' agreement controls the features of a partnership.

law of the place. (1947) Under the Federal Tort Claims Act, the state law applicable to the place where the injury occurred. • Under the Act, the federal government waives its sovereign immunity for specified injuries, including certain wrongful acts or omissions of a government employee causing injury that the United States, if it were a private person, would be liable for under the law of the state where the incident occurred. 28 USCA § 1346(b).

law of the road. The collective statutes, rules, and customs that regulate travel on public highways and streets.

law of the sea. The body of international law governing how nations use and control the sea and its resources. Cf. GENERAL MARITIME LAW; MARITIME LAW.

law of the trial. A legal theory or court ruling that is not objected to and is used or relied on in a trial <neither party objected to the court's jury instruction, so it became the law of the trial>. Cf. LAW OF THE CASE.

law of things. The law pertaining to things; the law that is determined by changes in the nature of things. • This is also commonly known as the *jus rerum*, a shortened form of *jus quod ad res pertinet* ("the law that pertains to things"). See JUS RERUM.

law practice. (17c) An attorney's professional business, including the relationships that the attorney has with clients and the goodwill associated with those relationships. Cf. PRACTICE OF LAW.

law question. See QUESTION OF LAW.

law reform. (1846) The process of, or a movement dedicated to, streamlining, modernizing, or otherwise improving a body of law generally or the code governing a particular branch of the law; specif., the investigation and discussion of the law on a topic (e.g., bankruptcy), usu. by a commission or expert committee, with the goal of formulating proposals for change to improve the operation of the law. — Also termed *science of legislation*; *censorial jurisprudence*.

law report. See REPORT (3).

law reporter. See REPORT (3).

law review. (1845) **1.** A journal containing scholarly articles, essays, and other commentary on legal topics by professors, judges, law students, and practitioners. ● Law reviews are usu. published at law schools and edited by law students <law reviews are often grossly overburdened with substantive footnotes>. **2.** The law-student staff and editorial board of such a journal <she made law review>. — Abbr. L. Rev. — Also termed *law journal.* See LAW JOURNAL.

law Salique (sə-**leek**). See SALIC LAW.

law school. (17c) An institution for formal legal education and training. ● Graduates who complete the standard program, usu. three years in length, receive a Juris Doctor (or, formerly, a Bachelor of Laws).

  accredited law school. (1905) A law school approved by the state and the Association of American Law Schools, or by the state and the American Bar Association. ● In all states except California, only graduates of an accredited law school may take the bar examination.

Law School Admissions Test. A standardized examination purporting to measure the likelihood of success in law school. ● Most American law schools use the results of this examination in admissions decisions. — Abbr. LSAT.

Law Society. A professional organization in England, chartered in 1845, governing the education, practice, and conduct of articled clerks and solicitors. ● A clerk or solicitor must be enrolled with the Law Society to be admitted to the legal profession.

Law Society of Scotland. A professional organization established by statute in 1949, governing the admission, conduct, and practice of solicitors enrolled to practice in Scotland.

laws of the several states. State statutes and state-court decisions on questions of general law.

laws of Visby (**vis**-bee). A code of maritime customs and decisions adopted on the island of Gothland (in the Baltic Sea), where Visby was the principal port. ● Most scholars believe that this code postdates the laws of Oléron. The code was influential throughout northern Europe. In recognition of the ancient code, the Visby Protocol to amend the Hague Rules was signed in Visby. The Hague–Visby Rules govern most of the world's liner trade. — Also spelled *laws of Wisby.* — Also termed *Gothland sea laws.*

laws of war. *Int'l law.* The rules and principles agreed on by most nations for regulating matters inherent in or incident to the conduct of a public war, such as the relations of neutrals and belligerents, blockades, captures, prizes, truces and armistices, capitulations, prisoners, and declarations of war and peace. Cf. GENEVA CONVENTIONS OF 1949.

laws of Wisby. See LAWS OF VISBY.

law spiritual. See ECCLESIASTICAL LAW.

lawsuit, *n.* See SUIT.

lawsuit, *vb. Archaic.* To proceed against (an adversary) in a lawsuit; to sue.

law-talk, *n.* **1.** LEGALESE. **2.** Discussion that is heavily laced with lawyers' concerns and legal references.

law writer. (1852) A person who writes on legal subjects, usu. from a technical, nonpopular point of view.

lawyer, *n.* (14c) One who is licensed to practice law. Cf. ATTORNEY. — **lawyerly, lawyerlike,** *adj.* — **lawyerdom,** *n.*

  certified military lawyer. A person qualified to act as counsel in a general court-martial. ● To be qualified, the person must be (1) a judge advocate of the Army, Navy, Air Force, or Marine Corps, or a law specialist of the Coast Guard, (2) a graduate of an accredited law school, or a member of a federal-court bar or the bar of the highest court of a state, and (3) certified as competent to perform such duties by the Judge Advocate General of the armed force that the person is a member of.

  criminal lawyer. (18c) A lawyer whose primary work is to represent criminal defendants. ● This term is rarely if ever applied to prosecutors despite their integral involvement in the criminal-justice system.

  guardhouse lawyer. See JAILHOUSE LAWYER.

  headnote lawyer. *Slang.* A lawyer who relies on the headnotes of judicial opinions rather than taking the time to read the opinions themselves.

  jailhouse lawyer. See JAILHOUSE LAWYER.

  public-interest lawyer. An attorney whose practice is devoted to advocacy on behalf of a public institution or nongovernmental organization, or to advising and representing indigent clients and others who have limited access to legal aid. ● Public-interest lawyers often practice in fields such as civil rights and immigration law.

  transactional lawyer. (1990) A lawyer who works primarily on transactions such as licensing agreements, mergers, acquisitions, joint ventures, and the like.

lawyer, *vb.* (18c) **1.** To practice as a lawyer <associates often spend their days and nights lawyering, with little time for recreation>. **2.** To supply with lawyers <the large law-school class will certainly help lawyer the state>. — **lawyering,** *n.*

lawyer–client privilege. See *attorney–client privilege* under PRIVILEGE (3).

lawyer-referral and information service. See LAWYER-REFERRAL SERVICE.

lawyer-referral service. A program, usu. offered by a bar association, that helps nonindigent clients clarify their legal problems and provides either contact information for lawyers who practice in the appropriate field or information about government agencies or consumer organizations that may be able to provide services. — Also termed *lawyer referral and information service.*

lawyer-witness rule. (1982) The principle that an attorney who will likely be called as a fact witness at trial may not participate as an advocate in the case, unless the testimony will be about an uncontested matter or the amount of attorney's fees in the case, or if disqualifying the attorney would create a substantial hardship for the client. • The rule permits an attorney actively participating in the case to be a witness on merely formal matters but discourages testimony on other matters on behalf of a client. *Model Rules of Professional Conduct* Rule 3.7 (1983). — Also termed *advocate-witness rule*; *attorney-witness rule.*

lay, *adj.* (14c) **1.** Not ecclesiastical; not of the clergy. **2.** Not expert, esp. with reference to law or medicine; nonprofessional.

lay, *n. Maritime law.* A share of the profits of a fishing or whaling trip, akin to wages, allotted to the officers and seamen.

lay, *vb.* (14c) To allege or assert.

layaway. An agreement between a retail seller and a consumer to hold goods for future sale. • The seller sets the goods aside and agrees to sell them to the consumer at an agreed price in the future. The consumer deposits with the seller some portion of the price of the goods, and may agree to other conditions with the seller, such as progress payments. The consumer receives the goods once the full purchase price has been paid.

lay corporation. See CORPORATION.

lay damages, *vb.* To allege damages, esp. in the complaint. See AD DAMNUM CLAUSE.

layday. *Maritime law.* A day allowed by a voyage charterparty for the charterer to load or unload cargo. • If more time is used, the vessel's owner is entitled to compensation for the delay, usu. in the form of demurrage. If less time is used, the owner may pay dispatch. — Also written *lay day.* See DEMURRAGE; DISPATCH; LAYTIME. Cf. *day of demurrage* under DAY.

lay fee. See FEE (2).

laying a foundation. *Evidence.* Introducing evidence of certain facts needed to render later evidence relevant, material, or competent. • For example, propounding a hypothetical question to an expert is necessary before the expert may render an opinion.

laying of the venue. (18c) A statement in a complaint naming the district or county in which the plaintiff proposes that any trial of the matter should occur. See VENUE.

lay investiture. *Eccles. law.* The ceremony by which a layperson places a bishop in possession of lands, money revenues, and other diocesan temporalities.

lay judge. See JUDGE.

layman. (15c) **1.** A person who is not a member of the clergy. **2.** A person who is not a member of a profession or an expert on a particular subject. — Also termed *layperson.*

layoff. (1868) The termination of employment at the employer's instigation; esp., the termination — either temporary or permanent — of many employees in a short time. — Also termed *reduction in force.* — **lay off,** *vb.*

mass layoff. *Labor law.* Under the Worker Adjustment and Retraining Notification Act, a reduction in force that results in the loss of work at a single site, of 30 days or more, for at least 500 full-time employees, or 50 or more full-time employees if they make up at least 33% of the employees at that site. 29 USCA § 2101(a)(3). See WORKER ADJUSTMENT AND RETRAINING NOTIFICATION ACT.

layoff bet. See BET.

layoff bettor. A bookmaker who accepts layoff bets from other bookmakers. See *layoff bet* under BET.

lay on the table. *Parliamentary law.* **1.** To postpone the consideration of (a matter before a deliberative assembly); TABLE. • Some parliamentary writers prefer the form "to lay on the table" and disapprove of the form "to table." **2.** *British English.* To schedule for consideration.

lay opinion testimony. See TESTIMONY.

layperson. 1. See LAYMAN. **2.** *Hist.* See JUROR.

lay system. *Maritime law.* A system in which a fishing vessel's catch is sold by contract or at auction, and after costs are paid and the shipowner is compensated, the net profits are divided among the crew members according to agreed-on percentages.

lay tenure. See TENURE.

laytime. *Maritime law.* Time allowed by a voyage charterparty for the charterer to load or unload cargo. • If more time is used, the vessel's owner is entitled to compensation for the delay, usu. in the form of demurrage. If less time is used, the owner may pay dispatch. — See DEMURRAGE; DISPATCH; LAYDAY.

lay witness. See WITNESS.

LBO. See *leveraged buyout* under BUYOUT.

LC. *abbr.* **1.** LETTER OF CREDIT. **2.** LETTER OF CREDENCE. — Also written L/C.

L-Claim proceeding. (1997) A hearing under the Racketeer Influenced and Corrupt Organizations Act, intended to ensure that property ordered to be forfeited belongs solely to the defendant. • A petition for an L-Claim proceeding is filed by a third party who claims an interest in the property. The purpose is not to divide the assets among competing claimants, and general creditors of the defendant are not allowed to maintain an L-Claim petition. The name refers to its legal basis in subsection *l* of RICO's penalty provision. 18 USCA § 1963(*l*)(2).

LEAA. *abbr.* LAW ENFORCEMENT ASSISTANCE ADMINISTRATION.

leaching (leech-ing). (18c) The process by which moving fluid separates the soluble components of a material. • Under CERCLA, leaching is considered a release of contaminants. The term is sometimes used to describe the migration of contaminating materials, by rain or groundwater, from a fixed source, such as a landfill. 42 USCA § 9601(22).

lead counsel. See COUNSEL.

leader. See LOSS LEADER.

leading case. (17c) **1.** A judicial decision that first definitively settled an important legal rule or principle and that has since been often and consistently followed. • An example is *Miranda v. Arizona*, 384 U.S. 436, 86 S.Ct. 1602 (1966) (creating the exclusionary rule for evidence improperly obtained from a suspect being interrogated while in police custody). Cf. LANDMARK DECISION. **2.** An important, often the most important, judicial precedent on a particular legal issue. **3.** Loosely, a reported case that is cited as the dispositive authority on an issue being litigated. — Also termed (in sense 3) *ruling case.*

leading counsel. See *lead counsel* under COUNSEL.

leading economic indicator. See ECONOMIC INDICATOR.

leading indicator. See INDICATOR.

leading-object rule. See MAIN-PURPOSE RULE.

leading of a use. *Hist.* In a deed, the specification, before the levy of a fine of land, of the person to whose use the fine will inure. • If the deed is executed after the fine, it "declares" the use.

leading question. (1824) A question that suggests the answer to the person being interrogated; esp., a question that may be answered by a mere "yes" or "no." • Leading questions are generally allowed only in cross-examination. — Also termed *cat-egorical question; suggestive question; suggestive interrogation.*

lead-lag study. A survey used to determine the amount of working capital that a utility company must reserve and include in its rate base, by comparing the time the company has to pay its bills and the time taken by its customers to pay for service. • The term comes from the phrases "lead time" and "lag time." Lead time is the average number of days between the company's receipt and payment of invoices it receives. Lag time is the average number of days between the company's billing of its customers and its receipt of payment. By analyzing the difference in timing between inward cash flow and outward cash flow, the company can calculate the amount of necessary reserves.

leads doctrine. *Tax.* In a tax-evasion case, the rule that the government must investigate all the taxpayer's leads that are reasonably accessible and that, if true, would establish the taxpayer's innocence, or the government risks having the trial judge presume that any leads not investigated are true and exonerating.

league. (15c) **1.** A covenant made by nations, groups, or individuals for promoting common interests or ensuring mutual protection. **2.** An alliance or association of nations, groups, or individuals formed by such a covenant. **3.** A unit of distance, usu. measuring about three miles (chiefly, nautical).

> **marine league.** A geographical measure of distance equal to one-twentieth part of a degree of latitude, or three nautical miles.

League of Nations. An organization of nations formed in 1919 to promote international cooperation and peace. • President Woodrow Wilson endorsed the League in an address to Congress, but the United States never joined. The League dissolved in 1946 and turned its assets over to the United Nations.

leakage. (15c) **1.** The waste of a liquid caused by its leaking from a storage container. **2.** An allowance against duties granted by customs to an importer of liquids for losses sustained by this waste. **3.** *Intellectual property.* Loss in value of a piece of intellectual property because of unauthorized copying. • The types of intellectual property most susceptible to leakage are recordable media such as compact discs and videotapes.

lean, *vb.* (bef. 12c) **1.** To incline or tend in opinion or preference. • A court is sometimes said to "lean toward" or "lean against" an advocate's position, meaning that the court regards that position favorably or unfavorably. **2.** To yield; to submit.

leapfrog development. (1976) An improvement of land that requires the extension of public facilities from their current stopping point, through undeveloped land that may be scheduled for future development, to the site of the improvement.

learned (lər-nid), *adj.* (14c) **1.** Having a great deal of learning; erudite. • A lawyer might refer to an adversary as a "learned colleague" or "learned opponent" — a comment that, depending on the situation and tone of voice, may be either a genuine compliment or a sarcastic slight. **2.** Well-versed in the law and its history. • Statutes sometimes require that judges be "learned in the law," a phrase commonly construed as meaning that they must have earned a law degree and been admitted to the bar.

learned intermediary. See *informed intermediary* under INTERMEDIARY.

learned-intermediary doctrine. The principle that a prescription-drug manufacturer fulfills its duty to warn of a drug's potentially harmful effects by informing the prescribing physician, rather than the end-user, of those effects.

learned-treatise rule. (1946) *Evidence.* An exception to the hearsay rule, by which a published text may be established as authoritative, either by expert testimony or by judicial notice. • Under the Federal Rules of Evidence, a statement in a published treatise, periodical, or pamphlet on sciences or arts (such as history or medicine) can be established as authoritative — and thereby admitted into evidence for the purpose of examining or cross-examining an expert witness — by expert testimony or by the court's taking judicial notice of the authoritative nature or reliability of the text. If the statement is admitted into evidence, it may be read into the trial record, but it may not be received as an exhibit. Fed. R. Evid. 803(18).

learning, *n.* **1.** *Hist.* Legal doctrine. **2.** The act of acquiring knowledge.

lease, *n.* (14c) **1.** A contract by which a rightful possessor of real property conveys the right to use and occupy the property in exchange for consideration, usu. rent. • The lease term can be for life, for a fixed period, or for a period terminable at will. **2.** Such a conveyance plus all covenants attached to it. **3.** The written instrument memorializing such a conveyance and its covenants. — Also termed *lease agreement*; *lease contract*. **4.** The piece of real property so conveyed. **5.** A contract by which the rightful possessor of personal property conveys the right to use that property in exchange for consideration.

assignable lease. (1915) A lease that the lessee can transfer to a successor. See SUBLEASE.

building lease. A long-term lease of land that includes a covenant to erect or alter a building or other improvement. Cf. *ground lease.*

capital lease. See LEASE-PURCHASE AGREEMENT.

commercial lease. (1909) A lease for business purposes.

community lease. (1919) A lease in which a number of lessors owning interests in separate tracts execute a lease in favor of a single lessee.

concurrent lease. (1946) A lease that begins before a previous lease ends, entitling the new lessee to be paid all rents that accrue on the previous lease after the new lease begins, and to remedies against the holding tenant.

consumer lease. (1972) **1.** A lease of goods by a person who is in the business of selling or leasing a product primarily for the lessee's personal or household use. UCC § 2A-103(1)(e). **2.** A residential — rather than commercial — lease.

derivative lease. See SUBLEASE.

durable lease. (1816) A lease that reserves a rent payable annually, usu. with a right of reentry for nonpayment.

edge lease. *Oil & gas.* A lease located on the edge of a field.

finance lease. (1966) A fixed-term lease used by a business to finance capital equipment. • The lessor's service is usu. limited to financing the asset, and the lessee pays maintenance costs and taxes and has the option of purchasing the asset at lease-end for a nominal price. Finance leases strongly resemble security agreements and are written almost exclusively by financial institutions as a way to help a commercial customer obtain an expensive capital item that the customer might not otherwise be able to afford. UCC § 2A-103(1)(g). — Also termed *full payout lease*; *tripartite lease.*

full-service lease. (1967) A lease in which the lessor agrees to pay all maintenance expenses, insurance premiums, and property taxes.

graduated lease. (1930) A lease in which rent varies depending on future contingencies, such as operating expenses or gross income.

gross lease. (1939) A lease in which the lessee pays a flat amount for rent, out of which the lessor pays all the expenses (such as fuel, water, and electricity).

ground lease. (1840) A long-term (usu. 99-year) lease of land only. • Such a lease typically involves commercial property, and any improvements built by the lessee usu. revert to the lessor. — Also termed *ground-rent lease*; *land lease.*

headlease. See HEADLEASE.

index lease. A lease that provides for increases in rent according to the increases in the consumer price index.

land lease. See *ground lease.*

leveraged lease. (1972) A lease that is collateral for the loan through which the lessor acquired the leased asset, and that provides the lender's only recourse for nonpayment of the debt; a lease in which a creditor provides nonrecourse financing to the lessor (who has substantial leverage in the property) and in which the lessor's net investment in the lease, apart from nonrecourse financing, declines during the early years and increases in later years. — Also termed *third-party equity lease; tax lease.*

master lease. (1935) A contract that establishes a leasehold's basic terms and conditions applicable to all related contracts for rental properties.

mineral lease. A lease in which the lessee has the right to explore for and extract oil, gas, or other minerals. • The rent usu. is based on the amount or value of the minerals extracted.

mining lease. A lease of a mine or mining claim, in which the lessee has the right to work the mine or claim, usu. with conditions on the amount and type of work to be done. • The lessor is compensated with either fixed rent or royalties based on the amount of ore mined.

month-to-month lease. (1914) A tenancy with no written contract. • Rent is paid monthly, and usu. one month's notice by the landlord or tenant is required to terminate the tenancy. See *periodic tenancy* under TENANCY.

net lease. A lease in which the lessee pays rent plus property expenses (such as taxes and insurance).

net-net-net lease. A lease in which the lessee pays all the expenses, including mortgage interest and amortization, leaving the lessor with an amount free of all claims. — Also termed *triple net lease.*

oil-and-gas lease. (1892) A lease granting the right to extract oil and gas from a specified piece of land. • Although called a "lease," this interest is typically considered a determinable fee in the minerals rather than a grant of possession for a term of years.

operating lease. A lease of property (esp. equipment) for a term that is shorter than the property's useful life. • Under an operating lease, the lessor is typically responsible for paying taxes and other expenses on the property. Cf. *capital lease*; LEASE-PURCHASE AGREEMENT.

"or" lease. *Oil & gas.* A mineral lease with a drilling-delay rental clause structured so that the lessee promises to start drilling operations or to pay delay rentals from time to time during the primary term. • If the lessee fails to do one or the other, the lease does not automatically

terminate, but the lessee is liable for the delay-rental amount.

parol lease (pǝ-**rohl** *or* **par**-ǝl). A lease based on an oral agreement; an unwritten lease.

percentage lease. A lease in which the rent is based on a percentage of gross (or net) sales or profits, typically with a set minimum rent.

perpetual lease. 1. An ongoing lease not limited in duration. **2.** A grant of lands in fee with a reservation of a rent in fee; a fee farm.

proprietary lease. A lease between a cooperative apartment association and a tenant.

reversionary lease. A lease that will take effect when a prior lease terminates.

sandwich lease. (1976) A lease in which the lessee subleases the property to a third party, esp. for more rent than under the original lease.

short lease. (17c) A lease of brief duration, often less than six months.

sublease. See SUBLEASE.

synthetic lease. A method for financing the purchase of real estate, whereby the lender creates a special-purpose entity that buys the property and then leases it to the ultimate user (usu. a corporation). • A synthetic lease is treated as a loan for tax purposes and as an operating lease for accounting purposes, so that the "lessee" can deduct the property's depreciation and the loan's interest yet keep both the asset and the debt off its balance sheet.

tax lease. 1. The instrument or estate given to the purchaser of land at a tax sale when the law does not permit the sale of an estate in fee for nonpayment of taxes but instead directs the sale of an estate for years. **2.** See *leveraged lease.*

third-party equity lease. See *leveraged lease.*

timber lease. (1853) A real-property lease that contemplates that the lessee will cut timber on the leased premises.

top lease. *Oil & gas.* A lease granted on property already subject to an oil-and-gas lease. • Generally, any rights granted by a top lease grants are valid only if the existing lease ends.

tripartite lease. See *finance lease.*

triple net lease. See *net-net-net lease.*

"unless" lease. *Oil & gas.* An oil-and-gas lease with a drilling-delay rental clause structured as a special limitation to the primary term. • Unless delay rentals are paid or drilling operations are started from time to time as specified, an "unless" lease automatically terminates, and the lessee has no liability for its failure to perform.

lease, *vb.* (16c) **1.** To grant the possession and use of (land, buildings, rooms, movable property, etc.) to another in return for rent or other consideration

<the city leased the stadium to the football team>. **2.** To take a lease of; to hold by a lease <Carol leased the townhouse from her uncle>.

lease agreement. See LEASE (3).

lease and release. *Hist.* A method of transferring seisin without livery, whereby the owner and the transferee would enter into a lease for a term of years, to take effect only when the transferee entered the property, whereupon the owner would release all interest in the property to the transferee by written instrument. • Once the transferee owned both the term and the freehold interest, the two interests would merge to form one estate in fee simple. This lease-and-release procedure was fully acceptable to the courts, on the theory that livery of seisin to one already occupying the land was unnecessary.

leaseback, *n.* (1947) The sale of property on the understanding, or with the express option, that the seller may lease the property from the buyer immediately upon the sale. — Also termed *sale and leaseback*; *sale-leaseback*.

lease contract. See LEASE (3).

lease for life. *Hist.* A lease of land for the duration of a specified number of lives instead of for a specified term of years. • Unlike a tenant for a term of years, a lessee for life could recover the land if dispossessed.

lease for years. See *tenancy for a term* under TENANCY.

leasehold, *n.* (18c) A tenant's possessory estate in land or premises, the four types being the tenancy for years, the periodic tenancy, the tenancy at will, and the tenancy at sufferance. • Although a leasehold has some of the characteristics of real property, it has historically been classified as a chattel real. — Also termed *leasehold estate*; *leasehold interest*. See TENANCY. Cf. FREEHOLD.

leaseholder royalty. See *landowner's royalty* under ROYALTY (2).

leasehold improvements. (1845) Beneficial changes to leased property (such as a parking lot or driveway) made by or for the benefit of the lessee. • The phrase is used in a condemnation proceeding to determine the share of compensation to be allocated to the lessee.

leasehold interest. (18c) **1.** LEASEHOLD; esp., for purposes of eminent domain, the lessee's interest in the lease itself, measured by the difference between the total remaining rent and the rent the lessee would pay for similar space for the same period. **2.** A lessor's or lessee's interest under a lease contract. UCC § 2A-103.

leasehold mortgage. See MORTGAGE.

leasehold-mortgage bond. See BOND (3).

leasehold royalty. See *landowner's royalty* under ROYALTY (2).

leasehold value. The value of a leasehold interest. • This term usu. applies to a long-term lease when the rent paid under the lease is lower than current market rates. Some states permit the lessee to claim the leasehold interest from the landlord in a condemnation proceeding, unless the lease prohibits such a claim. Other states prohibit these claims by statute. See LEASEHOLD INTEREST; NO-BONUS CLAUSE.

lease insurance. See INSURANCE.

lease-lend. See LEND-LEASE.

lease option. See OPTION.

lease-purchase agreement. (1939) A rent-to-own purchase plan under which the buyer takes possession of the goods with the first payment and takes ownership with the final payment; a lease of property (esp. equipment) by which ownership of the property is transferred to the lessee at the end of the lease term. • Such a lease is usu. treated as an installment sale. Under a capital lease, the lessee is responsible for paying taxes and other expenses on the property. — Also termed *lease-to-purchase agreement*; *hire-purchase agreement*; *capital lease*. Cf. *operating lease* under LEASE.

lease with an option to purchase. See *lease option* under OPTION.

least-intrusive-means doctrine. (1978) A doctrine requiring the government to exhaust all other investigatory means before seeking sensitive testimony, as by compelling an attorney to testify before a grand jury on matters that may be protected by the attorney–client privilege.

least-intrusive-remedy doctrine. (1989) The rule that a legal remedy should provide the damaged party with appropriate relief, without unduly penalizing the opposing party or the jurisdiction's legal system, as by striking only the unconstitutional portion of a challenged statute while leaving the rest intact.

least-restrictive educational environment. See LEAST-RESTRICTIVE ENVIRONMENT.

least-restrictive environment. Under the Individuals with Disabilities Education Act, the school setting that, to the greatest extent appropriate, educates a disabled child together with children who are not disabled. 20 USCA § 1412(5). — Also termed *least-restrictive-educational environment*. Cf. MAINSTREAMING.

least-restrictive-means test. (1972) The rule that a law or governmental regulation should be crafted in a way that will protect individual civil liberties as much as possible and should be only as restrictive as necessary to accomplish a legitimate governmental purpose.

leave, *n.* (bef. 12c) **1.** Departure; the act of going away <took his leave>. **2.** Extended absence for which one has authorization; esp., a voluntary vacation from military duties with the chance to visit home; furlough <on a three-month leave from the Army>. **3.** Permission <by leave of court>.

leave, *vb.* (bef. 12c) **1.** To give by will; to bequeath or devise <she left her ranch to her stepson>. • This usage has historically been considered loose by the courts, and it is not always given testamentary effect. **2.** To be survived by <he left no brothers or sisters>. **3.** To depart; voluntarily go away; quit (a place). **4.** To depart willfully with the intent not to return <Nelson left Texas and became a resident of Massachusetts>. **5.** To deliver (a summons, money, an article, etc.) by dropping off at a certain place, esp. to await the return of someone; esp., to post (a copy of a writ, etc.).

leave and license. In an action for trespass to land, the defense that the plaintiff consented to the defendant's presence.

leave no issue, *vb.* (16c) To die without any surviving child or other descendant. • The spouse of a deceased child is usu. not issue. See FAILURE OF ISSUE.

leave of absence. (18c) A worker's temporary absence from employment or duty with the intention to return. • Salary level and seniority typically are unaffected by a leave of absence.

leave of court. (18c) Judicial permission to follow a nonroutine procedure <the defense sought leave of court to allow the defendant to exit the courtroom when the autopsy photographs are shown>. — Often shortened to *leave.*

leave to sit. *Parliamentary law.* Permission from a deliberative assembly for a committee or other subordinate body to meet while the assembly is meeting.

LEC. *abbr.* LOCAL-EXCHANGE CARRIER.

lecture method. See HORNBOOK METHOD.

ledger (**lej**-ər). (16c) **1.** A book or series of books used for recording financial transactions in the form of debits and credits. — Also termed *general ledger.* **2.** *Archaic.* A resident ambassador or agent. — Also termed (in sense 2) *leger; lieger.*

leet (leet). *Hist.* A criminal court. • The last leets were abolished in England in 1977.

left-handed marriage. See *morganatic marriage* under MARRIAGE (1).

legacy (**leg**-ə-see), *n.* (15c) A gift by will, esp. of personal property and often of money. Cf. BEQUEST; DEVISE.

   absolute legacy. A legacy given without condition and intended to vest immediately. Cf. *vested legacy.*

   accumulated legacy. A legacy that has not yet been paid to a legatee.

   accumulative legacy. See *additional legacy.*

   additional legacy. A second legacy given to a legatee in the same will (or in a codicil to the same will) that gave another legacy. • An additional legacy is supplementary to another and is not considered merely a repeated expression of the same gift. — Also termed *accumulative legacy; cumulative legacy.*

   alternate legacy. (1983) A legacy by which the testator allows the legatee to choose one of two or more items.

   conditional legacy. (17c) A legacy that will take effect or be defeated subject to the occurrence or nonoccurrence of an event.

   contingent legacy. (18c) A legacy that depends on an uncertain event and thus has not vested. • An example is a legacy given to one's granddaughter "if she attains the age of 21.

   cumulative legacy. See *additional legacy.*

   demonstrative legacy (di-**mon**-strə-tiv). (18c) A legacy paid from a particular source if that source has enough money. • If it does not, the amount of the legacy not paid from that source is taken from the estate's general assets.

   failed legacy. See *lapsed legacy.*

   general legacy. (18c) **1.** A gift of personal property that the testator intends to come from the estate's general assets, payable in money or items indistinguishable from each other, such as shares of publicly traded stock. **2.** *Civil law.* A testator's gift of a fraction or proportion of the estate remaining after particular legacies have been satisfied. **3.** *Civil law.* A testator's gift of all, a fraction, or a proportion of one of certain categories of property, as specified by statute. See La. Civ. Code arts. 1586, 3506(28). — Also termed *legacy under a general title.* Cf. *particular legacy; universal legacy.*

   lapsed legacy. (18c) A legacy to a legatee who dies either before the testator dies or before the legacy is payable. • It falls into the residual estate unless the jurisdiction has an antilapse statute. — Also termed *failed legacy; failed gift.* See ANTILAPSE STATUTE.

   legacy under a general title. See *general legacy.*

   legacy under a particular title. See *particular legacy.*

   legacy under a universal title. *Louisiana law.* A testamentary disposition of all immovable property, or all movable property, or a fixed proportion of all immovable property or of all movable property. La. Civ. Code art. 1612. Cf. *general legacy; particular legacy; universal legacy.*

modal legacy (**moh**-dəl). A legacy accompanied by directions about the manner in which it will be applied to the legatee's benefit <a modal legacy for the purchase of a business>.

particular legacy. *Civil law.* A testamentary gift that is not expressed as a fraction or proportion and is less than all the estate; any testamentary gift that does not meet the definition of a general legacy or a universal legacy. *See* La. Civ. Code arts. 1587, 3506(28). — Also termed *legacy under a particular title.* Cf. *general legacy; universal legacy.*

pecuniary legacy (pi-**kyoo**-nee-er-ee). (18c) A legacy of a sum of money.

residuary legacy (ri-**zij**-oo-er-ee). (18c) A legacy of the estate remaining after the satisfaction of all claims and all specific, general, and demonstrative legacies.

special legacy. See *specific legacy.*

specific legacy. (18c) A legacy of a specific or unique item of property, such as any real estate or a particular piece of furniture. — Also termed *special legacy.*

substitutional legacy. (1894) A legacy that replaces a different legacy already given to a legatee.

trust legacy. A legacy of personal property to trustees to be held in trust, with the income usu. paid to a specified beneficiary.

universal legacy. *Louisiana law.* A testamentary disposition of all property, movable and immovable, to one or more persons. La. Civ. Code art. 1585. Cf. *general legacy; legacy under a universal title; particular legacy.*

vested legacy. (18c) A legacy given in such a way that the legatee has a fixed, indefeasible right to its payment. • A legacy is said to be vested when the testator's words making the bequest convey a transmissible interest, whether present or future, to the legatee. Thus, a legacy to be paid when the legatee reaches the age of 21 is a vested legacy because it is given unconditionally and absolutely. Although the legacy is vested, the legatee's enjoyment of it is deferred. Cf. *absolute legacy; contingent legacy.*

void legacy. (18c) A legacy that never had any legal existence. • The subject matter of such a legacy is treated as a part of the estate and passes under the residuary clause of a will or (in the absence of a residuary clause) under the rules for intestate succession.

legacy duty. See *legacy tax* under TAX.

legacy tax. See TAX.

legal, *adj.* (15c) **1.** Of or relating to law; falling within the province of law <pro bono legal services>. **2.** Established, required, or permitted by law; LAWFUL <it is legal to carry a concealed handgun in some states>. **3.** Of or relating to law as opposed to equity.

legal act. (15c) **1.** Any act not condemned as illegal. • For example, a surgeon's incision is a legal act, while stabbing is an illegal one. **2.** An action or undertaking that creates a legally recognized obligation; an act that binds a person in some way. **3.** See *act in the law* under ACT. **4.** See *act of the law* under ACT.

legal-acumen doctrine (**lee**-gəl ə-**kyoo**-mən). (1905) The principle that if a defect in, or the invalidity of, a claim to land cannot be discovered without legal expertise, then equity may be invoked to remove the cloud created by the defect or invalidity.

legal-advice exception. 1. The rule that an attorney may withhold as privileged the client's identity and information regarding fees, if there is a strong probability that disclosing the information would implicate the client in the criminal activity for which the attorney was consulted. **2.** An exemption contained in open-meetings legislation, permitting a governmental body to meet in closed session to consult with its attorney about certain matters.

legal age. (18c) **1.** See *age of capacity* under AGE. **2.** See *age of majority* (1) under AGE.

legal aid. (1890) Free or inexpensive legal services provided to those who cannot afford to pay full price. • Legal aid is usu. administered locally by a specially established organization. See LEGAL SERVICES CORPORATION.

legal analyst. See PARALEGAL.

legal asset. See ASSET.

legal assistant. (1939) **1.** PARALEGAL. **2.** A legal secretary.

legal benefit. See BENEFIT (2).

legal brief. See BRIEF (1).

legal capital. See CAPITAL.

legal cause. See *proximate cause* under CAUSE (1).

legal centralism. The theory suggesting that state-constructed legal entities form the center of legal life and control lesser normative systems (such as the family or business networks) that define appropriate behavior and social relationships. — Also termed *legal centrism; legocentrism* (lee-goh-**sen**-triz-əm).

legal-certainty test. (1964) *Civil procedure.* A test designed to determine whether the amount in controversy satisfies the minimum needed to establish the court's jurisdiction. • The amount claimed in the complaint will control unless there is a "legal certainty" that the claim is actually less than the minimum amount. See AMOUNT IN CONTROVERSY.

legal citology (si-**tol**-ə-jee). (1996) The study of citations (esp. in footnotes) and their effect on legal scholarship. — Often shortened to *citology*. — **legal citologist** (si-**tol**-ə-jist), *n.*

Legal Code. See CODE (2).

legal conclusion. (17c) A statement that expresses a legal duty or result but omits the facts creating or supporting the duty or result. Cf. CONCLUSION OF LAW; CONCLUSION OF FACT; FINDING OF FACT.

legal consideration. See *valuable consideration* under CONSIDERATION (1).

legal correlative. A legal status that has a corresponding or reciprocal status, such as a right that corresponds to a duty. ● Wesley Newcomb Hohfeld of Yale Law School first introduced the bases for the concept of legal correlatives in two articles published in the *Yale Law Journal* in 1913 and 1917. He polished the concept in the book *Fundamental Legal Conceptions, as Applied in Judicial Reasoning and Other Legal Essays*, published posthumously in 1919.

legal cruelty. See CRUELTY.

legal custody. 1. See CUSTODY (2). **2.** See CUSTODY (3). **3.** See DECISION-MAKING RESPONSIBILITY.

legal custom. See CUSTOM.

legal death. 1. See *brain death* under DEATH. **2.** See *civil death* (2) under DEATH. **3.** See *civil death* (3) under DEATH.

legal debt. See DEBT.

legal defense. See DEFENSE (1).

legal demand. See DEMAND (1).

legal dependent. See DEPENDENT.

legal description. (18c) A formal description of real property, including a description of any part subject to an easement or reservation, complete enough that a particular piece of land can be located and identified. ● The description can be made by reference to a government survey, metes and bounds, or lot numbers of a recorded plat. — Also termed *land description*.

legal detriment. See DETRIMENT (2).

legal discretion. See *judicial discretion* under DISCRETION.

legal distributee. See DISTRIBUTEE.

legal drafting. See DRAFTING.

legal duty. See DUTY (1).

legal-elements test. (1980) *Criminal law.* A method of determining whether one crime is a lesser included offense in relation to another crime, by examining the components of the greater crime to analyze whether a person who commits the greater crime necessarily commits the lesser one too. — Also termed *same-elements test*.

legal entity. (18c) A body, other than a natural person, that can function legally, sue or be sued, and make decisions through agents. ● A typical example is a corporation. Cf. *artificial person* under PERSON (3).

legalese (lee-gə-**leez**). (1914) The jargon characteristically used by lawyers, esp. in legal documents <the partner chided the associate about the rampant legalese in the draft sublease>. — Also termed *law-talk*. See PLAIN-LANGUAGE MOVEMENT.

legal estate. See ESTATE (1).

legal estoppel. See ESTOPPEL.

legal ethics. (1828) **1.** Standards of professional conduct applicable to members of the legal profession. ● Ethical rules consist primarily of the ABA Model Rules of Professional Conduct and the earlier ABA Model Code of Professional Responsibility, together with related regulatory judgments and opinions. The Model Rules of Professional Conduct have been enacted into law, often in a modified form, in most states. **2.** The study of such standards. **3.** A lawyer's practical observance of or conformity to established standards of professional conduct. See MODEL RULES OF PROFESSIONAL CONDUCT.

legal etiquette. The professional courtesy that lawyers have traditionally observed in their professional conduct, shown through civility and a strong sense of honor. — Also termed *etiquette of the profession*.

legal evidence. See EVIDENCE.

legal excuse. See EXCUSE (2).

legal fact. See FACT.

legal father. See FATHER.

legal fence. See LAWFUL FENCE.

legal fiction. (17c) An assumption that something is true even though it may be untrue, made esp. in judicial reasoning to alter how a legal rule operates; specif., a device by which a legal rule or institution is diverted from its original purpose to accomplish indirectly some other object. ● The constructive trust is an example of a legal fiction. — Often shortened to *fiction*. — Also termed *fiction of law*; *fictio juris*.

legal force. See *reasonable force* under FORCE.

legal formalism, *n.* (1895) The theory that law is a set of rules and principles independent of other political and social institutions. ● Legal formalism was espoused by such scholars as Christopher Columbus Langdell and Lon Fuller. Cf. LEGAL REALISM. — **legal formalist,** *n.*

legal fraud. See *constructive fraud* (1) under FRAUD.

legal heir. See HEIR (1).

legal holiday. (1867) A day designated by law as exempt from court proceedings, issuance of process, and the like. ● Legal holidays vary from state to state. — Sometimes shortened to *holiday*. — Also termed *nonjudicial day*.

legal hybrid. *Property.* A cooperative housing unit in which the same person holds a lease and also owns stock in the cooperative association that owns or leases the unit.

legal impossibility. See IMPOSSIBILITY.

legal inconsistency. See *legally inconsistent verdict* under VERDICT.

legal injury. See INJURY.

legal-injury rule. (1956) The doctrine that the statute of limitations on a claim does not begin to run until the claimant has sustained some legally actionable damage. ● Under this rule, the limitations period is tolled until the plaintiff has actually been injured. — Also termed *damage rule*.

legal innocence. See INNOCENCE.

legal insanity. See INSANITY.

legal instrument. See INSTRUMENT (1).

legal interest. 1. INTEREST (2). **2.** INTEREST (3).

legal interruption. See INTERRUPTION.

legal intromission. See INTROMISSION.

legal investments. See LEGAL LIST.

legalism, *n.* (1928) **1.** Formalism carried almost to the point of meaninglessness; an inclination to exalt the importance of law or formulated rules in any area of action. **2.** A mode of expression characteristic of lawyers; a jargonistic phrase characteristic of lawyers, such as "pursuant to."

legal issue. See ISSUE (1).

legalist, *n.* (1829) A person who views things from a legal or formalistic standpoint; esp., one who believes in strict adherence to the letter of the law rather than its spirit.

legalistic, *adj.* (17c) Characterized by legalism; exalting the importance of law or formulated rules in any area of action <a legalistic argument>.

legality. (15c) **1.** Strict adherence to law, prescription, or doctrine; the quality of being legal. **2.** The principle that a person may not be prosecuted under a criminal law that has not been previously published. — Also termed (in sense 2) *principle of legality*.

legalize, *vb.* (18c) **1.** To make lawful; to authorize or justify by legal sanction <the bill to legalize marijuana never made it to the Senate floor>. **2.** To imbue with the spirit of the law; to make legalistic <as religions age, they tend to become legalized>. — **legalization,** *n.*

legalized nuisance. See NUISANCE.

legal jeopardy. See JEOPARDY.

legal jointure. See JOINTURE (2).

legal liability. See LIABILITY (1).

legal life estate. See *life estate* under ESTATE (1).

legal life tenant. See LIFE TENANT.

legal list. A group of investments in which institutions and fiduciaries (such as banks and insurance companies) may legally invest according to state statutes. ● States usu. restrict the legal list to low-risk securities meeting certain specifications. — Also termed *approved list*; *legal investments*.

legally, *adv.* (16c) In a lawful way; in a manner that accords with the law.

legally determined, *adj.* (17c) (Of a claim, issue, etc.) decided by legal process <liability for the accident was legally determined>.

legally incapacitated person. (1919) A person, other than a minor, who is temporarily or permanently impaired by mental illness, mental deficiency, physical illness or disability, or alcohol or drug use to the extent that the person lacks sufficient understanding to make or communicate responsible personal decisions or to enter into contracts. — Abbr. LIP. — Also termed *legally incompetent person*; *incompetent*, n.

legally inconsistent verdict. See VERDICT.

legally liable. See LIABLE.

legally protected interest. See INTEREST (2).

legally sufficient consideration. See *sufficient consideration* under CONSIDERATION (1).

legal malice. See *implied malice* under MALICE.

legal malpractice. See MALPRACTICE.

legal maxim. See MAXIM.

legal memory. (1882) The period during which a legal right or custom can be determined or established. ● Traditionally, common-law legal memory began in the year 1189, but in 1540 it became a steadily moving period of 60 years. Cf. TIME IMMEMORIAL (1).

legal mind. (18c) The intellect, legal capacities, and attitudes of a well-trained lawyer — often used as a personified being <although this distinction occurs naturally to the legal mind, it is too technical to be satisfactory>.

legal monopoly. See MONOPOLY.

legal moralism. (1963) The theory that a government or legal system may prohibit conduct that is considered immoral.

legal mortgage. See MORTGAGE.

legal name. See NAME.

legal negligence. See *negligence per se* under NEGLIGENCE.

legal newspaper. See NEWSPAPER.

legal notice. See NOTICE.

legal obligation. See OBLIGATION.

legal officer. See OFFICER (2).

legal opinion. See OPINION (2).

legal order. (16c) **1.** Traditionally, a set of regulations governing a society and those responsible for enforcing them. **2.** Modernly, such regulations and officials plus the processes involved in creating, interpreting, and applying the regulations.

legal owner. See OWNER.

legal parent. See PARENT (1).

legal paternalism. (1913) The theory that a government or legal system is justified in controlling the individual and private affairs of citizens. • This theory is often associated with legal positivists. See PATERNALISM; LEGAL POSITIVISM.

legal person. See *artificial person* under PERSON (3).

legal personality. See PERSONALITY (1).

legal–personal representative. See REPRESENTATIVE.

legal philosophy. See *general jurisprudence* (2) under JURISPRUDENCE.

legal portion. See LEGITIME.

legal positivism, *n.* (1939) The theory that legal rules are valid only because they are enacted by an existing political authority or accepted as binding in a given society, not because they are grounded in morality or in natural law. • Legal positivism has been espoused by such scholars as H.L.A. Hart. See POSITIVE LAW. Cf. LOGICAL POSITIVISM. — **legal positivist,** *n.*

legal possessor. See POSSESSOR.

legal practice. See PRACTICE OF LAW.

legal practitioner. 1. A lawyer. **2.** In the traditional English system, a member of one of the recognized branches of practice.

legal prejudice. See PREJUDICE.

legal presumption. See *presumption of law* under PRESUMPTION.

legal proceeding. (17c) Any proceeding authorized by law and instituted in a court or tribunal to acquire a right or to enforce a remedy.

legal process. See PROCESS.

legal question. See QUESTION OF LAW.

legal rate. See INTEREST RATE.

legal realism, *n.* (1930) The theory that law is based, not on formal rules or principles, but instead on judicial decisions that should derive from social interests and public policy. • American legal realism — which flourished in the early 20th century — was espoused by such scholars as John Chipman Gray, Oliver Wendell Holmes, and Karl Llewellyn. Cf. LEGAL FORMALISM. — **legal realist,** *n.*

legal regime. See REGIME.

legal relation. The connection in law between one person or entity and another; VINCULUM JURIS.

legal remedy. See REMEDY.

legal representative. See REPRESENTATIVE.

legal rescission. See RESCISSION.

legal research. (18c) **1.** The finding and assembling of authorities that bear on a question of law. **2.** The field of study concerned with the effective marshaling of authorities that bear on a question of law.

legal reserve. See RESERVE.

legal residence. See DOMICILE (2).

legal right. See RIGHT.

legal ruling. See RULING.

legal science. (18c) The field of study that, as one of the social sciences, deals with the institutions and principles that particular societies have developed (1) for defining the claims and liabilities of persons against one another in various circumstances, and (2) for peaceably resolving disputes and controversies in accordance with principles accepted as fair and right in the particular community at a given time.

legal secretary. (1897) An employee in a law office whose responsibilities include typing legal documents and correspondence, keeping records and files, and performing other duties supportive of the employer's law practice. • Legal secretaries are usu. more highly skilled, and therefore more highly compensated, than secretaries in general business.

legal seisin. See *seisin in law* under SEISIN.

legal separation. 1. See SEPARATION (1). **2.** See SEPARATION (2). **3.** See *divorce a mensa et thoro* under DIVORCE.

Legal Services Corporation. A nonprofit federal corporation that provides financial aid in civil cases to those who cannot afford legal assistance through grants to legal-aid and other organizations and by contracting with individuals, firms, corporations, and organizations to provide legal services. • The agency was created by the Legal Services Corporation Act of 1974. 42 USCA § 2996.

legal servitude. See SERVITUDE (2).

legal signature. See SIGNATURE.

legal subdivision. See SUBDIVISION.

legal subrogation. See SUBROGATION.

legal succession. 1. See SUCCESSION (2). **2.** See DESCENT.

legal tender. (18c) The money (bills and coins) approved in a country for the payment of debts, the purchase of goods, and other exchanges for value. See TENDER (5).

legal theory. (1804) **1.** See *general jurisprudence* under JURISPRUDENCE. **2.** The principle under which a litigant proceeds, or on which a litigant bases its claims or defenses in a case.

legal title. See TITLE (2).

legal tutorship. See TUTORSHIP.

legal-unities doctrine. *Hist.* The common-law rule that a wife had no separate existence from her husband. — Also termed *doctrine of legal unities*; *unities doctrine of marriage.* See MARRIED WOMEN'S PROPERTY ACTS; SPOUSAL-UNITY DOCTRINE.

legal usufruct. See USUFRUCT.

legal value. See BENEFIT (2).

legal vote. See VOTE (1).

legal voter. See VOTER (2).

legal willfulness. See WILLFULNESS.

Legal Writing Institute. A nonprofit corporation founded in 1984 to promote the exchange of information and ideas about the teaching of legal writing. ● It is composed mainly of legal-writing teachers at American law schools. Like its sister organization, the Association of Legal Writing Directors, it seeks to improve the teaching of legal writing through research and scholarship, a biennial conference, an annual survey of legal-writing programs, an active listserv, and publications that include a journal called *Legal Writing.* — Abbr. LWI.

legal wrong. See WRONG.

legantine. See LEGATINE.

legatary (leg-ə-ter-ee), *n. Archaic.* See LEGATEE.

legate (leg-it), *n.* [fr. Latin *legare* "to send as an envoy"] (12c) **1.** *Roman law.* An official who undertakes a special mission for the emperor, or an official or body such as a municipality. **2.** *Roman law.* A person deputed to assist or act for the emperor, a governor, or a general in a military or administrative activity. **3.** A papal representative who may or may not have both diplomatic and ecclesiastical status; a diplomatic agent of the Vatican. Cf. NUNCIO (1); INTERNUNCIO (3).

legate a latere (ay lat-ə-ree). See *legatus a latere* under LEGATUS.

legate missus (mis-əs). See *legatus missus* under LEGATUS.

legate natus (nay-təs). See *legatus natus* under LEGATUS.

4. A representative of a state or the highest authority in a state; an ambassador; a person commissioned to represent a country in a foreign country. — Also termed *legatus.* — **legatine,** *adj.*

legate (lə-gayt), *vb.* To give or leave as a legacy; to make a testamentary gift of (property); BEQUEATH.

legatee (leg-ə-tee). (17c) **1.** One who is named in a will to take personal property; one who has received a legacy or bequest. **2.** Loosely, one to whom a devise of real property is given. — Also termed (archaically) *legatary.* Cf. DEVISEE.

general legatee. A person whose bequest is of a specified quantity to be paid out of the estate's personal assets.

residuary legatee (ri-zij-oo-er-ee). (18c) A person designated to receive the residue of a decedent's estate. See *residuary estate* under ESTATE (3).

specific legatee. (18c) The recipient, under a will, of designated property that is transferred by the owner's death.

universal legatee. A residuary legatee that receives the entire residuary estate.

legatine (leg-ə-teen *or* -tin), *adj.* Of or relating to a legate. — Also termed (erroneously) *legantine.*

legatine court. See COURT.

legation (lə-gay-shən). (14c) *Int'l law.* **1.** The act or practice of sending a diplomat to another country; a diplomatic mission. **2.** A body of diplomats sent to a foreign country and headed by an envoy extraordinary or a minister plenipotentiary. **3.** The official residence of a diplomatic minister in a foreign country. Cf. EMBASSY.

legator (lə-gay-tər *or* leg-ə-tor), *n. Rare.* One who bequeaths a legacy; TESTATOR.

legatory (leg-ə-tor-ee), *n. Hist.* The one-third portion of a freeman's estate in land that he could dispose of by will. ● The other two portions of the estate were subject to claims of the wife and children.

legatum (lə-gay-təm), *n.* [Latin fr. *legare* "to bequeath"] **1.** *Roman law.* A special bequest; a gift left by a deceased person to be paid from the estate by the heir. ● Unlike an heir, a legatee acquired a benefit and no duties attached. **2.** *Hist.* A legacy or bequest to the church, esp. for tithes not paid while the donor lived. See MORTUARY.

legatus (lə-gay-təs), *n.* A legate. Pl. *legati* (lə-gay-tI) See LEGATE.

legatus a latere (ay lat-ə-ree). [Latin "legate from the (Pope's) side"] A papal legate (esp. a cardinal) appointed for a special diplomatic mission and not as a permanent representative. ● This is a type of *legatus missus.* — Also termed *legate a latere.* Cf. NUNCIO.

legatus datus (day-təs). See *legatus missus.*

legatus missus (mis-əs). [Latin "legate sent"] A legate sent on a special mission. — Also termed *legate missus; legatus datus* (day-təs).

legatus natus (**nay**-təs). [Latin "legate born"] A bishop or archbishop who claims to be a legate by virtue of office in an important see, such as Canterbury. — Also termed *legate natus*.

leges (**lee**-jeez), *n. pl.* [Latin] **1.** See LEX. **2.** See LEGES PUBLICAE.

leges Angliae (**lee**-jeez **ang**-glee-ee). [Latin] *Hist.* The laws of England, as distinguished from the civil law and other legal systems.

leges barbarorum (**lee**-jeez bahr-bə-**ror**-əm). [Latin "laws of the barbarians"] *Hist.* The customary laws of medieval European law; esp., the customary laws of Germanic tribes during the Middle Ages. ● These include the *lex romana Visigothorum*, the *lex Burgundionum*, and the *lex Salica*. — Also termed *folk laws*. See SALIC LAW.

leges imperii (**lee**-jeez im-**peer**-ee-I). [Latin] *Roman law.* Laws conferring lawmaking and other powers on the emperor. — Also termed *leges de imperio*.

leges Juliae (**lee**-jeez **joo**-lee-ee). See *lex Julia judiciorum publicorum* under LEX JULIA.

leges publicae (**lee**-jeez **pəb**-lə-see). [Latin] *Roman law.* Statutes passed by the vote of the Roman people in popular assemblies. ● Most *leges publicae* were of temporary political interest but some, such as the *lex Aquilia* or the *lex Falcidia*, had a long life. — Often shortened to *leges*.

legis actio (**lee**-jis **ak**-shee-oh). *Roman law.* A legal or lawful action; an action at law requiring the use of a fixed form of words. ● These actions were abolished by the *leges Juliae*. — Also termed *actio legis*. Pl. *legis actiones* (**lee**-jis ak-shee-**oh**-neez).

legislate, *vb.* (180) **1.** To make or enact laws <the role of our lawmakers is to legislate, not to adjudicate>. **2.** To bring (something) into or out of existence by making laws; to attempt to control (something) by legislation <virtually every attempt to legislate morality has failed>.

legislation. (17c) **1.** The process of making or enacting a positive law in written form, according to some type of formal procedure, by a branch of government constituted to perform this process. — Also termed *lawmaking*; *statute-making*. **2.** The law so enacted. **3.** The whole body of enacted laws.

ancillary legislation. (1860) Legislation that is auxiliary to principal legislation.

antideficiency legislation. **1.** Legislation enacted to provide revenue to cover a budget deficiency. **2.** Legislation enacted to limit the rights of secured creditors to recover in excess of the security. — Also termed (in sense 2) *antideficiency statute*.

bare-bones legislation. See *skeletal legislation*.

class legislation. See *local and special legislation*.

general legislation. (18c) Legislation that applies to the community at large.

judicial legislation. (18c) The making of new legal rules by judges; JUDGE-MADE LAW (2).

local and special legislation. (1853) Legislation that affects only a specific geographic area or a particular class of persons. ● Such legislation is unconstitutional if it arbitrarily or capriciously distinguishes between members of the same class. — Also termed *class legislation*.

pork-barrel legislation. (1961) Legislation that favors a particular local district by allocating funds or resources to projects (such as constructing a highway or a post office) of economic value to the district and of political advantage to the district's legislator.

skeletal legislation. Basic legislation that broadly states objectives and standards rather than prescribing precise and definite rules, usu. with the expectation that it will be amplified by a body other than the legislature. ● Administrative and regulatory agencies are usu. authorized to interpret the legislation and create rules and regulations for its application and enforcement. But the executive branch may also be called upon to flesh out the law. — Also termed *skeleton legislation*; *bare-bones legislation*.

subordinate legislation. (18c) **1.** Legislation that derives from any authority other than the sovereign power in a state and that therefore depends for its continued existence and validity on some superior or supreme authority. **2.** REGULATION (3).

supreme legislation. (17c) Legislation that derives directly from the supreme or sovereign power in a state and is therefore incapable of being repealed, annulled, or controlled by any other legislative authority.

4. A proposed law being considered by a legislature <gun-control legislation was debated in the House>. **5.** The field of study concentrating on statutes.

legislative, *adj.* Of or relating to lawmaking or to the power to enact laws.

legislative apportionment. See APPORTIONMENT (3).

legislative assembly. See LEGISLATURE.

legislative branch. (18c) The branch of government responsible for enacting laws; LEGISLATURE. Cf. EXECUTIVE BRANCH; JUDICIAL BRANCH.

legislative committee. See COMMITTEE.

legislative council. **1.** A state agency that studies legislative problems and plans legislative strategy between regular legislative sessions. **2.** In some

English-speaking jurisdictions, the upper house of a legislature (corresponding to an American Senate). **3.** In some English-speaking jurisdictions, the lower house of a legislature (corresponding to an American House of Representatives).

legislative counsel. (1839) A person or group charged with helping legislators fulfill their legislative duties, such as by performing research, drafting bills, and the like.

legislative court. See COURT.

legislative day. See DAY.

legislative district. See DISTRICT.

legislative districting. (1962) The process of dividing a state into territorial districts to be represented in the state or federal legislature. See APPORTIONMENT (3); REAPPORTIONMENT; GERRYMANDERING. Cf. MALAPPORTIONMENT.

legislative divorce. See DIVORCE.

legislative-equivalency doctrine. (2003) The rule that a law should be amended or repealed only by the same procedures that were used to enact it.

legislative fact. See FACT.

legislative function. 1. The duty to determine legislative policy. **2.** The duty to form and determine future rights and duties. See LEGISLATIVE POWER.

legislative history. (1844) The background and events leading to the enactment of a statute, including hearings, committee reports, and floor debates. • Legislative history is sometimes recorded so that it can later be used to aid in interpreting the statute.

legislative immunity. See IMMUNITY (1).

legislative intent. (1812) The design or plan that the legislature had at the time of enacting a statute. — Also termed *intention of the legislature*; *intent of the legislature*; *congressional intent*; *parliamentary intent*.

   dormant legislative intent. The intent that the legislature would have had if a given ambiguity, inconsistency, or omission had been called to the legislators' minds. — Sometimes shortened to *dormant intent.* — Also termed *latent intent*; *latent intention*.

legislative investigation. A formal inquiry conducted by a legislative body incident to its legislative authority. • A legislature has many of the same powers as a court to support a legislative inquiry, including the power to subpoena and cross-examine a witness and to hold a witness in contempt.

legislative jurisdiction. See JURISDICTION.

legislative law. See STATUTORY LAW.

legislative officer. See OFFICER (1).

legislative power. (17c) *Constitutional law.* The power to make laws and to alter them; a legislative body's exclusive authority to make, amend, and repeal laws. • Under federal law, this power is vested in Congress, consisting of the House of Representatives and the Senate. A legislative body may delegate a portion of its lawmaking authority to agencies within the executive branch for purposes of rulemaking and regulation. But a legislative body may not delegate its authority to the judicial branch, and the judicial branch may not encroach on legislative duties.

legislative privilege. See PRIVILEGE (1).

Legislative Reference Service. *Hist.* See CONGRESSIONAL RESEARCH SERVICE.

legislative rule. An administrative rule created by an agency's exercise of delegated quasi-legislative authority. • A legislative rule has the force of law. — Also termed *substantive rule.* Cf. INTERPRETATIVE RULE.

legislative veto. See VETO.

legislator, *n.* (17c) One who makes laws within a given jurisdiction; a member of a legislative body. — Also termed *lawmaker.* — **legislatorial** (lej-is-lə-**tor**-ee-əl), *adj.*

legislature. (17c) The branch of government responsible for making statutory laws. • The federal government and most states have bicameral legislatures, usu. consisting of a house of representatives and a senate. — Also termed *legislative assembly.* Cf. EXECUTIVE (1); JUDICIARY (1).

legisprudence (lee-jis-**proo**-dənts). (1950) The systematic analysis of statutes within the framework of jurisprudential philosophies about the role and nature of law.

legist (**lee**-jist). (15c) **1.** One learned or skilled in the law; a lawyer. **2.** JURIST. — Formerly also termed *legister.*

legitimacy. (17c) **1.** Lawfulness. **2.** The status of a person who is born within a lawful marriage or who acquires that status by later action of the parents; legal kinship between a child and its parent or parents. Cf. ILLEGITIMACY.

legitimacy presumption. See PRESUMPTION OF PATERNITY.

legitimate (lə-**jit**-ə-mət), *adj.* (15c) **1.** Complying with the law; lawful <a legitimate business>. **2.** Genuine; valid <a legitimate complaint>. **3.** Born of legally married parents <a legitimate child>.

legitimate child. See CHILD.

legitimate heir. See HEIR (1).

legitimate portion. See LEGITIME.

legitimation, *n.* (16c) **1.** The act of making something lawful; authorization. **2.** The act or process of authoritatively declaring a person legitimate, esp. a child whose parentage has been unclear. **3.**

Hist. Proof of a person's identity and of legal permission to reside in a certain place or engage in a certain occupation. Cf. ADOPTION. — **legitimate** (lə-**jit**-ə-mayt), *vb.*

legitime (**lej**-ə-tim), *n. Civil law.* The part of a testator's property that his or her children (and occasionally other heirs) are legally entitled to regardless of the will's terms. See La. Civ. Code art. 1494. ● The legitime cannot be denied the children without legal cause. In Roman law, the amount of the legitime was one-fourth of the claimant's share on intestacy. — Also spelled (esp. in Scotland) *legitim.* — Also termed *legal portion*; *legitimate portion*; *forced portion.* See *forced heir* under HEIR.

legocentrism. See LEGAL CENTRALISM.

lego-literary (lee-goh-**lit**-ər-er-ee), *adj. Rare.* Of or relating to law and literature. See LAW AND LITERATURE.

leguleian (leg-yə-**lee**-ən), *n. Rare.* A pettifogging lawyer. — Also termed *leguleius* (leg-yoo-**lee**-əs). — **leguleian,** *adj.*

LEIN. *abbr.* LAW ENFORCEMENT INFORMATION NETWORK.

lemon law. (18c) **1.** A statute designed to protect a consumer who buys a substandard automobile, usu. by requiring the manufacturer or dealer either to replace the vehicle or to refund the full purchase price. ● Almost all states have lemon laws in effect. — Also termed *lemon protection.* **2.** By extension, a statute designed to protect a consumer who buys any product of inferior quality. — Also termed (in sense 2) *quality-of-products legislation.*

***Lemon* test.** (1971) A legal standard for judging the state's violation of the Establishment Clause of the First Amendment. ● The *Lemon* test has most often been used in school-related cases. It employs a three-pronged test to determine the state's action: (1) Does the state's action have a religious purpose? (2) Does the state's action have the primary effect of either promoting or inhibiting religion? (3) Does the state's action create an "excessive entanglement" between church and state? *Lemon v. Kurtzman*, 403 U.S. 602, 91 S.Ct. 2105 (1971). In recent years, the Court has not overturned *Lemon* but has declined to apply it when deciding Establishment Clause cases.

lend, *vb.* (bef. 12c) **1.** To allow the temporary use of (something), sometimes in exchange for compensation, on condition that the thing or its equivalent be returned. **2.** To provide (money) temporarily on condition of repayment, usu. with interest.

lender. A person or entity from which something (esp. money) is borrowed.

lending right. *Copyright.* The power of a copyright owner to control the use of copies of the work beyond the first sale, when that use involves offering the copy to the public for temporary use with no consideration required. ● Lending rights are recognized among members of the European Union.

lend-lease. (1941) A mutually beneficial exchange made between friendly parties; esp., an arrangement made in 1941, under the Lend-Lease Act, whereby U.S. destroyers were lent to Great Britain in exchange for Britain's leasing of land to the United States for military bases. — Also termed *lease-lend.*

lenient, *adj.* Tolerant; mild; merciful <lenient sentence>.

lenient test. (1996) The principle that the attorney–client privilege applicable to a document or other communication will be waived only by a knowing or intentional disclosure, and will not usu. be waived by an inadvertent disclosure. Cf. *strict test*; *Hydraflow test.*

lenity (**len**-ə-tee). (16c) The quality or condition of being lenient; mercy or clemency. See RULE OF LENITY.

lenity rule. See RULE OF LENITY.

leonine contract (lee-ə-nin). See *adhesion contract* under CONTRACT.

lese majesty (leez **maj**-əs-tee). [Law French "injured majesty"] (16c) **1.** A crime against the state, esp. against the ruler. — Also termed *laesa majestas*; *crimen laesae majestatis*; *crimen majestatis.* See *crimen majestatis* under CRIMEN; *high treason* under TREASON. **2.** An attack on a custom or traditional belief. — Also spelled *lèse-majesté*; *lèse majesty*; *leze majesty.*

lesion (**lee**-zhən). (15c) **1.** An injury or wound; esp., an area of wounded tissue. **2.** *Civil law.* Loss from another's failure to perform a contract; the injury suffered by one who did not receive the equivalent value of what was bargained for. La. Civ. Code art. 2589. — Also spelled (in sense 2) *lésion.* **3.** See LAESIO ENORMIS.

less-developed country. See DEVELOPING COUNTRY.

lessee (le-**see**). (15c) One who has a possessory interest in real or personal property under a lease; TENANT.

   lessee in the ordinary course of business. A person that, in good faith and without knowledge that the lease is in violation of a third party's ownership rights, security interest, or leasehold interest, leases in the ordinary course from a person in the business of selling or leasing goods of that kind. UCC § 2A-102(a)(26). ● The UCC specifically excludes pawnbrokers from the definition.

merchant lessee. A lessee who is a merchant of goods similar to those being leased. UCC § 2A-102(a)(31).

lessee's interest. The appraised value of leased property from the lessee's perspective for purposes of assignment or sale. • The value is usu. the property's market value minus the lessor's interest. Cf. LESSOR'S INTEREST.

lesser-evils defense. See DEFENSE (1).

lesser included offense. See OFFENSE (1).

lesser-interest clause. *Oil & gas.* A provision in an oil-and-gas lease allowing the lessee to reduce payments proportionately if the lessor turns out to own less than 100% of the mineral interest. — Also termed *proportionate-reduction clause.*

lesser offense. See *lesser included offense* under OFFENSE (1).

less-lethal, *n. Jargon.* A weapon that inflicts pain or discomfort short of death, as by firing bean bags or rubber bullets, or by discharging electromagnetic, acoustic, or other energy so that the target may be incapacitated but usu. not seriously injured. — Also termed *less-lethal force*; *nonlethal weapon*; *nondeadly weapon.*

less-lethal force. See LESS-LETHAL.

lessor (les-or *or* le-**sor**). (14c) One who conveys real or personal property by lease; esp., LANDLORD.

lessor of the plaintiff. *Hist.* The true party in interest prosecuting an action for ejectment. • At common law, an ejectment action theoretically was only for the recovery of the unexpired term of the lease. Conventions of pleadings at the time required the true plaintiff to grant a fictitious lease, thereby becoming a lessor, to an equally fictitious plaintiff in whose name the action would be prosecuted.

lessor's interest. (1821) The present value of the future income under a lease, plus the present value of the property after the lease expires. Cf. LESSEE'S INTEREST.

let, *n.* (12c) An impediment or obstruction <free to act without let or hindrance>.

let, *vb.* (bef. 12c) **1.** To allow or permit <the court, refusing to issue an injunction, let the nuisance continue>. **2.** To offer (property) for lease; to rent out <the hospital let office space to several doctors>. **3.** To award (a contract), esp. after bids have been submitted <the federal agency let the project to the lowest bidder>.

lethal, *adj.* (16c) Deadly; fatal <a lethal drug>.

lethal injection. (1898) An injection of a deadly substance into a prisoner in order to carry out a sentence of capital punishment.

lethal weapon. See *deadly weapon* under WEAPON.

letter. (13c) **1.** A written communication that is usu. enclosed in an envelope, sealed, stamped, and delivered (esp., an official written communication) <an opinion letter>. **2.** (*usu. pl.*) A written instrument containing or affirming a grant of some power or right <letters testamentary>. **3.** Strict or literal meaning <the letter of the law>. • This sense is based on the sense of a letter of the alphabet. Cf. SPIRIT OF THE LAW.

letter-book. A merchant's book for holding correspondence.

letter contract. See CONTRACT.

letter missive. 1. *Hist.* A letter from the king (or queen) to the dean and chapter of a cathedral, containing the name of the person whom the king wants elected as bishop. **2.** *Hist.* After a lawsuit is filed against a peer, peeress, or lord of Parliament, a request sent to the defendant to appear and answer the suit. **3.** *Civil law.* The appellate record sent by a lower court to a superior court. — Also termed *letter dimissory.*

letter of advice. *Commercial law.* A notice that a draft has been sent by the drawer to the drawee. UCC § 3-701.

letter of attorney. 1. See POWER OF ATTORNEY (1). **2.** See ATTORNEY (1).

letter of attornment. A grantor's letter to a tenant, stating that the leased property has been sold and directing the tenant to pay rent to the new owner. See ATTORNMENT (1).

letter of comfort. See COMFORT LETTER.

letter of comment. See DEFICIENCY LETTER.

letter of commitment. See COMMITMENT LETTER.

letter of credence. *Int'l law.* A document that accredits a diplomat to the government of the country to which he or she is sent. — Abbr. LC; L/C. — Also termed *letters of credence.*

letter of credit. (17c) *Commercial law.* An instrument under which the issuer (usu. a bank), at a customer's request, agrees to honor a draft or other demand for payment made by a third party (the *beneficiary*), as long as the draft or demand complies with specified conditions, and regardless of whether any underlying agreement between the customer and the beneficiary is satisfied. • Letters of credit are governed by Article 5 of the UCC. — Abbr. LC; L/C. — Often shortened to *credit.* — Also termed *circular letter of credit; circular note; bill of credit.*

clean letter of credit. A letter of credit that is payable on its presentation. • No document needs to be presented along with it. — Also termed *suicide letter of credit.* Cf. *documentary letter of credit.*

commercial letter of credit. A letter of credit used as a method of payment in a sale of goods (esp. in an international transaction), with the buyer being the issuer's customer and the seller being the beneficiary, so that the seller can obtain payment directly from the issuer instead of from the buyer.

confirmed letter of credit. A letter of credit that directly obligates a financing agency (such as a bank) doing business in the seller's financial market to a contract of sale. UCC § 2-325(3).

documentary letter of credit. A letter of credit that is payable when presented with another document, such as a certificate of title or invoice. — Abbr. DL/C. Cf. *clean letter of credit.*

export letter of credit. A commercial letter of credit issued by a foreign bank, at a foreign buyer's request, in favor of a domestic exporter.

general letter of credit. A letter of credit addressed to any and all persons without naming anyone in particular. Cf. *special letter of credit.*

guaranty letter of credit. See *standby letter of credit.*

import letter of credit. A commercial letter of credit issued by a domestic bank, at an importer's request, in favor of a foreign seller.

irrevocable letter of credit (i-**rev**-ə-kə-bəl). **1.** A letter of credit that the issuing bank guarantees will not be withdrawn or canceled before the expiration date. **2.** A letter of credit that cannot be modified or revoked without the customer's consent. **3.** A letter of credit that cannot be modified or canceled without the consent of all parties.

negotiation letter of credit. A letter of credit in which the issuer's engagement runs to drawers and indorsers under a standard negotiation clause.

open letter of credit. A letter of credit that can be paid on a simple draft without the need for documentary title.

revocable letter of credit (**rev**-ə-kə-bəl). A letter of credit in which the issuing bank reserves the right to cancel and withdraw from the transaction upon appropriate notice. • The letter cannot be revoked if the credit has already been paid by a third party.

revolving letter of credit. A letter of credit that self-renews by providing for a continuing line of credit that the beneficiary periodically draws on and the bank customer periodically repays. • A revolving letter of credit is used when there will be multiple drafts under a single transaction or multiple transactions under a single credit. — Abbr. RL/C.

special letter of credit. A letter of credit addressed to a particular individual, firm, or corporation. Cf. *general letter of credit.*

standby letter of credit. A letter of credit used to guarantee either a monetary or a nonmonetary obligation (such as the performance of construction work), whereby the issuing bank agrees to pay the beneficiary if the bank customer defaults on its obligation. — Abbr. SL/C. — Also termed *guaranty letter of credit.*

straight letter of credit. A letter of credit requiring that drafts drawn under it be presented to a specified party.

suicide letter of credit. See *clean letter of credit.*

time letter of credit. A letter of credit that is duly honored by the issuer accepting drafts drawn under it. — Also termed *acceptance credit; usance credit.*

transferable letter of credit. A letter of credit that authorizes the beneficiary to assign the right to draw under it.

traveler's letter of credit. 1. A letter of credit addressed to a correspondent bank, from which one can draw credit by identifying oneself as the person in whose favor the credit is drawn. **2.** A letter of credit used by a person traveling abroad, by which the issuing bank authorizes payment of funds to the holder in the local currency by a local bank. • The holder signs a check on the issuing bank, and the local bank forwards it to the issuing bank for its credit.

letter of exchange. See DRAFT (1).

letter of intent. (1942) A written statement detailing the preliminary understanding of parties who plan to enter into a contract or some other agreement; a noncommittal writing preliminary to a contract. • A letter of intent is not meant to be binding and does not hinder the parties from bargaining with a third party. Business people typically mean not to be bound by a letter of intent, and courts ordinarily do not enforce one; but courts occasionally find that a commitment has been made. — Abbr. LOI. — Also termed *memorandum of intent; memorandum of understanding; term sheet; commitment letter.* Cf. *precontract* under CONTRACT.

letter of license. *English law.* An agreement signed by all the creditors of a financially troubled business that does the following: (1) grants the debtor more time to pay debts, (2) permits the debtor to continue business in the hope of overcoming its financial distress, and (3) protects the debtor from arrest, lawsuit, or other interference while the letter is in effect. See ARRANGEMENT WITH CREDITORS.

letter of recall. 1. A document sent from one nation's executive to that of another, summoning a minister back to his or her own country. **2.** A manufacturer's letter to a buyer of a particular product, asking the buyer to bring the product back to the dealer for repair or replacement. — Also termed *recall letter.*

letter of recredentials (ree-krə-**den**-shəlz). A formal letter from a host country's diplomatic secretary of state to a minister or ambassador who has been recalled by his or her own country. ● The letter officially accredits the foreign minister back to his or her home country.

letter of request. 1. A document issued by one court to a foreign court, requesting that the foreign court (1) take evidence from a specific person within the foreign jurisdiction or serve process on an individual or corporation within the foreign jurisdiction and (2) return the testimony or proof of service for use in a pending case. *See* Fed. R. Civ. P. 28. — Also termed *letter rogatory* (**rog**-ə-tor-ee); *rogatory letter; requisitory letter* (ri-**kwiz**-ə-tor-ee). Cf. COMMISSION TO EXAMINE A WITNESS. **2.** An instrument by which an inferior court withdraws or waives jurisdiction so that a matter can be heard in the court immediately above. Pl. **letters of request.**

letter of the law. (17c) The strictly literal meaning of the law, rather than the intention or policy behind it. — Also termed *litera legis.* Cf. SPIRIT OF THE LAW.

letter of undertaking. An agreement by which a shipowner — to avoid having creditors seize the ship and release it on bond — agrees to post security on the ship, and to enter an appearance, acknowledge ownership, and pay any final decree entered against the vessel whether it is lost or not. ● A letter of undertaking is often issued by the shipowner's liability insurer.

letter rogatory. See LETTER OF REQUEST.

letter ruling. (1950) *Tax.* A written statement issued by the IRS to an inquiring taxpayer, explaining the tax implications of a particular transaction. — Also termed *private letter ruling.*

letters. (16c) *Wills & estates.* A court order giving official authority to a fiduciary to conduct appointed tasks. ● Examples are letters of administration, letters of conservatorship, letters of guardianship, and letters testamentary. Unif. Probate Code § 1-201(23). See LETTER (2).

letters close. See LETTERS SECRET.

letter security. See *restricted security* under SECURITY.

letters of absolution. *Hist.* Letters issued by an abbot releasing a member of his order from his vows of obedience to that order, thus permitting entry into another order.

letters of administration. (16c) A formal document issued by a probate court to appoint the administrator of an estate. ● Letters of administration originated in the Probate of Testaments Act of 1357 (31 Edw. 3, ch. 4), which provided that in case of intestacy the ordinary (a high-ranking ecclesiastical official within a territory) should depute the decedent's closest friends to administer the estate; a later statute, the Executors Act of 1529 (21 Hen. 8, ch. 4), authorized the ordinary to grant administration to the surviving spouse, to next of kin, or to both of them jointly. — Also termed *administration letters.* See ADMINISTRATION (4). Cf. LETTERS TESTAMENTARY.

letters of administration c.t.a. (1894) Letters of administration appointing an administrator *cum testamento annexo* (with the will annexed) either because the will does not name an executor or because the named executor does not qualify. See *administration cum testamento annexo* under ADMINISTRATION.

letters of administration d.b.n. (1877) Letters of administration appointing an administrator *de bonis non* (concerning goods not yet administered) because the named executor failed to complete the estate's probate. See *administration de bonis non* under ADMINISTRATION.

letters of credence. See LETTER OF CREDENCE.

letters of guardianship. (18c) A court order appointing a guardian to care for the well-being, property, and affairs of a minor or an incapacitated adult. ● It defines the scope of the guardian's rights and duties, including the extent of control over the ward's education and medical issues. See GUARDIAN.

letters of marque (mahrk). A license authorizing a private citizen to engage in reprisals against citizens or vessels of another nation. ● Congress has the exclusive power to grant letters of marque (U.S. Const. art. I, § 8, cl. 11), but it has done so only once since the 19th century. — Also termed *letters of marque and reprisal.*

letters of safe conduct. *Hist.* Formal written permission from the English sovereign to a citizen of a nation at war with England, permitting that person to travel and ship goods, to England or on the high seas, without risk of seizure. ● Passports or licenses from foreign ambassadors now may serve the same purpose. See SAFE CONDUCT.

letters patent. (15c) **1.** *Hist.* A document granting some right or privilege, issued under governmental seal but open to public inspection. — Also termed *literae patentes* (lit-ər-ee pə-**ten**-teez). Cf. LETTERS SECRET. **2.** A governmental grant of the exclusive right to use an invention or design. — Also termed (in both senses) *patent deed.* See PATENT (2).

letters rogatory. See LETTER OF REQUEST.

letters secret. *Hist.* A governmental document that is issued to a private person, closed and sealed, and thus not made available for public inspection. — Also termed *letters close.* Cf. LETTERS PATENT (1).

letters testamentary. (17c) A probate-court order approving the appointment of an executor under a will and authorizing the executor to administer the estate. Cf. LETTERS OF ADMINISTRATION.

ancillary letters testamentary. Letters testamentary issued at a place where the testator owned property but did not have a domicile. ● The executor or administrator is not authorized to act outside the issuing court's territorial jurisdiction.

domiciliary letters testamentary. Letters testamentary issued at the place where the testator was domiciled.

letter stock. See *restricted security* under SECURITY.

levari facias (lə-**vair**-ɪ **fay**-shee-əs). [Law Latin "that you cause to be levied"] A writ of execution ordering a sheriff to seize a judgment debtor's goods and income from lands until the judgment debt is satisfied. ● This writ is now used chiefly in Delaware. Cf. FIERI FACIAS.

levari facias damna de disseisitoribus (lə-**vair**-ɪ **fay**-shee-əs **dam**-nə dee dis-see-zə-**tor**-ə-bəs), *n.* [Law Latin "that you cause to be levied the damages from the disseisors"] *Hist.* A writ directing the sheriff to levy property to pay damages owed to one wrongfully dispossessed of a freehold estate. See DISSEISIN.

levari facias quando vicecomes returnavit quod non habuit emptores (lə-**vair**-ɪ **fay**-shee-əs **kwon**-doh vɪ-see-**koh**-meez ree-tər-**nay**-vit kwod non **hay**-byoo-it emp-**tor**-eez), *n.* [Law Latin "that you cause to be levied when the sheriff has returned that it had no buyers"] *Hist.* A writ directing a sheriff, who had already seized some of the debtor's property and found it unsalable, to sell as much additional property as necessary to pay the entire debt.

levari facias residuum debiti (lə-**vair**-ɪ **fay**-shee-əs ri-**zij**-oo-əm **deb**-ə-tɪ), *n.* [Law Latin "that you cause to be levied the rest of the debt"] *Hist.* A writ directing the sheriff to levy upon a debtor's lands or goods to pay the remainder of a partially satisfied debt.

levee (lev-ee), *n.* (17c) **1.** An embankment constructed along the edge of a river to prevent flooding. **2.** A landing place on a body of navigable water for loading and unloading goods or receiving and delivering passengers and boats.

levee district. See DISTRICT.

levée en masse. See LEVY EN MASSE.

level of abstraction. *Copyright.* The degree to which a work describes an idea or process in a general rather than concrete way. ● Judge Learned Hand posited that from any work one can restate the idea in more and more abstract ways, omitting more and more details, until one is left with an uncopyrightable idea rather than a protectable work of originality. See *Nichols v. Universal Pictures Corp.*, 45 F.2d 119 (1930).

level-premium insurance. See INSURANCE.

level-rate legal-reserve policy. See INSURANCE POLICY.

leverage, *n.* (1830) **1.** Positional advantage; effectiveness. **2.** The use of credit or borrowed funds (such as buying on margin) to improve one's speculative ability and to increase an investment's rate of return. **3.** The advantage obtained from using credit or borrowed funds rather than equity capital. **4.** The ratio between a corporation's debt and its equity capital. — Also termed *leverage ratio.* **5.** The effect of this ratio on common-stock prices.

leverage, *vb.* (1957) **1.** To provide (a borrower or investor) with credit or funds to improve speculative ability and to seek a high rate of return. **2.** To supplement (available capital) with credit or outside funds. **3.** To fund (a company) with debt as well as shareholder equity. **4.** *Antitrust.* To use power in one market to gain an unfair advantage in another market. **5.** *Insurance.* To manipulate two coverages, as by an insurer's withholding settlement of one claim to influence a claim arising under another source of coverage.

leverage contract. (1975) An agreement for the purchase or sale of a contract for the future delivery of a specified commodity, usu. silver, gold, or another precious metal, in a standard unit and quantity, for a particular price, with no right to a particular lot of the commodity. ● A leverage contract operates much like a futures contract, except that there is no designated contract market for leverage contracts. The market sets the uniform terms of a futures contract. But in a leverage contract, the individual merchant sets the terms, does not guarantee a repurchase market, and does not guarantee to continue serving or acting as the broker for the purchaser. Leverage contracts are generally forbidden for agricultural commodities. 7 USCA § 23(a). Cf. FUTURES CONTRACT.

leveraged buyout. See BUYOUT.

leveraged lease. See LEASE.

leveraged recapitalization. See RECAPITALIZATION.

leverage fund. See *dual fund* under MUTUAL FUND.

leverage ratio. See LEVERAGE (4).

leveraging up. See *leveraged recapitalization* under RECAPITALIZATION.

leviable (**lev**-ee-ə-bəl), *adj.* **1.** Able to be levied; assessable <the fine is leviable on each offense>. **2.** Able to be levied upon; seizable in execution of a judgment <leviable goods>.

levis (**lee**-vis), *adj.* [Latin] *Hist.* Light; trifling.

levis culpa. See CULPA.

levissima culpa. See CULPA.

levy (**lev**-ee), *n.* (13c) **1.** The imposition of a fine or tax; the fine or tax so imposed. — Also termed *tax levy.* **2.** The enlistment of soldiers into the military; the soldiers so enlisted. **3.** The legally sanctioned seizure and sale of property; the money obtained from such a sale. — Also termed (in sense 3) *levy of execution.*

> **wrongful levy.** (18c) A levy on a third party's property that is not subject to a writ of execution.

levy, *vb.* (14c) **1.** To impose or assess (a fine or a tax) by legal authority <levy a tax on gasoline>. **2.** To enlist for service in the military <the troops were quickly levied>. **3.** To declare or wage (a war) <the rival clans levied war against each other>. **4.** To take or seize property in execution of a judgment <the judgment creditor may levy on the debtor's assets>.

levy court. See COURT.

levy en masse. A large conscription or mobilization of troops, esp. in response to a threatened invasion. — Also spelled *levée en masse*; *levy in mass.*

levy of execution. See LEVY (3).

lewd, *adj.* (14c) Obscene or indecent; tending to moral impurity or wantonness <lewd behavior>.

lewd and lascivious cohabitation. See *illicit cohabitation* under COHABITATION.

lewd house. See DISORDERLY HOUSE (2).

lewdness. (16c) Gross, wanton, and public indecency that is outlawed by many state statutes; a sexual act that the actor knows will likely be observed by someone who will be affronted or alarmed by it. See Model Penal Code § 251.1. — Also termed *open lewdness.* Cf. INDECENT EXPOSURE; OBSCENITY.

lex (leks), *n.* [Latin "law"] **1.** Law, esp. statutory law. **2.** Positive law, as opposed to natural law. • Strictly speaking, *lex* is a statute, whereas *jus* is law in general (as well as a right). **3.** A system or body of laws, written or unwritten, that are peculiar to a jurisdiction or to a field of human activity. **4.** A collection of uncodified laws within a jurisdiction. **5.** LEX PUBLICA. **6.** LEX PRIVATA. **7.** *Civil law.* A legislative bill. Pl. *leges* (**lee**-jeez). Cf. JUS. **8.** The acquisition of property under some specific law, when the property is made over by a magistrate to the claimant. **9.** A term of a contract, treaty, or other agreement.

lex actus (leks **ak**-təs). See LEX LOCI ACTUS.

lex aeterna (leks ee-**tər**-nə). [Latin] Eternal law. See NATURAL LAW (1).

lex Angliae (leks **ang**-glee-ee), *n.* [Latin] *Hist.* The law of England; the common law.

lex apparens (leks ə-**par**-enz), *n.* [Law Latin "apparent law"] *Hist.* The legal processes of trial by ordeal or wager of battle. • The plaintiff could not summon the defendant for trial by these processes before establishing a clear or apparent right through testimony. See ORDEAL.

lex Aquilia (leks ə-**kwil**-ee-ə). [Latin "Aquilian law"] *Roman law.* A Roman statute imposing liability for pecuniary loss tortiously caused and generally regulating loss caused by damage to property, including compensation to be paid for injury to another's slave or livestock. • A loss had to be financially measurable and caused wrongfully. If the liable party denied liability, then damages were doubled. This law applied to negligence as well as *dolus.* The law, enacted around 287 B.C., superseded the earlier provisions of the Twelve Tables. — Also termed *Aquilian law.* See DAMNUM INJURIA DATUM; DOLUS. See *actio legis Aquiliae* under ACTIO.

lex Atinia (leks ə-**tin**-ee-ə). [Latin] *Roman law.* A law declaring that a prescriptive right cannot be acquired in stolen property. • It was enacted in the late third or early second century B.C. — Also termed *Atinian law.*

lex barbara (leks **bahr**-bə-rə). [Latin] *Roman law.* The law of barbarian nations, i.e., those that were not subject to the Roman Empire.

lex causae (leks **kaw**-zee). [Latin] The legal system that governs a dispute.

lex commercii (leks kə-**mər**-shee-I), *n.* [Latin] The law of business or commerce; commercial law. — Also termed *lex commissoria* (leks kom-ə-**sor**-ee-ə).

lex communis (leks kə-**myoo**-nis), *n.* [Latin] The common law. See JUS COMMUNE.

lex contractus (leks kən-**trak**-təs). See LEX LOCI CONTRACTUS.

lex delicti (leks də-**lik**-tI). See LEX LOCI DELICTI.

lex domicilii (leks dom-ə-**sil**-ee-I). [Latin] (18c) **1.** The law of the country where a person is domiciled. **2.** The determination of a person's rights by establishing where, in law, that person is domiciled. See Restatement (Second) of Conflict of Laws §§ 11 et seq. (1971).

Lex Duodecim Tabularum (leks d[y]oo-ə-**des**-əm tab-yə-**lair**-əm). See TWELVE TABLES.

lex Falcidia (leks fal-**sid**-ee-ə). See FALCIDIAN LAW.

lex fori (leks **for**-ɪ). [Latin] (1803) The law of the forum; the law of the jurisdiction where the case is pending <the *lex fori* governs whether the death penalty is a possible punishment for a first-degree-murder conviction>. — Also termed *lex ordinandi.* Cf. LEX LOCI (1).

lexical definition. See DEFINITION.

LEXIS (**lek**-sis). A proprietary online computer service that provides access to databases of legal information, including federal and state caselaw, statutes, and secondary materials.

lex loci (leks **loh**-sɪ). [Latin] (18c) **1.** The law of the place; local law. Cf. LEX FORI. **2.** LEX LOCI CONTRACTUS.

lex loci actus (leks **loh**-sɪ **ak**-təs). [Law Latin] The law of the place where an act is done or a transaction is completed. — Often shortened to *lex actus.*

lex loci celebrationis (leks **loh**-sɪ sel-ə-bray-shee-**oh**-nis). [Latin "law of the place of the ceremony"] The law of the place where a contract, esp. of marriage, is made. • This law usu. governs when the validity of a marriage is at issue. Restatement (Second) of Conflict of Laws § 283(2) (1971).

lex loci contractus (leks **loh**-sɪ kən-**trak**-təs). [Latin] The law of the place where a contract is executed or to be performed. • *Lex loci contractus* is often the proper law by which to decide contractual disputes. — Often shortened to *lex loci*; *lex contractus.*

lex loci delicti (leks **loh**-sɪ də-**lik**-tɪ). [Latin] The law of the place where the tort or other wrong was committed. — Often shortened to *lex delicti.* — Also termed *lex loci delictus; lex loci delicti commissi; place-of-wrong rule; place-of-wrong law.* Cf. LOCUS DELICTI.

lex loci solutionis (leks **loh**-sɪ sə-loo-shee-**oh**-nis). [Latin "law of the place of solution"] The law of the place where a contract is to be performed (esp. by payment). — Often shortened to *lex solutionis.*

lex mercatoria (leks mər-kə-**tor**-ee-ə). [Latin "mercantile law"] See LAW MERCHANT.

lex merciorum (leks mər-shee-**or**-əm). See MERCENLAGE.

lex naturae (leks nə-**tyoor**-ee). See NATURAL LAW.

lex naturale (leks nach-ə-**ray**-lee). [Law Latin] See NATURAL LAW.

lex non scripta (leks non **skrip**-tə). [Latin "unwritten law"] See *unwritten law* under LAW. Pl. *leges non scriptae.*

lex ordinandi (leks or-də-**nan**-dɪ). See LEX FORI.

lex patriae (leks **pay**-tree-ee *or* **pa**-tree-ee). [Latin] National law; the law of one's country. See PERSONAL LAW.

lex privata (leks prɪ-**vay**-tə). [Latin "private law"] *Roman law.* A term in a private contract. — Sometimes shortened to *lex.*

lex publica (leks **pəb**-li-kə). [Latin "public law"] *Roman law.* **1.** A law passed by a popular assembly and binding on all people. **2.** A written law. — Sometimes shortened to *lex.*

lex Salica (leks **sal**-ə-kə). [Latin] See SALIC LAW.

lex scripta (leks **skrip**-tə). [Latin "written law"] See *unwritten law* under LAW. Pl. *leges scriptae.*

lex situs (leks **sɪ**-təs. [Law Latin] The law of the place where property is located. — Also termed *lex loci rei sitae. See* Restatement (Second) of Conflict of Laws §§ 222 et seq. (1971).

lex solutionis. See LEX LOCI SOLUTIONIS.

lex talionis (leks tal-ee-**oh**-nis). [Law Latin] The law of retaliation, under which punishment should be in kind — an eye for an eye, a tooth for a tooth, and so on — but no more. — Also termed *eye for an eye; jus talionis; principle of retribution.*

lex terrae (leks **ter**-ee). [Law Latin] See LAW OF THE LAND.

ley (lay), *n.* [Law French] *Hist.* Law.

ley de terre (lay də **tair**). [Law French] See LAW OF THE LAND.

leze majesty. See LESE MAJESTY.

L.F. *abbr.* LAW FRENCH.

LHWCA. *abbr.* LONGSHORE AND HARBOR WORKERS' COMPENSATION ACT.

liability, *n.* (18c) **1.** The quality or state of being legally obligated or accountable; legal responsibility to another or to society, enforceable by civil remedy or criminal punishment <liability for injuries caused by negligence>. — Also termed *legal liability; subjection.* Cf. FAULT. **2.** (*often pl.*) A financial or pecuniary obligation; DEBT <tax liability> <assets and liabilities>.

absolute liability. See *strict liability.*

accomplice liability. (1958) Criminal responsibility of one who acts with another before, during, or (in some jurisdictions) after a crime. *See* 18 USCA § 2.

accrued liability. (1877) A debt or obligation that is properly chargeable in a given accounting period but that is not yet paid.

alternative liability. (1929) Liability arising from the tortious acts of two or more parties — when the plaintiff proves that one of the defendants has caused harm but cannot prove which one caused it — resulting in a shifting of the burden of proof to each defendant. Restatement (Second) of Torts § 433B(3) (1965).

civil liability. (1817) **1.** Liability imposed under the civil, as opposed to the criminal, law. **2.**

The state of being legally obligated for civil damages.

contingent liability. (18c) A liability that will occur only if a specific event happens; a liability that depends on the occurrence of a future and uncertain event. • In financial statements, contingent liabilities are usu. stated in footnotes.

current liability. A business liability that will be paid or otherwise discharged with current assets or by creating other current liabilities within the next year (or operating cycle). — Also termed *short-term debt.*

derivative liability. (1886) Liability for a wrong that a person other than the one wronged has a right to redress. • Examples include liability to a widow in a wrongful-death action and liability to a corporation in a shareholder's derivative suit.

enterprise liability. (1941) **1.** Liability imposed on each member of an industry responsible for manufacturing a harmful or defective product, allotted by each manufacturer's market share of the industry. — Also termed *industry-wide liability.* See *market-share liability.* **2.** Criminal liability imposed on a business (such as a corporation or partnership) for certain offenses, such as public-welfare offenses or offenses for which the legislature specifically intended to impose criminal sanctions. *See* Model Penal Code § 2.07. See *public-welfare offense* under OFFENSE (1).

fault liability. Liability based on some degree of blameworthiness. — Also termed *fault-based liability.* Cf. *strict liability.*

joint and several liability. (1819) Liability that may be apportioned either among two or more parties or to only one or a few select members of the group, at the adversary's discretion. • Thus, each liable party is individually responsible for the entire obligation, but a paying party may have a right of contribution and indemnity from nonpaying parties. See *solidary liability.*

joint liability. (18c) Liability shared by two or more parties.

liability in solido. See *solidary liability.*

liability without fault. See *strict liability.*

limited liability. (1833) Liability restricted by law or contract; esp., the liability of a company's owners for nothing more than the capital they have invested in the business.

market-share liability. (1980) Liability that is imposed, usu. severally, on each member of an industry, based on each member's share of the market or respective percentage of the product that is placed on the market. • This theory of liability usu. applies only in the situation in which a plaintiff cannot trace the harmful exposure to a particular product, as when several products contain a fungible substance. For example, it is sometimes applied to a claim that the plaintiff was harmed by exposure to asbestos. See *enterprise liability.*

official liability. Liability of an officer or receiver for a breach of contract or a tort committed during the officer's or receiver's tenure, but not involving any personal liability.

penal liability. Liability arising from a proceeding intended at least partly to penalize a wrongdoer. Cf. *remedial liability.*

personal liability. (18c) Liability for which one is personally accountable and for which a wronged party can seek satisfaction out of the wrongdoer's personal assets.

premises liability. See PREMISES LIABILITY.

primary liability. (1834) Liability for which one is directly responsible, as opposed to secondary liability.

products liability. See PRODUCTS LIABILITY.

remedial liability. Liability arising from a proceeding whose object contains no penal element. • The two types of proceedings giving rise to this liability are specific enforcement and restitution. Cf. *penal liability.*

secondary liability. (1830) Liability that does not arise unless the primarily liable party fails to honor its obligation.

several liability. (1819) Liability that is separate and distinct from another's liability, so that the plaintiff may bring a separate action against one defendant without joining the other liable parties.

shareholder's liability. **1.** The statutory, added, or double liability of a shareholder for a corporation's debts, despite full payment for the stock. **2.** The liability of a shareholder for any unpaid stock listed as fully owned on the stock certificate, usu. occurring either when the shareholder agrees to pay full par value for the stock and obtains the certificate before the stock is paid for, or when partially paid-for stock is intentionally issued by a corporation as fully paid, the consideration for it being entirely fictitious. — Also termed *stockholder's liability.*

solidary liability (sol-ə-dair-ee). *Civil law.* The liability of any one debtor among two or more joint debtors to pay the entire debt if the creditor so chooses. La. Civ. Code art. 1794. • This is equivalent to joint and several liability in the common law. — Also termed *liability in solido.* See *joint and several liability.*

statutory liability. Liability that is created by a statute (or regulation) as opposed to common law.

stockholder's liability. See *shareholder's liability.*

strict liability. (1844) Liability that does not depend on actual negligence or intent to harm, but that is based on the breach of an absolute duty to make something safe. ● Strict liability most often applies either to ultrahazardous activities or in products-liability cases. — Also termed *absolute liability; liability without fault.* Cf. *fault liability;* OUTCOME RESPONSIBILITY.

tortious liability. Liability that arises from the breach of a duty that (1) is fixed primarily by the law, (2) is owed to persons generally, and (3) when breached, is redressable by an action for unliquidated damages.

vicarious liability (vi-**kair**-ee-əs). (1890) Liability that a supervisory party (such as an employer) bears for the actionable conduct of a subordinate or associate (such as an employee) based on the relationship between the two parties. See RESPONDEAT SUPERIOR.

liability bond. See BOND (2).

liability dividend. See *scrip dividend* under DIVIDEND.

liability in solido. See *solidary liability* under LIABILITY.

liability insurance. See INSURANCE.

liability limit. *Insurance.* The maximum amount of coverage that an insurance company will provide on a single claim under an insurance policy. — Also termed *limit of liability; policy limits.*

liability without fault. See *strict liability* under LIABILITY.

liable (lI-ə-bəl *also* lI-bəl), *adj.* (15c) **1.** Responsible or answerable in law; legally obligated. **2.** (Of a person) subject to or likely to incur (a fine, penalty, etc.). — Also termed *legally liable.* See LIABILITY.

liar's loan. See LOAN.

libel (lI-bəl), *n.* (14c) **1.** A defamatory statement expressed in a fixed medium, esp. writing but also a picture, sign, or electronic broadcast. ● Libel is classified as both a crime and a tort but is no longer prosecuted as a crime. — Also termed *defamatory libel.* **2.** The act of making such a statement; publication of defamatory matter by written or printed words, by its embodiment in physical form or by any other form of communication that has the potentially harmful qualities characteristic of written or printed words. See DEFAMATION. Cf. SLANDER.

criminal libel. At common law, a malicious libel that is designed to expose a person to hatred, contempt, or ridicule and that may subject the author to criminal sanctions. ● Because of con-stitutional protections of free speech, libel is no longer criminally prosecuted.

false-implication libel. Libel that creates a false implication or impression even though each statement in the article, taken separately, is true. See FALSE LIGHT; INVASION OF PRIVACY.

group libel. (1940) Libel that defames a class of persons, esp. because of their race, sex, national origin, religious belief, or the like. ● Civil liability for group libel is rare because the plaintiff must prove that the statement applied particularly to him or her. Cf. *hate speech* under SPEECH.

libel per quod (pər **kwod**). (1927) **1.** Libel that is actionable only on allegation and proof of special damages. ● Most jurisdictions do not recognize libel per quod, holding instead that general damages from libel are presumed. **2.** Libel in which the defamatory meaning is not apparent from the statement on its face but rather must be proved from extrinsic circumstances. See INNUENDO (2).

libel per se (pər say). (1843) **1.** Libel that is actionable in itself, requiring no proof of special damages. ● Most jurisdictions do not distinguish between libel per se and libel per quod, holding instead that general damages from libel are presumed. **2.** Libel that is defamatory on its face, such as the statement "Frank is a thief."

obscene libel. Hist. **1.** The common-law crime of publishing, with the intent to corrupt, material (esp. sexual words or pictures) that tends to deprave or corrupt those whose minds are open to immoral influences. **2.** A writing, book, picture, or print that is so obscene that it shocks the public sense of decency.

seditious libel. Libel made with the intent of inciting sedition. ● Like other forms of criminal libel, seditious libel is no longer prosecuted. See SEDITION.

trade libel. Trade defamation that is written or recorded. See *trade defamation* under DEFAMATION; DISPARAGEMENT (3). Cf. *trade slander* under SLANDER.

3. The complaint or initial pleading in an admiralty or ecclesiastical case. — Also termed (in sense 3) *libel of information.*

libel, *vb.* (16c) **1.** To defame (someone) in a permanent medium, esp. in writing. **2.** *Hist. Maritime law.* To sue in admiralty or ecclesiastical court. ● This use of the term was eliminated with the merging of the Admiralty Rules into the Federal Rules of Civil Procedure in 1986.

libelant (lI-bəl-ənt). (16c) **1.** The party who institutes a suit in admiralty or ecclesiastical court by filing a libel. **2.** LIBELER. — Also spelled *libellant.*

libelee (lı-bəl-**ee**). The party against whom a libel has been filed in admiralty or ecclesiastical court. — Also spelled *libellee*.

libeler. One who publishes a written defamatory statement. — Also spelled *libeller*. — Also termed *libelant*.

libellary procedure (lı-bəl-er-ee). *Roman law.* The preliminary proceedings in a lawsuit, initiated by a plaintiff's written claims (in a *libellus*) to the magistrate.

libellous, *adj.* See LIBELOUS.

libellus (lə-**bel**-əs), *n.* [Latin] **1.** *Roman law.* A small book; a written statement to a court; a petition. **2.** *Hist.* An instrument conveying all or part of land. **3.** Any one of a number of legal petitions or documents, such as a bill of complaint.

libel of information. *Maritime law.* See LIBEL (3).

libel of review. *Maritime law.* A new proceeding attacking a final decree after the right to appeal has expired. See LIBEL (3).

libelous, *adj.* Constituting or involving libel; defamatory <a libelous newspaper story>. — Also spelled *libellous*.

libel per quod. See LIBEL.

libel per se. See LIBEL.

liber (lı-bər), *adj.* [Latin "free"] **1.** (Of courts, public places, etc.) open and accessible. **2.** (Of a person) having the state or condition of a freeman. **3.** (Of a person) free from another's service or authority.

liber (lı-bər), *n.* [Latin "book"] **1.** A book of records, esp. of deeds. **2.** A main division of a literary or professional work.

libera eleemosyna (**lib**-ər-ə el-ə-**mos**-ə-nə). See FRANKALMOIN.

liberal, *adj.* (14c) **1.** (Of a condition, state, opinion, etc.) not restricted; expansive; tolerant <liberal policy>. **2.** (Of a person or entity) opposed to conservatism; advocating expansive freedoms and individual expression <liberal party>. **3.** (Of an act, etc.) generous <a liberal gift>. **4.** (Of an interpretation, construction, etc.) not strict or literal; loose <a liberal reading of the statute>.

liberal construction. See CONSTRUCTION.

liberal interpretation. See INTERPRETATION.

liberam legem amittere (**lib**-ər-əm **lee**-jəm ə-**mit**-ə-ree). [Latin] *Hist.* To lose one's free law. ● This phrase refers to falling, by crime or infamy, from the status of *libera lex*. By what was known as a "villenous judgment," a person would be discredited as juror and witness, would forfeit goods and chattels and lands for life, would have his houses razed and trees uprooted, and would go to prison. This was the ancient punishment of a conspirator and of a party involved in a wager of battle who cried "craven." — Also termed *amittere liberam*

legem; *amittere legem terrae* ("to lose the law of the land"). See VILLENOUS JUDGMENT.

libera piscaria (**lib**-ər-ə pis-**kair**-ee-ə). See *free fishery* under FISHERY (1).

liberate (lib-ə-**ray**-tee), *n.* [Law Latin] *Hist.* **1.** A chancery writ to the Exchequer ordering the payment of an annual pension or other sum. **2.** A writ to the sheriff authorizing delivery of any property given as bond and then taken when a defendant forfeited a recognizance. **3.** A writ to a jailer ordering delivery of a prisoner who had paid bail. **4.** A writ to a sheriff commanding him to deliver to the plaintiff lands or goods pledged as part of a commercial trade loan arrangement (a statute staple) available in certain merchant towns in England. ● If a debtor defaulted on this obligation, the creditor could obtain a writ of extent, which directed the sheriff to take an inventory and entitled the creditor to keep the debtor's property for a time until the rentals on the property equaled the amount due. The writ of *liberate* was issued after the inventory had been performed under the writ of extent. See EXTENT; STAPLE (1), (2).

liberate, *vb.* (17c) To set (a person) free, as from slavery, bondage, or hostile control.

liberation. (15c) **1.** The act or an instance of freeing someone or something. **2.** *Civil law.* Final payment under a contract, thereby extinguishing the debt.

liberation movement. *Int'l law.* An organized effort to achieve the political independence of a particular nation or people.

liberative, *adj.* Serving or tending to free or release.

liberative prescription. See PRESCRIPTION.

liberticide (lə-**bər**-tə-sīd), *n.* **1.** The destruction of liberty. **2.** A destroyer of liberty. — **liberticidal,** *adj.*

liberties. *Hist.* **1.** Privileged districts exempt from the sheriff's jurisdiction. **2.** In American colonial times, laws. **3.** Political subdivisions of Philadelphia.

liberty. (14c) **1.** Freedom from arbitrary or undue external restraint, esp. by a government <give me liberty or give me death>. **2.** A right, privilege, or immunity enjoyed by prescription or by grant; the absence of a legal duty imposed on a person <the liberties protected by the Constitution>.

civil liberty. See CIVIL LIBERTY.

individual liberty. See *personal liberty*.

natural liberty. (16c) The power to act as one wishes, without any restraint or control, unless by nature.

personal liberty. (16c) One's freedom to do as one pleases, limited only by the government's right to regulate the public health, safety, and welfare. — Also termed *individual liberty*.

political liberty. (17c) A person's freedom to participate in the operation of government, esp. in elections and in the making and administration of laws.

religious liberty. (17c) Freedom — as guaranteed by the First Amendment — to express, without external control other than one's own conscience, any or no system of religious opinion and to engage in or refrain from any form of religious observance or public or private religious worship, as long as it is consistent with the peace and order of society.

Liberty Clause. (1971) The Due Process Clause in the 14th Amendment to the U.S. Constitution. See DUE PROCESS CLAUSE.

liberty interest. See INTEREST (2).

liberty not. See NO-DUTY.

liberty of a port. *Marine insurance.* A license incorporated in a marine policy allowing the vessel to dock and trade at a designated port other than the principal port of destination.

liberty of contract. See FREEDOM OF CONTRACT.

liberty of speech. See FREEDOM OF SPEECH.

liberty of the globe. *Marine insurance.* A license incorporated in a marine policy authorizing the vessel to go to any part of the world, rather than be confined to a particular port of destination.

liberty of the press. See FREEDOM OF THE PRESS.

liberum maritagium (lib-ər-əm mar-ə-**tay**-jee-əm). See FRANKMARRIAGE.

liberum tenementum (lib-ər-əm ten-ə-**men**-təm), *n.* [Law Latin] *Hist.* **1.** A plea of freehold; a defensive common-law pleading in an action for trespass to lands. • The defendant pleaded either ownership of the land in question or authorization from the freehold owner. **2.** FREEHOLD.

librarian. *Parliamentary law.* An officer charged with custody of an organization's books, periodicals, and other published matter, and sometimes of the organization's own archives and files as well.

Library of Congress. A library on the U.S. Capitol grounds responsible for conducting research for members of Congress and congressional committees. • The Library maintains collections of materials that in many areas are the world's most extensive. Headed by a Librarian appointed by the President with the advice and consent of the Senate, it was established in 1860. 2 USCA §§ 131 et seq.

license, *n.* (15c) **1.** A permission, usu. revocable, to commit some act that would otherwise be unlawful; esp., an agreement (not amounting to a lease or profit à prendre) that it is lawful for the licensee to enter the licensor's land to do some act that would otherwise be illegal, such as hunting game. See SERVITUDE (1). **2.** The certificate or document evidencing such permission. — **license,** *vb.*

artistic license. An open-source license that prohibits the sale of modified software unless it is included in a package with other software.

bare license. (17c) A license in which no property interest passes to the licensee, who is merely not a trespasser. • It is revocable at will. — Also termed *naked license*; *mere license*.

blanket license. *Copyright.* A license granted by a performing-rights society, such as ASCAP or BMI, to use all works in the society's portfolio in exchange for a fixed percentage of the user's revenues.

box-top license. See *shrink-wrap license*.

BSD license. A form of open-source license that allows users to incorporate the source code into proprietary products as long as the names of the original creator or contributors are not used to endorse or promote the products without permission. • It was originally created for the Berkeley Software Distribution operating system developed at the University of California. — Also termed *BSD-style license*.

click-wrap license. See POINT-AND-CLICK AGREEMENT.

compulsory license. **1.** *Copyright.* A statutorily created license that allows certain parties to use copyrighted material without the explicit permission of the copyright owner in exchange for a specified royalty. — Also termed *equitable remuneration*. **2.** *Patents.* A statutorily created license that allows certain people to pay a royalty and use an invention without the patentee's permission. • While some nations currently recognize compulsory licenses, the United States never has.

cross-license. *Patents.* An agreement between two or more patentees to exchange licenses for their mutual benefit and use of the licensed products.

distribution license. A marketing license, usu. limited by geography.

exclusive license. (18c) A license that gives the licensee the sole right to perform the licensed act, often in a defined territory, and that prohibits the licensor from performing the licensed act and from granting the right to anyone else; esp., such a license of a copyright, patent, or trademark right.

general-public license. See *open-source license*.

implied license. A royalty-free license arising from a property owner's conduct regarding another person's use of the property even though the owner has not expressly consented to the property's use. • In a patent context, for example, the circumstances surrounding the conduct give rise to an affirmative grant of consent or permission to infringe a patent's claims. For example, the conduct of a patentee who encourages the manufacture of infringing products may be construed as an implied license to use the patent. An implied license may also arise when a patentee authorizes the sale or express grant of a license to a buyer, who then resells the license to a third party; the third party is the patentee's implied licensee.

implied license by acquiescence. An implied license that arises from the patentee's tacit or passive acceptance of or implied consent to an otherwise infringing act.

implied license by conduct. An implied license based on the patentee's course of conduct, including language, from which another person could properly infer that the patentee consented to the other's use of the patent. See *implied license by equitable estoppel*; *implied license by legal estoppel*.

implied license by equitable estoppel. An implied license usu. based on the patentee's failure to take timely action to enforce patent rights against an infringer after objecting to the infringer's actions, thereby misleading the infringer to believe that the patentee will not act. See *A.C. Aukerman Co. v. R.L. Chaides Constr. Co.*, 960 F.2d 1020, 1042–43 (Fed. Cir.1992).

implied license by legal estoppel. An implied license usu. based on the patentee's broadcast grant of a right or interest that cannot be derogated by the patentee's later acts.

label license. A notice on an item's package granting the purchaser a license to practice the process by using the item without additional payments to the licensor.

license coupled with an interest. (1836) An irrevocable license in real estate that confers the right (not the mere permission) to perform an act or acts upon the property; esp., a license incidental to the ownership of an interest in a chattel located on the land with respect to which the license exists. • This type of license is considered an interest in the land itself. An injunction may be obtained to prevent the wrongful revocation of such a license. — Also termed *license coupled with the grant of an interest*.

limited license. A license that is narrow in scope or narrower than another license granted for the same purpose, or a license subject to conditions or limitations.

mechanical license. A grant of the right to produce and release a copyrighted work in exchange for a royalty based on the number of units manufactured and sold.

mere license. See *bare license*.

Mozilla public license. An open-source license that allows software users to modify and publicly distribute the software, but requires users to release the changed software under the same copyright as the original source code, and to release all claims to patent rights. • The Mozilla public license was developed for the Netscape and Netscape Communicator browsers but is not limited to use with them. — Abbr. MPL.

naked license. 1. A license allowing a licensee to use a trademark on any goods and services the licensee chooses. **2.** See *bare license*.

nonexclusive license. A license of intellectual-property rights that gives the licensee a right to use, make, or sell the licensed item on a shared basis with the licensor and possibly other licensees.

nonmetered license. *Patents.* An agreement to allow a patent's use in exchange for a flat percentage of sales, regardless of how much the patent is actually used. • The Supreme Court rejected a nonmetered license as patent misuse, saying the buyer has a right to insist on paying only for actual use. *Zenith Radio Co. v. Hazeltine Research, Inc.*, 395 U.S. 100, 89 S.Ct. 1562 (1969). See PATENT-MISUSE DOCTRINE.

off-sale license. A state-issued permit to sell alcoholic beverages that may be taken away from and consumed off the premises. — Also termed *off-premises license*. Cf. *on-sale license*.

on-sale license. A state-issued permit to sell alcoholic beverages to be consumed on the premises only. — Also termed *on-premises license*. Cf. *off-sale license*.

open-source license. A license that allows open-source software users to copy, distribute, or modify the source code, and publicly distribute derived works based upon the source code. • Open-source licenses usu. do not require royalty or other fees on distribution. The license typically requires a user who redistributes original or modified software that was received under an open-source license to provide the original license terms, including all disclaimers, to all future users, and to distribute the source code with any machine-executable software. It is unclear who has the right or power to enforce the terms of an open-source license. — Sometimes termed *general-public license*.

proprietary license. A license that restricts a software user's ability to copy, distribute, or modify the software.

shrink-wrap license. (1984) A license printed on the outside of a software package to advise the buyer that by opening the package, the buyer becomes legally bound to abide by the terms of the license. • Shrink-wrap licenses usu. seek to (1) prohibit users from making unauthorized copies of the software, (2) prohibit modifications to the software, (3) limit use of the software to one computer, (4) limit the manufacturer's liability, and (5) disclaim warranties. — Also written *shrinkwrap license*. — Also termed *box-top license*; *tear-me-open license*. See POINT-AND-CLICK AGREEMENT.

site license. *Copyright.* A software license that allows a company to install a set number of copies on individual computers within the company.

synchronization license. A license to reproduce and synchronize a copyrighted musical composition with visual images that are not covered by the musical work's copyright. • Synchronization rights are commonly associated with audiovisual productions, such as music videos or movies.

tear-me-open license. See *shrink-wrap license*.

use-based license. An open-source software license to which the user assents by acting according to the license's terms, namely by using, modifying, or distributing the licensed software. • Unlike a point-and-click agreement, the user does not have to expressly declare acceptance of the license terms before using the software.

license bond. See BOND (2).

license coupled with the grant of an interest. See *license coupled with an interest* under LICENSE.

licensee. (1864) **1.** One to whom a license is granted. **2.** One who has permission to enter or use another's premises, but only for one's own purposes and not for the occupier's benefit. • The occupier has a duty to warn the licensee of any dangerous conditions known to the occupier but unknown to the licensee. An example of a licensee is a social guest. Cf. INVITEE; TRESPASSER.

bare licensee. (1864) A licensee whose presence on the premises the occupier tolerates but does not necessarily approve, such as one who takes a shortcut across another's land. — Also termed *naked licensee*; *mere licensee*.

licensee by invitation. (1894) One who is expressly or impliedly permitted to enter another's premises to transact business with the owner or occupant or to perform an act benefiting the owner or occupant.

licensee by permission. (1894) One who has the owner's permission or passive consent to enter the owner's premises for one's own convenience, curiosity, or entertainment.

licensee with an interest. See INVITEE.

mere licensee. See *bare licensee*.

naked licensee. See *bare licensee*.

license fee. 1. A monetary charge imposed by a governmental authority for the privilege of pursuing a particular occupation, business, or activity. — Also termed *license tax*. **2.** A charge of this type accompanied by a requirement that the licensee take some action, or be subjected to regulations or restrictions.

license in amortization. *Hist.* A license authorizing the conveyance of property otherwise invalid under the statutes of mortmain. See MORTMAIN.

licenser. See LICENSOR.

license tax. See LICENSE FEE (1).

licensing. (15c) **1.** The sale of a license authorizing another to use something (such as computer software) protected by copyright, patent, or trademark. **2.** A governmental body's process of issuing a license. — Also termed *licensure*.

licensor. One who grants a license to another. — Also spelled *licenser*.

licensure. See LICENSING (2).

licentiate (lı-**sen**-shee-ət), *n.* (16c) One who has obtained a license or authoritative permission to exercise some function, esp. to practice a profession <a licentiate in law should be held to high ethical standards>.

licentious (lı-**sen**-shəs), *adj.* (16c) Lacking or ignoring moral or legal restraint, esp. in sexual activity; lewd; lascivious. — **licentiousness,** *n.*

licit (**lis**-it), *adj.* (15c) Not forbidden by law; permitted; legal. — **licitly,** *adv.*

licitation (lis-ə-**tay**-shən). (17c) **1.** The offering for sale or bidding for purchase at an auction; esp., in civil law, a judicial sale of property held in common. See La. Civ. Code art. 811. **2.** CANT.

Lidford law (**lid**-fərd). *Hist.* A form of lynch law permitting a person to be punished first and tried later. • The term took its name from the English town of Lidford (now Lydford) where this type of action supposedly took place. Cf. *Jedburgh justice* under JUSTICE (1).

lie, *vb.* (bef. 12c) **1.** To tell an untruth; to speak or write falsely <she lied on the witness stand>. See PERJURY. Cf. FABRICATE. **2.** To have foundation in the law; to be legally supportable, sustainable, or proper <in such a situation, an action lies in tort>. **3.** To exist; to reside <final appeal lies with the Supreme Court>.

Lieber Code. A codification of rules and customs of warfare, which set out the humane and ethical treatment of persons. • It was first developed by Francis Lieber during the American Revolution, formally adopted as law by Abraham Lincoln during the Civil War, and used as the basis for the first codified international rules of law at The Hague Peace Conference of 1899. The rules were extended and refined in another Hague convention in 1907, and became known as the Law of The Hague. See LAW OF THE HAGUE.

lie detector. See POLYGRAPH.

liege (leej), *adj.* (14c) *Hist.* **1.** Entitled to feudal allegiance and service. **2.** Bound by feudal tenure to a lord paramount; owing allegiance and service. **3.** Loyal; faithful. — Also termed *ligius*.

liege, *n. Hist.* **1.** A vassal bound to feudal allegiance. — Also termed *liege man; liege woman.* **2.** A loyal subject of a monarch or other sovereign. **3.** A feudal lord entitled to allegiance and service; a sovereign or superior lord. — Also termed (in sense 3) *liege lord.*

liegeance. See LIGEANCE.

liege homage, *n. Hist.* Homage paid by one sovereign to another, including pledges of loyalty and services.

liege lord, *n. Hist.* See LIEGE (3).

liege man, *n. Hist.* See LIEGE (1).

liege woman, *n. Hist.* See LIEGE (1).

lie in franchise, *vb. Hist.* (Of wrecks, waifs, strays, etc.) to be seizable without judicial action.

lie in grant, *vb. Hist.* (Of incorporeal hereditaments) to be passable by deed or charter without the ceremony of livery of seisin.

lie in livery, *vb. Hist.* (Of corporeal hereditaments) to be passable by livery of seisin rather than by deed.

lien (leen *or* lee-ən), *n.* (16c) A legal right or interest that a creditor has in another's property, lasting usu. until a debt or duty that it secures is satisfied. ● Typically, the creditor does not take possession of the property on which the lien has been obtained. Cf. PLEDGE (3). — **lien,** *vb.* — **lienable, liened,** *adj.*

accountant's lien. The right of an accountant to retain a client's papers until the accountant's fees have been paid.

agent's lien. A lien against property of the estate, in favor of an agent, to secure the agent's compensation as well as all necessary expenses incurred under the agent's power.

agister's lien (ə-jis-tərz). A lien on the animals under an agister's care, to secure payment of the agister's fee. See AGISTER; AGISTMENT.

agricultural lien. **1.** A statutory lien that protects a seller of farming equipment by giving the seller a lien on crops grown with the equipment. **2.** *Secured transactions.* An interest (other than a security interest) in farm products having three characteristics: (1) it must secure payment or performance of an obligation for goods or services furnished in connection with a debtor's farming operation, or of an obligation for rent on real property leased by a debtor in connection with farming; (2) it must be created by statute in favor of a person either who in the ordinary course of business furnished goods or services to a debtor in connection with the debtor's farming, or who leased real property to a debtor in connection with the debtor's farming; and (3) the effectiveness of the interest must not depend on the person's possession of the personal property. UCC § 9-102(a)(5).

architect's lien. A statutory lien on real property in favor of an architect who has drawn the plans for and supervised the construction of improvements on the property.

artisan's lien. See *mechanic's lien.*

attachment lien. A lien on property seized by prejudgment attachment. ● Such a lien is initially inchoate but becomes final and perfected upon entry of a judgment for the attaching creditor and relates back to the date when the lien first arose. — Also termed *lien of attachment.* See ATTACHMENT.

attorney's lien. The right of an attorney to hold or retain a client's money or property (a *retaining lien*) or to encumber money payable to the client (a *charging lien*) until the attorney's fees have been properly determined and paid.

banker's lien. The right of a bank to satisfy a customer's matured debt by seizing the customer's money or property in the bank's possession.

blanket lien. A lien that gives a creditor the entitlement to take possession of any or all of the debtor's real property to cover a delinquent loan.

carrier's lien. A carrier's right to retain possession of cargo until the owner of the cargo pays its shipping costs.

charging lien. **1.** An attorney's lien on a claim that the attorney has helped the client perfect, as through a judgment or settlement. **2.** A lien on specified property in the debtor's possession.

chattel lien. See *mechanic's lien.*

choate lien (koh-it). A lien in which the lienholder, the property, and the monetary amount are established so that the lien is perfected and nothing else needs to be done to make it enforceable.

common-law lien. **1.** A lien granted by the common law, rather than by statute, equity, or agreement by the parties. **2.** The right of one person to retain possession of property belonging to another until certain demands of the possessing party are met. ● This type of lien, unlike an equitable lien, cannot exist without possession.

concurrent lien. One of two or more liens of equal priority attaching to the same property.

construction lien. See *mechanic's lien.*

consummate lien (kən-**səm**-it). A judgment lien arising after the denial of a motion for a new trial. Cf. *inchoate lien.*

conventional lien. A lien that is created by the express agreement of the parties, in circumstances in which the law would not create a lien.

deferred lien. A lien effective at a future date, as distinguished from a present lien that is currently possessory.

demurrage lien (di-**mər**-ij). A carrier's lien on goods for any unpaid demurrage charges. See DEMURRAGE.

dragnet lien. A lien that is enlarged to cover any additional credit extended to the debtor by the same creditor.

equitable lien. A right, enforceable only in equity, to have a demand satisfied from a particular fund or specific property, without having possession of the fund or property. • It arises mainly in four circumstances: (1) when an occupant of land, believing in good faith to be the owner of that land, makes improvements, repairs, or other expenditures that permanently increase the land's value, (2) when one of two or more joint owners makes expenditures of that kind, (3) when a tenant for life completes permanent and beneficial improvements to the estate begun earlier by the testator, and (4) when land or other property is transferred subject to the payment of debts, legacies, portions, or annuities to third persons. — Also termed *equitable levy.*

execution lien. A lien on property seized by a levy of execution. • Such a lien gives the execution creditor priority over later transferees of the property and over prior unrecorded conveyances of interests in the property. See EXECUTION (3).

factor's lien. A lien, usu. statutory, on property held on consignment by a factor. • It allows the factor to keep possession of the property until the account has been settled. *See* UCC § 9-102(2). See FACTOR (2).

first lien. A lien that takes priority over all other charges or encumbrances on the same property and that must be satisfied before other charges may share in proceeds from the property's sale.

floating lien. **1.** A lien that is expanded to cover any additional property obtained by the debtor while the debt is outstanding. **2.** A lien that continues to exist even when the collateral changes in character, classification, or location. — Also termed *floating charge.*

garnishment lien. A lien on a debtor's property held by a garnishee. • Such a lien attaches in favor of the garnishing creditor when a garnishment summons is served and also impounds any credits the garnishee owes the debtor so that they must be paid to the garnishing creditor. — Also termed *lien of garnishment.* See GARNISHMENT.

general lien. A possessory lien by which the lienholder may retain any of the debtor's goods in the lienholder's possession until any debt due from the debtor, whether in connection with the retained goods or otherwise, has been paid. • Factors, insurance brokers, packers, stockbrokers, and bankers have a general lien over the property of their clients or customers. Cf. *particular lien.*

grantor's lien. See *vendor's lien* (1).

healthcare lien. A statutory lien asserted by an HMO, insurer, medical group, or independent practice association against those liable to the patient for damages, to recover money paid or claim money payable for healthcare services provided under a healthcare service plan or a disability insurance policy. — Also termed *medical lien.* Cf. *hospital lien; workers'-compensation lien.*

hospital lien. A statutory lien asserted by a hospital to recover the costs of emergency and ongoing medical and other services. • The lien applies against any judgment, compromise, or settlement received by a hospital patient either from a third person who caused the patient's injuries or from the third person's insurer. See *healthcare lien.*

hotelkeeper's lien. A possessory or statutory lien allowing an innkeeper to hold, as security for payment, personal property that a guest brought into the hotel. — Also termed *innkeeper's lien.*

inchoate lien (in-**koh**-it). A judgment lien that may be defeated if the judgment is vacated or a motion for new trial is granted. Cf. *consummate lien.*

innkeeper's lien. See *hotelkeeper's lien.*

involuntary lien. A lien arising without the debtor's consent.

judgment lien. A lien imposed on a judgment debtor's nonexempt property. • This lien gives the judgment creditor the right to attach the judgment debtor's property. — Also termed *lien of judgment.* See EXEMPT PROPERTY.

judicial lien. A lien obtained by judgment, levy, sequestration, or other legal or equitable process or proceeding. • If a debtor is adjudged to owe money to a creditor and the judgment has not been satisfied, the creditor can ask the court to impose a lien on specific property owned and possessed by the debtor. After the court imposes the lien, it usu. issues a writ directing the local sheriff to seize the property, sell it, and turn over the proceeds to the creditor.

junior lien. A lien that is subordinate to one or more other liens on the same property.

laborer's lien. See *mechanic's lien*.

landlord's lien. 1. At common law, a lien that gave a landlord the right to seize a tenant's property and sell it publicly to satisfy overdue rent. See DISTRESS. **2.** Generally, a statutory lien on a tenant's personal property at the leased premises in favor of a landlord who receives preferred-creditor status on that property. ● Such a lien usu. secures the payment of overdue rent or compensation for damage to the premises.

lien of attachment. See *attachment lien*.

lien of factor at common law. *Hist.* A lien not created by statute; a common-law lien.

lien of garnishment. See *garnishment lien*.

lien of judgment. See *judgment lien*.

manufacturer's lien. A statutory lien that secures payment for labor or materials expended in producing goods for another.

maritime lien. A lien on a vessel, given to secure the claim of a creditor who provided maritime services to the vessel or who suffered an injury from the vessel's use. — Also termed *tacit hypothecation*.

mechanic's lien. A statutory lien that secures payment for labor or materials supplied in improving, repairing, or maintaining real or personal property, such as a building, an automobile, or the like. — Also termed *artisan's lien*; *chattel lien* (for personal property); *construction lien* (for labor); *garageman's lien* (for repaired vehicles); *laborer's lien* (for labor); *materialman's lien* (for materials).

medical lien. See *healthcare lien*.

mortgage lien. A lien on the mortgagor's property securing the mortgage.

municipal lien. A lien by a municipal corporation against a property owner for the owner's proportionate share of a public improvement that specially and individually benefits the owner.

particular lien. A possessory lien by which the possessor of goods has the right to retain specific goods until a debt incurred in connection with those goods has been paid. — Also termed *special lien*. Cf. *general lien*.

possessory garageman's lien. A lien on a vehicle in the amount of the repairs performed by the garage.

possessory lien. A lien allowing the creditor to keep possession of the encumbered property until the debt is satisfied. ● A power of sale may or may not be combined with this right of possession. Examples include pledges of chattels, the liens of innkeepers, garageman's liens, and vendor's liens. See PLEDGE.

prior lien. A lien that is superior to one or more other liens on the same property, usu. because it was perfected first. — Also termed *priority lien*.

retaining lien. An attorney's right to keep a client's papers until the client has paid for the attorney's services. ● The attorney's retaining lien is not recognized in some states.

second lien. A lien that is next in rank after a first lien on the same property and therefore is next entitled to satisfaction out of the proceeds from the property's sale.

secret lien. A lien not appearing of record and unknown to purchasers; a lien reserved by the vendor and kept hidden from third parties, to secure the payment of goods after delivery.

senior lien. A lien that has priority over other liens on the same property.

special lien. See *particular lien*.

specific lien. A lien secured on a particular thing by a contract or by a judgment, execution, attachment, or other legal proceeding.

statutory lien. 1. A lien arising solely by force of statute, not by agreement of the parties. ● Examples are federal tax liens and mechanic's liens. **2.** *Bankruptcy.* Either of two types of liens: (1) a lien arising solely by force of a statute on specified circumstances or conditions, or (2) a lien of distress for rent, whether or not statutory. ● For bankruptcy purposes, a statutory lien does not include a security interest or judicial lien, whether or not the interest or lien arises from or is made effective by a statute.

superlien. See SUPERLIEN.

tax lien. 1. A lien on property, and all rights to property, imposed by the federal government for unpaid federal taxes. **2.** A lien on real estate in favor of a state or local government that may be foreclosed for nonpayment of taxes. ● A majority of states have adopted the Uniform Federal Tax Lien Registration Act.

vendee's lien. *Real estate.* A buyer's lien on the purchased land as security for repayment of purchase money paid in, enforceable if the seller does not or cannot convey good title.

vendor's lien. 1. *Real estate.* A seller's lien on land as security for the purchase price. ● This lien may be foreclosed in the same way as a mortgage: the buyer usu. has a redemption period within which to pay the full purchase price. — Also termed *grantor's lien*. **2.** A lien held by a seller of goods, who retains possession of the goods until the buyer has paid in full.

voluntary lien. A lien created with the debtor's consent.

warehouser's lien. A lien covering storage charges for goods stored with a bailee. — Also termed *warehouseman's lien.*

workers'-compensation lien. **1.** A statutory lien, asserted by a healthcare provider, to recover the costs of emergency and ongoing medical and other services. • The lien applies against any workers'-compensation benefits paid to a patient. **2.** A statutory lien, asserted by a workers'-compensation insurance carrier, against an insured worker's recovery from a third-party tortfeasor, to recover benefits paid to the injured worker. — Also termed *workers'-compensation subrogation lien.* Cf. *healthcare lien.*

lienable, *adj.* (Of property) legally amenable to a lien; capable of being subject to a lien.

lien account. See ACCOUNT.

lien avoidance. *Bankruptcy.* A debtor's depriving a creditor of a security interest in an asset of the bankruptcy estate. 11 USCA §§ 506(d), 522(f).

lien creditor. See CREDITOR.

lienee (leen-ee *or* lee-ən-ee). **1.** One whose property is subject to a lien. **2.** An encumbrancer who holds a lien; LIENHOLDER.

lienholder. (1830) A person having or owning a lien. — Also termed *lienor; lienee.*

lien of a covenant. (1916) The beginning portion of a covenant, stating the names of the parties and the character of the covenant.

lien of attachment. See *attachment lien* under LIEN.

lien of factor at common law. See LIEN.

lien of garnishment. See *garnishment lien* under LIEN.

lien of judgment. See *judgment lien* under LIEN.

lienor. See LIENHOLDER.

lien-stripping. *Bankruptcy.* The practice of splitting a mortgagee's secured claim into secured and unsecured components and reducing the claim to the market value of the debtor's residence, thereby allowing the debtor to modify the terms of the mortgage and reduce the amount of the debt. • The U.S. Supreme Court has prohibited lien-stripping in all Chapter 7 cases (*Nobelman v. American Savs. Bank*, 508 U.S. 324, 113 S.Ct. 2106 (1993)) and in Chapter 13 cases involving a debtor's principal residence (*Dewsnup v. Timm*, 502 U.S. 410, 112 S.Ct. 773 (1992)), and the Bankruptcy Reform Act of 1994 modified the Bankruptcy Code to prohibit lien-stripping in Chapter 11 cases involving an individual's principal residence.

lien theory. (1882) The idea that a mortgage resembles a lien, so that the mortgagee acquires only a lien on the property and the mortgagor retains both legal and equitable title unless a valid foreclosure occurs. • Most American states — commonly called *lien states, lien jurisdictions,* or *lien-theory jurisdictions* — have adopted this theory. Cf. TITLE THEORY.

lien waiver. See WAIVER (2).

lieu land. See LAND.

lieutenancy. The rank, office, or commission of a lieutenant. See COMMISSION OF LIEUTENANCY.

lieutenant. (14c) **1.** A deputy of or substitute for another; one acting by vicarious authority <he sent his chief lieutenant to the meeting>. **2.** A composite part of the title of many government and military officials who are subordinate to others, esp. when the duties of the higher official may devolve to the subordinate <lieutenant governor>. **3.** In the U.S. Army, a commissioned officer next below captain. **4.** In the U.S. Navy, an officer next below lieutenant commander.

lieutenant colonel. (16c) In the U.S. military, an officer next below colonel and above major.

lieutenant commander. (1839) In the U.S. Navy, an officer next below commander and above lieutenant.

lieutenant general. (16c) In the U.S. Army, an officer next below four-star general and above major general.

lieutenant governor. (16c) A deputy or subordinate governor, sometimes charged with such duties as presiding over the state legislature, but esp. important as the governor's successor if the governor dies, resigns, or becomes disabled.

life annuity. See ANNUITY.

life beneficiary. See BENEFICIARY.

life-care contract. (1950) An agreement in which one party is assured of care and maintenance for life in exchange for transferring property to the other party.

life estate. See ESTATE (1).

life estate pur autre vie. See ESTATE (1).

life expectancy. **1.** The period that a person of a given age and sex is expected to live, according to actuarial tables. **2.** The period that a given person is expected to live, taking into account individualized characteristics such as heredity, past and present diseases, and other relevant medical data. See ACTUARIAL TABLE; LIFE TABLE.

life-hold. See *life land* under LAND.

life in being. (1836) Under the rule against perpetuities, anyone alive when a future interest is created, whether or not the person has an interest in the estate. See IN BEING; RULE AGAINST PERPETUITIES. Cf. MEASURING LIFE.

life-income period-certain annuity. See ANNUITY.

life insurance. (1809) An agreement between an insurance company and the policyholder to pay a specified amount to a designated beneficiary on the insured's death. — Also termed (in Britain) *assurance.* See ASSURANCE (2).

    corporate-owned life insurance. A life-insurance policy bought by a company on an employee's life, naming the company as beneficiary. — Abbr. COLI.

    credit life insurance. Life insurance on a borrower, usu. in a consumer installment loan, in which the amount due is paid if the borrower dies.

    decreasing-term life insurance. See *decreasing term insurance* under INSURANCE.

    endowment life insurance. Life insurance that is payable either to the insured at the end of the policy period or to the insured's beneficiary if the insured dies before the period ends. — Also termed *endowment insurance.*

    industrial life insurance. Life insurance characterized by (1) a small death benefit (usu. $2,000 or less), (2) premium payments that are due weekly, biweekly, or monthly and that are collected at home by the insurer's representative, and (3) no required medical examination of the insured. — Sometimes shortened to *industrial insurance.*

    joint life insurance. (1920) Life insurance on two or more persons, payable to the survivor or survivors when one of the policyholders dies.

    key-employee life insurance. Life insurance taken out by a company on an essential or valuable employee, with the company as beneficiary. — Also termed *key-employee insurance; key-man insurance; key-person insurance; key-executive insurance.*

    last-survivor life insurance. Life insurance on two or more persons, payable after all the insureds have died. — Also termed *last-survivor insurance.*

    limited-payment life insurance. Life insurance that requires premium payments for less than the life of the agreement.

    national-service life insurance. Life insurance available to a person in active U.S. military service on or after October 8, 1940, and issuable at favorable rates. • This insurance was established by the National Service Life Insurance Act of 1940, and is regulated by the Administrator of Veterans Affairs. 38 USCA §§ 1901–1929.

    ordinary life insurance. 1. Life insurance having an investment-sensitive cash value, such as whole life insurance or universal life insurance. • Ordinary insurance is one of three main categories of life insurance. — Often shortened to *ordinary insurance.* Cf. *group insurance;*

industrial life insurance. 2. See *whole life insurance.*

    partnership life insurance. See *partnership insurance* (1) under INSURANCE.

    single-premium life insurance. Life insurance that is paid for in one installment rather than a series of premiums over time. — Also termed *single-premium insurance.*

    split-dollar life insurance. An arrangement between two people (often an employer and employee) by which life insurance is written on the life of one, though both share the premium payments. • On the insured's death or other event terminating the plan, the noninsured person receives the cash value of the insurance as reimbursement, and the beneficiary named by the insured is entitled to the remainder. — Also termed *split-dollar insurance.*

    straight life insurance. See *whole life insurance.*

    term life insurance. Life insurance that covers the insured for only a specified period. • It pays a fixed benefit to a named beneficiary upon the insured's death but is not redeemable for a cash value during the insured's life. Cf. *whole life insurance.*

    universal life insurance. Term life insurance in which the premiums are paid from the insured's earnings from a money-market fund.

    variable life insurance. Life insurance in which the premiums are invested in securities and whose death benefits thus depend on the securities' performance, though there is a minimum guaranteed death benefit.

    whole life insurance. Life insurance that covers an insured for life, during which the insured pays fixed premiums, accumulates savings from an invested portion of the premiums, and receives a guaranteed benefit upon death, to be paid to a named beneficiary. • Such a policy may provide that at a stated time, premiums will end or benefits will increase. — Also termed *ordinary life insurance; straight life insurance.* Cf. *term life insurance.*

life-insurance trust. See TRUST.

life interest. (18c) An interest in real or personal property measured by the duration of the holder's or another named person's life. See *life estate* under ESTATE (1).

life land. See LAND.

lifelode. See LIVELODE.

life of a writ. The effective period during which a writ may be levied. • That period usu. ends on the day that the law or the writ itself provides that it must be returned to court.

life-owner. See LIFE TENANT.

life policy. See INSURANCE POLICY.

life-prolonging procedure. See LIFE-SUSTAINING PROCEDURE.

life-qualified jury. See JURY.

lifer. See NONREMOVABLE INMATE.

life sentence. See SENTENCE.

life settlement. See *viatical settlement* under SETTLEMENT.

life-sustaining procedure. (1976) A medical procedure that uses mechanical or artificial means to sustain, restore, or substitute for a vital function and that serves only or mainly to postpone death. — Also termed *life-prolonging procedure.*

life table. An actuarial table that gives the probable proportions of people who will live to different ages. Cf. ACTUARIAL TABLE.

life tenancy. See *life estate* under ESTATE (1).

life tenant. (16c) A person who, until death, is beneficially entitled to property; the holder of a life estate. — Also termed *tenant for life; life-owner.* See *life estate* under ESTATE (1).

   equitable life tenant. (1880) A life tenant not automatically entitled to possession but who makes an election allowed by law to a person of that status — such as a spouse — and to whom a court will normally grant possession if security or an undertaking is given.

   legal life tenant. (1886) A life tenant who is automatically entitled to possession by virtue of a legal estate.

lifetime gift. See *inter vivos gift* under GIFT.

LIFO (lı-foh). *abbr.* LAST-IN, FIRST-OUT.

lift, *vb.* (16c) **1.** To stop or put an end to; to revoke or rescind <lift the stay>. **2.** To discharge or pay off (a debt or obligation) <lift a mortgage>. **3.** *Slang.* To steal <lift a purse>.

lifting costs. *Oil & gas.* The cost of producing oil and gas after drilling is complete but before the oil and gas is removed from the property, including transportation costs, labor, costs of supervision, supplies, costs of operating the pumps, electricity, repairs, depreciation, certain royalties payable to the lessor, gross-production taxes, and other incidental expenses.

ligeance (lı-jənts *or* lee-jənts). *Hist.* **1.** The obedience of a citizen to the citizen's sovereign or government; allegiance. **2.** The territory of a state or sovereign. — Also spelled *liegeance.* See LIEGE.

light-and-air easement. See EASEMENT.

lighterage (lı-tər-ij). **1.** The loading and unloading of goods between a ship and a smaller vessel, called a lighter, that is able to use a restricted port or dock. **2.** The compensation paid for this service. **3.** The loading and unloading of freight between a railroad car and a ship's side.

light most favorable. (1861) The standard of scrutinizing or interpreting a verdict by accepting as true all evidence and inferences that support it and disregarding all contrary evidence and inferences <in reviewing the defendant's motion for judgment notwithstanding the verdict, the court reviewed the evidence in the light most favorable to the verdict>. — Also termed *most favorable light.*

lights, ancient. See ANCIENT-LIGHTS DOCTRINE.

light work. See WORK (1).

ligius (lee-jee-əs), *n.* [Law Latin] *Hist.* A person bound to another by solemn relationship, as between subject and sovereign. See LIEGE.

like, *adj.* (12c) **1.** Equal in quantity, quality, or degree; corresponding exactly <like copies>. **2.** Similar or substantially similar <like character>.

like-kind exchange. (1963) An exchange of trade, business, or investment property (except inventory or securities) for property of the same kind, class, or character. • Such an exchange is not taxable unless cash or other property is received. IRC (26 USCA) § 1031).

like-kind property. (1946) *Tax.* Property that is of such a similar kind, class, or character to other property that a gain from an exchange of the property is not recognized for federal income-tax purposes. See LIKE-KIND EXCHANGE.

likelihood-of-confusion test. *Trademarks.* A test for trademark infringement, based on the probability that a substantial number of ordinarily prudent buyers will be misled or confused about the source of a product.

likelihood-of-success-on-the-merits test. *Civil procedure.* The rule that a litigant who seeks a preliminary injunction, or seeks to forestall the effects of a judgment during appeal, must show a reasonable probability of success in the litigation or appeal.

limbo time. The period when an employee is neither on duty nor off duty, as a railroad worker awaiting transportation from a duty assignment to the place of final release. 49 USCA § 21103(b)(4); *Brotherhood of Locomotive Eng'rs v. Atchison, Topeka & Santa Fe R.R.*, 516 U.S. 152, 116 S.Ct. 595 (1996).

limine. See IN LIMINE.

limine out (lim-ə-nee), *vb.* (1997) (Of a court) to exclude (evidence) by granting a motion in limine <the trial judge limined out most of the plaintiff's medical records>.

limit, *n.* (14c) **1.** A restriction or restraint. **2.** A boundary or defining line. **3.** The extent of power, right, or authority. — **limit,** *vb.* — **limited,** *adj.*

limitation. (14c) **1.** The act of limiting; the state of being limited. **2.** A restriction. **3.** A statutory period after which a lawsuit or prosecution cannot be brought in court. — Also termed *limitations period*; *limitation period*; *limitation of action* See STATUTE OF LIMITATIONS. Cf. LACHES. **4.** *Property.* The restriction of the extent of an estate; the creation by deed or devise of a lesser estate out of a fee simple. See WORDS OF LIMITATION.

collateral limitation. *Hist.* A limitation that makes the duration of an estate dependent on another event (other than the life of the grantee), such as an estate to A until B turns 21.

conditional limitation. (18c) **1.** See *executory limitation.* **2.** A lease provision that automatically terminates the lease if a specified event occurs, such as if the lessee defaults.

executory limitation. (18c) A restriction that causes an estate to automatically end and revest in a third party upon the happening of a specified event. • This type of limitation, which was not recognized at common law, can be created only as a shifting use or an executory devise. It is a condition subsequent in favor of someone other than the transferor. — Also termed *conditional limitation.* See *fee simple subject to an executory limitation* under FEE SIMPLE.

limitation over. (17c) An additional estate created or contemplated in a conveyance, to be enjoyed after the first estate expires or is exhausted. • An example of language giving rise to a limitation over is "to A for life, remainder to B."

special limitation. (17c) A restriction that causes an estate to end automatically and revert to the grantor upon the happening of a specified event. See *fee simple determinable* under FEE SIMPLE.

supplanting limitation. A limitation involving a secondary gift that is expressed in a clause following the original gift and that is typically introduced by the words "but if," "and if," or "in case."

5. ELEMENT (2).

limitation of action. See LIMITATION (3).

limitation of assize. *Hist.* A period prescribed by statute within which a person is required to allege that the person was properly seised of lands sued for under a writ of assize.

limitation-of-damages clause. (1933) A contractual provision by which the parties agree on a maximum amount of damages recoverable for a future breach of the agreement. Cf. LIQUIDATED-DAMAGES CLAUSE.

limitation-of-liability act. (1897) A federal or state law that limits the type of damages that may be recovered, the liability of particular persons or groups, or the time during which an action may be brought. See FEDERAL TORT CLAIMS ACT; *sovereign immunity* under IMMUNITY (1).

limitation-of-remedies clause. (1974) A contractual provision that restricts the remedies available to the parties if a party defaults. • Under the UCC, such a clause is valid unless it fails of its essential purpose or it unconscionably limits consequential damages. Cf. LIQUIDATED-DAMAGES CLAUSE; PENALTY CLAUSE.

limitation on indebtedness. See DEBT LIMITATION.

limitation period. See LIMITATION (3).

limitations, statute of. See STATUTE OF LIMITATIONS.

limitations period. **1.** See LIMITATION (3). **2.** See STATUTE OF LIMITATIONS.

limit debate. *Parliamentary law.* To set a limit on how long debate may continue, or on the number and length of speeches. See DEBATE. Cf. CLOSE DEBATE; EXTEND DEBATE.

limited administration. See ADMINISTRATION.

limited admissibility. See ADMISSIBILITY.

limited appeal. See APPEAL.

limited appearance. See *special appearance* under APPEARANCE.

limited-capacity well. See WELL.

limited certiorari. See *narrow certiorari* under CERTIORARI.

limited company. See COMPANY.

limited court. See COURT.

limited debate. See DEBATE.

limited defense. See *personal defense* under DEFENSE (4).

limited-dividend housing association. An independent entity formed by housing developers and used for borrowing funds from a public agency. • The developers invest in the association, agree to limit the return on their investment to a prescribed percentage, and rent a defined portion of the housing units to persons of low and moderate income. In exchange the government lender charges a below-market interest rate, subsidizes rents or interest rates, and may grant other tax benefits.

limited divorce. See DIVORCE.

limited executor. See EXECUTOR.

limited fee. See *base fee* under FEE (2).

limited guaranty. See GUARANTY.

limited interdict. See INTERDICT (2).

limited interdiction. See *partial interdiction* under INTERDICTION (3).

limited interpretation. See *restrictive interpretation* under INTERPRETATION.

limited jurisdiction. See JURISDICTION.

limited liability. See LIABILITY.

limited-liability company. See COMPANY.

limited-liability corporation. See *limited-liability company* under COMPANY.

limited-liability partnership. See PARTNERSHIP.

limited license. See LICENSE (2).

limited-market property. See *special-purpose property* under PROPERTY.

limited member. See *nonvoting member* under MEMBER.

limited monarchy. See MONARCHY.

limited owner. See OWNER.

limited partner. See PARTNER.

limited partnership. See PARTNERSHIP.

limited partnership association. See PARTNERSHIP ASSOCIATION.

limited-payment life insurance. See LIFE INSURANCE.

limited policy. See INSURANCE POLICY.

limited-policy insurance. See INSURANCE.

limited power of appointment. See POWER OF APPOINTMENT.

limited publication. See PUBLICATION.

limited public forum. See *designated public forum* under PUBLIC FORUM.

limited-purpose marriage. See MARRIAGE (1).

limited-purpose public figure. See PUBLIC FIGURE.

limited trust. See TRUST.

limited veto. See *qualified veto* under VETO.

limited voting. See VOTING.

limited warranty. See WARRANTY (2).

limit of liability. See LIABILITY LIMIT.

limit order. See ORDER (8).

Lincoln's Inn. One of the Inns of Court. See INN OF COURT (1).

Lindbergh Act. See FEDERAL KIDNAPPING ACT.

line, *n.* (14c) **1.** A demarcation, border, or limit <the line between right and wrong>. **2.** A person's occupation or business <what line of business is Watson in?>. **3.** In manufacturing, a series of closely related products. **4.** The ancestry of a person; lineage <the Fergusons came from a long line of wheat farmers>.

   collateral line. (16c) A line of descent connecting persons who are not directly related to each other as ascendants or descendants, but who are descendants of a common ancestor.

   direct line. (17c) A line of descent traced through only those persons who are related to each other directly as ascendants or descendants.

   maternal line. (17c) A person's ancestry or relationship with another traced through the mother.

   paternal line. (17c) A person's ancestry or relationship with another traced through the father.

lineage (lin-ee-əj). (14c) Ancestry and progeny; family, ascending or descending.

lineal (lin-ee-əl), *adj.* (15c) Derived from or relating to common ancestors, esp. in a direct line; hereditary. Cf. COLLATERAL (2).

lineal, *n.* (18c) A lineal descendant; a direct blood relative.

lineal ascendant. See ASCENDANT.

lineal consanguinity. See CONSANGUINITY.

lineal descendant. See DESCENDANT.

lineal descent. See DESCENT.

lineal heir. See HEIR.

lineal warranty. See WARRANTY (1).

line item. See ITEM.

line-item veto. See VETO.

line of credit. (1917) The maximum amount of borrowing power extended to a borrower by a given lender, to be drawn upon by the borrower as needed. — Also termed *credit line*.

line of demarcation. See DEMARCATION LINE.

line of title. See CHAIN OF TITLE (1).

lines and corners. See METES AND BOUNDS.

lineup. (1915) A police identification procedure in which a criminal suspect and other physically similar persons are shown to the victim or a witness to determine whether the suspect can be identified as the perpetrator of the crime. — Also termed (in BrE) *identification parade*. Cf. SHOWUP.

Lingle test. *Labor law.* A test for determining whether a union member's state-law claim against the employer is preempted by the Labor–Management Relations Act, the controlling principle being that if the state-law claim can be resolved without interpreting the collective-bargaining agreement, then there is no preemption. *Lingle v. Norge Division of Magic Chef, Inc.,* 486 U.S. 399, 108 S.Ct. 1877 (1988). See MARCUS MODEL; WHITE MODEL.

linguistic profiling. Profiling based on vocal characteristics that suggest a speaker's race, sex, or national, ethnic, or regional origin. ● This type of profiling occurs when the speaker is not visible but can be heard, as in a telephone conversation or voice message. Cf. RACIAL PROFILING.

link, *n.* (15c) **1.** A unit in a connected series; something that binds separate things <link in the chain

of title>. **2.** A unit of land measurement <one link equals 7.92 inches>. **3.** See HYPERLINK.

link financing. See FINANCING.

link-in-chain principle. (1962) *Criminal procedure.* The principle that a criminal defendant's Fifth Amendment right against self-incrimination protects the defendant not only from answering directly incriminating questions but also from giving answers that might connect the defendant to criminal activity in the chain of evidence.

LIP. *abbr.* LEGALLY INCAPACITATED PERSON.

liquid, *adj.* (1879) **1.** (Of an asset) capable of being readily converted into cash. **2.** (Of a person or entity) possessing assets that can be readily converted into cash.

liquid asset. See *current asset* under ASSET.

liquidate, *vb.* (16c) **1.** To settle (an obligation) by payment or other adjustment; to extinguish (a debt). **2.** To ascertain the precise amount of (debt, damages, etc.) by litigation or agreement. **3.** To determine the liabilities and distribute the assets of (an entity), esp. in bankruptcy or dissolution. **4.** To convert (a nonliquid asset) into cash. **5.** To wind up the affairs of (a corporation, business, etc.). **6.** *Slang.* To get rid of (a person), esp. by killing.

liquidated, *adj.* (18c) **1.** (Of an amount or debt) settled or determined, esp. by agreement. **2.** (Of an asset or assets) converted into cash.

liquidated account. See ACCOUNT.

liquidated amount. A figure readily computed, based on an agreement's terms.

liquidated claim. See CLAIM (3).

liquidated damages. See DAMAGES.

liquidated-damages clause. (1873) A contractual provision that determines in advance the measure of damages if a party breaches the agreement. ● Traditionally, courts have upheld such a clause unless the agreed-on sum is deemed a penalty for one of the following reasons: (1) the sum grossly exceeds the probable damages on breach, (2) the same sum is made payable for any variety of different breaches (some major, some minor), or (3) a mere delay in payment has been listed among the events of default. Cf. LIMITATION-OF-REMEDIES CLAUSE; PENALTY CLAUSE.

liquidated debt. See DEBT.

liquidated demand. See *liquidated claim* under CLAIM (3).

liquidating distribution. See DISTRIBUTION.

liquidating dividend. See *liquidation dividend* under DIVIDEND.

liquidating partner. See PARTNER.

liquidating price. See *redemption price* under PRICE.

liquidating trust. See TRUST.

liquidation, *n.* (16c) **1.** The act of determining by agreement or by litigation the exact amount of something (as a debt or damages) that before was uncertain. **2.** The act of settling a debt by payment or other satisfaction. **3.** The act or process of converting assets into cash, esp. to settle debts.

> *one-month liquidation.* A special election, available to certain shareholders, that determines how the distributions received in liquidation by electing shareholders will be treated for federal income-tax purposes. ● To qualify for the election, the corporation must be completely liquidated within one month. IRC § 333.

> *partial liquidation.* A liquidation that does not completely dispose of a company's assets; esp., a liquidation occurring when some corporate assets are distributed to shareholders (usu. on a pro rata basis) and the corporation continues to operate in a restricted form.

> *twelve-month liquidation.* A liquidation occurring within 12 months from adoption of the liquidation plan to complete liquidation, subject to a tax law prohibiting the company from recognizing any gains or losses on property sold within that time frame. ● Generally, inventory will not be included unless a bulk sale occurs. IRC § 337.

4. *Bankruptcy.* The process — under Chapter 7 of the Bankruptcy Code — of collecting a debtor's nonexempt property, converting that property to cash, and distributing the cash to the various creditors. ● Upon liquidation, the debtor hopes to obtain a discharge, which releases the debtor from any further personal liability for prebankruptcy debts. See CHAPTER 7. Cf. REHABILITATION (3).

liquidation bankruptcy. See CHAPTER 7 (2).

liquidation court. See COURT.

liquidation dividend. See DIVIDEND.

liquidation preference. See PREFERENCE.

liquidation price. See PRICE.

liquidation value. See VALUE (2).

liquidator. (1858) A person appointed to wind up a business's affairs, esp. by selling off its assets. See LIQUIDATION (3), (4). Cf. RECEIVER.

liquid debt. See DEBT.

liquidity. 1. The quality or state of being readily convertible to cash. **2.** *Securities.* The characteristic of having enough units in the market that large transactions can occur without substantial price variations. ● Most stocks traded on the New York Stock Exchange, for example, have liquidity.

liquidity ratio. The ratio between a person's or entity's assets that are held in cash or liquid form and the amount of the person's or entity's current liabilities, indicating the ability to pay current debts as they come due.

liquor offense. See OFFENSE (1).

lis (lis). [Latin] (17c) A piece of litigation; a controversy or dispute.

lis alibi pendens (lis **al**-ə-bı **pen**-dənz). [Latin] **1.** A lawsuit pending elsewhere. **2.** *Hist.* A preliminary defense that a case involving the same parties and the same subject is pending in another court. See LIS PENDENS.

lis pendens (lis **pen**-dənz). [Latin] (17c) **1.** A pending lawsuit. **2.** The jurisdiction, power, or control acquired by a court over property while a legal action is pending. **3.** A notice, recorded in the chain of title to real property, required or permitted in some jurisdictions to warn all persons that certain property is the subject matter of litigation, and that any interests acquired during the pendency of the suit are subject to its outcome. — Also termed (in sense 3) *notice of lis pendens*; *notice of pendency.* Cf. PENDENTE LITE.

list, *n.* (13c) **1.** A roll or register, as of names. **2.** A docket of cases ready for hearing or trial. See CALENDAR (2); DOCKET.

list, *vb.* (bef. 12c) **1.** To set down or enter (information) in a list. **2.** To register (a security) on an exchange so that it may be publicly traded. **3.** To place (property) for sale under an agreement with a real-estate agent or broker.

listed security. See SECURITY.

listed security exchange. An organized secondary security market operating at a designated location, such as the New York Stock Exchange.

listed species. See *candidate species* under SPECIES (1).

listed stock. See *listed security* under SECURITY.

lister. A person authorized to compile lists of taxable property for assessment and appraisal; an assessor.

listing. (1891) **1.** *Real estate.* An agreement between a property owner and an agent, whereby the agent agrees to try to secure a buyer or tenant for a specific property at a certain price and terms in return for a fee or commission. — Also termed *listing agreement; authorization to sell.*

   exclusive-agency listing. A listing providing that one agent has the right to be the only person, other than the owner, to sell the property during a specified period. — Also termed *exclusive listing; exclusive-authorization-to-sell listing.*

   general listing. See *open listing.*

   multiple listing. A listing providing that the agent will allow other agents to try to sell the property. • Under this agreement, the original agent gives the selling agent a percentage of the commission or some other stipulated amount.

   net listing. A listing providing that the agent agrees to sell the owner's property for a set minimum price, any amount over the minimum being retained by the agent as commission. — Also termed *net sale contract.*

   open listing. A listing that allows selling rights to be given to more than one agent at a time, obligates the owner to pay a commission when a specified broker makes a sale, and reserves the owner's right to personally sell the property without paying a commission. — Also termed *nonexclusive listing; general listing; simple listing.*

2. *Securities.* The contract between a firm and a stock exchange by which the trading of the firm's securities on the exchange is handled. See *listed security* under SECURITY.

   dual listing. The listing of a security on more than one exchange.

3. *Tax.* The creation of a schedule or inventory of a person's taxable property; the list of a person's taxable property.

listing agent. See AGENT (2).

listing agreement. See LISTING (1).

list of creditors. (1818) A schedule giving the names and addresses of creditors, along with amounts owed them. • This list is required in a bankruptcy proceeding.

list price. See PRICE.

litem (**lı**-tem *or* -təm). See AD LITEM.

lite pendente (**lı**-tee pen-**den**-tee). [Latin] See PENDENTE LITE.

literacy test. *Hist.* A test of one's ability to read and write, formerly required in some states as a condition for registering to vote. • Literacy tests were abused at various times in United States history to preclude minorities from exercising the right to vote. This practice was prohibited by the Voting Rights Act of 1965. 42 USCA §§ 1971–1974. *See South Carolina v. Katzenbach*, 383 U.S. 301, 86 S.Ct. 8 (1966).

literae patentes (**lit**-ər-ee pə-**ten**-teez), *n.* [Latin "open letters"] *Hist.* A public grant from the sovereign to a subject, conferring the right to land, a franchise, a title, liberty, or some other endowment. • The modern "patent" and, more closely, "letters patent" derive from this term. See LETTERS PATENT (1).

literal, *adj.* (16c) According to expressed language. • Literal performance of a condition requires exact compliance with its terms.

literal canon. See *strict constructionism* under CONSTRUCTIONISM.

literal construction. See *strict construction* under CONSTRUCTION.

literal contract. See CONTRACT.

litera legis. See LETTER OF THE LAW.

literal infringement. See INFRINGEMENT.

literal interpretation. See *strict construction* under CONSTRUCTION.

literal proof. See PROOF.

literal rule. See *strict constructionism* under CONSTRUCTIONISM.

literary, *adj.* Of or relating to literature or other written forms of expression.

literary composition. A written expression involving mental effort, arranged in a purposeful order. Cf. *literary work* under WORK (2).

literary executor. See EXECUTOR.

literary property. 1. The physical property in which an intellectual production is embodied, such as a book, screenplay, or lecture. **2.** An owner's exclusive right to possess, use, and dispose of such a production. See COPYRIGHT; INTELLECTUAL PROPERTY.

literary work. See WORK (2).

literate, *adj.* (15c) **1.** Able to read and write a language. **2.** Knowledgeable and educated. — **literacy,** *n.*

litigable (**lit**-ə-gə-bəl), *adj.* (18c) Able to be contested or disputed in court <litigable claims>. — **litigability,** *n.*

litigant. (17c) A party to a lawsuit.

   institutional litigant. See INSTITUTIONAL LITIGANT.

   self-represented litigant. See PRO SE.

   vexatious litigant. A litigant who repeatedly files frivolous lawsuits. • Many jurisdictions have statutes or local rules requiring a vexatious litigant to obtain the court's permission to file any further lawsuits or pleadings. The litigant may also be subject to sanctions.

litigation, *n.* (17c) **1.** The process of carrying on a lawsuit <the attorney advised his client to make a generous settlement offer in order to avoid litigation>. **2.** A lawsuit itself <several litigations pending before the court>. — **litigate,** *vb.* — **litigatory, litigational,** *adj.*

   complex litigation. Litigation involving several parties who are separately represented, and usu. involving multifarious factual and legal issues.

litigation costs. See COST (3).

litigation hold. See HOLD.

litigation-hold letter. A writing that orders the segregation and retention of certain documents and data that are or may be relevant to a threatened or pending litigation or an official investigation.

   internal litigation-hold letter. A litigation-hold letter sent by a company, directly or through its attorneys, to its own employees.

litigation privilege. See PRIVILEGE (1).

litigator. (16c) **1.** A trial lawyer. **2.** A lawyer who prepares cases for trial, as by conducting discovery and pretrial motions, trying cases, and handling appeals. **3.** *Archaic.* A party to a lawsuit; a litigant.

litigious (li-**tij**-əs), *adj.* (14c) **1.** Prone to legal disputes; contentious <our litigious society>. **2.** *Archaic.* Of or relating to the subject of a lawsuit <the litigious property>. **3.** *Archaic.* Of or relating to lawsuits; litigatory <they couldn't settle the litigious dispute>. — **litigiousness, litigiosity** (li-tij-ee-**os**-ə-tee), *n.*

litigious right. *Civil law.* A right that cannot be exercised without first being determined in a lawsuit. La. Civ. Code art. 2652. • If the right is sold, it must be in litigation at the time of sale to be considered a litigious right.

litispendence (li-tis-**pen**-dənts). *Archaic.* The time during which a lawsuit is pending.

Little FTC Act. See UNFAIR TRADE PRACTICES AND CONSUMER PROTECTION LAW.

littoral (**lit**-ər-əl), *adj.* (17c) Of or relating to the coast or shore of an ocean, sea, or lake <the littoral right to limit others' consumption of the water>. Cf. RIPARIAN. — **littoral,** *n.*

livelihood. (15c) A means of supporting one's existence, esp. financially.

livelode. *Archaic.* Livelihood; maintenance. — Also termed *lifelode.*

livery (**liv**-ə-ree *or* **liv**-ree). (15c) **1.** The delivery of the possession of real property. Cf. DELIVERY. **2.** *Hist.* An heir's writ, upon reaching the age of majority, to obtain seisin of his lands from the king. **3.** The boarding and care of horses for a fee. **4.** A business that rents vehicles.

livery in chivalry. *Hist.* The delivery of possession of real property from a guardian to a ward in chivalry when the ward reached majority.

livery office. An office designated for the delivery of lands.

livery of seisin. *Hist.* The ceremony by which a grantor conveyed land to a grantee. • Livery of seisin involved either (1) going on the land and having the grantor symbolically deliver possession of the land to the grantee by handing over a twig, a clod of dirt, or a piece of turf (called *livery in deed*) or (2) going within sight of the land and having the grantor tell the grantee that possession was being given, followed by the grantee's entering the land (called *livery in law*). See INVESTITURE; SEISIN.

lives in being. See LIFE IN BEING.

livestock, *n.* (18c) Domestic animals and fowls that (1) are kept for profit or pleasure, (2) can normally be confined within boundaries without seriously impairing their utility, and (3) do not normally intrude on others' land in such a way as to harm the land or growing crops.

live storage. The storage of cars in active daily use, rather than cars put away for an extended period. • A garage owner's responsibility sometimes depends on whether a car is in live or dead storage. Cf. DEAD STORAGE.

live thalweg. See THALWEG.

living, *n.* One's source of monetary support or resources; esp., one's employment.

living separate and apart. (18c) Of spouses) living away from each other, along with at least one spouse's intent to dissolve the marriage. • One basis for no-fault divorce in many states exists if the spouses have lived apart for a specified period. — Sometimes shortened to *separate and apart.*

living-together agreement. See COHABITATION AGREEMENT.

living trust. See *inter vivos trust* under TRUST.

living will. (1972) An instrument, signed with the formalities statutorily required for a will, by which a person directs that his or her life not be artificially prolonged by extraordinary measures when there is no reasonable expectation of recovery from extreme physical or mental disability. • Most states have living-will legislation. — Also termed *declaration of a desire for a natural death; directive to physicians.* See NATURAL-DEATH ACT; UNIFORM HEALTH-CARE DECISION ACT. Cf. ADVANCE DIRECTIVE (1), (2); INSTRUCTION DIRECTIVE.

L.J. *abbr.* 1. Law Judge. 2. LAW JOURNAL. 3. LORD JUSTICE OF APPEAL.

L.JJ. *abbr.* Lords justices. See LORD JUSTICE OF APPEAL.

L.L. *abbr.* LAW LATIN.

L.Lat. *abbr.* LAW LATIN.

LL.B. *abbr.* Bachelor of Laws. • This was formerly the law degree ordinarily conferred by American law schools. It is still the normal degree in British law schools. Cf. JURIS DOCTOR.

L.L.C. See *limited-liability company* under COMPANY.

LL.D. *abbr.* DOCTOR OF LAWS.

LL.J. *abbr.* Lords justices. See LORD JUSTICE OF APPEAL.

LL.M. *abbr.* MASTER OF LAWS.

Lloyd's. See LLOYD'S OF LONDON.

Lloyd's association. See LLOYD'S UNDERWRITERS.

Lloyd's bond. See BOND (3).

Lloyd's insurance. See INSURANCE.

Lloyd's of London. *Insurance.* 1. A London insurance mart where individual underwriters gather to quote rates and write insurance on a wide variety of risks. 2. A voluntary association of merchants, shipowners, underwriters, and brokers formed not to write policies but instead to issue a notice of an endeavor to members who may individually underwrite a policy by assuming shares of the total risk of insuring a client. • The names of the bound underwriters and the attorney-in-fact appear on the policy. — Also termed *Lloyd's; London Lloyd's.*

Lloyd's underwriters. An unincorporated association of underwriters who, under a common name, engage in the insurance business through an attorney-in-fact having authority to obligate the underwriters severally, within specified limits, on insurance contracts that the attorney makes or issues in the common name. — Also termed *Lloyd's association; American Lloyd's.*

L.L.P. See *limited-liability partnership* under PARTNERSHIP.

load, *n.* An amount added to a security's price or to an insurance premium in order to cover the sales commission and expenses <the mutual fund had a high front-end load>. — Also termed *sales load; acquisition cost.*

load factor. 1. The ratio of a utility customer's usage levels during a given period compared to the customer's demand during peak periods. 2. An analysis of the number of passengers on an airplane or other common carrier compared to available capacity.

load fund. See MUTUAL FUND.

loading. *Insurance.* An amount added to a life-insurance premium to cover the insurer's business expenses and contingencies. — Also termed *expense loading.* See *gross premium* (1) under PREMIUM (1).

load line. *Maritime law.* 1. The depth to which a safely loaded ship will sink in salt water. 2. One of a set of graduated marks on the side of a ship, indicating the depth to which the ship can be loaded in varying waters (such as salt water or freshwater) and weather conditions. • Load lines must, by law in most maritime countries, be cut and painted amidships. — Also termed (in sense 2) *load-line marks; Plimsoll marks.*

loadmanage. *Hist.* 1. The fee paid to loadsmen, who sail in small vessels acting as pilots for larger ships. 2. The hiring of a pilot for a vessel. 3. A pilot's or loadsman's skill. — Also spelled *lodemanage; lode manage.*

loadsman. *Hist.* 1. A person who directs a ship's course from a small boat traveling in front of the larger ship rather than from the ship itself. • The loadsmen had a monopoly on piloting in the cinque ports. See CINQUE PORTS. **2.** A person who took the ship to a berth after a pilot had brought it into port. — Also spelled *loadman; lodeman; lodesman.*

loan, *n.* (12c) **1.** An act of lending; a grant of something for temporary use <Turner gave the laptop as a loan, not a gift>. **2.** A thing lent for the borrower's temporary use; esp., a sum of money lent at interest <Hull applied for a car loan>.

accommodation loan. (1834) A loan for which the lender receives no consideration in return. See ACCOMMODATION.

add-on loan. (1972) A loan in which the interest is calculated at the stated rate for the loan agreement's full term for the full principal amount, and then the interest is added to the principal before installment payments are calculated, resulting in an interest amount higher than if it were calculated on the monthly unpaid balance. • Consumer loans are typically add-on loans. — Also termed *contract loan.* See *add-on interest* under INTEREST (3).

amortized loan. (1930) A loan calling for periodic payments that are applied first to interest and then to principal, as provided by the terms of the note. See AMORTIZATION (1).

back-to-back loan. A loan arrangement by which two firms lend each other funds denominated in different currencies for a specified period. • The purpose is usu. to protect against fluctuations in the currencies' exchange rates.

balloon loan. An installment loan in which one or more of the later repayments are much larger than earlier payments; esp., a loan featuring a string of payments that are too small to amortize the entire loan within the loan period, coupled with a large final lump-sum payment of the outstanding balance.

below-market loan. See *interest-free loan.*

bridge loan. A short-term loan that is used to cover costs until more permanent financing is arranged or to cover a portion of costs that are expected to be covered by an imminent sale. — Also termed *bridge financing; swing loan.*

broker call loan. See *call loan.*

building loan. A type of bridge loan used primarily for erecting a building. • The loan is typically advanced in parts as work progresses and is used to pay the contractor, subcontractors, and material suppliers. — Also termed *construction loan.* See *interim financing* under FINANCING.

call loan. (1869) A loan for which the lender can demand payment at any time, usu. with 24 hours' notice, because there is no fixed maturity date. — Also termed *broker call loan; demand loan.* Cf. *term loan.*

character loan. A loan made in reliance on the borrower's character and stable earnings. • Character loans are usu. secured by a mortgage or by other property, but sometimes they are unsecured.

clearing loan. A loan made to a bond dealer pending the sale of a bond issue.

collateral loan. See *secured loan.*

commercial loan. (1875) A loan that a financial institution gives to a business, generally for 30 to 90 days.

commodity loan. A loan secured by a commodity (such as cotton or wool) in the form of a warehouse receipt or other negotiable instrument.

consolidation loan. (1875) A loan whose proceeds are used to pay off other individual loans, thereby creating a more manageable debt.

construction loan. See *building loan.*

consumer loan. (1957) A loan that is given to an individual for family, household, personal, or agricultural purposes and that is generally governed by truth-in-lending statutes and regulations.

contract loan. See *add-on loan.*

Crown loan. *Tax.* An interest-free demand loan, usu. from parent to child, in which the borrowed funds are invested and the income from the investment is taxed at the child's rate. • This type of loan is named for one Harry Crown of Chicago, reputedly one of the first persons to use it. See *kiddie tax* under TAX.

day loan. A short-term loan to a broker to finance daily transactions.

demand loan. See *call loan.*

discount loan. A loan in which interest is deducted in advance, at the time the loan is made.

doorstep loan. A loan offered by a door-to-door solicitor, usu. for home repairs at a high interest rate and under misleading or fraudulent terms. • The term is used primarily in the United Kingdom.

GI loan. See *veteran's loan.*

home-equity loan. (1984) A line of bank credit given to a homeowner, using as collateral the homeowner's equity in the home. — Often shortened to *equity loan.* — Also termed *home-equity line of credit.* See EQUITY (7).

installment loan. (1916) A loan that is to be repaid in usu. equal portions over a specified period.

interest-free loan. (1946) Money loaned to a borrower at no charge or, under the Internal Revenue Code, with a charge that is lower than the market rate. IRC (26 USCA) § 7872. — Also termed (in the IRC) *below-market loan.*

interest-only loan. A loan for which the borrower pays only the interest on the principal balance of the loan for a stated period, usu. a few years. • At the end of the stated period, the principal balance is unchanged. An interest-only loan features low initial payments in return for significantly larger payments later or a balloon payment at the end of the term.

liar's loan. 1. A loan that involves no background check and can be obtained by claiming that one meets the lender's income and other requirements. **2.** See *no-doc loan* (1). **3.** See *stated-income loan* (1). Cf. *NINJA loan.*

maritime loan. A loan providing that a lender will not be repaid if the cargo is damaged or lost because of a navigational peril, but that the lender will be repaid plus interest if the cargo arrives safely or is damaged because of the carrier's negligence. — Also termed *marine loan.*

mortgage loan. (1846) A loan secured by a mortgage or deed of trust on real property.

NINJA loan. *abbr.* No-income, no-job, no-assets loan. Cf. *liar's loan* (1); *no-doc loan* (1); *stated-income loan* (1).

no-doc loan. 1. A loan for which a borrower provides only minimal proof of ability to repay. • The name is short for "no documentation." **2.** See *liar's loan* (1). Cf. *NINJA loan.*

nonperforming loan. (1984) An outstanding loan that is not being repaid.

nonrecourse loan. (1941) A secured loan that allows the lender to attach only the collateral, not the borrower's personal assets, if the loan is not repaid.

participation loan. (1928) A loan issued by two or more lenders. See LOAN PARTICIPATION.

policy loan. An insurer's loan to an insured, secured by the policy's cash reserve.

precarious loan. 1. A loan that may be recalled at any time. **2.** A loan in danger of not being repaid.

premium loan. A loan made to an insured by the insurer to enable the insured to pay further premiums. • The reserve value of the policy serves as collateral.

recourse loan. A loan that allows the lender, if the borrower defaults, not only to attach the collateral but also to seek judgment against the borrower's (or guarantor's) personal assets.

revolver loan. (1985) A single loan that a debtor takes out in lieu of several lines of credit or other loans from various creditors, and that is subject to review and approval at certain intervals. • A revolver loan is usu. taken out in an attempt to resolve problems with creditors. Cf. *revolving credit* under CREDIT (4).

revolving loan. (1927) A loan that is renewed at maturity.

scratch-and-dent loan. A loan made to a borrower who was able to repay when the loan was made but has since fallen behind on payments.

secured loan. (1862) A loan that is secured by property or securities. — Also termed *collateral loan.*

short-term loan. (1902) A loan with a due date of less than one year, usu. evidenced by a note.

signature loan. An unsecured loan based solely on the borrower's promise or signature. • To obtain such a loan, the borrower must usu. be highly creditworthy.

stated-income loan. 1. A loan extended to a borrower who claimed a certain income but has not verified the claim. **2.** See *liar's loan* (1). Cf. *NINJA loan.*

subprime loan. A loan, esp. a mortgage or home-equity loan, made to one whose financial condition and creditworthiness are poor, creating a high risk of default. • A subprime loan usu. has an adjustable interest rate that is low at inception, to help a financially weak borrower qualify, then rises over the life of the loan.

swing loan. See *bridge loan.*

term loan. A loan with a specified due date, usu. of more than one year. • Such a loan typically cannot be repaid before maturity without incurring a penalty. — Also termed *time loan.* Cf. *call loan.*

veteran's loan. A federally guaranteed loan extended to armed-forces veterans for the purchase of a home. — Also written *veterans' loan; veteran loan.* — Also termed *VA loan; GI loan.*

loan, *vb.* To lend, esp. money.

loan-amortization schedule. (1958) A schedule that divides each loan payment into an interest component and a principal component. • Typically, the interest component begins as the largest part of each payment and declines over time. See AMORTIZATION (1).

loan association. See SAVINGS-AND-LOAN ASSOCIATION.

loan broker. See BROKER.

loan-brokerage fee. See MORTGAGE DISCOUNT.

loan certificate. A certificate that a clearinghouse issues to a borrowing bank in an amount equal to a specified percentage of the value of the borrowing bank's collateral on deposit with the clearinghouse's loan committee.

loan commitment. (1940) A lender's binding promise to a borrower to lend a specified amount of money at a certain interest rate, usu. within a specified period and for a specified purpose (such as buying real estate). See MORTGAGE COMMITMENT.

loaned employee. See *borrowed employee* under EMPLOYEE.

loaned servant. See *borrowed employee* under EMPLOYEE.

loan for consumption. (1840) An agreement by which a lender delivers goods to a borrower who consumes them and who is obligated to return goods of the same quantity, type, and quality.

loan for exchange. (1915) A contract by which a lender delivers personal property to a borrower who agrees to return similar property, usu. without compensation for its use.

loan for use. (1837) An agreement by which a lender delivers an asset to a borrower who must use it according to its normal function or according to the agreement, and who must return it when finished using it. • No interest is charged.

loanland. *Hist.* A tenancy involving the loan of land by one person to another. — Also spelled *laenland*. Cf. BOOKLAND; FOLKLAND.

loan-origination fee. See FEE.

loan participation. (1934) The coming together of multiple lenders to issue a large loan (called a *participation loan*) to one borrower, thereby reducing each lender's individual risk.

loan ratio. See LOAN-TO-VALUE RATIO.

loan-receipt agreement. (1943) *Torts.* A settlement agreement by which the defendant lends money to the plaintiff interest-free, the plaintiff not being obligated to repay the loan unless he or she recovers money from other tortfeasors responsible for the same injury.

loansharking, *n.* (1914) The practice of lending money at excessive and esp. usurious rates, and often using threats or extortion to enforce repayment. — Also termed *extortionate credit transaction*. — **loan-shark,** *vb.* — **loan shark,** *n.*

loan-to-value ratio. The ratio, usu. expressed as a percentage, between the amount of a mortgage loan and the value of the property pledged as security for the mortgage. • For example, an $80,000 loan on property worth $100,000 results in a loan-to-value ratio of 80% — which is usu. the highest ratio that lenders will agree to without requiring the debtor to buy mortgage insurance. — Often shortened to *LTV ratio*. — Also termed *loan ratio*.

loan value. *Insurance.* **1.** The maximum amount that may be lent safely on property or life insurance without jeopardizing the lender's need for protection from the borrower's default. **2.** The

amount of money an insured can borrow against the cash value of his or her life-insurance policy.

lobby, *vb.* (1837) **1.** To talk with or curry favor with a legislator, usu. repeatedly or frequently, in an attempt to influence the legislator's vote <she routinely lobbies for tort reform in the state legislature>. **2.** To support or oppose (a measure) by working to influence a legislator's vote <the organization lobbied the bill through the Senate>. **3.** To try to influence (a decision-maker) <the lawyer lobbied the judge for a favorable ruling>. — **lobbying,** *n.* — **lobbyist,** *n.*

lobbying act. (1948) A federal or state law governing the conduct of lobbyists, usu. by requiring them to register and file activity reports. • An example is the Federal Regulation of Lobbying Act, 12 USCA § 261.

lobby vote. See VOTE (4).

local act. 1. See LOCAL LAW (1). **2.** See LOCAL LAW (2).

local action. See ACTION (4).

local administrator. See ADMINISTRATOR (1).

local agency. See AGENCY (3).

local agent. 1. See AGENT (2). **2.** See *special agent* under INSURANCE AGENT.

local allegiance. See *actual allegiance* under ALLEGIANCE.

local and special legislation. See LEGISLATION.

local assessment. See ASSESSMENT.

local bar association. See BAR ASSOCIATION.

local chattel. See CHATTEL.

local concern. (1833) An activity conducted by a municipality in its proprietary capacity.

local counsel. See COUNSEL.

local court. See COURT.

local custom. See CUSTOM.

local-exchange carrier. *Telecommunications law.* An entity that provides telephone service, usu. on a local basis, through a local-exchange network. 47 USCA § 153(26). — Abbr. LEC. See LOCAL-EXCHANGE NETWORK.

local-exchange network. *Telecommunications law.* A system for providing telephone service on a local basis. • A local-exchange network usu. consists of such elements as switches, local loops, and transport trunks, and capabilities such as billing databases and operator services. Switches are pieces of equipment that direct calls to the appropriate destination. Local loops are the wires that connect telephones to the switches. Transport trunks are the wires that carry calls from switch to switch. All the elements of a local-exchange network are often referred to as a bundle, and there are federal requirements that a local-exchange carrier who controls a local-exchange network permit competition by selling some access, including unbundled access, to its local-exchange network. 47 USCA § 251(c). See LOCAL-EXCHANGE CARRIER; UNBUNDLING RULES.

local government. See GOVERNMENT.

local improvement. See IMPROVEMENT.

local-improvement assessment. See *local assessment* under ASSESSMENT.

locality, *n.* (17c) **1.** A definite region; vicinity; neighborhood; community. **2.** *Hist. Scots law.* The land held by a widow in usufruct under the terms of her marriage contract. ● If a widow has locality lands, she cannot assert her statutory claim to a one-third share of her husband's real property.

locality of a lawsuit. (1939) The place where a court may exercise judicial authority.

locality-plus test. *Maritime law.* The requirement that, for a federal court to exercise admiralty tort jurisdiction, not only must the alleged wrong occur on navigable waters, it must also relate to a traditional maritime activity *Executive Jet Aviation, Inc. v. Cleveland*, 409 U.S. 249, 93 S.Ct. 493 (1972). — Also termed *locality-plus rule; maritime-connection doctrine.*

locality rule. 1. The doctrine that, in a professional-malpractice suit, the standard of care applicable to the professional's conduct is the reasonable care exercised by similar professionals in the same vicinity and professional community. **2.** The doctrine that, in determining the appropriate amount of attorney's fees to be awarded in a suit, the proper basis is the rate charged by similar attorneys for similar work in the vicinity.

locality test. *Maritime law.* The requirement that, for a federal court to exercise admiralty tort jurisdiction, the alleged wrong must have occurred on navigable waters. ● The test was replaced by the locality-plus test in *Executive Jet Aviation, Inc. v. Cleveland*, 409 U.S. 249, 93 S.Ct. 493 (1972). — Also termed *locality rule.* See LOCALITY-PLUS TEST.

localization doctrine. The doctrine that a foreign corporation, by doing sufficient business in a state, will subject itself to that state's laws.

local law. 1. A statute that relates to or operates in a particular locality rather than the entire state. **2.** A statute that applies to particular persons or things rather than an entire class of persons or things. — Also termed (in senses 1 & 2) *local act; local statute.* **3.** The law of a particular jurisdiction, as opposed to the law of a foreign state. — Also termed *internal law.* **4.** *Conflict of laws.* The body of standards, principles, and rules — excluding conflict-of-laws rules — that the state courts apply to controversies before them. Restatement (Second) of Conflict of Laws § 4(1) (1971).

local-law theory. *Conflict of laws.* The view that, although a court of the forum recognizes and enforces a local right (that is, one created under its own law), in a foreign-element case it does not necessarily apply the rule that would govern an analogous case of a purely domestic character, but instead takes into account the law of the foreign country by fashioning a local right as nearly as possible upon the law of the country in which the decisive facts have occurred. ● This theory is credited to Walter Wheeler Cook, who expounded it in the first chapter of his *Logical and Legal Bases of the Conflict of Laws* (1949).

local option. An option that allows a municipality or other governmental unit to determine a particular course of action without the specific approval of state officials. — Also termed *local veto.* Cf. HOME RULE.

local receiver. See RECEIVER.

local rule. (1819) **1.** A rule based on the physical conditions of a state and the character, customs, and beliefs of its people. **2.** A rule by which an individual court supplements the procedural rules applying generally to all courts within the jurisdiction. ● Local rules deal with a variety of matters, such as requiring extra copies of motions to be filed with the court or prohibiting the reading of newspapers in the courtroom. Fed. R. Civ. P. 83.

local statute. 1. See LOCAL LAW (1). **2.** See LOCAL LAW (2).

local union. See UNION.

local usage. See USAGE.

local veto. See LOCAL OPTION.

locatio (lə-**kay**-shee-oh), *n.* [Latin] *Roman & civil law.* Any contract by which the use of the thing bailed, or the use of the labor or services, is agreed to be given for a compensation. ● This type of contract benefits both parties. — Also termed *lease; hiring.* Cf. ABLOCATION. Pl. ***locationes*** (lə-kay-shee-**oh**-neez).

locatio conductio (lə-**kay**-shee-oh kən-**duk**-shee-oh). [Latin] *Roman law.* A letting for hire; specif., a contract by which one person agreed to give to another the use, or the use and enjoyment, of a thing or of services or labor in return for remuneration, usu. money. ● In Roman law, it covered a broad range of circumstances in return for a *merces* or rent.

locatio custodiae (lə-**kay**-shee-oh kəs-**toh**-dee-ee). [Latin] *Roman law.* The hiring of care or service, as when the bailee is to protect the thing bailed.

locatio mercium vehendarum. See *locatio operis mercium vehendarum.*

locatio operarum (lə-**kay**-shee-oh op-ə-**rair**-əm). [Latin "the letting of services"] *Roman & civil* *law.* A contract of employment; specif., contract in which someone, usu. a day laborer, hires out his services for a specified price. — Also termed *locatio operis faciendi.*

locatio operis faciendi (lə-**kay**-shee-oh **op**-ə-ris fay-shee-**en**-dı). [Latin "the letting of a job to be done"] *Roman law.* A contract by which someone hires a contractor (*conductor*) to undertake work (e.g., to build a home or teach a slave to read) on behalf of the hirer. — Sometimes shortened to *locatio operis.* See *locatio operarum.*

locatio operis mercium vehendarum (lə-**kay**-shee-oh **op**-ə-ris **mər**-shee-əm vee-hən-**dair**-əm). [Latin "the letting of the job of carrying goods"] *Roman law.* A bailment in which goods are delivered to the bailee for transport elsewhere, esp. by sea. — Also termed *locatio mercium vehendarum.*

locatio rei (lə-**kay**-shee-oh **ree**-ı). [Latin "letting of a thing"] *Roman law.* The hiring of a thing for use, by which the hirer gains the temporary use of the thing for a fee.

location. (16c) **1.** The specific place or position of a person or thing. **2.** The act or process of locating. **3.** *Real estate.* The designation of the boundaries of a particular piece of land, either on the record or on the land itself. **4.** *Mining law.* The act of appropriating a mining claim. — Also termed *mining location.* See MINING CLAIM. **5.** The claim so appropriated. **6.** *Civil law.* A contract for the temporary use of something for hire; a leasing for hire. See LOCATIO.

location-damage clause. See SURFACE-DAMAGE CLAUSE.

locative calls (lok-ə-tiv). (1807) *Property.* In land descriptions, specific descriptions that fix the boundaries of the land. • Locative calls may be marks of location, landmarks, or other physical objects. If calls in a description conflict, locative calls control over those indicating a general area of a boundary. See CALL (5); DIRECTORY CALLS.

locator (loh-**kay**-tər), *n.* [Latin] **1.** *Roman law.* (usu. ital.) One who lets out property or services for reward, or who contracts to have another person (the *conductor*) perform work for reward; a lessor or landlord. See CONDUCTOR (2).

Lochnerize (lok-nər-ız), *vb.* (1976) To examine and strike down economic legislation under the guise of enforcing the Due Process Clause, esp. in the manner of the U.S. Supreme Court during the early 20th century. • The term takes its name from the decision in *Lochner v. New York,* 198 U.S. 45, 25 S.Ct. 539 (1905), in which the Court invalidated New York's maximum-hours law for bakers. — **Lochnerization,** *n.*

lockbox. (1872) **1.** A secure box, such as a post-office box, strongbox, or safe-deposit box. **2.** A facility offered by a financial institution for quickly collecting and consolidating checks and other funds from a party's customers.

lockdown. (1977) The temporary confinement of prisoners in their cells during a state of heightened alert caused by an escape, riot, or other emergency.

Lockeanism. See LOCKEAN LABOR THEORY.

Lockean labor theory. The philosopher John Locke's justification of private property, based on the natural right of one's ownership of one's own labor, and the right to nature's common property to the extent that one's labor can make use of it. • Locke's theory, from the fifth chapter of his *Second Treatise on Civil Government,* is often used to analyze the natural rights of inventors, authors, and artists in their own creations. — Also termed *labor theory; Lockeanism.* Cf. PERSONALITY THEORY; UTILITARIANISM.

locked in, *adj.* **1.** (Of a person) unable to sell appreciated securities and realize the gain because of liability for capital gains taxes <my accountant advised me not to sell the stock because I am locked in>. **2.** (Of a price, rate, etc.) staying the same for a given period <the 7% mortgage rate is locked in for 30 days>.

locked-in rate. See *lock rate* under INTEREST RATE.

lockout. (1854) **1.** An employer's withholding of work and closing of a business because of a labor dispute.

defensive lockout. A lockout that is called to prevent imminent and irreparable financial harm to the company or to protect a legal right. • Defensive lockouts were legal, but the U.S. Supreme Court abolished the distinction between defensive and offensive lockouts in favor of a balancing test. *American Ship Bldg. Co. v. NLRB,* 380 U.S. 300, 85 S.Ct. 955 (1965).

offensive lockout. A lockout called by management to assert economic pressure on workers and thereby gain a bargaining advantage over a union. • Offensive lockouts were illegal before the U.S. Supreme Court abolished the legal distinction between offensive and defensive lockouts in favor of a balancing test. *American Ship Bldg. Co. v. NLRB,* 380 U.S. 300, 85 S.Ct. 955 (1965).

2. Loosely, an employee's refusal to work because the employer unreasonably refuses to abide by an expired employment contract while a new one is being negotiated. Cf. STRIKE; BOYCOTT; PICKETING.

lock rate. See INTEREST RATE.

lockup, *n.* **1.** See JAIL. **2.** See LOCKUP OPTION.

lockup agreement. *Securities.* A contract between an underwriter and a corporation's insiders that prohibits the insiders from selling any personal stockholdings for a specified time after the corporation makes a public offering of securities.

lockup option. A defense against a corporate takeover, in which a friendly party is entitled to buy parts of a corporation for a set price when a person or group acquires a certain percentage of the corporation's shares. ● An agreement of this kind may be illegal, to the extent it is not undertaken to serve the best interests of the shareholders. — Often shortened to *lockup.*

loco parentis. See IN LOCO PARENTIS.

locus (**loh**-kəs). [Latin "place"] (18c) The place or position where something is done or exists. — Abbr. L. See SITUS.

locus actus (**loh**-kəs **ak**-təs). [Latin "place of the act"] The place where an act was done; the place of performance.

locus contractus (**loh**-kəs kən-**trak**-təs). [Latin "place of the contract"] The place where a contract was made. Cf. LEX LOCI CONTRACTUS.

locus criminis (**loh**-kəs **krim**-ə-nis), *n.* [Latin] The place where a crime was committed.

locus delicti (**loh**-kəs də-**lik**-tɪ). [Latin "place of the wrong"] The place where an offense was committed; the place where the last event necessary to make the actor liable occurred. Cf. LEX LOCI DELICTI.

locus in quo (**loh**-kəs in **kwoh**). [Latin "place in which"] (18c) The place where something is alleged to have occurred.

locus partitus (**loh**-kəs pahr-**tɪ**-təs), *n.* [Latin "a place divided"] *Hist.* The act of dividing two towns or counties to determine which of them contains the land or place in question.

locus poenitentiae (**loh**-kəs pen-ə-**ten**-shee-ee). [Latin "place of repentance"] **1.** A point at which it is not too late for one to change one's legal position; the possibility of withdrawing from a contemplated course of action, esp. a wrong, before being committed to it. **2.** The opportunity to withdraw from a negotiation before finally concluding the contract.

locus publicus (**loh**-kəs **pəb**-li-kəs). [Latin] *Roman law.* A public place.

locus regit actum (**loh**-kəs **ree**-jit **ak**-təm), *n.* [Latin "the place rules the act"] *Int'l law.* The rule that a transaction complying with the legal formalities of the country where it is created will be considered valid in the country where it is to be effective, even if that country requires additional formalities.

locus rei sitae (**loh**-kəs **ree**-ɪ **sɪ**-tee), *n.* [Latin "place where a thing is situated"] *Civil law.* The rule that the place where the land is located is the proper forum in a case involving real estate.

locus solutionis (**loh**-kəs sə-loo-shee-**oh**-nis). [Latin] *Hist.* The place of performance.

locus standi (**loh**-kəs **stan**-dɪ *or* -dee). [Latin "place of standing"] (1835) The right to bring an action or to be heard in a given forum; STANDING.

lode, *n.* **1.** MINERAL LODE. **2.** LADE.

lode claim. See MINING CLAIM.

lodeman. See LOADSMAN.

lodemanage, *n.* See LOADMANAGE.

lodesman. See LOADSMAN.

lodestar. (14c) **1.** A guiding star; an inspiration or model. **2.** A reasonable amount of attorney's fees in a given case, usu. calculated by multiplying a reasonable number of hours worked by the prevailing hourly rate in the community for similar work, and often considering such additional factors as the degree of skill and difficulty involved in the case, the degree of its urgency, its novelty, and the like. ● Most statutes that authorize an award of attorney's fees use the lodestar method for computing the award.

lodge. See FILE (1).

lodger. (16c) **1.** A person who rents and occupies a room in another's house. **2.** A person who occupies a designated area in another's house but acquires no property interest in that area, which remains in the owner's legal possession.

log, *n.* **1.** See ARREST RECORD. **2.** JOURNAL (1).

logbook. (17c) **1.** A ship's or aircraft's journal containing an account of each trip, often with a history of events during the voyage; JOURNAL (1). **2.** Any journal or record of events.

logical-cause doctrine. (1980) The principle that, if the plaintiff proves that an injury occurred and proves a logical cause of it, a party desiring to defeat the claim cannot succeed merely by showing that there is another imaginable cause, but must also show that the alternative cause is more probable than the cause shown by the plaintiff.

logical interpretation. See INTERPRETATION.

logical positivism. (1931) A philosophical system or movement requiring that meaningful statements be in principle verifiable. Cf. LEGAL POSITIVISM.

logical-relationship standard. (1976) *Civil procedure.* A test applied to determine whether a defendant's counterclaim is compulsory, by examining whether both claims are based on the same operative facts or whether those facts activate additional rights, otherwise dormant, for the defendant. ● One of the most important factors considered is whether hearing the claims together would promote judicial economy and efficiency. Fed. R. Civ. P. 13(a).

logic bomb. Destructive or disruptive computer software that is planted on a computer, server, or network and waits until a certain time to activate itself.

logrolling, *n.* (1812) **1.** The exchanging of political favors; esp., the trading of votes among legislators to gain support of measures that are beneficial to each legislator's constituency. **2.** The legislative practice of including several propositions in one measure or proposed constitutional amendment so that the legislature or voters will pass all of them, even though these propositions might not have passed if they had been submitted separately. • Many state constitutions have single-subject clauses that prohibit this practice. — **logroll,** *vb.*

LOI. *abbr.* LETTER OF INTENT.

loitering, *n.* (14c) The criminal offense of remaining in a certain place (such as a public street) for no apparent reason. • Loitering statutes are generally held to be unconstitutionally vague. Cf. VAGRANCY. — **loiter,** *vb.*

lollipop syndrome. (1986) *Family law.* A situation in which one or both parents, often in a custody battle, manipulate the child with gifts, fun, good times, and minimal discipline in an attempt to win over the child. See *Disneyland parent* under PARENT. Cf. RESCUE SYNDROME.

Lombard law. A Germanic customary law based primarily on a code called the Edict of Rothar, published in A.D. 643. • Rothar was the King of the Lombards at the time (A.D. 636–652), and his code (written in Latin) was more complete than the Germanic *leges barbarorum.* — Also termed *law of Lombardy; law of Langobardi.* Cf. LEGES BARBARORUM.

London commodity option. An agreement to buy or sell a futures contract for a commodity traded on the London markets, for a particular price and within a particular time.

London Lloyd's. See LLOYD'S OF LONDON.

Lone Pine **order.** A case-management order in a toxic-tort lawsuit involving many plaintiffs, establishing procedures and deadlines for discovery, including requiring the plaintiffs to timely produce evidence and expert opinions to substantiate each plaintiff's exposure to the hazardous substance, the injury suffered, and the cause of the injury. *Lore v. Lone Pine Corp.,* No. L-33606-85 (N.J. Super. Ct. Nov. 18, 1986). • Although the *Lone Pine* opinion is unreported, it has become famous for the kind of case-management order involved, in part because the plaintiffs' claims were dismissed for failure to timely provide expert opinions.

long, *adj.* **1.** Holding a security or commodity in anticipation of a rise in price <a buyer long on pharmaceutical stock>. **2.** Of or relating to a purchase of securities or commodities in anticipation of rising prices <a long position>. Cf. SHORT.

long, *adv.* By a long purchase; into or in a long position <bought the wheat long>.

long account. See ACCOUNT.

long-arm, *adj.* Of, relating to, or arising from a long-arm statute <long-arm jurisdiction>.

long-arm jurisdiction. See JURISDICTION.

long-arm statute. (1951) A statute providing for jurisdiction over a nonresident defendant who has had contacts with the territory where the statute is in effect. • Most state long-arm statutes extend this jurisdiction to its constitutional limits. — Also termed *single-act statute.* See *long-arm jurisdiction* under JURISDICTION.

long-firm fraud. See FRAUD.

long-form bill of lading. See BILL OF LADING.

Long Parliament. *Hist.* **1.** The English Parliament of Charles I meeting between 1640 and 1653, dissolved by Oliver Cromwell in 1653, then recalled and finally dissolved in 1660. **2.** The English Parliament that met between 1661 and 1678, after the restoration of the monarchy. • This Parliament is sometimes called the "Long Parliament of Charles II" to distinguish it from that of sense 1.

long robe. *Hist.* The legal profession <gentlemen of the long robe>. See ROBE.

long-run incremental cost. *Antitrust.* A cost threshold for determining whether predatory pricing has occurred, consisting of all costs that, over a several-year period, would not be incurred if the product in question were not offered. • It differs from average variable cost because it includes some costs that do not vary in the short run but that do vary over a longer period, depending on whether a particular product is offered. — Abbr. LRIC. Cf. *average variable cost* under COST (1).

Longshore and Harbor Workers' Compensation Act. A federal law designed to provide workers'-compensation benefits to persons, other than seamen, who work in maritime occupations, esp. stevedoring and ship service. 33 USCA § 901–50. — Abbr. LHWCA.

longshoreman. (1811) A maritime laborer who works on the wharves in a port; esp., a person who loads and unloads ships. Cf. STEVEDORE.

long-term capital gain. See CAPITAL GAIN.

long-term capital loss. See LOSS.

long-term debt. See DEBT.

long-term foster care. See FOSTER CARE.

long-term security. See SECURITY.

long title. See TITLE (3).

long ton. See TON.

look and feel. See TRADE DRESS.

look-and-feel protection. Copyright protection of the images generated or revealed when one activates a computer program.

lookout, *n.* (17c) A careful, vigilant watching <the motorist's statutory duty of proper lookout>.

look-through principle. (1993) *Tax.* A doctrine for allocating transfer-gains taxes on real estate by looking beyond the entity possessing legal title to identify the beneficial owners of the property.

loophole. (17c) An ambiguity, omission, or exception (as in a law or other legal document) that provides a way to avoid a rule without violating its literal requirements; esp., a tax-code provision that allows a taxpayer to legally avoid or reduce income taxes.

loopification, *n.* (1982) In critical legal studies, the collapse of a legal distinction resulting when the two ends of a continuum become so similar that they become indistinguishable <it may be impossible to distinguish "public" from "private" because of loopification>. — **loopify,** *vb.*

loose construction. See *liberal construction* under CONSTRUCTION.

loose constructionism. See *liberal constructionism* under CONSTRUCTIONISM.

loose constructionist. See *liberal constructionist* under CONSTRUCTIONIST.

looseleaf service. (1927) A type of lawbook having pages that are periodically replaced with updated pages, designed to cope with constant change and increasing bulk.

lord. (bef. 12c) **1.** A title of honor or nobility belonging properly to a baron but applied also to anyone who attains the rank of a peer. — Abbr. L. **2.** (*cap. & pl.*) HOUSE OF LORDS. **3.** A property owner whose land is in a tenant's possession; LANDLORD (1).

temporal lord (**tem**-pə-rəl). One of the English peers (other than ecclesiastical) who sit in Parliament.

lord-and-master rule. See HEAD-AND-MASTER RULE.

Lord Campbell's Act. 1. The 1846 English statute that created a wrongful-death claim for the relatives of a decedent when the decedent would have had a claim if he or she had been merely injured and not killed. • Technically known as the Fatal Accidents Act of 1846, this statute changed the earlier rule, under which a tortfeasor who would have been liable to another escaped liability if the victim died. Cf. WRONGFUL-DEATH ACTION. **2.** An American state's wrongful-death statute patterned after the original English act.

Lord Chamberlain. The second officer of the royal household in England, who serves as a peer, a privy councilor, and a member of the ruling government. — Also termed *Lord Chamberlain of the Household.*

Lord Chancellor. The highest judicial officer in England. • The Lord Chancellor sits as speaker of the House of Lords, is a member of the Cabinet, and presides at appellate judicial proceedings. — Also termed *Lord High Chancellor; Keeper of the King's Conscience.*

Lord Chief Justice of England. The chief judge of the Queen's Bench Division of the High Court of Justice. • The Lord Chief Justice also serves on the Court of Appeal, and ranks second only to the Lord Chancellor in the English judicial hierarchy. — Formerly termed *Chief Justice of England.* Cf. CHIEF JUSTICE OF THE COMMON PLEAS.

Lord Denman's Act. See DENMAN'S ACT (1).

Lord High Chancellor. See LORD CHANCELLOR.

Lord High Steward. *Hist.* The speaker *pro tempore* and presiding officer in the House of Lords during a criminal trial of a peer for a felony or for treason. • The privilege of peerage in criminal proceedings was abolished in 1948.

Lord High Treasurer. *Hist.* An officer in charge of the royal revenues and customs duties, and of leasing the Crown lands. • The functions of the Lord High Treasurer are now vested in the lords commissioners of the treasury.

lord in gross. *Hist.* A lord holding the title not by virtue of a manor; a lord without a manor.

Lord Justice. See LORD JUSTICE OF APPEAL.

Lord Justice-Clerk. *Scots law.* The second highest judicial officer in Scotland, historically with special responsibility for criminal law. • The Lord Justice-Clerk presides over the Second Division of the Inner House of the Court of Session.

Lord Justice General. *Scots law.* The highest judicial officer in Scotland, and head of the High Court of Justiciary. • The Lord Justice General also holds the office of Lord President of the Court of Session.

Lord Justice of Appeal. A judge of the English Court of Appeal. — Often shortened to *lord justice.* — Abbr. L.J. (or, in pl., either LL.J. or L.JJ.).

Lord Keeper. See KEEPER OF THE GREAT SEAL.

Lord Keeper of the Great Seal. See KEEPER OF THE GREAT SEAL.

Lord Keeper of the Privy Seal. See LORD PRIVY SEAL.

Lord Langdale's Act. See WILLS ACT (2).

Lord Lieutenant. 1. An honorary officeholder who is the Queen's representative in a county and the principal military officer there, originally appointed to muster the inhabitants to defend the country. **2.** *Hist.* The former viceroy of the Crown in Ireland.

Lord Lyndhurst's Act. See LYNDHURST'S ACT.

Lord Mansfield's rule. The principle that neither spouse may testify about whether the husband had access to the wife at the time of a child's conception. ● In effect, this rule — which has been abandoned by most states — made it impossible to bastardize a child born during a marriage.

Lord Mayor. 1. *Hist.* The chief officer of the corporation of the city of London, so called because the fourth charter of Edward III conferred on that officer the honor of having maces carried before him by the sergeants. **2.** The title of the principal magistrate of a city, the office of which has been conferred by letters patent.

lord mayor's court. See COURT.

Lord of Appeal. A member of the House of Lords, of whom at least three must be present for the hearing and determination of appeals, and including the Lord Chancellor, the Lords of Appeal in Ordinary, and the peers that have held high judicial offices, such as ex-chancellors and judges of the superior court in Great Britain and Ireland.

Lord of Appeal in Ordinary. A person appointed and salaried to aid the House of Lords in the hearing of appeals. ● These lords rank as barons for life, and sit and vote in the House of Lords even after retirement. Cf. LAW LORD.

Lord of Parliament. A member of the House of Lords.

Lord President. *Scots law.* The highest judicial officer in Scotland, heading the Court of Session and the First Division of the Upper House. ● The Lord President also holds the office of Lord Justice-General of Scotland.

Lord Privy Seal (**priv**-ee). *English law.* An officer who has custody of the privy seal and who authenticates either a state document before it passes to receive the Great Seal or a document that does not require the Great Seal because of its minor importance. ● The Lord Privy Seal has nominal official duties but is often made a member of the British cabinet. — Also termed *Keeper of the Privy Seal*; *Lord Keeper of the Privy Seal*; *Privy Seal.*

Lords. See HOUSE OF LORDS.

Lord's Day Act. See BLUE LAW.

lordship. 1. Dominion. **2.** An honorary title used for a nobleman other than a duke. **3.** A customary title for a judge or some other public official.

lord spiritual. An archbishop or bishop who is a member of the House of Lords.

lord temporal. A House of Lords member who is not an ecclesiastic.

Lord Tenterden's rule. See EJUSDEM GENERIS.

loser-pays rule. See ENGLISH RULE.

loss. (bef. 12c) **1.** An undesirable outcome of a risk; the disappearance or diminution of value, usu. in an unexpected or relatively unpredictable way. ● When the loss is a decrease in value, the usual method of calculating the loss is to ascertain the amount by which a thing's original cost exceeds its later selling price. **2.** *Tax.* The excess of a property's adjusted value over the amount realized from its sale or other disposition. IRC (26 USCA) § 1001. — Also termed *realized loss.* **3.** *Insurance.* The amount of financial detriment caused by an insured person's death or an insured property's damage, for which the insurer becomes liable. **4.** The failure to maintain possession of a thing.

actual loss. (18c) A loss resulting from the real and substantial destruction of insured property.

actual total loss. **1.** See *total loss.* **2.** *Marine insurance.* The total loss of a vessel covered by an insurance policy (1) by its real and substantive destruction, (2) by injuries that destroy its existence as a distinct individual of a particular class, (3) by its being reduced to a wreck irretrievably beyond repair, or (4) by its being placed beyond the insured's control and beyond the insured's power of recovery.

business loss. See *ordinary loss.*

capital loss. (1921) The loss realized upon selling or exchanging a capital asset. Cf. CAPITAL GAIN.

casualty loss. (1934) For tax purposes, the total or partial destruction of an asset resulting from an unexpected or unusual event, such as an automobile accident or a tornado.

consequential loss. (1829) A loss arising from the results of damage rather than from the damage itself. ● A consequential loss is proximate when the natural and probable effect of the wrongful conduct, under the circumstances, is to set in operation the intervening cause from which the loss directly results. When the loss is not the natural and probable effect of the wrongful conduct, the loss is remote. — Also termed *indirect loss; consequential injury.* Cf. *direct loss.*

constructive total loss. (1805) **1.** Such serious damage to the insured property that the cost of repairs would exceed the value of the thing repaired. — Also termed *constructive loss.* **2.** *Marine underwriting.* According to the traditional American rule, such serious damage to the insured property that the cost of repairs would exceed half the value of the thing repaired. See *total loss.*

direct loss. (18c) A loss that results immediately and proximately from an event. Cf. *consequential loss.*

disaster loss. A casualty loss sustained in a geographic area that the President designates as a disaster area. • It may be treated as having occurred during the previous tax year so that a victim may receive immediate tax benefits.

economic loss. See ECONOMIC LOSS.

extraordinary loss. (17c) A loss that is both unusual and infrequent, such as a loss resulting from a natural disaster.

general average loss. *Marine underwriting.* A loss at sea usu. incurred when cargo is thrown overboard to save the ship; a loss due to the voluntary and intentional sacrifice of part of a venture (usu. cargo) to save the rest of the venture from imminent peril. • Such a loss is borne equally by all the interests concerned in the venture. See AVERAGE (3).

hobby loss. A nondeductible loss arising from a personal hobby, as contrasted with an activity engaged in for profit. • The law generally presumes that an activity is engaged in for profit if profits are earned during at least three of the last five years. IRC (26 USCA) § 183.

indirect loss. See *consequential loss.*

long-term capital loss. A loss on a capital asset held for an extended period, usu. at least 12 months.

net loss. The excess of all expenses and losses over all revenues and gains.

net operating loss. (1921) The excess of operating expenses over revenues, the amount of which can be deducted from gross income if other deductions do not exceed gross income. — Abbr. NOL.

ordinary loss. (1850) *Tax.* A loss incurred from the sale or exchange of an item that is used in a trade or business. • The loss is deductible from ordinary income, and thus is more beneficial to the taxpayer than a capital loss. — Also termed *business loss.*

out-of-pocket loss. (1921) The difference between the value of what the buyer paid and the market value of what was received in return. • In breach-of-contract cases, out-of-pocket loss is used to measure restitution damages.

paper loss. (1924) A loss that is realized only by selling something (such as a security) that has decreased in market value. — Also termed *unrealized loss.*

partial loss. A loss of part of the insured property; damage not amounting to a total loss. Cf. *total loss.*

particular average loss. *Marine underwriting.* A loss suffered by and borne alone by particular interests in a maritime venture. • Such a loss is usu. a partial loss.

passive loss. A loss, with limited tax deductibility, from an activity in which the taxpayer does not materially participate, from a rental activity, or from a tax-shelter activity.

pecuniary loss. A loss of money or of something having monetary value.

product-liability loss. The total of a taxpayer's product-liability expenses up to the amount of the taxpayer's net operating loss. IRC (26 USCA) § 172(j)(1). — Abbr. PLL. See *net operating loss.*

progressive loss. 1. Loss that spreads or becomes more expensive to repair over time. **2.** Late-manifesting harm that is related to an event that caused immediate harm, worsens over time, and is not catalyzed by any additional causative agent. • A classic example is asbestosis, a disease that manifests long after exposure to asbestos fibers.

recognized loss. *Tax.* The portion of a loss that is subject to income taxation. IRC (26 USCA) § 1001(c).

salvage loss. 1. Generally, a loss that presumptively would have been a total loss if certain services had not been rendered. **2.** *Marine underwriting.* The difference between the salvage value, less the salvage charges, and the original value of the insured property.

total loss. (1924) The complete destruction of insured property so that nothing of value remains and the subject matter no longer exists in its original form. • Generally, a loss is total if, after the damage occurs, no substantial remnant remains standing that a reasonably prudent uninsured owner, desiring to rebuild, would use as a basis to restore the property to its original condition. — Also termed *actual total loss.* Cf. *partial loss; constructive total loss.*

unrealized loss. See *paper loss.*

loss carryback. See CARRYBACK.

loss carryforward. See CARRYOVER.

loss carryover. See CARRYOVER.

loss insurance. See INSURANCE.

loss leader. (1922) A good or commodity sold at a very low price, usu. below cost, to attract customers to buy other items. — Sometimes shortened to *leader.* See BAIT AND SWITCH.

loss-of-bargain damages. See *benefit-of-the-bargain damages* under DAMAGES.

loss-of-bargain rule. (1903) The doctrine that damages for a breach of a contract should put the injured party in the position it would have been in if both parties had performed their contractual duties.

loss-of-chance doctrine. (1987) A rule in some states providing a claim against a doctor who has engaged in medical malpractice that, although it does not result in a particular injury, decreases or eliminates the chance of surviving or recovering from the preexisting condition for which the doctor was consulted. — Also termed *lost-chance doctrine*; *increased-risk-of-harm doctrine*.

loss of consortium (kən-**sor**-shee-əm). (1878) **1.** A loss of the benefits that one spouse is entitled to receive from the other, including companionship, cooperation, aid, affection, and sexual relations. • Loss of consortium can be recoverable as damages from a tortfeasor in a personal-injury or wrongful-death action. Originally, only the husband could sue for loss of consortium. But in 1950, nearly a century after the enactment of the married women's property acts, a wife's action for negligent impairment of consortium was first recognized. *Hitaffer v. Argonne Co.*, 183 F.2d 811 (D.C. Cir. 1950). Today 48 states and the District of Columbia recognize both a husband's and a wife's right to sue for loss of consortium (Utah and Virginia do not). **2.** A similar loss of benefits that one is entitled to receive from a parent or child. See CONSORTIUM.

loss-of-use exclusion. See *failure-to-perform exclusion* under EXCLUSION (3).

loss-payable clause. *Insurance.* An insurance-policy provision that authorizes the payment of proceeds to someone other than the named insured, esp. to someone who has a security interest in the insured property. • Typically, a loss-payable clause either designates the person as a beneficiary of the proceeds or assigns to the person a claim against the insurer, but the clause usu. does not treat the person as an additional insured. See MORTGAGE CLAUSE.

loss payee. *Insurance.* A person or entity named in an insurance policy (under a loss-payable clause) to be paid if the insured property suffers a loss.

loss ratio. 1. *Insurance.* The ratio between premiums paid and losses incurred during a given period. **2.** A bank's loan losses compared to its loan assets; a business's receivable losses compared to its receivables.

loss reserve. See RESERVE.

lost, *adj.* (16c) **1.** (Of property) beyond the possession and custody of its owner and not locatable by diligent search <lost at sea> <lost papers>. **2.** (Of a person) missing <lost child>. **3.** *Parliamentary law.* (Of a motion) rejected; not adopted <the motion is lost>.

lost boundary. See BOUNDARY.

lost-chance doctrine. (1985) **1.** LOSS-OF-CHANCE DOCTRINE. **2.** A rule permitting a claim, in limited circumstances, against someone who fails to come to the aid of a person who is in imminent danger of being injured or killed. Cf. GOOD SAMARITAN DOCTRINE.

lost corner. See CORNER.

lost earning capacity. (1908) A person's diminished earning power resulting from an injury. • This impairment is recoverable as an element of damages in a tort action. Cf. *lost earnings* under EARNINGS.

lost earnings. See EARNINGS.

lost-expectation damages. See *expectation damages* under DAMAGES.

lost or not lost. *Marine insurance.* A policy provision fixing the effective date of the policy to a time preceding the policy date, even if the insured ship has already been lost when the policy is executed, as long as neither party then knows, or has means of knowing, that the ship has been lost.

lost profits. 1. *Contracts.* A measure of damages that allows a seller to collect the profits that would have been made on the sale if the buyer had not breached. UCC § 2-708(2). **2.** *Patents.* A measure of damages set by estimating the net amount lost by a plaintiff-inventor because of the infringing defendant's actions. • The plaintiff can ask for a lost-profits recovery by showing that the patent is in demand, that the plaintiff is able to meet the demand, and that there are no acceptable non-infringing alternatives on the market. — Also termed (redundantly) *lost-profits damages.*

lost-profits damages. See LOST PROFITS (1).

lost property. See PROPERTY.

lost-sales-of-unpatented-items theory. *Patents.* A theory of lost-profits remedy whereby compensation is sought for sales of unpatented items that the plaintiff would have sold along with patented items but for the defendant's infringement.

lost-volume seller. (1974) A seller of goods who, after a buyer has breached a sales contract, resells the goods to a different buyer who would have bought identical goods from the seller's inventory even if the original buyer had not breached. • Such a seller is entitled to lost profits, rather than contract price less market price, as damages from the original buyer's breach. UCC § 2-708(2).

lost will. See WILL.

lot. (bef. 12c) **1.** A tract of land, esp. one having specific boundaries or being used for a given purpose.

> *minimum lot.* A lot that has the least amount of square footage allowed by a local zoning law.

nonconforming lot. A previously lawful lot that now violates an amended or newly adopted zoning ordinance.

2. An article that is the subject of a separate sale, lease, or delivery, whether or not it is sufficient to perform the contract. UCC §§ 2-105(5); 2A-103(1)(s). **3.** A specified number of shares or a specific quantity of a commodity designated for trading.

odd lot. A number of shares of stock or the value of a bond that is less than a round lot.

round lot. The established unit of trading for stocks and bonds. ● A round lot of stock is usu. 100 shares, and a round lot of bonds is usu. $1,000 or $5,000 par value. — Also termed *even lot; board lot.*

lot line. (1829) A land boundary that separates one tract from another <from the street to the alley, the lot line is 150 feet>.

lottery. (16c) A method of raising revenues, esp. state-government revenues, by selling tickets and giving prizes (usu. cash prizes) to those who hold tickets with winning numbers that are drawn at random. — Also termed *lotto.*

Dutch lottery. A lottery in which tickets are drawn from classes, and the number and value of prizes are fixed and increasing with each class. ● This type of lottery originated in Holland in the 16th century. — Also termed *class lottery.*

Genoese lottery (jen-oh-**eez** *or* -**ees**). A lottery in which, out of 90 consecutive numbers, five are drawn by lot, each player wagering that one or more of the numbers they have chosen will be drawn. ● This type of lottery originated in Genoa in about 1530. — Also termed *number lottery; numerical lottery.*

love day. See DAY.

Lovely claim. *Hist. Property.* An entitlement to settle on and take ownership of public land in Arkansas, created by the federal government for Lovely County settlers who were displaced by an 1828 treaty that gave the settlers' land to the Cherokee nation. ● The term gets its name from Lovely County in the Arkansas territory, which straddled what is now the Oklahoma–Arkansas border. The treaty divided the county, granted the portion west of the Mississippi River to the Cherokee nation, and required the settlers in that territory to relocate. On May 24, 1828, Congress passed an act granting relief to Lovely County settlers who were forced to leave the Cherokee land and granted them land on the eastern side of the river. *Lovely claims* are found in chains of title in Arkansas.

lowbote (loh-boht). *Hist.* Compensation paid for the death of one killed in a disturbance.

low diligence. See *slight diligence* under DILIGENCE.

lower chamber. See CHAMBER.

lower court. 1. See *court below* under COURT. **2.** See *inferior court* under COURT.

lower estate. See *servient estate* under ESTATE (4).

lower low tide. See TIDE.

lower-of-cost-or-market method. (1958) A means of pricing or costing inventory by which inventory value is set at either acquisition cost or market cost, whichever is lower.

lower scale. See SCALE.

lowest responsible bidder. (1844) A bidder who has the lowest price conforming to the contract specifications and who is financially able and competent to complete the work, as shown by the bidder's prior performance.

low-grade security. See SECURITY.

low justice. See JUSTICE (3).

low-total voting. See VOTING.

low-water mark. See WATERMARK.

loyalty, *n.* (15c) Faithfulness or allegiance to a person, cause, duty, or government. — **loyal,** *adj.*

loyalty oath. See *oath of allegiance* under OATH.

L.P. See *limited partnership* under PARTNERSHIP.

L.R. *abbr.* Law Reports. See REPORT (3).

LRIC. *abbr.* LONG-RUN INCREMENTAL COST.

L.S. *abbr.* LOCUS SIGILLI.

LSAT. *abbr.* LAW SCHOOL ADMISSIONS TEST.

Ltd. *abbr.* Limited — used in company names to indicate limited liability.

LTV ratio. See LOAN-TO-VALUE RATIO.

lucid, *adj.* (16c) **1.** Understandable. **2.** Rational. **3.** Sane.

lucid interval. (17c) **1.** A brief period during which an insane person regains sanity sufficient to have the legal capacity to contract and act on his or her own behalf. **2.** A period during which a person has enough mental capacity to understand the concept of marriage and the duties and obligations it imposes. **3.** A period during which an otherwise incompetent person regains sufficient testamentary capacity to execute a valid will. — Also termed *lucid moment.*

lucid moment. See LUCID INTERVAL.

lucrative (loo-krə-tiv), *adj.* (15c) **1.** Profitable; remunerative <a lucrative business>. **2.** *Civil law.* Acquired or held without accepting burdensome conditions or giving consideration <lucrative ownership>.

lucrative bailment. See *bailment for hire* under BAILMENT.

lucrative office. See OFFICE.

lucrative title. See TITLE (2).

lucre (**loo**-kər), *n.* Monetary gain; profit.

lucri causa (**loo**-krɪ **kaw**-zə). [Latin] For the sake of gain. • *Lucri causa* was formerly an essential element of larceny, but today the thief's intent to deprive the possessor of property is generally sufficient. See LARCENY.

lukewarm bench. See BENCH.

lumping. *Criminal procedure.* The imposition of a general sentence on a criminal defendant. See *general sentence* under SENTENCE.

lumping sale. See SALE.

lump-sum agreement. *Int'l law.* An agreement for one nation that caused injuries to another nation's citizens to make a single payment to the other nation to settle outstanding claims for those injuries. • The recipient nation has the power to decide how the settlement funds should be distributed. This method of settling claims has become increasingly common since the mid-20th century as an alternative to submitting the claims to an international tribunal.

lump-sum alimony. See *alimony in gross* under ALIMONY.

lump-sum payment. See PAYMENT.

lunacy. See INSANITY.

lunar month. See MONTH (3).

lunatic, *n. Archaic.* An insane person. See INSANE.

lunch-hour rule. The doctrine that an employer is not responsible for injuries suffered or caused by an employee who takes a lunch break off work premises and, during the break, is not performing tasks in the course of the employment.

luxury tax. See TAX.

LWI. *abbr.* LEGAL WRITING INSTITUTE.

lying by. The act or fact of being present at a transaction affecting one's interests but remaining silent. • Courts often treat a person who was "lying by" at a transaction as having agreed to it and as being prevented from objecting to it.

lying in wait. *Criminal law.* The series of acts involved in watching, waiting for, and hiding from someone, with the intent of killing or inflicting serious bodily injury on that person. • Because lying in wait shows premeditation and deliberation, it can result in an increased sentence.

lynch, *vb.* (1836) (Of a mob) to kill (somebody) without legal authority, usu. by hanging.

lynch law. (1811) The administration of summary punishment, esp. death, for an alleged crime, without legal authority. — Also termed (through personification) *Judge Lynch*.

lynching law. See ANTILYNCHING LAW.

Lyndhurst's Act. *Hist.* An English statute that rendered marriages within certain degrees of kinship null and void. Marriage Act of 1835, 5 & 6 Will. 4, ch. 54. — Also termed *Lord Lyndhurst's Act*.

M

M. 1. *abbr.* MORTGAGE. **2.** *Hist.* A letter engraved on a treasury note to show that the note bears interest at the rate of one mill per centum. **3.** *Hist.* A brand placed on the left thumb of a person convicted of manslaughter who claimed the benefit of clergy.

M1. A measure of the money supply including cash, checking accounts, and travelers' checks.

M2. A measure of the money supply including M1 items, plus savings and time deposits, money-market accounts, and overnight-repurchase agreements.

M3. A measure of the money supply including M2 items, plus large time deposits and money-market funds held by institutions.

mace. (14c) **1.** *Hist.* A weapon used in warfare, consisting of a staff topped by a heavy head, usu. of metal. **2.** A scepter; an ornamental form of weapon used as an emblem of the dignity of an office, as in Parliament and the U.S. House of Representatives. • In the House of Commons, it is laid on the table when the Speaker is in the chair. In the U.S. House of Representatives, it is usu. placed to the right of the Speaker and is borne upright by the sergeant-at-arms on extraordinary occasions, as when necessary to quell a disturbance or bring refractory members to order. **3.** (*cap.*) The trademarked name of a chemical liquid that can be sprayed in a person's face to cause dizziness and temporary immobilization.

mace-bearer. A person who carries a mace before an official, usu. one of high rank. See MACE (2).

mace-proof, *vb.* To exempt from an arrest; to secure against an arrest.

machination (mak-ə-**nay**-shən). (15c) **1.** An act of planning a scheme, esp. for an evil purpose. **2.** The scheme so planned.

machine. (16c) *Patents.* A device or apparatus consisting of fixed and moving parts that work together to perform some function. • Machines are one of the statutory categories of inventions that can be patented. — Also termed *apparatus*; *device.* Cf. MANUFACTURE; PROCESS (3).

Machinists preemption. See PREEMPTION.

MACRS. *abbr.* Modified Accelerated Cost Recovery System. See ACCELERATED COST RECOVERY SYSTEM.

made land. See LAND.

made law. See POSITIVE LAW.

Madison Amendment. See TWENTY-SEVENTH AMENDMENT.

Mad Parliament. In 1258, a commission of 24 barons summoned to Oxford by Henry III to carry out certain reforms and settle differences between the king and the barons. • The assembly was called the Mad Parliament because it ultimately abridged the king's power and gave unprecedented powers to the barons. The commission produced the Provisions of Oxford. — Also termed *parliamentum insanum.* See PROVISIONS OF OXFORD.

Madrid Agreement. *Trademarks.* **1.** An 1890 treaty establishing a system for the international registration of trademarks. • The agreement's official name is the Madrid Arrangement Concerning the International Registration of Marks. A product of the Madrid Revision Conference of the Paris Convention in 1890, it was last revised in 1967. Under this treaty's registration system, called the *Madrid Union*, a mark registered in a treaty nation that is also registered (in French) with the World Intellectual Property Organization receives equal protection in all signatory nations. The United States ratified the treaty in 2002. **2.** An 1890 treaty designed to discourage false indications of geographic source by permitting member nations to seize falsely marked imported goods. — Also termed *Madrid Arrangement*; *Madrid Registration of Marks Treaty*; *Madrid Union.* • Also a product of the Madrid Revision Conference of the Paris Convention in 1890, the treaty's official name is the Madrid Arrangement Concerning the Prevention of False or Deceptive Indications of Source. It applies to manufactured and handmade goods, and agricultural products. — Also termed (in sense 2) *Madrid Agreement for the Repression of False or Deceptive Indications of Source of Goods.*

Madrid Protocol. *Trademarks.* **1.** A 1996 international agreement that allows citizens of a Madrid Agreement signatory nation to apply for a single international trademark through the World Intellectual Property Organization instead of registering the trademark in each individual nation. • An applicant must apply for the trademark's registration in a treaty-member nation before applying for international trademark protection. **2.** A 1989 international trademark-registration agreement that supplements the Madrid Agreement on trademark registration, harmonizes the Agreement's registration system with that of the European Union, and allows citizens of nonmember nations to apply for international trademark registration without first registering the trademark in a member nation. • When referred to along with the Madrid Registration of Marks Treaty, it is sometimes also termed the *Madrid System*. See MADRID AGREEMENT (1).

Madrid Registration of Marks Treaty. See MADRID AGREEMENT (1).

Madrid System. See MADRID PROTOCOL (2).

Madrid Union. See MADRID AGREEMENT (1).

magisterial (maj-ə-steer-ee-əl), *adj.* (17c) Of or relating to the character, office, powers, or duties of a magistrate. — Also termed *magistral*; *magistratic*.

magisterial district. See *magisterial precinct* under PRECINCT.

magisterial precinct. See PRECINCT.

magistracy (maj-ə-strə-see). (16c) **1.** The office, district, or power of a magistrate. **2.** A body of magistrates.

magistral, *adj.* (16c) **1.** Of or relating to a master or masters <an absolutely magistral work>. **2.** Formulated by a physician <a magistral ointment>. **3.** MAGISTERIAL.

magistrate (maj-ə-strayt), *n.* (14c) **1.** The highest-ranking official in a government, such as the king in a monarchy, the president in a republic, or the governor in a state. — Also termed *chief magistrate*; *first magistrate*. **2.** A local official who possesses whatever power is specified in the appointment or statutory grant of authority. **3.** A judicial officer with strictly limited jurisdiction and authority, often on the local level and often restricted to criminal cases. Cf. JUSTICE OF THE PEACE. **4.** See *judicial officer* (3) under OFFICER. — **magisterial** (maj-ə-stir-ee-əl), *adj.*

committing magistrate. (18c) A judicial officer who conducts preliminary criminal hearings and may order that a defendant be released for lack of evidence, sent to jail to await trial, or released on bail. See *examining court* under COURT.

district-court magistrate. (1932) In some states, a quasi-judicial officer given the power to set bail, accept bond, accept guilty pleas, impose sentences for traffic violations and similar offenses, and conduct informal hearings on civil infractions.

federal magistrate. See UNITED STATES MAGISTRATE JUDGE.

investigating magistrate. (1908) A quasi-judicial officer responsible for examining and sometimes ruling on certain aspects of a criminal proceeding before it comes before a judge.

metropolitan stipendiary magistrate (stɪ-pen-dee-er-ee). *English law.* A stipendiary magistrate with jurisdiction in inner London areas. • Under the Access to Justice Act 1999, these magistrates have been renamed *district judges (magistrates' courts).* See *stipendiary magistrate.*

police magistrate. (18c) A judicial officer who has jurisdiction to try minor criminal offenses, breaches of police regulations, and similar violations. — Also termed *police justice.*

stipendiary magistrate (stɪ-**pen**-dee-er-ee). *English law.* A salaried magistrate that performs either in the place of or along with Justices of the Peace, and is appointed from barristers and solicitors of seven years standing.

U.S. Magistrate. See UNITED STATES MAGISTRATE JUDGE.

Magistrate Judge, U.S. See UNITED STATES MAGISTRATE JUDGE.

magistrate's court. See COURT.

magistratic, *adj.* See MAGISTERIAL.

Magna Carta (mag-nə kahr-tə). [Latin "great charter"] The English charter that King John granted to the barons in 1215 and that Henry III and Edward I later confirmed. • It is generally regarded as one of the great common-law documents and as the foundation of constitutional liberties. The other three great charters of English liberty are the Petition of Right (3 Car. (1628)), the Habeas Corpus Act (31 Car. 2 (1679)), and the Bill of Rights (1 Will. & M. (1689)). — Also spelled *Magna Charta.*

magna culpa (mag-nə kəl-pə). [Latin "great fault"] *Roman law.* Gross fault. • This is sometimes equivalent to *dolus.* See DOLUS.

magna neglegentia. See *gross negligence* under NEGLIGENCE.

Magnuson–Moss Warranty Act (mag-nə-sən–maws *or* –mos). A federal statute requiring that a written warranty of a consumer product fully and conspicuously disclose, in plain language, the terms and conditions of the warranty, including whether the warranty is full or limited, according to standards given in the statute. 15 USCA §§ 2301–2312.

mahr, *n. Islamic law.* A gift of money or property that must be made by a man to the woman he marries. • The parties agree to the mahr's amount and time of payment before marrying. If the time of payment is indefinite or if the mahr's outstanding balance is not paid sooner, the agreed amount or outstanding balance becomes due on divorce or the husband's death. Despite the religious basis for a mahr, secular courts may uphold the agreement if its secular terms are enforceable as a prenuptial contract. — Also termed *sadaq.* Cf. NIKAH.

maiden. (bef. 12c) **1.** A young unmarried woman. **2.** *Scots law.* An instrument used to behead criminals. • The Earl of Morton, who had introduced the instrument to Scotland, was the first to be executed by it, in 1581. It was the prototype of the guillotine. Hence, "*to kiss the maiden* was to be put to death." H. Percy Smith, *Glossary of Terms and Phrases* 307 (1883).

maiden assize. See ASSIZE (1).

maiden name. See NAME.

mail, *n.* (13c) **1.** One or more items that have been properly addressed, stamped with postage, and deposited for delivery in the postal system. **2.** An official system for delivering such items; the postal system. **3.** One or more written or oral messages sent electronically (e.g., through e-mail or voicemail).

   certified mail. Mail for which the sender requests proof of delivery in the form of a receipt signed by the addressee. ● The receipt (a green card, which is usu. referred to as such) must be signed before the mail will be delivered. — Also termed *certified mail, return receipt requested.*

   registered mail. Mail that the U.S. Postal Service records at the time of mailing and at each point on its route so as to guarantee safe delivery.

mail, *vb.* (1827) **1.** To deposit (a letter, package, etc.) with the U.S. Postal Service; to ensure that a letter, package, etc. is properly addressed, stamped, and placed into a receptacle for mail pickup. **2.** To deliver (a letter, package, etc.) to a private courier service that undertakes delivery to a third person, often within a specified time.

mailable, *adj.* (Of a letter or package) lawful to send through a postal service.

mailbox rule. (1975) **1.** *Contracts.* The principle that an acceptance becomes effective — and binds the offeror — once it has been properly mailed. ● The mailbox rule does not apply, however, if the offer specifies that an acceptance is not effective until received. **2.** The principle that when a pleading or other document is filed or served by mail, filing or service is deemed to have occurred on the date of mailing. ● The mailbox rule varies from jurisdiction to jurisdiction. It may apply only to certain types of filings, or it may apply to the use of an overnight courier instead of the U.S. mail. — Also termed *dispatch rule.*

mail cover. (1959) A process by which the U.S. Postal Service provides a government agency with information on the face of an envelope or package (such as a postmark) for the agency's use in locating a fugitive, identifying a coconspirator, or obtaining other evidence necessary to solve a crime.

mail fraud. See FRAUD.

mail-order divorce. See DIVORCE.

maim, *n.* (14c) *Archaic.* The type of strength-diminishing injury required to support a charge of mayhem; esp., serious injury to a body part that is necessary for fighting. — Also termed *maihem; maihemium.* See MAYHEM. — **maim,** *vb.*

main channel. See CHANNEL.

main demand. See DEMAND (1).

main motion. See MOTION (2).

main opinion. See *majority opinion* under OPINION (1).

mainpernable (mayn-pər-nə-bəl), *adj.* Capable of being bailed (mainprised); bailable. See MAINPRISE (2).

mainpernor (mayn-pər-nər), *n.* [Law French, fr. Old French *main* "hand" + *pernor* "taker"] *Hist.* **1.** A surety for a prisoner's appearance; one who gives mainprise for another. — Also termed *mainpriser.* **2.** A form of bail taken under a writ of mainprise. — Also termed *manucaptor* (man-yoo-**kap**-tər). See MAINPRISE.

main pot. *Tax.* A step in evaluating tax liability in which qualified transactions are compared to determine whether a net gain or loss has occurred. IRC (26 USCA) § 1231. — Also termed *big pot; hotchpot; hodgepodge.* Cf. CASUALTY POT.

mainprise (mayn-priz), *n.* [Law French, fr. Old French *main* "hand" + *prise* "taking"] *Hist.* **1.** Delivery of a prisoner to the mainpernor. **2.** A suretyship undertaking that makes the surety responsible for a prisoner's appearance in court on a specified date and time. **3.** A writ ordering the sheriff to take the security of a mainpernor for the prisoner's appearance and release the prisoner. — Also spelled *mainprize.* — Also termed *writ of mainprise; manucaption* (man-yoo-**kap**-shən).

mainprise, *vb.* *Hist.* To release (a prisoner) on the surety of a mainpernor.

main-purpose rule. *Contracts.* The doctrine that if a promise to guarantee another's debt is made primarily for the promisor's own benefit, then the statute of frauds does not apply and the promise need not be in writing to be enforceable. — Also termed *main-purpose doctrine; leading-object rule.*

main-relief rule. A doctrine by which venue for a lawsuit may be founded on the primary relief sought by the plaintiff, even if other claims, which alone would not support venue, are included in the suit.

main-rent. See VASSALAGE (2).

main sea. See SEA.

mainstreaming. (1973) The practice of educating a disabled student in classes with students who are not disabled, in a regular-education setting, as opposed to a special-education class. Cf. LEAST-RESTRICTIVE ENVIRONMENT.

maintain, *vb.* (14c) **1.** To continue (something). **2.** To continue in possession of (property, etc.). **3.** To assert (a position or opinion); to uphold (a position or opinion) in argument. **4.** To care for (property) for purposes of operational productivity or appearance; to engage in general repair and up-keep. **5.** To support (someone) financially; esp. to pay alimony to. **6.** (Of a third party to a lawsuit) to assist a litigant in prosecuting or defending a lawsuit; to meddle in someone else's litigation.

maintainor. (15c) *Criminal law.* A person who meddles in someone else's litigation by providing money or other assistance; a person who is guilty of maintenance. — Also spelled *maintainer.* See MAINTENANCE (6).

maintenance, *n.* (14c) **1.** The continuation of something, such as a lawsuit. **2.** The continuing possession of something, such as property. **3.** The assertion of a position or opinion; the act of up-holding a position in argument. **4.** The care and work put into property to keep it operating and productive; general repair and upkeep. **5.** Financial support given by one person to another, usu. paid as a result of a legal separation or divorce; esp. ALIMONY. • Maintenance may end after a specified time or upon the death, cohabitation, or remarriage of the receiving party.

   maintenance in gross. (1914) A fixed amount of money to be paid upon divorce by one former spouse to the other, in a lump sum or in installments. • Typically, the total amount is unmodifiable regardless of any change in either person's circumstances.

   separate maintenance. (17c) Money paid by one married person to another for support if they are no longer living together as husband and wife. • This type of maintenance is often mandated by a court order. An action for separate maintenance is not maintainable after the marriage has been dissolved. — Also termed *separate support.*

6. Improper assistance in prosecuting or defending a lawsuit given to a litigant by someone who has no bona fide interest in the case; meddling in someone else's litigation. Cf. CHAMPERTY.

maintenance and cure. *Maritime law.* Compensation provided to a sailor who becomes sick or injured while a member of a vessel's crew. • The obligation is broader than what would be covered under workers' compensation, as it applies to illness or injury whether or not arising out of shipboard duties. See CURE (2).

maintenance assessment. See ASSESSMENT.

maintenance bond. See BOND (2).

maintenance call. See *margin call* under CALL (2).

maintenance fee. 1. A periodic payment required to maintain a privilege, such as a license. **2.** A charge for keeping an improvement in working condition or a residential property in habitable condition. — Also termed *maintenance assessment.* **3.** A fee charged for reinvesting earnings

and dividends in mutual funds. **4.** *Patents.* The periodic charge a patentee must pay the U.S. Patent and Trademark Office in order to keep the patent in force. • U.S. maintenance fees are due 3½, 7, and 11½ years from the date the patent is issued.

maintenance in gross. See MAINTENANCE.

maintenance margin requirement. See MARGIN REQUIREMENT.

maister (**may**-stər). *Archaic.* A master.

maitre (**may**-trə *or* **mayt**-ər), *n.* [French] *French law.* A master, esp. of a vessel.

majestas (mə-**jes**-tas), *n.* [Latin "supreme power"] *Roman law.* **1.** The majesty, sovereign authority, or supreme prerogative of the state or sovereign; the supreme power of the people, esp. as represented by their highest representatives, the consuls, or the emperor. **2.** The crime of high treason. See *crimen majestatis* under CRIMEN.

major (**may**-jər). [Latin] (17c) **1.** *Roman law.* An older person, esp. one older than 25 and hence of full capacity. **2.** *Roman law.* An ascendant; an ancestor. **3.** *Hist.* A mayor. **4.** ADULT. **5.** In the U.S. Army, U.S. Air Force, or U.S. Marine Corps, a commissioned officer who ranks above a captain and below a lieutenant-colonel.

major action. *Environmental law.* An undertaking that may have a significant impact on the environment, triggering the need for an environmental assessment under the National Environmental Policy Act and some state laws. Cf. MAJOR-FEDERAL ACTION.

major-and-minor fault rule. See MAJOR-MINOR FAULT RULE.

major annus (**may**-jər **an**-əs). [Latin "the greater year"] A leap year, made up of 366 days.

major crime. See FELONY (1).

major disaster. A catastrophe, such as a hurricane, tornado, storm, flood, earthquake, drought, or fire, so severe that it warrants disaster assistance from the federal government. • When the President declares a major disaster, the federal government supplements the efforts and resources of states, local governments, and relief organizations to alleviate the damage, loss, hardship, and suffering caused by the catastrophe. 40 CFR § 109.

major dispute. See DISPUTE.

major federal action. *Environmental law.* An undertaking, either carried out by a federal agency or approved by a federal agency, that may have a significant impact on the environment. • Examples include constructing an aqueduct or dam, constructing a highway through wetlands, or adopting certain agency regulations. • Under the National Environmental Policy Act, a federal agency that plans to take a major federal action that may significantly affect the environment is required to prepare and file an environmental-impact statement, along with any public comments, with the Environmental Protection Agency. 40 CFR §§ 1506.9, 1508.

majority. (16c) **1.** The status of one who has attained the age (usu. 18) at which one is entitled to full civic rights and considered legally capable of handling one's own affairs. See AGE OF MAJORITY. Cf. MINORITY (1). **2.** A number that is more than half of a total; a group of more than 50 percent <the candidate received 50.4 percent of the votes — barely a majority>. • A majority always refers to more than half of some defined or assumed set. In parliamentary law, that set may be all the members or some subset, such as all members present or all members voting on a particular question. A "majority" without further qualification usu. means a simple majority. See *simple majority.* Cf. PLURALITY; MINORITY (2); HALF PLUS ONE.

  absolute majority. A majority of all those who are entitled to vote in a particular election, regardless of how many voters actually cast ballots. See QUORUM.

  constitutional majority. See *majority of all the members.*

  extraordinary majority. See *supermajority.*

  majority of all the members. A majority of all the actual members, disregarding vacancies. — Also termed *constitutional majority; majority of the entire membership; majority of the membership.*

  majority of all the memberships. A majority of all the possible memberships, including vacancies. — Also termed *majority of the fixed membership.*

  majority of the entire membership. See *majority of all the members.*

  majority of the fixed membership. See *majority of all the memberships.*

  majority of the membership. See *majority of all the members.*

  ordinary majority. See *simple majority.*

  plural majority. See PLURALITY.

  simple majority. A numerical majority of those actually voting. • Absent members, members who are present but do not vote, blanks, and abstentions are not counted. — Also termed *ordinary majority.*

  supermajority. A fixed proportion greater than half (often two-thirds or a percentage greater than 50%), required for a measure to pass. • Such a majority is needed for certain extraordinary actions, such as ratifying a constitutional amendment or approving a fundamental corporate change. — Also termed *extraordinary majority.*

  veto-proof majority. A legislative majority large enough that it can override an executive veto.

majority-consent procedure. *Corporations.* A statutory provision allowing shareholders to avoid a shareholders' meeting and to act instead by written consent of the holders of a majority of shares. • Delaware and a few other states have enacted such procedures.

majority-minority district. See DISTRICT.

majority opinion. See OPINION (1).

majority report. See REPORT (1).

majority rule. (1848) **1.** The principle that a majority of a group has the power to make decisions that bind the group; the principle that in the choice of alternatives, the one preferred by the greater number is selected. • It is governance by the majority of those who actually participate, regardless of the number entitled to participate. **2.** The constitutional principle "that a majority of the people of a State . . . elect a majority of that State's legislators," *Reynolds v. Sims,* 377 U.S. 533, 583–84, 84 S.Ct. 1362, 1393 (1964), from which it follows that each voter is entitled to a share of the franchise equal to that of each other voter. See ONE-PERSON, ONE-VOTE RULE. **3.** *Corporations.* The common-law principle that a director or officer owes no fiduciary duty to a shareholder with respect to a stock transaction. • This rule has been restricted by both federal insider-trading rules and state-law doctrine. Cf. SPECIAL-FACTS RULE.

majority shareholder. See SHAREHOLDER.

majority verdict. See VERDICT.

majority vote. See MAJORITY.

majority voting. See VOTING.

major life activity. (1979) A basic activity that an average person in the general population can perform with little or no difficulty, such as seeing, hearing, sleeping, eating, walking, traveling, or working. • A person who is substantially limited in a major life activity is protected from discrimination under a variety of disability laws, most significantly the Americans with Disabilities Act and the Rehabilitation Act. 42 USCA § 12102(2); 29 USCA § 705(9)(B). See AMERICANS WITH DISABILITIES ACT.

major-minor fault rule. *Maritime law.* The principle that if the fault of one vessel in a collision is uncontradicted and sufficient to account for the accident, then the other vessel is presumed not to have been at fault and therefore not to have contributed to the accident. • The elimination of the divided-damages rule has made this rule obsolete. — Also termed *major-and-minor fault rule.*

major offense. See OFFENSE (1).

major trend. See TREND.

make, *vb.* (bef. 12c) **1.** To cause (something) to exist <to make a record>. **2.** To enact (something) <to make law>. **3.** To acquire (something) <to make money on execution>. **4.** To legally perform, as by executing, signing, or delivering (a document) <to make a contract>.

make default. 1. DEFAULT (1). **2.** DEFAULT (2).

make law. 1. To legislate. **2.** To issue a legal precedent, esp. a judicial decision, that establishes a new rule of law on a particular subject. **3.** *Hist.* To deny a plaintiff's charge under oath, in open court, with compurgators.

make purpart (pər-pahrt), *vb.* To divide and apportion property formerly held in common. See PURPART.

maker. (14c) **1.** One who frames, promulgates, or ordains (as in *lawmaker*). **2.** A person who signs a promissory note. See NOTE (1). Cf. COMAKER. **3.** DRAWER.

accommodation maker. (1829) One who signs a note as a surety. See ACCOMMODATION (2); *accommodation indorser* under INDORSER.

prime maker. (1972) The person who is primarily liable on a note or other negotiable instrument.

makeup gas. *Oil & gas.* Natural gas that has been paid for by the purchaser, usu. under a take-or-pay contract, but that is to be delivered in the years following payment. See *take-or-pay contract* under CONTRACT.

make-whole doctrine. *Insurance.* The principle that, unless the insurance policy provides otherwise, an insurer will not receive any of the proceeds from the settlement of a claim, except to the extent that the settlement funds exceed the amount necessary to fully compensate the insured for the loss suffered.

mal (mal), *adj.* [Law French "bad; wrong; against"] Bad; wrong. • In Law French, *mal* was a separable word, equivalent to the Latin *male* ("badly"). In its modern uses, *mal-* is a prefix in terms such as *maladministration* and *malpractice.*

mala antiqua (mal-ə an-tɪ-kwə). Old crimes; offenses that date back to antiquity.

maladministration. Poor management or regulation by a public officer; specif., an official's abuse of power. — Also termed *misadministration; breach of trust.*

mala fides (mal-ə fɪ-deez), *n.* See BAD FAITH (1).

mala in se (mal-ə in **say** or **see**). See MALUM IN SE.

malapportionment, *n.* (1959) The improper or unconstitutional apportionment of a legislative district. See APPORTIONMENT (3); GERRYMANDERING; LEGISLATIVE DISTRICTING. — **malapportion,** *vb.*

mala prohibita (mal-ə proh-**hib**-i-tə). See MALUM PROHIBITUM.

malconduct in office. See *official misconduct* under MISCONDUCT.

malediction (mal-ə-**dik**-shən). *Hist.* A curse placed on property donated to a church to protect it against anyone attempting to violate the church's rights.

malefaction (mal-ə-**fak**-shən), *n.* [Latin *malefacere* "to do evil"] (15c) *Archaic.* An evil deed; a crime or offense. — Also termed *maleficium.* — **malefactory,** *adj.*

malefactor (mal-ə-**fak**-tər), *n.* [Latin] (15c) A wrongdoer; a criminal.

maleson. See MALISON.

malesworn (**mayl**-sworn), *p.pl.* Forsworn. — Also spelled *malsworn.*

malfeasance (mal-**fee**-zənts), *n.* (17c) A wrongful or unlawful act; esp. wrongdoing or misconduct by a public official; MISFEASANCE IN PUBLIC OFFICE. Cf. MISFEASANCE; NONFEASANCE. — **malfeasant** (mal-**fee**-zənt), *adj.* — **malfeasor** (mal-**fee**-zər), *n.*

malfunction theory. (1979) *Products-liability law.* A principle permitting a products-liability plaintiff to prove that a product was defective by proving that the product malfunctioned, instead of requiring the plaintiff to prove a specific defect. • A plaintiff relying on the malfunction theory usu. must also prove that the product was not misused, and must disprove all reasonable explanations for the occurrence other than a defect.

malice, *n.* (14c) **1.** The intent, without justification or excuse, to commit a wrongful act. **2.** Reckless disregard of the law or of a person's legal rights. **3.** Ill will; wickedness of heart. • This sense is most typical in nonlegal contexts.

actual malice. (18c) **1.** The deliberate intent to commit an injury, as evidenced by external circumstances. — Also termed *express malice; malice in fact.* Cf. *implied malice.* **2.** *Defamation.* Knowledge (by the person who utters or publishes a defamatory statement) that a statement is false, or reckless disregard about whether the statement is true. • To recover for defamation, a plaintiff who is a public official or public figure must overcome the defendant's qualified privilege by proving the defendant's actual malice. And for certain other types of claims, a plaintiff must prove actual malice to recover presumed or punitive damages. — Also termed *New York Times malice; constitutional malice; common-law malice.*

common-law malice. See *actual malice* (2).

constructive malice. See *implied malice.*

express malice. (17c) **1.** *Criminal law.* The intent to kill or seriously injure arising from a deliberate, rational mind. **2.** See *actual malice* (1). **3.** *Defamation.* The bad-faith publication of defamatory material.

general malice. (17c) Malice that is necessary for any criminal conduct; malice that is not directed at a specific person. Cf. *particular malice.*

implied malice. (17c) Malice inferred from a person's conduct. — Also termed *constructive malice; legal malice; malice in law.* Cf. *actual malice* (1).

malice in fact. See *actual malice* (1).

particular malice. (16c) Malice that is directed at a particular person. — Also termed *special malice.*

transferred malice. (1961) Malice directed to one person or object but instead harming another in the way intended for the first.

universal malice. (17c) The state of mind of a person who determines to take a life on slight provocation, without knowing or caring who may be the victim.

malice aforethought. (17c) The requisite mental state for common-law murder, encompassing any one of the following: (1) the intent to kill, (2) the intent to inflict grievous bodily harm, (3) extremely reckless indifference to the value of human life (the so-called "abandoned and malignant heart"), or (4) the intent to commit a dangerous felony (which leads to culpability under the felony-murder rule). — Also termed *premeditated malice; preconceived malice; malice prepense; malitia praecogitata.*

malice exception. (1977) A limitation on a public official's qualified immunity, by which the official can face civil liability for willfully exercising discretion in a way that violates a known or well-established right. See *qualified immunity* under IMMUNITY (1).

malice in fact. See *actual malice* (1) under MALICE.

malice in law. See *implied malice* under MALICE.

malice prepense. See MALICE AFORETHOUGHT.

malicious, *adj.* (13c) **1.** Substantially certain to cause injury. **2.** Without just cause or excuse.

malicious abandonment. See ABANDONMENT (3).

malicious abuse of legal process. See ABUSE OF PROCESS.

malicious abuse of process. See ABUSE OF PROCESS.

malicious accusation. See ACCUSATION.

malicious act. (17c) An intentional, wrongful act done willfully or intentionally against another without legal justification or excuse.

malicious arrest. See ARREST.

malicious assault with a deadly weapon. See ASSAULT.

malicious bankruptcy. See BANKRUPTCY.

malicious damage. See MALICIOUS MISCHIEF.

malicious defense. See DEFENSE (2).

malicious execution. See EXECUTION.

malicious injury. See INJURY.

malicious institution of civil proceedings. See MALICIOUS PROSECUTION.

malicious killing. (17c) An intentional killing without legal justification or excuse. — Also termed *killing with malice.* Cf. ACCIDENTAL KILLING.

maliciously damaging the property of another. See MALICIOUS MISCHIEF.

malicious mischief. (18c) The common-law misdemeanor of intentionally destroying or damaging another's property. • Although modern statutes predominantly make this offense a misdemeanor, a few make it a felony (depending on the nature of the property or its value). See Model Penal Code § 220.3. — Also termed *malicious mischief and trespass; malicious injury; malicious trespass; malicious damage; maliciously damaging the property of another;* (in the Model Penal Code) *criminal mischief.*

malicious motive. See MOTIVE.

malicious prosecution. (17c) **1.** The institution of a criminal or civil proceeding for an improper purpose and without probable cause. • The tort requires proof of four elements: (1) the initiation or continuation of a lawsuit; (2) lack of probable cause for the lawsuit's initiation; (3) malice; and (4) favorable termination of the original lawsuit. Restatement (Second) of Torts §§ 674–81B (1977). **2.** The tort claim resulting from the institution of such a proceeding. • Once a wrongful prosecution has ended in the defendant's favor, he or she may sue for tort damages. — Also termed (in the context of civil proceedings) *malicious use of process;* (archaically) *malicious institution of civil proceedings.* Cf. ABUSE OF PROCESS; VEXATIOUS SUIT; MALICIOUS DEFENSE.

malicious technology. Any electronic or mechanical means, esp. software, used to monitor or gain access to another's computer system without authorization for the purpose of impairing or disabling the system. • Examples of malicious technology are Trojan horses, time-outs, keystroke logging, and data-scrambling devices. — Also termed *malware.*

malicious trespass. See MALICIOUS MISCHIEF.

malicious use of process. See MALICIOUS PROSECUTION.

malinger, *vb.* (1820) To feign illness or disability, esp. in an attempt to avoid an obligation or to continue receiving disability benefits.

malison (mal-ə-zən *or* -sən). [fr. Latin *malum* "evil" + *sonus* "a sound"] *Hist.* A curse. — Also spelled *maleson*.

malitia praecogitata (pree-koj-ə-**tay**-tə). See MALICE AFORETHOUGHT. — Also termed *malitia excogitata*.

malleable, *adj.* (14c) **1.** (Of an object) capable of extension by hammering <the metal was malleable>. **2.** (Of a person) capable of being influenced <the young student was malleable>.

Mallory **rule.** See MCNABB–MALLORY RULE.

Maloney Act. A 1938 amendment to the Securities Exchange Act of 1934, providing for broker registration in over-the-counter markets.

malpractice (mal-**prak**-tis). (17c) An instance of negligence or incompetence on the part of a professional. • To succeed in a malpractice claim, a plaintiff must also prove proximate cause and damages. — Also termed *professional negligence.*

legal malpractice. A lawyer's failure to render professional services with the skill, prudence, and diligence that an ordinary and reasonable lawyer would use under similar circumstances. — Also termed *attorney malpractice.*

medical malpractice. A doctor's failure to exercise the degree of care and skill that a physician or surgeon of the same medical specialty would use under similar circumstances. — Often shortened to *med. mal.*

malpractice insurance. See INSURANCE.

malsworn. See MALESWORN.

maltreatment. (18c) Bad treatment (esp. improper treatment by a surgeon) resulting from ignorance, neglect, or willfulness. See MALPRACTICE.

malum (**mal**-əm *also* **may**-ləm), *n.* [Latin] Something bad or evil. Pl. *mala.*

malum in se (**mal**-əm in **say** *or* **see**), *n.* [Latin "evil in itself"] (17c) A crime or an act that is inherently immoral, such as murder, arson, or rape. — Also termed *malum per se.* Cf. MALUM PROHIBITUM. Pl. *mala in se.* — *malum in se, adj.*

malum prohibitum (**mal**-əm proh-**hib**-i-təm), *n.* [Latin "prohibited evil"] (18c) An act that is a crime merely because it is prohibited by statute, although the act itself is not necessarily immoral. • Misdemeanors such as jaywalking and running a stoplight are *mala prohibita,* as are many regulatory violations. Cf. MALUM IN SE. Pl. *mala prohibita.* — *malum prohibitum, adj.*

malum regimen (**mal**-əm **rej**-ə-men). [Law Latin] *Scots law.* Bad medical treatment. • A defendant in a homicide case may assert as a defense that the decedent actually died as a result of bad medical treatment, not the defendant's actions.

malversation (mal-vər-**say**-shən), *n.* [French "ill behavior"] Official corruption; misbehavior by an official in the exercise of the duties of the office. — **malverse,** *vb.*

malware. (1990) *Slang.* See MALICIOUS TECHNOLOGY.

man. (bef. 12c) **1.** An adult male. **2.** Humankind. — Also termed *mankind.* **3.** A human being. **4.** *Hist.* A vassal; a feudal tenant.

manacle (**man**-ə-kəl). (14c) A shackle; a handcuff.

managed care. (1982) A system of comprehensive healthcare provided by a health-maintenance organization, a preferred-provider organization, or a similar group.

managed-care organization. An association of professional healthcare providers that offers healthcare-service plans to subscribers. Cf. HEALTH-MAINTENANCE ORGANIZATION; PREFERRED-PROVIDER ORGANIZATION.

management. (16c) The people in an organization who are vested with a certain amount of discretion and independent judgment in managing its affairs.

middle management. People who exercise some discretion and independent judgment in carrying out top management's directives.

top management. The highest level of a company's management, at which major policy decisions and long-term business plans are made. — Also termed *upper management.*

management buyout. See BUYOUT.

management company. See COMPANY.

Management Directorate. The division of the Department of Homeland Security responsible for handling the Department's financial and personnel affairs.

management fee. See FEE (1).

manager. (16c) **1.** A person who administers or supervises the affairs of a business, office, or other organization.

general manager. A manager who has overall control of a business, office, or other organization, including authority over other managers. • A general manager is usu. equivalent to a president or chief executive officer of a corporation.

2. A legislator appointed to a conference committee charged with adjusting differences in a bill passed by both houses in different versions. — Also termed *conferee; manager of a conference.* **3.** *Parliamentary law.* A member who displays the evidence against another member who is charged with misconduct and faces possible disciplinary action. **4.** A representative appointed by the House of Representatives to prosecute an impeachment before the Senate. **5.** A member of a board of managers; DIRECTOR (2). See BOARD OF DIRECTORS. **6.** A court-of-equity appointee responsible for carrying on a business for the benefit of creditors or other beneficiaries.

manager of a conference. See MANAGER (2).

managing agent. See AGENT (2).

managing conservator. See CONSERVATOR.

managing conservatorship. See CUSTODY (2).

Manahan-type carried interest. *Oil & gas.* A transaction in which the owner of a lease assigns all the working interest to someone else — who takes on specified costs of drilling and development — and the assignor retains a reversionary interest in part of the working interest, which reverts to the assignor once the assignee has recovered the specified costs during the payout period. *Manahan Oil Co. v. Commissioner,* 8 T.C. 1159 (1947).

manbote. See BOTE (2).

mancipation (man-si-**pay**-shən), *n.* [fr. Latin *mancipatio* "hand-grasp"] **1.** *Roman law.* A legal formality for transferring property by either an actual or a simulated purchase; a formal conveyance in the guise of a sale. • The formality required the presence of the thing being conveyed (*res mancipi*), and of five adult male citizens acting as witnesses. Another person (the *libripens*) held the bronze scales with which the purchase price had been weighed out. The buyer made an assertion of ownership, struck the scales with a piece of bronze or copper, then gave the metal piece to the seller as a symbolic price. In Roman classical law, either this procedure or *cessio in jure* was necessary to pass legal title. This form of sale was abolished by Justinian. **2.** A similar form used for making a will, adoption, emancipation of children, etc. — Also termed *mancipatio.* Cf. EMANCIPATION. — **mancipate,** *vb.* — **mancipatory** (man-si-pə-**tohr**-ee), *adj.*

M & A. *abbr.* Mergers and acquisitions. See MERGER.

mandamus (man-**day**-məs), *n.* [Latin "we command"] (16c) A writ issued by a court to compel performance of a particular act by a lower court or a governmental officer or body, usu. to correct a prior action or failure to act. — Also termed *writ of mandamus; mandate;* (in BrE) *order.* Pl. **mandamuses.** — **mandamus,** *vb.*

alternative mandamus. A writ issued upon the first application for relief, commanding the defendant either to perform the act demanded or to appear before the court at a specified time to show cause for not performing it.

peremptory mandamus. An absolute and unqualified command to the defendant to do the act in question. • It is issued when the defendant defaults on, or fails to show sufficient cause in answer to, an alternative mandamus.

mandans (**man**-danz), *n.* [Latin] *Roman law.* The principal for whom a mandated person undertakes to perform a gratuitous service. See MANDATOR (2).

mandatary (**man**-də-ter-ee), *n.* (15c) **1.** A person to whom a mandate is given. See MANDATE (5). **2.** An agent, esp. one who acts gratuitously but is entitled to be indemnified for expenses incurred in carrying out the mandate. — Also termed (in Roman law) *mandatarius.* **3.** *Civil law.* The person who is employed to a mandator in a gratuitous agency. — Also termed *mandatee; mandatarius.* See MANDATE (5). — **mandatary,** *adj.*

mandate, *n.* (16c) **1.** An order from an appellate court directing a lower court to take a specified action. — Also termed (in BrE) *order.* See MANDAMUS. **2.** A judicial command directed to an officer of the court to enforce a court order. **3.** In politics, the electorate's overwhelming show of approval for a given political candidate or platform. **4.** *Roman & civil law.* A written command given by a principal to an agent; specif., a commission or contract by which one person (the *mandator*) requests someone (the *mandatary*) to perform some service gratuitously, the commission becoming effective when the mandatary agrees. La. Civ. Code art. 2989. • In this type of contract, no liability is created until the service requested has begun. The mandatary is bound to use reasonable care in performance, while the mandator is bound to indemnify against loss incurred in performing the service. — Also termed *mandatum.* **5.** *Louisiana law.* A contract by which one person, the principal, confers authority on another person, the mandatary, to transact one or more affairs for the principal. La. Civ. Code arts. 2989 et seq. • The contract of mandate may be either onerous or gratuitous. It is gratuitous if the parties do not state otherwise. **6.** *Hist. Int'l law.* An authority given by the League of Nations to certain governments to take over the administration and development of designated territories. Cf. TRUSTEESHIP (2). — **mandate,** *vb.*

mandate rule. (1958) The doctrine that, after an appellate court has remanded a case to a lower court, the lower court must follow the decision that the appellate court has made in the case, unless new evidence or an intervening change in the law dictates a different result.

mandator (man-**day**-tər *or* man-day-tər). (17c) **1.** A person who delegates the performance of a mandate to another. **2.** *Civil law.* The person who employs another (called a *mandatary* or *man-*

datarius) in a gratuitous agency. See MANDATE (5). — Also termed *mandant*. **3.** BAILOR (1).

mandatory, *adj.* (15c) Of, relating to, or constituting a command; required; preemptory.

mandatory commitment. See COMMITMENT.

mandatory injunction. See INJUNCTION.

mandatory instruction. See JURY INSTRUCTION.

mandatory joinder. See *compulsory joinder* under JOINDER.

mandatory penalty. See *mandatory sentence* under SENTENCE.

mandatory power. See POWER (5).

mandatory presumption. See *conclusive presumption* under PRESUMPTION.

mandatory punishment. See *mandatory sentence* under SENTENCE.

mandatory rule. See RULE (1).

mandatory sentence. See SENTENCE.

mandatory sentencing. See SENTENCING.

mandatory statute. See STATUTE.

mandatory subject of bargaining. *Labor law.* A topic that is required by the National Labor Relations Act to be discussed in good faith by the parties during labor negotiations; an essential employment matter, including wages, hours, and other terms and conditions of employment, about which management and the union are required to negotiate in good faith, and that can lawfully form the basis of a collective-bargaining impasse. 29 USCA § 158(d). — Often shortened to *mandatory subject.* Cf. PERMISSIVE SUBJECT OF BARGAINING.

mandatory trust. See TRUST.

mandatory waiver. The mandatory transfer, without judicial discretion, of a case from juvenile court to criminal court once the prosecutor has charged a juvenile with one of certain statutorily enumerated serious crimes. See TRANSFER STATUTE. Cf. STATUTORY EXCLUSION.

mandatum (man-**day**-təm). *Roman & civil law.* A bailment in which the bailee will, without recompense, perform some service relating to the goods; MANDATE (4). ● This type of bailment is for the sole benefit of the bailor.

man-endangering state of mind. See PERSON-ENDANGERING STATE OF MIND.

manhood. (13c) **1.** A male person's majority. **2.** *Hist.* A ceremony of a vassal paying homage to the vassal's lord. — Also termed *homagium.*

manifest, *n.* (16c) A document listing the cargo or passengers carried on a ship, airplane, or other vehicle; esp., a shipping or warehousing document containing a list of the contents, value,

origin, carrier, and destination of the goods. Cf. CONTENT.

manifestation of intention. (1826) *Wills & estates.* The external expression of the testator's intention, as distinguished from an undisclosed intention. — Also termed *manifestation of intent.*

manifestation theory. *Insurance.* The doctrine that coverage for an injury or disease falls to the policy in effect when the symptoms of the covered injury or disease first appear. Cf. EXPOSURE THEORY; ACTUAL-INJURY TRIGGER; TRIPLE TRIGGER.

manifest constitutional error. See ERROR (2).

manifest-disregard doctrine. (1983) The principle that an arbitration award will be vacated if the arbitrator knows the applicable law and deliberately chooses to disregard it, but will not be vacated for a mere error or misunderstanding of the law.

manifest error. See ERROR (2).

manifest-error-or-clearly-wrong rule. (1981) In some jurisdictions, the doctrine that an appellate court cannot set aside a trial court's finding of fact unless a review of the entire record reveals that the finding has no reasonable basis.

manifest injustice. A direct, obvious, and observable error in a trial court, such as a defendant's guilty plea that is involuntary or is based on a plea agreement that the prosecution has rescinded.

manifest intent. See INTENT (1).

manifest necessity. See NECESSITY.

manifesto. (17c) A written statement publicly declaring the issuer's principles, policies, or intentions; esp. a formal document explaining why a state or nation declared war or took some other significant international action.

manifest weight of the evidence. A deferential standard of review under which a verdict will be reversed or disregarded only if another outcome is obviously correct and the verdict is clearly unsupported by the evidence. Cf. WEIGHT OF THE EVIDENCE.

manipulation. *Securities.* (1888) The illegal practice of raising or lowering a security's price by creating the appearance of active trading. ● Manipulation is prohibited by section 10(b) of the Securities Exchange Act of 1934. 15 USCA § 78j(b). — Also termed *market manipulation; stock manipulation.*

mankind. See MAN (2).

Mann Act. A federal law, enacted originally in 1910, making it illegal to transport an individual in interstate or foreign commerce for prostitution or other criminal sexual activity. ● It is named its sponsor, Rep. James Robert Mann. 18 USCA § 2421–2424. — Also termed *White Slave Traffic Act.*

manor. (14c) **1.** A feudal estate, usu. granted by the king to a lord or other high person and cultivated as a unit. ● In more ancient times, the lord's manor included a village community, usu. composed of serfs.

    reputed manor. A manor in which the lands not granted in tenancy but reserved for the lord's own use (demesne lands) and services become absolutely separated. ● The manor is no longer a manor in actuality, only in reputation. — Also termed *seigniory in gross.*

2. A jurisdictional right over tenants of an estate, usu. exercised through a court baron. **3.** *Hist.* In the United States, a tract of land occupied by tenants who pay rent to a proprietor. **4.** A mansion on an estate.

manorial system. The medieval system of land ownership in which serfs and some freemen cultivated the soil of a manor in return for a lord's protection. See MANOR (1).

manse (mans), *n.* [Law Latin] *Hist.* **1.** A portion of land large enough to maintain one family.; a sufficient amount of land to be worked by a yoke of oxen for a year. **2.** A house without land; MESSUAGE. **3.** The residence of a minister, esp. a Presbyterian minister. **4.** A large, imposing residence. — Also termed *mansus.*

Mansfield rule. (1968) The doctrine that a juror's testimony or affidavit about juror misconduct may not be used to challenge the verdict. ● This Mansfield rule is intended to ensure that jurors are heard through their verdict, not through their postverdict testimony. In practice, the rule lessens the possibility that losing parties will seek to penetrate the secrets of the jury room. The rule was first announced in *Vaise v. Delaval*, 99 Eng. Rep. 944 (K.B. 1785), in an opinion by William Murray, first Earl of Mansfield, the Lord Chief Justice of the Court of King's Bench.

mansion-house. 1. *Hist.* The residence of the lord of a manor. **2.** DWELLING-HOUSE.

mansion-house rule. The doctrine that a tract of land lying in two counties will be assessed, for property-tax purposes, in the county in which the house is located.

manslaughter, *n.* (15c) The unlawful killing of a human being without malice aforethought. — Also termed (in some jurisdictions) *culpable homicide.* Cf. MURDER. — **manslaughter,** *vb.*

    first-degree manslaughter. See *voluntary manslaughter.*

    intentional manslaughter. See *voluntary manslaughter.*

    intoxication manslaughter. An unintentional homicide committed by an intoxicated person while operating a vehicle or some other type of machinery.

    involuntary manslaughter. (18c) Homicide in which there is no intention to kill or do grievous bodily harm, but that is committed with criminal negligence or during the commission of a crime not included within the felony-murder rule. — Also termed *negligent manslaughter; second-degree manslaughter; manslaughter in the second degree.* Cf. ACCIDENTAL KILLING.

    manslaughter in the first degree. See *voluntary manslaughter.*

    manslaughter in the second degree. See *involuntary manslaughter.*

    misdemeanor manslaughter. (1947) Unintentional homicide that occurs during the commission of a misdemeanor (such as a traffic violation).

    negligent manslaughter. See *involuntary manslaughter.*

    second-degree manslaughter. See *involuntary manslaughter.*

    voluntary manslaughter. (18c) An act of murder reduced to manslaughter because of extenuating circumstances such as adequate provocation (arousing the "heat of passion") or diminished capacity. — Also termed *intentional manslaughter; first-degree manslaughter; manslaughter in the first degree; unintentional murder.*

manstealing. See KIDNAPPING.

mansus. See MANSE.

manticulate (man-**tik**-yə-layt), *vb.* To pick pockets. — **manticulation,** *n.*

mantle child. See CHILD.

mantrap. See TRAP.

manual, *adj.* Used or performed by hand <manual labor>.

manual delivery. Delivery of personal property by actual and corporeal change in possession.

Manual for Courts-Martial. A manual that implements the Uniform Code of Military Justice. ● It was adopted in 1969 by presidential executive order.

manual gift. See GIFT.

manual labor. Work performed chiefly through muscular exertion, with or without tools or machinery.

Manual of Classification. *Patents.* The U.S. Patent and Trademark Office's official looseleaf publication describing the patent classification system and giving brief explanations of each class and subclass within the system.

Manual of Patent Examining Procedure. The book of substantive law (judicial and administrative-law precedents) and procedural rules for patent examiners at the U.S. Patent and Trademark Office. ● The MPEP is the primary resource that patent examiners use to process patent applications. — Abbr. MPEP.

Manual of the Judge Advocate General. The Secretary of the Navy's directive on military justice, with minor variations between rules applicable to the Navy and those applicable to the Marine Corps. — Also termed *JAG Manual*.

manual-rating insurance. See INSURANCE.

manucaption (man-yoo-**kap**-shən), *n. Hist.* **1.** MAINPRISE. **2.** A writ ordering someone to produce an alleged felon in court.

manucaptor. See MAINPERNOR (2).

manufacture, *n.* (16c) *Patents.* A thing that is made or built by a human being (or by a machine), as distinguished from something that is a product of nature; esp. any material form produced by a machine from an unshaped composition of matter. • Manufactures are one of the statutory categories of inventions that can be patented. Examples of manufactures are chairs and tires. 35 USCA § 101. — Also termed *article of manufacture*. Cf. MACHINE; PROCESS (3).

manufactured diversity. See DIVERSITY OF CITIZENSHIP.

manufactured home. See HOME.

manufacturer. (17c) A person or entity engaged in producing or assembling new products. • A federal law has broadened the definition to include those who act for (or are controlled by) any such person or entity in the distribution of new products, as well as those who import new products for resale. 42 USCA § 4902(6).

manufacturer's liability. See PRODUCTS LIABILITY.

manufacturer's lien. See LIEN.

manufacturing clause. *Hist.* **1.** A component of the Copyright Act of 1976 prohibiting imports of more than 2,000 copies of a nondramatic English-language literary work by an American author, unless the material was manufactured in Canada or the U.S. • The manufacturing clause expired in 1986. **2.** A component of the Copyright Act of 1909 limiting copyright protection for English-language books and periodicals to those printed in the U.S.

manufacturing cost. See COST (1).

manufacturing defect. See DEFECT.

manumission (man-yə-**mish**-ən), *n.* [Latin *manumissio* "I send out of hand"] (15c) *Roman law.* The granting of freedom to a slave. • In the Republic and early Empire, there were three usual methods, all of which made the freed slave a citizen. These were (1) *manumission vindicta* (by the rod), a fictitious lawsuit in which a liberator touched the slave with a wand or rod in the presence of the praetor and alleged that he was free; (2)

manumission censu, by which the slave's name was enrolled in the census as a citizen; and (3) *manumission testamento,* by will. Under Justinian, a grant of freedom in any form (except in fraud of creditors) made the slave free and a citizen. — Also termed *manumissio.*

manumit (man-yə-**mit**), *vb.* To free (a slave). — **manumitter,** *n.*

manuscript. (16c) An unpublished writing; an author's typescript or written work product that is proposed for publication.

manuscript policy. See INSURANCE POLICY.

***Mapp* hearing.** (1971) *Criminal procedure.* A hearing held to determine whether evidence implicating the accused was obtained as the result of an illegal search and seizure, and should therefore be suppressed. *Mapp v. Ohio,* 367 U.S. 643, 81 S.Ct. 1684 (1961).

maquiladora (mah-kee-lə-**dohr**-ə), *n.* [fr. Spanish *maquilar* "gristmill"] (1976) A Mexican corporation, esp. one that holds a permit to operate under a special customs regime that temporarily allows the corporation to import duty-free into Mexico various raw materials, equipment, machinery, replacement parts, and other items needed for the assembly or manufacture of finished goods for export. — Often shortened to *maquila.*

maraud (mə-**rawd**), *vb.* (18c) To rove about to pillage or plunder; to loot. — **marauder,** *n.*

march-in rights. *Patents.* The government's right to step in and grant a new license or revoke an existing license if the owner of a federally funded invention (or the owner's licensee) has not adequately developed or applied the invention within a reasonable time. 35 USCA § 203.

Marcus model. *Labor law.* A method for determining whether a union member's state-law claim against the employer is preempted by federal law, by focusing on whether the state-law claim can be maintained independently of an interpretation of the collective-bargaining agreement. • In *Lingle v. Norge Div. of Magic Chef, Inc.,* 486 U.S. 399, 108 S.Ct. 1877 (1988), the Supreme Court held that a union member's state-law retaliatory-discharge claim was not preempted by the Labor-Management Relations Act because the claim could be resolved without interpreting the collective-bargaining agreement. There are at least two models for applying the *Lingle* test: the White model, which focuses on whether the claim is negotiable or nonnegotiable (that is, whether state law allows the claim to be waived by a private contract), and the Marcus model, which focuses on the independence of the claim in relation to the collective-bargaining agreement. Under the Marcus model, if the claim can be maintained separately from an interpretation of the collective-bargaining agreement, it is not preempted regardless of whether the claim is generally waivable in contract. The Marcus model is named for the author of the law-review note in which it was proposed. Stephanie R. Marcus, Note, *The Need for a New Approach to Federal Preemption of Union Members' State Law Claims*, 99 Yale L.J. 209 (1989). See LINGLE TEST. Cf. WHITE MODEL.

mare (**mair**-ee *or* **mahr**-ee), *n. Hist.* [Latin] The sea. See SEA.

mare clausum (**mair**-ee *or* **mahr**-ee klaw-zəm). [Latin "closed sea"] A sea or other body of navigable water that is under the jurisdiction of a particular nation and is closed to other nations.

mare liberum (**mair**-ee *or* **mahr**-ee lib-ər-əm *or* **lɪ**-bər-əm). [Latin "free sea"] **1.** A sea or other body of navigable water that is open to all nations. **2.** FREEDOM OF THE SEAS.

margin, *n.* (14c) **1.** A boundary or edge. **2.** A measure or degree of difference. **3.** PROFIT MARGIN. **4.** The difference between a loan's face value and the market value of the collateral that secures the loan. **5.** Cash or collateral required to be paid to a securities broker by an investor to protect the broker against losses from securities bought on credit. **6.** The amount of an investor's equity in securities bought on credit through the broker. — **margin,** *vb.* — **marginal, margined,** *adj.*

good-faith margin. The amount of margin that a creditor exercising good judgment would customarily require for a specified security position. • This amount is established without regard to the customer's other assets or securities positions held with respect to unrelated transactions.

marginable security. See SECURITY.

margin account. See ACCOUNT.

marginal cost. See COST (1).

marginal note. A brief notation, in the nature of a subheading, placed in the margin of a printed statute to give a brief indication of the matters dealt with in the section or subsection beside which it appears. • For ease of reference, marginal notes are usu. in distinctive print. Many jurisdictions hold that notes of this kind cannot be used as the basis for an argument about the interpretation of a statute. — Also termed *sidenote.*

marginal release. See RELEASE (2).

marginal revenue. See REVENUE.

marginal tax rate. See TAX RATE.

margin call. See CALL (2).

margin deficiency. *Securities.* The extent to which the amount of the required margin exceeds the equity in a margin account.

margined security. See SECURITY.

margin list. A Federal Reserve Board list limiting the loan value of a particular bank's stock to a certain percentage (e.g., 50%) of its market value. • When a bank is not on the list, no limit is placed on the loan value of stock used as collateral.

margin requirement. *Securities.* The percentage of the purchase price that a buyer must deposit with a broker to buy a security on margin. • This percentage of the purchase price is set and adjusted by the Federal Reserve Board.

initial margin requirement. The minimum percentage of the purchase price that a buyer must deposit with a broker. • The Federal Reserve Board establishes minimum margin requirements to prevent excessive speculation and price volatility.

maintenance margin requirement. The minimum equity that a buyer must keep in a margin account, expressed as a percentage of the account value.

margin stock. See *marginable security* under SECURITY.

margin transaction. A securities or commodities transaction made through a broker on a margin account. — Also termed *buying on margin.* See MARGIN (5).

mariage de convenance. See *marriage of convenience* under MARRIAGE (1).

marine, *adj.* (15c) **1.** Of or relating to the sea <marine life>. **2.** Of or relating to sea navigation or commerce <marine insurance> <marine interest>.

marine belt. See *territorial waters* under WATER.

marine carrier. See CARRIER.

marine contract. See *maritime contract* under CONTRACT.

Marine Court in the City of New York. The New York City court, originally created to resolve seamen's disputes, that was the predecessor of the City Court of New York.

marine insurance. See INSURANCE.

marine interest. See MARITIME INTEREST.

marine league. See LEAGUE.

marine loan. See *maritime loan* under LOAN.

marine peril. See PERIL OF THE SEA.

marine protest. A writing attested by a justice of the peace, a notary public, or a consul, made or verified by the master of a vessel, stating that the vessel has suffered a severe voyage and that the master has engaged in neither misconduct nor negligence. See PROTEST.

mariner. (14c) A person employed on a vessel in sea navigation; SEAMAN.

marine-rescue doctrine. The rule that when a person on a ship goes overboard, the ship must use all reasonable means to retrieve the person from the water if the person can be seen, and, if the person cannot be seen, must search for the person as long as it is reasonably possible that the person is still alive.

marine risk. See PERIL OF THE SEA.

mariner's will. See *soldier's will* under WILL.

marine rule. The doctrine that if the cost of restoring damaged property would exceed one-half the value of the property before the damage, then the property is deemed to be totally destroyed. ● The marine rule developed in the context of applying marine insurance to damaged ships, but it has also been applied to other property, including buildings.

mariner's hypothec. See HYPOTHEC.

marine service. See MARITIME SERVICE.

maritagium (mar-ə-**tay**-jee-əm), *n.* [Law Latin] *Hist.* **1.** A lord's right to arrange a marriage for his infant ward; specif., the power of a feudal lord to give his infant ward or a vassal's heiress, minor heir, or widow in marriage, or to extract a fine from a vassal upon the vassal's marriage. **2.** *Hist.* The income derived from fines paid by vassals for the lord's permission to marry. **3.** DOWER. **4.** A marriage gift; DOWRY. — Also termed (in sense 4) *maritage*.

marital, *adj.* (17c) Of or relating to the marriage relationship <marital property>.

marital agreement. (1866) An agreement between spouses or two people engaged to be married concerning the division and ownership of marital property during marriage or upon dissolution by death or divorce; esp. a premarital contract or separation agreement primarily concerned with dividing marital property in the event of divorce. — Also termed *marriage settlement; property settlement.* See PRENUPTIAL AGREEMENT; POSTNUPTIAL AGREEMENT.

marital-communications privilege. See *marital privilege* (1) under PRIVILEGE (3).

marital deduction. See DEDUCTION.

marital-deduction trust. See TRUST.

marital dissolution. See DIVORCE.

marital domicile. See *matrimonial domicile* under DOMICILE.

marital estate. See *marital property* under PROPERTY.

marital home. See FAMILY HOME.

marital immunity. See *husband–wife immunity* under IMMUNITY (2).

marital life-estate trust. See *bypass trust* under TRUST.

marital misconduct. Any of the various statutory grounds for a fault divorce, such as adultery or cruelty. See *fault divorce* under DIVORCE.

marital portion. 1. *Civil law.* The portion of a deceased spouse's estate to which the surviving spouse is entitled. **2.** *Louisiana law.* The portion of a deceased spouse's estate to which the surviving spouse is entitled if the spouse died "rich in comparison with the surviving spouse." La. Civ. Code art. 2432.

marital-privacy doctrine. A principle that limits governmental intrusion into private family matters, such as those involving sexual relations between married persons. ● The marital-privacy doctrine was first recognized in *Griswold v. Connecticut*, 381 U.S. 479, 85 S.Ct. 1678 (1965). The doctrine formerly deterred state intervention into incidents involving domestic violence. Today, with the trend toward individual privacy rights, the doctrine does not discourage governmental protection from domestic violence. — Also termed *doctrine of marital privacy.*

marital privilege. See PRIVILEGE (3).

marital property. See PROPERTY.

marital rape. See RAPE.

marital residence. See FAMILY HOME.

marital rights. (18c) Rights and incidents (such as property or cohabitation rights) arising from the marriage contract.

marital settlement agreement. See DIVORCE AGREEMENT.

marital status. The condition of being single, married, legally separated, divorced, or widowed.

marital tort. See TORT.

mariticide. (1992) **1.** The murder of one's husband. **2.** A woman who murders her husband. Cf. UXORICIDE. — **mariticidal,** *adj.*

maritime (mar-i-tim), *adj.* (16c) **1.** Connected with or situated near the sea. **2.** Of or relating to sea navigation or commerce.

Maritime Administration. A unit in the U.S. Department of Transportation responsible for subsidizing certain costs of operating ships under the U.S. flag; constructing or supervising the construction of merchant-type ships for the U.S. government; administering the War Risk Insurance Program; and operating the Merchant Marine Academy, which trains merchant-marine officers. — Abbr. MARAD.

maritime belt. See *territorial waters* under WATER.

Maritime Commission. See FEDERAL MARITIME COMMISSION.

maritime-connection doctrine. See LOCALITY-PLUS TEST.

maritime contract. See CONTRACT.

maritime court. See ADMIRALTY (1).

maritime employment. Under the Longshoremen's and Harbor Workers' Compensation Act, a job that is related to the loading, unloading, construction, or repair of a vessel. 33 USCA § 902(3).

maritime flavor. The relation of a given case to shipping concerns. ● This is a factor used in determining federal admiralty jurisdiction over a particular matter by analyzing whether the matter sufficiently relates to marine and shipping concerns and whether there is need for a federal response.

maritime interest. Interest charged on a loan secured by a sea vessel or its cargo, or both. ● Because of the lender's considerable risk, the interest rate may be extraordinarily high. — Also termed *marine interest.*

maritime jurisdiction. See ADMIRALTY AND MARITIME JURISDICTION.

maritime law. The body of law governing marine commerce and navigation, the carriage at sea of persons and property, and marine affairs in general; the rules governing contract, tort, and workers'-compensation claims or relating to commerce on or over water. — Also termed *admiralty; admiralty law; sea law.* Cf. GENERAL MARITIME LAW; LAW OF THE SEA.

maritime lien. See LIEN.

maritime loan. See LOAN.

maritime peril. A danger or risk arising from navigating or being at sea.

maritime service. *Maritime law.* Work performed in connection with a ship or commerce on navigable waters, such as service to preserve a ship's crew, cargo, or equipment. — Also termed *marine service.*

maritime state. *Hist.* The collective officers and mariners of the British navy.

maritime tort. See TORT.

mark, *n.* (bef. 12c) **1.** A symbol, impression, or feature on something, usu. to identify it or distinguish it from something else. **2.** TRADEMARK (1). **3.** SERVICEMARK.

benchmark. See BENCHMARK.

certification mark. See *certification trademark* under TRADEMARK.

collective mark. See *collective trademark* under TRADEMARK.

markdown. A reduction in a selling price.

marked money. (1883) Money that bears a telltale mark so that the money can be traced, usu. to a perpetrator of a crime, as when marked money is given to a kidnapper as ransom.

market, *n.* (bef. 12c) **1.** A place of commercial activity in which goods or services are bought and sold <the farmers' market>. — Also termed *mart.* **2.** A geographic area or demographic segment considered as a place of demand for particular goods or services; esp. prospective purchasers of goods, wherever they are <the foreign market for microchips>. **3.** *Hist.* The privilege of having a public market. **4.** The opportunity for buying and selling goods or services; the extent of economic demand <a strong job market for accountants>. **5.** A securities or commodities exchange <the stock market closed early because of the blizzard>. **6.** The business of such an exchange; the enterprise of buying and selling securities or commodities <the stock market is approaching an all-time high>. **7.** The price at which the buyer and seller of a security or commodity agree <the market for wheat is $8 per bushel>.

advancing market. See *bull market.*

aftermarket. See *secondary market.*

auction market. A market (such as the New York Stock Exchange) in which securities are bought and sold by competitive bidding through brokers. Cf. *negotiated market.*

bear market. A securities market characterized by falling prices over a prolonged period. — Also termed *down market; receding market.*

black market. An illegal market for goods that are controlled or prohibited by the government, such as the underground market for prescription drugs.

bull market. A securities market characterized by rising prices over a prolonged period. — Also termed *advancing market; strong market.*

buyer's market. A market in which supply significantly exceeds demand, resulting in lower prices.

capital market. A securities market in which stocks and bonds with long-term maturities are traded. See *financial market.*

common market. An economic association formed by several nations to reduce or eliminate trade barriers among them, and to establish uniform trade barriers against nonmembers; esp. (*usu. cap.*), EUROPEAN UNION.

currency market. See *foreign-exchange market.*

derivative market. A market for the exchange of derivative instruments. — Also termed *paper market.* See DERIVATIVE.

discount market. The portion of the money market in which banks and other financial institutions trade commercial paper.

down market. See *bear market.*

financial market. A market for the exchange of capital and debt instruments. See *capital market*; *money market*.

foreign-exchange market. A market where various currencies are traded internationally. • Foreign-exchange markets take the form of spot, futures, and options markets. — Also termed *currency market*. See *futures market*; *spot market*.

forward market. See *futures market*.

free market. See *open market*.

Friday market. The normal tendency for stock-prices to decline on Fridays. • The tendency occurs because many investors balance their accounts before the weekend to avoid any adverse changes in market prices over the weekend.

futures market. A commodity exchange in which futures contracts are traded; a market for a trade (e.g., commodities futures contracts and stock options) that is negotiated at the current price but calls for delivery at a future time. — Also termed *forward market*. See FUTURES CONTRACT.

geographic market. *Antitrust.* The part of a relevant market that identifies the regions in which a firm might compete. • If a firm can raise prices or cut production without causing a quick influx of supply to the area from outside sources, that firm is operating in a distinct geographic market.

gray market. A market in which the seller uses legal but sometimes unethical methods to avoid a manufacturer's distribution chain and thereby sell goods (esp. imported goods) at prices lower than those envisioned by the manufacturer. See PARALLEL IMPORTS.

institutional market. The demand among large investors and corporations for short-term funds and commercial paper.

market overt. An open, legally regulated public market where buyers, with some exceptions, acquire good title to products regardless of any defects in the seller's title. Cf. FAIR.

money market. The financial market for dealing in short-term negotiable instruments such as commercial paper, certificates of deposit, banker's acceptances, and U.S. Treasury securities. See *financial market*.

negotiated market. A market (such as an over-the-counter securities market) in which buyers and sellers seek each other out and negotiate prices. Cf. *auction market*.

open market. A market in which any buyer or seller may trade and in which prices and product availability are determined by free competition. — Also termed *free market*.

original market. See *primary market*.

over-the-counter market. See OVER-THE-COUNTER MARKET.

paper market. See *derivative market*.

primary market. The market for goods or services that are newly available for buying and selling; esp. the securities market in which new securities are issued by corporations to raise capital. — Also termed *original market*.

product market. *Antitrust.* The part of a relevant market that applies to a firm's particular product by identifying all reasonable substitutes for the product and by determining whether these substitutes limit the firm's ability to affect prices.

public market. A market open to both buyers and sellers.

receding market. See *bear market*.

recognized market. A market where the items bought and sold are numerous and similar, where competitive bidding and bartering are not prevalent, and where prices paid in sales of comparable items are publicly quoted. • Examples of recognized markets include stock and commodities exchanges. Under the UCC, a secured creditor may, upon the debtor's default, sell the collateral in a recognized market without notifying the debtor. Such a sale is presumed to be commercially reasonable.

relevant market. *Antitrust.* A market that is capable of being monopolized — that is, a market in which a firm can raise prices above the competitive level without losing so many sales that the price increase would be unprofitable. • The relevant market includes both the *product market* and the *geographic market*.

secondary market. The market for goods or services that have previously been available for buying and selling; esp. the securities market in which previously issued securities are traded among investors. — Also termed *aftermarket*.

seller's market. A market in which demand exceeds (or approaches) supply, resulting in raised prices.

soft market. A market (esp. a stock market) characterized by falling or drifting prices and low volume.

spot market. A market (esp. in commodities) in which payment or delivery is immediate <the spot market in oil>.

strong market. See *bull market*.

thin market. A market in which the number of bids or offerings is relatively low.

marketability. (1877) Salability; the probability of selling property, goods, securities, or services at specified times, prices, and terms.

marketability test. *Mining law.* The principle that, for someone to obtain a patent on a mining claim on federal land, there must be a showing that a reasonably prudent person could extract and market the claimed mineral at a profit, and that at the time of discovery, a large enough market for the mineral existed to attract the efforts of a reasonably prudent person.

marketable, *adj.* (16c) Of commercially acceptable quality; fit for sale and in demand by buyers. — Also termed *merchantable.*

marketable-product rule. *Oil & gas.* For royalty-calculation purposes, the doctrine that "production" occurs when oil or gas is pumped up, stored, and made marketable through processing. • Until producing a marketable product, the lessee bears all costs of capturing and handling oil and gas. Cf. CAPTURE-AND-HOLD RULE.

marketable security. See SECURITY.

marketable title. See TITLE (2).

marketable-title act. (1957) A state statute providing that a person can establish good title to land by searching the public records only back to a specified time (such as 40 years). See *marketable title* under TITLE (2).

market activity. See MARKET VOLUME.

market approach. (1958) A method of appraising real property, by surveying the market and comparing the property to similar pieces of property that have been recently sold, and making appropriate adjustments for differences between the properties, including location, size of the property, and the dates of sale. — Also termed *comparative-sales approach*; *market-comparison approach*; *market-data approach*; *market-comparables analysis*; *comparable-sales approach*; *comparables analysis.* Cf. COST APPROACH; INCOME APPROACH.

market average. A price level for a specific group of stocks.

market-comparables analysis. See MARKET APPROACH.

market-comparison approach. See MARKET APPROACH.

market correction. See DOWN REVERSAL.

market-data approach. See MARKET APPROACH.

market equity. The percentage of the total market value that a particular company's securities account for, represented by each class of security. Cf. BOOK EQUITY.

marketing, *n.* (16c) **1.** The act or process of promoting and selling, leasing, or licensing products or services. **2.** The part of a business concerned with meeting customers' needs. **3.** The area of study concerned with the promotion and selling of products or services.

marketing contract. See CONTRACT.

marketing covenant. *Oil & gas.* In a mineral lease, the implied promise that the lessee will market the production from the lease within a reasonable time and at a reasonable price. See REASONABLY-PRUDENT-OPERATOR STANDARD.

marketing defect. See DEFECT.

market intermediary. *Securities.* A person whose business is to enter into transactions on both sides of the market. Investment Company Act, 15 USCA § 80a-3(c)(2)(B)(i).

market-maker. *Securities.* One who helps establish a market for securities by reporting bid-and-asked quotations. • A market-maker is typically a specialist permitted to act as a dealer, a dealer acting in the capacity of block positioner, or a dealer who, with respect to a security, routinely enters quotations in an interdealer communication system or otherwise and is willing to buy and sell securities for the dealer's own account.

market-making, *n.* The practice of establishing prices for over-the-counter securities by reporting bid-and-asked quotations. • A broker-dealer engaged in this practice, which is regulated by both the NASD and the SEC, buys and sells securities as a principal for its own account, and thus accepts two-way bids (both to buy and to sell). See BID AND ASKED.

market manipulation. See MANIPULATION.

market order. See ORDER (8).

market-out clause. *Oil & gas.* A contract provision permitting a pipeline-purchaser of natural gas to lower the purchase price if market conditions make it uneconomical to continue buying at the contract price, and permitting the well owner to respond by accepting the lower price or by rejecting it and canceling the contract. • Market-out clauses often refer to competing fuels such as fuel oil. — Also termed *economic-out clause.*

market overt. See MARKET.

market-participant doctrine. (1983) The principle that, under the Commerce Clause, a state does not discriminate against interstate commerce by acting as a buyer or seller in the market, by operating a proprietary enterprise, or by subsidizing private business. • Under the Dormant Commerce Clause principle, the Commerce Clause — art. I, § 8, cl. 3 of the U.S. Constitution — disallows most state regulation of, or discrimination against, interstate commerce. But if the state is participating in the market instead of regulating it, the Dormant Commerce Clause analysis does not apply, and the state activity will generally stand. See *Dormant Commerce Clause* under COMMERCE CLAUSE.

marketplace of ideas. (1949) A forum in which expressions of opinion can freely compete for acceptance without governmental restraint. • Although Justice Oliver Wendell Holmes was the first jurist to discuss the concept as a metaphor for explaining freedom of speech, the phrase *marketplace of ideas* dates in American caselaw only from 1954.

market portfolio. See PORTFOLIO.

market power. (1915) The ability to reduce output and raise prices above the competitive level — specif., above marginal cost — for a sustained period, and to make a profit by doing so. • In antitrust law, a large amount of market power may constitute monopoly power. See MONOPOLIZATION. Cf. MARKET SHARE.

market price. See PRICE.

market quotation. See QUOTATION.

market-recovery program. See JOB-TARGETING PROGRAM.

market share. (1954) The percentage of the market for a product that a firm supplies, usu. calculated by dividing the firm's output by the total market output. • In antitrust law, market share is used to measure a firm's market power, and if the share is high enough — generally 70% or more — then the firm may be guilty of monopolization. See MONOPOLIZATION. Cf. MARKET POWER.

market-share liability. See LIABILITY.

market-share theory. *Antitrust.* **1.** A method of determining damages for lost profits by calculating the impact of the defendant's violation on the plaintiff's output or market share. Cf. BEFORE-AND-AFTER THEORY; YARDSTICK THEORY. **2.** *Patents.* A theory of lost-profits remedy offered when the patentee and the infringer share the market with a noninfringing competitor. • Using this method, the court assumes that the percentage of the market that the patentee holds is the same as the percentage of the infringer's market that the patentee would have captured but for the infringement.

market stand-off agreement. *Securities.* A provision in a stock-purchase contract in which the stockholder promises not to sell or otherwise transfer any securities during a specified period after the corporation makes a public stock offering. Cf. LOCKUP AGREEMENT.

market structure. The broad organizational characteristics of a particular market, including seller concentration, product differentiation, and barriers to entry.

market trend. See TREND.

market value. See *fair market value* under VALUE (2).

market value at the well. *Oil & gas.* The value of oil or gas at the place where it is sold, minus the reasonable cost of transporting it and processing it to make it marketable.

market volume. 1. The total number of shares traded on one day on a stock exchange. **2.** The total number of shares of one stock traded on one day. — Also termed *market activity*.

***Mark Hopkins* doctrine.** The principle that when an employee leaves a job because of a labor dispute, any later employment the employee has must be bona fide and intended as permanent for the employee to avoid a labor-dispute disqualification from unemployment benefits if the employee leaves the later job. *Mark Hopkins, Inc. v. Employment Comm'n,* 151 P.2d 229 (Cal. 1944).

marking estoppel. See ESTOPPEL.

***Markman* hearing.** (1996) *Patents.* A hearing at which the court receives evidence and argument concerning the construction to be given to terms in a patent claim at issue. *Markman v. Westview Instruments, Inc.,* 52 F.3d 967, 984-85 (Fed. Cir. 1995) (en banc), aff'd, 517 U.S. 370, 116 S.Ct.1384 (1996). • In the namesake decision, the Federal Circuit Court of Appeals held that the construction of patent claims — and therefore the scope of the patentee's rights — is a question of law. In a *Markman* hearing, the court interprets the claims before the question of infringement is submitted to the fact-finder.

markon. An amount (usu. expressed as a percentage) initially added to a product's cost to obtain the list price. • Further increases or decreases in price are called *markups* or *markdowns*, respectively.

marksman. 1. A person who signs documents with some kind of character or symbol instead of writing his or her name. **2.** A highly skilled shooter.

***Marks* rule.** The doctrine that, when the U.S. Supreme Court issues a fractured, plurality opinion, the opinion of the justices concurring in the judgment on the narrowest grounds — that is, the legal standard with which a majority of the Court would agree — is considered the Court's holding. *Marks v. United States,* 430 U.S. 188, 97 S.Ct. 990 (1977).

mark-to-market accounting method. See *fair-value accounting method* under ACCOUNTING METHOD.

mark up, *vb.* (1868) **1.** To increase (the price of goods, etc.) **2.** To revise or amend (a legislative bill, a rule, etc.). **3.** To place (a case) on the trial calendar.

markup, *n.* (1916) **1.** An amount added to an item's cost to determine its selling price. See PROFIT MARGIN. **2.** A session of a congressional committee during which a bill is revised and put into final form before it is reported to the appropriate house.

Markush claim. See PATENT CLAIM.

Markush doctrine (mahr-kəsh). *Patents.* An exception to the policy against the use of alternative language in claims, by which in certain claims (esp. those involving chemical components) a claimant can use an alternative, subgeneric phrase when there is no applicable, commonly accepted generic expression. ● Characterized by a phrase such as "selected from the group consisting of," the claim includes a group of substances any one of which could serve the same function in the process. The term *Markush* comes from Dr. Eugene A. Markush, who was granted a dye-preparation patent in 1923. *Ex parte Markush*, 1925 Dec. Comm'r Pat. 126. See MARKUSH GROUP.

Markush group. *Patents.* A limited form of generic claim that recites an element, states the element is a member of a group, and names the other group members, any of which could substitute for the first recited element. ● All Markush group members must have at least one common property that is mainly responsible for their function in the claimed relationship. Although each material in the group is different, each must be able to serve the same function. See MARKUSH DOCTRINE.

marque (mahrk). *Archaic.* Reprisal. See LETTERS OF MARQUE.

marque, law of. *Archaic.* A reprisal entitling one who has been wronged and is unable to receive ordinary justice to take the goods of the wrongdoer (if they can be found within one's own precinct) in satisfaction for the wrong. See LETTERS OF MARQUE.

marquis (mahr-kwis *or* mahr-**kee**). (14c) An English nobleman below and next in order to a duke. — Also termed *marquess.*

marriage, *n.* (13c) **1.** The legal union of a couple as spouses. ● The essentials of a valid marriage are (1) parties legally capable of contracting to marry, (2) mutual consent or agreement, and (3) an actual contracting in the form prescribed by law. Marriage has important consequences in many areas of the law, such as torts, criminal law, evidence, debtor–creditor relations, property, and contracts. — Also termed *matrimony; conjugal union.*

attempted marriage. See *void marriage.*

clandestine marriage (klan-**des**-tin). **1.** A marriage that rests merely on the agreement of the parties. **2.** A marriage entered into in a secret way, as one solemnized by an unauthorized person or without all required formalities. See *Fleet marriage.*

common-law marriage. (17c) A marriage that takes legal effect, without license or ceremony, when two people capable of marrying live together as husband and wife, intend to be

married, and hold themselves out to others as a married couple. ● The common-law marriage traces its roots to the English ecclesiastical courts, which until 1753 recognized a kind of informal marriage known as *sponsalia per verba de praesenti*, which was entered into without ceremony. Today a common-law marriage, which is the full equivalent of a ceremonial marriage, is authorized in 11 states and in the District of Columbia. If a common-law marriage is established in a state that recognizes such marriages, other states, even those that do not authorize common-law marriage, must give full faith and credit to the marriage. A common-law marriage can be dissolved only by annulment, divorce, or death. — Also termed *consensual marriage; informal marriage.* See *common-law husband* under HUSBAND; *common-law wife* under WIFE.

confidential marriage. In some jurisdictions (such as California), a marriage between a man and a woman in which only the two parties and the officiant are present at the ceremony. ● Confidential marriages are neither witnessed nor recorded in public records. They are recorded in nonpublic records. Although rarely performed, they are generally legal. To obtain a confidential marriage, the parties must each be at least 18, must be of the opposite sex, and usu. must have lived together for an extended period. In ecclesiastical law, such a marriage is termed an *occult marriage* or, if performed in the strictest secrecy, a *marriage of conscience.*

consensual marriage. Marriage by consent alone, without any formal process. See *common-law marriage.*

consular marriage. A marriage solemnized in a foreign country by a consul or diplomatic official of the United States. ● Consular marriages are recognized in some jurisdictions.

covenant marriage. (1990) A special type of marriage in which the parties agree to more stringent requirements for marriage and divorce than are otherwise imposed by state law for ordinary marriages. ● In the late 1990s, several states (beginning with Louisiana: see Acts 1997, No. 1380, § 5) passed laws providing for covenant marriages. The requirements vary, but most of these laws require couples who opt for covenant marriage to undergo premarital counseling. A divorce will be granted only after the couple has undergone marital counseling and has been separated for a specified period (usu. at least 18 months). The divorce prerequisites typically can be waived with proof that a spouse has committed adultery, been convicted of a felony, abandoned the family for at least one year, or physically or sexually abused the other spouse or a child. — Also termed (in slang) *high-test marriage.*

cross-marriage. A marriage by a brother and sister to two people who are also brother and sister.

dead marriage. A marriage whose substance has disintegrated; a marriage that has irretrievably broken down.

de facto marriage (di **fak**-toh). A marriage that, despite the parties' living as husband and wife, is defective for some reason.

defunct marriage. A marriage in which both parties, by their conduct, indicate their intent to no longer be married.

Fleet marriage. *Hist.* **1.** A clandestine ceremonial marriage performed in the 17th or 18th century in the Fleet prison in London by a chaplain who had been imprisoned for debt. **2.** A clandestine ceremonial marriage performed by an unscrupulous itinerant clergymen in the area in London near the Fleet Prison. • Parliament attempted to stop the practice, but it was not until the statute of 26 George 2, ch. 33, declaring marriages performed outside public chapels or churches to be void and punishable as a felony, that the practice ceased.

fraudulent marriage. A marriage based on a misrepresentation regarding some issue of fundamental importance to the innocent party, who relies on the misrepresentation in the decision to marry. • The misrepresentation must concern something of fundamental importance to a marriage, such as religious beliefs, the ability to have sexual relations, or the ability or desire to have children. Cf. *sham marriage.*

green-card marriage. *Slang.* A sham marriage in which a U.S. citizen marries a foreign citizen for the sole purpose of allowing the foreign citizen to become a permanent U.S. resident. • The Marriage Fraud Amendments were enacted to regulate marriages entered into for the purpose of circumventing U.S. immigration laws. 8 USCA §§ 1154 (h), 1255(e). See *sham marriage.*

Gretna-Green marriage. A marriage entered into in a jurisdiction other than where the parties reside to avoid some legal impediment that exists where they live; a runaway marriage. • Gretna Green, a Scottish village close to the English border, served as a convenient place for eloping English couples to wed since in Scots law parties over 16 did not need parental consent.

handfast marriage. **1.** *Hist.* A marriage, often lacking only solemnization by clergy, characterized by the couple's joining of hands to conclude a marriage contract. **2.** *Hist.* A betrothal with all the binding effects of a marriage, including conjugal rights and cohabitation, followed by a later formal ceremony. **3.** A trial or probationary marriage wherein the couple agrees to cohabit and behave as spouses for a definite period, usu. one year, at the end of which they will mutually decide to separate or go through a permanently binding marriage. • The legal status of such a marriage is unsettled, as many such trial marriages are initiated with a ritual ceremony including an exchange of vows before a presiding officer legally empowered to perform marriages, yet the couple intends to remain free to end the relationship without legal proceedings. Cf. *marriage in jest; common-law marriage.* **4.** A binding form of marriage practiced by some modern pagan religions. • Unlike in sense 3, such marriages are entered into with the expectation of permanent duration. — Also termed (in senses 3 and 4) *handfasting.*

high-test marriage. See *covenant marriage.*

homosexual marriage. See *same-sex marriage.*

informal marriage. See *common-law marriage.*

in-marriage. Marriage between relatives; inbreeding.

left-handed marriage. See *morganatic marriage.*

limited-purpose marriage. A marriage in which the parties agree to be married only for certain reasons. • An example is a marriage in which the parties agree to marry so that a child will not be born illegitimate but agree not to live together or to have any duties toward each other. Courts have usu. found these marriages to be binding for all purposes. Cf. *sham marriage; green card-marriage.*

marriage by habit and repute. *Scots law.* An irregular marriage created by cohabitation that implies a mutual agreement to be married. • This type of marriage is still recognized in Scotland. See *Scotch marriage.*

marriage in jest. A voidable marriage in which the parties lack the requisite intent to marry.

marriage of conscience. *Eccles. law.* See *confidential marriage.*

marriage of convenience. (18c) **1.** A marriage entered into for social or financial advantages rather than out of mutual love. — Also termed *mariage de convenance.* **2.** Loosely, an ill-considered marriage that, at the time, is convenient for the parties involved.

marriage of the left hand. See *morganatic marriage.*

marriage per verba de futuro subsequente copula. *Scots law. Hist.* An irregular marriage created by a promise to marry in the future followed by an act of sexual intercourse. • Originally medieval canon law, this type of marriage was recognized in Scotland until 1940. See *Scotch marriage.*

marriage per verba de praesenti. *Scots law. Hist.* An irregular marriage created at the time of a mutual agreement to be married. • Originally medieval canon law, this type of marriage was recognized in Scotland until 1940. See *Scotch marriage.*

mixed marriage. See MISCEGENATION.

morganatic marriage (mor-gə-**nat**-ik). *Hist.* A marriage between a man of superior status to a woman of inferior status, with the stipulation that the wife and her children have no claims to the husband's title or possessions. • By extension, the term later referred to the marriage of a woman of superior status to a man of inferior status. The concept is now limited to royal marriages. — Also termed *left-handed marriage*; *marriage of the left hand*; *salic marriage.*

occult marriage. *Eccles. law.* See *confidential marriage.*

plural marriage. (1862) A marriage in which one spouse is already married to someone else; a bigamous or polygamous union; POLYGAMY.

putative marriage (**pyoo**-tə-tiv). A marriage in which either the husband or the wife believes in good faith that the two are married, but for some technical reason they are not formally married (as when the ceremonial official was not authorized to perform a marriage). • A putative marriage is typically treated as valid to protect the innocent spouse. The concept of a putative marriage was adopted from the Napoleonic Code in those states having a civil-law tradition, such as California, Louisiana, and Texas. This type of marriage is also recognized in the Uniform Marriage and Divorce Act. The legal rule by which putative marriages exist is sometimes referred to as the *putative-spouse doctrine.* — Also termed *putative matrimony.*

salic marriage. See *morganatic marriage.*

same-sex marriage. The ceremonial union of two people of the same sex; a marriage or marriage-like relationship between two women or two men. • The United States government and most American states do not recognize same-sex marriages, even if legally contracted in other countries such as Canada, so couples usu. do not acquire the legal status of spouses. But in some states same-sex couples have successfully challenged the laws against same-sex marriage on constitutional grounds. *See Goodridge v. Dept. of Pub. Health*, 798 N.E.2d 941 (Mass. 2003). *Cf. Baehr v. Lewin*, 852 P.2d 44 (Haw. 1993); *Baehr v. Miike*, 994 P.2d 566 (Haw. 1999); *Baker v. State*, 744 A.2d 864 (Vt. 1999). — Also termed *gay marriage*; *homosexual marriage.* Cf. CIVIL

COMMITMENT (2); CIVIL UNION; DOMESTIC PARTNERSHIP.

Scotch marriage. *Scots law.* A marriage by consensual contract, without the necessity of a formal ceremony. • Until 1940, Scots law retained the medieval canon-law forms of marriage *per verba de praesenti* and *per verba de futuro subsequente copula.* These promises constituted irregular but valid marriages. Scots law still retains the irregular marriage by cohabitation with habit and repute. No ceremony needs to be proved but, after the death of one spouse, the surviving spouse or any child can obtain a court's confirmation that a marriage existed, based on the general belief of neighbors, friends, and family.

sham marriage. (18c) A purported marriage in which all the formal requirements are met or seemingly met, but in which the parties go through the ceremony with no intent of living together as husband and wife. Cf. *green-card marriage*; *fraudulent marriage*; *limited-purpose marriage.*

valid marriage. See MARRIAGE (1).

voidable marriage. (1845) A marriage that is initially invalid but that remains in effect unless terminated by court order. • For example, a marriage is voidable if either party is underage or otherwise legally incompetent, or if one party used fraud, duress, or force to induce the other party to enter the marriage. The legal imperfection in such a marriage can be inquired into only during the lives of both spouses, in a proceeding to obtain a judgment declaring it void. A voidable marriage can be ratified once the impediment to a legal marriage has been removed.

void marriage. (17c) A marriage that is invalid from its inception, that cannot be made valid, and that can be terminated by either party without obtaining a divorce or annulment. • For example, a marriage is void if the parties are too closely related or if either party is already married. A void marriage does not exist, has never existed, and needs no formal act to be dissolved — although a judicial declaration may be obtained. — Also termed *attempted marriage.* See NULLITY OF MARRIAGE (1).

2. *Roman law.* A consensual agreement between a man and a woman to be married. • The consent of both parties and of any paterfamilias was necessary. Other requirements were the attainment of puberty and legal capacity (*conubium*). If either or both withdrew consent to be married, the marriage ended in divorce; no specific grounds were necessary. In the Christian empire, divorce without adequate grounds was penalized. **3.** MARRIAGE CEREMONY. — **marital,** *adj.*

ceremonial marriage. (1876) A wedding that follows all the statutory requirements and that has been solemnized before a religious or civil official.

civil marriage. (17c) A wedding ceremony conducted by an official, such as a judge, or by some other authorized person — as distinguished from one solemnized by a member of the clergy.

double-proxy marriage. A wedding in which both parties to a marriage are absent but represented by stand-ins. ● Only Montana allows this type of marriage.

proxy marriage. (1924) A wedding in which someone stands in for an absent bride or groom, as when one party is stationed overseas in the military. ● Proxy marriages are prohibited in most states.

marriage article. (1831) A premarital stipulation between spouses who intend to incorporate the stipulation in a postnuptial agreement.

marriage bonus. *Tax.* The difference between the reduced income-tax liability owed by a married couple filing a joint income-tax return and the greater amount they would have owed had they been single and filed individually. — Also termed *singles' penalty.* Cf. MARRIAGE PENALTY.

marriage broker. One who arranges a marriage in exchange for consideration. ● A marriage broker may be subject to criminal liability.

marriage-brokerage contract. An agreement under which a person, acting for compensation, procures someone for a marriage. ● Traditionally, these contracts have been void as being against public policy.

marriage ceremony. (17c) The religious or civil proceeding that solemnizes a marriage. — Sometimes shortened to *marriage.* — Also termed *wedding.*

marriage certificate. (1821) A document that is executed by the religious or civil official presiding at a marriage ceremony and filed with a public authority (usu. the county clerk) as evidence of the marriage. — Also termed *certificate of marriage.* Cf. MARRIAGE LICENSE.

marriage contract. See CONTRACT.

marriage license. (17c) A document, issued by a public authority, that grants a couple permission to marry. Cf. MARRIAGE CERTIFICATE.

marriage mill. A place that facilitates hasty, often secret, marriages by requiring few or no legal formalities. ● Marriage-mill unions may be voidable but are rarely void in the absence of absolute impediments to marriage.

marriage-notice book. An English registry of marriage applications and licenses.

marriage penalty. *Tax.* The difference between the greater income-tax liability owed by a married couple filing a joint income-tax return and the lesser amount they would owe had they been single and filed individually. ● A marriage penalty exists whenever a married couple is treated disadvantageously under a tax code in comparison with an unmarried couple. Cf. MARRIAGE BONUS.

marriage portion. See DOWRY.

marriage promise. See PROMISE.

marriage records. Government or church records containing information on prospective couples (such as a woman's maiden name and address) and on wedding services performed.

marriage settlement. 1. See MARITAL AGREEMENT. **2.** See PRENUPTIAL AGREEMENT.

married woman's separate estate in equity. *Hist.* At common law, a trust that a rich family could set up for a daughter so that she would not lose control of her own money and property to her husband. ● The daughter could escape the severe limits of coverture by having her family establish a separate estate in equity, allowing her the benefit of income that was not controlled by her husband even if the husband was named as trustee. See COVERTURE; MARRIED WOMEN'S PROPERTY ACTS.

married women's property acts. (*sometimes cap.*) Statutes enacted to remove a married woman's legal disabilities; esp. statutes that abolished the common-law prohibitions against a married woman's contracting, suing and being sued, or acquiring, holding, and conveying property in her own right, free from any restrictions by her husband. ● In addition, these acts abolished the spousal-unity doctrine. In actual usage, the term almost always appears in the plural form (*acts*, not *act*), except when referring to a particular statute. — Also termed *married women's acts*; *married woman's property acts*; *married woman's acts*; *emancipation acts*; *married women's emancipation acts.* See MERGER DOCTRINE OF HUSBAND AND WIFE; LEGAL-UNITIES DOCTRINE.

***Marsden* motion.** A criminal defendant's request that a court dismiss or replace a court-appointed attorney on grounds that the attorney is not completely or adequately representing the defendant. *People v. Marsden*, 465 P.2d 44 (Cal. 1970).

marshal, *n.* (13c) **1.** A law-enforcement officer with duties similar to those of a sheriff. **2.** A judicial officer who provides court security, executes process, and performs other tasks for the court. — **marshalship,** *n.*

United States Marshal. A federal official who carries out the orders of a federal court. ● U.S. Marshals are employees of the executive branch of government.

marshal, *vb.* (15c) **1.** To arrange or rank in order <the brief effectively marshaled the appellant's arguments>. **2.** To arrange (assets, etc.) according to their liability or availability for payment of debts. **3.** To fix the order of (creditors) according to their priority.

marshaling assets, rule of. See RULE OF MARSHALING ASSETS.

marshaling doctrine. The principle that, when a senior creditor has recourse to two or more funds to satisfy its debt, and a junior creditor has recourse to only one fund to satisfy its debt, the senior creditor must satisfy its debt out of the funds in which the junior creditor has no interest. See RULE OF MARSHALING ASSETS.

marshaling the evidence. (1892) **1.** Arranging all of a party's evidence in the order that it will be presented at trial. **2.** The practice of formulating a jury charge so that it arranges the evidence to give more credence to a particular interpretation.

mart. See MARKET (1).

martial law (**mahr**-shəl). (1933) **1.** The law by which during wartime the army, instead of civil authority, governs the country because of a perceived need for military security or public safety. ● The military assumes control purportedly until civil authority can be restored. **2.** A body of firm, strictly enforced rules that are imposed because of a perception by the country's rulers that civil government has failed, or might fail, to function. ● Martial law is usu. imposed when the rulers foresee an invasion, insurrection, economic collapse, or other breakdown of the rulers' desired social order.

> *absolute martial law.* The carrying on of government functions entirely by military agencies, as a result of which the authority of civil agencies is superseded.

> *qualified martial law.* The carrying on of government functions partly by military agencies, as a result of which the authority of some civil agencies is superseded.

3. The law by which the army in wartime governs foreign territory that it occupies. **4.** Loosely, MILITARY LAW.

Martindale-Hubbell Law Directory. A series of books, published annually, containing a roster and ratings of lawyers and law firms in most cities of the United States, corporate legal departments, government lawyers, foreign lawyers, and lawyer-support providers, as well as a digest of the laws of the states, the District of Columbia, and territories of the United States, and a digest of the laws of many foreign jurisdictions, including Canada and its provinces.

Martinez **report.** A report that a court may require a pro se party to file in order to clarify a vague or incomprehensible complaint. *Martinez v. Aaron,* 570 F.2d 317 (10th Cir. 1978).

Mary Carter agreement. (1972) A contract (usu. a secret one) by which one or more, but not all, codefendants settle with the plaintiff and obtain a release, along with a provision granting them a portion of any recovery from the nonparticipating codefendants. ● In a Mary Carter agreement, the participating codefendants agree to remain parties to the lawsuit and, if no recovery is awarded against the nonparticipating codefendants, to pay the plaintiff a settled amount. Such an agreement is void as against public policy in some states but is valid in others if disclosed to the jury. *Booth v. Mary Carter Paint Co.,* 202 So. 2d 8 (Fla. Dist. Ct. App. 1967). Cf. GALLAGHER AGREEMENT.

Mary Major. See JANE DOE.

masking, *n.* In critical legal studies, the act or an instance of concealing something's true nature <being a crit, Max contends that the legal system is merely an elaborate masking of social injustices>. — **mask,** *vb.*

mask work. *Copyright.* A three-dimensional pattern of metallic insulation or semiconducting material present or removed from the layers of a computer chip. ● Mask works are protected under the Semiconductor Chip Protection Act of 1984. 17 USCA §§ 902 et seq.

Massachusetts ballot. See BALLOT (4).

Massachusetts trust. See *business trust* under TRUST (4).

mass-action theory. The principle that, as long as a labor union is functioning, it is vicariously liable for the joint acts of its members.

mass-appraisal method. A technique for valuing large areas of land by studying market data to determine the price that similar property would sell for, without engaging in a parcel-by-parcel analysis.

mass asset. See ASSET.

Massiah **rule.** (1966) The principle that an attempt to elicit incriminating statements (usu. not during a formal interrogation) from a suspect whose right to counsel has attached but who has not waived that right violates the Sixth Amendment. *Massiah v. United States,* 377 U.S. 201, 84 S.Ct. 1199 (1964). See DELIBERATE ELICITATION.

mass layoff. See LAYOFF.

mass meeting. See MEETING.

mass murder. See MURDER.

mass tort. See TORT.

mast. 1. *Military law.* A Navy disciplinary proceeding at which the commanding officer of a unit considers minor offenses charged against enlisted personnel. ● The charges may be dismissed, the accused person may receive a punishment prescribed by military law, or the matter may be referred to a court-martial. The proceeding is not officially a trial, and no conviction or acquittal results. Traditionally, when a ship's captain disciplines crew members at sea, the hearing is held and the discipline announced (and sometimes carried out) at the ship's mainmast or *at the mast*. Depending on the rank of the presiding officer, it may be also termed a *captain's mast, admiral's mast*, or (for an admiral) *flag mast*. **2.** On board a ship, the usual place of assembly for a court hearing, public sale, etc. ● On sailing ships, the place is the mainmast. On all other vessels, the captain designates a place as the "mast." Cf. (in sense 2) MAST SELLING.

mast, at the. See MAST (1).

master, *n.* (bef. 12c) **1.** One who has personal authority over another's services; specif., a principal who employs another to perform one or more services and who controls or has the right to control the physical conduct of the other in the performance of the services; EMPLOYER <the law of master and servant>. **2.** A parajudicial officer (such as a referee, an auditor, an examiner, or an assessor) specially appointed to help a court with its proceedings. ● A master may take testimony, hear and rule on discovery disputes, enter temporary orders, and handle other pretrial matters, as well as computing interest, valuing annuities, investigating encumbrances on land titles, and the like — usu. with a written report to the court. Fed. R. Civ. P. 53. — Also termed *special master*.

special master. (1833) A master appointed to assist the court with a particular matter or case.

standing master. (1848) A master appointed to assist the court on an ongoing basis.]

master agreement. *Labor law.* An agreement between a union and industry leaders, the terms of which serve as a model for agreements between the union and individual companies within the industry.

master and servant. (16c) The relation between two persons, one of whom (the master) has authority over the other (the servant), with the power to direct the time, manner, and place of the services. ● This relationship is similar to that of principal and agent, but that terminology applies to employments in which the employee has some discretion, while the servant is almost completely under the control of the master. Also, an agent usu. acts for the principal in business relations with third parties, while a servant does not. See *master–servant relationship* under RELATIONSHIP.

master lease. See LEASE.

master limited partnership. See *publicly traded partnership* under PARTNERSHIP.

master of a ship. *Maritime law.* A commander of a merchant vessel; a captain of a ship. ● The master is responsible for the vessel's navigation and the safety and care of the crew and cargo. — Also termed *shipmaster*.

Master of Laws. A law degree conferred on those completing graduate-level legal study, beyond the J.D. or LL.B. — Abbr. LL.M. Cf. JURIS DOCTOR; LL.B.; DOCTOR OF LAWS.

Master of the Pells. See CLERK OF THE PELLS.

Master of the Rolls. The president of the Court of Appeal in England. ● Formerly, the Master of the Rolls was an assistant judge to a court of chancery, responsible for keeping the rolls and chancery records. In recent times, the most famous Master of the Rolls was Lord Denning (who lived from 1899 to 1999).

Master of the Supreme Court. An official of the Queen's Bench and Chancery Divisions of the Supreme Court who fills the several positions of master in the common-law courts, the Queen's Coroner and Attorney, the Master of the Crown Office, record and writ clerks, and associates.

master plan. (1914) *Land-use planning.* A municipal plan for housing, industry, and recreation facilities, including their projected environmental impact. See PLANNED-UNIT DEVELOPMENT.

master policy. See INSURANCE POLICY.

master's draft. *Maritime law.* A contract for money loaned to a ship's master to cover necessary disbursements, payable from the first freight the ship receives, and secured by the vessel and freight. See BOTTOMRY BOND.

master–servant relationship. See RELATIONSHIP.

master--servant rule. See RESPONDEAT SUPERIOR.

master's report. A master's formal report to a court, usu. containing a recommended decision in a case as well as findings of fact and conclusions of law.

mast selling. *Hist.* The practice of selling the goods of a dead seaman at the mast. See MAST (2).

matched order. See ORDER (8).

matching-acceptance rule. See MIRROR-IMAGE RULE.

matching principle. (1979) *Tax.* A method for handling expense deductions, by which the depreciation in a given year is matched by the associated tax benefit.

mate. (14c) **1.** A spouse or other long-term life partner. **2.** A second-in-command officer on a merchant vessel. **3.** A petty officer who assists a warrant officer. **4.** A friend or companion.

materia (mə-**teer**-ee-ə), *n.* [Latin] **1.** Materials, esp. for building, as distinguished from the form given to something by the exercise of labor or skill. **2.** Matter; substance.

material, *adj.* (14c) **1.** Of or relating to matter; physical <material goods>. **2.** Having some logical connection with the consequential facts <material evidence>. **3.** Of such a nature that knowledge of the item would affect a person's decision-making; significant; essential <material alteration of the document>. Cf. RELEVANT. — **materiality,** *n.*

material adverse information. See MATERIAL INFORMATION.

material allegation. See ALLEGATION.

material alteration. See ALTERATION (2).

material breach. See BREACH OF CONTRACT.

material change in circumstances. See CHANGE IN CIRCUMSTANCES.

material evidence. See EVIDENCE.

material fact. See FACT.

material fallacy. See FALLACY.

material information. *Securities.* Information that would be important to a reasonable investor in making an investment decision. • In the context of an "efficient" market, materiality translates into information that alters the price of a firm's stock. Securities Exchange Act of 1934 § 10(b), 15 USCA § 78j(b); 17 CFR § 240.10b-5.

  material adverse information. *Securities.* Material information that is likely to make an investment less attractive.

material issue. See ISSUE (1).

materialman. A person who supplies materials used in constructing or repairing a structure or vehicle. — Also termed *material supplier.*

materialman's lien. See *mechanic's lien* under LIEN.

material misrepresentation. See MISREPRESENTATION.

material representation. See REPRESENTATION (1).

material supplier. See MATERIALMAN.

material term. See TERM (2).

material witness. See WITNESS.

material-witness arrest. See ARREST.

maternal, *adj.* (15c) Of, relating to, or coming from one's mother <maternal property>. Cf. PATERNAL.

maternal line. See LINE.

maternal-line descent. See DESCENT.

maternal-preference presumption. *Family law.* The belief that custody of a child, regardless of age, should generally be awarded to the mother in a divorce unless she is found to be unfit. • Most jurisdictions no longer adhere to the maternal-preference presumption. — Also termed *maternal-preference doctrine.* Cf. PRIMARY-CAREGIVER DOCTRINE; TENDER-YEARS DOCTRINE.

maternal property. See PROPERTY.

maternity (mə-tər-ni-tee). (17c) **1.** The state or condition of being a mother, esp. a biological one; motherhood. Cf. FILIATION. **2.** The section of a hospital devoted to the care of mothers and infants during and after childbirth. **3.** ATTRIBUTION RIGHT.

maternity presumption. See PRESUMPTION OF MATERNITY.

mathematical-algorithm exception. See ALGORITHM EXCEPTION.

mathematical evidence. See EVIDENCE.

***Mathews v. Eldridge* test.** (1980) *Constitutional law.* The principle for determining whether an administrative procedure provides due-process protection, by analyzing (1) the nature of the private interest that will be affected by the governmental action, (2) the risk of an erroneous deprivation through the procedure used, (3) the probable value of additional or substitute procedural safeguards, (4) the governmental function involved, and (5) the administrative burden and expense that would be created by requiring additional or substitute procedural safeguards. *Mathews v. Eldridge,* 424 U.S. 319, 96 S.Ct. 893 (1976).

matricide (ma-trə-sɪd), *n.* (16c) **1.** The act of killing one's own mother. **2.** One who kills his or her mother. — **matricidal,** *adj.*

matriculate, *vb.* (16c) To enroll or register (in a university, college, etc.) — **matriculation,** *n.*

matrimonial action. See ACTION (4).

matrimonial cohabitation. See COHABITATION.

matrimonial domicile. See DOMICILE.

matrimonial home. See *matrimonial domicile* under DOMICILE.

matrimonial res. (1893) **1.** The marriage estate. **2.** The state of marriage; the legal relationship between married persons, as opposed to the property and support obligations arising from the marriage.

matrimonium (ma-trə-**moh**-nee-əm), *n.* [Latin] *Roman law.* Marriage. — Also termed *nuptiae* (nəp-shee-ee).

matrimony, *n.* (14c) The ceremony or state of being married; MARRIAGE (1). — **matrimonial,** *adj.*

matrix (**may**-triks), *n.* [Latin] **1.** *Hist.* Mother. **2.** *Civil law.* The original legal instrument, from which all copies must be made. **3.** A list of the parties to a lawsuit, including the addresses at which pleadings and notices can be served. • A matrix is commonly used to list the names and addresses of creditors and other parties in a bankruptcy case.

Many bankruptcy courts have specific rules on how to prepare the matrix.

matter, *n.* (13c) **1.** A subject under consideration, esp. involving a dispute or litigation; CASE (1) <this is the only matter on the court's docket today>. **2.** Something that is to be tried or proved; an allegation forming the basis of a claim or defense <the matters raised in the plaintiff's complaint are not actionable under state law>.

matter in deed. **1.** A matter that can be proved by a writing under seal. **2.** See *matter of fact.*

matter in pais (in **pay**). A matter of fact that has not been recorded in writing and that must therefore be proved by parol evidence.

matter of fact. (16c) A matter involving a judicial inquiry into the truth of alleged facts. — Also termed *matter in deed.*

matter of form. A matter concerned only with formalities or noncritical characteristics <the objection that the motion was incorrectly titled related to a matter of form>. Cf. *matter of substance.*

matter of law. A matter involving a judicial inquiry into the applicable law.

matter of record. A matter that has been entered on a judicial or other public record and therefore can be proved by producing that record.

matter of substance. A matter concerning the merits or critical elements, rather than mere formalities <the party objected because the motion was based on a repealed statute that related to a matter of substance>. Cf. *matter of form.*

new matter. **1.** A litigant's claim or defense that goes beyond the issues raised in the original litigation, either by raising a new issue with new facts to be proved or by raising a defense that does not implicate an element of the original claims. ● A typical example of new matter is an affirmative defense. **2.** See NEW MATTER (2).

special matter. *Common-law pleading.* Out-of-the-ordinary evidence that a defendant is allowed to enter, after notice to the plaintiff, under a plea of the general issue.

matter in controversy. See AMOUNT IN CONTROVERSY.

matter of. See IN RE.

matter of course. (17c) Something done as a part of a routine process or procedure.

mature, *vb.* (1861) (Of a debt or obligation) to become due <the bond matures in ten years>. — **maturity,** *n.* — **mature,** *adj.*

matured claim. See CLAIM (3).

mature-minor doctrine. *Family law.* A rule holding that an adolescent, though not having reached the age of majority, may make decisions about his or her health and welfare if the adolescent demonstrates an ability to articulate reasoned preferences on those matters. ● The mature-minor doctrine was recognized as constitutionally protected in medical decisions (abortion rights) in *Planned Parenthood of Cent. Missouri v. Danforth,* 428 U.S. 52, 96 S.Ct. 2831 (1976). Not all states recognize the common-law mature-minor doctrine. Cf. PARENTAL-CONSENT STATUTE.

maturity date. See *date of maturity* under DATE.

maturity value. The amount that is due and payable on an obligation's maturity date.

maxim (**mak**-sim). (16c) A traditional legal principle that has been frozen into a concise expression. ● Examples are "possession is nine-tenths of the law" and *caveat emptor* ("let the buyer beware"). — Also termed *legal maxim.*

maximalist retributivism. See RETRIBUTIVISM.

maximum cure. *Maritime law.* The point at which a seaman who is injured or sick has stabilized, and no additional medical treatment will improve the seaman's condition. ● A shipowner's obligation to provide maintenance and cure to a sick or injured seaman usu. continues until the seaman has reached maximum cure. *Farrell v. United States,* 336 U.S. 511, 69 S.Ct. 707 (1949); *Vella v. Ford Motor Co.,* 421 U.S. 1, 95 S.Ct. 1381 (1975). See CURE (2); MAINTENANCE AND CURE.

maximum medical improvement. (1955) The point at which an injured person's condition stabilizes, and no further recovery or improvement is expected, even with additional medical intervention. ● This term is most often used in the context of a workers'-compensation claim. An injured employee usu. receives temporary benefits until reaching maximum medical improvement, at which time a determination can be made about any permanent disability the employee has suffered and any corresponding benefits the employee should receive. — Abbr. MMI.

maximum sentence. See SENTENCE.

may, *vb.* (bef. 12c) **1.** To be permitted to <the plaintiff may close>. **2.** To be a possibility <we may win on appeal>. Cf. CAN. **3.** Loosely, is required to; shall; must <if two or more defendants are jointly indicted, any defendant who so requests may be tried separately>. ● In dozens of cases, courts have held *may* to be synonymous with *shall* or *must,* usu. in an effort to effectuate legislative intent.

mayhem (**may**-hem), *n.* (15c) **1.** The crime of maliciously injuring a person's body, esp. to impair or destroy the victim's capacity for self-defense. ● Modern statutes usu. treat this as a form of aggravated battery. See BATTERY. Cf. *serious bodily injury* under INJURY. **2.** Violent destruction. **3.**

Rowdy confusion or disruption. — **maim** (for sense 1), *vb.*

May it please the court. (17c) An introductory phrase that lawyers use when first addressing a court, esp. when presenting oral argument to an appellate court.

mayor, *n.* (14c) An official who is elected or appointed as the chief executive of a city, town, or other municipality. — **mayoral** (**may**-ər-əl), *adj.*

mayoralty (**may**-ər-əl-tee). (14c) The office or dignity of a mayor. — Also termed *mayorship.*

mayor of the staple. *Hist.* A person appointed to take recognizances of debt between staple merchants, and to hear disputes arising between merchants. See STAPLE (1), (2).

mayor's court. See COURT.

mayorship. See MAYORALTY.

MBDA. *abbr.* MINORITY BUSINESS DEVELOPMENT AGENCY.

MBE. See *Multistate Bar Examination* under BAR EXAMINATION.

MBO. See *management buyout* under BUYOUT.

MC. *abbr.* MEMBER OF CONGRESS.

McCarran Act. A federal law requiring, among other things, members of the Communist party to register with the Attorney General and requiring Communist organizations to provide the government with a list of its members. ● The Act was passed in 1950, during the Cold War. Over the years, the U.S. Supreme Court declared various portions of the Act unconstitutional, but it was not fully repealed until 1993. *See, e.g., United States v. Spector*, 343 U.S. 169, 72 S.Ct. 591 (1952); *Aptheker v. Secretary of State*, 378 U.S. 500, 84 S.Ct. 1659 (1964); *United States v. Robel*, 389 U.S. 258, 88 S.Ct. 419 (1967). — Also termed *McCarran Internal Security Act; Subversive Activities Control Act of 1950.*

McCarran–Ferguson Act. *Insurance.* A federal law allowing a state to regulate insurance companies doing business in that state, and also to levy a tax on them. 15 USCA §§ 1011–1015.

McCarran Internal Security Act. See MCCARRAN ACT.

McClanahan presumption. The presumption that the states do not have jurisdiction to tax members of a Native American tribe who live or work on tribal land. ● The presumption is not limited to tribal members who live or work on a formal reservation. Instead, it includes those who live or work on informal reservations, in dependent tribal communities, and on tribal allotments. *McClanahan v. Arizona Tax Comm'n*, 411 U.S. 164, 93 S.Ct. 1257 (1973).

McDonnell Douglas test. *Employment law.* The principle for applying a shifting burden of proof in employment-discrimination cases, essentially requiring the plaintiff to come forward with evidence of discrimination and the defendant to come forward with evidence showing that the employment action complained of was taken for nondiscriminatory reasons. ● Under this test, the plaintiff must first establish a prima facie case of discrimination, as by showing that the plaintiff is a member of a protected group and suffered an adverse employment action. If the plaintiff satisfies that burden, then the defendant must articulate a legitimate, nondiscriminatory reason for the employment action complained of. If the defendant satisfies that burden, then the plaintiff must prove that the defendant's stated reason is just a pretext for discrimination and that discrimination was the real reason for the employment action. *McDonnell Douglas Corp. v. Green*, 411 U.S. 792, 93 S.Ct. 1817 (1973). Cf. *burden-shifting analysis.*

mcf. *Abbr. Oil & gas.* One thousand cubic feet, one of the standard units for measuring natural gas.

McNabb–Mallory rule. *Criminal procedure.* The doctrine that a confession is inadmissible if obtained during an unreasonably long detention period between arrest and a preliminary hearing. ● Because of the broader protections afforded under the *Miranda* rule, the *McNabb–Mallory* rule is rarely applied in modern cases. *McNabb v. United States*, 318 U.S. 332, 63 S.Ct. 608 (1943); *Mallory v. United States*, 354 U.S. 449, 77 S.Ct. 1356 (1957). — Often shortened to *Mallory rule.*

McNaghten rules (mik-**nawt**-ən). (1917) *Criminal law.* The doctrine that a person is not criminally responsible for an act when a mental disability prevented the person from knowing either (1) the nature and quality of the act or (2) whether the act was right or wrong. ● The federal courts and most states have adopted this test in some form. *McNaghten's Case*, 8 Eng. Rep. 718 (H.L. 1843). — Also spelled *McNaughten rules; M'Naghten rules; M'Naughten rules.* — Also termed *right-and-wrong test; right-wrong test.* See INSANITY DEFENSE.

McNary comity. The principle that a U.S. district court should not hear a taxpayer's civil-rights challenge to the administration of a state's tax system. *Fair Assessment in Real Estate Ass'n v. McNary*, 454 U.S. 100, 102 S.Ct. 177 (1981).

M.D. *abbr.* (15c) **1.** Middle District, usu. in reference to U.S. judicial districts. **2.** Doctor of medicine.

MDA. *abbr.* MISSILE DEFENSE AGENCY.

MDL. *abbr.* MULTIDISTRICT LITIGATION.

MDP. *abbr.* MULTIDISCIPLINARY PRACTICE.

MDV. *abbr.* MOTION FOR DIRECTED VERDICT.

mean, *adj.* (14c) **1.** Of or relating to an intermediate point between two points or extremes <a mean position>. **2.** Medium in size <a mean height>. **3.** (Of a value, etc.) average <a mean score>. Cf. MEDIAN.

meander line (mee-**an**-dər). (1865) A survey line (not a boundary line) on a portion of land, usu. following the course of a river or stream.

mean high tide. See TIDE.

meaning. (14c) The sense of anything, but esp. of words; that which is conveyed (or intended to be conveyed) by a written or oral statement or other communicative act. ● The word ordinarily includes a mistaken but reasonable understanding of a communication. Cf. AMBIGUITY.

> *objective meaning.* The meaning that would be attributed to an unambiguous document (or portion of a document) by a disinterested reasonable person who is familiar with the surrounding circumstances. ● A party to a contract is often held to its objective meaning, which it is considered to have had reason to know, even if the party subjectively understood or intended something else.

> *plain meaning.* The meaning attributed to a document (usu. by a court) by giving the words their ordinary sense, without referring to extrinsic indications of the author's intent. — Also termed *ordinary meaning.* See PLAIN-MEANING RULE.

> *subjective meaning.* The meaning that a party to a legal document attributes to it when the document is written, executed, or otherwise adopted.

mean lower low tide. See TIDE.

mean low tide. See TIDE.

mean reserve. See RESERVE.

means, *n.* (14c) **1.** Available resources, esp. for the payment of debt; income. — Also termed *means of support.* **2.** Something that helps to attain an end; an instrument; a cause.

means-combination claim. See PATENT CLAIM.

means of support. See MEANS (1).

means-plus-function clause. *Patents.* An element in a patent claim, usu. in a claim for an apparatus patent, asserting that the claim element is a way to perform a given function or is a step in the process of performing a given function. ● The claim will be interpreted as including the structure or means stated in the patent specification and equivalents at the time of interpretation or infringement, but not all possible means of achieving the same function. 35 USCA § 112 ¶ 6. — Also termed *means-plus-function element; means-plus-function claim.* See *combination patent* under PATENT (3).

mean trading price. See PRICE.

mearstone. See MERESTONE.

measure of damages. (18c) The basis for calculating damages to be awarded to someone who has suffered an injury. ● For example, the measure of damages in an action on a penal bond is compensation for the actual loss, not exceeding the established penalty.

measuring life. (1922) Under the rule against perpetuities, the last beneficiary to die who was alive at the testator's death and who usu. holds a preceding interest. ● A measuring life is used to determine whether an interest will vest under the rule against perpetuities. See RULE AGAINST PERPETUITIES. Cf. LIFE IN BEING.

mechanical license. See LICENSE.

mechanical rights. *Copyright.* The right to reproduce a song in a phonorecord form, such as audiotape or compact disc. ● The right is obtained by paying a statutory royalty; it is not necessary to obtain the songwriter's express permission. See MECHANICAL ROYALTY. Cf. PERFORMANCE RIGHTS.

mechanical royalty. *Copyright.* The payment to which a songwriter is entitled each time a mechanical-right holder reproduces a song on a phonorecord. ● Mechanical-royalty rates are statutory, and payable per song or per minute (whichever is higher). If an artist is willing to pay the statutory rate, the songwriter's permission is not needed before a recording is made. If they choose to, artists and songwriters may negotiate lower royalty rates. 37 CFR § 255. — Also termed *statutory rate.*

mechanic's lien. See LIEN.

MED. *abbr.* OFFICE OF MEDICAL SERVICES.

median, *adj.* (15c) Located in or related to the precise midpoint in a range of values or quantities, such that half of them fall above the midpoint and half below. Cf. MEAN.

mediate descent. See DESCENT.

mediated settlement agreement. See SETTLEMENT (2).

mediate evidence. See *secondary evidence* under EVIDENCE.

mediate possession. See POSSESSION.

mediate powers (mee-dee-it). (1820) Subordinate powers incidental to primary powers, esp. as given by a principal to an agent; powers necessary to accomplish the principal task <adjusting debt is a mediate power to collecting debt>. Cf. PRIMARY POWERS.

mediate testimony. See *secondary evidence* under EVIDENCE.

mediation (mee-dee-**ay**-shən), *n.* (14c) **1.** A method of nonbinding dispute resolution involving a neutral third party who tries to help the disputing parties reach a mutually agreeable solution; CONCILIATION. — Also termed *case evaluation*; *facilitated negotiation.* Cf. COLLABORATIVE LAW; COOPERATIVE LAW. **2.** *Int'l law.* A process whereby a neutral country helps other countries peacefully resolve disputes between them. Cf. ARBITRATION. — **mediate** (**mee**-dee-ayt), *vb.* — **mediatory** (**mee**-dee-ə-tor-ee), *adj.*

Mediation and Conciliation Service. A federal agency that tries to prevent the interruption of commerce resulting from labor disputes, by assisting parties in settling their disputes through mediation and conciliation. • The agency can intervene on its own motion or on the motion of a party to the dispute. — Also termed *Federal Mediation and Conciliation Service.* 29 USCA §§ 172, 173.

mediator (**mee**-dee-ay-tər), *n.* (14c) A neutral person who tries to help disputing parties reach an agreement. Cf. ARBITRATOR.

mediators of questions. *Hist.* Six persons authorized by 27 Edw. 3, St. 2, ch. 24 to settle disputes between merchants.

Medicaid. (1966) A cooperative federal–state program that pays for medical expenses for qualifying individuals who cannot afford private medical services. • The program is authorized under the Social Security Act. — Also termed *Medical Assistance*; (in California) *MediCal.* Cf. MEDICARE.

Medicaid-qualifying trust. See TRUST.

medical directive. See ADVANCE DIRECTIVE (2).

medical-emergency exception. (1975) *Criminal law.* The principle that a police officer does not need a warrant to enter a person's home if the entrance is made to render aid to someone whom the officer reasonably believes to be in need of immediate assistance.

medical evidence. See EVIDENCE.

medical examiner. (1820) A public official who investigates deaths, conducts autopsies, and helps the state prosecute homicide cases. • Medical examiners have replaced coroners in many states. — Sometimes shortened to *examiner.* See CORONER.

medical expense. See EXPENSE.

medical-expense reimbursement plan. See EMPLOYEE BENEFIT PLAN.

medical jurisprudence. See FORENSIC MEDICINE.

medical lien. See *healthcare lien* under LIEN.

medical malpractice. See MALPRACTICE.

medical neglect. See NEGLECT.

medical probability. See REASONABLE MEDICAL PROBABILITY.

medicals. See *medical expense* (2) under EXPENSE.

Medicare. (1953) A federal program — established under the Social Security Act — that provides health insurance for the elderly and the disabled. Cf. MEDICAID; MEDIGAP INSURANCE.

medicolegal (med-i-koh-**lee**-gəl), *adj.* (1835) Involving the application of medical science to law <the coroner's medicolegal functions>. See FORENSIC MEDICINE.

medigap insurance. (1975) *Slang.* A private insurance policy for Medicare patients to cover the costs not covered by Medicare. Cf. MEDICARE.

medium of exchange. (18c) Anything generally accepted as payment in a transaction and recognized as a standard of value <money is a medium of exchange>. Cf. EXCHANGE (2); CURRENCY; LEGAL TENDER.

med. mal. See *medical malpractice* under MALPRACTICE.

meeting, *n.* (14c) *Parliamentary law.* The gathering of people to discuss or act on matters in which they have a common interest; esp. the convening of a deliberative assembly to transact business. • A deliberative assembly's meeting begins with a call to order and continues until the assembly adjourns. See *call to order* under CALL (1); ADJOURN (2). Cf. SESSION. — **meet,** *vb.*

adjourned meeting. 1. See *continued meeting*. **2.** A meeting that has adjourned. • These two senses are opposite in meaning, so the term "continued meeting" is preferable for sense 1.

annual meeting. A yearly meeting to elect or install officers or directors and to conduct other routine organizational business. • An organization's governing documents usu. specify the time and place of such a meeting.

business meeting. A formal meeting called for considering business, as opposed to a purely educational or social event. • A business meeting may fall within a program that also includes social and informational events. See PROGRAM (1).

called meeting. See *special meeting*.

continued meeting. A meeting that will be or has been resumed after a recess (or a so-called adjournment, which may last for several days but is still technically a recess, since it does not end the meeting). • A continued meeting is technically not an "adjourned meeting," and an "adjourned meeting" may also mean a meeting that has adjourned, so the term "continued meeting" is preferable. — Also loosely termed *adjourned meeting.* See RECESS (2).

creditors' meeting. *Bankruptcy.* The first meeting of a debtor's creditors and equity security holders, presided over by the U.S. Trustee and at which a bankruptcy trustee may be elected and the debtor may be examined under oath. 11 USCA § 341. — Also termed *meeting of creditors*; *341 meeting*; *first meeting of creditors.*

mass meeting. A meeting of an unorganized body called to discuss a particular issue or to organize for a particular purpose and usu. open to anyone interested in that issue or purpose.

organizational meeting. **1.** A mass meeting that establishes a permanent or ongoing organization. **2.** A meeting that begins an ongoing organization's proceedings under its regular order, such as adopting governing documents and electing officers, usu. following a mass meeting and an interval when the organization operates under provisional officers while its governing documents are drafted. ● If the organizational meeting is for a corporation and the articles of incorporation name the initial directors, the directors hold the meeting. Otherwise, the incorporator holds the meeting. **3.** The first meeting after a dissolution, at which a newly reconstituted deliberative assembly — such as a legislative body or a convention whose members are assuming the seats to which they have been elected or re-elected for a new term — elects officers, adopts rules, and otherwise organizes for the new session.

regular meeting. A periodic meeting held at a time set in an organization's governing documents or under a standing rule or schedule that the deliberative assembly has adopted. — Also termed *stated meeting.* Cf. *special meeting.*

special meeting. A meeting that is not a regular meeting; a meeting called for a particular purpose, usu. between regular meetings. — Also termed *called meeting.* Cf. *regular meeting.*

stated meeting. See *regular meeting.*

341 meeting. See *creditors' meeting.*

meeting-competition defense. *Antitrust.* A defense to a charge of price discrimination whereby the defendant shows that the lower price was a good-faith attempt to match what it believed to be a competitor's equally low offer.

meeting of creditors. See *creditors' meeting* under MEETING.

meeting of the minds. (1830) *Contracts.* Actual assent by both parties to the formation of a contract, meaning that they agree on the same terms, conditions, and subject matter. ● This was required under the traditional subjective theory of assent, but modern contract doctrine requires only objective manifestations of assent. — Also termed

mutuality of assent; *aggregatio mentium*; *assensio mentium.* See *mutual assent.* under ASSENT.

megalopolis (meg-ə-**lop**-ə-lis). A heavily populated, continuous urban area that is one vast city or composed of several cities and towns.

Megan's law (**meg**-ənz *or* **may**-gənz). (1994) A statute that requires sex offenders who are released from prison to register with a local board and that provides the means to disseminate information about the registrants to the community in which they dwell. ● Although many of these statutes were enacted in the late 1980s, they took their popular name from Megan Kanka of New Jersey, a seven-year-old who in 1994 was raped and murdered by a twice-convicted sex offender who lived across the street from her house. All states have these laws, but only some require community notification (as by publishing offenders' pictures in local newspapers); in others, people must call a state hotline or submit names of persons they suspect. The federal version of Megan's law may be found at 42 USCA § 14071. — Also termed *registration and community-notification law*; *community-notification law.* Cf. JACOB WETTERLING CRIMES AGAINST CHILDREN AND SEXUALLY VIOLENT OFFENDER REGISTRATION ACT.

Melson formula. *Family law.* A method of calculating a noncustodial parent's child-support obligation to ensure that (1) neither parent falls below the poverty level in meeting child-support obligations, and (2) a child of a wealthier noncustodial parent shares in that parent's higher standard of living. ● Named for Judge Elwood F. Melson of Delaware Family Court, the formula has been adopted in several states, such as Delaware, Hawaii, Montana, and West Virginia. The formula works as follows. A self-support reserve is first deducted from the parent-obligor's net income. Next, a primary support amount per child is calculated at an established subsistence level, added to actual work-related child-care expenses, and allocated between the parents. After deducting the support obligor's self-support reserve and pro rata share of the child's adjusted primary support amount, a percentage of the obligor's remaining income is allocated to additional child support as a cost-of-living adjustment. Total child support is determined by adding together the noncustodial parent's share of primary support and the standard-of-living allowance.

member. (14c) **1.** *Parliamentary law.* One of the individuals of whom an organization or a deliberative assembly consists, and who enjoys the full rights of participating in the organization — including the rights of making, debating, and voting on motions — except to the extent that the organization reserves those rights to certain classes of membership.

charter member. A member who was a member when the charter was granted or adopted; a founder.

full member. See *voting member.*

informational member. See *nonvoting member.*

limited member. See *nonvoting member.*

member ex officio. A member who serves (on a board or committee) by virtue of holding an office, and whose membership will therefore pass with the office to his or her successor. — Also termed *ex officio member.* See EX OFFICIO.

nonvoting member. A member whose rights do not include the right of voting on the organization's or assembly's business. — Also termed *informational member.*

voting member. A fully enfranchised member, as distinguished from a nonvoting member. — Also termed *full member.*

2. *Military law.* A person assigned to a court-martial to determine guilt and punishment.

member bank. See BANK.

member firm. *Securities.* A brokerage firm with at least one director, officer, or general partner who holds a seat in an organized securities exchange. — Also termed (if organized as a corporation) *member corporation.*

member of a crew. See SEAMAN.

member of Congress. An elected official who sits in either the U.S. Senate or the House of Representatives. • The official may be appointed to fill an unexpired term. — Abbr. MC.

member of Parliament. A person with the right to sit in one of the two houses of Parliament. — Abbr. MP.

membership committee. See COMMITTEE.

membrana (mem-**bray**-nə), *n.* [Latin "parchment"] *Hist.* **1.** A skin of parchment. **2.** A notebook of leaves of parchment. • The English rolls were made of several types of parchment and the term *membrana* was used in referring to them.

membrum (**mem**-brəm), *n.* [Latin "limb"] A division of something, esp. a slip or small piece of land.

memorandum. (15c) **1.** An informal written note or record outlining the terms of a transaction or contract <the memorandum indicated the developer's intent to buy the property at its appraised value>. • To satisfy the statute of frauds, a memorandum can be written in any form, but it must (1) identify the parties to the contract, (2) indicate the contract's subject matter, (3) contain the contract's essential terms, and (4) contain the signature of the party against whom enforcement is sought. — Also termed *memorial*; *note.* See STATUTE OF FRAUDS. **2.** An informal written

communication used esp. in offices <the firm sent a memorandum reminding all lawyers to turn in their timesheets>. — Often shortened to *memo.* **3.** A party's written statement of its legal arguments presented to the court, usu. in the form of a brief <memorandum of law>. Pl. **memoranda, memorandums.**

analytical memorandum. See *research memorandum.*

closed memorandum. A memorandum prepared by a law student using only given facts and the materials, usu. a collection of cases, in a packet provided to the student. — Also termed *closed memo*; *closed-universe memo.*

open memorandum. A memorandum prepared by a law student based on a given set of facts and using any available resources for research. — Also termed *open memo.*

persuasive memorandum. A memorandum written to sway the reader to accept the writer's position on a stated problem.

research memorandum. A memorandum whose purpose is analyze a legal issue and inform the reader about possible approaches and outcomes. • This type of memorandum is usu. an in-house document. — Also termed *analytical memorandum.*

memorandum articles. *Marine insurance.* Goods described in the memorandum clause. See MEMORANDUM CLAUSE.

memorandum check. See CHECK.

memorandum clause. A marine-insurance clause protecting underwriters from liability for injury to goods that are particularly perishable, or for minor damages.

memorandum decision. See *memorandum opinion* under OPINION (1).

memorandum disposition. See *memorandum opinion* under OPINION (1).

memorandum in error. A document alleging a factual error, usu. accompanied by an affidavit of proof.

memorandum of alteration. *English law.* A patentee's disclaimer of certain rights — such as rights to part of an invention that is not new and useful — to avoid losing the whole patent. • Until the mid-19th century, if a single patent was granted for two inventions, one of which was not new and useful, the entire patent would be defective.

memorandum of association. *English law.* A legal document setting up a corporation — either with or without limited liability — and including the company's name, purpose, and duration. See ARTICLES OF INCORPORATION.

memorandum of intent. See LETTER OF INTENT.

memorandum of understanding. See LETTER OF INTENT. — Abbr. MOU.

memorandum opinion. See OPINION (1).

memorandum sale. See SALE.

memorial, *n.* (17c) **1.** An abstract of a legal record, esp. a deed; MEMORANDUM (1). **2.** A written statement of facts presented to a legislature or executive as a petition.

menacing, *n.* (14c) An attempt to commit common-law assault. • The term is used esp. in jurisdictions that have defined assault to include battery. See ASSAULT.

mendacity (men-**das**-ə-tee), *n.* (16c) **1.** The quality of being untruthful. **2.** A lie; falsehood. — **mendacious** (men-**day**-shəs), *adj.*

mend-the-hold doctrine. The principle that a nonperforming party's defense in a breach-of-contract action must be raised before the close of evidence. • A minority of courts limit a defendant to the first defense raised after litigation begins, unless the defendant can show a good-faith basis for a new defense. Most courts allow the defendant to raise several defenses as long as each defense is based on the reason given for nonperformance when the breach occurred. The term comes from 19-century wrestling jargon, "mend the hold" meaning "get a better grip on your opponent."

men of straw. *Hist.* False witnesses who wandered around courts and were paid to give untrue testimony. • They stuffed straw into their shoes so that advocates could recognize them. See STRAW MAN (4).

mens (menz), *n.* [Latin] Mind; intention; will.

mensa et thoro (**men**-sə et **thor**-oh). [Latin] Bed and board. See A MENSA ET THORO; *divorce a mensa et thoro* under DIVORCE.

mens rea (**menz** ree-ə). [Law Latin "guilty mind"] (1861) The state of mind that the prosecution, to secure a conviction, must prove that a defendant had when committing a crime; criminal intent or recklessness <the *mens rea* for theft is the intent to deprive the rightful owner of the property>. • *Mens rea* is the second of two essential elements of every crime at common law, the other being the *actus reus.* — Also termed *mental element; criminal intent; guilty mind.* Pl. **mentes reae** (**men**-teez ree-ee). Cf. ACTUS REUS.

mental abuse. See *emotional abuse* under ABUSE.

mental anguish. See EMOTIONAL DISTRESS.

mental capacity. See CAPACITY (3).

mental cruelty. See CRUELTY.

mental distress. See EMOTIONAL DISTRESS.

mental element. See MENS REA.

mental evaluation. 1. See INDEPENDENT MENTAL EVALUATION. **2.** See PSYCHIATRIC EXAMINATION.

mental examination. See PSYCHIATRIC EXAMINATION.

mental illness. (1847) **1.** A disorder in thought or mood so substantial that it impairs judgment, behavior, perceptions of reality, or the ability to cope with the ordinary demands of life. **2.** Mental disease that is severe enough to necessitate care and treatment for the afflicted person's own welfare or the welfare of others in the community.

mental incompetence. See INCOMPETENCY.

mental-process privilege. See DELIBERATIVE-PROCESS PRIVILEGE.

mental reservation. (17c) One party's silent understanding or exception to the meaning of a contractual provision.

mental shock. See SHOCK.

mental suffering. See EMOTIONAL DISTRESS.

mentition (men-**tish**-ən), *n.* [fr. Latin *mentitio* "lying"] (17c) The act of lying.

mentor judge. See JUDGE.

MEPA. *abbr.* MULTIETHNIC-PLACEMENT ACT OF 1994.

mercantile (**mər**-kən-teel *or* -tɪl *or* -til), *adj.* (17c) Of or relating to merchants or trading; commercial <the mercantile system>.

mercantile agent. See AGENT (2).

mercantile law. See COMMERCIAL LAW (1).

Mercantile Law Amendment Acts. The Mercantile Law Amendment Act of 1856 (19 & 20 Vict., chs. 60, 97) and the Mercantile Law Amendment Act (Scotland) of 1856, passed primarily to reconcile parts of the mercantile laws of England, Scotland, and Ireland.

mercantile paper. See *commercial paper* (1) under PAPER.

mercedary (**mər**-sə-**der**-ee), *n.* [Latin] An employer; one who hires.

mercenary (**mər**-sə-ner-ee). (14c) *Int'l law.* A professional soldier hired by someone other than his or her own government to fight in a foreign country.

mercenlage (**mər**-sən-law). [fr. Saxon *myrcnalag*] The law of the Mercians. • This was one of the three principal legal systems prevailing in England at the beginning of the 11th century. It was observed in many midland counties and those bordering on Wales. — Also spelled *merchenlage* (**mər**-shən-law). — Also termed *lex merciorum* (leks mər-shee-**or**-əm); *Mercian law* (**mər**-shee-ən *or* **mər**-shən). See DANELAW; WEST SAXON LAW.

merchandise (mər-chən-dız *also* -dıs). (13c) **1.** In general, a movable object involved in trade or traffic; that which is passed from one person to another by purchase and sale. **2.** In particular, that which is dealt in by merchants; an article of trading or the class of objects in which trade is carried on by physical transfer; collectively, mercantile goods, wares or commodities, or any subjects of regular trade, animate as well as inanimate. ● This definition generally excludes real estate, ships, intangibles such as software, and the like, and does not apply to money, stocks, bonds, notes, or other mere representatives or measures of actual commodities or values. — Also termed (in senses 1 and 2) *article of merchandise.* **3.** Purchase and sale; trade; traffic, dealing, or advantage from dealing.

merchandise broker. See BROKER.

merchant. (13c) One whose business is buying and selling goods for profit; esp. a person or entity that holds itself out as having expertise peculiar to the goods in which it deals and is therefore held by the law to a higher standard of expertise than that of a nonmerchant. ● Because the term relates solely to goods, a supplier of services is not considered a merchant.

merchantable (mər-chənt-ə-bəl), *adj.* (15c) Fit for sale in the usual course of trade at the usual selling prices; MARKETABLE. — Also termed *salable.* See *implied warranty of merchantability* under WARRANTY (2). — **merchantability,** *n.*

merchantable title. See *marketable title* under TITLE (2).

merchant appraiser. An expert appointed by a customs officer to reexamine and revalue imported goods for customs purposes. ● The appraiser is usu. an experienced merchant who deals in or has dealt in goods of the character and quality of those at issue. An appraiser is appointed only when an importer requests one.

merchant exception. (1973) *Contracts.* In a sale of goods, an exemption from the statute of frauds whereby a contract between merchants is enforceable if, within a reasonable time after they reach an oral agreement, a written confirmation of the terms is sent, to which the recipient does not object within ten days of receiving it. ● The only effect of failing to object to the written confirmation is that the recipient will be precluded from relying on the statute of frauds — or the lack of a formal, written agreement — as a defense to a breach-of-contract claim. The party seeking to enforce an agreement must still prove that an agreement was reached. UCC § 2-201.

merchant lessee. See LESSEE.

merchantman. *Archaic.* A vessel employed in foreign or interstate commerce or in the merchant service.

merchant's accounts. Current, mutual accounts between merchants showing debits and credits for merchandise.

merchant's defense. (1972) The principle that a store owner will not be held liable for reasonably detaining a suspected shoplifter, to facilitate an investigation by a law-enforcement officer, if probable cause exists to suspect the detained person of wrongfully removing merchandise from the store.

merchant seaman. See SEAMAN.

merchant's firm offer. See *irrevocable offer* under OFFER.

Merchant Shipping Acts. English statutes to improve shipping conditions by, among other things, vesting the supervision of merchant shipping in the board of trade.

merciament (mər-see-ə-mənt). *Archaic.* See AMERCEMENT.

Mercian law. See MERCENLAGE.

mercy. (13c) Compassionate treatment, as of criminal offenders or of those in distress; esp. imprisonment, rather than death, imposed as punishment for capital murder. See CLEMENCY.

mercy killing. See EUTHANASIA.

mercy rule. (1981) *Evidence.* The principle that a defendant is entitled to offer character evidence as a defense to a criminal charge. ● This type of evidence is often offered by the defendant's friends and relatives. Fed. R. Evid. 404(a)(1).

mere-continuation doctrine. A principle under which a successor corporation will be held liable for the acts of a predecessor corporation, if only one corporation remains after the transfer of assets, and both corporations share an identity of stock, shareholders, and directors. — Also termed *continuity-of-entity doctrine.* Cf. SUBSTANTIAL-CONTINUITY DOCTRINE.

mere-evidence rule. *Criminal procedure.* The former doctrine that a search warrant allows seizure of the instrumentalities of the crime (such as a murder weapon) or the fruits of the crime (such as stolen goods), but does not permit the seizure of items that have evidentiary value only (such as incriminating documents). ● The Supreme Court has abolished this rule, and today warrants may be issued to search for and seize all evidence of a crime. *Warden v. Hayden,* 387 U.S. 294, 87 S.Ct. 1642 (1967); Fed. R. Crim. P. 41(b).

mere license. See *bare license* under LICENSE.

mere licensee. See *bare licensee* under LICENSEE.

mere right. An abstract right in property, without possession or even the right of possession. — Also termed *jus merum; merum jus; meer dreit.*

merestone (**meer**-stohn). *Archaic.* A stone that marks land boundaries. — Also spelled *mearstone*.

meretricious (mer-ə-**trish**-əs), *adj.* (17c) **1.** Involving prostitution <a meretricious encounter>. **2.** (Of a romantic relationship) involving either unlawful sexual connection or lack of capacity on the part of one party <a meretricious marriage>. **3.** Superficially attractive but fake nonetheless; alluring by false show <meretricious advertising claims>.

meretricious relationship. *Archaic.* A stable, marriage-like relationship in which the parties cohabit knowing that a lawful marriage between them does not exist.

mergee (mər-**jee**). A participant in a corporate merger.

merger. (18c) **1.** The act or an instance of combining or uniting. **2.** *Contracts.* The substitution of a superior form of contract for an inferior form, as when a written contract supersedes all oral agreements and prior understandings. See IN-TEGRATION (2). **3.** *Contracts.* The replacement of a contractual duty or of a duty to compensate with a new duty between the same parties, based on different operative facts, for the same performance or for a performance differing only in liquidating a duty that was previously unliquidated. **4.** *Property.* The absorption of a lesser estate into a greater estate when both become the same person's property. Cf. SURRENDER (3). **5.** *Criminal law.* The absorption of a lesser included offense into a more serious offense when a person is charged with both crimes, so that the person is not subject to double jeopardy. ● For example, a defendant cannot be convicted of both attempt (or solicitation) and the completed crime — though merger does not apply to conspiracy and the completed crime. — Also termed *merger of offenses.* **6.** *Civil procedure.* The effect of a judgment for the plaintiff, which absorbs any claim that was the subject of the lawsuit into the judgment, so that the plaintiff's rights are confined to enforcing the judgment. Cf. BAR (5). **7.** The joining of the procedural aspects of law and equity. **8.** The absorption of one organization (esp. a corporation) that ceases to exist into another that retains its own name and identity and acquires the assets and liabilities of the former. ● Corporate mergers must conform to statutory formalities and usu. must be approved by a majority of the outstanding shares. — Also termed *corporate merger.* Cf. CONSOLIDATION (4); BUYOUT.

bust-up merger. A merger in which the acquiring corporation sells off lines of business owned by the target corporation to repay the loans used in the acquisition.

cash merger. A merger in which shareholders of the target company must accept cash for their shares. — Also termed *cash-out merger; freeze-out merger.*

conglomerate merger. A merger between unrelated businesses that are neither competitors nor customers or suppliers of each other.

de facto merger (di **fak**-toh). A transaction that has the economic effect of a statutory merger but that is cast in the form of an acquisition or sale of assets or voting stock. ● Although such a transaction does not meet the statutory requirements for a merger, a court will generally treat it as a statutory merger for purposes of the appraisal remedy.

downstream merger. A merger of a parent corporation into its subsidiary.

forward triangular merger. See *triangular merger.*

freeze-out merger. See *cash merger.*

horizontal merger. A merger between two or more businesses that are on the same market level because they manufacture similar products in the same geographic region; a merger of direct competitors. — Also termed *horizontal integration.*

product-extension merger. A merger in which the products of the acquired company are complementary to those of the acquiring company and may be produced with similar facilities, marketed through the same channels, and advertised by the same media.

reverse triangular merger. A merger in which the acquiring corporation's subsidiary is absorbed into the target corporation, which becomes a new subsidiary of the acquiring corporation. — Also termed *reverse subsidiary merger.*

short-form merger. A statutory merger that is less expensive and time-consuming than an ordinary statutory merger, usu. permitted when a subsidiary merges into a parent that already owns most of the subsidiary's shares. ● Such a merger is generally accomplished when the parent adopts a merger resolution, mails a copy of the plan to the subsidiary's record shareholders, and files the executed articles of merger with the secretary of state, who issues a certificate of merger.

statutory merger. A merger provided by and conducted according to statutory requirements.

stock merger. A merger involving one company's purchase of another company's capital stock.

triangular merger. A merger in which the target corporation is absorbed into the acquiring corporation's subsidiary, with the target's shareholders receiving stock in the parent corporation. — Also termed *subsidiary merger; forward triangular merger.*

upstream merger. A merger of a subsidiary corporation into its parent.

vertical merger. A merger between businesses occupying different levels of operation for the same product, such as between a manufacturer and a retailer; a merger of buyer and seller.

9. The merger of rights and duties in the same person, resulting in the extinction of obligations; esp. the blending of the rights of a creditor and debtor, resulting in the extinguishment of the creditor's right to collect the debt. • As originally developed in Roman law, a merger resulted from the marriage of a debtor and creditor, or when a debtor became the creditor's heir. — Also termed *confusion; confusion of debts; confusion of rights.* Cf. CONFUSION OF TITLES. **10.** The absorption of a contract into a court order, so that an agreement between the parties (often a marital agreement incident to a divorce or separation) loses its separate identity as an enforceable contract when it is incorporated into a court order.

merger clause. See INTEGRATION CLAUSE.

merger doctrine. 1. *Copyright.* The principle that since an idea cannot be copyrighted, neither can an expression that must inevitably be used in order to express the idea. • When the idea and expression are very difficult to separate, they are said to merge. For example, courts have refused copyright protection for business-ledger forms (*Baker v. Selden*, 101 U.S. 99 (1879)), and for contest rules that were copied almost verbatim (*Morrissey v. Procter & Gamble*, 379 F.2d 675 (1st Cir. 1967)). — Also termed *Baker v. Selden doctrine.* **2.** *Hist. Family law.* The common-law principle that, upon marriage, the husband and wife combined to form one legal entity. — Often shortened to *merger; merger doctrine.* See SPOUSAL-UNITY DOCTRINE; LEGAL-UNITIES DOCTRINE.

merger of offenses. See MERGER (5).

meritorious (mer-ə-**tor**-ee-əs), *adj.* (15c) **1.** (Of an act, etc.) meriting esteem or reward <meritorious trial performance>. **2.** (Of a case, etc.) meriting a legal victory; having legal worth <meritorious claim>.

meritorious consideration. See *good consideration* under CONSIDERATION (1).

meritorious defense. See DEFENSE (1).

merit regulation. Under state blue-sky laws, the practice of requiring securities offerings not only to be accompanied by a full and adequate disclosure but also to be substantively fair, just, and equitable.

merits. (18c) **1.** The elements or grounds of a claim or defense; the substantive considerations to be taken into account in deciding a case, as opposed to extraneous or technical points, esp. of procedure <trial on the merits>. **2.** EQUITY (3) <on questions of euthanasia, the Supreme Court has begun to concern itself with the merits as well as the law>.

merits brief. See *brief on the merits* under BRIEF.

merits discovery. See DISCOVERY.

merit system. (1879) The practice of hiring and promoting employees, esp. government employees, based on their competence rather than political favoritism. Cf. SPOILS SYSTEM.

Merit Systems Protection Board. The independent federal agency that oversees personnel practices of the federal government and hears and decides appeals from adverse personnel actions taken against federal employees. • It has five regional offices and five field offices. Its functions were transferred from the former Civil Service Commission under Reorganization Plan No. 2 of 1978. — Abbr. MSPB. See CIVIL SERVICE COMMISSION.

MERP. *abbr.* Medical-expense reimbursement plan. See EMPLOYEE BENEFIT PLAN.

Merrill doctrine. The principle that the government cannot be estopped from disavowing an agent's unauthorized act. *Federal Crop Ins. Corp. v. Merrill*, 332 U.S. 380, 68 S.Ct. 1 (1947).

merum (**meer**-əm). [Latin] *Hist.* Mere; naked.

merum jus (**meer**-əm jəs). See MERE RIGHT.

mesne (meen), *adj.* (16c) **1.** Occupying a middle position; intermediate or intervening, esp. in time of occurrence or performance <the mesne encumbrance has priority over the third mortgage, but is subordinate to the first mortgage>. **2.** *Hist.* Of or relating to a lord who holds land of a superior while himself having a tenant.

mesne agreement. A transfer of intellectual-property rights through an intermediary, usu. an assignee, rather than directly from the property's creator.

mesne assignment. See ASSIGNMENT (2).

mesne conveyance. See CONVEYANCE.

mesne encumbrance. See ENCUMBRANCE.

mesne lord. *Hist.* A feudal lord who stood between a tenant and the chief lord, and held land from a superior lord. See LORD (3).

mesne process. See PROCESS.

mesne profits. See PROFIT (1).

mesonomic (mes-ə-**nom**-ik *also* mee-zə), *adj.* Of, relating to, or involving an act that, although it does not affect a person's physical freedom, has legal consequences in its evolution. • This term was coined by the philosopher Albert Kocourek in his book *Jural Relations* (1927). Cf. ZYGNOMIC.

message. (14c) A written or oral communication, often sent through a messenger or other agent, or electronically (e.g., through e-mail or voice-mail).

annual message. A message from the President or a governor given at the opening of an annual legislative session.

Presidential message. A communication from the President to the U.S. Congress on matters pertaining to the state of the union, esp. of matters requiring legislative consideration. U.S. Const. art. II, § 3. — Also termed *State of the Union.*

special message. A message from the President or a governor relating to a particular matter.

veto message. See VETO MESSAGE.

message from the Crown. An official communication from the sovereign to Parliament.

messenger. (14c) **1.** One who conveys a communication; esp. one employed to deliver telegrams or other communications. **2.** *Hist.* An officer who performs certain ministerial duties, such as taking temporary charge of assets of an insolvent estate.

messuage (mes-wij). (14c) A dwelling house together with the curtilage, including any outbuildings. See CURTILAGE.

meta (mee-tə), *n.* [Latin] **1.** *Roman law.* The mark where a racecourse ends or around which chariots turn; by extension, a limit in space or time. **2.** *Hist.* A boundary; a border.

metadata. Secondary data that organize, manage, and facilitate the use and understanding of primary data. ● Metadata are evaluated when conducting and responding to electronic discovery. If privileged documents or final versions of computer files may contain metadata, they might be "scrubbed" before release. See Fed. R. Civ. P. 26(b)(2)(B).

metalaw (met-ə-law). (1956) A hypothetical set of legal principles based on the rules of existing legal systems and designed to provide a framework of agreement for these different systems.

metatag. A word or phrase in HTML computer code that usu. identifies the subject of a web page and acts as a hidden keyword for Internet search engines. ● A person who uses a trademark as a metatag without permission may infringe on the trademark owner's rights.

metayer system (me-**tay**-yər *or* met-ə-**yay**). An agricultural system in which land is divided into small farms among single families who pay a landlord a fixed portion — usu. half — of the produce and the landlord provides the stock. ● The system was formerly prevalent in parts of France and Italy, and in the southern part of the United States. — Also written *métayer system.*

mete out, *vb.* (bef. 15c) To dispense or measure out (justice, punishment, etc.) <shortly after the jury returned its verdict, the judge meted out an appropriate punishment>.

meter. 1. A metric unit of length equal to 39.368 inches. **2.** An instrument of measurement used to measure use or consumption, esp. used by a utility company to measure utility consumption <a gas meter> <a water meter> <a parking meter>.

meter rate. A rate that a utility company applies to determine a charge for service <meter rate based on kilowatt-hours of electricity>.

metes and bounds (meets). (15c) The territorial limits of real property as measured by distances and angles from designated landmarks and in relation to adjoining properties. ● Metes and bounds are usu. described in deeds and surveys to establish the boundary lines of land. — Also termed *running description*; *butts and bounds*; *lines and corners.* See CALL (5).

metewand (**meet**-wahnd). *Archaic.* A measuring staff of varying lengths.

meteyard (**meet**-yahrd). *Archaic.* A metewand that is one yard long.

method. (15c) A mode of organizing, operating, or performing something, esp. to achieve a goal <method of election> <method of performing a job>.

method claim. See PATENT CLAIM.

method patent. See PATENT (3).

metric system. (1864) A decimal system for measuring length, weight, area, or volume, based on the meter as a unit length and the kilogram as a unit mass.

metropolitan, *adj.* (14c) Of or relating to a city or metropolis.

metropolitan, *n. Eccles. law.* An archbishop; the head of a province <the Archbishop of Canterbury is a metropolitan>.

metropolitan council. An official or quasi-official body appointed or elected by voters of a metropolitan area to provide for the unified administration of services (such as sewage disposal or public transportation) to the cities and towns within the metropolitan area.

metropolitan district. See DISTRICT.

metropolitan magistrate. See *metropolitan stipendiary magistrate* under MAGISTRATE.

metus (mee-təs), *n.* [Latin] *Roman law.* **1.** Fear of imminent danger; apprehension of serious danger, esp. in the form of duress to force a person to do something; the use of threats to bring about some end. ● *Metus* was more comprehensive than duress is in Anglo-American law. It included fear of any evil that was serious enough to affect a reasonable person. **2.** A threat that diminishes the value of another's property. • In both senses, a victim was allowed to seek fourfold damages against the perpetrator. Cf. DOLUS.

Mexican divorce. See DIVORCE.

MFN. *abbr.* MOST FAVORED NATION.

MFN clause. See MOST-FAVORED-NATION CLAUSE.

MFN treatment. *abbr.* MOST-FAVORED-NATION TREATMENT.

Michaelmas sittings (**mik-əl-məs**). In England, a term of court running from November 2 to November 25. • Until 1875, this was also called the *Michaelmas term.* The division of the legal year into terms was abolished by the Judicature Act of 1873. — Also termed *Michaelmas term.* Cf. EASTER SITTINGS; HILARY SITTINGS; TRINITY SITTINGS.

Midcal **test.** *Antitrust.* The doctrine that the anticompetitive acts of a private party will be considered state acts — and thereby protected from liability under the antitrust laws — if the acts are within a clearly articulated and affirmatively expressed policy of the state, and if the conduct is actively supervised by the state. *California Retail Liquor Dealers Ass'n v. Midcal Aluminum, Inc.,* 445 U.S. 97, 100 S.Ct. 937 (1980). See STATE-ACTION DOCTRINE; ACTIVE SUPERVISION.

mid-channel. See MIDDLE LINE OF MAIN CHANNEL.

middle burden of proof. See BURDEN OF PROOF.

middle-level scrutiny. See INTERMEDIATE SCRUTINY.

middle line of main channel. The equidistant point in the main channel of the river between the well-defined banks on either shore; the middle thread of a river's current. — Also termed *mid-channel*; *middle of the river.*

middleman. (17c) An intermediary or agent between two parties; esp. a dealer (such as a wholesaler) who buys from producers and sells to retailers or consumers.

middle management. See MANAGEMENT.

middle of the river. See MIDDLE LINE OF MAIN CHANNEL.

middle-of-the-road test. See HYDRAFLOW TEST.

middle thread. The center line of something; esp. an imaginary line drawn lengthwise through the middle of a stream's current.

mid-level scrutiny. See INTERMEDIATE SCRUTINY.

midnight deadline. A time limit for doing something, ending at midnight on a particular day. • For a bank, the midnight deadline is midnight on the next banking day following the day on which the bank receives the relevant item or from

which the time for taking action begins to run, whichever is later. UCC § 4-104(a)(10).

midnight judge. *Hist.* A federal judicial nominee appointed by President John Adams just before his term expired, in an effort to pack the judiciary with Federalist Party sympathizers. • The Judiciary Act of 1801, passed and signed into law a few weeks before Adams's term expired, led to the appointment of 84 federal judges and countless marshals, clerks, attorneys, registers of wills, and justices of the peace, all of whom were affiliated with the Federalists. The Senate approved nominations and granted commissions up until its final adjournment just before Thomas Jefferson's inauguration. More than half of the commissions had not been delivered by the end of inauguration day. Secretary of State James Madison, acting at Jefferson's direction, barred their delivery and treated them as void. This led William Marbury to seek a federal court order to compel Madison to deliver Marbury's commission as justice of the peace. See *Marbury v. Madison,* 5 U.S. 137 (1803).

midshipman. (17c) A naval cadet; a student at the U.S. Naval Academy.

midway. See THALWEG.

Midwest Piping **rule.** *Labor law.* The doctrine that an employer may not recognize multiple unions during a period in which there are conflicting claims of representation. *Midwest Piping & Supply Co.,* 63 NLRB Dec. (CCH) 1060 (1945).

migrant worker. **1.** *Int'l law.* A person who works seasonally as an agricultural laborer in a foreign country, esp. in agricultural labor. **2.** A person who works seasonally as a laborer in a different part of his or her own country.

migration. (17c) Movement (of people or animals) from one country or region to another.

migratory corporation. See CORPORATION.

migratory divorce. See DIVORCE.

Mike O'Connor **rule.** *Labor law.* The doctrine that unilateral changes that an employer makes after a union victory in an initial-representation election — but before the employer's objections have been resolved — are automatic violations of the National Labor Relations Act if the employer's objections are rejected. • If the employer's objections are sustained, any failure-to-bargain charge will be dismissed because the employer had no duty to bargain. But if the employer's objections are rejected, the employer is considered to have been under a duty to bargain as of the date of the election, which is why the unilateral changes are automatic violations of the Act. *Mike O'Connor Chevrolet-Buick-GMC Co.,* 209 NLRB Dec. (CCH) 701 (1974).

mild exigency. (1984) A circumstance that justifies a law-enforcement officer's departure from the knock-and-announce rule, such as the likelihood that the building's occupants will try to escape, resist arrest, or destroy evidence. See KNOCK-AND-ANNOUNCE RULE.

mile. (bef. 12c) **1.** A measure of distance equal to 5,280 feet. — Also termed *statute mile.* **2.** NAUTICAL MILE.

mileage. (18c) **1.** The distance in miles between two points. **2.** The distance a vehicle has traveled as reflected by an odometer. **3.** An allowance paid for travel expenses, as of a witness or public employee.

military, *adj.* (15c) **1.** Of or relating to the armed forces <military base>. **2.** Of or relating to war <military action>.

military, *n.* (18c) The armed forces.

military allotment. *Family law.* A child-support deduction from the salary of an obligor parent on active duty in the United States military and paid to the obligee parent. See *attachment of wages* under ATTACHMENT (1).

military board. A group of persons appointed to act as a fact-finding agency or as an advisory body to the appointing military authority.

military bounty land. Land offered to members of the military as a reward for services. See *donation land, bounty land* under LAND; BOUNTY-LAND WARRANT.

military commission. A court, usu. composed of both civilians and military officers, that is modeled after a court-martial and that tries and decides cases concerning martial-law violations. See COURT-MARTIAL.

military-contract defense. See GOVERNMENT-CONTRACTOR DEFENSE.

military-contractor defense. See GOVERNMENT-CONTRACTOR DEFENSE.

military court. See COURT.

military court of inquiry. See COURT.

military draft. See DRAFT (2).

military government. *Int'l law.* The control of all or most public functions within a country, or the assumption and exercise of governmental functions, by military forces or individual members of those forces; government exercised by a military commander under the direction of the executive or sovereign, either externally during a foreign war or internally during a civil war. • A military government's actions supersede all local law. See MARTIAL LAW.

military judge. See JUDGE.

military judge alone. *Military law.* A court-martial presided over by a single judge with no other court-martial members present.

military jurisdiction. The three types of governmental power given the military by the U.S. Constitution — specif., jurisdiction under military law, jurisdiction under military government, and jurisdiction under martial law.

military justice. A structure of punitive measures designed to foster order, morale, and discipline within the military. See MILITARY LAW.

military law. The branch of public law governing military discipline and other rules regarding service in the armed forces. • It is exercised both in peacetime and in war, is recognized by civil courts, and includes rules far broader than for the punishment of offenders. — Also termed *military justice.* — Sometimes loosely termed *martial law.* Cf. MARTIAL LAW.

military leave. A policy contained in employment policies or collective-bargaining agreements allowing a long-term leave of absence — without an accompanying loss of benefits — for a person in active service in the U.S. armed forces.

military necessity. *Int'l law.* A principle of warfare allowing coercive force to achieve a desired end, as long as the force used is not more than is called for by the situation. • This principle dates from the Hague Convention on Laws and Customs of War on Land of October 18, 1907, which prohibits the destruction or seizure of enemy property "unless such destruction or seizure be imperatively demanded by the necessities of war."

military objective. *Int'l law.* An object that by its nature, location, or use contributes to military action, and is thus susceptible to attack. • Under Geneva Convention Protocol 1 (1977), only military — rather than civilian — objects are proper targets.

military offense. An offense, such as desertion, that lies within the jurisdiction of a military court. See COURT-MARTIAL.

military officer. See OFFICER (2).

Military Rules of Evidence. The rules of evidence applicable to military law and courts-martial. — Abbr. MRE.

military tenure. See TENURE.

military testament. See *soldier's will* under WILL.

militate (mil-ə-tayt), *vb.* (16c) To exert a strong influence <the evidence of police impropriety militates against a conviction>. Cf. MITIGATE.

militia (mə-lish-ə), *n.* (16c) **1.** A body of citizens armed and trained, esp. by a state, for military service apart from the regular armed forces. • The Constitution recognizes a state's right to form a "well-regulated militia" but also grants Congress the power to activate, organize, and govern a federal militia. U.S. Const. amend. II; U.S. Const. art. I, § 8, cl. 15–16. See NATIONAL GUARD.

reserve militia. All persons who are not exempt from military service and not actively serving in the armed forces or national guard.

2. *Roman law.* Military service.

Militia Clause. (1918) One of two clauses of the U.S. Constitution giving Congress the power to call forth, arm, and maintain a military force to enforce compliance with its laws, suppress insurrections, and repel invasions. U.S. Const. art. I, § 8, cls. 15 and 16.

mill. (bef. 12c) **1.** A machine that grinds corn, grain, or other substances, esp. using a wheel and circular motion. • The substance ground in a mill is sometimes called grist, esp. when it is a grain. Courts sometimes refer to the grinding process as a metaphor for the judicial process <suits to collect on promissory notes are grist for the summary-judgment mill because the material facts in such cases are often undisputed>. **2.** The building in which the grinding is performed, along with the site, dam, or other items connected with the mill. **3.** A monetary unit equal to one-tenth of a cent. • Mills are a money of account used in the United States and Canada, esp. to reckon tax rates.

millage rate. See MILL RATE.

Miller Act. A federal law requiring the posting of performance and payment bonds before an award is made for a contract for construction, alteration, or repair of a public work or building. 40 USCA §§ 270a–270d-1.

Miller **trust.** See TRUST.

Miller–Tydings Act. A federal law, enacted in 1937 as an amendment to the Sherman Act, exempting fair-trade laws from the application of the Sherman Act and legalizing resale-price-maintenance agreements between producers and retailers of products. • The Act was repealed by the Consumer Goods Pricing Act of 1975.

Miller v. Shugart **agreement.** A settlement in which an insured consents to a judgment in favor of the plaintiff, on the condition that the plaintiff will satisfy the judgment only out of proceeds from the insured's policy, and will not seek recovery against the insured personally. • Although the phrase takes its name from a Minnesota case, it is used in other jurisdictions as well. *Miller v. Shugart*, 316 N.W.2d 729 (Minn. 1982).

milling in transit. An arrangement in which a shipment is temporarily detained at an intermediate point, usu. for the application of some manufacturing process, with or without an increase of a freight charge by the carrier.

mill power. A unit of water power used in defining quantities and weights of water available to a lessee.

mill privilege. The right of a mill-site owner to construct a mill and to use power from a stream to operate it, with due regard to the rights of other owners along the stream's path.

mill rate. A tax applied to real property whereby each mill represents $1 of tax assessment per $1,000 of the property's assessed value <the mill rate for taxes in this county is 10 mills, so for a home valued at $100,000, the owner will pay $1,000 in property taxes>. — Also termed *millage rate.*

mill site. 1. A small tract of land on or contiguous to a watercourse, suitable for the erection and operation of a mill. **2.** *Mining law.* A small parcel of nonmineral public land (not exceeding five acres) claimed and occupied by an owner of a mining claim because the extra space is needed for mining or ore-reduction operations. 30 USCA § 42.

Mimms **order.** (1993) A police officer's command for a motorist to get out of the vehicle. • A *Mimms* order need not be independently justified if the initial stop was lawful. *Pennsylvania v. Mimms*, 434 U.S. 106, 98 S.Ct. 330 (1977).

mind. (bef. 12c) **1.** The source of thought and intellect; the seat of mental faculties. **2.** The ability to will, direct, or assent. — Also termed *sound mind.* **3.** Memory.

mind and memory. *Archaic.* A testator's mental capacity to make a will <she argued that her uncle was not of sound mind and memory when executing the will because he had Alzheimer's disease>. • This phrase was generally used as part of the phrase *of sound mind and memory,* referring to the capacity of a testator to make a will. See CAPACITY (2).

mine. (14c) **1.** An underground excavation used to obtain minerals, ores, or other substances. **2.** A mineral deposit; a place containing a mineral deposit.

mineral, *n.* (15c) **1.** Any natural inorganic matter that has a definite chemical composition and specific physical properties that give it value <most minerals are crystalline solids>. **2.** A subsurface material that is explored for, mined, and exploited for its useful properties and commercial value. **3.** Any natural material that is defined as a mineral by statute or caselaw.

mineral acre. *Oil & gas.* The full mineral interest in one acre of land.

mineral deed. See DEED.

mineral district. See DISTRICT.

mineral easement. See EASEMENT.

mineral entry. (1882) The right of entry on public land to mine valuable mineral deposits.

mineral interest. *Oil & gas.* The right to search for, develop, and remove minerals from land or to receive a royalty based on the production of minerals. ● Mineral interests are granted by an oil-and-gas lease. — Also termed *mineral right*. See FEE INTEREST; SUBSURFACE INTEREST; SURFACE INTEREST.

mineral land. See LAND.

mineral lease. See LEASE.

mineral lode. (1870) A mineral bed of rock with definite boundaries in a general mass of a mountain; any belt of mineralized rock lying within boundaries that clearly separate it from neighboring rock. — Also termed *lode*.

mineral right. See MINERAL INTEREST.

mineral royalty. See ROYALTY (2).

mineral servitude. See SERVITUDE (2).

Minerals Management Service. A unit in the U.S. Department of the Interior responsible for entering into and managing leases for the recovery of minerals on the outer continental shelf and for collecting and distributing royalty and other payments due the U.S. and Indian tribes from mineral production.

miner's inch. A measurement of water discharge, equaling nine-gallons per minute from a one-inch square pipe. ● The precise measurement of a miner's inch varies in different localities.

Mine Safety and Health Administration. A unit in the U.S. Department of Labor responsible for preventing mine accidents and occupational diseases in the nation's mining industry. ● It sets mandatory safety and health standards, assesses fines for their violation, and investigates mine accidents. Its programs are operated through regional administrators located in the nation's mining regions. — Abbr. MSHA.

minimal contacts. See MINIMUM CONTACTS.

minimalist retributivism. See RETRIBUTIVISM.

minimal participant. (1987) *Criminal law*. Under the federal sentencing guidelines, a defendant who is among the least culpable of a group of criminal actors, as when the defendant does not understand the scope or structure of the criminal enterprise or the actions of the other members of the group. ● The offense level for a crime of a minimal participant can be decreased by four levels. U.S. Sentencing Guidelines Manual § 3B1.2(a). Cf. MINOR PARTICIPANT.

minimal scrutiny. See RATIONAL-BASIS TEST.

mini-maxi, *n*. An underwriting arrangement for a securities transaction, whereby a broker is required to sell the minimum number of securities on an all-or-none basis and the balance on a best-efforts basis. See UNDERWRITING (2).

miniment (min-ə-mənt). See MUNIMENT.

mini-*Miranda* requirement. *Debtor–creditor law*. A debt collector's obligation when communicating with a debtor to inform the debtor that (1) the communication is from a debt collector seeking to collect a debt and (2) any information received will be used for that purpose. ● This disclosure is required by the Fair Debt Collection Practices Act.

minimization requirement. (1972) *Criminal law*. The mandate that police officers acting under an eavesdropping warrant must use the wiretap in a way that will intercept the fewest possible conversations that are not subject to the warrant.

minimum, *adj*. (17c) Of, relating to, or constituting the smallest acceptable or possible quantity in a given case <minimum charge to a customer of a public utility>.

minimum contacts. (1945) A nonresident defendant's forum-state connections, such as business activity or actions foreseeably leading to business activity, that are substantial enough to bring the defendant within the forum-state court's personal jurisdiction without offending traditional notions of fair play and substantial justice. *International Shoe Co. v. Washington*, 326 U.S. 310, 66 S.Ct. 154 (1945). — Also termed *minimal contacts*.

minimum-fee schedule. *Hist*. A list of the lowest fees that a lawyer may charge, set by a state bar association. ● The courts held that minimum-fee schedules, now defunct, violated antitrust laws.

minimum lot. See LOT (1).

minimum-royalty clause. *Patents*. A royalty-agreement provision that prescribes a fixed payment by the licensee to the patentee, regardless of whether the invention is actually used.

minimum sale. See EXHIBITION VALUE.

minimum scrutiny. See RATIONAL-BASIS TEST.

minimum sentence. See SENTENCE.

minimum tax. See *alternative minimum tax* under TAX.

minimum wage. See WAGE.

mining. The process of extracting ore or minerals from the ground; the working of a mine. ● This term also encompasses oil and gas drilling.

mining claim. A parcel of land that contains precious metal in its soil or rock and that is appropriated by a person according to established rules and customs known as the process of *location*. See LOCATION (4), (5).

    lode claim. A mining claim (on public land) to a well-defined vein embedded in rock; a mining claim to a mineral lode.

    placer claim. A mining claim that is not a lode claim; a claim where the minerals are not located in veins or lodes within rock, but are usu. in softer ground near the earth's surface.

mining lease. See LEASE.

mining location. 1. See LOCATION (4). **2.** See LOCATION (5).

mining partnership. An association of persons to jointly share a mining business, including the profits, expenses, and losses. • The partnership has features of both a tenancy in common and an ordinary commercial partnership.

mining rent. Consideration given for a mining lease, whether the lease creates a tenancy, conveys a fee, or grants a mere license or incorporeal right.

minister, *n.* (14c) **1.** A person acting under another's authority; an agent. **2.** A prominent government officer appointed to manage an executive or administrative department. **3.** A diplomatic representative, esp. one ranking below an ambassador.

> *foreign minister.* **1.** A minister of foreign affairs, who in many countries is equivalent to the U.S. Secretary of State. **2.** An ambassador, minister, or envoy from a foreign government.

> *minister plenipotentiary* (plen-ə-pə-**ten**-shee-er-ee). A minister ranking below an ambassador but possessing full power and authority as a governmental representative, esp. as an envoy of a sovereign ruler. • This officer is often regarded as the personal representative of a head of state.

> *public minister.* A high diplomatic representative such as an ambassador, envoy, or resident, but not including a commercial representative such as a consul.

4. A person authorized by a Christian church to perform religious functions.

ministerial, *adj.* (16c) Of or relating to an act that involves obedience to instructions or laws instead of discretion, judgment, or skill <the court clerk's ministerial duties include recording judgments on the docket>.

ministerial act. See ACT.

ministerial duty. 1. See *ministerial act* under ACT. **2.** See DUTY (2).

ministerial-function test. (1990) The principle that the First Amendment bars judicial resolution of a Title VII employment-discrimination claim based on a religious preference, if the employee's responsibilities are religious in nature, as in spreading faith, supervising a religious order, and the like. 42 USCA § 2000e-1(a). See TITLE VII OF THE CIVIL RIGHTS ACT OF 1964.

ministerial office. See OFFICE.

ministerial officer. See OFFICER (1).

ministerial trust. See *passive trust* under TRUST.

minister plenipotentiary. See MINISTER.

ministrant (**min**-ə-strənt). **1.** One who ministers; a dispenser. **2.** *Hist. Eccles. law.* A party who cross-examines a witness.

minitrial. (1990) A private, voluntary, and informal form of dispute resolution in which each party's attorney presents an abbreviated version of its case to a neutral third party and to the opponent's representatives, who have settlement authority. • The third party may render an advisory opinion on the anticipated outcome of litigation. Cf. *summary jury trial* under TRIAL.

minor, *n.* (16c) **1.** A person who has not reached full legal age; a child or juvenile. — Also termed *infant.* Cf. ADULT.

> *emancipated minor.* (1817) A minor who is self-supporting and independent of parental control, usu. as a result of a court order. See EMANCIPATION.

> *minor in need of supervision.* See *child in need of supervision* under CHILD. — Abbr. MINS.

2. *Roman law.* A person who is past puberty but less than 25 years old. — Also termed *minor quam 25 annis.*

minor crime. See MISDEMEANOR.

minor dispute. See DISPUTE.

minor fact. See FACT.

minority. (15c) **1.** The state or condition of being under legal age. • In Scots law, legal minority begins at the end of puberty; until then, a person is a *pupil.* — Also termed *infancy; nonage; immaturity.* Cf. MAJORITY (1). **2.** A group having fewer than a controlling number of votes. Cf. MAJORITY (2). **3.** A group that is different in some respect (such as race or religious belief) from the majority and that is sometimes treated differently as a result; a member of such a group. • Some courts have held that the term *minority,* in this sense, is not limited to a group that is outnumbered. It may also be applied to a group that has been traditionally discriminated against or socially suppressed, even if its members are in the numerical majority in an area.

Minority Business Development Agency. A unit in the U.S. Department of Commerce responsible for developing and coordinating a national program for minority business enterprise. — Abbr. MBDA.

minority discount. A reduction in the value of a closely held business's shares that are owned by someone who has only a minority interest in the business. • The concept underlying a minority discount is recognition that controlling shares — those owned by someone who can control the business — are worth more in the market than noncontrolling shares. But when dissenting shareholders object to a corporate act, such as a merger, and become entitled to have their shares appraised and bought by the corporation, many courts hold that incorporating a minority discount into the valuation of the dissenters' shares is inequitable and is not permitted. See APPRAISAL REMEDY.

minority opinion. See *dissenting opinion* under OPINION (1).

minority report. See REPORT (1).

minority shareholder. See SHAREHOLDER.

minor participant. (1960) *Criminal law.* Under the federal sentencing guidelines, a defendant who is less culpable for a crime than the other members of the group committing the crime, but who has more culpability than a minimal participant. ● A defendant who is a minor participant can have the offense level for the crime decreased by two levels. U.S. Sentencing Guidelines Manual § 3B1.2(b). Cf. MINIMAL PARTICIPANT.

minor's estate. See ESTATE (1).

minor's trust. See *2503(c) trust* under TRUST.

MINS. *abbr.* Minor in need of supervision. See *child in need of supervision* under CHILD.

mint, *n.* (15c) **1.** A government-authorized place for coining money. **2.** A large supply, esp. of money.

mintage. (16c) **1.** The mint's charge for coining money. **2.** The product of minting; money.

mint-mark. An authorized mark on a coin showing where it was minted.

minuend (**min**-yoo-end). (18c) In a mathematical equation, the number from which another number (the subtrahend) is subtracted to arrive at a remainder or balance. ● The term is used in law in a variety of accounting and mathematical contexts. Cf. SUBTRAHEND.

minute book. (16c) **1.** A book in which a court clerk enters minutes of court proceedings. **2.** A record of the subjects discussed and actions taken at a corporate directors' or shareholders' meeting. — Also termed *minutes book.*

minute entry. See *minute order* (1) under ORDER (2).

minute order. See ORDER (2).

minutes. (15c) **1.** Memoranda or notes of a transaction, proceeding, or meeting. **2.** *Parliamentary law.* The formal record of a deliberative assembly's proceedings, approved (as corrected, if necessary) by the assembly. — Also termed *journal; record; report.* See DISPENSE WITH THE READING OF THE MINUTES; SPREAD UPON THE MINUTES. **3.** *Scots law.* Written forms for preserving evidence.

minutes book. See MINUTE BOOK.

Miranda hearing (mə-**ran**-də). (1966) A pretrial proceeding held to determine whether the *Miranda* rule has been followed and thus whether the prosecutor may introduce into evidence the defendant's statements to the police made after arrest. See MIRANDA RULE.

Miranda rule. (1966) The doctrine that a criminal suspect in police custody must be informed of certain constitutional rights before being interrogated. ● The suspect must be advised of the right to remain silent, the right to have an attorney present during questioning, and the right to have an attorney appointed if the suspect cannot afford one. If the suspect is not advised of these rights or does not validly waive them, any evidence obtained during the interrogation cannot be used against the suspect at trial (except for impeachment purposes). *Miranda v. Arizona*, 384 U.S. 436, 86 S.Ct. 1602 (1966).

Miranda warning. See MIRANDA RULE.

Mirandize (mə-**ran**-dɪz), *vb.* (1971) *Slang.* To read or recite (to an arrestee) rights under the *Miranda* rule <the suspect was arrested, Mirandized, and interrogated>. See MIRANDA RULE.

mirror-image rule. (1972) *Contracts.* The doctrine that the acceptance of a contractual offer must be positive, unconditional, unequivocal, and unambiguous, and must not change, add to, or qualify the terms of the offer; the common-law principle that for a contract to be formed, the terms of an acceptance must correspond exactly with those of the offer. ● In modern commercial contexts, the mirror-image rule has been replaced by a UCC provision that allows parties to enforce their agreement despite minor discrepancies between the offer and the acceptance. The rule still applies to international sales contracts governed by the UN Convention on Contracts for the International Sales of Goods (article 19). — Also termed *ribbon-matching rule.* See BATTLE OF THE FORMS.

misadministration. See MALADMINISTRATION.

misadventure. (13c) **1.** A mishap or misfortune. **2.** Homicide committed accidentally by a person doing a lawful act and having no intent to injure; ACCIDENTAL KILLING.

misallege, *vb.* To erroneously assert (a fact, a claim, etc.).

misapplication, *n.* (17c) The improper or illegal use of funds or property lawfully held. — **misapply,** *vb.*

misappropriation, *n.* (18c) **1.** The application of another's property or money dishonestly to one's own use. See EMBEZZLEMENT. Cf. APPROPRIATION; EXPROPRIATION (1). **2.** *Intellectual property.* The common-law tort of using the noncopyrightable information or ideas that an organization collects and disseminates for a profit to compete unfairly against that organization, or copying a work whose creator has not yet claimed or been granted exclusive rights in the work. *Int'l News*

Serv. v. Associated Press, 248 U.S. 215, 29 S.Ct. 68 (1918). • The elements of misappropriation are: (1) the plaintiff must have invested time, money, or effort to extract the information, (2) the defendant must have taken the information with no similar investment, and (3) the plaintiff must have suffered a competitive injury because of the taking. **3.** The doctrine giving rise to such a tort claim. — **misappropriate,** *vb.*

misappropriation theory. *Securities.* The doctrine that a person who wrongfully uses confidential information to buy or sell securities in violation of a duty owed to the one who is the information source is guilty of securities fraud.

misbehavior in office. See *official misconduct* under MISCONDUCT.

misbranding, *n.* The act or an instance of labeling one's product falsely or in a misleading way. • Misbranding is prohibited by federal and state law. — **misbrand,** *vb.*

miscarriage. (16c) Spontaneous and involuntary premature expulsion of a nonviable fetus. — Also termed *spontaneous abortion.*

    criminal miscarriage. Hist. See ABORTION (1).

miscarriage of justice. (1862) A grossly unfair outcome in a judicial proceeding, as when a defendant is convicted despite a lack of evidence on an essential element of the crime. — Also termed *failure of justice.*

miscegenation (mi-sej-ə-**nay**-shən). (1863) A marriage between persons of different races, formerly considered illegal in some jurisdictions. • In 1967, the U.S. Supreme Court held that laws banning interracial marriages are unconstitutional. *Loving v. Virginia*, 388 U.S. 1, 87 S.Ct. 1817 (1967). But for years, such laws technically remained on the books in some states. The last remaining state-law ban on interracial marriages was a provision in the Alabama constitution. The Alabama legislature voted to repeal the ban, subject to a vote of the state's citizens, in 1999; the repeal became effective in 2000. — Also termed *mixed marriage; interracial marriage.*

miscellaneous itemized deduction. See DEDUCTION.

mischarge. (1939) An erroneous jury instruction that may be grounds for reversing a verdict. — Also termed *misdirection.*

mischief (**mis**-chəf). (14c) **1.** A condition in which a person suffers a wrong or is under some hardship, esp. one that a statute seeks to remove or for which equity provides a remedy <this legislation seeks to eliminate the mischief of racially restrictive deed covenants>. **2.** Injury or damage caused by a specific person or thing <the vandals were convicted of criminal mischief>. **3.** The act

causing such injury or damage <their mischief damaged the abbey>.

mischief rule. (1974) In statutory construction, the doctrine that a statute should be interpreted by first identifying the problem (or "mischief") that the statute was designed to remedy and then adopting a construction that will suppress the problem and advance the remedy. — Also termed *rule in Heydon's Case; purpose approach.* Cf. GOLDEN RULE; PLAIN-MEANING RULE; EQUITY-OF-THE-STATUTE RULE.

misconduct (mis-**kon**-dəkt). (17c) **1.** A dereliction of duty; unlawful or improper behavior.

    affirmative misconduct. (1897) **1.** An affirmative act of misrepresentation or concealment of a material fact; intentional wrongful behavior. • Some courts hold that there must be an ongoing pattern of misrepresentation or false promises, as opposed to an isolated act of providing misinformation. **2.** With respect to a claim of estoppel against the federal government, a misrepresentation or concealment of a material fact by a government employee — beyond a merely innocent or negligent misrepresentation.

    juror misconduct. (1954) A juror's violation of the court's charge or the law, committed either during trial or in deliberations after trial, such as (1) communicating about the case with outsiders, witnesses, attorneys, bailiffs, or judges, (2) bringing into the jury room information relating to the case but not in evidence, and (3) conducting experiments regarding theories of the case outside the court's presence.

    misconduct in office. See *official misconduct.*

    official misconduct. (1830) A public officer's corrupt violation of assigned duties by malfeasance, misfeasance, or nonfeasance. — Also termed *misconduct in office; misbehavior in office; malconduct in office; misdemeanor in office; corruption in office; official corruption; political corruption.*

    wanton misconduct. (1844) An act, or a failure to act when there is a duty to do so, in reckless disregard of another's rights, coupled with the knowledge that injury will probably result. — Also termed *wanton and reckless misconduct.*

    willful and wanton misconduct. (1866) Conduct committed with an intentional or reckless disregard for the safety of others, as by failing to exercise ordinary care to prevent a known danger or to discover a danger. — Also termed *willful indifference to the safety of others.*

    willful misconduct. (1804) Misconduct committed voluntarily and intentionally.

    willful misconduct of an employee. (1884) The deliberate disregard by an employee of the employer's interests, including its work rules and standards of conduct, justifying a denial of unemployment compensation if the employee is terminated for the misconduct.

2. An attorney's dishonesty or attempt to persuade a court or jury by using deceptive or reprehensible methods.

miscontinuance. (16c) A continuance erroneously ordered by a court.

miscreant (**mis**-kree-ənt). (14c) **1.** A wrongdoer. **2.** An apostate; an unbeliever.

misdate. (16c) To erroneously date (a document, etc.).

misdelivery. (1867) Delivery not according to contractual specifications; esp. delivery to the wrong person or delivery of goods in a damaged condition. ● This concept applies to contracts of carriage and contracts of sale, lease, etc., requiring delivery in some form.

misdemeanant (mis-də-**mee**-nənt), *n.* (1819) A person who has been convicted of a misdemeanor.

misdemeanor (mis-di-**mee**-nər). (16c) **1.** A crime that is less serious than a felony and is usu. punishable by fine, penalty, forfeiture, or confinement (usu. for a brief term) in a place other than prison (such as a county jail). — Also termed *minor crime*; *summary offense*. Cf. FELONY (1).

   gross misdemeanor. (18c) A serious misdemeanor, though not a felony. — Also termed *high misdemeanor.*

   high misdemeanor. **1.** *Hist. English law.* A crime that ranked just below high treason in seriousness. ● In English law, the term was essentially synonymous with crime. Examples of crimes called high misdemeanors are riot and conspiracy. In early American law, the term had the same meaning as in English law and was used in defining crimes such as sedition. **2.** See *gross misdemeanor.* **3.** See *serious misdemeanor.*

   serious misdemeanor. (1893) One of a class of misdemeanors having more severe penalties than most other misdemeanors. ● Conduct rising to the level of a serious misdemeanor can, in some jurisdictions, be charged as either a felony or a misdemeanor. — Also termed *high misdemeanor*; *indictable misdemeanor*; *penitentiary misdemeanor*; *aggravated misdemeanor.*

   treasonable misdemeanor. See TREASONABLE MISDEMEANOR.

2. *Archaic.* Any crime, including a felony.

misdemeanor in office. See *official misconduct* under MISCONDUCT.

misdemeanor manslaughter. See MANSLAUGHTER.

misdemeanor-manslaughter rule. (1967) The doctrine that a death occurring during the commission of a misdemeanor (or sometimes a nondangerous felony) is involuntary manslaughter. ● Many states and the Model Penal Code have abolished this rule. Cf. FELONY-MURDER RULE.

misdescription. (1848) **1.** A contractual error or falsity that deceives, injures, or materially misleads one of the contracting parties. **2.** A bailee's inaccurate identification, in a document of title, of goods received from the bailor. **3.** An inaccurate legal description of land in a deed.

misdirection. See MISCHARGE.

misericordia (miz-ə-ri-**kor**-dee-ə). [Law Latin] *Hist.* **1.** Mercy. **2.** An arbitrary fine as a punishment. **3.** An exemption from a fine.

misfeasance (mis-**fee**-zənts), *n.* (16c) **1.** A lawful act performed in a wrongful manner. **2.** More broadly, a transgression or trespass; MALFEASANCE. Cf. NONFEASANCE. — **misfeasant,** *adj.* — **misfeasor,** *n.*

misfeasance in public office. (1880) The tort of excessive, malicious, or negligent exercise of statutory powers by a public officer. — Also termed *malfeasance.*

misjoinder (mis-**joyn**-dər). (18c) **1.** The improper union of parties in a civil case. See JOINDER. Cf. DISJOINDER; NONJOINDER. **2.** The improper union of offenses in a criminal case.

mislaid property. See PROPERTY.

mislay, *vb.* (15c) To deposit (property, etc.) in a place not afterwards recollected; to lose (property, etc.) by forgetting where it was placed. See *mislaid property* under PROPERTY.

misleading, *adj.* (16c) (Of an instruction, direction, etc.) delusive; calculated to be misunderstood.

misnomer (mis-**noh**-mər). (15c) A mistake in naming a person, place, or thing, esp. in a legal instrument. ● In federal pleading — as well as in most states — misnomer of a party can be corrected by an amendment, which will relate back to the date of the original pleading. Fed. R. Civ. P. 15(c)(3).

misperformance. (17c) A faulty attempt to discharge an obligation (esp. a contractual one). Cf. PERFORMANCE; NONPERFORMANCE.

mispleading. (16c) Pleading incorrectly. ● A party who realizes that its pleading is incorrect can usu. amend the pleading, as a matter of right, within a certain period, and can thereafter amend with the court's permission.

misprision (mis-**prizh**-ən). (15c) **1.** Concealment or nondisclosure of a serious crime by one who did not participate in the crime.

   clerical misprision. (18c) A court clerk's mistake or fraud that is apparent from the record.

   misprision of felony. (16c) Concealment or nondisclosure of someone else's felony. See 18 USCA § 4.

misprision of treason. (16c) Concealment or non-disclosure of someone else's treason.

negative misprision. (18c) The wrongful concealment of something that should be revealed <misprision of treason>.

positive misprision. (18c) The active commission of a wrongful act <seditious conduct against the government is positive misprision>.

2. Seditious conduct against the government. **3.** An official's failure to perform the duties of public office. **4.** Misunderstanding; mistake.

misprisor (mis-**prī**-zər). One who commits misprision of felony.

misreading. An act of fraud in which a person incorrectly reads the contents of an instrument to an illiterate or blind person with the intent to deceitfully obtain that person's signature.

misrecital. (16c) An incorrect statement of a factual matter in a contract, deed, pleading, or other instrument.

misrepresentation, *n.* (17c) **1.** The act of making a false or misleading assertion about something, usu. with the intent to deceive. • The word denotes not just written or spoken words but also any other conduct that amounts to a false assertion. **2.** The assertion so made; an assertion that does not accord with the facts. — Also termed *false representation*; (redundantly) *false misrepresentation*. Cf. REPRESENTATION (1). — **misrepresent,** *vb.*

fraudulent misrepresentation. (18c) A false statement that is known to be false or is made recklessly — without knowing or caring whether it is true or false — and that is intended to induce a party to detrimentally rely on it. — Also termed *fraudulent representation*; *deceit.*

innocent misrepresentation. (1809) A false statement that the speaker or writer does not know is false; a misrepresentation that, though false, was not made fraudulently.

material misrepresentation. (18c) **1.** *Contracts.* A false statement that is likely to induce a reasonable person to assent or that the maker knows is likely to induce the recipient to assent. **2.** *Torts.* A false statement to which a reasonable person would attach importance in deciding how to act in the transaction in question or to which the maker knows or has reason to know that the recipient attaches some importance. See Restatement (Second) of Torts § 538 (1979).

misrepresentation of source. See PASSING OFF.

negligent misrepresentation. (1888) A careless or inadvertent false statement in circumstances where care should have been taken.

misrepresentee. A person to whom a fact has been misrepresented.

misrepresenter. A person who misrepresents a fact to another. — Also spelled *misrepresentor.*

Missile Defense Agency. A unit in the U.S. Department of Defense responsible for developing and deploying a missile-defense system capable of protecting the United States, its armed forces, and others from missile attack. — Abbr. MDA.

missing-evidence rule. (1981) The doctrine that, when a party fails at trial to present evidence that the party controls and that would have been proper to present, the jury is entitled to infer that the evidence would have been unfavorable to that party.

missing person. 1. Someone whose whereabouts are unknown and, after a reasonable time, seem to be unascertainable. **2.** Someone whose continuous and unexplained absence entitles the heirs to petition a court to declare the person dead and to divide up the person's property. See SEVEN-YEARS'-ABSENCE RULE. Cf. DISAPPEARED PERSON.

missing ship. *Maritime law.* A vessel that has been gone for an unreasonably long time, leading to the presumption that it is lost at sea; esp. a vessel that has been gone longer than the average time it takes a vessel to make a similar voyage in the same season.

missing-witness rule. (1961) The doctrine that, when a party fails at trial to present a witness who is available only to that party and whose testimony would have been admissible, the jury is entitled to infer that the witness's testimony would have been unfavorable to that party.

mistake, *n.* (17c) **1.** An error, misconception, or misunderstanding; an erroneous belief. See ERROR. **2.** *Contracts.* The situation in which either (1) the parties to a contract did not mean the same thing, or (2) at least one party had a belief that did not correspond to the facts or law. • As a result, the contract may be voidable.

basic mistake. A mistake of fact or of law constituting the basis on which a transaction rests.

bilateral mistake. See *mutual mistake* (1).

collateral mistake. See *unessential mistake.*

common mistake. See *mutual mistake* (2).

essential mistake. (1818) *Contracts.* A mistake serious enough that no real consent could have existed, so that there was no real agreement.

inessential mistake. See *unessential mistake.*

mistake of fact. (1808) **1.** A mistake about a fact that is material to a transaction; any mistake other than a mistake of law. — Also termed *error in fact*; *error of fact.* **2.** The defense asserting that a criminal defendant acted from an innocent misunderstanding of fact rather than from a criminal purpose.

mistake of law. (18c) **1.** A mistake about the legal effect of a known fact or situation. — Also termed *error in law*; *error of law*. **2.** The defense asserting that a defendant did not understand the criminal consequences of certain conduct. • This defense is generally not as effective as a mistake of fact.

mutual mistake. (18c) **1.** A mistake in which each party misunderstands the other's intent. — Also termed *bilateral mistake*. **2.** A mistake that is shared and relied on by both parties to a contract. • A court will often revise or nullify a contract based on a mutual mistake about a material term. — Also termed (in sense 2) *common mistake*.

nonessential mistake. See *unessential mistake*.

unessential mistake. (1928) *Contracts*. A mistake that does not relate to the nature of the contents of an agreement, but only to some external circumstance, so that the mistake has no effect on the validity of the agreement. — Also termed *inessential mistake*; *nonessential mistake*; *collateral mistake*.

unilateral mistake. (1885) A mistake by only one party to a contract. • A unilateral mistake is generally not as likely to be a ground for voiding the contract as is a mutual mistake.

mistrial. (17c) **1.** A trial that the judge brings to an end, without a determination on the merits, because of a procedural error or serious misconduct occurring during the proceedings. **2.** A trial that ends inconclusively because the jury cannot agree on a verdict. — Also termed *abortive trial*.

misunderstanding. (13c) **1.** A flawed interpretation of meaning or significance. **2.** A situation in which the words or acts of two people suggest assent, but one or both of them in fact intend something different from what the words or acts express. **3.** A quarrel; an instance of usu. mild wrangling.

misuse, *n.* (14c) **1.** *Products liability*. A defense alleging that the plaintiff used the product in an improper, unintended, or unforeseeable manner. **2.** *Patents*. The use of a patent either to improperly extend the granted monopoly to nonpatented goods or to violate antitrust laws.

misuser. (17c) An abuse of a right or office, as a result of which the person having the right might lose it <it is an act of misuser to accept a bribe>. Cf. USER.

mitigate (mit-ə-gayt), *vb.* (15c) To make less severe or intense <the fired employee mitigated her damages for wrongful termination by accepting a new job>. Cf. MILITATE. — **mitigation,** *n.* — **mitigatory** (mit-ə-gə-tor-ee), *adj.*

mitigating circumstance. See CIRCUMSTANCE.

mitigation cost. See COST (1).

mitigation-of-damages doctrine. (1978) The principle requiring a plaintiff, after an injury or breach of contract, to make reasonable efforts to alleviate the effects of the injury or breach. • If the defendant can show that the plaintiff failed to mitigate damages, the plaintiff's recovery may be reduced. — Also termed *avoidable-consequences doctrine*. Cf. DOCTRINE OF CONSTRUCTIVE SERVICE (2).

mitigation of punishment. (18c) *Criminal law*. A reduction in punishment due to mitigating circumstances that reduce the criminal's level of culpability, such as the existence of no prior convictions. See *mitigating circumstance* under CIRCUMSTANCE.

mitigator. A factor tending to show that a criminal defendant, though guilty, is less culpable than the act alone would indicate <the fact that he was coerced into taking part in the robbery may have been a mitigator in the minds of the jurors>. Cf. AGGRAVATOR.

mittimus (mit-ə-məs). [Law Latin "we send"] *Hist.* **1.** A court order or warrant directing a jailer to detain a person until ordered otherwise; COMMITMENT (4). **2.** A certified transcript of a prisoner's conviction or sentencing proceedings. **3.** A writ directing the transfer of records from one court to another. Pl. **mittimuses.**

mixed action. See ACTION (4).

mixed blood. See BLOOD.

mixed cognation. See COGNATION.

mixed condition. See CONDITION (2).

mixed contract. See CONTRACT.

mixed cost. See COST (1).

mixed government. See GOVERNMENT.

mixed insurance company. See INSURANCE COMPANY.

mixed interpretation. See *liberal interpretation* under INTERPRETATION.

mixed jury. See JURY.

mixed larceny. See LARCENY.

mixed law. A law concerning both persons and property.

mixed marriage. See MISCEGENATION.

mixed-motive doctrine. *Employment law*. The principle that, when the evidence in an employment-discrimination case shows that the complained-of employment action was based in part on a nondiscriminatory reason and in part on a discriminatory reason, the plaintiff must show that discrimination was a motivating factor for the employment action and, if the plaintiff makes that showing, then the defendant must show that it would have taken the same action without regard to the discriminatory reason.

mixed nuisance. See NUISANCE.

mixed policy. See INSURANCE POLICY.

mixed presumption. See PRESUMPTION.

mixed property. See PROPERTY.

mixed question. (18c) **1.** MIXED QUESTION OF LAW AND FACT. **2.** An issue involving conflicts of foreign and domestic law.

mixed question of law and fact. (1805) An issue that is neither a pure question of fact nor a pure question of law. ● Mixed questions of law and fact are typically resolved by juries. — Often shortened to *mixed question.* — Also termed *mixed question of fact and law.*

mixed tithes. See TITHE.

mixed treaty. See TREATY (1).

mixed trust. See TRUST.

mixed war. See WAR.

mixtion (**miks**-chən). *Archaic.* **1.** The process of mixing products together so that they can no longer be separated. **2.** The product of mixing.

MJOA. *abbr.* MOTION FOR JUDGMENT OF ACQUITTAL.

MLA. *abbr.* MOTION FOR LEAVE TO APPEAL.

MMBtu. *Abbr. Oil & gas.* One million British thermal units, one of the standard units for measuring natural gas.

MMI. *abbr.* MAXIMUM MEDICAL IMPROVEMENT.

***M'Naghten* rules.** See MCNAGHTEN RULES.

***M'Naughten* rules.** See MCNAGHTEN RULES.

M.O. *abbr.* MODUS OPERANDI.

mobile goods. See GOODS.

***Mobile–Sierra* doctrine.** The principle that the Federal Energy Regulatory Commission may not grant a rate increase to a natural-gas producer unless the producer's contract authorizes a rate increase, or unless the existing rate is so low that it may adversely affect the public interest (as by threatening the continued viability of the public utility to continue its service). *United Gas Pipe Line Co. v. Mobile Gas Serv. Corp.*, 350 U.S. 332, 76 S.Ct. 373 (1956); *Federal Power Comm'n v. Sierra Pac. Power Co.*, 350 U.S. 348, 76 S.Ct. 368 (1956). — Also termed *Sierra–Mobile doctrine.*

mobilia (moh-**bil**-ee-ə), *n. pl.* [Latin "movables"] *Roman law.* Movable things. ● The term primarily refers to inanimate objects but sometimes also refers to slaves and animals.

mobilia sequuntur personam (moh-**bil**-ee-ə si-**kwən**-tər pər-**soh**-nəm). [Latin] *Int'l law.* Movables follow the person — i.e., the law of the person. ● This is the general principle that rights of ownership and transfer of movable property are determined by the law of the owner's domicile.

mock trial. (18c) **1.** A fictitious trial organized to allow law students, or sometimes lawyers, to practice the techniques of trial advocacy. **2.** A fictitious trial, arranged by a litigant's attorney, to assess trial strategy, to estimate the case's value or risk, and to evaluate the case's strengths and weaknesses. ● In this procedure, people from the relevant jury pool are hired to sit as mock jurors who, after a condensed presentation of both sides, deliberate and reach a verdict (often while being observed by the participants behind a one-way glass). The jurors may later be asked specific questions about various arguments, techniques, and other issues. Because the mock jurors usu. do not know which side has hired them, their candid views are thought to be helpful in formulating trial strategies. Cf. MOOT COURT.

modal legacy. See LEGACY.

mode. (17c) A manner of doing something <mode of proceeding> <mode of process>.

model act. (1931) A statute drafted by the National Conference of Commissioners on Uniform State Laws and proposed as guideline legislation for the states to borrow from or adapt to suit their individual needs. ● Examples of model acts include the Model Employment Termination Act and the Model Punitive Damages Act. Cf. UNIFORM LAW; UNIFORM ACT.

Model Code of Professional Responsibility. A set of guidelines for lawyers, organized in the form of canons, disciplinary rules, and ethical considerations. ● Published by the ABA in 1969, this code has been replaced in most states by the Model Rules of Professional Conduct as the ethical standards by which lawyers are regulated and disciplined, although the Model Code continues to be used to interpret and apply the Model Rules.

model jury charge. See *model jury instruction* under JURY INSTRUCTION.

model jury instruction. See JURY INSTRUCTION.

Model Marriage and Divorce Act. See UNIFORM MARRIAGE AND DIVORCE ACT.

Model Penal Code. A proposed criminal code drafted by the American Law Institute and used as the basis for criminal-law revision by many states. — Abbr. MPC.

Model Penal Code test. See SUBSTANTIAL-CAPACITY TEST.

Model Putative Fathers Act. See UNIFORM PUTATIVE AND UNKNOWN FATHERS ACT.

Model Rules of Professional Conduct. A set of ethical guidelines for lawyers, organized in the form of 52 rules — some mandatory, some discretionary — together with explanatory comments. ● Published by the ABA in 1983, these rules have generally replaced the Model Code of Professional Responsibility and have been adopted as law, sometimes with modifications, by most states. The Model Code of Professional Responsibility is sometimes used to interpret and apply the Model Rules.

Model State Trademark Bill. A proposed statute intended to standardize trademark laws among the states. • The bill was first promulgated by the International Trademark Association (then called the United States Trademark Association) in 1949. — Abbr. MSTB.

model statute. See *uniform statute* under STATUTE.

moderate force. See *nondeadly force* under FORCE.

moderator. (16c) **1.** One who presides at a meeting or assembly. See CHAIR (1). **2.** *Scots law.* The person who presides in a public assembly; specif., the elected chair of the General Assembly of the Church of Scotland or another Presbyterian church, of a presbytery, or of a kirk session.

modification. (17c) **1.** A change to something; an alteration <a contract modification>. **2.** A qualification or limitation of something <a modification of drinking habits>. **3.** *Parliamentary law.* A change in a motion that its mover initiates or accepts, usu. before the chair has stated the motion. • The mover controls a motion only until the chair states the question, after which the motion belongs to the assembly and the mover cannot modify it without the assembly's permission. See *request for permission to modify a motion* under REQUEST.

modification order. *Family law.* A post-divorce order that changes the terms of child support, custody, visitation, or alimony. • A modification order may be agreed to by the parties or may be ordered by the court. The party wishing to modify an existing order must show a material change in circumstances from the time when the order sought to be modified was entered. See CHANGE IN CIRCUMSTANCES.

Modified Accelerated Cost Recovery System. See ACCELERATED COST RECOVERY SYSTEM.

modified-comparative-negligence doctrine. See 50-PERCENT RULE.

modus (moh-dəs), *n.* [Latin "mode"] **1.** *Criminal procedure.* The part of a charging instrument describing the manner in which an offense was committed. **2.** *Roman & civil law.* Mode; manner; consideration, esp. the manner in which a gift, bequest, servitude, etc. is to be employed. **3.** *Eccles. law.* Cf. MODUS OPERANDI.

modus operandi (moh-dəs op-ə-ran-di *or* -dee). [Latin "a manner of operating"] (17c) A method of operating or a manner of procedure; esp. a pattern of criminal behavior so distinctive that investigators attribute it to the work of the same person <staging a fight at the train station was part of the pickpocket's modus operandi>. — Abbr. M.O. Pl. **modi operandi.**

modus vivendi (moh-dəs vi-ven-di *or* -dee). [Latin "means of living (together)"] *Int'l law.* A temporary, provisional arrangement concluded between subjects of international law and giving rise to binding obligations on the parties.

moiety (moy-ə-tee). (15c) **1.** A half of something (such as an estate). — Also termed *mediety.* **2.** A portion less than half; a small segment. **3.** In federal customs law, a payment made to an informant who assists in the seizure of contraband, the payment being no more than 25% of the contraband's net value (up to a maximum of $250,000). 19 USCA § 1619.

moiety act. (1875) *Criminal law.* A law providing that a portion (such as half) of an imposed fine will inure to the benefit of the informant.

mole. (1922) A person who uses a long affiliation with an organization to gain access to and betray confidential information.

molestation. (15c) **1.** The persecution or harassment of someone <molestation of a witness>. **2.** The act of making unwanted and indecent advances to or on someone, esp. for sexual gratification <sexual molestation>. — **molest,** *vb.* — **molester,** *n.*

   child molestation. (1951) Any indecent or sexual activity on, involving, or surrounding a child, usu. under the age of 14. See Fed. R. Evid. 414(d).

Molineux **rule.** *New York law.* The principle that evidence of prior crimes is inadmissible when offered to prove the defendant's bad character and to show that the defendant is therefore more likely than not to have committed the crime charged. • The evidence is admissible if offered to prove something other than criminal propensity, such as motive, identity, absence of mistake or accident, intent, or the existence of a common scheme or plan. The rule was first handed down in *People v. Molineux,* 61 N.E. 286 (N.Y. 1901).

monarchy. (14c) A government in which a single person rules, with powers varying from absolute dictatorship to the merely ceremonial.

   limited monarchy. A monarchical form of government in which the monarch's power is subject to constitutional or other restraints. — Also termed *constitutional monarchy.*

monetarism (mon-i-tə-riz-əm). An economic theory claiming that the money supply is the basic influence on the economy. • The theory was originated by Milton Friedman in the late 1960s.

monetary, *adj.* **1.** Of or relating to money <monetary value> <monetary damages>. **2.** Financial <monetary services> <monetary investments>.

monetary bequest. See *pecuniary bequest* under BEQUEST.

money. (14c) **1.** The medium of exchange authorized or adopted by a government as part of its currency; esp. domestic currency <coins and currency are money>. UCC § 1-201(24). **2.** Assets that can be easily converted to cash <demand deposits are money>. **3.** Capital that is invested or traded as a commodity <the money market> **4.** (*pl.*) Funds; sums of money <investment moneys>. — Also spelled (in sense 4) *monies.* See MEDIUM OF EXCHANGE; LEGAL TENDER.

 current money. Money that circulates throughout a country; currency.

 e-money. Money or a money substitute that is transformed into information stored on a computer or computer chip so that it can be transferred over information systems such as the Internet. Cf. *e-check* under CHECK. — Also termed *digital cash; electronic cash; electronic currency; Internet scrip; on-line scrip.*

 fiat money. Paper currency not backed by gold or silver. — Also termed *flat money.*

 hard money. **1.** Coined money, in contrast to paper currency. **2.** Cash.

 lawful money. Money that is legal tender for the payment of debts.

 paper money. Paper documents that circulate as currency; bills drawn by a government against its own credit.

 real money. **1.** Money that has metallic or other intrinsic value, as distinguished from paper currency, checks, and drafts. **2.** Current cash, as opposed to money on account.

money bequest. See *pecuniary bequest* under BEQUEST.

money bill. See *revenue bill* under BILL (3).

money broker. See BROKER.

money changer. One whose primary business is exchanging currencies.

money claim. *Hist.* Under the English Judicature Act of 1875, money claimed as damages, as for breaches of contract and rent arrearages.

money count. See COUNT.

money demand. (1821) A claim for a fixed, liquidated sum, as opposed to a damage claim that must be assessed by a jury.

moneyed capital. See CAPITAL.

moneyed corporation. See CORPORATION.

money had and received. See *action for money had and received* under ACTION (4).

money judgment. See JUDGMENT.

money land. Money held in a trust providing for its conversion into land.

money-laundering, *n.* (1974) The act of transferring illegally obtained money through legitimate people or accounts so that its original source cannot be traced. • Money-laundering is a federal crime. 18 USCA § 1956. It is also addressed by state governments, e.g., through the Uniform Money Services Act. Because some money-laundering is conducted across national borders, enforcement of money-laundering laws often requires international cooperation, fostered by organizations such as Interpol.

money made. A sheriff's return on a writ of execution signifying that the sum stated on the writ was collected.

money market. See MARKET.

money-market account. An interest-bearing account at a bank or other financial institution. • Such an account usu. pays interest competitive with money-market funds but allows a limited number of transactions per month. See *money market* under MARKET.

money-market fund. See MUTUAL FUND.

money order. (1802) A negotiable draft issued by an authorized entity (such as a bank, telegraph company, post office, etc.) to a purchaser, in lieu of a check to be used to pay a debt or otherwise transmit funds upon the credit of the issuer.

money paid. See *action for money paid* under ACTION (4).

money-purchase plan. See EMPLOYEE BENEFIT PLAN.

money scrivener. A money broker; one who obtains money for mortgages or other loans.

money service business, *n.* A nonbank entity that provides mechanisms for people to make payments or to obtain currency or cash in exchange for payment instruments. • Money service businesses do not accept deposits or make loans. They include money transmitters, payment instrument sellers, stored-value providers, check cashers, and currency exchangers. – Also termed *nonbank financial institution; nondepository provider of financial services.*

money supply. The total amount of money in circulation in the economy. See M1; M2; M3.

monger (məng-gər). *Archaic.* A seller of goods; a dealer <moneymonger>.

monies. See MONEY (4).

moniment. *Archaic.* A memorial; a monument.

monition (mə-**nish**-ən), *n.* (14c) **1.** Generally, a warning or caution; ADMONITION. **2.** *Civil & maritime law.* A summons to appear in court as a defendant or to answer contempt charges. **3.** *Eccles. law.* A formal notice from a bishop demanding that an offense within the clergy be corrected or avoided. — **monish** (**mon**-ish), *vb.* — **monitory** (**mon**-ə-tor-ee), *adj.*

monitory letter. *Eccles. law.* Admonitory communications sent from an ecclesiastical judge to staff members in response to reported abuses or scandals.

monocracy (mə-**nok**-rə-see). A government by one person.

monocrat (**mon**-ə-krat). A monarch who governs alone.

monogamy (mə-**nog**-ə-mee), *n.* (18c) **1.** The custom prevalent in most modern cultures restricting a person to one spouse at a time. **2.** The fact of being married to only one spouse. Cf. BIGAMY; POLYGAMY. — **monogamous,** *adj.* — **monogamist,** *n.*

monomachy (mə-**nom**-ə-kee). *Hist.* See DUEL (2).

monomania (mon-ə-**may**-nee-ə). (1823) Insanity about some particular subject or class of subjects, usu. manifested by a single insane delusion. ● A will made by someone suffering from this condition is usu. held valid unless the evidence shows that particular provisions in the will were influenced by the insane delusion. — **monomaniacal,** *adj.* — **monomaniac,** *n.*

monopolist (mə-**nop**-ə-list), *n.* **1.** One who has a monopoly; specif., a seller or combination of sellers who can alter the price of a product in the market by changing the quantity sold. ● By reducing output, a monopolist can raise the price above the cost of supplying the market. **2.** A proponent of a monopoly.

monopolization, *n.* (18c) The act or process of obtaining a monopoly. ● In federal antitrust law, monopolization is an offense with two elements: (1) the possession of monopoly power — that is, the power to fix prices and exclude competitors — within the relevant market, and (2) the willful acquisition or maintenance of that power, as distinguished from growth or development as a consequence of a superior product, business acumen, or historical accident. *United States v. Grinnell Corp.*, 384 U.S. 563, 86 S.Ct. 1698 (1966). — **monopolize,** *vb.*

attempted monopolization. The effort to monopolize any part of interstate or foreign commerce, consisting in (1) a specific intent to control prices or destroy competition in the relevant market, (2) predatory or anticompetitive conduct, and (3) a "dangerous probability" of success in achieving monopoly in the relevant market.

monopoly, *n.* (16c) **1.** Control or advantage obtained by one supplier or producer over the commercial market within a given region. Cf. OLIGOPOLY. **2.** The market condition existing when only one economic entity produces a particular product or provides a particular service. ● The term is now commonly applied also to situations that approach but do not strictly meet this definition. — **monopolistic,** *adj.* — **monopolist,** *n.*

bilateral monopoly. A hypothetical market condition in which there is only one buyer and one seller, resulting in transactional delays because either party can hold out for a better deal without fearing that the other party will turn to a third party.

legal monopoly. The exclusive right granted by government to business to provide utility services that are, in turn, regulated by the government.

natural monopoly. A monopoly resulting from a circumstance over which the monopolist has no power, as when the market for a product is so limited that only one plant is needed to meet demand.

3. *Patents.* The exclusive right of a patentee to make, use, sell, offer for sale, or import an invention for a certain period of time, subject to the rights of the owners of other patents that would be infringed.

monopoly leveraging. A theory of liability holding that a party violates the antitrust laws when it exploits its monopoly power in one market to gain a competitive advantage in another market.

monopoly power. The power to control prices or to exclude competition. ● The size of the market share is a primary determinant of whether monopoly power exists.

monopsony (mə-**nop**-sə-nee), *n.* (1933) A market situation in which one buyer controls the market. — **monopsonistic,** *adj.*

Monroe Doctrine. The principle that the United States will allow no intervention or domination in the Western Hemisphere by any non-American nation. ● This principle, which has some recognition in international law (though not as a formal doctrine), was first announced by President James Monroe in 1823.

Montevideo Treaty. *Copyright.* An 1889 copyright treaty among Western Hemisphere nations, based on the Berne Convention but affording less copyright protection.

month. (18c) (bef. 12c) **1.** One of the twelve periods of time in which the calendar is divided <the month of March>. — Also termed *calendar month; civil month.* **2.** Any time period approximating 30 days <due one month from today>. **3.** At common law, a period of 28 days; the period of one revolution of the moon <a lunar month>. — Also termed *lunar month.* **4.** One-twelfth of a tropical year; the time it takes the sun to pass through one sign of the zodiac, usu. approximating 30 days <a solar month> — Also termed *solar month.*

month-to-month lease. See LEASE.

month-to-month tenancy. See *periodic tenancy* under TENANCY.

Montreal Agreement. A private agreement, signed by most international airlines, waiving both the Warsaw Convention's limitation on liability for death and personal-injury cases (currently about $20,000) and the airline's due-care defenses, raising the liability limit per passenger to $75,000, and providing for absolute liability on the part of the carrier (in the absence of passenger negligence) for all flights originating, stopping, or terminating in the United States. • The Montreal Agreement was the result of negotiations in 1965 and 1966 following the United States' denunciation of the Warsaw Convention, based primarily on its low liability limits. — Also termed *Agreement Relating to Liability Limitation of the Warsaw Convention and the Hague Protocol.*

monument, *n.* (15c) **1.** A written document or record, esp. a legal one. **2.** Any natural or artificial object that is fixed permanently in land and referred to in a legal description of the land. — **monumental,** *adj.*

mural monument. A monument set into or otherwise made part of a wall.

natural monument. A nonartificial permanent thing on land, such as a tree, river, or beach. — Also termed *natural object.*

Moody's Investor's Service. An investment-analysis and advisory service. • Moody's rates the financial strength of businesses from Aaa (strongest) to Aa, A, Baa, and so on to C. The grade may also be modified with a 1, 2, or 3 according to the business's relative strength among similar companies. — Often shortened to *Moody's.*

moonlighting. (1957) The fact or practice of working at a second job after the hours of a regular job. — Also termed *dual employment; multiple job-holding.*

moonshine. (18c) *Slang.* A distilled alcoholic beverage, esp. whiskey, that is illegally manufactured.

moorage. **1.** An act of mooring a vessel at a wharf. **2.** A mooring charge.

moored in safety. *Marine insurance.* (Of a vessel) located in a usual place for landing or loading cargo, free from any imminent peril insured against.

moot, *adj.* (16c) **1.** *Archaic.* Open to argument; debatable. **2.** Having no practical significance; hypothetical or academic <the question on appeal became moot once the parties settled their case>. — **mootness,** *n.*

moot, *vb.* (bef. 12c) **1.** *Archaic.* To raise or bring forward (a point or question) for discussion. **2.** To render (a question) moot or of no practical significance.

moot case. A matter in which a controversy no longer exists; a case that presents only an abstract question that does not arise from existing facts or rights.

moot court. (18c) **1.** A fictitious court held usu. in law schools to argue moot or hypothetical cases, esp. at the appellate level. **2.** A practice session for an appellate argument in which a lawyer presents the argument to other lawyers, who first act as judges by asking questions and who later provide criticism on the argument. — Also termed *practice court.* Cf. MOCK TRIAL.

mootness doctrine. (1963) The principle that American courts will not decide moot cases — that is, cases in which there is no longer any actual controversy. Cf. RIPENESS.

moral absolutism. The view that a person's action can always properly be seen as right or wrong, regardless of the situation or the consequences. — Also termed *ethical absolutism; objective ethics.* Cf. MORAL RELATIVISM.

moral certainty. (17c) Absolute certainty. • Moral certainty is not required to sustain a criminal conviction. See REASONABLE DOUBT; *proof beyond a reasonable doubt* under PROOF.

moral coercion. See UNDUE INFLUENCE (1).

moral consideration. See *good consideration* (1) under CONSIDERATION (1).

moral depravity. See MORAL TURPITUDE (1).

moral duress. See DURESS.

moral duty. See DUTY (1).

moral evidence. See EVIDENCE.

moral fraud. See *actual fraud* under FRAUD.

moral hazard. See HAZARD (2).

morality. (14c) **1.** Conformity with recognized rules of correct conduct. **2.** The character of being virtuous, esp. in sexual matters. **3.** A system of duties; ethics.

private morality. (18c) A person's ideals, character, and private conduct, which are not valid governmental concerns if the individual is to be considered sovereign over body and mind and if the need to protect the individual's physical or moral well-being is insufficient to justify governmental intrusion. • In his essay *On Liberty* (1859), John Stuart Mill distinguished between conduct or ideals that affect only the individual from conduct that may do harm to others. Mill argued that governmental intrusion is justified only to prevent harm to others, not to influence a person's private morality.

public morality. (18c) **1.** The ideals or general moral beliefs of a society. **2.** The ideals or actions of an individual to the extent that they affect others.

moral law. (15c) A collection of principles defining right and wrong conduct; a standard to which an action must conform to be right or virtuous.

moral necessity. See NECESSITY.

moral obligation. See OBLIGATION.

moral person. See *artificial person* under PERSON (3).

moral relativism. The view that there are no absolute or constant standards of right and wrong. — Also termed *ethical relativism; subjective ethics.* Cf. MORAL ABSOLUTISM.

moral right. (*usu. pl.*) *Copyright.* The right of an author or artist, based on natural-law principles, to guarantee the integrity of a creation despite any copyright or property-law right of its owner. • Moral rights include rights of (1) attribution (also termed "paternity"): the right to be given credit and to claim credit for a work, and to deny credit if the work is changed; (2) integrity: the right to ensure that the work is not changed without the artist's consent; (3) publication: the right not to reveal a work before its creator is satisfied with it; and (4) retraction: the right to renounce a work and withdraw it from sale or display. Moral rights are recognized by law in much of Europe. Limited moral rights are recognized in the United States in 17 USCA § 106A. Cf. INTEGRITY RIGHT; ATTRIBUTION RIGHT.

moral suasion. The act or effort of persuading by appeal to principles of morality.

moral turpitude. (17c) **1.** Conduct that is contrary to justice, honesty, or morality. • In the area of legal ethics, offenses involving moral turpitude — such as fraud or breach of trust — traditionally make a person unfit to practice law. — Also termed *moral depravity.* **2.** *Military law.* Any conduct for which the applicable punishment is a dishonorable discharge or confinement not less than one year.

moral wrong. See WRONG.

moral-wrong doctrine. (1962) The doctrine that if a wrongdoer acts on a mistaken understanding of the facts, the law will not exempt the wrongdoer from culpability when, if the facts had been as the actor believed them to be, his or her conduct would nevertheless be immoral.

moratorium (mor-ə-**tor**-ee-əm). (1875) **1.** An authorized postponement, usu. a lengthy one, in the deadline for paying a debt or performing an obligation. **2.** The period of this delay. **3.** The suspension of a specific activity. Pl. **moratoriums, moratoria.**

moratory (mor-ə-tor-ee), *adj.* (1891) Of or relating to a delay; esp. of or relating to a moratorium.

moratory damages. See DAMAGES.

moratory interest. See *prejudgment interest* under INTEREST (3).

more or less. (Of a quantity) larger or smaller. • This phrase often appears in deeds <the property contains 120 acres, more or less> and sometimes in contracts <seller's wheat field will produce 50 bushels per acre, more or less>. It qualifies a good-faith representation of quantity. By using the phrase, the parties mutually acknowledge that the true circumstances may differ from what the parties believe they are when the contract is made, and accept a risk that the true quantity will be slightly different. When the qualifying phrase is present, neither party can recover for a surplus or deficiency.

morganatic marriage. See MARRIAGE (1).

Morgan Nick Alert. See AMBER ALERT.

Morgan presumption. (1948) A presumption that shifts the burden of proof by requiring the person against whom it operates to produce sufficient evidence to outweigh the evidence that supports the presumed fact, as in requiring a criminal defendant who was arrested while in possession of an illegal substance — and is thereby presumed to have knowingly possessed it — to produce sufficient evidence to entitle the jury to find that the defendant's evidence outweighs the evidence of knowing possession. *See* Edmund M. Morgan, *Instructing the Jury Upon Presumptions and Burdens of Proof,* 47 Harv. L. Rev. 59, 82–83 (1933). Cf. THAYER PRESUMPTION.

morsel of execration. See *ordeal of the morsel* under ORDEAL.

mors naturalis (**morz** nach-ə-**ray**-lis). See *natural death* under DEATH.

mortality factor. *Insurance.* In life-insurance rate-making, an estimate of the average number of deaths that will occur each year at each specific age, calculated by using an actuarial table. • The mortality factor is one element that a life insurer uses to calculate premium rates. See ACTUARIAL TABLE; PREMIUM RATE. Cf. INTEREST FACTOR; RISK FACTOR.

mortality table. See ACTUARIAL TABLE.

mortgage (**mor**-gij), *n.* (15c) **1.** A conveyance of title to property that is given as security for the payment of a debt or the performance of a duty and that will become void upon payment or performance according to the stipulated terms. — Also termed (archaically) *dead pledge.* **2.** A lien against property that is granted to secure an obligation (such as a debt) and that is extinguished upon payment or performance according to stipulated terms. **3.** An instrument (such as a deed or contract) specifying the terms of such a transaction. **4.** Loosely, the loan on which such a transaction is based. **5.** The mortgagee's rights conferred by such a transaction. **6.** Loosely, any real-property security transaction, including a deed of trust. — Abbr. M. — **mortgage,** *vb.*

adjustable-rate mortgage. A mortgage in which the lender can periodically adjust the mortgage's interest rate in accordance with fluctuations in some external market index. — Abbr. ARM. — Also termed *variable-rate mortgage*; *flexible-rate mortgage*. Cf. *exploding adjustable-rate mortgage*.

all-inclusive mortgage. See *wraparound mortgage*.

amortized mortgage. A mortgage in which the mortgagor pays the interest as well as a portion of the principal in the periodic payment. • At maturity, the periodic payments will have completely repaid the loan. — Also termed *self-liquidating mortgage*. See AMORTIZATION (1). Cf. *straight mortgage*.

balloon-payment mortgage. A mortgage requiring periodic payments for a specified time and a lump-sum payment of the outstanding balance at maturity.

blanket mortgage. A mortgage covering two or more properties that are pledged to support a debt.

bulk mortgage. 1. A mortgage of personal property in bulk; a pledge of an aggregate of goods in one location. **2.** A mortgage of more than one real-estate parcel.

chattel mortgage (**chat**-əl). A mortgage on goods purchased on installment, whereby the seller transfers title to the buyer but retains a lien securing the unpaid balance. • Chattel mortgages have generally been replaced by security agreements, which are governed by Article 9 of the UCC. Cf. *retail installment contract* under CONTRACT.

closed-end mortgage. A mortgage that does not permit either prepayment or additional borrowing against the collateral. Cf. *open-end mortgage*. — Also termed *closed mortgage*.

closed mortgage. See *closed-end mortgage*.

collateral mortgage. *Civil law.* A mortgage securing a promissory note pledged as collateral security for a principal obligation.

common-law mortgage. See *deed of trust* under DEED.

consolidated mortgage. A mortgage created by combining two or more mortgages.

construction mortgage. A mortgage used to finance a construction project.

contingent-interest mortgage. A mortgage whose interest rate is directly related to the economic performance of the pledged property.

conventional mortgage. A mortgage, not backed by government insurance, by which the borrower transfers a lien or title to the lending bank or other financial institution. • These mortgages, which feature a fixed periodic payment of principal and interest throughout the mortgage term, are typically used for home financing. — Also termed *conventional loan*.

direct-reduction mortgage. An amortized mortgage in which the principal and interest payments are paid at the same time — usu. monthly in equal amounts — with interest being computed on the remaining balance. — Abbr. DRM.

dry mortgage. A mortgage that creates a lien on property but does not impose on the mortgagor any personal liability for any amount that exceeds the value of the premises.

equitable mortgage. A transaction that has the intent but not the form of a mortgage, and that a court of equity will treat as a mortgage. Cf. *technical mortgage*.

exploding adjustable-rate mortgage. An adjustable-rate mortgage for which the lender resets the interest rate so high that the borrower can no longer make payments. — Sometimes shortened to *exploding ARM*. Cf. *adjustable-rate mortgage*.

extended first mortgage. See *wraparound mortgage*.

FHA mortgage. A mortgage that is insured fully or partially by the Federal Housing Administration.

first mortgage. A mortgage that is senior to all other mortgages on the same property.

fixed-rate mortgage. A mortgage with an interest rate that remains the same over the life of the mortgage regardless of market conditions. — Abbr. FRM.

flexible-rate mortgage. 1. See *adjustable-rate mortgage*. **2.** See *renegotiable-rate mortgage*.

flip mortgage. A graduated-payment mortgage allowing the borrower to place all or some of the down payment in a savings account and to use the principal and interest to supplement lower mortgage payments in the loan's early years.

future-advances mortgage. A mortgage in which part of the loan proceeds will not be paid until a future date.

general mortgage. *Civil law.* A blanket mortgage against all the mortgagor's present and future property. La. Civ. Code art. 3285.

graduated mortgage. See *graduated-payment mortgage*.

graduated-payment adjustable-rate mortgage. A mortgage combining features of the graduated-payment mortgage and the adjustable-rate mortgage. — Abbr. GPARM. — Also termed *graduated mortgage.*

graduated-payment mortgage. A mortgage whose initial payments are lower than its later payments. • The payments are intended to gradually increase, as the borrower's income increases over time.

growing-equity mortgage. A mortgage that is fully amortized over a significantly shorter term than the traditional 25- to 30-year mortgage, with increasing payments each year. — Abbr. GEM.

indemnity mortgage. See *deed of trust* under DEED.

interest-only mortgage. A balloon-payment mortgage on which the borrower must at first make only interest payments, but must make a lump-sum payment of the full principal at maturity. — Abbr. IO mortgage. — Also termed *standing mortgage; straight-term mortgage.*

joint mortgage. A mortgage given to two or more mortgagees jointly.

judicial mortgage. *Civil law.* A judgment lien created by a recorded legal judgment.

jumbo mortgage. A mortgage loan in a principal amount that exceeds the dollar limits for a government guarantee.

junior mortgage. A mortgage that is subordinate to another mortgage on the same property. — Also termed *puisne mortgage.*

leasehold mortgage. A mortgage secured by a lessee's leasehold interest.

legal mortgage. *Civil law.* A creditor's mortgage arising by operation of law on the debtor's property. — Also termed *tacit mortgage.*

open-end mortgage. A mortgage that allows the mortgagor to borrow additional funds against the same property. Cf. *closed-end mortgage.*

package mortgage. A mortgage that includes both real and incidental personal property, such as a refrigerator or stove.

participation mortgage. **1.** A mortgage that permits the lender to receive profits of the venture in addition to the normal interest payments. **2.** A mortgage held by more than one lender.

price-level-adjusted mortgage. A mortgage with a fixed interest rate but the principal balance of which is adjusted to reflect inflation. — Abbr. PLAM.

puisne mortgage. See *junior mortgage.*

purchase-money mortgage. A mortgage that a buyer gives the seller, when the property is conveyed, to secure the unpaid balance of the purchase price. — Abbr. PMM. See SECURITY AGREEMENT.

renegotiable-rate mortgage. A government-sponsored mortgage that requires the mortgagee to renegotiate its terms every three to five years, based on market conditions. — Also termed *flexible-rate mortgage; rollover mortgage.*

reverse annuity mortgage. A mortgage in which the lender disburses money over a long period to provide regular income to the (usu. elderly) borrower, and in which the loan is repaid in a lump sum when the borrower dies or when the property is sold. — Abbr. RAM. — Also termed *reverse mortgage.*

rollover mortgage. See *renegotiable-rate mortgage.*

second mortgage. A mortgage that is junior to a first mortgage on the same property, but that is senior to any later mortgage.

self-liquidating mortgage. See *amortized mortgage.*

senior mortgage. A mortgage that has priority over another mortgage (a junior mortgage) on the same property.

shared-appreciation mortgage. A mortgage giving the lender the right to recover (as contingent interest) an agreed percentage of the property's appreciation in value when it is sold or at some other specified, future date. — Abbr. SAM.

shared-equity mortgage. A mortgage in which the lender shares in the profits from the property's resale. • The lender must usu. first purchase a portion of the property's equity by providing a portion of the down payment.

special mortgage. *Civil law.* A mortgage burdening only particular, specified property of the mortgagor. La. Civ. Code art. 3285.

standing mortgage. See *interest-only mortgage.*

straight mortgage. A mortgage in which the mortgagor is obligated to pay interest during the mortgage term along with a final payment of principal at the end of the term. Cf. *amortized mortgage.*

straight-term mortgage. See *interest-only mortgage.*

submortgage. A mortgage created when a person holding a mortgage as security for a loan procures another loan from a third party and pledges the mortgage as security; a loan to a mortgagee who puts up the mortgage as collateral or security for the loan.

tacit mortgage. See *legal mortgage.*

technical mortgage. A traditional, formal mortgage, as distinguished from an instrument having the character of an equitable mortgage. Cf. *equitable mortgage.*

VA mortgage. A veteran's mortgage that is guaranteed by the Veterans Administration.

variable-rate mortgage. See *adjustable-rate mortgage.*

Welsh mortgage. A type of mortgage, formerly common in Wales and Ireland, by which the mortgagor, without promising to pay the debt, transfers title and possession of the property to the mortgagee, who takes the rents and profits and applies them to the interest, often with a stipulation that any surplus will reduce the principal. ● The mortgagee cannot compel the mortgagor to redeem, and cannot foreclose the right to redeem, because no time is fixed for payment. The mortgagor is never in default, but may redeem at any time.

wraparound mortgage. A second mortgage issued when a lender assumes the payments on the borrower's low-interest first mortgage (usu. issued through a different lender) and lends additional funds. ● Such a mortgage covers both the outstanding balance of the first mortgage and the additional funds loaned. 12 CFR § 226.17 cmt. 6. — Also termed *extended first mortgage*; *all-inclusive mortgage.*

zero-rate mortgage. A mortgage with a large down payment but no interest payments, with the balance paid in equal installments.

mortgage-backed security. See SECURITY.

mortgage banker. An individual or organization that originates real-estate loans for a fee, resells them to other parties, and services the monthly payments.

mortgage bond. See BOND (3).

mortgage broker. See BROKER.

mortgage certificate. (1843) A document evidencing part ownership of a mortgage.

mortgage clause. An insurance-policy provision that protects the rights of a mortgagee when the insured property is subject to a mortgage. ● Such a clause usu. provides that any insurance proceeds must be allocated between the named insured and the mortgagee "as their interests may appear." — Also termed *mortgagee clause.* See LOSS-PAYABLE CLAUSE; ATIMA.

open mortgage clause. A mortgage clause that does not protect the mortgagee if the insured mortgagor does something to invalidate the policy (such as committing fraud). ● This type of clause has been largely superseded by the mortgage-loss clause, which affords the mortgagee more protection. — Also termed *simple mortgage clause.* Cf. MORTGAGE-LOSS CLAUSE.

standard mortgage clause. A mortgage clause that protects the mortgagee's interest even if the insured mortgagor does something to invalidate the policy. ● In effect, this clause creates a separate contract between the insurer and the mortgagee. — Also termed *union mortgage clause.*

mortgage commitment. (1939) A lender's written agreement with a borrower stating the terms on which it will lend money for the purchase of specified real property, usu. with a time limitation.

mortgage company. A company that makes mortgage loans and then sells or assigns them to investors.

mortgage-contingency clause. (1965) A real-estate-sale provision that conditions the buyer's performance on obtaining a mortgage loan.

mortgage deed. See DEED.

mortgage discount. (1928) The difference between the mortgage principal and the amount the mortgage actually sells for; the up-front charge by a lender at a real-estate closing for the costs of financing. ● Although usu. paid by the buyer, the discount is sometimes paid by the seller when required by law, as with a VA mortgage. — Also termed *point*; *mortgage point*; *loan-brokerage fee*; *new-loan fee.*

mortgagee (mor-gə-**jee**). (16c) One to whom property is mortgaged; the mortgage creditor, or lender. — Also termed *mortgage-holder.*

mortgagee in possession. (18c) A mortgagee who takes control of mortgaged land by agreement with the mortgagor, usu. upon default of the loan secured by the mortgage.

mortgagee clause. See MORTGAGE CLAUSE.

mortgagee policy. A title-insurance policy that covers only the mortgagee's title and not the owner's title. Cf. OWNER'S POLICY.

mortgage foreclosure. See FORECLOSURE.

mortgage-guarantee insurance. Insurance provided by the Mortgage Guarantee Insurance Company to mortgage lenders that grant mortgages to parties having less than a 20% down payment. ● The cost of the insurance is included in the closing costs.

mortgage-holder. See MORTGAGEE.

mortgage insurance. See INSURANCE.

mortgage lien. See LIEN.

mortgage loan. See LOAN.

mortgage-loss clause. A mortgage clause providing that title insurance will not be invalidated by the mortgagor's acts. ● Thus, even if the mortgagor does an act that would otherwise make the policy void, the act merely voids the policy as against the mortgagor, but it remains in full force for the benefit of the mortgagee. — Also termed *New York standard clause*; *union-loss clause.* Cf. *open mortgage clause* under MORTGAGE CLAUSE.

mortgage market. The conditions that provide the demand for new mortgage loans and the later resale of those loans in the secondary mortgage market.

primary mortgage market. The national market in which mortgages are originated.

secondary mortgage market. The national market in which existing mortgages are bought and sold, usu. on a package basis.

mortgage note. See NOTE (1).

mortgage point. 1. See POINT (3). **2.** See MORTGAGE DISCOUNT.

mortgager. See MORTGAGOR.

mortgage servicing. The administration of a mortgage loan, including the collection of payments, release of liens, and payment of property insurance and taxes. • Servicing is usu. performed by the lender or the lender's agent, for a fee.

mortgage warehousing. An arrangement in which a mortgage company holds loans for later resale at a discount.

mortgaging out. The purchase of real property by financing 100% of the purchase price.

mortgagor (mor-gə-**jor** *or* mor-gə-jər). One who mortgages property; the mortgage-debtor, or borrower. — Also spelled *mortgager; mortgageor.*

mortification. (14c) The act of disposing of or contributing property for religious, charitable, or public purposes.

mortis causa (mor-tis **kaw**-zə). See *gift causa mortis* under GIFT.

mortmain (**mort**-mayn). [French "deadhand"] (15c) The condition of lands or tenements held in perpetuity by an ecclesiastical or other corporation. • Land alienated in mortmain is not inalienable, but it will never escheat or pass by inheritance (and thus no inheritance taxes will ever be paid) because a corporation does not die. See AMORTIZE (3); DEADHAND CONTROL.

mortmain statute. (1839) A law that limits gifts and other dispositions of land to corporations (esp. charitable ones) and that prohibits corporations from holding land in perpetuity. • In England, laws such as the Provisions of Westminster and Magna Carta essentially required the Crown's authorization before land could vest in a corporation. The object was to prevent lands from being held by religious corporations in perpetuity. Although this type of restriction was not generally part of the common law in the United States, it influenced the enactment of certain state laws restricting the amount of property that a corporation could hold for religious or charitable purposes. — Also termed *mortmain act; statute of mortmain.*

mortuary. (16c) **1.** A place where cadavers are prepared for burial; a place where dead bodies are held before burial. **2.** A burial place.

mortuary table. See ACTUARIAL TABLE.

mortuum vadium (mor-choo-əm **vay**-dee-əm). See *vadium mortuum* under VADIUM.

mortuus (mor-choo-əs), *adj.* [Latin] *Hist.* **1.** Dead. **2.** A sheriff's return that the named party is dead.

most favorable light. See LIGHT MOST FAVORABLE.

most favored nation. A treaty status granted to a nation, usu. in international trade, allowing it to enjoy the privileges that the other party accords to other nations under similar circumstances. • The primary effect of most-favored-nation status is lower trade tariffs. — Sometimes shortened to *favored nation.* Abbr. MFN. — Also termed *most-favored-nation status.*

most-favored-nation clause. 1. A clause in an agreement between two nations providing that each will treat the other as well as it treats any other nation that is given preferential treatment. **2.** By extension, such a clause in any contract, but esp. an oil-and-gas contract. — Often shortened to *favored-nation clause; MFN clause.* — Also termed *most-favored-nations clause.* Cf. *preferential tariff* under TARIFF (2).

most-favored-nation status. See MOST FAVORED NATION.

most-favored-nation treatment. *Intellectual property.* The practice or policy of automatically and unconditionally granting any intellectual-property protection, advantage, favor, privilege, or immunity that by treaty is extended to nationals of any member country to the nationals of all member countries. • This treatment is incorporated into the TRIPs agreement. — Abbr. MFN treatment.

most-favored-tenant clause. (1962) A commercial-lease provision ensuring that the tenant will be given the benefit of any negotiating concessions given to other tenants.

most-significant-contacts test. See MOST-SIGNIFICANT-RELATIONSHIPS TEST.

most-significant-relationship test. (1968) *Conflict of laws.* The doctrine that, to determine the state law to apply to a dispute, the court should determine which state has the most substantial connection to the occurrence and the parties. • For example, in a tort case, the court should consider where the injury occurred, where the conduct that caused the injury occurred, the residence, place of business, or place of incorporation of the parties, and the place where the relationship between the parties, if any, is centered. Restatement (Second) of Conflict of Laws § 145 (1971). In a case involving a contract, the court should consider where the contract was made, where the contract was negotiated, where the contract was to be performed, and the domicile, place of business, or place of incorporation of the parties. *Id.* § 188. — Also termed *most-significant-contacts test.*

most suitable use. See *highest and best use* under USE (1).

most-suitable-use value. See *optimal-use value* under VALUE (2).

mother. (bef. 12c) A woman who has given birth to, provided the egg for, or legally adopted a child. • The term is sometimes interpreted as including a pregnant woman who has not yet given birth.

adoptive mother. See *adoptive parent* under PARENT.

biological mother. (1965) The woman who provides the egg that develops into an embryo. • With today's genetic-engineering techniques, the biological mother may not be the birth mother, but she is usu. the legal mother. — Also termed *genetic mother; natural mother.*

birth mother. (1958) The woman who carries an embryo during the gestational period and who delivers the child. • When a child is conceived through artificial insemination, the birth mother may not be the genetic or biological mother. And she may not be the legal mother. — Also termed *gestational mother.* See *surrogate mother; natural mother; biological mother.*

de facto mother. See *de facto parent* under PARENT.

foster mother. See *foster parent* under PARENT.

genetic mother. See *biological mother.*

gestational mother. See *birth mother.*

godmother. See GODPARENT.

intentional mother. See *intentional parent* under PARENT.

natural mother. 1. See *birth mother.* 2. See *biological mother.*

psychological mother. See *psychological parent* under PARENT.

stepmother. (bef. 12c) The wife of one's father by a later marriage.

surrogate mother. (1914) 1. A woman who carries out the gestational function and gives birth to a child for another; esp. a woman who agrees to provide her uterus to carry an embryo throughout pregnancy, typically on behalf of an infertile couple, and who relinquishes any parental rights she may have upon the birth of the child. • A surrogate mother may or may not be the genetic mother of a child. — Often shortened to *surrogate.* — Also termed *surrogate parent; gestational surrogate; gestational carrier; surrogate carrier.* 2. A person who performs the role of a mother.

mother country. A colonizing nation; a colonial power. See COLONY.

Mother Hubbard clause. (1939) 1. A clause stating that a mortgage secures all the debts that the mortgagor may at any time owe to the mortgagee. — Also termed *anaconda clause; dragnet clause.* 2. *Oil & gas.* A provision in an oil-and-gas lease protecting the lessee against errors in the description of the property by providing that the lease covers all the land owned by the lessor in the area. • A Mother Hubbard clause is sometimes combined with an after-acquired-title clause. — Also termed *cover-all clause.* 3. A court's written declaration that any relief not expressly granted in a specific ruling or judgment is denied.

mother-in-law. (14c) The mother of a person's spouse.

motion. (18c) 1. A written or oral application requesting a court to make a specified ruling or order.

calendar motion. (1930) A motion relating to the time of a court appearance • Examples include motions to continue, motions to advance, and motions to reset.

contradictory motion. *Civil law.* A motion that is likely to be contested or that the nonmoving side should have an opportunity to contest. Cf. *contradictory judgment* under JUDGMENT.

cross-motion. A competing request for relief or orders similar to that requested by another party against the cross-moving party, such as a motion for summary judgment or for sanctions.

dilatory motion (**dil**-ə-tor-ee). (18c) 1. A motion made solely for the purpose of delay or obstruction. 2. A motion that delays the proceedings.

enumerated motion. *Archaic.* A motion directly related to the proceeding or the merits of the case.

ex parte motion (eks **pahr**-tee). (1831) A motion made to the court without notice to the adverse party; a motion that a court considers and rules on without hearing from all sides. — Also termed *ex parte application.*

motion for reduction. *Family law.* A motion to lessen the amount of child-support payments. • This is a type of motion to modify.

motion for resettlement. A request to clarify or correct the form of an order or judgment that does not correctly state the court's decision. • The motion cannot be used to request a substantial change to or amplification of the court's decision.

motion of course. A party's request that the court may grant as a matter of routine, without investigating or inquiring further.

motion to modify. A post-final-decree motion asking the court to change one of its earlier orders; esp. a request to change child support or visitation. — Also termed *complaint for modification*; *motion for modification*.

omnibus motion. (1889) A motion that makes several requests or asks for multiple forms of relief.

posttrial motion. (1889) A motion made after judgment is entered, such as a motion for new trial.

show-cause motion. A motion filed with the court requesting that a litigant be required to appear and explain why that litigant has failed to comply with a legal requirement.

speaking motion. (1935) A motion that addresses matters not raised in the pleadings.

special motion. (16c) A motion specifically requiring the court's discretion upon hearing, as distinguished from one granted as a matter of course.

2. *Parliamentary law.* A proposal made in a meeting, in a form suitable for its consideration and action, that the meeting (or the organization for which the meeting is acting) take a certain action or view. • A motion may be a *main motion* or a *secondary motion.* A motion technically becomes a "question" when the chair states it for the meeting's consideration. But for most purposes, the parliamentary terms "motion" and "question" are interchangeable. Cf. REQUEST.

coexisting motion. *Parliamentary law.* A main motion, such as one raising a question of privilege, that is pending at the same time as another main motion of lower precedence.

immediately pending motion. The pending motion directly under consideration; the pending motion last stated by the chair and next in line for a vote. See *pending motion*; PRECEDENCE (4).

improper motion. A motion that is out of order. See OUT OF ORDER.

incidental main motion. A main motion that relates to a procedural rather than a substantive matter; an otherwise secondary motion, made when no main motion is pending.— Also termed *procedural main motion*; *quasi-main motion*; *specific main motion.* See *main motion.* Cf. *original main motion.*

incidental motion. A secondary motion that relates to the procedure under which other business is considered. See *secondary motion.*

main motion. A motion that brings business before a meeting. • A main motion may be an *original main motion* or an *incidental main motion.* — Also termed *principal motion*; *proposition.*

ordinary main motion. See *original main motion.*

original main motion. A main motion that relates to a substantive rather than a procedural matter; a main motion that is not an incidental main motion. — Also termed *ordinary main motion*; *substantive main motion*; *substantive motion.* See *main motion.* Cf. *incidental main motion.*

parliamentary motion. 1. Any motion that is not an original main motion — that is, any motion that is either a secondary motion or an incidental main motion. 2. A motion under parliamentary law; MOTION (2).

pending motion. A motion under consideration, even though other pending motions of higher rank may have taken precedence over it. Cf. *immediately pending motion.*

principal motion. See *main motion.*

privileged motion. A secondary motion that does not relate to other business, but rather to the organization, the meeting, its members, and their rights and privileges, and is thus entitled to prompt attention in preference over other pending business. See *secondary motion*; PRIVILEGE (6).

procedural main motion. See *incidental main motion.*

procedural motion. A motion that relates to the manner in which a meeting conducts its business, rather than to the business itself. • A procedural motion may be either an *incidental motion* (including an *incidental main motion*) or a *privileged motion.*

quasi-main motion. See *incidental main motion.*

restorative motion. A motion that renews consideration of a question already disposed of. — Also termed *restoratory motion.*

restoratory motion. See *restorative motion.*

secondary motion. A motion that does not itself bring business before the meeting, and is therefore in order when a main motion is pending. • A secondary motion may be either an *incidental motion* (although not an *incidental main motion*), a *privileged motion*, or a *subsidiary motion.* Cf. *main motion.*

specific main motion. See *incidental main motion.*

subsidiary motion. A secondary motion that directly affects the main motion's form or consideration. See *secondary motion.*

substantive main motion. See *original main motion.*

substantive motion. See *original main motion.*

motion for a directed verdict. See MOTION FOR DIRECTED VERDICT.

motion for a more definite statement. See MOTION FOR MORE DEFINITE STATEMENT.

motion for a new trial. See MOTION FOR NEW TRIAL.

motion for a protective order. See MOTION FOR PROTECTIVE ORDER.

motion for directed verdict. (1904) A party's request that the court enter judgment in its favor before submitting the case to the jury because there is no legally sufficient evidentiary foundation on which a reasonable jury could find for the other party. ● Under the Federal Rules of Civil Procedure, the equivalent court paper is known as a motion for judgment as a matter of law. — Abbr. MDV. — Also termed *motion for a directed verdict*. See MOTION FOR JUDGMENT AS A MATTER OF LAW; *directed verdict* under VERDICT.

motion for j.n.o.v. See MOTION FOR JUDGMENT NOTWITHSTANDING THE VERDICT.

motion for judgment as a matter of law. (1956) A party's request that the court enter a judgment in its favor before the case is submitted to the jury, or after a contrary jury verdict, because there is no legally sufficient evidentiary basis on which a jury could find for the other party. ● Under the Federal Rules of Civil Procedure, a party may move for judgment as a matter of law anytime before the case has been submitted to the jury. This kind of motion was formerly known as a *motion for directed verdict* (and still is in many jurisdictions). If the motion is denied and the case is submitted to the jury, resulting in an unfavorable verdict, the motion may be renewed within ten days after entry of the judgment. This aspect of the motion replaces the court paper formerly known as a *motion for judgment notwithstanding the verdict*. Fed. R. Civ. P. 50.

motion for judgment notwithstanding the verdict. (1822) A party's request that the court enter a judgment in its favor despite the jury's contrary verdict because there is no legally sufficient evidentiary basis for a jury to find for the other party. ● Under the Federal Rules of Civil Procedure, this procedure has been replaced by the provision for a motion for judgment as a matter of law, which must be presented before the case has been submitted to the jury but can be reasserted if it is denied and the jury returns an unfavorable verdict. Fed. R. Civ. P. 50. — Also termed *motion for j.n.o.v.* See MOTION FOR JUDGMENT AS A MATTER OF LAW.

motion for judgment of acquittal. (1923) A criminal defendant's request, at the close of the government's case or the close of all evidence, to be acquitted because there is no legally sufficient evidentiary basis on which a reasonable jury could return a guilty verdict. ● If the motion is granted,

the government has no right of appeal. Fed. R. Crim. P. 29(a). — Abbr. MJOA.

motion for judgment on the pleadings. (1923) A party's request that the court rule in its favor based on the pleadings on file, without accepting evidence, as when the outcome of the case rests on the court's interpretation of the law. Fed. R. Civ. P. 12(c).

motion for leave to appeal. (1874) A request that an appellate court review an interlocutory order that meets the standards of the collateral-order doctrine. — Abbr. MLA. See COLLATERAL-ORDER DOCTRINE.

motion for modification. See *motion to modify* under MOTION (1).

motion for more definite statement. (1904) A party's request that the court require an opponent to amend a vague or ambiguous pleading to which the party cannot reasonably be required to respond. Fed. R. Civ. P. 12(e). — Also termed *motion for a more definite statement*.

motion for new trial. (18c) A party's postjudgment request that the court vacate the judgment and order a new trial for such reasons as factually insufficient evidence, newly discovered evidence, and jury misconduct. ● In many jurisdictions, this motion is required before a party can raise such a matter on appeal. — Also termed *motion for a new trial*.

motion for protective order. (1948) A party's request that the court protect it from potentially abusive action by the other party, usu. relating to discovery, as when one party seeks discovery of the other party's trade secrets. ● A court will sometimes craft a protective order to protect one party's trade secrets by ordering that any secret information exchanged in discovery be used only for purposes of the pending suit and not be publicized. — Also termed *motion for a protective order*.

motion for reduction. See MOTION (1).

motion for relief from stay. See MOTION TO LIFT THE STAY.

motion for relief from the judgment. (1867) A party's request that the court correct a clerical mistake in the judgment — that is, a mistake that results in the judgment's incorrectly reflecting the court's intentions — or relieve the party from the judgment because of such matters as (1) inadvertence, surprise, or excusable neglect, (2) newly discovered evidence that could not have been discovered through diligence in time for a motion for new trial, (3) the judgment's being the result of fraud, misrepresentation, or misconduct by the other party, or (4) the judgment's being void or having been satisfied or released. Fed. R.

Civ. P. 60. Cf. MOTION TO ALTER OR AMEND THE JUDGMENT.

motion for repleader. (18c) *Common-law pleading.* An unsuccessful party's posttrial motion asking that the pleadings begin anew because the issue was joined on an immaterial point. ● The court never awards a repleader to the party who tendered the immaterial issue. Cf. REPLEADER.

motion for resettlement. See MOTION (1).

motion for summary judgment. (1842) A request that the court enter judgment without a trial because there is no genuine issue of material fact to be decided by a fact-finder — that is, because the evidence is legally insufficient to support a verdict in the nonmovant's favor. ● In federal court and in most state courts, the movant-defendant must point out in its motion the absence of evidence on an essential element of the plaintiff's claim, after which the burden shifts to the nonmovant-plaintiff to produce evidence raising a genuine fact issue. But if a party moves for summary judgment on its own claim or defense, then it must establish each element of the claim or defense as a matter of law. Fed. R. Civ. P. 56. — Abbr. MSJ. — Also termed *summary-judgment motion; motion for summary disposition.* See SUMMARY JUDGMENT.

motion in arrest of judgment. (17c) **1.** A defendant's motion claiming that a substantial error appearing on the face of the record vitiates the whole proceeding and the judgment. **2.** A postjudgment motion in a criminal case claiming that the indictment is insufficient to sustain a judgment or that the verdict is somehow insufficient.

motion in limine (in **lim**-ə-nee). (18c) A pretrial request that certain inadmissible evidence not be referred to or offered at trial. ● Typically, a party makes this motion when it believes that mere mention of the evidence during trial would be highly prejudicial and could not be remedied by an instruction to disregard. If, after the motion is granted, the opposing party mentions or attempts to offer the evidence in the jury's presence, a mistrial may be ordered. A ruling on a motion in limine does not always preserve evidentiary error for appellate purposes. To raise such an error on appeal, a party may be required to formally object when the evidence is actually admitted or excluded during trial.

motion of course. See MOTION (1).

motion to alter or amend the judgment. (1950) A party's request that the court correct a substantive error in the judgment, such as a manifest error of law or fact. ● Under the Federal Rules of Civil Procedure, a motion to alter or amend the judgment must be filed within ten days after the judgment is entered. It should not ordinarily be used to correct clerical errors in a judgment.

Those types of errors — that is, errors that result in the judgment not reflecting the court's intention — may be brought in a motion for relief from the judgment, which does not have the ten-day deadline. A motion to alter or amend the judgment is usu. directed to substantive issues regarding the judgment, such as an intervening change in the law or newly discovered evidence that was not available at trial. Fed. R. Civ. P. 59(e). Cf. MOTION FOR RELIEF FROM THE JUDGMENT.

motion to compel discovery. (1960) A party's request that the court force the party's opponent to respond to the party's discovery request (as to answer interrogatories or produce documents). Fed. R. Civ. P. 37(a). — Often shortened to *motion to compel.* — Also termed *motion to enforce discovery.*

motion to correct inventorship. *Patents.* A request in an interference proceeding to add one or more unnamed coinventors to the patent application. ● The motion will be granted unless the unnamed coinventor acted with the intent to deceive.

motion to dismiss. (18c) A request that the court dismiss the case because of settlement, voluntary withdrawal, or a procedural defect. ● Under the Federal Rules of Civil Procedure, a plaintiff may voluntarily dismiss the case (under Rule 41(a)) or the defendant may ask the court to dismiss the case, usu. based on one of the defenses listed in Rule 12(b). These defenses include lack of personal or subject-matter jurisdiction, improper venue, insufficiency of process, the plaintiff's failure to state a claim on which relief can be granted, and the failure to join an indispensable party. A defendant will frequently file a motion to dismiss for failure to state a claim, which is governed by Rule 12(b)(6), claiming that even if all the plaintiff's allegations are true, they would not be legally sufficient to state a claim on which relief might be granted. — Abbr. MTD. See DEMURRER.

motion to dissolve interference. *Patents.* A request by the senior party to dismiss challenges to its priority as the first inventor.

motion to enforce discovery. See MOTION TO COMPEL DISCOVERY.

motion to lift the stay. (1969) *Bankruptcy.* A party's request that the bankruptcy court alter the automatic bankruptcy stay to allow the movant to act against the debtor or the debtor's property, as when a creditor seeks permission to foreclose on a lien because its security interest is not adequately protected. — Also termed *motion for relief from stay; motion to modify the stay.*

motion to modify. See MOTION (1).

motion to modify the stay. See MOTION TO LIFT THE STAY.

motion to quash (kwahsh). (18c) A party's request that the court nullify process or an act instituted by the other party, as in seeking to nullify a subpoena.

motion to remand. (1816) In a case that has been removed from state court to federal court, a party's request that the federal court return the case to state court, usu. because the federal court lacks jurisdiction or because the procedures for removal were not properly followed. 28 USCA § 1447(c).

motion to strike. (1806) **1.** *Civil procedure.* A party's request that the court delete insufficient defenses or immaterial, redundant, impertinent, or scandalous statements from an opponent's pleading. Fed. R. Civ. P. 12(f). **2.** *Evidence.* A request that inadmissible evidence be deleted from the record and that the jury be instructed to disregard it.

motion to suppress. (18c) A request that the court prohibit the introduction of illegally obtained evidence at a criminal trial.

motion to transfer venue. (1934) A request that the court transfer the case to another district or county, usu. because the original venue is improper under the applicable venue rules or because of local prejudice. See VENUE; CHANGE OF VENUE.

motion to withdraw. 1. An attorney's request for a court's permission to cease representing a client in a lawsuit. **2.** A defendant's formal request for a court's permission to change the defendant's plea or strike an admission. — Also termed (in sense 2) *motion to withdraw a plea.*

motion to withdraw a plea. See MOTION TO WITHDRAW (2).

motive. (14c) Something, esp. willful desire, that leads one to act. — Also termed *ulterior intent.* Cf. INTENT.

bad motive. (18c) A person's knowledge that an act is wrongful while the person commits the act.

malicious motive. (18c) A motive for bringing a prosecution, other than to do justice.

Motor Carrier Act. A federal statute, originally enacted in 1935 (49 USCA §§ 502–507), subjecting commercial motor carriers of freight and passengers in interstate commerce to the regulations of the Interstate Commerce Commission, now the U.S. Department of Transportation. • The Act was repealed in the 1980s.

MOU. *abbr.* MEMORANDUM OF UNDERSTANDING.

movable, *n.* (*usu. pl.*) (15c) **1.** Property that can be moved or displaced, such as personal goods; a tangible or intangible thing in which an interest constitutes personal property; specif., anything that is not so attached to land as to be regarded as a part of it as determined by local law. — Also termed *movable property*; *movable thing.*

intangible movable. A physical thing that can be moved but that cannot be touched in the usual sense. • Examples are light and electricity.

2. *Scots law.* A nonheritable right. — Also spelled (in BrE) *moveable.* Cf. IMMOVABLE. — **movable,** *adj.*

movable estate. See *personal property* (1) under PROPERTY.

movable fixture. See *tenant's fixture* under FIXTURE.

movable freehold. See FREEHOLD.

movable property. See MOVABLE (1).

movable thing. See MOVABLE (1).

movant (moov-ənt). (1875) One who makes a motion to the court or a deliberative body. — Formerly also spelled *movent.* — Also termed *moving party*; *mover.* — Also termed *moving party*; *mover.*

move, *vb.* (15c) **1.** To make an application (to a court) for a ruling, order, or some other judicial action <the appellant moved the court for a new trial>. **2.** To make a motion <the senator moved that a vote be taken>. See MOTION (2).

moveable. See MOVABLE.

movent. See MOVANT.

mover, *n.* **1.** *Slang.* A stock that experiences spectacular market price changes; a very unstable stock. **2.** MOVANT.

moving expense. See EXPENSE.

moving papers. The papers that constitute or support a motion in a court proceeding. — Also termed *motion papers.*

moving part. *Patents.* A separate component of an apparatus that works together with another to produce the intended useful result. • Moving parts and a rule of operation generally distinguish an apparatus from an article of manufacture.

moving party. See MOVANT.

moving violation. (1954) An infraction of a traffic law while the vehicle is in motion.

Mozilla public license. See LICENSE.

MP. *abbr.* Member of Parliament. See PARLIAMENT.

MPC. *abbr.* MODEL PENAL CODE.

MPC test. See SUBSTANTIAL-CAPACITY TEST.

MPEP. *abbr.* MANUAL OF PATENT EXAMINING PROCEDURE.

MPL. *abbr.* Mozilla public license. See *Mozilla public license* under LICENSE.

Mr. Denman's Act. See DENMAN'S ACT (2).

MRE. *abbr.* MILITARY RULES OF EVIDENCE.

MSA. *abbr.* See *mediated settlement agreement* under SETTLEMENT (2).

MSHA. *abbr.* MINE SAFETY AND HEALTH ADMINISTRATION.

MSJ. *abbr.* MOTION FOR SUMMARY JUDGMENT.

m.s.p. *abbr.* MORTUUS SINE PROLE.

MSPB. *abbr.* MERIT SYSTEMS PROTECTION BOARD.

MSTB. *abbr.* MODEL STATE TRADEMARK BILL.

MTD. *abbr.* MOTION TO DISMISS.

MUD. *abbr.* See *municipal utility district* under DISTRICT.

mug book. (1947) A collection of mug shots of criminal suspects maintained by law-enforcement agencies (such as the FBI and police departments) to be used in identifying criminal offenders.

mug shot. (1950) A photograph of a person's face taken after the person has been arrested and booked.

mulct (məlkt), *n.* (16c) A fine or penalty.

mulct, *vb.* (17c) **1.** To punish by a fine. **2.** To deprive or divest of, esp. fraudulently.

mulct law. *Hist.* An Iowa law that allowed some saloons to pay the state a sum of money and continue to operate despite a statewide prohibition against alcohol sales. • While the money paid was called a mulct, it was effectively a licensing tax rather than a criminal penalty because continuing violations of the liquor law were not prosecuted.

mule. *Slang.* A person hired to smuggle contraband, esp. a controlled substance, and deliver it to the distributor at a destination point. • For example, a drug mule might carry cocaine through a security checkpoint by concealing it beneath a suitcase's false bottom.

multicraft union. See UNION.

multidisciplinary practice. A fee-sharing association of lawyers and nonlawyers in a firm that delivers both legal and nonlegal services. • Rule 5.4 of the Model Rules of Professional Conduct effectively bars multidisciplinary practice. Under this rule, a lawyer cannot (1) share legal fees with nonlawyers, (2) form a partnership involving the practice of law with nonlawyers, (3) form a law firm in which a nonlawyer has an interest, or (4) allow a nonlawyer to direct the lawyer's professional judgment. — Abbr. MDP. — Sometimes termed *multidisciplinary practice of law.*

multidistrict litigation. (1966) *Civil procedure.* Federal-court litigation in which civil actions pending in different districts and involving common fact questions are transferred to a single district for coordinated pretrial proceedings, after which the actions are returned to their original districts for trial. • Multidistrict litigation is governed by the Judicial Panel on Multidistrict Litigation, which is composed of seven circuit and district judges appointed by the Chief Justice of the United States. 28 USCA § 1407. — Abbr. MDL.

Multiethnic Placement Act of 1994. A model statute intended to (1) decrease the length of time that a child awaits adoption, (2) identify and recruit adoptive and foster parents who can meet the needs of available children, and (3) eliminate adoption discrimination based on race, color, or national origin of the child or the adoptive parents. — Abbr. MEPA.

multifarious (məl-tə-**fair**-ee-əs), *adj.* (16c) **1.** (Of a single pleading) improperly joining distinct matters or causes of action, and thereby confounding them. **2.** Improperly joining parties in a lawsuit. **3.** Diverse; many and various. — **multifariousness,** *n.*

multifarious issue. See ISSUE (1).

multilateral, *adj.* (1827) Involving more than two parties <a multilateral agreement>.

multilateral advance pricing agreement. See ADVANCE PRICING AGREEMENT.

multilevel-distribution program. See PYRAMID SCHEME.

multimaturity bond. See *put bond* under BOND (3).

multimodal shipping. The transportation of freight using more means of carriage and usu. more than one carrier. • For example, a cargo may be carried first by air or sea, then by rail or truck to its destination. — Also termed *intermodal transport; multimodal carriage.*

multinational corporation. See CORPORATION.

multipartite, *adj.* (17c) (Of a document, etc.) divided into many parts.

multiperil policy. See INSURANCE POLICY.

multiple access. See ACCESS (4).

multiple admissibility. See ADMISSIBILITY.

multiple-class application. See *combined application* under TRADEMARK APPLICATION.

multiple counts. See COUNT.

multiple damages. See DAMAGES.

multiple-dependent claim. See PATENT CLAIM.

multiple evidence. See EVIDENCE.

multiple hearsay. See *double hearsay* under HEARSAY.

multiple interest. See INTEREST (2).

multiple job-holding. See MOONLIGHTING.

multiple listing. See LISTING (1).

multiple offense. See OFFENSE (1).

multiple-party account. See ACCOUNT.

multiple sentences. See SENTENCE.

multiplicity (məl-tə-**plis**-i-tee), *n. Criminal procedure.* The improper charging of the same offense in more than one count of a single indictment or information. • Multiplicity violates the Fifth Amendment protection against double jeopardy. — **multiplicitous** (məl-tə-**plis**-i-təs), *adj.*

multiplicity of actions. (17c) The existence of two or more lawsuits litigating the same issue against the same defendant. — Also termed *multiplicity of suits*; *multiplicity of proceedings*. See PIECE-MEAL LITIGATION.

multiplicity of claims. See AGGREGATION OF CLAIMS.

multiplied damages. See *multiple damages* under DAMAGES.

Multistate Bar Examination. See BAR EXAMINATION.

multistate corporation. See CORPORATION.

multital (**məl**-ti-təl), *adj.* (1917) **1.** Of or relating to legal relations that exist among three or more people, esp. a multitude of people. Cf. UNITAL. **2.** *Rare.* See IN REM.

Munchausen syndrome by proxy (mən-chow-zən). A condition in which a caregiver, usu. a parent, fabricates or induces a child's medical condition and seeks medical treatment for the child on the basis of the fabrications or induced condition. • This syndrome is a kind of child abuse, esp. when the victim is subjected to repeated medical examinations and treatment, often of an invasive nature, and sometimes even to physical injuries that induce symptoms consistent with the falsified medical condition. The parent is usu. emotionally deprived and fabricates or causes the child's illness or medical condition as an attention-getting device.

muni (**myoo**-nee), *n.* See *municipal bond* under BOND (3).

municipal, *adj.* (16c) **1.** Of or relating to a city, town, or local governmental unit. **2.** Of or relating to the internal government of a state or nation (as contrasted with *international*).

municipal, *n.* See *municipal bond* under BOND (3).

municipal action. Any authorized exercise of governmental power by a municipal officer, board, agency, or other municipal body.

municipal affairs. The matters relating to the local government of a municipality.

municipal aid. Financial or other assistance provided by a municipality to a private business, usu. to encourage it to relocate to the municipality.

municipal attorney. See CITY ATTORNEY.

municipal bond. See BOND (3).

municipal charter. See CHARTER (2).

municipal corporation. A city, town, or other local political entity formed by charter from the state and having the autonomous authority to administer the state's local affairs; esp., a public corporation created for political purposes and endowed with political powers to be exercised for the public good in the administration of local civil government. — Also termed *municipality*. Cf. *quasi-corporation* under CORPORATION.

municipal corporation de facto. A corporation recognized to exist, although it has not fully complied with statutory requirements, when there is (1) a valid law authorizing its incorporation, (2) a colorable and bona fide attempt to organize under that law, and (3) an assumption of powers conferred under that law.

municipal court. See COURT.

municipal domicile. See DOMICILE.

municipal election. See ELECTION (3).

municipal function. The duties and responsibilities that a municipality owes its members.

municipal government. See *local government* under GOVERNMENT.

municipality. (18c) **1.** MUNICIPAL CORPORATION. **2.** The governing body of a municipal corporation.

municipal judge. See JUDGE.

municipal law. 1. The ordinances and other laws applicable within a city, town, or other local governmental entity. **2.** The internal law of a nation, as opposed to international law.

municipal lien. See LIEN.

municipal officer. See OFFICER (1).

municipal ordinance. See ORDINANCE.

municipal security. See *municipal bond* under BOND (3).

municipal utility district. See DISTRICT.

municipal warrant. See WARRANT (2).

muniment (**myoo**-nə-mənt). (15c) A document (such as a deed or charter) evidencing the rights or privileges of a person, family, or corporation. — Also termed (archaically) *miniment*.

muniment house. *Hist.* A place (such as a room in a castle or cathedral) where titles, deeds, and other evidences of title are stored.

muniment of title. (1806) Documentary evidence of title, such as a deed or a judgment regarding the ownership of property. — Also termed *common assurance*. See CHAIN OF TITLE.

murder, *n.* (bef. 12c) The killing of a human being with malice aforethought. • At common law, the crime of murder was not subdivided, but many state statutes have adopted the degree structure outlined below, though the Model Penal Code has not. Model Penal Code § 210.2. See MALICE AFORETHOUGHT. Cf. MANSLAUGHTER. — **murder,** *vb.* — **murderous,** *adj.*

constructive murder. See *felony murder.*

depraved-heart murder. (1975) A murder resulting from an act so reckless and careless of the safety of others that it demonstrates the perpetrator's complete lack of regard for human life. — Also termed *depraved-indifference murder; unintentional murder.*

felony murder. (1926) Murder that occurs during the commission of a dangerous felony (often limited to rape, kidnapping, robbery, burglary, and arson). — Also termed *unintentional murder;* (in English law) *constructive murder.* See FELONY-MURDER RULE.

first-degree murder. (1895) Murder that is willful, deliberate, or premeditated, or that is committed during the course of another dangerous felony. • All murder perpetrated by poisoning or by lying in wait is considered first-degree murder. All types of murder not involving willful, deliberate, and premeditated killing are usu. considered second-degree murder. — Also termed *murder of the first degree; murder one.*

mass murder. (1917) A murderous act or series of acts by which a criminal kills many victims at or near the same time, usu. as part of one act or plan. Cf. *serial murder.*

murder by torture. (1901) A murder preceded by the intentional infliction of pain and suffering on the victim.

murder of the first degree. See *first-degree murder.*

murder of the second degree. See *second-degree murder.*

murder of the third degree. See *third-degree murder.*

murder one. See *first-degree murder.*

murder three. See *third-degree murder.*

murder two. See *second-degree murder.*

second-degree murder. (1909) Murder that is not aggravated by any of the circumstances of first-degree murder. — Also termed *murder of the second degree; murder two.*

serial murder. (1977) A murder in which a criminal kills one of many victims over time, often as part of a pattern in which the criminal targets victims who have some similar characteristics. Cf. *mass murder.*

third-degree murder. (1933) A wrong that did not constitute murder at common law. • Only a few states have added to their murder statutes a third degree of murder. The other states classify all murders in two degrees. Manslaughter is

not a degree of the crime of murder, but instead is a distinct offense. — Also termed *murder of the third degree; murder three.*

unintentional murder. **1.** A killing for which malice is implied because the person acted with intent to cause serious physical injury or knew that the conduct was substantially certain to cause death or serious physical injury. • In some jurisdictions, this term is applied generally to several grades of killings without express intent. **2.** See *depraved-heart murder.* **3.** See *felony murder.* **4.** See *voluntary manslaughter* under MANSLAUGHTER.

willful murder. (16c) The unlawful and intentional killing of another without excuse or mitigating circumstances.

murder clause. A contract provision that imposes onerous — often unreasonable — obligations on one party. • Murder clauses are usu. found in construction contracts.

muster, *vb.* (14c) *Military law.* **1.** To assemble together (troops) for inspection or service. **2.** To assemble together (potential troops) for enlistment.

muster roll. *Maritime law.* A shipmaster's account listing the name, age, national character, and quality of every employee on the ship. • In wartime, it is used in ascertaining a ship's neutrality.

must-pass bill. See BILL (3).

mutation, *n.* A significant and basic alteration; esp. in property law, the alteration of a thing's status, such as from separate property to community property. — **mutate,** *vb.* — **mutational,** *adj.*

mutation of libel. *Maritime law.* An amendment to a complaint. See LIBEL (3).

mutatis mutandis (myoo-**tay**-tis myoo-**tan**-dis). [Latin] (16c) All necessary changes having been made; with the necessary changes <what was said regarding the first contract applies *mutatis mutandis* to all later ones>.

mute, *n.* (17c) **1.** A person who cannot speak. **2.** A person (esp. a prisoner) who stands silent when required to answer or plead. • Formerly, if a prisoner stood mute, a jury was empaneled to determine whether the prisoner was intentionally mute or mute by an act of God. By the Criminal Law Act of 1827 (7 & 8 Geo. 4, ch. 28), if a prisoner was mute by malice, the officer automatically entered a plea of not guilty and the trial proceeded. If adjudicated to be insane, the prisoner was kept in custody until the Crown determined what should be done.— Also termed (in sense 2) *standing mute.*

mutilation, *n.* (16c) **1.** The act or an instance of rendering a document legally ineffective by subtracting or altering — but not completely destroying — an essential part through cutting, tearing, burning, or erasing. **2.** *Criminal law.* The act of cutting off or permanently damaging a body part, esp. an essential one. See MAYHEM. — **mutilate,** *vb.* — **mutilator,** *n.*

mutiny (**myoo**-tə-nee), *n.* (16c) **1.** An insubordination or insurrection of armed forces, esp. sailors, against the authority of their commanders; a forcible revolt by members of the military against constituted authority, usu. their commanding officers. **2.** Loosely, any uprising against authority. — Also termed (in both senses) *inciting revolt.* — **mutinous,** *adj.*

Mutiny Act. *Hist.* An English statute enacted annually from 1689 to 1879 to provide for a standing army and to punish mutiny, desertion, and other military offenses. ● It was merged into the Army Discipline and Regulation Act of 1879 (ch. 33).

mutual, *adj.* (16c) **1.** Generally, directed by each toward the other or others; reciprocal. **2.** (Of a condition, credit covenant, promise, etc.) reciprocally given, received, or exchanged. **3.** (Of a right, etc.) belonging to two parties; common. — **mutuality,** *n.*

mutual account. See ACCOUNT.

mutual affray. See MUTUAL COMBAT.

mutual-agreement program. (1978) A prisoner-rehabilitation plan in which the prisoner agrees to take part in certain self-improvement activities to receive a definite parole date.

mutual assent. See ASSENT.

mutual association. A mutually owned, cooperative savings and loan association, with the deposits being shares of the association. ● A mutual association is not allowed to issue stock and is usu. regulated by the Office of Thrift Supervision, an agency of the U.S. Treasury Department. — See SAVINGS-AND-LOAN ASSOCIATION.

mutual-benefit association. A fraternal or social organization that provides benefits for its members, usu. on an assessment basis.

mutual-benefit insurance. Benefits provided by a mutual-benefit association upon the occurrence of a loss.

mutual combat. (17c) A consensual fight on equal terms — arising from a moment of passion but not in self-defense — between two persons armed with deadly weapons. ● A murder charge may be reduced to voluntary manslaughter if death occurred by mutual combat. — Also termed *mutual affray.* Cf. DUEL.

mutual company. See COMPANY.

mutual contract. See *bilateral contract* under CONTRACT.

mutual debts. See DEBT.

mutual demands. (17c) Countering demands between two parties at the same time <a claim and counterclaim in a lawsuit are mutual demands>.

mutual fund. (1934) **1.** An investment company that invests its shareholders' money in a usu. diversified selection of securities. — Often shortened to *fund.* **2.** Loosely, a share in such a company.

  balanced fund. A mutual fund that maintains a balanced investment in stocks and bonds, investing a certain percentage in senior securities.

  bond fund. A mutual fund that invests primarily in specialized corporate bonds or municipal bonds.

  closed-end fund. A mutual fund having a fixed number of shares that are traded on a major securities exchange or an over-the-counter market.

  common-stock fund. A mutual fund that invests only in common stock.

  dual fund. A closed-end mutual fund that invests in two classes of stock — stock that pays dividends and stock that increases in investment value without dividends. ● A dual fund combines characteristics of an income fund and a growth fund. — Also termed *dual-purpose fund; leverage fund; split fund.*

  fully managed fund. A mutual fund whose policy allows reasonable discretion in trading securities in combination or quantity.

  global fund. A mutual fund that invests in stocks and bonds throughout the world, including the U.S. — Also termed *world fund.* Cf. *single-country fund; international fund.*

  growth fund. A mutual fund that typically invests in well-established companies whose earnings are expected to increase. ● Growth funds usu. pay small dividends but offer the potential for large share-price increases.

  hedge fund. See HEDGE FUND.

  income fund. A mutual fund that typically invests in securities that consistently produce a steady income, such as bonds or dividend-paying stocks.

  index fund. A mutual fund that invests in the stock of companies constituting a specific market index, such as Standard & Poor's 500 stocks, and thereby tracks the stock average.

  international fund. A mutual fund that invests in stocks and bonds of companies outside the U.S., but not those within. Cf. *global fund; single-country fund.*

  leverage fund. See *dual fund.*

  load fund. A mutual fund that charges a commission, usu. ranging from 4 to 9%, either when shares are purchased (a *front-end load*) or when they are redeemed (a *back-end load*).

money-market fund. A mutual fund that invests in low-risk government securities and short-term notes.

no-load fund. A mutual fund that does not charge any sales commission (although it may charge fees to cover operating costs).

open-end fund. A mutual fund that continually offers new shares and buys back existing shares on demand. • An open-end fund will continue to grow as more shareholders invest because it does not have a fixed number of shares outstanding.

performance fund. A mutual fund characterized by an aggressive purchase of stocks expected to show near-term growth.

regional fund. A mutual fund that concentrates its investments in a specific geographic area or a particular economic area.

single-country fund. A mutual fund that invests in an individual nation outside the U.S. Cf. *global fund*; *international fund*.

split fund. See *dual fund*.

utility fund. A mutual fund that invests only in public-utility securities.

value fund. A mutual fund that invests in stocks that its manager believes to be priced below their true market value.

vulture fund. An investment company that purchases bankrupt or insolvent companies to reorganize them in hopes of reselling them at a profit.

world fund. See *global fund*.

mutual-fund wrap account. See ACCOUNT.

mutual insurance. See INSURANCE.

mutual insurance company. See INSURANCE COMPANY.

mutuality. (16c) The state of sharing or exchanging something; a reciprocation; an interchange <mutuality of obligation>.

mutuality doctrine. (1926) The collateral-estoppel requirement that, to bar a party from relitigating an issue determined against that party in an earlier action, both parties must have been in privity with one another in the earlier proceeding. — Also termed *mutuality of parties*.

mutuality of assent. See MEETING OF THE MINDS.

mutuality of benefits. See RECIPROCITY (2).

mutuality of contract. See MUTUALITY OF OBLIGATION.

mutuality of debts. *Bankruptcy.* For purposes of setoff, the condition in which debts are owed between parties acting in the same capacity, even though the debts are not of the same character and did not arise out of the same transaction.

mutuality of estoppel. (1852) The collateral-estoppel principle that a judgment is not conclusively in favor of someone unless the opposite decision would also be conclusively against that person.

mutuality of obligation. (1838) The agreement of both parties to a contract to be bound in some way. — Also termed *mutuality of contract*. See *mutual assent* under ASSENT.

mutuality of parties. See MUTUALITY DOCTRINE.

mutuality of remedy. (1819) The availability of a remedy, esp. equitable relief, to both parties to a transaction, sometimes required before either party can be granted specific performance. See SPECIFIC PERFORMANCE.

mutual mistake. See MISTAKE.

mutual promises. See PROMISE.

mutual release. See RELEASE.

mutual rescission. See RESCISSION (2).

mutual savings bank. See BANK.

mutual testament. See *mutual will* under WILL.

mutual will. See WILL.

mutuant (**myoo**-choo-ənt). The provider of property in a mutuum. See MUTUUM. Cf. MUTUARY.

mutuary (**myoo**-choo-er-ee). (1839) The recipient of property in a mutuum. See MUTUUM. Cf. MUTUANT.

mutuum (**myoo**-choo-əm), *n.* (15c) **1.** A transaction (sometimes referred to as a bailment) in which goods are delivered but, instead of being returned, are replaced by other goods of the same kind. • At common law such a transaction is regarded as a sale or exchange, not as a bailment, because the particular goods are not returned. **2.** *Roman law.* A real contract in which money or fungible goods were delivered from the lender to the borrower, who was strictly liable to return an equivalent amount. • Because the contract was gratuitous, any interest had to be demanded by stipulation. This was one of the real contracts, along with the loan for use (*commodatum* (kom-ə-**day**-təm)) and deposit and pledge (*pignoratio* (pig-nə-**ray**-shee-oh)).

mysterious disappearance. A loss of property under unknown or baffling circumstances that are difficult to understand or explain. • The term is used in insurance policies covering theft.

mystic testament. See *mystic will* under WILL.

mystic will. See WILL.

N

n.a. *abbr.* (1947) **1.** (*cap.*) National Association. See *national bank* under BANK. **2.** Not applicable. **3.** Not available. **4.** Not allowed.

NAA. *abbr.* NEUTRON-ACTIVATION ANALYSIS.

NAFTA (**naf**-tə). *abbr.* NORTH AMERICAN FREE TRADE AGREEMENT.

naked, *adj.* (14c) (Of a legal act or instrument) lacking confirmation or validation <naked ownership of property>.

naked assignment. See *assignment-in-gross* under ASSIGNMENT (2).

naked authority. See AUTHORITY (1).

naked bailment. See *gratuitous bailment* under BAILMENT.

naked confession. See CONFESSION.

naked contract. See NUDUM PACTUM.

naked debenture. See DEBENTURE (3).

naked deposit. 1. See *gratuitous bailment* under BAILMENT. **2.** See DEPOSIT (5).

naked expectancy. See *naked possibility* under POSSIBILITY.

naked land trust. See *land trust* under TRUST.

naked license. See LICENSE.

naked licensee. See *bare licensee* under LICENSEE.

naked option. See OPTION.

naked owner. See OWNER.

naked ownership. See *imperfect ownership* under OWNERSHIP.

naked possession. See POSSESSION.

naked possibility. See POSSIBILITY.

naked power. See POWER (3).

naked promise. See *gratuitous promise* under PROMISE.

naked trust. See *passive trust* under TRUST.

name, *n.* (bef. 12c) A word or phrase identifying or designating a person or thing and distinguishing that person or thing from others.

assumed name. See ASSUMED NAME.

brand name. See TRADENAME.

Christian name. See *personal name.*

corporate name. The registered name under which a corporation conducts legal affairs such as suing, being sued, and paying taxes; the name that a corporation files with a state authority (usu. the secretary of state) as the name under which the corporation will conduct its affairs. • A corporate name usu. includes, and in many states is required to include, the word "corporation," "incorporated," or "company," or an abbreviation of one of those words. Cf. ASSUMED NAME.

distinctive name. A name, esp. a tradename, that clearly distinguishes one thing from another. • To maintain an action for tradename infringement, the plaintiff must prove, among other things, that it owns a distinctive name.

fictitious name. **1.** See ASSUMED NAME. **2.** See ALIAS. **3.** See JOHN DOE.

first name. See *personal name.*

full name. An individual's personal name, second or middle names or initials (if any), and surname arranged in a customary order. • In Western cultures, the traditional order is usu. personal name, middle names or initials, and surname. In many other cultures, the order is surname first, followed by one or more personal names.

generic name. See GENERIC NAME.

geographic name. A name that designates a geographic location or area. — Also termed *geographical name.*

given name. See PERSONAL NAME.

legal name. A person's full name as recognized in law. • A legal name is usu. acquired at birth or through a court order. There are no rules governing a legal name's length or constitution; it may be a single name (e.g., Prince) or include words not generally used in human names (e.g., Moon Unit).

maiden name. A woman's childhood surname (which may or may not remain her surname for life). • Normally the term is used only in reference to a woman who has married and changed her last name.

nickname. See NICKNAME.

personal name. An individual's name or names given at birth, as distinguished from a family name. — Also termed *given name*; (in the Western tradition) *first name*; (in the Christian tradition) *Christian name.* Cf. *surname.*

proprietary name. *Trademarks.* A nondescriptive name that may be owned and registered as a trademark.

street name. See STREET NAME.

surname. The family name automatically bestowed at birth, acquired by marriage, or adopted by choice. • Although in many cultures a person's surname is traditionally the father's surname, a person may take the mother's surname or a combination of the parents' surnames.

tradename. See TRADENAME.

name-and-arms clause. *Hist.* A clause (usu. in a will or settlement transferring property) providing that the property's recipient must assume and continue using the testator's or settlor's surname and coat-of-arms, or else the property will pass to another person.

named additional insured. See *additional insured* under INSURED.

named insured. See INSURED.

named-insured exclusion. See EXCLUSION (3).

named partner. See *name partner* under PARTNER.

named-perils policy. See *multiperil policy* under INSURANCE POLICY.

named plaintiff. See *class representative* under REPRESENTATIVE.

namely, *adv.* By name or particular mention; that is to say <the plaintiff asserted two claims, namely wrongful termination and slander>. ● The term indicates what is to be included by name. By contrast, *including* implies a partial list and indicates that something is not listed. See INCLUDE.

name partner. See PARTNER.

nanny tax. See TAX.

NAPABA. *abbr.* NATIONAL ASIAN PACIFIC AMERICAN BAR ASSOCIATION.

Napoleonic Code. 1. (*usu. pl.*) The codification of French law commissioned by Napoleon in the 19th century, including the *Code civil* (1804), the *Code de procédure civil* (1806), the *Code de commerce* (1807), the *Code pénal* (1810), and the *Code d'instruction crimenelle* (1811). — Sometimes shortened to *Napoléon*. — Also termed *Code Napoléon* (abbr. CN). **2.** Loosely, CIVIL CODE (2).

NAR. *abbr.* NATIONAL ASSOCIATION OF REALTORS.

NARA. *abbr.* NATIONAL ARCHIVES AND RECORDS ADMINISTRATION.

narcoanalysis (nahr-koh-ə-**nal**-ə-sis). (1936) The process of injecting a "truth-serum" drug into a patient to induce semiconsciousness, and then interrogating the patient. ● This process has been utilized to enhance the memory of a witness.

narcotic, *n.* (14c) **1.** An addictive drug, esp. an opiate, that dulls the senses and induces sleep. **2.** (*usu. pl.*) A drug that is controlled or prohibited by law. — **narcotic,** *adj.*

narr. *abbr.* NARRATIO.

narr-and-cognovit law (nahr-and-kahg-**noh**-vit). [Latin *narratio* "declaration" and *cognovit*

"the person has conceded"] *Hist.* A law providing that a plaintiff will be granted judgment on a note through an attorney's confession that the amount shown on the note, together with interest and costs, constitutes a legal and just claim. Cf. *cognovit judgment* under JUDGMENT; CONFESSION OF JUDGMENT.

narratio (nə-**ray**-shee-oh), *n.* [Latin "narrative"] *Hist.* A declaration, complaint, or petition in which the plaintiff sets out the facts of a case; an oral narrative by the plaintiff of the facts and legal arguments on which the claim is based. ● The term has also been called the "conte" or "tale." — Abbr. *narr.*

narrative recital. See RECITAL.

narrator (na-**ray**-tor *or* na-**ray**-tər), *n.* [Law Latin] *Hist.* A pleader or counter; a person who prepares pleadings (i.e., *narrs*). ● For example, a serjeant-at-law was also known as *serviens narrator.* Pl. **narratores** (na-rə-**tor**-eez).

narrow certiorari. See CERTIORARI.

narrow-channel rule. The navigational requirement that a vessel traveling down a slim fairway must keep as near to the fairway wall on the vessel's starboard side as is safe and practicable. 33 USCA § 2009(a)(i).

narrowly tailored, *adj.* (1972) (Of a content-neutral restriction on the time, place, or manner of speech in a designated public forum) being only as broad as is reasonably necessary to promote a substantial governmental interest that would be achieved less effectively without the restriction; no broader than absolutely necessary. See *designated public forum* under PUBLIC FORUM.

narrow sea. (*often pl.*) A sea running between two coasts that are close to each another. ● The English Channel, for example, is a narrow sea.

NASA. *abbr.* NATIONAL AERONAUTICS AND SPACE ADMINISTRATION.

NASD. *abbr.* NATIONAL ASSOCIATION OF SECURITIES DEALERS.

NASDAQ (**naz**-dak). *abbr.* NATIONAL ASSOCIATION OF SECURITIES DEALERS AUTOMATED QUOTATIONS.

NASS. *abbr.* NATIONAL AGRICULTURAL STATISTICS SERVICE.

nation, *n.* (14c) **1.** A large group of people having a common origin, language, and tradition and usu. constituting a political entity. ● When a nation is coincident with a state, the term *nation-state* is often used. — Also termed *nationality.* **2.** A community of people inhabiting a defined territory and organized under an independent government; a sovereign political state. Cf. STATE.

national, *adj.* (16c) **1.** Of or relating to a nation <national anthem>. **2.** Nationwide in scope <national emergency>.

national, *n.* **1.** A member of a nation. **2.** A person owing permanent allegiance to and under the protection of a state. 8 USCA § 1101(a)(21).

> **national of the United States.** A citizen of the United States or a noncitizen who owes permanent allegiance to the United States. 8 USCA § 1101(a)(22). — Also termed *U.S. national*; *U.S. citizen.*

National Aeronautics and Space Act. A 1958 federal statute that created the National Aeronautics and Space Administration (NASA). 42 USCA §§ 2451–2484.

National Aeronautics and Space Administration. The independent federal agency that conducts research into space flight and that builds and flies space vehicles. • NASA was created by the National Aeronautics and Space Act of 1958. 42 USCA §§ 2451–2484. — Abbr. NASA.

National Agricultural Statistics Service. An agency in the U.S. Department of Agriculture responsible for compiling statistical information and estimating agricultural production, supply, price, chemical use, and other related statistics. • Most of the data come from farmers, ranchers, and agribusinesses. — Abbr. NASS.

national airspace. See AIRSPACE.

National Archives and Records Administration. An independent federal agency that sets procedures for preserving governmental records that are important for legal and historical reasons; helps federal agencies manage their records; provides record-storage access; and manages the Presidential Libraries system. • The agency, run by the Archivist of the United States, retains only a small percentage of the federal records produced each year. It publishes the *United States Statutes at Large*, the *Federal Register*, the *Code of Federal Regulations*, the weekly *Compilation of Presidential Documents*, the annual *Public Papers of the President*, and the *United States Government Manual*. It is a successor to the National Archives Establishment, created in 1934, that was made a unit of the General Services Administration in 1949. It became an independent agency in 1984. — Abbr. NARA. See FEDERAL REGISTER.

National Asian Pacific American Bar Association. A professional association of Asian Pacific American attorneys, judges, law professors, and law students, emphasizing civil rights and immigration issues. — Abbr. NAPABA.

national association. See *national bank* under BANK.

National Association of Realtors. An association of real-estate brokers and agents promoting education, professional standards, and modernization in areas of real estate such as brokerage, appraisal, and property management. — Abbr. NAR.

National Association of Securities Dealers. A group of brokers and dealers empowered by the SEC to regulate the over-the-counter securities market. — Abbr. NASD.

National Association of Securities Dealers Automated Quotations. A computerized system for recording transactions and displaying price quotations for a group of actively traded securities on the over-the-counter market. — Abbr. NASDAQ.

National Association of Women Lawyers. An organization, formed in 1899, devoted to the interests of female lawyers and their families. — Abbr. NAWL.

national bank. See BANK.

National Bar Association. An organization of primarily African-American lawyers, founded in 1925 to promote education, professionalism, and the protection of civil rights. — Abbr. NBA.

National Capital Parks Commission. See NATIONAL CAPITAL PLANNING COMMISSION.

National Capital Planning Commission. A 12-member federal commission that plans the development of federal lands and facilities in the National Capital region, an area that includes the District of Columbia and six nearby counties — two in Maryland and four in Virginia. • The Commission was originally established as the National Capital Park Commission, a park-planning agency, in 1924. — Abbr. NCPC.

National Capital Region. The District of Columbia and six nearby counties: Montgomery and Prince George's in Maryland. and Fairfax, Loudoun, Prince William, and Arlington in Virginia. — Abbr. NCR.

National Cemetery Administration. A unit in the U.S. Department of Veterans Affairs responsible for operating national cemeteries, providing headstones for unmarked graves of veterans worldwide, and making grants to states for establishing and caring for veterans' cemeteries. — Abbr. NCA.

National Conference of Black Lawyers. An organization of African American attorneys formed in 1969, active esp. in civil rights. — Abbr. NCBL.

National Conference of Commissioners on Uniform State Laws. An organization that drafts and proposes statutes for adoption by individual states, with the goal of making the laws on various subjects uniform among the states. • Founded in 1892 and composed of representatives from all 50 states, the Conference has drafted more than 200 uniform laws, including the Uniform

Commercial Code. — Abbr. NCCUSL. — Also termed *Uniform Law Commissioners.* See UNIFORM ACT; MODEL ACT; UNIFORM LAW.

National Council of Juvenile and Family Court Judges. An organization of judges and hearing officers who exercise jurisdiction over abuse, neglect, divorce, custody and visitation, support, domestic-violence, and other family-law cases. ● Founded in 1937, the Council has an educational and support facility located near Reno, Nevada. It provides training, technical support, and professional assistance in improving courtroom operations.

National Credit Union Administration. An independent federal agency that charters, insures, supervises, and examines federal credit unions; administers the National Credit Union Share Insurance Fund and the Community Development Revolving Loan Fund; and manages the Central Liquidity Facility, a separate mixed-ownership government corporation that supplies emergency loans to member credit unions. ● The agency was established in 1970 and reorganized in 1978. — Abbr. NCUA.

national currency. See CURRENCY.

National Daily Quotation Service. See PINK SHEET.

national debt. (18c) The total financial obligation of the federal government, including such instruments as Treasury bills, notes, and bonds, as well as foreign debt.

national defense. 1. All measures taken by a nation to protect itself against its enemies. ● A nation's protection of its collective ideals and values is included in the concept of national defense. **2.** A nation's military establishment.

National Disaster Medical System. A unit of the Federal Emergency Management Agency in the U.S. Department of Homeland Security responsible for training, equipping, and deploying teams of emergency medical responders and for coordinating the transportation of people affected by emergencies. ● The agency was transferred from the U.S. Department of Health and Human Services in 2003. — Abbr. NDMS.

national domicile. See DOMICILE.

National Economic Council. See OFFICE OF POLICY DEVELOPMENT.

national emergency. A state of national crisis or a situation requiring immediate and extraordinary national action.

National Endowment for the Arts. An independent federal agency that promotes involvement in the arts by making grants to organizations, honoring artists for their achievements, expanding artistic resources, preserving cultural heritage, and funding projects that educate children and adults in the arts. — Abbr. NEA. See NATIONAL FOUNDATION ON THE ARTS AND THE HUMANITIES.

National Endowment for the Humanities. An independent federal agency that supports research, education, and public programs in the humanities through grants to individuals, groups, and institutions. — Abbr. NEH. See NATIONAL FOUNDATION ON THE ARTS AND THE HUMANITIES.

National Environmental Policy Act. A 1969 federal statute establishing U.S. environmental policy. ● The statute requires federal agencies to submit an environmental-impact statement with every proposal for a program or law that would affect the environment. 42 USCA §§ 4321–4347 — Abbr. NEPA. See ENVIRONMENTAL-IMPACT STATEMENT.

National Environmental Satellite, Data, and Information Service. See NATIONAL OCEANIC AND ATMOSPHERIC ADMINISTRATION.

National Firearms Act. A 1934 federal statute that governs the manufacture, possession, and transfer of certain types of firearms and other weapons. ● In its original form, the act banned gangster-type weapons, such as machine guns and sawn-off shotguns. It has been expanded by amendments to cover most rifles and handguns, and also "destructive devices" such as grenades and land mines. 26 USCA §§ 5801 et seq.

National Foundation on the Arts and the Humanities. An independent federal foundation that encourages and supports progress in the humanities and the arts by supporting the National Endowment for the Arts, the National Endowment for the Humanities, and the Institute of Museum and Library Services. ● The agency was created by act of Congress in 1965. See NATIONAL ENDOWMENT FOR THE ARTS; NATIONAL ENDOWMENT FOR THE HUMANITIES; INSTITUTE OF MUSEUM AND LIBRARY SERVICES.

national government. The government of an entire country, as distinguished from that of a province, state, subdivision, or territory of the country and as distinguished from an international organization. See *federal government* (2) under GOVERNMENT.

National Guard. The U.S. militia, which is maintained as a reserve for the U.S. Army and Air Force. ● Its members are volunteers, recruited and trained on a statewide basis and equipped by the federal government. A state may request the National Guard's assistance in quelling disturbances, and the federal government may order the National Guard into active service in times of war or other national emergency. See MILITIA.

National Highway Traffic Safety Administration. A unit in the U.S. Department of Transportation responsible for regulating the safety of motor vehicles and their equipment. • The agency's work focuses on matters such as theft prevention, speed limits, truthful odometer readings, and fuel consumption. It was established by the Highway Safety Act of 1970. 23 USCA §§ 101 et seq. — Abbr. NHTSA.

National Imaging and Mapping Agency. A unit in the U.S. Department of Defense responsible for providing the armed forces and intelligence officers with up-to-date and accurate geospatial information, esp. in the form of photographs, maps, and charts. — Abbr. NIMA.

National Institute for Literacy. A federally aided institute that leads national efforts to achieve universal literacy. — Abbr. NIFL.

National Institute of Corrections. A federal organization (established within the Bureau of Prisons) whose responsibilities include helping federal, state, and local authorities improve correctional programs, conducting research on correctional issues such as crime prevention, and conducting workshops for law-enforcement personnel, social workers, judges, and others involved in treating and rehabilitating offenders. 18 USCA §§ 4351–4353. See BUREAU OF PRISONS.

National Institute of Standards and Technology. See TECHNOLOGY ADMINISTRATION.

nationality. (17c) **1.** NATION (1). **2.** The relationship between a citizen of a nation and the nation itself, customarily involving allegiance by the citizen and protection by the state; membership in a nation. • This term is often used synonymously with *citizenship*. See CITIZENSHIP. **3.** The formal relationship between a ship and the nation under whose flag the ship sails. See FLAG STATE.

Nationality Act. See IMMIGRATION AND NATIONALITY ACT.

nationality theory. The jurisdictional principle that citizens are subject to the laws of their country, no matter where the citizens are.

nationalization, *n.* (1847) **1.** The act of bringing an industry under governmental control or ownership. **2.** The act of giving a person the status of a citizen. See NATURALIZATION.

nationalize, *vb.* (1809) **1.** To bring (an industry) under governmental control or ownership. **2.** To give (a person) the status of a citizen; NATURALIZE.

National Labor Relations Act. A federal statute regulating the relations between employers and employees and establishing the National Labor Relations Board. 29 USCA §§ 151–169. • The statute is also known as the Wagner Act of 1935. It was amended by the Taft–Hartley Act of 1947 and the Landrum–Griffin Act of 1959. — Abbr. NLRA. — Also termed *Wagner Act*.

National Labor Relations Board. An independent five-member federal board created to prevent and remedy unfair labor practices and to safeguard employees' rights to organize into labor unions. • The board hears complaints of unfair labor practices and issues orders that can be reviewed or enforced by a U.S. court of appeals. The agency was created by the National Labor Relations Act of 1935. 29 USCA § 153. — Abbr. NLRB. — Often shortened to *Labor Relations Board*.

National Lawyers Guild. An association of lawyers, law students, and legal workers dedicated to promoting a left-wing political and social agenda. • Founded in 1937, it now comprises some 4,000 members. Cf. FEDERALIST SOCIETY.

National Marine Fisheries Service. — Abbr. NMFS. See NATIONAL OCEANIC AND ATMOSPHERIC ADMINISTRATION.

National Mediation Board. An independent federal board that mediates labor–management disputes in the airline and railroad industries and provides administrative and financial support in adjusting grievances in the railroad industry. • The agency was created by the Railway Labor Act of 1934 to prevent interruptions in service. 45 USCA §§ 154–163. — Abbr. NMB. Cf. FEDERAL MEDIATION AND CONCILIATION SERVICE.

national monument. (1879) An object or structure and the land on which it is situated, publicly proclaimed by the U.S. President to be of historic or scientific interest. *See* 16 USCA § 341.

National Motor Vehicle Theft Act. See DYER ACT.

National Oceanic and Atmospheric Administration. A unit in the U.S. Department of Commerce responsible for monitoring the environment in order to make accurate and timely weather forecasts and to protect life, property, and the environment. • It was established in 1970 under Reorganization Plan No. 4 of 1970 and operates through several agencies: the National Weather Service (NWS); the National Environmental Satellite, Data, and Information Service (NESDIS); the National Marine Fisheries Service (NMFS); the National Ocean Service (NOS); and the Office of Oceanic and Atmospheric Research (OAR). It also maintains a fleet of ships and aircraft for research. — Abbr. NOAA.

National Ocean Service. See NATIONAL OCEANIC AND ATMOSPHERIC ADMINISTRATION.

national of the United States. See NATIONAL.

National Organ Transplant Act. A 1984 federal law banning the sale of human organs. 42 USCA §§ 273–274. — Abbr. NOTA.

national origin. (1880) The country in which a person was born, or from which the person's ancestors came. • This term is used in several antidiscrimination statutes, including Title VII of the Civil Rights Act of 1964, which prohibits discrimination because of an individual's "race, color, religion, sex, or national origin." 42 USCA § 2000e-2.

national park. (1868) A scenic, natural, historic, and recreational area owned by the United States and set aside for permanent protection. • Yellowstone National Park was declared the first national park in 1872. *See* 16 USCA § 1a-1.

National Park Service. A unit in the U.S. Department of the Interior responsible for managing the nation's national parks, monuments, scenic parkways, preserves, trails, river ways, seashores, lakeshores, recreational areas, and historic sites commemorating movements, events, and personalities of America's past. • The Service was established in 1916. 16 USCA § 1.

National Priorities List. *Environmental law.* The Environmental Protection Agency's list of the most serious uncontrolled or abandoned hazardous-waste sites that are identified for possible long-term remediation as Superfund sites. 40 CFR § 35.6015. — Abbr. NPL.

National Quotation Bureau. A company that publishes daily price quotations (*pink sheets*) of over-the-counter securities.

National Railroad Passenger Corporation. A federally chartered corporation created by the Rail Passenger Service Act of 1970 to provide intercity rail passenger service. • The corporation owns or leases railroad stations and operates passenger trains over tracks that are almost entirely owned by others. — Abbr. NRPC. — Usu. termed *Amtrak.*

National Reporter System. A series of lawbooks, published by the West Group, containing every published appellate decision of the federal and state courts in the United States. • For federal courts, the system includes the *Supreme Court Reporter, Federal Reporter, Federal Claims Reporter, Federal Supplement, Federal Rules Decisions, Bankruptcy Reporter, Military Justice Reporter,* and *Veterans Appeals Reporter.* For state courts, the system includes the *Atlantic Reporter, California Reporter, New York Supplement, North Eastern Reporter, North Western Reporter, Pacific Reporter, South Eastern Reporter, Southern Reporter,* and *South Western Reporter.*

National Response Center. *Environmental law.* A nationwide communication center located in Washington, D.C., responsible for receiving, and relaying to appropriate federal officials, all notices of oil discharges and other releases of hazardous substances. 40 CFR § 310.11.

national river. See RIVER.

National Science Foundation. An independent federal foundation that promotes progress in science and engineering through grants, contracts, and other agreements awarded to universities, colleges, academic consortia, and nonprofit and small-business institutions. • It was created by the National Science Foundation Act of 1950. — Abbr. NSF.

National Security Agency. A unit in the U.S. Department of Defense responsible for protecting U.S. information systems as well as producing foreign intelligence information. • The agency uses code makers and code breakers. — Abbr. NSA.

National Security Council. An agency in the Executive Office of the President responsible for advising the President on national-security matters. • It was created by the National Security Act of 1947. 50 USCA § 402. — Abbr. NSC.

national-security letter. A document that is issued by an FBI official, or by a senior official of another federal agency, and that functions as a subpoena requiring the recipient, usu. a business, to turn over specific business documents. • The Department of Justice provides guidelines for the issuance of a national-security letter, which is not typically reviewed by a court or magistrate. Federal law prohibits the letter's recipient from disclosing the existence of the letter, except to an attorney. — Abbr. NSL.

national-security privilege. See *state-secrets privilege* under PRIVILEGE (3).

national-service life insurance. See LIFE INSURANCE.

National Stolen Property Act. A federal statute that makes it a crime to transport, transmit, or transfer in interstate or foreign commerce goods or money worth $5,000 or more if the person knows that the money or goods were obtained unlawfully. 18 USCA §§ 2311 et seq. — Abbr. NSPA.

national synod. See SYNOD.

National Technical Information Service. See TECHNOLOGY ADMINISTRATION.

National Technical Institute for the Deaf. A federally aided institute, located in Rochester, New York, responsible for educating large numbers of deaf students on a college campus designed primarily for students who can hear. • Established by Congress in 1965, the institute is a part of the Rochester Institute for Technology. — Abbr. NTID.

National Telecommunications and Information Administration. A unit in the U.S. Department of Commerce responsible for advising the President on telecommunications and information policy; conducting research through its Institute for Telecommunications Sciences; and making grants to support advanced infrastructures and to increase ownership by women and minorities. — Abbr. NTIA.

National Transportation Safety Board. An independent five-member federal board that investigates air, rail, water, highway, pipeline, and hazardous-waste accidents; conducts studies; and makes recommendations to government agencies, the transportation industry, and others on safety measures and practices. ● The agency was created in 1966. 49 USCA §§ 1101–1155. — Abbr. NTSB.

national treatment. *Intellectual property.* The policy or practice of a country that accords the citizens of other countries the same intellectual-property protection as it gives its own citizens, with no formal treaty of reciprocity required. ● The principle of national treatment underlay the first international intellectual-property treaties in the 19th century, the Paris and Berne Conventions, and is also embodied in the TRIPs Agreement. Cf. RECIPROCITY; UNIVERSALITY.

national-treatment clause. A provision contained in some treaties, usu. commercial ones, according foreigners the same rights, in certain respects, as those accorded to nationals.

national union. See UNION.

National Weather Service. See NATIONAL OCEANIC AND ATMOSPHERIC ADMINISTRATION.

nations, law of. See INTERNATIONAL LAW.

nation-state. See NATION (1).

native, *n.* (16c) **1.** A person who is a citizen of a particular place, region, or nation by virtue of having been born there. **2.** A person whose national origin derives from having been born within a particular place. **3.** Loosely, a person born abroad whose parents are citizens of the nation and are not permanently residing abroad. **4.** Loosely, a person or thing belonging to a group indigenous to a particular place. ● The term *Native American* is sometimes shortened to *native.*

Native American law. The body of law dealing with American Indian tribes and their relationships to federal and state governments, private citizens, and each other. — Also termed *American Indian law; Indian law.*

native-born, *adj.* **1.** Born within the territorial jurisdiction of a country. **2.** Born of parents who convey rights of citizenship to their offspring, regardless of the place of birth.

native title. See *aboriginal title* (1) under TITLE (2).

natural, *adj.* (14c) **1.** In accord with the regular course of things in the universe and without accidental or purposeful interference <a natural death as opposed to murder>. **2.** Normal; proceeding from the regular character of a person or thing <it is natural for a duck to fly south in the winter>. **3.** Brought about by nature as opposed to

artificial means <a natural lake>. **4.** Inherent; not acquired or assumed <natural talent>. **5.** Indigenous; native <the original or natural inhabitants of a country>. **6.** Of or relating to birth <natural child as distinguished from adopted child>. **7.** Untouched by civilization; wild <only a small part of the forest remains in its natural state>. — **naturally,** *adv.*

natural, *n.* (16c) **1.** A person who is native to a place. See NATIVE; *natural-born citizen* under CITIZEN. **2.** A person or thing well suited for a particular endeavor.

natural-accumulation doctrine. The rule that a governmental entity or other landowner is not required to remove naturally occurring ice or snow from public property, such as a highway, unless the entity has, by taking some affirmative action (such as highway construction), increased the travel hazard to the public.

natural affection. (16c) The love naturally existing between close relatives, such as parent and child. ● Natural affection is not consideration for a contract. See CONSIDERATION (1); *executory contract* under CONTRACT.

natural allegiance. See ALLEGIANCE.

natural and probable consequence. See NATURAL CONSEQUENCE.

natural-born citizen. See CITIZEN.

Natural Born Citizen Clause. (1988) The clause of the U.S. Constitution barring persons not born in the United States from the presidency. U.S. Const. art. II, § 1, cl. 5.

natural boundary. See BOUNDARY.

natural channel. See CHANNEL.

natural child. See CHILD.

natural cognation. See COGNATION.

natural consequence. (16c) Something that predictably occurs as the result of an act <plaintiff's injuries were the natural consequence of the car wreck>. — Also termed *natural and probable consequence.*

natural day. See DAY (2).

natural death. See DEATH.

natural-death act. (1977) A statute that allows a person to prepare a living will instructing a physician to withhold life-sustaining procedures if the person should become terminally ill. See ADVANCE DIRECTIVE; LIVING WILL.

natural domicile. See *domicile of origin* under DOMICILE.

natural duty. See *moral duty* under DUTY (1).

natural equity. See EQUITY (3).

natural father. See *biological father* under FATHER.

natural flood channel. See CHANNEL.

natural fruit. See FRUIT.

natural gas. See DISTILLATE (1).

natural guardian. See GUARDIAN.

natural heir. See HEIR.

natural infancy. See INFANCY.

natural interruption. See INTERRUPTION.

naturalization. (16c) The granting of citizenship to a foreign-born person under statutory authority.

Naturalization Clause. (1849) The constitutional provision stating that every person born or naturalized in the United States is a citizen of the United States and of the state of residence. U.S. Const. amend. XIV, § 1. See JUS SOLI.

naturalization court. A court having jurisdiction to hear and decide naturalization petitions. • Naturalization courts were abolished as a result of the Immigration Act of 1990. Under current U.S. law, the Attorney General has the sole authority to naturalize citizens. But after a hearing before an immigration officer, an applicant may seek review of the denial of an application for naturalization in the federal district court for the district in which the applicant resides. If an applicant is certified to be eligible for naturalization, the oath of allegiance may be administered by the Attorney General, a federal district court, or a state court of record. See *oath of allegiance* under OATH.

naturalize, *vb.* (16c) To grant the rights, privileges, and duties of citizenship to (one previously a noncitizen); to make (a noncitizen) a citizen under statutory authority. — **naturalization,** *n.*

naturalized citizen. See CITIZEN.

natural justice. See JUSTICE (1).

natural law. (15c) 1. A physical law of nature <gravitation is a natural law>. 2. A philosophical system of legal and moral principles purportedly deriving from a universalized conception of human nature or divine justice rather than from legislative or judicial action; moral law embodied in principles of right and wrong <many ethical teachings are based on natural law>. — Also termed *law of nature*; *natural justice*; *lex aeterna*; *eternal law*; *lex naturae*; *lex naturalae*; *divine law*; *jus divinum*; *jus naturale*; *jus naturae*; (in sense 2) *normative jurisprudence*; *jure naturae*. Cf. FUNDAMENTAL LAW; POSITIVE LAW; DIVINE LAW.

natural liberty. See LIBERTY.

natural life. (15c) A person's physical life span.

natural monopoly. See MONOPOLY.

natural monument. See MONUMENT.

natural mother. 1. See *birth mother* under MOTHER. 2. See *biological mother* under MOTHER.

natural object. 1. A person likely to receive a portion of another person's estate based on the nature and circumstances of their relationship. — Also termed *natural object of bounty*; *natural object of one's bounty*; *natural object of testator's bounty*. 2. See *natural boundary* under BOUNDARY. 3. See *natural monument* under MONUMENT.

natural obligation. See OBLIGATION.

natural person. See PERSON (1).

natural possession. See POSSESSION.

natural premium. See PREMIUM (1).

natural presumption. See PRESUMPTION.

natural resource. (1870) 1. Any material from nature having potential economic value or providing for the sustenance of life, such as timber, minerals, oil, water, and wildlife. 2. Environmental features that serve a community's well-being or recreational interests, such as parks.

Natural Resources Conservation Service. An agency in the U.S. Department of Agriculture responsible for providing information and financial assistance to farmers and ranchers for voluntary conservation programs. • The Service was formerly known as the Soil Conservation Service. — Abbr. NRCS.

natural right. See RIGHT.

natural servitude. See SERVITUDE (2).

natural succession. See SUCCESSION (2).

natural watercourse. See WATERCOURSE.

natural wear and tear. See WEAR AND TEAR.

natural wrong. See *moral wrong* under WRONG.

natural year. See YEAR.

nature. (14c) 1. A fundamental quality that distinguishes one thing from another; the essence of something. 2. A wild condition, untouched by civilization. 3. A disposition or personality of someone or something. 4. Something pure or true as distinguished from something artificial or contrived. 5. The basic instincts or impulses of someone or something. 6. The elements of the universe, such as mountains, plants, planets, and stars.

nautical, *adj.* (16c) Of or relating to ships or shipping, carriage by sea, or navigation.

nautical assessor. A person skilled in maritime matters who is summoned in an admiralty case to assist the judge on points requiring special expertise.

nautical mile. (1834) A measure of distance for air and sea navigation, equal to one minute of arc of a great circle of the earth. • Different measures have been used by different countries because the earth is not a perfect sphere. Since 1959, however, the United States has used an international measure for a nautical mile, set by the Hydrographic

Bureau, equal to 6,076.11549 feet, or 1,852 meters.

NAV. *abbr.* NET ASSET VALUE.

naval, *adj.* (15c) **1.** Of or relating to ships or shipping. **2.** Of or relating to a navy. See NAVY.

naval law. A system of regulations governing naval forces. See CODE OF MILITARY JUSTICE.

navigable (**nav**-i-gə-bəl), *adj.* (15c) **1.** Capable of allowing vessels or vehicles to pass, and thereby usable for travel or commerce <the channel was barely navigable because it was so narrow>.

navigable in fact, *adj.* Naturally usable for travel or commerce in the present condition. • A stream is navigable in fact if, in its natural and ordinary state, it can be used for travel or commerce. For admiralty jurisdiction, the water must be capable of being used as a route in interstate or international commerce in customary modes of travel.

2. Capable of being steered <navigable aircraft>. — Also termed *boatable.* See NAVIGABLE WATER.

navigable airspace. See AIRSPACE.

navigable sea. *Int'l law.* The ocean waters divided into three zones of control among nations: (1) the inland waters, which are near a nation's shores and over which a nation has complete sovereignty; (2) territorial waters, which are measured from the seaward edge of the inland waters, over which a nation has extensive control but over which innocent parties must be allowed to travel to other nations; and (3) the high seas, which are international waters not subject to the domain of any single nation.

navigable water. 1. At early common law, any body of water affected by the ebb and flow of the tide. • This test was first adopted in England because most of England's in-fact navigable waters are influenced by the tide, unlike the large inland rivers that are capable of supporting commerce in the United States. — Also termed *boatable water.* **2.** (*usu. pl.*) A body of water that is used, or typically can be used, as a highway for commerce with ordinary modes of trade and travel on water. • Under the Commerce Clause, Congress has broad jurisdiction over all navigable waters of the United States.

navigable water of the United States. Navigable water that alone — or in combination with other waters — forms a continuous highway for commerce with other states or foreign countries.

navigate, *vb.* (16c) **1.** To travel or sail in a vessel on water <to navigate from New York to Bermuda>. **2.** To steer <to navigate the plane>. **3.** To make way through, on, or about something <the plaintiff was unable to navigate the stairs in the dark>.

navigation. (16c) **1.** The act of sailing vessels on water. **2.** The process and business of directing the course of a vessel from one place to another. See RULES OF NAVIGATION.

navigation easement. See EASEMENT.

navigation servitude. See SERVITUDE (2).

navy. (14c) **1.** A fleet of ships. **2.** The military sea force of a country, including its collective ships and its corps of officers and enlisted personnel; esp. (*usu. cap.*), the division of the U.S. armed services responsible primarily for seagoing forces. • The U.S. Constitution gives Congress the power to establish a navy and make laws governing the naval forces. U.S. Const. art. I, § 8, cl. 13–14.

Navy Department. A division of the Department of Defense that oversees the operation and efficiency of the Navy, including the Marine Corps component (and the U.S. Coast Guard when operating as a naval service). • Established in 1798, the Department is headed by the Secretary of the Navy, who is appointed by the President and reports to the Secretary of Defense. — Also termed *Department of the Navy.*

navy yard. (18c) The land on which ships are built for the U.S. Navy and the contiguous waters that are necessary to float the ships.

NAWL. *abbr.* NATIONAL ASSOCIATION OF WOMEN LAWYERS.

nay, *n. Parliamentary law.* A negative vote.

N.B. *abbr.* [Latin *nota bene*] (17c) Note well; take notice — used in documents to call attention to something important.

NBA. *abbr.* NATIONAL BAR ASSOCIATION.

NBFI. *abbr.* Nonbank financial institution. See MONEY SERVICE BUSINESS.

NCA. *abbr.* NATIONAL CEMETERY ADMINISTRATION.

NCBL. *abbr.* NATIONAL CONFERENCE OF BLACK LAWYERS.

NCCUSL (nə-**k**[**y**]**oo**-səl). *abbr.* NATIONAL CONFERENCE OF COMMISSIONERS ON UNIFORM STATE LAWS.

n.c.d. *abbr.* NEMINE CONTRADICENTE.

NCPC. *abbr.* NATIONAL CAPITAL PLANNING COMMISSION.

NCR. *abbr.* NATIONAL CAPITAL REGION.

NCUA. *abbr.* NATIONAL CREDIT UNION ADMINISTRATION.

N.D. *abbr.* **1.** Northern District, in reference to a U.S. judicial district. **2.** NEMINE DISSENTIENTER.

NDMS. *abbr.* NATIONAL DISASTER MEDICAL SYSTEM.

NDP. *abbr.* Nondepository provider of financial services. See MONEY SERVICE BUSINESS.

N.E. *abbr.* NORTH EASTERN REPORTER.

N/E. See NOTICE OF ALLOWABILITY/EXAMINER'S AMENDMENT.

NEA. *abbr.* NATIONAL ENDOWMENT FOR THE ARTS.

neap tide. See TIDE.

near, *adv. & adj.* (13c) **1.** Close to; not far away, as a measure of distance <the neighbors' houses are near one another>. **2.** Almost; close in degree <a near miss>. **3.** Closely tied by blood <my brother is a near relative>. **4.** Familiar; intimate <a near friend>.

nearly closed-ended claim. See PATENT CLAIM.

near money. See *current asset* under ASSET.

neat, *adj.* (bef. 12c) **1.** Clean; pure. **2.** Free from extraneous matter.

neat weight. See *net weight* under WEIGHT.

necessaries. (14c) **1.** Things that are indispensable to living <an infant's necessaries include food, shelter, and clothing>. ● Necessaries include whatever food, medicine, clothing, shelter, and personal services are usu. considered reasonably essential for the preservation and enjoyment of life, to the extent that a person having a duty of protection must furnish them. — Also termed *necessities; necessities of life.* **2.** Things that are essential to maintaining the lifestyle to which one is accustomed <a multimillionaire's necessaries may include a chauffeured limousine and a private chef>. ● The term includes whatever is reasonably needed for subsistence, health, comfort, and education, considering the person's age, station in life, and medical condition, but it excludes (1) anything purely ornamental, (2) anything solely for pleasure, (3) what the person is already supplied with, (4) anything that concerns someone's estate or business as opposed to personal needs, and (5) borrowed money. Under the common law, a husband was required to pay debts incurred by his wife or children for necessaries. Beginning in the late 1960s, most states began to change their statutes regarding the obligation to provide necessaries to include both husband and wife. See DOCTRINE OF NECESSARIES; FAMILY-EXPENSE STATUTE. **3.** *Maritime law.* Supplies and services needed for the maintenance and operation of a vessel, including repairs, tow fees, and the costs of loading and unloading. ● Authorized provision of necessaries automatically confers a maritime lien to the provider under the Federal Maritime Lien Act, 42 USCA § 971–93.

necessarily included offense. See *lesser included offense* under OFFENSE (1).

necessary and proper, *adj.* (16c) Being appropriate and well adapted to fulfilling an objective.

Necessary and Proper Clause. (1926) The clause of the U.S. Constitution permitting Congress to make laws "necessary and proper" for the execution of its enumerated powers. U.S. Const. art. I, § 8, cl. 18. ● The Supreme Court has broadly interpreted this clause to grant Congress the implied power to enact any law reasonably designed to achieve an express constitutional power. *McCulloch v. Maryland*, 17 U.S. (4 Wheat.) 316 (1819). — Also termed *Basket Clause; Coefficient Clause; Elastic Clause; Sweeping Clause.*

necessary damages. See *general damages* under DAMAGES.

necessary deposit. See DEPOSIT (5).

necessary diligence. See DILIGENCE.

necessary domicile. See DOMICILE.

necessary implication. See IMPLICATION.

necessary improvement. See IMPROVEMENT.

necessary inference. (17c) A conclusion that is unavoidable if the premise on which it is based is taken to be true.

necessary intromission. See INTROMISSION.

necessary party. See PARTY (2).

necessary repair. (16c) An improvement to property that is both needed to prevent deterioration and proper under the circumstances.

necessary way. See *easement by necessity* under EASEMENT.

necessities. (14c) **1.** Indispensable things of any kind. **2.** NECESSARIES (1).

necessities of life. See NECESSARIES (1).

necessitous, *adj.* (17c) Living in a state of extreme want; hard up.

necessitous circumstances. (17c) The situation of one who is very poor; extreme want.

necessity. 1. *Criminal law.* A justification defense for a person who acts in an emergency that he or she did not create and who commits a harm that is less severe than the harm that would have occurred but for the person's actions. ● For example, a mountain climber lost in a blizzard can assert necessity as a defense to theft of food and blankets from another's cabin. — Also termed *choice of evils; duress of circumstances; lesser-evils defense.* See *lesser-evils defense* under DEFENSE (1). **2.** *Torts.* A privilege that may relieve a person from liability for trespass or conversion if that person, having no alternative, harms another's property in an effort to protect life or health.

manifest necessity. (17c) A sudden and overwhelming emergency, beyond the court's and parties' control, that makes conducting a trial or reaching a fair result impossible and that therefore authorizes the granting of a mistrial. ● The standard of manifest necessity must be met to preclude a defendant from successfully raising a plea of former jeopardy after a mistrial.

military necessity. See MILITARY NECESSITY.

moral necessity. (17c) A necessity arising from a duty incumbent on a person to act in a particular way.

physical necessity. (17c) A necessity involving an actual, tangible force that compels a person to act in a particular way.

private necessity. (16c) *Torts.* A necessity that involves only the defendant's personal interest and thus provides only a limited privilege. ● For example, if the defendant harms the plaintiff's dock by keeping a boat moored to the dock during a hurricane, the defendant can assert private necessity but must compensate the plaintiff for the dock's damage.

public necessity. (16c) *Torts.* A necessity that involves the public interest and thus completely excuses the defendant's liability. ● For example, if the defendant destroys the plaintiff's house to stop the spread of a fire that threatens the town, the defendant can assert public necessity.

3. RULE OF NECESSITY.

necessity defense. See JUSTIFICATION (2).

neck verse. *Hist.* A verse, usu. consisting of the opening verse of Psalm 51 (*Miserere mei, Deus* "Have mercy on me, O God"), which was used as a literacy test for an accused who claimed benefit of clergy. ● An accused who read the passage satisfactorily would not receive the maximum sentence (the person's neck would be saved). Although judges could assign any passage, they usu. chose Psalm 51, so that for many years criminals memorized this verse and pretended to read it. Still, the records show that many accused persons failed the test. The reading of the neck verse was abolished in 1707. See BENEFIT OF CLERGY.

necropsy (**nek**-rop-see). See AUTOPSY (1).

née (nay), *adj.* [French] (17c) (Of a woman) born. ● This term is sometimes used after a married woman's name to indicate her maiden name <Mrs. Robert Jones, née Thatcher>. The masculine form (not common in English) is *né.* — Also spelled *nee.*

need, *n.* (bef. 12c) **1.** The lack of something important; a requirement. **2.** Indigence. — **need,** *vb.*

needy, *adj.* (12c) **1.** Needful; necessary. **2.** Indigent; very poor. ● *Needy* implies a more permanent and less urgent condition than *necessitous.* See NECESSITOUS.

ne exeat (nee **ek**-see-ət [*or* **ek**-see-at]). [Latin "that he not depart"]. **1.** A writ restraining a person from leaving the republic; specif., an equitable writ ordering the person to whom it is addressed not to leave the jurisdiction of the court or the state. ● *Ne exeat* writs are usu. issued to ensure the satisfaction of a claim against the defendant. The full phrase is *ne exeat republica* (nee **ek**-see-ət [*or* **ek**-see-at] ri-**pəb**-li-kəh) [Latin "let him not go out of the republic"]. **2.** *Family law.* An equitable writ restraining a person from leaving, or removing a child or property from, the jurisdiction. ● A *ne exeat* is often issued to prohibit a person from removing a child or property from the jurisdiction — and sometimes from leaving the jurisdiction. — Also termed *writ of ne exeat; ne exeat republica; ne exeat regno.*

negate, *vb.* (17c) **1.** To deny. **2.** To nullify; to render ineffective.

negative, *adj.* (15c) **1.** Of or relating to something bad; not positive <a negative attitude>. **2.** Of or relating to refusal of consent; not affirmative <a negative answer>.

negative, *n.* (16c) **1.** A word or phrase of denial or refusal <"no" and "not" are negatives>. **2.** A word expressing the opposite of the positive <two negatives and one positive>. **3.** The original plate or film of a photograph, on which light and shadows are the opposite of the positive images later created and printed <not only the pictures, but also the negatives, were required to be returned>. **4.** *Archaic.* The power of veto <the king's negative has eroded>.

negative, *vb.* (18c) To negate; to deny, nullify, or render ineffective <the jury negatived fraud>.

negative act. See ACT.

negative amortization. See AMORTIZATION.

negative averment. See AVERMENT.

negative cash flow. See CASH FLOW.

negative causation. See CAUSATION.

Negative Commerce Clause. See *Dormant Commerce Clause* under COMMERCE CLAUSE.

negative condition. See CONDITION (2).

negative contingent fee. See *reverse contingent fee* under CONTINGENT FEE.

negative covenant. See COVENANT (1).

negative defense. See DEFENSE (1).

negative disinheritance. See DISINHERITANCE.

negative duty. See DUTY (1).

negative easement. See EASEMENT.

negative equity. See EQUITY (7).

negative evidence. See EVIDENCE.

negative externality. See EXTERNALITY.

negative limitation. *Patents.* In a patent application, a claim that describes what the element is not or does not do, rather than what it is or does. ● Although older caselaw held that a negative limitation rendered a claim indefinite, more recent decisions allow those that define a clear alternative as long as the claim is not overbroad.

negative misprision. See MISPRISION.

negative plea. See PLEA (3).

negative-pledge clause. (1935) **1.** A provision requiring a borrower, who borrows funds without giving security, to refrain from giving future lenders any security without the consent of the first lender. **2.** A provision, usu. in a bond indenture, stating that the issuing entity will not pledge its assets if it will result in less security to the bondholders under the indenture agreement.

negative pregnant. (17c) A denial implying its affirmative opposite by seeming to deny only a qualification of the allegation and not the allegation itself. • An example is the statement, "I didn't steal the money last Tuesday," the implication being that the theft might have happened on another day. — Also termed *negative pregnant with an affirmative.* Cf. AFFIRMATIVE PREGNANT.

negative prescription. See PRESCRIPTION (4).

negative proof. See PROOF.

negative reprisal. See REPRISAL.

negative right. See RIGHT.

negative servitude. See SERVITUDE (2).

negative statute. See STATUTE.

negative testimony. See *negative evidence* under EVIDENCE.

negative veto. See *qualified veto* under VETO.

neglect, *n.* (16c) **1.** The omission of proper attention to a person or thing, whether inadvertent, negligent, or willful; the act or condition of disregarding. **2.** The failure to give proper attention, supervision, or necessities, esp. to a child, to such an extent that harm results or is likely to result. Cf. ABUSE. — **neglect,** *vb.* — **neglectful,** *adj.*

   child neglect. (1930) The failure of a person responsible for a minor to care for the minor's emotional or physical needs. • Child neglect is a form of child abuse. Local child-welfare departments investigate reports of child neglect. In a severe case, criminal charges may be filed against a person suspected of child neglect.

   culpable neglect. (18c) Censurable or blameworthy neglect; neglect that is less than gross carelessness but more than the failure to use ordinary care.

   developmental neglect. Failure to provide necessary emotional nurturing and physical or cognitive stimulation, as a result of which a child could suffer from serious developmental delays.

   educational neglect. Failure to ensure that a child attends school in accordance with state law.

   excusable neglect. (1855) A failure — which the law will excuse — to take some proper step at the proper time (esp. in neglecting to answer a lawsuit) not because of the party's own carelessness, inattention, or willful disregard of the court's process, but because of some unexpected or unavoidable hindrance or accident or because of reliance on the care and vigilance of the party's counsel or on a promise made by the adverse party.

   inexcusable neglect. (18c) Unjustifiable neglect; neglect that implies more than unintentional inadvertence. • A finding of inexcusable neglect in, for example, failing to file an answer to a complaint will prevent the setting aside of a default judgment.

   medical neglect. Failure to provide medical, dental, or psychiatric care that is necessary to prevent or to treat serious physical or emotional injury or illness. • In determining whether a parent's refusal to consent to medical treatment is neglectful, courts use any of three approaches: (1) an ad hoc test, (2) a best-interests-of-the-child test, or (3) a balancing test that weighs the interests of the parents, the child, and the state. Cf. FAITH-HEALING EXEMPTION.

   physical neglect. Failure to provide necessaries, the lack of which has caused or could cause serious injury or illness.

   willful neglect. (18c) Intentional or reckless failure to carry out a legal duty, esp. in caring for a child.

neglected child. See CHILD.

neglect hearing. See HEARING.

neglegentia (neg-li-jen-shee-ə), *n.* [Latin] *Roman law.* Carelessness; inattentive omission. • *Neglegentia* can be of varying degrees, which may or may not result in actionable liability. — Also spelled *negligentia.* See CULPA.

   lata neglegentia (lay-tə neg-li-jen-shee-ə). Extreme negligence resulting from an unawareness of something that the actor should have known.

   magna neglegentia (mag-nə neg-li-jen-shee-ə). See *gross negligence* under NEGLIGENCE.

negligence, *n.* (14c) **1.** The failure to exercise the standard of care that a reasonably prudent person would have exercised in a similar situation; any conduct that falls below the legal standard established to protect others against unreasonable risk of harm, except for conduct that is intentionally, wantonly, or willfully disregardful of others' rights. • The term denotes culpable carelessness. The Roman-law equivalents are *culpa* and *neglegentia*, as contrasted with *dolus* (wrongful intention). — Also termed *actionable negligence; ordinary negligence; simple negligence.* **2.** A tort grounded in this failure, usu. expressed in terms of the following elements: duty, breach of duty, causation, and damages.

active negligence. (1875) Negligence resulting from an affirmative or positive act, such as driving through a barrier. Cf. *passive negligence*.

advertent negligence. (1909) Negligence in which the actor is aware of the unreasonable risk that he or she is creating; RECKLESSNESS. — Also termed *willful negligence*; *supine negligence*.

casual negligence. A plaintiff's failure to (1) pay reasonable attention to his or her surroundings, so as to discover the danger created by the defendant's negligence, (2) exercise reasonable competence, care, diligence, and skill to avoid the danger once it is perceived, or (3) prepare as a reasonable person would to avoid future dangers.

collateral negligence. An independent contractor's negligence, for which the employer is generally not liable. See COLLATERAL-NEGLIGENCE DOCTRINE.

comparative negligence. (1862) A plaintiff's own negligence that proportionally reduces the damages recoverable from a defendant. — Also termed *comparative fault*. See COMPARATIVE-NEGLIGENCE DOCTRINE.

concurrent negligence. (1831) The negligence of two or more parties acting independently but causing the same damage. Cf. *joint negligence*.

contributory negligence. (1822) **1.** A plaintiff's own negligence that played a part in causing the plaintiff's injury and that is significant enough (in a few jurisdictions) to bar the plaintiff from recovering damages. • In most jurisdictions, this defense has been superseded by comparative negligence. See CONTRIBUTORY-NEGLIGENCE DOCTRINE; DISTRACTION DOCTRINE. **2.** *Rare.* The negligence of a third party — neither the plaintiff nor the defendant — whose act or omission played a part in causing the plaintiff's injury.

criminal negligence. (1838) Gross negligence so extreme that it is punishable as a crime. • For example, involuntary manslaughter or other negligent homicide can be based on criminal negligence, as when an extremely careless automobile driver kills someone. — Also termed *culpable negligence*; *gross negligence*.

culpable negligence. (17c) **1.** Negligent conduct that, while not intentional, involves a disregard of the consequences likely to result from one's actions. See *criminal negligence*. **2.**

gross negligence. (16c) **1.** A lack of slight diligence or care. **2.** A conscious, voluntary act or omission in reckless disregard of a legal duty and of the consequences to another party, who may typically recover exemplary damages. — Also termed *reckless negligence*; *wanton negligence*; *willful negligence*; *willful and wanton negligence*;

hazardous negligence; *magna neglegentia*. **3.** See *criminal negligence*.

hazardous negligence. **1.** Careless or reckless conduct that exposes someone to extreme danger of injury or to imminent peril. **2.** See *gross negligence* (2).

imputed negligence. (18c) Negligence of one person charged to another; negligence resulting from a party's special relationship with another party who is originally negligent — so that, for example, a parent might be held responsible for some acts of a child.

inadvertent negligence. (18c) Negligence in which the actor is not aware of the unreasonable risk that he or she is creating, but should have foreseen and avoided it. — Also termed *simple negligence*.

joint negligence. (18c) The negligence of two or more persons acting together to cause an accident. Cf. *concurrent negligence*.

legal negligence. See *negligence per se*.

negligence in law. Failure to observe a duty imposed by law. See *negligence per se*; *legal negligence*.

negligence per se. (1841) Negligence established as a matter of law, so that breach of the duty is not a jury question. • Negligence per se usu. arises from a statutory violation. — Also termed *legal negligence*.

ordinary negligence. (16c) **1.** Lack of ordinary diligence; the failure to use ordinary care. • The term is most commonly used to differentiate between *negligence* and *gross negligence*. **2.** NEGLIGENCE (1).

passive negligence. (18c) Negligence resulting from a person's failure or omission in acting, such as failing to remove hazardous conditions from public property. Cf. *active negligence*.

professional negligence. See MALPRACTICE.

reckless negligence. See *gross negligence*.

simple negligence. **1.** See *inadvertent negligence*. **2.** See NEGLIGENCE (1).

slight negligence. (18c) The failure to exercise the great care of an extraordinarily prudent person, resulting in liability in special circumstances (esp. those involving bailments or carriers) in which lack of ordinary care would not result in liability; lack of great diligence.

subsequent negligence. (1827) The negligence of the defendant when, after the defendant's initial negligence and the plaintiff's contributory negligence, the defendant discovers — or should have discovered — that the plaintiff was in a position of danger and fails to exercise due care in preventing the plaintiff's injuries. — Also termed *supervening negligence.* See LAST-CLEAR-CHANCE DOCTRINE.

supine negligence. See *advertent negligence.*

tax negligence. Negligence arising out of the disregard of tax- payment laws, for which the Internal Revenue Service may impose a penalty — 5% of the amount underpaid. IRC (26 USCA) § 6651(a).

wanton negligence. See *gross negligence.*

willful and wanton negligence. See *gross negligence.*

willful negligence. **1.** See *advertent negligence.* **2.** See *gross negligence.*

negligence rule. (1914) *Commercial law.* The principle that if a party's negligence contributes to an unauthorized signing or a material alteration in a negotiable instrument, that party is estopped from raising this issue against later parties who transfer or pay the instrument in good faith. ● Examples of negligence include leaving blanks or spaces on the amount line of the instrument, erroneously mailing the instrument to a person with the same name as the payee, and failing to follow internal procedures designed to prevent forgeries.

negligent, *adj.* (14c) Characterized by a person's failure to exercise the degree of care that someone of ordinary prudence would have exercised in the same circumstance <the negligent driver went through the stop sign> <negligent construction caused the bridge to collapse>. — **negligently,** *adv.*

negligent act. See ACT.

negligent conversion. See *technical conversion* under CONVERSION (2).

negligent entrustment. (1944) The act of leaving a dangerous article (such as a gun or car) with a person who the lender knows, or should know, is likely to use it in an unreasonably risky manner.

negligent escape. See ESCAPE (3).

negligent hiring. *Torts.* An employer's lack of care in selecting an employee who the employer knew or should have known was unfit for the position, thereby creating an unreasonable risk that another person would be harmed.

negligent homicide. See HOMICIDE.

negligentia (neg-li-**jen**-shee-ə), *n.* [Latin] *Roman law.* See NEGLEGENTIA.

negligent infliction of emotional distress. (1970) The tort of causing another severe emotional distress through one's negligent conduct. ● Most courts will allow a plaintiff to recover damages for emotional distress if the defendant's conduct results in physical contact with the plaintiff or, when no contact occurs, if the plaintiff is in the zone of danger. See EMOTIONAL DISTRESS; ZONE-

OF-DANGER RULE. — Abbr. NIED. Cf. INTENTIONAL INFLICTION OF EMOTIONAL DISTRESS.

negligent manslaughter. See *involuntary manslaughter* under MANSLAUGHTER.

negligent misrepresentation. See MISREPRESENTATION.

negligent offense. See OFFENSE (1).

negligent tort. See TORT.

negotiability. (18c) The capability of commercial paper to have its title transferred by indorsement and delivery, or by delivery alone, so that the transferee has a rightful claim on it. ● Negotiability (which pertains to commercial paper) differs from assignability (which pertains to contracts in general) because an assignee traditionally takes title subject to all equities, and an assignment is not complete without notice to the debtor, whereas an indorsee takes free of all equities and without any notice to the debtor.

negotiable, *adj.* (18c) **1.** (Of a written instrument) capable of being transferred by delivery or indorsement when the transferee takes the instrument for value, in good faith, and without notice of conflicting title claims or defenses. **2.** (Of a deal, agreement, etc.) capable of being accomplished. **3.** (Of a price or deal) subject to further bargaining and possible change. Cf. NONNEGOTIABLE; ASSIGNABLE.

negotiable bill of lading. See BILL OF LADING.

negotiable bond. See BOND (2).

negotiable certificate of deposit. See CERTIFICATE OF DEPOSIT.

negotiable document of title. See DOCUMENT OF TITLE.

negotiable instrument. (18c) A written instrument that (1) is signed by the maker or drawer, (2) includes an unconditional promise or order to pay a specified sum of money, (3) is payable on demand or at a definite time, and (4) is payable to order or to bearer. UCC § 3-104(a). — Also termed *negotiable paper; negotiable note.* ● Among the various types of negotiable instruments are bills of exchange, promissory notes, bank checks, certificates of deposit, and other negotiable securities.

negotiable note. See NEGOTIABLE INSTRUMENT.

negotiable order of withdrawal. A negotiable instrument (such as a check) payable on demand and issued against funds deposited with a financial institution. — Abbr. NOW.

negotiable-order-of-withdrawal account. See *NOW account* under ACCOUNT.

negotiable paper. See NEGOTIABLE INSTRUMENT.

negotiable words. (1819) The terms and phrases that make a document a negotiable instru-

ment. — Also termed *words of negotiability*. See
NEGOTIABLE INSTRUMENT.

negotiate, *vb.* (16c) **1.** To communicate with another party for the purpose of reaching an understanding <they negotiated with their counterparts
for weeks on end>. **2.** To bring about by discussion or bargaining <she negotiated a software license agreement>. **3.** To transfer (an instrument)
by delivery or indorsement, whereby the transferee takes the instrument for value, in good faith,
and without notice of conflicting title claims or
defenses <Jones negotiated the check at the neighborhood bank>.

negotiated agreement. A settlement that disputing parties reach between themselves, usu. with
the help of their attorneys, but without benefit
of formal mediation. — Also termed *negotiated
settlement.*

negotiated market. See MARKET.

negotiated offering. See OFFERING.

negotiated plea. See PLEA (1).

negotiating bank. See BANK.

negotiation, *n.* (16c) **1.** A consensual bargaining
process in which the parties attempt to reach
agreement on a disputed or potentially disputed matter. • Negotiation usu. involves complete
autonomy for the parties involved, without the
intervention of third parties. **2.** (*usu. pl.*) Dealings conducted between two or more parties for
the purpose of reaching an understanding. **3.** The
transfer of an instrument by delivery or indorsement whereby the transferee takes it for value,
in good faith, and without notice of conflicting title claims or defenses. See HOLDER IN DUE
COURSE. — **negotiate,** *vb.* — **negotiable,** *adj.* —
negotiability, *n.*

  due negotiation. The transfer of a negotiable
  document of title so that the transferee takes
  it free of certain claims enforceable against the
  transferor. • This is the good-faith-purchase exception to the doctrine of derivative title. UCC
  §§ 7-501(4); 7-502(1).

negotiation letter of credit. See LETTER OF CRED-
IT.

negotiorum gestio (ni-goh-shee-**or**-əm **jes**-chee-
oh), *n.* [Latin "management of another's affairs"]
Roman & civil law. A quasi-contractual situation
in which an actor (*negotiorum gestor*) manages or
interferes in the business transaction of another
person (*dominus negotii*) in that person's absence,
without authority but out of concern or friendship. La. Civ. Code art. 2292. • By such conduct,
the actor is bound to conduct the matter to a conclusion and to deliver the transaction's proceeds
to the person, who likewise must reimburse the
actor for any expenses incurred. La. Civ. Code
art. 2297. A *negotiorum gestio* does not exist if

the *gestor* acted self-interestedly or if the owner
expressly forbade the *gestor* from acting on the
owner's behalf. See *actio negotiorum gestorum*
under ACTIO.

negotiorum gestor (ni-goh-shee-**or**-əm **jes**-tor), *n.*
[Latin "a manager of another's affairs"] *Roman
& civil law.* A person who acts without authority
to protect another person's interests, in the reasonable belief that the owner would approve the
action if made aware of the circumstances. La.
Civ. Code art. 2292. • The actor has a claim to be
compensated by the owner for the trouble taken,
and the owner has a claim for any loss that results
from the *negotiorum gestor*'s fault. — Sometimes
shortened to *gestor*. See NEGOTIORUM GESTIO. Pl.
negotiorum gestores.

NEH. *abbr.* NATIONAL ENDOWMENT FOR THE HU-
MANITIES.

n.e.i. abbr. NON EST INVENTUS.

neighbor, *n.* (bef. 12c) **1.** A person who lives near
another <Jensen's neighbor spotted the fire>. **2.** A
person or thing situated near something <Can-
ada is the United States' neighbor to the north>.
3. A person in relation to humankind <love thy
neighbor>.

neighborhood. (15c) **1.** The immediate vicinity;
the area near or next to a specified place. **2.** People living in a particular vicinity, usu. forming
a community within a larger group and having
similar economic statuses and social interests. **3.**
The condition of being close together.

neighborhood effect. See EXTERNALITY.

neighboring right. (*usu. pl.*) *Copyright.* An intellectual-property right of a performer or of an
entrepreneur such as a publisher, broadcaster, or
producer, as distinguished from a moral right belonging to an author or artist as the work's creator. • In civil-law systems, neighboring rights
and moral rights are typically protected by different laws, while in common-law systems both
are typically protected by the same copyright
laws. — Also termed *related right; entrepreneurial right;* (in French) *droit voisins;* (in German)
Leistungsschutzrecht; (in Italian) *diritto connessi.*
Cf MORAL RIGHTS.

neighbor principle. (1963) The doctrine that one
must take reasonable care to avoid acts or omissions that one can reasonably foresee will be likely
to injure one's neighbor. • According to this principle, *neighbor* includes all persons who are so
closely and directly affected by the act that the
actor should reasonably think of them when engaging in the act or omission in question.

neither party. A docket entry reflecting the parties'
agreement not to continue to appear to prosecute
and defend a lawsuit. • This entry is equivalent
to a dismissal.

nem. con. *abbr.* NEMINE CONTRADICENTE.

nem. dis. *abbr.* NEMINE DISSENTIENTE.

nemine contradicente (**nem**-i-nee kahn-trə-di-**sen**-tee). [fr. Latin *nemo* "nobody" + *contradicere* "contradict"] Without opposition or dissent. ● This phrase expresses the lack of opposition by members of a court, legislative body, or other group to a resolution or vote <the motion passed *nemine contradicente*>. It is used in the British House of Commons. — Abbr. *nem. con.*; *n.c.d.* — Also termed *nemine dissentiente*. Cf. NEMINE DISSENTIENTE.

nemine dissentiente (**nem**-i-nee di-sen-shee-**en**-tee). [fr. Latin *nemo* "nobody" + *dissentio* "dissents"] Without opposition or dissent; NEMINE CONTRADICENTE. ● This phrase is used in the British House of Lords. — Abbr. *nem dis.*; *n.d.* Cf. NEMINE CONTRADICENTE.

nemo (**nee**-moh), *n.* [Latin] No one; no man. ● This term is the first word of many Latin maxims, such as *nemo est supra leges* ("no one is above the law").

neonatal (nee-oh-**nayt**-əl), *adj.* (1902) Of or relating to the first four weeks of life. — **neonate** (**nee**-oh-nayt or **nee**-ə-nayt), *n.*

neonaticide. See INFANTICIDE (1).

neonatology (nee-oh-nay-**tol**-ə-jee or nee-ə-nə-**tol**-ə-jee), *n.* The branch of medicine dealing with the development of newborn children, as well as various disorders of early infancy. — **neonatological** (nee-oh-nay-tə-**loj**-i-kəl or nee-ə-), *adj.* — **neonatologist** (nee-oh-nay-**tol**-ə-jist or nee-ə-nə-**tol**-ə-jist), *n.*

NEPA (**nee**-pə). *abbr.* NATIONAL ENVIRONMENTAL POLICY ACT.

nephew. (14c) **1.** The son of a person's brother or sister; sometimes understood to include the son of a person's brother-in-law or sister-in-law. ● This term is extended in some wills to include a grand-nephew. Cf. NIECE.

half nephew. The son of one's half brother or half sister.

2. *Hist.* A grandchild. **3.** *Hist.* A descendant.

nepotism (**nep**-ə-tiz-əm), *n.* (17c) Bestowal of official favors on one's relatives, esp. in hiring. — **nepotistic** (nep-ə-**tis**-tik), *adj.*

nerve-center test. A method courts sometimes use to determine the location of a company's principal place of business by examining where the company's central decision-making authority lies. ● Factors include the locations where the corporate officers, directors, and (sometimes) shareholders reside, and where they direct and control the corporation's activities.

NESDIS. *abbr.* National Environmental Satellite, Data, and Information Service. See NATIONAL OCEANIC AND ATMOSPHERIC ADMINISTRATION.

net, *n.* (15c) **1.** An amount of money remaining after a sale, minus any deductions for expenses, commissions, and taxes. **2.** The gain or loss from a sale of stock. **3.** See *net weight* under WEIGHT.

net assets. See *net worth* under WORTH.

net asset value. The market value of a share in a mutual fund, computed by deducting any liabilities of the fund from its total assets and dividing the difference by the number of outstanding fund shares. — Abbr. NAV. — Also termed *asset value.* See MUTUAL FUND.

net balance. See *net proceeds* under PROCEEDS.

net book cost. See COST (1).

net book value. See OWNER'S EQUITY.

net-capital rules. *Securities.* Basic financial-responsibility standards adopted by the Securities and Exchange Commission under the Securities Exchange Act of 1934. ● Under these rules, securities brokers are required to maintain a minimum level of capitalization and to maintain aggregate indebtedness at a level less than a specified multiple of the broker's net capital. 15 USCA § 780(c)(3); SEC Rule 15c3-1 (17 CFR § 240.15c3-1.

net cash flow. See CASH FLOW.

net cost. See COST (1).

net earnings. See *net income* under INCOME.

net estate. See *net probate estate* under PROBATE ESTATE.

net gain. See GAIN (3).

net income. See INCOME.

net investment. See INVESTMENT.

net lease. See LEASE.

net level annual premium. See PREMIUM (1).

net listing. See LISTING (1).

net loss. See LOSS.

net national product. The total value of goods and services produced in a country during a specific period, after deducting capital replacement costs.

net-net-net lease. See LEASE.

net operating asset. See ASSET.

net operating income. See INCOME.

net operating loss. See LOSS.

net position. 1. The difference between long and short contracts held by a securities or commodities trader. **2.** The amount gained or lost because of a change in the value of a stock or commodity.

net premium. See PREMIUM (1).

net present value. See PRESENT VALUE.

net price. See PRICE.

net probate estate. See PROBATE ESTATE.

net proceeds. See PROCEEDS.

net profit. See PROFIT (1).

net-profits interest. *Oil & gas.* A share of production free of the costs of production. • Like a royalty, the interest is expressed as a fraction or a percentage of production. But unlike a royalty, it is payable only if there is a net profit, and the costs that are used to calculate the net profit depend on what is negotiated.

net quick assets. 1. See ASSET. **2.** See QUICK-ASSET RATIO.

net realizable value. 1. For a receivable, the amount of cash expected from the collection of present customer balances. **2.** For inventory, the selling price less the completion and disposal costs. **3.** An accounting method requiring the value of scrap or by-products to be treated as a reduction in the cost of the primary products.

net rent. See RENT (1).

net rental. See RENTAL.

net return. See RETURN.

net revenue. See *net profit* under PROFIT (1).

net sale. See SALE.

net sale contract. See *net listing* under LISTING (1).

net single premium. See PREMIUM (1).

netspionage. [fr. (Inter)net + espionage] *Slang.* Spying that is enabled by and carried out through computer networks, esp. for the purpose of appropriating or misappropriating data.

net tangible worth. See WORTH.

net tonnage. See TONNAGE (1).

net valuation premium. See *net premium* under PREMIUM (1).

net value. See VALUE (2).

net weight. See WEIGHT.

network element. *Telecommunications.* A facility or piece of equipment used to provide telecommunications service, as by a local-exchange network, and each feature, function, or capability of the service. 47 USCA § 153(29).

net worth. See WORTH.

net-worth method. The procedure the Internal Revenue Service uses to determine the taxable income of a taxpayer who does not keep adequate records. • The change in net worth for the year determines the taxpayer's gross income, after taking into account nontaxable receipts and nondeductible expenses.

net yield. See YIELD.

neutral, *adj.* (15c) **1.** Indifferent. **2.** (Of a judge, mediator, arbitrator, or actor) refraining from taking sides in a dispute. **3.** Impartial; unbiased. • The term frequently applies to statutes that regulate or restrict speech.

    content-neutral. (Of a regulation or discrimination) applicable to all speech, regardless of viewpoint and subject matter. See TIME-PLACE-OR-MANNER RESTRICTION. Cf. *subject-matter-neutral; viewpoint-neutral.*

    subject-matter-neutral. (Of a regulation or discrimination) not based on the topic or subject of speech. See TIME-PLACE-OR-MANNER RESTRICTION. Cf. *content-neutral; viewpoint-neutral.*

    viewpoint-neutral. (Of a regulation or discrimination) not based on a point of view or an ideology. • Viewpoint neutrality was first addressed in *Rosenberger v. Visitors of Univ. of Va.*, 515 U.S. 819, 115 S.Ct. 2510 (1989). See TIME-PLACE-OR-MANNER RESTRICTION. Cf. *content-neutral; subject-matter-neutral.*

neutral, *n.* (15c) **1.** A person or country taking no side in a dispute; esp., a country that is at peace and is committed to aid neither of two or more belligerents. Cf. BELLIGERENT. **2.** A nonpartisan arbitrator typically selected by two other arbitrators — one of whom has been selected by each side in the dispute.

neutrality, *n.* (15c) **1.** The state or quality of being impartial or unbiased. **2.** The condition of a nation that in time of war takes no part in the dispute but continues peaceful dealings with the belligerents. — **neutral,** *adj.*

    armed neutrality. A condition of neutrality that the neutral state is willing to maintain by military force.

neutrality law. *Int'l law.* An act that prohibits a nation from militarily aiding either of two or more belligerent powers with which the nation is at peace; esp., a federal statute forbidding acts — such as the equipping of armed vessels or the enlisting of troops — designed to assist either of two belligerents that are at peace with the United States. 22 USCA §§ 441–457.

neutrality proclamation. *Int'l law.* At the outbreak of a war between two nations, an announcement by the President that the United States is neutral and that its citizens may not violate the neutrality laws, as in the Neutrality Proclamation of 1793, issued during the war between France and Great Britain.

neutralization. (1817) **1.** The act of making something ineffective. **2.** *Int'l law.* The process by which a country's integrity has been permanently guaranteed by international treaty, conditionally on its maintaining a perpetual neutrality except in its own defense. • Switzerland is the only remaining example, having been neutralized by the Treaty of Vienna in 1815 — a provision reaffirmed by the Treaty of Versailles in 1919. **3.** The act of declaring certain persons or property neutral and safe from capture. See NEUTRAL PROPERTY. **4.** *Evidence.* The cancellation of unexpected harmful testimony from a witness by showing, usu. by cross-examination, that the witness has made conflicting statements. • For example, a prosecutor may attempt to neutralize testimony of a state witness who offers unexpected adverse testimony. See IMPEACHMENT (2).

neutral principles. (1959) *Constitutional law.* Rules grounded in law, as opposed to rules based on personal interests or beliefs. • In this context, the phrase was popularized by Herbert Wechsler. See *Toward Neutral Principles of Constitutional Law,* 73 Harv. L. Rev. 1 (1959).

neutral property. Things belonging to citizens of a country that is not a party to a war, as long as the things are properly used and labeled. • For example, harmless neutral property aboard a captured belligerent ship would not normally be subject to seizure. But the hiding of explosives in otherwise neutral property could allow the property to be seized as contraband.

neutron-activation analysis. (1951) A method of identifying and analyzing physical evidence by measuring gamma rays emitted by a sample of material after that material has been bombarded with neutrons in a nuclear reactor. • This technique can be used, for example, to detect gunshot residue on the hand of someone who recently fired a gun. The analysis is usu. expensive to perform, but most courts allow the results into evidence. — Abbr. NAA.

Nevada trust. See *asset-protection trust* (1) under TRUST (3).

never indebted, plea of. (1880) A common-law traverse — or denial — by which the defendant in an action on a contract debt denies that an express or implied contract existed. — Also termed *non debit.* See TRAVERSE.

new, *adj.* **1.** (Of a person, animal or thing) recently come into being <the new car was shipped from the factory this morning>. **2.** (Of any thing) recently discovered <a new cure for cancer>. **3.** (Of a person or condition) changed from the former state <she has a new state of mind>. **4.** Unfamiliar; unaccustomed <she asked for directions because she was new to the area>. **5.** Beginning afresh <a new day in court>.

new acquisition. See ACQUISITION.

new and useful. *Patents.* Two of the requirements for an invention to be patentable — namely, that the invention be novel and that it have practical utility. 35 USCA § 101. See PATENT (3).

new asset. See ASSET.

new assignment. See ASSIGNMENT (7).

newborn-kidnapping by cesarean section. See *kidnapping by cesarean* under KIDNAPPING.

new business. See BUSINESS.

new-business rule. The principle precluding an award of damages for lost profits to a business with no recent record of profitability, because the damages would be too speculative.

new cause of action. See CAUSE OF ACTION.

new-contract dispute. See *major dispute* under DISPUTE.

new court commitment. See COMMITMENT.

new debtor. See DEBTOR.

new-debtor syndrome. Conduct showing a debtor's bad faith in filing for bankruptcy, as a result of which the court may dismiss the bankruptcy petition. • An example is the debtor's formation of a corporation, immediately before the bankruptcy filing, solely to take advantage of the bankruptcy laws.

new drug. See DRUG.

new-for-old. 1. *Marine insurance.* In adjusting a partial marine-insurance loss, the principle that old materials apply toward payment of the new, so that the old material's value is deducted from the total repair expenses, and then from that balance one-third of the cost of repairs (one-third of the new materials for the old on the balance) is deducted and charged against the insured shipowner. — Also termed *deduction for new.* **2.** The principle that a party whose property has been damaged is entitled to recover only the amount necessary to restore the property to the condition it was in before the damage, instead of acquiring a new item to replace one that was old and depreciated.

New Inn. *Hist. English law.* One of the Inns of Chancery (collegiate houses) in which law students were placed before entering the Inns of Court. • This practice continued until approximately 1650, when the buildings began to be used only by barristers and solicitors. See INN OF CHANCERY. Cf. INN OF COURT.

new issue. See ISSUE (2).

new-loan fee. See MORTGAGE DISCOUNT.

newly discovered evidence. See EVIDENCE.

new matter. 1. See MATTER. **2.** *Patents.* Additional information in an amended patent application that adds to the original disclosure. • Since the new matter was reduced to practice after the application was filed, it cannot carry the same filing date. Rather, it must be included in a continuation-in-part application. — Also termed *disconformity.*

new-matter rejection. See REJECTION.

new promise. See PROMISE.

new-rule principle. (1989) *Criminal procedure.* A doctrine barring federal courts from granting habeas corpus relief to a state prisoner because of a rule, not dictated by existing precedent, announced after the prisoner's conviction and sentence became final. — Also termed *nonretroactivity principle.* See HABEAS CORPUS.

new ruling. (1931) *Criminal procedure.* A Supreme Court ruling not dictated by precedent existing when the defendant's conviction became final and thus not applicable retroactively to habeas cases. ● For example, when the Court in *Ford v. Wainwright,* 477 U.S. 399, 106 S.Ct. 2595 (1986), ruled that the Eighth Amendment prohibits execution of insane prisoners, this new ruling was nonretroactive because it departed so widely from prior doctrine. *Teague v. Lane,* 489 U.S. 288, 109 S.Ct. 1060 (1989). See HABEAS CORPUS.

New Rules. See HILARY RULES.

new series. See N.S.

newsman's privilege. See *journalist's privilege* (1) under PRIVILEGE (3).

newspaper. (17c) A publication for general circulation, usu. in sheet form, appearing at regular intervals, usu. daily or weekly, and containing matters of general public interest, such as current events.

  daily newspaper. A newspaper customarily published five to seven days every week. — Often shortened to *daily.*

  legal newspaper. A newspaper containing matters of legal interest including summaries of cases, legal advertisements, legislative or regulatory changes, and local bankruptcy notices.

  newspaper of general circulation. (1838) A newspaper that contains news and information of interest to the general public, rather than to a particular segment, and that is available to the public within a certain geographic area. ● Legal notices (such as a class-action notice) are often required by law to be published in a newspaper of general circulation.

  official newspaper. A newspaper designated to contain all the public notices, resolves, acts, and advertisements of a state or municipal legislative body.

newspaper prospectus. See PROSPECTUS.

new style. The modern system for ordering time according to the Gregorian method, introduced by Pope Gregory XIII in 1582 and adopted in England and the American colonies in 1752. ● Because the Julian calendar year was slightly longer than the astronomical year, the vernal equinox over time had been displaced by ten days. Pope Gregory reformed the calendar by announcing that October 5, 1582 would be called October 15. And, while generally retaining a leap year for years divisible by 4, he skipped leap years in years divisible by 100 (such as 1800 and 1900), but retained leap years for years divisible by 400 (such as 2000). Thus, the years 2000, 2004, 2008, etc. are leap years, but 2100 is not. — Abbr. n.s. — Also termed *Gregorian calendar.* Cf. OLD STYLE.

new trial. See TRIAL.

new-use claim. See PATENT CLAIM.

new-use invention. See INVENTION.

new value. See VALUE (2).

new-value defense. See DEFENSE (1).

new works. See WORKS.

New York interest. See *Boston interest* under INTEREST (3).

New York standard clause. See MORTGAGE-LOSS CLAUSE.

New York Stock Exchange. An association of member firms that handle the purchase and sale of securities both for themselves and for customers. ● This exchange, the dominant one in the United States, trades in only large companies having at least one million outstanding shares. — Abbr. NYSE.

New York Supplement. A set of regional lawbooks, part of the West Group's National Reporter System, containing every published appellate decision from intermediate and lower courts of record in New York, from 1888 to date. ● The first series ran from 1888 to 1937; the second series is the current one. — Abbr. N.Y.S.; N.Y.S.2d.

New York Times **malice.** See *actual malice* (2) under MALICE.

New York Times **rule.** A commonsense rule of ethical conduct holding that one should not do anything arguably newsworthy — in public or in private — that one would mind having reported on the front page of a major newspaper. ● In various communities, a local newspaper is substituted for the *Times.*

next devisee. See DEVISEE.

next eventual estate. See ESTATE (1).

next friend. (16c) A person who appears in a lawsuit to act for the benefit of an incompetent or minor plaintiff, but who is not a party to the lawsuit and is not appointed as a guardian. — Also termed *prochein ami.* Cf. *guardian ad litem* under GUARDIAN.

next-in, first-out. A method of inventory valuation (but not a generally accepted accounting principle) whereby the cost of goods is based on their replacement cost rather than their actual cost. —

Abbr. NIFO. Cf. FIRST-IN, FIRST-OUT; LAST-IN, FIRST-OUT.

next of kin. (18c) **1.** The person or persons most closely related to a decedent by blood or affinity. Cf. RELATIVE. **2.** An intestate's heirs — that is, the person or persons entitled to inherit personal property from a decedent who has not left a will. See HEIR.

next presentation. See PRESENTATION.

nexus, *n.* (17c) **1.** A connection or link, often a causal one <cigarette packages must inform consumers of the nexus between smoking and lung cancer>. Pl. **nexuses; nexus**. **2.** *Roman law.* (*ital.*) In very early times, a debtor given in bondage to creditors until the debts have been paid. Pl. *nexi*.

nexus test. (1975) The standard by which a private person's act is considered state action — and may give rise to liability for violating someone's constitutional rights — if the conduct is so closely related to the government's conduct that the choice to undertake it may fairly be said to be that of the state. ● While similar to the symbiotic-relationship test, the nexus test focuses on the particular act complained of, instead of on the overall relationship of the parties. Still, some courts use the terms and analyses interchangeably. — Also termed *close-nexus test.* Cf. SYMBIOTIC-RELATIONSHIP TEST. See JOINT PARTICIPATION; STATE-COMPULSION TEST.

NGO. *abbr.* NONGOVERNMENTAL ORGANIZATION.

NGRI. See *not guilty by reason of insanity* under NOT GUILTY.

NHTSA. *abbr.* NATIONAL HIGHWAY TRAFFIC SAFETY ADMINISTRATION.

Nickerson letter. In New York City, a document issued by the Board of Education offering to pay the tuition of a disabled child who has been admitted to a state-approved private school and whose educational needs cannot be met in a public school. ● Nickerson letters are named for Judge Eugene P. Nickerson, who presided over the class-action suit that led to their creation. See *Jose P. v. Ambach,* 669 F.2d 865 (2d Cir. 1982); *see also Jose P. v. Ambach,* 557 F. Supp. 1230 (E.D.N.Y. 1983).

nickname, *n.* (15c) **1.** A shortened version of a person's name <"Bill" is William's nickname>. **2.** A descriptive or alternative name, in addition to or instead of the actual name <David Smith's nickname is "Red">.

niece. (14c) The daughter of a person's brother or sister; sometimes understood to include the daughter of a person's brother-in-law or sister-in-law. ● This term is extended in some wills to include a grandniece. Cf. NEPHEW.

half niece. The daughter of one's half brother or half sister.

NIED. *abbr.* NEGLIGENT INFLICTION OF EMOTIONAL DISTRESS.

NIFL. *abbr.* NATIONAL INSTITUTE FOR LITERACY.

NIFO (nı-foh). *abbr.* NEXT-IN, FIRST-OUT.

night. (bef. 12c) **1.** The time from sunset to sunrise. **2.** Darkness; the time when a person's face is not discernible. ● This definition was used in the common-law definition of certain offenses, such as burglary. **3.** Thirty minutes after sunset and thirty minutes before sunrise, or a similar definition as set forth by statute, as in a statute requiring specific authorization for night searches. **4.** Evening. — Also termed *nighttime.* Cf. DAY.

nightwalker. 1. *Hist.* A person who suspiciously wanders about at night and who might disturb the peace. ● Nightwalking was an example of a "common" offense requiring no specific facts to be asserted in the indictment. **2.** A prostitute who walks the streets at night; streetwalker. **3.** A sleepwalker.

nihil. See NIHIL EST.

nihil dicit (nı-hil dı-sit), *n.* [Latin "he says nothing"] **1.** The failure of a defendant to answer a lawsuit. **2.** See *nil dicit default judgment* under DEFAULT JUDGMENT.

nihil dicit default judgment. See *nil dicit default judgment* under DEFAULT JUDGMENT.

nihil est (nı-hil est). [Latin "there is nothing"] A form of return by a sheriff or constable who was unable to serve a writ because nothing was found to levy on. — Often shortened to *nihil.* Cf. NULLA BONA.

nihilism (nı-əl-iz-əm *or* nee-). (1812) **1.** A doctrine maintaining that there is no rational justification for moral principles and that there is no objective truth. **2.** The view that traditional beliefs are unfounded and that life is meaningless and useless. **3.** A theory that the existing economic, social, or political institutions should be destroyed, regardless of the result, because of the basic undesirability of those institutions. ● This theory, featured by Ivan Turgenev in his 1861 novel *Fathers and Sons,* was popular among Russian extremists until the collapse of the czarist government.

nihilist, *n.* A person who advocates nihilism. See NIHILISM.

nikah. *Islamic law.* A prenuptial contract, witnessed by at least two men, recording the parties' mutual agreement to marry, the husband's promise to give his wife a certain sum of money or property, and possibly other terms about the parties' rights in and expectations from the marriage. ● The contract may be enforceable under general contract-law principles. — Also termed *nikah nama.* Cf. MAHR.

nil (nil). [Latin] (16c) Nothing. ● This word is a contracted form of *nihil.* See NIHIL EST.

nil debet (nil **deb**-ət). [Latin "he owes nothing"] *Hist.* A general denial in a debt action on a simple contract.

***nil dicit* default judgment.** See DEFAULT JUDGMENT.

NIMA. *abbr.* NATIONAL IMAGING AND MAPPING AGENCY.

nimble dividend. See DIVIDEND.

nimmer. (14c) A petty thief; pilferer; pickpocket.

1908 Berlin Act. See BERLIN ACT.

1909 Copyright Act. See COPYRIGHT ACT OF 1909.

1971 Paris Act of the Berne Convention. See BERNE PARIS ACT.

1976 Copyright Act. See COPYRIGHT ACT OF 1976.

Nineteenth Amendment. The constitutional amendment, ratified in 1920, providing that a citizen's right to vote cannot be denied or abridged by the United States, or by any state within it, on the basis of sex. — Also termed *Women's Suffrage Amendment.*

1933 Act. See SECURITIES ACT OF 1933.

1934 Act. See SECURITIES EXCHANGE ACT OF 1934.

ninety-day letter. (1933) Statutory notice of a tax deficiency sent by the IRS to a taxpayer. ● During the 90 days after receiving the notice, the taxpayer must pay the taxes (and, if desired, seek a refund) or challenge the deficiency in tax court. IRC (26 USCA) §§ 6212, 6213. — Also written *90-day letter.* — Also termed *notice of deficiency; deficiency notice; tax-deficiency notice.* Cf. THIRTY-DAY LETTER.

NINJA loan. See LOAN.

Ninth Amendment. The constitutional amendment, ratified with the Bill of Rights in 1791, providing that rights listed in the Constitution must not be construed in a way that denies or disparages unlisted rights, which are retained by the people.

nisi (**nı**-sı), *adj.* [Latin "unless"] (18c) (Of a court's ex parte ruling or grant of relief) having validity unless the adversely affected party appears and shows cause why it should be withdrawn <a decree *nisi*>. See *decree nisi* under DECREE.

nisi decree. See *decree nisi* under DECREE.

nisi prius (**nı**-sı **prı**-əs). [Latin "unless before then"] (16c) A civil trial court in which, unlike in an appellate court, issues are tried before a jury. ● The term is obsolete in the United States except in New York and Oklahoma. — Abbr. n.p. — Also termed *nisi prius court.*

nisi prius clause. An entry to the record authorizing a jury trial in the designated county. See NISI PRIUS.

***nisi prius* court.** See NISI PRIUS.

***nisi prius* record.** A civil-trial record. See RECORD (4).

nisi prius roll. The transcript of a case at nisi prius. — Also termed *nisi prius record.*

NIST. *abbr.* National Institute of Standards and Technology. See TECHNOLOGY ADMINISTRATION.

nitroglycerine charge. See ALLEN CHARGE.

n.l. *abbr.* NON LIQUET.

NLRA. *abbr.* NATIONAL LABOR RELATIONS ACT.

NLRB. *abbr.* NATIONAL LABOR RELATIONS BOARD.

NMB. *abbr.* NATIONAL MEDIATION BOARD.

NMFS. *abbr.* NATIONAL MARINE FISHERIES SERVICE.

NMI. *abbr.* No middle initial.

NMN. *abbr.* No middle name.

NOA. *abbr. Slang.* **1.** No oral argument. ● This notation is used esp. in an appellate case in which oral argument is not granted <since the case was NOA, the court relied exclusively on the briefs>. **2.** See NOTICE OF APPEARANCE.

NOAA. *abbr.* NATIONAL OCEANIC AND ATMOSPHERIC ADMINISTRATION.

no-action clause. An insurance-policy provision that bars suit against the insurer until the liability of the insured has been determined by a judgment.

no-action letter. (1959) A letter from the staff of a governmental agency stating that if the facts are as represented in a person's request for an agency ruling, the staff will advise the agency not to take action against the person. ● Typically, a no-action letter is requested from the SEC on such matters as shareholder proposals, resales of stock, and marketing techniques.

no actus reus (noh **ak**-təs **ree**-əs). A plea in which a criminal defendant either denies involvement with a crime or asserts that the harm suffered is too remote from the criminal act to be imputable to the defendant.

no-answer default judgment. See DEFAULT JUDGMENT.

no arrival, no sale. A delivery term, included in some sales contracts, by which the seller assumes the duty to deliver the goods to a specified place, and assumes the risk of loss for the goods while they are in transit. ● If the goods arrive damaged or late, the buyer can either avoid the contract or accept the goods at a discount.

no award. In an action to enforce an award, the defendant's plea denying that an award was made.

nobility, *n. pl.* (14c) **1.** Persons of social or political preeminence, usu. derived by inheritance or from the sovereign. • In English law, there are various degrees of nobility, or peerage, such as dukes, marquises, earls, viscounts, and barons, and their female counterparts. Nobility is generally created either by a writ of summons to sit in Parliament or by a royal grant through letters patent, and was once usu. accompanied by a large land grant. Nobility by writ descended to a person's bodily heirs. The modern practice is to grant nobility by letters patent, which provide limitations as to future heirs. The U.S. Constitution prohibits granting a title of nobility. U.S. Const. art. I, § 9, cl. 8. **2.** Persons of high or noble character. **3.** The collective body of persons making up the noble class.

no bill, *n.* (18c) A grand jury's notation that insufficient evidence exists for an indictment on a criminal charge <the grand jury returned a no bill instead of the indictment the prosecutors expected>. <the grand jury no-billed three of the charges>. Cf. TRUE BILL. — **no-bill,** *vb.*

no-bonus clause. *Landlord–tenant law.* A lease provision that takes effect upon governmental condemnation, limiting the lessee's damages to the value of any improvements to the property and preventing the lessee from recovering the difference between the lease's fixed rent and the property's market rental value. See CONDEMNATION.

no cause of action. See *take-nothing judgment* under JUDGMENT.

nocent (noh-sənt), *adj.* [fr. Latin *nocere* "harm"] *Archaic.* **1.** Injurious; harmful. **2.** Guilty; criminal. • This word is the little-used antonym of *innocent.*

nocent (noh-sənt), *n.* [fr. Latin *nocere* "harm"] *Hist.* A person who is guilty.

no-claim, *n.* The lack of a claim. • Legal philosophers devised this term to denote the opposite of a claim. As one jurisprudent has said apologetically, "there is no word in English which expresses the lack of a claim and therefore the rather barbarous 'no-claim' has been suggested." George Whitecross Paton, *A Textbook of Jurisprudence* 291 (G.W. Paton & David P. Derham eds., 4th ed. 1972).

no-confidence vote. (1840) The formal legal method by which a legislative body, by a majority vote, forces the resignation of a cabinet or ministry. — Also termed *vote of no confidence.*

no-contact order. See STAY-AWAY ORDER.

no contest. (1931) A criminal defendant's plea that, while not admitting guilt, the defendant will not dispute the charge. • This plea is often preferable to a guilty plea, which can be used against the defendant in a later civil lawsuit. — Also termed *no-contest plea; nolo contendere; non vult contendere.*

no-contest clause. (1929) A provision designed to threaten one into action or inaction; esp., a testamentary provision that threatens to dispossess any beneficiary who challenges the terms of the will. — Also termed *in terrorem clause; noncontest clause; terrorem clause; anticontest clause; forfeiture clause.*

no cure, no pay. *Maritime law.* The common-law principle that compensation for salvage must come from the material salvaged, and that if no material is salvaged there can be no compensation. • By contrast, civil-law tradition awards compensation even for a failed effort. Cf. ASSISTANCE.

no-doc loan. See LOAN.

no-duty, *n.* Liberty not to do an act. — Also termed *liberty not.*

no-duty doctrine. (1966) *Torts.* **1.** The rule that a defendant who owes no duty to the plaintiff is not liable for the plaintiff's injury. **2.** The rule that the owner or possessor of property has no duty to warn or protect an invitee from known or obvious hazards.

***Noerr–Pennington* doctrine.** (1967) The principle that the First Amendment shields from liability (esp. under antitrust laws) companies that join together to lobby the government. • The doctrine derives from a line of Supreme Court cases beginning with *Eastern R.R. Presidents Conference v. Noerr Motor Freight, Inc.*, 365 U.S. 127, 81 S.Ct. 523 (1961), and *United Mine Workers v. Pennington*, 381 U.S. 657, 85 S.Ct. 1585 (1965).

no evidence. (15c) **1.** The lack of a legally sufficient evidentiary basis for a reasonable fact-finder to rule in favor of the party who bears the burden of proof <there is no evidence in the record about his whereabouts at midnight>. • Under the Federal Rules of Civil Procedure, a party can move for judgment as a matter of law to claim that the other party — who bears the burden of proof — has been fully heard and has not offered sufficient evidence to prove one or more essential elements of the suit or defense. Fed. R. Civ. P. 50. Though such a contention is usu. referred to as a no-evidence motion, the issue is not whether there was actually no evidence, but rather whether the evidence was sufficient for the fact-finder to be able to reasonably rule in favor of the other party. **2.** Evidence that has no value in an attempt to prove a matter in issue <that testimony is no evidence of an alibi>.

no-eyewitness rule. (1956) *Torts.* The largely defunct principle that if no direct evidence shows what a dead person did to avoid an accident, the jury may infer that the person acted with ordinary care for his or her own safety. • In a jurisdiction where the rule persists, a plaintiff in a survival or wrongful-death action can assert the rule to counter a defense of contributory negligence.

no-fault, *adj.* (1967) Of or relating to a claim that is adjudicated without any determination that a party is blameworthy <no-fault divorce>.

no-fault auto insurance. See INSURANCE.

no-fault divorce. See DIVORCE.

no funds. An indorsement marked on a check when there are insufficient funds in the account to cover the check.

no-further-representation clause. A contractual provision, usu. in a settlement agreement, prohibiting the plaintiff's attorney from representing future clients who have the same or a similar claim against the defendant. • Such a clause is thought to be void as against public policy.

no goods. See NULLA BONA.

NOIBN. *abbr.* NOT OTHERWISE INDEXED BY NAME.

no-knock search. See SEARCH.

no-knock search warrant. See SEARCH WARRANT.

NOL. See *net operating loss* under LOSS.

Nolan Act. *Hist. Patents.* A statute, passed after World War I, that extended the U.S. patenting deadlines for citizens of former enemy nations. • A similar measure, the Boykin Act, was passed after World War II.

nolens volens (**noh**-lenz **voh**-lenz), *adv. & adj.* [Latin] (16c) Willing or unwilling <*nolens volens*, the school district must comply with the court's injunction>.

no-limit order. See ORDER (8).

nolition (noh-**lish**-ən). (17c) The absence of volition; unwillingness.

nolle prosequi (**nahl**-ee **prahs**-ə-kwı), *n.* [Latin "not to wish to prosecute"] (17c) **1.** A legal notice that a lawsuit or prosecution has been abandoned. **2.** A docket entry showing that the plaintiff or the prosecution has abandoned the action. — Often shortened to *nolle*.

nolle prosequi (**nahl**-ee **prahs**-ə-kwı), *vb.* (1875) To abandon (a suit or prosecution); to have (a case) dismissed by a *nolle prosequi* <the state *nolle prosequied* the charges against Johnson>. — Often shortened to *nolle pros*; *nol-pros*; *nol-pro*.

no-load fund. See MUTUAL FUND.

nolo contendere (**noh**-loh kən-**ten**-də-ree). [Latin "I do not wish to contend"] (1829) NO CONTEST. — Often shortened to *nolo*.

nolo plea. See PLEA (1).

no man's land. *Labor law.* The lack of clear jurisdiction between a state government and the federal government over labor disputes. • This term was common in the 1950s, but its use has declined as later laws have clarified jurisdictional issues.

NOM clause. *abbr.* NO-ORAL-MODIFICATION CLAUSE.

no-merit brief. See *Anders brief* under BRIEF.

nominal (**nahm**-ə-nəl), *adj.* (17c) **1.** Existing in name only <he was the nominal leader but had no real authority>. **2.** (Of a price or amount) trifling, esp. as compared to what would be expected <the lamp sold for a nominal price of ten cents>. **3.** Of or relating to a name or term <a nominal definition>. — **nominally,** *adv.*

nominal account. See ACCOUNT.

nominal asset. See ASSET.

nominal capital. See CAPITAL.

nominal consideration. See CONSIDERATION (1).

nominal damages. See DAMAGES.

nominal defendant. See *nominal party* under PARTY (2).

nominal director. See *dummy director* under DIRECTOR.

nominal partner. See PARTNER.

nominal party. See PARTY (2).

nominal-payee rule. *Commercial law.* The rule that validates any person's indorsement of an instrument (such as a check) when the instrument's drawer intended for the payee to have no interest in the instrument. UCC § 3-404(b).

nominal plaintiff. See *nominal party* under PARTY (2).

nominal rate. See INTEREST RATE.

nominal sentence. See SENTENCE.

nominal trust. See *passive trust* under TRUST.

nominal value. See PAR VALUE.

nominal yield. See *coupon yield* under YIELD.

nominate (**nom**-ə-nət), *adj. Civil law.* Classified; having a special name or designation. See *nominate contract* under CONTRACT.

nominate, *vb.* (16c) **1.** To propose (a person) for election or appointment <Steven nominated Jane for president>. **2.** To name or designate (a person) for a position <the testator nominated an executor, who later withdrew because he couldn't perform his duties>.

nominate action. See ACTION (4).

nominate contract. See CONTRACT.

nominating and reducing. *Hist.* A method used, esp. in London, to obtain special jurors from which to select a jury panel. • Under this method, a number representing each person on a sheriff's list is drawn from a box until 48 unchallenged people have been nominated. Each party then strikes 12 people and the remaining 24 constitute the panel.

nominating committee. See COMMITTEE.

nomination.(15c) **1.** The act of proposing a person for election or appointment. **2.** The act of naming or designating a person for an office, membership, award, or like title or status. • Under parliamentary law, each nomination is effectively a proposal for filling the blank in the question, "*Resolved, That* ——— *is elected.*" See BLANK (2). See CLOSE NOMINATIONS; OPEN NOMINATIONS.

nomination paper. (*usu. pl.*) A document filed by an independent political group — usu. one not qualifying as a political party or able to hold primary elections — to place one or more nominees on a general-election ballot.

nomination to a living. *Eccles. law.* The right of an advowson owner to present a clerk to the bishop for induction to a benefice. • The owner of an advowson can grant the right to another but is then bound to present whomever the grantee chooses.

nominee (nom-i-**nee**), *n.* (17c) **1.** A person who is proposed for an office, membership, award, or like title or status. • An individual seeking nomination, election, or appointment is a *candidate*. A candidate for election becomes a *nominee* after being formally nominated. See CANDIDATE. **2.** A person designated to act in place of another, usu. in a very limited way. **3.** A party who holds bare legal title for the benefit of others or who receives and distributes funds for the benefit of others.

nominee account. See ACCOUNT.

nominee trust. See TRUST.

nomocanon (nə-**mok**-ə-non *or* noh-mə-**kan**-ən). (1908) **1.** A collection of canon and imperial laws applicable to ecclesiastical matters in the orthodox churches. • The first nomocanon is falsely ascribed to Johannes Scholasticus, patriarch of Constantinople, in 553. Later canons consist primarily of the canons of the Quinisext and the ecclesiastical laws of Justinian. **2.** A collection of the ancient canons of the apostles, councils, and fathers, without regard to imperial constitutions.

nomogenetics. See COMPARATIVE NOMOGENETICS.

nomographer (nə-**mog**-rə-fər). (17c) **1.** A person who drafts laws. **2.** A person skilled in nomography.

nomography (nə-**mog**-rə-fee). (1832) **1.** The art of drafting laws. **2.** A treatise on the drafting of laws.

nomoscopy. See COMPARATIVE NOMOSCOPY.

non (non). [Latin] (14c) Not; no. • This term negates, sometimes as a separate word and sometimes as a prefix.

nonability. (17c) **1.** The lack of legal capacity, esp. to sue on one's own behalf. **2.** A plea or exception raising a lack of legal capacity.

nonacceptance. (17c) **1.** The refusal or rejection of something, such as a contract offer; REJECTION (1). **2.** A buyer's rejection of goods because they fail to conform to contractual specifications. See UCC § 2-601(a). **3.** A drawee's failure or refusal to receive and pay a negotiable instrument.

nonaccess. *Family law.* (17c) Absence of opportunity for sexual intercourse. • Nonaccess is often used as a defense by the alleged father in paternity cases. Cf. *multiple access* under ACCESS.

nonacquiescence (non-ak-wee-**es**-ənts). *Administrative law.* An agency's policy of declining to be bound by lower-court precedent that is contrary to the agency's interpretation of its organic statute, but only until the Supreme Court has ruled on the issue.

nonactuarially sound retirement system. A retirement plan that uses current contributions and assets to pay current benefit obligations, instead of investing contributions to pay future benefits. Cf. ACTUARIALLY SOUND RETIREMENT SYSTEM.

nonadmission. (16c) **1.** The failure to acknowledge something. **2.** The refusal to allow something, such as evidence in a legal proceeding.

nonadmitted asset. See ASSET.

nonage (**non**-ij). **1.** MINORITY (1). **2.** NONAGIUM.

nonaggression pact. *Int'l law.* A treaty in which two or more countries agree not to engage in aggressive military operations against one another. — Also termed *nonaggression treaty.*

nonaligned state. *Int'l law.* A (usu. less developed) country that has banded together with other similarly situated countries to enhance its political and economic position in the world. • The movement of nonaligned states formally began at a summit in 1961, and during the Cold War these countries declared their independence from both the western and the Soviet blocs.

nonancestral estate. See ESTATE (1).

nonancestral property. See *nonancestral estate* under ESTATE (1).

nonapparent easement. See *discontinuous easement* under EASEMENT.

nonapparent servitude. See SERVITUDE (2).

nonappearance. (15c) The failure to appear in court, esp. to prosecute or defend a lawsuit. See DEFAULT; NONSUIT.

nonapportionment rule. *Oil & gas.* The majority doctrine that royalties accrued under a mineral lease on land that is later subdivided during the lease term are not shared by the owners of the subdivisions, but belong exclusively to the owner of the land where the producing well is located. • For example, if Grey granted a lease to Wainwright, then sold one-half of the land to Svenson, and a well on Wainwright's half began producing minerals, only Wainwright would be entitled to the royalty. Cf. APPORTIONMENT RULE.

nonart rejection. See *formal rejection* under REJECTION.

nonassertion letter. *Patents.* A patentee's written declaration that the holder does not intend to enforce the right to exclude others from practicing specified claims of a patent. • The patentee may choose to waive the right entirely or specify a time limit for the waiver.

nonassertive conduct. See CONDUCT.

nonassessable insurance. See INSURANCE.

nonassessable stock. See STOCK.

non assumpsit (non ə-**səm**[**p**]-sit). [Latin "he did not undertake"] *Hist.* A general denial in an action of assumpsit. See ASSUMPSIT.

non assumpsit infra sex annos (non ə-**səm**[**p**]-sit in-frə seks an-ohs), *n.* [Latin "he did not undertake within six years"] *Hist.* The specific pleading form for the statute-of-limitations defense in an action of assumpsit.

nonbailable, *adj.* (1811) **1.** (Of a person) not entitled to bail <the defendant was nonbailable because of a charge of first-degree murder>. **2.** (Of an offense) not admitting of bail <murder is a nonbailable offense>.

nonbank, *adj.* Of, relating to, or being an entity other than a bank <a nonbank depositor> <a nonbank creditor>.

nonbank bank. See BANK.

nonbank financial institution. See MONEY SERVICE BUSINESS.

nonbillable time. (1947) An attorney's or paralegal's time that is not chargeable to a client. Cf. BILLABLE TIME.

nonbinding minitrial. See *summary jury trial* under TRIAL.

nonbinding summary jury trial. See *summary jury trial* under TRIAL.

noncallable bond. See *noncallable security* under SECURITY.

noncallable security. See SECURITY.

noncancelability clause. An insurance-policy provision that prevents the insurer from canceling the policy after an insured's loss, as long as the premium has been paid.

noncapital, *adj.* (1865) (Of a crime) not involving or deserving of the death penalty <noncapital murder>.

noncareer vice-consul. See VICE-CONSUL.

noncash charge. See CHARGE.

noncircumvention agreement. A contractual provision or separate contract containing mutual promises to use confidential information only for certain purposes and only while the contract is in force. — Also termed *noncircumvent agreement.*

noncitable, *adj.* Not authorized by a court to be used as legal precedent. • In general, unpublished opinions are noncitable, although court rules vary. — Also termed *uncitable.* Cf. CITABLE.

noncitizen. (1850) A person who is not a citizen of a particular place. See ALIEN.

nonclaim. (15c) A person's failure to pursue a right within the legal time limit, resulting in that person's being barred from asserting the right. See STATUTE OF LIMITATIONS.

nonclaim statute. See STATUTE.

noncode state. *Hist.* A state that, at a given time, had not procedurally merged law and equity, so that equity was still administered as a separate system. • The term was current primarily in the early to mid-20th century. — Also termed *common-law state.* Cf. CODE STATE.

noncombatant, *adj.* (1826) **1.** Not serving in a fighting capacity <noncombatant personnel>. **2.** Not designed for combat <noncombatant vehicle>.

noncombatant, *n.* (1811) **1.** An armed-service member who serves in a non-fighting capacity. **2.** A civilian in wartime.

noncommercial partnership. See *nontrading partnership* under PARTNERSHIP.

noncommercial use. See USE (1).

noncommissioned officer. See OFFICER (2).

noncompete covenant. See *noncompetition covenant* under COVENANT (1).

noncompetition agreement. See *noncompetition covenant* under COVENANT (1).

noncompetition covenant. See COVENANT (1).

non compos mentis (non kom-pəs men-tis), *adj.* [Latin "not master of one's mind"] (17c) **1.** Insane. **2.** Incompetent. Cf. COMPOS MENTIS.

nonconforming goods. See GOODS.

nonconforming lot. See LOT (1).

nonconforming use. See USE (1).

nonconformist. (17c) A person who refuses to follow established customs, practices, beliefs, or ideas.

nonconformity. (17c) The failure to comply with something, as in a contract specification.

nonconsensual, *adj.* (1920) Not occurring by mutual consent <nonconsensual sexual relations>.

nonconsent. (1844) **1.** Lack of voluntary agreement. **2.** *Criminal law.* In the law of rape, the refusal to engage willingly in sexual intercourse. See CONSENT.

non constat (non **kon**-stat). [Latin "it is not settled"] It is not certain or agreed. • The phrase is generally used to state that some conclusion does not necessarily follow although it might appear on its face to follow. Cf. NON SEQUITUR.

nonconstitutional, *adj.* (1879) Of or relating to some legal basis or principle other than those of the U.S. Constitution or a state constitution <the appellate court refused — on nonconstitutional procedural grounds — to hear the defendant's argument about cruel and unusual punishment>. Cf. UNCONSTITUTIONAL.

nonconsumable, *n.* (1902) A thing (such as land, a vehicle, or a share of stock) that can be enjoyed without any change to its substance other than a natural diminution over time; NONFUNGIBLE. Cf. CONSUMABLE. — **nonconsumable,** *adj.*

noncontestability clause. See INCONTESTABILITY CLAUSE.

noncontest clause. See NO-CONTEST CLAUSE.

noncontinuing guaranty. See *limited guaranty* under GUARANTY.

noncontinuous easement. See *discontinuous easement* under EASEMENT.

noncontract, *adj.* See NONCONTRACTUAL.

noncontract demurrage. See DEMURRAGE.

noncontractual, *adj.* (1883) Not relating to or arising from a contract <a noncontractual obligation>. — Also termed *noncontract.*

noncontractual duty. See DUTY (1).

noncontribution clause. A fire-insurance-policy provision stating that only the interests of the property owner and the first mortgagee are protected under the policy.

noncontributory, *adj.* (1907) **1.** Not involved in something. **2.** (Of an employee benefit plan) funded solely by the employer.

noncontributory pension plan. See PENSION PLAN.

noncore proceeding. See RELATED PROCEEDING.

noncovered wages. See WAGE.

non culpabilis (non kəl-**pay**-bə-ləs). [Latin] Not guilty. — Abbr. *non cul.*

noncumulative approach. See DUALITY OF ART.

noncumulative dividend. See DIVIDEND.

noncumulative preferred stock. See STOCK.

noncumulative stock. See *noncumulative preferred stock* under STOCK.

noncumulative voting. See VOTING.

noncustodial, *adj.* **1.** (1960) (Of an interrogation, etc.) not taking place while a person is in custody. **2.** Of or relating to someone, esp. a parent, who does not have sole or primary custody.

noncustodial interrogation. See INTERROGATION.

noncustodial parent. See PARENT.

noncustodial sentence. See SENTENCE.

nondeadly force. See FORCE.

nondeadly weapon. See LESS-LETHAL.

non debit. See NEVER INDEBTED, PLEA OF.

nondelegable (non-**del**-ə-gə-bəl), *adj.* (1902) (Of a power, function, etc.) not capable of being entrusted to another's care <the duty to maintain the premises is a nondelegable duty>.

nondelegable duty. See DUTY (1).

nondelegation doctrine. See DELEGATION DOCTRINE.

nondelivery. (18c) A failure to transfer or convey something, such as goods. Cf. DELIVERY.

nondepository provider of financial services. See MONEY SERVICE BUSINESS.

nondirection. (18c) The failure of a judge to properly instruct a jury on a necessary point of law.

nondischargeable debt. See DEBT.

nondisclosure. (1908) **1.** The failure or refusal to reveal something that either might be or is required to be revealed. Cf. CONCEALMENT. **2.** NONDISCLOSURE AGREEMENT.

nondisclosure agreement. *Trade secrets.* A contract or contractual provision containing a person's promise not to disclose any information shared by or discovered from a trade-secret holder, including all information about trade secrets, procedures, or other internal or proprietary matters. • Employees and some nonemployees, such as beta-testers and contractors, are frequently required to sign nondisclosure agreements. — Often shortened to *nondisclosure.* — Abbr. NDA. — Also termed *confidentiality agreement.*

nondisclosure clause. See *confidentiality clause* under CLAUSE.

nondiscretionary trust. See *fixed trust* under TRUST.

nondisparagement clause. See CLAUSE.

nondiverse, *adj.* (1947) **1.** Of or relating to similar types <the attorney's practice is nondiverse: she handles only criminal matters>. **2.** (Of a person or entity) having the same citizenship as the party or parties on the other side of a lawsuit <the parties are nondiverse because both plaintiff and defendant are California citizens>. See *diversity jurisdiction* under JURISDICTION.

nonelected claim. See PATENT CLAIM.

nonenablement. *Patents.* In a patent application's specification, the quality of not being clear or complete enough to teach a of ordinary person skill in the art how to make and use the invention without undue experimentation. — Also termed *lack of enablement.*

nonenablement rejection. See REJECTION.

nonessential mistake. See *unessential mistake* under MISTAKE.

nonessential term. See *nonfundamental term* under TERM (2).

non-Euclidean zoning. See ZONING.

nonexclusive easement. See *common easement* under EASEMENT.

nonexclusive license. See LICENSE.

nonexclusive listing. See *open listing* under LISTING (1).

nonexecutive right. *Oil & gas.* A mineral interest that does not confer the right to lease. • Nonexclusive rights include royalty interests and nonexecutive mineral interests.

nonexempt property. A debtor's holdings and possessions that a creditor can attach to satisfy a debt. Cf. EXEMPT PROPERTY (1).

nonfeasance (non-**feez**-ənts), *n.* (16c) The failure to act when a duty to act existed. Cf. MALFEASANCE; MISFEASANCE; FEASANCE. — **nonfeasant,** *adj.* — **nonfeasor,** *n.*

nonfelonious homicide. See HOMICIDE.

nonfiler. *Tax.* See *illegal tax protester* under TAX PROTESTER.

nonforfeitable, *adj.* (1871) Not subject to forfeiture. See FORFEITURE.

nonforfeiture option. See OPTION.

nonfreehold estate. See ESTATE (1).

nonfunctional, *n. Trademarks.* A feature of a good that, although it might identify or distinguish the good from others, is unrelated to the product's use.

nonfunded deferred-compensation plan. See *nonqualified deferred-compensation plan* under EMPLOYEE BENEFIT PLAN.

nonfundamental term. See TERM (2).

nonfungible (non-**fən**-jə-bəl), *adj.* Not commercially interchangeable with other property of the same kind <a piece of land is regarded as nonfungible>. — **nonfungible,** *n.*

nongermane amendment. See AMENDMENT (3).

nongovernmental organization. *Int'l law.* Any scientific, professional, business, or public-interest organization that is neither affiliated with nor under the direction of a government; an international organization that is not the creation of an agreement among countries, but rather is composed of private individuals or organizations. • Examples of nongovernmental organizations, which are often granted consultative status with the United Nations, include Amnesty International, Greenpeace, and the International Committee of the Red Cross. — Abbr. NGO. — Also termed *private voluntary organization.*

nongrantor-owner trust. See TRUST (3).

noninfamous crime. See CRIME.

noninstallment credit. See CREDIT (4).

noninsurable risk. See RISK.

nonintercourse. 1. The refusal of one country to deal commercially with another. • For example, the Non-Intercourse Act of 1809, a congressional act, prohibited the importation of British or French goods. **2.** The lack of access, communication, or sexual relations between husband and wife. Cf. NONACCESS.

nonintercourse act. *Int'l law.* A statute that suspends commercial or other relations between nations.

non-interest-bearing bond. See *discount bond* under BOND (3).

noninterpretivism, *n.* (1978) In constitutional interpretation, the doctrine holding that judges are not confined to the Constitution's text or preratification history but may instead look to evolving social norms and values as the basis for constitutional judgments. Cf. INTERPRETIVISM; ORIGINALISM. — **noninterpretivist,** *n.*

nonintervention. (1831) *Int'l law.* The principle that a country should not interfere in the internal affairs of another country. • The U.N. Charter binds it from intervening "in matters which are essentially within the domestic jurisdiction of any state . . . ." U.N. Charter art. 2(7). — Also termed *principle of nonintervention.*

nonintervention executor. See *independent executor* under EXECUTOR.

nonintervention will. See WILL.

nonissuable plea. See PLEA (3).

nonjoinder. (1823) **1.** The failure to bring a person who is a necessary party into a lawsuit. Fed. R. Civ. P. 12(b)(7), 19. See JOINDER. Cf. MISJOINDER (1); DISJOINDER (1). **2.** *Patents.* Failure to name a coinventor in a patent application.

nonjudicial day. See DAY.

nonjudicial foreclosure. See FORECLOSURE.

nonjudicial oath. See OATH.

nonjudicial punishment. See PUNISHMENT.

nonjuridical (non-juu-**rid**-i-kəl), *adj.* (1853) **1.** Not of or relating to judicial proceedings or to the administration of justice <the dispute was nonjuridical>. **2.** Not of or relating to the law; not legal

<a natural person is a nonjuridical entity>. Cf. JURIDICAL.

nonjuror. (17c) **1.** Someone who is not serving as a juror. **2.** *Hist.* A person who refused to pledge allegiance to the sovereign; specif., in England and Scotland, a clergyman who, after 1688, refused to break the oath to James II and his heirs and successors, and to recognize William of Orange as king. ● In Scotland, a nonjuror was also recognized by the Presbyterian Church as a clergyman who refused to renounce the Episcopal Church when it was disestablished in 1690 in favor of Presbyterianism.

nonjury, *adj.* Of or relating to a matter determined by a judicial officer, such as a judge, rather than a jury <the plaintiff asked for a nonjury trial>.

nonjury trial. See *bench trial* under TRIAL.

nonjusticiable (non-jəs-**tish**-ee-ə-bəl *or* non-jəs-**tish**-ə-bəl), *adj.* (1915) Not proper for judicial determination <the controversy was nonjusticiable because none of the parties had suffered any harm>.

nonjusticiable question. See POLITICAL QUESTION.

nonlapse statute. See ANTILAPSE STATUTE.

nonlawyer. A person who is not a lawyer.

nonlethal weapon. See LESS-LETHAL.

nonleviable (non-**lev**-ee-ə-bəl), *adj.* (1860) (Of property or assets) exempt from execution, seizure, forfeiture, or sale, as in bankruptcy. See HOMESTEAD LAW.

non liquet (non **lI**-kwet *or* **li**-kwet). [Latin "it is not clear"] **1.** *Civil law.* The principle that a decision-maker may decline to decide a dispute on the ground that the matter is unclear. ● Even British judges formerly sometimes said *Non liquet* and found for the defendant. **2.** *Int'l law.* A tribunal's nondecision resulting from the unclarity of the law applicable to the dispute at hand. ● In modern usage, the phrase appears almost always in passages stating what a court must not do: tribunals are routinely disallowed from declaring a *non liquet.* — Abbr. *n.l.*

nonliquidating distribution. See DISTRIBUTION.

nonliteral infringement. See DOCTRINE OF EQUIVALENTS.

nonmailable, *adj.* Of or relating to a letter or parcel that cannot be transported by mail for a particular reason such as the package's size, contents, or obscene label.

nonmarital child. See *illegitimate child* under CHILD.

nonmarketable security. See SECURITY.

nonmedical policy. See INSURANCE POLICY.

nonmember bank. See BANK.

nonmerchantable title. See *unmarketable title* under TITLE (2).

nonmetered license. See LICENSE.

nonmonetary item. (1965) An asset or liability whose price fluctuates over time (such as land, equipment, inventory, and warranty obligations).

nonmovant (non-**moov**-ənt). (1955) A litigating party other than the one that has filed the motion currently under consideration <the court, in ruling on the plaintiff's motion for summary judgment, properly resolved all doubts in the nonmovant's favor>.

nonmutual collateral estoppel. See COLLATERAL ESTOPPEL.

nonnavigable, *adj.* **1.** (Of a body of water) unaffected by the tide. **2.** (Of a body of water) incapable of allowing vessels to pass for travel or commerce. **3.** (Of any vessel) incapable of being steered. Cf. NAVIGABLE.

nonnegotiable, *adj.* (1859) **1.** (Of an agreement or term) not subject to change <the kidnapper's demands were nonnegotiable>. **2.** (Of an instrument or note) incapable of transferring by indorsement or delivery. Cf. NEGOTIABLE.

nonnegotiable bill of lading. See *straight bill of lading* under BILL OF LADING.

nonnegotiable document of title. See DOCUMENT OF TITLE.

non obstante (non ahb-**stan**-tee *or* əb-**stan**-tee), *n.* [Latin "notwithstanding"]. **1.** *Hist.* A doctrine used by the Crown of England to give effect to certain documents, such as grants or letters patent, despite any laws to the contrary. ● This doctrine was abolished by the Bill of Rights. **2.** A phrase used in documents to preclude any interpretation contrary to the stated object or purpose. **3.** NON OBSTANTE VEREDICTO.

non obstante veredicto (non ahb-**stan**-tee [*or* əb-**stan**-tee] ver-ə-**dik**-toh). [Latin] (15c) Notwithstanding the verdict. — Often shortened to *non obstante.* — Abbr. n.o.v.; NOV. See *judgment notwithstanding the verdict* under JUDGMENT.

nonobviousness. *Patents.* **1.** An invention's quality of being sufficiently different from the prior art that, at the time the invention was made, it would not have been obvious to a person having ordinary skill in the art relevant to the invention. **2.** The requirement that this quality must be demonstrated for an invention to be patentable. ● Nonobviousness may be demonstrated with evidence concerning prior art or with other objective evidence, such as commercial success or professional approval. The test of obviousness involves examining the scope and content of the prior art, the differences between the prior art and the patent claims, and the level of ordinary skill in the art. 35 USCA § 103. See GRAHAM FACTORS. Cf. NOVELTY.

nonoccupant visitor. (1996) *Criminal procedure.* A person who owns, co-owns, is employed by, or is a patron of a business enterprise where a search is being conducted in accordance with a search warrant.

nonoccupational, *adj.* (1918) **1.** Not relating to one's job. **2.** Of or relating to a general-disability policy providing benefits to an individual whose disability prevents that individual from working at any occupation.

nonoccupier. (1958) One who does not occupy a particular piece of land; esp., an entrant on land who is either an invitee or a licensee. See INVITEE; LICENSEE (2).

nonoperating income. See INCOME.

nonoperative performance bond. See PERFORMANCE BOND.

nonoriginal bill. See BILL (2).

nonownership theory. *Oil & gas.* A characterization of oil-and-gas rights used in a minority of jurisdictions, holding that the owner of a severed mineral interest does not have a present right to possess the oil and gas in place, but only to search for, develop, and produce it. ● Because there is no right to present possession, the interest of such an owner in a nonownership-theory state is akin to a profit a prendre: a right to use the land and remove items of value from it. This theory is used in California, Wyoming, Louisiana, and Oklahoma. Cf. OWNERSHIP-IN-PLACE THEORY.

nonparticipating, *adj.* (1859) Of or relating to not taking part in something; specif., not sharing or having the right to share in profits or surpluses. — Often shortened to *nonpar.*

nonparticipating preferred stock. See STOCK.

nonparticipating royalty. See ROYALTY (2).

nonpayment. (15c) Failure to deliver money or other valuables, esp. when due, in discharge of an obligation. Cf. PAYMENT (1).

nonpecuniary damages. See DAMAGES.

nonpecuniary injury. See *irreparable injury* under INJURY.

nonperformance. (16c) Failure to discharge an obligation (esp. a contractual one). Cf. PERFORMANCE; MISPERFORMANCE.

nonperforming loan. See LOAN.

nonpersonal action. See ACTION (4).

nonprivity (non-**priv**-ə-tee). (1902) The fact or state of not being in privity of contract with another; lack of privity. See PRIVITY (1).

horizontal nonprivity. (1982) The lack of privity occurring when the plaintiff is not a buyer within the distributive chain, but one who consumes, uses, or is otherwise affected by the goods. ● For example, a houseguest who becomes ill after eating meat that her host bought from the local deli is in horizontal nonprivity with the deli.

vertical nonprivity. (1982) The lack of privity occurring when the plaintiff is a buyer within the distributive chain who did not buy directly from the defendant. ● For example, someone who buys a drill from a local hardware store and later sues the drill's manufacturer is in vertical nonprivity with the manufacturer.

nonprobate, *adj.* (1919) **1.** Of or relating to some method of transmitting property at death other than by a gift by will <nonprobate distribution>. **2.** Of or relating to the property so disposed <nonprobate assets>. See *nonprobate asset* under ASSET.

nonprobate asset. See ASSET.

nonprobate property. See *nonprobate asset* under ASSET.

nonprofit association. See ASSOCIATION.

nonprofit corporation. See CORPORATION.

Nonproliferation Bureau. See BUREAU OF NONPROLIFERATION.

nonproliferation treaty. See TREATY (1).

non pros (non prahs). *abbr.* NON PROSEQUITUR.

nonprosecution, affidavit of. See *affidavit of nonprosecution* under AFFIDAVIT.

non prosequitur (non prə-**sek**-wə-tər *or* proh-). [Latin "he does not prosecute"] (18c) The judgment rendered against a plaintiff who has not pursued the case. — Often shortened to *non pros.*

nonpublic forum. (1978) *Constitutional law.* Public property that is not designated or traditionally considered an arena for public communication, such as a jail or a military base. ● The government's means of regulating a nonpublic forum need only be reasonable and viewpoint-neutral to be constitutional. Cf. PUBLIC FORUM.

non-purchase-money, *adj.* (1941) Not pertaining to or being an obligation secured by property obtained by a loan <non-purchase-money mortgage>. Cf. *purchase-money mortgage* under MORTGAGE.

nonqualified deferred-compensation plan. See EMPLOYEE BENEFIT PLAN.

nonqualified executive-compensation plan. See *nonqualified deferred-compensation plan* under EMPLOYEE BENEFIT PLAN.

nonqualified pension plan. See PENSION PLAN.

nonqualified stock option. See STOCK OPTION.

nonrecognition. (1932) *Int'l law.* The refusal of one government to recognize the legitimacy of another government. Cf. RECOGNITION (6).

nonrecognition provision. (1932) *Tax.* A statutory rule that allows all or part of a realized gain or loss not to be recognized for tax purposes. ● Generally, this type of provision only postpones the recognition of the gain or loss. See RECOGNITION (4).

nonrecourse, *adj.* (1926) Of or relating to an obligation that can be satisfied only out of the collateral securing the obligation and not out of the debtor's other assets.

nonrecourse loan. See LOAN.

nonrecourse note. See NOTE (1).

nonrecurring dividend. See *extraordinary dividend* under DIVIDEND.

nonrefoulement (non-ri-**fowl**-mənt). [French] A refugee's right not to be expelled from one state to another, esp. to one where his or her life or liberty would be threatened. Cf. REFOULEMENT.

nonrefund annuity. See ANNUITY.

nonremovable inmate. An alien who, having been detained, would ordinarily be deportable but cannot be deported because the United States does not maintain diplomatic ties with the alien's country of origin. — Also termed *indefinite detainee*; *lifer*.

nonrenewal. (1819) A failure to renew something, such as a lease or an insurance policy.

nonreporting issuer. See ISSUER.

nonresidence, *n.* (16c) **1.** The status of living outside the limits of a particular place. **2.** *Eccles. law.* The absence of a spiritual person from the benefice. ● This was an offense punishable by sequestering the benefice and forfeiting part of its income.

nonresident, *n.* (16c) One who does not live within the jurisdiction in question. — Abbr. n.r. — **nonresident,** *adj.*

nonresident alien. See ALIEN.

nonresident decedent. See DECEDENT.

nonresidential parent. See *noncustodial parent* under PARENT.

nonresident-motorist statute. A state law governing the liabilities and obligations of nonresidents who use the state's highways.

nonresponsive, *adj.* **1.** (Of a reply to a question, esp. from a witness under oath) not directly answering the question asked. **2.** *Patents.* (Of a patent applicant's answer) not addressing every rejection, objection, and requirement contained in a patent examiner's office action. ● A nonresponsive reply may render an application abandoned. 37 CFR 1.111.

nonresponsive answer. See *unresponsive answer* under ANSWER (2).

nonretroactivity principle. See NEW-RULE PRINCIPLE.

nonrun time. See *dead time* under TIME.

non-self-governing territory. See TERRITORY.

non sequitur (non **sek**-wə-tər). [Latin "it does not follow"] (16c) **1.** An inference or conclusion that does not logically follow from the premises. **2.** A remark or response that does not logically follow from what was previously said. Cf. NON CONSTAT.

nonservant agent. See AGENT (2).

nonservice. (18c) The failure to serve a summons, warrant, or other process in a civil or criminal case.

nonshareholder constituency. A group of nonstockholders, such as employees or the public, who have an interest in the corporation's business — an interest that the corporation may legally consider, in addition to shareholders' interests, in making major policy decisions. — Also termed *alternative constituency.*

nonskip person. (1988) *Tax.* A person who is not a skip person for purposes of the generation-skipping transfer tax. IRC (26 USCA) § 2613(b). See SKIP PERSON.

nonsolicitation agreement. A promise, usu. in a contract for the sale of a business, a partnership agreement, or an employment contract, to refrain, for a specified time, from either (1) enticing employees to leave the company, or (2) trying to lure customers away.

nonsovereign state. See STATE.

nonstaple. *Patents.* An unpatented thing or material that is a component of a patented product or is used in a patented process, but that has little or no other practical use. ● Patentees have a limited right to control the market for nonstaples through tying agreements. But if the thing supplied is a staple, the tying agreement is restraint of trade. 35 USCA § 271(d). Cf. STAPLE (3).

nonstatutory, *adj.* **1.** Enforceable by some legal precept other than enacted law, such as precedent or trade custom. **2.** *Patents.* Unpatentable for not meeting some statutory requirement, e.g., novelty, utility, nonobviousness, or enabling description. **3.** *Patents.* Of or relating to an equitable defense to an infringement claim, esp. estoppel, inequitable conduct, or laches.

nonstatutory bond. See *voluntary bond* under BOND (3).

nonstatutory claim. See *omnibus claim* under PATENT CLAIM.

nonstatutory subject matter. *Patents.* A thing that does not fit into any of the categories of things that by law can be patented. ● Examples include works of nature, abstract ideas, human movements. 35 USCA § 101.

nonstock corporation. See CORPORATION.

non sui juris (non **s[y]oo**-ɪ *or* **soo**-ee **joor**-is), *adj.* [Latin "not of one's own right"] Lacking legal age or capacity. Cf. SUI JURIS.

nonsuit, *n.* (15c) **1.** A plaintiff's voluntary dismissal of a case or of a defendant, without a decision on the merits. ● Under the Federal Rules of Civil Procedure, a voluntary dismissal is equivalent to a nonsuit. Fed. R. Civ. P. 41(a). — Also termed *voluntary discontinuance.* **2.** A court's dismissal of a case or of a defendant because the plaintiff has failed to make out a legal case or to bring forward sufficient evidence. — Also termed *involuntary nonsuit; compulsory nonsuit.* See *judgment of nonsuit* under JUDGMENT. — **nonsuit,** *vb.*

nonsupport. (1909) *Family law.* The failure to support a person for whom one is legally obliged to provide, such as a child, spouse, or other dependent. ● Nonsupport is a crime in most states. — Also termed *criminal nonsupport; criminal neglect of family; abandonment of minor children; abandonment of children.* Cf. SUPPORT.

nontariff barrier. An official policy, other than a tariff, that restricts international trade, esp. by limiting imports or exports. — Abbr. NTB. Cf. NONTARIFF MEASURE.

nontariff measure. An official policy, other than a tariff, that affects international-trade conditions, including a policy that increases trade as well as one that restricts it. — Abbr. NTM. Cf. NONTARIFF BARRIER.

nontenure (non **ten**-yər). *Hist.* A general denial in a real action, whereby the defendant denies holding some or all of the land in question.

nontestifying expert. See *consulting expert* under EXPERT.

nontrading partnership. See PARTNERSHIP.

nontraditional public forum. See *designated public forum* under PUBLIC FORUM.

nonunion, *adj.* (1863) **1.** (Of a person or thing) not belonging to or affiliated with a labor union <a nonunion worker> <a nonunion contract>. **2.** (Of a position or belief) not favoring labor unions <she will not alter her nonunion stance>. **3.** (Of a product) not made by labor-union members <the equipment was of nonunion manufacture>.

nonuse. (16c) **1.** The failure to exercise a right <nonuse of the easement>. **2.** The condition of not being put into service <the equipment was in nonuse>. **3.** *Intellectual property.* See ABANDONMENT (8)–(10).

nonuser. The failure to exercise a right (such as a franchise or easement), as a result of which the person having the right might lose it <the government may not revoke a citizen's voting right because of nonuser>. Cf. USER (1).

nonverbal testimony. See TESTIMONY.

non-vessel-operating common carrier. See CARRIER.

nonvital term. See *nonfundamental term* under TERM (2).

nonvoluntary euthanasia. See EUTHANASIA.

nonvoting member. See MEMBER.

nonvoting stock. See STOCK.

non vult contendere (non vəlt kən-**ten**-də-ree). [Latin "he will not contest it"] NO CONTEST.

nonwaiver agreement. *Insurance.* A contract (supplementing a liability-insurance policy) in which the insured acknowledges that the insurer's investigation or defense of a claim against the insured does not waive the insurer's right to contest coverage later. Cf. RESERVATION-OF-RIGHTS LETTER.

nook of land. *Hist.* A variable quantity of land, often 12.5 acres.

no-oral-modification clause. (1969) A contractual provision stating that the parties cannot make any oral modifications or alterations to the agreement. — Abbr. NOM clause. See INTEGRATION CLAUSE; ZIPPER CLAUSE.

no par. See *no-par stock* under STOCK.

no-par stock. See STOCK.

no-par-value stock. See *no-par stock* under STOCK.

no-pass, no-play rule. (1984) A state law requiring public-school students who participate in extracurricular activities (such as sports or band) to maintain a minimum grade-point average or else lose the privilege to participate.

no progress. See WANT OF PROSECUTION.

no recourse. 1. The lack of means by which to obtain reimbursement from, or a judgment against, a person or entity <the bank had no recourse against the individual executive for collection of the corporation's debts>. **2.** A notation indicating that such means are lacking <the bill was indorsed "no recourse">. See *nonrecourse loan* under LOAN; WITHOUT RECOURSE.

No Religious Test Clause. See RELIGIOUS TEST CLAUSE.

no-retreat rule. (1973) *Criminal law.* The doctrine that the victim of a murderous assault may use deadly force in self-defense if there is no reasonable alternative to avoid the assailant's threatened harm. ● A majority of American jurisdictions have adopted this rule. Cf. RETREAT RULE.

no-right, *n.*(1913) The absence of right against another in some particular respect. ● A no-right is the correlative of a privilege. — Also termed *liability.*

norm. (1821) **1.** A model or standard accepted (voluntarily or involuntarily) by society or other large group, against which society judges someone or something. ● An example of a norm is the standard for right or wrong behavior. **2.** An actual or set standard determined by the typical or most frequent behavior of a group.

basic norm. In the legal theory of Hans Kelsen, the law from which all the other laws in a society derive. ● Kelsen's "pure theory of law" maintains that laws are norms. Therefore, a society's legal system is made up of its norms, and each legal norm derives its validity from other legal norms. Ultimately, the validity of all laws is tested against the "basic norm," which may be as simple as the concept that all pronouncements of the monarch are to be obeyed. Or it may be an elaborate system of lawmaking, such as a constitution. — Also termed *grundnorm.* See PURE THEORY.

normal, *adj.* (15c) **1.** According to a regular pattern; natural <it is normal to be nervous in court>. ● The term describes not just forces that are constantly and habitually operating but also forces that operate periodically or with some degree of frequency. In this sense, its common antonyms are *unusual* and *extraordinary.* **2.** According to an established rule or norm <it is not normal to deface statues>. **3.** Setting a standard or norm <a normal curriculum was established in the schools>.

normal balance. A type of debit or credit balance that is usu. found in ledger accounts. ● For example, assets usu. have debit balances and liabilities usu. have credit balances.

normal college. See NORMAL SCHOOL.

normalized earnings. See EARNINGS.

normalized financial statement. See FINANCIAL STATEMENT.

normal law. (1904) The law as it applies to persons who are free from legal disabilities.

normal market. See CONTANGO (1).

normal mind. (1887) A mental capacity that is similar to that of the majority of people who can handle life's ordinary responsibilities.

normal school. A training school for public-school teachers. ● Normal schools first appeared in the United States in the 1800s and were two-year post-high-school training programs for elementary-school teachers. At the turn of the century, normal schools expanded into four-year teaching colleges. Most of these institutions have developed into liberal arts colleges offering a wider variety of education and teaching programs. — Also termed *normal college.*

Norman French. A language that was spoken by the Normans and became the official language of English courts after the Norman Conquest in 1066. ● The language deteriorated into Law French and continued to be used until the late 17th century. English became the official language of the courts in 1731.

normative, *adj.* (1852) Establishing or conforming to a norm or standard <Rawls's theory describes normative principles of justice>.

normative jurisprudence. See NATURAL LAW.

Norris–La Guardia Act (nor-is lə-**gwahr**-dee-ə). A 1932 federal law that forbids federal courts from ruling on labor policy and that severely limits their power to issue injunctions in labor disputes. ● The statute was passed to curb federal-court abuses of the injunctive process, to declare the government's neutrality on labor policy, to curtail employers' widespread use of injunctions to thwart union activity, and to promote the use of collective bargaining to resolve disputes. 29 USCA §§ 101–115. — Also termed *Labor Disputes Act; Anti-Injunction Act.*

North American Free Trade Agreement. A 1994 agreement between the United States, Canada, and Mexico, designed to phase out all tariffs and eliminate many nontariff barriers (such as quotas) inhibiting the free trade of goods between the participating nations. ● Among other provisions, it set minimum standards for intellectual-property protection afforded other members' citizens. Negotiated at the same time as the GATT talks that produced TRIPs, NAFTA borrowed from many TRIPs provisions on intellectual-property protection, as by as protecting computer software and databases by copyright. While NAFTA incorporates by reference the Berne Convention standards of intellectual-property rights, it exempts the U.S. from recognizing Berne's moral rights. — Abbr. NAFTA.

North Eastern Reporter. A set of regional lawbooks, part of the West Group's National Reporter System, containing every published appellate decision from Illinois, Indiana, Massachusetts, New York, and Ohio, from 1885 to date. ● The first series ran from 1885 to 1936; the second series is the current one. — Abbr. N.E.; N.E.2d.

North Western Reporter. A set of regional lawbooks, part of the West Group's National Reporter System, containing every published appellate decision from Iowa, Michigan, Minnesota, Nebraska, North Dakota, South Dakota, and Wisconsin, from 1879 to date. ● The first series ran from 1879 to 1941; the second series is the current one. — Abbr. N.W.; N.W.2d.

Northwest Territory. *Hist.* The first possession of the United States, being the geographical region south of the Great Lakes, north of the Ohio River, and east of the Mississippi River, as designated by the Continental Congress in the late 1700s. ● This area includes the present states of Ohio, Indiana, Illinois, Michigan, Wisconsin, and the eastern part of Minnesota.

NOS. *abbr.* National Ocean Service. See NATIONAL OCEANIC AND ATMOSPHERIC ADMINISTRATION.

noscitur a sociis (nos-ə-tər ay [*or* ah] soh-shee-is). [Latin "it is known by its associates"] (18c) A canon of construction holding that the meaning of an unclear word or phrase should be determined by the words immediately surrounding it. Cf. EJUSDEM GENERIS; EXPRESSIO UNIUS EST EXCLUSIO ALTERIUS; RULE OF RANK.

nose coverage. See PRIOR-ACTS COVERAGE.

no-setoff certificate. See WAIVER OF DEFENSES.

no-shop provision. A stipulation prohibiting one or more parties to a commercial contract from pursuing or entering into a more favorable agreement with a third party.

no-strike clause. A labor-agreement provision that prohibits employees from striking for any reason and establishes instead an arbitration system for resolving labor disputes.

NOTA. *abbr.* NATIONAL ORGAN TRANSPLANT ACT.

nota bene (noh-tə ben-ee *or* bee-nee *or* ben-ay). See N.B.

no-talk provision. See *confidentiality clause* under CLAUSE.

notarial, *adj.* (15c) Of or relating to the official acts of a notary public <a notarial seal>. — Also spelled (in Scots law) *notorial.* See NOTARY PUBLIC.

notarial act. (18c) An official function of a notary public, such as placing a seal on an affidavit. See NOTARY PUBLIC.

notarial protest certificate. See PROTEST CERTIFICATE.

notarial record. See JOURNAL OF NOTARIAL ACTS.

notarial register. See JOURNAL OF NOTARIAL ACTS.

notarial seal. See NOTARY SEAL.

notarial will. See WILL.

notarize, *vb.* (Of a notary public) to attest to the authenticity of (a signature, mark, etc.).

notary public (noh-tə-ree), *n.* (16c) A person authorized by a state to administer oaths, certify documents, attest to the authenticity of signatures, and perform official acts in commercial matters, such as protesting negotiable instruments. — Often shortened to *notary.* — Abbr. n.p. Pl. **notaries public.** — **notarize,** *vb.* — **notarial,** *adj.*

notary record book. See JOURNAL OF NOTARIAL ACTS.

notary's certificate. A notary's signed and sealed or stamped statement attesting to the time and place that the specified acts and documents were authenticated.

notary seal. (18c) **1.** The imprint or embossment made by a notary public's seal. **2.** A device, usu. a stamp or embosser, that makes an imprint on a notarized document. — Also termed *notarial seal.*

   embossed seal. (1959) **1.** A notary seal that is impressed onto a document, raising the impression above the surface. • An embossed seal clearly identifies the original document because the seal is only faintly reproducible. For this reason, this type of seal is required in some states and on some documents notarized for federal purposes. **2.** The embossment made by this seal.

   rubber-stamp seal. (1948) **1.** In most states, a notary public's official seal, which is ink-stamped onto documents and is therefore photographically reproducible. • It typically includes the notary's name, the state seal, the words "Notary Public," the name of the county where the notary's bond is filed, and the expiration date of the notary's commission. **2.** The imprint made by this seal.

notation credit. (1956) A letter of credit specifying that anyone purchasing or paying a draft or demand for payment made under it must note the amount of the draft or demand on the letter. See LETTER OF CREDIT.

note, *n.* (17c) **1.** A written promise by one party (the *maker*) to pay money to another party (the *payee*) or to bearer. • A note is a two-party negotiable instrument, unlike a draft (which is a three-party instrument). — Also termed *promissory note.* Cf. DRAFT (1).

   accommodation note. A note that an accommodating party has signed and thereby assumed secondary liability for; ACCOMMODATION PAPER.

   approved indorsed note. A note indorsed by a person other than the maker to provide additional security.

   balloon note. A note requiring small periodic payments but a very large final payment. • The periodic payments usu. cover only interest, while the final payment (the balloon payment) represents the entire principal.

   banker's note. A promissory note given by a private banker or an unincorporated banking institution.

   banknote. See BANKNOTE.

   blue note. A note that maintains a life-insurance policy in effect until the note becomes due.

   bought note. A written memorandum of a sale delivered to the buyer by the broker responsible for the sale.

circular note. See LETTER OF CREDIT.

coal note. *Hist.* A promissory note written according to a statute that required payment for coal out of any vessel in the port of London to be in cash or by promissory note containing the words "value received in coal." • Noncompliance with the statute resulted in a fine of £100.

cognovit note. See COGNOVIT NOTE.

collateral note. See *secured note.*

coupon note. A note with attached interest coupons that the holder may present for payment as each coupon matures.

demand note. A note payable whenever the creditor wants to be paid. See *call loan* under LOAN.

executed note. A note that has been signed and delivered.

floating-rate note. A note carrying a variable interest rate that is periodically adjusted within a predetermined range, usu. every six months, in relation to an index, such as Treasury bill rates. — Also termed *floater.*

hand note. A note that is secured by a collateral note.

installment note. A note payable at regular intervals. — Also termed *serial note.*

inverse-floating-rate note. A note structured in such a way that its interest rate moves in the opposite direction from the underlying index (such as the London Interbank Offer Rate). • Many such notes are risky investments because if interest rates rise, the securities lose their value and their coupon earnings fall. — Also termed *inverse floater.*

joint and several note. A note for which multiple makers are jointly and severally liable for repayment, meaning that the payee may legally look to all the makers, or any one of them, for payment of the entire debt. See *joint and several liability* under LIABILITY.

joint note. A note for which multiple makers are jointly, but not severally, liable for repayment, meaning that the payee must legally look to all the makers together for payment of the debt. See *joint liability* under LIABILITY.

mortgage note. A note evidencing a loan for which real property has been offered as security.

negotiable note. See NEGOTIABLE INSTRUMENT.

nonrecourse note. A note that may be satisfied upon default only by means of the collateral securing the note, not by the debtor's other assets. Cf. *recourse note.*

note of hand. See *promissory note.*

post note. See *time note.*

premium note. A promissory note given by an insured to an insurance company for part or all of the premium.

promissory note. (18c) An unconditional written promise, signed by the maker, to pay absolutely and in any event a certain sum of money either to, or to the order of, the bearer or a designated person. — Also termed *note of hand.*

recourse note. A note that may be satisfied upon default by pursuing the debtor's other assets in addition to the collateral securing the note. Cf. *nonrecourse note.*

reissuable note. A note that may again be put into circulation after having once been paid.

renewal note. A note that continues an obligation that was due under a prior note.

sale note. A broker's memorandum on the terms of a sale, given to the buyer and seller.

savings note. A short-term, interest-bearing paper issued by a bank or the U.S. government.

secured note. A note backed by a pledge of real or personal property as collateral. — Also termed *collateral note.*

self-canceling installment note. A debt obligation that is automatically extinguished at the creditor's death. • Any remaining balance on the note becomes uncollectible. Self-canceling notes are typically used in estate planning. — Abbr. SCIN.

serial note. See *installment note.*

sold note. A written memorandum of sale delivered to the seller by the broker responsible for the sale, and usu. outlining the terms of the sale. See CONFIRMATION SLIP.

stock note. A note that is secured by securities, such as stocks or bonds.

tax-anticipation note. A short-term obligation issued by state or local governments to finance current expenditures and that usu. matures once the local government receives individual and corporate tax payments. — Abbr. TAN.

time note. A note payable only at a specified time and not on demand. — Also termed *post note.*

treasury note. See TREASURY NOTE.

unsecured note. A note not backed by collateral.

2. A scholarly legal essay shorter than an article and restricted in scope, explaining or criticizing a particular set of cases or a general area of the law, and usu. written by a law student for publication in a law review. — Also termed *comment; lawnote.* Cf. ANNOTATION. **3.** A minute or memorandum intended for later reference; MEMORANDUM (1).

broker's note. A memorandum, usu. one authorizing a broker to act as a principal's agent, that is prepared by the broker and a copy given to the principal.

note, *vb.* (13c) **1.** To observe carefully or with particularity <the defendant noted that the plaintiff seemed nervous>. **2.** To put down in writing <the court reporter noted the objection in the record>. **3.** *Archaic.* To brand <as punishment, the criminal was noted>. See NOTA.

note broker. See BROKER.

note of hand. See *promissory note* under NOTE (1). Pl. **notes of hand.**

note of protest. A notary's preliminary memo, to be formalized at a later time, stating that a negotiable instrument was neither paid nor accepted upon presentment. See PROTEST.

note payable. See *account payable* under ACCOUNT.

note receivable. See *account receivable* under ACCOUNT.

no-term lease. *Oil & gas.* A mineral lease with a drilling-delay rental clause that allows the lessee to extend the primary term indefinitely by paying delay rentals. ● No-term leases were common at the end of the 19th century. Some courts refused to enforce them on the ground that they created a mere estate at will, terminable at the will of either the lessor or the lessee. Other courts upheld them, but with the stipulation that the lessee had an obligation to either test or release the lease within a reasonable time.

note verbal (noht vər-bəl). *Int'l law.* An unsigned diplomatic note, usu. written in the third person, that sometimes accompanies a diplomatic message or note of protest to further explain the country's position or to request certain action. — Also spelled *note verbale* (vair-**bahl**).

not-for-profit corporation. See *nonprofit corporation* under CORPORATION.

not found. Words placed on a bill of indictment, meaning that the grand jury has insufficient evidence to support a true bill. See IGNORAMUS; NO BILL. Cf. TRUE BILL.

not guilty. (15c) **1.** A defendant's plea denying the crime charged. **2.** A jury verdict acquitting the defendant because the prosecution failed to prove the defendant's guilt beyond a reasonable doubt. Cf. INNOCENT.

not guilty by reason of insanity. (1844) **1.** A not-guilty verdict, based on mental illness, that usu. does not release the defendant but instead results in commitment to a mental institution. **2.** A criminal defendant's plea of not guilty that is based on the insanity defense. — Abbr. NGRI. — Also termed *not guilty on the ground of insanity.* See INSANITY DEFENSE.

3. *Common-law pleading.* A defendant's plea denying both an act of trespass alleged in a plaintiff's declaration and the plaintiff's right to possess the property at issue.

not guilty by statute. *Hist.* Under certain acts of Parliament, the pleading form for a defendant's general denial in a civil action. ● This pleading form allowed a public officer to indicate action under a statute. The officer had to write the words "by statute" in the margin along with the year, chapter, and section of the applicable statute, and the defendant could not file any other defense without leave of court. The right to plead "not guilty by statute" was essentially removed by the Public Authorities Protection Act of 1893.

4. A general denial in an ejectment action.

not-guilty plea. See PLEA (1).

nothous (**noh**-thəs), *adj.* *Archaic.* Spurious; illegitimate.

nothus (**noh**-thəs), *n.* [Latin fr. Greek *nothos* "false"] *Roman law.* An illegitimate child; one of base birth. ● If the child's mother was a Roman citizen, the child was also a Roman citizen. — Also termed *spurius.*

notice, *n.* (16c) **1.** Legal notification required by law or agreement, or imparted by operation of law as a result of some fact (such as the recording of an instrument); definite legal cognizance, actual or constructive, of an existing right or title <under the lease, the tenant must give the landlord written notice 30 days before vacating the premises>. ● A person has notice of a fact or condition if that person (1) has actual knowledge of it; (2) has received information about it; (3) has reason to know about it; (4) knows about a related fact; or (5) is considered as having been able to ascertain it by checking an official filing or recording. **2.** The condition of being so notified, whether or not actual awareness exists <all prospective buyers were on notice of the judgment lien>. Cf. KNOWLEDGE. **3.** A written or printed announcement <the notice of sale was posted on the courthouse bulletin board>.

actual notice. (18c) **1.** Notice given directly to, or received personally by, a party. — Also termed *express notice.* **2.** *Property.* Notice given by open possession and occupancy of real property.

adequate notice. See *due notice.*

commercial-law notice. Under the UCC, notice of a fact arising either as a result of actual knowledge or notification of the fact, or as a result of circumstances under which a person would have reason to know of the fact. UCC § 1-201(25).

constructive notice. (18c) Notice arising by presumption of law from the existence of facts and circumstances that a party had a duty to take notice of, such as a registered deed or a pending lawsuit; notice presumed by law to have been acquired by a person and thus imputed to that person. — Also termed *legal notice*.

direct notice. (17c) Actual notice of a fact that is brought directly to a party's attention. — Also termed *positive notice*.

due notice. (17c) Sufficient and proper notice that is intended to and likely to reach a particular person or the public; notice that is legally adequate given the particular circumstance. — Also termed *adequate notice*; *legal notice*.

express notice. (18c) Actual knowledge or notice given to a party directly, not arising from any inference, duty, or inquiry. See *actual notice*.

fair notice. (17c) **1.** Sufficient notice apprising a litigant of the opposing party's claim. **2.** The requirement that a pleading adequately apprise the opposing party of a claim. • A pleading must be drafted so that an opposing attorney of reasonable competence would be able to ascertain the nature and basic issues of the controversy and the evidence probably relevant to those issues. **3.** FAIR WARNING.

immediate notice. 1. Notice given as soon as possible. **2.** More commonly, and esp. on notice of an insurance claim, notice that is reasonable under the circumstances.

implied notice. (18c) Notice that is inferred from facts that a person had a means of knowing and that is thus imputed to that person; actual notice of facts or circumstances that, if properly followed up, would have led to a knowledge of the particular fact in question. — Also termed *indirect notice*; *presumptive notice*.

imputed notice. (1831) Information attributed to a person whose agent, having received actual notice of the information, has a duty to disclose it to that person. • For example, notice of a hearing may be imputed to a witness because it was actually disclosed to that witness's attorney of record.

indirect notice. See *implied notice*.

inquiry notice. (1945) Notice attributed to a person when the information would lead an ordinarily prudent person to investigate the matter further; esp., the time at which the victim of an alleged securities fraud became aware of facts that would have prompted a reasonable person to investigate.

judicial notice. See JUDICIAL NOTICE.

legal notice. 1. See *constructive notice*. **2.** See *due notice*.

notice by publication. See *public notice*.

personal notice. (17c) Oral or written notice, according to the circumstances, given directly to the affected person.

positive notice. See *direct notice*.

presumptive notice. See *implied notice*.

public notice. (16c) Notice given to the public or persons affected, usu. by publishing in a newspaper of general circulation. • This notice is usu. required, for example, in matters of public concern. — Also termed *notice by publication*.

reasonable notice. Notice that is fairly to be expected or required under the particular circumstances.

record notice. (1855) Constructive notice of the contents of an instrument, such as a deed or mortgage, that has been properly recorded.

short notice. Notice that is inadequate or not timely under the circumstances.

4. *Intellectual property.* A formal sign attached to items that embody or reproduce an intellectual property right. • Notice of patent is made by placing the word "patent" (or its abbreviation, "pat.") and the item's patent number on an item made by a patentee or licensee. There are three statutory notice forms for U.S. trademark and servicemark registration. The most common is the symbol with the letter R (®) but "Reg. U.S. Pat. & Tm. Off." or "Registered in U.S. Patent and Trademark Office" affords the same legal protection. A copyright notice also takes several forms. The first part may be the symbol with the letter C in a circle (©), or the word "Copr." or "Copyright." It must be followed by the copyright owner's name and the year that the work was first published. Informal signs, such as "Brand," "TM," "Trademark," "SM," and "Service Mark," adjacent to words or other symbols considered to be protectable marks are not legal notices of exclusive rights. **5.** *Parliamentary law.* A meeting's published call. See *call of a meeting* under CALL (1). **6.** *Parliamentary law.* A formal statement that certain business may come before a meeting, usu. made at an earlier meeting or published with the call of the meeting that will consider the business, and made as a prerequisite to the business's consideration. See *call of a meeting* under CALL (1). — Also termed *previous notice*.

notice, *vb.* (15c) **1.** To give legal notice to or of <the plaintiff's lawyer noticed depositions of all the experts that the defendant listed>. **2.** To realize or give attention to <the lawyer noticed that the witness was leaving>.

notice act. See NOTICE STATUTE.

notice-and-comment period. *Administrative law.* The statutory time frame during which an administrative agency publishes a proposed regulation and receives public comment on the regulation. •

The regulation cannot take effect until after this period expires. — Often shortened to *comment period.*

notice-and-comment rulemaking. See *informal rulemaking* under RULEMAKING.

notice-based quorum. See QUORUM.

notice by publication. See *public notice* under NOTICE.

notice doctrine. (1924) The equitable doctrine that when a new owner takes an estate with notice that someone else had a claim on it at the time of the transfer, that claim may still be asserted against the new owner even if it might have been disregarded at law. — Also termed *doctrine of notice.*

notice filing. The perfection of a security interest under Article 9 of the UCC by filing only a financing statement, as opposed to a copy or abstract of the security agreement. • The financing statement must contain (1) the debtor's signature, (2) the secured party's name and address, (3) the debtor's name and mailing address, and (4) a description of the types of, or items of, collateral.

notice of abandonment. 1. The formal notification that an action will no longer be pursued, such as notice from a plaintiff to a defendant that litigation will be nonsuited. **2.** *Property.* A formal announcement, usu. in writing and recorded, that a person is relinquishing a claim to personal or real property. **3.** *Patents.* A written declaration from the United States Patent Office to a patent applicant that the application has been terminated because the applicant failed to pursue prosecution. **4.** *Construction law.* A builder's or contractor's announcement that work on unfinished property is being discontinued. See ABANDONMENT.

notice-of-alibi rule. (1969) The principle that, upon written demand from the government, a criminal defendant who intends to call an alibi witness at trial must give notice of who that witness is and where the defendant claims to have been at the time of the alleged offense. • The government is, in turn, obligated to give notice to the defendant of any witness it intends to call to rebut the alibi testimony. *See* Fed. R. Crim. P. 12.1.

notice of allowability. *Patents.* Notification from the U.S. Patent and Trademark Office that at least one claim in a patent application has been approved on their merits. • This notice is followed by the Notice of Allowance. The notice may also be issued if at least one claim is allowable but the application is under a secrecy order. It may include examiner's amendments incorporating some formal changes.

notice of allowance. 1. *Patents.* The formal notification from the U.S. Patent and Trademark Office that a patent application has been approved and that a patent can be issued. • The patent itself is not issued until the applicant has paid the issue fee. **2.** *Trademarks.* The formal notification from the U.S. Patent and Trademark Office that a trademark may be placed on the Principal Register if it is actually used in commerce.

notice of appeal. (18c) A document filed with a court and served on the other parties, stating an intention to appeal a trial court's judgment or order. • In most jurisdictions, filing a notice of appeal is the act by which the appeal is perfected. For instance, the Federal Rules of Appellate Procedure provide that an appeal is taken by filing a notice of appeal with the clerk of the district court from which the appeal is taken, and that the clerk is to send copies of the notice to all the other parties' attorneys, as well as the court of appeals. Fed. R. App. P. 3(a), (d). — Also termed *claim of appeal.* See APPEAL.

notice of appearance. (1844) **1.** *Procedure.* A party's written notice filed with the court or oral announcement on the record informing the court and the other parties that the party wants to participate in the case. **2.** *Bankruptcy.* A written notice filed with the court or oral announcement in open court by a person who wants to receive all pleadings in a particular case. • This notice is usu. filed by an attorney for a creditor who wants to be added to the official service list. **3.** A pleading filed by an attorney to notify the court and the other parties that he or she represents one or more parties in the lawsuit. — Abbr. NOA.

notice of completion. *Construction law.* A written and recorded announcement that a building project is finished, thereby limiting the time for filing mechanic's liens against the property. • The time for filing a lien begins to run when the notice of completion is filed.

notice of copyright. See COPYRIGHT NOTICE.

notice of deficiency. See NINETY-DAY LETTER.

notice of dishonor. (1804) Notice to the indorser of an instrument that acceptance or payment has been refused. • This notice — along with presentment and actual dishonor — is a condition of an indorser's secondary liability. UCC § 3-503(a). — Also termed *certificate of protest; certificate of dishonor.*

notice of incomplete application. *Patents.* A notice sent to the applicant by the U.S. Patent and Trademark Office when a patent application lacks a required document or the filing fee. • The applicant generally has two months to complete the application, with an extension available upon payment of a surcharge.

notice of lis pendens. See LIS PENDENS (3).

notice of motion. (18c) Written certification that a party to a lawsuit has filed a motion or that a motion will be heard or considered by the court at a particular time. ● Under the Federal Rules of Civil Procedure, the requirement that a motion be made in writing is fulfilled if the motion is stated in a written notice of the hearing on the motion. Also, the courts in most jurisdictions require all motions to include a certificate, usu. referred to as a certificate of service, indicating that the other parties to the suit have been given notice of the motion's filing. Notice of any hearing or other submission of the motion must usu. be provided to all parties by the party requesting the hearing or submission. Fed. R. Civ. P. 5(d), 7(b)(1); Fed. R. Civ. P. Form 19.

notice of nonresponsibility. *Construction law.* A written disclaimer that, if posted conspicuously and recorded, relieves a property owner from liability for work or materials used on the property without the owner's authorization. ● It protects an owner against mechanic's liens that could arise when repairs or improvements are made by a tenant or other person in possession.

notice of orders or judgments. (1854) Written notice of the entry of an order or judgment, provided by the court clerk or one of the parties. ● Notice of a judgment is usu. provided by the clerk of the court in which the judgment was entered. If the court does not provide notice, a party is usu. required to provide it. Under the Federal Rules of Civil Procedure and the Federal Rules of Criminal Procedure, the clerk is required to provide immediate notice of any order or judgment to any party to the case who is not in default. Fed. R. Civ. P. 77(d); Fed. R. Crim. P. 49(c).

notice of pendency. See LIS PENDENS (3).

notice of prior-art references. *Patents.* Notification from a patent examiner of the previously issued patents used in rejecting one or more of the applicant's claims.

notice of protest. 1. A statement, given usu. by a notary public to a drawer or indorser of a negotiable instrument, that the instrument was neither paid nor accepted; information provided to the drawer or indorser that protest was made for nonacceptance or nonpayment of a note or bill. See PROTEST (2). **2.** A shipowner's or crew's declaration under oath that damages to their vessel or cargo were the result of perils of the sea and that the shipowner is not liable for the damages. See PERIL OF THE SEA.

notice of removal. (1892) The pleading by which the defendant removes a case from state court to federal court. ● A notice of removal is filed in the federal district court in the district and division in which the suit is pending. The notice must contain a short and plain statement of the grounds for removal and must include a copy of all process, pleadings, and orders that have been served on the removing party while the case has been pending. The removing party must also notify the state court and other parties to the suit that the notice of removal has been filed. A notice of removal must be filed, if at all, within 30 days after the defendant is served with process in the suit. 28 USCA § 1446; *Murphy Bros., Inc. v. Michetti Pipe Stringing, Inc.*, 526 U.S. 344, 119 S.Ct. 1322 (1999).

notice of trial. (17c) A document issued by a court informing the parties of the date on which the lawsuit is set for trial. ● While the court typically provides the notice to all parties, it may instead instruct one party to send the notice to all others.

notice pleading. See PLEADING (2).

notice-prejudice rule. A doctrine barring an insurer from using late notice as a reason to deny an insured's claim unless the insurer can show that it was prejudiced by the untimely notice.

notice-race statute. See RACE-NOTICE STATUTE.

notice statute. (1864) A recording act providing that the person with the most recent valid claim, and who purchased without notice of an earlier, unrecorded claim, has priority. ● About half the states have notice statutes. — Also termed *notice act.* Cf. RACE STATUTE; RACE-NOTICE STATUTE.

notice to admit. See REQUEST FOR ADMISSION.

notice to all the world. A general public announcement regarding a lawsuit, esp. to persons within the jurisdiction where a lawsuit is pending.

notice to appear. (17c) A summons or writ by which a person is cited to appear in court. ● This is an informal phrase sometimes used to refer to the summons or other initial process by which a person is notified of a lawsuit. The Federal Rules of Civil Procedure require the summons to state that the defendant must appear and defend within in a given time and that failure to do so will result in a default judgment. Fed. R. Civ. P. 4(a). See PROCESS; SUMMONS; DEFAULT JUDGMENT; NOTICE TO PLEAD.

notice to creditors. *Bankruptcy.* A formal notice to creditors that a creditors' meeting will be held, that proofs of claim must be filed, or that an order for relief has been granted.

notice to pay rent or quit. See NOTICE TO QUIT.

notice to plead. (18c) A warning to a defendant, stating that failure to file a responsive pleading within a prescribed time will result in a default judgment. ● The Federal Rules of Civil Procedure require the summons to notify the defendant that failure to appear and defend within a prescribed time will result in a default judgment. Fed. R. Civ. P. 4(a). See PROCESS; SUMMONS; DEFAULT JUDGMENT; NOTICE TO APPEAR.

notice to produce. See REQUEST FOR PRODUCTION.

notice to quit. (18c) **1.** A landlord's written notice demanding that a tenant surrender and vacate the leased property, thereby terminating the tenancy. **2.** A landlord's notice to a tenant to pay any back rent within a specified period (often seven days) or else vacate the leased premises. — Also termed *notice to pay rent or quit.*

notification. (15c) **1.** *Int'l law.* A formal announcement of a legally relevant fact, action, or intent, such as notice of an intent to withdraw from a treaty. **2.** NOTICE. ● A person receives notification if someone else (1) informs the person of the fact or of other facts from which the person has reason to know or should know the fact, or (2) does an act that, under the rules applicable to the transaction, has the same effect on the legal relations of the parties as the acquisition of knowledge. *Restatement of Agency* § 9(2).

notify, *vb.* (14c) **1.** To inform (a person or group) in writing or by any method that is understood <I notified the court of the change in address>. **2.** *Archaic.* To give notice of; to make known <to notify the lawsuit to all the defendants>. See NOTICE.

noting protest. See PROTEST (2).

not in order. See OUT OF ORDER (1).

not law. A judicial decision regarded as wrong by the legal profession.

notoriety. (16c) **1.** The state of being generally, and often unfavorably, known and spoken of <the company executive achieved notoriety when she fled the country to avoid paying taxes>. **2.** A person in such a state <the notoriety gave a rare interview>.

notorious, *adj.* (15c) **1.** Generally known and spoken of, usu. unfavorably. **2.** (Of the possession of property) so conspicuous as to impute notice to the true owner. — Also termed (in sense 2) *open and notorious.* See ADVERSE POSSESSION.

notorious cohabitation. See COHABITATION.

notorious possession. See POSSESSION.

not otherwise indexed by name. A phrase used in shipping and tariff construction, usu. to show a classification of something generally rather than specifically. ● For example, a shipment of aircraft and boat engines merely labeled "other articles" is *not otherwise indexed by name.* — Abbr. NOIBN.

not possessed. *Common-law pleading.* In an action in trover, the defendant's plea denying possession of the articles allegedly converted. See TROVER.

not proven. An archaic jury verdict — now used only in Scots criminal law — equivalent in result to not guilty, but carrying with it a strong suspicion of guilt not fully proved. — Also termed *Scotch verdict.*

not satisfied. A form of return by a sheriff or constable, on a writ of execution, indicating only that the amount due on a judgment was not paid. ● A general return of this type is usu. viewed as technically deficient because it does not state why the writ was not satisfied. Cf. NULLA BONA.

not sufficient funds. (1845) The notation of dishonor (of a check) indicating that the drawer's account does not contain enough money to cover payment. — Abbr. NSF. — Also termed *insufficient funds.*

notwithstanding, *prep.* (15c) Despite; in spite of <notwithstanding the conditions listed above, the landlord can terminate the lease if the tenant defaults>.

n.o.v. *abbr.* NON OBSTANTE VEREDICTO.

novation (noh-**vay**-shən), *n.* (16c) **1.** The act of substituting for an old obligation a new one that either replaces an existing obligation with a new obligation or replaces an original party with a new party. ● A novation may substitute (1) a new obligation between the same parties, (2) a new debtor, or (3) a new creditor. **2.** A contract that (1) immediately discharges either a previous contractual duty or a duty to make compensation, (2) creates a new contractual duty, and (3) includes as a party one who neither owed the previous duty nor was entitled to its performance. — Also termed *substituted agreement;* (Scots law) *innovation.;* (Roman law) *novatio* (noh-**vay**-shee-oh). See *substituted contract* under CONTRACT; ACCORD (2). — **novate** (noh-**vayt** *or* noh-vayt), *vb.* — **novatory** (noh-və-tor-ee), *adj.*

  objective novation. *Civil law.* A novation involving the substitution of a new obligation for an old one.

  subjective novation. *Civil law.* A novation involving the substitution of a new obligor for a previous obligor who has been discharged by the obligee.

novel assignment. See *new assignment* under ASSIGNMENT (7).

novel disseisin (nov-əl dis-**see**-zin), *n.* A recent disseisin. See DISSEISIN; *assize of novel disseisin* under ASSIZE (8).

Novellae (nə-**vel**-ee). See NOVELS.

Novels. A collection of 168 constitutions issued by the Roman emperor Justinian and his immediate successors. ● Taken together, the Novels make up one of four component parts of the *Corpus Juris Civilis.* — Also termed *Novellae; Novellae Constitutiones.* See CORPUS JURIS CIVILIS.

novelty. (14c) **1.** *Trade secrets.* The newness of information that is generally unused or unknown and that gives its owner a competitive advantage in a business field. ● In the law of trade secrets, novelty does not require independent conception or even originality. A rediscovered technique with marketable applications can qualify as a novelty and be protected as a trade secret. **2.** *Patents.* Newness of an invention both in form and in function or performance; the strict statutory requirement that this originality be demonstrated before an invention is patentable. • Proving novelty is one purpose of the rigorous and expensive examination process. If the invention has been previously patented, described in a publication, known or used by others, or sold, it is not novel. 35 USCA § 102. Cf. NONOBVIOUSNESS.

absolute novelty. *Patents.* The rule in most countries, but not in the United States, that an inventor must always file a patent application before the invention is publicly used, placed on sale, or disclosed. • Under U.S. law, an inventor is given a one-year grace period — beginning on the date of any public use, sale, offer of sale, or publication by the inventor or the inventor's agent — in which to file a patent application. After that, the patent is barred. Canada and Mexico also give the first inventor or the inventor's assignees a one-year grace period for filing, but they bar a patent for the first inventor if the invention is independently developed and disclosed by someone else during that time. — Also termed *absolute-novelty requirement.* Cf. BAR DATE.

novus actus interveniens (noh-vəs **ak**-təs in-tər-**vee**-nee-ənz). See *intervening cause* under CAUSE (1).

NOW. *abbr.* **1.** NEGOTIABLE ORDER OF WITHDRAWAL. **2.** National Organization for Women.

NOW account. See ACCOUNT.

now comes. See COMES NOW.

noxal (nok-səl), *adj. Archaic.* Of or relating to a claim against a father or owner for damage done by a son, a slave, or an animal.

noxal action. [fr. Latin *actio noxalis* "injurious action"] **1.** *Roman law.* The claim against an owner or father for a tort committed by a son, a slave, or an animal. • The head of the family could be sued either to pay a penalty due or to surrender the tortfeasor to the injured party. Roman law also provided for the surrender of animals that caused damage under the *actio de pauperie.* **2.** *Hist.* A person's claim to recover for damages committed by a person's son, slave, or animal.

noxious (nok-shəs), *adj.* (15c) **1.** Harmful to health; injurious. **2.** Unwholesome; corruptive. **3.** *Archaic.* Guilty.

n.p. *abbr.* **1.** NISI PRIUS. **2.** NOTARY PUBLIC.

NPL. *abbr.* NATIONAL PRIORITIES LIST.

NPV. See *net present value* under PRESENT VALUE.

NQDC. *abbr.* See *nonqualified deferred-compensation plan* under EMPLOYEE BENEFIT PLAN.

NQSO. *abbr.* See *nonqualified stock option* under STOCK OPTION.

n.r. *abbr.* **1.** New reports. **2.** Not reported. **3.** NONRESIDENT.

NRC. *abbr.* NUCLEAR REGULATORY COMMISSION.

NRCS. *abbr.* NATURAL RESOURCES CONSERVATION SERVICE.

NRPC. *abbr.* NATIONAL RAILROAD PASSENGER CORPORATION.

n.s. *abbr.* **1.** New series. • This citation form indicates that a periodical has been renumbered in a new series. **2.** NEW STYLE.

NSA. *abbr.* NATIONAL SECURITY AGENCY.

NSC. *abbr.* NATIONAL SECURITY COUNCIL.

NSF. *abbr.* **1.** NATIONAL SCIENCE FOUNDATION. **2.** NOT SUFFICIENT FUNDS.

NSL. *abbr.* See NATIONAL-SECURITY LETTER.

NSPA. *abbr.* NATIONAL STOLEN PROPERTY ACT.

NTB. *abbr.* NONTARIFF BARRIER.

NTIA. *abbr.* NATIONAL TELECOMMUNICATIONS AND INFORMATION ADMINISTRATION.

NTID. *abbr.* NATIONAL TECHNICAL INSTITUTE FOR THE DEAF.

NTIS. *abbr.* National Technical Information Service. See TECHNOLOGY ADMINISTRATION.

NTM. *abbr.* NONTARIFF MEASURE.

NTSB. *abbr.* NATIONAL TRANSPORTATION SAFETY BOARD.

nuclear-nonproliferation treaty. See *nonproliferation treaty* under TREATY (1).

Nuclear Regulatory Commission. An independent federal agency that licenses and regulates civilian use of nuclear energy. • The agency was created by the Energy Reorganization Act of 1974. Executive Order 11834 of 1975 gave it additional functions previously performed by the Atomic Energy Commission. — Abbr. NRC.

nude, *adj.* (15c) **1.** Naked; unclothed. **2.** Lacking in consideration or in some essential particular. See NUDUM PACTUM. **3.** Mere; lacking in description or specification.

nude contract. See NUDUM PACTUM.

nude matter. A mere allegation.

nude pact. See NUDUM PACTUM.

nudum pactum (n[y]oo-dəm **pak**-təm). [Latin "bare agreement"] (17c) **1.** *Roman law.* An informal agreement that is not legally enforceable, because it does not fall within the specific classes of agreements that can support a legal action. • But a *pactum* could create an exception to or modification of an existing obligation. **2.** An agreement that is unenforceable as a contract because it is not "clothed" with consideration. — Also termed *naked contract*; *nude contract*; *nude pact*.

nugatory (**n**[y]**oo**-gə-tor-ee), *adj.* (17c) Of no force or effect; useless; invalid <the Supreme Court rendered the statute nugatory by declaring it unconstitutional>.

nuisance. (14c) **1.** A condition, activity, or situation (such as a loud noise or foul odor) that interferes with the use or enjoyment of property; esp., a nontransitory condition or persistent activity that either injures the physical condition of adjacent land or interferes with its use or with the enjoyment of easements on the land or of public highways. • Liability might or might not arise from the condition or situation. — Formerly also termed *annoyance*. **2.** Loosely, an act or failure to act resulting in an interference with the use or enjoyment of property. • In this sense, the term denotes the action causing the interference, rather than the resulting condition <the Slocums' playing electric guitars in their yard constituted a nuisance to their neighbors>. **3.** The class of torts arising from such conditions, acts, or failures to act when they occur unreasonably. — Also termed *actionable nuisance*.

abatable nuisance. (1871) **1.** A nuisance so easily removable that the aggrieved party may lawfully cure the problem without notice to the liable party, such as overhanging tree branches. **2.** A nuisance that reasonable persons would regard as being removable by reasonable means.

absolute nuisance. (18c) **1.** Interference with a property right that a court considers fixed or invariable, such as a riparian owner's right to use a stream in its natural condition. **2.** See *nuisance per se*. **3.** Interference in a place where it does not reasonably belong, even if the interfering party is careful.

anticipatory nuisance. A condition that, although not yet at the level of a nuisance, is very likely to become one, so that a party may obtain an injunction prohibiting the condition. — Also termed *prospective nuisance*.

attractive nuisance. (1901) A dangerous condition that may attract children onto land, thereby causing a risk to their safety. See ATTRACTIVE-NUISANCE DOCTRINE. Cf. ALLUREMENT.; *dangerous condition* (2) under CONDITION (4).

cognate nuisance. *Rare.* Interference with an easement.

common nuisance. See *public nuisance*.

continuing nuisance. (1837) A nuisance that is either uninterrupted or frequently recurring. • It need not be constant or unceasing, but it must occur often enough that it is almost continuous.

legalized nuisance. A nuisance sanctioned by legislative, executive, or other official action and therefore immune from liability, such as a city park.

mixed nuisance. (1894) A condition that is both a private nuisance and a public nuisance, so that it is dangerous to the community at large but also causes particular harm to private individuals.

nuisance at law. See *nuisance per se*.

nuisance dependent on negligence. See *qualified nuisance*.

nuisance in fact. (1855) A nuisance existing because of the circumstances of the use or the particular location. • For example, a machine emitting high-frequency sound may be a nuisance only if a person's dog lives near enough to the noise to be disturbed by it. — Also termed *nuisance per accidens*.

nuisance per se (pər **say**). (186) Interference so severe that it would constitute a nuisance under any circumstances; a nuisance regardless of location or circumstances of use, such as a leaky nuclear-waste storage facility. — Also termed *nuisance at law*; *absolute nuisance*.

permanent nuisance. (18c) A nuisance that cannot readily be abated at reasonable expense. Cf. *temporary nuisance*.

private nuisance. (18c) A condition that interferes with a person's enjoyment of property; esp., a structure or other condition erected or put on nearby land, creating or continuing an invasion of the actor's land and amounting to a trespass to it. • The condition constitutes a tort for which the adversely affected person may recover damages or obtain an injunction.

prospective nuisance. See *anticipatory nuisance*.

public nuisance. (17c) An unreasonable interference with a right common to the general public, such as a condition dangerous to health, offensive to community moral standards, or unlawfully obstructing the public in the free use of public property. • Such a nuisance may lead to a civil injunction or criminal prosecution. — Also termed *common nuisance*.

qualified nuisance. (1944) A condition that, though lawful in itself, is so negligently permitted to exist that it creates an unreasonable risk of harm and, in due course, actually results in injury to another. • It involves neither an intentional act nor a hazardous activity. — Also termed *nuisance dependent on negligence*. Cf. *absolute nuisance*.

recurrent nuisance. A nuisance that occurs from time to time with distinct intervals between occurrences, rather than being continuous or only briefly interrupted.

temporary nuisance. (1879) A nuisance that can be corrected by a reasonable expenditure of money or labor. Cf. *permanent nuisance.*

nuisance money. See *nuisance settlement* under SETTLEMENT (2).

nuisance per accidens. See *nuisance in fact* under NUISANCE.

nuisance prior art. See ART.

nuisance settlement. See SETTLEMENT (2).

nuke. *Slang.* See DENIAL-OF-SERVICE ATTACK.

nul (nəl). [Law French] No; none. • This negative particle begins many phrases, such as *nul tiel.*

null, *adj.* (16c) Having no legal effect; without binding force; VOID <the contract was declared null and void>. • The phrase *null and void* is a common redundancy.

nulla bona (nəl-ə **boh**-nə). [Latin "no goods"] (18c) A form of return by a sheriff or constable upon an execution when the judgment debtor has no seizable property within the jurisdiction. Cf. NIHIL EST.

nulla poena sine lege (nəl-ə **pee**-nə **sɪ**-nee **lee**-jee *or* **sin**-ay **lay**-gay). [Latin] No punishment without a law authorizing it.

nullification (nəl-i-fi-**kay**-shən), *n.* (18c) **1.** The act of making something void; specif., the action of a state in abrogating a federal law, on the basis of state sovereignty. **2.** The state or condition of being void. See JURY NULLIFICATION.

nullification doctrine. The theory — espoused by southern states before the Civil War — advocating a state's right to declare a federal law unconstitutional and therefore void.

nullify, *vb.* To make void; to render invalid.

nullity (nəl-ə-tee). (16c) **1.** Something that is legally void <the forged commercial transfer is a nullity>. **2.** The fact of being legally void <she filed a petition for nullity of marriage>.

absolute nullity. Civil law. **1.** An act that is void because it is against public policy, law, or order. • The nullity is noncurable. It may be invoked by any party or by the court. *See* La. Civ. Code arts 7, 2030. **2.** The state of such a nullity. See NULLITY OF MARRIAGE.

relative nullity. Civil law. **1.** A legal nullity that can be cured by confirmation because the object of the nullity is valid. • The nullity may be invoked only by those parties for whose interest it was established. *See* La. Civ. Code art. 2031. **2.** The state of such a nullity.

nullity of marriage. 1. The invalidity of a presumed or supposed marriage because it is void on its face or has been voided by court order. • A void marriage, such as an incestuous marriage, is invalid on its face and requires no formality to end. See *void marriage* under MARRIAGE (1). **2.** A suit brought to nullify a marriage. — Also termed *nullity suit.* See ANNULMENT.

nullity suit. See NULLITY OF MARRIAGE (2).

nul tiel (nəl teel). [Law Latin] No such. • This phrase typically denotes a plea that denies the existence of something.

nul tiel corporation, n. [Law French "no such corporation exists"] A plea denying the existence of an alleged corporation. • The defense of *nul tiel corporation* must usu. be affirmatively pleaded by a defendant before a plaintiff is required to prove its corporate existence.

nul tiel record, n. [Law French "no such record"] A plea denying the existence of the record on which the plaintiff bases a claim. • Evidence may generally be introduced to invalidate the record only, not the statements in the record. See *trial by record* under TRIAL.

number lottery. See *Genoese lottery* under LOTTERY.

numbers game. A type of lottery in which a person bets that on a given day a certain series of numbers will appear from some arbitrarily chosen source, such as stock-market indexes or the U.S. Treasury balance. • The game creates a fund from which the winner's share is drawn and is subject to regulation as a lottery. Cf. NUMBERS RACKET.

numbers racket. An illegal lottery in which the players typically choose a series of numbers and win if their chosen numbers match a series of randomly drawn numbers. • Numbers rackets have historically been operated in poor neighborhoods and have permitted players to bet small amounts or even to bet on credit. An additional element of their historical attraction was the players' avoidance of paying income tax on winnings. Numbers rackets are often associated with organized crime, and because of their odds (about 1:1,000), they are noted for being rigged and making large profits for racketeers. Cf. NUMBERS GAME.

numerical lottery. See *Genoese lottery* under LOTTERY.

numerosity (n[y]oo-mər-**ahs**-ə-tee). (1958) The requirement in U.S. district courts that, for a case to be certified as a class action, the party applying for certification must show, among other things, that the class of potential plaintiffs is so large that the joinder of all of them into the suit is impracticable. See CLASS ACTION.

nuncio (nən-shee-oh), *n.* [Italian, fr. Latin *nunciare* "to announce"] **1.** A papal ambassador to a foreign court or government; a representative of the Vatican in a country that maintains diplomatic relations with it. — Also termed *nuncius; nuntio.* Cf. *legatus a latere* under LEGATUS; INTERNUNCIO (3); LEGATE (3). **2.** *Archaic.* A messenger.

nunc pro tunc (nəngk proh **t**əngk *or* **nuungk** proh **tuungk**). [Latin "now for then"] Having retroactive legal effect through a court's inherent power <the court entered a *nunc pro tunc* order to correct a clerical error in the record>.

nunc pro tunc **amendment.** See AMENDMENT (2).

nunc pro tunc **judgment.** See JUDGMENT.

nuncupate (**n**əng-kyə-payt), *vb.* [fr. Latin *nuncupare* "call by name"] **1.** *Hist.* To designate or name. **2.** To vow or declare publicly and solemnly. **3.** To declare orally, as a will. **4.** To dedicate or inscribe (a work).

nuncupative (**n**əng-kyə-pay-tiv *or* nəng-**kyoo**-pə-tiv), *adj.* [fr. Latin *nuncupare* "to name"] (15c) Stated by spoken word; declared orally.

nuncupative testament by public act. See *nuncupative will by public act* under WILL.

nuncupative will. See WILL.

nuncupative will by public act. See WILL.

nuptiae (**n**əp-shee-ee). See MATRIMONIUM.

nuptial (**n**əp-shəl), *adj.* (15c) Of or relating to marriage.

Nuremberg defense (**n**[y]ər-əm-bərg). The defense asserted by a member of the military that the soldier was following orders given by superiors. ●

The term derives from the Nuremberg war-crimes trials after World War II.

nurture, *vb.* (14c) **1.** To supply with nourishment. **2.** To train, educate, or develop.

nurturing-parent doctrine. *Family law.* The principle that, although a court deciding on child support generally disregards a parent's motive in failing to maximize earning capacity, the court will not impute income to a custodial parent who remains at home or works less than full-time in order to provide a better environment for a child. ● The doctrine is fact-specific; courts apply it case by case.

NVOCC. *abbr.* See *non-vessel-operating common carrier* under CARRIER.

N.W. *abbr.* NORTH WESTERN REPORTER.

NWS. *abbr.* National Weather Service. See NATIONAL OCEANIC AND ATMOSPHERIC ADMINISTRATION.

NYS. *abbr.* NEW YORK SUPPLEMENT.

NYSE. *abbr.* NEW YORK STOCK EXCHANGE.

nystagmus (ni-**stag**-məs). A rapid, involuntary jerking or twitching of the eyes, sometimes caused by ingesting drugs or alcohol. See HORIZONTAL-GAZE NYSTAGMUS TEST.

O

OAR. *abbr.* Office of Oceanic and Atmospheric Research. See NATIONAL OCEANIC AND ATMOSPHERIC ADMINISTRATION.

OASDHI. *abbr.* Old Age, Survivors, Disability, and Health Insurance. See OLD-AGE AND SURVIVORS' INSURANCE.

OASDI. *abbr.* Old Age, Survivors, and Disability Insurance. See OLD-AGE AND SURVIVORS' INSURANCE.

OASI. *abbr.* OLD-AGE AND SURVIVORS' INSURANCE.

oath. (bef. 12c) **1.** A solemn declaration, accompanied by a swearing to God or a revered person or thing, that one's statement is true or that one will be bound to a promise. ● The person making the oath implicitly invites punishment if the statement is untrue or the promise is broken. The legal effect of an oath is to subject the person to penalties for perjury if the testimony is false. **2.** A statement or promise made by such a declaration. **3.** A form of words used for such a declaration. **4.** A formal declaration made solemn without a swearing to God or a revered person or thing; AFFIRMATION. Cf. PLEDGE (1).

assertory oath (ə-sər-tə-ree). (18c) An oath by which one attests to some factual matter, rather than making a promise about one's future conduct. ● A courtroom witness typically takes such an oath.

corporal oath (kor-pər-əl). (16c) An oath made solemn by touching a sacred object, esp. the Bible. — Also termed *solemn oath; corporale sacramentum.*

decisive oath. *Civil law.* An oath by a party in a lawsuit, used to decide the case because the party's adversary, not being able to furnish adequate proof, offered to refer the decision of the case to the party. — Also termed *decisory oath.*

extrajudicial oath. (17c) An oath that, although formally sworn, is taken outside a legal proceeding or outside the authority of law. — Also termed *nonjudicial oath.*

false oath. See PERJURY.

judicial oath. (17c) An oath taken in the course of a judicial proceeding, esp. in open court.

loyalty oath. See *oath of allegiance.*

nonjudicial oath. 1. An oath taken out of court, esp. before an officer ex parte. — Also termed *voluntary oath.* **2.** See *extrajudicial oath.*

oath ex officio (eks ə-**fish**-ee-oh). *Hist.* At common law, an oath under which a person accused of a crime swore to answer questions before an ecclesiastical court.

oath in litem (lI-tem *or* -təm). *Civil law.* An oath taken by a plaintiff in testifying to the value of the thing in dispute when there is no evidence of value or when the defendant has fraudulently suppressed evidence of value.

oath of allegiance. An oath by which one promises to maintain fidelity to a particular sovereign or government. ● This oath is most often administered to a high public officer, to a soldier or sailor, or to an alien applying for naturalization. — Also termed *loyalty oath; test oath.*

oath of office. (16c) An oath taken by a person about to enter into the duties of public office, by which the person promises to perform the duties of that office in good faith.

oath purgatory. See *purgatory oath.*

oath suppletory. See *suppletory oath.*

pauper's oath. (1844) An affidavit or verification of poverty by a person requesting public funds or services. See *poverty affidavit* under AFFIDAVIT; IN FORMA PAUPERIS.

promissory oath. (15c) An oath that binds the party to observe a specified course of conduct in the future. ● Both the oath of office and the oath of allegiance are types of promissory oaths.

purgatory oath. An oath taken to clear oneself of a charge or suspicion. — Also termed *oath purgatory.*

solemn oath. See *corporal oath.*

suppletory oath (səp-lə-tor-ee). **1.** *Civil law.* An oath administered to a party, rather than a witness, in a case in which a fact has been proved by only one witness. ● In a civil-law case, two witnesses are needed to constitute full proof. See HALF-PROOF. **2.** An oath administered to a party to authenticate or support some piece of documentary evidence offered by the party. — Also termed *oath suppletory.*

test oath. See *oath of allegiance.*

voluntary oath. See *nonjudicial oath* (1).

oath against an oath. See SWEARING MATCH.

oath-helper. See COMPURGATOR.

oath of abjuration. See ABJURATION.

Oath or Affirmation Clause. (1974) The clause of the U.S. Constitution requiring members of Congress and the state legislatures, and all members of the executive or judicial branches — state or local — to pledge by oath or affirmation to support the Constitution. U.S. Const. art. VI, cl. 3.

oath-rite. The form or ceremony used when taking an oath.

oathworthy, *adj.* Legally capable of making an oath.

obedience. Compliance with a law, command, or authority.

obediential obligation. See OBLIGATION.

obiit (oh-bee-it). [Latin] He died; she died.

obiit sine prole (oh-bee-it **si**-nee **proh**-lee *also* sin-ay **prohl**). [Latin] He died without issue. — Abbr. *o.s.p.*

obit. (14c) **1.** *Archaic.* A memorial service on the anniversary of a person's death. **2.** A record or notice of a person's death; an obituary.

obiter (oh-bit-ər), *adv.* [Latin "by the way"] (16c) Incidentally; in passing <the judge said, obiter, that a nominal sentence would be inappropriate>.

obiter, n. See OBITER DICTUM.

obiter dictum (ob-i-tər **dik**-təm). [Latin "something said in passing"] (18c) A judicial comment made while delivering a judicial opinion, but one that is unnecessary to the decision in the case and therefore not precedential (although it may be considered persuasive). — Often shortened to *dictum* or, less commonly, *obiter.* Pl. **obiter dicta.** See DICTUM. Cf. HOLDING (1); RATIO DECIDENDI.

obiter ex post facto (ob-i-tər eks post **fak**-toh). A court's holding that, according to a later court, was expressed in unnecessarily broad terms. • Some authorities suggest that this is not, properly speaking, a type of obiter dictum at all.

object (**ob**-jekt), *n.* (15c) **1.** A person or thing to which thought, feeling, or action is directed <the natural object of one's bounty>. See NATURAL OBJECT.

object of a power. A person appointable by a donee. See POWER OF APPOINTMENT.

2. Something sought to be attained or accomplished; an end, goal, or purpose <the financial objects of the joint venture>.

object of an action. The legal relief that a plaintiff seeks; the remedy demanded or relief sought in a lawsuit. Cf. SUBJECT OF AN ACTION.

object of a statute. The aim or purpose of legislation; the end or design that a statute is meant to accomplish.

object (əb-**jekt**), *vb.* (15c) **1.** To state in opposition; to put forward as an objection <the prosecution objected that the defendant's discovery requests were untimely>. **2.** To state or put forward an objection, esp. to something in a judicial proceeding <the defense objected to the testimony on the ground that it was privileged>. — **objector,** *n.*

objectant. See CONTESTANT (1).

object code. *Copyright.* The machine-readable language compiled from a computer programmer's source code. • Object code is difficult to reverse-engineer, so publicly available software is always in this form. Object code is protected by copyright law and may also be protected by patent law. Because people cannot read or understand it, object code is deposited with the U.S. Copyright Office more often than source code. Cf. SOURCE CODE.

objection, *n.* (1837) **1.** A formal statement opposing something that has occurred, or is about to occur, in court and seeking the judge's immediate ruling on the point. • The party objecting must usu. state the basis for the objection to preserve the right to appeal an adverse ruling.

continuing objection. (1940) A single objection to all the questions in a given line of questioning. • A judge may allow a lawyer to make a continuing objection when the judge has overruled an objection applicable to many questions, and the lawyer wants to preserve the objection for the appellate record. — Also termed *running objection.*

general objection. (18c) An objection made without specifying any grounds in support of the objection. • A general objection preserves only the issue of relevancy. — Also termed *broadside objection.*

speaking objection. (1958) An objection that contains more information (often in the form of argument) than needed by the judge to sustain or overrule it. • Many judges prohibit lawyers from using speaking objections, and sometimes even from stating the grounds for objections, because of the potential for influencing the jury.

specific objection. (1894) An objection that is accompanied by a statement of one or more grounds in support of the objection.

2. *Parliamentary law.* A motion that suppresses a main motion, esp. one that will or may inflame controversy, immediately and without debate. • The motion, because it disposes of the main motion without any debate, usu. requires a supermajority. — Also termed *question of consideration; objection to consideration of a question.* **3.** *Parliamentary law.* A negative vote, esp. one that defeats a request for general consent. **4.** *Patents.* An examiner's action identifying a defect in the form of a patent application, usu. in the specification or a drawing. • An objection does not raise questions about the merit of the claims. An examiner might object, for instance, to a defective oath or to a trademark appearing on the drawings. Cf. REJECTION (4).

objectionable, *adj.* (18c) Open to opposition, esp. adverse reason or contrary argument. — Also termed *exceptionable.*

objection in point of law. (17c) A defensive pleading by which the defendant admits the facts alleged by the plaintiff but objects that they do not make out a legal claim.

objection to consideration of a question. See OBJECTION (2).

objective, *adj.* (17c) **1.** Of, relating to, or based on externally verifiable phenomena, as opposed to an individual's perceptions, feelings, or intentions <the objective facts>. **2.** Without bias or prejudice; disinterested <because her son was involved, she felt she could not be objective>. Cf. SUBJECTIVE.

objective but-for test. See BUT-FOR MATERIALITY.

objective entrapment. See ENTRAPMENT.

objective ethics. See MORAL ABSOLUTISM.

objective impossibility. See IMPOSSIBILITY.

objective meaning. See MEANING.

objective method. See HYPOTHETICAL-PERSON DEFENSE.

objective novation. See NOVATION.

objective standard. See STANDARD.

objective theory of contract. (1904) The doctrine that a contract is not an agreement in the sense of a subjective meeting of the minds but is instead a series of external acts giving the objective semblance of agreement. — Often shortened to *objective theory.* Cf. SUBJECTIVE THEORY OF CONTRACT; MEETING OF THE MINDS.

object of a power. See *permissible appointee* under APPOINTEE.

object of a right. (1880) The thing in respect of which a right exists; the subject matter of a right. — Also termed *subject of a right.* See SUBJECT OF A RIGHT.

object offense. See OFFENSE (1).

object of the power. See *permissible appointee* under APPOINTEE.

object of the power of appointment. See *permissible appointee* under APPOINTEE.

oblation (ah-**blay**-shən). (15c) An offering or sacrifice, esp. one in a religious or ritualistic ceremony. — **oblatory,** *adj.*

obligate, *vb.* (16c) **1.** To bind by legal or moral duty. **2.** To commit (funds, property, etc.) to meet or secure an obligation.

obligation, *n.* (18c) **1.** A legal or moral duty to do or not do something. ● The word has many wide and varied meanings. It may refer to anything that a person is bound to do or forbear from doing, whether the duty is imposed by law, contract, promise, social relations, courtesy, kindness, or morality. **2.** A formal, binding agreement or acknowledgment of a liability to pay a certain amount or to do a certain thing for a particular person or set of persons; esp., a duty arising by contract. — Also termed (in sense 2) *civil obligation.* See DUTY (1); LIABILITY (1). **3.** *Civil law.* A legal relationship in which one person, the obligor, is bound to render a performance in favor of another, the obligee. La. Civ. Code art. 1756.

absolute obligation. (17c) An obligation requiring strict fulfillment according to the terms of the engagement, without any alternatives to the obligor.

accessory obligation. (17c) **1.** An obligation that is incidental to another obligation. ● For example, a mortgage to secure payment of a bond is an accessory obligation. The primary obligation is to pay the bond itself. Cf. *primary obligation* (1). **2.** See *secondary obligation.*

alternative obligation. (18c) An obligation that can be satisfied in at least two different ways, at the choice of the obligor. — Also termed *disjunctive obligation.*

bifactoral obligation (bī-**fak**-tər-əl). An obligation created by two parties.

civil obligation. 1. See *conventional obligation.* **2.** OBLIGATION (2).

community obligation. A debt or other obligation incurred by either spouse after marriage in a community-property state. ● Such an obligation is presumed to be an obligation of the community and not of the individual spouse.

conditional obligation. (17c) An obligation that depends on an uncertain event.

conjunctive obligation. An obligation composed of multiple performances that can be separately rendered or enforced; esp., an obligation in which several objects are connected by *and* (not *or*) or are in some other way clearly meant to be separately included in the contract. ● For example, a loan agreement's conjunctive obligation may require payment of four loan installments and delivery of a deed of trust. Each loan installment and the deed's delivery is a separate, enforceable performance.

contractual obligation. An obligation arising from a contract or agreement.

conventional obligation. (18c) An obligation that results from agreement of the parties; a contractual obligation. — Also termed *express obligation; civil obligation.* Cf. *obediential obligation.*

correal obligation (**kor**-ee-əl *or* kə-**ree**-əl). *Roman & civil law.* A joint and several obligation.

current obligation. (18c) An obligation that is presently enforceable, but not past due.

determinate obligation. An obligation that has a specific thing as its object. • For example, an obligation to deliver the 1491 Venice edition of *Vocabularium Iuris* that once belonged to H.L.A. Hart can be discharged only by delivering the specified book. Cf. *indeterminate obligation*.

disjunctive obligation. See *alternative obligation*.

divisible obligation. An obligation that can be divided without the consent of the parties. • Either the performing party or the receiving party may unilaterally divide the obligation.

express obligation. See *conventional obligation*.

heritable obligation. (18c) An obligation that may be enforced by a successor of the creditor or against a successor of the debtor. — Also termed *inheritable obligation*.

imperfect obligation. See *moral obligation*.

implied obligation. See *obediential obligation*.

indeterminate obligation. 1. An obligation by which the obligor is bound to deliver one of a certain species of items. • For example, an obligation to deliver a pre-1509 edition of *Vocabularium Iuris* can be discharged by delivering any edition published before that date. **2.** An obligation that is not specific in amount or form, or is subject to being changed by a third party. Cf. *determinate obligation*.

inheritable obligation. See *heritable obligation*.

joint obligation. (18c) **1.** An obligation that binds two or more debtors to a single performance for one creditor. **2.** An obligation that binds one debtor to a single performance for two or more creditors.

moral obligation. (18c) A duty that is based only on one's conscience and that is not legally enforceable; an obligation with a purely moral basis, as opposed to a legal one. • In contract law, moral obligation may support a promise in the absence of traditional consideration, but only if the promisor has previously received some actual benefit from the promisee. — Also termed *imperfect obligation*; *natural obligation*.

natural obligation. 1. *Civil law.* A moral duty that is not enforceable by judicial action. • Natural obligations are recognized in civil-law jurisdictions. While they are not enforceable by judicial action, something that has been performed under a natural obligation may not be reclaimed. For example, if an indigent patient in a hospital has no legal obligation to pay for the treatment but does so anyway, that person cannot later reclaim the payments voluntarily made. — Also termed *obligatio naturalis*. **2.** See *moral obligation*.

obediential obligation (ə-bee-dee-**en**-shəl). (18c) An obligation imposed on a person because of a situation or relationship, such as an obligation of parents to care for their children. — Also termed *implied obligation*. Cf. *conventional obligation*.

perfect obligation. A legally enforceable obligation; one that is recognized and sanctioned by positive law.

personal obligation. 1. An obligation performable only by the obligor, not by the obligor's heirs or representatives. **2.** An obligation in which the obligor is bound to perform without encumbering his or her property for its performance.

primary obligation. (17c) **1.** An obligation that arises from the essential purpose of the transaction between the parties. Cf. *accessory obligation* (1). **2.** A fundamental contractual term imposing a requirement on a contracting party from which other obligations may arise. — Also termed *principal obligation*.

primitive obligation. The obligation designated as the first to be satisfied.

principal obligation. See *primary obligation* (2).

pure obligation. *Scots law.* An absolute obligation already due and immediately enforceable. — Also termed *pure debt*.

secondary obligation. (17c) A duty, promise, or undertaking that is incident to a primary obligation; esp., a duty to make reparation upon a breach of contract. — Also termed *accessory obligation*.

several obligation. 1. An obligation that binds two or more debtors to separate performances for one creditor. **2.** An obligation that binds one debtor to separate performances for two or more creditors.

simple obligation. (17c) An obligation that does not depend on an outside event; an unconditional obligation.

single obligation. (17c) An obligation with no penalty attached for nonperformance, as when one party simply promises to pay 20 dollars to another.

solidary obligation (**sol**-ə-der-ee). *Roman & civil law.* An obligation that binds each of two or more debtors for the entire performance at the option of the creditor. • Solidary obligations are analogous to common-law joint and several obligations.

statutory obligation. (18c) An obligation — whether to pay money, perform certain acts, or discharge duties — that is created by or arises out of a statute, rather than based on an independent contractual or legal relationship.

substitute obligation. Civil law. An obligation that takes the place of an extinguished obligation by novation. See NOVATION.

unifactoral obligation (yoo-nə-**fak**-tər-əl). An obligation created by one party.

obligation, mutuality of. See MUTUALITY OF OBLIGATION.

obligational. See OBLIGATORY.

obligation bond. See *general obligation bond* under BOND (3).

obligationes innominati. See INNOMINATE OBLIGATIONS.

Obligation of Contracts Clause. See CONTRACTS CLAUSE.

obligations, law of. See LAW OF OBLIGATIONS.

obligatory (ə-**blig**-ə-tor-ee), *adj.* (14c) **1.** Legally or morally binding <an obligatory promise>. **2.** Required; mandatory <attendance is not obligatory>. **3.** Creating or recording an obligation <a writing obligatory>. — Also termed (rarely) *obligational.*

oblige (ə-**blıj**), *vb.* (14c) **1.** To bind by legal or moral duty; OBLIGATE. **2.** To bind by doing a favor or service.

obligee (ob-lə-**jee**). (16c) **1.** One to whom an obligation is owed; a promisee, creditor, or donor beneficiary. **2.** Under the Uniform Interstate Family Support Act, any person to whom a duty of support is owed. **3.** *Archaic.* One who is obliged to do something; OBLIGOR (1).

obligor (ob-lə-**gor** *or* ob-lə-gor). (16c) **1.** One who has undertaken an obligation; a promisor or debtor. UCC § 9-102(a)(59). **2.** Under the Uniform Interstate Family Support Act, any person who owes a duty of support. **3.** *Archaic.* One who obliges another to do something; OBLIGEE (1).

principal obligor. A person who is under a duty of indemnity.

oblique (oh-**bleek** *or* ə-**bleek**), *adj.* (15c) **1.** Not direct in descent; collateral <an oblique heir>. **2.** Indirect; circumstantial <oblique evidence>.

oblique evidence. See *circumstantial evidence* (1) under EVIDENCE.

obliterate, *vb.* (16c) **1.** To wipe out, rub off, or erase (a writing or other markings). **2.** To remove from existence; to destroy all traces of. — **obliteration,** *n.*

obliterated corner. See CORNER.

oblivion. (14c) **1.** The act or fact of forgetting or having forgotten <the oblivion of sleep>. **2.** The state of being completely forgotten or unknown <a once-famous politician now in oblivion>. **3.** An official disregard of an offense; pardon; amnesty <an act of oblivion by Parliament>.

obloquy (**ob**-lə-kwee). (15c) **1.** Abusive or defamatory language; CALUMNY. **2.** The state or condition of being ill spoken of; disgrace or bad repute.

obnoxious, *adj.* (16c) **1.** Offensive; objectionable <obnoxious behavior>. **2.** Contrary; opposed <a practice obnoxious to the principle of equal protection under the law>. **3.** *Archaic.* Exposed to harm; liable to something undesirable <actions obnoxious to criticism>.

obreption (ob-**rep**-shən). (15c) The fraudulent obtaining of a gift or dispensation, esp. from a sovereign or ecclesiastical authority.

obrogate (**ob**-rə-gayt), *vb.* (17c) *Civil law.* To modify or repeal (a law) in whole or in part by passing a new law. Cf. ABROGATE. — **obrogation,** *n.*

obscene, *adj.* (16c) Extremely offensive under contemporary community standards of morality and decency; grossly repugnant to the generally accepted notions of what is appropriate. ● Under the Supreme Court's three-part test, material is legally obscene — and therefore not protected under the First Amendment — if, taken as a whole, the material (1) appeals to the prurient interest in sex, as determined by the average person applying contemporary community standards; (2) portrays sexual conduct, as specifically defined by the applicable state law, in a patently offensive way; and (3) lacks serious literary, artistic, political, or scientific value. *Miller v. California,* 413 U.S. 15, 93 S.Ct. 2607 (1973).

obscene libel. See LIBEL.

obscenity, *n.* (16c) **1.** The characteristic or state of being morally abhorrent or socially taboo, esp. as a result of referring to or depicting sexual or excretory functions. **2.** Something (such as an expression or act) that has this characteristic. See CONTEMPORARY COMMUNITY STANDARDS. Cf. INDECENCY.

commercialized obscenity. (1956) Obscenity produced and marketed for sale to the public.

observe, *vb.* (14c) To adhere to or abide by (a law, rule, or custom) <a traffic citation for failing to observe the speed limit>.

observer. *Int'l law.* (1925) A representative of a country or international organization who attends meetings of an international body (such as the United Nations) to which the observer's country does not belong. ● Observers do not vote or sign documents, but they are sometimes allowed to participate in discussions.

obsignation, *n.* A formal ratification or confirmation, esp. by an official seal. — **obsignatory** (ob-**sig**-nə-tor-ee), *adj.*

obsolescence (ob-sə-**les**-ənts). (1832) **1.** The process or state of falling into disuse or becoming obsolete. **2.** A diminution in the value or usefulness of property, esp. as a result of technological advances. • For tax purposes, obsolescence is usu. distinguished from physical deterioration. Cf. DEPRECIATION.

economic obsolescence. Obsolescence that results from external economic factors, such as decreased demand or changed governmental regulations. — Also termed *external obsolescence*. Cf. *functional obsolescence*.

external obsolescence. See *economic obsolescence*.

functional obsolescence. Obsolescence that results either from inherent deficiencies in the property, such as inadequate equipment or design, or from technological improvements available after the use began. Cf. *economic obsolescence*.

planned obsolescence. A system or policy of deliberately producing consumer goods that will wear out or become outdated after limited use, thus inducing consumers to buy new items more frequently. — Also termed *built-in obsolescence*.

obsolescent, *adj.* (18c) Going out of use; becoming obsolete.

obsolete, *adj.* (17c) No longer in general use; out-of-date.

obstacle preemption. See PREEMPTION.

obstante (ob-**stan**-tee *or* əb-). [Latin] Withstanding; hindering. See NON OBSTANTE VEREDICTO.

obstinate desertion. See DESERTION.

obstrict (əb-**strikt**), vb. To coerce. — **obstrictive,** *adj.* — **obstrictiveness,** *n.*

obstriction. *Archaic.* Obligation; bond.

obstructing process. See OBSTRUCTION OF PROCESS.

obstruction. (16c) **1.** Something that impedes or hinders, as in a street, river, or design; an obstacle. **2.** The act of impeding or hindering something; interference. **3.** *Oil & gas.* A common-law doctrine that suspends the running of time under an oil-and-gas lease or extends the lease for a reasonable period of time if rights granted under the lease are interfered with by the lessor or someone claiming through the lessor.

obstruction of justice. (1854) Interference with the orderly administration of law and justice, as by giving false information to or withholding evidence from a police officer or prosecutor, or by harming or intimidating a witness or juror. • Obstruction of justice is a crime in most jurisdictions. — Also termed *obstructing justice*; *obstructing public justice*.

obstruction of process. Interference of any kind with the lawful service or execution of a writ, warrant, or other process. • Most jurisdictions make

this offense a crime. — Also termed *obstructing process*; *resisting process*.

obtaining property by false pretenses. See FALSE PRETENSES.

obtain the floor. *Parliamentary law.* To receive recognition from the chair after claiming the floor.

obtest (ob- *or* əb-**test**), *vb.* (16c) **1.** To call to or invoke as a witness. **2.** To ask for earnestly; beseech; implore. **3.** To protest.

obvention (ob- *or* əb-**ven**-shən). *Eccles. law.* An incoming fee or revenue, esp. one that comes occasionally or incidentally.

obviate (**ob**-vee-ayt), *vb.* (16c) **1.** To dispose of or do away with (a thing); to anticipate and prevent from arising <they obviated the growing problem through legislation>. **2.** To make unnecessary <the movant obviated the all-night drafting session by getting the opponent to agree to an extension>. — **obviation,** *n.* — **obviator,** *n.*

obvious error. A standard of review that applies to unobjected-to actions and omissions at trial that are so seriously prejudicial as to result in manifest injustice.

obviousness, *n.* (1921) *Patents.* The quality or state of being easily apparent to a person with ordinary skill in a given art, considering the scope and content of the prior art, so that the person could reasonably believe that, at the time it was conceived, the invention was to be expected. • An invention that is determined to be obvious cannot be patented. Although an obviousness inquiry is rife with questions of fact, the ultimate conclusion is a question of law. See 35 USCA 5103. Cf. NONOBVIOUSNESS. — **obvious,** *adj.*

obviousness double patenting. See DOUBLE PATENTING.

obviousness-type double patenting. 1. DOUBLE PATENTING. **2.** See *judicially created double patenting* under DOUBLE PATENTING (2).

obviousness-type double-patenting rejection. See *judicially created double-patenting rejection* under REJECTION.

o.c. *abbr.* **1.** OPE CONSILIO. **2.** Orphan's court. See *probate court* under COURT.

OCC. *abbr.* OFFICE OF THE COMPTROLLER OF THE CURRENCY.

occasional sale. See SALE.

occult marriage. See *confidential marriage* under MARRIAGE (1).

occupancy. (16c) **1.** The act, state, or condition of holding, possessing, or residing in or on something; actual possession, residence, or tenancy, esp. of a dwelling or land. • In this sense, the term denotes whatever acts are done on the land to manifest a claim of exclusive control and to indicate to the public that the actor has appropriated the land. Hence, erecting and maintaining a substantial enclosure around a tract of land usu. constitutes occupancy of the whole tract.

   constructive occupancy. A manifest intent to occupy property physically, followed within a reasonable time by actual occupancy.

2. The act of taking possession of something that has no owner (such as abandoned property) so as to acquire legal ownership. See ADVERSE POSSESSION. **3.** The period or term during which one owns, rents, or otherwise occupies property. **4.** The state or condition of being occupied. **5.** The use to which property is put.

occupant. (16c) **1.** One who has possessory rights in, or control over, certain property or premises. **2.** One who acquires title by occupancy.

   general occupant. (18c) A person who occupies land in the interim arising after the death of a *pur autre vie* tenant but before the death of the person who serves as the measuring life for the estate. ● The *pur autre vie* tenant does not state who may occupy the land after the death of the first tenant; the land can be occupied by the first possessor of the land. — Also termed *common occupant.* Cf. CESTUI QUE VIE.

   special occupant. (18c) A person specifically designated in a conveyance as being entitled to a life estate if the conveyee dies before the end of the life estate; specif., a *pur autre vie* tenant's heir who occupies land in the interim between the death of the tenant and the death of the person who serves as the measuring life for the estate. ● A special occupancy can arise when the grant to the *pur autre vie* tenant provides that possession is for the life of the tenant, then to the tenant's heirs.

occupant statute. See BETTERMENT ACT.

occupatio (ok-yə-**pay**-shee-oh), *n. Roman law.* A mode of acquisition by which a person obtains absolute title by first possessing a thing that previously belonged to no one, such as a wild bird or pearls on the shore. Cf. RULE OF CAPTURE (2).

occupation. (14c) **1.** An activity or pursuit in which a person is engaged; esp., a person's usual or principal work or business.

   dangerous occupation. An occupation that involves an appreciable risk of death or serious bodily injury.

2. The possession, control, or use of real property; OCCUPANCY. **3.** The seizure and control of a territory by military force; the condition of territory that has been placed under the authority of a hostile army. **4.** The period during which territory seized by military force is held.

occupational crime. See CRIME.

occupational-disability insurance. See INSURANCE.

occupational disease. (1901) A disease that is contracted as a result of exposure to debilitating conditions or substances in the course of employment. ● Employees who suffer from occupational diseases are eligible for workers' compensation. Courts have construed the term to include a variety of ailments, including lung conditions (such as asbestosis or black lung), hearing loss, and carpal tunnel syndrome. — Also termed *industrial disease.*

occupational hazard. See HAZARD (1).

Occupational Safety and Health Act of 1970. A federal statute that requires employers to (1) keep the workplace free from recognized hazards that cause or are likely to cause death or serious physical harm to employees, and (2) comply with standards promulgated by the Secretary of Labor. 29 USCA §§ 651–678. — Abbr. OSHA (**oh**-shə).

Occupational Safety and Health Administration. A unit in the U.S. Department of Labor responsible for setting and enforcing workplace safety and health standards and for helping employers comply with them. ● It was created under the Occupational Safety and Health Act of 1970. There are ten regional offices. — Abbr. OSHA.

Occupational Safety and Health Review Commission. An independent, quasi-judicial commission that resolves allegations of unsafe or unhealthy working conditions. ● It was established by the Occupational Safety and Health Act of 1970. — Abbr. OSHRC.

occupational tax. See *occupation tax* under TAX.

occupation tax. See TAX.

occupying claimant. (1801) A person who claims the right under a statute to recover for the cost of improvements done to land that is later found not to belong to the person.

occupying-claimant act. See BETTERMENT ACT.

occurrence. (1978) Something that happens or takes place; specif., an accident, event, or continuing condition that results in personal injury or property damage that is neither expected nor intended from the standpoint of an insured party. ● This specific sense is the standard definition of the term under most liability policies.

occurrence-based liability insurance. See INSURANCE.

occurrence policy. See INSURANCE POLICY.

occurrence rule. *Civil procedure.* The rule that a limitations period begins to run when the alleged wrongful act or omission occurs, rather than when the plaintiff discovers the injury. ● This rule applies, for example, to most breach-of-contract claims. See STATUTE OF LIMITATIONS. Cf. DISCOVERY RULE.

ocean. (14c) **1.** The continuous body of salt water that covers more than 70% of the earth's surface; the high seas; the open sea. Cf. SEA. **2.** Any of the principal geographic divisions of this body. • There are generally considered to be five oceans: Atlantic, Pacific, Indian, Arctic, and Antarctic.

ocean bill of lading. See BILL OF LADING.

ocean marine insurance. See INSURANCE.

OCHAMPUS. *abbr.* OFFICE OF CIVILIAN HEALTH AND MEDICAL PROGRAMS OF THE UNIFORMED SERVICES.

octroy (ok-troy), *vb.* (Of a sovereign) to grant or concede as a privilege.

o/d. *abbr.* **1.** OVERDRAFT (1). **2.** OVERDRAFT (2).

OD. *abbr.* **1.** Overdose. **2.** OVERDRAFT (1). **3.** OVERDRAFT (2). **4.** See *ordinary seaman* under SEAMAN.

odd lot. See LOT (3).

odd-lot, *adj.* Of, relating to, or designating a worker who is so substantially disabled as to be unable to find stable employment in the ordinary labor market, and thus is considered totally disabled and entitled to workers'-compensation benefits under the odd-lot doctrine <an odd-lot worker who could find only sporadic employment>.

odd-lot doctrine. *Workers' compensation.* The doctrine that permits a finding of total disability for an injured claimant who, though able to work sporadically, cannot obtain regular employment and steady income and is thus considered an "odd lot" in the labor market.

odium (oh-dee-əm). (17c) **1.** The state or fact of being hated. **2.** A state of disgrace, usu. resulting from detestable conduct. **3.** Hatred or strong aversion accompanied by loathing or contempt. — **odious,** *adj.*

ODP. *abbr.* OFFICE OF DOMESTIC PREPAREDNESS.

OEQ. *abbr.* OFFICE OF ENVIRONMENTAL QUALITY.

OES. *abbr.* BUREAU OF OCEANS AND INTERNATIONAL ENVIRONMENTAL AND SCIENTIFIC AFFAIRS.

OFCCP. *abbr.* OFFICE OF FEDERAL CONTRACT COMPLIANCE PROGRAMS.

of counsel. See COUNSEL.

of course. (16c) **1.** Following the ordinary procedure <the writ was issued as a matter of course>. **2.** Naturally; obviously; clearly <we'll appeal that ruling, of course>.

off-board, *adj.* Outside a major exchange; over-the-counter or between private parties <an off-board securities transaction>. — Also termed *off-the-board.* See OVER-THE-COUNTER.

offender. (15c) A person who has committed a crime.

> ***adult offender.*** (1831) **1.** A person who has committed a crime after reaching the age of majority. **2.** A person who, having committed a crime while a minor, has been convicted after reaching the age of majority. **3.** A juvenile who has committed a crime and is tried as an adult rather than as a juvenile.

> ***career offender.*** (1965) Under the federal-sentencing guidelines, an adult who, after being convicted of two violent felonies or controlled-substance felonies, commits another such felony. U.S. Sentencing Guidelines Manual § 4B1.1.

> ***first offender.*** (1884) A person who authorities believe has committed a crime but who has never before been convicted of a crime. • First offenders are often treated leniently at sentencing or in plea negotiations.

> ***habitual offender.*** **1.** A person who commits the same or a similar offense a certain number of times in a certain period, as set by statute, and is therefore eligible for an enhanced sentence. **2.** RECIDIVIST.

> ***prior and persistent offender.*** *Missouri law.* See RECIDIVIST.

> ***repeat offender.*** (1956) A person who has been convicted of a crime more than once; RECIDIVIST.

> ***situational offender.*** (1945) A first-time offender who is unlikely to commit future crimes.

> ***status offender.*** (1967) A youth who engages in conduct that — though not criminal by adult standards — is considered inappropriate enough to bring a charge against the youth in juvenile court; a juvenile who commits a status offense. Cf. *youthful offender;* JUVENILE DELINQUENT.

> ***youthful offender.*** (1885) **1.** A person in late adolescence or early adulthood who has been convicted of a crime. • A youthful offender is often eligible for special programs not available to older offenders, including community supervision, the successful completion of which may lead to erasing the conviction from the offender's record. **2.** JUVENILE DELINQUENT. — Also termed *young offender; youth offender.* Cf. *status offender.*

offense (ə-**fents**). (14c) **1.** A violation of the law; a crime, often a minor one. See CRIME. — Also termed *criminal offense.*

> ***acquisitive offense.*** (1981) An offense characterized by the unlawful appropriation of another's property. • This is a generic term that refers to a variety of crimes (such as larceny) rather than a particular one.

> ***allied offense.*** (1896) A crime with elements so similar to those of another that the commission of the one is automatically the commission of the other.

> ***anticipatory offense.*** See *inchoate offense.*

arrestable offense. *English law.* An offense for which the punishment is fixed by law or for which a statute authorizes imprisonment for five years, or an attempt to commit such an offense. • This statutory category, created in 1967, abolished the traditional distinction between felonies and misdemeanors. — Also spelled (esp. in BrE) *arrestable offence.*

bailable offense. (18c) A criminal charge for which a defendant may be released from custody after providing proper security <misdemeanor theft is a bailable offense>.

capital offense. (16c) A crime for which the death penalty may be imposed. — Also termed *capital crime.*

civil offense. See *public tort* under TORT.

cognate offense. (1866) A lesser offense that is related to the greater offense because it shares several of the elements of the greater offense and is of the same class or category. • For example, shoplifting is a cognate offense of larceny because both crimes require the element of taking property with the intent to deprive the rightful owner of that property. Cf. *lesser included offense.*

compound offense. An offense composed of one or more separate offenses. • For example, robbery is a compound offense composed of larceny and assault.

continuing offense. (18c) A crime (such as a conspiracy) that is committed over a period of time, so that the last act of the crime controls when the statute of limitations begins to run.

cumulative offense. (1833) An offense committed by repeating the same act at different times.

divisible offense. (1847) A crime that includes one or more crimes of lesser grade. • For example, murder is a divisible offense comprising assault, battery, and assault with intent to kill.

extraneous offense. (1881) An offense beyond or unrelated to the offense for which a defendant is on trial.

graded offense. (1891) A crime that is divided into various degrees of severity with corresponding levels of punishment, such as murder (first-degree and second-degree) or assault (simple and aggravated). See DEGREE (2).

impeachable offense. See IMPEACHABLE OFFENSE.

inchoate offense. (1809) A step toward the commission of another crime, the step in itself being serious enough to merit punishment. • The three inchoate offenses are attempt, conspiracy, and solicitation. The term is sometimes criticized (see quot. below). — Also termed *anticipatory offense; inchoate crime; preliminary crime.*

included offense. See *lesser included offense.*

index offense. (1980) One of eight classes of crimes reported annually by the FBI in the Uniform Crime Report. • The eight classes are murder (and nonnegligent homicide), rape, robbery, aggravated assault, burglary, larceny-theft, arson, and auto theft. — Also termed *index crime.*

indictable offense. (18c) A crime that can be prosecuted only by indictment. • In federal court, such an offense is one punishable by death or by imprisonment for more than one year or at hard labor. Fed. R. Crim. P. 7(a). See INDICTMENT.

international offense. See INTERNATIONAL CRIME.

joint offense. (18c) An offense (such as conspiracy) committed by the participation of two or more persons.

lesser included offense. (1908) A crime that is composed of some, but not all, of the elements of a more serious crime and that is necessarily committed in carrying out the greater crime <battery is a lesser included offense of murder>. • For double-jeopardy purposes, a lesser included offense is considered the "same offense" as the greater offense, so that acquittal or conviction of either offense precludes a separate trial for the other. — Also termed *included offense; necessarily included offense; predicate offense; predicate act.* Cf. *cognate offense.*

liquor offense. Any crime involving the inappropriate use or sale of intoxicating liquor. See DRAM-SHOP LIABILITY; DRIVING WHILE INTOXICATED.

major offense. An offense the commission of which involves one or more lesser included offenses, as murder may include assault and battery.

military offense. See MILITARY OFFENSE.

multiple offense. (1908) An offense that violates more than one law but that may require different proof so that an acquittal or conviction under one statute does not exempt the defendant from prosecution under another.

necessarily included offense. See *lesser included offense.*

negligent offense. A violation of law arising from a defective discharge of duty or from criminal negligence. See *criminal negligence* under NEGLIGENCE.

object offense. The crime that is the object of the defendant's attempt, solicitation, conspiracy, or complicity. • For example, murder is the object offense in a charge of attempted murder. — Also termed *target offense.*

offense against property. (1837) A crime against another's personal property. • The common-law offenses against property were larceny, embez-zlement, cheating, cheating by false pretenses, robbery, receiving stolen goods, malicious mis-chief, forgery, and uttering forged instruments. Although the term *crimes against property*, a common term in modern usage, includes crimes against real property, the term *offense against property* is traditionally restricted to personal property. Cf. CRIMES AGAINST PROPERTY.

offense against public justice and authority. A crime that impairs the administration of jus-tice. • The common-law offenses of this type were obstruction of justice, barratry, mainte-nance, champerty, embracery, escape, prison breach, rescue, misprision of felony, compound-ing a crime, subornation of perjury, bribery, and misconduct in office.

offense against the habitation. (1849) A crime against another's house — traditionally either arson or burglary.

offense against the person. (1854) A crime against the body of another human being. • The common-law offenses against the person were murder, manslaughter, mayhem, rape, assault, battery, robbery, false imprisonment, abortion, seduction, kidnapping, and abduc-tion. Cf. CRIMES AGAINST PERSONS.

offense against the public health, safety, comfort, and morals. A crime traditionally viewed as en-dangering the whole of society. • The common-law offenses of this type were nuisance, bigamy, adultery, fornication, lewdness, illicit cohabita-tion, incest, miscegenation, sodomy, bestiality, buggery, abortion, and seduction.

offense against the public peace. (18c) A crime that tends to disturb the peace. • The common-law offenses of this type were riot, unlawful as-sembly, dueling, rout, affray, forcible entry and detainer, and libel on a private person.

petty offense. (17c) A minor or insignificant crime. 18 USCA § 19. Cf. *serious offense.*

political offense. See POLITICAL OFFENSE.

predicate offense. 1. An earlier offense that can be used to enhance a sentence levied for a later conviction. • Predicate offences are defined by statute and are not uniform from state to state. **2.** See *lesser included offense.*

public offense. (16c) An act or omission forbid-den by law.

public-welfare offense. (1933) A minor offense that does not involve moral delinquency and is prohibited only to secure the effective regula-tion of conduct in the interest of the commu-nity. • An example is driving a car with one brake-light missing. — Also termed *regulatory offense*; *contravention.*

regulatory offense. 1. A statutory crime, as op-posed to a common-law crime. **2.** See *public-welfare offense.*

same offense. 1. For double-jeopardy purposes, the same criminal act, omission, or transaction for which the person has already stood trial. See DOUBLE JEOPARDY. **2.** For sentencing and en-hancement-of-punishment purposes, an offense that is quite similar to a previous one.

second offense. An offense committed after con-viction for a first offense. • The previous convic-tion, not the indictment, forms the basis of the charge of a second offense.

separate offense. (18c) **1.** An offense arising out of the same event as another offense but contain-ing some differences in elements of proof. • A person may be tried, convicted, and sentenced for each separate offense. **2.** An offense arising out of a different event entirely from another offense under consideration.

serious offense. (18c) An offense not classified as a petty offense and usu. carrying at least a six-month sentence. — Also termed *serious crime.* Cf. *petty offense.*

sexual offense. (1885) An offense involving un-lawful sexual conduct, such as prostitution, indecent exposure, incest, pederasty, and bes-tiality.

status offense. (1960) **1.** See *status crime* under CRIME. **2.** A minor's violation of the juvenile code by doing some act that would not be con-sidered illegal if an adult did it, but that indi-cates that the minor is beyond parental control. • Examples include running away from home, truancy, and incorrigibility. See JUVENILE DE-LINQUENCY.

strict-liability offense. An offense for which the action alone is enough to warrant a convic-tion, with no need to prove a mental state. • For example, illegal parking is a strict-liability offense.

substantive offense (səb-stən-tiv). (18c) A crime that is complete in itself and is not dependent on another crime for one of its elements. — Also termed *substantive crime*; *substantive felony.*

summary offense. (1928) An offense (such as a petty misdemeanor) that can be prosecuted without an indictment. Cf. *indictable offense.*

target offense. See *object offense.*

unnatural offense. See SODOMY.

unrelated offense. (1896) A crime that is indepen-dent from the charged offense.

violent offense. (1965) A crime characterized by extreme physical force, such as murder, forcible rape, and assault and battery with a dangerous weapon. — Also termed *violent felony.*

2. *Civil law.* An intentional unlawful act that causes injury or loss to another and that gives rise to a claim for damages. La. Civ. Code art. 2315. ● This sense of *offense* is essentially the same as the common-law intentional tort.

> **quasi-offense.** *Civil law.* A negligent unlawful act that causes injury or loss to another and that gives rise to a claim for damages. ● This is equivalent to the common-law tort of negligence. — Also termed *quasi-delict.*

3. *Parliamentary law.* A breach of order or other misconduct for which the applicable rules subject a member to a penalty.

offensive (ə-**fen**-siv), *adj.* (16c) **1.** Of or for attack <an offensive weapon>. **2.** Unpleasant or disagreeable to the senses; obnoxious <an offensive odor>. **3.** Causing displeasure, anger, or resentment; esp., repugnant to the prevailing sense of what is decent or moral <patently offensive language and photographs>. See OBSCENE.

offensive and defensive league. *Int'l law.* A league binding the parties not only to aid one another when attacked but also to support one another when attacking in offensive warfare.

offensive collateral estoppel. See COLLATERAL ESTOPPEL.

offensive lockout. See LOCKOUT.

offensive strike. See STRIKE.

offensive treaty. See TREATY (1).

offensive-use waiver. (1993) An exemption from the attorney–client privilege, whereby a litigant is considered to have waived the privilege by seeking affirmative relief, if the claim relies on privileged information that would be outcome-determinative and that the opposing party has no other way to obtain. Cf. AT-ISSUE WAIVER.

offer, *n.* (15c) **1.** The act or an instance of presenting something for acceptance <the prosecutor's offer of immunity>. **2.** A promise to do or refrain from doing some specified thing in the future, conditioned on an act, forbearance, or return promise being given in exchange for the promise or its performance; a display of willingness to enter into a contract on specified terms, made in a way that would lead a reasonable person to understand that an acceptance, having been sought, will result in a binding contract <she accepted the $750 offer on the Victorian armoire>. Cf. ACCEPTANCE.

> **irrevocable offer** (i-**rev**-ə-kə-bəl). (1885) An offer that includes a promise to keep it open for a specified period, during which the offer cannot be withdrawn without the offeror's becoming subject to liability for breach of contract. ● Traditionally, this type of promise must be supported by consideration to be enforceable, but under UCC § 2-205, a merchant's signed, written offer giving assurances that it will be held open — but

lacking consideration — is nonetheless irrevocable for the stated period (or, if not stated, for a reasonable time not exceeding three months). — Also termed (in the UCC) *firm offer*; (specif.) *merchant's firm offer.*

> **offer to all the world.** (1861) An offer, by way of advertisement, of a reward for the rendering of specified services, addressed to the public at large. ● As soon as someone renders the services, a contract is made. — Also termed *public offer.*

> **offer to chaffer.** See INVITATION TO NEGOTIATE.

> **public-exchange offer.** A takeover attempt in which the bidder corporation offers to exchange some of its securities for a specified number of the target corporation's voting shares. Cf. TENDER OFFER.

> **public offer.** See *offer to all the world.*

> **standing offer.** (1842) An offer that is in effect a whole series of offers, each of which is capable of being converted into a contract by a distinct acceptance.

> **tender offer.** See TENDER OFFER.

> **two-tier offer.** See TWO-TIER OFFER.

3. A price at which one is ready to buy or sell; BID <she lowered her offer to $200>. **4.** ATTEMPT (2) <an offer to commit battery>. — **offer,** *vb.* — **offeror,** *n.*

offeree (ah-fər-**ee**). (1882) One to whom an offer is made.

offer for sale by tender. See *Dutch auction* (4) under AUCTION.

offer in compromise. See OFFER OF COMPROMISE.

offering, *n.* (15c) **1.** The act of making an offer; something offered for sale. **2.** The sale of an issue of securities. — Also termed (in BrE) *flotation.* See ISSUE (2).

> **all-or-none offering.** An offering that allows the issuer to terminate the distribution if the entire block of offered securities is not sold.

> **initial public offering.** A company's first public sale of stock; the first offering of an issuer's equity securities to the public through a registration statement. — Abbr. IPO.

> **negotiated offering.** A securities offering in which the terms (including the underwriters' compensation) have been negotiated between the issuer and the underwriters.

> **primary offering.** An offering of newly issued securities.

> **private offering.** An offering made only to a small group of interested buyers. — Also termed *private placement.*

> **public offering.** An offering made to the general public.

registered offering. A public offering of securities registered with the SEC and with appropriate state securities commissions. — Also termed *registered public offering.*

rights offering. An issue of stock-purchase rights allowing shareholders to buy newly issued stock at a fixed price, usu. below market value, and in proportion to the number of shares they already own. — Also termed *privileged subscription.* Cf. PREEMPTIVE RIGHT.

secondary offering. **1.** Any offering by an issuer of securities after its initial public offering. **2.** An offering of previously issued securities by persons other than the issuer. See *secondary distribution* (1) under DISTRIBUTION.

special offering. An offering of a large block of stock that, because of its size and the market in the particular issue, is specially handled on the floor of the stock exchange.

undigested offering. A public offering of securities that remain unsold because there is insufficient demand at the offered price.

offering circular. A document, similar to a prospectus, that provides information about a private securities offering. — Also termed *offering statement.*

offering price. See *asking price* under PRICE.

offering statement. See OFFERING CIRCULAR.

offer of compromise. (18c) An offer by one party to settle a dispute amicably (usu. by paying money) to avoid or end a lawsuit or other legal action. • An offer of compromise is usu. not admissible at trial as evidence of the offering party's liability but may be admissible for other purposes. — Also termed *offer in compromise*; *offer of settlement.*

offer of judgment. (1971) A settlement offer by one party to allow a specified judgment to be taken against the party. • In federal procedure (and in many states), if the adverse party rejects the offer, and if a judgment finally obtained by that party is not more favorable than the offer, then that party must pay the costs incurred after the offer was made. Fed. R. Civ. P. 68.

offer of performance. (18c) *Contracts.* One party's reasonable assurance to the other, through words or conduct, of a present ability to fulfill contractual obligations. • When performances are to be exchanged simultaneously, each party is entitled to refuse to proceed with the exchange until the other party makes an appropriate offer of performance. Cf. TENDER (1).

offer of proof. (17c) *Procedure.* A presentation of evidence for the record (but outside the jury's presence) usu. made after the judge has sustained an objection to the admissibility of that evidence, so that the evidence can be preserved on the record for an appeal of the judge's ruling. • An offer of proof, which may also be used to persuade the court to admit the evidence, consists of three parts: (1) the evidence itself, (2) an explanation of the purpose for which it is offered (its relevance), and (3) an argument supporting admissibility. Such an offer may include tangible evidence or testimony (through questions and answers, a lawyer's narrative description, or an affidavit). Fed. R. Evid. 103(a)(2). — Also termed *avowal.*

offer of settlement. See OFFER OF COMPROMISE.

offeror (ah-fər-**or**). (1882) One who makes an offer.

offer to all the world. See OFFER.

offer to chaffer. See INVITATION TO NEGOTIATE.

office. (13c) **1.** A position of duty, trust, or authority, esp. one conferred by a governmental authority for a public purpose <the office of attorney general>. **2.** (*often cap.*) A division of the U.S. government ranking immediately below a department <the Patent and Trademark Office>. **3.** A place where business is conducted or services are performed <a law office>.

alienation office. *English law.* An office for the recovery of fines levied upon writs of covenant and entries.

lucrative office. **1.** A position that produces fee revenue or a salary to the office holder. **2.** A position that yields a salary adequate to the services rendered and exceeding incidental expenses; a position whose pay is tied to the performance of the office's duties.

ministerial office. An office that does not include authority to exercise judgment, only to carry out orders given by a superior office, or to perform duties or acts required by rules, statutes, or regulations.

office of honor. An uncompensated public position of considerable dignity and importance to which public trusts or interests are confided.

Office action. *Patents & Trademarks.* A patent examiner's communication with a patent applicant, usu. to state the reasons for denying an application.

advisory Office action. An office action in which the patent examiner replies to an applicant's response following final rejection of the application. • An advisory action addresses the status of an amendment made in the applicant's response to the final rejection, indicates the status of the claims for appeal, addresses an affidavit or exhibit, or responds to a request for reconsideration. — Also termed *advisory action.*

final Office action. A patent examiner's determination that an application is not allowable. • The applicant may file a continuation application, appeal the decision, or request continued prosecution. Cf. *first office action.*

first Office action. A patent examiner's initial reply to a patent application. ● If the examiner's first report is a rejection of all or most of the application's claims, it is termed a *shotgun rejection.* To avoid abandoning the prosecution, the applicant must respond by answering the examiner's reasons for rejection, amending the claims, or both. Cf. *final office action.*

office audit. See AUDIT.

office-block ballot. See BALLOT (4).

office classification. See CLASSIFICATION OF PATENTS.

office expense. See OVERHEAD.

office grant. See GRANT.

office hours. *Military law.* See *nonjudicial punishment* under PUNISHMENT.

office lawyer. See OFFICE PRACTITIONER.

office of child-support enforcement. *Family law.* A state or federal agency established under Title IV(D) of the Social Security Act to help custodial parents collect child support. 42 USCA § 651 et seq. ● State offices of child-support enforcement generally come under the aegis of the Department of Human Resources. The federal Office of Child Support Enforcement has established the Parent-Locator Service.

Office of Civilian Health and Medical Programs of the Uniformed Services. A unit in the U.S. Department of Defense responsible for administering a civilian health and medical care program for the spouses and dependent children of active members of the armed forces and for retired military personnel, their spouses and children. — Abbr. OCHAMPUS.

Office of Community Planning and Development. A unit in the U.S. Department of Housing and Urban Development responsible for administering grant programs to help communities plan and finance their growth and development, increase their capacity to govern, and provide shelter and services for homeless people. — Abbr. CPD.

Office of Counterintelligence. An office in the U.S. Department of Energy responsible for conducting counterintelligence programs involving industrial intelligence activities of foreigners and foreign governments.

Office of Domestic Preparedness. A unit in the U.S. Department of Homeland Security responsible for helping state and local governments train and equip emergency responders, plan and conduct disaster drills, and offer other technical assistance to prevent, plan for, and respond to acts of terrorism. ● The Office was transferred from the U.S. Department of Justice in 2003. — Abbr. ODP.

Office of Enrollment and Discipline. *Patents.* The division of the U.S. Patent and Trademark Office charged with licensing patent attorneys and patent agents, and with hearing complaints involving their misconduct. ● The office is authorized to sanction practitioners, and to suspend or disbar them from practice before the PTO. Its authority is concurrent with state disciplinary procedures. — Abbr. OED.

Office of Environmental Quality. An office in the Executive Office of the President responsible for supporting the Council on Environmental Quality. — Abbr. OEQ. See COUNCIL ON ENVIRONMENTAL QUALITY.

Office of Fair Housing and Equal Opportunity. A unit in the U.S. Department of Housing and Urban Development responsible for administering the fair-housing laws and regulations that prohibit discrimination in public and private housing. — Abbr. FHEO.

Office of Federal Contract Compliance Programs. The division of the Employment Standards Administration in the U.S. Department of Labor responsible for enforcing contractors' compliance with Executive Order 11246, which prohibits job discrimination on the basis of race, color, gender, religion, or national origin. — Abbr. OFCCP. See EMPLOYMENT STANDARDS ADMINISTRATION; DEPARTMENT OF LABOR.

Office of Federal Housing Enterprise Oversight. A unit in the U.S. Department of Housing and Urban Development responsible for overseeing the financial safety and soundness of the Federal National Mortgage Association (Fannie Mae) and the Federal Home Loan Mortgage Corporation (Freddie Mac). — Abbr. OFHEO.

Office of Government Ethics. An independent agency in the executive branch responsible for issuing rules and regulations about ethical conduct and financial disclosure, providing training in ethics, monitoring the ethics of practices in departments and agencies, and giving guidance on matters of ethics. ● The agency was established under the Ethics in Government Act of 1978 and became a separate agency in 1988. — Abbr. OGE.

Office of Healthy Homes and Lead Hazard Control. A unit office in the U.S. Department of Housing and Urban Development responsible for informing the public about the dangers of lead poisoning, esp. by lead-based paint; developing methods of detection and abatement; encouraging states and local governments to develop prevention programs; and implementing the Department's Healthy Home Initiative to warn the public of other potential household hazards. — Abbr. OHHLHC.

office of honor. See OFFICE.

Office of Housing. A unit in the U.S. Department of Housing and Urban Development responsible for administering aid for building and financing new and rehabilitated housing and for preserving existing housing.

Office of Initial Patent Examination. The section of the U.S. Patent and Trademark Office that determines whether a new patent application is in the correct form, whether the claims are dependent or independent, how much the application fee should be, and to which examining group the application should be assigned. — Abbr. OIPE.

Office of Labor-Management Standards. The division of the Employment Standards Administration in the U.S. Department of Labor responsible for enforcing the Labor–Management Reporting and Disclosure Act of 1959, which establishes standards for labor-union management and financial operations. • The Act sets out a list of union-members' rights, including the right to fair elections of union leaders, the right to know about the union's administrative policies and financial transactions, and the right to have union funds safeguarded. — Abbr. OLMS. See EMPLOYMENT STANDARDS ADMINISTRATION.

Office of Management and Budget. An office in the Executive Office of the President responsible for helping the President prepare the annual federal budget and supervising its administration. • It was originally established by Reorganization Plan No.1 of 1939 as the Bureau of the Budget. — Abbr. OMB.

Office of Medical Services. A unit in the U.S. Department of State responsible for providing primary healthcare services for the Department's overseas employees and their eligible family members. — Abbr. MED.

Office of National Drug Control Policy. An office in the Executive Office of the President responsible for coordinating efforts at federal, state, and local levels to control illegal drug abuse and for devising national antidrug activities. • The office was created by the National Narcotics Leadership Act of 1988. 21 USCA §§ 1701–1713. — Abbr. ONDCP.

Office of Oceanic and Atmospheric Research. See NATIONAL OCEANIC AND ATMOSPHERIC ADMINISTRATION.

Office of Passport Services. See BUREAU OF CONSULAR AFFAIRS.

Office of Personnel Management. The independent federal agency that administers the personnel system of the government by helping agencies recruit and evaluate employees; manage retirement and health-benefit systems; coordinate temporary assignments; conduct investigations; and develop leadership in the federal executive service. • The agency was established by Reorganization Plan No. 2 of 1978 and given various functions of the former U.S. Civil Service Commission by Executive Order 12107 of 1978. — Abbr. OPM. See CIVIL SERVICE COMMISSION.

Office of Policy Development. An office in the Executive Office of the President comprising the Domestic Policy Council and the National Economic Council. • It was established in 1993 by Executive Order 12859. — Abbr. OPD.

Office of Private Sector Liaison. A unit in the U.S. Department of Homeland Security responsible for working with individual businesses through trade associations and other nongovernmental organizations on matters of security.

Office of Protocol. A unit in the U.S. Department of State responsible for advising the President, the Vice President, the Secretary of State, and other U.S. officials on matters of custom and decorum, and for planning and hosting state dinners and other affairs, esp. involving foreign heads of state and other diplomats. • The Office also manages the Blair House, where diplomatic visitors often stay. It is run by the Chief of Protocol.

Office of Public and Indian Housing. A unit in the U.S. Department of Housing and Urban Development responsible for providing technical assistance and operating subsidies to public-housing agencies and Indian housing authorities in developing low-income housing. — Abbr. PIH.

Office of Science and Technology Policy. An office in the Executive Office of the President responsible for advising the President on scientific, engineering, and technological development and for coordinating research and development programs. • The office was created by the National Science and Technology Policy, Organization, and Priorities Act of 1976. — Abbr. OSTP.

Office of Special Counsel. An independent federal agency that investigates activities prohibited by the civil-service laws, rules, and regulations and, if the investigation warrants it, litigates the matter before the Merit Systems Protection Board. • The agency was established by Reorganization Plan No. 2 of 1978. — Abbr. OSC.

Office of Special Investigations. A component of the criminal division of the Department of Justice that identifies and investigates suspected perpetrators of human-rights violations abroad, after the suspects have entered, or tried to enter, the United States. • Originally created in 1948 to seek out Nazi and Axis persecutors, the Office's mission has since been expanded to include other transgressors of human rights. — Abbr. OSI.

Office of State and Local Government Coordination. A unit in the U.S. Department of Homeland Security responsible for coordinating security matters with state and local governments.

Office of Surface Mining Reclamation and Enforcement. A unit in the U.S. Department of the Interior responsible for protecting against the adverse effects of surface coal mining by enforcing laws relating to surface mining and restoration and by assisting states and local governments, which have primary responsibility in this area. — Abbr. OSM.

Office of Tax-Shelter Analysis. An office in the U.S. Internal Revenue Service responsible for identifying and investigating questionable tax shelters. • The office was created in 2000. — Abbr. OTSA.

Office of Technology Assessment. A former office in the legislative branch of the federal government responsible for analyzing public-policy issues relating to science and technology. • The Office was active from 1972 to 1995. — Abbr. OTA.

Office of Technology Policy. See TECHNOLOGY ADMINISTRATION.

Office of the Comptroller of the Currency. An office in the U.S. Department of the Treasury responsible for regulating approximately 2,600 national banks by examining them; approving or denying applications for bank charters, branches, or mergers; closing banks that fail to follow rules and regulations; and regulating banking practices. — Abbr. OCC.

Office of the United States Trade Representative. An office in the Executive Office of the President responsible for setting and administering overall trade policy. • It was established under Reorganization Plan No. 3 of 1979. 19 USCA § 2171.

Office of Thrift Supervision. An office in the U.S. Department of the Treasury responsible for regulating and examining thrift institutions to ensure that they are financially sound. — Abbr. OTS.

Office of Workers' Compensation Programs. The division of the Employment Standards Administration in the U.S. Department of Labor responsible for processing and adjudicating claims under the Federal Employees' Compensation Act, the Longshore and Harbor Workers' Compensation Act, the Black Lung Benefits Reform Act, and similar worker-benefits statutes and regulations. — Abbr. OWCP. See EMPLOYMENT STANDARDS ADMINISTRATION.

office practice. (1872) A law practice that primarily involves handling matters outside of court, such as negotiating and drafting contracts, preparing wills and trusts, setting up corporations and partnerships, and advising on tax or employment issues; a transactional-law practice.

office practitioner. (1933) A lawyer who does not litigate; an attorney whose work is accomplished primarily in the office, without court appearances. — Also termed *office lawyer*; *transactional lawyer*.

officer. (14c) **1.** A person who holds an office of trust, authority, or command. • In public affairs, the term refers esp. to a person holding public office under a national, state, or local government, and authorized by that government to exercise some specific function. In corporate law, the term refers esp. to a person elected or appointed by the board of directors to manage the daily operations of a corporation, such as a CEO, president, secretary, or treasurer. Cf. DIRECTOR (2).

acting officer. One performing the duties of an office — usu. temporarily — but who has no claim of title to the office.

administrative officer. **1.** An officer of the executive department of government, usu. of inferior rank. **2.** A ministerial or executive officer, as distinguished from a judicial officer. **3.** *Family law.* An official, other than a judge, who is appointed to preside over child-support matters. See CHILD-SUPPORT-ENFORCEMENT AGENCY. Cf. MASTER (2); JUDGE.

attendance officer. See TRUANCY OFFICER.

chief executive officer. See CHIEF EXECUTIVE OFFICER.

constitutional officer. A government official whose office is created by a constitution, rather than by a statute; one whose term of office is fixed and defined by a constitution.

corporate officer. An officer of a corporation, such as a CEO, president, secretary, or treasurer.

county officer. An officer whose authority and jurisdiction are confined to the limits of the county served.

court officer. See OFFICER OF THE COURT.

de facto officer. See *officer de facto*.

de jure officer. See *officer de jure*.

escrow officer. See *escrow agent* under AGENT (2).

executive officer. See EXECUTIVE (2).

fiscal officer. **1.** The person (such as a state or county treasurer) charged with the collection and distribution of public money. **2.** The person (such as a chief financial officer) whose duties are to oversee the financial matters of a corporation or business.

health officer. See HEALTH OFFICER.

hearing officer. **1.** ADMINISTRATIVE-LAW JUDGE. **2.** See *judicial officer* (3).

inferior officer. **1.** An officer who is subordinate to another officer. **2.** A United States officer appointed by the President, by a court, or by the head of a federal department. • Senate confirmation is not required. See *United States officer*.

judicial officer. (17c) **1.** A judge or magistrate. **2.** Any officer of the court, such as a bailiff or court reporter. **3.** A person, usu. an attorney, who serves in an appointive capacity at the pleasure of an appointing judge, and whose actions and decisions are reviewed by that judge. — Also termed *magistrate; referee; special master; commissioner; hearing officer.*

juvenile officer. (1911) A juvenile-court employee, sometimes a social worker or probation officer, who works with the judge to direct and develop the court's child-welfare work. — Also termed *county agent.*

law-enforcement officer. See LAW-ENFORCEMENT OFFICER.

legislative officer. **1.** A member of a federal, state, or municipal legislative body. **2.** A government official whose duties relate primarily to the enactment of laws, such as a federal or state senator, representative, or assembly member. • State and federal constitutions generally restrict legislative officers' duties to the enactment of legislation. But legislative officers occasionally exercise judicial functions, such as presenting or hearing cases of impeachment of other government officers.

ministerial officer. An officer who primarily executes mandates issued by the officer's superiors. • One who performs specified legal duties when the appropriate conditions have been met, but who does not exercise personal judgment or discretion in performing those duties.

municipal officer. A person who occupies a municipal office — usu. mandated by statute or charter — and who may be required to take an oath and exercise sovereign authority in carrying out public duties, with compensation incident to the office irrespective of the actual services rendered.

officer de facto (di **fak**-toh). **1.** An officer who exercises the duties of an office under color of an appointment or election, but who has failed to qualify for office for any one of various reasons, as by being under the required age, having failed to take the oath, having not furnished a required bond, or having taken office under a statute later declared unconstitutional. **2.** *Corporations.* One who is acting under color of right and with apparent authority, but who is not legally a corporate officer. • The corporation is bound by all acts and contracts of an officer de facto in the same way as it is with those of an officer de jure. — Also termed *de facto officer.*

officer de jure (di **juur**-ee). **1.** An officer who exercises the duties of an office for which the holder has fulfilled all the qualifications. **2.** A duly authorized corporate officer. — Also termed *de jure officer.*

peace officer. See PEACE OFFICER.

police officer. See POLICE OFFICER.

presiding officer. See PRESIDING OFFICER (3) under OFFICER (2).

principal officer. **1.** An officer with the most authority of the officers being considered for some purpose. **2.** A United States officer appointed by the President with the advice and consent of the Senate. — Also termed *primary officer.* See *United States officer.*

probation officer. A government officer who supervises the conduct of a probationer.

recording officer. See SECRETARY (3).

safety officer. An OSHA employee responsible for investigating the safety practices and procedures at a place of business. See OCCUPATIONAL SAFETY AND HEALTH ACT OF 1970.

state officer. **1.** A person whose authority or jurisdiction extends to the general public or state as a whole, as distinguished from an officer whose authority and jurisdiction are confined to the limits of a particular political subdivision. **2.** An officer exercising authority under a state — rather than the federal — government.

subordinate officer. **1.** An officer ranking below and performing under the direction of another officer. **2.** An independent officer subject only to statutory direction.

truancy officer. See TRUANCY OFFICER.

trust officer. A trust-company official responsible for administering funds held by the company as a trustee.

United States officer. An officer appointed under the authority of the federal government; specif., an officer appointed in the manner described in Article II, section 2, of the U.S. Constitution.

2. *Military law.* One who holds a commission in the armed services, or a military post higher than that of the lowest ranks; a person who has a command in the armed forces. — Also termed *military officer.*

brevet officer (brə-**vet** *or* **brev**-it). A military officer who holds a nominal rank above that for which the person is paid.

commissioned officer. An officer in the armed forces who holds grade and office under a presidential commission.

general officer. A military officer whose command extends to a body of forces composed of several regiments. • Examples are generals, lieutenant-generals, major-generals, and brigadiers.

legal officer. **1.** The officer responsible for handling military justice within a command. **2.** The adviser and assistant to a commanding officer on military-law matters. **3.** Any commissioned officer of the Navy, Marine Corps, or Coast Guard who has been designated to perform legal duties for a command.

noncommissioned officer. An enlisted person in the Army, Air Force, or Marine Corps in certain pay grades above the lowest pay grade. ● Examples are sergeants and corporals.

officer of the day. An officer who has charge, for the time being, of the guard, prisoners, and police of a military force or camp. — Also termed *orderly officer*.

officer of the guard. A commissioned officer whose detail is to command the guard of a military force or camp. ● The officer of the guard is under the command of the officer of the day.

orderly officer. See *officer of the day*.

petty officer. An enlisted person in the Navy or Coast Guard with a pay-grade of E-4 or higher.

preliminary-inquiry officer. The person, usu. an officer, who conducts a preliminary inquiry.

presiding officer. 1. The president of the court in a special court-martial that does not have a military judge. **2.** In a court-martial with a military judge, the military judge. **3.** An officer who presides, esp. over a civilian court or deliberative assembly. See CHAIR (1); PRESIDE.

superior commissioned officer. A commissioned officer who is superior in command or rank.

warrant officer. 1. A person who holds a commission or warrant in a warrant-officer grade. ● A warrant officer's rank is below a second lieutenant or ensign but above cadets, midshipmen, and enlisted personnel. **2.** See SERGEANT-AT-ARMS (4).

officer of the court. (16c) A person who is charged with upholding the law and administering the judicial system. ● Typically, *officer of the court* refers to a judge, clerk, bailiff, sheriff, or the like, but the term also applies to a lawyer, who is obliged to obey court rules and who owes a duty of candor to the court. — Also termed *court officer*.

officer of the peace. See PEACE OFFICER.

officer's report. See REPORT.

official (ə-**fish**-əl), *adj.* (16c) **1.** Of or relating to an office or position of trust or authority <official duties>. **2.** Authorized or approved by a proper authority <a company's official policy>.

official, *n.* (14c) **1.** One who holds or is invested with a public office; a person elected or appointed to carry out some portion of a government's sovereign powers. — Also termed *public official*. **2.** One authorized to act for a corporation or organization, esp. in a subordinate capacity. **3.** (*usu. cap.*) OFFICIAL PRINCIPAL.

official bond. See BOND (2).

official-capacity suit. See SUIT.

official corruption. See *official misconduct* under MISCONDUCT.

Official Gazette. *Patents & Trademarks.* Either of two weekly publications of the U.S. Patent and Trademark Office: one for patents, publishing abstracts of new patents; and one for trademarks, publishing samples of trademarks proposed for registration. — Abbr. OG.

official liability. See LIABILITY.

official misconduct. See MISCONDUCT.

official newspaper. See NEWSPAPER.

official principal. (*usu. cap.*) *Eccles. law.* A person appointed by an archbishop, bishop, or archdeacon to exercise jurisdiction in and preside over an ecclesiastical court. — Sometimes shortened to *official*.

official privilege. See PRIVILEGE (1).

official report. See REPORT (3).

official shorthand writer. See COURT REPORTER (1).

official use. See USE (4).

officio. See EX OFFICIO.

officious intermeddler (ə-**fish**-əs). (18c) A person who confers a benefit on another without being requested or having a legal duty to do so, and who therefore has no legal grounds to demand restitution for the benefit conferred. — Sometimes shortened to *intermeddler*. — Also termed (archaically) *volunteer*.

officiousness (ə-**fish**-əs-nəs), *n.* (16c) Interference in the affairs of others without justification under the circumstances. — **officious,** *adj.*

officious testament. See TESTAMENT.

officious will. See *officious testament* under TESTAMENT.

off-label use. Use of prescription medicine or medical products for conditions and in circumstances not approved by the Food and Drug Administration.

off point. (1951) Not discussing the precise issue at hand; irrelevant. Cf. ON POINT.

off-premises license. See *off-sale license* under LICENSE (2).

off-sale license. See LICENSE (2).

offset, *n.* (18c) Something (such as an amount or claim) that balances or compensates for something else; SETOFF.

offset, *vb.* (17c) To balance or calculate against; to compensate for <the gains offset the losses>.

offset account. See ACCOUNT.

offshore asset-protection trust. See *asset-protection trust* (1) under TRUST (3).

offshore trust. See *foreign-situs trust* under TRUST.

offspring. (bef. 12c) Children; issue; progeny.

off-the-board, *adj.* See OFF-BOARD.

off the record. 1. (Of a statement, comment, or testimony) not recorded as official evidence of a proceeding, such as a trial or deposition. **2.** (Of a statement) not intended for quotation or attribution. • In either sense, whenever the phrase appears before the noun it modifies, it should be hyphenated <off-the-record comments>. Cf. ON THE RECORD.

off-year election. See ELECTION (3).

OFHEO. *abbr.* OFFICE OF FEDERAL HOUSING ENTERPRISE OVERSIGHT.

OFR. *abbr.* Office of Federal Register. See FEDERAL REGISTER.

of record. (16c) **1.** Recorded in the appropriate records <counsel of record>. See *attorney of record* under ATTORNEY. **2.** (Of a court) that has proceedings taken down stenographically or otherwise documented <court of record>. See *court of record* under COURT.

of the essence. (18c) (Of a contractual requirement) so important that if the requirement is not met, the promisor will be held to have breached the contract and a rescission by the promisee will be justified <time is of the essence>.

OG. *abbr.* OFFICIAL GAZETTE.

OGE. See OFFICE OF GOVERNMENT ETHICS.

OHHLHC. *abbr.* OFFICE OF HEALTHY HOMES AND LEAD HAZARD CONTROL.

OID. *abbr.* ORIGINAL-ISSUE DISCOUNT.

oil-and-gas lease. See LEASE.

OIPE. *abbr.* OFFICE OF INITIAL PATENT EXAMINATION.

Oireachtas (air-ək-thəs *or* eer-ək-təs). The Parliament of the Republic of Ireland.

Old-Age and Survivors' Insurance. (1935) A system of insurance, subsidized by the federal government, that provides retirement benefits for persons who reach retirement age and payments to survivors upon the death of the insured. • This was the original name for the retirement and death benefits established by the Social Security Act of 1935. As the scope of these benefits expanded, the name changed to Old Age, Survivors, and Disability Insurance (OASDI), and then to Old Age, Survivors, Disability, and Health Insurance (OASDHI). Today, the system is most often referred to as *Social Security.* — Abbr. OASI. See SOCIAL SECURITY ACT.

old business. See *unfinished business* under BUSINESS.

old combination. See COMBINATION.

old-combination rejection. See REJECTION.

old-soldier's rule. See EGGSHELL-SKULL RULE.

old style. The system of ordering time according to the Julian method, introduced by Julius Caesar in 46 B.C., by which all years have 365 days except the years divisible by 4, which have 366 days. • This differs from the modern calendar in that it assumes that there are exactly 365.25 days in a year. But there are actually slightly less than 365.25 days in a solar year, so the old-style calendar adds too many days over time. The Julian calendar was reformed by Pope Gregory XIII in 1582. — Abbr. o.s. — Also termed *Julian calendar.* Cf. NEW STYLE.

oligarchy (ol-ə-gahr-kee), *n.* (16c) A government in which a small group of persons exercises control; the persons who constitute such a government. — **oligarchic, oligarchical,** *adj.*

oligopolistic price coordination. See CONSCIOUS PARALLELISM.

oligopoly (ol-ə-gop-ə-lee), *n.* (1895) Control or domination of a market by a few large sellers, creating high prices and low output similar to those found in a monopoly. Cf. MONOPOLY. — **oligopolistic,** *adj.* — **oligopolist,** *n.*

oligopsony (ol-ə-gop-sə-nee), *n.* Control or domination of a market by a few large buyers or customers. — **oligopsonistic,** *adj.* — **oligopsonist,** *n.*

OLMS. *abbr.* OFFICE OF LABOR-MANAGEMENT STANDARDS.

olograph, *n.* See HOLOGRAPH. — **olographic,** *adj.*

olographic will. See *holographic will* under WILL.

OMB. *abbr.* OFFICE OF MANAGEMENT AND BUDGET.

ombudsman (om-bədz-mən). (1872) **1.** An official appointed to receive, investigate, and report on private citizens' complaints about the government. **2.** A similar appointee in a nongovernmental organization (such as a company or university). — Often shortened to *ombuds.*

omission, *n.* (14c) **1.** A failure to do something; esp., a neglect of duty <the complaint alleged that the driver had committed various negligent acts and omissions>. **2.** The act of leaving something out <the contractor's omission of the sales price rendered the contract void>. **3.** The state of having been left out or of not having been done <his omission from the roster caused no harm>. **4.** Something that is left out, left undone, or otherwise neglected <the many omissions from the list were unintentional>. — Formerly also termed *omittance.* — **omit,** *vb.* — **omissive, omissible,** *adj.*

omittance. *Archaic.* OMISSION.

omnibus (om-ni-bəs), *adj.* (1842) Relating to or dealing with numerous objects or items at once; including many things or having various purposes.

omnibus bill. See BILL (3).

omnibus claim. See PATENT CLAIM.

omnibus clause. (1880) **1.** A provision in an automobile-insurance policy that extends coverage to all drivers operating the insured vehicle with the owner's permission.

> *statutory omnibus clause. Insurance.* An omnibus clause provided by statute.

2. RESIDUARY CLAUSE.

omnibus count. See COUNT.

omnibus hearing. See HEARING.

omnibus motion. See MOTION (1).

omnium (om-nee-əm), *n.* (18c) The total amount or value of the items in a combined fund or stock. ● The term is used primarily in mercantile law and in Great Britain.

OMVI. *abbr.* Operating a motor vehicle while intoxicated. See DRIVING UNDER THE INFLUENCE.

OMVUI. *abbr.* Operating a motor vehicle while under the influence. See DRIVING UNDER THE INFLUENCE.

on all fours. (Of a law case) squarely on point (with a precedent) on both facts and law; nearly identical in all material ways <our client's case is on all fours with the Supreme Court's most recent opinion>. Cf. WHITEHORSE CASE.

onboard bill of lading. See BILL OF LADING.

ONDCP. See OFFICE OF NATIONAL DRUG CONTROL POLICY.

on demand. (17c) When presented or upon request for payment <this note is payable on demand>. — Also termed *on call.* See PAYABLE.

one-action rule. In debtor-creditor law, the principle that when a debt is secured by real property, the creditor must foreclose on the collateral before proceeding against the debtor's unsecured assets.

one-book rule. The requirement or practice that only one version of the Sentencing Guidelines be used to calculate all aspects of a defendant's sentence.

one-court-of-justice doctrine. A principle in some states holding that there is but a single court in the state and that this court is composed of several divisions, such as the supreme court, the courts of appeals, and district courts, probate courts, and any other legislatively created courts. ● Michigan, for example, has embodied this doctrine in its constitution (art. VI, § 1). — Also termed *one court of justice.*

one-day, one-trial method. (1976) A system of summoning and using jurors whereby a person answers a jury summons and participates in the venire for one day only, unless the person is actually empaneled for a trial, in which event the juror's service lasts for the entire length of the trial. ● This system, which is used in several states, reduces the average term of service and expands the number of individual jurors called.

one-half plus one. See HALF PLUS ONE.

180-day rule. *Criminal procedure.* **1.** A rule that, in some jurisdictions, allows a person charged with a felony to be released on personal recognizance if the person has been in jail for 180 days without being brought to trial, and if the delay has not resulted from the defendant's own actions. **2.** A rule requiring all pending charges against a prison inmate to be brought to trial in 180 days or to be dismissed with prejudice.

one-month liquidation. See LIQUIDATION.

one-party consent rule. The principle that one party to a telephone or other conversation may secretly record the conversation. ● This principle applies in most but not all states.

one-person, one-vote rule. (1965) *Constitutional law.* The principle that the Equal Protection Clause requires legislative voting districts to have about the same population. *Reynolds v. Sims,* 377 U.S. 533, 84 S.Ct. 1362 (1964). — Also termed *one-man, one-vote rule.* See APPORTIONMENT.

onerous (oh-nər-əs *or* on-ər-əs), *adj.* (14c) **1.** Excessively burdensome or troublesome; causing hardship <onerous discovery requests>. **2.** Having or involving obligations that outweigh the advantages <onerous property>. **3.** *Civil law.* Done or given in return for something of equivalent value; supported by consideration <an onerous contract>. Cf. GRATUITOUS (1). — **onerousness**, *n.*

onerous cause. *Civil law.* An advantage obtained in exchange for a contractual obligation. See La. Civ. Code arts. 1909, 1967.

onerous contract. See CONTRACT.

onerous deed. See DEED.

onerous donation. See DONATION.

onerous gift. See GIFT.

onerous title. See TITLE (2).

onerous trust. See TRUST.

one-satisfaction rule. (1965) The principle that a plaintiff is only entitled to only one recovery for a particular harm, and that the plaintiff must elect a single remedy if the jury has awarded more than one. ● This rule is, for example, one of the foundations of a defendant's right to have a jury verdict reduced by the amount of any settlements the plaintiff has received from other entities for the same injury. — Also termed *single-recovery rule*.

one-subject rule. The principle that a statute should embrace only one topic, which should be stated in its title.

one-time charge. See *special charge* under CHARGE.

one-way ratchet theory. See RATCHET THEORY.

one-year rule. *Patents.* The statutory requirement that a patent application must be filed within one year after any publication, public use, sale, or offer for sale of the invention. ● If an inventor waits longer than a year, the patent is blocked by this "statutory bar." 35 USCA §§ 102(b).

ongoing earnings. See *operating earnings* under EARNINGS.

online scrip. See *Internet scrip* under SCRIP.

onomastic (on-ə-**mas**-tik), *adj.* (16c) **1.** Of or relating to names or nomenclature. **2.** (Of a signature on an instrument) in a handwriting different from that of the body of the document; esp., designating an autograph signature alone, as distinguished from the main text in a different hand or in typewriting. Cf. HOLOGRAPH; SYMBOLIC. — **onomastics** (for sense 1), *n.*

on or about. (17c) Approximately; at or around the time specified. ● This language is used in pleading to prevent a variance between the pleading and the proof, usu. when there is any uncertainty about the exact date of a pivotal event. When used in nonpleading contexts, the phrase is mere jargon.

on pain of. (14c) Or else suffer punishment for noncompliance. ● This phrase usu. follows a command or condition <ordered to cease operations on pain of a $2,000 fine>.

on point. (1927) Discussing the precise issue now at hand; apposite <this opinion is not on point as authority in our case>. — Also termed *in point*. Cf. OFF POINT.

on-premises license. See *on-sale license* under LICENSE (2).

on-sale bar. *Patents.* A statutory bar prohibiting patent eligibility if an invention was sold or offered for sale more than one year before the patent application is filed. 35 USCA § 102(b).

on-sale license. See LICENSE (2).

onset date. The beginning of a period of disability for purposes of disability payments by the Social Security Administration.

on the brief. (Of a lawyer) having participated in preparing a given brief. ● The names of all the lawyers on the brief are typically listed on the front cover.

on the floor. *Parliamentary law.* **1.** (Of a motion) under consideration; PENDING (2) <the motion is on the floor>. **2.** (Of a member) physically present at a meeting and attending to its deliberations <the senator is on the floor>.

on the merits. (18c) (Of a judgment) delivered after the court has heard and evaluated the evidence and the parties' substantive arguments.

on the pleadings. (18c) (Of a judgment) rendered for reasons that are apparent from the faces of the complaint and answer, without hearing or evaluating the evidence or the substantive arguments. See SUMMARY JUDGMENT.

on the record. 1. (Of a statement, comment, or testimony) recorded as official evidence of a proceeding, such as a trial or deposition. **2.** (Of a statement) intended for quotation or attribution. ● In either sense, whenever the phrase appears before the noun it modifies, it should be hyphenated <an on-the-record statement>. Cf. OFF THE RECORD.

onus (**oh**-nəs). (17c) **1.** A burden; a load. **2.** A disagreeable responsibility; an obligation. **3.** ONUS PROBANDI.

onus probandi (**oh**-nəs prə-**ban**-dı). [Latin] (18c) BURDEN OF PROOF. — Often shortened to *onus*.

OOH-DNR. *abbr.* See *out-of-hospital do-not-resuscitate order* under DO-NOT-RESUSCITATE ORDER.

op. *abbr.* (*often cap.*) **1.** OPINION (1). **2.** Opinions.

OPD. *abbr.* OFFICE OF POLICY DEVELOPMENT.

OPEC (**oh**-pek). *abbr.* Organization of Petroleum Exporting Countries.

open, *adj.* (bef. 12c) **1.** Manifest; apparent; notorious. **2.** Visible; exposed to public view; not clandestine. **3.** Not closed, settled, fixed, or terminated.

open account. See ACCOUNT.

open adoption. See ADOPTION.

open and notorious. (16c) **1.** NOTORIOUS (2). **2.** (Of adultery) known and recognized by the public and flouting the accepted standards of morality in the community.

open and notorious adultery. See ADULTERY.

open and notorious cohabitation. See *notorious cohabitation* under COHABITATION.

open and notorious possession. See *notorious possession* under POSSESSION.

open bid. See BID (2).

open brief. See BRIEF.

open check. See CHECK.

open closed shop. See SHOP.

open court. (15c) **1.** A court that is in session, presided over by a judge, attended by the parties and their attorneys, and engaged in judicial business.

● *Open court* usu. refers to a proceeding in which formal entries are made on the record. The term is distinguished from a court that is hearing evidence in camera or from a judge that is exercising merely magisterial powers. **2.** A court session that the public is free to attend. ● Most state constitutions have open-court provisions guaranteeing the public's right to attend trials.

open credit. See *revolving credit* under CREDIT (4).

open diplomacy. See DIPLOMACY.

open-door law. See SUNSHINE LAW.

open-end, *adj.* (1931) **1.** Allowing for future changes or additions <open-end credit plan>. **2.** Continually issuing or redeeming shares on demand at the current net asset value <open-end investment company>. — Also termed *open-ended*.

open-end credit plan. See CREDIT PLAN.

open-ended claim. See PATENT CLAIM.

open-end fund. See MUTUAL FUND.

open-end mortgage. See MORTGAGE.

open-end mortgage bond. See BOND (3).

open entry. See ENTRY (1).

open-fields doctrine. (1963) *Criminal procedure.* The rule permitting a warrantless search of the area outside a property owner's curtilage. ● Unless there is some other legal basis for the search, it must exclude the home and any adjoining land (such as a yard) that is within an enclosure or otherwise protected from public scrutiny. — Also termed *open-field doctrine; open-fields rule.* Cf. PLAIN-VIEW DOCTRINE.

open forum. 1. GOOD OF THE ORDER. **2.** PUBLIC FORUM.

open guaranty. See *continuing guaranty* under GUARANTY.

opening a judgment. A court's grant of a motion for a rehearing on the merits but keeping the court's decision in effect.

opening bidding. See OPENING THE BIDDING.

opening brief. See BRIEF.

opening brief on the merits. See *opening brief* under BRIEF.

opening statement. (1848) At the outset of a trial, an advocate's statement giving the fact-finder a preview of the case and of the evidence to be presented. ● Although the opening statement is not supposed to be argumentative, lawyers — purposefully or not — often include some form of argument. The term is thus sometimes referred to as *opening argument.*

opening the bidding. In a sheriff's sale of real property, the unethical practice of setting aside the concluded sale to accept a better post-sale offer. — Also termed *opening bidding.*

open letter of credit. See LETTER OF CREDIT.

open lewdness. See LEWDNESS.

open listing. See LISTING (1).

open market. See MARKET.

open-meeting law. See SUNSHINE LAW.

open memorandum. See MEMORANDUM.

open microphone. See GOOD OF THE ORDER.

open mortgage clause. See MORTGAGE CLAUSE.

open nominations. *Parliamentary law.* To begin taking nominations from the floor upon passage of a motion.

open order. See ORDER (8).

open-perils policy. See INSURANCE POLICY.

open policy. See *unvalued policy* under INSURANCE POLICY.

open possession. See *notorious possession* under POSSESSION.

open price. See PRICE.

open-public-records act. See OPEN-RECORDS ACT.

open-records act. A statute providing for public access to view and copy government records maintained by public agencies. — Also termed *open-public-records act.*

open seas. See *high seas* under SEA.

open season. (1846) A specific time of year when it is legal to hunt or catch game or fish.

open session. See SESSION (1).

open shop. See SHOP.

open-shop–closed-shop operation. See DOUBLE-BREASTED OPERATION.

open source, *adj.* (1998) Of or related to software that includes human-readable source code and can be freely revised.

open-source license. See LICENSE.

open-source software. (1998) Software that is usu. not sold for profit, includes both human-readable source code and machine-readable object code, and allows users to freely copy, modify, or distribute the software. ● Even though open-source software is made widely available for free, it may be protected by federal trademark law. *See Planetary Motion Inc. v. Techplosion Inc.,* 261 F.3d 1188 (11th Cir. 2001).

open space. (17c) Undeveloped (or mostly undeveloped) urban or suburban land that is set aside and permanently restricted to agricultural, recreational, or conservational uses. ● The land may be publicly or privately owned. Access may be restricted or unrestricted. Open spaces are not necessarily in a natural state: the term includes land used for public parks, gardens, farms, and pastures. But it does not include structures such as parking lots, swimming pools, or tennis courts.

open town. *Int'l law.* An undefended city in a combat zone that is laid open to the grasp of the attacking forces.

open union. See UNION.

open verdict. See VERDICT.

operability. *Patents.* The ability of an invention to work as described. ● A patent examiner may challenge the operability of an invention and require some proof, such as a demonstration of a working model.

operating agreement. *Oil & gas.* A contract among owners of the working interest in a producing oil or gas well setting forth the parties' agreements about drilling, development, operations, and accounting.

operating a motor vehicle under the influence. See DRIVING UNDER THE INFLUENCE.

operating a motor vehicle while intoxicated. See DRIVING UNDER THE INFLUENCE.

operating-cost ratio. The ratio between the net sales of a business and its operating costs.

operating earnings. See EARNINGS.

operating expense. See EXPENSE.

operating income. See *ordinary income* (1) under INCOME.

operating interest. See WORKING INTEREST.

operating lease. See LEASE.

operating profit. See PROFIT (1).

operating under the influence. See DRIVING UNDER THE INFLUENCE.

operating while intoxicated. See DRIVING UNDER THE INFLUENCE.

operational, *adj.* (1922) **1.** Engaged in operation; able to function. **2.** Ministerial.

operation of law. (17c) The means by which a right or a liability is created for a party regardless of the party's actual intent <because the court didn't rule on the motion for rehearing within 30 days, it was overruled by operation of law>.

operations clause. *Oil & gas.* A provision in an oil-and-gas lease specifying that the lease will not expire as long as oil-and-gas development continues on the leased property. See CONTINUOUS-OPERATIONS CLAUSE; WELL-COMPLETION CLAUSE.

operative, *adj.* (15c) **1.** Being in or having force or effect; esp., designating the part of a legal instrument that gives effect to the transaction involved <the operative provision of the contract>. **2.** Having principal relevance; essential to the meaning of the whole <*may* is the operative word of the statute>.

operative clause. See CLAUSE.

operative construction. 1. The interpretation of a writing or agreement, esp. a contract, statute, or regulation, that is being relied on by the parties, a court, or an administrative agency. **2.** *Patents.* A working embodiment of an invention, usu. used to conceptualize the invention and how it will work rather than to create a working model. **3.** The doctrine that the interpretation of a statute or regulation made by an administrative agency charged with enforcing it is entitled to judicial deference unless it is arbitrary and capricious.

operative fact. See FACT.

operative performance bond. See PERFORMANCE BOND.

operative trust. See *active trust* under TRUST.

operative words. In a transactional document, the words that actually effect the transaction.

OPIC. *abbr.* OVERSEAS PRIVATE INVESTMENT CORPORATION.

opinion. (14c) **1.** A court's written statement explaining its decision in a given case, usu. including the statement of facts, points of law, rationale, and dicta. — Abbr. op. — Also termed *judicial opinion.* See DECISION. Cf. JUDGMENT (1); RULING(1).

advisory opinion. (1837) **1.** A nonbinding statement by a court of its interpretation of the law on a matter submitted for that purpose. ● Federal courts are constitutionally prohibited from issuing advisory opinions by the case-or-controversy requirement, but other courts, such as the International Court of Justice, render them routinely. See CASE-OR-CONTROVERSY REQUIREMENT. **2.** A written statement, issued only by an administrator of an employee benefit plan, that interprets ERISA and applies it to a specific factual situation. ● Only the parties named in the request for the opinion can rely on it, and its reliability depends on the accuracy and completeness of all material facts.

concurring opinion. See CONCURRENCE (3).

depublished opinion. An intermediate appellate court's opinion that has been struck from the official reports, esp. by the highest court.

dissenting opinion. (1817) An opinion by one or more judges who disagree with the decision reached by the majority. — Often shortened to *dissent.* — Also termed *minority opinion.*

extrajudicial opinion. **1.** An opinion that is beyond the court's authority to render. ● Such opinions are void. **2.** A judge's personal or scholarly opinion expressed in a medium other than a judicial opinion.

majority opinion. (1882) An opinion joined in by more than half the judges considering a given case. — Also termed *main opinion*.

memorandum opinion. (1912) A unanimous appellate opinion that succinctly states the decision of the court; an opinion that briefly reports the court's conclusion, usu. without elaboration because the decision follows a well-established legal principle or does not relate to any point of law. — Also termed *memorandum decision*; *memorandum disposition*; (slang) *memdispo*.

minority opinion. See *dissenting opinion*.

per curiam opinion (pər **kyoor**-ee-əm). (1860) An opinion handed down by an appellate court without identifying the individual judge who wrote the opinion. — Sometimes shortened to *per curiam*.

plurality opinion. (1908) An opinion lacking enough judges' votes to constitute a majority, but receiving more votes than any other opinion.

qualified opinion. See QUALIFIED OPINION.

seriatim opinions (seer-ee-**ay**-tim). (1832) A series of opinions written individually by each judge on the bench, as opposed to a single opinion speaking for the court as a whole.

slip opinion. 1. A court opinion that is published individually after being rendered and then collectively in advance sheets before being released for publication in a reporter. • Unlike an unpublished opinion, a slip opinion can usu. be cited as authority. — Also termed *slipsheet*. Cf. ADVANCE SHEETS. **2.** *Archaic.* A preliminary draft of a court opinion not yet ready for publication. — Also termed *slip decision*. Cf. *unpublished opinion*.

unpublished opinion. (1849) An opinion that the court has specifically designated as not for publication. • Court rules usu. prohibit citing an unpublished opinion as authority. Such an opinion is considered binding only on the parties to the particular case in which it is issued. Cf. *slip opinion*.

2. A formal expression of judgment or advice based on an expert's special knowledge; esp., a document, usu. prepared at a client's request, containing a lawyer's understanding of the law that applies to a particular case. — Also termed *opinion letter*.

adverse opinion. An outside auditor's opinion that a company's financial statements do not conform with generally accepted accounting principles or do not accurately reflect the company's financial position.

audit opinion. A certified public accountant's opinion regarding the audited financial statements of an entity.

comfort opinion. *Securities.* An attorney's written opinion that there is no reason to believe that the registration statement contains any material misrepresentations or omissions that would violate section 11 of the Securities Act of 1933. • The attorney usu. participates in the registration statement's preparation and confers with the securities issuer's representatives, underwriters, and public accountants before writing the opinion. The comfort opinion's purpose is to reassure the parties that the registration statement complies with securities laws; it is not part of the statement and is usu. not included.

coverage opinion. A lawyer's opinion on whether a particular event is covered by a given insurance policy.

infringement opinion. *Patents.* A patent attorney's opinion about the probable outcome of an infringement hearing or trial on whether a particular product or process infringes one or more claims of another's patent.

legal opinion. (18c) A written document in which an attorney provides his or her understanding of the law as applied to assumed facts. • The attorney may be a private attorney or attorney representing the state or other governmental entity. Private attorneys frequently render legal opinions on the ownership of real estate or minerals, insurance coverage, and corporate transactions. A party may be entitled to rely on a legal opinion, depending on factors such as the identity of the parties to whom the opinion was addressed, the nature of the opinion, and the law governing the opinion. See *coverage opinion*.

patentability opinion. *Patents.* A patent attorney's or patent agent's opinion on the patent office's probable holding about the allowability of a patent application's claims. • The opinion is almost a mini-examination report because it is based on consideration of the invention's subject matter, prior art, etc.

title opinion. (1927) A lawyer's or title company's opinion on the state of title for a given piece of real property, usu. describing whether the title is clear and marketable or whether it is encumbered. See TITLE SEARCH.

unqualified opinion. An audit opinion given by an accountant who is satisfied that the financial statements reviewed were fairly presented and consistent with the previous year, and that the audit was performed in accordance with generally accepted auditing standards.

validity opinion. *Patents.* A patent attorney's opinion about the likelihood that a patent or patent claim will be invalidated in light of evidence suggesting obviousness, lack of invention, unenforceability, etc.

3. A person's thought, belief, or inference, esp. a witness's view about a facts in dispute, as opposed to personal knowledge of the facts themselves. — Also termed (in sense 3) *conclusion*. See *opinion evidence* under EVIDENCE.

expert opinion. An opinion offered by a witness whose knowledge, skill, experience, training, and education qualify the witness to help a fact-finder understand the evidence or decide a factual dispute. See *expert witness* under WITNESS.

fixed opinion. (1807) A bias or prejudice that disqualifies a potential juror.

opinion evidence. See EVIDENCE.

opinion letter. See OPINION (2).

opinion rule. (1896) *Evidence.* The principle that a witness should testify to facts, not opinions, and that a nonexpert witness's opinions are often excludable from evidence. ● Traditionally, this principle is regarded as one of the important exclusionary rules in evidence law. It is based on the idea that a witness who has observed data should provide the most factual evidence possible, leaving the jury to draw inferences and conclusions from the evidence. Under this system, the witness's opinion is unnecessary. Today, opinions are admissible if rationally based on a witness's perceptions and helpful to the fact-finder.

opinion testimony. See TESTIMONY.

opinion work product. See WORK PRODUCT.

OPM. *abbr.* OFFICE OF PERSONNEL MANAGEMENT.

oppignorate (ə-**pig**-nə-rayt), *vb. Archaic.* To pawn or pledge. — Also spelled *oppignerate.* Cf. PIGNORATE.

opponent. (16c) **1.** An adverse party in a contested matter. **2.** A party that is challenging the admissibility of evidence. ● In this sense, the word is an antonym of *proponent.* **3.** *Parliamentary law.* A member who speaks against a pending motion. Cf. PROPONENT (3).

opportunity. The fact that the alleged doer of an act was present at the time and place of the act.

opportunity cost. See COST (1).

opportunity to be heard. (17c) The chance to appear in a court or other tribunal and present evidence and argument before being deprived of a right by governmental authority. ● The opportunity to be heard is a fundamental requirement of procedural due process. It ordinarily includes the right to receive fair notice of the hearing, to secure the assistance of counsel, and to cross-examine adverse witnesses. See *procedural due process* under DUE PROCESS.

opposer. 1. *Intellectual property.* One who formally seeks to prevent the grant of a patent or the registration of a trademark. **2.** *Hist.* APPOSER.

opposition. 1. *Patents.* An action or procedure by which a third party can request a patent application's refusal or an issued patent's annulment. ● Most countries allow opposition in some form. **2.** *Trademarks.* A procedure by which a third party can contest a trademark after it has been approved but before it has been placed on the Principal Register. Cf. CANCELLATION.

oppression. (14c) **1.** The act or an instance of unjustly exercising authority or power. **2.** An offense consisting in the abuse of discretionary authority by a public officer who has an improper motive, as a result of which a person is injured. ● This offense does not include extortion, which is typically a more serious crime. **3.** *Contracts.* Coercion to enter into an illegal contract. ● Oppression is grounds for the recovery of money paid or property transferred under an illegal contract. See DURESS; UNCONSCIONABILITY. **4.** *Corporations.* Unfair treatment of minority shareholders (esp. in a close corporation) by the directors or those in control of the corporation. — Also termed (in sense 4) *shareholder oppression.* See FREEZEOUT. — **oppress**, *vb.* — **oppressive**, *adj.*

oppressive child labor. See CHILD LABOR.

oppressor. (14c) A public official who unlawfully or wrongfully exercises power under color of authority in a way that causes a person harm; one who commits oppression.

OPRA. *abbr.* OPTIONS PRICE REPORTING AUTHORITY.

optimal-use value. See VALUE (2).

opt in, *vb.* (1966) To choose to participate in (something) <when the choice of settling or not settling came, the Joneses opted in, hoping to avoid a lengthy trial>.

option, *n.* (17c) **1.** The right or power to choose; something that may be chosen <the lawyer was running out of options for settlement>. **2.** An offer that is included in a formal or informal contract; esp., a contractual obligation to keep an offer open for a specified period, so that the offeror cannot revoke the offer during that period <the option is valid because it is supported by consideration>. — Also termed *option contract;* (redundantly) *time option.* See *irrevocable offer* under OFFER; OPTION AGREEMENT. **3.** The right conveyed by such a contract <Pitts declined to exercise his option to buy the house>. **4.** The right (but not the obligation) to buy or sell a given quantity of securities, commodities, or other assets at a fixed price within a specified time <trading stock options is a speculative business>. Cf. FUTURES CONTRACT.

American option. An option that can be exercised on any day, including its expiration date. — Also termed *American-style option.* Cf. *European option.*

call option. An option to buy something (esp. securities) at a fixed price even if the market rises; the right to require another to sell. — Often shortened to *call*.

cash-value option. The right of a life-insurance policyholder to surrender the policy for its cash value at a specified time or at any time.

commodity option. An option to buy or sell a commodity.

European option. An option that can be exercised only on its expiration date. — Also termed *European-style option.* Cf. *American option.*

futures option. An option to buy or sell a futures contract.

lease option. In a contract for rental property, a clause that gives the renter the right to buy the property at a fixed price, usu. at or after a fixed time. — Also termed *lease with an option to purchase.*

naked option. A call option that grants another the right to buy stock even though the option-giver does not own the stock to back up that commitment. — Also termed *uncovered option.*

nonforfeiture option. A policyholder's option, upon the lapse of premium payments, to continue an insurance policy for a shorter period than the original term, to surrender the policy for its cash value, to continue the policy for a reduced amount, or to take some other action rather than forfeit the policy.

option to purchase real property. A contract by which an owner of realty enters an agreement with another allowing the latter to buy the property at a specified price within a specified time, or within a reasonable time in the future, but without imposing an obligation to purchase upon the person to whom it is given.

put option. An option to sell something (esp. securities) at a fixed price even if the market declines; the right to require another to buy. — Often shortened to *put.* Cf. *put bond* under BOND (3).

seller's option. A special stock-exchange transaction that gives the seller the right to deliver the security within a specified period, usu. 5 to 60 days.

settlement option. *Insurance.* A life-insurance-policy clause providing choices in the method of paying benefits to a beneficiary, as by lump-sum payment or periodic installments.

stock option. See STOCK OPTION.

uncovered option. See *naked option.*

option, *vb.* (1888) To grant or take an option on (something) <Ward optioned his first screenplay to the studio for $50,000>.

option agreement. *Corporations.* A share-transfer restriction that commits the shareholder to sell, but not the corporation or other shareholders to buy, the shareholder's shares at a fixed price when a specified event occurs. Cf. BUY–SELL AGREEMENT (2); OPTION (2).

optional bond. See BOND (3).

optional completeness, rule of. See RULE OF OPTIONAL COMPLETENESS.

optional-completeness doctrine. See RULE OF OPTIONAL COMPLETENESS.

optional writ. See WRIT.

option contract. See OPTION (2).

optionee (op-shə-**nee**). One who receives an option from another. — Also termed *option-holder.*

optionor (**op**-shə-nər *or* op-shə-**nor**). One who grants an option to another. — Also spelled *optioner.* — Also termed *option-giver.*

option premium. See PREMIUM (4).

option spread. *Securities.* The difference between the option price and the market price of the underlying stock when the option is exercised. See SPREAD.

Options Price Reporting Authority. A national market-system plan approved by the SEC for collecting and disseminating last-sale and quotation information on options traded on a five-member exchange consisting of the American Stock Exchange, the Chicago Board of Options Exchange, the New York Stock Exchange, the Pacific Stock Exchange, and the Philadelphia Stock Exchange. — Abbr. OPRA.

option tender bond. See *put bond* under BOND (3).

option to purchase real property. See OPTION.

opt out, *vb.* (1922) To choose not to participate in (something) <with so many plaintiffs opting out of the class, the defendant braced itself for multiplicitous lawsuits>.

opt-out class. See CLASS (4).

opt-out statute. *Bankruptcy.* A state law that limits the exemptions that a debtor who has filed for bankruptcy can claim to those provided by state and local bankruptcy laws, and nonbankruptcy federal law. ● The federal bankruptcy code includes an "opt-out" provision that allows states to choose not to adopt the federal exemptions. 11 U.S.C. § 522(b). — Also termed *opt-out legislation.*

opus (**oh**-pəs), *n.* [Latin "work"] (18c) A product of work or labor; esp., an artistic, literary, or musical work or composition. Pl. **opuses, opera** (**ah**-pə-rə *or* **oh**-pə-rə).

opus novum (**oh**-pəs **noh**-vəm). [Latin "new work"] *Civil law*. A structure newly built on land. Pl. *opera nova*. See NOVI OPERIS NUNTIATIO.

O.R. *abbr*. Own recognizance; on one's own recognizance <the prosecutor agreed not to object to releasing the suspect O.R.>. See RECOGNIZANCE; RELEASE ON RECOGNIZANCE.

oral, *adj*. (17c) Spoken or uttered; not expressed in writing. Cf. PAROL.

oral argument. (1823) An advocate's spoken presentation before a court (esp. an appellate court) supporting or opposing the legal relief at issue. — Also termed (in BrE) *hearing*.

oral confession. See CONFESSION.

oral contract. See *parol contract* (1) under CONTRACT.

oral deposition. See DEPOSITION.

oral evidence. See *testimonial evidence* under EVIDENCE.

oral trust. See TRUST.

oral will. See WILL.

Orange Book. *Patents*. A list of patents on drugs or drug products for which generic-drug applications may be submitted to the Food and Drug Administration. • The expiration dates of the patents are also listed. An applicant may submit a generic-drug application at any time, but the applicant must either accept deferral of FDA approval until the patent expires or contest the validity of the patent. The Orange Book's official title is *Approved Drug Products With Therapeutic Equivalence Evaluations*.

orator (**or**-ə-tər), *n*. (15c) **1.** *Roman law*. (*ital*.) An advocate or pleader. **2.** *Hist*. A plaintiff or petitioner in an action in chancery.

ordeal. (bef. 12c) *Hist*. A primitive form of trial in which an accused person was subjected to a usu. dangerous or painful physical test, the result being considered a divine revelation of the person's guilt or innocence. • The participants believed that God would reveal a person's culpability by protecting an innocent person from some or all consequences of the ordeal. The ordeal was commonly used in Europe until the 13th century, but only sporadically after 1215, when the Fourth Lateran Council forbade the clergy from participating in ordeals. — Also termed *trial by ordeal*; *judicium Dei* ("judgment of God"); *vulgaris purgatio*.

bread-and-cheese ordeal. See *ordeal of the morsel*.

ordeal by fire. An ordeal in which the accused person was forced to hold a piece of hot metal or to walk barefoot across a hot surface, the judgment of guilt or innocence depending on how quickly and cleanly the person's hands or feet healed. • Typically the person's hand was bandaged and, upon the bandage's removal three days later, was examined for festers (indicating guilt). — Also termed *fire ordeal*; *ordeal by hot iron*; *ordeal of fire*.

ordeal by hot iron. See *ordeal by fire*.

ordeal by water. **1.** An ordeal in which guilt or innocence depended on whether the accused person floated or sank after being submerged in cold water. • A priest would first consecrate the pool of water, adjuring it to receive the innocent but reject the guilty. An accused who sank was declared innocent; one who floated was adjudged guilty because floating revealed the water's (and therefore God's) rejection of the person. This type of ordeal was used esp. in witchcraft trials. — Also termed *ordeal by cold water*; *cold-water ordeal*; *ordeal of cold water*; (in ecclesiastical law) *aquae frigidae judicium*. **2.** An ordeal in which guilt or innocence was determined by how quickly the accused person's arm healed after being placed in boiling water. • Often the person was forced to retrieve a stone from the bottom of a pot of boiling water. The person's hand and arm were then bandaged and, upon the bandage's removal three days later, were examined for festers (indicating guilt). — Also termed (in sense 2) *ordeal by hot water*; *hot-water ordeal*; *ordeal of hot water*; (in both senses) *water ordeal*; *ordeal of water*; (in ecclesiastical law) *aquae ferventis judicium*; *aenum*.

ordeal of the morsel. An ordeal in which the person who was to make the proof was given a one-ounce piece of bread or cheese that a priest had solemnly charged to stick in the throat of the guilty. • A person who choked was declared guilty; a person who did not was declared innocent. — Also termed *corsnaed*; *corsned*; *trial by corsnaed*; *judicial morsel*; *morsel of execration*.

single ordeal. An ordeal prescribed for someone accused of a less serious crime and involving less risk or torture than a triple ordeal. • For example, a single ordeal by fire required the accused to pick up a red-hot piece of iron weighing one pound, while a triple ordeal involved a piece of iron weighing three pounds.

triple ordeal. An ordeal prescribed for someone accused of a more serious crime and involving more risk or torture than a single ordeal. • For example, a triple ordeal by water required the accused to submerge an arm into boiling water up to the elbow, while a single ordeal required the arm to be submerged only to the wrist. — Also termed *threefold ordeal*.

order, *n*. (16c) **1.** A command, direction, or instruction. See MANDATE (1). **2.** A written direction or command delivered by a court or judge. • The word generally embraces final decrees as well as interlocutory directions or commands. — Also termed *court order*; *judicial order*. See MANDAMUS.

administrative order. 1. An order issued by a government agency after an adjudicatory hearing. **2.** An agency regulation that interprets or applies a statutory provision.

affiliation order. See *filiation order*.

alternative order. An order commanding the person to whom it is directed either to do a specific thing or to show cause why the court should not order it to be done.

antiharassment order. A type of restraining order available to victims of harassment or stalking, usu. forbidding a person to contact, surveil, or approach the victim.

blanket order. See BLANKET ORDER (1).

common order. See *conditional judgment* under JUDGMENT.

decretal order (di-**kree**-təl). A court of chancery's interlocutory order that is issued on motion of a party and has the effect of a final decree. See *decree nisi* under DECREE.

dismissal order. A court order ending a lawsuit without a decision on the merits. — Also termed *order of dismissal*.

docket order. A court order memorialized only as an entry on the docket sheet.

ex parte order (eks **pahr**-tee). (18c) An order made by the court upon the application of one party to an action without notice to the other.

filiation order. *Family law.* A court's determination of paternity, usu. including a direction to pay child support. ● Governments usu. seek filiation orders so that some or all of the public funds spent on the child's welfare can be recovered from a nonmarital child's father. Until the early 20th century, municipalities, not the state, had the legal duty to support the poor, including unwed mothers and their children. In some states, two judges had to determine who an unacknowledged child's father was before the municipality could recover its expenditures. — Also termed *affiliation order*; *order of filiation*.

final order. (16c) An order that is dispositive of the entire case. See *final judgment* under JUDGMENT.

foreign support order. See SUPPORT ORDER.

health-insurance order. See HEALTH-INSURANCE ORDER.

income-withholding order. See INCOME-WITHHOLDING ORDER.

interim order. 1. A temporary court decree that remains in effect for a specified time or until

a specified event occurs. **2.** See *interlocutory order*.

interlocutory order (in-tər-**lok**-yə-tor-ee). (17c) An order that relates to some intermediate matter in the case; any order other than a final order. ● Most interlocutory orders are not appealable until the case is fully resolved. But by rule or statute, most jurisdictions allow some types of interlocutory orders (such as preliminary injunctions and class-certification orders) to be immediately appealed. — Also termed *interlocutory decision*; *interim order*; *intermediate order*. See *appealable decision* under DECISION; COLLATERAL-ORDER DOCTRINE.

minute order. 1. An order recorded in the minutes of the court rather than directly on a case docket. ● Although practice varies, traditionally when a trial judge is sitting officially, with or without a court reporter, a clerk or deputy clerk keeps minutes. When the judge makes an oral order, the only record of that order may be in the minutes. It is therefore referred to as a minute order. — Also termed *minute entry*. **2.** A court order not directly relating to a case, such as an order adopting a local rule of court. ● In this sense, the court is not a single judge acting in an adjudicatory capacity, but a chief judge, or a group of two or more judges, acting for a court in an administrative or some other nonadjudicatory capacity.

modification order. See MODIFICATION ORDER.

order of dismissal. See *dismissal order*.

order to pay. 1. *Commercial law.* A written order to a person to deliver money, usu. out of funds on deposit with that person, to a third party on demand. **2.** A court order directing a person to deliver money that the person owes or for which the person is responsible.

preclusion order. (1921) An order barring a litigant from presenting or opposing certain claims or defenses for failing to comply with a discovery order.

pretrial order. See PRETRIAL ORDER.

protective order. See PROTECTIVE ORDER.

qualified domestic-relations order. See QUALIFIED DOMESTIC-RELATIONS ORDER.

receiving order. A court's direction to a bankruptcy receiver to take some action.

restraining order. See RESTRAINING ORDER.

separation order. A court order granting a married person's request for a legal separation. See SEPARATION AGREEMENT (1).

show-cause order. (1925) An order directing a party to appear in court and explain why the party took (or failed to take) some action or why the court should or should not grant some relief. — Also termed *order to show cause; rule to show cause; show-cause rule.*

standing order. A forward-looking order that applies to all cases pending before a court. • Some individual judges issue a standing order on a subject when there is no local rule bearing on it, often because a rule would not be acceptable to other judges on the court. Standing orders are frequently criticized because they undermine uniformity of procedural rules, esp. at the local level. Cf. *standing rule* under RULE (3).

supervision order. *Family law.* A court's order placing a child or young person under the supervision of a child-welfare agency or a probation officer in a case of neglect, abuse, or delinquency.

support order. See SUPPORT ORDER.

temporary order. A court order issued during the pendency of a suit, before the final order or judgment has been entered.

temporary restraining order. See TEMPORARY RESTRAINING ORDER.

turnover order. An order by which the court commands a judgment debtor to surrender certain property to a judgment creditor, or to the sheriff or constable on the creditor's behalf. • Such an order is usu. directed to property that is difficult to acquire by the ordinary judgment-collection process, such as share certificates and accounts receivable.

umbrella order. See BLANKET ORDER (1).

visitation order. See VISITATION ORDER.

3. *Parliamentary law.* The principles and practices of parliamentary law; the conduct of business according to those principles and practices; DECORUM. See IN ORDER; OUT OF ORDER. 4. *Parliamentary law.* An item of business, or an agenda or series of such items <call for the orders of the day>. See AGENDA.

general order. An order of the day other than a special order. See *order of the day* (1). Cf. *special order.*

order of business. 1. AGENDA. 2. The sequence in which a meeting considers its business.

order of the day. 1. An item of business scheduled for consideration at a certain upcoming meeting, at a certain time, or in a certain order. • An order of the day is either a *general order* or a *special order.* 2. The daily order of business. See *order of business.*

special order. An order of the day scheduled for consideration at a certain time, and which outranks and interrupts any other business except another special order scheduled earlier for the same time. See TIME CERTAIN.

5. *Parliamentary law.* A vote that assigns a duty to an officer, employee, or other agent, customarily in the form, "*Ordered*, That . . . ." 6. *Parliamentary law.* RULE (3). 7. *Commercial law.* The words in a draft (such as a check) directing one person to pay money to or deliver something to a designated person. • An order should appear to be the demand of a right as opposed to the request for a favor. See *order paper* under PAPER. 8. *Securities.* A customer's instructions to a broker about how and when to buy or sell securities.

all-or-none order. An order to buy a security to be executed either in its entirety or not at all.

alternative order. An order to buy a security by either of two alternatives (e.g., buy a stock at a limited price or buy on a stop order). — Also termed *either-or order.*

buy order. An investor's instruction to purchase stock.

day order. An order to buy or sell on one particular day only. Cf. *open order.*

discretionary order. An order to buy or sell at any price acceptable to the broker.

either-or order. See *alternative order.*

fill-or-kill order. An order that must be executed as soon as it reaches the trading floor. • If the order is not filled immediately, it is canceled.

limit order. An order to buy or sell at a specified price, regardless of market price. Cf. *no-limit order.*

market order. An order to buy or sell at the best price immediately available on the market. — Also termed *order at the market.*

matched order. An order to buy and sell the same security, at about the same time, in about the same quantity, and at about the same price.

no-limit order. An order to buy or sell securities with no limits on price. Cf. *limit order.*

open order. An order that remains in effect until filled by the broker or canceled by the customer. Cf. *day order.*

order at the market. See *market order.*

percentage order. An order to buy or sell a stated amount of a certain stock after a fixed number of shares of the stock have traded.

scale order. An order to buy or sell a security at varying price ranges.

sell order. An investor's instruction to sell stock.

split order. An order directing a broker to sell some stock at one price and some stock at another price.

stop order. An order to buy or sell when the security's price reaches a specified level (the *stop price*) on the market. • By fixing the price beforehand, the investor is cushioned against stock fluctuations. — Also termed *stop-loss order*; *stop-limit order*.

time order. An order that becomes a market or limited-price order at a specified time.

order absolute. See *decree absolute* under DECREE.

order assigning residue. A probate court's order naming the persons entitled to receive parts of an estate and allotting that share to each.

order at the market. See *market order* under ORDER (8).

order bill of lading. See BILL OF LADING.

order document. See *order paper* under PAPER.

ordered, adjudged, and decreed. (17c) The traditional words used to introduce a court decision <It is therefore ordered, adjudged, and decreed that Martin must return the overpayment to Hurley>.

order instrument. See *order paper* under PAPER.

orderly officer. See *officer of the day* under OFFICER (2).

order nisi. See *decree nisi* under DECREE.

order of business. See ORDER (4).

order of dismissal. See *dismissal order* under ORDER.

order of filiation. See *filiation order* under ORDER (2).

Order of the Coif (koyf). **1.** Formerly, the order of serjeants-at-law, the highest order of counsel at the English Bar. • The last serjeant was appointed to the Order in 1875. **2.** An honorary legal organization whose members are selected on the basis of their law-school grades. See COIF.

order of the day. See ORDER (4).

order paper. See PAPER.

order to pay. See ORDER (2).

Order, Resolution, or Vote Clause. U.S. Const. , art. I, § 7, cl. 3.

order to show cause. See *show-cause order* under ORDER (2).

ordinance (or-də-nənts). (14c) An authoritative law or decree; esp., a municipal regulation. • Municipal governments can pass ordinances on matters that the state government allows to be regulated at the local level. A municipal ordinance carries the state's authority and has the same effect within the municipality's limits as a state statute. — Also termed *bylaw*; *municipal ordinance*.

ordinarily prudent person. See REASONABLE PERSON.

ordinary, *adj.* (15c) **1.** Occurring in the regular course of events; normal; usual. Cf. EXTRAORDINARY. **2.** (Of a judge) having jurisdiction by right of office rather than by delegation. **3.** (Of

jurisdiction) original or immediate, as opposed to delegated.

ordinary, *n.* **1.** *Eccles. law.* A high-ranking official who has immediate jurisdiction over a specified territory, such as an archbishop over a province or a bishop over a diocese. **2.** *Civil law.* A judge having jurisdiction by right of office rather than by delegation. **3.** A probate judge. • The term is used in this sense only in some U.S. states.

ordinary ambassador. See *resident ambassador* under AMBASSADOR.

ordinary and necessary business expense. See *ordinary and necessary expense* under EXPENSE.

ordinary and necessary expense. See EXPENSE.

ordinary annuity. See ANNUITY.

ordinary assembly. See ASSEMBLY.

ordinary care. See *reasonable care* under CARE.

ordinary committee. See COMMITTEE.

ordinary course of business. See COURSE OF BUSINESS.

ordinary diligence. See DILIGENCE.

ordinary gain. See GAIN (3).

ordinary goods. See GOODS.

ordinary high tide. See *mean high tide* under TIDE.

ordinary income. See INCOME.

ordinary insurance. See *ordinary life insurance* under LIFE INSURANCE.

ordinary law. See STATUTORY LAW.

ordinary life insurance. 1. See LIFE INSURANCE. **2.** See *whole life insurance* under LIFE INSURANCE.

ordinary loss. See LOSS.

ordinary main motion. See *original main motion* under MOTION (2).

ordinary majority. See *simple majority* under MAJORITY.

ordinary meaning. See *plain meaning* under MEANING.

ordinary-meaning rule. 1. The rule that when a word is not defined in a statute or other legal instrument, the court normally construes it in accordance with its ordinary or natural meaning. **2.** PLAIN-MEANING RULE.

ordinary negligence. See NEGLIGENCE.

ordinary-observer test. See AUDIENCE TEST.

ordinary's court. See *probate court* under COURT.

ordinary seaman. See SEAMAN.

ordinary shares. See *common stock* under STOCK.

ordinary skill. 1. See SKILL. **2.** See ORDINARY SKILL IN THE ART.

ordinary skill in the art. *Patents.* The level of technical knowledge, experience, and expertise possessed by a typical engineer, scientist, designer, etc. in a technology that is relevant to an invention.

ordinary standing rule. See *standing rule* (1) under RULE (3).

ordinary work product. See *fact work product* under WORK PRODUCT.

ore tenus (or-ee **tee**-nəs *or* **ten**-əs), *adv. & adj.* [Latin "by word of mouth"] (17c) **1.** Orally; by word of mouth; VIVA VOCE <pleading carried on ore tenus>. **2.** Made or presented orally <ore tenus evidence>.

ore tenus rule. (1964) The presumption that a trial court's findings of fact are correct and should not be disturbed unless clearly wrong or unjust.

organic act. See *organic statute* under STATUTE.

organic disease. See DISEASE.

organic law. (1831) **1.** The body of laws (as in a constitution) that define and establish a government; FUNDAMENTAL LAW. **2.** *Civil law.* Decisional law; CASELAW.

organic statute. See STATUTE.

organization. (15c) **1.** A body of persons (such as a union or corporation) formed for a common purpose. — Also termed *society.* **2.** See UNION.

organizational crime. See *corporate crime* under CRIME.

organizational expense. See EXPENSE.

organizational meeting. See MEETING.

organizational picketing. See PICKETING.

organizational strike. See *recognition strike* under STRIKE.

organized crime. (1867) **1.** Widespread criminal activities that are coordinated and controlled through a central syndicate. See RACKETEERING. **2.** Persons involved in these criminal activities; a syndicate of criminals who rely on their unlawful activities for income. See SYNDICATE.

organized labor. **1.** Workers who are affiliated by membership in a union. **2.** A union, or unions collectively, considered as a political force.

organ trafficking. See TRAFFICKING.

original. See *original writ* under WRIT.

original acquisition. See ACQUISITION.

original administration. See ADMINISTRATION.

original bill. See BILL (2).

original contractor. See *general contractor* under CONTRACTOR.

original conveyance. See *primary conveyance* under CONVEYANCE.

original cost. See *acquisition cost* (1) under COST (1).

original-document rule. See BEST-EVIDENCE RULE.

original domicile. See *domicile of origin* under DOMICILE.

original drawing. See DRAWING.

original estate. See ESTATE (1).

original evidence. See EVIDENCE.

original intent. See INTENT (2).

originalism. (1980) *Constitutional law.* The theory that the U.S. Constitution should be interpreted according to the intent of those who drafted and adopted it. Cf. INTERPRETIVISM; NONINTERPRETIVISM.

original issue. See ISSUE (2).

original-issue discount. The difference between a bond's face value and the price at which it is initially sold. — Abbr. OID.

originality. (18c) *Copyright.* **1.** The quality or state of being the product of independent creation and having a minimum degree of creativity. ● Originality is a requirement for copyright protection. But this is a lesser standard than that of novelty in patent law: to be original, a work does not have to be novel or unique. Cf. NOVELTY. **2.** The degree to which a product claimed for copyright is the result of an author's independent efforts. Cf. CREATIVITY.

original jurisdiction. See JURISDICTION.

original main motion. See MOTION (2).

original market. See *primary market* under MARKET.

original-package doctrine. *Constitutional law.* The principle that imported goods are exempt from state taxation as long as they are unsold and remain in the original packaging. ● The Supreme Court abolished this doctrine in 1976, holding that states can tax imported goods if the tax is nondiscriminatory. See IMPORT-EXPORT CLAUSE.

original precedent. See PRECEDENT.

original process. See PROCESS.

original promise. See PROMISE.

original receiver. See *principal receiver* under RECEIVER.

original source. The person or persons who first disclosed fraud to the government, derived from direct and indirect information on which a qui tam complaint is based under the False Claims Act or a similar state law.

original title. See TITLE (2).

original writ. See WRIT.

original-writing rule. See BEST-EVIDENCE RULE.

origination clause. (*often cap.*) (1984) **1.** The constitutional provision that all bills for increasing taxes and raising revenue must originate in the House of Representatives, not the Senate (U.S. Const. art. I, § 7, cl. 1). • The Senate may, however, amend revenue bills. **2.** A provision in a state constitution requiring that revenue bills originate in the lower house of the state legislature.

origination fee. See FEE (1).

originator. The entity that initiates a funds transfer subject to UCC article 4A. UCC § 4A-104(c).

"or" lease. See LEASE.

ornamental fixture. See FIXTURE.

ornest. *Hist.* See TRIAL BY COMBAT.

ORP. *abbr.* Ordinary, reasonable, and prudent — the standard on which negligence cases are based.

orphan, *n.* (15c) **1.** A child whose parents are dead. **2.** A child with one dead parent and one living parent. — More properly termed *half orphan.* **3.** A child who has been deprived of parental care and has not been legally adopted; a child without a parent or guardian.

orphan drug. See DRUG.

orphan's court. See *probate court* under COURT.

OS. See *ordinary seaman* under SEAMAN.

o.s. *abbr.* OLD STYLE.

OSC. *abbr.* OFFICE OF SPECIAL COUNSEL.

OSHA (oh-shə). *abbr.* **1.** OCCUPATIONAL SAFETY AND HEALTH ACT OF 1970. **2.** OCCUPATIONAL SAFETY AND HEALTH ADMINISTRATION.

OSHRC. *abbr.* OCCUPATIONAL SAFETY AND HEALTH REVIEW COMMISSION.

OSI. *abbr.* See OFFICE OF SPECIAL INVESTIGATIONS.

OSM. *abbr.* OFFICE OF SURFACE MINING RECLAMATION AND ENFORCEMENT.

o.s.p. *abbr.* OBIIT SINE PROLE.

ostensible (ah-**sten**-sə-bəl), *adj.* (18c) Open to view; declared or professed; apparent.

ostensible agency. See *agency by estoppel* under AGENCY (1).

ostensible agent. See *apparent agent* under AGENT (2).

ostensible authority. See *apparent authority* under AUTHORITY (1).

ostensible partner. See *nominal partner* under PARTNER.

OSTP. See OFFICE OF SCIENCE AND TECHNOLOGY POLICY.

ostrich defense. See DEFENSE (1).

ostrich instruction. See JURY INSTRUCTION.

OTA. *abbr.* OFFICE OF TECHNOLOGY ASSESSMENT.

OTC. *abbr.* OVER-THE-COUNTER.

OTC market. *abbr.* OVER-THE-COUNTER MARKET.

other consideration. See CONSIDERATION (1).

other good and valuable consideration. See *other consideration* under CONSIDERATION.

other income. See INCOME.

other-insurance clause. An insurance-policy provision that attempts to limit coverage if the insured has other coverage for the same loss. • The three major other-insurance clauses are the pro rata clause, the excess clause, and the escape clause. See ESCAPE CLAUSE; EXCESS CLAUSE; PRO RATA CLAUSE.

other-property rule. The principle that tort recovery is unavailable if the only damage caused by a product defect is to the product itself. See *East River S.S. Corp. v. Transamerica Delaval, Inc.,* 476 U.S. 858, 106 S. Ct. 2295 (1986).

OTP. *abbr.* Office of Technology Policy. See TECHNOLOGY ADMINISTRATION.

OTS. *abbr.* OFFICE OF THRIFT SUPERVISION.

OTSA. *abbr.* OFFICE OF TAX-SHELTER ANALYSIS.

OUI. *abbr.* Operating under the influence. See DRIVING UNDER THE INFLUENCE.

our federalism. (*often cap.*) (1971) The doctrine holding that a federal court must refrain from hearing a constitutional challenge to state action if federal adjudication would be considered an improper intrusion into the state's right to enforce its own laws in its own courts. Cf. ABSTENTION; FEDERALISM.

oust, *vb.* (15c) To put out of possession; to deprive of a right or inheritance.

ouster. (16c) **1.** The wrongful dispossession or exclusion of someone (esp. a cotenant) from property (esp. real property); DISPOSSESSION. **2.** The removal of a public or corporate officer from office. Cf. EJECTMENT.

outbuilding. (17c) A detached building (such as a shed or garage) within the grounds of a main building.

outcome-determinative test. (1959) *Civil procedure.* A test used to determine whether an issue is substantive for purposes of the *Erie* doctrine by examining the issue's potential effect on the outcome of the litigation. See ERIE DOCTRINE.

outcome responsibility. The view that those who cause harm are responsible for it even in the absence of fault. Cf. *strict liability* under LIABILITY.

outer bar. *English law.* A group of junior barristers who sit outside the dividing bar in the court. • These barristers rank below the King's Counsel or Queen's Counsel. — Also termed *utter bar*. Cf. INNER BAR.

outer barrister. See BARRISTER.

outer space. (1842) **1.** The known and unknown areas of the universe beyond airspace. ● The boundary between airspace and outer space is not fixed or precise. Cf. AIRSPACE. **2.** *Int'l law.* The space surrounding the planet that by United Nations treaty is not subject to claim of appropriation by any national sovereignty. ● The treaty does not expressly define *outer space*. See OUTER SPACE TREATY.

Outer Space Treaty. *Int'l law.* The short title of the United Nations Treaty on Principles Governing the Activities of States in the Exploration and Use of Outer Space, Including the Moon and Other Celestial Bodies, 18 U.S.T. pt. 3, at 2410 (Jan. 27, 1967). ● This treaty stipulates that, because space exploration is in the interest of all humanity, no nation may claim territory, establish military bases, or station weapons on any other planet or a moon. The treaty also declares that international law and the United Nations charter apply in space. See OUTER SPACE.

outlaw, *n.* (bef. 12c) **1.** A person who has been deprived of the benefit and protection of the law; a person under a sentence of outlawry. **2.** A lawless person or habitual criminal; esp., a fugitive from the law. **3.** *Int'l law.* A person, organization, or nation under a ban or restriction because it is considered to be in violation of international law or custom.

outlaw, *vb.* (18c) **1.** To deprive (someone) of the benefit and protection of the law; to declare an outlaw <outlaw the fugitive>. **2.** To make illegal <outlaw fireworks within city limits>. **3.** To remove from legal jurisdiction or enforcement; to deprive of legal force <outlaw a claim under the statute>.

outlawry. 1. *Hist.* The act or process of depriving someone of the benefit and protection of the law. **2.** The state or condition of being outlawed; the status of an outlaw. **3.** Disregard or disobedience of the law.

outlaw strike. See *wildcat strike* under STRIKE.

outline form. *Patents.* A style of writing patent claims that uses a numbered or lettered subparagraph for each element. Cf. COLON-SEMICOLON FORM; SINGLE-PARAGRAPH FORM; SUBPARAGRAPH FORM.

out-of-court, *adj.* (1950) Not done or made as part of a judicial proceeding <an out-of-court settlement> <an out-of-court statement that was not under oath>. See EXTRAJUDICIAL.

out-of-court settlement. See SETTLEMENT (2).

out-of-home placement. *Family law.* The placing of a child in a living arrangement outside the child's home (as in foster care or institutional care), usu. as the result of abuse or neglect; specif., in a child-abuse or child-neglect case, state action that removes a child from a parent's or custodian's home and places the child in foster care or with a relative, either temporarily or for an extended period. Cf. FOSTER-CARE PLACEMENT.

out-of-hospital do-not-resuscitate order. See DO-NOT-RESUSCITATE ORDER.

out of order. (18c) **1.** (Of a motion) not in order <the motion is out of order because it conflicts with the bylaws>. See IN ORDER. ● A motion may be "out of order" because it is inherently inappropriate for the deliberative assembly's consideration at any time (e.g., because it proposes an unlawful action). A motion that is not appropriate simply because it is brought before the meeting at the wrong time but that may be appropriate for consideration at another time is more precisely referred to as "not in order." **2.** (Of a person) guilty of a breach of decorum or other misconduct during a meeting <the member is out of order>.

out-of-pocket expense. See EXPENSE.

out-of-pocket loss. See LOSS.

out-of-pocket rule. (1940) The principle that a defrauded buyer may recover from the seller as damages the difference between the amount paid for the property and the actual value received. Cf. BENEFIT-OF-THE-BARGAIN RULE (2).

out of the money, *adj.* (Of a creditor) unpaid because a debtor has insufficient assets to pay the claim.

out of the state. See BEYOND SEAS (2).

out of time. After a deadline; too late <because the statute of limitations expired before the action's filing, this lawsuit is out of time and should be dismissed>.

output, *n.* (1841) **1.** A business's production of goods or materials; the quantity or amount produced. **2.** The process or fact of producing goods or materials.

output contract. See CONTRACT.

outrage, *n.* See INTENTIONAL INFLICTION OF EMOTIONAL DISTRESS.

outrageous conduct. See CONDUCT.

outside director. See DIRECTOR.

outside financing. See FINANCING.

outside party. See THIRD PARTY.

outsourcing agreement. An agreement between a business and a service provider in which the service provider promises to provide necessary services, esp. data processing and information management, using its own staff and equipment, and usu. at its own facilities.

outstanding, *adj.* (18c) **1.** Unpaid; uncollected <outstanding debts>. **2.** Publicly issued and sold <outstanding shares>.

outstanding capital stock. See *outstanding stock* under STOCK.

outstanding security. See SECURITY.

outstanding stock. See STOCK.

outstanding warrant. See WARRANT (1).

over, *adj.* (bef. 12c) (Of a property interest) intended to take effect after the failure or termination of a prior estate; preceded by some other possessory interest <a limitation over> <a gift over>.

overage, *n.* (1909) **1.** An excess or surplus, esp. of goods or merchandise. **2.** A percentage of retail sales paid to a store's landlord in addition to fixed rent.

overbreadth doctrine. (1970) *Constitutional law.* The doctrine holding that if a statute is so broadly written that it deters free expression, then it can be struck down on its face because of its chilling effect — even if it also prohibits acts that may legitimately be forbidden. • The Supreme Court has used this doctrine to invalidate a number of laws, including those that would disallow peaceful picketing or require loyalty oaths. Cf. VAGUENESS DOCTRINE.

overdraft. (1843) **1.** A withdrawal of money from a bank in excess of the balance on deposit. **2.** The amount of money so withdrawn. — Abbr. (in senses 1 & 2) OD; o/d. **3.** A line of credit extended by a bank to a customer (esp. an established or institutional customer) who might overdraw on an account.

overdraw, *vb.* (18c) To draw on (an account) in excess of the balance on deposit; to make an overdraft.

overhead, *n.* (1907) Business expenses (such as rent, utilities, or support-staff salaries) that cannot be allocated to a particular product or service; fixed or ordinary operating costs. — Also termed *administrative expense; office expense.*

overheated economy. See ECONOMY.

overinclusive, *adj.* (1949) (Of legislation) extending beyond the class of persons intended to be protected or regulated; burdening more persons than necessary to cure the problem <an overinclusive classification>.

overinsurance. 1. Insurance (esp. from the purchase of multiple policies) that exceeds the value of the thing insured. **2.** Excessive or needlessly duplicative insurance.

overissue, *n.* An issue of securities beyond the authorized amount of capital or credit.

overlapping jurisdiction. See *concurrent jurisdiction* under JURISDICTION.

overplus. See SURPLUS.

overreaching, *n.* (16c) **1.** The act or an instance of taking unfair commercial advantage of another, esp. by fraudulent means. **2.** The act or an instance of defeating one's own purpose by going too far. — **overreach,** *vb.*

overridden veto. See VETO.

override (oh-vər-**rid**), *vb.* (14c) To prevail over; to nullify or set aside <Congress mustered enough votes to override the President's veto>.

override (**oh**-vər-rid), *n.* (1931) **1.** A commission paid to a manager on a sale made by a subordinate. **2.** A commission paid to a real-estate broker who listed a property when, within a reasonable amount of time after the expiration of the listing, the owner sells that property directly to a buyer with whom the broker had negotiated during the term of the listing. **3.** ROYALTY (2).

overriding royalty. See ROYALTY (2).

overrule, *vb.* (16c) **1.** To rule against; to reject <the judge overruled all of the defendant's objections>. **2.** (Of a court) to overturn or set aside (a precedent) by expressly deciding that it should no longer be controlling law <in *Brown v. Board of Education*, the Supreme Court overruled *Plessy v. Ferguson*>. Cf. VACATE (1).

overseas bill of lading. See BILL OF LADING.

Overseas Private Investment Corporation. A federally chartered corporation that promotes private investment in developing countries by making or guaranteeing loans; supporting private funds that invest in foreign nations; insuring investments against political risks; and engaging in outreach activities. • It was established as an independent agency by the Foreign Affairs Reform and Restructuring Act of 1998. The agency is self-sustaining. — Abbr. OPIC.

oversubscription. A situation in which there are more subscribers to a new issue of securities than there are securities available for purchase.

overt, *adj.* (14c) Open and observable; not concealed or secret <the conspirators' overt acts>.

overt act. (17c) *Criminal law.* **1.** An act that indicates an intent to kill or seriously harm another person and thus gives that person a justification to use self-defense. **2.** An outward act, however innocent in itself, done in furtherance of a conspiracy, treason, or criminal attempt. • An overt act is usu. a required element of these crimes. **3.** See ACTUS REUS. — Also termed *positive act.*

over-the-counter, *adj.* **1.** Not listed or traded on an organized securities exchange; traded between brokers and dealers who negotiate directly <over-the-counter stocks>. **2.** (Of drugs) sold legally without a doctor's prescription <over-the-counter cough medicine>. — Abbr. OTC.

over-the-counter market. The market for securities that are not traded on an organized exchange. • Over-the-counter (OTC) trading usu. occurs through telephone or computer negotiations between buyers and sellers. Many of the more actively traded OTC stocks are listed on NASDAQ. — Abbr. OTC market.

overtime. 1. The hours worked by an employee in excess of a standard day or week. • Under the Fair Labor Standards Act, employers must pay extra wages (usu. 1½ times the regular hourly rate) to certain employees (usu. nonsalaried ones) for each hour worked in excess of 40 hours per week. **2.** The extra wages paid for excess hours worked.

overtry, *vb.* (1911) (Of a trial lawyer) to try a lawsuit by expending excessive time, effort, and other resources to explore minutiae, esp. to present more evidence than the fact-trier can assimilate, the result often being that the adversary gains arguing points by disputing the minutiae.

overturn, *vb.* (1842) To overrule or reverse <the court overturned a long-established precedent>.

OWCP. *abbr.* OFFICE OF WORKERS' COMPENSATION PROGRAMS.

owelty (oh-əl-tee). (16c) **1.** Equality as achieved by a compensatory sum of money given after an exchange of parcels of land having different values or after an unequal partition of real property. **2.** The sum of money so paid.

OWI. *abbr.* Operating while intoxicated. See DRIVING UNDER THE INFLUENCE.

owing, *adj.* (15c) That is yet to be paid; owed; due <a balance of $5,000 is still owing>.

own, *vb.* (bef. 12c) To rightfully have or possess as property; to have legal title to.

owned-property exclusion. See EXCLUSION (3).

owner. (bef. 12c) One who has the right to possess, use, and convey something; a person in whom one or more interests are vested. • An owner may have complete property in the thing or may have parted with some interests in it (as by granting an easement or making a lease). See OWNERSHIP.

    adjoining owner. (18c) A person who owns land abutting another's; ABUTTER.

    beneficial owner. (18c) **1.** One recognized in equity as the owner of something because use and title belong to that person, even though legal title may belong to someone else; esp., one for whom property is held in trust. — Also termed *equitable owner.* **2.** A corporate shareholder who has the power to buy or sell the shares, but who is not registered on the corporation's books as the owner. **3.** *Intellectual property.* A person or entity who is entitled to enjoy the rights in a patent, trademark, or copyright even though legal title is vested in someone else. • The beneficial owner has standing to sue for infringement. A corporation is typically a beneficial owner if it has a contractual right to the assignment of the patent but the employee who owns the patent has failed to assign it. Similarly, a patent or copyright owner who has transferred title as collateral to secure a loan would be a beneficial owner entitled to sue for infringement.

    copyright owner. See COPYRIGHT OWNER.

    equitable owner. See *beneficial owner* (1).

    general owner. (18c) One who has the primary or residuary title to property; one who has the ultimate ownership of property. Cf. *special owner.*

    legal owner. (17c) One recognized by law as the owner of something; esp., one who holds legal title to property for the benefit of another. See TRUSTEE (1).

    limited owner. (1836) A tenant for life; the owner of a life estate. See *life estate* under ESTATE (1).

    naked owner. *Civil law.* A person whose property is burdened by a usufruct. • The naked owner has the right to dispose of the property subject to the usufruct, but not to derive its fruits. See USUFRUCT.

    owner of record. See *record owner.*

    owner pro hac vice (proh hahk **vee**-chay). See *bareboat charter* under CHARTER (8).

    record owner. (1863) **1.** A property owner in whose name the title appears in the public records. **2.** STOCKHOLDER OF RECORD.

    sole and unconditional owner. (1871) *Insurance.* The owner who has full equitable title to, and exclusive interest in, the insured property.

    special owner. (18c) One (such as a bailee) with a qualified interest in property. Cf. *general owner.*

owners' association. (1968) **1.** The basic governing entity for a condominium or planned unit developments. • It is usu. an unincorporated association or a nonprofit corporation. — Also termed *homeowners' association.* **2.** See *homeowners' association* under ASSOCIATION.

owners' equity. (1935) The aggregate of the owners' financial interests in the assets of a business entity; the capital contributed by the owners plus any retained earnings. • Owners' equity is calculated as the difference in value between a business entity's assets and its liabilities. — Also termed *owner's equity; book value; net book value;* (in a corporation) *shareholders' equity; stockholders' equity.*

ownership. (16c) The bundle of rights allowing one to use, manage, and enjoy property, including the right to convey it to others. • Ownership implies the right to possess a thing, regardless of any actual or constructive control. Ownership rights are general, permanent, and heritable. Cf. POS-SESSION; TITLE (1).

bare ownership. See *trust ownership.*

beneficial ownership. (18c) **1.** A beneficiary's interest in trust property. — Also termed *equitable ownership.* **2.** A corporate shareholder's power to buy or sell the shares, though the shareholder is not registered on the corporation's books as the owner.

bonitary ownership (bahn-ə-**tair**-ee). *Roman law.* A type of equitable ownership recognized by the praetor when the property was conveyed by an informal transfer, or by a formal transfer by one not the true owner. — Also termed *bonitarian ownership; in bonis habere.*

complete ownership. *Hist. Louisiana law.* See *perfect ownership.*

contingent ownership. (1886) Ownership in which title is imperfect but is capable of becoming perfect on the fulfillment of some condition; conditional ownership.

corporeal ownership. (1894) The actual ownership of land or chattels.

equitable ownership. See *beneficial ownership* (1).

full ownership. *Hist. Louisiana law.* See *perfect ownership.*

imperfect ownership. *Louisiana law.* Ownership of property subject to a usufruct interest held by another. See La. Civ. Code art. 478. — Also termed *naked ownership.*

incorporeal ownership. (1931) The ownership of rights in land or chattels.

joint ownership. (18c) Undivided ownership shared by two or more persons. • Typically, an owner's interest, at death, passes to the surviving owner or owners by virtue of the right of survivorship.

naked ownership. *Louisiana law.* See *imperfect ownership.*

ownership in common. (1838) Ownership shared by two or more persons whose interests are divisible. • Typically their interests, at death, pass to the dead owner's heirs or successors.

perfect ownership. *Hist. Louisiana law.* The complete bundle of rights to use, enjoy, and dispose of property without limitation. — Also termed *full ownership; complete ownership.*

qualified ownership. (18c) Ownership that is shared, restricted to a particular use, or limited in the extent of its enjoyment.

trust ownership. (1893) A trustee's interest in trust property. — Also termed *bare ownership.*

unqualified ownership. Absolute ownership.

vested ownership. (1867) Ownership in which title is perfect; absolute ownership.

ownership-in-place theory. *Oil & gas.* A characterization of oil-and-gas rights used in a majority of jurisdictions, holding that the owner has the right to present possession of the oil and gas in place as well as the right to use the land surface to search, develop, and produce from the property, but that the interest in the minerals terminates if the oil and gas flows out from under the owner's land. • This theory is used in Texas, New Mexico, Kansas, Mississippi, and other major producing states. The rights of a severed-mineral-interest owner to oil and gas in these states are often described as an estate in fee simple absolute, but ownership of specific oil-and-gas molecules is subject to the rule of capture. See also NONOWN-ERSHIP THEORY.

owner's policy. *Real estate.* A title-insurance policy covering the owner's title as well as the mortgagee's interest. Cf. MORTGAGEE POLICY.

own-product exclusion. See EXCLUSION (3).

own-work exclusion. See EXCLUSION (3).

oyer (**oy**-ər *or* **oh**-yər). [fr. Old French *oïr* "to hear"] (15c) *Hist.* **1.** A criminal trial held under a commission of oyer and terminer. See COMMISSION OF OYER AND TERMINER. **2.** The reading in open court of a document (esp. a deed) that is demanded by one party and read by the other. **3.** *Common-law pleading.* A prayer to the court by a party opposing a profert, asking to have the instrument on which the opponent relies read aloud. • Oyer can be demanded only when a profert has been properly made, but it is disallowed for a private writing under seal.

oyer, demand of. See DEMAND OF OYER.

oyer and terminer (**oy**-ər an[d] **tər**-mə-nər). [Law French *oyer et terminer* "to hear and determine"] (15c) **1.** See COMMISSION OF OYER AND TERMINER. **2.** COURT OF OYER AND TERMINER (2).

oyez (**oh**-yes *or* **oh**-yez *or* **oh**-yay). [Law French] (15c) Hear ye. • The utterance *oyez, oyez, oyez* is usu. used in court by the public crier to call the courtroom to order when a session begins or when a proclamation is about to be made.

P

P. *abbr.* PACIFIC REPORTER.

P.A. *abbr.* See *professional association* under AS-SOCIATION.

PAC (pak). *abbr.* POLITICAL-ACTION COMMITTEE.

PACER. *abbr.* PUBLIC ACCESS TO COURT ELEC-TRONIC RECORDS.

pacification (pas-ə-fi-**kay**-shən), *n.* (15c) *Int'l law.* The act of making peace between two belligerent nations. — **pacify** (**pas**-ə-fɪ), *vb.*

pacific blockade. See BLOCKADE.

pacificist. See PACIFIST.

Pacific Reporter. A set of regional lawbooks, part of the West Group's National Reporter System, containing every officially published appellate decision from Alaska, Arizona, California, Colorado, Hawaii, Idaho, Kansas, Montana, Nevada, New Mexico, Oklahoma, Oregon, Utah, Washington, and Wyoming, from 1883 to date. • The first series ran from 1883 to 1931; the second series ran until 2000; the third series is the current one. — Abbr. P.; P.2d; P.3d.

pacifism (**pas**-ə-fiz-əm). (1902) *Int'l law.* The advocacy of peaceful methods rather than war as a means of solving disputes.

pacifist (**pas**-ə-fist), *n.* (1906) A person who is opposed to war; a person who believes in pacifism. — Also termed *pacificist.* Cf. CONSCIENTIOUS OBJECTOR.

pack, *vb.* (16c) To choose or arrange (a tribunal, jurors, etc.) to accomplish a desired result <pack a jury>.

package mortgage. See MORTGAGE.

package policy. See INSURANCE POLICY.

packing, *n.* A gerrymandering technique in which a dominant political or racial group minimizes minority representation by concentrating the minority into as few districts as possible. Cf. CRACK-ING; STACKING (2).

packing a jury. See JURY-PACKING.

Pac-Man defense (**pak**-man). An aggressive antitakeover defense by which the target company attempts to take over the bidder company by making a cash tender offer for the bidder company's shares. • The name derives from a video game popular in the 1980s, the object of which was to gobble up the enemy. This defense is seldom used today. Cf. CROWN-JEWEL DEFENSE; SCORCHED-EARTH DEFENSE.

pact. (15c) An agreement between two or more parties; esp., an agreement (such as a treaty) between two or more nations or governmental entities.

pacta sunt servanda (**pak**-tə sənt sər-**van**-də). [Latin "agreements must be kept"] The rule that agreements and stipulations, esp. those contained in treaties, must be observed <the Quebec courts have been faithful to the *pacta sunt servanda* principle>.

paction (**pak**-shən). **1.** PACTIO. **2.** *Int'l law.* An agreement between two nations to be performed by a single act.

pactional, *adj.* Relating to or generating an agreement. — **pactionally,** *adv.*

Pact of Paris. See KELLOGG–BRIAND PACT.

pactum (**pak**-təm), *n.* [Latin] *Roman & civil law.* An agreement or convention, usu. falling short of a contract; a pact. — Also termed *pactum conventum.* Pl. **pacta.**

pad, *vb.* (1831) *Slang.* (Of a lawyer, paralegal, etc.) to overstate the number of (billable hours worked). See BILLABLE HOUR. — **padding,** *n.*

padded-payroll rule. See FICTITIOUS-PAYEE RULE.

paid-in capital. See CAPITAL.

paid-in fund. See FUND (1).

paid-in surplus. See SURPLUS.

paid-up insurance. See INSURANCE.

paid-up lease. *Oil & gas.* A mineral lease that does not provide for delay-rental payments and does not subject the lessor to any covenant to drill. • In effect, the lessor makes all delay-rental payments, and perhaps a bonus, when the lease is signed. A paid-up lease may be used to lease a small area or a fractional interest, or for a short primary term or for small delay rentals. The lease is effective through the primary term.

paid-up policy. See INSURANCE POLICY.

paid-up stock. See *full-paid stock* under STOCK.

pain and suffering. (1825) Physical discomfort or emotional distress compensable as an element of noneconomic damages in torts. See DAMAGES.

pain of, on. See ON PAIN OF.

pains and penalties, bill of. See BILL OF PAINS AND PENALTIES.

pair. *Parliamentary law.* Two voters, usu. legislators, on opposite sides of an issue who agree that they will abstain if either cannot vote on the issue. • A pair is usu. announced and recorded.

paired vote. See VOTE (1).

pais (pay *or* pays). See IN PAIS.

palimony (pal-ə-moh-nee). [Portmanteau word from *pal* + *alimony*] (1977) **1.** A court's award of post-relationship support or compensation for services, money, and goods contributed during a long-term nonmarital relationship, esp. where a common-law marriage cannot be established. ● Though not recognized under most state statutes, caselaw in some jurisdictions authorizes palimony claims. The term originated in the press coverage of *Marvin v. Marvin*, 557 P.2d 106 (Cal. 1976). Cf. ALIMONY. **2.** Loosely, child support. ● This sense is esp. common in the United Kingdom.

Palmer's Act. An English statute, enacted in 1856, giving a person accused of a crime falling outside the jurisdiction of the Central Criminal Court the right to have the case tried in that court. St. 19 & 20 Vict., ch. 16. — Also termed *Central Criminal Court Act.* See CENTRAL CRIMINAL COURT.

palming off. See PASSING OFF.

***Palsgraf* rule** (pawlz-graf). (1932) *Torts.* The principle that negligent conduct resulting in injury will lead to liability only if the actor could have reasonably foreseen that the conduct would cause the injury. ● In *Palsgraf v. Long Island R.R.*, 162 N.E. 99 (N.Y. 1928), two railroad attendants negligently dislodged a package of fireworks from a man they were helping board a train. The package exploded on impact and knocked over some scales that fell on Mrs. Palsgraf. The New York Court of Appeals, in a 4–3 majority opinion written by Chief Justice Benjamin Cardozo, held that the attendants could not have foreseen the possibility of injury to Palsgraf and therefore did not breach any duty to her. In the dissenting opinion, Justice William S. Andrews asserted that the duty to exercise care is owed to all, and thus a negligent act will subject the actor to liability to all persons proximately harmed by it, whether or not the harm is foreseeable. Both opinions have been widely cited to support the two views expressed in them.

Pan-American Convention. *Copyright.* One of a series of copyright conventions held among Western Hemisphere countries to negotiate treaties patterned after the Berne Convention. ● The first Convention was held in 1902, the last in 1946. The largest was the 1910 Pan American Convention in Buenos Aires.

pandect (pan-dekt). **1.** A complete legal code, esp. of a nation or a system of law, together with commentary. **2.** (*cap. & pl.*) The 50 books constituting Justinian's *Digest* (one of the four works making up the *Corpus Juris Civilis*), first published in A.D. 533. ● The substance of 2,000 treatises was distilled into this abridgment. One estimate is that 3 million lines were reduced to 150,000. This prodigious amount of work was carried out in three short years (A.D. 530–533) by a commission of 17 jurists headed by Tribonian. — Also termed (in sense 2) *Digest.* — Also spelled (in reference to German law) *pandekt.* Pl. **pandects, pandectae.** See CORPUS JURIS CIVILIS.

pander, *n.* (15c) One who engages in pandering. — Also termed *panderer.* See PIMP.

pandering (pan-dər-ing), *n.* (17c) **1.** The act or offense of recruiting a prostitute, finding a place of business for a prostitute, or soliciting customers for a prostitute. — Also termed *promoting prostitution.* **2.** The act or offense of selling or distributing textual or visual material (such as magazines or videotapes) openly advertised to appeal to the recipient's sexual interest. ● Although the concept of pandering was invoked by the U.S. Supreme Court in *Ginzburg v. United States*, 383 U.S. 463, 86 S.Ct. 942 (1966), it has seldom been discussed by the Court since then. — **pander,** *vb.*

***Panduit* test.** *Patents.* A four-factor test for measuring profits lost because of patent infringement. ● The patentee must prove (1) that there was a demand for the product; (2) that the patentee had the manufacturing and marketing capacity to meet that demand; (3) that there were no acceptable noninfringing alternatives on the market; and (4) how much was lost in profits. *Panduit Corp. v. Stahlin Bros. Fibre Works, Inc.*, 575 F.2d 1152 (6th Cir. 1978).

P & L. *abbr.* Profit and loss. See INCOME STATEMENT.

panel. (14c) **1.** A list of persons summoned as potential jurors; VENIRE. **2.** A group of persons selected to serve on a jury; JURY. **3.** A set of judges selected from a complete court to decide a specific case; esp., a group of three judges designated to sit for an appellate court. **4.** *Scots law.* A person indicted in a crime; the accused. — Also spelled (in sense 4) *pannel.*

panelation (pan-əl-**ay**-shən). (2003) The act of empaneling a jury. — Also spelled *panellation.*

panel attorney. See ATTORNEY.

panel-shopping. (1974) The practice of choosing the most favorable group of judges to hear an appeal.

panhandling. The act or practice of approaching or stopping strangers and begging for money or food. — **panhandler,** *n.* — **panhandle,** *vb.*

papal law (**pay**-pəl). See CANON LAW.

paper. (14c) **1.** Any written or printed document or instrument. **2.** A negotiable document or instrument evidencing a debt; esp., commercial documents or negotiable instruments considered as a group. See NEGOTIABLE INSTRUMENT. **3.** (*pl.*) COURT PAPERS.

accommodation paper. See ACCOMMODATION PAPER.

bankable paper. Notes, checks, bank bills, drafts, and other instruments received as cash by banks.

bearer paper. An instrument payable to the person who holds it rather than to the order of a specific person. • Bearer paper is negotiated simply by delivering the instrument to a transferee. — Also termed *bearer document; bearer instrument.*

chattel paper (chat-əl). See CHATTEL PAPER.

commercial paper. 1. An instrument, other than cash, for the payment of money. • Commercial paper — typically existing in the form of a draft (such as a check) or a note (such as a certificate of deposit) — is governed by Article 3 of the UCC. But even though the UCC uses the term *commercial paper* when referring to negotiable instruments of a particular kind (drafts, checks, certificates of deposit, and notes as defined by Article 3), the term long predates the UCC as a business and legal term in common use. Before the UCC, it was generally viewed as synonymous with *negotiable paper* or *bills and notes.* It was sometimes applied even to nonnegotiable instruments. — Also termed *mercantile paper; company's paper.* See NEGOTIABLE INSTRUMENT. **2.** Such instruments collectively. — Also termed *bills and notes.* **3.** Loosely, a short-term unsecured promissory note, usu. issued and sold by one company to meet another company's immediate cash needs.

commodity paper. An instrument representing a loan secured by a bill of lading or warehouse receipt.

order paper. An instrument payable to a specific payee or to any person that the payee designates. — Also termed *order document; order instrument.*

paper loss. See LOSS.

paper market. See *derivative market* under MARKET.

paper money. See MONEY.

paper patent. See PATENT (3).

paper profit. See PROFIT (1).

papers. See COURT PAPERS.

paper standard. A monetary system based entirely on paper; a system of currency that is not convertible into gold or other precious metal. Cf. GOLD STANDARD.

paper street. See STREET.

paper title. See *record title* under TITLE (2).

par. See PAR VALUE.

parade-of-horrors objection. See WEDGE PRINCIPLE.

parajudge. See UNITED STATES MAGISTRATE JUDGE.

paralegal, *n.* (1967) **1.** A person who has some education in law and assists a lawyer in duties related to the practice of law but who is not a licensed attorney. — Also termed *legal assistant; legal analyst.* **2.** *Canadian law.* A nonlawyer who is legally qualified through experience or special training and is licensed to provide limited legal services in certain fields. • Paralegals may assist in representing clients in both civil and criminal matters. — Also termed (in sense 2) *law clerk.* — **paralegal,** *adj.*

paralegalize, *vb. Slang.* To proofread, cite-check, and otherwise double-check the details in (a legal document).

parallel citation. See CITATION (3).

parallel imports. Goods bearing valid trademarks that are manufactured abroad and imported into the United States to compete with domestically manufactured goods bearing the same valid trademarks. • Domestic parties commonly complain that parallel imports compete unfairly in the U.S. market. But U.S. trademark law does not prohibit the sale of most parallel imports. — Also termed *gray-market goods.* See *gray market* under MARKET.

parallel parenting. See PARENTING.

parallel research. *Intellectual property.* The coincident but independent development of similar information or ideas by more than one person. • Parallel research may be offered to establish an independent-conception defense. If more than one person independently reaches the same result, each may protect the product as a trade secret.

paramount title. See TITLE (2).

parapherna (par-ə-fər-nə), *n.* [Greek "things brought on the side"] **1.** *Roman law.* Property of a wife not forming part of her dowry. See DOS (1). **2.** *Scots law.* A married woman's personal property, such as clothing, jewelry, and intimate possessions, which a husband did not acquire by virtue of marriage.

paraphernal property. See *extradotal property* under PROPERTY.

Paraphrase of Theophilus. See INSTITUTE (4).

parcel, *n.* (15c) **1.** A small package or bundle. **2.** A tract of land; esp., a continuous tract or plot of land in one possession, no part of which is separated from the rest by intervening land in another's possession.

parcel, *vb.* (15c) To divide and distribute (goods, land, etc.) • This verb is often used with *out* <the land is parceled out in allotments> or, rarely, *off* <the father arranged to have a 10.474-acre tract of his farm parceled off and retitled to his children as joint tenants>.

parcenary (pahr-sə-ner-ee). See COPARCENARY.

parcener (**pahr**-sə-nər). See COPARCENER.

pardon, *n.* (14c) The act or an instance of officially nullifying punishment or other legal consequences of a crime. ● A pardon is usu. granted by the chief executive of a government. The President has the sole power to issue pardons for federal offenses, and state governors have the power to issue pardons for state crimes. — Also termed *executive pardon.* See CLEMENCY. Cf. COMMUTATION (2); REPRIEVE. — **pardon,** *vb.*

   absolute pardon. A pardon that releases the wrongdoer from punishment and restores the offender's civil rights without qualification. — Also termed *full pardon; unconditional pardon.*

   conditional pardon. A pardon that does not become effective until the wrongdoer satisfies a prerequisite or that will be revoked upon the occurrence of some specified act.

   faultless pardon. A pardon granted because the act for which the person was convicted was not a crime.

   general pardon. See AMNESTY.

   partial pardon. A pardon that exonerates the offender from some but not all of the punishment or legal consequences of a crime.

   unconditional pardon. See *absolute pardon.*

pardon attorney. A Justice Department lawyer who considers applications for federal pardons and forwards those of promising candidates for review by the President.

parens patriae (**par**-enz **pay**-tree-ee *or* pa-tree-I). [Latin "parent of his or her country"] (18c) **1.** *Roman law.* The emperor as the embodiment of the state. **2.** The state regarded as a sovereign; the state in its capacity as provider of protection to those unable to care for themselves <the attorney general acted as *parens patriae* in the administrative hearing>. **3.** A doctrine by which a government has standing to prosecute a lawsuit on behalf of a citizen, esp. on behalf of someone who is under a legal disability to prosecute the suit <*parens patriae* allowed the state to institute proceedings>. ● The state ordinarily has no standing to sue on behalf of its citizens, unless a separate, sovereign interest will be served by the suit. — Also termed *doctrine of parens patriae.*

parent. (15c) **1.** The lawful father or mother of someone. ● In ordinary usage, the term denotes more than responsibility for conception and birth. The term commonly includes (1) either the natural father or the natural mother of a child, (2) either the adoptive father or the adoptive mother of a child, (3) a child's putative blood parent who has expressly acknowledged paternity, and (4) an individual or agency whose status as guardian has been established by judicial decree. In law, parental status based on any criterion may be terminated by judicial decree. In other words, a person ceases to be a legal parent if that person's status as a parent has been terminated in a legal proceeding. — Also termed *legal parent.*

   absent parent. See *noncustodial parent.*

   adoptive parent. (18c) A parent by virtue of legal adoption. See ADOPTION (1).

   biological parent. The woman who provides the egg or the man who provides the sperm to form the zygote that grows into an embryo. — Also termed *genetic parent.*

   birth parent. Either the biological father or the mother who gives birth to a child. — Sometimes written *birthparent.*

   constructive parent. See *equitable parent.*

   custodial parent. The parent awarded physical custody of a child in a divorce. See PHYSICAL CUSTODY (2). Cf. *noncustodial parent.*

   de facto parent. An adult who (1) is not the child's legal parent, (2) has, with consent of the child's legal parent, resided with the child for a significant period, and (3) has routinely performed a share of the caretaking functions at least as great as that of the parent who has been the child's primary caregiver without any expectation of compensation for this care. ● Because the status of de facto parent is subordinate to that of legal parent, a person who expects to be afforded the status of parent should, if possible, adopt the child. The primary function of this conceptual status is to provide courts with a means for maintaining a relationship between a child and an adult who has functioned as a parent when that adult is prohibited from legally adopting the child. The status is usu. limited to a person who has assumed the role of parent with the knowledge and consent, either express or implied, of the legal parent. But it may also arise when there is a total failure or inability of the legal parent to perform parental duties. Cf. *equitable parent; psychological parent.*

   Disneyland parent. A noncustodial parent who indulges his or her child with gifts and good times during visitation and leaves most or all disciplinary responsibilities to the other parent; esp., a noncustodial parent who provides luxuries that the custodial parent cannot afford but performs no disciplinary duties, in an effort to gain or retain the child's affection. See LOLLIPOP SYNDROME.

   domiciliary parent. A parent with whom a child lives.

   dual-residential parent. A parent who shares primary residential responsibility for a child with the other parent when each provides a residence that is substantially a primary residence. ● In many jurisdictions, dual residence is referred to as joint physical custody. See RESIDENTIAL RESPONSIBILITY; CUSTODY (2). Cf. *residential parent.*

equitable parent. **1.** A husband who, though not the biological father, is treated by the court as the father in an action for custody or visitation, usu. when the husband (1) has treated the child as his own while married to the child's mother, (2) is the only father the child has ever known, and (3) seeks the rights of fatherhood. **2.** A mother or father, not by blood or adoption, but by virtue of the close parent-like relationship that exists between that person and a child. • The status of equitable parent is a legal fiction that is used as an equitable remedy. Most commonly, the status of equitable parent arises when a person, living with the child and one of his or her legal or natural parents, forms a close bond with the child and assumes the duties and responsibilities of a parent. — Also termed *constructive parent.* See *adoption by estoppel* under ADOPTION. Cf. *psychological parent; de facto parent.*

foster parent. (17c) An adult who, though without blood ties or legal ties, cares for and rears a child, esp. an orphaned or neglected child who might otherwise be deprived of nurture, usu. under the auspices and direction of an agency and for some compensation or benefit. • Foster parents sometimes give care and support temporarily until a child is legally adopted by others. See FOSTER CARE. Cf. *foster child* under CHILD.

genetic parent. See *biological parent.*

godparent. See GODPARENT.

intended parent. See *intentional parent.*

intentional parent. The person whose idea it is to have and raise a child and who (1) enters into a surrogacy contract with a surrogate mother, and (2) is the legal parent of the child regardless of any genetic link to the child. — Also termed *intended parent.* See *intended child* under CHILD.

noncustodial parent. In the child-custody laws of some states, a parent without the primary custody rights of a child; esp., the parent not awarded physical custody of a child in a divorce. • The noncustodial parent is typically awarded visitation with the child. — Also termed *nonresidential parent; possessory conservator; absent parent.* See PHYSICAL CUSTODY (2). Cf. *custodial parent.*

nonresidential parent. See *noncustodial parent.*

parent by estoppel. A man who, though not a child's legal father, is estopped from denying liability for child support. • This estoppel usu. arises when the man (1) has lived with the child for at least two years, (2) has believed in good faith that he was the child's father, (3) has accepted parental responsibilities, and (4) has entered into a coparenting agreement with the child's mother — and when the court finds that recognition of the status of parent is in the child's best interests. See ESTOPPEL.

primary domiciliary parent. In a joint-custody arrangement, the parent who exercises primary physical custody. See *joint custody* under CUSTODY (2).

psychological parent. A person who, on a continuing and regular basis, provides for a child's emotional and physical needs. • The psychological parent may be the biological parent, a foster parent, a guardian, a common-law parent, or some other person unrelated to the child.

residential parent. A parent who has primary residential responsibility for a child and who is not a dual-residential parent. See RESIDENTIAL RESPONSIBILITY. Cf. *dual-residential parent.*

stepparent. (1840) The spouse of one's mother or father by a later marriage.

surrogate parent. (1972) **1.** A person who carries out the role of a parent by court appointment or the voluntary assumption of parental responsibilities. **2.** See *surrogate mother* (2) under MOTHER.

2. See *parent corporation* under CORPORATION.

parentage (**pair**-ən-tij *or* **par**-). (15c) The state or condition of being a parent; kindred in the direct ascending line.

parentage action. See PATERNITY SUIT.

parental access. See VISITATION (2).

parental-alienation syndrome. See PARENT-ALIENATION SYNDROME.

parental-autonomy doctrine. The principle that a parent has a fundamental right to raise his or her child and to make all decisions regarding that child free from governmental intervention, unless (1) the child's health and welfare are jeopardized by the parent's decisions, or (2) public health, welfare, safety, and order are threatened by the parent's decisions. • The Supreme Court first recognized the doctrine of parental autonomy over the family in *Meyer v. Nebraska*, 262 U.S. 390, 43 S.Ct. 625 (1923). — Also termed *family-autonomy doctrine.* Cf. PARENTAL-PRIVILEGE DOCTRINE.

parental consent. See CONSENT (1).

parental-consent statute. A statute that requires a minor to obtain his or her parent's consent before receiving elective medical treatment, such as an abortion. • Without parental consent, a physician or other medical professional commits a battery upon a child when giving nonemergency medical treatment. To pass constitutional muster, a parental-consent statute must include a judicial-bypass provision. *Planned Parenthood of Southeastern Pa. v. Casey*, 505 U.S. 833, 112 S. Ct. 2791 (1992). — Also termed *parental-consent treatment statute*. See JUDICIAL-BYPASS PROVISION. Cf. PARENTAL-NOTIFICATION STATUTE; MATURE-MINOR DOCTRINE.

parental-consent treatment statute. See PARENTAL-CONSENT STATUTE.

parental consortium. See CONSORTIUM.

parental-discipline privilege. A parent's right to use reasonable force or to impose reasonable punishment on a child in a way that is necessary to control, train, and educate. ● Several factors are used to determine the reasonableness of the action, including whether the actor is the parent; the child's age, sex, and physical and mental state; the severity and foreseeable consequences of the punishment; and the nature of the misconduct. Cf. PARENTAL-PRIVILEGE DOCTRINE.

parental functions. See PARENTING FUNCTIONS.

parent-alienation syndrome. A situation in which one parent has manipulated a child to fear or hate the other parent; a condition resulting from a parent's actions that are designed to poison a child's relationship with the other parent. ● Some mental-health specialists deny that this phenomenon amounts to a "psychological syndrome." — Also termed *parental-alienation syndrome*.

parental immunity. See IMMUNITY (2).

parental-immunity doctrine. See *parental immunity* (1) under IMMUNITY (2).

parental kidnapping. See KIDNAPPING.

Parental Kidnapping Prevention Act. A federal law, enacted in 1980, providing a penalty for child-kidnapping by a noncustodial parent and requiring states to recognize and enforce a child-custody order rendered by a court of another state. 28 USCA § 1738A; 42 USCA §§ 654, 655, 663. — Abbr. PKPA. Cf. UNIFORM CHILD CUSTODY JURISDICTION ACT; FEDERAL KIDNAPPING ACT.

parental-liability statute. (1963) A law obliging parents to pay damages for torts (esp. intentional ones) committed by their minor children. ● All states have these laws, but most limit the parents' monetary liability to about $3,000 per tort. Parents can also be held criminally liable for the acts of their children. One group of laws is aimed at contributing to the delinquency and endangering the welfare of a minor. More recently, the laws have been directed at improper supervision and failure to supervise. The first law aimed at punishing parents for the acts of their children was enacted in Colorado in 1903. By 1961 all but two states had enacted similar laws. At least five states make it a felony for a parent to intentionally, knowingly, and recklessly provide a firearm to a child, or permit the child to handle a firearm,

when the parent is aware of a substantial risk that the child will use the weapon to commit a crime. — Also termed *parental-responsibility statute*; *failure-to-supervise statute*. Cf. PARENTAL-RESPONSIBILITY STATUTE.

parental-notification statute. A law that requires a physician to notify a minor's parent of her intention to have an abortion. Cf. PARENTAL-CONSENT STATUTE.

parental-preference doctrine. (1974) The principle that custody of a minor child should ordinarily be granted to a fit parent rather than another person. ● The preference can be rebutted by proof that the child's best interests are to the contrary. — Also termed *parental-rights doctrine*; *parental-superior-rights doctrine*; *parental-presumption rule*. Cf. BEST INTERESTS OF THE CHILD.

parental-presumption rule. See PARENTAL-PREFERENCE DOCTRINE.

parental-privilege doctrine. The parent's right to discipline his or her child reasonably, to use reasonable child-rearing practices free of governmental interference, and to exercise decision-making authority over the child. Cf. PARENTAL-AUTONOMY DOCTRINE; PARENTAL-DISCIPLINE PRIVILEGE.

parental-responsibility statute. (1956) **1.** A law imposing criminal sanctions (such as fines) on parents whose minor children commit crimes as a result of the parents' failure to exercise sufficient control over them. — Also termed *control-your-kid law*. **2.** PARENTAL-LIABILITY STATUTE.

parental rights. (18c) A parent's rights to make all decisions concerning his or her child, including the right to determine the child's care and custody, the right to educate and discipline the child, and the right to control the child's earnings and property. See TERMINATION OF PARENTAL RIGHTS.

parental-rights doctrine. See PARENTAL-PREFERENCE DOCTRINE.

parental-superior-rights doctrine. See PARENTAL-PREFERENCE DOCTRINE.

parent application. See PATENT APPLICATION.

parent by estoppel. See PARENT.

parent-child immunity. See *parental immunity* (1) under IMMUNITY (2).

parent–child relationship. See RELATIONSHIP.

parent committee. See COMMITTEE.

parent company. See *parent corporation* under CORPORATION.

parent corporation. See CORPORATION.

parentela (par-ən-**tee**-lə), *n. pl.* [Law Latin] (15c) Persons who can trace descent from a common ancestor.

parentelic method (par-ən-**tee**-lik *or* -**tel**-ik). (1935) A scheme of computation used to determine the paternal or maternal collaterals entitled to inherit when a childless intestate decedent is not survived by parents or their issue. • Under this method, the estate passes to grandparents and their issue; if there are none, to great-grandparents and their issue; and so on down each line until an heir is found. The Uniform Probate Code uses a limited parentelic system: it looks first to the grandparents and their issue, but if no heir is found in that line, the search ends and the estate escheats to the state. See DEGREE (5). Cf. GRADUAL METHOD.

parent filing date. See *effective filing date* under DATE.

parenticide (pə-**ren**-tə-sɪd). (17c) **1.** The act of murdering one's parent. **2.** A person who murders his or her parent. — **parenticidal,** *adj.*

parenting, *n.* **1.** Performance of the functions of a parent. **2.** One or more methods of child-rearing.

    parallel parenting. A situation in which divorced parents, although disagreeing on some aspects of child-rearing, allow each other to handle discipline and daily regimens in their own individual ways when with the child.

    shared parenting. Cooperation between divorced parents in child-rearing.

parenting agreement. See PARENTING PLAN.

parenting function. A task that serves the direct or day-to-day needs of a child or of a child's family. • Parenting functions include providing necessaries, making decisions about the child's welfare, and maintaining the family residence. Cf. CARETAKING FUNCTIONS.

parenting plan. A plan that allocates custodial responsibility and decision-making authority for what serves the child's best interests and that provides a mechanism for resolving any later disputes between parents. — Also termed *parenting agreement.* See CUSTODY (2); CUSTODIAL RESPONSIBILITY; DECISION-MAKING RESPONSIBILITY.

parenting time. See VISITATION.

parent–subsidiary freezeout. See FREEZEOUT.

Pareto optimality (pə-**ray**-toh *or* pə-**ret**-oh), *n.* An economic situation in which no person can be made better off without making someone else worse off. • The term derives from the work of Vilfredo Pareto (1848–1923), an Italian economist and sociologist. — **Pareto-optimal,** *adj.*

Pareto superiority, *n.* An economic situation in which an exchange can be made that benefits someone and injures no one. • When such an exchange can no longer be made, the situation becomes one of Pareto optimality. — **Pareto-superior,** *adj.*

pari delicto, in. See IN PARI DELICTO.

pari materia, in. See IN PARI MATERIA.

parimutuel betting (par-i-**myoo**-choo-əl). A system of gambling in which bets placed on a race are pooled and then paid (less a management fee and taxes) to those holding winning tickets.

pari passu (**pahr**-ee **pahs**-oo *or* **pair**-ɪ, **pair**-ee, *or* **par**-ee **pas**-[y]oo). [Latin "by equal step"] Proportionally; at an equal pace; without preference <creditors of a bankrupt estate will receive distributions *pari passu*>.

Paris Additional Act. *Copyright.* An 1896 amendment to the Berne Convention extending copyright protection to photographs as derivative works.

Paris Convention. See PARIS CONVENTION FOR THE PROTECTION OF INDUSTRIAL PROPERTY.

Paris Convention for the Protection of Industrial Property. A treaty designed to unify and streamline patent prosecutions and trademark applications among the signatories. • The Convention eased the harsh effects of the first-to-file priority rule by allowing an applicant in any member country one year in which to apply in other member countries while maintaining the application's original priority date. It also banned patent-protection discrimination against residents of other member nations. Now administered by the World Intellectual Property Organization, an agency of the United Nations, the Convention was first signed in 1883, revised most recently in 1967, and amended in 1970. — Also termed *Paris Industrial Property Convention.* — Often shortened to *Paris Convention.*

parish. (14c) **1.** In Louisiana, a governmental subdivision analogous to a county in other U.S. states. **2.** *Eccles. law.* A division of a town or district, subject to the ministry of one pastor.

    district parish. *Eccles. law.* A geographical division of an English parish made by the Crown's commissioners for the building of new churches for worship, celebration of marriages, christenings, and burials.

parish court. See *county court* under COURT.

Paris Industrial Property Convention. See PARIS CONVENTION FOR THE PROTECTION OF INDUSTRIAL PROPERTY.

par item. See ITEM.

Parker **doctrine.** See STATE-ACTION DOCTRINE.

parking. (1983) **1.** The sale of securities subject to an agreement that the seller will buy them back at a later time for a similar price. • Parking is illegal if done to circumvent securities regulations or tax laws. It is often a method of evading the net-capital requirements of the National Association of Securities Dealers (NASD), which requires a brokerage firm to discount the value of any stock it holds in its own account when it files its monthly report about its net-capital condition. To reach technical compliance with the NASD's net-capital requirements, a brokerage firm "sells" stock from its own account to a customer at market price, thereby avoiding the discount for reporting purposes. Having filed its report, it can then "buy" the shares back from the customer, usu. at the same price at which it "sold" the stock, plus interest. **2.** The placement of assets in a safe, short-term investment while other investment opportunities are being considered. — Also termed (in sense 1) *stock-parking*.

parking-lot rule. The principle that workers'-compensation insurance covers the injuries suffered by an employee on the employer's premises when the employee is arriving at or leaving work. — Also termed *premises rule*.

parliament. (12c) The supreme legislative body of some nations; esp. (*cap.*), in the United Kingdom, the national legislature consisting of the monarch, the House of Lords, and the House of Commons.

parliamentarian. (17c) *Parliamentary law.* A consultant trained in parliamentary law who advises the chair and others on matters of parliamentary law and procedure. • The parliamentarian, who is often a professional, only advises and never "rules" on procedural issues. See *parliamentary law* under PARLIAMENTARY (2); *parliamentary procedure* under PARLIAMENTARY (2).

parliamentary, *adj.* (17c) **1.** Of or relating to a parliament. **2.** *Parliamentary law.* Of or relating to rules of order for the conduct of business in deliberative assemblies.

parliamentary authority. A parliamentary manual that an organization has adopted for its deliberations, and whose provisions govern the organization in every case to which they apply, as long as they are consistent with law and with the organization's governing documents. See PARLIAMENTARY MANUAL.

parliamentary diplomacy. See DIPLOMACY.

parliamentary divorce. See *legislative divorce* under DIVORCE.

parliamentary inquiry. See INQUIRY.

parliamentary intent. See LEGISLATIVE INTENT.

parliamentary law. The body of rules and precedents governing the proceedings of legislative bodies and other deliberative assemblies. — Also termed *parliamentary procedure*.

    common parliamentary law. **1.** See *general parliamentary law.* **2.** The common law as applied to parliamentary law; parliamentary law as it is found in judicial decisions.

    general parliamentary law. The basic principles and practices of parliamentary law, as commonly understood among a meeting's members based on their experience in other deliberative assemblies, that apply in the absence of adopted rules of order. • A parliamentary manual is evidence of the general parliamentary law. — Also termed *common parliamentary law.*

parliamentary manual. A code or reference, usu. a commercially published book, that contains parliamentary rules and is offered for adoption by organizations as their parliamentary authority. • The leading parliamentary manuals in print in the United States are *Robert's Rules of Order Newly Revised* for nonlegislative bodies, and *Mason's Manual of Legislative Procedure* for state legislatures. Cf. PARLIAMENTARY AUTHORITY.

parliamentary motion. See MOTION (2).

parliamentary practice. See PARLIAMENTARY PROCEDURE.

parliamentary privilege. See PRIVILEGE (1).

parliamentary procedure. 1. PARLIAMENTARY LAW. **2.** Parliamentary law as applied in a particular organization, including the parliamentary authority and other rules that the organization adopts. — Also termed *parliamentary practice.*

parliamentary will. See WILL.

parody. (16c) *Intellectual property.* A transformative use of a well-known work for purposes of satirizing, ridiculing, critiquing, or commenting on the original work, as opposed to merely alluding to the original to draw attention to the later work. • In constitutional law, a parody is protected as free speech. In copyright law, a work must meet the definition of a parody and be a fair use of the copyrighted material, or else it may constitute infringement. See FAIR USE.

par of exchange. The recognized standard value of one country's currency expressed in terms of that of another.

parol (pə-**rohl** *or* **par**-əl), *adj.* (16c) **1.** Oral; unwritten <parol evidence>. **2.** Not under seal <parol contract>.

parol (pə-**rohl** *or* **par**-əl), *n.* (15c) **1.** An oral statement or declaration. **2.** *Hist.* The oral pleadings in a case.

parol agreement. See *parol contract* (1) under CONTRACT.

parol arrest. See ARREST.

parol contract. See CONTRACT.

parol demurrer. See DEMURRER.

parole (pə-**rohl**), *n.* (17c) The conditional release of a prisoner from imprisonment before the full sentence has been served. • Although not available under some sentences, parole is usu. granted for good behavior on the condition that the parolee regularly report to a supervising officer for a specified period. Cf. PARDON; PROBATION (1). — **parole,** *vb.*

bench parole. See *bench probation* under PROBATION.

juvenile parole. The conditional release of a juvenile offender from confinement. — Also termed *aftercare.*

parole board. (1898) A governmental body that decides whether prisoners may be released from prison before completing their sentences. — Also termed *board of parole; parole commission.*

parolee (pə-roh-**lee**). (1903) A prisoner who is released on parole.

parole revocation. (1930) The administrative or judicial act of returning a parolee to prison because of the parolee's failure to abide by the conditions of parole (as by committing a new offense).

parol evidence. See EVIDENCE.

parol-evidence rule. (1893) *Contracts.* The common-law principle that a writing intended by the parties to be a final embodiment of their agreement cannot be modified by evidence of earlier or contemporaneous agreements that might add to, vary, or contradict the writing. ● This rule usu. operates to prevent a party from introducing extrinsic evidence of negotiations that occurred before or while the agreement was being reduced to its final written form. See INTEGRATION (2); MERGER (2). Cf. FOUR-CORNERS RULE.

parol lease. See LEASE.

parol trust. See *oral trust* (1) under TRUST.

***Parratt–Hudson* doctrine.** (1986) The principle that a state actor's random, unauthorized deprivation of someone's property does not amount to a due-process violation if the state provides an adequate postdeprivation remedy. *Parratt v. Taylor,* 451 U.S. 527, 101 S.Ct. 1908 (1984); *Hudson v. Palmer,* 468 U.S. 517, 104 S.Ct. 3194 (1984).

parricide (par-ə-sɪd), *n.* (16c) **1.** The act of killing a close relative, esp. a parent. **2.** One who kills such a relative. Cf. PATRICIDE. — **parricidal,** *adj.*

partial account. See ACCOUNT.

partial assignment. See ASSIGNMENT (2).

partial average. See *particular average* under AVERAGE.

partial-birth abortion. See ABORTION.

partial breach. See BREACH OF CONTRACT.

partial defense. See DEFENSE (1).

partial dependent. See DEPENDENT.

partial disability. See DISABILITY (2).

partial emancipation. See EMANCIPATION.

partial eviction. See EVICTION.

partial evidence. See EVIDENCE.

partial failure of consideration. See FAILURE OF CONSIDERATION.

partial guardian. See GUARDIAN.

partial insanity. See *diminished capacity* under CAPACITY (3).

partial integration. See INTEGRATION (2).

partial interdiction. See INTERDICTION (3).

partial intestate. See INTESTATE.

partial law. See LAW.

partial limitation. *Insurance.* A policy provision in which the insurer agrees to pay a total loss if the actual loss exceeds a specified amount.

partial liquidation. See LIQUIDATION.

partial loss. See LOSS.

partially disclosed principal. See PRINCIPAL (1).

partially integrated contract. See INTEGRATED CONTRACT.

partial pardon. See PARDON.

partial release. See RELEASE.

partial-release clause. See CLAUSE.

partial responsibility. See *diminished capacity* under CAPACITY (3).

partial summary judgment. See SUMMARY JUDGMENT.

partial truce. See *special truce* under TRUCE.

partial verdict. See VERDICT.

partial zoning. See ZONING.

particeps (**pahr**-tə-seps), *n.* [Latin] **1.** A participant. **2.** A part owner.

particeps criminis (**pahr**-tə-seps **krim**-ə-nis), *n.* [Latin "partner in crime"] (17c) **1.** An accomplice or accessory. See ACCESSORY. Pl. ***participes criminis*** (pahr-**tis**-ə-peez). **2.** The doctrine that one participant in an unlawful activity cannot recover in a civil action against another participant in the activity. ● This is a civil doctrine only, having nothing to do with criminal responsibility. Cf. IN PARI DELICTO DOCTRINE.

participating bond. See BOND (3).

participating insurance. See INSURANCE.

participating policy. See INSURANCE POLICY.

participating preferred stock. See STOCK.

participation, *n.* (14c) **1.** The act of taking part in something, such as a partnership, a crime, or a trial. **2.** The right of an employee to receive part of a business's profits; profit-sharing. See JOINT PARTICIPATION. — **participate,** *vb.*

participation loan. See LOAN.

participation mortgage. See MORTGAGE.

participation stock. See STOCK.

particular average. See AVERAGE.

particular average loss. See LOSS.

particular custom. See *local custom* under CUSTOM.

particular damages. See *special damages* under DAMAGES.

particular estate. See ESTATE (1).

particular jurisprudence. See JURISPRUDENCE.

particular legacy. See LEGACY.

particular lien. See LIEN.

particular malice. See MALICE.

particular partnership. See PARTNERSHIP.

particular power. See *special power* under POWER (3).

particular recital. See RECITAL.

particulars, bill of. See BILL OF PARTICULARS.

particulars of sale. (18c) A document that describes the various features of a thing (such as a house) that is for sale.

particular successor. See SUCCESSOR.

particular tenant. See TENANT.

particular title. See TITLE (2).

partition, *n.* (15c) **1.** Something that separates one part of a space from another. **2.** The act of dividing; esp., the division of real property held jointly or in common by two or more persons into individually owned interests. — Also termed *partition in kind.*

> **definitive partition.** A partition that is irrevocable.

> **partition of succession.** *Louisiana law.* The division of an estate among an intestate's heirs. See La. Civ. Code art. 1293.

> **provisional partition.** A temporary partition, often made before the remainder of the property can be divided.

3. *Oil & gas.* The division of an undivided mineral interest by voluntary agreement or judicial action. — **partition,** *vb.* — **partible,** *adj.*

partition in kind. See PARTITION (2).

partner. (13c) **1.** One who shares or takes part with another, esp. in a venture with shared benefits and shared risks; an associate or colleague <partners in crime>. **2.** One of two or more persons who jointly own and carry on a business for profit <the firm and its partners were sued for malpractice>. See PARTNERSHIP. **3.** One of two persons who are married or who live together; a spouse or companion <my partner in life>.

> **dormant partner.** See *silent partner.*

> **general partner.** (1804) A partner who ordinarily takes part in the daily operations of the business, shares in the profits and losses, and is personally responsible for the partnership's debts and other liabilities. — Also termed *full partner.*

> **junior partner.** (18c) A partner whose participation is limited with respect to both profits and management.

> **limited partner.** (1822) A partner who receives profits from the business but does not take part in managing the business and is not liable for any amount greater than his or her original investment. — Also termed *special partner;* (in civil law) *partner in commendam.* See *limited partnership* under PARTNERSHIP.

> **liquidating partner.** (1825) The partner appointed to settle the accounts, collect the assets, adjust the claims, and pay the debts of a dissolving or insolvent firm.

> **name partner.** (1945) A partner whose name appears in the name of the partnership <Mr. Tibbs is a name partner in the accounting firm of Gibbs & Tibbs>. — Also termed *named partner; title member.*

> **nominal partner.** (18c) A person who is held out as a partner in a firm or business but who has no actual interest in the partnership. — Also termed *ostensible partner; partner by estoppel.*

> **ostensible partner.** See *nominal partner.*

> **partner by estoppel.** See *nominal partner.*

> **partner in commendam** (in kə-**men**-dəm). See *limited partner.*

> **quasi-partner.** (1809) A person who joins others in an enterprise that appears to be, but is not, a partnership. ● A joint venturer, for example, is a quasi-partner.

> **secret partner.** (18c) A partner whose connection with the firm is concealed from the public. — Also termed *sleeping partner.*

> **senior partner.** (18c) A high-ranking partner, as in a law firm.

> **silent partner.** (18c) A partner who shares in the profits but who has no active voice in management of the firm and whose existence is often not publicly disclosed. — Also termed *dormant partner.*

> **sleeping partner.** See *secret partner.*

> **special partner.** See *limited partner.*

> **surviving partner.** (17c) The partner who, upon the partnership's dissolution because of another partner's death, serves as a trustee to administer the firm's remaining affairs.

partnership. (16c) A voluntary association of two or more persons who jointly own and carry on a business for profit. ● Under the Uniform Partnership Act, a partnership is presumed to exist if the persons agree to share proportionally the business's profits or losses. Cf. JOINT VENTURE; STRATEGIC ALLIANCE.

collapsible partnership. (1962) *Tax.* A partnership formed by partners who intend to dissolve it before they realize any income. • Any partner's gain resulting from unrealized receivables or inventory that has increased substantially in value will be treated by the IRS as ordinary income rather than as capital gain. IRC (26 USCA) § 751. Cf. *collapsible corporation* under CORPORATION.

commercial partnership. See *trading partnership*.

family partnership. (1902) A business partnership in which the partners are related. IRC (26 USCA) § 704(e). • In this phrase, the term *family* includes a person's spouse, ancestors, lineal descendants, siblings, and any trusts established primarily for the benefit of those persons. See FAMILY-PARTNERSHIP RULES.

general partnership. (18c) A partnership in which all partners participate fully in running the business and share equally in profits and losses (though the partners' monetary contributions may vary).

implied partnership. See *partnership by estoppel*.

limited-liability partnership. (1910) A partnership in which a partner is not liable for a negligent act committed by another partner or by an employee not under the partner's supervision. • All states have enacted statutes that allow a business (typically a law firm or accounting firm) to register as this type of partnership. — Abbr. L.L.P.

limited partnership. (18c) A partnership composed of one or more persons who control the business and are personally liable for the partnership's debts (called *general partners*), and one or more persons who contribute capital and share profits but who cannot manage the business and are liable only for the amount of their contribution (called *limited partners*). • The chief purpose of a limited partnership is to enable persons to invest their money in a business without taking an active part in managing the business, and without risking more than the sum originally contributed, while securing the cooperation of others who have ability and integrity but insufficient money. — Abbr. L.P. — Also termed *special partnership*; (in civil law) *partnership in commendam*.

master limited partnership. See *publicly traded partnership*.

nontrading partnership. A partnership that does not buy and sell but instead is a partnership of employment or occupation. — Also termed

noncommercial partnership. • This type of partnership offers services rather than goods.

particular partnership. A partnership in which the members unite to share the benefits of a single transaction or enterprise.

partnership at will. (1849) A partnership that any partner may dissolve at any time without thereby incurring liability. Cf. *partnership for a term*.

partnership by estoppel. (1872) A partnership implied by law when one or more persons represent themselves as partners to a third party who relies on that representation. • A person who is deemed a partner by estoppel becomes liable for any credit extended to the partnership by the third party. — Also termed *implied partnership*.

partnership for a term. A partnership that exists for a specified duration or until a specified event occurs. • Such a partnership can be prematurely dissolved by any partner, but that partner may be held liable for breach of the partnership agreement. Cf. *partnership at will*.

partnership in commendam. See *limited partnership*.

publicly traded partnership. A partnership whose interests are traded either over-the-counter or on a securities exchange. • These partnerships may be treated as corporations for income-tax purposes. IRC (26 USCA) § 7704(a). — Abbr. PTP. — Also termed *master limited partnership*.

special partnership. 1. See *limited partnership*. **2.** A partnership formed only for a single venture.

subpartnership. An arrangement between a firm's partner and a nonpartner to share the partner's profits and losses in the firm's business, but without forming a legal partnership between the partner and the nonpartner.

tiered partnership. An ownership arrangement consisting of one parent partnership that is a partner in one or more subsidiary partnerships.

trading partnership. A partnership whose usual business involves buying and selling. — Also termed *commercial partnership*.

umbrella limited partnership. A limited partnership used by a real-estate investment trust to acquire investment properties in exchange for shares in the partnership. See *umbrella-partnership real-estate investment trust* under REAL-ESTATE INVESTMENT TRUST.

universal partnership. A partnership formed by persons who agree to contribute all their individually owned property — and to devote all their skill, labor, and services — to the partnership.

partnership agreement. (1802) A contract defining the partners' rights and duties toward one another — not the partners' relationship with third parties. — Also termed *articles of partnership*.

partnership association. (1812) A business organization that combines the features of a limited partnership and a close corporation. ● Partnership associations are statutorily authorized in only a few states. — Also termed *statutory partnership association*; *limited partnership association*.

partnership at will. See PARTNERSHIP.

partnership certificate. A document that evidences the participation of the partners in a partnership. ● The certificate is often furnished to financial institutions when the partnership borrows money.

partnership distribution. See DISTRIBUTION.

partnership insurance. See INSURANCE.

partner's lien. (1870) A partner's right to have the partnership property applied in payment of the partnership's debts and to have whatever is due the firm from fellow partners deducted from what would otherwise be payable to them for their shares.

partnership life insurance. See *partnership insurance* (1) under INSURANCE.

part payment. See PAYMENT.

part performance. 1. See PERFORMANCE. **2.** See PART-PERFORMANCE DOCTRINE.

part-performance doctrine. (1935) The equitable principle by which a failure to comply with the statute of frauds is overcome by a party's execution, in reliance on an opposing party's oral promise, of a substantial portion of an oral contract's requirements. — Sometimes shortened to *part performance*. See *part performance* under PERFORMANCE.

part-sovereign state. See SOVEREIGN STATE.

party. (13c) **1.** One who takes part in a transaction <a party to the contract>.

party of the first part. (18c) *Archaic.* The party named first in a contract; esp., the owner or seller.

party of the second part. (18c) *Archaic.* The party named second in a contract; esp., the buyer.

2. One by or against whom a lawsuit is brought <a party to the lawsuit>. ● For purposes of res judicata, a party to a lawsuit is a person who has been named as a party and has a right to control the lawsuit either personally, or, if not fully competent, through someone appointed to protect the person's interests.

adverse party. (15c) A party whose interests are opposed to the interests of another party to the action. Cf. *hostile witness* under WITNESS.

aggrieved party. (17c) A party entitled to a remedy; esp., a party whose personal, pecuniary, or property rights have been adversely affected by another person's actions or by a court's decree or judgment. — Also termed *party aggrieved*; *person aggrieved*.

coparty. See COPARTY.

fictitious party. A person who is named in a writ, complaint, or record as a party in a suit, but who does not actually exist, or a person who is named as a plaintiff but is unaware of the suit and did not consent to be named.

formal party. See *nominal party*.

indispensable party. (1821) A party who, having interests that would inevitably be affected by a court's judgment, must be included in the case. ● If such a party is not included, the case must be dismissed. Fed. R. Civ. P. 19(b). Cf. *necessary party*.

innocent party. (16c) A party who did not consciously or intentionally participate in an event or transaction.

interested party. (17c) A party who has a recognizable stake (and therefore standing) in a matter. — Abbr. IP.

joint party. See COPARTY.

necessary party. (18c) A party who, being closely connected to a lawsuit, should be included in the case if feasible, but whose absence will not require dismissal of the proceedings. See *compulsory joinder* under JOINDER. Cf. *indispensable party*.

nominal party. (18c) A party to an action who has no control over it and no financial interest in its outcome; esp., a party who has some immaterial interest in the subject matter of a lawsuit and who will not be affected by any judgment, but who is nonetheless joined in the lawsuit to avoid procedural defects. ● An example is the disinterested stakeholder in a garnishment action. — Also termed *formal party*. Cf. *real party in interest*.

party aggrieved. See *aggrieved party*.

party cast. The losing party in a lawsuit.

party in interest. See *real party in interest*.

party opponent. (18c) An adversary in a legal proceeding. — Sometimes written *party-opponent*.

party to be charged. (1923) A defendant in an action to enforce a contract falling within the statute of frauds.

prevailing party. (17c) A party in whose favor a judgment is rendered, regardless of the amount of damages awarded <in certain cases, the court will award attorney's fees to the prevailing party>. — Also termed *successful party*. See *Buckhannon Bd. & Care Home, Inc. v. West Va. Dep't of Health & Human Res.*, 532 U.S. 598, 603, 121 S.Ct. 1835, 1839 (2001) (relying on the seventh edition of *Black's Law Dictionary* [1999]).

proper party. (1823) A party who may be joined in a case for reasons of judicial economy but whose presence is not essential to the proceeding. See *permissive joinder* under JOINDER.

real party in interest. (1804) A person entitled under the substantive law to enforce the right sued upon and who generally, but not necessarily, benefits from the action's final outcome. — Also termed *party in interest*; (archaically) *interessee*. Cf. *nominal party*.

successful party. See *prevailing party*.

third party. See THIRD PARTY.

3. POLITICAL PARTY.

party-column ballot. See BALLOT (4).

party wall. See WALL.

par value. The value of an instrument or security as shown on its face; esp., the arbitrary dollar amount assigned to a stock share by the corporate charter, or the principal of a bond at maturity. — Often shortened to *par*. — Also termed *face value*; *nominal value*; *stated value*.

par-value stock. See STOCK.

pass, *vb.* (14c) **1.** To pronounce or render an opinion, ruling, sentence, or judgment <the court refused to pass on the constitutional issue, deciding the case instead on procedural grounds>. **2.** To transfer or be transferred <the woman's will passes title to the house to her nephew, much to her husband's surprise>. **3.** To enact (a legislative bill or resolution); to adopt <Congress has debated whether to pass a balanced-budget amendment to the Constitution>. See ADOPTION (5). **4.** To approve or certify (something) as meeting specified requirements <the mechanic informed her that the car had passed inspection>. **5.** To publish, transfer, or circulate (a thing, often a forgery) <he was found guilty of passing counterfeit bills>. **6.** To forgo or proceed beyond <the case was passed on the court's trial docket because the judge was presiding over a criminal trial>. **7.** ABSTAIN (1).

passage, *n.* **1.** ADOPTION (5); esp., the passing of a legislative measure into law. **2.** A right, privilege, or permission to cross land or water; an easement to travel through another's property. **3.** The process of traveling, esp. in transit <safe passage>. **4.** The act of coming and going <right of passage>.

pass-along, *adj.* See PASS-THROUGH.

passbook. A depositor's book in which a bank records all the transactions on an account. — Also termed *bankbook*.

passed dividend. See DIVIDEND.

passim (**pas**-im), *adv.* [Latin] (17c) Here and there; throughout (the cited work). • In modern legal writing, the citation signal *see generally* is preferred to *passim* as a general reference, although *passim* can be useful in a brief's index of authorities to show that a given authority is cited throughout the brief.

passing off, *n.* (1900) *Intellectual property.* The act or an instance of falsely representing one's own product as that of another in an attempt to deceive potential buyers. • Passing off is actionable in tort under the law of unfair competition. It may also be actionable as trademark infringement. — Also termed *palming off*; *misrepresentation of source*. Cf. MISAPPROPRIATION. — **pass off,** *vb.*

reverse passing off. The act or an instance of falsely representing another's product as one's own in an attempt to deceive potential buyers. — Also termed *reverse palming off*.

passing on. See *pass-on defense* under DEFENSE (1).

passive, *adj.* Not involving active participation; esp., of or relating to a business enterprise in which an investor does not have immediate control over the activity that produces income.

passive activity. (1962) *Tax.* A business activity in which the taxpayer does not materially participate and therefore does not have immediate control over the income. • A typical example is the ownership and rental of real property by someone not in the real-property business.

passive adoption-registry statute. See ADOPTION-REGISTRY STATUTE.

passive bond. See BOND (3).

passive breach of contract. See BREACH OF CONTRACT.

passive concealment. See CONCEALMENT.

passive conduct. See CONDUCT.

passive debt. See DEBT.

passive duty. See *negative duty* under DUTY (1).

passive euthanasia. See EUTHANASIA.

passive income. See INCOME.

passive investment income. See INCOME.

passive loss. See LOSS.

passive mercy killing. See DYATHANASIA.

passive negligence. See NEGLIGENCE.

passive trust. See TRUST.

pass-on defense. See DEFENSE (1).

passport. 1. A formal document certifying a person's identity and citizenship so that the person may travel to and from a foreign country. **2.** SEA LETTER. **3.** SAFE CONDUCT.

Passport Office. See BUREAU OF CONSULAR AFFAIRS.

pass the witness. See TAKE THE WITNESS.

pass-through, *adj.* (1951) (Of a seller's or lessor's costs) chargeable to the buyer or lessee. — Also termed *pass-along.*

pass-through security. See SECURITY.

pass-through taxation. See TAXATION.

past consideration. See CONSIDERATION (1).

past recollection recorded. *Evidence.* A document concerning events that a witness once knew about but can no longer remember. • The document itself is evidence and, despite being hearsay, may be admitted and read into the record if it was prepared or adopted by the witness when the events were fresh in the witness's memory. Fed. R. Evid. 803(5). — Also termed *recorded recollection; past recorded recollection.* Cf. PRESENT RECOLLECTION REFRESHED.

***Pasula–Robinette* test.** The principle that if a miner establishes a prima facie case of retaliation for filing a claim under the Mine Safety and Health Act, the mine operator can still prevail by proving, as an affirmative defense, that (1) the miner did not engage in a protected activity, (2) the adverse action was based on the miner's unprotected activity, and (3) the mine operator would have taken the same action based solely on the unprotected activity. • To establish a prima facie case of retaliation, the evidence must show that the miner engaged in a protected activity and that an adverse employment action occurred based at least in part on that activity. 30 USCA § 815(c); *Secretary ex rel. Pasula v. Consolidation Coal Co.,* 2 FMSHRC 2786 (1980); *Secretary ex rel. Robinette v. United Coal Co.,* 3 FMSHRC 802 (1981).

pat-down, *n.* See FRISK.

***Pate* hearing.** A proceeding in which the trial court seeks to determine whether a criminal defendant is competent to stand trial. *Pate v. Robinson,* 383 U.S. 375, 86 S.Ct. 836 (1966); 18 USCA § 4241. — Also termed *competency hearing; incompetency hearing.*

patent (**pay**-tənt), *adj.* (14c) Obvious; apparent <a patent ambiguity>. Cf. LATENT.

patent (**pat**-ənt), *n.* (14c) **1.** The governmental grant of a right, privilege, or authority. **2.** The official document so granting. — Also termed *public grant.* See LETTERS PATENT.

   call patent. A land patent in which the corners have been staked but the boundary lines have not been run out at the time of the grant.

   escheat patent. See *escheat grant* under GRANT.

   land patent. An instrument by which the government conveys a grant of public land to a private person.

   lapse patent. A land patent substituting for an earlier patent to the same land that lapsed because the previous patentee did not claim it.

3. The right to exclude others from making, using, marketing, selling, offering for sale, or importing an invention for a specified period (20 years from the date of filing), granted by the federal government to the inventor if the device or process is novel, useful, and nonobvious. 35 USCA §§ 101–103. • The holding of a patent alone does not by itself grant any right to make, use, or sell anything if that activity would infringe another's blocking patent. — Also termed *patent right; patent grant.*

   basic patent. See *pioneer patent.*

   blocking patent. One of two patents, neither of which can be effectively practiced without infringing the other. • For example, if *A* patents an improvement of *B*'s patented invention, *A* cannot practice the improvement without infringing *B*'s patent. Nor can *B* use the improvement without infringing *A*'s patent. Owners of blocking patents often cross-license each other. See *fencing patent;* DOMINATION.

   broadened reissue patent. *Patents.* A patent that is issued again, having broader claims than the original, surrendered patent. • Under 35 USCA § 251, a patent may be reissued, under certain circumstances, with broader claims than the original patent if the reissue application is filed within two years of the grant of the original patent. See INTERVENING RIGHTS.

   business-method patent. A U.S. patent that describes and claims a series of process steps that, as a whole, constitutes a method of doing business. • Until 1998, methods for doing business were not expressly recognized as being patentable. In that year, the Federal Circuit Court of Appeals held in *State Street Bank & Trust Co. v. Signature Fin. Group, Inc.,* 140 F.3d 1368 (Fed. Cir. 1998), that business methods are subject to the same legal requirements for patentability as any other process or method. — Also termed *cyberpatent.*

   combination patent. A patent granted for an invention that unites existing components in a novel and nonobvious way.

   Community patent. An international patent issued by the European Patent Office. • Community patents are good for 20 years from the application date. They may be registered in any nation in the European Union and other EPC signatories.

copending patent. A patent whose application is being prosecuted at or near the same time as another, similar patent. • Continuing applications must be copending with an existing patent application. A copending patent may affect another patent's validity if it discloses the same invention, or discloses some part of the invention that, combined with other prior art, results in anticipation (esp. if the copending patent is issued before the affected patent). A copending patent may be shown to be an unpatentable improvement on another copending patent's invention. 35 USCA § 102(e). See COPENDING.

cyberpatent. 1. See *business-method patent*. **2.** See *Internet patent*.

design patent. A patent granted for a new, original, and ornamental design for an article of manufacture; a patent that protects a product's appearance or nonfunctional aspects. • Design patents — which, unlike utility patents, have a term of only 14 years from the date the patent is granted — are similar to copyrights. 36 USCA § 171.

dominating patent. See *fencing patent*.

fencing patent. A patent procured for some aspect of an invention that the inventor does not intend to produce but that the inventor wants to prevent competitors from using in making improvements. • By making a claim whose only purpose is to protect other claims, the inventor seeks to "fence in" any such competing improvements. Courts disfavor fencing claims. — Also termed *dominating patent*.

improvement patent. A patent having claims directed to an improvement on a preexisting invention. • If the preexisting invention is patented by another, the owner of the improvement patent may need a license to practice the invention covered by the claims of the improvement patent. Similarly, the owner of the preexisting invention's patent may need a license to practice the invention in the improvement patent. Cf. *pioneer patent*.

in-force patent. A patent that has not expired or been ruled invalid.

Internet patent. A type of utility patent granted on an invention that combines business methods and software programs for Internet applications. — Also termed *cyberpatent*.

method patent. A patent having method or process claims that define a series of actions leading to a tangible physical result. — Also termed *process patent*.

paper patent. A patent granted for a discovery or invention that has never been used commercially. • A paper patent may receive less protection under the law than a patent granted for a device that is actually used in industry. As a prior-art reference, a paper patent may carry less weight with examiners than one for an invention that has been commercially exploited, because it may suggest that the invention did not work as claimed.

pioneer patent. A patent covering a function or a major technological advance never before performed, a wholly novel device, or subject matter of such novelty and importance as to mark a distinct step in the progress of the art, as distinguished from a mere improvement or perfection of what had gone before. • Under U.S. law, the claims of a pioneer patent are entitled to broader interpretation and to be given a broader range of equivalents. A pioneer patent is usu. the first one documented by a patent-tracking service, although it may not be the first patent published by a national registry, such as the PTO. — Cf. *improvement patent*.

plant patent. A patent granted for the invention or discovery of a new and distinct variety of asexually reproducing plant. 36 USCA § 161.

process patent. A patent for a method of treating specified materials to produce a certain result; a patent outlining a means of producing a physical result independently of the producing mechanism. • The result might be brought about by chemical action, by applying some element or power of nature, by mixing certain substances together, or by heating a substance to a certain temperature. See *method patent*.

reissue patent. A patent that is issued to correct unintentional or unavoidable errors in an original patent, such as to revise the specification or to fix an invalid claim. • A reissue may correct patent defects that might call the validity of the patent into question. It is also used, although rarely, to make the claims broader or narrower. The patentee risks the possibility that previously allowed claims may be rejected. It does not change the term of the patent. 35 USCA § 251. — Sometimes shortened to *reissue*.

submarine patent. *Slang.* A patent that is delayed in prosecution by the applicant in order to let an infringing user continue to develop its business, with the intention of taking in later-invented technology once the patent finally "surfaces" from the U.S. Patent and Trademark Office. • Typically, the patent applicant is aware of the developments and consciously delays the PTO's issuance of a patent, so that the invention's unwitting users will be forced to pay license fees. As of 29 November 2000, most patent applications must be published within 18 months of filing, so submarine patents are relatively rare now. See CONTINUATION-APPLICATION LACHES DOCTRINE.

utility-model patent. See UTILITY MODEL.

utility patent. A patent granted for one of the following types of inventions: a process, a machine, a manufacture, or a composition of matter (such as a new chemical). • Utility patents are the most commonly issued patents. 35 USCA § 101.

patentability opinion. See OPINION (2).

patentability search. An inventor's research into a field's state of the art to determine whether an invention will qualify for patent protection. Cf. INFRINGEMENT SEARCH; VALIDITY SEARCH.

patentable, *adj.* Capable of being patented <patentable processes>.

patentable combination. A series of process steps, mechanical elements, or a mixture of materials that produce a desirable result or effect that is not obvious from the qualities of the individual components or steps.

patentable subject matter. Things that by law can be patented; any machine, process, manufacture, or material composition, or an improvement to such things, that (1) is discovered or invented, (2) is new and useful, and (3) meets the statutory conditions and requirements to qualify for a patent. • Patents may be issued for "any new and useful process, machine, manufacture, or composition of matter, or any new and useful improvement thereof." 35 USCA § 101. Patents may not be issued for laws of nature, naturally occurring materials, physical phenomena, or abstract ideas and formulas. But if a naturally occurring material is processed in a way that gives it a new use, that process may be patentable. — Often shortened to *subject matter.* — Also termed *statutory subject matter.*

Patent Act. The current federal statute governing patent registrations and rights, enacted in 1952. 35 USCA §§ 1 et seq. • The Act reversed several Supreme Court doctrines of patentability by eliminating the synergism and "flash of genius" requirements for combination patents (§ 103), making "means-plus-function" claims valid once again (§ 112), and narrowing the patent-misuse doctrine of contributory infringement (§ 271). — Also termed *Patent Act of 1952.*

Patent Act of 1790. *Hist.* The first U.S. patent statute, establishing a board to examine patent applications, specifications, and drawings to determine whether the invention is "sufficiently useful and important" to justify the granting of a patent. • The examining board, comprising the Secretary of State, the Secretary of War, and the Attorney General, was abolished three years later in favor of a simple registration system.

Patent Act of 1793. *Hist.* An early U.S. patent law that (1) abandoned the examination process in favor of simple registration (2) established the infringement defenses of invalidity for lack of novelty or public use; and (3) articulated the four categories of patentable subject matter as machine, manufacture, composition of matter, and art (now called *process*). • The State Department handled the registration of patents, and their question of their validity was left up to the courts.

Patent Act of 1836. *Hist.* The U.S. statute that charged the Patent Office with examining patent applications for novelty and utility, and that first required claims in patent applications.

Patent Act of 1870. A U.S. statute that shifted the burden of disclosing the exact nature of an invention to the patent applicant by requiring a rigorous listing of distinct claims. • Before the Act was passed, patent claims were less important than the description and drawings, and the scope of the patent grant was often ambiguous.

Patent Act of 1952. See PATENT ACT.

patent agent. See AGENT (2).

patent ambiguity. See AMBIGUITY.

Patent and Copyright Clause. (1929) The constitutional provision granting Congress the authority to promote the advancement of science and the arts by establishing a national system for patents and copyrights. U.S. Const. art. I, § 8, cl. 8.

Patent and Trademark Depository Library. A library that has been designated by the U.S. Patent and Trademark Office as an official repository for information to aid in a patent or trademark search. — Abbr. PTDL.

Patent and Trademark Law Amendments Act. See BAYH-DOLE ACT.

Patent and Trademark Office. The Department of Commerce agency that examines patent and trademark applications, issues patents, registers trademarks, and furnishes patent and trademark information and services to the public. — Abbr. PTO.

patent application. An inventor's request for a patent, filed with the U.S. Patent and Trademark Office and accompanied by a specification (ending with at least one claim), drawings, the filing fee, and (except for a provisional patent application) an oath or a declaration.

allowed application. A patent application for which the U.S. Patent and Trademark Office examiner has determined that at least one pending claim meets the conditions for patentability. • When an application is allowed, the PTO notifies the applicant through a Notice of Allowability and a Notice of Allowance. Once a patent application is allowed, a patent normally issues after the applicant has paid the required issue fee.

application for a reissue patent. An application by a patentee to change the scope of a patent that has already been issued, or to correct clerical or technological errors in the issued patent. • The scope of the claims can be broadened only if the application is made within two years of the date the patent was issued. See *reissue patent* under PATENT (3). Cf *certificate of correction.*

child application. A later-filed application in a chain of continuing applications filed during the pendency of an earlier application and sharing common subject matter. • The first-filed application is called the parent application. Cf. *parent application.*

continued-prosecution application. A request to abandon a patent application after final rejection and reopen a new case with the same file wrapper as the parent application. • CPAs are authorized in 37 CFR § 1.53(d). — Abbr. CPA. — Also termed *Rule 1.53(d) application.* Cf. REQUEST FOR CONTINUED EXAMINATION.

continuing application. A patent application that is filed while the parent application is pending and that carries on prosecution of some or all of the original application. • Continuation, continuation-in-part, divisional, and reissue applications are all forms of continuing applications.

Convention application. A patent application filed in accordance with the terms of an international patent treaty such as the Paris Convention or the Patent Cooperation Treaty.

divisional application. A patent application based on the same disclosure as the original application but claiming a different invention. • If an examiner finds that a disclosure reveals two or more distinct inventions, the applicant must restrict the original application to claiming one of the inventions. A divisional application can then be filed on any nonelected invention, and it will keep the same filing date as the parent application. — Often shortened to *divisional.* — Also termed *restriction application.*

file-wrapper continuation application. 1. See CONTINUATION. **2.** See CONTINUATION-IN-PART.

grandparent application. The first-filed application in a chain of at least three continuation or continuation-in-part patent applications.

informal application. A patent application that is not in the correct form as required by the U.S. Patent and Trademark Office. • According to the Manual of Patent Examining Procedure, an application is informal if it is printed on both sides of the paper, or is not permanent, legible, or reproducible. An informal application may be corrected and still retain the original filing date.

international application. An application under the Patent Cooperation Treaty for patent protection in specified member nations. • A PCT filing may be added as long as 31 months after the initial filing in a national patent office. It allows for simultaneous patent searches and examinations in multiple countries. — Also termed *PCT application*; *PCT filing.* See PATENT COOPERATION TREATY.

international application designating the United States. An international-patent application that is filed in accordance with the Patent Cooperation Treaty and specifically seeks patent protection in the United States. • The application may be filed in any nation, including the U.S., that is a party to the treaty.

international application originating in the United States. An international-patent application that is filed in the U.S. Patent and Trademark Office in accordance with the Patent Cooperation Treaty. • Under the treaty, the PTO acts as a receiving office for international applications. The applicant may or may not be seeking patent protection in the U.S.

parent application. The first-filed application in a chain of later-filed continuation or continuation-in-part applications. • An application becomes the parent application when another type of application (such as continuation, divisional, or substitute) is filed. The term "parent" is generally not used to refer to a provisional application. Cf. *child application.*

provisional application. An application that can be filed up to a year before the patent application itself, in order to establish a date for prior art and constructive reduction to practice. • The PPA must include a full description of the invention, but claims, drawings and prior-art disclosures are not required. — Also termed *provisional patent application.* — Abbr. PPA.

restriction application. See *divisional application.*

Rule 1.53 application. See *continued-prosecution application.*

substitute application. A duplicate application filed after the response period for a first office action has expired and the first application has been deemed abandoned. • A substitute application carries some danger for the applicant: the original filing date is lost, and any developments since that date become prior art that the examiner must consider before granting the patent.

patent-application amendment. A modification to a patent application, usu. narrowing or eliminating some claims in response to an examiner's rejection.

amendment after allowance. An amendment submitted to the U.S. Patent and Trademark Office after the PTO has mailed notice of a patent application's approval. • Once a notice of allowance has been mailed, prosecution of the application is closed on the merits, and the entry of any amendment is within the discretion of the patent examiner. Amendments after allowance commonly address such matters as an amendment to the specification or claims, a change in the drawings or the list of inventors, and the submission of prior art. Amendments that merely correct formal matters in the specification or drawings, change the claims without changing their scope, or cancel a claim are typically approved by the Office. Amendments of greater significance require approval of the supervisory examiner under policies established by the group director. CFR § 1.312. — Also termed *312 amendment*; *Rule 312 amendment*. See *amendment after payment of issue fee.*

amendment after appeal. An amendment made after an appeal is taken from a patent application's final rejection. • Such an amendment is not made as a matter of right but is frequently allowed if it puts the case in better form for consideration on appeal or helps implement an examiner's recommendation.

amendment after final action. An amendment made after final rejection of the patent application. • The amendment may drop claims but not add them. To be entered, it may make changes in form, but may not raise new issues for the examiner. CFR § 1.116. — Also termed *Rule 116 amendment.*

amendment after payment of issue fee. An amendment made by the applicant after the application has been allowed and the issue fee paid. • Such an amendment is not made as a matter of right but is governed by 37 CFR § 1.312. It must be accompanied by a petition to the Commissioner showing good and sufficient reasons why the amendment was not presented earlier. See *amendment after allowance.*

amendment before first action. See *preliminary amendment.*

amendment in excess of filing fee. An amendment to a patent application that increases the number of claims in the original application and requires payment of an additional fee.

preliminary amendment. An amendment filed before the U.S. Patent and Trademark Office issues an office action on a patent application. • Amendments that are not filed with the original application are not considered part of the original disclosure. — Also termed *amendment before first action.*

Rule 116 amendment. See *amendment after final action.*

Rule 312 amendment. See *amendment after allowance.*

312 amendment. See *amendment after allowance.*

patent attorney. A lawyer who drafts and prosecutes patent applications, and who represents inventors in infringement suits and interference hearings. • In addition to a law license, a patent attorney must have a scientific or technical background, pass the patent bar examination, and be licensed by the U.S. Patent and Trademark Office.

patent claim. A formal statement describing the novel features of an invention and defining the scope of the patent's protection <claim #3 of the patent describes an electrical means for driving a metal pin>. Cf. SPECIFICATION (3).

apparatus claim. A patent claim on a mechanical device, explaining how the components are connected and function together. • The preamble of an apparatus claim typically states the function of the machine; the body explains its elements and how they work together.

appendant claim. See *dependent claim.*

closed-ended claim. A patent claim that expressly limits its scope to a list of elements, typically introduced by the phrase "consisting of." Cf. *nearly closed-ended claim*; *open-ended claim.*

coined-name claim. A chemical-patent claim consisting only of the name of the new material. • A coined-name claim is allowed by the U.S. Patent and Trademark Office only on the rare occasion when the name is established in the field before the patent is applied for. The chemical composition, its physical properties, and the process for making it must still be disclosed in the specification.

dependent claim. A patent claim that refers to and further limits another claim or set of claims in the same patent application. — Also termed *appendant claim.*

design claim. The single claim allowed in an application for a design patent, incorporating by reference the drawing and other specifications. • The brief claim typically starts with "an ornamental design for" and ends with "as shown" or "as shown and described." Cf. *omnibus claim.*

fingerprint claim. A chemical-patent claim that differentiates the material from prior art in terms of some physical feature, such as melting point or spectrum, rather than its chemical composition. • Fingerprint claims are allowed only when the chemical composition cannot be determined or cannot be distinguished from prior art.

generic claim. A claim that encompasses a class of elements, any of which could function as equivalents. • For a generic claim to be valid, the specific elements it encompasses must have a definable feature in common that makes them fit for the purpose. — Also termed *genus claim.* Cf. *species claim.*

improvement claim. See *Jepson claim.*

independent claim. A patent claim that does not refer to any other claim.

Jepson claim. An improvement-patent claim characterized by a preamble setting forth the current state of the art, followed by the phrase "the improvement comprising" and a description of the claimed patentable improvement. • The name comes from *Ex parte Jepson*, 1917 C.D. 62, 243 O.G. 526 (Ass't Comm'r Pat. 1917), in which this type of claim was first approved and sanctioned by the Commissioner of Patents. — Also termed *improvement claim.*

Markush claim. A patent claim that includes elements listing alternative chemicals, materials, or steps in a process. • A Markush claim typically has language such as "selected from the group consisting of." The alternatives must all give the same result, rather than patentably distinct products. The name derives from *Ex parte Markush*, 1925 Dec. Comm'r Pat. 126. See MARKUSH DOCTRINE.

means-combination claim. A type of claim in a patent application that includes multiple limitations, at least one of which is in means-plus-function or step-plus-function form. • Means-combination claims are acceptable to examiners.

means-plus-function claim. See MEANS-PLUS-FUNCTION CLAUSE.

method claim. A patent claim that describes what is done to a workpiece in order to achieve the useful result claimed. • A method claim is the same thing as a process claim, but "method" is used more often in applications for mechanical and electrical devices.

multiple-dependent claim. A dependent claim that refers to more than one other preceding claim.

nearly closed-ended claim. A patent claim that limits its scope to a list of elements but does not expressly exclude close analogues. The claim is typically introduced by a phrase such as "consisting essentially of." Cf. *closed-ended claim*; *open-ended claim.*

new-use claim. A method claim for a new way of using an existing invention.

nonelected claim. A claim that has been withdrawn from consideration based on the examiner's finding that the application claims more than one invention. • The applicant must elect to prosecute one invention. Other claims may either be abandoned or else be prosecuted separately under a divisional application. See RESTRICTION (4).

nonstatutory claim. See *omnibus claim.*

omnibus claim. A claim in a patent application that does not distinctly narrate a means to carry out a function but rather refers to the drawings or description with phrases such as "as described and shown." • Omnibus claims are rejected in the United States but are accepted elsewhere. — Also termed *nonstatutory claim.* Cf. *design claim.*

open-ended claim. A patent claim that contains a nonexclusive list of elements, typically introduced by the phrase "consisting of." • A later patent applicant cannot avoid infringement by merely adding an analogue to the list. Cf. *closed-ended claim*; *nearly closed-ended claim.*

plant-patent claim. The single claim in a plant-patent application, describing the principal distinguishing characteristics of the plant.

process claim. A patent claim that describes by steps what is done to the subject matter, usu. a substance, in order to achieve a useful result. • A process claim is the same thing as a method claim, but "process" is used more often in applications for chemical patents.

product-by-process claim. A patent claim defining a product through the process by which it is made. • The product-by-process claim is most often used to define new chemical compounds, such as drugs.

product claim. A patent claim that covers the structure, apparatus, or composition of a product.

single-means claim. A type of claim in a patent application that indicates a process, result, or function but does not describe the method of reaching that end <a method of curing cancer>. • Where no other method is obvious, such an assertion claims rights to all possible ways of achieving the result — ways not specified in the application and even ways that have not yet been invented. Single-means claims are rejected as too broad. — Also termed *single-element means claim.* Cf. MEANS-PLUS-FUNCTION CLAUSE.

species claim. A claim that is limited to a single apparatus, process, composition of matter, or article of manufacture, rather than to a range of similar and related items. Cf *generic claim.*

Squires claim. A utility-patent claim that incorporates a drawing or table by reference. • This claim is allowed by the U.S. Patent and Trademark Office only if there is no practical way to define the invention in words, but the invention is simple to illustrate with the drawing or table. See SQUIRES DOCTRINE.

subcombination claim. A patent claim, usu. on a device, describing a subsystem of a larger combination. ● A subcombination may be patented separately if it has its own utility.

Patent Cooperation Treaty. A 1970 treaty that streamlined the process of securing patents in multiple countries by establishing a single filing date and providing for a single preliminary patent search. ● An inventor who wants to qualify for patents from several member countries files a standard application in one country, thus preserving the priority date, then submits a PCT filing that designates which other countries' patents are being applied for. WIPO, the United Nations' World Intellectual Property Organization, administers the treaty. — Often shortened to PCT. See *international application* under PATENT APPLICATION.

patent danger. See *apparent danger* (1) under DANGER.

patent deed. See LETTERS PATENT (2).

patent defect. See DEFECT.

patent disclaimer. See *statutory disclaimer* under DISCLAIMER.

patentee (pat-ən-**tee**). One who either has been granted a patent or has succeeded in title to a patent. ● Although it might seem helpful to distinguish a patentee as a person to whom a patent is issued and a patent-holder as the owner of a patent, including the original grantee's assigns, the Patent Act explicitly includes all title-holders under the term "patentee." 35 USCA § 100(d). — Also termed *patent-holder*; *patent-owner*.

patent-exhaustion doctrine. *Patents.* The rule that the unconditioned sale of a patented article ends the patentee's monopoly right to control its use. ● That control may still be exercised by limitations in a contract or license, as long as it does not amount to anticompetitive patent misuse. *Adams v. Burke*, 84 U.S. (17 Wall.) 453 (1874). See FIRST-SALE DOCTRINE.

patent grant. See PATENT (3).

patent-holder. See PATENTEE.

patent infringement. See INFRINGEMENT.

patent insurance. See INSURANCE.

patent marking. The incorporation or affixation of a patent number to a patented article's surface or surrounding packaging. ● Affixing the patent number to a product gives constructive notice of patent rights to infringers. Without the number in place, a patentee can not recover losses that occur before the infringer has actual notice of the patent. 35 USCA § 287. See PATENT NUMBER.

patent medicine. A packaged drug that is protected by trademark and is available without prescription.

patent-misuse doctrine. An equitable rule that patentees should not be allowed to use their patent to effectively broaden the scope of their monopoly in restraint of trade or otherwise against the public interest. ● Two common examples of anticompetitive broadening are (1) using a patent to restrain competition from an unpatented product or process, and (2) employing the patent beyond its lifespan to exclude others from gaining commercial advantages by using the product or process. The practical effect of finding patent misuse is the loss of patent protection. The doctrine operates independently of antitrust law but overlaps it in many ways and arose in the same era, at the turn of the 20th century. It has been described as an application of the equitable rule of "unclean hands." See *nonmetered license* under LICENSE.

patent number. *Patents.* The unique eight-character number assigned by the U.S. Patent and Trademark Office to a patent upon issuance. See PATENT MARKING.

Patent Office. See UNITED STATES PATENT AND TRADEMARK OFFICE.

Patent Office Reports. *Hist.* The former official publication of the U.S. Patent and Trademark Office. ● It was replaced in 1872 by the Official Gazette of the United States Patent and Trademark Office.

patentor (pat-ən-tər *or* pat-ən-**tor**). One who grants a patent.

patent-owner. See PATENTEE.

patent pending. (1917) The designation given to an invention while the Patent and Trademark Office is processing the patent application. ● No protection against infringement exists, however, unless an actual patent is granted. — Abbr. pat. pend.

patent pooling. The cross-licensing of patents among patentees. ● Patent pooling does not violate antitrust laws unless it is done to suppress competition or control an industry.

patent-prosecution process. See PROSECUTION (4).

patent right. 1. See PATENT (3). **2.** See RIGHT.

patent-right dealer. A person who buys and sells or brokers the sale or purchase of patent rights.

patent search. 1. See INFRINGEMENT SEARCH. **2.** See PATENTABILITY SEARCH. **3.** See VALIDITY SEARCH.

patent solicitor. See *patent agent* under AGENT (2).

patent suppression. The deliberate nonuse of a patent, esp. in order to deny the public or competitors the benefit of the invention. ● Patent suppression is a rich source of urban legend, such as the rumor of oil companies sitting on inventions that would greatly improve gas mileage, or pantyhose companies suppressing a patent on no-run nylon. But the stories are not always fictional: in 1942 Standard Oil admitted trying to delay synthetic-rubber technology in order to protect its market in natural rubber.

patent term. The period during which a patent is in force.

patent-term adjustment. A compulsory extension of the time a utility or plant patent remains in force, following administrative delays in prosecuting the application. • A provision of the American Inventors' Protection Act of 1999, the extension is available for new applications, continuation applications, and divisional applications filed since May 29, 2000. — Abbr. PTA. Cf. PATENT-TERM EXTENSION.

patent-term extension. A lengthening of the time a patent remains in force, given to compensate inventors for time lost because of administrative delays such as interferences, secrecy orders, or appeals. • The extension applies to original utility and plant patents issued after June 7, 1995 and before May 29, 2000. Its maximum length is five years. Cf. PATENT-TERM ADJUSTMENT.

patent-term guarantee. An inventor's statutory right to extend the term of a patent if the application was delayed by the U.S. Patent and Trademark Office. • The term can be extended up to five years if the application was delayed because of an interference proceeding or appellate review, or if the PTO missed a statutory deadline for certain steps in the prosecution, or failed to grant the patent within three years of the filing date. The guarantee took effect May 29, 2000.

patent watch. A system for continually monitoring published patent applications and newly issued patents in a particular scientific or technological field to detect or ensure against infringements.

patent writ. See WRIT.

paterfamilias (pay-tər-fə-**mil**-ee-əs *or* pah-tər-), *n.* [Latin] *Roman law.* The male head of a family or household, the senior ascendant male; esp., one invested with *potestas* (power) over another. — Also termed *homo sui juris.* See *patria potestas* under POTESTAS.

paternal, *adj.* (15c) Of, relating to, or coming from one's father <paternal property>. Cf. MATERNAL.

paternalism, *n.* (1873) A government's policy or practice of taking responsibility for the individual affairs of its citizens, esp. by supplying their needs or regulating their conduct in a heavyhanded manner. — **paternalistic,** *adj.*

paternal line. See LINE.

paternal-line descent. See DESCENT.

paternal property. See PROPERTY.

paternity (pə-**tər**-ni-tee). (15c) **1.** The state or condition of being a father, esp. a biological one; fatherhood. Cf. FILIATION. **2.** ATTRIBUTION RIGHT.

paternity action. See PATERNITY SUIT.

paternity presumption. See PRESUMPTION OF PATERNITY.

paternity suit. (1945) A court proceeding to determine whether a person is the father of a child (esp. one born out of wedlock), usu. initiated by the mother in an effort to obtain child support. — Also termed *paternity action; parentage action; bastardy proceeding; bastardy process.*

paternity test. (1926) A test, usu. involving DNA identification or tissue-typing, for determining whether a given man is the biological father of a particular child. See DNA IDENTIFICATION; HUMAN-LEUKOCYTE ANTIGEN TEST; BLOOD-GROUPING TEST.

pathological intoxication. See INTOXICATION.

pathology (pə-**thol**-ə-jee), *n.* (17c) The branch of medical study that examines the origins, symptoms, and nature of diseases. — **pathological** (path-ə-**loj**-i-kəl), *adj.* — **pathologist** (pə-**thol**-ə-jist), *n.*

patient, *n.* A person under medical or psychiatric care.

patient-litigant exception. (1951) An exemption from the doctor–patient privilege, whereby the privilege is lost when the patient sues the doctor for malpractice.

patient–physician privilege. See *doctor–patient privilege* under PRIVILEGE (3).

patient's bill of rights. (1973) A general statement of patient rights voluntarily adopted by a healthcare provider or mandated by statute, covering such matters as access to care, patient dignity and confidentiality, personal safety, consent to treatment, and explanation of charges.

pat. pend. *abbr.* PATENT PENDING.

patria (**pay**-tree-ə *or* **pa**-tree-ə), *n.* [Latin] **1.** *Roman law.* The fatherland; a person's home area. **2.** *Hist.* The country or the area within it, such as a county or neighborhood. **3.** *Hist.* A jury, as when a defendant "puts himself upon the country" (*ponit se super patriam*). See CONCLUSION TO THE COUNTRY; GOING TO THE COUNTRY; PAYS.

patria potestas. See POTESTAS.

patricide (**pa**-trə-sɪd), *n.* (16c) **1.** The act of killing one's own father. **2.** One who kills his or her father. Cf. PARRICIDE. — **patricidal,** *adj.*

patrimonial (pa-trə-**moh**-nee-əl), *adj.* Of or relating to an inheritance, esp. from a male ancestor.

patrimony (**pa**-trə-moh-nee). (14c) **1.** An estate inherited from one's father or other ancestor;

legacy or heritage. **2.** *Civil law.* All of a person's assets and liabilities that are capable of monetary valuation and subject to execution for a creditor's benefit. **3.** PATRIMONIUM.

Patriot Act. See USA PATRIOT ACT.

patron. (15c) **1.** A regular customer or client of a business. **2.** A licensee invited or permitted to enter leased land for the purpose for which it is leased. **3.** A person who protects or supports some person or thing.

patronage (**pay**-trə-nij). (16c) **1.** The giving of support, sponsorship, or protection. **2.** All the customers of a business; clientele. **3.** The power to appoint persons to governmental positions or to confer other political favors. — Also termed (in sense 3) *political patronage.* See SPOILS SYSTEM.

patronizing a prostitute. (1956) The offense of requesting or securing the performance of a sex act for a fee; PROSTITUTION. Cf. SOLICITATION (3).

pattern, *n.* (1883) A mode of behavior or series of acts that are recognizably consistent <a pattern of racial discrimination>.

pattern jury charge. See *model jury instruction* under JURY INSTRUCTION.

pattern jury instruction. See *model jury instruction* under JURY INSTRUCTION.

pattern of racketeering activity. (1972) Two or more related criminal acts that amount to, or pose a threat of, continued criminal activity. • This phrase derives from the federal Racketeer Influenced and Corrupt Organizations Act. See RACKETEERING.

pattern-or-practice case. A lawsuit, often a class action, in which the plaintiff attempts to show that the defendant has systematically engaged in discriminatory activities, esp. by means of policies and procedures. • Typically, such a case involves employment discrimination, housing discrimination, or school segregation. A plaintiff must usu. show that a defendant's behavior forms a pattern of actions or is embedded in routine practices but inferences of executive or official complicity may be drawn from a consistent failure to respond to complaints or implement corrective measures.

pattern similarity. See *comprehensive nonliteral similarity* under SIMILARITY.

pauper. (16c) A very poor person, esp. one who receives aid from charity or public funds; INDIGENT. See IN FORMA PAUPERIS.

pauper's affidavit. See *poverty affidavit* under AFFIDAVIT.

pauper's oath. See OATH.

pawn, *n.* (15c) **1.** An item of personal property deposited as security for a debt; a pledge or guarantee. • In modern usage, the term is usu. restricted to the pledge of jewels and other personal chattels

to pawnbrokers as security for a small loan. **2.** The act of depositing personal property in this manner. **3.** The condition of being held on deposit as a pledge. **4.** PIGNUS (1). Cf. BAILMENT (1); PIGNUS (4). — **pawn,** *vb.*

pawnbroker, *n.* One who lends money, usu. at a high interest rate, in exchange for personal property that is deposited as security by the borrower. — **pawnbroking,** *n.*

pawnee. One who receives a deposit of personal property as security for a debt.

pawnor. One who deposits an item of personal property as security for a debt. — Also spelled *pawner.*

payable, *adj.* (14c) (Of a sum of money or a negotiable instrument) that is to be paid. • An amount may be payable without being due. Debts are commonly payable long before they fall due.

> **payable after sight.** (18c) Payable after acceptance or protest of nonacceptance. See *sight draft* under DRAFT.

> **payable on demand.** (17c) Payable when presented or upon request for payment; payable at any time.

> **payable to bearer.** (18c) Payable to anyone holding the instrument.

> **payable to order.** (17c) Payable only to a specified payee.

payable, *n.* See *account payable* under ACCOUNT.

payable date. See DATE.

pay any bank. A draft indorsement that permits only banks to acquire the rights of a holder until the draft is either returned to the customer initiating collection or specially indorsed by a bank to a person who is not a bank. UCC § 4-201(b).

payback method. An accounting procedure that measures the time required to recover a venture's initial cash investment.

payback period. The length of time required to recover a venture's initial cash investment, without accounting for the time value of money.

paydown, *n.* A loan payment in an amount less than the total loan principal.

payee. (18c) One to whom money is paid or payable; esp., a party named in commercial paper as the recipient of the payment. Cf. PAYOR.

payer. See PAYOR.

pay-if-paid clause. See CLAUSE.

paying quantities. *Oil & gas.* An amount of mineral production from a single well sufficient to justify a reasonably prudent operator to continue producing from that well. • Most jurisdictions interpret the language "for so long thereafter as oil and gas is produced" in habendum clauses to mean so long as paying quantities are produced. See HABENDUM CLAUSE.

payment. (14c) **1.** Performance of an obligation by the delivery of money or some other valuable thing accepted in partial or full discharge of the obligation. **2.** The money or other valuable thing so delivered in satisfaction of an obligation.

advance payment. (16c) A payment made in anticipation of a contingent or fixed future liability or obligation.

balloon payment. (1935) A final loan payment that is usu. much larger than the preceding regular payments and that discharges the principal balance of the loan. See *balloon note* under NOTE (1).

conditional payment. (17c) Payment of an obligation only on condition that something be done. ● Generally, the payor reserves the right to demand the payment back if the condition is not met.

constructive payment. (1827) A payment made by the payor but not yet credited by the payee. ● For example, a rent check mailed on the first of the month is a constructive payment even though the landlord does not deposit the check until ten days later.

direct payment. (18c) **1.** A payment made directly to the payee, without using an intermediary, such as a child-support payment made directly to the obligee parent rather than through the court. **2.** A payment that is absolute and unconditional on the amount, the due date, and the payee.

down payment. (1926) The portion of a purchase price paid in cash (or its equivalent) at the time the sale agreement is executed. Cf. BINDER (2); EARNEST MONEY.

indefinite payment. **1.** A stream of payments with no termination date, or a single payment with no specified due date. **2.** A payment that does not specify to which debt it should be applied when it is made to a single creditor who holds several of the payor's debts.

installment payment. One of a series of periodic payments made under an installment plan. See INSTALLMENT SALE.

involuntary payment. (18c) A payment obtained by fraud or duress.

lump-sum payment. (1914) A payment of a large amount all at once, as opposed to a series of smaller payments over time. Cf. *periodic payment*.

part payment. A buyer's delivery of money or other thing of value to the seller, and its acceptance by the seller, when the money or the value of the thing does not equal the full sum owed.

periodic payment. One of a series of payments made over time instead of a one-time payment for the full amount. Cf. *lump-sum payment.*

two-party payment. A single payment made by check to two people, usu. for the sum of the amount due to each person.

unofficious payment. A payment made by a person who has an interest in seeing that it should be made.

payment bond. See BOND (2).

payment date. See DATE.

payment in due course. (1816) A payment to the holder of a negotiable instrument at or after its maturity date, made by the payor in good faith and without notice of any defect in the holder's title. See HOLDER IN DUE COURSE.

payment intangible. See INTANGIBLE.

payment into court. (1829) A party's money or property deposited with a court for distribution after a proceeding according to the parties' settlement or the court's order. See INTERPLEADER.

payoff. See KICKBACK.

payola (pay-oh-lə). (1937) An indirect and secret payment for a favor, esp. one relating to business; a bribe.

pay-on-death account. See ACCOUNT.

pay-on-death bank account. See *pay-on-death account* under ACCOUNT.

payor. (16c) One who pays; esp., a person responsible for paying a negotiable instrument. — Also spelled *payer*. See DRAWEE; PAYEE.

payor bank. See BANK.

pay-or-play contract. See CONTRACT.

payout period. The time required for an asset to produce enough revenue to pay back the initial investment; esp., in oil-and-gas law, the time required for a well to produce a sufficient amount of oil or gas to pay back the investment in the well.

payout ratio. The ratio between a corporation's dividends per share and its earnings per share. Cf. COMMON-STOCK RATIO.

payroll. **1.** A list of employees to be paid and the amount due to each of them. **2.** The total compensation payable to a company's employees for one pay period.

payroll tax. See TAX.

pays (pay *or* pays), *n.* [Law French] The country; a jury. See PATRIA.

pay-when-paid clause. See CLAUSE.

PBGC. *abbr.* PENSION BENEFIT GUARANTY CORPORATION.

PBS. *abbr.* **1.** PUBLIC BUILDINGS SERVICE. **2.** Public Broadcasting Service.

P.C. *abbr.* **1.** See *professional corporation* under CORPORATION. **2.** POLITICAL CORRECTNESS. **3.** PRIVY COUNCILLOR.

PCA. *abbr.* POSSE COMITATUS ACT.

PCR action. See POSTCONVICTION-RELIEF PROCEEDING.

PCT. *abbr.* PATENT COOPERATION TREATY.

PCT application. See *international application* under PATENT APPLICATION.

PCT filing. See *international application* under PATENT APPLICATION.

PCT filing date. *Patents.* The date of an international application under the Patent Cooperation Treaty. — Also termed *international filing date*. See PATENT COOPERATION TREATY; PCT FILING.

P.D. *abbr.* **1.** PUBLIC DEFENDER. **2.** Police department.

PDA. See PREGNANCY-DISCRIMINATION ACT.

peace, *n.* **1.** A state of public tranquility; freedom from civil disturbance or hostility <breach of the peace>. **2.** The termination or absence of armed conflict between nations. See *peace treaty* under TREATY. — **peaceable,** *adj.* — **peaceful,** *adj.*

   armed peace. A situation in which two or more nations, while at peace, are actually armed for possible or probable hostilities.

peace, justice of the. See JUSTICE OF THE PEACE.

peaceable possession. See POSSESSION.

peace bond. See BOND (2).

Peace Corps. An independent federal agency that promotes peace and friendship in the world by sending volunteers to other countries to work in education, agriculture, health, small-business development, urban development, the environment, and information technology. • The agency was established by the Peace Corps Act of 1961 and became independent in 1988.

peacemaker's court. See COURT.

peace officer. A civil officer (such as a sheriff or police officer) appointed to maintain public tranquility and order; esp., a person designated by public authority to keep the peace and arrest persons guilty or suspected of crime. • This term may also include a judge who hears criminal cases or another public official (such as a mayor) who may be statutorily designated as a peace officer for limited purposes. — Also termed *officer of the peace*; *conservator of the peace*.

peacetime. A period in which a country has declared neither a war nor a national emergency, even if the country is involved in a conflict or quasi-conflict.

peace treaty. See TREATY (1).

peace warrant. See WARRANT (1).

peak demand. The point (during some specified period) at which customer use results in the highest level of demand for a utility.

peculation (pek-yə-**lay**-shən), *n.* (17c) Embezzlement, esp. by a public official. Cf. DEPECULATION. — **peculate** (**pek**-yə-layt), *vb.* — **peculative** (**pek**-yə-lə-tiv), *adj.* — **peculator** (**pek**-yə-lay-tər), *n.*

peculiar, *adj.* Special; particular <peculiar benefit>.

peculiar benefit. See *special benefit* under BENEFIT.

peculiar-risk doctrine. (1958) The principle that an employer will be liable for injury caused by an independent contractor if the employer failed to take reasonable precautions against a risk that is peculiar to the contractor's work and that the employer should have recognized. — Also termed *peculiar-risk exception*.

pecuniary (pi-**kyoo**-nee-er-ee), *adj.* (16c) Of or relating to money; monetary <a pecuniary interest in the lawsuit>.

pecuniary ability. Income from any source or sources sufficient to meet or pay an obligation, or for some other purpose, such as providing suitable maintenance for a spouse.

pecuniary benefit. See BENEFIT.

pecuniary bequest. See BEQUEST.

pecuniary damages. See DAMAGES.

pecuniary devise. See DEVISE.

pecuniary gain. See GAIN (1).

pecuniary injury. See INJURY.

pecuniary interest. See *financial interest* under INTEREST (2).

pecuniary legacy. See LEGACY.

pecuniary loss. See LOSS.

pedal possession. See POSSESSION.

pederasty (**ped**-ər-as-tee), *n.* (17c) Anal intercourse between a man and a boy. • Pederasty is illegal in all states. Cf. SODOMY. — **pederast** (**ped**-ə-rast), *n.*

pedigree. A history of family succession; ancestry or lineage.

pedophile. One who engages in pedophilia.

pedophilia. (1906) **1.** A sexual disorder consisting in the desire for sexual gratification by molesting children, esp. prepubescent children. **2.** An adult's act of child molestation. • Pedophilia can but does not necessarily involve intercourse. The American Psychiatric Association applies both senses to perpetrators who are at least 16 years old and at least five years older than their victims. Cf. PEDERASTY.

Peeping Tom. (18c) A person who spies on another (as through a window), usu. for sexual pleasure; VOYEUR. — Also termed *peeper*.

peer, *n.* **1.** A person who is of equal status, rank, or character with another. **2.** A member of the British nobility (such as a duchess, marquis, earl, viscount, or baroness). — **peerage** (**peer**-ij), *n.*

peer-reviewed journal. (1980) A publication whose practice is to forward submitted articles to disinterested experts who screen them for scholarly or scientific reliability so that articles actually published have already withstood expert scrutiny and comment.

peer-review organization. (1978) A governmental agency that monitors health-regulation compliance by private hospitals requesting public funds (such as Medicare payments). — Abbr. PRO.

peer-review privilege. See PRIVILEGE (3).

peine forte et dure (**pen for** tay **door** *or* **payn fort** ay **dyoor**). [French "strong and hard punishment"] *Hist.* The punishment of an alleged felon who refused to plead, consisting of pressing or crushing the person's body under heavy weights until the accused either pleaded or died.

pell. See CLERK OF THE PELLS.

penal (**pee**-nəl), *adj.* (15c) Of, relating to, or being a penalty or punishment, esp. for a crime.

penal action. See ACTION (4).

penal bill. See *penal bond* under BOND (2).

penal bond. See BOND (2).

penal clause. See PENALTY CLAUSE.

penal code. (18c) A compilation of criminal laws, usu. defining and categorizing the offenses and setting forth their respective punishments. — Also termed *criminal code.* See MODEL PENAL CODE.

penal colony. A remote place of detention for convicts and political prisoners, usu. in an isolated part of a nation or in a nation's extraterritorial holdings. • Historical examples include the Soviet Union's gulags in Siberia and France's penal colony on Devil's Island off the coast of Guiana.

penal custody. See CUSTODY (1).

penal institution. See PRISON.

penal law. 1. See *penal statute* under STATUTE. **2.** See CRIMINAL LAW.

penal liability. See LIABILITY.

penal redress. See REDRESS.

penal sanction. See *criminal sanction* under SANCTION.

penal servitude. Confinement in prison with hard labor. See HARD LABOR. Cf. IMPRISONMENT.

penal statute. See STATUTE.

penal sum. (17c) The monetary amount specified as a penalty in a penal bond. See *penal bond* under BOND (2).

penalty. (15c) **1.** Punishment imposed on a wrongdoer, usu. in the form of imprisonment or fine; esp., a sum of money exacted as punishment for either a wrong to the state or a civil wrong (as distinguished from compensation for the injured party's loss). • Though usu. for crimes, penalties are also sometimes imposed for civil wrongs.

civil penalty. (17c) A fine assessed for a violation of a statute or regulation <the EPA levied a civil penalty of $10,000 on the manufacturer for exceeding its pollution limits>.

statutory penalty. (18c) A penalty imposed for a statutory violation; esp., a penalty imposing automatic liability on a wrongdoer for violation of a statute's terms without reference to any actual damages suffered.

2. An extra charge against a party who violates a contractual provision.

prepayment penalty. (1948) A charge assessed against a borrower who elects to pay off a loan before it is due.

3. Excessive stipulated damages that a contract purports to impose on a party that breaches. • If the damages are excessive enough to be considered a penalty, a court will usu. not enforce that particular provision of the contract. Some contracts specify that a given sum of damages is intended "as liquidated damages and not as a penalty" — but even that language is not foolproof. **4.** PENALTY CLAUSE.

penalty clause. (1843) A contractual provision that assesses against a defaulting party an excessive monetary charge unrelated to actual harm. • Penalty clauses are generally unenforceable. — Often shortened to *penalty.* — Also termed *penal clause.* Cf. LIQUIDATED-DAMAGES CLAUSE; LIMITATION-OF-REMEDIES CLAUSE.

penalty phase. (1959) The part of a criminal trial in which the fact-finder determines the punishment for a defendant who has been found guilty. — Also termed *sentencing phase.* Cf. GUILT PHASE.

penalty point. A punishment levied for a traffic offense and accumulated on the driver's record. • If a driver receives a statutorily set number of points, the driver's license may be restricted, suspended, or terminated.

penance. *Eccles. law.* A punishment assessed by an ecclesiastical court for some spiritual offense.

pend, *vb.* (18c) (Of a lawsuit) to be awaiting decision or settlement.

pendency (**pen**-dən-see), *n.* (17c) The state or condition of being pending or continuing undecided.

pendens. See LIS PENDENS.

pendent (**pen**-dənt), *adj.* (18c) **1.** Not yet decided; pending <a pendent action>. **2.** Of or relating to pendent jurisdiction or pendent-party jurisdiction <pendent parties>. **3.** Contingent; dependent <pendent upon a different claim>.

pendent-claim jurisdiction. See *pendent jurisdiction* under JURISDICTION.

pendente lite (pen-**den**-tee lI-tee), *adv.* [Latin "while the action is pending"] During the proceeding or litigation; in a manner contingent on the outcome of litigation. — Also termed *lite pendente*. Cf. LIS PENDENS.

pendente lite administration. See *administration pendente lite* under ADMINISTRATION.

pendent jurisdiction. See JURISDICTION.

pendent-party jurisdiction. See JURISDICTION.

pendent-venue doctrine. The principle that once venue is established for a federal claim, proof of venue for additional federal claims, cross-claims, and counterclaims is unnecessary.

pending, *prep.* (17c) **1.** Throughout the continuance of; during <in escrow pending arbitration>. **2.** While awaiting; until <the injunction was in force pending trial>.

pending, *adj.* (17c) **1.** Remaining undecided; awaiting decision <a pending case>. **2.** *Parliamentary law.* (Of a motion) under consideration; moved by a member and stated by the chair as a question for the meeting's consideration. See CONSIDERATION (2); ON THE FLOOR. ● A motion may be immediately pending, meaning that it is directly under consideration, being the last motion stated by the chair and next in line for a vote; or it may be pending subject to other motions of higher rank that have taken precedence over it. See *immediately pending motion* and *pending motion* under MOTION (2).

pending motion. See MOTION (2).

pending-ordinance doctrine. The principle that a municipality may properly deny an application for a property use that, although it would satisfy existing law, would violate a law that is pending when the application is made. ● This doctrine was judicially created, mainly to short-circuit landowners' attempts to circumvent a new ordinance by applying for a nonconforming use on the eve of its approval.

penetration, *n.* **1.** *Criminal law.* The entry of the penis or some other part of the body or a foreign object into the vagina or other bodily orifice. ● This is the typical meaning today in statutes defining sexual offenses. — Also termed *intromission.* See RAPE (1). **2.** The depth reached by a bullet or other projectile in something against which the projectile is fired. **3.** The act of piercing or passing something into or through a body or object. — **penetrate,** *vb.*

penetration pricing. Pricing of a new product below its anticipated market price to enter a mar-

ket and capture market share by breaking down existing brand loyalties.

penitentiary (pen-ə-**ten**-shə-ree), *n.* (1807) A correctional facility or other place of long-term confinement for convicted criminals; PRISON. — **penitentiary,** *adj.*

penitentiary misdemeanor. See *serious misdemeanor* under MISDEMEANOR.

***Pennoyer* rule** (pə-**noy**-ər). (1968) The principle that a court may not issue a personal judgment against a defendant over whom it has no personal jurisdiction. *Pennoyer v. Neff,* 95 U.S. 714 (1877).

***Pennsylvania* rule.** *Torts.* The principle that a tortfeasor who violates a statute in the process of causing an injury has the burden of showing that the violation did not cause the injury. *The Pennsylvania,* 86 U.S. (19 Wall.) 125, 136 (1874).

penny stock. See STOCK.

penology (pee-**nol**-ə-jee), *n.* (1838) The study of penal institutions, crime prevention, and the punishment and rehabilitation of criminals, including the art of fitting the right treatment to an offender. Cf. CRIMINOLOGY. — **penological** (pee-nə-**loj**-i-kəl), *adj.* — **penologist** (pee-**nol**-ə-jist), *n.*

pen register. (1953) A mechanical device that logs dialed telephone numbers by monitoring electrical impulses. ● Because a pen register does not record the telephone conversation, it may not constitute a Fourth Amendment search requiring a search warrant (though it does need a court order). Some states, however, do consider the use of a pen register invasive enough to require a search warrant. Cf. WIRETAPPING.

pension. (16c) A fixed sum paid regularly to a person (or to the person's beneficiaries), esp. by an employer as a retirement benefit. Cf. ANNUITY (3).

vested pension. A pension in which an employee (or employee's estate) has rights to benefits purchased with the employer's contributions to the plan, even if the employee is no longer employed by this employer at the time of retirement. ● The vesting of qualified pension plans is governed by ERISA. See EMPLOYEE RETIREMENT INCOME SECURITY ACT.

Pension and Welfare Benefits Administration. A unit in the U.S. Department of Labor that was responsible for regulating employee pension plans under the Employees Retirement Income Security Act (ERISA) and for enforcing the Act through its field offices. ● It has been replaced by the Employee Benefits Security Administration. — Abbr. PWBA.

Pension Benefit Guaranty Corporation. A self-financing federal corporation that guarantees payment of pension benefits in covered benefit pension plans. — *Abbr.* PBGC.

pensioner. A recipient or beneficiary of a pension plan.

pension plan. 1. Under ERISA, any plan, fund, or program established or maintained by an employer or an employee organization that provides retirement income to employees or results in a deferral of income by employees extending to the termination of employment or beyond. 29 USCA § 1002(2)(A). **2.** Under the Internal Revenue Code, an employer's plan established and maintained primarily to provide systematically for the payment of definitely determinable benefits to employees over a period of years, usu. for life, after retirement. See EMPLOYEE RETIREMENT INCOME SECURITY ACT. Cf. EMPLOYEE BENEFIT PLAN.

   contributory pension plan. A pension plan funded by both employer and employee contributions.

   defined-benefit pension plan. A pension plan in which an employer commits to paying an employee a specific benefit for life beginning at retirement. • The amount of the benefit is based on factors such as age, earnings, and years of service.

   defined-contribution pension plan. See *defined-contribution plan* under EMPLOYEE BENEFIT PLAN.

   defined pension plan. A pension plan in which the employer promises specific benefits to each employee. — Also termed *fixed-benefit plan.*

   noncontributory pension plan. A pension plan funded solely by the employer's contributions.

   nonqualified pension plan. A deferred-compensation plan in which an executive increases retirement benefits by annual additional contributions to the company's basic plan.

   qualified pension plan. A pension plan that complies with federal law (ERISA) and thus allows the employee to receive tax benefits for contributions and tax-deferred investment growth. — Often shortened to *qualified plan.*

   top-hat pension plan. An unfunded pension plan that is maintained by an employer primarily for the purpose of providing deferred compensation for a select group of managers or highly paid employees. • Top-hat plans are generally not subject to the broad remedial provisions of ERISA because Congress recognized that certain individuals, by virtue of position or compensation level, can substantially influence the design or operation of their deferred-compensation plans. — Often shortened to *top-hat plan.*

pension trust. See TRUST.

Pentagon Force Protection Agency. A unit in the U.S. Department of Defense responsible for operating the Pentagon police force and providing basic law enforcement and security for the Pentagon and other military installations in the Washington, D.C. area. • The Agency was formed after the Pentagon was attacked on 11 September 2001. — *Abbr.* PFPA.

penumbra (pi-**nəm**-brə), *n.* (18c) A surrounding area or periphery of uncertain extent. • In constitutional law, the Supreme Court has ruled that the specific guarantees in the Bill of Rights have penumbras containing implied rights, esp. the right of privacy. Pl. **penumbras, penumbrae** (pi-**nəm**-bree). — **penumbral** (pi-**nəm**-brəl), *adj.*

peonage (**pee**-ə-nij), *n.* (1844) Illegal and involuntary servitude in satisfaction of a debt. — **peon,** *n.*

people. (*usu. cap.*) (1801) The citizens of a state as represented by the prosecution in a criminal case <*People v. Snyder*>.

people's court. (1912) **1.** A court in which individuals can resolve small disputes. See *small-claims court* under COURT. **2.** *Hist.* (*cap.*) In Nazi Germany, a tribunal that dealt with political offenses. • In German, *Volksgerichtshof.*

people-smuggling. The crime of helping a person enter a country illegally in return for a fee. Cf. *human trafficking* under TRAFFICKING; SMUGGLING.

peppercorn. A small or insignificant thing or amount; nominal consideration <the contract was upheld despite involving mere peppercorn>. See *nominal consideration* under CONSIDERATION; *peppercorn rent* under RENT.

peppercorn rent. See RENT.

per (pər), *prep.* [Latin] (14c) **1.** Through; by <the dissent, per Justice Thomas>. **2.** For each; for every <55 miles per hour>. **3.** In accordance with the terms of; according to <per the contract>.

perambulation. The act or custom of walking around the boundaries of a piece of land, either to confirm the boundaries or to preserve evidence of them.

per annum (pər **an**-əm), *adv.* [Latin] (16c) By, for, or in each year; annually <interest of eight percent per annum>.

P/E ratio. *abbr.* PRICE-EARNINGS RATIO.

per autre vie. See PUR AUTRE VIE.

per capita (pər **kap**-i-tə), *adj.* [Latin "by the head"] (17c) **1.** Divided equally among all individuals, usu. in the same class <the court will distribute the property to the descendants on a per capita basis>. Cf. PER STIRPES.

   per capita with representation. (1935) Divided equally among all members of a class of takers, including those who have predeceased the testator, so that no family stocks are cut off by the prior death of a taker. • For example, if T (the testator) has three children — A, B, and C — and C has two children but predeceases T, C's children will still take C's share when T's estate is distributed.

2. Allocated to each person; possessed by each individual <the average annual per capita income has increased over the last two years>. — **per capita**, *adv.*

per capita tax. See *poll tax* under TAX.

percentage depletion. *Oil & gas.* A method of allowing a taxpayer who owns an economic interest in a producing oil or gas well to deduct a specified percentage of the gross income from the well in lieu of depleting the actual basis. 26 USCA § 611. Cf. COST DEPLETION.

percentage game. See GAME.

percentage lease. See LEASE.

percentage-of-completion method. See ACCOUNTING METHOD.

percentage order. See ORDER (8).

perception. **1.** An observation, awareness, or realization, usu. based on physical sensation or experience; appreciation or cognition. • The term includes both the actor's knowledge of the actual circumstances and the actor's erroneous but reasonable belief in the existence of nonexistent circumstances. **2.** *Roman & civil law.* The act of taking into possession (as rents, profits, etc.), esp. by a bona fide possessor or usufructuary. — Also termed (in Roman law) *perceptio* (pər-**sep**-shee-oh).

percipient witness. See WITNESS.

percolating water. See WATER.

per contra (pər **kon**-trə). [Latin] (16c) On the other hand; to the contrary; by contrast.

per curiam (pər **kyoor**-ee-əm), *adv. & adj.* [Latin] (15c) By the court as a whole.

per curiam, *n.* See *per curiam opinion* under OPINION (1).

per curiam opinion. See OPINION (1).

per diem (pər **dɪ**-əm *or* **dee**-əm), *adv.* [Latin] (15c) By the day; for each day. Cf. IN DIEM.

per diem, *adj.* (18c) Based on or calculated by the day <per diem interest>.

per diem, *n.* (1812) **1.** A monetary daily allowance, usu. to cover expenses. **2.** A daily fee.

perdurable (pər-**d[y]uur**-ə-bəl), *adj.* (15c) (Of an estate in land) lasting or enduring; durable; permanent.

perempt (pər-**empt**), *vb.* **1.** *Civil law.* To quash, do away with, or extinguish. **2.** *Slang.* To exercise a peremptory challenge.

peremption (pər-**emp**-shən), *n. Civil law.* A period of time fixed by statute for the existence of a right. • If the right is not exercised during this period, it is extinguished. Whereas prescription simply bars a specific remedy, peremption bars the action itself. Cf. PRESCRIPTION (1). See STATUTE OF REPOSE.

peremptory (pər-**emp**-tə-ree), *adj.* (15c) **1.** Final; absolute; conclusive; incontrovertible <the king's peremptory order>. **2.** Not requiring any shown cause; arbitrary <peremptory challenges>.

peremptory, *n.* See *peremptory challenge* under CHALLENGE (2).

peremptory challenge. See CHALLENGE (2).

peremptory day. See DAY.

peremptory defense. See DEFENSE (1).

peremptory exception. See EXCEPTION (1).

peremptory instruction. See JURY INSTRUCTION.

peremptory mandamus. See MANDAMUS.

peremptory norm. See JUS COGENS (2).

peremptory plea. See PLEA (3).

peremptory rule. See RULE (1).

peremptory strike. See *peremptory challenge* under CHALLENGE (2).

peremptory writ. See WRIT.

perfect (pər-**fekt**), *vb.* (14c) To take all legal steps needed to complete, secure, or record (a claim, right, or interest); to provide necessary public notice in final conformity with the law <perfect a security interest> <perfect the title>.

perfect attestation clause. (1875) A testamentary provision asserting that all actions required to make a valid testamentary disposition have been performed.

perfect competition. See COMPETITION.

perfect defense. See DEFENSE (1).

perfect duty. See DUTY (1).

perfected security interest. See SECURITY INTEREST.

perfect equity. See EQUITY.

perfect grant. See GRANT.

perfecting amendment. See AMENDMENT (3).

perfect instrument. See INSTRUMENT (3).

perfection. Validation of a security interest as against other creditors, usu. by filing a statement with some public office or by taking possession of the collateral. Cf. ATTACHMENT (4).

automatic perfection. The self-operative perfection of a purchase-money security interest without filing or without possession of the collateral. • The security interest is perfected simply by the attachment of the security interest, without any additional steps. See *purchase-money security interest* under SECURITY INTEREST.

temporary perfection. The continuous perfection of a security interest for a limited period. • For example, a security interest in proceeds from the original collateral is perfected for ten days after the debtor receives the proceeds; the interest will become unperfected after this ten-day period unless certain statutory requirements are met. On most instruments, a secured party who advances new value under a written security agreement obtains a 21-day perfection period, even if the secured party does not file a financing statement and the collateral remains with the debtor. UCC § 9-304(4).

perfect obligation. See OBLIGATION.

perfect ownership. See OWNERSHIP.

perfect right. See RIGHT.

perfect self-defense. See SELF-DEFENSE.

perfect tender. See TENDER (3).

perfect-tender rule. (1970) *Commercial law.* The principle that a buyer may reject a seller's goods if the quality, quantity, or delivery of the goods fails to conform precisely to the contract. • Although the perfect-tender rule was adopted by the UCC (§ 2-601), other Code provisions — such as the seller's right to cure after rejection — have softened the rule's impact. Cf. SUBSTANTIAL-PERFORMANCE DOCTRINE.

perfect title. See TITLE (2).

perfect trial. See TRIAL.

perfect usufruct. See USUFRUCT.

perfect war. See WAR.

perfidy (pər-fə-dee). *Int'l law.* A combatant's conduct that creates the impression that an adversary is entitled to, or is obliged to accord, protection under international law, when in fact the conduct is a ruse to gain an advantage. • Acts of perfidy include feigning an intent to negotiate under a flag of truce, or feigning protected status by using signs, emblems, or uniforms of the United Nations or of a neutral country.

performance, *n.* (16c) **1.** The successful completion of a contractual duty, usu. resulting in the performer's release from any past or future liability; EXECUTION (2). — Also termed *full performance.* Cf. NONPERFORMANCE; MISPERFORMANCE.

defective performance. (1832) A performance that, whether partial or full, does not wholly comply with the contract. • One example is late performance.

future performance. (17c) Performance in the future of an obligation that will become due under a contract.

misperformance. See MISPERFORMANCE.

nonperformance. See NONPERFORMANCE.

part performance. (18c) **1.** The accomplishment of some but not all of one's contractual obligations. **2.** A party's execution, in reliance on an opposing party's oral promise, of enough of an oral contract's requirements that a court may hold the statute of frauds not to apply. **3.** PART-PERFORMANCE DOCTRINE.

specific performance. See SPECIFIC PERFORMANCE.

substantial performance. (18c) Performance of the primary, necessary terms of an agreement. See SUBSTANTIAL-PERFORMANCE DOCTRINE.

vicarious performance. Performance carried by an employee, agent, or other nominee.

2. The equitable doctrine by which acts consistent with an intention to fulfill an obligation are construed to be in fulfillment of that obligation, even if the party was silent on the point. **3.** A company's earnings. **4.** The ability of a corporation to maintain or increase earnings.

performance bond. **1.** A bond given by a surety to ensure the timely performance of a contract. • In major international agreements, performance bonds are typically issued by banks, but sometimes also by insurance companies. The face amount of the bond is typically 2% of the value of performance, but occasionally as much as 5%. **2.** A third party's agreement to guarantee the completion of a construction contract upon the default of the general contractor. — Also termed *completion bond; surety bond; contract bond.* Cf. *common-law bond* under BOND (2).

nonoperative performance bond. A performance bond that is not currently in effect but is activated upon the issuance of the buyer's letter of credit or other approved financing.

operative performance bond. A performance bond that has been activated by the issuance of the buyer's letter of credit or other approved financing.

revolving performance bond. A performance bond that is in effect on a continuing basis for the duration of the contract, usu. plus an additional number of days (often 45).

up-front performance bond. A performance bond given before the issuance of the buyer's letter of credit or other financing.

performance bonus. See BONUS.

performance contract. See CONTRACT.

performance fund. See MUTUAL FUND.

performance plan. A bonus compensation plan in which executives are paid according to the company's growth.

performance right. A copyright holder's exclusive right to recite, play, act, show, or otherwise render the protected work publicly, whether directly or by technological means (as by broadcasting the work on television). • Every public performance of a copyrighted work requires authorization from the copyright owner or its representative, unless a statutory ephemeral-recording exemption applies. — Also termed *public-performance right.*

performance shares. Stock given to an executive when the corporation meets a performance objective.

performance specification. See STATEMENT OF WORK.

performance stock. See *glamour stock* under STOCK.

peril. (13c) 1. Exposure to the risk of injury, damage, or loss <the perils of litigation>.

inescapable peril. (1933) A danger that one cannot avoid without another's help. See LAST-CLEAR-CHANCE DOCTRINE.

2. *Insurance.* The cause of a risk of loss to person or property; esp., the cause of a risk such as fire, accident, theft, forgery, earthquake, flood, or illness <insured against all perils>. Cf. RISK (3).

peril of the sea. An action of the elements at sea of such force as to overcome the strength of a well-founded ship and the normal precautions of good marine practice. • A peril of the sea may relieve a carrier from liability for the resulting losses. — Also termed *danger of navigation; danger of river; marine peril; marine risk;* (in regard to the Great Lakes) *perils of the lakes; danger of the sea.*

per incuriam (pər in-**kyoor**-ee-əm), *adj.* (Of a judicial decision) wrongly decided, usu. because the judge or judges were ill-informed about the applicable law.

periodic alimony. See *permanent alimony* under ALIMONY.

periodic audit. See AUDIT.

periodic estate. See *periodic tenancy* under TENANCY.

periodic payment. See PAYMENT.

periodic-payment-plan certificate. See STOCK CERTIFICATE.

periodic tenancy. See TENANCY.

period of prescription. The period fixed by local law as sufficient for obtaining or extinguishing a right through lapse of time. • In addition to a fixed number of years, the period includes whatever further time is allowed by local law because

of infancy, insanity, coverture, and other like circumstances. See PRESCRIPTIVE RIGHT; PRESCRIPTION (3), (4), (5).

peripheral right. See RIGHT.

periphrasis (pə-**rif**-rə-sis), *n.* (16c) A roundabout way of writing or speaking; circumlocution. — **periphrastic** (per-ə-**fras**-tik), *adj.*

perishable-food-disparagement act. See AGRICULTURAL-DISPARAGEMENT LAW.

perjury (**pər**-jər-ee), *n.* (14c) The act or an instance of a person's deliberately making material false or misleading statements while under oath. — Also termed *false swearing; false oath;* (archaically) *forswearing.* — **perjure** (**pər**-jər), *vb.* — **perjured** (**pər**-jərd), **perjurious** (pər-**juur**-ee-əs), *adj.* — **perjuror** (**pər**-jər-ər), *n.*

perjury-trap doctrine. (1989) The principle that a perjury indictment against a person must be dismissed if the prosecution secures it by calling that person as a grand-jury witness in an effort to obtain evidence for a perjury charge, esp. when the person's testimony does not relate to issues material to the grand-jury's ongoing investigation.

perk, *n.* See PERQUISITE.

Perlman **doctrine.** The principle that a discovery order directed at a disinterested third party is immediately appealable on the theory that the third party will not risk contempt by refusing to comply. • The doctrine originated in *Perlman v. United States,* 247 U.S. 7, 13, 38 S.Ct. 417, 420 (1918). The Court reasoned that the third party's ability to protect his or her rights would be thwarted if the party could not appeal immediately.

permanency hearing. See HEARING.

permanency plan. A proposed written strategy for the eventual permanent placement of a child who has been removed from his or her parents. • A permanency plan, ideally, provides either for the child's safe return to one or both parents or for the child's adoption. If neither of these alternatives is possible, then the plan will provide for long-term foster care, relative care, or guardianship. Under the Adoption and Safe Families Act, long-term foster care is the choice of last resort. — Also termed *permanent plan.*

permanency-planning hearing. See *permanency hearing* under HEARING.

permanent abode. See DOMICILE (1).

permanent alimony. See ALIMONY.

permanent allegiance. See ALLEGIANCE.

permanent chargé d'affaires. See CHARGÉ D'AFFAIRES.

permanent committee. See *standing committee* under COMMITTEE.

permanent damages. See DAMAGES.

permanent disability. See DISABILITY (2).

permanent employment. See EMPLOYMENT.

permanent financing. See FINANCING.

permanent fixture. See FIXTURE.

permanent injunction. See INJUNCTION.

permanent injury. See INJURY.

permanent law. See LAW.

permanent nuisance. See NUISANCE.

permanent plan. See PERMANENCY PLAN.

permanent policy. See INSURANCE POLICY.

permanent protective order. See PROTECTIVE ORDER.

permanent statute. See *perpetual statute* under STATUTE.

permanent taking. See TAKING (2).

permanent treaty. See TREATY (1).

permanent trespass. See TRESPASS.

permanent ward. See WARD.

per minas. See *duress per minas* under DURESS.

permissible appointee. See APPOINTEE.

permissible-repair doctrine. See REPAIR DOCTRINE.

permission. (15c) **1.** The act of permitting. **2.** A license or liberty to do something; authorization.

> *express permission.* Permission that is clearly and unmistakably granted by actions or words, oral or written.

> *implied permission.* **1.** Permission that is inferred from words or actions. **2.** See *implied consent* under CONSENT.

3. Conduct that justifies others in believing that the possessor of property is willing to have them enter if they want to do so. Cf. INVITATION.

permissive abstention. See ABSTENTION.

permissive counterclaim. See COUNTERCLAIM.

permissive inference. See *permissive presumption* under PRESUMPTION.

permissive joinder. See JOINDER.

permissive presumption. See PRESUMPTION.

permissive statute. See STATUTE.

permissive subject of bargaining. *Labor law.* An employment or collective-bargaining issue, other than a basic employment issue, that is not required to be the subject of collective bargaining but that cannot be implemented by management without union approval. ● For example, altering the scope of the bargaining unit does not affect a term or condition of employment, so it is a permissive, instead of mandatory, subject of bargaining. Disagreement on a permissive subject of bargaining cannot be used as the basis for an impasse in negotiating a collective-bargaining agreement, unlike a mandatory subject of bargaining. — Often shortened to *permissive subject.* Cf. MANDATORY SUBJECT OF BARGAINING.

permissive tenant. See *tenant at sufferance* under TENANT.

permissive use. See USE (4).

permissive waste. See WASTE (1).

permit (pər-mit), *n.* (17c) A certificate evidencing permission; a license <a gun permit>.

permit (pər-mit), *vb.* (15c) **1.** To consent to formally <permit the inspection to be carried out>. **2.** To give opportunity for <lax security permitted the escape>. **3.** To allow or admit of <if the law so permits>.

permit bond. See *license bond* under BOND (2).

permit card. *Labor law.* A document issued by a union to a nonunion member to allow the person to work on a job covered by a union contract.

permittee (pər-mi-**tee**). One who has permission to do something.

> *subpermittee.* A person who receives permission to act from a permittee.

permutation. *Civil law.* Barter; exchange.

perp (pərp), *n. Slang.* Perpetrator <the police brought in the perp for questioning>. See PERPETRATOR.

perparts. See PURPART.

perpetrate, *vb.* (16c) To commit or carry out (an act, esp. a crime) <find whoever perpetrated this heinous deed>. — **perpetration,** *n.*

perpetrator. (16c) A person who commits a crime or offense.

perpetual bond. See *annuity bond* under BOND (3).

perpetual edict. See *edictum perpetuum* under EDICTUM.

perpetual freehold. See FREEHOLD.

perpetual injunction. See *permanent injunction* under INJUNCTION.

perpetual lease. See LEASE.

perpetually renewable lease. See LEASE.

perpetual policy. See INSURANCE POLICY.

perpetual statute. See STATUTE.

perpetual succession. See SUCCESSION (4).

perpetual trust. See TRUST.

perpetuation of testimony. The means or procedure for preserving for future use witness testimony that might otherwise be unavailable at trial.

perpetuities, rule against. See RULE AGAINST PERPETUITIES.

perpetuity (pər-pə-t[y]oo-ə-tee). **1.** The state of continuing forever. **2.** *Hist.* An unbarrable entail. **3.** *Hist.* An inalienable interest. **4.** An interest that does not take effect or vest within the period prescribed by law. • In reference to the rule against perpetuities, only sense 4 is now current. See RULE AGAINST PERPETUITIES.

per procurationem (pər prok-yə-ray-shee-**oh**-nəm). [Latin] By proxy. — Abbr. *per pro.*; *p. proc.*; *p. pro.*; *p.p.* — Also termed *per procuration*.

perp walk. *Slang.* The act of making a suspect in custody walk before an audience, esp. members of the media. • *Perp* is short for *perpetrator*.

perquisite (pər-kwi-zit). (16c) A privilege or benefit given in addition to one's salary or regular wages. — Often shortened to *perk*.

per quod (pər **kwod**), *adv. & adj.* [Latin "whereby"] (17c) Requiring reference to additional facts; (of libel or slander) actionable only on allegation and proof of special damages. See *actionable per quod* under ACTIONABLE; *libel per quod* under LIBEL; *slander per quod* under SLANDER.

Perringer release. See *Pierringer release* under RELEASE (2).

per se (pər say), *adv. & adj.* [Latin] (16c) **1.** Of, in, or by itself; standing alone, without reference to additional facts. See *actionable per se* under ACTIONABLE; *libel per se* under LIBEL; *slander per se* under SLANDER. **2.** As a matter of law.

persecution, *n.* Violent, cruel, and oppressive treatment directed toward a person or group of persons because of their race, religion, sexual orientation, politics, or other beliefs. See *hate crime* under CRIME. — **persecute,** *vb.*

per se deadly weapon. See *deadly weapon per se* under WEAPON.

per se rule. *Antitrust.* The judicial principle that a trade practice violates the Sherman Act simply if the practice is a restraint of trade, regardless of whether it actually harms anyone. See SHERMAN ANTITRUST ACT. Cf. RULE OF REASON.

per se violation. *Antitrust.* A trade practice (such as price-fixing) that is considered inherently anticompetitive and injurious to the public without any need to determine whether it has actually injured market competition.

persistent price discrimination. See PRICE DISCRIMINATION.

person. (13c) **1.** A human being. — Also termed *natural person.*

> **absent person.** *Louisiana law.* A person who has no representative in the state and whose whereabouts are not known and cannot be ascertained by diligent effort. La. Civ. Code art. 47.

> **adult disabled person.** A child over the age of 18 for whom a parent continues to have a duty of support.

> **associated person.** See ASSOCIATED PERSON.

> **disabled person.** (1872) A person who has a mental or physical impairment. See DISABILITY.

> **disappeared person.** See DISAPPEARED PERSON.

> **displaced person.** A person who remains within an internationally recognized state border after being forced to flee a home or place of habitual residence because of armed conflict, internal strife, the government's systematic violations of human rights, or a natural or man-made disaster. — Also termed *internally displaced person.* Cf. EVACUEE; REFUGEE.

> **interested person.** (1844) A person having a property right in or claim against a thing, such as a trust or decedent's estate. • The meaning may expand to include an entity, such as a business that is a creditor of a decedent. — Abbr. IP.

> **person in loco parentis** (in **loh**-koh pə-**ren**-tis). (1827) A person who acts in place of a parent, either temporarily (as a schoolteacher does) or indefinitely (as a stepparent does); a person who has assumed the obligations of a parent without formally adopting the child. See IN LOCO PARENTIS.

> **person in need of supervision.** See *child in need of supervision* under CHILD. — Abbr. PINS.

> **person not deceased.** A person who is either living or has not yet been born.

> **person of incidence.** (1880) The person against whom a right is enforceable; a person who owes a legal duty. • The meaning may expand to include an entity, such as an insurance company.

> **person of inherence** (in-**heer**-ənts). (1909) The person in whom a legal right is vested; the owner of a right. • The meaning may expand to include an entity.

> **person of interest.** A person who is the subject of a police investigation but who has not been identified by investigators as being suspected of committing the crime itself.

> **person of opposite sex sharing living quarters.** See POSSLQ.

> **person with ordinary skill in the art.** See PERSON WITH ORDINARY SKILL IN THE ART.

> **private person. 1.** A person who does not hold public office or serve in the military. **2.** *Civil law.* An entity such as a corporation or partnership that is governed by private law.

> **protected person. 1.** A person for whom a conservator has been appointed or other protective order has been made. **2.** *Int'l law.* A person who is protected by a rule of international law; esp., one who is in the hands of an occupying force

during a conflict. • Protected persons are entitled to a standard of treatment (including a prohibition on coercion and corporal punishment) under the Geneva Convention Relative to the Protection of Civilian Persons in Time of War (1949). **3.** *English law.* An inhabitant of a protectorate of the United Kingdom. • Though not a British subject, such a person is given diplomatic protection by the Crown.

2. The living body of a human being <contraband found on the smuggler's person>. **3.** An entity (such as a corporation) that is recognized by law as having most of the rights and duties of a human being. • In this sense, the term includes partnerships and other associations, whether incorporated or unincorporated.

artificial person. (17c) An entity, such as a corporation, created by law and given certain legal rights and duties of a human being; a being, real or imaginary, who for the purpose of legal reasoning is treated more or less as a human being. • An entity is a person for purposes of the Due Process and Equal Protection Clauses but is not a citizen for purposes of the Privileges and Immunities Clauses in Article IV § 2 and in the Fourteenth Amendment. — Also termed *fictitious person; juristic person; juridical person; legal person; moral person.* Cf. LEGAL ENTITY.

control person. See CONTROL PERSON.

fictitious person. See *artificial person.*

international person. See INTERNATIONAL PERSON.

juridical person. See *artificial person.*

juristic person. See *artificial person.*

legal person. See *artificial person.*

moral person. See *artificial person.*

private person. See *private person* (2) under PERSON (1).

personable, *adj.* (16c) Having the status of a legal person (and thus the right to plead in court, enter into contracts, etc.) <a personable entity>.

person aggrieved. See *aggrieved party* under PARTY (2).

persona grata (pər-**soh**-nə **gray**-tə *or* **grah**-tə *or* **grat**-ə), *n.* [Latin] An acceptable person; esp., a diplomat who is acceptable to a host country. Pl. **personae gratae** (pər-**soh**-nee **gray**-tee *or* **grah**-tee *or* **grat**-ee). Cf. PERSONA NON GRATA.

personal, *adj.* (14c) **1.** Of or affecting a person <personal injury>. **2.** Of or constituting personal property <personal belongings>. See IN PERSONAM.

personal action. See ACTION (4).

personal asset. See ASSET.

personal bond. See BOND (2).

personal-capacity suit. See SUIT.

personal chattel. See *chattel personal* under CHATTEL.

personal check. See CHECK.

personal-comfort doctrine. The principle that the course of employment is not interrupted by certain acts relating to the employee's personal comfort, typically short breaks for eating, drinking, using the restroom, and the like. — Also termed *personal-comfort rule.*

personal-condition crime. See *status crime* under CRIME.

personal contract. See CONTRACT.

personal covenant. See COVENANT (4).

personal crime. See CRIME.

personal defense. See DEFENSE (4).

personal demand. See DEMAND (3).

personal effects. See EFFECTS.

personal estate. See *personal property* (1) under PROPERTY.

personal evidence. See TESTIMONY.

personal exemption. See EXEMPTION.

personal goodwill. See GOODWILL.

personal history. An individual's background; the particular experiences and events that shape a person's life.

personal holding company. See COMPANY.

personal-holding-company tax. See *holding-company tax* under TAX.

personal income. See INCOME.

personal indignity. See INDIGNITY.

personal injury. See INJURY.

personality. (1870) **1.** The legal status of one regarded by the law as a person; the legal conception by which the law regards a human being or an artificial entity as a person. — Also termed *legal personality.* **2.** *Parliamentary law.* (usu. pl.) An improper reference to a member by name or in his or her personal capacity.

personality theory. *Intellectual property.* A rationalization of intellectual-property laws, esp. copyright, drawing on the philosophy of G.W.F. Hegel, holding that personal expression is a form of self-actualization that gives the creator inalienable moral rights in the creations. • As a way of analyzing intellectual-property rights, personality theory takes the point of view of the individual inventor, author, or artist rather than that of society as a whole. Cf. LOCKEAN LABOR THEORY; UTILITARIANISM.

personal judgment. See JUDGMENT.

personal jurisdiction. See JURISDICTION.

personal justice. See JUSTICE (1).

personal knowledge. See KNOWLEDGE.

personal law. (18c) The law that governs a person's family matters, usu. regardless of where the person goes. • In common-law systems, personal law refers to the law of the person's domicile. In civil-law systems, it refers to the law of the individual's nationality (and so is sometimes called *lex patriae*). Cf. TERRITORIAL LAW.

personal liability. See LIABILITY.

personal liberty. See LIBERTY.

personal name. See NAME.

personal notice. See NOTICE.

personal obligation. See OBLIGATION.

personal privilege. See PRIVILEGE (5).

personal property. See PROPERTY.

personal-property tax. See TAX.

personal recognizance. See RECOGNIZANCE.

personal replevin. See REPLEVIN.

personal representative. See REPRESENTATIVE.

personal reputation. See REPUTATION.

personal-residence trust. See TRUST.

Personal Responsibility and Work Opportunity Reconciliation Act. A 1996 federal law that overhauled the welfare system, as well as requiring states to provide a means for collecting child support by (1) imposing liens on a child-support obligor's assets, and (2) facilitating income-withholding. • The Act did away with Aid to Families with Dependent Children in favor of Temporary Assistance to Needy Families. It also limited the length of time that persons could receive welfare and tied states' receipt of federal child-support funds to their implementing enhanced paternity-establishment services. — Also termed *Welfare Reform Act*. See AID TO FAMILIES WITH DEPENDENT CHILDREN; TEMPORARY ASSISTANCE TO NEEDY FAMILIES. — Abbr. PRWORA.

personal right. See RIGHT.

personal security. See SECURITY.

personal service. (16c) **1.** Actual delivery of the notice or process to the person to whom it is directed. — Also termed *actual service*. **2.** An act done personally by an individual. • In this sense, a personal service is an economic service involving either the intellectual or manual personal effort of an individual, as opposed to the salable product of the person's skill.

personal servitude. See SERVITUDE (2).

personal statute. See STATUTE.

personal suretyship. See SURETYSHIP.

personal tithe. See TITHE.

personal tort. See TORT.

personal treaty. See TREATY (1).

personal trust. See *private trust* under TRUST.

personalty (**pars**-ən-əl-tee). (16c) Personal property as distinguished from real property. See *personal property* (1) under PROPERTY.

  quasi-personalty. Things that are considered movable by the law, though fixed to real property either actually (as with a fixture) or fictitiously (as with a lease for years).

personal warrandice. See WARRANDICE.

personal warranty. See WARRANTY (2).

personal wrong. See WRONG.

personam. See IN PERSONAM.

persona non grata (pər-**sohn**-ə non **grah**-də), *n.* [Latin] An unwanted person; esp., a diplomat who is not acceptable to a host country. Pl. **personae non gratae.** Cf. PERSONA GRATA.

personation. See IMPERSONATION.

person-endangering state of mind. (1990) An intent to kill, inflict great bodily injury, act in wanton disregard of an unreasonable risk to others, or perpetrate a dangerous felony. — Also termed *man-endangering state of mind*.

person *in loco parentis.* See PERSON (1).

person in need of supervision. See *child in need of supervision* under CHILD. — Abbr. PINS.

person not deceased. See PERSON (1).

person of incidence. See PERSON (1).

person of inherence. See PERSON (1).

person of interest. See PERSON (1).

person of opposite sex sharing living quarters. See POSSLQ.

person with ordinary skill in the art. *Patents.* A fictional construct of the patent laws, denoting someone who has reasonably developed abilities in the field of the invention at issue. • The patent application must be clear and complete enough to teach a person skilled in the art how to make and use the invention without undue experimentation.

per stirpes (pər **stər**-peez), *adv.* & *adj.* [Latin "by roots or stocks"] (17c) Proportionately divided between beneficiaries according to their deceased ancestor's share. — Also termed *in stirpes*; *per stirpem.* Cf. PER CAPITA.

persuade, *vb.* To induce (another) to do something <Steve persuaded his neighbor to sign the release after the accident>.

persuaded confession. See CONFESSION.

persuasion. (14c) The act of influencing or attempting to influence others by reasoned argument; the act of persuading.

  fair persuasion. Argument, exhortation, or persuasion that does not involve harassment, threats, or misrepresentations.

persuasion burden. See BURDEN OF PERSUASION.

persuasive authority. See AUTHORITY (4).

persuasive memorandum. See MEMORANDUM.

persuasive precedent. See PRECEDENT.

pertain, *vb.* To relate to; to concern.

pertinent, *adj.* (15c) Pertaining to the issue at hand; relevant <pertinent testimony>.

pertinent art. 1. See *analogous art* under ART. **2.** See *relevant art* under ART.

perverse verdict. See VERDICT.

petit (pet-ee *or* pet-it), *adj.* [Law French "minor, small"] (15c) See PETTY.

petite assize. See ASSIZE (5).

Petite **policy.** The Department of Justice rule forbidding a federal prosecution after a previous state or federal prosecution based on the same acts unless (1) an Assistant Attorney General has approved the prosecution, (2) a substantial federal interest supports the prosecution, (3) the previous prosecution failed to vindicate the federal interest, and (4) there is sufficient evidence to sustain a conviction. United States Attorneys' Manual § 9–2.031 (Sept. 1997); *Petite v. United States*, 361 U.S. 529, 80 S.Ct. 450 (1960).

petition, *n.* (15c) **1.** A formal written request presented to a court or other official body.

   bankruptcy petition. See *voluntary petition.*

   certiorari petition. A petition seeking discretionary review from an appellate court. See CERTIORARI.

   debtor's petition. See *voluntary petition.*

   involuntary petition. (1868) A petition filed in a bankruptcy court by a creditor seeking to declare a debtor bankrupt. ● This petition may be filed only under Chapter 7 or Chapter 11 of the Bankruptcy Code.

   juvenile petition. (1945) A juvenile-court petition alleging delinquent conduct by the accused. ● The accusations made in a juvenile petition are sometimes tried in an adjudication hearing. See *adjudication hearing* (3) under HEARING.

   petition for probate. A written application by which a party requests that a court admit a will to probate.

   petition in error. See APPEAL (1).

   voluntary petition. (1842) A petition filed with a bankruptcy court by a debtor seeking protection from creditors. — Also termed *bankruptcy petition*; *debtor's petition.*

2. In some states, the first pleading in a lawsuit; COMPLAINT. **3.** *Patents.* A patent applicant's request to a patent office's administrative head for supervision of a procedural or jurisdictional matter related to the patent application. — **petition,** *vb.*

petition de droit. See PETITION OF RIGHT.

petitioner. (15c) A party who presents a petition to a court or other official body, esp. when seeking relief on appeal. — Also termed (archaically) *plaintiff in error.* Cf. RESPONDENT (2).

petition for access. *Patents.* Application to inspect a patent application, made by someone who does not usu. have the authority to do so. ● The petition must demonstrate a special need for access, and show that the applicant has been notified of the petition. The patent applicant is entitled to a hearing before access is granted.

petition in bankruptcy. A formal written request, presented to a bankruptcy court, seeking protection for an insolvent debtor. ● The debtor (in a voluntary bankruptcy) or the debtor's creditors (in an involuntary bankruptcy) can file such a petition to initiate a bankruptcy proceeding.

petition of right. 1. (*cap.*) One of the four great charters of English liberty (3 Car. I (1628)), establishing that "no man be compelled to make or yield any gift, loan, benevolence, tax, or such like charge, without common consent by act of parliament." ● The other three great charters are Magna Carta, the Habeas Corpus Act (31 Car. 2 (1679)), and the Bill of Rights (1 W. & M. (1689)). **2.** *Hist.* A proceeding in chancery by which a subject claims that a debt is owed by the Crown or that the Crown has broken a contract or wrongfully detained the subject's property. ● Although the petition is addressed directly to the Crown, the courts adjudicate the claim just as in an action between private parties. — Also termed *petition de droit.*

petition to make special. *Patents.* A petition asking the U.S. Patent and Trademark Office to expedite a patent prosecution. ● Special processing is available, for example, in favored areas of science (such as cancer research and energy conservation), where the inventor is sick or elderly, and where infringement is already taking place.

petit juror. See JUROR.

petit jury. See JURY.

petit larceny. See LARCENY.

petit offense. See OFFENSE.

petit officer. See OFFICER.

petitorium (pet-ə-**tor**-ee-əm). See *petitory action* under ACTION (4).

petitory action. See ACTION (4).

petitory suit. See *petitory action* under ACTION (4).

petit serjeanty. See SERJEANTY.

petit treason. See *petty treason* under TREASON.

petroleum-conservation law. *Oil & gas.* A state law that limits the rule of capture and defines the correlative-rights doctrine by regulating the drilling and operation of oil-and-gas wells. • Petroleum-conservation laws are intended to prevent waste and protect correlative rights.

pettifogger (pet-i-fog-ər), *n.* (16c) **1.** A lawyer lacking in education, ability, sound judgment, or common sense. **2.** A lawyer who clouds an issue with insignificant details. — **pettifoggery** (pet-i-**fog**-ər-ee), *n.*

pet trust. See TRUST.

petty, *adj.* (16c) Relatively insignificant or minor <a petty crime>. Cf. GRAND.

petty assize. See ASSIZE (6).

petty average. See *particular average* under AVERAGE.

petty cash. See CASH.

petty jury. See *petit jury* under JURY.

petty larceny. See *petit larceny* under LARCENY.

petty offense. See OFFENSE (1).

petty officer. See OFFICER (2).

petty patent. See UTILITY MODEL.

petty theft. See THEFT.

petty treason. See TREASON.

PFPA. *abbr.* PENTAGON FORCE PROTECTION AGENCY.

PGS. *abbr.* See *pictorial, graphic, and sculptural work* under WORK (2).

phantom jury. See *shadow jury* under JURY.

phantom stock. See STOCK.

phantom stock plan. A long-term benefit plan under which a corporate employee is given units having the same characteristics as the employer's stock shares. • It is termed a "phantom" plan because the employee does not actually hold any shares but instead holds the right to the value of those shares. — Also termed *shadow stock plan.*

phenotype. *Patents.* A living organism's physical characteristics and behavior. • A patent on living matter must disclose its genetic makeup rather than just describe its phenotype. Cf. GENOTYPE.

Philadelphia lawyer. (1788) A shrewd and learned lawyer. • This term can have positive or negative connotations today, but when it first appeared (in colonial times), it carried only a positive sense deriving from Philadelphia's position as America's center of learning and culture.

philosophie du droit. See *ethical jurisprudence* under JURISPRUDENCE.

philosophy of law. See *general jurisprudence* (2) under JURISPRUDENCE.

phishing, *n. Slang.* The sending of a fraudulent electronic communication that appears to be a genuine message from a legitimate entity or business for the purpose of inducing the recipient to disclose sensitive personal information. Cf. BOILER-ROOM TRANSACTION; TELESCAM.

Phonograms Convention. See GENEVA PHONOGRAMS CONVENTION.

phonorecord (foh-noh-rek-ərd). (1968) A physical object (such as a phonographic record, cassette tape, or compact disc) from which fixed sounds can be perceived, reproduced, or otherwise communicated directly or with a machine's aid. • The term is fairly common in copyright contexts since it is defined in the U.S. Copyright Act of 1976 (17 USCA § 101).

photofit. See IDENTIKIT.

p.h.v. *abbr.* PRO HAC VICE.

phylacist (fɪ-lə-sist), *n. Archaic.* A jailer. — Also spelled *phylasist.*

physical child endangerment. See CHILD ENDANGERMENT.

physical cruelty. See CRUELTY.

physical custody. (1884) **1.** Custody of a person (such as an arrestee) whose freedom is directly controlled and limited. **2.** *Family law.* The right to have the child live with the person awarded custody by the court. — Also termed *residential custody.* **3.** Possession of a child during visitation.

physical diagnosis. See DIAGNOSIS.

physical disability. See DISABILITY (2).

physical endangerment. See *physical child endangerment* under CHILD ENDANGERMENT.

physical evidence. See *real evidence* (1) under EVIDENCE.

physical fact. See FACT.

physical-facts rule. (1923) *Evidence.* The principle that oral testimony may be disregarded when it is inconsistent or irreconcilable with the physical evidence in the case. — Also termed *doctrine of incontrovertible physical facts; incontrovertible-physical-facts doctrine.*

physical force. See *actual force* under FORCE.

physical harm. See HARM.

physical hazard. See HAZARD (2).

physical-impact rule. See IMPACT RULE.

physical impossibility. See *factual impossibility* under IMPOSSIBILITY.

physical incapacity. See IMPOTENCE.

physical injury. See *bodily injury* under INJURY.

physical-inventory accounting method. See ACCOUNTING METHOD.

physical necessity. See NECESSITY.

physical neglect. See NEGLECT.

physical-proximity test. (1955) *Criminal law.* A common-law test for the crime of attempt, focusing on how much more the defendant would have needed to do to complete the offense. See ATTEMPT (2).

physical shock. See SHOCK.

physical taking. See TAKING (2).

physician-assisted suicide. See *assisted suicide* under SUICIDE.

physician–client privilege. See *doctor–patient privilege* under PRIVILEGE (3).

physician–patient privilege. See *doctor–patient privilege* under PRIVILEGE (3).

physician's directive. See ADVANCE DIRECTIVE (2).

P.I. *abbr.* **1.** See *personal injury* under INJURY. **2.** Private investigator.

picaroon (pik-ə-**roon**). A robber or plunderer.

picketing. (1832) The demonstration by one or more persons outside a business or organization to protest the entity's activities or policies and to pressure the entity to meet the protesters' demands; esp., an employees' demonstration aimed at publicizing a labor dispute and influencing the public to withhold business from the employer. • Picketing is usu. considered a form of fair persuasion of third persons if access to the place of business is not materially obstructed. Cf. BOYCOTT; STRIKE.

common-situs picketing. The illegal picketing by union workers of a construction site, stemming from a dispute with one of the subcontractors.

informational picketing. Picketing to inform the public about a matter of concern to the union.

organizational picketing. Picketing by a union in an effort to persuade the employer to accept the union as the collective-bargaining agent of the employees; esp., picketing by members of one union when the employer has already recognized another union as the bargaining agent for the company's employees.— Also termed *recognition picketing.*

secondary picketing. The picketing of an establishment with which the picketing party has no direct dispute in order to pressure the party with which there is a dispute. See *secondary boycott* under BOYCOTT; *secondary strike* under STRIKE.

unlawful picketing. Picketing carried on in violation of law, as when the picketers use threats or violence to dissuade other employees from returning to work.

pickpocket. (16c) A thief who steals money or property from the person of another, usu. by stealth but sometimes by physical diversion such as bumping into or pushing the victim.

pickpocketing, *n.* See *larceny from the person* under LARCENY.

pickup tax. See TAX.

pictorial, graphic, and sculptural work. See WORK (2).

piecemeal zoning. See *partial zoning* under ZONING.

piecework. Work done or paid for by the piece or job.

piercing the corporate veil. (1928) The judicial act of imposing personal liability on otherwise immune corporate officers, directors, or shareholders for the corporation's wrongful acts. — Also termed *disregarding the corporate entity*; *veil-piercing.* See CORPORATE VEIL.

Pierringer **release.** See RELEASE (2).

pigeon drop. See JAMAICAN SWITCH.

piggyback registration rights. See REGISTRATION RIGHTS.

pignorate (**pig**-nə-rayt), *vb.* (17c) **1.** To give over as a pledge; to pawn. **2.** To take in pawn. Cf. OPPIGNORATE. — **pignorative,** *adj.*

pignorative contract. See CONTRACT.

pignus (**pig**-nəs), *n.* [Latin "pledge"] **1.** *Roman & civil law.* (*ital.*) A bailment in which goods are delivered to secure the payment of a debt or performance of an engagement, accompanied by a power of sale in case of default. • This type of bailment is for the benefit of both parties. — Also termed *pawn*; *pledge.* **2.** A lien. Pl. *pignora* or *pignera.*

PIH. *abbr.* OFFICE OF PUBLIC AND INDIAN HOUSING.

pilferage (**pil**-fər-ij), *n.* (18c) **1.** The act or an instance of stealing. **2.** The item or items stolen. See LARCENY; THEFT. — **pilfer** (**pil**-fər), *vb.*

pill. See POISON PILL.

pillage (**pil**-ij), *n.* **1.** The forcible seizure of another's property, esp. in war; esp., the wartime plundering of a city or territory. **2.** The property so seized or plundered; BOOTY. — Also termed *plunder.* — **pillage,** *vb.*

pillory (**pil**-ə-ree), *n. Hist.* A punishment instrument consisting of a wooden framework with holes through which an offender's head and hands are placed and secured. • A person put in a pillory usu. had to stand rather than sit (as with the stocks). Cf. STOCKS.

finger pillory. Hist. Eccles. law. A miniature stock used to confine the fingers of a person who misbehaved during church services.

pilot. 1. A person in control of an airplane. **2.** *Maritime law.* A person in control of a vessel.

bar pilot. See BRANCH PILOT.

branch pilot. A pilot, esp. one who is trained and licensed to navigate rivers and their tributaries.

• The term originated in England when pilots were licensed to navigate the River Thames and its tributaries. — Also termed *bar pilot*. See TRINITY HOUSE.

compulsory pilot. A ship pilot entitled by law to guide a ship for a particular purpose, such as piloting the ship into harbor. • The compulsory nature of the appointment relieves the vessel's owner of personal liability if the pilot causes a collision. Cf. *voluntary pilot*.

voluntary pilot. A ship pilot who controls a ship with the permission of the vessel's owner. • The vessel's owner is personally liable for damage resulting from a collision caused by a voluntary pilot. Cf. *compulsory pilot*.

pilotage (pɪ-lə-tij). **1.** The navigating of vessels; the business of navigating vessels. **2.** Compensation that a pilot receives for navigating a vessel, esp. into and out of harbor or through a channel or passage.

compulsory pilotage. A requirement, imposed by law in some jurisdictions, that vessels approaching or leaving a harbor must take on a licensed pilot to guide the vessel into or out of the harbor.

half-pilotage. Compensation equaling half the value of services that a pilot has offered to perform. • Shipowners can avoid compulsory pilotage in some jurisdictions by payment of half-pilotage.

pimp, *n.* (17c) A person who solicits customers for a prostitute, usu. in return for a share of the prostitute's earnings. See PANDERING (1). Cf. BAWD. — **pimp,** *vb.* — **pimping,** *n.*

pincite. See *pinpoint citation* under CITATION (3).

pinkerton. *Slang.* A private detective or security guard, usu. one who is armed. • The name comes from the Pinkerton Detective Agency, the first private detective agency in the United States, established in 1852.

Pinkerton rule. (1979) *Criminal law.* The doctrine imposing liability on a conspirator for all offenses committed in furtherance of the conspiracy, even if those offenses are actually performed by coconspirators. *Pinkerton v. United States*, 328 U.S. 640, 66 S.Ct. 1180 (1946).

pink sheet. A daily publication listing over-the-counter stocks, their market-makers, and their prices. • Printed on pink paper, pink sheets are published by the National Quotation Bureau, a private company. — Also termed *National Daily Quotation Service*.

pink slip. *Slang.* A notice of employment termination given to an employee by an employer.

pinpoint citation. See CITATION (3).

PINS. *abbr.* PERSON IN NEED OF SUPERVISION.

pioneer drug. See DRUG.

pioneer patent. See PATENT (3).

pious gift. See *charitable gift* under GIFT.

pious use. See USE (1).

Pipe Rolls. *Hist.* The Exchequer's records of royal revenue, including revenue from feudal holdings, judicial fees, and tax revenue collected by the sheriffs. • The Pipe Rolls comprise 676 rolls, covering the years 1131 and 1156 to 1833 (except for gaps in 1216 and 1403). — Also termed *Great Rolls of the Exchequer*.

PIR. *abbr.* PRESENTENCE INVESTIGATION REPORT.

piracy, *n.* (16c) **1.** Robbery, kidnapping, or other criminal violence committed at sea. **2.** A similar crime committed aboard a plane or other vehicle. **3.** HIJACKING.

air piracy. (1948) The crime of using force or threat to seize control of an aircraft; the hijacking of an aircraft, esp. one in flight. — Also termed *aircraft piracy*.

4. The unauthorized and illegal reproduction or distribution of materials protected by copyright, patent, or trademark law. See INFRINGEMENT. — **pirate,** *vb.* — **piratical** (pɪ-rat-ə-kəl), *adj.* — **pirate,** *n.*

video piracy. The illegal copying and sale or rental of copyrighted motion pictures.

pirate recording. *Copyright.* An unauthorized copy of the sounds on a copyright-protected recording, including digital duplication made available over the Internet. — Sometimes also termed *bootleg recording*.

piscary. 1. See FISHERY (1). **2.** See *common of piscary* under COMMON (1).

pit and gallows. *Hist. Scots law.* An ancient form of capital punishment for theft by which a condemned woman was drowned in a pit and a condemned man was hanged on a gallows.

PITI. *abbr.* Principal, interest, taxes, and insurance — the components of a monthly mortgage payment.

P.J. See *presiding judge* under JUDGE.

PKPA. *abbr.* PARENTAL KIDNAPPING PREVENTION ACT.

pl. *abbr.* PLACITUM (8).

P.L. *abbr.* PUBLIC LAW.

placard (plak-ahrd *or* plak-ərd). **1.** *Hist.* An official document, such as a license or permit. **2.** An advertisement posted in a public place.

place land. See INDEMNITY LAND.

placement. 1. The act of selling a new issue of securities or arranging a loan or mortgage. **2.** The act of finding employment for a person, esp. as done by an employment agency.

place of abode. (16c) A person's residence or domicile. See ABODE; RESIDENCE; DOMICILE.

place of business. (16c) A location at which one carries on a business. Cf. DOMICILE (2).

principal place of business. (1825) The place of a corporation's chief executive offices, which is typically viewed as the "nerve center.

place of contracting. (18c) The country or state in which a contract is entered into. • The place of contracting is not necessarily the place where the document is signed; another location may be designated in the contract.

place of delivery. (17c) The place where goods sold are to be sent by the seller. • If no place is specified in the contract, the seller's place of business is usu. the place of delivery. UCC § 2-308.

place of employment. (17c) The location at which work done in connection with a business is carried out; the place where some process or operation related to the business is conducted.

place of performance. The place where a promise is to be performed, either by specific provision or by interpretation of the language of the promise.

place of wrong. The place, esp. the state, where the last event necessary to make an actor liable for an alleged tort takes place.

place-of-wrong law. See LEX LOCI DELICTI.

place-of-wrong rule. See LEX LOCI DELICTI.

placer claim. See MINING CLAIM.

plagiarism. (17c) The deliberate and knowing presentation of another person's original ideas or creative expressions as one's own. • Generally, plagiarism is immoral but not illegal. If the expression's creator gives unrestricted permission for its use and the user claims the expression as original, the user commits plagiarism but does not violate copyright laws. If the original expression is copied without permission, the plagiarist may violate copyright laws, even if credit goes to the creator. And if the plagiarism results in material gain, it may be deemed a passing-off activity that violates the Lanham Act. It can also be a criminal act under 17 USCA § 5-6. Cf. INFRINGEMENT. — **plagiarize** (play-jə-rɪz), *vb.* — **plagiarist** (play-jə-rist), *n.*

plagium (play-jee-əm), *n.* [Latin] *Roman law.* The act of kidnapping, esp. a slave or child, which included harboring another's slave. — Also termed *crimen plagii.*

plain bond. See DEBENTURE (3).

plain error. See ERROR (2).

plain-feel doctrine. (1984) *Criminal procedure.* The principle that a police officer, while conducting a legal pat-down search, may seize any contraband that the officer can immediately and clearly identify, by touch but not by manipulation, as being illegal or incriminating. — Also termed *plain-touch doctrine.*

plain-language law. (1978) Legislation requiring nontechnical, readily comprehensible language in consumer contracts such as residential leases or insurance policies. • Many of these laws have genuinely simplified the needlessly obscure language in which consumer contracts have traditionally been couched.

plain-language movement. (1978) **1.** The loosely organized campaign to encourage legal writers and business writers to write clearly and concisely — without legalese — while preserving accuracy and precision. **2.** The body of persons involved in this campaign.

plain meaning. See MEANING.

plain-meaning rule. (1937) **1.** The rule that if a writing, or a provision in a writing, appears to be unambiguous on its face, its meaning must be determined from the writing itself without resort to any extrinsic evidence. • Though often applied, this rule is often condemned as simplistic because the meaning of words varies with the verbal context and the surrounding circumstances, not to mention the linguistic ability of the users and readers (including judges). Cf. GOLDEN RULE; MISCHIEF RULE; EQUITY-OF-THE STATUTE RULE. **2.** ORDINARY-MEANING RULE.

plain-sight rule. See PLAIN-VIEW DOCTRINE.

plaint. **1.** *Archaic.* A complaint, esp. one filed in a replevin action. See COMPLAINT (1). **2.** *Civil law.* A complaint or petition, esp. one intended to set aside an allegedly invalid testament.

plaintiff. (14c) The party who brings a civil suit in a court of law. — Abbr. pltf. Cf. DEFENDANT.

involuntary plaintiff. A plaintiff who is joined in a lawsuit by court order when the party's joinder is imperative for the litigation and the party is subject to the court's jurisdiction but refuses to join the suit voluntarily. • Under Federal Rule of Civil Procedure 19(a), a party is usu. joined as a defendant but may be joined as an involuntary plaintiff in "a proper case."

use plaintiff. See USE PLAINTIFF.

plaintiff in error. (17c) *Archaic.* **1.** See APPELLANT. **2.** See PETITIONER.

plaintiff's-viewpoint rule. The principle that courts should measure the amount in controversy in a case by analyzing only the amount of damages claimed by the plaintiff.

plain-touch doctrine. See PLAIN-FEEL DOCTRINE.

plain-vanilla swap. See INTEREST-RATE SWAP.

plain-view doctrine. (1963) *Criminal procedure.* The rule permitting a police officer's warrantless seizure and use as evidence of an item seen in plain view from a lawful position or during a legal search when the officer has probable cause to believe that the item is evidence of a crime. — Also termed *clear-view doctrine*; *plain-sight rule*. Cf. OPEN-FIELDS DOCTRINE.

PLAM. See *price-level-adjusted mortgage* under MORTGAGE.

plan, *n.* **1.** BANKRUPTCY PLAN. **2.** EMPLOYEE BENEFIT PLAN.

planned obsolescence. See OBSOLESCENCE.

planned-unit development. A land area zoned for a single-community subdivision with flexible restrictions on residential, commercial, and public uses. — Abbr. PUD. Cf. RESIDENTIAL CLUSTER.

planning board. A local government body responsible for approving or rejecting proposed building projects. ● In most jurisdictions, the planning board's decisions are subject to the review of the city council. — Also termed *planning commission.*

plan of arrangement. *Bankruptcy.* An insolvent debtor's written proposal for partially or completely settling outstanding debts.

plan of rehabilitation. See BANKRUPTCY PLAN.

plan of reorganization. See BANKRUPTCY PLAN.

plan-of-the-convention doctrine. The principle that each U.S. state, by ratifying the U.S. Constitution, has consented to the possibility of being sued by each of the other states, and has no immunity from such a suit under the 11th Amendment.

plant patent. See PATENT (3).

Plant Patent Act. *Patents.* The 1930 federal law that extended patent protection for developing "any distinct and new" varieties of asexually reproducing plants. ● Before passage of the Act, plant patents were rejected because the subject matter was considered naturally occurring and therefore unpatentable. 35 USCA §§ 161–164. — Abbr. PPA.

plant-patent claim. See PATENT CLAIM.

Plant Variety Protection Act. *Patents.* The 1970 federal law that extended patent-like protection for developing new and distinct varieties of seed-producing plants. ● A Certificate of Plant Variety Protection gives the holder exclusive rights to sell, reproduce, and develop further hybrids from the plant. 7 USCA §§ 2321–2582. — Abbr. PVPA.

plat. (15c) **1.** A small piece of land; PLOT (1). **2.** A map describing a piece of land and its features, such as boundaries, lots, roads, and easements.

platform. A statement of principles and policies adopted by a political party as the basis of the party's appeal for public support.

platform committee. See COMMITTEE.

plat map. (1941) A document that gives the legal descriptions of pieces of land by lot, street, and block number. ● A plat map is usu. drawn after the property has been described by some other means, such as a government survey. Once a plat map is prepared, property descriptions are defined by referring to the map. Plat maps are usu. recorded by a government agency.

plea, *n.* (13c) **1.** An accused person's formal response of "guilty," "not guilty," or "no contest" to a criminal charge. — Also termed *criminal plea.*

Alford plea. See ALFORD PLEA.

blind plea. (1972) A guilty plea made without the promise of a concession from either the judge or the prosecutor. Cf. *negotiated plea.*

conditional plea. A plea of guilty or nolo contendere entered with the court's approval and the government's consent, the defendant reserving the right to appeal any adverse determinations on one or more pretrial motions. ● If an appeal is successful, the plea is withdrawn and a new one entered. Fed. R. Crim. P. 11(a)(2).

guilty plea. (1942) An accused person's formal admission in court of having committed the charged offense. ● A guilty plea must be made voluntarily and only after the accused has been informed of and understands his or her rights. It ordinarily has the same effect as a guilty verdict and conviction after a trial on the merits. A guilty plea is usu. part of a plea bargain.

insanity plea. See INSANITY DEFENSE.

negotiated plea. (1956) The plea agreed to by a criminal defendant and the prosecutor in a plea bargain. See PLEA BARGAIN. Cf. *blind plea.*

no-contest plea. See NO CONTEST.

nolo plea. A plea by which the defendant does not contest or admit guilt. *See* Fed. R. Crim. P. 11(b); NOLO CONTENDERE.

not-guilty plea. (1912) An accused person's formal denial in court of having committed the charged offense. ● The prosecution must then prove all elements of the charged offense beyond a reasonable doubt if the defendant is to be convicted.

provident plea. *Military law.* A plea that is entered knowingly, intelligently, and consciously, and is legally and factually consistent and accurate.

2. At common law, the defendant's responsive pleading in a civil action. Cf. DECLARATION (7). **3.** A factual allegation offered in a case; a pleading. See DEMURRER.

affirmative plea. See *pure plea.*

anomalous plea. (1851) An equitable plea in which a party states new facts and negates some of the opponent's stated facts. ● Partly confession and avoidance and partly traverse, the plea is appropriate when the plaintiff, in the bill, has anticipated the plea, and the defendant then traverses the anticipatory matters. — Also termed *plea not pure*. Cf. *pure plea*.

common plea. (17c) **1.** A common-law plea in a civil action as opposed to a criminal prosecution. — Also termed *common cause*; *common suit*. **2.** *Hist.* A plea made by a commoner.

dilatory plea (**dil**-ə-tor-ee). (16c) A plea that does not challenge the merits of a case but that seeks to delay or defeat the action on procedural grounds.

double plea. (16c) A plea consisting in two or more distinct grounds of complaint or defense for the same issue. Cf. *alternative pleading* under PLEADING (2); DUPLICITY (2).

general plea. See *general denial* under DENIAL.

issuable plea. (17c) A plea on the merits presenting a cognizable complaint to the court. Cf. *issuable defense* under DEFENSE (1).

jurisdictional plea. (1900) A plea asserting that the court lacks jurisdiction either over the defendant or over the subject matter of the case. — Also termed *plea to the jurisdiction*.

negative plea. (16c) A plea that traverses some material fact or facts stated in the bill. — Also termed *plea to the action*.

nonissuable plea. (1841) A plea on which a court ruling will not decide the case on the merits, such as a plea in abatement.

peremptory plea. (18c) A plea that responds to the merits of the plaintiff's claim.

plea in abatement. (17c) A plea that objects to the place, time, or method of asserting the plaintiff's claim but does not dispute the claim's merits. • A defendant who successfully asserts a plea in abatement leaves the claim open for continuation in the current action or reassertion in a later action if the defect is cured. — Also termed *abater*.

plea in bar. See PLEA IN BAR.

plea in confession and avoidance. See CONFESSION AND AVOIDANCE.

plea in discharge. (18c) A plea that the defendant has previously satisfied and discharged the plaintiff's claim.

plea in equity. (17c) A special defense relying on one or more reasons why the suit should be dismissed, delayed, or barred. • The various kinds are (1) pleas to the jurisdiction, (2) pleas to the person, (3) pleas to the form of the bill, and (4) pleas in bar of the bill. Pleas in equity generally fall into two classes: *pure pleas* and *anomalous pleas*.

plea in estoppel. (1831) *Common-law pleading.* A plea that neither confesses nor avoids but rather pleads a previous inconsistent act, allegation, or denial on the part of the adverse party to preclude that party from maintaining an action or defense.

plea in reconvention. *Civil law.* A plea that sets up a new matter, not as a defense, but as a cross-complaint, setoff, or counterclaim.

plea in suspension. (1875) A plea that shows some ground for not proceeding in the suit at the present time and prays that the proceedings be stayed until that ground is removed, such as a party's being a minor or the plaintiff's being an alien enemy.

plea not pure. See *anomalous plea*.

plea of confession and avoidance. See CONFESSION AND AVOIDANCE.

plea of privilege. (17c) A plea that raises an objection to the venue of an action. See CHANGE OF VENUE.

plea of release. (18c) A plea that admits the claim but sets forth a written discharge executed by a party authorized to release the claim. See RELEASE (2).

plea puis darrein continuance (**pwis dar**-ayn kən-**tin**-yoo-ənts). [Law French "plea since the last continuance"] (18c) A plea that alleges new defensive matter that has arisen during a continuance of the case and that did not exist at the time of the defendant's last pleading.

plea to further maintenance to the action. *Hist.* A defensive plea asserting that events occurring after the commencement of the action necessitate its dismissal. • The plea is obsolete because of the pleading requirements in federal and state rules of civil procedure.

plea to the action. See *negative plea*.

plea to the declaration. (1820) A plea in abatement that objects to the declaration and applies immediately to it. — Also termed *plea to the count*.

plea to the jurisdiction. See *jurisdictional plea*.

plea to the person of the defendant. (1872) A plea in abatement alleging that the defendant has a legal disability to be sued.

plea to the person of the plaintiff. (1821) A plea in abatement alleging that the plaintiff has a legal disability to sue.

plea to the writ. (17c) A plea in abatement that objects to the writ (summons) and applies (1) to the form of the writ for a matter either apparent on the writ's face or outside the writ, or (2) to the way in which the writ was executed or acted on.

pure plea. (18c) An equitable plea that affirmatively alleges new matters that are outside the bill. • If proved, the effect is to end the controversy by dismissing, delaying, or barring the suit. A pure plea must track the allegations of the bill, not evade it or mistake its purpose. Originally, this was the only plea known in equity. — Also termed *affirmative plea.* Cf. *anomalous plea.*

rolled-up plea. (1929) *Defamation.* A defendant's plea claiming that the statements complained of are factual and that, to the extent that they consist of comment, they are fair comment on a matter of public interest. See FAIR COMMENT.

special plea. (16c) A plea alleging one or more new facts rather than merely disputing the legal grounds of the action or charge. • All pleas other than general issues are special pleas. See *general issue* under ISSUE (1).

plea bargain, *n.* (1963) A negotiated agreement between a prosecutor and a criminal defendant whereby the defendant pleads guilty to a lesser offense or to one of multiple charges in exchange for some concession by the prosecutor, usu. a more lenient sentence or a dismissal of the other charges. — Also termed *plea agreement; negotiated plea; sentence bargain.* — **plea-bargain,** *vb.* — **plea-bargaining,** *n.*

charge bargain. (1890) A plea bargain in which a prosecutor agrees to drop some of the counts or reduce the charge to a less serious offense in exchange for a plea of either guilty or no contest from the defendant.

sentence bargain. (1973) A plea bargain in which a prosecutor agrees to recommend a lighter sentence in exchange for a plea of either guilty or no contest from the defendant.

plead, *vb.* (13c) **1.** To make a specific plea, esp. in response to a criminal charge <he pleaded not guilty>. **2.** To assert or allege in a pleading <fraud claims must be pleaded with particularity>. **3.** To file or deliver a pleading <the plaintiff hasn't pleaded yet>.

pleader. (13c) **1.** A party who asserts a particular pleading. **2.** A person who pleads in court on behalf of another. **3.** *Hist.* At common law, a person who (though not an attorney) specialized in preparing pleadings for others. — Also termed *special pleader.* **4.** *Hist.* NARRATOR.

pleading, *n.* (16c) **1.** A formal document in which a party to a legal proceeding (esp. a civil lawsuit) sets forth or responds to allegations, claims, denials, or defenses. • In federal civil procedure, the main pleadings are the plaintiff's complaint and the defendant's answer.

accusatory pleading. (1908) An indictment, information, or complaint by which the government begins a criminal prosecution.

amended pleading. (1809) A pleading that replaces an earlier pleading and that contains matters omitted from or not known at the time of the earlier pleading. Cf. *supplemental pleading.*

anomalous pleading. (1845) A pleading that is partly affirmative and partly negative in its allegations.

argumentative pleading. A pleading that states allegations rather than facts, and thus forces the court to infer or hunt for supporting facts. • Conclusory statements in court papers are a form of argumentative pleading. — Also termed *inferential pleading.*

articulated pleading. (1953) A pleading that states each allegation in a separately numbered paragraph.

defective pleading. (17c) A pleading that fails to meet minimum standards of sufficiency or accuracy in form or substance.

hypothetical pleading. A pleading asserting that if a certain fact is true, then a certain result must follow. • Hypothetical pleadings are generally improper.

inferential pleading. See *argumentative pleading.*

pleading to the merits. A responsive pleading that addresses the plaintiff's cause of action, in whole or in part.

responsive pleading. (1833) A pleading that replies to an opponent's earlier pleading. See ANSWER.

sham pleading. (1825) An obviously frivolous or absurd pleading that is made only for purposes of vexation or delay. — Also termed *sham plea; false plea;* (archaically) *deceitful plea.*

shotgun pleading. (1964) A pleading that encompasses a wide range of contentions, usu. supported by vague factual allegations.

supplemental pleading. (1841) A pleading that either corrects a defect in an earlier pleading or addresses facts arising since the earlier pleading was filed. • Unlike an amended pleading, a supplemental pleading merely adds to the earlier pleading and does not replace it. Cf. *amended pleading.*

2. A system of defining and narrowing the issues in a lawsuit whereby the parties file formal documents alleging their respective positions.

alternative pleading. (1868) A form of pleading whereby the pleader alleges two or more independent claims or defenses that are not necessarily consistent with each other, such as alleging both intentional infliction of emotional distress and negligent infliction of emotional distress based on the same conduct. Fed. R. Civ. P. 8(e)(2). — Also termed *pleading in the alternative*. Cf. DUPLICITY (2); *double plea* under PLEA (3).

artful pleading. (1950) A plaintiff's disguised phrasing of a federal claim as solely a state-law claim in order to prevent a defendant from removing the case from state court to federal court.

code pleading. (1860) A procedural system requiring that the pleader allege merely the facts of the case giving rise to the claim or defense, not the legal conclusions necessary to sustain the claim or establish the defense. — Also termed *fact pleading*. Cf. *issue pleading*.

common-law pleading. The system of pleading historically used in the three common-law courts of England (the King's Bench, the Common Pleas, and the Exchequer) up to 1873.

equity pleading. (18c) The system of pleading used in courts of equity. • In most jurisdictions, rules unique to equity practice have been largely supplanted by one set of rules of court, esp. where law courts and equity courts have merged.

fact pleading. See *code pleading*.

issue pleading. (1916) The common-law method of pleading, the main purpose of which was to frame an issue. Cf. *code pleading*.

notice pleading. (1918) A procedural system requiring that the pleader give only a short and plain statement of the claim showing that the pleader is entitled to relief, and not a complete detailing of all the facts. Fed. R. Civ. P. 8(a).

pleading in the alternative. See *alternative pleading*.

special pleading. See SPECIAL PLEADING.

3. The legal rules regulating the statement of the plaintiff's claims and the defendant's defenses <today, pleading is a much simpler subject than it was in former years>.

pleading the baby act. See BABY ACT, PLEADING THE.

pleading the Fifth. See TAKE THE FIFTH.

plead over, *vb.* (17c) **1.** To fail to notice a defective allegation in an opponent's pleading before responding to the pleading. **2.** *Hist.* To plead the general issue after a defendant has had a dilatory plea overruled. See AIDER BY PLEADING OVER.

plead the Fifth. See TAKE THE FIFTH.

plea in abatement. See PLEA (3).

plea in avoidance. See *affirmative defense* under DEFENSE (1).

plea in bar. (17c) A plea that seeks to defeat the plaintiff's or prosecutor's action completely and permanently.

general plea in bar. (18c) A criminal defendant's plea of not guilty by which the defendant denies every fact and circumstance necessary to be convicted of the crime charged.

special plea in bar. (17c) A plea that, rather than addressing the merits and denying the facts alleged, sets up some extrinsic fact showing why a criminal defendant cannot be tried for the offense charged. • Examples include the plea of *autrefois acquit* and the plea of pardon.

plea in confession and avoidance. See CONFESSION AND AVOIDANCE.

plea in discharge. See PLEA (3).

plea in equity. See PLEA (3).

plea in estoppel. See PLEA (3).

plea in justification. See *affirmative defense* under DEFENSE (1).

plea in reconvention. See PLEA (3).

plea in suspension. See PLEA (3).

plea not pure. See *anomalous plea* under PLEA (3).

plea of confession and avoidance. See CONFESSION AND AVOIDANCE.

plea of privilege. See PLEA (3).

plea of release. See PLEA (3).

plea of sanctuary. See DECLINATORY PLEA.

plea of tender. (18c) At common law, a pleading asserting that the defendant has consistently been willing to pay the debt demanded, has offered it to the plaintiff, and has brought the money into court ready to pay the plaintiff. See TENDER.

plea puis darrein continuance. See PLEA (3).

pleasure appointment. See APPOINTMENT (1).

plea to further maintenance to the action. See PLEA (3).

plea to the action. See *negative plea* under PLEA (3).

plea to the count. See *plea to the declaration* under PLEA (3).

plea to the declaration. See PLEA (3).

plea to the jurisdiction. See *jurisdictional plea* under PLEA (3).

plea to the person of the defendant. See PLEA (3).

plea to the person of the plaintiff. See PLEA (3).

plea to the writ. See PLEA (3).

plebiscite (**pleb**-ə-sit *or* **pleb**-ə-sit), *n.* (1860) **1.** A binding or nonbinding referendum on a proposed law, constitutional amendment, or significant public issue. Cf. REFERENDUM; INITIATIVE. **2.** *Int'l law.* A direct vote of a country's electorate to decide a question of public importance, such as union with another country or a proposed change to the constitution. — **plebiscitary** (plə-**bi**-sə-ter-ee), *adj.*

plebs (plebz), *n.* [Latin] *Roman law.* The common people in ancient Rome; the general body of citizens, excluding the patricians. Pl. **plebes** (plee-beez).

pledge, *n.* (14c) **1.** A formal promise or undertaking. Cf. OATH. **2.** The act of providing something as security for a debt or obligation. **3.** A bailment or other deposit of personal property to a creditor as security for a debt or obligation; PAWN (2). See *contract to pledge* under CONTRACT. Cf. LIEN (1). **4.** The item of personal property so deposited; PAWN (1). **5.** The thing so provided. — Formerly also termed *safe-pledge*. **6.** A security interest in personal property represented by an indispensable instrument, the interest being created by a bailment or other deposit of personal property for the purpose of securing the payment of a debt or the performance of some other duty. **7.** *Hist.* A person who acts as a surety for the prosecution of a lawsuit. ● In early practice, pledges were listed at the end of the declaration. Over time the listing of pledges became a formality, and fictitious names (such as "John Doe" or "Richard Roe") were allowed. — **pledge,** *vb.* — **pledgeable,** *adj.*

pledged account. See ACCOUNT.

pledgee. One with whom a pledge is deposited.

pledgor. One who gives a pledge to another. — Also spelled *pledger*.

plenary (plee-nə-ree *or* plen-ə-ree), *adj.* (15c) **1.** Full; complete; entire <plenary authority>. **2.** (Of an assembly) intended to have the attendance of all members or participants <plenary session>.

plenary action. See ACTION (4).

plenary confession. See CONFESSION.

plenary guardianship. See GUARDIANSHIP.

plenary jurisdiction. See JURISDICTION.

plenary power. See POWER (3).

plenary review. See JUDICIAL REVIEW.

plenary session. See SESSION (1).

plenary suit. See SUIT.

plenipotentiary (plen-ə-pə-ten-shee-er-ee). A person who has full power to do a thing; a person fully commissioned to act for another. See *minister plenipotentiary* under MINISTER.

plevin (plev-in), *n. Archaic.* An assurance or warrant; a pledge.

Plimsoll marks. See LOAD LINE (2).

PLL. *abbr.* See *product-liability loss* under LOSS.

plot, *n.* (bef. 12c) **1.** A measured piece of land; LOT (1). Cf. PLAT (1). **2.** A plan forming the basis of a conspiracy.

plot plan. (1925) A plan that shows a proposed or present use of a plot of land, esp. of a residential area.

plottage. (1916) The increase in value achieved by combining small, undeveloped tracts of land into larger tracts.

plow back, *vb.* To reinvest earnings and profits into a business instead of paying them out as dividends or withdrawals.

plowbote. See BOTE (1).

plowman's fee. See FEE (2).

PLR. *abbr.* PUBLIC-LENDING RIGHT.

pltf. *abbr.* PLAINTIFF.

plunder. See PILLAGE.

plunderage. *Maritime law.* The embezzling of goods on a ship.

plurality. (1803) The greatest number (esp. of votes), regardless of whether it is a simple or an absolute majority <a four-member plurality of the Supreme Court agreed with this view, which received more votes than any other>. — Also termed *plural majority*. Cf. MAJORITY (2).

plurality opinion. See OPINION (1).

plurality vote. See PLURALITY.

plurality voting. 1. See PLURALITY. **2.** See VOTING.

plural majority. See PLURALITY.

plural marriage. 1. See MARRIAGE (1). **2.** See POLYGAMY.

plural wife. See WIFE.

pluries (pluur-ee-eez), *n.* [Latin "many times"] (15c) A third or subsequent writ issued when the previous writs have been ineffective; a writ issued after an alias writ. — Also termed *pluries writ*.

plurinational administrative institution. *Int'l law.* An entity designed to perform transnational administrative activities when politically oriented international organizations and traditional international agreements are unsuitable. ● These institutions usu. arise in fields where transnational arrangements are necessary (such as natural-resource management, transportation, or utilities), and they are often organized as international corporations, national agencies, or private corporations.

plus factor. A fact that supports finding that a specified legal test has been satisfied.

p.m. *abbr.* POST MERIDIEM.

PM. *abbr.* **1.** POSTMASTER. **2.** PRIME MINISTER. **3.** BUREAU OF POLITICAL–MILITARY AFFAIRS.

PMI. *abbr.* Private mortgage insurance. See *mortgage insurance* under INSURANCE.

PMM. See *purchase-money mortgage* under MORTGAGE.

PMRT. See *purchase-money resulting trust* under TRUST.

PMSI. See *purchase-money security interest* under SECURITY INTEREST.

pneumoconiosis. Chronic lung disease and related conditions characterized by respiratory and pulmonary impairments and caused or aggravated by coal-dust exposure during coal-mine employment.● The disease is usu. latent and often does not manifest until after coal-dust exposure has ended. 20 CFR § 718.201. — Also termed *black-lung disease.*

clinical pneumoconiosis. Any medically recognized condition caused by coal-dust exposure while working in a coal mine and characterized by large, permanent deposits of particulate matter in the lungs, coupled with the lung tissue's fibrotic reaction. ● Some examples of clinical pneumoconioses are silicosis or silicotuberculosis, massive pulmonary fibrosis, and anthrosilicosis. Cf. *legal pneumoconiosis.*

legal pneumoconiosis. Any chronic restrictive or obstructive pulmonary disease or impairment and related conditions arising out of coal-mine employment. Cf. *clinical pneumoconiosis.*

P.O. *abbr.* **1.** Post office. **2.** PURCHASE ORDER.

poaching, *n.* The illegal taking or killing of fish or game on another's land. — **poach,** *vb.*

pocket immunity. See IMMUNITY (3).

pocket money. See HAT MONEY.

pocket part. (1931) A supplemental pamphlet inserted usu. into the back inside cover of a lawbook, esp. a treatise or code, to update the material in the main text until the publisher issues a new edition of the entire work. ● Legal publishers frequently leave a little extra room inside their hardcover books so that pocket parts may later be added. — Also termed *cumulative supplement.*

pocket veto. See VETO.

P.O.D. *abbr.* Pay on delivery.

POD account. See *pay-on-death account* under ACCOUNT.

poena (**pee**-nə). [Latin] (1859) Punishment; penalty.

point, *n.* (13c) **1.** A pertinent and distinct legal proposition, issue, or argument <point of error>. **2.** *Parliamentary law.* Any of several kinds of requests made in a deliberative body. See REQUEST.

point of clarification. A question about procedure or substance.

point of information. An inquiry asking a question about a motion's merits or effect. ● A point of information can be made only to seek information, not to volunteer information. It may request an objective fact or an expert opinion, but may not request anyone — including the chair or the mover — to speculate about how

he or she expects or intends that the present or future leadership will interpret or apply a motion. See INQUIRY (2). — Also termed *question of information.*

point of order. A request suggesting that the meeting or a member is not following the applicable rules and asking the chair enforce the rules. ● Some organizations use the term "point of order" as a generic term that also includes a parliamentary inquiry and a question of privilege. — Also termed *question of order.* See *parliamentary inquiry* under INQUIRY; *question of privilege* under QUESTION (3).

point of privilege. A motion that raises a question of privilege. See *question of privilege* under QUESTION (3); RAISE A QUESTION OF PRIVILEGE.

procedural point. A request that raises a personal privilege relating to a member's ability to participate effectively in the meeting, such as the member's ability to see or hear the proceedings. See *personal privilege* under PRIVILEGE (5).

3. One percent of the face value of a loan (esp. a mortgage loan), paid up front to the lender as a service charge or placement fee <the borrower hoped for only a two-point fee on the mortgage>. — Also termed *mortgage point.* See MORTGAGE DISCOUNT. **4.** A unit used for quoting stock, bond, or commodity prices <the stock closed up a few points today>. **5.** A payment to secure a loan, stated as a percentage of the loan's face amount.

point-and-click agreement. (2000) An electronic version of a shrink-wrap license in which a computer user agrees to the terms of an electronically displayed agreement by pointing the cursor to a particular location on the screen and then clicking. ● Point-and-click agreements usu. require express acceptance only once but may include a clause providing for a user's ongoing-acceptance of any changes to the agreement's terms, whether or not the user is notified of the changes. See *shrink-wrap license* under LICENSE. — Also termed *e-contract*; *click-wrap license*; *click-wrap agreement*; *user agreement*; *website-user agreement*; *web-wrap agreement.* Cf. E-CONTRACT.

point of attachment. *Copyright.* A connection with a copyright-convention member nation sufficient to make a work eligible for protection under that convention. ● For example, a work is eligible for Berne Convention protection if the author is a citizen of a Berne member nation or if the work originated in a Berne member nation. — Also termed *connecting factor.*

point of error. (18c) An alleged mistake by a lower court asserted as a ground for appeal. See ERROR (2); WRIT OF ERROR.

point of fact. A discrete factual proposition at issue in a case.

point of law. (16c) A discrete legal proposition at issue in a case.

    reserved point of law. (1821) An important or difficult point of law that arises during trial but that the judge sets aside for future argument or decision so that testimony can continue. — Also termed *point reserved.*

point reserved. See *reserved point of law* under POINT OF LAW.

points-and-authorities brief. See *brief on the merits* under BRIEF (1).

point source. *Environmental law.* The discernible and identifiable source from which pollutants are discharged.

point system. (1955) *Criminal law.* A system that assigns incremental units to traffic violations, the accumulation of a certain number within a year resulting in the automatic suspension of a person's driving privileges.

poisonous-tree doctrine. See FRUIT-OF-THE-POISONOUS-TREE DOCTRINE.

poison pill. A corporation's defense against an unwanted takeover bid whereby shareholders are granted the right to acquire equity or debt securities at a favorable price to increase the bidder's acquisition costs. — Often shortened to *pill.* See TAKEOVER DEFENSE; SHARK REPELLANT. Cf. PORCUPINE PROVISION.

Polaroid test. *Trademarks.* A judicial test for trademark infringement, analyzing eight factors: (1) strength of the mark, (2) similarity between the marks, (3) proximity of the products' markets, (4) effects on market expansion (ability to "bridge the gap"), (5) actual confusion, (6) the defendant's good or bad faith, (7) quality of the products, and (8) sophistication of the buyer. *Polaroid Corp. v. Polarad Electronics Corp.*, 287 F.2d 492, 495 (2d Cir. 1961).

police, *n.* **1.** The governmental department charged with the preservation of public order, the promotion of public safety, and the prevention and detection of crime. **2.** The officers or members of this department. — **police,** *vb.*

police action. See ARMED CONFLICT.

police-assisted suicide. See *suicide-by-cop* under SUICIDE.

police blotter. See ARREST RECORD.

police chief. The head of a police department.

police court. See *magistrate's court* (1) under COURT.

police jury. *Louisiana law.* The governing body of a parish.

police justice. See *police magistrate* under MAGISTRATE.

police magistrate. See MAGISTRATE.

police officer. A peace officer responsible for preserving public order, promoting public safety, and preventing and detecting crime. Cf. PEACE OFFICER.

police power. (1821) **1.** The inherent and plenary power of a sovereign to make all laws necessary and proper to preserve the public security, order, health, morality, and justice. ● It is a fundamental power essential to government, and it cannot be surrendered by the legislature or irrevocably transferred away from government. **2.** A state's Tenth Amendment right, subject to due-process and other limitations, to establish and enforce laws protecting the public's health, safety, and general welfare, or to delegate this right to local governments. **3.** Loosely, the power of the government to intervene in the use of privately owned property, as by subjecting it to eminent domain. See EMINENT DOMAIN.

police science. See CRIMINAL JUSTICE (2).

police state. See STATE.

policy. (14c) **1.** The general principles by which a government is guided in its management of public affairs. See PUBLIC POLICY. **2.** A document containing a contract of insurance; INSURANCE POLICY. **3.** A type of lottery in which bettors select numbers to bet on and place the bet with a "policy writer."

policy court. See COURT.

policyholder. One who owns an insurance policy, regardless of whether that person is the insured party. — Also termed *policyowner.*

policy limits. See LIABILITY LIMIT.

policy loan. See LOAN.

policy of insurance. See INSURANCE POLICY.

policy of the law. See PUBLIC POLICY (1).

policyowner. See POLICYHOLDER.

policy proof of interest. *Insurance.* Evidence — shown by possession of a policy — that a person making a claim has an insurable interest in the loss. — Abbr. PPI.

policy reserve. See RESERVE.

policy stacking. See STACKING.

policy value. *Insurance.* The amount of cash available to a policyholder on the surrender or cancellation of the insurance policy.

policy year. *Insurance.* The year beginning on the date that a policy becomes effective. Cf. ANNIVERSARY DATE.

political, *adj.* Pertaining to politics; of or relating to the conduct of government.

political-action committee. (1839) An organization formed by a special-interest group to raise and contribute money to the campaigns of political candidates who the group believes will promote its interests. — Abbr. PAC.

political assessment. See ASSESSMENT.

political asylum. See ASYLUM (2).

political corporation. See *public corporation* (2) under CORPORATION.

political correctness, *n.* (1979) **1.** The inclination to avoid language and practices that might offend anyone's political sensibilities, esp. in racial or sexual matters. **2.** An instance in which a person conforms to this inclination. — Abbr. P.C. — **politically correct,** *adj.*

political corruption. See *official misconduct* under MISCONDUCT.

political crime. See POLITICAL OFFENSE.

political economy. See ECONOMY.

political gerrymandering. See GERRYMANDERING (1).

political law. See POLITICAL SCIENCE.

political liberty. **1.** See LIBERTY. **2.** See *political right* under RIGHT.

Political–Military Affairs Bureau. See BUREAU OF POLITICAL–MILITARY AFFAIRS.

political offense. (18c) A crime directed against the security or government of a nation, such as treason, sedition, or espionage. ● Under principles of international law, the perpetrator of a political offense cannot be extradited. — Also termed *political crime.*

political party. An organization of voters formed to influence the government's conduct and policies by nominating and electing candidates to public office. ● The United States has traditionally maintained a two-party system, which today comprises the Democratic and Republican parties. — Often shortened to *party.*

political patronage. See PATRONAGE (3).

political power. The power vested in a person or body of persons exercising any function of the state; the capacity to influence the activities of the body politic. — Also termed *civil power.*

   sovereign political power. Power that is absolute and uncontrolled within its own sphere. ● Within its designated limits, its exercise and effective operation do not depend on, and are not subject to, the power of any other person and cannot be prevented or annulled by any other power recognized within the constitutional system. — Often shortened to *sovereign power.* — Also termed *supreme power.*

   subordinate political power. Power that, within its own sphere of operation, is subject in some degree to external control because there exists some superior constitutional power that can prevent, restrict, direct, or annul its operation. — Often shortened to *subordinate power.*

political question. (1808) A question that a court will not consider because it involves the exercise of discretionary power by the executive or legislative branch of government. — Also termed *nonjusticiable question.* Cf. JUDICIAL QUESTION.

political-question doctrine. The judicial principle that a court should refuse to decide an issue involving the exercise of discretionary power by the executive or legislative branch of government.

political right. See RIGHT.

political science. (17c) The branch of learning concerned with the study of the principles and conduct of government. — Also termed *political law.*

political society. See STATE (1).

political subdivision. (1827) A division of a state that exists primarily to discharge some function of local government.

political trial. See TRIAL.

political-vote privilege. See PRIVILEGE (3).

politics. **1.** The science of the organization and administration of the state. **2.** The activity or profession of engaging in political affairs.

polity (**pol**-ə-tee). (16c) **1.** The total governmental organization as based on its goals and policies. **2.** A politically organized body or community.

polity approach. (1975) A method of resolving church-property disputes by which a court examines the structure of the church to determine whether the church is independent or hierarchical, and then resolves the dispute in accordance with the decision of the proper church-governing body.

poll, *n.* (18c) **1.** A sampling of opinions on a given topic, conducted randomly or obtained from a specified group. **2.** The act or process of voting at an election. **3.** The result of the counting of votes. **4.** (*usu. pl.*) The place where votes are cast.

poll, *vb.* (17c) **1.** To ask how each member of (a group) individually voted <after the verdict was read, the judge polled the jury>. **2.** To question (people) so as to elicit votes, opinions, or preferences <the committee polled 500 citizens about their views>. **3.** To receive (a given number of votes) in an election <the third-party candidate polled only 250 votes in the county>.

pollicitation. *Contracts.* (15c) The offer of a promise.

poll tax. See TAX.

pollute, *vb.* To corrupt or defile; esp., to contaminate the soil, air, or water with noxious substances. — **pollution,** *n.* — **polluter,** *n.*

pollution exclusion. See EXCLUSION (3).

polyandry (pol-ee-an-dree). (17c) The condition or practice of having more than one husband at the same time. Cf. POLYGYNY.

polyarchy (pol-ee-ahr-kee). Government by many persons. — Also termed *polygarchy* (**pol**-ə-gahr-kee). Cf. MONARCHY. — **polyarchal,** *adj.*

polygamist (pə-**lig**-ə-məst). **1.** A person who has several spouses simultaneously. **2.** An advocate of polygamy.

polygamy (pə-**lig**-ə-mee), *n.* (16c) **1.** The state or practice of having more than one spouse simultaneously. — Also termed *simultaneous polygamy*; *plural marriage.* **2.** *Hist.* The fact or practice of having more than one spouse during one's lifetime, though never simultaneously. • Until the third century, polygamy included remarriage after a spouse's death because a valid marriage bond was considered indissoluble. — Also termed *successive polygamy*; *serial polygamy*; *sequential marriage.* Cf. BIGAMY; MONOGAMY. — **polygamous,** *adj.* — **polygamist,** *n.*

polygarchy. See POLYARCHY.

polygraph, *n.* (1923) A device used to evaluate truthfulness by measuring and recording involuntary physiological changes in the human body during interrogation. • Polygraph results are inadmissible as evidence in most states but are commonly used by the police as an investigative tool. — Also termed *lie detector.* — **polygraphic,** *adj.* — **polygraphy,** *n.*

polygyny (pə-**lij**-ə-nee). (18c) The condition or practice of having more than one wife at the same time. Cf. POLYANDRY.

pontiff. 1. *Roman law.* A member of the council of priests in ancient Rome. — Also termed *pontifex.* **2.** The leader of the Catholic Church; the Pope. See PONTIFEX.

pony homestead. See *constitutional homestead* under HOMESTEAD.

Ponzi scheme (**pon**-zee). (1920) A fraudulent investment scheme in which money contributed by later investors generates artificially high dividends or returns for the original investors, whose example attracts even larger investments. • Money from the new investors is used directly to repay or pay interest to earlier investors, usu. without any operation or revenue-producing activity other than the continual raising of new funds. This scheme takes its name from Charles Ponzi, who in the late 1920s was convicted for fraudulent schemes he conducted in Boston. See GIFTING CLUB. Cf. PYRAMID SCHEME.

pool, *n.* (1868) **1.** An association of individuals or entities who share resources and funds to promote their joint undertaking; esp., an association of persons engaged in buying or selling commodities. • If such an association is formed to eliminate competition throughout a single industry, it is a restraint of trade that violates federal antitrust laws. **2.** A gambling scheme in which numerous persons contribute stakes for betting on a particular event (such as a sporting event).

pool clerk. See CLERK (5).

pooled-income fund. A trust created and maintained by a public charity rather than a private person, whereby (1) the donor creates an irrevocable, vested remainder in the charitable organization that maintains the trust, (2) the property transferred by each donor is commingled with property transferred by other donors, (3) the fund cannot invest in tax-exempt securities, (4) no donor or income beneficiary can be a trustee, (5) the donor retains (either personally or for one or more named income beneficiaries) a life income interest, and (6) each income beneficiary is entitled to and receives a proportional share of the annual income based on the rate of return earned by the fund. IRC (26 USCA) § 642(c)(5).

pooled trust. See TRUST.

pooling, *n.* *Oil & gas.* The bringing together of small tracts of land or fractional mineral interests over a producing reservoir for the purpose of drilling an oil or gas well. • Pooling is usu. associated with collecting a large enough tract to meet well-spacing regulations. — Also termed *communitization.* Cf. UNITIZATION.

compulsory pooling. Pooling done by order of a regulatory agency. — Also termed *forced pooling.*

forced pooling. See *compulsory pooling.*

voluntary pooling. Pooling arranged by agreement of the owners of mineral interests.

pooling agreement. A contractual arrangement by which corporate shareholders agree that their shares will be voted as a unit. — Also termed *voting agreement*; *shareholder voting agreement*; *shareholder-control agreement.*

pooling clause. *Oil & gas.* A provision found in most oil-and-gas leases granting the lessee the right to combine part or all of the leased acreage with other properties for development or operation.

pooling of interests. A method of accounting used in mergers, whereby the acquired company's assets are recorded on the acquiring company's books at their cost when originally acquired. • No goodwill account is created under the pooling method.

poor relief. See WELFARE (2).

pop, *n. Telecommunications.* A calculation of the potential customer base for a mobile-phone-service provider, calculated by the number of people living in the area multiplied by the company's percentage ownership of the area's cellular service.

popular action. See QUI TAM ACTION.

popular election. See ELECTION (3).

popular justice. See JUSTICE (1).

popular sovereignty. See SOVEREIGNTY (1).

popular use. See USE (1).

porcupine provision. A clause in a corporation's charter or bylaws designed to prevent a takeover without the consent of the board of directors. Cf. SHARK REPELLENT; POISON PILL.

pork-barrel legislation. See LEGISLATION.

pornography, *n.* (1842) Material (such as writings, photographs, or movies) depicting sexual activity or erotic behavior in a way that is designed to arouse sexual excitement. • Pornography is protected speech under the First Amendment unless it is determined to be legally obscene. See OBSCENITY. — **pornographic,** *adj.*

    child pornography. (1967) Material depicting a person under the age of 18 engaged in sexual activity. • Child pornography is not protected by the First Amendment — even if it falls short of the legal standard for obscenity — and those directly involved in its distribution can be criminally punished.

    virtual child pornography. Material that includes a computer-generated image that appears to be a minor engaged in sexual activity but that in reality does not involve a person under the age of 18.

port. 1. A harbor where ships load and unload cargo. 2. Any place where persons and cargo are allowed to enter a country and where customs officials are stationed. — Also termed (in sense 2) *port of entry.*

    foreign port. 1. One exclusively within the jurisdiction of another country or state. 2. A port other than a home port.

    free port. A port located outside a country's customs frontier, so that goods may be delivered usu. free of import duties or taxes, without being subjected to customs-control procedures; FREE-TRADE ZONE.

    home port. The port that is either where a vessel is registered or where its owner resides.

    port of call. A port at which a ship stops during a voyage.

    port of delivery. The port that is the terminus of any particular voyage and where the ship unloads its cargo.

    port of departure. The port from which a vessel departs on the start of a voyage.

    port of destination. The port at which a voyage is to end. • This term generally includes any stopping places at which the ship receives or unloads cargo.

    port of discharge. The place where a substantial part of the cargo is discharged.

portable business. (1983) A portfolio of legal business that an attorney can take from one firm or geographic location to another, with little loss in client relationships. — Also termed *portable practice.*

port authority. (1870) A state or federal agency that regulates traffic through a port or that establishes and maintains airports, bridges, tollways, and public transportation.

portfolio. (1848) 1. The various securities or other investments held by an investor at any given time. • An investor will often hold several different types of investments in a portfolio for the purpose of diversifying risk.

    market portfolio. A value-weighted portfolio of every asset in a particular market.

2. The role within the government of a high official <minister without portfolio>.

portfolio income. See INCOME.

portfolio-pumping. *Securities.* The practice of purchasing additional shares of a stock near the end of a fiscal period in an attempt to improve an investment fund's apparent performance. — Also termed *window dressing.*

portion. A share or allotted part (as of an estate).

port of call. See PORT.

port of delivery. See PORT.

port of departure. See PORT.

port of destination. See PORT.

port of discharge. See PORT.

port of entry. See PORT (2).

port-risk insurance. See INSURANCE.

port-state control. *Maritime law.* The exercise of authority under international conventions for a state to stop, board, inspect, and when necessary detain vessels sailing under foreign flags while they are navigating in the port state's territorial waters or are in one of its ports. • The purpose is to ensure the safety of the vessels as well as to enforce environmental regulations. Cf. COASTAL-STATE CONTROL; FLAG-STATE CONTROL.

port toll. A duty paid for bringing goods into a port.

portwarden. An official responsible for the administration of a port.

posit, *vb.* **1.** To presume true or to offer as true. **2.** To present as an explanation.

position. The extent of a person's investment in a particular security or market.

positional-risk doctrine. The principle by which the workers'-compensation requirement that the injury arise out of employment is satisfied if the injured worker's employment required the worker to be at the place where the injury occurred at the time it occurred. — Also termed *positional risk analysis; positional risk test.*

position of the United States. (1981) The legal position of the federal government in a lawsuit, esp. in a case involving the Equal Access to Justice Act. ● Under the EAJA, the reasonableness of the position in light of precedent determines whether the government will be liable for the opposing party's attorney's fees.

positive act. 1. OVERT ACT. **2.** ACT (2).

positive condition. See CONDITION (2).

positive covenant. See COVENANT (1).

positive duty. See DUTY (1).

positive easement. See *affirmative easement* under EASEMENT.

positive evidence. See *direct evidence* (1) under EVIDENCE.

positive externality. See EXTERNALITY.

positive fraud. See *actual fraud* under FRAUD.

positive justice. See JUSTICE (1).

positive law. (14c) A system of law promulgated and implemented within a particular political community by political superiors, as distinct from moral law or law existing in an ideal community or in some nonpolitical community. ● Positive law typically consists of enacted law — the codes, statutes, and regulations that are applied and enforced in the courts. The term derives from the medieval use of *positum* (Latin "established"), so that the phrase *positive law* literally means law established by human authority. — Also termed *jus positivum; made law.* Cf. NATURAL LAW.

positive misprision. See MISPRISION.

positive notice. See *direct notice* under NOTICE.

positive prescription. See PRESCRIPTION (5).

positive proof. See PROOF.

positive reprisal. See REPRISAL.

positive right. See RIGHT.

positive servitude. See SERVITUDE (2).

positive testimony. See *affirmative testimony* under TESTIMONY.

positive wrong. See WRONG.

positivism. (1846) The doctrine that all true knowledge is derived from observable phenomena, rather than speculation or reasoning. See LEGAL POSITIVISM; LOGICAL POSITIVISM; *positivist jurisprudence* under JURISPRUDENCE.

positivistic, *adj.* Of or relating to legal positivism. See LEGAL POSITIVISM.

positivistic jurisprudence. See *positivist jurisprudence* under JURISPRUDENCE.

posse (pos-ee). [Latin] (16c) **1.** A possibility. See IN POSSE. Cf. IN ESSE. **2.** Power; ability. **3.** POSSE COMITATUS.

posse comitatus (pos-ee kom-ə-tay-təs), *n.* [Latin "power of the county"] (16c) A group of citizens who are called together to help the sheriff keep the peace or conduct rescue operations. — Often shortened to *posse.*

Posse Comitatus Act. A federal law that, with a few exceptions, prohibits the Army or Air Force from directly participating in civilian law-enforcement operations, as by making arrests, conducting searches, or seizing evidence. ● The Act was originally enacted in 1878. It does not usu. apply to members of the Navy, the National Guard, or the Coast Guard. 18 USCA § 1385. — Abbr. PCA.

possess, *vb.* (14c) To have in one's actual control; to have possession of.

possessio civilis (sə-vı-lis). [Latin] See *possession in law* under POSSESSION.

possession. (14c) **1.** The fact of having or holding property in one's power; the exercise of dominion over property. **2.** The right under which one may exercise control over something to the exclusion of all others; the continuing exercise of a claim to the exclusive use of a material object. **3.** *Civil law.* The detention or use of a physical thing with the intent to hold it as one's own. La. Civ. Code art. 3421(1). **4.** (*usu. pl.*) Something that a person owns or controls; PROPERTY (2). Cf. OWNERSHIP; TITLE (1). **5.** A territorial dominion of a state or nation.

actual possession. (16c) Physical occupancy or control over property. Cf. *constructive possession.*

adverse possession. See ADVERSE POSSESSION.

bona fide possession. (1815) Possession of property by a person who in good faith does not know that the property's ownership is disputed.

civil possession. 1. *Civil law.* Possession existing by virtue of a person's intent to own property even though the person no longer occupies or has physical control of it. **2.** *Louisiana law.* The continuation of possession through the possessor's presumed intent to continue holding the thing as his or her own, after the possessor' ceases to possess the thing corporeally. La. Civ. Code arts. 3431–32. ● Civil possession may be evidenced by such things as paying taxes on the property or granting rights of interest in it.

constructive possession. (18c) **1.** Control or dominion over a property without actual possession or custody of it. — Also termed *effective possession*. **2.** *Civil law.* Possession by operation of law of an entirety by virtue of corporeal possession of a part. ● When a possessor holds title to a property and physically possesses part of it, the law will deem the possessor to hold constructive possession of the rest of the property described in the title. La. Civ. Code art. 3426. — Also termed *possessio fictitia*; *possession in law*. Cf. *actual possession*.

corporeal possession. Possession of a material object, such as a farm or a coin. — Also termed *natural possession*; *possessio corporis*; (Ger.) *Sachenbesitz*.

criminal possession. (1811) The unlawful possession of certain prohibited articles, such as illegal drugs or drug paraphernalia, firearms, or stolen property.

derivative possession. (1851) Lawful possession by one (such as a tenant) who does not hold title.

direct possession. See *immediate possession*.

double possession. The doctrine that, in a bailment, both the bailor and the bailee have possession of the item that has been bailed. ● This doctrine does not apply in most Anglo-American jurisdictions.

effective possession. See *constructive possession*.

exclusive possession. (18c) The exercise of exclusive dominion over property, including the use and benefit of the property.

hostile possession. (1812) Possession asserted against the claims of all others, esp. the record owner. See ADVERSE POSSESSION.

immediate possession. (17c) Possession that is acquired or retained directly or personally. — Also termed *direct possession*.

immemorial possession. Possession that began so long ago that no one still living witnessed its beginning.

incorporeal possession. (1964) Possession of something other than a material object, such as an easement over a neighbor's land, or the access of light to the windows of a house. — Also termed *possessio juris*; *quasi-possession*.

indirect possession. See *mediate possession*.

insular possession. An island territory of the United States, such as Guam.

joint possession. Possession shared by two or more persons.

mediate possession (**mee**-dee-it). Possession of a thing through someone else, such as an agent. ● In every instance of mediate possession, there is a direct possessor (such as an agent) as well

as a mediate possessor (the principal). — Also termed *indirect possession*.

naked possession. (16c) The mere possession of something, esp. real estate, without any apparent right or colorable title to it.

natural possession. *Civil law.* The exercise of physical detention or control over a thing, as by occupying a building or cultivating farmland. ● Natural possession may be had without title, and may give rise to a claim of unlawful possession or a claim of ownership by acquisitive prescription. The term "natural possession" has been replaced by the term "corporeal possession" in the Louisiana Civil Code, by virtue of a 1982 revision. La. Civ. Code Ann. art. 3425. See *corporeal possession*; PRESCRIPTION (2).

notorious possession. (18c) Possession or control that is evident to others; possession of property that, because it is generally known by people in the area where the property is located, gives rise to a presumption that the actual owner has notice of it. ● Notorious possession is one element of adverse possession. — Also termed *open possession*; *open and notorious possession*. See ADVERSE POSSESSION.

open and notorious possession. See *notorious possession*.

open possession. See *notorious possession*.

peaceable possession. (16c) Possession (as of real property) not disturbed by another's hostile or legal attempts to recover possession; esp., wrongful possession that the rightful possessor has appeared to tolerate. Cf. *scrambling possession* (1); ADVERSE POSSESSION.

pedal possession. (1839) Actual possession, as by living on the land or by improving it. ● This term usu. appears in adverse-possession contexts.

possession animo domini. *Civil law.* Possession with the intent to own a thing, movable or immovable; possession as an owner. *See* La. Civ. Code art. 3427.

possession by relation of law. A person's legally recognized possession of land despite the person's not having actual possession after being improperly or unlawfully dispossessed by another.

possession in fact. (17c) Actual possession that may or may not be recognized by law. ● For example, an employee's possession of an employer's property is for some purposes not legally considered possession, the term *detention* or *custody* being used instead. — Also termed *possessio naturalis*.

possession in law. (16c) **1.** Possession that is recognized by the law either because it is a specific type of possession in fact or because the law for some special reason attributes the advantages and results of possession to someone who does not in fact possess. **2.** See *constructive possession*. — Also termed *possessio civilis*.

possession of a right. (17c) The continuing exercise and enjoyment of a right. ● This type of possession is often unrelated to an ownership interest in property. For example, a criminal defendant possesses the right to demand a trial by jury. — Also termed *possessio juris*; (Ger.) *Rechtsbesitz*.

precarious possession. *Civil law.* Detention of property by someone other than the owner or possessor on behalf of or with permission of the owner or possessor. ● A lessee has precarious possession of the leased property.

quasi-possession. See *incorporeal possession*.

scrambling possession. (1823) **1.** A wrongful possession that the rightful possessor has not appeared to tolerate. Cf. *peaceable possession*. **2.** Possession that is uncertain because it is in dispute. ● With scrambling possession, the dispute is over who actually has possession — not over whether a party's possession is lawful.

possession unity. See *unity of possession* under UNITY.

possessor. (15c) One who has possession of real or personal property; esp., a person who is in occupancy of land with the intent to control it or has been but no longer is in that position, but no one else has gained occupancy or has a right to gain it. — **possessorial** (pos-ə-**sor**-ee-əl), *adj.*

legal possessor. (17c) One with the legal right to possess property, such as a buyer under a conditional sales contract, as contrasted with the legal owner who holds legal title. See *legal owner* under OWNER.

possessor bona fide (**boh**-nə **fi**-dee). A possessor who believes that no other person has a better right to the possession.

possessor mala fide (**mal**-ə **fi**-dee). A possessor who knows that someone else has a better right to the possession.

possessorium (pos-ə-**sor**-ee-əm). See *possessory action* under ACTION (4).

possessory (pə-**zes**-ə-ree), *adj.* Of, relating to, or having possession.

possessory action. See ACTION (4).

possessory claim. (1833) Title to public land held by a claimant who has filed a declaratory statement but has not paid for the land.

possessory conservator. See *noncustodial parent* under PARENT.

possessory estate. See ESTATE (1).

possessory garageman's lien. See LIEN.

possessory interdict. See INTERDICT (1).

possessory interest. (18c) **1.** The present right to control property, including the right to exclude others, by a person who is not necessarily the owner. **2.** A present or future right to the exclusive use and possession of property.

possessory lien. See LIEN.

possessory warrant. See WARRANT (1).

possibility. (14c) **1.** An event that may or may not happen. **2.** A contingent interest in real or personal property.

bare possibility. See *naked possibility*.

naked possibility. (18c) A mere chance or expectation that a person will acquire future property. ● A conveyance of a naked possibility is usu. void for lack of subject matter, as in a deed conveying all rights to a future estate not yet in existence. — Also termed *bare possibility*; *naked expectancy*.

possibility coupled with an interest. (18c) An expectation recognized in law as an estate or interest, as occurs in an executory devise or in a shifting or springing use. ● This type of possibility may be sold or assigned. See *shifting use*, *springing use* under USE.

possibility on a possibility. See *remote possibility*.

remote possibility. (17c) A limitation dependent on two or more facts or events that are contingent and uncertain; a double possibility. — Also termed *possibility on a possibility*.

possibility of reverter. (18c) A reversionary interest that is subject to a condition precedent; specif., a future interest retained by a grantor after conveying a fee simple determinable, so that the grantee's estate terminates automatically and reverts to the grantor if the terminating event ever occurs. ● In this type of interest, the grantor transfers an estate whose maximum potential duration equals that of the grantor's own estate and attaches a special limitation that operates in the grantor's favor. — Often shortened to *reverter*. See *fee simple determinable* under FEE SIMPLE. Cf. REMAINDER (1); REVERSION.

possibility on a possibility. See *remote possibility* under POSSIBILITY.

POSSLQ (**pahs**-əl-kyoo). *abbr.* A person of opposite sex sharing living quarters. ● Although this term (which is used by the Census Bureau) is intended to include only a person's roommate of the opposite sex to whom the person is not married, the phrase literally includes those who are married. This overbreadth has occasionally been criticized. See CUPOS.

post. [Latin] (14c) After. Cf. ANTE.

post, *vb.* (17c) **1.** To publicize or announce by affixing a notice in a public place <foreclosure notice was posted at the county courthouse>. **2.** To transfer (accounting entries) from an original record to a ledger <post debits and credits>. **3.** To place in the mail <post a letter>. **4.** To make a payment or deposit; to put up <post bail>.

postal currency. See CURRENCY.

Postal Rate Commission. An independent federal agency that recommends changes in postage rates, fees, and mail classifications for the governors of the United States Postal Service. ● It was created by the Postal Reorganization Act. 39 USCA §§ 3601–04. — Abbr. PRC.

post-answer default judgment. See DEFAULT JUDGMENT.

post audit. See AUDIT.

post bail, *vb.* See GIVE BAIL.

postconviction-relief proceeding. (1964) A state or federal procedure for a prisoner to request a court to vacate or correct a conviction or sentence. — Also termed *postconviction-remedy proceeding; PCR action; postconviction proceeding.*

postdate, *vb.* (17c) To put a date on (an instrument, such as a check) that is later than the actual date. Cf. ANTEDATE; BACKDATE.

postdated check. See CHECK.

post diem (pohst **dɪ**-əm). [Latin] After the day. ● A plea of payment *post diem* is made after the day when the money becomes due.

posted water. See WATER.

posteriority (pah-steer-ee-**or**-ə-tee). The condition or state of being subsequent. ● This word was formerly used to describe the relationships existing between a tenant and the two or more lords the tenant held of; the tenant held the older tenancy "by priority" and the more recent one "by posteriority."

posterity, *n.* (14c) **1.** Future generations collectively. **2.** All the descendants of a person to the furthest generation.

post-expiration-sales theory. *Patents.* A theory of lost-profits remedy by which compensation is sought for sales lost after a patent expired, on the basis that infringement gave the competitor a head start on entering the market. — Also termed *accelerated reentry theory.*

post facto (pohst **fak**-toh). [Latin] After the fact. See EX POST FACTO.

postglossators (pohst-glah-**say**-tərz), *n. pl.* (*often cap.*) A group of mainly Italian jurisconsults who were active during the 14th and 15th centuries writing commentaries and treatises that related Roman law to feudal and Germanic law, canon law, and other contemporary bodies of law. ● The postglossators constituted the second wave

of Roman-law study after its revival in the 11th century, the first being that of the glossators. — Also termed *commentators.* See GLOSSATORS.

post hoc (pohst hok). [Latin fr. *post hoc, ergo propter hoc* "after this, therefore because of this"] (1844) **1.** *adv.* After this; subsequently. **2.** *adj.* Of or relating to the fallacy of assuming causality from temporal sequence; confusing sequence with consequence.

posthumous (pos-chə-məs), *adj.* Occurring or existing after death; esp., (of a child) born after the father's death.

posthumous adoption. See ADOPTION.

posthumous child. See CHILD.

posthumous work. See WORK (2).

posting. (17c) **1.** *Accounting.* The act of transferring an original entry to a ledger. **2.** The act of mailing a letter. **3.** A method of substituted service of process by displaying the process in a prominent place (such as the courthouse door) when other forms of service have failed. See SERVICE (1). **4.** A publication method, as by displaying municipal ordinances in designated localities. **5.** The act of providing legal notice, as by affixing notices of judicial sales at or on the courthouse door. **6.** The procedure for processing a check, including one or more of the following steps: (1) verifying any signature, (2) ascertaining that sufficient funds are available, (3) affixing a "paid" or other stamp, (4) entering a charge or entry to a customer's account, and (5) correcting or reversing an entry or erroneous action concerning the check.

post-issue activity. *Patents.* Any acts done during a patent's term, including making, using, or selling a patented invention or process, esp. without authorization.

postjudgment discovery. See DISCOVERY.

postliminium (pohst-lə-**min**-ee-əm), *n.* [fr. Latin *post* "after" + *limen* "threshold"] **1.** *Roman & civil law.* The reentering of one's residence. **2.** *Roman & civil law.* The doctrine that a restoration of a person's lost rights or status relates back to the time of the original loss or deprivation, esp. in regard to the restoration of the status of a prisoner of war. **3.** *Int'l law.* The act of invalidating all of an occupying force's illegal acts, and the post-occupation revival of all illegitimately modified legal relations to their former condition, esp. the restoration of property to its rightful owner. — Also termed *postliminy; jus postliminii.*

postmarital, *adj.* **1.** Of, relating to, or occurring after marriage. Cf. PREMARITAL. **2.** Of, relating to, or occurring after divorce.

postmark. An official mark put by the post office on an item of mail to cancel the stamp and to indicate the place and date of sending or receipt.

postmaster. A U.S. Postal Service official responsible for a local branch of the post office. — Abbr. PM.

Postmaster General. The head of the U.S. Postal Service.

post meridiem (pohst mə-**rid**-ee-əm). [Latin] After noon. — Abbr. p.m.; PM.

postmortem, *adj.* (1824) Done or occurring after death <a postmortem examination>.

postmortem, *n.* See AUTOPSY (1).

post note. A banknote payable at a future time rather than on demand. See *time note* under NOTE (1).

postnup, *n. Slang.* See POSTNUPTIAL AGREEMENT.

postnuptial (pohst-**nəp**-shəl), *adj.* (1807) Made or occurring during marriage <a postnuptial contract>. Cf. PRENUPTIAL.

postnuptial agreement (pohst-**nəp**-shəl). (1834) An agreement entered into during marriage to define each spouse's property rights in the event of death or divorce. ● The term commonly refers to an agreement between spouses during the marriage at a time when separation or divorce is not imminent. When dissolution is intended as the result, it is more properly called a *property settlement* or *marital agreement.* — Often shortened to *postnup.* — Also termed *postnuptial settlement.* Cf. PRENUPTIAL AGREEMENT.

postnuptial settlement. See POSTNUPTIAL AGREEMENT.

postnuptial will. See WILL.

post-obit agreement. See BOND (3).

post-obit bond. See BOND (3).

postpone, *vb.* (15c) **1.** To put off to a later time. **2.** To place lower in precedence or importance; esp., to subordinate (a lien) to a later one. **3.** *Parliamentary law.* To temporarily or permanently suppress a main motion. — **postponement,** *n.*

postpone definitely. To delay a main motion's consideration to a specified time or until a specified condition occurs, usu. by the next meeting — or to the next meeting as unfinished business. — Also termed *postpone to a certain time; postpone to a definite time; postpone to a time certain.* See TIME CERTAIN.

postpone indefinitely. To dispose of a main motion without taking a view on its merits while preventing its further consideration during the same session. ● This motion's ancient form in the English Parliament was to postpone consideration until "this day six months" (or "three months") — that is, some time beyond the current session, sufficiently remote that the body expected not to consider the matter again. — Also termed *indefinite postponement.*

postpone temporarily. See TABLE.

postpone to a certain time. See *postpone definitely.*

postpone to a definite time. See *postpone definitely.*

postpone to a time certain. See *postpone definitely.*

post-terminal sitting. A court session held after the normal term.

posttrial discovery. See *postjudgment discovery* under DISCOVERY.

posttrial motion. See MOTION (1).

posttrial proceeding. See PROCEEDING.

potentate (**poh**-tən-tayt). A ruler who possesses great power or sway; a monarch.

potential, *adj.* Capable of coming into being; possible <things having a potential existence may be the subject of mortgage, assignment, or sale>.

potentially responsible party. *Environmental law.* A person or entity that may be required to clean up a polluted site because the person or entity (1) owns or operates on the site, (2) arranged for the disposal of a hazardous substance on the site, (3) transported a hazardous substance to the site, or (4) contributed in any other way to contaminate the site. — Abbr. PRP. See SUPERFUND.

potential Pareto superiority. See WEALTH MAXIMIZATION.

potestas (pə-**tes**-təs *or* -tas), *n.* [Latin "power"] *Roman law.* Authority or power, such as the power of a magistrate to enforce the law, or the authority of an owner over a slave.

patria potestas (**pay**-tree-ə *or* **pa**-tree-ə). [Latin "paternal power"] The authority held by the male head of a family (the senior ascendant male) over his legitimate and adopted children, as well as further descendants in the male line, unless emancipated. ● Initially, the father had extensive powers over the family, including the power of life and death; until Justinian's time, the father alone in his *familia* had proprietary capacity but he could give a son or slave a *peculium.* Over time, the broad nature of the *patria potestas* gradually became more in the nature of a responsibility to support and maintain family members. But except in early Roman history, a wife did not fall into her husband's power but remained in her father's until she became *sui juris* by his death. — Also termed *fatherly power.*

potestative condition. See CONDITION (2).

pound, *n.* (12c) **1.** A place where impounded property is held until redeemed. **2.** A place for the detention of stray animals. **3.** A measure of weight equal to 16 avoirdupois ounces or 7,000 grains. **4.** The basic monetary unit of the United Kingdom, equal to 100 pence. ● A pound was worth

20 shillings until decimalization in 1968. — Also termed (in sense 4) *pound sterling*.

poundage fee. (18c) A percentage commission awarded to a sheriff for moneys recovered under judicial process, such as execution or attachment.

pound of land. (16c) An uncertain quantity of land, usu. thought to be about 52 acres.

pound sterling. See POUND (4).

pour out, *vb.* (1978) *Slang.* To deny (a claimant) damages or relief in a lawsuit <the plaintiff was poured out of court by the jury's verdict of no liability>.

pourover trust. See TRUST.

pourover will. See WILL.

pourpresture (poor-**pres**-chər). [Law French] See PURPRESTURE.

poverty. 1. The condition of being indigent; the scarcity of the means of subsistence <war on poverty>. **2.** Dearth of something desirable <a poverty of ideas>.

poverty affidavit. See AFFIDAVIT.

POW. *abbr.* PRISONER OF WAR.

Powell **doctrine.** See CORRUPT-MOTIVE DOCTRINE.

power. (13c) **1.** The ability to act or not act; esp., a person's capacity for acting in such a manner as to control someone else's responses. **2.** Dominance, control, or influence over another; control over one's subordinates. **3.** The legal right or authorization to act or not act; a person's or organization's ability to alter, by an act of will, the rights, duties, liabilities, or other legal relations either of that person or of another.

  agent's power. The ability of an agent or apparent agent to act on behalf of the principal in matters connected with the agency or apparent agency.

  concurrent power. (1812) A political power independently exercisable by both federal and state governments in the same field of legislation.

  congressional power. The authority vested in the U.S. Senate and House of Representatives to enact laws and take other constitutionally permitted actions. U.S. Const. art. I.

  delegated power. Power normally exercised by an authority that has temporarily conferred the power on a lower authority.

  derivative power. Power that arises only from a grant of authority. • Power may be derived, for example, by an agent from a principal, or by a head of state from constitutional or statutory provisions.

  discretionary power. A power that a person may choose to exercise or not, based on the person's judgment.

  enumerated power. (1805) A political power specifically delegated to a governmental branch by a constitution. — Also termed *express power*.

  implied power. (1807) A political power that is not enumerated but that nonetheless exists because it is needed to carry out an express power.

  incident power. (17c) A power that, although not expressly granted, must exist because it is necessary to the accomplishment of an express purpose. — Also termed *incidental power*.

  inherent power. (17c) A power that necessarily derives from an office, position, or status.

  institorial power (in-stə-**tor**-ee-əl). *Civil law.* The power given by a business owner to an agent to act in the owner's behalf.

  investigatory power (in-**ves**-tə-gə-tor-ee). (*usu. pl.*) The authority conferred on a governmental agency to inspect and compel disclosure of facts germane to an investigation.

  judicial power. See JUDICIAL POWER.

  mediate powers. See MEDIATE POWERS.

  naked power. (18c) The power to exercise rights over something (such as a trust) without having a corresponding interest in that thing. Cf. *power coupled with an interest.*

  particular power. See *special power*.

  plenary power (**plee**-nə-ree *or* **plen**-ə-ree). (16c) Power that is broadly construed; esp., a court's power to dispose of any matter properly before it.

  police power. See POLICE POWER.

  power coupled with an interest. (18c) A power to do some act, conveyed along with an interest in the subject matter of the power. • A power coupled with an interest is not held for the benefit of the principal, and it is irrevocable due to the agent's interest in the subject property. For this reason, some authorities assert that it is not a true agency power. — Also termed *power given as security*; *proprietary power*. See *irrevocable power of attorney* under POWER OF ATTORNEY. Cf. *naked power*.

  power given as security. See *power coupled with an interest.*

  power of acceptance. An offeree's power to bind an offeror to a contract by accepting the offer.

  power of revocation (rev-ə-**kay**-shən). (17c) A power that a person reserves in an instrument (such as a trust) to revoke the legal relationship that the person has created.

  power of sale. A power granted to sell the property that the power relates to. • The power's exercise is often conditioned on the occurrence of a specific event, such as the nonpayment of a debt.

power over oneself. See CAPACITY (2).

power over other persons. See AUTHORITY (1).

primary powers. See PRIMARY POWERS.

private power. A power vested in a person to be exercised for personal ends and not as an agent for the state.

proprietary power. See *power coupled with an interest.*

public power. A power vested in a person as an agent or instrument of the functions of the state. ● Public powers comprise the various forms of legislative, judicial, and executive authority.

quasi-judicial power. (152) An administrative agency's power to adjudicate the rights of those who appear before it.

quasi-legislative power. (1864) An administrative agency's power to engage in rulemaking. 5 USCA § 553.

reserved power. (1831) A political power that is not enumerated or prohibited by a constitution, but instead is reserved by the constitution for a specified political authority, such as a state government. See TENTH AMENDMENT.

restraining power. A power to restrict the acts of others.

resulting power. A political power derived from the aggregate powers expressly or impliedly granted by a constitution.

special power. (18c) **1.** An agent's limited authority to perform only specific acts or to perform under specific restrictions. — Also termed *particular power*. **2.** See *limited power of appointment* under POWER OF APPOINTMENT.

spending power. (1923) The power granted to a governmental body to spend public funds; esp., the congressional power to spend money for the payment of debt and provision of the common defense and general welfare of the United States. U.S. Const. art. I, § 8, cl. 1.

taxing power. (18c) The power granted to a governmental body to levy a tax; esp., the congressional power to levy and collect taxes as a means of effectuating Congress's delegated powers. U.S. Const. art. I, § 8, cl. 1. See SIXTEENTH AMENDMENT.

trust power. See *beneficial power.*

visitatorial power. The power to inspect or make decisions about an entity's operations. — Also termed *visitorial power.*

4. A document granting legal authorization. See AUTHORITY. **5.** An authority to affect an estate in land by (1) creating some estate independently of any estate that the holder of the authority possesses, (2) imposing a charge on the estate, or (3) revoking an existing estate. See POWER OF APPOINTMENT; PERMIT.

appendant power (ə-**pen**-dənt). (17c) **1.** A power that gives the donee a right to appoint estates that attach to the donee's own interest. **2.** A power held by a donee who owns the property interest in the assets subject to the power, and whose interest can be divested by the exercise of the power. ● The appendant power is generally viewed as adding nothing to the ownership and thus is not now generally recognized as a true power. — Also termed *power appendant*; *power appurtenant.*

avoiding power. *Bankruptcy.* The power of a bankrupt trustee or debtor in possession to void certain transfers made or obligations incurred by a debtor, including fraudulent conveyances, preferences transferred to creditors, unperfected security interests in personal property, and unrecorded mortgages. 11 USCA §§ 544–53.

beneficial power. (18c) A power that is executed for the benefit of the power's donee, as distinguished from a *trust power*, which is executed for the benefit of someone other than the power's donee (i.e., a trust beneficiary).

collateral power. A power created when the donee has no estate in the land, but simply the authority to appoint.

general power. See POWER OF APPOINTMENT.

limited power. See POWER OF APPOINTMENT.

mandatory power. A power that the donee must exercise and must do so only as instructed, without discretion.

power appendant. See *appendant power.*

power appurtenant. See *appendant power.*

power collateral. See *power in gross.*

power in gross. (18c) A power held by a donee who has an interest in the assets subject to the power but whose interest cannot be affected by the exercise of the power. ● An example is a life tenant with a power over the remainder. — Also termed *power collateral.*

power of appointment. See POWER OF APPOINTMENT.

relative power. A power that relates directly to land, as distinguished from a collateral power.

testamentary power. See POWER OF APPOINTMENT.

6. Physical strength. **7.** Moral or intellectual force. **8.** A person of influence <a power in the community>. **9.** One of the great nations of the world <one of the world's two great powers>. See PROTECTING POWER. **10.** The military or unit of it, such as a troop of soldiers.

power-delegating law. See LAW OF COMPETENCE.

power given as security. See *power coupled with an interest* under POWER (3).

power of alienation. (16c) The capacity to sell, transfer, assign, or otherwise dispose of property.

power of appointment. (18c) A power created or reserved by a person having property subject to disposition, enabling the donee of the power to designate transferees of the property or shares in which it will be received; esp., a power conferred on a donee by will or deed to select and determine one or more recipients of the donor's estate or income. • If the power is exercisable before the donee's death, it is exercisable wholly in favor of the donee. If the power is testamentary, it is exercisable wholly in favor of the donee's estate. — Often shortened to *power*. — Also termed *enabling power*.

general power of appointment. (18c) A power of appointment by which the donee can appoint — that is, dispose of the donor's property — in favor of anyone at all, including oneself or one's own estate; esp., a power that authorizes the alienation of a fee to any alienee. — Often shortened to *general power*.

limited power of appointment. (1830) A power of appointment that either does not allow the entire estate to be conveyed or restricts to whom the estate may be conveyed; esp., a power by which the donee can appoint to only the person or class specified in the instrument creating the power, but cannot appoint to oneself or one's own estate. — Often shortened to *limited power*. — Also termed *special power of appointment*.

special power of appointment. See *limited power of appointment*.

testamentary power of appointment (tes-tə-men-tə-ree *or* -tree). (1858) A power of appointment created by a will. — Often shortened to *testamentary power*.

power-of-appointment trust. See TRUST.

power of attorney. (18c) **1.** An instrument granting someone authority to act as agent or attorney-in-fact for the grantor. • An ordinary power of attorney is revocable and automatically terminates upon the death or incapacity of the principal. — Also termed *letter of attorney*; *warrant of attorney*. See ATTORNEY (1). **2.** The authority so granted; specif., the legal ability to produce a change in legal relations by doing whatever acts are authorized. Pl. **powers of attorney.**

durable power of attorney. (1980) A power of attorney that remains in effect during the grantor's incompetency. • Such instruments commonly allow an agent to make healthcare decisions for a patient who has become incompetent.

general power of attorney. (18c) A power of attorney that authorizes an agent to transact business for the principal. Cf. *special power of attorney*.

irrevocable power of attorney (i-rev-ə-kə-bəl). (18c) A power of attorney that the principal cannot revoke. — Also termed *power of attorney coupled with an interest*. See *power coupled with an interest* under POWER (3).

power of attorney coupled with an interest. See *irrevocable power of attorney*.

power of attorney for healthcare. See ADVANCE DIRECTIVE (1).

special power of attorney. (18c) A power of attorney that limits the agent's authority to only a specified matter. Cf. *general power of attorney*.

springing power of attorney. A power of attorney that becomes effective only when needed, at some future date or upon some future occurrence, usu. upon the principal's incapacity. — Also termed *springing durable power of attorney*. See *durable power of attorney*; ADVANCE DIRECTIVE.

power of revocation (rev-ə-**kay**-shən). See POWER (3).

power of sale. See POWER (3).

power-of-sale clause. (1883) A provision in a mortgage or deed of trust permitting the mortgagee or trustee to sell the property without court authority if the payments are not made.

power-of-sale foreclosure. See FORECLOSURE.

power of termination. (1919) A future interest retained by a grantor after conveying a fee simple subject to a condition subsequent, so that the grantee's estate terminates (upon breach of the condition) only if the grantor exercises the right to retake it. — Also termed *right of entry*; *right of reentry*; *right of entry for breach of condition*; *right of entry for condition broken*. See *fee simple subject to a condition subsequent* under FEE SIMPLE. Cf. POSSIBILITY OF REVERTER.

power over oneself. See CAPACITY (2).

power over other persons. See AUTHORITY (1).

power politics. *Int'l law.* An approach to foreign policy that encourages a nation to use its economic and military strength to enlarge its own power as an end in itself; a system in which a country is willing to bring its economic and (esp.) military strength to bear in an effort to increase its own power.

power to inspect. *Patents.* The authority of a third party to review a patent application. • The power may be given by the applicant or an assignee, often to a potential buyer. It must specify which application the person is authorized to see, and it becomes part of the record of the application. See ACCESS (4), (5).

p.p. *abbr.* **1.** PER PROCURATIONEM. **2.** PROPRIA PERSONA.

PPA. *abbr.* **1.** See *provisional application* under PATENT APPLICATION. **2.** PLANT PATENT ACT.

PPI. *abbr.* POLICY PROOF OF INTEREST.

PPO. *abbr.* **1.** PREFERRED-PROVIDER ORGANIZATION. **2.** See *permanent protective order* under PROTECTIVE ORDER.

p. pro. *abbr.* PER PROCURATIONEM.

p. proc. *abbr.* PER PROCURATIONEM.

PR. *abbr.* PUBLIC RELATIONS.

practicable, *adj.* (16c) (Of a thing) reasonably capable of being accomplished; feasible.

practicably irrigable acreage. Land that is susceptible to prolonged irrigation, at reasonable cost.

practical construction. See *contemporaneous construction* under CONSTRUCTION.

practical finality. The situation in which a court order directs immediate delivery of physical property, subjecting the losing party to irreparable harm if an immediate appeal were not possible. ● Practical finality provides an exception to the usual rule that interlocutory orders are not appealable. See FINALITY DOCTRINE.

practical interpretation. See *contemporaneous construction* under CONSTRUCTION.

practically avoidable. See AVOIDABLE.

practice, *n.* (15c) **1.** The procedural methods and rules used in a court of law <local practice requires that an extra copy of each motion be filed with the clerk>. **2.** PRACTICE OF LAW <where is your practice?>.

practice, *vb.* *Patents.* **1.** To make and use (a patented invention) <the employer had a shop right to practice the patent, but not to sell it>. **2.** To build a physical embodiment of an invention. See REDUCTION TO PRACTICE.

practice act. (1881) A statute governing practice and procedure in courts. ● Practice acts are usu. supplemented with court rules such as the Federal Rules of Civil Procedure.

practice book. (1873) A volume devoted to the procedures in a particular court or category of courts, usu. including court rules, court forms, and practice directions.

practice court. 1. MOOT COURT. **2.** (*cap.*) BAIL COURT.

practice goodwill. See GOODWILL.

practice guide. A written explanation of how to proceed in a particular area of law or in a particular court or locality.

practice of law. (17c) The professional work of a duly licensed lawyer, encompassing a broad range of services such as conducting cases in court, preparing papers necessary to bring about various transactions from conveying land to effecting corporate mergers, preparing legal opinions on various points of law, drafting wills and other estate-planning documents, and advising clients on legal questions. ● The term also includes activities that comparatively few lawyers engage in but that require legal expertise, such as drafting legislation and court rules. — Also termed *legal practice.* Cf. LAW PRACTICE.

multidisciplinary practice of law. See MULTIDISCIPLINARY PRACTICE.

unauthorized practice of law. (1928) The practice of law by a person, typically a nonlawyer, who has not been licensed or admitted to practice law in a given jurisdiction. — Abbr. UPL.

practitioner. (16c) A person engaged in the practice of a profession, esp. law or medicine.

praecipe (**pree**-sə-pee *or* **pres**-ə-pee), *n.* [Latin "command"] (15c) **1.** At common law, a writ ordering a defendant to do some act or to explain why inaction is appropriate. — Also termed *writ of praecipe.* **2.** A written motion or request seeking some court action, esp. a trial setting or an entry of judgment. — Also spelled *precipe.* — **praecipe,** *vb.*

praedial (**pree**-dee-əl), *adj.* See PREDIAL.

pratique (pra-**teek** *or* **prat**-ik). *Maritime law.* A license allowing a vessel to trade in a particular country or port after complying with quarantine requirements or presenting a clean bill of health.

praxis (**prak**-sis). [Greek "doing; action"] (1933) In critical legal studies, practical action; the practice of living the ethical life in conjunction and in cooperation with others.

prayer conference. See CHARGE CONFERENCE.

prayer for relief. (18c) A request addressed to the court and appearing at the end of a pleading; esp., a request for specific relief or damages. — Often shortened to *prayer.* — Also termed *demand for relief; request for relief.* See AD DAMNUM CLAUSE.

general prayer. (18c) A prayer for additional unspecified relief, traditionally using language such as, "Plaintiff additionally prays for such other and further relief to which she may show herself to be justly entitled." ● The general prayer typically follows a special prayer.

special prayer. (18c) A prayer for the particular relief to which a plaintiff claims to be entitled.

prayer in aid. See AID PRAYER.

prayer of process. (18c) A conclusion in a bill in equity requesting the issuance of a subpoena if the defendant fails to answer the bill.

PRC. *abbr.* POSTAL RATE COMMISSION.

preamble (**pree**-am-bəl), *n.* (14c) **1.** An introductory statement in a constitution, statute, or other document explaining the document's basis and objective; esp., a statutory recital of the inconveniences for which the statute is designed to provide a remedy. ● A preamble often consists of a series of clauses introduced by the conjunction *whereas.* Such a preamble is sometimes called the *whereas clauses.* **2.** *Patents.* The first words of a patent claim, often a single phrase indicating the field of art. ● The preamble is typically nonlimiting unless it "breathes life and meaning into the claims." *Corning Glass Works v. Sumitomo Elec. U.S.A., Inc.,* 868 F.2d 1251, 1257 (Fed. Cir. 1989). Elements, the later parts of the claim, narrow this broad identification more and more specifically. Cf. BODY OF A CLAIM; TRANSITION PHRASE. — **preambulary** (pree-**am**-byə-ler-ee), **preambular** (pree-**am**-byə-lər), *adj.*

preappointed evidence. See EVIDENCE.

preargument-conference attorney. See CIRCUIT MEDIATOR.

prebankruptcy, *adj.* Occurring before the filing of a bankruptcy petition <prebankruptcy transactions>.

prebend (**preb**-ənd), *n.* **1.** A stipend granted in a cathedral church for the support of the members of the chapter. **2.** The property from which the stipend comes.

prebendary (**preb**-ən-der-ee). A person serving on the staff of a cathedral who receives a stipend from the cathedral's endowment.

prebut (**pree**-bət), *vb. Slang.* To rebut an argument in advance of an opponent's making it.; to engage in anticipatory refutation.

precarious, *adj.* (17c) Dependent on the will or pleasure of another; uncertain.

precarious loan. See LOAN.

precarious possession. See POSSESSION.

precarious right. See RIGHT.

precarious trade. See TRADE.

precatory (**prek**-ə-tor-ee), *adj.* (17c) (Of words) requesting, recommending, or expressing a desire for action, but usu. in a nonbinding way. ● An example of precatory language is "it is my wish and desire to . . . ."

precatory trust. See TRUST.

precautionary appeal. See *protective appeal* under APPEAL.

precedence (**pres**-ə-dənts *or* prə-**seed**-ənts), *n.* (16c) **1.** The order or priority in place or time observed by or for persons of different statuses (such as political dignitaries) on the basis of rank during ceremonial events. **2.** Generally, the act or state of going before something else according to some system of priorities. **3.** *Parliamentary law.*

The ranked priority that determines whether a motion is in order while another motion is pending, or whether a pending motion yields to another motion. **4.** *Parliamentary law.* The priority in which a member is entitled to the floor. — Also termed *precedence in recognition; preference in being recognized.* **5.** The order in which persons may claim the right to administer an intestate's estate. ● The traditional order is (1) surviving spouse, (2) next of kin, (3) creditors, and (4) public administrator.

precedent (prə-**seed**-ənt *also* **pres**-ə-dənt), *adj.* (14c) Preceding in time or order <condition precedent>.

precedent (**pres**-ə-dənt), *n.* (16c) **1.** The making of law by a court in recognizing and applying new rules while administering justice. **2.** A decided case that furnishes a basis for determining later cases involving similar facts or issues. See STARE DECISIS. — **precedential,** *adj.*

binding precedent. (17c) A precedent that a court must follow. ● For example, a lower court is bound by an applicable holding of a higher court in the same jurisdiction. — Also termed *authoritative precedent; binding authority.* Cf. *imperative authority* under AUTHORITY (4).

declaratory precedent. (1900) A precedent that is merely the application of an already existing legal rule.

original precedent. (17c) A precedent that creates and applies a new legal rule.

persuasive precedent. (1905) A precedent that is not binding on a court, but that is entitled to respect and careful consideration. ● For example, if the case was decided in a neighboring jurisdiction, the court might evaluate the earlier court's reasoning without being bound to decide the same way.

precedent sub silentio (səb sə-**len**-shee-oh). (1825) A legal question that was neither argued nor explicitly discussed in a judicial decision but that seems to have been silently ruled on and might therefore be treated as a precedent.

superprecedent. **1.** A precedent that defines the law and its requirements so effectively that it prevents divergent holdings in later legal decisions on similar facts or induces disputants to settle their claims without litigation. ● This sense was posited by W. Landes and Richard Posner in *Legal Precedent: A Theoretical and Empirical Analysis,* 19 J. Law & Econ. 249, 251 (1976). **2.** A precedent that has become so established in the law by a long line of reaffirmations that it is very difficult to overturn it; specif., a precedent that has been reaffirmed many times and whose rationale has been extended to cover cases in which the facts are dissimilar, even wholly unrelated, to those of the precedent.

• For example, *Roe v. Wade* has been called a superprecedent because it has survived more than three dozen attempts to overturn it and has been relied on in decisions protecting gay rights and the right to die. Cf. *super stare decisis* under STARE DECISIS.

3. DOCTRINE OF PRECEDENT. **4.** A form of pleading or property-conveyancing instrument. • Precedents are often compiled in book form and used by lawyers as guides for preparing similar documents.

precept (**pree**-sept). (14c) **1.** A standard or rule of conduct; a command or principle <several legal precepts govern here>. **2.** A writ or warrant issued by an authorized person demanding another's action, such as a judge's order to an officer to bring a party before the court <the sheriff executed the precept immediately>.

preceptive statute. See STATUTE.

precinct. A geographical unit of government, such as an election district, a police district, or a judicial district.

magisterial precinct. (1894) A county subdivision that defines the territorial jurisdiction of a magistrate, constable, or justice of the peace. — Also termed *magisterial district*.

precipe (**pre**-sə-pee). See PRAECIPE.

précis (pray-**see** or **pray**-see), *n.* [French] (18c) A concise summary of a text's essential points; an abstract. Pl. **précis** (pray-**seez** or **pray**-seez).

preclusion order. See ORDER (2).

precompounded prescription drug. See DRUG.

preconceived malice. See MALICE AFORE-THOUGHT.

precondition. See CONDITION (1).

precontract. See CONTRACT.

predate, *vb.* See ANTEDATE.

predation. See PREDATORY PRICING.

predator. See SEXUAL PREDATOR.

predatory crime. See CRIME.

predatory intent. See INTENT (1).

predatory pricing. Unlawful below-cost pricing intended to eliminate specific competitors and reduce overall competition; pricing below an appropriate measure of cost for the purpose of eliminating competitors in the short run and reducing competition in the long run. — Also termed *predation*. See ANTITRUST.

predecease, *vb.* To die before (another) <she predeceased her husband>.

predecessor. 1. One who precedes another in an office or position. **2.** An ancestor.

predecisional, *adj.* Of, relating to, or occurring during the time before a decision.

predial (**pree**-dee-əl), *adj.* (15c) Of, consisting of, relating to, or attached to land <predial servitude>. — Also spelled *praedial*.

predial servitude. See *servitude appurtenant* under SERVITUDE (2).

predicate act. (1977) **1.** See *predicate offense* under OFFENSE (1). **2.** See *lesser included offense* under OFFENSE (1). **3.** Under RICO, one of two or more related acts of racketeering necessary to establish a pattern. See RACKETEER INFLUENCED AND CORRUPT ORGANIZATIONS ACT. **4.** See *predicate act* under ACT (2).

predicate fact. See FACT.

predicate offense. See *lesser included offense* under OFFENSE (1).

prediction theory. 1. See BAD-MAN THEORY. **2.** See PREDICTIVE THEORY OF LAW.

predictive theory of law. (1956) The view that the law is nothing more than a set of predictions about what the courts will decide in given circumstances. • This theory is embodied in Holmes's famous pronouncement, "The prophecies of what the courts will do in fact, and nothing more pretentious, are what I mean by the law." Oliver Wendell Holmes, *The Path of the Law*, 10 Harv. L. Rev. 457, 460–61 (1897). — Also termed *prediction theory*. Cf. BAD-MAN THEORY.

predisposition. (17c) A person's inclination to engage in a particular activity; esp., an inclination that vitiates a criminal defendant's claim of entrapment.

predominant-aspect test. See PREDOMINANT-PURPOSE TEST.

predominant-purpose test. An assessment of whether Article 2 of the UCC applies to an exchange, conducted by considering whether the exchange's chief aspect, viewed in light of all the circumstances, is the sale of goods. • If goods account for most of the exchange's value, it is probably a sale; if services account for most of the value, it probably is not. The leading case is *Bonebrake v. Cox*, 499 F.2d 951, 960 (8th Cir. 1974). — Also termed *predominant-aspect test*.

preemption (pree-**emp**-shən), *n.* (18c) **1.** The right to buy before others. See RIGHT OF PREEMPTION. **2.** The purchase of something under this right. **3.** An earlier seizure or appropriation. **4.** The occupation of public land so as to establish a preemptive title. **5.** *Constitutional law.* The principle (derived from the Supremacy Clause) that a federal law can supersede or supplant any inconsistent state law or regulation. — Also termed (in sense 5) *federal preemption*. See COMPLETE-PREEMPTION DOCTRINE. — **preempt,** *vb.* — **preemptive,** *adj.*

conflict preemption. See *obstacle preemption*.

Garmon preemption. *Labor law.* A doctrine prohibiting state and local regulation of activities that are actually or arguably (1) protected by the National Labor Relations Act's rules relating to the right of employees to organize and bargain collectively, or (2) prohibited by the National Labor Relations Act's provision that governs unfair labor practices. *San Diego Bldg. Trades Council v. Garmon*, 359 U.S. 236, 79 S.Ct. 773 (1959). — Also termed *Garmon doctrine*. See COLLECTIVE BARGAINING; UNFAIR LABOR PRACTICE.

Machinists preemption. *Labor law.* The doctrine prohibiting state regulation of an area of labor activity or management-union relations that Congress has intentionally left unregulated. *Lodge 76, Int'l Ass'n of Machinists v. Wisconsin Employment Relations Comm'n*, 427 U.S. 132, 96 S.Ct. 2548 (1976).

obstacle preemption. The principle that federal or state law can supersede or supplant state or local law that stands as an obstacle to accomplishing the full purposes and objectives of the overriding federal or state law. — Also termed *conflict preemption*.

preemption claimant. (1824) One who has settled on land subject to preemption, intending in good faith to acquire title to it.

preemption right. (18c) The privilege to take priority over others in claiming land subject to preemption. • The privilege arises from the holder's actual settlement of the land. See PREEMPTION (3).

preemptive right. A shareholder's privilege to purchase newly issued stock — before the shares are offered to the public — in an amount proportionate to the shareholder's current holdings in order to prevent dilution of the shareholder's ownership interest. • This right must be exercised within a fixed period, usu. 30 to 60 days. — Also termed *subscription privilege*. See SUBSCRIPTION RIGHT. Cf. *rights offering* under OFFERING.

preexisting condition. See CONDITION (2).

preexisting duty. See DUTY (1).

preexisting-duty rule. (1990) *Contracts.* The rule that if a party does or promises to do what the party is already legally obligated to do — or refrains or promises to refrain from doing what the party is already legally obligated to refrain from doing — the party has not incurred detriment. • This rule's result is that the promise does not constitute adequate consideration for contractual purposes. For example, if a builder agrees to construct a building for a specified price but later threatens to walk off the job unless the owner promises to pay an additional sum, the owner's new promise is not enforceable because, under the preexisting-duty rule, there is no consideration for that promise. — Also termed *preexisting-legal-duty rule*.

prefect (**pree**-fekt), *n.* **1.** A high official or magistrate put in charge of a particular command, department, or region. **2.** In New Mexico, a probate judge.

prefer, *vb.* (14c) **1.** To put forward or present for consideration; esp. (of a grand jury), to bring (a charge or indictment) against a criminal suspect <the defendant claimed he was innocent of the charges preferred against him>. **2.** To give priority to, such as to one creditor over another <the statute prefers creditors who are first to file their claims>.

preference. 1. The act of favoring one person or thing over another; the person or thing so favored. **2.** Priority of payment given to one or more creditors by a debtor; a creditor's right to receive such priority. **3.** *Bankruptcy.* PREFERENTIAL TRANSFER.

insider preference. A transfer of property by a bankruptcy debtor to an insider more than 90 days before but within one year after the filing of the bankruptcy petition.

liquidation preference. A preferred shareholder's right, once the corporation is liquidated, to receive a specified distribution before common shareholders receive anything.

voidable preference. See PREFERENTIAL TRANSFER.

preference case. See *preferred cause* under CAUSE (3).

preference cause. See *preferred cause* under CAUSE (3).

preference in being recognized. See PRECEDENCE (4).

preference shares. See *preferred stock* under STOCK.

preferential assignment. See PREFERENTIAL TRANSFER.

preferential ballot. See *preferential vote* under VOTE (1).

preferential debt. See DEBT.

preferential nonunion shop. See SHOP.

preferential rule. (1959) *Evidence.* A rule that prefers one kind of evidence to another. • It may work provisionally, as when a tribunal refuses to consider one kind of evidence until another kind (presumably better) is shown to be unavailable, or it may work absolutely, as when the tribunal refuses to consider anything but the better kind of evidence.

preferential shop. See *preferential union shop* under SHOP.

preferential tariff. See TARIFF (2).

preferential transfer. *Bankruptcy.* A prebankruptcy transfer made by an insolvent debtor to or for the benefit of a creditor, thereby allowing the creditor to receive more than its proportionate share of the debtor's assets; specif., an insolvent debtor's transfer of a property interest for the benefit of a creditor who is owed on an earlier debt, when the transfer occurs no more than 90 days before the date when the bankruptcy petition is filed or (if the creditor is an insider) within one year of the filing, so that the creditor receives more than it would otherwise receive through the distribution of the bankruptcy estate. ● Under the circumstances described in 11 USCA § 547, the bankruptcy trustee may recover — for the estate's benefit — a preferential transfer from the transferee. — Also termed *preference*; *voidable preference*; *voidable transfer*; *preferential assignment*. Cf. FRAUDULENT CONVEYANCE (2).

preferential union shop. See SHOP.

preferential vote. See VOTE (1).

preferential voting. See VOTING.

preferred, *adj.* Possessing or accorded a priority or privilege <a preferred claim>.

preferred cause. See CAUSE (3).

preferred creditor. See CREDITOR.

preferred dividend. See DIVIDEND.

preferred docket. See DOCKET (2).

preferred-provider organization. (1984) A group of healthcare providers (such as doctors, hospitals, and pharmacies) that agree to provide medical services at a discounted cost to covered persons in a given geographic area. — Abbr. PPO. Cf. HEALTH-MAINTENANCE ORGANIZATION; MANAGED-CARE ORGANIZATION.

preferred stock. See STOCK.

preferring of charges. *Military law.* The formal completion of a charge sheet, which includes signing and swearing to the charges and specifications. ● Only a person subject to the Uniform Code of Military Justice can prefer charges. Cf. INITIATION OF CHARGES.

prefiled bill. See BILL (3).

Pregnancy-Discrimination Act. A federal statute that prohibits workplace discrimination against a pregnant woman or against a woman affected by childbirth or a related medical condition. 42 USCA § 2000. ● The Pregnancy-Discrimination Act is part of Title VII of the Civil Rights Act of 1964. — Abbr. PDA.

pregnant chad. See *dimpled chad* under CHAD.

prehearing conference. (1946) An optional conference for the discussion of procedural and substantive matters on appeal, usu. held in complex civil, criminal, tax, and agency cases. ● Those attending are typically the attorneys involved in the case as well as a court representative such as a judge, staff attorney, or deputy clerk. Fed. R. App. P. 33.

prehire agreement. An employment contract between a union and an employer, in which the employer agrees to hire union members. See *closed shop* under SHOP.

prejudgment attachment. See ATTACHMENT (1).

prejudgment interest. See INTEREST (3).

prejudice, *n.* (14c) **1.** Damage or detriment to one's legal rights or claims. See *dismissal with prejudice* and *dismissal without prejudice* under DISMISSAL.

    legal prejudice. (18c) A condition that, if shown by a party, will usu. defeat the opposing party's action; esp., a condition that, if shown by the defendant, will defeat a plaintiff's motion to dismiss a case without prejudice. ● The defendant may show that dismissal will deprive the defendant of a substantive property right or preclude the defendant from raising a defense that will be unavailable or endangered in a second suit.

    undue prejudice. (17c) The harm resulting from a fact-trier's being exposed to evidence that is persuasive but inadmissible (such as evidence of prior criminal conduct) or that so arouses the emotions that calm and logical reasoning is abandoned.

2. A preconceived judgment formed with little or no factual basis; a strong bias. — **prejudice,** *vb.* — **prejudicial,** *adj.*

prejudicial error. See *reversible error* under ERROR (2).

prejudicial publicity. (1935) Extensive media attention devoted to an upcoming civil or criminal trial. ● Under the Due Process Clause, extensive coverage of a criminal trial may deprive the defendant of a fair trial.

preliminary, *adj.* Coming before and usu. leading up to the main part of something <preliminary negotiations>.

preliminary amendment. See PATENT-APPLICATION AMENDMENT.

preliminary availability search. *Trademarks.* A cursory or moderate search of registered trademarks and common-law uses of proposed-trademark names or phrases, done to narrow the list of names phrases before conducting a thorough search.

preliminary complaint. See COMPLAINT.

preliminary crime. See *inchoate offense* under OFFENSE (1).

preliminary evidence. See EVIDENCE.

preliminary examination. 1. See EXAMINATION (3). **2.** See PRELIMINARY HEARING.

preliminary hearing. A criminal hearing (usu. conducted by a magistrate) to determine whether there is sufficient evidence to prosecute an accused person. • If sufficient evidence exists, the case will be set for trial or bound over for grand-jury review, or an information will be filed in the trial court. — Also termed *preliminary examination*; *probable-cause hearing*; *bindover hearing*; *examining trial*. Cf. ARRAIGNMENT.

preliminary injunction. See INJUNCTION.

preliminary inquiry. *Military law.* The initial investigation of a reported or suspected violation of the Uniform Code of Military Justice. Cf. PRETRIAL INVESTIGATION.

preliminary-inquiry officer. See OFFICER (2).

preliminary letter. See INVITATION TO NEGOTIATE.

preliminary objection. *Int'l law.* In a case before an international tribunal, an objection that, if upheld, would render further proceedings before the tribunal impossible or unnecessary. • An objection to the court's jurisdiction is an example of a preliminary objection.

preliminary proof. See PROOF.

preliminary prospectus. See PROSPECTUS.

preliminary protective hearing. See *shelter hearing* under HEARING.

preliminary statement. (1834) The introductory part of a brief or memorandum in support of a motion, in which the advocate summarizes the essence of what follows. • In at least two jurisdictions, New York and New Jersey, the preliminary statement is a standard part of court papers. In many other jurisdictions, advocates do not routinely include it. But preliminary statements are typically allowed, even welcomed, though not required. — Also termed *summary of argument*.

preliminary warrant. See WARRANT (1).

premarital, *adj.* Of, relating to, or occurring before marriage. Cf. POSTMARITAL.

premarital agreement. See PRENUPTIAL AGREEMENT.

premarital asset. See ASSET.

prematurity. 1. The circumstance existing when the facts underlying a plaintiff's complaint do not yet create a live claim. Cf. RIPENESS. **2.** The affirmative defense based on this circumstance.

premeditated, *adj.* (16c) Done with willful deliberation and planning; consciously considered beforehand <a premeditated killing>.

premeditated malice. See MALICE AFORETHOUGHT.

premeditation, *n.* (15c) Conscious consideration and planning that precedes some act (such as committing a crime). — **premeditate,** *vb.*

premier serjeant. See SERJEANT-AT-LAW.

premise (prem-is), *n.* (14c) A previous statement or contention from which a conclusion is deduced. — Also spelled (in BrE) *premiss*. — **premise (prem-**is *or* pri-**mIz**), *vb.*

premises (prem-ə-siz). (15c) **1.** Matters (usu. preliminary facts or statements) previously referred to in the same instrument <wherefore, premises considered, the plaintiff prays for the following relief>. **2.** The part of a deed that describes the land being conveyed, as well as naming the parties and identifying relevant facts or explaining the reasons for the deed. **3.** A house or building, along with its grounds <smoking is not allowed on these premises>.

> *demised premises.* Leased property. — Also termed *premises demised*.

premises liability. (1950) A landowner's or landholder's tort liability for conditions or activities on the premises.

premises rule. See PARKING-LOT RULE.

premium, *n.* **1.** The periodic payment required to keep an insurance policy in effect. — Also termed *insurance premium*.

> *advance premium.* A payment made before the start of the period covered by the insurance policy.

> *earned premium.* The portion of an insurance premium applicable to the coverage period that has already expired. • For example, if the total premium for a one-year insurance policy is $1,200, the earned premium after three months is $300.

> *gross premium.* **1.** The net premium plus expenses (i.e., the loading), less the interest factor. See LOADING; INTEREST FACTOR. **2.** The premium for participating life insurance. See *participating insurance* under INSURANCE.

> *natural premium.* The actual cost of life insurance based solely on mortality rates. • This amount will be less than a net premium. See *net premium*.

> *net level annual premium.* A net premium that stays the same each year.

> *net premium.* **1.** Generally, the premium amount for an insurance policy less agent commissions. **2.** The portion of the premium that covers the estimated cost of claims. **3.** The money needed to provide benefits under an insurance policy. • The net premium in a life-insurance policy is calculated by using an assumed interest and mortality-table rate; it does not include additional expense amounts that will be charged to the policyholder. — Also termed *net valuation premium*.

> *net single premium.* The money that must be collected from a policyholder at one time to guarantee enough money to pay claims made

on an insurance policy. • This amount assumes that interest accrues at an expected rate and is based on a prediction of the likelihood of certain claims.

net valuation premium. See *net premium.*

unearned premium. The portion of an insurance premium applicable to the coverage period that has not yet occurred. • In the same example as above under *earned premium,* the unearned premium after three months is $900.

2. A sum of money paid in addition to a regular price, salary, or other amount; a bonus. **3.** The amount by which a security's market value exceeds its face value. — Also termed (specif.) *bond premium.* Cf. DISCOUNT (3).

control premium. A premium paid for shares carrying the power to control a corporation. • The control premium is often computed by comparing the aggregate value of the controlling block of shares with the cost that would be incurred if the shares could be acquired at the going market price per share.

4. The amount paid to buy a securities option. — Also termed (in sense 4) *option premium.*

premium bond. See BOND (3).

premium loan. See LOAN.

premium note. See NOTE (1).

premium on capital stock. See *paid-in surplus* under SURPLUS.

premium rate. *Insurance.* The price per unit of life insurance. • It is usu. expressed as a cost per thousands of dollars of coverage. Life insurers use three factors — the interest factor, the mortality factor, and the risk factor — to calculate premium rates. — Sometimes shortened to *rate.* See INTEREST FACTOR; MORTALITY FACTOR; RISK FACTOR.

premium stock. See STOCK.

premium tax. See TAX.

prenatal injury. Harm to a fetus or an embryo. Cf. BIRTH INJURY.

prenatal tort. See TORT.

prender. The right to take a thing before it is offered. — Also spelled *prendré.*

prenup, *n. Slang.* See PRENUPTIAL AGREEMENT.

prenuptial (pree-**nəp**-shəl), *adj.* (1857) Made or occurring before marriage; premarital. — Also termed *antenuptial* (an-tee-**nəp**-shəl). Cf. POSTNUPTIAL.

prenuptial agreement. (1882) An agreement made before marriage usu. to resolve issues of support and property division if the marriage ends in divorce or by the death of a spouse. — Also termed *antenuptial agreement; antenuptial contract; premarital agreement; premarital contract; marriage settlement.* — Sometimes shortened to *prenup.*

Cf. POSTNUPTIAL AGREEMENT; COHABITATION AGREEMENT.

prenuptial gift. See GIFT.

prenuptial will. See WILL.

prepaid card. See STORED-VALUE CARD.

prepaid expense. See EXPENSE.

prepaid income. See INCOME.

prepaid interest. See INTEREST (3).

prepaid legal services. (1963) An arrangement — usu. serving as an employee benefit — that enables a person to make advance payments for future legal services.

preparation. *Criminal law.* The act or process of devising the means necessary to commit a crime. Cf. ATTEMPT.

prepayment clause. (1935) A loan-document provision that permits a borrower to satisfy a debt before its due date. • Although any interest not yet due is waived, the lender may impose a penalty for prepayment.

prepayment penalty. See PENALTY (2).

prepense (**pree**-pens), *adj. Rare.* Planned; deliberate <malice prepense>.

prepetition (pree-pə-**tish**-ən), *adj.* (1938) Occurring before the filing of a petition (esp. in bankruptcy) <prepetition debts>.

preponderance (pri-**pon**-dər-ənts), *n.* (17c) Superiority in weight, importance, or influence. — **preponderate** (pri-**pon**-dər-ayt), *vb.* — **preponderant** (pri-**pon**-dər-ənt), *adj.*

preponderance of the evidence. (18c) The greater weight of the evidence, not necessarily established by the greater number of witnesses testifying to a fact but by evidence that has the most convincing force; superior evidentiary weight that, though not sufficient to free the mind wholly from all reasonable doubt, is still sufficient to incline a fair and impartial mind to one side of the issue rather than the other. • This is the burden of proof in most civil trials, in which the jury is instructed to find for the party that, on the whole, has the stronger evidence, however slight the edge may be. — Also termed *preponderance of proof; balance of probability.* See REASONABLE DOUBT. Cf. *clear and convincing evidence* under EVIDENCE.

prerogative (pri-**rog**-ə-tiv), *n.* (15c) An exclusive right, power, privilege, or immunity, usu. acquired by virtue of office. — **prerogative,** *adj.*

prerogative court. See COURT.

prerogative of mercy. The limited right of a chief executive to commute a death sentence or to pardon a convicted person, esp. one convicted of a capital crime.

prerogative writ. See *extraordinary writ* under WRIT.

presale. The sale of real property (such as condominium units) before construction has begun.

prescribable (pri-**skrıb**-ə-bəl), *adj.* (1890) (Of a right) that can be acquired or extinguished by prescription.

prescribe, *vb.* **1.** To dictate, ordain, or direct; to establish authoritatively (as a rule or guideline). **2.** To claim ownership through prescription. **3.** To invalidate or otherwise make unenforceable through prescription. **4.** To become invalid or otherwise unenforceable through prescription.

prescript, *adj.* Having the nature of a rule or command.

prescript, *n. Archaic.* A rule, law, command, or ordinance; PRESCRIPTION (2). ● A general term, *prescript* may also apply to an edict, a regulation, or any instructive guideline.

prescription, *n.* (15c) **1.** The act of establishing authoritative rules. Cf. PROSCRIPTION. **2.** A rule so established. — Also termed (archaically) *prescript.* **3.** The effect of the lapse of time in creating and destroying rights. **4.** The extinction of a title or right by failure to claim or exercise it over a long period. — Also termed *negative prescription*; *extinctive prescription.* **5.** The acquisition of title to a thing (esp. an intangible thing such as the use of real property) by open and continuous possession over a statutory period. — Also termed *positive prescription*; *acquisitive prescription.* Cf. ADVERSE POSSESSION. See (for senses 3–5) PERIOD OF PRESCRIPTION. **6.** *Int'l law.* The acquisition of a territory through a continuous and undisputed exercise of sovereignty over it. **7.** *Oil & gas.* A Louisiana doctrine that extinguishes unused mineral servitudes after ten years if there is no effort to discover or produce on the land or the land pooled with it.

acquisitive prescription (ə-**kwiz**-ə-tiv). **1.** PRESCRIPTION (5). **2.** *Civil law.* A mode of acquiring ownership or other legal rights through possession for a specified period of time.

liberative prescription (**lib**-ə-rə-tiv). *Civil law.* A bar to a lawsuit resulting from its untimely filing. La. Civ. Code art. 3447. ● This term is essentially the civil-law equivalent of a statute of limitations. See STATUTE OF LIMITATIONS.

prescription in a que estate (ah **kee**). [Law French "prescription in whose estate"] A claim of prescription based on the immemorial enjoyment of the right by the claimant and the former owners whose estate the claimant has succeeded to.

prescription of nonuse. *Civil law.* A mode of extinction of a real right other than ownership (such as a servitude) as a result of failure to exercise the right for a specified period of time.

prescriptive easement. See EASEMENT.

prescriptive right. (17c) A right obtained by prescription <after a nuisance has been continuously in existence for 20 years, a prescriptive right to continue it is acquired as an easement appurtenant to the land on which it exists>.

presence, *n.* **1.** The state or fact of being in a particular place and time <his presence at the scene saved two lives>. **2.** Close physical proximity coupled with awareness <the agent was in the presence of the principal>.

constructive presence. 1. *Criminal law.* Legal imputation of having been at a crime scene, based on having been close enough to the scene to have aided and abetted the crime's commission. See CONSPIRACY. **2.** *Wills & estates.* Legal imputation of a witness's having been in the room when a will was signed, based on the fact that the testator and the witness were able to see each other at the time of the signing. ● This principle was commonly employed until the 20th century, when the presence-of-the-testator rule became dominant. See PRESENCE-OF-THE-TESTATOR RULE.

presence-of-defendant rule. The principle that a felony defendant is entitled to be present at every major stage of the criminal proceeding. Fed. R. Crim. P. 43.

presence of the court. (18c) The company or proximity of the judge or other courtroom official. ● For purposes of contempt, an action is in the presence of the court if it is committed within the view of the judge or other person in court and is intended to disrupt the court's business.

presence-of-the-testator rule. The principle that a testator must be aware (through sight or other sense) that the witnesses are signing the will. ● Many jurisdictions interpret this requirement liberally, and the Uniform Probate Code has dispensed with it.

present, *adj.* (14c) **1.** Now existing; at hand <a present right to the property>. **2.** Being considered; now under discussion <the present appeal does not deal with that issue>. **3.** In attendance; not elsewhere <all present voted for him>.

present ability. See ABILITY.

present and voting. *Parliamentary law.* (Of a member) casting a vote. ● The result of a vote is ordinarily determined with reference to the members voting (often termed, somewhat redundantly, as "present and voting"). An answer of "present" when casting a vote amounts to an abstention because the voter is indicating that he or she is present but not voting. See ABSTAIN (1).

presentation. (15c) **1.** The delivery of a document to an issuer or named person for the purpose of initiating action under a letter of credit; PRESENTMENT (3). **2.** *Hist. Eccles. law.* A benefice patron's nomination of a person to fill a vacant benefice.

• If the bishop rejected the appointee, the patron could enforce the right to fill the vacancy by writ of *quare impedit* in the Court of Common Pleas. See QUARE IMPEDIT. Cf. ADVOWSON; INSTITUTION (5).

next presentation. *Hist. Eccles. law.* In the law of advowsons, the right to present to the bishop a clerk to fill the first vacancy that arises in a church or other ecclesiastical office.

present case. See *case at bar* under CASE.

present conveyance. See CONVEYANCE.

present covenant. See COVENANT (4).

presentence hearing. (1940) A proceeding at which a judge or jury receives and examines all relevant information regarding a convicted criminal and the related offense before passing sentence. — Also termed sentencing hearing.

presentence-investigation report. (1943) A probation officer's detailed account of a convicted defendant's educational, criminal, family, and social background, conducted at the court's request as an aid in passing sentence. See Fed. R. Crim. P. 32(c). — Abbr. PSI; PIR. — Often shortened to *presentence report*.

present enjoyment. See ENJOYMENT.

presenter. *Commercial law.* Any person presenting a document (such as a draft) to an issuer for honor. UCC § 5-102.

present estate. 1. ESTATE (1). **2.** See *present interest* under INTEREST (2).

presenting bank. See BANK.

presenting jury. See GRAND JURY.

present interest. See INTEREST (2).

presentment (pri-**zent**-mənt). (15c) **1.** The act of presenting or laying before a court or other tribunal a formal statement about a matter to be dealt with legally. **2.** *Criminal procedure.* A formal written accusation returned by a grand jury on its own initiative, without a prosecutor's previous indictment request. • Presentments are obsolete in the federal courts. **3.** The formal production of a negotiable instrument for acceptance or payment. — Also termed (in sense 3) *presentation*.

presentment for acceptance. (18c) Production of an instrument to the drawee, acceptor, or maker for acceptance. • This type of presentment may be made anytime before maturity, except that with bills payable at sight, after demand, or after sight, presentment must be made within a reasonable time.

presentment for payment. (18c) Production of an instrument to the drawee, acceptor, or maker for payment. • This type of presentment must be made on the date when the instrument is due.

presentment warranty. See WARRANTY (2).

present recollection refreshed. (1908) *Evidence.* A witness's memory that has been enhanced by showing the witness a document that describes the relevant events. • The document itself is merely a memory stimulus and is not admitted in evidence. Fed. R. Evid. 612. — Also termed *refreshing recollection; refreshing memory; present recollection revived.* Cf. PAST RECOLLECTION RECORDED.

presents, *n. pl.* (14c) *Archaic.* The instrument under consideration. • This is usu. part of the phrase *these presents,* which is part of the longer phrase *know all men by these presents* (itself a loan translation from the Latin *noverint universi per praesentes*). See KNOW ALL MEN BY THESE PRESENTS.

present sale. See SALE.

present sense impression. (1942) *Evidence.* One's perception of an event or condition, formed during or immediately after the fact. • A statement containing a present sense impression is admissible even if it is hearsay. Fed. R. Evid. 803(1). Cf. EXCITED UTTERANCE.

present use. See USE (4).

present value. The sum of money that, with compound interest, would amount to a specified sum at a specified future date; future value discounted to its value today. — Also termed *present worth.*

adjusted present value. An asset's value determined by adding together its present value and the value added by capital-structure effects. — Abbr. APV.

net present value. The present value of net cash flow from a project, discounted by the cost of capital. • This value is used to evaluate the project's investment potential. — Abbr. NPV.

preservation order. A direction to a property owner to maintain a historic building or conserve a natural habitat.

preside, *vb.* (15c) **1.** To occupy the place of authority, esp. as a judge during a hearing or trial <preside over the proceedings>. **2.** To exercise management or control <preside over the estate>.

president, *n.* **1.** The chief political executive of a government; the head of state. **2.** The chief executive officer of a corporation or other organization. **3.** CHAIR (1). **4.** CHAIR (3). See (in senses 3 & 4) *presiding officer* (3) under OFFICER (2). — **presidential,** *adj.*

immediate past president. The last president who held office before the incumbent. See EMERITUS.

president-elect. An officer who automatically succeeds to the presidency when the incumbent president's term expires. • If the organization's governing documents so provide, the president-elect may act as president in the incumbent president's absence, or may assume the presidency early if the incumbent does not finish the term.

president emeritus. See EMERITUS.

presidential elector. See ELECTOR (1).

Presidential message. See MESSAGE.

president judge. See *presiding judge* under JUDGE.

president of a court-martial. *Military law.* The senior member in rank present at a court-martial trial.

President of the United States. The highest executive officer of the federal government of the United States. • The President is elected to a four-year term by a majority of the presidential electors chosen by popular vote from each of the states. The President must be a natural citizen, must be at least 35 years old, and must have been a resident for 14 years within the United States. U.S. Const. art. II, § 1.

presiding judge. See JUDGE.

presiding juror. See JUROR.

presiding officer. See OFFICER (2).

press, *n.* **1.** The news media; print and broadcast news organizations collectively. **2.** *Hist.* A piece of parchment, as one sewed together to make up a roll or record of judicial proceedings.

Press Clause. The First Amendment provision that "Congress shall make no law . . . abridging the freedom . . . of the press." U.S. Const. amend I. — Also termed *Freedom of the Press Clause.*

prest (prest). *Hist.* A duty to be paid by the sheriff upon his account in the Exchequer or for money remaining in his custody.

prestation (pre-**stay**-shən). *Hist.* **1.** A payment (or *presting*) of money. **2.** The rendering of a service.

prest money. *Hist.* A monetary payment made to a soldier or sailor on enlistment.

presume, *vb.* To assume beforehand; to suppose to be true in the absence of proof.

presumed bias. See *implied bias* under BIAS.

presumed crime. See *constructive crime* under CRIME.

presumed fact. See FACT.

presumed father. See FATHER.

presumed-seller test. A method of imposing product liability on a manufacturer if the manufacturer, having full knowledge of the product's dangerous propensities, would be negligent in placing the product on the market.

presumption. (15c) A legal inference or assumption that a fact exists, based on the known or proven existence of some other fact or group of facts. • Most presumptions are rules of evidence calling for a certain result in a given case unless the adversely affected party overcomes it with other evidence. A presumption shifts the burden of production or persuasion to the opposing party, who can then attempt to overcome the presumption. See BURDEN OF PRODUCTION.

absolute presumption. See *conclusive presumption.*

adverse presumption. See *adverse inference* under INFERENCE.

artificial presumption. See *presumption of law.*

conclusive presumption. (18c) A presumption that cannot be overcome by any additional evidence or argument <it is a conclusive presumption that a child under the age of seven is incapable of committing a felony>. — Also termed *absolute presumption; irrebuttable presumption; mandatory presumption; presumption juris et de jure.* Cf. *rebuttable presumption.*

conditional presumption. See *rebuttable presumption.*

conflicting presumption. (1830) One of two or more presumptions that would lead to opposite results. — Also termed *inconsistent presumption.*

disputable presumption. See *rebuttable presumption.*

dry presumption. A presumption that has no probative value unless the party with the burden of proof presents evidence to support the presumption.

factual presumption. See *presumption of fact.*

heeding presumption. (1990) A rebuttable presumption that an injured product user would have followed a warning label had the product manufacturer provided one.

inconsistent presumption. See *conflicting presumption.*

irrebuttable presumption. See *conclusive presumption.*

legal presumption. See *presumption of law.*

mandatory presumption. See *conclusive presumption.*

McClanahan presumption. See MCCLANAHAN PRESUMPTION.

mixed presumption. (1838) A presumption containing elements of both law and fact.

Morgan presumption. See MORGAN PRESUMPTION.

natural presumption. (16c) A deduction of one fact from another, based on common experience.

permissive presumption. (1827) A presumption that a trier of fact is free to accept or reject from a given set of facts. — Also termed *permissive inference*.

presumption juris et de jure. See *conclusive presumption*.

presumption of a quorum. *Parliamentary law.* The presumption that a quorum, once established, is present until the chair or a member notices otherwise.

presumption of fact. A type of rebuttable presumption that may be, but as a matter of law need not be, drawn from another established fact or group of facts <the possessor of recently stolen goods is, by presumption of fact, considered the thief>. — Also termed *factual presumption*.

presumption of general application. A presumption that applies across the board to all legislation, as a result of which lawmakers need not list each such presumption in all bills.

presumption of innocence. See PRESUMPTION OF INNOCENCE.

presumption of intent. (18c) A permissive presumption that a criminal defendant who intended to commit an act did so.

presumption of law. (16c) A legal assumption that a court is required to make if certain facts are established and no contradictory evidence is produced <by presumption of law, a criminal defendant is considered innocent until proven guilty beyond a reasonable doubt>. — Also termed *legal presumption*; *artificial presumption*; *praesumptio juris*; *pseudopresumption of law*.

presumption of maternity. See PRESUMPTION OF MATERNITY.

presumption of natural and probable consequences. See PRESUMPTION OF NATURAL AND PROBABLE CONSEQUENCES.

presumption of paternity. See PRESUMPTION OF PATERNITY.

presumption of survivorship. See PRESUMPTION OF SURVIVORSHIP.

presumption of validity. See PRESUMPTIONO OF VALIDITY.

prima facie presumption. See *rebuttable presumption*.

procedural presumption. A presumption that may be rebutted by credible evidence.

pseudopresumption of law. See *presumption of law*.

rebuttable presumption. (1852) An inference drawn from certain facts that establish a prima facie case, which may be overcome by the introduction of contrary evidence. — Also termed *prima facie presumption*; *disputable

presumption*; *conditional presumption*; *praesumptio juris*. Cf. *conclusive presumption*.

statutory presumption. (1819) A rebuttable or conclusive presumption that is created by statute.

Thayer presumption. See THAYER PRESUMPTION.

presumption of death. (18c) A presumption that arises on the unexpected disappearance and continued absence of a person for an extended period, commonly seven years.

presumption-of-fertility rule. See FERTILE-OCTOGENARIAN RULE.

presumption-of-identity rule. The common-law rule that unless there is a specific, applicable statute in another state, a court will presume that the common law has developed elsewhere identically with how it has developed in the court's own state, so that the court may apply its own state's law. • Today this rule applies primarily in Georgia. See *Shorewood Packaging Corp. v. Commercial Union Ins.*, 865 F. Supp. 1577 (N.D. Ga. 1994).

presumption of innocence. (18c) *Criminal law.* The fundamental principle that a person may not be convicted of a crime unless the government proves guilt beyond a reasonable doubt, without any burden placed on the accused to prove innocence.

presumption of legitimacy. See PRESUMPTION OF PATERNITY.

presumption of maternity. *Family law.* The presumption that the woman who has given birth to a child is both the genetic mother and the legal mother of the child. — Also termed *maternity presumption*. Cf. PRESUMPTION OF PATERNITY.

presumption of natural and probable consequences. (1980) *Criminal law.* The presumption that *mens rea* may be derived from proof of the defendant's conduct.

presumption of paternity. (1829) *Family law.* The presumption that the father of a child is the man who (1) is married to the child's mother when the child was conceived or born (even though the marriage may have been invalid), (2) married the mother after the child's birth and agreed either to have his name on the birth certificate or to support the child, or (3) welcomed the child into his home and later held out the child as his own. — Also termed *paternity presumption*; *presumption of legitimacy*; *legitimacy presumption*. See *presumed father* under FATHER.

presumption of survivorship. (1844) The presumption that one of two or more victims of a common disaster survived the others, based on the supposed survivor's youth, good health, or other reason rendering survivorship likely.

presumption of validity. *Patents.* The doctrine that the holder of a patent is entitled to a statutory presumption that the patent is valid and that the burden is on a challenger to prove invalidity. See BORN VALID.

presumptive (pri-**zəmp**-tiv), *adj.* (15c) **1.** Giving reasonable grounds for belief or presumption. **2.** Based on a presumption. — **presumptively,** *adv.*

presumptive authority. See *implied authority* under AUTHORITY (1).

presumptive damages. See *punitive damages* under DAMAGES.

presumptive death. See DEATH.

presumptive evidence. See EVIDENCE.

presumptive heir. See *heir presumptive* under HEIR.

presumptive notice. See *implied notice* under NOTICE.

presumptive proof. See *conditional proof* under PROOF.

presumptive sentence. See SENTENCE.

presumptive sentencing. See SENTENCING.

presumptive taker. See TAKER.

presumptive title. See TITLE (2).

presumptive trust. See *resulting trust* under TRUST.

pret a usage. *Civil law.* A gratuitous loan for use.

pretax, *adj.* Existing or occurring before the assessment or deduction of taxes <pretax income>.

pretax earnings. See EARNINGS.

pretensive joinder. See JOINDER.

preterlegal (pree-tər-**lee**-gəl), *adj. Rare.* Beyond the range of what is legal; not according to law <preterlegal customs>.

pretermission (pree-tər-**mish**-ən). (18c) **1.** The condition of one who is pretermitted, as an heir of a testator. **2.** The act of omitting an heir from a will.

pretermission statute. See PRETERMITTED-HEIR STATUTE.

pretermit (pree-tər-**mit**), *vb.* (15c) **1.** To ignore or disregard purposely <the court pretermitted the constitutional question by deciding the case on procedural grounds>. **2.** To neglect, overlook, or omit accidentally <the third child was pretermitted in the will>. ● Although in ordinary usage sense 1 prevails, in legal contexts (esp. involving heirs) sense 2 is usual.

pretermitted child. See *pretermitted heir* under HEIR.

pretermitted defense. See DEFENSE (1).

pretermitted heir. See HEIR.

pretermitted-heir statute. (1955) A state law that, under certain circumstances, grants an omitted heir the right to inherit a share of the testator's estate, usu. by treating the heir as though the testator had died intestate. ● Most states have a pretermitted-heir statute, under which an omitted child or spouse receives the same share of the estate as if the testator had died intestate, unless the omission was intentional. The majority rule, and that found in the Uniform Probate Code, is that only afterborn children — that is, children born after the execution of a will — receive protection as pretermitted heirs. Under that circumstance, an inference arises that their omission was inadvertent rather than purposeful. — Also termed *pretermission statute.*

pretermitted spouse. See *pretermitted heir* under HEIR.

pretext (**pree**-tekst), *n.* (16c) A false or weak reason or motive advanced to hide the actual or strong reason or motive. — **pretextual** (pree-**teks**-choo-əl), *adj.*

pretextual arrest. See ARREST.

pretorial court (pri-**tor**-ee-əl). See COURT.

pretrial conference. (1938) An informal meeting at which opposing attorneys confer, usu. with the judge, to work toward the disposition of the case by discussing matters of evidence and narrowing the issues that will be tried. *See* Fed. R. Civ. P. 16; Fed. R. Crim. P. 17.1. ● The conference takes place shortly before trial and ordinarily results in a pretrial order. — Often shortened to *pretrial.* — Also termed *pretrial hearing.*

pretrial detention. See DETENTION.

pretrial discovery. See DISCOVERY.

pretrial diversion. See DIVERSION PROGRAM (1).

pretrial hearing. See PRETRIAL CONFERENCE.

pretrial intervention. 1. DIVERSION PROGRAM (1). **2.** See *deferred judgment* under JUDGMENT.

pretrial investigation. *Military law.* An investigation to decide whether a case should be recommended for forwarding to a general court-martial.

pretrial order. (1939) A court order setting out the claims and defenses to be tried, the stipulations of the parties, and the case's procedural rules, as agreed to by the parties or mandated by the court at a pretrial conference. *See* Fed. R. Civ. P. 16(e). ● In federal court, a pretrial order supersedes the pleadings.

prevail, *vb.* (17c) **1.** To obtain the relief sought in an action; to win a lawsuit <the plaintiff prevailed in the Supreme Court>. **2.** To be commonly accepted or predominant <it's unclear which line of precedent will prevail>.

prevailing party. See PARTY (2).

prevarication (pri-var-ə-**kay**-shən), *n.* (16c) The act or an instance of lying or avoiding the truth; equivocation. — **prevaricate** (pri-**var**-ə-kayt), *vb.*

prevaricator (pri-**var**-ə-kay-tər), *n.* [Latin] **1.** A liar; an equivocator. **2.** *Roman law.* One who betrays another's trust, such as an advocate who aids the opposing party by betraying the client. — Also spelled (in sense 2) *praevaricator.*

prevent, *vb.* To hinder or impede <a gag order to prevent further leaks to the press>.

preventative law. See PREVENTIVE LAW.

prevention. *Civil law.* The right of one of several judges having concurrent jurisdiction to exercise that jurisdiction over a case that the judge is first to hear.

prevention doctrine. (1979) *Contracts.* The principle that each contracting party has an implied duty to not do anything that prevents the other party from performing its obligation. — Also termed *prevention-of-performance doctrine.*

preventive custody. See CUSTODY (1).

preventive detention. See DETENTION.

preventive injunction. See INJUNCTION.

preventive justice. See JUSTICE (1).

preventive law. A practice of law that seeks to minimize a client's risk of litigation or secure more certainty with regard to the client's legal rights and duties. ● Emphasizing planning, counseling, and the nonadversarial resolution of disputes, preventive law focuses on the lawyer's role as adviser and negotiator. — Also termed (less correctly) *preventative law.*

preventive punishment. See PUNISHMENT.

previously taxed income. See INCOME.

previous notice. See NOTICE (6).

previous question. See CLOSE DEBATE.

price. The amount of money or other consideration asked for or given in exchange for something else; the cost at which something is bought or sold.

  agreed price. The price for a sale, esp. of goods, arrived at by mutual agreement. Cf. *open price.*

  arm's-length price. The price at which two unrelated, unaffiliated, and nondesperate parties would freely agree to do business. See *arm's-length transaction* under TRANSACTION; *fair market value* under VALUE.

  asked price. The lowest price at which a seller is willing to sell a security at a given time. See SPREAD (2).

  asking price. The price at which a seller lists property for sale, often implying a willingness to sell for less. — Also termed *ask price; offering price.*

  at-the-market price. A retail price that store owners in the same vicinity generally charge.

  bid price. The highest price that a prospective buyer is willing to pay for a security at a given time. See SPREAD (2).

  call price. **1.** The price at which a bond may be retired before its maturity. **2.** See *strike price.*

  ceiling price. **1.** The highest price at which a buyer is willing to buy. **2.** The highest price allowed by a government agency or by some other regulatory institution.

  closing price. The price of a security at the end of a given trading day. — Also termed *close.*

  exercise price. See *strike price.*

  ex-works price. The price of goods as they leave the factory. See EX WORKS.

  fixed price. A price that is agreed upon by a wholesaler and a retailer for the later sale or resale of an item. ● Agreements to fix prices are generally prohibited by state and federal statutes.

  floor price. The lowest price at which a seller is willing to sell.

  liquidating price. See *redemption price.*

  liquidation price. A price that is paid for property sold to liquidate a debt. ● Liquidation price is usu. below market price. — Also termed *liquidation value.*

  list price. A published or advertised price of goods; retail price.

  market price. The prevailing price at which something is sold in a specific market. See *fair market value* under VALUE (2).

  mean trading price. *Securities.* The average of the daily trading price of a security determined at the close of the market each day during a 90-day period.

  net price. The price of something, after deducting cash discounts.

  offering price. See *asking price.*

  open price. The price for a sale, esp. of goods, that has not been settled at the time of a sale's conclusion. UCC § 2-305. Cf. *agreed price.*

  predatory price. See PREDATORY PRICING.

  put price. See *strike price.*

  redemption price. **1.** The price of a bond that has not reached maturity, purchased at the issuer's option. **2.** The price of shares when a mutual-fund shareholder sells shares back to the fund. — Also termed *liquidating price; repurchase price.*

  reserve price. In an auction, the amount that a seller of goods stipulates as the lowest acceptable offer. ● The reserve price may or may not be announced. See WITH RESERVE; WITHOUT RESERVE.

sales price. The total amount for which property is sold, often including the costs of any services that are a part of the sale. • Under sales-tax statutes, the amount is typically valued in money even if the value is not received in money. — Also termed *selling price*.

spot price. The amount for which a commodity is sold in a spot market.

strike price. *Securities.* The price for which a security will be bought or sold under an option contract if the option is exercised. — Also termed *striking price; exercise price; call price; put price.* See OPTION.

subscription price. See SUBSCRIPTION PRICE.

suggested retail price. The sales price recommended to a retailer by a manufacturer of the product.

support price. A minimum price set by the federal government for a particular agricultural commodity.

target price. A price set by the federal government for particular agricultural commodities. • If the market price falls below the target price, farmers receive a subsidy from the government for the difference.

trade price. The price at which a manufacturer or wholesaler sells to others in the same business or industry.

transfer price. The price charged by one segment of an organization for a product or service supplied to another segment of the same organization; esp., the charge assigned to an exchange of goods or services between a corporation's organizational units.

unit price. A price of a food product expressed in a well-known measure such as ounces or pounds.

upset price. The lowest amount that a seller is willing to accept for property or goods sold at auction.

wholesale price. The price that a retailer pays for goods purchased (usu. in bulk) from a wholesaler for resale to consumers at a higher price.

price amendment. *Securities.* A change in a registration statement, prospectus, or prospectus supplement affecting the offering price, the underwriting and selling discounts or commissions, the amount of proceeds, the conversion rates, the call prices, or some other matter relating to the offering price.

price/cost analysis. A technique of determining, for antitrust purposes, whether predatory pricing has occurred by examining the relationship between a defendant's prices and either its average variable cost or its average total cost.

price discrimination. (1915) The practice of offering identical or similar goods to different buyers at different prices when the costs of producing the goods are the same. • Price discrimination can violate antitrust laws if it reduces competition. It may be either direct, as when a seller charges different prices to different buyers, or indirect, as when a seller offers special concessions (such as favorable credit terms) to some but not all buyers.

persistent price discrimination. A monopolist's systematic policy of obtaining different rates of return from different sales groupings.

price-earnings ratio. The ratio between a stock's current share price and the corporation's earnings per share for the last year. • Some investors avoid stocks with high price-earnings ratios because those stocks may be overpriced. — Abbr. P/E ratio. Cf. *earnings yield* under YIELD.

price-erosion theory. *Patents.* A theory of lost-profits remedy that measures the difference between what an item could have sold for with patent protection and what it actually sold for while having to compete against an infringing item.

price expectancy. See EXHIBITION VALUE.

price-fixing. (1889) The artificial setting or maintenance of prices at a certain level, contrary to the workings of the free market. • Price-fixing is usu. illegal per se under antitrust law. See FIX (3).

horizontal price-fixing. (1935) Price-fixing among competitors on the same level, such as retailers throughout an industry.

vertical price-fixing. (1936) Price-fixing among parties in the same chain of distribution, such as manufacturers and retailers attempting to control an item's resale price.

price index. An index of average prices as a percentage of the average prevailing at some other time (such as a base year). See CONSUMER PRICE INDEX; PRODUCER PRICE INDEX.

price leadership. (1942) A market condition in which an industry leader establishes a price that others in the field adopt as their own. • Price leadership alone does not violate antitrust laws without other evidence of an intent to create a monopoly.

price-level-adjusted mortgage. See MORTGAGE.

price memorandum. *Securities.* A document created by an underwriter to explain how securities are priced for a public offering and, typically, to show estimates and appraisals that are not allowed as part of the offering documents.

price-renegotiation clause. *Oil & gas.* A provision in a gas contract allowing for price renegotiation from time to time or upon election of one of the parties.

price squeeze. *Antitrust.* Discriminatory pricing practiced by a manufacturer or distributor who also supplies materials or products to a competitor, and charges a high wholesale price in an attempt to reduce or eliminate a competitor's ability to make a retail profit.

price support. (1927) The artificial maintenance of prices (as of a particular commodity) at a certain level, esp. by governmental action (as by subsidy).

price war. (1895) A period of sustained or repeated price-cutting in an industry (esp. among retailers), designed to undersell competitors or force them out of business.

priest–penitent privilege. See PRIVILEGE (3).

prima facie (**prI**-mə **fay**-shə *or* **fay**-shee), *adv.* [Latin] (15c) At first sight; on first appearance but subject to further evidence or information <the agreement is prima facie valid>.

prima facie, *adj.* (18c) Sufficient to establish a fact or raise a presumption unless disproved or rebutted <a prima facie showing>.

prima facie case. (1805) **1.** The establishment of a legally required rebuttable presumption. **2.** A party's production of enough evidence to allow the fact-trier to infer the fact at issue and rule in the party's favor.

prima facie evidence. See EVIDENCE.

prima facie presumption. See *rebuttable presumption* under PRESUMPTION.

prima facie privilege. See *qualified immunity* under IMMUNITY (1).

prima facie tort. See TORT.

primage (**prI**-mij). See HAT MONEY.

primary, *n.* See *primary election* under ELECTION (3).

primary activity. *Labor law.* Concerted action (such as a strike or picketing) directed against an employer with which a union has a dispute. Cf. SECONDARY ACTIVITY.

primary agent. See AGENT (2).

primary allegation. See ALLEGATION.

primary amendment. See AMENDMENT (3).

primary assumption of the risk. See ASSUMPTION OF THE RISK.

primary authority. See AUTHORITY (4).

primary beneficiary. See BENEFICIARY.

primary boycott. See BOYCOTT.

primary caregiver. *Family law.* **1.** The parent who has had the greatest responsibility for the daily care and rearing of a child. See TENDER-YEARS DOCTRINE; PRIMARY-CAREGIVER DOCTRINE. **2.** The person (including a nonparent) who has had the greatest responsibility for the daily care and rearing of a child. — Also termed *primary caretaker.*

primary-caregiver doctrine. *Family law.* The presumption that, in a custody dispute, the parent who is a child's main caregiver will be the child's custodian, assuming that he or she is a fit parent. ● This doctrine includes the quality and the quantity of care that a parent gives a child — but excludes supervisory care by others while the child is in the parent's custody. Under this doctrine, courts sometimes divide children into three age groups: those under the age of 6, those 6 to 14, and those 14 and older. For children under the age of 6, an absolute presumption exists in favor of the primary caretaker as custodian. For those 6 to 14, the trial court may hear the child's preference on the record but without the parents being present. For those 14 and older, the child may be allowed to choose which parent will be the custodian, assuming that both parents are fit. — Also termed *primary-caretaker doctrine; primary-caregiver presumption; primary-caretaker presumption; primary-caregiver preference.* Cf. MATERNAL-PREFERENCE PRESUMPTION; TENDER-YEARS DOCTRINE.

primary caretaker. See PRIMARY CAREGIVER.

primary cause. See *proximate cause* under CAUSE (1).

primary committee. *Bankruptcy.* A group of creditors organized to help the debtor draw up a reorganization plan.

primary conveyance. See CONVEYANCE.

primary devise. See DEVISE.

primary domiciliary parent. See PARENT.

primary-duty doctrine. *Maritime law.* The principle that a seaman cannot recover damages if the injury arose from an unseaworthy condition created by the seaman's breach of duty.

primary election. See ELECTION (3).

primary evidence. See *best evidence* under EVIDENCE.

primary fact. See FACT.

primary insurance. See INSURANCE.

primary insured. See INSURED.

primary insurer. See INSURER.

primary jurisdiction. See JURISDICTION.

primary-jurisdiction doctrine. A judicial doctrine whereby a court tends to favor allowing an agency an initial opportunity to decide an issue in a case in which the court and the agency have concurrent jurisdiction. See *primary jurisdiction* under JURISDICTION.

primary lease. See HEADLEASE.

primary liability. See LIABILITY.

primary-line competition. See *horizontal competition* under COMPETITION.

primary-line injury. *Antitrust.* Under the price-discrimination provisions of the Robinson-Patman Act, the practice of charging below-cost, predatory prices in an attempt to eliminate the seller's competition in the market. 15 USCA § 13(a). ● A primary-line injury, which hinders or seeks to hinder competition among the seller's competitors, is distinguishable from a secondary-line injury, which refers to discriminatory pricing that hinders or seeks to hinder competition among the seller's customers, by favoring one customer over another in the prices the seller charges. Cf. SECONDARY-LINE INJURY.

primary market. See MARKET.

primary mortgage market. See MORTGAGE MARKET.

primary obligation. See OBLIGATION.

primary offering. See OFFERING.

primary officer. See *principal officer* under OFFICER (1).

primary plea. See *primary allegation* under ALLEGATION.

primary powers. (1864) The chief powers given by a principal to an agent to accomplish the agent's tasks. Cf. MEDIATE POWERS.

primary purpose or effect. *Copyright.* The main reason for or consequence of using a product, as a test for whether its sale amounts to contributory infringement. ● The Supreme Court rejected the test in a landmark copyright case, but four justices said that if the primary purpose or effect of the product's sale or use infringes the copyrights of others, its manufacturer could be enjoined from selling the product or required to pay a reasonable royalty to the copyright owners. *Sony Corp. of Am. v. Universal City Studios, Inc.*, 464 U.S. 417, 457–500, 104 S.Ct. 774, 796–818 (1984) (Blackmun, J., dissenting). Cf. COMMERCIALLY SIGNIFICANT NONINFRINGING USE.

primary receiver. See *principal receiver* under RECEIVER.

primary reserve ratio. See RESERVE RATIO.

primary residential responsibility. See RESIDENTIAL RESPONSIBILITY.

primary right. See RIGHT.

primary term. *Oil & gas.* The option period — set by the habendum clause in an oil-and-gas lease — during which the lessee has the right to search, develop, and produce from the property. ● The primary term should be long enough to allow the lessee to evaluate the property and make arrangements to drill. In practice, the primary term may extend for 24 hours or 25 years, depending on how much competition there is for leases in the area. See HABENDUM CLAUSE. Cf. SECONDARY TERM.

primate (**prɪ**-mit). A chief ecclesiastic; an archbishop or bishop having jurisdiction over other bishops within a province.

prime, *n.* See *prime rate* under INTEREST RATE.

prime, *vb.* To take priority over <Watson's preferred mortgage primed Moriarty's lien>.

prime contractor. See *general contractor* under CONTRACTOR.

prime cost. See COST (1).

prime lending rate. See *prime rate* under INTEREST RATE.

prime maker. See MAKER.

prime minister. (*often cap.*) The chief executive of a parliamentary government; the head of a cabinet. — Abbr. PM.

primer (**prim**-ər *or* **prɪ**-mər). [Law French] First; primary <primer seisin>.

prime rate. See INTEREST RATE.

primer election. A first choice; esp., the eldest coparcener's pick of land on division of the estate. See ELECTION.

primer seisin. See SEISIN.

prime serjeant. See *premier serjeant* under SERJEANT-AT-LAW.

prime tenant. See TENANT.

primitiae (pri-**mish**-ee-ee). [fr. Latin *primus* "first"] See FIRST FRUITS (2). — **primitial** (pri-**mish**-əl), *adj.*

primitive obligation. See OBLIGATION.

primogeniture (prɪ-mə-**jen**-ə-chər). (15c) **1.** The state of being the firstborn child among siblings. **2.** The common-law right of the firstborn son to inherit his ancestor's estate, usu. to the exclusion of younger siblings. — Also termed (in sense 2) *primogenitureship*. See BOROUGH ENGLISH.

principal, *adj.* Chief; primary; most important.

principal, *n.* (14c) **1.** One who authorizes another to act on his or her behalf as an agent. Cf. AGENT (2).

  apparent principal. A person who, by outward manifestations, has made it reasonably appear to a third person that another is authorized to act as the person's agent.

  disclosed principal. (1858) A principal whose identity is revealed by the agent to a third party. ● A disclosed principal is always liable on a contract entered into by the agent with the principal's authority, but the agent is usu. not liable.

  partially disclosed principal. (1934) A principal whose existence — but not actual identity — is revealed by the agent to a third party.

undisclosed principal. (1835) A principal whose identity is kept secret by the agent; a principal for whom the other party has no notice that the agent is acting. ● An undisclosed principal and the agent are both liable on a contract entered into by the agent with the principal's authority.

2. One who commits or participates in a crime. Cf. ACCESSORY (2); ACCOMPLICE (2).

principal in the first degree. (18c) The perpetrator of a crime. — Also termed *first-degree principal.*

principal in the second degree. (18c) One who helped the perpetrator at the time of the crime. — Also termed *accessory at the fact; second-degree principal.* See ABETTOR.

3. One who has primary responsibility on an obligation, as opposed to a surety or indorser. **4.** The corpus of an estate or trust. **5.** The amount of a debt, investment, or other fund, not including interest, earnings, or profits.

principal action. See *main demand* under DEMAND (1).

principal challenge. See CHALLENGE (2).

principal contract. See CONTRACT.

principal covenant. See COVENANT (1).

principal creditor. See CREDITOR.

principal demand. See *main demand* under DEMAND (1).

principal fact. 1. See *fact in issue* under FACT. **2.** See *ultimate fact* under FACT.

principal in the first degree. See PRINCIPAL (2).

principal in the second degree. See PRINCIPAL (2).

principal motion. See *main motion* under MOTION (2).

principal obligation. See *primary obligation* (2) under OBLIGATION.

principal obligor. See OBLIGOR.

principal officer. See OFFICER (1).

principal place of business. See PLACE OF BUSINESS.

principal receiver. See RECEIVER.

Principal Register. *Trademarks.* The list of distinctive marks approved for federal trademark registration. ● The register is maintained by the U.S. Patent and Trademark Office. Only marks that are strong, distinctive, and famous are listed. 15 USCA § 1052. Cf. SUPPLEMENTAL REGISTER.

principal right. See RIGHT.

principle, *n.* A basic rule, law, or doctrine.

principle of finality. See FINALITY DOCTRINE.

principle of legality. See LEGALITY (2).

principle of nonintervention. See NONINTERVENTION.

principle of retribution. See LEX TALIONIS.

print. 1. *Copyright.* The impression made in a material by a die, mold, stamp, or the like; a distinctive stamped or printed mark or design. **2.** FINGERPRINT.

printed-matter doctrine. *Patents.* The rule that printed matter may not be patented unless it is a physical part of a patentable invention. ● For example, the doctrine has been used to deny patents for systems of representing sheet music and for methods of compiling directories. But it cannot be used to deny a patent for computer software.

Printers Ink Statute. A model statute drafted in 1911 and adopted in a number of states making it a misdemeanor to print an advertisement that contains a false or deceptive statement.

prior, *adj.* (17c) **1.** Preceding in time or order <under this court's prior order>. **2.** Taking precedence <a prior lien>.

prior, *n.* (1919) *Criminal law. Slang.* A previous conviction <because the defendant had two priors, the judge automatically enhanced his sentence>.

prior-acts coverage. *Insurance.* A claims-made professional-liability policy indorsement that makes the effective date retroactive and extends the policy's protection to claims made and lawsuits filed during the policy period for negligent acts that occurred before the policy was actually purchased. — Also termed *nose coverage.* Cf. TAIL COVERAGE.

prior and persistent offender. See RECIDIVIST.

prior-appropriation doctrine. (1959) The rule that, among the persons whose properties border on a waterway, the earliest users of the water have the right to take all they can use before anyone else has a right to it. Cf. RIPARIAN-RIGHTS DOCTRINE.

prior art. See ART.

prior-claim rule. The principle that before suing for a tax refund or abatement, a taxpayer must first assert the claim to the Internal Revenue Service.

prior consistent statement. See STATEMENT.

prior creditor. See CREDITOR.

prior-exclusive-jurisdiction doctrine. The rule that a court will not assume in rem jurisdiction over property that is already under the jurisdiction of another court of concurrent jurisdiction.

prior inconsistent statement. See STATEMENT.

priority. (15c) **1.** The status of being earlier in time or higher in degree or rank; precedence. **2.** *Commercial law.* An established right to such precedence; esp., a creditor's right to have a claim paid before other creditors of the same debtor receive payment. **3.** The doctrine that, as between two courts, jurisdiction should be accorded the court in which proceedings are first begun. **4.** *Patents & Trademarks.* The status of being first to invent something (and therefore be potentially eligible for patent protection) or to use a mark in trade (and therefore be potentially eligible for trademark registration).

priority of adoption. *Trademarks.* Priority in designing or creating a trademark. • Priority of adoption does not in itself confer the right to exclusive use of a mark if someone else was first to use it in commerce. — Also termed *priority of appropriation*; *priority of invention*. Cf. *priority of use.*

priority of appropriation. *Trademarks.* See *priority of adoption.*

priority of invention. 1. *Patents.* The determination that one among several patent applications, for substantially the same invention, should receive the patent when the U.S. Patent and Trademark Office has declared interference. • This determination depends on the date of conception, the date of reduction to practice, and diligence. **2.** *Trademarks.* See *priority of adoption.*

priority of use. *Trademarks.* Priority in using a mark in actual commerce. • The priority of use, not the priority of adoption, determines who has the right to protection. Cf. *priority of adoption.*

priority award. *Patents.* A final judgment by the U.S. Patent and Trademark Office designating one party in an interference contest as the first inventor. — Also termed *award in interference.*

priority claim. See CLAIM (5).

priority contest. See INTERFERENCE (3).

priority date. See DATE.

priority-jurisdiction rule. See FIRST-TO-FILE RULE.

priority lien. See *prior lien* under LIEN.

priority of liens. The ranking of liens in the order in which they are perfected.

prior lien. See LIEN.

prior preferred stock. See STOCK.

prior publication. *Patents.* Public disclosure of the basis for or existence of an invention, made before filing a patent application for the invention. • If the publication was made more than a year before the application is filed, the patent is barred by statute. Publication occurs when the information is made available to any member of the general public. See *limited publication* under PUBLICATION.

prior-relationship rape. See *relationship rape* under RAPE.

prior restraint. (1833) A governmental restriction on speech or publication before its actual expression. • Prior restraints violate the First Amendment unless the speech is obscene, is defamatory, or creates a clear and present danger to society.

prior sale. *Patents.* Sale or offer of sale of an invention before a patent is applied for. • If the sale occurred more than one year before the application is filed, the patent is barred by statute. 35 USCA § 102(b).

prior sentence. See SENTENCE.

prior-use bar. See PUBLIC-USE BAR.

prior-use doctrine. (1856) The principle that, without legislative authorization, a government agency may not appropriate property already devoted to a public use.

prior-user right. *Patents.* The right of a first inventor to continue using an invention after someone else has patented it. • This right protects first inventors in most countries from the harsh effects of a first-to-file system.

prison. (bef. 12c) A state or federal facility of confinement for convicted criminals, esp. felons. — Also termed *penitentiary*; *penal institution*; *adult correctional institution*. Cf. JAIL.

private prison. (1865) A prison that is managed by a private company, not by a governmental agency.

prison breach. (17c) A prisoner's forcible breaking and departure from a place of lawful confinement; the offense of escaping from confinement in a prison or jail. • *Prison breach* has traditionally been distinguished from *escape* by the presence of force, but some jurisdictions have abandoned this distinction. — Also termed *prison breaking*; *breach of prison*. Cf. ESCAPE (2).

prison camp. (1864) A usu. minimum-security camp for the detention of trustworthy prisoners who are often employed on government projects.

prisoner. 1. A person who is serving time in prison. **2.** A person who has been apprehended by a law-enforcement officer and is in custody, regardless of whether the person has yet been put in prison. Cf. CAPTIVE (1).

prisoner at the bar. (16c) *Archaic.* An accused person who is on trial.

prisoner of conscience. *Human-rights law.* A person who is imprisoned because of his or her beliefs, race, sex, ethnic origin, language, or religion. • The range of "beliefs" that fall within this definition is not settled but may include political ideologies and objections to military service, esp. in wartime.

prisoner of war. A person, usu. a soldier, who is captured by or surrenders to the enemy in

wartime. — Also termed *captive*. — Abbr.
POW.

prisoner's dilemma. A logic problem — often used
by law-and-economics scholars to illustrate the
effect of cooperative behavior — involving two
prisoners who are being separately questioned
about their participation in a crime: (1) if both
confess, they will each receive a 5-year sentence;
(2) if neither confesses, they will each receive a
3-year sentence; and (3) if one confesses but the
other does not, the confessing prisoner will receive a 1-year sentence while the silent prisoner
will receive a 10-year sentence. See EXTERNAL-
ITY.

Prison Litigation Reform Act. A federal statute
designed to reduce the number of frivolous lawsuits and petitions filed by prisoners and to reduce the power of federal courts over state prison
systems. 110 Stat. 1321-66–1321-77 (1996).

privacy. The condition or state of being free from
public attention to intrusion into or interference
with one's acts or decisions.

   autonomy privacy. An individual's right to control his or her personal activities or intimate
personal decisions without outside interference,
observation, or intrusion. ● If the individual's
interest in an activity or decision is fundamental,
the state must show a compelling public interest before the private interest can be overcome.
If the individual's interest is acknowledged to
be less than fundamental or is disputed, then a
court must apply a balancing test. *Hill v. NCAA*,
865 P.2d 633, 653, 654 (Cal. 1994).

   informational privacy. Tort. A private person's
right to choose to determine whether, how,
and to what extent information about oneself
is communicated to others, esp. sensitive and
confidential information.

privacy, invasion of. See INVASION OF PRIVACY.

privacy, right of. See RIGHT OF PRIVACY.

privacy act. See PRIVACY LAW (1).

Privacy Act of 1974. An act that regulates the government's creation, collection, use, and dissemination of records that can identify an individual
by name, as well as other personal information.
18 USCA § 552a.

privacy law. (1936) **1.** A federal or state statute that
protects a person's right to be left alone or that
restricts public access to personal information
such as tax returns and medical records. — Also
termed *privacy act.* **2.** The area of legal studies
dealing with a person's right to be left alone and
with restricting public access to personal information such as tax returns and medical records.

privacy privilege. See PRIVILEGE (3).

private, *adj.* (14c) **1.** Relating or belonging to
an individual, as opposed to the public or the
government. **2.** (Of a company) not having shares
that are freely available on an open market. **3.**
Confidential; secret.

private act. See *special statute* under STATUTE.

private action. See *civil action* under ACTION (4).

private adoption. See ADOPTION.

private agent. See AGENT (2).

private annuity. See ANNUITY.

private attorney. See ATTORNEY (1).

private-attorney-general doctrine. The equitable
principle that allows the recovery of attorney's
fees to a party who brings a lawsuit that benefits
a significant number of people, requires private
enforcement, and is important to society as a
whole.

private bank. See BANK.

private benefit. *Tax.* The use of a tax-exempt organization's assets primarily to further the interests
of a private individual or entity, rather than for a
public interest. ● Under most circumstances, this
type of benefit is prohibited. *See* IRC (26 USCA)
§ 501(c)(3). Cf. *private inurement* under INURE-
MENT.

   qualitatively incidental private benefit. A permissible private benefit arising from circumstances under which a benefit to the public
cannot be achieved without necessarily also
benefiting a private interest.

   quantitatively incidental private benefit. A permissible private benefit that is a necessary but
insubstantial concomitant to a public benefit.

private bill. See BILL (3).

private boundary. See BOUNDARY.

private brand. See BRAND.

private carrier. See CARRIER.

private contract. See CONTRACT.

private corporation. See CORPORATION.

private delict. See DELICT.

private easement. See EASEMENT.

privateer (prī-və-teer), *n.* **1.** A vessel owned and
operated by private persons, but authorized by a
nation on certain conditions to damage the commerce of the enemy by acts of piracy. **2.** A sailor
on such a vessel.

privateering, *n. Int'l law.* The practice of arming
privately owned merchant ships for the purpose of
attacking enemy trading ships. ● Before the practice was outlawed, governments commissioned
privateers by issuing letters of marque to their
merchant fleets. Privateering was prohibited by
the Declaration of Paris Concerning Naval Warfare of 1856, which has been observed by nearly
all nations since that time. — **privateer,** *vb.*

private fact. See FACT.

private foundation. See FOUNDATION.

private grant. See GRANT.

private injury. See *personal injury* (2) under IN-JURY.

private international law. See INTERNATIONAL LAW.

private inurement. See INUREMENT.

private judging. (1979) A type of alternative dispute resolution whereby the parties hire a private individual to hear and decide a case. ● This process may occur as a matter of contract between the parties or in connection with a statute authorizing such a process. — Also termed *rent-a-judging*.

private land grant. See LAND GRANT.

private law. (18c) **1.** The body of law dealing with private persons and their property and relationships. Cf. PUBLIC LAW (1). **2.** See *special law* under LAW.

private letter ruling. See LETTER RULING.

private morality. See MORALITY.

private mortgage insurance. See *mortgage insurance* under INSURANCE.

private necessity. See NECESSITY.

private nonoperating foundation. See *private foundation* under FOUNDATION.

private nuisance. See NUISANCE.

private offering. See OFFERING.

private operating foundation. See FOUNDATION.

private person. See PERSON (1).

private placement. 1. *Family law.* The placement of a child for adoption by a parent, lawyer, doctor, or private agency, rather than by a government agency. ● At least eight states have prohibited private-placement adoptions. — Also termed *direct placement.* **2.** *Securities.* See *private offering* under OFFERING.

private-placement adoption. See *private adoption* under ADOPTION.

private power. See POWER (3).

private prison. See PRISON.

private property. See PROPERTY.

private prosecution. See PROSECUTION.

private prosecutor. See PROSECUTOR (2).

private publication. See *limited publication* under PUBLICATION.

private reprimand. See REPRIMAND.

private right. See RIGHT.

private right-of-way. See EASEMENT.

private river. See RIVER.

private sale. See SALE.

private school. See SCHOOL.

private seal. See SEAL.

private search. See SEARCH.

private sector. (1930) The part of the economy or an industry that is free from direct governmental control. Cf. PUBLIC SECTOR.

private servitude. See SERVITUDE (2).

private signature. See SIGNATURE.

private statute. See *special statute* under STATUTE.

private stream. See STREAM.

private treaty. See TREATY (3).

private trust. See TRUST.

private-use exception. *Patents.* An exception to the public-use statutory bar, allowing the inventor to use the invention for personal benefit for more than one year without abandoning patent rights under the statutory bars. — Also termed *prior-user right.*

private voluntary organization. See NONGOVERNMENTAL ORGANIZATION.

private war. See WAR.

private water. See WATER.

private way. See WAY.

private wharf. See WHARF.

private wrong. See WRONG.

private zoning. See ZONING.

privation (prI-**vay**-shən). (15c) **1.** The act of taking away or withdrawing. **2.** The condition of being deprived.

privatization (prI-və-tə-**zay**-shən), *n.* (1942) The act or process of converting a business or industry from governmental ownership or control to private enterprise. Cf. DENATIONALIZATION (2). — **privatize,** *vb.*

privies (**priv**-eez). See PRIVY.

privilege. (bef. 12c) **1.** A special legal right, exemption, or immunity granted to a person or class of persons; an exception to a duty. ● A privilege grants someone the legal freedom to do or not to do a given act. It immunizes conduct that, under ordinary circumstances, would subject the actor to liability.

> *absolute privilege.* (18c) A privilege that immunizes an actor from suit, no matter how wrongful the action might be, and even though it is done with an improper motive. Cf. *qualified privilege.*

> *audit privilege.* See AUDIT PRIVILEGE.

> *conditional privilege.* See *qualified privilege.*

> *courtroom privilege.* See *judicial privilege.*

> *defamation privilege.* See *litigation privilege.*

deliberative-process privilege. (1977) A privilege permitting the government to withhold documents relating to policy formulation to encourage open and independent discussion among those who develop government policy.

judicial privilege. (1845) *Defamation.* **1.** The privilege protecting any statement made in the course of and with reference to a judicial proceeding by any judge, juror, party, witness, or advocate. **2.** See *litigation privilege.* — Also termed *courtroom privilege.*

judicial-proceedings privilege. See *litigation privilege.*

legislative privilege. (1941) *Defamation.* The privilege protecting (1) any statement made in a legislature by one of its members, and (2) any paper published as part of legislative business. — Also termed (in a parliamentary system) *parliamentary privilege.*

litigation privilege. A privilege protecting the attorneys and parties in a lawsuit against tort claims based on certain acts done and statements made when related to the litigation. • The privilege is most often applied to defamation claims but may be extended to encompass other torts, such as invasion of privacy and disclosure of trade secrets. The facts of each case determine whether the privilege applies and whether it is qualified or absolute. — Also termed *judicial-proceedings privilege*; *judicial privilege*; *defamation privilege.*

official privilege. (1927) The privilege immunizing from a defamation lawsuit any statement made by one state officer to another in the course of official duty.

parliamentary privilege. **1.** See *legislative privilege.* **2.** PRIVILEGE (5).

privilege from arrest. (1840) An exemption from arrest, as that enjoyed by members of Congress during legislative sessions. U.S. Const. art. I, § 6, cl. 1.

qualified privilege. (1865) A privilege that immunizes an actor from suit only when the privilege is properly exercised in the performance of a legal or moral duty. — Also termed *conditional privilege.* Cf. *absolute privilege.*

special privilege. (17c) **1.** A privilege granted to a person or class of persons to the exclusion of others and in derogation of the common right. **2.** See *personal privilege* under PRIVILEGE (5).

testimonial privilege. (1907) A right not to testify based on a claim of privilege; a privilege that overrides a witness's duty to disclose matters within the witness's knowledge, whether at trial or by deposition.

viatorial privilege (vI-ə-**tor**-ee-əl). (1904) A privilege that overrides a person's duty to attend court in person and to testify.

work-product privilege. See WORK-PRODUCT RULE.

2. An affirmative defense by which a defendant acknowledges at least part of the conduct complained of but asserts that the defendant's conduct was authorized or sanctioned by law; esp., in tort law, a circumstance justifying or excusing an intentional tort. See JUSTIFICATION (2). Cf. IMMUNITY (2). **3.** An evidentiary rule that gives a witness the option to not disclose the fact asked for, even though it might be relevant; the right to prevent disclosure of certain information in court, esp. when the information was originally communicated in a professional or confidential relationship. • Assertion of an evidentiary privilege can be overcome by proof that an otherwise privileged communication was made in the presence of a third party to whom the privilege would not apply.

accountant–client privilege. (1956) The protection afforded to a client from an accountant's unauthorized disclosure of materials submitted to or prepared by the accountant. • The privilege is not widely recognized.

antimarital-facts privilege. See *marital privilege* (2).

attorney–client privilege. (1934) The client's right to refuse to disclose and to prevent any other person from disclosing confidential communications between the client and the attorney. • The privilege is widely recognized. — Also termed *lawyer–client privilege*; *client's privilege.*

clergyman–penitent privilege. See *priest–penitent privilege.*

client's privilege. See *attorney–client privilege.*

doctor–patient privilege. (1954) The right to exclude from discovery and evidence in a legal proceeding any confidential communication that a patient makes to a physician for the purpose of diagnosis or treatment, unless the patient consents to the disclosure. — Also termed *patient–physician privilege*; *physician–patient privilege*; *physician–client privilege.*

editorial privilege. See *journalist's privilege* (2).

executive privilege. (1909) A privilege, based on the constitutional doctrine of separation of powers, that exempts the executive branch of the federal government from usual disclosure requirements when the matter to be disclosed involves national security or foreign policy. Cf. *executive immunity* under IMMUNITY (1).

husband–wife privilege. See *marital privilege.*

informant's privilege. (1962) The qualified privilege that a government can invoke to prevent disclosure of the identity and communications of its informants. ● In exercising its power to formulate evidentiary rules for federal criminal cases, the U.S. Supreme Court has consistently declined to hold that the government must disclose the identity of informants in a preliminary hearing or in a criminal trial. *McCray v. Illinois,* 386 U.S. 300, 312, 87 S.Ct. 1056, 1063 (1967). A party can, however, usu. overcome the privilege by demonstrating that the need for the information outweighs the public interest in maintaining the privilege. — Also termed *informer's privilege.*

joint-defense privilege. (1975) The rule that a defendant can assert the attorney–client privilege to protect a confidential communication made to a codefendant's lawyer if the communication was related to the defense of both defendants. — Also termed *common-interest doctrine; common-interest privilege; common-interest exception.*

journalist's privilege. (1970) **1.** A reporter's protection, under constitutional or statutory law, from being compelled to testify about confidential information or sources. — Also termed *reporter's privilege; newsman's privilege.* See SHIELD LAW (1). **2.** A publisher's protection against defamation lawsuits when the publication makes fair comment on the actions of public officials in matters of public concern. — Also termed *editorial privilege; common-interest privilege; common-interest exception.* See FAIR COMMENT.

lawyer–client privilege. See *attorney–client privilege.*

marital privilege. (1902) **1.** The privilege allowing a spouse not to testify, and to prevent another person from testifying, about confidential communications between the spouses during the marriage. — Also termed *marital-communications privilege.* **2.** The privilege allowing a spouse not to testify in a criminal case as an adverse witness against the other spouse, regardless of the subject matter of the testimony. — Also termed (in sense 2) *privilege against adverse spousal testimony; antimarital-facts privilege.* **3.** The privilege immunizing from a defamation lawsuit any statement made between husband and wife. — Also termed (in all senses) *spousal privilege; husband–wife privilege.*

national-security privilege. See *state-secrets privilege.*

newsman's privilege. See *journalist's privilege* (1).

patient–physician privilege. See *doctor–patient privilege.*

peer-review privilege. (1979) A privilege that protects from disclosure the proceedings and reports of a medical facility's peer-review committee, which reviews and oversees the patient care and medical services provided by the staff.

physician–client privilege. See *doctor–patient privilege.*

political-vote privilege. A privilege to protect from compulsory disclosure a vote cast in an election by secret ballot.

priest–penitent privilege. (1958) The privilege barring a clergy member from testifying about a confessor's communications. — Also termed *clergyman–penitent privilege.*

privacy privilege. A defendant's right not to disclose private information unless the plaintiff can show that (1) the information is directly relevant to the case, and (2) the plaintiff's need for the information outweighs the defendant's need for nondisclosure. ● This privilege is recognized in California but in few other jurisdictions.

privilege against adverse spousal testimony. See *marital privilege* (2).

privilege against self-incrimination. *Criminal law.* **1.** RIGHT AGAINST SELF-INCRIMINATION. **2.** A criminal defendant's right not to be asked any questions by the judge or prosecution unless the defendant chooses to testify. — Also termed *right not to be questioned.*

psychotherapist–patient privilege. (1968) A privilege that a person can invoke to prevent the disclosure of a confidential communication made in the course of diagnosis or treatment of a mental or emotional condition by or at the direction of a psychotherapist. ● The privilege can be overcome under certain conditions, as when the examination is ordered by a court. — Also termed *psychotherapist–client privilege.*

reporter's privilege. See *journalist's privilege* (1).

self-critical-analysis privilege. (1982) A privilege protecting individuals and entities from divulging the results of candid assessments of their compliance with laws and regulations, to the extent that the assessments are internal, the results were intended from the outset to be confidential, and the information is of a type that would be curtailed if it were forced to be disclosed. ● This privilege is founded on the public policy that it is beneficial to permit individuals and entities to confidentially evaluate their compliance with the law, so that they will monitor and improve their compliance with it. — Also termed *self-policing privilege; self-evaluation privilege.*

spousal privilege. See *marital privilege.*

state-secrets privilege. (1959) A privilege that the government may invoke against the discovery of a material that, if divulged, could compromise national security. — Also termed *national-security privilege*.

tax-return privilege. A privilege to refuse to divulge the contents of a tax return or certain related documents. ● The privilege is founded on the public policy of encouraging honest tax returns.

4. *Civil law.* A creditor's right, arising from the nature of the debt, to priority over the debtor's other creditors. **5.** *Parliamentary law.* The status of a motion as outranking other business because of its relationship to the meeting's or a member's rights. — Also termed *parliamentary privilege*. See *question of privilege* under QUESTION (3).

general privilege. A privilege that concerns the deliberative assembly as a body, rather than any particular member or members. — Also termed *privilege of the assembly*; *privilege of the house*. Cf. *personal privilege*.

parliamentary privilege. 1. A privilege under parliamentary law. **2.** See *legislative privilege* under PRIVILEGE (1).

personal privilege. A privilege that concerns an individual member or members (e.g., a member's reputation or physical ability to hear the proceedings) rather than the deliberative assembly generally. — Also termed *special privilege*. See *procedural point* under POINT. Cf. *general privilege*.

privilege of the assembly. See *general privilege*.

privilege of the floor. *Parliamentary law.* (*usu. pl.*) The right of entering, passing through, and sitting on the floor during a meeting. See FLOOR (1).

privilege of the house. See *general privilege*.

special privilege. See *personal privilege*.

privileged, *adj.* **1.** Not subject to the usual rules or liabilities; esp., not subject to disclosure during the course of a lawsuit <a privileged document>. **2.** Enjoying or subject to a privilege. See *privileged motion* under MOTION (2).

privileged communication. See COMMUNICATION.

privileged debt. See DEBT.

privileged evidence. See EVIDENCE.

privileged motion. See MOTION (2).

privileged question. See QUESTION (3).

privileged subscription. See *rights offering* under OFFERING.

privileged villeinage. See VILLEINAGE.

privilege from arrest. See PRIVILEGE (1).

Privileges and Immunities Clause. (1911) The constitutional provision (U.S. Const. art. IV, § 2, cl. 1) prohibiting a state from favoring its own citizens by discriminating against other states' citizens who come within its borders.

Privileges or Immunities Clause. (1918) The constitutional provision (U.S. Const. amend. XIV, § 1) prohibiting state laws that abridge the privileges or immunities of U.S. citizens. ● The clause was effectively nullified by the Supreme Court in the *Slaughter-House Cases*, 83 U.S. (16 Wall.) 36 (1873). Cf. DUE PROCESS CLAUSE; EQUAL PROTECTION CLAUSE.

privilege tax. See TAX.

privity (**priv-ə-tee**). (16c) **1.** The connection or relationship between two parties, each having a legally recognized interest in the same subject matter (such as a transaction, proceeding, or piece of property); mutuality of interest <privity of contract>.

horizontal privity. (1968) *Commercial law.* The legal relationship between a party and a nonparty who is related to the party (such as a buyer and a member of the buyer's family).

privity of blood. (16c) **1.** Privity between an heir and an ancestor. **2.** Privity between coparceners.

privity of contract. (17c) The relationship between the parties to a contract, allowing them to sue each other but preventing a third party from doing so. ● The requirement of privity has been relaxed under modern laws and doctrines of implied warranty and strict liability, which allow a third-party beneficiary or other foreseeable user to sue the seller of a defective product.

privity of estate. (17c) A mutual or successive relationship to the same right in property, as between grantor and grantee or landlord and tenant. — Also termed *privity of title*; *privity in estate*.

privity of possession. (1818) Privity between parties in successive possession of real property. ● The existence of this type of privity is often at issue in adverse-possession claims.

privity of title. See *privity of estate*.

vertical privity. (1968) **1.** *Commercial law.* The legal relationship between parties in a product's chain of distribution (such as a manufacturer and a seller). **2.** Privity between one who signs a contract containing a restrictive covenant and one who acquires the property burdened by it.

2. Joint knowledge or awareness of something private or secret, esp. as implying concurrence or consent <privity to a crime>.

privy (**priv-ee**), *n. pl.* (15c) A person having a legal interest of privity in any action, matter, or property; a person who is in privity with another. ● Traditionally, there were six types of privies: (1) *privies in blood*, such as an heir and an ancestor;

(2) *privies in representation*, such as an executor and a testator or an administrator and an intestate person; (3) *privies in estate*, such as grantor and grantee or lessor and lessee; (4) *privies in respect to a contract* — the parties to a contract; (5) *privies in respect of estate and contract*, such as a lessor and lessee where the lessee assigns an interest, but the contract between lessor and lessee continues because the lessor does not accept the assignee; and (6) *privies in law*, such as husband and wife. The term also appears in the context of litigation. In this sense, it includes someone who controls a lawsuit though not a party to it; someone whose interests are represented by a party to the lawsuit; and a successor in interest to anyone having a derivative claim. Pl. **privies.**

Privy Council. In Britain, the principal council of the sovereign, composed of the cabinet ministers and other persons chosen by royal appointment to serve as privy councillors. ● The functions of the Privy Council are now mostly ceremonial. See JUDICIAL COMMITTEE OF THE PRIVY COUNCIL.

Privy Councillor. A member of the Privy Council. — Abbr. P.C.

privy seal. 1. A seal used in making out grants or letters patent before they are passed under the great seal. **2.** (*cap.*) LORD PRIVY SEAL.

privy signet. *Hist.* The signet or seal used by the sovereign in making out grants and private letters.

privy verdict. See VERDICT.

prize. 1. Something of value awarded in recognition of a person's achievement. **2.** A vessel or cargo captured at sea or seized in port by the forces of a nation at war, and therefore liable to being condemned or appropriated as enemy property.

prize court. See COURT.

prize fighting. Fighting for a reward or prize; esp., professional boxing.

prize goods. See GOODS.

prize law. The system of laws applicable to the capture of prize at sea, dealing with such matters as the rights of captors and the distribution of the proceeds.

prize money. 1. A dividend from the proceeds of a captured vessel, paid to the captors. **2.** Money offered as an award.

PRM. *abbr.* BUREAU OF POPULATION, REFUGEES, AND MIGRATION.

PRO. *abbr.* PEER-REVIEW ORGANIZATION.

pro (proh). [Latin] (15c) For.

probable cause. (16c) **1.** *Criminal law.* A reasonable ground to suspect that a person has committed or is committing a crime or that a place contains specific items connected with a crime. ● Under the Fourth Amendment, probable cause — which amounts to more than a bare suspicion but less than evidence that would justify a conviction — must be shown before an arrest warrant or search warrant may be issued. — Also termed *reasonable cause; sufficient cause; reasonable grounds; reasonable excuse* Cf. *reasonable suspicion* under SUSPICION. **2.** *Torts.* A reasonable belief in the existence of facts on which a claim is based and in the legal validity of the claim itself. ● In this sense, probable cause is usu. assessed as of the time when the claimant brings the claim (as by filing suit). **3.** A reasonable basis to support issuance of an administrative warrant based on either (1) specific evidence of an existing violation of administrative rules, or (2) evidence showing that a particular business meets the legislative or administrative standards permitting an inspection of the business premises.

probable-cause hearing. 1. See PRELIMINARY HEARING. **2.** See *shelter hearing* under HEARING.

probable consequence. (16c) An effect or result that is more likely than not to follow its supposed cause.

probable-desistance test. (1974) *Criminal law.* A common-law test for the crime of attempt, focusing on whether the defendant has exhibited dangerous behavior indicating a likelihood of committing the crime. See ATTEMPT (2).

probable evidence. See *presumptive evidence* under EVIDENCE.

probandum (proh-**ban**-dəm), *n.* A fact to be proved. See *fact in issue* under FACT. Pl. **probanda.**

probate (proh-bayt), *n.* (15c) **1.** The judicial procedure by which a testamentary document is established to be a valid will; the proving of a will to the satisfaction of the court. ● Unless set aside, the probate of a will is conclusive upon the parties to the proceedings (and others who had notice of them) on all questions of testamentary capacity, the absence of fraud or undue influence, and due execution of the will. But probate does not preclude inquiry into the validity of the will's provisions or on their proper construction or legal effect. — Also termed *proof of will.*

independent probate. See *informal probate.*

informal probate. (1974) Probate designed to operate with minimal input and supervision of the probate court. ● Most modern probate codes encourage this type of administration, with an independent personal representative. — Also termed *independent probate.* Cf. *independent executor* under EXECUTOR.

probate in common form. Probate granted in the registry, without any formal procedure in court, on the executor's ex parte application. ●

The judgment is subject to being reopened by a party who has not been given notice.

probate in solemn form. Probate granted in open court, as a final decree, when all interested parties have been given notice. ● The judgment is final for all parties who have had notice of the proceeding, unless a later will is discovered.

small-estate probate. (2004) An informal procedure for administering small estates, less structured than the normal process and usu. not requiring the assistance of an attorney.

2. Loosely, a personal representative's actions in handling a decedent's estate. **3.** Loosely, all the subjects over which probate courts have jurisdiction. **4.** *Archaic.* A nonresident plaintiff's proof of a debt by swearing before a notary public or other officer that the debt is correct, just, and due, and by having the notary attach a jurat.

probate, *vb.* (18c) **1.** To admit (a will) to proof. **2.** To administer (a decedent's estate). **3.** To grant probation to (a criminal); to reduce (a sentence) by means of probation.

probate asset. See *legal asset* under ASSET.

probate bond. See BOND (2).

probate code. (1931) A collection of statutes setting forth the law (substantive and procedural) of decedents' estates and trusts.

probate court. See COURT.

probate distribution. See DISTRIBUTION.

probate duty. See DUTY (4).

probate estate. (1930) A decedent's property subject to administration by a personal representative. ● The probate estate comprises property owned by the decedent at the time of death and property acquired by the decedent's estate at or after the time of death. — Also termed *probate property.* See *decedent's estate* under ESTATE (3).

net probate estate. The probate estate after the following deductions: (1) family allowances, (2) exempt property, (3) homestead allowances, (4) claims against the estate, and (5) taxes for which the estate is liable. — Also termed *net estate.* Cf. *adjusted gross estate* (1) under ESTATE (3).

probate fee. See FEE (1).

probate homestead. See HOMESTEAD.

probate in common form. See PROBATE.

probate in solemn form. See PROBATE.

probate judge. See JUDGE.

probate jurisdiction. See JURISDICTION.

probate law. The body of statutes, rules, cases, etc. governing all subjects over which a probate court has jurisdiction.

probate property. See PROBATE ESTATE.

probate register. See REGISTER.

probation. (16c) **1.** A court-imposed criminal sentence that, subject to stated conditions, releases a convicted person into the community instead of sending the criminal to jail or prison. Cf. PAROLE. — **probationary,** *adj.*

bench probation. (1966) Probation in which the offender agrees to certain conditions or restrictions and reports only to the sentencing judge rather than a probation officer. — Also termed *bench parole; court probation.*

deferred-adjudication probation. See *deferred judgment* under JUDGMENT.

shock probation. (1972) Probation that is granted after a brief stay in jail or prison. ● Shock probation is intended to awaken the defendant to the reality of confinement for failure to abide by the conditions of probation. This type of probation is discretionary with the sentencing judge and is usu. granted within 180 days of the original sentence. — Also termed *split sentence.* Cf. *shock incarceration* under INCARCERATION.

2. The act of judicially proving a will. See PROBATE. — **probate,** *adj.*

probationary employee. See EMPLOYEE.

probation before judgment. See *deferred judgment* under JUDGMENT.

probationer. A convicted criminal who is on probation.

probation officer. See OFFICER (1).

probation termination. (1970) The ending of a person's status as a probationer by (1) the routine expiration of the probationary period, (2) early termination by court order, or (3) probation revocation.

probation-violation warrant. See *violation warrant* under WARRANT (1).

probation without judgment. See *deferred judgment* under JUDGMENT.

probative (proh-bə-tiv), *adj.* (17c) Tending to prove or disprove. ● Courts can exclude relevant evidence if its probative value is substantially outweighed by the danger of unfair prejudice. Fed. R. Evid. 403. — **probativeness, probativity,** *n.*

probative evidence. See EVIDENCE.

probative fact. See FACT.

probative similarity. See *substantial similarity* under SIMILARITY.

probator (proh-**bay**-tər), *n. Hist.* An accused person who confesses to a crime but asserts that another also participated in the crime. ● The probator had to undertake to prove the supposed accomplice's guilt.

probatory term. See *term probatory* (2) under TERM (5).

problem-oriented policing. (1986) A method that law-enforcement officers use to reduce crime by identifying and remedying the underlying causes of criminal incidents rather than merely seeking basic information (such as the identity of the perpetrator) about the crime being investigated.

problem-solving court. See COURT.

pro bono (proh **boh**-noh), *adv.* & *adj.* [Latin *pro bono publico* "for the public good"] (1966) Being or involving uncompensated legal services performed esp. for the public good <took the case pro bono> <50 hours of pro bono work each year>.

procedural consolidation. See JOINT ADMINISTRATION.

procedural-default doctrine. (1980) The principle that a federal court lacks jurisdiction to review the merits of a habeas corpus petition if a state court has refused to review the complaint because the petitioner failed to follow reasonable state-court procedures.

procedural due process. See DUE PROCESS.

procedural law. (1896) The rules that prescribe the steps for having a right or duty judicially enforced, as opposed to the law that defines the specific rights or duties themselves. — Also termed *adjective law.* Cf. SUBSTANTIVE LAW.

procedural main motion. See *incidental main motion* under MOTION (2).

procedural motion. See MOTION (2).

procedural point. See POINT.

procedural presumption. See PRESUMPTION.

procedural right. See RIGHT.

procedural unconscionability. See UNCONSCIONABILITY.

procedure. (16c) **1.** A specific method or course of action. **2.** The judicial rule or manner for carrying on a civil lawsuit or criminal prosecution. — Also termed *rules of procedure.* See CIVIL PROCEDURE; CRIMINAL PROCEDURE.

proceeding. (16c) **1.** The regular and orderly progression of a lawsuit, including all acts and events between the time of commencement and the entry of judgment. **2.** Any procedural means for seeking redress from a tribunal or agency. **3.** An act or step that is part of a larger action. **4.** The business conducted by a court or other official body; a hearing. **5.** *Bankruptcy.* A particular dispute or matter arising within a pending case — as opposed to the case as a whole.

adjudicatory proceeding. See *adjudication hearing* under HEARING.

administrative proceeding. See ADMINISTRATIVE PROCEEDING.

collateral proceeding. (18c) A proceeding brought to address an issue incidental to the principal proceeding.

competency proceeding. (1925) A proceeding to assess a person's mental capacity. ● A competency hearing may be held either in a criminal context to determine a defendant's competency to stand trial or as a civil proceeding to assess whether a person should be committed to a mental-health facility or should have a guardian appointed to manage the person's affairs.

contempt proceeding. (1859) A judicial or quasi-judicial hearing conducted to determine whether a person has committed contempt.

core proceeding. See CORE PROCEEDING.

criminal proceeding. (16c) A proceeding instituted to determine a person's guilt or innocence or to set a convicted person's punishment; a criminal hearing or trial.

ex parte proceeding (eks **pahr**-tee). (18c) A proceeding in which not all parties are present or given the opportunity to be heard. — Also termed *ex parte hearing.*

in camera proceeding (in **kam**-ə-rə). (1958) A proceeding held in a judge's chambers or other private place.

informal proceeding. (18c) A trial conducted in a more relaxed manner than a typical court trial, such as an administrative hearing or a trial in small-claims court.

involuntary proceeding. See *involuntary bankruptcy* under BANKRUPTCY.

judicial proceeding. (16c) Any court proceeding; any proceeding initiated to procure an order or decree, whether in law or in equity.

noncore proceeding. See RELATED PROCEEDING.

posttrial proceeding. Action on a case that occurs after the trial is completed.

proceeding in rem. A proceeding brought to affect all persons' interests in a thing that is subject to the power of a state.

proceeding quasi in rem. A proceeding brought to affect particular persons' interests in a thing.

quasi-criminal proceeding. *Procedure.* A civil proceeding that is conducted in conformity with the rules of a criminal proceeding because a penalty analogous to a criminal penalty may apply, as in some juvenile proceedings. ● For example, juvenile delinquency is classified as a civil offense. But like a defendant in a criminal trial, an accused juvenile faces a potential loss of liberty. So criminal procedure rules apply.

related proceeding. See RELATED PROCEEDING.

special proceeding. (18c) **1.** A proceeding that can be commenced independently of a pending action and from which a final order may be appealed immediately. **2.** A proceeding involving statutory or civil remedies or rules rather than the rules or remedies ordinarily available under rules of procedure; a proceeding providing extraordinary relief.

summary proceeding. (17c) A nonjury proceeding that settles a controversy or disposes of a case in a relatively prompt and simple manner. — Also termed *summary trial.* Cf. *plenary action* under ACTION (4).

supplementary proceeding. (17c) **1.** A proceeding held in connection with the enforcement of a judgment, for the purpose of identifying and locating the debtor's assets available to satisfy the judgment. **2.** A proceeding that in some way supplements another.

proceedings below. See STATEMENT OF THE CASE (1).

proceeds (**proh**-seedz), *n.* (13c) **1.** The value of land, goods, or investments when converted into money; the amount of money received from a sale <the proceeds are subject to attachment>. **2.** Something received upon selling, exchanging, collecting, or otherwise disposing of collateral. UCC § 9-102(a)(67). • Proceeds differ from other types of collateral because they constitute any collateral that has changed in form. For example, if a farmer borrows money and gives the creditor a security interest in the harvest, the harvested wheat is collateral. If the farmer then exchanges the harvest for a tractor, the tractor becomes the proceeds of the wheat.

net proceeds. (18c) The amount received in a transaction minus the costs of the transaction (such as expenses and commissions). — Also termed *net balance.*

proceeds and avails. The cash-surrender value of a life-insurance policy, together with values built up since the policy's issue date and the benefits payable on maturity and at the death of the insured.

process, *n.* (14c) **1.** The proceedings in any action or prosecution <due process of law>. **2.** A summons or writ, esp. to appear or respond in court <service of process>. — Also termed *judicial process; legal process.*

alias process. A process issued after an earlier process has failed for some reason. • Among the types of alias process are *alias execution, alias subpoena, alias summons,* and *alias writ.*

bailable process. A process instructing an officer to take bail after arresting a defendant. • The defendant's discharge is required by law after the tender of suitable security.

civil process. A process that issues in a civil lawsuit.

compulsory process. A process, with a warrant to arrest or attach included, that compels a person to appear in court as a witness.

criminal process. A process (such as an arrest warrant) that issues to compel a person to answer for a crime.

defective process. Void or voidable process. See *void process; voidable process.*

final process. A process issued at the conclusion of a judicial proceeding; esp., a writ of execution.

irregular process. A process not issued in accordance with prescribed practice. • Whether the process is void or merely voidable depends on the type of irregularity. Cf. *regular process.*

legal process. Process validly issued. — Also termed *lawful process.*

mesne process (meen). **1.** A process issued between the commencement of a lawsuit and the final judgment or determination. **2.** The procedure by which a contumacious defendant is compelled to plead. — Also termed *writ of mesne process; writ of mesne.*

original process. A process issued at the beginning of a judicial proceeding.

regular process. A process that issues lawfully according to prescribed practice. Cf. *irregular process.*

summary process. **1.** An immediate process, issuing and taking effect without intermediate applications or delays. **2.** A legal procedure used to resolve a controversy more efficiently and expeditiously than ordinary methods. **3.** The legal documents achieving such a result. **4.** A procedure for repossessing real property from a tenant upon default. See *summary eviction* under EVICTION. **5.** SHOW-CAUSE PROCEEDING.

trust process. In some states (particularly in New England), garnishment or foreign attachment.

voidable process. A defective process with a curable defect.

void process. Legal process that, in some material way, does not comply with the required form.

3. *Patents.* A method, operation, or series of actions intended to achieve some new and useful end or result by changing a material's chemical or physical characteristics. • Process is a statutory category of patentable invention. Cf. MACHINE; MANUFACTURE.

process, abuse of. See ABUSE OF PROCESS.

process agent. See AGENT (2).

process by foreign attachment. See FACTORIZING PROCESS.

process claim. See PATENT CLAIM.

processioning. The survey and inspection of land boundaries, performed esp. in the former English colonies along the southeastern seaboard, and analogous to the English *perambulation.*

process patent. See PATENT (3).

process server. (17c) A person authorized by law or by a court to formally deliver process to a defendant or respondent. See SERVICE (1).

procès-verbal (proh-**say**-vair-**bahl**). [French "official record of oral proceedings"] *Civil & int'l law.* A detailed, authenticated written report of a proceeding, esp. of an international conference; PROTOCOL (3). • A *procès-verbal* may be cast in various forms, according to the style a country prefers.

proclaim, *vb.* To declare formally or officially.

proclamation. A formal public announcement made by the government.

procompetitive, *adj.* Increasing, encouraging, or preserving competition. Cf. ANTICOMPETITIVE.

pro–con debate. See DEBATE.

pro–con divorce. See DIVORCE.

proconsul (proh-**kon**-səl), *n.* [Latin] *Roman law.* **1.** An ex-consul whose consular powers were extended by the Senate or emperor after leaving office. **2.** The governor of certain senatorial provinces.

proctor. 1. One appointed to manage the affairs of another. **2.** An advocate who represents clients in ecclesiastical courts; PROCURATOR (4). **3.** DIVORCE PROCTOR. **4.** An advocate who represents a party in the admiralty side of a district court. — Also termed (in sense 4) *proctor in admiralty.*

procuracy (**prok**-yə-rə-see). The document that grants power to an attorney-in-fact; a letter of agency.

procuration (prok-yə-**ray**-shən). **1.** The act of appointing someone as an agent or attorney-in-fact. **2.** The authority vested in a person so appointed; the function of an attorney. **3.** PROCUREMENT.

procurator (**prok**-yə-ray-tər), *n.* **1.** *Roman law.* A person informally appointed to represent another in a judicial proceeding. Cf. COGNITOR. **2.** *Roman law.* A government official, usu. subordinate in authority to a provincial governor; one of several imperial officers of the Roman Empire entrusted with the management of the financial affairs of the province and often having administrative powers in a province as agents of the emperor. **3.** *Hist. English law.* An agent, attorney, or servant. **4.** *Eccles. law.* An advocate of a religious house; a lawyer who represents a cleric or religious society in legal matters. — Also termed *proctor.* **5.** An agent or attorney-in-fact. **6.** *Scots law.* A solicitor who represents clients in the lower courts; formerly, any law agent.

procurement (proh-**kyoor**-mənt), *n.* (14c) **1.** The act of getting or obtaining something or of bringing something about. — Also termed *procuration.* **2.** The act of persuading or inviting another, esp. a woman or child, to have illicit sexual intercourse. — **procure,** *vb.*

procurement contract. See CONTRACT.

procurement of breach of contract. See TORTIOUS INTERFERENCE WITH CONTRACTUAL RELATIONS.

procurer. (15c) One who induces or prevails upon another to do something, esp. to engage in an illicit sexual act. See PIMP.

procuring agent. See AGENT (2).

procuring an abortion. See ABORTION.

procuring cause. See CAUSE (1).

prodigal (**prod**-ə-gəl), *n. Civil law.* A person whose affairs are managed by a curator because of the person's wasteful spending or other bad conduct. • In Roman law, the agnatic family of a prodigal (*prodigus*) or spendthrift could result in that person's being prohibited from engaging in certain legal transactions, and the person's estate being put in the charge of a curator. See *cura prodigi* under CURA.

produce (**proh**-doos), *n.* The product of natural growth, labor, or capital; esp., agricultural products.

produce (prə-**doos**), *vb.* (15c) **1.** To bring into existence; to create. **2.** To provide (a document, witness, etc.) in response to subpoena or discovery request. **3.** To yield (as revenue). **4.** To bring (oil, etc.) to the surface of the earth.

producer. See INSURANCE AGENT.

producer price index. An index of wholesale price changes, issued monthly by the U.S. Bureau of Labor Statistics. — Formerly also termed *wholesale price index.* Cf. CONSUMER PRICE INDEX.

producing cause. See *proximate cause* under CAUSE (1).

product. (1825) Something that is distributed commercially for use or consumption and that is usu. (1) tangible personal property, (2) the result of fabrication or processing, and (3) an item that has passed through a chain of commercial distribution before ultimate use or consumption. See ARTICLE OF MANUFACTURE; PRODUCTS LIABILITY.

   defective product. (1903) A product that is unreasonably dangerous for normal use, as when it is not fit for its intended purpose, inadequate instructions are provided for its use, or it is inherently dangerous in its design or manufacture.

product-by-process claim. See PATENT CLAIM.

product claim. See PATENT CLAIM.

product defect. See DEFECT.

product disparagement. See TRADE DISPARAGE-
MENT.

product-extension merger. See MERGER.

production burden. See BURDEN OF PRODUC-
TION.

production casing. See CASING.

production for commerce. The production of
goods that an employer intends for interstate
commerce. • This is one criterion by which an
employer may be subject to the Fair Labor Standards Act.

production of suit. (1830) *Common-law pleading.*
The plaintiff's burden to produce evidence to confirm the allegations made in the declaration.

production payment. *Oil & gas.* A share of oil-and-
gas production from property, free of the costs
of production, ending when an agreed sum has
been paid.

product liability. See PRODUCTS LIABILITY.

product-liability loss. See LOSS.

product-line exception. An exception from the
usual rule that a successor corporation is not liable for the acts of its predecessor, arising when
the successor acquired all the predecessor's assets,
held itself out as a continuation of the predecessor by producing the same product line under the
same or a similar name, and benefited from the
predecessor's goodwill.

product mark. See *product trademark* under
TRADEMARK.

product market. See MARKET.

product rule. A means of calculating the likelihood that a series of independent events will
occur jointly, done by multiplying together the
probability of each event.

products liability, *n.* (1925) **1.** A manufacturer's or
seller's tort liability for any damages or injuries
suffered by a buyer, user, or bystander as a result
of a defective product. • Products liability can be
based on a theory of negligence, strict liability, or
breach of warranty. **2.** The legal theory by which
liability is imposed on the manufacturer or seller
of a defective product. **3.** The field of law dealing
with this theory. — Also termed *product liability*;
(specif.) *manufacturer's liability.* See LIABILITY. —
products-liability, *adj.*

strict products liability. (1964) Products liability
arising when the buyer proves that the goods
were unreasonably dangerous and that (1) the
seller was in the business of selling goods, (2)
the goods were defective when they were in the
seller's hands, (3) the defect caused the plaintiff's injury, and (4) the product was expected to
and did reach the consumer without substantial
change in condition.

products-liability action. A lawsuit brought
against a manufacturer, seller, or lessor of a product — regardless of the substantive legal theory
or theories upon which the lawsuit is brought —
for personal injury, death, or property damage
caused by the manufacture, construction, design,
formulation, installation, preparation, or assembly of a product. — Also termed *product-liability
action.*

products-liability insurance. See INSURANCE.

product test. See DURHAM RULE.

product trademark. See TRADEMARK.

profane, *adj.* (Of speech or conduct) irreverent to
something held sacred.

profanity. Obscene, vulgar, or insulting language;
BLASPHEMY. • Profanity is distinguished from
mere vulgarity and obscenity by the additional
element of irreverence toward or mistreatment
of something sacred.

proferens (proh-**fer**-enz). [Latin] The party that
proposes a contract or a condition in a contract.
Pl. *proferentes* (proh-fə-**ren**-teez).

profert (**proh**-fərt). (18c) *Common-law pleading.*
A declaration on the record stating that a party
produces in court the deed or other instrument
relied on in the pleading.

profess, *vb.* (16c) To declare openly and freely; to
confess.

profession. (15c) **1.** A vocation requiring advanced
education and training; esp., one of the three traditional learned professions — law, medicine, and
the ministry. **2.** Collectively, the members of such
a vocation.

professional, *n.* (1846) A person who belongs to a
learned profession or whose occupation requires
a high level of training and proficiency.

professional association. See ASSOCIATION.

professional corporation. See CORPORATION.

professional goodwill. See *personal goodwill* under
GOODWILL.

professionalism. The practice of a learned art in
a characteristically methodical, courteous, and
ethical manner.

professional negligence. See MALPRACTICE.

professional relationship. See RELATIONSHIP.

proffer (**prof**-ər), *vb.* (14c) To offer or tender (something, esp. evidence) for immediate acceptance. —
proffer, *n.*

proffered evidence. See EVIDENCE.

profiling. 1. See RACIAL PROFILING. **2.** See LINGUIS-
TIC PROFILING.

profit, *n.* (13c) **1.** The excess of revenues over expenditures in a business transaction; GAIN (2). Cf.
EARNINGS; INCOME.

accumulated profit. Profit that has accrued but not yet been distributed; earned surplus. — Also termed *undivided profit*. See *retained earnings* under EARNINGS.

gross profit. Total sales revenue less the cost of the goods sold, no adjustment being made for additional expenses and taxes. Cf. *net profit*.

lost profits. See LOST PROFITS.

mesne profits. The profits of an estate received by a tenant in wrongful possession between two dates. — Also termed (archaically) *medium tempus*.

net profit. Total sales revenue less the cost of the goods sold and all additional expenses. — Also termed *net revenue*. Cf. *gross profit*.

operating profit. Total sales revenue less all operating expenses, no adjustment being made for any nonoperating income and expenses, such as interest payments.

paper profit. A profit that is anticipated but not yet realized. • Gains from stock holdings, for example, are paper profits until the stock is actually sold at a price higher than its original purchase price. — Also termed *unrealized profit*.

short-swing profits. See SHORT-SWING PROFITS.

surplus profit. *Corporations.* The excess of revenue over expenditures. • Some jurisdictions prohibit the declaration of a dividend from sources other than surplus profit.

undistributed profit. See *retained earnings* under EARNINGS.

undivided profit. See *accumulated profit*.

unrealized profit. See *paper profit*.

2. A servitude that gives the right to pasture cattle, dig for minerals, or otherwise take away some part of the soil; PROFIT À PRENDRE. • A profit may be either appurtenant or in gross. See SERVITUDE (1).

profit appendant (ə-**pen**-dənt). A profit annexed to land by operation of law; esp., a common of pasture. See *common appendant* under COMMON.

profit appurtenant (ə-**pərt**-ən-ənt). A profit, whether several or in common, attached to land, for the benefit of certain other identified land, by the act of the parties (as by grant or by prescription). See *common appurtenant* under COMMON.

profit in gross (in **grohs**). A profit exercisable by the owner independently of his or her ownership of land. See *common in gross* under COMMON.

profit pur cause de vicinage (pər **kawz** də **vis**-ə-nij). A profit arising when the holders of adjoining commons have allowed their cattle to stray on each other's lands. • A claim for this profit fails if one of the commoners fences off the common or has in the past driven off the other commoner's cattle.

profit-and-loss account. See ACCOUNT.

profit-and-loss statement. See INCOME STATEMENT.

profit à prendre (a **prawn**-drə *or* ah **prahn**-dər). [Law French "profit to take"] (*usu. pl.*) (17c) A right or privilege to go on another's land and take away something of value from its soil or from the products of its soil (as by mining, logging, or hunting). — Also termed *right of common*. Pl. **profits à prendre.** Cf. EASEMENT.

profiteering, *n.* (1814) The taking advantage of unusual or exceptional circumstances to make excessive profits, as in the selling of scarce goods at inflated prices during war. — **profiteer,** *vb.*

profit insurance. See INSURANCE.

profit margin. 1. The difference between the cost of something and the price for which it is sold. **2.** The ratio, expressed as a percentage, between this difference and the selling price. • For example, a widget costing a retailer $10 and selling for $15 has a profit margin of 33% ($5 difference divided by $15 selling price). — Often shortened to *margin*.

profit-sharing plan. An employee benefit plan that allows an employee to share in the company's profits. • ERISA governs the administration of many profit-sharing plans, which provide for discretionary employer contributions and provide a definite predetermination formula for allocating the contributions to the plan among the participants. Contributions are frequently allocated in proportion to each participant's compensation. See EMPLOYEE BENEFIT PLAN; EMPLOYEE RETIREMENT INCOME SECURITY ACT.

qualified profit-sharing plan. A plan in which an employer's contributions are not taxed to the employee until distribution. • The employer is allowed to deduct the contributions. IRC (26 USCA) § 401(a). — Often shortened to *qualified plan*.

pro forma (proh **for**-mə), *adj.* [Latin "for form"] (16c) **1.** Made or done as a formality. **2.** (Of an invoice or financial statement) provided in advance to describe items, predict results, or secure approval.

pro forma amendment. See AMENDMENT (3).

pro forma earnings. See *operating earnings* under EARNINGS.

pro forma session. See SESSION (1).

progeny (**proj**-ə-nee), *n. pl.* (14c) **1.** Children or descendants; offspring <only one of their progeny attended law school>. **2.** In a figurative sense, a line of precedents that follow a leading case <*Erie and its progeny*>.

prognosis (prog-**noh**-sis). (17c) **1.** The process of forecasting the probable outcome of a present medical condition (such as a disease). **2.** The forecast of such an outcome. Cf. DIAGNOSIS.

program. *Parliamentary law.* **1.** An agenda for a meeting or a convention, listing the order of business and possibly including educational or social events. See AGENDA; *business meeting* under MEETING. **2.** A speech or other presentation within a meeting offered for the assembly's information or for the members' education or entertainment, but not for their formal consideration or action as a deliberative assembly.

program committee. See COMMITTEE.

program trading. A form of computerized securities trading that usu. involves buying or selling large amounts of stocks while simultaneously selling or buying index futures in offsetting amounts.

progressive lawyering. See CAUSE LAWYERING.

progressive loss. See LOSS.

progressive tax. See TAX.

pro hac vice (proh hahk **vee**-chay *or* hak **vi**-see *also* hahk **vees**). [Latin] (17c) For this occasion or particular purpose. ● The phrase usu. refers to a lawyer who has not been admitted to practice in a particular jurisdiction but who is admitted there temporarily for the purpose of conducting a particular case. — Abbr. *p.h.v.* See *admission pro hac vice* under ADMISSION (2). For *owner pro hac vice,* see *demise charter* under CHARTER (8).

prohibit, *vb.* **1.** To forbid by law. **2.** To prevent or hinder.

prohibited and reserved trademarks. See TRADE-MARK.

prohibited degree. See DEGREE.

prohibited substitution. See SUBSTITUTION.

prohibition. (15c) **1.** A law or order that forbids a certain action. **2.** An extraordinary writ issued by an appellate court to prevent a lower court from exceeding its jurisdiction or to prevent a nonjudicial officer or entity from exercising a power. — Also termed (in sense 2) *writ of prohibition; inhibition;* (in Scots law) *inhibition.* Cf. WRIT OF CONSULTATION. **3.** (*cap.*) The period from 1920 to 1933, when the manufacture, transport, and sale of alcoholic beverages in the United States was forbidden by the 18th Amendment to the Constitution. ● The 18th Amendment was repealed by the 21st Amendment.

prohibitive statute. See STATUTE.

prohibitory injunction. See INJUNCTION.

prohibitory interdict. See INTERDICT (1).

project financing. See FINANCING.

projector. See PROMOTER.

proletariat (proh-lə-**tair**-ee-ət). The working class; those without capital who sell their labor to survive.

prolicide (**proh**-lə-sid). (1826) **1.** The killing of offspring; esp., the crime of killing a child shortly before or after birth. **2.** One who kills a child shortly before or after birth. Cf. INFANTICIDE. — **prolicidal,** *adj.*

prolixity (proh-**lik**-sə-tee). (14c) The unnecessary and superfluous stating of facts and legal arguments in pleading or evidence.

prolixity rejection. See REJECTION.

prolocutor (proh-**lok**-yə-tər). **1.** *Eccles. law.* The president or chair of a convocation. **2.** *Hist.* The speaker of the British House of Lords. ● This office now belongs to the Lord Chancellor. — Also termed (in sense 2) *forspeca.*

promise, *n.* (15c) **1.** The manifestation of an intention to act or refrain from acting in a specified manner, conveyed in such a way that another is justified in understanding that a commitment has been made; a person's assurance that the person will or will not do something. ● A binding promise — one that the law will enforce — is the essence of a contract. **2.** The words in a promissory note expressing the maker's intention to pay a debt. ● A mere written acknowledgment that a debt is due is insufficient to constitute a promise. — **promise,** *vb.*

aleatory promise (**ay**-lee-ə-tor-ee). A promise conditional on the happening of a fortuitous event, or on an event that the parties believe is fortuitous.

alternative promise. (17c) A contractual promise to do one of two or more things, any one of which qualifies as consideration.

bare promise. See *gratuitous promise.*

collateral promise. A promise to guarantee the debt of another, made primarily without benefit to the party making the promise. ● Unlike an original promise, a collateral promise must be in writing to be enforceable. See MAIN-PURPOSE RULE.

conditional promise. (16c) A promise that is conditioned on the occurrence of an event other than the lapse of time <she made a conditional promise to sell the gold on April 2 unless the price fell below $300 an ounce before that time>. ● A conditional promise is not illusory as long as the condition is not entirely within the promisor's control.

corresponding promise. A mutual promise calling for the performance of an act substantially similar to the act called for by the other mutual promise, both acts being in pursuit of a common purpose.

counterpromise. See COUNTERPROMISE.

dependent promise. (1829) A promise to be performed by a party only when another obligation has first been performed by another party.

divisible promises. Promises that are capable of being divided into independent parts.

false promise. A promise made with no intention of carrying it out. Cf. *promissory fraud* under FRAUD.

fictitious promise. See *implied promise*.

gratuitous promise. (17c) A promise made in exchange for nothing; a promise not supported by consideration. ● A gratuitous promise is not ordinarily legally enforceable. — Also termed *bare promise*; *naked promise*.

illusory promise. (1841) A promise that appears on its face to be so insubstantial as to impose no obligation on the promisor; an expression cloaked in promissory terms but actually containing no commitment by the promisor. ● An illusory promise typically, by its terms, makes performance optional with the promisor. For example, if a guarantor promises to make good on the principal debtor's obligation "as long as I think it's in my commercial interest," the promisor is not really bound.

implied promise. (18c) A promise created by law to render a person liable on a contract so as to avoid fraud or unjust enrichment. — Also termed *fictitious promise*.

independent promise. See *unconditional promise*.

marriage promise. *Family law.* A betrothal; an engagement to be married. — Also termed *agreement to marry*; *promise to marry*; *promise of marriage*.

mutual promises. (16c) Promises given simultaneously by two parties, each promise serving as consideration for the other. See *bilateral contract* under CONTRACT.

naked promise. See *gratuitous promise*.

new promise. A previously unenforceable promise that a promisor revives and agrees to fulfill, as when a debtor agrees to pay a creditor an amount discharged in the debtor's bankruptcy.

original promise. A promise to guarantee the debt of another, made primarily for the benefit of the party making the promise. ● An original promise need not be in writing to be enforceable. See MAIN-PURPOSE RULE.

promise implied in fact. (1909) A promise existing by inference from the circumstances or actions of the parties. See *implied promise*.

promise in consideration of marriage. A promise for which the actual performance of the marriage is the consideration, as when a man agrees to transfer property to a woman if she will marry him. ● A promise to marry, however, is not considered a promise in consideration of marriage.

promise in restraint of trade. A promise whose performance would limit competition in any business or restrict the promisor in the exercise of a gainful occupation. ● Such a promise is usu. unenforceable.

remedial promise. A seller's promise to repair or replace goods or to refund the price if the goods (1) do not conform to the contract or to a representation at the time of the delivery of the goods, (2) conform at the time of delivery but later fail to perform as agreed, or (3) contain a defect. UCC § 2-102(a)(31).

unconditional promise. (1802) A promise that either is unqualified or requires nothing but the lapse of time to make the promise presently enforceable. ● A party who makes an unconditional promise must perform that promise even though the other party has not performed according to the bargain. — Also termed *independent promise*.

voidable promise. A promise that one party may, under the law, declare void by reason of that party's incapacity or mistake, or by reason of the fraud, breach, or other fault of the other party.

promisee (prom-is-**ee**). (18c) One to whom a promise is made.

promise not to compete. See *noncompetition covenant* under COVENANT (1).

promise of marriage. See *marriage promise* under PROMISE.

promise to marry. See *marriage promise* under PROMISE.

promisor (prom-is-**or**). (17c) One who makes a promise; esp., one who undertakes a contractual obligation.

promissory, *adj.* (15c) Containing or consisting of a promise <the agreement's promissory terms>.

promissory condition. See CONDITION (2).

promissory estoppel. See ESTOPPEL.

promissory fraud. See FRAUD.

promissory note. See NOTE (1).

promissory oath. See OATH.

promissory representation. See REPRESENTATION (1).

promissory restraint. An attempt by an otherwise effective conveyance or contract to discourage a later conveyance by imposing contractual liability on anyone who makes a later conveyance.

promissory warranty. See WARRANTY (3).

promoter. (14c) **1.** A person who encourages or incites. **2.** A founder or organizer of a corporation or business venture; one who takes the entrepreneurial initiative in founding or organizing a business or enterprise. — Formerly also termed *projector.*

promoting prostitution. See PANDERING (1).

prompt, *vb.* To incite, esp. to immediate action.

promulgate (prə-**məl**-gayt *or* **prom**-əl-gayt), *vb.* (16c) **1.** To declare or announce publicly; to proclaim. **2.** To put (a law or decree) into force or effect. **3.** (Of an administrative agency) to carry out the formal process of rulemaking by publishing the proposed regulation, inviting public comments, and approving or rejecting the proposal. — **promulgation** (prom-əl-**gay**-shən *or* proh-məl-), *n.*

promulgation (prom-əl-**gay**-shən *or* proh-məl-). The official publication of a new law or regulation, by which it is put into effect.

pronotary (proh-**noh**-tə-ree), *n.* First notary.

pronounce, *vb.* (14c) To announce formally <pronounce judgment>.

pronunciation (prə-nən-see-**ay**-shən). *Archaic.* A sentence or decree.

proof, *n.* (13c) **1.** The establishment or refutation of an alleged fact by evidence; the persuasive effect of evidence in the mind of a fact-finder. **2.** Evidence that determines the judgment of a court. **3.** An attested document that constitutes legal evidence.

affirmative proof. (18c) Evidence establishing the fact in dispute by a preponderance of the evidence.

conditional proof. (1931) A fact that amounts to proof as long as there is no other fact amounting to disproof. — Also termed *presumptive proof.*

double proof. (1955) **1.** *Bankruptcy.* Proof of claims by two or more creditors against the same debt. ● This violates the general rule that there can be only one claim with respect to a single debt. **2.** *Evidence.* Corroborating government evidence (usu. by two witnesses) required to sustain certain convictions.

full proof. **1.** *Civil law.* Proof by two witnesses or by public instrument. **2.** Evidence that satisfies the minds of the jury of the truth of the fact in dispute beyond a reasonable doubt.

literal proof. *Civil law.* Written evidence. Cf. *testimonial proof.*

negative proof. (16c) Proof that establishes a fact by showing that its opposite is not or cannot be true. Cf. *positive proof.*

positive proof. (17c) Direct or affirmative proof. Cf. *negative proof.*

preliminary proof. *Insurance.* The first proof offered of a loss occurring under a policy, usu. sent in to the underwriters with a notification of the claim.

presumptive proof. See *conditional proof.*

proof beyond a reasonable doubt. (1834) Proof that precludes every reasonable hypothesis except that which it tends to support. See REASONABLE DOUBT. ● Formerly, this standard required evidence to "establish the truth of the fact to a reasonable and moral certainty" and "proof to a moral certainty as distinguished from an absolute certainty." *Moral certainty* is no longer a synonym for *proof beyond a reasonable doubt.* See *Victor v. Nebraska*, 511 U.S. 1, 8, 12, 114 S.Ct. 1239, 1244, 1246 (1994).

testimonial proof. *Civil law.* Proof by the evidence of witnesses, rather than proof by written instrument. Cf. *literal proof.*

4. *Scots law.* A bench trial.

proof, burden of. See BURDEN OF PROOF.

proof brief. See BRIEF.

proof of acknowledgment. (18c) An authorized officer's certification — based on a third party's testimony — that the signature of a person (who usu. does not appear before the notary) is genuine and was freely made. — Also termed *certificate of proof.* See ACKNOWLEDGMENT (5).

proof of claim. *Bankruptcy.* A creditor's written statement that is submitted to show the basis and amount of the creditor's claim. Pl. **proofs of claim.**

informal proof of claim. A proof of claim stating a creditor's demand for payment and intent to hold the debtor's bankruptcy estate liable, but that does not comply with the Bankruptcy Code's form for proofs of claim. ● A late-filed proof of claim may be given effect if the creditor had timely filed an informal proof of claim.

proof of debt. The establishment by a creditor of a debt in some prescribed manner (as by affidavit) as a first step in recovering the debt from an estate or property; PROOF OF CLAIM.

proof of loss. An insured's formal statement of loss required by an insurance company before it will determine whether the policy covers the loss.

proof of service. (18c) **1.** A document filed (as by a sheriff) in court as evidence that process has been successfully served on a party. — Also termed *return of service; return of process.* See SERVICE (1). **2.** CERTIFICATE OF SERVICE.

proof of will. See PROBATE (1).

propaganda. *Int'l law.* **1.** The systematic dissemination of doctrine, rumor, or selected information to promote or injure a particular doctrine, view, or cause. **2.** The ideas or information so disseminated. ● The word *propaganda* originated as an abbreviated form of *Congregatio de propaganda fide*, a committee (of cardinals) for propagating the (Christian) faith.

   defamatory propaganda. Propaganda used to promote dissatisfaction among a nation's citizens and undermine government authority. ● Defamatory propaganda is common in wartime but is also used in peacetime as a means of incitement.

   hostile propaganda. Propaganda employed by a nation to manipulate the people of another nation to support or oppose their government. — Also termed *ideological aggression.* See *subversive propaganda.*

   subversive propaganda. Propaganda calculated to incite a civil war or revolution. ● When the instigator is another nation, it is termed *hostile propaganda* or *ideological aggression.*

   war-mongering propaganda. Propaganda calculated to produce national support for a war and to encourage the government to declare or join in a war regardless of any legal constraints.

pro per., *adv. & adj.* See PRO PERSONA.

pro per., *n.* **1.** See PRO SE. **2.** See PROPRIA PERSONA.

proper care. See *reasonable care* under CARE.

proper evidence. See *admissible evidence* under EVIDENCE.

proper feud. See FEUD (1).

proper improbation. See IMPROBATION.

proper independent advice. See INDEPENDENT ADVICE.

proper law. *Conflict of laws.* The substantive law that, under the principles of conflict of laws, governs a transaction.

proper lookout, *n.* (1842) The duty of a vehicle operator to exercise caution to avoid collisions with pedestrians or other vehicles.

proper means. *Trade secrets.* Any method of discovering trade secrets that does not violate property-protection statutes or standards of commercial ethics. ● Proper means include independent invention, reverse engineering, observing the product in public, and studying published literature. RESTATEMENT OF TORTS § 757 cmt. f (1977).

proper party. See PARTY (2).

pro persona (proh pər-**soh**-nə), *adv. & adj.* [Latin] For one's own person; on one's own behalf <a pro *persona* brief>. — Sometimes shortened to *pro per.* See PRO SE.

property. (14c) **1.** The right to possess, use, and enjoy a determinate thing (either a tract of land or a chattel); the right of ownership <the institution of private property is protected from undue governmental interference>. — Also termed *bundle of rights.* **2.** Any external thing over which the rights of possession, use, and enjoyment are exercised <the airport is city property>.

   abandoned property. (1841) Property that the owner voluntarily surrenders, relinquishes, or disclaims. Cf. *lost property; mislaid property.*

   absolute property. Property that one has full and complete title to and control over.

   appointive property. A property interest that is subject to a power of appointment.

   common property. (17c) **1.** Real property that is held by two or more persons with no right of survivorship. Cf. *joint property.* **2.** COMMON AREA.

   community property. See COMMUNITY PROPERTY.

   complete property. The entirety of the rights, privileges, powers, and immunities that it is legally possible for a person to have with regard to land or any other thing, apart from those that all other members of society have in the land or thing.

   corporeal property. **1.** The right of ownership in material things. **2.** Property that can be perceived, as opposed to incorporeal property; tangible property.

   distressed property. (1927) Property that must be sold because of mortgage foreclosure or because it is part of an insolvent estate.

   domestic-partnership property. Property that would be marital property if the domestic partners were married to each other. See DOMESTIC PARTNERSHIP; DOMESTIC-PARTNERSHIP PERIOD.

   dotal property. *Civil law.* Separate property that the wife brings to the marriage to assist the husband with the marriage expenses. Cf. *extradotal property.*

   exempt property. See EXEMPT PROPERTY.

   extradotal property (ek-strə-**doh**-təl). *Civil law.* **1.** That portion of a wife's property over which she has complete control. **2.** All of a wife's effects that have not been settled on her as dowry; any property that a wife owns apart from her dowry. ● In Louisiana, after January 1, 1980, all property acquired by the wife that is not community is neither dotal nor extradotal; it is simply her separate property, as has always been true of the husband. La. Civ. Code art. 2341. — Also termed *paraphernal property.* Cf. *dotal property.*

general property. Property belonging to a general owner. See *general owner* under OWNER.

income property. Property that produces income, such as rental property.

incorporeal property. (18c) **1.** An in rem proprietary right that is not classified as corporeal property. • Incorporeal property is traditionally broken down into two classes: (1) *jura in re aliena* (encumbrances), whether over material or immaterial things, examples being leases, mortgages, and servitudes; and (2) *jura in re propria* (full ownership over immaterial things), examples being patents, copyrights, and trademarks. **2.** A legal right in property having no physical existence. • Patent rights, for example, are incorporeal property. — Also termed *incorporeal chattel; incorporeal thing.*

intangible property. (1843) Property that lacks a physical existence. • Examples include stock options and business goodwill. Cf. *tangible property.*

intellectual property. See INTELLECTUAL PROPERTY.

joint property. Real or personal property held by two or more persons with a right of survivorship. Cf. *common property.*

limited-market property. See *special-purpose property.*

literary property. See LITERARY PROPERTY.

lost property. (1810) Property that the owner no longer possesses because of accident, negligence, or carelessness, and that cannot be located by an ordinary, diligent search. Cf. *abandoned property; mislaid property.*

marital property. (1855) Property that is acquired during marriage and that is subject to distribution or division at the time of marital dissolution. • Generally, it is property acquired after the date of the marriage and before a spouse files for separation or divorce. The phrase *marital property* is used in equitable-distribution states and is roughly equivalent to *community property.* — Also termed *marital estate.* See COMMUNITY PROPERTY; EQUITABLE DISTRIBUTION.

maternal property. Property that comes from the mother of a party or other ascendants of the maternal stock.

mislaid property. (1915) Property that has been voluntarily relinquished by the owner with an intent to recover it later — but that cannot now be found. Cf. *abandoned property; lost property.*

mixed property. (18c) Property with characteristics of both real property and personal property — such as heirlooms and fixtures.

movable property. See MOVABLE (1).

neutral property. See NEUTRAL PROPERTY.

nonancestral property. See *nonancestral estate* under ESTATE (1).

nonexempt property. See NONEXEMPT PROPERTY.

paraphernal property. See *extradotal property.*

paternal property. Property that comes from the father of a party or other ascendants of the paternal stock.

personal property. (18c) **1.** Any movable or intangible thing that is subject to ownership and not classified as real property. — Also termed *personalty; personal estate; movable estate;* (in plural) *things personal.* Cf. *real property.* **2.** *Tax.* Property not used in a taxpayer's trade or business or held for income production or collection.

private property. (17c) Property — protected from public appropriation — over which the owner has exclusive and absolute rights.

public property. (17c) State- or community-owned property not restricted to any one individual's use or possession.

qualified property. A temporary or special interest in a thing (such as a right to possess it), subject to being totally extinguished by the occurrence of a specified contingency over which the qualified owner has no control.

qualified-terminable-interest property. (1982) Property that passes by a QTIP trust from a deceased spouse to the surviving spouse and that (if the executor so elects) qualifies for the marital deduction provided that the surviving spouse is entitled to receive all income in payments made at least annually for life and that no one has the power to appoint the property to anyone other than the surviving spouse. • The purpose of the marital deduction is to permit deferral of estate taxes until the death of the surviving spouse. But this property is included in the surviving spouse's estate at death, where it is subject to the federal estate tax. — Abbr. QTIP. See *QTIP trust* under TRUST.

quasi-community property. See COMMUNITY PROPERTY.

real property. (18c) Land and anything growing on, attached to, or erected on it, excluding anything that may be severed without injury to the land. • Real property can be either corporeal (soil and buildings) or incorporeal (easements). — Also termed *realty; real estate.* Cf. *personal property* (1).

scheduled property. Insurance. Property itemized on a list (usu. attached to an insurance policy) that records property values, which provide the basis for insurance payments in the event of a loss under an insurance policy.

separate property. See SEPARATE PROPERTY.

special-design property. See *special-purpose property.*

special property. Property that the holder has only a qualified, temporary, or limited interest in, such as (from a bailee's standpoint) bailed property.

special-purpose property. Property that has a unique design or layout, incorporates special construction materials, or has other features that limit the property's utility for purposes other than the one for which it was built. • Because of the property's specialized nature, the market for the property may be quite limited. — Also termed *limited-market property; special-design property.*

specialty property. See SPECIALTY (3).

tangible personal property. (1843) Corporeal personal property of any kind; personal property that can be seen, weighed, measured, felt, or touched, or is in any other way perceptible to the senses, such as furniture, cooking utensils, and books.

tangible property. (1802) Property that has physical form and characteristics. Cf. *intangible property.*

terminable property. Property (such as a leasehold) whose duration is not perpetual or indefinite but is limited in time or is liable to termination upon the occurrence of some specified event.

wasting property. (1853) **1.** Property that is consumed in its normal use, such as a wasting asset, a leasehold interest, or a patent right. **2.** A right to or an interest in such property.

property, law of. See LAW OF PROPERTY.

property crimes. See CRIMES AGAINST PROPERTY.

property-damage insurance. See *property insurance* under INSURANCE.

property dividend. See *asset dividend* under DIVIDEND.

property division. See PROPERTY SETTLEMENT (1).

property insurance. See INSURANCE.

property of the debtor. *Bankruptcy.* Property that is owned or (in some instances) possessed by the debtor, including property that is exempted from the bankruptcy estate. 11 USCA § 541(b). — Also termed *debtor's property.*

property of the estate. *Bankruptcy.* The debtor's tangible and intangible property interests (including both legal and equitable interests) that fall under the bankruptcy court's jurisdiction because they were owned or held by the debtor when the bankruptcy petition was filed. 11 USCA § 541. — Also termed *estate's property.*

property right. See RIGHT.

property settlement. 1. A judgment in a divorce case determining the distribution of the marital property between the divorcing parties. • A property settlement includes a division of the marital debts as well as assets. — Also termed *property division; division of property.* **2.** A contract that divides up the assets of divorcing spouses and is incorporated into a divorce decree. — Also termed *integrated property settlement; property settlement agreement.* Cf. DIVORCE AGREEMENT. **3.** MARITAL AGREEMENT.

property settlement agreement. See PROPERTY SETTLEMENT (2).

property tax. See TAX.

property tort. See TORT.

prophylactic (proh-fə-**lak**-tik), *adj.* (16c) Formulated to prevent something <a prophylactic rule>. — **prophylaxis** (proh-fə-**lak**-sis), **prophylactic,** *n.*

prophylactic cost. See COST (1).

propinquity (prə-**ping**-kwə-tee). (15c) The state of being near; specif., kindred or parentage <degrees of propinquity>.

propone (prə-**pohn**), *vb.* To put forward for consideration or adjudication <propone a will for probate>.

proponent, *n.* (16c) **1.** A person who puts forward a legal instrument for consideration or acceptance; esp., one who offers a will for probate. — Also termed *propounder.* **2.** A person who puts forward a proposal; one who argues in favor of something <a proponent of gun control>. **3.** *Parliamentary law.* A member who speaks in favor of a pending motion. Cf. OPPONENT (3).

proportionality. *Int'l law.* The principle that the use of force should be in proportion to the threat or grievance provoking the use of force.

proportionality review. (1976) *Criminal law.* An appellate court's analysis of whether a death sentence is arbitrary, capricious, or excessive by comparing the case in which it was imposed with similar cases in which the death penalty was approved or disapproved.

proportional quorum. See QUORUM.

proportional representation. 1. An electoral system that allocates legislative seats to each political group in proportion to its popular voting strength. **2.** See *proportional voting* under VOTING. • The term refers to two related but distinguishable concepts: proportional *outcome* (having members of a group elected in proportion to their numbers in the electorate) and proportional *involvement* (more precisely termed *proportional voting* and denoting the electoral system also known as *single transferable voting*).

proportional tax. See *flat tax* under TAX.

proportional voting. See VOTING.

proportionate-reduction clause. See LESSER-INTEREST CLAUSE.

proposal. Something offered for consideration or acceptance.

proposed agenda. See AGENDA.

proposed regulation. See REGULATION.

proposition. See *main motion* under MOTION (2).

propound (prə-**pownd**), *vb.* (16c) **1.** To offer for consideration or discussion. **2.** To make a proposal. **3.** To put forward (a will) as authentic.

propounder. An executor or administrator who offers a will or other testamentary document for admission to probate; PROPONENT.

prop. reg. *abbr.* See *proposed regulation* under REGULATION.

propria persona (**proh**-pree-ə pər-**soh**-nə), *adj. & adv.* [Latin] In his own person; PRO SE. — Sometimes shortened to *pro per.* — Abbr. *p.p.*

proprietary (prə-**prI**-ə-ter-ee), *adj.* (15c) **1.** Of or relating to a proprietor <the licensee's proprietary rights>. **2.** Of, relating to, or holding as property <the software designer sought to protect its proprietary data>.

proprietary act. See PROPRIETARY FUNCTION.

proprietary article. See ARTICLE.

proprietary capacity. See CAPACITY (1).

proprietary capital. See CAPITAL.

proprietary drug. See DRUG.

proprietary duty. See DUTY (2).

proprietary function. (1902) *Torts.* A municipality's conduct that is performed for the profit or benefit of the municipality, rather than for the benefit of the general public. • Generally, a municipality is not immune from tort liability for proprietary acts. But the distinction between proprietary acts and governmental functions has been abrogated by statute in many states. — Also termed *proprietary act.* Cf. GOVERNMENTAL FUNCTION.

proprietary government. See GOVERNMENT.

proprietary information. Information in which the owner has a protectable interest. See TRADE SECRET.

proprietary interest. See INTEREST (2).

proprietary lease. See LEASE.

proprietary license. See LICENSE.

proprietary name. See NAME.

proprietary power. See *power coupled with an interest* under POWER (3).

proprietary right. See RIGHT.

proprietary software. Software that cannot be used, redistributed, or modified without permission. • Proprietary software is usu. sold for profit, consists only of machine-readable code, and carries a limited license that restricts copying, modification, and redistribution. A user may usu. make a backup copy for personal use; but if the software is sold or given away, any backup copies must be passed on to the new user or destroyed. Cf. FREEWARE; SHAREWARE; SEMI-FREE SOFTWARE.

proprietary technology. *Intellectual property.* A body of knowledge or know-how that is owned or controlled by a person whose authorization is required before any other party may use that know-how or knowledge for commercial purposes. See TRADE SECRET.

proprietor, *n.* (16c) An owner, esp. one who runs a business. See SOLE PROPRIETORSHIP. — **proprietorship,** *n.*

propriety. *Hist.* Privately owned possessions; property.

proprio vigore (**proh**-pree-oh vi-**gor**-ee). [Latin] By its own strength.

propter (**prop**-tər). [Latin] For; on account of.

pro rata (proh **ray**-tə *or* **rah**-tə *or* **ra**-tə), *adv.* (16c) Proportionately; according to an exact rate, measure, or interest <the liability will be assessed pro rata between the defendants>. See RATABLE. — **pro rata,** *adj.*

pro rata clause. An insurance-policy provision — usu. contained in the "other insurance" section of the policy — that limits the insurer's liability to payment of the portion of the loss that the face amount of the policy bears to the total insurance available on the risk. — Also termed *pro rata distribution clause.* Cf. ESCAPE CLAUSE; EXCESS CLAUSE.

prorate (**proh**-rayt *or* proh-**rayt**), *vb.* (1858) To divide, assess, or distribute proportionately <prorate taxes between the buyer and the seller>. — **proration,** *n.*

prorogated jurisdiction. See JURISDICTION.

prorogation (proh-rə-**gay**-shən). (14c) **1.** The act of putting off to another day; esp., the discontinuance of a legislative session until its next term. **2.** *Civil law.* The extension of a court's or judge's jurisdiction by consent of the parties to a case that it would otherwise be incompetent to hear. — **prorogative,** *adj.*

tacit prorogation. *Civil law.* Consent to jurisdiction that arises when a party does not request recusal despite awareness that the judge is not qualified to try the case. Cf. *prorogated jurisdiction* under JURISDICTION.

prorogue (proh-**rohg** *or* prə-), *vb.* (15c) **1.** To postpone or defer. **2.** To discontinue a session of (a legislative assembly, esp. the British Parliament) without dissolution. **3.** To suspend or discontinue a legislative session.

proscribe, *vb.* (15c) **1.** To outlaw or prohibit; to forbid. **2.** *Roman & civil law.* To post or publish the name of (a person) as condemned to death and forfeiture of property.

proscription, *n.* (14c) **1.** The act of prohibiting; the state of being prohibited. **2.** A prohibition or restriction. Cf. PRESCRIPTION (1). — **proscriptive,** *adj.*

pro se (proh **say** *or* **see**), *adv. & adj.* [Latin] (1817) For oneself; on one's own behalf; without a lawyer <the defendant proceeded pro se> <a pro se defendant>. — Also termed *pro persona; in propria persona; propria persona; pro per.* See PROPRIA PERSONA.

pro se, *n.* (1857) One who represents oneself in a court proceeding without the assistance of a lawyer <the third case on the court's docket involving a pro se>. — Also termed *pro per; self-represented litigant;* (rarely) *pro se-er.*

prosecutable, *adj.* (Of a crime or person) subject to prosecution; capable of being prosecuted.

prosecute, *vb.* (15c) **1.** To commence and carry out a legal action <because the plaintiff failed to prosecute its contractual claims, the court dismissed the suit>. **2.** To institute and pursue a criminal action against (a person) <the notorious felon has been prosecuted in seven states>. **3.** To engage in; carry on <the company prosecuted its business for 12 years before going bankrupt>. — **prosecutory,** *adj.*

prosecuting attorney. See DISTRICT ATTORNEY.

prosecuting witness. See WITNESS.

prosecution. (16c) **1.** The commencement and carrying out of any action or scheme <the prosecution of a long, bloody war>. **2.** A criminal proceeding in which an accused person is tried <the conspiracy trial involved the prosecution of seven defendants>. — Also termed *criminal prosecution.*

> **deferred prosecution.** See *deferred judgment* under JUDGMENT.

> **private prosecution.** *Hist.* A criminal prosecution initiated by a privately employed attorney or by a layperson or private organization, rather than a district attorney or other government-employed prosecutor. • Until the 19th century, victims often had the burden of directly prosecuting criminals who had harmed them. With the rise of public-prosecution services, the need for private prosecutions declined. Though

uncommon, they are still sometimes permitted in England.

> **selective prosecution.** See SELECTIVE PROSECUTION.

> **sham prosecution.** (1903) A prosecution that seeks to circumvent a defendant's double-jeopardy protection by appearing to be prosecuted by another sovereignty, when it is in fact controlled by the sovereignty that already prosecuted the defendant for the same crime. • A sham prosecution is, in essence, a misuse of the dual-sovereignty doctrine. Under that doctrine, a defendant's protection against double jeopardy does not provide protection against a prosecution by a different sovereignty. For example, if the defendant was first tried in federal court and acquitted, that fact would not forbid the state authorities from prosecuting the defendant in state court. But a sham prosecution — for example, a later state-court prosecution that is completely dominated or manipulated by the federal authorities that already prosecuted the defendant, so that the state-court proceeding is merely a tool of the federal authorities — will not withstand a double-jeopardy challenge. See DUAL-SOVEREIGNTY DOCTRINE.

> **vindictive prosecution.** (1834) A prosecution in which a person is singled out under a law or regulation because the person has exercised a constitutionally protected right. Cf. SELECTIVE ENFORCEMENT.

3. The government attorneys who initiate and maintain a criminal action against an accused defendant <the prosecution rests>. **4.** *Patents.* The process of applying for a patent through the U.S. Patent and Trademark Office and negotiating with the patent examiner. — Also termed *patent-prosecution process.*

prosecution history. See FILE WRAPPER.

prosecution-history estoppel. See ESTOPPEL.

prosecution laches. See LACHES.

prosecution-laches doctrine. See CONTINUATION-APPLICATION LACHES DOCTRINE.

prosecutor, *n.* (16c) **1.** A legal officer who represents the state or federal government in criminal proceedings. See DISTRICT ATTORNEY; UNITED STATES ATTORNEY; ATTORNEY GENERAL. — Also termed *public prosecutor; state's attorney; public commissioner.*

> **public prosecutor. 1.** See PROSECUTOR (1). **2.** See DISTRICT ATTORNEY.

> **special prosecutor.** (1859) A lawyer appointed to investigate and, if justified, seek indictments in a particular case. See *independent counsel* under COUNSEL.

2. A private person who institutes and carries on a legal action, esp. a criminal action. — Also termed (in sense 2) *private prosecutor*. — **pros-ecutorial**, *adj.*

prosecutorial discretion. See DISCRETION (4).

prosecutorial immunity. See IMMUNITY.

prosecutorial misconduct. (1963) *Criminal law.* A prosecutor's improper or illegal act (or failure to act), esp. involving an attempt to avoid required disclosure or to persuade the jury to wrongly convict a defendant or assess an unjustified punishment. ● If prosecutorial misconduct results in a mistrial, a later prosecution may be barred under the Double Jeopardy Clause.

prosecutorial vindictiveness. *Criminal law.* The act or an instance of intentionally charging a more serious crime or seeking a more severe penalty in retaliation for a defendant's lawful exercise of a constitutional right.

prosecutrix (pros-ə-**kyoo**-triks). *Archaic.* A female prosecutor.

prosequi (**prahs**-ə-kwı), *vb.* [Latin] To follow up or pursue; to sue or prosecute. See NOLLE PROSE-QUI.

prosequitur (prə-**sek**-wə-tər *or* proh-). [Latin] He follows or pursues; he prosecutes.

prospectant evidence. See EVIDENCE.

prospective, *adj.* (18c) **1.** Effective or operative in the future <prospective application of the new statute>. Cf. RETROACTIVE. **2.** Anticipated or expected; likely to come about <prospective clients>.

prospective damages. See DAMAGES.

prospective heir. See HEIR.

prospective law. See *prospective statute* under STATUTE.

prospective nuisance. See *anticipatory nuisance* under NUISANCE.

prospective statute. See STATUTE.

prospective waiver. See WAIVER (1).

prospect theory. See INCENTIVE-TO-COMMERCIAL-IZE THEORY.

prospectus (prə-**spek**-təs). A printed document that describes the main features of an enterprise (esp. a corporation's business) and that is distributed to prospective buyers or investors; esp., a written description of a securities offering. ● Under SEC regulations, a publicly traded corporation must provide a prospectus before offering to sell stock in the corporation. Pl. **prospectuses.** See REGIS-TRATION STATEMENT. Cf. TOMBSTONE.

newspaper prospectus. A summary prospectus that the SEC allows to be disseminated through advertisements in newspapers, magazines, or other periodicals sent through the mails as second-class matter (though not distributed by the advertiser), when the securities involved are

issued by a foreign national government with which the United States maintains diplomatic relations.

preliminary prospectus. A prospectus for a stock issue that has been filed but not yet approved by the SEC. ● The SEC requires such a prospectus to contain a notice — printed in distinctive red lettering — that the document is not complete or final. That notice, which is usu. stamped or printed in red ink, typically reads as follows: "The information here given is subject to completion or amendment. A registration statement relating to these securities has been filed with the Securities and Exchange Commission. These securities cannot be sold — and offers to buy cannot be accepted — until the registration statement becomes effective. This prospectus does not constitute an offer to buy. And these securities cannot be sold in any state where the offer, solicitation, or sale would be unlawful before registration or qualification under the securities laws of that state." — Also termed *red-herring prospectus*; *red herring*.

prostitute, *n.* (16c) A person who engages in sexual acts in exchange for money or anything else of value.

child prostitute. A child who is offered or used for sex acts in exchange for money. ● Some people object to this phrase because the term "prostitute" suggests a degree of voluntariness or choice on the child's part, which is often not true. An alternative without those connotations is *prostituted child*.

prostituted child. See *child prostitute* under PROS-TITUTE.

prostitution, *n.* (16c) **1.** The act or practice of engaging in sexual activity for money or its equivalent; commercialized sex.

child prostitution. The act or practice of offering or using a minor for sex acts in exchange for money. See *child prostitute* under PROSTITUTE.

2. The act of debasing. — **prostitute,** *vb.* — **prostitute,** *n.*

pro tanto (proh **tan**-toh), *adv.* & *adj.* [Latin] (17c) To that extent; for so much; as far as it goes <the debt is pro tanto discharged> <a pro tanto payment>.

protected activity. (1918) Conduct that is permitted or encouraged by a statute or constitutional provision, and for which the actor may not legally be retaliated against. ● For example, Title VII of the Civil Rights Act prohibits an employer from retaliating against an employee who opposes a discriminatory employment practice or helps in investigating an allegedly discriminatory employment practice. An employee who is retaliated against for engaging in one of those activities has a claim against the employer. 42 USCA § 2000e-3(a).

protected class. See CLASS (1).

protected person. See PERSON (1).

protecting power. *Int'l law.* A country responsible for protecting another country's citizens and interests during a conflict or a suspension of diplomatic ties between the citizens' country and a third party. ● After a protecting power is accepted by both belligerents, it works to ensure the proper treatment of nationals who are in a belligerent's territory, esp. prisoners of war. If the parties cannot agree on a protecting power, the International Committee of the Red Cross is often appointed to this position.

protection, *n.* (14c) **1.** The act of protecting. **2.** PROTECTIONISM. **3.** COVERAGE (1). **4.** A document given by a notary public to sailors and other persons who travel abroad, certifying that the bearer is a U.S. citizen. — **protect,** *vb.*

Protection and Advocacy for Individuals with Mental Illness Act. A 1986 federal statute that provides funding for the state-level establishment of independent organizations dedicated to monitoring and protecting the rights of mentally ill citizens. 42 U.S.C. §§ 10801–10851. ● Formerly titled the *Protection and Advocacy for Mentally Ill Individuals Act,* this statute was renamed in the Children's Health Act of 2000 (114 Stat. 1101).

Protection and Advocacy for Mentally Ill Individuals Act. See PROTECTION AND ADVOCACY FOR INDIVIDUALS WITH MENTAL ILLNESS ACT.

protection covenant. *Oil & gas.* The implied promise in an oil-and-gas lease that the lessee will protect the property against the loss of oil and gas by drainage from the producing reservoir by drilling one or more offsetting wells. ● The covenant applies only if a reasonably prudent operator would drill the additional wells. — Also termed *covenant to protect against drainage.* See REASONABLY PRUDENT-OPERATOR STANDARD.

protectionism. (1844) The protection of domestic businesses and industries against foreign competition by imposing high tariffs and restricting imports. — **protectionist,** *adj.*

protection money. (18c) **1.** A bribe paid to an officer as an inducement not to interfere with the criminal activities of the briber. ● Examples include payments to an officer in exchange for the officer's releasing an arrestee, removing records of traffic violations from a court's files, and refraining from making a proper arrest. **2.** Money extorted from a business owner by one who promises to "protect" the business premises, with the implied threat that if the owner does not pay, the person requesting the payment will harm the owner or damage the premises.

protection order. See RESTRAINING ORDER (1).

protective appeal. See APPEAL.

protective committee. A group of security holders or preferred stockholders appointed to protect the interests of their group when the corporation is liquidated or reorganized.

protective custody. See CUSTODY (1).

protective order. (1884) **1.** A court order prohibiting or restricting a party from engaging in conduct (esp. a legal procedure such as discovery) that unduly annoys or burdens the opposing party or a third-party witness. **2.** RESTRAINING ORDER (1).

blanket protective order. A protective order that covers a broad subject or class. — Often shortened to *blanket order.* — Also termed *umbrella protective order.*

emergency protective order. A temporary protective order granted on an expedited basis, usu. after an ex parte hearing (without notice to the other side), most commonly to provide injunctive relief from an abuser in a domestic-violence case; esp., a short-term restraining order that is issued at the request of a law-enforcement officer in response to a domestic-violence complaint from a victim who is in immediate danger. ● A victim of domestic violence can obtain an EPO only through a law-enforcement officer. There is no notice requirement, but the abuser must be served with the order. The duration of an EPO varies from three to seven days, depending on state law. — Abbr. EPO. Cf. TEMPORARY RESTRAINING ORDER.

permanent protective order. A protective order of indefinite duration granted after a hearing with notice to both sides; esp., a court order that prohibits an abuser from contacting or approaching the protected person for a long period, usu. years. Despite the name, permanent orders often have expiration dates set by state law. An order may also require the abuser to perform certain acts such as attending counseling or providing financial support for the protected person. — Abbr. PPO.

protective principle. *Int'l law.* The doctrine that a sovereign state has the power to assert jurisdiction over a person whose conduct outside its boundaries threatens its security or could interfere with the operation of its government functions.

protective search. See SEARCH.

protective sweep. (1973) A police officer's quick and limited search — conducted after the officer has lawfully entered the premises — based on a reasonable belief that such a search is necessary to protect the officer or others from harm.

protective tariff. See TARIFF (2).

protective trust. See TRUST.

protector. **1.** An unrelated, disinterested overseer of a trust who possesses broader authority than a trustee. ● Protectors are usu. appointed to manage offshore trusts, but the concept is slowly being applied to domestic trusts. Protectors often possess broad powers to act for the benefit of the trust, as by removing trustees and clarifying or modifying trust terms to promote the settlor's objectives. For these reasons, a protector is generally not a trustee or beneficiary of the trust. Cf. TRUSTEE. **2.** A person who, having been named in an instrument creating a fee tail, has the responsibility of exercising discretion over whether the tenant in tail may bar the entail. — Also termed *protector of the settlement*.

protectorate (prə-**tek**-tə-rət). **1.** *Int'l law.* The relationship between a weaker nation and a stronger one when the weaker nation has transferred the management of its more important international affairs to the stronger nation. **2.** *Int'l law.* The weaker or dependent nation within such a relationship. **3.** (*usu. cap.*) The period in British history — from 1653 to 1659 — during which Oliver Cromwell and Richard Cromwell governed. **4.** The British government in the period from 1653 to 1659.

protégé. **1.** A person protected by or under the care or training of another person or an entity, esp. one who is established or influential. **2.** *International law.* A nation that is under the protection of another nation. **3.** *International law.* A person who is a citizen of a protected nation or otherwise recognized by treaty as a protected person.

pro tem. *abbr.* PRO TEMPORE.

pro tempore (proh **tem**-pə-ree), *adv.* & *adj.* [Latin] (15c) For the time being; appointed to occupy a position temporarily <a judge pro tempore>. — Abbr. pro tem.

protest, *n.* (15c) **1.** A formal statement or action expressing dissent or disapproval. ● Under some circumstances, a protest is lodged to preserve a claim or right. **2.** A notary public's written statement that, upon presentment, a negotiable instrument was neither paid nor accepted. — Also termed *initial protest*; *noting protest*. Cf. NOTICE OF DISHONOR. **3.** A formal statement, usu. in writing, disputing a debt's legality or validity but agreeing to make payment while reserving the right to recover the amount at a later time. ● The disputed debt is described as *under protest*. **4.** *Tax.* A taxpayer's statement to the collecting officer that payment is being made unwillingly because the taxpayer believes the tax to be invalid. **5.** *Int'l law.* A formal communication from one subject of international law to another objecting to conduct or a claim by the latter as violating international law. **6.** *Patents.* A proceeding in the U.S. Patent and Trademark Office to determine patentability of an invention after a third party has challenged

it in a petition. ● Unlike in a public use proceeding, the protestant has no right to participate in the proceeding beyond filing the petition and supporting documents. 37 CFR 1.291. Cf. PUBLIC-USE PROCEEDING. — **protest,** *vb.*

protestant. *Patents.* A person who files a protest petition with the U.S. Patent and Trademark Office challenging the patentability of an invention. See PROTEST.

protestation (prot-ə-**stay**-shən). (14c) **1.** *Common-law pleading.* A declaration by which a party makes an oblique allegation or denial of some fact, claiming that it does or does not exist or is or is not legally sufficient, while not directly affirming or denying the fact. **2.** *Scots law.* A defendant's act in a civil case to compel a pursuer (plaintiff) who has failed to take the necessary procedural steps either to proceed or to allow the action to fall.

protest certificate. A notarial certificate declaring (1) that a holder in due course has recruited the notary public to present a previously refused or dishonored negotiable instrument, (2) that the notary has presented the instrument to the person responsible for payment or acceptance (the *drawee*), (3) that the instrument was presented at a given time and place, and (4) that the drawee refused or dishonored the instrument. ● In former practice, the notary would issue a protest certificate, which could then be presented to the drawee and any other liable parties as notice that the holder could seek damages for the dishonored negotiable instrument. — Also termed *notarial protest certificate*. See NOTICE OF DISHONOR.

protest fee. A fee charged by a bank or other financial institution when an item (such as a check) is presented but cannot be collected.

prothonotary (prə-**thon**-ə-ter-ee or proh-thə-**noh**-tə-ree), *n.* A chief clerk in certain courts of law. — Also termed *protonotary*. — **prothonotarial,** *adj.*

protocol. **1.** A summary of a document or treaty. **2.** A treaty amending and supplementing another treaty. **3.** The formal record of the proceedings of a conference or congress. — Also termed *procès-verbal*. **4.** The minutes of a meeting, usu. initialed by all participants after confirming accuracy. **5.** The rules of diplomatic etiquette; the practices that nations observe in the course of their contacts with one another.

protonotary. See PROTHONOTARY.

protutor (proh-t[y]oo-tər). *Civil law.* A person who, though not legally appointed as a guardian, administers another's affairs.

provable, *adj.* (15c) Capable of being proved.

prove, *vb.* (13c) To establish or make certain; to establish the truth of (a fact or hypothesis) by satisfactory evidence.

prove up, *vb.* (1832) To present or complete the proof of (something) <deciding not to put a doctor on the stand, the plaintiff attempted to prove up his damages with medical records only>.

prove-up, *n.* The establishment of a prima facie claim. • A prove-up is necessary when a factual assertion is unopposed because even without opposition, the claim must be supported by evidence.

provided, *conj.* (15c) **1.** On the condition or understanding (that) <we will sign the contract provided that you agree to the following conditions>. **2.** Except (that) <all permittees must be at least 18 years of age, provided that those with a bona fide hardship must be at least 15 years of age>. **3.** And <a railway car must be operated by a full crew if it extends for more than 15 continuous miles, provided that a full crew must consist of at least six railway workers>.

provident plea. See PLEA (1).

province, *n.* **1.** An administrative district into which a country has been divided. **2.** A sphere of activity of a profession such as medicine or law.

provincial synod. See SYNOD.

provision. (15c) **1.** A clause in a statute, contract, or other legal instrument. **2.** A stipulation made beforehand. See PROVISO.

provisional, *adj.* (16c) **1.** Temporary <a provisional injunction>. **2.** Conditional <a provisional government>.

provisional alimony. See *temporary alimony* under ALIMONY.

provisional application. See PATENT APPLICATION.

provisional attachment. See ATTACHMENT (1).

provisional court. See COURT.

provisional director. See DIRECTOR.

provisional exit. *Criminal procedure.* A prisoner's temporary release from prison for a court appearance, hospital treatment, work detail, or other purpose requiring a release with the expectation of return.

provisional government. See GOVERNMENT.

provisional injunction. See *preliminary injunction* under INJUNCTION.

provisional partition. See PARTITION.

provisional patent application. See *provisional application* under PATENT APPLICATION.

provisional remedy. See REMEDY.

provisional right. *Patents.* The right to obtain a reasonable royalty for use of a patented invention

or process by an infringer with actual notice during the period between the publication of a patent application and the time a patent is issued. • The right is only available if the invention as claimed in the issued patent is substantially identical to the invention as claimed in the published application. 35 USCA § 154.

provisional seizure. See ATTACHMENT (1).

proviso (prə-**vɪ**-zoh). (15c) **1.** A limitation, condition, or stipulation upon whose compliance a legal or formal document's validity or application may depend. **2.** In drafting, a provision that begins with the words *provided that* and supplies a condition, exception, or addition.

provocation, *n.* (15c) **1.** The act of inciting another to do something, esp. to commit a crime. **2.** Something (such as words or actions) that affects a person's reason and self-control, esp. causing the person to commit a crime impulsively. — **provoke,** *vb.* — **provocative,** *adj.*

   adequate provocation. (1842) Something that would cause a reasonable person to act without self-control and lose any premeditated state of mind. • The usual form of adequate provocation is the heat of passion. Adequate provocation can reduce a criminal charge, as from murder to voluntary manslaughter. — Also termed *adequate cause; reasonable provocation.* See HEAT OF PASSION. Cf. SELF-DEFENSE.

   reasonable provocation. See *adequate provocation.*

provost marshal. *Military law.* A staff officer who supervises a command's military police and advises the commander.

proximate (**prok**-sə-mit), *adj.* (17c) **1.** Immediately before or after. **2.** Very near or close in time or space. Cf. IMMEDIATE. — **proximateness,** *n.*

proximate cause. See CAUSE (1).

proximate consequence. (1840) A result following an unbroken sequence from some (esp. negligent) event.

proximate damages. See DAMAGES.

proximity. (15c) The quality or state of being near in time, place, order, or relation.

proxy, *n.* (15c) **1.** One who is authorized to act as a substitute for another; esp., in corporate law, a person who is authorized to vote another's stock shares. Cf. *absentee vote* under VOTE (1). **2.** The grant of authority by which a person is so authorized. **3.** The document granting this authority. — Also termed (for sense 3 in Roman law) *procuratorium.*

proxy contest. A struggle between two corporate factions to obtain the votes of uncommitted shareholders. • A proxy contest usu. occurs when a group of dissident shareholders mounts a battle against the corporation's managers. — Also termed *proxy fight*.

proxy directive. A document that appoints a surrogate decision-maker for the declarant's healthcare decisions. Cf. ADVANCE DIRECTIVE; INSTRUCTION DIRECTIVE; LIVING WILL.

proxy marriage. See MARRIAGE (3).

proxy solicitation. A request that a corporate shareholder authorize another person to cast the shareholder's vote at a corporate meeting.

proxy statement. An informational document that accompanies a proxy solicitation and explains a proposed action (such as a merger) by the corporation.

PRP. *abbr.* POTENTIALLY RESPONSIBLE PARTY.

prudent, *adj.* (14c) Circumspect or judicious in one's dealings; cautious. — **prudence,** *n.*

prudent-investor rule. (1960) *Trusts.* The principle that a fiduciary must invest in only those securities or portfolios of securities that a reasonable person would buy. ● The origin of the prudent-investor rule is *Harvard College v. Amory,* 26 Mass. 446 (1830). This case stressed two points for a trustee to consider when making investments: probable income and probable safety. The trustee must consider both when making investments. Originally termed the *prudent-man rule,* the Restatement (Third) of Trusts changed the term to *prudent-investor rule.* — Also termed *prudent-person rule.*

prudent-operator standard. See REASONABLY-PRUDENT-OPERATOR STANDARD.

prudent person. See REASONABLE PERSON.

prudent-person rule. See PRUDENT-INVESTOR RULE.

prurient (**pruur**-ee-ənt), *adj.* (17c) Characterized by or arousing inordinate or unusual sexual desire <films appealing to prurient interests>. See OBSCENITY. — **prurience,** *n.*

PRWORA. *abbr.* PERSONAL RESPONSIBILITY AND WORK OPPORTUNITY RECONCILIATION ACT.

p.s. *abbr.* (*usu. cap.*) **1.** Public statute. See PUBLIC LAW (2). **2.** Postscript.

pseudo-foreign-corporation statute. A state law regulating foreign corporations that either derive a specified high percentage of their income from that state or have a high percentage of their stock owned by people living in that state.

pseudograph (**soo**-də-graf). A false writing; a forgery.

pseudo-guarantee treaty. See *guarantee treaty* under TREATY (1).

pseudonym (**sood**-ə-nim), *n.* A fictitious name or identity. Cf. ALIAS. — **pseudonymous** (soo-**don**-ə-məs), *adj.* — **pseudonymity** (sood-ə-**nim**-ə-tee), *n.*

pseudonymous work. See WORK (2).

pseudopresumption of law. See *presumption of law* under PRESUMPTION.

pseudo-stepparent adoption. See *second-parent adoption* under ADOPTION.

PSI. *abbr.* PRESENTENCE INVESTIGATION REPORT.

psychiatric (sɪ-kee-**at**-rik), *adj.* Of or relating to the study or treatment of mental, emotional, and behavioral disorders by medical doctors trained in the field of psychiatry.

psychiatric examination. *Criminal law.* An analysis performed by a psychiatrist to determine a defendant's mental state. ● A defendant in a criminal prosecution may undergo a psychiatric examination to determine competence to stand trial or to establish a defense based on some mental condition, such as insanity. — Also (more broadly) termed *mental examination.* See INSANITY DEFENSE; COMPETENCY (2). Cf. *competency proceeding* under PROCEEDING; SUBSTANTIAL-CAPACITY TEST. Cf. INDEPENDENT MENTAL EVALUATION.

psychological abuse. See *emotional abuse* under ABUSE.

psychological fact. See FACT.

psychological father. See *psychological parent* under PARENT.

psychological mother. See *psychological parent* under PARENT.

psychological parent. See PARENT.

psychopath (**sɪ**-kə-path), *n.* (1885) **1.** A person with a mental disorder characterized by an extremely antisocial personality that often leads to aggressive, perverted, or criminal behavior. ● The formal psychiatric term for the mental illness from which a psychopath suffers is *antisocial personality disorder.* **2.** Loosely, a person who is mentally ill or unstable. — Also termed *sociopath.* — **psychopathy** (sɪ-**kop**-ə-thee), *n.* — **psychopathic** (sɪ-kə-**path**-ik), *adj.*

psychotherapist–client privilege. See *psychotherapist-patient privilege* under PRIVILEGE (3).

psychotherapist–patient privilege. See PRIVILEGE (3).

PTA. *abbr.* PATENT-TERM ADJUSTMENT.

PTI. See *previously taxed income* under INCOME.

PTO. *abbr.* Patent and Trademark Office. See UNITED STATES PATENT AND TRADEMARK OFFICE.

PTO Code of Professional Responsibility. Disciplinary rules and canons of ethics for practicing before the U.S. Patent and Trademark Office. ● The Code is found at 37 CFR §§ 10.20-10.112. — Often shortened to PTO Code.

PTP. See *publicly traded partnership* under PARTNERSHIP.

puberty. 1. The stage of physical development in which a person takes on secondary sexual characteristics, when it becomes possible to reproduce. • In females, the beginning of this stage is marked by the menarche. **2.** *Hist.* The earliest age at which one could presumptively consent and to legally enter into a binding marriage. • At English common law, children became marriageable at the onset of legal puberty (age 12 for girls and 14 for boys). At French civil law, a marriage was invalid if contracted before the end of legal puberty (age 15 for girls and 18 for boys). An underage spouse had the power to void the marriage. — Also termed (in English common law) *age of discretion.*

Pub. L. *abbr.* PUBLIC LAW (2).

public, *adj.* (14c) **1.** Relating or belonging to an entire community, state, or nation. **2.** Open or available for all to use, share, or enjoy. **3.** (Of a company) having shares that are available on an open market.

public, *n.* (16c) **1.** The people of a nation or community as a whole <a crime against the public>. **2.** A place open or visible to the public <in public>.

Public Access to Court Electronic Records. A computer system by which subscribers can obtain online information from the federal courts, including information from a court's docket sheet about the parties, filing, and orders in a specific case. — Abbr. PACER.

public accommodation. See ACCOMMODATION.

public act. See PUBLIC LAW (2).

public action. See *civil action* under ACTION (4).

public administration. See ADMINISTRATION.

public administrator. See ADMINISTRATOR (2).

public advocate. See ADVOCATE.

public agency. See AGENCY (3).

public agent. See AGENT (2).

publican (pəb-li-kən). **1.** A person authorized by license to keep a public house for consumption of alcoholic beverages on or off the premises. **2.** PUBLICANUS.

public appointment. See APPOINTMENT (1).

publication, *n.* (14c) **1.** Generally, the act of declaring or announcing to the public. **2.** *Copyright.* The offering or distribution of copies of a work to the public. • At common law, publication marked the dividing line between state and federal protection, but the Copyright Act of 1976 superseded most of common-law copyright and thereby diminished the significance of publication. Under the Act, an original work is considered published only when it is first made publicly available without restriction.

divestitive publication. *Archaic.* The public distribution of an author's work on a scale large enough to divest the author of any claim to state common-law copyright protection. • The Copyright Act of 1976 preempted most common-law copyright. — Sometimes (erroneously) written *divestive publication.*

general publication. Distribution of an author's work to the public, as opposed to a selected group, whether or not restrictions are placed on the use of the work. • Before the Copyright Act of 1976, a general publication was generally held to divest common-law rights in a work. Rather, the author was deemed to have dedicated the work to the public. Cf. *limited publication.*

investitive publication. *Archaic.* The public distribution of an author's work on a scale large enough to qualify for federal statutory copyright protection. • Since 1976 copyright has protected works since their creation, rather than their publication.

limited publication. Distribution of copies of an author's work to a selected group for a limited purpose and with no permission to copy the work, at a time when copies are not available to the general public. • Before the Copyright Act of 1976 made publication irrelevant, courts distinguished between limited publication and general publication to decide whether federal copyright laws applied. Under that Act, a work published before January 1, 1978 without proper copyright notice entered the public domain unless the publication was limited. — Also termed *private publication.* Cf. *general publication.*

private publication. See *limited publication.*

3. *Defamation.* The communication of defamatory words to someone other than the person defamed. • The communication may be in any form, verbal or nonverbal. **4.** *Wills & estates.* The formal declaration made by a testator when signing the will that it is the testator's will. • There is no requirement that the provisions of the will or the identities of the beneficiaries be revealed to the witnesses.

publication-quality drawings. *Patents.* Illustrations or drawings filed with a patent application and capable of being scanned.

publication right. *Copyright.* The right of an author or artist to decide when to reveal or display a creative work. • Publication is one of the moral rights of artists recognized in civil-law countries and much of Europe, but largely unavailable in the United States. — Also termed *right of disclosure.*

public attorney. See ATTORNEY (2).

public authority. See AUTHORITY (3).

public-authority justification. See JUSTIFICATION.

public-benefit corporation. See *public corporation* (3) under CORPORATION.

public bill. See BILL (3).

public blockade. See BLOCKADE.

public boundary. See BOUNDARY.

public building. A building that is accessible to the public; esp., one owned by the government.

Public Buildings Service. A unit in the General Services Administration responsible for constructing federal buildings and managing federally owned and leased property through 11 regional offices. — Abbr. PBS.

public carrier. See *common carrier* under CARRIER.

public character. See PUBLIC FIGURE.

public commissioner. See PROSECUTOR (1).

public contract. See CONTRACT.

Public Contracts Act. See WALSH–HEALEY ACT.

public controversy. See CONTROVERSY.

public-convenience-and-necessity standard. (1964) A common criterion used by a governmental body to assess whether a particular request or project should be granted or approved.

public corporation. See CORPORATION.

public debt. See DEBT.

public defender. (1827) A lawyer or staff of lawyers, usu. publicly appointed and paid, whose duty is to represent indigent criminal defendants. — Often shortened to *defender*. — Abbr. P.D.

public delict. See DELICT.

public director. See DIRECTOR.

public disclosure of private facts. See DISCLOSURE (1).

public disturbance. See BREACH OF THE PEACE.

public document. See DOCUMENT.

public domain. (17c) **1.** Government-owned land. **2.** *Hist.* Government lands that are open to entry and settlement. • Today virtually all federal lands are off-limits to traditional entry and settlement. **3.** *Intellectual property.* The universe of inventions and creative works that are not protected by intellectual-property rights and are therefore available for anyone to use without charge. • When copyright, trademark, patent, or trade-secret rights are lost or expire, the intellectual property they had protected becomes part of the public domain and can be appropriated by anyone without liability for infringement.

public-duty doctrine. (1976) *Torts.* The rule that a governmental entity (such as a state or municipality) cannot be held liable for an individual plaintiff's injury resulting from a governmental officer's or employee's breach of a duty owed to the general public rather than to the individual plaintiff. — Also termed *public-duty rule*. See SPECIAL-DUTY DOCTRINE.

public easement. See EASEMENT.

public enemy. See ENEMY.

public entity. See ENTITY.

public-exchange offer. See OFFER.

public fact. See FACT.

public figure. (1871) A person who has achieved fame or notoriety or who has voluntarily become involved in a public controversy. • A public figure (or public official) suing for defamation must prove that the defendant acted with actual malice. *New York Times Co. v. Sullivan*, 376 U.S. 254, 84 S.Ct. 710 (1964). — Also termed *public character*.

   all-purpose public figure. A person who achieves such pervasive fame or notoriety that he or she becomes a public figure for all purposes and in all contexts. • For example, a person who occupies a position with great persuasive power and influence may become an all-purpose public figure whether or not the person actively seeks attention. *Gertz v. Robert Welch, Inc.*, 418 U.S. 323, 345, 94 S.Ct. 2997, 3009 (1974).

   limited-purpose public figure. (1979) A person who, having become involved in a particular public issue, has achieved fame or notoriety only in relation to that particular issue.

public forum. (1935) *Constitutional law.* A public place where people traditionally gather to express ideas and exchange views. • To be constitutional, the government's regulation of a public forum must be narrowly tailored to serve a significant government interest and must usu. be limited to time-place-or-manner restrictions. — Also termed *open forum*. See TIME-PLACE-OR-MANNER RESTRICTION. Cf. NONPUBLIC FORUM.

   designated public forum. (1985) Public property that has not traditionally been open for public assembly and debate but that the government has opened for use by the public as a place for expressive activity, such as a public-university facility or a publicly owned theater. • Unlike a traditional public forum, the government does not have to retain the open character of a designated public forum. Also, the subject matter of the expression permitted in a designated public forum may be limited to accord with the character of the forum; reasonable, content-neutral time, place, and manner restrictions are generally permissible. But any prohibition based on the content of the expression must be narrowly drawn to effectuate a compelling state interest, as with a traditional public forum. — Also termed *limited public forum*; *nontraditional public forum*.

traditional public forum. (1973) Public property that has by long tradition — as opposed to governmental designation — been used by the public for assembly and expression, such as a public street, public sidewalk, or public park. ● To be constitutional, the government's content-neutral restrictions of the time, place, or manner of expression must be narrowly tailored to serve a significant government interest, and leave open ample alternative channels of communication. Any government regulation of expression that is based on the content of the expression must meet the much higher test of being necessary to serve a compelling state interest. — Also termed *quintessential public forum*.

public-function doctrine. See PUBLIC-FUNCTION TEST.

public-function rationale. See GOVERNMENTAL-FUNCTION THEORY.

public-function test. (1966) In a suit under 42 USCA § 1983, the doctrine that a private person's actions constitute state action if the private person performs functions that are traditionally reserved to the state. — Also termed *public-function doctrine*; *public-function theory*.

public fund. See FUND (1).

public grant. See PATENT (2).

public ground. See *public land* under LAND.

public health. See HEALTH.

Public Health Service. The combined offices and units of the U.S. Department of Health and Human Services responsible for promoting the physical and mental health of American citizens.

public hearing. See HEARING.

public highway. See HIGHWAY.

public house. 1. *Archaic.* An inn. **2.** A tavern where alcoholic beverages may be bought and consumed on the premises. ● The British term *pub* is an abbreviation of *public house*. — Also termed (in sense 2) *tippling house*.

publici juris (pəb-li-sɪ **joor**-is), *adj.* [Latin] Of public right; of importance to or available to the public <a city holds title to its streets as property *publici juris*> <words that are in general or common use and that are merely descriptive are *publici juris* and cannot be appropriated as a trademark>.

public improvement. See IMPROVEMENT.

public injury. See INJURY.

public institution. See INSTITUTION (3).

public instrument. See PUBLIC WRITING.

public interest. (16c) **1.** The general welfare of the public that warrants recognition and protection.

2. Something in which the public as a whole has a stake; esp., an interest that justifies governmental regulation.

public-interest exception. (1957) The principle that an appellate court may consider and decide a moot case — although such decisions are generally prohibited — if (1) the case involves a question of considerable public importance, (2) the question is likely to arise in the future, and (3) the question has evaded appellate review.

public-interest law. Legal practice that advances social justice or other causes for the public good, such as environmental protection. ● Although public-interest law primarily encompasses private not-for-profit work, the term is sometimes used to include the work of government agencies such as public-defender offices. Cf. CAUSE LAWYERING; *social justice* under JUSTICE.

public-interest lawyer. See LAWYER.

public international law. See INTERNATIONAL LAW.

public intoxication. See INTOXICATION.

public invitee. See INVITEE.

publicist. 1. A public-relations specialist. **2.** An international-law scholar. ● The term applies to scholars of both public and private international law.

public-key encryption. See KEY ENCRYPTION.

public land. See LAND.

public law. (16c) **1.** The body of law dealing with the relations between private individuals and the government, and with the structure and operation of the government itself; constitutional law, criminal law, and administrative law taken together. Cf. PRIVATE LAW (1). **2.** A statute affecting the general public. ● Federal public laws are first published in *Statutes at Large* and are eventually collected by subject in the U.S. Code. — Abbr. Pub. L.; P.L. — Also termed *public statute* (abbr. P.S.); *general statute*; (esp. in BrE) *public act*. Cf. *general law* (1) under LAW; *general act* and *public act* under ACT (3). **3.** Constitutional law.

public-lending right. *Copyright.* In the U.K. and some other countries, the right of an author to a royalty for works that are lent out by a public library.

public-liability insurance. See *liability insurance* under INSURANCE.

publicly held corporation. See *public corporation* (1) under CORPORATION.

publicly traded partnership. See PARTNERSHIP.

public market. See MARKET.

public-meeting law. See SUNSHINE LAW.

public minister. See MINISTER.

public morality. See MORALITY.

public necessity. See NECESSITY.

public notice. See NOTICE.

public nuisance. See NUISANCE.

public offense. See OFFENSE (1).

public offer. See *offer to all the world* under OFFER.

public offering. See OFFERING.

public office. A position whose occupant has legal authority to exercise a government's sovereign powers for a fixed period.

public official. See OFFICIAL (1).

public passage. A right held by the public to pass over a body of water, whether the underlying land is publicly or privately owned.

public-performance right. See PERFORMANCE RIGHTS.

public person. A sovereign government, or a body or person delegated authority under it.

public place. Any location that the local, state, or national government maintains for the use of the public, such as a highway, park, or public building.

public policy. (16c) **1.** Broadly, principles and standards regarded by the legislature or by the courts as being of fundamental concern to the state and the whole of society. ● Courts sometimes use the term to justify their decisions, as when declaring a contract void because it is "contrary to public policy." — Also termed *policy of the law*. **2.** More narrowly, the principle that a person should not be allowed to do anything that would tend to injure the public at large.

public-policy limitation. (1961) *Tax.* A judicially developed principle that a person should not be allowed to deduct expenses related to an activity that is contrary to the public welfare. ● This principle is reflected in the Internal Revenue Code's specific disallowance provisions (such as for kickbacks and bribes).

public pond. See GREAT POND.

public power. See POWER (3).

public property. See PROPERTY.

public prosecutor. **1.** See DISTRICT ATTORNEY. **2.** See PROSECUTOR (1).

public purpose. (18c) An action by or at the direction of a government for the benefit of the community as a whole.

public record. See RECORD.

public-records doctrine. The principle, applicable in many states, that a third person acquiring or interested in real or immovable property may rely on the face of relevant public records and need not investigate further for unrecorded interests.

public-records exception. The exception from the hearsay rule for the contents of certain public records or the absence of a record where it would ordinarily be kept in public archives. Fed. R. Evid. 803(8)–(10).

public relations. **1.** The business of creating or maintaining a company's goodwill or good public image. **2.** A company's existing goodwill or public image. — Abbr. PR.

public reprimand. See REPRIMAND.

public revenue. See REVENUE.

public right. See RIGHT.

public right-of-way. See RIGHT-OF-WAY.

public safety. (16c) The welfare and protection of the general public, usu. expressed as a governmental responsibility <Department of Public Safety>.

public-safety exception. (1984) *Evidence.* An exception to the *Miranda* rule, allowing into evidence an otherwise suppressible statement by a defendant concerning information that the police needed at the time it was made in order to protect the public. ● If, for example, a victim tells the police that an assailant had a gun, and upon the suspect's arrest the police find a holster but no gun, they would be entitled immediately to ask where the gun is. Under the public-safety exception, the suspect's statement of the gun's location would be admissible.

public sale. See SALE.

public school. See SCHOOL.

public seal. See SEAL.

public sector. (1934) The part of the economy or an industry that is controlled by the government. Cf. PRIVATE SECTOR.

public security. See SECURITY.

public service. (16c) **1.** A service provided or facilitated by the government for the general public's convenience and benefit. **2.** Government employment; work performed for or on behalf of the government. **3.** Broadly, any work that serves the public good, including government work and public-interest law.

public-service commission. See COMMISSION (3).

public-service corporation. See CORPORATION.

public servitude. See SERVITUDE (2).

public session. See *open session* under SESSION (1).

public statute. **1.** See *general statute* under STATUTE. **2.** See PUBLIC LAW (2).

public stock. See STOCK.

public store. See STORE.

public tort. See TORT.

public trial. See TRIAL.

public trust. See *charitable trust* under TRUST.

public-trust doctrine. The principle that navigable waters are preserved for the public use, and that the state is responsible for protecting the public's right to the use.

publicum jus (pəb-li-kəm jəs). [Latin] See JUS PUBLICUM.

public use. See USE (1).

public-use bar. *Patents.* A statutory bar that prevents the granting of a patent for an invention that was publicly used or sold in the United States more than one year before the application date. 35 USCA § 102(b). • The doctrine can be invoked for any public use, any commercial use, any sale or offer of sale, or any private transfer made without a pledge of secrecy. Cf. PRIVATE-USE EXCEPTION. — Also termed *prior-use bar.*

public-use proceeding. *Patents.* An investigation into whether a patent is barred because the invention was publicly used or sold more than a year before the application was filed. • Rarely used, this procedure is instituted upon a petition by someone protesting the application. If the petition and supporting documents make out a prima facie case, the examiner will hold a hearing and issue a final decision, which is not reviewable. 37 CFR 1.292. — Abbr. PUP. Cf. PROTEST.

public utility. See UTILITY.

public utility district. See *municipal utility district* under DISTRICT.

Public Utility Holding Company Act. A federal law enacted in 1935 to protect investors and consumers from the economic disadvantages produced by the small number of holding companies that owned most of the nation's utilities. • The Act also sought to protect the public from deceptive security advertising. 15 USCA §§ 79 et seq. — Abbr. PUHCA.

public verdict. See VERDICT.

public vessel. See VESSEL.

Public Vessels Act. A federal law enacted in 1925 to allow claims against the United States for damages caused by one of its vessels. 46 USCA app. §§ 781–90. — Abbr. PVA.

public war. See WAR.

public water. See WATER.

public welfare. See WELFARE (1).

public-welfare offense. See OFFENSE (1).

public wharf. See WHARF.

public works. See WORKS.

public worship. See WORSHIP.

public writing. 1. The written acts or records of a government (or its constituent units) that are not constitutionally or statutorily protected from disclosure. • Laws and judicial records, for example, are public writings. A private writing that becomes part of a public record may be a public writing in some circumstances. **2.** *Rare.* A document prepared by a notary public in the presence of the parties who sign it before witnesses. — Also termed (in both senses) *public instrument*; (in sense 2) *escritura publica.*

public wrong. See WRONG.

publish, *vb.* (14c) **1.** To distribute copies (of a work) to the public. **2.** To communicate (defamatory words) to someone other than the person defamed. See INTENT TO PUBLISH. **3.** To declare (a will) to be the true expression of one's testamentary intent. **4.** To make (evidence) available to a jury during trial. See PUBLICATION.

PUC. *abbr.* Public Utilities Commission.

PUD. *abbr.* **1.** PLANNED-UNIT DEVELOPMENT. **2.** See *municipal utility district* under DISTRICT.

pueblo (**pweb**-loh). [Spanish] A town or village, esp. in the southwestern United States.

puerility (pyoo-ə-**ril**-ə-tee *or* pyuu-**ril**-ə-tee). *Civil law.* A child's status between infancy and puberty.

puffer. See BY-BIDDER.

puffing. (18c) **1.** The expression of an exaggerated opinion — as opposed to a factual misrepresentation — with the intent to sell a good or service. • Puffing involves expressing opinions, not asserting something as a fact. Although there is some leeway in puffing goods, a seller may not misrepresent them or say that they have attributes that they do not possess. — Also termed *puffery*; *sales puffery*; *dealer's talk.* **2.** Secret bidding at an auction by or on behalf of a seller; BY-BIDDING.

Pugh clause. *Oil & gas.* A provision in an oil-and-gas lease modifying the effect of most lease-pooling clauses by severing pooled portions of the lease from unpooled portions of the lease. • Drilling or production on a pooled portion will not maintain the lease for the unpooled portions. The clause is named for Lawrence G. Pugh, an attorney from Cowley, Louisiana, who drafted the first version in 1947. In Texas it is termed a Freestone rider. See POOLING.

PUHCA. *abbr.* PUBLIC UTILITY HOLDING COMPANY ACT.

puis darrein continuance (pwis dar-ayn kən-**tin**-yoo-ənts). [Law French "since the last continuance"] See *plea puis darrein continuance* under PLEA (3).

puisne (**pyoo**-nee), *adj.* [Law French] (16c) Junior in rank; subordinate.

puisne judge. See JUDGE.

puisne mortgage. See *junior mortgage* under MORTGAGE.

Pullman **abstention.** See ABSTENTION.

pulsator (pəl-**say**-tər). *Civil law.* A plaintiff or actor.

pumping unit. *Oil & gas.* Equipment used to pump oil to the surface when the pressure difference between the formation and the borehole is not strong enough to cause oil to rise to the surface. — Also termed *pumpjack; horsehead.*

pumpjack. See PUMPING UNIT.

punies (**pyoo**-neez). *Slang.* Punitive damages. See *punitive damages* under DAMAGES.

punishable, *adj.* (15c) **1.** (Of a person) subject to a punishment <there is no dispute that Jackson remains punishable for these offenses>. **2.** (Of a crime or tort) giving rise to a specified punishment <a felony punishable by imprisonment for up to 20 years>. — **punishability,** *n.*

punishment, *n.* (15c) **1.** A sanction — such as a fine, penalty, confinement, or loss of property, right, or privilege — assessed against a person who has violated the law. See SENTENCE.

   capital punishment. See CAPITAL PUNISHMENT.

   collective punishment. See COLLECTIVE PUNISHMENT.

   corporal punishment. (16c) Physical punishment; punishment that is inflicted upon the body (including imprisonment).

   cruel and unusual punishment. (17c) Punishment that is torturous, degrading, inhuman, grossly disproportionate to the crime in question, or otherwise shocking to the moral sense of the community. • Cruel and unusual punishment is prohibited by the Eighth Amendment.

   cumulative punishment. (1842) Punishment that increases in severity when a person is convicted of the same offense more than once.

   deterrent punishment. (1896) **1.** *Criminal law.* Punishment intended to deter the offender and others from committing crimes and to make an example of the offender so that like-minded people are warned of the consequences of crime. **2.** *Torts.* Punishment intended to deter a tortfeasor from repeating a behavior or failing to remove a hazard that led to an injury. • Punitive damages are usu. awarded as a deterrent punishment.

   excessive punishment. (17c) Punishment that is not justified by the gravity of the offense or the defendant's criminal record. See *excessive fine* (1) under FINE (5).

   infamous punishment. (16c) Punishment by imprisonment, usu. in a penitentiary. See *infamous crime* under CRIME.

   nonjudicial punishment. *Military law.* A procedure under which a commanding officer levies punishment against a minor offender who is subject to the Uniform Code of Military Justice. • In the Navy and Coast Guard, nonjudicial punishment is termed *captain's mast*; in the Marine Corps, it is termed *office hours*; and in the Army and Air Force, it is referred to as *Article 15.* Nonjudicial punishment is not a court-martial.

   preventive punishment. (1893) Punishment intended to prevent a repetition of wrongdoing by disabling the offender.

   reformative punishment. (1919) Punishment intended to change the character of the offender.

   retributive punishment. (1887) Punishment intended to satisfy the community's retaliatory sense of indignation that is provoked by injustice.

2. *Family law.* A negative disciplinary action administered to a minor child by a parent.

punitive, *adj.* (16c) Involving or inflicting punishment. — Also termed *punitory.*

punitive articles. Articles 77–134 of the Uniform Code of Military Justice. • These articles list the crimes in the military-justice system.

punitive damages. See DAMAGES.

punitive isolation. See *punitive segregation* under SEGREGATION (1).

punitive segregation. See SEGREGATION.

punitive statute. See *penal statute* under STATUTE.

punitory. See PUNITIVE.

punitory damages. See *punitive damages* under DAMAGES.

PUP. *abbr.* See PUBLIC-USE PROCEEDING.

pupil. *Scots & civil law.* A person who has not reached or completed puberty. See MINORITY (1).

pupillarity (pyoo-pi-**lair**-ə-tee). *Scots & Civil law.* The stage of a person's life that spans from infancy through puberty.

pupillary substitution (**pyoo**-pə-ler-ee). See SUBSTITUTION (5).

pur (pər *or* poor). [Law French] By; for.

pur autre vie (pər **oh**-trə [*or* **oh**-tər] vee). [Law French "for another's life"] For or during a period measured by another's life <a life estate *pur autre vie*>. — Also spelled *per autre vie.*

purchase, *n.* (15c) **1.** The act or an instance of buying. **2.** The acquisition of real property by one's own or another's act (as by will or gift) rather than by descent or inheritance. Cf. DESCENT (1). — **purchase,** *vb.*

   compulsory purchase. *Rare.* See EMINENT DOMAIN.

purchase, words of. See WORDS OF PURCHASE.

purchase accounting method. See ACCOUNTING METHOD.

purchase agreement. (1909) A sales contract. Cf. REPURCHASE AGREEMENT.

> **blanket purchase agreement.** See BLANKET ORDER (3).

purchase money. (17c) The initial payment made on property secured by a mortgage.

purchase-money interest. See *purchase-money security interest* under SECURITY INTEREST.

purchase-money mortgage. See MORTGAGE.

purchase-money resulting trust. See TRUST.

purchase-money security interest. See SECURITY INTEREST.

purchase order. (1916) A document authorizing a seller to deliver goods with payment to be made later. — Abbr. P.O.

> **blanket purchase order.** See BLANKET ORDER (3).

purchaser. (14c) **1.** One who obtains property for money or other valuable consideration; a buyer.

> **affiliated purchaser.** *Securities.* Any of the following: (1) a person directly or indirectly acting in concert with a distribution participant in connection with the acquisition or distribution of the securities involved; (2) an affiliate who directly or indirectly controls the purchases of those securities by a distribution participant, or whose purchases are controlled by such a participant, or whose purchases are under common control with those of such a participant; (3) an affiliate, who is a broker or a dealer (except a broker-dealer whose business consists solely of effecting transactions in "exempted securities," as defined in the Exchange Act); (4) an affiliate (other than a broker-dealer) who regularly purchases securities through a broker-dealer, or otherwise, for its own account or for the account of others, or recommends or exercises investment discretion in the purchase or sale of securities (with certain specified exceptions). SEC Rule 10b-18(a)(2) (17 CFR § 240.10b-18(a)(2)).

> **bona fide purchaser.** (18c) One who buys something for value without notice of another's claim to the property and without actual or constructive notice of any defects in or infirmities, claims, or equities against the seller's title; one who has in good faith paid valuable consideration for property without notice of prior adverse claims. • Generally, a bona fide purchaser for value is not affected by the transferor's fraud against a third party and has a superior right to the transferred property as against the transferor's creditor to the extent of the consideration that the purchaser has paid. — Abbr. BFP. — Also termed *bona fide purchaser for value*; *good-faith purchaser*; *purchaser in good faith*; *innocent purchaser*; *innocent purchaser for value.*

> **good-faith purchaser.** See *bona fide purchaser.*

> **innocent purchaser.** See *bona fide purchaser.*

> **innocent purchaser for value.** See *bona fide purchaser.*

> **purchaser for value.** A purchaser who pays consideration for the property bought.

> **purchaser in good faith.** See *bona fide purchaser.*

> **purchaser pendente lite.** One who buys an interest in something that is the subject of a pending lawsuit.

2. One who acquires real property by means other than descent, gift, or inheritance.

> **first purchaser.** An ancestor who first acquired an estate that still belongs to the family.

pure accident. See *unavoidable accident* under ACCIDENT.

pure annuity. See *nonrefund annuity* under ANNUITY.

pure-comparative-negligence doctrine. (1976) The principle that liability for negligence is apportioned in accordance with the percentage of fault that the fact-finder assigns to each party and that a plaintiff's percentage of fault reduces the amount of recoverable damages but does not bar recovery. See *comparative negligence* under NEGLIGENCE; APPORTIONMENT OF LIABILITY. Cf. 50-PERCENT RULE.

pure debt. See *pure obligation* under OBLIGATION.

pure easement. See *easement appurtenant* under EASEMENT.

pure freezeout. See FREEZEOUT.

pure mark. See *technical trademark* under TRADEMARK.

pure obligation. See OBLIGATION.

pure plea. See PLEA (3).

pure race statute. See RACE STATUTE.

pure risk. See RISK.

pure speech. See SPEECH.

pure theory. The philosophy of Hans Kelsen, in which he contends that a legal system must be "pure" — that is, self-supporting and not dependent on extralegal values. • Kelsen's theory, set out in such works as *General Theory of Law and the State* (1945) and *The Pure Theory of Law* (1934), maintains that laws are norms handed down by the state. Laws are not defined in terms of history, ethics, sociology, or other external factors. Rather, a legal system is an interconnected system of norms, in which coercive techniques are used to secure compliance. The validity of each law, or legal norm, is traced to another legal norm. Ultimately, all laws must find their validity in the society's basic norm (*grundnorm*), which may be as simple as the concept that the constitution was validly enacted. See *basic norm* under NORM.

pure trademark. See *technical trademark* under TRADEMARK.

pure villeinage. See VILLEINAGE.

purgation (pər-**gay**-shən). *Hist.* The act of cleansing or exonerating oneself of a crime or accusation by an oath or ordeal.

   canonical purgation. Purgation by oath-helpers in an ecclesiastical court. See COMPURGATION.

   vulgar purgation. Purgation by fire, hot irons, battle, or cold water; purgation by means other than by oath-helpers. • Vulgar purgation was so called because it was not sanctioned by the church after 1215.

purgatory oath. See OATH.

purge, *vb.* (13c) To exonerate (oneself or another) of guilt <the judge purged the defendant of contempt>.

purpart (pər-pahrt). A share of an estate formerly held in common; a part in a division; an allotment from an estate to a coparcener. — Formerly also termed *purparty*; *perparts*; *pourparty*.

purparty (pər-pahr-tee). See PURPART.

purport (pər-port), *n.* (15c) The idea or meaning that is conveyed or expressed, esp. by a formal document.

purport (pər-**port**), *vb.* (17c) To profess or claim, esp. falsely; to seem to be <the document purports to be a will, but it is neither signed nor dated>.

purported, *adj.* (1885) Reputed; rumored.

purpose. (13c) An objective, goal, or end; specif., the business activity that a corporation is chartered to engage in.

purpose approach. See MISCHIEF RULE.

purpose clause. An introductory clause to a statute explaining its background and stating the reasons for its enactment.

purposeful, *adj.* Done with a specific purpose in mind; deliberate.

purposive construction. See CONSTRUCTION.

purpresture (pər-**pres**-chər). (14c) An encroachment upon public rights and easements by appropriation to private use of that which belongs to the public. — Also spelled *pourpresture*.

purse, *n.* A sum of money available to the winner of a contest or event; a prize.

purser. A person in charge of accounts and documents on a ship.

purse-snatching. The stealing of a handbag or other similar item by seizing or grabbing it from a victim's physical possession and then fleeing, often without harm or threat of harm to the victim. • Purse-snatching is usu. a type of larceny.

But if the perpetrator uses great force to take the bag or injures or threatens to injure the victim, it may instead be classified as a robbery. Cf. LARCENY; ROBBERY.

pursuant to. (16c) **1.** In compliance with; in accordance with; under <she filed the motion pursuant to the court's order>. **2.** As authorized by; under <pursuant to Rule 56, the plaintiff moves for summary judgment>. **3.** In carrying out <pursuant to his responsibilities, he ensured that all lights had been turned out>.

pursuer. *Civil & Scots law.* A plaintiff.

pursuit. (14c) **1.** An occupation or pastime. **2.** The act of chasing to overtake or apprehend. See FRESH PURSUIT.

pursuit of happiness. (18c) The principle — announced in the Declaration of Independence — that a person should be allowed to pursue the person's desires (esp. in regard to an occupation) without unjustified interference by the government.

purview (pər-vyoo). (15c) **1.** Scope; area of application. **2.** The body of a statute following the preamble.

pusher. A person who sells illicit drugs.

Pushman **doctrine.** *Archaic.* The rule that transfer of an unpublished work transfers the common-law copyright to the work along with the work itself. • The name derives from *Pushman v. New York Graphic Soc'y, Inc.*, 39 N.E.2d (N.Y. 1942). The doctrine was rejected by § 202 of the Copyright Act of 1976, but it remains in effect for transfers completed before the provision's effective date of January 1, 1978.

put, *n.* See *put option* under OPTION.

putative (**pyoo**-tə-tiv), *adj.* (15c) Reputed; believed; supposed.

putative damages. See DAMAGES.

putative father. See FATHER.

putative-father registry. *Family law.* An official roster in which an unwed father may claim possible paternity of a child for purposes of receiving notice of a prospective adoption of the child.

Putative Fathers Act. See UNIFORM PUTATIVE AND UNKNOWN FATHERS ACT.

putative marriage. See MARRIAGE (1).

putative matrimony. See *putative marriage* under MARRIAGE (1).

putative spouse. See SPOUSE.

putative-spouse doctrine. See *putative marriage* under MARRIAGE (1).

put bond. See BOND (3).

put in, *vb.* (15c) To place in due form before a court; to place among the records of a court.

put on notice. See CHARGED WITH NOTICE.

put option. See OPTION.

put out. See EVICT (1).

put price. See *strike price* under PRICE.

puttable (**puut**-ə-bəl), *adj.* (Of a security) capable of being required by the holder to be redeemed by the issuing company.

put the question. (Of the chair) to formally state a question in its final form for the purpose of taking a vote. Cf. STATE THE QUESTION.

putting in fear. (17c) The threatening of another person with violence to compel the person to hand over property. ● These words are part of the common-law definition of robbery.

PVA. *abbr.* PUBLIC VESSELS ACT.

PVPA. *abbr.* PLANT VARIETY PROTECTION ACT.

PWBA. *abbr.* PENSION AND WELFARE BENEFITS ADMINISTRATION.

pyramid distribution plan. See PYRAMID SCHEME.

pyramiding. A speculative method used to finance a large purchase of stock or a controlling interest by pledging an investment's unrealized profit. See LEVERAGE; MARGIN.

pyramiding inferences. See INFERENCE-STACKING.

pyramiding inferences, rule against. (1959) *Evidence.* A rule prohibiting a fact-finder from piling one inference on another to arrive at a conclusion. ● Today this rule is followed in only a few jurisdictions. Cf. REASONABLE-INFERENCE RULE.

pyramid scheme. (1949) A property-distribution scheme in which a participant pays for the chance to receive compensation for introducing new persons to the scheme, as well as for when those new persons themselves introduce participants. ● Pyramid schemes are illegal in most states. — Also termed *endless-chain scheme*; *chain-referral scheme*; *multilevel-distribution program*; *pyramid distribution plan*. Cf. PONZI SCHEME.

Q

Q. *abbr.* (16c) QUESTION (1). • This abbreviation is almost always used in deposition and trial transcripts to denote each question asked by the examining lawyer.

Q-and-A. *abbr.* (1837) QUESTION-AND-ANSWER.

Q.B. *abbr.* QUEEN'S BENCH.

Q.B.D. *abbr.* QUEEN'S BENCH DIVISION.

Q.C. *abbr.* QUEEN'S COUNSEL.

qcf. *abbr.* QUARE CLAUSUM FREGIT.

QD. *abbr.* [Latin *quasi dicat*] (16c) As if he should say.

QDOT. *abbr.* QUALIFIED DOMESTIC TRUST.

QDRO (**kwah**-droh). *abbr.* QUALIFIED DOMESTIC-RELATIONS ORDER.

QED. *abbr.* [Latin *quod erat demonstrandum*] (17c) Which was to be demonstrated or proved.

QMCSO. *abbr.* QUALIFIED MEDICAL CHILD- SUPPORT ORDER.

QPRT. *abbr.* QUALIFIED PERSONAL-RESIDENCE TRUST.

qq.v. See Q.V.

QSST. *abbr.* See *qualified S-corporation trust* under TRUST (3).

Q.T. *abbr.* QUI TAM ACTION.

QTIP (**kyoo**-tip). *abbr.* QUALIFIED-TERMINABLE-INTEREST PROPERTY.

QTIP trust. See TRUST.

qua (kway *or* kwah). [Latin] (17c) In the capacity of; as <the fiduciary, qua fiduciary, is not liable for fraud, but he may be liable as an individual>.

quadriennium (kwah-dree-**en**-ee-əm), *n.* [Latin fr. *quatuor* "four" + *annus* "year"] **1.** *Roman law.* The four-year course of study required of law students before they were qualified to study the Code or collection of imperial constitutions. **2.** *Scots law.* See QUADRIENNIUM UTILE.

quadripartite, *adj. Hist.* (Of an indenture, etc.) drawn, divided, or executed in four parts.

quadripartite, *n.* A book or treatise divided into four parts.

quaere (**kweer**-ee), *vb.* [Latin] (17c) Inquire; query; examine. • This term was often used in the syllabus of a reported case to show that a point was doubtful or open to question.

quaestor (**kwes**-tər *or* **kwees**-tər), *n.* [Latin] **1.** *Roman law.* A magistrate, subordinate to the consuls or provincial governors, who maintained and administered the public money, performing tasks such as making necessary payments, receiving revenues, keeping accurate accounts, registering debts and fines, supervising the accommodation of foreign ambassadors, and financing the burials and monuments of distinguished citizens. **2.** *Hist.* An agent of the Pope who carried *quaesita* from door to door. — Also termed *quaesitor*; *questionarius.* Pl. **quaestores.** — **quaestorial,** *adj.* — **quaestorship,** *n.*

qualification. (16c) **1.** The possession of qualities or properties (such as fitness or capacity) inherently or legally necessary to make one eligible for a position or office, or to perform a public duty or function <voter qualification requires one to meet residency, age, and registration requirements>. **2.** A modification or limitation of terms or language; esp., a restriction of terms that would otherwise be interpreted broadly <the contract contained a qualification requiring the lessor's permission before exercising the right to sublet>. **3.** CHARACTERIZATION (1). — **qualify,** *vb.*

qualified, *adj.* (16c) **1.** Possessing the necessary qualifications; capable or competent <a qualified medical examiner>. **2.** Limited; restricted <qualified immunity>. — **qualify,** *vb.*

qualified acceptance. See ACCEPTANCE (1).

qualified corporation. See *admitted corporation* under CORPORATION.

qualified disclaimer. See DISCLAIMER.

qualified domestic-relations order. (1984) A state-court order or judgment that relates to alimony, child support, or some other state domestic-relations matter and that (1) recognizes or provides for an alternate payee's right to receive all or part of any benefits due a participant under a pension, profit-sharing, or other retirement benefit plan, (2) otherwise satisfies § 414 of the Internal Revenue Code, and (3) is exempt from the ERISA rule prohibiting the assignment of plan benefits. • Among other things, the QDRO must set out certain facts, including the name and last-known mailing address of the plan participant and alternate payee, the amount or percentage of benefits going to the alternate payee, and the number of payments to which the plan applies. The benefits provided under a QDRO are treated as income to the actual recipient. IRC (26 USCA) § 414(p)(1)(A); 29 USCA § 1056(d)(3)(D)(i). — Abbr. QDRO.

qualified domestic trust. See TRUST.

qualified elector. See ELECTOR.

qualified estate. See ESTATE (1).

qualified fee. 1. See *fee simple defeasible* under FEE SIMPLE. **2.** See *fee simple determinable* under FEE SIMPLE. **3.** See *base fee* under FEE (2).

qualified general denial. See DENIAL.

qualified immunity. See IMMUNITY (1).

qualified income trust. See *Miller trust* under TRUST.

qualified indorsement. See INDORSEMENT.

qualified institutional buyer. See BUYER.

qualified investor. See INVESTOR.

qualifiedly (kwah-lə-fɪd-lee *or* -fɪ-əd-lee), *adv.* In a fit or qualified manner <qualifiedly privileged>.

qualified martial law. See MARTIAL LAW.

qualified medical child-support order. A family-court order that enables a nonemployee custodial parent — without the employee parent's consent — to enroll the child, make claims, and receive payments as needed under the employee parent's group health plan, all at the employee parent's expense. ● The group-health-plan administrator must find that the order meets the requirements of a QMCSO, which are established by § 609(a) of the Employee Retirement Income Security Act, 29 USCA § 1169(a). — Abbr. QMCSO.

qualified nuisance. See NUISANCE.

qualified opinion. An audit-report statement containing exceptions or qualifications to certain items in the accompanying financial statement.

qualified ownership. See OWNERSHIP.

qualified pension plan. See PENSION PLAN.

qualified personal-residence trust. See TRUST.

qualified plan. 1. See *qualified pension plan* under PENSION PLAN. **2.** See *qualified profit-sharing plan* under PROFIT-SHARING PLAN.

qualified privilege. See PRIVILEGE (1).

qualified profit-sharing plan. See PROFIT-SHARING PLAN.

qualified property. See PROPERTY.

qualified residence interest. See INTEREST (3).

qualified S-corporation trust. See TRUST (3).

qualified stock option. See STOCK OPTION.

qualified subchapter-S corporation trust. See *qualified S-corporation trust* under TRUST (3).

qualified-terminable-interest property. See PROPERTY.

qualified veto. See VETO.

qualified voter. 1. See *qualified elector* under ELECTOR. **2.** VOTER (2).

qualified witness. See WITNESS.

qualifying event. Any one of several specified occasions that, but for the continuation-of-coverage provisions under the Consolidated Omnibus Budget Reconciliation Act of 1985 (COBRA), would result in a loss of benefits to a covered employee under a qualified benefit plan. ● These occasions include employment termination, a reduction in work hours, the employee's separation or divorce, the employee's death, and the employer's bankruptcy. IRC (26 USCA) § 4980B(f)(3).

qualifying share. See SHARE (2).

qualitatively incidental private benefit. See PRIVATE BENEFIT.

quality. 1. The particular character or properties of a person, thing, or act, often essential for a particular result <she has leadership quality> <greed is a negative quality>. **2.** The character or degree of excellence of a person or substance, esp. in comparison with others <the quality of work performed under the contract>.

quality of estate. (18c) **1.** The period when the right of enjoying an estate is conferred upon the owner, whether at present or in the future. **2.** The manner in which the owner's right of enjoyment of an estate is to be exercised, whether solely, jointly, in common, or in coparcenary.

quality-of-products legislation. See LEMON LAW (2).

quango (kwang-goh). See QUASI-AUTONOMOUS NONGOVERNMENTAL ORGANIZATION.

quantitatively incidental private benefit. See PRIVATE BENEFIT.

quantitative rule. (1919) An evidentiary rule requiring that a given type of evidence is insufficient unless accompanied by additional evidence before the case is closed. ● Such a rule exists because of the known danger or weakness of certain types of evidence. — Also termed *synthetic rule.*

quantity discount. See *volume discount* under DISCOUNT.

quantum (kwon-təm). [Latin "an amount"] The required, desired, or allowed amount; portion or share <a quantum of evidence>. Pl. **quanta** (kwon-tə).

quantum meruit (kwon-təm mer-oo-it). [Latin "as much as he has deserved"] (17c) **1.** The reasonable value of services; damages awarded in an amount considered reasonable to compensate a person who has rendered services in a quasi-contractual relationship. **2.** A claim or right of action for the reasonable value of services rendered. **3.** At common law, a count in an assumpsit action to recover payment for services rendered to another person. ● Quantum meruit is still used today as an equitable remedy to provide restitution for unjust enrichment. It is often pleaded as an alternative claim in a breach-of-contract case so that the plaintiff can recover even if the contract is unenforceable. See *implied-in-law contract* under CONTRACT.

quantum valebant (**kwon**-təm və-**lee**-bant *or* -bənt). [Latin "as much as they were worth"] (18c) **1.** The reasonable value of goods and materials. **2.** At common law, a count in an assumpsit action to recover payment for goods sold and delivered to another. • *Quantum valebant* — although less common than *quantum meruit* — is still used today as an equitable remedy to provide restitution for another's unjust enrichment.

quarantine. (17c) **1.** The isolation of a person or animal afflicted with a communicable disease or the prevention of such a person or animal from coming into a particular area, the purpose being to prevent the spread of disease. • Federal, state, and local authorities are required to cooperate in the enforcement of quarantine laws. 42 USCA § 243(a). **2.** A place where a quarantine is in force. **3.** *Hist.* A period of 40 days, esp. for the isolation and detention of ships containing persons or animals suspected of having or carrying a dangerous communicable disease, in order to prevent the spread of the disease. **4.** *Hist.* A widow's privilege to remain in her husband's house for 40 days after his death while her dower is being assigned. • This right was enforced by a writ *de quarantina habenda*. — Also spelled *quarentine*; *quarentene*. — **quarantine,** *vb.*

quare (**kwair**-ee). [Latin] Why; for what reason; on what account. • This was used in various common-law writs, esp. writs in trespass.

quare clausum fregit (**kwair**-ee **klaw**-zəm **free**-jit). [Latin] Why he broke the close. — Abbr. *qu. cl. fr.*; *q.c.f.* See TRESPASS QUARE CLAUSUM FREGIT.

quare impedit (**kwair**-ee **im**-pə-dit). [Latin "why he hinders"] *Hist. Eccles. law.* A writ or action to enforce a patron's right to present a person to fill a vacant benefice. — Also termed *writ of quare impedit.* See PRESENTATION (2); ADVOWSON.

quarentine. See QUARANTINE.

quarrel, *n.* **1.** An altercation or angry dispute; an exchange of recriminations, taunts, threats, or accusations between two persons. — **quarrel,** *vb.* **2.** *Archaic.* A complaint; a legal action.

quarta Falcidiana (**kwor**-tə fal-**sid**-ee-ə). [Latin "Falcidian fourth"] See FALCIDIAN PORTION.

quarter, *n.* **1.** In the law of war, the act of showing mercy to a defeated enemy by sparing lives and accepting a surrender <to give no quarter>. **2.** See *quarter section* under SECTION.

quarter day. See DAY.

quartering, *n. Hist.* **1.** The dividing of a criminal's body into quarters after execution, esp. as part of the punishment for a crime such as high treason. See HANGED, DRAWN, AND QUARTERED. **2.** The furnishing of living quarters to members of the military. • In the United States, a homeowner's consent is required before soldiers may be quartered in a private home during peacetime. During wartime, soldiers may be quartered in private homes only as prescribed by law. The Third Amendment generally protects U.S. citizens from being forced to use their homes to quarter soldiers. U.S. Const. amend. III. **3.** The dividing of a shield into four parts to show four different coats of arms. — **quarter,** *vb.*

quarterly report. A financial report issued by a corporation (and by most mutual funds and investment managers) every three months.

quartermaster. See TREASURER.

quarter seal. See SEAL.

quarter section. See SECTION.

quarter session. See SESSION (1).

quarters of coverage. The number of quarterly payments made by a person into the social-security fund as a basis for determining the person's entitlement to benefits.

quash (kwahsh), *vb.* (13c) **1.** To annul or make void; to terminate <quash an indictment> <quash proceedings>. **2.** To suppress or subdue; to crush <quash a rebellion>.

quashal (**kwahsh**-əl), *n.* The act of quashing something <quashal of the subpoena>.

quasi (**kway**-sɪ *or* **kway**-zɪ *also* **kwah**-zee). [Latin "as if"] (15c) Seemingly but not actually; in some sense or degree; resembling; nearly.

quasi-admission. See ADMISSION (1).

quasi-affinity. See AFFINITY.

quasi-autonomous nongovernmental organization. A semipublic administrative body (esp. in the United Kingdom) having some members appointed and financed by, but not answerable to, the government, such as a tourist authority, a university-grants commission, a price-and-wage commission, a prison or parole board, or a medical-health advisory panel. • This term is more commonly written as an acronym, *quango* (**kwang**-goh), without capital letters.

quasi committee of the whole. See COMMITTEE.

quasi-community property. See COMMUNITY PROPERTY.

quasi-contract. See *implied-in-law contract* under CONTRACT.

quasi-corporation. See CORPORATION.

quasi-crime. See CRIME.

quasi-criminal proceeding. See PROCEEDING.

quasi-delict. See DELICT.

quasi-deposit. See DEPOSIT (5).

quasi-derelict. See DERELICT.

quasi-deviation. See DEVIATION.

quasi-domicile. See *commercial domicile* under DOMICILE.

quasi-dwelling-house. See DWELLING-HOUSE.

quasi-easement. See EASEMENT.

quasi-enclave. See ENCLAVE.

quasi-entail. See ENTAIL.

quasi-estoppel. See ESTOPPEL.

quasi-fee. See FEE (2).

quasi-governmental agency. See AGENCY (3).

quasi-guarantee treaty. See *guarantee treaty* under TREATY (1).

quasi-guardian. See GUARDIAN.

quasi-individual. See *private corporation* under CORPORATION.

quasi in rem. See IN REM.

quasi-in-rem jurisdiction. See JURISDICTION.

quasi-insurer. See INSURER.

quasi-judicial, *adj.* (1820) Of, relating to, or involving an executive or administrative official's adjudicative acts. ● Quasi-judicial acts, which are valid if there is no abuse of discretion, often determine the fundamental rights of citizens. They are subject to review by courts.

quasi-judicial act. (1840) **1.** A judicial act performed by an official who is not a judge. **2.** An act performed by a judge who is not acting entirely in a judicial capacity. See *judicial act* under ACT.

quasi-judicial duty. See DUTY (1).

quasi-judicial function. See FUNCTION.

quasi-judicial power. See POWER (3).

quasi-legislative, *adj.* (1934) (Of an act, function, etc.) not purely legislative in nature <the administrative agency's rulemaking, being partly adjudicative, is not entirely legislative — that is, it is quasi-legislative>.

quasi-legislative power. See POWER (3).

quasi-main motion. See *incidental main motion* under MOTION (2).

quasi-municipal corporation. See *quasi-corporation* under CORPORATION.

quasi-national domicile. See DOMICILE.

quasi-offense. See OFFENSE (2).

quasi-partner. See PARTNER.

quasi-personalty. See PERSONALTY.

quasi-possession. See *incorporeal possession* under POSSESSION.

quasi-posthumous child. See CHILD.

quasi-public corporation. See CORPORATION.

quasi-pupillary substitution. See SUBSTITUTION (5).

quasi-realty. See REALTY.

quasi-rent. (*often pl.*) *Law and economics.* Value over and above one's opportunity cost or next best alternative; the excess of an asset's value over its salvage value. ● In the economic theory of marriage, a quasi-rent is a spouse's excess value of the marriage over the value of the next best option of not being in that specific marriage. The next best option may be separation, divorce, or divorce and remarriage, depending on the spouse's preferences and opportunities.

quasi-seisin. See SEISIN.

quasi-statute. See STATUTE.

quasi-suspect classification. See SUSPECT CLASSIFICATION.

quasi-tenant. See TENANT.

quasi-tort. See TORT.

quasi-trustee. See TRUSTEE (1).

quasi-usufruct. See USUFRUCT.

quayage (**kee-**əj). A toll or fee charged for lading or unlading goods on a quay or wharf. — Also written *keyage.*

***Quayle* action.** *Patents.* An office action telling the patent applicant that the claims are allowable on the merits but that the form of the application still needs to be amended. *Ex parte Quayle,* 25 USPQ (BNA) 74, 1935 C.D. 11, 453 O.G. 213 (Comm'r Pat. 1935). ● The applicant generally has two months to respond. A *Quayle* action ends the prosecution on the merits, and amendments that affect the merits will be treated in a manner similar to amendments after final rejection.

qu. cl. fr. *abbr.* QUARE CLAUSUM FREGIT.

queen. **1.** A woman who possesses, in her own right, the sovereignty and royal power in a monarchy. ● Among the most famous English queens are Queen Mary I, Queen Elizabeth I, Queen Victoria, and Queen Elizabeth II. — Also termed *queen regnant.* **2.** The wife of a reigning king. ● She has some royal prerogatives (such as having her own officers), but is in many ways legally no different from the rest of the king's subjects. — Also termed *queen consort.* **3.** A woman who rules in place of the actual sovereign (e.g., if the sovereign is a child). — Also termed *queen regent.* **4.** DOWAGER-QUEEN.

queen dowager. See DOWAGER-QUEEN.

queen mother. A queen who has children; esp., a dowager-queen whose child is the reigning monarch. See DOWAGER-QUEEN.

Queen's Bench. Historically, the highest common-law court in England, presided over by the reigning monarch. ● The jurisdiction of this court now lies with the Queen's Bench Division of the High Court of Justice; when a king begins to reign, the name automatically changes to *King's Bench.* —

Abbr. Q.B. — Also termed *Court of Queen's Bench.* Cf. KING'S BENCH.

Queen's Bench Division. The English court, formerly known as the Queen's Bench or King's Bench, that presides over tort and contract actions, applications for judicial review, and some magistrate-court appeals. — Abbr. Q.B.D.

Queen's Counsel. In the United Kingdom, Canada, and territories that have retained the rank, an elite, senior-level barrister or advocate. • Originally, a Queen's Counsel was appointed to serve as counsel to the reigning monarch. — Also termed *senior counsel.* — Abbr. Q.C. Cf. KING'S COUNSEL.

Queen's prison. A prison established in 1842 in Southwark, to be used for debtors and criminals confined under authority of the superior courts at Westminster, the highest court of admiralty, and the bankruptcy laws. • It replaced the Queen's Bench Prison, Fleet Prison, and Marshalsea Prison but was closed in 1862.

Queen's proctor. A solicitor who represents the Crown in domestic-relations, probate, and admiralty cases. • For example, in a suit for divorce or nullity of marriage, the Queen's proctor might intervene to prove collusion between the parties. — Also termed (when a king reigns) *King's proctor.*

question. (14c) **1.** A query directed to a witness. — Abbr. Q.

categorical question. (18c) **1.** LEADING QUESTION. **2.** (*often pl.*) One of a series of questions, on a particular subject, arranged in systematic or consecutive order.

cross-question. (17c) A question asked of a witness during cross-examination. — Abbr. XQ.

direct question. (17c) A question asked of a witness during direct examination.

hypothetical question. See HYPOTHETICAL QUESTION.

leading question. See LEADING QUESTION.

2. An issue in controversy; a matter to be determined.

certified question. See CERTIFIED QUESTION.

federal question. See FEDERAL QUESTION.

judicial question. See JUDICIAL QUESTION.

mixed question. See MIXED QUESTION.

mixed question of law and fact. See MIXED QUESTION OF LAW AND FACT.

nonjusticiable question. See POLITICAL QUESTION.

political question. See POLITICAL QUESTION.

question of fact. See QUESTION OF FACT.

question of law. See QUESTION OF LAW.

ultimate question. See *ultimate issue* under ISSUE (1).

3. *Parliamentary law.* A motion that the chair has stated for a meeting's consideration in a form that the meeting can adopt or reject; a pending motion. • A question is technically only a "motion" until the chair states it for the meeting's consideration. But for most purposes, the parliamentary terms "motion" and "question" are interchangeable. See MOTION (2); PUT THE QUESTION; STATE THE QUESTION.

privileged question. A privileged motion that that the chair has stated for a meeting's consideration. See *privileged motion* under MOTION (2). Cf. *question of privilege.*

question of consideration. See OBJECTION (2).

question of information. See *point of information* under POINT.

question of order. See *point of order* under POINT.

question of privilege. Any question that concerns the deliberative assembly's or a member's rights or privileges. See PRIVILEGE (6); RAISE A QUESTION OF PRIVILEGE. Cf. *privileged question.*

question-and-answer. (17c) **1.** The portion of a deposition or trial transcript in which evidence is developed through a series of questions asked by the lawyer and answered by the witness. — Abbr. Q-and-A. **2.** The method for developing evidence during a deposition or at trial, requiring the witness to answer the examining lawyer's questions, without offering unsolicited information. **3.** The method of instruction used in many law-school classes, in which the professor asks questions of one or more students and then follows up each answer with another question. — Also termed *Socratic method.* See SOCRATIC METHOD; QUESTION-AND-ANSWER METHOD.

question of consideration. See OBJECTION (2).

question of fact. (17c) **1.** An issue that has not been predetermined and authoritatively answered by the law. • An example is whether a particular criminal defendant is guilty of an offense or whether a contractor has delayed unreasonably in constructing a building. **2.** An issue that does not involve what the law is on a given point. **3.** A disputed issue to be resolved by the jury in a jury trial or by the judge in a bench trial. — Also termed *fact question.* See FACT-FINDER. **4.** An issue capable of being answered by way of demonstration, as opposed to a question of unverifiable opinion.

question of law. (17c) **1.** An issue to be decided by the judge, concerning the application or interpretation of the law <a jury cannot decide questions of law, which are reserved for the court>. **2.** A question that the law itself has authoritatively answered, so that the court may not answer it as a matter of discretion <the enforceability of an arbitration clause is a question of law>. **3.** An issue about what the law is on a particular point; an issue in which parties argue about, and the court must decide, what the true rule of law is <both parties appealed on the question of law>. **4.** An issue that, although it may turn on a factual point, is reserved for the court and excluded from the jury; an issue that is exclusively within the province of the judge and not the jury <whether a contractual ambiguity exists is a question of law>. — Also termed *legal question*; *law question*.

question of privilege. See QUESTION (3).

questman. *Hist.* **1.** An instigator of a lawsuit or prosecution. **2.** A person who was chosen to inquire into abuses, esp. those relating to weights and measures. **3.** A churchwarden; SIDESMAN. — Also termed *questmonger*.

quia (**kwɪ**-ə *or* **kwee**-ə). [Latin] *Hist.* Because; whereas. ● This term was used to point out the consideration in a conveyance.

Quia Emptores (**kwɪ**-ə *or* **kwee**-ə emp-**tor**-eez). [Latin "since purchasers"] *Hist.* A statute giving fee-simple tenants (other than those holding directly of the Crown) the power to alienate their land and bind the transferee to perform the same services for the lord as the transferor had been obliged to perform. ● The statute, enacted in 1290, tended to concentrate feudal lordships in the Crown by eliminating multiple layers of fealty. 18 Edw., ch. 1. — Also termed *Quia Emptores Terrarum*.

quia timet (**kwɪ**-ə **tɪ**-mət *or* **kwee**-ə **tim**-et). [Latin "because he fears"] (17c) A legal doctrine that allows a person to seek equitable relief from future probable harm to a specific right or interest.

quia-timet **injunction.** See INJUNCTION.

quick asset. See ASSET.

quick-asset ratio. The ratio between an entity's current or liquid assets (such as cash and accounts receivable) and its current liabilities. — Also termed *quick ratio*; *acid-test ratio*.

quick condemnation. See CONDEMNATION (2).

quick dispatch. See DISPATCH.

quickening. The first motion felt in the womb by the mother of the fetus, usu. occurring near the middle of the pregnancy.

quickie divorce. See DIVORCE.

quickie strike. See *wildcat strike* under STRIKE.

quick ratio. See QUICK-ASSET RATIO.

quick-take. See *quick condemnation* under CONDEMNATION (2).

quid pro quo (**kwid** proh **kwoh**), *n.* [Latin "something for something"] (16c) An action or thing that is exchanged for another action or thing of more or less equal value; a substitute <the discount was given as a quid pro quo for the extra business>. See RECIPROCITY (2). Cf. CONSIDERATION.

quid pro quo sexual harassment. See SEXUAL HARASSMENT.

quiet, *vb.* **1.** To pacify or silence (a person, etc.). **2.** To make (a right, position, title, etc.) secure or unassailable by removing disturbing causes or disputes.

quiet diplomacy. See *secret diplomacy* under DIPLOMACY.

quiet enjoyment. See ENJOYMENT.

quiet-title action. See *action to quiet title* under ACTION.

quietus (kwɪ-**ee**-təs), *adj.* [Law Latin] Quit; acquitted; discharged, esp. from a debt or obligation, or from serving as an executor. ● In England, this term was formerly used by the Clerk of the Pipe, in a discharge given to an accountant, usu. concluding with *abinde recessit quietus* ("hath gone quit thereof"), called *quietus est.* **2.** *Hist.* The removal of a judge from the bench.

quietus redditus (kwɪ-**ee**-təs **red**-ə-təs). [Law Latin] See QUIT RENT.

Quinquaginta Decisiones. See FIFTY DECISIONS.

quintal (**kwin**-təl). A weight of 100 pounds or 100 kilograms. — Also termed *kintal*.

quintessential public forum. See *traditional public forum* under PUBLIC FORUM.

Quiritarian (kwi-rə-**tair**-ee-ən), *adj. Roman law.* (In the context of ownership, with the full right available to citizens) legal as opposed to equitable; LEGAL (3). — Also termed *Quiritary.* Cf. BONITARIAN (1).

quit, *adj.* (13c) (Of a debt, obligation, or person) acquitted; free; discharged.

quit, *vb.* (15c) **1.** To cease (an act, etc.); to stop <he didn't quit stalking the victim until the police intervened>. **2.** To leave or surrender possession of (property) <the tenant received a notice to quit but had no intention of quitting the premises>.

qui tam action (**kwɪ** tam *or* **kee**-tam). [Latin *qui tam pro domino rege quam pro se ipso in hac parte sequitur* "who as well for the king as for himself sues in this matter"] (18c) An action brought under a statute that allows a private person to sue for a penalty, part of which the government or some specified public institution will receive. — Often shortened to *qui tam* (Q.T.). — Also termed *popular action.* See FALSE CLAIMS ACT.

quitclaim, *n.* (14c) **1.** A formal release of one's claim or right. **2.** See *quitclaim deed* under DEED.

quitclaim, *vb.* (14c) **1.** To relinquish or release (a claim or right). **2.** To convey all of one's interest in (property), to whatever extent one has an interest; to execute a quitclaim deed.

quitclaim deed. See DEED.

quit rent. *Hist.* A payment to a feudal lord by a freeholder or copyholder, so called because upon payment the tenant goes "quit and free" (discharged) of all other services. — Also spelled *quitrent.* — Also termed *quietus redditus.*

quittance. (13c) **1.** A release or discharge from a debt or obligation. **2.** The document serving as evidence of such a release. See ACQUITTANCE.

quoad (**kwoh**-ad). [Latin] As regards; with regard to <with a pledge, the debtor continues to possess *quoad* the world at large>.

quoad hoc (**kwoh**-ad hok). [Latin] (17c) As to this; with respect to this; so far as this is concerned. • A prohibition *quoad hoc* is a prohibition of certain things among others, such as matters brought in an ecclesiastical court that should have been brought in a temporal court.

quod erat demonstrandum (kwod **er**-ət dem-ən-**stran**-dəm). See Q.E.D.

quod nota (kwod **noh**-tə). [Latin] *Hist.* Which note; which mark. • This is a reporter's note directing attention to a point or rule.

quod permittat (kwod pər-**mit**-it), *n.* [Latin "that he permit"] *Hist.* A writ to prevent an interference in the exercise of a right, such as a writ for the heir of someone disseised of a common of pasture against the heir of the disseisor.

quod vide (kwod **vi**-dee *or* **vee**-day). See Q.V.

quo jure (kwoh **joor**-ee). [Law Latin "by what right"] *Hist.* A writ for someone holding land to which another claimed a common, to compel the latter to prove title. See COMMON (1).

quominus (**kwoh**-mə-nəs *or* kwoh-**mi**-nəs). [Latin *quo minus* "by which the less"] *Hist.* A 14th-century Exchequer writ alleging that the plaintiff had lent the defendant a sum of money and that the plaintiff was unable to repay a debt of similar amount to the Crown because of the debt to the defendant. • In effect, the plaintiff pleaded the fiction that he was a debtor of the king who could not repay that debt because of the defendant's failure to repay him. — Also termed *writ of quominus.*

quondam (**kwon**-dəm), *adj.* Having been formerly; former <the quondam ruler>.

quondam, *n. Archaic.* A person who once held an office or a position, esp. one who was involuntarily removed or deposed.

quorum, *n.* (17c) *Parliamentary law.* The minimum number of members (usu. a majority of all the members) who must be present for a deliberative assembly to legally transact business. Pl. **quorums.**

constituency-based quorum. See *interest-based quorum.*

disappearing quorum. A quorum whose presence may be more presumptive than actual. See *presumption of a quorum* under PRESUMPTION.

interest-based quorum. A quorum determined according to the presence or representation of various constituencies. — Also termed *constituency-based quorum.*

notice-based quorum. A quorum determined according to how far in advance of the meeting its call was circulated. • Under a notice-based quorum, the later the call gets sent out, the larger the quorum grows.

proportional quorum. A quorum calculated with reference to some defined or assumed set, usu. either the number of seats (including vacancies) or the number of sitting members (excluding vacancies).

registration-based quorum. A quorum determined according to how many members have checked in at the meeting, either at some fixed time or throughout the time since the meeting began.

quorum bonorum (**kwor**-əm bə-**nor**-əm). [Latin] *Roman law.* A praetorian interdict by which a person was allowed to take possession of an estate.

quorum call. See CALL (1).

quorumless, *adj.* Lacking a quorum. — **quorumlessness,** *n.*

quota. (17c) **1.** A proportional share assigned to a person or group; an allotment <the university's admission standards included a quota for in-state residents>. **2.** A quantitative restriction; a minimum or maximum number <Faldo met his sales quota for the month>.

export quota. A restriction on the products that can be sold to foreign countries. • In the United States, export quotas can be established by the federal government for various purposes, including national defense, price support, and economic stability.

import quota. A restriction on the volume of a certain product that can be brought into the country from a foreign country. • In the United States, the President may establish a quota on an item that poses a threat of serious injury to a domestic industry.

quotation. (17c) **1.** A statement or passage that is exactly reproduced, attributed, and cited. **2.** The amount stated as a stock's or commodity's current price.

market quotation. The most current price at which a security or commodity trades.

3. A contractor's estimate for a given job. — Sometimes shortened to *quote*.

quotient verdict. See VERDICT.

quo warranto (kwoh wə-**ran**-toh *also* kwoh **wahr**-ən-toh). [Law Latin "by what authority"] (15c) **1.** A common-law writ used to inquire into the authority by which a public office is held or a franchise is claimed. — Also termed *writ of quo warranto*. **2.** An action by which the state seeks to revoke a corporation's charter. ● The Federal Rules of Civil Procedure are applicable to proceedings for quo warranto "to the extent that the practice in such proceedings is not set forth in statutes of the United States and has therefore conformed to the practice in civil actions." Fed. R. Civ. P. 81(a)(2).

q.v. *abbr.* [Latin *quod vide*] (17c) Which see — used in non-*Bluebook* citations for cross-referencing. Pl. **qq.v.**

R

R. *abbr.* **1.** REX. **2.** REGINA. **3.** RANGE. **4.** *Trademarks.* When contained in a circle (and often superscripted), the symbol indicating that a trademark or servicemark is registered in the U.S. Patent and Trademark Office. See *registered trademark* under TRADEMARK; SERVICEMARK.

rabbicular trust. See TRUST (3).

rabbinical divorce. See DIVORCE.

rabbi trust. See TRUST (3).

race act. See RACE STATUTE.

race-notice statute. (1968) A recording law providing that the person who records first, without notice of prior unrecorded claims, has priority. • About half the states have race-notice statutes. — Also termed *race-notice act*; *notice-race statute.* Cf. RACE STATUTE; NOTICE STATUTE.

race of diligence. *Bankruptcy.* A first-come, first-served disposition of assets.

race statute. (1944) A recording act providing that the person who records first, regardless of notice, has priority. • Only Louisiana and North Carolina have race statutes. — Also termed *pure race statute*; *race act.* Cf. NOTICE STATUTE; RACE-NOTICE STATUTE.

race to the courthouse. (1961) **1.** *Bankruptcy.* The competition among creditors to make claims on assets, usu. motivated by the advantages to be gained by those who act first in preference to other creditors. • Chapter 11 of the Bankruptcy Code, as well as various other provisions, is intended to prevent a race to the courthouse and instead to promote equality among creditors. **2.** *Civil procedure.* The competition between disputing parties, both of whom know that litigation is inevitable, to prepare and file a lawsuit in a favorable or convenient forum before the other side files in one that is less favorable or less convenient. • A race to the courthouse may result after one party informally accuses another of breach of contract or intellectual-property infringement. When informal negotiations break down, both want to resolve the matter quickly, usu. to avoid further business disruption. While the accuser races to sue for breach of contract or infringement, the accused seeks a declaratory judgment that no breach or infringement has occurred. See ANTICIPATORY FILING.

racial discrimination. See DISCRIMINATION.

racial profiling. The law-enforcement practice of using race, national origin, or ethnicity as a salient basis for suspicion of criminal activity. • Originally, the term referred to the practice of stopping a disproportionate number of male African-American drivers on the assumption that they had a heightened likelihood of being involved in criminal activity. After the terrorist attacks of September 11, 2001, the term was frequently used in reference to searching and interrogating Middle Eastern men at airports. — Also termed *ethnic profiling*; *profiling.* Cf. LINGUISTIC PROFILING.

rack, *n. Hist.* An instrument of torture on which a person was slowly stretched, formerly used to interrogate someone charged with a crime.

racket, *n.* (1819) **1.** An organized criminal activity; esp., the extortion of money by threat or violence. **2.** A dishonest or fraudulent scheme, business, or activity.

racketeer, *n.* (1924) A person who engages in racketeering. — **racketeer,** *vb.*

Racketeer Influenced and Corrupt Organizations Act. A law designed to attack organized criminal activity and preserve marketplace integrity by investigating, controlling, and prosecuting persons who participate or conspire to participate in racketeering. 18 USCA §§ 1961–1968. • Enacted in 1970, the federal RICO statute applies only to activity involving interstate or foreign commerce. Since then, many states have adopted laws (sometimes called "little RICO" acts) based on the federal statute. The federal and most state RICO acts provide for enforcement not only by criminal prosecution but also by civil lawsuit, in which the plaintiff can sue for treble damages. — Abbr. RICO.

racketeering, *n.* (1897) **1.** A system of organized crime traditionally involving the extortion of money from businesses by intimidation, violence, or other illegal methods. **2.** A pattern of illegal activity (such as bribery, extortion, fraud, and murder) carried out as part of an enterprise (such as a crime syndicate) that is owned or controlled by those engaged in the illegal activity. • The modern sense (sense 2) derives from the federal RICO statute, which greatly broadened the term's original sense to include such activities as mail fraud, securities fraud, and the collection of illegal gambling debts. See 18 USCA §§ 1951–1960.

rack rent, *n.* Rent equal to or nearly equal to the full annual value of the property; excessively or unreasonably high rent. — **rack-rent,** *vb.* — **rack-renter,** *n.*

radical lawyering. See CAUSE LAWYERING.

raffle, *n.* A form of lottery in which each participant buys one or more chances to win a prize.

raid, *n.* **1.** A sudden attack or invasion by law-enforcement officers, usu. to make an arrest or to search for evidence of a crime. **2.** An attempt by a business or union to lure employees or members from a competitor. **3.** An attempt by a group of speculators to cause a sudden fall in stock prices by concerted selling.

raider. See CORPORATE RAIDER.

railroad, *vb.* **1.** To transport by train. **2.** To send (a measure) hastily through a legislature so that there is little time for consideration and debate. **3.** To convict (a person) hastily, esp. by the use of false charges or insufficient evidence.

railroad-aid bond. See BOND (3).

railroad company. See *railroad corporation* under CORPORATION.

railroad corporation. See CORPORATION.

Railroad Retirement Board. A three-member federal board that administers the program providing retirement, unemployment, and sickness benefits to retired railroad employees and their families. ● The Board was established by the Railroad Retirement Act of 1934. — Abbr. RRB.

Railway Labor Act. A 1926 federal law giving transportation employees the right to organize without management interference and establishing guidelines for the resolution of labor disputes in the transportation industry. ● In 1934, the law was amended to include the airline industry and to establish the National Mediation Board. 45 USCA §§ 151–188. See NATIONAL MEDIATION BOARD.

rainmaker, *n.* A lawyer who generates a large amount of business for a law firm, usu. through wide contacts within the business community <the law firm fell on hard times when the rainmaker left and took his clients with him>. — **rainmaking,** *n.*

raise, *vb.* (12c) **1.** To increase in amount or value <the industry raised prices>. **2.** To gather or collect <the charity raised funds>. **3.** To bring up for discussion or consideration; to introduce or put forward <the party raised the issue in its pleading>. **4.** To create or establish <the person's silence raised an inference of consent>. **5.** To increase the stated amount of (a negotiable instrument) by fraudulent alteration <the indorser raised the check>.

raise a question of privilege. To offer a question of privilege to be considered by the meeting or ruled on by the chair. See *question of privilege* under QUESTION (3).

raised check. See CHECK.

raising an instrument. The act of fraudulently altering a negotiable instrument, esp. a check, to increase the amount stated as payable. See *raised check* under CHECK.

rake-off, *n.* (1887) A percentage or share taken, esp. from an illegal transaction; an illegal bribe, payoff, or skimming of profits. — **rake off,** *vb.*

rally, *n.* A sharp rise in price or trading (as of stocks) after a declining market.

RAM. See *reverse annuity mortgage* under MORTGAGE.

Rambo lawyer. *Slang.* A lawyer, esp. a litigator, who uses aggressive, unethical, or illegal tactics in representing a client and who lacks courtesy and professionalism in dealing with other lawyers. — Often shortened to *Rambo.*

ram raid. *Slang.* The smashing of a shop window or other commercial premises with a vehicle in order to break in and steal cash or goods. ● The term is most common in Britain, Ireland, and Australia. — Also termed *crash-and-dash.* Cf. SMASH-AND-GRAB.

Ramseyer rule. A rule of the U.S. House of Representatives requiring any committee reporting a bill that amends legislation in force to show in its report what wording the bill would strike from or insert into the current law. ● The rule is named for Representative C. William Ramseyer (1875–1943) of Iowa, who proposed it. The analogous rule in the U.S. Senate is the Cordon rule. See CORDON RULE.

R and D. *abbr.* RESEARCH AND DEVELOPMENT.

range, *n. Land law.* In U.S. government surveys, a strip of public land running due north to south, consisting of a row of townships, at six-mile intervals. — Abbr. R.

ranger. 1. *Hist.* In England, an officer or keeper of a royal forest, appointed to patrol the forest, drive out stray animals, and prevent trespassing. **2.** An officer or warden who patrols and supervises the care and preservation of a public park or forest. **3.** One of a group of soldiers who patrol a given region; esp., in the U.S. military, a soldier specially trained for surprise raids and close combat. **4.** A member of a special state police force.

rank, *n.* **1.** A social or official position or standing, as in the armed forces <the rank of captain>. **2.** *Parliamentary law.* A motion's relative precedence. See PRECEDENCE (3).

rank and file. 1. The enlisted soldiers of an armed force, as distinguished from the officers. **2.** The general membership of a union.

rank-order voting. See *preferential voting* under VOTING.

ransom, *n.* (13c) **1.** Money or other consideration demanded or paid for the release of a captured person or property. See KIDNAPPING. **2.** The release of a captured person or property in exchange for payment of a demanded price.

ransom, *vb.* (14c) **1.** To obtain the release of (a captive) by paying a demanded price. **2.** To release (a captive) upon receiving such a payment. **3.** To hold and demand payment for the release of (a captive).

ransom bill. *Int'l law.* A contract by which a vessel or other property captured at sea during wartime is ransomed in exchange for release and safe conduct to a friendly destination. — Also termed *ransom bond.*

ransom factor. *Slang.* The costliness of litigation considered as a disincentive to vindicate one's rights in court. • The term is used mostly in England.

rap, *n.* (1903) *Slang.* **1.** Legal responsibility for a criminal act <he took the rap for his accomplices>. **2.** A criminal charge <a murder rap>. **3.** A criminal conviction; esp., a prison sentence <a 20-year rap for counterfeiting>.

rape, *n.* (15c) **1.** At common law, unlawful sexual intercourse committed by a man with a woman not his wife through force and against her will. • The common-law crime of rape required at least a slight penetration of the penis into the vagina. Also at common law, a husband could not be convicted of raping his wife. — Formerly termed *rapture; ravishment.* **2.** Unlawful sexual activity (esp. intercourse) with a person (usu. a female) without consent and usu. by force or threat of injury. • Most modern state statutes have broadened the definition along these lines. Rape includes unlawful sexual intercourse without consent after the perpetrator has substantially impaired his victim by administering, without the victim's knowledge or consent, drugs or intoxicants for the purpose of preventing resistance. It also includes unlawful sexual intercourse with a person who is unconscious. Marital status is now usu. irrelevant, and sometimes so is the victim's gender. — Also termed (in some statutes) *unlawful sexual intercourse; sexual assault; sexual battery; sexual abuse;* (in Latin) *crimen raptus.* Cf. *sexual assault* under ASSAULT; *sexual battery* under BATTERY.

acquaintance rape. (1980) Rape committed by someone known to the victim, esp. by the victim's social companion. Cf. *date rape; relationship rape.*

command rape. Coerced or forced sexual contact between a superior member and subordinate member of the armed forces.

date rape. (1975) Rape committed by a person who is escorting the victim on a social occasion. • Loosely, *date rape* also sometimes refers to what is more accurately called *acquaintance rape* or *relationship rape.*

marital rape. (1936) A husband's sexual intercourse with his wife by force or without her consent. • Marital rape was not a crime at common

law, but under modern statutes the marital exemption no longer applies, and in most jurisdictions a husband can be prosecuted for raping his wife. — Also termed *spousal rape.*

prior-relationship rape. See *relationship rape.*

rape by means of fraud. An instance of sexual intercourse that has been induced by fraud. • Authorities are divided on the question whether rape can occur when a woman is induced by fraudulent statements to have sexual intercourse. But the term *rape by means of fraud* is not uncommon in legal literature.

rape under age. See *statutory rape.*

relationship rape. (1999) Rape committed by someone with whom the victim has had a significant association, often (though not always) of a romantic nature. • This term encompasses all types of relationships, including family, friends, dates, cohabitants, and spouses, in which the victim has had more than brief or perfunctory interaction with the other person. Thus it does not extend to those with whom the victim has had only brief encounters or a nodding acquaintance. — Also termed *prior-relationship rape.* Cf. *date rape; acquaintance rape.*

spousal rape. See *marital rape.*

statutory rape. (1873) Unlawful sexual intercourse with a person under the age of consent (as defined by statute), regardless of whether it is against that person's will. • Generally, only an adult may be convicted of this crime. A person under the age of consent cannot be convicted. — Also termed *rape under age.* See *age of consent* under AGE.

3. *Archaic.* The act of seizing and carrying off a person (esp. a woman) by force; abduction. **4.** The act of plundering or despoiling a place. **5.** *Hist.* One of the six administrative districts into which Sussex, England was divided, being smaller than a shire and larger than a hundred.

rape, *vb.* **1.** To commit rape against. **2.** *Archaic.* To seize and carry off by force; abduct. **3.** To plunder or despoil. — **rapist, raper,** *n.*

rape shield law. See SHIELD LAW (2).

rape shield statute. See SHIELD LAW (2).

rape under age. See *statutory rape* under RAPE.

rapine (rap-in). **1.** Forcible seizure and carrying off of another's property; pillage or plunder. **2.** *Archaic.* Rape.

rapprochement (ra-prosh-**mahn**). [French] The establishment or restoration of cordial relations between two or more nations. — Also spelled *rapprochment.*

rap sheet. (1960) *Slang.* A person's criminal record.

rapture. *Archaic.* **1.** Forcible seizure and carrying off of another person (esp. a woman); abduction. **2.** RAPE (1).

RAR. *abbr.* REVENUE AGENT'S REPORT.

rasure (**ray**-zhər). **1.** The scraping or shaving of a document's surface to remove the writing from it; erasure. **2.** Obliteration. — **rase,** *vb.*

rat. *Slang.* See STOOL PIGEON (1).

ratable (**ray**-tə-bəl), *adj.* (16c) **1.** Proportionate <ratable distribution>. **2.** Capable of being estimated, appraised, or apportioned <because hundreds of angry fans ran onto the field at the same time, blame for the goalpost's destruction is not ratable>. **3.** Taxable <the government assessed the widow's ratable estate>. See PRO RATA.

ratchet theory. (1977) *Constitutional law.* The principle that Congress, in exercising its enforcement power under the 14th Amendment, can increase but not dilute the scope of 14th Amendment guarantees as previously defined by the Supreme Court. • The thought underlying the term is that the enabling clause works in only one direction, like a ratchet. The theory was stated by Justice Brennan in *Katzenbach v. Morgan*, 384 U.S. 641, 86 S.Ct. 1717 (1966), but was repudiated by the Supreme Court in *City of Boerne v. Flores*, 521 U.S. 507, 117 S.Ct.2157 (1997). — Also termed *one-way ratchet theory.*

rate, *n.* (15c) **1.** Proportional or relative value; the proportion by which quantity or value is adjusted <rate of inflation>. **2.** An amount paid or charged for a good or service <the rate for a business-class fare is $550>.

   class rate. A single rate applying to the transportation of several articles of the same general character.

   confiscatory rate. A utility rate set so low by the government that the utility company cannot realize a reasonable return on its investment.

   freight rate. A rate charged by a carrier for the transportation of cargo, usu. based on the weight, volume, or quantity of goods but sometimes also on the goods' value or the mileage.

   joint rate. A single rate charged by two or more carriers to cover a shipment of goods over a single route.

   union rate. The wage scale set by a union as a minimum wage to be paid and usu. expressed as an hourly rate or piecework rate.

3. INTEREST RATE <the rate on the loan increases by 2% after five years>. **4.** PREMIUM RATE. **5.** *English law.* A sum assessed or payable to the local government in the place where a ratepayer dwells or has property. See RATEPAYER. — **rate,** *vb.*

rate base. The investment amount or property value on which a company, esp. a public utility, is allowed to earn a particular rate of return.

rate-base value. See *net book cost* under COST (1).

rate of interest. See INTEREST RATE.

rate of return. The annual income from an investment, expressed as a percentage of the investment. See RETURN (5).

   fair rate of return. The amount of profit that a public utility is permitted to earn, as determined by a public utility commission.

   internal rate of return. *Accounting.* A discounted-cash-flow method of evaluating a long-term project, used to determine the actual return on an investment. — Abbr. IRR.

ratepayer. *English law.* A person who pays local taxes; a person liable to pay rates. See RATE (4).

ratification, *n.* (15c) **1.** Adoption or enactment, esp. where the act is the last in a series of necessary steps or consents <The Ratification of the Conventions of nine States, shall be sufficient for the Establishment of this Constitution between the States so ratifying the Same>. • In this sense, ratification runs the gamut of a formal approval of a constitutional amendment to rank-and-file approval of a labor union's collective-bargaining agreement with management. See ADOPTION (5). Cf. SANCTION (1). **2.** Confirmation and acceptance of a previous act, thereby making the act valid from the moment it was done <the board of directors' ratification of the president's resolution>. • This sense includes action taken by the legislature to make binding a treaty negotiated by the executive. **3.** *Contracts.* A person's binding adoption of an act already completed but either not done in a way that originally produced a legal obligation or done by a third party having at the time no authority to act as the person's agent <an adult's ratification of a contract signed during childhood is necessary to make the contract enforceable>. **4.** *Int'l law.* The final establishment of consent by the parties to a treaty to be bound by it, usu. including the exchange or deposit of instruments of ratification <the ratification of the nuclear-weapons treaty>. See INSTRUMENT OF RATIFICATION. Cf. CONFIRMATION. — **ratify,** *vb.* — **ratifiable,** *adj.*

rating. 1. *Marine insurance.* The determination of a vessel's state or condition as a factor of insurability. **2.** INSURANCE RATING.

ratio. See RATIO DECIDENDI.

ratiocination (rash-ee-os-ə-**nay**-shən), *n.* (16c) The process or an act of reasoning. — **ratiocinative** (rash-ee-**os**-ə-nay-tiv), *adj.* — **ratiocinate** (rash-ee-**os**-ə-nayt), *vb.*

ratio decidendi (**ray**-shee-oh des-ə-**den**-dɪ), *n.* [Latin "the reason for deciding"] (18c) **1.** The principle or rule of law on which a court's decision is founded <many poorly written judicial opinions do not contain a clearly ascertainable *ratio decidendi*>. **2.** The rule of law on which a later court thinks that a previous court founded its decision; a general rule without which a case must have been decided otherwise <this opinion recognizes the Supreme Court's *ratio decidendi* in the school desegregation cases>. — Often shortened to *ratio*. Pl. *rationes decidendi* (**ray**-shee-oh-neez des-ə-den-dɪ). Cf. OBITER DICTUM; HOLDING (1).

rational-basis test. (1947) *Constitutional law.* The criterion for judicial analysis of a statute that does not implicate a fundamental right or a suspect or quasi-suspect classification under the Due Process or Equal Protection Clause, whereby the court will uphold a law if it bears a reasonable relationship to the attainment of a legitimate governmental objective. ● Rational basis is the most deferential of the standards of review that courts use in due-process and equal-protection analysis. — Also termed *rational-purpose test*; *rational-relationship test*; *minimum scrutiny*; *minimal scrutiny*. Cf. STRICT SCRUTINY; INTERMEDIATE SCRUTINY.

rational-choice theory. (1979) The theory that behavioral choices, including the choice to engage in criminal activity, are based on purposeful decisions that the potential benefits outweigh the risks. Cf. CONTROL THEORY; ROUTINE-ACTIVITIES THEORY; STRAIN THEORY.

rational doubt. See REASONABLE DOUBT.

rational interpretation. See *logical interpretation* under INTERPRETATION.

rational-purpose test. See RATIONAL-BASIS TEST.

rational-relationship test. See RATIONAL-BASIS TEST.

ravishment, *n. Archaic.* **1.** Forcible seizure and carrying off of another person (esp. a woman); abduction. **2.** RAPE (1). ● In this sense the term is widely considered inappropriate for modern usage, given its romantic connotations (in other contexts) of ecstasy and delight. In the Restatement (First) of Torts § 65a, the word was defined as including not just rape but any carnal intercourse of a criminal nature. — **ravish,** *vb.*

RBS. *abbr.* RURAL BUSINESS-COOPERATIVE SERVICE.

RCE. *abbr.* REQUEST FOR CONTINUED EXAMINATION.

rDNA. *abbr.* RECOMBINANT DNA TECHNOLOGY.

re (ree *or* ray), *prep.* (18c) Regarding; in the matter of. ● In the title of a case, it usu. signifies a legal proceeding regarding the disposition of real or personal property or a change in legal status. In American caselaw, the abbreviation commonly used is *in re* <In re Estate of Kirk>. In business correspondence, the term signals the subject matter <re: Board Meeting>. See IN RE.

REA. *abbr.* RURAL ELECTRIFICATION ADMINISTRATION.

rea (ree-ə), *n.* [Latin] In civil and canon law, a defendant. Pl. **reae.**

reacquired stock. See *treasury stock* under STOCK.

reading. *Parliamentary law.* The recitation aloud of a bill or other main motion, sometimes by title only, usu. in a series of three such recitations necessary before a legislative body can pass a bill. See *reading clerk* under CLERK (7).

reading clerk. See CLERK (7).

read into, *vb.* See READ ON.

readjustment, *n.* (18c) Voluntary reorganization of a financially troubled corporation by the shareholders themselves, without a trustee's or a receiver's intervention. — **readjust,** *vb.*

read law. 1. To prepare for a legal career by working in a lawyer's office as a clerk while studying legal texts on one's own time. ● Most American lawyers in the 18th and 19th centuries obtained their legal educations solely by reading law. Today, few American states allow applicants to take the bar exam without attending law school. **2.** To study law at a law school.

read on, *vb. Patents.* **1.** (Of a patent claim) to contain all the same features of (a prior-art reference). ● If the patent claim reads on the prior art, the claim has been anticipated and the patent will be denied. See ANTICIPATED. **2.** (Of a patent claim) to describe an infringing product or process. ● If all the patent claims read on the other product, that product infringes the patent.

ready, willing, and able. (1829) (Of a prospective buyer) legally and financially capable of consummating a purchase.

reaffirmation, *n.* (1857) **1.** Approval of something previously decided or agreed to; renewal <the Supreme Court's reaffirmation of this principle is long overdue>. **2.** *Bankruptcy.* An agreement between the debtor and a creditor by which the debtor promises to repay a prepetition debt that would otherwise be discharged at the conclusion of the bankruptcy <the debtor negotiated a reaffirmation so that he could keep the collateral>. ● There are two main requirements for a reaffirmation to be enforceable: (1) the agreement must contain a clear and conspicuous provision stating that the debtor may rescind the reaffirmation agreement anytime before discharge or within 60 days after the agreement is filed with the court; and (2) for a debtor who is not represented by counsel, the court must determine that the reaffirmation is in the debtor's best interest and does not impose an undue hardship. 11 USCA § 524(c). — Also termed (in sense 2) *reaffirmation agreement.* — **reaffirm,** *vb.*

reaffirmation hearing. *Bankruptcy.* A hearing at which the debtor and a creditor present a reaffirmation of a dischargeable debt for the court's approval. • The reaffirmation hearing is usu. held simultaneously with the discharge hearing. See DISCHARGE HEARING.

real, *adj.* (15c) **1.** Of or relating to things (such as lands and buildings) that are fixed or immovable <real property> <a real action>. **2.** *Civil law.* Of, relating to, or attached to a thing (whether movable or immovable) rather than a person <a real right>. **3.** Actual; genuine; true <real authority>. **4.** (Of money, income, etc.) measured in terms of purchasing power rather than nominal value; adjusted for inflation <real wages>.

real account. See ACCOUNT.

real action. See ACTION (4).

real asset. See ASSET.

real authority. See *actual authority* under AUTHORITY (1).

real burden. See BURDEN (4).

real chattel. See *chattel real* under CHATTEL.

real contract. See CONTRACT.

real covenant. See *covenant running with the land* under COVENANT (4).

real damages. See *actual damages* under DAMAGES.

real defense. See DEFENSE (4).

real earnings. See EARNINGS.

real estate. See *real property* under PROPERTY.

real-estate agent. See AGENT (2).

real-estate broker. See BROKER.

real-estate investment trust. A company that invests in and manages a portfolio of real estate, with the majority of the trust's income distributed to its shareholders. • Such a trust may qualify for special income-tax treatment if it distributes 95% of its income to its shareholders. — Abbr. REIT. See *investment company* under COMPANY. Cf. REAL-ESTATE MORTGAGE TRUST.

   umbrella-partnership real-estate investment trust. A REIT that controls and holds most of its properties through an umbrella limited partnership, as a result of which the trust can acquire properties in exchange for the limited-partnership interests in the umbrella while triggering no tax obligations for certain sellers. • This is a structure that many REITs now use. — Abbr. UPREIT.

real-estate-mortgage investment conduit. An entity that holds a fixed pool of mortgages or mortgage-backed securities (such as collateralized

mortgage obligations), issues interests in itself to investors, and receives favorable tax treatment by passing its income through to those investors. • Real-estate-mortgage investment conduits were created by the Tax Reform Act of 1986. They can be organized as corporations, partnerships, or trusts. To qualify for tax-exempt status, the entity must meet two requirements: (1) almost all the entity's assets must be real-estate mortgages (though a few other cash-flow-maintaining assets are allowed); and (2) all interests in the entity must be classified as either regular interests (which entitle the holder to principal and interest income through debt or equity) or residual interests (which provide contingent income). — Abbr. REMIC.

real-estate mortgage trust. A real-estate investment trust that buys and sells the mortgages on real property rather than the real property itself. — Abbr. REMT. Cf. REAL-ESTATE INVESTMENT TRUST.

real estate owned. Property acquired by a lender, usu. through foreclosure, in satisfaction of a debt. — Abbr. REO.

Real Estate Settlement Procedures Act. A federal law that requires lenders to provide home buyers with information about known or estimated settlement costs. 12 USCA §§ 2601–2617. — Abbr. RESPA. See REGULATION X.

real-estate syndicate. A group of investors who pool their money to buy and sell real property. • Most real-estate syndicates operate as limited partnerships or real-estate investment trusts.

real evidence. See EVIDENCE.

realignment (ree-ə-līn-mənt), *n.* The process by which a court, usu. in determining diversity jurisdiction, identifies and rearranges the parties as plaintiffs and defendants according to their ultimate interests. — **realign,** *vb.*

real income. See INCOME.

realization, *n.* (18c) **1.** Conversion of noncash assets into cash assets. **2.** *Tax.* An event or transaction, such as the sale or exchange of property, that substantially changes a taxpayer's economic position so that income tax may be imposed or a tax allowance granted. Cf. RECOGNITION (4). — **realize,** *vb.*

realized gain. See GAIN (3).

realized loss. See LOSS (2).

real law. The law of real property; real-estate law.

real money. See MONEY.

real party in interest. See PARTY (2).

real-party-in-interest rule. The principle that the person entitled by law to enforce a substantive right should be the one under whose name the action is prosecuted. Fed. R. Civ. P. 17(a).

real property. See PROPERTY.

real rate. See INTEREST RATE.

real right. See RIGHT.

real security. See SECURITY.

real servitude. See *servitude appurtenant* under SERVITUDE (2).

real statute. See STATUTE.

real subrogation. See SUBROGATION.

real suretyship. See SURETYSHIP.

real things. (18c) Property that is fixed and immovable, such as lands and buildings; real property. — Also termed *things real*. See *real property* under PROPERTY. Cf. *chattel real* under CHATTEL.

realtor (reel-tər). **1.** (*cap.*) *Servicemark.* A real-estate agent who is a member of the National Association of Realtors. **2.** Loosely, any real-estate agent or broker.

real treaty. See TREATY (1).

realty. Land and anything growing on, attached to, or erected on it, that cannot be removed without injury to the land. — Also termed *real property*.

    quasi-realty. *Hist.* Things that the law treats as fixed to realty, but are themselves movable, such as title deeds.

realty trust. See *nominee trust* (2) under TRUST.

real wages. See WAGE.

real wrong. See WRONG.

reapportionment, *n.* (1874) Realignment of a legislative district's boundaries to reflect changes in population and ensure proportionate representation by elected officials. See U.S. Const. art. I, § 2, cl. 3. — Also termed *redistricting*. Cf. GERRYMANDERING. — **reapportion,** *vb.*

reargument, *n.* (18c) The presentation of additional arguments, which often suggest that a controlling legal principle has been overlooked, to a court (usu. an appellate court) that has already heard initial arguments. Cf. REHEARING. — **reargue,** *vb.*

rearrest. See ARREST.

reasonable, *adj.* (14c) **1.** Fair, proper, or moderate under the circumstances <reasonable pay>. **2.** According to reason <your argument is reasonable but not convincing>. **3.** (Of a person) having the faculty of reason <a reasonable person would have looked both ways before crossing the street>. **4.** *Archaic.* Human <criminal homicide is traditionally called the unlawful killing of a "reasonable person">. — **reasonableness,** *n.*

reasonable accommodation. See ACCOMMODATION.

reasonable-apprehension test. *Patents.* A judicial analysis to decide whether there is a justiciable controversy between a patentee and an alleged infringer. • The test has two elements: (1) the patent owner must make an explicit threat or take other action that makes another person reasonably believe that an infringement suit is likely, and (2) the other person must be engaged in an activity that could constitute infringement or must be intentionally preparing to engage in possibly infringing activity. If either element is prospective or uncertain, the court will not consider the complaint.

reasonable care. See CARE.

reasonable cause. See PROBABLE CAUSE (1).

reasonable-consumer test. The prevailing test for determining whether advertisement is deceptive, determined by asking whether the reasonable consumer would believe that the claim is true. Cf. FOOL'S TEST.

reasonable-development covenant. *Oil & gas.* The implied promise in an oil-and-gas lease that once production is obtained the lessee will continue to develop the property as would a reasonably prudent operator, as opposed to merely holding the lease by the production already obtained. See FURTHER-EXPLORATION COVENANT.

reasonable deviation. See DEVIATION.

reasonable diligence. See DILIGENCE.

reasonable doubt. (18c) The doubt that prevents one from being firmly convinced of a defendant's guilt, or the belief that there is a real possibility that a defendant is not guilty. • "Beyond a reasonable doubt" is the standard used by a jury to determine whether a criminal defendant is guilty. *See* Model Penal Code § 1.12. In deciding whether guilt has been proved beyond a reasonable doubt, the jury must begin with the presumption that the defendant is innocent. — Also termed *rational doubt*. See BURDEN OF PERSUASION. Cf. *clear and convincing evidence* under EVIDENCE; PREPONDERANCE OF THE EVIDENCE.

reasonable excuse. See PROBABLE CAUSE.

reasonable-expectations doctrine. The principle that an ambiguous or inconspicuous term in a contract should be interpreted to favor the weaker party's objectively reasonable expectations from the contract, even though the explicit language of the terms may not support those expectations. • This principle is most often applied when interpreting insurance policies, consumer contracts, and other types of adhesion contracts. — Also written *reasonable-expectation doctrine*.

reasonable force. See FORCE.

reasonable grounds. See PROBABLE CAUSE (1).

reasonable-inference rule. (1945) An evidentiary principle providing that a jury, in deciding a case, may properly consider any reasonable inference drawn from the evidence presented at trial. Cf. PYRAMIDING INFERENCES, RULE AGAINST.

reasonable man. See REASONABLE PERSON.

reasonable medical probability. (1949) In proving the cause of an injury, a standard requiring a showing that the injury was more likely than not caused by a particular stimulus, based on the general consensus of recognized medical thought. — Also termed *reasonable medical certainty*.

reasonable notice. See NOTICE.

reasonable person. 1. A hypothetical person used as a legal standard, esp. to determine whether someone acted with negligence; specif., a person who exercises the degree of attention, knowledge, intelligence, and judgment that society requires of its members for the protection of their own and of others' interests. ● The reasonable person acts sensibly, does things without serious delay, and takes proper but not excessive precautions. See Restatement (Second) of Torts § 283(b). — Also termed *reasonable man*; *prudent person*; *ordinarily prudent person*; *reasonably prudent person*; *highly prudent person*. See *reasonable care* under CARE. **2.** *Archaic.* A human being.

reasonable provocation. See *adequate provocation* under PROVOCATION.

reasonable royalty. See ROYALTY (1).

reasonable skill. See SKILL.

reasonable support. 1. See SUPPORT (1). **2.** See SUPPORT (2).

reasonable suspicion. See SUSPICION.

reasonable time. (1951) **1.** *Contracts.* The time needed to do what a contract requires to be done, based on subjective circumstances. ● If the contracting parties do not fix a time for performance, the law will usu. presume a reasonable time. **2.** *Commercial law.* The time during which the UCC permits a party to accept an offer, inspect goods, substitute conforming goods for rejected goods, and the like.

reasonable use. See USE (1).

reasonable-use theory. (1933) *Property.* The principle that owners of riparian land may make reasonable use of their water if this use does not affect the water available to lower riparian owners.

reasonably believe. See BELIEVE.

reasonably-prudent-operator standard. *Oil & gas.* The test generally applied to determine a lessee's compliance with implied lease covenants by considering what a reasonable, competent operator in the oil-and-gas industry would do under the circumstances, acting in good faith and with economic motivation, and taking into account the lessor's interests as well as that of the operator. — Also termed *reasonable-prudent-operator standard*; *prudent-operator standard*.

reasonably prudent person. See REASONABLE PERSON.

reasonably suspect. See SUSPECT.

reasons for allowance. See RULE 109 STATEMENT.

reason to know. Information from which a person of ordinary intelligence — or of the superior intelligence that the person may have — would infer that the fact in question exists or that there is a substantial enough chance of its existence that, if the person exercises reasonable care, the person can assume the fact exists.

reassurance. See REINSURANCE.

rebate, *n.* A return of part of a payment, serving as a discount or reduction. — **rebate,** *vb.*

rebellion. 1. Open, organized, and armed resistance to an established government or ruler. **2.** Open resistance or opposition to an authority or tradition. **3.** *Hist.* Disobedience of a legal command or summons.

rebus sic stantibus (**ree**-bəs sik **stan**-ti-bəs). [Latin "matters so standing"] *Civil law & Int'l law.* The principle that all agreements are concluded with the implied condition that they are binding only as long as there are no major changes in the circumstances. See CLAUSA REBUS SIC STANTIBUS.

rebut, *vb.* (14c) To refute, oppose, or counteract (something) by evidence, argument, or contrary proof <rebut the opponent's expert testimony> <rebut a presumption of negligence>.

rebuttable presumption. See PRESUMPTION.

rebuttal, *n.* (1830) **1.** In-court contradiction of an adverse party's evidence. **2.** The time given to a party to present contradictory evidence or arguments. Cf. CASE-IN-CHIEF. **3.** The arguments contained in a reply brief. See *reply brief* under BRIEF.

rebuttal evidence. See EVIDENCE.

rebuttal witness. See WITNESS.

rebutter. (16c) **1.** *Common-law pleading.* The defendant's answer to a plaintiff's surrejoinder; the pleading that followed the rejoinder and surrejoinder, and that might in turn be answered by the surrebutter. **2.** One who rebuts.

rebutting evidence. See *rebuttal evidence* under EVIDENCE.

recall, *n.* (1902) **1.** Removal of a public official from office by popular vote. **2.** A manufacturer's request to consumers for the return of defective products for repair or replacement. **3.** Revocation of a judgment for factual or legal reasons. — **recall,** *vb.*

recall election. See ELECTION (3).

recall exclusion. See *sistership exclusion* under EXCLUSION (3).

recall of mandate. The extraordinary action by an appellate court of withdrawing the order it issued to the trial court upon deciding an appeal, usu. after the deadline has passed for the losing party to seek a rehearing. • Because this action can interfere with trial-court proceedings on remand, and also because it clouds the waters that repose (the finality of a judgment) is meant to clear, courts are reluctant to use the power. But they will use it to correct clerical errors or to remedy a fraud on the court during the appeal. It has also been used when the original mandate would result in a grave injustice. See MANDATE (1).

recant (ri-**kant**), *vb.* (16c) **1.** To withdraw or renounce (prior statements or testimony) formally or publicly <the prosecution hoped the eyewitness wouldn't recant her corroborating testimony on the stand>. **2.** To withdraw or renounce prior statements or testimony formally or publicly <under grueling cross-examination, the witness recanted>. — **recantation**, *n.*

recapitalization, *n.* An adjustment or recasting of a corporation's capital structure — that is, its stocks, bonds, or other securities — through amendment of the articles of incorporation or merger with a parent or subsidiary. • An example of recapitalization is the elimination of unpaid preferred dividends and the creation of a new class of senior securities. Cf. REORGANIZATION (2). — **recapitalize**, *vb.*

   leveraged recapitalization. Recapitalization whereby the corporation substitutes debt for equity in the capital structure, usu. to make the corporation less attractive as a target for a hostile takeover. — Also termed *leveraging up.*

recaption. (17c) **1.** At common law, lawful seizure of another's property for a second time to secure the performance of a duty; a second distress. See DISTRESS. **2.** Peaceful retaking, without legal process, of one's own property that has been wrongfully taken.

recapture, *n.* **1.** The act or an instance of retaking or reacquiring; recovery. **2.** The lawful taking by the government of earnings or profits exceeding a specified amount; esp., the government's recovery of a tax benefit (such as a deduction or credit) by taxing income or property that no longer qualifies for the benefit. **3.** *Int'l law.* The retaking of a prize or booty so that the property is legally restored to its original owner. See POSTLIMINIUM (2). — **recapture**, *vb.*

recapture clause. 1. A contract provision that limits prices or allows for the recovery of goods if market conditions greatly differ from what the contract anticipated. **2.** A commercial-lease provision that grants the landlord both a percentage of the tenant's profits above a fixed amount of rent and the right to terminate the lease — and thus recapture the property — if those profits are too low.

recapture rule. *Patents.* The doctrine that a patentee cannot regain, in a reissue patent, a claim that the patentee previously abandoned in order to gain allowance of the patent application. • The rule provides a defense in an infringement action by allowing the defendant to attack the validity of a reissue patent. An attempt to recapture a strategically abandoned claim cannot meet the statutory requirement that the error be made without deceptive intent. 35 USCA § 251.

recede, *vb.* (Of a house in a bicameral legislature) to withdraw from an amendment in which the other house has not concurred. See CONCUR (3).

receding market. See *bear market* under MARKET.

receipt, *n.* (14c) **1.** The act of receiving something <my receipt of the document was delayed by two days>. **2.** A written acknowledgment that something has been received <keep the receipt for the gift>.

   accountable receipt. A receipt in which a person admits that goods or money were delivered to the person and that the person is obliged to deliver all or part of the goods or money to a third person.

   interim receipt. The written acknowledgment of a premium paid on an insurance policy that is pending final approval.

   warehouse receipt. See WAREHOUSE RECEIPT.

3. (*usu. pl.*) Something received; INCOME <post the daily receipts in the ledger>.

receipt, *vb.* (18c) **1.** To acknowledge in writing the receipt of (something, esp. money) <the bill must be receipted>. **2.** To give a receipt for (something, esp. money) <the bookkeeper receipted the payments>.

receipt clause. In a conveyancing document, a clause that acts as a receipt for the consideration given. • This clause typically appears to avoid the necessity of a separate receipt.

receiptor (ri-**see**-tər). (1814) A person who receives from a sheriff another's property seized in garnishment and agrees to return the property upon demand or execution.

receivable, *adj.* **1.** Capable of being admitted or accepted <receivable evidence>. **2.** Awaiting receipt of payment <accounts receivable>. **3.** Subject to a call for payment <a note receivable>.

receivable, *n.* (14c) An amount owed, esp. by a business's customer. See *account receivable* under ACCOUNT.

   unrealized receivable. (1957) An amount earned but not yet received. • Unrealized receivables have no income-tax basis for cash-basis taxpayers.

receiver. (18c) A disinterested person appointed by a court, or by a corporation or other person, for the protection or collection of property that is the subject of diverse claims (for example, because it belongs to a bankrupt or is otherwise being litigated). Cf. LIQUIDATOR.

ancillary receiver. One who is appointed as a receiver in a particular area to help a foreign receiver collect the assets of an insolvent corporation or other entity.

general receiver. See *principal receiver.*

judgment receiver. A receiver who collects or diverts funds from a judgment debtor to the creditor. • A judgment receiver is usu. appointed when it is difficult to enforce a judgment in any other manner. — Also termed *receiver in aid of execution.*

local receiver. *Conflict of laws.* A receiver appointed in the state where property is located or where an act is done.

principal receiver. A receiver who is primarily responsible for the receivership estate. • A principal receiver may ordinarily (1) act outside the state of appointment, (2) sue in a foreign court, (3) exercise broad powers of assignment, and (4) handle all distributions. — Also termed *primary receiver; general receiver; original receiver.*

receiver in aid of execution. See *judgment receiver.*

statutory receiver. A receiver whose appointment is provided for in a statute.

receiver general. A public official in charge of a government's receipts and treasury. Pl. **receivers general.**

receiver's certificate. *Bankruptcy.* An instrument issued by a receiver as evidence that the holder is entitled to receive payment from funds controlled by the bankruptcy court.

receivership. (15c) **1.** The state or condition of being in the control of a receiver. **2.** The position or function of being a receiver appointed by a court or under a statute. **3.** A proceeding in which a court appoints a receiver.

ancillary receivership. A receivership in which a further administrative proceeding is appointed in another state to help the principal receivership.

dry receivership. A receivership in which there is no equity available to pay general creditors.

receivership estate. The totality of the interests that the receivers of an association in one or more states are appointed to protect.

receiving, *n.* See RECEIVING STOLEN PROPERTY.

receiving order. See ORDER (2).

receiving state. See STATE.

receiving stolen property. (1847) The criminal offense of acquiring or controlling property known to have been stolen by another person. • Some

jurisdictions require the additional element of wrongful intent. In some jurisdictions it is a felony, but in others it is either a felony or a misdemeanor depending on the value of the property. *See* Model Penal Code §§ 223.1, 223.6. — Sometimes shortened to *receiving.* — Also termed *receiving stolen goods.* See FENCE (1).

reception. (1931) The adoption in whole or in part of the law of one jurisdiction by another jurisdiction. • In the legal idiom, it is most common to speak of the reception of Roman law.

receptitious (ree-sep-**tish**-əs), *adj. Roman law.* **1.** (Of a dowry) returnable by agreement to the donor upon the dissolution of the marriage. **2.** (Of property) retained by the wife and not included in the dowry.

recess (**ree**-ses), *n.* (17c) **1.** A brief break in judicial proceedings <the court granted a fifteen-minute recess so the attorney and plaintiff could confer>. Cf. CONTINUANCE (3). **2.** *Parliamentary law.* A motion that suspends but does not end a meeting, and that usu. provides for resumption of the meeting <the meeting had a 15-minute recess>. • The motion to recess, which merely suspends the meeting, differs from the motion to adjourn, which ends the meeting. Cf. ADJOURN. **3.** *Parliamentary law.* The interval between such a motion's adoption and the meeting's reconvening <Congress took a monthlong recess>. — **recess** (ri-**ses**), *vb.*

recess appointment. See APPOINTMENT.

recession. (1929) A period characterized by a sharp slowdown in economic activity, declining employment, and a decrease in investment and consumer spending. Cf. DEPRESSION.

recharacterization. A court's determination that an insider's loan to an entity in liquidation (such as a corporation or partnership) should be treated as a capital contribution, not as a loan, thereby entitling the insider to only part of the liquidation proceeds payable after all the business's debts have been discharged. • Factors influencing this determination include the amount of capital initially available, the ability of the entity to obtain loans from outside sources, how long the entity has existed, the treatment of the loan in the entity's business records, and past treatment of similar transactions made to that entity by an insider.

recidivate (ri-**sid**-ə-vayt), *vb.* To return to a habit of criminal behavior; to relapse into crime.

recidivation. *Archaic.* See RECIDIVISM.

recidivism (ri-**sid**-ə-viz-əm), *n.* (1886) A tendency to relapse into a habit of criminal activity or behavior. — Also termed (archaically) *recidivation.* — **recidivous, recidivist,** *adj.*

recidivist (ri-**sid**-ə-vist), *n.* (1880) One who has been convicted of multiple criminal offenses, usu.

similar in nature; a repeat offender <proponents of prison reform argue that prisons don't cure the recidivist>. — Also termed *habitual offender; habitual criminal; repeater; career criminal; prior and persistent offender.*

reciprocal (ri-**sip**-rə-kəl), *adj.* (16c) **1.** Directed by each toward the other or others; MUTUAL <reciprocal trusts>. **2.** BILATERAL <a reciprocal contract>. **3.** Corresponding; equivalent <reciprocal discovery>.

reciprocal contract. See *bilateral contract* under CONTRACT.

reciprocal dealing. A business arrangement in which a buyer having greater economic power than a seller agrees to buy something from the seller only if the seller buys something in return. ● Reciprocal dealing usu. violates antitrust laws. — Also termed *reciprocal-dealing arrangement.* Cf. TYING ARRANGEMENT.

reciprocal discovery. See *reverse Jencks material* under JENCKS MATERIAL.

reciprocal exchange. An association whose members exchange contracts and pay premiums through an attorney-in-fact for the purpose of insuring themselves and each other. ● A reciprocal exchange can consist of individuals, partnerships, trustees, or corporations, but the exchange itself is unincorporated. — Also termed *interinsurance exchange; reciprocal insurance exchange; reciprocal interinsurance exchange.* See *reciprocal insurance* under INSURANCE; EXCHANGE (5).

reciprocal insurance. See INSURANCE.

reciprocal insurance exchange. See RECIPROCAL EXCHANGE.

reciprocal interinsurance exchange. See RECIPROCAL EXCHANGE.

reciprocal negative easement. See EASEMENT.

reciprocal trade agreement. An agreement between two countries providing for the exchange of goods between them at lower tariffs and better terms than exist between one of the countries and other countries.

reciprocal trust. See TRUST.

reciprocal will. See *mutual will* under WILL.

reciprocity (res-ə-**pros**-i-tee). (18c) **1.** Mutual or bilateral action <the Arthurs stopped receiving social invitations from friends because of their lack of reciprocity>. **2.** The mutual concession of advantages or privileges for purposes of commercial or diplomatic relations <Texas and Louisiana grant reciprocity to each other's citizens in qualifying for in-state tuition rates>. — Also termed *mutuality of benefits; quid pro quo; equivalence of advantages.* **3.** *Intellectual property.* The recognition by one country of a foreign national's intellectual-property rights only if and only to

the extent that the other nation would recognize those same rights for the first country's citizens. ● Reciprocity is the most restrictive approach to international intellectual-property law rights. Cf. NATIONAL TREATMENT; UNIVERSALITY.

recision. See RESCISSION.

recission. See RESCISSION.

recital. (16c) **1.** An account or description of some fact or thing <the recital of the events leading up to the accident>. **2.** A preliminary statement in a contract or deed explaining the reasons for entering into it or the background of the transaction, or showing the existence of particular facts <the recitals in the settlement agreement should describe the underlying dispute>. ● Traditionally, each recital begins with the word *whereas.* — Also termed (in sense 2) *whereas clause.* — **recite,** *vb.*

   introductory recital. (*usu. pl.*) A recital explaining how and why the existing state of affairs is to be altered.

   narrative recital. (*usu. pl.*) A recital dealing with matters such as how the buyer and the seller came together.

   particular recital. A recital that states a fact definitely.

recite, *vb.* See READ ON.

reckless, *adj.* (bef. 12c) Characterized by the creation of a substantial and unjustifiable risk of harm to others and by a conscious (and sometimes deliberate) disregard for or indifference to that risk; heedless; rash. ● Reckless conduct is much more than mere negligence: it is a gross deviation from what a reasonable person would do. See RECKLESSNESS. Cf. CARELESS; WANTON. — **recklessly,** *adv.*

reckless disregard. See DISREGARD.

reckless driving. (1902) The criminal offense of operating a motor vehicle in a manner that shows conscious indifference to the safety of others.

reckless endangerment. (1968) The criminal offense of putting another person at substantial risk of death or serious injury. ● This is a statutory, not a common-law, offense.

reckless homicide. See HOMICIDE.

reckless indifference. See *deliberate indifference* under INDIFFERENCE.

reckless knowledge. See KNOWLEDGE.

reckless negligence. See *gross negligence* under NEGLIGENCE.

recklessness, *n.* (bef. 12c) **1.** Conduct whereby the actor does not desire harmful consequence but nonetheless foresees the possibility and consciously takes the risk. ● Recklessness involves a greater degree of fault than negligence but a lesser degree of fault than intentional wrongdoing. **2.**

The state of mind in which a person does not care about the consequences of his or her actions. — Also termed *heedlessness*. Cf. WANTONNESS.

reclamation (rek-lə-**may**-shən), *n.* (1848) **1.** The act or an instance of improving the value of economically useless land by physically changing the land, such as irrigating a desert. **2.** *Commercial law.* A seller's limited right to retrieve goods delivered to a buyer when the buyer is insolvent. UCC § 2-702(2). See STOPPAGE IN TRANSITU. **3.** The act or an instance of obtaining valuable materials from waste materials. — **reclaim,** *vb.*

reclusion (ri-**kloo**-zhən). *Civil law.* Incarceration as punishment for a crime; esp. solitary confinement or confinement at hard labor in a penitentiary.

recognition, *n.* (16c) **1.** Confirmation that an act done by another person was authorized. See RATIFICATION. **2.** The formal admission that a person, entity, or thing has a particular status; esp. a nation's act in formally acknowledging the existence of another nation or national government. **3.** *Parliamentary law.* The chair's acknowledgment that a member is entitled to the floor <the chair recognizes the delegate from Minnesota>. See PRECEDENCE (4). **4.** *Tax.* The act or an instance of accounting for a taxpayer's realized gain or loss for the purpose of income-tax reporting. Cf. NONRECOGNITION PROVISION; REALIZATION (2). **5.** An employer's acknowledgment that a union has the right to act as a bargaining agent for employees. **6.** *Int'l law.* Official action by a country acknowledging, expressly or by implication, *de jure* or *de facto*, the existence of a government or a country, or a situation such as a change of territorial sovereignty. **7.** RULE OF RECOGNITION. — **recognize,** *vb.*

recognition clause. *Real estate.* A clause providing that, when a tract of land has been subdivided for development, the ultimate buyers of individual lots are protected if the developer defaults on the mortgage. • Such a clause is typically found in a blanket mortgage or a contract for deed.

recognition picketing. See *organizational picketing* under PICKETING.

recognition strike. See STRIKE.

recognizance (ri-**kog**-nə-zənts). (14c) **1.** A bond or obligation, made in court, by which a person promises to perform some act or observe some condition, such as to appear when called, to pay a debt, or to keep the peace; specif., an in-court acknowledgment of an obligation in a penal sum, conditioned on the performance or nonperformance of a particular act. • Most commonly, a recognizance takes the form of a bail bond that guarantees an unjailed criminal defendant's return for a court date <the defendant was released on his own recognizance>. See RELEASE ON RECOGNIZANCE.

personal recognizance. (18c) The release of a defendant in a criminal case in which the court takes the defendant's word that he or she will appear for a scheduled matter or when told to appear. • This type of release dispenses with the necessity of the person's posting money or having a surety sign a bond with the court.

2. See *bail bond* under BOND (2).

recognized gain. See GAIN (3).

recognized loss. See LOSS.

recognized market. See MARKET.

recognizee (ri-kog-nə-**zee**). (16c) A person in whose favor a recognizance is made; one to whom someone is bound by a recognizance.

recognizor (ri-kog-nə-**zor**). (16c) A person who is obligated under a recognizance; one who is bound by a recognizance. — Also termed *recognitor.*

recollection, *n.* (17c) **1.** The action of recalling something to the mind, esp. through conscious effort. **2.** Something recalled to the mind. See PAST RECOLLECTION RECORDED; PRESENT RECOLLECTION REFRESHED. — **recollect,** *vb.*

recombinant (ri-**kom**-bə-nənt), *adj. Patents.* Of, relating to, or describing the introduction of DNA from one living organism into another.

recombinant DNA technology. *Patents.* The science of mutating organisms by splicing sections of one organism's DNA onto that of another. — Abbr. rDNA.

recommit. *Parliamentary law.* To refer (a motion) back to a committee that has considered it. • The motion is called "recommit" rather than "re-refer" for the sake of euphony. See REFER. Cf. *re-refer* under REFER. — **recommit,** *n.*

recompensable. See COMPENSABLE.

recompense (**rek**-əm-pents), *n.* (15c) Repayment, compensation, or retribution for something, esp. an injury or loss. — **recompense,** *vb.*

reconciliation (rek-ən-sil-ee-**ay**-shən), *n.* (14c) **1.** Restoration of harmony between persons or things that had been in conflict <a reconciliation between the plaintiff and the defendant is unlikely even if the lawsuit settles before trial>. **2.** *Family law.* Voluntary resumption, after a separation, of full marital relations between spouses <the court dismissed the divorce petition after the parties' reconciliation>. Cf. CONDONATION (2). **3.** *Accounting.* An adjustment of accounts so that they agree, esp. by allowing for outstanding items <reconciliation of the checking account and the bank statement>. — **reconcile** (**rek**-ən-sil), *vb.*

reconciliation agreement. *Family law.* A contract between spouses who have had marital difficulties but who now wish to save the marital relationship, usu. by specifying certain economic actions that might ameliorate pressures on the marriage. •

This type of agreement serves a limited purpose. In fact, many states have statutes prohibiting enforcement of contracts for domestic services, so if the agreement governs anything other than economic behavior, it may be unenforceable.

reconciliation statement. An accounting or financial statement in which discrepancies are adjusted.

reconduction, *n.* **1.** *Civil law.* The renewal of a lease. — Also termed *relocation.* See TACIT RELOCATION. **2.** *Int'l law.* The forcible return of aliens (esp. illegal aliens, destitute or diseased aliens, or alien criminals who have served their punishment) to their country of origin. — Also termed (in sense 2) *renvoi.* — **reconduct,** *vb.*

reconsider, *vb.* To discuss or take up (a matter) again <legislators voted to reconsider the bill>. • Under parliamentary law, a motion to reconsider sets aside a certain vote already taken and restores the motion on which the vote is being reconsidered to its status immediately before the vote occurred. Making a motion to reconsider suspends a vote already taken until the assembly decides whether to reconsider it. — **reconsideration,** *n.*

reconsider and enter on the minutes. *Parliamentary law.* To make a motion to reconsider for the purpose of suspending a vote already taken and bringing it back up at the next meeting. — Also termed *reconsider and enter; reconsider and have it entered on the minutes.*

reconsignment. (16c) A change in the terms of a consignment while the goods are in transit. See CONSIGNMENT.

reconstruction. **1.** The act or process of rebuilding, re-creating, or reorganizing something <an expert in accident reconstruction>. **2.** *Patents.* A rebuilding of a broken, worn-out, or otherwise inoperative patented article in such a way that a new article is created, thus resulting in an infringement <the replacement of the machine's essential parts was an infringing reconstruction rather than a permissible repair>. Cf. REPAIR DOCTRINE. **3.** *(cap.)* The process by which the Southern states that had seceded during the Civil War were readmitted into the Union during the years following the war (i.e., from 1865 to 1877) <the 13th, 14th, and 15th Amendments to the U.S. Constitution are a lasting legacy of Reconstruction>.

recontinuance. (16c) *Hist.* **1.** Resumption or renewal. **2.** The recovery of an incorporeal hereditament that had been wrongfully deprived.

reconvention. *Civil law.* The act or process of making a counterclaim. See COUNTERCLAIM.

reconventional demand. See DEMAND (1).

reconversion. The notional or imaginary process by which an earlier constructive conversion (a change of personal into real property or vice

versa) is annulled and the converted property restored to its original character. See *equitable conversion* under CONVERSION (1).

reconveyance, *n.* (16c) The restoration or return of something (esp. an estate or title) to a former owner or holder. — **reconvey,** *vb.*

record, *n.* (13c) **1.** A documentary account of past events, usu. designed to memorialize those events. **2.** Information that is inscribed on a tangible medium or that, having been stored in an electronic or other medium, is retrievable in perceivable form. UCC § 2A-102(a)(34). **3.** MINUTES (2). **4.** The official report of the proceedings in a case, including the filed papers, a verbatim transcript of the trial or hearing (if any), and tangible exhibits. — Also termed (in some jurisdictions) *clerk's record;* (in BrE) *bundle.* See DOCKET (1).

    defective record. (18c) **1.** A trial record that fails to conform to requirements of appellate rules. **2.** A flawed real-estate title resulting from a defect on the property's record in the registry of deeds.

    public record. (16c) A record that a governmental unit is required by law to keep, such as land deeds kept at a county courthouse. • Public records are generally open to view by the public. Cf. *public document* under DOCUMENT.

    reporter's record. In some jurisdictions, a trial transcript. — Also termed *stenographer's record.*

    silent record. *Criminal procedure.* A record that fails to disclose that a defendant voluntarily and knowingly entered a plea, waived a right to counsel, or took any other action affecting his or her rights.

    stenographer's record. See *reporter's record.*

record, *vb.* To deposit (an original or authentic official copy of a document) with an authority <she recorded the deed in the county property office>.

record agent. See INSURANCE AGENT.

recordal. See RECORDATION.

recordation (rek-ər-**day**-shən), *n.* The act or process of recording an instrument, such as a deed or mortgage, in a public registry. • Recordation generally perfects a person's interest in the property against later purchasers (including later mortgagees), but the effect of recordation depends on the type of recording act in effect. — Also termed *recordal.*

record date. See DATE.

recorded recollection. See PAST RECOLLECTION RECORDED.

recorder. (15c) **1.** *Hist.* A magistrate with criminal jurisdiction in some British cities or boroughs. **2.** A municipal judge with the criminal jurisdiction of a magistrate or a police judge and sometimes also with limited civil jurisdiction. **3.** A municipal or county officer who keeps public records such as deeds, liens, and judgments.

court recorder. (18c) A court official who records court activities using electronic recording equipment, usu. for the purpose of preparing a verbatim transcript. Cf. COURT REPORTER (1).

recorder of deeds. See *register of deeds* under REGISTER (1).

4. SECRETARY (3).

recorder's court. See COURT.

recording act. (1802) A law that establishes the requirements for recording a deed or other property interest and the standards for determining priorities between persons claiming interests in the same property (usu. real property). ● Recording acts — the three main types of which are the *notice statute*, the *race statute*, and the *race-notice statute* — are designed to protect bona fide purchasers from earlier unrecorded interests. — Also termed *recording statute*. See NOTICE STATUTE; RACE STATUTE; RACE-NOTICE STATUTE.

recording agent. See INSURANCE AGENT.

recording officer. See SECRETARY (3).

recording secretary. See SECRETARY (3).

recording statute. See RECORDING ACT.

record notice. See NOTICE.

record of decision. *Environmental law.* A public document, generated under CERCLA, describing a federal agency's decision regarding an environmental problem, identifying the remedies considered and which one is best, stating whether practical means to minimize or prevent environmental harms caused by the chosen remedy have been adopted, and summarizing a plan for monitoring and enforcing any measures required to mitigate environmental harm. — Abbr. ROD.

record on appeal. The record of a trial-court proceeding as presented to the appellate court for review. — Also termed *appellate record.* See RECORD (4).

record owner. See OWNER.

record title. See TITLE (2).

recoupment (ri-**koop**-mənt), *n.* (17c) **1.** The recovery or regaining of something, esp. expenses. **2.** The withholding, for equitable reasons, of all or part of something that is due. See EQUITABLE RECOUPMENT (1), (2). **3.** Reduction of a plaintiff's damages because of a demand by the defendant arising out of the same transaction. See EQUITABLE RECOUPMENT (3). Cf. SETOFF (2). **4.** The right of a defendant to have the plaintiff's claim reduced or eliminated because of the plaintiff's breach of contract or duty in the same transaction. **5.** An affirmative defense alleging such a

breach. **6.** *Archaic.* A counterclaim arising out of the same transaction or occurrence as the one on which the original action is based. ● In modern practice, the recoupment has been replaced by the compulsory counterclaim. — **recoup,** *vb.*

recourse (**ree**-kors *or* ri-**kors**). (14c) **1.** The act of seeking help or advice. **2.** Enforcement of, or a method for enforcing, a right. **3.** The right of a holder of a negotiable instrument to demand payment from the drawer or indorser if the instrument is dishonored. See WITH RECOURSE; WITHOUT RECOURSE. **4.** The right to repayment of a loan from the borrower's personal assets, not just from the collateral that secured the loan.

recourse loan. See LOAN.

recourse note. See NOTE (1).

recover, *vb.* (14c) **1.** To get back or regain in full or in equivalence <the landlord recovered higher operating costs by raising rent>. **2.** To obtain by a judgment or other legal process <the plaintiff recovered punitive damages in the lawsuit>. **3.** To obtain (a judgment) in one's favor <the plaintiff recovered a judgment against the defendant>. **4.** To obtain damages or other relief; to succeed in a lawsuit or other legal proceeding <the defendant argued that the plaintiff should not be allowed to recover for his own negligence>.

recoverable, *adj.* (14c) Capable of being recovered, esp. as a matter of law <court costs and attorney's fees are recoverable under the statute>. — **recoverability,** *n.*

recovered-memory syndrome. See REPRESSED-MEMORY SYNDROME.

recoveree. *Hist.* The party against whom a judgment is obtained in a common recovery. See COMMON RECOVERY.

recoveror. *Hist.* The demandant who obtains a judgment in a common recovery. See COMMON RECOVERY.

recovery. (15c) **1.** The regaining or restoration of something lost or taken away. **2.** The obtainment of a right to something (esp. damages) by a judgment or decree. **3.** An amount awarded in or collected from a judgment or decree.

double recovery. (1813) **1.** A judgment that erroneously awards damages twice for the same loss, based on two different theories of recovery. **2.** Recovery by a party of more than the maximum recoverable loss that the party has sustained.

recrimination (ri-krim-i-**nay**-shən), *n.* **1.** *Family law. Archaic.* In a divorce suit, a countercharge that the complainant has been guilty of an offense constituting a ground for divorce. ● When both parties to the marriage have committed marital misconduct that would be grounds for divorce, neither may obtain a fault divorce. Recriminations are now virtually obsolete because of the prevalence of no-fault divorce. See COMPARATIVE RECTITUDE. Cf. COLLUSION (2); CONNIVANCE (2); CONDONATION (2). **2.** *Criminal law.* An accused person's counteraccusation against the accuser. • The accusation may be for the same or a different offense. — **recriminatory,** *adj.*

recross-examination. (1869) A second cross-examination, after redirect examination. — Often shortened to *recross.* See CROSS-EXAMINATION.

rectification (rek-tə-fi-**kay**-shən), *n.* (18c) **1.** A court's equitable correction of a contractual term that is misstated; the judicial alteration of a written contract to make it conform to the true intention of the parties when, in its original form, it did not reflect this intention. • As an equitable remedy, the court alters the terms as written so as to express the true intention of the parties. The court might do this when the rent is wrongly recorded in a lease or when the area of land is incorrectly cited in a deed. **2.** A court's slight modification of words of a statute as a means of carrying out what the court is convinced must have been the legislative intent. • For example, courts engage in rectification when they read *and* as *or* or *shall* as *may,* as they frequently must do because of unfastidious drafting. See REFORMATION. — **rectify,** *vb.*

recurrent nuisance. See NUISANCE.

recusable (ri-**kyoo**-zə-bəl), *adj.* (1863) **1.** (Of an obligation) arising from a party's voluntary act and that can be avoided. Cf. IRRECUSABLE. **2.** (Of a judge) capable of being disqualified from sitting on a case. **3.** (Of a fact) providing a basis for disqualifying a judge from sitting on a case.

recusal (ri-**kyoo**-zəl), *n.* (1949) Removal of oneself as judge or policy-maker in a particular matter, esp. because of a conflict of interest. — Also termed *recusation; recusement.* Cf. DISQUALIFICATION.

recusant (**rek**-yə-zənt *or* ri-**kyoo**-zənt), *adj.* (16c) Refusing to submit to an authority or comply with a command <a recusant witness>.

recusant (**rek**-yə-zənt *or* ri-**kyoo**-zənt), *n.* **1.** *Eccles. law.* A person (esp. a Roman Catholic) who refuses to attend the services of the established Church of England. **2.** A person who refuses to submit to an authority or comply with a command.

recusation (rek-yə-**zay**-shən). **1.** *Civil law.* An objection, exception, or appeal; esp. an objection alleging a judge's prejudice or conflict of interest. **2.** RECUSAL.

recuse (ri-**kyooz**), *vb.* (16c) **1.** To remove (oneself) as a judge in a particular case because of prejudice or conflict of interest <the judge recused himself from the trial>. **2.** To challenge or object to (a judge) as being disqualified from hearing a case because of prejudice or a conflict of interest

<the defendant filed a motion to recuse the trial judge>.

recusement. See RECUSAL.

redaction (ri-**dak**-shən), *n.* (18c) **1.** The careful editing of a document, esp. to remove confidential references or offensive material. **2.** A revised or edited document. — **redactional,** *adj.* — **redact,** *vb.*

red-cow case. See WHITEHORSE CASE.

reddendo singula singulis (ri-**den**-doh **sing**-gyə-lə **sing**-gyə-lis). [Latin "by rendering each to each"] Assigning or distributing separate things to separate persons, or separate words to separate subjects. • This was used as a rule of construction designed to give effect to the intention of the parties who drafted the instrument. — Also termed *referendo singula singulis.*

reddendum (ri-**den**-dəm). [Latin "that must be given back or yielded"] (17c) A clause in a deed by which the grantor reserves some new thing (esp. rent) out of what had been previously granted.

reddition (ri-**dish**-ən). *Hist.* An acknowledgment in court that one is not the owner of certain property being demanded, and that it in fact belongs to the demandant.

redeemable bond. See BOND (3).

redeemable ground rent. See *ground rent* (1) under RENT (1).

redeemable security. See SECURITY.

redeemable stock. See STOCK.

redelivery. (15c) An act or instance of giving back or returning something; restitution.

redelivery bond. See *replevin bond* under BOND (2).

redemise, *n.* (18c) An act or instance of conveying or transferring back (an estate) already demised. See DEMISE. — **redemise,** *vb.*

redemption, *n.* (16c) **1.** The act or an instance of reclaiming or regaining possession by paying a specific price. **2.** *Bankruptcy.* A debtor's right to repurchase property from a buyer who obtained the property at a forced sale initiated by a creditor. **3.** *Securities.* The reacquisition of a security by the issuer. • Redemption usu. refers to the repurchase of a bond before maturity, but it may also refer to the repurchase of stock and mutual-fund shares. — Also termed (in reference to stock) *stock redemption; stock repurchase.* **4.** *Property.* The payment of a defaulted mortgage debt by a borrower who does not want to lose the property. — Also termed *dismortgage.* See EQUITY OF REDEMPTION. — **redeemable, redemptive, redemptional** *adj.* — **redeem,** *vb.*

statutory redemption. (1851) The statutory right of a defaulting mortgagor to recover property, within a specified period, after a foreclosure or tax sale, by paying the outstanding debt or charges. • The purpose is to protect against the sale of property at a price far less than its value. See REDEMPTION PERIOD.

tax redemption. (1867) A taxpayer's recovery of property taken for nonpayment of taxes, accomplished by paying the delinquent taxes and any interest, costs, and penalties.

redemption agreement. See STOCK-REDEMPTION AGREEMENT.

redemptioner. A person who redeems; esp. one who redeems real property under the equity of redemption or the right of redemption. See EQUITY OF REDEMPTION; STATUTORY RIGHT OF REDEMPTION.

redemption period. The statutory period during which a defaulting mortgagor may recover property after a foreclosure or tax sale by paying the outstanding debt or charges.

redemption price. See PRICE.

red herring. (1884) **1.** An irrelevant legal or factual issue, usu. intended to distract or mislead <law students should avoid discussing the red herrings that professors raise in exams>. **2.** See *preliminary prospectus* under PROSPECTUS.

red-herring prospectus. See *preliminary prospectus* under PROSPECTUS.

redhibition (red-[h]i-**bish**-ən), *n. Civil law.* The voidance of a sale as the result of an action brought on account of some defect in a thing sold, on grounds that the defect renders the thing either useless or so imperfect that the buyer would not have originally purchased it. La. Civ. Code art. 2531. — **redhibitory** (red-**hib**-ə-tor-ee), *adj.*

redhibitory action. See ACTION (4).

redhibitory defect. *Civil law.* A fault or imperfection in something sold, as a result of which the buyer may return the item and demand back the purchase price. La. Civ. Code art. 2520. — Also termed *redhibitory vice.*

redirect examination. (1865) A second direct examination, after cross-examination, the scope ordinarily being limited to matters covered during cross-examination. — Often shortened to *redirect.* — Also termed (in England) *reexamination.* See DIRECT EXAMINATION.

rediscount, *n.* **1.** The act or process of discounting a negotiable instrument that has already been discounted, as by a bank. **2.** (*usu. pl.*) A negotiable instrument that has been discounted a second time. See DISCOUNT. — **rediscount,** *vb.*

rediscount rate. See INTEREST RATE.

redisseisin (ree-dis-**see**-zin), *n.* (16c) **1.** A disseisin by one who has already dispossessed the same person of the same estate. **2.** A writ to recover an estate that has been dispossessed by

redisseisin. — Also spelled *redisseizin.* See DISSEISIN. — **redisseise** (ree-dis-**seez**), *vb.*

redistribution. The act or process of distributing something again or anew <redistribution of wealth>.

redistrict, *vb.* To organize into new districts, esp. legislative ones; reapportion.

redistricting. See REAPPORTIONMENT.

red-light abatement laws. An ordinance or statute intended to eliminate and prohibit sex-oriented businesses, usu. on grounds that they are public nuisances. • Brothels were once typically identified by a red light displayed in a window or in the front yard.

redlining, *n.* (1973) **1.** Credit discrimination (usu. unlawful discrimination) by an institution that refuses to provide loans or insurance on properties in areas that are considered to be poor financial risks or to the people who live in those areas. **2.** The process, usu. automated, of creating, for an existing document, an interim version that shows, through strike-outs and other typographical features, all deletions and insertions made in the most recent revision. — **redline,** *vb.*

redraft, *n.* (17c) A second negotiable instrument offered by the drawer after the first instrument has been dishonored. — **redraft,** *vb.*

redress (ri-**dres** *or* ree-dres), *n.* (14c) **1.** Relief; remedy <money damages, as opposed to equitable relief, is the only redress available>. **2.** A means of seeking relief or remedy <if the statute of limitations has run, the plaintiff is without redress>. — **redressable,** *adj.* — **redress** (ri-**dres**), *vb.*

penal redress. A form of penal liability requiring full compensation of the injured person as an instrument for punishing the offender; compensation paid to the injured person for the full value of the loss (an amount that may far exceed the wrongdoer's benefit). See RESTITUTION.

restitutionary redress. Money paid to one who has been injured, the amount being the pecuniary value of the benefit to the wrongdoer. See RESTITUTION.

red tape. A bureaucratic procedure required to be followed before official action can be taken; esp. rigid adherence to time-consuming rules and regulations; excessive bureaucracy. • The phrase originally referred to the red ribbons that lawyers and government officials once used to tie their papers together.

reductio ad absurdum (ri-**dək**-shee-oh *or* ri-**dək**-tee-oh ad ab-**sər**-dəm). [Latin "reduction to the absurd"] (18c) In logic, disproof of an argument by showing that it leads to a ridiculous conclusion.

reduction in force. See LAYOFF.

reduction to practice. *Patents.* The embodiment of the concept of an invention, either by physical construction and operation or by filing a patent application with a disclosure adequate to teach a person reasonably skilled in the art how to make and work the invention without undue experimentation. • The date of reduction to practice is critical in determining priority between inventors competing for a patent on the same invention. See INVENTION.

> **actual reduction to practice.** The empirical demonstration that an invention performs its intended purpose and is therefore complete for patent purposes; the use of an idea or invention — as by testing it — to establish that the idea or invention will perform its intended purpose. *Brunswick Corp. v. U.S.*, 34 Fed. Cl. 532, 584 (1995).

> **constructive reduction to practice.** The documented demonstration that an invention will perform its intended purpose, contained in a patent application that provides enough detail that a person skilled in the art could make and test the invention; the filing of a patent application for an invention or design. *Brunswick Corp. v. U. S.*, 34 Fed. Cl. 532, 584 (1995).

> **vicarious reduction to practice.** A doctrine that treats one party's actual reduction to practice of an invention as the opposing (usu. complaining) party's actual reduction to practice. • In a two-party interference, proof of derivation is usu. sufficient; showing an actual reduction to practice is unnecessary. The doctrine is more important in a three-party interference.

reenactment rule. (1941) In statutory construction, the principle that when reenacting a law, the legislature implicitly adopts well-settled judicial or administrative interpretations of the law.

reentry, *n.* (15c) **1.** The act or an instance of retaking possession of land by someone who formerly held the land and who reserved the right to retake it when the new holder let it go. **2.** A landlord's resumption of possession of leased premises upon the tenant's default under the lease. See POWER OF TERMINATION — **reenter,** *vb.*

reeve (reev). *Hist.* **1.** A ministerial officer of high rank having local jurisdiction; the chief magistrate of a hundred. • The reeve executed process, kept the peace, and enforced the law by holding court within the hundred. **2.** A minor officer serving the Crown at the hundred level; a bailiff or deputy-sheriff. **3.** An overseer of a manor, parish, or the like. — Also spelled *reve.* — Also termed *greve.*

> **shire-reeve.** The reeve of a shire. • The *shire-reeve* was a forerunner of the sheriff. — Also spelled *shire-reve.* — Also termed *shire-gerefa.*

reexamination, *n.* (17c) **1.** REDIRECT EXAMINATION <the attorney focused on the defendant's alibi during reexamination>. **2.** *Patents.* A proceeding by the U.S. Patent and Trademark Office to determine whether prior art renders one or more claims of an already-issued patent invalid; specif., an administrative procedure by which a party can seek review of a patent on the basis of prior art by the PTO <the alleged infringer, hoping to avoid liability, sought reexamination of the patent to narrow its scope>. • A reexamination may be sought by anyone, even the patentee or an anonymous informant, at any time during the life of a patent. Only patents and publications may be considered as prior art. 35 USCA §§ 301–05. — **reexamine,** *vb.*

> **ex parte reexamination.** A reexamination procedure, created in the early 1980s, that allows a challenger to initiate a review by producing prior art and responding to a patentee's statements regarding the new prior art, but that excludes the challenger from further participation in the examination process. • Ex parte reexamination does not employ discovery mechanisms and witnesses are not examined. The challenger also has no right to participate in an appeal. See 35 USCA §§ 302–07. Cf. *inter partes reexamination.*

> **inter partes reexamination.** A reexamination procedure, created in 1999, that allows a challenger to initiate a review by producing prior art, to respond to a patentee's statements regarding the new prior art, to address the patentee's responses to any office actions, and to request a hearing. • Both parties must serve each other with documents filed in the proceeding, but there is no discovery and witnesses are not examined. Either party may appeal the PTO's final decision on patentability. Inter partes reexamination is available to patents that issue from original applications that were filed on or after November 29, 1999. See 35 USCA §§ 311–318. Cf. *ex parte reexamination.*

reexamination certificate. *Patents.* A certificate issued by the U.S. Patent and Trademark Office at the conclusion of a reexamination proceeding, confirming that a patent has been reexamined and the claims have been found to be patentable, confirming that claims determined to be unpatentable have been canceled, or incorporating into the patent any amended or new claims determined to be patentable. 35 USCA § 307.

reexchange, *n.* **1.** A second or new exchange. **2.** The process of recovering the expenses that resulted from the dishonor of a bill of exchange in a foreign country. **3.** The expenses themselves.

reexecution. (18c) The equitable remedy by which a lost or destroyed deed or other instrument is replaced. • Equity compels the party or parties to execute a new deed or instrument if a claimant properly proves a right under one that has been lost or destroyed.

reexport, *n.* **1.** The act of exporting again something imported. **2.** A good or commodity that is exported again. — **reexport,** *vb.*

refection. *Civil law.* Repair or restoration, as of a building.

refer. *Parliamentary law.* To send (a motion) to a committee for its consideration or investigation, with a view to a report from the committee back to the referring body. — Also termed *commit.* Cf. RECOMMIT; DISCHARGE (9).

re-refer. (Of the U.S. House of Representatives) to refer a bill to a different committee from the one it was originally referred to.

referee. (17c) **1.** A type of master appointed by a court to assist with certain proceedings. • In some jurisdictions, referees take testimony before reporting to the court. See MASTER (2). **2.** See *judicial officer* (3) under OFFICER.

referee in bankruptcy. A federal judicial officer who administers bankruptcy proceedings. • Abolished by the Bankruptcy Reform Act of 1978, these referees were replaced by bankruptcy judges. — Also termed *register in bankruptcy.* See *bankruptcy judge* under JUDGE.

reference, *n.* (16c) **1.** The act of sending or directing to another for information, service, consideration, or decision; specif., the act of sending a case to a master or referee for information or decision.

general reference. (18c) A court's reference of a case to a referee, usu. with all parties' consent, to decide all issues of fact and law. • The referee's decision stands as the judgment of the court.

special reference. (1831) A court's reference of a case to a referee for decisions on specific questions of fact. • The special referee makes findings and reports them to the trial judge, who treats them as advisory only and not as binding decisions.

2. An order sending a case to a master or referee for information or decision. **3.** Mention or citation of one document or source in another document or source. **4.** *Patents.* Information — such as that contained in a publication, another patent, or another patent application — that a patent examiner considers to be anticipatory prior art or proof of unpredictability in the art that forms a basis for one or more of an applicant's claims to be rejected. See CITATION (4). — **refer,** *vb.*

reference case. See CASE.

reference committee. See *resolutions committee* under COMMITTEE.

reference statute. See STATUTE.

referendo singula singulis. See REDDENDO SINGULA SINGULIS.

referendum. (1847) **1.** The process of referring a state legislative act, a state constitutional amendment, or an important public issue to the people for final approval by popular vote. **2.** A vote taken by this method. **3.** *Int'l law.* An ambassador's request for instructions on subject matter that the ambassador does not have sufficient power to address. Pl. **referendums, referenda.** Cf. INITIATIVE; PLEBISCITE.

referral. (1927) The act or an instance of sending or directing to another for information, service, consideration, or decision <referral of the client to an employment-law specialist> <referral of the question to the board of directors>.

referral sales contract. A dual agreement consisting of an agreement by the consumer to purchase goods or services (usu. at an inflated price) and an agreement by the seller to compensate the consumer for each customer (or potential customer) referred to the seller. — Also termed *referral sales agreement.* Cf. PYRAMID SCHEME.

refinancing, *n.* An exchange of an old debt for a new debt, as by negotiating a different interest rate or term or by repaying the existing loan with money acquired from a new loan. — **refinance,** *vb.*

reformation (ref-ər-**may**-shən), *n.* (1829) An equitable remedy by which a court will modify a written agreement to reflect the actual intent of the parties, usu. to correct fraud or mutual mistake in the writing, such as an incomplete property description in a deed. • In cases of mutual mistake, the actual intended agreement must usu. be established by clear and convincing evidence. In cases of fraud, there must be clear evidence of what the agreement would have been but for the fraud. See RECTIFICATION. — **reform,** *vb.*

reformation condition. See *conditional bequest* under BEQUEST.

reformative punishment. See PUNISHMENT.

reformatory, *n.* (1834) A penal institution in which young offenders, esp. minors, are disciplined and trained or educated. — Also termed *reform school.*

refoulement (ri-**fowl**-mənt). [French] Expulsion or return of a refugee from one state to another. Cf. NONREFOULEMENT.

refreshing memory. See PRESENT RECOLLECTION REFRESHED.

refreshing recollection. See PRESENT RECOLLECTION REFRESHED.

refugee. A person who flees or is expelled from a country, esp. because of persecution, and seeks haven in another country. Cf. *displaced person* under PERSON (1); EVACUEE.

refugeeism. The state of being a refugee.

refund, *n.* **1.** The return of money to a person who overpaid, such as a taxpayer who overestimated tax liability or whose employer withheld too much tax from earnings. **2.** The money returned to a person who overpaid. **3.** The act of refinancing, esp. by replacing outstanding securities with a new issue of securities. — **refund,** *vb.*

refund annuity. See ANNUITY.

refunding. See FUNDING (2).

refunding bond. See BOND (2).

re-funding bond. See BOND (3).

refusal. (15c) **1.** The denial or rejection of something offered or demanded <the lawyer's refusal to answer questions was based on the attorney–client privilege>. **2.** An opportunity to accept or reject something before it is offered to others; the right or privilege of having this opportunity <she promised her friend the first refusal on her house>. See RIGHT OF FIRST REFUSAL.

refusal to deal. A company's decision not to do business with another company. • A business has the right to refuse to deal only if it is not accompanied by an illegal restraint of trade.

refusal to pay. See VEXATIOUS DELAY.

refus de justice (ruu-**foo** də zhoos-**tees**). See DENIAL OF JUSTICE.

refute, *vb.* (16c) **1.** To prove (a statement) to be false. **2.** To prove (a person) to be wrong. Cf. REBUT.

Reg. *abbr.* **1.** REGULATION. **2.** REGISTER.

reg, *n.* (*usu. pl.*) (1904) *Slang.* REGULATION (3) <review not only the tax code but also the accompanying regs>.

regale episcoporum (ri-**gay**-lee ə-pis-kə-**por**-əm). *Eccles. law.* The temporal rights and privileges of a bishop.

regalia (ri-**gay**-lee-ə). **1.** *Hist.* Rights and privileges held by the Crown under feudal law. • *Regalia* is a shortened form of *jura regalia.*

regard, *n.* (14c) **1.** Attention, care, or consideration <without regard for the consequences>. **2.** *Hist.* In England, an official inspection of a forest to determine whether any trespasses have been committed. **3.** *Hist.* The office or position of a person appointed to make such an inspection.

regardant (ri-**gahr**-dənt), *adj. Hist.* Attached or annexed to a particular manor <a villein regardant>. See VILLEIN.

regarder. An official who inspects a forest to determine whether any trespasses have been committed. — Also termed *regarder of the forest.*

regency. 1. The office or jurisdiction of a regent or body of regents. **2.** A government or authority by regents. **3.** The period during which a regent or body of regents governs.

regent. 1. A person who exercises the ruling power in a kingdom during the minority, absence, or other disability of the sovereign. **2.** A governor or ruler. **3.** A member of the governing board of an academic institution, esp. a state university. **4.** *Eccles. law.* A master or professor of a college.

Reg. FD. See REGULATION FAIR DISCLOSURE.

regicide (**rej**-ə-sɪd). **1.** The killing or murder of a king. **2.** One who kills or murders a king, esp. to whom one is subject. — **regicidal,** *adj.*

regime (rə-**zheem** *or* ray-**zheem**). (18c) **1.** A system of rules, regulations, or government <the community-property regime>. **2.** A particular administration or government, esp. an authoritarian one. — Also spelled *régime.*

international regime. A set of norms of behavior and rules and policies that cover international issues and that facilitate substantive or procedural arrangements among countries.

legal regime. A set of rules, policies, and norms of behavior that cover any legal issue and that facilitate substantive or procedural arrangements for deciding that issue.

régime dotal (ray-**zheem** doh-**tahl**). *Hist. Civil law.* The right and power of a husband to administer his wife's dotal property, the property being returned to the wife when the marriage is dissolved by death or divorce. See *dotal property* under PROPERTY.

régime en communauté (ray-**zheem** on koh-moo-noh-**tay** *or* kom-yoo-). *Hist. Civil law.* The community of property between husband and wife arising automatically upon their marriage, unless excluded by marriage contract.

regina (ri-**jɪ**-nə). (*usu. cap.*) **1.** A queen. **2.** The official title of a queen. **3.** In a monarchy ruled by a queen, the prosecution side in criminal proceedings. — Abbr. R. Cf. REX.

regional fund. See MUTUAL FUND.

regional securities exchange. See SECURITIES EXCHANGE.

regional stock exchange. See *regional securities exchange* under SECURITIES EXCHANGE.

register, *n.* (16c) **1.** A governmental officer who keeps official records <each county employs a register of deeds and wills>. Cf. REGISTRAR.

probate register. (1887) One who serves as the clerk of a probate court and, in some jurisdictions, as a quasi-judicial officer in probating estates.

register of deeds. (18c) A public official who records deeds, mortgages, and other instruments affecting real property. — Also termed *registrar of deeds; recorder of deeds.*

register of land office. *Hist.* A federal officer appointed for each federal land district to take charge of the local records and to administer the sale, preemption, or other disposition of public lands within the district.

register of wills. (18c) A public official who records probated wills, issues letters testamentary and letters of administration, and serves generally as clerk of the probate court. • The register of wills exists only in some states.

2. See *probate judge* under JUDGE. **3.** A book in which all docket entries are kept for the various cases pending in a court. — Also termed (in sense 3) *register of actions.* **4.** *Eccles. law.* A record book of significant events occurring in a parish, including marriages, births, christenings, and burials. • Registers became required in England around 1530. — Abbr. Reg.

register, *vb.* (14c) **1.** To enter in a public registry <register a new car>. **2.** To enroll formally <five voters registered yesterday>. **3.** To make a record of <counsel registered three objections>. **4.** (Of a lawyer, party, or witness) to check in with the clerk of court before a judicial proceeding <please register at the clerk's office before entering the courtroom>. **5.** To file (a new security issue) with the Securities and Exchange Commission or a similar state agency <the company hopes to register its securities before the end of the year>.

registered agent. See AGENT (2).

registered bond. 1. See BOND (2). **2.** See BOND (3).

registered broker. See BROKER.

registered check. See CHECK.

registered corporation. See CORPORATION.

registered dealer. See DEALER.

registered mail. See MAIL.

registered mark. See *registered trademark* under TRADEMARK.

registered offering. See OFFERING.

registered organization. An organization created under state or federal law, for which the state or federal government must maintain a public record showing that the organization has been duly organized. UCC § 9-102(a)(47).

registered patent agent. See *patent agent* under AGENT (2).

registered public offering. See *registered offering* under OFFERING.

registered representative. See REPRESENTATIVE.

registered security. See SECURITY.

registered stock. See *registered security* under SECURITY.

registered tonnage. See REGISTER TONNAGE.

registered trademark. See TRADEMARK.

registered voter. See VOTER.

register in bankruptcy. See *referee in bankruptcy* under REFEREE.

register of actions. See REGISTER (3).

Register of Copyrights. The federal official who is in charge of the U.S. Copyright Office, which issues regulations and processes applications for copyright registration. — Also termed (erroneously) *Registrar of Copyrights.*

register of deeds. See REGISTER (1).

register of land office. See REGISTER (1).

register of ships. *Maritime law.* A record kept by a customs collector containing the names and owners of commercial vessels and other key information about the vessels. • When a ship logs in with customs, it receives a certificate of registry. Cf. REGISTRY (2).

Register of the Treasury. An officer of the U.S. Treasury whose duty is to keep accounts of receipts and expenditures of public money, to record public debts, to preserve adjusted accounts with vouchers and certificates, to record warrants drawn on the Treasury, to sign and issue government securities, and to supervise the registry of vessels under federal law. 31 USCA § 161.

register of wills. See REGISTER (1).

register's court. See COURT.

register tonnage. The volume of a vessel available for commercial use, officially measured and entered in a record for purposes of taxation. — Also termed *registered tonnage.*

registrant. (1890) One who registers; esp., one who registers something for the purpose of securing a right or privilege granted by law upon official registration.

registrar. (17c) A person who keeps official records; esp., a school official who maintains academic and enrollment records. Cf. REGISTER (1).

Registrar of Copyrights. See REGISTER OF COPYRIGHTS.

registrar of deeds. See *register of deeds* under REGISTER (1).

registration, *n.* **1.** The act of recording or enrolling <the county clerk handles registration of voters>.

criminal registration. The requirement in some communities that any felon who spends any time in the community must register his or her name with the police. • Since the late 1980s, many states have adopted strict registration laws for convicted sex offenders. See MEGAN'S LAW.

special registration. Voter registration for a particular election only.

2. *Securities.* The complete process of preparing to sell a newly issued security to the public <the

security is currently in registration>. — **register**, *vb*.

shelf registration. Registration with the SEC of securities to be sold over time, the purpose being to avoid the delays and market uncertainties of individual registration.

registration and community-notification law. See MEGAN'S LAW.

registration-based quorum. See QUORUM.

registration rights. *Securities.* A securities owner's entitlement to have the securities registered for public sale or to participate in a public sale or resale of securities by the issuer or by another securities owner.

demand registration rights. A securities holder's right to force the issuing company to register all or part of the securities so that the holder can resell them.

piggyback registration rights. A securities holder's option to require the issuing company to include all or part of the holder's securities in a registration of other securities of the same class when a third party, such as a lender, requests the registration.

registration statement. A document containing detailed information required by the SEC for the public sale of corporate securities. • The statement includes the prospectus to be supplied to prospective buyers. See PROSPECTUS.

registration system. *Patents.* A patent system in which an invention is given patent protection when it is registered, without being subjected to official examination. • The United States operated under a registration system from 1790 until 1793. Cf. EXAMINATION SYSTEM.

registry. 1. See *probate judge* under JUDGE. 2. REGISTER (2). 3. *Maritime law.* The list or record of ships subject to a particular country's maritime regulations. • A ship is listed under the nationality of the flag it flies. See CERTIFICATE OF REGISTRY. Cf. REGISTER OF SHIPS; *enrollment of vessels* under ENROLLMENT.

regnal (reg-nəl), *adj.* Of or relating to a monarch's reign <the regnal years of Henry II are 1154–1159>.

regnal year. A year of a monarch's reign, marked from the date or anniversary of the monarch's accession. • Before 1962, British statutes were cited by the regnal years in which they were enacted. Since 1962, British statutes have been cited by calendar year rather than regnal year. (A table of British regnal years is listed in Appendix F of this book.)

regnant (reg-nənt), *adj.* Exercising rule, authority, or influence; reigning <a queen regnant>.

regrant, *n.* The act or an instance of granting something again; the renewal of a grant (as of property). — **regrant**, *vb*.

regrating, *n. Hist.* 1. The purchase of market commodities (esp. necessary provisions) for the purpose of reselling them in or near the same market at a higher price. 2. The resale of commodities so purchased. • In England, regrating was a criminal offense. — **regrater**, *n.*— **regrate**, *vb*.

regress, *n.* (14c) 1. The act or an instance of going or coming back; return or reentry <free entry, egress, and regress>. 2. The right or liberty of going back; reentry. Cf. EGRESS; INGRESS. 3. *Hist.* The right to repayment or compensation; recourse. — **regress** (ri-**gres**), *vb*.

regressive tax. See TAX.

regular army. See ARMY.

regular course of business. See COURSE OF BUSINESS.

regular election. See *general election* (1) under ELECTION (3).

regular income. See INCOME.

regular life policy. See *life policy* under INSURANCE POLICY.

regular meeting. See MEETING.

regular process. See PROCESS.

regular session. See SESSION (1).

regular term. See TERM (5).

regular use. See USE (1).

regulation, *n.* (17c) 1. The act or process of controlling by rule or restriction <the federal regulation of the airline industry>.

self-regulation. The process by which an identifiable group of people, such as licensed lawyers, govern or direct their own activities by rules; specif., an organization's or industry's control, oversight, or direction of itself according to rules and standards that it establishes. • Self-regulation is often subject to the oversight of various governmental agencies, such as the Securities Exchange Commission and the Commodities Futures Trading Commission.

2. BYLAW (1) <the CEO referred to the corporate regulation>. 3. A rule or order, having legal force, usu. issued by an administrative agency <Treasury regulations explain and interpret the Internal Revenue Code>. — Abbr. (usu. cap.) reg. — Also termed (in sense 3) *agency regulation*; *subordinate legislation*; *delegated legislation*. See MERIT REGULATION. — **regulatory, regulable**, *adj.* — **regulate**, *vb*.

proposed regulation. A draft administrative regulation that is circulated among interested parties for comment. — Abbr. prop. reg.

Regulation A. An SEC regulation that exempts stock offerings of up to $5 million from certain registration requirements.

Regulation D. An SEC regulation that exempts certain stock offerings (such as those offered by private sale) from registration under the Securities Act of 1933.

Regulation Fair Disclosure. An October 2000 SEC rule requiring companies to disclose material information to all investors at the same time. • The regulation is intended to prevent some investors from receiving advance information about earnings, mergers and acquisitions, product discoveries, changes in auditors, and any other information that a reasonable investor would consider in making an investment decision. — Often shortened to *Regulation FD*; *Reg. FD*.

Regulation FD. See REGULATION FAIR DISCLOSURE.

Regulation J. A Federal Reserve Board regulation that governs the collection of checks by and the transfer of funds through member banks.

Regulation Q. A Federal Reserve Board regulation that sets interest-rate ceilings and regulates advertising of interest on savings accounts. • The Banking Act of 1933 is the basis of this regulation, which applies to all commercial banks.

Regulation T. A Federal Reserve Board regulation that limits the amount of credit that a securities broker or dealer may extend to a customer, and that sets initial margin requirements and payment rules for securities transactions. • The credit limit and margin rules usu. require the customer to provide between 40 and 60% of the purchase price.

Regulation U. A Federal Reserve Board regulation that limits the amount of credit that a bank may extend to a customer who buys or carries securities on margin.

Regulation X. A HUD regulation that implements the provisions of the Real Estate Settlement Procedures Act. See REAL ESTATE SETTLEMENT PROCEDURES ACT.

Regulation Z. A Federal Reserve Board regulation that implements the provisions of the federal Consumer Credit Protection Act for member banks. See CONSUMER CREDIT PROTECTION ACT.

regulatory agency. See AGENCY (3).

regulatory offense. See OFFENSE (1).

regulatory-out clause. See FERC-OUT CLAUSE.

regulatory search. See *administrative search* under SEARCH.

rehabilitation, *n.* (1940) **1.** *Criminal law.* The process of seeking to improve a criminal's character and outlook so that he or she can function in society without committing other crimes

<rehabilitation is a traditional theory of criminal punishment, along with deterrence and retribution>. Cf. DETERRENCE; RETRIBUTION (1). **2.** *Evidence.* The restoration of a witness's credibility after the witness has been impeached <the inconsistencies were explained away during the prosecution's rehabilitation of the witness>. **3.** *Bankruptcy.* The process of reorganizing a debtor's financial affairs — under Chapter 11, 12, or 13 of the Bankruptcy Code — so that the debtor may continue to exist as a financial entity, with creditors satisfying their claims from the debtor's future earnings <the corporation's rehabilitation was successful>. — Also termed *debtor rehabilitation.* Cf. LIQUIDATION (4). — **rehabilitative,** *adj.* — **rehabilitate,** *vb.*

rehabilitative alimony. See ALIMONY.

rehearing. (17c) A court's second or subsequent hearing of a case, a motion, or an appeal, usu. to consider an alleged error or omission in the court's judgment or opinion <the appellant, dissatisfied with the appellate court's ruling, filed a motion for rehearing>. — Abbr. reh'g. Cf. REARGUMENT.

reh'g. *abbr.* REHEARING.

rei (**ree**-ɪ). *pl.* REUS.

reification (ree-ə-fi-**kay**-shən), *n.* (1846) **1.** Mental conversion of an abstract concept into a material thing. **2.** *Civil procedure.* Identification of the disputed thing in a nonpersonal action and attribution of an in-state situs to it for jurisdictional purposes. **3.** *Commercial law.* Embodiment of a right to payment in a writing (such as a negotiable instrument) so that a transfer of the writing also transfers the right. — **reify** (**ree**-ə-fɪ *or* **ray**-), *vb.*

reimbursement, *n.* **1.** Repayment. **2.** Indemnification. — **reimburse,** *vb.*

reimbursement alimony. See ALIMONY.

reinscription, *n.* *Civil law.* A second or renewed recordation of a mortgage or other title document. — **reinscribe,** *vb.*

reinstate, *vb.* To place again in a former state or position; to restore <the judge reinstated the judgment that had been vacated>. — **reinstatement,** *n.*

reinsurance. Insurance of all or part of one insurer's risk by a second insurer, who accepts the risk in exchange for a percentage of the original premium. — Also termed *reassurance.*

excess reinsurance. Reinsurance in which a reinsurer assumes liability only for an amount of insurance that exceeds a specified sum. See *excess insurance* under INSURANCE.

facultative reinsurance. Reinsurance of an individual risk at the option (the "faculty") of the reinsurer.

flat reinsurance. Reinsurance (esp. of marine insurance) that cannot be canceled or modified.

treaty reinsurance. Reinsurance under a broad agreement of all risks in a given class as soon as they are insured by the direct insurer.

reinsurance treaty. A contract of reinsurance (usu. long-term) covering different classes or lines of business of the reinsured (such as professional liability, property, etc.) and obligating the reinsurer in advance to accept the cession of covered risks. ● Rather than receive individual notice of each specific claim covered, the treaty reinsurer will generally receive periodic reports providing basic information on the losses paid. — Also termed *treaty of reinsurance.* See BORDEREAU. Cf. FACULTATIVE CERTIFICATE.

reinsured, *n.* An insurer that transfers all or part of a risk it underwrites to a reinsurer, usu. along with a percentage of the original premium. — Also termed *cedent; cedant.*

reinsurer. An insurer that assumes all or part of a risk underwritten by another insurer, usu. in exchange for a percentage of the original premium.

reinvested dividend. See DIVIDEND.

reinvestment. 1. The addition of interest earned on a monetary investment to the principal sum. **2.** A second, additional, or repeated investment; esp., the application of dividends or other distributions toward the purchase of additional shares (as of a stock or a mutual fund).

reissuable error. *Patents.* A type of nondeceptive mistake in a patent that may be corrected in a reissue patent. 35 USCA § 252.

reissuable note. See NOTE (1).

reissue. 1. An abstractor's certificate attesting to the correctness of an abstract. ● A reissue is an important precaution when the abstract comprises an original abstract brought down to a certain date and then several later continuations or extensions. **2.** See *reissue patent* under PATENT (3).

reissue patent. See PATENT (3).

REIT (reet). *abbr.* REAL-ESTATE INVESTMENT TRUST.

reject, assume or. See ASSUME OR REJECT.

rejecting, *n.* A parent's or caregiver's pattern of refusing to acknowledge a child's worth or legitimate needs. Cf. ISOLATING; IGNORING.

rejection. (16c) **1.** A refusal to accept a contractual offer. **2.** A refusal to accept tendered goods as contractual performance. ● Under the UCC, a buyer's rejection of nonconforming goods must be made within a reasonable time after tender or delivery, and notice of the rejection must be given to the seller. Cf. REPUDIATION (2); RESCISSION; REVOCATION (1). **3.** *Parliamentary law.* Failure of adoption

or ratification. See LOST (3). **4.** *Patents.* A patent examiner's finding in an office action that a claim in an application is unpatentable. Cf. OBJECTION (4); RESTRICTION (4). — **reject,** *vb.*

aggregation rejection. Rejection of a patent claim on the ground that it is a list of unrelated elements that, taken together, do not assert a claim.

alternativeness rejection. Rejection of a patent claim on the ground that it seeks a broad monopoly on the invention as disclosed and on other unspecified variations. ● For example, a claim using a phrase such as "and similar materials" would probably be too broad to be allowed.

duplicate-claiming rejection. The nonart rejection of a patent claim because it is not substantially different from another claim.

exhausted-combination rejection. See *old-combination rejection.*

failure-to-disclose-best-mode rejection. Rejection of a patent application on the ground that the inventor has not disclosed the best way to use the invention. ● To warrant rejection, the examiner must find deliberate concealment or a description so poorly drafted as to amount to concealment.

final rejection. A patent examiner's finding, in a second or subsequent office action, that a claim in an application is unpatentable on the merits. ● A final rejection is made in the final office action. Despite the misleading name, a final rejection need not end the prosecution. The rejection can be appealed, or the application can be reexamined or continued in another application. A rejection may also be appealed to the Board of Patent Appeals and Interferences. A decision of that Board may be reviewed by the U.S. District Court for the District of Columbia or appealed to the U.S. Court of Appeals for the Federal Circuit. 35 USCA §§ 141–45.

formal rejection. Rejection of a patent claim because of an error in format rather than substance. ● A formal rejection is actually an objection rather than a rejection, since it requires no substantive change in the claim. — Also termed *nonart rejection.*

functional rejection. Rejection of a patent claim on the grounds that it broadly claims a function but does not disclose enough structure to account for achieving that function. Cf. FUNCTIONAL LIMITATION.

inaccuracy rejection. Rejection of a patent claim on the ground that it is not consistent with the description.

incompleteness rejection. Rejection of a patent application on the ground that an element of the device or a step in the process has been left out.

interference-estoppel rejection. Rejection of a patent claim on the ground that the applicant failed to bring the claim into a previous interference contest where its priority could have been determined.

judicially-created-double-patenting rejection. Rejection of a patent application on the ground that the invention is an obvious variation of another patented invention by the same inventor. — Also termed *obviousness-type double-patenting rejection.*

lack-of-antecedent-basis rejection. Rejection of a patent application on the ground that a reference either in the specification or in the claim is missing.

lack-of-enablement rejection. See *nonenablement rejection.*

lack-of-utility rejection. Rejection of a patent claim on the ground that the invention is inoperative, frivolous, fraudulent, or against the public interest. ● The classic examples are perpetual-motion machines (inoperative), cures for the common cold (frivolous because believed impossible, and also probably fraudulent), and gambling devices (formerly seen as against the public interest).

new-matter rejection. Rejection of a patent claim on the ground that an amendment contains new matter.

nonart rejection. See *formal rejection.*

nonenablement rejection. Rejection of a patent application claim on the ground that its specification does not teach enough to enable a person skilled in the art to make and use the invention. — Also termed *lack-of-enablement rejection.*

obviousness-type double-patenting rejection. See *judicially created double-patenting rejection.*

old-combination rejection. Rejection of a patent claim on the ground that, despite the fact that one or more elements perform in a different way, all the elements perform the same function as a previously patented invention. ● The improved element may be patentable, but the combination may not be. — Also termed *exhausted-combination rejection.*

prolixity rejection. Rejection of a patent application on the ground that the language is so wordy and tedious that it tends more to hide than to disclose the invention.

rejection on issues of interference. Rejection of a patent claim on the ground that the applicant has lost a final judgment of priority regarding the claim in an interference contest.

same-invention double patenting rejection. See *statutory double patenting rejection.*

Section 101 rejection. Rejection of a patent application on the ground that it is based on nonstatutory subject matter. 35 USCA § 101.

Section 102 rejection. Rejection of a patent application for lack of novelty. 35 USCA § 102.

Section 103 rejection. Rejection of a patent application for obviousness. 35 USCA § 103.

Section 112 rejection. See *vague-and-indefinite rejection.*

shotgun rejection. *Slang.* Denial of all or almost all claims in a patent application by the U.S. Patent and Trademark Office, esp. in the first office action.

statutory double patenting rejection. Rejection of a patent application on the ground that the invention is the same subject matter as an already-patented invention by the same inventor. ● This rejection is based on 35 USCA § 101. — Also termed *same-invention double patenting rejection.*

undue-breadth rejection. Rejection of a patent claim on the ground that it seeks a patent monopoly on more than the invention. ● For instance, a functional claim is too broad if it purports to include every other possible way of accomplishing that function. A claim on a chemical is more likely to be rejected for undue breadth than a claim on a machine, because future discoveries are less predictable.

undue-multiplicity-of-claims rejection. Rejection of a patent application on the ground that it makes an unreasonable number of claims. See AGGREGATION OF CLAIMS.

vague-and-indefinite rejection. Rejection of a patent claim on the ground that a person of ordinary skill in the art could not clearly understand it. ● For example, terms used in more than one sense could make the meaning unclear. — Also termed *Section 112 rejection.*

rejoinder, *n.* (15c) *Common-law pleading.* The defendant's answer to the plaintiff's reply (or replication). — **rejoin,** *vb.*

related good. *Trademarks.* A good that infringes a trademark because it appears to come from the same source as the marked good, despite not competing with the marked good. ● For example, a cutting tool named "McKnife" might infringe the "McDonald's" trademark as a related good.

related proceeding. *Bankruptcy.* A proceeding that involves a claim that will affect the administration of the debtor's estate (such as a tort action between the debtor and a third party), but that does not arise under bankruptcy law and could be adjudicated in a state court. ● A related proceeding must be adjudicated in federal district court unless the parties consent to bankruptcy-court jurisdiction or unless the district court refers the matter to the bankruptcy court or to state court. — Also termed *noncore proceeding*. Cf. CORE PROCEEDING (1).

related right. See NEIGHBORING RIGHT.

relation. See RELATIVE.

relation back, *n.* (18c) **1.** The doctrine that an act done at a later time is, under certain circumstances, treated as though it occurred at an earlier time. • In federal civil procedure, an amended pleading may relate back, for purposes of the statute of limitations, to the time when the original pleading was filed. Fed. R. Civ. P. 15(c). **2.** A judicial application of that doctrine. — Also termed *doctrine of relation back*. Cf. NUNC PRO TUNC. — **relate back,** *vb.*

relationship. The nature of the association between two or more people; esp., a legally recognized association that makes a difference in the participants' legal rights and duties of care.

   attorney–client relationship. The formal legal representation of a person by a lawyer. • An attorney–client relationship may be found, for disciplinary purposes, without any formal agreement.

   confidential relationship. 1. See *fiduciary relationship*. **2.** *Trade secrets.* A relationship in which one person has a duty to the other not to disclose proprietary information. • A confidential relationship can be expressly established, as by the terms of an employment contract. It can also be implied when one person knows or should know that the information is confidential, and the other person reasonably believes that the first person has consented to keep the information confidential. A confidential relationship might be implied, for instance, between two people negotiating the sale of a business.

   doctor–patient relationship. The association between a medical provider and one who is being diagnosed or treated. • The relationship imposes a duty on the doctor to ensure that the patient gives informed consent for treatment.

   employer–employee relationship. The association between a person employed to perform services in the affairs of another, who in turn has the right to control the person's physical conduct in the course of that service. • At common law, the relationship was termed "master-servant." That term is still used often, but "employer–employee" dominates in modern legal usage.

   fiducial relationship. See *trust relationship*.

   fiduciary relationship. (1846) A relationship in which one person is under a duty to act for the benefit of another on matters within the scope of the relationship. • Fiduciary relationships — such as trustee–beneficiary, guardian–ward, principal–agent, and attorney–client — require an unusually high degree of care. Fiduciary relationships usu. arise in one of four situations: (1) when one person places trust in the faithful integrity of another, who as a result gains superiority or influence over the first, (2) when one person assumes control and responsibility over another, (3) when one person has a duty to act for or give advice to another on matters falling within the scope of the relationship, or (4) when there is a specific relationship that has traditionally been recognized as involving fiduciary duties, as with a lawyer and a client or a stockbroker and a customer. — Also termed *fiduciary relation; confidential relationship*. Cf. *special relationship*.

   master–servant relationship. The association between one in authority and a subordinate, esp. between an employer and an employee. • At common law, this term also designated the husband–wife relationship for purposes of analyzing loss of consortium, but that usage is now obsolete. — Also termed *employer-employee relationship*. See MASTER AND SERVANT.

   parent–child relationship. The association between an adult and a minor in the adult's care, esp. an offspring or an adoptee. • The relationship imposes a high duty of care on the adult, including the duties to support, to rescue, to supervise and control, and to educate.

   professional relationship. An association that involves one person's reliance on the other person's specialized training. • Examples include one's relationship with a lawyer, doctor, insurer, banker, and the like.

   special relationship. A nonfiduciary relationship having an element of trust, arising esp. when one person trusts another to exercise a reasonable degree of care and the other knows or ought to know about the reliance. Cf. *fiduciary relationship*.

   trust relationship. An association based on one person's reliance on the other person's specialized training. — Also termed *fiducial relationship*.

relationship rape. See RAPE.

relative, *n.* (14c) A person connected with another by blood or affinity; a person who is kin with another. — Also termed *relation; kinsman*. Cf. NEXT OF KIN (1).

   blood relative. (1863) One who shares an ancestor with another.

   collateral relative. (18c) A relative who is not in the direct line of descent, such as a cousin.

   relative by affinity. (1821) A person who is related solely as the result of a marriage and not by blood or adoption. • A person is a relative by affinity (1) to any blood or adopted relative of his or her spouse, and (2) to any spouse of his or her blood and adopted relatives. Based on the theory that marriage makes two people one, the relatives of each spouse become the other spouse's relatives by affinity. See AFFINITY.

relative of the half blood. A collateral relative who shares one common ancestor. • A half brother, for example, is a relative of the half blood. See *half blood* under BLOOD.

relative confession. See CONFESSION.

relative-convenience doctrine. The principle that an injunction or other equitable relief may be denied if granting it would cause one party great inconvenience but denying it would cause the other party little or no inconvenience.

relative fact. See FACT.

relative nullity. See NULLITY.

relative power. See POWER (5).

relative-responsibility statute. A law requiring adult children to support or provide basic necessities for their indigent elderly parents.

relative right. See RIGHT.

relative simulated contract. See CONTRACT.

relator. (17c) **1.** The real party in interest in whose name a state or an attorney general brings a lawsuit. See EX REL. **2.** The applicant for a writ, esp. a writ of mandamus, prohibition, or quo warranto. **3.** A person who furnishes information on which a civil or criminal case is based; an informer.

relatrix (ri-**lay**-triks). *Archaic.* A female relator.

release, *n.* (14c) **1.** Liberation from an obligation, duty, or demand; the act of giving up a right or claim to the person against whom it could have been enforced <the employee asked for a release from the noncompete agreement>. — Also termed *discharge; surrender.* **2.** The relinquishment or concession of a right, title, or claim <Benson's effective release of the claim against Thompson's estate precluded his filing a lawsuit>. **3.** A written discharge, acquittance, or receipt; specif., a writing — either under seal or supported by sufficient consideration — stating that one or more of the worker's contractual or compensatory rights are discharged <Jones signed the release before accepting the cash from Hawkins>. • Beneficiaries of an estate are routinely required to sign a release discharging the estate from further liability before the executor or administrator distributes the property. **4.** A written authorization or permission for publication <the newspaper obtained a release from the witness before printing his picture on the front page>. **5.** The act of conveying an estate or right to another, or of legally disposing of it <the release of the easement on February 14>. **6.** A deed or document effecting a conveyance

<the legal description in the release was defective>. See *deed of release* under DEED. **7.** The action of freeing or the fact of being freed from restraint or confinement <he became a model citizen after his release from prison>. **8.** A document giving formal discharge from custody <after the sheriff signed the release, the prisoner was free to go>. — **release,** *vb.*

conditional release. (18c) **1.** A discharge from an obligation based on some condition, the failure of which defeats the release. **2.** An early discharge of a prison inmate, who is then subject to the rules and regulations of parole.

marginal release. *Property.* An entry made in the margin of a property record by the recorder of deeds to show that a claim against the property has been satisfied.

mutual release. A simultaneous exchange of releases of legal claims held by two or more parties against each other.

partial release. (1837) A release of a portion of a creditor's claims against property; esp., a mortgagee's release of specified parcels covered by a blanket mortgage.

Pierringer release. A release that allows a defendant in a negligence suit to settle with the plaintiff for a share of the damages and insulates the settling defendant against contribution claims by nonsettling defendants. • This type of release was first described in *Pierringer v. Hoger,* 124 N.W.2d 106, 110–11 (Wis. 1963). It is used in some jurisdictions that do not have contribution statutes. — Also spelled (incorrectly) *Perringer release.*

study release. (1970) A program that allows a prisoner to be released for a few hours at a time to attend classes at a nearby college or technical institution. — Also termed *study furlough.*

unconditional release. (1871) The final discharge of a prison inmate from custody.

9. *Environmental law.* The injection of contaminants or pollutants into the environment as a side effect of operations such as manufacturing, mining, or farming.

release clause. *Real estate.* **1.** A blanket-mortgage provision that enables the mortgagor to obtain a release from the mortgage of a specific portion of the property upon paying a specific (usu. more than pro rata) portion of the loan. • Mortgagees commonly include a clause that disallows a partial release if the mortgagor is in default on any part of the mortgage. **2.** A purchase-agreement provision that allows a seller who has accepted an offer containing a contingency to continue to market the property and accept other offers. • If the seller accepts another buyer's offer, the original buyer typically has a specified time (such as

72 hours) to waive the contingency (such as the sale of the buyer's present house) or to release the seller from the agreement.

release deed. See DEED.

releasee. 1. One who is released, either physically or by contractual discharge. **2.** One to whom an estate is released.

release of mortgage. A written document that discharges a mortgage upon full payment by the borrower and that is publicly recorded to show that the borrower has full equity in the property.

release on recognizance. (1913) The pretrial release of an arrested person who promises, usu. in writing but without supplying a surety or posting bond, to appear for trial at a later date. — Abbr. ROR. — Also termed *release on own recognizance.* See RECOGNIZANCE.

releaser. See RELEASOR.

release to uses. (1830) Conveyance of property, by deed of release, by one party to another for the benefit of the grantor or a third party. See *deed of release* under DEED; STATUTE OF USES; USE (4).

releasor. (17c) One who releases property or a claim to another. — Also spelled *releaser.*

relegation, *n.* (16c) **1.** Banishment or exile, esp. a temporary one. **2.** Assignment or delegation. — **relegate,** *vb.*

relevance. The fact, quality, or state of being relevant; relation or pertinence to the issue at hand. — Also termed *relevancy.*

relevancy. See RELEVANCE.

relevant, *adj.* (16c) Logically connected and tending to prove or disprove a matter in issue; having appreciable probative value — that is, rationally tending to persuade people of the probability or possibility of some alleged fact. Cf. MATERIAL (2), (3).

relevant art. See ART.

relevant evidence. See EVIDENCE.

relevant market. See MARKET.

reliance, *n.* (17c) Dependence or trust by a person, esp. when combined with action based on that dependence or trust. — **rely,** *vb.*

detrimental reliance. (1941) Reliance by one party on the acts or representations of another, causing a worsening of the first party's position. ● Detrimental reliance may serve as a substitute for consideration and thus make a promise enforceable as a contract. See *promissory estoppel* under ESTOPPEL.

reliance damages. See DAMAGES.

reliance interest. See INTEREST (2).

reliance-loss damages. See DAMAGES.

reliance materials. See EXPERT-RELIANCE MATERIALS.

reliction (ri-**lik**-shən). (17c) **1.** A process by which a river or stream shifts its location, causing the recession of water from its bank. **2.** The alteration of a boundary line because of the gradual removal of land by a river or stream. See ACCRETION; DERELICTION (2).

relief. (14c) **1.** A payment made by an heir of a feudal tenant to the feudal lord for the privilege of succeeding to the ancestor's tenancy. **2.** Aid or assistance given to those in need, esp., financial aid provided by the state. **3.** The redress or benefit, esp. equitable in nature (such as an injunction or specific performance), that a party asks of a court. — Also termed *remedy.* Cf. REMEDY.

affirmative relief. (1842) The relief sought by a defendant by raising a counterclaim or cross-claim that could have been maintained independently of the plaintiff's action.

alternative relief. (1851) Judicial relief that is mutually exclusive with another form of judicial relief. ● In pleading, a party may request alternative relief, as by asking for both specific performance and damages that would be averted by specific performance. Fed. R. Civ. P. 8(a). Cf. ELECTION OF REMEDIES.

coercive relief. (1886) Judicial relief, either legal or equitable, in the form of a personal command to the defendant that is enforceable by physical restraint.

declaratory relief. A unilateral request to a court to determine the legal status or ownership of a thing.

extraordinary relief. Judicial relief that exceeds what is typically or customarily granted but is warranted by the unique or extreme circumstances of a situation. ● The types of extraordinary relief most frequently sought are injunctions and extraordinary writs, esp. mandamus. See INJUNCTION; MANDAMUS. Cf. *extraordinary writ* under WRIT.

interim relief. (1886) Relief that is granted on a preliminary basis before an order finally disposing of a request for relief.

therapeutic relief. (1889) The relief, esp. in a settlement, that requires the defendant to take remedial measures as opposed to paying damages. ● An example is a defendant-corporation (in an employment-discrimination suit) that agrees to undergo sensitivity training. — Often shortened to *therapeutics.*

religion. A system of faith and worship usu. involving belief in a supreme being and usu. containing a moral or ethical code; esp., such a system recognized and practiced by a particular church, sect, or denomination. ● In construing the protections under the Establishment Clause and the Free Exercise Clause, courts have interpreted the term *religion* quite broadly to include a wide variety of theistic and nontheistic beliefs.

state religion. A religion promoted, taught, or enforced by a government's acts to the exclusion of other religions.

religion, freedom of. See FREEDOM OF RELIGION.

Religion Clause. In the Bill of Rights, the provision stating that "Congress shall make no law respecting an establishment of religion or prohibiting the free exercise thereof." U.S. Const. amend. I. • Some writers use the plural form, "Religion Clauses," to mean both the Establishment Clause and the Free Exercise Clause, thus emphasizing the asserted common purpose of the two provisions.

religious-affinity fraud. See FRAUD.

religious corporation. See CORPORATION.

religious-exemption statute. See FAITH-HEALING EXEMPTION.

religious liberty. See LIBERTY.

Religious Test Clause. The clause of the U.S. Constitution that prohibits the use of a religious test as a qualification to serve in any office or public trust. U.S. Const. art. VI, par. 3, cl. 2. — Also termed *No Religious Test Clause*.

relinquishment, *n.* (15c) The abandonment of a right or thing. — **relinquish,** *vb.*

relitigate, *vb.* (1826) To litigate (a case or matter) again or anew <relitigate the issue in federal court>. — **relitigation,** *n.*

relocation. 1. Removal and establishment of someone or something in a new place. **2.** *Mining law.* Appropriation of a new tract of land for a mining claim, as by an owner who wishes to change the boundaries of the original tract or by a stranger who wishes to claim an abandoned or forfeited tract. **3.** *Civil law.* RECONDUCTION (1).

rem. See IN REM.

remainder. (15c) *Property.* **1.** A future interest arising in a third person — that is, someone other than the estate's creator, its initial holder, or the heirs of either — who is intended to take after the natural termination of the preceding estate. • For example, if a grant is "to A for life, and then to B," B's future interest is a remainder. If there is only one preceding estate and the remainder vests on that estate's expiration, the remainder is also termed an *executed estate*. — Also termed *remainder estate; estate in remainder.* Cf. EXECUTORY INTEREST; REVERSION; POSSIBILITY OF REVERTER.

accelerated remainder. (1901) A remainder that has passed to the remainderman, as when the gift to the preceding beneficiary fails.

alternative remainder. (1830) A remainder in which the disposition of property is to take effect only if another disposition does not take effect.

charitable remainder. (1932) A remainder, usu. from a life estate, that is given to a charity; for example, "to Jane for life, and then to the American Red Cross.

contingent remainder. (18c) A remainder that is either given to an unascertained person or made subject to a condition precedent. • An example is "to A for life, and then, if B has married before A dies, to B." — Also termed *executory remainder; remainder subject to a condition precedent.*

cross-remainder. (18c) A future interest that results when particular estates are given to two or more persons in different parcels of land, or in the same land in undivided shares, and the remainders of all the estates are made to vest in the survivor or survivors. • Two examples of devises giving rise to cross-remainders are (1) "to A and B for life, with the remainder to the survivor and her heirs," and (2) "Blackacre to A and Whiteacre to B, with the remainder of A's estate to B on A's failure of issue, and the remainder of B's estate to A on B's failure of issue." • If no tenants or issue survive, the remainder vests in a third party (sometimes known as the *ulterior remainderman*). Each tenant in common has a reciprocal, or *cross*, remainder in the share of the others. This type of remainder could not be created by deed unless expressly stated. It could, however, be implied in a will.

defeasible remainder. (18c) A vested remainder that will be destroyed if a condition subsequent occurs. • An example is "to A for life, and then to B, but if B ever sells liquor on the land, then to C." — Also termed *remainder subject to divestment.*

executed remainder. See *vested remainder.*

executory remainder. See *contingent remainder.*

indefeasible remainder. (1898) A vested remainder that is not subject to a condition subsequent; specif., a remainder in which the remainderman is certain to acquire a present interest sometime in the future and will be entitled to retain the interest permanently. — Also termed *indefeasibly vested remainder; remainder indefeasibly vested.*

remainder subject to a condition precedent. See *contingent remainder.*

remainder subject to divestment. See *defeasible remainder.*

remainder subject to open. (1838) A vested remainder that is given to a class of persons whose numbers may change over time and that is to be shared equally by each member of the class. • An example is "to A for life, and then equally to all of B's children." The class must have at least one member, but more can be added over time. — Also termed *remainder subject to partial divestment*; *remainder vested subject to open*.

vested remainder. (18c) A remainder that is given to an ascertained person and that is not subject to a condition precedent. • An example is "to A for life, and then to B." — Also termed *executed remainder*.

2. The property in a decedent's estate that is not otherwise specifically devised or bequeathed in a will. See *residuary estate* under ESTATE (3).

remainder bequest. See *residuary bequest* under BEQUEST.

remainderer. See REMAINDERMAN.

remainder estate. See REMAINDER (1).

remainder indefeasibly vested. See *indefeasible remainder* under REMAINDER.

remainder interest. (1815) The property that passes to a beneficiary after the expiration of an intervening income interest. • For example, if a grantor places real estate in trust with income to A for life and remainder to B upon A's death, then B has a remainder interest.

remainderman. (18c) A person who holds or is entitled to receive a remainder. — Also termed *remainderer*; *remainderperson*; *remainor*.

ulterior remainderman. A third party whose future interest in a property vests only if all the preceding reciprocal interests expire. See *cross-remainder* under REMAINDER.

remainder subject to partial divestment. See *remainder subject to open* under REMAINDER.

remainder vested subject to open. See *remainder subject to open* under REMAINDER.

remainor, *n.* See REMAINDERMAN.

remake rights. *Copyright.* The rights to produce one or more additional movies or screenplays based on what is substantially the same story as is contained in the original movie or screenplay for which the rights have been granted.

remand (ri-**mand** *also* **ree**-mand), *n.* (18c) **1.** The act or an instance of sending something (such as a case, claim, or person) back for further action. **2.** An order remanding a case, claim, or person.

fourth-sentence remand. In a claim for social-security benefits, a court's decision affirming, reversing, or modifying the decision of the Commissioner of Social Security. • This type of remand is called a fourth-sentence remand because it is based on the fourth sentence of 42 USCA § 405(g): "The court shall have power to enter, upon the pleadings and transcript of the

record, a judgment affirming, modifying, or reversing the decision of the Commissioner of Social Security, with or without remanding the cause for a rehearing." *See Melkonyan v. Sullivan*, 501 U.S. 89, 111 S.Ct. 2157 (1991).

sixth-sentence remand. In a claim for social-security benefits, a court's decision that the claim should be reheard by the Commissioner of Social Security because new evidence is available, which was not available before, that might change the outcome of the proceeding. • This type of remand is called a sixth-sentence remand because it is based on the sixth sentence of 42 USCA § 405(g): "The court may, on motion of the Commissioner of Social Security made for good cause shown before the Commissioner files the Commissioner's answer, remand the case to the Commissioner of Social Security for further action by the Commissioner of Social Security, and it may at any time order additional evidence to be taken before the Commissioner of Social Security, but only upon a showing that there is new evidence which is material and that there is good cause for the failure to incorporate such evidence into the record in a prior proceeding . . . ." *See Melkonyan v. Sullivan*, 501 U.S. 89, 111 S.Ct. 2157 (1991).

remand (ri-**mand**), *vb.* (15c) **1.** To send (a case or claim) back to the court or tribunal from which it came for some further action <the appellate court reversed the trial court's opinion and remanded the case for new trial>. Cf. REMOVAL (2). **2.** To recommit (an accused person) to custody after a preliminary examination <the magistrate, after denying bail, remanded the defendant to custody>.

remanet (**rem**-ə-net). (16c) **1.** A case or proceeding whose hearing has been postponed. **2.** A remainder or remnant.

remargining, *n.* *Securities.* The act or process of depositing additional cash or collateral with a broker when the equity in a margin account falls to an insufficient level. See *margin account* under ACCOUNT. — **remargin,** *vb.*

remarry, *vb.* To marry a second or later time, after a divorce or the death of one's spouse.

remediable, *adj.* (15c) Capable of being remedied, esp. by law <remediable wrongs>. — **remediability,** *n.*

remedial, *adj.* (17c) **1.** Affording or providing a remedy; providing the means of obtaining redress <a remedial action>. **2.** Intended to correct, remove, or lessen a wrong, fault, or defect <a remedial statute>. **3.** Of or relating to a means of enforcing an existing substantive right <a remedial right>.

remedial action. 1. *Environmental law.* An action intended to bring about or restore long-term environmental quality; esp., under CERCLA, a measure intended to permanently alleviate pollution when a hazardous substance has been released or might be released into the environment, so as to prevent or minimize any further release of hazardous substances and thereby minimize the risk to public health or to the environment. 42 USCA § 9601(24); 40 CFR § 300.6. — Also termed *remedy*. See CERCLA. Cf. REMOVAL ACTION. **2.** See *personal action* (1) under ACTION (4).

remedial enforcement. See *secondary right* under RIGHT.

remedial law. (17c) **1.** A law providing a means to enforce rights or redress injuries. **2.** A law that corrects or modifies an existing law; esp., a law providing a new or different remedy when the existing remedy, if any, is inadequate.

remedial liability. See LIABILITY.

remedial promise. See PROMISE.

remedial right. See RIGHT.

remedial statute. See STATUTE.

remedial trust. See *constructive trust* under TRUST.

remediation. *Environmental law.* The restoration of polluted land, water, or air to its former state, or as nearly so as is practical.

remedies, *n.* The field of law dealing with the means of enforcing rights and redressing wrongs.

remedy, *n.* (13c) **1.** The means of enforcing a right or preventing or redressing a wrong; legal or equitable relief. — Also termed *civil remedy.* **2.** REMEDIAL ACTION. Cf. RELIEF. — Also termed (in both senses) *law of remedy.* — **remedy,** *vb.*

> **adequate remedy at law.** (18c) A legal remedy (such as an award of damages) that provides sufficient relief to the petitioning party, thus preventing the party from obtaining equitable relief. See IRREPARABLE INJURY RULE.

> **administrative remedy.** (1880) A nonjudicial remedy provided by an administrative agency. ● Ordinarily, if an administrative remedy is available, it must be exhausted before a court will hear the case. See EXHAUSTION OF REMEDIES.

> **civil remedy.** See REMEDY (1).

> **concurrent remedy.** (18c) One of two or more legal or equitable actions available to redress a wrong.

> **cumulative remedy.** (18c) A remedy available to a party in addition to another remedy that still remains in force.

> **equitable remedy.** (18c) A remedy, usu. a nonmonetary one such as an injunction or specific performance, obtained when available legal remedies, usu. monetary damages, cannot adequately redress the injury. ● Historically, an

equitable remedy was available only from a court of equity. — Also termed *equitable relief.* See IRREPARABLE-INJURY RULE.

> **extrajudicial remedy.** A remedy not obtained from a court, such as repossession. — Also termed *self-help remedy.*

> **extraordinary remedy.** (16c) A remedy — such as a writ of mandamus or habeas corpus — not available to a party unless necessary to preserve a right that cannot be protected by a standard legal or equitable remedy. ● Because there is no agreed list of extraordinary remedies, some standard remedies — such as preliminary and permanent injunctions — are sometimes described as extraordinary.

> **judicial remedy.** (18c) A remedy granted by a court.

> **legal remedy.** (17c) A remedy historically available in a court of law, as distinguished from a remedy historically available only in equity. ● After the merger of law and equity, this distinction remained relevant in some ways, such as in determining the right to jury trial and the choice between alternate remedies.

> **provisional remedy.** (18c) A temporary remedy awarded before judgment and pending the action's disposition, such as a temporary restraining order, a preliminary injunction, a prejudgment receivership, or an attachment. ● Such a remedy is intended to maintain the status quo by protecting a person's safety or preserving property.

> **remedy over.** (18c) A remedy that arises from a right of indemnification or subrogation. ● For example, if a city is liable for injuries caused by a defect in a street, the city has a "remedy over" against the person whose act or negligence caused the defect.

> **self-help remedy.** See *extrajudicial remedy.*

> **specific remedy.** (18c) A remedy whereby the injured party is awarded the very performance that was contractually promised or whereby the injury threatened or caused by a tort is prevented or repaired. ● A court awards a specific remedy by ordering a defaulting seller of goods to deliver the specified goods to the buyer (as opposed to paying damages).

> **speedy remedy.** (18c) A remedy that, under the circumstances, can be pursued expeditiously before the aggrieved party has incurred substantial detriment. ● "Speedy remedy" is an informal expression with no fixed meaning — that is, what is considered speedy in one context may not be considered speedy in other contexts. For example, the Federal Tax Injunction Act requires a "plain, speedy, and efficient remedy" in state courts. But the Act does not require

preliminary or injunctive relief — or even interest for delay.

substitutional remedy. (1987) A remedy intended to give the promisee something as a replacement for the promised performance or to give the plaintiff something in lieu of preventing or repairing an injury. • A court awards a substitutional remedy by ordering a defaulting seller of goods to pay the buyer damages (as opposed to delivering the promised goods). — Also termed *substitutionary remedy.*

remedy, mutuality of. See MUTUALITY OF REMEDY.

REMIC (**rem**-ik *or* **ree**-mik). *abbr.* REAL-ESTATE-MORTGAGE INVESTMENT CONDUIT.

remise (ri-**mIz**), *vb.* (15c) To give up, surrender, or release (a right, interest, etc.) <the quitclaim deed provides that the grantor remises any rights in the property>.

remission. (13c) **1.** A cancellation or extinguishment of all or part of a financial obligation; a release of a debt or claim.

conventional remission. *Civil law.* A remission expressly granted to a debtor by a creditor having capacity to alienate. La. Civ. Code art. 1840.

tacit remission. *Civil law.* A remission arising by operation of law, as when a creditor surrenders an original title to the debtor. La. Civ. Code art. 1888.

2. A pardon granted for an offense. **3.** Relief from a forfeiture or penalty. **4.** A diminution or abatement of the symptoms of a disease.

remit, *vb.* (14c) **1.** To pardon or forgive <the wife could not remit her husband's infidelity>. **2.** To abate or slacken; to mitigate <the receipt of money damages remitted the embarrassment of being fired>. **3.** To refer (a matter for decision) to some authority, esp. to send back (a case) to a lower court <the appellate court remitted the case to the trial court for further factual determinations>. See REMAND. **4.** To send or put back to a previous condition or position <a landlord's breach of a lease does not justify the tenant's refusal to pay rent; instead, the tenant is remitted to the right to recover damages>. **5.** To transmit (as money) <upon receiving the demand letter, she promptly remitted the amount due>. — **remissible** (for senses 1–4), *adj.* — **remittable** (for sense 5), *adj.*

remittance. (18c) **1.** A sum of money sent to another as payment for goods or services. **2.** An instrument (such as a check) used for sending money. **3.** The action or process of sending money to another person or place.

remittance advice. See ADVICE.

remittee. (18c) One to whom payment is sent.

remitter. (16c) **1.** The principle by which a person having two titles to an estate, and entering on it by the later or more defective title, is deemed to hold the estate by the earlier or more valid title. **2.** The act of sending back a case to a lower court. **3.** One who sends payment to someone else. — Also spelled (in sense 3) *remittor.*

remitting bank. See BANK.

remittitur (ri-**mit**-i-tər). (18c) **1.** An order awarding a new trial, or a damages amount lower than that awarded by the jury, and requiring the plaintiff to choose between those alternatives <the defendant sought a remittitur of the $100 million judgment>. **2.** The process by which a court requires either that the case be retried, or that the damages awarded by the jury be reduced. Cf. ADDITUR.

remittitur of record. (1848) The action of sending the transcript of a case back from an appellate court to a trial court; the notice for doing so.

remittor. See REMITTER (3).

remnants and surpluses. *Maritime law.* The proceeds remaining from the sale of a ship after claims for seamen's wages, bottomry bonds, salvage services, and supplies have been paid.

remonetization, *n.* The restoration of a precious metal (such as gold or silver) to its former use as legal tender. — **remonetize,** *vb.*

remonstrance (ri-**mon**-strənts), *n.* (16c) **1.** A presentation of reasons for opposition or grievance. **2.** A formal document stating reasons for opposition or grievance. **3.** A formal protest against governmental policy, actions, or officials. — **remonstrate** (ri-**mon**-strayt), *vb.*

remote, *adj.* (15c) **1.** Far removed or separated in time, space, or relation. **2.** Slight. **3.** *Property.* Beyond the 21 years after some life in being by which a devise must vest. See RULE AGAINST PERPETUITIES.

remote cause. See CAUSE (1).

remote damages. See *speculative damages* (1) under DAMAGES.

remoteness of consequence. *Torts.* The lack of proximate causation with respect to an alleged act by a defendant. • Even if the plaintiff proves every other element for tortious liability, the defendant will not be liable if the harm suffered by the plaintiff is too far removed from the defendant's conduct. — Also termed *remoteness of damage.*

remote possibility. See POSSIBILITY.

removal, *n.* (16c) **1.** The transfer or moving of a person or thing from one location, position, or residence to another. **2.** The transfer of an action from state to federal court. • In removing a case to federal court, a litigant must timely file the removal papers and must show a valid basis for federal-court jurisdiction. 28 USCA § 1441. Cf. REMAND (1). — **remove,** *vb.*

civil-rights removal. (1964) Removal of a case from state to federal court because a person: (1) has been denied or cannot enforce a civil right in the state court, (2) is being sued for performing an act under color of authority derived from a law providing for equal rights, or (3) is being sued for refusing to perform an act that would be inconsistent with equal rights.

removal action. *Environmental law.* An action, esp. under CERCLA, intended to bring about the short-term abatement and cleanup of pollution (as by removing and disposing of toxic materials). See CERCLA. Cf. REMEDIAL ACTION.

removal bond. See BOND (2).

REMT. *abbr.* REAL-ESTATE MORTGAGE TRUST.

remuneration (ri-myoo-nə-**ray**-shən), *n.* (15c) **1.** Payment; compensation. **2.** The act of paying or compensating. — **remunerative,** *adj.* — **remunerate,** *vb.*

remunerative donation. See DONATION.

rencounter (ren-**kown**-tər). (16c) A hostile meeting or contest; a battle or combat. — Also spelled *rencontre* (ren-**kon**-tər).

render, *n.* (14c) *Hist.* **1.** A payment in money, goods, or services made by a feudal tenant to the landlord. **2.** A return conveyance made by the grantee to the grantor in a fine. See FINE (1).

render, *vb.* **1.** To transmit or deliver <render payment>. **2.** (Of a judge) to deliver formally <render a judgment>. **3.** (Of a jury) to agree on and report formally <render a verdict>. **4.** To pay as due <render an account>.

rendezvous, *n.* **1.** A place designated for meeting or assembly, esp. of troops or ships. **2.** The meeting or assembly itself.

rendition, *n.* (17c) **1.** The action of making, delivering, or giving out, such as a legal decision. **2.** The return of a fugitive from one state to the state where the fugitive is accused or was convicted of a crime. — Also termed (in sense 2) *interstate rendition.* Cf. EXTRADITION.

erroneous rendition. See EXTRAORDINARY RENDITION.

extraordinary rendition. The transfer, without formal charges, trial, or court approval, of a person suspected of being a terrorist or supporter of a terrorist group to a foreign nation for imprisonment and interrogation on behalf of the transferring nation. ● When an innocent person is subjected to extraordinary rendition, it is also termed *erroneous extradition.* When a transfer is made to a nation notorious for human-rights violations, it may be colloquially termed *torture by proxy* or *torture flight.*

rendition of judgment. (18c) The judge's oral or written ruling containing the judgment entered. Cf. ENTRY OF JUDGMENT.

rendition warrant. See WARRANT (1).

renege (ri-**nig** *or* ri-**neg**), *vb.* (16c) To fail to keep a promise or commitment; to back out of a deal.

renegotiable-rate mortgage. See MORTGAGE.

renegotiation, *n.* (1934) **1.** The act or process of negotiating again or on different terms; a second or further negotiation. **2.** The reexamination and adjustment of a government contract to eliminate or recover excess profits by the contractor. — **renegotiate,** *vb.*

renewable term insurance. See INSURANCE.

renewal, *n.* (17c) **1.** The act of restoring or reestablishing. **2.** *Parliamentary law.* The introduction or consideration of a question already disposed of. — Also termed *renewal of a motion.* See *restorative motion* under MOTION (2). Cf. RECONSIDER. **3.** The re-creation of a legal relationship or the replacement of an old contract with a new contract, as opposed to the mere extension of a previous relationship or contract. Cf. EXTENSION (1); REVIVAL (1). — **renew,** *vb.*

renewal note. See NOTE (1).

renewal of a motion. See RENEWAL (2).

renounce, *vb.* (14c) **1.** To give up or abandon formally (a right or interest); to disclaim <renounce an inheritance>. **2.** To refuse to follow or obey; to decline to recognize or observe <renounce one's allegiance>.

rent, *n.* (13c) **1.** Consideration paid, usu. periodically, for the use or occupancy of property (esp. real property).

ceiling rent. The maximum rent that can be charged under a rent-control regulation.

double rent. Twice the amount of rent agreed to; specif., a penalty of twice the amount of rent against a tenant who holds possession of the leased property after the date provided in the tenant's notice to quit. ● The penalty was provided by the Distress for Rent Act, 1737, 11 Geo. 2., ch. 19, § 13.

dry rent. **1.** Rent reserved without a distress clause allowing the rent to be collected by distress; rent that can be collected only by an ordinary legal action. — Formerly also termed *rent seck.* **2.** See *rent seck* under RENT (2).

economic rent. See ECONOMIC RENT.

ground rent. **1.** Rent paid by a tenant under a long-term lease for the use of undeveloped land, usu. for the construction of a commercial building. — Also termed *redeemable ground rent.* See *ground lease* under LEASE. **2.** A heritable interest, in rental income from land, reserved by a grantor who conveys the land in fee simple. ●

This type of ground rent is found primarily in Maryland and Pennsylvania. — Also termed (in Scots law) *irredeemable ground rent*; *ground annual*.

irredeemable ground rent. See *ground rent* (2).

net rent. The rental price for property after payment of expenses, such as repairs, utilities, and taxes.

rack-rent. See RACK-RENT.

redeemable ground rent. See *ground rent* (1).

2. *Hist.* A compensation or return made periodically by a tenant or occupant for the possession and use of lands or corporeal hereditaments; money, chattels, or services issuing usu. annually out of lands and tenements as payment for use.

peppercorn rent. A nominal rent that is far below the market rate. • The rent may be a mere token payment. Historically in English law, some lease agreements called for a token annual rent payment of a single dried berry of black pepper. See PEPPERCORN.

quit rent. See QUIT RENT.

rent charge. The right to receive an annual sum from the income of land, usu. in perpetuity, and to retake possession if the payments are in arrears. — Also spelled *rent-charge*; *rentcharge*. — Also termed *fee-farm rent*.

rent seck. *Hist.* A rent reserved by deed but without any clause of distress. — Also spelled *rent-seck*; *rent-sec*. — Also termed *dry rent*. Pl. **rents seck.**

rent service. A rent with some corporeal service incident to it (as by fealty) and with a right of distress. — Also written *rent-service*.

3. *Civil law.* A contract by which one party conveys to another party a tract of land or other immovable property, to be held by the other party as owner and in perpetuity, in exchange for payment of an annual sum of money or quantity of fruits. • Under Louisiana law, the rent is essentially redeemable even though stipulated to be perpetual. The seller may set the terms of the redemption, which must take place after a stipulated time (not to exceed 30 years) La. Civ. Code art. 2788. See FRUIT (2). — Also termed *rent of lands*. **4.** The difference between the actual return from a commodity or service and the cost of supplying it; the difference between revenue and opportunity cost. — **rent,** *vb.*

rentage. (17c) Rent or rental.

rent-a-judging. See PRIVATE JUDGING.

rental, *n.* (14c) **1.** The amount received as rent.

crescendo rental. A rent payment that gradually increases at fixed periods during the lease term.

delay rental. *Oil & gas.* A periodic payment made by an oil-and-gas lessee to postpone exploration during the primary lease term. See DRILLING-DELAY RENTAL CLAUSE; *"or" lease, "unless" lease* under LEASE; PAID-UP LEASE.

net rental. The amount remaining after deducting all expenses from the gross rental income.

2. The income received from rent. **3.** A record of payments received from rent. — **rental,** *adj.*

rent, *vb.* **1.** To pay for the use of another's property. **2.** *Hist. Slang.* EXTORT (2).

Rental and Related Rights Directive. See DIRECTIVE ON RENTAL, LENDING AND CERTAIN NEIGHBORING RIGHTS.

Rental Directive. See DIRECTIVE ON RENTAL, LENDING AND CERTAIN NEIGHBORING RIGHTS.

rental division order. *Oil & gas.* A stipulation signed by those entitled to delay rentals, stating what interest each owns and how much rental each is to receive.

rental right. *Copyright.* The power of a copyright owner to control the use of copies of the work beyond the first sale, when that use involves offering the copy to the public for temporary use for a fee (as at a store renting DVDs and videotapes) or some other commercial advantage (as at a hotel offering the loan of DVDs or videotapes). • Rental rights are recognized among members of the European Commission and under TRIPs. The right also applies to the rental of computer software.

rentcharge. The right to receive an annual sum from the income of land, usu. in perpetuity, and to retake possession if the payments are in arrears. — Also spelled *rent-charge*; *rent charge*. — Also termed *fee-farm rent*.

rent control. (1931) A restriction imposed, usu. by municipal legislation, on the maximum rent that a landlord may charge for rental property, and often on a landlord's power of eviction.

rentee. *Rare.* A tenant.

rent of lands. See RENT (3).

rent seck. See RENT (2).

rent-seeking, *n.* Economic behavior motivated by an incentive to overproduce goods that will yield a return greater than the cost of production. • The term is often used in the field of law and economics. See RENT (4).

rent service. See RENT (2).

rents, issues, and profits. (17c) The total income or profit arising from the ownership or possession of property.

rent strike. (1964) A refusal by a group of tenants to pay rent until grievances with the landlord are heard or settled.

renunciation (ri-nən-see-**ay**-shən), *n.* (14c) **1.** The express or tacit abandonment of a right without transferring it to another. **2.** *Wills & estates.* The act of waiving a right under a will. • At one time, one *renounced* an inheritance by intestacy and *disclaimed* a gift by will. Today *disclaim* is common in both situations. — Also termed (in sense 2) *disclaimer.* See RIGHT OF ELECTION. Cf. DISCLAIMER. **3.** *Criminal law.* Complete and voluntary abandonment of criminal purpose — sometimes coupled with an attempt to thwart the activity's success — before a crime is committed. • Renunciation can be an affirmative defense to attempt, conspiracy, and the like. Model Penal Code § 5.01(4). — Also termed *withdrawal; abandonment.* **4.** See *anticipatory repudiation* under REPUDIATION. — **renunciative, renunciatory,** *adj.* — **renounce,** *vb.*

renvoi (ren-**voy**), *n.* [French "sending back"] **1.** The doctrine under which a court in resorting to foreign law adopts as well the foreign law's conflict-of-laws principles, which may in turn refer the court back to the law of the forum. **2.** The problem arising when one state's rule on conflict of laws refers a case to the law of another state, and that second state's conflict-of-law rule refers the case either back to the law of the first state or to a third state. See CONFLICT OF LAWS. **3.** RECONDUCTION (2).

REO. *abbr.* REAL ESTATE OWNED.

reopen. (Of a court) to review (an otherwise final and nonappealable judgment) for the purpose of possibly granting or modifying relief. • A court will reopen a judgment or case only in highly unusual circumstances. *See* Fed. R. Civ. P. 60.

reorganization, *n.* **1.** *Bankruptcy.* A financial restructuring of a corporation, esp. in the repayment of debts, under a plan created by a trustee and approved by a court. See CHAPTER 11.

haircut reorganization. A restructuring that reduces the principal amount of indebtedness owed to creditors. • The more common usage is simply *haircut* <we took a haircut on that deal>.

2. *Tax.* A restructuring of a corporation, as by a merger or recapitalization, in order to improve its tax treatment under the Internal Revenue Code. • The Code classifies the various types of reorganizations with different letters. IRC (26 USCA) § 368(a)(1). Cf. RECAPITALIZATION.

A reorganization. A reorganization involving a merger or consolidation under a specific state statute.

B reorganization. A reorganization in which one corporation exchanges its voting shares for another corporation's voting shares.

C reorganization. A reorganization in which one corporation exchanges its voting shares for substantially all the assets of another corporation.

D reorganization. A reorganization in which the corporation transfers some or all of its assets to another corporation that is controlled by the transferor or its shareholders, and then the stock of the transferee corporation is distributed.

E reorganization. A reorganization involving a recapitalization.

F reorganization. A reorganization involving a mere change in a corporation's identity, form, or place of organization.

G reorganization. A reorganization involving a transfer of all or part of the corporation's assets to another corporation in a bankruptcy or similar proceeding.

reorganization bond. See *adjustment bond* under BOND (3).

reorganization plan. *Bankruptcy.* A plan of restructuring submitted by a corporation for approval by the court in a Chapter 11 case. See CHAPTER 11.

rep. *abbr.* **1.** REPORT. **2.** REPORTER. **3.** REPRESENTATIVE. **4.** REPUBLIC.

repair-and-replace provision. A contractual clause providing that a product's defect will be remedied by repairing or replacing the defective part or product.

repair doctrine. *Patents.* The rule that a licensee who is authorized to produce, use, or distribute a patented device also has the right to repair and replace unpatented components. — Also termed *permissible-repair doctrine.* Cf. RECONSTRUCTION.

reparable injury. See INJURY.

reparation (rep-ə-**ray**-shən). (14c) **1.** The act of making amends for a wrong. **2.** (*usu. pl.*) Compensation for an injury or wrong, esp. for wartime damages or breach of an international obligation.

reparative injunction. See INJUNCTION.

reparole. (1916) A second release from prison on parole, served under the same sentence for which the parolee served the first term of parole.

repeal, *n.* (16c) RESCIND (3); esp., abrogation of an existing law by legislative act. — **repeal,** *vb.*

express repeal. (17c) Repeal by specific declaration in a new statute or main motion.

implied repeal. (18c) Repeal by irreconcilable conflict between an old law or main motion and a more recent law or motion. — Also termed *repeal by implication.*

repeal by implication. See *implied repeal.*

repealer. 1. A legislative act abrogating an earlier law. — Also termed *repealing act*. **2.** One who repeals.

repealing clause. (17c) A statutory provision that repeals an earlier statute.

repealing statute. See STATUTE.

repeater. See RECIDIVIST.

repeat offender. See OFFENDER.

repetition. *Civil law.* A demand or action for restitution or repayment.

replacement cost. See COST (1).

replacement-cost depreciation method. See DEPRECIATION METHOD.

replacement insurance. See INSURANCE.

replead, *vb.* (16c) **1.** To plead again or anew; to file a new pleading, esp. to correct a defect in an earlier pleading. **2.** To make a repleader.

repleader (ree-**plee**-dər). (17c) *Common-law pleading.* A court order or judgment — issued on the motion of a party who suffered an adverse judgment — requiring the parties to file new pleadings because of some defect in the original pleadings. — Also termed *judgment of repleader.* See MOTION FOR REPLEADER.

repleviable (ri-**plev**-ee-ə-bəl), *adj.* (16c) Capable of being replevied; recoverable by replevin <repleviable property>. — Also spelled *replevisable* (ri-**plev**-ə-sə-bəl). Cf. IRREPLEVIABLE.

replevin (ri-**plev**-in), *n.* (17c) **1.** An action for the repossession of personal property wrongfully taken or detained by the defendant, whereby the plaintiff gives security for and holds the property until the court decides who owns it. — Also termed *claim and delivery.* **2.** A writ obtained from a court authorizing the retaking of personal property wrongfully taken or detained. — Also termed (in sense 2) *writ of replevin.* Cf. DETINUE; TROVER.

personal replevin. (1844) At common law, an action to replevy a person out of prison or out of another's custody. ● Personal replevin has been largely superseded by the writ of habeas corpus as a means of investigating the legality of an imprisonment. See HABEAS CORPUS.

replevin in cepit (in **see**-pit). (18c) An action for the repossession of property that is both wrongfully taken and wrongfully detained.

replevin in detinet (in **det**-i-net). (18c) An action for the repossession of property that is rightfully taken but wrongfully detained.

replevin, *vb.* Archaic. REPLEVY.

replevin bond. See BOND (2).

replevisable. See REPLEVIABLE.

replevisor (ri-**plev**-ə-sər). The plaintiff in a replevin action.

replevy (ri-**plev**-ee), *n.* Archaic. REPLEVIN.

replevy, *vb.* (16c) **1.** To recover possession of (goods) by a writ of replevin. **2.** To recover (goods) by replevin. **3.** *Archaic.* To bail (a prisoner).

replevy bond. See *replevin bond* under BOND (2).

repliant (ri-**plI**-ənt). (16c) A party who makes a replication (i.e., a common-law reply). — Also termed *replicant.*

replication (rep-lə-**kay**-shən). (15c) A plaintiff's or complainant's reply to a defendant's plea or answer; REPLY (2).

anticipatory replication. Equity pleading. In an original bill, the denial of defensive matters that the defendant might assert. ● A defendant who relies on the anticipated defense must traverse the anticipatory matter in addition to setting up the defense.

general replication. Equity pleading. A replication consisting of a general denial of the defendant's plea or answer and an assertion of the truth and sufficiency of the bill.

replication de injuria. Common-law pleading. A traverse occurring only in the replication whereby the plaintiff is permitted to traverse the whole substance of a plea consisting merely of legal excuse, when the matter does not involve a title or interest in land, authority of law, authority of fact derived from the opposing party, or any matter of record. — Also termed *replication de injuria sua propria, absque tali causa.*

replication per fraudem. Common-law pleading. A replication asserting that the discharge pleaded by the defendant was obtained by fraud.

special replication. Equity pleading. A replication that puts in issue a new fact to counter a new matter raised in the defendant's plea or answer.

reply, *n.* (18c) **1.** *Civil procedure.* In federal practice, the plaintiff's response to the defendant's counterclaim (or, by court order, to the defendant's or a third party's answer). Fed. R. Civ. P. 7(a). **2.** *Common-law pleading.* The plaintiff's response to the defendant's plea or answer. ● The reply is the plaintiff's second pleading, and it is followed by the defendant's rejoinder. — Also termed (in sense 2) *replication.* — **reply,** *vb.*

reply brief. See BRIEF.

repo (**ree**-poh). **1.** REPOSSESSION. **2.** REPURCHASE AGREEMENT.

report, *n.* (14c) **1.** A formal oral or written presentation of facts or a recommendation for action <according to the treasurer's report, there is $300 in the bank>.

committee report. *Parliamentary law.* A report from a committee to a deliberative assembly on business referred to the committee or on a matter otherwise under its charge.

informational report. *Parliamentary law.* A report without a recommendation for action.

insider report. *Securities.* A monthly report that must be filed with the SEC when more than 10% of a company's stock is traded.

majority report. *Parliamentary law.* A committee report, as distinguished from a minority report. See *committee report.* Cf. *minority report.*

minority report. *Parliamentary law.* A report by a member or members who dissent from a committee report, setting forth their views, and sometimes proposing an alternative recommendation. • Some organizations require that a minority must reach a certain size (or obtain permission) before it can file a report. A typical minimum is one-fourth of the committee's members, which guarantees that not more than one minority report will result.

officer's report. *Parliamentary law.* A report from an officer to an organization or deliberative assembly on business relating to the officer's duties or on a matter otherwise under the officer's charge.

report with recommendation. *Parliamentary law.* A report accompanied by a recommendation for action.

2. A written account of a court proceeding and judicial decision <the law clerk sent the court's report to counsel for both sides>. **3.** (*usu. pl.*) A published volume of judicial decisions by a particular court or group of courts <U.S. Reports>. • Generally, these decisions are first printed in temporary paperback volumes, and then printed in hardbound reporter volumes. Law reports may be either official (published by a government entity) or unofficial (published by a private publisher). Court citations frequently include the names of both the official and unofficial reports. — Also termed *reporter; law report; law reporter.* Cf. ADVANCE SHEETS.

official report. (*usu. pl.*) The governmentally approved set of reported cases within a given jurisdiction.

4. (*usu. pl.*) A collection of administrative decisions by one or more administrative agencies. **5.** MINUTES (2). — Abbr. rep. — **report,** *vb.*

report agenda. See *report calendar* under CALENDAR (4).

report calendar. See CALENDAR (4).

reporter. (14c) **1.** A person responsible for making and publishing a report; esp., a lawyer-consultant who prepares drafts of official or semi-official writings such as court rules or Restatements

<the reporter to the Advisory Committee on Bankruptcy Rules explained the various amendments>. **2.** REPORTER OF DECISIONS. **3.** REPORT (3) <Supreme Court Reporter>. — Abbr. rep.; rptr.

reporter of decisions. (1839) The person responsible for publishing a court's opinions. • The position began historically — in the years before systematic reporting of decisions was introduced — when lawyers attended the sessions of particular courts, were accredited to them by the judges, and reported the decisions of that court. Today, the reporter of decisions holds an administrative post as a court employee. The reporter often has duties that include verifying citations, correcting spelling and punctuation, and suggesting minor editorial improvements before judicial opinions are released or published. — Often shortened to *reporter.* — Also termed *court reporter.* See COURT REPORTER.

reporter's privilege. See *journalist's privilege* (1) under PRIVILEGE (3).

reporter's record. 1. See RECORD. **2.** See TRANSCRIPT.

reporter's syllabus. See HEADNOTE.

reporting company. See COMPANY.

report of proceedings. See TRANSCRIPT.

reports, *n.* See REPORT.

Reports, The. A series of 13 volumes of caselaw published in the 17th century by Sir Edward Coke.

report with recommendation. See REPORT (1).

repose (ri-**pohz**), *n.* (16c) **1.** Cessation of activity; temporary rest. **2.** A statutory period after which an action cannot be brought in court, even if it expires before the plaintiff suffers any injury. See STATUTE OF REPOSE.

repository (ri-**poz**-ə-tor-ee). (15c) A place where something is deposited or stored; a warehouse or storehouse.

repossession, *n.* (15c) The act or an instance of retaking property; esp., a seller's retaking of goods sold on credit when the buyer has failed to pay for them. — Often shortened to *repo.* Cf. FORECLOSURE; RESCUE (3). — **repossess,** *vb.*

representation, *n.* (16c) **1.** A presentation of fact — either by words or by conduct — made to induce someone to act, esp. to enter into a contract; esp., the manifestation to another that a fact, including a state of mind, exists <the buyer relied on the seller's representation that the roof did not leak>. Cf. MISREPRESENTATION.

affirmative representation. (1842) A representation asserting the existence of certain facts pertaining to a given subject matter.

false representation. See MISREPRESENTATION.

material representation. (18c) A representation to which a reasonable person would attach importance in deciding his or her course of action in a transaction. • Material representation is a necessary element of an action for fraud.

promissory representation. (1842) A representation about what one will do in the future; esp., a representation made by an insured about what will happen during the time of coverage, stated as a matter of expectation and amounting to an enforceable promise.

2. The act or an instance of standing for or acting on behalf of another, esp. by a lawyer on behalf of a client <Clarence Darrow's representation of John Scopes>.

concurrent representation. The simultaneous representation of more than one person in the same matter. See CONFLICT OF INTEREST (2).

3. The fact of a litigant's having such a close alignment of interests with another person that the other is considered as having been present in the litigation <the named plaintiff provided adequate representation for the absent class members>.

adequate representation. (1939) A close alignment of interests between actual parties and potential parties in a lawsuit, so that the interests of potential parties are sufficiently protected by the actual parties. • The concept of adequate representation is often used in procedural contexts. For example, if a case is to be certified as a class action, there must be adequate representation by the named plaintiffs of all the potential class members. Fed. R. Civ. P. 23(a)(4). And if a nonparty is to intervene in a lawsuit, there must not already be adequate representation of the nonparty by an existing party. Fed. R. Civ. P. 24(a)(2).

virtual representation. (1934) A party's maintenance of an action on behalf of others with a similar interest, as a class representative does in a class action. See VIRTUAL-REPRESENTATION DOCTRINE.

4. The assumption by an heir of the rights of his or her predecessor <each child takes a share by representation>. See PER STIRPES. **5.** (*usu. pl.*) *Int'l law.* A friendly but firm statement of a perceived wrong. • This is the mildest form of complaint that one nation can make to another. — Also termed *diplomatic representation*. — **represent,** *vb.*

representation, estoppel by. See *estoppel by representation* under ESTOPPEL.

representation election. See ELECTION (3).

representative, *n.* (17c) **1.** One who stands for or acts on behalf of another <the owner was the football team's representative at the labor negotiations>. See AGENT (2).

accredited representative. (1846) A person with designated authority to act on behalf of another person, group, or organization, usu. by being granted that authority by law or by the rules of the group or organization <as an officer of the union, she was the accredited representative of the employees in the wage dispute>.

class representative. (1942) A person who sues on behalf of a group of plaintiffs in a class action. — Also termed *named plaintiff*. See CLASS ACTION.

independent personal representative. See *personal representative*.

lawful representative. (17c) **1.** A legal heir. **2.** An executor, administrator, or other legal representative. — Also termed *legal representative*. See *personal representative*.

legal–personal representative. (18c) **1.** When used by a testator referring to personal property, an executor or administrator. **2.** When used by a testator referring to real property, one to whom the real estate passes immediately upon the testator's death. **3.** When used concerning the death of a mariner at sea, the public administrator, executor, or appointed administrator in the seaman's state of residence.

legal representative. 1. See *lawful representative*. **2.** See *personal representative*.

personal representative. (18c) A person who manages the legal affairs of another because of incapacity or death, such as the executor of an estate. • Technically, an executor is a personal representative named in a will, while an administrator is a personal representative not named in a will. — Also termed *independent personal representative*; *legal representative*.

registered representative. (1945) A person approved by the SEC and stock exchanges to sell securities to the public. — Formerly also termed *customer's man*; *customer's person*.

2. A member of a legislature, esp. of the lower house <one senator and one representative attended the rally>. — Abbr. rep.

representative action. (1911) **1.** CLASS ACTION. **2.** DERIVATIVE ACTION (1).

representative capacity. See CAPACITY (1).

representee. One to whom a representation is made.

representor. One who makes a representation.

repressed-memory syndrome. A memory disorder characterized by an intermittent and extensive inability to recall important personal information, usu. following or concerning a traumatic or highly stressful occurrence, when the memory lapses cannot be dismissed as normal forgetfulness. • The theoretical basis for this syndrome was proposed by Sigmund Freud in 1895. The American Psychiatric Association has recognized the syndrome officially by the medical term *dissociative amnesia*. Although the APA has affirmed that some people suffering partial or total dissociative amnesia may later recover some or all of the memory of the traumatic or stressful event, the existence of the syndrome is controversial. Some studies indicate that "repressed" memories, at least in some patients, may be a product of suggestions made by mental-health therapists rather than of any actual experience. — Abbr. RMS. — Also termed *recovered-memory syndrome*; *dissociative amnesia*. Cf. FALSE-MEMORY SYNDROME.

repressive tax. See *sin tax* under TAX.

reprieve (ri-**preev**), *n.* (16c) Temporary postponement of the carrying out of a criminal sentence, esp. a death sentence. Cf. COMMUTATION (2); PARDON. — **reprieve,** *vb.*

reprimand, *n.* (17c) In professional responsibility, a form of disciplinary action — imposed after trial or formal charges — that declares the lawyer's conduct improper but does not limit his or her right to practice law; a mild form of lawyer discipline that does not restrict the lawyer's ability to practice law. — **reprimand,** *vb.*

   private reprimand. An unpublished communication between a disciplinary agency and a wrongdoing attorney, admonishing the attorney about the improper conduct. • Sometimes a published reprimand that does not identify the lawyer by name is considered a private reprimand.

   public reprimand. A published notice, appearing usu. in a legal newspaper or bar journal, admonishing the attorney about improper conduct and describing the impropriety for the benefit of other members of the legal profession.

reprisal (ri-**pri**-zəl). **1.** (*often pl.*) *Int'l law.* The use of force, short of war, against another country to redress an injury caused by that country.

   general reprisal. A reprisal by which a nation directs all its military officers and citizens to redress an injury caused by another nation. • An example is a command to seize the property of the offending nation wherever it is found.

   negative reprisal. A reprisal by which a nation refuses to perform an obligation to another nation, such as the fulfillment of a treaty.

   positive reprisal. A reprisal by which a nation forcibly seizes another nation's property or persons.

   special reprisal. A reprisal by which a nation authorizes an aggrieved private citizen to redress an injury caused by another nation. • An example is an authorization for a private citizen to seize a particular vessel of the offending nation. See LETTERS OF MARQUE.

2. (*often pl.*) *Int'l law.* An act of forceful retaliation for injury or attack by another country; formerly, in war, the killing of prisoners in response to an enemy's war crimes (now unlawful). Cf. RETORSION. **3.** Any act or instance of retaliation, as by an employer against a complaining employee.

reprise (ri-**priz**), *n.* An annual deduction, duty, or payment out of a manor or estate, such as an annuity.

reprobation (rep-rə-**bay**-shən). The act of raising an objection or exception, as to the competency of a witness or the sufficiency of evidence. — **reprobationary** (rep-rə-**bay**-shə-ner-ee), **reprobative** (**rep**-rə-bay-tiv), *adj.* — **reprobate** (**rep**-rə-bayt), *vb.*

reproduction right. *Copyright.* A copyright holder's exclusive right to make copies or phonorecords of the protected work. • Unauthorized copying constitutes infringement. — Also termed *right of reproduction*.

reproductive rights. A person's constitutionally protected rights relating to the control of his or her procreative activities; specif., the cluster of civil liberties relating to pregnancy, abortion, and sterilization, esp. the personal bodily rights of a woman in her decision whether to become pregnant or bear a child. • The phrase includes the idea of being able to make reproductive decisions free from discrimination, coercion, or violence. Human-rights scholars increasingly consider many reproductive rights to be protected by international human-rights law.

republic, *n.* A system of government in which the people hold sovereign power and elect representatives who exercise that power. • It contrasts on the one hand with a pure democracy, in which the people or community as an organized whole wield the sovereign power of government, and on the other with the rule of one person (such as a king or dictator) or of an elite group (such as an oligarchy, aristocracy, or junta). — Abbr. rep. Cf. DEMOCRACY. — **republican,** *adj.*

republican government. See GOVERNMENT.

republication, *n.* (18c) **1.** The act or an instance of publishing again or anew. **2.** *Wills & estates.* Reestablishment of the validity of a previously revoked will by repeating the formalities of execution or by using a codicil. • The result is to make the old will effective from the date of republication. — Also termed *revalidation*. Cf. REVIVAL (2). **3.** *Defamation.* The act or an instance of repeating or spreading more widely a defamatory statement. — **republish,** *vb.*

repudiate, *vb.* (16c) **1.** To reject or renounce (a duty or obligation); esp., to indicate an intention not to perform (a contract). **2.** *Hist.* To divorce or disown (one's wife).

repudiatee (ri-pyoo-dee-ə-**tee**). A party to a contract that has been repudiated by the other party.

repudiation (ri-pyoo-dee-**ay**-shən), *n.* (16c) **1.** *Eccles. law. Rare.* A person's refusal to accept a benefice. **2.** A contracting party's words or actions that indicate an intention not to perform the contract in the future; a threatened breach of contract. Cf. REJECTION (1), (2); RESCISSION; REVOCATION (1). — **repudiatory** (ri-**pyoo**-dee-ə-tor-ee), **repudiable** (ri-**pyoo**-dee-ə-bəl), *adj.*

anticipatory repudiation. (1913) Repudiation of a contractual duty before the time for performance, giving the injured party an immediate right to damages for total breach, as well as discharging the injured party's remaining duties of performance. • This type of repudiation occurs when the promisor unequivocally disavows any intention to perform when the time for performance comes. Once the repudiation occurs, the nonrepudiating party has three options: (1) treat the repudiation as an immediate breach and sue for damages; (2) ignore the repudiation, urge the repudiator to perform, wait for the specified time of performance, and sue if the repudiating party does not perform; or (3) cancel the contract. — Also termed *renunciation.* See *anticipatory breach* under BREACH OF CONTRACT.

total repudiation. (1859) An unconditional refusal by a party to perform the acts required by a contract. • This type of repudiation justifies the other party in refraining from performance.

repudiator (ri-**pyoo**-dee-ay-tər). One who repudiates; esp., a party who repudiates a contract.

repugnancy (ri-**pəg**-nən-see). (1865) An inconsistency or contradiction between two or more parts of a legal instrument (such as a contract or statute).

repugnant (ri-**pəg**-nənt), *adj.* (14c) Inconsistent or irreconcilable with; contrary or contradictory to <the court's interpretation was repugnant to the express wording of the statute>.

repugnant verdict. See VERDICT.

repurchase, *n.* The act or an instance of buying something back or again; esp., a corporation's buying back of some or all of its stock at market price. See REDEMPTION. — **repurchase,** *vb.*

repurchase agreement. A short-term loan agreement by which one party sells a security to another party but promises to buy back the security on a specified date at a specified price. — Often shortened to *repo.*

repurchase price. See *redemption price* under PRICE.

reputation, *n.* (14c) The esteem in which a person is held by others. • Evidence of reputation may be introduced as proof of character whenever character evidence is admissible. Fed. R. Evid. 405. — Also termed *personal reputation.* See *character evidence* under CHARACTER. — **reputational,** *adj.*

reputational evidence. See *reputation evidence* under EVIDENCE.

reputation evidence. See EVIDENCE.

reputed manor. See MANOR.

request, *n. Parliamentary law.* A motion by which a member invokes a right, seeks permission for the exercise of a privilege, or asks a question. Cf. MOTION (2); DEMAND (2); INQUIRY (2); POINT (2).

request for leave to modify a motion. See *request for permission to modify a motion.*

request for leave to withdraw a motion. See *request for permission to withdraw a motion.*

request for permission to modify a motion. A motion by which the mover seeks an amendment to his or her own motion after the chair has stated the motion. • The mover controls a motion only until the chair states the question. After that, the motion belongs to the assembly and the mover cannot modify it without the assembly's permission. See *friendly amendment* under AMENDMENT (3). — Also termed *request for leave to modify a motion.*

request for permission to withdraw a motion. A motion by the mover to end consideration of the motion without reaching a decision on its merits. See *request for permission to modify a motion.* — Also termed *request for leave to withdraw a motion.*

request to be excused from a duty. A motion seeking relief from a duty that an officer or other member has been charged with.

request to read papers. **1.** A motion asking permission to read aloud from printed matter. • Reading aloud is generally not allowed without permission. **2.** A motion asking that the chair or secretary read aloud a document for the mover's or the assembly's information.

request for admission. (1939) *Civil procedure.* In pretrial discovery, a party's written factual statement served on another party who must admit, deny, or object to the substance of the statement. • Ordinarily, many requests for admission appear in one document. The admitted statements, along with any statements not denied or objected to, will be treated by the court as established and therefore do not have to be proved at trial. Fed. R. Civ. P. 36. — Abbr. RFA. — Also termed *request for admissions; request to admit; notice to admit.*

request for continued examination. *Patents.* A means of negating the final action on a patent so that the applicant can file amendments, new claims, etc. to show that the invention is patentable as of the original application date. • Unlike a continuation application, a request for continued examination keeps a patent alive as if no final decision had been made. It allows prosecution of claims that have been rejected in a final office action to continue. — Abbr. RCE. Cf. CONTINUATION.

request for instructions. (1942) *Procedure.* During trial, a party's written request that the court instruct the jury on the law as set forth in the request. *See* Fed. R. Civ. P. 51. — Abbr. RFI. — Also termed *request to charge.*

request for leave to withdraw a motion. See REQUEST.

request for leave to modify a motion. See REQUEST.

request for permission to withdraw a motion. See REQUEST.

request for permission to modify a motion. See REQUEST.

request for production. (1944) *Procedure.* In pretrial discovery, a party's written request that another party provide specified documents or other tangible things for inspection and copying. Fed. R. Civ. P. 34. — Abbr. RFP. — Also termed *document request; request for production of documents; notice to produce; demand for document inspection.*

request for proposal. An invitation to prospective suppliers or contractors to submit proposals or bids to provide goods or services. ● Unlike most invitations for bids, an RFP requires bidders to give more information than the proposed price. For instance, bidders may have to provide evidence of good financial condition, acceptable technical capability, stock availability, and customer satisfaction. — Abbr. RFP.

request for reconsideration. *Patents.* An applicant's submission of further arguments after a patent claim's rejection.

request for reexamination. *Patents.* A formal process of asking the Patent and Trademark Office to review an in-force patent's validity in light of prior-art references. ● Anyone, including the patent owner or an infringer, may request a patent's reexamination.

request for relief. See PRAYER FOR RELIEF.

request to admit. See REQUEST FOR ADMISSION.

request to be excused from a duty. See REQUEST.

request to charge. See REQUEST FOR INSTRUCTIONS.

request to read papers. See REQUEST.

required-records doctrine. (1945) The principle that the privilege against self-incrimination does not apply when one is being compelled to produce business records that are kept in accordance with government regulations and that involve public aspects. ● Some courts have held that certain medical records and tax forms fall within this doctrine and are thus not protected by the privilege against self-incrimination.

required-request law. A law mandating that hospital personnel discuss with a deceased patient's relatives the possibility of an anatomical gift. ● The Uniform Anatomical Gift Act (not in effect in some states) mandates a required-request law.

required reserve. See RESERVE.

requirement for division. See RESTRICTION (4).

requirement for restriction. See RESTRICTION (4).

requirements contract. See CONTRACT.

requirements testing. See ACCEPTANCE TESTING.

requisition (rek-wə-**zish**-ən), *n.* **1.** An authoritative, formal demand <a state governor's requisition for another state's surrender of a fugitive>. **2.** A governmental seizure of property <the state's requisition of the shopping center during the weather emergency>. See TAKING (2). — **requisition,** *vb.*

requisitionist. One who makes a formal demand (as for the performance of an obligation or the return of a fugitive). See REQUISITION (1).

requisitory letter. See LETTER OF REQUEST.

re-refer. See REFER.

res (rays *or* reez *or* rez), *n.* [Latin "thing"] (17c) **1.** An object, interest, or status, as opposed to a person <jurisdiction of the res — the real property in Colorado>. **2.** The subject matter of a trust; CORPUS (1) <the stock certificate is the res of the trust>. Pl. **res.**

res accessoria (rays ak-ses-**or**-ee-ə). [Latin] *Civil law.* An accessory thing; a thing that is related to a principal thing. Pl. **res accessoriae.**

res adjudicata (rays ə-joo-di-**kay**-tə *or* -**kah**-tə). See RES JUDICATA.

resale, *n.* (17c) **1.** The act of selling goods or property — previously sold to a buyer who breached the sales contract — to someone else. UCC § 2-706. **2.** A retailer's selling of goods, previously purchased from a manufacturer or wholesaler, usu. to consumers or to someone else further down the chain of distribution. — **resell,** *vb.*

resale-price maintenance. A form of price-fixing in which a manufacturer forces or persuades several different retailers to sell the manufacturer's product at the same price, thus preventing competition. ● Resale-price maintenance is not per se illegal under antitrust law, but it is illegal if it produces anticompetitive effects under the rule of reason. A manufacturer may suggest a retail price as long as it does not compel retailers to sell at that price. See RULE OF REASON; *vertical price-fixing* under PRICE-FIXING.

res caduca (rays kə-**d[y]oo**-kə). [Latin] *Civil law.* A fallen thing; an escheat. Pl. *res caducae.*

resceit (ri-**seet**). *Hist.* The admittance of an interested third party to plead in a case between two others; intervention.

rescind (ri-**sind**), *vb.* (17c) **1.** To abrogate or cancel (a contract) unilaterally or by agreement. **2.** To make void; to repeal or annul <rescind the legislation>. **3.** *Parliamentary law.* To void, repeal, or nullify a main motion adopted earlier. — Also termed *annul; repeal.* — **rescindable,** *adj.*

rescind and expunge. See EXPUNGE (2).

rescission (ri-**sizh**-ən), *n.* (17c) **1.** A party's unilateral unmaking of a contract for a legally sufficient reason, such as the other party's material breach, or a judgment rescinding the contract; VOIDANCE. ● Rescission is generally available as a remedy or defense for a nondefaulting party and is accompanied by restitution of any partial performance, thus restoring the parties to their precontractual positions. — Also termed *avoidance.* **2.** An agreement by contracting parties to discharge all remaining duties of performance and terminate the contract. — Also spelled *recision; recission.* — Also termed (in sense 2) *agreement of rescission; mutual rescission; abandonment.* Cf. REJECTION (2); REPUDIATION (2); REVOCATION (1). — **rescissory** (ri-**sis**-ə-ree *or* ri-**siz**-), *adj.*

equitable rescission. (1889) Rescission that is decreed by a court of equity.

legal rescission. (1849) **1.** Rescission that is effected by the agreement of the parties. **2.** Rescission that is decreed by a court of law, as opposed to a court of equity.

rescissory action. See ACTION (4).

rescissory damages. See DAMAGES.

res communes (rays kə-**myoo**-neez), *n. pl.* [Latin "common things"] *Civil law.* Things common to all; things that cannot be owned or appropriated, such as light, air, and the sea. La. Civ. Code art. 449.

res corporales (rays kor-pə-**ray**-leez), *n. pl.* [Latin] *Civil law.* Corporeal things; tangible things that are perceptible to the senses. La. Civ. Code art. 461. See *corporeal thing* under THING.

rescous (res-kəs). **1.** RESCUE (2). **2.** RESCUE (3).

rescript (**ree**-skript), *n.* (17c) **1.** A judge's written order to a court clerk explaining how to dispose of a case. **2.** An appellate court's written decision, usu. unsigned, that is sent down to the trial court. **3.** A Roman emperor's or a Pope's written answer to a legal inquiry or petition. Cf. PRECES. — Also termed (when the reply is to a private citizen) *annotation; subnotation; subscription;* (when the reply is to an official body) *epistle.* **4.** A duplicate or counterpart; a rewriting.

rescue, *n.* (14c) **1.** The act or an instance of saving or freeing someone from danger or captivity. **2.** The forcible and unlawful freeing of a person from arrest or imprisonment. **3.** The forcible retaking by the owner of goods that have been lawfully distrained. — Also termed (in senses 2 & 3) *rescous.* Cf. REPOSSESSION. **4.** *Int'l law.* The retaking of a prize by persons captured with it, so that the property is legally restored to its original owner. See POSTLIMINIUM (3). — **rescue,** *vb.*

rescue clause. See SUE-AND-LABOR CLAUSE.

rescue doctrine. (1926) *Torts.* The principle that a tortfeasor who negligently endangered a person is liable for injuries to someone who reasonably attempted to rescue the person in danger. ● The rationale for this doctrine is that an attempted rescue of someone in danger is always foreseeable. Thus, if the tortfeasor is negligent toward the rescuee, the tortfeasor is also negligent toward the rescuer. — Also termed *danger-invites-rescue doctrine.* Cf. EMERGENCY DOCTRINE; GOOD SAMARITAN DOCTRINE.

rescue syndrome. *Family law.* A situation in which a child in a custody battle expresses a preference for the parent perceived by the child to be the "weaker" of the two, in the belief that the parent needs the child. ● This is a form of parent-alienation syndrome. One parent may overtly or subtly act increasingly dependent on the child, leading the child to believe that he or she is responsible for the parent's comfort, happiness, and protection. The child may also believe that one parent is actively harming the other and attempt to protect the "weaker" parent by choosing to stay with that parent, even if the child would actually prefer to live with the "stronger" parent. Cf. LOLLIPOP SYNDROME; PARENT-ALIENATION SYNDROME.

res derelicta (rays der-ə-**lik**-tə). [Latin] A thing thrown away or forsaken by its owner; abandoned property.

research and development. An effort (as by a company or business enterprise) to create or improve products or services, esp. by discovering new technology or advancing existing technology. — Abbr. R and D; R & D.

Research and Special Programs Administration. A unit in the U.S. Department of Transportation responsible for conducting research and engaging in special programs through several offices, including the Office of Hazardous Materials Safety, the Office of Pipeline Safety, the Transportation Systems Center, the Office of Emergency Transportation, the Office of Program Management and Administration, and the Office of Aviation Information Management. — Abbr. RSPA.

research attorney. See ATTORNEY.

research memorandum. See MEMORANDUM.

resentencing, *n.* (1878) The act or an instance of imposing a new or revised criminal sentence. — **resentence,** *vb.*

reservation. (15c) **1.** The creation of a new right or interest (such as an easement), by and for the grantor, in real property being granted to another. Cf. EXCEPTION (3).

implied reservation. (1867) An implied easement that reserves in a landowner an easement across a portion of sold land, such as a right-of-way over land lying between the seller's home and the only exit. ● An implied reservation arises only if the seller could have expressly reserved an easement, but for some reason failed to do so. See *implied easement* under EASEMENT.

2. The establishment of a limiting condition or qualification; esp., a nation's formal declaration, upon signing or ratifying a treaty, that its willingness to become a party to the treaty is conditioned on the modification or amendment of one or more provisions of the treaty as applied in its relations with other parties to the treaty. **3.** A tract of public land that is not open to settlers but is set aside for a special purpose; esp., a tract of land set aside for use by indigenous peoples. — Also termed (in sense 3) *reserve; reserved land; withdrawn land.*

reservation-of-rights letter. *Insurance.* A notice of an insurer's intention not to waive its contractual rights to contest coverage or to apply an exclusion that negates an insured's claim. — Also termed *reservation of rights.*

reserve, *n.* **1.** Something retained or stored for future use; esp., a fund of money set aside by a bank or an insurance company to cover future liabilities.

amortization reserve. An account created for bookkeeping purposes to extinguish an obligation gradually over time.

bad-debt reserve. A reserve to cover losses on uncollectible accounts receivable.

excess reserve. The portion of a bank's reserve against deposits in excess of the amount of reserve required by law.

legal reserve. The minimum amount of liquid assets that a bank or an insurance company must maintain by law to meet depositors' or claimants' demands.

loss reserve. **1.** An insurance company's reserve that represents the estimated value of future payments, as for losses incurred but not yet reported. **2.** A bank's reserve set aside to cover possible losses, as from defaulting loans.

mean reserve. In insurance, the average of the beginning reserve (after the premium has been paid for the policy year) and the ending reserve of the policy year.

policy reserve. An insurance company's reserve that represents the difference between net premiums and expected claims for a given year. ● This type of reserve is kept esp. by life-insurance companies.

required reserve. The minimum amount of money, as required by the Federal Reserve Board, that a bank must hold in the form of vault cash and deposits with regional Federal Reserve Banks.

sinking-fund reserve. A reserve used to pay long-term debt. See *sinking fund* under FUND (1).

unearned-premium reserve. An insurance company's reserve that represents premiums that have been received in advance but not yet applied to policy coverage. ● If a policyholder cancels coverage before the policy expires but has already paid a premium for the full policy period, the insurance company refunds the policyholder out of this reserve.

2. RESERVATION (3). **3.** See *net value* under VALUE (2). — **reserve,** *vb.*

reserve account. See *impound account* under ACCOUNT.

reserve bank. See *member bank* under BANK.

Reserve Board. See FEDERAL RESERVE BOARD OF GOVERNORS.

reserve clause. A clause in a professional athlete's contract restricting the athlete's right to change teams, even after the contract expires. ● Reserve clauses are uncommon in modern professional sports. Cf. FREE AGENCY.

reserved easement. See EASEMENT.

reserved land. See RESERVATION (3).

reserved point of law. See POINT OF LAW.

reserved power. See POWER (3).

Reserved Power Clause. See TENTH AMENDMENT.

reserved surplus. See *appropriated surplus* (1) under SURPLUS.

reserve militia. See MILITIA.

reserve price. See PRICE.

reserve ratio. The Federal Reserve Board's measurement of a member bank's required reserves. See *required reserve* under RESERVE.

primary reserve ratio. The ratio between a bank's required reserves (cash in vault plus deposits with Federal Reserve Banks) and its demand and time deposits.

secondary reserve ratio. The ratio between a bank's government securities and its demand and time deposits.

resettlement, *n.* (17c) **1.** The settlement of one or more persons in a new or former place. See

SETTLEMENT (6). **2.** The reopening of an order or decree for the purpose of correcting a mistake or adding something omitted. — **resettle,** *vb.*

res gestae (rays **jes**-tee *also* **jes**-tı), *n. pl.* [Latin "things done"] (17c) The events at issue, or other events contemporaneous with them. • In evidence law, words and statements about the res gestae are usu. admissible under a hearsay exception (such as present sense impression or excited utterance). Where the Federal Rules of Evidence or state rules fashioned after them are in effect, the use of *res gestae* is now out of place. *See* Fed. R. Evid. 803(1), (2). — Also termed *res gesta*.

res gestae witness. *See* WITNESS.

resiance (**rez**-ee-ənts). *Archaic.* Residence; abode.

resiant (**rez**-ee-ənt), *adj. Archaic.* Continually dwelling or abiding in a place; resident.

residence. (14c) **1.** The act or fact of living in a given place for some time <a year's residence in New Jersey>. — Also termed *residency*. **2.** The place where one actually lives, as distinguished from a domicile <she made her residence in Oregon>. • *Residence* usu. just means bodily presence as an inhabitant in a given place; *domicile* usu. requires bodily presence plus an intention to make the place one's home. A person thus may have more than one residence at a time but only one domicile. Sometimes, though, the two terms are used synonymously. Cf. DOMICILE (2). **3.** A house or other fixed abode; a dwelling <a three-story residence>. **4.** The place where a corporation or other enterprise does business or is registered to do business <Pantheon Inc.'s principal residence is in Delaware>.

habitual residence. 1. *Family law.* A person's customary place of residence; esp., a child's customary place of residence before being removed to some other place. • The term, which appears as an undefined term in the Hague Convention, is used in determining the country having a presumed paramount interest in the child. **2.** *Copyright.* An established place, esp. a country, in which one lives for the long term, usu. without being a citizen of the place. • The Berne Convention makes habitual residence an alternative to legal domicile in a member country to qualify for copyright protection but leaves the exact definition of the term to member countries.

residency. (14c) **1.** A place of residence, esp. an official one <the diplomat's residency>. **2.** RESIDENCE (1) <one year's residency to be eligible for in-state tuition>.

resident, *adj.* **1.** Affiliated with or working for a particular person or company <resident agent>. **2.** Dwelling in a place other than one's home on a long-term basis <the hospital's resident patient>.

resident, *n.* (15c) **1.** A person who lives in a particular place. **2.** A person who has a home in a particular place. • In sense 2, a resident is not necessarily either a citizen or a domiciliary. Cf. CITIZEN (1); DOMICILIARY.

resident agent. *See registered agent* under AGENT (2).

resident alien. *See* ALIEN.

resident ambassador. *See* AMBASSADOR.

residential care. *Family law.* Foster-care placement involving residence in a group home or institution. • This type of foster care is most commonly used for adolescents who have been adjudged to be delinquents or status offenders.

residential cluster. *Land-use planning.* An area of land developed as a unit with group housing and open common space. Cf. PLANNED-UNIT DEVELOPMENT.

residential community treatment center. *See* HALFWAY HOUSE.

residential custody. *See* PHYSICAL CUSTODY (2).

residential parent. *See* PARENT.

residential responsibility. Overnight responsibility for a child. *See Principles of the Law of Family Dissolution: Analysis and Recommendations* § 3.02 (2000). *See* CUSTODY; *dual-residential parent, residential parent* under PARENT.

primary residential responsibility. Predominant overnight responsibility for a child.

residential time. *See* VISITATION (2).

residua (ri-**zij**-oo-ə). *pl.* RESIDUUM.

residual, *adj.* (16c) Of, relating to, or constituting a residue; remaining; leftover <a residual claim> <a residual functional disability>.

residual, *n.* **1.** A leftover quantity; a remainder. **2.** (*often pl.*) A disability remaining after an illness, injury, or operation. **3.** (*usu. pl.*) A fee paid to a composer or performer for each repeated broadcast (esp. on television) of a film, program, or commercial.

residual estate. *See residuary estate* under ESTATE (3).

residual value. *See salvage value* under VALUE (2).

residuary (ri-**zij**-oo-er-ee), *adj.* (18c) Of, relating to, or constituting a residue; residual <a residuary gift>.

residuary, *n.* **1.** *See residuary estate* under ESTATE (3). **2.** *See residuary legatee* under LEGATEE.

residuary bequest. *See* BEQUEST.

residuary clause. (18c) *Wills & estates.* A testamentary clause that disposes of any estate property remaining after the satisfaction of all other gifts. — Also termed *omnibus clause*.

residuary devise. *See* DEVISE.

residuary devisee. See DEVISEE.

residuary estate. See ESTATE (3).

residuary legacy. See LEGACY.

residuary legatee. See LEGATEE.

residue. (14c) **1.** Something that is left over after a part is removed or disposed of; a remainder. **2.** See *residuary estate* under ESTATE (3).

residuum (ri-**zij**-oo-əm). (17c) **1.** That which remains; a residue. **2.** See *residuary estate* under ESTATE (3). Pl. **residua** (ri-**zij**-oo-ə).

residuum rule. *Administrative law.* The principle that an agency decision based partly on hearsay evidence will be upheld on judicial review only if the decision is founded on at least some competent evidence. ● The residuum rule has generally been rejected by federal and state courts.

resignation, *n.* (14c) **1.** The act or an instance of surrendering or relinquishing an office, right, or claim. **2.** A formal notification of relinquishing an office or position. **3.** *Hist.* The surrender to the lord of the vassal's interest in land. — **resign,** *vb.*

resile (ri-**zil**), *vb.* **1.** To retract (a statement, allegation, etc.). **2.** To draw back (from an agreement, contract, etc.). **3.** To return to one's original position.

res immobiles (rays i-**moh**-bə-leez), *n. pl.* [Latin] *Civil law.* Immovable things; chattels real.

res incorporales (rays in-kor-pə-**ray**-leez), *n. pl.* [Latin] *Civil law.* Incorporeal things; intangible things that are not perceptible to the senses. See *incorporeal thing* under THING.

res integra (rays **in**-tə-grə *also* in-**teg**-rə). [Latin "an entire thing"] See RES NOVA.

res inter alios acta (rays **in**-tər **ay**-lee-ohs **ak**-tə). [Latin "a thing done between others"] **1.** *Contracts.* The common-law doctrine holding that a contract cannot unfavorably affect the rights of a person who is not a party to the contract. **2.** *Evidence.* The rule prohibiting the admission of collateral facts into evidence.

res ipsa loquitur (rays **ip**-sə **loh**-kwə-tər). [Latin "the thing speaks for itself"] (17c) *Torts.* The doctrine providing that, in some circumstances, the mere fact of an accident's occurrence raises an inference of negligence that establishes a prima facie case. — Often shortened to *res ipsa.*

res ipsa loquitur test (rays **ip**-sə **loh**-kwə-tər). (1962) A method for determining whether a defendant has gone beyond preparation and has actually committed an attempt, based on whether the defendant's act itself would have indicated to an observer what the defendant intended to do. — Also termed *equivocality test.* See ATTEMPT (2).

resisting arrest. (1851) The crime of obstructing or opposing a police officer who is making an arrest. — Also termed *resisting lawful arrest.*

resisting process. See OBSTRUCTION OF PROCESS.

resisting unlawful arrest. (1905) The act of opposing a police officer who is making an unlawful arrest. ● Most jurisdictions have accepted the Model Penal Code position prohibiting the use of force to resist an unlawful arrest when the person arrested knows that a police officer is making the arrest. But some jurisdictions allow an arrestee to use nondeadly force to prevent the arrest. See Model Penal Code § 3.

res judicata (rays joo-di-**kay**-tə *or* -**kah**-tə). [Latin "a thing adjudicated"] (17c) **1.** An issue that has been definitively settled by judicial decision. **2.** An affirmative defense barring the same parties from litigating a second lawsuit on the same claim, or any other claim arising from the same transaction or series of transactions and that could have been — but was not — raised in the first suit. ● The three essential elements are (1) an earlier decision on the issue, (2) a final judgment on the merits, and (3) the involvement of the same parties, or parties in privity with the original parties. Restatement (Second) of Judgments §§ 17, 24 (1982). — Also termed *res adjudicata; claim preclusion; doctrine of res judicata.* Cf. COLLATERAL ESTOPPEL.

res litigiosae (rays li-tij-ee-**oh**-see), *n. pl.* [Latin] *Civil law.* Things that are in litigation; property or rights that are the subject of a pending action.

res mobiles (rays **moh**-bə-leez), *n. pl.* [Latin] *Civil law.* Movable things; chattels personal.

res nova (rays **noh**-və). [Latin "new thing"] **1.** An undecided question of law. **2.** A case of first impression. — Also termed *res integra.* See *case of first impression* under CASE.

res nullius (rays nə-**li**-əs). [Latin "thing of no one"] A thing that can belong to no one; an ownerless chattel.

resolution. (17c) **1.** *Parliamentary law.* A main motion that formally expresses the sense, will, or action of a deliberative assembly (esp. a legislative body). ● A resolution is a highly formal kind of main motion, often containing a preamble, and one or more resolving clauses in the form, "*Resolved,* That . . . ."

  concurrent resolution. (17c) A resolution passed by one house and agreed to by the other. ● It expresses the legislature's opinion on a subject but does not have the force of law.

  joint resolution. (17c) A legislative resolution passed by both houses. ● It has the force of law and is subject to executive veto.

  simple resolution. (18c) A resolution passed by one house only. ● It expresses the opinion or affects the internal affairs of the passing house, but it does not have the force of law.

2. Formal action by a corporate board of directors or other corporate body authorizing a particular act, transaction, or appointment. — Also termed *corporate resolution.*

   shareholder resolution. A resolution by shareholders, usu. to ratify the actions of the board of directors.

3. A document containing such an expression or authorization.

resolutions committee. See COMMITTEE.

Resolution Trust Corporation. A federal agency established to act as a receiver for insolvent federal savings-and-loan associations and to transfer or liquidate those associations' assets. ● The agency was created when the Federal Savings and Loan Insurance Corporation was abolished in 1989. — Abbr. RTC. See FEDERAL SAVINGS AND LOAN INSURANCE CORPORATION.

resolutive condition. See *resolutory condition* under CONDITION (2).

resolutory (ri-**zahl**-yə-tor-ee), *adj.* (1818) Operating or serving to annul, dissolve, or terminate <a resolutory clause>.

resolutory condition. See CONDITION (2).

resolving clause. See CLAUSE.

resort, *n.* Something that one turns to for aid or refuge <the court of last resort>. — **resort,** *vb.*

RESPA (**res**-pə). *abbr.* REAL ESTATE SETTLEMENT PROCEDURES ACT.

respite (**res**-pit), *n.* (14c) **1.** A period of temporary delay; an extension of time. **2.** A temporary suspension of a death sentence; a reprieve. **3.** A delay granted to a jury or court for further consideration of a verdict or appeal. **4.** *Civil law.* An agreement between a debtor and several creditors for an extension of time to repay the various debts. La. Civ. Code art. 3084. — **respite,** *vb.*

   forced respite. A respite in which some of the creditors are compelled by a court to give the same extension of time that the other creditors have agreed to.

   voluntary respite. A respite in which all the creditors agree to the debtor's proposal for an extension of time.

respondeat ouster (ri-**spon**-dee-at **ow**-stər). [Law Latin "let him make further answer"] An interlocutory judgment or order that a party who made a dilatory plea that has been denied must now plead on the merits. — Also termed *judgment respondeat ouster.*

respondeat superior (ri-**spon**-dee-at soo-**peer**-ee-ər or sə-peer-ee-**or**). [Law Latin "let the superior make answer"] (17c) *Torts.* The doctrine holding an employer or principal liable for the employee's or agent's wrongful acts committed within the scope of the employment or agency. — Also termed *master–servant rule.* See SCOPE OF EMPLOYMENT.

respondent. (16c) **1.** The party against whom an appeal is taken; APPELLEE. ● In some appellate courts, the parties are designated as *petitioner* and *respondent.* In most appellate courts in the United States, the parties are designated as *appellant* and *appellee.* Often the designations depend on whether the appeal is taken by writ of certiorari (or writ of error) or by direct appeal. **2.** The party against whom a motion or petition is filed. Cf. PETITIONER. **3.** At common law, the defendant in an equity proceeding. **4.** *Civil law.* One who answers for another or acts as another's security.

respondent bank. See BANK.

respondentia (ree-spon-**den**-shee-ə *or* res-pon-). [Law Latin fr. Latin *respondere* "to answer"] A loan secured by the cargo on one's ship rather than the ship itself. Cf. BOTTOMRY.

respondentia bond. See BOND (2).

responsa prudentium (ri-**spon**-sə proo-**den**-shee-əm). [Latin "the answers of the learned"] *Roman law.* The opinions and judgments of eminent lawyers or jurists on questions of law addressed to them. ● The *responsa prudentium* originally constituted part of the early Roman civil law. Roman citizens seeking legal advice, as well as magistrates and judges, often referred legal questions to leading jurists so as to obtain their opinions (*responsa*). The *responsa* of some leading jurists were collected, much in the manner of caselaw digests, and many of them passed into Justinian's Digest. The phrase *responsa prudentium* gradually migrated to the common law, but today it is of primarily historical use. — Also spelled *responsa prudentum.*

response. *Patents.* A patent applicant's answer to an office action, usu. countering the examiner's rejections and objections and often amending the claims.

responsibility, *n.* (18c) **1.** LIABILITY (1). **2.** *Criminal law.* A person's mental fitness to answer in court for his or her actions. See COMPETENCY. **3.** *Criminal law.* Guilt. — Also termed (in senses 2 & 3) *criminal responsibility.* — **responsible,** *adj.*

responsible broker-dealer. See BROKER.

responsive, *adj.* (15c) Giving or constituting a response; answering <the witness's testimony is not responsive to the question>.

responsive action. *Patents.* A patent applicant's answer to an examiner rejections in an office action. ● To be responsive, the answer must address all of the examiner's issues in detail, rather than merely submitting substitute claims.

responsive pleading. See PLEADING (1).

responsive verdict. See VERDICT.

res privatae (rays pri-**vay**-tee), *n. pl.* [Latin "private things"] *Roman & civil law.* Things that can be owned by individuals or by the state and its political subdivisions in their capacity as private citizens. La. Civ. Code art. 450. — Also termed *res in privatorum patrimonio.*

res publicae (rays **pəb**-li-see), *n. pl.* [Latin "public things"] *Roman & civil law.* Things that cannot be individually owned because they belong to the public, such as the sea, navigable waters, and highways. • Public things are owned by the state and its political subdivisions in their capacity as public persons. La. Civ. Code art. 449.

res quotidianae (rays kwoh-tid-ee-**ay**-nee), *n. pl.* [Latin] *Civil law.* Everyday matters; familiar points or questions.

res religiosae (rays ri-lij-ee-**oh**-see), *n. pl.* [Latin] *Civil law.* Religious things; esp., burial places.

res sanctae (rays **sangk**-tee), *n. pl.* [Latin "sacred things"] *Roman law.* The walls of a city. • The Romans considered maintenance of city walls so important that damage to a city's walls was a capital offense.

res singulorum (rays sing-gyə-**lor**-əm). [Latin] *Hist.* The property of individuals.

res sua (rays s[y]**oo**-ə). [Latin] *Hist.* One's own property.

rest, *vb.* (1905) **1.** (Of a litigant) to voluntarily conclude presenting evidence in a trial <after the police officer's testimony, the prosecution rested>. **2.** (Of a litigant) to voluntarily conclude presenting evidence in (a trial) <the defense rested its case after presenting just two witnesses>. • In sense 1, the verb is intransitive; in sense 2, it is transitive.

Restatement. One of several influential treatises published by the American Law Institute describing the law in a given area and guiding its development. • The Restatements use a distinctive format of black-letter rules, official comments, illustrations, and reporter's notes. Although the Restatements are frequently cited in cases and commentary, a Restatement provision is not binding on a court unless it has been officially adopted as the law by that jurisdiction's highest court. Restatements have been published in the following areas of law: Agency, Conflict of Laws, Contracts, Employment Law, Foreign Relations Law of the United States, Judgments, Law Governing Lawyers, Property, Restitution, Security, Suretyship and Guaranty, Torts, Trusts, and Unfair Competition. — Also termed *Restatement of the Law.*

restater. (1955) An author or reporter of a Restatement.

restaur (res-**tor**). **1.** The recourse that insurers (esp. marine underwriters) have against each other according to the date of their insurance. **2.** The recourse that marine insurers have against a ship's master if a loss occurs through the master's fault or negligence. **3.** The recourse that one has against a guarantor or other person under a duty to indemnify. — Also spelled *restor.*

restitution, *n.* (13c) **1.** A body of substantive law in which liability is based not on tort or contract but on the defendant's unjust enrichment. See UNJUST ENRICHMENT. **2.** The set of remedies associated with that body of law, in which the measure of recovery is usu. based not on the plaintiff's loss, but on the defendant's gain. Cf. COMPENSATION; DAMAGES. **3.** Return or restoration of some specific thing to its rightful owner or status. **4.** Compensation for loss; esp., full or partial compensation paid by a criminal to a victim, not awarded in a civil trial for tort, but ordered as part of a criminal sentence or as a condition of probation. — **restitutionary,** *adj.*

restitutionary redress. See REDRESS.

restitution damages. See DAMAGES.

restitution interest. See INTEREST (2).

restitutory interdict. See INTERDICT (1).

restitutory right. See RIGHT.

restor. See RESTAUR.

restorative justice. An alternative delinquency sanction focused on repairing the harm done, meeting the victim's needs, and holding the offender responsible for his or her actions. • Restorative-justice sanctions use a balanced approach, producing the least restrictive disposition while stressing the offender's accountability and providing relief to the victim. The offender may be ordered to make restitution, to perform community service, or to make amends in some other way that the court orders.

restorative motion. See MOTION (2).

restoratory motion. See *restorative motion* under MOTION (2).

restraining order. (1876) **1.** A court order prohibiting family violence; esp., an order restricting a person from harassing, threatening, and sometimes merely contacting or approaching another specified person. • This type of order is issued most commonly in cases of domestic violence. A court may grant an ex parte restraining order in a family-violence case if it is necessary to (1) achieve the government's interest in protecting victims of family violence from further abuse, (2) ensure prompt action where there is an immediate threat of danger, and (3) provide governmental control by ensuring that judges grant such orders only where there is an immediate danger of such abuse. *Fuentes v. Shevin,* 407 U.S. 67, 92 S.Ct. 1983

(1972). — Also termed *protection order; protective order; stay-away order.* See *ex parte motion* under MOTION. **2.** TEMPORARY RESTRAINING ORDER. **3.** A court order entered to prevent the dissipation or loss of property.

restraining power. See POWER (3).

restraining statute. See *disabling statute* under STATUTE.

restraint, *n.* (15c) **1.** Confinement, abridgment, or limitation <a restraint on the freedom of speech>. See PRIOR RESTRAINT. **2.** Prohibition of action; holding back <the victim's family exercised no restraint — they told the suspect exactly what they thought of him>. **3.** RESTRAINT OF TRADE. **4.** FORFEITURE RESTRAINT.

restraint of marriage. (16c) A condition (esp. in a gift or bequest) that nullifies the grant to which it applies if the grantee marries or remarries. • Restraints of marriage are usu. void if they are general or unlimited in scope.

restraint of princes. *Archaic.* An embargo. • The phrase still occasionally appears in marine-insurance contexts. — Also termed *restraint of princes and rulers; restraint of princes, rulers, and people.* See EMBARGO.

restraint of trade. 1. A limitation on business dealings or professional or gainful occupations. **2.** *Antitrust.* An agreement between two or more businesses or a combination of businesses intended to eliminate competition, create a monopoly, artificially raise prices, or otherwise adversely affect the free market. • Restraints of trade are usu. illegal, but may be declared reasonable if they are in the best interests of both the parties and the public. — Often shortened to *restraint.* — Also termed *conspiracy in restraint of trade.* See PER SE RULE; RULE OF REASON.

   horizontal restraint. A restraint of trade imposed by agreement between competitors at the same level of distribution. • The restraint is horizontal not because it has horizontal effects, but because it is the product of a horizontal agreement. — Also termed *horizontal agreement.*

   unreasonable restraint of trade. A restraint of trade that produces a significant anticompetitive effect and thus violates antitrust law.

   vertical restraint. A restraint of trade imposed by agreement between firms at different levels of distribution (as between manufacturer and retailer).

restraint on alienation. (18c) **1.** A restriction, usu. in a deed of conveyance, on a grantee's ability to sell or transfer real property; a provision that conveys an interest and that, even after the interest has become vested, prevents or discourages the owner from disposing of it at all or from disposing of it in particular ways or to particular persons. • Restraints on alienation are generally unenforceable as against public policy favoring the free alienability of land. — Also termed *unreasonable restraint on alienation.* **2.** A trust provision that prohibits or penalizes alienation of the trust corpus.

restricted indorsement. See *conditional indorsement* under INDORSEMENT.

restricted interpretation. See *restrictive interpretation* under INTERPRETATION.

restricted security. See SECURITY.

restricted stock. See *restricted security* under SECURITY.

restricted surplus. See SURPLUS.

restricted visitation. See *supervised visitation* under VISITATION.

restriction. (15c) **1.** A limitation or qualification. **2.** A limitation (esp. in a deed) placed on the use or enjoyment of property. See *restrictive covenant* under COVENANT (4).

   conservation restriction. See *conservation easement* under EASEMENT.

3. *Military law.* A deprivation of liberty involving moral and legal, rather than physical, restraint. • A military restriction is imposed as punishment either by a commanding officer's nonjudicial punishment or by a summary, special, or general court-martial. Restriction is a lesser restraint because it permits the restricted person to perform full military duties. See *nonjudicial punishment* under PUNISHMENT.

   restriction in lieu of arrest. A restriction in which a person is ordered to stay within specific geographical limits, such as a base or a ship, and is permitted to perform full military duties.

4. *Patents.* A patent examiner's ruling that a patent application comprises two or more patentably distinct or independent inventions; the requirement that the applicant elect one invention to continue prosecuting under the original application by abandoning some of the original claims. • The applicant may defend the claims by traversing the requirement, abandon any nonelected invention, or continue prosecuting any nonelected invention under a separate divisional application. — Also termed *requirement for restriction; restriction requirement; division.* Cf. OBJECTION (2); REJECTION (4).

restriction application. See *divisional application* under PATENT APPLICATION.

restriction requirement. See RESTRICTION (4).

restrictive condition. See *negative condition* under CONDITION (2).

restrictive covenant. 1. See *noncompetition covenant* under COVENANT (1). **2.** See COVENANT (4).

restrictive covenant in equity. See *restrictive covenant* under COVENANT (4).

restrictive indorsement. See INDORSEMENT.

restrictive interpretation. See INTERPRETATION.

restrictive principle of sovereign immunity. The doctrine by which a foreign nation's immunity does not apply to claims arising from the nation's private or commercial acts, but protects the nation only from claims arising from its public functions. See COMMERCIAL-ACTIVITY EXCEPTION; JURE GESTIONIS; JURE IMPERII.

restrictive title. See TITLE (3).

resulting power. See POWER (3).

resulting trust. See TRUST.

resulting use. See USE (4).

resume consideration. See *take from the table* under TABLE.

resummons. (15c) A second or renewed summons to a party or witness already summoned. See SUMMONS.

resumption. 1. The taking back of property previously given up or lost. **2.** *Hist.* The retaking by the Crown or other authority of lands or rights previously given to another (as because of false suggestion or other error).

retail, *n.* The sale of goods or commodities to ultimate consumers, as opposed to the sale for further distribution or processing. — **retail,** *adj.* Cf. WHOLESALE. — **retail,** *vb.*

retailer, *n.* A person or entity engaged in the business of selling personal property to the public or to consumers, as opposed to selling to those who intend to resell the items.

retail installment contract. See CONTRACT.

retail installment contract and security agreement. See *retail installment contract* under CONTRACT.

retail installment sale. See INSTALLMENT SALE.

retail sales tax. See *sales tax* under TAX.

retainage (ri-**tayn**-ij). (1901) A percentage of what a landowner pays a contractor, withheld until the construction has been satisfactorily completed and all mechanic's liens are released or have expired. — Also termed *retained fund.*

retained earnings. See EARNINGS.

retained fund. See RETAINAGE.

retained income trust. See *grantor-retained income trust* under TRUST.

retainer, *n.* (18c) **1.** A client's authorization for a lawyer to act in a case <the attorney needed an express retainer before making a settlement offer>. **2.** A fee that a client pays to a lawyer simply to be available when the client needs legal help during a specified period or on a specified matter.

3. A lump-sum fee paid by the client to engage a lawyer at the outset of a matter. — Also termed *engagement fee.* **4.** An advance payment of fees for work that the lawyer will perform in the future. — Also termed *retaining fee.* Cf. ATTORNEY'S FEES. — **retain,** *vb.*

general retainer. (18c) A retainer for a specific length of time rather than for a specific project.

special retainer. (18c) A retainer for a specific case or project.

retaining fee. See RETAINER (4).

retaining lien. See LIEN.

retaliatory discharge. See DISCHARGE (7).

retaliatory eviction. See EVICTION.

retaliatory law. (1820) A state law restraining another state's businesses — as by levying taxes — in response to similar restraints imposed by the second state on the first state's businesses.

retaliatory tariff. See TARIFF (2).

retinue. A group of persons who are retained to follow and attend to a sovereign, noble, or other distinguished person.

retired stock. See *treasury stock* under STOCK.

retirement, *n.* (16c) **1.** Termination of one's own employment or career, esp. upon reaching a certain age or for health reasons; retirement may be voluntary or involuntary. **2.** Withdrawal from action or for privacy <Carol's retirement to her house by the lake>. **3.** Withdrawal from circulation; payment of a debt <retirement of a series of bonds>. See REDEMPTION. — **retire,** *vb.*

compulsory retirement. Mandatory retirement based on a person's age, esp. as specified in a union contract, by corporate policy, or by statute.

retirement annuity. See ANNUITY.

Retirement Equity Act of 1984. A federal law that requires private pension plans to comply with the court-ordered division of a pension between spouses and permits the plan administrator to pay all or part of a worker's pensions and survivor benefits directly to a former spouse if the plan has been served with a court order that meets the federal requirements for a qualified domestic-relations order. 29 USCA § 1056(d)(3). See QUALIFIED DOMESTIC-RELATIONS ORDER.

retirement-income insurance. See INSURANCE.

retirement plan. See EMPLOYEE BENEFIT PLAN.

retorsion (ri-**tor**-shən). *Int'l law.* An act of lawful retaliation in kind for another nation's unfriendly or unfair act. ● Examples of retorsion include suspending diplomatic relations, expelling foreign nationals, and restricting travel rights. — Also spelled *retortion.* Cf. REPRISAL (2).

retraction, *n.* (14c) **1.** The act of taking or drawing back <retraction of anticipatory repudiation before breach of contract>. **2.** The act of recanting; a statement in recantation <retraction of a defamatory remark>. **3.** *Wills & estates.* A withdrawal of a renunciation <because of her retraction, she took property under her uncle's will>. See RENUNCIATION (3). **4.** *Copyright.* The right of authors and artists to renounce their creative works and to forbid their sale or display. ● Retraction is one of the moral rights of artists recognized in civil-law countries and much of Europe, but largely unavailable in the United States. — Also termed (in sense 4) *withdrawal.* — **retract,** *vb.*

retraxit (ri-**trak**-sit). [Latin "he has withdrawn"] A plaintiff's voluntary withdrawal of a lawsuit in court so that the plaintiff forever forfeits the right of action. ● In modern practice, retraxit is called *voluntary dismissal with prejudice.* A dismissal without prejudice does not operate as a retraxit. See *judgment of retraxit* under JUDGMENT.

retreat rule. (1935) *Criminal law.* The doctrine holding that the victim of an assault has a duty to retreat instead of resorting to deadly force in self-defense, unless (1) the victim is at home or in his or her place of business (the so-called *castle doctrine*), or (2) the assailant is a person whom the victim is trying to arrest. ● A minority of American jurisdictions have adopted this rule. Cf. NO-RETREAT RULE.

retrial, *n.* (18c) A new trial of an action that has already been tried. See *trial de novo* under TRIAL. — **retry,** *vb.*

retribution, *n.* (14c) **1.** *Criminal law.* Punishment imposed as repayment or revenge for the offense committed; requital. Cf. DETERRENCE; REHABILITATION (1). **2.** Something justly deserved; repayment; reward. — **retributive,** *adj.* — **retribute,** *vb.*

retributive danger. See DANGER.

retributive punishment. See PUNISHMENT.

retributivism (ri-**trib**-yə-tə-viz-əm). (1966) The legal theory by which criminal punishment is justified, as long as the offender is morally accountable, regardless of whether deterrence or other good consequences <would result. ● According to retributivism, a criminal is thought to have a debt to pay to society, which is paid by punishment. The punishment is also sometimes said to be society's act of paying back the criminal for the wrong done. Opponents of retributivism sometimes refer to it as "vindictive theory." Cf. *hedonistic utilitarianism* under UTILITARIANISM; UTILITARIAN-DETERRENCE THEORY.

maximalist retributivism. The classical form of retributivism, espoused by scholars such as Immanuel Kant, under which it is argued that society has a duty, not just a right, to punish a criminal who is guilty and culpable, that is, someone who has no justification or excuse for the illegal act.

minimalist retributivism. The more contemporary form of retributivism, which maintains that no one should be punished in the absence of guilt and culpability (that is, unless punishment is deserved), and that a judge may absolve the offender from punishment, wholly or partially, when doing so would further societal goals such as rehabilitation or deterrence.

retroactive, *adj.* (17c) (Of a statute, ruling, etc.) extending in scope or effect to matters that have occurred in the past. — Also termed *retrospective.* Cf. PROSPECTIVE (1). — **retroactivity,** *n.*

retroactive law. (18c) A legislative act that looks backward or contemplates the past, affecting acts or facts that existed before the act came into effect. ● A retroactive law is not unconstitutional unless it (1) is in the nature of an ex post facto law or a bill of attainder, (2) impairs the obligation of contracts, (3) divests vested rights, or (4) is constitutionally forbidden. — Also termed *retrospective law; retroactive statute; retrospective statute.*

retrocession. (17c) **1.** The act of ceding something back (such as a territory or jurisdiction). **2.** The return of a title or other interest in property to its former or rightful owner. **3.** The process of transferring all or part of a reinsured risk to another reinsurance company; reinsurance of reinsurance. ● Subsequent retrocessions are referred to as *first retrocession, second retrocession,* and so on. **4.** The amount of risk that is so transferred.

retrocessionaire. *Reinsurance.* A reinsurer of a reinsurer. See RETROCESSION.

retrocessional agreement. An agreement providing for reinsurance of reinsurance.

retrospectant evidence. See EVIDENCE.

retrospective, *adj.* See RETROACTIVE.

retrospective law. See RETROACTIVE LAW.

retrospective statute. See RETROACTIVE LAW.

return, *n.* (15c) **1.** A court officer's bringing back of an instrument to the court that issued it; RETURN OF WRIT <a sheriff's return of citation>. **2.** A court officer's indorsement on an instrument brought back to the court, reporting what the officer did or found <a return of *nulla bona*>. See FALSE RETURN (1). **3.** TAX RETURN <file your return before April 15>. **4.** (*usu. pl.*) An official report of voting results <election returns>. **5.** Yield or profit <return on an investment>. See RATE OF RETURN. — **return,** *vb.*

capital return. *Tax.* Revenue that represents the repayment of cost or capital and thus is not taxable as income. — Also termed *return of capital.*

fair return on investment. The usual or reasonable profit in a business, esp. a public utility.

net return. The profit on an investment after deducting all investment expenses.

return of capital. See *capital return.*

return date. See *return day* under DAY.

return day. See DAY.

returnee. A refugee whom authorities have returned to the country of origin; one who has fled from the home country and then been sent back.

returning board. An official body or commission that canvasses election returns.

return of process. See PROOF OF SERVICE.

return of service. See PROOF OF SERVICE.

return of writ. (18c) The sheriff's bringing back a writ to the court that issued it, with a short written account (usu. on the back) of the manner in which the writ was executed. — Often shortened to *return.* See RETURN (1).

reunification. The return of a child who has been removed from his or her parents because of abuse or neglect by one or both of them. • When a child has been removed from the home because of abuse or neglect, the state's primary goal is family reunification as long as this is in the best interests of the child. The state is required, in most instances, to provide the parent or parents with services that will enable them to provide adequately for their child upon his or her return. After the enactment of the Adoption and Safe Families Act in 1997, states became more concerned with limiting the time that children are in foster care and less concerned with lengthy reunification plans. — Also termed *family reunification.* See ADOPTION AND SAFE FAMILIES ACT; PERMANENCY PLAN; ADOPTION ASSISTANCE AND CHILD WELFARE ACT. — **reunify,** *vb.*

re-up, *vb.* **1.** To reenlist in one of the armed forces <the soldier re-upped the day after being discharged>. **2.** To sign an extension to a contract, esp. an employment agreement <the star athlete re-upped in a three-year deal worth $12 million>.

reus (**ree**-əs). [Latin] *Roman & civil law.* **1.** A defendant. Cf. ACTOR (3). **2.** A party to a suit, whether plaintiff or defendant. **3.** A party to a contract or transaction, esp. one assuming a debt or obligation. **4.** *Roman law.* In criminal law, an accused or convicted person. Pl. *rei.* Fem. *rea,* pl. *reae.*

revalidation. See REPUBLICATION (2).

revaluation, *n.* An increase in the value of one currency in relation to another currency. Cf. DEVALUATION. — **revalue,** *vb.*

revaluation surplus. See SURPLUS.

rev'd. *abbr.* Reversed.

reve (reev). *Hist.* The bailiff of a franchise or manor. See REEVE.

revendication, *n.* **1.** The recovery or claiming back of something by a formal claim or demand. **2.** *Civil law.* An action to recover real rights in and possession of property that is wrongfully held by another. • This is analogous to the common-law replevin. — **revendicate,** *vb.*

revendicatory action. See *petitory action* under ACTION (4).

revenue. (15c) Gross income or receipts.

general revenue. The income stream from which a state or municipality pays its obligations unless a law calls for payment from a special fund. See *general fund* under FUND (1).

land revenue. Revenue derived from lands owned by the Crown in Great Britain. • Since, over the years, crown lands have been largely granted to subjects, they are now transferred within very narrow limits. See *Crown land* under LAND.

marginal revenue. The amount of revenue earned from the sale of one additional unit.

public revenue. A government's income, usu. derived from taxes, levies, and fees.

revenue agent's report. A report indicating any adjustments made to a tax return as a result of an IRS audit. • After an audit, this report is mailed to the taxpayer along with a thirty-day letter. — Abbr. RAR. See THIRTY-DAY LETTER.

revenue bill. See BILL (3).

revenue bond. See BOND (3).

Revenue Procedure. An official statement by the IRS regarding the administration and procedures of the tax laws. — Abbr. Rev. Proc.

Revenue Ruling. An official interpretation by the IRS of the proper application of the tax law to a specific transaction. • Revenue Rulings carry some authoritative weight and may be relied on by the taxpayer who requested the ruling. — Abbr. Rev. Rul.

revenue stamp. (1862) A stamp used as evidence that a tax has been paid.

revenue tariff. See TARIFF (2).

reversal, *n.* (15c) **1.** An appellate court's overturning of a lower court's decision. **2.** *Securities.* A change in a security's near-term market-price trend.

reverse, *vb.* To overturn (a judgment) on appeal. • Sometimes, the verb is used without a direct object <We reverse>. The equivalent expression in British English is *to allow the appeal.*

reverse annuity mortgage. See MORTGAGE.

reverse bear hug. See BEAR HUG.

reverse bonus. See *reverse contingent fee* under CONTINGENT FEE.

reverse condemnation. See *inverse condemnation* under CONDEMNATION.

reverse confusion. See CONFUSION.

reverse-confusion doctrine. *Intellectual property.* The rule that it is unfair competition if the defendant's use of a title that is confusingly similar to the one used by the plaintiff leads the public to believe that the plaintiff's work is the same as the defendant's, or that it is derived from or associated in some manner with the defendant. • Under the conventional passing-off form of unfair competition, similarity of titles leads the public to believe that the defendant's work is the same as the plaintiff's work, or is in some manner derived from the plaintiff. But in reverse confusion, the unfair competition results from the confusion created about the origin of the plaintiff's work.

reverse consensus. *Intellectual property.* In a dispute-settlement procedure under TRIPs, an agreement between the parties that a dispute should not be submitted to a World Trade Organization panel for adjudication. • Before TRIPs, any party could delay formation of a WTO panel or adoption of its report by withholding consensus. Under TRIPs, each process is automatic unless all parties agree not to go forward.

reverse contingent fee. See CONTINGENT FEE.

reverse discovery. See *reverse Jencks material* under JENCKS MATERIAL.

reverse discrimination. See DISCRIMINATION.

reverse doctrine of equivalents. See DOCTRINE OF EQUIVALENTS.

reverse-engineering. *Intellectual property.* The process of discovering how an invention works by inspecting and studying it, esp. by taking it apart in order to learn how it works and how to copy it and improve it. • Reverse engineering is a proper means of discovering trade secrets, according to the Uniform Trade Secrets Act, and is a defense against a suit for misappropriation of trade secrets. But it is not a defense in a suit for patent infringement. — **reverse-engineer,** *vb.*

reverse Erie doctrine. 1. The rule that a state court must apply federal law when state law is preempted by federal law or federal law prevails by an *Erie*-like balancing of the facts in situations not already regulated by Congress or the Constitution. **2.** *Maritime law.* The principle that a state court hearing an admiralty or maritime case must apply federal admiralty law even if that law conflicts with the law of the state. — Often shortened to *reverse Erie.* — Also termed *converse-Erie doctrine*; *inverse-Erie doctrine.* Cf. ERIE DOCTRINE.

reverse FOIA suit (foy-ə). A lawsuit by the owner of a trade secret or other information exempt from disclosure under a freedom-of-information act to prevent a governmental entity from making that information available to the public. See FREEDOM OF INFORMATION ACT.

reverse Jencks. See *reverse Jencks material* under JENCKS MATERIAL.

reverse mortgage. See *reverse annuity mortgage* under MORTGAGE.

reverse palming off. See PASSING OFF.

reverse passing off. See PASSING OFF.

reverse spot zoning. See ZONING.

reverse stock split. See STOCK SPLIT.

reverse subsidiary merger. See *reverse triangular merger* under MERGER.

reverse transfer statute. See TRANSFER STATUTE.

reverse triangular merger. See MERGER.

reversible error. See ERROR (2).

reversion, *n.* (15c) **1.** The interest that is left after subtracting what the transferor has parted with from what the transferor originally had; specif., a future interest in land arising by operation of law whenever an estate owner grants to another a particular estate, such as a life estate or a term of years, but does not dispose of the entire interest. • A reversion occurs automatically upon termination of the prior estate, as when a life tenant dies. — Also termed *reversionary estate*; *estate in reversion*; *equitable reversion.* **2.** Loosely, REMAINDER. Cf. POSSIBILITY OF REVERTER; REMAINDER. — **reversionary,** *adj.* — **revert,** *vb.*

reversionary estate. See REVERSION.

reversionary interest. See INTEREST (2).

reversionary lease. See LEASE.

reversioner. (17c) **1.** One who possesses the reversion to an estate; the grantor or heir in reversion. **2.** Broadly, one who has a lawful interest in land but not the present possession of it.

reverter. See POSSIBILITY OF REVERTER.

reverter guarantee. *Real estate.* A mortgage clause protecting the mortgagee against a loss occasioned by the occurrence of a terminating event under a possibility of reverter. See POSSIBILITY OF REVERTER.

revest, *vb.* (16c) To vest again or anew <revesting of title in the former owner>.

rev'g. *abbr.* Reversing.

review, *n.* (15c) **1.** Consideration, inspection, or reexamination of a subject or thing. **2.** Plenary power to direct and instruct an agent or subordinate, including the right to remand, modify, or vacate any action by the agent or subordinate, or to act directly in place of the agent or subordinate <Subject to the Assembly's review, the Council

enjoys the same powers of review and delegation as the Assembly.>. — **review,** *vb.*

administrative review. (1928) **1.** Judicial review of an administrative proceeding. **2.** Review of an administrative proceeding within the agency itself.

appellate review. (1837) Examination of a lower court's decision by a higher court, which can affirm, reverse, modify, or vacate the decision.

discretionary review. (1914) The form of appellate review that is not a matter of right but that occurs only with the appellate court's permission. See CERTIORARI.

judicial review. See JUDICIAL REVIEW.

reviewable issue. See *appealable decision* under DECISION.

review hearing. See HEARING.

revised statutes. See STATUTE.

revision, *n.* (17c) **1.** A reexamination or careful review for correction or improvement. **2.** *Parliamentary law.* A general and thorough rewriting of a governing document, in which the entire document is open to amendment <bylaws revision>. **3.** *Military law.* The reconvening of a general or special court-martial to revise its action or to correct the record because of an improper or inconsistent action concerning the findings or the sentence. • A revision can occur only if it will not materially prejudice the accused. **4.** An altered version of a work.

revival, *n.* (17c) **1.** Restoration to current use or operation; esp., the act of restoring the validity or legal force of an expired contract, an abandoned patent, or a dormant judgment. — Also termed (for a dormant judgment) *revival of judgment.* Cf. RENEWAL (2). **2.** *Wills & estates.* The reestablishment of the validity of a revoked will by revoking the will that invalidated the original will or in some other way manifesting the testator's intent to be bound by the earlier will. Cf. REPUBLICATION (2). **3.** *Patents.* Renewal of a patent prosecution that has been deemed abandoned because the applicant did not respond to an office action within the statutory period. • The applicant can petition for revival on the basis of unavoidable or unintentional delay. 37 CFR § 1.137. — **revive,** *vb.*

revival statute. See STATUTE.

revivor. (18c) A proceeding to revive an action ended because of either the death of one of the parties or some other circumstance.

***Revlon* duty.** *Delaware law.* The obligation of a company's board of directors, upon deciding to sell the company or when the sale of the company becomes inevitable, to act reasonably in seeking out and accepting a transaction that offers the best value to shareholders. • This duty was first applied in *Revlon v. MacAndrews & Forbes Holdings Inc.*, 506 A.2d 173, 181–82 (Del. 1986).

revocable (**rev**-ə-kə-bəl), *adj.* (15c) Capable of being canceled or withdrawn <a revocable transfer>.

revocable guaranty. See GUARANTY.

revocable letter of credit. See LETTER OF CREDIT.

revocable trust. See TRUST.

revocation (rev-ə-kay-shən), *n.* (15c) **1.** An annulment, cancellation, or reversal, usu. of an act or power. **2.** *Contracts.* Withdrawal of an offer by the offeror. Cf. REPUDIATION (2); RESCISSION; REJECTION (1). **3.** *Wills & estates.* Invalidation of a will by the testator, either by destroying the will or by executing a new one. • A will, or parts of a will, may be revoked by operation of law. For example, most states have a statute providing for the revocation, upon divorce, of all provisions relating to the testator's former spouse. — **revoke,** *vb.*

revocation hearing. See HEARING.

revocatory action (**rev**-ə-kə-tor-ee *or* ri-**vok**-ə-tor-ee). *Civil law.* An action brought by a creditor to annul a contract that has been entered into by the debtor and that will increase the debtor's insolvency. La. Civ. Code art. 2036.

revolution, *n.* An overthrow of a government, usu. resulting in fundamental political change; a successful rebellion. — **revolutionary,** *adj.* & *n.* — **revolt,** *vb.*

revolver loan. See LOAN.

revolving charge account. See *revolving credit* under CREDIT (4).

revolving credit. See CREDIT (4).

revolving fund. See FUND (1).

revolving letter of credit. See LETTER OF CREDIT.

revolving loan. See LOAN.

revolving performance bond. See PERFORMANCE BOND.

Rev. Proc. *abbr.* REVENUE PROCEDURE.

Rev. Rul. *abbr.* REVENUE RULING.

Rev. Stat. See *revised statutes* under STATUTE.

reward, *n.* **1.** Something of value, usu. money, given in return for some service or achievement, such as recovering property or providing information that leads to the capture of a criminal. Cf. BOUNTY (1). **2.** SALVAGE (3). — **reward,** *vb.*

rewritten specification. See *substitute specification* under SPECIFICATION (3).

rex (reks). (*usu. cap.*) **1.** A king. **2.** The official title of a king. **3.** The prosecution side (as representatives of the king) in criminal proceedings in a monarchy. — Abbr. R. Cf. REGINA.

rezone, *vb.* (1951) To change the zoning boundaries or restrictions of (an area) <rezone the neighborhood>. See ZONING.

RFA. *abbr.* REQUEST FOR ADMISSION.

RFI. *abbr.* REQUEST FOR INSTRUCTIONS.

RFP. *abbr.* **1.** REQUEST FOR PRODUCTION. **2.** See REQUEST FOR PROPOSAL.

rhadamanthine (rad-ə-**man**-thin), *adj.* (*often cap.*) (1840) (Of a judge) rigorous and inflexible <the judge's rhadamanthine interpretation of procedural requirements makes it essential to study the local rules before appearing in court>.

Rhodian law (**roh**-dee-ən). As legend would have it, the earliest known system or code of maritime law, supposedly dating from 900 B.C. and adopted intact by the Romans. ● Rhodian law was purportedly developed by the people of the island Rhodes, located in the Aegean Sea and now belonging to Greece. The ancient inhabitants of Rhodes are said to have controlled the seas because of their commercial prosperity and naval superiority. Despite the uncertainties about its history, Rhodian law has often been cited as a source of admiralty and maritime law.

RHS. *abbr.* RURAL HOUSING SERVICE.

ribbon-matching rule. See MIRROR-IMAGE RULE.

Richard Roe. A fictitious name for a male party to a legal proceeding, used because the party's true identity is unknown or because his real name is being withheld; esp., the second of two such parties. Cf. JOHN DOE.

RICO (**ree**-koh). *abbr.* (1972) RACKETEER INFLUENCED AND CORRUPT ORGANIZATIONS ACT.

RICO person. Under the Racketeer Influenced and Corrupt Organizations Act, any individual or entity capable of holding a legal or beneficial interest in property and posing a continuous threat of engaging in the acts of racketeering.

rider. An attachment to some document, such as a legislative bill or an insurance policy, that amends or supplements the document. ● A rider to a legislative bill often addresses subject matter unrelated to the main purpose of the bill.

RIF. *abbr.* Reduction in force. See LAYOFF.

rif, *vb. Slang.* To lay off (a worker). ● The word derives from the acronym for *reduction in force.*

rigging the market. The practice of artificially inflating stock prices, by a series of bids, so that the demand for those stocks appears to be high and investors will therefore be enticed into buying the stocks. See MANIPULATION.

right, *n.* (bef. 12c) **1.** That which is proper under law, morality, or ethics <know right from wrong>. **2.** Something that is due to a person by just claim, legal guarantee, or moral principle <the right of liberty>. **3.** A power, privilege, or immunity secured to a person by law <the right to dispose of one's estate>. **4.** A legally enforceable claim that another will do or will not do a given act;

a recognized and protected interest the violation of which is a wrong <a breach of duty that infringes one's right>. **5.** (*often pl.*) The interest, claim, or ownership that one has in tangible or intangible property <a debtor's rights in collateral> <publishing rights>. **6.** The privilege of corporate shareholders to purchase newly issued securities in amounts proportionate to their holdings. **7.** The negotiable certificate granting such a privilege to a corporate shareholder.

absolute right. 1. A right that belongs to every human being, such as the right of personal liberty; a natural right. **2.** An unqualified right; specif., a right that cannot be denied or curtailed except under specific conditions <freedom of thought is an absolute right>. ● For example, a plaintiff has an absolute right to voluntarily nonsuit a case before it is finally submitted; after final submission, the court has discretion to grant or deny a voluntary nonsuit. Cf. *relative right.*

accessory right. A supplementary right that has been added to the main right that is vested in the same owner. ● For example, the right in a security is accessory to the right that is secured; a servitude is accessory to the ownership of the land for whose benefit the servitude exists. Cf. *principal right.*

accrued right. A matured right; a right that is ripe for enforcement (as through litigation).

acquired right. A right that a person does not naturally enjoy, but that is instead procured, such as the right to own property.

civil right. See CIVIL RIGHT.

conditional right. A right that depends on an uncertain event; a right that may or may not exist. ● For example, parents have the conditional right to punish their child, the condition being that the punishment must be reasonable.

conjugal rights. See CONJUGAL RIGHTS.

equitable right. A right cognizable within a court of equity. ● If a legal right and an equitable right conflict, the legal right ordinarily prevails over and destroys the equitable right even if the legal right arose after the equitable right. Breaches of equitable rights are remedied by means other than monetary damages, such as an injunction or specific performance. With the merger of law and equity in federal and most state courts, the procedural differences between legal and equitable rights have been largely abolished. Cf. *legal right* (1), (2).

expectant right. A right that is contingent on the occurrence of some future event; a contingent right.

fundamental right. See FUNDAMENTAL RIGHT.

imperfect right. A right that is recognized by the law but is not enforceable. • Examples include time-barred claims and claims exceeding the local limits of a court's jurisdiction.

imprescriptible right. A right that cannot be lost to prescription.

inalienable right. A right that cannot be transferred or surrendered; esp., a natural right such as the right to own property. — Also termed *inherent right*.

incorporeal right. A right to intangible, rather than tangible, property. • A right to a legal action (a *chose in action*) is an incorporeal right. See *chose in action* under CHOSE.

inherent right. See *inalienable right*.

legal right. 1. A right created or recognized by law. • The breach of a legal right is usu. remediable by monetary damages. **2.** A right historically recognized by common-law courts. Cf. *equitable right*. **3.** The capacity of asserting a legally recognized claim against one with a correlative duty to act.

natural right. A right that is conceived as part of natural law and that is therefore thought to exist independently of rights created by government or society, such as the right to life, liberty, and property. See NATURAL LAW.

negative right. A right entitling a person to have another refrain from doing an act that might harm the person entitled. Cf. *positive right*.

patent right. A right secured by a patent.

perfect right. A right that is recognized by the law and is fully enforceable.

peripheral right. A right that surrounds or springs from another right.

personal right. 1. A right that forms part of a person's legal status or personal condition, as opposed to the person's estate. **2.** See *right in personam*.

political right. The right to participate in the establishment or administration of government, such as the right to vote or the right to hold public office. — Also termed *political liberty*.

positive right. A right entitling a person to have another do some act for the benefit of the person entitled. Cf. *negative right*.

precarious right. A right enjoyed at the pleasure of another; a right that can be revoked at any time.

primary right. A right prescribed by the substantive law, such as a right not to be defamed or assaulted. • The enforcement of a primary right is termed *specific enforcement*.

principal right. A right to which has been added a supplementary right in the same owner. Cf. *accessory right*.

private right. A personal right, as opposed to a right of the public or the state. Cf. *public right*.

procedural right. (1911) A right that derives from legal or administrative procedure; a right that helps in the protection or enforcement of a substantive right. Cf. *substantive right*.

property right. (1853) A right to specific property, whether tangible or intangible.

proprietary right. A right that is part of a person's estate, assets, or property, as opposed to a right arising from the person's legal status.

public right. A right belonging to all citizens and usu. vested in and exercised by a public office or political entity. Cf. *private right*.

real right. 1. *Civil law.* A right that is connected with a thing rather than a person. • Real rights include ownership, use, habitation, usufruct, predial servitude, pledge, and real mortgage. **2.** JUS IN RE. **3.** See *right in rem*.

relative right. A right that arises from and depends on someone else's right, as distinguished from an absolute right. Cf. *absolute right*.

remedial right. The secondary right to have a remedy that arises when a primary right is broken. See *secondary right*.

restitutory right. A right to restitution.

right in personam (in pər-**soh**-nəm). An interest protected solely against specific individuals. — Also termed *personal right*; *jus in personam*. See IN PERSONAM.

right in rem (in **rem**). A right, often negative, exercisable against the world at large. — Also termed *real right*; *jus in rem*. See IN REM.

secondary right. A right prescribed by procedural law to enforce a substantive right, such as the right to damages for a breach of contract. • The enforcement of a secondary right is variously termed *secondary enforcement*, *remedial enforcement*, or *sanctional enforcement*. — Also termed *remedial right*; *sanctioning right*.

substantial right. (18c) An essential right that potentially affects the outcome of a lawsuit and is capable of legal enforcement and protection, as distinguished from a mere technical or procedural right.

substantive right (səb-stən-tiv). (18c) A right that can be protected or enforced by law; a right of substance rather than form. Cf. *procedural right*.

vested right. A right that so completely and definitely belongs to a person that it cannot be impaired or taken away without the person's consent.

right against self-incrimination. (1911) A criminal defendant's or a witness's constitutional right — under the Fifth Amendment, but waivable under certain conditions — guaranteeing that a person cannot be compelled by the government to testify if the testimony might result in the person's being criminally prosecuted. • Although this right is most often asserted during a criminal prosecution, a person can also "plead the Fifth" in a civil, legislative, administrative, or grand-jury proceeding. — Also termed *privilege against self-incrimination*; *right to remain silent*. See SELF-INCRIMINATION.

right-and-wrong test. See MCNAGHTEN RULES.

rightful, *adj.* **1.** (Of an action) equitable; fair <a rightful dispossession>. **2.** (Of a person) legitimately entitled to a position <a rightful heir>. **3.** (Of an office or piece of property) that one is entitled to <her rightful inheritance>.

right heir. See HEIR.

right in personam. See RIGHT.

right in re aliena. See JUS IN RE ALIENA.

right in rem. See RIGHT.

right in re propria. See JUS IN RE PROPRIA.

right not to be questioned. See *privilege against self-incrimination* under PRIVILEGE (3).

right of action. 1. The right to bring a specific case to court. **2.** A right that can be enforced by legal action; a chose in action. Cf. CAUSE OF ACTION.

right of angary. See ANGARY.

right of approach. *Int'l law.* The right of a warship on the high seas to draw near another vessel to determine its nationality.

right of assembly. The constitutional right — guaranteed by the First Amendment — of the people to gather peacefully for public expression of religion, politics, or grievances. — Also termed *freedom of assembly*; *right to assemble.* Cf. FREEDOM OF ASSOCIATION; *unlawful assembly* under ASSEMBLY.

right of audience. A right to appear and be heard in a given court. • The term is chiefly used in England to denote the right of a certain type of lawyer to appear in a certain type of court.

right of common. See PROFIT À PRENDRE.

right-of-conscience law. A statute allowing healthcare professionals to refuse to provide services that they find morally objectionable.

right of contribution. See CONTRIBUTION (1).

right of dissent and appraisal. See APPRAISAL REMEDY.

right of election. *Wills & estates.* A surviving spouse's statutory right to choose either the gifts given by the deceased spouse in the will or a forced share or a share of the estate as defined in the probate statute. — Also termed *widow's election.* See ELECTION (2); *augmented estate* under ESTATE (3).

right of entry. 1. The right of taking or resuming possession of land or other real property in a peaceable manner. **2.** POWER OF TERMINATION. **3.** The right to go into another's real property for a special purpose without committing trespass. • An example is a landlord's right to enter a tenant's property to make repairs. **4.** The right of an alien to go into a jurisdiction for a special purpose. • An example is an exchange student's right to enter another country to attend college.

right of entry for breach of condition. See POWER OF TERMINATION.

right of entry for condition broken. See POWER OF TERMINATION.

right of exoneration. See EQUITY OF EXONERATION.

right of family integrity. A fundamental and substantive due-process right for a family unit to be free of unjustified state interference. • While not specifically mentioned in the U.S. Constitution, this right is said to emanate from it. The contours of the right are nebulous and incompletely defined, but it at least includes the right to bear children, to rear them, and to guide them according to the parents' beliefs, as well as the right of children to be raised by their parents free of unwarranted interference by state officials. The right restricts state action under the Fourteenth Amendment. Interference is not permitted in the absence of a compelling state interest and is reviewed under a strict-scrutiny standard. Most courts require a state to establish by clear and convincing evidence that interference in a familial relationship is justified. — Also termed *right to family integrity.* See PARENTAL-AUTONOMY DOCTRINE; PARENTAL-PRIVILEGE DOCTRINE. Cf. *freedom of intimate association* under FREEDOM OF ASSOCIATION.

right of first publication. See *common-law copyright* under COPYRIGHT.

right of first refusal. 1. A potential buyer's contractual right to meet the terms of a third party's higher offer. • For example, if Beth has a right of first refusal on the purchase of Sam's house, and if Terry offers to buy the house for $300,000, then Beth can match this offer and prevent Terry from buying it. Cf. RIGHT OF PREEMPTION. **2.** *Family law.* The right of a parent to be offered the opportunity to have custody of a child other than during a usual visitation period before the other parent turns to a third-party caregiver. • The right may be exercised by either parent, and may exist in circumstances that are foreseeable (e.g., a business trip) or unforeseeable (e.g., an illness).

right of fishery. See FISHERY (1).

right of innocent passage. See INNOCENT PASSAGE.

right of occupancy. See INDIAN TITLE.

right of petition. See RIGHT TO PETITION.

right of possession. The right to hold, use, occupy, or otherwise enjoy a given property; esp., the right to enter real property and eject or evict a wrongful possessor.

right of preemption. A potential buyer's contractual right to have the first opportunity to buy, at a specified price, if the seller chooses to sell within the contracted period. • For example, if Beth has a right of preemption on Sam's house for five years at $100,000, Sam can either keep the house for five years (in which case Beth's right expires) or, if he wishes to sell during those five years, offer the house to Beth, who can either buy it for $100,000 or refuse to buy. If Beth refuses, Sam can sell to someone else. — Also termed *first option to buy*. Cf. RIGHT OF FIRST REFUSAL.

right of privacy. 1. The right to personal autonomy. • The U.S. Constitution does not explicitly provide for a right of privacy or for a general right of personal autonomy, but the Supreme Court has repeatedly ruled that a right of personal autonomy is implied in the "zones of privacy" created by specific constitutional guarantees. **2.** The right of a person and the person's property to be free from unwarranted public scrutiny or exposure. — Also termed *right to privacy*. See INVASION OF PRIVACY.

right of publicity. The right to control the use of one's own name, picture, or likeness and to prevent another from using it for commercial benefit without one's consent.

right of redemption. 1. See EQUITY OF REDEMPTION. **2.** See STATUTORY RIGHT OF REDEMPTION.

right of reentry. See POWER OF TERMINATION.

right of reproduction. See REPRODUCTION RIGHT.

right of rescission. See RIGHT TO RESCIND.

right of retainer. A trustee's power to withhold trust funds or property from distribution, exercisable when the beneficiary owes money to the trust.

right of retention. See RETENTION.

right of revolution. The inherent right of a people to cast out its rulers, change its polity, or effect radical reforms in its system of government or institutions, by force or general uprising, when the legal and constitutional methods of making such changes have proved inadequate or are so obstructed as to be unavailable.

right of search. *Int'l law.* The right to stop, visit, and examine vessels on the high seas to discover whether they or the goods they carry are liable to capture; esp., a belligerent state's right to stop any merchant vessel of a neutral state on the high seas and to search as reasonably necessary to determine whether the ship has become liable to capture under the international law of naval warfare. • This right carries with it no right to destroy without full examination, unless those on a given vessel actively resist. — Also termed *right of visit*; *right of visit and search*; *right of visitation*; *right of visitation and search*. See VISIT.

right of subrogation. 1. See SUBROGATION. **2.** See EQUITY OF SUBROGATION.

right of suit. A person's right to seek redress in a court.

right of support. *Property.* **1.** A landowner's right to have the land supported by adjacent land and by the underlying earth. **2.** A servitude giving the owner of a house the right to rest timber on the walls of a neighboring house.

right of survivorship. A joint tenant's right to succeed to the whole estate upon the death of the other joint tenant. — Also termed *jus accrescendi*. See SURVIVORSHIP; *joint tenancy* under TENANCY.

right of termination. A remedy involving the ending of contractual relations, accorded to a party to a contract when the other party breaches a duty that arises under the contract. • The right of termination is contrasted with a right to rescind, which arises when the other party breaches a duty that arises independently of the contract. — Also termed *right to terminate*.

right of transit passage. See TRANSIT PASSAGE.

right of visit. See RIGHT OF SEARCH.

right of visit and search. See RIGHT OF SEARCH.

right of visitation. 1. VISITATION RIGHT. **2.** RIGHT OF SEARCH.

right of visitation and search. See RIGHT OF SEARCH.

right-of-way. 1. The right to pass through property owned by another. • A right-of-way may be established by contract, by longstanding usage, or by public authority (as with a highway). Cf. EASEMENT. **2.** The right to build and operate a railway line or a highway on land belonging to another, or the land so used. **3.** The right to take precedence in traffic. **3.** The strip of land subject to a nonowner's right to pass through. — Also written *right of way*. Pl. **rights-of-way.**

private right-of-way. See EASEMENT.

public right-of-way. The right of passage held by the public in general to travel on roads, freeways, and other thoroughfares.

right of wharfing out. A right to the exclusive use of submerged lands, as by establishing a permanent structure or wharf on the land to dock oceangoing vessels.

rights arbitration. See *grievance arbitration* under ARBITRATION.

rights-consciousness. See CLAIMS-CONSCIOUS-NESS.

rights-management information. *Intellectual property.* Information about an intellectual-property right, affixed to the subject matter when it is communicated to the public, esp. in electronic form, and identifying the right's owner, terms of use, indexing numbers or codes, or other identifying information. • The information facilitates contracting with the owner of the rights. In digital technology, laws may ban the removal or alteration of rights-management information as a form of intellectual-property protection.

rights of attribution. See ATTRIBUTION RIGHTS.

rights off. See EX RIGHTS.

rights offering. See OFFERING.

rights on. See CUM RIGHTS.

right to assemble. See RIGHT OF ASSEMBLY.

right to assistance of counsel. See RIGHT TO COUNSEL.

right to bear arms. The constitutional right of persons to own firearms. U.S. Const. amend II. See SECOND AMENDMENT.

right to choose. See FREEDOM OF CHOICE.

right-to-convey covenant. See *covenant of seisin* under COVENANT (4).

right to counsel. 1. *Criminal law.* A criminal defendant's constitutional right, guaranteed by the Sixth Amendment, to representation by a court-appointed lawyer if the defendant cannot afford to hire one. • The Supreme Court has recognized a juvenile delinquent defendant's right to counsel. *In re Gault,* 387 U.S. 1, 87 S.Ct. 1428 (1967). — Also termed *benefit of counsel*; *right to assistance of counsel.* **2.** *Family law.* The right of a defendant in a suit for termination of parental rights to representation by a court-appointed lawyer if the defendant cannot afford to hire one. • Although some states appoint counsel for indigent defendants in a suit for termination of parental rights, the Supreme Court has held that the Constitution does not require that counsel be appointed for indigent defendants in all termination suits, but if a criminal charge may be made, the right to counsel may attach. *Lassiter v. Department of Soc. Servs.,* 452 U.S. 18, 101 S.Ct. 2153 (1981). — Also termed (in both senses) *access to counsel.* See ASSISTANCE OF COUNSEL.

right to die. The right of a terminally ill person to refuse life-sustaining treatment. — Also termed *right to refuse treatment.* See ADVANCE DIRECTIVE.

right to exclude. *Patents.* A patentee's right to prevent others from making, using, selling, or offering for sale the patentee's invention.

right to family integrity. See RIGHT OF FAMILY INTEGRITY.

right-to-know act. A federal or state statute requiring businesses (such as chemical manufacturers) that produce hazardous substances to disclose information about the substances both to the community where they are produced or stored and to employees who handle them. — Also termed *right-to-know statute.*

right to petition. (17c) The constitutional right — guaranteed by the First Amendment — of the people to make formal requests to the government, as by lobbying or writing letters to public officials. — Also termed *right of petition*; *freedom of petition.*

right to privacy. See RIGHT OF PRIVACY.

right to pursue happiness. See HAPPINESS, RIGHT TO PURSUE.

right to refuse treatment. See RIGHT TO DIE.

right to remain silent. See RIGHT AGAINST SELF-INCRIMINATION.

right to rescind. The remedy accorded to a party to a contract when the other party breaches a duty that arises independently of the contract. • The right to rescind is contrasted with a right of termination, which arises when the other party breaches a duty that arises under the contract. — Also termed *right of rescission.*

right to terminate. See RIGHT OF TERMINATION.

right to travel. (1838) A person's constitutional right — guaranteed by the Privileges and Immunities Clause — to travel freely between states.

right to vote. See SUFFRAGE (1).

right-to-work law. (1958) A state law that prevents labor–management agreements requiring a person to join a union as a condition of employment. See *open shop* under SHOP.

right-wrong test. See MCNAGHTEN RULES.

rigid constitution. See CONSTITUTION.

rigor juris (**rig**-ər **joor**-is). [Latin] Strictness of law.

rigor mortis (**rig**-ər **mor**-tis). The temporary stiffening of a body's joints and muscles after death. • The onset of rigor mortis can vary from 15 minutes to several hours after death, depending on the body's condition and on atmospheric factors.

ringing out. See RINGING UP.

ringing the changes. Fraud consisting in the offender's using a large bill to pay for a small purchase, waiting for the shopkeeper to put change on the counter, and then, by a series of maneuvers involving changes of mind — such as asking for some other article of little value or for smaller change for some of the money on the counter — creating a confused situation in which the offender picks up more the money than due.

ringing up. A method by which commodities dealers cooperate to discharge contracts for future delivery in advance by using offsets, cancellations, and price adjustments, thus saving the cost of actual delivery and change of possession. — Also termed *ringing out*.

riot, *n.* (14c) **1.** An assemblage of three or more persons in a public place taking concerted action in a turbulent and disorderly manner for a common purpose (regardless of the lawfulness of that purpose). **2.** An unlawful disturbance of the peace by an assemblage of usu. three or more persons acting with a common purpose in a violent or tumultuous manner that threatens or terrorizes the public or an institution. Cf. *unlawful assembly* under ASSEMBLY; CIVIL COMMOTION; ROUT; AFFRAY. — **riotous,** *adj.* — **riot,** *vb.*

Riot Act. A 1714 English statute that made it a capital offense for 12 or more rioters to remain together for an hour after a magistrate has officially proclaimed that rioters must disperse. • This statute was not generally accepted in the United States and did not become a part of American common law. It did, however, become a permanent part of the English language in the slang phrase *reading the riot act* (meaning "to reprimand vigorously"), which originally referred to the official command for rioters to disperse.

riotous assembly. See ASSEMBLY.

riparian (ri-**pair**-ee-ən *or* rī-), *adj.* (1841) Of, relating to, or located on the bank of a river or stream (or occasionally another body of water, such as a lake) <riparian land> <a riparian owner>. Cf. LITTORAL.

riparian land. See LAND.

riparian proprietor. (1808) A person who is in possession of riparian land or who owns an estate in it; a landowner whose property borders on a stream or river. See *riparian land* under LAND.

riparian right. (*often pl.*) (1860) The right of a landowner whose property borders on a body of water or watercourse. • Such a landowner traditionally has the right to make reasonable use of the water. — Also termed *water right*.

riparian-rights doctrine. (1921) The rule that owners of land bordering on a waterway have equal rights to use the water passing through or by their property. Cf. PRIOR-APPROPRIATION DOCTRINE.

ripeness, *n.* **1.** The state of a dispute that has reached, but has not passed, the point when the facts have developed sufficiently to permit an intelligent and useful decision to be made. **2.** The requirement that this state must exist before a court

will decide a controversy. See JUSTICIABILITY. Cf. MOOTNESS DOCTRINE; PREMATURITY (1). — **ripe,** *adj.* — **ripen,** *vb.*

ripper act. *Slang.* A statute that gives a government's chief executive broad powers to appoint and remove department heads or other subordinate officials.

rise, *vb.* **1.** (Of a court) to adjourn finally at the end of a term. **2.** (Of spectators and participants in a courtroom) to stand when the judge enters or exits. **3.** (Of a court) to take a recess or temporary break, as at the end of a day. **4.** *Parliamentary law.* (Of a special committee that has exhausted its business) to dissolve and send a report to the referring body. • A committee's rising is equivalent to a deliberative assembly's adjourning sine die. — Also termed *rise and report*. Cf. *adjourn sine die* under ADJOURN (2).

rising vote. See VOTE (4).

rising vote of thanks. See *rising vote* under VOTE (4).

risk, *n.* (17c) **1.** The uncertainty of a result, happening, or loss; the chance of injury, damage, or loss; esp., the existence and extent of the possibility of harm <many feel that skydiving is not worth the risk>. See ASSUMPTION OF THE RISK. **2.** Liability for injury, damage, or loss if it occurs <the consumer-protection statute placed the risk on the manufacturer instead of the buyer>. **3.** *Insurance.* The chance or degree of probability of loss to the subject matter of an insurance policy <the insurer undertook the risk in exchange for a premium>. Cf. PERIL (2). **4.** *Insurance.* The amount that an insurer stands to lose <the underwriter took steps to reduce its total risk>. **5.** *Insurance.* A person or thing that an insurer considers a hazard; someone or something that might be covered by an insurance policy <she's a poor risk for health insurance>. **6.** *Insurance.* The type of loss covered by a policy; a hazard from a specified source <this homeowner's policy covers fire risks and flood risks>. — **risk,** *vb.*

absorbable risk. A potential loss that a corporation believes that it can cover either with available capital or with self-insurance.

assigned risk. One who is a poor risk for insurance but whom an insurance company is forced to insure because of state law. • For example, an accident-prone driver is an assigned risk in a state with a compulsory motor-vehicle-insurance statute.

classified risk. In life- and health-insurance policies, the risk created by a policyholder's substandard health or other peril.

noninsurable risk. A risk for which insurance will not be written because the risk is too uncertain to be the subject of actuarial analysis.

pure risk. A risk that can only result in a loss. • Insurance protects only against pure risks. Cf. *speculative risk.*

shifting risk. The changing risk covered under an insurance policy insuring a stock of goods or similar property that varies in amount and composition in the course of trade.

speculative risk. A risk that can result in either a loss or a gain. Cf. *pure risk.*

risk arbitrage. See ARBITRAGE.

risk assessment. *Family law.* A process for ascertaining the likelihood that a person, usu. a parent, will harm a child. • Before a child can be removed from his or her family by a governmental entity, a risk assessment should be performed to determine the likelihood of the child's being harmed in the future.

risk-averse, *adj.* (Of a person) uncomfortable with volatility or uncertainty; not willing to take risks; very cautious <a risk-averse investor>.

risk-benefit test. See RISK-UTILITY TEST.

risk capital. See CAPITAL.

risk-capital test. *Securities.* A test of whether a transaction constitutes the sale of a security (and is thus subject to securities laws) based on whether the seller is soliciting risk capital with which to develop a business venture. Cf. CAPITAL-RISK TEST.

risk distribution. The method by which a legal system allocates the risk of harm between the person who suffers it and the loss.

risk factor. *Insurance.* In life-insurance ratemaking, the estimated cost of present and future claims, based on a mortality table. • The risk factor is one element that a life insurer uses to calculate premium rates. See PREMIUM RATE. Cf. INTEREST FACTOR; MORTALITY FACTOR.

risk management. The procedures or systems used to minimize accidental losses, esp. to a business.

Risk Management Agency. An agency in the U.S. Department of Agriculture responsible for administering the programs of the Federal Crop Insurance Corporation and for overseeing other programs relating to the risk management of crops and commodities. — Abbr. RMA.

risk of jury doubt. See BURDEN OF PERSUASION.

risk of loss. (18c) **1.** The danger or possibility of damage to, destruction of, or misplacement of goods or other property <commercial transportation always carries some risk of loss>. **2.** Responsibility for bearing the costs and expenses of such damage, destruction, or misplacement <the contract specifies who assumes the risk of loss>.

risk of nonpersuasion. See BURDEN OF PERSUASION.

risk-stops-here rule. See DOCTRINE OF SUPERIOR EQUITIES.

risk-utility test. (1982) A method of imposing product liability on a manufacturer if the evidence shows that a reasonable person would conclude that the benefits of a product's particular design versus the feasibility of an alternative safer design did not outweigh the dangers inherent in the original design. — Also termed *danger-utility test*; *risk-benefit test.* Cf. CONSUMER-CONTEMPLATION TEST.

RIT. *abbr.* Rochester Institute of Technology. See NATIONAL TECHNICAL INSTITUTE FOR THE DEAF.

river. A natural, flowing body of water that empties into another body of water, such as a lake, sea, or channel.

international river. A river that flows through or between two or more countries.

national river. A river wholly contained within a single country. • That country has exclusive territorial rights over the river.

private river. A river to which a riparian owner may claim ownership of the riverbed because the river is unnavigable or navigable only by vessels with shallow drafts. • A navigable private river is not wholly owned by a private person and cannot be closed to public use; people may still make ordinary use of the river for transportation and navigation.

RL/C. See *revolving letter of credit* under LETTER OF CREDIT.

RMA. *abbr.* RISK MANAGEMENT AGENCY.

RMS. *abbr.* REPRESSED-MEMORY SYNDROME.

roadstead. *Maritime law.* A convenient or safe place where vessels usu. anchor.

robbery, *n.* (12c) The illegal taking of property from the person of another, or in the person's presence, by violence or intimidation; aggravated larceny. • Robbery is usu. a felony, but some jurisdictions classify some robberies as high misdemeanors. — Also termed (in Latin) *crimen roberiae.* See LARCENY; THEFT. Cf. BURGLARY. — **rob,** *vb.*

aggravated robbery. (1878) Robbery committed by a person who either carries a dangerous weapon — often called *armed robbery* — or inflicts bodily harm on someone during the robbery. • Some statutes also specify that a robbery is aggravated when the victim is a member of a protected class, such as children or the elderly.

armed robbery. (1926) Robbery committed by a person carrying a dangerous weapon, regardless of whether the weapon is revealed or used. • Most states punish armed robbery as an aggravated form of robbery rather than as a separate crime.

conjoint robbery (kən-**joynt**). A robbery committed by two or more persons.

highway robbery. 1. Robbery committed against a traveler on or near a public highway. **2.** Figuratively, a price or fee that is unreasonably high; excessive profit or advantage.

simple robbery. (18c) Robbery that does not involve an aggravating factor or circumstance.

robe. (18c) **1.** The gown worn by a judge while presiding over court. • In the U.S., judges generally wear plain black gowns. In the U.K., judicial robes vary in color and adornment, depending on the judge's rank, the season, and the court, and are traditionally worn with white horsehair wigs. — Also termed *judicial robe.* **2.** (*often cap.*) The legal or judicial profession <eminent members of the robe>.

Robert's Rules. 1. A parliamentary manual titled *Robert's Rules of Order*, originally written in 1875–76 by Henry M. Robert (1837–1923). • The manual went through three editions under its original title and three more (beginning in 1915) under the title *Robert's Rules of Order Revised*. Since 1970 it has been titled *Robert's Rules of Order Newly Revised*. It is the best selling and most commonly adopted parliamentary manual in the United States. **2.** Any parliamentary manual that includes "Robert's Rules" in its title. • The copyright on the first several editions has expired, and many imitators have adapted those editions in varying degrees of faithfulness to the original. **3.** (*sing.*) RULE (3). See PARLIAMENTARY MANUAL.

Robinson–Patman Act. A federal statute (specif., an amendment to the Clayton Act) prohibiting price discrimination that hinders competition or tends to create a monopoly. 15 USCA § 13. See ANTITRUST LAW; CLAYTON ACT.

Rochin **rule.** The now-rejected principle that unconstitutionally obtained evidence is admissible against the accused unless the evidence was obtained in a manner that shocks the conscience (such as pumping the stomach of a suspect to obtain illegal drugs that the suspect has swallowed, as occurred in the *Rochin v. California* case). • The Supreme Court handed down *Rochin* before the Fourth Amendment exclusionary rule applied to the states. *Rochin v. California*, 342 U.S. 165, 72 S.Ct. 205 (1952).

rocket docket. (1987) **1.** An accelerated dispute-resolution process. **2.** A court or judicial district known for its speedy disposition of cases. **3.** A similar administrative process, in which disputes must be decided within a specified time (such as 60 days).

ROD. *abbr.* See RECORD OF DECISION.

rogatio testium. The production of a witness who can testify to the making of a nuncupative will. • The witness must confirm that the testator declared or expressed that the words spoken were a will. See *nuncupative will* under WILL.

rogatory letter (**rog**-ə-tor-ee). See LETTER OF REQUEST.

rogue court. See COURT.

rogue jury. See JURY.

roll, *n.* (14c) **1.** A record of a court's or public office's proceedings. **2.** An official list of the persons and property subject to taxation. — Also termed (in sense 2) *tax roll; tax list; assessment roll.* Cf. TAXPAYERS' LISTS. **3.** *Parliamentary law.* The roster of those entitled to vote. — Also termed *roll of delegates; roll of members.*

roll call. See CALL (1).

roll-call vote. See VOTE (4).

rolled-up plea. See PLEA (3).

rolling stock. Movable property, such as locomotives and rail cars, owned by a railroad.

roll of delegates. See ROLL (3).

roll of members. See ROLL (3).

rollover, *n.* **1.** The extension or renewal of a short-term loan; the refinancing of a maturing loan or note. **2.** The transfer of funds (such as IRA funds) to a new investment of the same type, esp. so as to defer payment of taxes. — **roll over,** *vb.*

rollover mortgage. See *renegotiable-rate mortgage* under MORTGAGE.

Roman–Dutch law. A system of law in Holland from the mid-15th century to the early 19th century, based on a mixture of Germanic customary law and Roman law as interpreted in medieval and Renaissance lawbooks. • This law forms the basis of modern South African law, the law of several other countries in southern Africa, and the law of Sri Lanka.

Romanesque law. See CIVIL LAW (1).

Romanist, *n.* One who is versed in or practices Roman law; a Roman-law specialist.

Roman law. (16c) The legal system of the ancient Romans, forming the basis of the modern civil law; CIVIL LAW (1).

Rome Act. *Copyright.* A 1928 revision of the Berne Convention adding the moral rights of attribution and integrity to the minimum standards of protection that member nations must recognize, creating a compulsory license of recorded performances for radio broadcasting, and specifying that the term of protection for joint works must be measured from the death of the last surviving coauthor. — Also termed *Rome Act of 1928; 1928 Rome Act.*

Rome Convention. See ROME CONVENTION ON RELATED RIGHTS.

Rome Convention on Related Rights. *Copyright.* A 1961 treaty setting minimum standards for neighboring rights of performers, producers, and broadcasters. • The United States is not a signatory. Neighboring rights were not protected under the Paris Convention or the Berne Convention. They are part of the copyright protection under the Agreement on Trade-Related Aspects of Intellectual Property (TRIPs). — Also termed *Convention for the Protection of Performers, Producers of Phonograms and Broadcasting Organizations.* — Often shortened to *Rome Convention.* See NEIGHBORING RIGHT.

Rooker–Feldman doctrine. The rule that a federal court cannot consider claims actually decided by a state court or claims inextricably intertwined with an earlier state-court judgment. *Rooker v. Fidelity Trust Co.,* 263 U.S. 413, 415–16, 44 S.Ct. 149, 150 (1923); *District of Columbia Ct. of App. v. Feldman,* 460 U.S. 462, 476, 103 S.Ct. 1303, 1311 (1983). • This doctrine precludes "a party losing in state court . . . from seeking what in substance would be appellate review of [a] state judgment in a United States district court, based on the losing party's claim that the state judgment itself violates the loser's federal rights." *Johnson v. De Grandy,* 512 U.S. 997, 1005–06, 114 S.Ct. 2647, 2654 (1994).

root. *Civil law.* A descendant.

root of title. (1846) The recorded land transaction, usu. at least 40 years old, that is used to begin a title search. See CHAIN OF TITLE; TITLE SEARCH.

ROR. *abbr.* RELEASE ON RECOGNIZANCE.

Roth IRA. See INDIVIDUAL RETIREMENT ACCOUNT.

round lot. See LOT (3).

round-up. See *dragnet arrest* under ARREST.

rout (rowt), *n.* (15c) The offense that occurs when an unlawful assembly makes some move toward the accomplishment of its participants' common purpose. Cf. RIOT.

routine-activities theory. (1985) The theory that criminal acts occur when (1) a person is motivated to commit the offense, (2) a vulnerable victim is available, and (3) there is insufficient protection to prevent the crime. Cf. CONTROL THEORY; RATIONAL-CHOICE THEORY; STRAIN THEORY.

Royal Marriages Act. A 1772 statute (12 Geo. 3, ch. 1) forbidding members of the royal family from marrying without the sovereign's permission, except on certain conditions.

royalty. (1839) **1.** *Intellectual property.* A payment — in addition to or in place of an up-front payment — made to an author or inventor for each copy of a work or article sold under a copyright or patent. • Royalties are often paid per item made, used, or sold, or per time elapsed.

  established royalty. A royalty set at an agreed-on price. • In the absence of an established royalty, a court will determine a remedy for infringement based on what a reasonable royalty would have been.

  reasonable royalty. A royalty that a licensee would be willing to pay the holder of the thing's intellectual-property rights while still making a reasonable profit from its use. • The reasonable-royalty standard often serves as the measure of damages in a claim of patent, copyright, or trademark infringement, or for misappropriation of trade secrets. In deciding what royalty is reasonable in a trade-secrets suit, courts consider the unique circumstances of the case, as well as (1) how the use affected the parties' ability to compete; (2) the cost of past licenses; (3) the cost to develop the secret and its present value; (4) how the defendant intends to use the information; and (5) the availability of alternatives.

2. *Oil & gas.* A share of the product or profit from real property, reserved by the grantor of a mineral lease, in exchange for the lessee's right to mine or drill on the land. — Also termed (in sense 2) *override.*

  haulage royalty. A royalty paid to a landowner for moving coal via a subterranean passageway under the landowner's land from a mine located on an adjacent property. • The payment is calculated at a certain amount per ton of coal.

  landowner's royalty. A share of production or revenues provided for the lessor in the royalty clause of the oil-and-gas lease and paid at the well free of any costs of production. • Traditionally, except in California, the landowner's royalty has been 1/8 of gross production for oil and 1/8 of the proceeds received from the sale of gas. But today the size is often negotiated. — Also termed *leaseholder royalty.*

  mineral royalty. A right to a share of income from mineral production.

  nonparticipating royalty. A share of production — or of the revenue from production free its costs — carved out of the mineral interest. • A nonparticipating-royalty holder is entitled to the stated share of production or cash without regard to the terms of any lease. Nonparticipating royalties are often retained by mineral-interest owners who sell their rights.

  overriding royalty. A share of either production or revenue from production (free of the costs of production) carved out of a lessee's interest under an oil-and-gas lease. • Overriding-royalty interests are often used to compensate those who have helped structure a drilling venture.

An overriding-royalty interest ends when the underlying lease terminates.

shut-in royalty. A payment made by an oil-and-gas lessee to the lessor to keep the lease in force when a well capable of producing is not utilized because there is no market for the oil or gas. • Generally, without such a payment, the lease will terminate at the end of the primary term unless actual production has begun.

royalty interest. *Oil & gas.* A share of production — or the value or proceeds of production, free of the costs of production — when and if there is production. • A royalty interest is usu. expressed as a fraction (such as 1/6). A royalty-interest owner has no right to operate the property and therefore no right to lease the property or to share in bonuses or delay rentals. In some states a royalty owner has the right of ingress and egress to take the royalty production. Authorities are split over what costs are costs of production. Several different but related kinds of royalty interests are commonly encountered. See ROYALTY (2).

rptr. *abbr.* REPORTER.

RRB. *abbr.* RAILROAD RETIREMENT BOARD.

R.S. See *revised statutes* under STATUTE.

RSPA. *abbr.* RESEARCH AND SPECIAL PROGRAMS ADMINISTRATION.

RTC. *abbr.* RESOLUTION TRUST CORPORATION.

rubber check. See *bad check* under CHECK.

rubber-stamp seal. See NOTARY SEAL.

rubric (roo-brik). **1.** The title of a statute or code <the rubric of the relevant statute is the Civil Rights Act of 1964>. **2.** A category or designation <assignment of rights falls under the rubric of contract law>. **3.** An authoritative rule, esp. for conducting a public worship service <the rubric dictates whether the congregation should stand or kneel>. **4.** An introductory or explanatory note; a preface <a well-known scholar wrote the rubric to the book's fourth edition>. **5.** An established rule, custom, or law <what is the rubric in the Northern District of Texas regarding appearance at docket call?>.

rule, *n.* (13c) **1.** Generally, an established and authoritative standard or principle; a general norm mandating or guiding conduct or action in a given type of situation.

default rule. A legal principle that fills a gap in a contract in the absence of an applicable express provision but remains subject to a contrary agreement. Cf. GAP-FILLER.

general rule. A rule applicable to a class of cases or circumstances.

mandatory rule. A legal rule that is not subject to a contrary agreement. • For example, the UCC

obligation of good faith and fair dealing cannot be disclaimed.

peremptory rule. A court order that must be obeyed without an opportunity to respond. • No objections may be lodged or arguments made.

special rule. See SPECIAL RULE (1).

2. A regulation governing a court's or an agency's internal procedures. **3.** *Parliamentary law.* A procedural rule (sense 1) for the orderly conduct of business in a deliberative assembly. — Also termed *rule of order (often pl.).*

Cordon rule. See CORDON RULE.

joint rule. A rule adopted by both houses of a bicameral legislature for the conduct of business or relations between them, such as when they meet in joint session, or for other matters in which they share an interest. See *joint session* under SESSION (1).

ordinary standing rule. See *standing rule* (1).

Ramseyer rule. See RAMSEYER RULE.

special rule. 1. See SPECIAL RULE (2). **2.** See SPECIAL RULE (3).

standing rule. 1. A rule that relates to an organization's administration or operation rather than to its procedure in meetings. • For example, a rule about the time and place of regular meetings, or about a committee's jurisdiction, is a standing rule. — Also termed *ordinary standing rule.* **2.** A special rule of continuing force. • Many conventions and other deliberative assemblies collect both their administrative and procedural rules into a set titled "standing rules." See *special rule* (1).

rule, *vb.* (13c) **1.** To command or require; to exert control <the dictator ruled the country>. **2.** To decide a legal point <the court ruled on the issue of admissibility>.

rule, the. An evidentiary and procedural rule by which all witnesses are excluded from the courtroom while another witness is testifying <invoking "the rule">. • The phrase "the rule" is used chiefly in the American South and Southwest, but it is a common practice to exclude witnesses before they testify.

rule against vitiation of a claim element. See ALL-ELEMENTS RULE.

Rule in Queen Caroline's Case. The common-law principle that a witness who is impeached with a prior inconsistent statement on cross-examination must be given the opportunity to admit, explain, repudiate, or deny it before the statement is admissible into evidence. • In American law, Federal Rule of Evidence 613 embodies this principle, with some variations. The original rule is found in *Queen Caroline's Case*, (1820) 129 Eng. Rep. 976.

Rule 1.53 application. See *continued-prosecution application* under PATENT APPLICATION.

Rule 10b-5. The SEC rule that prohibits deceptive or manipulative practices (such as material misrepresentations or omissions) in the buying or selling of securities. — Also termed *antifraud rule*.

Rule 11. *Civil procedure.* **1.** In federal practice, the procedural rule requiring the attorney of record or the party (if not represented by an attorney) to sign all pleadings, motions, and other papers filed with the court and — by this signing — to represent that the paper is filed in good faith after an inquiry that is reasonable under the circumstances. ● This rule provides for the imposition of sanctions, upon a party's or the court's own motion, if an attorney or party violates the conditions stated in the rule. Fed. R. Civ. P. 11. **2.** In Texas practice, the procedural rule requiring agreements between attorneys or parties concerning a pending suit to be in writing, signed, and filed in the court's record or made on the record in open court. Tex. R. Civ. P. 11.

Rule 109 statement. *Patents.* A statement by a patent examiner of the reasons for allowing a patent claim. ● An examiner may file a Rule 109 statement at any time if it appears that the record does not adequately reflect the reasons for allowance. It should state how the claim differs from prior art and why that difference is nonobvious. PTO Reg. § 1.109; 37 CFR § 1.104(e). — Also termed *Reasons for Allowance*.

Rule 116 amendment. See *amendment after final action* under PATENT-APPLICATION AMENDMENT.

Rule 312 amendment. See *amendment after allowance* under PATENT-APPLICATION AMENDMENT.

rule absolute. See *decree absolute* under DECREE.

rule against accumulations. See ACCUMULATIONS, RULE AGAINST.

rule against inalienability. The principle that property must not be made nontransferable. — Also termed *rule against trusts of perpetual duration*. Cf. RULE AGAINST PERPETUITIES.

rule against perpetuities. (*sometimes cap.*) (18c) *Property.* The common-law rule prohibiting a grant of an estate unless the interest must vest, if at all, no later than 21 years (plus a period of gestation to cover a posthumous birth) after the death of some person alive when the interest was created. ● The purpose of the rule was to limit the time that title to property could be suspended out of commerce because there was no owner who had title to the property and who could sell it or exercise other aspects of ownership. If the

terms of the contract or gift exceeded the time limits of the rule, the gift or transaction was void. See MEASURING LIFE. Cf. ACCUMULATIONS, RULE AGAINST.

rule against trusts of perpetual duration. See RULE AGAINST INALIENABILITY.

rule day. See *return day* (3) under DAY.

rule in Heydon's case. See MISCHIEF RULE.

Rule in Shelley's Case. (18c) *Property.* The rule that if — in a single grant — a freehold estate is given to a person and a remainder is given to the person's heirs, the remainder belongs to the named person and not the heirs, so that the person is held to have a fee simple absolute. ● The rule, which dates from the 14th century but draws its name from the famous 16th-century case, has been abolished in most states. *Wolfe v. Shelley*, 76 Eng. Rep. 206 (K.B. 1581).

Rule in Wild's Case. (1842) *Property.* The rule construing a grant to "A and A's children" as a fee tail if A's children do not exist at the effective date of the instrument, and as a joint tenancy if A's children do exist at the effective date. ● The rule has been abolished along with the fee tail in most states.

rulemaking, *n.* (1926) The process used by an administrative agency to formulate, amend, or repeal a rule or regulation. — Also termed *administrative rulemaking*. Cf. ADMINISTRATIVE ADJUDICATION; INFORMAL AGENCY ACTION. — **rulemaking,** *adj.*

   formal rulemaking. (1960) Agency rulemaking that, when required by statute or the agency's discretion, must be on the record after an opportunity for an agency hearing, and must comply with certain procedures, such as allowing the submission of evidence and the cross-examination of witnesses. Cf. *informal rulemaking.*

   informal rulemaking. (1968) Agency rulemaking in which the agency publishes a proposed regulation and receives public comments on the regulation, after which the regulation can take effect without the necessity of a formal hearing on the record. ● Informal rulemaking is the most common procedure followed by an agency in issuing its substantive rules. — Also termed *notice-and-comment rulemaking.* See NOTICE-AND-COMMENT PERIOD. Cf. *formal rulemaking.*

rule nisi. See *decree nisi* under DECREE.

rule of capture. 1. The doctrine that if the donee of a general power of appointment manifests an intent to assume control of the property for all purposes and not just for the purpose of appointing it to someone, the donee captures the property and the property goes to the donee's estate. ● One common way for the donee to show an intent to assume control for all purposes is to include provisions in his or her will blending the appointing property with the donee's own property. **2.** *Property.* The principle that wild animals belong to the person who captures them, regardless of whether they were originally on another person's land. **3.** *Water law.* The principle that a surface landowner can extract and appropriate all the groundwater beneath the land by drilling or pumping, even if doing so drains away groundwaters to the point of drying up springs and wells from which other landowners benefit. • This doctrine has been widely abolished or limited by legislation. **4.** *Oil & gas.* A fundamental principle of oil-and-gas law holding that there is no liability for drainage of oil and gas from under the lands of another so long as there has been no trespass and all relevant statutes and regulations have been observed. — Also termed *doctrine of capture*; *law of capture.* Cf. AD COELUM DOCTRINE.

rule of completeness. See RULE OF OPTIONAL COMPLETENESS.

rule of construction. See *canon of construction* under CANON (1).

rule of court. (17c) A rule governing the practice or procedure in a given court <federal rules of court>. See LOCAL RULE.

rule of decision. (18c) A rule, statute, body of law, or prior decision that provides the basis for deciding or adjudicating a case.

rule of doubt. 1. *Copyright.* The doctrine that unreadable or incomprehensible identifying material deposited with the U.S. Copyright Office may not be protected under copyright law because it cannot easily be examined to determine whether it qualifies. • This rule usu. applies to computer object code. • Unlike a Certificate of Registration, a filing under the rule of doubt is not prima facie evidence of a valid copyright. **2.** *Patents.* An abandoned judicial doctrine holding that when there is doubt whether an invention is patentable, the patent should be issued so that the inventor can test its validity in court.

rule of evidence. See EVIDENCE (4).

rule of four. (1949) The convention that for certiorari to be granted by the U.S. Supreme Court, four justices must vote in favor of the grant. See CERTIORARI.

rule of inconvenience. (1934) The principle of statutory interpretation holding that a court should not construe a statute in a way that will jeopardize an important public interest or produce a serious hardship for anyone, unless that interpretation is unavoidable. — Often shortened to *inconvenience.*

rule of interpretation. See *canon of construction* under CANON (1).

rule of justice. A jurisprudential principle that determines the sphere of individual liberty in the pursuit of individual welfare, so as to confine that liberty within limits that are consistent with the general welfare of humankind.

rule of law. (18c) **1.** A substantive legal principle <under the rule of law known as respondeat superior, the employer is answerable for all wrongs committed by an employee in the course of the employment>. **2.** The supremacy of regular as opposed to arbitrary power <citizens must respect the rule of law>. — Also termed *supremacy of law.* **3.** The doctrine that every person is subject to the ordinary law within the jurisdiction <all persons within the United States are within the American rule of law>. **4.** The doctrine that general constitutional principles are the result of judicial decisions determining the rights of private individuals in the courts <under the rule of law, Supreme Court caselaw makes up the bulk of what we call "constitutional law">. **5.** Loosely, a legal ruling; a ruling on a point of law <the *ratio decidendi* of a case is any rule of law reached by the judge as a necessary step in the decision>.

rule of lenity (**len**-ə-tee). The judicial doctrine holding that a court, in construing an ambiguous criminal statute that sets out multiple or inconsistent punishments, should resolve the ambiguity in favor of the more lenient punishment. — Also termed *lenity rule.*

rule of marshaling assets. An equitable doctrine that requires a senior creditor, having two or more funds to satisfy its debt, to first dispose of the fund not available to a junior creditor. • It prevents the inequity that would result if the senior creditor could choose to satisfy its debt out of the only fund available to the junior creditor and thereby exclude the junior creditor from any satisfaction. — Also termed *marshaling doctrine*; *rule of marshaling securities*; *rule of marshaling remedies.*

rule of marshaling liens. See INVERSE-ORDER-OF-ALIENATION DOCTRINE.

rule of marshaling remedies. See RULE OF MARSHALING ASSETS.

rule of marshaling securities. See RULE OF MARSHALING ASSETS.

rule of necessity. A rule requiring a judge or other official to hear a case, despite bias or conflict of interest, when disqualification would result in the lack of any competent court or tribunal. — Often shortened to *necessity.*

rule of operation. *Patents.* A method of using a machine to produce its intended useful result. • A rule of operation and moving parts generally distinguish a machine from an article of manufacture.

rule of optional completeness. (1983) The evidentiary rule providing that when a party introduces part of a writing or an utterance at trial, the opposing party may require that the remainder of the passage be read to establish the full context. • The rule has limitations: first, no utterance can be received if it is irrelevant, and second, the remainder of the utterance must explain the first part. In many jurisdictions, the rule applies to conversations, to an opponent's admissions, to confessions, and to all other types of writings — even account books. But the Federal Rules of Evidence limit the rule to writings and recorded statements. Fed. R. Evid. 106. In most jurisdictions, including federal, the remainder is admissible unless its admission would be unfair or misleading. — Also termed *rule of completeness*; *doctrine of completeness*; *doctrine of optional completeness*; *completeness doctrine*; *optional-completeness rule*; *optional-completeness doctrine.*

rule of order. See RULE (3).

rule of rank. A doctrine of statutory construction holding that a statute dealing with things or persons of an inferior rank cannot by any general words be extended to things or persons of a superior rank. • Blackstone gives the example of a statute dealing with deans, prebendaries, parsons, vicars, *and others* having spiritual promotion. According to Blackstone, this statute is held not to extend to bishops, even though they have spiritual promotion, because deans are the highest persons named, and bishops are of a higher order. Cf. EJUSDEM GENERIS; EXPRESSIO UNIUS EST EXCLUSIO ALTERIUS; NOSCITUR A SOCIIS.

rule of reason. *Antitrust.* The judicial doctrine holding that a trade practice violates the Sherman Act only if the practice is an unreasonable restraint of trade, based on the totality of economic circumstances. See SHERMAN ANTITRUST ACT; RESTRAINT OF TRADE. Cf. PER SE RULE.

rule of recognition. In the legal theory of H.L.A. Hart, a legal system's fundamental rule, by which all other rules are identified and understood. • In *The Concept of Law* (1961), Hart contends that a society's legal system is centered on rules. There are primary rules of obligation, which prescribe how a person should act in society, and secondary rules, by which the primary rules are created, identified, changed, and understood. A "rule of recognition" is a secondary rule, and serves to instruct citizens on when a pronouncement or societal principle constitutes a rule of obligation. — Sometimes shortened to *recognition.* Cf. RULES OF CHANGE; *basic norm* under NORM.

rule of right. (18c) The source of a right; the rule that gives rise to a right.

rule of 72. A method for determining how many years it takes to double money invested at a compound interest rate. • For example, at a compound rate of 6%, it takes 12 years (72 divided by 6) for principal to double.

rule of 78. A method for computing the amount of interest that a borrower saves by paying off a loan early, when the interest payments are higher at the beginning of the loan period. • For example, to determine how much interest is saved by prepaying a 12-month loan after 6 months, divide the sum of the digits for the remaining six payments (21) by the sum of the digits for all twelve payments (78) and multiply that percentage by the total interest. — Also termed *rule of the sum of the digits.*

rule of the floating subtrahend. The common-law doctrine that a plaintiff whose damage was not caused entirely by the defendant must prove the amount of damage that is not attributable to the defendant (the subtrahend) or else recover nothing. • The reasoning behind the rule is that damage is an essential element of a tort claim, and the plaintiff has the burden of proof. If proved, the subtrahend is subtracted from the total damage to determine the plaintiff's recovery.

rule of the last antecedent. (1919) An interpretative principle by which a court determines that qualifying words or phrases modify the words or phrases immediately preceding them and not words or phrases more remote, unless the extension is necessary from the context or the spirit of the entire writing. • For example, an application of this rule might mean that, in the phrase *Texas courts, New Mexico courts, and New York courts in the federal system,* the words *in the federal system* might be held to modify only *New York courts* and not *Texas courts* or *New Mexico courts.* — Also termed *doctrine of the last antecedent*; *doctrine of the last preceding antecedent.*

rule of the shorter term. *Copyright.* A provision of the Universal Copyright Convention stating that no member country is required to extend a longer term of protection than the work receives in the country where it is first published. — Also termed *shorter-term rule.*

rule of the sum of the digits. See RULE OF 78.

rule of universal inheritance. See UNIVERSAL-INHERITANCE RULE.

rules committee. See COMMITTEE.

rules of change. In the legal theory of H.L.A. Hart, the fundamental rules by which a legal system's other rules are altered. • In Hart's theory, a legal system's primary rules are subject to identification and change by secondary rules. Among those rules are "rules of change," which prescribe how laws are altered or repealed. Cf. RULE OF RECOGNITION.

rules of court. See COURT RULES.

Rules of Decision Act. A federal statute (28 USCA § 1652) providing that a federal court, when exercising diversity jurisdiction, must apply the substantive law of the state in which the court sits. See *diversity jurisdiction* under JURISDICTION.

rules of evidence. See EVIDENCE (4); FEDERAL RULES OF EVIDENCE.

rules of navigation. *Maritime law.* The principles and regulations that govern the steering and sailing of vessels to avoid collisions. ● Examples include the International Rules governing conduct on the high seas and the Inland Rules governing navigation on the inland waters of the United States and U.S. vessels on the Canadian waters of the Great Lakes. 33 USCA §§ 1602–1608, 2001–2073.

rules of order. See RULE (3).

rules of procedure. See PROCEDURE (2).

rule to show cause. 1. See SHOW-CAUSE PROCEEDING. **2.** See *show-cause order* under ORDER (2).

ruling, *n.* (16c) **1.** The outcome of a court's decision either on some point of law or on the case as a whole. — Also termed *legal ruling.* Cf. JUDGMENT (1); OPINION (1). **2.** *Parliamentary law.* The chair's decision on a point of order. — **rule,** *vb.*

ruling case. See LEADING CASE (3).

ruling letter. See DETERMINATION LETTER.

RULPA. *abbr.* Revised Uniform Limited Partnership Act. See UNIFORM LIMITED PARTNERSHIP ACT.

run, *vb.* (bef. 12c) **1.** To expire after a prescribed period <the statute of limitations had run, so the plaintiff's lawsuit was barred>. **2.** To accompany a conveyance or assignment of (land) <the covenant runs with the land>. **3.** To apply <the injunction runs against only one of the parties in the dispute>.

runaway. (16c) **1.** A person who is fleeing or has escaped from custody, captivity, restraint, or control; esp., a minor who has voluntarily left home without permission and with no intent to return. Cg. THROWAWAY. **2.** An animal or thing that is out of control or has escaped from confinement. — **run away,** *vb.*

runaway grand jury. See GRAND JURY.

runner. (18c) **1.** A law-office employee who delivers papers between offices and files papers in court. **2.** One who solicits personal-injury cases for a lawyer. — Also termed *capper.* **3.** A smuggler. **4.** *BrE. Slang.* An escape; flight (from something); a voluntary disappearance.

running account. See ACCOUNT.

running description. See METES AND BOUNDS.

running-down clause. *Marine insurance.* A provision for the hull insurer's paying a proportion of the damages sustained by the other vessel in a collision.

running objection. See *continuing objection* under OBJECTION.

running policy. See *floating policy* under INSURANCE POLICY.

running with the land. *Property law.* See *covenant running with the land* under COVENANT (4).

runoff election. See ELECTION (3).

Rural Business-Cooperative Service. An agency in the U.S. Department of Agriculture responsible for making loans and grants to public agencies and private parties to develop rural businesses. — Abbr. RBS.

Rural Electrification Administration. A former agency in the U.S. Department of Agriculture responsible for making or guaranteeing loans to rural electric and telephone utilities. ● Its duties were transferred to the Rural Utilities Service in 1994. — Abbr. REA. See RURAL UTILITIES SERVICE.

Rural Housing Service. An agency in the U.S. Department of Agriculture responsible for making or guaranteeing loans for rural housing. — Abbr. RHS.

rural servitude. See SERVITUDE (2).

Rural Utilities Service. An agency in the U.S. Department of Agriculture responsible for making or guaranteeing loans to rural electric and telecommunication utilities. ● The agency is the successor to the Rural Electrification Administration. — Abbr. RUS.

RUS. *abbr.* RURAL UTILITIES SERVICE.

S

s. *abbr.* **1.** STATUTE. **2.** SECTION (1). **3.** (*usu. cap.*) SENATE.

S-1. An SEC form that a company usu. must file before listing and trading its securities on a national exchange. ● Used primarily by first-time issuers of securities, this form is the basic, full-length registration statement that requires a great deal of information about the issuer and the securities being sold. The SEC has also adopted modified forms for smaller enterprises, such as Forms SB-1 and SB-2. — Also termed *Form S-1.*

Sabbath-breaking. The violation of laws or rules on observing the Sabbath; esp., the violation of a blue law.

Sabbath law. See BLUE LAW.

sabotage (**sab**-ə-tahzh), *n.* (1910) **1.** The destruction, damage, or knowingly defective production of materials, premises, or utilities used for national defense or for war. 18 USCA §§ 2151 et seq. **2.** The willful and malicious destruction of an employer's property or interference with an employer's normal operations, esp. during a labor dispute. — **sabotage,** *vb.*

saboteur (sab-ə-**tər**), *n.* (1921) A person who commits sabotage.

sacrilege (**sak**-rə-lij). **1.** The act or an instance of desecrating or profaning a sacred thing. **2.** *Hist.* Larceny of sacred objects, as from a church.

sacristy (**sak**-ri-stee). See VESTRY (1).

SAET. *abbr.* SUBSTANCE-ABUSE EVALUATION AND TREATMENT.

safe, *adj.* **1.** Not exposed to danger; not causing danger <driving at a safe limit of speed>. **2.** Unlikely to be overturned or proved wrong.

safe-berth clause. *Maritime law.* A provision in a voyage or time charterparty obligating the charterer to choose a berth for loading and unloading the chartered ship where the ship will be safe from damage. ● The ship's master can refuse to enter the berth without breaching the charter. But if the master reasonably enters the berth and the ship is damaged, the charterer is liable. Cf. SAFE-PORT CLAUSE.

safe blower. One who uses explosives to open a safe, esp. for the purpose of stealing the contents. Cf. SAFE CRACKER.

safe breaker. See SAFE CRACKER.

safe conduct. *Int'l law.* **1.** A privilege granted by a belligerent allowing an enemy, a neutral, or some other person to travel within or through a designated area for a specified purpose. **2.** A

document conveying this privilege. — Sometimes written *safe-conduct.* — Also termed *safeguard; passport.*

safe cracker. One who breaks into a safe, esp. for the purpose of stealing the contents. — Also termed *safe breaker.* Cf. SAFE BLOWER.

safe-deposit box. (1874) A lockbox stored in a bank's vault to secure a customer's valuables. ● It usu. takes two keys (one held by the bank and one held by the customer) to open the box. — Often shortened to *deposit box.* — Also termed *safety-deposit box.*

safe-deposit company. See DEPOSITARY (1).

safe harbor. (1960) **1.** An area or means of protection. **2.** A provision (as in a statute or regulation) that affords protection from liability or penalty. ● SEC regulations, for example, provide a safe harbor for an issuer's business forecasts that are made in good faith. — Also termed *safe-harbor clause; safe-harbor provision.*

safe-haven law. *Family law.* A statute that protects a parent who abandons a baby at a designated place such as a hospital, a physician's office, or a fire station, where it can receive emergency medical assistance as needed. ● The law typically stipulates that a parent who leaves a baby at such a place will not be publicly identified or prosecuted. Such laws have been enacted in many states in response to a perceived increase in incidents of child abandonment. — Also termed *Baby Moses law.*

safe house. A residence where people live under protection, usu. in anonymity. ● Safe houses are operated for a range of purposes, both legal and illegal. Shelters for abused spouses and runaway children are safe houses. Law-enforcement agencies keep safe houses for undercover operations and to protect witnesses who have been threatened. Lawbreakers use them to shield criminal activity such as drug manufacturing.

safekeeping. 1. The act of protecting something in one's custody. **2.** Under the Securities Investors Protection Act, the holding of a security on behalf of the investor or broker that has paid for it. 15 USCA § 78lll(2).

safe-pledge. See PLEDGE (5).

safe-port clause. *Maritime law.* A provision in a voyage or time charterparty obligating the charterer to choose a port where the ship will be safe from damage. ● The ship's master can refuse to enter the port without breaching the charter. But if the master reasonably enters the port and the ship is damaged, the charterer is liable. Cf. SAFE-BERTH CLAUSE.

safe-storage statute. A law that prohibits persons from leaving firearms unattended in places where children may gain access to them. — Also termed *child-access prevention statute.*

Safety Appliance Act. A federal law regulating the safety of equipment used by railroads in interstate commerce. 49 USCA §§ 20301 et seq.

safety-deposit box. See SAFE-DEPOSIT BOX.

safety engineering. The inspection and study of potentially dangerous conditions, usu. in an industrial environment, so that precautionary measures can be taken.

safety officer. See OFFICER (1).

safe workplace. A place of employment in which all dangers that should reasonably be removed have been removed; a place of employment that is reasonably safe given the nature of the work performed. See OCCUPATIONAL SAFETY AND HEALTH ADMINISTRATION.

said, *adj.* (13c) Aforesaid; above-mentioned. • The adjective *said* is obsolescent in legal drafting, its last bastion being patent claims. But even in that context the word is giving way to the ordinary word *the*, which if properly used is equally precise. See AFORESAID.

sailor's will. See *soldier's will* under WILL.

Saint Lawrence Seaway Development Corporation. A wholly-owned corporation in the U.S. Department of Transportation responsible for developing, operating, and maintaining a part of the St. Lawrence Seaway from Montreal to Lake Erie. • It charges tolls at rates negotiated with the St. Lawrence Seaway Authority of Canada. — Abbr. SLSDC.

salable (**say**-lə-bəl *or* **sayl**-ə-bəl), *adj.* (16c) Fit for sale in the usual course of trade at the usual selling price; MERCHANTABLE. — **salability** (say-lə-**bil**-ə-tee *or* sayl-ə-**bil**-ə-tee), *n.*

salable value. See *fair market value* under VALUE (2).

salary. (13c) An agreed compensation for services — esp. professional or semiprofessional services — usu. paid at regular intervals on a yearly basis, as distinguished from an hourly basis. • Salaried positions are usu. exempt from the requirements of the Fair Labor Standards Act (on overtime and the like) but are subject to state regulation. Cf. WAGE.

   accrued salary. A salary that has been earned but not yet paid.

sale, *n.* (bef. 12c) **1.** The transfer of property or title for a price. See UCC § 2-106(1). **2.** The agreement by which such a transfer takes place. • The four elements are (1) parties competent to contract, (2)

mutual assent, (3) a thing capable of being transferred, and (4) a price in money paid or promised.

   absolute sale. A sale in which possession and title to the property pass to the buyer immediately upon the completion of the bargain. Cf. *conditional sale.*

   approval sale. See *sale on approval.*

   auction sale. See AUCTION.

   average gross sales. The amount of total sales divided by the number of sales transactions in a specific period.

   bona fide sale. A sale made by a seller in good faith, for valuable consideration, and without notice of a defect in title or any other reason not to hold the sale.

   bootstrap sale. **1.** A sale in which the purchase price is financed by earnings and profits of the thing sold; esp., a leveraged buyout. See BUYOUT. **2.** A seller's tax-saving conversion of a business's ordinary income into a capital gain from the sale of corporate stock.

   bulk sale. See BULK SALE.

   cash-against-documents sale. See *documentary sale.*

   cash sale. **1.** A sale in which cash payment is concurrent with the receipt of the property sold. **2.** A securities transaction on the stock-exchange floor requiring cash payment and same-day delivery.

   compulsory sale. The forced sale of real property in accordance with either an eminent-domain order or an order for a judicial sale arising from nonpayment of taxes.

   conditional sale. **1.** A sale in which the buyer gains immediate possession but the seller retains title until the buyer performs a condition, esp. payment of the full purchase price. See *retail installment contract* under CONTRACT. **2.** A sale accompanied by an agreement to resell upon specified terms. Cf. *absolute sale.*

   consignment sale. A sale of an owner's property (such as clothing or furniture) by a third party entrusted to make the sale. UCC § 9-102(a)(20). See CONSIGNMENT.

   consumer-credit sale. A sale in which the seller extends credit to the consumer. • A consumer-credit sale includes a lease in which the lessee's rental payments equal or exceed the retail value of the item rented.

   credit sale. A sale of goods to a buyer who is allowed to pay for the goods at a later time.

   distress sale. **1.** A form of liquidation in which the seller receives less for the goods than what would be received under normal sales conditions; esp., a going-out-of-business sale. **2.** A foreclosure or tax sale.

dock sale. A sale in which a purchaser takes possession of the product at the seller's shipping dock, esp. for transportation outside the state.

documentary sale. A sale in which the buyer pays upon the seller's tender of documents of title covering the goods, plus a sight draft requiring the buyer to pay "at sight." • This type of sale typically occurs before delivery of the goods, which might be en route when the buyer pays. — Also termed *cash-against-documents sale*.

exclusive sale. A sale made by a broker under an exclusive-agency listing. See *exclusive-agency listing* under LISTING.

execution sale. A forced sale of a debtor's property by a government official carrying out a writ of execution. — Also termed *forced sale*; *judgment sale*; *sheriff's sale*. See EXECUTION.

executory sale. A sale agreed upon in principle but with a few minor details remaining.

fair sale. A foreclosure sale or other judicial sale conducted with fairness toward the rights and interests of the affected parties.

fire sale. 1. A sale of merchandise at reduced prices because of fire or water damage. **2.** Any sale at greatly reduced prices, esp. due to an emergency. • Fire sales are often regulated to protect the public from deceptive sales practices.

forced sale. 1. See *execution sale*. **2.** A hurried sale by a debtor because of financial hardship or a creditor's action. Cf. *voluntary sale*.

foreclosure sale. The sale of mortgaged property, authorized by a court decree or a power-of-sale clause, to satisfy the debt. See FORECLOSURE.

fraudulent sale. A sale made to defraud the seller's creditors by converting into cash property that should be used to satisfy the creditors' claims.

gross sales. Total sales (esp. in retail) before deductions for returns and allowances. — Also termed *sales in gross*.

installment sale. See INSTALLMENT SALE.

isolated sale. An infrequent or one-time sale that does not carry an implied warranty of merchantability because the seller is not a merchant with respect to goods of that kind. UCC § 2-314(1).

judgment sale. See *execution sale*.

judicial sale. A sale conducted under the authority of a judgment or court order, such as an execution sale. — Also termed *sheriff's sale*.

lumping sale. A court-ordered sale in which several distinct pieces of property are sold together for a single sum.

memorandum sale. A conditional sale in which the buyer takes possession but does not accept title until approving the property.

net sale. The amount of money remaining from a sale, after deducting returns, allowances, rebates, discounts, and other expenses.

present sale. Under the UCC, a sale accomplished by the making of a contract. UCC § 2-106(1).

private sale. An unadvertised sale negotiated and concluded directly between the buyer and seller, not through an agent.

public sale. 1. A sale made after public notice, such as an auction or sheriff's sale; specif., a sale to which the public has been invited by advertisement to appear and bid at auction for the items to be sold. **2.** *Patents.* An actual exchange for value or an offer through some medium (e.g., a sales brochure) of an article, product, or process to a member of the general public.

retail installment sale. See INSTALLMENT SALE.

sale against the box. See *short sale against the box*.

sale and leaseback. See LEASEBACK.

sale and return. See *sale or return*.

sale as is. A sale in which the buyer accepts the property in its existing condition unless the seller has misrepresented its quality. — Also termed *sale with all faults*.

sale by sample. A sale in which the parties understand that the goods exhibited constitute the standard with which the goods not exhibited correspond and to which all deliveries should conform. • Any sample that is made part of the basis of the bargain creates an express warranty that the whole of the goods will conform to the sample or model. UCC § 9-102(a)(20). — Also termed *sample sale*.

sale in gross. 1. A sale of a tract of land made with no guarantee about the exact amount or size of the land being sold. **2.** (*pl.*) See *gross sales*.

sale-leaseback. See LEASEBACK.

sale on approval. A sale in which completion hinges on the buyer's satisfaction, regardless of whether the goods conform to the contract. • Title and risk of loss remain with the seller until the buyer approves. UCC § 2-326(1)(a). — Also termed *approval sale*.

sale on credit. A sale accompanied by delivery of possession, but with payment deferred to a later date.

sale or return. A sale in which the buyer may return the goods to the seller, regardless of whether they conform to the contract, if the goods were delivered primarily for resale. • This transaction is a type of consignment in which the seller (usu. a distributor) sells goods to the buyer (often a retailer), who then tries to resell the goods, but a buyer who cannot resell is allowed to return them to the seller. Title and risk of loss are with the buyer until the goods are returned. UCC § 2-326(1)(b). — Also termed *sale and return*. Cf. SALES GUARANTEED.

sale per aversionem (pər ə-vər-zhee-**oh**-nəm). *Civil law.* A conveyance of all immovable property that falls within the boundaries stated in a purchase agreement, as opposed to a specified amount of acreage. • The sales price will not be modified because of a surplus or shortage in the amount of property that is exchanged, because the boundary description is the binding definition of the property conveyed. La. Civ. Code art. 2495.

sale positive. A sale with no reserve price.

sales in gross. See *gross sales*.

sale short. See *short sale*.

sale with all faults. See *sale as is*.

sale with right of redemption. A sale in which the seller reserves the right to retake the goods by refunding the purchase price.

sample sale. See *sale by sample*.

sheriff's sale. 1. See *execution sale*. 2. See *judicial sale*.

short sale. *Securities.* A sale of a security that the seller does not own or has not contracted for at the time of sale, and that the seller must borrow to make delivery. • Such a sale is usu. made when the seller expects the security's price to drop. If the price does drop, the seller can make a profit on the difference between the price of the shares sold and the lower price of the shares bought to pay back the borrowed shares. — Also termed *sale short*.

short sale against the box. *Securities.* A short sale of a security by a seller who owns enough shares of the security to cover the sale but borrows shares anyway because the seller wants to keep ownership a secret or because the owned shares are not easily accessible. • Delivery may be made with either the owned or the borrowed shares, so it is less risky than an ordinary short sale. The phrase *against the box* refers to the owned shares that are in safekeeping; formerly, the "box" was a container used to store stock certificates. — Often shortened to *sale against the box*.

similar sales. *Eminent domain.* Sales of like property in the same locality and time frame, admissible in a condemnation action to determine the market value of the particular property at issue.

simulated sale. A sale in which no price or other consideration is paid or intended to be paid, and in which there is no intent to actually transfer ownership. • Simulated sales are usu. done in an attempt to put property beyond the reach of creditors. — Also termed *simulated transaction*.

tax sale. A sale of property because of nonpayment of taxes. See *tax deed* under DEED.

voluntary sale. A sale made freely with the seller's consent. Cf. *forced sale*.

wash sale. *Securities.* A sale of securities made at about the same time as a purchase of the same securities (such as within 30 days), resulting in no change in beneficial ownership. • A loss from a wash sale is usu. not tax-deductible. And securities laws prohibit a wash sale made to create the false appearance of market activity. — Also termed *wash transaction*.

sale and exchange. See SALE OR EXCHANGE.

sale and leaseback. See LEASEBACK.

sale and return. See *sale or return* under SALE.

sale-leaseback. See LEASEBACK.

sale note. See NOTE (1).

sale-of-business doctrine. The outmoded rule holding that the transfer of stock incident to the sale of a business does not constitute a transfer of securities. • This doctrine was rejected by the U.S. Supreme Court in *Landreth Timber Co. v. Landreth*, 471 U.S. 681, 105 S.Ct. 2297 (1985), and its companion case, *Gould v. Ruefenacht*, 471 U.S. 701, 105 S.Ct. 2308 (1985).

sale of land. A transfer of title to real estate from one person to another by a contract of sale. • A transfer of real estate is often referred to as a conveyance rather than a sale.

sale on approval. See SALE.

sale on credit. See SALE.

sale or exchange. (1905) 1. *Tax.* A voluntary transfer of property for value (as distinguished from a gift) resulting in a gain or loss recognized for federal tax purposes. 2. A transfer of property; esp., a situation in which proceeds of a sale are to be vested in another estate of the same character and use. — Also termed (in both senses) *sale and exchange*.

sale or return. See SALE.

sale per aversionem. See SALE.

sale positive. See SALE.

sales agreement. (1920) A contract in which ownership of property is presently transferred, or will be transferred in the future, from a seller to a buyer for a fixed sum. UCC § 2-106(1).

sales-assessment-ratio study. A method for calculating the assessment level for taxable property in a jurisdiction, by comparing the assessed value and the actual sales price of a statistically reliable sample of the property in the jurisdiction, to determine the percentage by which the assessed values are above or below the sales prices.

sales finance company. See FINANCE COMPANY.

sale short. See *short sale* under SALE.

sales in gross. See *gross sales* under SALE.

sales invoice. See INVOICE.

sales journal. A book used to record sales of merchandise on account.

sales load. See LOAD.

sales mix. The relative combination of individual-product sales to total sales.

sales price. See PRICE.

sales puffery. See PUFFING (1).

sales tax. See TAX.

sale with all faults. See *sale as is* under SALE.

sale with right of redemption. See SALE.

Salic law (**sal**-ik *or* **say**-lik). An influential early medieval Frankish code of law that originated with the Salian Franks and that deals with a variety of civil property and family issues but is primarily a penal code listing the punishments for various crimes. ● Salic law is the principal compilation of the early Germanic laws known collectively as *leges barbarorum* ("laws of the barbarians"). Salic law also designated a rule barring females from the line of succession to the throne, as a result of which references to *Salic law* have sometimes referred only to the code provision excluding women from inheriting certain lands (which probably existed only because military duties were connected with the inheritance). In the late 19th century, Oliver Wendell Holmes revived scholarly interest in Salic law by referring to it throughout *The Common Law* (1881). — Also termed *Salique law*; *law Salique* (sə-**leek** *or* **sal**-ik); *lex Salica* (leks **sal**-ə-kə).

salic marriage. See *morganatic marriage* under MARRIAGE (1).

salting, *n. Labor law.* A union tactic that involves a paid union employee going to work for a targeted nonunion employer with the intention of organizing the workforce. ● The union agent (known as a *salt*) is considered an employee of the nonunion company and is protected by the National Labor Relations Act.

salvage (**sal**-vij), *n.* **1.** The rescue of imperiled property. **2.** The property saved or remaining after a fire or other loss, sometimes retained by an insurance company that has compensated the owner for the loss. **3.** Compensation allowed to a person who, having no duty to do so, helps save a ship or its cargo. — Also termed (in sense 3) *salvage award*; *reward*. — **salvage,** *vb.*

salvage award. See SALVAGE (3).

salvage charges. *Insurance.* Costs necessarily incurred in salvage.

salvage loss. See LOSS.

salvager. See SALVOR.

salvage service. The aid or rescue given, either voluntarily or by contract, to a vessel in need of assistance because of present or apprehended danger. ● Although salvage may involve towing, it is distinguished from *towing service*, which is rendered merely to expedite a voyage, not to respond to dangerous circumstances.

salvage value. See VALUE (2).

salvo (**sal**-voh). [Latin fr. *salvus* "safe"] *Hist.* **1.** Saving; excepting. ● This term was used in deeds. **2.** Safely.

salvo jure (**sal**-voh **joor**-ee). [Latin "the rule being safe"] Without prejudice to.

salvor (**sal**-vər), *n.* [Law Latin] A person who saves a vessel and its cargo from danger or loss; a person entitled to salvage. — Also termed *salvager*.

SAM. See *shared-appreciation mortgage* under MORTGAGE.

same, *pron.* (14c) The very thing just mentioned or described; it or them <two days after receiving the goods, Mr. Siviglio returned same>.

same-actor inference. *Employment law.* The doctrine that when an employee is hired and fired by the same person, and the termination occurs a reasonably short time after the hiring, the termination will be presumed not to be based on a discriminatory reason.

same-conduct test. *Criminal law.* A test for determining whether a later charge arising out of a single incident is barred by the Double Jeopardy Clause; specif., an analysis of whether the later charge requires the state to prove the same conduct that it was required to prove in a previous trial against the same defendant. ● The Supreme Court abandoned the *Blockburger* test and adopted the same-conduct test in 1990 (*Grady v. Corbin*, 495 U.S. 508, 110 S.Ct. 2084), but overruled that decision and revived *Blockburger* three years later (*U.S. v. Dixon*, 509 U.S. 688, 113 S.Ct. 2849 (1993)). Cf. BLOCKBURGER TEST; SAME-TRANSACTION TEST.

same-elements test. 1. See BLOCKBURGER TEST. **2.** See LEGAL-ELEMENTS TEST.

same-evidence test. See BLOCKBURGER TEST.

same invention. *Patents.* **1.** A second invention claiming the identical subject matter as a previous invention. **2.** Within a reissue statute, the invention described in the original patent.

same-invention double patenting. See *statutory double patenting* under DOUBLE PATENTING.

same-invention double patenting rejection. See *statutory double patenting rejection* under REJECTION.

same offense. See OFFENSE (1).

same-sex harassment. See *same-sex sexual harassment* under SEXUAL HARASSMENT.

same-sex marriage. See MARRIAGE (1).

same-sex sexual harassment. See SEXUAL HARASSMENT.

same-transaction test. *Criminal law.* A double-jeopardy test, never adopted, that would require the government to bring all charges arising out of a single incident against a defendant in one prosecution. ● Justice Brennan advocated the same-transaction test in a case involving a conviction for felony-murder and a later prosecution for the underlying felony. *Harris v. Okla.*, 433 U.S. 682, 97 S.Ct. 2912 (1977). Cf. BLOCKBURGER TEST; SAME-CONDUCT TEST.

sample sale. See *sale by sample* under SALE.

sampling, *n. Copyright.* The process of taking a small portion of a sound recording and digitally manipulating it as part of a new recording. ● Sampling may infringe the copyright of the sample's source, esp. the musical-works and sound-recording copyrights. — Also termed *digital sampling.*

S&T. *abbr.* SCIENCE AND TECHNOLOGY DIRECTORATE.

sanction (**sangk**-shən), *n.* (15c) **1.** Official approval or authorization <the committee gave sanction to the proposal>. Cf. RATIFICATION (1). **2.** A penalty or coercive measure that results from failure to comply with a law, rule, or order <a sanction for discovery abuse>. Cf. DISCIPLINE.

   criminal sanction. (1872) A sanction attached to a criminal conviction, such as a fine or restitution. — Also termed *penal sanction.*

   death-penalty sanction. (1991) *Civil procedure.* A court's order dismissing the suit or entering a default judgment in favor of the plaintiff because of extreme discovery abuses by a party or because of a party's action or inaction that shows an unwillingness to participate in the case. ● Such a sanction is rarely ordered, and is usu. preceded by orders of lesser sanctions that have not been complied with or that have not remedied the problem. — Often shortened to *death penalty.*

   shame sanction. (1991) A criminal sanction designed to stigmatize or disgrace a convicted offender, and often to alert the public about the offender's conviction. ● A shame sanction usu. publicly associates the offender with the crime that he or she committed. An example is being required to post a sign in one's yard stating, "Convicted Child Molester Lives Here." — Also

termed *shame sentence; shaming sanction; shaming sentence; scarlet-letter punishment; scarlet-letter sentence.*

   3. *Int'l law.* An economic or military coercive measure taken by one or more countries toward another to force it to comply with international law <U.N. sanctions against a renegade nation>.

sanction, *vb.* (18c) **1.** To approve, authorize, or support <the court will sanction the trust disposition if it is not against public policy>. **2.** To penalize by imposing a sanction <the court sanctioned the attorney for violating the gag order>.

sanctionable, *adj.* (18c) (Of conduct or action) meriting sanctions; likely to be sanctioned.

sanctional enforcement. See *secondary right* under RIGHT.

sanctioning right. See *secondary right* under RIGHT.

sanctions tort. A means of recovery for another party's discovery abuse, whereby the judge orders the abusive party to pay a fine to the injured party for the discovery violation. ● This is not a tort in the traditional sense, but rather a form of punishment that results in monetary gain for the injured party.

sanctity of contract. (1831) The principle that the parties to a contract, having duly entered into it, must honor their obligations under it.

sanctuary. (14c) **1.** A safe place, esp. where legal process cannot be executed; asylum. **2.** A holy area of a religious building; esp., the area in a church or temple where the main altar or tabernacle is located.

sandbagging, *n.* **1.** A trial lawyer's remaining cagily silent when a possible error occurs at trial, with the hope of preserving an issue for appeal if the court does not correct the problem. ● Such a tactic does not usu. preserve the issue for appeal because objections must be promptly made to alert the trial judge of the possible error. **2.** *Corporations.* An antitakeover tactic wherein the target company delays a hostile bidder's final offer by agreeing to negotiate then prolonging bad-faith negotiations as long as possible. — **sandbag,** *vb.*

S & L. *abbr.* SAVINGS-AND-LOAN ASSOCIATION.

sandpapering, *n.* A lawyer's general preparation of a witness before a deposition or trial. Cf. HORSESHEDDING.

sandwich lease. See LEASE.

sane, *adj.* (17c) Having a relatively sound and healthy mind; capable of reason and of distinguishing right from wrong.

sane memory. See CAPACITY (3).

sanitary code. A set of ordinances regulating the food and healthcare industries.

sanity. (15c) The state or condition of having a relatively sound and healthy mind. Cf. INSANITY.

sanity hearing. (1925) **1.** An inquiry into the mental competency of a person to stand trial. See COMPETENCY. **2.** A proceeding to determine whether a person should be institutionalized.

sans jour (sawn **zhoor** *or* sanz **joor**). [Law French] *Hist.* Without day; SINE DIE.

sans recours (sawn rə-**koor** *or* sanz ri-**kuur**). See WITHOUT RECOURSE.

sap, *n.* A club, a blackjack, a hose containing rocks in the middle, or any other object generally used as a bludgeon.

SAPJ. See *senior administrative patent judge* under JUDGE.

SAR. *abbr.* **1.** STOCK-APPRECIATION RIGHT. **2.** SUSPICIOUS-ACTIVITY REPORT.

satellite litigation. (1983) **1.** One or more lawsuits related to a major piece of litigation that is being conducted in another court <the satellite litigation in state court prevented the federal judge from ruling on the issue>. **2.** Peripheral skirmishes involved in the prosecution of a lawsuit <the plaintiffs called the sanctions "satellite litigation," drummed up by the defendants to deflect attention from the main issues in the case>.

satellite state. See *client state* under STATE.

satisfaction, *n.* (14c) **1.** The giving of something with the intention, express or implied, that it is to extinguish some existing legal or moral obligation. ● Satisfaction differs from performance because it is always something given as a substitute for or equivalent of something else, while performance is the identical thing promised to be done. — Also termed *satisfaction of debt.* **2.** The fulfillment of an obligation; esp., the payment in full of a debt. **3.** SATISFACTION PIECE. **4.** *Wills & estates.* The payment by a testator, during the testator's lifetime, of a legacy provided for in a will; ADVANCEMENT. Cf. ADEMPTION. **5.** *Wills & estates.* A testamentary gift intended to satisfy a debt owed by the testator to a creditor. See ACCORD AND SATISFACTION. — **satisfy,** *vb.*

satisfaction contract. See CONTRACT.

satisfaction of debt. See SATISFACTION (1).

satisfaction of judgment. (17c) **1.** The complete discharge of obligations under a judgment. **2.** The document filed and entered on the record indicating that a judgment has been paid.

satisfaction of lien. (1833) **1.** The fulfillment of all obligations made the subject of a lien. **2.** The document signed by the lienholder releasing the property subject to a lien.

satisfaction of mortgage. (18c) **1.** The complete payment of a mortgage. **2.** A discharge signed by the mortgagee or mortgage holder indicating that the property subject to the mortgage is released or that the mortgage debt has been paid and the mortgage conditions have been fully satisfied.

satisfaction piece. (1831) A written statement that one party (esp. a debtor) has discharged its obligation to another party, who accepts the discharge. — Also termed *certificate of discharge*; *satisfaction.*

satisfactory evidence. See EVIDENCE.

satisfactory proof. See *satisfactory evidence* under EVIDENCE.

satisfied term. See TERM (4).

Saturday-night special. (1959) **1.** A handgun that is easily obtained and concealed. **2.** *Corporations.* A surprise tender offer typically held open for a limited offering period (such as one week) to maximize pressure on a shareholder to accept. ● These tender offers are now effectively prohibited by section 14(e) of the Williams Act. 15 USCA § 78n(e).

SAUSA. *abbr.* Special assistant to the united states attorney. See UNITED STATES ATTORNEY.

save, *vb.* **1.** To preserve from danger or loss <save a ship in distress>. **2.** To lay up; to hoard <save money>. **3.** To toll or suspend (the operation, running, etc.) of something <save a statute of limitations>. **4.** To except, reserve, or exempt (a right, etc.) <to save vested rights>. **5.** To lessen or avoid (a cost, resource, etc.) <save labor>.

save harmless. See HOLD HARMLESS.

save-harmless agreement. See HOLD-HARMLESS AGREEMENT.

save-harmless clause. See INDEMNITY CLAUSE.

saving, *n.* An exception; a reservation.

saving clause. (17c) **1.** A statutory provision exempting from coverage something that would otherwise be included. ● A saving clause is generally used in a repealing act to preserve rights and claims that would otherwise be lost. **2.** SAVING-TO-SUITORS CLAUSE. **3.** SEVERABILITY CLAUSE. — Also termed *savings clause.*

savings account. A savings-bank depositor's account usu. bearing interest or containing conditions (such as advance notice) to the right of withdrawal.

savings-account trust. See *Totten trust* under TRUST.

savings-and-loan association. (1884) A financial institution — often organized and chartered like a bank — that primarily makes home-mortgage loans but also usu. maintains checking accounts and provides other banking services. — Often shortened to S & L. — Also termed *savings-and-loan bank*; *loan association*; *thrift institution*; *thrift.* Cf. BUILDING-AND-LOAN ASSOCIATION.

savings bank. See BANK.

savings-bank trust. See *Totten trust* under TRUST.

savings bond. See BOND (3).

savings clause. See SAVING CLAUSE.

savings note. See NOTE (1).

saving-to-suitors clause. *Maritime law.* In the federal statutory provision granting admiralty and maritime jurisdiction to the federal courts, a clause that preserves the option to file suit in a nonadmiralty court. 28 USCA § 1333(1). • The nonadmiralty court is typically either a state court or a law-side federal court. Under the reverse-*Erie* doctrine, the nonadmiralty court is required to apply the same law that the admiralty court would have used. — Also termed *saving clause.*

savor, *vb.* (16c) To partake of the character of or bear affinity to (something). • In traditional legal idiom, an interest arising from land is said to "savor of the realty." — Also spelled *savour.*

S.B. See *senate bill* under BILL (3).

SBA. *abbr.* SMALL BUSINESS ADMINISTRATION.

SBIC. *abbr.* SMALL- BUSINESS INVESTMENT COMPANY.

sc. *abbr.* SCILICET.

S.C. *abbr.* **1.** SUPREME COURT. **2.** Same case. • In former practice, when put between two citations, the abbreviation indicated that the same case was reported in both places. **3.** SENATUS CONSULTUM.

scab. (18c) A person who works under conditions contrary to a union contract; esp., a worker who crosses a union picket line to replace a union worker during a strike. — Also termed *strikebreaker.*; (in BrE) *black-leg labor.*

scale, *n.* **1.** A progression of degrees; esp., a range of wage rates. **2.** A wage according to a range of rates. **3.** An instrument for weighing. **4.** *Hist.* In the practice of the English Supreme Court of Judicature, the fee charged by a solicitor for a particular type of case. • Unless the court ordered otherwise, the *lower scale* applied to all causes and matters assigned by the Judicature Acts to the King's Bench, or the Probate, Divorce, and Admiralty divisions; to all actions for debt, contract, or tort; and to almost all causes and matters assigned by the acts to the Chancery division and in which the amount in controversy was less than £1,000. The *higher scale* applied in all other cases, and in actions falling under one of the lower-scale classes if the principal relief sought was injunctive.

scale order. See ORDER (8).

scale tolerance. The nominal variation of the mass or weight of the same goods on different scales.

scalper. **1.** A seller who buys something (esp. a ticket) at face value (or less) and then tries to resell it for a higher price. — Also termed *ticket speculator.* **2.** An investment adviser who buys a security before recommending it to clients. **3.** A market-maker who puts an excessive markup or markdown on a transaction.

scalping, *n.* **1.** The practice of selling something (esp. a ticket) at a price above face value once it becomes scarce (usu. just before a high-demand event begins). **2.** The purchase of a security by an investment adviser before the adviser recommends that a customer buy the same security. • This practice is usu. considered unethical because the customer's purchase will increase the security's price, thus enabling the investment adviser to sell at a profit. **3.** The excessive markup or markdown on a transaction by a market-maker. • This action violates National Association of Securities Dealers guidelines. — **scalp,** *vb.*

scandal. **1.** Disgraceful, shameful, or degrading acts or conduct. **2.** Defamatory reports or rumors; esp., slander. See SCANDALOUS MATTER.

scandalous matter. (17c) *Civil procedure.* A matter that is both grossly disgraceful (or defamatory) and irrelevant to the action or defense. • A federal court — upon a party's motion or on its own — can order a scandalous matter struck from a pleading. Fed. R. Civ. P. 12(f). Cf. IMPERTINENT MATTER.

scandalous subject matter. *Trademarks.* A word, phrase, symbol, or graphic depiction that the U.S. Patent and Trademark Office may refuse to register because it is shockingly offensive to social mores. • Although the Lanham Act uses the phrase "immoral, deceptive, or scandalous subject matter," courts have not distinguished "scandalous" from "immoral."

scarlet-letter punishment. See *shame sanction* under SANCTION.

scarlet-letter sentence. See *shame sanction* under SANCTION.

scatter-point analysis. (1993) A method for studying the effect that minority-population changes have on voting patterns, involving a plotting of the percentage of votes that candidates receive to determine whether voting percentages increase or decrease as the percentages of voters of a particular race increase or decrease.

schedule, *n.* (15c) A written list or inventory; esp., a statement that is attached to a document and that gives a detailed showing of the matters referred to in the document <Schedule B to the title policy lists the encumbrances on the property>. — **schedule,** *vb.* — **scheduled,** *adj.*

scheduled injury. See INJURY.

scheduled property. See PROPERTY.

scheme 1148

scheme. (16c) **1.** A systemic plan; a connected or orderly arrangement, esp. of related concepts <legislative scheme>. **2.** An artful plot or plan, usu. to deceive others <a scheme to defraud creditors>.

schism (siz-əm *or* skiz-əm). (14c) **1.** A breach or rupture; a division, esp. among members of a group, as of a union. **2.** A separation of beliefs and doctrines by persons of the same organized religion, religious denomination, or sect.

school, *n.* **1.** An institution of learning and education, esp. for children.

common school. See *public school.*

district school. A public school contained in and maintained by a school district. See SCHOOL DISTRICT.

private school. A school maintained by private individuals, religious organizations, or corporations, funded, at least in part, by fees or tuition, and open only to pupils selected and admitted based on religious affiliations or other particular qualifications.

public school. An elementary, middle, or high school established under state law, regulated by the local state authorities in the various political subdivisions, funded and maintained by public taxation, and open and free to all children of the particular district where the school is located. — Also termed *common school.*

2. The collective body of students under instruction in an institution of learning. **3.** A group of people adhering to the same philosophy or system of beliefs.

school board. An administrative body, made up of a number of directors or trustees, responsible for overseeing public schools within a city, county, or district. Cf. BOARD OF EDUCATION.

school bond. See BOND (3).

school district. A political subdivision of a state, created by the legislature and invested with local powers of self-government, to build, maintain, fund, and support the public schools within its territory and to otherwise assist the state in administering its educational responsibilities.

consolidated school district. A public-school district in which two or more existing schools have consolidated into a single district.

school land. See LAND.

Schumer box. In a credit-card agreement, a table that summarizes all the costs for which the cardholder is liable, so that the cardholder can more easily compare credit-card agreements. • The term derives from the name of Senator Charles Schumer, who proposed the disclosure requirements. The box must contain the information listed in 15 USCA § 1637(c)(1)(A)–(B). — Also termed *Schumer's box.*

Science and Technology Directorate. The division of the Department of Homeland Security responsible for coordinating research and development, including preparing for and responding to terrorist threats involving weapons of mass destruction. • The Directorate also works with the Chemical, Biological, Radiological, and Nuclear Countermeasures Program and the Environmental Measurements Lab in the Department of Energy, the National BW (biological warfare) Defense Analysis Center in the Department of Defense, and the Plum Island Animal Disease Center — Abbr. S&T.

science of legislation. See LAW REFORM.

scienter (sɪ-en-tər *or* see-), *n.* [Latin "knowingly"] (1824) **1.** A degree of knowledge that makes a person legally responsible for the consequences of his or her act or omission; the fact of an act's having been done knowingly, esp. as a ground for civil damages or criminal punishment. See KNOWLEDGE; MENS REA. **2.** A mental state consisting in an intent to deceive, manipulate, or defraud. • In this sense, the term is used most often in the context of securities fraud. The Supreme Court has held that to establish a claim for damages under Rule 10b-5, a plaintiff must prove that the defendant acted with scienter. *Ernst & Ernst v. Hochfelder,* 425 U.S. 185, 96 S.Ct. 1375 (1976).

scienter action. A lawsuit in which the plaintiff must prove that the defendant acted knowingly or knew of the danger — e.g., at common law an action for damage caused by a domestic animal. See SCIENTER.

scientific creationism. See CREATIONISM.

scientific evidence. See EVIDENCE.

scientific knowledge. See KNOWLEDGE.

scientific method. An analytical technique by which a hypothesis is formulated and then systematically tested through observation and experimentation.

sci. fa. abbr. SCIRE FACIAS.

scil. abbr. SCILICET.

scilicet (sil-ə-set *or* -sit). [fr. Latin *scire licet* "that you may know"] (14c) That is to say; namely; VIDELICET. • Like *videlicet,* this word is used in pleadings and other instruments to introduce a more particular statement of matters previously mentioned in general terms. It has never been quite as common, however, as *videlicet.* — Abbr. sc.; scil.; (erroneously) ss.

SCIN. *abbr.* See *self-canceling installment note* under NOTE (1).

scintilla (sin-til-ə). (13c) A spark or trace <the standard is that there must be more than a scintilla of evidence>. Pl. **scintillas** (sin-til-əz).

scintilla-of-evidence rule. (1896) A common-law doctrine holding that if even the slightest amount of relevant evidence exists on an issue, then a motion for summary judgment or for directed verdict cannot be granted and the issue must go to the jury. • Federal courts do not follow this rule, but some states apply it. — Also termed *scintilla rule.*

scire facias (sɪ-ree **fay**-shee-əs). [Law Latin "you are to make known, show cause"] (15c) A writ requiring the person against whom it is issued to appear and show cause why some matter of record should not be annulled or vacated, or why a dormant judgment against that person should not be revived. — Abbr. *sci. fa.*

   amicable scire facias to revive a judgment. A written agreement in which a person against whom a revival of an action is sought agrees to the entry of an adverse judgment.

   scire facias ad audiendum errores (sɪ-ree **fay**-shee-əs ad aw-dee-**en**-dəm e-**ror**-eez). [Law Latin "that you cause to know to hear errors"] *Hist.* A common-law writ allowing a party who had assigned error to compel the opposing party to plead. • It was abolished in 1875.

   scire facias ad disprobandum debitum (sɪ-ree **fay**-shee-əs ad dis-proh-**ban**-dəm **deb**-ə-təm). [Law Latin "that you cause to know to disprove the debt"] *Hist.* A writ allowing a defendant in a foreign attachment against the plaintiff to disprove or avoid the debt recovered by the plaintiff, within a year and a day from the time of payment.

   scire facias ad rehabendam terram (sɪ-ree **fay**-shee-əs ad re-hə-**ben**-dəm **ter**-əm), *n.* [Law Latin "that you cause to know to recover the land"] *Hist.* A writ allowing a judgment debtor to recover lands taken in execution after the debtor has satisfied the judgment.

   scire facias quare restitutionem non (sɪ-ree **fay**-shee-əs **kwair**-ee res-tə-t[y]oo-shee-**oh**-nəm non), *n.* [Law Latin "that you cause to know why (there is not) restitution"] *Hist.* A writ for restitution after an execution on a judgment is levied but not paid and the judgment is later reversed on appeal.

   scire facias sur mortgage (sɪ-ree **fay**-shee-əs sər **mor**-gij), *n.* [Law Latin "that you cause to know on mortgage"] *Hist.* A writ ordering a defaulting mortgagor to show cause why the mortgage should not be foreclosed and the property sold in execution.

   scire facias sur municipal claim (sɪ-ree **fay**-shee-əs sər myoo-**nis**-ə-pəl **klaym**), *n.* [Law Latin "that you cause to know on municipal claim"] *Hist.* A writ compelling the payment of a municipal claim out of the property to which a municipal lien is attached.

scire feci (sɪ-ree **fee**-sɪ). [Latin "I have caused to know"] *Hist.* The sheriff's return to a writ of scire facias, indicating that notice was given to the parties against whom the writ was issued.

***scire fieri* inquiry** (sɪ-ree **fɪ**-ə-rɪ), *n.* [Law Latin] *Hist.* A writ to ascertain the location of a testator's property from an executor, when the sheriff returned nulla bona to a writ of execution *fieri facias de bonis testatoris.* See FIERI FACIAS.

scofflaw (**skof**-law). (1924) **1.** A person who treats the law with contempt; esp., one who avoids various laws that are not easily enforced <some scofflaws carry mannequins in their cars in order to drive in the carpool lane>. **2.** *Hist.* A person who consumes illegally made or obtained alcoholic beverages. • This was the original meaning.

scold, *n. Hist.* A person who regularly breaks the peace by scolding people, increasing discord, and generally being a public nuisance to the neighborhood. • This behavior was formerly punishable in various ways, including having an iron bridle fitted to the person's mouth. — Also termed *common scold; objurgatrix.*

scope note. (1903) In a digest, a précis appearing after a title and showing concisely what subject matter is included and what is excluded.

scope of a patent. *Patents.* The limits of a patent's protection, as defined by the allowed claims.

scope of authority. (1805) *Agency.* The range of reasonable power that an agent has been delegated or might foreseeably be delegated in carrying out the principal's business. See SCOPE OF EMPLOYMENT; RESPONDEAT SUPERIOR.

scope of business. The range of activities that are reasonably necessary to operate a commercial venture successfully, as determined by the nature of the venture and the activities of others engaged in the same occupation in the same area.

scope of employment. (1836) The range of reasonable and foreseeable activities that an employee engages in while carrying out the employer's business; the field of action in which a servant is authorized to act in the master–servant relationship. See RESPONDEAT SUPERIOR. Cf. COURSE OF EMPLOYMENT; ZONE OF EMPLOYMENT.

scope-of-work clause. A contractual provision that highlights in summary fashion what work is to be performed under the contract.

scorched-earth defense. *Corporations.* An antitakeover tactic by which a target corporation sells its most valuable assets or divisions in order to reduce its value after acquisition and thus try to defeat a hostile bidder's tender offer. Cf. CROWN-JEWEL DEFENSE; PAC-MAN DEFENSE.

S corporation. See CORPORATION.

scot. *Hist.* A payment; esp., a customary tax.

scot and lot. *Hist.* **1.** The customary payment of a share of taxes based on one's ability. **2.** A municipal tax on the right to vote.

Scotch marriage. See MARRIAGE (1).

Scotch verdict. See NOT PROVEN.

SCPA. *abbr.* SEMICONDUCTOR CHIP PROTECTION ACT.

scrambling possession. See POSSESSION.

scrap value. See *salvage value* under VALUE (2).

scratch-and-dent loan. See LOAN.

scratching the ticket. A party member's rejection of a candidate on a regular party ticket by canceling the candidate's name or by voting for one or more nominees of the opposing political party.

scrawl. See SCROLL (3).

screening committee. See COMMITTEE.

screening grand jury. See GRAND JURY.

screening mechanism. See ETHICAL WALL.

screen-scraping, *n. Intellectual property.* The practice of extracting data directly from one website and displaying it on another website. ● The source website's database is not used — only the display. Screen-scraping may infringe the extracted website-owner's copyright in the contents. — **screen-scrape,** *vb.*

scribe. See SECRETARY (3).

Scribes. See AMERICAN SOCIETY OF WRITERS ON LEGAL SUBJECTS.

scrip.(18c) **1.** A document that entitles the holder to receive something of value. See LAND SCRIP. **2.** Money, esp. paper money, that is issued for temporary use.

Internet scrip. **1.** Value that may be exchanged over the Internet but may not be exchanged for money. ● Internet scrip is analogous to coupons or bonus points that can be exchanged by a consumer for goods or services but that have no cash value. **2.** See *e-money* under MONEY. — Also termed *online scrip.*

on-line scrip. See *Internet scrip.*

scrip dividend. See DIVIDEND.

script. (14c) **1.** An original or principal writing. **2.** Handwriting.

scrivener (skriv-[ə]-nər). (14c) A writer; esp., a professional drafter of contracts or other documents.

money scrivener. See MONEY SCRIVENER.

scrivener's error. See *clerical error* under ERROR (2).

scrivener's exception. (1978) An exemption from the attorney–client privilege whereby the privilege does not attach if the attorney is retained solely to perform a ministerial task for the client, such as preparing a statutory-form deed.

scroll, *n.* (15c) **1.** A roll of paper, esp. one containing a writing; a list. **2.** A draft or outline to be completed at a later time. **3.** A written mark; esp., a character affixed to a signature in place of a seal. — Also termed (in sense 3) *scrawl.*

S.Ct. *abbr.* **1.** SUPREME COURT. **2.** Supreme Court Reporter.

scutage (**skyoo**-tij), *n.* [fr. Latin *scutum* "a shield"] *Hist.* **1.** A monetary payment levied by the king on barons as a substitute for some or all of the knights to be supplied to the king by each baron. ● This payment seems to date from the 12th century, Henry II (1154–1189) having levied five scutages in the first 11 years of his reign. **2.** A fee paid by a tenant-in-chief by knight-service in lieu of serving in a war. **3.** A tax on a knight's estate to help furnish the army. — Also termed *escuage.*

S.D. *abbr.* Southern District, in reference to U.S. judicial districts.

s/d b/l. *abbr.* Sight draft with bill of lading attached. See *sight draft* under DRAFT.

S.E. *abbr.* SOUTH EASTERN REPORTER.

sea. **1.** The ocean <on the sea>. **2.** A large land-locked part of the ocean; a large body of salt water smaller than a regular ocean <the Mediterranean Sea>. **3.** The ocean swell <a rough sea>. **4.** An extremely large or extended quantity <a sea of documents>.

free seas. See *high seas.*

high seas. The seas or oceans beyond the jurisdiction of any country. ● Under traditional international law, the high seas began 3 miles from the coast; today the distance is generally accepted as 12 miles. Under the 1982 U.N. Convention on the Law of the Sea, coastal shores now have a 200-mile exclusive economic zone. — Also termed *free seas; open seas; main sea.*

main sea. Archaic. The open ocean; high seas.

navigable sea. See NAVIGABLE SEA.

open seas. See *high seas.*

territorial sea. See *territorial waters* under WATER.

seabed. The sea floor; the ground underlying the ocean, over which nations may assert sovereignty, esp. if underlying their territorial waters.

sea brief. See SEA LETTER.

seagoing vessel. See VESSEL.

seal, *n.* (13c) **1.** A fastening that must be broken before access can be obtained; esp., a device or substance that joins two things, usu. making the seam impervious. — Also termed *common-law seal.* **2.** A piece of wax, a wafer, or some other substance affixed to the paper or other material on which a promise, release, or conveyance is written, together with a recital or expression of intention by which the promisor, releasor, or grantor manifests that a piece of wax, wafer, or other substance is a seal. • The purpose of a seal is to secure or prove authenticity. **3.** A design embossed or stamped on paper to authenticate, confirm, or attest; an impression or sign that has legal consequence when applied to an instrument.

corporate seal. (18c) A seal adopted by a corporation for executing and authenticating its corporate and legal instruments.

great seal. **1.** The official seal of the United States, of which the Secretary of State is the custodian. — Also termed *seal of the United States.* **2.** The official seal of a particular state. — Also termed *seal of the state; state seal.* **3.** The official seal of Great Britain, of which the Lord Chancellor is the custodian.

notary seal. See NOTARY SEAL.

private seal. (16c) A corporate or individual seal, as distinguished from a public seal.

public seal. (16c) A seal used to certify documents belonging to a public authority or government bureau.

quarter seal. A seal (originally a quarter section of the great seal) maintained in the Scotch chancery to be used on particular grants from the Crown. See *great seal* (3).

seal of the state. See *great seal* (2).

seal of the United States. See *great seal* (1).

state seal. See *great seal* (2).

wafer seal. A plastic or paper disk, usu. red or gold, affixed to a legal document as a substitute for a wax seal. • Wafers are more common in the U.K. than in the U.S. — Sometimes shortened to *wafer.*

seal, *vb.* (14c) **1.** To authenticate or execute (a document) by use of a seal. **2.** To close (an envelope, etc.) tightly; to prevent access to (a document, record, etc.).

sealed and delivered. See SIGNED, SEALED, AND DELIVERED.

sea lane. *Int'l & maritime law.* A designated course or regularly used route for ships, esp. in restricted waters such as harbors and straits. • Although sea lanes have obvious safety advantages, they were long resisted by sea captains, who saw them as a threat to their freedom to navigate.

sea law. See MARITIME LAW.

sealed bid. See BID (2).

sealed-container rule. (1961) *Products liability.* The principle that a seller is not liable for a defective product if the seller receives the product from the manufacturer and sells it without knowing of the defect or having a reasonable opportunity to inspect the product.

sealed contract. See *contract under seal* under CONTRACT.

sealed instrument. (17c) At common law and under some statutes, an instrument to which the bound party has affixed a personal seal, usu. recognized as providing indisputable evidence of the validity of the underlying obligations. • The common-law distinction between sealed and unsealed instruments do not apply to contracts for the sale of goods or negotiable instruments. UCC § 2-203. See *contract under seal* under CONTRACT.

sealed-record statute. See CONFIDENTIALITY STATUTE.

sealed testament. See *mystic will* under WILL.

sealed verdict. See VERDICT.

sealed will. See *mystic will* under WILL.

sea letter. *Hist.* A manifest issued during a war by authorities of a port where a neutral vessel is fitted, certifying the vessel's nationality, specifying the nature of and destination of the vessel's cargo, and allowing the vessel to sail under the neutral flag of its owner. • The last sea letter was issued at the Port of New York in 1806, and the use of sea letters was discontinued by proclamation of President James Madison. — Also spelled *sea-letter.* — Also termed *sea brief; sea pass; passport.*

sealing of records. (1953) The act or practice of officially preventing access to particular (esp. juvenile-criminal) records, in the absence of a court order. Cf. EXPUNGEMENT OF RECORD.

seal of the state. See *great seal* (2) under SEAL.

seal of the United States. See *great seal* (1) under SEAL.

seaman. *Maritime law.* Under the Jones Act and the Longshore and Harbor Workers' Compensation Act, a person who is attached to a navigating vessel as an employee below the rank of officer and contributes to the function of the vessel or the accomplishment of its mission. • Seamen's injuries are covered under the Jones Act and the general maritime law. — Also termed *crew member; mariner; member of a crew.* See JONES ACT. Cf. STEVEDORE.

able-bodied seaman. An experienced seaman who is qualified for all seaman's duties and certified by an inspecting authority. — Abbr. AB; ABS. — Also termed *able seaman; bluewater seaman.*

merchant seaman. A sailor employed by a private vessel, as distinguished from one employed in public or military service.

ordinary seaman. A seaman who has some experience but who is not proficient enough to be classified as an able-bodied seaman. — Abbr. OS; OD.

seaman's will. See *soldier's will* under WILL.

sea pass. See SEA LETTER.

search, *n.* (14c) **1.** *Criminal procedure.* An examination of a person's body, property, or other area that the person would reasonably be expected to consider as private, conducted by a law-enforcement officer for the purpose of finding evidence of a crime. • Because the Fourth Amendment prohibits unreasonable searches (as well as seizures), a search cannot ordinarily be conducted without probable cause.

administrative search. (1963) A search of public or commercial premises carried out by a regulatory authority to enforce compliance with health, safety, or security regulations. • The probable cause required for an administrative search is less stringent than that required for a search incident to a criminal investigation. — Also termed *regulatory search*; *inspection search.*

border search. (1922) **1.** A search conducted at the border of a country, esp. at a checkpoint, to exclude illegal aliens and contraband. **2.** Loosely, a search conducted near the border of a country. • Generally, searches near the U.S. border are treated no differently from those conducted elsewhere in the country.

checkpoint search. (1973) **1.** A search anywhere on a military installation. **2.** A search in which police officers set up roadblocks and stop motorists to ascertain whether the drivers are intoxicated.

Chimel search. See *protective search.*

consent search. (1965) A search conducted after a person with the authority to do so voluntarily waives Fourth Amendment rights. • The government has the burden to show that the consent was given freely — not under duress. *Bumper v. North Carolina*, 391 U.S. 543, 548–49, 88 S.Ct. 1788, 1792 (1968). — Also termed *consensual search.*

constructive search. A subpoena of a corporation's records.

emergency search. (1971) A warrantless search conducted by a police officer who has probable cause and reasonably believes that, because of a need to protect life or property, there is not enough time to obtain a warrant. See EMERGENCY DOCTRINE (3).

exigent search (eks-ə-jənt). (1974) A warrantless search carried out under exigent circumstances, such as an imminent danger to human life or a risk of the destruction of evidence. See *exigent circumstances* under CIRCUMSTANCE.

illegal search. See *unreasonable search.*

inventory search. (1966) A complete search of an arrestee's person before that person is booked into jail. • All possessions found are typically held in police custody.

no-knock search. (1970) A search of property by the police without knocking and announcing their presence and purpose before entry. • A no-knock search warrant may be issued under limited circumstances, as when a prior announcement would probably lead to the destruction of the objects searched for, or would endanger the safety of the police or another person.

private search. A search conducted by a private person rather than by a law-enforcement officer. • Items found during a private search are generally admissible in evidence if the person conducting the search was not acting at the direction of a law-enforcement officer.

protective search. (1967) A search of a detained suspect and the area within the suspect's immediate control, conducted to protect the arresting officer's safety (as from a concealed weapon) and often to preserve evidence. • A protective search can be conducted without a warrant. *Chimel v. California*, 395 U.S. 752, 89 S.Ct. 2034 (1969). — Also termed *search incident to arrest*; *Chimel search* (shə-**mel**).

regulatory search. See *administrative search.*

search incident to arrest. See *protective search.*

sector search. See *zone search.*

shakedown search. (1952) A usu. unannounced and warrantless search for illicit or contraband material (such as weapons or drugs) in a prisoner's cell. — Often shortened to *shakedown.*

strip search. (1955) A search of a person conducted after that person's clothes have been removed, the purpose usu. being to find any contraband the person might be hiding.

unreasonable search. (18c) A search conducted without probable cause or other considerations that would make it legally permissible. — Also termed *illegal search.*

voluntary search. (1936) A search in which no duress or coercion was applied to obtain the defendant's consent. See *consent search.*

warranted search. (1968) A search conducted under authority of a search warrant.

warrantless search. (1950) A search conducted without obtaining a proper warrant. • Warrantless searches are permissible under exigent circumstances or when conducted incident to an arrest. See *exigent circumstances* under CIRCUMSTANCE; *protective search*.

zone search. A search of a crime scene (such as the scene of a fire or explosion) by dividing it up into specific sectors. — Also termed *sector search*.

2. An examination of public documents or records for information; esp., TITLE SEARCH. **3.** *Int'l law.* The wartime process of boarding and examining the contents of a merchant vessel for contraband. ● A number of treaties regulate the manner in which the search must be conducted. See RIGHT OF SEARCH.

search-and-seizure warrant. See SEARCH WARRANT.

search book. (1912) A lawbook that contains no statements of the law but instead consists of lists or tables of cases, statutes, and the like, used simply to help a researcher find the law. ● Most indexes, other than index-digests, are search books.

search committee. See COMMITTEE.

search incident to arrest. See *protective search* under SEARCH.

search of patentability. See PATENTABILITY SEARCH.

search report. *Patents.* A list of prior-art documents cited by the patent examiner during the patent application's preliminary examination.

search warrant. (18c) *Criminal law.* A judge's written order authorizing a law-enforcement officer to conduct a search of a specified place and to seize evidence. See Fed. R. Crim. P. 41. — Also termed *search-and-seizure warrant.* See WARRANT (1).

anticipatory search warrant. (1912) A search warrant based on an affidavit showing probable cause that evidence of a certain crime (such as illegal drugs) will be located at a specific place in the future.

blanket search warrant. (1921) **1.** A single search warrant that authorizes the search of more than one area. **2.** An unconstitutional warrant that authorizes the seizure of everything found at a given location, without specifying which items may be seized.

covert-entry search warrant. A warrant authorizing law-enforcement officers to clandestinely enter private premises in the absence of the owner or occupant without prior notice, and to search the premises and collect intangible evidence, esp. photographs and eyewitness information. ● Although previously used in federal criminal investigations, these types of warrants were first given express statutory authority by the USA Patriot Act. 18 USCA § 3103a. Information gathered while executing a sneak-and-peek warrant can later be used to support a search warrant under which physical evidence can be

seized. — Also termed *sneak-and-peek search warrant*; *surreptitious-entry search warrant*.

no-knock search warrant. (1972) A search warrant that authorizes the police to enter premises without knocking and announcing their presence and purpose before entry because a prior announcement would lead to the destruction of the objects searched for or would endanger the safety of the police or another person. Cf. KNOCK-AND-ANNOUNCE RULE.

sneak-and-peek search warrant. See *covert-entry search warrant*

surreptitious-entry search warrant. See *covert-entry search warrant*

search-warrant affidavit. See AFFIDAVIT.

sea rover. 1. A person who roves the sea for plunder; a pirate. **2.** A pirate vessel.

***Sears–Compco* doctrine.** The principle that Congress, by passing copyright, trademark, and patent laws, has preempted some state-law protection of information that is not protected by those statutes. *Sears, Roebuck & Co. v. Stiffel Co.*, 376 U.S. 225, 84 S.Ct. 784 (1964); *Compco Corp. v. Day-Brite Lighting, Inc.*, 376 U.S. 234, 84 S.Ct. 779 (1964). ● The doctrine reflects a congressional policy decision that public access to information outweighs private economic incentives to collect and disseminate it. It limits how far states may protect against misappropriation.

seasonable, *adj.* (15c) Within the time agreed on; within a reasonable time <seasonable performance of the contract>.

seasonal employment. See EMPLOYMENT.

seat, *n.* **1.** Membership and privileges in an organization; esp., membership on a securities or commodities exchange <her seat at the exchange dates back to 1998>. **2.** The center of some activity <the seat of government>.

seated land. See LAND.

seat of government. The nation's capital, a state capital, a county seat, or other location where the principal offices of the national, state, and local governments are located.

seaworthy, *adj.* (Of a vessel) properly equipped and sufficiently strong and tight to resist the perils reasonably incident to the voyage for which the vessel is insured. ● An implied condition of marine-insurance policies, unless otherwise stated, is that the vessel will be seaworthy. — **seaworthiness,** *n.*

seaworthy vessel. See VESSEL.

sec. *abbr.* **1.** (all cap.) SECURITIES AND EXCHANGE COMMISSION. **2.** Section. See SECTION (1).

secession. The process or act of withdrawing, esp. from a religious or political association <the seces-

sion from the established church> <the secession of 11 states at the time of the Civil War>.

second, *n. Parliamentary law.* **1.** A statement by a member other than a motion's maker that the member also wants the assembly to consider the motion <Is there a second to the motion?>. **2.** *Criminal law.* A person who directs, assists, or supports another engaged in a duel. See DUEL (2). — **second,** *vb.*

Second Amendment. The constitutional amendment, ratified with the Bill of Rights in 1791, guaranteeing the right to keep and bear arms as necessary for securing freedom through a well-regulated militia. See RIGHT TO BEAR ARMS.

secondary, *adj.* (14c) (Of a position, status, use, etc.) subordinate or subsequent.

secondary abuse. See ABUSE.

secondary activity. *Labor law.* A union's picketing or boycotting of a secondary or neutral party, with the goal of placing economic pressure on that party so that it will stop doing business with the employer that is the primary subject of the labor dispute. ● Secondary activities are forbidden by the Labor–Management Relations Act. 29 USCA § 158(b)(4). See *secondary boycott* under BOYCOTT; *secondary picketing* under PICKETING. Cf. PRIMARY ACTIVITY.

secondary affinity. See AFFINITY.

secondary amendment. See AMENDMENT (3).

secondary assumption of risk. See ASSUMPTION OF THE RISK.

secondary authority. See AUTHORITY (4).

secondary beneficiary. See *contingent beneficiary* (2) under BENEFICIARY.

secondary boycott. See BOYCOTT.

secondary consideration. See SECONDARY FACTOR.

secondary conveyance. See CONVEYANCE.

secondary creditor. See CREDITOR.

secondary devise. See *alternative devise* under DEVISE.

secondary distribution. See DISTRIBUTION.

secondary easement. See EASEMENT.

secondary-effects test. A court's analysis of a regulation affecting free-speech interests to determine whether it is actually intended to diminish or eliminate an indirect harm flowing from the regulated expression. ● The test is used to distinguish content-specific regulation from content-neutral regulation. A regulation that is facially content-specific may be treated as content-neutral if its purpose is to diminish or eliminate a secondary effect of the speech, such as a zoning regulation for adult theaters when it is intended to limit crime. The test was first enunciated in *City*

of Renton v. Playtime Theatres, Inc., 475 U.S. 41, 106 S.Ct. 925 (1986).

secondary enforcement. See *secondary right* under RIGHT.

secondary evidence. See EVIDENCE.

secondary factor. (*usu. pl.*) *Patents.* Objective evidence that courts consider in determining a patent claim's nonobviousness. ● Secondary factors include "commercial success, long-felt but unsolved need, failure of others, and unexpected results." *Graham v. John Deere Co.*, 383 U.S. 1, 17–18 (1966). — Also termed *secondary consideration.*

secondary insured. See *additional insured* under INSURED.

secondary insurer. See *excess insurer* under INSURER.

secondary invention. *Patents.* An invention that uses or incorporates established elements or combinations to achieve a new and useful result.

secondary lender. A wholesale mortgage buyer who purchases first mortgages from banks and savings-and-loan associations, enabling them to restock their money supply and loan more money.

secondary liability. See LIABILITY.

secondary-line competition. See *vertical competition* under COMPETITION.

secondary-line injury. *Antitrust.* Under the price-discrimination provisions of the Robinson-Patman Act, the act of hindering or seeking to hinder competition among a seller's customers by selling substantially the same products at favorable prices to one customer, or a select group of customers, to the detriment of others. 15 USCA § 13(a). ● A secondary-line injury, which refers to competition among the seller's customers, is distinguishable from a primary-line injury, which refers to the anticompetitive effects that predatory pricing has on the direct competitors of the seller. Cf. PRIMARY-LINE INJURY.

secondary market. See MARKET.

secondary meaning. *Intellectual property.* A special sense that a trademark or tradename for a business, goods, or services has acquired even though the trademark or tradename was originally merely descriptive and therefore not protectable. ● The term does not refer to a subordinate or rare meaning, but rather to a later meaning that has been added to the original one borne by the mark or name and that has now become in the market its usual and primary meaning. — Also termed *special meaning; trade meaning.*

secondary mortgage market. See MORTGAGE MARKET.

secondary motion. See MOTION (2).

secondary obligation. See OBLIGATION.

secondary offering. See OFFERING.

secondary party. *Commercial law.* **1.** A party not primarily liable under an instrument, such as a guarantor. **2.** The drawer or indorser of a negotiable instrument.

secondary picketing. See PICKETING.

secondary register. See SUPPLEMENTAL REGISTER.

secondary reserve ratio. See RESERVE RATIO.

secondary right. See RIGHT.

secondary strike. See STRIKE.

secondary term. *Oil & gas.* The term of an oil-and-gas lease after production has been established, typically lasting "as long thereafter as oil and gas is produced from the premises." See HABENDUM CLAUSE; PRIMARY TERM.

secondary trading. See TRADING.

secondary use. See *shifting use* under USE (4).

second chair, *n.* (1968) A lawyer who helps the lead attorney in court, usu. by examining some of the witnesses, arguing some of the points of law, and handling parts of the voir dire, opening statement, and closing argument <the young associate was second chair for the fraud case>. — **second-chair,** *vb.*

second-collision doctrine. See CRASHWORTHINESS DOCTRINE.

second cousin. See COUSIN.

second-degree amendment. See *secondary amendment* under AMENDMENT (3).

second-degree manslaughter. See *involuntary manslaughter* under MANSLAUGHTER.

second-degree murder. See MURDER.

second-degree principal. See *principal in the second degree* under PRINCIPAL (2).

second deliverance. See DELIVERANCE.

second delivery. See DELIVERY.

second distress. See DISTRESS.

secondhand evidence. See HEARSAY.

second-impact doctrine. See CRASHWORTHINESS DOCTRINE.

second lien. See LIEN.

second-look doctrine. (1962) **1.** WAIT-AND-SEE PRINCIPLE. **2.** An approach that courts use to monitor the continuing effectiveness or validity of an earlier order. ● For example, a family court may reconsider a waiver of alimony, and a federal court may reconsider a law that Congress has passed a second time after the first law was struck down as unconstitutional.

second mortgage. See MORTGAGE.

second offense. See OFFENSE (1).

second-parent adoption. See ADOPTION.

second-permittee doctrine. *Insurance.* The principle that, when a third person is allowed to use an insured's car by permission granted by someone else to whom the insured gave permission to use the car, the third person's use of the car will be a permissive use, under the insured's automobile-liability-insurance policy, as long as that use falls within the scope of the permission originally given by the insured.

seconds, *n.* *Commercial law.* Goods that are defective or nonconforming because they do not meet a recognized standard.

second-step freezeout. See FREEZEOUT.

second surcharge. See SURCHARGE.

second-tier patent. See UTILITY MODEL.

second user. See JUNIOR USER.

secrecy. The state or quality of being concealed, esp. from those who would be affected by the concealment; hidden.

secret, *n.* (14c) **1.** Something that is kept from the knowledge of others or shared only with those concerned. See STATE SECRET; TRADE SECRET. **2.** Information that cannot be disclosed without a breach of trust; specif., information that is acquired in the attorney–client relationship and that either (1) the client has requested be kept private or (2) the attorney believes would be embarrassing or likely to be detrimental to the client if disclosed. ● Under the ABA Code of Professional Responsibility, a lawyer usu. cannot reveal a client's secret unless the client consents after full disclosure. DR 4–101. Cf. CONFIDENCE (3).

secretary. 1. An administrative assistant. **2.** A corporate officer in charge of official correspondence, minutes of board meetings, and records of stock ownership and transfer. — Also termed *clerk of the corporation.* **3.** *Parliamentary law.* An officer charged with recording a deliberative assembly's proceedings. — Also termed *clerk; recorder; recording secretary; recording officer; scribe.*

corresponding secretary. An officer in charge of an organization's correspondence, usu. including notices to members.

financial secretary. **1.** An officer in charge of billing, collecting, and accounting for dues from the members. **2.** TREASURER.

Secretary General. The chief administrative officer of the United Nations, nominated by the Security Council and elected by the General Assembly.

Secretary of Agriculture. The member of the President's cabinet who heads the U.S. Department of Agriculture.

Secretary of Commerce. The member of the President's cabinet who heads the U.S. Department of Commerce.

Secretary of Defense. The member of the President's cabinet who heads the U.S. Department of Defense.

Secretary of Education. The member of the President's cabinet who heads the U.S. Department of Education.

secretary of embassy. A diplomatic officer appointed as secretary or assistant, usu. to an ambassador or minister plenipotentiary.

Secretary of Energy. The member of the President's cabinet who heads the U.S. Department of Energy.

Secretary of Health and Human Services. The member of the President's cabinet who heads the U.S. Department of Health and Human Services.

Secretary of Homeland Security. The member of the President's cabinet who heads the U.S. Department of Homeland Security.

Secretary of Housing and Urban Development. The member of the President's cabinet who heads the U.S. Department of Housing and Urban Development.

Secretary of Labor. The member of the President's cabinet who heads the U.S. Department of Labor.

secretary of legation. An officer employed to attend a foreign mission and perform certain clerical duties.

Secretary of State. (18c) **1.** The member of the President's cabinet who heads the U.S. Department of State. ● The Secretary is the first-ranking member of the cabinet and is also a member of the National Security Council. He or she is fourth in line of succession to the presidency after the Vice President, the Speaker of the House, and the President pro tempore of the Senate. **2.** A state government official who is responsible for the licensing and incorporation of businesses, the administration of elections, and other formal duties. ● The secretary of state is elected in some states and appointed in others.

Secretary of the Interior. The member of the President's cabinet who heads the U.S. Department of the Interior.

Secretary of the Treasury. The member of the President's cabinet who heads the U.S. Department of the Treasury.

Secretary of Transportation. The member of the President's cabinet who heads the U.S. Department of Transportation.

Secretary of Veterans Affairs. The member of the President's cabinet who heads the U.S. Department of Veterans Affairs.

secret ballot. See BALLOT (2).

secret detainee. See DETAINEE.

secret detention. See DETENTION.

secret diplomacy. See DIPLOMACY.

secrete (si-**kreet**), *vb.* (17c) To conceal or secretly transfer (property, etc.), esp. to hinder or prevent officials or creditors from finding it.

secret equity. See *latent equity* under EQUITY.

secret evidence. See EVIDENCE.

secretion of assets. The hiding of property, usu. for the purpose of defrauding an adversary in litigation or a creditor.

secret lien. See LIEN.

secret partner. See PARTNER.

Secret Service. See UNITED STATES SECRET SERVICE.

secret session. See *executive session* under SESSION (1).

secret testament. See *mystic will* under WILL.

secret trust. See TRUST.

secret will. See *mystic will* under WILL.

sectarian, *adj.* Of or relating to a particular religious sect <sectarian college>.

section. (16c) **1.** A distinct part or division of a writing, esp. a legal instrument. — Abbr. §; sec.; s. **2.** *Real estate.* A piece of land containing 640 acres, or one square mile. ● Traditionally, public lands in the United States were divided into 640-acre squares, each one called a "section." — Also termed *section of land.*

half section. A piece of land containing 320 acres, laid off either by a north-and-south or by an east-and-west line; half a section of land.

quarter section. A piece of land containing 160 acres, laid off by a north-south or east-west line; one quarter of a section of land, formerly the amount usu. granted to a homesteader. — Often shortened to *quarter.*

Section 8 affidavit. See DECLARATION OF USE.

Section 8 and 15 affidavit. See COMBINED § 8 AND § 15 AFFIDAVIT.

Section 8 and 15 declaration. See COMBINED § 8 AND § 15 AFFIDAVIT.

Section 8 declaration. See DECLARATION OF USE.

Section 8(f) agreement. *Labor law.* A labor contract that is negotiated between an employer in the construction business and a union that cannot demonstrate that it represents a majority of the employees at the time the contract is executed. 29 USCA § 158(f). ● This is an exception to the general rule that an employer need only negotiate with a union that can demonstrate majority status. It was enacted in part because of the nature of the construction industry, in which the employers may have several different jobs in different parts of the country, the jobs are typically completed in a relatively short time, and the workforce is often transient. Since the workforce often does not have sufficient ties to a particular employer to petition for a certification election, section 8(f) agreements provide a certain level of protection in recognition of that fact. But section 8(f) agreements are not equivalent to collective-bargaining agreements. For example, the employer can legally repudiate the agreement at any time, and the employees may not legally picket to enforce the agreement. The main protection such an agreement provides is a monetary obligation, which can be enforced, if necessary, in federal court. And if the union achieves majority status, the section 8(f) agreement will essentially become a fully enforceable collective-bargaining agreement.

Section 15 affidavit. See DECLARATION OF INCONTESTABILITY.

Section 15 declaration. See DECLARATION OF INCONTESTABILITY.

Section 43(a) action. *Trademarks.* A private cause of action codified in the Lanham Trademark Act and covering a broad spectrum of deceptive trade practices, including passing off, false advertising, trade-dress infringement, trademark dilution, and cyperpiracy. 15 USCA § 1125(a).

Section 101 rejection. See REJECTION.

Section 102 rejection. See REJECTION.

Section 103 rejection. See REJECTION.

Section 112 rejection. See *vague-and-indefinite rejection* under REJECTION.

section of land. See SECTION (2).

sector search. See *zone search* under SEARCH.

secular, *adj.* Worldly, as distinguished from spiritual <secular business>.

secular clergy. 1. Clergy who have no particular religious affiliation or do not belong to a particular religious denomination. **2.** Clergy who live in their parishes and minister there, as contrasted with regular clergy who live in monasteries.

secular trust. See TRUST (3).

secured, *adj.* (1875) **1.** (Of a debt or obligation) supported or backed by security or collateral. **2.** (Of a creditor) protected by a pledge, mortgage, or other encumbrance of property that helps ensure financial soundness and confidence. See SECURITY.

secured bond. See BOND (3).

secured claim. See CLAIM (5).

secured creditor. See CREDITOR.

secured debt. See DEBT.

secured loan. See LOAN.

secured note. See NOTE (1).

secured party. See *secured creditor* under CREDITOR.

secured transaction. (1936) A business arrangement by which a buyer or borrower gives collateral to the seller or lender to guarantee payment of an obligation. ● Article 9 of the UCC deals with secured transactions. See SECURITY AGREEMENT.

securities act. (1933) A federal or state law protecting the public by regulating the registration, offering, and trading of securities. See SECURITIES ACT OF 1933; SECURITIES EXCHANGE ACT OF 1934; BLUE-SKY LAW.

Securities Act of 1933. The federal law regulating the registration and initial public offering of securities, with an emphasis on full public disclosure of financial and other information. 15 USCA §§ 77a–77aa. — Also termed *Securities Act*; *1933 Act.*

securities analyst. A person, usu. an employee of a bank, brokerage, or mutual fund, who studies a company and reports on the company's securities, financial condition, and prospects.

Securities and Exchange Commission. The five-member federal agency that regulates the issuance and trading of securities to protect investors against fraudulent or unfair practices. ● The Commission was established by the Securities Exchange Act of 1934. —- Abbr. SEC.

Securities and Investment Board. See FINANCIAL SERVICES AGENCY. — Abbr. SIB.

securities broker. See BROKER.

securities exchange. (1909) **1.** A marketplace or facility for the organized purchase and sale of securities, esp. stocks. **2.** A group of people who organize themselves to create such a marketplace; EXCHANGE (5). — Often shortened to *exchange.* — Also termed *stock exchange.*

    regional securities exchange. A securities exchange that focuses on stocks and bonds of local interest, such as the Boston, Philadelphia, and Midwest stock exchanges. — Also termed *regional stock exchange.*

Securities Exchange Act of 1934. The federal law regulating the public trading of securities. ● This law provides for periodic disclosures by issuers of securities and for the registration and supervision of securities exchanges and brokers, and regulates proxy solicitations. The Act also established the SEC. 15 USCA §§ 78a et seq. — Also termed *Exchange Act*; *1934 Act.*

Securities Investor Protection Act. A 1970 federal law establishing the Securities Investor Protection

Corporation that, although not a governmental agency, is designed to protect investors whose brokers and dealers are in financial trouble. — Abbr. SIPA. 15 USCA §§ 78aaa et seq.

Securities Investor Protection Corporation. A federally chartered corporation established under the Securities Investor Protection Act to protect investors and help brokers in financial trouble. — Abbr. SIPC. See SECURITIES INVESTOR PROTECTION ACT.

securities-offering distribution. See DISTRIBUTION.

securitizable, *adj.* **1.** Of, relating to, or constituting the class of obligations that a creditor (originator) may package and sell to others for corporate purposes. **2.** (Of an asset) capable of being rapidly converted to cash, as with commercial-loan receivables and trade accounts receivable.

securitize, *vb.* To convert (assets) into negotiable securities for resale in the financial market, allowing the issuing financial institution to remove assets from its books, and thereby improve its capital ratio and liquidity, and to make new loans with the security proceeds if it so chooses. — **securitized,** *adj.* — **securitization,** *n.*

security, *n.* (15c) **1.** Collateral given or pledged to guarantee the fulfillment of an obligation; esp., the assurance that a creditor will be repaid (usu. with interest) any money or credit extended to a debtor. **2.** A person who is bound by some type of guaranty; SURETY. **3.** The state of being secure, esp. from danger or attack. **4.** An instrument that evidences the holder's ownership rights in a firm (e.g., a stock), the holder's creditor relationship with a firm or government (e.g., a bond), or the holder's other rights (e.g., an option). • A security indicates an interest based on an investment in a common enterprise rather than direct participation in the enterprise. Under an important statutory definition, a security is any interest or instrument relating to finances, including a note, stock, treasury stock, bond, debenture, evidence of indebtedness, certificate of interest or participation in a profit-sharing agreement, collateral trust certificate, preorganization certificate or subscription, transferable share, investment contract, voting trust certificate, certificate of deposit for a security, fractional undivided interest in oil, gas, or other mineral rights, or certificate of interest or participation in, temporary or interim certificate for, receipt for, guarantee of, or warrant or right to subscribe to or purchase any of these things. A security also includes any put, call, straddle, option, or privilege on any security, certificate of deposit, group or index of securities, or any such device entered into on a national securities exchange, relating to foreign currency. 15 USCA § 77b(1). — Also termed (in sense 4) *evi-*

dence of indebtedness; evidence of debt. Cf. SHARE (2); STOCK (4).

adjustment security. A stock or bond that is issued during a corporate reorganization. • The security holders' relative interests are readjusted during this process.

assessable security. A security on which a charge or assessment covering the obligations of the issuing company is made. • Bank and insurance-company stock may be assessable.

asset-backed security. A debt security (such as a bond) that is secured by assets that have been pooled and secured by the assets from the pool.

bearer security. An unregistered security payable to the holder. Cf. *bearer bond* under BOND (3).

callable security. See *redeemable security.*

certificated security. A security that is a recognized investment vehicle, belongs to or is divisible into a class or series of shares, and is represented on an instrument payable to the bearer or a named person. UCC § 8-102(1)(4).

collateral security. 1. A security, subordinate to and given in addition to a primary security, that is intended to guarantee the validity or convertibility of the primary security. **2.** COLLATERAL (2).

consolidated security. (usu. pl.) A security issued in large enough numbers to provide the funds to retire two or more outstanding issues of debt securities.

conversion security. The security into which a convertible security may be converted, usu. common stock.

convertible security. A security (usu. a bond or preferred stock) that may be exchanged by the owner for another security, esp. common stock from the same company, and usu. at a fixed price on a specified date. — Also termed (specif.) *convertible debt; convertible stock.*

coupon security. A security with detachable interest coupons that the holder must present for payment as they mature. • Coupon securities are usu. in denominations of $1,000, and they are negotiable.

debt security. A security representing funds borrowed by the corporation from the holder of the debt obligation; esp., a bond, note, or debenture. • Generally, a debt security is any security that is not an equity security. See BOND (3).

dematerialized security. See *uncertificated security.*

derivative security. See DERIVATIVE.

divisional security. A special type of security issued to finance a particular project.

equity security. A security representing an ownership interest in a corporation (such as a share of stock) rather than a debt interest (such as a bond); any stock or similar security, or any security that is convertible into stock or similar security or carrying a warrant or right to subscribe to or purchase stock or a similar security, and any such warrant or right.

exempt security. A security that need not be registered under the provisions of the Securities Act of 1933 and is exempt from the margin requirements of the Securities Exchange Act of 1934.

fixed-income security. A security that pays a fixed rate of return, such as a bond with a fixed interest rate or a preferred stock with a fixed dividend.

government security. A security issued by a government, a government agency, or a government corporation; esp., a security (such as a Treasury bill) issued by a U.S. government agency, with the implied backing of Congress. — Also termed *government-agency security*; *agency security*; *government bond.*

heritable security. *Scots law.* A debt instrument secured by a charge on heritable property. — Also termed *inheritable security.* See *heritable bond* under BOND (2).

high-grade security. A security issued by a company of sound financial condition and having the ability to maintain good earnings (e.g., a utility company security).

hybrid security. A security with features of both a debt instrument (such as a bond) and an equity interest (such as a share of stock). ● An example of a hybrid security is a convertible bond, which can be exchanged for shares in the issuing corporation and is subject to stock-price fluctuations.

investment security. An instrument issued in bearer or registered form as a type commonly recognized as a medium for investment and evidencing a share or other interest in the property or enterprise of the issuer.

junior security. A security that is subordinate to a senior security. ● Junior securities have a lower priority in claims on assets and income.

landed security. A mortgage or other encumbrance affecting land.

letter security. See *restricted security.*

listed security. A security accepted for trading on a securities exchange. ● The issuing company must have met the SEC's registration requirements and complied with the rules of the particular exchange. — Also termed *listed stock.* See DELISTING.

long-term security. **1.** A new securities issue with an initial maturity of ten years or more. **2.** On a balance sheet, a security with a remaining maturity of one year or more.

low-grade security. A security with low investment quality. ● Low-grade securities usu. offer higher yields to attract capital. See *high-yield bond* under BOND (3).

marginable security. A security that can be bought on margin. — Also termed *margin stock.* See MARGIN.

margined security. A security that is bought on margin and that serves as collateral in a margin account. See MARGIN.

marketable security. A security that the holder can readily sell on a stock exchange or an over-the-counter market.

mortgage-backed security. A security (esp. a pass-through security) backed by mortgages. ● The cash flow from these securities depends on principal and interest payments from the pool of mortgages. See *stripped mortgage-backed security.*

municipal security. See *municipal bond* under BOND (3).

noncallable security. A security that cannot be redeemed, or bought back, at the issuer's option. — Also termed (specif.) *noncallable bond.*

nonmarketable security. **1.** A security that cannot be sold on the market and can be redeemed only by the holder. **2.** A security that is not of investment quality.

outstanding security. A security that is held by an investor and has not been redeemed by the issuing corporation.

pass-through security. A security that passes through payments from debtors to investors. ● Pass-through securities are usu. assembled and sold in packages to investors by private lenders who deduct a service fee before passing the principal and interest payments through to the investors.

personal security. **1.** An obligation for the repayment of a debt, evidenced by a pledge or note binding a natural person, as distinguished from property. **2.** A person's legal right to enjoy life, health, and reputation.

public security. A negotiable or transferable security that is evidence of government debt.

real security. The security of mortgages or other liens or encumbrances upon land. See COLLATERAL (2).

redeemable security. Any security, other than a short-term note, that, when presented to the issuer, entitles the holder to receive a share of the issuer's assets or the cash equivalent. — Also termed *callable security*.

registered security. 1. A security whose owner is recorded in the issuer's books. ● The issuer keeps a record of the current owners for purposes of sending dividends, interest payments, proxies, and the like. **2.** A security that is to be offered for sale and for which a registration statement has been submitted. — Also termed (specif.) *registered stock*.

restricted security. A security that is not registered with the SEC and therefore may not be sold publicly unless specified conditions are met. ● A restricted security is usu. acquired in a nonpublic transaction in which the buyer gives the seller a letter stating the buyer's intent to hold the stock as an investment rather than resell it. — Also termed *restricted stock*; *letter security*; *letter stock*; *unregistered security*.

senior security. A security of a class having priority over another class as to the distribution of assets or the payment of dividends. 15 USCA § 77r(d)(4).

shelf security. A security that is set aside for shelf registration.

short-term security. A bond or note that matures and is payable within a brief period (often one year).

speculative security. A security that, as an investment, involves a risk of loss greater than would usu. be involved; esp., a security whose value depends on proposed or promised future promotion or development, rather than on present tangible assets or conditions.

stripped mortgage-backed security. A derivative security providing distributions to classes that receive different proportions of either the principal or interest payments from a pool of mortgage-backed securities. — Abbr. SMBS. See *mortgage-backed security*.

structured security. (*usu. pl.*) **1.** A security whose cash-flow characteristics depend on one or more indexes, or that has an embedded forward or option. **2.** A security for which an investor's investment return and the issuer's payment obligations are contingent on, or highly sensitive to, changes in the value of the underlying assets, indexes, interest rates, or cash flows. SEC Rule 434(h) (17 CFR § 230.434(h)).

treasury security. See *treasury stock* under STOCK.

uncertificated security. A share or other interest in property or an enterprise, or an obligation of the issuer that is not represented by an instrument but is registered on the issuer's books. UCC § 8-102(a)(18). ● This term was called *uncertified*

security in earlier versions of the UCC. — Also termed (in BrE) *dematerialized security*.

unlisted security. An over-the-counter security that is not registered with a stock exchange. — Also termed *unlisted stock*.

unregistered security. See *restricted security*.

voting security. See *voting stock* under STOCK.

when-issued security. A security that can be traded even though it has not yet been issued. ● Any transaction that takes place does not become final until the security is issued.

worthless security. A security that has lost its value, for which a loss (usu. capital) is allowed for tax purposes. IRC (26 USCA) § 165.

zero-coupon security. A security (esp. a bond) that is issued at a large discount but pays no interest. ● The face value of the bond is payable at maturity.

security agreement. An agreement that creates or provides for an interest in specified real or personal property to guarantee the performance of an obligation. ● It must provide for a security interest, describe the collateral, and be signed by the debtor. The agreement may include other important covenants and warranties.

Security Council. A principal organ of the United Nations, consisting of five permanent members (China, France, Russia, the United Kingdom, and the United States) and ten additional members elected at stated intervals, charged with the responsibility of maintaining international peace and security, and esp. of preventing or halting wars by diplomatic, economic, or military action. ● The nonpermanent members are elected from each of the world's major regions, based on a distribution formula.

security deposit. See DEPOSIT (3).

security for costs. (17c) Money, property, or a bond given to a court by a plaintiff or an appellant to secure the payment of court costs if that party loses.

security grade. See SECURITY RATING.

security grading. See SECURITY RATING.

security interest. (1951) A property interest created by agreement or by operation of law to secure performance of an obligation (esp. repayment of a debt). ● Although the UCC limits the creation of a security interest to personal property, the Bankruptcy Code defines the term to mean "a lien created by an agreement." 11 USCA § 101(51).

perfected security interest. (1955) A security interest that complies with the statutory requirements for achieving priority over a trustee in bankruptcy and unperfected interests. ● A perfected interest may also have priority over another interest that was perfected later in time. See PERFECT.

purchase-money security interest. (1957) A security interest that is created when a buyer uses the lender's money to make the purchase and immediately gives the lender security by using the purchased property as collateral (UCC § 9-107); a security interest that is either (1) taken or retained by the seller of the collateral to secure all or part of its price or (2) taken by a person who by making advances or incurring an obligation gives value to enable the debtor to acquire rights in or the use of collateral if that value is in fact so used. • If a buyer's purchase of a boat, for example, is financed by a bank that loans the amount of the purchase price, the bank's security interest in the boat that secures the loan is a purchase-money security interest. — Abbr. PMSI. — Also termed *purchase-money interest.*

unperfected security interest. (1957) A security interest held by a creditor who has not established priority over any other creditor. • The only priority is over the debtor.

security rating. 1. The system for grading or classifying a security by financial strength, stability, or risk. • Firms such as *Standard and Poor's* and *Moody's* grade securities. — Also termed *security grade; security grading; security rate.* **2.** The classification that a given security is assigned to under this system.

secus (**see**-kəs). [Latin] Otherwise; to the contrary.

se defendendo (**see** def-en-**den**-doh), *adv.* [Law Latin] In self-defense; in defending oneself <homicide *se defendendo*>.

sedentary work. See WORK (1).

sedge flat. A tract of land below the high-water mark.

sedition, *n.* (14c) **1.** An agreement, communication, or other preliminary activity aimed at inciting treason or some lesser commotion against public authority. **2.** Advocacy aimed at inciting or producing — and likely to incite or produce — imminent lawless action. • At common law, sedition included defaming a member of the royal family or the government. The difference between *sedition* and *treason* is that the former is committed by preliminary steps, while the latter entails some overt act for carrying out the plan. But if the plan is merely for some small commotion, even accomplishing the plan does not amount to treason. Cf. TREASON. — **seditious,** *adj.*

Sedition Act. *Hist.* A 1798 federal statute that prohibited the malicious publication of defamatory material about the government, Congress, or the President. • The act expired in 1801.

seditious conspiracy. See CONSPIRACY.

seditious libel. See LIBEL.

seditious speech. See SPEECH.

seduction. (16c) The offense that occurs when a man entices a woman of previously chaste character to have unlawful intercourse with him by means of persuasion, solicitation, promises, or bribes, or other means not involving force. • Many states have abolished this offense for persons over the age of legal consent. Traditionally, the parent of a young woman had an action to recover damages for the loss of her services. But in measuring damages, the jury could consider not just the loss of services but also the distress and anxiety that the parent had suffered in being deprived of her comfort and companionship. Though seduction was not a crime at common law, many American states made it a statutory crime until the late 20th century.

see, *n.* The area or district of a bishop's jurisdiction <the see of Canterbury>.

seed money. Start-up money for a business venture. — Also termed *front money; front-end money.*

seeming danger. See DANGER.

segregation, *n.* (16c) **1.** The act or process of separating.

punitive segregation. (1958) The act of removing a prisoner from the prison population for placement in separate or solitary confinement, usu. for disciplinary reasons. — Also termed *punitive isolation.*

2. The unconstitutional policy of separating people on the basis of color, nationality, religion, or the like. — **segregate,** *vb.* — **segregative,** *adj.*

de facto segregation. (1958) Segregation that occurs without state authority, usu. on the basis of socioeconomic factors.

de jure segregation. (1963) Segregation that is permitted by law.

seignior (**seen**-yər), *n.* [Law French] *Hist.* An owner of something; a lord of a fee or manor. — Also spelled *seigneur* (**seen**- or sayn-**yər**); *seignor.* See SEIGNIORY.

seigniorage (**seen**-yər-ij), *n.* [Law French] **1.** *Hist.* The tenure existing between lord and vassal. **2.** *Hist.* A prerogative of the Crown; specif., the charge for coining bullion into money; mintage. **3.** A royalty. **4.** A profit.

seigniory (**seen**-yər-ee), *n.* [Law French] *Hist.* **1.** The rights and powers of a lord; esp., a grantor's retained right to have the grantee perform services in exchange for the transfer of land. **2.** A lord's dominions; a feudal or manor lordship; esp., land held subject to such a retained right in the grantor. — Also spelled *seignory.*

seigniory in gross (**seen**-yər-ee in **grohs**). See *re-puted manor* under MANOR.

seise (seez), *vb.* To invest with seisin or establish as a holder in fee simple; to put in possession <he became seised of half a section of farmland near Amarillo>.

seised to uses. See STANDING SEISED TO USES.

seisin (**see**-zin), *n.* (14c) **1.** *Hist.* Completion of the ceremony of feudal investiture, by which the tenant was admitted into freehold. **2.** Possession of a freehold estate in land; ownership. **3.** *Louisiana law.* The right that the law accords universal successors to own and possess a person's estate directly and immediately upon that person's death. La. Civ. Code arts. 935 *et seq.* — Also spelled *seizin.* — Also termed *vesture; seisina;* (in Scots law) *sasine.*

actual seisin. See *seisin in deed.*

constructive seisin. See *seisin in law.*

covenant of seisin. See COVENANT (4).

customary seisin. See *quasi-seisin.*

equitable seisin. 1. Possession or enjoyment of a property interest or right enforceable in equity. **2.** See *seisin in law.*

fictitious seisin. See *seisin in law.*

legal seisin. See *seisin in law.*

livery of seisin. See LIVERY OF SEISIN.

primer seisin (**prim**-ər *or* **prɪ**-mər **see**-zin). *Hist.* A right of the Crown to receive, from the heir of a tenant who died in possession of a knight's fee, one year's profits of the inherited estate (or half a year's profits if the estate was in reversion); FIRST FRUITS (1).

quasi-seisin. A copyholder's possession of lands, the freehold possession being in the lord. — Also termed *customary seisin.*

seisin in deed. (17c) Actual possession of a freehold estate in land, by oneself or by one's tenant or agent, as distinguished from legal possession. — Also termed *seisin in fact; actual seisin.*

seisin in fact. See *seisin in deed.*

seisin in law. (17c) The right to immediate possession of a freehold estate in land, as when an heir inherits land but has not yet entered it. — Also termed *legal seisin; constructive seisin; equitable seisin; fictitious seisin.*

seize, *vb.* (13c) **1.** To forcibly take possession (of a person or property). **2.** To place (someone) in possession. **3.** To be in possession (of property). **4.** To be informed of or aware of (something). See SEISIN; SEIZURE.

seizin. See SEISIN.

seizure, *n.* (15c) The act or an instance of taking possession of a person or property by legal right or process; esp., in constitutional law, a confiscation or arrest that may interfere with a person's reasonable expectation of privacy.

constructive seizure. A manifest intent to seize and take possession of another person's property, usu. either by lawfully acquiring actual custody and control of the property or by posting notice of the property's pending foreclosure.

select committee. See *special committee* under COMMITTEE.

select council. See COUNCIL.

selective disclosure. (1963) The act of divulging part of a privileged communication, or one of several privileged communications, usu. because the divulged portion is helpful to the party giving the information, while harmful portions of the communication are withheld. • Such a disclosure can result in a limited waiver of the privilege for all communications on the same subject matter as the divulged portion.

selective-draft law. A statute empowering the federal government to conscript citizens for military duty. • The constitutionality of the first selective-draft law was challenged and upheld in the Selective-Draft-Law Cases. *See Arver v. United States,* 245 U.S. 366, 38 S.Ct. 159 (1918).

selective enforcement. (1958) The practice of law-enforcement officers who use wide or even unfettered discretion about when and where to carry out certain laws; esp., the practice of singling a person out for prosecution or punishment under a statute or regulation because the person is a member of a protected group or because the person has exercised or is planning to exercise a constitutionally protected right. — Also termed *selective prosecution.* Cf. *vindictive prosecution* under PROSECUTION.

selective incorporation. See INCORPORATION.

selective prosecution. (1967) **1.** SELECTIVE ENFORCEMENT. **2.** The practice or an instance of a criminal prosecution brought at the discretion of a prosecutor rather than one brought as a matter of course in the normal functioning of the prosecuting authority's office. • Selective prosecution violates the Equal Protection Clause of the Fourteenth Amendment if a defendant is singled out for prosecution when others similarly situated have not been prosecuted and the prosecutor's reasons for doing so are impermissible.

selective prospectivity. (1991) A court's decision to apply a new rule of law in the particular case in which the new rule is announced, but to apply the old rule in all other cases pending at the time the new rule is announced or in which the facts predate the new rule's announcement.

Selective Service System. The federal agency that registers all persons 18–26 who are eligible for military service military service and provides personnel to the Armed Forces during emergencies. ● It was established in 1940 as a part of the War Manpower Commission and became independent in 1943. — Abbr. SSS.

selectman. A municipal officer elected annually in some New England towns to transact business and perform some executive functions.

self-applying, *adj.* (1894) (Of a statute, ordinance, etc.) requiring no more for interpretation than a familiarity with the ordinary meanings of words.

self-authentication. See AUTHENTICATION.

self-canceling installment note. See NOTE (1).

self-crimination. See SELF-INCRIMINATION.

self-critical-analysis privilege. See PRIVILEGE (3).

self-dealing, *n.* (1940) Participation in a transaction that benefits oneself instead of another who is owed a fiduciary duty. ● For example, a corporate director might engage in self-dealing by participating in a competing business to the corporation's detriment. Cf. FAIR DEALING (1), (2). — **self-deal,** *vb.*

self-defense, *n.* (1651) **1.** The use of force to protect oneself, one's family, or one's property from a real or threatened attack. ● Generally, a person is justified in using a reasonable amount of force in self-defense if he or she reasonably believes that the danger of bodily harm is imminent and that force is necessary to avoid this danger. — Also termed *defense of self.* Cf. *adequate provocation* under PROVOCATION.

　imperfect self-defense. (1882) The use of force by one who makes an honest but unreasonable mistake that force is necessary to repel an attack. ● In some jurisdictions, such a self-defender will be charged with a lesser offense than the one committed.

　perfect self-defense. (1883) The use of force by one who accurately appraises the necessity and the amount of force to repel an attack.

2. *Int'l law.* The right of a state to defend itself against a real or threatened attack. *See* United Nations Charter, art. 51 (59 Stat. 1031). — Also spelled (esp. in BrE) *self-defence.* — **self-defender,** *n.*

self-destruct clause. A provision in a trust for a condition that will automatically terminate the trust. ● Discretionary trusts, esp. supplemental-needs trusts, often include a self-destruct provision. For example, a trust to provide for the needs of a disabled person may terminate if the beneficiary becomes ineligible for a government-benefits program such as Medicaid.

self-destruction. See SUICIDE (1).

self-determination contract. See CONTRACT.

self-determination election. See GLOBE ELECTION.

self-employed retirement plan. See KEOGH PLAN.

self-employment tax. See TAX.

self-evaluation privilege. See *self-critical-analysis privilege* under PRIVILEGE (3).

self-executing, *adj.* (1857) (Of an instrument) effective immediately without the need of any type of implementing action <the wills had self-executing affidavits attached>. ● Legal instruments may be self-executing according to various standards. For example, treaties are self-executing under the Supremacy Clause of the U.S. Constitution (art. VI, § 2) if textually capable of judicial enforcement and intended to be enforced in that manner.

self-help, *n.* (1831) An attempt to redress a perceived wrong by one's own action rather than through the normal legal process. ● The UCC and other statutes provide for particular self-help remedies (such as repossession) if the remedy can be executed without breaching the peace. UCC § 9-609. — Also termed *self-redress; extrajudicial enforcement.*

self-help remedy. See *extrajudicial remedy* under REMEDY.

self-incrimination. (1853) The act of indicating one's own involvement in a crime or exposing oneself to prosecution, esp. by making a statement. — Also termed *self-crimination; self-inculpation.* See RIGHT AGAINST SELF-INCRIMINATION.

Self-Incrimination Clause. (1925) The clause of the Fifth Amendment to the U.S. Constitution barring the government from compelling criminal defendants to testify against themselves.

self-inculpation. See SELF-INCRIMINATION.

self-induced frustration. See FRUSTRATION.

self-induced intoxication. See *voluntary intoxication* under INTOXICATION.

self-insurance. See INSURANCE.

self-insured retention. *Insurance.* The amount of an otherwise-covered loss that is not covered by an insurance policy and that usu. must be paid before the insurer will pay benefits <the defendant had a $1 million CGL policy to cover the loss, but had to pay a self-insured retention of $100,000, which it had agreed to so that the policy premium would be lower>. — Abbr. SIR. Cf. DEDUCTIBLE.

self-killing. See SUICIDE (1).

self-liquidating mortgage. See *amortized mortgage* under MORTGAGE.

self-murder. See SUICIDE (1).

self-policing privilege. See *self-critical-analysis privilege* under PRIVILEGE (3).

self-proved will. See WILL.

self-proving affidavit. See AFFIDAVIT.

self-redress. See SELF-HELP.

self-regulation. See REGULATION (1).

self-regulatory organization. A nongovernmental organization that is statutorily empowered to regulate its members by adopting and enforcing rules of conduct, esp. those governing fair, ethical, and efficient practices. — Abbr. SRO.

self-represented litigant. See PRO SE.

self-serving declaration. See DECLARATION (6).

self-settled trust. See TRUST.

self-slaughter. See SUICIDE (1).

self-stultification. (1862) The act or an instance of testifying about one's own deficiencies. See STULTIFY.

sell, *vb.* (bef. 12c) To transfer (property) by sale.

seller. (13c) **1.** A person who sells or contracts to sell goods; a vendor. UCC § 2-103(1)(d). **2.** Generally, a person who sells anything; the transferor of property in a contract of sale.

seller's market. See MARKET.

seller's option. See OPTION.

selling agent. See AGENT (2).

selling price. See *sales price* under PRICE.

sell-off, *n.* A period when heavy pressure to sell causes falling stock-market prices.

sell order. See ORDER (8).

semble (**sem**-bəl). [Law French] (1817) It seems; it would appear <semble that the parties' intention was to create a binding agreement>. • This term is used chiefly to indicate an obiter dictum in a court opinion or to introduce an uncertain thought or interpretation. — Abbr. sem.; semb.

Semiconductor Chip Protection Act. *Intellectual property.* A 1984 statute protecting manufacturers against the unauthorized copying or use of semiconductor chips and the mask works used to manufacture them. • Semiconductor chips do not qualify for patent protection since technological advancements are small and usu. obvious. Mask works are multi-layered, three-dimensional templates used to produce semiconductor chips. Mask-work design is more functional than expressive and so traditional copyright protection was inapplicable until 1984. The Act provides copyright protection to the mask works for a period of ten years. 17 USCA §§ 901–914. — Abbr. SCPA.

semi-free software. Software that does not include source code but comes with permission for individuals to use, copy, modify, and distribute the software for nonprofit purposes. Cf. FREEWARE; PROPRIETARY SOFTWARE; SHAREWARE.

seminary. **1.** An educational institution such as a college, academy, or other school; esp., one that trains students for the clergy. **2.** The building in which the institution performs its functions.

semi-secret trust. See TRUST.

semi-skilled work. See WORK (1).

senate. (13c) **1.** The upper chamber of a bicameral legislature. **2.** (*cap.*) The upper house of the U.S. Congress, composed of 100 members — two from each state — who are elected to six-year terms. — Abbr. S.

senate bill. See BILL (3).

senator. (13c) A person who is a member of a senate.

senatorial courtesy. (1884) **1.** The tradition that the President should take care in filling a high-level federal post (such as a judgeship) with a person agreeable to the senators from the nominee's home state, lest the senators defeat confirmation. **2.** Loosely, civility among senators <a decline of senatorial courtesy>.

sending state. See STATE.

senility. (18c) Mental feebleness or impairment caused by old age. • A senile person (in the legal, as opposed to the popular, sense) is incompetent to enter into a binding contract or to execute a will. — Also termed *senile dementia* (**see**-nɪl di-**men**-shee-ə). — **senile,** *adj.*

senior, *adj.* (14c) **1.** (Of a debt, etc.) first; preferred, as over junior obligations. **2.** (Of a person) older than someone else. **3.** (Of a person) higher in rank or service. **4.** (Of a man) elder, as distinguished from the man's son who has the same name.

senior administrative patent judge. See JUDGE.

senior counsel. 1. See *lead counsel* under COUNSEL. **2.** See KING'S COUNSEL; QUEEN'S COUNSEL.

senior debt. See DEBT.

senior interest. See INTEREST (2).

seniority. (15c) **1.** The preferential status, privileges, or rights given to an employee based on the employee's length of service with an employer. • Employees with seniority may receive additional or enhanced benefit packages and obtain competitive advantages over fellow employees in lay-off and promotional decisions. **2.** The status of being older or senior.

seniority system. *Employment law.* Any arrangement that recognizes length of service in making decisions about job layoffs and promotions or other advancements.

senior judge. See JUDGE.

senior lien. See LIEN.

senior mortgage. See MORTGAGE.

senior partner. See PARTNER.

senior party. *Intellectual property.* In an interference proceeding, the first person to file an application for a property's legal protection, e.g., an invention patent or a trademark registration. • In the United States, merely being the first to file does not entitle the party to the protection. The proceeding's administrator also takes other factors into account. For instance, in a patent-interference proceeding the invention's conception date and the inventor's diligence in reducing the invention to practice are relevant factors. Priority in the filing date is prima facie evidence that the senior party is the first inventor, so the challenger has the burden of proof. Cf. JUNIOR PARTY.

senior security. See SECURITY.

senior status. (1970) The employment condition of a semiretired judge who continues to perform certain judicial duties that the judge is willing and able to undertake.

senior user. *Trademarks.* The first person to use a mark. • That person is usu. found to be the mark's owner. — Also termed *first user.* Cf. JUNIOR USER.

sensitivity training. (1956) One or more instructional sessions for management and employees, designed to counteract the callous treatment of others, esp. women and minorities, in the workplace.

sentence, *n.* (14c) The judgment that a court formally pronounces after finding a criminal defendant guilty; the punishment imposed on a criminal wrongdoer <a sentence of 20 years in prison>. *See* Fed. R. Crim. P. 32. — Also termed *judgment of conviction.* — **sentence,** *vb.*

   accumulative sentences. See *consecutive sentences.*

   aggregate sentence. (1917) A sentence that arises from a conviction on multiple counts in an indictment.

   alternative sentence. (1841) A sentence other than incarceration. • Examples include community service and victim restitution. — Also termed *creative sentence.*

   blended sentence. In a juvenile-delinquency disposition, a sanction that combines delinquency sanctions and criminal punishment.

   concurrent sentences. (1905) Two or more sentences of jail time to be served simultaneously. • For example, if a convicted criminal receives concurrent sentences of 5 years and 15 years, the total amount of jail time is 15 years.

   conditional sentence. (1843) A sentence of confinement if the convicted criminal fails to perform the conditions of probation.

   consecutive sentences. (1844) Two or more sentences of jail time to be served in sequence. • For example, if a convicted criminal receives consecutive sentences of 20 years and 5 years, the total amount of jail time is 25 years. — Also termed *cumulative sentences; accumulative sentences.*

   consolidated sentence. See *general sentence.*

   creative sentence. See *alternative sentence.*

   death sentence. (1811) A sentence that imposes the death penalty. See Model Penal Code § 210.6. — Also termed *judgment of blood.* See DEATH PENALTY.

   deferred sentence. (1915) A sentence that will not be carried out if the convicted criminal meets certain requirements, such as complying with conditions of probation.

   delayed sentence. (1906) A sentence that is not imposed immediately after conviction, thereby allowing the convicted criminal to satisfy the court (usu. by complying with certain restrictions or conditions during the delay period) that probation is preferable to a prison sentence.

   determinate sentence. (1885) A sentence for a fixed length of time rather than for an unspecified duration. — Also termed *definite sentence; definitive sentence; fixed sentence; flat sentence; straight sentence.*

   excessive sentence. (1879) A sentence that gives more punishment than is allowed by law.

   fixed sentence. **1.** See *determinate sentence.* **2.** See *mandatory sentence.*

   flat sentence. See *determinate sentence.*

   general sentence. (1891) An undivided, aggregate sentence in a multicount case; a sentence that does not specify the punishment imposed for each count. • General sentences are prohibited. — Also termed *consolidated sentence.*

   indeterminate sentence. (1885) **1.** A sentence of an unspecified duration, such as one for a term of 10 to 20 years. **2.** A maximum prison term that the parole board can reduce, through statutory authorization, after the inmate has served the minimum time required by law. — Also termed *indefinite sentence.* See INDETERMINATE SENTENCING.

   intermittent sentence. (1964) A sentence consisting of periods of confinement interrupted by periods of freedom. — Also termed (when served on weekends) *weekend sentence.*

   life sentence. (1878) A sentence that imprisons the convicted criminal for life — though in some jurisdictions the prisoner may become eligible for release on good behavior, rehabilitation, or the like.

mandatory sentence. (1926) A sentence set by law with no discretion for the judge to individualize punishment. — Also termed *mandatory penalty*; *mandatory punishment*; *fixed sentence.*

maximum sentence. (1898) The highest level of punishment provided by law for a particular crime.

minimum sentence. (1891) The least amount of time that a convicted criminal must serve in prison before becoming eligible for parole.

multiple sentences. (1938) Concurrent or consecutive sentences, if a convicted criminal is found guilty of more than one offense.

nominal sentence. (1852) A criminal sentence in name only; an exceedingly light sentence.

noncustodial sentence. (1971) A criminal sentence (such as probation) not requiring prison time.

presumptive sentence. (1978) An average sentence for a particular crime (esp. provided under sentencing guidelines) that can be raised or lowered based on the presence of mitigating or aggravating circumstances.

prior sentence. (1863) A sentence previously imposed on a criminal defendant for a different offense, whether by a guilty verdict, a guilty plea, or a *nolo contendere.*

split sentence. (1927) A sentence in which part of the time is served in confinement — to expose the offender to the unpleasantness of prison — and the rest on probation. See *shock probation* under PROBATION.

straight sentence. See *determinate sentence.*

suspended sentence. (1919) A sentence postponed so that the convicted criminal is not required to serve time unless he or she commits another crime or violates some other court-imposed condition. ● A suspended sentence, in effect, is a form of probation. — Also termed *withheld sentence.*

weekend sentence. See *intermittent sentence.*

sentence bargain. See PLEA BARGAIN.

sentence cap. *Military law.* A pretrial plea agreement in a court-martial proceeding by which a ceiling is placed on the maximum penalty that can be imposed.

sentenced to time served. (1959) A sentencing disposition whereby a criminal defendant is sentenced to the same jail time that the defendant is credited with serving while in custody awaiting trial. ● The sentence results in the defendant's release from custody. Cf. BALANCE OF SENTENCE SUSPENDED.

sentence-factor manipulation. See *sentencing entrapment* under ENTRAPMENT.

sentence-package rule. (1996) *Criminal procedure.* The principle that a defendant can be resentenced on an aggregate sentence — that is, one arising from a conviction on multiple counts in an indictment — when the defendant successfully challenges part of the conviction, as by successfully challenging some but not all of the counts.

sentencing. The judicial determination of the penalty for a crime.

determinate sentencing. See *mandatory sentencing.*

discretionary sentencing. See *indeterminate sentencing.*

fixed sentencing. See *mandatory sentencing.*

indeterminate sentencing. Sentencing that is left up to the court, with few or very flexible guidelines. — Also termed *discretionary sentencing.*

mandatory sentencing. A statutorily specified penalty that automatically follows a conviction for the offense, often with a minimum mandatory term. — Also termed *determinate sentencing*; *fixed sentencing.*

presumptive sentencing. A statutory scheme that prescribes a sentence or range of sentences for an offense but allows the court some flexibility in atypical cases.

sentencing council. (1973) A panel of three or more judges who confer to determine a criminal sentence. ● Sentencing by a council occurs less frequently than sentencing by a single trial judge.

sentencing entrapment. See ENTRAPMENT.

sentencing guidelines. (1970) A set of standards for determining the punishment that a convicted criminal should receive, based on the nature of the crime and the offender's criminal history. ● The federal government and several states have adopted sentencing guidelines in an effort to make judicial sentencing more consistent.

sentencing hearing. See PRESENTENCE HEARING.

sentencing phase. See PENALTY PHASE.

Sentencing Reform Act of 1984. A federal statute enacted to bring greater uniformity to punishments assessed for federal crimes by creating a committee of federal judges and other officials (the United States Sentencing Commission) responsible for producing sentencing guidelines to be used by the federal courts. 28 USCA § 994(a)(1).

Sentencing Table. A reference guide used by federal courts to calculate the appropriate punishment under the sentencing guidelines by taking into account the gravity of the offense and the convicted person's criminal history.

SEP. *abbr.* See *simplified employee pension plan* under EMPLOYEE BENEFIT PLAN.

separability. *Copyright.* An element of various judicial tests used to determine whether a design in a functional article is a copyrightable work of applied art, or an uncopyrightable industrial design, the test being based on whether the beholder separates the work's artistic appearance from its useful function. • Some courts use a strict physical separability test, but most look at whether the work's two roles are conceptually separate.

separability clause. See SEVERABILITY CLAUSE.

separable, *adj.* (14c) Capable of being separated or divided <a separable controversy>.

separable controversy. See CONTROVERSY.

separate, *adj.* (15c) (Of liability, cause of action, etc.) individual; distinct; particular; disconnected.

separate action. See ACTION (4).

separate and apart. See LIVING SEPARATE AND APART.

separate-but-equal doctrine. (1950) The now-defunct doctrine that African-Americans could be segregated if they were provided with equal opportunities and facilities in education, public transportation, and jobs. • This rule was established in *Plessy v. Ferguson*, 163 U.S. 537, 16 S.Ct. 1138 (1896), and overturned in *Brown v. Board of Education*, 347 U.S. 483, 74 S.Ct. 686 (1954).

separate caucus. See CAUCUS.

separate count. See COUNT.

separate covenant. See *several covenant* under COVENANT (1).

separate demise. See DEMISE.

separate estate. See ESTATE (1).

separate examination. (18c) 1. The private interrogation of a witness, apart from the other witnesses in the same case. 2. The interrogation of a wife outside the presence of her husband by a court clerk or notary for the purpose of acknowledging a deed or other instrument. • This was done to ensure that the wife signed without being coerced to do so by her husband.

separate goodwill. See *personal goodwill* under GOODWILL.

separate maintenance. See MAINTENANCE.

separate offense. See OFFENSE (1).

separate property. (18c) 1. Property that a spouse owned before marriage or acquired during marriage by inheritance or by gift from a third party, and in some states property acquired during marriage but after the spouses have entered into a separation agreement and have begun living apart or after one spouse has commenced a divorce action. — Also termed *individual property*. Cf. COMMUNITY PROPERTY; *marital property* under PROPERTY. 2. In some common-law states, property titled to one spouse or acquired by one spouse individually during marriage. 3. Property acquired during the marriage in exchange for separate property (in sense 1 or sense 2).

separate-property state. See COMMON-LAW STATE (2).

separate return. See TAX RETURN.

separate-sovereigns rule. (1995) *Criminal procedure.* The principle that a person may be tried twice for the same offense — despite the Double Jeopardy Clause — if the prosecutions are conducted by separate sovereigns, as by the federal government and a state government or by two different states. See DOUBLE JEOPARDY.

separate-spheres doctrine. *Hist. Family law.* The common-law doctrine that wives were limited to control of the home — the personal or domestic sphere — and that husbands had control of the public sphere. • Under this-early-19th century doctrine, the wife was to tend to the home and family and the husband was to be the breadwinner. — Also termed *doctrine of separate spheres*.

separate support. See *separate maintenance* under MAINTENANCE.

separate trading of registered interest and principal of securities. A treasury security by which the owner receives either principal or interest, but usu. not both. — Abbr. STRIP.

separate trial. See TRIAL.

separation. (17c) 1. An arrangement whereby a husband and wife live apart from each other while remaining married, either by mutual consent (often in a written agreement) or by judicial decree; the act of carrying out such an arrangement. — Also termed *separation from bed and board*. See *divorce a mensa et thoro* under DIVORCE. 2. The status of a husband and wife having begun such an arrangement, or the judgment or contract that brought about the arrangement. — Also termed (in both senses) *legal separation*; *judicial separation*. 3. Cessation of a contractual relationship, esp. in an employment situation. — **separate,** *vb.*

separation agreement. (1886) 1. An agreement between spouses in the process of a divorce or legal separation concerning alimony, maintenance, property division, child custody and support, and the like. — Also termed *separation order* (if approved or sanctioned judicially). See *temporary order* under ORDER. 2. DIVORCE AGREEMENT.

separation a mensa et thoro. See *divorce a mensa et thoro* under DIVORCE.

separation from bed and board. 1. SEPARATION (1). 2. See *divorce a mensa et thoro* under DIVORCE.

separation of patrimony. *Civil law.* The act of providing creditors of a succession the right to collect against the class of estate property from which the creditors should be paid, by separating certain succession property from property rights belonging to the heirs.

separation of powers. (1896) The division of governmental authority into three branches of government — legislative, executive, and judicial — each with specified duties on which neither of the other branches can encroach; a constitutional doctrine of checks and balances designed to protect the people against tyranny. Cf. DIVISION OF POWERS.

separation of witnesses. (1819) The exclusion of witnesses (other than the plaintiff and defendant) from the courtroom to prevent them from hearing the testimony of others.

separation order. 1. See SEPARATION AGREEMENT. **2.** See ORDER (2).

separation pay. See SEVERANCE PAY.

separator, *n. Oil & gas.* Equipment used at a well site to separate oil, water, and gas produced in solution with oil. ● Basic separators simply heat oil to speed the natural separation process. More complex separators may use chemicals.

SEP-IRA. See *simplified employee pension plan* under EMPLOYEE BENEFIT PLAN.

sequence listing. *Patents.* A description of the nucleotide or amino-acid chain in a biotechnological invention.

sequential journal. See JOURNAL OF NOTARIAL ACTS.

sequential marriage. See BIGAMY (2).

sequester (si-**kwes**-tər), *n.* (14c) **1.** An across-the-board cut in government spending. **2.** A person with whom litigants deposit property being contested until the case has concluded; a sequestrator.

sequester, *vb.* (15c) **1.** To seize (property) by a writ of sequestration. **2.** To segregate or isolate (a jury or witness) during trial. **3.** *Eccles. law.* To excommunicate. See EXCOMMUNICATION. — Also (erroneously) termed *sequestrate.*

sequestered account. See ACCOUNT.

sequesterer. See SEQUESTRATOR.

sequestrate, *vb.* See SEQUESTER.

sequestration (see-kwes-**tray**-shən), *n.* (16c) **1.** The process by which property is removed from the possessor pending the outcome of a dispute in which two or more parties contend for it. Cf. ATTACHMENT (1); GARNISHMENT.

   conventional sequestration. The parties' voluntary deposit of the property at issue in a lawsuit.

   judicial sequestration. The court-ordered deposit of the property at issue in a lawsuit.

2. The setting apart of a decedent's personal property when no one has been willing to act as a personal representative for the estate. **3.** The process by which a renounced interest is subjected to judicial management and is distributed as the testator would have wished if he or she had known about the renunciation. **4.** A judicial writ commanding the sheriff or other officer to seize the goods of a person named in the writ. ● This writ is sometimes issued against a civil defendant who has defaulted or has acted in contempt of court. **5.** The court-ordered seizure of a bankrupt's estate for the benefit of creditors. **6.** *Int'l law.* The seizure by a belligerent power of enemy assets. **7.** The freezing of a government agency's funds; SEQUESTER (1). **8.** Custodial isolation of a trial jury to prevent tampering and exposure to publicity, or of witnesses to prevent them from hearing the testimony of others. — Also termed (in sense 8) *jury sequestration.*

sequestrator (see-kwes-tray-tər). (15c) **1.** An officer appointed to execute a writ of sequestration. **2.** A person who holds property in sequestration. — Also termed *sequesterer.*

serendipity doctrine. (1989) *Criminal procedure.* The principle that all evidence discovered during a lawful search is eligible to be admitted into evidence at trial.

serf. *Hist.* A person in a condition of feudal servitude, bound to labor at the will of a lord; a villein. ● Serfs differed from slaves in that they were bound to the native soil rather than being the absolute property of a master.

sergeant. 1. *Hist.* A person who is not a knight but holds lands by tenure of military service. **2.** *Hist.* A municipal officer performing duties for the Crown. **3.** *Hist.* A bailiff. **4.** SERGEANT-AT-ARMS. **5.** A noncommissioned officer in the armed forces ranking a grade above a corporal. **6.** An officer in the police force ranking below a captain or lieutenant. — Also spelled *serjeant.*

sergeant-at-arms. 1. *Hist.* An armed officer attending a sovereign. **2.** An officer the Crown assigns to attend a session of Parliament. **3.** A legislative officer charged with maintaining order and serving notices and process on behalf of the legislative body and its committees. **4.** *Parliamentary law.* An officer charged with helping keep order in a meeting under the chair's direction. — Also spelled (in senses 1, 2, & 4) *serjeant-at-arms.* — Also termed (in sense 4) *warden; warrant officer.*

sergeantry. See SERJEANTY.

Sergeant Schultz defense. *Slang.* An assertion by a criminal or civil defendant who claims that he or she was not an active participant in an alleged scheme or conspiracy, and that he or she knew nothing, saw nothing, and heard nothing. ● This defense is named after a character from the television series *Hogan's Heroes*, in which Sergeant Schultz, a German guard in charge of prisoners of war during World War II, would avoid responsibility for the prisoners' schemes by proclaiming that he saw nothing and knew nothing.

sergeanty. See SERJEANTY.

serial bond. See BOND (3).

serial consideration. See *consideration seriatim* under CONSIDERATION (2).

serial murder. See MURDER.

serial note. See *installment note* under NOTE (1).

serial number. 1. A number assigned to a specific thing, esp. a product, to identify it from other things of the same kind. • While serial numbers are usually assigned in numerical order, they may also be random. **2.** *Patents & Trademarks.* An identifying number assigned to a completed patent or trademark application. • The serial number is assigned when the application is received or completed. See APPLICATION NUMBER.

serial polygamy. See POLYGAMY (2).

serial right. The right of publication; esp., a right reserved in a publishing contract giving the author or publisher the right to publish the manuscript in installments (as in a magazine) before or after the publication of the book.

serial violation. (1989) *Civil-rights law.* The practice by an employer of committing a series of discriminatory acts against an employee, all of which arise out of the same discriminatory intent or animus. • Such a series of discriminatory acts will usu. be considered a continuing violation. For a claim on the violation to be timely, at least one of the discriminatory acts must have taken place within the time permitted to assert the claim (e.g., 300 days for a Title VII claim). Cf. SYSTEMATIC VIOLATION.

seriatim (seer-ee-**ay**-tim), *adj.* Occurring in a series.

seriatim, *adv.* [Latin] One after another; in a series; successively <the court disposed of the issues seriatim>. See *consideration seriatim* under CONSIDERATION. — Also termed *seriately* (**seer**-ee-ət-lee).

seriatim opinions. See OPINION (1).

series bonds. See BOND (3).

series code. *Patents & Trademarks.* A numerical designation assigned to any of a group of applications for patent or trademark registration filed in the U.S. Patent and Trademark Office. • The series code is part of an application number and is followed by a slash. For example, if the application number is 09/445,323, then 09 is the series code, and the application is the 445,323rd application in that batch. For ordinary patent applications, series codes are assigned for a group of applications filed during a particular period. Nonprovisional patent applications are assigned series codes from 01 to 10, depending on the period during which the application was filed. The series code for design applications is 29, for provisional applications 60, for ex parte reexamination proceedings 90, and for *inter partes* reexamination proceedings 95. For trademark applications, the series code usu. begins with numbers between 70 and 75. — Also termed *batch number.*

serious, *adj.* **1.** (Of conduct, opinions, etc.) weighty; important <serious violation of rules>. **2.** (Of an injury, illness, accident, etc.) dangerous; potentially resulting in death or other severe consequences <serious bodily harm>.

serious and willful misconduct. *Workers' compensation.* An intentional act performed with the knowledge that it is likely to result in serious injury or with a wanton and reckless disregard of its probable consequences.

serious bodily harm. See *serious bodily injury* under INJURY.

serious bodily injury. See INJURY.

serious crime. 1. See *serious offense* under OFFENSE (1). **2.** See FELONY (1).

serious felony. See FELONY.

serious health condition. Under the Family and Medical Leave Act, an illness, injury, or physical or mental state that involves in-patient care or continuing treatment by a healthcare provider for several days. • Excluded from the definition are cosmetic treatments and minor illnesses that are not accompanied by medical complications.

serious illness. *Insurance.* A disorder that permanently or materially impairs, or is likely to permanently or materially impair, the health of the insured or an insurance applicant.

seriously harmful behavior. See HARMFUL BEHAVIOR.

serious misdemeanor. See MISDEMEANOR.

serious offense. See OFFENSE (1).

serjeant. 1. See SERGEANT. **2.** See SERJEANT-AT-LAW.

serjeant-at-arms. See SERGEANT-AT-ARMS.

serjeant-at-law. *Hist. English law.* A barrister of superior grade; one who had achieved the highest degree of the legal profession, having (until 1846) the exclusive privilege of practicing in the Court of Common Pleas. • Every judge of the common-law courts was required to be a serjeant-at-law until the Judicature Act of 1873. The rank was gradually superseded by that of Queen's Counsel. — Often shortened to *serjeant.* — Also termed *serjeant at the law*; *serjeant of the law*; *serjeant of the coif*; *serviens narrator.*

serjeanty (**sahr**-jən-tee). *Hist.* A feudal lay tenure requiring some form of personal service to the king. • The required service was not necessarily military. Many household officers of the Crown, even those as humble as bakers and cooks, held lands in serjeanty. — Also spelled *sergeanty*. — Also termed *sergeantry*.

> **grand serjeanty.** *Hist.* Serjeanty requiring the tenant to perform a service relating to the country's defense. • The required service could be as great as fielding an army or as small as providing a fully equipped knight. Sometimes the service was ceremonial or honorary, such as carrying the king's banner or serving as an officer at the coronation.

> **petit serjeanty** (**pet**-ee). *Hist.* Serjeanty requiring only a minor service of small value, usu. with military symbolism. • Examples include presenting an arrow or an unstrung bow to the king.

serological test (seer-ə-**loj**-ə-kəl). (1931) A blood examination to detect the presence of antibodies and antigens, as well as other characteristics, esp. as indicators of disease. • Many states require serological tests to determine the presence of venereal disease in a couple applying for a marriage license. See BLOOD TEST.

serpentine vote. See VOTE (4).

servage (sər-vij). *Hist.* A feudal service that a serf was required to perform for the lord or else pay the equivalent value in kind or money.

servant. (13c) A person who is employed by another to do work under the control and direction of the employer. • A servant, such as a full-time employee, provides personal services that are integral to an employer's business, so a servant must submit to the employer's control of the servant's time and behavior. See EMPLOYEE. Cf. MASTER (1).

> **fellow servant.** See FELLOW SERVANT.

> **indentured servant.** *Hist.* A servant who contracted to work without wages for a fixed period in exchange for some benefit, such as learning a trade or cancellation of a debt or paid passage to another country, and the promise of freedom when the contract period expired. • Indentured servitude could be voluntary or involuntary. A contract usu. lasted from four to ten years, but the servant could terminate the contract sooner by paying for the unexpired time. Convicts transported to the colonies were often required to serve as indentured servants as part of their sentences.

serve, *vb.* (15c) **1.** To make legal delivery of (a notice or process) <a copy of the pleading was served on all interested parties>. **2.** To present (a person) with a notice or process as required by law <the defendant was served with process>.

service, *n.* (15c) **1.** The formal delivery of a writ, summons, or other legal process <after three attempts, service still had not been accomplished>. — Also termed *service of process*. **2.** The formal delivery of some other legal notice, such as a pleading <be sure that a certificate of service is attached to the motion>.

> **actual service.** See PERSONAL SERVICE (1).

> **constructive service.** (1808) **1.** See *substituted service*. **2.** Service accomplished by a method or circumstance that does not give actual notice.

> **personal service.** See PERSONAL SERVICE (1).

> **service by publication.** (1826) The service of process on an absent or nonresident defendant by publishing a notice in a newspaper or other public medium.

> **sewer service.** *Slang.* The fraudulent service of process on a debtor by a creditor seeking to obtain a default judgment.

> **substituted service.** (1840) Any method of service allowed by law in place of personal service, such as service by mail. — Also termed *constructive service*.

3. The act of doing something useful for a person or company, usu. for a fee <your services were no longer required>.

> **personal service.** See PERSONAL SERVICE (2).

4. A person or company whose business is to do useful things for others <a linen service>.

> **civil service.** See CIVIL SERVICE.

> **salvage service.** See SALVAGE SERVICE.

5. An intangible commodity in the form of human effort, such as labor, skill, or advice <contract for services>.

service, *vb.* (1927) To provide service for; specif., to make interest payments on (a debt) <service the deficit>.

service by publication. See SERVICE (2).

service charge. 1. A charge assessed for performing a service, such as the charge assessed by a bank against the expenses of maintaining or servicing a customer's checking account. **2.** The sum of (1) all charges payable by the buyer and imposed by the seller as an incident to the extension of credit and (2) charges incurred for investigating the collateral or creditworthiness of the buyer or for commissions for obtaining the credit. UCCC § 2.109. — Also termed (in sense 2) *credit service charge*.

service contract. See CONTRACT.

service establishment. Under the Fair Labor Standards Act, an establishment that, although having the characteristics of a retail store, primarily furnishes services to the public, such as a barber shop, laundry, or automobile-repair shop.

service life. The period of an asset's expected usefulness. • It may or may not coincide with the asset's depreciable life for income-tax purposes.

servicemark. (1945) *Trademarks.* A name, phrase, or other device used to identify and distinguish the services of a certain provider. • Servicemarks identify and afford protection to intangible things such as services, as distinguished from the protection already provided for marks affixed to tangible things such as goods and products. — Often shortened to *mark.* — Also spelled *service mark*; *service-mark.* Cf. TRADEMARK (1); *registered trademark* under TRADEMARK.

servicemark application. See TRADEMARK APPLICATION.

service-occupation tax. See TAX.

service of process. See SERVICE (1).

serviens narrator (sər-vee-enz nə-**ray**-tər). See SERJEANT-AT-LAW.

servient (sər-vee-ənt), *adj.* (17c) (Of an estate) subject to a servitude or easement. See *servient estate* under ESTATE (4).

servient estate. See ESTATE (4).

servient property. See *servient estate* under ESTATE (4).

servient tenant. See TENANT.

servient tenement. See *servient estate* under ESTATE (4).

servitude. (16c) **1.** An encumbrance consisting in a right to the limited use of a piece of land or other immovable property without the possession of it; a charge or burden on an estate for another's benefit <the easement by necessity is an equitable servitude>. • Servitudes include easements, irrevocable licenses, profits, and real covenants. See EASEMENT; LICENSE; PROFIT (2); *covenant running with the land* under COVENANT (4). **2.** *Roman & civil law.* The right exercised by a dominant tenement over a servient tenement, either adjoining or neighboring. • This right was perpetual except for personal servitudes; the land, rather than its owner, enjoyed the right. Although a servitude could not be possessed because it was incorporeal, it could be protected by interdict. Generally, a servitude had to be exercised *civiliter,* with as little inconvenience as possible. There was never a closed list of what constituted a servitude; for example, Justinian classed personal rights *in re aliena* as personal servitude. See SERVITUS (2).

    acquired servitude. (1971) A servitude requiring a special mode of acquisition before it comes into existence.

    additional servitude. (18c) A servitude imposed on land taken under an eminent-domain proceeding for a different type of servitude, as when a highway is constructed on land condemned for a public sidewalk. • A landowner whose land is burdened by an additional servitude is entitled to further compensation.

    affirmative servitude. *Civil law.* See *positive servitude.*

    apparent servitude. (1834) *Civil law.* A servitude appurtenant that is manifested by exterior signs or constructions, such as a roadway. Cf. *nonapparent servitude.*

    conservation servitude. See *conservation easement* under EASEMENT.

    continuous servitude. *Louisiana law.* See *continuous easement* under EASEMENT. La. Civ. Code art. 646.

    conventional servitude. *Civil law.* A servitude established by agreement or through acquisitive prescription.

    discontinuous servitude. See *discontinuous easement* under EASEMENT.

    equitable servitude. See *restrictive covenant* under COVENANT (4).

    landed servitude. See *servitude appurtenant.*

    legal servitude. (18c) *Civil law.* A limitation that the law imposes on the use of an estate for the benefit of the general public or of a particular person or persons. • Examples of legal servitudes are restrictions on certain uses of the shores of navigable rivers, and the obligation of a landowner to provide a passage to an enclosed estate.

    mineral servitude. (1931) *Louisiana law.* A servitude granting the right to enter another's property to explore for and extract minerals; specif., under the Louisiana Mineral Code, a charge on land in favor of a person or another tract of land, creating a limited right to use the land to explore for and produce minerals. • The servitude is generally equivalent to the severed mineral interest in a common-law state.

    natural servitude. (18c) **1.** A servitude naturally appurtenant to land, requiring no special mode of acquisition. • An example is the right of land, unencumbered by buildings, to the support of the adjoining land. **2.** *Civil law.* A servitude imposed by law because of the natural situation of the estates. • An example of a natural servitude is a lower estate that is bound to receive waters flowing naturally from a higher estate.

    navigation servitude. **1.** An easement allowing the federal government to regulate commerce on navigable water without having to pay compensation for interfering with private ownership rights. See NAVIGABLE WATER. **2.** An easement, based on the state police power or public-trust doctrine, that allows a state to regulate commerce on navigable water and provide limited compensation for interference with private ownership rights. • A state servitude is inferior to the federal servitude.

negative servitude. *Civil law.* A servitude appurtenant allowing a dominant landowner to prohibit the servient landowner from exercising a right. • For example, a negative servitude, such as *jus ne luminibus officiatur,* prevents a landowner from building in a way that blocks light from reaching another person's house.

nonapparent servitude. *Civil law.* A servitude appurtenant that is not obvious because there are no exterior signs of its existence. • An example is a prohibition against building above a certain height. Cf. *apparent servitude.*

personal servitude. (17c) **1.** A servitude granting a specific person certain rights in property. **2.** *Roman law.* A specific person's right over the property of another, regardless of who the owner might be. • A personal servitude lasted for the person's lifetime. **3.** *Louisiana law.* A servitude that benefits a person or an immovable. La. Civ. Code art. 534.

positive servitude. *Civil law.* A real servitude allowing a person to lawfully do something on the servient landowner's property, such as entering the property. — Also termed *affirmative servitude.*

predial servitude. See *servitude appurtenant.*

private servitude. (1922) A servitude vested in a particular person. • Examples include a landowner's personal right-of-way over an adjoining piece of land or a right granted to one person to fish in another's lake.

public servitude. (1805) A servitude vested in the public at large or in some class of indeterminate individuals. • Examples include the right of the public to use a highway over privately owned land and the right to navigate a river the bed of which is privately owned.

real servitude. See *servitude appurtenant.*

rural servitude. *Roman law.* A servitude chiefly affecting agricultural land or land in the country. • The four oldest types, *iter, actus, via,* and *aqueductus* were all *res mancipi* despite being incorporeal. Most rural servitudes were easements, but some were profits. — Also termed *rustic servitude; praedium rusticum; jus rusticorum praediorum.*

servitude appurtenant. (1893) A servitude that is not merely an encumbrance of one piece of land but is accessory to another piece; the right of using one piece of land for the benefit of another, such as the right of support for a building. — Also termed *real servitude; predial* (or *praedial*) *servitude; landed servitude.* La. Civ. Code art. 646.

servitude in gross. (1884) A servitude that is not accessory to any dominant estate for whose benefit it exists but is merely an encumbrance on a given piece of land.

servitude of drip. *Louisiana law.* A servitude appurtenant that binds the servient estate's owner to maintain a roof so that rainwater does not drip or drain onto the dominant estate. La. Civ. Code art. 664. — Also termed *servitude of drip and drain.*

servitude of view. *Louisiana law.* The dominant estate owner's right to enjoy a view through the servient estate and to prevent its obstruction. La. Civ. Code art. 701.

urban servitude. (1831) **1.** A servitude appertaining to the building and construction of houses in a city, such as the right to light and air. **2.** *Roman law.* A servitude that primarily affects buildings or urban land. • With the exception of *oneris ferendi,* urban servitudes were passive. They could be affected by planning legislation. — Also termed (in sense 2) *praedium urbanum; jus urbanorum praediorum.*

3. The condition of being a servant or slave <under the 15th Amendment, an American citizen's right to vote cannot be denied on account of race, color, or previous condition of servitude>. **4.** The condition of a prisoner who has been sentenced to forced labor <penal servitude>.

involuntary servitude. (18c) The condition of one forced to labor — for pay or not — for another by coercion or imprisonment.

servitude of drip and drain. See *servitude of drip* under SERVITUDE (2).

session. (15c) **1.** *Parliamentary law.* A meeting or series of related meetings throughout which a court, legislature, or other deliberative assembly conducts business in a continuing sequence <the court's spring session>. — Also termed (for a court) *sitting.* See TERM (5).

biennial session. (1854) A legislative session held every two years. • Most state legislatures have biennial sessions, usu. held in odd-numbered years.

closed session. (1956) **1.** See *executive session.* **2.** A session to which parties not directly involved are not admitted. **3.** *Military law.* A period during a court-martial when the members (or the judge, if trial is before a military judge) deliberate alone. — Also termed *closed court.*

executive session. A meeting, usu. held in secret, that only the members and invited nonmembers may attend. • The term originated in the United States Senate, which until 1929 sat behind closed doors when it advised the President about executive business such as appointments and treaties. — Also termed *closed session; secret session.*

extraordinary session. See *special session.*

extra session. See *special session.*

joint session. (1853) The combined meeting of two legislative bodies (such as the House of Representatives and the Senate) to pursue a common agenda.

lame-duck session. (1924) A post-election legislative session in which some of the participants are voting during their last days as elected officials. See LAME DUCK.

open session. (1810) **1.** A session to which parties not directly involved are admitted. — Also termed *public session.* **2.** *Military law.* The period during a court-martial in which all participants are in the courtroom. ● Generally, the public may attend a court-martial's open session.

plenary session. (1936) A meeting of all the members of a deliberative assembly, not just a committee.

pro forma session. A legislative session held not to conduct business but only to satisfy a constitutional provision that neither house may adjourn for longer than a certain time (usu. three days) without the other house's consent.

public session. See *open session* (1).

regular session. (18c) A session that takes place at fixed intervals or specified times.

secret session. See *executive session.*

special session. (17c) A legislative session, usu. called by the executive, that meets outside its regular term to consider a specific issue or to reduce backlog. — Also termed *extra session; extraordinary session.*

2. The period within any given day during which such a body is assembled and performing its duties <court is in session>. ● The terms "meeting" and "session" have opposite but sometimes interchangeable meanings. An organization's annual convention may consist of several consecutive meetings that it calls "sessions," such as a morning session and an afternoon session, or a Friday session and a Saturday session, which are technically meetings rather than sessions. Likewise, the organization may call its convention an "annual meeting," which technically comprises several meetings that constitute a single session. Cf. MEETING. **3.** A trading day in a stock market.

triple witching session. A stock-market session on the third Friday in March, June, September, and December during which stock options, index options and futures contracts all expire. ● Stock-market volatility and share volume are often high on these days

session laws. (18c) **1.** A body of statutes enacted by a legislature during a particular annual or biennial session. **2.** The softbound booklets containing these statutes. — Also termed *acts of assembly; blue books; sheet acts.*

set-aside, *n.* (1943) Something (such as a percentage of funds) that is reserved or put aside for a specific purpose.

set aside, *vb.* (18c) (Of a court) to annul or vacate (a judgment, order, etc.) <the judge refused to set aside the default judgment>.

setback, *n.* (1916) *Real estate.* The minimum amount of space required between a lot line and a building line <a 12-foot setback>. ● Typically contained in zoning ordinances or deed restrictions, setbacks are designed to ensure that enough light and ventilation reach the property and to keep buildings from being erected too close to property lines. See BUSINESS LINE.

setback requirement. See BUILDING LINE.

set down, *vb.* (18c) To schedule (a case) for trial or hearing, usu. by making a docket entry.

set forth. See SET OUT.

seti (**set**-ee). *Mining law.* A lease.

set of exchange. *Commercial law.* A single bill of lading drawn in a set of parts, each of which is valid only if the goods have not been delivered against any other part. ● Bills may be drawn in duplicate or triplicate, the first part being "first of exchange," the second part being "second of exchange," and so on. When one part has been paid, the other parts become void.

setoff, *n.* (18c) **1.** A defendant's counterdemand against the plaintiff, arising out of a transaction independent of the plaintiff's claim. **2.** A debtor's right to reduce the amount of a debt by any sum the creditor owes the debtor; the counterbalancing sum owed by the creditor. — Also written *set-off.* — Also termed (in civil law) *compensation; stoppage.* See COUNTERCLAIM; OFFSET. Cf. RECOUPMENT (3). **3.** The balancing of mutual liabilities with respect to a pledge relationship. — **set off,** *vb.*

set out, *vb.* (16c) To recite, explain, narrate, or incorporate (facts or circumstances) <set out the terms of the contract>. — Also termed *set forth.*

set over, *vb.* (16c) To transfer or convey (property) <to set over the land to the purchaser>.

setting, *n.* The date and time established by a court for a trial or hearing <the plaintiff sought a continuance of the imminent setting>.

special setting. (1916) A preferential setting on a court's calendar, usu. reserved for older cases or cases given priority by law, made either on a party's motion or on the court's own motion. ● For example, some jurisdictions authorize a special setting for cases involving a party over the age of 70. — Also termed *special trial setting; trial-setting preference.*

settled estate. See ESTATE (1).

settled insanity. See DELIRIUM TREMENS.

settled land. See LAND.

settlement, *n.* (17c) **1.** The conveyance of property — or of interests in property — to provide for one or more beneficiaries, usu. members of the settlor's family, in a way that differs from what the beneficiaries would receive as heirs under the statutes of descent and distribution <in marriage settlements, historically, the wife waived her right to claim dower or to succeed to her husband's property>.

   strict settlement. *Hist.* A property settlement that aimed to keep the estate within the family by creating successive interests in tail and shielding remainders from destruction by the interposition of a trust. Cf. *trader's settlement.*

   trader's settlement. *Hist.* A property settlement in which the land is put into a trust for sale, the proceeds to be either paid out to beneficiaries over time or divided among the settlor's heirs. Cf. *strict settlement.*

   voluntary settlement. A property settlement made without valuable consideration — other than psychological or emotional consideration such as love and affection — from the beneficiary.

2. An agreement ending a dispute or lawsuit <the parties reached a settlement the day before trial>.— Also termed *settlement agreement.*

   derivative settlement. 1. The negotiated outcome of a derivative action. See DERIVATIVE ACTION. **2.** A person's legal-residence status that is acquired though another person, as with a child through one or both parents.

   final settlement. A court order discharging an executor's duties after an estate's execution.

   full settlement. A settlement and release of all pending claims between the parties.

   judicial settlement. The settlement of a civil case with the help of a judge who is not assigned to adjudicate the dispute. ● Parties sometimes find this procedure advantageous because it capitalizes on judicial experience in evaluating the settlement value of a claim.

   mediated settlement agreement. A settlement agreement arrived at through mediation. — Abbr. MSA.

   nuisance settlement. A settlement in which the defendant pays the plaintiff purely for economic reasons — as opposed to any notion of responsibility — because without the settlement the defendant would spend more money in legal fees and expenses caused by protracted litigation than in paying the settlement amount. ● The money paid in such a settlement is often termed *nuisance money.*

   out-of-court settlement. The settlement and termination of a pending suit, arrived at without the court's participation.

   structured settlement. A settlement in which the defendant agrees to pay periodic sums to the plaintiff for a specified time.

3. Payment, satisfaction, or final adjustment <the seller shipped the goods after confirming the buyer's settlement of the account>.

   viatical settlement (vī-**at**-ə-kəl). [fr. Latin *viaticus* "relating to a road or journey"] A transaction in which a terminally or chronically ill person sells the benefits of a life-insurance policy to a third party in return for a lump-sum cash payment equal to a percentage of the policy's face value. ● Viatical settlements are common with AIDS patients, many of whom sell their policies at a 20% to 40% discount, depending on life expectancy. When the insured (called the "viator") dies, the investor receives the insurance benefit. — Also termed *life settlement.*

4. CLOSING <the settlement on their first home is next Friday>. **5.** *Wills & estates.* The complete execution of an estate by the executor <the settlement of the estate was long and complex>. **6.** The establishment of a legal residence. ● This sense was frequently used in poor-relief contexts. Cf. (in sense 6) STATUS OF IRREMOVABILITY. — **settle,** *vb.*

settlement agent. 1. See AGENT (2). **2.** See *settlement attorney* under ATTORNEY.

settlement agreement. See SETTLEMENT (2).

settlement attorney. See ATTORNEY.

settlement class. See CLASS (4).

settlement counsel. See CIRCUIT MEDIATOR.

settlement credit. (1979) *Civil procedure.* A court's reduction of the amount of a jury verdict — or the effect of the verdict on nonsettling defendants — to account for settlement funds the plaintiff has received from former defendants or from other responsible parties.

settlement date. See DATE.

settlement-first method. (1996) A means by which to apply a settlement credit to a jury verdict, by first reducing the amount of the verdict by subtracting the amount of all settlements the plaintiff has received on the claim, then reducing the remainder by the percentage of the plaintiff's comparative fault. See SETTLEMENT CREDIT. Cf. FAULT-FIRST METHOD.

settlement option. See OPTION.

settlement right. *Hist.* A government-issued certificate granting land to a settler.

settlement sheet. See CLOSING STATEMENT (2).

settlement statement. See CLOSING STATEMENT (2).

settlement value. See VALUE (2).

settler. (17c) **1.** A person who occupies property with the intent to establish a residence. • The term is usu. applied to an early resident of a country or region. **2.** SETTLOR.

settle up, *vb.* (1884) To collect, pay, and turn over debts and property (e.g., of a decedent, bankrupt, or insolvent business).

settlor (**set**-lər). (18c) **1.** A person who makes a settlement of property; esp., one who sets up a trust. — Also termed *creator*; *donor*; *trustor*; *grantor*; *founder*. **2.** A party to an instrument. — Also spelled (in both senses) *settler*.

set up, *vb.* To raise (a defense) <the defendant set up the insanity defense on the murder charge>.

Seventeenth Amendment. The constitutional amendment, ratified in 1913, transferring the power to elect U.S. senators from the state legislatures to the states' voters.

Seventh Amendment. The constitutional amendment, ratified with the Bill of Rights in 1791, guaranteeing the right to a jury trial in federal civil cases that are traditionally considered to be suits at common law and that have an amount in controversy exceeding $20.

72 COLREGS. See INTERNATIONAL RULES OF THE ROAD.

seven-years'-absence rule. (1920) The principle that a person who has been missing without explanation for at least seven years is legally presumed dead. Cf. ENOCH ARDEN LAW.

severability. See BLUE-PENCIL TEST.

severability clause. (1935) A provision that keeps the remaining provisions of a contract or statute in force if any portion of that contract or statute is judicially declared void, unenforceable, or unconstitutional. — Also termed *saving clause*; *separability clause*. See *severable contract* under CONTRACT; *severable statute* under STATUTE.

severable contract. See CONTRACT.

severable statute. See STATUTE.

several, *adj.* (15c) **1.** (Of a person, place, or thing) more than one or two but not a lot <several witnesses>. **2.** (Of liability, etc.) separate; particular; distinct, but not necessarily independent <a several obligation>. **3.** (Of things, etc.) different; various <several settlement options>.

several action. See *separate action* under ACTION (4).

several contract. See *severable contract* under CONTRACT.

several count. See COUNT.

several covenant. See COVENANT (1).

several demise. See DEMISE.

several fishery. See FISHERY (1).

several inheritance. See INHERITANCE.

several liability. See LIABILITY.

severally, *adj.* Distinctly; separately <severally liable>.

several obligation. See OBLIGATION.

several-remedies rule. (1975) A procedural rule that tolls a statute of limitations for a plaintiff who has several available forums (such as a workers'-compensation proceeding and the court system) and who timely files in one forum and later proceeds in another forum, as long as the defendant's right and claims are not affected.

several tail. See TAIL.

several tenancy. See TENANCY.

severalty (**sev**-[ə]-rəl-tee). (15c) The state or condition of being separate or distinct <the individual landowners held the land in severalty, not as joint tenants>.

severance, *n.* (15c) **1.** The act of cutting off; the state of being cut off. **2.** *Civil procedure.* The separation, by the court, of the claims of multiple parties either to permit separate actions on each claim or to allow certain interlocutory orders to become final. — Also termed *severance of actions*; *severance of claims*. See *bifurcated trial* under TRIAL. Cf. CONSOLIDATION (3). **3.** The termination of a joint tenancy, usu. by converting it into a tenancy in common. **4.** The removal of anything (such as crops or minerals) attached or affixed to real property, making it personal property rather than a part of the land. • Mineral rights are frequently severed from surface rights on property that may contain oil and gas or other minerals. **5.** See SEVERANCE PAY. — **sever,** *vb.* — **severable,** *adj.*

severance damages. See DAMAGES.

severance of actions. See SEVERANCE (2).

severance of claims. See SEVERANCE (2).

severance pay. Money (apart from back wages or salary) paid by an employer to a dismissed employee. • The payment may be made in exchange for a release of any claims that the employee might have against the employer. — Sometimes shortened to *severance*. — Also termed *separation pay*; *dismissal compensation*.

severance tax. See TAX.

sewer service. See SERVICE (2).

sex. (14c) **1.** The sum of the peculiarities of structure and function that distinguish a male from a female organism; gender. **2.** Sexual intercourse. **3.** SEXUAL RELATIONS (2).

sex change. See SEX REASSIGNMENT.

sex discrimination. See DISCRIMINATION.

sex-offender registry. A publicly available list of the names and addresses of sex offenders who have been released from prison. • The registries were started by state statutes known as "Megan's laws." The lists are often posted on the Internet, and some states require publication of the offender's photograph, name, and address in local newspapers. See MEGAN'S LAW.

sex reassignment. Medical treatment intended to effect a sex change; surgery and hormonal treatments designed to alter a person's gender. — Also termed *sex change*.

sexual abuse. 1. See ABUSE. **2.** See RAPE.

sexual activity. See SEXUAL RELATIONS.

sexual assault. 1. See ASSAULT. **2.** See RAPE.

sexual assault by contact. See *sexual assault* (2) under ASSAULT.

sexual battery. 1. See BATTERY. **2.** See RAPE.

sexual exploitation. The use of a person, esp. a child, in prostitution, pornography, or other sexually manipulative activity that has caused or could cause serious emotional injury. — Sometimes shortened to *exploitation*.

sexual harassment. (1973) A type of employment discrimination consisting in verbal or physical abuse of a sexual nature. See HARASSMENT.

hostile-environment sexual harassment. (1986) Sexual harassment in which a work environment is created where an employee is subject to unwelcome verbal or physical sexual behavior that is either severe or pervasive. • This type of harassment might occur, for example, if a group of coworkers repeatedly e-mailed pornographic pictures to a colleague who found the pictures offensive.

quid pro quo sexual harassment. (1982) Sexual harassment in which an employment decision is based on the satisfaction of a sexual demand. • This type of harassment might occur, for example, if a boss fired or demoted an employee who refused to go on a date with the boss.

same-sex sexual harassment. Sexual harassment by a supervisor of an employee of the same sex. — Also termed *same-sex harassment*.

sexually dangerous person. See SEXUAL PREDATOR.

sexually transmitted disease. A disease transmitted only or chiefly by engaging in sexual acts with an infected person. • Common examples are syphilis and gonorrhea. — Abbr. STD. — Also termed *venereal disease*.

sexually violent predator. See SEXUAL PREDATOR.

sexual offense. See OFFENSE (1).

sexual orientation. (1931) A person's predisposition or inclination toward a particular type of sexual activity or behavior; heterosexuality, homosexuality, or bisexuality. • There has been a trend in recent years to make sexual orientation a protected class, esp. in employment and hate-crime statutes.

sexual predator. A person who has committed many violent sexual acts or who has a propensity for committing violent sexual acts. — Also termed *predator*; *sexually dangerous person*; *sexually violent predator*.

sexual relations. (1909) **1.** Sexual intercourse. — Also termed *carnalis copula*. **2.** Physical sexual activity that does not necessarily culminate in intercourse. • Sexual relations usu. involve the touching of another's breast, vagina, penis, or anus. Both persons (the toucher and the person touched) are said to engage in sexual relations. — Also termed *sexual activity*.

SF. See *sinking fund* under FUND (1).

S/F. *abbr.* STATUTE OF FRAUDS.

SG. *abbr.* **1.** SOLICITOR GENERAL. **2.** SURGEON GENERAL.

shadow economy. Collectively, the unregistered economic activities that contribute to a country's gross national product. • A shadow economy may involve the legal and illegal production of goods and services, including gambling, prostitution, and drug-dealing, as well as barter transactions and unreported incomes. — Also termed *black economy*; *black market*; *underground economy*.

shadow jury. See JURY.

shadow stock plan. See PHANTOM STOCK PLAN.

shakedown. (1902) **1.** An extortion of money using threats of violence or, in the case of a police officer, threats of arrest. **2.** See *shakedown search* under SEARCH.

shakedown search. See SEARCH.

shaken-baby syndrome. The medical condition of a child who has suffered forceful shaking, with resulting brain injury. • The syndrome was first identified in the early 1970s. Common injuries include retinal hemorrhage and subdural and subarachnoid hemorrhage, with minimal or no signs of external cranial trauma. Many victims suffer blindness or death.

shakeout, *n.* An elimination of weak or nonproductive businesses in an industry, esp. during a period of intense competition or declining prices.

shall, *vb.* (bef. 12c) **1.** Has a duty to; more broadly, is required to <the requester shall send notice> <notice shall be sent>. • This is the mandatory sense that drafters typically intend and that courts typically uphold. **2.** Should (as often interpreted by courts) <all claimants shall request mediation>. **3.** May <no person shall enter the building without

first signing the roster>. • When a negative word such as *not* or *no* precedes *shall* (as in the example in angle brackets), the word *shall* often means *may*. What is being negated is permission, not a requirement. **4.** Will (as a future-tense verb) <the corporation shall then have a period of 30 days to object>. **5.** Is entitled to <the secretary shall be reimbursed for all expenses>. • Only sense 1 is acceptable under strict standards of drafting.

sham, *n.* (17c) **1.** Something that is not what it seems; a counterfeit. **2.** A person who pretends to be something that he or she is not; a faker. — **sham,** *vb.* — **sham,** *adj.*

sham action. See ACTION (4).

sham affidavit. See AFFIDAVIT.

sham defense. See DEFENSE (1).

shame sanction. See SANCTION.

shame sentence. See *shame sanction* under SANCTION.

sham exception. (1969) An exception to the *Noerr–Pennington* doctrine whereby a company that petitions the government will not receive First Amendment protection or an exemption from the antitrust laws if its intent in petitioning the government for favorable government action or treatment is really an effort to harm its competitors. See NOERR–PENNINGTON DOCTRINE; *sham action* under ACTION (4).

shaming sentence. See *shame sanction* under SANCTION.

sham lawsuit. See *sham action* under ACTION (4).

sham litigation. See *sham action* under ACTION (4).

sham marriage. See MARRIAGE (1).

sham petitioning. See *sham action* under ACTION (4).

sham plea. See *sham pleading* under PLEADING (1).

sham pleading. See PLEADING (1).

sham prosecution. See PROSECUTION.

sham suit. See *sham action* under ACTION (4).

sham transaction. (1937) An agreement or exchange that has no independent economic benefit or business purpose and is entered into solely to create a tax advantage (such as a deduction for a business loss). • The Internal Revenue Service is entitled to ignore the purported tax benefits of a sham transaction.

shanghaiing (shang-**hi**-ing). The act or an instance of coercing or inducing someone to do something by fraudulent or other wrongful means; specif., the practice of drugging, tricking, intoxicating, or otherwise illegally inducing a person to work aboard a vessel, usu. to secure advance money or

a premium. — Also termed *shanghaiing sailors.* 18 USCA § 2194.

share, *n.* (14c) **1.** An allotted portion owned by, contributed by, or due to someone <each partner's share of the profits>.

intestate share. The share that the renouncer of a will would take in the decedent's assets if the decedent had left no will affecting in any way the distribution of assets.

2. One of the definite number of equal parts into which the capital stock of a corporation or joint-stock company is divided <the broker advised his customer to sell the stock shares when the price reaches $29>. • A share represents an equity or ownership interest in the corporation or joint-stock company. Cf. STOCK (4); SECURITY (4).

American share. *Securities.* A share of stock in a foreign corporation issued directly to U.S. investors through a transfer agent.

qualifying share. A share of common stock purchased by someone in order to become a director of a corporation that requires its directors to be shareholders.

share, *vb.* (16c) **1.** To divide (something) into portions. **2.** To enjoy or partake of (a power, right, etc.).

share account. See *share-draft account* under ACCOUNT.

share acquisition. The acquisition of a corporation by purchasing all or most of its outstanding shares directly from the shareholders; TAKEOVER. — Also termed *share-acquisition transaction*; *stock acquisition*; *stock-acquisition transaction.* Cf. ASSET ACQUISITION.

share and share alike. To divide (assets, etc.) in equal shares or proportions; to engage in per capita division. See PER CAPITA.

share certificate. See STOCK CERTIFICATE.

sharecropping. An agricultural arrangement in which a landowner leases land to a tenant who, in turn, gives the landlord a portion of the crop as rent. • The landlord usu. provides the seed, fertilizer, and equipment. — **sharecropper,** *n.*

shared-appreciation mortgage. See MORTGAGE.

shared custody. See *joint custody* under CUSTODY (2).

shared-equity mortgage. See MORTGAGE.

shared parenting. See PARENTING.

share draft. See DRAFT.

share-draft account. See ACCOUNT.

shared residency. See *joint physical custody* under CUSTODY.

shareholder. (1832) One who owns or holds a share or shares in a company, esp. a corporation. — Also termed *shareowner*; (in a corporation) *stockholder*.

controlling shareholder. A shareholder who can influence the corporation's activities because the shareholder either owns a majority of outstanding shares or owns a smaller percentage but a significant number of the remaining shares are widely distributed among many others.

dummy shareholder. A shareholder who owns stock in name only for the benefit of the true owner, whose identity is usu. concealed.

interested shareholder. A person who owns enough of a corporation's stock to affect corporate decision-making, usu. at least 15–20% of the corporation's outstanding stock. — Also termed *interested stockholder*.

majority shareholder. A shareholder who owns or controls more than half the corporation's stock.

minority shareholder. A shareholder who owns less than half the total shares outstanding and thus cannot control the corporation's management or singlehandedly elect directors.

shareholder-control agreement. See POOLING AGREEMENT.

shareholder derivative suit. See DERIVATIVE ACTION (1).

shareholder oppression. See OPPRESSION (4).

shareholder proposal. A proposal by one or more corporate stockholders to change company policy or procedure. ● Ordinarily, the corporation informs all stockholders about the proposal before the next shareholder meeting.

shareholder resolution. See RESOLUTION (2).

shareholders' equity. See OWNERS' EQUITY.

shareholder's liability. See LIABILITY.

shareholder voting agreement. See POOLING AGREEMENT.

shareowner. See SHAREHOLDER.

shares outstanding. See *outstanding stock* under STOCK.

share split. See STOCK SPLIT.

shareware. Software that can be redistributed but not modified and requires all users to pay a license fee. ● The license fee applies to both originals and distributed copies. Cf. FREEWARE; PROPRIETARY SOFTWARE; SEMI-FREE SOFTWARE.

share-warrant to bearer. A warrant providing that the bearer is entitled to a certain amount of fully paid stock shares. ● Delivery of the warrant operates as a transfer of the shares of stock.

Sharia (shə-**ree**-ə). The body of Islamic religious law applicable to police, banking, business, contracts, and social issues. ● Sharia is a system of

laws, rather than a codification of laws, based on the Koran and other Islamic sources.

shark repellent. 1. TAKEOVER DEFENSE. **2.** More specifically, a charter or bylaw provision designed to impede hostile bids to acquire a controlling interest in a corporation.

sharp, *adj.* (1886) (Of a clause in a mortgage, deed, etc.) empowering the creditor to take immediate and summary action upon the debtor's default. See DROP-DEAD PROVISION.

sharp practice. (1836) Unethical action and trickery, esp. by a lawyer. — Also termed (archaically) *unhandsome dealing.* — **sharp practitioner,** *n.*

shave, *vb.* (1832) **1.** To purchase (a negotiable instrument) at a greater than usual discount rate. **2.** To reduce or deduct from (a price).

sheer, *n. Maritime law.* A vessel's sudden deviation from its line of course; a swerve.

sheet acts. See SESSION LAWS.

shelf company. See COMPANY.

shelf corporation. See *shelf company* under COMPANY.

shelf issue. See ISSUE (2).

shelf registration. See REGISTRATION (2).

shelf security. See SECURITY.

shell corporation. See CORPORATION.

Shelley's Case, Rule in. See RULE IN SHELLEY'S CASE.

shell game. A sleight-of-hand game that uses three cups or thimble-like objects, one of which has a pea, ball, or other small object underneath. ● This is a game of chance in which one player bets that he or she can remember under which cup the object is. The cups are moved around so quickly that the player finds it difficult to remember where the object is. When played casually on public streets the shell game is usu. a swindle because the operator palms the object rather than leaving it under a cup, so the player has no chance of winning. — Also termed *thimblerig; thimbles and balls.* See GAME OF CHANCE.

shelter, *n.* **1.** A place of refuge providing safety from danger, attack, or observation.

homeless shelter. A privately or publicly operated residential facility providing overnight accommodation free of charge to homeless people. ● Most homeless shelters accept occupants on a first-come-first-served basis and are open only from early evening to early morning. Those that serve homeless families may remain open throughout the day to women and children. Some shelters offer occupants help such as advice on finding and applying for public assistance, employment, and medical care.

women's shelter. A privately or publicly operated residential facility providing women (and their children) who are victims of domestic violence with temporary lodging, food, and other services such as employment assistance, counseling, and medical care. — Also termed *family shelter.*

youth shelter. **1.** A privately or publicly operated residential facility offering young runaway or throwaway children and homeless young people a safe place to stay, usu. for a short time. ● The residents enter the shelter voluntarily and can leave anytime they wish. Some shelters offer long-term transitional training so that young people can leave street life and eventually lead independent, productive lives. **2.** An alternative type of juvenile-detention center that is less physically restrictive than a jail or boot camp. ● Delinquent juveniles are usu. brought to these shelters by police or ordered to reside there by a court. Residents attend school or work in the daytime and may be permitted weekend visits at their family homes.

2. See TAX SHELTER <the shelter saved the taxpayer over $2,000 in taxes>. — **shelter,** *vb.*

shelter-care hearing. See *shelter hearing* under HEARING.

shelter doctrine. (1955) *Commercial law.* The principle that a person to whom a holder in due course has transferred commercial paper, as well as any later transferee, will succeed to the rights of the holder in due course. ● As a result, transferees of holders in due course are generally not subject to defenses against the payment of an instrument. This doctrine ensures the free transferability of commercial paper. Its name derives from the idea that the transferees "take shelter" in the rights of the holder in due course.

shelter hearing. See HEARING.

shelving. *Patents.* The failure to begin or the stopping of commercial use of a patent during a specified period, usu. the term of the license. ● A licensor may place an anti-shelving provision in a license to ensure the licensed product's manufacture and sale. The term usu. applies to patented inventions, but licenses for trademarked products may also address shelving.

shepardize, *vb.* (1928) **1.** (*often cap.*) To determine the subsequent history and treatment of (a case) by using a printed or computerized version of *Shepard's Citators.* **2.** Loosely, to check the precedential value of (a case) by the same or similar means. — **shepardization, shepardizing,** *n.*

sheriff. [Middle English *shire reeve* from Anglo-Saxon *scirgerefa*] A county's chief peace officer, usu. elected, who in most jurisdictions acts as custodian of the county jail, executes civil and criminal process, and carries out judicial mandates within the county. — Also termed *high sheriff; vice-comes.*

deputy sheriff. An officer who, acting under the direction of a sheriff, may perform most of the duties of the sheriff's office. ● Although *undersheriff* is broadly synonymous with *deputy sheriff,* writers have sometimes distinguished between the two, suggesting that a deputy is appointed for a special occasion or purpose, while an undersheriff is permanent. — Also termed *undersheriff; general deputy; vice-sheriff.*

sheriff's court. See COURT.

sheriff's deed. See DEED.

sheriff's jury. See JURY.

sheriff's sale. See SALE.

Sherman Antitrust Act. A federal statute, passed in 1890, that prohibits direct or indirect interference with the freely competitive interstate production and distribution of goods. ● This Act was amended by the Clayton Act in 1914. 15 USCA §§ 1–7. — Often shortened to *Sherman Act.* — Also termed *the Antitrust Law.*

Sherman–Sorrells doctrine. (1998) The principle that a defendant may claim as an affirmative defense that he or she was not disposed to commit the offense until a public official (often an undercover police officer) encouraged the defendant to do so. ● This entrapment defense, which is recognized in the federal system and a majority of states, was developed in *Sherman v. United States,* 356 U.S. 369, 78 S.Ct. 819 (1958), and *Sorrells v. United States,* 287 U.S. 435, 53 S.Ct. 210 (1932). — Also termed *subjective method.* See ENTRAPMENT. Cf. HYPOTHETICAL-PERSON DEFENSE.

shield law. (1971) **1.** A statute that affords journalists the privilege not to reveal confidential sources. See *journalist's privilege* under PRIVILEGE (3). **2.** A statute that restricts or prohibits the use, in rape or sexual-assault cases, of evidence about the victim's past sexual conduct. — Also termed (in sense 2) *rape shield law; rape shield statute.*

shifting, *adj.* (1874) (Of a position, place, etc.) changing or passing from one to another <a shifting estate>.

shifting clause. (1813) At common law, a clause under the Statute of Uses prescribing a substituted mode of devolution in the settlement of an estate. See STATUTE OF USES.

shifting executory interest. See EXECUTORY INTEREST.

shifting ground. *Patents.* The broadening of a patent application in an amendment by claiming a feature of the invention that was disclosed but not claimed in the original application.

shifting inheritance. See INHERITANCE.

shifting risk. See RISK.

shifting stock of merchandise. Merchandise inventory subject to change by purchases and sales in the course of trade.

shifting the burden of proof. (1805) In litigation, the transference of the duty to prove a fact from one party to the other; the passing of the duty to produce evidence in a case from one side to another as the case progresses, when one side has made a prima facie showing on a point of evidence, requiring the other side to rebut it by contradictory evidence. See BURDEN OF PROOF.

shifting trust. See TRUST.

shifting use. See USE (4).

shill. 1. A person who poses as an innocent bystander at a confidence game but actually serves as a decoy for the perpetrators of the scheme. 2. BY-BIDDER. — **shill,** *vb.*

shilling, *n.* 1. The practice of fraudulently bidding on items at an auction solely to drive up the price. • The seller might collude with another person to bid or might act alone and anonymously. Cf. BIDDING UP; BY-BIDDING. 2. *Hist.* An English coin equal to 12 pence or 1/20th of a pound. • Shillings were revalued as five pence and phased out when decimalization was adopted in the early 1970s. The modern five-pence coin, like its predecessor equal to 1/20th of a pound, is sometimes nostalgically referred to as a shilling.

shingle. A small, usu. dignified sign that marks the office door of a lawyer or other professional.

shingle theory. *Securities.* The notion that a broker-dealer must be held to a high standard of conduct because by engaging in the securities business ("hanging out a shingle"), the broker-dealer implicitly represents to the world that the conduct of all its employees will be fair and meet professional norms.

shin plaster. *Hist. Slang.* 1. A bank note that has greatly depreciated in value; esp., the paper money of the Republic of Texas in relation to the U.S. dollar. 2. Paper money in denominations less than one dollar.

ship, *n.* A type of vessel used or intended to be used in navigation. See VESSEL.

  chartered ship. 1. A ship specially hired to transport the goods of only one person or company. 2. A ship on which a shipper has chartered space for a cargo.

  general ship. A ship that is set for a particular voyage to carry the goods of any persons willing to ship goods on it for that voyage.

ship, *vb.* To send (goods, documents, etc.) from one place to another, esp. by delivery to a carrier for transportation.

ship broker. *Maritime law.* 1. The business agent of a shipowner or charterer; an intermediary between an owner or charterer and a shipper. 2. One who negotiates the purchase and sale of a ship.

ship channel. *Maritime law.* The part of a navigable body of water where the water is deep enough for large vessels to travel safely.

shipmaster. See MASTER OF A SHIP.

shipment. 1. The transportation of goods; esp., the delivery of goods to a carrier and subsequent issuance of a bill of lading. 2. The goods so shipped; an order of goods.

shipment contract. See CONTRACT.

Ship Mortgage Act. A federal law regulating mortgages on ships registered as U.S. vessels by, among other things, providing for enforcement of maritime liens in favor of those who furnish supplies or maintenance to the vessels. 46 USCA §§ 30101, 31301–43.

shipowner-negligence doctrine. The principle that a shipowner is liable for an assault on a crew member if the crew member was assaulted by a superior, during an activity undertaken for the benefit of the ship's business, and if the ship's officers could reasonably have foreseen the assault.

shipper. 1. One who ships goods to another. 2. One who contracts with a carrier for the transportation of cargo. • As a legal term of art, the shipper may not be the person who owns the cargo, but an agent or an independent contractor. Cf. CARRIER (1).

shipping articles. *Maritime law.* A document (provided by a master of a vessel to the mariners) detailing voyage information, such as the voyage term, the number of crew, and the wage rates. 46 USCA § 10302.

shipping commissioner. An officer, appointed by the secretary of the treasury, who is posted at a port of entry, and vested with general supervisory authority over seamen's contracts and welfare. • In 1993, the term was changed to "master or individual in charge." See Pub. L. 103-206 § 403.

shipping document. Any paper that covers a shipment in trade, such as a bill of lading or letter of credit.

shipping law. See LAW OF SHIPPING.

shipping order. A copy of the shipper's instructions to a carrier regarding the disposition of goods to be transported.

ship's husband. *Maritime law.* A person appointed to act as general agent of all the coowners of a ship, as by contracting for all necessary services, equipment, and supplies. Cf. EXERCITOR.

ship's papers. *Maritime law.* The papers that a vessel is required to carry to provide the primary evidence of the ship's national character, ownership, nature and destination of cargo, and compliance with navigation laws. ●These papers includes certificates of health, charter-party, muster-rolls, licenses, and bills of lading.

shipwreck. *Maritime law.* **1.** A ship's wreckage. **2.** The injury or destruction of a vessel because of circumstances beyond the owner's control, rendering the vessel incapable of carrying out its mission.

shire. A county in Great Britain (esp. England), originally made up of many hundreds but later consisting of larger divisions set off by metes and bounds.

shire-reeve. See REEVE.

Shively **presumption** (shɪv-lee). The doctrine that any prestatehood grant of public property does not include tidelands unless the grant specifically indicates otherwise. *Shively v. Bowlby*, 152 U.S. 1, 14 S.Ct. 548 (1894); *United States v. Holt State Bank*, 270 U.S. 49, 46 S.Ct. 197 (1925). See EQUAL-FOOTING DOCTRINE.

shock, *n.* A profound and sudden disturbance of the physical or mental senses; a sudden and violent physical or mental impression depressing the body's vital forces, as by a sudden injury or medical procedure.

   mental shock. Shock caused by agitation of the mental senses and resulting in extreme grief or joy, as by witnessing the horrific death of a family member or winning the lottery. Cf. EMOTIONAL DISTRESS.

   physical shock. Shock caused by agitation of the physical senses, as from a sudden violent blow, impact, collision, or concussion.

shock incarceration. See INCARCERATION.

shock probation. See PROBATION.

shock the conscience. To cause intense ethical or humanitarian discomfort. ● This phrase is used as an equitable standard for gauging whether (1) state action amounts to a violation of a person's substantive-due-process rights, (2) a jury's award is excessive, (3) a fine, jail term, or other penalty is disproportionate to the crime, or (4) a contract is unconscionable. See CONSCIENCE OF THE COURT (2).

shop, *n.* (13c) A business establishment or place of employment; a factory, office, or other place of business.

   agency shop. A shop in which a union acts as an agent for the employees, regardless of their union membership. ● Nonunion members must pay union dues because it is presumed that any collective bargaining will benefit nonunion as well as union members.

   closed nonunion shop. A shop in which the employer restricts employment to workers who are unaffiliated with any labor union.

   closed shop. A shop in which the employer, by agreement with a union, employs only union members in good standing. ● Closed shops were made illegal under the federal Labor-Management Relations Act. — Also termed *closed union shop.* See PREHIRE AGREEMENT. Cf. *closed union* under UNION.

   open closed shop. A shop in which the employer hires nonunion workers on the understanding that they will become union members within a specified period. — Also termed *open shop.*

   open shop. **1.** A shop in which the employer hires workers without regard to union affiliation. See RIGHT-TO-WORK LAW. Cf. *open union* under UNION. **2.** See *open closed shop.*

   preferential nonunion shop. A shop in which nonunion members are given preference over main members in employment matters.

   preferential shop. See *preferential union shop.*

   preferential union shop. A shop in which union members are given preference over nonunion members in employment matters. — Also termed *preferential shop.*

   union shop. A shop in which the employer may hire nonunion employees on the condition that they join a union within a specified time (usu. at least 30 days).

shop-book rule. (1898) *Evidence.* An exception to the hearsay rule permitting the admission into evidence of original bookkeeping records if the books' entries were made in the ordinary course of business and the books are authenticated by somebody who maintains them.

shop books. (17c) Records of original entry maintained in the usual course of business by a shopkeeper, trader, or other businessperson. — Also termed *books of account; account books.*

shop committee. A union committee that resolves employee complaints within a union shop. See *union shop* under SHOP.

shoplifting, *n.* (17c) Theft of merchandise from a store or business; specif., larceny of goods from a store or other commercial establishment by willfully taking and concealing the merchandise with the intention of converting the goods to one's personal use without paying the purchase price. See LARCENY. — **shoplift,** *vb.*

shop right. (1879) *Patents.* An employer's right to an irrevocable, nonassignable, nonexclusive, royalty-free license in an employee's invention, if the employee conceived and developed the invention during the course of employment and used company funds and materials. ● The term derives from the idea that the right belongs to the shop, not to the employee. Employment contracts frequently contain patent-assignment clauses, but the employer is entitled to the license even if the employee retains the patent. If the employee or consultant was hired to invent, then the employer owns the resulting inventions. If an employee develops an invention independently, the employee is its sole owner. But if an employees uses the employer's resources to make the invention, courts use the shop-right doctrine to order the employee to compensate the employer.

shop steward. See STEWARD (2).

shore. (14c) **1.** Land lying between the lines of high- and low-water mark; lands bordering on the shores of navigable waters below the line of ordinary high water. **2.** Land adjacent to a body of water regardless of whether it is below or above the ordinary high- or low-water mark. — Also termed *shore land*.

short, *adj.* **1.** Not holding at the time of sale the security or commodity that is being sold in anticipation of a fall in price <the trader was short at the market's close>. **2.** Of or relating to a sale of securities or commodities not in the seller's possession at the time of sale <a short position>. See *short sale* under SALE. Cf. LONG.

short, *adv.* By a short sale <sold the stock short>. See *short sale* under SALE.

short, *vb.* To sell (a security or commodity) by a short sale <shorted 1,000 shares of Pantheon stock>. See *short sale* under SALE.

short cause. See CAUSE (3).

short-cause calendar. See CALENDAR (2).

short-cause trial. See *short cause* under CAUSE (3).

shortened statutory period. *Patents.* An amount of time less than 6 months, but not less than 30 days, given in certain circumstances to a patent applicant to respond to an office action. ● The period for most responses can be extended up to the statutory period of 6 months. MPEP 710.02.

shorter-term rule. See RULE OF THE SHORTER TERM.

short-form agreement. *Labor law.* A contract usu. entered into by a small independent contractor whereby the contractor agrees to be bound by a collective-bargaining agreement negotiated between a union and a multiemployer bargaining unit.

short-form bill of lading. See BILL OF LADING.

short-form merger. See MERGER.

short interest. *Securities.* In a short sale, the number of shares that have not been purchased for return to lenders. See *short sale* under SALE.

short lease. See LEASE.

short notice. See NOTICE.

short position. The position of an investor who borrowed stock to make a short sale but has not

yet purchased the stock to repay the lender. See *short sale* under SALE.

short sale. See SALE.

short sale against the box. See SALE.

short-shipped, *adj. Commercial law.* Partially filled; containing fewer units than requested or paid for.

short summons. See SUMMONS.

short-swing profits. Profits made by a corporate insider on the purchase and sale (or sale and purchase) of company stock within a six-month period. ● These profits are subject to being returned to the company.

short-term alimony. See *rehabilitative alimony* under ALIMONY.

short-term capital gain. See CAPITAL GAIN.

short-term debt. **1.** See DEBT. **2.** See *current liability* under LIABILITY.

short-term loan. See LOAN.

short-term security. See SECURITY.

short-term trading. See TRADING.

short-term trust. See *Clifford trust* under TRUST.

short title. See TITLE (3).

short ton. See TON.

shotgun instruction. See ALLEN CHARGE.

shotgun pleading. See PLEADING (1).

shotgun rejection. See REJECTION.

show, *vb.* (12c) To make (facts, etc.) apparent or clear by evidence; to prove.

show cause. To produce a satisfactory explanation or excuse, usu. in connection with a motion or application to a court.

show-cause motion. See MOTION.

show-cause order. See ORDER (2).

show-cause proceeding. (1922) A usu. expedited proceeding on a show-cause order. — Also termed *rule to show cause*; *summary process*; *summary procedure*; *expedited proceeding*.

show-cause rule. See *show-cause order* under ORDER (2).

shower (shoh-ər), *n.* A person commissioned by a court to take jurors to a place so that they may observe it as they consider a case on which they are sitting. See VIEW (3).

showing, *n.* (1857) The act or an instance of establishing through evidence and argument; proof <a prima facie showing>.

show of hands. See *vote by show of hands* under VOTE (4).

show-stopper. *Corporations.* An antitakeover tactic by which the target company seeks an injunction barring the takeover offer, usu. because the proposed merger violates antitrust laws.

show trial. (1937) A trial, usu. in a nondemocratic country, that is staged primarily for propagandistic purposes, with the outcome predetermined.

showup, *n.* (1929) A pretrial identification procedure in which a suspect is confronted with a witness to or the victim of a crime. • Unlike a lineup, a showup is a one-on-one confrontation. Cf. LINEUP.

shrinkage. (1961) The reduction in inventory caused by theft, breakage, or waste.

shrink-wrap license. See LICENSE.

SHU. *abbr.* SPECIAL HOUSING UNIT.

shutdown. (1884) A cessation of work production, esp. in a factory.

shut-in royalty. See ROYALTY (2).

shut-in royalty clause. *Oil & gas.* A provision in an oil-and-gas lease allowing the lessee to maintain the lease while there is no production from the property because wells capable of production are shut in. • The lessee pays the lessor a shut-in royalty in lieu of production.

shuttle diplomacy. See DIPLOMACY.

shyster (**shıs**-tər). (1843) A person (esp. a lawyer) whose business affairs are unscrupulous, deceitful, or unethical.

SIB. *abbr.* **1.** Securities and Investment Board. See FINANCIAL SERVICES AGENCY. **2.** See *survivor-income benefit plan* under EMPLOYEE BENEFIT PLAN.

sibling. A brother or sister.

sibship. 1. The quality or state of being a blood relative, esp. a sibling. See DEGREE. **2.** A group of blood relatives; kindred.

sic (sik). [Latin "so, thus"] (1859) Spelled or used as written. • *Sic*, invariably bracketed and usu. set in italics, is used to indicate that a preceding word or phrase in a quoted passage is reproduced as it appeared in the original document <"that case peeked [*sic*] the young lawyer's interest">.

sick leave. 1. An employment benefit allowing a worker time off for sickness, either with or without pay, but without loss of seniority or other benefits. **2.** The time so taken by an employee.

sickness and accident insurance. See *health insurance* under INSURANCE.

side, *n.* (13c) **1.** The position of a person or group opposing another <the law is on our side>. **2.** Either of two parties in a transaction or dispute <each side put on a strong case>. **3.** *Archaic.* The field of a court's jurisdiction <equity side> <law side>. **4.** *Property.* In a description of more or less rectangularly shaped land, either of the two long boundary lines.

side agreement. See AGREEMENT.

sidebar. (1856) **1.** A position at the side of a judge's bench where counsel can confer with the judge beyond the jury's earshot <the judge called the attorneys to sidebar>. **2.** SIDEBAR CONFERENCE <during the sidebar, the prosecutor accused the defense attorney of misconduct>. **3.** A short, secondary article within or accompanying a main story in a publication <the sidebar contained information on related topics>. **4.** SIDEBAR COMMENT.

sidebar comment. (1922) An unnecessary, often argumentative remark made by an attorney or witness, esp. during a trial or deposition <the witness paused after testifying, then added a sidebar>. — Often shortened to *sidebar*. — Also termed *sidebar remark*.

sidebar conference. (1925) **1.** A discussion among the judge and counsel, usu. over an evidentiary objection, outside the jury's hearing. — Also termed *bench conference*. **2.** A discussion, esp. during voir dire, between the judge and a juror or prospective juror. — Often shortened to *sidebar*.

sidebar remark. See SIDEBAR COMMENT.

side judge. See JUDGE.

side lines. 1. The margins of something, such as property. **2.** A different type of business or goods than one principally engages in or sells. **3.** *Mining law.* The boundary lines of a mining claim not crossing the vein running on each side of it. — Also written *sidelines*. Cf. END LINES.

sidenote. See MARGINAL NOTE.

side reports. (1943) **1.** Unofficial volumes of case reports. **2.** Collections of cases omitted from the official reports.

sidesman. *Eccles. law.* A church officer who originally reported to the bishop on clerical and congregational misdeeds, including heretical acts, and later became a standing officer whose duties gradually devolved by custom on the churchwarden. — Also termed *synodsman; questman.*

Sierra–Mobile **doctrine.** See MOBILE–SIERRA DOCTRINE.

sight. (1810) A drawee's acceptance of a draft <payable after sight>. • The term *after sight* means "after acceptance."

sight draft. See DRAFT.

sight strike. See STRIKE (2).

sigil (sij-əl), *n.* A seal or an abbreviated signature used as a seal; esp., a seal formerly used by civil-law notaries.

sigla (**sig**-lə), *n. pl.* [Latin] Abbreviations and signs used in writing, esp. by the Glossators.

sign, *vb.* (15c) **1.** To identify (a record) by means of a signature, mark, or other symbol with the intent to authenticate it as an act or agreement of the person identifying it <both parties signed the contract>. **2.** To agree with or join <the commissioner signed on for a four-year term>.

signal. (1949) **1.** A means of communication, esp. between vessels at sea or between a vessel and the shore. • The international code of signals assigns arbitrary meanings to different arrangements of flags or light displays. **2.** In the citation of legal authority, an abbreviation or notation supplied to indicate some basic fact about the authority. • For example, according to the *Bluebook*, the signal *See* means that the cited authority plainly supports the proposition, while *Cf.* means that the cited authority supports a proposition analogous to (but in some way different from) the main proposition. For these and other signals, see *The Bluebook: A Uniform System of Citation* § 1.2, at 22–24 (17th ed. 2000). — Also termed (in sense 2) *citation signal.*

signatory (sig-nə-tor-ee), *n.* (1866) A person or entity that signs a document, personally or through an agent, and thereby becomes a party to an agreement <eight countries are signatories to the treaty>. — **signatory,** *adj.*

signatory authority. 1. License to make a decision, esp. to withdraw money from an account or to transfer a negotiable instrument. **2.** *Patents.* In the U.S. Patent and Trademark Office, the power of an examiner to approve an office action.

signature. (16c) **1.** A person's name or mark written by that person or at the person's direction. — Also termed *sign manual.* **2.** *Commercial law.* Any name, mark, or writing used with the intention of authenticating a document. UCC §§ 1-201(37), 3-401(b). — Also termed *legal signature.*

digital signature. (1978) A secure, digital code attached to an electronically transmitted message that uniquely identifies and authenticates the sender. • A digital signature consists of a "hashed" number combined with a number assigned to a document (a private-encryption key). Generating a signature requires the use of private- and public-key-encryption software, and is often activated by a simple command or act, such as clicking on a "place order" icon on a retailer's website. Digital signatures are esp. important for electronic commerce and are a key component of many electronic message-authentication schemes. Several states have passed legislation recognizing the legality of digital signatures. See E-COMMERCE; KEY ENCRYPTION.

electronic signature. An electronic symbol, sound, or process that is either attached to or logically associated with a document (such as a contract or other record) and executed or adopted by a person with the intent to sign the document. • Types of electronic signatures include a typed name at the end of an email, a digital image of a handwritten signature, and the click of an "I accept" button on an e-commerce site. The term *electronic signature* does not suggest or require the use of encryption, authentication, or identification measures. A document's integrity (unaltered content), authenticity (sender's identity), and confidentiality (of the signer's identity or document's contents) are not ensured merely because an electronic signature is provided for.

facsimile signature. (1892) **1.** A signature that has been prepared and reproduced by mechanical or photographic means. **2.** A signature on a document that has been transmitted by a facsimile machine. See FAX.

private signature. *Civil law.* A signature made on a document (such as a will) that has not been witnessed or notarized.

unauthorized signature. (1859) A signature made without actual, implied, or apparent authority. • It includes a forgery. UCC § 1-201(43).

signature card. (1902) A financial-institution record consisting of a customer's signature and other information that assists the institution in monitoring financial transactions, as by comparing the signature on the record with signatures on checks, withdrawal slips, and other documents.

signature crime. See CRIME.

signature evidence. See EVIDENCE.

signature loan. See LOAN.

signed, sealed, and delivered. (17c) In a certificate of acknowledgment, a statement that the instrument was executed by the person acknowledging it. — Often shortened to *sealed and delivered.*

signed writing. See WRITING.

signet. 1. *Civil law.* An elaborate hand-drawn symbol (usu. incorporating a cross and the notary's initials) formerly placed at the base of notarial instruments, later replaced by a seal. **2.** *Scots law.* A seal used to authenticate summonses in civil matters before the Court of Session. • Originally, this was the monarch's personal seal.

significant-connection jurisdiction. See JURISDICTION.

significant-connection/substantial-evidence jurisdiction. See *significant-connection jurisdiction* under JURISDICTION.

significant-relationship theory. See CENTER-OF-GRAVITY DOCTRINE.

significavit (sig-ni-fi-kay-vit), *n.* [Latin "he has signified"] *Eccles. law.* **1.** A bishop's certificate that a person has been in a state of excommunication for more than 40 days. **2.** A notice to the Crown in chancery, based on the bishop's certificate, whereby a writ *de contumace capiendo* (or, earlier, a writ *de excommunicato capiendo*) would issue for the disobedient person's arrest and imprisonment.

sign manual. 1. See SIGNATURE (1). **2.** A symbol or emblem, such as a trademark, representing words or an idea.

silence, *n.* (13c) **1.** A restraint from speaking. • In criminal law, silence includes an arrestee's statements expressing the desire not to speak and requesting an attorney. **2.** A failure to reveal something required by law to be revealed. See *estoppel by silence* under ESTOPPEL. — **silent,** *adj.*

silent confirmation. See CONFIRMATION.

silent partner. See PARTNER.

silent record. See RECORD.

silent-witness theory. (1973) *Evidence.* A method of authenticating and admitting evidence (such as a photograph), without the need for a witness to verify its authenticity, upon a sufficient showing of the reliability of the process of producing the evidence, including proof that the evidence has not been altered.

silk gown. 1. The professional robe worn by a Queen's Counsel. **2.** One who is a Queen's Counsel. — Often shortened (in sense 2) to *silk.* Cf. STUFF GOWN.

silver certificate. *Hist.* A banknote issued by the United States Treasury from 1878 to 1963 and redeemable in silver. • The notes represented that a certain amount of silver was on deposit with the government and would be paid to the bearer on demand. Originally, these notes were not legal tender and could be used only to pay taxes and other public obligations. In 1967, Congress abolished redemption in silver after June 1968. Silver certificates now have the same status as Federal Reserve notes, which are not redeemable for precious metal. Cf. FEDERAL RESERVE NOTE; GOLD CERTIFICATE.

silver parachute. See TIN PARACHUTE.

silver-platter doctrine. (1958) *Criminal procedure.* The principle that a federal court could admit evidence obtained illegally by a state police officer as long as a federal officer did not participate in or request the search. • The Supreme Court rejected this doctrine in *Elkins v. United States*, 364 U.S. 206, 80 S.Ct. 1437 (1960).

similar happenings. *Evidence.* Events that occur at a time different from the time in dispute and are therefore usu. inadmissible except to the extent that they provide relevant information on issues that would be fairly constant, such as the control of and conditions on land on the day in question.

similarity. *Intellectual property.* The resemblance of one trademark or copyrighted work to another. • How closely a trademark must resemble another to amount to infringement depends on the nature of the product and how much care the typical buyer would be expected to take in making the selection in that particular market. It is a question of overall impression rather than an element-by-element comparison of the two marks. — Also termed *imitation; colorable imitation.* Cf. SUBSTANTIAL SIMILARITY.

comprehensive nonliteral similarity. Copyright. Similarity evidenced by the copying of the protected work's general ideas or structure (such as a movie's plot) without using the precise words or phrases of the work. — Also termed *pattern similarity.*

fragmented literal similarity. Copyright. Similarity evidenced by the copying of verbatim portions of the protected work.

substantial similarity. Copyright. A strong resemblance between a copyrighted work and an alleged infringement, thereby creating an inference of unauthorized copying. • The standard for substantial similarity is whether an ordinary person would conclude that the alleged infringement has appropriated nontrivial amounts of the copyrighted work's expressions. — Also termed *probative similarity.* See *derivative work* under WORK (2).

similar sales. See SALE.

similiter (si-**mil**-i-tər). [Latin "similarly"] *Common-law pleading.* A party's written acceptance of an opponent's issue or argument; a set form of words by which a party accepts or joins in an issue of fact tendered by the other side. See *joinder of issue* (2) under JOINDER.

simony (**sim**-ə-nee *or* **si**-mə-nee), *n.* [fr. Latin *simonia* "payment for things spiritual," fr. the proper name *Simon Magus* (see below)] *Hist. Eccles. law.* The unlawful practice of giving or receiving money or gifts in exchange for spiritual promotion; esp., the unlawful buying or selling of a benefice or the right to present clergy to a vacant benefice.

simple, *adj.* (16c) **1.** (Of a crime) not accompanied by aggravating circumstances. Cf. AGGRAVATED (1). **2.** (Of an estate or fee) heritable by the owner's heirs with no conditions concerning tail. **3.** (Of a contract) not made under seal.

simple agreement. See AGREEMENT.

simple assault. 1. See ASSAULT (1). **2.** See ASSAULT (2).

simple average. See *particular average* under AVERAGE.

simple battery. See BATTERY.

simple blockade. See BLOCKADE.

simple bond. See BOND (2).

simple contract. 1. See *informal contract* (1) under CONTRACT. **2.** See *parol contract* (2) under CONTRACT.

simple-contract debt. See DEBT.

simple interest. See INTEREST (3).

simple kidnapping. See KIDNAPPING.

simple larceny. See LARCENY.

simple listing. See *open listing* under LISTING (1).

simple majority. See MAJORITY.

simple mortgage clause. See *open mortgage clause* under MORTGAGE CLAUSE.

simple negligence. See *inadvertent negligence* under NEGLIGENCE.

simple obligation. See OBLIGATION.

SIMPLE plan. See EMPLOYEE BENEFIT PLAN.

simple resolution. See RESOLUTION (1).

simple robbery. See ROBBERY.

simple state. See *unitary state* under STATE.

simple-tool rule. The principle that an employer has no duty to warn its employees of dangers that are obvious to everyone involved, and has no duty to inspect a tool that is within the exclusive control of an employee when that employee is fully acquainted with the tool's condition.

simple trust. 1. See *mandatory trust* under TRUST. **2.** See *passive trust* under TRUST.

simplex dictum. See DICTUM.

simpliciter (sim-**plis**-i-tər), *adv.* [Latin] (16c) **1.** In a simple or summary manner; simply. **2.** Absolutely; unconditionally; per se.

simplified employee pension plan. See EMPLOYEE BENEFIT PLAN.

simulated contract. See CONTRACT.

simulated fact. See FACT.

simulated judgment. See JUDGMENT.

simulated sale. See SALE.

simulated transaction. See *simulated sale* under SALE.

simulation. 1. An assumption of an appearance that is feigned, false, or deceptive. **2.** *Civil law.* A feigned, pretended act, usu. to mislead or deceive. **3.** See *simulated contract* under CONTRACT.

simultaneous death. See DEATH.

simultaneous-death act. See UNIFORM SIMULTANEOUS DEATH ACT.

simultaneous-death clause. (1953) A testamentary provision mandating that if the testator and beneficiary die in a common disaster, or the order of their deaths is otherwise unascertainable, the testator is presumed to have survived the beneficiary. • If the beneficiary is the testator's spouse, an express exception is often made so that the

spouse with the smaller estate is presumed to have survived. See *simultaneous death* under DEATH. Cf. SURVIVAL CLAUSE.

simultaneous polygamy. See POLYGAMY (1).

sine (**sI**-nee or **sin**-ay), *prep.* [Latin] Without.

sinecure (**sI**-nə-kyoor or **sin**-ə-kyoor). [fr. Latin *sine cura* "without duties"] *Hist.* A post without any duties attached; an office for which the holder receives a salary but has no responsibilities. — **sinecural** (**sI**-nə-kyoor-əl or sI-nə-**kyoor**-əl), *adj.*

sine die (**sI**-nee **dI**-ee or **dI**- or **sin**-ay **dee**-ay). [Latin "without day"] (17c) With no day being assigned (as for resumption of a meeting or hearing). See *adjourn sine die* under ADJOURN (2); GO HENCE WITHOUT DAY.

sine prole (**sI**-nee **proh**-lee). [Latin] Without issue. • This phrase was used primarily in genealogical tables. — Abbr. s.p.

sine qua non (**sI**-nee kway **non** or **sin**-ay kwah **nohn**), *n.* [Latin "without which not"] (17c) An indispensable condition or thing; something on which something else necessarily depends. — Also termed *conditio sine qua non.*

single, *adj.* **1.** Unmarried <single tax status>. **2.** Consisting of one alone; individual <single condition> <single beneficiary>.

single-act statute. See LONG-ARM STATUTE.

single adultery. See ADULTERY.

single-asset real estate. *Bankruptcy.* A single piece of real property (apart from residential property with fewer than four residential units) that a debtor operates for business purposes, that provides the debtor with substantially all his or her gross income, and that carries aggregate, liquidated, noncontingent secured debts of $4 million or less. 11 USCA § 101(51B).

single bill. See *bill single* under BILL (7).

single bond. See *bill obligatory* under BILL (7).

single combat. See DUEL (2).

single condition. See CONDITION (2).

single-controversy doctrine. See ENTIRE-CONTROVERSY DOCTRINE.

single-country fund. See MUTUAL FUND.

single creditor. See CREDITOR.

single-criminal-intent doctrine. See SINGLE-LARCENY DOCTRINE.

single-date-of-removal doctrine. *Civil procedure.* The principle that the deadline for removing a case from state court to federal court is 30 days from the day that any defendant receives a copy of the state-court pleading on which the removal is based. • If a later-served defendant seeks to remove a case to federal court more than 30 days after the day any other defendant received the pleading, the removal is untimely even if effectuated within 30 days after the removing defendant received the pleading. One theory underlying this doctrine is that all defendants must consent to remove a case to federal court, and a defendant who has waited longer than 30 days to remove does not have the capacity to consent to removal. 28 USCA § 1446(b). See NOTICE OF REMOVAL.

single demise. See DEMISE.

single-element means claim. See *single-means claim* under PATENT CLAIM.

single-entry bookkeeping. See BOOKKEEPING.

single-filing rule. *Civil-rights law.* The principle that an administrative charge filed by one plaintiff in a civil-rights suit (esp. a Title VII suit) will satisfy the administrative-filing requirements for all coplaintiffs who are making claims for the same act of discrimination. • But this rule will not usu. protect a coplaintiff's claims if the coplaintiff also filed an administrative charge, against the same employer, in which different discriminatory acts were complained of, because the administrative agency (usu. the EEOC) and the employer are entitled to rely on the allegations someone makes in an administrative charge.

single-impulse plan. See SINGLE-LARCENY DOCTRINE.

single-juror instruction. See JURY INSTRUCTION.

single-larceny doctrine. (1969) *Criminal law.* The principle that the taking of different items of property belonging to either the same or different owners at the same time and place constitutes one act of larceny if the theft is part of one larcenous plan, as when it involves essentially one continuous act or if control over the property is exercised simultaneously. • The thief's intent determines the number of occurrences. — Also termed *single-impulse plan*; *single-larceny rule*; *single-criminal-intent doctrine.*

single-means claim. See PATENT CLAIM.

single-name paper. A negotiable instrument signed by only one maker and not backed by a surety.

single obligation. See OBLIGATION.

single ordeal. See ORDEAL.

single original. (1815) An instrument executed singly, not in duplicate.

single-paragraph form. *Patents.* A style of writing patent claims that uses a colon after the introductory phrase and a semicolon between each element. Cf. COLON-SEMICOLON FORM; OUTLINE FORM; SUBPARAGRAPH FORM.

single-premium deferred annuity. See ANNUITY.

single-premium insurance. See *single-premium life insurance* under LIFE INSURANCE.

single-premium life insurance. See LIFE INSURANCE.

single-publication rule. The doctrine that a plaintiff in a libel suit against a publisher has only one claim for each mass publication, not a claim for every book or issue in that run.

single-purpose project. A facility that is designed, built, and used for one reason only, such as to generate electricity. • This term most often refers to large, complex, expensive projects such as power plants, chemical-processing plants, mines, and toll roads. Projects of this type are often funded through project financing, in which a special-purpose entity is established to perform no function other than to develop, own, and operate the facility, the idea being to limit the number of the entity's creditors and thus provide protection for the project's lenders. See *project financing* under FINANCING; SPECIAL-PURPOSE ENTITY; BANKRUPTCY-REMOTE ENTITY.

single-recovery rule. See ONE-SATISFACTION RULE.

single-registration rule. *Copyright.* The U.S. Copyright Office doctrine that permits only one registration for each original work. • Exceptions to the rule are routinely made for unpublished works that are later published. Generally, revised works cannot be registered a second time if the revisions are not substantial, but the creator may be allowed to file a supplemental registration.

single-source requirement. Under the common-law tort of false advertising, the necessity to show that the plaintiff is the only supplier of the genuine goods in question and that buyers would have bought the plaintiff's goods if the true nature of the defendant's goods had been known. *Ely-Norris Safe Co. v. Mosler Safe Co.*, 7 F.2d 603 (2d Cir. 1925). • This is a narrow exception to the common-law rule that the tort of false advertising applies only in instances of passing off, trade defamation, or trade disparagement.

singles' penalty. See MARRIAGE BONUS.

single transferable vote. See VOTE (1).

singular, *adj.* **1.** Individual; each <all and singular>. **2.** *Civil law.* Of or relating to separate interests in property, rather than the estate as a whole <singular succession>.

singular successor. See SUCCESSOR.

singular title. See TITLE (2).

sinking fund. See FUND (1).

sinking-fund bond. See BOND (3).

sinking-fund debenture. See DEBENTURE.

sinking-fund depreciation method. See DEPRECIATION METHOD.

sinking-fund reserve. See RESERVE.

sinking-fund tax. See TAX.

sin tax. See TAX.

SIPA (**see**-pə). *abbr.* SECURITIES INVESTOR PROTECTION ACT.

SIPC. *abbr.* SECURITIES INVESTOR PROTECTION CORPORATION.

SIR. *abbr.* **1.** SELF-INSURED RETENTION. **2.** STATUTORY INVENTION REGISTRATION.

sister. (bef. 12c) A female who has one parent or both parents in common with another person.

    consanguine sister (kahn-**sang**-gwin *or* kən-**san**-gwin). *Civil law.* A sister who has the same father, but a different mother.

    half sister. A sister who has the same father or the same mother, but not both.

    sister-german. A full sister; the daughter of both of one's parents. See GERMAN.

    stepsister. (15c) The daughter of one's stepparent.

    uterine sister (**yoo**-tər-in). *Civil law.* A sister who has the same mother, but a different father.

sister corporation. See CORPORATION.

sisterhood. See GIFTING CLUB.

sister-in-law. (15c) The sister of one's spouse or the wife of one's brother. • The wife of one's spouse's brother is also sometimes considered a sister-in-law. Pl. **sisters-in-law.**

sistership exclusion. See EXCLUSION (3).

sistren, *n.* Sisters, esp. those considered spiritual kin (such as female colleagues on a court). Cf. BRETHREN.

sit, *vb.* (14c) **1.** (Of a judge) to occupy a judicial seat <Judge Wilson sits on the trial court for the Eastern District of Arkansas>. **2.** (Of a judge) to hold court or perform official functions <is the judge sitting this week?>. **3.** (Of a court or legislative body) to hold proceedings <the U.S. Supreme Court sits from October to June>.

sit-and-squirm test. A judicial doctrine, used esp. by administrative-law judges in disability-claim cases, whereby a court subjectively determines a set of traits that it expects the claimant to exhibit and denies relief if the claimant fails to exhibit those traits. • The doctrine is adhered to only in some federal circuits and has been expressly rejected in others. Generally, an administrative-law judge may observe a claimant's demeanor in evaluating the credibility of the complaint. Yet it is error for the judge to base a judgment solely on personal observation and not on the record as a whole.

sit-down strike. See STRIKE.

site. 1. A place or location; esp., a piece of property set aside for a specific use. **2.** SCITE.

site assessment. See *transactional audit* under AUDIT.

site license. See LICENSE.

site plan. (1937) An illustrated proposal for the development or use of a particular piece of real property. • The illustration is usu. a map or sketch of how the property will appear if the proposal is accepted. Some zoning ordinances require a developer to present a site plan to the city council and to receive council approval before certain projects may be completed.

sit-in, *n.* An organized, passive demonstration in which participants usu. sit (or lie) down and refuse to leave a place as a means of protesting against policies or activities. • Sit-ins originated as a communal act of protesting racial segregation. People who were discriminated against would sit in places that were prohibited to them and refuse to leave. Later the term came to refer to any group protest, as with anti–Vietnam War protests and some labor strikes. Cf. *sit-down strike* under STRIKE.

sitting, *n.* (14c) A court session; esp., a session of an appellate court. See SESSION (1).

    en banc sitting. (1944) A court session in which all the judges (or a quorum) participate. See EN BANC.

    in camera sitting. (1976) A court session conducted by a judge in chambers or elsewhere outside the courtroom. See IN CAMERA.

situation. 1. Condition; position in reference to circumstances <dangerous situation>. **2.** The place where someone or something is occupied; a location <situation near the border>.

situational offender. See OFFENDER.

situation of danger. See DANGEROUS SITUATION.

situs (**SI**-təs). [Latin] (1834) The location or position (of something) for legal purposes, as in *lex situs*, the law of the place where the thing in issue is situated. See LOCUS.

    tax situs. See TAX SITUS.

678 trust. See *nongrantor-owner trust* under TRUST (3).

Sixteenth Amendment. The constitutional amendment, ratified in 1913, allowing Congress to tax income.

Sixth Amendment. The constitutional amendment, ratified with the Bill of Rights in 1791, guaranteeing in criminal cases the right to a speedy and public trial by jury, the right to be informed of the nature of the accusation, the right to confront witnesses, the right to counsel, and the right to compulsory process for obtaining favorable witnesses.

sixth-sentence remand. See REMAND.

sixty clerks. See SWORN CLERKS IN CHANCERY.

sixty-day notice. *Labor law.* Under the Taft-Hartley Act, the 60-day advance notice required for either party to a collective-bargaining agreement to reopen or terminate the contract. • During this period, strikes and lockouts are prohibited. 29 USCA § 158(d)(1).

S.J.D. See DOCTOR OF JURIDICAL SCIENCE.

SJI. See STATE JUSTICE INSTITUTE.

skeletal legislation. See LEGISLATION.

skeleton bill. See BILL (7).

skeleton bill of exceptions. See BILL (2).

skeleton legislation. See *skeletal legislation* under LEGISLATION.

skill. Special ability and proficiency; esp., the practical and familiar knowledge of the principles and processes of an art, science, or trade, combined with the ability to apply them appropriately, with readiness and dexterity. • Skill is generally considered more than mere competence. It is a special competence that is not a part of the reasonable person's ordinary equipment, but that results from aptitude cultivated through special training and experience.

> *ordinary skill.* The skill of a typical person who performs a given task or job.

> *reasonable skill.* The skill ordinarily possessed and used by persons engaged in a particular business.

skilled artisan. See ARTISAN.

skilled witness. See *expert witness* under WITNESS.

skilled work. See WORK (1).

skip bail. See JUMP BAIL.

skip person. (1988) *Tax.* A beneficiary who is more than one generation removed from the transferor and to whom assets are conveyed in a generation-skipping transfer. IRC (26 USCA) § 2613(a). See GENERATION-SKIPPING TRANSFER.

skippeson. See ESKIPPESON.

skiptracing agency. (1984) A service that locates persons (such as delinquent debtors, missing heirs, witnesses, stockholders, bondholders, etc.) or missing assets (such as bank accounts).

skyjack, *vb. Slang.* To hijack an aircraft. See HIJACK (1). — **skyjacking,** *n.*

S.L. *abbr.* **1.** Session law. See SESSION LAWS. **2.** Statute law.

slack tax. See *pickup tax* under TAX.

slamming. The practice by which a long-distance telephone company wrongfully appropriates a customer's service from another company, usu. through an unauthorized transfer or by way of a transfer authorization that is disguised as something else, such as a form to sign up for a free vacation.

slander, *n.* (13c) **1.** A defamatory assertion expressed in a transitory form, esp. speech. • Damages for slander — unlike those for libel — are not presumed and thus must be proved by the plaintiff (unless the defamation is slander per se). **2.** The act of making such a statement. See DEFAMATION. Cf. LIBEL (1). — **slander,** *vb.* — **slanderous,** *adj.*

> *slander per quod.* (18c) Slander that does not qualify as slander per se, thus forcing the plaintiff to prove special damages.

> *slander per se.* (1841) Slander for which special damages need not be proved because it imputes to the plaintiff any one of the following: (1) a crime involving moral turpitude, (2) a loathsome disease (such as a sexually transmitted disease), (3) conduct that would adversely affect one's business or profession, or (4) unchastity (esp. of a woman).

> *trade slander.* Trade defamation that is spoken but not recorded. See *trade defamation* under DEFAMATION. Cf. *trade libel* under LIBEL.

slanderer, *n.* (13c) One who commits slander.

slander of goods. See DISPARAGEMENT.

slander of title. (18c) A false statement, made orally or in writing, that casts doubt on another person's ownership of property. — Also termed *jactitation of title.* See DISPARAGEMENT.

slander per quod. See SLANDER.

slander per se. See SLANDER.

SLAPP (slap). *abbr.* A strategic lawsuit against public participation — that is, a suit brought by a developer, corporate executive, or elected official to stifle those who protest against some type of high-dollar initiative or who take an adverse position on a public-interest issue (often involving the environment). — Also termed *SLAPP suit.*

slate. A list of candidates, esp. for political office or a corporation's board of directors, that usu. includes as many candidates for election as there are representatives being elected.

slavery. 1. A situation in which one person has absolute power over the life, fortune, and liberty of another. **2.** The practice of keeping individuals in such a state of bondage or servitude. • Slavery was outlawed by the 13th Amendment to the U.S. Constitution.

slavery, badge of. See BADGE OF SLAVERY.

slay, *vb.* To kill (a person), esp. in battle.

slayer rule. (1986) The doctrine that neither a person who kills another nor the killer's heirs can share in the decedent's estate. — Also termed *slayer's rule.*

slayer statute. *Slang.* A statute that prohibits a person's killer from taking any part of the decedent's estate through will or intestacy. • The Uniform Probate Code and nearly all jurisdictions have a slayer-statute provision.

SL/C. See *standby letter of credit* under LETTER OF CREDIT.

SLC. *abbr.* SPECIAL LITIGATION COMMITTEE.

sleeper. A security that has strong market potential but is underpriced and lacks investor interest.

sleeping on rights. See LACHES (1).

sleeping partner. See *secret partner* under PARTNER.

sleepwalking defense. See AUTOMATISM.

sliding scale. A pricing method in which prices are determined by a person's ability to pay.

slight care. See CARE.

slight diligence. See DILIGENCE.

slight evidence. See EVIDENCE.

slight-evidence rule. (1936) **1.** The doctrine that if evidence establishes the existence of a conspiracy between at least two other people, the prosecution need only offer slight evidence of a defendant's knowing participation or intentional involvement in the conspiracy to secure a conviction. • This rule was first announced in *Tomplain v. United States*, 42 F.2d 202, 203 (5th Cir. 1930). In the decades after *Tomplain*, other circuits adopted the rule, but not until the 1970s did the rule become widespread. Since then, the rule has been widely criticized and, in most circuits, abolished. *See, e.g., United States v. Durrive*, 902 F.2d 1379, 1380 n.* (7th Cir. 1990). But its vitality remains undiminished in some jurisdictions. **2.** The doctrine that only slight evidence of a defendant's participation in a conspiracy need be offered in order to admit a coconspirator's out-of-court statement under the coconspirator exception to the hearsay rule. *See* Fed. R. Evid. 801(d)(2)(E).

slight negligence. See NEGLIGENCE.

slip-and-fall case. (1952) **1.** A lawsuit brought for injuries sustained in slipping and falling, usu. on the defendant's property. **2.** Loosely, any minor case in tort.

slip decision. See *slip opinion* under OPINION (1).

slip law. (1922) An individual pamphlet in which a single enactment is printed immediately after its passage but before its inclusion in the general laws (such as the session laws or the *U.S. Statutes at Large*). — Also termed *slip-law print*.

slip opinion. See OPINION (1).

slippery-slope principle. See WEDGE PRINCIPLE.

slipsheet. See *slip opinion* under OPINION (1).

slot charter. See CHARTER (8).

slough. 1. (sloo) An arm of a river, separate from the main channel. **2.** (slow) A bog; a place filled with deep mud.

slowdown. An organized effort by workers to decrease production to pressure the employer to take some desired action.

slowdown strike. See STRIKE (1).

SLSDC. *abbr.* SAINT LAWRENCE SEAWAY DEVELOPMENT CORPORATION.

slump, *n.* A temporary downturn in the economy and particularly in the stock market, characterized by falling market prices.

slush fund. Money that is set aside for undesignated purposes, often corrupt ones, and that is not subject to financial procedures designed to ensure accountability.

SM. *abbr.* SERVICEMARK.

Small Business Administration. A federal agency that helps small businesses by assuring them a fair share of government contracts, guaranteeing their loans or lending them money directly, and providing disaster relief. • The agency was established by the Small Business Act of 1953. — Abbr. SBA.

small-business concern. A business qualifying for an exemption from freight undercharges because it is independently owned and operated and is not dominant in its field of operation, with limited numbers of employees and business volume. 15 USCA § 632. — Often shortened to *small business*.

small-business corporation. See CORPORATION.

Small Business Investment Act. A federal law, originally enacted in 1958, under which investment companies may be formed and licensed to supply long-term equity capital to small businesses. • The statute is implemented by the Small Business Administration. 15 USCA §§ 661 et seq.

small-business investment company. A corporation created under state law to provide long-term equity capital to small businesses, as provided under the Small Business Investment Act and regulated by the Small Business Administration. 15 USCA §§ 661 et seq. — Abbr. SBIC.

small claim. A claim for damages at or below a specified monetary amount. See *small-claims court* under COURT.

small-claims court. See COURT.

small-debts court. See *small-claims court* under COURT.

small entity. *Patents.* An independent inventor, a nonprofit organization, or a company with 500 or fewer employees. • A small entity is usu. charged a lower fee for patent applications and related expenses as long as the patent rights are not assigned or licensed to a large entity (a for-profit organization with more than 500 employees). 37 CFR § 1.27.

small-estate probate. See PROBATE.

small invention. See UTILITY MODEL.

small-loan act. A state law fixing the maximum legal interest rate and other terms on small, short-term loans by banks and finance companies.

small-loan company. See *consumer finance company* under FINANCE COMPANY.

smart card. See STORED-VALUE CARD.

smart money. 1. Funds held by sophisticated, usu. large investors who are considered capable of minimizing risks and maximizing profits <the smart money has now left this market>. **2.** See *punitive damages* under DAMAGES <although the jury awarded only $7,000 in actual damages, it also awarded $500,000 in smart money>.

smash-and-grab. *Slang.* The act of breaking a window or other glass barrier in order to seize goods beyond it before fleeing. ● In a smash-and-grab, the criminal usu. breaks a shop window or a glass display case with a handheld tool and seizes whatever merchandise is nearest. Cf. RAM RAID.

SMBS. *abbr.* See *stripped mortgage-backed security* under SECURITY.

Smith Act. A 1948 federal antisedition law that criminalizes advocating the forcible or violent overthrow of the government. 18 USCA § 2385.

Smithsonian Institution. An independent trust of the United States responsible for conducting scientific and scholarly research; publishing its results; maintaining over 140 million artifacts, works of art, and scientific specimens for study, display, and circulation throughout the nation; and engaging in educational programming and international cooperative research. ● It was created in 1846 to give effect to the terms of the will of a British scientist, James Smithson, who left his entire estate to the United States.

smoking gun. (1974) A piece of physical or documentary evidence that conclusively impeaches an adversary on an outcome-determinative issue or destroys the adversary's credibility.

Smoot–Hawley Tariff Act. *Hist.* A 1930 protectionist statute that raised tariff rates on most articles imported into the U.S., and provoked U.S. trading partners to institute comparable tariff increases. ● This act is often cited as a factor in precipitating and spreading the Great Depression. The Act was named for the legislators who sponsored it, Senator Reed Smoot of Utah and Representative Willis C. Hawley of Oregon. It is sometimes called the *Grundy Tariff* for Joseph Grundy, who was president of the Pennsylvania Manufacturers Association and the chief lobbyist supporting the Act. — Also termed *Tariff Act of 1930*.

smuggling, *n.* (17c) The crime of importing or exporting illegal articles or articles on which duties have not been paid. See CONTRABAND. Cf. PEOPLE-SMUGGLING; TRAFFICKING. — **smuggle,** *vb.*

alimentary-canal smuggling. Smuggling carried out by swallowing packets, usu. balloons, filled with contraband, which stays in the smuggler's stomach or intestines during the crossing of a border.

smurf, *n. Slang.* **1.** A person who participates in a money-laundering operation by making transactions of less than $10,000 (the amount that triggers federal reporting requirements) at each of many banks. ● The name derives from a cartoon character of the 1980s. **2.** See CURRENCY-TRANSACTION REPORT.

sneak-and-peek search warrant. See *covert-entry search warrant* under SEARCH WARRANT.

SNS. *abbr.* STRATEGIC NATIONAL STOCKPILE.

So. *abbr.* SOUTHERN REPORTER.

sober, *adj.* (14c) **1.** (Of a person) not under the influence of drugs or alcohol. **2.** (Of a person) regularly abstinent or moderate in the use of intoxicating liquors. **3.** (Of a situation, person, etc.) serious; grave. **4.** (Of facts, arguments, etc.) basic; unexaggerated. **5.** (Of a person) rational; having self-control.

sober house. See SOBER-LIVING RESIDENCE.

sober-living residence. A transitional form of group housing for people recovering from alcoholism or drug abuse. ● The residents typically receive counseling about how to function without mind-altering substances. — Sometimes shortened to *sober living.* — Also termed *sober-living housing; sober house.*

sobriety checkpoint. (1984) A part of a roadway at which police officers maintain a roadblock to stop motorists and ascertain whether the drivers are intoxicated.

sobriety test. (1931) A method of determining whether a person is intoxicated. ● Common sobriety tests are coordination tests and the use of mechanical devices to measure the blood alcohol content of a person's breath sample. See BREATHALYZER; HORIZONTAL-GAZE NYSTAGMUS TEST.

field sobriety test. (1956) A motor-skills test administered by a peace officer during a stop to determine whether a suspect has been driving while intoxicated. ● The test usu. involves checking the suspect's speaking ability or coordination (as by reciting the alphabet or walking in a straight line). — Abbr. FST.

socage (sok-ij). *Hist.* A type of lay tenure in which a tenant held lands in exchange for providing the lord husbandry-related (rather than military) service. ● Socage, the great residuary tenure, was any free tenure that did not fall within the definition of knight-service, serjeanty, or frankalmoin. Cf. KNIGHT-SERVICE; VILLEINAGE.

free socage. Socage in which the services were both certain and honorable. • By the statute 12 Car. 2, ch. 24 (1660), all the tenures by knight-service were, with minor exceptions, converted into free socage. — Also termed *free and common socage*; *liberum socagium.*

villein socage (vil-ən). Socage in which the services, though certain, were of a baser nature than those provided under free socage.

socager (sok-ij-ər). A tenant by socage; SOCMAN.

social contract. (1837) The express or implied agreement between citizens and their government by which individuals agree to surrender certain freedoms in exchange for mutual protection; an agreement forming the foundation of a political society. • The term is primarily associated with political philosophers, such as Thomas Hobbes, John Locke, and esp. Jean Jacques Rousseau, though it can be traced back to the Greek Sophists.

social cost. See COST (1).

social guest. See GUEST.

social harm. See HARM.

social insurance. See INSURANCE.

social justice. See JUSTICE (1).

social restriction. 1. The curtailment of individuals' liberties ostensibly for the general benefit. **2.** A governmental measure that has this effect.

Social Security Act. A federal law, originally enacted in 1935 in response to the Great Depression, creating a system of benefits, including old-age and survivors' benefits, and establishing the Social Security Administration. 42 USCA §§ 401–433.

Social Security Administration. A federal agency in the executive branch responsible for administering the nation's retirement program and its survivors- and disability-insurance program. • The agency was established under the Social Security Act of 1935 and became independent in 1995. — Abbr. SSA.

Social Security Disability Insurance. A benefit for adults with disabilities, paid by the Social Security Administration to wage-earners who have accumulated enough quarters of coverage and then become disabled. • Benefits are also available to disabled adult children and to disabled widows and widowers of qualified wage-earners. — Abbr. SSDI.

social-service state. See STATE.

social study. See HOME-STUDY REPORT.

social value. See VALUE (1).

society. (16c) **1.** A community of people, as of a state, nation, or locality, with common cultures, traditions, and interests.

civil society. The political body of a state or nation; the body politic.

2. An association or company of persons (usu. unincorporated) united by mutual consent, to deliberate, determine, and act jointly for a common purpose; ORGANIZATION (1). **3.** The general love, affection, and companionship that family members share with one another.

sociological jurisprudence. See JURISPRUDENCE.

sociology of law. See *sociological jurisprudence* under JURISPRUDENCE.

sociopath, *n.* See PSYCHOPATH. — **sociopathy,** *n.* — **sociopathic,** *adj.*

socius (soh-shee-əs), *n.* [Latin] *Roman law.* **1.** A partner. **2.** An accomplice; an accessory. **3.** A political ally. Pl. *socii* (soh-shee-I).

socius criminis (soh-shee-əs krim-ə-nis). An associate in crime; an accomplice.

Socratic method. (18c) A technique of philosophical discussion — and of law-school instruction — by which the questioner (a law professor) questions one or more followers (the law students), building on each answer with another question, esp. an analogy incorporating the answer. • This method takes its name from the Greek philosopher Socrates, who lived in Athens from about 469–399 B.C. His method is a traditional one in law schools, primarily because it forces law students to think through issues rationally and deductively — a skill required in the practice of law. Most law professors who employ this method call on students randomly, an approach designed to teach students to think quickly, without stage fright. — Also termed *question-and-answer method.* See QUESTION-AND-ANSWER (3). Cf. CASEBOOK METHOD; HORNBOOK METHOD.

SODDI defense (sahd-ee). *Slang.* The some-other-dude-did-it defense; a claim that somebody else committed a crime, usu. made by a criminal defendant who cannot identify the third party.

sodomy (sod-ə-mee), *n.* (13c) **1.** Oral or anal copulation between humans, esp. those of the same sex. **2.** Oral or anal copulation between a human and an animal; bestiality. — Also termed *buggery*; *crime against nature*; *abominable and detestable crime against nature*; *unnatural offense*; *unspeakable crime*; (archaically) *sodomitry*; (in Latin) *crimen innominatum.* Cf. PEDERASTY. — **sodomize,** *vb.* — **sodomitic,** *adj.* — **sodomist, sodomite,** *n.*

aggravated sodomy. (1965) Criminal sodomy that involves force or results in serious bodily injury to the victim in addition to mental injury and emotional distress. • Some laws provide that sodomy involving a minor is automatically aggravated sodomy.

SOF. *abbr.* STATUTE OF FRAUDS.

SOFA. *abbr.* See STATEMENT OF FINANCIAL AFFAIRS.

soft currency. See CURRENCY.

soft dollars. 1. *Securities.* The credits that brokers give their clients in return for the clients' stock-trading business. **2.** The portion of an equity investment that is tax-deductible in the first year. Cf. HARD DOLLARS.

soft goods. See GOODS.

soft law. 1. Collectively, rules that are neither strictly binding nor completely lacking in legal significance. **2.** *Int'l law.* Guidelines, policy declarations, or codes of conduct that set standards of conduct but are not legally binding.

soft market. See MARKET.

soft positivism. See INCORPORATIONISM.

soft sell. A low-key sales practice characterized by sincerity and professionalism. Cf. HARD SELL.

software beta-test agreement. See BETA-TEST AGREEMENT.

software-based invention. See INVENTION.

Software Directive. See DIRECTIVE ON THE LEGAL PROTECTION OF COMPUTER PROGRAMS.

Software Patent Institute. A Kansas-based non-profit institute that collects and organizes non-patented prior-art software references in a database for patent researchers.

soil bank. A federal agricultural program in which farmers are paid to not grow crops or to grow noncommercial vegetation, to preserve the quality of the soil and stabilize commodity prices by avoiding surpluses. See LAND BANK (2).

Soil Conservation Service. See NATURAL RESOURCES CONSERVATION SERVICE.

sojourn (soh-jərn), *n.* A temporary stay by someone who is not just passing through a place but is also not a permanent resident <she set up a three-month sojourn in France>. — **sojourn** (soh-jərn *or* soh-jərn), *vb.* — **sojourner** (soh-jər-nər *or* soh-jər-nər), *n.*

solar day. See DAY.

solar easement. See EASEMENT.

solar month. See MONTH (4).

Soldiers' and Sailors' Civil Relief Act. A federal law, originally enacted in 1940, protecting the civil rights of persons in military service, as by modifying their civil liability, placing limits on interest rates charged against their obligations, and prescribing specific procedures for claims made against them. 50 USCA app. §§ 501 et seq.

soldier's and sailor's will. See *soldier's will* under WILL.

soldier's will. See WILL.

sold note. 1. See NOTE (1). **2.** See CONFIRMATION SLIP.

sole-actor doctrine. (1923) *Agency.* The rule charging a principal with knowledge of the agent's actions, even if the agent acted fraudulently.

sole and separate use. See *entire use* under USE (4).

sole and unconditional owner. See OWNER.

sole cause. See CAUSE (1).

sole corporation. See CORPORATION.

sole custody. See CUSTODY (2).

sole discretion. See DISCRETION (2).

solemn admission. See *judicial admission* under ADMISSION (1).

solemnity (sə-lem-nə-tee). (14c) **1.** A formality (such as a ceremony) required by law to validate an agreement or action <solemnity of marriage>. **2.** The state of seriousness or solemn respectfulness or observance <solemnity of contract>.

solemnity of contract. (1812) The concept that two people may enter into any contract they wish and that the resulting contract is enforceable if formalities are observed and no defenses exist.

solemnization. The performance of a formal ceremony (such as a marriage ceremony) before witnesses, as distinguished from a clandestine ceremony.

solemnize (sol-əm-nɪz), *vb.* (14c) To enter into (a marriage, contract, etc.) by a formal act, usu. before witnesses.

solemn oath. See *corporal oath* under OATH.

solemn occasion. In some states, the serious and unusual circumstance in which the supreme court is constitutionally permitted to render advisory opinions to the remaining branches of government, as when the legislature doubts the legality of proposed legislation and a determination must be made to allow the legislature to exercise its functions. ● Some factors that have been considered in determining whether a solemn occasion exists include whether an important question of law is presented, whether the question is urgent, whether the matter is ripe for an opinion, and whether the court has enough time to consider the question.

solemn war. See WAR.

sole practitioner. (1946) A lawyer who practices law without any partners or associates. — Often shortened to *solo.* — Also termed *solo practitioner.*

sole proprietorship. (1860) **1.** A business in which one person owns all the assets, owes all the liabilities, and operates in his or her personal capacity. **2.** Ownership of such a business. — Also termed *individual proprietorship.*

sole selling agency. See *exclusive agency* under AGENCY (1).

sole-source rule. In a false-advertising action at common law, the principle that a plaintiff may not recover unless it can demonstrate that it has a monopoly in the sale of goods possessing the advertised trait, because only then is it clear that the plaintiff would be harmed by the defendant's advertising.

sole use. See *entire use* under USE (4).

solicitation, *n.* (16c) **1.** The act or an instance of requesting or seeking to obtain something; a request or petition <a solicitation for volunteers to handle at least one pro bono case per year>. **2.** The criminal offense of urging, advising, commanding, or otherwise inciting another to commit a crime <convicted of solicitation of murder>. ● Solicitation is an inchoate offense distinct from the solicited crime. Under the Model Penal Code, a defendant is guilty of solicitation even if the command or urging was not actually communicated to the solicited person, as long as it was designed to be communicated. Model Penal Code § 5.02(2). — Also termed *criminal solicitation; incitement.* Cf. ATTEMPT (2). **3.** An offer to pay or accept money in exchange for sex <the prostitute was charged with solicitation>. — Also termed *soliciting.* Cf. PATRONIZING A PROSTITUTE. **4.** An attempt or effort to gain business <the attorney's solicitations took the form of radio and television ads>. ● The Model Rules of Professional Conduct place certain prohibitions on lawyers' direct solicitation of potential clients. **5.** *Securities.* A request for a proxy; a request to execute, not execute, or revoke a proxy; the furnishing of a form of proxy; or any other communication to security holders under circumstances reasonably calculated to result in the procurement, withholding, or revocation of a proxy. — **solicit,** *vb.*

solicitation for bids. See INVITATION TO NEGOTIATE.

solicitation of a bribe. The crime of asking or enticing another to commit bribery. 18 USCA § 201. See BRIBERY.

solicitee. One who is solicited. See SOLICITATION.

soliciting, *n.* See SOLICITATION (3).

soliciting agent. See AGENT (2).

solicitor. (15c) **1.** A person who seeks business or contributions from others; an advertiser or promoter. **2.** A person who conducts matters on another's behalf; an agent or representative. **3.** The chief law officer of a governmental body or a municipality. **4.** In the United Kingdom, a lawyer who consults with clients and prepares legal documents but is not generally heard in High Court or (in Scotland) Court of Session unless specially licensed. Cf. BARRISTER. **5.** See *special agent* under INSURANCE AGENT. **6.** A prosecutor (in some jurisdictions, such as South Carolina). **7.** See *special agent* under INSURANCE AGENT.

solicitor general. (*usu. cap.*) (17c) The second-highest-ranking legal officer in a government (after the attorney general); esp., the chief courtroom lawyer for the executive branch. — Abbr. SG. Pl. **solicitors general.**

solicitor's hypothec. See HYPOTHEC.

solidarity. (1875) The state of being jointly and severally liable (as for a debt). See *solidary obligation* under OBLIGATION. — **solidarily,** *adv.*

solidary (sol-ə-der-ee), *adj.* (Of a liability or obligation) joint and several. See JOINT AND SEVERAL.

solidary liability. See LIABILITY.

solidary obligation. See OBLIGATION.

solitary confinement. (17c) Separate confinement that gives a prisoner extremely limited access to other people; esp., the complete isolation of a prisoner.

solo, *n.* See SOLE PRACTITIONER.

Solomon Amendment. A federal law authorizing the Secretary of Defense to withhold federal funding from schools that do not allow military recruiters on their campuses or deny access equal to that enjoyed by other types of recruiters. ● The amendment is named for Representative Gerald B.H. Solomon of New York. 10 USCA § 983.

solo practitioner. See SOLE PRACTITIONER.

solvency, *n.* (18c) The ability to pay debts as they come due. Cf. INSOLVENCY. — **solvent,** *adj.*

somnambulism (sahm-nam-byə-liz-əm). (18c) Sleepwalking. ● Generally, a person will not be held criminally responsible for an act performed while in this state. See AUTOMATISM.

somnolentia (sahm-nə-len-shee-ə). (1879) **1.** The state of drowsiness. **2.** A condition of incomplete sleep resembling drunkenness, during which part of the faculties are abnormally excited while the others are dormant; the combined condition of sleeping and wakefulness producing a temporary state of involuntary intoxication. ● To the extent that it destroys moral agency, somnolentia may be a defense to a criminal charge.

son. 1. A person's male child, whether natural or adopted; a male of whom one is the parent. **2.** An immediate male descendant. **3.** *Slang.* Any young male person.

son-in-law. The husband of one's daughter.

Sonny Bono Copyright Term Extension Act. *Copyright.* A federal law extending the copyright term by 20 years for all works published in the U.S. after January 1, 1978, and settling the copyright term for works created before 1978 as 95 years from the original copyright date. • Before the extension, the copyright term was the life of the author plus 50 years. Pub. L. 105-298, 112 Stat. 2827.

Son-of-Sam law. (1981) A state statute that prohibits a convicted criminal from profiting by selling his or her story rights to a publisher or filmmaker. • State law usu. authorizes prosecutors to seize royalties from a convicted criminal and to place the money in an escrow account for the crime victim's benefit. This type of law was first enacted in New York in 1977, in response to the lucrative book deals that publishers offered David Berkowitz, the serial killer who called himself "Son of Sam." In 1992, the U.S. Supreme Court declared New York's Son-of-Sam law unconstitutional as a content-based speech regulation, prompting many states to amend their laws in an attempt to avoid constitutionality problems. *Simon & Schuster, Inc. v. New York State Crime Victims Bd.*, 502 U.S. 105, 112 S.Ct. 501 (1992).

Sony doctrine. See COMMERCIALLY SIGNIFICANT NONINFRINGING USE.

sophisticated investor. See INVESTOR.

sororicide (sə-ror-ə-sɪd). (17c) **1.** The act of killing one's own sister. **2.** A person who kills his or her sister. Cf. FRATRICIDE. — **sororicidal,** *adj.*

sound, *adj.* (12c) **1.** (Of health, mind, etc.) good; whole; free from disease or disorder. **2.** (Of property) good; marketable. **3.** (Of discretion) exercised equitably under the circumstances. — **soundness,** *n.*

sound, *vb.* (18c) **1.** To be actionable (in) <her claims for physical injury sound in tort, not in contract>. **2.** To be recoverable (in) <his tort action sounds in damages, not in equitable relief>.

sound health. *Insurance.* **1.** A policy applicant's good mental and physical condition; a state of health characterized by a lack of grave impairment or disease, or of any ailment that seriously affects the applicant's health. **2.** GOOD HEALTH.

sound mind. 1. MIND (2). **2.** See *testamentary capacity* under CAPACITY (3).

Sound Recording Amendment of 1972. A Copyright Act of 1909 amendment that established copyright protection for sound recordings.

source, *n.* The originator or primary agent of an act, circumstance, or result <she was the source of the information> <the side business was the source of income>.

source code. *Copyright.* The nonmachine language used by a computer programmer to create a program. • If it is not included with the software sold to the public, source code is protected by trade secret laws as well as copyright and patent laws. Source code may be deposited with the U.S. Copyright Office but, because of the need to protect a trade secret, and because a skilled programmer could figure out how to duplicate the source code's functions without necessarily copying it, strategic parts may be blacked out. Cf. OBJECT CODE.

source of law. (1892) Something (such as a constitution, treaty, statute, or custom) that provides authority for legislation and for judicial decisions; a point of origin for law or legal analysis. — Also termed *fons juris.*

South Eastern Reporter. A set of regional lawbooks, part of the West Group's National Reporter System, containing every published appellate decision from Georgia, North Carolina, South Carolina, Virginia, and West Virginia, from 1887 to date. • The first series ran from 1887 to 1939; the second series is the current one. — Abbr. S.E.; S.E.2d.

Southern Reporter. A set of regional lawbooks, part of the West Group's National Reporter System, containing every published appellate decision from Alabama, Florida, Louisiana, and Mississippi, from 1887 to date. • The first series ran from 1887 to 1941; the second series is the current one. — Abbr. So.; So.2d.

South Western Reporter. A set of regional lawbooks, part of the West Group's National Reporter System, containing every published appellate decision from Arkansas, Kentucky, Missouri, Tennessee, and Texas, from 1886 to date. • The first series ran from 1886 to 1928; the second series ran until 1999; the third series is the current one. — Abbr. S.W.; S.W.2d.; S.W.3d.

sovereign, *adj.* (Of a state) characteristic of or endowed with supreme authority <sovereign nation> <sovereign immunity>.

sovereign, *n.* (13c) **1.** A person, body, or state vested with independent and supreme authority. **2.** The ruler of an independent state. — Also spelled *sovran.* See SOVEREIGNTY.

sovereign equality. *Int'l law.* The principle that nations have the right to enjoy territorial integrity and political independence, free from intervention by other nations,. • The United Nations "is based on the principle of the sovereign equality of all its Members." UN Charter art. 2, ¶ 1.

sovereign immunity. See IMMUNITY (1).

sovereign people. (17c) The political body consisting of the collective number of citizens and qualified electors who possess the powers of sovereignty and exercise them through their chosen representatives.

sovereign political power. See POLITICAL POWER.

sovereign power. (15c) **1.** The power to make and enforce laws. **2.** See *sovereign political power* under POLITICAL POWER.

sovereign right. (16c) A unique right possessed by a state or its agencies that enables it to carry out its official functions for the public benefit, as distinguished from certain proprietary rights that it may possess like any other private person.

sovereign state. (17c) **1.** A state that possesses an independent existence, being complete in itself, without being merely part of a larger whole to whose government it is subject. **2.** A political community whose members are bound together by the tie of common subjection to some central authority, whose commands those members must obey. — Also termed *independent state*. Cf. *client state*, *nonsovereign state* under STATE.

> **part-sovereign state.** A political community in which part of the powers of external sovereignty are exercised by the home government, and part are vested in or controlled by some other political body or bodies. • Such a state is not fully independent because by the conditions of its existence it is not allowed full freedom of action in external affairs.

sovereignty (**sahv**-[ə-]rin-tee). (18c) **1.** Supreme dominion, authority, or rule.

> **popular sovereignty.** A system of government in which policy choices reflect the preferences of the majority of citizens.

> **state sovereignty.** See STATE SOVEREIGNTY.

2. The supreme political authority of an independent state. **3.** The state itself.

> **external sovereignty.** The power of dealing on a nation's behalf with other national governments.

> **internal sovereignty.** The power enjoyed by a governmental entity of a sovereign state, including affairs within its own territory and powers related to the exercise of external sovereignty.

sovran. See SOVEREIGN.

SOW. *Abbr.* STATEMENT OF WORK.

s.p. *abbr.* **1.** SINE PROLE. **2.** Same principle; same point. • This notation, when inserted between two citations, indicates that the second involves the same principles as the first.

space arbitrage. See ARBITRAGE.

space charter. See CHARTER (8).

spacial jurisdiction. See JURISDICTION.

spam. Unsolicited commercial e-mail.

SPD. *abbr.* SUMMARY PLAN DESCRIPTION.

SPDA. See *single-premium deferred annuity* under ANNUITY.

SPE. *abbr.* SPECIAL-PURPOSE ENTITY.

speaker. **1.** One who speaks or makes a speech <the slander claim was viable only against the speaker>. **2.** The presiding officer of a large deliberative assembly, esp. a legislature's more numerous house, such as the House of Representatives <Speaker of the House>. See CHAIR (1).

speaking a vessel. *Maritime law.* A pilot's offer of services.

speaking demurrer. See DEMURRER.

speaking motion. See MOTION (1).

speaking objection. See OBJECTION.

speaking statute. See STATUTE.

spec. *abbr.* SPECIFICATION.

special, *adj.* (13c) **1.** Of, relating to, or designating a species, kind, or individual thing. **2.** (Of a statute, rule, etc.) designed for a particular purpose. **3.** (Of powers, etc.) unusual; extraordinary.

special acceptance. See ACCEPTANCE (4).

special act. See *special law* under LAW.

special administration. See ADMINISTRATION.

special administrator. See ADMINISTRATOR (2).

special advocate. See *guardian ad litem* under GUARDIAN.

special agency. See AGENCY (1).

special agent. **1.** See AGENT (2). **2.** See INSURANCE AGENT.

special agreement. See *ad hoc compromis* under COMPROMIS.

special allocatur. See ALLOCATUR.

special allowance. See ALLOWANCE (4).

special appearance. See APPEARANCE.

special assessment. See ASSESSMENT.

special-assessment bond. See *special-tax bond* under BOND (3).

Special Assistant to the United States Attorney. See UNITED STATES ATTORNEY.

special assumpsit. See ASSUMPSIT.

special attorney. See *special counsel* under COUNSEL.

special authority. See AUTHORITY (1).

special bail. See *bail to the action* under BAIL (4).

special bailiff. See BAILIFF.

special benefit. See BENEFIT.

special calendar. See CALENDAR (2).

special case. See *case reserved* (1) under CASE.

special charge. **1.** See *special instruction* under JURY INSTRUCTION. **2.** See CHARGE.

special charter. See CHARTER (3).

special circumstances. See *exigent circumstances* under CIRCUMSTANCE.

special-circumstances rule. See SPECIAL-FACTS RULE.

special committee. See COMMITTEE.

special contract. See CONTRACT.

special-contract debt. See DEBT.

special counsel. See COUNSEL.

special count. See COUNT.

special court-martial. See COURT-MARTIAL.

special covenant against encumbrances. See COVENANT (4).

special custom. See *local custom* under CUSTOM.

special damages. See DAMAGES.

special demurrer. See DEMURRER.

special deposit. See DEPOSIT (2).

special deputy. See DEPUTY.

special-design property. See *special-purpose property* under PROPERTY.

special deterrence. See DETERRENCE.

special diligence. See DILIGENCE.

special district. See DISTRICT.

special dividend. See *extraordinary dividend* under DIVIDEND.

special-duty doctrine. (1980) *Torts.* The rule that a governmental entity (such as a state or municipality) can be held liable for an individual plaintiff's injury when the entity owed a duty to the plaintiff but not to the general public. • This is an exception to the public-duty doctrine. The special-duty doctrine applies only when the plaintiff has reasonably relied on the governmental entity's assumption of the duty. — Also termed *special-duty exception.* See PUBLIC-DUTY DOCTRINE.

special-duty exception. 1. SPECIAL-DUTY DOCTRINE. **2.** SPECIAL-ERRAND DOCTRINE.

special election. See ELECTION (3).

special employee. See *borrowed employee* under EMPLOYEE.

special employer. See EMPLOYER.

special-errand doctrine. The principle that workers' compensation covers an employee's injuries occurring while the employee is on a journey or special duty for the employer away from the workplace. • This is an exception to the general rule that an employee is not covered for injuries occurring away from work. — Also termed *special-duty exception; special-mission exception.* See GOING-AND-COMING RULE. Cf. SPECIAL-HAZARD RULE.

special exception. 1. A party's objection to the form rather than the substance of an opponent's claim, such as an objection for vagueness or ambiguity.

See DEMURRER. Cf. *general exception* (1) under EXCEPTION (1). **2.** An allowance in a zoning ordinance for special uses that are considered essential and are not fundamentally incompatible with the original zoning regulations. — Also termed (in sense 2) *conditional use; special use.* Cf. VARIANCE (2).

special execution. See EXECUTION.

special executor. See EXECUTOR.

special-facts rule. *Corporations.* The principle that a director or officer has a fiduciary duty to disclose material inside information to a shareholder when engaging in a stock transaction under special circumstances, as when the shareholder lacks business acumen, the shares are closely held with no readily ascertainable market value, or the director or officer instigated the transaction. • This is an exception to the "majority rule." — Also termed *special-circumstances rule.* Cf. MAJORITY RULE (2).

special finding. See FINDING OF FACT.

special-form drawing. See DRAWING.

special franchise. See FRANCHISE (2).

special grand jury. See GRAND JURY.

special guaranty. See GUARANTY.

special guardian. See GUARDIAN.

special-hazard rule. The principle that workers' compensation covers an employee for injuries received while traveling to or from work if the route used contains unique risks or hazards and is not ordinarily used by the public except in dealing with the employer. • This is an exception to the general rule that an employee is not covered for injuries occurring during the employee's commute. See GOING-AND-COMING RULE. Cf. SPECIAL-ERRAND DOCTRINE.

special housing unit. A block of cells used to house inmates who have been separated from the general prison population, usu. for disciplinary purposes but sometimes for safety reasons. • Inmates in special housing units typically have fewer privileges than other inmates. — Abbr. SHU.

special imparlance. See IMPARLANCE.

special indorsement. See INDORSEMENT.

special injunction. See INJUNCTION.

special instruction. See JURY INSTRUCTION.

special-interest group. An organization that seeks to influence legislation or government policy in favor of a particular interest or issue, esp. by lobbying. — Also termed *special interest.*

special interrogatory. See INTERROGATORY.

special issue. 1. See ISSUE (1). **2.** See *special interrogatory* under INTERROGATORY.

specialist. 1. A lawyer who has been board-certified in a specific field of law. See BOARD OF LEGAL SPECIALIZATION. **2.** *Securities.* A securities-exchange member who makes a market in one or more listed securities. ● The exchange assigns securities to various specialists and expects them to maintain a fair and orderly market as provided by SEC standards.

special judge. See JUDGE.

special jurisdiction. See *limited jurisdiction* under JURISDICTION.

special jury. See JURY.

special law. See LAW.

special legacy. See *specific legacy* under LEGACY.

special letter of credit. See LETTER OF CREDIT.

special lien. See *particular lien* under LIEN.

special limitation. See LIMITATION.

special litigation committee. *Corporations.* A committee of independent corporate directors assigned to investigate the merits of a shareholder derivative suit and, if appropriate, to recommend maintaining or dismissing the suit. — Abbr. SLC. — Also termed *independent investigation committee; authorized committee.* See DERIVATIVE ACTION.

specially accredited agent. See AGENT (2).

special malice. See *particular malice* under MALICE.

special master. 1. MASTER. **2.** See *judicial officer* (3) under OFFICER.

special matter. See MATTER.

special meaning. See SECONDARY MEANING.

special meeting. See MEETING.

special message. See MESSAGE.

special-mission exception. See SPECIAL-ERRAND DOCTRINE.

special mortgage. See MORTGAGE.

special motion. See MOTION (1).

special-needs analysis. (1989) *Criminal procedure.* A balancing test used by the Supreme Court to determine whether certain searches (such as administrative, civil-based, or public-safety searches) impose unreasonably on individual rights.

special-needs child. See CHILD.

special-needs trust. See *supplemental-needs trust* under TRUST.

special occupant. See OCCUPANT.

special offering. See OFFERING.

special order. See ORDER (4).

special-order agenda. See *special-order calendar* under CALENDAR (4).

special-order calendar. See CALENDAR (4).

special owner. See OWNER.

special partner. See *limited partner* under PARTNER.

special partnership. See PARTNERSHIP.

special permit. See SPECIAL-USE PERMIT.

special plea. See PLEA (3).

special pleader. See PLEADER.

special pleading. (17c) **1.** The common-law system of pleading that required the parties to exchange a series of court papers (such as replications, rebutters, and surrebutters) setting out their contentions in accordance with hypertechnical rules before a case could be tried. ● Often, therefore, cases were decided on points of pleading and not on the merits. **2.** The art of drafting pleadings under this system. **3.** An instance of drafting such a pleading. **4.** A responsive pleading that does more than merely deny allegations, as by introducing new matter to justify an otherwise blameworthy act. **5.** An argument that is unfairly slanted toward the speaker's viewpoint because it omits unfavorable facts or authorities and develops only favorable ones.

special plea in bar. See PLEA IN BAR.

special plea in error. At common law, a plea alleging some extraneous matter as a ground for defeating a writ of error (such as a release or expiration of the time within which error can be brought), to which the plaintiff in error must reply or demur.

special power. 1. See POWER (3). **2.** See *limited power of appointment* under POWER OF APPOINTMENT.

special power of appointment. See *limited power of appointment* under POWER OF APPOINTMENT.

special power of attorney. See POWER OF ATTORNEY.

special prayer. See PRAYER FOR RELIEF.

special privilege. See PRIVILEGE (1).

special proceeding. See PROCEEDING.

special property. See PROPERTY.

special prosecutor. See PROSECUTOR.

special-purpose entity. A business established to perform no function other than to develop, own, and operate a large, complex project (usu. called a *single-purpose project*), esp. so as to limit the number of creditors claiming against the project. ● A special-purpose entity provides additional protection for project lenders, which are usu. paid only out of the money generated by the entity's business, because there will be fewer competing claims for that money and because the entity will be less likely to be forced into bankruptcy. A special-purpose entity will sometimes issue securities instead of just receiving a direct loan. — Abbr. SPE. — Also termed *special-purpose vehicle* (SPV). See BANKRUPTCY-REMOTE ENTITY; SINGLE-PURPOSE PROJECT; *project financing* under FINANCING.

special-purpose property. See PROPERTY.

special-purpose vehicle. See SPECIAL-PURPOSE ENTITY.

special reference. See REFERENCE.

special registration. See REGISTRATION (1).

special relationship. See RELATIONSHIP.

special-relationship doctrine. (1981) The theory that if a state has assumed control over an individual sufficient to trigger an affirmative duty to protect that individual (as in an involuntary hospitalization or custody), then the state may be liable for the harm inflicted on the individual by a third party. ● This is an exception to the general principle prohibiting members of the public from suing state employees for failing to protect them from third parties. — Also termed *special-relationship exception.* Cf. DANGER-CREATION DOCTRINE.

special relief. *Copyright.* A variance from a formal requirement for copyright registration or deposit granted by the U.S. Copyright Office when an applicant shows a good reason for the variance.

special replication. See REPLICATION.

special reprisal. See REPRISAL.

special retainer. See RETAINER.

special retention. See RETENTION.

special rule. 1. A rule applicable to a particular case or circumstance only. See RULE (1). **2.** A deliberative assembly's rule that supplements or supersedes its parliamentary authority. See PARLIAMENTARY AUTHORITY. **3.** A rule that applies only to a particular matter, such as a specific bill. In senses 2 & 3, see RULE (2), (3).

specials. See *special damages* under DAMAGES.

special-sensitivity rule. See EGGSHELL-SKULL RULE.

special session. See SESSION (1).

special setting. See SETTING.

special statute. See STATUTE.

special stock. See STOCK.

special tail. See *tail special* under TAIL.

special tax. See TAX.

special-tax bond. See BOND (3).

special term. See TERM (5).

Special 301. *Intellectual property.* A provision of the Omnibus Trade and Competitiveness Act of 1988 directing the U.S. Trade Representative to report annually on countries that do not provide adequate and effective protection against the pirating of goods protected by U.S. intellectual-property rights. ● Countries that fail the annual audit are put on a watch list and may face trade sanctions. 19 USCA §§ 2411 et seq.

special traverse. See TRAVERSE.

special trial setting. See *special setting* under SETTING.

special truce. See TRUCE.

special trust. See *active trust* under TRUST.

specialty. 1. See *contract under seal* under CONTRACT. **2.** DOCTRINE OF SPECIALTY. **3.** *Eminent domain.* Unique property (such as a church or cemetery) that is essentially not marketable, so that its value for condemnation purposes is determined by measuring the property's reproduction cost less any depreciation. — Also termed (in sense 3) *specialty property.*

specialty bar. See BAR.

specialty contract. See *contract under seal* under CONTRACT.

specialty creditor. See CREDITOR.

specialty debt. See *special-contract debt* under DEBT.

specialty doctrine. See DOCTRINE OF SPECIALTY.

specialty property. See SPECIALTY (3).

special use. See SPECIAL EXCEPTION (2).

special-use permit. A zoning board's authorization to use property in a way that is identified as a special exception in a zoning ordinance. ● Unlike a variance, which is an authorized violation of a zoning ordinance, a special-use permit is a permitted exception. — Abbr. SUP. — Also termed *conditional-use permit; special permit.* See SPECIAL EXCEPTION (2). Cf. VARIANCE (2).

special-use valuation. See VALUATION.

special venire. See VENIRE.

special verdict. See VERDICT.

special warranty. See WARRANTY (1).

special warranty deed. See DEED.

specie (spee-shee). See IN SPECIE.

species (spee-sheez). **1.** A taxonomic class of organisms uniquely distinguished from other classes by shared characteristics and usu. by an inability to interbreed with members of other classes.

    candidate species. Environmental law. Plants and animals identified by the Fish and Wildlife Service or National Marine Fisheries Service as potentially endangered or threatened but not of high enough priority to develop a proposed listing regulation under the Endangered Species Act. ● Candidate species are not protected by federal law. — Also termed *listed species.*

    endangered species. A species in danger of becoming extinct; esp., under federal law, a species that is in danger of extinction throughout all or a significant part of its range. ● Federal law excludes from the definition a species of the class Insecta if the Environmental Protection Agency determines that it constitutes a pest whose protection would present a significant risk to the human population. 50 CFR § 81.

listed species. See *candidate species.*

threatened species. A species that, within the foreseeable future, is likely to become an endangered species throughout all or a significant part of its range. 16 USCA § 1532(20).

2. A specific class or kind of thing within a larger, general class. ● For example, *tort* refers to a general class or genus. *Slander* refers to a specific kind of tort. Cf. GENUS. **3.** *Patents.* An element, usu. one of several mutually exclusive alternatives, that may be used in an invention to achieve a desired result <magnetic metals, including iron and steel>. ● Species may be structures, steps, parts, compounds, and so on.

ultimate species. A species that has been fully and narrowly defined. ● For example, a species may be defined generally as "magnetic metals, including iron and steel," or particularly, such as "sodium chloride."

species claim. See PATENT CLAIM.

specific, *adj.* **1.** Of, relating to, or designating a particular or defined thing; explicit <specific duties>. **2.** Of or relating to a particular named thing <specific item>. **3.** Conformable to special requirements <specific performance>. — **specificity** (spes-ə-**fis**-i-tee), *n.* — **specifically,** *adv.*

specific appropriation. See APPROPRIATION (2).

specification. (17c) **1.** The act of making a detailed statement, esp. of the measurements, quality, materials, or other items to be provided under a contract. **2.** The statement so made. **3.** *Patents.* The part of a patent application describing how an invention is made and used, the best mode of operation of the claimed invention, and the inventor's claims. ● The specification must be clear and complete enough to enable a person of ordinary skill in the art to make and use the invention. It must also disclose the best mode of working the invention. The term may also refer to the description as separate from the claims. — Abbr. spec. Cf. PATENT CLAIM.

substitute specification. A patent specification that is rewritten (1) to include amendments made to the specification after filing; (2) to replace an illegible or unreadable original; or (3) to prepare the papers for printing. ● A substitute specification must be accompanied by a statement that it contains no new matter, and by a copy showing what has been added and deleted since the original specification. Substitute specifications

are allowed under 37 CFR 1.125. — Also termed *rewritten specification.*

4. A statement of charges against one who is accused of an offense, esp. a military offense. **5.** The acquisition of title to materials belonging to another person by converting those materials into a new and different form, as by changing grapes into wine, lumber into shelving, or corn into liquor. ● The effect is that the original owner of the materials loses the property rights in them and is left with a right of action for their original value. — Abbr. spec.

specific bequest. See BEQUEST.

specific denial. See DENIAL.

specific deposit. See *special deposit* under DEPOSIT (2).

specific devise. See DEVISE.

specific duty. See DUTY (4).

specific enforcement. See *primary right* under RIGHT.

specific example. See EXAMPLE.

specific guaranty. See GUARANTY.

specific intent. See INTENT (1).

specific-intent defense. *Criminal law.* A defendant's claim that he or she did not have the capacity (often supposedly because of intoxication or mental illness) to form the intent necessary for committing the crime alleged.

specific jurisdiction. See JURISDICTION.

specific legacy. See LEGACY.

specific legatee. See LEGATEE.

specific lien. See LIEN.

specific main motion. See *incidental main motion* under MOTION (2).

specific objection. See OBJECTION.

specific performance. (18c) The rendering, as nearly as practicable, of a promised performance through a judgment or decree; specif., a court-ordered remedy that requires precise fulfillment of a legal or contractual obligation when monetary damages are inappropriate or inadequate, as when the sale of real estate or a rare article is involved. ● Specific performance is an equitable remedy that lies within the court's discretion to award whenever the common-law remedy is insufficient, either because damages would be inadequate or because the damages could not possibly be established. — Also termed *specific relief.*

specific personal jurisdiction. See JURISDICTION.

specific policy. See *basic-form policy* under INSURANCE POLICY.

specific-purpose rule. *Insurance.* The principle that a nonowner driver of a vehicle is treated as an omnibus insured under the vehicle owner's liability coverage only if the driver's actual use of the vehicle at the time of the accident is the exact use that the owner contemplated when granting permission or consent to the nonowner driver. • The time at which the bailment of the vehicle was to expire must not have passed, the place where the vehicle was being used must be as specified or contemplated by the insured, and the use of the vehicle must comport with the type of use that the insured had in mind when the bailment was created. Otherwise, the permittee's use of the vehicle will be regarded as a conversion. — Also termed *conversion rule*; *strict rule*.

specific relief. See SPECIFIC PERFORMANCE.

specific remedy. See REMEDY.

specific tax. See TAX.

specific traverse. See *common traverse* under TRAVERSE.

specimen. An actual sample of something; esp., an example of a trademark as it is used in commerce. • In the field of trademarks, a specimen typically consists of a label, a container, a display, or a photograph of the mark used for selling or advertising the goods or services.

specious, *adj.* Falsely appearing to be true, accurate, or just <specious argument>.

spectrograph. (1884) An electromagnetic machine that analyzes sound, esp. a human voice, by separating and mapping it into elements of frequency, time lapse, and intensity (represented by a series of horizontal and vertical bar lines) to produce a final voiceprint. See VOICEPRINT.

speculation, *n.* (14c) **1.** The buying or selling of something with the expectation of profiting from price fluctuations <he engaged in speculation in the stock market>. **2.** The act or practice of theorizing about matters over which there is no certain knowledge <the public's speculation about the assassination of John F. Kennedy>. — **speculate,** *vb.* — **speculative,** *adj.*

speculative damages. See DAMAGES.

speculative risk. See RISK.

speculative security. See SECURITY.

speculator. A knowledgeable, aggressive investor who trades securities to profit from fluctuating market prices.

speech. (bef. 12c) **1.** The expression or communication of thoughts or opinions in spoken words; something spoken or uttered. See FREEDOM OF SPEECH.

commercial speech. (1963) Communication (such as advertising and marketing) that involves only the commercial interests of the speaker and the audience, and is therefore afforded lesser First Amendment protection than social, political, or religious speech. Cf. *pure speech*.

corporate speech. (1959) Speech deriving from a corporation and protected under the First Amendment. • It does not lose protected status simply because of its corporate source.

hate speech. (1988) Speech that carries no meaning other than the expression of hatred for some group, such as a particular race, esp. in circumstances in which the communication is likely to provoke violence. Cf. *hate crime* under CRIME; *group libel* under LIBEL.

pure speech. (1943) Words or conduct limited in form to what is necessary to convey the idea. • This type of speech is given the greatest constitutional protection. Cf. *commercial speech*; *symbolic speech*.

seditious speech. (1920) Speech advocating the violent overthrow of government. See SEDITION.

speech-plus. See *symbolic speech*.

symbolic speech. (1966) Conduct that expresses opinions or thoughts, such as a hunger strike or the wearing of a black armband. • Symbolic speech does not enjoy the same constitutional protection that pure speech does. — Also termed *speech-plus*. Cf. *pure speech*.

2. *English law.* An opinion delivered by a Law Lord; JUDGMENT (2). **3.** *Parliamentary law.* The unit of debate; specif., one statement, usu. subject to a time limit, on one question by one member. • When finished, the speaker must relinquish the floor and ordinarily cannot yield it to another member.

Speech Clause. The First Amendment provision that "Congress shall make no law . . . abridging the freedom of speech." U.S. Const. amend I. — Also termed *Freedom of Speech Clause*.

Speech or Debate Clause. (1965) The clause of the U.S. Constitution giving members of Congress immunity for statements made during debate in either the House or the Senate. • This immunity is extended to other areas where it is necessary to prevent impairment of deliberations and other legitimate legislative activities, such as subpoenaing bank records for an investigation. U.S. Const. art. I, § 6., cl. 1. — Also termed *Speech and Debate Clause*. See *congressional immunity* under IMMUNITY (1).

speech-plus. See *symbolic speech* under SPEECH.

speedy execution. See EXECUTION.

speedy remedy. See REMEDY.

speedy trial. (18c) *Criminal procedure.* A trial that the prosecution, with reasonable diligence, begins promptly and conducts expeditiously. • The Sixth Amendment secures the right to a speedy trial. In deciding whether an accused has been deprived of that right, courts generally consider the length of and reason for the delay, and the prejudice to the accused.

Speedy Trial Act of 1974. A federal statute establishing time limits for carrying out the major events (such as information, indictment, arraignment, and trial commencement) in the prosecution of federal criminal cases. 18 USCA §§ 3161–3174.

spending bill. See *appropriations bill* under BILL (3).

spending power. See POWER (3).

spendthrift, *n.* One who spends lavishly and wastefully; a profligate. — **spendthrift,** *adj.*

spendthrift trust. See TRUST.

spent bill of lading. See BILL OF LADING.

sperate (**speer**-ət), *adj. Archaic.* (Of a debt) recoverable; not hopeless. • In determining whether a debt could be collected, consideration was formerly given to whether the debt was *desperate* or *sperate.*

Spielberg **doctrine.** *Labor law.* The policy of the National Labor Relations Board to defer to an arbitrator's decision regarding a contract dispute if (1) the decision is not repugnant to the NLRB, (2) the arbitration proceedings provided a hearing as fair as would have been provided before the NLRB, and (3) the contract requires binding arbitration. *Spielberg Mfg. Co.,* 112 NLRB Dec. (CCH) 86 (1955). Cf. COLLYER DOCTRINE.

spillover. See EXTERNALITY.

spillover theory. (1985) The principle that a severance must be granted only when a defendant can show that a trial with a codefendant would substantially prejudice the defendant's case, as when the jury might wrongly use evidence against the defendant. See BRUTON ERROR.

spinning. *Securities.* The giving of shares or preferred opportunities to buy shares in an initial public offering to key investment-banking clients in order to solicit or retain profitable business in the future.

spin-off, *n.* **1.** A corporate divestiture in which a division of a corporation becomes an independent company and stock of the new company is distributed to the corporation's shareholders. **2.** The company created by this divestiture. — Also written *spinoff.* Cf. SPLIT-OFF; SPLIT-UP.

spirit of the law. (16c) The general meaning or purpose of the law, as opposed to its literal content. Cf. LETTER OF THE LAW.

spiritual, *adj.* Of or relating to ecclesiastical rather than secular matters <spiritual corporation>.

spiritual corporation. See CORPORATION.

spiritual court. See *ecclesiastical court* under COURT.

spiritual lord. An archbishop or bishop having a seat in the House of Lords.

spiritual tenure. See TENURE.

spiritual-treatment exemption. See FAITH-HEALING EXEMPTION.

spital (**spit**-əl). *Archaic.* A hospital. — Also termed *spittle.*

spite fence. (1901) A fence erected solely to annoy a neighbor, as by blocking the neighbor's view or preventing the neighbor from acquiring an easement of light <the court temporarily enjoined the completion of the 25-foot spite fence>. Cf. LAWFUL FENCE.

split, *vb.* **1.** To divide (a cause of action) into segments or parts. **2.** To issue two or more shares for each old share without changing the shareholder's proportional ownership interest. See STOCK SPLIT; SPLIT-INTEREST PURCHASE OF PROPERTY.

split custody. See CUSTODY (2).

split-dollar life insurance. See LIFE INSURANCE.

split fund. See *dual fund* under MUTUAL FUND.

split-funded plan. See EMPLOYEE BENEFIT PLAN.

split gift. See GIFT.

split income. See INCOME.

split-interest purchase of property. An arrangement between two parties to purchase an asset whereby one party (often a parent) purchases a life estate and the other party (often a child or grandchild of the life tenant) purchases a remainder interest. • Each party to a split pays the actuarial value of the interest purchased. — Often shortened to *split.* — Also termed *joint-interest purchase.*

split-interest trust. See *charitable-remainder trust* under TRUST.

split-level statute. See STATUTE.

split-off, *n.* **1.** The creation of a new corporation by an existing corporation that gives its shareholders stock in the new corporation in return for their stock in the original corporation. **2.** The corporation created by this process. — Also written *splitoff.* Cf. SPIN-OFF; SPLIT-UP.

split order. See ORDER (8).

split sentence. See SENTENCE.

splitting a cause of action. (1850) Separating parts of a demand and pursuing it piecemeal; presenting only a part of a claim in one lawsuit, leaving the rest for a second suit. • This practice has long been considered procedurally impermissible.

split-up, *n.* The division of a corporation into two or more new corporations. • The shareholders in the original corporation typically receive shares in the new corporations, and the original corporation goes out of business. — Also written *split-up.* Cf. SPIN-OFF; SPLIT-OFF.

split verdict. See VERDICT.

spoiled ballot. See BALLOT (2).

spoils of war. See BOOTY (1).

spoils system. The practice of awarding government jobs to supporters and friends of the victorious political party. Cf. MERIT SYSTEM.

spoliation (spoh-lee-**ay**-shən), *n.* (18c) **1.** The intentional destruction, mutilation, alteration, or concealment of evidence, usu. a document. ● If proved, spoliation may be used to establish that the evidence was unfavorable to the party responsible. **2.** The seizure of personal or real property by violent means; the act of pillaging. **3.** The taking of a benefit properly belonging to another. **4.** *Eccles. law.* The wrongful deprivation of a cleric of his benefice. — **spoliate** (**spoh**-lee-ayt), *vb.* — **spoliator** (**spoh**-lee-ay-tər), *n.*

sponge tax. See *pickup tax* under TAX.

sponsion (**spon**-shən), *n.* [fr. Latin *spondere* "to engage"] **1.** The formal pledge by which a person becomes a surety. **2.** *Int'l law.* An ultra vires promise of an official agent (such as a general in wartime), requiring later ratification by the principal. **3.** *Roman law.* A form of guarantee accessory to an oral contract. ● Only Roman citizens could make this type of guarantee. See ADPROMISSION (1). — **sponsional** (**spon**-shən-əl), *adj.*

sponsor. 1. One who acts as a surety for another. **2.** A legislator who proposes a bill. **3.** *Civil law.* One who voluntarily intervenes for another without being requested to do so. **4.** GODPARENT.

spontaneous abortion. See MISCARRIAGE.

spontaneous crime. See CRIME.

spontaneous declaration. (1840) *Evidence.* A statement that is made without time to reflect or fabricate and is related to the circumstances of the perceived occurrence. — Also termed *spontaneous statement; spontaneous exclamation; spontaneous utterance.* See EXCITED UTTERANCE; PRESENT SENSE IMPRESSION.

sports franchise. See FRANCHISE (4).

spot, *adj.* Made, paid, or delivered immediately <a spot sale> <spot commodities>.

spot market. See MARKET.

spot price. See PRICE.

spot zoning. See ZONING.

spousal abuse. See ABUSE.

spousal allowance. See ALLOWANCE (1).

spousal consortium. See CONSORTIUM.

spousal-impoverishment provision. A section of the Medicare Catastrophic Coverage Act allowing the stay-at-home spouse of a person residing in a nursing home to retain certain assets and some joint income, and to earn income without jeopardizing the institutionalized spouse's eligibility for Medicaid. ● Before the provision was enacted

in 1988, almost all of a couple's joint assets and the noninstitutionalized spouse's income had to go toward the cost of the nursing-home resident's care before Medicaid provided any support. 42 USCA § 1396r-5.

spousal labor. *Family law.* Work by either spouse during the marriage. ● This term is typically used in community-property states.

spousal privilege. See *marital privilege* under PRIVILEGE (3).

spousal rape. See *marital rape* under RAPE.

spousals. *Hist.* Mutual promises to marry.

spousal support. See ALIMONY.

spousal-unity doctrine. *Hist.* **1.** *Family law.* The common-law rule that a husband and wife were a legal unity. ● Under the spousal-unity doctrine, the husband had all rights to the possession, management, control, and alienation of property. The wife had no interests in property. — Also termed *doctrine of spousal unity.* Cf. LEGAL-UNITIES DOCTRINE. See MARRIED WOMEN'S PROPERTY ACTS. **2.** *Tax.* The rule that a person and that person's spouse are treated as one. ● This rule has been repealed. — Also termed *spousal-unity rule.*

spouse. One's husband or wife by lawful marriage; a married person.

   innocent spouse. (1924) *Tax.* A spouse who may be relieved of liability for taxes on income that the other spouse did not include on a joint tax return. ● The innocent spouse must prove that the other spouse omitted the income, that the innocent spouse did not know and had no reason to know of the omission, and that it would be unfair under the circumstances to hold the innocent spouse liable.

   putative spouse. *Family law.* A spouse who believes in good faith that his or her invalid marriage is legally valid. See *putative marriage* under MARRIAGE (1).

   surviving spouse. A spouse who outlives the other spouse.

spouse-breach. See ADULTERY.

spray trust. See *sprinkle trust* under TRUST.

spread, *n.* **1.** *Banking.* The difference between the interest rate that a financial institution must pay to attract deposits and the rate at which money can be loaned. **2.** *Securities.* The difference between the highest price a buyer will pay for a security (the *bid price*) and the lowest price at which a seller will sell a security (the *asked price*). **3.** *Securities.* The simultaneous buying and selling of one or more options or futures contracts on the same security in order to profit from the price difference. **4.** In investment banking, the difference between the price the underwriter pays the issuer of the security and the price the public paid in the initial offering. • The spread compensates the underwriter for its services; it comprises the manager's fee, the underwriter's discount, and the selling-group concession or discount. — Also termed (in sense 4) *gross spread; underwriting spread.*

spread eagle. See STRADDLE.

spreadsheet. A multicolumn worksheet used esp. by accountants and auditors to summarize and analyze financial transactions.

springing durable power of attorney. See *springing power of attorney* under POWER OF ATTORNEY.

springing executory interest. See EXECUTORY INTEREST.

springing power of attorney. See POWER OF ATTORNEY.

springing use. See USE (4).

spring tide. See TIDE.

sprinkle power. In a sprinkle trust, the trustee's discretion about when and how much of the trust principal and income are to be distributed to the beneficiaries. See *sprinkle trust* under TRUST.

sprinkle trust. See TRUST.

spurious (spyoor-ee-əs), *adj.* (16c) **1.** Deceptively suggesting an erroneous origin; fake <spurious trademarks>. **2.** Of doubtful or low quality <spurious goods that fell apart>. **3.** *Archaic.* Of illegitimate birth <spurious offspring>.

spurious bank bill. See *spurious banknote* under BANKNOTE.

spurious banknote. See BANKNOTE.

spurious class action. See CLASS ACTION.

spurius (spyuur-ee-əs), *n.* [Latin] *Roman law.* A bastard; the offspring of unlawful intercourse. Pl. *spurii* (spyuur-ee-ı). See NOTHUS.

SPV. *abbr.* Special-purpose vehicle. See SPECIAL-PURPOSE ENTITY.

spy. One who secretly observes and collects secret information or intelligence about what another government or company is doing or plans to do; one who commits espionage. See ESPIONAGE.

square, *n.* (17c) **1.** A certain portion of land within a city limit. — Also termed *block.* **2.** A space set apart for public use. **3.** In a government survey, an area measuring 24 by 24 miles.

squatter. (18c) **1.** A person who settles on property without any legal claim or title. **2.** A person who settles on public land under a government regulation allowing the person to acquire title upon fulfilling specified conditions.

squatter's rights. (1855) The right to acquire title to real property by adverse possession, or by preemption of public lands. See ADVERSE POSSESSION.

squeeze-out, *n.* An action taken in an attempt to eliminate or reduce a minority interest in a corporation. Cf. FREEZE-OUT.

Squires **claim.** See PATENT CLAIM.

Squires **doctrine.** *Patents.* A rule of the U.S. Patent and Trademark Office that a utility-patent claim may incorporate drawings or tables by reference, but only when there is no practical way to express the information in words, and when referring to the artwork is a concise way to communicate the information. • The namesake case involved a numerical font designed to be readable in the dim red light inside a submarine. It is allowed only when necessary, and is not available just for the convenience of an applicant. *Ex parte Squires*, 133 USPQ (BNA) 598 (Bd. App. 1961).

SRO. *abbr.* See SELF-REGULATORY ORGANIZATION.

ss. *abbr.* **1.** Sections. **2.** *Subscripsi* (i.e., signed below). **3.** Sans (i.e., without). **4.** (Erroneously) scilicet.

SSA. *abbr.* SOCIAL SECURITY ADMINISTRATION.

SSDI. *abbr.* SOCIAL SECURITY DISABILITY INSURANCE.

SSI. *abbr.* SUPPLEMENTAL SECURITY INCOME.

SSS. *abbr.* SELECTIVE SERVICE SYSTEM.

stabilize, *vb.* **1.** To make firm or steadfast <to stabilize the ship>. **2.** To maintain a particular level or amount <stabilize prices>.

stacking. (1982) **1.** *Insurance.* The process of obtaining benefits from a second policy on the same claim when recovery from the first policy alone would be inadequate.

judicial stacking. The principle that a court can construe insurance policies to permit stacking, under certain circumstances, when the policies do not specifically allow stacking but public policy is best served by permitting it.

policy stacking. Stacking that is permitted by the express terms of an insurance policy.

2. A gerrymandering technique in which a large political or racial group is combined in the same district with a larger opposition group. Cf. CRACKING; PACKING.

staff attorney. 1. See ATTORNEY. **2.** See CLERK (5).

staff director. See EXECUTIVE DIRECTOR.

staff judge advocate. See JUDGE ADVOCATE.

stagflation (stag-flay-shən), *n.* A period of slow economic growth or recession characterized by high inflation, stagnant consumer demand, and high unemployment. — **stagflationary,** *adj.*

staggered board of directors. See BOARD OF DIRECTORS.

stake, *n.* (bef. 12c) **1.** Something (such as property) deposited by two or more parties with a third party pending the resolution of a dispute; the subject matter of an interpleader. **2.** An interest or share in a business venture. **3.** Something (esp. money) bet in a wager, game, or contest. **4.** A boundary marker used in land surveys.

stakeholder. (18c) **1.** A disinterested third party who holds money or property, the right to which is disputed between two or more other parties. See INTERPLEADER. **2.** A person who has an interest or concern in a business or enterprise, though not necessarily as an owner. **3.** One who holds the money or valuables bet by others in a wager.

stale check. See CHECK.

stale claim. See CLAIM (3).

Stalingrad defense. See DEFENSE (2).

stalking. (bef. 12c) **1.** The act or an instance of following another by stealth. **2.** The offense of following or loitering near another, often surreptitiously, to annoy or harass that person or to commit a further crime such as assault or battery. • Some statutory definitions include an element that the person being stalked must reasonably feel harassed, alarmed, or distressed about personal safety or the safety of one or more persons for whom that person is responsible. And some definitions include acts such as telephoning another and remaining silent during the call. Cf. CYBERSTALKING.

stamp, *n.* (15c) An official mark or seal placed on a document, esp. to indicate that a required tax (such as duty or excise tax) has been paid.

stamp acts. English statutes requiring and regulating stamps on deeds, contracts, legal papers, bills, or other documents.

stamp duty. *Hist.* A tax raised by requiring stamps sold by the government to be affixed to designated documents, thus forming part of the perpetual revenue. See *stamp tax* under TAX.

stamp tax. See TAX.

stand. See WITNESS STAND.

stand adjourned. (Of a meeting or proceeding) to be in a state of adjournment <this court stands adjourned until 10:00 a.m. tomorrow>. • This status is usu. announced by a judge or other presiding officer concerning the business scheduled to continue at a later time. — Often shortened to *adjourned.*

standard, *n.* (15c) **1.** A model accepted as correct by custom, consent, or authority <what is the standard in the ant-farm industry?>. **2.** A criterion for measuring acceptability, quality, or accuracy <the attorney was making a nice living — even by New York standards>. — **standard,** *adj.*

objective standard. (1915) A legal standard that is based on conduct and perceptions external to a particular person. • In tort law, for example, the reasonable-person standard is considered an objective standard because it does not require a determination of what the defendant was thinking.

subjective standard. (1915) A legal standard that is peculiar to a particular person and based on the person's individual views and experiences. • In criminal law, for example, a subjective standard applies to determine premeditation because it depends on the defendant's mental state.

Standard & Poor's. An investment-analysis and -advisory service. • Standard & Poor's rates the financial strength of businesses from AAA (strongest) to AA, A, BBB, and so on to CCC. Most grades may also be modified with a plus- or minus-sign according to the business's relative strength among similar companies. A rating of R means that the company is the subject of some regulatory action.

standard characteristics. See STANDARD DESCRIPTIVE CHARACTERISTICS.

standard deduction. See DEDUCTION.

standard descriptive characteristics. *Parliamentary law.* The basic rules that apply to and define a motion. • The characteristics include when the motion is in order; its rank — that is, what it takes precedence over, and what yields to it; whether making it may interrupt a speaker; whether it needs a second; whether it is debatable; whether it is amendable; what vote its adoption takes; and whether it can be reconsidered. — Also termed *standard characteristics.*

standard-form contract. See CONTRACT.

standard instruction. See JURY INSTRUCTION.

standardized contract. See *standard-form contract* under CONTRACT.

standard mortgage clause. See MORTGAGE CLAUSE.

standard of care. (1890) *Torts.* In the law of negligence, the degree of care that a reasonable person should exercise. See CARE (2).

standard of need. In public-assistance law, the total subsistence resources required by an individual or family unit as determined by a state and, when unsatisfied by available resources, entitles the individual or family unit to public assistance.

standard of proof. (1922) The degree or level of proof demanded in a specific case, such as "beyond a reasonable doubt" or "by a preponderance of the evidence." See BURDEN OF PERSUASION.

standard of review. The criterion by which an appellate court exercising appellate jurisdiction measures the constitutionality of a statute or the propriety of an order, finding, or judgment entered by a lower court.

standard policy. See INSURANCE POLICY.

standard-setting organization. A body that sets, describes, or documents uniform operating, technological, or other norms for participants in a particular field or industry. — Also termed *standards body*.

Standards for Imposing Lawyer Sanctions. The ABA's 1986 supplement to the Standards for Lawyer Discipline, prescribing a range of sanctions and guidelines for applying them. ● Sanctions range from reprimands to disbarment.

Standards for Lawyer Discipline. A set of model rules, created by the ABA in 1979, establishing procedures for disciplining lawyers who violate ethics rules or commit crimes. ● The rules stress that the process is an inquiry to determine an attorney's fitness to practice, not to determine a punishment.

stand at ease. *Parliamentary law.* To take an informal pause during a meeting without taking a recess, at the instance of the chair.

standby charge. A property levy, often based on acreage, imposed on the mere availability of a service, whether or not the service is actually used.

standby commitment. An arrangement between an underwriter and an issuer of securities whereby the underwriter agrees, for a fee, to buy any unsold shares remaining after the public offering. — Also termed *standby underwriting agreement*.

standby counsel. See COUNSEL.

standby guardian. See GUARDIAN.

standby guardianship. See GUARDIANSHIP.

standby letter of credit. See LETTER OF CREDIT.

standby trust. See TRUST.

standby underwriting. See UNDERWRITING.

standby underwriting agreement. See STANDBY COMMITMENT.

standing, *n.* (1924) A party's right to make a legal claim or seek judicial enforcement of a duty or right. ● To have standing in federal court, a plaintiff must show (1) that the challenged conduct has caused the plaintiff actual injury, and (2) that the interest sought to be protected is within the zone of interests meant to be regulated by the statutory or constitutional guarantee in question. — Also termed *standing to sue*. Cf. JUSTICIABILITY.

third-party standing. (1968) Standing held by someone claiming to protect the rights of others. ● For example, in most jurisdictions, only a parent has standing to bring a suit for custody or visitation; in some, however, a third party — for

instance, a grandparent or a person with whom the child has substantial contacts — may have standing to bring an action for custody or visitation. See GRANDPARENT RIGHTS.

standing aside a juror. The prosecution practice of provisionally placing a juror aside until the panel is exhausted, without providing a reason, instead of challenging the juror or showing cause. ● The practice originally developed as a method of avoiding the Challenge of Jurors Act (1305), which prohibited the Crown from challenging a juror without showing cause. A similar practice was formerly used in Pennsylvania.

standing by. (14c) **1.** The awaiting of an opportunity to respond, as with assistance. **2.** Silence or inaction when there is a duty to speak or act; esp., the tacit possession of knowledge under circumstances requiring the possessor to reveal the knowledge. See *estoppel by silence* under ESTOPPEL.

standing committee. See COMMITTEE.

Standing Committee on Rules of Practice and Procedure. A group of judges, lawyers, and legal scholars appointed by the Chief Justice of the United States to advise the Judicial Conference of the United States on possible amendments to the procedural rules in the various federal courts and on other issues relating to the operation of the federal courts. 28 USCA § 331.

standing crops. See CROPS.

standing division. See *standing vote* under VOTE (4).

standing master. See MASTER.

standing mortgage. See *interest-only mortgage* under MORTGAGE.

standing mute. See MUTE (2).

standing offer. See OFFER.

standing order. See ORDER (2).

standing rule. See RULE (3).

standing seised to uses. The holding of title for the benefit or use of another, such as a relative in consideration of blood or marriage. ● A covenant to stand seised to uses is a type of conveyance that depends on the Statute of Uses for its effect. — Often shortened to *seised to uses*. See STATUTE OF USES.

standing to sue. See STANDING.

standing vote. See VOTE (4).

stand mute. (16c) **1.** (Of a defendant) To refuse to enter a plea to a criminal charge. ● Standing mute is treated as a plea of not guilty. **2.** (Of any party) to raise no objections.

standstill agreement. (1934) Any agreement to refrain from taking further action; esp., an agreement by which a party agrees to refrain from further attempts to take over a corporation (as by making no tender offer) for a specified period, or by which financial institutions agree to call bonds or loans when due.

stand trial. (17c) To submit to a legal proceeding, esp. a criminal prosecution.

staple (**stay**-pəl). **1.** A key commodity such as wool, leather, tin, lead, butter, or cheese (collectively termed *the staple*). **2.** *Hist.* A town appointed by the Crown as an exclusive market for staple products. See STATUTE STAPLE. **3.** *Patents.* An unpatented thing or material that is a component of a patented product or is used in a patented process, but also has other practical uses. ● Patentees may not gain control of the market for staples through tying agreements. Cf. NONSTAPLE.

Star Chamber. 1. *Hist.* An English court having broad civil and criminal jurisdiction at the king's discretion and noted for its secretive, arbitrary, and oppressive procedures, including compulsory self-incrimination, inquisitorial investigation, and the absence of juries. ● The Star Chamber was abolished in 1641 because of its abuses of power. — Also termed *Court of Star Chamber*; *Camera Stellata.* **2.** (*usu. l.c.*) Any secretive, arbitrary, or oppressive tribunal or proceeding.

stare decisis (**stahr**-ee di-**sı**-sis *or* **stair**-ee), *n.* [Latin "to stand by things decided"] (18c) The doctrine of precedent, under which a court must follow earlier judicial decisions when the same points arise again in litigation. See PRECEDENT; NON QUIETA MOVERE. Cf. RES JUDICATA; LAW OF THE CASE; (in civil law) *jurisprudence constante* under JURISPRUDENCE.

> ***horizontal stare decisis.*** The doctrine that a court, esp. an appellate court, must adhere to its own prior decisions, unless it finds compelling reasons to overrule itself.

> ***super stare decisis.*** The theory that courts must follow earlier court decisions without considering whether those decisions were correct. ● Critics argue that strict adherence to old decisions can result in grave injustices and cite as an example the repudiation of *Plessy v. Ferguson*, 163 U.S. 537, 16 S.Ct. 1138 (1896) by *Brown v. Board of Education*, 347 U.S. 483, 74 S.Ct. 686 (1954).

> ***vertical stare decisis.*** The doctrine that a court must strictly follow the decisions handed down by higher courts within the same jurisdiction.

star paging, *n.* (1873) **1.** A method of referring to a page in an earlier edition of a book, esp. a legal source. ● This method correlates the pagination of the later edition with that of the earlier (usu. the first) edition. **2.** By extension, the method of displaying on a computer screen the page breaks that occur in printed documents such as

law reports and law reviews. — Also termed *star pagination.* — **star page,** *n.*

stash, *vb.* To hide or conceal (money or property).

stat. *abbr.* STATUTE.

state, *n.* (16c) **1.** The political system of a body of people who are politically organized; the system of rules by which jurisdiction and authority are exercised over such a body of people <separation of church and state>. — Also termed *political society.* Cf. NATION.

> ***client state.*** A country that is obliged in some degree to cede some of the control of its external relations to some foreign power or powers. — Also termed *satellite state.* Cf. SOVEREIGN STATE.

> ***composite state.*** A state that comprises an aggregate or group of constituent states.

> ***dependent state.*** See *nonsovereign state.*

> ***federal state.*** A composite state in which the sovereignty of the entire state is divided between the central or federal government and the local governments of the several constituent states; a union of states in which the control of the external relations of all the member states has been surrendered to a central government so that the only state that exists for international purposes is the one formed by the union. Cf. *confederation of states* under CONFEDERATION.

> ***imperial state.*** *Archaic.* A composite state in which a common or central government possesses in itself the entire sovereignty, so that the constituent states possess no portion of this sovereignty.

> ***nonsovereign state.*** A state that is a constituent part of a greater state that includes both it and one or more others, and to whose government it is subject; a state that is not complete and self-existent. ● Among other things, a nonsovereign state has no power to engage in foreign relations. — Also termed *dependent state.* Cf. SOVEREIGN STATE.

> ***part-sovereign state.*** See SOVEREIGN STATE.

> ***police state.*** A state in which the political, economic, and social life of its citizens is subject to repressive governmental control and arbitrary uses of power by the ruling elite, which uses the police as the instrument of control; a totalitarian state.

> ***receiving state.*** The country to which a diplomatic agent or consul is sent by the country represented by that agent. Cf. *sending state.*

> ***satellite state.*** See *client state.*

> ***sending state.*** The country from which a diplomatic agent or consul is sent abroad. Cf. *receiving state.*

> ***simple state.*** See *unitary state.*

social-service state. A state that uses its power to create laws and regulations to provide for the welfare of its citizens.

sovereign state. See SOVEREIGN STATE.

unitary state. A state that is not made up of territorial divisions that are states themselves. — Also termed (archaically) *simple state.*

2. An institution of self-government within a larger political entity; esp., one of the constituent parts of a nation having a federal government <the 50 states>. **3.** (*often cap.*) The people of a state, collectively considered as the party wronged by a criminal deed; esp., the prosecution as the representative of the people <the State rests its case>.

state action. (1893) Anything done by a government; esp., in constitutional law, an intrusion on a person's rights (esp. civil rights) either by a governmental entity or by a private requirement that can be enforced only by governmental action (such as a racially restrictive covenant, which requires judicial action for enforcement).

state-action doctrine. *Antitrust.* The principle that the antitrust laws do not prohibit a state's anticompetitive acts, or official acts directed by a state. *Parker v. Brown*, 317 U.S. 341, 63 S.Ct. 307 (1943). — Also termed *Parker doctrine.* See MID-CAL TEST.

state agency. See AGENCY (3).

state-all-facts interrogatory. See *identification interrogatory* under INTERROGATORY.

state appeal. See APPEAL.

state auditor. See AUDITOR.

state bank. See BANK.

state bar association. See BAR ASSOCIATION.

state body. See *state agency* under AGENCY (3).

state bond. See BOND (3).

state-compulsion test. (1978) *Civil-rights law.* The rule that a state is responsible for discrimination that a private party commits while acting under the requirements of state law, as when a restaurant owner is required by state law to refuse service to minorities. *Adickes v. S.H. Kress & Co.*, 398 U.S. 144, 90 S.Ct. 1598 (1970). See SYMBIOTIC-RELA-TIONSHIP TEST; NEXUS TEST.

state court. See COURT.

state criminal. See CRIMINAL.

stated, *adj.* **1.** Fixed; determined; settled <at the stated time> <settlement for a stated amount>. **2.** Expressed; declared <stated facts>.

stated account. See *account stated* under AC-COUNT.

stated capital. See CAPITAL.

State Department. See DEPARTMENT OF STATE.

stated-income loan. See LOAN.

stated interest rate. See *nominal rate* under INTER-EST RATE.

stated meeting. See *regular meeting* under MEET-ING.

stated rate. See *nominal rate* under INTEREST RATE.

stated term. See *general term* under TERM (5).

stated value. See PAR VALUE.

state government. See GOVERNMENT.

state jurisdiction. See JURISDICTION.

State Justice Institute. A nonprofit federal corporation charged with improving judicial administration in state courts. ● It was created by the State Justice Institute Act of 1984. 42 USCA §§ 10701–10713. — Abbr. SJI.

state law. (18c) A body of law in a particular state consisting of the state's constitution, statutes, regulations, and common law. Cf. FEDERAL LAW.

stateless person. *Int'l law.* A natural person who is not considered a national by any country. ● The Convention Relating to Status of Stateless Persons (1954) provides these people with certain protections and obliges them to abide by the laws of the country where they reside.

statement. (18c) **1.** *Evidence.* A verbal assertion or nonverbal conduct intended as an assertion. **2.** A formal and exact presentation of facts. — Also termed (for plaintiff) *statement of cause of action.* **3.** *Criminal procedure.* An account of a person's knowledge of a crime, taken by the police during their investigation of the offense. Cf. CONFES-SION.

consonant statement. (1889) A witness's previous declaration, testified to by a person to whom the declaration was made and allowed into evidence only after the witness's testimony has been impeached. ● This type of evidence would, but for the impeachment of the witness, be inadmissible hearsay. Cf. *prior consistent statement.*

false statement. (18c) **1.** An untrue statement knowingly made with the intent to mislead. See PERJURY. **2.** Any one of three distinct federal offenses: (1) falsifying or concealing a material fact by trick, scheme, or device; (2) making a false, fictitious, or fraudulent representation; and (3) making or using a false document or writing. 18 USCA § 1001.

financial statement. See FINANCIAL STATE-MENT.

incriminating statement. (1896) A statement that tends to establish the guilt of someone, esp. the person making it.

prior consistent statement. (1883) A witness's earlier statement that is consistent with the witness's testimony at trial. ● A prior consistent statement is not hearsay if it is offered to rebut a charge that the testimony was improperly influenced or fabricated. Fed. R. Evid. 801(d)(1)(B). Cf. *consonant statement*.

prior inconsistent statement. (1885) A witness's earlier statement that conflicts with the witness's testimony at trial. • In federal practice, extrinsic evidence of an unsworn prior inconsistent statement is admissible — if the witness is given an opportunity to explain or deny the statement — for impeachment purposes only. Fed. R. Evid. 613(b). Sworn statements may be admitted for all purposes. Fed. R. Evid. 801(d)(1)(A).

sworn statement. (1831) **1.** A statement given under oath; an affidavit. Cf. AFFIDAVIT; DECLARATION (8). **2.** A contractor-builder's listing of suppliers and subcontractors, and their respective bids, required by a lending institution for interim financing.

voluntary statement. (1817) A statement made without the influence of duress, coercion, or inducement.

Statement and Account Clause. (1975) The clause of the U.S. Constitution requiring the regular publication of the receipts and expenditures of the federal government. U.S. Const. art. I, § 9, cl. 7.

statement of account. 1. A report issued periodically (usu. monthly) by a bank to a customer, providing certain information on the customer's account, including the checks drawn and cleared, deposits made, charges debited, and the account balance. — Also termed *bank statement*. See ACCOUNT (4). **2.** A report issued periodically (usu. monthly) by a creditor to a customer, providing certain information on the customer's account, including the amounts billed, credits given, and the balance due. — Also termed *account statement*.

statement of affairs. 1. STATEMENT OF FINANCIAL AFFAIRS. **2.** A balance sheet showing immediate liquidation values (rather than historical costs), usu. prepared when insolvency or bankruptcy is imminent.

statement of cause of action. See STATEMENT (2).

statement of claim. 1. COMPLAINT (1). **2.** *English law.* A plaintiff's initial pleading in a civil case; DECLARATION (7).

statement of condition. See BALANCE SHEET.

statement of confession. See CONFESSION OF JUDGMENT.

statement of defense. The assertions by a defendant; esp., in England, the defendant's answer to the plaintiff's statement of claim.

statement of fact. A form of conduct that asserts or implies the existence or nonexistence of a fact. • The term includes not just a particular statement that a particular fact exists or has existed, but also

an assertion that, although perhaps expressed as an opinion, implies the existence of some fact or facts that have led the assertor to hold the opinion in question. See *affirmative testimony* under TESTIMONY.

statement of facts. (18c) A party's written presentation of the facts leading up to or surrounding a legal dispute, usu. recited toward the beginning of a brief. Cf. STATEMENT OF THE CASE.

    agreed statement of facts. A narrative statement of facts that is stipulated to be correct by the parties and is submitted to a tribunal for a ruling. • When the narrative statement is filed on appeal instead of a report of the trial proceedings, it is called an *agreed statement on appeal*.

statement of financial affairs. *Bankruptcy.* A document that an individual or corporate debtor must file to answer questions about the debtor's past and present financial status. — Also termed *statement of affairs*.

statement of financial condition. See BALANCE SHEET.

statement of financial position. See BALANCE SHEET.

statement of income. See INCOME STATEMENT.

statement of intention. *Bankruptcy.* A preliminary statement filed by an individual debtor in a chapter 7 case, in which the debtor details, among other things, whether property of the bankruptcy estate securing any debt will be retained or surrendered and whether the property is claimed as exempt. • The statement must be filed on or before the date of the first creditors' meeting or within 30 days after the bankruptcy petition is filed, whichever is earlier. 11 USCA § 521 (a)(2).

statement of particulars. See BILL OF PARTICULARS.

statement of principle. In legislative drafting, a sentence or paragraph that explains the legislature's purpose in passing a statute. • Although a statement of principle often resembles a preamble (usu. both do not appear in a single statute), it differs in that it typically appears in a numbered section of the statute.

statement of prior-art references. See INFORMATION-DISCLOSURE STATEMENT.

statement of the case. In an appellate brief, a short review of what has happened procedurally in the lawsuit and how it reached the present court. • The statement introduces the reviewing court to the case by reciting the facts, procedures, decisions of the court or courts below as they are relevant to the appeal, and the reasons for those decisions. — Also termed *proceedings below*. Cf. STATEMENT OF FACTS.

statement of use. See *amendment to allege use* under TRADEMARK-APPLICATION AMENDMENT.

statement of utility. *Patents.* The portion of a patent-application disclosure statement that explains how the invention is useful.

statement of work. A contractual provision or exhibit that defines what one party (e.g., the seller) is going to do for the other (e.g., the buyer). • The statement of work often covers such terms as (1) inspection and acceptance, (2) quality-assurance requirements, (3) packing and marking, (4) data requirements, and (5) training. There are generally two types of specifications in a statement of work: a performance specification establishing the minimum requirements for items to be supplied, and a design specification establishing the methods to be used in meeting those minimum requirements. — Also termed *statement-of-work clause.* — Abbr. SOW.

state of art. See STATE OF THE ART.

state officer. See OFFICER (1).

state of mind. (17c) **1.** The condition or capacity of a person's mind; MENS REA. **2.** Loosely, a person's reasons or motives for committing an act, esp. a criminal act.

state-of-mind exception. (1949) *Evidence.* The principle that an out-of-court declaration of an existing motive is admissible, even when the declarant cannot testify in person. • This principle is an exception to the general rule that hearsay is inadmissible.

state of nature. (16c) The lack of a politically organized society. • The term is a hypothetical construct for the period in human history predating any type of political society.

state of the art. (1910) *Products liability.* The level of pertinent scientific and technical knowledge existing at the time of a product's manufacture, and the best technology reasonably available at the time the product was sold. — Also termed *state of art.* — **state-of-the-art,** *adj.*

state of the case. The posture of litigation as it develops, as in discovery, at trial, or on appeal.

State of the Union. See *Presidential message* under MESSAGE.

state of war. A situation in which war has been declared or armed conflict is in progress. See WAR.

state paper. 1. A document prepared by or relating to a state or national government and affecting the administration of that government in its political or international relations. **2.** A newspaper officially designated for the publication of public statutes, resolutions, notices, and advertisements.

state paper office. *Hist.* An office established in London in 1578, headed by the Clerk of the Papers, to maintain custody of state documents.

state police. (1843) The department or agency of a state government empowered to maintain order, as by investigating and preventing crimes, and making arrests.

state police power. (1849) The power of a state to enforce laws for the health, welfare, morals, and safety of its citizens, if enacted so that the means are reasonably calculated to protect those legitimate state interests.

state religion. See RELIGION.

state's attorney. 1. See DISTRICT ATTORNEY. **2.** See PROSECUTOR (1).

state seal. See *great seal* (2) under SEAL.

state secret. (1822) A governmental matter that would be a threat to the national defense or diplomatic interests of the United States if revealed; information possessed by the government and of a military or diplomatic nature, the disclosure of which would be contrary to the public interest. • State secrets are privileged from disclosure by a witness in an ordinary judicial proceeding. — Also termed *governmental secret; government secret.* See *executive privilege* & *state-secrets privilege* under PRIVILEGE (3).

state-secrets privilege. See PRIVILEGE (3).

state's evidence. See EVIDENCE.

state's evidence, turn. See TURN STATE'S EVIDENCE.

state sovereignty. (18c) The right of a state to self-government; the supreme authority exercised by each state.

state-sponsored terrorism. See TERRORISM.

states' rights. (1839) Under the Tenth Amendment, rights neither conferred on the federal government nor forbidden to the states.

State Street Bank. *Patents.* A landmark 1998 decision in the Federal Circuit that made it easier to get patents on computer software, and also rejected the long-accepted notion that business methods are per se unpatentable. • The court struck down *per se* rules against patenting mathematical algorithms (the soul of software), focusing instead on whether the ultimate result was useful, concrete, and tangible in practice. *State Street Bank & Trust C. v. Signature Fin. Group, Inc.,* 149 F.3d 1368 (Fed. Cir. 1998).

state's ward. See *ward of the state* under WARD.

state tax. See TAX.

state terrorism. See TERRORISM.

state the question. *Parliamentary procedure.* (Of the chair) to formally state a motion as in order and ready for consideration. Cf. PUT THE QUESTION.

state trial. See TRIAL.

stateway, *n.* A governmental policy or law. • This term is formed on the analogy of *folkway.*

station. 1. Social position or status. See STATUS. **2.** A place where military duties are performed or military goods are stored. **3.** A headquarters, as of a police department. **4.** A place where both freight and passengers are received for transport or delivered after transport. **5.** *Civil law.* A place where ships may safely travel.

Stationers' Company. *Hist.* An association of stationers and their successors, formed in London in 1403 and granted a royal charter in 1557, entrusted, by order of the Privy Council, with censorship of the press. • This company was the holder of the first rights we associate today with copyright.

stationhouse. 1. A police station or precinct. **2.** The lockup at a police precinct.

stationhouse bail. See *cash bail* under BAIL (1).

station-in-life test. *Family law.* An analysis performed by a court to determine the amount of money reasonably needed to maintain a particular person's accustomed lifestyle. • The elements were first set forth in *Canfield vs. Security-First Nat'l Bank*, 87 P.2d 830, 840 (Cal. 1939). The court takes into account the person's station in society and the costs of the person's support in that station, including housing and related expenses, medical care, further education, and other reasonably necessary expenses, but not including luxuries or extravagant expenditures. See NECESSARIES (1), (2).

statist (stay-tist). **1.** *Archaic.* A statesman; a politician. **2.** A statistician.

statistical-decision theory. (1966) A method for determining whether a panel of potential jurors was selected from a fair cross section of the community, by calculating the probabilities of selecting a certain number of jurors from a particular group to analyze whether it is statistically probable that the jury pool was selected by mere chance. • This method has been criticized because a pool of potential jurors is not ordinarily selected by mere chance; potential jurors are disqualified for many legitimate reasons. See FAIR-CROSS-SECTION REQUIREMENT; ABSOLUTE DISPARITY; COMPARATIVE DISPARITY; DUREN TEST.

status. (17c) **1.** A person's legal condition, whether personal or proprietary; the sum total of a person's legal rights, duties, liabilities, and other legal relations, or any particular group of them separately considered <the status of a landowner>. **2.** A person's legal condition regarding personal rights but excluding proprietary relations <the status of a father> <the status of a wife>. **3.** A person's capacities and incapacities, as opposed to other elements of personal status <the status of minors>. **4.** A person's legal condition insofar as it is imposed by the law without the person's consent, as opposed to a condition that the person has acquired by agreement <the status of a slave>.

status, law of. See LAW OF STATUS.

STAT-USA. A unit in the U.S. Department of Commerce responsible for disseminating economics and trade information compiled by other federal agencies to businesses and individuals through subscription services and federal depository libraries. • STAT-USA is an agency within the Department's Economics and Statistics Administration.

status crime. See CRIME.

status offender. See OFFENDER.

status offense. See OFFENSE (1).

status-offense jurisdiction. See JURISDICTION.

status quo (stay-təs *or* stat-əs kwoh). [Latin "state in which"] (1807) The situation that currently exists.

status quo ante (stay-təs kwoh an-tee). [Latin "state in which previously"] (1877) The situation that existed before something else (being discussed) occurred.

statutable (stach-ə-tə-bəl), *adj.* (17c) **1.** Prescribed or authorized by statute. **2.** Conforming to the legislative requirements for quality, size, amount, or the like. **3.** (Of an offense) punishable by law. See STATUTORY.

statute. (14c) A law passed by a legislative body; specif., legislation enacted by any lawmaking body, including legislatures, administrative boards, and municipal courts. • The term *act* is interchangeable as a synonym. For each of the subentries listed below, *act* is sometimes substituted for *statute.* — Abbr. s.; stat.

affirmative statute. (16c) A law requiring that something be done; one that directs the doing of an act. Cf. *negative statute.*

always-speaking statute. See *speaking statute.*

antideficiency statute. See *antideficiency legislation* under LEGISLATION.

codifying statute. (1908) A law that purports to be exhaustive in restating the whole of the law on a particular topic, including prior caselaw as well as legislative provisions. • Courts generally presume that a codifying statute supersedes prior caselaw. Cf. *consolidating statute.*

compiled statutes. Laws that have been arranged by subject but have not been substantively changed; COMPILATION (2). Cf. *revised statutes.*

consolidating statute. (1886) A law that collects the legislative provisions on a particular subject and embodies them in a single statute, often with minor amendments and drafting improvements. • Courts generally presume that a consolidating statute leaves prior caselaw intact. Cf. *codifying statute.*

construction statute. A legislative directive included in a statute, intended to guide or direct a court's interpretation of the statute. • A construction act can, for example, be a simple statement such as "The word 'week' means seven consecutive days" or a broader directive such as "Words and phrases are to be read in context and construed according to the rules of grammar and common usage. Words and phrases that have acquired a technical or particular meaning, whether by legislative definition or otherwise, are to be construed accordingly."

criminal statute. (18c) A law that defines, classifies, and sets forth punishment for one or more specific crimes. See PENAL CODE.

curative statute. 1. An act that corrects an error in a statute's original enactment, usu. an error that interferes with interpreting or applying the statute. Cf. *validating statute.* 2. See *remedial statute.*

declaratory statute. (17c) A law enacted to clarify prior law by reconciling conflicting judicial decisions or by explaining the meaning of a prior statute. — Also termed *expository statute.*

directory statute. (1834) A law that indicates only what should be done, with no provision for enforcement. Cf. *mandatory statute; permissive statute.*

disabling statute. (18c) A law that limits or curbs certain rights.

enabling statute. (18c) A law that permits what was previously prohibited or that creates new powers; esp., a congressional statute conferring powers on an executive agency to carry out various delegated tasks.

expository statute. See *declaratory statute.*

general statute. (16c) A law pertaining to an entire community or all persons generally. — Also termed *public statute.* See PUBLIC LAW (2).

imperfect statute. (1847) A law that prohibits, but does not render void, an objectionable transaction. • Such a statute provides a penalty for disobedience without depriving the violative transaction of its legal effect.

local statute. 1. See LOCAL LAW (1). 2. See LOCAL LAW (2).

mandatory statute. (18c) A law that requires a course of action as opposed to merely permitting it. Cf. *directory statute; permissive statute.*

model statute. See *uniform statute.*

negative statute. (16c) A law prohibiting something; a law expressed in negative terms. Cf. *affirmative statute.*

nonclaim statute. (18c) 1. STATUTE OF LIMITATIONS. 2. A law that sets a time limit for creditors to bring claims against a decedent's estate.

• Unlike a statute of limitations, a nonclaim statute is usu. not subject to tolling and is not waivable.

organic statute. (1856) A law that establishes an administrative agency or local government. — Also termed *organic act.* Cf. ORGANIC LAW.

penal statute. (16c) A law that defines an offense and prescribes its corresponding fine, penalty, or punishment. — Also termed *penal law; punitive statute.*

permanent statute. See *perpetual statute.*

permissive statute. A statute that allows certain acts but does not command them. • A permissive statute creates a license or privilege, or allows discretion in performing an act. Cf. *directory statute; mandatory statute.*

perpetual statute. (16c) A law containing no provision for repeal, abrogation, or expiration. — Also termed *permanent statute.* Cf. *temporary statute* (1).

personal statute. *Civil law.* A law that primarily affects a person's condition or status (such as a statute relating to capacity or majority) and affects property only incidentally.

preceptive statute. A statute that is prescriptive, general, definite, and complete. • In form, a preceptive statute is similar to a rule.

private statute. See *special statute.*

prohibitive statute. A statute that forbids all acts that disturb society's peace or forbids certain acts on other grounds. • An example of a noncriminal prohibitive statute is one forbidding the execution of a mentally retarded criminal because a person who lacks mental capacity cannot understand the reason for the punishment.

prospective statute. (1831) A law that applies to future events.

public statute. See PUBLIC LAW (2).

punitive statute. See *penal statute.*

quasi-statute. An executive or administrative order, or a regulation promulgated by a governmental agency, that has the binding effect of legislation.

real statute. *Civil law.* A law primarily affecting the operation, status, and condition of property, and addressing persons only incidentally.

recording statute. See RECORDING ACT.

reference statute. A law that incorporates and adopts by reference provisions of other laws.

remedial statute. (18c) A law that affords a remedy. — Also termed *curative statute.*

repealing statute. A statute that revokes, and sometimes replaces, an earlier statute. • A repealing statute may work expressly or by implication.

restraining statute. See *disabling statute.*

retroactive statute. See RETROACTIVE LAW.

retrospective statute. See RETROACTIVE LAW.

revised statutes. (18c) Laws that have been collected, arranged, and reenacted as a whole by a legislative body. — Abbr. Rev. Stat.; R.S. See CODE (1). Cf. *compiled statutes.*

revival statute. (1899) A law that provides for the renewal of actions, of wills, and of the legal effect of documents. • A revival statute cannot resurrect a time-barred criminal prosecution. *Stegner v. California,* 539 U.S. 607, 123 S.Ct. 2446 (2003).

severable statute. (1930) A law that remains operative in its remaining provisions even if a portion of the law is declared unconstitutional.

single-act statute. See LONG-ARM STATUTE.

speaking statute. (2000) A statute to be interpreted in light of the understanding of its terms prevailing at the time of interpretation. — Also termed *always-speaking statute.*

special statute. (17c) A law that applies only to specific individuals, as opposed to everyone. — Also termed *private statute.*

split-level statute. (1980) A law that includes officially promulgated explanatory materials in addition to its substantive provisions, so that courts are left with two levels of documents to construe.

statute of descent and distribution. See STATUTE OF DISTRIBUTION.

statute of distribution. See STATUTE OF DISTRIBUTION.

statute of frauds. See STATUTE OF FRAUDS.

temporary statute. (17c) **1.** A law that specifically provides that it is to remain in effect for a fixed, limited period. Cf. *perpetual statute.* **2.** A law (such as an appropriation statute) that, by its nature, has only a single and temporary operation.

uniform statute. A law drafted with the intention that it will be adopted by all or most of the states; esp., UNIFORM LAW. — Also termed *model statute; uniform act.* Cf. MODEL ACT.

validating statute. (1882) A law that is amended either to remove errors or to add provisions to conform to constitutional requirements. — Also termed *validation statute.* Cf. *curative statute.*

statute book. (16c) A bound collection of statutes, usu. as part of a larger set of books containing a complete body of statutory law, such as the United States Code Annotated.

statute law. See STATUTORY LAW.

statute-making. See LEGISLATION (1).

statute merchant. *Hist.* **1.** (*cap.*) One of two 13th-century statutes establishing procedures to better secure and recover debts by, among other things, providing for a commercial bond that, if not timely paid, resulted in swift execution on the debtor's lands, goods, and body. 13 Edw. I, ch. 6 (1283); 15 Edw. I, ch. 6 (1285).• These statutes were repealed in 1863. — Also termed *pocket judgment.* **2.** The commercial bond so established. Cf. STATUTE STAPLE.

statute mile. See MILE (1).

Statute of Accumulations. *Hist.* A statute forbidding the accumulation, beyond a certain period, of property settled by deed or will. 39 & 40 Geo. 3, ch. 98 (1800).

Statute of Anne. *Hist. English law.* **1.** The Copyright Act of 1709, which first granted copyright protection to book authors. 8 Anne, ch. 19 (1709). **2.** The statute that modernized the English bankruptcy system and first introduced the discharge of the debtor's existing debts. 4 Anne, ch. 17 (1705).

statute of distribution. (18c) A state law regulating the distribution of an estate among an intestate's heirs and relatives. • Historically, the statute specified separate, and often different, patterns for distributing an intestate's real property and personal property. Generally, land descended to the heirs and personalty descended to the next of kin. — Also termed *statute of descent and distribution.*

Statute of Elizabeth. *Hist. English law.* A 1571 penal statute that contained provisions against conveyances made to defraud creditors. 13 Eliz., ch. 5. • The fundamental provisions of this statute formed the basis for modern laws against fraudulent conveyances.

statute of frauds. (18c) **1.** *Hist.* (*cap.*) A 1677 English statute that declared certain contracts judicially unenforceable (but not void) if they were not committed to writing and signed by the party to be charged. • The statute was entitled "An Act for the Prevention of Frauds and Perjuries" (29 Car. 2, ch. 3). — Also termed *Statute of Frauds and Perjuries.* **2.** A statute (based on the English Statute of Frauds) designed to prevent fraud and perjury by requiring certain contracts to be in writing and signed by the party to be charged. • Statutes of frauds traditionally apply to the following types of contracts: (1) a contract for the sale or transfer of an interest in land, (2) a contract that cannot be performed within one year of its making, (3) a contract for the sale of goods valued at $500 or more, (4) a contract of an executor or administrator to answer for a decedent's debt, (5) a contract to guarantee the debt or duty of another, and (6) a contract made in consideration of marriage. UCC § 2-201. — Abbr. S/F; SOF.

Statute of Frauds and Perjuries. See STATUTE OF FRAUDS (1).

statute of limitations. (18c) **1.** A law that bars claims after a specified period; specif., a statute establishing a time limit for suing in a civil case, based on the date when the claim accrued (as when the injury occurred or was discovered). ● The purpose of such a statute is to require diligent prosecution of known claims, thereby providing finality and predictability in legal affairs and ensuring that claims will be resolved while evidence is reasonably available and fresh. — Also termed *nonclaim statute*; *limitations period*. **2.** A statute establishing a time limit for prosecuting a crime, based on the date when the offense occurred. — Abbr. S/L; SOL. Cf. STATUTE OF REPOSE.

Statute of Monopolies. *Hist.* A 1624 act of the English Parliament banning the Crown's practice of granting monopolies with the single exception of letters patent, which gave an inventor the exclusive right to make and use the invention for 14 years. 21 Jac. 1, ch. 3.

statute of mortmain. See MORTMAIN STATUTE.

statute of repose. (18c) A statute barring any suit that is brought after a specified time since the defendant acted (such as by designing or manufacturing a product), even if this period ends before the plaintiff has suffered a resulting injury. Cf. STATUTE OF LIMITATIONS.

Statute of Uses. *Hist.* An English statute of 1535 that converted the equitable title held by a cestui que use (i.e., a beneficiary) to a legal one in order to make the cestui que use liable for feudal dues, as only a legal owner (the *feoffee to uses*) could be. 27 Hen. 8, ch. 10. ● This statute was the culmination of a series of enactments designed by the Tudors to stop the practice of creating uses in land that deprived feudal lords of the valuable incidents of feudal tenure. The statute discouraged the granting of property subject to another's use by deeming the person who enjoys the use to have legal title with the right of absolute ownership and possession. So after the statute was enacted, if A conveyed land to B subject to the use of C, then C became the legal owner of the land in fee simple. Ultimately, the statute was circumvented by the courts' recognition of the use of equitable trusts in land-conveyancing. See CESTUI QUE USE; GRANT TO USES; USE (4).

statute of wills. (17c) **1.** (*cap.*) An English statute (enacted in 1540) that established the right of a person to devise real property by will. — Also termed *Wills Act*. **2.** A state statute, usu. derived from the English statute, providing for testamentary disposition and if certain requirements for valid execution in that jurisdiction are met.

statute roll. *Hist.* A roll upon which a statute was formally entered after receiving the royal assent.

Statutes at Large. An official compilation of the acts and resolutions that become law from each session of Congress, printed in chronological order.

statutory (**stach**-ə-tor-ee), *adj.* (18c) **1.** Of or relating to legislation <statutory interpretation>. **2.** Legislatively created <the law of patents is purely statutory>. **3.** Conformable to a statute <a statutory act>.

statutory action. See ACTION (4).

statutory agent. See AGENT (2).

statutory arson. See ARSON (2).

statutory bar. *Patents.* A patent law provision that denies patent protection to inventors who wait too long to apply. ● This "loss of right" may occur when an inventor publishes an article about the work, sells it, offers it for sale, or makes public use of the invention. The inventor has one year after the disclosure to apply for a patent. See BAR (7). Cf. GRACE PERIOD (2).

statutory bond. 1. See BOND (2). **2.** See BOND (3).

statutory burglary. See BURGLARY (2).

statutory construction. (1813) **1.** The act or process of interpreting a statute. **2.** Collectively, the principles developed by courts for interpreting statutes. — Also termed *statutory interpretation*. See CONSTRUCTION (2).

statutory contract. See CONTRACT.

statutory crime. See CRIME.

statutory damages. See DAMAGES.

statutory dedication. See DEDICATION.

statutory deed. See DEED.

statutory disclaimer. See DISCLAIMER.

statutory double patenting. See DOUBLE PATENTING.

statutory double-patenting rejection. See REJECTION.

statutory employee. See EMPLOYEE.

statutory employer. See EMPLOYER.

statutory exception. See EXCEPTION (2).

statutory exclusion. *Criminal procedure.* The removal, by law, of certain crimes from juvenile-court jurisdiction. ● Many states now remove certain particularly serious crimes committed by older juveniles from the jurisdiction of the juvenile courts. In this kind of case, the juvenile court never has jurisdiction, so a transfer hearing is not required or necessary. Cf. MANDATORY WAIVER.

statutory exposition. (1854) A statute's special interpretation of the ambiguous terms of a previous statute <the statute contained a statutory exposition of the former act>.

statutory extortion. See EXTORTION.

statutory forced share. See ELECTIVE SHARE.

statutory foreclosure. See *power-of-sale foreclosure* under FORECLOSURE.

statutory guardian. See GUARDIAN.

statutory homestead. See *constitutional homestead* under HOMESTEAD.

statutory insolvency. See BANKRUPTCY (3).

statutory instrument. A British administrative regulation or order; an order or regulation issued by an authority empowered by statute to do so, usu. to give detailed effect to the statute.

statutory interpretation. See STATUTORY CONSTRUCTION.

statutory invention registration. *Patents.* An official procedure for placing an invention in the public domain by publishing the patent abstract (which is included with the invention's original application) in the U.S. Patent and Trademark Office's Official Gazette, thus making the abstract a prior-art reference as of the application's filing date. ● The process results in abandonment of the patent application. If an alternative form of disclosure is used, the prior-art references's effective date is the date of publication. 35 USCA § 157. — Abbr. SIR. See DEFENSIVE DISCLOSURE.

statutory law. (17c) The body of law derived from statutes rather than from constitutions or judicial decisions. — Also termed *statute law*; *legislative law*; *ordinary law.* Cf. COMMON LAW (1); CONSTITUTIONAL LAW.

statutory liability. See LIABILITY.

statutory lien. See LIEN.

statutory merger. See MERGER.

statutory obligation. See OBLIGATION.

statutory omnibus clause. See OMNIBUS CLAUSE.

statutory partnership association. See PARTNERSHIP ASSOCIATION.

statutory penalty. See PENALTY (1).

statutory period. 1. A time limit specified in a statute; esp., the period prescribed in the relevant statute of limitations. ● This period includes, in addition to a fixed number of years, whatever time local law allows because of infancy, insanity, coverture, and other like circumstances. 2. *Patents.* The time available to a patent applicant to answer an examiner's office action. ● Since the six-month period is set by statute, it cannot be extended but it can be shortened to as few as 30 days. 35 USCA § 133. Cf. SHORTENED STATUTORY PERIOD.

statutory presumption. See PRESUMPTION.

statutory rape. See RAPE.

statutory rate. See MECHANICAL ROYALTY.

statutory receiver. See RECEIVER.

statutory redemption. See REDEMPTION.

statutory release. *Hist.* A conveyance superseding the compound assurance by lease and release, created by the Conveyance by Release Without Lease Act of 1841 (St. 4 & 5 Vict., ch. 21).

statutory right of redemption. (1857) The right of a mortgagor in default to recover property after a foreclosure sale by paying the principal, interest, and other costs that are owed, together with any other measure required to cure the default. ● This statutory right exists in many states but is not uniform. See EQUITY OF REDEMPTION; REDEMPTION (4).

statutory share. See ELECTIVE SHARE.

statutory subject matter. See PATENTABLE SUBJECT MATTER.

statutory successor. See SUCCESSOR.

statutory tenant. See TENANT.

Statutum de Nova Custuma (stə-t[y]oo-təm dee noh-və kəs-chə-mə or kəs-tyə-mə). See CARTA MERCATORIA.

stay, *n.* (16c) 1. The postponement or halting of a proceeding, judgment, or the like. 2. An order to suspend all or part of a judicial proceeding or a judgment resulting from that proceeding. — Also termed *stay of execution*; *suspension of judgment.* — **stay,** *vb.* — **stayable,** *adj.*

   automatic stay. *Bankruptcy.* A bar to all judicial and extrajudicial collection efforts against the debtor or the debtor's property, subject to specific statutory exceptions. 11 USCA §§ 362 (a)–(b). ● The policy behind the automatic stay, which is effective upon the filing of the bankruptcy petition, is that all actions against the debtor should be halted pending the determination of creditors' rights and the orderly administration of the debtor's assets free from creditor interference. — Also termed *automatic suspension.*

stay-away order. 1. In a domestic-violence case, an order forbidding the defendant to contact the victim. ● A stay-away order usu. prohibits the defendant from coming within a certain number of feet of the victim's home, school, work, or other specific place. Stay-away orders are most often issued in criminal cases. 2. RESTRAINING ORDER (1). 3. In a juvenile-delinquency case, an order prohibiting a youthful offender from frequenting the scene of the offense or from being in the company of certain persons. — Also termed *no-contact order*; *stay-away order of protection.*

stay of execution. See STAY.

stay of mandate. 1. The suspension of a lower court's order of execution, imposed by a higher court. 2. An appellate court's suspension of its own judgment for reconsideration.

stay-put rule. *School law.* The principle that a child must remain in his or her current educational placement while an administrative claim under the Individuals with Disabilities Education Act (usu. for an alternative placement or for mainstreaming) is pending. 20 USCA § 1415(j).

STB. *abbr.* SURFACE TRANSPORTATION BOARD.

STD. *abbr.* SEXUALLY TRANSMITTED DISEASE.

steady course. *Maritime law.* A ship's path that can be readily ascertained either because the ship is on a straight heading or because the ship's future positions are easy to plot based on the ship's current position and movements.

steal, *vb.* (bef. 12c) **1.** To take (personal property) illegally with the intent to keep it unlawfully. **2.** To take (something) by larceny, embezzlement, or false pretenses.

stealth. 1. *Hist.* Theft; an act or instance of stealing. • Etymologically, this term is the noun corresponding to the verb *steal.* **2.** Surreptitiousness; furtive slyness.

stealth juror. See JUROR.

steganography (steg-ə-**nog**-rə-fee), *n.* A cryptographic method that digitally embeds or encodes one item of information within another. • Because digitized audio or visual files usu. have unused data areas, indelible (and nearly undetectable) information can be added without altering the file's quality. Copyright or trademark tags can be hidden in every fragment of a digital work, making disassociation almost impossible. — Also termed *digital fingerprinting; digital watermarking.*

stenographer's record. See *reporter's record* under RECORD.

stepbrother. See BROTHER.

stepchild. See CHILD.

stepfather. See FATHER.

step-in-the-dark rule. (1955) *Torts.* The contributory-negligence rule that a person who enters a totally unfamiliar area in the darkness has a duty, in the absence of unusual stress, to refrain from proceeding until first ascertaining whether any dangerous obstacles exist. See *contributory negligence* under NEGLIGENCE.

stepmother. See MOTHER.

stepparent. See PARENT.

stepparent adoption. See ADOPTION.

stepped-up basis. See BASIS.

stepped-up visitation. See VISITATION.

step-rate-premium insurance. See INSURANCE.

stepsister. See SISTER.

step-transaction doctrine. A method used by the Internal Revenue Service to determine tax liability by viewing the transaction as a whole, and disregarding one or more nonsubstantive, intervening transactions taken to achieve the final result. — Also termed *step-transaction approach.*

sterilization. 1. The act of making (a person or other living thing) permanently unable to reproduce. **2.** The act of depriving (a person or other living thing) of reproductive organs; esp., castration. — Also termed (in both senses) *asexualization.*

sterling, *adj.* **1.** Of or conforming to a standard of national value, esp. of English money or metal <a pound sterling>. **2.** (Of an opinion, value, etc.) valuable; authoritative <a sterling report>.

stet (stet), *n.* [Latin "let it stand"] (18c) **1.** An order staying legal proceedings, as when a prosecutor determines not to proceed on an indictment and places the case on a stet docket. • The term is used chiefly in Maryland. **2.** An instruction to leave a text as it stands.

stevedore (**stee**-və-dor). *Maritime law.* A person or company that hires longshore and harbor workers to load and unload ships. Cf. SEAMAN; LONGSHOREMAN.

steward. 1. A person appointed to manage the affairs of another. **2.** A union official who represents union employees and who oversees the performance of union contracts. — Also termed (in sense 2) *union steward; shop steward.*

steward of all England. *Hist.* An officer vested with various powers, including the power to preside over the trial of peers.

steward of a manor. *Hist.* An officer who handles the business matters of a manor, including keeping the court rolls and granting admittance to copyhold lands.

stickering. *Securities.* The updating of a prospectus by affixing stickers that contain the new or revised information. • Stickering avoids the expense of reprinting an entire prospectus.

stickler. *Hist.* An arbitrator.

stickup. (1904) An armed robbery in which the victim is threatened by the use of weapons. — Also termed *holdup.* See *armed robbery* under ROBBERY.

stiffening note. *Maritime law.* A permit, issued by a customs collector to the ship's master, that authorizes the receipt and loading of heavy goods necessary to ballast a vessel before the inward-bound cargo has been completely unloaded.

stifling of a prosecution. An illegal agreement, in exchange for money or other benefit, to abstain from prosecuting a person.

stigma-plus doctrine. The principle that defamation by a government official is not actionable as a civil-rights violation unless the victim suffers not only embarrassment but also the loss of a property interest (such as continued employment in a government job).

still, *n.* An instrument or apparatus used for making distilled liquor or alcohol.

stillborn, *adj.* (Of an infant) born dead. — Also termed *deadborn*.

sting. (1976) An undercover operation in which law-enforcement agents pose as criminals to catch actual criminals engaging in illegal acts.

stipend (stɪ-pend *or* -pənd). **1.** A salary or other regular, periodic payment. **2.** A tribute to support the clergy, usu. consisting of payments in money or grain.

stipendiary estate (stɪ-**pen**-dee-er-ee). See ESTATE (1).

stipendiary magistrate. See MAGISTRATE.

stipital (**stip**-i-təl), *adj.* See STIRPITAL.

stipulated authority. See *express authority* under AUTHORITY (1).

stipulated damages. See *liquidated damages* under DAMAGES.

stipulated judgment. See *agreed judgment* under JUDGMENT.

stipulation (stip-yə-**lay**-shən), *n.* (18c) **1.** A material condition or requirement in an agreement; esp., a factual representation that is incorporated into a contract as a term <breach of the stipulation regarding payment of taxes>. ● Such a contractual term often appears in a section of the contract called "Representations and Warranties." **2.** A voluntary agreement between opposing parties concerning some relevant point; esp., an agreement relating to a proceeding, made by attorneys representing adverse parties to the proceeding <the plaintiff and defendant entered into a stipulation on the issue of liability>. ● A stipulation relating to a pending judicial proceeding, made by a party to the proceeding or the party's attorney, is binding without consideration. **3.** *Roman law.* A formal contract by which a promisor (and only the promisor) became bound by oral question and answer. ● By the third century A.D., stipulations were always evidenced in writing. — **stipulate** (**stip**-yə-layt), *vb.* — **stipulative** (**stip**-yə-lə-tiv), *adj.*

stipulative definition. See DEFINITION.

stipulator. 1. One who makes a stipulation. **2.** *Civil law.* The promisee in a stipulation pour autrui, accepting the promise of a benefit to a third party.

stirpal (**stɪr**-pəl), *adj.* See STIRPITAL.

stirpes (**stɪr**-peez). (*pl.*) See STIRPS.

stirpital (**stɪr**-pə-təl), *adj.* (1886) Of or relating to per stirpes distribution. — Also termed *stipital*; *stirpal*. See PER STIRPES.

stirps (stərps), *n.* [Latin "stock"] (17c) A branch of a family; a line of descent. Pl. **stirpes** (**stɪr**-peez). See PER STIRPES.

stock, *n.* (14c) **1.** The original progenitor of a family; a person from whom a family is descended; BRANCH (1) <George Harper, Sr. was the stock of the Harper line>. **2.** A merchant's goods that are kept for sale or trade <the car dealer put last year's models on sale to reduce its stock>. **3.** The capital or principal fund raised by a corporation through subscribers' contributions or the sale of shares <Acme's stock is worth far more today than it was 20 years ago>. **4.** A proportional part of a corporation's capital represented by the number of equal units (or shares) owned, and granting the holder the right to participate in the company's general management and to share in its net profits or earnings <Julia sold her stock in Pantheon Corporation>. See SHARE (2). Cf. SECURITY (4).

adjustable-rate preferred stock. Preferred stock whose dividend is periodically changed according to changes in a benchmark interest rate, such as that of Treasury bills.

assented stock. Stock that an owner deposits with a third person according to an agreement by which the owner voluntarily accepts a change in the corporation's securities.

assessable stock. Stock that is subject to resale by the issuer if the holder fails to pay any assessment levied on it.

authorized stock. See *capital stock* (1).

bailout stock. Nontaxable preferred stock issued to stockholders as a dividend. ● Bailout stock is issued to gain favorable tax rates by distributing corporate earnings at capital gains rates rather than by distributing capital dividends at ordinary income rates. This practice is now prohibited by the Internal Revenue Code. IRC (26 USCA) § 306.

barometer stock. A stock whose price fluctuates according to market conditions; an individual stock considered to be indicative of the strength of the market in general. — Also termed *bellwether stock*.

blank stock. Securities. Stock with voting powers and rights set by the issuer's board of directors after the stock has been sold.

blue-chip stock. See BLUE CHIP.

bonus stock. A stock share that is issued for no consideration, as an enticement to buy some other type or class of security. ● It is considered a type of watered stock. — Also termed *bonus share*.

book-value stock. Stock offered to executives at a book-value price, rather than at its market value. ● The stock is offered with the understanding that when its book value has risen, the company will buy back the stock at the increased price or will make payments in stock equal to the increased price.

callable preferred stock. Preferred stock that may be repurchased by the issuing corporation at a prestated price, usu. at or slightly above par value.

capital stock. 1. The total number of shares of stock that a corporation may issue under its charter or articles of incorporation, including both common stock and preferred stock. • A corporation may increase the amount of capital stock if the owners of a majority of the outstanding shares consent. — Also termed *authorized stock*; *authorized capital stock*; *authorized stock issue*; *authorized shares.* **2.** The total par value or stated value of this stock; CAPITALIZATION (4). **3.** See *common stock.*

cheap stock. Stock or stock options issued to the issuer's directors, employees, consultants, promoters, and the like at a price lower than the public-offering price up to 12 months before the offering.

common stock. A class of stock entitling the holder to vote on corporate matters, to receive dividends after other claims and dividends have been paid (esp. to preferred shareholders), and to share in assets upon liquidation. • Common stock is often called *capital stock* if it is the corporation's only class of stock outstanding. — Also termed *ordinary shares.* Cf. *preferred stock.*

convertible stock. See *convertible security* under SECURITY.

corporate stock. An equity security issued by a corporation.

cumulative preferred stock. Preferred stock that must receive dividends in full before common shareholders may receive any dividend. • If the corporation omits a dividend in a particular year or period, it is carried over to the next year or period and must be paid before the common shareholders receive any payment. — Also termed *cumulative stock*; *cumulative preference share.*

deferred stock. Stock whose holders are entitled to dividends only after the corporation has met some other specified obligation, such as the discharge of a liability or the payment of a dividend to preferred shareholders.

discount stock. A stock share issued for less than par value. • Discount stock is considered a type of watered stock, the issuance of which may impose liability on the recipient for the difference between the par value and the cash amount paid. — Also termed *discount share.*

donated stock. Stock donated to a charity or given to a corporation by its own stockholders, esp. for resale.

equity stock. Stock of any class having unlimited dividend rights, regardless of whether the stock is preferred.

floating stock. Stock that is offered for sale on the open market and that has not yet been purchased; the number of outstanding shares available for trading.

full-paid stock. Stock on which no further payments can be demanded by the issuing company. — Also termed *paid-up stock.*

glamour stock. See *growth stock* (2).

growth stock. 1. Stock issued by a growth company. • Because a growth company usu. reinvests a large share of its income back into the company, growth stock pays relatively low dividends, though its price usu. has a relatively high appreciation in market value over time. **2.** Stock that has produced or is expected to produce above-average returns and usu. receives small or no dividends. — Also termed *glamour stock.*

guaranteed stock. Preferred stock on which a dividend is guaranteed by someone (usu. a parent corporation) other than the issuer.

guarantee stock. A fixed, nonwithdrawal investment in a building-and-loan association. • This type of stock guarantees to all other investors in the association a fixed dividend or interest rate. See BUILDING-AND-LOAN ASSOCIATION.

guaranty stock. A savings-and-loan association's stock yielding dividends to the holders after dividends have been paid to the depositors.

hot stock. See *hot issue* under ISSUE (2).

inactive stock. A low-volume stock.

income stock. A stock with a history of high yields or dividend payments (e.g., public utilities and well-established corporations).

issued stock. Capital stock that has been authorized and sold to subscribers, but may be reacquired, such as treasury stock.

joint stock. Capital invested in an unincorporated business and divided into shares proportionate to the size of each investment.

letter stock. See *restricted security* under SECURITY.

listed stock. See *listed security* under SECURITY.

margin stock. See *marginable security* under SECURITY.

nonassessable stock. Stock owned by a holder whose potential liability is limited to the amount paid for the stock and who cannot be charged additional funds to pay the issuer's debts. • Stock issued in the United States is usu. nonassessable.

noncumulative preferred stock. Preferred stock that does not have to be paid dividends that are in arrears. • Once a periodic dividend is omitted, it will not be paid. — Also termed *noncumulative stock.*

nonparticipating preferred stock. Preferred stock that does not give the shareholder the right to additional earnings — usu. surplus common-stock dividends — beyond those stated in the preferred contract.

nonvoting stock. Stock that has no voting rights under most situations.

no-par stock. Stock issued without a specific value assigned to it. • For accounting purposes, it is given a legal or stated value that has little or no connection to the stock's actual value. — Sometimes shortened to *no par.* — Also termed *no-par-value stock.*

outstanding stock. Stock that is held by investors and has not been redeemed by the issuing corporation. — Also termed *outstanding capital stock; shares outstanding.*

paid-up stock. See *full-paid stock.*

participating preferred stock. Preferred stock whose holder is entitled to receive stated dividends and to share with the common shareholders in any additional distributions of earnings.

participation stock. Stock permitting the holder to participate in profits and surplus.

par-value stock. Stock originally issued for a fixed value derived by dividing the total value of capital stock by the number of shares to be issued. • The par value does not bear a necessary relation to the actual stock value because surplus plays a role in the valuation.

penny stock. An equity security that is not traded in established markets, represents no tangible assets, or has average revenues less than required for trading on an exchange. • Typically, a penny stock is highly speculative and can be purchased for less than $5 a share.

performance stock. See *glamour stock.*

phantom stock. Imaginary stock that is credited to a corporate executive account as part of the executive's compensation package. See PHANTOM STOCK PLAN.

preferred stock. A class of stock giving its holder a preferential claim to dividends and to corporate assets upon liquidation but that usu. carries no voting rights. — Also termed *preference shares.* Cf. *common stock.*

premium stock. Stock that carries a premium for trading, as in the case of short-selling.

prior preferred stock. Preferred stock that has preference over another class of preferred stock from the same issuer. • The preference usu. relates to dividend payments or claims on assets.

public stock. 1. See *public security* under SECURITY. **2.** Stock of a publicly traded corporation.

reacquired stock. See *treasury stock.*

redeemable stock. Preferred stock that can be called by the issuing corporation and retired.

registered stock. See *registered security* under SECURITY.

restricted stock. See *restricted security* under SECURITY.

retired stock. See *treasury stock.*

subscribed stock. A stockholder's equity account showing the capital that will be contributed when the subscription price is collected. See SUBSCRIPTION (2).

tainted stock. Stock owned or transferred by a person disqualified from serving as a plaintiff in a derivative action. • A good-faith transferee is also disqualified from filing a derivative action.

treasury stock. Stock issued by a company but then reacquired and either canceled or held. • Some states have eliminated this classification and treat such stock as if it is authorized but unissued. — Also termed *treasury security; treasury share; reacquired stock; retired stock.*

unissued stock. Stock that is authorized by the corporate charter but not yet distributed.

unlisted stock. See *unlisted security* under SECURITY.

volatile stock. Stock subject to wide and rapid fluctuations in price. — Also termed *yo-yo stock.*

voting stock. Stock that entitles the holder to vote in the corporation's election of directors and on other matters that are put to a vote. — Also termed *voting security.*

watered stock. Stock issued for less than par value.

whisper stock. The stock of a company that is rumored to be the target of a takeover attempt.

yo-yo stock. See *volatile stock.*

stock acquisition. See SHARE ACQUISITION.

stock-appreciation right. (*usu. pl.*) A right, typically granted in tandem with a stock option, to be paid the option value (usu. in cash) when exercised along with the simultaneous cancellation of the option. — Abbr. SAR.

stock association. See *joint-stock company* under COMPANY.

stock attribution. See ATTRIBUTION.

stock bailout. A stock redemption in the form of a preferred stock dividend.

stock/bond power. See STOCK POWER.

stock bonus plan. A special type of profit-sharing plan in which the distribution of benefits consists of the employer-company's own stock.

stockbroker. One who buys or sells stock as agent for another. — Also termed *account executive*; *account representative*.

stock certificate. An instrument evidencing ownership of shares of stock. — Also termed *certificate of stock*; *share certificate*.

   face-amount certificate. **1.** A certificate, investment contract, or other security representing an obligation by its issuer to pay a stated or determinable sum, at a fixed or determinable date or dates more than 24 months after the date of issuance, in consideration of the payment of periodic installments of a stated or determinable amount. — Also termed *face-amount certificate of the installment type.* **2.** A security representing a similar obligation on the part of the issuer of a face-amount certificate, the consideration for which is the payment of a single lump sum. See 15 USCA § 80a-2(a)(15). — Also termed *fully paid face-amount certificate.*

   periodic-payment-plan certificate. A certificate, investment contract, or other security providing for a series of periodic payments by the holder and representing an undivided interest in certain specified securities or in a unit or fund of securities purchased wholly or partly with the proceeds of those payments. ● The term also includes any security whose issuer is also issuing the certificates described above and whose holder has substantially the same rights and privileges as those holders have upon completing the periodic payments for which the securities provide. See 15 USCA § 80a-2(a)(27).

stock clearing. The actual exchange of money and stock between buyer and seller, typically performed by a clearing corporation.

stock clearing corporation. A New York Stock Exchange subsidiary that is a central agency for securities deliveries and payments between member firms.

stock control. A system of inventory management by which a business maintains perpetual records of its inventory.

stock corporation. See CORPORATION.

stock dividend. See DIVIDEND.

stock exchange. See SECURITIES EXCHANGE.

stock-for-assets exchange. *Mergers & acquisitions.* A merger in which one corporation agrees to dissolve and transfers all or most of its assets to another corporation, which then distributes shares of its own stock to the dissolving corporation's shareholders.

stock-for stock exchange. See *stock swap* under SWAP.

stockholder. See SHAREHOLDER.

stockholder derivative suit. See DERIVATIVE ACTION (1).

stockholder of record. The person who is listed in the issuer's books as the owner of stock on the record date. — Also termed *holder of record*; *owner of record*; *record owner*. See *record date* under DATE.

stockholders' equity. See OWNERS' EQUITY.

stockholder's liability. See *shareholder's liability* under LIABILITY.

stock insurance company. See INSURANCE COMPANY.

stock in trade. **1.** The inventory carried by a retail business for sale in the ordinary course of business. **2.** The tools and equipment owned and used by a person engaged in a trade. **3.** The equipment and other items needed to run a business.

stock issue. See ISSUE (2).

stockjobber. See JOBBER (2).

stockjobbing, *n.* The business of dealing in stocks or shares; esp., the buying and selling of stocks and bonds by jobbers who operate on their own account. — Also termed *stockjobbery*.

stock-law district. See DISTRICT.

stock life-insurance company. See INSURANCE COMPANY.

stock manipulation. See MANIPULATION.

stock market. **1.** See MARKET (5). **2.** See MARKET (6).

stock merger. See MERGER.

stock note. See NOTE (1).

stock option. **1.** An option to buy or sell a specific quantity of stock at a designated price for a specified period regardless of shifts in market value during the period. **2.** An option that allows a corporate employee to buy shares of corporate stock at a fixed price or within a fixed period. ● Such an option is usu. granted as a form of compensation and can qualify for special tax treatment under the Internal Revenue Code. — Also termed (in sense 2) *employee stock option*; *incentive stock option* (ISO).

   nonqualified stock option. A stock-option plan that does not receive capital-gains tax treatment, thus allowing a person to buy stock for a period (often ten years) at or below the market price. — Abbr. NQSO.

   qualified stock option. A now-rare stock-option plan that allows a person to buy stock for a period (often five years) at the market price, the stock being subject to capital-gains tax treatment.

stock-option contract. See CONTRACT.

stock-parking, *n.* See PARKING (2).

stock power. A power of attorney permitting a person, other than the owner, to transfer ownership of a security to a third party. — Also termed *stock/bond power.*

stock-purchase plan. An arrangement by which an employer corporation allows employees to purchase shares of the corporation's stock.

stock redemption. See REDEMPTION (3).

stock-redemption agreement. An agreement between a corporation's individual owners and the corporation itself, whereby the corporation agrees to purchase (i.e., redeem) the stock of a withdrawing or deceased owner. — Often shortened to *redemption agreement.* — Also termed *stock-retirement agreement.*

stock repurchase. See REDEMPTION (3).

stock-repurchase plan. A program by which a corporation buys back its own shares in the open market, usu. when the corporation believes the shares are undervalued.

stock-retirement agreement. See STOCK-REDEMPTION AGREEMENT.

stock right. See SUBSCRIPTION RIGHT.

stocks, *n.* A punishment device consisting of two boards that together form holes for trapping an offender's feet and hands. — Formerly also termed *cippi.* Cf. PILLORY.

stock sale. *Mergers & acquisitions.* A takeover in which the acquiring corporation buys stock directly from the target corporation's shareholders until it controls all or a majority of the target's stock.

stock split. The issuance of two or more new shares in exchange for each old share without changing the proportional ownership interests of each shareholder. ● For example, a 3-for-1 split would give an owner of 100 shares a total of 300 shares, or 3 shares for each share previously owned. A stock split lowers the price per share and thus makes the stock more attractive to potential investors. — Also termed *share split.*

> **reverse stock split.** A reduction in the number of a corporation's shares by calling in all outstanding shares and reissuing fewer shares having greater value.

stock subscription. See SUBSCRIPTION (2).

stock swap. See SWAP.

stock-transfer agent. See AGENT (2).

stock-transfer tax. See TAX.

stock warrant. See WARRANT (4).

stolen property. (18c) Goods acquired by larceny, robbery, or theft.

stonewall, *vb.* To persistently refuse to cooperate in an investigation; esp., to refuse to testify or to hand over requested material until every available legal challenge has been exhausted. — **stonewalling,** *n.*

stool pigeon. *Slang.* **1.** An informant, esp. a police informant. **2.** A person who acts as a decoy, esp. on behalf of a gambler or swindler, or for the police to help make an arrest. — Also termed (in sense 1) *rat*; (in sense 2) *capper.*

stop, *n.* (16c) Under the Fourth Amendment, a temporary restraint that prevents a person from walking away.

stop and frisk, *n.* (1963) A police officer's brief detention, questioning, and search of a person for a concealed weapon when the officer reasonably suspects that the person has committed or is about to commit a crime. ● The stop and frisk, which can be conducted without a warrant or probable cause, was held constitutional by the Supreme Court in *Terry v. Ohio,* 392 U.S. 1, 88 S.Ct. 1868 (1968). — Also termed *investigatory stop*; *investigatory detention*; *Terry stop*; *field stop.* See *reasonable suspicion* under SUSPICION.

stopgap tax. See TAX.

stopgap zoning. See *interim zoning* under ZONING.

stop-limit order. See *stop order* under ORDER (8).

stop-list. *Antitrust.* An illegal means by which manufacturers sometimes attempt to enforce price maintenance, by having suppliers agree among themselves not to supply any party who competes actively and breaks anticompetitive price "rules."

stop-loss insurance. See INSURANCE.

stop-loss order. See *stop order* under ORDER (8).

stop-notice statute. (1963) A law providing an alternative to a mechanic's lien by allowing a contractor, supplier, or worker to make a claim against the construction lender and, in some instances, the owner for a portion of the undisbursed construction-loan proceeds. See *mechanic's lien* under LIEN.

stop order. 1. See ORDER (8). **2.** An SEC order that suspends a registration statement containing false, incomplete, or misleading information. **3.** A bank customer's order instructing the bank not to honor one of the customer's checks. — Also termed (in sense 3) *stop-payment order.*

stoppage, *n.* (15c) **1.** An obstruction or hindrance to the performance of some act <stoppage of goods or persons in transit for inspection>. **2.** *Civil law.* SETOFF <stoppage in pay for money owed>.

stoppage *in transitu* (in **tran**-si-t[y]oo *or* tranz-i-t[y]oo). (18c) The right of a seller of goods to regain possession of those goods from a common carrier under certain circumstances, even though the seller has already parted with them under a contract for sale. ● This right traditionally applies when goods are consigned wholly or partly on credit from one person to another, and the consignee becomes bankrupt or insolvent before the goods arrive — in which event the consignor may direct the carrier to deliver the goods to someone other than the consignee (who can no longer pay for them). — Also termed *stoppage in transit*. See RECLAMATION (2).

stop-payment order. See STOP ORDER (3).

store, *n.* (13c) **1.** A place where goods are deposited for purchase or sale. **2.** (*usu. pl.*) A supply of articles provided for the subsistence and accommodation of a ship's crew and passengers. **3.** A place where goods or supplies are stored for future use; a warehouse.

> *public store.* A government warehouse administratively maintained, as for the storage of imported goods or military supplies.

store, *vb.* (13c) To keep (goods, etc.) in safekeeping for future delivery in an unchanged condition.

stored-value card. A device that provides access to a specified amount of funds for making payments to others, is the only means of routine access to the funds, and does not have an associated account in the name of the holder. ● Typically, a consumer pays a bank or merchant money in exchange for a stored-value card; the consumer uses the card rather than paper currency to purchase goods and services. — Also termed *smart card*; *prepaid card*; *value-added card*.

store-receiver exemption. See AIKEN EXEMPTION.

stowage (**stoh**-ij). *Maritime law.* **1.** The storing, packing, or arranging of cargo on a vessel to protect the goods from friction, bruising, or water damage during a voyage. ● The bill of lading will often prescribe the method of stowage to be used. **2.** The place (such as a ship's hull) where goods are stored. **3.** The goods so stored. **4.** A fee paid for the storage of goods; a storage fee.

stowaway. A person who hides on board an outgoing or incoming vessel or aircraft to obtain free passage. 18 USCA § 2199.

STR. *abbr.* SUSPICIOUS-TRANSACTION REPORT.

straddle, *n.* In securities and commodities trading, a situation in which an investor holds contracts to buy and to sell the same security or commodity, thus ensuring a loss on one of the contracts. ● The aim of this strategy is to defer gains and use losses to offset other taxable income. — Also termed *spread eagle*; *combination.* — **straddle,** *vb.*

straight annuity. See ANNUITY.

straight bankruptcy. See CHAPTER 7 (2).

straight bill of lading. See BILL OF LADING.

straight deductible. See DEDUCTIBLE.

straight letter of credit. See LETTER OF CREDIT.

straight life annuity. See *nonrefund annuity* under ANNUITY.

straight life insurance. See *whole life insurance* under LIFE INSURANCE.

straight-line depreciation method. See DEPRECIATION METHOD.

straight-line interest. See *simple interest* under INTEREST (3).

straight mortgage. See MORTGAGE.

straight sentence. See *determinate sentence* under SENTENCE.

straight-term mortgage. See *interest-only mortgage* under MORTGAGE.

straight up. See S.U.

straight voting. See *noncumulative voting* under VOTING.

strain theory. (18c) The theory that people commit crimes to alleviate stress created by the disjunction between their station in life and the station to which society has conditioned them to aspire. Cf. CONTROL THEORY; RATIONAL-CHOICE THEORY; ROUTINE-ACTIVITIES THEORY.

strand, *n.* (bef. 12c) A shore or bank of an ocean, lake, river, or stream.

stranding, *n. Maritime law.* A ship's drifting, driving, or running aground on a strand. ● The type of stranding that occurs determines the method of apportioning the liability for any resulting losses.

> *accidental stranding.* Stranding caused by natural forces, such as wind and waves. — Also termed *involuntary stranding.* See *general average* and *particular average* under AVERAGE.

> *voluntary stranding.* Stranding to avoid a more dangerous fate or for fraudulent purposes.

stranger. (14c) **1.** One who is not party to a given transaction; esp., someone other than a party or the party's employee, agent, tenant, or immediate family member. **2.** One not standing toward another in some relation implied in the context; esp., one who is not in privity. **3.** A person who voluntarily pays another person's debt even though the payor cannot be held liable for the debt and the payor's property is not affected by the creditor's rights. ● Subrogation does not apply to a stranger if the debtor did not agree to or assign subrogation rights.

stranger in blood. (17c) **1.** One not related by blood, such as a relative by affinity. **2.** Any person not within the consideration of natural love and affection arising from a relationship.

stratagem. (15c) A trick or deception to obtain an advantage, esp. in a military conflict.

strategic alliance. (1983) A coalition formed by two or more persons in the same or complementary businesses to gain long-term financial, operational, or marketing advantages without jeopardizing competitive independence <through their strategic alliance, the manufacturer and distributor of a co-developed product shared development costs>. Cf. ALLIANCE (1); JOINT VENTURE; PARTNERSHIP.

Strategic National Stockpile. A national repository of medicines and healthcare supplies maintained jointly by the U.S. Department of Homeland Security and the U.S. Department of Health and Human Services to respond to public-health emergencies. • Created as the National Pharmaceutical Stockpile in 1999, the agency caches antibiotics, chemical antidotes, antitoxins, life-support medications, IV administration, airway maintenance supplies, and medical supplies. — Abbr. SNS.

stratocracy (strə-**tok**-rə-see). A military government.

straw bail. See *bail common* under BAIL (4).

straw bond. See BOND (2).

straw man. (1896) **1.** A fictitious person, esp. one that is weak or flawed. **2.** A tenuous and exaggerated counterargument that an advocate makes for the sole purpose of disproving it. — Also termed *straw-man argument*. **3.** A third party used in some transactions as a temporary transferee to allow the principal parties to accomplish something that is otherwise impermissible. **4.** A person hired to post a worthless bail bond for the release of an accused. — Also termed *stramineus homo*. Cf. DUMMY.

straw-man scam. *Criminal law.* A scheme in which an innocent third person is hired to receive fraudulently obtained money and wire it to a location outside the country.

straw poll. A nonbinding vote, taken as a way of informally gauging support or opposition but usu. without a formal motion or debate.

stray remarks. *Employment law.* Statements to or about an employee by a coworker or supervisor, concerning the employee's race, sex, age, national origin, or other status, that are either objectively or subjectively offensive, but that do not represent harassment or discrimination by the employer because of (1) their sporadic, unsystematic, and unofficial nature, (2) the circumstances in which they were made, or (3) their not showing any intention to hamper the employee's continued employment. — Also termed *stray comments*.

stream. Anything liquid that flows in a line or course; esp., a current of water consisting of a bed, bank, and watercourse, usu. emptying into other bodies of water but not losing its character even if it breaks up or disappears.

    private stream. A watercourse, the bed, channel, or waters of which are exclusively owned by private parties.

stream-of-commerce theory. (1942) **1.** The principle that a state may exercise personal jurisdiction over a defendant if the defendant places a product in the general marketplace and the product causes injury or damage in the forum state, as long as the defendant also takes other acts to establish some connection with the forum state, as by advertising there or by hiring someone to serve as a sales agent there. *Asahi Metal Indus. Co., Ltd. v. Superior Court of Cal.*, 480 U.S. 102, 107 S.Ct. 1026 (1987). **2.** The principle that a person who participates in placing a defective product in the general marketplace is strictly liable for harm caused by the product. Restatement (Second) of Torts § 402A (1979).

street. A road or public thoroughfare used for travel in an urban area, including the pavement, shoulders, gutters, curbs, and other areas within the street lines.

    paper street. A thoroughfare that appears on plats, subdivision maps, and other publicly filed documents, but that has not been completed or opened for public use.

street crime. See CRIME.

street gang. See GANG.

street name. A brokerage firm's name in which securities owned by another are registered. • A security is held by a broker in street name (at the customer's request) to simplify trading because no signature on the stock certificate is required. A street name may also be used for securities purchased on margin. The word "street" in this term is a reference to Wall Street.

street-name security. See *nominee account* under ACCOUNT.

street sweep. *Mergers & acquisitions. Slang.* A bidder's cancellation of a tender offer followed by the open-market purchase of large blocks of stock in the target corporation.

street time. *Criminal law.* The period between a person's release from prison on parole and a court's revocation of that parole.

strict, *adj.* (15c) **1.** Narrow; restricted <strict construction>. **2.** Rigid; exacting <strict statutory terms>. **3.** Severe <strict punishment>. **4.** Absolute; requiring no showing of fault <strict liability>.

strict construction. See CONSTRUCTION.

strict constructionism. See CONSTRUCTIONISM.

strict constructionist. See CONSTRUCTIONIST.

strict foreclosure. See FORECLOSURE.

stricti juris (**strik**-tɪ **joor**-is). [Latin] **1.** Of strict right of law; according to the exact law, without extension or enhancement in interpretation. ● This term was often applied to servitudes because they are a restriction on the free exercise of property rights. **2.** *Roman law.* (Of a contract) required to be interpreted strictly on its terms, regardless of circumstances. See BONA FIDES (2).

strict interpretation. See INTERPRETATION.

strictissimi juris (strik-**tis**-ə-mɪ **joor**-is). [Latin] Of the strictest right or law; to be interpreted in the strictest manner. ● This term was usu. applied to certain statutes, esp. those imposing penalties or restraining natural liberties.

strict liability. See LIABILITY.

strict-liability crime. See CRIME.

strict-liability offense. See OFFENSE (1).

strict products liability. See PRODUCTS LIABILITY.

strict rule. See SPECIFIC-PURPOSE RULE.

strict scrutiny. (1941) *Constitutional law.* The standard applied to suspect classifications (such as race) in equal-protection analysis and to fundamental rights (such as voting rights) in due-process analysis. ● Under strict scrutiny, the state must establish that it has a compelling interest that justifies and necessitates the law in question. See COMPELLING-STATE-INTEREST TEST; SUSPECT CLASSIFICATION; FUNDAMENTAL RIGHT. Cf. INTERMEDIATE SCRUTINY; RATIONAL-BASIS TEST.

strict settlement. See SETTLEMENT (1).

strict test. *Evidence.* The principle that disclosure of a privileged document, even when inadvertent, results in a waiver of the attorney–client privilege regarding the document, unless all possible precautions were taken to protect the document from disclosure. Cf. LENIENT TEST; HYDRAFLOW TEST.

strict underwriting. See *standby underwriting* under UNDERWRITING.

strike, *n.* (1810) **1.** An organized cessation or slowdown of work by employees to compel the employer to meet the employees' demands; a concerted refusal by employees to work for their employer, or to work at their customary rate of speed, until the employer grants the concessions that they seek. — Also termed *walkout.* Cf. LOCKOUT; BOYCOTT; PICKETING.

ca'canny strike. See *slowdown strike.*

economic strike. A strike resulting from an economic dispute with the employer (such as a wage dispute); a dispute for reasons other than

unfair labor practices. ● An employer can permanently replace an economic striker but cannot prevent the worker from coming back to an unreplaced position simply because the worker was on strike.

general strike. A strike organized to affect an entire industry.

illegal strike. **1.** A strike using unlawful procedures. **2.** A strike to obtain unlawful objectives, as in a strike to force an employer to stop doing business with a particular company.

jurisdictional strike. A strike resulting from a dispute between members of different unions over work assignments.

organizational strike. See *recognition strike.*

outlaw strike. See *wildcat strike.*

quickie strike. See *wildcat strike.*

recognition strike. A strike by workers seeking to force their employer to acknowledge the union as their collective-bargaining agent. ● After the National Labor Relations Act was passed in 1935, recognition strikes became unnecessary. Under the Act, the employer is required to recognize an NLRB-certified union for bargaining purposes. — Also termed *organizational strike.*

secondary strike. A strike against an employer because that employer has business dealings with another employer directly involved in a dispute with the union. See *secondary boycott* under BOYCOTT; *secondary picketing* under PICKETING.

sit-down strike. A strike in which employees occupy the workplace but do not work. See SIT-IN.

slowdown strike. A strike in which the workers remain on the job but work at a slower pace to reduce their output. — Also termed *ca'canny strike.*

sympathy strike. A strike by union members who have no grievance against their own employer but who want to show support for another union involved in a labor dispute.

whipsaw strike. A strike against some but not all members of a multiemployer association, called for the purpose of pressuring all the employees to negotiate a labor contract. ● Employers whose workers are not on strike have the right to lock out employees to exert counterpressure on the union.

wildcat strike. A strike not authorized by a union or by a collective-bargaining agreement. — Also termed *outlaw strike*; *quickie strike.*

2. The removal of a prospective juror from the jury panel <a peremptory strike>. See CHALLENGE (2).

sight strike. The elimination of a veniremember based solely on appearance. See *peremptory challenge* under CHALLENGE (2).

3. A failure or disadvantage, as by a criminal conviction <a strike on one's record>. **4.** *Parliamentary law.* A form of the motion to amend by deleting one or more words. See *amendment by striking out* under AMENDMENT (3).

strike, *vb.* (14c) **1.** (Of an employee or union) to engage in a strike <the flight attendants struck to protest the reduction in benefits>. **2.** To remove (a prospective juror) from a jury panel by a peremptory challenge or a challenge for cause <the prosecution struck the panelist who indicated an opposition to the death penalty>. See *peremptory challenge* under CHALLENGE (2). **3.** To expunge, as from a record <motion to strike the prejudicial evidence>. **4.** *Parliamentary law.* To amend by deleting one or more words. See *amendment by striking out* under AMENDMENT (3). — Also termed (in sense 4) *strike out.*

strikebreaker. See SCAB.

strike down. (1894) To invalidate (a statute); to declare void.

strike fund. A union fund that provides benefits to its members who are on strike, esp. for subsistence while the members are not receiving wages.

strike off. 1. (Of a court) to order (a case) removed from the docket. **2.** (Of an auctioneer or sheriff) to announce, usu. by the falling of the hammer, that an item of personal or real property has been sold.

strike out. See STRIKE (4).

strike price. See PRICE.

strike suit. See SUIT.

strike zone. *Slang.* The period in jury selection in which veniremembers are subject to being struck by peremptory challenge before the jury is seated. ● If a court requires 12 jurors and allows each side 10 peremptory strikes, the strike zone would be the first 32 veniremembers.

striking a jury. (1859) The selecting of a jury out of all the candidates available to serve on the jury; esp., the selecting of a special jury. See *struck jury, special jury* under JURY.

striking off the roll. See DISBARMENT.

striking price. See *strike price* under PRICE.

string of title. See CHAIN OF TITLE (1).

strip, *n.* (16c) **1.** The act of separating and selling a bond's coupons and corpus separately. **2.** The act of a tenant who, holding less than the entire fee in land, spoils or unlawfully takes something from the land.

STRIP (strip). *abbr.* SEPARATE TRADING OF REGISTERED INTEREST AND PRINCIPAL OF SECURITIES.

stripped mortgage-backed security. See SECURITY.

stripper well. See WELL.

strip search. See SEARCH.

strong-arm clause. See CLAUSE.

strongly corroborated. (18c) (Of testimony) supported from independent facts and circumstances that are powerful, satisfactory, and clear to the court and jury.

strong mark. See *strong trademark* under TRADEMARK.

strong market. See *bull market* under MARKET.

strong trademark. See TRADEMARK.

struck jury. See JURY.

struck off. 1. Removed from an active docket, usu. because of a want of prosecution or jurisdiction.

structural alteration. See ALTERATION (1).

structural takeover defense. See TAKEOVER DEFENSE.

structural unemployment. See UNEMPLOYMENT.

structure. (15c) **1.** Any construction, production, or piece of work artificially built up or composed of parts purposefully joined together <a building is a structure>. **2.** The organization of elements or parts <the corporate structure>. **3.** A method of constructing parts <the loan's payment structure was a financial burden>.

structured security. See SECURITY.

structured settlement. See SETTLEMENT (2).

student-benefit theory. A principle that allows state funds to be provided to private-school pupils if the allotment can be justified as benefiting the child. ● The Supreme Court upheld a Louisiana law that allowed the purchase of textbooks for all children throughout the state — even those in private schools — under this theory. *Cochran v. Louisiana State Bd. of Educ.*, 281 U.S. 370, 50 S.Ct. 335 (1930). — Also termed *child-benefit theory.*

study furlough. See *study release* under RELEASE.

study release. See RELEASE.

stuff gown. 1. The professional robe worn by barristers of the outer bar who have not been appointed Queen's Counsel. **2.** A junior barrister. Cf. SILK GOWN.

stultify, *vb.* (18c) **1.** To make (something or someone) appear stupid or foolish <he stultified opposing counsel's argument>. **2.** To testify about one's own lack of mental capacity. **3.** To contradict oneself, as by denying what one has already alleged.

stumpage (stəmp-ij). (1835) **1.** The timber standing on land. **2.** The value of the standing timber. **3.** A license to cut the timber. **4.** The fee paid for the right to cut the timber.

STV. See *single transferable vote* under VOTE (1).

style, *n.* **1.** A case name or designation <the style of the opinion is *Connor v. Gray*>. — Also termed *title.* Cf. CAPTION (1). **2.** *Scots law.* A form of writ or deed used in conveyancing. • A book of styles is essentially a formbook; a typical Scottish example is John Hendry's *Styles of Deeds and Instruments* (2d ed. 1862).

stylized drawing. See *special-form drawing* under DRAWING.

s.u. *abbr.* Straight up. • When a prosecutor writes this on a defendant's file, it usu. means that the prosecutor plans to try the case — that is, not enter into a plea bargain.

suable, *adj.* (17c) **1.** Capable of being sued <a suable party>. **2.** Capable of being enforced <a suable contract>. — **suability,** *n.*

sua sponte (s[y]oo-ə **spon**-tee). [Latin "of one's own accord; voluntarily"] Without prompting or suggestion; on its own motion <the court took notice sua sponte that it lacked jurisdiction over the case>.

sub (səb). [Latin] Under; upon.

sub. See *subsidiary corporation* under CORPORATION.

subagent. See AGENT (2).

subaltern (səb-**awl**-tərn), *n.* An inferior or subordinate officer.

subassignee. See ASSIGNEE.

subchapter-C corporation. See *C corporation* under CORPORATION.

subchapter-S corporation. See *S corporation* under CORPORATION.

subcombination claim. See PATENT CLAIM.

subcommittee. See COMMITTEE.

subcontract. See CONTRACT.

subcontractor. (1834) One who is awarded a portion of an existing contract by a contractor, esp. a general contractor. • For example, a contractor who builds houses typically retains subcontractors to perform specialty work such as installing plumbing, laying carpet, making cabinetry, and landscaping — each subcontractor is paid a somewhat lesser sum than the contractor receives for the work.

subdivision, *n.* (15c) **1.** The division of a thing into smaller parts. **2.** A parcel of land in a larger development. — **subdivide,** *vb.*

illegal subdivision. The division of a tract of land into smaller parcels in violation of local subdivision regulations, as when a developer begins laying out streets, installing sewer and utility lines, and constructing houses without the local planning commission's authorization.

legal subdivision. The governmentally approved division of a tract of land into smaller parcels using ordinary and legally recognized methods for surveying and platting land and publicly recording the results.

subdivision exaction. A charge that a community imposes on a subdivider as a condition for permitting recordation of the subdivision map and sale of the subdivided parcels.

subdivision map. (1887) A map that shows how a parcel of land is to be divided into smaller lots, and generally showing the layout and utilities.

subjacent (səb-**jay**-sənt), *adj.* (16c) Located underneath or below <the land's subjacent support>.

subjacent support. See SUPPORT (4).

subject, *adj.* Referred to above; having relevance to the current discussion <the subject property was then sold to Smith>.

subject, *n.* (14c) **1.** One who owes allegiance to a sovereign and is governed by that sovereign's laws <the monarchy's subjects>. **2.** The matter of concern over which something is created <the subject of the statute>. — Also termed (in sense 2) *subject matter.*

subject, *adj.* Referred to above; having relevance to the current discussion <the subject property was then sold to Smith>.

subjection. (14c) **1.** The act of subjecting someone to something <their subjection to torture was unconscionable>. **2.** The condition of a subject in a monarchy; the obligations surrounding such a person <a subject, wherever residing, owes fidelity and obedience to the Crown, while an alien may be released at will from all such ties of subjection>. **3.** The condition of being subject, exposed, or liable; liability <the defendants' subjection to the plaintiffs became clear shortly after the trial began>. — Also termed (in sense 3) *liability*; *susceptibility.*

subjective, *adj.* (18c) **1.** Based on an individual's perceptions, feelings, or intentions, as opposed to externally verifiable phenomena <the subjective theory of contract — that the parties must have an actual meeting of the minds — is not favored by most courts>. **2.** Personal; individual <subjective judgments about popular music>. Cf. OBJECTIVE.

subjective ethics. See MORAL RELATIVISM.

subjective impossibility. See IMPOSSIBILITY.

subjective meaning. See MEANING.

subjective method. See SHERMAN–SORRELLS DOCTRINE.

subjective novation. See NOVATION.

subjective standard. See STANDARD.

subjective theory of contract. (1928) The doctrine (now largely outmoded) that a contract is an agreement in which the parties have a subjective meeting of the minds. — Often shortened to *subjective theory.* See MEETING OF THE MINDS. Cf. OBJECTIVE THEORY OF CONTRACT.

subject matter. (16c) **1.** The issue presented for consideration; the thing in which a right or duty has been asserted; the thing in dispute. **2.** PATENTABLE SUBJECT MATTER. — Sometimes written (as a noun) *subject-matter.* See SUBJECT (2); CORPUS (1). — **subject-matter,** *adj.*

subject-matter jurisdiction. See JURISDICTION.

subject-matter-neutral. See NEUTRAL.

subject-matter test. (1974) A method of determining whether an employee's communication with a corporation's lawyer was made at the direction of the employee's supervisors and in the course and scope of the employee's employment, so as to be protected under the attorney–client privilege, despite the fact that the employee is not a member of the corporation's control group. *Harper & Row Pubs., Inc. v. Decker,* 423 F.2d 487 (7th Cir. 1970), *aff'd per curiam by equally divided Court,* 400 U.S. 348, 91 S.Ct. 479 (1971). — Also termed *Decker test.* Cf. CONTROL-GROUP TEST.

subject-matter waiver. See WAIVER (1).

subject of an action. The right or property at issue in a lawsuit; the basis of a legal claim. Cf. *object of an action* under OBJECT (2).

subject of a right. (1876) **1.** The owner of a right; the person in whom a legal right is vested. **2.** OBJECT OF A RIGHT.

subject to liability, *adj.* (Of a person) susceptible to a lawsuit that would result in an adverse judgment; specif., having engaged in conduct that would make the actor liable for another's injury because the actor's conduct is the legal cause of the injury, the injured party having no disability for bringing the lawsuit.

subject to open. (1906) Denoting the future interest of a class of people when this class is subject to a possible increase or decrease in number.

sub judice (səb **joo**-di-see *also* suub **yoo**-di-kay), *adv.* [Latin "under a judge"] (17c) Before the court or judge for determination; at bar <in the case sub judice, there have been no out-of-court settlements>. • Legal writers sometimes use "case sub judice" where "the present case" would be more comprehensible.

sublease, *n.* A lease by a lessee to a third party, conveying some or all of the leased property for a term shorter than or equal to that of the lessee, who retains a reversion in the lease. — Also termed *subtenancy; derivative lease;* and (esp. in England) *underlease.* — **sublease, sublet,** *vb.*

sublessee. (1882) A third party who receives by lease some or all of the leased property from a lessee. — Also termed *subtenant* and (esp. in England) *undertenant.*

sublessor. (1884) A lessee who leases some or all of the leased property to a third party. — Also termed (esp. in England) *underlessor.*

sublicense. (1880) A license or contract granting to a third party a portion or all of the rights granted to the licensee under an original license.

submarine patent. See PATENT (3).

submission, *n.* (14c) **1.** A yielding, or readiness to yield, to the authority or will of another <his resistance ended in an about-face: complete submission>. **2.** A contract in which the parties agree to refer their dispute to a third party for resolution <in their submission to arbitration, they referred to the rules of the American Arbitration Association>. **3.** An advocate's argument <neither the written nor the oral submissions were particularly helpful>. — **submit,** *vb.*

submission bond. See BOND (2).

submission date. See DATE.

submission of controversy. **1.** The completion of the series of acts by which the parties to a particular dispute place any matter of real controversy existing between them before a court with jurisdiction for a final determination. **2.** A statutory action in which the parties submit their dispute to a court that has jurisdiction, agree on and sign a statement of facts, swear that the controversy is real, and swear that the suit is brought in good faith.

submission to a finding. The admission to facts sufficient to warrant a finding of guilt. — Also termed *admission to sufficient facts.*

submission to the jury. (1818) The process by which a judge gives a case to the jury for its consideration and verdict, usu. after all evidence has been presented, arguments have been completed, and jury instructions have been given.

submit, *vb.* To end the presentation of further evidence in (a case) and tender a legal position for decision <case submitted, Your Honor>.

submortgage. See MORTGAGE.

sub nomine (səb **nom**-ə-nee). [Latin] (1861) Under the name of. • This phrase, typically in abbreviated form, is often used in a case citation to indicate that there has been a name change from one stage of the case to another, as in *Guernsey Memorial Hosp. v. Secretary of Health and Human Servs.,* 996 F.2d 830 (6th Cir. 1993), *rev'd sub nom. Shalala v. Guernsey Memorial Hosp.,* 514 U.S. 87, 115 S.Ct. 1232 (1995). — Abbr. *sub nom.*

subordinate (sə-**bor**-də-nit), *adj.* (15c) **1.** Placed in or belonging to a lower rank, class, or position <a

subordinate lien>. **2.** Subject to another's authority or control <a subordinate lawyer>.

subordinate (sə-**bor**-də-nayt), *vb.* (17c) To place in a lower rank, class, or position; to assign a lower priority to <subordinate the debt to a different class of claims>.

subordinated bond. See *junior bond* under BOND (3).

subordinate debenture. See DEBENTURE.

subordinate debt. See DEBT.

subordinate legislation. See LEGISLATION.

subordinate officer. See OFFICER (1).

subordinate political power. See POLITICAL POWER.

subordination, *n.* **1.** The act or an instance of moving something (such as a right or claim) to a lower rank, class, or position <subordination of a first lien to a second lien>. **2.** *Parliamentary law.* The status and relation of a lower-ranking governing document to a higher-ranking one. • A higher-ranking document supersedes and controls a subordinate document if there is any inconsistency between them. See *governing document* under DOCUMENT. — **subordinate,** *adj.*

subordination clause. 1. In a legal instrument, a clause that explicitly acknowledges the one party's claim of interest is inferior to that of another party. **2.** A covenant in a junior mortgage enabling the first lien to keep its priority in case of renewal or refinancing. **3.** In a legal instrument, a clause that explicitly subjects its provisions to those in a higher-ranking document.

subordination agreement. See AGREEMENT.

suborn (sə-**born**), *vb.* [Latin *subonare,* from *sub* "secretly + *ornare* "to furnish; equip"] (16c) **1.** To induce (a person) to commit an unlawful or wrongful act, esp. in a secret or underhanded manner. **2.** To induce (a person) to commit perjury. **3.** To obtain (perjured testimony) from another. — **subornation** (səb-or-**nay**-shən), *n.* — **suborner** (sə-**bor**-nər), *n.*

subornation of perjury. (16c) The crime of persuading another to commit perjury. — Sometimes shortened to *subornation.*

subparagraph form. A style of legal drafting that uses indented subparagraphs for enumerated items; esp., a style of drafting patent claims in this form so as to distinguish clearly between each of the claimed elements. — Also termed *tabular form.* Cf. COLON-SEMICOLON FORM; OUTLINE FORM; SINGLE-PARAGRAPH FORM.

subpartnership. See PARTNERSHIP.

subpoena (sə-**pee**-nə), *n.* [Latin "under penalty"] (15c) A writ or order commanding a person to appear before a court or other tribunal, subject

to a penalty for failing to comply. — Also spelled *subpena.* Pl. **subpoenas.**

accommodation subpoena. See *friendly subpoena.*

administrative subpoena. A subpoena issued by an administrative agency to compel an individual to provide information to the agency. • The subpoena may take the form of a *subpoena ad testificandum* or a *subpoena duces tecum.*

alias subpoena (ay-lee-əs sə-**pee**-nə). (18c) A second subpoena issued after an initial subpoena has failed.

deposition subpoena. **1.** A subpoena issued to summon a person to make a sworn statement in a time and place other than a trial. **2.** In some jurisdictions, a subpoena duces tecum.

friendly subpoena. A subpoena issued to a person or entity that is willing to testify or produce documents, but only if legally required to do so. • The subpoena may protect the information provider from retaliation from others because the provider is required to comply. — Also termed *accommodation subpoena.*

subpoena ad testificandum (sə-**pee**-nə ad tes-tə-fi-**kan**-dəm). [Law Latin] (1807) A subpoena ordering a witness to appear and give testimony.

subpoena duces tecum (sə-**pee**-nə d[y]oo-seez **tee**-kəm *also* **doo**-səz **tay**-kəm). [Law Latin] (18c) A subpoena ordering the witness to appear in court and to bring specified documents, records, or things. — Also termed *deposition subpoena duces tecum.*

subpoena, *vb.* (17c) **1.** To serve with a subpoena to appear before a court or other tribunal <subpoena the material witnesses>. **2.** To order the production of (documents or other things) by subpoena duces tecum <subpoena the corporate records>. — Also spelled *subpena.*

subpoenal (sə-**pee**-nəl), *adj.* (1969) Required or done under penalty, esp. in compliance with a subpoena.

subprime loan. See LOAN.

subrogate (**səb**-rə-gayt), *vb.* (15c) To substitute (a person) for another regarding a legal right or claim.

subrogation (səb-rə-**gay**-shən), *n.* (15c) **1.** The substitution of one party for another whose debt the party pays, entitling the paying party to rights, remedies, or securities that would otherwise belong to the debtor. • For example, a surety who has paid a debt is, by subrogation, entitled to any security for the debt held by the creditor and the benefit of any judgment the creditor has against the debtor, and may proceed against the debtor as the creditor would. Subrogation most commonly arises in relation to insurance policies. **2.** The equitable remedy by which such a substitution takes place. **3.** The principle under which an insurer that has paid a loss under an insurance policy is entitled to all the rights and remedies belonging to the insured against a third party with respect to any loss covered by the policy. See EQUITY OF SUBROGATION; ANTISUBROGATION RULE.

conventional subrogation. Subrogation that arises by contract or by an express act of the parties.

legal subrogation. Subrogation that arises by operation of law or by implication in equity to prevent fraud or injustice. ● Legal subrogation usu. arises when (1) the paying party has a liability, claim, or fiduciary relationship with the debtor, (2) the party pays to fulfill a legal duty or because of public policy, (3) the paying party is a secondary debtor, (4) the paying party is a surety, or (5) the party pays to protect its own rights or property. — Also termed *equitable subrogation.*

real subrogation. *Civil law.* The substitution of one thing for another.

subrogation clause. 1. *Insurance.* A provision in a property- or liability-insurance policy whereby the insurer acquires certain rights upon paying a claim for a loss under the policy. ● These rights include (1) taking legal action on behalf of the insured to recover the amount of the loss from the party who caused the loss, and (2) receiving a full or proportionate amount of the benefits (such as disability compensation) paid to the insured under a statutory plan. **2.** *Oil & gas.* A provision in an oil-and-gas lease permitting the lessee to pay taxes, mortgages, or other encumbrances on the leased property and to recover those payments out of future proceeds under the lease.

subrogative (**sǝb**-rǝ-gay-tiv), *adj.* Of or relating to subrogation <subrogative rights>. — Also termed *subrogatory; subrogational.*

subrogee (sǝb-rǝ-**gee**). One who is substituted for another in having a right, duty, or claim; esp., the person or entity that assumes the right to attempt to collect on another's claim against a third party by paying the other's claim-related debts or expenses. ● An insurance company frequently becomes a subrogee after paying a policy claim, as a result of which it is then in a position to sue a tortfeasor who injured the insured or otherwise caused harm.

subrogor (sǝb-rǝ-**gor**). One who allows another to be substituted for oneself as creditor, with a transfer of rights and duties; esp., one who transfers a legal right to collect a claim to another in return for payment of the transferor's claim-related debts or expenses.

subscribed capital. See CAPITAL.

subscribed stock. See STOCK.

subscribing witness. See WITNESS.

subscription, *n.* (15c) **1.** The act of signing one's name on a document; the signature so affixed. **2.** *Securities.* A written contract to purchase newly issued shares of stock or bonds. — Also termed (in connection with stock) *stock subscription.* **3.** An oral or a written agreement to contribute a sum of money or property, gratuitously or with consideration, to a specific person or for a specific purpose. — Also termed *subscription contract.* **4.** RESCRIPT (3). — **subscribe,** *vb.* — **subscriber,** *n.*

subscription contract. See SUBSCRIPTION (3).

subscription list. An enumeration of subscribers to an agreement, periodical, or service.

subscription price. The fixed price at which investors can buy shares in a new stock offering before the shares are offered to the public.

subscription privilege. See PREEMPTIVE RIGHT.

subscription right. A certificate evidencing a shareholder's right (known as a *preemptive right*) to purchase newly issued stock before the stock is offered to the public. ● Subscription rights have a market value and are actively traded because they allow the holder to purchase stock at favorable prices. — Also termed *stock right.* See PREEMPTIVE RIGHT.

subscription warrant. See WARRANT (4).

subsequent, *adj.* (15c) (Of an action, event, etc.) occurring later; coming after something else.

subsequent-advance rule. *Bankruptcy.* The principle that a preferential transfer by the debtor will not be avoided or rescinded by the debtor's bankruptcy trustee if (1) the creditor extended new value to the debtor after receiving the preferential transfer, (2) the new value is unsecured, and (3) the new value remains unpaid after its transfer. 11 USCA § 547(c)(4).

subsequent creditor. See CREDITOR.

subsequent negligence. See NEGLIGENCE.

subsequent-negligence doctrine. See LAST-CLEAR-CHANCE DOCTRINE.

subsequent remedial measure. (*usu. pl.*) (1956) *Evidence.* An action taken after an event, which, if taken before the event, would have reduced the likelihood of the event's occurrence. ● Evidence of subsequent remedial measures, such as repairs made after an accident or the installation of safety equipment, is not admissible to prove negligence, but it may be admitted to prove ownership, control, feasibility, or the like. Fed. R. Evid. 407.

subservant. See *subagent* under AGENT (2).

subsidence (sǝb-**sɪd**-ǝn[t]s), *n.* Any downward movement of the soil from its natural position; esp., a sinking of soil.

subsidiary (sǝb-**sid**-ee-er-ee), *adj.* Subordinate; under another's control. See *subsidiary corporation* under CORPORATION.

subsidiary, *n.* See *subsidiary corporation* under CORPORATION.

subsidiary corporation. See CORPORATION.

subsidiary merger. See *triangular merger* under MERGER.

subsidiary motion. See MOTION (2).

subsidy (sǝb-sǝ-dee), *n.* (14c) **1.** A grant, usu. made by the government, to any enterprise whose promotion is considered to be in the public interest. • Although governments sometimes make direct payments (such as cash grants), subsidies are usu. indirect. They may take the form of research-and-development support, tax breaks, provision of raw materials at below-market prices, or low-interest loans or low-interest export credits guaranteed by a government agency. — Also termed *grant.* **2.** A specific financial contribution by a foreign government or public entity conferring a benefit on exporters to the United States. • Such a subsidy is countervailable under 19 USCA §§ 1671, 1677.

countervailable subsidy (kown-tǝr-**vayl**-ǝ-bǝl). A foreign government's subsidy on the manufacture of goods exported to another country, giving rise to the importing country's entitlement to impose a countervailing duty on the goods if their import caused or threatens to cause material injury to domestic industry. See *countervailing duty* under DUTY (4).

3. *Int'l law.* Financial assistance given by one nation to another to preserve the receiving nation's neutrality or to support it in a war, even if the donor nation does not directly participate. — **subsidize,** *vb.*

sub silentio (sǝb si-**len**-shee-oh). [Latin] (17c) Under silence; without notice being taken; without being expressly mentioned (such as precedent *sub silentio*).

subsistence. (17c) Support; means of support. See NECESSARIES.

substance. (14c) **1.** The essence of something; the essential quality of something, as opposed to its mere form <matter of substance>. **2.** Any matter, esp. an addictive drug <illegal substance> <abuse of a substance>.

substance-abuse evaluation and treatment. (1983) A drug offender's court-ordered participation in a drug rehabilitation program. • This type of treatment is esp. common in DUI cases. — Abbr. SAET.

substantial-capacity test. (1968) *Criminal law.* The Model Penal Code's test for the insanity defense, stating that a person is not criminally responsible for an act if, as a result of a mental disease or defect, the person lacks substantial capacity either to appreciate the criminality of the conduct or to conform the conduct to the law. • This test combines elements of both the *McNaghten* rules and the irresistible-impulse test by allowing consideration of both volitional and cognitive weaknesses. This test was formerly used by the federal courts and many states, but since 1984 many jurisdictions (including the federal courts) — in response to the acquittal by reason of insanity of would-be presidential assassin John Hinckley — have narrowed the insanity defense and adopted a new test resembling the *McNaghten* rules, although portions of the substantial-capacity test continue to be used. Model Penal Code § 4.01. — Also termed *Model Penal Code test*; *MPC test*; *American Law Institute test*; *ALI test*. See INSANITY DEFENSE.

substantial-cause test. (1929) *Torts.* The principle that causation exists when the defendant's conduct is an important or significant contributor to the plaintiff's injuries. — Also termed *substantial-factor test*. Cf. BUT-FOR TEST.

substantial-certainty test. *Copyright.* The test for deciding whether a second work was copied from the first. • The question is whether a reasonable observer would conclude with substantial certainty that the second work is a copy.

substantial change in circumstances. See CHANGE IN CIRCUMSTANCES.

substantial-compliance rule. See SUBSTANTIAL-PERFORMANCE DOCTRINE.

substantial-continuity doctrine. A principle for holding a successor corporation liable for the acts of its predecessor corporation, if the successor maintains the same business as the predecessor, with the same employees, doing the same jobs, for the same supervisors, under the same working conditions, and using the same production processes to produce the same products for the same customers. — Also termed *continuity-of-enterprise doctrine*. Cf. MERE-CONTINUATION DOCTRINE.

substantial damages. See DAMAGES.

substantial equivalent. *Patents.* A device or process that falls outside a patent claim's literal scope but performs the same function in substantially the same way. — Also termed *substantial equivalent of a patented device*. See **tripartite test.**

substantial error. See ERROR (2).

substantial evidence. See EVIDENCE.

substantial-evidence jurisdiction. See *significant-connection jurisdiction* under JURISDICTION.

substantial-evidence rule. (1938) The principle that a reviewing court should uphold an administrative body's ruling if it is supported by evidence on which the administrative body could reasonably base its decision.

substantial-factor test. (1929) See SUBSTANTIAL-CAUSE TEST.

substantial justice. See JUSTICE (1).

substantially justified. (Of conduct, a position, etc.) having a reasonable basis in law and in fact. • Under the Equal Access to Justice Act, a prevailing party in a lawsuit against the government will be unable to recover its attorney's fees if the government's position is substantially justified.

substantial new question of patentability. *Patents.* A significant, freshly arisen issue relating to the validity of a patent, triggering the statutory threshold required for the Director of the U.S. Patent and Trademark Office to order that a patent's validity be reexamined. • An examination cannot be reopened solely on issues of prior art and issues that came up during the original examination. The Director's determination is final and not appealable. 35 USCA §§ 303–04.

substantial noninfringing use. See COMMERCIALLY SIGNIFICANT NONINFRINGING USE.

substantial performance. See PERFORMANCE.

substantial-performance doctrine. (1936) The rule that if a good-faith attempt to perform does not precisely meet the terms of an agreement or statutory requirements, the performance will still be considered complete if the essential purpose is accomplished, subject to a claim for damages for the shortfall. • Under the Uniform Probate Code, a will that is otherwise void because some formality has not been followed may still be valid under the substantial-performance doctrine. But this rule is not widely followed. — Also termed *substantial-compliance rule.* Cf. PERFECT-TENDER RULE.

substantial right. See RIGHT.

substantial similarity. See SIMILARITY.

substantial-step test. (1980) *Criminal law.* The Model Penal Code's test for determining whether a person is guilty of attempt, based on the extent of the defendant's preparation for the crime, the criminal intent shown, and any statements personally made that bear on the defendant's actions. Model Penal Code § 5.01(1)(c). See ATTEMPT.

substantiate, *vb.* (17c) To establish the existence or truth of (a fact, etc.), esp. by competent evidence; to verify.

substantive consolidation. See CONSOLIDATION.

substantive crime. See *substantive offense* under OFFENSE (1).

substantive due process. See DUE PROCESS.

substantive evidence. See EVIDENCE.

substantive examination. *Patents.* A patent examiner's in-depth study of a patent application to determine whether a patent should be granted.

substantive felony. See *substantive offense* under OFFENSE (1).

substantive law (səb-stən-tiv). (18c) The part of the law that creates, defines, and regulates the rights,

duties, and powers of parties. Cf. PROCEDURAL LAW.

substantive main motion. See *original main motion* under MOTION (2).

substantive motion. See *original main motion* under MOTION (2).

substantive offense. See OFFENSE (1).

substantive right. See RIGHT.

substantive rule. See LEGISLATIVE RULE.

substantive unconscionability. See UNCONSCIONABILITY.

substitute, *n.* **1.** One who stands in another's place <a substitute for a party>. See SUBSTITUTION OF PARTIES; SUBROGATION. **2.** *Civil law.* A person named in a will as heir to an estate after the estate has been held and then passed on by another specified person (called the *institute*). See INSTITUTE (5). **3.** *Parliamentary law.* A form of the motion to amend by replacing one or more words with others. See *amendment by substituting* under AMENDMENT (3). **4.** *Scots law.* A deputy. — **substitute,** *vb.*

substitute amendment. See AMENDMENT (3).

substitute application. See PATENT APPLICATION.

substituted agreement. See NOVATION.

substituted basis. See BASIS.

substituted complaint. See *amended complaint* under COMPLAINT.

substituted contract. See CONTRACT.

substituted executor. See EXECUTOR.

substituted-judgment doctrine. (1967) A principle that allows a surrogate decision-maker to attempt to establish, with as much accuracy as possible, what healthcare decision an incompetent patient would make if he or she were competent to do so. • The standard of proof is by clear and convincing evidence. Generally, the doctrine is used for a person who was once competent but no longer is. — Also termed *doctrine of substituted judgment.* Cf. SPIRITUAL-TREATMENT EXEMPTION; *medical neglect* under NEGLECT.

substitute drawing. See DRAWING.

substituted service. See SERVICE (2).

substitute gift. See GIFT.

substitute information in lieu of indictment. See INFORMATION.

substitute obligation. See OBLIGATION.

substitute specification. See SPECIFICATION (3).

substitution. (14c) **1.** A designation of a person or thing to take the place of another person or thing. **2.** The process by which one person or thing takes the place of another person or thing. **3.** *Parliamentary law.* An amendment by replacing one or more words with others. See *amendment by* *substituting* under AMENDMENT (3). **4.** *Roman law.* The nomination of a person to take the place of a previously named heir who has refused or failed to accept an inheritance. — Also termed *common substitution; vulgar substitution.* **5.** *Roman law.* The nomination of a person to take the place of, or to succeed, a descendant who is under the age of puberty and in the *potestas* of the testator, if the descendant has died before reaching puberty. • This type of substitution was known as a *pupillary substitution.* If a descendant of any age failed to take by reason of lunacy, the substitution was known as an *exemplary substitution* or *quasi-pupillary substitution.* **6.** *Roman law.* A testator's designation of a person to whom the property was to be given by the person named as heir, or by the heir of that person. — Also termed *fideicommissary substitution.* See FIDEICOMMISSUM. **7.** *Civil law.* The designation of a person to succeed another as beneficiary of an estate, usu. involving a fideicommissum. — Also termed (in senses 6 & 7) *fideicommissary substitution.*

prohibited substitution. *Louisiana law.* The designation of a person who is not a trustee to take full ownership of property and deliver it to another designated person at death. • The first donee is called the *institute,* the second the *substitute.* See INSTITUTE (5); SUBSTITUTE (2).

substitutional, *adj.* (14c) Capable of taking or supplying the position of another <substitutional executor> <substitutional issue>. — Also termed *substitutionary.*

substitutional gift. See *substitute gift* under GIFT.

substitutional legacy. See LEGACY.

substitutional remedy. See REMEDY.

substitutionary. See SUBSTITUTIONAL.

substitutionary evidence. See *secondary evidence* under EVIDENCE.

substitutionary remedy. See REMEDY.

substitution-of-judgment doctrine. 1. *Administrative law.* The standard for reviewing an agency's decision, by which a court uses its own independent judgment in interpreting laws and administrative regulations — rather than deferring to the agency — when the agency's interpretation is not instructive or the regulations do not involve matters requiring the agency's expertise. **2.** *Wills & estates.* The principle that a guardian, conservator, or committee of an incompetent person may make gifts out of that person's estate.

substitution of parties. The replacement of one litigant by another because of the first litigant's death, incompetency, transfer of interest, or, when the litigant is a public official, separation from office.

substraction (səb-**strak**-shən), *n.* (1814) The secret misappropriation of property, esp. from a decedent's estate.

subsume (səb-**s[y]oom**), *vb.* (1825) To judge as a particular instance governed by a general principle; to bring (a case) under a broad rule. — **subsumption** (səb-**səmp**-shən), *n.*

subsurety (səb-**shuur**[-ə]-tee). (1916) A person whose undertaking is given as additional security, usu. conditioned not only on nonperformance by the principal but also on nonperformance by an earlier promisor as well; a surety with the lesser liability in a subsuretyship.

subsuretyship (səb-**shuur**[-ə]-tee-ship). (1967) The relation between two (or more) sureties, in which a principal surety bears the burden of the whole performance that is due from both sureties; a relationship in which one surety acts as a surety for another.

subsurface interest. 1. A landowner's right to the minerals and water below the property. **2.** A similar right held by another through grant by, or purchase from, a landowner. Cf. SURFACE INTEREST; MINERAL INTEREST.

subtenancy. See SUBLEASE.

subtenant. See SUBLESSEE.

subterfuge (**səb**-tər-fyooj). (16c) A clever plan or idea used to escape, avoid, or conceal something <a subterfuge to avoid liability under a statute>.

subterfuge arrest. See ARREST.

subterranean water. See WATER.

subtraction. 1. The process of deducting one number from another number to determine the difference. **2.** *Hist.* The act of neglecting a duty or service that one party owes to another, esp. one that arises out of land tenure.

subtrahend (**səb**-trə-hend). In a mathematical equation, the amount subtracted from another number (the minuend) to arrive at a remainder or balance. • The term is used in law in a variety of accounting contexts. Cf. MINUEND.

subvention (səb-**ven**-shən). A grant of financial aid or assistance; a subsidy.

subversion. (14c) The process of overthrowing, destroying, or corrupting <subversion of legal principles> <subversion of the government>.

Subversive Activities Control Act of 1950. See MC-CARRAN ACT.

subversive activity. (1939) A pattern of acts designed to overthrow a government by force or other illegal means.

subversive propaganda. See PROPAGANDA.

success fee. See FEE (1).

successful party. See *prevailing party* under PARTY (2).

succession, *n.* (14c) **1.** The act or right of legally or officially taking over a predecessor's office, rank, or duties. **2.** The acquisition of rights or property by inheritance under the laws of descent and distribution; DESCENT (1). — **succeed,** *vb.*

   hereditary succession. See *intestate succession.*

   intestate succession. (18c) **1.** The method used to distribute property owned by a person who dies without a valid will. **2.** Succession by the common law of descent. — Also termed *hereditary succession; descent and distribution.* See DESCENT (1). Cf. *testate succession.*

   irregular succession. (17c) Succession by special laws favoring certain persons or the state, rather than heirs (such as testamentary heirs) under the ordinary laws of descent.

   legal succession. (18c) The succession established by law, usu. in favor of the nearest relation of a deceased person.

   natural succession. (18c) Succession between natural persons, as in descent on the death of an ancestor.

   testamentary succession. Civil law. Succession resulting from the designation of an heir in a testament executed in the legally required form.

   testate succession. (18c) The passing of rights or property by will. Cf. *intestate succession.*

   universal succession. Succession to an entire estate of another at death. ● This type of succession carries with it the predecessor's liabilities as well as assets. Originally developed by Roman law and later continued by civil law, this concept has now been widely adopted as an option endorsed and authorized by the Uniform Probate Code. La. Civ. Code art. 3506(28).

   vacant succession. Civil law. **1.** A succession that fails either because there are no known heirs or because the heirs have renounced the estate. **2.** An estate that has suffered such a failure. See ESCHEAT.

3. The right by which one group, in replacing another group, acquires all the goods, movables, and other chattels of a corporation. **4.** The continuation of a corporation's legal status despite changes in ownership or management. — Also termed *artificial succession.*

   perpetual succession. The continuous succession of a corporation — despite changes in shareholders and officers — for as long as the corporation legally exists.

successional, *adj.* (14c) Of or relating to acquiring rights or property by inheritance under the laws of descent and distribution.

succession duty. See DUTY (4).

succession tax. See *inheritance tax* (1) under TAX.

successive, *adj.* **1.** *Archaic.* (Of an estate) hereditary. **2.** (Of persons, things, appointments, etc.) following in order; consecutive.

successive polygamy. See POLYGAMY (2).

successive tortfeasors. See TORTFEASOR.

successive-writ doctrine. (1987) *Criminal procedure.* The principle that a second or supplemental petition for a writ of habeas corpus may not raise claims that were heard and decided on the merits in a previous petition. Cf. ABUSE-OF-THE-WRIT DOCTRINE.

successor. (14c) **1.** A person who succeeds to the office, rights, responsibilities, or place of another; one who replaces or follows a predecessor. **2.** A corporation that, through amalgamation, consolidation, or other assumption of interests, is vested with the rights and duties of an earlier corporation.

   particular successor. Civil law. One who succeeds to rights and obligations that pertain only to the property conveyed.

   singular successor. One who succeeds to a former owner's rights in a single piece of property.

   statutory successor. One who succeeds to the assets of a corporation upon its dissolution; specif., the person to whom all corporate assets pass upon a corporation's dissolution according to the statute of the state of incorporation applicable at the time of the dissolution. See Restatement (Second) of Conflict of Laws § 388 cmt. a (1971).

   universal successor. **1.** One who succeeds to all the rights and powers of a former owner, as with an intestate estate or an estate in bankruptcy. **2.** *Louisiana law.* An heir or legatee who succeeds in the entire estate of the deceased or a specified portion of it, rather than by particular title as legatee of a specific thing. ● A universal successor succeeds in all of the decedent's rights and charges, whereas the particular legatee succeeds only to the rights and charges pertaining to the bequeathed thing. La. Civ. Code art. 3506(28).

successor agent. See AGENT (2).

successor fiduciary. See FIDUCIARY.

successor guardian. See GUARDIAN.

successor in interest. (1832) One who follows another in ownership or control of property. ● A successor in interest retains the same rights as the original owner, with no change in substance.

successor trustee. See TRUSTEE (1).

such, *adj.* (bef. 12c) **1.** Of this or that kind <she collects a variety of such things>. **2.** That or those; having just been mentioned <a newly discovered Fabergé egg will be on auction next week; such egg is expected to sell for more than $500,000>.

sudden-and-accidental pollution exclusion. See *pollution exclusion* under EXCLUSION (3).

sudden-death jurisdiction. *Wills & estates.* A jurisdiction in which a will once revoked cannot be revived, and instead must be reexecuted. See REVIVAL (2).

sudden-emergency doctrine. See EMERGENCY DOCTRINE (1).

sudden heat. See HEAT OF PASSION.

sudden heat of passion. See HEAT OF PASSION.

sudden-onset rule. (1981) The principle that medical testimony is unnecessary to prove causation of the obvious symptoms of an injury that immediately follows a known traumatic incident.

sudden passion. See HEAT OF PASSION.

sudden-peril doctrine. See EMERGENCY DOCTRINE (1).

sudden-peril rule. See EMERGENCY DOCTRINE (1).

sue, *vb.* To institute a lawsuit against (another party).

sue-and-labor clause. *Marine insurance.* A provision in property- and marine-insurance policies requiring the insured to protect damaged property against further loss. ● The clause generally requires the insured to "sue and labor" to protect the insured party's interests. — Also termed *rescue clause.*

sue facts. (1980) Facts that determine whether a party should bring a lawsuit; esp., facts determining whether a shareholder-derivative action should be instituted under state law.

sue out, *vb.* (15c) **1.** To apply to a court for the issuance of (a court order or writ). **2.** To serve (a complaint) on a defendant.

suffer, *vb.* (14c) **1.** To experience or sustain physical or emotional pain, distress, or injury <suffer grievously><suffer damages>. **2.** To allow or permit (an act, etc.) <to suffer a default>.

sufferance (**səf**-ər-ənts *or* **səf**-rənts). (14c) **1.** Toleration; passive consent. **2.** The state of one who holds land without the owner's permission. See *tenancy at sufferance* under TENANCY. **3.** A license implied from the omission to enforce a right.

sufficiency of disclosure. See ADEQUACY OF DISCLOSURE.

sufficiency-of-evidence test. (1972) *Criminal procedure.* **1.** The guideline for a grand jury considering whether to indict a suspect: if all the evidence presented were uncontradicted and unexplained, it would warrant a conviction by the fact-trier. **2.** A standard for reviewing a criminal conviction on appeal, based on whether enough evidence exists to justify the fact-trier's finding of guilt beyond a reasonable doubt. — Also termed *sufficiency-of-the-evidence test.*

sufficient, *adj.* Adequate; of such quality, number, force, or value as is necessary for a given purpose <sufficient consideration> <sufficient evidence>.

sufficient cause. 1. See *good cause* under CAUSE (2). **2.** PROBABLE CAUSE.

sufficient consideration. See CONSIDERATION (1).

sufficient evidence. See *satisfactory evidence* under EVIDENCE.

suffragan (**səf**-rə-gən *or* -jən). A titular bishop ordained to assist a bishop of the diocese in the church business; a deputy or assistant bishop. ● Suffragans were originally appointed only to replace absent bishops and were called *chorepiscopi* ("bishops of the county"), as distinguished from the regular bishops of the city or see.

suffrage (**səf**-rij). (14c) **1.** The right or privilege of casting a vote at a public election. — Also termed *right to vote.* **2.** A vote; the act of voting.

suggested retail price. See PRICE.

suggestibility, *n.* The readiness with which a person accepts another's suggestion. — **suggestible,** *adj.*

suggestio falsi (səg-**jes**-tee-oh **fal**-sɪ *or* **fawl**-sɪ). [Latin] A false representation or misleading suggestion. Cf. SUPPRESSIO VERI.

suggestion, *n.* (14c) **1.** An indirect presentation of an idea <the client agreed with counsel's suggestion to reword the warranty>. **2.** *Procedure.* A statement of some fact or circumstance that will materially affect the further proceedings in the case <suggestion for rehearing en banc>. **3.** *Archaic. Wills & estates.* UNDUE INFLUENCE. — **suggest** (for senses 1 & 2), *vb.*

suggestion of bankruptcy. (1869) A pleading by which a party notifies the court that the party has filed for bankruptcy and that, because of the automatic stay provided by the bankruptcy laws, the court cannot take further action in the case.

suggestion of death. (18c) A pleading filed by a party, or the party's representatives, by which the court is notified that a party to a suit has died.

suggestion of error. (1811) An objection made by a party to a suit, indicating that the court has committed an error or that the party wants a rehearing of a particular issue.

suggestion on the record. A formal written or oral statement informing the court of an important fact that may require a stay of proceedings or affect the court's decision. ● Suggestions on the record include suggestion of bankruptcy, suggestion of death, and suggestion of error.

suggestive interrogation. See LEADING QUESTION.

suggestive mark. See *suggestive trademark* under TRADEMARK.

suggestive name. See *suggestive trademark* under TRADEMARK.

suggestive question. See LEADING QUESTION.

suggestive trademark. See TRADEMARK.

suicide, *n.* (17c) **1.** The act of taking one's own life. — Also termed *self-killing; self-destruction; self-slaughter; self-murder; felony-de-se; death by one's own hand.*

    assisted suicide. (1976) The intentional act of providing a person with the medical means or the medical knowledge to commit suicide. — Also termed *assisted self-determination;* (when a doctor provides the means) *physician-assisted suicide.* Cf. EUTHANASIA.

    attempted suicide. (1880) An unsuccessful suicidal act.

    physician-assisted suicide. See *assisted suicide.*

    police-assisted suicide. See *suicide-by-cop.*

    suicide-by-cop. *Slang.* A form of suicide in which the suicidal person intentionally engages in life-threatening behavior to induce a police officer to shoot the person. • Frequently, the decedent attacks the officer or otherwise threatens the officer's life, but occasionally a third person's life is at risk. A suicide-by-cop is distinguished from other police shootings by three elements. The person must: (1) evince an intent to die; (2) consciously understand the finality of the act; and (3) confront a law enforcement official with behavior so extreme that it compels that officer to act with deadly force. — Also termed *police-assisted suicide; victim-precipitated homicide.*

    2. A person who has taken his or her own life. — Also termed *felo-de-se; felon-de-se; felon of oneself.* — **suicidal,** *adj.*

suicide clause. *Insurance.* A life-insurance-policy provision either excluding suicide as a covered risk or limiting the insurer's liability in the event of a suicide to the total premiums paid.

suicide letter of credit. See *clean letter of credit* under LETTER OF CREDIT.

sui generis (s[y]oo-ɪ *or* soo-ee jen-ə-ris). [Latin "of its own kind"] (18c) Of its own kind or class; unique or peculiar. • The term is used in intellectual-property law to describe a regime designed to protect rights that fall outside the traditional patent, trademark, copyright, and trade-secret doctrines. For example, a database may not be protected by copyright law if its content is not original, but it could be protected by a sui generis statute designed for that purpose.

sui juris (s[y]oo-ɪ *or* soo-ee joor-is). [Latin "of one's own right; independent"] (17c) **1.** Of full age and capacity. **2.** Possessing full social and civil rights.

3. *Roman law.* Of or relating to anyone of any age, male or female, not in the *postestas* of another, and therefore capable of owning property and enjoying private law rights. • As a status, it was not relevant to public law.

suit. (14c) Any proceeding by a party or parties against another in a court of law; CASE (1). — Also termed *lawsuit; suit at law.* See ACTION (4).

    ancillary suit (an-sə-ler-ee). (1845) An action, either at law or in equity, that grows out of and is auxiliary to another suit and is filed to aid the primary suit, to enforce a prior judgment, or to impeach a prior decree. — Also termed *ancillary bill; ancillary proceeding; ancillary process.*

    blackmail suit. (1892) A suit filed by a party having no genuine claim but hoping to extract a favorable settlement from a defendant who would rather avoid the expense and inconvenience of litigation.

    class suit. See CLASS ACTION.

    derivative suit. See DERIVATIVE ACTION (1).

    frivolous suit. (1837) A lawsuit having no legal basis, often filed to harass or extort money from the defendant.

    official-capacity suit. A lawsuit that is nominally against one or more individual state employees but that has as the real party in interest the state or a local government. Cf. *personal-capacity suit.*

    personal-capacity suit. An action to impose personal, individual liability on a government officer. Cf. *official-capacity suit.*

    petitory suit. See *petitory action* under ACTION (4).

    plenary suit (plee-nə-ree *or* plen-ə-ree). (1817) An action that proceeds on formal pleadings under rules of procedure. Cf. *summary proceeding* under PROCEEDING.

    sham suit. See *sham action* under ACTION (4).

    strike suit. (1902) A suit (esp. a derivative action), often based on no valid claim, brought either for nuisance value or as leverage to obtain a favorable or inflated settlement.

    suit at law. A suit conducted according to the common law or equity, as distinguished from statutory provisions. • Under the current rules of practice in federal and most state courts, the term *civil action* embraces an action both at law and in equity. Fed. R. Civ. P. 2. See *action at law* under ACTION (4).

    suit in equity. A civil suit stating an equitable claim and asking for an exclusively equitable remedy. — Also termed *action in equity.*

    suit of a civil nature. A civil action. See *civil action* under ACTION (4).

suitable, *adj.* (Of goods, etc.) fit and appropriate for their intended purpose.

suit for exoneration. (1928) A suit in equity brought by a surety to compel the debtor to pay the creditor. • If the debtor has acted fraudulently and is insolvent, a suit for exoneration may include further remedies to ensure that the debtor's assets are applied equitably to the debtor's outstanding obligations. — Also termed *suit to compel payment.*

suit money. (1846) Attorney's fees and court costs allowed or awarded by a court; esp., in some jurisdictions, a husband's payment to his wife to cover her reasonable attorney's fees in a divorce action.

suitor. (16c) **1.** A party that brings a lawsuit; a plaintiff or petitioner. **2.** An individual or company that seeks to take over another company.

Suitors' Deposit Account. *English law.* An account consisting of suitors' fees paid in the Court of Chancery that, by the Chancery Act of 1872, were to be invested in government securities bearing interest at 2% per annum on behalf of the investing suitor, unless the suitor directed otherwise.

suit papers. See COURT PAPERS.

Suits in Admiralty Act. A 1920 federal law giving injured parties the right to sue the government in admiralty. 46 USCA app. §§ 741–52.

suit to compel payment. See SUIT FOR EXONERATION.

sum. 1. A quantity of money. **2.** *English law.* A legal summary or abstract; a compendium; a collection. • Several treatises are called *sums.*

sum certain. (16c) **1.** Any amount that is fixed, settled, or exact. **2.** *Commercial law.* In a negotiable instrument, a sum that is agreed on in the instrument or a sum that can be ascertained from the document.

summary, *adj.*(15c) **1.** Short; concise <a summary account of the events on March 6>. **2.** Without the usual formalities; esp., without a jury <a summary trial>. **3.** Immediate; done without delay <the new weapon was put to summary use by the military>. — **summarily** (səm-ər-ə-lee *or* sə-**mair**-ə-lee), *adv.*

summary, *n.* (16c) **1.** An abridgment or brief. **2.** A short application to a court without the formality of a full proceeding.

summary adjudication. See *partial summary judgment* under SUMMARY JUDGMENT.

summary conviction. See CONVICTION.

summary court-martial. See COURT-MARTIAL.

summary disposition. See SUMMARY JUDGMENT.

summary eviction. See EVICTION.

summary judgment. (18c) A judgment granted on a claim or defense about which there is no genuine issue of material fact and upon which the movant is entitled to prevail as a matter of law. • The court considers the contents of the pleadings, the motions, and additional evidence adduced by the parties to determine whether there is a genuine issue of material fact rather than one of law. This procedural device allows the speedy disposition of a controversy without the need for trial. Fed. R. Civ. P. 56. — Also termed *summary disposition; judgment on the pleadings.* See JUDGMENT.

   partial summary judgment. (1924) A summary judgment that is limited to certain issues in a case and that disposes of only a portion of the whole case. — Also termed *summary adjudication.*

summary-judgment motion. See MOTION FOR SUMMARY JUDGMENT.

summary jurisdiction. See JURISDICTION.

summary jury trial. See TRIAL.

summary of argument. See SUMMARY OF THE ARGUMENT.

Summary of Commentary on Current Economic Conditions by Federal Reserve District. See BEIGE BOOK.

summary offense. 1. See OFFENSE (1). **2.** See MISDEMEANOR (1).

summary of the argument. The part of a brief, esp. an appellate brief, in which the advocate condenses the argument to a précis or synopsis, directing the court to the heart of the argument on each point. • A summary typically runs from one to four pages. — Also termed *summary of argument.*

summary of the invention. *Patents.* In a U.S. patent application, the section that describes the nature, operation, and purpose of the invention in enough detail that the examiner and anyone searching the patent literature for prior art can understand the unique character of the invention.

summary plan description. Under the Employee Retirement Security Act (ERISA), an outline of an employee benefit plan, containing such information as the identity of the plan administrator, the requirements for eligibility and participation in the plan, circumstances that may result in disqualification or denial of benefits, and the identity of any insurers responsible for financing or administering the plan. • A summary plan description must generally be furnished to all employee-benefit-plan participants and beneficiaries. 29 USCA § 1022. — Abbr. SPD.

summary procedure. See SHOW-CAUSE PROCEEDING.

summary proceeding. See PROCEEDING.

summary process. See PROCESS.

summary trial. See *summary proceeding* under PROCEEDING.

summation. See CLOSING ARGUMENT.

summer associate. See CLERK (4).

summer clerk. See CLERK (4).

summing up. 1. CLOSING ARGUMENT. **2.** *English law.* A judge's review of the key points of evidence presented in a case and instructions to the jury on the law it is to apply to the evidence. • The judge's summing up follows the advocates' closing speeches. — **sum up,** *vb.*

summon, *vb.* (13c) To command (a person) by service of a summons to appear in court. — Also termed *summons.*

summons, *n.* (13c) **1.** A writ or process commencing the plaintiff's action and requiring the defendant to appear and answer. **2.** A notice requiring a person to appear in court as a juror or witness. **3.** *Hist.* A writ directing a sheriff to summon a defendant to appear in court. **4.** *English law.* The application to a common-law judge upon which an order is made. Pl. **summonses.**

alias summons. A second summons issued after the original summons has failed for some reason.

John Doe summons. **1.** A summons to a person whose name is unknown at the time of service. **2.** *Tax.* A summons from the Internal Revenue Service to a third party to provide information on an unnamed, unknown taxpayer with potential tax liability. — Also termed *third-party record-custodian summons.*

judgment summons. A process used by a judgment creditor to start an action against a judgment debtor to enforce the judgment.

short summons. A summons having a response time less than that of an ordinary summons, usu. served on a fraudulent or nonresident debtor.

third-party record-custodian summons. See *John Doe summons.*

summons, *vb.* (17c) **1.** SUMMON. **2.** To request (information) by summons.

summum bonum (səm-əm boh-nəm *also* suum-uum baw-nuum). [Latin] The greatest good.

summum jus (səm-əm jəs). [Latin] The highest law.

sum-of-the-years'-digits depreciation method. See DEPRECIATION METHOD.

sum payable. (17c) An amount due; esp., the amount for which the maker of a negotiable instrument becomes liable and must tender in full satisfaction of the debt.

sumptuary law (səmp-choo-er-ee). **1.** A statute, ordinance, or regulation that limits the expenditures that people can make for personal gratification or ostentatious display. **2.** More broadly, any law whose purpose is to regulate conduct thought to be immoral, such as prostitution, gambling, or drug abuse.

Sunday-closing law. See BLUE LAW.

Sunday law. See BLUE LAW.

sundries (sən-dreez). Miscellaneous items that may be considered together, without being separately specified or identified.

sundry (sən-dree), *adj.* Separate; diverse; various.

sunk cost. See COST (1).

sunna. See FEMALE GENITAL MUTILATION.

sunset law. (1976) A statute under which a governmental agency or program automatically terminates at the end of a fixed period unless it is formally renewed.

sunset legislation. See SUNSET LAW.

sunshine committee. (2000) An official or quasi-official committee whose proceedings and work are open to public access.

sunshine law. (1972) A statute requiring a governmental department or agency to open its meetings or its records to public access. — Also termed *open-meeting law; public-meeting law; open-door law.*

SUP. *abbr.* SPECIAL-USE PERMIT.

sup. ct. *abbr.* SUPREME COURT.

super (s[y]oo-pər). [Latin] Above; over; higher.

supercargo. *Maritime law.* A person specially employed and authorized by a cargo owner to sell cargo that has been shipped and to purchase returning cargo, at the best possible prices; the commercial or foreign agent of a merchant.

superficies (s[y]oo-pər-**fish**-ee-eez *or* -**fish**-eez), *n.* [Latin "surface"] *Roman & civil law.* **1.** The surface of the ground. **2.** An improvement that stands on the surface of the ground, such as a building, other construction, trees, plants, or crops.

Superfund. (1977) **1.** The program that funds and administers the cleanup of hazardous-waste sites through a trust fund (financed by taxes on petroleum and chemicals and a tax on certain corporations) created to pay for cleanup pending reimbursement from the liable parties. **2.** The popular name for the act that established this program — the Comprehensive Environmental Response, Compensation, and Liability Act of 1980 (CERCLA). See CERCLA.

superintendent. A person with the power to direct activities; a manager.

superintending control. See CONTROL.

superior, *adj.* (14c) (Of a rank, office, power, etc.) higher; elevated; possessing greater power or authority; entitled to exert authority or command over another <superior estate> <superior force> <superior agent>. — **superior,** *n.*

superior agent. See *high-managerial agent* under AGENT (2).

superior commissioned officer. See OFFICER (2).

superior court. See COURT.

superior fellow servant. See FELLOW SERVANT.

superior force. **1.** See FORCE MAJEURE. **2.** See ACT OF GOD. **3.** See VIS MAJOR.

superior knowledge. See KNOWLEDGE.

superior-knowledge rule. The doctrine that when a property owner knows or should know that a hazardous condition exists on the property, and the condition is not obvious to a person exercising reasonable care, the owner must make the premises reasonably safe or else warn others of the hazardous condition. • An exception to the rule is sometimes allowed for obvious dangers or dangers of which the invitee is aware. Restatement (Second) of Torts § 343A. But the exception is neither automatic nor absolute. See *id.* § 343A(1) & cmt. f. — Also termed *equal-or-superior-knowledge rule.*

superior servant. See *superior fellow servant* under FELLOW SERVANT.

superior-servant doctrine. See FELLOW-SERVANT RULE.

superlien. (1984) A government's lien that is imposed on a property whose condition violates environmental and public-health and public-safety rules and that has priority over all other liens, so that the government can recover public funds spent on cleanup operations. • A statutory lien is superior to all existing liens and all later-filed liens on the same property. Superliens are sometimes granted to a state's environmental-protection agency. Several states — including Arkansas, Connecticut, Massachusetts, New Hampshire, New Jersey, and Tennessee — have enacted statutes creating superliens on property owned by a party responsible for environmental cleanup. See LIEN.

supermajority. See MAJORITY.

supermajority provision. A clause in a corporation's articles of incorporation requiring more than a simple majority of shareholders to vote in favor of a merger or substantial sale of assets.

supernumerary witness. See WITNESS.

superprecedent. See PRECEDENT.

superpriority. *Bankruptcy.* The special priority status granted by the court to a creditor for extending credit to a debtor or trustee that cannot obtain unsecured credit from a willing lender. • This priority may be either an administrative claim outranking other administrative claims or, if certain statutory requirements are met, a security interest in property. 11 USCA § 364(c)(1).

supersede, *vb.* (17c) **1.** To annul, make void, or repeal by taking the place of <the 1996 statute supersedes the 1989 act>. **2.** To invoke or make applicable the right of supersedeas against (an award of damages) <what is the amount of the bond necessary to supersede the judgment against her?>. — **supersession** (for sense 1), *n.*

supersedeas (soo-pər-**seed**-ee-əs), *n.* [Latin "you shall desist"] (14c) **1.** A writ or bond that suspends a judgment creditor's power to levy execution, usu. pending appeal. — Also termed *writ of supersedeas.* **2.** See *supersedeas bond* under BOND (2). Pl. **supersedeases** (soo-pər-**see**-dee-əs-iz).

supersedeas bond. See BOND (2).

superseding cause. See CAUSE (1).

super stare decisis. See STARE DECISIS.

superstitious use. See USE (1).

supervening cause. See *intervening cause* under CAUSE (1).

supervening impossibility. See IMPOSSIBILITY.

supervening negligence. See *subsequent negligence* under NEGLIGENCE.

supervening-negligence doctrine. See LAST-CLEAR-CHANCE DOCTRINE.

supervised visitation. See VISITATION.

supervision, *n.* The act of managing, directing, or overseeing persons or projects. — **supervise,** *vb.* — **supervisory** (soo-pər-**VI**-zə-ree), *adj.*

supervision order. See ORDER (2).

supervisor, *n.* (15c) **1.** One having authority over others; a manager or overseer. • Under the National Labor Relations Act, a supervisor is any individual having authority to hire, transfer, suspend, lay off, recall, promote, discharge, discipline, and handle grievances of other employees, by exercising independent judgment. **2.** The chief administrative officer of a town or county. — **supervisorial** (soo-pər-VI-**zor**-ee-əl), *adj.*

supervisory authority. *Military law.* An officer who, exercising general court-martial jurisdiction, reviews summary and special court-martial trial records after the convening authority has reviewed them.

supervisory control. The control exercised by a higher court over a lower court, as by prohibiting the lower court from acting extrajurisdictionally and by reversing its extrajurisdictional acts. See MANDAMUS.

supine negligence. See *advertent negligence* under NEGLIGENCE.

supplanting limitation. See LIMITATION.

supplemental, *adj.* (17c) Supplying something additional; adding what is lacking <supplemental rules>.

supplemental affidavit. See AFFIDAVIT.

supplemental agreement. See *side agreement* under AGREEMENT.

supplemental bill. See BILL (2).

supplemental bill in the nature of a bill of review. See *bill in the nature of a bill of review* under BILL (2).

supplemental claim. See CLAIM (4).

supplemental complaint. See COMPLAINT.

supplemental declaration. *Patents.* A sworn document, filed after the U.S. Patent and Trademark Office allows a patent's issuance. See SUPPLEMENTAL OATH.

supplemental jurisdiction. See JURISDICTION.

supplemental-needs trust. See TRUST.

supplemental pleading. See PLEADING (1).

supplemental register. *Trademarks.* A roll of trademarks that are ineligible for listing on the Principal Register because they are not distinctive. ● Marks on the supplemental register are not protected by trademark law, except to the extent that the listing may bar the registration of a similar mark. The listing may be required, however, for the mark to be registered in other countries. 15 USCA § 1091. Cf. PRINCIPAL REGISTER. — Also termed *secondary register.*

Supplemental Rules for Certain Maritime and Admiralty Claims. A supplement to the Federal Rules of Civil Procedure, setting out procedures for suits in admiralty and maritime law.

Supplemental Security Income. A welfare or needs-based program providing monthly income to the aged, blind, or disabled. ● It is authorized by the Social Security Act. — Abbr. SSI.

supplemental surety. See SURETY.

supplementary proceeding. See PROCEEDING.

suppletory oath (səp-lə-tor-ee). See OATH.

suppliant (səp-lee-ənt). (15c) One who humbly requests something; specif., the actor in a petition of right.

supplier, *n.* **1.** A person engaged, directly or indirectly, in the business of making a product available to consumers. **2.** A person who gives possession of a chattel for another's use or allows someone else to use or occupy it while it is in the person's possession or control.

supplies, *n.* **1.** Means of provision or relief; stores available for distribution. **2.** In parliamentary proceedings, the annual grant voted on by the House of Commons for maintaining the Crown and various public services.

supply, *n.* The amount of goods produced or available at a given price.

   aggregate supply. The total amount of goods and services generated in an economy during a specific period.

supply curve. A line on a price-output graph showing the relationship between a good's price and the quantity supplied at a given time.

support, *n.* (14c) **1.** Sustenance or maintenance; esp., articles such as food and clothing that allow one to live in the degree of comfort to which one is accustomed. See MAINTENANCE; NECESSARIES. **2.** One or more monetary payments to a current or former family member for the purpose of helping the recipient maintain an acceptable standard of living. — Also termed (in both senses) *reasonable support.* See ALIMONY. Cf. NONSUPPORT; MAINTENANCE (5).

   child support. See CHILD SUPPORT.

   family support. See FAMILY SUPPORT.

   spousal support. See ALIMONY.

3. Basis or foundation. **4.** The bracing of land so that it does not cave in because of another landowner's actions. — **support,** *vb.*

   lateral support. Support by the land that lies next to the land under consideration. — Also termed *easement of natural support.*

   subjacent support. Support by the earth that lies underneath the land under consideration.

support agreement. *Oil & gas.* A contract between people or entities in the oil-and-gas industry to promote exploratory operations. ● Generally, one party agrees to contribute money or property to another if the other will drill a well on leases that it holds and provide the contributing party with information from tests conducted. For the contributing party, a support agreement is a purchase of geological or technological information. For the party receiving the support, the contribution lessens the cost or the risk of drilling operations. — Also termed *contribution agreement.* See DRY-HOLE AGREEMENT; BOTTOM-HOLE AGREEMENT; ACREAGE-CONTRIBUTION AGREEMENT.

support deed. See DEED.

support obligation. (1938) A secondary obligation or letter-of-credit right that supports the payment or performance of an account, chattel paper, general intangible, document, healthcare-insurance receivable, instrument, or investment property. UCC § 9-102(a)(53).

support order. (1948) A court decree requiring a party (esp. one in a divorce or paternity proceeding) to make payments to maintain a child or spouse, including medical, dental, and educational expenses.

foreign support order. An out-of-state support order.

support price. See PRICE.

support trust. See TRUST.

supposition (səp-ə-**zish**-ən), *n.* An assumption that something is true, without proof of its veracity; the act of supposing. — **suppose,** *vb.* — **supposable,** *adj.*

suppress, *vb.* To put a stop to, put down, or prohibit; to prevent (something) from being seen, heard, known, or discussed <the defendant tried to suppress the incriminating evidence>. — **suppression,** *n.* — **suppressible, suppressive,** *adj.*

suppression hearing. See HEARING.

suppression of evidence. (18c) **1.** A trial judge's ruling that evidence offered by a party should be excluded because it was illegally acquired. **2.** The destruction of evidence or the refusal to give evidence at a criminal proceeding. ● This is usu. considered a crime. See OBSTRUCTION OF JUSTICE. **3.** The prosecution's withholding from the defense of evidence that is favorable to the defendant.

suppressio veri (sə-**pres**[**h**]-ee-oh **veer**-ɪ). [Latin] Suppression of the truth; a type of fraud. Cf. SUGGESTIO FALSI.

supra (s[y]oo-prə). [Latin "above"] (15c) Earlier in this text; used as a citational signal to refer to a previously cited authority. Cf. INFRA.

supralegal, *adj.* Above or beyond the law <a supralegal sovereign>.

supranational, *adj.* Free of the political limitations of nations.

supra protest. (Of a debt) under protest. See PROTEST (3).

supra riparian (**soo**-prə ri-**pair**-ee-ən *or* rɪ-). (1857) Upper riparian; higher up the stream. ● This phrase describes the estate, rights, and duties of a riparian owner whose land is situated nearer the source of a stream than the land it is compared to.

supremacy. (16c) The position of having the superior or greatest power or authority.

Supremacy Clause. (1940) The clause in Article VI of the U.S. Constitution declaring that the Constitution, all laws made in furtherance of the Constitution, and all treaties made under the authority of the United States are the "supreme law of the land" and enjoy legal superiority over any conflicting provision of a state constitution or law. See PREEMPTION.

supremacy of law. See RULE OF LAW (2).

supreme, *adj.* (16c) (Of a court, power, right, etc.) highest; superior to all others.

supreme court. (17c) **1.** (*cap.*) SUPREME COURT OF THE UNITED STATES. **2.** An appellate court existing in most states, usu. as the court of last resort. **3.** In New York, a court of general jurisdiction with trial and appellate divisions. ● The Court of Appeals is the court of last resort in New York. **4.** SUPREME COURT OF JUDICATURE. — Abbr. S.C.; S.Ct.; Sup. Ct.

Supreme Court of Appeals. The highest court in West Virginia.

Supreme Court of Judicature. The highest court in England and Wales, consisting of the High Court of Justice, the Court of Appeal, and the Crown Court. ● The Supreme Court was created under the Judicature Act of 1873 that consolidated the existing superior courts, including the High Court of Chancery, the court of Queen's Bench, the court of Exchequer, the High Court of Admiralty, the court of Probate, and the London court of Bankruptcy. — Sometimes shortened to *Supreme Court.*

Supreme Court of the United States. The court of last resort in the federal system, whose members are appointed by the President and approved by the Senate. ● The Court was established in 1789 by Article III of the U.S. Constitution, which vests the Court with the "judicial power of the United States." — Often shortened to *Supreme Court.* — Also termed *United States Supreme Court.*

Supreme Judicial Court. See COURT.

supreme law of the land. (18c) **1.** The U.S. Constitution. **2.** Acts of Congress made in accordance with the U.S. Constitution. **3.** U.S. treaties. See SUPREMACY CLAUSE.

supreme legislation. See LEGISLATION.

supreme power. See *sovereign political power* under POLITICAL POWER.

sur (sər). [Law French] *Hist.* Upon. ● This term appears in various phrases, such as *sur cognizance de droit* ("upon acknowledgment of right").

surcharge, *n.* **1.** An additional tax, charge, or cost, usu. one that is excessive. **2.** An additional load or burden. **3.** A second or further mortgage. **4.** The omission of a proper credit on an account. **5.** The amount that a court may charge a fiduciary that has breached its duty. **6.** An overprint on a stamp, esp. one that changes its face value. **7.** The overstocking of an area with animals. — **surcharge,** *vb.*

surcharge, *vb.* (15c) **1.** To impose an additional (usu. excessive) tax, charge, or cost. **2.** To impose an additional load or burden. **3.** (Of a court) to impose a fine on a fiduciary for breach of duty. **4.** To overstock (an area) with animals.

second surcharge. To overstock (a common) a second time for which a writ of second surcharge was issued.

surcharge and falsify. To scrutinize particular items in an account to show items that were not credited as required (to surcharge) and to prove that certain items were wrongly inserted (to falsify). • The courts of chancery usu. granted plaintiffs the opportunity to surcharge and falsify accounts that the defendant alleged to be settled.

surety (**shuur**[-ə]-tee). (14c) **1.** A person who is primarily liable for paying another's debt or performing another's obligation. • Although a surety is similar to an insurer, one important difference is that a surety often receives no compensation for assuming liability. A surety differs from a guarantor, who is liable to the creditor only if the debtor does not meet the duties owed to the creditor; the surety is directly liable. Cf. GUARANTOR.

accommodation surety. See *voluntary surety.*

compensated surety. A surety who is paid for becoming obliged to the creditor; esp., one that engages in the business of executing suretyship contracts in exchange for premiums, which are determined by an actuarial computation of risks. • A bonding company is a typical example of a compensated surety. — Also termed *commercial surety.*

cosurety. See COSURETY.

gratuitous surety. A surety who is not compensated for becoming obliged to the creditor. • Perhaps the most common example is the parent who signs as a surety for a child.

subsurety. See SUBSURETY.

supplemental surety. A surety for a surety.

surety of the peace. *Hist.* A surety responsible for ensuring that a person will not commit a future offense. • It is required of one against whom there are probable grounds to suspect future misbehavior.

voluntary surety. A surety who receives no consideration for the promise to act as a surety. — Also termed *accommodation surety.*

2. A formal assurance; esp., a pledge, bond, guarantee, or security given for the fulfillment of an undertaking.

surety and fidelity insurance. See *fidelity insurance* under INSURANCE.

surety bond. See PERFORMANCE BOND.

surety company. See COMPANY.

surety insurance. See *guaranty insurance* under INSURANCE.

suretyship. 1. The legal relation that arises when one party assumes liability for a debt, default, or other failing of a second party. • The liability of both parties begins simultaneously. In other words, under a contract of suretyship, a surety becomes a party to the principal obligation. **2.** The lending of credit to aid a principal who does not have sufficient credit. • The purpose is to guard

against loss if the principal debtor were to default. **3.** The position or status of a surety.

involuntary suretyship. A suretyship that arises incidentally, when the chief object of the contract is to accomplish some other purpose.

personal suretyship. A suretyship in which the surety is answerable in damages.

real suretyship. A suretyship in which specified property can be taken, but the surety is not answerable in damages.

suretyship by operation of law. A suretyship that the law creates when a third party promises a debtor to assume and pay the debt that the debtor owes to a creditor.

voluntary suretyship. A suretyship in which the chief object of the contract is to make one party a surety.

surface. 1. The top layer of something, esp. of land. **2.** *Mining law.* An entire portion of land, including mineral deposits, except those specifically reserved. • The meaning of the term varies, esp. when used in legal instruments, depending on the language used, the intention of the parties, the business involved, and the nature and circumstances of the transaction. **3.** *Mining law.* The part of the geologic section lying over the minerals in question.

surface casing. See CASING.

surface-damage clause. *Oil & gas.* A lease provision requiring the lessee to pay the lessor or the surface-interest owner for all or for a specified kind or degree of damage to the surface that results from oil-and-gas operations. — Also termed *location-damage clause; damages clause.*

surface interest. *Oil & gas.* Every right in real property other than the mineral interest. • The surface-interest owner has the right to the surface subject to the right of the mineral-interest owner to use the surface. The surface-interest owner is entitled to all whatever nonmineral substances are found in or under the soil. — Also termed *surface right.* Cf. MINERAL INTEREST; SUBSURFACE INTEREST.

surface issue. See ISSUE (1).

Surface Transportation Board. A unit in the U.S. Department of Transportation responsible for the economic regulation of interstate surface transportation, primarily railroads. • Its jurisdiction includes railroad-rate and -service issues, railroad-company mergers and related labor matters; certain truck and ocean shipping rates; certain intercity bus-company structures; and certain pipeline matters not regulated by the Federal Energy Regulatory Commission. — Abbr. STB.

surface water. See WATER.

Surgeon General. (18c) **1.** The chief medical officer of the U.S. Public Health Service or of a state public-health agency. **2.** The chief officer of the medical departments in the armed forces. — Abbr. SG.

surmise (sər-**mIz**), *n.* (18c) **1.** An idea based on weak evidence; conjecture. **2.** *Hist.* A suggestion, esp. to a court. **3.** *Hist. Eccles. law.* An allegation in the complaint. • A collateral surmise is a surmise of a fact not contained in the libel. See LIBEL (3).

surname. See NAME.

surplice fees (sər-plis **feez**). *Eccles. law.* Fees paid to clergy for performing occasional duties, such as marriages, funerals, and baptisms.

surplus. **1.** The remainder of a thing; the residue or excess. **2.** The excess of receipts over disbursements. **3.** Funds that remain after a partnership has been dissolved and all its debts paid. **4.** A corporation's net worth, beyond the par value of capital stock. — Also termed *overplus.*

accumulated surplus. Earnings in excess of a corporation's capital and liabilities.

acquired surplus. The surplus gained by the purchase of another business.

actuarial surplus. See ACTUARIAL SURPLUS.

appreciation surplus. See *revaluation surplus.*

appropriated surplus. **1.** The portion of surplus earmarked for a specific purpose. — Also termed *reserved surplus.* **2.** See *appropriated retained earnings* under EARNINGS.

capital surplus. **1.** All surplus (such as paid-in surplus or donated surplus) not arising from the accumulation of profits; a company's surplus other than earned surplus, usu. created by financial reorganization or gifts. **2.** See *paid-in surplus.*

donated surplus. **1.** Assets (such as stock) contributed to a corporation. **2.** The increase in the shareholders' equity account resulting from such a contribution.

earned surplus. See *retained earnings* under EARNINGS.

initial surplus. The surplus that appears on the financial statement at the beginning of an accounting period, but that does not reflect the operations for the statement's period.

paid-in surplus. The surplus gained by the sale, exchange, or issuance of capital stock at a price above par value. — Also termed *capital surplus; premium on capital stock.*

reserved surplus. See *appropriated surplus* (1).

restricted surplus. A surplus with a limited or restricted use; esp., the portion of retained earnings that cannot be distributed as dividends. • The restriction is usu. due to preferred dividends in arrears, a covenant in a loan agreement, or some decision of the board of directors. See *retained earnings* under EARNINGS.

revaluation surplus. Surplus that is gained when assets are reappraised at a higher value. — Also termed *appreciation surplus.*

trade surplus. The excess of merchandise exports over merchandise imports during a specific period. Cf. *trade deficit* under DEFICIT.

unearned surplus. *Corporations.* The total of amounts assigned to shares in excess of stated capital, surplus arising from a revaluation of assets above cost, and contributions other than for shares, whether from shareholders or others.

surplusage (sər-**pləs**-ij). (15c) **1.** Redundant words in a statute or legal instrument; language that does not add meaning <the court must give effect to every word, reading nothing as mere surplusage>. **2.** Extraneous matter in a pleading <allegations that are irrelevant to the case will be treated as surplusage>.

surplus earnings. See EARNINGS.

surplus-lines insurance. See INSURANCE.

surplus profit. See PROFIT (1).

surplus revenue. See *appropriated retained earnings* under EARNINGS.

surplus water. See WATER.

surprise. (15c) An occurrence for which there is no adequate warning or that affects someone in an unexpected way. • In a trial, the procedural rules are designed to limit surprise — or trial by ambush — as much as possible. For example, the parties in a civil case are permitted to conduct discovery, to determine the essential facts of the case and the identities of possible witnesses, and to inspect relevant documents. At trial, if a party calls a witness who has not been previously identified, the witness's testimony may be excluded if it would unfairly surprise and prejudice the other party. And if a party has diligently prepared the case and is nevertheless taken by surprise on a material point at trial, that fact can sometimes be grounds for a new trial or for relief from the judgment under Rules 59 and 60 of the Federal Rules of Civil Procedure.

surrebuttal (sər-ri-**bət**-əl). (1853) The response to the opposing party's rebuttal in a trial or other proceeding; a rebuttal to a rebuttal <called two extra witnesses in surrebuttal>.

surrebutter (sər-ri-**bət**-ər). *Common-law pleading.* (17c) The plaintiff's answer of fact to the defendant's rebutter.

surrejoinder (sər-ri-**joyn**-dər). *Common-law pleading.* (16c) The plaintiff's answer to the defendant's rejoinder. See REPLICATION.

surrender, *n.* (15c) **1.** The act of yielding to another's power or control. **2.** The giving up of a right or claim; RELEASE (1). **3.** The return of an estate to the person who has a reversion or remainder, so as to merge the estate into a larger estate. Cf. MERGER (4). **4.** *Commercial law.* The delivery of an instrument so that the delivery releases the deliverer from all liability. **5.** A tenant's relinquishment of possession before the lease has expired, allowing the landlord to take possession and treat the lease as terminated. — Also termed (in sense 5) *surrender of term.* — **surrender,** *vb.*

surrender by bail. (18c) A surety's delivery of a prisoner, who had been released on bail, into custody.

surrender by operation of law. (1836) An act that is an equivalent to an agreement by a tenant to abandon property and the landlord to resume possession, as when the parties perform an act so inconsistent with the landlord–tenant relationship that surrender is presumed, or when a tenant performs some act that would not be valid if the estate continued to exist.

surrender clause. *Oil & gas.* A provision commonly found in oil-and-gas leases authorizing a lessee to release its rights to all or any portion of the leased property at any time and to be relieved of further obligations on the acreage surrendered.

surrenderee. One to whom a surrender is made. See SURRENDER.

surrenderer. See SURRENDEROR.

surrender of a criminal. An officer's delivery of a prisoner to the authorities in the appropriate jurisdiction. See EXTRADITION; RENDITION.

surrender of a preference. *Bankruptcy.* The yielding of a voidable conveyance, transfer, assignment, or encumbrance by a creditor to the trustee as a condition of allowing the creditor's claim.

surrender of charter. *Corporations.* The dissolution of a corporation by a formal yielding of its charter to the state under which it was created and the subsequent acceptance of that charter by the state.

surrender of term. See SURRENDER (5).

surrenderor. One who surrenders; esp., one who yields up a copyhold estate for conveyance. — Also spelled *surrenderer.* See COPYHOLD.

surrender value. See *cash surrender value* under VALUE (2).

surreply. A movant's second supplemental response to another party's opposition to a motion. — Sometimes written *sur-reply.*

surreptitious (sər-əp-**tish**-əs), *adj.* (15c) (Of conduct) unauthorized and clandestine; stealthily and usu. fraudulently done <surreptitious interception of electronic communications is prohibited under wiretapping laws>.

surreptitious-entry search warrant. See *covert-entry search warrant* under SEARCH WARRANT.

surreptitious-entry warrant. See WARRANT (1).

surrogacy. 1. The act of performing some function in the place of someone else. **2.** The process of carrying and delivering a child for another person.

   gestational surrogacy. A pregnancy in which one woman (the genetic mother) provides the egg, which is fertilized, and another woman (the surrogate mother) carries the fetus and gives birth to the child.

   traditional surrogacy. A pregnancy in which a woman provides her own egg, which is fertilized by artificial insemination, and carries the fetus and gives birth to a child for another person.

surrogacy contract. See SURROGATE-PARENTING AGREEMENT.

surrogate (sər-ə-git), *n.* (17c) **1.** A substitute; esp., a person appointed to act in the place of another <in his absence, Sam's wife acted as a surrogate>. See SURROGACY; *surrogate mother* under MOTHER. **2.** A probate judge <the surrogate held that the will was valid>. See *probate judge* under JUDGE. **3.** One who acts in place of another. — **surrogate,** *adj.* — **surrogacy** (sər-ə-gə-see), **surrogateship,** *n.*

surrogate carrier. See *surrogate mother* (1) under MOTHER.

surrogate court. See *probate court* under COURT.

surrogate mother. See MOTHER.

surrogate parent. 1. See PARENT. **2.** See *surrogate mother* under MOTHER.

surrogate-parenting agreement. (1985) A contract between a woman and typically an infertile couple under which the woman provides her uterus to carry an embryo throughout pregnancy; esp., an agreement between a person (the intentional parent) and a woman (the surrogate mother) providing that the surrogate mother will (1) bear a child for the intentional parent, and (2) relinquish any and all rights to the child. ● If the surrogate mother is married, her husband must also consent to the terms of the surrogacy contract. The agreement usu. provides that the woman will relinquish to the couple any parental rights she may have upon the birth of the child. Complex issues arise concerning who is the parent of the resulting child: the genetic donor of egg or sperm, a spouse of either donor, the surrogate, or the person intending to care for the resulting child? American jurisdictions are split on the interpretation and enforceability of these contracts. — Also termed *surrogacy contract.* See *surrogate mother* under MOTHER; *intended child* under CHILD; *intentional parent* under PARENT.

surrogate's court. See *probate court* under COURT.

surrounding circumstances. (1828) The facts underlying an act, injury, or transaction — usu. one at issue in a legal proceeding.

surtax. See TAX.

surtax exemption. (18c) **1.** An exclusion of an item from a surtax. **2.** An item or an amount not subject to a surtax. See *surtax* under TAX.

surveillance (sər-**vay**-ləns), *n.* (1802) Close observation or listening of a person or place in the hope of gathering evidence. — **surveil** (sər-**vayl**), *vb.*

survey, *n.* (16c) **1.** A general consideration of something; appraisal <a survey of the situation>. **2.** The measuring of a tract of land and its boundaries and contents; a map indicating the results of such measurements <the lender requires a survey of the property before it will issue a loan>.

　government survey. A survey made by a governmental entity of tracts of land (as of townships and sections and quarter-sections of land). — Also termed (when conducted by the federal government) *congressional survey.*

　inclusive survey. A survey that includes within the described boundaries land that is owned or claimed by others and excluded from the survey's computed area.

　topographical survey. A survey that determines a property's elevation above sea level.

3. A governmental department that carries out such measurements <please obtain the boundaries from survey>. **4.** A poll or questionnaire, esp. one examining popular opinion <the radio station took a survey of the concert audience>. **5.** *Maritime law.* A written assessment of the current condition of a vessel or cargo. — Also termed (in sense 5) *survey of a vessel.* — **survey,** *vb.*

survey of a vessel. See SURVEY (5).

surveyor (sər-**vay**-ər), *n.* One who surveys land and buildings. — **surveyorship,** *n.*

surveyor of the port. *Hist.* A U.S. customs revenue officer appointed for each principal port of entry to oversee the inspection and valuation of imports. ● The office was abolished in 1953.

survival action. (1938) A lawsuit brought on behalf of a decedent's estate for injuries or damages incurred by the decedent immediately before dying. ● A survival action derives from the claim that a decedent would have had — such as for pain and suffering — if he or she had survived. In contrast is a claim that the beneficiaries may have in a wrongful-death action, such as for loss of consortium or loss of support from the decedent. Cf. WRONGFUL-DEATH ACTION.

survival clause. *Wills & estates.* A testamentary provision conditioning a bequest on a beneficiary's living for a specified period, often 60 days, after the testator's death. ● If the beneficiary dies within the stated period, the testamentary gift usu. accrues to the residuary estate. — Also termed *survivorship clause.* Cf. SIMULTANEOUS-DEATH CLAUSE.

survival statute. (1892) A law that modifies the common law by allowing certain actions to continue in favor of a personal representative after the death of the party who could have originally brought the action; esp., a law that provides for the estate's recovery of damages incurred by the decedent immediately before death. Cf. DEATH STATUTE.

survivance. The right of succession (as to an office or to an estate) of a survivor named before the death of the incumbent or the holder.

surviving, *adj.* (16c) Remaining alive; living beyond the happening of an event so as to entitle one to a distribution of property or income <surviving spouse>. See SURVIVAL ACTION.

surviving corporation. See CORPORATION.

surviving partner. See PARTNER.

surviving spouse. See SPOUSE.

survivor. (15c) **1.** One who outlives another. **2.** A trustee who administers a trust after the cotrustee has been removed, has refused to act, or has died.

survivor-income benefit plan. See EMPLOYEE BENEFIT PLAN.

survivorship. (17c) **1.** The state or condition of being the one person out of two or more who remains alive after the others die. **2.** The right of a surviving party having a joint interest with others in an estate to take the whole. See RIGHT OF SURVIVORSHIP.

survivorship annuity. See ANNUITY.

survivorship clause. See SURVIVAL CLAUSE.

survivorship policy. See INSURANCE POLICY.

susceptibility. See SUBJECTION (3).

suspect, *n.* (14c) A person believed to have committed a crime or offense.

suspect, *vb.* **1.** To consider (something) to be probable. **2.** To consider (something) possible. **3.** To consider (a person) as having probably committed wrongdoing, but without certain truth.

　reasonably suspect. **1.** To consider (something) to be probable under circumstances in which a reasonable person would be led to that conclusion. **2.** To consider (someone) as having probably committed wrongdoing under circumstances in which a reasonable person would be led to that conclusion.

suspect class. (1952) A group identified or defined in a suspect classification.

suspect classification. (1949) *Constitutional law.* A statutory classification based on race, national origin, or alienage, and thereby subject to strict scrutiny under equal-protection analysis. ● Examples of laws creating suspect classifications are those permitting only U.S. citizens to receive welfare benefits and setting quotas for the government's hiring of minority contractors. See STRICT SCRUTINY. Cf. FUNDAMENTAL RIGHT.

> **quasi-suspect classification.** A statutory classification based on gender or legitimacy, and therefore subject to intermediate scrutiny under equal-protection analysis. ● Examples of laws creating a quasi-suspect classification are those permitting alimony for women only and providing for an all-male draft. See INTERMEDIATE SCRUTINY.

suspend, *vb.* (14c) **1.** To interrupt; postpone; defer <the fire alarm suspended the prosecutor's opening statement>. **2.** To temporarily keep (a person) from performing a function, occupying an office, holding a job, or exercising a right or privilege <the attorney's law license was suspended for violating the Model Rules of Professional Conduct>.

> **suspend the rules.** *Parliamentary law.* To pass a motion that overrides an agenda or other procedural rule, for a limited time and purpose, so that the deliberative assembly may take some otherwise obstructed action.

suspended sentence. See SENTENCE.

suspended trading. See TRADING HALT.

suspense. (15c) The state or condition of being suspended; temporary cessation <a suspense of judgment>.

suspense account. See ACCOUNT.

suspense reserve. See *appropriated retained earnings* under EARNINGS.

suspension. (15c) **1.** The act of temporarily delaying, interrupting, or terminating something <suspension of business operations> <suspension of a statute>. **2.** The state of such delay, interruption, or termination <corporate transfers were not allowed because of the suspension of business>. **3.** The temporary deprivation of a person's powers or privileges, esp. of office or profession; esp., a fairly stringent level of lawyer discipline that prohibits the lawyer from practicing law for a specified period, usu. from several months to several years <suspension of the bar license>. ● Suspension may entail requiring the lawyer to pass a legal-ethics bar examination, or to take one or more ethics courses as continuing legal education, before being readmitted to active practice. **4.** The temporary withdrawal from employment, as distinguished from permanent severance <suspension from teaching without pay>. **5.** *Eccles.*

law. An ecclesiastical censure that can be temporary or permanent, and partial or complete. See DEPRIVATION. **6.** *Scots law.* The process of staying a judgment pending an appeal to the Supreme Court.

suspension of arms. See TRUCE.

suspension of judgment. See STAY.

suspension of trading. The temporary cessation of all trading of a particular stock on a stock exchange because of some abnormal market condition.

suspensive appeal. See APPEAL.

suspensive condition. See CONDITION (2).

suspensive veto. See *suspensory veto* under VETO.

suspensory veto. See VETO.

suspicion. (14c) The apprehension or imagination of the existence of something wrong based only on inconclusive or slight evidence, or possibly even no evidence.

> **reasonable suspicion.** (18c) A particularized and objective basis, supported by specific and articulable facts, for suspecting a person of criminal activity. ● A police officer must have a reasonable suspicion to stop a person in a public place. See STOP AND FRISK. Cf. PROBABLE CAUSE.

suspicious-activity report. (1996) A form that, as of 1996, a financial institution must complete and submit to federal regulatory authorities if it suspects that a federal crime has occurred in the course of a monetary transaction. ● This form superseded two earlier forms, the criminal-referral form and the suspicious-transaction report. — Abbr. SAR.

suspicious character. (18c) In some states, a person who is strongly suspected or known to be a habitual criminal and therefore may be arrested or required to give security for good behavior.

suspicious-transaction report. (1993) A checkbox on IRS Form 4789 formerly (1990–1995) requiring banks and other financial institutions to report transactions that might be relevant to a violation of the Bank Secrecy Act or its regulations or that might suggest money-laundering or tax evasion. ● This checkbox, like the criminal-referral form, has since been superseded by the suspicious-activity report. — Abbr. STR.

sustain, *vb.* (13c) **1.** To support or maintain, esp. over a long period <enough oxygen to sustain life>. **2.** To nourish and encourage; lend strength to <she helped sustain the criminal enterprise>. **3.** To undergo; suffer <Charles sustained third-degree burns>. **4.** (Of a court) to uphold or rule in favor of <objection sustained>. **5.** To substantiate or corroborate <several witnesses sustained Ms. Sipes's allegation>. **6.** To persist in making (an effort) over a long period <he sustained his vow of

silence for the last 16 years of his life>. — **sustainment, sustentation,** *n.* — **sustainable,** *adj.*

suzerain (**soo**-zə-rin *or* -rayn), *n.* [Law French] **1.** *Hist.* A Crown tenant; a tenant *in capite* holding an estate immediately of the Crown. **2.** *Int'l law.* A nation that exercises control over another nation's foreign relations. — Also spelled *suzereign.*

suzerainty (**soo**-zə-rin-tee *or* -rayn-tee). **1.** *Hist.* The power of a feudal overlord to whom fealty is due. See FEALTY. **2.** *Int'l law.* The dominion of a nation that controls the foreign relations of another nation but allows it autonomy in its domestic affairs.

suzereign. See SUZERAIN.

S.W. *abbr.* SOUTH WESTERN REPORTER.

swamp and overflowed land. See LAND.

swap, *n. Commercial law.* **1.** An exchange of one security for another. **2.** A financial transaction between two parties, usu. involving an intermediary or dealer, in which payments or rates are exchanged over a specified period and according to specified conditions.

    currency swap. An agreement to swap specified payment obligations denominated in one currency for specified payment obligations denominated in a different currency.

    stock swap. In a corporate reorganization, an exchange of one corporation's stock for another corporation's stock. — Also termed *stock-for-stock exchange.*

swatting, *n. Slang.* The act of falsely telephoning a report of a serious crime or emergency in progress in order to provoke a response from a law-enforcement agency, esp. the dispatch of a SWAT (Special Weapons and Tactics) team. ● Swatting schemes are often elaborate, involving the use of electronic tools to mask the caller's true identity and location, such as voice-changing devices, fake caller-IDs, and the like. — **swatter,** *n.*

swear, *vb.* (bef. 12c) **1.** To administer an oath to (a person). **2.** To take an oath. **3.** To use obscene or profane language.

swearing behind. *Patents.* A patent applicant's showing that an invention was conceived of or reduced to practice before the effective date of a prior-art reference cited by a patent examiner as grounds for rejecting an application. 37 CFR § 1.131. — Also termed *swearing behind the reference.* See ANTEDATING OF A PRIOR-ART REFERENCE. — **swear behind,** *vb.*

swearing contest. See SWEARING MATCH.

swearing-in, *n.* (1900) The administration of an oath to a person who is taking office or testifying in a legal proceeding. See OATH.

swearing match. (1907) A dispute in which determining a vital fact involves the credibility choice between one witness's word and another's — the two being irreconcilably in conflict and there being no other evidence. ● In such a dispute, the fact-finder is generally thought to believe the more reputable witness, such as a police officer over a convicted drug-dealer. — Also termed *swearing contest; oath against an oath.*

swear out, *vb.* (1850) To obtain the issue of (an arrest warrant) by making a charge under oath <Franklin swore out a complaint against Sutton>.

sweat equity. (1966) Financial equity created in property by the owner's labor in improving the property <the lender required the homeowner to put 300 hours of sweat equity into the property>.

sweating. (1824) *Criminal procedure.* The illegal interrogation of a prisoner by use of threats or similar means to extort information.

sweat-of-the-brow doctrine. *Copyright.* The now-discarded principle that copyrights can protect the labor and expense that went into a work, rather than the work's originality. ● The Supreme Court rejected the sweat-of-the-brow doctrine in *Feist Pubs., Inc. v. Rural Tel. Servs. Co.,* 499 U.S. 340, 111 S.Ct. 1282 (1991). Cf. SWEATWORK.

sweatshop. (1890) *Slang.* A business where the employees are overworked and underpaid in extreme conditions; esp., in lawyer parlance, a law firm that requires associates to work so hard that they barely (if at all) maintain a family or social life — though the firm may, in return, pay higher salaries.

sweatwork. *Slang.* A compilation, esp. a searchable computer database, that does not qualify for U.S. copyright protection because the underlying facts are not copyrightable and the compilation is not a nontrivial arrangement. ● New forms of intellectual-property laws are aimed at protecting the "sweat-of-the-brow" investment that goes into compiling databases. Cf. SWEAT-OF- THE-BROW DOCTRINE.

sweeping, *adj.* **1.** Comprehensive in scope <a sweeping objection><sweeping legislation>. **2.** Overwhelming <sweeping voter turnout>.

Sweeping Clause. See NECESSARY AND PROPER CLAUSE.

sweepstakes. 1. A race (esp. a horse race) in which the winner's prize is the sum of the stakes contributed by the various competitors. **2.** A contest, often for promotional purposes, that awards prizes based on the random selection of entries. ● State and federal laws prohibit conducting a sweepstakes as a scheme to obtain money or property through the mail by false representations. 39 USCA § 3005.

sweetener. 1. An inducement offered to a brokerage firm to enter into an underwriting arrangement with an issuer. **2.** A special stock feature (such as convertibility) that enhances the stock's marketability.

sweetheart deal. A collusive agreement; esp., a collective-bargaining agreement made as a result of collusion between an employer and a union representative, usu. allowing the employer to pay lower wages in exchange for payoffs to the union representative.

swell, *n.* **1.** An expansion in the bulk of something <a swell resulting from defective canning procedures>. **2.** A gradual rise of something <a swell of damages>. **3.** A large, unbroken wave; the collective waves, particularly following a storm <a rough swell caused the shipwreck>.

swift witness. See *zealous witness* under WITNESS.

swindle, *vb.* (18c) To cheat (a person) out of property <Johnson swindled Norton out of his entire savings> <Johnson swindled Norton's entire savings out of him>. — **swindle,** *n.* — **swindling,** *n.*

swindler. A person who willfully defrauds or cheats another.

swinging-door chad. See CHAD.

swing loan. See *bridge loan* under LOAN.

swing vote. (1962) The vote that determines an issue when all other voting parties, such as appellate judges, are evenly split.

swipe, *vb.* **1.** To strike or try to strike with a swinging blow <the cat swiped its claws across my hand>. **2.** To steal <the thief swiped the ring out of the display case>. **3.** To pass a card with a magnetic stripe through a machine that reads the stripe <I swiped my credit card through the pay phone's reader and made my call>. — Sometimes termed (in sense 3) *wipe.*

switching. In mutual funds, the practice of selling shares in one fund to buy shares in another.

sworn statement. See STATEMENT.

SYD. *abbr.* Sum of the years' digits. See *sum-of-the-years'-digits depreciation method* under DEPRECIATION METHOD.

SYD method. See *sum-of-the-year's-digits depreciation method* under DEPRECIATION METHOD.

syllabus (**sil**-ə-bəs). **1.** An abstract or outline of a topic or course of study. **2.** A case summary appearing before the printed judicial opinion in a law report, briefly reciting the facts and the holding of the case. ● The syllabus is ordinarily not part of the court's official opinion. — Sometimes termed *headnote.* Cf. HEADNOTE. Pl. **syllabuses, syllabi** (**sil**-ə-bɪ).

symbiotic-relationship test. (1973) The standard by which a private person may be considered a state actor — and may be liable for violating someone's constitutional rights — if the relationship between the private person and the government is so close that they can fairly be said to be acting jointly. ● Private acts by a private person do not generally create liability for violating someone's constitutional rights. But if a private person violates someone's constitutional rights while engaging in state action, the private person, and possibly the government, can be held liable. State action may be shown by proving that the private person and the state have a mutually dependent (symbiotic) relationship. For example, a restaurant in a public parking garage was held to have engaged in discriminatory state action by refusing to serve African-Americans. *Burton v. Wilmington Parking Authority*, 365 U.S. 715, 81 S.Ct. 856 (1961). There, the Court found a symbiotic relationship because the restaurant relied on the garage for its existence and significantly contributed to the municipal parking authority's ability to maintain the garage. But the symbiotic-relationship test is strictly construed. For example, the fact that an entity receives financial support from — or is heavily regulated by — the government is probably insufficient to show a symbiotic relationship. Thus, although a state had granted a partial monopoly to a public utility, the Court refused to find a symbiotic relationship between them. *Jackson v. Metropolitan Edison Co.*, 419 U.S. 345, 95 S.Ct. 449 (1974). See JOINT-PARTICIPATION TEST. Cf. STATE-COMPULSION TEST; NEXUS TEST.

symbolaeography (sim-bə-lee-**og**-rə-fee). The art of drafting legal instruments.

symbolic, *adj.* (Of a signature) consisting of a symbol or mark. Cf. ONOMASTIC (2); HOLOGRAPH.

symbolic delivery. See DELIVERY.

symbolic speech. See SPEECH.

sympathy strike. See STRIKE.

synallagmatic contract. See CONTRACT.

synchronization license. See LICENSE.

syndic (**sin**-dik), *n.* [French "governmental representative"] **1.** An agent (esp. of a government or corporation) appointed to transact business for others. **2.** *Civil law.* A bankruptcy trustee.

syndicalism (**sin**-di-kə-liz-əm), *n.* A direct plan or practice implemented by trade-union workers seeking to control the means of production and distribution, esp. by using a general strike. — **syndicalist,** *n.*

   criminal syndicalism. Any doctrine that advocates or teaches the use of illegal methods to change industrial or political control.

syndicate (**sin**-di-kit), *n.* (17c) A group organized for a common purpose; esp., an association formed to promote a common interest, carry out a particular business transaction, or (in a negative sense) organize criminal enterprises. See ORGANIZED CRIME. — **syndicate** (sin-di-kayt), *vb.* — **syndication** (sin-di-**kay**-shən), *n.* — **syndicator** (**sin**-di-kay-tər), *n.*

buying syndicate. A group of investment bankers who share the risk in underwriting a securities issue.

syndicate book. *Securities.* A list of investors who have expressed an interest in purchasing shares in a forthcoming public offering. ● The lead managing underwriter of the offering compiles and maintains the list during the offering.

syndicating. 1. The act or process of forming a syndicate. 2. The gathering of materials for newspaper publication from various writers and distribution of the materials at regular intervals to newspapers throughout the country for publication on the same day.

synergism (**sin**-ər-jiz-əm), *n. Patents.* 1. A combination of known elements or functions that create a result greater than the sum of the individual elements or functions. ● Demonstrating that synergism exists is sometimes useful in proving nonobviousness. The U.S. Supreme Court held that synergism was a requirement for a combination patent in *Great Atl. & Pac. Tea Co. v. Supermarket Equip. Corp.*, 340 U.S. 147 (1950). But that holding was overturned by the Patent Act of 1952. 35 USCA § 103. 2. A patentable device that produces a new or different function or an unusual or surprising consequence. — Also termed *synergy; synergistic result.* — **synergistic** (sin-ər-**jis**-tik), **synergetic** (sin-ər-**jet**-ik), *adj.*

synod (**sin**-əd). *Eccles. law.* An ecclesiastical council lawfully assembled to determine church matters; esp., a meeting of several adjoining presbyteries in the Presbyterian church.

diocesan synod (dy-**os**-ə-sən). A synod composed of clergy from one diocese.

general synod. A synod composed of bishops from all nations. — Also termed *universal synod.*

national synod. A synod composed of clergy from a single nation.

provincial synod. A synod composed of clergy from a single province. — Also termed *convocation.*

synodal (**sin**-ə-dəl), *n.* 1. A collection of ordinances of diocesan synods. 2. A tribute of money given by clergy to a bishop at the Easter visitation.

synodsman. See SIDESMAN.

synopsis (si-**nop**-sis), *n.* (17c) A brief or partial survey; a summary or outline; HEADNOTE. — **synopsize** (si-**nop**-siz), *vb.*

synthetic lease. See LEASE.

synthetic rule. See QUANTITATIVE RULE.

systematic jurisprudence. See *expository jurisprudence* under JURISPRUDENCE.

systematic violation. (1980) *Civil-rights law.* An employer's policy or procedure that discriminates against an employee. ● Such a policy or procedure will usu. be considered a continuing violation. So an employee's claim of unlawful discrimination will not be barred as untimely as long as some discriminatory effect of the policy or procedure occurs within the limitations period (e.g., 300 days for a Title VII claim). Cf. SERIAL VIOLATION.

T

T. *Hist.* **1.** A letter branded on the base of the thumb of a person who claimed the benefit of clergy to prevent the person from claiming it again. • This practice was formally abolished by the Criminal Statutes (England) Repeal Act of 1827. **2.** In Pennsylvania, a letter sewn onto the left sleeve of a convicted thief. • This letter — required by a 1698 statute — had to be at least four inches high and of a different color from the rest of the garment.

TAB. *abbr.* TAX-ANTICIPATION BILL.

table, *n.* **1.** A synopsized representation, esp. in columnar form, of the particulars of a subject, usu. to present diverse items in a way that can be more easily understood. • Examples include actuarial tables, genealogical tables (which show the names and relationships of all the persons constituting a family), and interest tables. **2.** A formulation of laws inscribed on tablets, such as the Twelve Tables of Roman law. See TWELVE TABLES. **3.** *Parliamentary law.* The secretary's desk.

table, *vb.* (1849) *Parliamentary law.* (Of a deliberative assembly) to set aside the pending business until the assembly votes to resume its consideration. • A matter that has been tabled may be brought up again by a vote of the assembly. — Also termed *lay on the table; postpone temporarily.* **2.** *English law.* To put forward (a bill, proposal, resolution, etc.) for consideration and discussion by a legislative or deliberative assembly.

tableau of distribution. *Civil law.* A list of creditors of an estate, stating what each is entitled to. See *judgment homologating the tableau* under JUDGMENT.

table of authorities. See INDEX OF AUTHORITIES.

table of cases. (18c) **1.** An alphabetical list of the cases cited in a brief or lawbook, usu. prefixed or appended to it, with one or more page or section numbers showing where in the text each case is cited. **2.** INDEX OF AUTHORITIES.

Tablets of Amalfi. See AMALPHITAN CODE.

tabula rasa (tab-yə-lə rah-sə *or* -zə). [Latin "scraped tablet"] (16c) A blank tablet ready for writing; a clean slate. Pl. ***tabulae rasae*** (tab-yə-lee-**rahs**-ı).

tabular form. See SUBPARAGRAPH FORM.

T-account. An accounting form shaped like the letter *T*, with the account's name above the horizontal line, debits listed to the left of the vertical line, and credits to the right.

tacit (**tas**-it), *adj.* (17c) **1.** Implied but not actually expressed; implied by silence or silent acquiescence <a tacit understanding> <a tacit admission>. **2.**

Civil law. Arising by operation of law; constructive <a tacit mortgage> <tacit relocation>. La. Civ. Code art. 3506(30). — **tacitly,** *adv.*

tacit acceptance. *Civil law.* **1.** An acceptance of an offer indicated by circumstances or operation of law rather than express words. La. Civ. Code art. 1927. **2.** An acceptance of an inheritance, indicated by the heir's doing some act that shows an intent to accept it and that the heir would have no right to do except in that capacity.

tacit admission. See *implied admission* under ADMISSION (1).

tacit collusion. See CONSCIOUS PARALLELISM.

tacit contract. See CONTRACT.

tacit dedication. See DEDICATION.

tacit hypothecation. See HYPOTHECATION.

tacit law. See LAW.

tacit mortgage. **1.** See *legal mortgage* under MORTGAGE. **2.** See *tacit hypothecation* under HYPOTHECATION.

tacit prorogation. See PROROGATION.

tacit relocation. The implied or constructive renewal of a lease, usu. on a year-to-year basis, when the landlord and tenant have failed to indicate their intention to have the lease terminated at the end of the original term.

tacit-relocation doctrine. The principle under which a lease is presumed to continue (usu. for a one-year period) beyond its expiration date because of the parties' failure to indicate that the agreement should terminate at the stipulated date.

tacit remission. See REMISSION.

tack, *vb.* **1.** To add (one's own period of land possession) to a prior possessor's period to establish continuous adverse possession for the statutory period. **2.** To annex (a junior lien) to a first lien to acquire priority over an intermediate lien.

tacking. (18c) **1.** The joining of consecutive periods of possession by different persons to treat the periods as one continuous period; esp., the adding of one's own period of land possession to that of a prior possessor to establish continuous adverse possession for the statutory period. See ADVERSE POSSESSION. **2.** The joining of a junior lien with the first lien in order to acquire priority over an intermediate lien.

Taft–Hartley Act. See LABOR–MANAGEMENT RELATIONS ACT.

Taft–Hartley fund. See *joint-welfare fund* under FUND (1).

tail, *n.* (14c) The limitation of an estate so that it can be inherited only by the fee owner's issue or class of issue. See FEE TAIL; ENTAIL. — Also termed (in Scots law) *tailzie* (**tay**-lee).

> *several tail.* A tail that designates two separate heirs or classes of heirs who are eligible to inherit.

> *tail female.* (18c) A limitation to female heirs.

> *tail general.* (15c) **1.** A tail limited to the issue of a particular person, but not to that of a particular couple. — Also termed *general tail.* **2.** See *tail male.*

> *tail male.* (17c) A limitation to male heirs. — Also termed *tail general.*

> *tail special.* (15c) A tail limited to specified heirs of the donee's body. — Also termed *special tail.*

tail coverage. *Insurance.* An extension of a claims-made professional-liability policy to protect against claims and lawsuits filed after the end of the policy period but based on negligent acts that occurred during the policy period. — Also termed *extended-reporting-period endorsement.* Cf. PRIOR-ACTS COVERAGE.

taint, *n.* (16c) **1.** A conviction of felony. **2.** A person so convicted. See ATTAINDER.

taint, *vb.* (14c) **1.** To imbue with a noxious quality or principle. **2.** To contaminate or corrupt. **3.** To tinge or affect slightly for the worse. — **taint,** *n.*

tainted evidence. See EVIDENCE.

tainted stock. See STOCK.

take, *vb.* (bef. 12c) **1.** To obtain possession or control, whether legally or illegally <it's a felony to take that property without the owner's consent>. **2.** To seize with authority; to confiscate or apprehend <take the suspect into custody>. **3.** To acquire (property) for public use by eminent domain; (of a governmental entity) to seize or condemn property <the state took the land under its eminent-domain powers>. **4.** To acquire possession by virtue of a grant of title, the use of eminent domain, or other legal means; esp., to receive property by will or intestate succession <the probate code indicates the proportions according to which each heir will take>. See TAKING. **5.** To claim one's rights under <she took the Fifth Amendment>.

take a default judgment. To reduce to final judgment a defendant's failure to timely answer a lawsuit. ● The process usu. involves informing the court of the defendant's failure to answer, proving damages, and submitting a proposed judgment for the judge to sign. See DEFAULT JUDGMENT.

take a deposition. To obtain the testimony of a witness by deposition. See DEPOSITION (1).

take away, *vb. Hist.* To entice or persuade (a female under the age of 18) to leave her family for purposes of marriage, prostitution, or illicit sex. See ABDUCTION (2).

take back, *vb.* (18c) To revoke; to retract.

take by stealth. (16c) To steal (personal property); to pilfer or filch.

take care of. (16c) **1.** To support or look after (a person). **2.** To pay (a debt). **3.** To attend to (some matter).

take delivery. (1829) To receive something purchased or ordered; esp., to receive a commodity under a futures contract or spot-market contract, or to receive securities recently purchased.

take effect, *vb.* (14c) **1.** To become operative or executed. **2.** To be in force; to go into operation.

take from the table. *Parliamentary law.* To resume consideration of (business previously tabled). — Also termed *resume consideration.*

take-home pay. Gross wages or salary reduced by deductions such as income taxes, social-security taxes, voluntary contributions, and union dues; the net amount of a paycheck.

take-it-or-leave-it contract. See *adhesion contract* under CONTRACT.

take-nothing judgment. See JUDGMENT.

take-or-pay contract. See CONTRACT.

takeover. The acquisition of ownership or control of a corporation. ● A takeover is typically accomplished by a purchase of shares or assets, a tender offer, or a merger.

> *friendly takeover.* A takeover that is approved by the target corporation.

> *hostile takeover.* A takeover that is resisted by the target corporation. — Also termed *unfriendly takeover.*

> *unfriendly takeover.* See *hostile takeover.*

takeover agreement. See AGREEMENT.

takeover bid. An attempt by outsiders to wrest control from the incumbent management of a target corporation. — Also termed *tender offer.* See TENDER OFFER.

takeover defense. A measure taken by a corporation to discourage hostile takeover attempts. — Often shortened to *defense.* — Also termed *shark repellent.*

> *structural takeover defense.* A legal mechanism adopted by a corporation to thwart any future takeover bid without having any financial or operational effect on the target corporation.

> *transactional takeover defense.* A financial or operational transaction designed to make a

present or future takeover bid more difficult by raising a company's share price, paying off the bidder, or reducing a bidder's profit. • Examples include issuing new shares of stock, acquiring expensive assets, and adopting a poison-pill defense. See POISON PILL; PORCUPINE PROVISION.

takeover offer. See TENDER OFFER.

taker, *n.* (18c) A person who acquires; esp., one who receives property by will, by power of appointment, or by intestate succession.

   first taker. (18c) A person who receives an estate that is subject to a remainder or executory devise.

   presumptive taker. A person who would take under the applicable provisions if the takers were to be finally ascertained at the present moment.

   taker in default. (1911) A person who will receive property not effectively appointed; esp., a person designated by a donor to receive property under a power of appointment if the donee fails to exercise that power.

take the Fifth. (1952) To assert one's right against self-incrimination under the Fifth Amendment. • A common but loose variant of the phrase is *plead the Fifth*; invoking the right is not a plea. See RIGHT AGAINST SELF-INCRIMINATION.

take the witness. You may now question the witness. • This phrase is a lawyer's courtroom announcement that ends one side's questioning and prompts the other side to begin its questioning. Synonymous phrases are *your witness* and *pass the witness.*

take up, *vb.* **1.** To pay or discharge (a note). **2.** To retire (a negotiable instrument); to discharge one's liability on (a negotiable instrument), esp. the liability of an indorser or acceptor. **3.** To purchase (a note).

taking, *n.* (14c) **1.** *Criminal & tort law.* The act of seizing an article, with or without removing it, but with an implicit transfer of possession or control.

   constructive taking. (1843) An act that does not equal an actual appropriation of an article but that does show an intention to convert it, as when a person entrusted with the possession of goods starts using them contrary to the owner's instructions.

2. *Constitutional law.* The government's actual or effective acquisition of private property either by ousting the owner or by destroying the property or severely impairing its utility. • There is a taking of property when government action directly interferes with or substantially disturbs the owner's use and enjoyment of the property. — Also termed *constitutional taking.* See CONDEMNATION (2); EMINENT DOMAIN.

actual taking. See *physical taking.*

de facto taking (di **fak**-toh). (1921) **1.** Interference with the use or value or marketability of land in anticipation of condemnation, depriving the owner of reasonable use and thereby triggering the obligation to pay just compensation. **2.** A taking in which an entity clothed with eminent-domain power substantially interferes with an owner's use, possession, or enjoyment of property.

permanent taking. A government's taking of property with no intention to return it. • The property owner is entitled to just compensation.

physical taking. A physical appropriation of an owner's property by an entity clothed with eminent-domain authority. — Also termed *actual taking.*

temporary taking. A government's taking of property for a finite time. • The property owner may be entitled to compensation and damages for any harm done to the property.

taking a case from the jury. See *directed verdict* under VERDICT.

Takings Clause. (1955) The Fifth Amendment provision that prohibits the government from taking private property for public use without fairly compensating the owner. — Also termed *Just Compensation Clause.* See EMINENT DOMAIN.

taking the Fifth. See TAKE THE FIFTH.

tales (**tay**-leez *or* taylz). [Latin, pl. of *talis* "such," in the phrase *tales de circumstantibus* "such of the bystanders"] (15c) **1.** A supply of additional jurors, usu. drawn from the bystanders at the courthouse, summoned to fill a panel that has become deficient in number because of juror challenges or exemptions. **2.** A writ or order summoning these jurors.

tales-juror. See TALESMAN.

talesman (**taylz**-mən *or* **tay**-leez-mən). *Archaic.* **1.** A person selected from among the bystanders in court to serve as a juror when the original jury panel has become deficient in number. **2.** VENIREMEMBER. — Also termed *tales-juror.*

talisman (**tal**-is-mən), *n.* A charm, amulet, or other physical thing supposedly capable of working wonders <private property is not some sacred talisman that can never be touched by the state — it can be taken for public use as long as the owner is justly compensated>. — **talismanic** (tal-is-**man**-ik), *adj.*

tally. 1. *Hist.* A stick cut into two parts and marked with notches to show what was due between a debtor and creditor. **2.** Anything used to record an account. **3.** An account; a score.

Talmud (**tahl**-muud *or* **tal**-məd), *n.* A work embodying the civil and canonical law of the Jewish people. — **Talmudic** (tahl-**moo**-dik *or* tal-), *adj.*

TAM. *abbr.* TECHNICAL ADVICE MEMORANDUM.

tame, *adj.* (Of an animal) domesticated; accustomed to humans. See *domestic animal* under ANIMAL.

tamper, *vb.* (16c) **1.** To meddle so as to alter (a thing); esp., to make changes that are illegal, corrupting, or perverting. **2.** To interfere improperly; to meddle.

tampering, *n.* (17c) **1.** The act of altering a thing; esp., the act of illegally altering a document or product, such as written evidence or a consumer good. *See* Model Penal Code §§ 224.4, 241.8; 18 USCA § 1365. **2.** The act or an instance of engaging in improper or underhanded dealings, esp. in an attempt to influence. • Tampering with a witness or jury is a criminal offense. See WITNESS TAMPERING; OBSTRUCTION OF JUSTICE; EMBRACERY.

TAN. See *tax-anticipation note* under NOTE (1).

TANF. *abbr.* TEMPORARY ASSISTANCE TO NEEDY FAMILIES.

tangible, *adj.* (16c) **1.** Having or possessing physical form; CORPOREAL. **2.** Capable of being touched and seen; perceptible to the touch; capable of being possessed or realized. **3.** Capable of being understood by the mind.

tangible asset. See ASSET.

tangible chattel paper. See CHATTEL PAPER.

tangible cost. See COST (1).

tangible damages. See *actual damages* under DAMAGES.

tangible evidence. See EVIDENCE.

tangible medium of expression. *Copyright.* Any material form in which a work can be expressed and communicated, either directly or through a machine. • A requirement for copyright is that the work be fixed in a tangible medium of expression.

tangible personal property. See PROPERTY.

tangible-personal-property memorandum. A handwritten or signed document that lists items of tangible personal property (such as jewelry, artwork, or furniture) and the persons who should receive the property upon the owner's death. • This memorandum is a separate document from the property owner's will, and if referred to by the will, it is a valid testamentary disposition. Unif. Probate Code § 2-513. — Abbr. TPPM.

tangible property. See PROPERTY.

tangible thing. See *corporeal thing* under THING.

tangible worth. See WORTH.

tapper, *n.* (1930) **1.** A person who approaches another for money; a beggar. **2.** By extension, a thief.

tapping, *n.* See WIRETAPPING.

tare (tair), *n.* **1.** A deficiency in the weight or quantity of merchandise resulting from including its container's weight in the total. **2.** An allowance or abatement of a certain weight or quantity that a seller makes to the buyer because of the container's weight. Cf. TRET.

target benefit plan. See EMPLOYEE BENEFIT PLAN.

target corporation. See CORPORATION.

target defendant. See DEFENDANT.

target offense. See *object offense* under OFFENSE (1).

target price. See PRICE.

target witness. See WITNESS.

tariff, *n.* **1.** A schedule or system of duties imposed by a government on imported or exported goods. • In the United States, tariffs are imposed on imported goods only. **2.** A duty imposed on imported or exported goods under such a system. See DUTY (4).

> ***ad valorem tariff.*** A tariff set as a percentage of the imported goods' value. • This is the primary method used to calculate customs duties.

> ***antidumping tariff.*** A tariff equaling the difference between the price at which the product is sold in the exporting country and the price at which the importer will sell the product in the importing country. • These tariffs are designed to prevent foreign businesses from artificially lowering their prices and gaining unfair advantages outside their home market. — Also termed *antidumping duty.* See ANTIDUMPING LAW.

> ***autonomous tariff.*** A tariff set by legislation rather than by commercial treaty.

> ***common external tariff.*** A tariff rate that members of a customs union, common market, or economic union uniformly apply to imports from nonmember nations. — Abbr. CXT. — Also termed *tariff exterior commun.*

> ***discriminatory tariff.*** A tariff containing duties that are applied unequally to different countries or manufacturers.

> ***preferential tariff.*** A tariff that favors the products of one country over those of another. Cf. MOST-FAVORED-NATION CLAUSE.

> ***protective tariff.*** A tariff designed primarily to give domestic manufacturers economic protection against price competition from abroad, rather than to generate revenue.

retaliatory tariff. A tariff imposed to pressure another country into removing its own tariffs or making trade concessions.

revenue tariff. A tariff enacted solely or primarily to raise revenue.

tariff exterior commun. [French] See *common external tariff.* — Abbr. TEC.

3. A fee that a public utility or telecommunications company may assess for its services. ● The tariffs that a provider may charge are limited by statute. **4.** A schedule listing the rates charged for services provided by a public utility, the U.S. Postal Service, or a business (esp. one that must by law file its rates with a public agency). **5.** A scale of sentences and damages for crimes and injuries, arranged by severity. — **tariff,** *vb.*

joint tariff. A rate schedule established by two or more carriers covering shipments between places requiring the use of facilities owned by those carriers.

Tariff Act of 1930. See SMOOT–HAWLEY TARIFF ACT.

tarnishment. *Trademarks.* A form of dilution that occurs when a trademark's unauthorized use degrades the mark and diminishes its distinctive quality. Cf. BLURRING.

task order. See *task-order contract* under CONTRACT.

task-order contract. See CONTRACT.

tax, *n.* (14c) A charge, usu. monetary, imposed by the government on persons, entities, transactions, or property to yield public revenue. ● Most broadly, the term embraces all governmental impositions on the person, property, privileges, occupations, and enjoyment of the people, and includes duties, imposts, and excises. Although a tax is often thought of as being pecuniary in nature, it is not necessarily payable in money. — **tax,** *vb.*

accrued tax. (1872) A tax that has been incurred but not yet paid or payable.

accumulated-earnings tax. (1957) A penalty tax imposed on a corporation that has retained its earnings in an effort to avoid the income-tax liability arising once the earnings are distributed to shareholders as dividends. — Also termed *undistributed-earnings tax.*

additional tax. See *stopgap tax.*

admission tax. A tax imposed as part of the price of being admitted to a particular event.

ad valorem tax. (1810) A tax imposed proportionally on the value of something (esp. real property), rather than on its quantity or some other measure.

alternative minimum tax. (1972) A tax, often a flat rate, potentially imposed on corporations and higher-income individuals to ensure that those taxpayers do not avoid too much (or all) income-tax liability by legitimately using exclusions, deductions, and credits. — Abbr. AMT. — Also termed *minimum tax.*

amusement tax. A tax on a ticket to a concert, sporting event, or the like. ● The tax is usu. expressed as a percentage of the ticket price.

back tax. (*oft. pl.*) A tax that, though assessed for a previous year or years, remains due and unpaid.

betterment tax. See BETTERMENT TAX.

capital-gains tax. (1930) A tax on income derived from the sale of a capital asset. ● The federal income tax on capital gains typically has a more favorable tax rate — for example, 20% for an individual and 34% for a corporation — than the otherwise applicable tax rate on ordinary income. See CAPITAL GAIN.

capital-stock tax. **1.** A tax on capital stock in the hands of a stockholder. **2.** A state tax for conducting business in the corporate form, usu. imposed on out-of-state corporations for the privilege of doing business in the state. ● The tax is usu. assessed as a percentage of the par or assigned value of a corporation's capital stock.

capitation tax. See *poll tax.*

child's income tax. See *kiddie tax.*

classified tax. A tax system in which different rates are assessed against different types of taxed property.

collateral-inheritance tax. A tax levied on the transfer of property by will or intestate succession to a person other than the spouse, a parent, or a descendant of the decedent. Cf. *legacy tax.*

commutation tax. **1.** A combination of two or more taxes that is or can be substituted for something else that could be imposed, such as a demand for other taxes or the performance of personal services. ● For example, an excise or franchise tax may be combined with a local tax in lieu of all other taxes related to the subject matter. **2.** *Hist.* A tax imposed on shipowners, requiring them to post a bond or remit a payment per foreign passenger. ● In the 19th-century, the tax was used to discourage immigration and to raise revenue to defray the costs of supporting indigent immigrants who had remained in the U.S. **3.** *Hist.* A 1784 tax intended to reduce tea-smuggling and increase tax revenue by cutting the tax on tea and raising the tax on windows. ● To avoid payment of the tax, many people boarded up their windows.

consumption tax. A tax imposed on sale of goods or services to be consumed.

death tax. **1.** See *estate tax.* **2.** See *inheritance tax.*

delinquent tax. A tax not paid when due.

direct tax. (18c) A tax that is imposed on property, as distinguished from a tax on a right or privilege. • A direct tax is presumed to be borne by the person upon whom it is assessed, and not "passed on" to some other person. Ad valorem and property taxes are direct taxes.

documentary-stamp transfer tax. See *stamp tax.*

erroneous tax. **1.** A tax levied without statutory authority. **2.** A tax on property not subject to taxation. **3.** A tax levied by an officer who lacks authority to levy the tax. — Also termed *illegal tax.*

estate tax. (1928) A tax imposed on the transfer of property by will or by intestate succession. — Also termed *death tax; death duty.* Cf. *inheritance tax.*

estimated tax. (1926) A tax paid quarterly by a taxpayer not subject to withholding (such as a self-employed person) based on either the previous year's tax liability or an estimate of the current year's tax liability.

excess-profits tax. (1918) A tax levied on profits that are beyond a business's normal profits. • This type of tax is usu. imposed only in times of national emergency (such as war) to discourage profiteering.

excise lieu property tax. A tax on the gross premiums received and collected by designated classes of insurance companies.

excise tax. See EXCISE.

export tax. A tax levied on merchandise and goods shipped or to be shipped out of a country.

flat tax. (1952) A tax whose rate remains fixed regardless of the amount of the tax base. • Most sales taxes are flat taxes. — Also termed *proportional tax.* Cf. *progressive tax; regressive tax.*

floor tax. A tax imposed on distilled spirits stored in a warehouse.

franchise tax. A tax imposed on the privilege of carrying on a business (esp. as a corporation), usu. measured by the business's income. See FRANCHISE.

general tax. (16c) **1.** A tax that returns no special benefit to the taxpayer other than the support of governmental programs that benefit all. **2.** A property tax or an ad valorem tax that is imposed for no special purpose except to produce public revenue. Cf. *special assessment* under ASSESSMENT.

generation-skipping tax. (1977) A tax on a property transfer that skips a generation. • The tax limits the use of generation-skipping techniques as a means of avoiding estate taxes.

generation-skipping transfer tax. (1984) A gift or estate tax imposed on a generation-skipping transfer or a generation-skipping trust. IRC (26 USCA) §§ 2601–2663. — Sometimes shortened to *generation-skipping tax; transfer tax.* See DIRECT SKIP; GENERATION-SKIPPING TRANSFER; *generation-skipping trust* under TRUST; TAXABLE DISTRIBUTION.

gift tax. (1925) A tax imposed when property is voluntarily and gratuitously transferred. • Under federal law, the gift tax is imposed on the donor, but some states tax the donee.

graduated tax. **1.** A tax employing a rate schedule with higher marginal rates for larger taxable bases (income, property, transfer, etc.) **2.** See *progressive tax.*

gross-income tax. (1916) A tax on gross income, possibly after the deduction for costs of goods sold, rather than on net profits; an income tax without allowance for expenses or deductions. See *gross income* under INCOME.

gross-receipts tax. A tax on a business's gross receipts, without a deduction for costs of goods sold, or allowance for expenses or deductions. See GROSS RECEIPTS.

head tax. **1.** See *poll tax.* **2.** HEAD MONEY (3).

hidden tax. (1935) A tax that is paid, often unknowingly, by someone other than the person or entity on whom it is levied; esp., a tax imposed on a manufacturer or seller (such as a gasoline producer) who passes it on to consumers in the form of higher sales prices.

highway tax. A tax raised to pay for the construction, repair, and maintenance of highways.

holding-company tax. A federal tax imposed on undistributed personal-holding-company income after allowing deductions for such things as dividends paid. IRC (26 USCA) § 545. — Also termed *personal-holding-company tax.*

illegal tax. **1.** A tax that violates the law, esp. the constitution. • For an example, see *poll tax.* **2.** See *erroneous tax.*

income tax. (18c) A tax on an individual's or entity's net income. • The federal income tax — set forth in the Internal Revenue Code — is the federal government's primary source of revenue, and most states also have income taxes. Cf. *property tax;* EXCISE.

indirect tax. (18c) A tax on a right or privilege, such as an occupation tax or franchise tax. • An indirect tax is often presumed to be partly or wholly passed on from the nominal taxpayer to another person.

inheritance tax. (18c) **1.** A tax imposed on a person who inherits property from another (unlike an estate tax, which is imposed on the decedent's estate). • There is no federal inheritance tax, but some states have an inheritance tax (though it is creditable or deductible under the federal estate tax). — Also termed *succession tax*; *death tax*. Cf. *estate tax*. **2.** Loosely, an estate tax.

in lieu tax. A tax imposed as a substitute for another.

intangible tax. A state tax imposed on the privilege of owning, transferring, devising, or otherwise dealing with intangible property.

interest-equalization tax. A tax imposed on a U.S. citizen's acquisition of stock issued by a foreign issuer or a debt obligation of a foreign obligor, but only if the obligation did not mature within a year. • This tax was repealed in the mid-1970s. IRC (26 USCA) § 4911.

kiddie tax. (18c) *Slang.* A federal tax imposed on a child's unearned income (above an exempt amount) at the parents' tax rate if the parents' rate is higher and if the child is under 18 years old. — Also termed *child's income tax*.

land tax. See *property tax*.

legacy tax. A tax on a legacy, often with the provision that the rate increases as the relationship of the legatee becomes more remote from the testator. • In English law, this tax was known as a *legacy duty*; it was abolished in 1949. Cf. *collateral-inheritance tax*.

luxury tax. (1925) An excise tax imposed on high-priced items that are not deemed necessities (such as cars costing more than a specified amount). Cf. *sin tax*.

minimum tax. See *alternative minimum tax*.

nanny tax. (1993) *Slang.* A federal social-security tax imposed on the employer of a domestic employee if the employer pays that employee more than a specified amount in total wages in a year. • The term, which is not a technical legal phrase, was popularized in the mid-1990s, when several of President Clinton's nominees were found not to have paid the social-security tax for their nannies.

occupation tax. (1879) An excise tax imposed for the privilege of carrying on a business, trade, or profession. • For example, many states require lawyers to pay an occupation tax. — Also termed *occupational tax*.

payroll tax. (1936) **1.** A tax payable by an employer based on its payroll (such as a social-security tax or an unemployment tax). **2.** A tax collected by an employer from its employees' gross pay (such as an income tax or a social-security tax). See *withholding tax*.

per capita tax. See *poll tax*.

personal-holding-company tax. See *holding-company tax*.

personal-property tax. (1863) A tax on personal property (such as jewelry or household furniture) levied by a state or local government.

pickup tax. *Slang.* A state death tax levied in an amount equal to the federal death-tax credit. — Also termed *sponge tax*; *slack tax*.

poll tax. (17c) A fixed tax levied on each person within a jurisdiction. • The 24th Amendment prohibits the federal and state governments from imposing poll taxes as a condition for voting. — Also termed *per capita tax*; *capitation tax*; *capitation*; *head tax*.

premium tax. A state tax paid by an insurer on premiums paid by the insured.

privilege tax. A tax on the privilege of carrying on a business or occupation for which a license or franchise is required.

progressive tax. (1886) **1.** A tax structured so that the effective tax rate increases more than proportionately as the tax base increases, or so that an exemption remains flat or diminishes. • With this type of tax, the percentage of income paid in taxes increases as the taxpayer's income increases. Most income taxes are progressive, so that higher incomes are taxed at a higher rate. But a tax can be progressive without using graduated rates. — Also termed *graduated tax*. Cf. *regressive tax*; *flat tax*. **2.** See *graduated tax*.

property tax. (1808) A tax levied on the owner of property (esp. real property), usu. based on the property's value. • Local governments often impose property taxes to finance school districts, municipal projects, and the like. — Also termed (specif.) *land tax*. Cf. *income tax*; EXCISE.

proportional tax. See *flat tax*.

regressive tax. (1893) A tax structured so that the effective tax rate decreases as the tax base increases. • With this type of tax, the percentage of income paid in taxes decreases as the taxpayer's income increases. A flat tax (such as the typical sales tax) is usu. considered regressive — despite its constant rate — because it is more burdensome for low-income taxpayers than high-income taxpayers. A growing exemption also produces a regressive tax effect. Cf. *progressive tax*; *flat tax*.

repressive tax. See *sin tax*.

sales tax. (1921) A tax imposed on the sale of goods and services, usu. measured as a percentage of their price. — Also termed *retail sales tax*. See *flat tax*.

self-employment tax. The Social-Security and Medicare tax imposed on the net earnings of a self-employed person.

service-occupation tax. A tax imposed on persons who sell services, usu. computed as a percentage of net cost of the tangible personal property (e.g., materials and goods) transferred as an incident to the sale.

severance tax. A tax imposed on the value of oil, gas, timber, or other natural resources extracted from the earth.

sinking-fund tax. A tax to be applied to the repayment of a public loan.

sin tax. (1971) An excise tax imposed on goods or activities that are considered harmful or immoral (such as cigarettes, liquor, or gambling). — Also termed *repressive tax.* Cf. *luxury tax.*

slack tax. See *pickup tax.*

special tax. (18c) **1.** A tax levied for a unique purpose. **2.** A tax (such as an inheritance tax) that is levied in addition to a general tax.

specific tax. (18c) A tax imposed as a fixed sum on each article or item of property of a given class or kind without regard to its value.

sponge tax. See *pickup tax.*

stamp tax. (18c) A tax imposed by requiring the purchase of a revenue stamp that must be affixed to a legal document (such as a deed or note) before the document can be recorded. — Also termed *documentary-stamp transfer tax.*

state tax. (18c) **1.** A tax — usu. in the form of a sales or income tax — earmarked for state, rather than federal or municipal, purposes. **2.** A tax levied under a state law.

stock-transfer tax. A tax levied by the federal government and by some states on the transfer or sale of shares of stock. — Often shortened to *transfer tax.*

stopgap tax. A tax, usu. temporary, levied during the term of a budget to cover an unexpected deficit. — Also termed *additional tax.*

succession tax. See *inheritance tax* (1).

surtax. (1881) An additional tax imposed on something being taxed or on the primary tax itself.

tonnage tax. See *tonnage duty* under DUTY (4).

transfer tax. (1890) **1.** A tax imposed on the transfer of property, esp. by will, inheritance, or gift. **2.** See *stock-transfer tax.* **3.** See *generation-skipping transfer tax.*

undistributed-earnings tax. See *accumulated-earnings tax.*

unemployment tax. (1937) A tax imposed on an employer by state or federal law to cover the cost of unemployment insurance. ● The Federal Unemployment Tax Act (FUTA) provides for a tax based on a percentage of employee earnings but allows a credit for amounts paid in state unemployment taxes.

unified transfer tax. The federal transfer tax imposed equally on property transferred during life or at death. ● Until 1977, gift-tax rates were lower than estate taxes. — Also termed *unified estate-and-gift tax.*

unitary tax. A tax of income earned locally by a business that transacts business through an affiliated company outside the state or country. See UNITARY BUSINESS.

unrelated-business-income tax. (1962) A tax levied on a not-for-profit organization's taxable income, such as advertising revenue from a publication.

use tax. A tax imposed on the use of certain goods that are bought outside the taxing authority's jurisdiction. ● Use taxes are designed to discourage the purchase of products that are not subject to the sales tax.

value-added tax. (1935) A tax assessed at each step in the production of a commodity, based on the value added at each step by the difference between the commodity's production cost and its selling price. ● A value-added tax — which is levied in several European countries — effectively acts as a sales tax on the ultimate consumer. — Abbr. VAT.

windfall-profits tax. (1973) A tax imposed on a business or industry as a result of a sudden increase in profits. ● An example is the tax imposed on oil companies in 1980 for profits resulting from the Arab oil embargo of the 1970s.

withholding tax. (1927) A portion of income tax that is subtracted from salary, wages, dividends, or other income before the earner receives payment. ● The most common example is the income tax and social-security tax withheld by an employer from an employee's pay.

taxable, *adj.* (16c) **1.** Subject to taxation <interest earned on a checking account is taxable income>. **2.** (Of legal costs or fees) assessable <expert-witness fees are not taxable court costs>.

taxable cost. See COST (3).

taxable distribution. (1927) A generation-skipping transfer from a trust to the beneficiary (i.e., the skip person) that is neither a direct skip nor a taxable termination. See GENERATION-SKIPPING TRANSFER; *generation-skipping transfer tax* under TAX; *generation-skipping trust* under TRUST; SKIP PERSON.

taxable estate. See ESTATE (3).

taxable gift. See GIFT.

taxable income. See INCOME.

taxable termination. (1988) A taxable event that occurs when (1) an interest in a generation-skipping trust property terminates (as on the death of a skip person's parent who possessed the interest), (2) no interest in the trust is held by a nonskip person, and (3) a distribution may be made to a skip person. ● Before the creation of taxable terminations in 1976, a taxpayer could create a trust that paid income to a child for life, then to that child's child for life, and so on without incurring an estate or gift tax liability at the death of each generation's beneficiary. See GENERATION-SKIPPING TRANSFER; *generation-skipping transfer tax* under TAX; *generation-skipping trust* under TRUST; SKIP PERSON.

taxable year. See *tax year* under YEAR.

tax accounting. The accounting rules and methods used in determining a taxpayer's liability.

tax-anticipation bill. A short-term obligation issued by the U.S. Treasury to meet the cash-flow needs of the government. ● Corporations can tender these bills at par value to make quarterly tax payments. — Abbr. TAB.

tax-anticipation note. See NOTE (1).

tax-anticipation warrant. See WARRANT (2).

tax-apportionment clause. A testamentary provision directing how inheritance and estate taxes should be paid.

tax assessment. See ASSESSMENT (3).

tax assessor. See ASSESSOR (1).

taxation. (14c) **1.** The imposition or assessment of a tax; the means by which the state obtains the revenue required for its activities.

double taxation. (18c) **1.** The imposition of two taxes on the same property during the same period and for the same taxing purpose. **2.** The imposition of two taxes on one corporate profit; esp., the structure of taxation employed by Subchapter C of the Internal Revenue Code, under which corporate profits are taxed twice, once to the corporation when earned and once to the shareholders when the earnings are distributed as dividends. **3.** *Int'l law.* The imposition of comparable taxes in two or more states on the same taxpayer for the same subject matter or identical goods. — Also termed *duplicate taxation.*

duplicate taxation. See *double taxation.*

equal and uniform taxation. A tax system in which no person or class of persons in the taxing district — whether it be a state, city, or county — is taxed at a different rate from others in the same district on the same value or thing.

pass-through taxation. (1998) The taxation of an entity's owners for the entity's income without taxing the entity itself. ● Partnerships and S corporations are taxed under this method. So are limited liability companies and limited liability partnerships unless they elect to be taxed as corporations by "checking the box" on their income tax returns. The election is made on Form 8832 (Entity Classification Election). See

Treas. Reg. § 301.7701-(3)(b)(1). — Also termed *conduit taxation.*

2. TAXATION OF COSTS.

taxation of costs. The process of fixing the amount of litigation-related expenses that a prevailing party is entitled to be awarded. — Sometimes shortened to *taxation.*

tax audit. See AUDIT.

tax avoidance. (1927) The act of taking advantage of legally available tax-planning opportunities in order to minimize one's tax liability. Cf. TAX EVASION.

tax base. The total property, income, or wealth subject to taxation in a given jurisdiction; the aggregate value of the property being taxed by a particular tax. Cf. BASIS (2).

tax basis. See BASIS (2).

tax-benefit doctrine. See TAX-BENEFIT RULE.

tax-benefit rule. (1942) The principle that if a taxpayer recovers a loss or expense that was deducted in a previous year, the recovery must be included in the current year's gross income to the extent that it was previously deducted. — Also termed *tax-benefit doctrine.*

tax bracket. (1923) A categorized level of income subject to a particular tax rate under federal or state law <28% tax bracket>.

tax certificate. An instrument issued to the buyer of property at a tax sale, certifying the sale and entitling the buyer to a tax deed and possession of the property upon the expiration of the redemption period. ● If the property is redeemed, the tax certificate is voided. See REDEMPTION PERIOD; *tax sale* under SALE. Cf. *tax deed* under DEED.

tax court. (1841) **1.** TAX COURT, U.S. **2.** In some states, a court that hears appeals in nonfederal tax cases and can modify or change any valuation, assessment, classification, tax, or final order that is appealed.

Tax Court, U.S. A federal court that hears appeals by taxpayers from adverse IRS decisions about tax deficiencies. ● The Tax Court was created in 1942, replacing the Board of Tax Appeals. — Abbr. T.C.

tax credit. (1946) An amount subtracted directly from one's total tax liability, dollar for dollar, as opposed to a deduction from gross income. — Often shortened to *credit.* Cf. DEDUCTION (2).

child- and dependent-care tax credit. (2001) A tax credit available to a person who is employed full-time and who maintains a household for a dependent child or a disabled spouse or dependent.

earned-income credit. (1927) A refundable federal tax credit on the earned income of a low-income worker with dependent children. ● The credit is paid to the taxpayer even if it exceeds the total tax liability. See IRC (26 USCA) § 32. — Abbr. EIC.

foreign tax credit. (1928) A tax credit against U.S. income taxes for a taxpayer who earns income overseas and has paid foreign taxes on that income. See FOREIGN-EARNED-INCOME EXCLUSION.

investment tax credit. (1965) A tax credit intended to stimulate business investment in capital goods by allowing a percentage of the purchase price as a credit against the taxpayer's income taxes. • The Tax Reform Act of 1986 generally repealed this credit retroactively for most property placed in service after January 1, 1986. — Abbr. ITC.

unified credit. See *unified estate-and-gift tax credit.*

unified estate-and-gift tax credit. (1988) A tax credit applied against the federal unified transfer tax. IRC (26 USCA) § 2001(c)(2). — Often shortened to *unified credit.* — Also termed *applicable exclusion credit.*

tax deduction. See DEDUCTION (2).

tax deed. See DEED.

tax-deferred, *adj.* (1948) Not taxable until a future date or event <a tax-deferred retirement plan>.

tax-deferred account. See ACCOUNT.

tax-deferred annuity. See *403(b) plan* under EMPLOYEE BENEFIT PLAN.

tax deficiency. See DEFICIENCY (2).

tax-deficiency notice. See NINETY-DAY LETTER.

tax denier. See TAX PROTESTER.

tax evasion. (1922) The willful attempt to defeat or circumvent the tax law in order to illegally reduce one's tax liability. • Tax evasion is punishable by both civil and criminal penalties. — Also termed *tax fraud.* Cf. TAX AVOIDANCE.

tax-exempt, *adj.* (1923) **1.** By law not subject to taxation <a tax-exempt charity>. **2.** Bearing interest that is free from income tax <tax-exempt municipal bonds>. — Also termed *tax-free.*

tax-exempt bond. See BOND (3).

tax ferret. A private person engaged in the business of searching for taxable property that has somehow not been taxed.

tax foreclosure. See FORECLOSURE.

tax fraud. See TAX EVASION.

tax-free, *adj.* See TAX-EXEMPT.

tax-free exchange. (1927) A transfer of property for which the tax law specifically defers (or possibly exempts) income-tax consequences. • For example, a transfer of property to a controlled corporation under IRC (26 USCA) § 351(a) and a like-kind exchange under IRC (26 USCA) § 1031(a). — Also termed *1031 exchange.* Cf. 1031 EXCHANGE.

tax haven. (18c) A jurisdiction, esp. a country, that imposes little or no tax on the profits from transactions carried on there or on persons resident there.

tax home. (18c) A taxpayer's principal business location, post, or station. • Travel expenses are tax-deductible only if the taxpayer is traveling away from home.

tax-identification number. A nine-digit tracking number assigned by the Internal Revenue Service to the tax accounts of businesses and also to entities or individuals who are required to file business tax returns. — Abbr. TIN. — Often shortened to *tax i.d.* — Also termed *employer-identification number* (EIN); *federal-employer-identification number* (FEIN).

tax incentive. (18c) A governmental enticement, through a tax benefit, to engage in a particular activity, such as the contribution of money or property to a qualified charity.

tax-increment financing. A technique used by a municipality to finance commercial developments usu. involving issuing bonds to finance land acquisition and other up-front costs, and then using the additional property taxes generated from the new development to service the debt. — Abbr. TIF.

taxing district. See DISTRICT.

taxing power. See POWER (3).

tax injunction act. A federal law prohibiting a federal court from interfering with the assessment or collection of any state tax where the state affords a plain, speedy, and efficient remedy in its own courts. 28 USCA § 1341.

tax law. (18c) **1.** INTERNAL REVENUE CODE. **2.** The statutory, regulatory, constitutional, and common-law rules that constitute the law applicable to taxation. **3.** The area of legal study dealing with taxation.

tax lease. See LEASE.

tax levy. See LEVY (1).

tax liability. (1932) The amount that a taxpayer legally owes after calculating the applicable tax; the amount of unpaid taxes.

tax lien. See LIEN.

tax list. An official schedule listing the taxable items within a jurisdiction; ROLL (2).

tax loophole. See LOOPHOLE.

tax-loss carryback. See CARRYBACK.

tax-loss carryforward. See CARRYOVER.

tax-loss carryover. See CARRYOVER.

tax negligence. See NEGLIGENCE.

tax-option corporation. See *S corporation* under CORPORATION.

taxpayer. One who pays or is subject to a tax. Cf. TAX PROTESTER.

taxpayers' bill of rights. (1988) Federal legislation granting taxpayers specific rights when dealing with the Internal Revenue Service, such as the right to have representation and the right to receive written notice of a levy 30 days before enforcement.

taxpayers' lists. Written exhibits required of taxpayers in some taxing districts, listing all property owned by them and subject to taxation, used as a basis for assessment and valuation. Cf. ROLL (2).

taxpayer-standing doctrine. (1977) *Constitutional law.* The principle that a taxpayer has no standing to sue the government for allegedly misspending the public's tax money unless the taxpayer can demonstrate a personal stake and show some direct injury.

tax-preference items. (1971) Certain items that, even though lawfully deducted in arriving at taxable income for regular tax purposes, must be considered in calculating a taxpayer's alternative minimum tax. See *alternative minimum tax* under TAX.

tax protest. A taxpayer's formal, usu. written, statement that he or she does not acknowledge a legal or just basis for the tax or a duty to pay it. ● The purpose of the protest is to make clear that any payment is made "under protest" and to avoid waiving the right to recover the money paid if the tax is later invalidated.

tax protester. **1.** One who files a tax protest. **2.** A person who opposes tax laws and seeks or employs ways, often illegal, to avoid the laws' effects; esp., a person who refuses to pay a tax on grounds that the government has no authority to levy the tax. — Sometimes spelled *tax protestor.* — Also termed *tax denier.* Cf. TAXPAYER.

illegal tax protester. *Hist.* The name once used by the IRS to designate a person believed to have used illegal means to avoid or reduce tax liability. ● In the Internal Revenue Service Restructuring and Reform Act of 1998, Congress forbade the IRS to continue using the label. Today the term *nonfiler* is typically used instead.

tax-protest scheme. A plan designed to avoid or express dissatisfaction with tax laws, usu. by unlawful means. ● The most common schemes involve illegally evading or reducing tax liabilities, or interfering with the administration of the tax laws.

tax rate. (1876) A mathematical figure for calculating a tax, usu. expressed as a percentage.

average tax rate. (1895) A taxpayer's tax liability divided by the amount of taxable income. — Also called *effective tax rate.*

marginal tax rate. (1939) In a tax scheme, the rate applicable to the last dollar of income earned by the taxpayer. ● This concept is useful in calculating the tax effect of receiving additional income or claiming additional deductions. See TAX BRACKET.

tax-rate schedule. (1951) A schedule used to determine the tax on a given level of taxable income and based on a taxpayer's status (for example, married filing a joint income-tax return). — Also termed *tax table.*

tax rebate. See TAX REFUND.

tax redemption. See REDEMPTION.

tax refund. Money that a taxpayer overpaid and is thus returned by the taxing authority. — Also termed *tax rebate.*

tax return. (1870) An income-tax form on which a person or entity reports income, deductions, and exemptions, and on which tax liability is calculated. — Often shortened to *return.* — Also termed *income-tax return.*

amended return. (1861) A return filed after the original return, usu. to correct an error in the original.

consolidated return. A return that reflects combined financial information for a group of affiliated corporations.

false return. See FALSE RETURN (2).

information return. (1920) A return, such as a W-2, filed by an entity to report some economic information related to, but other than, tax liability.

joint return. (1930) A return filed together by spouses. ● A joint return can be filed even if only one spouse had income, but each spouse is usu. individually liable for the tax payment.

separate return. (1913) A return filed by each spouse separately, showing income and liability. ● Unlike with a joint return, each spouse is individually liable only for taxes due on the separate return.

tax-return privilege. See PRIVILEGE (3).

tax roll. See ROLL (2).

tax sale. See SALE.

tax shelter, *n.* (1952) A financial operation or investment strategy (such as a partnership or real-estate investment trust) that is created primarily for the purpose of reducing or deferring income-tax payments. ● The Tax Reform Act of 1986 — by restricting the deductibility of passive losses — sharply limited the effectiveness of tax shelters. — Often shortened to *shelter.* — **tax-sheltered,** *adj.*

tax-sheltered annuity. See *403(b) plan* under EM-PLOYEE BENEFIT PLAN.

tax situs (SI-təs). A state or other jurisdiction that has a substantial connection with assets that are subject to taxation.

tax-straddle rule. A rule preventing undue deferral of tax on income or conversion of ordinary income or short-term capital gain into long-term capital gain by disallowing the premature deduction of a loss on sale or disposition of one leg of a straddle position while retaining the other, offsetting leg or position. ● For example, in a straddle position a promise to sell may be offset by a promise to buy, such as in a futures contract. This practice has been greatly restricted by the requirement that gains and losses on commodities transactions must be reported based on their value at year end. IRC (26 USCA) § 165(c)(2). See STRADDLE.

tax table. See TAX-RATE SCHEDULE.

tax title. See TITLE (2).

tax warrant. See WARRANT (1).

tax write-off. (1955) A deduction of depreciation, loss, or expense from taxable income.

tax year. See YEAR.

TBC. *abbr.* Trial before the court. See *bench trial* under TRIAL.

T-bill. *abbr.* TREASURY BILL.

T-bond. *abbr.* TREASURY BOND.

T.C. *abbr.* See TAX COURT, U.S.

T.C.M. See T.C. MEMO.

T.C. memo. *abbr.* A memorandum decision of the U.S. Tax Court. — Also abbreviated T.C.M.

TDA. *abbr.* UNITED STATES TRADE AND DEVELOPMENT AGENCY.

teach, *vb. Patents.* **1.** (Of a patent specification) to instruct (a person of ordinary skill in the art how to make and use an invention). **2.** (Of a prior-art reference) to anticipate (the invention being examined) by discussing, describing, or analyzing the invention's essential elements or technology. ● In this sense, prior art that discourages an inventor from pursuing an invention "teaches away from" that invention. A teaching raises a statutory bar to an invention's patentability.

teamwork. (1828) Work done by a team; esp., work by a team of animals as a substantial part of one's business, such as farming, express carrying, freight hauling, or transporting material. ● In some jurisdictions, animals (such as horses) that work in teams are exempt from execution on a civil judgment.

tear-me-open license. See *shrink-wrap license* under LICENSE.

TEAS. *abbr.* TRADEMARK ELECTRONIC APPLICATION SYSTEM.

TEC. *abbr.* Tariff exterior commun. See *common external tariff* under TARIFF (2).

TECA (**tee**-kə). *abbr.* TEMPORARY EMERGENCY COURT OF APPEALS.

technical adjustment. A brief change in the general upward or downward trend of stock-market prices, such as a short rally during a bear market.

Technical Advice Memorandum. (1967) A publication issued by the national office of the IRS, usu. at a taxpayer's request, to explain some complex or novel tax-law issue. — Abbr. TAM.

technical conversion. See CONVERSION (2).

technical error. See *harmless error* under ERROR (2).

technical estoppel. See ESTOPPEL.

technical mark. See *technical trademark* under TRADEMARK.

technical mortgage. See MORTGAGE.

technical trademark. See TRADEMARK.

technical trust. See *passive trust* under TRUST.

Technology Administration. A unit in the U.S. Department of Commerce responsible for working with industry on ways to use technology to stimulate economic growth. ● The agency also carries out technology programs and disseminates information about technology. It has three offices: the Office of Technology Policy (OTP), the National Institute of Standards and Technology (NIST), and the National Technical Information Service (NTIS). It was established in 1988. 15 USCA § 3704.

technology transfer. **1.** The sale or licensing of intellectual property. **2.** The field involving the sale and licensing of intellectual property. ● Many major universities have an office of technology transfer to control the university's intellectual property and generate income from it.

teen court. See COURT.

telecopier. See FAX (2).

teleological interpretation. See *purposive construction* under CONSTRUCTION.

telescam. A fraud committed by using telemarketing to induce the victim to disclose sensitive personal information or send money to the perpetrator. Cf. BOILER-ROOM TRANSACTION; PHISHING.

teller. **1.** A bank clerk who deals directly with customers by receiving and paying out money. **2.** *Parliamentary law.* A member of a tellers committee; esp., a vote-counter at an election. See *tellers committee* under COMMITTEE.

Teller in Parliament. One of the members of the British House of Commons — two from government and two from the opposition — appointed by the Speaker to count votes.

teller's check. See CHECK.

tellers committee. See COMMITTEE.

teller vote. See *lobby vote* under VOTE (4).

temperance. **1.** Habitual moderation regarding the indulgence of the natural appetites and passions; restrained or moderate indulgence (esp. of alcoholic beverages). **2.** Abstinence.

temporality. **1.** Civil or political power, as distinguished from ecclesiastical power. **2.** (*usu. pl.*) The secular properties or revenues of an ecclesiastic.

temporal jurisdiction. See JURISDICTION.

temporal lord. See LORD.

temporary, *adj.* Lasting for a time only; existing or continuing for a limited (usu. short) time; transitory.

temporary administration. See ADMINISTRATION.

temporary alimony. See ALIMONY.

temporary allegiance. See ALLEGIANCE.

Temporary Assistance to Needy Families. A combined state and federal program that provides limited financial assistance to families in need. 42 USCA §§ 601–603a. • This program replaced Aid to Families with Dependent Children. TANF differs from AFDC because families are limited to no more than five years of assistance, and states have more control over eligibility requirements. — Abbr. TANF.

temporary-cessation-of-production doctrine. *Oil & gas.* The rule that an oil-and-gas lease term "for so long thereafter as oil and gas are produced" will not terminate once production is attained unless the cessation of production is for an unreasonable length of time. See CESSATION-OF-PRODUCTION CLAUSE.

temporary committee. See *special committee* under COMMITTEE.

temporary damages. See DAMAGES.

temporary detention. See *pretrial detention* under DETENTION.

temporary disability. See DISABILITY (2).

Temporary Emergency Court of Appeals. *Hist.* A special U.S. court created in 1971 with exclusive jurisdiction over appeals from federal district courts in cases arising under the wage-and-price-control program of the Economic Stabilization Act of 1970. • The court consisted of nine district and circuit judges appointed by the Chief Justice. This court was abolished in 1992. — Abbr. TECA. Cf. EMERGENCY COURT OF APPEALS.

temporary employment. See EMPLOYMENT.

temporary executor. See *acting executor* under EXECUTOR.

temporary fiduciary. See FIDUCIARY.

temporary frustration. See FRUSTRATION.

temporary injunction. See *preliminary injunction* under INJUNCTION.

temporary injury. See INJURY.

temporary insanity. See INSANITY.

temporary insider. See INSIDER.

temporary judge. See *visiting judge* under JUDGE.

temporary nuisance. See NUISANCE.

temporary order. See ORDER (2).

temporary perfection. See PERFECTION.

temporary restraining order. (1861) **1.** A court order preserving the status quo until a litigant's application for a preliminary or permanent injunction can be heard. • A temporary restraining order may sometimes be granted without notifying the opposing party in advance. Cf. *emergency protective order* under PROTECTIVE ORDER. **2.** See *ex parte injunction* under INJUNCTION. — Often shortened to *restraining order.* — Abbr. TRO.

temporary statute. See STATUTE.

temporary taking. See TAKING (2).

temporary total disability. See DISABILITY (2).

temporary ward. See WARD.

tenancy. (16c) **1.** The possession or occupancy of land under a lease; a leasehold interest in real estate. **2.** The period of such possession or occupancy. See ESTATE (1). **3.** The possession of real or personal property by right or title, esp. under a conveying instrument such as a deed or will.

at-will tenancy. See *tenancy at will.*

common tenancy. See *tenancy in common.*

cotenancy. (1875) A tenancy with two or more cowners who have unity of possession. • Examples are a joint tenancy and tenancy in common.

entire tenancy. (17c) A tenancy possessed by one person, as opposed to a joint or common tenancy. See *estate by entirety* under ESTATE (1).

general tenancy. (18c) A tenancy that is not of fixed duration under the parties' agreement.

holdover tenancy. See *tenancy at sufferance.*

joint tenancy. (17c) A tenancy with two or more cowners who take identical interests simultaneously by the same instrument and with the same right of possession. • A joint tenancy differs from a tenancy in common because each joint tenant has a right of survivorship to the other's share (in some states, this right must be clearly expressed in the conveyance — otherwise, the tenancy will be presumed to be a tenancy in common). See RIGHT OF SURVIVORSHIP. Cf. *tenancy in common.*

life tenancy. See *life estate* under ESTATE (1).

periodic tenancy. (1891) A tenancy that automatically continues for successive periods — usu. month to month or year to year — unless terminated at the end of a period by notice. • A typical example is a month-to-month apartment lease. This type of tenancy originated through court rulings that, when the lessor received a periodic rent, the lease could not be terminated without reasonable notice. — Also termed *tenancy from period to period; periodic estate; estate from period to period;* (more specif.) *month-to-month tenancy* (or *estate); year-to-year tenancy* (or *estate).*

several tenancy. (17c) A tenancy that is separate and not held jointly with another person.

tenancy at sufferance. (18c) A tenancy arising when a person who has been in lawful possession of property wrongfully remains as a holdover after his or her interest has expired. • A tenancy at sufferance takes the form of either a tenancy at will or a periodic tenancy. — Also termed *holdover tenancy; estate at sufferance.* See HOLDING OVER (1).

tenancy attendant on the inheritance. A tenancy for a term that is vested in a trustee in trust for the owner of the inheritance. • The tenancy is a form of personal property to the trustee. — Also termed *tenancy attendant on an inheritance; term attendant on the inheritance.*

tenancy at will. (17c) A tenancy in which the tenant holds possession with the landlord's consent but without fixed terms (as for duration or rent); specif., a tenancy that is terminable at the will of either the transferor or the transferee and that has no designated period of duration. • Such a tenancy may be terminated by either party upon fair notice. — Also termed *at-will tenancy; estate at will.*

tenancy by the entirety (en-tɪ-ər-tee). See *estate by entirety* under ESTATE (1).

tenancy by the rod. See COPYHOLD.

tenancy by the verge. See COPYHOLD.

tenancy for a term. (17c) A tenancy whose duration is known in years, weeks, or days from the moment of its creation. — Also termed *tenancy for a period; tenancy for years; term for years; term of years; estate for a term; estate for years; lease for years.*

tenancy from period to period. See *periodic tenancy.*

tenancy in common. (17c) A tenancy by two or more persons, in equal or unequal undivided shares, each person having an equal right to possess the whole property but no right of survivorship. — Also termed *common tenancy; estate in common.* Cf. *joint tenancy.*

tenancy in coparcenary. See COPARCENARY.

tenancy in fee. See FEE SIMPLE.

tenancy in gross. (1860) A tenancy for a term that is outstanding — that is, one that is unattached to or disconnected from the estate or inheritance, such as one that is in the hands of some third party having no interest in the inheritance.

tenancy in tail. See FEE TAIL.

tenancy par la verge. See COPYHOLD.

year-to-year tenancy. See *periodic tenancy.*

tenant, *n.* (14c) **1.** One who holds or possesses lands or tenements by any kind of right or title. See TENANCY.

copyhold tenant. See *customary tenant.*

customary tenant. A tenant holding by the custom of the manor. • Over time, customary tenants became known as *copyhold tenants.* See COPYHOLD.

dominant tenant. The person who holds a dominant estate and therefore benefits from an easement. Cf. *servient tenant.*

holdover tenant. A person who remains in possession of real property after a previous tenancy (esp. one under a lease) expires, thus giving rise to a tenancy at sufferance. — Sometimes shortened to *holdover.* See *tenancy at sufferance* under TENANCY.

hypothetical tenant. See HYPOTHETICAL TENANT.

illusory tenant. **1.** A fictitious person who, as the landlord's alter ego, subleases an apartment to permit the landlord to circumvent rent-law regulations. **2.** A tenant whose business is to sublease rent-controlled apartments.

joint tenant. See *joint tenancy* under TENANCY.

life tenant. See LIFE TENANT.

particular tenant. A tenant of a limited estate taken out of a fee. See *particular estate* under ESTATE (1).

prime tenant. A commercial or professional tenant with an established reputation that leases substantial, and usu. the most preferred, space in a commercial development. • A prime tenant is important in securing construction financing and in attracting other desirable tenants.

quasi-tenant. A sublessee that the new tenant or reversioner allows to hold over.

servient tenant. The person who holds a servient estate and is therefore burdened by an easement. Cf. *dominant tenant.*

statutory tenant. A person who is legally entitled to remain on property after the tenancy expires.

tenant at sufferance. A tenant who has been in lawful possession of property and wrongfully remains as a holdover after the tenant's interest has expired. • The tenant may become either a tenant at will or a periodic tenant. — Also termed *permissive tenant.* See *tenancy at will; periodic tenancy.*

tenant by elegit. See ELEGIT.

tenant by the curtesy. A life tenant who receives the estate from his deceased wife by whom he has had legitimate children. • The children hold the remainder interest. See CURTESY.

tenant by the verge. See COPYHOLDER.

tenant for a term. A tenant whose tenancy is for a defined number of years, months, weeks, or days, set when the tenancy is created.

tenant for life. See LIFE TENANT.

tenant in chief. Hist. A person who held land directly of the king. — Also termed *tenant in capite.* See IN CAPITE.

tenant in common. One of two or more tenants who hold the same land by unity of possession but by separate and distinct titles, with each person having an equal right to possess the whole property but no right of survivorship. See *tenancy in common* under TENANCY.

tenant in demesne (di-**mayn** or di-**meen**). A feudal tenant who holds land of, and owes services to, a tenant in service. Cf. *tenant in service.*

tenant in dower. A life tenant who is entitled to hold and use one-third of all the real property owned by her deceased husband. See DOWER.

tenant in fee. The owner of land held in fee. — Also termed *tenant in fee simple.*

tenant in service. A feudal tenant who grants an estate to another (a *tenant in demesne*) and is therefore entitled to services from the latter. Cf. *tenant in demesne.*

undertenant. See SUBLESSEE.

2. One who pays rent for the temporary use and occupation of another's land under a lease or similar arrangement. See LESSEE. **3.** *Archaic.* The defendant in a real action (the plaintiff being called a *demandant*). See *real action* under ACTION (4).

tenancy by the curtesy. See CURTESY.

tenantable repair. (17c) A repair that will render premises fit for present habitation. See HABITABILITY.

tenantlike, *adj.* In accordance with the rights and obligations of a tenant, as in matters of repairs, waste, etc.

tenant par la verge. See COPYHOLDER.

tenantry. A body or group of tenants.

tenant's fixture. See FIXTURE.

tend, *vb.* **1.** To be disposed toward (something). **2.** To serve, contribute, or conduce in some degree or way; to have a more or less direct bearing or effect. **3.** To be directed or have a tendency to (an end, object, or purpose).

ten-day rule. The doctrine that one who sells goods on credit and then learns that the buyer is insolvent has ten days after the buyer receives the goods to demand their return. • The seller has even longer to demand return if the buyer has made a written representation of solvency to the seller within three months before delivery.

tender, *n.* (16c) **1.** A valid and sufficient offer of performance; specif., an unconditional offer of money or performance to satisfy a debt or obligation <a tender of delivery>. • The tender may save the tendering party from a penalty for nonpayment or nonperformance or may, if the other party unjustifiably refuses the tender, place the other party in default. Cf. OFFER OF PERFORMANCE; CONSIGNATION.

tender of delivery. (1821) A seller's putting and holding conforming goods at the buyer's disposition and giving the buyer any notification reasonably necessary to take delivery. • The manner, time, and place for tender are determined by the agreement and by Article 2 of the Uniform Commercial Code.

tender of performance. (18c) An obligor's demonstration of readiness, willingness, and ability to perform the obligation; esp., a buyer's demonstration of readiness, willingness, and ability to pay the purchase money, or a seller's offer to deliver merchantable title.• An offer to perform is usu. necessary to hold the defaulting party to a contract liable for breach.

2. Something unconditionally offered to satisfy a debt or obligation. **3.** *Contracts.* Attempted performance that is frustrated by the act of the party for whose benefit it is to take place. • The performance may take the form of either a tender of goods or services, or a tender of payment. Although this sense is quite similar to sense 1, it differs in making the other party's refusal part of the definition itself.

perfect tender. (18c) A seller's tender that meets the contractual terms entered into with the buyer concerning the quality and specifications of the goods sold. See PERFECT-TENDER RULE.

4. An offer or bid put forward for acceptance <a tender for the construction contract>. **5.** Something that serves as a means of payment, such as coin, banknotes, or other circulating medium; money <legal tender>. — **tender,** *vb.*

tender, plea of. See PLEA OF TENDER.

tender offer. A public offer to buy a minimum number of shares directly from a corporation's shareholders at a fixed price, usu. at a substantial premium over the market price, in an effort to take control of the corporation. — Also termed *takeover offer; takeover bid.* Cf. *public-exchange offer* under OFFER.

    cash tender offer. A tender offer in which the bidder offers to pay cash for the target's shares, as opposed to offering other corporate shares in exchange. ● Most tender offers involve cash.

    creeping tender offer. See *creeping acquisition* under ACQUISITION.

tender of issue. (1811) *Common-law pleading.* A form attached to a traverse, by which the traversing party refers the issue to the proper mode of trial.

tender-years doctrine. (1954) *Family law.* The doctrine holding that custody of very young children (usu. five years of age and younger) should generally be awarded to the mother in a divorce unless she is found to be unfit. ● This doctrine has been rejected in most states and replaced by a presumption of joint custody. See MATERNAL-PREFERENCE DOCTRINE; PRIMARY-CAREGIVER DOCTRINE.

tender-years hearsay exception. See HEARSAY EXCEPTION.

tenement. (14c) **1.** Property (esp. land) held by freehold; an estate or holding of land.

    dominant tenement. See *dominant estate* under ESTATE (4).

    servient tenement (sər-vee-ənt). See *servient estate* under ESTATE (4).

2. A house or other building used as a residence. **3.** An apartment. **4.** TENEMENT HOUSE.

tenement house. (1858) A low-rent apartment building, usu. in poor condition and at best meeting only minimal safety and sanitary conditions. — Sometimes shortened to *tenement.*

tenendum (tə-**nen**-dəm). [Latin "to be held"] (17c) A clause in a deed designating the kind of tenure by which the things granted are to be held. — Also termed *tenendum clause;* (in Scots law) *tenendas.* See HABENDUM ET TENENDUM. Cf. HABENDUM CLAUSE (1).

10-K. A financial report filed annually with the SEC by a registered corporation. ● The report typically includes an audited financial statement, a description of the corporation's business and financial condition, and summaries of other financial data. — Also termed *Form 10-K.* Cf. 8-K; 10-Q.

Tennessee Valley Authority. A government-owned corporation, created in 1933, that conducts a unified program of resource development to advance economic growth in the Tennessee Valley region.

● The Authority's activities include flood control, navigation development, electric-power production, fertilizer development, recreation improvement, and forestry-and-wildlife development. Though its power program is financially self-supporting, the Authority's other programs are financed primarily by congressional appropriations. — Abbr. TVA.

tenor, *n.* **1.** An exact copy of an instrument. **2.** The exact words of a legal document, esp. as cited in a pleading. **3.** The meaning of a legal document.

ten-percent bond. See BOND (2).

10-Q. An unaudited financial report filed quarterly with the SEC by a registered corporation. ● The 10-Q is less detailed than the 10-K. — Also termed *Form 10-Q.* Cf. 10-K.

tentative agenda. See *proposed agenda* under AGENDA.

tentative trust. See *Totten trust* under TRUST.

Tenth Amendment. The constitutional amendment, ratified as part of the Bill of Rights in 1791, providing that any powers not constitutionally delegated to the federal government, nor prohibited to the states, are reserved for the states or the people. — Also termed *Reserved Power Clause.*

1031 exchange (ten-thər-tee-wən). (1972) **1.** An exchange of like-kind property that is exempt from income-tax consequences under IRC (26 USCA) § 1031. Cf. TAX-FREE EXCHANGE. **2.** See TAX-FREE EXCHANGE.

tenure (**ten**-yər), *n.* (15c) **1.** A right, term, or mode of holding lands or tenements in subordination to a superior. ● In feudal times, real property was held predominantly as part of a tenure system. **2.** A particular feudal mode of holding lands, such as socage, gavelkind, villeinage, and frankalmoign.

    base tenure. Hist. The holding of property in villeinage rather than by military service or free service. See VILLEINAGE.

    copyhold tenure. See COPYHOLD.

    lay tenure. Hist. Any tenure not held through religious service, such as a base tenure or a freehold tenure. ● The three historical types of lay tenures are *knight-service, socage,* and *serjeanty.* See KNIGHT-SERVICE; SOCAGE; SERJEANTY. Cf. *tenure by divine service.*

    military tenure. A tenure that bears some relation to military service, such as knight-service, grand serjeanty, and cornage. — Also termed *tenure in chivalry.*

    spiritual tenure. A tenure that bears some relation to religious exercises, such as frankalmoign and tenure by divine service.

    tenure by divine service. Hist. A tenure obligating the tenant to perform an expressly defined divine service, such as singing a certain number of masses or distributing a fixed sum of alms. Cf. *lay tenure.*

tenure in chivalry. See *military tenure.*

villein tenure. See VILLEINAGE.

3. A status afforded to a teacher or professor as a protection against summary dismissal without sufficient cause. • This status has long been considered a cornerstone of academic freedom. **4.** More generally, the legal protection of a long-term relationship, such as employment. — **tenurial** (ten-**yuur**-ee-əl), *adj.*

tenured faculty. The members of a school's teaching staff who hold their positions for life or until retirement, and who may not be discharged except for cause.

tenure in capite. See IN CAPITE.

tenure in chivalry. See *military tenure* under TENURE.

tepid bench. See *lukewarm bench* under BENCH.

teratogen (tə-**rat**-ə-jən), *n.* An agent, usu. a chemical, that causes injury to a fetus or causes any of various birth defects <alcohol is a teratogen to the developing brain of a fetus>. — **teratogenic** (tə-rat-ə-**jen**-ik), *adj.*

term, *n.* (14c) **1.** A word or phrase; esp., an expression that has a fixed meaning in some field <term of art>. **2.** A contractual stipulation <the delivery term provided for shipment within 30 days>. See CONDITION (3).

essential term. See *fundamental term.*

fundamental term. (1873) **1.** A contractual provision that must be included for a contract to exist; a contractual provision that specifies an essential purpose of the contract, so that a breach of the provision through inadequate performance makes the performance not only defective but essentially different from what had been promised. **2.** A contractual provision that must be included in the contract to satisfy the statute of frauds. — Also termed *essential term; vital term.*

implied term. (18c) A provision not expressly agreed to by the parties but instead read into the contract by a court as being implicit. • An implied term should not, in theory, contradict the contract's express terms.

material term. (1839) A contractual provision dealing with a significant issue such as subject matter, price, payment, quantity, quality, duration, or the work to be done.

nonessential term. See *nonfundamental term.*

nonfundamental term. (1969) Any contractual provision that is not regarded as a fundamental term. — Also termed *nonessential term; nonvital term.*

vital term. See *fundamental term.*

3. (*pl.*) Provisions that define an agreement's scope; conditions or stipulations <terms of sale>. **4.** A fixed period of time; esp., the period for which an estate is granted <term of years>.

attendant term. (1983) A long period (such as 1,000 years) specified as the duration of a mortgage, created to protect the mortgagor's heirs' interest in the land by not taking back title to the land once it is paid for, but rather by assigning title to a trustee who holds the title in trust for the mortgagor and the mortgagor's heirs. • This arrangement gives the heirs another title to the property in case the interest they inherited proves somehow defective. These types of terms have been largely abolished. See *tenancy attendant on the inheritance* under TENANCY.

satisfied term. (18c) A term of years in land that has satisfied the purpose for which it was created before the term's expiration.

term for deliberating. (1843) The time given a beneficiary to decide whether to accept or reject an inheritance or other succession.

term in gross. (1852) A term that is unattached to an estate or inheritance. See *tenancy in gross* under TENANCY.

term of years. **1.** A fixed period covering a precise number of years. — Also termed *tenancy for a term.* **2.** *English law.* A fixed period covering less than a year, or a specified number of years and a fraction of a year. • This sense applies under a seminal English statute — the Law of Property Act of 1925.

unexpired term. The remainder of a period prescribed by law or by agreement.

5. The period or session during which a court conducts judicial business <the most recent term was busy indeed>. — Also termed (in sense 5) *term of court.* See SESSION.

additional term. A distinct, added term to a previous term.

adjourned term. (18c) A continuance of a previous or regular term but not a separate term; the same term prolonged.

appearance term. The regular judicial term in which a party is required to appear, usu. the first one after legal service has been made.

civil term. The period during which a civil court hears cases.

criminal term. A term of court during which indictments are found and returned, and criminal trials are held.

equity term. (1836) The period during which a court tries only equity cases.

general term. A regular term of court — that is, the period during which a court ordinarily sits. — Also termed *stated term*.

regular term. (1820) A term of court begun at the time appointed by law and continued, in the court's discretion, until the court lawfully adjourns.

special term. (1803) A term of court scheduled outside the general term, usu. for conducting extraordinary business.

stated term. See *general term*.

term probatory. *Eccles. law.* **1.** The period given to the promoter of an ecclesiastical suit to produce witnesses and prove the case. **2.** *Hist.* The time assigned for taking testimony. — Sometimes termed (in sense 2) *probatory term*.

term to conclude. *Eccles. law.* A deadline imposed by the judge for all parties to renounce any further exhibits and allegations.

term to propound all things. *Eccles. law.* A deadline imposed by the judge for the parties to exhibit all evidence supporting their positions.

6. *Hist. English law.* One of the four periods in a year during which the courts are in session to conduct judicial business. ● Terms came into use in the 13th century, and their dates varied. The four terms — Hilary, Easter, Trinity, and Michaelmas — were abolished by the Judicature Acts of 1873–1875, and the legal year was divided into sittings and vacations. Terms are still maintained by the Inns of Court to determine various time periods and dates, such as a call to the bar or observance of a Grand Day.

term annuity. See *annuity certain* under ANNUITY.

term attendant on the inheritance. See *tenancy attendant on the inheritance* under TENANCY.

term bond. See BOND (3).

term clause. See HABENDUM CLAUSE.

term day. See *quarter day* under DAY.

term deposit. See *time deposit* under DEPOSIT.

term for deliberating. See TERM (4).

term for years. See *tenancy for a term* under TENANCY.

terminable interest. See INTEREST (2).

terminable property. See PROPERTY.

terminal disclaimer. See DISCLAIMER.

terminate, *vb.* **1.** To put an end to; to bring to an end. **2.** To end; to conclude.

termination, *n.* (15c) **1.** The act of ending something; EXTINGUISHMENT <termination of the partnership by winding up its affairs>.

termination of conditional contract. The act of putting an end to all unperformed portions of a conditional contract.

termination of employment. The complete severance of an employer–employee relationship.

2. The end of something in time or existence; conclusion or discontinuance <the insurance policy's termination left the doctor without liability coverage>. — **terminate,** *vb.* — **terminable,** *adj.*

termination clause. See CANCELLATION CLAUSE.

termination fee. A fee paid if a party voluntarily backs out of a deal to sell or purchase a business or a business's assets. ● Termination fees are usu. negotiated and agreed on as part of corporate merger or acquisition negotiations. The fee is designed to protect the prospective buyer and to deter the target corporation from entertaining bids from other parties. — Also termed *break-up fee*.

termination-for-convenience clause. A contractual provision allowing the government to terminate all or a portion of a contract when it chooses. ● Among the governmental contracts that often include a termination-for-convenience clause are service contracts, research-and-development contracts, and fixed-price contracts. See 48 CFR § 52.249-1--52.249-2.

termination hearing. See *termination-of-parental-rights hearing* under HEARING.

termination of parental rights. (1939) *Family law.* The legal severing of a parent's rights, privileges, and responsibilities regarding his or her child. ● Termination of a parent's rights frees the child to be adopted by someone else. — Abbr. TPR. See *termination-of-parental-rights hearing* under HEARING; PARENTAL RIGHTS.

termination-of-parental-rights hearing. See HEARING.

termination proceeding. (1939) An administrative action to end a person's or entity's status or relationship. ● For example, the International Banking Act authorizes the International Banking Board to institute a termination proceeding when a foreign bank or its U.S. agency or branch is convicted of money-laundering. 12 USCA § 3105(e).

terminer. See OYER AND TERMINER.

term in gross. See TERM (4).

term interest. *Oil & gas.* A mineral interest or royalty interest that is not perpetual. ● A term interest may be for a fixed term (e.g., for 25 years) or defeasible (e.g., for 25 years and so long thereafter as there is production from the premises).

term life insurance. See LIFE INSURANCE.

term loan. See LOAN.

term of art. (17c) **1.** A word or phrase having a specific, precise meaning in a given specialty, apart from its general meaning in ordinary contexts. ● Examples in law include *and his heirs* and *res* *ipsa loquitur.* **2.** Loosely, a jargonistic word or phrase. — Also termed *word of art.*

term-of-art canon. (1994) In statutory construction, the principle that if a term has acquired a technical or specialized meaning in a particular context, the term should be presumed to have that meaning if used in that context.

term of court. See TERM (5).

term of office. The period during which an elected officer or appointee may hold office, perform its functions, and enjoy its privileges and emoluments.

term of years. 1. See TERM (4). **2.** See *tenancy for a term* under TENANCY.

termor (**tər**-mər). (14c) A person who holds lands or tenements for a term of years or for life.

term policy. See INSURANCE POLICY.

term probatory. See TERM (5).

terms. See YEAR BOOKS.

term sheet. *Securities.* **1.** A document setting forth all information that is material to investors about the offering but is not disclosed in the accompanying prospectus or the confirmation. **2.** LETTER OF INTENT.

  abbreviated term sheet. A term sheet that includes (1) the description of the securities as required by Item 202 of SEC Regulation S-K, or a good summary of that information; and (2) all material changes to the issuer's affairs required to be disclosed on SEC Form S-3 or F-3, as applicable.

termtime. The time of the year when a court is in session.

term to conclude. See TERM (5).

term to propound all things. See TERM (5).

terra nullius (**ter**-ə **nəl**-ee-əs), *n.* [Latin "the land of no one"] A territory not belonging to any particular country.

terre-tenant (**tair** ten-ənt). (15c) **1.** One who has actual possession of land; the occupant of land. **2.** One who has an interest in a judgment debtor's land after the judgment creditor's lien has attached to the land (such as a subsequent purchaser). — Also spelled *tertenant* (**tər**-ten-ənt). — Also termed *land-tenant.*

territorial, *adj.* Having to do with a particular geographical area.

territorial court. See COURT.

territorialism. (1977) The traditional approach to choice of law, whereby the place of injury or of contract formation determines which state's law will be applied in a case. See CHOICE OF LAW.

territoriality. *Int'l law.* The principle that a nation has the right of sovereignty within its borders.

territorial jurisdiction. See JURISDICTION.

territorial law. The law that applies to all persons within a given territory regardless of their citizenship or nationality. Cf. PERSONAL LAW.

territorial property. Land and water over which a state has jurisdiction and control, whether the legal title is held by the state or by a private individual or entity. ● Lakes and waters wholly within a state are generally its property, as is the marginal sea within the three-mile limit, but bays and gulfs are not always recognized as state property.

territorial sea. See *territorial waters* under WATER.

territorial waters. See WATER.

territory, *n.* (14c) **1.** A geographical area included within a particular government's jurisdiction; the portion of the earth's surface that is in a state's exclusive possession and control. Cf. INSULAR AREA.

  non-self-governing territory. *Int'l law.* A territory that is governed by another country. ● These types of territories are rarely allowed representation in the governing country's legislature.

  trust territory. *Int'l law.* A territory to which the United Nations' international trusteeship system formerly applied; a territory once administered by the United Nations or a member state for the political, economic, educational, and social advancement of its inhabitants. ● All territories that were subject to this system either became independent nations or opted to become part of another nation.

2. A part of the United States not included within any state but organized with a separate legislature (such as Guam and the U.S. Virgin Islands). Cf. COMMONWEALTH (2); DEPENDENCY (1). — **territorial,** *adj.*

territory of a judge. (18c) The territorial jurisdiction of a particular court. See JURISDICTION (3).

terrorem clause. See NO-CONTEST CLAUSE.

terrorism, *n.* (18c) The use or threat of violence to intimidate or cause panic, esp. as a means of affecting political conduct. See 18 USCA § 2331. See also *terroristic threat* under THREAT; *terrorism insurance* under INSURANCE. — **terrorist,** *adj. & n.*

  bioterrorism. Terrorism involving the intentional release of harmful biological agents, such as bacteria or viruses, into the air, food, or water supply, esp. of humans. — Also termed *biological terrorism.*

  cyberterrorism. Terrorism committed by using a computer to make unlawful attacks and threats of attack against computers, networks, and electronically stored information, and actually causing the target to fear or experience harm.

domestic terrorism. **1.** Terrorism that occurs primarily within the territorial jurisdiction of the United States. 18 USCA § 2331(5). **2.** Terrorism that is carried out against one's own government or fellow citizens.

ecoterrorism. Terrorism related to environmental issues or animal rights. — Also termed *enviroterrorism; ecological terrorism; environmental terrorism; ecosabotage; ecovandalism.*

international terrorism. Terrorism that occurs primarily outside the territorial jurisdiction of the United States, or that transcends national boundaries by the means in which it is carried out, the people it is intended to intimidate, or the place where the perpetrators operate or seek asylum. 18 USCA § 2331(1). Cf. *state-sponsored terrorism.*

state-sponsored terrorism. **1.** International terrorism supported by a sovereign government to pursue strategic and political objectives. **2.** See *state terrorism* (1). Cf. *international terrorism.*

state terrorism. **1.** Terrorism practiced by a sovereign government, esp. against its own people. ● Under international legal principles of sovereignty, a government's conduct that has effects only within its borders is generally not subject to interference from other nations. **2.** See *state-sponsored terrorism* (1).

terrorism insurance. See INSURANCE.

terroristic threat. See THREAT.

terrorizing, *n. Family law.* A parent's or caregiver's act of orally assaulting, bullying, or frightening a child, or causing the child to believe that the world is a hostile place.

Terry **stop.** See STOP AND FRISK.

tertenant. See TERRE-TENANT.

tertius gaudens (tǝr-shee-ǝs **gaw**-denz). [Latin "a rejoicing third"] A third party who profits when two others dispute.

testable, *adj.* (17c) **1.** Capable of being tested <a testable hypothesis>. **2.** Capable of being transferred by will <today virtually all property is considered testable>. **3.** Capable of making a will <an 18-year-old person is testable in this state>. **4.** Legally qualified to testify as a witness or give evidence <the witness is testable about the statement>.

test action. See *test case* (2) under CASE.

testacy. The state or condition of a person having died with a valid will. Cf. INTESTACY.

testament (tes-tǝ-mǝnt). (14c) **1.** Traditionally, a will disposing of personal property. Cf. DEVISE (4). **2.** WILL (2).

closed testament. See *mystic will* under WILL.

inofficious testament. Civil law. A will that does not dispose of property to the testator's natural heirs; esp., a will that deprives the heirs of a portion of the estate to which they are entitled by law. — Also termed *inofficious will; unofficious will.* See *forced heir* under HEIR.

military testament. See *soldier's will* under WILL.

mutual testament. See *mutual will* under WILL.

mystic testament. See *mystic will* under WILL.

officious testament. Civil law. A will that disposes of property to the testator's family; a will that reserves the legitime for the testator's children and other natural heirs. — Also termed *officious will.* See LEGITIME.

sealed testament. See *mystic will* under WILL.

secret testament. See *mystic will* under WILL.

testamentary (tes-tǝ-**men**-tǝ-ree *or* -tree), *adj.* (14c) **1.** Of or relating to a will or testament <testamentary intent>. **2.** Provided for or appointed by a will <testamentary guardian>. **3.** Created by a will <testamentary gift>.

testamentary capacity. See CAPACITY (3).

testamentary class. See CLASS (3).

testamentary condition. See CONDITION (2).

testamentary disposition. See DISPOSITION (1).

testamentary gift. See GIFT.

testamentary guardian. See GUARDIAN.

testamentary heir. See HEIR.

testamentary instrument. See WILL.

testamentary intent. See INTENT (1).

testamentary power of appointment. See POWER OF APPOINTMENT.

testamentary succession. See SUCCESSION (2).

testamentary transfer. See TRANSFER.

testamentary trust. See TRUST.

testamentary trustee. See TRUSTEE (1).

testate (**tes**-tayt), *adj.* (15c) Having left a will at death <she died testate>. Cf. INTESTATE.

testate, *n.* See TESTATOR.

testate succession. See SUCCESSION (2).

testation (te-**stay**-shǝn). **1.** The disposal of property by will; the power to dispose of property by will. **2.** *Archaic.* Attestation; a witnessing.

testator (**tes**-tay-tǝr *also* te-**stay**-tǝr). (14c) A person who has made a will; esp., a person who dies leaving a will. ● Because this term is usu. interpreted as applying to both sexes, *testatrix* has become archaic. — Also termed *testate.* Cf. INTESTATE.

testatrix (te-**stay**-triks *or* tes-tǝ-triks). *Archaic.* A female testator. ● In modern usage, a person who leaves a will is called a testator, regardless of sex. Pl. **testatrixes, testatrices.**

test case. See CASE.

teste (**tes**-tee). [Latin *teste meipso* "I myself being a witness"] **1.** In drafting, the clause that states the name of a witness and evidences the act of witnessing. — Also termed *teste of process*; *teste of writ*. **2.** The final clause in a royal writ naming the person who authorizes the affixing of the king's seal. ● The clause generally contains the place and date of the sealing. When the monarch authenticates the sealing, the clause begins with the phase *teste meipso* ("by my own witness"). Otherwise, the authenticator states his or her name and office.

testifier. One who testifies; WITNESS. — Also termed (archaically) *testificator* (**tes**-tə-fi-kay-tər).

testify, *vb.* (14c) **1.** To give evidence as a witness <she testified that the Ford Bronco was at the defendant's home at the critical time>. **2.** (Of a person or thing) to bear witness <the incomplete log entries testified to his sloppiness>.

testifying expert. See EXPERT.

testimonial evidence. 1. See TESTIMONY. **2.** See EVIDENCE.

testimonial immunity. See IMMUNITY (3).

testimonial incapacity. See INCAPACITY.

testimonial privilege. See PRIVILEGE (1).

testimonial proof. See PROOF.

testimonium clause. (1823) A provision at the end of an instrument (esp. a will) reciting the date when the instrument was signed, by whom it was signed, and in what capacity. ● This clause traditionally begins with the phrase "In witness whereof." — Also termed *testatum clause*; *witness clause*. Cf. ATTESTATION CLAUSE.

testimony, *n.* (14c) Evidence that a competent witness under oath or affirmation gives at trial or in an affidavit or deposition. — Also termed *testimonial evidence*; *personal evidence*. — **testimonial,** *adj.*

  affirmative testimony. (1806) Testimony about whether something occurred or did not occur, based on what the witness saw or heard at the time and place in question. — Also termed *positive testimony*; (formerly) *statement of fact*. See *direct evidence* under EVIDENCE.

  cumulative testimony. (1818) Identical or similar testimony by more than one witness, and usu. by several, offered by a party usu. to impress the jury with the apparent weight of proof on that party's side. ● The trial court typically limits cumulative testimony.

  dropsy testimony. (1970) *Slang.* A police officer's false testimony that a fleeing suspect dropped an illegal substance that was then confiscated by the police and used as probable cause for arresting the suspect. ● Dropsy testimony is sometimes given when an arrest has been made without probable cause, as when illegal substances have been found through an improper search.

  expert testimony. See *expert evidence* under EVIDENCE.

  false testimony. (16c) Testimony that is untrue. ● This term is broader than *perjury*, which has a state-of-mind element. Unlike perjury, false testimony does not denote a crime. — Also termed *false evidence*.

  interpreted testimony. Testimony translated because the witness cannot communicate in the language of the tribunal.

  lay opinion testimony. (1942) Evidence given by a witness who is not qualified as an expert but who testifies to opinions or inferences. ● In federal court, the admissibility of this testimony is limited to opinions or inferences that are rationally based on the witness's perception and that will be helpful to a clear understanding of the witness's testimony or the determination of a fact in issue. Fed. R. Evid. 701.

  mediate testimony. See *secondary evidence* under EVIDENCE.

  negative testimony. See *negative evidence* under EVIDENCE.

  nonverbal testimony. (1922) A photograph, drawing, map, chart, or other depiction used to aid a witness in testifying. ● The witness need not have made it, but it must accurately represent something that the witness saw. See *demonstrative evidence* under EVIDENCE.

  opinion testimony. (1925) Testimony based on one's belief or idea rather than on direct knowledge of the facts at issue. ● Opinion testimony from either a lay witness or an expert witness may be allowed in evidence under certain conditions. See *opinion evidence* under EVIDENCE.

  positive testimony. See *affirmative testimony*.

  testimony de bene esse (dee **bee**-nee **es**-ee *also* day **ben**-ay es-ay). (1805) Testimony taken because it is in danger of being lost before it can be given at a trial or hearing, usu. because of the impending death or departure of the witness. ● Such testimony is taken in aid of a pending case, while testimony taken under a bill to perpetuate testimony is taken in anticipation of future litigation. See *deposition de bene esse* under DEPOSITION.

  written testimony. (17c) **1.** Testimony given out of court by deposition or affidavit. ● The recorded writing, signed by the witness, is considered testimony. **2.** In some administrative agencies and courts, direct narrative testimony that is reduced to writing, to which the witness swears at a hearing or trial before cross-examination takes place in the traditional way.

test oath. See *oath of allegiance* under OATH.

test paper. A writing that has been proved genuine and submitted to a jury as a standard by which to determine the authenticity of other writings. • The court decides the test paper's authenticity as a matter of law before it is used by the jury. Direct evidence, such as a witness to the writing's creation or an admission by the party, is preferred, but strong circumstantial evidence is usu. acceptable. In Pennsylvania, a paper or instrument shown to the jury as evidence is still called a *test paper* (sometimes written *test-paper*).

Texas ballot. See BALLOT (4).

textbook digest. (1922) A legal text whose aim is to set forth the law of a subject in condensed form, with little or no criticism or discussion of the authorities cited, and no serious attempt to explain or reconcile apparently conflicting decisions.

textual citation. See CITATION (4).

textualism. See *strict constructionism* under CONSTRUCTIONISM.

thalweg (**tahl**-vayk *or* -veg). (1831) **1.** A line following the lowest part of a (usu. submerged) valley. **2.** The middle of the primary navigable channel of a waterway, constituting the boundary between states. — Also spelled *talweg*. — Also termed *midway*.

> **live thalweg.** The part of a river channel that is most followed, usu. at the middle of the principal channel. *Louisiana v. Mississippi*, 466 U.S. 96, 104 S.Ct. 1645 (1984).

Thayer presumption. (1958) A presumption that allows the party against whom the presumption operates to come forward with evidence to rebut the presumption, but that does not shift the burden of proof to that party. *See* James B. Thayer, *A Preliminary Treatise on Evidence* 31–44 (1898). • Most presumptions that arise in civil trials in federal court are interpreted in this way. Fed. R. Evid. 301. Cf. MORGAN PRESUMPTION.

The Federalist. See FEDERALIST PAPERS.

theft, *n.* (bef. 12c) **1.** The wrongful taking and removing of another's personal property with the intent of depriving the true owner of it; larceny. **2.** Broadly, any act or instance of stealing, including larceny, burglary, embezzlement, and false pretenses. • Many modern penal codes have consolidated such property offenses under the name "theft." — Also termed (in Latin) *crimen furti*. See LARCENY. Cf. ROBBERY.

> ***cybertheft.*** See CYBERTHEFT.

> ***identity theft.*** See IDENTITY THEFT.

> ***petty theft.*** A theft of a small quantity of cash or of low-value goods or services. • This offense is usu. a misdemeanor.

> ***theft by deception.*** (1930) The use of trickery to obtain another's property, esp. by (1) creating or reinforcing a false impression (as about value), (2) preventing one from obtaining information that would affect one's judgment about a transaction, or (3) failing to disclose, in a property transfer, a known lien or other legal impediment. Model Penal Code § 223.

> ***theft by extortion.*** (1969) Larceny in which the perpetrator obtains property by threatening to (1) inflict bodily harm on anyone or commit any other criminal offense, (2) accuse anyone of a criminal offense, (3) expose any secret tending to subject any person to hatred, contempt, or ridicule, or impair one's credit or business reputation, (4) take or withhold action as an official, or cause an official to take or withhold action, (5) bring about or continue a strike, boycott, or other collective unofficial action, if the property is not demanded or received for the benefit of the group in whose interest the actor purports to act, (6) testify or provide information or withhold testimony or information with respect to another's legal claim or defense, or (7) inflict any other harm that would not benefit the actor. Model Penal Code § 223.4. — Also termed *larceny by extortion*. See EXTORTION.

> ***theft by false pretext.*** The use of a false pretext to obtain another's property.

> ***theft of property lost, mislaid, or delivered by mistake.*** (1973) Larceny in which one obtains control of property the person knows to be lost, mislaid, or delivered by mistake (esp. in the amount of property or identity of recipient) and fails to take reasonable measures to restore the property to the rightful owner. Model Penal Code § 223.5. — Also termed *larceny of property lost, mislaid, or delivered by mistake*.

> ***theft of services.*** (1946) The act of obtaining services from another by deception, threat, coercion, stealth, mechanical tampering, or using a false token or device. See Model Penal Code § 223.7.

theftbote. (**theft**-boht) See BOTE (2).

theftuous (**thef**-choo-əs), *adj.* **1.** (Of an act) characterized by theft. **2.** (Of a person) given to stealing. — Also spelled *theftous*.

thence, *adv.* (13c) **1.** From that place; from that time. • In surveying, and in describing land by courses and distances, this word, preceding each course given, implies that the following course is continuous with the one before it <south 240 feet to an iron post, thence west 59 feet>. **2.** On that account; therefore.

thence down the river. (16c) With the meanders of a river. • This phrase appears in the field notes of patent surveyors, indicating that the survey follows a meandering river unless evidence shows that the meander line as written was where the surveyor in fact ran it. Meander lines show the general course of the river and are used in estimating acreage, but are not necessarily boundary lines. See MEANDER LINE.

theocracy (thee-**ok**-rə-see). (17c) **1.** Government of a state by those who are believed to be or represent that they are acting under the immediate direction of God or some other divinity. **2.** A state in which power is exercised by ecclesiastics.

Theodosian Code (thee-ə-**doh**-shən). *Roman law.* A compilation of imperial enactments prepared at the direction of the emperor Theodosius II and published in A.D. 438. • The Theodosian Code replaced all other imperial legislation from the time of Constantine I (A.D. 306–337), and remained the basis of Roman law until it was superseded by the first Justinian Code in A.D. 529. — Also termed (in Latin) *Codex Theodosianus* (**koh**-deks thee-ə-doh-shee-**ay**-nəs).

theory of law. The legal premise or set of principles on which a case rests.

theory-of-pleading doctrine. (1956) The principle — now outmoded — that one must prove a case exactly as pleaded. • Various modern codes and rules of civil procedure have abolished this strict pleading-and-proof requirement. For example, Fed. R. Civ. P. 15 allows amendment of pleadings to conform to the evidence.

theory of the case. (1800) A comprehensive and orderly mental arrangement of principles and facts, conceived and constructed for the purpose of securing a judgment or decree of a court in favor of a litigant; the particular line of reasoning of either party to a suit, the purpose being to bring together certain facts of the case in a logical sequence and to correlate them in a way that produces in the decision-maker's mind a definite result or conclusion favored by the advocate. See CAUSE OF ACTION (1).

therapeutic abortion. See ABORTION.

therapeutic jurisprudence. See JURISPRUDENCE.

therapeutic relief. See RELIEF.

therapeutics. See *therapeutic relief* under RELIEF.

thereabouts, *adv.* (bef. 12c) Near that time or place <Schreuer was seen in Rudolf Place or thereabouts>. — Also termed *thereabout.*

thereafter, *adv.* (bef. 12c) Afterward; later <Skurry was thereafter arrested>.

thereat, *adv.* (bef. 12c) **1.** At that place or time; there. **2.** Because of that; at that occurrence or event.

thereby, *adv.* (bef. 12c) By that means; in that way <Blofeld stepped into the embassy and thereby found protection>.

therefor, *adv.* (bef. 12c) For it or them; for that thing or action; for those things or actions <she lied to Congress but was never punished therefor>.

therefore, *adv.* (14c) **1.** For that reason; on that ground or those grounds <a quorum was not present; therefore, no vote was taken>. **2.** To that end <she wanted to become a tax lawyer, and she therefore applied for the university's renowned LL.M. program in taxation>. — Also termed *thereupon.*

therefrom, *adv.* (13c) From that, it, or them <Hofer had several financial obligations to Ricks, who refused to release Hofer therefrom>.

therein, *adv.* (bef. 12c) **1.** In that place or time <the Dallas/Fort Worth metroplex has a population of about 3 million, and some 20,000 lawyers practice therein>. **2.** Inside or within that thing; inside or within those things <there were 3 school buses with 108 children therein>. **3.** In that regard, circumstance, or particular <therein lies the problem>.

thereinafter, *adv.* (1818) Later in that thing (such as a speech or document) <the book's first reference was innocuous, but the five references thereinafter were libelous per se>.

thereof, *adv.* (bef. 12c) Of that, it, or them <although the disease is spreading rapidly, the cause thereof is unknown>.

thereon, *adv.* (bef. 12c) On that or them <Michaels found the online reports of the cases and relied thereon instead of checking the printed books>. — Also termed *thereupon.*

thereto, *adv.* (bef. 12c) To that place, thing, issue, or the like <the jury awarded $750,000 in actual damages, and it added thereto another $250,000 in punitive damages>. — Also termed *thereunto.*

theretofore, *adv.* (14c) Until that time; before that time <theretofore, the highest award in such a case has been $450,000>.

thereunder, *adv.* (bef. 12c) Under that or them <on the top shelf were three books, and situated thereunder was the missing banknote> <section 1988 was the relevant fee statute, and the plaintiffs were undeniably proceeding thereunder>.

thereunto, *adv.* See THERETO.

thereupon, *adv.* (13c) **1.** Immediately; without delay; promptly <the writ of execution issued from the court, and the sheriff thereupon sought to find the judgment debtor>. **2.** THEREON. **3.** THEREFORE.

***Thibodaux* abstention** (tib-ə-doh). See ABSTENTION.

thief. (bef. 12c) One who steals, esp. without force or violence; one who commits theft or larceny. See THEFT.

   common thief. (16c) A thief who has been convicted of theft or larceny more than once. — Also termed *common and notorious thief.*

thieve, *vb.* (bef. 12c) To steal; to commit theft or larceny. See THEFT.

thievery. The act or practice of stealing.

thimblerig. See SHELL GAME.

thimbles and balls. See SHELL GAME.

thin capitalization. See CAPITALIZATION.

thin corporation. See CORPORATION.

thing. (bef. 12c) **1.** The subject matter of a right, whether it is a material object or not; any subject matter of ownership within the sphere of proprietary or valuable rights. ● Things are divided into three categories: (1) things real or immovable, such as land, tenements, and hereditaments, (2) things personal or movable, such as goods and chattels, and (3) things having both real and personal characteristics, such as a title deed and a tenancy for a term. The civil law divided things into corporeal (*tangi possunt*) and incorporeal (*tangi non possunt*). La. Civ. Code art. 461.

   accessory thing. A thing that stands in a dependency relationship with another thing (the principal thing). ● An accessory thing ordinarily serves the economic or other purpose of the principal thing and shares its legal fate in case of transfer or encumbrance.

   corporeal thing. (17c) The subject matter of corporeal ownership; a material object. — Also termed *res corporales; tangible thing.*

   immovable thing. See IMMOVABLE.

   incorporeal thing. (17c) The subject matter of incorporeal ownership; any proprietary right apart from the right of full dominion over a material object. — Also termed *res incorporale; intangible thing.*

   movable thing. See MOVABLE (1).

   real things. See REAL THINGS.

   thing in action. See *chose in action* under CHOSE.

   thing in possession. See *chose in possession* under CHOSE.

2. Anything that is owned by someone as part of that person's estate or property. — Also termed *res; chose.*

thing in action. See *chose in action* under CHOSE.

thing in possession. See *chose in possession* under CHOSE.

things personal. See *personal property* (1) under PROPERTY.

things real. See REAL THINGS.

thin market. See MARKET.

thin-skull rule. See EGGSHELL-SKULL RULE.

Third Amendment. The constitutional amendment, ratified as part of the Bill of Rights in 1791, prohibiting the quartering of soldiers in private homes except during wartime.

third cousin. See COUSIN.

third degree, *n.* (1900) The process of extracting a confession or information from a suspect or prisoner by prolonged questioning, the use of threats, or physical torture <the police gave the suspect the third degree>.

third-degree instruction. See ALLEN CHARGE.

third-degree murder. See MURDER.

third estate. *Property.* A landowner's right to have the land supported below the surface against subsidence when it is undermined by tunnels, such as those made for mining operations. ● The phrase appears most frequently in Pennsylvania, where the common law traditionally recognizes three estates in land: the surface (first or surface estate), the minerals (second or mineral estate), and an estate in the support of the surface (the third estate). The third estate originated with the common-law duty of miners to support the surface estate.

third opposition. *Civil law.* A species of intervention, usu. in a real-property case, in which the third party asserts a claim of ownership or other real right to seized property, and the claim does not depend on the outcome of the original suit between the plaintiff and the defendant. La. Code Civ. Proc. art. 1092. *See, e.g., Atkins v. Smith,* 15 So. 2d 855 (La. 1943). See INTERVENTION (1).

third party, *n.* (1818) A person who is not a party to a lawsuit, agreement, or other transaction but who is usu. somehow implicated in it; someone other than the principal parties. — Also termed *outside party; third person.* See PARTY. — **third-party,** *adj.*

third-party, *vb.* (1965) To bring (a person or entity) into litigation as a third-party defendant <seeking indemnity, the defendant third-partied the surety>.

third-party action. See ACTION (4).

third-party beneficiary. See BENEFICIARY.

third-party-beneficiary contract. See CONTRACT.

third-party business-buyout agreement. See AGREEMENT.

third-party check. (1904) A check that the payee indorses to another party — for example, a customer check that the payee indorses to a supplier. ● A person who takes a third-party check in good faith and without notice of a security interest can be a holder in due course.

third-party complaint. See COMPLAINT.

third-party consent. (1942) A person's agreement to official action (such as a search of premises) that affects another person's rights or interests. • To be effective for a search, third-party consent must be based on the consenting person's common authority over the place to be searched or the items to be inspected. See COMMON-AUTHORITY RULE.

third-party defendant. (1927) A party brought into a lawsuit by the original defendant.

third-party equity lease. See *leveraged lease* under LEASE.

third-party insurance. See *liability insurance* under INSURANCE.

third-party logistical service provider. See FREIGHT FORWARDER. — Abbr. TPL.

third-party plaintiff. (1857) A defendant who files a pleading in an effort to bring a third party into the lawsuit. See *third-party complaint* under COMPLAINT.

third-party practice. See IMPLEADER.

third-party record-custodian summons. See *John Doe summons* under SUMMONS.

third-party standing. See STANDING.

third person. See THIRD PARTY.

third possessor. *Civil law.* A person who acquires mortgaged property but is not personally bound by the obligation secured by the mortgage.

Third World. *Int'l law.* **1.** DEVELOPING COUNTRY. **2.** The group of nations (esp. in Africa and Asia) not aligned with major powers, whether Western democracies (i.e., the *First* — or *Free* — *World*) or countries that were formerly part of the Soviet bloc (i.e., the *Second World*). • Although Third World nations are often underdeveloped, the term *Third World* may denote only their political rather than their economic status.

Third World country. See DEVELOPING COUNTRY.

Thirteenth Amendment. The constitutional amendment, ratified in 1865, that abolished slavery and involuntary servitude.

30(b)(6) deposition. See DEPOSITION.

thirty-day letter. (1929) A letter that accompanies a revenue agent's report issued as a result of an Internal Revenue Service audit or the rejection of a taxpayer's claim for refund and that outlines the taxpayer's appeal procedure before the Internal Revenue Service. • If the taxpayer does not request any such procedure within the 30-day period, the IRS will issue a statutory notice of deficiency. Cf. NINETY-DAY LETTER.

threat, *n.* (bef. 12c) **1.** A communicated intent to inflict harm or loss on another or on another's property, esp. one that might diminish a person's freedom to act voluntarily or with lawful consent <a kidnapper's threats of violence>.

    terroristic threat. (1959) A threat to commit any crime of violence with the purpose of (1) terrorizing another, (2) causing the evacuation of a building, place of assembly, or facility of public transportation, (3) causing serious public inconvenience, or (4) recklessly disregarding the risk of causing such terror or inconvenience. Model Penal Code § 211. See TERRORISM.

    2. An indication of an approaching menace <the threat of bankruptcy>. **3.** A person or thing that might well cause harm <Mrs. Harrington testified that she had never viewed her husband as a threat>. — **threaten,** *vb.* — **threatening,** *adj.*

threatened species. See SPECIES (1).

threat of continuing harm. See CONTINUING THREAT OF HARM.

threat of continuing injury. See CONTINUING THREAT OF HARM.

three estates, the. See ESTATES OF THE REALM (1).

threefold ordeal. See *triple ordeal* under ORDEAL.

312 amendment. See *amendment after allowance* under PATENT-APPLICATION AMENDMENT.

341 meeting. See *creditors' meeting* under MEETING.

three-judge court. See COURT.

three-mile limit. The distance of one marine league or three miles offshore, usu. recognized as the limit of territorial jurisdiction.

three-step test. *Copyright.* An analysis of an infringement defense under TRIPs and the Berne Convention, looking at whether the defendant's use of a protected work (1) is inherently limited to special cases, (2) did not conflict with the owner's normal exploitation of the work, and (3) did not unreasonably prejudice the legitimate interests of the owner. • The test is analogous to the analysis under the fair-use doctrine in U.S. law.

three-strikes law. (1984) *Slang.* A statute prescribing an enhanced sentence, esp. life imprisonment, for a repeat offender's third felony conviction. • About half the states have enacted a statute of this kind. — Also termed *three-strikes-and-you're-out law.*

three wicked sisters. *Slang.* The three doctrines — contributory negligence, the fellow-servant rule, and assumption of the risk — used by 19th-century courts to deny recovery to workers injured on the job.

threshold. *Parliamentary law.* The number or proportion of votes needed for election.

threshold confession. See CONFESSION.

thrift institution. See SAVINGS-AND-LOAN ASSO-
CIATION.

through bill of lading. See BILL OF LADING.

through lot. A lot that abuts a street at each end.

through rate. The total shipping cost when two or
more carriers are involved. • The carriers agree
in advance on a through rate, which is typically
lower than the sum of the separate rates.

throwaway, *n. Slang.* **1.** An unemancipated minor
whose parent or caregiver has forced him or her to
leave home. **2.** A runaway whose parent or caregiver refuses to allow him or her to return home.
Cf. RUNAWAY.

throwback rule. (1972) *Tax.* **1.** In the taxation of
trusts, a rule requiring that an amount distributed in any tax year that exceeds the year's distributable net income must be treated as if it had
been distributed in the preceding year. • The beneficiary is taxed in the current year although the
computation is made as if the excess had been distributed in the previous year. If the trust did not
have undistributed accumulated income in the
preceding year, the amount of the throwback is
tested against each of the preceding years. IRC (26
USCA) §§ 665–668. **2.** A taxation rule requiring
a sale that would otherwise be exempt from state
income tax (because the state to which the sale
would be assigned for apportionment purposes
does not have an income tax, even though the
seller's state does) to be attributed to the seller's
state and thus subjected to a state-level tax. • This
rule applies only if the seller's state has adopted
a throwback rule.

throw out, *vb.* (1817) To dismiss (a claim or lawsuit).

thrust-upon conflict. See CONFLICT OF INTER-
EST.

thumbprint. See FINGERPRINT.

ticket, *n.* **1.** A certificate indicating that the person
to whom it is issued, or the holder, is entitled to
some right or privilege <she bought a bus ticket
for Miami>. **2.** CITATION (2) <he got a speeding
ticket last week>. **3.** BALLOT (2) <they all voted a
straight-party ticket>.

ticket of leave. *Archaic.* The English equivalent of
parole.

ticket-of-leave man. A convict who has obtained
a ticket of leave.

ticket speculator. A person who buys tickets and
then resells them for more than their face value;
in slang, a scalper. See SCALPER (1).

tidal, *adj.* Affected by or having tides. • For a river
to be "tidal" at a given spot, the water need not
necessarily be salt, but the spot must be one where
the tide, in the ordinary and regular course of
things, flows and reflows.

tide. The rising and falling of seawater that is produced by the attraction of the sun and moon,
uninfluenced by special winds, seasons, or other
circumstances that create meteorological and atmospheric meteorological tides; the ebb and flow
of the sea. • Tides are used to measure a shore's
upland boundary.

> *lower low tide.* The lowest point of the daily
> tide.

> *mean high tide.* The average of all high tides, esp.
> over a period of 18.6 years. — Also termed *or-
> dinary high tide.*

> *mean lower low tide.* The average of lower low
> tides over a fixed period.

> *mean low tide.* The average of all low tides — both
> low and lower low — over a fixed period.

> *neap tide* (neep). A tide, either high tide or low
> tide, that is lower than average because it oc-
> curs during the first or last quarter of the moon,
> when the sun's attraction partly counteracts the
> moon's.

> *ordinary high tide.* See *mean high tide.*

> *spring tide.* A tide, either high tide or low tide,
> that is higher than average because it occurs
> during the new moon and full moon.

tideland. (18c) Land between the lines of the ordinary high and low tides, covered and uncovered
successively by the ebb and flow of those tides;
land covered and uncovered by the ordinary
tides.

tidewater. (18c) Water that falls and rises with the
ebb and flow of the tide. • The term is not usu.
applied to the open sea, but to coves, bays, and
rivers.

tideway. (18c) Land between high- and low-water
marks.

tie, *n.* **1.** An equal number of votes for two candidates in an election. **2.** An equal number of votes
cast for and against a particular measure by a legislative or deliberative body. • In the U.S. Senate,
the Vice President has the deciding vote in the
event of a tie. U.S. Const. art. I, § 3. See *tie vote*
under VOTE.

tied product. See TYING ARRANGEMENT (1).

tied service. See TYING ARRANGEMENT (1).

tie-in arrangement. See TYING ARRANGEMENT.

tiered partnership. See PARTNERSHIP.

tie vote. See VOTE (3).

TIF. *abbr.* TAX-INCREMENT FINANCING.

tight, *adj. Slang.* (Of a note, bond, mortgage, lease,
etc.) characterized by summary and stringent
clauses providing the creditor's remedies in case
of default.

TILA. *abbr.* Truth in Lending Act. See CONSUMER CREDIT PROTECTION ACT.

tillage (til-ij), *n.* (15c) A place tilled or cultivated; land under cultivation as opposed to land lying fallow or in pasture.

till-tapping. (1893) *Slang.* Theft of money from a cash register.

timber easement. See EASEMENT.

timber lease. See LEASE.

timber rights. See *timber easement* under EASEMENT.

time. (bef. 12c) **1.** A measure of duration. **2.** A point in or period of duration at or during which something is alleged to have occurred. **3.** *Slang.* A convicted criminal's period of incarceration.

    dead time. (1909) Time that does not count for a particular purpose, such as time not included in calculating an employee's wages or time not credited toward a prisoner's sentence. • The time during which a prisoner has escaped, for example, is not credited toward the prisoner's sentence. — Also termed *nonrun time.*

    earned time. A credit toward a sentence reduction awarded to a prisoner who takes part in activities designed to lessen the chances that the prisoner will commit a crime after release from prison. • Earned time, which is usu. awarded for taking educational or vocational courses, working, or participating in certain other productive activities, is distinct from good time, which is awarded simply for refraining from misconduct. Cf. *good time.*

    flat time. (1943) A prison term that is to be served without the benefit of time-reduction allowances for good behavior and the like.

    good time. (1886) The credit awarded to a prisoner for good conduct, which can reduce the duration of the prisoner's sentence. Cf. GOOD BEHAVIOR; *earned time.*

    jail-credit time. See JAIL CREDIT.

    nonrun time. See *dead time.*

    street time. The time that a convicted person spends on parole or on other conditional release. • If the person's parole is revoked, this time may or may not be credited toward the person's sentence, depending on the jurisdiction and the particular conditions of that person's parole. See *dead time.*

time agreement. 1. A pact made by the party leaders in the U.S. Senate to limit the time allowed for debate on a bill or amendment. **2.** See UNANIMOUS-CONSENT AGREEMENT.

time arbitrage. See ARBITRAGE.

time-bar, *n.* (1881) A bar to a legal claim arising from the lapse of a defined length of time, esp. one contained in a statute of limitations. — **time-barred,** *adj.*

time-bargain. See FUTURES CONTRACT.

time bill. See *time draft* under DRAFT.

time certain. 1. A definite, specific date and time. Cf. DATE CERTAIN. **2.** *Parliamentary law.* A specified time or condition for which a matter's consideration is scheduled or to which its consideration is postponed. See *postpone definitely* under POSTPONE (3); *special order* under ORDER (4).

time charter. See CHARTER (8).

time check. See TIMESHEET.

time deposit. See DEPOSIT (2).

time draft. See DRAFT.

time immemorial. (17c) **1.** A point in time so far back that no living person has knowledge or proof contradicting the right or custom alleged to have existed since then. • At common law, that time was fixed as the year 1189, the year that Henry II of England died. — Also termed *time out of memory; time out of mind; time of memory.* **2.** A point in time beyond which legal memory cannot go. See LEGAL MEMORY. **3.** A very long time.

time insurance. See INSURANCE.

time is of the essence. See OF THE ESSENCE.

time-is-of-the-essence clause. *Contracts.* A contractual provision making timely performance a condition.

time letter of credit. See LETTER OF CREDIT.

time loan. See *term loan* under LOAN.

time note. See NOTE (1).

time of memory. *Archaic.* See TIME IMMEMORIAL (1).

time option. See OPTION (2).

time order. See ORDER (8).

time out of memory. See TIME IMMEMORIAL.

time out of mind. See TIME IMMEMORIAL.

time-place-or-manner restriction. (1974) *Constitutional law.* A government's limitation on when, where, or how a public speech or assembly may occur, but not on the content of that speech or assembly. • As long as such restrictions are narrowly tailored to achieve a legitimate governmental interest, they do not violate the First Amendment. — Also written *time, place, or manner restriction.* — Also termed *time-place-and-manner restriction.* See PUBLIC FORUM.

time policy. See INSURANCE POLICY.

time-price differential. 1. A figure representing the difference between the current cash price of an item and the total cost of purchasing it on credit. **2.** The difference between a seller's price for immediate cash payment and a different price when payment is made later or in installments.

time-price doctrine. The rule that if a debt arises out of a purchase and sale, the usury laws do not apply. ● If a higher price is charged for a deferred payment than for an immediate payment, the difference between the time price and the cash price is deemed compensation to the seller for the risk that the buyer will default and for the interest that the seller could have earned on an immediate payment. Because the buyer can usu. choose to postpone a purchase and save up the cash price, the buyer does not have the same status as a needy borrower who must deal with a potentially predatory lender.

time-sharing, *n.* (1976) Joint ownership or rental of property (such as a vacation condominium) by several persons who take turns occupying the property. — Also termed *time-share.* — **time-share,** *vb.*

timesheet. (1970) **1.** An employee's record of time spent on the job. **2.** An attorney's daily record of billable and nonbillable hours, used to generate clients' bills. — Also termed (formerly) *time check.* See BILLABLE HOUR.

time-shifting. The practice of recording a broadcast for viewing at a later time. ● Time-shifting was found to be a noninfringing fair use of videotape recorders in *Sony Corp. v. Universal Studios, Inc.,* 464 U.S. 417, 104 S.Ct. 774 (1984).

time unity. See *unity of time* under UNITY.

time value. The price associated with the length of time that an investor must wait until an investment matures or the related income is earned. Cf. YIELD TO MATURITY.

timocracy (ti-**mok**-rə-see). (15c) **1.** An aristocracy of property; government by propertied, relatively rich people. **2.** A government in which the rulers' primary motive is the love of honor.

TIN. *abbr.* See TAX-IDENTIFICATION NUMBER.

tin parachute. An employment-contract provision that grants a corporate employee (esp. one below the executive level) severance benefits in the event of a takeover. ● These benefits are typically less lucrative than those provided under a golden parachute. — Also termed *silver parachute.* Cf. GOLDEN PARACHUTE.

tip, *n.* **1.** A piece of special information; esp., in securities law, advance or inside information passed from one person to another. See INSIDE INFORMATION; INSIDER TRADING. **2.** A gratuity for service given. ● Tip income is taxable. IRC (26 USCA) § 61(a).

tippee. *Securities.* A person who acquires material nonpublic information from someone in a fiduciary relationship with the company to which that information pertains.

tipper. *Securities.* A person who is in a fiduciary relationship with a company that the person possesses material inside information about, and who selectively discloses that information for trading or other personal purposes <the tippee traded 5,000 shares after her conversation with the tipper>.

tippling house. See PUBLIC HOUSE.

TIPS. *abbr.* See *TIPS bond* under TREASURY BOND.

tipstaff. A court crier. ● The name derives from the crier's former practice of holding a staff tipped with silver as a badge of office. See CRIER. Pl. **tipstaves, tipstaffs.**

tithe (tith), *n.* **1.** A tenth of one's income, esp. in reference to a religious or charitable gift or obligation. **2.** *Hist.* A small tax or assessment, esp. in the amount of one-tenth. — **tithe,** *vb.* — **tithable,** *adj.*

> **great tithe.** (*usu. pl.*) A tithe paid in kind and therefore considered more valuable than other tithes. ● The great tithes often consisted of corn, peas, beans, hay, and wood.

> **mixed tithes.** A tithe consisting of a natural product, such as milk or wool, obtained or cultivated by human effort.

> **personal tithe.** A tithe of profits from manual occupations or trades.

> **predial tithe.** A tithe of crops (such as corn). — Also spelled *praedial tithe.*

> **vicarial tithe** (vI-**kair**-ee-əl). A small tithe payable to a vicar.

tithing. See DECENARY.

title. (15c) **1.** The union of all elements (as ownership, possession, and custody) constituting the legal right to control and dispose of property; the legal link between a person who owns property and the property itself <no one has title to that land>. Cf. OWNERSHIP; POSSESSION. **2.** Legal evidence of a person's ownership rights in property; an instrument (such as a deed) that constitutes such evidence <record your title with the county clerk>.

> **aboriginal title. 1.** Land ownership, or a claim of land ownership, by an indigenous people in a place that has been colonized. — Also termed *native title.* **2.** INDIAN TITLE.

> **absolute title.** (17c) An exclusive title to land; a title that excludes all others not compatible with it. See *fee simple absolute* under FEE SIMPLE.

> **adverse title.** (18c) A title acquired by adverse possession. See ADVERSE POSSESSION.

> **after-acquired title.** (1810) Title held by a person who bought property from a seller who acquired title only after purporting to sell the property to the buyer. See AFTER-ACQUIRED-TITLE DOCTRINE. Cf. *title by estoppel.*

> **apparent title.** See COLOR OF TITLE.

bad title. **1.** See *defective title.* **2.** See *unmarketable title.*

clear title. (17c) **1.** A title free from any encumbrances, burdens, or other limitations. **2.** See *marketable title.* — Also termed *good title.*

defeasible title. (17c) A title voidable on the occurrence of a contingency, but not void on its face.

defective title. (17c) A title that cannot legally convey the property to which it applies, usu. because of some conflicting claim to that property. — Also termed *bad title.*

derivative title. (17c) **1.** A title that results when an already existing right is transferred to a new owner. **2.** The general principle that a transferee of property acquires only the rights held by the transferor and no more.

dormant title. (17c) A title in real property held in abeyance.

doubtful title. (17c) A title that exposes the party holding it to the risk of litigation with an adverse claimant. See *unmarketable title.*

equitable title. (17c) A title that indicates a beneficial interest in property and that gives the holder the right to acquire formal legal title. • Before the Statute of Uses (1536), an equitable title was enforceable only in a court of chancery, not of law. Cf. *legal title.*

good title. (16c) **1.** A title that is legally valid or effective. **2.** See *clear title* (1). **3.** See *marketable title.*

imperfect title. (18c) A title that requires a further exercise of the granting power to pass land in fee, or that does not convey full and absolute dominion.

Indian title. See INDIAN TITLE.

just title. In a case of prescription, a title that the possessor received from someone whom the possessor honestly believed to be the real owner, provided that the title was to transfer ownership of the property.

legal title. (17c) A title that evidences apparent ownership but does not necessarily signify full and complete title or a beneficial interest. • Before the Statute of Uses (1536), a legal title was enforceable only in a court of law, not chancery. Cf. *equitable title.*

lucrative title. *Civil law.* A title acquired without giving anything in exchange for the property; title by which a person acquires anything that comes as a clear gain, as by gift, descent, or devise. • Because lucrative title is usu. acquired by gift or inheritance, it is treated as the separate property of a married person. Cf. *onerous title.*

marketable title. (18c) A title that a reasonable buyer would accept because it appears to lack any defect and to cover the entire property that the seller has purported to sell; a title that enables a purchaser to hold property in peace during the period of ownership and to have it accepted by a later purchaser who employs the same standards of acceptability. — Also termed *good title; merchantable title; clear title.*

native title. See *aboriginal title* (1).

nonmerchantable title. See *unmarketable title.*

onerous title (on-ər-əs). **1.** *Civil law.* A title acquired by giving valuable consideration for the property, as by paying money or performing services. **2.** A title to property that is acquired during marriage through a spouse's skill or labor and is therefore treated as community property. Cf. *lucrative title.*

original title. A title that creates a right for the first time.

paper title. See *record title.*

paramount title. (18c) **1.** *Archaic.* A title that is the source of the current title; original title. **2.** A title that is superior to another title or claim on the same property.

particular title. *Civil law.* A title acquired from an ancestor by purchase, gift, or inheritance before or after the ancestor's death.

perfect title. **1.** FEE SIMPLE. **2.** A grant of land that requires no further act from the legal authority to constitute an absolute title to the land. **3.** A title that does not disclose a patent defect that may require a lawsuit to defend it. **4.** A title that is good both at law and in equity. **5.** A title that is good and valid beyond all reasonable doubt.

presumptive title. (17c) A title of the lowest order, arising out of the mere occupation or simple possession of property without any apparent right, or any pretense of right, to hold and continue that possession.

record title. (18c) A title as it appears in the public records after the deed is properly recorded. — Also termed *title of record; paper title.*

singular title. (17c) The title by which one acquires property as a singular successor.

tax title. (1831) A title to land purchased at a tax sale.

title by descent. (17c) A title that one acquires by law as an heir of the deceased owner.

title by devise. (1819) A title created by will.

title by estoppel. Title acquired from a person who did not have title at the time of a purported conveyance with a warranty but later acquired the title, which then inures to the benefit of the grantee. Cf. *after-acquired title.*

title by prescription. (17c) A title acquired by prescription. See PRESCRIPTION (5).

title defective in form. (1836) A title for which some defect appears on the face of the deed, as opposed to a defect that arises from circumstances or extrinsic evidence. • Title defective in form cannot be the basis of prescription. See PRESCRIPTION (5).

title of entry. (16c) The right to enter upon lands.

title of record. See *record title.*

universal title. (17c) A title acquired by a conveyance causa mortis of a stated portion of all the conveyor's property interests so that on the conveyor's death the recipient stands as a universal successor.

unmarketable title. (18c) A title that a reasonable buyer would refuse to accept because of possible conflicting interests in or litigation over the property. — Also termed *bad title; unmerchantable title; nonmerchantable title.*

3. The heading of a statute or other legal document <the title of the contract was "Confidentiality Agreement">.

general title. A statute's name that broadly and comprehensively identifies the subject matter addressed by the legislature. Cf. *restrictive title.*

long title. The full, formal title of a statute, usu. containing a brief statement of legislative purpose.

short title. The abbreviated title of a statute by which it is popularly known; a statutory nickname.

4. A subdivision of a statute or code <Title IX>.

restrictive title. A statute's name that narrowly identifies the particular subject matter addressed by the legislature. Cf. *general title.*

5. The name by which a court case or other legal proceeding is distinguished from others; STYLE (1). **6.** An appellation of office, dignity, or distinction <after the election, he bore the title of mayor for the next four years>.

title, abstract of. See ABSTRACT OF TITLE.

title, action to quiet. See *action to quiet title* under ACTION (4).

title, chain of. See CHAIN OF TITLE.

title, cloud on. See CLOUD ON TITLE.

title, color of. See COLOR OF TITLE.

title, covenant for. See *covenant for title* under COVENANT (4).

title, document of. See DOCUMENT OF TITLE.

title, indicia of. See INDICIA OF TITLE.

title, muniment of. See MUNIMENT OF TITLE.

title, root of. See ROOT OF TITLE.

title, warranty of. See *warranty of title* under WARRANTY (2).

Title VII of the Civil Rights Act of 1964. A federal law that prohibits employment discrimination and harassment on the basis of race, sex, pregnancy, religion, and national origin, as well as prohibiting retaliation against an employee who opposes illegal harassment or discrimination in the workplace. • This term is often referred to simply as Title VII. 42 USCA §§ 2000e et seq.

Title IX of the Educational Amendments of 1972. A federal statute generally prohibiting sex discrimination and harassment by educational facilities that receive federal funds. • This term is often referred to simply as Title IX. 20 USCA §§ 1681 et seq.

title clearance. The removal of impediments to the marketability of land, esp. through title examinations.

title company. See COMPANY.

title deed. See DEED.

title division. *Archaic.* A common-law system for dividing property acquired during marriage upon the dissolution of the marriage, the divisions being based on who holds legal title to the property. • Under title division, when a marriage ends in divorce, property purchased during the marriage is awarded to the person who holds title to the property. Cf. COMMUNITY PROPERTY; EQUITABLE DISTRIBUTION.

title-guaranty company. See *title company* under COMPANY.

title insurance. See INSURANCE.

title jurisdiction. See TITLE THEORY.

title member. See *name partner* under PARTNER.

title-object clause. See CLAUSE.

title of entry. See TITLE (2).

title of record. See *record title* under TITLE (2).

title of right. (1917) A court-issued decree creating, transferring, or extinguishing rights. • Examples include a decree of divorce or judicial separation, an adjudication of bankruptcy, a discharge in bankruptcy, a decree of foreclosure against a mortgagor, an order appointing or removing a trustee, and a grant of letters of administration. In all the examples listed, the judgment operates not as a remedy but as a title of right.

title opinion. See OPINION (2).

title registration. (1971) A system of registering title to land with a public registry, such as a county clerk's office. See TORRENS SYSTEM.

title retention. (1936) A form of lien, in the nature of a chattel mortgage, to secure payment of a loan given to purchase the secured item.

title search. (1965) An examination of the public records to determine whether any defects or encumbrances exist in a given property's chain of title. ● A title search is typically conducted by a title company or a real-estate lawyer at a prospective buyer's or mortgagee's request.

title standards. (1938) Criteria by which a real-estate title can be evaluated to determine whether it is defective or marketable. ● Many states, through associations of conveyancers and real-estate attorneys, still adhere to title standards.

title state. See TITLE THEORY.

title theory. (1907) *Property law.* The idea that a mortgage transfers legal title of the property to the mortgagee, who retains it until the mortgage has been satisfied or foreclosed. ● Only a few American states — known as *title states, title jurisdictions,* or *title-theory jurisdictions* — have adopted this theory. Cf. LIEN THEORY.

title transaction. (1939) A transaction that affects title to an interest in land.

title unity. See *unity of title* under UNITY.

TM. *abbr.* TRADEMARK. ● Typically used as a superscript after a mark (^TM), it signals only that someone claims ownership of the mark; it does not mean that the mark is registered.

TMEP. *abbr.* TRADEMARK MANUAL OF EXAMINING PROCEDURE.

T-note. *abbr.* TREASURY NOTE.

to-have-and-to-hold clause. See HABENDUM CLAUSE (1).

token, *n.* (bef. 12c) **1.** A sign or mark; a tangible evidence of the existence of a fact. **2.** A sign or indication of an intention to do something, as when a buyer places a small order with a vendor to show good faith with a view toward later placing a larger order. **3.** A coin or other legal tender. ● Although *token* most commonly refers to a piece of metal, the term may also denote a bill or other medium of exchange.

false token. A counterfeit coin, bill, or the like.

toleration, *n.* **1.** The act or practice of permitting or enduring something not wholly approved of; the act or practice of allowing something in a way that does not hinder. **2.** The allowance of opinions and beliefs, esp. religious ones, that differ from prevailing norms. **3.** *Archaic.* Legal permission or authorization; LICENSE (1). — **tolerate,** *vb.*

toll, *n.* **1.** A tax or due paid for the use of something; esp., the consideration paid either to use a public road, highway, or bridge, or to maintain a booth for the sale of goods at a fair or market. **2.** A right to collect such a tax or due. **3.** The privilege of being free from such a tax or due. **4.** A charge for a long-distance telephone call.

toll, *vb.* (15c) **1.** To annul or take away <toll a right of entry>. **2.** (Of a time period, esp. a statutory one) to stop the running of; to abate <toll the limitations period>. See EQUITABLE TOLLING. **3.** *Hist.* To raise or collect a tax or due for the use of something.

tollage (**toh**-lij). **1.** Payment of a toll. **2.** Money charged or paid as a toll. **3.** The liberty or franchise of charging a toll.

tolling agreement. (1934) An agreement between a potential plaintiff and a potential defendant by which the defendant agrees to extend the statutory limitations period on the plaintiff's claim, usu. so that both parties will have more time to resolve their dispute without litigation.

tolling statute. (1899) A law that interrupts the running of a statute of limitations in certain situations, as when the defendant cannot be served with process in the forum jurisdiction.

tolt (tohlt). *Hist.* A writ for removing a case pending in a court baron to a county court. — Also termed *writ of tolt.* See COURT BARON; *county court* under COURT.

tombstone. *Securities.* An advertisement (esp. in a newspaper) for a public securities offering, describing the security and identifying the sellers. ● The term gets its name from the ad's traditional black border and plain print. — Also termed *tombstone advertisement; tombstone ad.* Cf. PROSPECTUS.

ton. A measure of weight fixed at either 2,000 pounds avoirdupois or 20 hundredweights, each hundredweight being 112 pounds avoirdupois.

long ton. Twenty long hundredweight (2,240 pounds), or 1.016 metric tons.

short ton. Twenty short hundredweight (2,000 pounds), or 0.907 metric tons.

ton mile. In transportation, a measure equal to the transportation of one ton of freight one mile.

tonnage (**tən**-ij). **1.** The capacity of a vessel for carrying freight or other loads, calculated in tons. — Also termed *net tonnage.* **2.** The total shipping tonnage of a country or port. **3.** See *tonnage duty* under DUTY (4).

tonnage duty. See DUTY (4).

tonnage-rent. A rent reserved by a mining lease or similar transaction, consisting of a royalty on every ton of minerals extracted from the mine.

tonnage tax. See *tonnage duty* under DUTY (4).

tontine (**ton**-teen *or* ton-**teen**), *n.* **1.** A financial arrangement in which a group of participants share in the arrangement's advantages until all but one has died or defaulted, at which time the whole goes to that survivor. **2.** A financial arrangement in which an entire sum goes to the contributing participants still alive and not in default at the end of a specified period.

tontine policy. See INSURANCE POLICY.

top-hat pension plan. See PENSION PLAN.

top lease. See LEASE.

top management. See MANAGEMENT.

topographical survey. See SURVEY.

torpedo doctrine. See ATTRACTIVE-NUISANCE DOCTRINE.

Torrens system (tor-ənz *or* tahr-ənz). (1863) A system for establishing title to real estate in which a claimant first acquires an abstract of title and then applies to a court for the issuance of a title certificate, which serves as conclusive evidence of ownership. • This system — named after Sir Robert Torrens, a 19th-century reformer of Australian land laws — has been adopted in the United States by several counties with large metropolitan areas. — Also termed *Torrens title system.* See CAVEAT (3).

tort (tort). (16c) **1.** A civil wrong, other than breach of contract, for which a remedy may be obtained, usu. in the form of damages; a breach of a duty that the law imposes on persons who stand in a particular relation to one another. **2.** (*pl.*) The branch of law dealing with such wrongs.

business tort. A tort that impairs some aspect of an economic interest or business relationship and causes economic loss rather than property damage or bodily harm. • Business torts include tortious interference with contractual relations, intentional interference with prospective economic advantage, unfair business practices, misappropriation of trade secrets, and product disparagement.

constitutional tort. (1966) A violation of one's constitutional rights by a government officer, redressable by a civil action filed directly against the officer. • A constitutional tort committed under color of state law (such as a civil-rights violation) is actionable under 42 USCA § 1983. — Sometimes (informally) shortened to *contort.*

dignitary tort (**dig**-nə-tair-ee). (1996) A tort involving injury to one's reputation or honor. • In the few jurisdictions in which courts use the phrase *dignitary tort* (such as Maine), defamation is commonly cited as an example. — Also (erroneously) termed *dignatory tort.*

environmental tort. A tort involving exposure to disagreeable or harmful environmental conditions or harm to and degradation of an environment (e.g., the pouring of acid on golf greens). • An environmental tort is usu. harmful to land rather than people, though people may find it unpleasant (e.g., odors from a landfill). By contrast, toxic torts involve exposure to harmful

substances that cause personal physical injury or disease. Cf. *toxic tort.*

government tort. (1945) A tort committed by the government through an employee, agent, or instrumentality under its control. • The tort may or may not be actionable, depending on whether the government is entitled to sovereign immunity. A tort action against the U.S. government is regulated by the Federal Tort Claims Act, while a state action is governed by the state's tort claims act. See FEDERAL TORT CLAIMS ACT; *sovereign immunity* under IMMUNITY (1).

intentional tort. (1860) A tort committed by someone acting with general or specific intent. • Examples include battery, false imprisonment, and trespass to land. — Also termed *willful tort.* Cf. NEGLIGENCE.

marital tort. A tort by one spouse against the other. • Since most jurisdictions have abolished interspousal tort immunity, courts have had to decide which tort claims to recognize between married persons. Among those that some, but not all, courts have chosen to recognize are assault and battery, including claims for infliction of sexually transmitted disease, and intentional and negligent infliction of emotional distress. — Also termed *domestic tort.* Cf. *husband–wife immunity* under IMMUNITY.

maritime tort. Any tort within the admiralty jurisdiction.

mass tort. (1940) A civil wrong that injures many people. • Examples include toxic emissions from a factory, the crash of a commercial airliner, and contamination from an industrial-waste-disposal site. Cf. *toxic tort.*

negligent tort. (1865) A tort committed by failure to observe the standard of care required by law under the circumstances. See NEGLIGENCE.

personal tort. (17c) A tort involving or consisting in an injury to one's person, reputation, or feelings, as distinguished from an injury or damage to real or personal property.

preconception tort. A tort that is committed before the victim has been conceived.

prenatal tort. (1960) **1.** A tort committed against a fetus. • If born alive, a child can sue for injuries resulting from tortious conduct predating the child's birth. **2.** Loosely, any of several torts relating to reproduction, such as those giving rise to wrongful-birth actions, wrongful-life actions, and wrongful-pregnancy actions.

prima facie tort (pri-mə **fay**-shee-ee *or* -shee *or* -shə). (1938) An unjustified, intentional infliction of harm on another person, resulting in damages, by one or more acts that would otherwise be lawful. • Some jurisdictions have established this tort to provide a remedy for malicious deeds — esp. in business and trade contexts — that are not actionable under traditional tort law.

property tort. (1898) A tort involving damage to property.

public tort. (1949) A minor breach of the law (such as a parking violation) that, although it carries a criminal punishment, is considered a civil offense rather than a criminal one because it is merely a prohibited act (*malum prohibitum*) and not inherently reprehensible conduct (*malum in se*). — Also termed *civil offense.* Cf. *civil wrong* under WRONG; *public delict* under DELICT.

quasi-tort. (1809) A wrong for which a nonperpetrator is held responsible; a tort for which one who did not directly commit it can nonetheless be found liable, as when an employer is held liable for a tort committed by an employee. — Also spelled *quasi tort.* See *vicarious liability* under LIABILITY; RESPONDEAT SUPERIOR.

sanctions tort. See SANCTIONS TORT.

toxic tort. (1979) A civil wrong arising from exposure to a toxic substance, such as asbestos, radiation, or hazardous waste. ● A toxic tort can be remedied by a civil lawsuit (usu. a class action) or by administrative action. Cf. *mass tort; environmental tort.*

willful tort. See *intentional tort.*

tortfeasor (**tort**-fee-zər). (17c) One who commits a tort; a wrongdoer.

concurrent tortfeasors. (1921) Two or more tortfeasors whose simultaneous actions cause injury to a third party. ● Such tortfeasors are jointly and severally liable.

consecutive tortfeasors. (1955) Two or more tortfeasors whose actions, while occurring at different times, combine to cause a single injury to a third party. ● Such tortfeasors are jointly and severally liable.

joint tortfeasors. (1822) Two or more tortfeasors who contributed to the claimant's injury and who may be joined as defendants in the same lawsuit. See *joint and several liability* under LIABILITY.

successive tortfeasors. (1954) Two or more tortfeasors whose negligence occurs at different times and causes different injuries to the same third party.

tortious (**tor**-shəs), *adj.* (16c) **1.** Constituting a tort; wrongful <tortious conduct>. **2.** In the nature of a tort <tortious cause of action>.

tortious act. See ACT (2).

tortious battery. See BATTERY (2).

tortious conduct. See CONDUCT.

tortious interference with a business advantage. See TORTIOUS INTERFERENCE WITH PROSPECTIVE ADVANTAGE.

tortious interference with contractual relations. (1954) A third party's intentional inducement of a contracting party to break a contract, causing damage to the relationship between the contracting parties. — Also termed *unlawful interference with contractual relations; interference with a contractual relationship; interference with contract; inducement of breach of contract; procurement of breach of contract.*

tortious interference with economic relations. See TORTIOUS INTERFERENCE WITH PROSPECTIVE ADVANTAGE.

tortious interference with prospective advantage. (1973) An intentional, damaging intrusion on another's potential business relationship, such as the opportunity of obtaining customers or employment. — Also termed *interference with a business relationship; tortious interference with a business advantage; tortious interference with economic relations.*

tortious liability. See LIABILITY.

tort-of-another doctrine. *Torts.* The principle that a party who must bring or defend an action against a third person based on a tort committed by another person is entitled to seek litigation-related damages from that other person.

tort reform. (1974) A movement to reduce the amount of tort litigation, usu. involving legislation that restricts tort remedies or that caps damages awards (esp. for punitive damages). ● Advocates of tort reform argue that it lowers insurance and healthcare costs and prevents windfalls, while opponents contend that it denies plaintiffs the recovery they deserve for their injuries.

torture, *n.* (16c) The infliction of intense pain to the body or mind to punish, to extract a confession or information, or to obtain sadistic pleasure. — **torture,** *vb.*

torture by proxy. See *extraordinary rendition* under RENDITION.

torture flight. See *extraordinary rendition* under RENDITION.

total, *adj.* (14c) **1.** Whole; not divided; full; complete. **2.** Utter; absolute.

total assignment. See ASSIGNMENT (2).

total breach. See BREACH OF CONTRACT.

total disability. See DISABILITY (2).

total-disability insurance. See *general-disability insurance* under INSURANCE.

total eviction. See EVICTION.

total failure of consideration. See FAILURE OF CONSIDERATION.

total incorporation. See INCORPORATION.

totality-of-the-circumstances test. (1959) *Criminal procedure.* A standard for determining whether hearsay (such as an informant's tip) is sufficiently reliable to establish probable cause for an arrest or search warrant. • Under this test — which replaced *Aguilar–Spinelli*'s two-pronged approach — the reliability of the hearsay is weighed by focusing on the entire situation as described in the probable-cause affidavit, and not on any one specific factor. *Illinois v. Gates*, 462 U.S. 213, 103 S.Ct. 2317 (1983). Cf. AGUILAR–SPINELLI TEST.

total loss. See LOSS.

total-offset rule. *Torts.* A theory of damages holding that the eroding effect of inflation offsets the accrual of interest on an award and makes it unnecessary to discount future damages to their present value.

total repudiation. See REPUDIATION.

Totten trust. See TRUST.

touch, *vb. Marine insurance.* To stop at a port, usu. for a brief period.

touch and stay. *Marine insurance.* A right, granted by an insurer to an insured vessel, to stop and remain at certain designated points in the course of the voyage. • A vessel that has the power to touch and stay at a place must confine itself strictly to the terms of the permission given, and any deviation during a stay — for example, by shipping or landing goods — will discharge the underwriters, unless the vessel has permission to trade as well as to touch and stay.

Touhy regulations. The rules governing procedures for document production by federal agencies for purposes of litigation. 28 C.F.R. 16.21 et seq. • The term comes from *United States ex rel. Touhy v. Ragen*, 340 U.S. 462, 71 S.Ct. 416 (1951). In that case, an FBI agent refused to produce certain records under a subpoena duces tecum because a departmental regulation expressly stated that the Attorney General was the only person with authority to produce the documents. The United States Supreme Court upheld the regulation's validity.

touting, *n.* The solicitation of business by highly recommending a security or product, esp. when the recommendation's basis is largely puffery.

towage (**toh**-ij), *n.* **1.** The act or service of towing ships and vessels, usu. by means of a small vessel called a *tug.* **2.** The charge for such a service.

toward, *adj.* **1.** In the direction of; on a course or line leading to (some place or something). **2.** Coming soon; not long before.

to wit (too **wit**), *adv.* (14c) *Archaic.* That is to say; namely <the district attorney amended the complaint to include embezzlement, to wit, "stealing money that the company had entrusted to the accused">. — Sometimes spelled *to-wit; towit.*

town. 1. A center of population that is larger and more fully developed than a village, but that (traditionally speaking) is not incorporated as a city. **2.** The territory within which this population lives. **3.** Collectively, the people who live within this territory. Cf. CITY.

town-bonding act. A law authorizing a town, county, or other municipal corporation to issue its corporate bonds for the purpose of aiding in construction, often of railroads. — Also termed *town-bonding law.*

town clerk. See CLERK (1).

town collector. A town officer charged with collecting the taxes assessed by a town.

town commissioner. See COMMISSIONER.

town hall. A building that houses the offices of a town's government.

townhouse. A dwelling unit having usu. two or three stories and often connected to a similar structure by a common wall and (particularly in a planned-unit development) sharing and owning in common the surrounding grounds. — Also termed *townhome.*

town meeting. 1. A legal meeting of a town's qualified voters for the administration of local government or the enactment of legislation. • Town meetings of this type are common in some New England states. **2.** More generally, any assembly of a town's citizens for the purpose of discussing political, economic, or social issues. **3.** Modernly, a televised event in which one or more politicians meet and talk with representative citizens about current issues.

town order. An official written direction by the auditing officers of a town, directing the treasurer to pay a sum of money. — Also termed *town warrant.*

town purpose. A municipal project or expenditure that concerns the welfare and advantage of the town as a whole.

township. 1. In a government survey, a square tract six miles on each side, containing thirty-six square miles of land. **2.** In some states, a civil and political subdivision of a county. — Abbr. tp.

township trustee. See TRUSTEE (1).

townsite. A portion of the public domain segregated by proper authority and procedure as the site for a town.

town treasurer. An officer responsible for maintaining and disbursing town funds.

town warrant. See TOWN ORDER.

toxic, *adj.* Having the character or producing the effects of a poison; produced by or resulting from a poison; poisonous. — Also termed *toxical.*

toxicant (**tok**-si-kənt), *n.* (1879) A poison; a toxic agent; any substance capable of producing toxication or poisoning.

toxic asset. See *troubled asset* under ASSET.

toxicate, *vb.* Archaic. To poison. See INTOXICATION.

toxic convert. See DEATH-SPIRAL DEAL.

toxicology (tok-si-**kol**-ə-jee). (18c) The branch of medicine that concerns poisons, their effects, their recognition, their antidotes, and generally the diagnosis and therapeutics of poisoning; the science of poisons. — **toxicological** (tok-si-kə-loj-i-kəl), *adj.*

toxic tort. See TORT.

toxic waste. See WASTE (2).

toxin, *n.* (1886) **1.** Broadly, any poison or toxicant. **2.** As used in pathology and medical jurisprudence, any diffusible alkaloidal substance — such as the ptomaines, abrin, brucin, or serpent venoms — and esp. the poisonous products of disease-producing bacteria.

tp. *abbr.* TOWNSHIP.

TPL. *abbr.* Third-party logistical service provider. See FREIGHT FORWARDER.

TPPM. *abbr.* TANGIBLE-PERSONAL-PROPERTY MEMORANDUM.

TPR. *abbr.* TERMINATION OF PARENTAL RIGHTS.

traces, *n.* See *retrospectant evidence* under EVIDENCE.

tracing, *n.* (16c) **1.** The process of tracking property's ownership or characteristics from the time of its origin to the present <tracing the vehicle's history>. • Parties in a divorce will be expected to trace the origins of property in existence at the time of marital dissolution in order to characterize each asset as separate or marital property (or as community property in some states). — Also termed *tracing of funds; tracing of property.* Cf. COMMINGLE. **2.** The act of discovering and following a person's actions or movements <tracing the robber's steps>.

tract. (14c) A specified parcel of land <a 40-acre tract>.

tract index. See INDEX (1).

trade, *n.* (14c) **1.** The business of buying and selling or bartering goods or services; COMMERCE.

inland trade. Trade wholly carried on within a country, as distinguished from foreign commerce.

precarious trade. Int'l law. Trade by a neutral country between two belligerent powers, allowed to exist at the latter's sufferance.

2. A transaction or swap. **3.** A business or industry occupation; a craft or profession. — **trade,** *vb.*

trade acceptance. See ACCEPTANCE (4).

trade agreement. 1. An agreement — such as the North American Free Trade Agreement — between two or more nations concerning the buying and selling of each nation's goods. **2.** COLLECTIVE-BARGAINING AGREEMENT.

trade and commerce. Every business occupation carried on for subsistence or profit and involving the elements of bargain and sale, barter, exchange, or traffic.

Trade and Development Program. See UNITED STATES TRADE AND DEVELOPMENT AGENCY.

trade association. See ASSOCIATION.

trade council. A central labor union; the central organization of a local trade union. — Also termed *trades council.* See UNION.

trade defamation. See DEFAMATION.

trade deficit. See DEFICIT.

trade discount. See DISCOUNT.

trade disparagement. The common-law tort of belittling someone's business, goods, or services with a remark that is false or misleading but not necessarily defamatory. • To succeed at the action, a plaintiff must prove that (1) the defendant made the disparaging remark; (2) the defendant either intended to injure the business, knew the statement was false, or recklessly disregarded whether it was true; and (3) the statement resulted in special damages to the plaintiff, usu. by passing off. — Also termed *commercial disparagement; product disparagement; injurious falsehood.* Cf. *trade defamation* under DEFAMATION.

trade dispute. 1. *Int'l law.* A dispute between two or more countries arising from tariff rates or other matters related to international commerce. **2.** *Labor law.* A dispute between an employer and employees over pay, working conditions, or other employment-related matters. • An employee who leaves during a trade dispute is not entitled to benefits under the Unemployment Insurance Act.

trade draft. See DRAFT.

trade dress. *Trademarks.* The overall appearance and image in the marketplace of a product or a commercial enterprise. • For a product, trade dress typically comprises packaging and labeling. For an enterprise, it typically comprises design and decor. If a trade dress is distinctive and nonfunctional, it may be protected under trademark law. — Also termed *get-up; look and feel.*

trade embargo. See EMBARGO (3).

trade fixture. See FIXTURE.

trade gap. See *trade deficit* under DEFICIT.

trade guild. See GUILD (1).

trade libel. Trade defamation that is written or recorded. See LIBEL; *trade defamation* under DEFAMATION; DISPARAGEMENT (3). Cf. *trade slander* under SLANDER.

trademark, *n.* (1838) 1. A word, phrase, logo, or other graphic symbol used by a manufacturer or seller to distinguish its product or products from those of others. • The main purpose of a trademark is to designate the source of goods or services. In effect, the trademark is the commercial substitute for one's signature. To receive federal protection, a trademark must be (1) distinctive rather than merely descriptive or generic; (2) affixed to a product that is actually sold in the marketplace; and (3) registered with the U.S. Patent and Trademark Office. In its broadest sense, the term *trademark* includes a servicemark. Unregistered trademarks are protected under common-law only, and distinguished with the mark "TM." — Often shortened to *mark*. Cf. SERVICEMARK. 2. The body of law dealing with how businesses distinctively identify their products. — Abbr. TM. See LANHAM ACT. Cf. SERVICEMARK; *registered trademark*; BRAND; TRADENAME.

abandoned trademark. A mark whose owner has discontinued using it and has no intent to resume using it in the ordinary course of trade, or has allowed it to become a generic term or otherwise to lose its distinctive significance. • Under § 45 of the Lanham Act, nonuse of a mark for three consecutive years is prima facie evidence of abandonment. The owner of an abandoned mark has no trademark rights to exclude others from using it. — Also termed *abandoned mark*.

arbitrary trademark. A trademark containing common words that do not describe or suggest any characteristic of the product to which the trademark is assigned. • Because arbitrary marks are neither descriptive nor suggestive of the goods or services in connection with which they are used, they are inherently distinctive, require no proof of secondary meaning, and are entitled to strong legal protection. A name that would be generic if used with one product may be arbitrary if used with another. For example, "Bicycle" may be registered to identify playing cards, but it could not be protected as a mark to identify bicycles. — Also termed *arbitrary mark*; *arbitrary name*.

certification trademark. A word, symbol, or device used on goods or services to certify the place of origin, material, mode of manufacture, quality, or other characteristic. See 15 USCA § 1127. — Also termed *certification mark*. Cf. *collective trademark*.

coined trademark. See *fanciful trademark*.

collective trademark. (1941) A trademark or servicemark used by an association, union, or other group either to identify the group's products or services or to signify membership in the group. • Collective marks — such as "Realtor" or "American Peanut Farmers" — can be federally registered under the Lanham Act. — Also termed *collective mark*. Cf. *certification trademark*.

Community trademark. A trademark registered with the European Union Trademark Office and recognized in all EU countries. — Also termed *Community mark*.

composite trademark. (kəm-**poz**-it mahrk). A trademark or servicemark made up of several words that form a distinctive whole, even if the individual words are ordinary. • Advertising slogans are often protectable as composite marks. A trademark registrant can establish ownership in the whole mark, but must disclaim ownership in any unregistrable parts. — Also termed *composite mark*; *hybrid mark*; *hybrid trademark*.

counterfeit trademark. A spurious mark that is identical to, or substantially indistinguishable from, a registered trademark. 15 USCA § 1116(d)(1)(B). — Also termed *counterfeit mark*.

descriptive trademark. A trademark that is a meaningful word in common usage or that merely describes or suggests a product. • This type of trademark is entitled to protection only if it has acquired distinctiveness over time. — Also termed *descriptive mark*; *weak mark*; *weak trademark*. See SECONDARY MEANING.

disparaging trademark. A trademark that tends to bring a person or class of people into contempt or disrepute. • Section 2(a) of the Lanham Act prohibits the registration of disparaging marks. 15 USCA § 1052(a). — Also termed *disparaging mark*. See *prohibited and reserved trademark*.

distinctive trademark. A very strong trademark, one that consumers immediately and consistently associate with specific goods and services. • Distinctive trademarks are usu. fanciful, arbitrary, or suggestive, but descriptive trademarks and common names can become distinctive if they become so well known as to acquire a secondary meaning. — Also termed *distinctive mark*.

evocative trademark. See *suggestive trademark*.

famous trademark. A trademark that not only is distinctive but also has been used and heavily advertised or widely accepted in the channels of trade over a long time, and is so well known that consumers immediately associate it with one specific product or service. • Only famous marks are protected from dilution. Eight non-exclusive statutory factors are often used in determining whether a particular mark is famous. See 15 USCA § 1125 (c)(1)(A)–(H). — Also termed *famous mark*.

fanciful trademark. A trademark consisting of a made-up or coined word; a distinctive trademark or tradename having no independent meaning. • This type of mark is considered inherently distinctive and thus protected at common law, and is eligible for trademark registration from the time of its first use. — Also termed *fanciful mark*; *fanciful term*; *coined trademark*; *coined mark*; *coined term*.

geographically descriptive trademark. A trademark that uses a geographic name to indicate where the goods are grown or manufactured. • This type of mark is protected at common law, and can be registered only on proof that it has acquired distinctiveness over time. — Also termed *geographically descriptive mark*. See SECONDARY MEANING.

house trademark. A trademark that identifies a company, a division of a company, or a company's product line as the source of a product or service. • A house mark and a product mark often appear together on a label. — Also termed *house mark*. Cf. *product trademark*.

hybrid trademark. See *composite trademark*.

product trademark. A trademark that identifies a single good or service, rather than the producing company, a division of a company, or a product line. • A product mark and a house mark often appear together on a label. — Also termed *product mark*. Cf. *house trademark*.

prohibited and reserved trademark. A mark that is not protected under the Lanham Act because it either fall into an expressly excluded category or else is similar to a mark granted by statute to another. 15 USCA § 1052. — Also termed *prohibited and reserved mark*.

pure trademark. See *technical trademark*.

registered trademark. A trademark that has been filed and recorded with the Patent and Trademark Office. • A federally registered trademark is usu. marked by the symbol "®" or a phrase such as "Registered U.S. Patent & Trademark Office" so that the trademark owner can potentially collect treble damages or the defendant's profits for an infringement. If the symbol is not used, the owner can collect these damages or profits only by proving that the defendant actually knew that the mark was registered. — Also termed *registered mark*. Cf. SERVICEMARK.

strong trademark. An inherently distinctive trademark that is used — usu. by the owner only — in a fictitious, arbitrary, and fanciful manner, and is therefore given greater protection than a weak mark under the trademark laws. — Also termed *strong mark*.

suggestive trademark. A trademark that suggests rather than describes the particular characteristics of a product, thus requiring a consumer to use imagination to draw a conclusion about the nature of the product. • A suggestive trademark is entitled to protection without proof of secondary meaning. — Also termed *evocative mark*; *suggestive mark*; *suggestive name*. See SECONDARY MEANING.

technical trademark. A mark that satisfies all the elements of a common-law trademark. • The essential elements of a technical trademark are as follows: (1) its use to designate a commercial source would not interfere with anyone else's right to use the mark; (2) it must primarily identify the source, rather than the product's category or grade of quality; (3) it must be attached to the product, label, or collateral materials rather than merely used in advertising; and (4) its use must not undermine some public policy, as by being scandalous or deceptive. — Also termed *pure trademark*; *technical mark*; *true trademark*.

true trademark. See *technical trademark*.

weak trademark. See *descriptive trademark*.

Trademark Act of 1946. See LANHAM ACT.

trademark application. A mark owner's written request, filed with the U.S. Patent and Trademark Office, for federal registration of a mark, accompanied by a sample of the mark to be protected and the filing fee. • The application may describe either an existing mark that is in use or a proposed mark. — Also termed *servicemark application*.

combined application. An application to register a mark to be used in more than one class of goods or services. • A combined application is given a single serial number, but it is examined as if it were a set of distinct single applications. Separate filing fees must be paid for each class. — Also termed *multiple-class application*.

intent-to-use application. An application filed with the U.S. Patent and Trademark Office to protect a trademark or servicemark that is not currently in commercial use but whose owner has a bona fide intent to use the mark commercially in the foreseeable future. • Trademark rights have traditionally been restricted to marks actually used in trade, but a 1988 amendment to the Lanham Act permitted applications to be filed before actual use begins if the mark otherwise qualifies for the Principal Register. 15 USCA § 1051(b). See PRINCIPAL REGISTER.

multiple-class application. See *combined application.*

trademark-application amendment. A proposed modification to a registered trademark or to an application for trademark registration.

   amendment of registration. *Trademarks.* Amendment of an existing trademark registration to make minor changes in the design of a mark to reflect how the mark is actually used. • The U.S. Patent and Trademark Office permits an amendment of registration only if it does not materially alter the character of the mark. The PTO amends a registration by attaching to the printed registration a printed certificate showing the amendment. — Also termed *amendment of mark in registration.*

   amendment to allege use. *Trademarks.* A supplement to a trademark applicant's intent-to-use application filed to inform the U.S. Patent and Trademark Office that a trademark is actually in use in interstate commerce. • The form is titled "Allegation of Use for Intent to Use Application." — Abbr. AAU. — Also termed *statement of use; allegation of use.* See DECLARATION OF USE.

   amendment to different register. *Trademarks.* An amendment to an application for registration on the Principal Register, requesting that the mark instead be placed on the supplemental register.

trademark class. Any one of 42 international trademark-protection categories, each comprising similar goods or services. • There are 34 goods classes and 8 services classes. A trademark is protected in each class that is relevant to the product's or service's business area.

Trademark Cyberpiracy Prevention Act. See ANTICYBERSQUATTING CONSUMER PROTECTION ACT.

Trademark Electronic Application System. A method of applying to the U.S. Patent and Trademark Office for a trademark over the Internet. • The system is available at http://www.uspto.gov/teas/index.html. — Abbr. TEAS.

trademark infringement. See INFRINGEMENT.

Trademark Law Treaty. A 1994 treaty that reduces barriers to applying for and registering trademarks internationally, and establishes a model international-trademark-registration form acceptable by all signatory nations. • The United States is a party to the treaty.

Trademark Manual of Examining Procedure. *Trademarks.* The U.S. Patent and Trademark Office book containing guidelines and procedures for trademark examiners. — Abbr. TMEP.

Trademark Office. See UNITED STATES PATENT AND TRADEMARK OFFICE.

trademark-registration notice. A notice that a mark is protected by registration with the U.S. Patent and Trademark Office, shown by placing a symbol next to the mark. • In the U.S., the R-within-a-circle symbol (®) is common but the legend "Reg. U.S. Pat. Off." is acceptable. Only federally registered marks may use this notice.

Trademark Trial and Appeal Board. An administrative body that hears and decides disputes involving trademark ownership, conflicts between marks, and registrability of marks. — Abbr. TTAB.

trade meaning. See SECONDARY MEANING.

tradename. *Intellectual property.* **1.** A name, style, or symbol used to distinguish a company, partnership, or business (as opposed to a product or service); the name under which a business operates. • A tradename is a means of identifying a business — or its products or services — to establish goodwill. It symbolizes the business's reputation. Cf. BRAND; D/B/A; TRADEMARK. **2.** A trademark that was not originally susceptible to exclusive appropriation but has acquired a secondary meaning. — Also termed *brand name; commercial name.*

trade or business. *Tax.* Any business or professional activity conducted by a taxpayer with the objective of earning a profit. • If the taxpayer can show that the primary purpose and intention is to make a profit, the taxpayer may deduct certain expenses as trade-or-business expenses under the Internal Revenue Code.

trade practice. A customary way of doing business; esp., a method of using specifications for size, thickness, shape, or quality adopted within a given industry.

trade price. See PRICE.

trader. **1.** A merchant; a retailer; one who buys goods to sell them at a profit. **2.** One who sells goods substantially in the form in which they are bought; one who has not converted them into another form of property by skill and labor. **3.** One who, as a member of a stock exchange, buys and sells securities on the exchange floor either for brokers or on his or her own account. **4.** One who buys and sells commodities and commodity futures for others or for his or her own account in anticipation of a speculative profit.

Trade-Related Aspects of Intellectual Property Rights. See TRIPS.

trader's settlement. See SETTLEMENT (1).

trades council. See TRADE COUNCIL.

trade secret. (1862) **1.** A formula, process, device, or other business information that is kept confidential to maintain an advantage over competitors;

information — including a formula, pattern, compilation, program, device, method, technique, or process — that (1) derives independent economic value, actual or potential, from not being generally known or readily ascertainable by others who can obtain economic value from its disclosure or use, and (2) is the subject of reasonable efforts, under the circumstances, to maintain its secrecy. • This definition states the majority view, which is found in the Uniform Trade Secrets Act. **2.** Information that (1) is not generally known or ascertainable, (2) provides a competitive advantage, (3) has been developed at the plaintiff's expense and is used continuously in the plaintiff's business, and (4) is the subject of the plaintiff's intent to keep it confidential. • This definition states the minority view, which is found in the Restatement of Torts § 757 cmt. b (1939).

trade slander. See SLANDER.

tradesman (**traydz**-mən), *n*. **1.** One who buys and sells things for profit; esp., a shopkeeper. **2.** A shopkeeper's employee. **3.** A mechanic or artisan whose livelihood depends on manual labor; one who is skilled in a trade. — Also termed *tradesperson*.

trade surplus. See SURPLUS.

trade union. See UNION.

trade usage. See USAGE.

trading. The business of buying and selling, esp. of commodities and securities.

  day trading. The act or practice of buying and selling stock shares or other securities on the same day, esp. over the Internet, usu. for the purpose of making a quick profit on the difference between the buying price and the selling price.

  secondary trading. The buying and selling of securities in the market between members of the public, involving neither the issuer nor the underwriter of the securities.

  short-term trading. Investment in securities only to hold them long enough to profit from market-price fluctuations.

trading corporation. See CORPORATION.

trading curb. A temporary restriction on trading in a particular security to curtail dramatic price movements. — Sometimes shortened to *curb.* Cf. TRADING HALT.

trading halt. A temporary suspension of trading in a particular security for a specific reason, such as an order imbalance or a pending news announcement. • Options can be exercised during a trading halt, and open orders may be canceled. — Also termed *suspended trading.* Cf. TRADING CURB.

trading partnership. See PARTNERSHIP.

trading voyage. See VOYAGE.

trading with the enemy. The federal offense of carrying on commerce with a nation or with a subject or ally of a nation with which the United States is at war.

traditio brevi manu (trə-**dish**-ee-oh **bree**-vɪ **man**-yoo). [Latin] *Roman law.* The surrender of the mediate possession of a thing to the person who is already in immediate possession of it. • This is a type of constructive delivery in which a delivery to the mediate possessor and redelivery to the immediate possessor are unnecessary. See BREVI MANU. For the other two types of constructive delivery, see ATTORNMENT; CONSTITUTUM POSSESSORIUM.

tradition. (14c) **1.** Past customs and usages that influence or govern present acts or practices. **2.** The delivery of an item or an estate.

traditional public forum. See PUBLIC FORUM.

traditional surrogacy. See SURROGACY.

traditionary evidence. See EVIDENCE.

traduce (trə-**d[y]oos**), *vb.* (16c) To slander; calumniate. — **traducement,** *n.*

traffic, *n.* (16c) **1.** Commerce; trade; the sale or exchange of such things as merchandise, bills, and money. **2.** The passing or exchange of goods or commodities from one person to another for an equivalent in goods or money. **3.** People or things being transported along a route. **4.** The passing to and fro of people, animals, vehicles, and vessels along a transportation route.

traffic, *vb.* To trade or deal in (goods, esp. illicit drugs or other contraband) <trafficking in heroin>. — **trafficking,** *n.* — **trafficker,** *n.*

traffic balance. The balance of moneys collected in payment for transporting passengers and freight.

traffic court. See COURT.

trafficking. The act of transporting, trading, or dealing, esp. in people or illegal goods. Cf. PEOPLE-SMUGGLING; SMUGGLING.

  drug trafficking. The act of illegally producing, importing, selling, or supplying significant amounts of a controlled substance.

  human trafficking. The illegal recruitment, transportation, transfer, harboring, or receipt of a person, esp. one from another country, with the intent to hold the person captive or exploit the person for labor, services, or body parts. • Human-trafficking offenses include forced prostitution, forced marriages, sweat-shop labor, slavery, and harvesting organs from unwilling donors. — Also termed *trafficking in persons.* Cf. PEOPLE-SMUGGLING; *organ trafficking.*

  organ trafficking. Illegal trafficking in human body parts, esp. transplantable organs that are offered to the highest bidder or that have been harvested without the consent of the donor or the donor's next of kin. • In international law, organ trafficking is broadly included in the offense of human trafficking. — Also termed *trafficking in persons*. Cf. *human trafficking*.

trafficking in persons. 1. See *human trafficking*. 2. See *organ trafficking*.

trafficking in persons. See TRAFFICKING.

traffic regulation. A prescribed rule of conduct for traffic; a rule intended to promote the orderly and safe flow of traffic.

trailer clause. An employee's promise to assign to the employer the rights to all inventions developed while employed and for a specified time afterward. • For the covenant to be enforceable, the time restriction must be reasonable. — Also termed *holdover clause*.

traitor, *n.* 1. A person who commits treason against his or her country. 2. One who betrays a person, a cause, or an obligation. — **traitorous,** *adj.*

tramp, *n.* 1. A person who roams about from place to place, begging or living without labor or visible means of support; a vagrant. 2. TRAMP STEAMER.

tramp corporation. See CORPORATION.

tramp steamer. A ship that is not scheduled to sail between prearranged ports of call but that stops at those ports for which it has cargo. • A tramp steamers typically carries bulk cargoes such as oil, grain, coal, steel, iron ore, or lumber, and is contracted with a charterparty rather than a bill of lading. — Often shortened to *tramp*.

tranche (transh), *n.* [French "slice"] *Securities.* 1. A bond issue derived from a pooling of similar debt obligations. • A tranche usu. differs from other issues by maturity date or rate of return. 2. A block of bonds designated for sale in a foreign country. — Also spelled *tranch; trench.* See COLLATERALIZED MORTGAGE OBLIGATION.

transact, *vb.* 1. To carry on or conduct (negotiations, business, etc.) to a conclusion <transact business>. 2. *Civil law.* To settle (a dispute) by mutual concession. See TRANSACTION (4). 3. To carry on or conduct negotiations or business <refuses to transact with the enemy>.

transaction, *n.* (17c) 1. The act or an instance of conducting business or other dealings; esp., the formation, performance, or discharge of a contract. 2. Something performed or carried out; a business agreement or exchange. 3. Any activity involving two or more persons. 4. *Civil law.* An agreement that is intended by the parties to prevent or end a dispute and in which they make reciprocal concessions. La. Civ. Code art. 3071. — **transactional,** *adj.*

arm's-length transaction. 1. A transaction between two unrelated and unaffiliated parties.

2. A transaction between two parties, however closely related they may be, conducted as if the parties were strangers, so that no conflict of interest arises.

closed transaction. *Tax.* A transaction in which an amount realized on a sale or exchange can be established for the purpose of stating a gain or loss.

colorable transaction. (18c) A sham transaction having the appearance of authenticity; a pretended transaction <the court set aside the colorable transaction>.

transactional audit. See AUDIT.

transactional immunity. See IMMUNITY (3).

transactional lawyer. 1. See LAWYER. 2. See OFFICE PRACTITIONER.

transactional takeover defense. See TAKEOVER DEFENSE.

transaction causation. See CAUSATION.

transaction cost. See COST (1).

transaction-or-occurrence test. (1957) A test used to determine whether, under Fed. R. Civ. P. 13(a), a particular claim is a compulsory counterclaim. • Four different tests have been suggested: (1) Are the legal and factual issues raised by the claim and counterclaim largely the same? (2) Would res judicata bar a later suit on the counterclaim in the absence of the compulsory-counterclaim rule? (3) Will substantially the same evidence support or refute both the plaintiff's claim and the counterclaim? (4) Are the claim and counterclaim logically related? See *compulsory counterclaim* under COUNTERCLAIM.

transaction slip. See CONFIRMATION SLIP.

transcarceration. (1987) The movement of prisoners or institutionalized mentally ill persons from facility to facility, rather than from a prison or an institution back to the community, as when a prisoner is transferred to a halfway house or to a drug-treatment facility.

transcribe, *vb.* (16c) To make a written or typed copy of (spoken material, esp. testimony).

transcript, *n.* (14c) A handwritten, printed, or typed copy of testimony given orally; esp., the official record of proceedings in a trial or hearing, as taken down by a court reporter. — Also termed *report of proceedings; reporter's record.*

transcription. (16c) 1. The act or process of transcribing. 2. Something transcribed; a transcript.

transcript of proceedings. A compilation of all documents relating to a bond issue, typically including the notices, affidavits of notices, a bond resolution (or bond ordinance), official statement, trust indenture and loan agreements, and minutes of meetings of all authorizing bodies.

transfer, *n.* (14c) **1.** Any mode of disposing of or parting with an asset or an interest in an asset, including a gift, the payment of money, release, lease, or creation of a lien or other encumbrance. • The term embraces every method — direct or indirect, absolute or conditional, voluntary or involuntary — of disposing of or parting with property or with an interest in property, including retention of title as a security interest and foreclosure of the debtor's equity of redemption. **2.** Negotiation of an instrument according to the forms of law. • The four methods of transfer are by indorsement, by delivery, by assignment, and by operation of law. **3.** A conveyance of property or title from one person to another.

   colorable transfer. A sham transfer having the appearance of authenticity; a pretended transfer. See ILLUSORY-TRANSFER DOCTRINE.

   constructive transfer. (1852) A delivery of an item — esp. a controlled substance — by someone other than the owner but at the owner's direction.

   incomplete transfer. Tax. A decedent's inter vivos transfer that is not completed for federal estate-tax purposes because the decedent retains significant powers over the property's possession or enjoyment. • Because the transfer is incomplete, some or all of the property's value will be included in the transferor's gross estate. IRC (26 USCA) §§ 2036–2038.

   inter vivos transfer (**in**-tər **vi**-vohs *or* **vee**-vohs). (1930) A transfer of property made during the transferor's lifetime.

   testamentary transfer. A transfer made in a will. • The transfer may be of something less than absolute ownership. Cf. *testamentary gift* under GIFT.

   transfer in contemplation of death. See *gift causa mortis* under GIFT.

   transfer in fraud of creditors. (1883) A conveyance of property made in an attempt to prevent the transferor's creditors from making a claim to it.

transfer, *vb.* (14c) **1.** To convey or remove from one place or one person to another; to pass or hand over from one to another, esp. to change over the possession or control of. **2.** To sell or give.

transferable (trans-**fər**-ə-bəl), *adj.* (14c) Capable of being transferred, together with all rights of the original holder.

transferable letter of credit. See LETTER OF CREDIT.

transferable vote. See *single transferable vote* under VOTE (1).

transfer agent. See AGENT (2).

transfer-agent-run dividend-reinvestment plan. See DIVIDEND-REINVESTMENT PLAN.

transferee. One to whom a property interest is conveyed.

transferee liability. (1951) *Tax.* The liability of a transferee to pay taxes owed by the transferor. • This liability is limited to the value of the asset transferred. The Internal Revenue Service can, for example, force a donee to pay the gift tax when the donor who made the transfer cannot pay it. IRC (26 USCA) §§ 6901–6905.

transfer hearing. See HEARING.

transfer in fraud of creditors. See TRANSFER.

transfer of a case. (1843) The removal of a case from the jurisdiction of one court or judge to another by lawful authority. — Also termed *transfer of a cause.* See REMOVAL (2).

transfer of venue. See CHANGE OF VENUE.

transferor. (1875) One who conveys an interest in property.

transfer payment. (*usu. pl.*) (1945) A governmental payment to a person who has neither provided goods or services nor invested money in exchange for the payment. • Examples include unemployment compensation and welfare payments.

transfer price. See PRICE.

transferred intent. See INTENT (1).

transferred-intent doctrine. (1957) The rule that if one person intends to harm a second person but instead unintentionally harms a third, the first person's criminal or tortious intent toward the second applies to the third as well. • Thus, the offender may be prosecuted for an intent crime or sued by the third person for an intentional tort. See INTENT.

transferred malice. See MALICE.

transfer statute. A provision that allows or mandates the trial of a juvenile as an adult in a criminal court for a criminal act. • Every state has some form of transfer statute. The Supreme Court has held that a juvenile cannot be transferred to criminal court under a discretionary statute "without ceremony — without hearing, without effective assistance of counsel, without a statement of reasons." *Kent v. United States,* 383 U.S. 541, 554, 86 S.Ct. 1045, 1053–54 (1966).

   automatic-transfer statute. A law requiring the transfer from delinquency court to criminal court for certain statutorily enumerated offenses if certain statutory requirements are met.

   discretionary-transfer statute. A law that allows, but does not mandate, the transfer from delinquency court to criminal court for certain statutorily enumerated offenses if certain statutory requirements are met. • The prosecutor has discretion to request the transfer, and the judge has discretion to order the transfer.

reverse transfer statute. A provision that allows a criminal court to return certain cases to juvenile court.

Transfers to Minors Act. See UNIFORM TRANSFERS TO MINORS ACT.

transfer tax. See *generation-skipping transfer tax* under TAX.

transfer warranty. See WARRANTY (2).

transformative use. *Copyright.* The use of copyrighted material in a manner, or for a purpose, that differs from the original use in such a way that the expression, meaning, or message is essentially new. • The term was coined by Judge Pierre N. Leval in a 1990 law-review article entitled *Toward a Fair Use Standard*, 103 Harv. L. Rev. 1105, 1111 (1990). The concept was first applied by the U.S. Supreme Court in *Campbell v. Acuff-Rose Music, Inc.*, 510 U.S. 569, 114 S.Ct. 1164 (1994). The Court held that the transformative use in that case was a fair, noninfringing use of the plaintiff's copyright.

transgenic (tranz-**jen**-ik), *adj. Patents.* Of, relating to, or describing a living organism that has been genetically altered by introducing recombinant DNA from another organism.

transgress, *vb.* **1.** To exceed the limits of (a law, rule, regulation, etc.); to break or violate. **2.** To pass over (limits, boundaries, etc.). — **transgressor,** *n.*

transgression. *Archaic.* See MISDEMEANOR.

transgressive trust. See TRUST.

transient (tran-shənt), *adj.* (16c) Temporary; impermanent; passing away after a short time.

transient, *n.* **1.** A person or thing whose presence is temporary or fleeting. **2.** TRANSIENT PERSON.

transient foreigner. One who visits a country without the intent to remain.

transient jurisdiction. See JURISDICTION.

transient merchant. A trader who sells merchandise at a temporary location without intending to become a permanent merchant in that place.

transient person. (18c) One who has no legal residence within a jurisdiction for the purpose of a state venue statute. — Also termed *transient*.

transit, *n.* (15c) **1.** The transportation of goods or persons from one place to another. **2.** Passage; the act of passing.

transitional alimony. See *rehabilitative alimony* under ALIMONY.

transition phrase. *Patents.* In a patent claim, the word or phrase that relates the preamble to the body. • The transition is often the term "comprising," "having," "including," "consisting of,"

or "consisting essentially of." Cf. PREAMBLE (2); BODY OF A CLAIM.

transitive covenant. See COVENANT (1).

transitory (**tran**-sə-tor-ee *or* tran-zə-), *adj.* (14c) Passing from place to place; capable of passing or being changed from one place to another.

transitory action. See ACTION (4).

transitory treaty. See TREATY (1).

transitory wrong. See WRONG.

transit passage. *Int'l law.* The right of a vessel or airplane to exercise freedom of navigation and overflight solely for the purpose of continuous and expeditious transit between one part of the high seas or an exclusive economic zone and another part of the high seas or an exclusive economic zone. — Also termed *right of transit passage.* Cf. INNOCENT PASSAGE.

translation, *n.* **1.** The transformation of language from one form to another; esp., the systematic rendering of the language of a book, document, or speech into another language. **2.** *Archaic.* The transfer of property. **3.** *Eccles. law.* The removal of a bishop from one diocese to another.

translative (trans- *or* tranz-**lay**-tiv), *adj.* Making or causing a transfer or conveyance.

translative fact. See FACT.

transmission. *Civil law.* The passing of an inheritance to an heir.

transmit, *vb.* (15c) **1.** To send or transfer (a thing) from one person or place to another. **2.** To communicate.

transmittal letter. (1914) A nonsubstantive letter that establishes a record of delivery, such as a letter to a court clerk advising that a particular pleading is enclosed for filing. • Lawyers have traditionally opened transmittal letters with the phrase "Enclosed please find," even though that phrasing has been widely condemned in business-writing handbooks since the late 19th century. A transmittal letter may properly begin with a range of openers as informal as "Here is" to the more formal "Enclosed is." — Also termed *cover letter.*

transmutation. A change in the nature of something; esp., in family law, the transformation of separate property into marital property, or of marital property into separate property.

transnational adoption. See *international adoption* under ADOPTION.

transnational corporation. See *multinational corporation* under CORPORATION.

transnational law. 1. The amalgam of common principles of domestic and international law dealing esp. with problems arising from agreements made between sovereign states and foreign private parties. **2.** The problems to which such principles apply. Cf. INTERNATIONAL LAW.

transparency. Openness; clarity; lack of guile and attempts to hide damaging information. • The word is used of financial disclosures, organizational policies and practices, lawmaking, and other activities where organizations interaction with the public.

transport, *vb.* To carry or convey (a thing) from one place to another.

transportation, *n.* (16c) **1.** The movement of goods or persons from one place to another by a carrier. **2.** *Criminal law.* A type of punishment that sends the criminal out of the country to another place (usu. a penal colony) for a specified period. Cf. DEPORTATION.

Transportation Security Administration. The federal agency charged with promoting safety and security of air, water, rail, and highway transportation. • The agency was created in the Department of Transportation after the terrorist attacks of September 11, 2001, and was transferred to the Department of Homeland Security in 2002.

transracial adoption. See ADOPTION.

transsexual. A person born with the physical characteristics of one sex but who has undergone, or is preparing to undergo, sex-change surgery. See SEX REASSIGNMENT.

transshipment. *Maritime law.* The act of taking cargo out of one ship and loading it on another. • Transshipment may also involve transfer of cargo to another mode of transportation, such as rail or truck. — **transship,** *vb.*

transvestitive fact. See FACT.

trap, *n.* (bef. 12c) **1.** A device for capturing living creatures, such as a pitfall, snare, or machine that shuts suddenly.

mantrap. A booby-trap; esp., a device to catch a trespasser or burglar. • A mantrap is not illegal if it is designed merely to sound an alarm and not cause bodily harm. Illegal mantraps include manufactured devices such as spring guns, and dangerous hidden conditions (manufactured or natural) that can injure a person, such as pitfalls. — Also spelled *man-trap.*

2. Any device or contrivance by which one may be caught unawares; stratagem; snare. **3.** *Torts.* An ultrahazardous hidden peril of which the property owner or occupier, but not a licensee, has knowledge. • A trap can exist even if it was not designed or intended to catch or entrap anything.

trashing. DECONSTRUCTION.

trauma-pricing. See DRAMA-PRICING.

travel-accident insurance. See INSURANCE.

Travel Act. A federal law, enacted in 1961, that prohibits conduct intended to promote, direct, or manage illegal business activities in interstate commerce. • This statute was enacted to create federal jurisdiction over many criminal activities traditionally handled by state and local governments to help those jurisdictions cope with increasingly complex interstate criminal activity. 18 USCA § 1952.

traveled place. (1894) A place where the public has, in some manner, acquired the legal right to travel.

traveler, *n.* A person who passes from place to place, for any reason.

traveler's check. See CHECK.

traveler's letter of credit. See LETTER OF CREDIT.

travel expense. See EXPENSE.

traverse (trav-ərs), *n.* (15c) *Common-law pleading.* A formal denial of a factual allegation made in the opposing party's pleading <Smith filed a traverse to Allen's complaint, asserting that he did not knowingly provide false information>. See DENIAL. — **traverse** (trav-ərs *or* trə-**vərs**), *vb.*

common traverse. (1841) A traverse consisting of a tender of issue — that is, a denial accompanied by a formal offer for decision of the point denied — with a denial that expressly contradicts the terms of the allegation traversed. — Also termed *specific traverse.*

cumulative traverse. (1848) A traverse that analyzes a proposition into its constituent parts and traverses them cumulatively. • It amounts to the same thing as traversing the one entire proposition, since the several parts traversed must all make up one entire proposition or point.

general traverse. (17c) A denial of all the facts in an opponent's pleading.

special traverse. (18c) A denial of one material fact in an opponent's pleading; a traverse that explains or qualifies the denial. • The essential parts of a special traverse are an inducement, a denial, and a verification.

specific traverse. See *common traverse.*

traverse jury. See *petit jury* under JURY.

traverser, *n.* (14c) One who traverses or denies a pleading.

traverse the requirement, *vb.* *Patents.* To (1) respond in detail to a patent examiner's decision that the patent application claims more than one invention and (2) ask that the restriction requirement be reconsidered. • The traverse must specifically explain why restriction should not be required, not merely assert that the requirement is wrong. Failure to traverse a requirement forfeits any rights to appeal the decision.

treachery, *n.* A deliberate and willful betrayal of trust and confidence.

treason, *n.* (13c) The offense of attempting to overthrow the government of the state to which one owes allegiance, either by making war against the state or by materially supporting its enemies. — Also termed *high treason; alta proditio.* Cf. SEDITION. — **treasonable, treasonous,** *adj.*

    constructive treason. **1.** Speech that manifests a desire or intent to make war against the state or materially support an enemy, even though the speech is unaccompanied by acts that further the desire or intent. ● There is no crime of constructive treason in U.S. law because treason requires an affirmative act, and intent alone cannot substitute for an act. Cf. SEDITION. **2.** *Hist.* Speech that is critical of the government. ● This sense arose during the reign of Henry VIII of England. Critical speech remained a capital crime until the early 18th century.

    petty treason. *Archaic.* Murder of one's employer or husband. ● Until 1828, this act was considered treason under English law. — Also spelled *petit treason.*

Treas. Reg. *abbr.* TREASURY REGULATION.

treasurer. An organization's chief financial officer. ● The treasurer's duties typically include prudently depositing (or, if authorized, investing) and safeguarding the organization's funds and otherwise managing its finances; monitoring compliance with any applicable law relating to such finances and filing any required report; disbursing money as authorized; and reporting to the organization on the state of the treasury. — Also termed *finance officer; financial secretary; quartermaster.*

    city treasurer. A local officer who is responsible for managing municipal funds.

Treasurer of the United States. The officer in the U.S. Department of the Treasury responsible for overseeing the operations of the Bureau of Engraving and Printing and the U.S. Mint.

treasure trove. [Law French "treasure found"] (16c) Valuables (usu. gold or silver) found hidden in the ground or other private place, the owner of which is unknown. ● At common law in the United States, the finder of a treasure trove can usu. claim good title against all except the true owner. But until 1996, any treasure trove found in the United Kingdom belonged to the Crown.

Treasuries. (1922) Debt obligations of the federal government backed by the full faith and credit of the government. See TREASURY BILL; TREASURY BOND; TREASURY CERTIFICATE; TREASURY NOTE.

treasury. 1. A place or building in which stores of wealth are kept; esp., a place where public revenues are deposited and kept and from which money is disbursed to defray government expenses. **2.** (*cap.*) DEPARTMENT. OF THE TREASURY.

Treasury Bench. In the British House of Commons, the first row of seats on the right hand of the speaker. ● The Treasury Bench is occupied by the First Lord of the Treasury or principal minister of the Crown.

Treasury bill. (18c) A short-term debt security issued by the federal government, with a maturity of 13, 26, or 52 weeks. ● These bills — auctioned weekly or quarterly — pay interest in the form of the difference between their discounted purchase price and their par value at maturity. — Abbr. T-bill.

Treasury bond. (1858) A long-term debt security issued by the federal government, with a maturity of 10 to 30 years. ● These bonds are considered risk-free, but they usu. pay relatively little interest. — Abbr. T-bond.

    TIPS bond. A treasury bond whose face value is adjusted to keep pace with the inflation rate. ● The acronym TIPS stands for *Treasury inflation-protected securities.* — Abbr. TIPS.

treasury certificate. An obligation of the federal government maturing in one year and on which interest is paid on a coupon basis.

Treasury Department. See DEPARTMENT OF THE TREASURY.

Treasury inflation-protected securities. See *TIPS bond* under TREASURY BOND.

Treasury note. (18c) An intermediate-term debt security issued by the federal government, with a maturity of two to ten years. ● These notes are considered risk-free, but they usu. pay relatively little interest. — Abbr. T-note.

Treasury Regulation. (1860) A regulation promulgated by the U.S. Treasury Department to explain or interpret a section of the Internal Revenue Code. ● Treasury Regulations are binding on all taxpayers. — Abbr. Treas. Reg.

treasury security. See *treasury stock* under STOCK.

treasury share. See *treasury stock* under STOCK.

treasury stock. See STOCK.

treasury warrant. See WARRANT (2).

treating-physician rule. The principle that a treating physician's diagnoses and findings about the degree of a social-security claimant's impairment are binding on an administrative-law judge in the absence of substantial contrary evidence.

treaty. 1. An agreement formally signed, ratified, or adhered to between two nations or sovereigns; an international agreement concluded between two or more states in written form and governed by international law. — Also termed *accord;*

convention; *covenant*; *declaration*; *pact*. Cf. EX-
ECUTIVE AGREEMENT.

commercial treaty. A bilateral or multilateral
treaty concerning trade or other mercantile
activities. • Such a treaty may be general in
nature, as by supplying the framework of long-
term commercial relations. Or it may be specific, as by detailing the conditions of particular
branches of trade or other commercial transactions. Sometimes a treaty of this kind deals
with an individual project, such as a guaranty
agreement.

defensive treaty. A treaty in which each party
agrees to come to the other's aid if one is attacked by another nation. See *treaty of alliance*.

dispositive treaty (dis-**poz**-ə-tiv). A treaty by
which a country takes over territory by impress-
ing a special character on it, creating something
analogous to a servitude or easement in private
law.

guarantee treaty. An agreement between countries directly or indirectly establishing a unilateral or reciprocal guarantee. — Also spelled
guaranty treaty. — Also termed *treaty of guarantee*; *quasi-guarantee treaty*; *pseudo-guarantee
treaty*.

mixed treaty. A treaty with characteristics of different types of treaties, esp. contrasting types
(e.g., permanent and transitory, or personal and
real).

nonaggression treaty. See NONAGGRESSION
PACT.

nonproliferation treaty. A treaty forbidding the
transfer of nuclear weapons from a country with
a nuclear arsenal to one that does not have nuclear-weapons capability. • The first such treaty
was concluded in 1968, and now more than 100
nations have agreed to its terms. — Also termed
nuclear-nonproliferation treaty.

offensive treaty. A treaty in which the parties
agree to declare war jointly on another nation
and join forces to wage the war. See *treaty of
alliance*.

peace treaty. A treaty signed by heads of state to
end a war. — Also termed *treaty of peace*. Cf.
TRUCE.

permanent treaty. A treaty that contemplates
ongoing performance (as with a treaty of neutrality).

personal treaty. *Hist.* A treaty relating exclusively
to the contracting sovereign as a person. • Examples of personal treaties are family alliances
and treaties guaranteeing the throne to a particular sovereign and his or her family. With the
advent of constitutional government in Europe,
personal treaties have lost their importance.

pseudo-guarantee treaty. See *guarantee treaty*.

quasi-guarantee treaty. See *guarantee treaty*.

real treaty. A treaty relating solely to the subject
matter of the compact, independently of the
persons of the contracting sovereigns. • Real
treaties continue to bind the state even when
the heads of government change.

transitory treaty. A treaty carried into effect once
and for all, so that it is complete when the act has
been performed (as with a treaty of cession).

treaty of alliance. A treaty establishing mutual
and reciprocal support obligations. • A treaty
of alliance may be for support in defense, aggression, or both. See *defensive treaty*; *offensive
treaty*.

treaty of guarantee. See *guarantee treaty*.

treaty of neutrality. A treaty in which the parties agree not to engage in any aggressive action against one another, whether individually
or jointly with others, and not to interfere with
the other party's affairs. • There is no commitment to aid another party in the event of war —
only to refrain from becoming involved.

treaty of peace. See *peace treaty*.

2. A contract or agreement between insurers
providing for treaty reinsurance. See *treaty reinsurance* under REINSURANCE. **3.** A negotiated
contract or agreement between private persons.

private treaty. An agreement to convey property negotiated by the buyer and seller or their
agents. • This term is esp. common in the U.K.

Treaty Clause. The constitutional provision giving the President the power to make treaties, with
the advice and consent of the Senate. U.S. Const.
art. II, § 2.

treaty-created law. See CONVENTIONAL LAW.

treaty-made law. See CONVENTIONAL LAW.

treaty of reinsurance. See REINSURANCE TREATY.

treaty power. (1835) The President's constitutional
authority to make treaties, with the advice and
consent of the Senate. See TREATY CLAUSE.

treaty reinsurance. See REINSURANCE.

treble damages. See DAMAGES.

trebucket (**tree**-bək-it). See CASTIGATORY.

trend. A price pattern in the stock market generally
or in a particular stock.

major trend. A long-term trend of the stock market; a general increase or decrease of stock prices
over an extended period. — Also termed *fundamental trend*.

market trend. The direction of stock-market prices over a several-month period.

trespass (**tres**-pəs *or* **tres**-pas), *n.* (13c) **1.** An unlawful act committed against the person or property

of another; esp., wrongful entry on another's real property. Cf. *unlawful entry* under ENTRY (1). **2.** At common law, a legal action for injuries resulting from an unlawful act of this kind. **3.** *Archaic.* MISDEMEANOR. — **trespass,** *vb.* — **trespassory** (**tres**-pə-sor-ee), *adj.*

constructive trespass. See *trespass to chattels.*

continuing trespass. A trespass in the nature of a permanent invasion on another's rights, such as a sign that overhangs another's property.

criminal trespass. 1. A trespass on property that is clearly marked against trespass by signs or fences. **2.** A trespass in which the trespasser remains on the property after being ordered off by a person authorized to do so.

innocent trespass. A trespass committed either unintentionally or in good faith.

joint trespass. A trespass that two or more persons have united in committing, or that some have actually committed while others commanded, encouraged, or directed it.

permanent trespass. A trespass consisting of a series of acts, done on consecutive days, that are of the same nature and that are renewed or continued from day to day, so that the acts in the aggregate form one indivisible harm.

trespass ab initio (ab i-**nish**-ee-oh). An entry on land that, though begun innocently or with a privilege, is deemed a trespass from the beginning because of conduct that abuses the privilege.

trespass by relation. A trespass committed when the plaintiff had a right to immediate possession of land but had not yet exercised that right. • When the plaintiff takes possession, a legal fiction treats the plaintiff as having had possession ever since the accrual of the right of entry. This is known as *trespass by relation* because the plaintiff's possession relates back to the time when the plaintiff first acquired a right to possession.

trespass de bonis asportatis (dee **boh**-nis as-pər-**tay**-tis). [Latin "trespass for carrying goods away"] **1.** A wrongful taking of chattels. • This type of trespassory taking was also an element of common-law larceny. **2.** At common law, an action to recover damages for the wrongful taking of chattels. — Abbr. trespass d.b.a. — Often shortened to *trespass de bonis.* — Also termed *trespass to personal property.*

trespass on the case. (15c) At common law, an action to recover damages that are not the immediate result of a wrongful act but rather a later consequence. • This action was the precursor to a variety of modern-day tort claims, including negligence, nuisance, and business torts. — Often shortened to *case.* — Also termed

action on the case; breve de transgressione super casum.

trespass quare clausum fregit (**kwair**-ee-**klaw**-zəm-**free**-jit). [Latin "why he broke the close"] (17c) **1.** A person's unlawful entry on another's land that is visibly enclosed. • This tort consists of doing any of the following without lawful justification: (1) entering upon land in the possession of another, (2) remaining on the land, or (3) placing or projecting any object upon it. **2.** At common law, an action to recover damages resulting from another's unlawful entry on one's land that is visibly enclosed. — Abbr. trespass q.c.f. — Also termed *trespass to real property; trespass to land; quare clausum querentis fregit.* See *trespass vi et armis.*

trespass to chattels. (1843) The act of committing, without lawful justification, any act of direct physical interference with a chattel possessed by another. • The act must amount to a direct forcible injury. — Also termed *trespass to goods; constructive trespass.*

trespass to goods. See *trespass to chattels.*

trespass to land. See *trespass quare clausum fregit* (2).

trespass to personal property. See *trespass de bonis asportatis.*

trespass to real property. See *trespass quare clausum fregit* (2).

trespass to try title. (1826) **1.** In some states, an action for the recovery of property unlawfully withheld from an owner who has the immediate right to possession. **2.** A procedure under which a claim to title may be adjudicated.

trespass vi et armis (VI et **ahr**-mis). [Latin "with force and arms"] (17c) **1.** At common law, an action for damages resulting from an intentional injury to person or property, esp. if by violent means; trespass to the plaintiff's person, as in illegal assault, battery, wounding, or imprisonment, when not under color of legal process, or when the battery, wounding, or imprisonment was in the first instance lawful, but unnecessary violence was used or the imprisonment continued after the process had ceased to be lawful. • This action also lay for injury to relative rights, such as menacing tenants or servants, beating and wounding a spouse, criminal conversation with or seducing a wife, or debauching a daughter or servant. **2.** See *trespass quare clausum fregit.* • In this sense, the "force" is implied by the "breaking" of the close (that is, an enclosed area), even if no real force is used.

trespass d.b.a. See *trespass de bonis asportatis* under TRESPASS.

trespasser. (14c) One who commits a trespass; one who intentionally and without consent or privilege enters another's property. • In tort law, a landholder owes no duty to unforeseeable trespassers. Cf. INVITEE; LICENSEE (2).

innocent trespasser. (1888) One who enters another's land unlawfully, but either inadvertently or believing in a right to do so.

trespass q.c.f. See *trespass quare clausum fregit* under TRESPASS.

tret (tret), *n.* An allowance or abatement of a certain weight or quantity that a seller makes to a buyer because of water or dust that may be mixed with a commodity. Cf. TARE.

triable, *adj.* (15c) Subject or liable to judicial examination and trial <a triable offense>.

trial. (15c) A formal judicial examination of evidence and determination of legal claims in an adversary proceeding.

abortive trial. See MISTRIAL.

bench trial. (1954) A trial before a judge without a jury. • The judge decides questions of fact as well as questions of law. — Also termed *trial to the bench; nonjury trial; court trial; trial before the court* (abbr. TBC); *judge trial.*

bifurcated trial. (1945) A trial that is divided into two stages, such as for guilt and punishment or for liability and damages. — Also termed *two-stage trial.* Cf. SEVERANCE (2).

closed trial. A trial that is not open to the public, usu. because of some overriding concern such as a need to protect a child's anonymity or for security.

court trial. See *bench trial.*

fair trial. See FAIR TRIAL.

joint trial. (18c) A trial involving two or more parties; esp., a criminal trial of two or more persons for the same or similar offenses.

judge trial. See *bench trial.*

jury trial. (18c) A trial in which the factual issues are determined by a jury, not by the judge. — Also termed *trial by jury.*

mock trial. See MOCK TRIAL.

new trial. (16c) A postjudgment retrial or reexamination of some or all of the issues determined in an earlier judgment. • The trial court may order a new trial by motion of a party or on the court's own initiative. Also, when an appellate court reverses the trial court's judgment, it may remand the case to the trial court for a new trial on some or all of the issues on which the reversal is based. *See* Fed. R. Civ. P. 59; Fed. R. Crim. P. 33. See MOTION FOR NEW TRIAL; REMAND.

nonbinding minitrial. See *summary jury trial.*

nonbinding summary jury trial. See *summary jury trial.*

nonjury trial. See *bench trial.*

perfect trial. A trial free from all error.

political trial. (18c) A trial (esp. a criminal prosecution) in which either the prosecution or the defendant (or both) uses the proceedings as a platform to espouse a particular political belief; a trial of a person for a political crime. See SHOW TRIAL.

public trial. A trial that anyone may attend or observe.

separate trial. (18c) **1.** *Criminal procedure.* The individual trial of each of several persons jointly accused of a crime. Fed. R. Crim. P. 14. **2.** *Civil procedure.* Within a single action, a distinct trial of a separate claim or issue — or of a group of claims or issues — ordered by the trial judge, usu. to conserve resources or avoid prejudice. Fed. R. Civ. P. 42(b). Cf. SEVERANCE (2).

short-cause trial. See *short cause* under CAUSE (3).

show trial. See SHOW TRIAL.

speedy trial. See SPEEDY TRIAL.

state trial. A trial for a political offense.

summary jury trial. (1984) A settlement technique in which the parties argue before a mock jury, which then reaches a nonbinding verdict that will assist the parties in evaluating their positions. — Also termed *nonbinding summary jury trial; nonbinding minitrial.* Cf. MOCK TRIAL.

trial at bar. *Hist.* A trial before all the judges of the court in which the proceedings take place. — Also termed *trial at the bar.*

trial at nisi prius (ni-si pri-əs). *Hist.* A trial before the justices of assize and nisi prius in the county where the facts are alleged to have occurred, and from which county the jurors have been summoned.

trial before the court. See *bench trial.*

trial by battle. See TRIAL BY COMBAT.

trial by combat. See TRIAL BY COMBAT.

trial by duel. See TRIAL BY COMBAT.

trial by jury. See *jury trial.*

trial by ordeal. See ORDEAL.

trial by record. *Hist.* A trial in which, a record having been pleaded by one party and denied by the other, the record is inspected in order to decide the dispute, no other evidence being admissible. See NUL TIEL RECORD.

trial by the country. See *trial per pais.*

trial de novo (dee *or* di noh-voh). (18c) A new trial on the entire case — that is, on both questions of fact and issues of law — conducted as if there had been no trial in the first instance.

trial in absentia. A trial held without the accused being present. • In the United States, a trial may be held *in absentia* only if the accused has either voluntarily left after the trial has started else has so disrupted the proceedings that the judge orders the accused's removal as a last resort.

trial on the merits. (18c) A trial on the substantive issues of a case, as opposed to a motion hearing or interlocutory matter.

trial per pais (pər **pay** *or* **pays**). [Law French "trial by the country"] (17c) Trial by jury. — Also termed *trial by the country.* Cf. CONCLUSION TO THE COUNTRY; GOING TO THE COUNTRY; PATRIA (3).

trial to the bench. See *bench trial.*

trifurcated trial. (1959) A trial that is divided into three stages, such as for liability, general damages, and special damages.

two-stage trial. See *bifurcated trial.*

trial brief. See BRIEF.

trial by combat. *Hist.* A trial that is decided by personal battle between the disputants, common in Europe and England during the Middle Ages; specif., a trial in which the person accused fought with the accuser, the idea being that God would give victory to the person in the right. • This method was introduced into England by the Normans after 1066, but it was a widely detested innovation and was little used. It became obsolete several centuries before being formally abolished in 1818, having been replaced in practice by the grand assize and indictment. — Also termed *trial by battle*; *trial by wager of battle*; *trial by duel*; *judicial combat*; *duel*; *duellum*; *wager of battle*; *ornest*; *vadiatio duelli*; *wehading.* See JUDICIUM DEI.

trial by corsnaed. See *ordeal of the morsel* under ORDEAL.

trial by duel. See TRIAL BY COMBAT.

trial by oath. See COMPURGATION.

trial by ordeal. See ORDEAL.

trial by wager of battle. See TRIAL BY COMBAT.

trial calendar. See DOCKET (2).

trial counsel. See COUNSEL.

trial court. See COURT.

trial de novo. See TRIAL.

trial examiner. See ADMINISTRATIVE-LAW JUDGE.

trial franchise. See FRANCHISE (4).

trial judge. See JUDGE.

trial jury. See *petit jury* under JURY.

trial of right of property. 1. INTERVENTION (1). 2. INTERVENTION (2).

trial per pais. See TRIAL.

trial-setting preference. See *special setting* under SETTING.

trial-type hearing. See ADMINISTRATIVE PROCEEDING.

triangular merger. See MERGER.

Tribal Court. Under the Indian Child Welfare Act, a court with child-custody jurisdiction that is (1) a Court of Indian Offenses, (2) a court established and operated under an Indian tribe's code or custom, or (3) any other tribal administrative body that is vested with authority over child-custody proceedings. • The Tribal Court is composed of tribal members, is usu. situated on the reservation, and varies in its characteristics from tribe to tribe. It is not part of any state's judicial system, instead operating more or less as a judicial system of a foreign nation. See INDIAN CHILD WELFARE ACT.

tribal-exhaustion doctrine. The general principle that when an Indian tribal court, original or appellate, has personal and subject-matter jurisdiction, the parties must pursue all remedies available under tribal law before turning to nontribal courts. • A federal court may review a challenge to jurisdiction only after the tribal court has established it has jurisdiction and determined the case on the merits. See *National Farmer's Union Ins. Co. v. Crow Tribe*, 471 U.S. 845, 856–57, 105 S.Ct. 2447, 2454 (1985).

tribal land. A part of an Indian reservation that is not allotted to or occupied by individual Indians but is held as the tribe's common land. Cf. INDIAN LAND.

tribunal (trɪ-**byoo**-nəl). (15c) **1.** A court or other adjudicatory body. **2.** The seat, bench, or place where a judge sits.

tributary (**trib**-yə-ter-ee), *n.* (14c) A stream flowing directly or indirectly into a river.

tribute (**trib**-yoot), *n.* (14c) **1.** An acknowledgment of gratitude or respect. **2.** A contribution that a sovereign raises from its subjects to defray the expenses of state. **3.** Money paid by an inferior sovereign or state to a superior one to secure the latter's friendship and protection.

tri-chad. See CHAD.

trier of fact. See FACT-FINDER.

trifurcated trial. See TRIAL.

trigamy (**trig**-ə-mee), *n.* (17c) The act of marrying a person while legally married to someone else and bigamously married to yet another.

triggering condition. See CONDITION (2).

Trinity House. *Maritime law.* A British corporation chartered in 1514 to train and license pilots and officially regulate pilotage. • Trinity House has also erected and maintained aids to navigation, such as lighthouses and buoys, on the coasts of Great Britain.

Trinity sittings. *English law.* A term of court beginning on May 22 of each year and ending on June 12. • This was known until 1875 as *Trinity term.* Cf. EASTER SITTINGS; HILARY SITTINGS; MICHAELMAS SITTINGS.

tripartite (trī-**pahr**-tīt), *adj.* (15c) Involving, composed of, or divided into three parts or elements <a tripartite agreement>.

tripartite lease. See *finance lease* under LEASE.

tripartite test. *Patents.* A judicial test for determining patent infringement by looking at whether a challenged device or process, though outside the literal scope of the patent claims, performs the function in substantially the same way. See SUBSTANTIAL EQUIVALENT.

triple damages. See *treble damages* under DAMAGES.

triple net lease. See *net-net-net lease* under LEASE.

triple ordeal. See ORDEAL.

triple trigger. *Insurance.* (1981) A theory of coverage providing that all insurers on a risk must cover a loss from the day a claimant is first exposed to an injury-producing product (such as asbestos) to the date of diagnosis or death, whichever occurs first. • This term was first used in *Keene Corp. v. Insurance Co. of N. Am.*, 667 F.2d 1034 (D.C. Cir. 1981), *cert denied*, 445 U.S. 1007, 102 S.Ct. 1644 (1982). — Also termed *continuous trigger.* Cf. ACTUAL-INJURY TRIGGER; EXPOSURE THEORY; MANIFESTATION THEORY.

TRIPs. *abbr. Intellectual property.* The Agreement on Trade-Related Aspects of Intellectual Property Rights, a treaty that harmonized and strengthened the intellectual-property laws of its signatories by linking the obligation to protect the intellectual-property rights of other members' citizens with a mechanism for settling international trade disputes. • TRIPs was negotiated at the 1994 Uruguay Round of the General Agreement on Tariffs and Trade (GATT). More than 150 nations are parties to the agreement. In the field of patents, TRIPs standardized patentable subject matter to include medicines, required testing for nonobviousness and utility, and protected patentees from infringing imports. In response to the agreement Congress (1) changed patent terms to 20 years from the date of application, rather than 17 years from the date of issue; (2) allowed foreign filers to prove priority by inventive efforts that preceded filing; (3) widened the definition of infringement to cover offering for sale and importing; and (4) permitted provisional applications, with brief descriptions and no claims, to establish priority. 33 I.L.M. 1197. In the field of copyrights, TRIPs incorporates most of the provisions of the Berne Convention for the Protection of Literary or Artistic Works, and sets the length of copyright protection as the life of the author plus 50 years. In the field of trademarks, TRIPs sets the initial term of a trademark registration as not less than seven years, and makes it renewable indefinitely. Nations subject to TRIPs may make registrability dependent on use but may not require use as a condition for filing an application. — Also written TRIPS. — Also termed *TRIPs Agreement.*

tristis successio (**tris**-tis sək-**ses**[h]-ee-oh). See *hereditas luctuosa* under HEREDITAS.

trivial, *adj.* (16c) Trifling; inconsiderable; of small worth or importance.

TRO (tee-ahr-**oh**). *abbr.* TEMPORARY RESTRAINING ORDER.

troubled asset. See ASSET.

trover (**troh**-vər). (16c) A common-law action for the recovery of damages for the conversion of personal property, the damages generally being measured by the property's value. — Also termed *trover and conversion.* Cf. DETINUE; REPLEVIN.

truancy (**troo**-ən-see), *n.* (18c) The act or state of shirking responsibility; esp., willful and unjustified failure to attend school by one who is required to attend. — **truant,** *adj. & n.*

truancy officer. An official responsible for enforcing laws mandating school attendance for minors of specified ages (usu. 16 and under). — Also termed *truant officer; attendance officer.*

truant, *n.* A person who without permission is absent from work or school or who shirks a duty.

truce. *Int'l law.* A suspension or temporary cessation of hostilities by agreement between belligerent powers. — Also termed *armistice; ceasefire; suspension of arms.* Cf. *peace treaty* under TREATY (1). — **trucial,** *adj.*

> **general truce.** A truce suspending hostilities in all places.

> **special truce.** A truce referring only to operations before a specific fortress or in a district, or between certain detachments of armies. — Also termed *partial truce.*

true admission. See *judicial admission* under ADMISSION (1).

true and correct. Authentic; accurate; unaltered <we have forwarded a true and correct copy of the expert's report>. — Also termed *true and exact.*

true bill, *n.* (18c) A grand jury's notation that a criminal charge should go before a petty jury for trial <the grand jury returned a true bill, and the state prepared to prosecute>. — Also termed *billa vera.* Cf. NO BILL.

true-bill, *vb.* To make or deliver a true bill on <the grand jury true-billed the indictment>.

true copy. See COPY.

true defense. See DEFENSE (1).

true legal impossibility. See *legal impossibility* (1) under IMPOSSIBILITY.

true mark. See *technical trademark* under TRADEMARK.

true residue. See CLEAR RESIDUE.

true trademark. See *technical trademark* under TRADEMARK.

true value. See *fair market value* under VALUE (2).

true-value rule. The rule requiring that one who subscribes for and receives corporate stock must pay par value for it, in either money or its equivalent, so that a corporation's real assets square with its books. • If true value is less than par value, the stock is deemed unpaid for to the full extent of the difference, and the affected shareholder is liable to creditors for the difference, notwithstanding the directors' good faith.

true verdict. See VERDICT.

trust, *n.* (15c) **1.** The right, enforceable solely in equity, to the beneficial enjoyment of property to which another person holds the legal title; a property interest held by one person (the *trustee*) at the request of another (the *settlor*) for the benefit of a third party (the *beneficiary*). • For a trust to be valid, it must involve specific property, reflect the settlor's intent, and be created for a lawful purpose. The two primary types of trusts are *private trusts* and *charitable trusts* (see below). **2.** A fiduciary relationship regarding property and charging the person with title to the property with equitable duties to deal with it for another's benefit; the confidence placed in a trustee, together with the trustee's obligations toward the property and the beneficiary. • A trust arises as a result of a manifestation of an intention to create it. See *fiduciary relationship* under RELATIONSHIP. **3.** The property so held; CORPUS (1).

A-B-Q trust. See *bypass trust*.

A-B trust. See *bypass trust*.

accumulation trust. A trust in which the trustee must accumulate income and gains from sales of trust assets for ultimate disposition with the principal when the trust terminates. • Many states restrict the time over which accumulations may be made or the amount that may be accumulated.

active trust. A trust in which the trustee has some affirmative duty of management or administration besides the obligation to transfer the property to the beneficiary. — Also termed *express active trust*; *special trust*; *operative trust*. Cf. *passive trust*.

Alaska trust. See *asset-protection trust* (1).

alimony trust. A trust in which the payor spouse transfers to the trustee property from which the payee spouse, as beneficiary, will be supported after a divorce or separation.

annuity trust. A trust from which the trustee must pay a sum certain annually to one or more beneficiaries for their respective lives or for a term of years, and must then either transfer the remainder to or for the use of a qualified charity or retain the remainder for such a use. • The sum certain must not be less than 5% of the initial fair market value of the property transferred to the trust by the donor. A qualified annuity trust must comply with the requirements of IRC (26 USCA) § 664.

asset-protection trust. 1. A trust designed specifically to insulate assets from the settlor's creditors. • When the trust is created using the law of a state, it is also termed a *domestic asset-protection trust*. It may also be referred to by the name of the specific state, e.g., *Alaska trust*, *Delaware trust*, or *Nevada trust*. If it is created under foreign law, even though the assets are within the United States, it is also termed an *offshore asset-protection trust*. **2.** See *self-settled trust*.

bank-account trust. See *Totten trust*.

blended trust. A trust in which the beneficiaries are a group, with no member of the group having a separable individual interest. • Courts rarely recognize these trusts.

blind trust. (1969) A trust in which the settlor places investments under the control of an independent trustee, usu. to avoid a conflict of interest. • The beneficiary has no knowledge of the trust's holdings and no right to participate in the trust's management.

bond trust. A trust whose principal consists of bonds that yield interest income.

bypass trust. (1981) A trust into which just enough of a decedent's estate passes, so that the estate can take advantage of the unified credit against federal estate taxes. See 26 USCA § 2010. — Also termed *credit-shelter trust*; *A-B trust*; *A-B-Q trust*; *marital life-estate trust*. See *unified estate-and-gift tax credit* under TAX CREDIT.

charitable lead trust. An irrevocable trust made in favor of a charity and allowing the charity to receive income from the trust property for a specified period, after which the property reverts to the settlor's estate.

charitable-remainder annuity trust. A charitable-remainder trust in which the beneficiaries receive for a specified period a fixed payment of 5% or more of the fair market value of the original principal, after which the remaining principal passes to charity. — Abbr. CRAT. — Also termed *charitable-remainder-trust retirement fund.*

charitable-remainder trust. A trust consisting of assets that are designated for a charitable purpose and paid over to the trust after the expiration of a life estate or intermediate estate. — Abbr. CRT. — Also termed *split-interest trust.*

charitable-remainder-trust retirement fund. See *charitable-remainder annuity trust.*

charitable trust. (18c) A trust created to benefit a specific charity, specific charities, or the general public rather than a private individual or entity. ● Charitable trusts are often eligible for favorable tax treatment. If the trust's terms do not specify a charity or a particular charitable purpose, a court may select a charity. See Uniform Trust Act § 405. — Also termed *public trust*; *charitable use.* See *charitable deduction* under DEDUCTION; CY PRES. Cf. *private trust.*

Claflin trust. See *indestructible trust.*

Clifford trust. (1941) An irrevocable trust, set up for at least ten years and a day, whereby income from the trust property is paid to the beneficiary but the property itself reverts back to the settlor when the trust expires. ● These trusts were often used by parents — with their children as beneficiaries — to shelter investment income, but the Tax Reform Act of 1986 eliminated the tax advantage by imposing the kiddie tax and by taxing the income of settlors with a reversionary interest that exceeds 5% of the trust's value. This term gets its name from *Helvering v. Clifford*, 309 U.S. 331, 60 S.Ct. 554 (1940). — Also termed *short-term trust.*

common-law trust. See *business trust* under TRUST (4).

community trust. See COMMUNITY TRUST.

complete voluntary trust. See *executed trust.*

complex trust. 1. A trust having elaborate provisions. **2.** See *discretionary trust.*

constructive trust. (18c) An equitable remedy that a court imposes against one who has obtained property by wrongdoing. ● A constructive trust, imposed to prevent unjust enrichment, creates no fiduciary relationship. Despite its name, it is not a trust at all. — Also termed *implied trust*; *involuntary trust*; *trust de son tort*; *trust ex delicto*; *trust ex maleficio*; *remedial trust*; *trust in invitum.* See *trustee de son tort* under TRUSTEE. Cf. *resulting trust.*

contingent trust. An express trust depending for its operation on a future event.

credit-shelter trust. See *bypass trust.*

Crummey trust. A trust in which the trustee has the power to distribute or accumulate income and to give the beneficiary the right to withdraw an amount equal to the annual gift exclusion (or a smaller sum) within a reasonable time after the transfer. ● This type of trust can have multiple beneficiaries and is often used when the beneficiaries are minors. Gifts to a *Crummey* trust qualify for the annual gift exclusion regardless of the age of the beneficiaries. The trust assets are not required to be distributed to the beneficiaries at age 21. The validity of this type of trust was established in *Crummey v. Commissioner*, 397 F.2d 82 (9th Cir. 1968). — Also termed *discretionary trust.* See CRUMMEY POWER; *annual exclusion* under EXCLUSION. Cf. *2503(c) trust.*

custodial trust. A revocable trust for which a custodial trustee is named to manage the assets for an incapacitated or disabled beneficiary. ● The beneficiary does not have to be disabled or incapacitated at the time the trust is created. An adult beneficiary who is not disabled or incapacitated may terminate the trust at any time before his or her disability, incapacity, or death.

declared trust. See *express trust.*

defective trust. A trust that is treated, for income-tax purposes, as if it were the same entity as the grantor, but for estate-tax purposes is treated as an entity separate from the grantor. ● Typically a trust is an independent entity that is taxed separately from the settlor. Because trust income is taxed at higher rates than individual income, the settlor may intentionally create a defect in the trust terms so that the trust's income will be taxable to the grantor. This is achieved by violating the grantor-trust rules of IRC §§ 671–677 in a way that does not affect the completeness of the gift under IRC §§ 2035–2042. A violation renders the trust "defective" because the settlor must recognize the income even if the settlor does not actually receive it. The attribution of tax liability and payment of taxes on trust income do not give the grantor an ownership in the trust, which remains separate from the settlor's estate and is not subject to estate taxes.

Delaware trust. See *asset-protection trust.*

destructible trust. (1953) A trust that can be destroyed by the happening of an event or by operation of law.

directory trust. 1. A trust that is not completely and finally settled by the instrument creating it, but only defined in its general purpose and to be carried into detail according to later specific directions. **2.** See *fixed trust.*

direct trust. See *express trust.*

discretionary trust. (1837) **1.** A trust in which the settlor has delegated nearly complete or limited discretion to the trustee to decide when and how much income or property is distributed to a beneficiary. ● This is perhaps the most common type of trust used in estate planning. **2.** See *Crummey trust.* Cf. *mandatory trust;* CRUMMEY POWER.

domestic asset-protection trust. See *asset-protection trust* (1).

donative trust. A trust that establishes a gift of a beneficial interest in property for a beneficiary. • Most trusts are donative trusts. — Also termed *gratuitous trust.*

donor-advised trust. A trust set up by a public charity using cash or other assets donated by a person who will act as a director of the trust. IRC (26 USCA) § 4966(d)(2). — Also termed *donor-advised fund.*

dry trust. 1. A trust that merely vests legal title in a trustee and does not require that trustee to do anything. **2.** See *passive trust.*

dynasty trust. A generation-skipping trust funded with the amount that is permanently exempt from generation-skipping tax and designed to last more than two generations. • In 2000, a settlor could contribute $1 million to a dynasty trust. Almost half the states allow dynasty trusts, despite their potential for lasting more than 100 years. — Also termed *GST supertrust.*

educational trust. 1. A trust to found, endow, or support a school. **2.** A trust to support someone's education.

electing small-business trust. A trust of which the beneficiaries are individuals, estates, certain charitable organizations, or certain governmental entities, who did not purchase an interest in the trust, and for which the trustee has elected to be taxed under special rules. IRC (26 USCA) § 1391(e)(1). — Abbr. ESBT.

equipment trust. See EQUIPMENT TRUST.

estate trust. A trust that is established to qualify a deceased spouse's property for the marital deduction. • The trustee may be given discretion to distribute principal or income to the donor's spouse if the donor also provides that, at the surviving spouse's death, any accumulated income and remaining principal must be distributed to the surviving spouse's estate. See *marital deduction* under DEDUCTION.

ex delicto trust (də-**lik**-toh). A trust that is created for an illegal purpose, esp. to prevent the settlor's creditors from collecting their claims out of the trust property.

executed trust. A trust in which the estates and interests in the subject matter of the trust are completely limited and defined by the instrument creating the trust and require no further instruments to complete them. — Also termed *complete voluntary trust.*

executory trust (eg-**zek**-yə-tor-ee). (18c) A trust in which the instrument creating the trust is intended to be provisional only, and further conveyances are contemplated by the trust instrument before the terms of the trust can be carried out. — Also termed *imperfect trust.*

express active trust. See *active trust.*

express private passive trust. A trust in which land is conveyed to or held by one person in trust for another, without any power being expressly or impliedly given to the trustee to take actual possession of the land or exercise any ownership rights over it, except at the beneficiary's direction.

express trust. (18c) A trust created with the settlor's express intent, usu. declared in writing; an ordinary trust as opposed to a resulting trust or a constructive trust. — Also termed *direct trust; declared trust.*

family-pot trust. A trust in which all the assets are kept in a single fund for the trustee to use for multiple beneficiaries (usu. children). • Family-pot trusts are typically testamentary and used to administer a donor's property until the donor's minor children have completed their education.

family trust. A trust created to benefit persons who are related to one another by blood, affinity, or law.

fixed trust. A trust in which the trustee may not exercise any discretion over the trust's management or distributions. — Also termed *directory trust; nondiscretionary trust.*

foreign-situs trust (**sI**-təs). A trust created under foreign law. • This type of trust usu. has no significant income-tax benefits and is subject to greater reporting requirements than a domestic trust. Because creditors cannot easily reach the foreign trust's assets, it is frequently used as a means of asset-protection. — Also termed *foreign trust; offshore trust.*

general trust. See *passive trust.*

generation-skipping trust. (1976) A trust that is established to transfer (usu. principal) assets to a skip person (a beneficiary more than one generation removed from the settlor). • The transfer is often accomplished by giving some control or benefits (such as trust income) of the assets to a nonskip person, often a member of the generation between the settlor and skip person. This type of trust is subject to a generation-skipping transfer tax. IRC (26 USCA) §§ 2601 et seq. See DEEMED TRANSFEROR; GENERATION-SKIPPING TRANSFER; *generation-skipping transfer tax* under TAX; SKIP PERSON. Cf. *dynasty trust.*

governmental trust. 1. A type of charitable trust established to provide a community with facilities ordinarily supplied by the government, esp. by a municipality, and to promote purposes that are sufficiently beneficial to the community to justify permitting the property to be perpetually devoted to those purposes. • Examples of such facilities include public buildings, bridges, streets, parks, schools, and hospitals. **2.** A type of charitable trust established for general governmental or municipal purposes, such as defraying the expenses of a governmental entity or paying the public debt. Restatement (Second) of Trusts §§ 373, 374 (1959).

grantor-retained annuity trust. An irrevocable trust into which the grantor transfers property in exchange for the right to receive fixed payments at least annually, based on original fair market value of the property transferred. • At the end of the specified time, the principal passes to a noncharitable beneficiary such as the grantor's child or grandchild. Essentially, the grantor makes to the remainderman a current gift of the right to trust assets at a specified date in the future. — Abbr. GRAT.

grantor-retained income trust. A trust in which a gift's value can be reduced by the grantor's retaining an income interest, for a specified time, in the gifted property. • At the end of the specified time, the principal passes to a noncharitable beneficiary such as the grantor's child or grandchild. Essentially, the grantor makes to the remainderman a current gift of the right to trust assets at a specified date in the future. — Sometimes shortened to *retained income trust.* — Abbr. GRIT.

grantor-retained unitrust. An irrevocable trust into which the grantor transfers property in exchange for the right to receive annual payments, the amount of which fluctuates based on the increase or decrease in the value of the property transferred. — Abbr. GRUT. Cf. *grantor-retained annuity trust.*

grantor trust. A trust in which the settlor retains control over the trust property or its income to such an extent that the settlor is taxed on the trust's income. • The types of controls that result in such tax treatment are set out in IRC (26 USCA) §§ 671–677. An example is the revocable trust.

gratuitous trust. See *donative trust.*

GST supertrust. See *dynasty trust.*

honorary trust. (1844) A noncharitable trust that is of doubtful validity because it lacks a beneficiary capable of enforcing the trust. • Examples include trusts for the care and support of specific animals, or for the care of certain graves. The modern trend is to recognize the validity of such trusts, if the trustee is willing to accept the responsibility. If the trustee fails to carry out the duties, however, a resulting trust arises in favor of the settlor's residuary legatees or next of kin.

Illinois land trust. See *land trust.*

illusory trust. (1939) An arrangement that looks like a trust but, because of powers retained in the settlor, has no real substance and is not a completed trust.

imperfect trust. See *executory trust.*

implied trust. **1.** See *constructive trust.* **2.** See *resulting trust.*

indestructible trust. (1909) A trust that, because of the settlor's wishes, cannot be prematurely terminated by the beneficiary. — Also termed *Claflin trust.*

insurance trust. A trust whose principal consists of insurance policies or their proceeds.

inter vivos trust (in-tər VI-vohs *or* vee-vohs). (1921c) A trust that is created and takes effect during the settlor's lifetime. — Also termed *living trust.* Cf. *testamentary trust.*

investment trust. See *investment company* under COMPANY.

involuntary trust. See *constructive trust.*

irrevocable trust (i-rev-ə-kə-bəl). (1837) A trust that cannot be terminated by the settlor once it is created. • In most states, a trust will be deemed irrevocable unless the settlor specifies otherwise.

land trust. A land-ownership arrangement by which a trustee holds both legal and equitable title to land while the beneficiary retains the power to direct the trustee, manage the property, and draw income from the trust. — Also termed *Illinois land trust; naked land trust.*

life-insurance trust. A trust consisting of one or more life-insurance policies payable to the trust when the insured dies.

limited trust. A trust created for a limited period. Cf. *perpetual trust.*

liquidating trust. A trust designed to be liquidated as soon as possible. • An example is a trust into which a decedent's business is placed to safeguard the business until it can be sold.

living trust. See *inter vivos trust.*

mandatory trust. A trust in which the trustee must distribute all the income generated by the trust property to one or more designated beneficiaries. — Also termed *simple trust.* Cf. *discretionary trust.*

marital-deduction trust. (1953) A testamentary trust created to take full advantage of the marital deduction; esp., a trust entitling a spouse to lifetime income from the trust and sufficient control over the trust to include the trust property in the spouse's estate at death. See *marital deduction* under DEDUCTION.

marital life-estate trust. See *bypass trust.*

Massachusetts trust. See *business trust* under TRUST (4).

Medicaid-qualifying trust. (1989) A trust deemed to have been created in an effort to reduce someone's assets so that the person may qualify for Medicaid, and that will be included as an asset for purposes of determining the person's eligibility. • A person who wants to apply and qualify for Medicaid, but who has too many assets to qualify, will sometimes set up a trust — or have a spouse or custodian set up a trust — using the applicant's own assets, under which the applicant may be the beneficiary of all or part of the payments from the trust, which are distributed by a trustee with discretion to make trust payments to the applicant. Such a trust may be presumed to have been established for the purpose of attempting to qualify for Medicaid, and may be counted as an asset of the applicant, resulting in a denial of benefits and the imposition of a penalty period during which the applicant cannot reapply. Nonetheless, Medicaid rules allow three types of trusts that do not impair Medicaid eligibility, since the trust assets are not considered the beneficiary's property: *Miller trust*, *pooled trust*, and *under-65 trust*.

Miller trust. An irrevocable trust funded with the income of an incompetent beneficiary who seeks to qualify for Medicaid in a state with an income cap. • Funding is strictly limited to the beneficiary's income (from any source). The assets in the trust are not included in the beneficiary's estate for Medicaid purposes if the trust assets will be used to reimburse the state after the beneficiary's death. Trust distributions are kept below the income cap in order to preserve the beneficiary's Medicaid eligibility. This type of trust was first judicially sanctioned in *Miller v. Ibarra*, 746 F.Supp. 19 (D. Colo. 1990). — Also termed *Miller's trust*; *qualified income trust*.

ministerial trust. See *passive trust*.

minor's trust. See *2503(c) trust*.

mixed trust. A trust established to benefit both private individuals and charities.

naked land trust. See *land trust*.

naked trust. See *passive trust*.

Nevada trust. See *asset-protection trust* (1).

nominal trust. See *passive trust*.

nominee trust. **1.** A trust in which the beneficiaries have the power to direct the trustee's actions regarding the trust property. **2.** An arrangement for holding title to real property under which one or more persons or corporations, under a written declaration of trust, declare that they will hold any property that they acquire as trustees for the benefit of one or more undis-

closed beneficiaries. — Also termed (in sense 2) *realty trust*.

nondiscretionary trust. See *fixed trust*.

nongrantor-owner trust. A trust in which the beneficiary has an unrestricted power to vest the principal or interest in him or herself. IRC (26 USCA) § 678. — Also termed *678 trust*.

offshore asset-protection trust. See *asset-protection trust* (1).

offshore trust. See *foreign-situs trust*.

onerous trust. A trust that places exceptionally heavy and time-consuming duties of responsibility and care on the trustee, often without providing for compensation. • Because of the burden and inequity of requiring the trust to be administered voluntarily, courts often grant a trustee a reasonable sum for the tasks performed.

oral trust. **1.** A trust created by the settlor's spoken statements as opposed to a written agreement. • Trusts of real property must usu. be in writing (because of the statute of frauds). Trusts of personal property may be created orally but require clear and convincing evidence to show that an oral trust was created. Uniform Trust Act § 8407. — Also termed *parol trust*. **2.** A trust created by operation of law, such as a resulting trust or a constructive trust.

parol trust. See *oral trust* (1).

passive trust. A trust in which the trustee has no duty other than to transfer the property to the beneficiary. — Also termed *dry trust*; *general trust*; *nominal trust*; *simple trust*; *naked trust*; *ministerial trust*; *technical trust*. See *bare trustee* under TRUSTEE. Cf. *active trust*.

pension trust. An employer-funded pension plan; esp., a pension plan in which the employer transfers to trustees amounts sufficient to cover the benefits payable to the employees.

perpetual trust. A trust that is to continue as long as the need for it continues, such as for the lifetime of a beneficiary or the term of a particular charity. Cf. *limited trust*.

personal-residence trust. An irrevocable trust to which the settlor transfers ownership of his or her personal residence while retaining the right to live there for a specified term of years. • The trust cannot hold any assets other than the residence and proceeds resulting from damage to or destruction of the residence. Cf. *qualified personal-residence trust*.

personal trust. See *private trust*.

pet trust. An honorary trust that is established for the care and maintenance of a particular animal or group of animals. • Pet trusts are generally invalid because animals are incapable of compelling a trustee to act, and animals have no standing in law. Effectively, the trust has no beneficiary. But some states (e.g., Colorado) statutorily recognize these trusts as valid. Pet trusts are covered in the Uniform Trust Code (§ 408).

pooled-income fund. See POOLED-INCOME FUND.

pooled trust. An irrevocable, discretionary trust that (1) is established and managed by a nonprofit association, (2) is funded with the assets of disabled persons, and (3) maintains a separate trust account for each beneficiary, but (4) pools the trust assets for investment purposes. ● If the trust provides for distribution of a deceased beneficiary's interest to the state in reimbursement of Medicaid expenditures, a pooled-trust beneficiary may be eligible for Medicaid benefits. The assets contributed to the trust for the individual's benefit are not treated as the beneficiary's property. — Also termed *pooled-assets trust.*

pourover trust. (1981) An inter vivos trust that receives property (usu. the residual estate) from a will upon the testator's death. Cf. *pourover will* under WILL.

power-of-appointment trust. (1848) A trust in which property is left in trust for the surviving spouse. ● The trustee must distribute income to the spouse for life, and the power of appointment is given to the spouse or to his or her estate. A power-of-appointment trust is commonly used to qualify property for the marital deduction. See *marital deduction* under DEDUCTION.

precatory trust (**prek**-ə-tor-ee). (1878) A trust that the law will recognize to carry out the wishes of the testator or grantor even though the statement in question is in the nature of an entreaty or recommendation rather than a command.

presumptive trust. See *resulting trust.*

private trust. A trust created for the financial benefit of one or more designated beneficiaries rather than for the public benefit; an ordinary trust as opposed to a charitable trust. ● Three elements must be present for a private trust: (1) the demonstrated intent of the settlor, (2) trust property (as *res*), and (3) a certain beneficiary capable of enforcing the trust. — Also termed *personal trust.* Cf. *charitable trust.*

protective trust. A trust that is designed to protect the trust property to ensure the continued support of the beneficiary.

public trust. See *charitable trust.*

purchase-money resulting trust. A resulting trust that arises when one person buys property but directs the seller to transfer the property and its title to another. ● Although a purchase-money

resulting trust is properly understood as a court-imposed equitable remedy rather than as a true trust, the buyer is occasionally referred to as the "beneficiary" and the titleholder as the "trustee." — Abbr. PMRT.

QTIP trust (**kyoo**-tip). (1985) A trust that is established to qualify for the marital deduction. ● Under this trust, the assets are referred to as qualified-terminable-interest property, or QTIP. See *qualified-terminable-interest property* under PROPERTY. Cf. *qualified domestic trust.*

qualified domestic trust. A trust for a noncitizen spouse qualifying for the marital deduction. See 26 USCA § 2056(d). — Abbr. QDOT. See *marital deduction* under DEDUCTION. Cf. *QTIP trust.*

qualified income trust. See *Miller trust.*

qualified personal-residence trust. An irrevocable trust that is funded with cash and the personal residence of the grantor, who retains the right to dwell in the residence for a specified term of years. ● The trust may receive and hold additional cash to pay for trust expenses, mortgage installments, and improvements to the residence. — Abbr. QPRT. Cf. *personal-residence trust.*

qualified S-corporation trust. A trust that (1) owns stock in one or more S corporations, (2) distributes all income to one individual (who must be a United States citizen or resident), (3) requires only one beneficiary at a time, and (4) requires the income-beneficiary-elect to have the trust qualify as a QSST. ● The trust is rarely termed a *qualified subchapter-S corporation trust* but the common abbreviation is *QSST*, not *QSCT.*

rabbicular trust. A rabbi trust that protects the trust assets against the claims of the employer's creditors by converting to a secular trust if the employer funding the trust becomes insolvent. ● The term is a portmanteau word from *rabbi* and *secular.* Cf. *rabbi trust; secular trust.*

rabbi trust. *Slang.* An irrevocable grantor trust whose assets remain subject to the claims of the grantor's general creditors, and from which benefits are paid to the grantor's employees if a stipulated event occurs. ● A rabbi trust is a form of nonqualified deferred-compensation plan. Because the trust can be reached by creditors, the participants can avoid being taxed on the constructive receipt of the benefits held in the trust. Its name derives from the IRS letter ruling that approved its use by a synagogue. Priv. Ltr. Rul. 81-13-107 (Dec. 31, 1980). Cf. *rabbicular trust; secular trust.*

real-estate investment trust. See REAL-ESTATE INVESTMENT TRUST.

real-estate mortgage trust. See REAL-ESTATE MORTGAGE TRUST.

realty trust. See *nominal trust* (2).

reciprocal trust. A trust arrangement between two parties in which one party is beneficiary of a trust established by the other party, and vice versa. • Such trusts are common between husband and wife.

remedial trust. See *constructive trust*.

resulting trust. (18c) A remedy imposed by equity when property is transferred under circumstances suggesting that the transferor did not intend for the transferee to have the beneficial interest in the property. — Also termed *implied trust*; *presumptive trust*. Cf. *constructive trust*.

retained income trust. See *grantor-retained income trust*.

revocable trust (**rev**-ə-kə-bəl). A trust in which the settlor reserves the right to terminate the trust and recover the trust property and any undistributed income.

savings-account trust. See *Totten trust*.

savings-bank trust. See *Totten trust*.

secret trust. An instrument, usu. a will, that appears to give an absolute gift to another although the donee has orally agreed with the grantor that he or she is to use the property for the benefit of some third party. • Courts admit evidence of the promise to prevent unjust enrichment and enforce it by imposing the remedy of a constructive trust upon the reneging "trustee." Cf. *semi-secret trust*.

secular trust. An irrevocable trust, funded by an employer, that protects an employee-beneficiary's deferred compensation from the claims of creditors during an employer's bankruptcy or insolvency. • The trust provides the employee-beneficiary with exclusive rights. The employee enjoys security since the trust is funded and the funds are beyond the reach of creditors and immune from forfeiture, but the employee cannot defer income recognition. Cf. *rabbicular trust*; *rabbi trust*.

self-settled trust. (1969) A trust in which the settlor is also the person who is to receive the benefits from the trust, usu. set up in an attempt to protect the trust assets from creditors. • In most states, such a trust will not protect trust assets from the settlor's creditors. Restatement (Second) of Trusts § 156 (1959). — Also termed *asset-protection trust*.

semi-secret trust. An instrument that indicates who is to serve as a trustee but fails to identify either the beneficiary or the terms of the trust, or both. • Traditionally, this trust was deemed to fail for want of an ascertainable beneficiary. But the modern view is to provide the same relief as that given for a secret trust: to receive evidence of the donor's intent, including the intended beneficiary, and impose a constructive trust in his or her favor. Cf. *secret trust*.

shifting trust. An express trust providing that, upon a specified contingency, it may operate in favor of an additional or substituted beneficiary.

short-term trust. See *Clifford trust*.

simple trust. 1. See *mandatory trust*. 2. See *passive trust*.

678 trust. See *nongrantor-owner trust*.

special-needs trust. See *supplemental-needs trust*.

special trust. See *active trust*.

spendthrift trust. (1878) **1.** A trust that prohibits the beneficiary's interest from being assigned and also prevents a creditor from attaching that interest; a trust by the terms of which a valid restraint is imposed on the voluntary or involuntary transfer of the beneficiary's interest. **2.** A similar trust in which the restraint on alienation results from a statute rather than from the settlor's words in the trust instrument. **split-interest trust.** See *charitable-remainder trust*.

spray trust. See *sprinkle trust*.

sprinkle trust. A trust in which the trustee has discretion to decide how much will be given to each beneficiary. — Also termed *spray trust*. See SPRINKLE POWER.

standby trust. A trust created to manage a person's assets while he or she is out of the country or disabled.

supplemental-needs trust. A trust established to provide supplemental income for a disabled beneficiary who is receiving or may be eligible to receive government benefits. • This type of irrevocable trust is often used by parents of disabled children to ensure the beneficiary's eligibility for government benefits by expressly prohibiting distributions that may be used for the beneficiary's food, shelter, or clothing.

support trust. (1946) A discretionary trust in which the settlor authorizes the trustee to pay to the beneficiary as much income or principal as the trustee believes is needed for support, esp. for "comfortable support" or "support in accordance with the beneficiary's standard of living." • The beneficiary's interest cannot be voluntarily transferred, but creditors who provide necessaries can usu. reach it; general creditors cannot.

technical trust. See *passive trust*.

tentative trust. See *Totten trust*.

testamentary trust (tes-tə-**men**-tə-ree *or* -tree). (1832) A trust that is created by a will and takes effect when the settlor (testator) dies. — Also termed *trust under will*. Cf. *inter vivos trust*.

Totten trust. (1931) A revocable trust created by one's deposit of money, typically in a savings account, in the depositor's name as trustee for another. • A Totten trust is an early form of "pay on death" account, since it creates no interest in the beneficiary unless the account remained at the depositor's death. Its name derives from the earliest decision in which the court approved the concept, even though the formalities of will execution were not satisfied: *In re Totten*, 71 N.E. 748 (N.Y. 1904). A Totten trust is commonly used to indicate a successor to the account without having to create a will, and thus it is a will substitute. — Also termed *tentative trust*; *bank-account trust*; *savings-account trust*; *savings-bank trust*; *trustee bank account*.

transgressive trust. A trust that violates the rule against perpetuities. See RULE AGAINST PERPETUITIES.

trust de son tort (də sawn [*or* son] **tor**[t]). See *constructive trust*.

trust ex delicto. See *constructive trust*.

trust ex maleficio. See *constructive trust*.

trust for support. A trust that, by its terms, provides that the trustee must pay or apply only as much of the income and principal as is necessary for the education and support of the beneficiary.

trust in invitum. See *constructive trust*.

trust under will. See *testamentary trust*.

2503(b) trust. A trust that requires a distribution of income to the beneficiary at least annually, and provides that gifts to the trust qualifying as gifts of a present interest become eligible for the annual gift-tax exclusion. • It is named after the section of the IRS code on which it is based. IRC (26 USCA) § 2503(b).

2503(c) trust. A trust with only one beneficiary, who must be a minor and must have the power to withdraw all assets from the trust upon attaining the age of 21. • This type of trust derives its name from the requirements set forth in IRC (26 USCA) § 2503(c). Although the trust may continue after the beneficiary turns 21, gifts to the trust will no longer qualify for the annual exclusion if the beneficiary has no immediate right to withdraw the gift. — Also termed *minor's trust*.

under-65 trust. A discretionary trust established for the sole benefit of a Medicaid recipient who is under the age of 65. • This type of trust may be established by anyone except the beneficiary, who must be less than 65 years old at the time of creation. The assets in trust will not be included in the beneficiary's estate for purposes of determining Medicaid eligibility. The beneficiary may receive distributions from the trust during life, but any balance remaining in the trust must be used to reimburse the state for the beneficiary's Medicaid expenditures.

unit-investment trust. 1. A trust in which funds are pooled and invested in income-producing securities. • Units of the trust are sold to investors, who maintain an interest in the trust in proportion to their investment. **2.** An investment company that gives a shareholder an undivided interest in a fixed pool of securities held by the trustee. • This type of company can be organized in several ways (as by trust indenture, contract of custodianship or agency, or similar instrument), but is most commonly organized with a trust indenture. Such a company does not have a board of directors and issues only redeemable securities, each of which represents an undivided interest in a unit of specified securities. 15 USCA § 80a-4. See *investment company* under COMPANY.

unitrust. (1971) A trust from which a fixed percentage of the fair market value of the trust's assets, valued annually, is paid each year to the beneficiary.

voluntary trust. 1. A trust that is not founded on consideration. • One having legal title to property may create a voluntary trust by (1) declaring that the property is to be held in trust for another, and (2) transferring the legal title to a third person who acts as trustee. **2.** An obligation arising out of a personal confidence reposed in, and voluntarily accepted by, one for the benefit of another.

voting trust. A trust used to hold shares of voting stock in a closely held corporation, usu. transferred from a parent to a child, and empowering the trustee to exercise the right to vote. • The trust acts as custodian of the shares but is not a stockholder. Cf. VOTING GROUP.

wasting trust. A trust in which the trust property is gradually depleted by periodic payments to the beneficiary.

4. A business combination that aims at monopoly. See ANTITRUST LAW.

business trust. A form of business organization, similar to a corporation, in which investors receive transferable certificates of beneficial interest instead of stock shares. — Also termed *Massachusetts trust*; *common-law trust*.

common-law trust. See *business trust*.

Massachusetts trust. See *business trust*.

trust account. See CLIENT TRUST ACCOUNT.

trust agreement. See *declaration of trust* (2) under DECLARATION (1).

trustbuster, *n.* A person — esp. a federal officer — who seeks the dissolution of business trusts under the antitrust laws. See *business trust* under TRUST (4).

trust certificate. See EQUIPMENT TRUST CERTIFICATE.

trust company. See COMPANY.

trust corporation. See *trust company* under COMPANY.

trust deed. 1. See *declaration of trust* (2) under DECLARATION (1). **2.** See *deed of trust* under DEED.

trust de son tort (də sawn [*or* son] **tor**[t]). See *constructive trust* under TRUST.

trust distribution. See DISTRIBUTION.

trustee (trəs-**tee**), *n.* (17c) **1.** One who stands in a fiduciary or confidential relation to another; esp., one who, having legal title to property, holds it in trust for the benefit of another and owes a fiduciary duty to that beneficiary. ● Generally, a trustee's duties are to convert to cash all debts and securities that are not qualified legal investments, to reinvest the cash in proper securities, to protect and preserve the trust property, and to ensure that it is employed solely for the beneficiary, in accordance with the directions contained in the trust instrument.

    bare trustee. A trustee of a passive trust. ● A bare trustee has no duty other than to transfer the property to the beneficiary. See *passive trust* under TRUST.

    corporate trustee. (1852) A corporation that is empowered by its charter to act as a trustee, such as a bank or trust company.

    indenture trustee. A trustee named in a trust indenture and charged with holding legal title to the trust property; a trustee under an indenture.

    joint trustee. See COTRUSTEE.

    judicial trustee. (18c) A trustee appointed by a court to execute a trust.

    quasi-trustee. (1830) One who benefits from a breach of a trust to a great enough degree to become liable as a trustee.

    successor trustee. (1866) A trustee who succeeds an earlier trustee, usu. as provided in the trust agreement.

    testamentary trustee (tes-tə-**men**-tə-ree *or* -tree). (1811) A trustee appointed by or acting under a will; one appointed to carry out a trust created by a will.

    township trustee. One of a board of officers to whom, in some states, a township's affairs are entrusted.

    trustee ad litem (ad **lI**-tem *or* -təm). (1921) A trustee appointed by the court.

    trustee de son tort (də sawn [*or* son] **tor**[t]). (1857) A person who, without legal authority, administers a living person's property to the detriment of the property owner. See *constructive trust* under TRUST.

    trustee ex maleficio (eks mal-ə-**fish**-ee-oh). (1837) A person who is guilty of wrongful or fraudulent conduct and is held by equity to the duty of a trustee, in relation to the subject matter, to prevent him or her from profiting from the wrongdoing.

2. *Bankruptcy.* A person appointed by the U.S. Trustee or elected by creditors or appointed by a judge to administer the bankruptcy estate during a bankruptcy case. ● The trustee's duties include (1) collecting and reducing to cash the assets of the estate, (2) operating the debtor's business with court approval if appropriate to preserve the value of business assets, (3) examining the debtor at a meeting of creditors, (4) filing inventories and making periodic reports to the court on the financial condition of the estate, (5) investigating the debtor's financial affairs, (6) examining proofs of claims and objecting to improper claims, (7) furnishing information relating to the bankruptcy to interested parties, and (8) opposing discharge through bankruptcy, if advisable. A trustee is appointed or elected in every Chapter 7 case, and is appointed in every Chapter 12 and Chapter 13 case under the Bankruptcy Code. A trustee is not appointed or elected in a Chapter 11 case unless the court finds that a trustee is needed and appoints one. In most Chapter 11 cases, the bankruptcy estate is administered by the debtor in possession, rather than by a trustee. The role of a bankruptcy trustee varies depending on the type of bankruptcy case. 11 USCA §§ 701–03, 1104, 1202. — Also termed (in sense 2) *bankruptcy trustee; trustee in bankruptcy.* See UNITED STATES TRUSTEE.

    interim trustee. A bankruptcy trustee appointed to perform all the functions and duties of a trustee until the regular trustee is selected and qualified. ● Before the meeting of creditors, the interim trustee often preliminarily investigates the debtor's assets and financial affairs.

3. DIRECTOR (2). **4.** *Parliamentary law.* An officer who audits an organization's finances.

trustee, *vb.* (1818) **1.** To serve as trustee. **2.** To place (a person or property) in the hands of one or more trustees. **3.** To appoint (a person) as trustee, often of a bankrupt's estate in order to restrain a creditor from collecting moneys due. **4.** To attach (the effects of a debtor) in the hands of a third person.

trustee, U.S. See UNITED STATES TRUSTEE.

trustee bank account. See *Totten trust* under TRUST.

trustee in bankruptcy. See TRUSTEE (2).

trustee process. See FACTORIZING PROCESS.

trusteeship. 1. The office, status, or function of a trustee. **2.** *Int'l law.* Administration or supervision of a territory by one or more countries, esp. under a U.N. trusteeship council. Cf. MANDATE (6).

trust estate. See CORPUS (1).

trust ex delicto. See *constructive trust* under TRUST.

trust ex maleficio. See *constructive trust* under TRUST.

trust fund. (18c) The property held in a trust by a trustee; CORPUS (1).

　common trust fund. (1852) A trust fund set up within a trust department to combine the assets of numerous small trusts to achieve greater investment diversification. ● Common trust funds are regulated by state law.

　pooled-income fund. See POOLED-INCOME FUND.

trust-fund doctrine. (1892) The principle that the assets of an insolvent company, including paid and unpaid subscriptions to the capital stock, are held as a trust fund to which the company's creditors may look for payment of their claims. ● The creditors may follow the property constituting this fund, and may use it to reduce the debts, unless it has passed into the hands of a bona fide purchaser without notice. — Also termed *trust-fund theory.*

trust indenture. See INDENTURE.

Trust Indenture Act. A federal law, enacted in 1939, designed to protect investors of certain types of bonds by requiring that (1) the SEC approve the trust indenture, (2) the indenture include certain protective clauses and exclude certain exculpatory clauses, and (3) the trustees be independent of the issuing company. 15 USCA §§ 77aaa et seq. ● The Act is administered by the U.S. Securities and Exchange Commission.

trust indorsement. See INDORSEMENT.

trust in invitum (in in-VI-təm). See *constructive trust* under TRUST.

trust instrument. See *declaration of trust* (2) under DECLARATION (1).

trust legacy. See LEGACY.

trust officer. See OFFICER (1).

trustor. (1855) One who creates a trust; SETTLOR (1).

trust ownership. See OWNERSHIP.

trust power. See *beneficial power* under POWER (5).

trust process. See PROCESS.

trust property. See CORPUS (1).

trust receipt. 1. A pre-UCC security device — now governed by Article 9 of the Code — consisting of a receipt stating that the wholesale buyer has possession of the goods for the benefit of the financier. ● Today there must usu. be a security agreement coupled with a filed financing statement. **2.** A method of financing commercial transactions by which title passes directly from the manufacturer or seller to a banker or lender, who as owner delivers the goods to the dealer on whose behalf the banker or lender is acting, and to whom title ultimately goes when the banker's or lender's primary right has been satisfied.

trust relationship. See RELATIONSHIP.

trust res (reez *or* rays). See CORPUS (1).

trust territory. See TERRITORY.

trust under will. See *testamentary trust* under TRUST.

trusty, *n.* (1855) A convict or prisoner who is considered trustworthy by prison authorities and therefore given special privileges.

truth. (bef. 12c) **1.** A fully accurate account of events; factuality. **2.** *Defamation.* An affirmative defense by which the defendant asserts that the alleged defamatory statement is substantially accurate.

Truth in Lending Act. See CONSUMER CREDIT PROTECTION ACT. — Abbr. TILA.

truth-seeker. One who strives to reveal the truth <the trial lawyer should be a truth-seeker>.

truth, the whole truth, and nothing but the truth. The words used in the common oath administered to a witness who is about to testify <do you swear or affirm that you shall tell the truth, the whole truth and nothing but the truth?>. ● The purpose of the second part of the oath is to preclude the possibility of *supressio veri*; the purpose of the third part is to preclude the possibility of *suggestio falsi*. See SUPPRESSIO VERI; SUGGESTIO FALSI.

try, *vb.* (13c) To examine judicially; to examine and resolve (a dispute) by means of a trial.

try title. The judicial examination of a title. See TRESPASS TO TRY TITLE; *action to quiet title* under ACTION (4).

TSCA. *abbr.* Toxic Substances Control Act. 42 USCA §§ 2601 et seq.

TTB. *abbr.* ALCOHOL AND TOBACCO TAX AND TRADE BUREAU.

Tucker Act. A federal law enacted in 1887 to ameliorate the inadequacies of the original authority of the Court of Claims by extending that court's jurisdiction to include (1) claims founded on the Constitution, a federal statute, or a federal regulation, and (2) damage claims in cases not arising in tort.

turncoat witness. See WITNESS.

turnkey, *adj.* (1927) **1.** (Of a product) provided in a state of readiness for immediate use <a turnkey computer network>. **2.** Of, relating to, or involving a product provided in this manner <a turnkey contract>.

turnkey, *n.* A jailer; esp., one charged with keeping the keys to a jail or prison.

turnkey contract. See *engineering, procurement, and construction contract* under CONTRACT.

turnkey drilling contract. See DRILLING CONTRACT.

turnover duty. *Maritime law.* A shipowner's obligation to provide safe working conditions and to give notice of any nonobvious hazards regarding instruments and areas that the shipowner turns over to the stevedore and longshoremen while the ship is being loaded or unloaded. Cf. ACTIVE-OPERATIONS DUTY; INTERVENTION DUTY.

turnover order. See ORDER (2).

turn state's evidence, *vb.* (1846) To cooperate with prosecutors and testify against other criminal defendants <after hours of intense negotiations, the suspect accepted a plea bargain and agreed to turn state's evidence>.

turntable doctrine. See ATTRACTIVE-NUISANCE DOCTRINE.

turpitude (tər-pə-t[y]ood). See MORAL TURPITUDE.

tutelage (t[y]oo-tə-lij), *n.* **1.** The act of protecting or guiding; guardianship. **2.** *Int'l law.* The state of being under the care and management of an international organization such as the League of Nations or United Nations. • This term applies, for example, to the status of a people who do not yet benefit from a fully operational government of their own — such as people displaced by war and living in a territory that will in the future be given its autonomy.

tutor, *n.* **1.** One who teaches; esp., a private instructor. Pl. **tutors. 2.** *Roman & civil law.* A guardian of a minor; a person appointed to have the care of the minor's person and estate. • The guardian of a minor past the age of puberty is called a *curator* and has duties somewhat different from those of a tutor. Pl. ***tutores.***

> **undertutor.** *Civil law.* A person appointed by a court to represent a minor under the care of a tutor when the interests of the minor conflict with that of the tutor. See TUTORSHIP.

tutorship. *Civil law.* The office and power of a tutor; the power that an individual has, *sui juris,* to take care of one who cannot care for himself or herself. • The four types of tutorship are (1) tutorship by

nature, (2) tutorship by will, (3) tutorship by the effect of the law, and (4) tutorship by judicial appointment. La. Civ. Code art. 247.

> **dative tutorship.** *Civil law.* Tutorship that arises from a court's appointment, usu. on the advice of the family. — Also termed *dative curatorship; tutorship by judicial appointment.*

> **legal tutorship.** *Civil law.* Tutorship that is bestowed by statute and does not require a court's or family's approval. • For example, a spouse has the legal tutorship of the incompetent spouse. — Also termed *tutorship by the effect of the law.*

> **tutorship by judicial appointment.** *Civil law.* See *dative tutorship.*

> **tutorship by nature. 1.** Tutorship of a minor child that belongs by right to a surviving parent. **2.** Tutorship of a minor child that belongs to the parent under whose care the child has been placed following divorce or judicial separation. • If the parents are awarded joint custody, both have cotutorship and equal authority, privileges, and responsibilities. La. Civ. Code art. 250.

> **tutorship by the effect of the law.** *Civil law.* See *legal tutorship.*

> **tutorship by will.** Tutorship that is created (1) by the will of the parent who dies last, or (2) by any declaration of the surviving father or mother (or the parent who is the curator of the other spouse), executed before a notary and two witnesses. La. Civ. Code art. 257.

TVA. *abbr.* TENNESSEE VALLEY AUTHORITY.

Twelfth Amendment. The constitutional amendment, ratified in 1804, that altered the electoral-college system by separating the balloting for presidential and vice-presidential candidates. • In 1800, members of the Electoral College could cast votes only for the office of President, and Thomas Jefferson and his running mate Aaron Burr each received the same number of votes. The House of Representatives had to break the tie.

twelve-day rule. *Criminal procedure.* A rule in some jurisdictions requiring that a person charged with a felony be given a preliminary examination no later than 12 days after the arraignment on the original warrant.

twelve-month liquidation. See LIQUIDATION.

Twelve Tables. *Roman law.* The earliest surviving legislation enacted by the Romans, written on 12 tablets in the 5th century B.C. • The Tables set out many rights and duties of Roman citizens, including debtors' rights, family law, wills, torts, civil procedure, and some public law. They substituted a written body of laws, easily accessible and binding on all citizens of Rome, for an unwritten usage accessible to only a few. The law of the Twelve Tables was also known as the *Lex Duodecim Tabularum*.

Twentieth Amendment. The constitutional amendment, ratified in 1933, that changed the date of the presidential and vice-presidential inaugurations from March 4 to January 20, and the date for congressional convention from March 4 to January 3, thereby eliminating the short session of Congress, during which a number of members sat who had not been reelected to office. — Also termed *lame-duck amendment*.

Twenty-fifth Amendment. The constitutional amendment, ratified in 1967, that established rules of succession for the presidency and vice presidency in the event of death, resignation, or incapacity. • Article II, § 1 of the Constitution provides for the Vice President to assume the President's powers and duties but does not clearly state that the Vice President also assumes the title of President.

Twenty-first Amendment. The constitutional amendment, ratified in 1933, that repealed the 18th Amendment (which established national Prohibition) and returned the power to regulate alcohol to the states.

2503(b) trust. See TRUST (3).

2503(c) trust. See TRUST (3).

Twenty-fourth Amendment. The constitutional amendment, ratified in 1964, that prohibits the federal and state governments from restricting the right to vote in a federal election because of one's failure to pay a poll tax or other tax.

Twenty-second Amendment. The constitutional amendment, ratified in 1951, that prohibits a person from being elected President more than twice (or, if the person succeeded to the office with more than half the predecessor's term remaining, more than once).

Twenty-seventh Amendment. The constitutional amendment, ratified in 1992, that prevents a pay raise for senators and representatives from taking effect until a new Congress convenes. • This amendment was proposed as part of the original Bill of Rights in 1789, but it took 203 years for the required three-fourths of the states to ratify it. — Also termed *Madison Amendment*.

Twenty-sixth Amendment. The constitutional amendment, ratified in 1971, that sets the minimum voting age at 18 for all state and federal elections.

Twenty-third Amendment. The constitutional amendment, ratified in 1961, that allows District of Columbia residents to vote in presidential elections.

twist, *n. Slang.* An informant who provides testimony in exchange for leniency in sentencing, rather than for money. See INFORMANT.

twisting, *n.* An insurance agent's or company's misrepresenting or misstating facts, or giving an incomplete comparison of policies, to induce an insured to give up a policy in one company and buy another company's policy.

two-controlled-studies standard. The requirement by the Federal Trade Commission that before the maker of an over-the-counter painkiller can advertise that it is better or has fewer side effects than another brand, the maker must verify the claim in two scientifically controlled studies.

two-dismissal rule. (1944) The rule that a notice of voluntary dismissal operates as an adjudication on the merits — not merely as a dismissal without prejudice — when filed by a plaintiff who has already dismissed the same claim in another court.

245(i) waiver. *Immigration law.* An Immigration and Nationality Act provision that allows certain qualified aliens who are otherwise ineligible for adjustment of their status to pay a penalty for the convenience of having their status adjusted to permanent-resident status without having to leave the United States. 8 USCA § 1255(i). Cf. ADJUSTMENT OF STATUS.

two-issue rule. (1929) The rule that if multiple issues were submitted to a trial jury and at least one of them is error-free, the appellate court should presume that the jury based its verdict on the proper issue — not on an erroneous one — and should therefore affirm the judgment.

two-party payment. See PAYMENT.

two-round voting. See VOTING.

two-stage trial. See *bifurcated trial* under TRIAL.

two-tier offer. A two-step technique by which a bidder tries to acquire a target corporation, the first step involving a cash tender offer and the second usu. a merger in which the target company's remaining shareholders receive securities from the bidder (these securities ordinarily being less favorable than the cash given in the first step).

two-witness rule. (1900) **1.** The rule that, to support a perjury conviction, two independent witnesses (or one witness along with corroborating evidence) must establish that the alleged perjurer gave false testimony. **2.** The rule, as stated in the U.S. Constitution, that no person may be convicted of treason without two witnesses to the same overt act — or unless the accused confesses in open court. U.S. Const. art. IV, § 2, cl. 2.

tying, *adj. Antitrust.* Of or relating to an arrangement whereby a seller sells a product to a buyer only if the buyer purchases another product from the seller <tying agreement>.

tying arrangement. *Antitrust.* (1953) A seller's agreement to sell one product or service only if the buyer also buys a different product or service; a seller's refusal to sell one product or service unless the buyer also buys a different product or service. • The product or service that the buyer wants to buy is known as the *tying product* or *tying service*; the different product or service that the seller insists on selling is known as the *tied product* or *tied service*. Tying arrangements may be illegal under the Sherman or Clayton Act if their effect is too anticompetitive. — Also termed *tying agreement*; *tie-in*; *tie-in arrangement*. Cf. RECIPROCAL DEALING.

tying product. See TYING ARRANGEMENT.

tying service. See TYING ARRANGEMENT.

typed drawing. See DRAWING.

typed-form drawing. See *typed drawing* under DRAWING.

tyranny. **1.** The severe deprivation of a natural right. **2.** The accumulation of all powers — the legislative, executive, and judicial — in the same hands (whether few or many). • Sense 2 expresses the Madisonian view of tyranny, to be found in *The Federalist*, No. 47. **3.** Arbitrary or despotic government; the severe and autocratic exercise of sovereign power, whether vested constitutionally in one ruler or usurped by that ruler by breaking down the division and distribution of governmental powers. — **tyrannical, tyrannous,** *adj.*

tyrant, *n.* A sovereign or ruler, legitimate or not, who wields power unjustly and arbitrarily to oppress the citizenry; a despot.

U

U3C. *abbr.* UNIFORM CONSUMER CREDIT CODE.

UAA. *abbr.* UNIFORM ADOPTION ACT.

UAGA. *abbr.* UNIFORM ANATOMICAL GIFT ACT.

U.B. *abbr.* Upper Bench.

uberrimae fidei (yoo-**ber**-ə-mee **fi**-dee-ɪ). [Latin] (1850) Of the utmost good faith. See *contract uberrimae fidei* under CONTRACT.

uberrima fides (yoo-**ber**-ə-mə **fɪ**-deez), *n.* [Latin] Utmost good faith <a contract requiring *uberrima fides*>.

ubi (**yoo**-bɪ *or* **oo**-bee). [Latin] Where.

ubi supra (**yoo**-bɪ **s[y]oo**-prə). [Latin] Where stated above.

UCC. *abbr.* **1.** UNIFORM COMMERCIAL CODE. **2.** UNIVERSAL COPYRIGHT CONVENTION.

UCC battle of the forms. See BATTLE OF THE FORMS.

UCCC. *abbr.* UNIFORM CONSUMER CREDIT CODE.

UCCJA. *abbr.* UNIFORM CHILD CUSTODY JURISDICTION ACT.

UCCJEA. *abbr.* UNIFORM CHILD CUSTODY JURISDICTION AND ENFORCEMENT ACT.

UCE. *abbr.* Unsolicited commercial e-mail. See SPAM.

UCITA. *abbr.* UNIFORM COMPUTER INFORMATION TRANSACTIONS ACT.

UCMJ. *abbr.* UNIFORM CODE OF MILITARY JUSTICE.

UCP. *abbr.* UNIFORM CUSTOMS AND PRACTICE FOR COMMERCIAL DOCUMENTARY CREDITS.

UCR. *abbr.* UNIFORM CRIME REPORTS.

UDITPA. *abbr.* UNIFORM DIVISION OF INCOME FOR TAX PURPOSES ACT.

UDRA. *abbr.* UNIFORM DIVORCE RECOGNITION ACT.

UDRP. *abbr.* UNIFORM DOMAIN-NAME DISPUTE-RESOLUTION POLICY.

UDTPA. *abbr.* UNIFORM DECEPTIVE TRADE PRACTICES ACT.

UETA. *abbr.* UNIFORM ELECTRONIC TRANSACTIONS ACT.

UFCA. *abbr.* UNIFORM FRAUDULENT CONVEYANCES ACT.

UFTA. *abbr.* UNIFORM FRAUDULENT TRANSFER ACT.

UGMA. *abbr.* Uniform Gifts to Minors Act. See UNIFORM TRANSFERS TO MINORS ACT.

UHCDA. *abbr.* UNIFORM HEALTH-CARE DECISION ACT.

UIFSA. *abbr.* UNIFORM INTERSTATE FAMILY SUPPORT ACT.

UIJC. *abbr.* UNIFORM INTERSTATE JUVENILE COMPACT.

UJCA. *abbr.* UNIFORM JUVENILE COURT ACT.

U.K. *abbr.* UNITED KINGDOM.

ukase (yoo-**kays** *or* **yoo**-kays). (18c) A proclamation or decree, esp. of a final or arbitrary nature. ● This term originally referred to a decree issued by a Russian czar.

ullage (ə-lij), *n.* The degree to which a container of liquid falls short of being full.

ullage, *vb.* To determine the amount of ullage in a container holding liquid.

ULPA. *abbr.* UNIFORM LIMITED PARTNERSHIP ACT.

ulterior intent. See INTENT (1).

ulterior remainderman. See REMAINDERMAN.

ultima ratio (əl-ti-mə **ray**-shee-oh). [Latin] **1.** The final argument; the last resort; the means last to be resorted to. **2.** A final sanction.

ultimate fact. See FACT.

ultimate issue. See ISSUE (1).

ultimate question. See *ultimate issue* under ISSUE (1).

ultimate species. See SPECIES (2).

ultimatum (əl-tə-**may**-təm), *n.* (18c) The final and categorical proposal made in negotiating a treaty, contract, or the like. ● An ultimatum implies that a rejection might lead to a break-off in negotiations or, in international law, to a cessation of diplomatic relations or even to war. Pl. **ultimatums.**

ultimus heres (əl-ti-məs **heer**-eez). See HERES.

ultrahazardous. See EXTRAHAZARDOUS.

ultrahazardous activity. See ABNORMALLY DANGEROUS ACTIVITY.

ultra mare (əl-trə **mair**-ee *or* **mahr**-ee). [Latin] See BEYOND SEAS.

ultra reprises (əl-trə ri-**prɪz**-iz). After deduction of expenses; net.

ultra vires (əl-trə **vɪ**-reez *also* **veer**-eez), *adj.* [Latin "beyond the powers (of)"] (18c) Unauthorized; beyond the scope of power allowed or granted by a corporate charter or by law <the officer was liable for the firm's ultra vires actions>. — Also termed *extra vires*. Cf. INTRA VIRES. — **ultra vires,** *adv.*

ultroneous witness. See WITNESS.

umbrella insurance. See INSURANCE.

umbrella limited partnership. See PARTNERSHIP.

umbrella order. See BLANKET ORDER (1).

umbrella-partnership real-estate investment trust. See REAL-ESTATE INVESTMENT TRUST.

umbrella policy. See INSURANCE POLICY.

umbrella protective order. See *blanket protective order* under PROTECTIVE ORDER.

UMDA. *abbr.* UNIFORM MARRIAGE AND DIVORCE ACT.

umpirage (əm-pIr-ij). **1.** The office or authority of an umpire. **2.** The decision (such as an arbitral award) of an umpire.

umpire. (15c) An impartial person appointed to make an award or a final decision, usu. when a matter has been submitted to arbitrators who have failed to agree. ● An arbitral submission may provide for the appointment of an umpire. — Also termed (in Scots law) *oversman*. — **umpire,** *vb.*

UMTA. *abbr.* URBAN MASS TRANSIT ADMINISTRATION.

un-, *prefix.* (bef. 12c) **1.** Not <unassignable>. **2.** Contrary to; against <unconstitutional>.

U.N. *abbr.* UNITED NATIONS.

unaccrued, *adj.* Not due, as rent on a lease.

una cum. [Latin] Together with.

unalienable, *adj.* See INALIENABLE.

unanimous (yoo-**nan**-ə-məs), *adj.* (17c) **1.** Agreeing in opinion; being in complete accord <the judges were unanimous in their approval of the recommendation>. **2.** Arrived at by the consent of all <a unanimous verdict>. See *unanimous consent* under CONSENT (2); *unanimous vote* under VOTE. Cf. *without objection* under OBJECTION (3).

unanimous consent. See CONSENT (2).

unanimous-consent agenda. See *consent calendar* under CALENDAR (4).

unanimous-consent agreement. *Parliamentary law.* An agreement, negotiated between opposing sides debating a motion, regarding the procedure under which the assembly will consider the motion. ● The unanimous-consent agreement is a common practice in the U.S. Senate. — Also termed *time agreement.* See *unanimous consent* under CONSENT (2).

unanimous-consent calendar. See *consent calendar* under CALENDAR (4).

unanimous vote. See VOTE (3).

unascertained duty. See DUTY (4).

unauthorized, *adj.* (16c) Done without authority; specif. (of a signature or indorsement), made without actual, implied, or apparent authority. UCC § 1-201(43).

unauthorized completion. *Commercial law.* The act of filling in missing information in a negotiable instrument either without any authority to do so or without adequate authority. ● Unauthorized completion is a personal defense, so it can be raised against any later holder of the instrument who does not have the rights of a holder in due course. See *personal defense* under DEFENSE (4).

unauthorized indorsement. See INDORSEMENT.

unauthorized practice of law. See PRACTICE OF LAW.

unauthorized signature. See SIGNATURE.

unauthorized use of a vehicle. See JOYRIDING.

unavailability, *n.* (1855) The status or condition of not being available, as when a witness is exempted by court order from testifying. ● Unavailability is recognized under the Federal Rules of Evidence as an exemption to the hearsay rule. Fed. R. Evid. 804.

una voce (**yoo**-nə **voh**-see). [Latin] With one voice; unanimously; without dissent.

unavoidable accident. See ACCIDENT.

unavoidable-accident doctrine. (1961) *Torts.* The rule holding no party liable for an accident that was not foreseeable and that could not have been prevented by the exercise of reasonable care. ● The modern trend is for courts to ignore this doctrine and to rely instead on the basic concepts of duty, negligence, and proximate cause. — Also termed *inevitable-accident doctrine.*

unavoidable casualty. See *unavoidable accident* under ACCIDENT.

unavoidable cause. See CAUSE (1).

unavoidable danger. See DANGER.

unbanked, *adj.* Lacking a formal relationship with a bank or other financial institution. ● Unbanked consumers are the most frequent users of money services businesses.

unborn beneficiary. See BENEFICIARY.

unborn child. See CHILD.

unborn-widow rule. (1957) The legal fiction, assumed under the rule against perpetuities, that a beneficiary's widow is not alive at the testator's death, and thus a succeeding life estate to her voids any remainders because the interest would not vest within the perpetuities period. See RULE AGAINST PERPETUITIES.

unbroken, *adj.* (14c) Not interrupted; continuous <unbroken possession by the adverse possessor>.

unbundling rules. *Telecommunications.* Regulations passed by the Federal Communications Commission to effectuate the local-competition requirements of the Telecommunications Act of 1996, which requires local-exchange carriers to provide access to elements of local-exchange networks on an unbundled (i.e., separated) basis. 47 USCA § 251; 47 CFR pt. 51. See NETWORK ELEMENT.

uncertain damages. See DAMAGES.

uncertificated security. See SECURITY.

uncertified security. See *uncertificated security* under SECURITY.

uncitable. See NONCITABLE.

UNCITRAL Rules. The Arbitration Rules of the United Nations Commission on International Trade Law, applicable to all international commercial arbitrations except as prohibited by the local law where the arbitration takes place.

unclean bill of lading. See BILL OF LADING.

unclean-hands doctrine. See CLEAN-HANDS DOCTRINE.

uncollected funds. A credit, such as an increase in the balance of a checking or other deposit account in a financial institution, given on the basis of a check or other right to payment that has not yet been received from the drawee or other payor.

unconditional, *adj.* (17c) Not limited by a condition; not depending on an uncertain event or contingency; absolute.

unconditional delivery. See DELIVERY.

unconditional discharge. See DISCHARGE (5).

unconditional heir. See HEIR.

unconditional pardon. See *absolute pardon* under PARDON.

unconditional promise. See PROMISE.

unconditional release. See RELEASE.

unconscionability (ən-kon-shə-nə-**bil**-ə-tee). (16c) **1.** Extreme unfairness. ● Unconscionability is normally assessed by an objective standard: (1) one party's lack of meaningful choice, and (2) contractual terms that unreasonably favor the other party. **2.** The principle that a court may refuse to enforce a contract that is unfair or oppressive because of procedural abuses during contract formation or because of overreaching contractual terms, esp. terms that are unreasonably favorable to one party while precluding meaningful choice for the other party. ● Because unconscionability depends on circumstances at the time the contract is formed, a later rise in market price is irrelevant.

procedural unconscionability. (1973) Unconscionability resulting from improprieties in contract formation (such as oral misrepresentations or disparities in bargaining position) rather than from the terms of the contract itself.

substantive unconscionability. (1973) Unconscionability resulting from actual contract terms that are unduly harsh, commercially unreasonable, and grossly unfair given the existing circumstances.

unconscionable (ən-**kon**-shə-nə-bəl), *adj.* (16c) **1.** (Of a person) having no conscience; unscrupulous <an unconscionable used-car salesman>. **2.** (Of an act or transaction) showing no regard for conscience; affronting the sense of justice, decency, or reasonableness <the contract is void as unconscionable>. Cf. CONSCIONABLE.

unconscionable agreement. See AGREEMENT.

unconscionable bargain. See *unconscionable agreement* under AGREEMENT.

unconscionable contract. See *unconscionable agreement* under AGREEMENT.

unconscious, *adj.* Without awareness; not conscious. ● A person who commits a criminal act while unconscious may be relieved from liability for the act.

unconsciousness defense. See AUTOMATISM.

unconstitutional, *adj.* (18c) Contrary to or in conflict with a constitution, esp. the U.S. Constitution <the law is unconstitutional because it violates the First Amendment's free-speech guarantee>. Cf. NONCONSTITUTIONAL.

unconstitutional-conditions doctrine. *Constitutional law.* **1.** The rule that the government cannot condition a person's receipt of a governmental benefit on the waiver of a constitutionally protected right (esp. a right under the First Amendment). ● For example, a television station that receives public funds cannot be forced to refrain from endorsing political candidates. **2.** The rule that the government cannot force a defendant to choose between two constitutionally protected rights. — Also termed *doctrine of unconstitutional conditions.*

unconstitutionally vague. See VAGUE.

uncontestable clause. See INCONTESTABILITY CLAUSE.

uncontested divorce. See DIVORCE.

uncontested hearing. See HEARING.

uncontrollable, *adj.* Incapable of being controlled.

uncontrollable impulse. See IMPULSE.

uncontrolled-securities-offering distribution. See *securities-offering distribution* (2) under DISTRIBUTION.

uncopyrightable, *adj.* (Of a work) ineligible for copyright protection either because the work lacks originality or because it is an idea, concept, process, or other abstraction that is not included in one of the eight covered classifications of copyrightable works. 17 USCA §§ 101–106.

uncorrectability defense. *Patents.* An affirmative defense in an infringement suit, established by showing (1) that a coinventor's name was omitted from a patent, and (2) that the patent cannot be corrected because the named coinventor acted with deceptive intent.

uncounseled, *adj.* Without the benefit or participation of legal counsel <an uncounseled conviction> <an uncounseled defendant>.

uncovered option. See *naked option* under OPTION.

UNCRC. *abbr.* UNITED NATIONS CONVENTION ON THE RIGHTS OF THE CHILD.

undercapitalization. See CAPITALIZATION.

undercover agent. See AGENT.

undercurrent of surface stream. Water that moves slowly through the bed of a stream or the lands under or immediately adjacent to the stream. • This water is considered part of the surface stream. — Also termed *underflow of surface stream.*

underdeveloped country. See DEVELOPING COUNTRY.

underflow of surface stream. See UNDERCURRENT OF SURFACE STREAM.

underground economy. See SHADOW ECONOMY.

underground recording. See BOOTLEG RECORDING (1).

underinsurance. An agreement to indemnify against property damage up to a certain amount but for less than the property's full value.

underinsured-motorist coverage. Insurance that pays for the insured's losses and injuries negligently caused by a driver does not have enough liability insurance to cover the damages. Cf. UNINSURED-MOTORIST COVERAGE.

underlease. See SUBLEASE.

underlessor. See SUBLESSOR.

under one's hand. (Of a person's signature) affixed manually, as opposed to printed or stamped.

under protest. See PROTEST (3).

Undersecretary of Commerce for Intellectual Property. See DIRECTOR OF THE UNITED STATES PATENT AND TRADEMARK OFFICE.

undersheriff. See *deputy sheriff* under SHERIFF.

undersigned, *n.* (17c) A person whose name is signed at the end of a document <the undersigned agrees to the terms and conditions set forth above>.

under-65 trust. See TRUST.

understand, *vb.* To apprehend the meaning of; to know <the testator did not understand what he was signing>.

understanding, *n.* (bef. 12c) **1.** The process of comprehending; the act of a person who understands something. **2.** One's personal interpretation of an event or occurrence. **3.** An agreement, esp. of an implied or tacit nature.

under submission. (18c) Being considered by the court; under advisement <the case was under submission in the court of appeals for more than two years>.

undertake, *vb.* (13c) **1.** To take on an obligation or task <he has undertaken to chair the committee on legal aid for the homeless>. **2.** To give a formal promise; guarantee <the merchant undertook that the goods were waterproof>. **3.** To act as surety for (another); to make oneself responsible for (a person, fact, or the like) <her husband undertook her appearance in court>.

undertaking, *n.* (14c) **1.** A promise, pledge, or engagement. **2.** A bail bond.

undertenant. See SUBLESSEE.

under the influence. (1879) (Of a driver, pilot, etc.) deprived of clearness of mind and self-control because of drugs or alcohol. See DRIVING UNDER THE INFLUENCE.

undertutor. See TUTOR.

underwriter. 1. INSURER. **2.** One who buys stock from the issuer with an intent to resell it to the public; a person or entity, esp. an investment banker, who guarantees the sale of newly issued securities by purchasing all or part of the shares for resale to the public.

> *chartered life underwriter.* An underwriter who has satisfied the requirements set forth by The American College (formerly The American College of Life Underwriters) to be designated a life insurance underwriter. — Abbr. CLU.

> *insurance underwriter.* **1.** INSURER. — Also termed *writer.* **2.** An insurance-company employee who is responsible for determining whether to issue a policy and the amount to charge for the coverage provided.

underwriting, *n.* **1.** The act of assuming a risk by insuring it; the insurance of life or property. See INSURANCE. **2.** The act of agreeing to buy all or part of a new issue of securities to be offered for public sale. — **underwrite,** *vb.*

> *best-efforts underwriting.* Underwriting in which an investment banker agrees to direct, but not guarantee, the public sale of the issuer's securities. • The underwriter, or underwriting group, sells the securities as agent for the issuer, and unsold securities are never issued.

firm-commitment underwriting. Underwriting in which the underwriter agrees to buy and sell all the shares to be issued and assumes full financial responsibility for any unsold securities. • The underwriter, or underwriting group, buys the securities from the issuer and resells them as principal. In this type of underwriting, securities that are not sold to the public are owned by the underwriter, and the issuer is paid for those securities as well as the others.

standby underwriting. Underwriting in which the underwriter agrees, for a fee, to buy from the issuer any unsold shares remaining after the public offering. — Also termed *strict underwriting.*

underwriting agreement. See AGREEMENT.

underwriting spread. See SPREAD (4).

undesirable discharge. See DISCHARGE (8).

undigested offering. See OFFERING.

undisclosed agency. See AGENCY (1).

undisclosed principal. See PRINCIPAL (1).

undisputed, *adj.* Not questioned or challenged; uncontested.

undisputed fact. See FACT.

undistributed-earnings tax. See *accumulated-earnings tax* under TAX.

undistributed profit. See *retained earnings* under EARNINGS.

undivided interest. See INTEREST (2).

undivided profit. See *accumulated profit* under PROFIT (1).

undivided right. See *undivided interest* under INTEREST (2).

undivided title. See *undivided interest* under INTEREST (2).

undocumented alien. See *illegal alien* under ALIEN.

undue, *adj.* (14c) **1.** *Archaic.* Not yet owed; not currently payable <an undue debt>. **2.** Excessive or unwarranted <undue burden> <undue influence>. — **unduly,** *adv.*

undue-breadth rejection. See REJECTION.

undue burden, *n.* See BURDEN.

undue-burden test. (1992) *Constitutional law.* The Supreme Court test stating that a law regulating abortion will be struck down if it places a substantial obstacle in the path of a woman's right to obtain an abortion. • This test replaced the "trimester analysis" set forth in *Roe v. Wade,* in which the state's ability to restrict abortion increased after each trimester of pregnancy. *Planned Parenthood of Southeastern Pa. v. Casey,* 505 U.S. 833, 112 S.Ct. 2791 (1992).

undue experimentation. *Patents.* An unreasonable amount of research and testing that would be required for a person skilled in the appropriate art to make and work an invention from the specification in the patent application. • If undue experimentation would be required, the application fails the embodiment requirement of 35 USCA § 112. See WANDS TEST.

undue hardship. See HARDSHIP.

undue influence. (18c) **1.** The improper use of power or trust in a way that deprives a person of free will and substitutes another's objective. • Consent to a contract, transaction, or relationship or to conduct is voidable if the consent is obtained through undue influence. — Also termed *implied coercion; moral coercion.* **2.** *Wills & estates.* Coercion that destroys a testator's free will and substitutes another's objectives in its place. • When a beneficiary actively procures the execution of a will, a presumption of undue influence may be raised, based on the confidential relationship between the influencer and the person influenced. — Also termed *improper influence;* (formerly, in both senses) *suggestion.* See COERCION; DURESS.

undue multiplicity of claims. See AGGREGATION OF CLAIMS.

undue-multiplicity-of-claims rejection. See REJECTION.

undue prejudice. See PREJUDICE.

unduly dangerous conduct. See *unreasonably dangerous conduct* under CONDUCT.

undutiful will. See *unnatural will* under WILL.

unearned income. See INCOME.

unearned increment. See INCREMENT.

unearned interest. See INTEREST (3).

unearned premium. See PREMIUM (1).

unearned-premium reserve. See RESERVE.

unearned surplus. See SURPLUS.

unemployment. The state or condition of not having a job even though available for work and perhaps seeking it.

structural unemployment. Unemployment resulting from a shift in the demand for a particular product or service.

unemployment compensation. See *unemployment insurance* under INSURANCE; COMPENSATION.

unemployment insurance. See INSURANCE.

unemployment tax. See TAX.

unenacted law. See LAW.

unencumbered (ən-in-kəm-bərd), *adj.* Without any burdens or impediments <unencumbered title to property>.

unenforceable, *adj.* (1804) (Of a contract) valid but incapable of being enforced. Cf. VOID; VOIDABLE.

unenforceable contract. See CONTRACT.

UNEP. *abbr.* UNITED NATIONS ENVIRONMENT PROGRAMME.

unequal, *adj.* (16c) Not equal in some respect; uneven <unequal treatment under the law>.

unequivocal (ən-i-**kwiv**-ə-kəl), *adj.* (18c) Unambiguous; clear; free from uncertainty.

unerring (ən-**ər**-ing *also* ən-**er**-ing), *adj.* Incapable of error; infallible.

UNESCO. *abbr.* UNITED NATIONS EDUCATIONAL, SCIENTIFIC, AND CULTURAL ORGANIZATION.

unessential mistake. See MISTAKE.

unethical, *adj.* (1871) Not in conformity with moral norms or standards of professional conduct. See LEGAL ETHICS.

unexpected, *adj.* Happening without warning; not expected.

unexpired term. See TERM (4).

unfair competition. (1876) **1.** Dishonest or fraudulent rivalry in trade and commerce; esp., the practice of endeavoring to pass off one's own goods or products in the market for those of another by means of imitating or counterfeiting the name, brand, size, shape, or other distinctive characteristic of the article or its packaging. **2.** The body of law encompassing various business and privacy torts, all generally based on deceitful trade practices, including passing off, false advertising, commercial disparagement, and misappropriation.

unfair hearing. See HEARING.

unfair labor practice. Any conduct prohibited by state or federal law governing the relations among employers, employees, and labor organizations. • Examples of unfair labor practices by an employer include (1) interfering with protected employee rights, such as the right to self-organization, (2) discriminating against employees for union-related activities, (3) retaliating against employees who have invoked their rights, and (4) refusing to engage in collective bargaining. Examples of unfair labor practices by a labor organization include causing an employer to discriminate against an employee, engaging in an illegal strike or boycott, causing an employer to pay for work not to be performed (i.e., featherbedding), and refusing to engage in collective bargaining. 29 USCA §§ 151–169.

unfair persuasion. (1931) *Contracts.* A type of undue influence in which a stronger party achieves a result by means that seriously impair the weaker party's free and competent exercise of judgment. • Unfair persuasion is a lesser form of undue influence than duress and misrepresentation. The two primary factors to be considered are the unavailability of independent advice and the susceptibility of the person persuaded. See UNDUE INFLUENCE (1).

unfair surprise. (1815) A situation in which a party, having had no notice of some action or proffered evidence, is unprepared to answer or refute it.

unfair trade. An inequitable business practice; esp., the act or an instance of a competitor's repeating of words in a way that conveys a misrepresentation that materially injures the person who first used the words, by appropriating credit of some kind earned by the first user.

Unfair Trade Practices and Consumer Protection Law. A model statute patterned on the Federal Trade Commission Act and proposed by the FTC in 1967 for adoption by the states; a state law providing consumer-protection remedies, including private causes of action, for deceptive trade practices and false advertising. • The Act gives the state attorney general power to regulate unfair and deceptive trade practices. It also gives consumers a right to sue offenders directly. — Abbr. UTPCPL. — Also termed *Little FTC Acts.*

unfinished business. See BUSINESS.

unfinished business and general orders. See BUSINESS.

unfit, *adj.* (16c) **1.** Unsuitable; not adapted or qualified for a particular use or service <the buyer returned the unfit goods to the seller and asked for a refund>. **2.** *Family law.* Morally unqualified; incompetent <the judge found the mother unfit and so found that awarding custody of the child to the father was in the child's best interests>.

unfitness of a parent. *Family law.* A parent's failure to exhibit a reasonable concern for, interest in, or responsibility for a child's welfare. • Regardless of the specific ground for an allegation of unfitness, a court considers the parent's actions and the circumstances surrounding the conduct in deciding whether unfitness has been demonstrated.

unforeseen, *adj.* Not foreseen; not expected <unforeseen circumstances>.

unfriendly suitor. See CORPORATE RAIDER.

unfriendly takeover. See *hostile takeover* under TAKEOVER.

unfunded deferred-compensation plan. See EMPLOYEE BENEFIT PLAN.

unhandsome dealing. *Archaic.* See SHARP PRACTICE.

unharmed, *adj.* Not injured or damaged.

unifactoral obligation. See OBLIGATION.

unified bar. See *integrated bar* under BAR.

unified credit. See *unified estate-and-gift tax credit* under TAX CREDIT.

unified estate-and-gift tax. See *unified transfer tax* under TAX.

unified estate-and-gift tax credit. See TAX CREDIT.

unified family court. See COURT.

unified transfer tax. See TAX.

uniform, *adj.* Characterized by a lack of variation; identical or consistent.

uniform act. 1. A law drafted with the intention that it will be adopted by all or most of the states; esp., a uniform law. See UNIFORM LAW. Cf. MODEL ACT. **2.** See *uniform statute* under STATUTE.

Uniform Adoption Act. A 1994 model statute aimed at achieving uniformity in adoption laws. ● The current version of the Act was promulgated in 1994 by the National Conference of Commissioners on Uniform State Laws. State adoption has been largely unsuccessful. Earlier versions, in 1953 and 1971, were amended many times but were enacted in only a few states. — Abbr. UAA.

Uniform Anatomical Gift Act. A 1968 model statute that created protocols that govern the giving and receiving of anatomical gifts. ● Under the Act, persons may donate their body or parts of their body for purposes of transplantation, therapy, research, or education. The original Act has been adopted in some form in all 50 states and the District of Columbia. It was revised in 1987, and the revised version has been adopted in some form in at least 22 states. — Abbr. UAGA.

Uniform Child Custody Jurisdiction Act. A 1968 model statute that sets out a standard (based on the child's residence in and connections with the state) by which a state court determines whether it has jurisdiction over a particular child-custody matter or whether it must recognize a custody decree issued by another state's court. ● The Uniform Child Custody Jurisdiction Act was replaced in 1997 by the Uniform Child Custody Jurisdiction and Enforcement Act. — Abbr. UCCJA. See HOME STATE. Cf. PARENTAL KIDNAPPING PREVENTION ACT; UNIFORM CHILD CUSTODY JURISDICTION AND ENFORCEMENT ACT.

Uniform Child Custody Jurisdiction and Enforcement Act. A 1997 model statute that provides uniform methods of expedited interstate custody and visitation orders. ● This Act was promulgated as a successor to the Uniform Child Custody Jurisdiction Act. The UCCJEA brings the Uniform Child Custody Jurisdiction Act into conformity with the Parental Kidnapping Prevention Act and the Violence Against Women Act. The Act revises child-custody jurisdiction, giving clearer standards for original jurisdiction and a standard for continuing jurisdiction. The Act also provides a remedial process for enforcing interstate child custody and visitation. — Abbr. UCCJEA. Cf. UNIFORM CHILD CUSTODY JURISDICTION ACT.

Uniform Code of Military Justice. 1. CODE OF MILITARY JUSTICE. **2.** A model code promulgated by the National Conference of Commissioners on Uniform State Laws to govern state military forces when not in federal service. 11 U.L.A. 335 et seq. (1974). — Abbr. UCMJ.

Uniform Commercial Code. A uniform law that governs commercial transactions, including sales of goods, secured transactions, and negotiable instruments. ● The Code has been adopted in some form by every state and the District of Columbia. — Abbr. UCC.

Uniform Computer Information Transactions Act. A model law that regulates software licensing and computer-information transactions. ● The act draws upon contract law and the Uniform Commercial Code to create a regulatory scheme for licensing, rather than sales or lease, transactions. Among other things, UCITA applies to contracts for the licensing or purchase of software, contracts for software development, and contracts for access to databases through the Internet. It does not cover goods or services contracts within the scope of the UCC. — Abbr. UCITA.

Uniform Consumer Credit Code. A uniform law designed to simplify and modernize the consumer credit and usury laws, to improve consumer understanding of the terms of credit transactions, to protect consumers against unfair practices, and the like. ● This Code has been adopted by only a few states. — Abbr. UCCC; U3C. — Also termed *Consumer Credit Code.* See CONSUMER CREDIT PROTECTION ACT.

Uniform Controlled Substances Act. A uniform act, adopted by many states and the federal government, governing the sale, use, and distribution of drugs. 21 USCA §§ 801 et seq.

Uniform Crime Reports. A series of annual criminological studies (each entitled *Crime in the United States*) prepared by the FBI. ● The reports include data on eight index offenses, statistics on arrests, and information on offenders, crime rates, and the like. — Abbr. UCR.

Uniform Customs and Practice for Commercial Documentary Credits. A publication of the International Chamber of Commerce that codifies widespread customs of bankers and merchants relating to the mechanics and operation of letters of credit. ● Courts use this publication to supplement and help interpret primary sources of credit law, such as UCC Article 5. — Abbr. UCP.

Uniform Deceptive Trade Practices Act. A 1964 model state statute that codified many common-law intellectual-property torts, such as trademark infringement, passing off, trade disparagement, and false advertising, and that provided additional consumer protection against other forms of commercial deception. ● The Act provides a laundry list of prohibited practices, all involving misrepresentation. — Abbr. UDTPA. See BABY FTC ACT.

Uniform Determination of Death Act. A 1978 model statute that provides a comprehensive basis for determining death. • This is a technical act that merely defines death clinically and does not deal with suicide, assisted suicide, or the right to die. The Act was revised in 1980. It has been adopted in almost all states.

Uniform Disposition of Community Property at Death Act. A 1971 model statute designed for non-community-property states to preserve the rights of each spouse in property that was community property before the spouses moved to non-community-property states, unless they have severed or altered their community-property rights.

Uniform Division of Income for Tax Purposes Act. A uniform law, adopted by some states, that provides criteria to assist in assigning the total taxable income of a multistate corporation among the various states. — Abbr. UDITPA.

Uniform Divorce Recognition Act. A 1947 model code adopted by some states regarding full-faith-and-credit issues that arise in divorces. — Abbr. UDRA.

Uniform Durable Power of Attorney Act. A 1979 model statute that provides a simple way for a person to deal with his or her property by providing a power of attorney that will survive after the incompetence of the principal. • The Act was revised in 1987 and has been adopted in almost every state.

Uniformed Services Former Spouses' Protection Act. A federal statute that governs the disposition of military pension benefits to former spouses of persons in the armed services. 10 USCA §§ 1401 et seq. • The Act permits state courts to treat military-retirement pay as marital property and to order payment of up to 50% of the retirement pay directly to the former spouse if the spouses were married for at least ten years while the employee served in the military. — Abbr. USFSPA.

Uniform Electronic Transactions Act. A 1999 model law designed to support electronic commerce by providing means for legally recognizing and retaining electronic records, establishing how parties can bind themselves in an electronic transaction, and providing for the use of electronic records by governmental agencies. • UETA covers electronic records and digital signatures but applies only if all parties agree to do business electronically. — Abbr. UETA.

Uniform Enforcement of Foreign Judgments Act. A uniform state law giving the holder of a foreign judgment the right to levy and execute as if it were a domestic judgment.

Uniform Fraudulent Conveyances Act. A model act adopted in 1918 to deal with issues arising from fraudulent conveyances by insolvent persons. • This act differentiated between conduct that was presumed fraudulent and conduct that required an actual intent to commit fraud. — Abbr. UFCA.

Uniform Fraudulent Transfer Act. A model act designed to bring uniformity among the states regarding the definition of, and penalties for, fraudulent transfers. • This act was adopted in 1984 to replace the Uniform Fraudulent Conveyances Act. — Abbr. UFTA.

Uniform Gifts to Minors Act. See UNIFORM TRANSFERS TO MINORS ACT. — Abbr. UGMA.

Uniform Health-Care Decisions Act. A 1993 model statute that facilitates and encourages adults to make advance directives. — Abbr. UHCDA. See ADVANCE DIRECTIVE; LIVING WILL.

Uniform Interstate Family Support Act. A 1992 model statute establishing a one-order system by which an alimony or child-support decree issued by one state can be enforced against a former spouse who resides in another state. • This statute has been adopted in every state and is the basis of jurisdiction in child-support suits. The purpose of the Act is to make the pursuit of interstate child support and paternity more effective, consistent, and efficient by requiring all states to recognize and enforce consistently support orders issued in other states. Before its enactment, there was considerable disparity among the states in the way they handled interstate child-support proceedings, since each state had differing versions of the earlier uniform law, the Uniform Reciprocal Enforcement of Support Act. The Act was revised in 1996 and again in 2001. — Abbr. UIFSA.

Uniform Interstate Juvenile Compact. An agreement that regulates the treatment of juveniles who are not under proper supervision or control, or who have run away or escaped, and who are likely to endanger their own or others' health, morals, or welfare. • The Compact is relied on by the state to transport juvenile runaways back to their home states. It has now been universally adopted in the United States, but not always in its entirety. — Abbr. UIJC.

Uniformity Clause. (1881) The clause of the U.S. Constitution requiring the uniform collection of federal taxes. U.S. Const. art. I, § 8, cl. 1.

Uniform Juvenile Court Act. A 1968 model statute designed to (1) provide for the care, protection, and moral, mental, and physical development of the children who come under its provisions, (2) provide juvenile delinquents with treatment, training, and rehabilitation rather than criminal punishment, (3) attempt to keep families together unless separation of parents and children is necessary for the children's welfare or is in the public interest, (4) provide a judicial procedure for a fair hearing and protection of juvenile delinquents' constitutional and other legal rights, and (5) provide simple interstate procedures to carry out cooperative measures among the juvenile courts of different states. — Abbr. UJCA.

uniform law. An unofficial law proposed as legislation for all the states to adopt exactly as written, the purpose being to promote greater consistency among the states. • All the uniform laws are promulgated by the National Conference of Commissioners on Uniform State Laws. For a complete collection, see *Uniform Laws Annotated*. See *uniform statute* under STATUTE. Cf. MODEL ACT.

Uniform Law Commissioners. See NATIONAL CONFERENCE OF COMMISSIONERS ON UNIFORM STATE LAWS.

Uniform Limited Partnership Act. A model law promulgated in 1916 for adoption by state legislatures to govern the relationship between the partners of a limited partnership. • At one time it was adopted in all states except Louisiana. The National Conference of Commissioners on Uniform State Laws promulgated the Revised Uniform Limited Partnership Act (RULPA) in 1976, and made substantial amendments to it in 1985. The amended RULPA has been adopted by most states. — Abbr. ULPA.

Uniform Mandatory Disposition of Detainers Act. A 1958 model statute requiring a state to timely dispose of any untried charges against a prisoner in that state, on the prisoner's written request. • The Act has been adopted by several states. See INTERSTATE AGREEMENT ON DETAINERS ACT.

Uniform Marriage and Divorce Act. A 1970 model statute that defines marriage and divorce. • Extensively amended in 1973, the Act was an attempt by the National Conference of Commissioners on Uniform State Laws to make marriage and divorce laws more uniform. The Act's greatest significance is that it introduced, as the sole ground for divorce, irreconcilable differences. Although the UMDA has been enacted in part in only a handful of states, it has had an enormous impact on marriage and divorce laws in all states. — Abbr. UMDA. — Also termed *Model Marriage and Divorce Act*. See IRRECONCILABLE DIFFERENCES.

Uniform Parentage Act. A 1973 model statute that provides a means for determining parenthood for the general welfare of the child and for assigning child support. • The Act abolishes distinctions between legitimate and illegitimate status for children. Instead, it directs courts to determine rights and responsibilities based on the existence of a parent–child relationship. The Act has been adopted in all states. The Act was revised in 2000 and amended in 2002. Among other changes, the revisions provided frameworks for establishing the parentage (esp. paternity) of children born to married or unmarried couples, and set standards and rules for genetic testing. A minority of states have enacted a version of the revised Act.

Uniform Partnership Act. A 1914 model statute intended to bring uniformity to state laws governing general and limited partnerships. • The Act was adopted by almost all the states, but has been superseded in several of them by the Revised Uniform Partnership Act (1994). — Abbr. UPA.

Uniform Premarital Agreement Act. A 1983 model statute that governs the drafting of prenuptial contracts and provides a more certain framework for drafting complete and enforceable agreements. • Under the UPAA, a premarital agreement must be in writing and signed by the parties. It becomes effective only upon marriage. The agreement may govern the parties' assets, support, and obligations during the marriage, at death, and upon divorce. The UPAA has been adopted in some form in about one-third of the states. — Abbr. UPAA.

Uniform Principal and Income Act. A uniform code adopted by some states governing allocation of principal and income in trusts and estates.

Uniform Probate Code. A 1969 model statute that modernizes the rules and doctrines governing intestate succession, probate, and the administration of estates. • It has been extensively amended many times since 1969 and has been enacted in a majority of states. — Abbr. UPC.

Uniform Prudent Investor Act. A 1994 model statute that sets a standard for the acts of a trustee, adopts a prudent-investor standard, and prefers a modern portfolio approach to investing. • Under the Uniform Prudent Investor Act, the trustee is given significant power to delegate the selection of investments. The prudent-investor standard replaces the prudent-person standard of investing. The portfolio approach provides that no investment will be viewed in isolation; rather, it will be viewed as part of the entire portfolio. Under this theory, even though an investor loses trust assets on an investment, if there is an overall positive return, the investor will not be liable to the beneficiaries. — Abbr. UPIA. See PRUDENT-INVESTOR RULE.

Uniform Putative and Unknown Fathers Act. A 1988 model statute aimed at codifying Supreme Court decisions on the rights of an unwed father in relation to his child. • The Act deals primarily with an unwed father's right to notice of a termination and adoption proceeding, to adjudication of paternity, to visitation, and to custody. — Abbr.

UPUFA. — Also termed *Model Putative Fathers Act*; *Putative Fathers Act*.

Uniform Reciprocal Enforcement of Support Act. A 1950 model statute (now superseded) that sought to unify the way in which interstate support matters were processed and the way in which one jurisdiction's orders were given full faith and credit in another jurisdiction. ● This Act, which was amended in 1958 and 1960, was replaced in 1997 with the Uniform Interstate Family Support Act. — Abbr. URESA. See UNIFORM INTERSTATE FAMILY SUPPORT ACT.

Uniform Simultaneous Death Act. A 1940 model statute creating a rule that a person must survive a decedent by at least 120 hours in order to avoid disputes caused by simultaneous deaths (as in a common disaster) or by quickly successive deaths of persons between whom property or death benefits pass on the death of one survived by the other. ● In the absence of the 120-hour period of survival, each person is presumed to have survived the other for purposes of distributing their respective estates. The Act was revised in 1993 and has been adopted in some form by almost every state. See COMMORIENTES.

Uniform Status of Children of Assisted Conception Act. A 1988 model statute aimed at ensuring certainty of legal parentage when assisted conception has been used. ● The adopting state has the option of regulating or prohibiting contracts with surrogate mothers.

uniform statute. See STATUTE.

Uniform Trade Secrets Act. A 1979 model statute, enacted by most states, defining *trade secret* differently from the common law by being at once broader (because there is no continuous-use requirement) and narrower (because information "readily ascertainable by proper means" cannot qualify). ● The Act has three elements: (1) the information must qualify as a trade secret; (2) it must be misappropriated, either through wrongful means or by breaching a duty of confidentiality; and (3) the owner must have taken reasonable precautions to keep the information secret. — Abbr. UTSA. — Also termed *Uniform Trade Secrets Protection Act*.

Uniform Transfers to Minors Act. A 1983 model statute providing for the transfer of property to a minor and permitting a custodian who acts in a fiduciary capacity to manage investments and apply the income from the property to the minor's support. ● The Act has been adopted in most states. It was revised in 1986. — Abbr. UTMA. — Also termed *Transfers to Minors Act*. — Formerly also termed *Uniform Gifts to Minors Act*; *Gifts to Minors Act*.

unify, *vb.* To cause to become one; to form into a single unit.

unigeniture (yoo-nə-**jen**-ə-chər). *Archaic.* The fact of being an only child.

unilateral (yoo-nə-**lat**-ər-əl), *adj.* (1802) One-sided; relating to only one of two or more persons or things <unilateral mistake>.

unilateral act. See ACT (2).

unilateral advance pricing agreement. See ADVANCE PRICING AGREEMENT.

unilateral contract. See CONTRACT.

unilateral mistake. See MISTAKE.

unimproved land. See LAND.

unincorporated association. See ASSOCIATION (3).

unindicted coconspirator. See COCONSPIRATOR.

unindicted conspirator. See *unindicted coconspirator* under COCONSPIRATOR.

uninstructed delegate. See DELEGATE.

uninsured-motorist coverage. Insurance that pays for the insured's injuries and losses negligently caused by a driver who has no liability insurance. Cf. UNDERINSURED-MOTORIST COVERAGE.

unintelligible vote. See VOTE (1).

unintentional act. See ACT (2).

unintentional murder. See MURDER.

uninterrupted-adverse-use principle. See CONTINUOUS-ADVERSE-USE PRINCIPLE.

unio (yoo-**nee**-oh). *Eccles. law.* A consolidation of two churches into one.

union, *n.* An organization formed to negotiate with employers, on behalf of workers collectively, about job-related issues such as salary, benefits, hours, and working conditions. ● Unions generally represent skilled workers in trades and crafts. — Also termed *labor union*; *labor organization*; *organization*. See TRADE COUNCIL. — **unionize,** *vb.* — **unionist,** *n.*

closed union. A union with restrictive membership requirements, such as high dues and long apprenticeship periods. Cf. *closed shop* under SHOP.

company union. 1. A union whose membership is limited to the employees of a single company. **2.** A union under company domination.

craft union. A union composed of workers in the same trade or craft, such as carpentry or plumbing, regardless of the industry in which they work. — Also termed *horizontal union*.

federal labor union. A local union directly chartered by the AFL-CIO. See AMERICAN FEDERATION OF LABOR AND CONGRESS OF INDUSTRIAL ORGANIZATIONS.

horizontal union. See *craft union*.

independent union. A union that is not affiliated with a national or international union.

industrial union. A union composed of workers in the same industry, such as shipbuilding or automobile manufacturing, regardless of their particular trade or craft. — Also termed *vertical union.*

international union. A parent union with affiliates in two or more countries.

local union. A union that serves as the local bargaining unit for a national or international union.

multicraft union. A union composed of workers in different industries.

national union. A parent union with locals in various parts of the United States.

open union. A union with minimal membership requirements. Cf. *open shop* under SHOP.

trade union. A union composed of workers of the same or of several allied trades; a craft union.

vertical union. See *industrial union.*

union certification. A determination by the National Labor Relations Board or a state agency that a particular union qualifies as the bargaining representative for a segment of a company's workers — a bargaining unit — because it has the support of a majority of the workers in the unit. — Also termed *certification of bargaining agent; certification of labor union.*

union contract. See COLLECTIVE-BARGAINING AGREEMENT.

union givebacks. See CONCESSION BARGAINING.

Union Jack. The common name of the national flag of the United Kingdom, combining the national flags of England, Scotland, and Ireland. • The Union Jack was originally a small union flag flown from the jack-staff at the bow of a vessel. It is different from the Royal Standard, which bears the royal arms and is the Queen's personal flag.

union-loss clause. See MORTGAGE-LOSS CLAUSE.

union mortgage clause. See *standard mortgage clause* under MORTGAGE CLAUSE.

union rate. See RATE.

union-security clause. A provision in a union contract intended to protect the union against employers, nonunion employees, and competing unions.

union shop. See SHOP.

union steward. See STEWARD (2).

unique chattel. See CHATTEL.

unissued stock. See STOCK.

unit. The number of shares, often 100, in which a given stock is normally traded.

unital (yoo-nə-təl), *adj.* (1860) Of or relating to legal relations that exist between only two persons. Cf. MULTITAL.

unitary business (yoo-nə-ter-ee). *Tax.* A business that has subsidiaries in other states or countries and that calculates its state income tax by determining what portion of a subsidiary's income is attributable to activities within the state, and paying taxes on that percentage.

unitary state. See STATE.

unitary tax. See TAX.

unit cost. See COST (1).

unit depreciation method. See DEPRECIATION METHOD.

unite, *vb.* **1.** To combine or join to form a whole. **2.** To act in concert or in a common cause.

United Kingdom. A country in Europe comprising England, Scotland, Wales, and Northern Ireland, but not the Isle of Man or the Channel Islands. — Abbr. U.K.

United Nations. An international organization established in 1945 to promote and ensure international peace and security, to promote friendly relations between nations, and to contribute in resolving international problems related to economic, social, cultural, and humanitarian conditions. — Abbr. U.N.

United Nations Convention on the Rights of the Child. An international instrument covering children's civil, political, economic, social, and cultural rights. • The Convention was adopted by the United Nations General Assembly on November 20, 1989. Only a few nations, including the United States, have not ratified the convention. — Abbr. UNCRC.

United Nations Educational, Scientific, and Cultural Organization. The arm of the United Nations charged with promoting the exchange of educational, scientific, and cultural enterprises among nations. • Its Copyright Law Division administers the Universal Copyright Convention. — Abbr. UNESCO.

United Nations Environment Programme. An organization created in 1972 to encourage education in and employment of environmentally sound practices in all nations. — Abbr. UNEP.

United Nations Treaty on Principles Governing the Activities of States in the Exploration and Use of Outer Space. See OUTER SPACE TREATY.

United States. Abbr. U.S. See UNITED STATES OF AMERICA.

United States Agency for International Development. The independent federal agency that administers U.S. foreign-aid programs to give economic and humanitarian assistance to developing nations. • The agency became independent by the Foreign Affairs and Restructuring Act of 1998, although its administrator is under the direct authority and foreign-policy guidance of the Secretary of State. — Abbr. AID; USAID.

United States Air Force. The aviation branch of the United States armed forces, made up of the Regular Air Force (standing air force), the Air Force Reserve, and the Air National Guard. ● The United States Air Force is under the authority of the U.S. Department of the Air Force. — Abbr. USAF.

United States Air Force Academy. An institution of higher learning in the United States Department of the Air Force responsible for educating and training commissioned officers for service in the United States Air Force. ● Founded in 1954, the academy is located near Colorado Springs, Colorado. — Abbr. USAFA. — Occasionally also termed (informally) the *Colorado Air Force School.*

United States Arbitration Act. See FEDERAL ARBITRATION ACT. — Abbr. USAA.

United States Army. The land-combat and land-operations branch of the United States armed forces. ● This branch includes supporting air- and water-transport services such as the Army Air Corps. The Army includes the Regular Army (the standing force), the Army Reserve, and the Army National Guard when in active federal service, as in time of war or other national emergency. The United States Army is under the authority of the U.S. Department of the Army. — Also termed *land forces.* — Abbr. USA.

United States Attorney. A lawyer appointed by the President to represent, under the direction of the Attorney General, the federal government in civil and criminal cases in a federal judicial district. ● One U.S. Attorney is assigned to each of the federal judicial districts, except for the Northern Mariana Islands and Guam. — Abbr. USA. — Also termed *United States District Attorney.* Cf. DISTRICT ATTORNEY.

Assistant United States Attorney. A lawyer appointed by the Attorney General to act under the direction of the United States Attorney and represent the federal government in civil and criminal cases filed in federal courts. — Abbr. AUSA.

Special Assistant to the United States Attorney. An attorney appointed by the Attorney General for a limited period to assist a United States Attorney in specific cases. 28 USCA § 543. — Abbr. SAUSA.

United States Bankruptcy Court. See BANKRUPTCY COURT.

United States Botanic Garden. An enclosed garden on the U.S. Capitol grounds where plants are cultivated for ceremonial use, public display, and research. ● Many rare botanical specimens are available for study by students and scientists at the Garden.

United States Claims Court. See UNITED STATES COURT OF FEDERAL CLAIMS.

United States Coast Guard. A military service and armed-forces branch that enforces the federal laws applicable to waters subject to U.S. jurisdiction, administers laws and promulgates regulations for the safety of lives and property on waters under U.S. jurisdiction, carries out maritime rescue operations, performs oceanographic research, and at times serves as a specialized branch of the Navy. ● The Coast Guard was established in 1915. 14 USCA § 1. It has been part of the U.S. Department of the Treasury and the U.S. Department of Transportation. Today it is part of the U.S. Department of Homeland Security during peacetime, and the U.S. Department of Defense during wartime. — Abbr. USCG.

United States Coast Guard Academy. An institution of higher learning responsible for educating and training commissioned officers for service in the United States Coast Guard. ● The academy began in 1876 as the School of Instruction of the Revenue Cutter Service near New Bedford, Massachusetts. In 1915, the academy acquired its current name and, in 1932, moved to New London, Connecticut. — Abbr. USCGA.

United States Code. A multivolume published codification of federal statutory law. — Abbr. U.S.C.; USC.

United States Code Annotated. A multivolume publication of the complete text of the United States Code with historical notes, cross-references, and casenotes of federal and state decisions construing specific Code sections. — Abbr. USCA.

United States Commissioner. See COMMISSIONER.

United States Commission on Civil Rights. The agency that compiles information about discrimination based on race, color, religion, sex, age, disability, or national origin, and about the denial of equal protection of the laws in voting, education, employment, and housing. ● The agency makes findings and recommendations to Congress but has no enforcement power. It was established by the Civil Rights Act of 1957. — Abbr. CCR.

United States Copyright Office. A branch of the Library of Congress that is responsible for implementing federal copyright laws. ● In addition to processing applications for copyrights, the U.S. Copyright Office stores deposited copyrighted materials and issues opinions (by request) on questions of copyright protection. Materials deposited with this agency are not automatically added to the Library of Congress collection; a separate and direct submission to the Library may be required. The Office also administers various licensing provisions of the statute, including collecting and distributing royalties.

United States court. See *federal court* under COURT.

United States Court of Appeals. A federal appellate court having jurisdiction to hear cases in one of the 13 judicial circuits of the United States (the First Circuit through the Eleventh Circuit, plus the District of Columbia Circuit and the Federal Circuit). — Also termed *circuit court.*

United States Court of Appeals for the Armed Forces. The primary civilian appellate tribunal responsible for reviewing court-martial convictions from all the military services. 10 USCA §§ 941–950. — Formerly also termed *Court of Military Appeals.*

United States Court of Appeals for the Federal Circuit. An intermediate-level appellate court with jurisdiction to hear appeals in patent cases, various actions against the United States to recover damages, cases from the U.S. Court of Federal Claims, the U.S. Court of International Trade, the U.S. Court of Appeals for Veterans Claims, the Merit Systems Protection Board, and some administrative agencies. ● The Court originated in the 1982 merger of the Court of Customs and Patent Appeals and the U.S. Court of Claims (although the trial jurisdiction of the Court of Claims was given to a new U.S. Claims Court). Among the purposes of its creation were ending forum-shopping in patent suits, settling differences in patent-law doctrines among the circuits, and allowing a single forum to develop the expertise needed to rule on complex technological questions that arise in patent suits. — Abbr. CAFC, Fed. Cir. — Often shortened to *Federal Circuit.*

United States Court of Appeals for Veterans Claims. An Article I federal appellate court that has exclusive jurisdiction to review decisions of the Board of Veterans Appeals. ● The Court was created in 1988 as the United States Court of Veterans Appeals; its name was changed in 1998. Its seven judges are appointed by the President and confirmed by the Senate; they serve 15-year terms. Appeals from its decisions are to the U.S. Court of Appeals for the Federal Circuit. 38 USCA §§ 7251 et seq. — Also termed *United States Court of Veterans Appeals.*

United States Court of Federal Claims. A specialized federal court created under Article I of the Constitution in 1982 (with the name *United States Claims Court*) as the successor to the Court of Claims, and renamed in 1992 as the United States Court of Federal Claims. ● It has original, nationwide jurisdiction to render a money judgment on any claim against the United States founded on the Constitution, a federal statute, a federal regulation, an express or implied-in-fact contract with the United States, or any other claim for damages not sounding in tort. — Abbr. Cl. Ct.; (formerly) Ct. Cl. — Also termed *Court of Claims.*

United States Court of International Trade. A court with jurisdiction over any civil action against the United States arising from federal laws governing import transactions or the eligibility of workers, firms, and communities for adjustment assistance under the Trade Act of 1974 (19 USCA §§ 2101–2495). ● Its exclusive jurisdiction also includes actions to recover customs duties, to recover on a customs bond, and to impose certain civil penalties for fraud or negligence. See 28 USCA §§ 1581–1584. — Abbr. USCIT; CIT. — Also termed *International Trade Court*; *Court of International Trade*; (formerly) *U.S. Customs Court.*

United States Court of Veterans Appeals. See UNITED STATES COURT OF APPEALS FOR VETERANS CLAIMS.

United States currency. See CURRENCY.

United States Customs Court. A court that formerly heard cases involving customs and duties. ● Abolished in 1980, its responsibilities have been taken over by the United States Court of International Trade. See UNITED STATES COURT OF INTERNATIONAL TRADE.

United States Customs Service. An agency in the U.S. Department of Homeland Security responsible for collecting import duties on goods, wares, and merchandise, and for enforcing customs and related laws. ● The Customs Service was created in 1863. 12 Stat. 665. It was transferred from the Department of the Treasury in 2003. — Also termed *Bureau of Customs.*

United States District Attorney. See UNITED STATES ATTORNEY.

United States District Court. A federal trial court having jurisdiction to hear civil and criminal cases within its judicial district. ● The United States is divided into nearly 100 federal judicial districts. Each state has at least one judicial district. Also, the District of Columbia, Puerto Rico, Guam, the Virgin Islands, and the Northern Mariana Islands each have one district. — Abbr. U.S.D.C.

United States Fish and Wildlife Service. A unit in the U.S. Department of the Interior responsible for managing more than 93 million acres of land and water consisting of more than 500 national wildlife refuges and thousands of small wetlands. ● It also administers or enforces laws relating to migratory birds, endangered species, certain marine mammals, and sports fisheries. — Abbr. FWS; USFWS.

United States Foreign Intelligence Surveillance Court. An 11-judge court that hears requests from the Attorney General for surveillance warrants under the Foreign Intelligence Surveillance Act. • The court's proceedings and records are normally closed to the public. Its rulings may be reviewed by the Foreign Intelligence Court of Review. — Abbr. FISC.

United States Foreign Intelligence Surveillance Court of Review. A panel comprising three federal judges appointed by the Chief Justice to review decisions of the United States Intelligence Surveillance Court. • The Court was established in 1978 by the Foreign Intelligence Surveillance Act.

United States Foreign Service. A division of the State Department responsible for maintaining diplomatic and consular offices and personnel in foreign countries. — Often shortened to *Foreign Service*.

United States Geological Survey. A unit in the U.S. Department of the Interior responsible for preparing and publishing maps, technical reports, and fact sheets, and for compiling information about energy and mineral resources and the use and quality of the nation's water resources. — Abbr. USGS.

United States Institute of Peace. An independent federal institution created to develop and disseminate knowledge about international peace and conflict resolution. • The Institute was established in 1984.

United States International Trade Commission. An independent federal agency that compiles information on international trade and tariffs; reports its findings and recommendations to the President, the U.S. Trade Representative, and Congressional Committees; and conducts investigations into international-trade relief. — Abbr. USITC.

United States Magistrate Judge. A federal judicial officer who hears civil and criminal pretrial matters and who may conduct civil trials or criminal misdemeanor trials. 28 USCA §§ 631–639. • Magistrate judges are appointed to renewable eight-year terms under Article I of the U.S. Constitution. — Also termed *federal magistrate*; (before 1990) *United States Magistrate*; *parajudge*.

United States Marine Corps. The military service within the United States Navy whose forces are trained for land, sea, and air combat. • The United States Marine Corps is a separate service within the United States Navy under the authority of the U.S. Department of the Navy. — Abbr. USMC.

United States Marshal. See MARSHAL.

United States Marshals Service. The unit in the U.S. Department of Justice responsible for protecting federal courts and ensuring effective operation of the judicial system. • U.S. marshals make arrests, serve court papers, and enforce court orders. — Abbr. USMS.

United States Merchant Marine Academy. A military-affiliated institution of higher learning responsible for educating and training commissioned officers for service on civilian merchant vessels or in the armed forces. • The academy was founded in 1938, and since 1943 has been located at King's Point, New York. — Abbr. USMMA.

United States Military Academy. An institution of higher learning in the U.S. Department of the Army responsible for educating and training officers for service in the U.S. Army. • Founded in 1802, the academy is located on the Hudson River in West Point, New York. — Abbr. USMA. — Often termed *West Point*.

United States Mint. A unit in the U.S. Department of the Treasury responsible for producing coins to be used in trade and commerce, numismatic coins, gold and silver coins, and national medals. • It also operates the gold-storage facility at Fort Knox, Kentucky. It was formerly termed the Bureau of the Mint.

United States Naval Academy. An institution of higher learning in the United States Department of the Navy responsible for educating and training commissioned officers for service in the United States Navy and the United States Marine Corps. • Founded in 1845, the academy is located in Annapolis, Maryland. — Abbr. USNA. — Often also termed (informally) *Annapolis*.

United States Navy. The naval-operations branch of the United States armed forces, including naval aviation and the United States Marine Corps, and the United States Coast Guard when operating as a service in the Navy. • The United States Navy is under the authority of the U.S. Department of the Navy. — Abbr. USN.

United States of America. A federal republic formed after the War of Independence and made up of 48 conterminous states, plus the state of Alaska and the District of Columbia in North America, plus the state of Hawaii in the Pacific. — Abbr. USA; U.S.

United States officer. See OFFICER (1).

United States Patent and Trademark Office. The Department of Commerce agency that examines patent and trademark applications, issues patents, registers trademarks, and furnishes patent and trademark information and services to the public. — Abbr. PTO; USPTO. — Often shortened to *Patent Office*; *Trademark Office*.

United States person. A U.S. resident or national (except a national living outside the United States who is employed by someone other than a United States person), a domestic American concern, and any foreign subsidiary or affiliate of a domestic concern with operations controlled by the domestic concern. • Under antiboycott regulatory controls, no United States person may participate in a secondary boycott or discrimination against Jews and others by members of the League of Arab States. 50 USCA app. § 2415(2).

United States Postal Service. An independent establishment in the executive branch responsible for operating post offices, safeguarding and delivering mail, and enforcing the laws affecting the integrity and security of the mail. • The Postal Reorganization Act of 1970 replaced the cabinet-level Post Office Department with the United States Postal Service. 39 USCA § 101 et seq. — Abbr. USPS.

United States Reports. The official printed record of U.S. Supreme Court cases. • In a citation, it is abbreviated as U.S., as in 388 U.S. 14 (1967).

United States Secret Service. A law-enforcement agency in the U.S. Department of Homeland Security responsible for providing security for the President, Vice President, certain other government officials, and visiting foreign diplomats, and for protecting U.S. currency by enforcing the laws relating to counterfeiting, forgery, and credit-card fraud. • The Service was transferred from the Department of the Treasury in 2003. — Often shortened to *Secret Service.*

United States Sentencing Commission. An independent commission in the judicial branch of the federal government responsible for setting and regulating guidelines for criminal sentencing in federal courts and for issuing policy statements about their application. • The President appoints its members with the advice and consent of the Senate. It was created under the Sentencing Reform Act 1984. 28 USCA § 991.

United States Sentencing Guidelines. A detailed set of instructions for judges to determine appropriate sentences for federal crimes. — Abbr. USSG. — Also termed *federal sentencing guidelines.*

United States Supreme Court. See SUPREME COURT OF THE UNITED STATES.

United States Tax Court. See TAX COURT, U.S.

United States Trade and Development Agency. An independent federal agency in the executive branch responsible for promoting trade between the United States and developing countries to create jobs in the United States and to promote economic progress in poorer nations. • It was established in 1961 as the Trade and Development

Program and was renamed in 1992. — Abbr. TDA; USTDA.

United States Trade Representative. The top U.S. trade negotiator and adviser to the President on foreign-trade policy. • The Cabinet-level office is responsible for making annual reports on nations that do not act diligently to stop piracy of copyrighted material. The Trade Representative holds the rank of ambassador. — Abbr. USTR. See OFFICE OF THE UNITED STATES TRADE REPRESENTATIVE; SPECIAL 301.

United States trustee. A federal official who is appointed by the Attorney General to perform administrative tasks in the bankruptcy process, such as appointing bankruptcy trustees in Chapter 7 and Chapter 11 cases. See TRUSTEE (2).

unities doctrine of marriage. See LEGAL-UNITIES DOCTRINE.

Uniting and Strengthening America by Providing Appropriate Tools Required to Intercept and Obstruct Terrorism. See USA PATRIOT ACT.

unit-investment trust. See TRUST.

unitization. *Oil & gas.* The collection of producing wells over a reservoir for joint operations such as enhanced-recovery techniques. • Unitization is usu. carried out after primary production has begun to fall off substantially, in order to permit efficient secondary-recovery operations. It is also done to comply with well-spacing requirements established by state law or regulation. Pooling, by contrast, is usu. associated with drilling a single well and operating that well by primary-production techniques. Cf. POOLING. — **unitize** (yoo-nə-tiz), *vb.*

   compulsory unitization. Unitization done by order of a regulatory agency. — Also termed *forced unitization.*

   forced unitization. See *compulsory unitization.*

   voluntary unitization. Unitization arranged by agreement of the owners of mineral interests.

unitization clause. *Oil & gas.* A provision in an oil-and-gas lease granting the lessee the right to unitize the leased premises, generally for enhanced-recovery operations.

unit-ownership act. A state law governing condominium ownership.

unit price. See PRICE.

unit pricing. A system in which contract items are priced per unit rather than on the basis of a flat contract price.

unit rule. 1. *Securities.* A method of valuing securities by multiplying the total number of shares held by the sale price of one share sold on a licensed stock exchange, ignoring all other facts about value. 2. *Parliamentary law.* A convention's rule that lets a delegation's majority cast the entire delegation's votes. Cf. *instructed delegate* under DELEGATE.

unitrust. See TRUST.

units-of-output depreciation method. See DEPRE-CIATION METHOD.

units-of-production method. *Tax.* An accounting method in which the depreciation provision is computed at a fixed rate per product unit, based on an estimate of the total number of units that the property will produce during its service life. • This method is used in the oil-and-gas industry when the total number of units of production (i.e., barrels in a reserve) can be accurately estimated.

unity, *n.* (13c) **1.** The fact or condition of being one in number; oneness. **2.** Jointness in interest, possession, time, or title. • At common law, all four of these unities were required for the creation of a joint tenancy. See *joint tenancy* under TENANCY. — **unitary,** *adj.*

unity of interest. (18c) The requirement that all joint tenants' interests must be identical in nature, extent, and duration. — Also termed *interest unity.*

unity of possession. (18c) The requirement that each joint tenant must be entitled to possession of the whole property. — Also termed *possession unity.*

unity of time. (18c) The requirement that all joint tenants' interests must vest at the same time. — Also termed *time unity.*

unity of title. (18c) The requirement that all joint tenants must acquire their interests under the same instrument. — Also termed *title unity.*

unity of art. *Copyright.* The inseparable nature of utilitarian and functional aspects of applied art. • France uses the unity-of-art approach to applied art and industrial design, but stops short of protecting strictly utilitarian design under copyright. — Also termed *cumulative approach.* Cf. DUALITY OF ART.

unity of seisin (**see**-zin). (1800) The merging of seisin in one person, brought about when the person becomes seised of a tract of land on which he or she already has an easement.

universal agency. See *general agency* under AGENCY (1).

universal agent. See AGENT.

Universal Copyright Convention. A 1952 treaty binding signatories to give citizens of other member nations the same copyright protection that their own citizens receive. 25 U.S.T. 1341, T.I.A.S. No. 7868. • Administered by the United Nations Educational, Scientific, and Cultural Organization, the Convention does not apply between nations that are also signatories of the Berne Convention. The United States signed the treaty in 1955. — Abbr. UCC.

Universal Declaration of Human Rights. An international bill of rights proclaimed by the United Nations in December 1948, being that body's first general enumeration of human rights and fundamental freedoms. • The preamble states that "recognition of the inherent dignity and of the equal and inalienable rights of all members of the human family is the foundation of freedom, justice and peace in the world." The Declaration contains a lengthy list of rights and fundamental freedoms. For the full text of the Declaration, see Appendix C.

universal defense. See *real defense* under DEFENSE (4).

universal inheritance. See INHERITANCE.

universal-inheritance rule. *Wills & estates.* A doctrine holding that an intestate estate escheats to the state only if the decedent leaves no surviving relatives, no matter how distant. • Through the first half of the 20th century, this rule was broadly followed in American jurisdictions. The Uniform Probate Code abandons the universal-inheritance rule and provides that if no member of the third or a nearer parentela survives the decedent, the intestate estate escheats to the state. — Also termed *rule of universal inheritance.* See PARENTELA. Cf. *laughing heir* under HEIR; GRADUAL METHOD.

universalist movement. *Copyright.* A 19th-century campaign in Europe to recognize a worldwide copyright law based on an author's moral rights.

universal legacy. See LEGACY.

universal legatee. See LEGATEE.

universal life insurance. See LIFE INSURANCE.

universal malice. See MALICE.

universal partnership. See PARTNERSHIP.

universal succession. See SUCCESSION (2).

universal successor. See SUCCESSOR.

universal synod. See *general synod* under SYNOD.

universal title. See TITLE (2).

unjudicial, *adj.* (16c) Not becoming of or appropriate to a judge.

unjust, *adj.* (14c) Contrary to justice; not just.

unjust enrichment. (1897) **1.** The retention of a benefit conferred by another, without offering compensation, in circumstances where compensation is reasonably expected. **2.** A benefit obtained from another, not intended as a gift and not legally justifiable, for which the beneficiary must make restitution or recompense. **3.** The area of law dealing with unjustifiable benefits of this kind.

unlaw, *n.* **1.** A violation of law; an illegality. **2.** Lawlessness.

unlawful, *adj.* (14c) **1.** Not authorized by law; illegal <in some cities, jaywalking is unlawful>. **2.** Criminally punishable <unlawful entry>. **3.** Involving moral turpitude <the preacher spoke to the congregation about the unlawful activities of gambling and drinking>. — **unlawfully,** *adv.*

unlawful act. (16c) Conduct that is not authorized by law; a violation of a civil or criminal law.

unlawful arrest. See ARREST.

unlawful assembly. See ASSEMBLY.

unlawful condition. See CONDITION (2).

unlawful detainer. See DETAINER.

unlawful-detainer proceeding. (1879) An action to return a wrongfully held tenancy (as one held by a tenant after the lease has expired) to its owner. See *unlawful detainer* under DETAINER.

unlawful entry. See ENTRY (1).

unlawful force. See FORCE.

unlawful interest. See USURY.

unlawful interference with contractual relations. See TORTIOUS INTERFERENCE WITH CONTRACTUAL RELATIONS.

unlawful picketing. See PICKETING.

unlawful sexual conduct with a minor. See IMPAIRING THE MORALS OF A MINOR.

unlawful sexual intercourse. See RAPE.

"unless" lease. See LEASE.

unlimited, *adj.* Without restriction or limitation.

unliquidated, *adj.* (18c) Not previously specified or determined <unliquidated damages>.

unliquidated claim. See CLAIM (3).

unliquidated damages. See DAMAGES.

unliquidated debt. See DEBT.

unlisted security. See SECURITY.

unlisted stock. See *unlisted security* under SECURITY.

unlivery. *Maritime law.* The unloading of cargo at its intended destination.

unmarketable title. See TITLE (2).

unmarried, *adj.* Not married; single.

unmerchantable title. See *unmarketable title* under TITLE (2).

unnatural offense. See SODOMY.

unnatural will. See WILL.

unnavigable, *adj.* See INNAVIGABLE.

unnecessary, *adj.* Not required under the circumstances; not necessary.

unnecessary hardship. See HARDSHIP (4).

unoccupied, *adj.* **1.** (Of a building) not occupied; vacant. **2.** (Of a person) not busy; esp., unemployed.

unofficious payment. See PAYMENT.

unofficious will. See *inofficious testament* under TESTAMENT.

unpaid dividend. See DIVIDEND.

unpatentable over art. *Patents.* (Of an invention) ineligible for patent protection because of obviousness or the lack of novelty.

unperfected security interest. See SECURITY INTEREST.

unprecedented (ən-**pres**-ə-den-tid), *adj.* Never before known; without any earlier example.

unpremeditation. The lack of premeditation; the absence of planning.

unprofessional conduct. See CONDUCT.

unpublished opinion. See OPINION (1).

unqualified indorsement. See INDORSEMENT.

unqualified opinion. See OPINION (2).

unqualified ownership. See OWNERSHIP.

unrealized loss. See *paper loss* under LOSS.

unrealized profit. See *paper profit* under PROFIT (1).

unrealized receivable. See RECEIVABLE.

unreasonable, *adj.* (14c) **1.** Not guided by reason; irrational or capricious. **2.** Not supported by a valid exception to the warrant requirement <unreasonable search and seizure>.

unreasonable compensation. See COMPENSATION.

unreasonable decision. See DECISION.

unreasonable deviation. See DEVIATION.

unreasonable refusal to submit to operation. *Workers' compensation.* An injured employee's refusal to submit to a necessary surgical procedure. ● This refusal is grounds for terminating the employee's workers'-compensation benefits.

unreasonable restraint of trade. See RESTRAINT OF TRADE.

unreasonable restraint on alienation. See RESTRAINT ON ALIENATION (1).

unreasonable search. See SEARCH.

unreasonably dangerous conduct. See CONDUCT.

unrebuttable, *adj.* Not rebuttable <an unrebuttable presumption>.

unrecorded, *adj.* (16c) Not recorded; esp., not filed in the public record <unrecorded deed>.

unregistered security. See *restricted security* under SECURITY.

unrelated-business income. See INCOME.

unrelated-business-income tax. See TAX.

unrelated-business taxable income. See *unrelated-business income* under INCOME.

unrelated offense. See OFFENSE (1).

unresponsive answer. See ANSWER (2).

unrestricted indorsement. See *unrestrictive indorsement* under INDORSEMENT.

unrestrictive indorsement. See INDORSEMENT.

unrestrictive interpretation. See INTERPRETATION.

unreviewable, *adj.* (1877) Not subject to legal or judicial review <the claim is unreviewable on appeal>.

unsafe, *adj.* (Of a verdict or judgment) likely to be overturned on appeal because of a defect.

unsatisfied-judgment fund. See FUND (1).

unseated, *adj.* (Of land) vacant and neither developed nor cultivated.

unseaworthy, *adj.* (Of a vessel) unable to withstand the perils of an ordinary voyage. Cf. SEAWORTHY.

unsecured bail bond. See BOND (2).

unsecured bond. See DEBENTURE (3).

unsecured claim. See CLAIM (5).

unsecured creditor. See CREDITOR.

unsecured debt. See DEBT.

unsecured note. See NOTE (1).

unskilled work. See WORK (1).

unsolemn war. See WAR (1).

unsolemn will. See WILL.

unsolicited commercial e-mail. See SPAM. — Abbr. UCE.

unsound, *adj.* (14c) **1.** Not healthy; esp., not mentally well <unsound mind>. **2.** Not firmly made; impaired <unsound foundation>. **3.** Not valid or well founded <unsound argument>.

unspeakable crime. See SODOMY.

unsworn, *adj.* (16c) Not sworn <an unsworn statement>.

unsworn declaration under penalty of perjury. See DECLARATION (8).

untenantable (ən-**ten**-ən-tə-bəl), *adj.* (17c) Not capable of being occupied or lived in; not fit for occupancy <the city closed the untenantable housing project>.

unthrift. *Archaic.* A prodigal; a spendthrift.

untimely, *adj.* (13c) Not timely <an untimely answer>; at an inappropriate time, either too soon or too late.

untrue, *adj.* **1.** (Of something said) not correct; inaccurate. **2.** (Of a person) not faithful or true (to a standard or belief).

unus nullus **rule** (**yoo**-nəs **nəl**-əs). [Latin "one is nobody" + rule] *Civil law.* The evidentiary principle that the testimony of only one witness is given no weight. Cf. HALF-PROOF (1).

unusual charge. See *special charge* under CHARGE.

unvalued policy. See INSURANCE POLICY.

unworthy, *adj. Civil law.* (Of an heir) not entitled to inherit from a person because of a failure in a duty to that person.

unwritten constitution. See CONSTITUTION.

unwritten evidence. See EVIDENCE.

unwritten law. See LAW.

unwritten will. See *nuncupative will* under WILL.

UPA. *abbr.* UNIFORM PARTNERSHIP ACT.

UPAA. *abbr.* UNIFORM PREMARITAL AGREEMENT ACT.

up before. *Informal.* In the presence of (a particular court or judge) <for the bail hearing you'll come up before Judge Franklin>.

UPC. *abbr.* UNIFORM PROBATE CODE.

up-front performance bond. See PERFORMANCE BOND.

UPIA. *abbr.* UNIFORM PRUDENT INVESTOR ACT.

UPL. *abbr.* Unauthorized practice of law <the state bar's UPL committee>. See *unauthorized practice of law* under PRACTICE OF LAW.

upper chamber. See CHAMBER.

upper court. See *court above* under COURT.

upper estate. See *dominant estate* under ESTATE (4).

upper management. See *top management* under MANAGEMENT.

UPREIT (əp-rit). See *umbrella-partnership real-estate investment trust* under REAL-ESTATE INVESTMENT TRUST.

upset bid. See BID (1).

upset price. See PRICE.

upside. *Securities.* **1.** An upward movement in stock prices. **2.** The potential of an upward movement in stock prices. Cf. DOWNSIDE.

upstream guaranty. See GUARANTY.

upstreaming. A parent corporation's use of a subsidiary's cash flow or assets for purposes unrelated to the subsidiary.

upstream merger. See MERGER.

UPUFA. *abbr.* UNIFORM PUTATIVE AND UNKNOWN FATHERS ACT.

upward departure. See DEPARTURE.

urban, *adj.* Of or relating to a city or town; not rural.

urban-fear syndrome. See URBAN-SURVIVAL SYNDROME.

Urban Mass Transit Administration. A unit in the U.S. Department of Transportation responsible for making grants to help states, regional and local governmental bodies, and public agencies to acquire or improve capital equipment and facilities for urban mass-transit systems; for providing technical assistance and funds for demonstration projects; for making educational grants for urban mass-transit research and training; and for making training grants to mass-transit systems for training. ● The agency also awards grants for transit operations in nonurban areas. — Abbr. UMTA.

urban planning. See LAND-USE PLANNING.

urban-psychosis defense. See URBAN-SURVIVAL SYNDROME.

urban renewal. (1954) The process of redeveloping urban areas by demolishing or repairing existing structures or by building new facilities on areas that have been cleared in accordance with an overall plan.

urban servitude. See SERVITUDE (2).

urban-survival syndrome. A self-defense theory holding that a defendant who uses unreasonable force may be acquitted if the defendant lives in a dangerous environment that heightens the defendant's fears of injury to life or limb so much that the force used seemed reasonable and necessary to the defendant. — Also termed *urban-survival defense*; *urban-fear syndrome*; *urban-psychosis defense*; *inner-city post-traumatic-stress defense*.

URESA (yə-**ree**-sə). *abbr.* UNIFORM RECIPROCAL ENFORCEMENT OF SUPPORT ACT.

urgent deficiency bill. See *deficiency bill* under BILL (3).

Uruguay Round. The 1994 negotiations of the General Agreement on Tariffs and Trade. ● The negotiations resulted in the TRIPs agreement that established the World Trade Organization and made member nations' patent laws more uniform. See TRIPS.

U.S. *abbr.* **1.** United States. See UNITED STATES OF AMERICA. **2.** UNITED STATES REPORTS.

USA. *abbr.* **1.** UNITED STATES OF AMERICA. **2.** UNITED STATES ARMY. **3.** UNITED STATES ATTORNEY.

USAA. *abbr.* United States Arbitration Act. See FEDERAL ARBITRATION ACT.

USAF. *abbr.* UNITED STATES AIR FORCE.

USAFA. *abbr.* See UNITED STATES AIR FORCE ACADEMY.

usage. (13c) **1.** A well-known, customary, and uniform practice, usu. in a specific profession or business. See CUSTOM (1). Cf. CONVENTION (6).

　　custom and usage. See CUSTOM AND USAGE.

　　general usage. (16c) A usage that prevails throughout a country or particular trade or profession; a usage that is not restricted to a local area.

　　immemorial usage. (17c) A usage that has existed for a very long time; longstanding custom. See TIME IMMEMORIAL.

　　local usage. (18c) A practice or method regularly observed in a particular place, sometimes considered by a court in interpreting a document. UCC § 1-205(2)(3). See CUSTOM AND USAGE.

　　trade usage. (1864) A practice or method of dealing having such regular observance in a region, vocation, or trade that it justifies an expectation that it will be observed in a given transaction; a customary practice or set of practices relied on by persons conversant in, or connected with, a trade or business. ● While a course of performance or a course of dealing can be established by the parties' testimony, a trade usage is usu. established by expert testimony. — Also termed *usage of trade*; *course of trade*. Cf. COURSE OF DEALING; COURSE OF PERFORMANCE. **2.** See *conventional custom* under CUSTOM.

USAID. *abbr.* UNITED STATES AGENCY FOR INTERNATIONAL DEVELOPMENT.

usance (**yoo**-zənts). The time allowed for the payment of a foreign bill of exchange, sometimes set by custom but now usu. by law.

usance credit. See *time letter of credit* under LETTER OF CREDIT.

USA Patriot Act. A statute enacted in response to the terrorist attacks of September 11, 2001, giving law-enforcement agencies broader authority to collect information on suspected terrorists, to share that information among domestic and foreign intelligence agencies, to make the country's borders more secure, to detain suspects on new types of criminal charges using new criminal procedures, and to give the Treasury Department more authority to investigate and regulate financial institutions that participate in foreign money-laundering. ● The title is an acronym of Uniting and Strengthening America by Providing Appropriate Tools Required to Intercept and Obstruct Terrorism. — Often shortened to *Patriot Act.*

USC. *abbr.* UNITED STATES CODE.

USCA. *abbr.* UNITED STATES CODE ANNOTATED.

USCG. *abbr.* UNITED STATES COAST GUARD.

USCGA. *abbr.* See UNITED STATES COAST GUARD ACADEMY.

USCIS. *abbr.* U.S. CITIZENSHIP AND IMMIGRATION SERVICE.

USCIT. *abbr.* See UNITED STATES COURT OF INTERNATIONAL TRADE.

U.S. citizen. See *national of the United States* under NATIONAL.

U.S. Citizenship and Immigration Service. A unit in the U.S. Department of Homeland Security responsible for enforcing the nation's immigration laws. • Its functions were transferred from the former Immigration and Naturalization Service of the U.S. Department of Justice in 2003. — Abbr. USCIS.

USDA. *abbr.* DEPARTMENT OF AGRICULTURE.

U.S.D.C. *abbr.* UNITED STATES DISTRICT COURT.

use (yoos), *n.* (bef. 12c) **1.** The application or employment of something; esp., a long-continued possession and employment of a thing for the purpose for which it is adapted, as distinguished from a possession and employment that is merely temporary or occasional <the neighbors complained to the city about the owner's use of the building as a dance club>.

accessory use. *Zoning.* A use that is dependent on or pertains to a main use.

adverse use. A use without license or permission. Cf. ADVERSE POSSESSION.

beneficial use. *Property.* The right to use property and all that makes that property desirable or habitable, such as light, air, and access, even if someone else owns the legal title to the property.

collateral use. *Intellectual property.* The legal use of a trademark by someone other than the trademark owner, whereby the other party must clearly identify itself, the use of the trademark, and the absence of affiliation with the trademark owner.

commercial use. A use that is connected with or furthers an ongoing profit-making activity. Cf. *noncommercial use.*

conditional use. *Zoning.* A use of property subject to special controls and conditions. • A conditional use is one that is suitable to a zoning district, but not necessarily to every location within that district. — Also termed *special exception.* See SPECIAL EXCEPTION (2).

conforming use. *Zoning.* The use of a structure or of the land in conformity with the uses permitted under the zoning classifications of a particular area, such as the building of a single-family dwelling in a residential zone.

double use. *Patents.* An application of a known principle or process to a new use without leading to a new result or product.

exclusive use. 1. *Trademarks.* The right to use a specific mark without exception, and to prevent another from using a confusingly similar mark. **2.** *Property.* The right of an adverse user to a property, exercised independently of any similar rights held by others; one of the elements of a prescriptive easement. See USER.

experimental use. *Patents.* **1.** The use or sale of an invention by the inventor for experimental

purposes. **2.** A defense to liability for patent infringement when the infringement took place only to satisfy curiosity or to complete an experiment, rather than for profit.

highest and best use. *Real estate.* In valuing property, the use that will generate the most profit. • This standard is used esp. to determine the fair market value of property subject to eminent domain. — Often shortened to *best use.* — Also termed *most suitable use.*

incidental use. *Zoning.* Land use that is dependent on or affiliated with the land's primary use.

most suitable use. See *highest and best use.*

noncommercial use. A use for private pleasure or business purposes that non involving the generation of income or bestowing a reward or other compensation. Cf. *commercial use.*

nonconforming use. *Zoning.* Land use that is impermissible under current zoning restrictions but that is allowed because the use existed lawfully before the restrictions took effect.

pious use. The designation and actual use of property for recognized religious or charitable purposes. Cf. *superstitious use.*

popular use. A person's imperfect right to enjoy public land. • A popular use is not legally enforceable. It is dependent on the government's will to allow access to the land.

public use. 1. *Property.* The public's beneficial right to use property or facilities subject to condemnation. See CONDEMNATION (2). **2.** *Patents.* Any use of or offer to use a completed or operative invention in a nonsecret, natural, and intended manner. • A patent is invalid if the invention was in public use more than one year before the patent's application date.

reasonable use. Use of one's property for an appropriate purpose that does not unreasonably interfere with another's use of property. See REASONABLE-USE THEORY.

regular use. *Insurance.* A use that is usual, normal, or customary, as opposed to an occasional, special, or incidental use. • This term often appears in automobile-insurance policies in the definition of a *nonowned automobile* — that is, an automobile not owned by or furnished for the regular use of the insured. Nonowned automobiles are excluded from coverage under most liability policies.

superstitious use. A designation or use of property for religious purposes not legally recognized or tolerated (such as gifts either favoring an unrecognized religion or supporting the saying of prayers for the dead). Cf. *pious use.*

2. A habitual or common practice <drug use>. **3.** A purpose or end served <the tool had several

uses>. **4.** A benefit or profit; esp., the right to take profits from land owned and possessed by another; the equitable ownership of land to which another person holds the legal title <cestui que use>. See CESTUI QUE USE. — **use** (yooz), *vb.*

contingent use. (17c) A use that would be a contingent remainder if it had not been limited by way of use. ● An example is a transfer "to A, to the use of B for life, with the remainder to the use of C's heirs." — Also termed *future use.*

entire use. A use of property solely for the benefit of a married woman. ● When used in the habendum of a trust deed for the benefit of a married woman, this phrase operates to keep her husband from taking anything under the deed. — Also termed *entire benefit; sole use; sole and separate use.*

executed use. *Hist.* A use resulting from combining the equitable title and legal title of an estate, done to comply with the Statute of Uses' mandate that the holder of an estate be vested with legal title to ensure the holder's liability for feudal dues. See STATUTE OF USES.

executory use. See *springing use.*

future use. See *contingent use.*

official use. *Hist.* A use imposing a duty on a person holding legal title to an estate on behalf of another, such as a requirement that a feoffee to uses sell the estate and apportion the proceeds among several beneficiaries. ● The Statute of Uses eliminated this type of use.

permissive use. *Hist.* A passive use resorted to before passage of the Statute of Uses in 1535 to avoid an oppressive feudal law (such as mortmain) by naming one person as the legal owner of property while allowing another to possess the property and enjoy the benefits arising from it.

present use. *Hist.* A use that has an immediate existence and is subject to the Statute of Uses.

resulting use. (18c) A use created by implication and remaining with the grantor when the conveyance lacks consideration.

secondary use. See *shifting use.*

shifting use. (18c) A use arising from the occurrence of a certain event that terminates the preceding use. ● In the following example, C has a shifting use that arises when D makes the specified payment: "to A for the use of B, but then to C when D pays $1,000 to E." This is a type of conditional limitation. — Also termed *secondary use.* See *conditional limitation* under LIMITATION.

sole and separate use. See *entire use.*

springing use. (17c) A use arising on the occurrence of a future event. ● In the following

example, B has a springing use that vests when B marries: "to A for the use of B when B marries." — Also termed *executory use.*

use-based license. See LICENSE.

use/derivative-use immunity. See *use immunity* under IMMUNITY (3).

usee. See USE PLAINTIFF.

useful, *adj. Patents.* (Of an invention) having a practical application.

useful-article doctrine. See APPLIED-ART DOCTRINE.

useful life. (1923) The estimated length of time that depreciable property will generate income. ● Useful life is used to calculate depreciation and amortization deductions. — Also termed *depreciable life.* See DEPRECIATION METHOD.

use immunity. See IMMUNITY (3).

use in commerce. *Trademarks.* Actual use of a trademark in the advertising, marketing, promotion, sale, or distribution of goods or services. ● Use of a trademark in commerce is a prerequisite to trademark registration. Regular use demonstrates that the trademark has become associated with currently available goods or services, as contrasted with a token use intended to reserve some right to use the trademark in the future. For goods, a trademark is used in commerce if it is displayed on or with goods offered for sale, or placed on documents related to the goods. For services, a mark is used in commerce if it appears in advertising or on documents related to the services. In addition, the goods must be used or the services rendered in more than one state, because use of a trademark in interstate commerce is a prerequisite to federal trademark registration.

useless-gesture exception. (1970) *Criminal procedure.* An exception to the knock-and-announce rule whereby police are excused from having to announce their purpose before entering the premises to execute a warrant when it is evident from the circumstances that people inside the premises are of aware of the police officers' authority and purpose. See KNOCK-AND-ANNOUNCE RULE.

use plaintiff. *Common-law pleading.* A plaintiff for whom an action is brought in another's name. ● For example, when the use plaintiff is an assignee ("A") of a chose in action and sues in the assignor's name ("B"), the assignor's name appears first on the petition's title: "B for the Use of A against C." — Also termed *usee.*

user (yooz-ər). (15c) **1.** The exercise or employment of a right or property <the neighbor argued that an easement arose by his continuous user over the last 15 years>. Cf. NONUSER.

user de action (yoo-zər dak-shən). [Law French] The pursuing or bringing of an action.

2. Someone who uses a thing <the stapler's last user did not put it away>.

end user. (1963) The ultimate consumer for whom a product is designed.

user agreement. See POINT-AND-CLICK AGREEMENT.

user confusion. See CONSUMER CONFUSION.

user fee. (1967) A charge assessed for the use of a particular item or facility.

Uses, Statute of. See STATUTE OF USES.

use tax. See TAX.

use value. See VALUE (2).

use variance. See VARIANCE (2).

use zoning. See *Euclidean zoning* under ZONING.

USFSPA. *abbr.* UNIFORMED SERVICES FORMER SPOUSE PROTECTION ACT.

USFWS. *abbr.* UNITED STATES FISH AND WILDLIFE SERVICE.

USGS. *abbr.* UNITED STATES GEOLOGICAL SURVEY.

usher, *n. English law.* A court officer responsible for maintaining silence and order in some English courts, swearing in jurors and witnesses, and otherwise aiding the judge.

USIP. *abbr.* UNITED STATES INSTITUTE OF PEACE.

USITC. *abbr.* UNITED STATES INTERNATIONAL TRADE COMMISSION.

USMA. *abbr.* UNITED STATES MILITARY ACADEMY.

U.S. Magistrate. See UNITED STATES MAGISTRATE JUDGE.

USMC. *abbr.* UNITED STATES MARINE CORPS.

USMMA. *abbr.* See UNITED STATES MERCHANT MARINE ACADEMY.

USMS. *abbr.* UNITED STATES MARSHALS SERVICE.

USN. *abbr.* UNITED STATES NAVY.

USNA. *abbr.* See UNITED STATES NAVAL ACADEMY.

U.S. national. See *national of the United States* under NATIONAL.

U.S.-owned foreign corporation. See CORPORATION.

USPS. *abbr.* UNITED STATES POSTAL SERVICE.

USPTO. *abbr.* UNITED STATES PATENT AND TRADEMARK OFFICE.

usque ad coelum (əs-kwee ad **see**-ləm). [Latin] Up to the sky <the owner of land also owns the space above the surface *usque ad coelum*>.

USSG. *abbr.* UNITED STATES SENTENCING GUIDELINES.

USTDA. *abbr.* UNITED STATES TRADE AND DEVELOPMENT AGENCY.

USTR. *abbr.* UNITED STATE TRADE REPRESENTATIVE.

usual, *adj.* (14c) **1.** Ordinary; customary. **2.** Expected based on previous experience, or on a pattern or course of conduct to date.

usuary (**yoo**-zhoo-er-ee), *n. Civil law.* A person who has the use (*usus*) of a thing to satisfy personal and family needs; a beneficiary. — Also termed (in Roman law) *usuarius*.

usufruct (yoo-zə-frəkt), *n.* [fr. Latin *usufructus*] *Roman & civil law.* A right for a certain period to use and enjoy the fruits of another's property without damaging or diminishing it, but allowing for any natural deterioration in the property over time. ● In Roman law, the usufruct was considered a personal servitude, resulting in a real right. In modern civil law, the owner of the usufruct is similar to a life tenant, and the owner of the property burdened is known as the *naked owner*. La. Civ. Code art. 535. — Also termed *perfect usufruct*; *usufructus*; (in Scots law) *liferent*. Cf. HABITATION (3).

   legal usufruct. A usufruct established by operation of law, such as the right of a surviving spouse to property owned by the deceased spouse. La. Civ. Code art. 890.

   quasi-usufruct. **1.** A right to use property that cannot be used without being expended or consumed, such as money or food. ● Unlike an ordinary usufruct, a quasi-usufruct actually involves alteration and diminution of the property used. — Also termed *imperfect usufruct*. **2.** *Louisiana law.* A usufruct over consumable things, such as money or harvested crops, the value of which must be delivered to the naked owner at the end of the usufruct's term. La. Civ. Code art. 538. ● The usufructuary has the right to consume or alienate the consumables and, at the end of the usufruct, to deliver to the naked owner either the value that the things had when the usufruct began or things of the same quantity and quality.

usufructuary (yoo-zə-**frək**-choo-er-ee), *adj. Roman & civil law.* Of or relating to a usufruct; of the nature of a usufruct.

usufructuary, *n. Roman & civil law.* One having the right to a usufruct; specif., a person who has the right to the benefits of another's property; a life-renter.

usurious (yoo-z[y]**oor**-ee-əs *or* yoo-**zhuu**-ree-əs), *adj.* (17c) **1.** Practicing usury <a usurious lender>. **2.** Characterized by usury <a usurious contract>.

usurpation (yoo-sər-**pay**-shən *or* yoo-zər-**pay**-shən), *n.* (14c) The unlawful seizure and assumption of another's position, office, or authority. — **usurp** (yoo-**sərp** *or* yoo-**zərp**), *vb.*

usury (**yoo**-zhə-ree), *n.* (14c) **1.** Historically, the lending of money with interest. **2.** Today, the charging of an illegal rate of interest as a condition to lending money. **3.** An illegally high rate of interest. — Also termed *illegal interest*; *unlawful interest*. — **usurer** (**yoo**-zhər-ər), *n.*

usury law. A law prohibiting moneylenders from charging illegally high interest rates.

uterine (**yoo**-tər-in), *adj.* Born of the same mother but having different biological fathers.

uterine brother. See BROTHER.

uterine sister. See SISTER.

utilitarian-deterrence theory. (1983) The legal theory that a person should be punished only if the punishment benefits society — that is, only if the punishment would help to deter future harmful conduct. See *hedonistic utilitarianism* under UTILITARIANISM. Cf. RETRIBUTIVISM.

utilitarianism. (1827) The philosophical and economic doctrine that the best social policy is that which does the most good for the greatest number of people; esp., an ethical theory that judges the rightness or wrongness of actions according to the pleasure they create or the pain they inflict and recommends whatever action creates the greatest good for the greatest number of people. ● This is a type of consequentialism. For example, utilitarianism analyzes intellectual-property rights from the point of view of society rather than the individual inventor, author, or artist, and justifies the rights as an incentive for social and technological progress. See CONSEQUENTIALISM. Cf. LOCKEAN LABOR THEORY; PERSONALITY THEORY. — **utilitarian,** *adj.* & *n.*

    hedonistic utilitarianism. (1943) The theory that the validity of a law should be measured by determining the extent to which it promotes the greatest happiness to the greatest number of citizens. ● This theory is found most prominently in the work of Jeremy Bentham, whose "Benthamite utilitarianism" greatly influenced legal reform in nineteenth-century Britain. Hedonistic utilitarianism generally maintains that pleasure is intrinsically good and pain intrinsically bad. Therefore, inflicting pain on an individual, as by punishing a criminal, is justified only if it results in a net increase of pleasure for society by deterring future harmful behavior. — Also termed *Benthamism.* See *utilitarian-deterrence theory;* BENTHAMITE. Cf. RETRIBUTIVISM.

utility. (14c) **1.** The quality of serving some function that benefits society; meritoriousness. **2.** *Patents.* Capacity to perform a function or attain a result for which the patent applicant or holder claims protection as intellectual property. ● In patent law, utility is one of the three basic requirements of patentability, the others being nonobviousness and novelty. In the calculation of damages for patent infringement, utility is the benefit or advantage of the patented product or process over the products or processes, if any, that previously had been used to produce similar results. **3.** A business enterprise that performs an essential pub-lic service and that is subject to governmental regulation.

public utility. (1895) **1.** A company that provides necessary services to the public, such as telephone lines and service, electricity, and water. ● Most utilities operate as monopolies but are subject to governmental regulation. **2.** A person, corporation, or other association that carries on an enterprise for the accommodation of the public, the members of which are entitled as a matter of right to use the enterprises's facilities.

utility fund. See MUTUAL FUND.

utility model. *Patents.* A system of patent registration giving patent-like rights in some countries, usu. for a shorter term than a patent but with little or no search required. ● Utility-model registration is not available in the U.S. or Great Britain, but is offered in Japan and many European countries, including Germany and France. They are available for machines only, and not for chemicals. — Also termed *petty patent; second-tier patent; small invention.*

utility patent. See PATENT (3).

ut infra (ət **in**-frə *also* uut). [Latin] *Hist.* As below.

UTMA. *abbr.* UNIFORM TRANSFERS TO MINORS ACT.

utmost care. See *great care* under CARE.

UTSA. *abbr.* UNIFORM TRADE SECRETS ACT.

ut supra (ət **s**[**y**]**oo**-prə *also* uut). [Latin] *Hist.* As above.

utter, *adj.* (15c) Complete; absolute; total <an utter denial>.

utter, *vb.* (15c) **1.** To say, express, or publish <don't utter another word until your attorney is present>. **2.** To put or send (a document) into circulation; esp., to circulate (a forged note) as if genuine <she uttered a counterfeit $50 bill at the grocery store>. — **utterance** (for sense 1), **uttering** (for sense 2), *n.*

utter bar. See OUTER BAR.

utter barrister. See *outer barrister* under BARRISTER.

uttering. (18c) The crime of presenting a false or worthless instrument with the intent to harm or defraud. — Also termed *uttering a forged instrument.* See FORGERY.

uxor (ək-sor), *n.* [Latin] Wife. — Abbr. *ux.* See ET UXOR. Cf. VIR.

uxorial (ək-**sor**-ee-əl *or* əg-**zor**-), *adj.* Of, relating to, or characteristic of a wife <uxorial property>.

uxoricide (ək-**sor**-ə-sɪd *or* əg-**zor**-), *n.* (18c) **1.** The murder of one's wife. **2.** A man who murders his wife. Cf. MARITICIDE. — **uxoricidal,** *adj.*

V

v. *abbr.* **1.** VERSUS. — Also abbreviated *vs.* **2.** Volume. — Also abbreviated *vol.* **3.** Verb. — Also abbreviated *vb.* **4.** (*cap.*) Victoria — the Queen of England from 1837 to 1901. **5.** *Vide.* ● This Latin term, meaning "see," is used in phrases such as *quod vide* ("which see," abbreviated *q.v.*). **6.** *Voce* (**voh**-see). ● This Latin term means "voice."

VA. *abbr.* DEPARTMENT OF VETERANS AFFAIRS.

vacancy, *n.* **1.** The state or fact of a lack of occupancy in an office, post, or piece of property. **2.** The time during which an office, post, or piece of property is not occupied. **3.** An unoccupied office, post, or piece of property; an empty place. ● Although the term sometimes refers to an office or post that is temporarily filled, the more usual reference is to an office or post that is unfilled even temporarily. An officer's misconduct does not create a vacancy even if a suspension occurs; a vacancy, properly speaking, does not occur until the officer is officially removed.

vacancy clause. *Insurance.* A special indorsement allowing premises to be unoccupied beyond the period stipulated in the original insurance policy, so that the insurance remains in effect during policy extensions, often for a reduced amount.

vacant, *adj.* (13c) **1.** Empty; unoccupied <a vacant office>. ● Courts have sometimes distinguished *vacant* from *unoccupied*, holding that *vacant* means completely empty while *unoccupied* means not routinely characterized by the presence of human beings. **2.** Absolutely free, unclaimed, and unoccupied <vacant land>. **3.** (Of an estate) abandoned; having no heir or claimant. — The term implies either abandonment or nonoccupancy for any purpose.

vacantia (və-**kan**-sh[ee]-ə). See *bona vacantia* under BONA.

vacantia bona (və-**kan**-sh[ee]-ə **boh**-nə). See *bona vacantia* under BONA.

vacant succession. See SUCCESSION (2).

vacate, *vb.* (17c) **1.** To nullify or cancel; make void; invalidate <the court vacated the judgment>. Cf. OVERRULE. **2.** To surrender occupancy or possession; to move out or leave <the tenant vacated the premises>.

vacatio (və-**kay**-shee-oh). *Civil law.* Exemption; immunity; privilege; dispensation.

vacation, *n.* (15c) **1.** The act of vacating <vacation of the office> <vacation of the court's order>. **2.** The period between the end of one term of court and the beginning of the next; the space of time during which a court holds no sessions. ● The

traditional vacations in England were Christmas vacation, beginning December 24 and ending January 6; Easter vacation, beginning Good Friday and ending Easter Tuesday; Whitsun vacation, beginning on the Saturday immediately before and ending the Tuesday immediately after Whitsunday (i.e., Pentecost, the seventh Sunday after Easter); and the long vacation, beginning August 13 and ending October 23. **3.** Loosely, any time when a given court is not in session. **4.** *Eccles. law.* The act or process by which a church or benefice becomes vacant, as on the death or resignation of the incumbent, until a successor is appointed. — Also termed (in sense 4) *vacatura*.

vacation barrister. See BARRISTER.

vacatur (və-**kay**-tər), *n.* [Law Latin "it is vacated"] (17c) **1.** The act of annulling or setting aside. **2.** A rule or order by which a proceeding is vacated.

vadimonium (vad-ə-**moh**-nee-əm), *n.* *Roman law.* **1.** A guarantee (originally backed by sureties) that a litigant would appear in court. **2.** A solemn promise to this effect. — Also termed *vadimony.*

vadium (**vay**-dee-əm), *n.* [Law Latin "pledge, bail, security"] *Hist.* **1.** Security by a pledge of property.

vadium mortuum (**vay**-dee-əm **mor**-choo-əm). [Law Latin "dead pledge"] A mortgage. ● This was considered a "dead pledge" because an estate was given as security by the borrower, who granted to the lender the estate in fee, on the condition that if the money were not repaid at the specified time, the pledged estate would continue as the lender's — it would be gone from, or "dead" to, the borrower (mortgagor). — Also termed *mortuum vadium.* See MORTGAGE.

vadium vivum (**vay**-dee-əm **vi**-vəm). [Law Latin "live pledge"] A living pledge, which exists when an estate is granted by a borrower to a lender until a debt is paid out of the estate's proceeds. ● The pledge was so called because neither the money nor the lands were lost; it was a "living pledge" because the profits of the land were constantly paying off the debt. — Also termed *vivum vadium; vif-gage.*

2. Wages; salary.

vagabond (**vag**-ə-bond), *n.* *Archaic.* A homeless wanderer without any means or an honest livelihood; VAGRANT. ● This term became archaic over the course of the 20th century, as vagrants won the right not to be forcibly removed from cities in such cases as *Papachristou v. City of Jacksonville,* 405 U.S. 156, 92 S.Ct. 839 (1972). In the 1980s and 1990s, vagabonds came to be known as *street* *people* and *homeless people*, or *the homeless.* — Also termed *vagabundus* (vag-ə-**bən**-dəs).

vagabondage (vag-ə-bon-dij). **1.** The condition of a vagabond. **2.** Vagabonds as a class. — Also termed (in sense 1) *vagabondism*; (in senses 1 & 2) *vagabondry.*

vagrancy (vay-grən-see), *n.* (17c) **1.** The state or condition of wandering from place to place without a home, job, or means of support. • Vagrancy is generally considered a course of conduct or a manner of living, rather than a single act. But under some statutes, a single act has been held sufficient to constitute vagrancy. One court held, for example, that the act of prowling about and creeping up on parked cars and their occupants at night, under circumstances suggesting an intent to commit a crime, constitutes vagrancy. See *Smith v. Drew,* 26 P.2d 1040 (Wash. 1933). Many state laws prohibiting vagrancy have been declared unconstitutionally vague. — Also termed *vagrantism.* **2.** An instance of such wandering. Cf. LOITERING.

vagrant, *adj.* (15c) **1.** Of, relating to, or characteristic of a vagrant; inclined to vagrancy. **2.** Nomadically homeless.

vagrant, *n.* (15c) **1.** At common law, anyone belonging to the several classes of idle or disorderly persons, rogues, and vagabonds. **2.** One who, not having a settled habitation, strolls from place to place; a homeless, idle wanderer. • The term often refers to one who spends time in idleness, lacking any property and without any visible means of support. Under some statutes, a vagrant is an offender against or menace to the public peace, usu. liable to become a public burden. Cf. VAGABOND.

vagrantism. See VAGRANCY.

vague, *adj.* (16c) **1.** Imprecise; not sharply outlined; indistinct; uncertain.

    unconstitutionally vague. **1.** (Of a penal legislative provision) so unclear and indefinite as not to give a person of ordinary intelligence the opportunity to know what is prohibited, restricted, or required. **2.** (Of a statute) impermissibly delegating basic policy matters to administrators and judges so such a degree as to lead to arbitrary and discriminatory application.

2. (Of language) describing a distribution around a central norm, as opposed to a neatly bounded class; broadly indefinite; not clearly or concretely expressed. **3.** Characterized by haziness of thought.

vague-and-indefinite rejection. See REJECTION.

vagueness. (18c) **1.** Uncertain breadth of meaning <the phrase "within a reasonable time" is plagued by vagueness — what is reasonable?>. • Though common in writings generally, vagueness raises due-process concerns if legislation does not provide fair notice of what is required, restricted, or prohibited, because enforcement may become arbitrary. **2.** Loosely, ambiguity. See AMBIGUITY.

vagueness doctrine. (1957) *Constitutional law.* The doctrine — based on the Due Process Clause — requiring that a criminal statute state explicitly and definitely what acts are prohibited or restricted, so as to provide fair warning and preclude arbitrary enforcement. — Also termed *void-for-vagueness doctrine.* See *void for vagueness* under VOID. Cf. OVERBREADTH DOCTRINE.

valid, *adj.* (16c) **1.** Legally sufficient; binding <a valid contract>. **2.** Meritorious <that is a valid conclusion based on the facts presented in this case>. — **validate,** *vb.* — **validation, validity,** *n.*

valid agreement. See *valid contract* under CONTRACT.

validating statute. See STATUTE.

valid contract. See CONTRACT.

validity opinion. See OPINION (2).

validity search. An exhaustive search for prior art or any other facts that can be used to invalidate a patent. See BREAKING A PATENT. Cf. INFRINGEMENT SEARCH; PATENTABILITY SEARCH.

valid judgment. See JUDGMENT.

valid marriage. See MARRIAGE (1).

valid warrant. See WARRANT (1).

valise diplomatique (və-**lees** di-ploh-ma-**teek**). See DIPLOMATIC POUCH.

Vallescura rule. *Maritime law.* The holding that when a maritime loss is due to more than one cause, and the carrier is exempt from liability for at least one of them, the burden is on the carrier to prove what loss is due to the exempt cause. • If the carrier fails to prove the exemption, it is liable for the entire loss. *Schnell v. The Vallescura,* 293 U.S. 296, 55 S.Ct. 194 (1934).

VA loan. See *veteran's loan* under LOAN.

valor (**val**-ər), *n.* [Latin] *Hist.* Value; worth; rate; a valuation. — Also spelled (esp. in BrE) *valour.* See AD VALOREM.

valuable, *adj.* Worth a good price; having financial or market value.

valuable consideration. See CONSIDERATION (1).

valuable improvement. See IMPROVEMENT.

valuable papers. Documents that, upon a person's death, are important in carrying out the decedent's wishes and in managing the estate's affairs. • Examples include a will, title documents, stock certificates, powers of attorney, letters to be opened on one's death, and the like. Some statutes require that, to be effective, a holographic will devising realty must be found among the decedent's valuable papers.

valuable-papers insurance. See INSURANCE.

valuation, *n.* (16c) **1.** The process of determining the value of a thing or entity. **2.** The estimated worth of a thing or entity. — **value, valuate,** *vb.*

assessed valuation. (1825) The value that a taxing authority gives to property and to which the tax rate is applied.

special-use valuation. (1976) An executor's option of valuating real property in an estate, esp. farmland, based on its current use rather than for its highest potential value.

valuation date. See ALTERNATE VALUATION DATE.

valuation list. *Hist.* An inventory of all the ratable hereditaments in a parish, each item in the inventory recording the name of the occupier, the owner, the property, the extent of the property, the gross estimated rental, and the ratable value. • The list was traditionally prepared by the overseers of each parish.

value, *n.* (14c) **1.** The significance, desirability, or utility of something.

social value. The significance, desirability, or utility of something to the general public.

2. The monetary worth or price of something; the amount of goods, services, or money that something commands in an exchange.

actual cash value. *Insurance.* **1.** Replacement cost minus normal depreciation. **2.** See *fair market value.*

actual market value. See *fair market value.*

actual value. See *fair market value.*

agreed value. A property's value that is fixed by agreement of the parties, esp. the property's owner and the person or entity valuating the property. • An example is a list of property values contained in an insurance policy.

annual value. 1. The net yearly income derivable from a given piece of property. **2.** One year's rental value of property, less the costs and expenses of maintaining the property.

assessed value. The value of an asset as determined by an appraiser for tax purposes.

book value. See BOOK VALUE.

cash surrender value. *Insurance.* The amount of money payable when an insurance policy having cash value, such as a whole-life policy, is redeemed before maturity or death. — Abbr. CSV. — Also termed *surrender value; cash value.*

cash value. 1. See *fair market value.* **2.** See *full cash value.* **3.** See *cash surrender value.*

clear annual value. The net annual value of property, after payment of taxes, interest on mortgages, and other charges.

clear market value. See *fair market value.*

clear value. *Tax.* For purposes of an inheritance tax, whatever remains of an estate after all claims against it have been paid.

commuted value (kə-**myoo**-tid). **1.** In the assessment of damages, the present value of a future interest in property. **2.** The value of future payments when discounted to their present value.

enterprise value. A measure of a company's market value, calculated by aggregating the value of the company's market capitalization, debt, and preferred stock, and subtracting cash and cash equivalents.

exchange value. The amount of money for which property or services could be exchanged or procured if there is a ready market continually resorted to by traders — or, in the absence of such a market, the amount that could be obtained in the usual course of finding a purchaser or hirer of similar property or services.

fair market value. (18c) The price that a seller is willing to accept and a buyer is willing to pay on the open market and in an arm's-length transaction; the point at which supply and demand intersect. — Abbr. FMV. — Also termed *actual value; actual cash value; actual market value; cash value; clear market value; fair and reasonable value; fair cash market value; fair cash value; fair market price; fair value; full value; just value; market value; salable value; true value.*

fair value. See *fair market value.*

full cash value. Market value for property tax purposes; estimated value derived by standard appraisal methods. — Also termed *cash value.*

full value. See *fair market value.*

future value. The value, at some future time, of a present sum or a series of monetary payments, calculated at a specific interest rate.

going-concern value. The value of a commercial enterprise's assets or of the enterprise itself as an active business with future earning power, as opposed to the liquidation value of the business or of its assets. • Going-concern value includes, for example, goodwill. — Also termed *going value.* Cf. GOODWILL.

highest proved value. In a trover action, the greatest value (as proved by the plaintiff) that the converted property reached from the time of the conversion until trial. • It is the highest amount that a plaintiff is entitled to recover.

insurable value. See INSURABLE VALUE.

intrinsic value. The inherent value of a thing, without any special features that might alter its market value. • The intrinsic value of a silver coin, for example, is simply the value of the silver within it.

just value. See *fair market value.*

liquidation value. 1. The value of a business or of an asset when it is sold in liquidation, as opposed to being sold in the ordinary course of business. **2.** See *liquidation price* under PRICE.

market value. See *fair market value.*

most-suitable-use value. See *optimal-use value.*

net value. 1. *Insurance.* The excess of a policyholder payments over the yearly cost of insurance; the part of an insured's annual premium that, according to actuarial tables, the insurer must set aside to meet the insurer's obligations to the insured. — Also termed *reserve.* **2.** The fair market value of shares of stock.

new value. 1. A value that is newly given or freshly calculated. **2.** The value obtained by taking a security, such as collateral, for any debt other than a preexisting one.

optimal-use value. *Tax.* The highest and best use of a thing from an economic standpoint. • If a farm would be worth more as a shopping center than as a farm, the shopping-center value will control even if the transferee (that is, a donee or heir) continues to use the property as a farm. — Also termed *most-suitable-use value.*

par value. See PAR VALUE.

policy value. See POLICY VALUE.

present value. See PRESENT VALUE.

residual value. See *salvage value.*

salable value. See *fair market value.*

salvage value. (1917) The value of an asset after it has become useless to the owner; the amount expected to be obtained when a fixed asset is disposed of at the end of its useful life. • Salvage value is used, under some depreciation methods, to determine the allowable tax deduction for depreciation. And under the UCC, when a buyer of goods breaches or repudiates the contract of sale, the seller may, under certain circumstances, either complete the manufacture of any incomplete goods or cease the manufacture and sell the partial product for scrap or salvage value. UCC § 2-704(2). — Also termed *residual value; scrap value.* See DEPRECIATION.

scrap value. See *salvage value.*

settlement value. The value of a claim if the claimant settles immediately as opposed to pursuing the claim further through litigation.

surrender value. See *cash surrender value.*

true value. See *fair market value.*

use value. A value established by the utility of an object instead of its sale or exchange value.

value received. See VALUE RECEIVED.

3. Sufficient contractual consideration. — **value,** *vb.* — **valuation,** *n.*

value-added card. See STORED-VALUE CARD.

value-added model. See LABOR-DESERT MODEL.

value-added tax. See TAX.

value date. The date when the proceeds of a bill of exchange (e.g., a check) or of a foreign-exchange transaction (e.g., a sale of dollars for euros) become available for use. — Also termed *here and there.*

valued policy. See INSURANCE POLICY.

valued-policy law. A statute requiring insurance companies to pay the full amount of the insurance to the insured in the event of a total loss, regardless of the true value of the property at the time of loss.

value fund. See MUTUAL FUND.

valuer. See APPRAISER.

value received. (17c) Consideration that has been delivered. • This phrase is commonly used in a bill of exchange or promissory note to show that it was supported by consideration.

VA mortgage. See MORTGAGE.

vandal. [fr. Latin *Vandalus*, a member of the Germanic tribe known as Vandals] (17c) A malicious destroyer or defacer of works of art, monuments, buildings, or other property.

vandalism, *n.* (18c) **1.** Willful or ignorant destruction of public or private property, esp. of artistic, architectural, or literary treasures. **2.** The actions or attitudes of one who maliciously or ignorantly destroys or disfigures public or private property; active hostility to anything that is venerable or beautiful. — **vandalize,** *vb.* — **vandalistic,** *adj.*

vara (**vah**-rah). *Spanish-Am. law.* A measure of length equal to about 33 inches. • Local usage varies, so that a vara may sometimes be more and sometimes less than 33 inches. In Mexican land grants, the measure is equal to 32.9927 inches. The term is often found in old land grants in states that were formed from land governed by Spain or Mexico.

variable annuity. See ANNUITY.

variable annuity contract. See CONTRACT.

variable cost. See COST (1).

variable life insurance. See LIFE INSURANCE.

variable rate. See INTEREST RATE.

variable-rate mortgage. See *adjustable-rate mortgage* under MORTGAGE.

variance. (14c) **1.** A difference or disparity between two statements or documents that ought to agree; esp., in criminal procedure, a difference between the allegations in a charging instrument and the proof actually introduced at trial. — Also termed *variation*.

fatal variance. (18c) A variance that either deprives the defendant of fair notice of the charges or exposes the defendant to the risk of double jeopardy. • A fatal variance is grounds for reversing a conviction.

immaterial variance. (18c) A variance too slight to mislead or prejudice the defendant and is thus harmless error.

2. A license or official authorization to depart from a zoning law. — Also termed (in sense 2) *zoning variance*. See HARDSHIP (4). Cf. SPECIAL EXCEPTION (2); SPECIAL-USE PERMIT.

area variance. A variance permitting deviation from zoning requirements about construction and placement, but not from requirements about use.

use variance. A variance permitting deviation from zoning requirements about use.

vassal (vas-əl), *n.* [fr. Law Latin *vassallus*] *Hist.* The grantee of a fief, feud, or fee; a feudal tenant. Cf. FREEMAN (5).

arriere vassal (a-ree-**air** vas-əl). *Hist.* The vassal of a vassal.

vassalage (vas-əl-ij), *n. Hist.* **1.** The state of being a vassal or feudatory. — Also termed *vasseleria*. **2.** The service required of a vassal. — Also termed *vassaticum; main-rent*. **3.** The territory held by a vassal; a fief or fee. **4.** Vassals collectively. **5.** The dominion or authority of a feudal superior over vassals. **6.** Political servility; subjection.

vassal state. *Int'l law.* A state that possesses only those rights and privileges that have been granted to it by a more powerful state.

vastum (vas-təm), *n. Hist.* WASTE.

VAT. See *value-added tax* under TAX.

Vaughn index. A comprehensive list of all documents that the government wants to shield from disclosure in Freedom of Information Act (FOIA) litigation, each document being accompanied by a statement of justification for nondisclosure. • Supported by one or more affidavits, a *Vaughn* index has three purposes: (1) forcing the government to scrutinize all material withheld; (2) enabling the trial court to fulfill its duty of ruling on the factual basis of each claimed FOIA exemption; and (3) enabling the adversary system to operate by giving the requester as much information as possible. 5 USCA § 552 et seq. The name derives from *Vaughn v. Reese*, 484 F.2d 820 (D.C. Cir. 1973).

VAWA. *abbr.* VIOLENCE AGAINST WOMEN ACT.

VC. *abbr.* VICE-CHANCELLOR.

v.e. *abbr.* VENDITIONI EXPONAS.

vectigal (vek-**tı**-gəl), *n. Roman & civil law.* **1.** A tax, esp. an import or export duty, paid to the state. **2.** An annual ground rent paid in kind or in money. Pl. **vectigalia** (vek-tə-**gay**-lee-ə).

vectigal judiciarium (vek-**tı**-gəl joo-dish-ee-**air**-ee-əm), *n.* A tax or fine to defray the expenses of maintaining courts of justice. Pl. **vectigalia judiciaria.**

veggie-libel law. *Slang.* See AGRICULTURAL-DISPARAGEMENT LAW.

vehicle (vee-ə-kəl), *n.* **1.** An instrument of transportation or conveyance. **2.** Any conveyance used in transporting passengers or things by land, water, or air.

vehicular (vee-**hik**-yə-lər), *adj.* Of, relating to, or caused by a vehicle or vehicles.

vehicular homicide. See HOMICIDE.

veil-piercing. See PIERCING THE CORPORATE VEIL.

vein, *n. Mining law.* A continuous body of mineral or mineralized rock, filling a seam or fissure in the earth's crust, within defined boundaries that clearly separate it from surrounding rock.

discovery vein. The primary vein for the purpose of locating a mining claim.

vel non (vel **non**). [Latin "or not"] (1895) Or the absence of it (or them) <this case turns solely on the finding of discrimination vel non>.

venal (vee-nəl), *adj.* (17c) **1.** (Of a person) capable of being bribed. **2.** Ready to sell one's services or influence for money or other valuable consideration, usu. for base motives. **3.** Of, relating to, or characterized by corrupt bargaining. **4.** Broadly, purchasable; for sale.

vend, *vb.* (17c) **1.** To transfer to another for money or something else of value. • The term is not commonly applied to real estate, although its derivatives (*vendor* and *vendee*) are. **2.** To make an object of trade, esp. by hawking or peddling. **3.** To utter publicly; to say or state; to publish broadly.

vendee. (16c) A purchaser, usu. of real property; a buyer.

vendee's lien. See LIEN.

vendetta (ven-**det**-ə), *n.* (1855) A private blood feud in which family members seek revenge on one or more persons outside the family (often members of another family); esp., a private war in which the nearest of kin seek revenge for the slaying of a relative.

vend. ex. *abbr.* VENDITIONI EXPONAS.

vendible, *adj.* Salable; fit or suitable to be sold.

vendition, *n.* The act of selling; a sale. — Also termed *venditio*.

venditioni exponas (ven-dish-ee-**oh**-nı eks-**poh**-nəs). [Latin "you are to expose for sale"] A writ of execution requiring a sale of particular goods to be made. • The writ is directed to a sheriff who has levied upon goods under a *fieri facias* but has reported that the goods remain unsold for lack of buyers. In some jurisdictions, a *venditioni exponas* is issued to require a sale of property seized under an earlier writ, after the property has been condemned or passed upon by inquisition. — Abbr. *vend. ex.*; *v.*

venditor (ven-də-tər), *n. Hist.* See VENDOR.

vendor. A seller, usu. of real property. — Also termed *venditor.*

itinerant vendor. A vendor who travels from place to place selling goods.

vendor's lien. See LIEN.

vendue (ven-**d[y]oo** *or* **ven**-d[y]oo). *Hist.* **1.** A sale; esp., a sale at public auction. **2.** See *execution sale* under SALE.

venereal disease. See SEXUALLY TRANSMITTED DISEASE.

venery (**ven**-ə-ree). *Archaic.* **1.** Hunting. **2.** Sexual intercourse.

Venetian patent statute. *Hist.* A law enacted in Venice in 1474, giving an inventor the exclusive right to make and use an invention for 10 years. • This was the first known patent law, with procedures for securing and enforcing the inventor's right to exclude others from working, using, or benefiting from the invention.

venial (**vee**-nee-əl), *adj.* (14c) (Of a transgression) forgivable; pardonable.

venire (və-**nɪ**-ree *or* -**neer**-ee *or* -**nɪr** *or* -**neer**). (1807) **1.** A panel of persons selected for jury duty and from among whom the jurors are to be chosen. — Also termed *array*; *jury panel*; *jury pool.*

special venire. A panel of citizens summoned when there is an unexpected need for a larger pool from which to select jurors, or a panel summoned for a particular (usu. capital) case.

2. VENIRE FACIAS.

venire de novo. See *venire facias de novo* under VENIRE FACIAS.

venire facias (və-**nɪ**-ree [*or* -**neer**-ee *or* -**nɪr** *or* -**neer**] **fay**-shee-əs). (15c) A writ directing a sheriff to assemble a jury. — Often shortened to *venire.* — Also termed *venire facias juratores* (juur-ə-**tor**-eez).

venire facias ad respondendum (ad ree-spon-**den**-dəm). A writ requiring a sheriff to summon a person against whom an indictment for a misdemeanor has been issued. • A warrant is now more commonly used.

venire facias de novo (dee *or* di **noh**-voh). (18c) A writ for summoning a jury panel anew because of some impropriety or irregularity in the original jury's return or verdict such that a judgment

cannot be entered on it. • The result of a new venire is a new trial. In substance, the writ is a motion for a new trial, but when the party objects to the verdict because of a procedural error (and not an error on the merits), the form of motion was traditionally for a venire facias de novo. — Often shortened to *venire de novo.*

veniremember (və-**nɪ**-ree-mem-bər *or* və-**neer**-ee- *or* və-**neer**-). (1966) A prospective juror; a member of a jury panel. — Also termed *venireman; venireperson; talesman.* See TALESMAN.

venit et dicit (**vee**-nit et **dɪ**-sit). [Latin] Comes and says. • The phrase appeared in old-style pleadings. Remnants of the phrase still occur in some American jurisdictions: *Now comes the plaintiff, and respectfully says . . . .*

venter (**ven**-tər), *n.* [Latin "womb"] **1.** The womb of a wife or mother. **2.** One of two or more women who are sources of the same man's offspring.

venture. (16c) An undertaking that involves risk; esp., a speculative commercial enterprise. Cf. JOINT VENTURE.

venture capital. See CAPITAL.

venturer, *n.* (16c) **1.** One who risks something, and hopes to gain more, in a business enterprise. **2.** One who participates in an association of two or more parties in a business enterprise. See JOINT VENTURE.

venue (**ven**-yoo). [Law French "coming"] (16c) *Procedure.* **1.** The proper or a possible place for a lawsuit to proceed, usu. because the place has some connection either with the events that gave rise to the lawsuit or with the plaintiff or defendant. **2.** The territory, such as a country or other political subdivision, over which a trial court has jurisdiction. Cf. JURISDICTION (1), (2). **3.** Loosely, the place where a conference or meeting is being held. **4.** In a pleading, the statement establishing the place for trial. **5.** In an affidavit, the designation of the place where it was made.

venue, change of. See CHANGE OF VENUE.

venue facts. (1936) Facts that need to be pleaded or established in a hearing to determine whether venue is proper in a given court.

veracious (və-**ray**-shəs), *adj.* (17c) Truthful; accurate. — Also termed *veridical.*

veracity (və-**ras**-ət-ee), *n.* (17c) **1.** Truthfulness <the witness's fraud conviction supports the defense's challenge to his veracity>. **2.** Accuracy <you called into question the veracity of Murphy's affidavit>. — **veracious** (və-**ray**-shəs), *adj.*

verbal, *adj.* (15c) **1.** Of, relating to, or expressed in words. **2.** Loosely, of, relating to, or expressed in spoken words.

verbal abuse. See ABUSE.

verbal act. See ACT (2).

verbal-act doctrine. (1901) The rule that utterances accompanying conduct that might have legal effect are admissible when the conduct is material to the issue and is equivocal in nature, and when the words help give the conduct its legal significance.

verbal contract. See *parol contract* (1) under CONTRACT.

verbal note. *Diplomacy.* An unsigned memorandum informally reminding an official of a pending request, an unanswered question, or the like.

vertical stare decisis. See STARE DECISIS.

verbal will. See *nuncupative will* under WILL.

verbatim (vər-**bay**-təm), *adj.* & *adv.* [fr. Latin *verbum* "word"] Word for word. ● Courts have repeatedly held that, in the context of the requirement that a trial record must be "verbatim," absolute word-for-word accuracy is not necessary — and insubstantial omissions do not make a transcript "nonverbatim."

verdict. (15c) **1.** A jury's finding or decision on the factual issues of a case. **2.** Loosely, in a nonjury trial, a judge's resolution of the issues of a case.

chance verdict. (1820) A now-illegal verdict, arrived at by hazard or lot. — Also termed *gambling verdict*; *verdict by lot.*

compromise verdict. (1851) A verdict reached when jurors, to avoid a deadlock, concede some issues so that other issues will be resolved as they want.

defective verdict. (18c) A verdict on which a judgment cannot be based because of irregularities or legal inadequacies.

directed verdict. (1912) A ruling by a trial judge taking a case from the jury because the evidence will permit only one reasonable verdict. — Also termed *instructed verdict.*

excessive verdict. (1817) A verdict resulting from the jury's passion or prejudice and thereby shocks the court's conscience.

false verdict. *Archaic.* A verdict so contrary to the evidence and so unjust that the judge may set it aside.

gambling verdict. See *chance verdict.*

general verdict. (17c) A verdict by which the jury finds in favor of one party or the other, as opposed to resolving specific fact questions. Cf. *special verdict.*

general verdict subject to a special case. *Archaic.* A court's verdict rendered without regard to the jury's general verdict, given when a party does not want to put the legal question on the record but merely wants the court to decide on the basis of a written statement of all the facts in the case, prepared for the opinion of the court by counsel on either side, according to the principles of a special verdict, whereupon the court decides the special case submitted and gives judgment accordingly.

general verdict with interrogatories. (1878) A general verdict accompanied by answers to written interrogatories on one or more issues of fact that bear on the verdict.

guilty verdict. (18c) A jury's finding that a defendant is guilty of the offense charged.

instructed verdict. See *directed verdict.*

joint verdict. (1825) A verdict covering two or more parties to a lawsuit.

legally inconsistent verdict. (1975) A verdict in which the same element is found to exist and not to exist, as when a defendant is acquitted of one offense and convicted of another, even though the offenses arise from the same set of facts and an element of the second offense requires proof that the first offense has been committed. — Also termed *legal inconsistency.* Cf. *repugnant verdict.*

majority verdict. A verdict agreed to by all but one or two jury members. ● In some jurisdictions, a civil verdict supported by 10 of 12 jurors is acceptable.

open verdict. A verdict of a coroner's jury finding that the subject "came to his death by means to the jury unknown" or "came to his death at the hands of a person or persons to the jury unknown." ● This verdict leaves open either the question whether any crime was committed or the identity of the criminal.

partial verdict. (1829) A verdict by which a jury finds a criminal defendant not guilty of some charges and guilty of other charges.

perverse verdict. (1870) A jury verdict so contrary to the evidence that it justifies the granting of a new trial.

privy verdict (**priv**-ee). *Hist.* A verdict given after the judge has left or adjourned the court, and the jury, having agreed, obtains leave to give its verdict privately to the judge out of court so that the jurors can be delivered from their confinement. ● Such a verdict was of no force unless afterwards affirmed in open court. This practice has been superseded by that of rendering a sealed verdict. See *sealed verdict.*

public verdict. (17c) A verdict delivered by the jury in open court.

quotient verdict. (1867) An improper damage verdict that a jury arrives at by totaling what each juror would award and dividing by the number of jurors.

repugnant verdict. (1883) A verdict that contradicts itself in that the defendant is convicted and acquitted of different crimes having identical elements. • Sometimes the inconsistency occurs in a single verdict (*repugnant verdict*), and sometimes it occurs in two separate verdicts (*repugnant verdicts*). Both terms are used mainly in New York. Cf. *legally inconsistent verdict.*

responsive verdict. *Civil law.* A verdict that properly answers the indictment with specific findings prescribed by statute, the possible findings being guilty, not guilty, and guilty of a lesser included offense.

sealed verdict. (18c) A written verdict put into a sealed envelope when the jurors have agreed on their decision but court is not in session or the jury is continuing to deliberate other counts. • Upon delivering a sealed verdict, the jurors may separate. When court convenes again, this verdict is officially returned with the same effect as if the jury had returned it in open court before separating.

special verdict. (17c) A verdict in which the jury makes findings only on factual issues submitted to them by the judge, who then decides the legal effect of the verdict. *See* Fed. R. Civ. P. 49. Cf. *general verdict.*

split verdict. (1886) **1.** A verdict in which one party prevails on some claims, while the other party prevails on others. **2.** *Criminal law.* A verdict finding a defendant guilty on one charge but not guilty on another. **3.** *Criminal law.* A verdict of guilty for one defendant and of not guilty for a codefendant.

true verdict. (16c) A verdict that is reached voluntarily — even if one or more jurors freely compromise their views — and not as a result of an arbitrary rule or order, whether imposed by the jurors themselves, the court, or a court officer.

verdict by lot. See *chance verdict.*

verdict contrary to law. (18c) A verdict that the law does not authorize a jury to render because the conclusion drawn is not justified by the evidence. — Also termed *wrong verdict.* Cf. JURY NULLIFICATION.

verdict subject to opinion of court. (1820) A verdict that is subject to the court's determination of a legal issue reserved to the court upon the trial, so that judgment is ultimately entered depending on the court's ruling on a point of law.

wrong verdict. See *verdict contrary to law.*

veredicto. See NON OBSTANTE VEREDICTO.

veredictum (ver-ə-**dik**-təm), *n. Hist.* A verdict; a declaration of the truth of a matter in issue, submitted to a jury for trial.

verge (vərj), *n. Hist.* **1.** The area within 12 miles of the place where the king held his court and within which the king's peace was enforced. •

This area was commonly referred to as being *in the verge.* The verge got its name from the staff (called a "verge") that the marshal bore. **2.** The compass of the royal court, within which the lord steward and marshal of the king's household had special jurisdiction. — Also termed (in senses 1 & 2) *Court of Verge.* **3.** The neighborhood of Whitehall, the section of London in which British government offices have traditionally been located. **4.** An uncertain quantity of land from 15 to 30 acres. **5.** A stick or rod by which a person, after holding the stick and swearing fealty, is admitted as a tenant to a copyhold estate. — Also spelled *virge.* For *tenant by the verge,* see COPYHOLDER.

verger, *n.* One who carries a verge (a rod) as an emblem of office; esp., an attendant on a bishop or justice.

veridical (və-**rid**-ə-kəl). See VERACIOUS.

verification, *n.* (16c) **1.** A formal declaration made in the presence of an authorized officer, such as a notary public, or (in some jurisdictions) under oath but not in the presence of such an officer, whereby one swears to the truth of the statements in the document. • Traditionally, a verification is used as a conclusion for all pleadings that are required to be sworn. Cf. ACKNOWLEDGMENT (4). — Also termed *affidavit of verification.* **2.** An oath or affirmation that an authorized officer administers to an affiant or deponent. **3.** Loosely, ACKNOWLEDGMENT (5). **4.** See *certified copy* under COPY. **5.** CERTIFICATE OF AUTHORITY (1). **6.** Any act of notarizing. Cf. JURAT (1). — **verify,** *vb.* — **verifier,** *n.*

verified copy. See *certified copy* under COPY.

verify, *vb.* **1.** To prove to be true; to confirm or establish the truth or truthfulness of; to authenticate. **2.** To confirm or substantiate by oath or affidavit; to swear to the truth of.

verily, *adv. Archaic.* Truly; in fact; certainly.

verity (**ver**-ə-tee). (14c) Truth; truthfulness; conformity to fact.

versus, *prep.* (15c) Against. — Abbr. v.; vs.

vertical competition. See COMPETITION.

vertical equality. In per capita distribution of an estate, parity of distribution among children's families. See PER CAPITA. Cf. HORIZONTAL EQUALITY.

vertical integration. See INTEGRATION (5).

vertical merger. See MERGER.

vertical nonprivity. See NONPRIVITY.

vertical price-fixing. See PRICE-FIXING.

vertical privity. See PRIVITY.

vertical restraint. See RESTRAINT OF TRADE.

vertical stare decisis. See STARE DECISIS.

vertical trust. *Antitrust.* A combination that gathers together under a single ownership a number of businesses or plants engaged in successive stages of production or marketing.

vertical union. See *industrial union* under UNION.

very heavy work. See WORK (1).

VESA. *abbr.* VIDEO ELECTRONICS STANDARDS ASSOCIATION.

vessel. A ship, brig, sloop, or other craft used — or capable of being used — to navigate on water. • To qualify as a vessel under the Jones Act, the structure's purpose must to some reasonable degree be to transport passengers, cargo, or equipment from place to place across navigable waters.

foreign vessel. A vessel owned by residents of, or sailing under the flag of, a foreign nation.

Jones Act vessel. A vessel whose crew members can qualify as seamen under the Jones Act; esp., a craft designed or used for transporting cargo or people on navigable waters, or that was being used for navigation at the time of a worker's injury. See JONES ACT.

public vessel. A vessel owned and used by a nation or government for its public service, whether in its navy, its revenue service, or otherwise. See PUBLIC VESSELS ACT.

seagoing vessel. A vessel that — considering its design, function, purpose, and capabilities — is normally expected both to carry passengers for hire and to engage in substantial operations beyond the boundary line (set by the Coast Guard) dividing inland waters from the high seas. • Typically excluded from the definition are pleasure yachts, tugs and towboats, fishing boats, and other vessels that do not carry passengers for hire.

seaworthy vessel. A vessel that can withstand the ordinary stress of the wind, waves, and other weather that seagoing vessels might ordinarily be expected to encounter. • In some legal contexts, the question whether a vessel is seaworthy includes the question whether it is fit to carry an intended cargo properly. Under federal maritime law, a vessel's owner has the duty to provide a crew with a seaworthy vessel. See SEAWORTHY.

vest, *vb.* (15c) **1.** To confer ownership (of property) upon a person. **2.** To invest (a person) with the full title to property. **3.** To give (a person) an immediate, fixed right of present or future enjoyment. **4.** *Hist.* To put (a person) into possession of land by the ceremony of investiture. — **vesting,** *n.*

vested, *adj.* (18c) Having become a completed, consummated right for present or future enjoyment; not contingent; unconditional; absolute <a vested interest in the estate>.

vested in interest. (18c) Consummated in a way that will result in future possession and use. • Reversions, vested remainders, and any other future use or executory devise that does not depend on an uncertain period or event are all said to be vested in interest.

vested in possession. (18c) Consummated in a way that has resulted in present enjoyment.

vested estate. See ESTATE (1).

vested gift. See GIFT.

vested interest. See INTEREST (2).

vested legacy. See LEGACY.

vested ownership. See OWNERSHIP.

vested pension. See PENSION.

vested remainder. See REMAINDER.

vested right. See RIGHT.

vested-rights doctrine. *Constitutional law.* The rule that the legislature cannot take away a right that has been vested by a court's judgment; specif., the principle that it is beyond the province of Congress to reopen a final judgment issued by an Article III court. — Also termed *doctrine of vested rights.*

vestigial words (ve-**stij**-ee-əl). Statutory words and phrases that, through a succession of amendments, have been made useless or meaningless. • Courts do not allow vestigial words to defeat the fair meaning of a statute.

vestigium (ve-**stij**-ee-əm). *Archaic.* A vestige, mark, or sign; a trace, track, or impression left by a person or a physical object.

vesting order. (1873) A court order passing legal title in lieu of a legal conveyance.

vestitive fact (**ves**-tə-tiv). See *dispositive fact* (1) under FACT.

vestry (**ves**-tree). *Eccles. law.* **1.** The place in a church where the priest's robes are kept. — Also termed *sacristy.* **2.** An assembly of the minister, church wardens, and parishioners to conduct church business.

vestry clerk. *Eccles. law.* An officer appointed to attend a vestry and to take minutes of the proceedings.

vesture (**ves**-chər). *Hist.* **1.** The corn, grass, underwood, stubble, or other growth — apart from trees — that covers the land. — Also termed *vestura* (ves-**t**[**y**]**oor**-ə); *vestura terrae* (**ter**-ee); *vesture of land.* **2.** Seisin; investiture.

veteran. A person who has been honorably discharged from military service.

Veterans Administration. See DEPARTMENT OF VETERANS AFFAIRS.

Veterans Affairs, Department of. See DEPARTMENT OF VETERANS AFFAIRS.

Veterans Appeals, U.S. Court of. See UNITED STATES COURT OF APPEALS FOR VETERANS CLAIMS.

Veterans Benefits Administration. A unit in the U.S. Department of Veterans Affairs responsible for advising and assisting veterans and their families who apply for veterans' benefits.

Veterans' Employment and Training Service. A unit in the U.S. Department of Labor responsible for administering various programs relating to veterans' employment and training. ● The agency protects the reemployment rights of veterans and the employment and retention rights of members of the Reserve and National Guard. Its regional administrators work with state employment-security agencies and with recipients of grants under the Job Training Partnership Act to ensure that veterans are provided the priority services required by law. — Abbr. VETS.

Veterans Health Administration. A unit in the U.S. Department of Veterans Affairs responsible for providing hospital, nursing-home, and medical care to eligible veterans of military service.

veteran's loan. See LOAN.

vetitive (vet-ə-tiv), *adj.* Of, relating to, or having the power to veto.

veto (vee-toh), *n.* [Latin "I forbid"] (17c) **1.** A power of one governmental branch to prohibit an action by another branch; esp., a chief executive's refusal to sign into law a bill passed by the legislature. **2.** VETO MESSAGE. *Pl.* **vetoes.** — **veto,** *vb.*

absolute veto. (1852) An unrestricted veto that is not subject to being overridden.

item veto. See *line-item veto.*

legislative veto. (1850) *Hist.* A veto allowing Congress to block a federal executive or agency action taken under congressionally delegated authority. ● The Supreme Court held the legislative veto unconstitutional in *INS v. Chadha,* 462 U.S. 919, 103 S.Ct. 2764 (1983). See DELEGATION DOCTRINE.

liberum veto (lib-ər-əm). *Hist.* Formerly in Poland, the right of any single member of the diet to invalidate a measure.

limited veto. See *qualified veto.*

line-item veto. (1858) The executive's power to veto some provisions in a legislative bill without affecting other provisions. ● The U.S. Supreme Court declared the presidential line-item veto unconstitutional in 1998. See *Clinton v. City of New York,* 524 U.S. 417, 118 S.Ct. 2091 (1998). — Also termed *item veto.*

negative veto. See *qualified veto.*

overridden veto. (1971) A veto that the legislature has superseded by again passing the vetoed act, usu. by a supermajority of legislators. ● In the federal government, a bill vetoed by the President must receive a two-thirds majority in Congress to override the veto and enact the measure into law.

pocket veto. (1842) A veto resulting from the President's failure to sign a bill passed within the last ten days of the congressional session.

qualified veto. (1853) A veto that is conclusive unless overridden by an extraordinary majority of the legislature. ● This is the type of veto power that the President of the United States has. — Also termed *limited veto; negative veto.*

suspensory veto (sə-**spen**-sə-ree). (1911) A veto that suspends a law until the legislature reconsiders it and then allows the law to take effect if repassed by an ordinary majority. — Also termed *suspensive veto.*

vetoer, *n.* One who vetoes. — Also termed *vetoist.*

veto message. (1830) A statement communicating the reasons for the executive's refusing to sign into law a bill passed by the legislature. — Sometimes shortened to *veto.*

veto power. (1883) An executive's conditional power to prevent a bill that has passed the legislature from becoming law.

veto-proof majority. See MAJORITY.

VETS. *abbr.* VETERANS' EMPLOYMENT AND TRAINING SERVICE.

vetus jus (vee-təs jəs). *Roman & civil law.* **1.** The law of the Twelve Tables. See TWELVE TABLES. **2.** Long-established or ancient law. **3.** A law in force before the passage of a later law.

vex, *vb.* (15c) **1.** To harass, disquiet, or annoy. **2.** To cause physical or emotional distress. — **vexatious,** *adj.* — **vexation,** *n.*

vexata quaestio (vek-**say**-tə kwes-chee-oh). See VEXED QUESTION.

vexation. (15c) The damage that results from trickery or malice.

vexatious (vek-**say**-shəs), *adj.* (16c) (Of conduct) without reasonable or probable cause or excuse; harassing; annoying.

vexatious delay. An insurance company's unjustifiable refusal to satisfy an insurance claim, esp. based on a mere suspicion but no hard facts that the claim is ill-founded. — Also termed *vexatious refusal to pay; refusal to pay.*

vexatious lawsuit. See VEXATIOUS SUIT.

vexatious litigant. See LITIGANT.

vexatious proceeding. See VEXATIOUS SUIT.

vexatious refusal to pay. See VEXATIOUS DELAY.

vexatious suit. (17c) A lawsuit instituted maliciously and without good grounds, meant to create trouble and expense for the party being sued. — Also termed *vexatious lawsuit; vexatious* *litigation; vexatious proceeding.* Cf. MALICIOUS PROSECUTION.

vexed question. (17c) **1.** A question often argued about but seemingly never settled. **2.** A question or point that has been decided differently by different tribunals and has therefore been left in doubt. — Also termed *vexata quaestio* (vek-**say**-tə kwes-tee-oh).

via (**VI**-ə), *n.* [Latin "way, road"] *Roman & civil law.* **1.** A road, way, or right-of-way.

via publica (**VI**-ə **pəb**-li-kə). [Latin] *Roman & civil law.* A public way or road. ● The land itself belongs to the public.

2. *Roman law.* A type of rural servitude that gave the holder the right to walk, ride, or drive over another's land; SERVITUS VIAE. ● It was broader than and included the *servitus itineris* and the *servitus actus*; that is, *via* encompassed both *iter* (a footpath) and *actus* (a driveway). **3.** *Civil law.* The way in which legal procedures are followed.

via executiva (**VI**-ə eg-zek-yə-**tI**-və). *Civil law.* Executory process by which the debtor's property is seized, without previous citation, for some reason specified by law, usu. because of an act or title amounting to a confession of judgment.

via juris (**VI**-ə **joor**-is). [Latin] *Hist.* By means of law; by means of legal process.

via ordinaria (**VI**-ə or-di-**nair**-ee-ə). *Civil law.* The ordinary way or process by which a citation is served and all the usual forms of law are followed.

viable (**VI**-ə-bəl), *adj.* (1832) **1.** Capable of living, esp. outside the womb <a viable fetus>. **2.** Capable of independent existence or standing <a viable lawsuit>. **3.** Capable of succeeding <a viable option>. — **viability** (**VI**-ə-**bil**-ə-tee), *n.*

viatical settlement. See SETTLEMENT (3).

viatication (**VI**-at-ə-**kay**-shən). [fr. Latin *viaticus* "relating to a road or journey"] The purchase of a terminally or chronically ill policyholder's life insurance in exchange for a lump-sum payment equal to a percentage of the policy's full value. See *viatical settlement* under SETTLEMENT.

viator (**VI**-ay-tər). **1.** APPARITOR (1). **2.** A terminally or chronically ill life-insurance policyholder who sells the policy to a third party in return for a lump-sum payment equal to a percentage of the policy's face value.

viatorial privilege. See PRIVILEGE (1).

vicar. **1.** One who performs the functions of another; a substitute. **2.** The incumbent of an ecclesiastical benefice. Cf. RECTOR.

vicarage (**vik**-ər-ij). **1.** The benefice of a vicar. **2.** The house or household of a vicar. **3.** VICARSHIP.

vicar general. An ecclesiastical officer who helps the bishop or archbishop in the discharge of his office.

vicarial tithe (vI-**kair**-ee-əl). See TITHE.

vicarious (vI-**kair**-ee-əs), *adj.* (17c) Performed or suffered by one person as substitute for another; indirect; surrogate.

vicarious disqualification. See DISQUALIFICATION.

vicarious exhaustion of remedies. See EXHAUSTION OF REMEDIES.

vicarious infringement. See INFRINGEMENT.

vicarious liability. See LIABILITY.

vicarious performance. See PERFORMANCE.

vicarious reduction to practice. See REDUCTION TO PRACTICE.

vicarship. The office, function, or duty of a vicar. — Also termed *vicarage.*

vice (vIs), *n.* (14c) **1.** A moral failing; an ethical fault. **2.** Wickedness; corruption. **3.** Broadly, any defect or failing.

vice (vI-see *or* vI-sə), *prep.* (18c) In the place of; in the stead of. ● As a prefix, *vice-* (vIs) denotes one who takes the place of.

vice-admiralty court. *Hist.* A tribunal established in British possessions beyond the seas, with jurisdiction over maritime cases, including those related to prize. ● The governor of the colony, in the capacity of "vice-admiral," exercised judicial authority in this court.

vice-chancellor. A judge appointed to act for the chancellor, esp. in a chancery court. — Abbr. VC.

vice-commercial agent. See AGENT.

vice-consul. A consular officer subordinate to a consul; esp., one who is substituted temporarily to fill the place of a consul who is absent or has been relieved from duty.

career vice-consul. A vice-consul who is a member of the Foreign Service. — Also termed *vice-consul of career.*

noncareer vice-consul. A vice-consul who is not a member of the Foreign Service and who is appointed without examination.

vice crime. See CRIME.

vice-dominus episcopi (vI-sə-**dom**-ə-nəs ə-**pis**-kə-pI). **1.** A vicar general. **2.** A commissary of a bishop.

vicegerent (vIs-**jeer**-ənt). A deputy; lieutenant.

vice-governor, *n.* A deputy or lieutenant governor.

vice-marshal. An officer appointed to assist the earl marshal. See EARL MARSHAL OF ENGLAND.

vice president, *n.* (16c) **1.** An officer selected in advance to fill the presidency if the president dies, resigns, is removed from office, or cannot or will not serve. ● The Vice President of the United States, who is elected at the same time as the President, serves as presiding officer of the Senate but may cast a vote only to break a tie. On the death, incapacity, resignation, or removal of the President, the Vice President succeeds to the presidency. **2.** A corporate officer of mid-level to high rank, usu. having charge of a department. — Abbr. V.P.; VP. — Also written *vice-president.* — **vice presidency,** *n.* — **vice-presidential,** *adj.*

vice principal. See FELLOW-SERVANT RULE.

viceregent, *n.* **1.** A deputy regent; esp., one who acts in the place of a ruler, governor, or sovereign. **2.** More broadly, an officer deputed by a superior or by proper authority to exercise the powers of the higher authority; one with delegated power.

viceroy, *n.* The governor of a kingdom or colony, who rules as the deputy of a monarch. — **viceroyal, viceregal,** *adj.*

vice-sheriff. See *deputy sheriff* under SHERIFF.

vice-treasurer, *n.* A deputy or assistant treasurer.

vicinage (vis-ə-nij). [Law French "neighborhood"] (14c) **1.** Vicinity; proximity. **2.** The place where a crime is committed or a trial is held; the place from which jurors are to be drawn for trial; esp., the locale from which the accused is entitled to have jurors selected. — Also termed *vicinetum* (vis-ə-**nee**-təm). **3.** A right of common that neighboring tenants have in a barony or fee.

vicious animal. See ANIMAL.

vicious intromission. See *vitious intromission* under INTROMISSION.

vicious propensity. (1835) An animal's tendency to endanger the safety of persons or property. See *vicious animal* under ANIMAL.

vicontiel (vi-**kon**-tee-əl), *adj.* (17c) **1.** Of or relating to a viscount. **2.** Of or relating to a sheriff. — Also spelled *vicountiel.* — Also termed *vicecomital.*

victim, *n.* (15c) A person harmed by a crime, tort, or other wrong. — **victimize,** *vb.* — **victimization,** *n.*

victim allocution. See ALLOCUTION.

victim-impact statement. (1981) A statement read into the record during sentencing to inform the judge or jury of the financial, physical, and psychological impact of the crime on the victim and the victim's family.

victimless crime. See CRIME.

victim-precipitated homicide. See HOMICIDE.

victim-related adjustment. An increase in punishment available under federal sentencing guidelines when the defendant knew or should have known that the victim bore a particular characteristic — e.g., the victim was unusually vulnerable (because of age or condition) — or was otherwise particularly susceptible to the criminal conduct. See USSG §§ 3A1.1, 1.2.

Victims of Child Abuse Laws. An organization of persons who claim to have been wrongly accused of sexually abusing children. — Abbr. VOCAL. Cf. FALSE MEMORY SYNDROME FOUNDATION.

victus (**vik**-təs). *Civil law.* Sustenance; support; a means of living.

vide (**vi**-dee *also* **vee**-day). [Latin] See. ● This is a citation signal still seen in some texts, esp. in the abbreviated form *q.v.* (*quod vide* "which see"). *Vide ante* or *vide supra* refers to a previous passage in a text; *vide post* or *vide infra* refers to a later passage.

videlicet (vi-**del**-ə-set *or* -sit). [Latin] (15c) To wit; that is to say; namely; SCILICET. ● The term is used primarily to point out, particularize, or make more specific what has been previously stated in general (or occas. obscure) language. One common function is to state the time, place, or manner when that is the essence of the matter at issue. — Abbr. *viz.* See VIZ.

Video Electronics Standards Association. A nonprofit organization that promotes and develops industry-wide standards for computers to ensure interoperability, and encourage innovation and market growth. — Abbr. VESA.

video piracy. See PIRACY (3).

Video Privacy Protection Act. A federal statute that bars video stores from disclosing to third parties the names of customers' rentals. 18 USCA § 2710.

viduity (vi-**d[y]oo**-ə-tee). *Archaic.* Widowhood.

vie (vee). [French] Life. ● The term occurs in such Law French phrases as *cestui que vie* and *pur autre vie.*

vi et armis (**vi** et **ahr**-mis). [Latin] *Hist.* By or with force and arms. See *trespass vi et armis* under TRESPASS.

view, *n.* **1.** The common-law right of prospect — that is, an outlook from the windows of one's house. **2.** An urban servitude that prohibits the obstruction of the outlook from a person's house. **3.** A jury's trip to inspect a place or thing relevant to the case it is considering; the act or proceeding by which a tribunal goes to observe an object that cannot be produced in court because it is immovable or inconvenient to remove. ● The appropriate procedures are typically regulated by state statute. At common law, and today in many civil cases, the trial judge's presence is not required. The common practice has been for the jury to be escorted by "showers" who are commissioned for this purpose. Parties and counsel are generally permitted to attend, although this is a matter typically within the trial judge's discretion. Cf. VIEW OF AN INQUEST. **4.** In a real action, a defendant's observation of the thing at issue to ascertain its identity and other circumstances surrounding it. Cf. DEMAND OF VIEW.

viewer. (15c) A person, usu. one of several, appointed by a court to investigate certain matters or to examine a particular locality (such as the proposed site of a new road) and to report to the court.

view of an inquest. (1837) A jury's inspection of a place or property to which an inquiry or inquest refers. Cf. VIEW (3).

viewpoint discrimination. See DISCRIMINATION.

viewpoint-neutral. See NEUTRAL.

vigil. *Eccles. law.* The day before any solemn feast.

vigilance. (16c) Watchfulness; precaution; a proper degree of activity and promptness in pursuing one's rights, in guarding them from infraction, and in discovering opportunities for enforcing one's lawful claims and demands.

vigilant, *adj.* (15c) Watchful and cautious; on the alert; attentive to discover and avoid danger.

vigilante (vij-ə-**lan**-tee). (1856) A person who seeks to avenge a crime by taking the law into his or her own hands.

vigilantism (vij-ə-**lan**-tiz-əm). The act of a citizen who takes the law into his or her own hands by apprehending and punishing suspected criminals.

village. 1. Traditionally, a modest assemblage of houses and buildings for dwellings and businesses. **2.** In some states, a municipal corporation with a smaller population than a city. — Also termed (in sense 2) *town; borough.*

villein (**vil**-ən). *Hist.* A person entirely subject to a lord or attached to a manor, but free in relation to all others; a serf. ● At the time of the Domesday Inquest (shortly after the Norman Conquest), about 40% of households were marked as belonging to villeins: they were the most numerous element in the English population. Cf. FREEMAN.

villein in gross. A villein who was annexed to the person of the lord, and transferable by deed from one owner to another.

villein regardant (ri-**gahr**-dənt). A villein annexed to the manor of land.

villeinage (**vil**-ə-nij). *Hist.* **1.** The holding of property through servitude to a feudal lord; a servile type of tenure in which a tenant was obliged to render base services to a lord. Cf. KNIGHT SERVICE; SOCAGE. **2.** A villein's status, condition, or service. — Also spelled *villenage; villainage; villanage.* — Also termed *villein tenure.*

privileged villeinage. Villeinage in which the services to be performed were certain, though of a base and servile nature.

pure villeinage. Villeinage in which the services were not certain, but the tenant was obliged to do whatever he was commanded whenever the command came.

villein in gross. See VILLEIN.

villein regardant. See VILLEIN.

villein service. *Hist.* A base service that a villein performed, such as working on the lord's land on certain days of the week (usu. two to four). ● These services were not considered suitable to a man of free and honorable rank. — Also termed *villein servitium.* See WEEK-WORK.

villein socage (**sok**-ij). See SOCAGE.

villenous judgment (**vil**-ə-nəs). *Hist.* A judgment that deprived a person of his *libera lex,* as a result of which he was discredited and disabled as a juror and witness, forfeited his goods and chattels and land, had his houses razed and trees uprooted, and went to prison. — Also spelled *villainous judgment.*

vinagium (vi-**nay-jee**-əm). A payment in kind of wine as rent for a vineyard.

vinculo (**ving**-kyə-loh), *n.* [Latin "by bond"] *Spanish law.* **1.** A tie or bond; esp., the bond of marriage. See *divorce a vinculo matrimonii* under DIVORCE. **2.** An entail.

vinculum juris (**ving**-kyə-ləm **joor**-is). [Latin "a bond of the law"] *Roman law.* The tie that legally binds one person to another; legal bond; obligation.

vindicate, *vb.* (16c) **1.** To clear (a person or thing) from suspicion, criticism, blame, or doubt <DNA tests vindicated the suspect>. **2.** To assert, maintain, or affirm (one's interest) by action <the claimants sought to vindicate their rights through a class-action suit>. **3.** To defend (one's interest) against interference or encroachment <the borrower vindicated its interest in court when the lender tried to foreclose>. **4.** *Roman & civil law.* To assert a legal right to (a thing); to seek recovery of (a thing) by legal process <Antony Honoratus attempted to vindicate the sword he had lent his cousin>. — **vindication,** *n.* — **vindicator,** *n.*

vindicatio (vin-di-**kay**-shee-oh), *n.* [Latin "claim"] *Roman law.* **1.** An action by the owner to claim property.

vindicatio servitutis (vin-di-**kay**-shee-oh sər-və-**t[y]oo**-tis). [Latin "claim of servitude"] *Roman law.* An action against the owner of land over which the plaintiff claims that a servitude exists. — Also termed *actio confessoria.*

2. The claiming of a thing as one's own; the assertion of a right in or title to a thing. Pl. *vindicationes* (vin-di-kay-shee-**oh**-neez).

vindicatory part (**vin**-də-kə-tor-ee). (1881) The portion of a statute setting forth the penalty for committing a wrong or neglecting a duty.

vindicta (vin-**dik**-tə), *n. Roman law.* **1.** A rod or wand. **2.** The assertion of freedom or ownership by symbolically touching the person or thing with a rod.

vindictive damages. See *punitive damages* under DAMAGES.

vindictive prosecution (vin-**dik**-tiv). See PROSECUTION.

violation, *n.* (15c) **1.** An infraction or breach of the law; a transgression. See INFRACTION. **2.** The act of breaking or dishonoring the law; the contravention of a right or duty. **3.** Rape; ravishment. **4.** Under the Model Penal Code, a public-welfare offense. ● In this sense, a violation is not a crime. See Model Penal Code § 1.04(5). — **violate,** *vb.* — **violative** (**vɪ**-ə-lay-tiv), *adj.* — **violator,** *n.*

violation warrant. See WARRANT (1).

violence. (14c) The use of physical force, usu. accompanied by fury, vehemence, or outrage; esp., physical force unlawfully exercised with the intent to harm. ● Some courts have held that violence in labor disputes is not limited to physical contact or injury, but may include picketing conducted with misleading signs, false statements, erroneous publicity, and veiled threats by words and acts.

   domestic violence. **1.** Violence between members of a household, usu. spouses; an assault or other violent act committed by one member of a household against another. See BATTERED-CHILD SYNDROME; BATTERED-WOMAN SYNDROME. **2.** The infliction of physical injury, or the creation of a reasonable fear that physical injury or harm will be inflicted, by a parent or a member or former member of a child's household, against a child or against another member of the household. — Also termed *domestic abuse; family violence.* **3.** *Archaic.* Insurrection or unlawful force fomented from within a country.

Violence Against Women Act. A federal statute that established a federal civil-rights action for victims of gender-motivated violence, without the need for a criminal charge. 42 USCA § 13981. ● In 2000, the Supreme Court invalidated the statute, holding that neither the Commerce Clause nor the Enforcement Clause of the 14th Amendment authorized Congress to enact the civil-remedy provision of this Act. *United States v. Morrison,* 120 S.Ct. 1740 (2000). — Abbr. VAWA.

violent, *adj.* (14c) **1.** Of, relating to, or characterized by strong physical force <violent blows to the legs>. **2.** Resulting from extreme or intense force <violent death>. **3.** Vehemently or passionately threatening <violent words>.

violent crime. See CRIME.

violent death. See DEATH.

violent felony. See *violent offense* under OFFENSE (1).

violent offense. See OFFENSE (1).

vir (veer), *n.* [Latin] **1.** An adult male; a man. **2.** A husband. ● In the Latin phrases and maxims that once pervaded English law, *vir* generally means "husband," as in the expression *vir et uxor* (husband and wife). See ET VIR. Cf. UXOR.

vires (**vɪ**-reez), *n.* (18c) **1.** Natural powers; forces. **2.** Granted powers, esp. when limited. See ULTRA VIRES; INTRA VIRES.

vir et uxor (**veer** et ək-sor). [Latin] Husband and wife.

virga (**vər**-gə). *Hist.* A rod or staff; esp., a rod as an ensign of office.

virgata (vər-**gay**-tə). **1.** A quarter of an acre of land. See ACRE. **2.** A quarter of a hide of land. See HIDE (1).

virge. See VERGE.

virile share. *Civil law.* An amount that an obligor owes jointly and severally with another. La. Civ. Code art. 1804. — Also termed *virile portion.*

virtual adoption. See *adoption by estoppel* under ADOPTION.

virtual child pornography. See PORNOGRAPHY.

virtual representation. See REPRESENTATION (3).

virtual-representation doctrine. (1945) The principle that a judgment may bind a person who is not a party to the litigation if one of the parties is so closely aligned with the nonparty's interests that the nonparty has been adequately represented by the party in court. ● Under this doctrine, for instance, a judgment in a case naming only the husband as a party can be binding on his wife as well. See RES JUDICATA.

virtue ethics. *Ethics.* An ethical theory that focuses on the character of the actor rather than on the nature of the act or its consequences. ● This approach received its first and perhaps its fullest expression in the works of Aristotle, esp. in his *Ethics.* Cf. CONSEQUENTIALISM.

vis (vis). [Latin "power"] (17c) **1.** Any force, violence, or disturbance relating to a person or property. **2.** The force of law. ● Thus *vim habere* ("to have force") is to be legally valid. Pl. *vires.*

visa (**vee**-zə). An official indorsement made on a passport, showing that it has been examined and that the bearer is permitted to proceed; a recognition by the country in which a passport-holder wishes to travel that the holder's passport is valid. ● A visa is generally required for the admission of aliens into the United States. 8 USCA §§ 1181, 1184. — Also termed (archaically) *visé* (**vee**-zay *or* vi-**zay**).

vis-à-vis (**veez**-ə-**vee**). [French "face to face"] (18c) In relation to; opposite to <the creditor established a preferred position vis-à-vis the other creditors>.

viscount (**vI**-kownt). **1.** The title of the fourth rank of European nobility. ● In the British peerage, viscount is placed between the dignity of earl and baron. **2.** *Hist.* A sheriff.

viscountess (**vI**-kown-tis). **1.** The wife of a viscount. — Also termed *vice-comitissa*. **2.** A woman who holds the rank of viscount in her own right.

vis divina (**vis** di-**vI**-nə), *n. Civil law.* Divine or superhuman force; ACT OF GOD; VIS MAJOR.

visé. See VISA.

visible, *adj.* **1.** Perceptible to the eye; discernible by sight. **2.** Clear, distinct, and conspicuous.

visible crime. See *street crime* under CRIME.

visible means of support. (1846) An apparent method of earning a livelihood. ● Vagrancy statutes have long used this phrase to describe those who have no ostensible ability to support themselves.

visit, *n. Int'l law.* A naval officer's boarding an ostensibly neutral merchant vessel from another state to exercise the right of search. ● This right is exercisable when suspicious circumstances exist, as when the vessel is suspected of involvement in piracy. — Also termed *visitation.* See RIGHT OF SEARCH.

visitation (viz-ə-**tay**-shən). (14c) **1.** Inspection; superintendence; direction; regulation. **2.** *Family law.* A relative's, esp. a noncustodial parent's, period of access to a child. — Also termed *parental access; access; parenting time; residential time.* **3.** The process of inquiring into and correcting corporate irregularities. **4.** VISIT.

grandparent visitation. A grandparent's court-approved access to a grandchild. ● The Supreme Court recently limited a grandparent's right to have visitation with his or her grandchild if the parent objects, citing a parent's fundamental right to raise his or her child and to make all decisions concerning the child free from state intervention absent a threat to the child's health and safety. *Troxel v. Granville,* 530 U.S. 57, 120 S.Ct. 2054 (2000).

restricted visitation. See *supervised visitation.*

stepped-up visitation. Visitation, usu. for a parent who has been absent from the child's life, that begins on a very limited basis and increases as the child comes to know the parent. — Also termed *step-up visitation.*

supervised visitation. Visitation, usu. court-ordered, in which a parent may visit with the child or children only in the presence of some other individual. ● A court may order supervised visitation when the visiting parent is known or believed to be prone to physical abuse, sexual abuse, or violence. — Also termed *restricted visitation.*

visitation books. *Hist.* Books compiled by the heralds, when royal progresses were solemnly and regularly made into every part of the kingdom, to inquire into the state of families and to register whatever marriages and descents were verified to them upon oath.

visitation credit. *Family law.* A child-support reduction that reflects the amount of time the child lives with the noncustodial parent.

visitation order. (1944) *Family law.* **1.** An order establishing the visiting times for a noncustodial parent with his or her child. **2.** An order establishing the visiting times for a child and a person with a significant relationship to the child. ● Such an order may allow for visitation between (1) a grandparent and a grandchild, (2) a child and another relative, (3) a child and a stepparent, or (4) occasionally, a child and the child's psychological parent. — Also termed *access order.*

visitation right. (1935) **1.** *Family law.* A noncustodial parent's or grandparent's court-ordered privilege of spending time with a child or grandchild who is living with another person, usu. the custodial parent. ● The noncustodial parent with visitation rights may sometimes be a parent from whose custody the child has been removed because of abuse or neglect. **2.** *Int'l law.* A belligerent nation's right to search a neutral vessel to find out whether it is carrying contraband or is otherwise engaged in nonneutral service. ● If the searched vessel is doing either of these things, the searchers may seize the contraband and carry out an appropriate punishment. — Also termed (in both senses) *right of visitation.*

visitatorial (viz-ə-tə-**tor**-ee-əl), *adj.* Of or relating to on-site inspection or supervision. — Also termed *visitorial.*

visitatorial power. See POWER (3).

visiting judge. See JUDGE.

visitor. 1. A person who goes or comes to a particular person or place.

business visitor. See BUSINESS VISITOR.

2. A person appointed to visit, inspect, inquire into, and correct corporate irregularities.

visitorial. See VISITATORIAL.

visitorial power. See *visitatorial power* under POWER (3).

visitor of manners. A regarder's office in the forest.

vis major (vis **may**-jər), *n.* [Latin "a superior force"] (17c) **1.** A greater or superior force; an irresistible or overwhelming force of nature; FORCE MAJEURE. Cf. ACT OF GOD. **2.** A loss resulting immediately from a natural cause without human intervention and that could not have been prevented by the exercise of prudence, diligence, and care. — Also termed *act of nature; act of providence; superior force; irresistible force; vis divina.*

VISTA (**vis**-tə). *abbr.* (1964) Volunteers in Service to America, a federal program established in 1964 to provide volunteers to help improve the living conditions of people in the poorest areas of the United States, its possessions, and Puerto Rico.

Visual Artists Rights Act. *Copyright.* A 1990 federal law giving a visual artist nontransferable moral rights of integrity and attribution in original and limited-edition creations. ● Passed in order to meet Berne Convention standards, the Act protects the original artist — not the owner of the copyright — by granting some rights to prevent the work from being changed or destroyed, and by guaranteeing that the artist may claim authorship of the original work but may deny authorship if the work is modified. 17 USCA §§ 106A, 113. — Abbr. VARA.

vital statistics. (1837) Public records — usu. relating to matters such as births, marriages, deaths, diseases, and the like — that are statutorily mandated to be kept by a city, state, or other governmental division or subdivision. ● On the admissibility of vital statistics, see Fed. R. Evid. 803(9).

vital term. See *fundamental term* under TERM (2).

vitiate (**vish**-ee-ayt), *vb.* (16c) **1.** To impair; to cause to have no force or effect <the new statute vitiates any common-law argument that the plaintiffs might have>. **2.** To make void or voidable; to invalidate either completely or in part <fraud vitiates a contract>. **3.** To corrupt morally <Mr. Lawrence complains that his children were vitiated by their governess>. — **vitiation,** *n.* — **vitiator,** *n.*

vitious intromission. See INTROMISSION.

viva voce (**vɪ**-və **voh**-see *also* **vee**-və **voh**-chay), *adv.* [Law Latin "with living voice"] (16c) By word of mouth; orally. ● In reference to votes, the term means a voice vote was held rather than a vote by ballot. In reference to the examination of witnesses, the term means that oral rather than written testimony was taken. See *voice vote* under VOTE (4).

viva voce vote. See *voice vote* under VOTE (4).

vivisection, *n.* **1.** Physiological or pathological experimentation on or investigation of living vertebrate animals using procedures likely to cause severe pain. **2.** By extension, questioning or criticism that is intense, minute, and merciless.

vivum vadium (**vɪ**-vəm **vay**-dee-əm). See *vadium vivum* under VADIUM.

viz. (viz). *abbr.* [Latin *videlicet*] (16c) Namely; that is to say <the defendant engaged in fraudulent activities, viz., misrepresenting his gross income, misrepresenting the value of his assets, and forging his wife's signature>. See VIDELICET.

VOCAL. *abbr.* VICTIMS OF CHILD ABUSE LAWS.

vocation. A person's regular calling or business; one's occupation or profession.

voice exemplar. (1954) A sample of a person's voice used for the purpose of comparing it with a recorded voice to determine whether the speaker is the same person. ● Although voiceprint identification was formerly inadmissible, the trend in recent years has been toward admissibility. *See* Fed. R. Evid. 901.

voiceprint. (1962) A distinctive pattern of curved lines and whorls made by a machine that measures human vocal sounds for the purpose of identifying an individual speaker. ● Like fingerprints, voiceprints are thought to be unique to each person.

voice vote. See VOTE (4).

void, *adj.* (14c) **1.** Of no legal effect; null. ● The distinction between *void* and *voidable* is often of great practical importance. Whenever technical accuracy is required, *void* can be properly applied only to those provisions that are of no effect whatsoever — those that are an absolute nullity. — **void, avoid,** *vb.* — **voidness,** *n.*

facially void. (1969) (Of an instrument) patently void upon an inspection of the contents. — Also termed *void on its face.*

void ab initio (ab i-**nish**-ee-oh). (17c) Null from the beginning, as from the first moment when a contract is entered into. ● A contract is void ab initio if it seriously offends law or public policy, in contrast to a contract that is merely voidable at the election of one party to the contract.

void for vagueness. (1814) **1.** (Of a deed or other instrument affecting property) having such an insufficient property description as to be unenforceable. **2.** (Of a penal statute) establishing a requirement or punishment without specifying what is required or what conduct is punishable, and therefore void because violative of due process. — Also termed *void for indefiniteness.* See VAGUENESS DOCTRINE.

2. VOIDABLE. • Although sense 1 above is the strict meaning of *void*, the word is often used and construed as bearing the more liberal meaning of "voidable."

voidable, *adj.* (15c) Valid until annulled; esp., (of a contract) capable of being affirmed or rejected at the option of one of the parties. • This term describes a valid act that may be voided rather than an invalid act that may be ratified. — Also termed *avoidable.* — **voidability,** *n.*

voidable agreement. See *voidable contract* under CONTRACT.

voidable contract. See CONTRACT.

voidable judgment. See JUDGMENT.

voidable marriage. See MARRIAGE (1).

voidable preference. See PREFERENTIAL TRANSFER.

voidable process. See PROCESS.

voidable promise. See PROMISE.

voidable transfer. See PREFERENTIAL TRANSFER.

void agreement. See *void contract* under CONTRACT.

voidance, *n.* (14c) The act of annulling, canceling, or making void. — Also termed *avoidance.*

void contract. See CONTRACT.

void for indefiniteness. See *void for vagueness* under VOID.

void for vagueness. See VOID.

void-for-vagueness doctrine. 1. See VAGUENESS DOCTRINE. **2.** See *void for vagueness* under VOID.

void judgment. See JUDGMENT.

void legacy. See LEGACY.

void marriage. See MARRIAGE (1).

void on its face. See *facially void* under VOID.

void process. See PROCESS.

voir dire (vwahr **deer** *also* vor **deer** *or* vor **dir**), *n.* [Law French "to speak the truth"] (17c) **1.** A preliminary examination of a prospective juror by a judge or lawyer to decide whether the prospect is qualified and suitable to serve on a jury. • Loosely, the term refers to the jury-selection phase of a trial. **2.** A preliminary examination to test the competence of a witness or evidence. **3.** *Hist.* An oath administered to a witness requiring that witness to answer truthfully in response to questions. — Also spelled *voire dire.* — Also termed *voir dire exam; examination on the voir dire.* — **voir dire,** *vb.*

voiture (vwah-t[y]oor), *n.* Carriage; transportation by carriage.

volatile stock. See STOCK.

volatility. In securities markets, the quality of having sudden and extreme price changes.

volens (**voh**-lenz), *adj.* [Latin] (1872) Willing. See NOLENS VOLENS.

volenti non fit injuria (voh-**len**-tɪ non fit in-**joor**-ee-ə). [Law Latin "to a willing person it is not a wrong," i.e., a person is not wronged by that to which he or she consents] (17c) The principle that a person who knowingly and voluntarily risks danger cannot recover for any resulting injury. • This is the type of affirmative defense that must be pleaded under Fed. R. Civ. P. 8(c). — Often shortened to *volenti.* See ASSUMPTION OF THE RISK.

volition (və-**lish**-ən *or* voh-), *n.* (17c) **1.** The ability to make a choice or determine something. **2.** The act of making a choice or determining something. **3.** The choice or determination that someone makes. — **volitional,** *adj.*

volitional test. See IRRESISTIBLE-IMPULSE TEST.

Volstead Act (**vol**-sted). A federal statute enacted in 1919 to prohibit the manufacture, sale, or transportation of liquor. • Sponsored by Andrew Joseph Volstead of Minnesota, a famous Prohibitionist, the statute was passed under the 18th Amendment to the U.S. Constitution. When the 21st Amendment repealed the 18th Amendment in 1933, the Volstead Act was voided.

volume discount. See DISCOUNT.

voluntarily, *adv.* Intentionally; without coercion.

voluntary, *adj.* (14c) **1.** Done by design or intention <voluntary act>. **2.** Unconstrained by interference; not impelled by outside influence <voluntary statement>. **3.** Without valuable consideration or legal obligation; gratuitous <voluntary gift>. **4.** Having merely nominal consideration <voluntary deed>. — **voluntariness,** *n.*

voluntary abandonment. See ABANDONMENT (3).

voluntary appearance. See APPEARANCE.

voluntary arbitration. See ARBITRATION.

voluntary assignment. See *general assignment* under ASSIGNMENT (2).

voluntary association. See ASSOCIATION (3).

voluntary assumption of the risk. See ASSUMPTION OF THE RISK.

voluntary bankruptcy. See BANKRUPTCY.

voluntary bar. See BAR.

voluntary bond. See BOND (3).

voluntary commitment. See COMMITMENT.

voluntary confession. See CONFESSION.

voluntary consent. See CONSENT (1).

voluntary contract. See *gratuitous contract* (2) under CONTRACT.

voluntary conveyance. See CONVEYANCE.

voluntary courtesy. (17c) An act of kindness performed by one person toward another, from the free will of the doer, without any previous request or promise of reward made by the person who is the object of the act. ● No promise of remuneration arises from such an act.

voluntary deposit. See DEPOSIT (5).

voluntary disclosure of offense. See DISCLOSURE (1).

voluntary discontinuance. See NONSUIT (1).

voluntary dismissal. See DISMISSAL (1).

voluntary dissolution. See DISSOLUTION.

voluntary escape. See ESCAPE (3).

voluntary euthanasia. See EUTHANASIA.

voluntary exposure to unnecessary danger. (1883) An intentional act that, from the standpoint of a reasonable person, gives rise to an undue risk of harm. ● The phrase suggests that the actor was consciously willing to take the risk.

voluntary ignorance. (1836) Willful obliviousness; an unknowing or unaware state resulting from the neglect to take reasonable steps to acquire important knowledge.

voluntary improvement. See IMPROVEMENT.

voluntary intoxication. See INTOXICATION.

voluntary jurisdiction. See JURISDICTION.

voluntary lien. See LIEN.

voluntary manslaughter. See MANSLAUGHTER.

voluntary oath. See *nonjudicial oath* (1) under OATH.

voluntary petition. See PETITION.

voluntary pilot. See PILOT.

voluntary pooling. See POOLING.

voluntary-registry law. See ADOPTION-REGISTRY STATUTE.

voluntary respite. See RESPITE.

voluntary sale. See SALE.

voluntary search. See SEARCH.

voluntary settlement. See SETTLEMENT (1).

voluntary statement. See STATEMENT.

voluntary stranding. See STRANDING.

voluntary surety. See SURETY.

voluntary suretyship. See SURETYSHIP.

voluntary trust. See TRUST.

voluntary unitization. See UNITIZATION.

voluntary waste. See WASTE (1).

volunteer. (16c) **1.** A voluntary actor or agent in a transaction; esp., a person who, without an employer's assent and without any justification from legitimate personal interest, helps an employee in the performance of the employer's business. **2.** The grantee in a voluntary conveyance; a person to whom a conveyance is made without any valuable consideration. See *voluntary conveyance* under CONVEYANCE. **3.** *Military law.* A person who enters military service voluntarily and is then subject to the same rules as other soldiers. Cf. DRAFT (2). **4.** *Archaic.* See OFFICIOUS INTERMEDDLER.

Volunteers in Service to America. See VISTA.

vote, *n.* (15c) **1.** The expression of one's preference or opinion in a meeting or election by ballot, show of hands, or other type of communication <the Republican candidate received more votes than the Democratic candidate>.

absentee vote. See *absentee voting* under VOTING.

bullet vote. A vote cast for fewer nominees than are being elected. ● A bullet vote slightly enhances the ballot's effect on the outcome. — Also termed *bullet ballot.*

casting vote. A deciding vote cast by the chair of a deliberative assembly when the votes are tied. ● The U.S. Constitution gives the Vice President the casting vote in the Senate. U.S. Const. art. I, § 3.

effective vote. A vote that counts toward a winning candidate, to the extent needed to win. ● A vote that goes to a winning candidate is "effective" to the extent needed to win, and "excess" beyond that point. For example, if a candidate needs 100 votes and gets 150, then 50 votes are excess votes and each vote is two-thirds effective and one-third excess. Cf. *excess vote; wasted vote.*

excess vote. A vote that counts toward a winning candidate, beyond the extent needed to win. Cf. *effective vote.*

exhausted vote. A preferential vote on which all the ranked candidates have already been elected or eliminated. — Also termed *exhausted ballot.*

illegal vote. A vote that does not count because it was cast by someone not entitled to vote or for an ineligible choice, or in a form or manner that does not comply with the applicable rules. See *spoiled ballot* under BALLOT (2).

legal vote. A vote cast in the proper form and manner for an eligible choice by someone entitled to vote.

paired vote. An abstention resulting from a pairing. See PAIR.

preferential vote. A vote that ranks the choices in order of preference. ● A preferential vote may be transferable or weighted. — Also termed *preferential ballot.* Cf. *single transferable vote; weighted vote.*

single transferable vote. A preferential vote that will migrate or "transfer" away from a candidate whom it will no longer help. ● Under transferable voting, a candidate wins if his or her first-choice votes reach the number need-ed to win, or the "threshold." If no candidate reaches the threshold, the least-preferred can-didate is dropped and his or her votes transfer to the next-preferred candidate on each ballot. If a candidate reaches the threshold with an excess, that excess still transfers — after being discounted by the non-excess fraction needed to reach the threshold — among the surviving candidates. Each transfer preserves each vote as long as at least one candidate that the voter ranked survives. The redistribution continues until enough candidates reach the threshold or the number of surviving candidates equals the number of representatives still to be elected. See DROOP QUOTA. — Also termed *STV*; *transferable vote*; *choice voting*.

transferable vote. See *single transferable vote*.

unintelligible vote. An otherwise legal vote cast in a form from which the tellers cannot ascer-tain the voter's intent. • On a secret ballot, no voter may properly claim an unintelligible vote for the purpose of explaining it since the vote may have been cast by another voter who cannot contradict the claimant without sacrificing his or her right to secrecy.

vote of no confidence. See NO-CONFIDENCE VOTE.

wasted vote. A vote that does not count toward any winning candidate. Cf. *effective vote*; *excess vote*.

weighted vote. A nontransferable preferential vote whose strength is allocated among the ranked preferences either by the voter or according to a series of fixed weights.

2. The total number of votes cast in an election <the incumbent received 60% of the vote>. **3.** The majority or supermajority needed for a certain question <a two-thirds vote>.

majority vote. See MAJORITY (2).

plurality vote. See PLURALITY.

tie vote. An equally divided vote. • A tie vote is not a deadlock unless the assembly is obliged to act, for example when electing an officer to an office that will otherwise be vacant. Cf. DEAD-LOCK.

unanimous vote. A vote in which every voter con-curs. See UNANIMOUS (2).

winner-take-all vote. An election in which the majority (or sometimes the plurality) elects all the representatives. Cf. UNIT RULE; PROPOR-TIONAL REPRESENTATION; *proportional voting* under VOTING.

4. The act of voting, usu. by a deliberative assem-bly <the Senate postponed the vote on the gun-control bill>. — **vote**, *vb.*

counted vote. *Parliamentary law.* A vote taken in a way that individually counts each voter. • Examples of a counted vote are a show of hands, a standing vote, a roll-call vote, or a written bal-lot. See DIVISION (1).

division vote. See DIVISION (1).

lobby vote. A counted vote taken by each voter passing through a lobby between tellers. — Also termed *teller vote*.

rising vote. 1. See *standing vote*. **2.** A vote of appreciation demonstrated by the members standing, sometimes silently but usu. with ap-plause. — Also termed *rising vote of thanks*.

roll-call vote. A counted vote by roll call, in which the secretary calls each member's name, in an-swer to which the member casts aloud his or her vote. • The U.S. Constitution provides that "the Yeas and Nays of the Members of either House on any question shall, at the Desire of one fifth of those Present, be entered on the Journal." U.S. Const. art. I, § 5, cl. 3. — Also termed *vote by yeas and nays*; *yeas and nays*. See *roll call* under CALL (1).

serpentine vote. A standing vote in which the voters count off and sit down, with the count progressing up one row and down the next until each member on the side of the question being counted has voted.

standing vote. A counted vote taken by each voter standing up when his or her side of the question is counted. — Also termed *rising vote*; *standing division*.

teller vote. See *lobby vote*.

viva voce vote. See *voice vote*.

voice vote. A vote taken by the voters collective-ly answering aloud, usu. with "aye" or "nay," when their side of the question is called. — Also termed *viva voce vote*.

vote by show of hands. A vote taken by the voters raising their hands when their side of the ques-tion is counted. — Often shortened to *show of hands*.

vote by yeas and nays. See *roll-call vote*.

vote dilution. See DILUTION (3).

vote immediately. See CLOSE DEBATE.

vote of no confidence. See NO-CONFIDENCE VOTE.

voter. (16c) **1.** A person who engages in the act of voting. **2.** A person who has the qualifications necessary for voting. — Also termed (in sense 2) *legal voter*; *qualified voter*.

registered voter. A person who is qualified to vote and whose name is recorded in the voting dis-trict where he or she resides.

voting. (16c) The casting of votes for the purpose of deciding an issue.

  absentee voting. (1932) **1.** Participation in an election by a qualified voter who is unable to appear at the polls on election day. **2.** The practice of allowing voters to participate in this way. — Also termed (in sense 1) *absentee ballot*; *absentee vote*. See *absentee ballot* under BALLOT (2). Cf. *early voting.*

  choice voting. See *single transferable vote* under VOTE (1).

  class voting. (1941) A method of shareholder voting in which different classes of shares vote separately on fundamental corporate changes that affect the rights and privileges of that class. — Also termed *voting by class*; *voting by voting group.*

  cumulative voting. (1884) A system in which each voter may cast more than one vote for the same candidate. • Cumulative voting helps a minority elect at least one representative. It is common in shareholder elections.

  early voting. (1984) Voting before the day of an election, esp. during a period designated for that purpose. • Unlike with absentee voting, taking advantage of early voting does not require the voter to swear to the inability to come to the polling place on election day. Cf. *absentee voting.*

  first-past-the-post voting. See *plurality voting.*

  Hare–Ware voting. See *instant-runoff voting.*

  instant-runoff voting. A system of preferential voting that mimics a runoff election by using each voter's ranked preferences instead of a second round of voting. See *runoff election* under ELECTION (3). — Also termed *Hare–Ware voting*; *West Australian plan.* Abbr. IRV.

  limited voting. A system in which each voter must cast fewer votes than the number of representatives being elected.

  low-total voting. A system of weighted preferential voting that adds up the ranked preferences — "1" for a first choice, "2" for a second choice, and so forth — so that the most-preferred candidate wins by having the lowest total. See *preferential voting*; *weighted vote* under VOTE (1).

  majority voting. A system in which each voter may cast one vote per representative being elected, and a simple majority is required for election.

  noncumulative voting. (1956) A corporate voting system in which a shareholder is limited in board elections to voting no more than the number of shares that he or she owns for a single candidate. • The result is that a majority shareholder will elect the entire board of directors. — Also termed *straight voting.*

  plurality voting. Election by plurality. See PLURALITY. — Also termed *first-past-the-post voting.*

  preferential voting. A system in which each voter ranks the choices in order of preference. • A preferential vote may be transferable or weighted. — Also termed *rank-order voting.* See *single transferable vote* under VOTE (1); *weighted vote* under VOTE (1).

  proportional voting. A system of transferable preferential voting in a multi-representative election. See *preferential vote* under VOTE (1); *single transferable vote* under VOTE (1). — Also termed *proportional representation.*

  rank-order voting. See *preferential voting.*

  straight voting. See *noncumulative voting.*

  two-round voting. A system in which the voting occurs in two rounds, with the first round determining the candidate's eligibility for the second round. • The second round may be a runoff between the top two candidates from the first round, an election by plurality among candidates who won their political parties' nominations in the first round, or an election by plurality among the candidates from the first round who reached a certain threshold. See *runoff election* under ELECTION (3).

  voting by class. See *class voting.*

  voting by voting group. See *class voting.*

  voting by yeas and nays. See *roll-call vote* under VOTE (4).

voting agreement. See POOLING AGREEMENT.

voting by class. See *class voting* under VOTING.

voting by voting group. See *class voting* under VOTING.

voting group. (1972) **1.** A classification of shareholders by the type of stock held for voting on corporate matters. **2.** Collectively, the shareholders falling within such a classification.

voting member. See MEMBER.

Voting Rights Act. The federal law that guarantees a citizen's right to vote, without discrimination based on race, color, or previous condition of servitude. 42 USCA §§ 1971–1974.

voting security. See *voting stock* under STOCK.

voting stock. See STOCK.

voting-stock rights. A stockholder's right to vote stock in the affairs of the company. • Typically, holders of common stock have one vote for each share. Holders of preferred stock usu. have the right to vote when preferred dividends are in default for a specified period.

voting trust. See TRUST.

voting-trust certificate. A certificate issued by a voting trustee to the beneficial holders of shares held by the voting trust. ● A voting-trust certificate may be as readily transferable as the underlying shares; it carries with it all the incidents of ownership except the power to vote. See *voting trust* under TRUST.

vouch, *vb.* (14c) **1.** To answer for (another); to personally assure <the suspect's mother vouched for him>. **2.** To call upon, rely on, or cite as authority; to substantiate with evidence <counsel vouched the mathematical formula for determining the statistical probability>. **3.** *Hist.* To call into court to warrant and defend, usu. in a fine and recovery. See FINE (1). **4.** *Hist.* To authenticate (a claim, etc.) by vouchers.

vouchee (vow-**chee**), *n. Hist.* **1.** A person vouched into court; one who has been vouched over. See VOUCH OVER. **2.** A person cited as authority in support of some fact.

voucher, *n.* (17c) **1.** Confirmation of the payment or discharge of a debt; a receipt. **2.** A written or printed authorization to disburse money. **3.** *Hist.* A person who calls on another person (the vouchee) as a witness, esp. in support of a warranty of title. **4.** *Hist.* The tenant in a writ of right.

voucher to warranty. *Hist.* The calling into court of a person who has warranted lands, by the person warranted, to come and defend a lawsuit.

vouching-in. (1849) **1.** At common law, a procedural device by which a defendant may give notice of suit to a third party who may be liable to the defendant on the subject-matter of the suit, so that the third party will be bound by the court's decision. ● Although this device has been largely replaced by third-party practice, it remains available under the Federal Rules of Civil Procedure. *Humble Oil & Refining Co. v. Philadelphia Ship Maintenance Co.,* 444 F.2d 727, 735 (3d Cir. 1971). **2.** The invitation of a person who is liable to a defendant in a lawsuit to intervene and defend so that, if the invitation is denied and the defendant later sues the person invited, the latter is bound by any determination of fact common to the two lawsuits. See UCC § 2-607. **3.** IMPLEADER.

vouch over, *vb.* (16c) To cite (a person) into court in one's stead. See VOUCHEE (1).

voyage. *Maritime law.* The passing of a vessel by sea from one place, port, or country to another. ● Courts generally hold that the term includes the entire enterprise, not just the route.

foreign voyage. A voyage to a port or place within the territory of a foreign nation. ● If the voyage is from one port in a foreign country to another port in the same country, it is considered a foreign voyage.

freighting voyage. A voyage that involves a vessel's transporting cargo between terminal points.

trading voyage. A voyage that contemplates a vessel's touching and stopping at various ports to traffic in, buy and sell, or exchange commodities on the owners' and shippers' account.

voyage charter. See CHARTER (8).

voyage insurance. See INSURANCE.

voyage policy. See INSURANCE POLICY.

voyeur (voy-**yər** *also* vwah-**yər**), *n.* (1900) A person who observes something without participating; esp., one who gains pleasure by secretly observing another's genitals or sexual acts.

voyeurism, *n.* (1900) Gratification derived from observing the genitals or sexual acts of others, usu. secretly. — **voyeuristic,** *adj.*

V.P. *abbr.* See VICE PRESIDENT.

vs. *abbr.* VERSUS.

vulgar abuse. See *verbal abuse* under ABUSE.

vulgar purgation. See PURGATION.

vulgar substitution. See SUBSTITUTION (4).

vulnerable adult. See ADULT.

vulture fund. See MUTUAL FUND.

W

W-2 form. (18c) (1948) *Tax.* A statement of earnings and taxes withheld (including federal, state, and local income taxes and FICA tax) during a given tax year. ● The W-2 is prepared by the employer, provided to each employee, and filed with the Internal Revenue Service. Cf. W-4 FORM.

W-4 form. (1955) *Tax.* A form indicating the number of personal exemptions an employee is claiming and that is used by the employer in determining the amount of income to be withheld from the employee's paycheck for federal-income tax purposes. — Also termed *Employee's Withholding Allowance Certificate.* Cf. W-2 FORM.

Wade hearing. (1969) *Criminal law.* A pretrial hearing in which the defendant contests the validity of his or her out-of-court identification. ● If the court finds that the identification was tainted by unconstitutional methods, the prosecution cannot use the identification and must link the defendant to the crime by other means. *United States v. Wade,* 388 U.S. 218, 87 S.Ct. 1926 (1967).

wage, *n.* (*usu. pl.*) (14c) Payment for labor or services, usu. based on time worked or quantity produced; specif., compensation of an employee based on time worked or output of production. ● Wages include every form of remuneration payable for a given period to an individual for personal services, including salaries, commissions, vacation pay, bonuses, and the reasonable value of board, lodging, payments in kind, tips, and any similar advantage received from the employer. An employer usu. must withhold income taxes from wages. Cf. SALARY.

    covered wages. Wages on which a person is required to pay social-security taxes.

    current wages. Wages for the current period; wages that are not past due.

    front wages. Prospective compensation paid to a victim of job discrimination until the denied position becomes available.

    minimum wage. The lowest permissible hourly rate of compensation for labor, as established by federal statute and required of employers engaged in interstate commerce. 29 USCA § 206.

    noncovered wages. Wages on which a person is not required to pay social-security taxes.

    real wages. Wages representing the true purchasing power of the dollar, derived by dividing a price index into money wages.

wage, *vb.* **1.** To engage in (a war, etc.). **2.** *Archaic.* To give security for (a performance, etc.). Cf. GAGE.

Wage and Hour Division. The division of the Employment Standards Administration in the U.S. Department of Labor responsible for enforcing the Fair Labor Standards Act, the Family and Medical Leave Act, the Employee Polygraph Protection Act, and other workplace-related statutes and regulations. — Abbr. WHD. See EMPLOYMENT STANDARDS ADMINISTRATION.

wage-and-hour law. A law (such as the federal Fair Labor Standards Act) governing minimum wages and maximum working hours for employees.

wage-and-price controls. A system of government-mandated maximum prices that can be charged for different goods and services or paid to various workers in different jobs.

wage-and-price freeze. See FREEZE.

wage assignment. 1. See *attachment of wages* under ATTACHMENT (1). **2.** INCOME-WITHHOLDING ORDER. **3.** ASSIGNMENT (2).

wage-assignment order. See INCOME-WITHHOLDING ORDER.

wage-earner's plan. See CHAPTER 13.

wager, *n.* (14c) **1.** Money or other consideration risked on an uncertain event; a bet or gamble. **2.** A promise to pay money or other consideration on the occurrence of an uncertain event. **3.** See *wagering contract* under CONTRACT. — **wager,** *vb.* — **wagerer,** *n.*

wagering contract. See CONTRACT.

wager of battle. See TRIAL BY COMBAT.

wager of law. *Hist.* A method of proof in which a person defends against a claim by swearing that the claim is groundless, and by enlisting others (*compurgators*) to swear to the defendant's credibility. — Also termed *gager del ley* (**gay**-jər del **lay**); *vadiatio legis* (vad-ee-**ay**-shee-oh **lee**-jis). See COMPURGATION.

wager policy. See INSURANCE POLICY.

wages. See WAGE.

wage-withholding. See *attachment of wages* under ATTACHMENT (1).

wage-withholding order. See INCOME-WITHHOLDING ORDER.

Wagner Act. See NATIONAL LABOR RELATIONS ACT.

wagonage (**wag**-ə-nij). **1.** Transportation by a wagon. **2.** The fee for carriage by wagon. **3.** A group of wagons.

waif, *n.* (14c) **1.** An abandoned article whose owner is unknown, esp. something stolen and thrown away by the thief in flight, usu. through fear of apprehension. • At common law, if a waif, whether stolen or merely abandoned, was seized before the owner reclaimed it, the title vested in the Crown. The owner was thus punished for leaving the property or for failing to pursue the thief and attempting to recover the property. Today, however, the general rule is that a waif passes to the state in trust for the true owner, who may regain it by proving ownership. **2.** *Hist.* A homeless person, esp. a woman or child; a social outcast.

wainable (**way**-nə-bəl), *adj. Archaic.* (Of land) plowable; tillable.

wainage (**way**-nij), *n. Hist.* **1.** The plow, team, and other implements used by a person (esp. a villein) to cultivate the soil; instruments of husbandry. **2.** Cultivated land or the profits from it. — Also termed *wainagium*; *waynagium* (way-**nay**-jee-əm); (in sense 2) *gainage.*

wainbote. See BOTE (1).

wait-and-see principle. (1989) A modification to the rule against perpetuities, under which a court may determine the validity of a contingent future interest based on whether it actually vests within the perpetuities period, rather than on whether it possibly could have vested outside the period. — Also termed *second-look doctrine.*

waiting period. (1897) A period that must expire before some legal right or remedy can be enjoyed or enforced. • For example, many states have waiting periods for the issuance of marriage licenses or the purchase of handguns.

waive, *n. Archaic.* A woman who has by her conduct deprived herself of the protection of the law; a female outlaw. • The term "outlaw" usu. referred only to a male. See OUTLAW (1), (2).

waive, *vb.* (14c) **1.** To abandon, renounce, or surrender (a claim, privilege, right, etc.); to give up (a right or claim) voluntarily. • Ordinarily, to waive a right one must do it knowingly — with knowledge of the relevant facts. **2.** To refrain from insisting on (a strict rule, formality, etc.); to forgo. **3.** *Hist.* To declare someone a waif. See WAIF (2).

waiver (**way**-vər), *n.* (17c) **1.** The voluntary relinquishment or abandonment — express or implied — of a legal right or advantage; FORFEITURE (2) <waiver of notice>. • The party alleged to have waived a right must have had both knowledge of the existing right and the intention of forgoing it. Cf. ESTOPPEL.

express waiver. (18c) A voluntary and intentional waiver.

implied waiver. (18c) A waiver evidenced by a party's decisive, unequivocal conduct reasonably inferring the intent to waive.

prospective waiver. (1889) A waiver of something that has not yet occurred, such as a contractual

waiver of future claims for discrimination upon settlement of a lawsuit.

subject-matter waiver. A waiver that may result when a party voluntarily discloses a communication or privileged material about a particular topic to a third party. • A party's voluntary disclosure may lead a court to find an implied waiver that extends to all other communications relating to the same subject matter.

waiver of notice. Parliamentary law. The waiver that occurs when a defective notice for a meeting is issued but every member attends and participates without objecting to the defect.

2. The instrument by which a person relinquishes or abandons a legal right or advantage <the plaintiff must sign a waiver when the funds are delivered>.

jury waiver. A form signed by a criminal defendant who relinquishes the right to have the trial conducted before a jury.

lien waiver. A written and signed waiver of a subcontractor's mechanic's lien rights, usu. submitted to enable the owner or general contractor to receive a draw on a construction loan.

waiver by election of remedies. (1873) A defense arising when a plaintiff has sought two inconsistent remedies and by a decisive act chooses one of them, thereby waiving the other.

waiver hearing. See *transfer hearing* under HEARING.

waiver of claims and defenses. (1975) **1.** The intentional relinquishment by a maker, drawer, or other obligor under a contract of the right to assert against the assignee any claims or defenses the obligor has against the assignor. **2.** The contractual clause providing for such a waiver.

waiver of counsel. (1870) A criminal defendant's intentional relinquishment of the right to legal representation. • To be valid, a waiver of counsel must be made voluntarily, knowingly, and intelligently.

waiver of defenses. *Real estate.* A document by which a mortgagor acknowledges that the mortgage is good and valid for the full amount of the mortgage note. • This document ensures that the mortgagor has no defenses to the mortgage. — Also termed *estoppel certificate*; *no-setoff certificate*; *declaration of no defenses.*

waiver of exemption. (1846) **1.** A debtor's voluntary relinquishment of the right to an exemption from a creditor's levy or sale of any part of the debtor's personal property by judicial process. **2.** The contractual clause expressly providing for such a waiver.

waiver of immunity. (1883) The act of giving up the right against self-incrimination and proceeding to testify. See IMMUNITY (3).

waiver of notice. See WAIVER (1).

waiver-of-premium clause. *Insurance.* A provision for a waiver of premium payments after the insured has been disabled for a specified length of time, such as six months.

waiver of protest. A relinquishment by a party to a negotiable instrument of the formality of protest in case of dishonor. See PROTEST (2).

waiver of service. A defendant's voluntary submission to the jurisdiction made by signing an acknowledgment of receipt of the petition and stating that he or she waives all further service.

waiver of tort. (1815) The election to sue in quasi-contract to recover the defendant's unjust benefit, instead of suing in tort to recover damages. See *implied-in-law contract* under CONTRACT.

walk, *vb.* (1958) *Slang.* **1.** To be acquitted <though charged with three thefts, Robinson walked each time>. **2.** To escape any type of real punishment <despite the seriousness of the crime, Selvidge paid only $750: he walked>.

Walker Process claim. *Patents.* A counterclaim in an infringement suit, seeking a declaratory judgment that the patent is invalid because its owner defrauded the Patent Office. • The claim is based on antitrust law, alleging that the patentee wrongfully tried to monopolize a market. *Walker Process Equip., Inc. v. Food Mach. & Chem.*, 382 U.S. 172, 86 S.Ct. 347 (1965). — Also termed *Walker Process defense.*

walkout. 1. STRIKE (1). **2.** The act of leaving a work assignment, meeting, or other event as a show of protest.

wall. An erection of stone, brick, or other material raised to varying heights, esp. inside or surrounding a building, for privacy, security, or enclosure.

    ancient wall. A party wall that has stood for at least 20 years, thus giving each party an easement right to refuse to allow the other party to remove or substantially change the wall.

    party wall. A wall that divides two adjoining, separately owned properties and that is shared by the two property owners as tenants in common. — Also termed *common wall.*

Walsh Act. A statute, originally enacted in 1926, giving federal courts the power to subpoena and compel the return, testimony, and (if requested) production of documents or other items of U.S. citizens or residents who are abroad. • The subpoena is available for criminal proceedings, including grand-jury proceedings. 28 USCA § 1783.

Walsh–Healey Act. A federal law, enacted in 1936, stipulating that government contractors must: (1) pay their workers no less than the prevailing minimum wage; (2) observe the eight-hour day and 40-hour workweek (with time-and-a-half for work exceeding those hours); (3) employ no convict labor and no females under 18 or males under 16 years of age; and (4) maintain sanitary working conditions. 41 USCA §§ 35 et seq. — Also termed *Public Contracts Act; Walsh–Healey Public Contracts Act.*

Wands test. *Patents.* A judicial test of "undue experimentation" for determining if a patent application's specification teaches one skilled in the art how to make and work the claimed invention. *In re Wands*, 858 F.2d 731 (Fed. Cir. 1988). • The test takes account of eight factors: (1) how much experimentation would be needed, (2) how much guidance is given, (3) whether there is a working example, (4) the nature of the invention, (5) the state of the prior art, (6) the level of skill of those in the art, (7) how predictable or unpredictable the art is, and (8) the breadth of the claims. The factors (often called *Wands factors*) are illustrative rather than mandatory. See UNDUE EXPERIMENTATION.

wantage (**wahnt**-ij), *n.* A deficiency of something; specif., a vessel's deficiency of not being full, due to leakage.

wanted person. A person sought by a law-enforcement agency because the person has escaped from custody or an arrest warrant has been issued for the person's arrest.

want of amicable demand. *Louisiana law.* A defensive pleading by a defendant who seeks to avoid, delay, or defeat the plaintiff's petition. • A defendant may (1) refuse to participate in the suit (a *declinatory exception*), (2) seek to delay the litigation in the suit (a *dilatory exception*), or (3) seek to dismiss or defeat the suit (a *peremptory exception*). See *declinatory exception, dilatory exception, peremptory exception* under EXCEPTION (1).

want of consideration. (18c) The lack of consideration for a contract. See CONSIDERATION (1). Cf. FAILURE OF CONSIDERATION.

want of jurisdiction. A court's lack of power to act in a particular way or to give certain kinds of relief. • A court may have no power to act at all, may lack authority over a person or the subject matter of a lawsuit, or may have no power to act until the prerequisites for its jurisdiction have been satisfied. — Also termed *lack of jurisdiction.* See JURISDICTION.

want of prosecution. (17c) Failure of a litigant to pursue the case <dismissal for want of prosecution>. — Also termed *lack of prosecution; no progress.* — Abbr. w.o.p.

want of repair. (17c) A defective condition, such as a condition on a highway making it unsafe for ordinary travel.

wanton (**wahn**-tən), *adj.* (14c) Unreasonably or maliciously risking harm while being utterly indifferent to the consequences. ● In criminal law, *wanton* usu. connotes malice (in the criminal-law sense), while *reckless* does not. Cf. RECKLESS; WILLFUL.

wanton and reckless misconduct. See *wanton misconduct* under MISCONDUCT.

wanton misconduct. See MISCONDUCT.

wanton negligence. See *gross negligence* under NEGLIGENCE.

wantonness, *n.* (14c) Conduct indicating that the actor is aware of the risks but indifferent to the results. ● Wantonness usu. suggests a greater degree of culpability than recklessness, and it often connotes malice in criminal-law contexts. Cf. RECKLESSNESS. — **wanton,** *adj.*

war. 1. Hostile conflict by means of armed forces, carried on between nations, states, or rulers, or sometimes between parties within the same nation or state; a period of such conflict <the Gulf War>. ● A state of war may also exist without armed conflict; for example, the treaty formally ending the World War II state of war between the United States and Japan was signed seven years after the fighting ended in 1945.

  civil war. An internal armed conflict between people of the same nation; esp. (usu. cap.), the war from 1861 to 1865, resulting from the Confederate states' attempted secession from the Union.

  imperfect war. A war limited in terms of places, persons, and things.

  mixed war. A war between a nation and private individuals.

  perfect war. A war involving an entire nation against another.

  private war. A war between private persons.

  public war. A war between two nations under authority of their respective governments.

  solemn war. A war formally declared — esp. by public declaration — by one country against another.

  war of aggression. A war that the attacking nation initiates for reasons other than self-defense. ● This type of war is considered a crime against international peace under customary international law.

2. A dispute or competition between adversaries <fare wars are common in the airline industry>. **3.** A struggle to solve a pervasive problem <America's war against drugs>.

War Clause. (1943) U.S. Const. art. I, § 8, cl. 11–14, giving Congress the power to declare war. — Also termed *War Powers Clause*. See WAR POWER.

war contribution. *Int'l law.* An extraordinary payment imposed by an occupying power on the population of an occupied territory during wartime. — Often shortened to *contribution*.

war crime. Conduct that violates international laws governing the conduct of international armed conflicts. ● Examples of war crimes are the killing of hostages, abuse of civilians in occupied territories, abuse of prisoners of war, and devastation that is not justified by military necessity.

ward. (15c) **1.** A person, usu. a minor, who is under a guardian's charge or protection. See GUARDIAN (1).

  permanent ward. (1927) A ward who has been assigned a permanent guardian, the rights of the natural parents having been terminated by a juvenile court.

  temporary ward. (1901) A minor who is under the supervision of a juvenile court but whose parents' parental rights have not been terminated.

  ward-in-chancery. *Hist.* An infant under the superintendence of the chancellor.

  ward of admiralty. A seaman — so called because of the legal view that a seaman, in contractual matters, should be treated as a beneficiary and the other contracting party as a fiduciary because of the perceived inequitability of their bargaining positions.

  ward of the state. (1832) A person who is housed by, and receives protection and necessities from, the government. — Also termed *state's ward*.

2. A territorial division in a city, usu. defined for purposes of city government. **3.** The act of guarding or protecting something or someone. **4.** *Archaic.* One who guards. **5.** CASTLE-GUARD. — Formerly also termed *warda*.

warden. (13c) **1.** A person in charge of something <game warden> <port warden>; esp., the official in charge of a prison, jail, or park <prison warden> <game warden>. **2.** SERGEANT-AT-ARMS (4).

ward-in-chancery. See WARD.

ward of admiralty. See WARD.

ward of the state. See WARD.

wardship. (15c) **1.** Guardianship of a person, usu. a minor. **2.** The condition of being a ward. **3.** *Hist.* The right of the feudal lord to guardianship of a deceased tenant's minor heir until the heir reached the age of majority. — Also termed (in senses 1 & 3) *guardage*.

wardship in chivalry. Wardship as a feudal incident to the tenure of knight-service.

wardship in copyholds. Wardship by which the lord is guardian of an infant tenant by special custom.

warehouse. A building used to store goods and other items.

> **bonded warehouse.** A special type of private warehouse used to store products subject to customs duties. See WAREHOUSE SYSTEM.

warehouse book. A book used by merchants to account for quantities of goods received, shipped, and in stock.

warehouseman. See WAREHOUSER.

warehouseman's lien. See *warehouser's lien* under LIEN.

warehouser. One who, as a business, keeps or stores the goods of another for a fee. ● The transaction in which a warehouser engages is a bailment for the benefit of both parties, and the bailee is liable for ordinary negligence. — Also termed *warehouseman*. See BAILEE.

warehouse receipt. A document evidencing title to goods stored with someone else; esp., a receipt issued by a person engaged in the business of storing goods for a fee. ● A warehouse receipt, which is considered a document of title, may be a negotiable instrument and is often used for financing with inventory as security. See BAILMENT.

warehouser's lien. See LIEN.

warehouse system. A system of maintaining bonded warehouses so that importers can either store goods for reexportation without paying customs duties or store the goods without paying duties until the goods are removed for domestic consumption. See *bonded warehouse* under WAREHOUSE.

warehouse-to-warehouse cover. Insurance coverage for goods protecting against damage at any time during the shipping process, including the loading and unloading of the goods. See COMPLETE-OPERATION RULE. Cf. COMING-TO-REST DOCTRINE.

warehousing. 1. A mortgage banker's holding of mortgages until the resale market improves. **2.** A corporation's giving of advance notice of a tender offer to institutional investors, who can then buy stock in the target company before public awareness of the takeover inflates the stock's price. See TENDER OFFER.

warfare. 1. The act of engaging in war or military conflict. See WAR. **2.** Loosely, the act of engaging in any type of conflict.

> **biological warfare.** The use of biological or infectious agents in war, usu. by delivering them via airplanes or ballistic missiles. Cf. *chemical warfare*.

> **biochemical warfare.** Warfare in which both biological and chemical weapons are used. See *biological warfare*, *chemical warfare*.

> **chemical warfare.** Warfare in which deadly chemical agents, such as nerve gas, are used as weapons, usu. by delivering the chemicals via shells, missiles, or bombs. ● Chemical weapons were first used in World War I. The first international treaty forbidding the use of both chemical and biological weapons, the Protocol for the Prohibition of the Use in War of Asphyxiating, Poisonous or Other Gases, and of Biological Methods of Warfare was signed in 1925 and came into force in 1928. The United States is a signatory but with reservations. Cf. *biological warfare*.

> **economic warfare. 1.** A hostile relationship between two or more countries in which at least one tries to damage the other's economy for economic, political, or military ends. **2.** The collective measures that might be taken to achieve such ends.

> **guerrilla warfare.** Hostilities that are conducted by individuals or small groups who are usu. not part of an organized army and who fight by means of surprise attacks, ambushes, and sabotage. ● Formerly, it was thought that the hostilities had to be conducted in enemy-occupied territory. Typically, guerrilla warfare is carried out only when geographical conditions are favorable and when the civilian population is at least partly cooperative.

> **land warfare.** Hostilities conducted on the ground, as opposed to at sea or in the air.

war-mongering propaganda. See PROPAGANDA.

WARN (worn). *abbr.* WORKER ADJUSTMENT AND RETRAINING NOTIFICATION ACT.

warning. (bef. 12c) The pointing out of a danger, esp. to one who would not otherwise be aware of it. ● State and federal laws (such as 21 USCA § 825) require warning labels to be placed on potentially dangerous materials, such as drugs and equipment.

> **adequate warning.** (1885) A warning that reasonably alerts a product's average user to a potential hazard, and the nature and extent of the danger. ● Four elements have been articulated as comprising an adequate warning: (1) notice that a severe hazard exists, (2) a description of the hazard's nature, (3) a description of the hazard's possible consequences, and (4) instructions on how to avoid the hazard. In addition, the warning must be prominently displayed, and may have to illustrate the nature and severity of the hazard with pictographs.

war of aggression. See WAR.

war power. (18c) The constitutional authority of Congress to declare war and maintain armed forces (U.S. Const. art. I, § 8, cls. 11–14), and of the President to conduct war as commander-in-chief (U.S. Const. art. II, § 2, cl. 1).

War Powers Clause. See WAR CLAUSE.

war-powers resolution. (1954) A resolution passed by Congress in 1973 (over the President's veto) restricting the President's authority to involve the United States in foreign hostilities without congressional approval, unless the United States or one of its territories is attacked. 50 USCA §§ 1541–1548.

warrant, *n.* (14c) **1.** A writ directing or authorizing someone to do an act, esp. one directing a law enforcer to make an arrest, a search, or a seizure.

> ***administrative warrant.*** (1951) A warrant issued by a judge at the request of an administrative agency. • This type of warrant is sought to conduct an administrative search. See *administrative search* under SEARCH. — Also termed *administrative search warrant.*

> ***anticipatory search warrant.*** See SEARCH WARRANT.

> ***arrest warrant.*** (1894) A warrant, issued only on probable cause, directing a law-enforcement officer to arrest and bring a person to court. — Also termed *warrant of arrest.*

> ***bench warrant.*** (17c) A writ issued directly by a judge to a law-enforcement officer, esp. for the arrest of a person who has been held in contempt, has been indicted, has disobeyed a subpoena, or has failed to appear for a hearing or trial. • A bench warrant is often issued for the arrest of a child-support obligor who is found in contempt for not having paid the support obligation.

> ***blanket search warrant.*** See SEARCH WARRANT.

> ***border warrant.*** A writ of arrest or other warrant concerning debts owed, issued on one side of a national border for execution on the other side; esp., such a warrant issued on either side of the border between England and Scotland.

> ***commitment warrant.*** See *warrant of commitment.*

> ***death warrant.*** (18c) A warrant authorizing a warden or other prison official to carry out a death sentence. • A death warrant typically sets the time and place for a prisoner's execution.

> ***distress warrant.*** (18c) **1.** A warrant authorizing a court officer to distrain property. See DISTRESS. **2.** A writ allowing an officer to seize a tenant's goods for failing to pay rent due to the landlord.

> ***escape warrant.*** (18c) **1.** A warrant directing a peace officer to rearrest an escaped prisoner. **2.** *Hist.* A warrant granted to retake a prisoner who had escaped from a royal prison after being committed there. • The warrant was obtained on affidavit from the judge of the court in which the action had been brought, and was directed to all sheriffs throughout England, commanding them to retake and commit the prisoner to the nearest jail.

> ***extradition warrant.*** (1876) A warrant for the return of a fugitive from one jurisdiction to another. Cf. *rendition warrant.*

> ***fugitive warrant.*** (1900) A warrant authorizing law-enforcement officers to take into custody a person who has fled from one state to another to avoid prosecution or punishment.

> ***general warrant.*** (16c) **1.** *Hist.* A warrant issued by the English Secretary of State for the arrest of the author, printer, or publisher of a seditious libel, without naming the persons to be arrested. • General warrants were banned by Parliament in 1766. **2.** A warrant giving a law-enforcement officer broad authority to search and seize unspecified places or persons; a search or arrest warrant that lacks a sufficiently particularized description of the person or thing to be seized or the place to be searched. • General warrants are unconstitutional because they fail to meet the Fourth Amendment's specificity requirements.

> ***John Doe warrant.*** (1900) A warrant for the arrest of a person whose name is unknown. • A John Doe warrant may be issued, for example, for a person known by sight but not by name. This type of warrant is permitted in a few states, but not in federal practice.

> ***justice's warrant.*** See *peace warrant.*

> ***landlord's warrant.*** (1824) A type of distress warrant from a landlord to seize the tenant's goods, to sell them at public sale, and to compel the tenant to pay rent or observe some other lease stipulation. See DISTRAIN; DISTRESS.

> ***no-knock search warrant.*** See SEARCH WARRANT.

> ***outstanding warrant.*** (1899) An unexecuted arrest warrant.

> ***peace warrant.*** (18c) A warrant issued by a justice of the peace for the arrest of a specified person. — Also termed *justice's warrant.*

> ***possessory warrant.*** (1850) A process, similar to a search warrant, used under certain circumstances by a plaintiff to search for and recover property wrongfully taken or held by another.

> ***preliminary warrant.*** (1859) A warrant to bring a person to court for a preliminary hearing on probable cause.

> ***probation-violation warrant.*** See *violation warrant.*

> ***rendition warrant.*** (1881) A warrant requesting the extradition of a fugitive from one jurisdiction to another. Cf. *extradition warrant.*

search warrant. See SEARCH WARRANT.

surreptitious-entry warrant. (1985) A warrant authorizing a law officer to enter and observe an ongoing criminal operation (such as an illegal drug lab).

tax warrant. (18c) An official process issued for collecting unpaid taxes and under which property may be seized and sold.

valid warrant. A warrant that is regular in form and is issued by a court, body, or official having both the authority to issue the warrant for the purpose stated and jurisdiction over the person named, all the requisite proceedings for its proper issuance having taken place.

violation warrant. A warrant issued for the arrest of a convict who has violated the terms of probation, parole, or supervised release. — Also termed (narrowly) *probation-violation warrant.*

warrant of arrest. See *arrest warrant.*

warrant of commitment. A warrant committing a person to custody. — Also termed *commitment warrant.*

warrant upon indictment or information. (1903) An arrest warrant issued at the request of the prosecutor for a defendant named in an indictment or information. Fed. R. Crim. P. 9.

2. A document conferring authority, esp. to pay or receive money.

deposit warrant. A warehouse receipt used as security for a loan.

dock warrant. See DOCK RECEIPT.

interest warrant. **1.** An order by a corporation directing a bank to pay the interest due on a note, bond, or other debt to a corporate creditor. **2.** A document by which a creditor, usu. a company, asks an insurer to pay all the interest due on the insurer's notes, bonds, or other debts held by the creditor.

municipal warrant. An order to draw money from a municipality's treasury for the payment of the municipality's expenses or debts.

tax-anticipation warrant. A warrant that is issued to raise public money and that is payable out of tax receipts when collected.

treasury warrant. An order in the form of a check on which government disbursements are paid.

3. An order by which a drawer authorizes someone to pay a particular sum of money to another.

county warrant. A warrant drawn by a county official, directing the county treasurer to pay a sum of money out of county funds to bearer, to a named individual, or to the named individual's order.

4. *Securities.* An instrument granting the holder a long-term (usu. a five- to ten-year) option to buy shares at a fixed price. ● It is commonly attached to preferred stocks or bonds. — Also termed *stock warrant; subscription warrant.*

warrant, *vb.* (14) **1.** To guarantee the security of (realty or personalty, or a person) <the store warranted the safety of the customer's jewelry>. **2.** To give warranty of (title); to give warranty of title to (a person) <the seller warrants the property's title to the buyer>. **3.** To promise or guarantee <warrant payment>. **4.** To justify <the conduct warrants a presumption of negligence>. **5.** To authorize <the manager warranted the search of the premises>.

warrant arrest. See *lawful arrest* under ARREST.

Warrant Clause. (1962) The clause of the Fourth Amendment to the U.S. Constitution requiring that warrants be issued only on probable cause.

warrant creditor. See CREDITOR.

warranted arrest. See ARREST.

warranted search. See SEARCH.

warrantee (wor-ən-**tee** *or* wahr-). A person to whom a warranty is given; esp., a person who receives a written warranty. ● The term also sometimes applies to the beneficiary of an implied warranty.

warrantless arrest. See ARREST.

warrantless search. See SEARCH.

warrant of arrest. See *arrest warrant* under WARRANT (1).

warrant of attorney. 1. POWER OF ATTORNEY (1). **2.** *Archaic.* Written authority given by a client to a lawyer to appear in court and to confess judgment in favor of a specified party. ● It usu. instructed the attorney not to bring any action, seek a writ of error, or file a bill in equity that might delay the judgment. The warrant was typically given as security for an obligation on which judgment was authorized. Cf. CONFESSION OF JUDGMENT; COGNOVIT.

warrant of commitment. See WARRANT (1).

warrant of confession. See CONFESSION OF JUDGMENT.

warrant officer. 1. OFFICER (2). **2.** SERGEANT-AT-ARMS (4).

warrantor (wor-ən-tor *or* -tər *or* wahr-). (15c) A person who gives a written warranty or becomes obligated under an implied warranty. See 15 USCA § 2301(5).

warrant recall, *n.* A procedure for removing from government computers information about canceled warrants in order to avoid repeated or mistaken arrests.

warrant to sue and defend. *Hist.* **1.** Written authority given by a client to a lawyer to authorize commencement or defense of a lawsuit. **2.** A special warrant from the Crown authorizing a party to appoint an attorney to sue or defend on the party's behalf.

warrant upon indictment or information. See WARRANT (1).

warranty (wor-ən-tee *or* wahr-), *n.* (14c) **1.** *Property.* A covenant by which the grantor in a deed promises to secure to the grantee the estate conveyed in the deed, and pledges to compensate the grantee if the grantee is evicted by someone having better title. ● The covenant is binding on the grantor's heirs. Historically, a warrantor was expected to turn over land. But cash compensation could be substituted. See COVENANT (4). Cf. *quitclaim deed* under DEED.

　collateral warranty. (16c) A warranty that is made by a stranger to the title, and that consequently runs only to the covenantee and not with the land.

　general warranty. (17c) A warranty against the claims of all persons.

　lineal warranty. *Hist.* A warranty existing when an heir derives title to land from the warrantor; a warranty from the same ancestor as the one from whom the land derived.

　special warranty. (17c) A warranty against any person's claim made by, through, or under the grantor or the grantor's heirs.

2. *Contracts.* An express or implied promise that something in furtherance of the contract is guaranteed by one of the contracting parties; esp., a seller's promise that the thing being sold is as represented or promised. ● Although a court may treat a misrepresentation as an implied warranty, in general a warranty differs from a representation in four principal ways: (1) a warranty is conclusively presumed to be material, while the burden is on the party claiming breach to show that a representation is material; (2) a warranty must be strictly complied with, while substantial truth is the only requirement for a representation; (3) a warranty is an essential part of a contract, while a representation is usu. only a collateral inducement; and (4) an express warranty is usu. written on the face of the contract, while a representation may be written or oral. Cf. CONDITION (2), (3); GUARANTEE (1).

　as-is warranty. (1976) A warranty that goods are sold with all existing faults. See AS IS.

　construction warranty. (1968) A warranty from the seller or building contractor of a new home that the home is free of structural, electrical, plumbing, and other defects and is fit for its intended purpose.

　deceptive warranty. (1975) A warranty containing false or fraudulent representations or promises.

　express warranty. (17c) A warranty created by the overt words or actions of the seller. ● Under the UCC, an express warranty is created by any of the following: (1) an affirmation of fact or promise made by the seller to the buyer relating to the goods that becomes the basis of the bargain; (2) a description of the goods that becomes part of the basis of the bargain; or (3) a sample or model made part of the basis of the bargain. UCC § 2-313.

　extended warranty. (1936) An additional warranty often sold with the purchase of consumer goods (such as appliances and motor vehicles) to cover repair costs not otherwise covered by a manufacturer's standard warranty, by extending either the standard-warranty coverage period or the range of defects covered. — Also termed *extended service warranty*; *extended service contract.*

　full warranty. A warranty that fully covers labor and materials for repairs. ● Under federal law, the warrantor must remedy the consumer product within a reasonable time and without charge after notice of a defect or malfunction. 15 USCA § 2304. See MAGNUSON–MOSS WARRANTY ACT. Cf. *limited warranty.*

　implied warranty. (18c) An obligation imposed by the law when there has been no representation or promise; esp., a warranty arising by operation of law because of the circumstances of a sale, rather than by the seller's express promise.

　implied warranty of fitness for a particular purpose. (1923) A warranty — implied by law if the seller has reason to know of the buyer's special purposes for the item — that the item is suitable for those purposes. — Sometimes shortened to *warranty of fitness.*

　implied warranty of habitability. (1900) In a residential lease, a warranty from the landlord to the tenant that the leased property is fit to live in and that it will remain so during the term of the lease. — Also termed *covenant of habitability.* ● This warranty usu. applies to residential property, but a few courts, esp. in Utah, have applied it to commercial property as well.

　implied warranty of merchantability. (1896) A merchant seller's warranty — implied by law — that the thing sold is fit for its ordinary purposes. ● Under the UCC, an implied warranty of merchantability arises whenever a merchant sells goods unless the agreement expressly provides otherwise. UCC 2-314. — Sometimes shortened to *warranty of merchantability.*

limited warranty. (1871) A warranty that does not fully cover labor and materials for repairs. • Under federal law, a limited warranty must be clearly labeled as such on the face of the warranty. See MAGNUSON–MOSS WARRANTY ACT. Cf. *full warranty.*

personal warranty. (18c) A warranty arising from an obligation to pay all or part of the debt of another.

presentment warranty. (1965) An implied promise concerning the title and credibility of an instrument, made to a payor or acceptor upon presentment of the instrument for payment or acceptance. UCC §§ 3-417, 3-418.

transfer warranty. (1964) **1.** An implied promise concerning the title and credibility of an instrument, made by a transferor to a transferee and, if the transfer is by indorsement, to remote transferees. UCC §§ 3-417, 4-207. **2.** A warranty made by a transferee of a document of title upon a transfer of the document for value to the immediate transferee. UCC § 7-507.

warranty ab initio (ab i-**nish**-ee-oh). (12006) An independent subsidiary promise whose breach does not discharge the contract, but gives to the injured party a right of action for the damage sustained as a result of the breach. • *Ab initio* means that the warranty existed from the contract's inception. Cf. *warranty ex post facto.*

warranty against infringement. A merchant's warranty that the goods being sold or licensed do not violate any patent, copyright, trademark, or other intellectual-property claim. • The warranty does not arise if the buyer provides the seller with the specifications for the goods purchased. Under § 2-312(3) of the Uniform Commercial Code, the warranty against infringement is a part of the warranty of title unless it is explicitly disclaimed.

warranty ex post facto (eks pohst **fak**-toh). (1961) A broken condition for which the injured party could void the contract, but decides instead to continue the contract, with a right of action for the broken condition (which amounts to a breached warranty). • The warranty is *ex post facto* because it was not originally part of the contract. It arises only after the injured party elects to continue the contract, thereby reducing the broken condition to a breached warranty. See CONDITION (2). Cf. *warranty ab initio.*

warranty of actual title. See *warranty of title.*

warranty of assignment. (18c) An assignor's implied warranty that he or she (1) has the rights assigned, (2) will do nothing to interfere with those rights, and (3) knows of nothing that impairs the value of the assignment.

warranty of authorship. Copyright. An author's contractual warranty that the work is an original work by that author.

warranty of fitness. See *implied warranty of fitness for a particular purpose.*

warranty of merchantability. See *implied warranty of merchantability.*

warranty of title. (18c) A warranty that the seller or assignor of property has title to that property, that the transfer is rightful, and that there are no liens or other encumbrances beyond those that the buyer or assignee is aware of at the time of contracting. • This warranty arises automatically whenever anyone sells goods. — Also termed *warranty of actual title.*

written warranty. (1807) A warranty made in writing; specif., any written affirmation or promise by a supplier of a consumer product to a buyer (for purposes other than resale), forming the basis of the bargain and providing that the material or workmanship is free of defects or will be repaired or replaced free of charge if the product fails to meet the required specifications. 15 USCA § 2301.

3. *Insurance.* A pledge or stipulation by the insured that the facts relating to the person insured, the thing insured, or the risk insured are as stated.

affirmative warranty. A warranty — express or implied — that facts are as stated at the beginning of the policy period. • An affirmative warranty is usu. a condition precedent to the policy taking effect.

executory warranty. A warranty that arises when an insured undertakes to perform some executory stipulation, such as a promise that certain acts will be done or that certain facts will continue to exist.

promissory warranty. A warranty that facts will continue to be as stated throughout the policy period, such that a failure of the warranty provides the insurer with a defense to a claim under the policy. — Also termed *continuing warranty.*

warranty clause. 1. A contractual clause containing a warranty. **2.** *Oil & gas.* A provision in an oil-and-gas lease by which the lessor guarantees that title is without defect and agrees to defend it. • If the warranty is breached, the lessor may be held liable to the lessee to the extent that the lessor has received payments under the lease. Presence of a warranty in an oil-and-gas lease may also cause after-acquired interests to pass from the lessor to the lessee by application of estoppel by deed.

warranty deed. See DEED.

warren (**wor**-ən *or* **wahr**-ən). **1.** A place for the preservation of certain wildlife (such as pheasants, partridges, or rabbits). **2.** A privilege to keep wild-life or game in a warren. **3.** The area to which the privilege extends.

free warren. A warren privilege giving the grant-ee the sole right to kill the wildlife to the extent of the grantee's warren area. — Also termed *libera warrena.*

war-risk insurance. See INSURANCE.

Warsaw Convention. *Int'l law.* A treaty (to which the United States is a party) negotiated in War-saw, Poland, in 1929, consisting of uniform rules governing claims made for personal injuries aris-ing out of international air travel. Cf. MONTREAL AGREEMENT.

warship. *Int'l law.* A ship commissioned by a na-tion's military, operating with a military com-mand and crew and displaying the nation's flag or other external marks indicating its country of origin. • Under international maritime laws, war-ships are not subject to many of the safety and environmental regulations that apply to shipping vessels and passenger ships.

war zone. *Int'l law.* A designated area, on land or at sea, within which the rights of neutral countries are not respected by belligerent countries.

wash, *n.* **1.** A situation in which two effects offset each other. • For example, if an event produces gross income and also a deduction in the same amount so that taxable income is unchanged, the event creates a wash. **2.** The shallow part of a river or the arm of a sea; the sand, rocks, and gravel washed down by a mountain stream and depos-ited on level land near the mouth of a canyon.

wash sale. See SALE.

wash transaction. See *wash sale* under SALE.

waste, *n.* (15c) **1.** Permanent harm to real property committed by a tenant (for life or for years) to the prejudice of the heir, the reversioner, or the remainderman. • In the law of mortgages, any of the following acts by the mortgagor may con-stitute waste: (1) physical damage, whether inten-tional or negligent, (2) failure to maintain and repair, except for repair of casualty damage or damage caused by third-party acts, (3) failure to pay property taxes or governmental assessments secured by a lien having priority over the mort-gage, so that the payments become delinquent, (4) the material failure to comply with mortgage cov-enants concerning physical care, maintenance, construction, demolition, or casualty insurance, or (5) keeping the rents to which the mortgagee has the right of possession. — Also termed *dev-astation; vastum.*

active waste. See *commissive waste.*

affirmative waste. See *commissive waste.*

ameliorating waste (ə-**meel**-yə-ray-ting). (1927) A lessee's unauthorized change to the physical character of a lessor's property — technically constituting waste, but in fact resulting in im-provement of the property. • Generally, equity will not enjoin such waste. — Also termed *ame-liorative waste.*

commissive waste (kə-**mis**-iv). (1868) Waste caused by the affirmative acts of the tenant. — Also termed *active waste; affirmative waste; vol-untary waste.*

double waste. *Hist.* The destruction occurring when a tenant having a duty to repair allows a house to deteriorate, and then unlawfully cuts down timber to repair it.

economic waste. See ECONOMIC WASTE.

equitable waste. (1842) Waste that abuses a privi-lege of nonimpeachability at common law, for which equity will restrain the commission of willful, destructive, malicious, or extravagant waste; esp., waste caused by a life tenant who, although ordinarily not responsible for permis-sive waste, flagrantly damages or destroys the property.

permissive waste. (17c) A tenant's failure to make normal repairs to property so as to protect it from substantial deterioration.

voluntary waste. (16c) Waste resulting from some positive act of destruction. See *commis-sive waste.*

2. Refuse or superfluous material, esp. that re-maining after a manufacturing or chemical pro-cess <toxic waste>.

hazardous waste. (1974) Waste that — because of its quantity, concentration, or physical, chemi-cal, or infectious characteristics — may cause or significantly contribute to an increase in mortality or otherwise harm human health or the environment. 42 USCA § 6903(5). — Also termed *hazardous substance.*

toxic waste. (1964) Hazardous, poisonous sub-stances, such as dichlorodiphenyltrichlo-roethane (DDT). • Most states regulate the handling and disposing of toxic waste, and sev-eral federal statutes (such as the Comprehen-sive Environmental Response Compensation and Liability Act of 1980 (CERCLA), 42 USCA §§ 9601–9657) regulate the use, transportation, and disposal of toxic waste.

waste book. A merchant's book for making rough entries of transactions before posting them into a journal. — Also termed *blotter.*

wasted vote. See VOTE (1).

wastewater. See WATER.

wasting asset. See ASSET.

wasting property. See PROPERTY.

wasting trust. See TRUST.

watch, *n. Maritime law.* **1.** A division of a ship's crew <port or starboard watch>. **2.** The division of the day into time periods of service by officers and the crew <four-hour watch>.

watch, *vb. Hist.* To stand guard during the night.

water. **1.** The transparent liquid that is a chemical compound of hydrogen and oxygen (H₂O). **2.** A body of this liquid, as in a stream, river, lake, or ocean.

    backwater. Water in a stream that, because of a dam or obstruction, cannot flow forward and sometimes flows back.

    coast water. Tidewater navigable by an ocean vessel; all water opening directly or indirectly into the ocean and navigable by a vessel coming in from the ocean. — Also termed *coastal water.*

    developed water. Water brought to the surface and made available for use by the party claiming the water rights.

    diffused surface water. Water, such as rainfall runoff, that collects and flows on the ground but does not form a watercourse. ● Surface water is usu. subject to different regulations from water flowing in a watercourse. — Often shortened to *surface water.* See COMMON-ENEMY DOCTRINE; WATERCOURSE.

    excess water. Water that is flowing in a stream in addition to what may be termed adjudicated waters; any water not needed for the reasonable beneficial uses of those having priority rights. — Also termed *surplus water.*

    floodwater. Water that escapes from a watercourse in large volumes and flows over adjoining property in no regular channel.

    foreign water. Water belonging to another nation or subject to another jurisdiction.

    groundwater. Water found in layers of permeable rock or soil.

    inland waters. See INTERNAL WATERS.

    internal waters. See INTERNAL WATERS.

    navigable water. See NAVIGABLE WATER.

    navigable water of the United States. See NAVIGABLE WATER.

    percolating water. Water that oozes or seeps through the soil without a defined channel (such as rainwater or other water that has lost its status as part of a stream). ● Percolating water usu. constitutes part of the land on which it is found.

    posted water. (*usu. pl.*) A body of water that is reserved for the exclusive use of the person who owns the land surrounding it. ● The owner secures the exclusive use by posting a notice prohibiting others from using the water.

    private water. Nonnavigable water owned and controlled by one or more individuals and not subject to public use. ● If a body of water is small and of little or no practical value for general public use, it is considered private.

    public water. Water adapted for purposes of navigation or public access.

    subterranean water. Water that lies or flows beneath the earth's surface and that is not artificially confined.

    surface water. **1.** Water lying on the surface of the earth but not forming part of a watercourse or lake. ● Surface water most commonly derives from rain, springs, or melting snow. **2.** See *diffused surface water.*

    surplus water. **1.** Water running off irrigated ground; water not consumed by the irrigation process. **2.** See *excess water.*

    territorial waters. The waters under a state's or nation's jurisdiction, including both inland waters and surrounding sea (traditionally within three miles of the coastline). — Also termed *territorial sea; marine belt; maritime belt.*

    tidewater. See TIDEWATER.

    wastewater. **1.** Water that escapes from the canals, ditches, or other receptacles of the lawful claimant; water that is not used by the appropriator and is permitted to run off the appropriator's property. **2.** Water that is left over, esp. after a chemical or manufacturing process.

waterboarding. A form of torture in which water is poured over the face of a supine, immobilized victim whose head is pulled back so that the victim cannot avoid inhaling water, and thus experiences the sensation of drowning. ● In some variations, fabric or plastic may be draped over the victim's face or the victim may be gagged before the water is poured. See TORTURE.

watercourse. (16c) A body of water, usu. of natural origin, flowing in a reasonably definite channel with bed and banks. ● The term includes not just rivers and creeks, but also springs, lakes, and marshes in which such flowing streams originate or through which they flow. — Also termed *waterway.*

    ancient watercourse. A watercourse in a channel that has existed from time immemorial.

    artificial watercourse. A man-made watercourse, usu. to be used only temporarily. ● If the watercourse is of a permanent character and has been maintained for a sufficient length of time, it may be considered a natural watercourse to which riparian rights can attach.

    natural watercourse. A watercourse with its origin in the forces of nature. ● A *natural watercourse* does not include surface water, which often flows intermittently and in an indefinite channel. In addition, a natural stream is distinguished from an artificial ditch or canal, which is typically not the subject of riparian rights. See RIPARIAN RIGHTS; WATER.

water district. See DISTRICT.

watered stock. See STOCK.

waterfront, *n.* Land or land with buildings fronting a body of water.

watergage, *n.* **1.** A seawall. **2.** An instrument used to measure the height of water.

watermark. 1. A mark indicating the highest or lowest point to which water rises or falls.

    high-water mark. **1.** The shoreline of a sea reached by the water at high tide. ● The high-water mark is usu. computed as a mean or average high tide and not as the extreme height of the water. **2.** In a freshwater lake created by a dam in an unnavigable stream, the highest point on the shore to which the dam can raise the water in ordinary circumstances. **3.** In a river not subject to tides, the line that the river impresses on the soil by covering it long enough to deprive it of agricultural value. — Also termed *high-water line.*

    low-water mark. **1.** The shoreline of a sea marking the edge of the water at the lowest point of the ordinary ebb tide. **2.** In a river, the point to which the water recedes at its lowest stage.

2. The transparent design or symbol seen when paper is held up to the light, usu. to indicate the genuineness of the document or the document's manufacturer.

water ordeal. See *ordeal by water* under ORDEAL.

waterpower. 1. The force obtained by converting water into energy. **2.** The riparian owner's right consisting of the fall in the stream as it passes over or through the riparian owner's land; the difference of the level between the surface where the stream first touches one's land and the surface where the water leaves the land.

water right. (*often pl.*) (18c) The right to use water from a natural stream or from an artificial canal for irrigation, power, domestic use, and the like; RIPARIAN RIGHT. — Also termed *aquatic right.*

waterscape, *n.* (1842) An aqueduct or passage for water.

waterway. See WATERCOURSE.

waveson (wayv-sən), *n. Hist.* Goods that float on the sea after a shipwreck. Cf. FLOTSAM; JETSAM; LAGAN (1).

way. (bef. 12c) **1.** A passage or path. **2.** A right to travel over another's property. See RIGHT-OF-WAY.

    private way. (17c) **1.** The right to pass over another's land. **2.** A way provided by local authorities primarily to accommodate particular individuals (usu. at the individual's expense) but also for the public's passage.

    way of necessity. See *implied easement* under EASEMENT.

waybill. *Maritime law.* A document acknowledging the receipt of goods by a carrier or by the shipper's agent and the contract for the transportation of those goods. ● Unlike a bill of lading, a waybill is not a document of title and is nonnegotiable. — Abbr. WB. Cf. BILL OF LADING.

    air waybill. A waybill for goods shipped by air. Cf. *overseas bill of lading* under BILL OF LADING.

way-going crop. A grain crop, formerly sown by a tenant during a tenancy (esp. in Pennsylvania), that did not ripen until after expiration of the lease. ● In the absence of an express agreement to the contrary, the tenant was entitled to the crop.

way-leave, *n.* (15c) **1.** A right-of-way (usu. created by an express grant) over or through land for the transportation of minerals from a mine or quarry. **2.** The royalty paid for such a right.

way of necessity. See *implied easement* under EASEMENT.

ways-and-means committee. (1840) A legislative committee that determines how money will be raised for various governmental purposes.

WB. *abbr.* WAYBILL.

WC. *abbr.* WORKERS' COMPENSATION.

WCT. *abbr.* WIPO COPYRIGHT TREATY.

W.D. *abbr.* Western District, in reference to U.S. judicial districts.

weak mark. See *descriptive trademark* under TRADEMARK.

weak trademark. See *descriptive trademark* under TRADEMARK.

wealreaf (weel-reef), *n. Archaic.* The robbery of a dead person in a grave.

wealth. 1. A large quantity of something. **2.** The state of having abundant financial resources; affluence.

wealth maximization. A situation resulting from a change in the allocation of resources if the change benefits the winner — i.e., the one who benefits from the change — more than it harms the loser. ● A situation in which all possible wealth-maximizing changes have occurred is described as *Kaldor-Hicks efficient* or as being *potentially Pareto superior.* See PARETO OPTIMALITY; PARETO SUPERIORITY.

weapon. (bef. 12c) An instrument used or designed to be used to injure or kill someone.

    concealed weapon. (1833) A weapon that is carried by a person but that is not visible by ordinary observation.

dangerous weapon. (17c) An object or device that, because of the way it is used, is capable of causing serious bodily injury.

deadly weapon. (16c) Any firearm or other device, instrument, material, or substance that, from the manner in which it is used or is intended to be used, is calculated or likely to produce death. ● In some states, the definition encompasses the likelihood of causing either death or serious physical injury. — Also termed *lethal weapon.* Cf. DANGEROUS INSTRUMENTALITY.

deadly weapon per se. (1872) A weapon that is deadly in and of itself or would ordinarily result in death by its use <a gun is a deadly weapon per se>. — Also termed *per se deadly weapon.*

lethal weapon. See *deadly weapon.*

nondeadly weapon. See LESS-LETHAL.

nonlethal weapon. See LESS-LETHAL.

weapon of mass destruction. (*usu. pl.*) A weapon that is intended to kill human beings, without discriminating between combatants and noncombatants, on a massive scale. ● Among the most frequently cited examples are nuclear weapons and chemical weapons. — Abbr. WMD.

wear and tear. (17c) Deterioration caused by ordinary use; the depreciation of property resulting from its reasonable use <the tenant is not liable for normal wear and tear to the leased premises>. — Also termed *fair wear and tear*; *natural wear and tear.*

Webb–Pomerene Act. A federal law, originally enacted in 1918, that provides a qualified exemption for an export business against the prohibitions of the antitrust laws. 15 USCA §§ 61 et seq.

website-user agreement. See POINT-AND-CLICK AGREEMENT.

web-wrap agreement. See POINT-AND-CLICK AGREEMENT.

wedding. See MARRIAGE CEREMONY.

wedge principle. (1951) The argument that relaxation of a constitutionally imposed restraint under specific circumstances may justify further relaxation in broader circumstances. ● This principle is most often raised in the context of legalized human euthanasia. But it has frequently been invoked in other contexts, such as the right to protection from unreasonable search and seizure. — Also termed *slippery-sloped principle*; *parade-of-horrors objection.*

wedlock. The state of being married; matrimony.

week. 1. A period of seven consecutive days beginning on either Sunday or Monday. **2.** Any consecutive seven-day period.

weekend sentence. See *intermittent sentence* under SENTENCE.

weighage (**way**-ij). A duty or other payment required in return for weighing merchandise.

weight. A measure of heaviness; a measure of the quantity of matter.

gross weight. The total weight of a thing, including its contents and any packaging.

net weight. The total weight of a thing, after deducting its container, its wrapping, and any other extraneous matter.— Also termed *neat weight.*

weighted vote. See VOTE (1).

weight of the evidence. (17c) The persuasiveness of some evidence in comparison with other evidence <because the verdict is against the great weight of the evidence, a new trial should be granted>. See BURDEN OF PERSUASION. Cf. MANIFEST WEIGHT OF THE EVIDENCE; PREPONDERANCE OF THE EVIDENCE.

Weingarten right. *Labor law.* A union member's right to have a union representative present during an employment meeting that the member reasonably believes will result in disciplinary action. *NLRB v. J. Weingarten, Inc.,* 420 U.S. 251, 95 S.Ct. 959 (1975). ● In July 2000, the NLRB extended *Weingarten* rights to nonunion employees.

welching. See WELSHING.

welfare. (14c) **1.** Well-being in any respect; prosperity.

general welfare. (17c) The public's health, peace, morals, and safety.

public welfare. (16c) A society's well-being in matters of health, safety, order, morality, economics, and politics.

2. A system of social insurance providing assistance to those who are financially in need, as by providing food stamps and family allowances. — Also termed (historically) *poor relief.*

corporate welfare. Governmental financial assistance given to a large company, usu. in the form of a subsidy.

Welfare Clause. See GENERAL WELFARE CLAUSE.

welfare plan. See EMPLOYEE BENEFIT PLAN.

welfare state. (1894) A nation in which the government undertakes various social insurance programs, such as unemployment compensation, old-age pensions, family allowances, food stamps, and aid to the blind or deaf. — Also termed *welfare-regulatory state.*

well, *adj. Marine insurance.* (Of a vessel) in good condition; safe and sound <the vessel was warranted well on January 1>.

well, *adv.* (bef. 12c) In a legally sufficient manner; unobjectionable <well-pleaded complaint>.

well, *n.* A hole or shaft sunk into the earth to obtain a fluid, such as water, oil, or natural gas.

limited-capacity well. An oil or gas well that is limited to producing only a portion of its monthly allowable because of market demand.

stripper well. An oil or gas well that produces only small quantities. • In some states, such as Kansas and Illinois, stripper wells are common.

well-completion clause. *Oil & gas.* A provision in an oil-and-gas lease specifying that a lessee who starts drilling before the lease terminates has the right to complete the well and to maintain the lease if the drilling achieves production. See OP-ERATIONS CLAUSE.

well-knowing, *adj.* (17c) Intentional <a well-knowing act or omission>. • This term was formerly used in a pleading to allege scienter. See SCIENTER.

well-pleaded complaint. See COMPLAINT.

welshing. (1857) **1.** The act or an instance of evading an obligation, esp. a gambling debt. **2.** The common-law act of larceny in which one receives a deposit to be paid back with additional money depending on the outcome of an event (such as a horse race) but at the time of the deposit the depositee intends to cheat and defraud the depositor by absconding with the money. • Although this term is sometimes thought to be a slur against those hailing from Wales, etymologists have not been able to establish this connection. Authoritative dictionaries record the origin of the term as being unknown. — Also termed *welching.* — **welsh,** *vb.* — **welsher,** *n.*

Welsh mortgage. See MORTGAGE.

West Australian plan. See *instant-runoff voting* under VOTING.

Westlaw. A West Group database for computer-assisted legal research, providing online access to legal resources, including federal and state caselaw, statutes, regulations, legal treatises, legal periodicals, and general and business news. — Abbr. WL.

West Point. See UNITED STATES MILITARY ACADEMY.

West-Saxon law. *Hist.* A system of rules introduced by the West Saxons and one of the three principal legal systems prevailing in England in the beginning of the 11th century. • It was observed primarily in southern English counties from Kent to Devonshire. — Also termed *West-Saxon lage.* See MERCENLAGE; DANELAW.

Wetterling Act. See JACOB WETTERLING CRIMES AGAINST CHILDREN AND SEXUALLY VIOLENT OFFENDER REGISTRATION ACT.

wharf. A structure on the shores of navigable waters, to which a vessel can be brought for loading or unloading.

private wharf. One that can be used only by its owner or lessee.

public wharf. One that can be used by the public.

Wharton's rule ([h]**wor**-tən). (1940) *Criminal law.* The doctrine that an agreement by two or more persons to commit a particular crime cannot be prosecuted as a conspiracy if the crime could not be committed except by the actual number of participants involved. • But if an additional person participates so as to enlarge the scope of the agreement, all the actors may be charged with conspiracy. The doctrine takes its name from the influential criminal-law author Francis Wharton (1820–1889). — Also termed *Wharton rule*; *concert-of-action rule.*

WHD. *abbr.* WAGE AND HOUR DIVISION.

wheelage ([h]**weel**-ij), *n. Hist.* A duty or toll for a vehicle to pass over certain property.

wheel conspiracy. See CONSPIRACY.

when-issued security. See SECURITY.

whereabouts, *n.* (17c) The general locale where a person or thing is <her whereabouts are unknown> <the Joneses' present whereabouts is a closely guarded secret>. • As the examples illustrate, this noun, though plural in form, may be construed with either a plural or a singular verb. — **whereabouts,** *adv. & conj.*

whereas, *conj.* (14c) **1.** While by contrast; although <McWilliams was stopped at 10:08 p.m. wearing a green hat, whereas the assailant had been identified at 10:04 p.m. wearing a black hat>. **2.** Given the fact that; since <Whereas, the parties have found that their 1994 agreement did not adequately address incidental expenses . . . ; and Whereas, the parties have now decided in an equitable sharing of those expenses . . . ; Now, Therefore, the parties agree to amend the 1994 agreement as follows . . . >. • In sense 2, *whereas* is used to introduce contractual recitals and the like, but modern drafters increasingly prefer a simple heading, such as "Recitals" or "Preamble," and in that way avoid the legalistic *whereas*es. — **whereas** (recital or preamble), *n.*

whereas clause. 1. See PREAMBLE (1). **2.** See RECITAL (2).

whereat, *conj.* (14c) **1.** At or toward which <the point whereat he was aiming>. **2.** As a result of which; whereupon <Pettrucione called Bickley a scurrilous name, whereat a fistfight broke out>.

whereby, *conj.* (13c) By which; through which; in accordance with which <the treaty whereby the warring nations finally achieved peace>.

wherefore, premises considered. (1867) For all these reasons; for the reason or reasons mentioned above. • The phrase is often used to begin the final paragraph of a motion, judgment, contract, or agreement.

wherefrom, *conj.* (14c) From which <the students sent two faxes to the president's office, wherefrom no reply ever came>.

wherein, *conj.* (14c) **1.** In which; where <the jurisdiction wherein Lynn practices>. **2.** During which <they listened intently at the concert, wherein both of them became convinced that the composer's "new" work was a fraud>. **3.** How; in what respect <Fallon demanded to know wherein she had breached any duty>. — **wherein,** *adv.*

whereof, *conj.* (13c) **1.** Of what <Judge Wald knows whereof she speaks>. **2.** Of which <citations whereof even the most responsible are far afield from the true issue>. **3.** Of whom <judges whereof only the most glowing words might be said>.

whereon, *conj.* (13c) On which <the foundation whereon counsel bases this argument>. — Also termed *whereupon.*

whereto, *conj.* (14c) To what place or time <at first, Campbell did not know whereto he was being taken>. — Also termed *whereunto.* — **whereto,** *adv.*

whereupon, *conj.* (14c) **1.** WHEREON <the precedent whereupon the defense bases its argument>. **2.** Soon after and as a result of which; and then <a not-guilty verdict was announced, whereupon a riot erupted>.

wherewith, *conj.* (14c) By means of which <the plaintiff lacked a form of action wherewith to state a compensable claim>.

whim. A passing fancy; an impulse <the jury was instructed to render a verdict based solely on the evidence, not on a whim>.

whipping, *n.* A method of corporal punishment formerly used in England and a few American states, consisting of inflicting long welts on the skin, esp. with a whip.

whipsaw strike. See STRIKE.

whisper stock. See STOCK.

whistleblower, *n.* (1970) An employee who reports employer wrongdoing to a governmental or law-enforcement agency. ● Federal and state laws protect whistleblowers from employer retaliation. — **whistleblowing,** *n.*

whistleblower act. (1984) A federal or state law protecting employees from retaliation for properly disclosing employer wrongdoing such as violating a law or regulation, mismanaging public funds, abusing authority, or endangering public health or safety. ● Federal laws containing whistleblower provisions include the Whistleblower Protection Act (5 USCA § 1211), the Occupational Safety and Health Act (29 USCA § 660), CERCLA (42 USCA § 9610), and the Air Pollution and Control Act (42 USCA § 7622).

Whiteacre. (17c) A fictitious tract of land used in legal discourse (esp. law-school hypotheticals) to discuss real-property issues. See BLACKACRE.

white book. 1. *Hist.* (*cap.*) ALBUS LIBER. **2.** A government report bound in white, common esp. in European and papal affairs.

whitecapping. (1900) *Criminal law.* The criminal act of threatening a person — usu. a member of a minority group — with violence in an effort to compel the person either to move away or to stop engaging in a certain business or occupation. ● Whitecapping statutes were originally enacted to curtail the activities of the Ku Klux Klan.

white-collar crime. (1940) A nonviolent crime usu. involving cheating or dishonesty in commercial matters. ● Examples include fraud, embezzlement, bribery, and insider trading.

whitehorse case. (1971) *Slang.* A reported case with facts virtually identical to those of the instant case, so that the disposition of the reported case should determine the outcome of the instant case. — Also termed *horse case; goose case; gray mule case; red-cow case.* Cf. ON ALL FOURS.

white knight. A person or corporation that rescues the target of an unfriendly corporate takeover, esp. by acquiring a controlling interest in the target corporation or by making a competing tender offer. — Also termed *friendly suitor.* See TAKEOVER. Cf. CORPORATE RAIDER.

Whiteley rule. See FELLOW-OFFICER RULE.

White model. *Labor law.* A method for determining whether a union member's state-law claim against the employer is preempted by federal law, by focusing on whether state law permits the claim to be waived by a private contract. ● In *Lingle v. Norge Division of Magic Chef, Inc.,* 486 U.S. 399, 108 S.Ct. 1877 (1988), the Supreme Court held that a union member's state-law retaliatory-discharge claim was not preempted by the Labor-Management Relations Act because the claim could be resolved without interpreting the collective-bargaining agreement. There are at least two models for applying the *Lingle* test: the White model, which focuses on whether the claim is negotiable or nonnegotiable (that is, whether state law allows the claim to be waived by a private contract) and the Marcus model, which focuses on the independence of the claim in relation to the collective-bargaining agreement. Under the White model, all negotiable claims (those waivable by private contract) are necessarily preempted because their resolution will require an interpretation of the collective-bargaining agreement. A nonnegotiable claims (one that state law does not permit to be waived by private contract) will be preempted only if its resolution requires an interpretation of the collective-bargaining agreement. The White model is named for the author of the law-review article in which it was proposed. Rebecca Homer White, *Section 301's Preemption of State Law Claims: A Model for Analysis*, 41 Ala. L. Rev. 377 (1990). See LINGLE TEST. Cf. MARCUS MODEL.

white rent. *Hist.* A feudal rent paid in silver, rather than in work, grain, or money baser than silver. Cf. BLACK RENT.

white slavery. The practice of forcing a female (or, rarely, a male) to engage in commercial prostitution. • Trafficking in persons for prostitution is prohibited by the Mann Act (18 USCA §§ 2421–2424).

White Slave Traffic Act. See MANN ACT.

whole blood. See *full blood* under BLOOD.

whole law. The law applied by a forum court in a multistate or multinational case after referring to its own choice-of-law rules.

whole life insurance. See LIFE INSURANCE.

wholesale, *n.* The sale of goods or commodities usu. to a retailer for resale, and not to the ultimate consumer. Cf. RETAIL. — **wholesale,** *vb.* — **wholesale,** *adj.*

wholesale arrest. See *dragnet arrest* under ARREST.

wholesale dealer. One who sells goods in gross to retail dealers rather than selling in smaller quantities directly to consumers.

wholesale price. See PRICE.

wholesale price index. See PRODUCER PRICE INDEX.

wholesaler. One who buys large quantities of goods and resells them in smaller quantities to retailers or other merchants, who in turn sell to the ultimate consumer.

whole-statute rule. The principle of statutory construction that a statute should be considered in its entirety, and that the words used within it should be given their ordinary meanings unless there is a clear indication to the contrary.

wholly, *adv.* Not partially; fully; completely.

wholly and permanently disabled, *adj. Insurance.* (Of an insured) completely and continuously unable to perform work for compensation or profit.

wholly dependent, *adj. Workers' compensation.* (Of a person) deriving full support from a worker's wages.

wholly destroyed, *adj. Insurance.* (Of a building) so damaged that it is no longer capable of being classified as a building, although some parts may remain intact.

wholly disabled, *adj. Insurance.* (Of a person) unable to perform the substantial and material acts necessary to carry on a business or occupation in the customary and usual manner.

whorehouse. See BROTHEL.

widow, *n.* A woman whose husband has died and who has not remarried.

widower, *n.* A man whose wife has died and who has not remarried.

widower's allowance. See *spousal allowance* under ALLOWANCE (1).

widow's allowance. See *spousal allowance* under ALLOWANCE (1).

widow's election. See RIGHT OF ELECTION.

wife. A married woman; a woman who has a lawful spouse living.

   common-law wife. **1.** The wife in a common-law marriage; a woman who contracts an informal marriage with a spouse and then holds herself out to the community as being married to that spouse. See *common-law marriage* under MARRIAGE (1). **2.** *Archaic.* Loosely, a concubine.

   plural wife. One of two or more women married simultaneously to the same spouse in a polygamous marriage.

wife beating. See *spousal abuse* under ABUSE.

wife's equity. See EQUITY TO A SETTLEMENT.

wife's settlement. See EQUITY TO A SETTLEMENT.

wild animal. See ANIMAL.

wildcat strike. See STRIKE.

wild creature. See *wild animal* under CREATURE.

wild deed. See DEED.

Wild's Case, Rule in. See RULE IN WILD'S CASE.

wilful. See WILLFUL.

will, *n.* (bef. 12c) **1.** Wish; desire; choice <employment at will>. **2.** The legal expression of an individual's wishes about the disposition of his or her property after death; esp., a document by which a person directs his or her estate to be distributed upon death <there was no mention of his estranged brother in the will>. — Also termed *testament; will and testament;* (archaically) *testamentary instrument.* — **will,** *vb.*

   ambulatory will. (1909) A will that can be altered during the testator's lifetime.

   antenuptial will. See *prenuptial will.*

   attested will. A will that has been signed by a witness.

   bogus will. An unauthentic will, esp. one involving fraud or unauthorized changes.

   closed will. See *mystic will.*

   conditional will. A will that depends on the occurrence of an uncertain event for the will to take effect. ● Most jurisdictions hold a conditional will valid even though the testator's death does not result from or on the occasion of the condition mentioned in the will. The courts generally hold that the condition is the inducement for making the will rather than a condition precedent to its operation. See *Eaton v. Brown*, 193 U.S. 411, 24 S.Ct. 487 (1904); *In re Will of Cohen*, 491 A.2d 1292 (N.J. Super. Ct. App. Div. 1985). Cf. *contingent will.*

conjoint will. See *joint will.*

contingent will. A will that takes effect only if a specified event occurs. Cf. *conditional will.*

counter will. See *mutual will.*

double will. See *mutual will.*

duplicate will. (1855) A will executed in duplicate originals by a testator who retains one copy and gives the second copy to another person. ● The rules applicable to wills apply to both wills, and upon application for probate, both copies must be tendered into the registry of the probate court.

holographic will (hol-ə-**graf**-ik). (1850) A will that is handwritten by the testator. ● Such a will is typically unattested. Holographic wills are rooted in the civil-law tradition, having originated in Roman law and having been authorized under the Napoleonic Code. French and Spanish settlers introduced holographic wills in America, primarily in the South and West. Today they are recognized in about half the states. — Also termed *olographic will.* See HOLOGRAPH.

inofficious will. See *inofficious testament* under TESTAMENT.

international will. A will that is executed according to formalities provided in an international treaty or convention, and that will be valid although it may be written in a foreign language by a testator domiciled in another country.

invalid will. (18c) A will that fails to make an effective disposition of property.

joint and mutual will. (1841) A single will executed by two or more people — to dispose of property they own separately, in common, or jointly — requiring the surviving testator to dispose of the property in accordance with the terms of the will. ● A joint and mutual will is drafted to be contractually binding on the survivor. The word "joint" indicates the form of the will. The word "mutual" describes the substantive provisions. — Also termed *joint and reciprocal will.*

joint and reciprocal will. See *joint and mutual will.*

joint will. (18c) A single will executed by two or more testators, usu. disposing of their common property by transferring their separate titles to one devisee. — Also termed *conjoint will.*

last will. (16c) The most recent will of a deceased; the instrument ultimately fixing the disposition of real and personal property at the testator's death. — Also termed *last will and testament.*

last will and testament. See *last will.*

living will. See LIVING WILL.

lost will. An executed will that cannot be found at the testator's death. ● Its contents can be proved by parol evidence in many jurisdictions. But the overwhelming majority of American jurisdictions follow the common-law presumption of revocation if a will is proved to have been in the possession of the testator and has since been lost.

mancipatory will (**man**-sip-i-tor-ee). *Roman law.* In early and classical law, a formal will sealed by seven witnesses and submitted to the praetor.

mariner's will. See *soldier's will.*

mutual will. (*usu. pl.*) (1837) One of two separate wills in which two persons, usu. a husband and wife, establish identical or similar testamentary provisions disposing of their estates in favor of each other. ● It is also possible (though rare) for the testators to execute a single mutual will, as opposed to separate ones. And it is possible (though, again, rare) for more than two parties to execute mutual wills. — Also termed *reciprocal will; counter will; double will; mutual testament.*

mystic will. *Civil law.* A secret will signed by the testator, sealed and delivered to a notary in the presence of three to seven witnesses, accompanied by the testator's declaration that it is a valid will. ● The notary is then required to indorse on the envelope containing the will a statement of all the facts surrounding the transaction, and this is signed by the notary and all the witnesses. — Also termed *mystic testament; secret will; secret testament; closed will; closed testament; sealed will; sealed testament.*

nonintervention will. A will that authorizes an independent executor. See *independent executor* under EXECUTOR.

notarial will. A will executed by a testator in the presence of two witnesses and a notary public.

nuncupative will (nəng-kyə-pay-tiv *or* nəng-**kyoo**-pə-tiv). (18c) An oral will made in contemplation of imminent death, esp. from a recent injury. ● Nuncupative wills are invalid in most states. Even in states allowing them, the amount that may be conveyed is usu. limited by statute. Traditionally, only personal property may be conveyed. — Also termed *oral will; unwritten will; verbal will.*

nuncupative will by public act. *Hist.* Louisiana law. A will dictated by the testator to a notary in the presence of a specified number of witnesses. • The notary had to read the will back to the testator. The testator and the witnesses then signed the will. If the testator was physically unable to sign, another person could sign in the testator's presence on the testator's behalf. The number of required witnesses varied depending on the circumstances. This type of will was abolished in 1997. *See* La. Civ. Code art. 1574. — Also termed *nuncupative testament by public act.*

olographic will. See *holographic will.*

oral will. (1853) A will made by the spoken declaration of the testator and usu. dependent on oral testimony for proof. See *nuncupative will.*

parliamentary will. *Slang.* The legislation that governs the distribution of an intestate's property. • The term arose because the legislature effectively makes an intestate's will by passing statutes regulating descent and distribution. The terms of the parliamentary will are gathered from the statutes in effect when the intestate died.

postnuptial will (pohst-**nəp**-shəl). A will executed after marriage.

pourover will (**por**-oh-vər). (1946) A will giving money or property to an existing trust. Cf. *pourover trust* under TRUST.

prenuptial will (pree-**nəp**-shəl). (1914) A will executed before marriage. • At common law, marriage automatically revoked a spouse's will, but modern statutes usu. provide that marriage does not revoke a will (although divorce does). But if this marriage was not contemplated by the will and there is nothing otherwise on its face to indicate that the testator intentionally left nothing to any future spouse, the pretermitted spouse may be entitled to a special forced share of the estate. Uniform Probate Code § 2-508. — Also termed *antenuptial will.*

reciprocal will. See *mutual will.*

sealed will. See *mystic will.*

seaman's will. See *soldier's will.*

secret will. See *mystic will.*

self-proved will. (1963) A will proved by a self-proving affidavit. See *self-proving affidavit* under AFFIDAVIT. • This method of proof, recognized in a growing number of states, eliminates the practical problems of obtaining the live testimony of witnesses.

soldier's will. A soldier's informal oral or written will that is usu. valid despite its noncompliance with normal statutory formalities, as long as the soldier was in actual service at the time the will was made. — Also termed *seaman's will;*

mariner's will; military testament; soldier's and sailor's will.

undutiful will. *Civil law.* See *unnatural will.*

unnatural will. (1854) A will that distributes the testator's estate to strangers rather than to the testator's relatives, without apparent reason. — Also termed (in civil law) *undutiful will.*

unofficious will. See *inofficious testament* under TESTAMENT.

unsolemn will. *Civil law.* A will in which an executor is not named.

unwritten will. See *nuncupative will.*

verbal will. See *nuncupative will.*

will and testament. See WILL.

will contest. *Wills & estates.* The litigation of a will's validity, usu. based on allegations that the testator lacked capacity or was under undue influence.

willful, *adj.* (13c) Voluntary and intentional, but not necessarily malicious. — Sometimes spelled *wilful.* Cf. WANTON. — **willfulness,** *n.*

willful and malicious injury. See INJURY.

willful and wanton misconduct. See MISCONDUCT.

willful and wanton negligence. See *gross negligence* under NEGLIGENCE.

willful blindness. (1927) Deliberate avoidance of knowledge of a crime, esp. by failing to make a reasonable inquiry about suspected wrongdoing despite being aware that it is highly probable. • A person acts with willful blindness, for example, by deliberately refusing to look inside an unmarked package after being paid by a known drug dealer to deliver it. Willful blindness creates an inference of knowledge of the crime in question. *See* Model Penal Code § 2.

willful-blindness instruction. See JURY INSTRUCTION.

willful, continued, and obstinate desertion. See *obstinate desertion* under DESERTION.

willful homicide. See HOMICIDE.

willful indifference to the safety of others. See *willful and wanton misconduct* under MISCONDUCT.

willful infringement. See INFRINGEMENT.

willful misconduct. See MISCONDUCT.

willful misconduct of an employee. See MISCONDUCT.

willful murder. See MURDER.

willful neglect. See NEGLECT.

willful negligence. **1.** See *advertent negligence* under NEGLIGENCE. **2.** See *gross negligence* (2) under NEGLIGENCE.

willfulness. (13c) **1.** The fact or quality of acting purposely or by design; deliberateness; intention. • Willfulness does not necessarily imply malice, but it involves more than just knowledge. **2.** The voluntary, intentional violation or disregard of a known legal duty. — Also termed *legal willfulness.*

willful tort. See *intentional tort* under TORT.

willful wrong. See *intentional wrong* under WRONG.

Williams Act. A federal statute, enacted in 1968, that amended the Securities Exchange Act of 1934 by requiring investors who own more than 5% of a company's stock to furnish certain information to the SEC and to comply with certain requirements when making a tender offer.

Wills Act. 1. STATUTE OF WILLS (1). **2.** An 1837 English statute that allowed people to dispose of every type of property interest by will and that had an elaborate set of requirements for valid execution. • Some states today continue to adhere to these stringent requirements. Cf. Uniform Probate Code § 2-502. — Also termed (in sense 2) *Lord Langdale's Act.*

will substitute. A document or instrument that allows a person, upon death, to dispose of an estate in the same or similar manner as a will but without the formalities and expense of a probate proceeding. • The most common will substitutes are trusts, life-insurance plans, and retirement-benefits contracts. The creation of will substitutes has been one of the most important developments in the area of decedents' estates in the past 50 years. Cf. *nonprobate asset* under ASSET.

Winchester measure. *Hist.* The standard weights and measures of England, originally kept at Winchester.

windfall. (15c) An unanticipated benefit, usu. in the form of a profit and not caused by the recipient.

windfall-profits tax. See TAX.

winding up, *n.* (1858) The process of settling accounts and liquidating assets in anticipation of a partnership's or a corporation's dissolution. Cf. DISSOLUTION (4). — **wind up,** *vb.* — **wind up,** *n.*

window-dressing. (1898) The deceptive arrangement of something, usu. facts or appearances, to make it appear more attractive or favorable. • The term is often used to describe the practice of some financial managers, esp. some managers of mutual funds, to sell certain positions at the end of a quarter to make an investment's quarterly performance appear better than it actually was.

winner-take-all vote. See VOTE (3).

wipe. See SWIPE (3).

WIPO. *abbr.* WORLD INTELLECTUAL PROPERTY ORGANIZATION.

WIPO Copyright Treaty. A 1996 treaty that made changes in the Berne Convention in light of the TRIPs Agreement and dealt with new copyright issues raised by the emergence of the Internet and other digital technology. • The WIPO Treaty expressly protects computer software and databases and expressly excludes from protection "ideas, procedures, methods of operation or mathematical concepts as such." The WIPO Copyright Treaty was adopted simultaneously with the WIPO Performances and Phonograms Treaty. — Abbr. WCT.

WIPO digital agenda. See DIGITAL AGENDA.

WIPO Performances and Phonograms Treaty. A 1996 treaty giving performers the rights of attribution and integrity in their performances, and giving producers the rights of reproduction, distribution, rental, and availability. — Abbr. WPPT.

wire fraud. See FRAUD.

wiretapping, *n.* (1904) Electronic or mechanical eavesdropping, usu. done by law-enforcement officers under court order, to listen to private conversations. • Wiretapping is regulated by federal and state law. — Often shortened to *tapping.* See BUGGING; EAVESDROPPING. Cf. PEN REGISTER. — **wiretap,** *vb.* — **wiretap,** *n.*

Wisby, laws of. See LAWS OF VISBY.

wish, *vb.* **1.** To desire; to hope. **2.** To will; to devise; to give.

witchcraft. The practices of a witch, esp. in black magic; sorcery. • Under the Witchcraft Act of 1541 (33 Hen. 8, ch. 8) and the Witchcraft Act of 1603 (1 Jac. ch. 12), witchcraft was a felony punishable by death without benefit of clergy. The last execution in England for witchcraft occurred in 1716. The Acts were repealed in 1736. In the United States, the most conspicuous (and nearly the last) persecution for witchcraft occurred in Salem, Massachusetts, where 19 people were hanged for this offense in 1692.

with all deliberate speed. See DELIBERATE SPEED, WITH ALL.

with all faults. See AS IS.

withdraw, *vb.* **1.** (*vt.*) To take back (something presented, granted, enjoyed, possessed, or allowed) <withdraw blame>. **2.** (*vt.*) To retract (one's words) <withdraw the objection>. **3.** (*vt.*) To refrain from prosecuting or proceeding with (an action) <withdraw the petition for divorce>. **4.** (*vi.*) (Of a lawyer) To terminate one's representation of a client before a matter is complete <withdraw from representation>. **5.** (*vt.*) To remove a juror <withdraw a biased juror>. **6.** (*vi.*) To leave or retire (from a community or society). **7.** (*vi.*) (Of a condition or immaterial thing) to vanish, depart.

withdrawal, *n.* (18c) **1.** The act of taking back or away; removal <withdrawal of consent>. **2.** The act of retreating from a place, position, or situation <withdrawal from the moot-court competition>. **3.** The removal of money from a depository <withdrawal of funds from the checking account>. **4.** RENUNCIATION (3) <withdrawal from the conspiracy to commit arson>. **5.** RETRACTION (4). **6.** *Parliamentary law.* A motion's removal from consideration by its mover. • The mover controls a motion only until the chair states the question, after which the motion belongs to the assembly and the mover cannot withdraw it without the assembly's permission. See *request for permission to withdraw a motion* under REQUEST. **7.** *Parliamentary law.* See DISCHARGE (9). — **withdraw,** *vb.*

withdrawal of charges. (1842) The removal of charges by the one bringing them, such as a prosecutor. See NOLLE PROSEQUI.

withdrawal of counsel. (1875) An attorney's termination of his or her role in representing a party in a case. • Normally, the attorney must have the court's permission to withdraw from a case. Permission is usu. sought by a written motion (1) explaining the reason for the requested withdrawal (often, a conflict between attorney and client over a matter such as strategy or fees), and (2) stating whether the client agrees. — Also termed *withdrawing of counsel.*

withdrawing a juror. (18c) The act or an instance of removing a juror, usu. to obtain a continuance in a case or, sometimes in English practice, to end the case, as when the case has settled, the parties are too anxious to proceed to verdict, or the judge recommends it because the action is not properly before the court.

withdrawing of record. 1. With the court's permission, taking the record or any portion of it out of the office of the clerk of the court. **2.** *Hist.* A plaintiff's removing of the *nisi prius* or trial record to prevent the case from being tried, usu. either before the jury is sworn or afterwards with the consent of defense counsel.

withdrawn land. 1. See *reserved land* under LAND. **2.** See RESERVATION (3).

withernam (with-ər-nahm), *n.* [fr. Saxon *weder* "other" + *naam* "a taking"] *Hist.* A reciprocal taking or distress in place of a previous one. See *capias in withernam* under WITHERNAM.

withersake (with-ər-sayk). *Archaic.* An enemy; esp., a deliberately faithless renegade.

with full power. See *committee with power* under COMMITTEE (1).

withheld sentence. See *suspended sentence* under SENTENCE.

withholding, *n.* (1940) **1.** The practice of deducting a certain amount from a person's salary, wages, dividends, winnings, or other income, usu. for tax purposes; esp., an employer's practice of taking out a portion of an employee's gross earnings and paying that portion to the government for income-tax and social-security purposes. **2.** The money so deducted. — Also termed *income-tax withholding.* — **withhold,** *vb.*

withholding of evidence. (1848) The act or an instance of obstructing justice by stifling or suppressing evidence knowing that it is being sought in an official investigation or a judicial proceeding. See OBSTRUCTION OF JUSTICE.

withholding tax. See TAX.

without day. See GO HENCE WITHOUT DAY.

without delay. (13c) **1.** Instantly; at once. **2.** Within the time reasonably allowed by law.

without dissent. See WITHOUT OBJECTION.

without impeachment of waste. (16c) (Of a tenant) not subject to an action for waste; not punishable for waste. • This clause is inserted in a lease to give a tenant the right to take certain actions (such as cutting timber) without being held liable for waste. But a tenant cannot abuse the right and will usu. be held liable for maliciously committing waste. — Also termed *absque impetitione vasti.*

without notice. (16c) Lacking actual or constructive knowledge. • To be a bona fide purchaser, one must buy something "without notice" of another's claim to the item or of defects in the seller's title. To be a holder in due course, one must take a bill or note "without notice" that it is overdue, has been dishonored, or is subject to a claim. UCC § 3-302(a)(2). See NOTICE; *bona fide purchaser* under PURCHASER.

without objection. With general consent. — Also termed *without dissent.* See *general consent* under CONSENT (2).

without prejudice, *adv.* (15c) Without loss of any rights; in a way that does not harm or cancel the legal rights or privileges of a party <dismissed without prejudice>. See *dismissal without prejudice* under DISMISSAL (1).

without recourse. (18c) (In an indorsement) without liability to subsequent holders. • With this stipulation, one who indorses an instrument indicates that he or she has no further liability to any subsequent holder for payment. — Also termed *sans recours.*

without reserve. Of or relating to an auction at which an item will be sold for the highest bid price.

without this, that. See ABSQUE HOC.

with power. See *committee with power* under COMMITTEE (1).

with prejudice, *adv.* With loss of all rights; in a way that finally disposes of a party's claim and bars any future action on that claim <dismissed with prejudice>. See *dismissal with prejudice* under DISMISSAL (1).

with recourse, *adv.* (In an indorsement) with liability to subsequent holders. • With this stipulation, one who indorses an instrument indicates that he or she remains liable to the holder for payment.

with reserve. Of or relating to an auction at which an item will not be sold unless the highest bid exceeds a minimum price.

with strong hand. With force. • In common-law pleading, this term implies a degree of criminal force, esp. as used in forcible-entry statutes.

witness, *n.* (bef. 12c) **1.** One who sees, knows, or vouches for something <a witness to a testator's signature>. **2.** One who gives testimony under oath or affirmation (1) in person, (2) by oral or written deposition, or (3) by affidavit <the witness to the signature signed the affidavit.>. • A witness must be legally competent to testify. — **witness,** *vb.*

accomplice witness. (1853) A witness who is an accomplice in the crime that the defendant is charged with. • A codefendant cannot be convicted solely on the testimony of an accomplice witness.

adverse witness. See *hostile witness.*

alibi witness. (1897) A witness who testifies that the defendant was in a location other than the scene of the crime at the relevant time; a witness who supports the defendant's alibi.

attesting witness. (18c) One who vouches for the authenticity of another's signature by signing an instrument that the other has signed <proof of the will requires two attesting witnesses>. — Also termed *subscribing witness.*

character witness. (1893) A witness who testifies about another person's character traits or community reputation. See *character evidence* under EVIDENCE.

competent witness. (17c) A witness who is legally qualified to testify. • A lay witness who has personal knowledge of the subject matter of the testimony is competent to testify. Fed. R. Evid. 601–602.

corroborating witness. (1853) A witness who confirms or supports someone else's testimony.

court witness. A witness called or re-called to testify by the judge. • The witness called to testify by the court usu. has expertise in the subject matter of the trial and is considered necessary to resolve a conflict in the testimony. The court's discretion to call its own witnesses exists in both civil and criminal cases.

credible witness. (16c) A witness whose testimony is believable.

disinterested witness. (18c) A witness who has no private interest in the matter at issue.

expert witness. (1858) A witness qualified by knowledge, skill, experience, training, or education to provide a scientific, technical, or other specialized opinion about the evidence or a fact issue. Fed. R. Evid. 702–706. — Also termed *skilled witness.* See EXPERT; DAUBERT TEST; *expert opinion* under OPINION (3).

going witness. *Archaic.* A witness who is about to leave a court's jurisdiction, but not the country. • An example is the witness who leaves one state to go to another.

grand-jury witness. (1947) A witness who is called to testify before a grand jury.

hostile witness. (1852) A witness who is biased against the examining party, who is unwilling to testify, or who is identified with an adverse party. • A hostile witness may be asked leading questions on direct examination. Fed. R. Evid. 611(c). — Also termed *adverse witness.* See *adverse party* under PARTY (2).

interested witness. (18c) A witness who has a direct and private interest in the matter at issue. • Most jurisdictions provide that a person witnessing a will may not be a devisee under the will. The Uniform Probate Code, however, has abrogated this rule.

lay witness. (1853) A witness who does not testify as an expert and who is therefore restricted to giving an opinion or making an inference that (1) is based on firsthand knowledge, and (2) is helpful in clarifying the testimony or in determining facts. Fed. R. Evid. 701.

material witness. (17c) A witness who can testify about matters having some logical connection with the consequential facts, esp. if few others, if any, know about those matters.

percipient witness. (1913) A witness who has perceived the things about which he or she testifies. See EYEWITNESS; EARWITNESS.

prosecuting witness. (1823) A person who files the complaint that triggers a criminal prosecution and whose testimony the prosecution usu. relies on to secure a conviction.

qualified witness. (1845) A witness who, by explaining the manner in which a business records are made and kept, is able to lay the foundation for the admission of those records under an exception to the hearsay rule. Fed. R. Evid. 803(6).

rebuttal witness. (1891) A witness who contradicts or attempts to contradict evidence previously presented.

res gestae witness. (1894) A witness who, having been at the scene of an incident, can give a firsthand account of what happened. See RES GESTAE.

skilled witness. **1.** See *expert witness.* **2.** A witness whose degree of knowledge in a particular subject or field is short of the standard for an expert but greater than the knowledge possessed by a typical layperson.

subscribing witness. (17c) One who witnesses the signatures on an instrument and signs at the end of the instrument to that effect. See *attesting witness.*

supernumerary witness. An unrequired witness, such as a third witness to a will where only two are required.

swift witness. See *zealous witness.*

target witness. (1965) **1.** The person who has the knowledge that an investigating body seeks. **2.** A witness who is called before a grand jury and against whom the government is also seeking an indictment.

turncoat witness. (1947) A witness whose testimony was expected to be favorable but who becomes (usu. during the trial) a hostile witness.

ultroneous witness. *Scots law.* A witness who comes forward without being summoned to appear in court.

zealous witness (**zel**-əs). (1868) A witness who shows partiality toward the litigant that called him or her to testify and who seems eager to help that side in the lawsuit. — Also termed *swift witness.*

witness box. See WITNESS STAND.

witness clause. See TESTIMONIUM CLAUSE.

witnesseth, *vb.* Shows; records. ● This term, usu. set in all capitals, commonly separates the preliminaries in a contract, up through the recitals, from the contractual terms themselves. Modern drafters increasingly avoid it as an antiquated relic. Traditionally, the subject of this verb was *This Agreement*: the sentence, boiled down, was *This Agreement witnesseth* [i.e., shows or records] *that, whereas* [*the parties have agreed to contract with one another*], *the parties therefore agree as follows* .... Many modern contracts erroneously retain the *Witnesseth* even though a new verb appears in the preamble: *This Agreement is between* [one party and the other party]. After the preamble is a period, followed by an all-capped WITNESSETH. It is an example of a form retained long after its utility, and most lawyers do not know what it means or even what purpose it once served.

witness fee. See FEE (1).

witnessing part. See ATTESTATION CLAUSE.

witness jurat. See JURAT.

witness-protection program. (1970) A federal or state program in which a person who testifies against a criminal is assigned a new identity and relocated to another part of the country to avoid retaliation by anyone convicted as a result of that testimony. ● The Federal Witness Protection Program was established by the Organized Crime Control Act of 1970 and is administered by the marshals of the U.S. Justice Department.

witness stand. (1853) The space in a courtroom, usu. a boxed area, occupied by a witness while testifying. — Often shortened to *stand.* — Also termed *witness box.*

witness-tampering. (1924) The act or an instance of obstructing justice by intimidating, influencing, or harassing a witness before or after the witness testifies. ● Several state and federal laws, including the Victim and Witness Protection Act of 1982 (18 USCA § 1512), provide criminal penalties for tampering with witnesses or other persons in the context of a pending investigation or official proceeding. See OBSTRUCTION OF JUSTICE.

W.L. *abbr.* WESTLAW.

wobbler. *Slang.* A crime that can be charged as either a felony or a misdemeanor.

Women's Bureau. A unit in the U.S. Department of Labor responsible for formulating policies and standards to promote the welfare of wage-earning women.

women's shelter. See SHELTER.

Women's Suffrage Amendment. See NINETEENTH AMENDMENT.

woodshedding. See HORSESHEDDING.

w.o.p. *abbr.* WANT OF PROSECUTION.

word of art. See TERM OF ART.

words actionable in themselves. (18c) Language that is libelous or slanderous per se. See *slander per se* under SLANDER; *libel per se* under LIBEL.

words of limitation. (16c) Language in a conveying instrument — often nonliteral language — describing the extent or quality of an estate. ● For example, under long-standing principles of property law, the phrase "to A and her heirs" creates a fee simple in A but gives nothing to A's heirs. See LIMITATION (4).

words of negotiability. See NEGOTIABLE WORDS.

words of procreation (proh-kree-**ay**-shən). (18c) Language in a deed essential to create an estate tail, such as an estate "to A and the heirs of his body."

words of purchase. (17c) Language in a deed or will designating the persons who are to receive the grant. ● For example, the phrase "to A for life with a remainder to her heirs" creates a life estate in A and a remainder in A's heirs. See PURCHASE (2).

words of severance. In a grant of lands, words showing that the tenants were each to take a distinct share in the property as opposed to undivided portions. • Typical words of severance are *share and share alike, to be divided among, equally,* and *between.*

work, *n.* **1.** Physical and mental exertion to attain an end, esp. as controlled by and for the benefit of an employer; labor.

additional work. 1. Work that results from a change or alteration in plans concerning the work required, usu. under a construction contract; added work necessary to meet the performance goals under a contract. **2.** See *extra work.*

extra work. In construction law, work not required under the contract; something done or furnished in addition to the contract's requirements; work entirely outside and independent of the contract and not contemplated by it. • A contractor is usu. entitled to charge for extra work consisting of labor and materials not contemplated by or subsumed within the original contract, at least to the extent that the property owner agrees to a change order. Materials and labor not contemplated by the contract, but that are required by later changes in the plans and specifications, are considered to be extra work. — Also termed *additional work.*

heavy work. Work involving frequent lifting and carrying of large items. • Under the Social Security Administration regulations for describing a worker's physical limitations, heavy work involves lifting no more than 100 pounds, with frequent lifting or carrying of objects weighing up to 50 pounds. 20 CFR § 404.

inherently dangerous work. Work that can be carried out only by the exercise of special skill and care and that involves a grave risk of serious harm if done unskillfully or carelessly.

light work. Work involving some limited lifting and moving. • Under the Social Security Administration regulations for describing a worker's physical limitations, light work includes walking, standing, sitting while pushing or pulling arm or leg controls, and lifting no more than 20 pounds, with frequent lifting or carrying of objects that weigh up to 10 pounds. 20 CFR § 404.

medium work. Work involving some frequent lifting and moving. • Under the Social Security Administration regulations for describing a worker's physical limitations, medium work includes lifting up to 50 pounds, with frequent lifting or carrying of objects weighing up to 25 pounds. 20 CFR § 404.

sedentary work. Work involving light lifting and only occasional walking or standing. • Under the Social Security Administration regulations for describing a worker's physical limitations, sedentary work involves lifting of no more than ten pounds, occasionally carrying small items such as docket files and small tools, and occasional standing or walking. 20 CFR § 404.

semi-skilled work. Work that may require some alertness and close attention, such as inspecting items or machinery for irregularities, or guarding property or people against loss or injury. 20 CFR § 404.1568(b). — Also written *semiskilled work.*

skilled work. Work requiring the worker to use judgment, deal with the public, analyze facts and figures, or work with abstract ideas at a high level of complexity. 20 CFR § 404.

unskilled work. Work requiring little or no judgment, and involving simple tasks that can be learned quickly on the job. 20 CFR § 404.

very heavy work. Work involving frequent lifting of very large objects and frequent carrying of large objects. • Under the Social Security Administration regulations for describing a worker's physical limitations, very heavy work involves lifting 100 pounds or more, and frequent lifting or carrying of objects weighing 50 pounds or more. 20 CFR § 404.1567(e).

work of necessity. Work reasonably essential to the public's economic, social, or moral welfare as determined by the community standards at a particular time, and (formerly) excepted from the operation of blue laws. See BLUE LAW.

2. *Copyright.* An original expression, in fixed or tangible form (such as paper, audiotape, or computer disk), that may be entitled to common-law or statutory copyright protection. • A work may take many different forms, including art, sculpture, literature, music, crafts, software, and photography.

anonymous work. A work that, on copies or phonorecords, does not identify any natural person as the author. 17 USCA § 101.

architectural work. The copyrightable design of a building, as fixed in tangible media such as plans, drawings, and the building itself. 17 USCA § 102(8). • Only the overall design is protected, not each design element. This category of works was added to U.S. law by the Berne Convention Implementation Act of 1988. It is one of eight categories eligible for copyright protection.

artistic work. Any visual representation, such as a painting, drawing, map, photograph, sculpture, engraving, or architectural plan.

audiovisual work. A work consisting of related images that are presented in a series, usu. with the aid of a machine, and accompanied by sound. • An example of an audiovisual work is a lecture illustrated with a film strip, or a movie with a soundtrack.

collective work. (1870) **1.** A publication (such as a periodical issue, anthology, or encyclopedia) in which several contributions, constituting separate and independent works in themselves, are assembled into a copyrightable whole. **2.** A selection and arrangement of brief portions of different movies, television shows, or radio shows into a single copyrightable work. • If the selecting and arranging involves any originality, the person who selects and arranges the clips may claim a copyright even if copyright cannot be claimed in the individual component parts. Cf. COMPILATION (1).

composite work (kəm-**poz**-it). (1910) An original publication that relates to a variety of subjects and includes discrete selections from many authors. • Although the distinguishable parts are separately protectable, the owner of the composite work — not the individual authors — owns the renewal term, if any. 17 USCA § 304(a).

creative work. See *work of authorship*.

derivative work. (1965) A copyrightable creation that is based on a preexisting product; a translation, musical arrangement, fictionalization, motion-picture version, abridgment, or any other recast or adapted form of an original work. • Only the holder of the copyright on the original form can produce or permit someone else to produce a derivative work. 17 USCA § 101. — Sometimes shortened to *derivative*. Cf. COMPILATION (1).

dramatic work. Any form of nonliterary work created for performance and viewing. • The term includes plays, scripts, films, choreographic works, and similar creations.

joint work. A work created or developed by two or more people whose contributions blend inseparably or interdependently into the whole work. • The cocreators have equal legal rights to register and enjoy the copyright, but this does not affect any other contractually unequal ownership arrangements.

literary work. (18c) A nonaudiovisual work that is expressed in verbal, numerical, or other symbols, such as words or musical notation, and embodied in some type of physical object. • Literary works are one of eight general categories that are eligible for copyright protection. 17 USCA § 102. Cf. LITERARY COMPOSITION.

pictorial, graphic, and sculptural work. Two- or three-dimensional works of graphic, fine, or applied art that are eligible for copyright protection. • This is one of eight general classifications covered by copyright law. Examples include globes, architectural drawings, photographs, and models. 17 USCA § 102. — Abbr. PGS.

posthumous work. The product of an author who died before publication.

pseudonymous work. A work done by an author who uses a fictitious name.

work for hire. A copyrightable work produced either by an employee within the scope of employment or by an independent contractor under a written agreement; esp., a work specially ordered or commissioned for use as (1) a contribution to a collective work, (2) a translation, (3) a supplementary work, (4) a part of a movie or other audiovisual work, (5) a compilation, (6) an instructional text, (7) a test, (8) answer material for a test, or (9) an atlas. • If the work is produced by an independent contractor, the parties must agree expressly in writing that the work will be a work for hire. The employer or commissioning party owns the copyright. 17 USCA § 101. — Also termed *work made for hire*.

work of authorship. The product of creative expression, such as literature, music, art, and graphic designs. • Copyright protects a work of authorship if it meets three criteria. First, the work must be original, not a copy. Second, the work must be presented in a fixed medium, such as a computer disk, a canvas, or paper. Finally, some creativity must have been involved in the work's creation, although the amount of creativity required depends on the particular work. — Also termed *creative work*.

work of the United States government. A work created by a U.S. government officer or employee in the course of performing official duties. • By statute, federal-government works may not be copyrighted.

work, *vb.* **1.** To exert effort; to perform, either physically or mentally <lawyers work long hours during trial>. **2.** To function properly; to produce a desired effect <the strategy worked>. **3.** *Patents.* To develop and use (a patented invention, esp. to make it commercially available) <the patentee failed to work the patent>. • Failure to work a patent in a specified amount of time is grounds for a compulsory license in some countries.

worker. 1. One who labors to attain an end; esp., a person employed to do work for another. **2.** A person who offers to perform services for compensation in the employ of another, whether or not the person is so employed at a given time.

Worker Adjustment and Retraining Notification Act. A federal law that requires an employer to provide notice of a plant closing or mass layoff, 60 days before the closing or layoff, to the employees, the state-dislocated-workers unit, and the chief elected official of the unit of local government where the plant closing or layoff is to occur. 29 USCA §§ 2101–2109. — Abbr. WARN.

workers' compensation. A system of providing benefits to an employee for injuries occurring in the scope of employment. • Most workers'-compensation statutes both hold the employer strictly liable and bar the employee from suing the employer in tort. — Abbr. WC. — Also termed *workmen's compensation; employers' liability.*

workers'-compensation act. A statute by which employers are made responsible for bodily harm to their workers arising out of and in the course of their employment, regardless of the fault of either the employee or the employer.

workers'-compensation board. An agency that reviews cases arising under workers'-compensation statutes and administers the related rules and regulations. — Also termed *workers'-compensation commission.*

workers'-compensation lien. See LIEN.

workers'-compensation subrogation lien. See *workers'-compensation lien* under LIEN.

workfare. (1969) A system of requiring a person receiving a public-welfare benefit to earn that benefit by performing a job provided by a government agency or undergoing job training.

work for hire. See WORK (2).

work furlough (fər-loh). (1960) A prison-treatment program allowing an inmate to be released during the day to work in the community. See WORK-RELEASE PROGRAM.

work-furlough program. See WORK-RELEASE PROGRAM.

workhouse. (17c) A jail for criminals who have committed minor offenses and are serving short sentences.

working capital. See CAPITAL.

working capital acceptance. See *finance bill* under BILL (6).

working control. See CONTROL.

working example. See EXAMPLE.

working interest. *Oil & gas.* The rights to the mineral interest granted by an oil-and-gas lease, so called because the lessee acquires the right to work on the leased property to search, develop, and produce oil and gas, as well as the obligation to pay all costs. See ROYALTY (2). — Also termed *leasehold interest; operating interest.*

working model. *Patents.* A sample of an invention, usu. built for testing and for displaying to potential buyers. • The building of a working model is called "actual reduction to practice." It is not required for a patent, but it can help the applicant to clarify the description and to establish a date of invention in the event of an interference.

working papers. 1. WORK PERMIT; esp., an employment certificate or permit required of an employer in some states before a minor may be hired. **2.** *Accounting.* The records kept by an independent auditor of the procedures followed, tests performed, information obtained, and conclusions reached in an audit. • A reviewer may evaluate the quality of an audit by examining the working papers.

work-in-process. A product being manufactured or assembled but not yet completed. — Abbr. WIP. — Also termed *work-in-progress.*

work made for hire. See *work for hire* under WORK (2).

workmen's compensation. See WORKERS' COMPENSATION.

work of authorship. See WORK (2).

work of necessity. See WORK (1).

work of the United States government. See WORK (2).

workout, *n.* **1.** The act of restructuring or refinancing overdue loans. **2.** *Bankruptcy.* A debtor's agreement, usu. negotiated with a creditor or creditors out of court, to reduce or discharge the debt. — **work out,** *vb.*

work permit. An alien's documentary work authorization from the Immigration and Naturalization Service. • Under the Immigration Reform and Control Act of 1986, it is illegal for an employer to hire an alien who lacks a work permit. 8 USCA § 1324a(a)(1). — Also termed *working papers.*

workpiece. *Patents.* The embodiment of an invention, usu. a device, as the patent claims describe how to make and use it.

workplace. A person's place of employment or work setting in general. See SAFE WORKPLACE.

work product. (1947) Tangible material or its intangible equivalent — in unwritten or oral form — that was either prepared by or for a lawyer or prepared for litigation, either planned or in progress. • Work product is generally exempt from discovery or other compelled disclosure. The term is also used to describe the products of a party's investigation or communications concerning the subject matter of a lawsuit if made (1) to assist in the prosecution or defense of a pending suit, or (2) in reasonable anticipation of litigation. Fed. R. Evid. 26. — Also termed *attorney work product.*

   core work product. See *opinion work product.*

   fact work product. A lawyer's tangible work product that includes facts but not the lawyer's mental impressions. • Fact work product is subject to a qualified privilege. It is not discoverable unless the party seeking discovery can show (1) a substantial need for the materials and (2) an inability to acquire the information by any other means without undue hardship. *See* Fed. R. Evid. 26(b)(3). — Also termed *ordinary work product.*

> **opinion work product.** A lawyer's opinions, mental impressions, conclusions, and legal theories arising from a client's case. ● An adversary usu. cannot gain access to this work product despite showing substantial need and undue hardship. Fed. R. Evid. 26(b)(3). — Also termed *core work product.*

> **ordinary work product.** See *fact work product.*

work-product rule. (1954) The rule providing for qualified immunity of an attorney's work product from discovery or other compelled disclosure. Fed. R. Civ. P. 26(b)(3). ● The exemption was primarily established to protect an attorney's litigation strategy. *Hickman v. Taylor,* 329 U.S. 495, 67 S.Ct. 385 (1947). — Also termed *work-product immunity; work-product privilege; work-product exemption; attorney-work-product privilege.*

work-release program. (1964) A correctional program allowing a prison inmate — primarily one being readied for discharge — to hold a job outside prison. — Also termed *work-furlough program.* See HALFWAY HOUSE.

works. 1. A mill, factory, or other establishment for manufacturing or other industrial purposes; a manufacturing plant; a factory. **2.** Any building or structure on land. ● Some states also include structures built in the sea, such as offshore-drilling platforms.

> **new works.** *Civil law.* A structure newly commenced on a particular estate. ● A denunciation of new works is a remedy allowed for an adjacent landowner whose property will be injured if the structure is completed.

> **public works.** Structures (such as roads or dams) built by the government for public use and paid for by public funds.

work stoppage. A cessation of work; STRIKE.

world. 1. The planet Earth <the world has limited natural resources>. **2.** All the Earth's inhabitants; the public generally <the world will benefit from this discovery>. **3.** All persons who have a claim or acquire an interest in a particular subject matter <a judgment *in rem* binds all the world>.

World Bank. A U.N. specialized agency established in 1945 to provide loans that aid in economic development, through economically sustainable enterprises. ● Its capital derives from both U.N. member states and loans on the open market. — Also termed *International Bank for Reconstruction and Development.*

World Court. See INTERNATIONAL COURT OF JUSTICE.

world fund. See *global fund* under MUTUAL FUND.

World Intellectual Property Organization. An agency of the United Nations Educational, Scientific, and Cultural Organization formed in 1967 to (1) promote intellectual-property protection worldwide through cooperation among nations, and (2) administer multilateral treaties dealing with legal and administrative aspects of intellectual property. ● The organization's headquarters are in Geneva, Switzerland. — Abbr. WIPO.

worldly, *adj.* Of or relating to the present state of existence; temporal; earthly <worldly possessions>. See SECULAR.

World Trade Organization. The body charged with enforcing intellectual-property provisions of the GATT treaty. ● WTO comprises the signatories of the Uruguay Round of GATT negotiations. — Abbr. WTO. See TRIPS.

worldwide military-locator service. A search service that locates the current duty station of a member of any branch of the United States military services, esp. for enforcing the service member's child-support obligations. ● Each branch of the armed forces maintains a worldwide locator service that is available to military and nonmilitary persons, their counsel, and Title IV-D agencies. Use of the locator service requires the member's full name and social-security number.

worship. 1. Any form of religious devotion, ritual, or service showing reverence, esp. for a divine being or supernatural power <freedom of worship>.

> **public worship. 1.** Worship conducted by a religious society according to the society's system of ecclesiastical authority, ritual propriety, and rules and regulations. **2.** Worship under public authority. **3.** Worship in a public place, without privacy or concealment. **4.** Worship allowed by all members of the public equally.

2. *English law.* A title of honor or dignity used in addressing certain magistrates or other high officers. ● The title is always preceded by a possessive pronoun, usu. *your* <your worship>.

wort (wərt), *n. Archaic.* A country farm; a curtilage. — Also termed *worth.*

worth, *n.* (bef. 12c) **1.** The monetary value of a thing; the sum of the qualities that render a thing valuable and useful, expressed in the current medium of exchange. **2.** The emotional or sentimental value of something. **3.** The total wealth held by a person or entity.

> **net tangible worth.** A corporation's net physical value, calculated by subtracting the liabilities from the value of the tangible assets then dividing by the number of outstanding shares.

net worth. A measure of one's wealth, usu. calculated as the excess of total assets over total liabilities. — Also termed *net assets*.

   tangible worth. The amount of wealth held in the form of physical, valuable assets, such as cash and equipment.

   4. WORT.

worthier-title doctrine. (1935) **1.** *Hist.* The common-law doctrine that if a beneficiary of a will would receive an identical interest as an heir under the laws of intestacy, the person takes the interest as an heir rather than as a beneficiary. ● The doctrine has been abolished in most states. **2.** *Property.* The doctrine that favors a grantor's intent by construing a grant as a reversion in the grantor instead of as a remainder in the grantor's heirs. — Also termed *doctrine of worthier title*. See REMAINDER; REVERSION.

worthiest of blood, *n. Hist.* Of or relating to males, because of the preference given them in the laws of descent. See PRIMOGENITURE.

worthless, *adj.* Totally lacking worth; of no use or value.

worthless check. See *bad check* under CHECK.

worthless person. *Archaic.* A person who owns nothing.

worthless security. See SECURITY.

worthy, *adj.* Having worth; possessing merit; valuable.

wounded feelings. (18c) Injuries resulting from insults, indignity, or humiliation, as distinguished from the usual mental pain and suffering consequent to physical injury.

wounding. (14c) **1.** An injury, esp. one involving a rupture of the skin. **2.** An injury to feelings or reputation. **3.** *Hist.* An aggravated type of assault and battery in which one person seriously injures another.

wrap account. See ACCOUNT.

wraparound mortgage. See MORTGAGE.

wrap-fee account. See *wrap account* under ACCOUNT.

wreck, *n.* **1.** SHIPWRECK. **2.** Goods cast ashore from a wrecked vessel and not claimed by the owner within a specified period (such as one year).

wreckfree, *adj.* (Of a port, etc.) exempt from the forfeiture of shipwrecked goods and vessels to the Crown.

writ (rit). (bef. 12c) A court's written order, in the name of a state or other competent legal authority, commanding the addressee to do or refrain from doing some specified act.

   alias writ. (18c) An additional writ issued after another writ of the same kind in the same case. ● It derives its name from a Latin phrase that formerly appeared in alias writs: *sicut alias praecipimus,* meaning "as we at another time commanded." Cf. *alias execution* under EXECUTION.

   alternative writ. (1827) A common-law writ commanding the person against whom it is issued either to do a specific thing or to show cause why the court should not order it to be done.

   close writ. *Hist.* **1.** A royal writ sealed because the contents were not deemed appropriate for public inspection. Cf. *patent writ*; CLAUSE ROLLS. **2.** A writ directed to a sheriff instead of to a lord.

   concurrent writ. A duplicate of an original writ (esp. a summons), issued either at the same time as the original writ or at any time while the original writ is valid.

   counterpart writ. (1841) A copy of an original writ, to be sent to a court in another county where the defendant is located.

   extraordinary writ. (17c) A writ issued by a court exercising unusual or discretionary power. ● Examples are certiorari, habeas corpus, mandamus, and prohibition. — Also termed *prerogative writ.* Cf. *extraordinary relief* under RELIEF.

   ground writ. *Hist.* A writ issued in a county having venue of an action in order to allow a writ of *capias ad satisfaciendum* or of *fieri facias* to be executed in a county where the defendant or the defendant's property was found. ● These two writs could not be executed in a county other than the county having venue of the action until a ground writ and then a *testatum* writ were first issued. This requirement was abolished in 1852.

   judicial writ. (16c) **1.** A writ issuing from the court to which the original writ was returnable; a writ issued under the private seal of the court and not under the great seal of England. Cf. *original writ.* **2.** Any writ issued by a court.

   junior writ. (1839) A writ issued at a later time than a similar writ, such as a later writ issued by a different party or a later writ on a different claim against the same defendant.

   optional writ. (18c) At common law, an original writ issued when the plaintiff seeks specific damages, such as payment of a liquidated debt. ● The writ commands the defendant either to do a specified thing or to show why the thing has not been done.

   original writ. (16c) A writ commencing an action and directing the defendant to appear and answer. ● In the United States, this writ has been largely superseded by the summons. At common law, this type of writ was a mandatory letter issuing from the court of chancery under the great seal, and in the king's name, directed to the sheriff of the county where the injury was alleged to have occurred, containing a summary statement of the cause of complaint, and requiring the sheriff in most cases to command the defendant to satisfy the claim or else appear in court to account for not satisfying it. — Sometimes shortened to *original*. See SUMMONS.

patent writ (**pay**-tənt). *Hist.* An open writ; one not closed or sealed up. Cf. *close writ.*

peremptory writ (pər-**emp**-tə-ree). (18c) At common law, an original writ issued when the plaintiff seeks only general damages, as in an action for trespass. • The writ, which is issued only after the plaintiff gives security for costs, directs the sheriff to have the defendant appear in court.

pluries writ. See PLURIES.

prerogative writ. See *extraordinary writ.*

vicontiel writ (vi-**kon**-tee-əl). *Hist.* A writ triable in the county court. • In the 13th–14th centuries, civil litigation could originate in the county court either by oral plaint or by a writ from the Chancery ordering the sheriff to do justice in a case. The writ that began such a proceeding was called *vicontiel* because it was addressed to the sheriff. See VICONTIEL (2).

writ of capias. See CAPIAS.

write down, *vb. Accounting.* To transfer part of the balance (of an asset account) to an expense or loss account to reflect the asset's diminished value.

write off, *vb. Accounting.* To transfer the entire balance (of an asset account) to an expense or loss account to reflect the asset's total loss of value <the partnership wrote off the bad debt>. — **write-off,** *n.* See TAX WRITE-OFF. — **write-off,** *n.*

writer. *Securities.* **1.** A person or institution that sells securities or futures option contracts. **2.** See *insurance underwriter* (1) under UNDERWRITER.

write-up, *n.* **1.** A memorandum of a conference between an employer and an employee, usu. held to discuss the employee's poor work performance or a disciplinary action against the employee. **2.** A publication (such as a newspaper article) about a particular person, thing, or event.

write-up, *vb. Accounting.* To increase the valuation of an asset in a financial statement to reflect current value. • With a few minor exceptions, this is generally not permitted.

writing, *n.* Any intentional recording of words that may be viewed or heard with or without mechanical aids. • This includes hard-copy documents, electronic documents on computer media, audio and videotapes, e-mails, and any other media on which words can be recorded.

signed writing. A writing to which a person's signature has been affixed in some form. See SIGNATURE.

writing obligatory, *n.* A bond; a written obligation, as technically described in a pleading.

writ of *ad quod damnum.* See AD QUOD DAMNUM.

writ of aiel (ay-əl). See AIEL (2).

writ of assistance. 1. A writ to enforce a court's decree transferring real property, the title of which has been previously adjudicated. **2.** *Hist.* A writ issued by the Court of Exchequer ordering the sheriff to assist in collecting a debt owed the Crown. **3.** *Hist.* In colonial America, a writ issued by a superior colonial court authorizing an officer of the Crown to enter and search any premises suspected of containing contraband. • The attempted use of this writ in Massachusetts — defeated in 1761 — was one of the acts that led to the American Revolution.

writ of attachment. See ATTACHMENT (3).

writ of capias. See CAPIAS.

writ of certiorari. See CERTIORARI.

writ of consultation. An extraordinary writ issued by an appellate court ordering a lower court to proceed in a matter that the lower court previously refused to hear. Cf. PROHIBITION (2).

writ of *coram nobis.* See CORAM NOBIS.

writ of *coram vobis.* See CORAM VOBIS.

writ of course. (17c) A writ issued as a matter of course or granted as a matter of right. — Also termed *writ of right; breve de cursu.*

writ of covenant. *Hist.* A writ for one claiming damages as a result of a breach of a promise under seal or other covenant. — Also termed *breve de conventione* (breev *or* **bree**-vee dee kən-ven-shee-**oh**-nee).

writ of debt. See DEBT (4).

writ of deliverance. See DELIVERANCE (3).

writ of detinue. (17c) A writ in an action for detinue. See DETINUE.

writ of ejectment. (17c) The writ in an action of ejectment for the recovery of land. See EJECTMENT.

writ of entry. (16c) A writ that allows a person wrongfully dispossessed of real property to enter and retake the property.

writ of error. (15c) **1.** A writ issued by an appellate court directing a lower court to deliver the record in the case for review. Cf. ASSIGNMENT OF ERROR.

writ of error coram nobis. See CORAM NOBIS.

writ of error coram vobis. See CORAM VOBIS.

2. *Hist.* A writ issued by a chancery court, at the request of a party who was unsuccessful at trial, directing the trial court either to examine the record itself or to send it to another court of appellate jurisdiction to be examined, so that some alleged error in the proceedings may be corrected.

writ of execution. See EXECUTION (4).

writ of extent. See EXTENT (2).

writ of false judgment. See FALSE JUDGMENT.

writ of formedon. See FORMEDON.

writ of habeas corpus. See HABEAS CORPUS.

writ of injunction. See INJUNCTION.

writ of inquiry. *Hist.* A writ ordering the sheriff to empanel a jury and act as judge in a trial held to determine the amount of damages suffered by a plaintiff who has won a default judgment on an unliquidated claim.

writ of mainprise. See MAINPRISE (3).

writ of mandamus. See MANDAMUS.

writ of mandate. See MANDATE (2).

writ of ne exeat. See NE EXEAT.

writ of possession. (17c) A writ issued to recover the possession of land.

writ of praecipe. See PRAECIPE (1).

writ of prevention. (17c) A writ to prevent the filing of a lawsuit. See QUIA TIMET.

writ of privilege. *Hist.* An action to enforce or maintain a privilege, usu. one granted by statute or by a court. ● Traditionally, the writ was used to protect legislators from arrest in civil suits during a legislative session. Parties and witnesses who did not reside within a court's jurisdiction were also privileged against service of process in civil suits while attending the court and while traveling to or from it.

writ of probable cause. See CERTIFICATE OF APPEALABILITY.

writ of proclamation. *Hist.* A writ, issued at the time an *exigent* was issued, ordering the sheriff of the county of a defendant's residence to make three proclamations of outlawry in a public and notorious place a month before the outlawry is declared. See OUTLAW.

writ of prohibition. See PROHIBITION (2).

writ of protection. (17c) **1.** A writ to protect a witness in a judicial proceeding who is threatened with arrest. **2.** A writ exempting anyone in the Crown's service from arrest in a civil proceeding for a year and a day.

writ of *quare impedit*. See QUARE IMPEDIT.

writ of quominus. See QUOMINUS.

writ of *quo warranto*. See QUO WARRANTO (1).

writ of rebellion. See COMMISSION OF REBELLION.

writ of recaption. *Hist.* A writ allowing a plaintiff to recover goods and damages from a defendant who makes a second distress while a replevin action for a previous distress is pending. See RECAPTION.

writ of replevin. See REPLEVIN (2).

writ of restitution. (17c) **1.** The process of enforcing a civil judgment in a forcible-entry-and-detainer action or enforcing restitution on a verdict in a criminal prosecution for forcible entry and detainer. **2.** A common-law writ issued when a judgment is reversed, whereby all that was lost as a result of the judgment is restored to the prevailing party.

writ of review. (18c) A general form of process issuing from an appellate court to bring up for review the record of the proceedings in the court below; the common-law writ of certiorari.

writ of right. See WRIT OF COURSE.

writ of second deliverance. See *second deliverance* under DELIVERANCE.

writ of sequestration. (18c) A writ ordering that a court be given custody of something or that something not be taken from the jurisdiction, such as the collateral for a promissory note. ● Such a writ is usu. issued during litigation, often so that the object will be available for attachment or execution after judgment.

writ of supersedeas. See SUPERSEDEAS.

writ of supervisory control. (1901) A writ issued to correct an erroneous ruling made by a lower court either when there is no appeal or when an appeal cannot provide adequate relief and the ruling will result in gross injustice.

writ of tolt (tohlt). See TOLT.

writ system. (1890) The common-law procedural system under which a plaintiff commences an action by obtaining the appropriate type of original writ.

written contract. See CONTRACT.

written description. See DESCRIPTION (5).

written directive. See ADVANCE DIRECTIVE (2).

written law. See LAW.

written testimony. See TESTIMONY.

written warranty. See WARRANTY (2).

wrong, *n.* (bef. 12c) Breach of one's legal duty; violation of another's legal right. — **wrong,** *vb.*

   civil wrong. (17c) A violation of noncriminal law, such as a tort, a breach of contract or trust, a breach of statutory duty, or a defect in performing a public duty; the breach of a legal duty treated as the subject matter of a civil proceeding. See TORT (1). Cf. CRIME.

   continuing wrong. (1846) An ongoing wrong that is capable of being corrected by specific enforcement. ● An example is the nonpayment of a debt.

intentional wrong. (18c) A wrong in which the *mens rea* amounts to intention, purpose, or design. — Also termed *willful wrong.*

legal wrong. (18c) An act that is a violation of the law; an act authoritatively prohibited by a rule of law.

moral wrong. (18c) An act that is contrary to the rule of natural justice. — Also termed *natural wrong.*

personal wrong. An invasion of a personal right.

positive wrong. (18c) A wrongful act willfully committed.

private wrong. (16c) An offense committed against a private person and dealt with at the instance of the person injured.

public wrong. (16c) An offense committed against the state or the community at large, and dealt with in a proceeding to which the state is itself a party. • Not all public wrongs are crimes. For example, a person that breaches a contract with the government commits a public wrong, but the offense is a civil one, not a criminal one.

real wrong. An injury to the freehold.

transitory wrong. (2004) A wrong that, once committed, belongs to the irrevocable past. • An example is defamation.

willful wrong. See *intentional wrong.*

wrong of negligence. (1902) A wrong in which the *mens rea* is a form of mere carelessness, as opposed to wrongful intent.

wrong of strict liability. (1986) A wrong in which a *mens rea* is not required because neither wrongful intent nor culpable negligence is a necessary condition of responsibility.

wrongdoer, *n.* (15c) One who violates the law <both criminals and tortfeasors are wrongdoers>. — **wrongdoing,** *n.*

wrongful, *adj.* (14c) **1.** Characterized by unfairness or injustice <wrongful military invasion>. **2.** Contrary to law; unlawful <wrongful termination>. **3.** (Of a person) not entitled to the position occupied <wrongful possessor>. — **wrongfully,** *adv.*

wrongful act. See *wrongful conduct* under CONDUCT.

wrongful adoption. 1. An adoption in which the adoption agency fails to provide adoptive parents with full or accurate information regarding the child's physical or psychological background. • The adoptive parents normally do not seek to nullify the adoption. Rather, they seek damages, usu. for medical care and for emotional distress. **2.** An adoptive parent's legal claim against an adoption agency for not fully or accurately disclosing the child's physical or psychological background. Cf. ABROGATION OF ADOPTION.

wrongful-birth action. (1972) A lawsuit brought by parents against a doctor for failing to advise them prospectively about the risks of their having a child with birth defects.

wrongful-conception action. See WRONGFUL-PREGNANCY ACTION.

wrongful conduct. See CONDUCT.

wrongful-death action. (1926) A lawsuit brought on behalf of a decedent's survivors for their damages resulting from a tortious injury that caused the decedent's death. — Also termed *death action; death case.* Cf. SURVIVAL ACTION.

wrongful-death statute. (1904) A statute authorizing a decedent's personal representative to bring a wrongful-death action for the benefit of certain beneficiaries. — Formerly also termed *death-damage statute.*

wrongful discharge. See DISCHARGE (7).

wrongful-discharge action. (1957) A lawsuit brought by an ex-employee against the former employer, alleging that the termination of employment violated a contract or was illegal. — Also termed *wrongful-termination action.*

wrongful dishonor, *n.* (1895) A refusal to accept or pay (a negotiable instrument) when it is properly presented and is payable. Cf. DISHONOR (1).

wrongful-eviction action. A lawsuit brought by a former tenant or possessor of real property against one who has put the plaintiff out of possession, alleging that the eviction was illegal.

wrongful garnishment. See GARNISHMENT.

wrongful levy. See LEVY.

wrongful-life action. (1963) A lawsuit brought by or on behalf of a child with birth defects, alleging that but for the doctor-defendant's negligent advice, the parents would not have conceived the child or, if they had, would have aborted the fetus to avoid the pain and suffering resulting from the child's congenital defects. • Most jurisdictions reject these claims.

wrongful-pregnancy action. (1979) A lawsuit brought by a parent for damages resulting from a pregnancy following a failed sterilization. — Also termed *wrongful-conception action.*

wrongful process. See ABUSE OF PROCESS.

wrongful-termination action. See WRONGFUL-DISCHARGE ACTION.

wrong of negligence. See WRONG.

wrong of strict liability. See WRONG.

wrong verdict. See *verdict contrary to law* under VERDICT.

WTO. See WORLD TRADE ORGANIZATION.

X

X. *abbr.* **1.** EX DIVIDEND. **2.** EX RIGHTS. **3.** EX DISTRIBUTION. **4.** EX WARRANTS.

X. 1. A mark serving as the signature of a person who is physically handicapped or illiterate. ● The signer's name usu. appears near the mark, and if the mark is to be notarized as a signature, two signing witnesses are ordinarily required in addition to the notary public. **2.** A symbol equivalent to "by" when used in giving dimensions, as in 3 x 5 inches. **3.** A mark placed on a document (such as an application) to indicate a selection, such as "yes" or "no"; esp., a mark on a ballot to indicate a vote.

XD. *abbr.* EX DIVIDEND.

XDIS. *abbr.* EX DISTRIBUTION.

xenodochium (zen-ə-də-**kɪ**-əm *or* -**dok**-ee-əm), *n.* [fr. Greek *xenos* "a guest" + *dochein* "to receive"] *Roman law.* **1.** An inn. **2.** A hospital. ● This was a charitable institution to which donations and legacies might validly be given. — Also termed *xenodochion*; *xenodocheum*; *xenodochy*.

X-patent. *Patents.* An early U.S. patent, granted before the numbering system set up in the Patent Act of 1836 and so named because an *X* was added to the numbers of existing patents to avoid duplicate numbers.

XQ. See *cross-question* under QUESTION (1).

XR. *abbr.* EX-RIGHTS.

XW. *abbr.* EX-WARRANTS.

xylon (**zɪ**-lon), *n.* [fr. Greek *xulon* "wood"] *Archaic.* A Greek punishment apparatus similar to stocks.

XYY-chromosome defense. *Criminal law.* A defense, usu. asserted as the basis for an insanity plea, whereby a male defendant argues that his criminal behavior is due to the genetic abnormality of having an extra Y chromosome, which causes him to have uncontrollable aggressive impulses. ● Most courts have rejected this defense because its scientific foundations are uncertain. — Also termed *XYY defense*. See INSANITY DEFENSE.

XYY syndrome. The abnormal presence of an extra Y chromosome in a male, theoretically resulting in increased aggressiveness and antisocial behavior sometimes resulting in criminal conduct. See XYY-CHROMOSOME DEFENSE.

Y

Y2K warranty. *abbr.* Year 2000 warranty; a warranty that software, hardware, or a product having computer hardware or software components will function properly on and after January 1, 2000. ● These warranties were common in the late 1990s.

yank-cheating, *n.* The illegal practice of inserting paper money into a vending machine, then pulling the money out again after the machine has recognized it, thereby retaining the cash and unlawfully obtaining merchandise.

yardstick theory. *Antitrust.* A method of determining damages for lost profits (and sometimes overcharges) whereby a corporate plaintiff identifies a company similar to the plaintiff but without the impact of the antitrust violation. Cf. BEFORE-AND-AFTER THEORY; MARKET-SHARE THEORY.

yea, *n. Parliamentary law.* An affirmative vote.

yea and nay (yay / nay). Yes and no. ● In old records, this was a mere assertion and denial without the necessity of an oath.

year. 1. Twelve calendar months beginning January 1 and ending December 31. — Also termed *calendar year.* **2.** A consecutive 365-day period beginning at any point; a span of twelve months.

   fiscal year. An accounting period of 12 consecutive months <the company's fiscal year is October 1 to September 30>. ● A fiscal year is often different from the calendar year, esp. for tax purposes. — Also termed *fiscal period.*

   half-year. In legal computation, a period of 182 days.

   natural year. Hist. The period of 365 days and about 6 hours, or the time it takes the earth to orbit the sun.

   tax year. The period used for computing federal or state income-tax liability, usu. either the calendar year or a fiscal year of 12 months ending on the last day of a month other than December. — Also termed *taxable year.*

Year 2000 warranty. See Y2K WARRANTY.

year and a day. The common-law time limit fixed for various purposes, such as claiming rights, exemptions, or property (such as rights to wreckage or estrays), or for prosecuting certain acts — so called because a year was formerly counted to include the first and last day, meaning that a year from January 1 was December 31, so a year and a day would then mean a full year from January 1 through January 1. — Also termed *year and day*; (formerly in Scots law) *zeir and day.* See YEAR-AND-A-DAY RULE; YEAR, DAY, AND WASTE.

year-and-a-day rule. (1876) *Criminal law.* The common-law principle that an act causing death is not homicide if the death occurs more than a year and a day after the act was committed. ● In Latin, the phrase *year and a day* was commonly rendered *annus et dies.*

year and day. See YEAR AND A DAY.

Year Books. *Hist.* Books of cases anonymously and fairly regularly reported covering primarily the period from the reign of Edward I to the time of Henry VIII. ● The title "Year Books" derives from their being grouped under the regnal years of the sovereigns in whose reigns the reported cases were cited. The reports were probably originally prepared by law teachers and students and later by professional reporters or scribes. — Also written *Year-Books; year-books; yearbooks.* — Also termed *terms.* Cf. ABBREVIATIO PLACITORUM.

year, day, and waste. *Hist.* A right of the Crown to the profits and waste for a year and a day of the land of persons convicted of petty treason or felony (unless the lord made redemption), after which the Crown had to restore the property to the lord of the fee. The right was abrogated by the Corruption of Blood Act of 1814. — Also termed (in Law French) *ann, jour, et wast*; (in Law Latin) *annus, dies, et vastum.*

year-end dividend. See DIVIDEND.

Year of Our Lord. See ANNO DOMINI.

year-to-year tenancy. See *periodic tenancy* under TENANCY.

yeas and nays. The affirmative and negative votes on a bill or resolution before a deliberative assembly. See *roll-call vote* under VOTE (4).

yellow-dog contract. An employment contract forbidding membership in a labor union. ● Such a contract is generally illegal under federal and state law.

yeoman (yoh-mən**). 1.** *Hist.* An attendant in a royal or noble household. **2.** *Hist.* A commoner; a freeholder (under the rank of gentleman) who holds land yielding 40 shillings per year. **3.** *English law.* One who owns and cultivates property. **4.** A petty officer performing clerical work in the U.S. Navy. — Also sometimes spelled *yoman.*

yeoman of the guard. A member of a corps of officers whose primary duties are to ceremonially guard the English royal household. ● A yeoman is usu. at least six feet tall, is of the best rank under the gentry, and is generally exempt from arrest on civil process. — Also termed *yeoman of the guard of the royal household.*

yeomanry (**yoh**-mən-ree). **1.** The collective body of yeomen. **2.** Volunteer cavalry units in Great Britain, later transferred to the Territorial Army.

***Yick Wo* doctrine** (yik **woh**). (1958) The principle that a law or ordinance giving a person or entity absolute discretion to give or withhold permission to carry on a lawful business violates the 14th Amendment to the U.S. Constitution. *Yick Wo v. Hopkins*, 118 U.S. 356, 6 S.Ct. 1064 (1886).

yield, *n.* (bef. 12c) Profit expressed as a percentage of the investment. — Also termed *yield on investment*; *return*. See RATE OF RETURN.

> ***coupon yield.*** The annual interest paid on a security (esp. a bond) divided by the security's par value. — Also termed *nominal yield.*

> ***current yield.*** The annual interest paid on a security (esp. a bond) divided by the security's current market price.

> ***discount yield.*** The yield on a security sold at a discount.

> ***earnings yield.*** The earnings per share of a security divided by its market price. ● The higher the ratio, the better the investment yield. — Also termed *earnings-price ratio.* Cf. PRICE-EARNINGS RATIO.

> ***net yield.*** The profit or loss on an investment after deducting all appropriate costs and loss reserves.

> ***nominal yield.*** See *coupon yield.*

yield, *vb.* **1.** To give up, relinquish, or surrender (a right, etc.) <yield the floor>. **2.** *Parliamentary law.* (Of a motion) to give way to a higher-ranking motion. Cf. PRECEDENCE (3). **3.** *Hist.* To perform a service owed by a tenant to a lord <yield and pay>. See YIELDING AND PAYING.

yield on investment. See YIELD.

yield spread. The differences in yield between various securities issues.

yield to maturity. The rate of return from an investment if the investment is held until it matures. — Abbr. YTM. Cf. TIME VALUE.

yoman. See YEOMAN.

York, Statute of. *Hist.* An English statute passed in York in the twelfth year of Edward II's reign, and including provisions on the subject of attorneys, witnesses, and the taking of inquests by nisi prius.

York–Antwerp rules. *Maritime law.* A set of rules relating to the settlement of maritime losses and disputes arising from bills of lading. ● Although these rules have no statutory authority, they are incorporated into almost all bills of lading. The Rules are maintained and updated by the Comité Maritime International (CMI).

***Younger* abstention.** See ABSTENTION.

younger-generation devise. See DEVISE.

young offender. See *youthful offender* under OFFENDER.

your Honor. (16c) A title customarily used when directly addressing a judge or other high official. Cf. HIS HONOR.

your witness. See TAKE THE WITNESS.

Youth Correction Authority Act. A model act, promulgated by the American Law Institute in 1940, that proposed the creation of central state commissions responsible for setting up appropriate agencies that would determine the proper treatment for each youthful offender committed to the agency by the courts. ● The Act is noteworthy for its emphasis on rehabilitating juvenile offenders, as opposed to punishing them.

youth court. See *teen court* under COURT.

youthful offender. 1. See OFFENDER. **2.** JUVENILE DELINQUENT.

youth shelter. See SHELTER.

yo-yo stock. See *volatile stock* under STOCK.

YTM. *abbr.* YIELD TO MATURITY.

Z

zap. See INTERSUBJECTIVE ZAP.

ZBA. *abbr.* ZERO-BRACKET AMOUNT.

Z-bond. See *accrual bond* under BOND (3).

zealous witness. See WITNESS.

zeir and day (yeer). See YEAR AND DAY. • *Zeir* is an obsolete graphic variant of *year*.

zero-bracket amount. A tax deduction formerly available to all individual taxpayers, regardless of whether they itemized their deductions. • In 1944 this was replaced by the standard deduction. — Abbr. ZBA. See *standard deduction* under DEDUCTION.

zero-coupon bond. See BOND (3).

zero-coupon security. See SECURITY.

zero-rate mortgage. See MORTGAGE.

zero-tolerance policy. (1990) An established plan or method of action stating that certain acts will not be permitted or condoned. • School districts often have a zero-tolerance policy regarding the use of drugs and alcohol on school premises or at school-sponsored functions. In 1995 Congress enacted a nationwide zero-tolerance statute to combat underage drinking.

zetetic (zi-**tet**-ik), *adj. Hist.* Proceeding by inquiry; investigative. — Also spelled *zetetick*.

ZIFT. *abbr.* ZYGOTE INTRAFALLOPIAN TRANSFER.

zipper clause. *Contracts.* A contractual provision that operates both as an integration clause and as a no-oral-modification clause. See INTEGRATION CLAUSE; NO-ORAL-MODIFICATION CLAUSE.

zone. 1. An area that is different or is distinguished from surrounding areas <zone of danger>. **2.** An area in a city or town that, through zoning regulations, is under particular restrictions as to building size, land use, and the like <the capitol is at the center of the height-restriction zone>.

   floating zone. An amount of land assigned for a particular use but in no particular location. • An applicant who owns the specified amount of land can apply for a use permit in a specific location. See *floating zoning* under ZONING.

   holding zone. Temporary, low-density zoning used until a community determines how the area should be rezoned.

zone-of-danger rule. (1966) *Torts.* The doctrine allowing the recovery of damages for negligent infliction of emotional distress if the plaintiff was both located in the dangerous area created by the defendant's negligence and frightened by the risk of harm.

zone of employment. *Workers' compensation.* The physical place of employment within which an employee, if injured there, can receive compensation. Cf. COURSE OF EMPLOYMENT; SCOPE OF EMPLOYMENT.

zone of interests. (1969) The class or type of interests or concerns that a statute or constitutional guarantee is intended to regulate or protect. • To have standing to challenge a ruling (esp. of an administrative agency), the plaintiff must show that the specific injury suffered comes within the zone of interests protected by the statute on which the ruling was based.

zone of privacy. (1964) *Constitutional law.* A range of fundamental privacy rights that are implied in the express guarantees of the Bill of Rights. See PENUMBRA; RIGHT OF PRIVACY.

zone search. See SEARCH.

zoning, *n.* (1912) The legislative division of a region, esp. a municipality, into separate districts with different regulations within the districts for land use, building size, and the like. — **zone,** *vb.*

   aesthetic zoning. Zoning designed to preserve the aesthetic features or values of an area.

   bonus zoning. See *incentive zoning.*

   cluster zoning. Zoning that favors planned-unit development by allowing a modification in lot size and frontage requirements under the condition that other land in the development be set aside for parks, schools, or other public needs. — Also termed *density zoning.* See PLANNED-UNIT DEVELOPMENT.

   conditional zoning. Zoning in which a governmental body (without definitively committing itself) grants a zoning change subject to conditions that are usu. not imposed on similarly zoned property.

   contextual zoning. An approach to zoning that considers appropriate use of a lot based on the scale and types of nearby buildings. • Contextual zoning has been used, for example, to prevent the destruction of older, smaller residences to make room for larger houses disparagingly called "monster homes" or "mc mansions." in established neighborhoods.

   contract zoning. **1.** Zoning according to an agreement, by which the landowner agrees to certain restrictions or conditions in exchange for more favorable zoning treatment. • This type of contract zoning is usu. considered an illegal restraint of the government's police power, because by private agreement, the government has committed itself to a particular type of zoning. **2.** Rezoning of property to a less restrictive classification subject to the landowner's agreement to observe specified limitations on the use and physical development of the property that are not imposed on other property in the zone. • This device is esp. used when property is located in a more restrictive zone that borders on a less restrictive zone.

cumulative zoning. A method of zoning in which any use permitted in a higher-use, less intensive zone is permissible in a lower-use, more intensive zone. • For example, under this method, a house could be built in an industrial zone but a factory could not be built in a residential zone.

density zoning. See *cluster zoning.*

Euclidean zoning (yoo-**klid**-ee-ən). Zoning by specific and uniform geographical division. • The purpose of Euclidean zoning is to ensure a municipality's orderly development by detailing what uses are permitted and where, and seeing that conflicting land uses are clearly separated. Its name comes from the Supreme Court case that approved it: *Village of Euclid v. Ambler Realty Co.,* 272 U.S. 365, 47 S.Ct. 114 (1926). — Also termed *use zoning.* Cf. *non-Euclidean zoning.*

exclusionary zoning. Zoning that excludes a specific class or type of business from a district.

floating zoning. Zoning that allots land for particular uses but does not specify the geographic locations for those uses. • This is a type of non-Euclidean zoning. It allows a zoning board to make individual rulings on every application for a particular use and take into account the community's current feelings about where or if the use should be allowed. See *non-Euclidean zoning.*

incentive zoning. A relaxation in zoning restrictions (such as density limits) that offers an incentive to a developer to provide certain public benefits (such as building low-income housing units). — Also termed *bonus zoning.*

interim zoning. Temporary emergency zoning pending revisions to existing ordinances or the development of a final zoning plan. — Also termed *stopgap zoning.*

inverse zoning. Zoning that attempts to disperse particular types of property use rather than concentrate them.

non-Euclidean zoning. Zoning that allows a mix of land uses in the same area if the uses are or can be made nonconflicting • For example, a business might be permitted to operate in a residential area if the business adopts a certain architecture to blend in with other structures and has sufficient landscaping and setback to guarantee that nearby residents will not suffer excessive noise, pollution, or other nuisances. Cf. *Euclidean zoning.*

partial zoning. Zoning that affects only a portion of a municipality's territory, and that is usu. invalid because it contradicts the comprehensive zoning plan. — Also termed *piecemeal zoning.*

private zoning. The use of restrictive covenants in private agreements to restrict the use and occupancy of real property. • Private zoning often covers such things as lot size, building lines, architectural specifications, and property uses.

reverse spot zoning. Zoning of a large area of land without regard for the zoning of a small piece of land within that area.

spot zoning. Zoning of a particular piece of land without regard for the zoning of the larger area surrounding the land.

stopgap zoning. See *interim zoning.*

use zoning. See *Euclidean zoning.*

zoning map. The map that is created by a zoning ordinance and shows the various zoning districts.

zoning ordinance. (1919) A city ordinance that regulates the use to which land within various parts of the city may be put. • It allocates uses to the various districts of a municipality, as by allocating residences to certain parts and businesses to other parts. A comprehensive zoning ordinance usu. regulates the height of buildings and the proportion of the lot area that must be kept free from buildings.

zoning variance. See VARIANCE (2).

zygnomic (zig-**noh**-mik), *adj.* Of, relating to, or involving an act whose evolution directly abridges the freedom of a person who bears a duty in the enjoyment of a legal advantage. • This rather abstract term was coined by the philosopher Albert Kocourek in his book *Jural Relations* (1927). Cf. MESONOMIC.

zygocephalum (zɪ-gə-**sef**-ə-ləm), *n.* [Greek fr. *zygo-* "yoke, pair" + *kephalos* "head"] *Hist.* A measure of land, esp. the amount that can be plowed in one day.

zygostates (zɪ-goh-**stay**-teez), *n.* [Greek] *Roman law.* An officer who resolved controversies over weight; a public weigher.

zygote. A two-celled organism formed by the joining of egg and sperm. Cf. EMBRYO; FETUS.

zygote intrafallopian transfer. A procedure in which mature eggs are fertilized in a test tube or petri dish and then injected into a woman's fallopian tubes. — Abbr. ZIFT. — Also termed *zygote intrafallopian-tube transfer.* Cf. ARTIFICIAL INSEMINATION; GAMETE INTRAFALLOPIAN TRANSFER; IN VITRO FERTILIZATION.

Constitution of the United States

We the People of the United States, in Order to form a more perfect Union, establish Justice, insure domestic Tranquility, provide for the common defence, promote the general Welfare, and secure the Blessings of Liberty to ourselves and our Posterity, do ordain and establish this Constitution for the United States of America.

Article I

Section 1. All legislative Powers herein granted shall be vested in a Congress of the United States, which shall consist of a Senate and House of Representatives.

Section 2. The House of Representatives shall be composed of Members chosen every second Year by the People of the several States, and the Electors in each State shall have the Qualifications requisite for Electors of the most numerous Branch of the State Legislature.

No Person shall be a Representative who shall not have attained to the Age of twenty five Years, and been seven Years a Citizen of the United States, and who shall not, when elected, be an Inhabitant of that State in which he shall be chosen.

Representatives and direct Taxes shall be apportioned among the several States which may be included within this Union, according to their respective Numbers, which shall be determined by adding to the whole Number of free Persons, including those bound to Service for a Term of Years, and excluding Indians not taxed, three fifths of all other Persons. The actual Enumeration shall be made within three Years after the first Meeting of the Congress of the United States, and within every subsequent Term of ten Years, in such Manner as they shall by Law direct. The Number of Representatives shall not exceed one for every thirty Thousand, but each State shall have at Least one Representative; and until such enumeration shall be made, the State of New Hampshire shall be entitled to chuse three, Massachusetts eight, Rhode Island and Providence Plantations one, Connecticut five, New York six, New Jersey four, Pennsylvania eight, Delaware one, Maryland six, Virginia ten, North Carolina five, South Carolina five, and Georgia three.

When vacancies happen in the Representation from any State, the Executive Authority thereof shall issue Writs of Election to fill such Vacancies.

The House of Representatives shall chuse their Speaker and other Officers; and shall have the sole Power of Impeachment.

Section 3. The Senate of the United States shall be composed of two Senators from each State, chosen by the Legislature thereof, for six Years; and each Senator shall have one Vote.

Immediately after they shall be assembled in Consequence of the first Election, they shall be divided as equally as may be into three Classes. The Seats of the Senators of the first Class shall be vacated at the Expiration of the second Year, of the second Class at the Expiration of the fourth Year, and the third Class at the Expiration of the sixth Year, so that one third may be chosen every second Year; and if Vacancies happen by Resignation, or otherwise, during the Recess of the Legislature of any State, the Executive thereof may make temporary Appointments until the next Meeting of the Legislature, which shall then fill such Vacancies.

No Person shall be a Senator who shall not have attained to the Age of thirty Years, and been nine Years a Citizen of the United States and who shall not, when elected, be an Inhabitant of that State for which he shall be chosen.

The Vice President of the United States shall be President of the Senate, but shall have no Vote, unless they be equally divided.

The Senate shall chuse their other Officers, and also a President pro tempore, in the Absence of the Vice President, or when he shall exercise the Office of President of the United States.

The Senate shall have the sole Power to try all Impeachments. When sitting for that Purpose, they shall be on Oath or Affirmation. When the President of the United States is tried, the Chief Justice shall preside: And no Person shall be convicted without the Concurrence of two thirds of the Members present.

Judgment in Cases of Impeachment shall not extend further than to removal from Office, and disqualification to hold and enjoy any Office of Honor, Trust or Profit under the United States: but the Party convicted shall nevertheless be liable and subject to Indictment, Trial, Judgment and Punishment, according to Law.

Section 4. The Times, Places and Manner of holding Elections for Senators and Representatives, shall be prescribed in each State by the Legislature thereof; but the Congress may at any time by Law make or alter such Regulations, except as to the Places of chusing Senators.

The Congress shall assemble at least once in every Year, and such Meeting shall be on the first Monday in December, unless they shall by Law appoint a different Day.

Section 5. Each House shall be the Judge of the Elections, Returns and Qualifications of its own Members, and a Majority of each shall constitute a Quorum to do Business; but a smaller Number may adjourn from day to day, and may be authorized to compel the Attendance of absent Members, in such Manner, and under such Penalties as each House may provide.

Each House may determine the Rules of its Proceedings, punish its Members for disorderly Behavior, and, with the Concurrence of two thirds, expel a Member.

Each House shall keep a Journal of its Proceedings, and from time to time publish the same, excepting such Parts as may in their Judgment require Secrecy; and the Yeas and Nays of the Members of either House on any question shall, at the Desire of one fifth of those Present, be entered on the Journal.

Neither House, during the Session of Congress, shall, without the Consent of the other, adjourn for more than three days, nor to any other Place than that in which the two Houses shall be sitting.

Section 6. The Senators and Representatives shall receive a Compensation for their Services, to be ascertained by Law, and paid out of the Treasury of the United States. They shall in all Cases, except Treason, Felony and Breach of the Peace, be privileged from Arrest during their Attendance at the Session of their respective Houses, and in going to and returning from the same; and for any Speech or Debate in either House, they shall not be questioned in any other Place.

No Senator or Representative shall, during the Time for which he was elected, be appointed to any civil Office under the Authority of the United States, which shall have been created, or the Emoluments whereof shall have been encreased during such time; and no Person holding any Office under the United States, shall be a Member of either House during his Continuance in Office.

Section 7. All Bills for raising Revenue shall originate in the House of Representatives; but the Senate may propose or concur with Amendments as on other Bills.

Every Bill which shall have passed the House of Representatives and the Senate, shall, before it become a Law, be presented to the President of the United States; If he approve he shall sign it, but if not he shall return it, with his Objections to the House in which it shall have originated, who shall enter the Objections at large on their Journal, and proceed to reconsider it. If after such Reconsideration two thirds of that House shall agree to pass the Bill, it shall be sent, together with the Objections, to the other House, by which it shall likewise be reconsidered, and if approved by two thirds of that House, it shall become a Law. But in all such Cases the Votes of both Houses shall be determined by yeas and nays, and the Names of the Persons voting for and against the Bill shall be entered on the Journal of each House respectively. If any Bill shall not be returned by the President within ten Days (Sundays excepted) after it shall have been presented to him, the Same shall be a Law, in like Manner as if he had signed it, unless the Congress by their Adjournment prevent its Return, in which Case it shall not be a Law.

Every Order, Resolution, or Vote to which the Concurrence of the Senate and House of Representatives may be necessary (except on a question of Adjournment) shall be presented to the President of the United States; and before the Same shall take Effect, shall be approved by him, or being disapproved by him, shall be repassed by two thirds of the Senate and House of Representatives, according to the Rules and Limitations prescribed in the Case of a Bill.

Section 8. The Congress shall have Power To lay and collect Taxes, Duties, Imposts and Excises, to pay the Debts and provide for the common Defence and general Welfare of the United States; but all Duties, Imposts and Excises shall be uniform throughout the United States;

To borrow Money on the credit of the United States;

To regulate Commerce with foreign Nations, and among the several States, and with the Indian Tribes;

To establish an uniform Rule of Naturalization, and uniform Laws on the subject of Bankruptcies throughout the United States;

To coin Money, regulate the Value thereof, and of foreign Coin, and fix the Standard of Weights and Measures;

To provide for the Punishment of counterfeiting the Securities and current Coin of the United States;

To establish Post Offices and post Roads;

To promote the Progress of Science and useful Arts, by securing for limited Times to Authors and Inventors the exclusive Right to their respective Writings and Discoveries;

To constitute Tribunals inferior to the supreme Court;

To define and punish Piracies and Felonies committed on the high Seas, and Offences against the Law of Nations;

To declare War, grant Letters of Marque and Reprisal, and make Rules concerning Captures on Land and Water;

To raise and support Armies, but no Appropriation of Money to that Use shall be for a longer Term than two Years;

To provide and maintain a Navy;

To make Rules for the Government and Regulation of the land and naval Forces;

To provide for calling forth the Militia to execute the Laws of the Union, suppress Insurrections and repel Invasions;

To provide for organizing, arming, and disciplining, the Militia, and for governing such Part of them as may be employed in the Service of the United States, reserving to the States respectively, the Appointment of the Officers, and the Authority of training the Militia according to the discipline prescribed by Congress;

To exercise exclusive Legislation in all Cases whatsoever, over such District (not exceeding ten Miles square) as may, by Cession of particular States, and the Acceptance of Congress, become the Seat of the Government of the United States, and to exercise like Authority over all Places purchased by the Consent of the Legislature of the State in which the Same shall be, for the Erection of Forts, Magazines, Arsenals, dock-Yards, and other needful Buildings;—And

To make all Laws which shall be necessary and proper for carrying into Execution the foregoing Powers, and all other Powers vested by this Constitution in the Government of the United States, or in any Department or Officer thereof.

Section 9. The Migration or Importation of such Persons as any of the States now existing shall think proper to admit, shall not be prohibited by the Congress prior to the Year one thousand eight hundred and eight, but a Tax or duty may be imposed on such Importation, not exceeding ten dollars for each Person.

The Privilege of the Writ of Habeas Corpus shall not be suspended, unless when in Cases of Rebellion or Invasion the public Safety may require it.

No Bill of Attainder or ex post facto Law shall be passed.

No Capitation, or other direct, Tax shall be laid, unless in Proportion to the Census or Enumeration herein before directed to be taken.

No Tax or Duty shall be laid on Articles exported from any State.

No Preference shall be given by any Regulation of Commerce or Revenue to the Ports of one State over those of another: nor shall Vessels bound to, or from, one State, be obliged to enter, clear or pay Duties in another.

No Money shall be drawn from the Treasury, but in Consequence of Appropriations made by Law; and a regular Statement and Account of Receipts and Expenditures of all public Money shall be published from time to time.

No Title of Nobility shall be granted by the United States: And no Person holding any Office of Profit or Trust under them, shall, without the Consent of the Congress, accept of any present, Emolument, Office, or Title, of any kind whatever, from any King, Prince, or foreign State.

Section 10. No State shall enter into any Treaty, Alliance, or Confederation; grant Letters of Marque and Reprisal; coin Money; emit Bills of Credit; make any Thing but gold and silver Coin a Tender in Payment of Debts; pass any Bill of Attainder, ex post facto Law, or Law impairing the Obligation of Contracts, or grant any Title of Nobility.

No State shall, without the Consent of the Congress, lay any Imposts or Duties on Imports or Exports, except what may be absolutely necessary for executing its inspection Laws: and the net Produce of all Duties and Imposts, laid by any State on Imports or Exports, shall be for the Use of the Treasury of the United States; and all such Laws shall be subject to the Revision and Controul of the Congress.

No State shall, without the Consent of Congress, lay any Duty of Tonnage, keep Troops, or Ships of War in time of Peace, enter into any Agreement or Compact with another State, or with a foreign Power, or engage in War, unless actually invaded, or in such imminent Danger as will not admit of delay.

Article II

Section 1. The executive Power shall be vested in a President of the United States of America. He shall hold his Office during the Term of four Years, and, together with the Vice President, chosen for the same Term, be elected, as follows:

Each State shall appoint, in such Manner as the Legislature thereof may direct, a Number of Electors, equal to the whole Number of Senators and Representatives to which the State may be entitled in the Congress: but no Senator or Representative, or Person holding an Office of Trust or Profit under the United States, shall be appointed an Elector.

The Electors shall meet in their respective States, and vote by Ballot for two Persons, of whom one at least shall not be an Inhabitant of the same State with themselves. And they shall make a List of all the Persons voted for, and of the Number of Votes for each; which List they shall sign and certify, and transmit sealed to the Seat of the Government of the United States, directed to the President of the Senate. The President of the Senate shall, in the Presence of the Senate and House of Representatives, open all the Certificates, and the Votes shall then be counted. The Person having the greatest Number of Votes shall be the President, if such Number be a Majority of the whole Number of Electors appointed; and if there be more than one who have such Majority, and have an equal Number of Votes, then the House of Representatives shall immediately chuse by Ballot one of them for President; and if no Person have a Majority, then from the five highest on the List the said House shall in like Manner chuse the President. But in chusing the President, the Votes shall be taken by States, the Representation from each State having one Vote; A quorum for this Purpose shall consist of a Member or Members from two thirds of the States, and a Majority of all the States shall be necessary to a Choice. In every Case, after the Choice of the President, the Person having the greatest Number of Votes of the Electors shall be the Vice President. But if there should remain two or more who have equal Votes, the Senate shall chuse from them by Ballot the Vice President.

The Congress may determine the Time of chusing the Electors, and the Day on which they shall give their Votes; which Day shall be the same throughout the United States.

No Person except a natural born Citizen, or a Citizen of the United States, at the time of the Adoption of this Constitution, shall be eligible to the Office of President; neither shall any Person be eligible to that Office who shall not have attained to the Age of thirty five Years, and been fourteen Years a Resident within the United States.

In Case of the Removal of the President from Office, or of his Death, Resignation, or Inability to discharge the Powers and Duties of the said Office, the Same shall devolve on the Vice President, and the Congress may by Law provide for the Case of Removal, Death, Resignation or Inability, both of the President and Vice President, declaring what Officer shall then act as President, and such Officer shall act accordingly, until the Disability be removed, or a President shall be elected.

The President shall, at stated Times, receive for his Services, a Compensation, which shall neither be increased nor diminished during the Period for which he shall have been elected, and he shall not receive within that Period any other Emolument from the United States, or any of them.

Before he enter on the Execution of his Office, he shall take the following Oath or Affirmation: "I do solemnly swear (or affirm) that I will faithfully execute the Office of President of the United States, and will to the best of my Ability, preserve, protect and defend the Constitution of the United States."

Section 2. The President shall be Commander in Chief of the Army and Navy of the United States, and of the Militia of the several States, when called into the actual Service of the United States; he may require the Opinion, in writing, of the principal Officer in each of the executive Departments, upon any Subject relating to the Duties of their respective Offices, and he shall have Power to grant Reprieves and Pardons for Offences against the United States, except in Cases of Impeachment.

He shall have Power, by and with the Advice and Consent of the Senate, to make Treaties, provided two thirds of the Senators present concur; and he shall nominate, and by and with the Advice and Consent of the Senate, shall appoint Ambassadors, other public Ministers and Consuls, Judges of the supreme Court, and all other Officers of the United States, whose Appointments are not herein otherwise provided for, and which shall be established by Law: but the Congress may by Law vest the Appointment of such inferior Officers, as they think proper, in the President alone, in the Courts of Law, or in the Heads of Departments.

The President shall have Power to fill up all Vacancies that may happen during the Recess of the Senate, by granting Commissions which shall expire at the End of their next Session.

Section 3. He shall from time to time give to the Congress Information of the State of the Union, and recommend to their Consideration such Measures as he shall judge necessary and expedient; he may, on extraordinary Occasions, convene both Houses, or either of them, and in Case of Disagreement between them, with Respect to the Time of Adjournment, he may adjourn them to such Time as he shall think proper; he shall receive Ambassadors and other public Ministers; he shall take Care that the Laws be faithfully executed, and shall Commission all the Officers of the United States.

Section 4. The President, Vice President and all civil Officers of the United States, shall be removed from Office on Impeachment for, and Conviction of, Treason, Bribery, or other high Crimes and Misdemeanors.

Article III

Section 1. The judicial Power of the United States, shall be vested in one supreme Court, and in such inferior Courts as the Congress may from time to time ordain and establish. The Judges, both of the supreme and inferior Courts, shall hold their Offices during good Behaviour, and shall, at stated Times, receive for their Services a Compensation, which shall not be diminished during their Continuance in Office.

Section 2. The judicial Power shall extend to all Cases, in Law and Equity, arising under this Constitution, the Laws of the United States, and Treaties made, or which shall be made, under their Authority;—to all Cases affecting Ambassadors, other public Ministers and Consuls;—to all Cases of admiralty and maritime Jurisdiction;—to Controversies to which the United States shall be a Party;—to Controversies between two or more States;—between a State and Citizens of another State;—between Citizens of different States;—between Citizens of the same State claiming Lands under the Grants of different States, and between a State, or the Citizens thereof, and foreign States, Citizens or Subjects.

In all Cases affecting Ambassadors, other public Ministers and Consuls, and those in which a State shall be a Party, the supreme Court shall have original Jurisdiction. In all the other Cases before mentioned, the supreme Court shall have appellate Jurisdiction, both as to Law and Fact, with such Exceptions, and under such Regulations as the Congress shall make.

The Trial of all Crimes, except in Cases of Impeachment, shall be by Jury; and such Trial shall be held in the State where the said Crimes shall have been committed; but when not committed within any State, the Trial shall be at such Place or Places as the Congress may by Law have directed.

Section 3. Treason against the United States, shall consist only in levying War against them, or in adhering to their Enemies, giving them Aid and Comfort. No Person shall be convicted of Treason unless on the Testimony of two Witnesses to the same overt Act, or on Confession in open Court.

The Congress shall have Power to declare the Punishment of Treason, but no Attainder of Treason shall work Corruption of Blood, or Forfeiture except during the Life of the Person attainted.

Article IV

Section 1. Full Faith and Credit shall be given in each State to the public Acts, Records, and judicial Proceedings of every other State. And the Congress may by general Laws prescribe the Manner in which such Acts, Records and Proceedings shall be proved, and the Effect thereof.

Section 2. The Citizens of each State shall be entitled to all Privileges and Immunities of Citizens in the several States.

A Person charged in any State with Treason, Felony, or other Crime, who shall flee from Justice, and be found in another State, shall on demand of the executive Authority of the State from which he fled, be delivered up, to be removed to the State having Jurisdiction of the Crime.

No Person held to Service or Labour in one State, under the Laws thereof, escaping into another, shall, in Consequence of any Law or Regulation therein, be discharged from such Service or Labour, but shall be delivered up on Claim of the Party to whom such Service or Labour may be due.

Section 3. New States may be admitted by the Congress into this Union; but no new State shall be formed or erected within the Jurisdiction of any other State; nor any State be formed by the Junction of two or more States, or Parts of States, without the Consent of the Legislatures of the States concerned as well as of the Congress.

The Congress shall have Power to dispose of and make all needful Rules and Regulations respecting the Territory or other Property belonging to the United States; and nothing in this Constitution shall be so construed as to Prejudice any Claims of the United States, or of any particular State.

Section 4. The United States shall guarantee to every State in this Union a Republican Form of Government, and shall protect each of them against Invasion; and on Application of the Legislature, or of the Executive (when the Legislature cannot be convened) against domestic Violence.

Article V

The Congress, whenever two thirds of both Houses shall deem it necessary, shall propose Amendments to this Constitution, or, on the Application of the Legislatures of two thirds of the several States, shall call a Convention for proposing Amendments, which, in either Case, shall be valid to all Intents and Purposes, as Part of this Constitution, when ratified by the Legislatures of three fourths of the several States, or by Conventions in three fourths thereof, as the one or the other Mode of Ratification may be proposed by the Congress; Provided that no Amendment which may be made prior to the Year One thousand eight hundred and eight shall in any Manner affect the first and fourth Clauses in the Ninth Section of the first Article; and that no State, without its Consent, shall be deprived of its equal Suffrage in the Senate.

Article VI

All Debts contracted and Engagements entered into, before the Adoption of this Constitution, shall be as valid against the United States under this Constitution, as under the Confederation.

This Constitution, and the Laws of the United States which shall be made in Pursuance thereof; and all Treaties made, or which shall be made, under the Authority of the United States, shall be the supreme Law of the Land; and the Judges in every State shall be bound thereby, any Thing in the Constitution or Laws of any State to the Contrary notwithstanding.

The Senators and Representatives before mentioned, and the Members of the several State Legislatures, and all executive and judicial Officers, both of the United States and of the several States, shall be bound by Oath or Affirmation, to support this Constitution; but no religious Test shall ever be required as a Qualification to any Office or public Trust under the United States.

Article VII

The Ratification of the Conventions of nine States, shall be sufficient for the Establishment of this Constitution between the States so ratifying the Same.

Articles in addition to, and amendment of, the Constitution of the United States of America, proposed by Congress, and ratified by the Legislatures of the Several States pursuant to the Fifth Article of the original Constitution.

Amendment I [1791]

Congress shall make no law respecting an establishment of religion, or prohibiting the free exercise thereof; or abridging the freedom of speech, or of the press; or the right of the people peaceably to assemble, and to petition the Government for a redress of grievances.

Amendment II [1791]

A well regulated Militia, being necessary to the security of a free State, the right of the people to keep and bear Arms, shall not be infringed.

Amendment III [1791]

No Soldier shall, in time of peace be quartered in any house, without the consent of the Owner, nor in time of war, but in a manner to be prescribed by law.

Amendment IV [1791]

The right of the people to be secure in their persons, houses, papers, and effects, against unreasonable searches and seizures, shall not be violated, and no Warrants shall issue, but upon probable cause, supported by Oath or affirmation, and particularly describing the place to be searched, and the persons or things to be seized.

Amendment V [1791]

No person shall be held to answer for a capital, or otherwise infamous crime, unless on a presentment or indictment of a Grand Jury, except in cases arising in the land or naval forces, or in the Militia, when in actual service in time of War or public danger; nor shall any person be subject for the same offence to be twice put in jeopardy of life or limb; nor shall be compelled in any criminal case to be a witness against himself, nor be deprived of life, liberty, or property, without due process of law; nor shall private property be taken for public use, without just compensation.

Amendment VI [1791]

In all criminal prosecutions, the accused shall enjoy the right to a speedy and public trial, by an impartial jury of the State and district wherein the crime shall have been committed, which district shall have been previously ascertained by law, and to be informed of the nature and cause of the accusation; to be confronted with the witnesses against him; to have compulsory process for obtaining witnesses in his favor, and to have the Assistance of Counsel for his defence.

Amendment VII [1791]

In Suits at common law, where the value in controversy shall exceed twenty dollars, the right of trial by jury shall be preserved, and no fact tried by jury, shall be otherwise re-examined in any Court of the United States, than according to the rules of the common law.

Amendment VIII [1791]

Excessive bail shall not be required, nor excessive fines imposed, nor cruel and unusual punishments inflicted.

Amendment IX [1791]

The enumeration in the Constitution, of certain rights, shall not be construed to deny or disparage others retained by the people.

Amendment X [1791]

The powers not delegated to the United States by the Constitution, nor prohibited by it to the States, are reserved to the States respectively, or to the people.

Amendment XI [1798]

The Judicial power of the United States shall not be construed to extend to any suit in law or equity, commenced or prosecuted against one of the United States by Citizens of another State, or by Citizens or Subjects of any Foreign State.

Amendment XII [1804]

The Electors shall meet in their respective states and vote by ballot for President and Vice-President, one of whom, at least, shall not be an inhabitant of the same state with themselves; they shall name in their ballots the person voted for as President, and in distinct ballots the person voted for as Vice-President, and they shall make distinct lists of all persons voted for as President, and of all persons voted for as Vice-President, and of the number of votes for each, which lists they shall sign and certify, and transmit sealed to the seat of the government of the United States, directed to the President of the Senate;—The President of the Senate shall, in the presence of the Senate and House of Representatives, open all the certificates and the votes shall then be counted;—The person having the greatest Number of votes for President, shall be the President, if such number be a majority of the whole number of Electors appointed; and if no person have such majority, then from the persons having the highest numbers not exceeding three on the list of those voted for as President, the House of Representatives shall choose immediately, by ballot, the President. But in choosing the President, the votes shall be taken by states, the representation from each state having one vote; a quorum for this purpose shall consist of a member or members from two-thirds of the states, and a majority of all the states shall be necessary to a choice. And if the House of Representatives shall not choose a President whenever the right of choice shall devolve upon them before the fourth day of March next following, then the Vice-President shall act as President, as in the case of the death or other constitutional disability of the President.—The person having the greatest number of votes as Vice-President, shall be the Vice-President, if such number be a majority of the whole number of Electors appointed, and if no person have a majority, then from the two highest numbers on the list, the Senate shall choose the Vice-President; a quorum for the purpose shall consist of two-thirds of the whole number of Senators, and a majority of the whole number shall be necessary to a choice. But no person constitutionally ineligible to the office of President shall be eligible to that of Vice-President of the United States.

Amendment XIII [1865]

Section 1. Neither slavery nor involuntary servitude, except as a punishment for crime whereof the party shall have been duly convicted, shall exist within the United States, or any place subject to their jurisdiction.

Section 2. Congress shall have power to enforce this article by appropriate legislation.

Amendment XIV [1868]

Section 1. All persons born or naturalized in the United States, and subject to the jurisdiction thereof, are citizens of the United States and of the State wherein they reside. No State shall make or enforce any law which shall abridge the privileges or immunities of citizens of the United States; nor shall any State deprive any person of life, liberty, or property, without due process of law; nor deny to any person within its jurisdiction the equal protection of the laws.

Section 2. Representatives shall be apportioned among the several States according to their respective numbers, counting the whole number of persons in each State, excluding Indians not taxed. But when the right to vote at any election for the choice of electors for President and Vice-President of the United States, Representatives in Congress, the Executive and Judicial officers of a State, or the members of the Legislature thereof, is denied to any of the male inhabitants of such State, being twenty-one years of age, and citizens of the United States, or in any way abridged, except for participation in rebellion, or other crime, the basis of representation therein shall be reduced in the proportion which the number of such male citizens shall bear to the whole number of male citizens twenty-one years of age in such State.

Section 3. No person shall be a Senator or Representative in Congress, or elector of President and Vice-President, or hold any office, civil or military, under the United States, or under any State, who, having previously taken an oath, as a member of Congress, or as an officer of the United States, or as a member of any State legislature, or as an executive or judicial officer of any State, to support the Constitution of the United States, shall have engaged in insurrection or rebellion against the same, or given aid or comfort to the enemies thereof. But Congress may by a vote of two-thirds of each House, remove such disability.

Section 4. The validity of the public debt of the United States, authorized by law, including debts incurred for payment of pensions and bounties for services in suppressing insurrection or rebellion, shall not be questioned. But neither the United States nor any State shall assume or pay any debt or obligation incurred in aid of insurrection or rebellion against the United States, or any claim for the loss or emancipation of any slave; but all such debts, obligations and claims shall be held illegal and void.

Section 5. The Congress shall have power to enforce, by appropriate legislation, the provisions of this article.

Amendment XV [1870]

Section 1. The right of citizens of the United States to vote shall not be denied or abridged by the United States or by any State on account of race, color, or previous condition of servitude.

Section 2. The Congress shall have power to enforce this article by appropriate legislation.

Amendment XVI [1913]

The Congress shall have power to lay and collect taxes on incomes, from whatever source derived, without apportionment among the several States, and without regard to any census or enumeration.

Amendment XVII [1913]

[1] The Senate of the United States shall be composed of two Senators from each State, elected by the people thereof, for six years; and each Senator shall have one vote. The electors in each State shall have the qualifications requisite for electors of the most numerous branch of the State legislatures.

[2] When vacancies happen in the representation of any State in the Senate, the executive authority of such State shall issue writs of election to fill such vacancies: *Provided*, That the legislature of any State may empower the executive thereof to make temporary appointments until the people fill the vacancies by election as the legislature may direct.

[3] This amendment shall not be so construed as to affect the election or term of any Senator chosen before it becomes valid as part of the Constitution.

Amendment XVIII [1919]

Section 1. After one year from the ratification of this article the manufacture, sale, or transportation of intoxicating liquors within, the importation thereof into, or the exportation thereof from the United States and all territory subject to the jurisdiction thereof for beverage purposes is hereby prohibited.

Section 2. The Congress and the several States shall have concurrent power to enforce this article by appropriate legislation.

Section 3. This article shall be inoperative unless it shall have been ratified as an amendment to the Constitution by the legislatures of the several States, as provided in the Constitution, within seven years from the date of the submission hereof to the States by the Congress.

Amendment XIX [1920]

[1] The right of citizens of the United States to vote shall not be denied or abridged by the United States or by any State on account of sex.

[2] Congress shall have power to enforce this article by appropriate legislation.

Amendment XX [1933]

Section 1. The terms of the President and Vice President shall end at noon on the 20th day of January, and the terms of Senators and Representatives at noon on the 3d day of January, of the years in which such terms would have ended if this article had not been ratified; and the terms of their successors shall then begin.

Section 2. The Congress shall assemble at least once in every year, and such meeting shall begin at noon on the 3d day of January, unless they shall by law appoint a different day.

Section 3. If, at the time fixed for the beginning of the term of the President, the President elect shall have died, the Vice President elect shall become President. If the President shall not have been chosen before the time fixed for the beginning of his term, or if the President elect shall have failed to qualify, then the Vice President elect shall act as President until a President shall have qualified; and the Congress may by law provide for the case wherein neither a President elect nor a Vice President elect shall have qualified, declaring who shall then act as President, or the manner in which one who is to act shall be selected, and such person shall act accordingly until a President or Vice President shall have qualified.

Section 4. The Congress may by law provide for the case of the death of any of the persons from whom the House of Representatives may choose a President whenever the right of choice shall have devolved upon them, and for the case of the death of any of the persons from whom the Senate may choose a Vice President whenever the right of choice shall have devolved upon them.

Section 5. Sections 1 and 2 shall take effect on the 15th day of October following the ratification of this article.

Section 6. This article shall be inoperative unless it shall have been ratified as an amendment to the Constitution by the legislatures of three-fourths of the several States within seven years from the date of its submission.

Amendment XXI [1933]

Section 1. The eighteenth article of amendment to the Constitution of the United States is hereby repealed.

Section 2. The transportation or importation into any State, Territory, or possession of the United States for delivery or use therein of intoxicating liquors, in violation of the laws thereof, is hereby prohibited.

Section 3. The article shall be inoperative unless it shall have been ratified as an amendment to the Constitution by conventions in the several States, as provided in the Constitution, within seven years from the date of the submission hereof to the States by the Congress.

Amendment XXII [1951]

Section 1. No person shall be elected to the office of the President more than twice, and no person who has held the office of President, or acted as President, for more than two years of a term to which some other person was elected President shall be elected to the office of the President more than once. But this Article shall not apply to any person holding the office of President when this Article was proposed by the Congress, and shall not prevent any person who may be holding the office of President, or acting as President, during the term within which this Article becomes operative from holding the office of President or acting as President during the remainder of such term.

Section 2. This article shall be inoperative unless it shall have been ratified as an amendment to the Constitution by the legislatures of three-fourths of the several States within seven years from the date of its submission to the States by the Congress.

Amendment XXIII [1961]

Section 1. The District constituting the seat of Government of the United States shall appoint in such manner as the Congress may direct:

A number of electors of President and Vice President equal to the whole number of Senators and Representatives in Congress to which the District would be entitled if it were a State, but in no event more than the least populous State; they shall be in addition to those appointed by the States, but they shall be considered, for the purposes of the election of President and Vice President, to be electors appointed by a State; and they shall meet in the District and perform such duties as provided by the twelfth article of amendment.

Section 2. The Congress shall have power to enforce this article by appropriate legislation.

Amendment XXIV [1964]

Section 1. The right of citizens of the United States to vote in any primary or other election for President or Vice President, for electors for President or Vice President, or for Senator or Representative in Congress, shall not be denied or abridged by the United States or any State by reason of failure to pay any poll tax or other tax.

Section 2. The Congress shall have power to enforce this article by appropriate legislation.

Amendment XXV [1967]

Section 1. In case of the removal of the President from office or of his death or resignation, the Vice President shall become President.

Section 2. Whenever there is a vacancy in the office of the Vice President, the President shall nominate a Vice President who shall take office upon confirmation by a majority vote of both Houses of Congress.

Section 3. Whenever the President transmits to the President pro tempore of the Senate and the Speaker of the House of Representatives his written declaration that he is unable to discharge the powers and duties of his office, and until he transmits to them a written declaration to the contrary, such powers and duties shall be discharged by the Vice President as Acting President.

Section 4. Whenever the Vice President and a majority of either the principal officers of the executive departments or of such other body as Congress may by law provide, transmit to the President pro tempore of the Senate and the Speaker of the House of Representatives their written declaration that the President is unable to discharge the powers and duties of his office, the Vice President shall immediately assume the powers and duties of the office as Acting President.

Thereafter, when the President transmits to the President pro tempore of the Senate and the Speaker of the House of Representatives his written declaration that no inability exists, he shall resume the powers and duties of his office unless the Vice President and a majority of either the principal officers of the executive department or of such other body as Congress may by law provide, transmit within four days to the President pro tempore of the Senate and the Speaker of the House of Representatives their written declaration that the President is unable to discharge the powers and duties of his office. Thereupon Congress shall decide the issue, assembling within forty-eight hours for that purpose if not in session. If the Congress, within twenty-one days after receipt of the latter written declaration, or, if Congress is not in session, within twenty-one days after Congress is required to assemble, determines by two-thirds vote of both Houses that the President is unable to discharge the powers and duties of his office, the Vice President shall continue to discharge the same as Acting President; otherwise, the President shall resume the powers and duties of his office.

Amendment XXVI [1971]

Section 1. The right of citizens of the United States, who are eighteen years of age or older, to vote shall not be denied or abridged by the United States or by any State on account of age.

Section 2. The Congress shall have power to enforce this article by appropriate legislation.

Amendment XXVII [1992]

No law, varying the compensation for the services of the Senators and Representatives, shall take effect, until an election of Representatives shall have intervened.